SPORT BIBLIOGRAPHY

The International Sport Bibliographical System

VOLUME 13

1984

Prepared by
Sport Information Resource Centre

Edited by
L. Wheeler
G. Chiasson
H. Nadeau
M. Rogers
R. Stark

Human Kinetics Publishers, Inc.

Champaign, Illinois

Managing Editor: Peg Goyette
Production Director: Ernie Noa
Typesetters: Angela Snyder and Sandra Meier
Text Layout: Leah Freedman
Cover Design: Julie Szamocki
Printed by: Braun Brumfield, Inc.

ISBN: 0-87322-104-4
ISSN: 0885-7180

Printed in the United States of America

10 9 8 7 6 5 4 3 2 1

Human Kinetics Publishers, Inc.
Box 5076, Champaign, IL 61820, USA

CONTENTS

Introduction   v

Acknowledgments   vi

Sport Bibliography volumes   vii

Key to abbreviations   viii

Sample entries   ix

Sport Bibliography   1

Index en français   535

Indice en español   536

Deutsches Inhaltsverzeichnis   538

Русский указатель   539

INTRODUCTION

The Sport Information Resource Centre (SIRC) is the largest resource center in the world, collecting and disseminating information in sport, physical education, physical fitness, and sports medicine. Established in 1973 by the Coaching Association of Canada, SIRC achieved the status of an incorporated nonprofit organization in 1985. SIRC is located in the National Sport and Recreation Centre, 333 River Road, Ottawa, Ontario, Canada K1L 8H9.

The original eight-volume set of the *Sport Bibliography*, published in 1981-1982, is the most comprehensive sport subject index ever printed. It contains over 70,000 sport and physical activity references to documents (books, periodical articles, theses, microforms, and conference proceedings) published in the years 1974 to 1980 inclusive, with a substantial but less comprehensive coverage prior to 1974.

In 1983, a two-volume update was published. This update contains over 28,000 references representing material published from 1979 to 1981-82 that had been added to the SIRC computerized retrieval system since the publication of the eight-volume series. The two-volume update should be considered as Volumes 9 and 10 in the *Sport Bibliography* series.

Volumes 11 and 12 of the *Sport Bibliography* each contain over 15,000 references. Volume 11 covers material published in 1982 and Volume 12 covers material published in 1983. French, German, Spanish, and Russian subject indices are located at the end of each volume.

Volume 13 in the *Sport Bibliography* series lists over 15,000 references to documentation published in 1984 that have been added to the SIRC computerized retrieval system.

Each document included in Volume 13 has been examined and classified under a specific subject heading. Because of the large volume of material, most citations are listed only once under the heading considered most appropriate to the specific subject content of the document. Within the literature concerning a particular sport or sport science topic, material can be further classified into alphabetically arranged subject headings that reflect specific aspects such as administration, biomechanics, coaching, medicine, and training. Arrangement of entries under a particular subject heading is alphabetical by personal author or editor. In the case of a work without an author, entries are alphabetized by title.

A comprehensive listing is provided for each document, including author(s), title, publisher, and place and date of publication. Other information, such as the International Standard Book Number (ISBN) or the Library of Congress card number, is provided when available. To assist users in choosing material most suited to their particular needs, the citation includes a code that represents its level of sophistication (basic, intermediate, or advanced). In addition, advanced or research-level citations are often accompanied by an English language abstract.

Although most of the material included is in English, limited foreign language references also are listed. For example, Volume 13 contains citations gathered through cooperative indexing with the Federal Institute of Sport Science in Cologne, West Germany, and with the Footscray Institute of Technology in Melbourne, Australia. Future volumes will contain contributions from additional foreign countries since SIRC's SPORT database has now been recognized as the international database for sport by the International Association of Sport Information (IASI) and by the International Council of Sport Science and Physical Education (ICSSPE). The language of each document is identified by an abbreviation in the citation. For foreign language periodical articles, the original language title is also accompanied by an English language translation of the title that appears in brackets. The article itself is never translated, but sometimes an English abstract is given. (Refer to the language note to find out the language of the article.)

A key to abbreviations used in *Sport Bibliography* appears on page viii, followed by sample citations on page ix that illustrate the various types of documents and that specify the significance of each component of the citation. All citations published in *Sport Bibliography* are indexed on the SPORT Database. Online access to the most current sport information is available through the following vendors: BRS, CAN/OLE, DIALOG, DIMDI, SDC.

Also available is *SportSearch*, a current awareness tool that complements the *Sport Bibliography*. *SportSearch* contains the table of contents of over 200 current sport journals with the added feature of several pages of abstracts of research articles. *SportSearch* is also published by SIRC. Write to Sport Information Resource Centre, 333 River Road, Ottawa, Ontario, Canada K1L 8H9, for current subscription price information.

ACKNOWLEDGMENTS

The editors wish to thank the Sport Information Resource Centre staff: Lynne Allain, Claire Bordeleau, Brian Drysdale, Suzanne Foisy, Jean-Michel Johnson, Christine Lalande, Francine Power, and especially Danielle Allain and Gail Shaver for their invaluable help.

Publication of the *Sport Bibliography* would not have been possible without the support of Fitness and Amateur Sport Canada.

SPORT BIBLIOGRAPHY VOLUMES

Volume	Topic
1	Aquatic sports, boating, ice sports, outdoor sports and activities, and winter sports
2	Bowling, golf, and team sports
3	Combat sports, gymnastics, dance, martial arts, racquet sports, track and field, weight lifting, and body building
4	Aeronautical sports, animal sports, equestrian sports, modern pentathlon, motor sports, roller skating and skateboarding, target sports, cycling, and throwing games
5	Coaching, training, and officiating
6	Events and national and international competitions
7	Humanities and social science
8	Science and medicine (Volumes 1-8 contain over 70,000 references to documentation published primarily in the years 1974 to 1980.)
9	Sport (all sport activities). Volume 9 contains references updating the sport topics covered in Volumes 1-4.
10	Sports medicine and sport science. Volume 10 contains references updating the topics covered in Volumes 5-8. (Originally Volumes 9 and 10 of *Sport Bibliography* were referred to as Update 1 and Update 2, respectively. Volumes 9 and 10 contain 28,000 references, updating the *Sport Bibliography* series for the period 1979 to 1981-82.)
11	All sport, sports medicine, and sport science topics. (Volume 11 contains 15,000 references to documentation published in 1982.)
12	All sport, sports medicine, and sport science topics. (Volume 12 contains references to documentation published in 1983.)
13	All sport, sports medicine, and sport science topics. (Volume 13 contains references to documentation published in 1984.)
14	All sport, sports medicine, and sport science topics. (Volume 14, available in 1987, will contain references to documentation published in 1985.)

ALL VOLUMES THAT HAVE BEEN PRINTED ARE AVAILABLE FROM
HUMAN KINETICS PUBLISHERS, INC.
BOX 5076
CHAMPAIGN, ILLINOIS 61820

KEY TO ABBREVIATIONS

ANNOT	Annotations
CONF	Conference
CORP	Corporate Author
DISS.ABST	Dissertation Abstract Number
EDRS	Eric Document Reproduction Service
ISBN	International Standard Book Number
LANG	Language

Afr	Afrikaans
Bul	Bulgarian
Bur	Burmese
Cat	Catalonese
Chi	Chinese
Cze	Czech
Dan	Danish
Dut	Dutch
Est	Estonian
Fin	Finnish
Fr	French
Ger	German
Gre	Greek
Heb	Hebrew
Hun	Hungarian
Ind	Indonesian
It	Italian
Jpn	Japanese
Kor	Korean
Lai	Lai
May	Malay
Nah	Nahuatl
Nor	Norwegian

Per	Persian
Pol	Polish
Por	Portuguese
Rum	Rumanian
Rus	Russian
Scr	Serbocroatian
Slo	Slovak
Slv	Slovene
Snd	Sindhi
Snh	Sinahalese
Spa	Spanish
Swa	Swahili
Swe	Swedish
Tur	Turkish
Ukr	Ukranian
Urd	Urdu
Vie	Vietnamese

LC CARD	Library of Congress Card Number
LEVEL: A	Advanced or research material
LEVEL: B	Basic, easy reading material
LEVEL: I	Intermediate-level material
NOTES	Additional information regarding a document provided whenever appropriate
REFS	Number of references given in the document
SIRC ARTICLE NO	SIRC Article Number

SAMPLE ENTRIES

BOOK

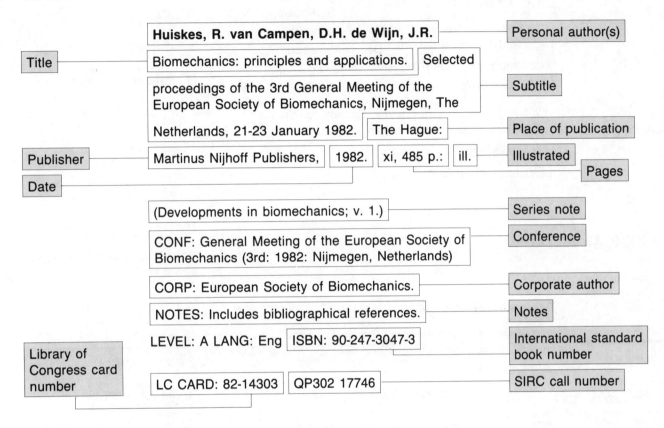

Personal author(s): **Huiskes, R. van Campen, D.H. de Wijn, J.R.**

Title: Biomechanics: principles and applications.

Subtitle: Selected proceedings of the 3rd General Meeting of the European Society of Biomechanics, Nijmegen, The Netherlands, 21-23 January 1982.

Place of publication: The Hague:

Publisher: Martinus Nijhoff Publishers,

Date: 1982.

Pages: xi, 485 p.:

Illustrated: ill.

Series note: (Developments in biomechanics; v. 1.)

Conference: CONF: General Meeting of the European Society of Biomechanics (3rd: 1982: Nijmegen, Netherlands)

Corporate author: CORP: European Society of Biomechanics.

Notes: NOTES: Includes bibliographical references.

LEVEL: A LANG: Eng

International standard book number: ISBN: 90-247-3047-3

Library of Congress card number: LC CARD: 82-14303

SIRC call number: QP302 17746

BOOK ANALYTIC

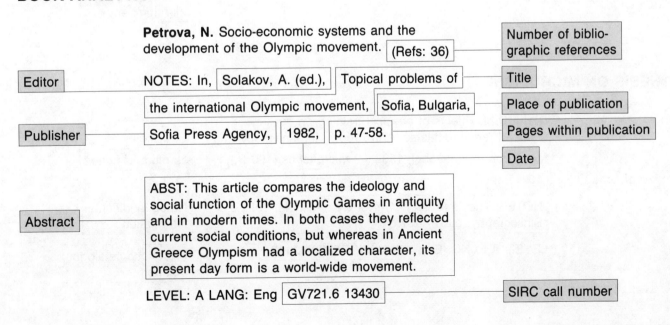

Petrova, N. Socio-economic systems and the development of the Olympic movement.

Number of bibliographic references: (Refs: 36)

Editor: NOTES: In, Solakov, A. (ed.),

Title: Topical problems of the international Olympic movement,

Place of publication: Sofia, Bulgaria,

Publisher: Sofia Press Agency,

Date: 1982,

Pages within publication: p. 47-58.

Abstract: ABST: This article compares the ideology and social function of the Olympic Games in antiquity and in modern times. In both cases they reflected current social conditions, but whereas in Ancient Greece Olympism had a localized character, its present day form is a world-wide movement.

LEVEL: A LANG: Eng

SIRC call number: GV721.6 13430

NON-PRINT MATERIAL

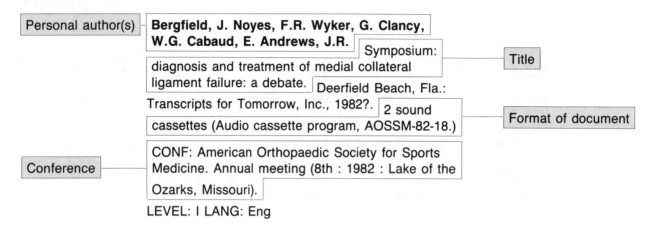

Personal author(s) — **Bergfield, J. Noyes, F.R. Wyker, G. Clancy, W.G. Cabaud, E. Andrews, J.R.**

Title — Symposium:

diagnosis and treatment of medial collateral ligament failure: a debate. Deerfield Beach, Fla.: Transcripts for Tomorrow, Inc., 1982?.

Format of document — 2 sound cassettes (Audio cassette program, AOSSM-82-18.)

Conference — CONF: American Orthopaedic Society for Sports Medicine. Annual meeting (8th : 1982 : Lake of the Ozarks, Missouri).

LEVEL: I LANG: Eng

PERIODICAL ARTICLE

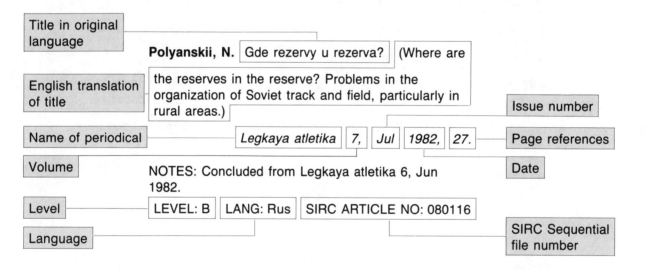

Title in original language

English translation of title

Polyanskii, N. Gde rezervy u rezerva? (Where are the reserves in the reserve? Problems in the organization of Soviet track and field, particularly in rural areas.)

Issue number

Name of periodical — Legkaya atletika 7, Jul 1982, 27. — Page references

Volume

Date

NOTES: Concluded from Legkaya atletika 6, Jun 1982.

Level — LEVEL: B LANG: Rus SIRC ARTICLE NO: 080116

Language

SIRC Sequential file number

THESIS ON MICROFICHE

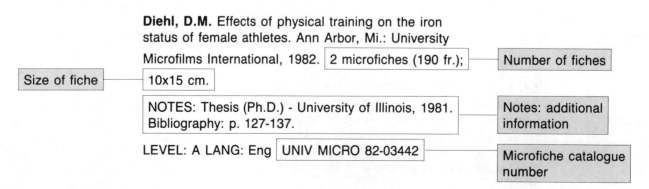

Diehl, D.M. Effects of physical training on the iron status of female athletes. Ann Arbor, Mi.: University Microfilms International, 1982. 2 microfiches (190 fr.); — Number of fiches

Size of fiche — 10x15 cm.

NOTES: Thesis (Ph.D.) - University of Illinois, 1981. Bibliography: p. 127-137. — Notes: additional information

LEVEL: A LANG: Eng UNIV MICRO 82-03442 — Microfiche catalogue number

ABNORMAL PSYCHOLOGY

Schneider, F.J. Die Auswirkungen einer Unterrichtseinheit 'Schoepferische Bewegung und Pantomime' und einer Unterrichtseinheit 'Badminton' auf die Gesamt-koerperkoordination aelterer legasthener Jungen. (Effects of classes in 'creative movement and pantomime' and 'badminton' on total-body coordination in older dyslexic boys.) *Rehabilitation (Stuttgart) 23(4), Nov 1984, 148-154.*
NOTES: English abstract.
LEVEL: A LANG: Ger

AUTISM

Kern, L. The influence of vigorous versus mild exercise on autistic stereotyped behaviors. *Journal of autism and developmental disorders (New York) 14(1), Mar 1984, 57-67.*
LEVEL: A LANG: Eng

Killian, K.J. Joyce-Petrovich, R.A. Menna, L. Arena, S.A. Measuring water orientation and beginner swim skills of autistic individuals. (Refs: 22)*Adapted physical activity quarterly (Champaign, Ill.) 1(4), 1984, 287-295.*
ABST: In this study, a checklist was used to record the responses of 37 autistic children and youth to water orientation and beginner swim activities. The data indicated that the autistic subjects responded in a predictable and apparently normal manner to a hierarchy of water skills. Also, the subjects displayed a low objection rate to water activities. Strong relationships were shown between age and water orientation and also between prior experience and water orientation. The findings support the literature in that the majority of subjects responded well to, or at least tolerated, water activities.
LEVEL: A LANG: Eng SIRC ARTICLE NO: 103966

EMOTIONAL DISORDERS

Forshaw, S.L. Incidence of inappropriate behavior by emotionally disturbed children during participation in cooperative game Eugene, Ore.: Microform Publications, University of Oregon, 1984. 1 microfiche : negative ; 11 x 15 cm.
NOTES: Thesis (M.A.) - Texas Women's University, 1983); (vii, 82 leaves); includes bibliography.
LEVEL: A LANG: Eng UO84 224

LEARNING DISORDERS

Pendergast, E.M. The relationships among perceptual-motor characteristics, physical fitness, and verbal and performance IQ scores of learning disabled and gifted children. Eugene, Ore.: Microform Publications, University of Oregon, 1984. 2 microfiches : negative ; 11 x 15 cm.
NOTES: Thesis (M.S.) - University of Kansas, 1981; (ix, 136 leaves); appendices B-E omitted; includes bibliography.
LEVEL: A LANG: Eng UO84 405-406

MENTAL DISORDERS

Donskaia, L.V. Izmeneniia EKG do i posle fizicheskoi nagruzki v sopostavlenii sekskretsiei katekholaminov u bol'nykh vegetativno-sosudistymi distoniiami. (ECG changes before and after physical loading compared to catecholamine excretion in patients with autonomic vascular dystonia.) *Terapevticheskii archiv (Moskva) 56(2), 1984, 118-121.*
LEVEL: A LANG: Rus

Revutskii, E.L. Federishko, S.S. Maznichenko, L.G. Kishenets, V.A. Previr, V.N. Fizicheskaia rabotosposobnost' u bol'nykh neirotsirkuliatornoi distoniei. (Physical work capacity in neurocirculatory dystonia.) *Vrachebnoe delo (Kiev) 1, Jan 1984, 75-79.*
LEVEL: A LANG: Rus

Suele, F. Turnovszky, E. Az autogen-trening es a psychotherapia kapcsolata fiatal sportolok essentialis hypertoniajanak kezeleseben. (Relations of autogenic training and psychotherapy in the treatment of the juvenile hypertony of young sportsmen and sportswomen.) (Refs: 15)*Sportorvosi szemle/Hungarian review of sports medicine (Budapest) 25(2), 1984, 117-123.*
ABST: The authors discuss the complex psychotherapy of the juvenile hypertony of young sportsmen which cannot be accounted for by other internal causes. They describe the finding that it is important to detect and treat the emerging psychosomatic disorder early because the complex therapy promises good results. The complex therapy consists of 3 to 6 months of autogenic training, and a period of explorative deeppsycho logical brief therapy. The findings are demonstrated with the analysis of a case. They found the most common problem to be the identification of the troubles of the patients and the resulting breakdown in their psychological development.
LEVEL: A LANG: Hun SIRC ARTICLE NO: 097264

ACROBATICS

Criley, D. What is sports acrobatics and how do I get into it? *International gymnast (Santa Monica, Calif.) 26(2), Feb 1984 61-63.*
LEVEL: B LANG: Eng SIRC ARTICLE NO: 094802

ADMINISTRATION

Applin, A.G. U.S. Sports Academy prepares future administrators. *Athletic administration (Cleveland, Oh.) 19(3), May 1984, 24-25.*
LEVEL: B LANG: Eng SIRC ARTICLE NO: 094176

Cobb, J.W. Sports administration: an interdisciplinary approach. *TAHPERD journal (Austin, Tex.) 53(1), Oct 1984, 10.*
LEVEL: B LANG: Eng SIRC ARTICLE NO: 109090

Garvie, G.T. Le principe de la pyramide dans l'administration du sport. *Science du sport: document de recherche et de technologie P-1, mars 1984, 1-3.*
LEVEL: B LANG: Fr SIRC ARTICLE NO: 092678

Garvie, G.T. The pyramid principle of sports administration: a focal point. *Sports: science periodical on research and technology in sport P-1, Mar 1984, 1-4.*
LEVEL: B LANG: Eng SIRC ARTICLE NO: 092679

Imlay, G. Life cycles in programs. *Journal of physical education and program (Columbus, Ohio) 81(7), Oct 1984, G7-G8.*
LEVEL: B LANG: Eng SIRC ARTICLE NO: 100453

Rice, H.C. Leadership for leaders. Part 2, time management start by determining exactly how you are utilizing every minute o your daily time. *Scholastic coach (New York) 54(3), Oct 1984, 44;46;75.*
LEVEL: B LANG: Eng SIRC ARTICLE NO: 100460

The AP&F guide to sports/fitness management programs. *Athletic purchasing and facilities (Madison, Wis.) 8(1), Jan 1984, 32-36.*
LEVEL: B LANG: Eng SIRC ARTICLE NO: 094175

BIBLIOGRAPHIES

Halphen, A. Psycho drame des presidents. Vous les connaissez. Peut-etre moins que Platini ou Prost, Rives ou Noah mais au fi de l'actualite, ils sont montes 'a la une' plusieurs fois au cours de leur carriere. *Equipe magazine 184, 3 mars 1984, 32-39.*
LEVEL: B LANG: Fr SIRC ARTICLE NO: 092681

BIOGRAPHY AND AUTOBIOGRAPHY

Burke, M. In outrageous good fortune. Boston: Little, Brown, 1984. 1v.
LEVEL: B LANG: Eng ISBN: 0316116793 LC CARD: 84-0144

McCormack, M.H. What they don't teach you at Harvard Business School. Toronto: Bantam, c1984. xvi, 256 p. (A John Boswell Associates book.)
LEVEL: I LANG: Eng ISBN: 0-553-05061-3 LC CARD: 84-45172 HD31 18356

COMMUNICATION

Meyer, D. Norman, R. Saunders, S. Organizational communication. A guide to effective communication for sports and recreation organizations. North Bay, Ont.: Northeastern Ontario Regional Sports Committee : Ministry of Tourism and Recreation, 1984. ii, 36 p. (Sport and recreation resource series for community groups; v.2.)
CORP: Northeastern Ontario Regional Sports Committee.
CORP: Ontario. Ministry of Tourism and Recreation. Field Services Office.
LEVEL: B LANG: Eng GV181.5 19015

News release checklist. *Sport administrator (Ottawa) 1(1), Sept/Oct 1984, 7-8.*
LEVEL: B LANG: Eng SIRC ARTICLE NO: 103809

Valeriote, T. Publishing a manual. Ottawa: New Traditions, c1984. 67 p. : ill.
NOTES: Bibliography: p. 65.
LEVEL: B LANG: Eng ISBN: 0-9691563-3-2 LC CARD: 84-90049-X GV713 17607

DATA PROCESSING

Cicciarella, C.F. Getting into the computer game: guidelines and pitfalls. *Journal of physical education, recreation & danc (Reston, Va.) 55(4), Apr 1984, 46-47.*
LEVEL: B LANG: Eng SIRC ARTICLE NO: 094177

Dodson, W.R. Computerization - why and how: part one. *Sport administrator (Ottawa) 1(1), Sept/Oct 1984, 1;4-5.*
LEVEL: B LANG: Eng SIRC ARTICLE NO: 103804

Frazier, C.S. Hatfield, A.B. Computerize your athletic office. *Texas coach (Austin, Tex.) 28(3), Oct 1984, 18-20.*
LEVEL: B LANG: Eng SIRC ARTICLE NO: 173200

ADMINISTRATION (continued)

Gilovich, T. Judgmental biases in the world of sports. (Refs: 27)*In, Straub, W.F. and Williams, J.M. (eds.), Cognitive spor psychology, Lansing, N.Y., Sport Science Associates, c1984, p. 31-41.* LEVEL: A LANG: Eng GV706.4 20099

Haggerty, T.R. The use of computers in sport administration. (Refs: 10)*CAHPER journal/Revue de l'ACSEPR (Vanier, Ont.) 50(3), Jan/Feb 1984, 20-23.* LEVEL: I LANG: Eng SIRC ARTICLE NO: 094179

Railey, D.C. Scheduling league games by computer. Having trouble finding the time or where-with-all to schedule league games This program could be for your sport. *Coaching review 7, Jan/Feb 1984, 34-35.* LEVEL: B LANG: Eng SIRC ARTICLE NO: 091272

Sharp, B. Paliczka, V. Computing in physical education. (Refs: 7)*Scottish journal of physical education (Glasgow, Scotland) 12(2), Apr 1984, 10-18.* ABST: This study presents the results of a survey of Scottish secondary school physical education teachers and their interest, knowledge and use of microcomputers. There was a large variety of applications of microcomputers in physical education. However for the most part they were used in record keeping applications and program planning. LEVEL: A LANG: Eng SIRC ARTICLE NO: 094532

Stabenow, D. The computer and competitive programming. *NIRSA journal (Corvallis, Ore.) 9(1), Fall 1984, 54-57.* LEVEL: B LANG: Eng SIRC ARTICLE NO: 105155

DECISION-MAKING

Moriarty, D. The theory and practice of participatory decision making. La theorie et la pratique de la prise de decision democratique. *CAHPER journal (Ottawa) 51(1), Sept/Oct 1984, 38-40.* NOTES: Part of a series of Administrative Tips prepared by the Administration Committee of CAHPER. Ces conseils en administration proviennent de la serie preparee par le comite d'administration de l'ACSEPL. LEVEL: B LANG: Eng Fr SIRC ARTICLE NO: 100457

Zeigler, E.F. One decision-making strategy: the case method approach. Une technique de prise de decision: l'etude des cas. *CAHPER journal/Revue de l'ACSEPR (Ottawa) 50(5), May/Jun 1984, 30-31.* NOTES: Some of these suggestions were taken from M.P. McNair and H.L. Hansen, Problems in marketing, New York: McGraw-Hill Book Co., 1949, p. 22-25. Certaines de ces suggestions sont extraites de M.P. McNair et H.L. Hansen, Problems in marketing, New York: McGraw-Hill Book Co., 1949, p. 22-25. LEVEL: B LANG: Eng Fr SIRC ARTICLE NO: 095709

INSURANCE

Fazey, I.H. The injury debate. The sports insurance battle. Sports injuries can be expensive as well as frustrating. In the fourth of his series, Ian Hamilton Fazey looks at the competing claims of two insurance schemes. *Running (London) 37, May 1984, 101-102.* LEVEL: B LANG: Eng SIRC ARTICLE NO: 095701

McNamara, S. Moriarty, D. Liability: ensure you're insured. (Refs: 23) NOTES: In, Brown, R. (ed.) et al., Sport, physical activity and the law, Ottawa, Canadian Association for Health, Physical Education, Recreation and Dance, c1984, p. 63-74. LEVEL: I LANG: Eng GV705 18324

INTERPERSONAL RELATIONS

Kahn, F. Kahn, G.N. One way to manage a boss. *Golf course management (Lawrence, Kans.) 52(11), Nov 1984, 66-68;70.* LEVEL: LANG: Eng SIRC ARTICLE NO: 172996

MANAGEMENT SYSTEMS

Chouinard, N. A systems approach to management. Les systemes lies a la gestion. (Refs: 2)*CAHPER journal/Revue de l'ACSEPR (Ottawa) 50(6), Jul/Aug-juil/aout 1984, 26-27;31-32.* NOTES: Part of a series of Administrative Tips prepared by the Administration Committee of CAHPER. Ces conseils en administration proviennent de la serie preparee par le Comite d'administration de l'ACSEPR. LEVEL: B LANG: Eng Fr SIRC ARTICLE NO: 098880

MARKETING

Kelley, L. Public relations and marketing in support of the local association. Toronto: The National Council of YMCAs of Canada, 1984?. 19 p. CORP: National Council of YMCAs of Canada. NOTES: Aussi publie en francais sous le titre, Relations publiques et marketing a l'intention des associations locales. LEVEL: B LANG: Eng GV713 17014

Kelley, L. Relations publiques et marketing a l'intention des associations locales. Toronto: Le Conseil national des YMCA du Canada, 1984?. 20 p. CORP: Conseil national des YMCA du Canada. NOTES: Also published in English under the title, Public relations and marketing in support of the local association. LEVEL: B LANG: Fr GV713 17015

Taylor, L. The marketing and sponsorship of sport in Australia: marketing is defined as having the right product, in the right place, at the right time, in the right quantities and at the right price. *Sports coach (Wembley, W. Aust.) 8(2), Oct 1984, 12-14.* LEVEL: B LANG: Eng SIRC ARTICLE NO: 103817

ORGANIZATION

Meyer, D. Norman, R. Saunders, S. A framework for organization. A guide to developing sports and recreation organizations. North Bay, Ont.: Northeastern Ontario Regional Sports Committee : Ministry of Tourism and Recreation, 1984. ca. 60 p. in various pagings (Sport and recreation resource series for community groups; v.1.) CORP: Northeastern Ontario Regional Sports Committee. CORP: Ontario. Ministry of Tourism and Recreation. Field Services Office. LEVEL: B LANG: Eng GV181.5 19014

Olafson, G.A. Structural variation and sport policy: a comparison of Canadian and British Sport Systems. (Refs: 22)*In, Ilmarinen, M. (ed.) et al., Sport and International Understanding: proceedings*

of the congress held in Helsinki, Finland, July 7-10, 1982, Berlin, Springer-Verlag, 1984, p. 352-357. CONF: Congress on Sport and International Understanding (1982 : Helsinki). LEVEL: A LANG: Eng GV706.8 18979

Savola, J. Organizational development and organizational change. (Refs: 34)*Physical educator (Indianapolis) 41(4), Dec 1984 209-214.* LEVEL: B LANG: Eng SIRC ARTICLE NO: 103814

Winkler, J. On the structural change in voluntary organisations: the case of the 'German Sports Association' ('DSB'). (Refs: 23)*International review for the sociology of sport (Munich) 19(1), 1984, 31-46.* ABST: Following the empiric example of sports associations in the Federal Republic of Germany, those structural changes are analyzed which a voluntary (associative) organization undergoes when its function changes. When an organization having a 'democratic-cooperative' basis, such as the Deutsche Sportbund (DSB), assumes quasi-public functions, its internal structure is changed. This, in addition to the existing honorary and 'democratic' elements, leads to a new hierarchical order of professional functionaries with completely new recruiting procedures and an extension of their decision-making and management functions. LEVEL: A LANG: Eng SIRC ARTICLE NO: 103822

PERSONNEL MANAGEMENT

Boucher, R.L. The psychology of making sound hiring decisions. (Refs: 19)*NIRSA journal (Corvallis, Ore.) 8(3), Spring 1984, 18-23.* LEVEL: I LANG: Eng SIRC ARTICLE NO: 097401

Boucher, R.L. The utility of the preemployment interview: insights for sport administrators. (Refs: 25)*Physical educator (Indianapolis) 41(4), Dec 1984, 195-199.* LEVEL: B LANG: Eng SIRC ARTICLE NO: 103801

Cooper, W.E. The desired work environment and the professional. Human resource development in a time of economic crisis. (Refs: 9)*Journal of physical education, recreation & dance (Reston, Va.) 55(5), May/Jun 1984, 27-31.* LEVEL: I LANG: Eng SIRC ARTICLE NO: 094178

Kelly, T.W. Getting the right person for the right job: staffing for professionalism. (Refs: 6)*NIRSA journal (Corvallis, Ore.) 8(3), Spring 1984, 14-16.* LEVEL: B LANG: Eng SIRC ARTICLE NO: 097408

Kelly, T.W. Evaluating staff performance: cure or curse? (Refs: 8)*In, Vendl, B.C. (ed.) et al., Interpretive aspects of intramural-recreational sports: selected proceedings from the Thirty-fifth Annual National Intramural-Recreational Sports Association Conference, Corvallis, Or., Oregon State University, c1984, p. 134-140.* CONF: National Intramural-Recreational Sports Association Conference (35th : 1984 : Fort Worth, Tex.). LEVEL: B LANG: Eng GV710 18914

PLANNING

Meyer, D. Norman, R. Avey, C. The basics of program planning. Program planning for sports and recreation groups. North Bay, Ont.: Northeastern Ontario Regional Sports Committee : Ministry of Tourism and Recreation, 1984. ii, 25 p. (Sport and recreation resource series for community groups; v.5.)

CORP: Northeastern Ontario Regional Sports Committee.
CORP: Ontario. Ministry of Tourism and Recreation. Field Services Office.
LEVEL: B LANG: Eng GV181.5 19018

POLICY

Kent, J. Strachan, D. Grandir dans le sport: un guide pour l'elaboration d'une perspective de developpement dans le sport. Ottawa: Condition physique et Sport amateur, 1984. vi, 105 feuillets
CORP: Canada. Condition physique et Sport amateur.
CORP: Canada. Fitness and Amateur Sport.
NOTES: Also published in English under the title: Growing in sport: a handbook for creating a sport development perspective. Bibliographie: feuillets 104-105. Comprend aussi: Modele de perfectionnement par etapes des volleyeurs, par Lorne Sawula et Terry Valeriote.
LEVEL: I LANG: Fr GV713 17283

Kent, J. Strachan, D. Growing in sport: a handbook for creating a sport development perspective. Ottawa: Fitness and Amateur Sport, 1984. vi, 99 leaves
CORP: Canada. Fitness and Amateur Sport.
CORP: Canada. Condition physique et Sport amateur.
NOTES: Egalement publie en francais sous le titre: Grandir dans le sport: un guide pour l'elaboration d'une perspective de developpement dans le sport. Bibliography: leaves 98-99. Includes: Volleyball development model, 2nd ed., by Lorne Sawula and Terry Valeriote, and Fair play codes for children in sport, by the National Task Force on Children's Play.
LEVEL: I LANG: Eng GV713 17282

White, A.G. Public administration, policy, and sports - franchise movement: a selected bibliography. Monticello, Ill.: Vance Bibliographies, 1984. 5 p. (Pub. admin. series; bibliography P1522.)
NOTES: ISSN: 0193-970X.
LEVEL: B LANG: Eng ISBN: 0-89028-102-5 GV713 18440

White, A.G. Public administration, policy, and sports - television and professional sports: a selected bibliography. Monticello, Ill.: Vance Bibliographies, 1984. 9 p. (Pub. admin. series; bibliography P1523.)
NOTES: ISSN: 0193-970X.
LEVEL: B LANG: Eng ISBN: 0-89028-103-3 GV713 18432

PROFESSIONAL DEVELOPMENT

Bauza, W.P. Values of field experiences. In, Zanger, B.K. and Parks, J.B. (eds.), Sport management curricula: the business and education nexus, Bowling Green, Ohio, Bowling Green State University, 1984, p. 93-94.
CONF: Bowling Green State University Sport Management Curriculum Symposium (1983 : Bowling Green, Ohio).
LEVEL: B LANG: Eng GV713 20087

Birk, T.J. Sport management field experiences with the Center for Health Promotion at Riverside Hospital. In, Zanger, B.K. and Parks, J.B. (eds.), Sport management curricula: the business and education nexus, Bowling Green, Ohio, Bowling Green State University, 1984, p. 89-90.

CONF: Bowling Green State University Sport Management Curriculum Symposium (1983 : Bowling Green, Ohio).
LEVEL: B LANG: Eng GV713 20087

Carey, D.M. Developing and training recreational sports staff through a retreat experience. NIRSA journal (Corvallis, Ore.) 8(3), Spring 1984, 27.
LEVEL: B LANG: Eng SIRC ARTICLE NO: 097402

DeSensi, J.T. What does academe need from business/agencies? Adjunct faculty. (Refs: 7)In, Zanger, B.K. and Parks, J.B. (eds.), Sport management curricula: the business and education nexus, Bowling Green, Ohio, Bowling Green State University, 1984, p. 36-41.
CONF: Bowling Green State University Sport Management Curriculum Symposium (1983 : Bowling Green, Ohio).
LEVEL: I LANG: Eng GV713 20087

Flynn, R.B. What does academe need from business/agencies? Advisory boards and beyond. (Refs: 29)In, Zanger, B.K. and Parks J.B. (eds.), Sport management curricula: the business and education nexus, Bowling Green, Ohio, Bowling Green State University, 1984, p. 42-49.
CONF: Bowling Green State University Sport Management Curriculum Symposium (1983 : Bowling Green, Ohio).
LEVEL: I LANG: Eng GV713 20087

Gregory, J. Coordinating the selection and assignment procedure for field experience student. In, Zanger, B.K. and Parks, J.B. (eds.), Sport management curricula: the business and education nexus, Bowling Green, Ohio, Bowling Green State University, 1984, p. 84-85.
CONF: Bowling Green State University Sport Management Curriculum Symposium (1983 : Bowling Green, Ohio).
LEVEL: B LANG: Eng GV713 20087

Hager, S.A. Curricular questions confronting sport management. A summary. In, Zanger, B.K. and Parks, J.B. (eds.), Sport management curricula: the business and education nexus, Bowling Green, Ohio, Bowling Green State University, 1984, p. 118-120.
CONF: Bowling Green State University Sport Management Curriculum Symposium (1983 : Bowling Green, Ohio).
LEVEL: B LANG: Eng GV713 20087

Kirbus, R.A. Sport management field experiences with Riverview Racquet Club. In, Zanger, B.K. and Parks, J.B. (eds.), Sport management curricula: the business and education nexus, Bowling Green, Ohio, Bowling Green State University, 1984, p. 91-93.
CONF: Bowling Green State University Sport Management Curriculum Symposium (1983 : Bowling Green, Ohio).
LEVEL: B LANG: Eng GV713 20087

Miller, R. Sport management field experiences with the Detroit Tigers Baseball Club. In, Zanger, B.K. and Parks, J.B. (eds.), Sport management curricula: the business and education nexus, Bowling Green, Ohio, Bowling Green State University, 1984, p. 86-88.
CONF: Bowling Green State University Sport Management Curriculum Symposium (1983 : Bowling Green, Ohio).
LEVEL: B LANG: Eng GV713 20087

Mullin, B.J. A graduate curriculum in sport management: considerations before taking the big

plunge. (Refs: 7)In, Zanger, B.K. and Parks, J.B. (eds.), Sport management curricula: the business and education nexus, Bowling Green, Ohio, Bowling Green State University, 1984, p. 110-117.
CONF: Bowling Green State University Sport Management Curriculum Symposium (1983 : Bowling Green, Ohio).
LEVEL: I LANG: Eng GV713 20087

Quain, R.J. The REM statement. (Refs: 6)In, Zanger, B.K. and Parks, J.B. (eds.), Sport management curricula: the business and education nexus, Bowling Green, Ohio, Bowling Green State University, 1984, p. 71-75.
CONF: Bowling Green State University Sport Management Curriculum Symposium (1983 : Bowling Green, Ohio).
LEVEL: B LANG: Eng GV713 20087

Reed, C. Advice to undergraduates. In, Zanger, B.K. and Parks, J.B. (eds.), Sport management curricula: the business and education nexus, Bowling Green, Ohio, Bowling Green State University, 1984, p. 94.
CONF: Bowling Green State University Sport Management Curriculum Symposium (1983 : Bowling Green, Ohio).
LEVEL: B LANG: Eng GV713 20087

Sidwell, J. The sport management field experience profile at Bowling Green State University. In, Zanger, B.K. and Parks, J.B. (eds.), Sport management curricula: the business and education nexus, Bowling Green, Ohio, Bowling Green State University, 1984, p. 79-83.
CONF: Bowling Green State University Sport Management Curriculum Symposium (1983 : Bowling Green, Ohio).
LEVEL: I LANG: Eng GV713 20087

Stotlar, D.K. What does academe need from business/agencies? Sites. (Refs: 7)In, Zanger, B.K. and Parks, J.B. (eds.), Sport management curricula: the business and education nexus, Bowling Green, Ohio, Bowling Green State University, 1984, p. 50-52.
CONF: Bowling Green State University Sport Management Curriculum Symposium (1983 : Bowling Green, Ohio).
LEVEL: I LANG: Eng GV713 20087

Thorpe, R.D. Hazeldine, R. Bunker, D. Guidelines for short courses for the training of sports leaders. Nottingham: Sports Council, East Midland Region, 1984. 44 p.
CORP: Sports Council. East Midland Region.
LEVEL: B LANG: Eng GV713 17826

van der Smissen, B. A process for success: sport management curricula - an idea whose time has come. (Refs: 16)In, Zanger, B.K. and Parks, J.B. (eds.), Sport management curricula: the business and education nexus, Bowling Green, Ohio, Bowling Green State University, 1984, p. 5-18.
CONF: Bowling Green State University Sport Management Curriculum Symposium (1983 : Bowling Green, Ohio).
LEVEL: I LANG: Eng GV713 20087

Vogt, K.E. The power of education and business. In, Zanger, B.K. and Parks, J.B. (eds.), Sport management curricula: the business and education nexus, Bowling Green, Ohio, Bowling Green State University, 1984, p. 19-25.
CONF: Bowling Green State University Sport Management Curriculum Symposium (1983 : Bowling Green, Ohio).
LEVEL: I LANG: Eng GV713 20087

ADMINISTRATION (continued)

Washburn, J.R. What does academe need from business/agencies? Supervision: a participatory activity. *In, Zanger, B.K. and Parks, J.B. (eds.), Sport management curricula: the business and education nexus, Bowling Green, Ohio, Bowling Green State University, 1984, p. 53-57.*
CONF: Bowling Green State University Sport Management Curriculum Symposium (1983 : Bowling Green, Ohio).
LEVEL: I LANG: Eng GV713 20087

Zanger, B.K. Sport management curriculum model. School of Health, Physical Education and Recreation, Bowling Green State University. *In, Zanger, B.K. and Parks, J.B. (eds.), Sport management curricula: the business and education nexus, Bowling Green, Ohio, Bowling Green State University, 1984, p. 97-109.*
CONF: Bowling Green State University Sport Management Curriculum Symposium (1983 : Bowling Green, Ohio).
LEVEL: I LANG: Eng GV713 20087

PROMOTION

Jacobs, B. Use closed schools to develop extension sites. *Journal of physical education and program (Columbus, Oh.) 81(4), Apr 1984, D14-D15.*
LEVEL: B LANG: Eng SIRC ARTICLE NO: 094296

Promotion of physical education and sport. *ACHPER national journal (Kingswood, Aust.) 104, Winter 1984, 28-29.*
LEVEL: B LANG: Eng SIRC ARTICLE NO: 100844

ROLE AND RESPONSIBILITY

Ostro, H. The importance of being earnest - and a good role model. *Scholastic coach (New York) 53(10), May/Jun 1984, 6;8;10;12.*
LEVEL: B LANG: Eng SIRC ARTICLE NO: 094184

SALARIES

Rosen, M. The sport 100: our annual salary report. *Sport (New York) 75(3), Mar 1984, 25-28;30-32.*
LEVEL: B LANG: Eng SIRC ARTICLE NO: 094763

TOURNAMENTS AND COMPETITIONS

Calendrier des competitions internationales sportives avril/septembre 1984. Calendar of international sports competitions April/September 1984. Monte-Carlo: GAISF : AGFIS, 1984. 423 p.
CORP: Association generale des federations internationales de sports.
CORP: General Association of International Sports Federations.
NOTES: Titre de la couverture: Calendrier international du sport mondial avril/septembre 1984. Cover title: International calendar of world sports April/September 1984.
LEVEL: B LANG: Eng Fr GV721 18519

Calendrier international du sport mondial, octobre/mars 1984/1985. International calendar of world sports, October/March 1984-1985. Monte-Carlo: AGFIS : GAISF, 1984. 311 p.
CORP: Association generale des federations internationales de sports.
CORP: General Association of International Sports Federations.
LEVEL: B LANG: Eng Fr GV721 18476

Tournaments and competitions: a guide for tournament organisers. *Sports coach (Wembley, Aust.) 8(1), 1984, 40-42;62.*
LEVEL: LANG: Eng SIRC ARTICLE NO: 095707

VOLUNTEERS

Drowatzky, J. Marcal, H. Volunteers in sport for the disabled: a case study. *In, Ilmarinen, M. (ed.) et al., Sport and International Understanding: proceedings of the congress held in Helsinki, Finland, July 7-10, 1982, Berlin, Springer-Verlag, 1984, p. 271-274.*
CONF: Congress on Sport and International Understanding (1982 : Helsinki).
LEVEL: B LANG: Eng GV706.8 18979

Heinz, U.S. Slack, T. Glassford, R.G. A model for the effective use of volunteers in amateur sport organizations. (Refs: 7) *CAHPER journal/Revue de l'ACSEPR (Vanier, Ont.) 50(3), Jan/Feb 1984, 16-19.*
LEVEL: I LANG: Eng SIRC ARTICLE NO: 094180

Heinz, U.S. Slack, T. Glassford, R.G. A model for the effective use of volunteers in amateur sport organizations. (Refs: 7) *CAHPER journal/Revue de l'ACSEPR (Ottawa) 50(4), Mar/Apr 1984, 19-22.*
LEVEL: I LANG: Eng SIRC ARTICLE NO: 095703

Imlay, G. YMCA volunteers: the endangered species. *Journal of physical education and program (Columbus, Oh.) 81(4), Apr 1984, D8-D9.*
LEVEL: B LANG: Eng SIRC ARTICLE NO: 094181

Remans, A. Le travail volontaire dans le sport. *Sport: Communaute francaise de Belgique (Bruxelles) 106, 1984, 106-110.*
LEVEL: B LANG: Fr SIRC ARTICLE NO: 097415

AEROBIC DANCE

Buchanan, L.K. Fitaerobics: a young sport is growing up. The showcase of aerobic dance is following in the footsteps of competitive figure skating - from pastime to prime time. *Runner's world presents (Mountain View, Calif.) 3, Jul 1984, 2-5.*
NOTES: Special issue: Fitaerobics.
LEVEL: B LANG: Eng SIRC ARTICLE NO: 105781

Grau, J. Guidelines: 17 questions to ask yourself before you sign up for your next class. *Shape (Woodland Hills, Calif.) 4(1), Sept 1984, 48-49.*
LEVEL: B LANG: Eng SIRC ARTICLE NO: 101197

Hills, S. Aerobics: are you making the right moves? *Canadian living (Toronto) 9(9), 8 Oct 1984, 86-87;89-90;93.*
LEVEL: B LANG: Eng SIRC ARTICLE NO: 108079

Rychlick, M. Aerobic dance... as a competitive sport. *Body talk (Springfield Gardens, N.Y.) 1, Spring 1984, 24-25.*
LEVEL: LANG: Eng SIRC ARTICLE NO: 102190

CERTIFICATION

Grau, J. Certification - how an industry is attempting to regulate itself. *Shape (Woodland Hills, Calif.) 4(1), Sept 1984, 74-75;143-145.*
LEVEL: B LANG: Eng SIRC ARTICLE NO: 101198

CLOTHING

Aerobic shoe update. *Fitness industry (Miami, Fl.) 2(7), Nov/Dec 1984, 50-51;56.*
LEVEL: B LANG: Eng SIRC ARTICLE NO: 102398

Califano, R. Davis, K. Shoes do more than just coddle your feet - select yours carefully. *Shape (Woodland Hills, Calif.) 4(1), Sept 1984, 52-53;145-146.*
LEVEL: B LANG: Eng SIRC ARTICLE NO: 101194

Feigel, W. Dancing feet. To step to the beat, you need to outfit your feet. *Runner's world presents (Mountain View, Calif.) 3, Jul 1984, 44-47.*
NOTES: Special issue: Fitaerobics.
LEVEL: B LANG: Eng SIRC ARTICLE NO: 105784

Let's dance: our second annual aerobic shoe survey takes the guesswork out of buying shoes. *Fit (Mountain View, Calif.) 4(4), 50;56-60;103-104.*
LEVEL: B LANG: ENG SIRC ARTICLE NO: 108553

INJURIES AND ACCIDENTS

Buickel, S. First aid to help you bounce back from injuries safely and quickly. *Shape (Woodland Hills, Calif.) 4(1), Sept 1984, 66-67;143.*
LEVEL: B LANG: Eng SIRC ARTICLE NO: 101193

Francis, L.L. Cautions: follow these safeguards to make your workouts injury and pain free. *Shape (Woodland Hills, Calif.) 4(1), Sept 1984, 64-65.*
LEVEL: B LANG: Eng SIRC ARTICLE NO: 101196

Kerr, K.A. Aerobic dance: a consumer's guide. *Journal of physical education, recreation & dance 55(2), Feb 1984, 50-51.*
LEVEL: B LANG: Eng SIRC ARTICLE NO: 092032

Linden, S. How to avoid aerobic injury. *Slimmer (Santa Monica, Calif.) 4(2), Apr 1984, 56-58;60-61.*
LEVEL: B LANG: Eng SIRC ARTICLE NO: 101203

Read, M.T.F. Runner's stress fracture produced by an aerobic dance routine. Case report. (Refs: 6)*British journal of sports medicine (Loughborough, Eng.) 18(1), Mar 1984, 40-41.*
LEVEL: I LANG: Eng SIRC ARTICLE NO: 096629

PHYSICAL FITNESS

Johnson, S. Berg, K. Latin, R. The effect of training frequency of aerobic dance on oxygen uptake, body composition and personality. (Refs: 50)*Journal of sports medicine and physical fitness (Torino, Italy) 24(4), Dec 1984, 290-298.*
ABST: The purpose of this investigation was to compare the effect of two training frequencies of aerobic dance on oxygen uptake, body composition, and personality. Subjects were 23 sedentary female students (ages 18-31 yrs) enrolled in two aerobic dance classes. Subjects trained at 70 percent of max HR for 30 min in week 1 and progressed to 90 min in week 13. One group trained twice weekly (2X) while the other group trained three times weekly (3X). It appears that aerobic dance performed two or three times weekly is effective in producing change in cardiorespiratory fitness and body composition when appropriate levels of intensity and duration are used. Furthermore, with the intensity and duration used, exercise frequencies of two and three weekly produce similar changes in these variables. Lastly, aerobic dance training results in favorable personality changes.
LEVEL: A LANG: Eng SIRC ARTICLE NO: 107152

Pool, J. Reflections on the bounce. Danser pour la forme? *CAHPER journal (Ottawa) 51(2), Nov/Dec 1984, 28-31.*
LEVEL: B LANG: Eng Fr SIRC ARTICLE NO: 102738

Stamford, B. Aerobic dance: good for fitness? *Physician and sportsmedicine 12(4), Apr 1984, 172.*
LEVEL: B LANG: Eng SIRC ARTICLE NO: 093386

Watterson, V.V. The effects of aerobic dance on cardiovascular fitness. (Refs: 11)*Physician and sportsmedicine (Minneapolis Minn.) 12(10), Oct 1984, 138-141;144-145.*
ABST: Body weight, resting and working heart rates, blood pressure, and distance covered on Cooper's 12-minute field performance test of 16 women were determined prior and following a 60-minute dance session three days a week for six weeks. This study concluded that aerobic dance training can improve cardiovascular fitness.
LEVEL: A LANG: Eng SIRC ARTICLE NO: 099525

PHYSIOLOGY

Clearly, M.L. Moffatt, R.J. Knutzen, K.M. The effects of two-and three-day-per-week aerobic dance programs on maximal oxygen uptake. (Refs: 11)*Research quarterly for exercise & sport (Reston, Va.) 55(2), Jun 1984, 172-174.*
ABST: This investigation determined the effect of a two- and three-day-per week aerobic dance program on the maximal oxygen uptake (VO2 max) of 18 college women. The women in the three-day-per week classes increased their VO2 max by 10%. The women in the two-day-per week classes did not increase their VO2 max significantly. These results suggest that aerobic dance classes should be held three days per week in order to obtain an increase in VO2 max of the participants.
LEVEL: A LANG: Eng SIRC ARTICLE NO: 096616

Deroanne, R. Mathy, J. Lognay, F. Schmitz, V. Evolution de la frequence cardiaque au cours de la seance d''aerobic'. *Revue de l'education physique (Liege, Belgique) 24(4), 1984, 39-44.*
LEVEL: A LANG: Fr SIRC ARTICLE NO: 104660

Hooper, P.L. Noland, B.J. Aerobic dance program improves cardiovascular fitness in men. (Refs: 4)*Physician and sportsmedicine (Minneapolis, Minn.), 12(5), May 1984, 132-135.*
LEVEL: I LANG: Eng SIRC ARTICLE NO: 094959

Rose, M.E. The caloric expenditure of aerobic dance. Eugene, Ore.: Microform Publications, University of Oregon, 1984. 1 microfiche : negative ; 11 x 15 cm.
NOTES: Thesis (M.S.) - Brigham Young University, 1982; (v, 47 leaves); includes bibliography.
LEVEL: A LANG: Eng UO84 272

White, M.K. Yeater, R.A. Martin, R.B. Rosenberg, B.S. Sherwood, L. Weber, K.C. Della-Giustina, D.E. Effects of aerobic dancing and walking on cardiovascular function and muscular strength in postmenopausal women. (Refs: 21)*Journal of sports medicine and physical fitness (Torino, Italy) 24(2), Jun 1984, 159-166.*
ABST: The effects of a six month aerobic dancing and walking program were examined in 51 postmenopausal women. A treadmill test to a heart rate of 145 bpm was used to assess changes in cardiovascular fitness. Analysis of variance indicated that both groups showed significant increases in treadmill time and work accomplished

while showing decreases in resting heart rate, rate-pressure products and recovery heart rates. The only significant group X test interaction occurred with heart rate during the third minute of recovery, where the members of the dancing group showed a 5% decrease while the walking group remained unchanged. ANOVAs indicated that significant increases occurred in knee extension and ankle plantar flexion strength. A significant group X test interaction for ankle plantar flexion indicated that greater improvement occurred in the walkers. On the other hand, the dancers showed greater improvement in elbow flexion strength (5% dancers, 2% walkers).
LEVEL: A LANG: Eng SIRC ARTICLE NO: 102751

PHYSIOLOGY - MUSCLE

Lucas, R.C. Koslow, R. Comparative study of static, dynamic, and proprioceptive neuromuscular facilitation stretching techniques on flexibility. (Refs: 8)*Perceptual and motor skills (Missoula, Mont.) 58(2), Apr 1984, 615-618.*
ABST: This report evaluates the effects of static, dynamic, and proprioceptive neuromuscular facilitating stretching techniques on the flexibility of the hamstring-gastrocnemius muscles. 63 college women enrolled in aerobic dance classes served as subjects. Pretest and posttest mean scores indicated significant improvements using all 3 methods of flexibility training.
LEVEL: A LANG: Eng SIRC ARTICLE NO: 094963

PSYCHOLOGY

Dielens, S. Narcissisme et activites physiques a la mode. Profil psychologique des pratiquants d'aerobic, de jogging et de bodybuilding. (Refs: 13)*Revue de l'education physique (Liege, Belgique) 24(1), 1984, 21-24.*
LEVEL: I LANG: Fr SIRC ARTICLE NO: 096321

TEACHING

Fenley, L. Dance-exercise guidelines planned. *Physician and sportsmedicine (Minneapolis, Minn.) 12(9), Sept 1984, 31-32.*
LEVEL: B LANG: Eng SIRC ARTICLE NO: 099517

Kramer, D. Dance is physical education too. (Refs: 2)*Journal of physical education, recreation & dance (Reston, Va.) 55(6), Aug 1984, 30-31;52.*
LEVEL: B LANG: Eng SIRC ARTICLE NO: 098038

Patano, P. Savage, L. Aerobics instruction: more than just a song and dance. *Fit (Mountain View, Calif.) 3(11), Apr 1984, 56-58;90.*
NOTES: Part 111 of a three-part series.
LEVEL: B LANG: Eng SIRC ARTICLE NO: 099521

Patano, P. Savage, L. Aerobics instruction: more than just a song and dance. *Fit (Mountain View, Calif.) 3(9), Feb 1984, 38-39;71-72.*
NOTES: Part 1 of a three-part series.
LEVEL: B LANG: Eng SIRC ARTICLE NO: 099522

TECHNIQUES AND SKILLS

Herman, S. Aerobic dance is a new competitive sport that you can enter and win. *Shape (Woodland Hills, Calif.) 4(1), Sept 1984, 70-71;146-147.*
LEVEL: B LANG: Eng SIRC ARTICLE NO: 101201

Kravitz, L. Creating a world-class routine. A fitaerobics champ tells you which moves set you apart from the rest. *Runner's world presents*

(Mountain View, Calif.) 3, Jul 1984, 62-65.
NOTES: Special issue: Fitaerobics.
LEVEL: B LANG: Eng SIRC ARTICLE NO: 105788

Patano, P. Savage, L. Aerobics instruction: more than just a song and dance. *Fit (Mountain View, Calif.) 3(10), Mar 1984, 28-29;77.*
NOTES: Part 11 of a three-part series.
LEVEL: B LANG: Eng SIRC ARTICLE NO: 099523

Theme and variation: the compulsory moves. Two accomplished fitaerobics competitors give you tips on how to put jazz in your jumping jack, quickness in your kick and spunk in your sit-up. *Runner's world presents (Mountain View, Calif.) 3, Jul 1984, 12-19.*
NOTES: Special issue: Fitaerobics.
LEVEL: B LANG: Eng SIRC ARTICLE NO: 105792

Weaver, G. Making fitness a career. *Fit (Mountain View, Calif.) 3(10), Mar 1984, 42-43;90-91.*
LEVEL: B LANG: Eng SIRC ARTICLE NO: 099526

Yessis, M. Don't do it wrong when you can do it right with these directions. *Shape (Woodland Hills, Calif.) 4(1), Sept 1984 56-63.*
LEVEL: B LANG: Eng SIRC ARTICLE NO: 101209

TRAINING AND CONDITIONING

Dayton, L. Training to win: stretching routine, strength training. Any athlete knows: it's not the spotlight that makes the star but the long hours of sweat and hard work. Make those long hours count, with a training program designed to bring out your best. *Runner's world presents (Mountain View, Calif.) 3, Jul 1984, 28-32.*
NOTES: Special issue: Fitaerobics.
LEVEL: B LANG: Eng SIRC ARTICLE NO: 105783

Getting up your degree of difficulty. Difficult moves put the polish on your routine - play your cards right and practice up. *Runner's world presents (Mountain View, Calif.) 3, Jul 1984, 20-27.*
NOTES: Special issue: Fitaerobics.
LEVEL: B LANG: Eng SIRC ARTICLE NO: 105786

Griffith, B.R. Davis, K. Using these seven easy steps, you can design your own aerobic-dance routines. *Shape (Woodland Hills, Calif.) 4(1), Sept 1984, 50-51;147.*
LEVEL: B LANG: Eng SIRC ARTICLE NO: 101199

Marsden, V. Upper body boogie. *Fitness leader (Ottawa) 2(8), Apr 1984, 15-16.*
LEVEL: B LANG: Eng SIRC ARTICLE NO: 100869

Strachan, D. Aerobic rhythmics: jump-kick. *Fitness leader (Ottawa) 2(9), May 1984, 17-18.*
LEVEL: B LANG: Eng SIRC ARTICLE NO: 100877

Strachan, D. Aerobic rhythmics: arm tease. *Fitness leader (Ottawa) 2(8), Apr 1984, 15-16.*
LEVEL: B LANG: Eng SIRC ARTICLE NO: 100878

Strachan, D. Let's dance: hands up. *Fitness leader (Ottawa) 2(8), Apr 1984, 15-16.*
LEVEL: B LANG: Eng SIRC ARTICLE NO: 100879

WOMEN

Lenskyj, H. Kidd, B. Selling sexercise. *Mudpie Dec 1984, 17.*
LEVEL: B LANG: Eng SIRC ARTICLE NO: 183317

White, M.K. The effects of walking and aerobic dancing on the skeletal and cardiovascular systems of post-menopausal females Eugene, Ore.: Microform Publications, University of Oregon, 1984. 2 microfiches : negative, ill. ; 11 x 15 cm.

AEROBIC DANCE (continued)

NOTES: Thesis (Ed.D.) - West Virginia University, 1981; (x, 156 leaves); vita; includes bibliography.
LEVEL: A LANG: Eng UO84 195-196

White, M.K. Martin, R.B. Yeater, R.A. Butcher, R.L. Radin, E.L. The effects of exercise on the bones of postmenopausal women (Refs: 36)*International orthopaedics (New York) 7(4), 1984, 209-214.*
ABST: The effects of walking and aerobic dancing on the bones of 73 recently postmenopausal women have been compared with a control group who did not exercise. The period of observation was six months. Results showed that the control group and the walking group lost statistically significant amounts of bone mineral content (1.6 per cent, and 1.7 per cent respectively), but that the dancing group did not (0.8 per cent). The control group did not show a significant increase in the bone width (0.9 per cent), but both the dancing (1.3 per cent) and walking (1.6 per cent) groups did.
LEVEL: A LANG: Eng SIRC ARTICLE NO: 104529

AERONAUTICAL SPORTS

EQUIPMENT

A collection of technical papers. AIAA 8th Aerodynamic Decelerator and Balloon Technology Conference, April 2-4, 1984/Hyannis, Massachusetts. New York: American Institute of Aeronautics and Astronautics, 1984. 266 p. : ill.
CONF: Aerodynamic Decelerator and Balloon Technology Conference (8th : 1984 : Hyannis, Mass.).
CORP: American Institute of Aeronautics and Astronautics.
NOTES: ISSN 0146-3705.
LEVEL: A LANG: Eng

AFRICA

Ajisafe, M.O. Co-operation between developing countries and advanced countries in respect of sport. (Refs: 4)*In, Ilmarinen, M. (ed.) et al., Sport and international Understanding: proceedings of the congress held in Helsinki, Finland, July 7-10, 1982, Berlin, Springer-Verlag, 1984, p. 298-303.*
CONF: Congress on Sport and International Understanding (1982 : Helsinki).
LEVEL: I LANG: Eng GV706.8 18979

AGE GROUP SWIMMING

CHILDREN

Christie, I. Children in competitive swimming - effects of hard physical training. (Refs: 38)*Physical educator (Indianapolis, Ind.) 3(41), Oct 1984, 121-129.*
ABST: The author reviews the literature on the anthropometric, physiological, structural and psychological aspects of children and adolescents participating in competitive swimming. Implications for training are discussed.
LEVEL: A LANG: Eng SIRC ARTICLE NO: 101544

COACHING

Holmes, T. Dream and reality. *Swim Canada (Toronto) 11(4), Apr 1984, 18-19.*
LEVEL: B LANG: Eng SIRC ARTICLE NO: 095304

Leonard, J. Parent, coach and athlete. A handbook for age group swimming parents. s.l.: s.n., 1984. 1 v.
LEVEL: B LANG: Eng GV838.53.A44 20735

PSYCHOLOGY

Cracklen, C. Martin, G.L. Earning fun with correct techniques: doling out fun indiscriminately might not be as effective as having kids learn to earn it. (Refs: 12)*Swimming technique (Los Angeles, Calif.) 20(3), Nov 1983/Jan 1984, 29-30;32.*
LEVEL: I LANG: Eng SIRC ARTICLE NO: 095290

Watson, G.G. Blanksby, B.A. Bloomfield, J. Reward systems in childrens sport - perceptions and evaluations of elite junior swimmers. (Refs: 35)*Journal of human movement studies (Edinburgh) 10(3), 1984, 123-156.*
LEVEL: A LANG: Eng SIRC ARTICLE NO: 098546

AGED

Activite physique, sport et vieillissement. *Lyon mediterranee medical (Lyon) 20(14), 1984, 9333-9338;9340-9344.*
CONF: Colloque de geriatrie (11e : 1983 : Lyon).
LEVEL: I LANG: Fr SIRC ARTICLE NO: 171190

Danigelis, N.L. Sport and the disabled elderly. (Refs: 27)*Arena review 8(1), Mar 1984, 68-79.*
NOTES: Special issue: spor and disability.
LEVEL: I LANG: Eng SIRC ARTICLE NO: 103712

De Vries, H.A. Drinkwater, B.L. Fox, S.M. Nicholas, J.A. Smith, E.L. L'exercice peut retarder le vieillissement. Quels sont les sports qui conviennent aux personnes agees? (Refs: 6)*Gazette medicale (Paris) 91(34), 1984, 83-84;87-88;91.*
LEVEL: I LANG: Fr SIRC ARTICLE NO: 171189

Larsson, B. Renstroem, P. Svaerdsudd, K. Welin, L. Grimby, G. Eriksson, H. Ohlson, L.O. Wilhelmsen, L. Bjoerntorp, P. Health and ageing characteristics of highly physically active 65-year-old men. (Refs: 5)*European heart journal (London) 5(Suppl E), Nov 1984, 31-35.*
ABST: A comparative study between 80 highly physically active 65-year-old men and controls in the same age group was the focus of this study. The well-trained subjects were characterized by low body fat, good health, lower plasma insulin, blood pressure, resting heart rate and ventilatory capacity than the controls.
LEVEL: A LANG: Eng SIRC ARTICLE NO: 109718

Strovas, J. Seniors walk away from sedentary life. *Physician and sportsmedicine 12(4), Apr 1984, 144-148;152.*
LEVEL: B LANG: Eng SIRC ARTICLE NO: 093236

PHYSICAL FITNESS

An annotated bibliography. 1983 update. Bibliographie annotee. Revisee 1983. Ottawa: Fitness and Amateur Sport : Condition physique et Sport amateur, 1984?. 33 p.
CORP: Canada. Fitness and Amateur Sport.

CORP: Canada. Condition physique et Sport amateur.
CORP: Secretariat for Fitness in the Third Age.
CORP: Secretariat pour la condition physique du troisieme age.
NOTES: Cover title. Titre de la couverture.
LEVEL: B LANG: Eng Fr GV482.6 20854

Biegel, L. Fitness: who, what, and why. (Refs: 16)
NOTES: In, Biegel, L. (ed.), Physical fitness and the older person: a guide to exercise for health care professionals, Rockville, Md., Aspen Systems Corp., 1984, p. 1-12.
LEVEL: I LANG: Eng GV482.6 17754

Bruynen, J. Physical education and the older adult. (Refs: 12)*Unpublished paper, Physical Education Graduating Seminar Conference, Australia, 1984, 1-6.*
CONF: Physical Education Graduating Seminar Conference (1984 : Footscray Institute of Technology).
LEVEL: B LANG: Eng SIRC ARTICLE NO: 096128

DiGilio, D.A. Howze, E.H. Fitness and full living for older adults. *Parks & recreation (Alexandria, Va.) 19(12), Dec 1984, 32-37;66.*
LEVEL: B LANG: Eng SIRC ARTICLE NO: 173248

Gauthier, P. L'activite physique et le vieillissement. *Kino-nouvelles (Quebec) 6(4), oct 1984, 4-5.*
LEVEL: I LANG: Fr SIR ARTICLE NO: 100857

Haber, P. Hoeniger, B. Klicpera, M. Niederberger, M. Ergebnisse eines 3monatigen Ausdauertrainings auf einem Fahrradergomete bei alten Menschen zwischen 67 und 76 Jahren. (Results of 3 months' endurance training on a bicycle ergometer in people between 67 and 76.) *Acta medica austriaca (Vienna) 11(3/4), 1984, 107-111.*
ABST: 8 healthy women and 4 men with a mean age 71.1 years, took part in a bicycle ergometer training, 3 times a week, for 12 weeks. In order to hold the training heart rate (HR) at the constant level of 60 per cent of maximum, the work load had to be increased systematically during the whole training period up to 180 per cent of the level at the beginning. The working time in each training session was increased from 2 x 10 minutes in the beginning up to 2 x 20 minutes from the 7th week on. The maximum work load and the maximum oxygen uptake increased significantly. The submaximal HR decreased significantly. This study concludes that in healthy people between 67-76 years a significant endurance effect is possible when the training is systematically increased in work load and working time.
LEVEL: A LANG: Ger

Harris, I. McCulloch, B. O'Neill, K. Aging in action. *Fitness leader (Ottawa) 3(4), Dec 1984, 13-16.*
LEVEL: B LANG: Eng SIRC ARTICLE NO: 105438

Heitmann, H.M. Status of older adult physical activity programs in Illinois. (Refs: 13)*Physical educator (Indianapolis, Ind.) 41(1), Mar 1984, 35-39.*
LEVEL: I LANG: Eng SIRC ARTICLE NO: 096191

La sante, les facteurs psychologiques et sociologiques. Bibliographie annotee. Health, psychological and social factors. An annotated bibliography. Vanier, Ont.: Secretariat for Fitness in the Third Age : Secretariat pour la condition physique du troisieme age, 1984. 24 p.
CORP: Secretariat for Fitness in the Third Age.

CORP: Secretariat pour la condition physique du troisieme age.
CORP: Canada. Fitness and Amateur Sport.
CORP: Canada. Condition physique et Sport amateur.
LEVEL: B LANG: Eng Fr ISBN: 0-919963-23-4 GV482.6 18730

Loennerblad, L. Exercises to promote independent living in older patients. *Geriatrics (New York) 39(2), Feb 1984, 93-101.*
LEVEL: B LANG: Eng

Macheath, J.A. Activity, health and fitness in old age. London ; New York: Croom Helm : St. Martin's Press, c1984. xx, 179 p
NOTES: Includes index. Bibliography: p. 139-152.
LEVEL: I LANG: Eng ISBN: 0-7099-1783-X LC CARD: 83-040128 GV482.6 17087

Meusel, H. Developing physical fitness through sports and exercise in the elderly. (Refs: 19)*International journal of physical education (Schorndorf, W. Germany) 21(1), 1984, 30-37.*
NOTES: Lecture on the 11th Annual Fitness, After Fifty Workshop Conference at the Center for the Study of Aging, Albany, N.Y., September 30-October 2, 1983.
LEVEL: I LANG: Eng SIRC ARTICLE NO: 093055

Meusel, H. Developing physical fitness for the elderly through sport and exercise. (Refs: 19)*British journal of sports medicine (Loughborough, Leicestershire) 18(1), Mar 1984, 4-12.*
CONF: Annual Fitness After Fifty Workshop Conference (11th : 1983 : Albany, N.Y.).
ABST: Physical activity is necessary to maintain and develop the motor ability and fitness of elderly people. However, this physical activity must be varied in order to develop an overall improvement of physical performance. The purpose of such a program should be to maintain the mobility and well-being of the elderly so that they can maintain their independence and satisfaction with life.
LEVEL: I LANG: Eng SIRC ARTICLE NO: 096193

Millar, A.P. Exercise for the elderly. (Refs: 4)*Australian family physician (Sydney) 13(8), Aug 1984, 592-593.*
LEVEL: I LANG: Eng SIRC ARTICLE NO: 173994

Miyoshi, H. (Physical training at a home for the aged. 3. The meaning of the 'life' for the aged.) *Kangogaku zasshi/Japanes journal of nursing (Tokyo) 48(7), Jul 1984, 813-816.*
LEVEL: B LANG: Jpn

Ogijima, H. Kondo, M. (Questions and answers on rehabilitation. 3. Activities for the aged to avoid the bedridden state.) *Kangogaku zasshi. Japanese journal of nursing (Tokyo) 48(6), Jun 1984, 697-700.*
LEVEL: B LANG: Jpn

Ostrow, A.C. Physical activity and the older adult; psychological perspectives. Princeton, N.J.: Princeton Book Co., c1984. xiii, 175 p
NOTES: Includes indexes and bibliographies.
LEVEL: A LANG: Eng ISBN: 0916622282 LC CARD: 83-063191 GV482.6 18993

Physical activity: annotated bibliography. Activite physique: bibliographie annotee. Ottawa: Secretariat for Fitness in the Third Age : Secretariat pour la condition physique du troisieme age, 1984. 28 p.
CORP: Secretariat for Fitness in the Third Age.
CORP: Secretariat pour la condition physique du troisieme age.

LEVEL: B LANG: Eng Fr ISBN: 0919963-20-X GV482.6 18463

Pirani, A. Neri, M. Belloi, L. Dinelli, M. Vecchi, G.P. Do mental and physical performances have different patterns in elderly? (Refs: 25)*Journal of sports medicine and physical fitness (Torino, Italy) 24(4), Dec 1984, 303-306.*
ABST: The goal of this study was to assess the importance of age, sex and physical fitness - separately and concurrently - in determining modifications of cognitive, psychomotor and emotional faculties in the elderly. The sample consisted of 126 male and female subjects (mean age: 67.3 years). Every subject underwent a scaled bicycle ergometer test (calibrated at 120 P.W.C.) for measuring physical fitness, and a battery of psycho-cognitive tests for measuring cognitive, emotional and psychomotor performance. The results show that: age influences cognitive performance; sex is a determining factor for a good preservation of emotional equilibrium; there is a clear separation between physical fitness and cognitive performance, but there is also a correlation between physical fitness and psychiatric disorders.
LEVEL: A LANG: Eng SIRC ARTICLE NO: 106736

Research and studies: an annotated bibliography. Recherche et communique: bibliographie annotee. Vanier, Ont.: Secretariat for Fitness in the Third Age : Secretariat pour la condition physique du troisieme age, 1984. 23 p.
CORP: Secretariat for Fitness in the Third Age.
CORP: Secretariat pour la condition physique du troisieme age.
LEVEL: A LANG: Eng Fr ISBN: 0-919963-20-X GV482.6 18462

Rockwell, R.E. Osborne, N.E. de Haas, E. Fitness and nutrition for seniors. Springfield, Ill.: Charles C. Thomas, c1984. ix, 153 p. : ill.
NOTES: Includes index. Includes bibliographical references.
LEVEL: B LANG: Eng ISBN: 0398049483 LC CARD: 83-018114 GV482.6 17995

Shephard, R.J. Physical activity for the senior: a role for pool exercises? (Refs: 33)*CAHPER journal/Revue de l'ACSEPR (Ottawa) 50(6), Jul/Aug 1984, 2-5;20.*
LEVEL: I LANG: Eng SIRC ARTICLE NO: 099206

Shephard, R.J. Management of exercise in the elderly. (Refs: 105)*Canadian journal of applied sport sciences/Journal canadie des sciences appliquees au sport (Windsor, Ont.) 9(3), Sept 1984, 109-120.*
ABST: The principles of exercise management in the elderly are reviewed from the standpoint of the practising physician. The fitness needs of the older individual are defined, and practical methods of assessment are suggested for both the healthy and the partially disabled senior citizen. The exercise prescription must include an adequate warm up and warm down. As condition permits, the aerobic component should be extended to 30 minutes of activity at 60% or more of maximum oxygen intake.
LEVEL: A LANG: Eng SIRC ARTICLE NO: 102745

Staples, M. I was tired of living scared. (interview) *Journal of gerontology nursing (Thorofare, N.J.) 10(7), Jul 1984, 38-39.*
LEVEL: B LANG: Eng SIRC ARTICLE NO: 104266

Thornton, E.W. Exercise and ageing: an unproven relationship. Liverpool: Liverpool University Press, c1984. ii, 31 p.
NOTES: Bibliography: p. 27-31.

LEVEL: I LANG: Eng ISBN: 0-85323-055-2 GV482.6 19048

Thornton, J.E. Collins, J.B. Patterns of leisure and physical activities in older adults: reasons, attitudes and meanings. Vancouver: University of British Columbia, 1984. 54 leaves
NOTES: This research was supported by a grant from Fitness and Amateur Sport, Canada, 7259-2. Bibliography: leaves 51-54.
LEVEL: A LANG: Eng GV184 17363

Vallbona, C. Baker, S.B. Physical fitness prospects in the elderly. (Refs: 47)*Archives of physical medicine and rehabilitation 65(4), Apr 1984, 194-200.*
LEVEL: I LANG: Eng SIRC ARTICLE NO: 093062

PHYSICAL FITNESS - PROGRAMS

Biegel, L. Physical fitness and the older person: a guide to exercise for health care professionals. Rockville, Md.: Aspen Systems Corp., 1984. xi, 165 p.
NOTES: Includes bibliographical references and index.
LEVEL: I LANG: Eng ISBN: 0894438948 LC CARD: 84-006328 GV482.6 17754

Biegel, L. Getting started and monitoring progress. (Refs: 1)
NOTES: In, Biegel, L. (ed.), Physical fitness and the older person: a guide to exercise for health care professionals, Rockville, Md., Aspen Systems Corp., 1984, p. 51-59.
LEVEL: I LANG: Eng GV482.6 17754

Buell, M.N. Psychosocial advantages of fitness programs for older people. (Refs: 17)
NOTES: In, Biegel, L. (ed.), Physical fitness and the older person: a guide to exercise for health care professionals, Rockville, Md., Aspen Systems Corp., 1984, p. 27-39.
LEVEL: I LANG: Eng GV482.6 17754

Cupelli, V. Brettoni, M. Attina, D.A. Laverone, E. Arcangeli, G. Cupelli, G. Bucchino, G. Bini, G. Giuliano, G. Cardiovascular response to maximal exercise in active elderly healthy people. (Refs: 28)*Journal of sports medicine and physical fitness (Torino, Italy) 24(4), Dec 1984, 273-279.*
ABST: The influence of variables (age, sport, degree of training, athletic seniority) on the cardiovascular responses of 216 subjects to maximal cycloergometer tests were examined. Systolic blood pressure (BP) was higher and efficiency (E) better in the groups of subjects over 50. The maximal work load, E and test duration were higher for aerobic sports, diastolic BP after exercise was higher for mixed sports. Trained subjects showed higher double product and better E in contrast to non-athletic subjects showing a higher systolic BP standard and reaching a lower work load. It is maintained that older subjects, particularly those with higher BP, must be started on aerobic sports which, if correctly calibrated, protect them from BP increases.
LEVEL: A LANG: Eng SIRC ARTICLE NO: 106694

Cureton, T.K. Rating the programs. (Refs: 11)
NOTES: In, Biegel, L. (ed.), Physical fitness and the older person: a guide to exercise for health care professionals, Rockville, Md., Aspen Systems Corp., 1984, p. 41-50.
LEVEL: I LANG: Eng GV482.6 17754

Donnet, K. The institutionalised elderly: updating the role of the physical educator. (Refs: 10)

CONF: Physical Education Graduating Seminar Conference (1984 : Footscray Institute of Technology).
NOTES: In, Physical education in Australia: past, present and future directions, s.l., Footscray Institute of Technology, 1984, p. 88-94.
LEVEL: I LANG: Eng SIRC ARTICLE NO: 096181

Exercise programs for the elderly. (Refs: 21)*JAMA: Journal of the American Medical Association* (Chicago) 252(4), 27 Jul 1984 544-546.
CORP: Council on Scientific Affairs.
NOTES: Council report.
LEVEL: B LANG: Eng SIRC ARTICLE NO: 102713

Ferrara, J. Le troisieme souffle. *Science et vie* (Paris) HS147, 1984, 139-141.
LEVEL: B LANG: Fr SIRC ARTICLE NO: 171091

Flatten, K. Outreach: recreation and exercise for the home-centered elderly. Alexandria, Va.: Computer Microfilm International, 1984. 1 microfiche (16 fr.)
LEVEL: I LANG: Eng EDRS: ED249202

Howze, E.H. Health education and physical fitness for older Americans. Alexandria, Va.: Computer Microfilm International, 1984. 1 microfiche (25 fr.)
CONF: Mid-Year Conference of the Society for Public Health Education (2nd : 1984 : Johnson City, Tenn.).
LEVEL: A LANG: Eng EDRS: ED248213

Miyoshi, H. (Physical training at homes for the aged. 1. Aging as a natural process.) *Kangogaku zasshi. Japanese journal of nursing* (Tokyo) 48(5), May 1984, 573-576.
LEVEL: I LANG: Jpn

O'Neill, K. Fitness for older adults: getting started. *Fitness leader* (Ottawa) 3(4), Dec 1984, 7-8.
LEVEL: B LANG: Eng SIRC ARTICLE NO: 105446

Palmer, P. The senior citizen's 10-minutes-a-day fitness plan. Babylon, N.Y.: Pilot Books, c1984. 39 p. : ill.
LEVEL: B LANG: Eng ISBN: 0875761070 LC CARD: 83-017331 GV482.6 17060

Piterman, L. Aerobic exercise. *Australian family physician* (Sydney) 13(6), June 1984, 450-451.
LEVEL: B LANG: Eng

Price, W.F. Lyon, L.B. A national directory of physical fitness programs for older adults. 2nd ed. Saranac Lake, N.Y.: North Country Community College Press : North Country Center for Human Development, c1984. 1v.
NOTES: Includes bibliography.
LEVEL: I LANG: Eng ISBN: 0940280116 LC CARD: 84-018919

Programming: an annotated bibliography. Programmation: bibliographie annotee. (Ottawa): Fitness and Amateur Sport. Secretariat for Fitness in the Third Age, 1984?. 18 p.
CORP: Canada. Fitness and Amateur Sport. Secretariat for Fitness in the Third Age.
CORP: Canada. Condition physique et Sport amateur. Secretariat pour la Condition physique du troisieme age.
LEVEL: B LANG: Eng Fr GV482.6 18203

Sager, K. Exercises to activate seniors. *Physician and sportsmedicine* (Minneapolis, Minn.) 12(5), May 1984, 144-151.
LEVEL: B LANG: Eng SIRC ARTICLE NO: 094572

Sandel, S.L. Kelleher, M. Dance/movement therapy. (Refs: 20)

NOTES: In, Biegel, L. (ed.), Physical fitness and the older person: a guide to exercise for health care professionals, Rockville, Md., Aspen Systems Corp., 1984, p. 101-118.
LEVEL: I LANG: Eng GV482.6 17754

Satterfield, M.J. Yasumara, K. Goodman, G. Impact of an engineered physical therapy program for the elderly. *International journal of rehabilitation research* (Rheinstetten) 7(2), 1984, 151-162.
LEVEL: A LANG: Eng

Wear, R.E. Calisthenics for active older individuals. (Refs: 1)
NOTES: In, Biegel, L. (ed.), Physical fitness and the older person: a guide to exercise for health care professionals, Rockville, Md., Aspen Systems Corp., 1984, p. 61-87.
LEVEL: I LANG: Eng GV482.6 17754

PSYCHOLOGY

Parent, C.J. Whall, A.L. Are physical activity, self-esteem, & depression related. (Refs: 12)*Journal of gerontology nursing* (Thorofare, N.J.) 10(9), Sept 1984, 8-11.
LEVEL: B LANG: Eng SIRC ARTICLE NO: 104416

Perri, S. Templer, D.I. The effects of an aerobic exercise program on psychological variables in older adults. *Internationa journal of aging and human development* (Farmingdale, N.Y.) 20(3), 1984/1985, 167-172.
LEVEL: A LANG: Eng

Regna, J.L. Physical fitness, self-concept, and life satisfaction in the older adult. (Refs: 24)*Florida journal of health, physical education, recreation and dance* (Gainsville, Fla.) 22(1), Feb 1984, 5-6.
LEVEL: I LANG: Eng SIRC ARTICLE NO: 096338

Spirduso, W.W. Exercise as a factor in aging motor behavior plasticity. (Refs: 47)*American Academy of Physical Education papers* (Champaign, Ill.) 17, 1984, 89-100.
CONF: American Academy of Physical Education. Annual Meeting (54th : 1983 : Minneapolis).
NOTES: Conference theme: Exercise and health.
LEVEL: A LANG: Eng SIRC ARTICLE NO: 104420

SOCIOLOGY

McPherson, B.D. Sport participation across the life cycle: a review of the literature and suggestions for future research. (Refs: 66)*Sociology of sport journal* (Champaign, Ill.) 1(3), 1984, 213-230.
ABST: To provide baseline information for futures studies pertaining to sport participation and aging, this paper summarizes the literature on sport participation patterns across the life cycle, briefly describes the importance of analyzing aging as a social process, and argues that alternative theoretical frameworks including a life-span developmental perspective should be utilized in future studies. The paper also introduces a number of theoretical and methodological issues that should be addressed concerning research in this area, and raises a variety of research questions that must be pursued in order to better understand sport phenomena from a life cycle perspective, especially during the middle and later years of life.
LEVEL: A LANG: Eng SIRC ARTICLE NO: 102911

AIKIDO

Devin, I. L'aikido: 'une ecole de vie'. *Loisirs sante* (Paris) 9, avr/mai 1984, 32-33.
LEVEL: B LANG: Fr SIRC ARTICLE NO: 101383

BIOGRAPHY AND AUTOBIOGRAPHY

Coleman, J. The Aikido Wizardry of Uyeshiba: his greatest years were his last. (Morihei Uyeshiba) *Black belt* (Burbank, Calif.) 22(6), Jun 1984, 26-31.
LEVEL: B LANG: Eng SIRC ARTICLE NO: 096733

Hommes, G. The martial magic of Morihei Uyeshiba: the fighting strategies of Aikido's founder. *Black belt magazine* (Burbank Calif.) 22(10), Oct 1984, 52-59;128.
LEVEL: B LANG: Eng SIRC ARTICLE NO: 107357

Ivan, D. Ivan, D. Gozo Shioda: the 'Little Giant' of Aikido. *Kick illustrated* (Burbank, Calif.) 5(4), Apr 1984, 34-36.
LEVEL: B LANG: Eng SIRC ARTICLE NO: 099801

CHILDREN

Linden, P. Aikido: a movement awareness approach to physical education. (Refs: 7)*Journal of physical education, recreation and dance* (Reston, Va.) 55(7), Sept 1984, 64-65.
LEVEL: B LANG: Eng SIRC ARTICLE NO: 101394

TECHNIQUES AND SKILLS

Hallander, J. Sword and staff: weapons of aikido. *Inside karate* (Burbank, Calif.) 5(11), Nov 1984, 49-54.
LEVEL: B LANG: Eng SIRC ARTICLE NO: 107354

Soulenq, M. Aikido, enseignements traditionnels. Paris: Editions Amphora, c1984. 222, (1) p. : ill. (Sports & loirsirs.)
NOTES: Bibliographie: p. (1).
LEVEL: B LANG: Fr ISBN: 2-85180-072-8 GV1114.35 17976

ALPINE SKIING

Conniff, C. The case for status quo: mountain signs used at ski areas in the United States are serving well. The question is will the more signs be an improvement or a detriment. *Ski area management* (New York) 23(2), Mar 1984, 56;77.
LEVEL: B LANG: Eng SIRC ARTICLE NO: 098469

Petrick, T. Tejada-Flores, L. Ski-tech: bump skiing and the establishment. *Powder* (Dana Point, Calif.) 12(6), Feb 1984, 21-22;24.
LEVEL: B LANG: Eng SIRC ARTICLE NO: 098475

Roessing, W. How not to feel like a fool on the slopes: surviving the ups and downs of learning to ski - or of learning to ski again. *New body* (New York) 4(1), Dec/Jan 1985, 57-59;70;72.
LEVEL: B LANG: Eng SIRC ARTICLE NO: 173292

Spencer, J. The case for standardized signs. Western Canada has adopted ski signs widely used in Europe. Other area operator throughout North America need to evaluate this system. *Ski area management* (New York) 23(2), Mar 1984, 53-55.
LEVEL: B LANG: Eng SIRC ARTICLE NO: 098479

ADMINISTRATION

Lang, E.J. The sponsorship dilemma. *Chimo magazine 7(2), Apr 1984, 6-7.*
LEVEL: B LANG: Eng SIRC ARTICLE NO: 092682

BIOGRAPHY AND AUTOBIOGRAPHY

Lang, P. What a gold medal is worth. *Ski 48(6), Feb 1984, 58;60;62.*
LEVEL: B LANG: Eng SIRC ARTICLE NO: 093723

West, T. Il etait une fois. Le premier 'Crazy Canuck'. (Jim Hunter) Looking back. The first 'Crazy Canuck'. (Jim Hunter) *Champion (Vanier, Ont.) 8(2), May/mai 1984, 50-51.*
LEVEL: B LANG: Fr Eng SIRC ARTICLE NO: 095242

BIOMECHANICS

Dorius, L.K. Hull, M.L. Dynamic simulation of the leg in torsion. (Refs: 24)*Journal of biomechanics (Elmsford, N.Y.) 17(1), 1984, 1-9.*
ABST: The authors investigate alpine skiing injuries with respect to the dynamic response of the leg in torsion.
LEVEL: A LANG: Eng SIRC ARTICLE NO: 096817

CHILDREN

Adamski, M. Common myths: are young children really 'fearless, natural learners'? Yes - and no... *Skiing 36(5), Jan 1984, 107-110.*
LEVEL: B LANG: Eng SIRC ARTICLE NO: 093700

Maclane, C. When should I start my child skiing? Answering that important question is never easy for any parent. Here are some useful guidelines to help you decide. *Skiing 36(5), Jan 1984, 97-98.*
LEVEL: B LANG: Eng SIRC ARTICLE NO: 093724

CLOTHING

Auran, J.H. Kids need good boots, too. As performance demands increase, children require quality boots; here's how to meet your growing child's boot needs without taking out stock in the company. *Skiing 36(5), Jan 1984, 100-102.*
LEVEL: B LANG: Eng SIRC ARTICLE NO: 093702

Auran, J.H. Racing boots: not just for racing. *Skiing (Boulder, Colo.) 37(3), Nov 1984, 136-138;140-142;144.*
LEVEL: B LANG: Eng SIRC ARTICLE NO: 098935

Goldsmith, D. Equipment; boot buyer's guide. *Survey ski (London) 5(52), Oct 1984, 52-56.*
LEVEL: B LANG: Eng SIRC ARTICLE NO: 098942

Henry, J. Women's boots. *Skiing (Los Angeles) 37(4), Dec 1984, 136-138;142;145;221.*
LEVEL: B LANG: Eng SIRC ARTICLE NO: 107502

Joubert, G. Gauer, J.-P. Le point de vue du bio-mecanicien: pour bien vous chausser, analysez votre 'canting'. *Ski magazine (Neuilly, Cedex) 65, nov 1984, 108-111.*
LEVEL: B LANG: Fr SIRC ARTICLE NO: 173522

Joubert, G. Lemoine, C. Face a face: 10/10 pour le rapport qualite-prix. *Ski magazine (Neuilly, Cedex) 65, nov 1984, 114-117.*
LEVEL: B LANG: Fr SIRC ARTICLE NO: 173523

Killham, D. Boots: rear-entry vs. front-entry.Are rear-entry boots more comfortable? Do front-entry boots yield higher performance? Our lab and slope comparison tests of three front- and four rear-entry models produced some surprising results. *Skiing (Los Angeles) 37(2), Oct 1984, 202-205;234.*
LEVEL: B LANG: Eng SIRC ARTICLE NO: 103436

Masia, S. Different strokes: the plastic boot ain't what it used to be. Unconventional entry options and fit controls put these 16 at the cutting edge of boot design. *Ski (New York) 49(3), Nov 1984, 194-196;198-199.*
LEVEL: B LANG: Eng SIRC ARTICLE NO: 098954

COACHING

Currie Chapman, head coach of the Canadian women's alpine ski team, believes that somewhere a kid is on the slopes figuring out, through trial and error, a new way to ski faster than the world has ever seen. *Coaching review 7, Jan/Feb 1984, 8-15.*
LEVEL: B LANG: Eng SIRC ARTICLE NO: 092363

Joubert, G. Roland Francey: un nouveau patron pour l'equipe de France. *Ski magazine (Neuilly, Cedex) 65, nov 1984, 25-28.*
LEVEL: B LANG: Fr SIRC ARTICLE NO: 173518

COUNTRIES AND REGIONS

Alpinfo. Vanier, Ont.: Canadian Ski Association - Alpine, 1984?. (26) p. (loose-leaf)
CORP: Canadian Ski Association-Alpine.
LEVEL: B LANG: Eng Fr GV854.8.C3 20225

Boon, M.A. Understanding skier behavior: an application of benefit segmentation market analysis to commercial recreation. (United States) (Refs: 13)*Loisir & societe/Society and leisure (Trois-Rivieres, Que.) 7(2), automne 1984, 397-406.*
ABST: Benefit segmentation is a recent approach to identifying ski markets which emerged from earlier market research. It advocates segmenting recreational markets according to benefits sought by client groups from the experience. The purpose of this study was (1) to identify the most important benefits sought by the southern downhill skier and (2) to demonstrate the utility of segmenting a commercial recreation market by combining information derived from benefits sought from the ski experience with selected sociodemographic variables. Results of this study support the need for continuous market analysis specific to regional destinations. Implications indicate that southern skiers differ from their western and midwestern counterparts in terms of overall benefits sought. This study demonstrates that a combination of sociodemographic variables with benefits sought from the downhill ski experience is a useful way to support ski market decision making. Information obtained from this study was used to identify differences within skier markets.
LEVEL: A LANG: Eng SIRC ARTICLE NO: 171331

DIRECTORIES

Lipton, A. Ski's 1984 guide to summer ski camps. *Ski (New York) 48(8), Apr 1984, 75-77;79.*
LEVEL: B LANG: Eng SIRC ARTICL NO: 099907

ECONOMICS

Fisher, M. Podborski won't spell it out, but he's probably millionaire. Trust fund earnings only tip of iceberg for skiers. *Globe and mail 141(41,913), 6 Apr 1984, 17.*
LEVEL: B LANG: Eng SIRC ARTICLE NO: 092366

EQUIPMENT

Caldwell, F. Bindings: a critical role in downhill ski safety. *Physician and sportsmedicine 12(1), Jan 1984, 148-150;155;158-159;162.*
LEVEL: B LANG: Eng SIRC ARTICLE NO: 092361

Campbell, S. The go-anywhere bunch. Do you really need a Ferrari when you spend your time off-road? *Ski (New York) 49(3), Nov 1984, 86-88;92;94-96.*
LEVEL: B LANG: Eng SIRC ARTICLE NO: 098937

Chaussures de ski: les modeles a entree arriere s'imposent. *Ski Quebec (Montreal) 10(2), nov 1984, 40-41;44-45;48;74.*
LEVEL B LANG: Fr SIRC ARTICLE NO: 179528

Choisir un ski pour les enfants. Votre enfant et le choix de ses bottes. *Ski Quebec (Montreal) 10(2), nov 1984, 78-79.*
LEVEL: B LANG: Fr SIRC ARTICLE NO: 179530

Dorworth, D. Ready for a racer? If you consider yourself a good all-around skier, a versatile recreational racing ski can pu new excitement in your skiing. *Ski (Los Angeles) 49(2), Oct 1984, 112-114;116;118;120;125-126.*
LEVEL: B LANG: Eng SIRC ARTICLE NO: 103432

Duquet, D. Ski alpin: la performance est de retour. *Ski Quebec (Montreal) 10(2), nov 1984, 33-35;38-39.*
LEVEL: B LANG: Fr SIRC ARTICLE NO: 179527

Ettlinger, C. The Ess variable: a new German binding system permits quick readjustment of boot location on the ski for changing conditions. *Skiing 36(6), Feb 1984, 121-123.*
LEVEL: B LANG: Eng SIRC ARTICLE NO: 093707

Ettlinger, C. Children's bindings. If anything, kids need well-engineered, properly adjusted bindings even more than do adults. Here's advice on how to outfit your child, together with test reports on the currently available models. *Skiing 36(5), Jan 1984, 116-118.*
LEVEL: B LANG: Eng SIRC ARTICLE NO: 093710

Ettlinger, C. Tyrolia's 390-290 series: the combination of diagonal heel piece and diagonal reflex toe piece provides this new series with a release capability unique among current bindings. *Skiing (Boulder, Colo.) 37(3), Nov 1984, 161-163.*
LEVEL: B LANG: Eng SIRC ARTICLE NO: 098940

Ettlinger, C. The Salomon 47 series: the new 747E, 747, and 647 provide consistent release functions under a broad range of conditions. (bindings) *Skiing (Los Angeles) 37(2), Oct 1984, 206-208.*
LEVEL: B LANG: Eng SIRC ARTICLE NO: 103433

Ettlinger, C. The new Gezes: force compensation has been adopted throughout this West Germany company's current line. (bindings) *Skiing (Los Angeles) 37(4), Dec 1984, 168-170.*
LEVEL: B LANG: Eng SIRC ARTICLE NO: 107490

Ettlinger, C. The Look 89RX and 49LX: two new models - a low-cost, lightweight turntable and a rugged but simple toe combine with an improved step-in heel - have been added to this French line. (bindings) *Skiing (Los Angeles) 37(4), Dec 1984, 196;198.*
LEVEL: B LANG: Eng SIRC ARTICLE NO: 107491

Ettlinger, C. The Marker M-26: with the new M-26 and its junior version, the M-16, Marker has added ruggedness, simplicity, and elasticity to the heel

ALPINE SKIING (continued)

piece while continuing the traditional, proven toe-piece design. (bindings) *Skiing (Los Angeles) 37(4), Dec 1984, 208;218.*
LEVEL: B LANG: Eng SIRC ARTICLE NO: 107492

Goldsmith, D. Twelve on test: ski survey tested twelve of this season's performance skis in Courchevel last March. *Ski survey (London) 5(53), Nov 1984, 55-57;59-63.*
LEVEL: B LANG: Eng SIRC ARTICLE NO: 173481

Grout, B. Sport skis. *Skiing (Boulder, Colo.) 37(1), Sept 1984, 92-97;282;284;286.*
LEVEL: B LANG: Eng SIRC ARTICLE NO: 098947

Grout, B. Recreational skis: here's a detailed look at 21 notable skis for the improving skier. *Skiing (Los Angeles) 37(2), Oct 1984, 190-193;196;198;200.*
LEVEL: B LANG: Eng SIRC ARTICLE NO: 103434

Grout, W. Choosing a ski for your child. In selecting a ski from among today's vastly improved junior models, ease of turnin and controllability are the two most important criteria. *Skiing 36(5), Jan 1984, 112-113.*
LEVEL: B LANG: Eng SIRC ARTICLE NO: 093714

Joubert, G. Face a face: skis competition... skis grand tourisme. *Ski (Paris) 62, janv 1984, 66-69.*
LEVEL: B LANG: Fr SIR ARTICLE NO: 099901

Kinsella, E.J. Control/communication wiring. The principles of this vital link in safe and efficient tramway operations are explained in detail, along with recommendations for aerial and underground installation. *Ski area management (New York) 23(2), Mar 1984, 57-59;86;89.*
LEVEL: I LANG: Eng SIRC ARTICLE NO: 098472

Masia, S. Soft touches: not all experts have the heft necessary to handle a racing ski. Here are 14 soft-flexing high-performance models that let lightweights turn in style. *Ski (New York) 48(7), Mar 1984, 54-57.*
LEVEL: B LANG: Eng SIRC ARTICLE NO: 098473

Masia, S. A champ who builds for champs. (Al Davignon) *Ski (Buyer's guide '85) (New York) 49(1), 31 Dec 1984, 87;90;92.*
LEVEL: B LANG: Eng SIRC ARTICLE NO: 100563

Masia, S. Founding son. (Georges Salomon) *Ski (Buyer's guide '85) (New York) 49(1), 31 Dec 1984, 162-163.*
LEVEL: B LANG: Eng SIRC ARTICLE NO: 100565

McLellan, R. Where are gondolas going? Increased capacity, length and vertical rise are the first steps in dramatic gondola developments. In the future watch for larger cabins and faster speeds. *Ski area management (North Salem, N.Y.) 23(5), Sept 1984, 72-73.*
LEVEL: B LANG: Eng SIRC ARTICLE NO: 103428

Petrick, T. A ski for all reasons. *Powder (San Juan Capistrano, Calif.) 13(1), Fall 1984, 88-92;97-98.*
LEVEL: B LANG: Eng SIRC ARTICLE NO: 098955

Polyethylene et polissage: la verite sur les semelles des skis. *Ski (Paris) 62, janv 1984, 62-65.*
LEVEL: I LANG: Fr SIRC ARTICLE NO: 099914

Poulet, G. Les fixations 83-84. *Ski (Paris) 62, janv 1984, 70-79.*
LEVEL: B LANG: Fr SIRC ARTICLE NO: 098956

Ungerholm, S. Gierup, J. Gustavsson, J. Lindsjoe, U. Skiing safety in children: adjustment and reliability of the bindings. (Refs: 20)*International journal of sports medicine (Stuttgart) 5(6), Dec 1984, 325-329.*
ABST: One-hundred children were picked at random from ski lift queues and were questioned as regards their skiing ability, experience, and ski equipment. The lateral toe release and recentering forces were recorded. We found, irrespective of to which reference system our results were correlated, a very low percentage of bindings with acceptable setting, lower than has been reported for adults. Sixty percent of the bindings did not have any space between the sole of the boot and the slip plate. Our results indicate the need for several improvements regarding children's release bindings, including factors such as mechanical function, adjustment, and testing.
LEVEL: A LANG: Eng SIRC ARTICLE NO: 104875

Weston, C. 7 steps to binding happiness. *Ski Canada magazine (Toronto) 13(3), Nov 1984, 66;68;70;72-73.*
LEVEL: B LANG: En SIRC ARTICLE NO: 098961

FACILITIES

Bull, H. Buildings for lifts and people. (gondola terminal) *Ski area management (North Salem, N.Y.) 23(6), Nov 1984, 63-66;109.*
LEVEL: B LANG: Eng SIRC ARTICLE NO: 107487

Hayter, B. Scale model snow control: simulating the natural movement of snow and wind on mini versions of ski areas permits planning and modifications of the environment. *Ski area management (North Salem, N.Y.) 23(5), Sept 1984, 64-65.*
LEVEL: B LANG: Eng SIRC ARTICLE NO: 102420

Mathews, P. Mount Allan: planned by computer. A new ski area is being created for the 1988 Winter Olympics in Calgary. Here is an inside look at why the site was selected and how the area was designed. *Ski area management (North Salem, N.Y.) 23(5), Sept 1984, 60-62;94-95.*
LEVEL: B LANG: Eng SIRC ARTICLE NO: 102421

Thibaudeau, G. Consolidate and innovate: Mont St-Sauveur was a mixed bag until retrofitting and high-tech management made it a major entertainment center in Quebec. *Ski area management (New York) 23(2), Mar 1984, 66-67.*
LEVEL: B LANG: Eng SIRC ARTICLE NO: 098480

Weston, G. Mont Ste-Anne: a mountain with the right stuff. *Ski Canada magazine (Toronto) 13(1), Sept 1984, 22-25;28;60.*
LEVEL: B LANG: Eng SIRC ARTICLE NO: 099916

FACILITIES - DESIGN, CONSTRUCTION AND PLANNING

Mathews, P. Mount Allan: part II; the facilities, the financing, the potential. *Ski area management (North Salem, N.Y.) 23 (6), Nov 1984, 76-78;107.*
LEVEL: B LANG: Eng SIRC ARTICLE NO: 106433

HUMOUR

LaTool, S. The accelerated LaTool teaching method. *Powder (San Juan Capistrano, Calif.) 13(1), Fall 1984, 36.*
LEVEL: B LANG: Eng SIRC ARTICLE NO: 099905

INJURIES AND ACCIDENTS

Bechtel, S.L. Ellman, B.R. Jordan, J.L. Skier's knee: the cruciate connection. (Refs: 18)*Physician and sportsmedicine (Minneapolis, Minn.) 12(11), Nov 1984, 50-54.*
LEVEL: I LANG: Eng SIRC ARTICLE NO: 101503

Blitzer, C.M. Johnson, R.J. Ettlinger, C.F. Aggeborn, K. Downhill skiing injuries in children. (Refs: 23)*American journal o sports medicine (Baltimore, Md.) 12(2), Mar/Apr 1984. 142-147.*
ABST: This study compared the number and type of injuries suffered by children to those suffered by adults in the 3182 injuries which occurred at one ski resort over a period of 9 years. Six hundred ninety-six (22%) of the injuries occurred in children 16 years of age or younger. The injury rate for children under 11 years of age was the same as the injury rate of adults. Adolescents had a higher injury rate. Tibia fractures and head and spine injuries were more prevalent in younger skiers than in adults.
LEVEL: A LANG: Eng SIRC ARTICLE NO: 095233

Duplan, B. Bourgeat, E. Menthonnex, P. Accidents de ski. Evolution de la gravite des accidents et de la mortalite du ski alpin. (Refs: 13)*Concours medical (Paris) 106(43), 1984, 4207-4210.*
LEVEL: B LANG: Fr

Metheny, J.A. Skiing arthosis for recurrent shoulder dislocation. (Refs: 3)*American journal of sports medicine (Baltimore, Md.) 12(1), Jan/Feb 1984, 82-83.*
ABST: In the competitive skier glenohumeral dislocations occur as a result of mild abduction and forceful external rotation. The skiing orthosis was developed for the young athlete who wishes to finish the ski season and prevent recurrent dislocations. It involves a pelvic band connected to a leather elbow cuff. The apparatus checks abduction and rotational torque.
LEVEL: A LANG: Eng SIRC ARTICLE NO: 095238

Oliver, J. Ski alpin et orthopedie: types de blessures et traitement. *Canadian Academy of Sport Medicine newsletter (Ottawa 5(4), 1984, 26-29.*
NOTES: Tire de: L'actualite medicale, 8 octobre 1984.
LEVEL: B LANG: Fr SIRC ARTICLE NO: 106046

Suckert, K. Pechlaner, S. Der WSandel des Verletzungsmusters im alpinen Schisport. Studie und Analyse von 16 421 Schiunfaellen. (Changes in the injury pattern in alpine skiing. Study and analysis of 16,421 ski accidents.) *Unfallheilkunde (Berlin) 87(12), Dec 1984, 506-511.*
LEVEL: A LANG: Ger

NUTRITION

Cohen, A. O'Shea, M. Behrens, J. Is exercise physiology reaching professional football? (Refs: 7)*Athletic training (Greenville, N.C.) 19(3), Fall 1984, 185-188.*
ABST: The athletic trainers of 28 professional football teams from the National Footbal Leage are surveyed on the administration of supplements before and after practice, on the administration of fluids during and after practice, on the administration of vitamin and protein supplements, and on the preferred equipment used for strength training and rehabilitation. Results indicate that 1)

salt tablets, K-Lyte, and Fosfree are used heavily before and after practice, 2) players are encouraged to drink during and after practice, 3) 62% of the teams give vitamins to all players, while 48% give out protein supplements, and 4) free weights are more frequently used for strength training and the Cybex and Orthotron machines for rehabilitation.
LEVEL: A LANG: Eng SIRC ARTICLE NO: 099566

PERCEPTUAL MOTOR PROCESSES

Bacharach, D. Skill acquisition and motor control in Alpine skiing. (Refs: 8)*Journal of professional ski coaching and instruction (Boulder, Colo.)* May 1984, 44-45.
LEVEL: I LANG: Eng SIRC ARTICLE NO: 096816

PHYSICAL FITNESS

Fitzgerald, J. Kopp, P. Shaping up with the national team. *Ski Canada magazine (Toronto)* 13(1), Sept 1984, 49-51;53;55.
LEVEL: B LANG: Eng SIRC ARTICLE NO: 099895

Pedersen, T. How to start the season right: the conditioning program outlined here, begun now, will give you the fitness you need. *Skiing (Los Angeles)* 37(2), Oct 1984, 230;232-233.
LEVEL: B LANG: Eng SIRC ARTICLE NO: 103441

PHYSIOLOGY

Grant, J.D. Max VO2: a significant physiological parameter that can be measured and monitered to maximize performance. (Refs 12)*Journal of professional ski coaching and instruction (Boulder, Colo.)* May 1984, 26-28.
LEVEL: I LANG: Eng SIRC ARTICLE NO: 096818

Karlsson, J. Profiles of cross-country and alpine skiers. (Refs: 30)*Clinics in sports medicine (Philadelphia)* 3(1), Jan 1984, 245-271.
NOTES: Symposium on profiling.
ABST: The profile of cross-country skiers shows an emphasis on endurance; whereas, the alpine profile shows an emphasis on leg muscle strength. The skiing profile can determine the potential for injury which can be partly prevented by training programs.
LEVEL: A LANG: Eng SIRC ARTICLE NO: 093694

PSYCHOLOGY

Petrick, T. Tejada-Flores, L. Fear: overcoming imaginary monsters. *Powder magazine (San Juan Capistrano, Calif.)* 13(3), Nov 1984, 22;24;26;30;32.
LEVEL: B LANG: Eng SIRC ARTICLE NO: 173196

PSYCHOLOGY - MENTAL TRAINING

Lund, M. A strong body and flawless technique are just two parts of a race-winning equation. A top racer completes the formula by setting his...mind over matter. *Ski (New York)* 49(3), Nov 1984, 185-186;188-189.
LEVEL: B LANG: Eng SIRC ARTICLE NO: 099908

SAFETY

Cuyler, L. Lift evacuation: no place for on-the-job training. *Ski area management (North Salem, N.Y.)* 23(3), May 1984, 97-99;138-140.
LEVEL: B LANG: Eng SIRC ARTICLE NO: 099893

SPORTING EVENTS

Mapping a strategy for the Calgary Olympics: the first of a six-part series. *Ski Canada magazine (Toronto)* 13(1), Sept 1984, 31-33;35.
LEVEL: B LANG: Eng SIRC ARTICLE NO: 099910

TEACHING

Fry, J. Future teach: a rap with PSIA's brain trust on how ski instruction will change. *Ski (Los Angeles)* 48(4), Dec 1984, 209;211;213-214;217.
LEVEL: B LANG: Eng SIRC ARTICLE NO: 107497

Haynes, J.B. A university on skis. *Virginia journal (Harrisonburg, Va.)* 7(1), Nov 1984, 17-18.
LEVEL: B LANG: Eng SIRC ARTICLE NO: 101505

Hofferber, M. Outlaw instruction: the old problem of who should be allowed to teach skiing has surfaced again. There's no wa to stop it, but it can be slowed down and should be watched. *Ski area management (New York)* 23(2), Mar 1984, 64-65;80-81.
LEVEL: B LANG: Eng SIRC ARTICLE NO: 098470

Jenkins, J. Neuro Linguistic Programming for ski instructors. (Refs: 4)*Journal of professional ski coaching and instructors (Boulder, Colo.)* May 1984, 23-25;28.
LEVEL: I LANG: Eng SIRC ARTICLE NO: 096809

Le ski alpin: les activites physiques de pleine nature a l'ecole elementaire. (Paris): Revue E.P.S., (1984). 61 p. : ill.
CORP: France. Education nationale.
LEVEL: B LANG: Fr ISBN: 2-86713-005-0

McCluggage, D. Teaching what skiing is: Weems Westfeldt is a ski school supervisor at Taos Ski valley, N.M. - and, to him, ski instruction doesn't end with a 'biomechanical cookie.' *Skiing (Boulder, Colo.)* 37(3), Nov 1984, 90;144.
LEVEL: B LANG: Eng SIRC ARTICLE NO: 099911

McCluggage, D. Learning to ski on Scorpians. *Skiing (Los Angeles)* 37(4), Dec 1984, 48;55.
LEVEL: B LANG: Eng SIRC ARTICLE NO: 107510

Milner, E.K. Baker, J.A.W. Collins, M.S. Skiing for credit: a concentrated program. (Refs: 1)*Journal of physical education, recreation & dance 55(1), Jan 1984, 50-51.
LEVEL: B LANG: Eng SIRC ARTICLE NO: 092376

Needham, D. The case for contemporary: has over-instruction left you with hard-to-kick habits? Ski like a racer and watch those long-ingrained glitches take flight. *Ski 48(6), Feb 1984, 81-83.
LEVEL: B LANG: Eng SIRC ARTICLE NO: 093730

Warren, J. The teaching blend. *Journal of professional ski coaching and instruction (Boulder, Colo.)* May 1984, 7-14.
LEVEL: B LANG: Eng SIRC ARTICLE NO: 096815

TECHNIQUES AND SKILLS

Bilodeau, D. Bust through the intermediate barrier. *Ski Canada magazine (Toronto)* 13(2), Oct 1984, 75;77;79;81;83.
LEVEL: LANG: Eng SIRC ARTICLE NO: 106038

Bruant, G. La rationalisation du geste sportif et ses enjeux. Un exemple a travers l'evolution des techniques du ski alpin. (Refs: 21)*Dans, Culture technique no. 13, Neuilly-sur-Seine, France, Centre de Recherche sur la Culture Technique, c1984, p.

284-297.
LEVEL: A LANG: Fr RC1235 20096

Campbell, S. Tippage: good or bad? How you tilt your upper body can help a lot in making cleaner turns. The question is where, when, and how much. *Ski 48(6), Feb 1984, 98-100;102.
LEVEL: B LANG: Eng SIRC ARTICLE NO: 093706

Campbell, S. 5 steps to expert skiing. *Ski (New York)* 48(7), Mar 1984, 37-41.
LEVEL: B LANG: Eng SIRC ARTICLE NO: 098468

Campbell, S. Ski your body type. *Ski (New York)* 49(3), Nov 1984, 74;76-79;82;84.
LEVEL: B LANG: Eng SIRC ARTICLE NO: 0998

Husted, J. Ryman, C. Grout, W. How to make molehills out of moguls: use this approach to mogul skiing to increase your skill level - and your confidence - step by step. *Skiing 36(6), Feb 1984, 111-113;116-117;119.
LEVEL: B LANG: Eng SIRC ARTICLE NO: 093718

Joubert, G. Initiez-vous a l'appui talon frein. *Ski flash magazine (Paris)* 64, mars/avr 1984, 64-67.
LEVEL: B LANG: Fr SIRC ARTICLE NO: 099902

Lundberg, M. Revolution in powder skiing. *Skiing (Boulder, Colo.)* 37(3), Nov 1984, 191-192;194;196;198;200.
LEVEL: B LANG Eng SIRC ARTICLE NO: 099909

TECHNIQUES AND SKILLS - START

Barros, J. Cutter, K. Getting a fast start. *Skiing 36(5), Jan 1984, 114.
LEVEL: B LANG: Eng SIRC ARTICLE NO: 093703

TRAINING AND CONDITIONING

Atkins, J.W. Hagerman, G.R. Alpine skiing. *National Strength & Conditioning Association journal 5(6), Jan 1984, 6-8.
LEVEL: B LANG: Eng SIRC ARTICLE NO: 090873

Jones, P.J. First get the motion, then add the angles. Becoming a fluid, dynamic skier is not that difficult, says the author, if you start with a key first step - getting sufficient vertical movement in the body. *Skiing 36(5), Jan 1984, 87-88;90;92;94.
LEVEL: B LANG: Eng SIRC ARTICLE NO: 093720

TRAINING AND CONDITIONING - DRILLS

Heggie, J. One hour to better balance. *Skiing (Boulder, Colo.)* 37(3), Nov 1984, 249-251.
LEVEL: B LANG: Eng SIRC ARTICLE NO: 099898

Jenkins, J. Eight progressions to better skiing: here are easy, step-by-step ways to increase your body awareness, flexibility, and responsiveness. *Skiing (Los Angeles)* 37(4), Dec 1984, 181-182;184;186-188;190.
LEVEL: B LANG: Eng SIRC ARTICLE NO: 107506

TRAINING AND CONDITIONING - DRYLAND TRAINING

Polastri, T. How to program yourself for better skiing. *Skiing (Boulder, Colo.)* 37(1), Sept 1984, 268;270;272;274.
LEVEL: LANG: Eng SIRC ARTICLE NO: 099913

ALPINE SKIING (continued)

TRAINING AND CONDITIONING - STRETCHING AND FLEXIBILITY EXERCISES

Jenkins, C. Lawrence, G. Pre-ski stretch. *Ski annual (London) 8(1), Sept 1984, 42-43.*
LEVEL: B LANG: Eng SIRC ARTICLE NO: 099900

TRAINING AND CONDITIONING - TRAINING CAMPS

Rotella, R. Gansneder, B. Margolies, M. Ojala, D. Specialized sports academies: are they good for athletes, education, and American sport? (Refs: 1)*Journal of professional ski coaching and instruction (Boulder, Colo.) May 1984, 17-19.*
LEVEL: B LANG: Eng SIRC ARTICLE NO: 096820

TRAINING AND CONDITIONING - WARM-UPS, WARM-DOWNS, LEAD-UP GAMES

Levine, C. How to start your skiing day: don't expect perfection on the first run, says the author; work toward peak performance gradually, using these basic steps. *Skiing (Los Angeles) 37(2), Oct 1984, 210-212;214;216.*
LEVEL: B LANG: Eng SIRC ARTICLE NO: 103438

TRAINING AND CONDITIONING - WEIGHT AND STRENGTH TRAINING

Nelson, J. Are bigger muscles the way to better skiing? Building strength through weight training can not only improve your skiing, it can also help you avoid injury. Here's how to get started. *Ski (Los Angeles) 49(2), Oct 1984, 149-150;152;154.*
LEVEL: B LANG: Eng SIRC ARTICLE NO: 103440

VARIATIONS

Gaimard, A. Le surf: une technique facile a decouvrir. *Ski flash magazine (Paris) 64, mars/avr 1984, 76-77.*
LEVEL: B LANG Fr SIRC ARTICLE NO: 099897

ANTHROPOLOGY

Barreau, J.J. Morne, J.J. Sport, experience corporelle et science de l'homme. Elements d'epistemologie et d'anthropologie de activities physiques et sportives. Paris: Editions Vigot, c1984. 458 p. (Collection Sport et enseignement; 72.)
NOTES: Comprend des bibliographies.
LEVEL: A LANG: Fr ISBN: 2-7114-0882-5 GV701 18685

GAMES

Chick, G.E. The cross-cultural study of games. (Refs: 104)*Exercise and sport sciences reviews (Lexington, Mass.) 12, 1984, 307-337.*
ABST: This paper deals with the cross-cultural comparative study of games, emphasizing those played by adults. The history, theoretical developments, and problems of cross-cultural comparative game research are addressed. The author believes that the cross-cultural study of games has reflected the changing theory, methods, and substantive interests of the field of anthropology over approximately the last century. The major finding of this research has been the observation of a positive correlation between the number and complexity of games in a culture and various measures of the complexity of the culture.
LEVEL: A LANG: Eng SIRC ARTICLE NO: 096390

Wasserman, M. Myth and cultus in sport - the case of the Aztec flying game. (Refs: 14)*Mankind quarterly (Washington) 24(3), 1984, 341-347.*
LEVEL: I LANG: Eng SIRC ARTICLE NO: 097562

ANTHROPOMETRY

Bhatnagar, D.P. Grewal, R. A comparative study of rural athletes of four states of India. (Refs: 13)*British journal of sports medicine (Loughborough, Leicestershire) 18(1), Mar 1984, 34-37.*
ABST: This descriptive study compared 22 male athletes from 4 Indian states on 23 anthropometric parameters. These parameters included weight, height, sitting height, six diameters, six circumferences and eight skin and subcutaneous tissue folds.
LEVEL: A LANG: Eng SIRC ARTICLE NO: 096223

Carter, J.E.L. Physical structure of Olympic athletes. Part II. Kinanthropometry of Olympic athletes. Basel: Karger, c1984. 245 p. (Medicine and sport science; v. 18.)
NOTES: Contents: pt 1. The Montreal Olympic Games Anthropological Project - pt 2. Kinanthropometry of Olympic athletes.
LEVEL: A LANG: Eng ISBN: 3-8055-3871-5 RC1235 12672

Carter, J.E.L. The kinanthropometric approach. (Refs: 21)
NOTES: In, Carter, J.E.L. (ed.), Physical structure of Olympic athletes. Part II. Kinanthropometry of Olympic athletes, Basel, Karger, c1984, p. 1-6.
LEVEL: I LANG: Eng RC1235 12672

Carter, J.E.L. Age and body size of Olympic athletes. (Refs: 23)
NOTES: In, Carter, J.E.L. (ed.), Physical structure of Olympic athletes. Part II. Kinanthropometry of Olympic athletes, Basel, Karger, c1984, p. 53-79.
LEVEL: A LANG: Eng RC1235 12672

Carter, J.E.L. Summary and future directions. (Refs: 6)
NOTES: In, Carter, J.E.L. (ed.), Physical structure of Olympic athletes. Part II. Kinanthropometry of Olympic athletes, Basel, Karger, c1984, p. 231-241.
LEVEL: A LANG: Eng RC1235 12672

Celentano, E.J. Nottrodt, J.W. Saunders, P.L. The relationship between size, strength and task demands. *Ergonomics (London) 27(5), May 1984, 481-488.*
LEVEL: A LANG: Eng SIRC ARTICLE NO: 104289

Heyters, C. Profil morpho-fonctionnel d'etudiantes en education physique. (Refs: 44)*Revue de l'education physique (Liege, Belgique) 24(1), 1984, 25-30.*
RESUME: Au cours de cette etude, l'auteur evalue les mensurations morphologiques, la capacite vitale, l'indice de Tiffeneau, le debit expiratoire de pointe, la ventilation maximale minute a la cadence de 80 respirations par minute, l'aptitude cardio-circulatoire et l'aptitude motrice d'etudiantes (agees en moyenne de 21.3 ans + - 1.5) en education physique. Les resultats obtenus sont compares a ceux provenant d'etudes realisees aupres de sportives de haut niveau et d'une population generale d'etudiantes.
LEVEL: A LANG: Fr SIRC ARTICLE NO: 096451

Ketkin, A.T. Varlamova, N.G. Evdokimov, V.G. Antropotricheskie pokazateli i fizicheskaia rabotosposobnost'. (Anthropometri indices and physical work capacity.) *Fiziologiya cheloveka (Moscow) 10(1), Jan/Feb 1984, 112-116.*
LEVEL: A LANG: Rus

King, H.A. Carter, J.E.L. Comparative factor analyses of anthropometric variables for athletes at the Mexico City and Montreal Olympic Games. (Refs: 13)
NOTES: In, Carter, J.E.L. (ed.), Physical structure of Olympic athletes. Part II. Kinanthropometry of Olympic athletes, Basel, Karger, c1984, p. 202-211.
LEVEL: A LANG: Eng RC1235 12672

Ross, W.D. Ward, R. Proportionality of Olympic athletes. (Refs: 24)
NOTES: In, Carter, J.E.L. (ed.), Physical structure of Olympic athletes. Part II. Kinanthropometry of Olympic athletes, Basel, Karger, c1984, p. 110-143.
LEVEL: A LANG: Eng RC1235 12672

Verit, J. Pasquis, P. Etude des performances de jeunes sportifs de section sport-etudes. (Refs: 5)*Medecine du sport (Paris) 58(2), 25 mars 1984, 27-29.*
RESUME: La morphologie et les performances de 42 filles et 62 garcons, ages de 12 a 18 ans, participants a des sections sport-etudes (soccer, handball olympique, tennis de table et gymnastique) sont etudiees. Les gymnastes et les joueurs de tennis sont plus petits. Dans tous les sports, l'auteur observe des puissances maximales et 170 ainsi que VO2 max kg-1 semblables. Les performances chez les garcons sont en moyenne 20% superieures a celles des filles.
LEVEL: A LANG: Fr SIRC ARTICLE NO: 094215

Watson, A.W.S. The physique of sportsmen: a study using factor analysis. (Refs: 33)*Medicine and science in sports and exercise (Indianapolis) 16(3), June 1984, 287-293.*
ABST: A range of anthropometric measurements was taken on 116 sportsmen who were successfully involved in a variety of sports. The measurements included 11 skeletal lengths, 4 bone widths, 4 trunk and limb circumferences, and 15 skinfold thicknesses. The greatest inter-subject variability occurred in the skinfold measurements. The variability of limb bone lengths and muscle circumferences was generally high, particularly in the case of lower thigh circumference and leg bone lengths. The variability of trunk length and biacromial diameter was low. Alpha factor analysis produced seven factors as follows (the percentage of the total variance explained is in parenthesis): 1) circumferences and bone (32 per cent), 2) skeletal lengths, particularly of limb bones (17 per cent), 3) skinfolds on the trunk (10 per cent), 4) leg and triceps skinfolds (8 per cent), 5) muscle size specific to the legs (6 per cent), 6) trunk length (5 per cent), and 7) pelvic depth (4 per cent).
LEVEL: A LANG: Eng SIRC ARTICLE NO: 108600

Watson, D.G. Check your talent, choose your sport.
NOTES: In, Cantu, R.C. (ed.), Clinical sports medicine, Lexington, Mass. ; Toronto, Collamore Press : D.C. Heath, c1984, p. 3-13.
LEVEL: I LANG: Eng RC1201 15964

BODY COMPOSITION

Body composition assessment and methodology in nonathletic and athletic adolescent and adult males and females. (Refs: 74) *Journal of orthopaedic and sports physical therapy (Baltimore, Md.) 5(6), May/Jun 1984, 336-347.*
ABST: The purpose of this review is to outline methodology for assessing body composition utilizing anthropometric and densitometric techniques. The objective of body composition assessment is to measure body fat and lean body mass. The quantity of these components varies due to growth, physical activity, dietary regimens, and aging. Anthropometric techniques incorporate selected skinfolds, circumferences, skeletal widths, or other variables to estimate body composition within 2-4 per cent. These techniques are adequate for field testing of groups of individuals, but are population specific. Densitometry measures body volume irrespective of physique, sex, or age. This laboratory technique estimates body composition within 1-2 percent, is more difficult to administer, but is not population specific. Some limitation exists with any present technique due to biological variability and incomplete research of reference body composition in children, females, and the aged.
LEVEL: A LANG: Eng SIRC ARTICLE NO: 100890

Bulbulian, R. The influence of somatotype on anthropometric prediction of body composition in young women. (Refs: 26) *Medicine and science in sports and exercise (Indianapolis) 16(4), Aug 1984, 389-397.*
ABST: The influence of somatotype on the validity of anthropometric prediction of body density (Db) in young women (N,92) was investigated. Three groups of predominantly endomorph (N,27), mesomorph (N,35), and ectomorph (N,30) women were identified by the Heath-Carter and Sheldon somatotyping methods. Discriminant analysis revealed a 100% accuracy in somatotype group determination. Thirteen diameters, 26 girths, and 8 skinfolds were measured and used in a STEPWISE regression analysis to derive somatotype-specific regression equations to predict body density. Combining all the measures provided very good prediction accuracy in all three groups with multiple correlation coefficients (R) of 0.98, 0.90, and the standard error of estimate (SEE) of 0.003, 0.005, and 0.005 for Db (gm.cc-1) in the endomorphs, mesomorphs, and ectomorphs, respectively.
LEVEL: A LANG: Eng SIRC ARTICLE NO: 102967

Buskirk, E.R. Mendez, J. Sports science and body composition analysis: emphasis on cell and muscle mass. (Refs: 53) *Medicine and science in sports and exercise (Indianapolis) 16(6), Dec 1984, 584-593.*
CONF: American College of Sports Medicine. Meeting (30th : 1983 : Montreal).
ABST: In order to extend our knowledge of body composition and to quantitatively ascertain the mass of skeletal muscle, some of the procedures for calculating cell and muscle mass are reviewed including total body potassium, total body nitrogen, creatinine excretion, and 3-methylhistidine excretion. These procedures reveal important information, but require further investigation before we are confident that we are measuring cell or muscle mass. The authors have focused on 3-methylhistidine excretion because preliminary investigation suggests that it may reveal differences in muscle mass not detected by densitometry.
LEVEL: A LANG: Eng SIRC ARTICLE NO: 104108

Carter, J.E.L. Yuhasz, M.S. Skinfolds and body composition of Olympic athletes. (Refs: 29)
NOTES: In, Carter, J.E.L. (ed.), Physical structure of Olympic athletes. Part II. Kinanthropometry of Olympic athletes, Basel, Karger, c1984, p. 144-182.
LEVEL: A LANG: Eng RC1235 12672

Cureton, K.J. A reaction to the manuscript of Jackson. (Refs: 7)*Medicine and science in sports and exercise (Indianapolis) 16(6), Dec 1984, 621-622.*
CONF: American College of Sports Medicine. Meeting (30th : 1983 : Montreal).
LEVEL: I LANG: Eng SIRC ARTICLE NO: 104111

Dey, A.N. Body composition and sports performance. (Refs: 12)*SNIPES journal (Patiala, India) 7(4), Oct 1984, 38-41.*
LEVEL I LANG: Eng SIRC ARTICLE NO: 171614

Hebbelinck, M. Borms, J. Review of studies on Olympic athletes. (Refs: 74)
NOTES: In, Carter, J.E.L. (ed.), Physical structure of Olympic athletes. Part II. Kinanthropometry of Olympic athletes, Basel, Karger, c1984, p. 7-27.
LEVEL: A LANG: Eng RC1235 12672

Heyters, C. Evolution de la morphologie et de la composition corporelle d'etudiants universitaires pratiquant des activites physiques pendant plusieurs annees. (Refs: 22)*Medecine du sport (Paris) 58(3), 25 mai 1984, 12-18.*
RESUME: Cette etude longitudinale portait sur l'evolution des mensurations corporelles (poids, longueurs, diametres, perimetres et graisse sous-cutanee) d'etudiants en kinesitherapie et education physique. 74 filles et 60 garcons furent testes avant et apres une periode de 3 a 4 annees d'activite physique pluri-disciplinaire, d'intensite moyenne ou plus importante. Aucune difference ne fut observee entre garcons et filles. L'auteur constate une augmentation du poids total avec un accroissement de la musculature et aucun changement ou simplement une legere diminution de la quantite de graisse sous-cutanee.
LEVEL: A LANG: Fr SIRC ARTICLE NO: 096251

Housh, T.J. Thorland, W.G. Johnson, G.O. Tharp, G.D. Body build and composition variables as discriminators of sports participation of elite adolescent male athletes. (Refs: 13)*Journal of sports medicine and physical fitness (Torino, Italy) 24(3), Sept 1984, 169-174.*
ABST: The purpose of this study was to determine the extent to which body build/composition characteristics discriminated between elite adolescent male athletes competing in different sports. One hundred sixty-three National Junior Olympic Championship participants volunteered for this study. The body build/composition variables included fat-free body (FFB), fat-free body/height body (FFB/Ht), body weight (BW) height (Ht), relative fat (RF), ponderal index (PI), and biacromial diameter/bi-iliac diameter (BA/BI). Multiple discriminant analysis revealed three significant discriminant functions. DF1 described primarily the body build/composition differences between the throwers and all other groups of athletes with the most potent discriminators being Ht, BW, PI, and FFB. The second function (DF2) described primarily the differences between the gymnasts/divers and swimmers. The most potent discriminators between these groups of athletes were Ht and FFB. DF3 represented primarily the body build/composition differences between the wrestlers and middle distance runners. Measures of muscularity (FFB and FFB/Ht) were the variables which best

discriminated between these groups of athletes.
LEVEL: A LANG: Eng SIRC ARTICLE NO: 105480

Jackson, A.S. Research design and analysis of data procedures for predicting body density. (Refs: 14)*Medicine and science i sports and exercise (Indianapolis) 16(6), Dec 1984, 616-620.*
CONF: American College of Sports Medicine. Meeting (30th : 1983 : Montreal).
ABST: Statistical methods used to develop body composition prediction equations are examined. Equations published in the 1960s and early 1970s have been called 'population-specific' equations because they were developed on homogeneous samples. A major limitation of population-specific equations was a low ratio of subjects per variable, which reduces validity. The more recent method has been to develop 'generalized' equations with large samples varying greatly in age and body fatness. The statistical models used for generalized equations were nonlinear regression analysis to account for the quadratic relation between body density and skinfold fat. Age was used as an independent variable to adjust for aging.
LEVEL: A LANG: Eng SIRC ARTICLE NO: 104118

Katch, F.I. Katch, V.L. The body composition profile: techniques of measurement and applications. (Refs: 43)*Clinics in sports medicine (Philadelphia) 3(1), Jan 1984, 31-63.*
NOTES: Symposium on profiling.
ABST: To determine the amount of the structural components (muscle, bone and body fat) of the body several techniques are used. Anthropometric data including skinfolds and diameters are collected; hydrostatic weighing is done to determine body density; ultrasound and radiography also give subcutaneous fat measurements at various sites on the body. Integrated with computer technology, this information provides a body composition profile, and aids in the prescription of an exercise and nutrition program for the athlete.
LEVEL: A LANG: Eng SIRC ARTICLE NO: 092937

Katch, F.I. Clarkson, P.M. Kroll, W. McBride, T. Wilcox, A. Effects of sit up exercise training on adipose cell size and adiposity. (Refs: 24)*Research quarterly for exercise & sport (Reston, Va.) 55(3), Sept 1984, 242-247.*
ABST: The present experiment evaluated the efffects of a 27-day sit up exercise training program on adipose cell size and adiposity. Fat biopsies were taken from the abdomen, subscapular, and gluteal sites by needle aspiration in 13 experimental and 6 control male subjects before and after a five days/week progressive training regimen. Day 1 consisted of 10 bouts of 10-sec exercise, 7 sit ups/bout, with 10-sec rest intervals; on day 27, 14 bouts of 30-sec exercise were performed, 24 sit ups/bout with 10-sec rest intervals. The results demonstrate that (1) the conventional sit up exercise does not preferentially reduce adipose cell size or subcutaneous fat thickness in the abdominal region to a greater extent compared to other adipose sites, and (2) significant changes in fat cell size may occur in the absence of changes in fatfolds, girths or total body composition.
LEVEL: A LANG: Eng SIRC ARTICLE NO: 102791

Katch, V.L. A reaction of laboratory methodology. (Refs: 6)*Medicine and science in sports and exercise (Indianapolis) 16(6) Dec 1984, 604-605.*
CONF: American College of Sports Medicine. Meeting (30th : 1983 : Montreal).
LEVEL: I LANG: Eng SIRC ARTICLE NO: 104120

Lohman, T.G. Preface to body composition assessment: a reevaluation of our past and a look toward the future. (Refs: 1) *Medicine and science in sports and exercise (Indianapolis) 16(6), Dec 1984, 578.*
CONF: American College of Sports Medicine. Meeting (30th : 1983 : Montreal).
LEVEL: B LANG: Eng SIRC ARTICLE NO: 104123

Lohman, T.G. Research progress in validation of laboratory methods of assessing body composition. (Refs: 52)*Medicine and science in sports and exercise (Indianapolis) 16(6), Dec 1984, 596-603.*
CONF: American College of Sports Medicine. Meeting (30th : 1983 : Montreal).
ABST: This paper presents various laboratory methods designed to estimate body composition and documents some of the progress in their validation. In addition to the well-known methods of densitometry, hydrometry, and spectrometry (40K), many other methods are reviewed briefly for their relation to body composition. Emphasis is given to validation principles which need to be followed if new methods are to be developed. The reliance of past research on the two-component model and reference man is reviewed, and the need for multicomponent approaches to the study of body composition is emphasized.
LEVEL: A LANG: Eng SIRC ARTICLE NO: 104124

Lohman, T.G. Boileau, R.A. Slaughter, M.H. Body composition in children and youth. (Refs: 83)*In, Boileau, R.A. (ed.), Advances in pediatric sport sciences. Volume 1: biological issues, Champaign, Ill., Human Kinetics Publishers, c1984, p. 29-57.*
LEVEL: A LANG: Eng RJ125 20044

Malina R.M. Comments on clinical methods of assessing body composition. (Refs: 16)*Medicine and science in sports and exercise (Indianapolis) 16(6), Dec 1984, 614-165.*
CONF: American College of Sports Medicine. Meeting (30th : 1983 : Montreal).
LEVEL: I LANG: Eng SIRC ARTICLE NO: 104125

Mechikoff, R.A. Francis, L. Social and demographic influences on the physique of the Olympic athlete. (Refs: 20)
NOTES: In, Carter, J.E.L. (ed.), Physical structure of Olympic athletes. Part II. Kinanthropometry of Olympic athletes, Basel, Karger, c1984, p. 39-52.
LEVEL: A LANG: Eng RC1235 12672

Ogawa, M. (Human body density to estimated by anthropometric factors -- with special reference to male college students.) *Nippon Eiseigsku zasshi/ Japanese journal of hygiene (Tokyo) 38(6), Feb 1984, 914-922.*
LEVEL: A LANG: Jpn

Pollock, M.L. Jackson, A.S. Research progress in validation of clinical methods of assessing body composition. (Refs: 75) *Medicine and science in sports and exercise (Indianapolis) 16(6), Dec 1984, 606-613.*
CONF: American College of Sports Medicine. Meeting (30th : 1983 : Montreal).
ABST: Anthropometry is the method of choice for estimating body composition in the clinical setting. The method can be accurate, and requires little time, space, equipment, or financial outlay. Although used extensively in epidemiological research, height/weight indices are not as accurate as skinfold and circumference measures for estimating body composition. The validity of estimating body density is enhanced by using a combination of skinfold and circumference measures in a multiple-regression model.
LEVEL: A LANG: Eng SIRC ARTICLE NO: 104136

Roche, A.F. Research progress in the field of body composition. (Refs: 37)*Medicine and science in sports and exercise (Indianapolis) 16(6), Dec 1984, 579-583.*
CONF: American College of Sports Medicine. Meeting (30th : 1983 : Montreal).
ABST: A broad review is presented of the changes in 'state of the art' in body composition between 1963 and 1983, together with suggestions for future research. Consideration is given to the development of equations to estimate body density from anthropometry with special reference to the limitations of the stepwise approach and the need to consider power functions. The advantages of the maximum R2 method and the potential of ridge regressions to extend the applicability of estimation equations is discussed.
LEVEL: A LANG: Eng SIRC ARTICLE NO: 104143

Sady, S.P. Freedson, P.S. Body composition and structural comparisons of female and male athletes. (Refs: 107)*Clinics in sports medicine (Philadelphia) 3(4), Oct 1984, 755-777.*
NOTES: Symposium on the athletic woman.
ABST: This article compares the body composition and physical structure of female and male athletes. A brief review of laboratory and field techniques used to assess body composition and structure is given. The contribution of body composition and physical structure to sex differences in performance and physiology is discussed.
LEVEL: I LANG: Eng SIRC ARTICLE NO: 100919

Sinning, W.E. Wilson, J.R. Validity of generalized equations for body composition analysis in woman athletes. *Research quarterly for exercise & sport (Reston, Va.) 55(2), Jun 1984, 153-160.*
ABST: This study investigated the validity of nine body composition equations based on skinfold measurements in assessing the body composition of woman athletes. The equations of Jackson et al. and Katch and McArdle were found to be acceptable if the ordinate values were adjusted to account for the higher density of women in athletes. The other equations were unacceptable.
LEVEL: A LANG: Eng SIRC ARTICLE NO: 096482

Telford, R. Tumulty, D. Damm, G. Skinfold measurements in well-performed Australian athletes. (Refs: 5)*Sports sciences & medicine quarterly (Australia) 1(2), Oct 1984, 13-16.*
LEVEL: I LANG: Eng SIRC ARTICLE NO: 102834

Thomas, T.R. Adeniran, S.B. Etheridge, G.L. Effects of different running programs on VO2 max, percent fat, and plasma lipids (Refs: 30)*Canadian journal of applied sport sciences/Journal canadien des sciences appliquees au sport (Windsor, Ont.) 9(2), Jun 1984, 55-62.*
ABST: The purpose of this study was to determine the effects of interval and continuous running on factors associated with cardiovascular health in 59 young men and women. The experimental subjects trained three times a week for 12 weeks using either an interval (90% maximal heart rate) or a continuous (75% maximal heart rate) program. All programs utilized approximately 500 cal/session. Only the interval group improved their VO2 max compared to the control group. All experimental groups decreased in percent fat with no method found to be superior to the others in decreasing percent fat. There were no changes in plasma lipids between groups.
LEVEL: A LANG: Eng SIRC ARTICLE NO: 096302

Timson, B.F. Coffman, J.L. Body composition by hydrostatic weighing at total lung capacity and residual volume. (Refs: 21) *Medicine and science in sports and exercise (Indianapolis) 16(4), Aug 1984, 411-414.*
ABST: Body density and percent fat were determined by hydrostatic weighing (HW) at residual volume (RV), total lung capacity measured on land (TLCL), and total lung capacity measured in water (TLCW) in 50 male and 50 female subjects. Body density was 1.0588 plus or minus 0.0215, l.0581 plus or minus 0.207, and 1.6034 plus or minus 0.0214 for males, and 1.0246 plus or minus 0.0219, 1.0242 plus or minus 0.0233, and 1.0276 plus or minus 0.0238 for females at RV, TLCW, and TLCL, respectively. Percent fat was 17.7 plus or minus 9.7, 18.0 plus or minus 9.3, and 15.7 plus or minus 9.5 for males, and 33.4 plus or minus 10.3, 33.5 plus or minus 10.8, and 32.0 plus or minus 11.0 for females at RV, TLCW, and TLCL, respectively. Body density and percent fat were similar when measured by HW at RV and by HW at TLCW. Body density and percent fat measured by HW at TLCL were different than when measured by HW at RV.
LEVEL: A LANG: Eng SIRC ARTICLE NO: 102836

Tremblay, A. Despres, J.P. Bouchard, C. Adipose tissue characteristics of ex-obese long-distance runners. *International journal of obesity (London) 8(6), 1984, 641-648.*
LEVEL: A LANG: Eng

Uppal, A.K. Dey, R.N. Singh, R. Comparison and relationship of percentage of body fat and body weight of physical education students belonging to different weight categories. (Refs: 6)*Snipes journal (Patiala, India) 7(3), Jul 1984, 26-29.*
ABST: The purpose of this study was to compare the relationship of percentage of fat to body weight of physical education male students. Subjects, aged between 17 and 25 years, were classified in three weight categories: below 55 kg, 56 kg to 65 kg, and above 65 kg. No significant relationship was observed among the three classes. The percentage of body fat of subjects belonging to the heaviest weight category was higher than the other subjects.
LEVEL: A LANG: Eng SIRC ARTICLE NO: 099109

Ward, G.M. Stager, J. Johnson, J.E. Body composition: methods of estimation and effect upon performance. (Refs: 56)*Clinics in sports medicine (Philadelphia) 3(3), Jul 1984, 705-722.*
NOTES: Symposium on nutritional aspects of exercise.
ABST: The assumption that is implicit in nearly all methods for determining body composition is that the fat-free body has a constant composition and that fat content can vary from some minimal amount to over 70 per cent. Fat estimations, however, are almost always indirect and are based upon estimating some fat-free component of the body. Some fifteen different methods are described in terms of the principle involved, the cost, and the applicability for routine use. A review is presented of a large number of regression equations that have been developed to predict body density from many types of anthropometric equations. The accuracy or comparative accuracy of body composition methods cannot be evaluated with human subjects. Methods can be validated only by using the method on an animal model, then performing chemical analyses

on the same animal. Data of this type are limited.
LEVEL: A LANG: Eng SIRC ARTICLE NO: 100933

Watson, A.W.S. Distribution of sub-cutaneous fat in sportsmen: relationship to anaerobic power-output. (Refs: 20)*Journal of sports medicine and physical fitness (Torino, Italy) 24(3), Sept 1984, 195-204.*
ABST: Seventeen skinfold thickness were measured on a group of 65 sportsmen. The vertical jump and Margaria test of anaerobic power output were also administered. Analysis of the skinfold data revealed considerable inter-individual differences in the distribution of subcutaneous fat. Factor analysis produced three fat factors. The first accounted for 81% of the total variance and corresponded to trunk fat. The second accounted for 13% of the variance and was highly loaded onto skinfolds on the lower limb and the triceps. The third factor was less specific but was associated with the other skinfolds on the upper limbs. Results of the vertical jump and power output tests were negatively related to skinfolds.
LEVEL: A LANG: Eng SIRC ARTICLE NO: 105499

Williams, D. Anderson, T. Currier, D. Underwater weighing using the Hubbard tank vs the standard tank. (Refs: 24)*Physical therapy (Alexandria, Va.) 64(5), May 1984, 658-664.*
ABST: The validity and reliability of underwater weighing in the Hubbard tank was assessed in this study. Thirty subjects, 14 men and 16 women, were weighed underwater in a standardized sit-in underwater weighing tank and in a Hubbard tank. Results show that correlations between weighing methods were very high, the difference of the coefficient of variation between the two methods was only 0.01 percent, and the interrater reliability was 99.9 per cent for the standard tank and 99.8 per cent for the Hubbard tank. The authors concluded that the Hubbard tank was a valid and reliable method for determining body composition.
LEVEL: A LANG: Eng SIRC ARTICLE NO: 094448

Wilmore, J.H. A reaction to the manuscripts of Roche and Buskirk. (Refs: 11)*Medicine and science in sports and exercise (Indianapolis) 16(6), Dec 1984, 594-595.*
CONF: American College of Sports Medicine. Meeting (30th : 1983 : Montreal).
LEVEL: I LANG: Eng SIRC ARTICLE NO: 104157

Yokoyama, S. Differences in body composition of athletes and non-athletes. *Annals of physiological anthropology 3(2), 1984, 146-148.*
LEVEL: I LANG: Eng

GROWTH AND DEVELOPMENT

Erbaugh, S.J. The relationship of stability performance and the physcial growth characteristics of preschool children. (Refs 30)*Research quarterly for exercise & sport (Reston, Va.) 55(1), Mar 1984, 8-16.*
ABST: The main purpose of this study was to investigate selected standard anthropometric indicators of physical growth as predicators of children's stability performance in two previously described tests: the elevated beam and the stabilometer. Among 42 children of three and four years of age, it was found that the given predictors (ie. estimated leg length/tibial height, foot length, minimum abdominal circumference, chest circumference, foot breadth, leg muscle area, and ectomorphy) accounted for 55% of the performance variation on the elevated beam test. For the

stabilometer test, the given predictors (ie. height/ age, biacromial diameter, maximum abdominal circumference, arm fatness/arm area, and ectomorphy) accounted for 28% of the performance variation. Thus, the major finding was that physical growth independently explained a significant percentage of performance variation in both stability tests for young children.
LEVEL: A LANG: Eng SIRC ARTICLE NO: 096015

Malina, R.M. Little, B.B. Bouchard, C. Carter, J.E.L. Hughes, P.C.R. Kunze, D. Ahmed, L. Growth status of Olympic athletes less than 18 years of age. (Refs: 14)
NOTES: In, Carter, J.E.L. (ed.), Physical structure of Olympic athletes. Part II. Kinanthropometry of Olympic athletes, Basel, Karger, c1984, p. 183-201.
LEVEL: A LANG: Eng RC1235 12672

Malina, R.M. Human growth, maturation, and regular physical activity. (Refs: 99)*In, Boileau, R.A. (ed.), Advances in pediatric sport sciences. Volume 1: biological issues, Champaign, Ill., Human Kinetics Publishers, c1984, p. 59-83.*
LEVEL: A LANG: Eng RJ125 20044

Malina, R.M. Physical growth and maturation. (Refs: 29)*In, Thomas, J.R. (ed.), Motor development during childhood and adolescence, Minneapolis, Minn., Burgess Publishing Co., 1984, p. 2-26.*
LEVEL: A LANG: Eng BF1 20187

Meszaros, J. Szmodis, I. Mohacsi, J. Szabo, T. Prediction of final stature at the age of 11 - 13 years. (Refs: 10)
CONF: Symposium of Paediatric Work Physiology (10th : 1981 : Joutsa, Finland).
NOTES: In, Ilmarinen, J. and Vaelimaeki, I. (eds.), Children and sport: paediatric work physiology, Berlin, Springer-Verlag, 1984, p. 31-36.
ABST: This study develops a method by which genuine age can be suitably estimated in Hungarian youth; further, by knowledge of this age, an attempt is made at predicting the expected final stature in a group of young subjects who were followed up for a longer period of time.
LEVEL: A LANG: Eng SIRC ARTICLE NO: 102336

Robin, M. Les parametres de la croissance. (Refs: 9)*Basketball (Paris) 492, fevr/mars/avr 1984, 23-24;33-36.*
LEVEL: I LANG: Fr SIRC ARTICLE NO: 097757

Rougier, G. Ottoz, H. Entrainement physique et croissance staturale. (Refs: 18)*Dans, Mandel, C. (ed.), Le medecin, l'enfant et le sport, Paris, (Vigot), c1984, p. 141-152.*
LEVEL: A LANG: Fr RC1218.C45 18886

Royer, P. Sports, activite physique et developpement. (Refs: 7)*Dans, Mandel, C. (ed.), Le medecin, l'enfant et le sport, Paris, (Vigot), c1984, p. 7-13.*
LEVEL: I LANG: Fr RC1218.C45 18886

Rutenfranz, J. Andersen, K.L. Seliger, V. Klimmer, F. Kylian, H. Ruppel, M. Ilmarinen, J. Maximal aerobic power affected by maturation and body growth during childhood and adolescence. (Refs: 27)
CONF: Symposium of Paediatric Work Physiology (10th : 1981 : Joutsa, Finland).
NOTES: In, Ilmarinen, J. and Vaelimaeki, I. (eds.), Children and sport: paediatric work physiology, Berlin, Springer-Verlag, 1984, p. 67-85.
ABST: This paper examines the maximal aerobic power and its rate of change as a function of

maturation and body growth in order to test the hypothesis that the differences in maximal aerobic power between the Norwegian and German children are primarily due to differences in growth and maturation.
LEVEL: A LANG: Eng SIRC ARTICLE NO: 102338

Sautkin, M.F. Zavisimost' godichnykh izmenenii dliny i massy tela ot stadii biologicheskoi zrelosti i urovnia dvigatel'noi aktivnosti shkol'nikov. (Annual changes in the body height and weight of schoolchildren as a function of their biological maturity and level of motor activity.) *Pediatriia (Moscow) 3, 1984, 55-56.*
LEVEL: A LANG: Rus

Szabo, T. Meszaros, J. Pinter, A. Szmodis, I. Somatotype, growth, and motor performance in 10-year-old girls taking part in elevated level physical education at school. (Refs: 3)
CONF: Symposium of Paediatric Work Physiology (10th : 1981 : Joutsa, Finland).
NOTES: In, Ilmarinen, J. and Vaelimaeki, I. (eds.), Children and sport: paediatric work physiology, Berlin, Springer-Verlag, 1984, p. 37-41.
ABST: This paper reports on a study of performance structure and the relationships between variables reflecting motor abilities and body build.
LEVEL: A LANG: Eng SIRC ARTICLE NO: 102342

MEASUREMENT

Battinelli, T. A simplistic approach to structural dysplasia assessment: description and validation. (Refs: 14)*British journal of sports medicine (Loughborough, Leicestershire) 18(1), Mar 1984, 22-25.*
ABST: This paper describes a simple method for assessing human structural dysplasia. The method is based on the anthropometric measurements of 222 University students. The results indicate that this method can objectively identify and qualify disharmonic morphological types and subtypes.
LEVEL: A LANG: Eng SIRC ARTICLE NO: 096219

DeLisio, M.J. Comparison of hydrostatic weighing at residual volume and total lung capacity in boys. Eugene, Ore.: Microform Publications, University of Oregon, 1984. 1 microfiche : negative ; 11 x 15 cm.
NOTES: Thesis (M.S.) - University of Wisconsin-La Crosse, 1982; (vi, 55 leaves); includes bibliography.
LEVEL: A LANG: Eng UO84 288

Farmosi, I. Testnevelesi Foiskola-i hallgatok testsurusege - a becsles lehetosegei. (Body density in physical education students and how to estimate it.) (Refs: 6)*Sportorvosi szemle/Hungarian review of sports medicine (Budapest) 25(2), 1984, 147-150.*
ABST: Body density was measured by the water immersion technique (hydrostatic weighing) in 39 female and 31 male students attending the first or second term in the Hungarian University of Physical Education, Budapest. Regression estimates for body density were also obtained in the same subjects by using formulae of four different authors. The statistical analysis of the results has led to the conclusion that for the males the measured values were best approximated by Parizkova's (1959) and Sloan's (1967) formulae while for the females the least difference was found when the formula of Maleski et al. (1982) was used. These regression estimates appear therefore suitable for estimating body density in regularly training Hungarian female

and male athletes.
LEVEL: A LANG: Hun SIRC ARTICLE NO: 097259

Jette, M. Hendricks, S. Kroetsch, D. Nielsen, H. Soucy, P. Guide for anthropometric measurements of Canadian adults. Montreal: C.T. Management & Consultant Inc., 1984?. 16 p.
NOTES: Cover title. Egalement publie en francais sous le titre: Guide de mesures anthropometriques des adultes canadiens. Bibliography: p. 15.
LEVEL: B LANG: Eng GV435 17380

Jette, M. Guide de mesures anthropometriques des adultes canadiens. Montreal: C.T. Gestion & Consultant, 1984?. 16 p.
NOTES Also available in English under the title: Guide for anthropometric measurements of Canadian adults. Comprend des references bibliographiques.
LEVEL: B LANG: Fr GV435 17716

Katch, F. Behnke, A.B. Arm x-ray assessment of percent body fat in men and women. (Refs: 27)*Medicine and science in sports and exercise (Indianapolis) 16(3), June 1984, 316-321.*
ABST: The present experiment determined the validity of arm radiography for quantifying total body fat in young and older men and women. One hundred subjects were measured for 1) body density by underwater weighing with correction for residual air volume to estimate percent body fat and 2) horizontal right upper arm x-ray at KV 76, exposure time 1/30th s, 300 MA, and focal length 72 inches. Total radiation was 10 millirems (mR). The width of fat on the x-ray was measured at three cross-sectional sites (FAT, x-ray). These results demonstrate that the new, arm radiogrammetric method is a reliable and valid technique for assessment of body composition in men and women ages 18-40 yr.
LEVEL: A LANG: Eng SIRC ARTICLE NO: 108605

Katch, F.I. Spiak, D.L. Validity of the Mellitis and Cheek method for body-fat estimation in relation to menstrual cycle status in athletes and non-athletes below 22 per cent fat. *Annals of human biology (London) 11(5), Sept/Oct 1984, 389-396.*
LEVEL: A LANG: Eng

Lohman, T.G. Pollock, M.L. Slaughter, M.H. Brandon, L.J. Boileau, R.A. Methodological factors and the prediction of body fat in female athletes. (Refs: 12)*Medicine and science in sports and exercise 16(1), 1984, 92-96.*
ABST: Body fat was measured on 16 college age female basketball players. Four skinfold calipers, four investigators and five prediction equations were used in studying these athletes. All these factors were found to affect the prediction of body fat in the female athletes. Depending on the combination of the three, the estimates of body fat ranged from 14.1-28.1% for this sample of female basketball players. Triceps and subscapular sites showed the least amount of variability. The authors conclude by calling for standardized body composition measurement procedures when studying specific population groups.
LEVEL: A LANG: Eng SIRC ARTICLE NO: 091744

Smith, K. The measure of body fat. La mesure du taux de graisse. (Refs: 4)*CAHPER journal/Revue de l'ACSEPR (Ottawa) 50(4), Mar/Apr 1984, 31-32.*
NOTES: Part of a series of fitness tips prepared by the Fitness Committee of CAHPER. Ces conseils en conditionnement physique proviennent de la serie preparee par le comite de la condition physique ACSEPR.

LEVEL: B LANG: Eng Fr SIRC ARTICLE NO: 096298

Thorland, W.G. Johnson, G.O. Tharp, G.D. Fagot, T.G. Hammer, R.W. Validity of anthropometric equations for the estimation of body density in adolescent athletes. (Refs: 23)*Medicine and science in sports and exercise 16(1), 1984, 77-81.*
ABST: Anthropometric measures were compared to underwater weighing using certain anthropometric equations. The tests were done on 274 adolescent male and female athletes. The equations showed a great deal of variability; however, the authors agreed that the quadratic and linear equations were the best predictors of body density for the males, while only the quadratic equations predicted well for females.
LEVEL: A LANG: Eng SIRC ARTICLE NO: 091782

Thorland, W.G. Johnson, G.O. Tharp, G.D. Housh, T.J. Cisar, C.J. Estimation of body density in adolescent athletes. *Human biology (Detroit) 56(3), Sept 1984, 439-448.*
LEVEL: A LANG: Eng

Volz, P.A. Ostrove, S.M. Evaluation of a portable ultrasonoscope in assessing the body composition of college-age women. (Refs: 25)*Medicine and science in sports and exercise 16(1), 1984, 97-102.*
ABST: The ultrasonoscope is a portable device using ultrasound to determine tissue thickness. To validate this device skinfold calipers and underwater weighing were also used in measuring the body composition of 66 females aged 18 to 26. The ultrasonoscope was found to be a useful device in measuring body composition. It gives more reliable results than the skinfold calipers, but is ten times as expensive.
LEVEL: A LANG: Eng SIRC ARTICLE NO: 091785

Weiss, L.W. Ultrasonic measurement of subcutaneous fat on the upper leg. (Refs: 13)*American corrective therapy journal (San Diego, Calif.) 38(2), Mar/Apr 1984, 40-43.*
ABST: This descriptive study investigated the efficacy of brightness-mode (B-mode) ultrasound in measuring the thickness of subcutaneous adipose tissue on the upper leg. The results indicate that the ultrasound sonogram is a very reliable measurement; exhibiting a correlation of .99-1.0 between multiple and single sonograms and a correlation of .99 between single sonograms repeated within 30 minutes. Furthermore, the sonogram is highly correlated with skinfold measurements (.88 for men, .83 for women). The results indicate that ultrasonic protocols may have a potential use in measuring body composition.
LEVEL: A LANG: Eng SIRC ARTICLE NO: 096309

OBESITY AND WEIGHT CONTROL

Aronson, V. Effective weight control: a complete diet plan for active weight loss. *Runner's world 19(2), Feb 1984, 74-83;120.*
LEVEL: B LANG: Eng SIRC ARTICLE NO: 090113

Barnes, L. Exercise is crucial in new weight-loss theory. *Physician and sportsmedicine 12(2), Feb 1984, 19.*
LEVEL: B LANG Eng SIRC ARTICLE NO: 091499

Creff, A.F. Le gain de poids chez le sportif. *Medecine du sport (Paris) 58(6), nov 1984, 26-30.*
LEVEL: I LANG: Fr SIRC ARTICLE NO: 102763

Despres, J.P. Bouchard, C. Savard, R. Tremblay, A. Marcotte, M. Theriault, G. The

effect of a 20-week endurance training program on adipose-tissue morphology and lipolysis in men and women. *Metabolism, clinical and experimental (New York) 33(3), Mar 1984, 235-239.*
ABST: 22 adult subjects participated in a 20 week ergocycle training program in order to evaluate the effect of endurance training on adipose tissue and lipolysis. Overall, training significantly reduced fat cell weight, percentage of fat, and increased adipocyte epinephrine maximal stimulated lipolysis. Though the exercise program significantly lowered the adiposity of men, in women training induced no significant changes in the fatness indicators.
LEVEL: A LANG: Eng SIRC ARTICLE NO: 099230

Fitness and fatness in Canada. La condition physique et l'obesite au Canada. *Highlights/Faits saillants (Ottawa) 39, Nov 1984 1-2.*
LEVEL: B LANG: Eng Fr SIRC ARTICLE NO: 102716

Hoerr, S.L. Exercise: an alternative to fad diets for adolescent girls. (Refs: 29)*Physician and sportsmedicine (Minneapolis Minn.) 12(2), Feb 1984, 76-83.*
LEVEL: I LANG: Eng SIRC ARTICLE NO: 091510

Smith, N.J. Weight control in the athlete. (Refs: 8)*Clinics in sports medicine (Philadelphia) 3(3), Jul 1984, 693-704.*
NOTES: Symposium on nutritional aspects of exercise.
ABST: Levels of fatness associated with elite performance in various sports have been identified. Such fatness levels can serve as guidelines for participants in various sport programs who wish to achieve a desired best competing weight. Steps to be taken to decrease body fat levels are detailed. In addition, modification of body composition by increasing weight through increases in muscle mass becomes important in many sports. A program of muscle weight gain is described.
LEVEL: I LANG: Eng SIRC ARTICLE NO: 100922

SEX FACTOR

Wilmore, J.H. Morphologic and physiologic differences between man and woman relevant to exercise. (Refs: 20)*International journal of sports medicine (Stuttgart) Suppl. 5, Nov 1984, 193-194.*
CONF: International Congress on Sports and Health (1983 : Maastricht, Netherlands).
LEVEL: A LANG: Eng SIRC ARTICLE NO: 104393

SOMATOTYPES

Bale, P. Colley, E. Mayhew, J. Size and somatotype correlates of strength and physiological performance in adult male students. (Refs: 25)*Australian journal of science & medicine in sport (Kingston, Aust.) 16(4), Dec 1984, 2-6.*
ABST: To evaluate the effect of physique on dynamic and explosive strength performance, 161 male students were measured on grip strength, trunk extension, leg lift, vertical jump, predicted VO2 max, and PWC170. Correlations between the physique, strength and performance variables were low to moderate. Multivariate analysis of variance and discriminant analysis isolated a combination of seven variables which significantly differentiated three of the four somatotype groups. The endo-mesomorphic group performed best in those aspects requiring strength and power, closely followed by mesomorphs. The best aerobic performance in relation to body weight was achieved by the balanced and ectomorphic groups

who were leanest and lightest.
LEVEL: A LANG: Eng SIRC ARTICLE NO: 105459

Carter, J.E.L. Somatotypes of Olympic athletes from 1948 to 1976. (Refs: 15)
NOTES: In, Carter, J.E.L. (ed.), Physical structure of Olympic athletes. Part II. Kinanthropometry of Olympic athletes, Basel, Karger, c1984, p. 80-109.
LEVEL: A LANG: Eng RC1235 12672

ANTIGUA

Butwin, D. Antigua: more than just another pretty place. *Physician and sportsmedicine 12(1), Jan 1984, 194-197.*
LEVEL: B LANG: Eng SIRC ARTICLE NO: 091864

AQUATIC SPORTS

DISABLED

Gehlsen, G.M. Grigsby, S.A. Winant, D.M. Effects of an aquatic fitness program on the muscular strength and endurance of patients with multiple sclerosis. (Refs: 19)*Physical therapy (Alexandria, Va.) 64(5), May 1984, 653-657.*
ABST: The authors determined the effects of a 10-week aquatic exercise program on muscular strength, endurance, work, and power of 10 multiple sclerosis patients. Overall, the program had a beneficial effect on the variables studied.
LEVEL: A LANG: Eng SIRC ARTICLE NO: 094314

Hall, L. Shelar, D. An aquatics program for the sensory impaired. *NIRSA journal (Corvallis, Ore.) 8(3), Spring 1984, 38-39.*
LEVEL: B LANG: Eng SIRC ARTICLE NO: 097538

Killian, K.J. Joyce-Petrovich, R.A. Menna, L. Arena, S.A. Measuring water orientation and beginner swim skills of autistic individuals. (Refs: 22)*Adapted physical activity quarterly (Champaign, Ill.) 1(4), 1984, 287-295.*
ABST: In this study, a checklist was used to record the responses of 37 autistic children and youth to water orientation and beginner swim activities. The data indicated that the autistic subjects responded in a predictable and apparently normal manner to a hierarchy of water skills. Also, the subjects displayed a low objection rate to water activities. Strong relationships were shown between age and water orientation and also between prior experience and water orientation. The findings support the literature in that the majority of subjects responded well to, or at least tolerated, water activities.
LEVEL: A LANG: Eng SIRC ARTICLE NO: 103966

Roberts, K. Water sports.
NOTES: In, Thomson, N. (ed.) et al., Sports and recreation provision for disabled people, London, Architectural Press, c1984, p. 61-62.
LEVEL: B LANG: Eng GV433.G7 17991

EQUIPMENT

Desmaris, H. A l'aventure des structures gonflables. *Alerte (Montreal) 18, sept 1984, 19-22.*
LEVEL: B LANG: Fr SIRC ARTICLE NO: 106387

FACILITIES - DESIGN, CONSTRUCTION AND PLANNING

Taillibert, R. The Kirchberg Swimming Centre, Luxembourg. Il centro per il nuoto di Kirchberg in Lussemburgo. *Industria Italiana del cemento (Rome) Jun 1984, 54(6), 366-379.*
LEVEL: I LANG: It Eng SIRC ARTICLE NO: 103941

INJURIES AND ACCIDENTS

Busby, J.D. Special problems of the water sports participant. (Refs: 24)
NOTES: In, Birrer, R.B. (ed.), Sports medicine for the primary care physician, Norwalk, Conn., Appleton-Century-Crofts, c1984, p. 279-286.
LEVEL: I LANG: Eng RC1210 17030

JUVENILE LITERATURE

Wallace, D. Petronella, M. Water sports basics. Englewood Cliffs, N.J.: Prentice-Hall, c1984. 1v.
LEVEL: B LANG: Eng ISBN: 013945957X LC CARD: 84-022294

LAW AND LEGISLATION

Sports nautiques. Prevention et reparation des accidents. *Particulier (France) 671, 1984, 5-9.*
LEVEL: B LANG: Fr

MEDICINE

Surfer's ears - external ear canal exostosis. *Sportsmedicine digest (Van Nuys, Calif.) 6(4), Apr 1984, 3.*
LEVEL: I LANG: En SIRC ARTICLE NO: 099958

TEACHING

Shields, D. Aquatic positions: do you qualify? (Refs: 7)*Florida journal of health, physical education, recreation and dance (Gainsville, Fla.) 22(2), May 1984, 9;12-13.*
LEVEL: B LANG: Eng SIRC ARTICLE NO: 096893

ARCHERY

Pszczola, L. Mussett, L.J. Vannier, M. Fait, H.F. Archery. 3rd ed. Philadelphia ; Montreal: Saunders College Pub., c1984. viii, 95 p. : ill. (Saunders physical activities series.)
NOTES: Bibliography: p. 95.
LEVEL: B LANG: Eng ISBN: 0030697115 LC CARD: 83-020098 GV1185 17174

ASSOCIATIONS

Sapp, R. Archery manufacturers look to the future. *Archery retailer (Minneapolis, Minn.) 8(6), Dec/Jan 1984, 56;59-61;73.*
LEVEL: B LANG: Eng SIRC ARTICLE NO: 097897

BIOGRAPHY AND AUTOBIOGRAPHY

Rohde, J. Fire, the wheel, and Rick McKinney. *Olympian (Colorado Springs, Colo.) 10(8), Mar 1984, 4-6.*
LEVEL: B LANG: Eng SIRC ARTICLE NO: 099383

Tir a l'arc: Linda Kazienko. Archery: Linda Kazienko. *Champion (Ottawa) 8(3), Aug 1984, 42-43.*
LEVEL: B LANG: Fr Eng SIRC ARTICLE NO: 096489

CERTIFICATION

Federation of Canadian Archers level IV technical coaching manual. (Ottawa): Federation of Canadian Archers, 1984. 1v. (loose-leaf) (National Coaching Certification Program.)
CORP: Federation of Canadian Archers.
NOTES: Cover title: Technical manual. Federation of Canadian Archers.
LEVEL: I LANG: Eng GV1185 18780

CHILDREN

Freed, D. The youth market: building sales now and for the future. *Archery retailer (Minnetonka, Minn.) 9(3), June 1984, 26-29;52-53;55-59.*
LEVEL: B LANG: Eng SIRC ARTICLE NO: 108436

Soar, D. Adolescence: five factors linked to elite performance. (Refs: 7)*Coaching review 7, Mar/Apr 1984, 58-59.*
LEVEL: B LANG: Eng SIRC ARTICLE NO: 093257

CLUBS

Kember-Smith, J. When is a club not a club? *British archer (Bracknell, Berkshire, Eng.) 35(5), Mar 1984, 197-198.*
ABST: The existence of a sport club does not insure its success. An archery club can be unsuccessful for a variety of reasons and symptoms such as a declining membership should be closely investigated by club administration. A club can be revitalized through the active promotion of its activities to the general public, increased cooperation with public authorities, as well as an active recruiting campaign followed by a good program of training and coaching of new members.
LEVEL: B LANG: Eng SIRC ARTICLE NO: 101057

COACHING

Coaching young people. *British archer (Berkshire) 36(1), Jul 1984, 7-9.*
LEVEL: B LANG: Eng SIRC ARTICLE NO: 104531

Coaching young people. *British archer (Berkshire, Eng.) 36(1), Jul 1984, 7-9.*
LEVEL: B LANG: Eng SIRC ARTICLE NO: 102126

Lightfoot, S.R. The game of time management: the how to. (Refs: 3)*4 for 20 (Willowdale, Ont.) Apr 1984, 24-25.*
LEVEL: B LANG: Eng SIRC ARTICLE NO: 099381

DIRECTORIES

Archery retailer: directory '85. *Archery retailer (Minnetonka, Minn.) 9(5), Oct 1984, 19-22;24-26;28-32.*
LEVEL: B LANG: Eng SIRC ARTICLE NO: 105637

ARCHERY (continued)

Product listing. *Archery retailer (Minnetonka, Minn.)* 9(5), Oct 1984, 34-46;48-74;79-87.
LEVEL: B LANG: Eng SIRC ARTICLE NO 105640

DISABLED

Heer, M. Elements of archery: Part 1 - getting started. *Sports 'n spokes (Phoenix, Ariz.)* 10(2), Jul/Aug 1984, 17-19.
NOTES: First in a series of three articles.
LEVEL: B LANG: Eng SIRC ARTICLE NO: 097539

Spraggs, S.S. Archery with the Sightless Sight System. *Palaestra (Macomb, Ill.)* 1(1), Fall 1984, 38-39.
LEVEL: B LANG: En SIRC ARTICLE NO: 171817

ENCYCLOPEDIAS

Paterson, W.F. Encyclopaedia of archery. London: R. Hale, c1984. 202 p. : ill.
NOTES: Bibliography: p. 201-202.
LEVEL: B LANG: Eng ISBN: 0-7090-1072-9 LC CARD: 84-198856 GV1184.5 18755

EQUIPMENT

Drouin, C. L'arc a poulies et l'arc a cames, une revolution technologique. *Archer au Quebec (Montreal)* 8(1/2), janv/fevr 1984, 12-13.
LEVEL: B LANG: Fr SIRC ARTICLE NO: 099379

Genge, R. Tillering: the art of bowyers. *Archery international (London, Eng.)* 4(1), Spring 1984, 14-15.
LEVEL: B LANG: En SIRC ARTICLE NO: 096486

Henderson, D. Bow report: Oneida Eagle. *Bow & arrow (Capistrano Beach, Calif.)* 22(4), Nov/Dec 1984, 66-70.
LEVEL: B LANG: Eng SIRC ARTICLE NO: 104532

Mullaney, N. York CNC-1: it shoots with crisp authority. *Archery world (Minnetonka, Minn.)* 33(5), Aug/Sept 1984, 92-96.
LEVEL: B LANG: Eng SIRC ARTICLE NO: 108439

Siatkowski, S. Everything you always wanted to know about archery... (fletching) *Canadian archer (Nobert, Man.)* Nov/Dec 1984, 42-48.
LEVEL: B LANG: Eng SIRC ARTICLE NO: 102986

Vittor, L.K. How to: create a custom compound bow cover. Create your own custom bow cover in less than three hours, and for as little as $6. *Bow & arrow (Capistrano Beach, Calif.)* 22(4), Nov/Dec 1984, 60-64.
LEVEL: B LANG: Eng SIRC ARTICLE NO: 105642

Wills, A. The compound bow...'kiss bow turning'. *Canadian archer (Norbert, Man.)* Mar/Apr 1984, 33-34.
LEVEL: B LANG: Eng SIRC ARTICLE NO: 099386

EQUIPMENT - RETAILING

Sapp, R. Cam bow accessories. *Archery retailer (Minnetonka, Minn.)* 9(4), Aug/Sept 1984, 18-20;22-23.
LEVEL: B LANG: Eng SIRC ARTICLE NO: 102985

What critical factors will influence the growth of the archery industry in 1984? With the 1984 Olympics in Los Angeles and the economy turning around, archery industry leaders are optimistic 1984 will be a profitable year. *Archery retailer (Minneapolis, Minn.)* 8(6), Dec/Jan 1984,30-31;90;92-93.
LEVEL: B LANG: Eng SIRC ARTICLE NO: 097898

HALLS OF FAME AND MUSEUMS

Usher, F. Archery museum proposal. Le musee de tir a l'arc. *Canadian archer (Norbert, Man.)* Mar/Apr 1984, 35-39.
LEVEL: B LANG: Eng Fr SIRC ARTICLE NO: 099385

HISTORY

Bergman, C. Gibbs, P. American composites in Britain. (Refs: 1)*Society of archer-antiquaries (London)* 27, 1984, 32-33.
LEVEL: B LANG: Eng SIRC ARTICLE NO: 108833

Elmy, D. The anatomy of a quiver. *Society of archer-antiquaries (London)* 27, 1984, 26-27.
LEVEL: B LANG: Eng SIRC ARTICLE NO: 108831

Elmy, D. Arrow moulds from Scythia and Luristan. (Refs: 7)*Society of archer-antiquaries (London)* 27, 1984, 45-47.
LEVEL: LANG: Eng SIRC ARTICLE NO: 108836

Fabian, G. An Avar bow. *Society of archer-antiquaries (London)* 27, 1984, 30-31.
LEVEL: B LANG: Eng SIRC ARTICLE NO: 10883

Hartley, P.D. Some speculations on the nature of longbowstrings. (Refs: 1)*Society of archer-antiquaries (London)* 27, 1984, 24-25.
LEVEL: I LANG: Eng SIRC ARTICLE NO: 108830

Holt, A. The Harrow Silver Arrow contest. (Refs: 11)*Society of archer-antiquaries (London)* 27, 1984, 36-40.
LEVEL: B LANG Eng SIRC ARTICLE NO: 108834

Massicotte, J.P. Lessard, C. Le tir a l'arc du XVIe au XIXe siecles. (Refs: 17)*Dans, Massicotte, J.P. et Lessard, C. (eds.) Histoire du sport de l'antiquite au XIXe siecle, Sillery, Que., Presses de l'Universite du Quebec, 1984, p. 243-254.*
LEVEL: A LANG: Fr GV571 18971

Tucker, W.E. Pilgrim 'archers'. (badges) *Society of archer-antiquaries (London)* 27, 1984, 41-42.
LEVEL: B LANG: Eng SIRC ARTICLE NO: 108835

PHILATELY, NUMISMATICS AND COLLECTIONS

Osborne, J. Toxophilately: recent archery tournaments & stamps. *British archer (Berkshire)* 36(2), Sept 1984, 53-54.
LEVEL B LANG: Eng SIRC ARTICLE NO: 104534

PHOTOGRAPHY

Powell, J. Shooting the shooters. *Archery international (London, Eng.)* 4(1), Spring 1984, 16-18.
LEVEL: B LANG: Eng SIRC ARTICLE NO: 096488

PHYSIOLOGY

Torrey, L. Science goes to the Olympics. *Canadian archer (Vanier, Ont.)* Sept/Oct 1984, 5-7.
LEVEL: B LANG: Eng SIRC ARTICLE NO: 173553

Torrey, L. Comment la science fabrique des gagnants. *Canadian archer (Vanier, Ont.)* Sept/Oct 1984, 7-8;11;37;;50.
LEVEL: LANG: Fr SIRC ARTICLE NO: 173554

PSYCHOLOGY - MENTAL TRAINING

Daniels, F. Relaxation training and imagery. Entrainement a la relaxation et projection mentale. *Canadian archer (Ottawa)* Jul/Aug 1984, 33-37.
LEVEL: B LANG: Eng Fr SIRC ARTICLE NO: 101056

Wiseman, H. Coach's clinic. (mental practice) *Canadian archer (Ottawa)* Jul/Aug 1984, 44-46.
LEVEL: B LANG: Eng SIRC ARTICLE NO: 101060

SPORTING EVENTS

Stump, W. The last archery Olympics...until now. Olympic archery early in this century was a haphazard event at best. *Canadian archer (Ottawa)* Jul/Aug 1984, 41-43.
NOTES: Reprinted from, Archery World Jan 1972.
LEVEL: B LANG: Eng SIRC ARTICLE NO: 101059

TEACHING

Brunelle, J. Ladouceur, M. L'enseignement du tir a l'arc. (Refs: 5)*Revue quebecoise de l'activite physique (Trois-Rivieres, Que.)* 3(1), oct 1984, 29-33.
LEVEL: I LANG: Fr SIRC ARTICLE NO: 101055

Strauf, D.L. Ring archery. *Journal of physical education, recreation and dance (Reston, Va.)* 55(8), Oct 1984, 71.
LEVEL: LANG: Eng SIRC ARTICLE NO: 101058

Virgilio, S.J. The effects of command and reciprocal teaching styles on the cognitive, affective and psychomotor behaviour o fifth grade pupils. (Refs: 26)*Australian journal of science & medicine in sport (Kingston, Aust.)* 16(3), Oct 1984, 16-19.
ABST: This study investigated the differential affects of two styles of teaching. Pre- and post-test measures were analysed in archery knowledge, self-concept and archery skill. The subjects were randomly assigned to one of four groups and the groups to one of two treatments. Results indicated significant gains in pre- to post-test measures. However, there were no significant differences when the teaching styles were compared. These results indicate that an individualised style (reciprocal) is as effective as the traditional style of teaching archery (command).
LEVEL: A LANG: Eng SIRC ARTICLE NO: 105641

TECHNIQUES AND SKILLS

Kember-Smith, J. String clearance. *British archer (Berkshire)* 36(2), Sept 1984, 55-57.
LEVEL: B LANG: Eng SIRC ARTICLE NO 104533

TECHNIQUES AND SKILLS - AIMING

Wiseman, H. Coach's clinic. (aiming) *Canadian archer (Nobert, Man.)* Nov/Dec 1984, 37-41.
LEVEL: B LANG: Eng SIRC ARTICLE NO: 102987

TESTING AND EVALUATION

Loiselle, E.J. Speed tester: the low cost model 900 custom chronograph. *Bow & arrow (Capistrano Beach, Calif.)* 21(6), Mar/Apr 1984, 48-51.
LEVEL: B LANG: Eng SIRC ARTICLE NO: 099382

TRAINING AND CONDITIONING - WEIGHT AND STRENGTH TRAINING

Elliott, M. Weight training for archery. *British archer (Bracknell, Birkshire, Eng.)* 35(6), May/Jun 1984, 246-247.
LEVEL: LANG: Eng SIRC ARTICLE NO: 099380

VISION

Guidelines for shooting and archery eyewear. *Sports mediscope (Colorado Springs)* 4(2), Summer 1984, 13-14.
CORP: United States. Olympic Committee. Vision Performance and Safety Advisory Committee.
LEVEL: B LANG: Eng SIRC ARTICLE NO: 096803

ARM AND WRIST WRESTLING

TRAINING AND CONDITIONING - WEIGHT AND STRENGTH TRAINING

Doherty, M. What every beginner should know. *Arm bender (Taylor, Pa.)* 8(1), Winter/Spring 1984, 1-2.
LEVEL: B LANG: Eng SIRC ARTICLE NO: 097857

ART AND SPORT

Becker, W. Sport in the visual arts in the twentieth century. *Olympic review (Lausanne)* 201/202, Jul/Aug 1984, 518-524.
NOTES: Published in the catalogue of 'Art and Sport' exhibition organized at the 'Musee des Beaux-Arts de Mons' (BEL) from 23rd March to 30th June 1984.
LEVEL: B LANG: Eng SIRC ARTICLE NO: 096404

Becker, W. Le sport dans les arts plastiques du XXe siecle. *Revue olympique (Lausanne)* 201/202, juil/aout 1984, 518-524.
NOTES: Article paru dans le catalogue de l'exposition 'Art et Sport' organisee au Musee des Beaux-arts de Mons (BEL) du 23 mars au 30 juin 1984. 'Swimmer Reflexion' est extraite du catalogue.
LEVEL: B LANG: Fr SIRC ARTICLE NO: 104483

Juli, R.B. Le sport dans l'oeuvre de Joan Miro. *Revue olympique (Lausanne)* 206, dec 1984, 986-988.
LEVEL: B LANG: Fr SIRC ARTICLE NO: 105594

ART

Becker, W. Le sport dans les arts plastiques du XXe siecle. *Revue olympique (Lausanne)* 201/202, juil/aout 1984, 518-524.
NOTES: Article paru dans le catalogue de l'exposition 'Art et Sport' organisee au Musee des Beaux-Arts de Mons (BEL) du 23 mars au 30 juin 1984. 'Swimmer Reflexion' est extraite de ce catalogue.
LEVEL: B LANG: Fr SIRC ARTICLE NO: 102133

Juli, R.B. The sport in the work of Joan Miro. *Olympic review (Lausanne)* 206, Dec 1984, 986-988.
LEVEL: B LANG: Eng SIRC ARTICLE NO: 105593

ASIAN GAMES

The 10th Asian Games, Seoul 1986, 20 September - 5 October. *Sports (Kallang, Singapore)* 12(10), Nov/Dec 1984, 24;31;33.
LEVEL: B LANG: Eng SIRC ARTICLE NO: 108994

KOREA

10th Asian Games, Seoul 1986. Seoul, Korea: Seoul Asian Games Organizing Committee, 1984?. 37 p. : ill.
CORP: Seoul Asian Games Organizing Committee.
NOTES: Cover title.
LEVEL: B LANG: Eng GV722.5.A7 17010

ASSOCIATIONS

Buggel, E. On some essential tasks of and prospects for international co-operation in sport science. *In, Ilmarinen, M. (ed. et al., Sport and International Understanding: proceedings of the congress held in Helsinki, Finland, July 7-10, 1982, Berlin, Springer-Verlag, 1984, p. 174-176.*
CONF: Congress on Sport and International Understanding (1982 : Helsinki).
LEVEL: B LANG: Eng GV706.8 18979

Expanding role of the AIS. *International swimmer* Jan/Feb 1984, 28-30.
LEVEL: I LANG: Eng SIRC ARTICLE NO: 097859

Hebbelinck, M. Borms, J. Sport international. *International journal of physical education (Schorndorf, W. Germany)* 21(1), 1984, 38.
LEVEL: B LANG: Eng SIRC ARTICLE NO: 093004

Hebbelinck, M. Organisations for sport sciences: developments and perspectives. (Refs: 8)*In, Ilmarinen, M. (ed.) et al., Sport and International Understanding: proceedings of the congress held in Helsinki, Finland, July 7-10, 1982, Berlin, Springer-Verlag, 1984, p. 167-173.*
CONF: Congress on Sport and International Understanding (1982 : Helsinki).
LEVEL: I LANG: Eng GV706.8 18979

Karvonen, M.J. Sport and health: an outline of the World Health Organization's position. (Refs: 9)*In, Ilmarinen, M. (ed.) e al., Sport and International Understanding: proceedings of the congress held in Helsinki, Finland, July 7-10, 1982, Berlin, Springer-Verlag, 1984, p. 177-179.*
CONF: Congress on Sport and International Understanding (1982 : Helsinki).
LEVEL: B LANG: Eng GV706.8 18979

ADMINISTRATION

Financement du fonctionnement des associations sportives: du normal aux exces. *Sport dans la cite (France)* 98, 1984, 38-55.
CONF: Journees nationales d'etudes (1983 : Bourges).
LEVEL: I LANG: Fr

Galasso, P.J. Sport and the law: intersections. (Refs: 6)
NOTES: In, Brown, R. (ed.) et al., Sport, physical activity and th law, Ottawa, Canadian Association for Health, Physical Education, Recreation and Dance, c1984, p. 1-7.
LEVEL: B LANG: Eng GV705 18324

Halphen, A. Psycho drame des presidents. Vous les connaissez. Peut-etre moins que Platini ou Prost, Rives ou Noah mais au fi de l'actualite, ils sont montes 'a la une' plusieurs fois au cours de leur carriere. *Equipe magazine 184, 3 mars 1984, 32-39.*
LEVEL: B LANG: Fr SIRC ARTICLE NO: 092681

Kelley, L. Public relations and marketing in support of the local association. Toronto: The National Council of YMCAs of Canada, 1984?. 19 p.
CORP: National Council of YMCAs of Canada.
NOTES: Aussi publie en francais sous le titre, Relations publiques et marketing a l'intention des associations locales.
LEVEL: B LANG: Eng GV713 17014

Kelley, L. Relations publiques et marketing a l'intention des associations locales. Toronto: Le Conseil national des YMCA du Canada, 1984?. 20 p.
CORP: Conseil national des YMCA du Canada.
NOTES: Also published in English under the title, Public relations and marketing in support of the local association.
LEVEL: B LANG: Fr GV713 17015

Meyer, D. Norman, R. Saunders, S. Avey, C. A guide to organizational effectiveness. The administrative function in sports an recreation organizations. North Bay, Ont.: Northeastern Ontario Regional Sports Committee : Ministry of Tourism and Recreation, 1984. ii, 36 p. (Sport and recreation resource series for community groups; v.4.)
CORP: Northeastern Ontario Regional Sports Committee.
CORP: Ontario. Ministry of Tourism and Recreation. Field Services Office.
LEVEL: B LANG: Eng GV181.5 19017

DIRECTORIES

Colgate, C. Freedman, S.J. National recreational, sporting & hobby organizations of the United States. 4th ed. Washington, D.C.: Columbia Books Inc., 1984. 136 p.
LEVEL: I LANG: Eng ISBN: 0910416486 LC CARD: 80-70429 GV53 10891

Directory of associations: here is an alphabetical listing of national organizations related to the administration of sports and recreation programs and facilities. *Athletic purchasing and facilities (Madison, Wis.)* 8(2), Feb 1984, 101-107.
NOTES: 1984 buyers guide.
LEVEL: B LANG: Eng SIRC ARTICLE NO: 108280

Wisconsin Association for Health, Physical Education, Recreation and Dance 1984-1985 directory. Madison, Wis.: Wisconsin Association for Health, Physical Education, Recreation and Dance, 1984. 69, 18 p.
CORP: Wisconsin Association for Health, Physical Education, Recreation and Dance.
NOTES: Cover title.
LEVEL: B LANG: Eng GV208 20182

HISTORY

Lachenicht, S. Historical background of the coordinating committee of IASI. *International bulletin of sports information (The Hague, Netherlands)* 6, 1984, 2.
LEVEL: B LANG: Eng SIRC ARTICLE NO: 095781

McQuaid, T. Cusack: man of vision, courage and dynamic energy. *Gaelic sport (Dublin)* 27(2), May/June 1984, 15;17;19.
LEVEL: B LANG: Eng SIRC ARTICLE NO: 173469

Ringli, K. Sport information- yesterday- today-tomorrow: the structure and tasks of the International Association for Sport Information (IASI). *International bulletin of sports information (The Hague, Neth.)* 6(4), 1984, 5-10.
LEVEL: B LANG: Eng SIRC ARTICLE NO: 104493

Ryan, S. Milestones of a century... *Gaelic sport (Dublin)* 27(2), May/June 1984, 32-35.
LEVEL: B LANG: Eng SIRC ARTICLE NO 173470

ATHLETIC TRAINER

Athletic training and sports medicine. 1st ed. Chicago, Ill.: American Academy of Orthopaedic Surgeons, c1984. vii, 602 p. : ill.
CORP: American Academy of Orthopaedic Surgeons.
LEVEL: I LANG: Eng ISBN: 0-89203-002-X RC1210 20089

Bell, G.W. Cardinal, R.A. Dooley, J.N. Athletic trainer manpower survey of selected Illinois High Schools. (Refs: 6)*Athleti training* 19(1), Spring 1984, 23-24.
LEVEL: I LANG: Eng SIRC ARTICLE NO: 091501

Gieck, J. Stress management and the athletic trainer. (Refs: 10)*Athletic training (Greenville, N.C.)* 19(2), Summer 1984, 115-119.
LEVEL: I LANG: Eng SIRC ARTICLE NO: 094643

Gillespie, C.A. Student trainers: essential link between athletes and coaches. *First aider (Gardner, Kan.)* 53(6), Mar 1984, 11.
LEVEL: B LANG: Eng SIRC ARTICLE NO: 094419

Kane, B. Trainer counseling to avoid three face-saving maneuvers. (Refs: 7)*Athletic training (Greenville, N.C.)* 19(3), Fall 1984, 171-174.
LEVEL: B LANG: Eng SIRC ARTICLE NO: 099093

Reasoner, A.E. A western states survey of certified athletic trainers' use of joint mobilization in treatment programs. Eugene, Ore.: Microform Publications, University of Oregon, 1984. 2 microfiches : negative, ill. ; 11 x 15 cm.
NOTES: Thesis (M.S.) - University of Oregon, 1982; (xiii, 112 leaves); vita; includes bibliography.
LEVEL: A LANG: Eng UO84 139-140

ADMINISTRATION

Dreese, T. The Lock Haven University Athletic Training Club. *Athletic training* 19(1), Spring 1984, 15.
LEVEL: B LANG: Eng SIRC ARTICLE NO: 091505

Proctor, D. Computers in the training room. Making practical use of new technology. *First aider (Gardner, Kans.)* 54(1), Sep 1984, 5.
LEVEL: B LANG: Eng SIRC ARTICLE NO: 105350

FACILITIES

Secor, M.R. Designing athletic training facilities or 'where do you want the outlets?' (Refs: 4)*Athletic training* 19(1), Spring 1984, 19-21.
LEVEL: I LANG: Eng SIRC ARTICLE NO: 091531

LAW AND LEGISLATION

Gieck, J. Lowe, J. Kenna, K. Trainer malpractice: a spleeping giant. (Refs: 14)*Athletic training* 19(1), Spring 1984, 41-46.
LEVEL: I LANG: Eng SIRC ARTICLE NO: 091507

Hales, C. Legal liability of Physical Therapists and Athletic Trainers. (Refs: 12)
NOTES: In, Brown, R. (ed.) et al., Sport, physical activity and the law, Ottawa, Canadian Association for Health, Physical Education, Recreation and Dance, c1984, p. 48-55.
LEVEL: I LANG: Eng GV705 18324

PROFESSIONAL PREPARATION

Kauth, B. The athletic training major. *Journal of physical education, recreation and dance (Reston, Va.)* 55(8), Oct 1984, 11-13.
LEVEL: B LANG: Eng SIRC ARTICLE NO: 100729

TAPING

Mattison, R. Comment on knee basketweave. *Sports physiotherapy division (Victoria, B.C.)* 9(1), Jan/Feb 1984, 24-30.
LEVEL I LANG: Eng SIRC ARTICLE NO: 099050

Myburgh, K.H. Vaughan, C.L. Isaacs, S.K. The effects of ankle guards and taping on joint motion before, during, and after a squash match. (Refs: 12)*American journal of sports medicine (Baltimore)* 12(6), Nov/Dec 1984, 441-446.
ABST: The effects of ankle guards and taping on joint motion before, during, and after exercise were studied. Twelve league squash players played two matches, each lasting 1 hour. Two different ankle guards, and two types of tape applied by the same method, served as supports. A specially designed goniometer with electronic digital display was used to determine joint range of motion: plantar-flexion and dorsiflexion, neutral inversion and eversion, plantar-flexed inversion and eversion. The results were statistically analyzed to determine the significance of the restriction provided by the supports. This revealed that the two ankle guards provided no significant support. The two tapes, however, provided significant support before exercise and after 10 minutes but not after 1 hour of exercise.
LEVEL: A LANG: Eng SIRC ARTICLE NO: 104907

TECHNIQUES

Reasoner, A.E. A Western States survey of certified athletic trainers' use of joint mobilization in treatment programs. (Refs: 18)*Athletic training (Greenville, N.C.)* 19(4), Winter 1984, 267-270;301.
LEVEL: I LANG: Eng SIRC ARTICLE NO: 104140

AUSTRALIA

Australian Sports Commission information and background: a report to national sporting and recreation organisations. s.l.: ACHP, 1984. 22 leaves (loose-leaf)
NOTES: Cover title.
ABST: The Australian Sports Commission was established to increase coordination and effectiveness of sports development policies and programs in Australia. 21 members have been appointed, many transferring from the Federal Dept.

of Sport, Recreation and Tourism. The objectives of the Commission are to sustain and improve on Australia's level of achievement in international sporting competition and to increase the level of participation in sport by all Australians. Legislation has been drafted to establish the commission as a statutory authority.
LEVEL: B LANG: Eng GV675 18660

Chenery, J. John Brown. *Sports world Australia* 1(1), Jul 1984, 18-21;78-79.
ABST: Topics covered in an interview with Federal Minister for Sport, Recreation and Tourism, include, government funding of sport and facilities, injuries, tobacco sponsorship, apartheid, politics in sport and amateurism.
LEVEL: I LANG: Eng SIRC ARTICLE NO: 102113

Davis, G. Aboriginals in recreation: Kununurra case study. *Recreation Australia* 3(4), Autumn 1984, 28;30.
LEVEL: I LANG: Eng SIRC ARTICLE NO: 097856

Matthews, I. Victorian Government Sporting Policy: towards a true 'sport for all'. (Refs: 7)
CONF: Physical Education Graduating Seminar Conference (1984 : Footscray Institute of Technology).
NOTES: In, Physical education in Australia: past, present and future directions, s.l., Footscray Institute of Technology, 1984, Suppl. p. 23-31.
LEVEL: I LANG: Eng SIRC ARTICLE NO: 096425

Mitchell, B. Working towards sport. (Refs: 11)
CONF: Physical Education Graduating Seminar Conference (1984 : Footscray Institute of Technology).
NOTES: In, Physical education in Australia: past, present and future directions, s.l., Footscray Institute of Technology, 1984, p. 64-69.
LEVEL: I LANG: Eng SIRC ARTICLE NO: 096157

Pearce, W. The Victorian Sports Institute, and its relationship with the existing physical education system in Victoria. (Refs: 3)
CONF: Physical Education Graduating Seminar Conference (1984 : Footscray Institute of Technology).
NOTES: In, Physical education in Australia: past, present and future directions, s.l., Footscray Institute of Technology, 1984, p. 51-54.
LEVEL: I LANG: Eng SIRC ARTICLE NO: 096163

Physical education in Australia: past, present and future directions. s.l.: Footscray Institute of Technology, 1984. 162, 31 p
CONF: Physical Education Graduating Seminar Conference (1984 : Footscray Institute of Technology).
CORP: Footscray Institute of Technology.
NOTES: Cover title. Includes bibliographies.
ABST: A collection of 29 papers on aspects of physical education in Australia, prepared by the June 1984 graduating class of the Dept. of Physical Education and Recreation of the Footscray Institute of Technology. Major themes of the papers include: history, children, special populations, legal liability, employment opportunities and future directions of physical education within the Australian context.
LEVEL: A LANG: Eng GV315 17673

Robertson, I. Sport in the lives of South Australian children. *Sports coach (Wembley, Australia)* 7(4), Mar 1984, 3-6.
LEVEL: I LANG: Eng SIRC ARTICLE NO: 094210

Taylor, L. The marketing and sponsorship of sport in Australia: marketing is defined as having the right

product, in the right place, at the right time, in the right quantities and at the right price. *Sports coach (Wembley, W. Aust.) 8(2), Oct 1984, 12-14.*
LEVEL: B LANG: Eng SIRC ARTICLE NO: 103817

The congress and where to from here? *Vicsport sportsview Apr 1984, 3.*
LEVEL: B LANG: Eng

HISTORY

Long, M. Physical education in Australian schools 1865-1965. (Refs: 4)
CONF: Physical Education Graduating Seminar Conferenc (1984 : Footscray Institute of Technology).
NOTES: In, Physical education in Australia: past, present and future directions, s.l., Footscray Institute of Technology, 1984, p. 21-26.
LEVEL: I LANG: Eng SIRC ARTICLE NO: 096148

McCormack, C. Pioneers in physical education in Australia. (Refs: 13)
CONF: Physical Education Graduating Seminar Conference (1984 : Footscray Institute of Technology).
NOTES: In, Physical education in Australia: past, present and future directions, s.l., Footscray Institute of Technology, 1984, p. 6-12.
LEVEL: I LANG: Eng SIRC ARTICLE NO: 096153

Myors, R. The impact of research on physical education. (Refs: 9)
CONF: Physical Education Graduating Seminar Conference (1984 : Footscray Institute of Technology).
NOTES: In, Physical education in Australia: past, present and future directions, s.l., Footscray Institute of Technology, 1984, p. 27-32.
LEVEL: I LANG: Eng SIRC ARTICLE NO: 096158

Roberts, M.J. The physical education time line past and present. (Refs: 6)
CONF: Physical Education Graduating Seminar Conference (1984 : Footscray Institute of Technology).
NOTES: In, Physical education in Australia: past, present and future directions, s.l., Footscray Institute of Technology, 1984, Suppl. p. 2-6.
LEVEL: I LANG: Eng SIRC ARTICLE NO: 096166

Ross, J.L. From informal to formal physical education. (Refs: 14)
CONF: Physical Education Graduating Seminar Conference (1984 : Footscray Institute of Technology).
NOTES: In, Physical education in Australia: past, present and future directions, s.l., Footscray Institute of Technology, 1984, p. 13-20.
LEVEL: I LANG: Eng SIRC ARTICLE NO: 096168

PHYSICAL FITNESS

Owen, N. Lee, C. Why people do and do not exercise. Recommendations for initiatives to promote regular, vigorous physical activity in Australia. (Adelaide): Department of Recreation and Sport, South Australia, c1984. vii, 79 p.
NOTES: On title page: Review and recommendations for Sport and Recreation Ministers' Council. Bibliography: p. 61-75.
ABST: An examination of why people do and do not exercise, based on theory, research and discussions with experts in the theoretical and practical aspects of exercise promotion. The 4 sections of the report are: (1) recommendations for government action; (2) key principles to be

considered when planning policy and programs; (3) a non-technical report describing the nature of the problem and approaches to it; (4) a technical and detailed review of the literature which supports the principles and recommendations.
LEVEL: B LANG: Eng ISBN: 0-7243-6426-9 GV481 17547

Van de Vlugt, M. Recent themes in the promotion health and fitness in Australians. (Refs: 8)
CONF: Physical Education Graduating Seminar Conference (1984 : Footscray Institute of Technology).
NOTES: In, Physical education in Australia: past, present and future directions, s.l., Footscray Institute of Technology, 1984, p. 56-63.
LEVEL: I LANG: Eng SIRC ARTICLE NO: 096208

Williams, P. Health related fitness - an Australian perspective. *British journal of physical education (London) 15(1), Jan/Feb 1984, 4;30.*
LEVEL: B LANG: Eng SIRC ARTICLE NO: 099216

AUSTRALIAN FOOTBALL

SOCIAL PSYCHOLOGY

Dunn, L. Jenkin, D. Junior football in Melbourne: the drop-out phenomenon. (Refs: 21)*Pelops 5, Feb 1984, 7-16.*
ABST: The results and background of a study conducted to determine the extent of the drop-out phenomenon in a popular junior sport, Australian Rules Football. Specifically the purpose of the study was to identify those factors influencing boys to withdraw from organised football with a junior club. Personal interviews were conducted with 68 boys. The results in accordance with Robinson's findings showed boys stopped playing with a junior club because of behaviour by coaches and inadequate coaching instruction, conflicting circumstances and interests.
LEVEL: A LANG: Eng SIRC ARTICLE NO: 097900

AUTOMOBILE RACING

Amadio, J. Race drivers should train like other athletes. *Auto racing digest (Des Moines, Iowa) 12(4), Jun/Jul 1984, 4-5.*
LEVEL: B LANG: Eng SIRC ARTICLE NO: 093260

Woodner, J. Cline, T. Real racing: an SCCA national champion tells why he left the circuit for the open road of pro rally. *Sports car (Englewood, Colo.) 42(7), Jul 1984, 25-27.*
LEVEL: B LANG: Eng SIRC ARTICLE NO: 101063

BIOGRAPHY AND AUTOBIOGRAPHY

Christensen, P. The last hero. *Chequered flag (Paddington, N.S.W.) 12(1), Jan 1984, 19-22.*
LEVEL: B LANG: Eng SIRC ARTICL NO: 097901

Ottum, B. A hunk hits the road: if you don't think life as a front man for a pizza chain can be beautiful, take a careful look at Indy-Car driver Danny Sullivan. *Sports illustrated (Chicago, Ill.) 60(20), 14 May 1984, 56;58;63-64;66.*
LEVEL: B LANG: Eng SIRC ARTICLE NO: 094812

Ottum, B. There's no way to put Darrell down. Darrell Waltrip has won more races than any driver in the past decade, and he' not easing off. *Sports*

illustrated *(Los Angeles, Calif.) 61(21), 5 Nov 1984, 34-37;40.*
LEVEL: B LANG: Eng SIRC ARTICLE NO: 101062

Rosen, K. Yesterday's heroes: Janet Guthrie didn't retire from racing willingly, despite the heat she faced as a woman drive *Auto racing digest (Des Moines, Iowa) 12(4), Jun/Jul 1984, 62-65.*
LEVEL: B LANG: Eng SIRC ARTICLE NO: 093261

Smiljanic, S. Soloing together. George & Dee Schweikle win by putting fun first. *Sports car (Santa Ana, Calif.) 42(6), Jun 1984, 24-27.*
LEVEL: B LANG: Eng SIRC ARTICLE NO: 102098

EQUIPMENT

Cooke, P. Indy's wings of victory. In, Schrier, E.W. and Allman, W.F. (eds.), Newton at the bat: the science in sports, New York, Scribner, c1984, p. 83-86.
LEVEL: B LANG: Eng RC1235 18609

Mitchell, B. Trans-AM 1984: an inside look at the technology. *Sports car (Englewood, Colo.) 42(7), Jul 1984, 17-22.*
LEVEL B LANG: Eng SIRC ARTICLE NO: 101061

Mitchell, B. How to be street prepared: a solo II handbook for bolting on some fun. *Sports car (Santa Ana, Calif.) 42(10), Oct 1984, 41-43.*
LEVEL: B LANG: Eng SIRC ARTICLE NO: 108780

HISTORY

O'Brien, L. Dirt track legends: a history of sprint car racing at the Iowa State Fairgrounds. Sioux City, Iowa: L. O'Brien, c1984. v. 1 : ill ; 20 cm.
NOTES: Vol. 1: 1907-1949.
LEVEL: I LANG: Eng LC CARD: 84-081653

INJURIES AND ACCIDENTS

Miller, J. How racing families cope when tragedy strikes. *Auto racing digest (Des Moines, Iowa) 12(1), Dec/Jan 1984, 28-31.*
LEVEL: B LANG: Eng SIRC ARTICLE NO: 173540

MEDICINE

Shyne, K. The Indianapolis 500: speed challenges medicine. *Physician and sportsmedicine (Minneapolis, Minn.) 12(5), May 1984, 166-168;170-171.*
LEVEL: B LANG: Eng SIRC ARTICLE NO: 094813

RULES AND REGULATIONS

Circuit routier: reglements. Road racing: rules. Montreal: Federation Auto-Quebec, 1984. 29 p.
CORP: Federation Auto-Quebec.
LEVEL: B LANG: Eng Fr LC CARD: 83-31729-5 GV1030 18503

Rallye: reglements. Montreal: Federation Auto-Quebec, 1984. 36, 10, 7 p.
CORP: Federation Auto-Quebec.
NOTES: Cover title.
LEVEL: B LANG: Fr GV1029.2 18504

Reglements tout-terrain. Montreal: Federation Auto-Quebec, 1984. 26 p.
CORP: Federation Auto-Quebec.
LEVEL: B LANG: Fr GV103 18502

Solo: reglements. Montreal: Federation Auto-Quebec, 1984. 21 p.
CORP: Federation Auto-Quebec.

AUTOMOBILE RACING (continued)

NOTES: Titre de la couverture.
LEVEL: B LANG: Fr GV1030 18507

SPORTING EVENTS

Donaldson, G. The Grand Prix of Canada.
Scarborough, Ont.: Avon Books, c1984. 128 p. : ill.
NOTES: Egalement publie en francais sous le titre:
Le Grand Prix du Canada.
LEVEL: B LANG: Eng ISBN: 0-380-87080-0 LC
CARD: C84-098556-8 GV1034.15 17630

Grand Prix Labatt du Canada, 15, 16 et 17 juin
1984. Montreal: Grand Prix Labatt du Canada,
1984. 80 p. : ill.
LEVEL: B LANG: Fr Eng LC CARD: 83-31725-2
GV1034.15.L3 17871

Hayes, D. Off the track. The death of Gilles
Villeneuve robbed auto racing of one of its most
talented drivers. It may also have marked the
beginning of the end for the Canadian Grand Prix.
Saturday night (Toronto) 99(6), Jun 1984, 69-70.
LEVEL: B LANG: Eng SIRC ARTICLE NO: 104536

BACKPACKING AND HIKING

Curtis, S. To get to the other side. River crossings
can be exhilarating. They can be dangerous too. An
expert tells you how to get over, around, or through
the water. *Backpacker (New York) 12(2), Mar 1984,
14;16;20-22.*
LEVEL: B LANG: Eng SIRC ARTICLE NO: 097903

Fletcher, C. Prince, V. The complete walker III: the
joys and techniques of hiking and backpacking. 3rd
ed., rev., enl. and updated. New York: Knopf, 1984.
xiv, 668 p. : ill.
NOTES: Includes index. Rev. ed. of: The new
complete walker, 2nd ed., rev., enl., and updated,
1974.
LEVEL: I LANG: Eng ISBN: 0394722647 LC CARD:
83-048870 GV199.6 18078

Hart, J. Walking softly in the wilderness: the Sierra
Club guide to backpacking. Rev. & updated. San
Francisco: Sierra Club Books, c1984. xii, 500 p. :
ill.
LEVEL: B LANG: Eng ISBN: 0-87156-813-6
GV199.6 18097

Jope, K.L. Shelby, B. Hiker behavior and the
outcome of interactions with grizzly bears. (Refs:
23)*Leisure sciences (New York) 6(3), 1984, 257-
271.*
ABST: Confrontations between hikers and grizzly
bears have led to management strategies intended
to allow people and grizzlies to coexist in national
park settings. Although several attitude studies
suggest that people support the continued presence
of bears in parks, the success of management
programs also requires knowledge of human and
bear behavior in potential conflict situations. This
study was based on hiker reports of encounters
with grizzly bears in Glacier National Park.
Variables measuring human behavior included level
of trail use, size of hiker party, the presence of bear
bells in the party, presence of horses, and people's
behavioral reaction to sighting the bear. Results
showed that bear bells reduced the likelihood of
charges by bears, greater trail use reduced the
chance of full charges, and the presence of horses
and group size had no effect.
LEVEL: A LANG: Eng SIRC ARTICLE NO: 102989

McNeish, C. The backpacker's manual. New York:
Times Books, c1984. 1v.
LEVEL: B LANG: Eng ISBN: 0812963385 LC
CARD: 84-0001

Wirth, B. Backpacking in the 80's. West Nyack,
N.Y.: Parker Pub. Co., c1984. 1v.
NOTES: Includes index.
LEVEL: B LANG: Eng ISBN: 0130567396 LC
CARD: 83-013249

CLOTHING

Chase, J. Looking for trouble. How do you know
your gear will hold up? Here's a sneak look at W.L.
Gore - one of the fussies product testing programs
anywhere. *Backpacker (New York) 12(3), May
1984, 72-76;78.*
LEVEL: B LANG: Eng SIRC ARTICLE NO: 100551

Coming to terms: when you need the right fabric
badly enough, words shouldn't get in the way.
Here's what some of the fancies terms really mean.
*Backpacker (New York) 12(3), May 1984,
14;16;19;99.*
LEVEL: B LANG: Eng SIRC ARTICLE NO: 100552

Conroy, C. Design and materials. (hiking boots)
*Great outdoors (Glasgow, Scotland) 7(8), Aug
1984, 51;53;55-56.*
LEVEL: B LANG: Eng SIRC ARTICLE NO: 098938

Eugenis, T. Take away DuPont. *Backpacker (New
York) 12(2), Mar 1984, 69-70;72;74.*
LEVEL: B LANG: Eng SIRC ARTICLE NO: 097484

McGowan, E. Green, S. Performance trailwear:
today's new trail clothes are engineered to keep
you warmer, drier, and more comfortable than ever
before. *Backpacker (Los Angeles) 12(5), Sept 1984,
48-54;56-58;92.*
LEVEL: B LANG: Eng SIRC ARTICLE NO: 102406

Woodward, B. The fast-moving world of
breathable rainwear. *Backpacker (New York) 12(2),
Mar 1984, 42-48;87.*
LEVEL: B LANG Eng SIRC ARTICLE NO: 097504

Woodward, B. Step-by-step boot care. *Backpacker
(New York) 12(3), May 1984, 41;71.*
LEVEL: B LANG: Eng SIRC ARTICLE NO: 100578

COUNTRIES AND REGIONS

Butwin, D. Take a hike. *Physician and
sportsmedicine (Minneapolis, Minn.) 12(5), May
1984, 155-156;158.*
LEVEL: B LANG: En SIRC ARTICLE NO: 094815

De Hart, A. Hiking the Old Dominion. San
Francisco: Sierra Club Books, 1984. 1v. (A Sierra
Club totebook.)
NOTES: Includes index.
LEVEL: B LANG: Eng ISBN: 0871568128 LC
CARD: 83-019586

De Hart, A. South Carolina hiking trails. Charlotte,
N.C.: East Woods Press, 1984. 1v.
LEVEL: B LANG: Eng ISBN: 0887420095 LC
CARD: 83-049035

Dickinson, G. The West Highland Way: potentials
and problems. (Refs: 3)*Scottish journal of physical
education (Glasgow, Scotland) 12(2), Apr 1984, 47-
49.*
LEVEL: B LANG: Eng SIRC ARTICLE NO: 094816

Dornan, P. Return to Kokoda. (Refs: 1)*Sport health
(Pennant Hills, Aust.) 2(1), 1984, 36-38.*
LEVEL: I LANG: Eng SIRC ARTICLE NO: 094817

Ehling, B. Fifty hikes in Central New York: hikes
and backpacks from the Western Adirondacks to
the Finger lakes. Woodstock, Vt.: Backcountry
Publications, c1984. 208 p.
LEVEL: B LANG: Eng ISBN: 0-942440-17-X LC
CARD: 84-070169

Fortunato, D.J. Miles on the Appalachian trail. s.l.:
s.n., c1984. 157 p. : ill.
NOTES: Bibliography: p. 156-157.
LEVEL: B LANG: Eng ISBN: 0961349409 LC
CARD: 84-209561

Fullerton, J. Backpacking in the Canyons of
Mexico. *NIRSA journal (Mt. Pleasant, Mich.) 8(20),
Winter 1984, 16-18.*
LEVEL: LANG: Eng SIRC ARTICLE NO: 097904

Jones, J.S. Tramping in Europe: a walking guide.
Englewood Cliffs, N.J.: Prentice-Hall, c1984. 1v.
NOTES: Includes index.
LEVEL: B LANG: Eng ISBN: 0139269800 LC
CARD: 83-019055

Smith, R. Hiking Maui: the valley isle. 3rd ed.
Berkeley: Wilderness Press, 1984. 132 p. : ill.
(Wilderness press trail guid series.)
NOTES: Includes index.
LEVEL: B LANG: Eng ISBN: 0899970370 LC
CARD: 83-051475

Strickland, R. Pacific Northwest trail guide.
Seattle, Wash.: Writing Works, c1984. 1v.
(Northwest collection.)
NOTES: Includes index.
LEVEL: B LANG: Eng ISBN: 0916076628 LC
CARD: 84-015304

DIRECTORIES

Ambrosi, J.G. Hiking Alberta's southwest.
Vancouver: Douglas & McIntyre, c1984. 166 p. : ill.
NOTES: Bibliography: p. 161-162. 'Sponsored by
Sierra Club of Western Canada (Alberta Group)'.
LEVEL: B LANG: Eng ISBN: 0-88894-426-8 LC
CARD: C84-91155-6 GV199.44.C3 17597

Martin, B. Hiking guide to Colorado's highest
passes. 1st ed. Boulder, Colo.: Pruett Pub. Co.,
c1984. 1v.
NOTES: Includes index.
LEVEL: B LANG: Eng ISBN: 0871086689 LC
CARD: 84-006893

Maughan, J.J. The hiker's guide to Idaho. Billings,
Mont.: Falcon Press, c1984. viii, 264 p. : ill., maps ;
24 cm.
LEVEL: B LANG: Eng ISBN: 0934318182 LC
CARD: 84-080089

Melius, M. The cloud peak primitive area: trail
guide, history and photo odyssey: an island
wilderness in the Big Horn Mountain range. 1st ed.
Aberdeen, S.D.: Tensleep Pub., 1984. 1v.
NOTES: Includes index.
LEVEL: B LANG: Eng ISBN: 096101301X LC
CARD: 84-050166

Robertson, D. The best hiking in Ontario.
Edmonton: Hurtig, c1984. 139 p. : ill.
NOTES: Bibliography: p. 137-139.
LEVEL: B LANG: Eng ISBN: 0-88830-256-8 LC
CARD: 84-91152-1 GV199.44.C3O5 17637

Rudner, R. Taking to the trail: eight great American
routes, from jungle to mountaintop. *Outside 9(4),
May 1984, 50-56;8-82.*
LEVEL: B LANG: Eng SIRC ARTICLE NO: 093632

ENVIRONMENT

Gordon, G. Understanding mountain weather. *Backpacker (New York) 12(1), Jan 1984, 14-15;22.* LEVEL: B LANG: Eng SIRC ARTICLE NO: 094819

Winning the bug war: did you ever feel like a bug's buffet in hiking boots? Here's how to disagree with something that eats yo *Backpacker (New York) 12(4), Jul 1984, 27-28;100.* LEVEL: B LANG: Eng SIRC ARTICLE NO: 102161

EQUIPMENT

Brewster, B. Pack preview. *Backpacker (New York) 12(1), Jan 1984, 26-28;30;32;34;36;41-45;90.* LEVEL: B LANG: Eng SIRC ARTICLE NO: 094814

Conroy, C. Chris Conroy advises on watching your weight. (hiking) *Great outdoors (Glasgow, Scotland) 7(7), Jul 1984, 71;73.* LEVEL: B LANG: Eng SIRC ARTICLE NO: 099387

Conroy, C. Kit check: Chris Conroy looks at the 'protection racket'. *Great outdoors (Glasgow, U.K.) 7(12), Dec 1984, 59-60.* LEVEL: B LANG: Eng SIRC ARTICLE NO: 173380

Eugenis, T.P. Good things in small packages. *Backpacker (New York) 12(1), Jan 1984, 62-67;75;81.* LEVEL: B LANG: Eng SIRC ARTICLE NO: 094818

Eugenis, T.P. Small wonders: that old surplus knapsack has come a long way. Look at the remarkable daypacks that are out now *Backpacker (New York) 12(2), Mar 1984, 82-87.* LEVEL: B LANG: Eng SIRC ARTICLE NO: 097485

McGowan, E. Behing the label: The North Face. After a quart of Scotch, the bold master plan: make nothing but the best, and people will pay for it. *Backpacker (New York) 12(4), Jul 1984, 60;102.* LEVEL: B LANG: Eng SIRC ARTICLE NO: 102162

Noble, C. Travel packs: convertible luggage for going in style. *Outside (Chicago, Ill.) 9(10), Nov 1984, 95-97.* LEVEL: B LANG: Eng SIRC ARTICLE NO: 173269

Reaney, J. Tully, C. Lack, T. Design and materials. Pt. II. *Great outdoors (Glasgow) 7(9), Sept 1984, 57-59.* LEVEL: B LANG: Eng SIRC ARTICLE NO: 109369

Rethmel, R.C. Rees, C.F. Backpacking. 7th ed. rev. and updated. Piscataway, N.J.: Winchester Press, c1984. 1v. NOTES: Includes index. LEVEL: I LANG: Eng ISBN: 0832903620 LC CARD: 84-016582

INJURIES AND ACCIDENTS

van Lear, D. Summer skin alert: no laughing matter. There's nothing funny about skin burns, itches, and chafes. A skin care expert thinks backpackers can do more to stay out of trouble. Here's what she suggests. *Backpacker (New York) 12(4), Jul 1984, 78;80;93.* LEVEL: B LANG: Eng SIRC ARTICLE NO: 102163

MEDICINE

Hiking medicine, part II: a personal wilderness medical kit. *American hiker (Washington, D.C.) Oct 1984, 4.* LEVEL: B LANG: Eng SIRC ARTICLE NO: 102988

Tully, C. Looking after your feet. *Great outdoors (Glasgow, Eng.) 7(3), Mar 1984, 76;78.* LEVEL: B LANG: Eng SIRC ARTICLE NO: 101066

NUTRITION

van Lear, D. Banquets in bags: camp food used to look like something that had fallen under the wheels of an Army jeep. No more. Here's a report on the pick of the fancy new compact cuisine. *Backpacker (New York) 12(4), Jul 1984, 81-86;89.* LEVEL: B LANG: Eng SIRC ARTICLE NO: 102166

PHYSICAL FITNESS

Ferstle, J. Taking fitness in hand: those little red handweights are showing up everywhere. Are their benefits real or imagined? *Backpacker (Los Angeles) 12(5), Sept 1984, 34;36;82.* LEVEL: B LANG: Eng SIRC ARTICLE NO: 102715

Ferstle, J. Rowing smart: here's a machine that not only conditions your backpacking muscles, but uses a little computer to help you along. *Backpacker (New York) 12(4), Jul 1984, 21-23.* LEVEL: B LANG: Eng SIRC ARTICLE NO: 102160

Jackson, P. Expanding your horizons. *Great outdoors (Glasgow, Eng.) 7(3), Mar 1984, 80.* LEVEL: B LANG: Eng SIRC ARTICLE NO: 101064

Noble, C. Running high: wilderness running may be the best way ever to build your power for backpacking. You can even do bot at once. *Backpacker (New York) 12(3), May 1984, 100-103.* LEVEL: B LANG: Eng SIRC ARTICLE NO: 101065

Rutstrum, C. Hiking. Merrillville, Ind.: ICS Books, 1984. 1v. LEVEL: B LANG: Eng ISBN: 0934802203 LC CARD: 83-026485

PHYSIOLOGY

Bensch, C. Deliac, P. Mirande, B. Fouillot, J.P. Ottoz, H. Evolution de frequences cardiaques de sujets non sportifs au cour de longues randonnees pedestres successives en moyenne altitude. (Refs: 11)*Medecine du sport (Paris) 58(3), 25 mai 1984, 26-31.* RESUME: Les variations de la frequence cardiaque dans trois groupes de trois sujets, heterogenes en age, sexe et aptitude physique, effectuant en moyenne altitude (inferieure a 3000 m) des randonnees pedestres au cours de trois journees consecutives furent enregistrees. La technique de Holter fut utilisee. L'evolution pour chaque sujet et tout au long de la randonnee, les variations individuelles au cours de la meme randonnee, ainsi que l'ensemble de l'evolution de la frequence cardiaque moyenne pour chaque groupe et chaque randonnee furent les aspects etudies. LEVEL: A LANG: Fr SIRC ARTICLE NO: 096493

TEACHING

Mentis, J. Backpacking: outdoor living skills series. Instructor manual. Jefferson City, Mo.: Missouri Dept. of Conservation 1984. 1 microfiche (110 fr.) (Outdoor living skills.) LEVEL: I LANG: Eng EDRS: ED247046

TECHNIQUES AND SKILLS

Fox, R. Fox, B. Loading a frame pack. *Adirondac (Glen Falls, N.Y.) 48(6), Jul 1984, 32-33.* NOTES: Reprinted from, January bulletin of Penn's Woods chapter. LEVEL: B LANG: Eng SIRC ARTICLE NO: 099388

BADMINTON

Krotee, M.L. Turner, E.T. Innovative theory and practice of badminton. Dubuque, Iowa: Kendall/Hunt, c1984. ix, 133 p. : ill. NOTES: Filmography: p. 117. Bibliography: p. 115-116. LEVEL: B LANG: Eng ISBN: 0840331525 LC CARD: 83-082051 GV1007 18242

Porteles, A.M. Le badminton, sport d'elite et sport populaire. *Macolin (Suisse) 4, avr 1984, 6-7.* LEVEL: B LANG: Fr SIRC ARTICLE NO: 101068

BIOGRAPHY AND AUTOBIOGRAPHY

Hales, G. Helen Tibbetts. *Badminton U.S.A. (Warwich, R.I.) 42(3), Jan 1984, 8.* LEVEL: B LANG: Eng SIRC ARTICLE NO: 097905

COACHING

Interview: the best of badminton. (Paul Whetnall) *Sports coach (Wembley, Australia) 7(4), Mar 1984, 16-18.* LEVEL: B LANG: E SIRC ARTICLE NO: 094820

EQUIPMENT

Badminton & squash: product action on the courts. *Sports trader (London) 145(1009), 19 Apr 1984, 14-15;17.* LEVEL: B LANG: E SIRC ARTICLE NO: 101872

EQUIPMENT - RETAILING

Getting to know you. Many sports shops specialise in a particular sport. We talked to one shop owner known in his area for badminton to find out what that means to business. *Sports trader (London) 145(1009), 19 Apr 1984, 22-23.* LEVEL: B LANG: Eng SIRC ARTICLE NO: 101874

No change at the top: our survey reveals that established names still dominate badminton and squash. *Sports trader (London) 145(1009), 19 Apr 1984, 10-11.* LEVEL: B LANG: Eng SIRC ARTICLE NO: 101871

The Pro's progress. Badminton & squash. (Pro-Kennex) *Sports trader (London) 145(1009), 19 Apr 1984, 19;22-23.* LEVEL: B LANG Eng SIRC ARTICLE NO: 101873

BADMINTON (continued)

FACILITIES

Badminton 1. *Sport & leisure (London, Eng.) Sept/Oct 1984, 55-58.*
NOTES: Technical sports data no 16.
LEVEL: B LANG: Eng SIRC ARTICLE NO: 108902

Jeannotat, Y. Centre de badminton Malley-Lausanne: un modele du genre. *Macolin (Suisse) 4, avr 1984, 4-5.*
LEVEL: B LANG: SIRC ARTICLE NO: 101067

Technical sports data - November 1984 no. 17: Badminton 2. *Sport and leisure (London) 25(5), Nov/Dec 1984, 49-50.*
CORP: England. Sports Council.
LEVEL: B LANG: Eng SIRC ARTICLE NO: 108966

INJURIES AND ACCIDENTS

Medhurst, D. McNaughton, L. Badminton injuries in Australia. (Refs: 13)*Sports coach (Wembley, W. Aust.) 8(2), Oct 1984, 10-11.*
LEVEL: B LANG: Eng SIRC ARTICLE NO: 104539

OFFICIATING

Serving judges. *World badminton (Moncton, N.B.) 12(3), Sept 1984, 12-13.*
LEVEL: B LANG: Eng SIRC ARTICLE NO: 102992

PERCEPTUAL MOTOR PROCESSES

Salapatas, N. Sports vision. *World badminton (Gloucestershire, Eng.) 12(1), Mar 1984, 10.*
LEVEL: B LANG: Eng SIRC ARTICLE NO: 097907

PSYCHOLOGY

Albury, K.W. Fear of failure and fear of success: the relationship of achievement motives to the motor performance of males and females. Eugene, Ore.: Microform Publications, University of Oregon, 1984. 1 microfiche : negative; 11 x 15 cm.
NOTES: Thesis (M.S.) - North Texas State University, 1982; (iv, 74 leaves); includes bibliography.
LEVEL: A LANG: Eng UO84 212

STRATEGY

Jian, H. Hao, L. How to choose a style of play. *World badminton (Gloucestershire, Eng.) 12(1), Mar 1984, 23.*
LEVEL: B LANG: Eng SIRC ARTICLE NO: 097906

TECHNIQUES AND SKILLS - STANCE

Smith, G. Badminton footwork. *Badminton review (Calgary Alta.) 21(6), Jun 1984, 4.*
LEVEL: B LANG: Eng SIRC ARTICLE NO: 097908

VARIATIONS

McTavish, B. McTavish, R. Pickle ball. *OPHEA: Ontario Physical and Health Education Association (London, Ont.) 10(2), Sprin 1984, 21-25.*
LEVEL: B LANG: Eng SIRC ARTICLE NO: 099345

BALLET

BIOGRAPHY AND AUTOBIOGRAPHY

Kareda, U. In a class of her own. Evelyn Hart is torn between her commitment to the Royal Winnipeg Ballet and her desire to be a world-class dancer. *Saturday night (Toronto) 99(11), Nov 1984, 65-67.*
LEVEL: B LANG: Eng SIRC ARTICLE NO: 104662

Smeltzer, D. Roberts, D. There is only the dance. Obsessive. Compulsive. Painful. The graceful world of dance has a hard edg to rival that of any sport. (Carla Stallings) *Ultrasport (Boston, Mass.) 1(2), Apr 1984, 38-39;42-45.*
LEVEL: B.LANG: Eng SIRC ARTICLE NO: 098042

BIOMECHANICS

Gray, M. Skinar, M.H. Support base use in two dance idioms. (Refs: 10)*Research quarterly for exercise & sport (Reston, Va.) 55(2), Jun 1984, 184-187.*
ABST: This study investigated the size of the bases of support used in ballet and modern dance classes. The authors indicate that dance literature suggests that ballet utilizes a narrow and non-supported base while modern dance utilizes wider and grounded bases of support. This study confirms this hypothesis for the warm-up phase of the two types of dance. Thus, the results indicate that there exist inherent similarities along with fundamental differences between ballet and modern dance.
LEVEL: A LANG: Eng SIRC ARTICLE NO: 096617

Woodruff, J. Plies - some food for thought. (Refs: 2)*Kinesiology for dance (Carlisle, Pa.) 7(1), Oct 1984, 8-9.*
LEVEL: I LANG: Eng SIRC ARTICLE NO: 108796

INJURIES AND ACCIDENTS

Klemp, P. Learmonth, I.D. Hypermobility and injuries in a professional ballet company. (Refs: 15)*British journal of sports medicine (Loughborough, Eng.) 18(3), Sept 1984, 143-148.*
ABST: A study was conducted on members of the Cape Performing Arts Board (CAPAB) professional ballet company to determine the prevalence of hypermobility and to document the injuries sustained over a ten year period. If forward flexion, which is acquired through training, is excluded as a parameter the difference in hypermobility between dancers and controls is not statistically significant. Considering the stresses imposed on the musculoskeletal system, the number of injuries was suprisingly low. Ligamentous injuries about the ankle and knee were both common and accounted for the major morbidity. There were minor differences in the nature of severity of injuries in the male and female dancers. Back injuries, fractures and osteoarthrosis were uncommon and shin splints was not recorded in any of the dancers.
LEVEL: A LANG: Eng SIRC ARTICLE NO: 103131

Tudisco, C. Pudd, G. Stenosing tenosynovitis of the flexor hallucis longus tendon in a classical ballet dancer. (Refs: 7) *American journal of sports medicine (Baltimore, Md.) 12(5), Sept/Oct 1984, 403-404.*
LEVEL: A LANG: Eng SIRC ARTICLE NO: 104670

MEDICINE

Barrack, R.L. Skinner, H.B. Cook, S.D. Proprioception of the knee joint. Paradoxical effect of training. (Refs: 30)*American journal of physical medicine (Baltimore) 63(4), Aug 1984, 175-181.*
ABST: Two tests frequently used to measure joint proprioception were performed on the knees of twelve members of a professional ballet company to determine the effect of extensive athletic training on this sensation. These tests measured the threshold of perception of joint motion and the ability of a subject to reproduce a joint position. A healthy, active age-matched control group was also tested. Results show that dancers performed significantly better on the threshold test and significantly worse when reproducing a joint position than the control group.
LEVEL: A LANG: Eng SIRC ARTICLE NO: 104658

Calabrese, L.H. Weight control in dance and gymnastics. Chicago: Teach'em Inc., 1984?. 1 sound cassette (Audio cassette series on sports medicine: Sportsmedicine for female athletes, SM-40.)
NOTES: Cassettes recorded and produced by Teach'em Inc. in cooperation with the Physician and Sportsmedicine.
LEVEL: I LANG: Eng

McQueen, C. The pointe shoe. (Refs: 6)*Kinesiology for dance (Carlisle, Pa.) 7(2), Dec 1984, 9-11.*
LEVEL: I LANG: Eng SIRC ARTICLE NO: 104665

Stoller, S.M. Hekmat, F. Kleiger, B. A comparative study of the frequency of anterior impingement exostoses of the ankle in dancers and nondancers. (Refs: 13)*Foot & ankle 4(4), Jan/Feb 1984, 201-203.*
ABST: This study compared the incidence of anterior impingement exostoses of the ankle in 100 nondancers and 32 professional or preprofessional (students) classical and modern ballet dancers. Findings show that 4% of the nondancers suffered from talar exostoses while 59.3% of the dancers had talar exostoses.
LEVEL: A LANG: Eng SIRC ARTICLE NO: 093387

PERCEPTUAL MOTOR PROCESSES

Barrack, R.L. Skinner, H.B. Cook, S.D. Proprioception of the knee joint; paradoxical effect of training. (Refs: 30)*American journal of physical medicine (Baltimore, Md.) 63(4), Aug 1984, 175-181.*
ABST: Knee joint proprioception of twelve members (average age 25 years old) of a professional ballet company and fourteen age-matched controls was measured in this study. Subjects were tested on the threshold of perception of joint motion and the ability to reproduce a joint position. Findings indicated that the test group was less accurate than the control group in reproducing angles (p0.05) while it performed better on the threshold test (p0.05).
LEVEL: A LANG: Eng SIRC ARTICLE NO: 098036

Barrack, R.L. Skinner, H.B. Brunet, M.E. Cook, S.D. Joint kinesthesia in the highly trained knee. (Refs: 10)*Journal of sports medicine and physical fitness (Torino) 24(1), Mar 1984, 18-20.*
ABST: 5 male and 7 female members of a professional ballet company were tested for their ability to small position changes in their knee joint.

An age-matched group of healthy active controls were also tested. The dancers were found to be more sensitive to the detection of the onset of motion at the knee joint. It is concluded that this sense of joint motion and position can be attributed to extensive athletic training.
LEVEL: A LANG: Eng SIRC ARTICLE NO: 099515

Clarkson, P.M. Kennedy, T.E. Flanagan, J. A study of three movements in classical ballet. (Refs: 6)*Research quarterly for exercise & sport (Reston, Va.) 55(2), Jun 1984, 175-179.*
ABST: This study examined and compared three simple ballet movements: releve, saute, and en pointe from first position. Total reaction time and angular degree of plie were analyzed for each of the movements. Twenty-three female students of ballet were studied. The results indicate that there is 'set' demi-plie which results from classical ballet training. This depth can be reached slowly or quickly depending on the type of movement being executed.
LEVEL: A LANG: Eng SIRC ARTICLE NO: 096615

PHYSICAL FITNESS

Kent, A. Camner, J. Camner, C. The dancers' body book. New York: Quill, 1984. 220 p. : ill.
NOTES: Bibliography: p. 219-220
LEVEL: B LANG: Eng ISBN: 0-688-01539-5 LC CARD: 83-17732 GV1787 17583

PHYSIOLOGY

Micheli, L.J. Gillespie, W.J. Walaszek, A. Physiologic profiles of female professional ballerinas. (Refs: 19)*Clinics in sports medicine (Philadelphia) 3(1), Jan 1984, 199-209.*
NOTES: Symposium on profiling.
ABST: Nine elite level ballerinas were tested and compared with elite ballet students. The profiles included an assessment of cardiovascular fitness, muscle strength and flexibility as well as the compilation of anthropometric data and an injury profile. With such information it may be possible to avoid future injuries and maximize performances. As well the profile can help to determine when a young dancer is ready for a specific technique.
LEVEL: A LANG: Eng SIRC ARTICLE NO: 093382

PHYSIOLOGY - MUSCLE

Kirkendall, D.T. Bergfeld, J.A. Calabrese, L. Lombardo, J.A. Street, G. Weiker, G.G. Isokinetic characteristics of ballet dancers and the response to a season of ballet training. (Refs: 19)*Journal of orthopaedic and sports physical therapy (Baltimore) 5(4), Jan/Feb 1984, 207-211.*
ABST: This study was undertaken to describe the upper leg, isokinetic strength of professional ballet dancers in the preseason and at the 'peak' of the season. Other selected isokinetic characteristics were also measured so that some normative data may be collected for the screening of dancers in a preventative setting. The data indicates that within the given period, significant training improvement in terms of torque generated occur only at higher speeds. It is also indicated that male dancers have characteristics similar to other athletes; that female dancers generate less relative torque than other female athletes; and that dance training affects torque only at functional velocities.
LEVEL: A LANG: Eng SIRC ARTICLE NO: 093380

BALLOONING

Landowner relations. *Ballooning (Cincinnati, Oh.) 17(3), Fall 1984, 13-14.*
NOTES: A chapter from the B.F.A.'s Education Committee project, Landowner Relations.
LEVEL: B LANG: Eng SIRC ARTICLE NO: 102995

ECONOMICS

Leon, V. To be or not to be (sponsored): that is the question facing the National Balloon Championships. *Ballooning (Cincinnati, Ohio) 17(1), Jan/Feb 1984, 7-8.*
LEVEL: B LANG: Eng SIRC ARTICLE NO: 097913

EQUIPMENT

Flying the Viva-65. *Ballooning (Cincinnati, Oh.) 17(3), Fall 1984, 6-7.*
LEVEL: B LANG: Eng SIRC ARTICLE NO: 102993

Haug, E. de Rouvray, A. Finite element design of a high pressure balloon with Pam-Lisa.
CONF: Aerodynamic Decelerator and Balloon Technology Conference (8th : 1984 : Hyannis, Mass.).
CORP: Engineering System International S.A..
NOTES: In, A collection of technical papers: AIAA 8th Aerodynamic Decelerator and Balloon Technology Conference, New York, American Institute of Aeronautics and Astronautics, 1984, p. 200-209.
ABST: The authors present a rational methodology for the engineering design of lightweight structures, such as balloons, parachutes, sails, tents, and other structures. This methodology effectively solves the steps of shape finding, optimal cutting pattern evaluation and load response analysis of fabric membranes. This methodology has been incorporated into a computer program called PAM-LISA. The present paper details the application of this methodology to the design of a high technology balloon.
LEVEL: A LANG: Eng SIRC ARTICLE NO: 097911

Leon, V. The wicker tradition. *Ballooning (Cincinnati, Ohio) 17(2), Mar/Apr 1984, 38-39;46-47.*
LEVEL: B LANG: Eng SIRC ARTICLE NO: 094822

Zierdt, C.H. Nelson, J.R. High wind balloon material test and launch concept description.
CONF: Aerodynamic Decelerator and Balloon Technology Conference (8th : 1984 : Hyannis, Mass.).
NOTES: In, A collection of technical papers: AIAA 8th Aerodynamic Decelerator and Balloon Technology Conference, New York, American Institute of Aeronautics and Astronautics, 1984, p. 39-44.
ABST: The authors detail the testing of a balloon in a 35 mph wind field which used a new Winzen film that can withstand twice the stress of existing polyethylene balloon film and is very resistant to abrasion. The results indicate this type of film an excellent material for use in windy launches.
LEVEL: A LANG: Eng SIRC ARTICLE NO: 097915

PHOTOGRAPHY

Leon, V. Building better balloon aloft. Part two: the camera aloft. *Ballooning (Cincinnati, Ohio.) 17(2), Mar/Apr 1984, 34-37.*
LEVEL: B LANG: Eng SIRC ARTICLE NO: 094821

Leon, V. Building better balloon photos. Part 1: shooting from terra firma. *Ballooning (Cincinnati, Ohio) 17(1), Jan/Feb 1984, 35-37.*
LEVEL: B LANG: Eng SIRC ARTICLE NO: 097914

WOMEN

Crouch, T. Fair voyagers: intrepid women in American ballooning. *Ballooning (Cincinnati, Ohio) 17(1), Jan/Feb 1984, 18-19;22.*
NOTES: Excerpts from, The Eagle aloft, by Dr. Tom Crouch.
LEVEL: B LANG: Eng SIRC ARTICLE NO: 097909

BANDY

COUNTRIES AND REGIONS

Johnson, A. Gilchrist, J. The ice-rink in contemporary society - a critical appraisal. (Refs: 187)*Momentum: a journal of human movement studies (Edinburgh) 9(2), Summer 1984, 26-70.*
LEVEL: I LANG: Eng SIRC ARTICLE NO: 098970

BASEBALL

Boswell, T. Why time begins on opening day. 1st ed. Garden City, N.Y.: Doubleday, 1984. 312 p.
LEVEL: B LANG: Eng ISBN: 0385184093 LC CARD: 82-046029

Coffey, F. The all-time baseball teams book. New York: St. Martin's Press, 1984. 1v.
LEVEL: B LANG: Eng ISBN: 0312020368 LC CARD: 83-023045

Fabianic, D. Managerial succession, organizational effectiveness and franchise relocation in professional baseball. (Refs: 1 *Journal of sport behavior (Mobile, Ala.) 7(1), Feb 1984, 3-12.*
ABST: The study sought to update earlier work concerning the relationship between managerial succession and organizational effectiveness. The results indicate that there is an inverse relationship between the two variables among franchises which have remained stable since 1951. Conversely there is a direct relationship between the two variables for the franchises added to the league since 1951.
LEVEL: A LANG: Eng SIRC ARTICLE NO: 096500

Fischler, S. Waltzman, R. Lippman, D. Stan Fischler's amazing trivia from the world of baseball. Markham, Ont.: Penguin Book Canada, c1984. 176 p. : ill.
LEVEL: B LANG: Eng ISBN: 0-14-007200-4 LC CARD: C84-98138-4 GV867.3 17533

Gordon, A. Foul balls: five years in the American League. Toronto: McClelland and Stewart Limited, c1984. 204 p.
LEVEL: B LANG: Eng ISBN: 0-7710-4325-3 LC CARD: C84-099239-4 GV875.A15 18114

Lloyd, M. Baseball lessons for nurses. *Nursing outlook (New York) 32(4), Jul/Aug 1984, 200-203.*
LEVEL: B LANG: Eng SIRC ARTICLE NO: 103009

Skipper, J.K. Baseball's 'Babes' - Ruth and others. *Baseball research journal (Cooperstown, N.Y.) 1984, 24-26.*
LEVEL: I LANG: Eng SIRC ARTICLE NO: 107007

Wolcott, B. Albrecht, R. Baseball and softball: a mid-season update. *Spotlight (East Lansing, Mich.)*

7(2), Summer 1984, 3-4.
LEVEL: B LANG: Eng SIRC ARTICLE NO: 097932

ADMINISTRATION

Chass, M. Bowie Kuhn: he gave baseball a corporate image. *Inside sports (Evanston, Ill.) 6, Nov 1984, 18-20;22;24.*
LEVEL: LANG: Eng SIRC ARTICLE NO: 102999

Fabianic, D. Organization effectiveness and managerial succession: an update of an old problem. (Refs: 18)*Journal of sport behavior (Mobile, Ala.) 7(4), Dec 1984, 139-152.*
ABST: An examination of midseason managerial successions in professional baseball between 1951-80 reveals that managerial replacements usually occur during a team slump, and team performance ordinarily improves in the period immediately following the managerial change. This finding is consistent with the common sense theory which suggests that team performance will improve following managerial replacement. However, when the effects of the prereplacement slump and recovery period are removed, the data are consistent with the ritual scapegoating explanation of succession which posits that managers have little effect on team performance. When team performances under new and old managers are compared in general, with no consideration of other variables, there is weak support for the common sense theory. The results of this study indicate that the relationship of organizational effectiveness and managerial succession is one that is dependent upon the time periods considered to discern team performance, and the character of the replacement process and origin of successor.
LEVEL: A LANG: Eng SIRC ARTICLE NO: 101069

Miller, R. Sport management field experiences with the Detroit Tigers Baseball Club. *In, Zanger, B.K. and Parks, J.B. (eds.), Sport management curricula: the business and education nexus, Bowling Green, Ohio, Bowling Green State University, 1984, p. 86-88.*
CONF: Bowling Green State University Sport Management Curriculum Symposium (1983 : Bowling Green, Ohio).
LEVEL: B LANG: Eng GV713 20087

Ringolsby, T. Sport interview: Calvin Griffith. *Sport (New York) 75(4), Apr 1984, 15;17-18;20-22.*
LEVEL: B LANG: Eng SIRC ARTICLE NO: 093290

AERODYNAMICS

Allman, W.F. Pitching rainbows: the untold physics of the curve ball. *In, Schrier, E.W. and Allman, W.F. (eds.), Newton at the bat: the science in sports, New York, Scribner, c1984, p. 3-14.*
LEVEL: I LANG: Eng RC1235 18609

Allman, W.F. What makes a knuckleball dance? *In, Schrier, E.W. and Allman, W.F. (eds.), Newton at the bat: the science in sports, New York, Scribner, c1984, p. 15-19.*
LEVEL: I LANG: Eng RC1235 18609

Smith, M.A. The effect of roughness elements on the Magnus characteristics of rotating spherical projectiles. Eugene, Ore.: Microform Publications, University of Oregon, 1984. 1 microfiche : negative, ill. ; 11 x 15 cm.
NOTES: Thesis (M.S.) - North Texas State University, 1982; (vi, 87 leaves); includes bibliography.
LEVEL: A LANG: Eng UO84 207

ASSOCIATIONS

Directory - Society for American Baseball Research. Cooperstown, N.Y.: Society for American Baseball Research, 1984. 96 p.
CORP: Society for American Baseball Research.
NOTES: Cover title: SABR 1984 directory.
LEVEL: B LANG: Eng GV862 18293

AUDIO VISUAL MATERIAL

Burroughs, W.A. Visual simulation training of baseball batters. (Refs: 8)*International journal of sport psychology (Rome, Italy) 15(2), 1984, 117-126.*
ABST: Visual simulation training films were developed by filming collegiate baseball pitchers throwing fastball and curves with the camera located in the right handed batter's box. Films were then edited into a series of learning trials in which subjects were required to respond to questions regarding the type of pitch and its location in the hitting area. Fifty-nine collegiate batters participated in two separate studies to evaluate batters' improvement in pitch recognition and location. The dependent variables were subjects' 1)recognition scores and 2) location scores on a real time three dimensional measure of their visual skills by means of its visual interruption system, an apparatus designed for use in a bullpen. Group comparisons by means of tests indicated significant gains in location scores and non significant changes in pitch recognition scores (probably due to initally high pretest levels). These gains occurred with the use of slow motion or real time films and most of the gains were maintained in a six week follow up posttest.
LEVEL: A LANG: Eng SIRC ARTICLE NO: 099434

BIOGRAPHY AND AUTOBIOGRAPHY

Alexander, C.C. Ty Cobb. New York: Oxford University Press, 1984. 272 p. : ill.
NOTES: Includes index. Bibliography: p. 254-259.
LEVEL: I LANG: Eng ISBN: 0195034147 LC CARD: 83-017409 GV865.C6 18085

Anderson, B. Yesterday: a former foundry worker forged a record by playing for 26 seasons. (James Thomas McGuire) *Sports illustrated (Chicago, Ill.) 61(8), 13 Aug 1984, 96;98.*
LEVEL: B LANG: Eng SIRC ARTICLE NO: 096494

Coffey, W. Sport interview: Dan Quisenberry. The ace relief pitcher with the screwy delivery keeps baseball in stiches. *Sport (New York) 75(5), May 1984, 21;23-25.*
LEVEL: B LANG: Eng SIRC ARTICLE NO: 093271

Conner, F. Snyder, J. Baseball's footnote players. South Bend, Ind.: Icarus Press, 1984. 1v.
NOTES: Includes index.
LEVEL: LANG: Eng ISBN: 089651059X LC CARD: 84-006559

Coplon, J. Soto: the year of living dangerously. For Mario Soto, his best season has been the worst of times. *Sport (New York) 75(10), Oct 1984, 62-64;67-72.*
LEVEL: B LANG: Eng SIRC ARTICLE NO: 099390

Creamer, R.W. Stengel: his life and times. New York: Simon and Schuster, c1984. 349 p. : ill.
NOTES: Includes index.
LEVEL B LANG: Eng ISBN: 0671224891 LC CARD: 83-017508 GV865.S8 16043

Derby, R. Mays' beaning of Chapman recounted. (Ray Chapman) *Baseball research journal (Cooperstown, N.Y.) 1984, 12-13.*
LEVEL: B LANG: Eng SIRC ARTICLE NO: 106968

Falk, B. Bibb Falk recalls the old Black Sox. Eddie Cicotte once told him there was nothing to rumours the club 'chrew' the 1919 series. *Baseball digest (Evanston, Ill.) 43(5), 68-72.*
LEVEL: B LANG: Eng SIRC ARTICLE NO: 094828

Feinstein, J. Darryl Strawberry: no big apple hype. *Inside sports (Evanston, Ill.) 6, Mar 1984, 26-31.*
LEVEL: B LANG: Eng SIRC ARTICLE NO: 108802

Fiffer, S. Tommy John: still some wins in that old rebuilt machine. *Inside sports (Evanston, Ill.) 6, Sept 1984, 20-24.*
LEVEL: B LANG: Eng SIRC ARTICLE NO: 097916

Fimbrite, R. He's done his daddy proud. (Cal Ripken Jr.) *Sports illustrated 60(14), 2 Apr 1984, 34-36;38;40;43.*
LEVEL: B LANG: Eng SIRC ARTICLE NO: 093275

Fimrite, R. Pete's out to prove he can pull his weight. At 42 going on 4,000, Pete Rose has a new team, the Expos, and a new challenge - lifting yet another club to the pennant. *Sports illustrated 60(7), 13 Feb 1984, 42-44;47.*
LEVEL: B LANG: Eng SIRC ARTICLE NO: 090448

Fimrite, R. Don't knock the rock. His drug problem behind him, Montreal centerfielder Tim (Rock) Raines is now one of baseball's best all-round players. *Sports illustrated (Los Angeles, Calif.) 60(26), 25 Jun 1984, 48-49;52;54;56.*
LEVEL: B LANG: Eng SIRC ARTICLE NO: 094829

Fimrite, R. Just call me slick, pal. (Billy Gardner) *Sports illustrated (Chicago, Ill.) 61(15), 24 Sept 1984, 46;48-49.*
LEVEL: B LANG: Eng SIRC ARTICLE NO: 099391

Fimrite, R. Armed to win the big ones. Detroit's Jack Morris is a complex character with a simple approach to post season play - dominate it. *Sports illustrated (Los Angeles, Calif.) 61(20), 29 Oct 1984, 42-45.*
LEVEL: B LANG: Eng SIRC ARTICLE NO: 099392

Fimrite, R. The happy hunter. After years of disappointment, Kirk Gibson, Detroit's hot-tempered rightfielder, unleashed his 'potential' and made '84 a season to remember. *Sports illustrated (Los Angeles, Calif.) 61(26), 10 Dec 1984, 88-92;94;96;98;100;102.*
LEVEL: B LANG: Eng SIRC ARTICLE NO: 103003

Gallagher, M. 50 years of Yankee all-stars. New York: Leisure Press, 1984. 1v.
LEVEL: B LANG: Eng ISBN: 0880111615 LC CARD: 84-002907

Garrity, J. Having a monster of a season: fun-loving Alan Trammell is a terror in the field and at the plate for the Tigers, who are winning so big this season that it's scary. *Sports illustrated (Chicago, Ill.) 60(21), 28 May 1984, 46-48;50;52-53.*
LEVEL: B LANG: Eng SIRC ARTICLE NO: 094833

Garrity, J. The trade that made the Cubs. Chicago was gambling when it got Rick Stucliffe from Cleveland, but the deal may have won the pennant. *Sports illustrated (Chicago) 61(11), 3 Sept 1984, 28-31.*
LEVEL: B LANG: Eng SIRC ARTICLE NO: 097917

Grace, K. 'Bushel Basket' Charlie Gould of Red Stockings. *Baseball research journal (Cooperstown,*

N.Y.) 1984, 82-84.
LEVEL: B LANG: Eng SIRC ARTICLE NO: 106975

Gunther, M. Basepaths: from the minor leagues to the majors and beyond. New York: Charles Scribner's Sons, c1984. ix, 224 p. : ill.
LEVEL: B LANG: Eng ISBN: 0-684-18175-4 LC CARD: 84-13881 GV863.A1 18177

Henkey, B. Joe Cronin, hall of fame player, exec. 1906-1984. *Sporting news (St. Louis, Mo.) 17 Sept 1984, 2.*
LEVEL: B LANG: Eng SIRC ARTICLE NO: 099393

Holway, J.B. Sam Streeter smartest pitcher in negro leagues. *Baseball research journal (Cooperstown, N.Y.) 1984, 71-72.*
LEVEL: B LANG: Eng SIRC ARTICLE NO: 106980

Jackson, R. Reggie. New York: Villard Books, 1984. 1v.
LEVEL: B LANG: Eng ISBN: 0394532430 LC CARD: 83-050863

Jacobs, B. Little big man: for 20 seasons Joe Morgan has proved he can hit, run, and play defense with anybody. The only thing he's bad at is losing. *Inside sports (Evanston, Ill.) 6, Nov 1984, 58-64.*
LEVEL: B LANG: Eng SIRC ARTICLE NO: 103006

Kram, M. The dark side of a loser: Denny McLain once seemed destined for the Hall of Fame - now it could be prison. *Inside sports (Evanston, Ill.) 6, Oct 1984, 66-68;70;72-73.*
LEVEL: B LANG: Eng SIRC ARTICLE NO: 104544

Langford, W.M. Travis Jackson: he captained John McGraw's giants. *Baseball digest (Evanston, Ill.) 43(9), Sept 1984, 89-90;92-95.*
LEVEL: B LANG: Eng SIRC ARTICLE NO: 097922

Linderman, L. Sport interview: Joe Morgan. Baseball's little big man has a curious habit - everywhere he goes, he wins. *Sport (New York) 75(6), Jun 1984, 19-23.*
LEVEL: B LANG: Eng SIRC ARTICLE NO: 093281

Nack, W. The perils of Darryl: a rugged apprenticeship behind him, Darryl Strawberry could be swinging into an amazin' futur *Sports illustrated (Chicago, Ill.) 60(17), 23 Apr 1984, 32-34;38-39.*
LEVEL: B LANG: Eng SIRC ARTICLE NO: 094839

Nettles, G. Golenbock, P. Balls. New York: Putnam, c1984. 1v.
LEVEL: B LANG: Eng ISBN: 0399128948 LC CARD: 84-001866

O'Neil, J. Unforgettable Satchel Paige. *Reader's digest (Montreal) Jul 1984, 66-70.*
LEVEL: B LANG: Eng SIRC ARTICLE NO: 107990

Overfield, J.M. Easter's Charisma, remarkable slugging captivated fans. (Luke Easter) *Baseball research journal (Cooperstown, N.Y.) 1984, 14-16.*
LEVEL: B LANG: Eng SIRC ARTICLE NO: 106999

Peterson, R. Only the ball was white: a history of legendary black players and all black professional teams. New York ; Montreal: McGraw-Hill, 1984. iv, 406 p. : ill. (Sports.)
NOTES: Reprint. Originally published: Englewood Cliffs, N.J.: Prentice-Hall, c1970.
LEVEL: I LANG: Eng ISBN: 0070495998 LC CARD: 83-026745 GV863.A1 18160

Robinson, J. Smith, W. Jackie Robinson's first spring training.
NOTES: In, Riess, S.A. (ed.), The American sporting experience: a historical anthology of sport

in America, New York, Leisure Press, c1984, p. 365-370. Excerpt from: Jackie Robinson: my own story, by Jack R. Robinson and Wendell Smith, New York, Greenberg, 1948, p. 65-68;70-75;79-80.
LEVEL: B LANG: Eng GV583 17631

Rosen, C. The last of the knuckleball brotherhood: throwing the knuckler is 'a sick way to make a living', says Charlie Hough. Yet, he and the brothers Nierko persist in the dying art, while major league hitters are struggling to bat .200 against the three of them. *Inside sports (Evanston, Ill.) 6, Oct 1984, 38-43;45.*
LEVEL: B LANG: Eng SIRC ARTICLE NO: 104551

Schoor, G. Tom Seaver: a baseball biography. 1st ed. Garden City, N.Y.: Doubleday, 1984. 1v.
NOTES: Includes index.
LEVEL: B LANG: Eng ISBN: 0385192169 LC CARD: 84-001532

Smith, L.T. Versions of defeat: baseball autobiographies. (Refs: 17)*Arete: the journal of sport literature (San Diego, Calif.) 2(1), Fall 1984, 141-158.*
LEVEL: A LANG: Eng SIRC ARTICLE NO: 108409

Stargell, W. Bird, T. Willie Stargell: an autobiography. 1st ed. New York: Harper & Row, c1984. 1v.
LEVEL: B LANG: Eng ISBN 0060152389 LC CARD: 83-048387

Stein, H. Brought to his knees: two years ago, Andre Dawson was hailed as the best in the game. Now he's been overtaken by a ruthless rival - his left knee. It's painful, for everybody. *Sport (New York) 75(9), Sept 1984, 61;63-67.*
LEVEL: B LANG: Eng SIRC ARTICLE NO: 103016

Tygiel, J. Baseball's great experiment: Jackie Robinson and his legacy. 1st Vintage Books ed. New York: Vintage Books, 1984, c1983. xii, 398 p. : ill.
NOTES: Includes bibliographical references and index.
LEVEL: I LANG: Eng ISBN: 039472593X LC CARD: 84-040024

Wuld, S. Knucksie hasn't lost his grip: unceremoniously booted out of Atlanta, 45-year-old Phil Niekro is starring for the Yankees. Indeed, his knuckleball is dancing with the sprightliness of a polka step. *Sports illustrated (Chicago, Ill.) 60(22), 4 Jun 1984, 90-94;96;98;100;102-104.*
LEVEL: B LANG: Eng SIRC ARTICLE NO: 094847

Wulf, S. His bad rep is a bad rap: so says Cincinnati's hot-tempered fireballer Mario Soto, who has already been suspended twice so far this year. *Sports illustrated (Chicago, Ill.) 61(5), 23 Jul 1984, 28-31.*
LEVEL: B LANG: Eng SIRC ARTICLE NO: 096508

BIOMECHANICS

Corzatt, R.D. Groppel, J.L. Pfautsch, E. Boscardin, J. The biomechanics of head-first versus feet-first sliding. (Refs: 5) *American journal of sports medicine (Baltimore) 12(3), May/Jun 1984, 229-232.*
ABST: The purpose of this study was to povide a biomechanical analysis and comparison of the head-first and feet-first sliding techniques, as performed by four professional baseball players, in game situations. Some descriptive kinematics of both techniques are given, but it was not determined which technique was faster. A

description and comparison of the techniques were given in each of four phases: the initial sprint, the attainment of the sliding position, the airborne phase, and the landing. It was suggested that the head-first slider may maximize his already present forward rotation, from the sprint, while the feet-first slider must change his angular momentum, and possibly decrease his velocity. The injury potentials of both techniques were also discussed.
LEVEL: A LANG: Eng SIRC ARTICLE NO: 103000

Jobe, F.W. Moynes, D.R. Tibone, J.E. Perry, J. An EMG analysis of the shoulder in pitching. (Refs: 4)*American journal of sports medicine (Baltimore) 12(3), May/Jun 1984, 218-220.*
CONF: American Orthopaedic Society for Sports Medicine. Annual Meeting (9th : 1983 : Williamsburg, Va.).
ABST: The purpose of this study was to produce an electromyographic (EMG) analysis of selected muscles of the upper extremity during baseball pitching. Indwelling electrodes received EMG signals from the biceps, long and lateral heads of the triceps, pectoralis major, latissimus dorsi, serratus anterior, and brachialis muscles of four professional baseball pitchers. The EMG records were synchronized with four phases of the pitch, as seen on high speed film, for analysis. Thus, the relative contribution of the various muscles was described throughout a pitch. The authors believe that a better understanding of the muscle activation patterns could lead to more effective conditioning and rehabilitation programs.
LEVEL: A LANG: Eng SIRC ARTICLE NO: 103008

Lawler, J. Jimmy Cooney in two unaided triple plays. *Baseball research journal (Cooperstown, N.Y.) 1984, 39-41.*
LEVEL: B LANG: Eng SIRC ARTICLE NO: 106986

Mahr, J. The biomechanics of base stealing. A good ball player - and more specifically, a good base stealer - should do his homework before walking onto the field. *Athletic journal 64(8), Mar 1984, 10;58-59.*
LEVEL: B LANG: Eng SIRC ARTICLE NO: 093282

McCarthy, J. In search of speed - dissecting the fastball. (biomechanics) *Coaching review (Ottawa, Ont.) 7, Jul/Aug 1984, 36-39.*
LEVEL: I LANG: Eng SIRC ARTICLE NO: 094838

Poole, W.H. The biomechanics of pitching. *Athletic journal 64(7), Feb 1984, 12-14;69.*
LEVEL: B LANG: Eng SIRC ARTICLE NO: 091923

CAREERS

Keteyian, A. Say 'he's out.' Not 'you're out.' or you're out. Joe Brinkman's school, where 9090 of aspiring umps get the thumb, is one of two routes to the pros. *Sports illustrated 60(11), 12 Mar 1984, 32-36;38.*
LEVEL: B LANG: Eng SIRC ARTICLE NO: 091920

CHILDREN

Jobe, F.W. Moynes, D.R. The official little league fitness guide. New York: Simon and Schuster, c1984. 96 p. : ill.
NOTES: Includes index.
LEVEL: B LANG: Eng ISBN: 0671507192 LC CARD: 84-001268 GV875.6 18087

Martens, R. Rivkin, F. Bump, L.A. A field study of traditional and nontraditional children's baseball. (Refs: 1)*Research quarterly for exercise and sport*

BASEBALL (continued)

(Reston, Va.) 55(4), Dec 1984, 351-355.
ABST: Nine- to 10-year-old children have difficulty playing baseball using adult rules because pitchers lack the ability to throw the ball over the plate with consistency and batters lack ability to hit erratically thrown balls. Thus a natural field experiment investigated a modification of adult baseball for 9- to 10-year-old children. Instead of one of the players on the opposing team pitching, the coach of the offensive team pitched to the batters. Teams in a league who played baseball by adult rules (traditional league) were compared with teams in a league who played the modified game (nontraditional league), and both these leagues were compared with 11- to 12-year-old teams (older league). Various offensive and defensive activities were recorded by two observers and satisfaction scores were obtained from the players after the games. More offensive and defensive activity occurred in the nontraditional league games than in the traditional and older league games.
LEVEL: A LANG: Eng SIRC ARTICLE NO: 104547

The little league way: making youth baseball safer. *Athletic business (Madison, Wis.) 8(3), Mar 1984, 24;26.*
LEVEL: B LANG: Eng SIRC ARTICLE NO: 175923

CLUBS AND TEAMS

1984 American Legion baseball: 59th consecutive season. Indianapolis, Ind.: American Legion, 1984. 64 p. : ill.
CORP: America Legion. National Americanism Commission.
LEVEL: B LANG: Eng GV875.A1 14875

Bilovsky, F. Westcott, R. The Phillies encyclopedia. New York: Leisure Press, 1984. 1v.
LEVEL: B LANG: Eng ISBN: 0880111216 LC CARD: 82-083945

Blue Jays 1984 yearbook. Toronto: Controlled Media Publications, 1984. 71 p. : ill.
LEVEL: B LANG: Eng LC CARD: 83-31941-7 GV875.T67 17672

Fleming, G.H. The dizziest season: the gashouse gang chases the pennant. 1st ed. New York: W. Morrow, 1984. 320 p. : ill.
NOTES: Includes index.
LEVEL: B LANG: Eng ISBN: 0688030971 LC CARD: 84-060213

Gewecke, C.G. Day by day in Dodgers history. New York: Leisure Press, c1984. 1v.
NOTES: Includes indexes.
LEVEL: B LANG: E ISBN: 0880111089 LC CARD: 84-007825

Golenbock, P. Bums - an oral history of the Brooklyn Dodgers. New York: Putnam, c1984. 1v.
NOTES: Includes index.
LEVEL: B LANG: Eng ISBN: 0399128468 LC CARD: 84-002167

Grimm, J. The next best thing to playing shortstop. *Chronicle, the quarterly magazine of the Historical Society of Michigan (Ann Arbor, Mich.) 20(1), Spring 1984, 2-7.*
ABST: A brief history of the ownership of the Detroit Tigers baseball team.
LEVEL: I LANG: Eng

Honig, D. The Boston Red Sox: an illustrated tribute. New York: St. Martin's Press, 1984. 1v.
LEVEL: B LANG: Eng ISBN: 0312093179 LC CARD: 83-019260

Lindberg, R. Sox: the complete record of Chicago White Sox baseball. New York: Macmillan, c1984. 1v.
LEVEL: B LANG: Eng ISBN: 0020294301 LC CARD: 84-003954

McGreal, J. Stamford team fielded six black players. *Baseball research journal (Cooperstown, N.Y.) 1984, 45-48.*
LEVEL: B LANG: Eng SIRC ARTICLE NO: 106991

Mix, S.A. The fabulous Detroit Tigers of 1934-35. *D.A.C. news (Detroit, Mich.) 69(7), Oct 1984, 14-16;18;20.*
LEVEL: B LANG: Eng SIRC ARTICLE NO: 101072

Patterson, T. Day-by-day in Orioles history. New York: Leisure Press, 1984. 1v.
LEVEL: B LANG: Eng ISBN: 0880112220 LC CARD 84-047516

Schoor, G. The complete Cardinals record book. New York: Facts on File Inc., (1984). 1v.
NOTES: Includes index.
LEVEL: B LANG: Eng ISBN: 0871961164 LC CARD: 82-015757

Schoor, G. The complete Yankees record book. New York: Facts on File Inc., (1984). 1v.
NOTES: Includes index.
LEVEL: B LANG: Eng ISBN: 0871961180 LC CARD: 82-015758

Stokes, G. Pinstripe Pandemonium: a season with the New York Yankees. 1st ed. New York: Harper & Row, c1984. 1v.
LEVEL: B LANG: Eng ISBN: 0060153113 LC CARD: 83-048806

Thornley, S. Millers topped minors in odd protested games. *Baseball research journal (Cooperstown, N.Y.) 1984, 79-81.*
LEVEL: B LANG: Eng SIRC ARTICLE NO: 107011

Wulf, S. It's the Maine attraction. The best little AAA park in the game has popped up in a clearing in a pine forest near the Atlantic Ocean. *Sports illustrated (Chicago, Ill.) 61(2), 9 Jul 1984, 42;44;53-54;56.*
LEVEL: B LANG: Eng SIRC ARTICLE NO: 094848

COACHING

Alston, W.E. Weiskopf, D. The complete baseball handbook: strategies and techniques for winning. 2nd ed. Boston ; Toronto: Allyn and Bacon, c1984. xiii, 530 p. : ill.
NOTES: Includes index.
LEVEL: B LANG: Eng ISBN: 0205081096 LC CARD: 83-025740 GV875.5 17531

Blount, R. Y.O.G.I.: as a reincarnated Yankee skipper, Yogi Berra is working for George Steinbrenner. Is Yogi worried about longevity? no. He knows a managing job, like a ball game, ain't over'til it's over. *Sports illustrated 60(14), 2 Apr 1984, 84-88;90;92-94;96-98.*
LEVEL: B LANG: Eng SIRC ARTICLE NO: 093270

Boros, S. Computers in the dugout. The former manager of the Oakland A's explains how electronic help would give the nationa pastime a valuable assist. *Discover (Los Angeles) 5(10), Oct 1984, 80-82.*
LEVEL: B LANG: Eng SIRC ARTICLE NO: 099389

Carrow, R. Infielder's 'top ten'. (training tips) *Coaching review (Ottawa, Ont.) 7, May/Jun 1984, 59.*
LEVEL: B LANG: Eng SIRC ARTICLE NO: 094827

Fiffer, S. Chicago's college of coaches: Tony LaRussa's Sox may not win the pennant, but they lead the league in computers, baseball theory, videotape, and coaching. *Inside sports (Harlan, Iowa) 6, May 1984, 34-40.*
LEVEL: B LANG: Eng SIRC ARTICLE NO: 093274

Fimrite, R. He goes where the in crowd goes. Buckle up your seat belt, because you're about to experience life in the Hollywood fast lane with Tommy Lasorda and some of his closest friends. *Sports illustrated 60(4), 30 Jan 1984, 64-68;70;72;74;76;78.*
LEVEL: B LANG: Eng SIRC ARTICLE NO: 090447

Fimrite, R. Sparky & George: the manager of the Tigers may be aptly nicknamed for his baseball persona, but away from the game, he's another fellow. *Sports illustrated (Chicago, Ill.) 60(24), 11 Jun 1984, 70-74;76-80;82;84.*
LEVEL: B LANG: Eng SIRC ARTICLE NO: 094830

Harp, R. McCullough, J. Tarkanian: countdown of a rebel. New York: Leisure Press, 1984. 1v.
LEVEL: B LANG: Eng ISBN: 0880112298 LC CARD: 84-000940

James, B. How they play the game. *Sport (New York) 75(7), Jul 1984, 51-52;54-55;57.*
LEVEL: B LANG: Eng SIRC ARTICLE NO: 103007

Kerrane, K. Diamonds in the rough. In 1984 the author went to an amateur baseball tournament in Johnstown, Pa. to research a book on baseball scouts. As this excerpt reveals, while the scouts discovered their gems on the playing field, he found his own off the field. *Sports illustrated 60(12), 19 Mar 1984, 76-80;82-84;86;88;90.*
LEVEL: B LANG: Eng SIRC ARTICLE NO: 091919

McCormack, J. Active pilots 20% over norm in titles won. *Baseball research journal (Cooperstown, N.Y.) 1984, 30-33.*
LEVEL I LANG: Eng SIRC ARTICLE NO: 106990

Mentus, R. Sign language: baseball's silent strategy code. *Baseball digest (Evanston, Ill.) 43(9), Sept 1984, 84-86.*
LEVEL: B LANG: Eng SIRC ARTICLE NO: 097926

Nightingale, D. Spies in the sky. Baseball is using super sleuths in the press box. *Sporting news (St. Louis, Mo.) 197(26), 25 Jun 1984, 12.*
LEVEL: B LANG: Eng SIRC ARTICLE NO: 094840

S.J. Picariello: basketball's best man. *Paraplegia news (Phoenix, Ariz.) 38(1), Jan 1984, 65.*
LEVEL: B LANG: Eng SIRC ARTICLE NO: 092825

Weaver, E. Pluto, T. Weaver on strategy. 1st Collier Books ed. New York: Collier Books, c1984. 1v.
LEVEL: B LANG: Eng ISBN: 0020296304 LC CARD: 83-025245

COUNTRIES AND REGIONS

Buck, R. Dominican real fan and talent hotbed. *Baseball research journal (Cooperstown, N.Y.) 1984, 3-6.*
LEVEL: B LANG: En SIRC ARTICLE NO: 106964

Shelley, F.M. Cantin, K.F. The geography of baseball fan support in the United States. (Refs: 3)*North American culture 1, 1984, 77-95.*
LEVEL: A LANG: Eng

DICTIONARIES AND TERMINOLOGY

Dallaire, P. Repertoire de termes de baseball. Glossary of baseball terms. Montreal ; Toronto: Les Entreprises Radio-Canada/CBC Enterprises, c1984. 110, 110 p. : ill.
LEVEL: B LANG: Fr Eng ISBN: 0-88794-150-8 LC CARD: C84-98859-1 GV867.3 18049

DIRECTORIES

1984 baseball blue book. St. Petersburg, Fla.: Baseball Blue Book, Inc., 1984. 807 p. : ill.
LEVEL: B LANG: Eng GV867 18379

Smalling, R.J. Eckes, D.W. Sport Americana baseball address list, no. 3. Laurel, Md. ; Lakewood, Ohio: Den's Collectors Den Edgewater Book Co., 1984. 156 p. : ill. (Sport Americana.)
LEVEL: B LANG: Eng ISBN: 0-937424-25-0 GV867.3 18158

DISABLED

Brandmeyer, G.A. Alexander, L.K. Physical impairment and psycho-social disability in professional baseball. (Refs: 13)*Arena review 8(1), Mar 1984, 46-53.*
NOTES: Special issue: sport and disability.
LEVEL: I LANG: Eng SIRC ARTICLE NO: 103710

DOCUMENTATION

Solomon, E. Jews, baseball, and the American novel. *Arete: the journal of sport literature (San Diego, Calif.) 1(2), Spring 1983, 43-66.*
ABST: This article reviews Jewish baseball novels such as Irving Shaw's Voices of a Summer Day (1965), Mark Harris's The Southpaw (1953) and Bang the Drum Slowly (1956), and Bernard Malamud's The Natural (1952).
LEVEL: A LANG: Eng SIRC ARTICLE NO: 097930

DRUGS, DOPING AND ERGOGENIC AIDS

Kaplan, J. Taking steps to solve the drug dilemma... *Sports illustrated (Chicago, Ill.) 60(21), 28 May 1984, 36-38;40;45.*
LEVEL: B LANG: Eng SIRC ARTICLE NO: 094835

Nightingale, D. Baseball's drug policy: still piecemeal. *Sporting news 197(15), 9 Apr 1984, 31.*
LEVEL: B LANG: Eng SIRC ARTICLE NO: 091922

ECONOMICS

Chass, M. Baseball salaries double in 3 years. *Sporting news 197(5), 30 Jan 1984, 16-17.*
LEVEL: B LANG: Eng SIRC ARTICLE NO: 090441

Hill, J.R. Spellman, W. Pay discrimination in baseball - data from the 70s. (Refs: 16)*Industrial relations (Berkley, Calif. 23(1), 1984, 103-112.*
LEVEL: A LANG: Eng SIRC ARTICLE NO: 096502

ENCYCLOPEDIAS

Whittingham, R. The World Series illustrated almanac. Chicago: Contemporary Books, c1984. 379 p. : ill.
NOTES: Includes index.
LEVEL: I LANG: Eng ISBN: 0809254891 LC CARD: 83-026295 GV863.A1 18084

EQUIPMENT

Hall, S.S. Baseball's dirty tricks. *In, Schrier, E.W. and Allman, W.F. (eds.), Newton at the bat: the science in sports, Ne York, Scribner, c1984, p. 20-24.*
LEVEL: B LANG: Eng RC1235 18609

LaMarre, T. From jeers to cheers: the evolution of the baseball glove. *Sports now (St. Louis, Mo.) 2(5), May 1984, 30.*
LEVEL: B LANG: Eng SIRC ARTICLE NO: 097921

EQUIPMENT - RETAILING

Brown, R. Boosting baseball sales. *Sports trade Canada (Downsview, Ont.) 12(2), Apr 1984, 24.*
LEVEL: B LANG: Eng SIRC ARTICLE NO: 102998

FACILITIES - DESIGN, CONSTRUCTION AND PLANNING

Ball fields. Winnipeg?: Department of Culture, Heritage and Recreation, (1984). 1 kit
CORP: Manitoba. Department of Culture, Heritage and Recreation.
NOTES: Cover title.
LEVEL: B LANG: Eng GV413 17371

Lipsitz, G. Sports stadia and urban development: a tale of three cities. (Refs: 63)*Journal of sport and social issues (Boston, Mass.) 8(2), Summer/Fall 1984, 1-18.*
ABST: Pressure by civic leaders and sports entrepreneurs led St. Louis, Los Angeles, and Houston to build new sports stadia in the 1960s. The use of public money for private profit-making ventures generated controversy at the time but won acceptance with promises of widely dispersed benefits. This article argues that two long range trends, the Warner Model of urban development and the accumulation of capital for private enterprise by the state, determined the nature of stadium building in these three cities and that those long range trends illumine the causes of current urban problems.
LEVEL: A LANG: Eng SIRC ARTICLE NO: 103936

HISTORY

Danehy, T. Yesterday. High stakes at high noon turned a baseball park into a battleground. *Sports illustrated 60(16), 16 Ap 1984, 90;92-93.*
LEVEL: B LANG: Eng SIRC ARTICLE NO: 093272

Dickey, G. Jackson, R. The history of the World Series since 1903. New York: Stein and Day, 1984. 1v.
NOTES: Includes index
LEVEL: B LANG: Eng ISBN: 0812829514 LC CARD: 83-040365

Feldman, J. Bluegrass baseball: barnstorming band and ball club. *Baseball research journal (Cooperstown, N.Y.) 1984, 18-19.*
LEVEL: B LANG: Eng SIRC ARTICLE NO: 106972

Gelber, S.M. Their hands are all out playing: business and amateur baseball, 1845-1917. *Journal of sport history (Seattle, Wash.) 11(1), Spring 1984, 5-27.*
ABST: The attitude of the American business community toward baseball from the 1840's to the 1910's is the focus of this article. Baseball was seen at first as a threat to workers' commitment to their job. In the 1880's, employer's attitudes

changed and company sponsored teams appeared. By the First World War, baseball was recognized as part of the industrial recreation programs of the progressive era.
LEVEL: A LANG: Eng SIRC ARTICLE NO: 096501

Levine, P. Business, missionary motives behind 1888-89 World Tour. *Baseball research journal (Cooperstown, N.Y.) 1984, 60-63.*
LEVEL: I LANG: Eng SIRC ARTICLE NO: 106987

Luse, V. Research of Minors yields major finds. *Baseball research journal (Cooperstown, N.Y.) 1984, 85-86.*
LEVEL: I LANG: Eng SIRC ARTICLE NO: 106989

Mott, M. The first pro sports league on the Prairies: the Manitoba Baseball League of 1886. (Refs: 42)*Canadian journal of history of sport/Revue canadienne de l'histoire des sports (Windsor, Ont.) 15(2), Dec 1984, 62-69.*
LEVEL: A LANG: Eng SIRC ARTICLE NO: 104548

Reidenbaugh, L. At first, John T. brushed off the suggestion of a World Series. *Sporting news (St. Louis, Mo.) 8 Oct 1984, 16.*
LEVEL: B LANG: Eng SIRC ARTICLE NO: 099399

Ritter, L.S. Honig, D. The image of their greatness: an illustrated history of baseball from 1900 to the present. Upd. ed. New York: Crown, c1984. ix, 406 p. : ill.
NOTES: Includes index.
LEVEL: B LANG: Eng ISBN: 0517554224 LC CARD: 84-007724 GV863.A1 18191

Ritter, L.S. The glory of their times: the story of the early days of baseball told by the men who played it. new enl. ed. New York: W. Morrow, 1984. xviii, 360 p. : ill., Ports. ; 25 cm.
NOTES: Includes index.
LEVEL: B LANG: Eng ISBN: 0688039014 LC CARD: 84-221549

Simpson, D. No player, only pilot of '39-40 Reds in Shrine. *Baseball research journal (Cooperstown, N.Y.) 1984, 64-66.*
LEVEL: B LANG: Eng SIRC ARTICLE NO: 107006

Stadler, K. The Pacific Coast League: one man's memories, 1938-1957. Los Angeles: Marbek Publications, c1984. 173, (2) p. : ill.
LEVEL: B LANG: Eng ISBN: 0931239001 LC CARD: 85-169952

Thorn, J. Rucker, M. A special pictorial issue: baseball in the nineteenth century. *National pastime: a review of baseball history (Cooperstown, N.Y.) 3(1), Spring 1984, 1-69;71-86.*
LEVEL: B LANG: Eng SIRC ARTICLE NO: 096507

HUMOUR

Nelson, K. Baseball's greatest insults: a humorous collection of the game's most outrageous, abusive, and irreverent remarks New York: Simon & Schuster, c1984. 1v. (A fireside book.)
NOTES: Includes index.
LEVEL: B LANG: Eng ISBN: 067147975X LC CARD: 84-001243

INJURIES AND ACCIDENTS

Allen, M.E. Stress fracture of the humerus. A case study. *American journal of sports medicine (Baltimore) 12(3), May/Jun 1984, 244-245.*
ABST: A 13-year-old male Little League pitcher sustained a displaced spiral fracture of the right midhumerus while in midpitch. Deep ache

BASEBALL (continued)

prodrome symptoms in the midhumerus at rest and during pitching occurred during the preceeding week, suggestive of a stress fracture that later completed to an overt fracture during the added stress of a forceful side-arm curve ball pitch, his specialty. Osteonal remodeling in stress fractures is discussed.
LEVEL: A LANG: Eng SIRC ARTICLE NO: 102997

Baskin, Y. Bauer's biomechanics aid arm ailments. *Physician and sportsmedicine (Minneapolis, Minn.) 12(7), Jul 1984, 136-138.*
LEVEL: B LANG: Eng SIRC ARTICLE NO: 096495

Cantu, R.C. Injury prevention and rehabilitation in baseball. (Refs: 17)
NOTES: In, Cantu, R.C. (ed.), Clinical sports medicine, Lexington, Mass. ; Toronto, Collamore Press : D.C. Heath, c1984, p. 179-191.
LEVEL: I LANG: Eng RC1201 15964

Dick, R. Baseball. *In, Adams, S.H. (ed.), et al., Catastrophic injuries in sports: avoidance strategies, Salinas, Calif., Cayote Press, c1984, p. 59-63.*
LEVEL: B LANG: Eng RD97 19088

English, W.R. Young, D.R. Moss, R.E. Raven, P.B. Chronic muscle overuse syndrome in baseball. (Refs: 8)*Physician and sportsmedicine 12(3), Mar 1984, 111-115.*
LEVEL: I LANG: Eng SIRC ARTICLE NO: 091917

Kitagawa, H. Kashimoto, T. Locking of the thumb at the interphalangeal joint by one of the sesamoid bones. A case report. *Journal of bone and joint surgery (Boston) 66(8), Oct 1984, 1300-1301.*
LEVEL: A LANG: Eng

Marks, M.W. Argenta, L.C. Dingman, R.O. Traumatic arteriovenous malformation of the external carotid arterial system. *Head neck surgery (Boston) 6(6), Jul/Aug 1984, 1054-1058.*
LEVEL: I LANG: Eng SIRC ARTICLE NO: 104057

McKeag, D. Shoulder soreness hard to diagnose. *Spotlight on youth sports (East Lansing, Mich.) 7(1), Spring 1984, 2.*
NOTES: Reprinted from, Lansing State Journal 7 Jun 1981. Fourth in a series.
LEVEL: B LANG: Eng SIRC ARTICLE NO: 103011

Posteromedial osteophyte in baseball pitcher's elbow. *Sportsmedicine digest (Van Nuys, Calif.) 6(2), Feb 1984, 7.*
LEVEL: I LANG: Eng SIRC ARTICLE NO: 099398

Selesnick, F.H. Dolitsky, B. Haskell, S.S. Fracture of the coronoid process requiring open reduction with internal fixation. A case report. *Journal of bone and joint surgery (Boston) 66(8), Oct 1984, 1304-1306.*
LEVEL: A LANG: Eng

Stacey, E. Pitching injuries to the shoulder: an understanding of the proper mechanics involved in pitching can aid in the prevention of shoulder injuries. (Refs: 7)*Athletic journal 64(6), Jan 1984, 44-47.*
LEVEL: I LANG: Eng SIRC ARTICLE NO: 090470

JUVENILE LITERATURE

Arnow, J. Louisville Slugger: the making of a baseball bat. New York: Pantheon Books, 1984. 1 v.
LEVEL: B LANG: Eng ISBN: 039486297X LC CARD: 84-007049

LATERALITY

Taking aim in baseball. (letter) *New England journal of medicine (Boston) 310(17), 26 Apr 1984, 1128-1129.*
LEVEL: I LANG: E SIRC ARTICLE NO: 101073

LAW AND LEGISLATION

Kozlowski, J.C. Fans catch more than baseball fever. *Parks & recreation (Arlington, Va.) 19(5), May 1984, 30-32;36-37;74-75.*
LEVEL: B LANG: Eng SIRC ARTICLE NO: 094837

Narol, M. Player injuries: baseball umps' potential liability. *Referee (Franksville, Wis.) 9(2), Feb 1984, 53.*
LEVEL: B LANG: Eng SIRC ARTICLE NO: 097927

Pennsylvania - student hit by ball batted by coach denied damages. *Sports and the courts (Winston-Salem, N.C.) 5(4), Fall 1984, 9.*
LEVEL: B LANG: Eng SIRC ARTICLE NO: 103014

MASS MEDIA

Rubin, B. TV baseball has always been played according to Coyle. (Harry Coyle) *Inside sports (Evanston, Ill.) 6, Nov 1984, 12;14-15.*
LEVEL: B LANG: Eng SIRC ARTICLE NO: 103015

Schottelkotte, J. Replay: time was when a baseball lensman was right in the thick of the action. *Sports illustrated (Chicago, Ill.) 61(9), 20 Aug 1984, 6;9-10;12.*
LEVEL: B LANG: Eng SIRC ARTICLE NO: 096505

MEDICINE

Duda, M. Baseball modernizes conditioning, care. *Physician and sportsmedicine (Minneapolis, Minn.) 12(7), Jul 1984, 133-134;135-136.*
LEVEL: B LANG: Eng SIRC ARTICLE NO: 096498

OFFICIATING

Harrington, D. Umpiring in the majors is a special calling. *Baseball digest (Evanston, Ill.) 43(5). May 1984 82-88.*
LEVEL B LANG: Eng SIRC ARTICLE NO: 094834

Hill, M.B. Computer dating. *Referee (Franksville, Wis.) 9(2), Feb 1984, 56-57.*
LEVEL: B LANG: Eng SIRC ARTICLE NO: 097920

Keteyian, A. Say 'he's out.' Not 'you're out.' or you're out. Joe Brinkman's school, where 9090 of aspiring umps get the thumb, is one of two routes to the pros. *Sports illustrated 60(11), 12 Mar 1984, 32-36;38.*
LEVEL: B LANG: Eng SIRC ARTICLE NO: 091920

Marazzi, R. Umpire interference. *Referee (Franksville, Wis.) 9(5), May 1984, 35-37.*
LEVEL: B LANG: Eng SIRC ARTICLE NO: 097925

Narol, M. A legal mine field for baseball umpires. *Referee (Franksville, Wis.) 9(5) May 1984, 53.*
LEVEL: B LANG: Eng SIRC ARTICLE NO: 097928

Wulf, S. The umpires strike back. *Sports illustrated 60(14), 2 Apr 1984, 68;70;73-74;76.*
LEVEL: B LANG: Eng SIRC ARTICLE NO: 093296

PERCEPTUAL MOTOR PROCESSES

Isaacs, L.D. Players' success in T-baseball. (Refs: 3)*Perceptual and motor skills (Missoula, Mont.) 59(3), Dec 1984, 852-854.*
ABST: This paper investigates success of 6 year old boys playing T-baseball. These boys were very proficient in batting the ball from a stationary tee, but 62% of all balls in play resulted in defensive errors.
LEVEL: A LANG: Eng SIRC ARTICLE NO: 103005

Lippert, B. Baseball card subsets checklist book (1951-1984). s.l.: s.n., (1984?). 69 leaves
NOTES: Cover title.
LEVEL: B LANG: Eng LC CARD: 84-154274

PHYSIOLOGY

Duda, M. Baseball modernizes conditioning, care. *Physician and sportsmedicine (Minneapolis, Minn.) 12(7), Jul 1984, 133-134;135-136.*
LEVEL: B LANG: Eng SIRC ARTICLE NO: 096498

PICTORIAL WORKS

Iooss, W. Angell, R. Baseball. New York: H.N. Abrams, 1984. 1v.
LEVEL: B LANG: Eng ISBN: 0810907119 LC CARD: 84-009268

Schoor, G. A pictorial history of the Dodgers. New York: Leisure Press, 1984. 1v.
LEVEL: B LANG: Eng ISBN: 0880110457 LC CARD: 84-009712

Thorn, J. Rucker, M. A special pictorial issue: baseball in the nineteenth century. *National pastime: a review of baseball history (Cooperstown, N.Y.) 3(1), Spring 1984, 1-69;71-86.*
LEVEL: B LANG: Eng SIRC ARTICLE NO: 096507

PSYCHOLOGY

Harris, J.C. Interpreting youth baseball: players' understandings of fun and excitement, danger, and boredom. (Refs: 14) *Research quarterly for exercise and sport (Reston, Va.) 55(4), Dec 1984, 379-382.*
LEVEL: A LANG: Eng SIRC ARTICLE NO: 104543

Nash, H.L. Baseball breaks from tradition in player care. *Physician and sportsmedicine (Minneapolis, Minn.) 12(7), Jul 1984 131-133.*
LEVEL: B LANG: Eng SIRC ARTICLE NO: 096504

Spiker, D.D. An assessment and treatment of precompetitive state anxiety among collegiate baseball players. Eugene, Ore.: Microform Publications, University of Oregon, 1984. 2 microfiches : negative, ill. ; 11 x 15 cm.
NOTES: Thesis (Ed.D.) - West Virginia University, 1982; (vii, 146 leaves); includes bibliography.
LEVEL: A LANG: Eng UO84 187-188

RACE RELATIONS

Clifton, M. Quebec loop broke color line in 1935. *Baseball research journal (Cooperstown, N.Y.) 1984, 67-68.*
LEVEL: B LANG: Eng SIRC ARTICLE NO: 106967

Fabianic, D. Minority managers in professional baseball. (Refs: 7)*Sociology of sport journal (Champaign, Ill.) 1(2), 1984, 163-171.*
ABST: A salient feature of professional baseball is the absence of minority members serving in

managerial positions. Traditionally, it has been argued that minority players did not occupy the playing positions from which managers were generally recruited, thus accounting for their lack of career mobility in baseball. However, examination of the distribution of minority players in major league baseball reveals that they generally appear in high interactor positions in proportion to their general percentage representation among all players. Although managers continue to be selected from high interactor positions, minority players are disregarded by ownership for managerial selection. This study generates an expected frequency of minority representation among managers, based on the positions from which managers are selected and the proportion of minority players occupying those positions.
LEVEL: A LANG: Eng SIRC ARTICLE NO: 103002

Papalas, A. Lil' Rastus Cobb's good luck charm. *Baseball research journal (Cooperstown, N.Y.)* 1984, 69-70.
LEVEL: B LANG: Eng SIRC ARTICLE NO: 107000

Walker, B. Discrimination in baseball. (letter) (Refs: 1)*Dissent (New York)* 31(3), 1984, 382.
LEVEL: B LANG: Eng SIRC ARTICLE NO: 097931

RULES AND REGULATIONS

LaRoche, R.L. Baseball League official rule book. Terre Haute, Ind.: L & L Activities, c1984. 12 p.
NOTES: Cover title.
LEVEL: B LANG: Eng GV1229 17009

Marazzi, R. Situations involving the batter. Part one. *Referee (Franksville, Wis.)* 9(3), Mar 1984, 34-36.
LEVEL: B LANG: Eng SIRC ARTICLE NO: 097923

Marazzi, R. Situations involving the batter: Part two. *Referee (Franksville, Wis.)* 9(4), Apr 1984, 36.
LEVEL: B LANG: Eng SIRC ARTICLE NO: 097924

Rebackoff, Z. Setlow, D. Tough calls: an illustrated book of official baseball rules. New York: Avon, c1984. 212 p. : ill.
LEVEL: B LANG: Eng ISBN: 0-380-86777-X LC CARD: 84-090892 GV877 19038

SOCIAL PSYCHOLOGY

Baumeister, R.F. Steinhilber, A. Paradoxical effects of supportive audiences on performance under pressure: the home field disadvantages in sports championships. (Refs: 30)*Journal of personality and social psychology (Washington, D.C.)* 47(1), Jul 1984, 85-93.
ABST: Results from baseball's World Series from 1924 to 1982 and from National Basketball Association (NBA) championship and semifinal series from 1967 to 1982 are used in this study. The authors set up to test the following hypothesis: the presence of supportive audiences is detrimental to performance in decisive contests. Findings corroborate the hypothesis. Results from both World Series and NBA series games show that home teams tend to win early games but lose final ones.
LEVEL: A LANG: Eng SIRC ARTICLE NO: 096496

Bruce, H.A. Baseball and the national life.
NOTES: In, Riess, S.A. (ed.), The American sporting experience: a historical anthology of sport in America, New York, Leisure Press, c1984, p. 264-270. Previously published in, Outlook 104, May

1913, p. 104-107.
LEVEL: I LANG: Eng GV583 17631

Nightingale, D. Baseball's superstitious. The diamond is, and always has been, a hotbed for omen-seekers. *Sporting news 197(17), 23 Apr 1984, 12-13.*
LEVEL: B LANG: Eng SIRC ARTICLE NO: 093287

SOCIOLOGY

Rhodes, R. Baseball, hot dogs, apple pie, and Chevrolets. (Refs: 8)*In, Cowan, W. (ed.), Paper of the fifteenth Algonquian Conference, Ottawa, Carleton University, 1984, p. 373-388.*
CONF: Algonquian Conference (15th : 1983 : Cambridge, Mass.).
LEVEL: A LANG: Eng GV585 18629

Skipper, J.K. The sociological significance of nicknames: the case of baseball players. (Refs: 28)*Journal of sport behavior (Mobile, Ala.) 7(1), Feb 1984, 28-38.*
NOTES: This is a revision of a paper presented at the 13th Annual Alpha Kappa Delta Research Symposium, Richmond, Virginia, February 18, 1983.
ABST: This paper seeks to increase awareness of the sociological meaning, usage, and significance of nicknames in American society. The author suggests that nicknames give sports fans a feeling of intimacy with the sports hero. Over the past three decades there has been a gradual decline in the number of nicknames given to major league baseball players. The author suggests that this trend is caused by a change in the fans' perceptions. The players are now considered entrepreneurs instead of folk heroes and thus are less deserving of nicknames.
LEVEL: A LANG: Eng SIRC ARTICLE NO: 096506

SPORTING EVENTS

Gulka, O.N. Report: sports event medical coverage. Medical services of the World Youth Baseball Championships 1984. *Canadia Academy of Sport Medicine newsletter (Ottawa) 5(4), 1984, 16-21.*
LEVEL: I LANG: Eng SIRC ARTICLE NO: 105650

SPORTSMANSHIP

Hertzel, B. Cheating frowned on, but still a part of baseball. *Baseball digest (Evanston, Ill.) 43(9), Sept 1984, 34-36.*
LEVEL: B LANG: Eng SIRC ARTICLE NO: 097919

Ray, R. Baseball or beanball? What's the game coming to? *Sporting news (St. Louis, Mo.) 198(11), 10 Sept 1984, 3;25.*
LEVEL: B LANG: Eng SIRC ARTICLE NO: 097929

STATISTICS AND RECORDS

Ault, A.B. Pitching, defense just slightly more important to team wins than offense. *Baseball research journal (Cooperstown N.Y.) 1984, 53-54.*
LEVEL: I LANG: Eng SIRC ARTICLE NO: 106961

Elstein, P. Swap to better, poorer team most helpful? *Baseball research journal (Cooperstown, N.Y.) 1984, 87-88.*
LEVEL: I LANG: Eng SIRC ARTICLE NO: 106971

Hofacker, C.F. Relationships between offense and defense in major league baseball. (Refs: 6)*Journal of sport behaviour (Mobile, Ala.) 7(2), Jun 1984,*

79-86.
ABST: While baseball fans are known for their penchant for statistics, the application of rational statistical methods to the results of baseball game is still a new phenomenon. The lack of quantitative research is all the more surprising when it is considered that almost every aspect of the sport has been religiously tabulated for over 100 years. In this study, the performance of baseball teams was analyzed in the same way one might scientifically look at the performance of any organization. The aspect chosen for analysis is fundamental to the nature of sports; the relationship between offense and defense in particular, the relative contribution to winning of scoring runs and preventing runs was explored. Second, the relationship between the ability of teams to score runs and the ability of teams to prevent runs was investigated. And last, historical data for each league taken as a whole were analyzed in order to look at the nature of changes in the relative balance between offense and defense.
LEVEL: A LANG: Eng SIRC ARTICLE NO: 099394

James, B. The Bill James baseball abstract 1984. 1st ed. New York: Ballantine Books, 1984. 273 p.
LEVEL: B LANG: Eng ISBN: 0-345-31155-8 LC CARD: 83-91165 GV877 17377

Kross, B. Is N.L. really better? Study raises doubts. *Baseball research journal (Cooperstown, N.Y.) 1984, 27-29.*
LEVEL: I LANG: Eng SIRC ARTICLE NO: 106985

Leconte, W. The ultimate New York Yankees record book. New York: Leisure Press, 1984. 1v.
LEVEL: B LANG: Eng ISBN: 08801123 LC CARD: 84-047520

Lowry, P.J. Late finishes leave fans limp but ecstatic. *Baseball research journal (Cooperstown, N.Y.) 1984, 55-59.*
LEVEL: LANG: Eng SIRC ARTICLE NO: 106988

Mead, A. Figuring probability fluctuations in baseball. *Baseball research journal (Cooperstown, N.Y.) 1984, 20-23.*
LEVEL: LANG: Eng SIRC ARTICLE NO: 106993

Munro, N. Rating results vs. total plate appearances. *Baseball research journal (Cooperstown, N.Y.) 1984, 36-38.*
LEVEL: I LANG: Eng SIRC ARTICLE NO: 106995

Polhamus, J. 95 enjoyed ten winning seasons; 19 for Alexander. *Baseball research journal (Cooperstown, N.Y.) 1984, 9-11.*
LEVEL: B LANG: Eng SIRC ARTICLE NO: 107001

Sutton, M. Basketball & baseball computer programs at John C. Calhoun State Community College. *Juco review (Hutchinson, Kans.) 36(3), Nov 1984, 4;6;8.*
LEVEL: B LANG: Eng SIRC ARTICLE NO: 173371

Thorn, J. Palmer, P. Reuther, D. The hidden game of baseball: a revolutionary approach to baseball and its statistics. Garde City, N.Y.: Doubleday, 1984. x, 419 p.
NOTES: Bibliography: p. 416-419.
LEVEL: I LANG: Eng ISBN: 0-385-18283-X LC CARD: 82-46043 GV867 18101

BASEBALL (continued)

STATISTICS AND RECORDS - PARTICIPATION

Baseball -- a game for the young? Le baseball -- un jeu pour les jeunes? *Highlights/Faits saillants (Ottawa) 30, Jun 1984, 1-2.*
CORP: Canada Fitness Survey.
CORP: Enquete condition physique Canada.
LEVEL: B LANG: Eng Fr SIRC ARTICLE NO: 094823

STRATEGY

Cardwell, J. Slocombe, S. The developing game of field hockey on artificial surfaces. Part 2 - set pieces. *Hockey field (Cornwall, U.K.) 72, 27 Oct 1984, 35-37.*
LEVEL: B LANG: Eng SIRC ARTICLE NO: 173372

STRATEGY - DEFENSIVE

Billerbeck, R. Fundamentals of defensive baseball. *Coaching clinic (Princeton, N.J.) 22(8), Apr 1984, 3-5.*
LEVEL: B LANG: Eng SIRC ARTICLE NO: 094825

Buntzen, G. Defending the squeeze play: a practicable approach. *Coaching clinic (Princeton, N.J.) 22(8), Apr 1984, 1-3.*
LEVEL: B LANG: Eng SIRC ARTICLE NO: 094826

Robards, L. Defending the double steal. Never allow the opponent to steal an uncontested base; if you haven't found a method of stopping the double steal, try this play. *Athletic journal (Evanston, Ill.) 64(10), May 1984, 30.*
LEVEL: B LANG: Eng SIRC ARTICLE NO: 094841

Stevens, D. Defending against the steal of second: with a little practice and strategy, there is no reason that a high schoo team can't learn to defend against the 'automatic' steal of second in a first and third situation. *Athletic journal 64(6), Jan 1984, 26;56-58.*
LEVEL: B LANG: Eng SIRC ARTICLE NO: 090471

STRATEGY - OFFENSIVE

Albo, B. Scoring from third base. *Coaching clinic 22(6), Feb 1984, 3-4.*
LEVEL: B LANG: Eng SIRC ARTICLE NO: 090434

TEACHING

Alexander-Hall, J. Teaching hockey to beginners: the small sided game. *Hockey field (Truro, Eng.) 72(1), 29 Sept 1984, 24-26.*
LEVEL: B LANG: Eng SIRC ARTICLE NO: 101224

TECHNIQUES AND SKILLS

Long, R. Baseball hints...tips for success. *Coaching clinic (Princeton, N.J.) 23(2), Oct 1984, 1-4.*
LEVEL: B LANG: Eng SIRC ARTICLE NO: 101071

Schultz, G. The little things really do count. *Coaching clinic 22(6), Feb 1984, 4-6.*
LEVEL: B LANG: Eng SIRC ARTICLE NO: 090466

TECHNIQUES AND SKILLS - BASERUNNING

Anderson, D. A baserunning drill for your team. *Coaching clinic 22(6), Feb 1984, 1-3.*
LEVEL: B LANG: Eng SIRC ARTICLE NO: 090436

Ford, D. Taking that extra base. *Scholastic coach 53(8), Mar 1984, 54-55;72-73.*
LEVEL: B LANG: Eng SIRC ARTICLE NO: 09327

Fox, P. Sliding to win. Proper sliding techniques can mean extra runs and possible wins for your team. *Athletic journal (Evanston, Ill.) 64(10), May 1984, 22;58-61.*
LEVEL: B LANG: Eng SIRC ARTICLE NO: 094831

Gray, B. Base running. *Coaching clinic 22(7), Mar 1984, 4-6.*
LEVEL: B LANG: Eng SIRC ARTICLE NO: 093277

Pellerin, G. Base stealing techniques. *Coaching clinic (Princeton, N.J.) 23(3), Nov 1984, 1-2.*
LEVEL: B LANG: Eng SIRC ARTICLE NO: 103013

TECHNIQUES AND SKILLS - BATTER AND BATTING

Beale, W. Hitting: the lost mechanics. *Athletic journal (Evanston, Ill.) 65(5), Dec 1984, 34;41.*
LEVEL: B LANG: Eng SIRC ARTICLE NO: 104540

Berson, M. Hitting: a fundamental approach. *Athletic journal 64(9), Apr 1984, 32-33.*
LEVEL: B LANG: Eng SIRC ARTICLE NO: 093269

Ferris, W. The role of bunting. To have a productive bunting game, you must know what type of bunt to execute in each situation. *Athletic journal 64(7), Feb 1984, 65;72;75-76.*
LEVEL: B LANG: Eng SIRC ARTICLE NO: 091918

Lane, M. Don't give up on the drag bunt: with proper practice, drag bunting can be a formidable offensive weapon. *Athletic journal 64(6), Jan 1984, 12-13;63.*
LEVEL: B LANG: Eng SIRC ARTICLE NO: 090458

Stockbridge, G. keep your head in there. *Scholastic coach 53(7), Feb 1984, 22-24.*
LEVEL: B LANG: Eng SIRC ARTICLE NO: 093312

Weiskopf, D. Batting styles of the '80s. Some of the top hitters in baseball demonstrate the styles and techniques that have made them successful. *Athletic journal 64(8), Mar 1984, 36-46;57.*
LEVEL: B LANG: Eng SIRC ARTICLE NO: 093294

Werbylo, R. Hitting angles. *Coaching clinic (Princeton, N.J.) 23(4), Dec 1984, 1-4.*
LEVEL: B LANG: Eng SIRC ARTICLE NO: 103018

TECHNIQUES AND SKILLS - CATCHER

McCarver, T. How a catcher calls a game. *Sport (New York) 75(8), Aug 1984, 55-56;59;61;63-65.*
LEVEL: B LANG: Eng SIRC ARTICLE NO: 103010

Thomas, H. Handling the high & the low pitches. *Scholastic coach (New York) 53(9), Apr 1984, 28-31;87.*
LEVEL: B LANG: Eng SIRC ARTICLE NO: 094846

TECHNIQUES AND SKILLS - INFIELDER

Delmonico, R. Six ways to get two at second: getting to the bag under control is of prime importance. *Scholastic coach 53(8), Mar 1984, 34-37;68.*
LEVEL: B LANG: Eng SIRC ARTICLE NO: 093273

Fox, P. The fundamentals of third base play. *Coaching clinic (Princeton, N.J.) 22(9), May 1984, 1-4.*
LEVEL: B LANG: Eng SIRC ARTICLE NO: 094832

TECHNIQUES AND SKILLS - OUTFIELDER

Winn, E. Ground ball mechanics for the outfielder. *Scholastic coach 53(7), Feb 1984, 60-61;76.*
LEVEL: B LANG: Eng SIRC ARTICLE NO: 093295

TECHNIQUES AND SKILLS - PITCHER AND PITCHING

Jordan, P. Handville, R. Sports Illustrated pitching. Rev. ed. New York: Harper & Row, c1984. 138 p. : ill.
LEVEL: B LANG: Eng ISBN: 0-06-091167-0 LC CARD: 84-047581 GV871 20835

Karn, B. Pick off techniques. *Coaching clinic (Princeton, N.J.) 23(1), Sept 1984, 1-3.*
LEVEL: B LANG: Eng SIRC ARTICLE NO 099397

McBee, B. McCullough, H. The common pitching flaws & what to do about them. *Scholastic coach 53(8), Mar 1984, 22-24;70-73.*
LEVEL: B LANG: Eng SIRC ARTICLE NO: 093284

Seaver, T. Lowenfish, L. The art of pitching. New York: Hearst Books, c1984. 223 p. : ill. (A Mountain Lion book.)
NOTES: Includes index. Bibliography: p. 211.
LEVEL: I LANG: Eng ISBN: 068802663X LC CARD: 83-083031 GV871 18373

Steenhuis, W. Command of curve ball will produce diamond success. *Coaching clinic (Princeton, N.J.) 22(8), Apr 1984, 5-7.*
LEVEL: B LANG: Eng SIRC ARTICLE NO: 094844

Weiskopf, D. Split finger fastball: growing in popularity, the split-finger fastball may become the pitch of the '80s. *Athletic journal 64(6), Jan 1984, 28-35.*
LEVEL: I LANG: Eng SIRC ARTICLE NO: 090478

Weiskopf, D. Keep 'em close. If a pitcher has an effective move to first, he will be able to hold the runner close and prevent many runs from scoring. *Athletic journal 64(7), Feb 1984, 40-47.*
LEVEL: B LANG: Eng SIRC ARTICLE NO: 091924

TRAINING AND CONDITIONING

Buttitta, B. Take me out to the Dojo. Many major league baseball players are discovering that the martial arts and baseball are quite a double-play combination. *Karate illustrated (Burbank, Calif.) 15(1), Jan 1984, 28-32;75.*
LEVEL: B LANG: Eng SIRC ARTICLE NO: 108120

Highley, R. A winning philosophy...playing championship baseball. *Coaching clinic (Princeton, N.J.) 23(2), Oct 1984, 4-6.*
LEVEL: B LANG: Eng SIRC ARTICLE NO: 101070

Jobe, F.W. Shoulder and arm exercises for baseball players. *Sports medicine digest (Van Nuys, Calif.) 6(1), Jan 1984, 6-7.*
LEVEL: B LANG: Eng SIRC ARTICLE NO: 099395

Miller, J. USIU power program for baseball. (Refs: 9)*National Strength & Conditioning Association journal (Lincoln, Neb.) 6(5), Oct/Nov 1984, 34-37.*
ABST: The power program at the United States International University is divided into the three phases of post-season, pre-season and in-season. The post-season program begins with low intensity

workouts which build toward the important pre-season phase in which power development is stressed since baseball requires short, quick and powerful movements. The in-season program is designed to maintain gains in the areas of strength, flexibility and speed. Detailed programs are described for all three phases of baseball training.
LEVEL: B LANG: Eng SIRC ARTICLE NO: 103012

Schreiber, K. Development program for pitchers. *Athletic journal 64(9), Apr 1984, 36;73-74.*
LEVEL: B LANG: Eng SIRC ARTICLE NO: 093291

TRAINING AND CONDITIONING - DRILLS

Easom, M. A productive practice. *Juco review (Hutchinson, Kan.) 35(8), Apr 1984, 20;24.*
LEVEL: B LANG: Eng SIRC ARTICLE NO: 096499

Hockenjos, T. Benedict, G. Indoor batting practice: a well-organized indoor batting practice session will help coaches avoid wasting valuable early season time. *Athletic journal 64(9), Apr 1984, 16;25.*
LEVEL: B LANG: Eng SIRC ARTICLE NO: 093279

Marchant, B. Baseball drills. *Texas coach 27(4), Jan 1984, 57.*
LEVEL: B LANG: Eng SIRC ARTICLE NO: 093283

Milliken, B. Inside practice in a small area. *Coaching clinic 22(7), Mar 1984, 3-4.*
LEVEL: B LANG: Eng SIRC ARTICLE NO: 093286

Potteiger, G. Defensive baseball. *Coaching clinic 22(7), Mar 1984, 6-7.*
LEVEL: B LANG: Eng SIRC ARTICLE NO: 093289

Smilowitz, J. Two helpful hitting drills. *Coaching clinic 22(7), Mar 1984, 1-3.*
LEVEL: B LANG: Eng SIRC ARTICLE NO: 09329

Sorensen, D. Successful baseball practice ideas. *Coaching clinic (Englewood Cliffs, N.J.) 22(10), Jun 1984, 3-4.*
LEVEL: B LANG: Eng SIRC ARTICLE NO: 094842

Sparks, H. Selection and practice for perfection. *Coaching clinic (Princeton, N.J.) 22(9), May 1984, 4-7.*
LEVEL: B LANG: Eng SIRC ARTICLE NO: 094843

Steinmiller, G.R. Offensive executive: the way to more run production in baseball. *Coaching clinic (Englewood Cliffs, N.J.) 22(10), Jun 1984, 1-2.*
LEVEL: B LANG: Eng SIRC ARTICLE NO: 094845

Young, C. Incorporating base running into the offensive workout. *Texas coach 27(4), Jan 1984, 54-55.*
LEVEL: B LANG: Eng SIRC ARTICLE NO: 093297

TRAINING AND CONDITIONING - WEIGHT AND STRENGTH TRAINING

Jobe, F.W. Shoulder and arm exercises for baseball players. *Sportsmedicine digest (Van Nuys, Calif.) 6(2), Feb 1984, 6-8.*
LEVEL: B LANG: Eng SIRC ARTICLE NO: 099396

Kephart, K. Strength training for baseball. *National Strength & Conditioning Association journal (Lincoln, Neb.) 6(2), Apr/May 1984, 36.*
LEVEL: B LANG: Eng SIRC ARTICLE NO: 094836

VISION

Hoffman, L.G. Polan, G. Powell, J. The relationship of contrast sensitivity functions to sports vision. *Journal of the American Optometric Association (St. Louis) 55(10), Oct 1984, 747-752.*
LEVEL: A LANG: Eng

WOMEN

Keenan, S. The umpress strikes back. Triple A umpire Pam Postema calls 'em as she sees 'em, not hears 'em. *Sports illustrated (Chicago, III.) 61(6), 30 Jul 1984, 44-45.*
LEVEL: B LANG: Eng SIRC ARTICLE NO: 096503

BASKETBALL

Busnel, R. Les problemes du futur. *Basketball (Paris) 493, supplement 5, 1 aout 1984, 265-268.*
NOTES: A suivre.
LEVEL: B LANG: Fr SIRC ARTICLE NO: 104564

Mezzulo, M. The intangibles. *Basketball clinic (Princeton, N.J.) 16(10), Jun 1984, 11-12.*
LEVEL: B LANG: Eng SIRC ARTICLE NO: 096525

Olin, K. Attitudes toward professional foreign players in Finnish Amateur Basketball. (Refs: 14)*International review for th sociology of sport (Warszawa, Poland) 19(3/4), 1984, 273-282.*
ABST: To determine the attitudes toward foreign professionals in various Finnish amateur basketball leagues, all clubs playing basketball in the three highest Finnish leagues were interviewed by mailed questionnaire. The results indicated that recruitment of foreign pros was held to effect negatively the team spirit and the play tactics, the economics of the club, the development of other sport branches in the club and the success of the national team. Positive effects were expected on the number of spectators, public relations of the club and the success of its team. For lower leagues foreign professionals were not recommended.
LEVEL: A LANG: Eng SIRC ARTICLE NO: 105695

Smiddly, J.L. Winning is no accident: it takes planning and hard work. *Women's coaching clinic 7(8), Apr 1984, 6-9.*
LEVEL B LANG: Eng SIRC ARTICLE NO: 093309

ADMINISTRATION

Busnel, R. The difficulties of the future. *International basketball (Budapest, Hungary) 24, 1984, 32-42.*
LEVEL: B LANG: E SIRC ARTICLE NO: 105665

Kieffer, M. Marketing your high school basketball program. *Texas coach (Austin, Tex.) 28(2), Sept 1984, 25-27.*
LEVEL: B LANG: Eng SIRC ARTICLE NO: 105681

Pingel, N. Running the basketball program. *Women's coaching clinic 7(7), Mar 1984, 5-6.*
LEVEL: B LANG: Eng SIRC ARTICLE NO: 091946

Shapiro, M. Dr. J' moves forward off the court. (Julius Erving) *Advertising age (Chicago, III.) 55(84), 10 Dec 1984, 38;40.*
LEVEL: B LANG: Eng SIRC ARTICLE NO: 103049

Wayne, J. League is trying to net Canadian basketball teams. *Financial post 78(1), 7 Jan 1984, 39.*
LEVEL: B LANG: Eng SIR ARTICLE NO: 089008

ANTHROPOMETRY

Walsh, F.K. Heyward, V.H. Schau, C.G. Estimation of body composition of female intercollegiate basketball players. (Refs: 32 *Physician and sportsmedicine (Minneapolis, Minn.) 12(11), Nov 1984, 74-81;85;89.*
ABST: The authors evaluated the applicability of the Jackson and Sloan equations to estimate body density of female intercollegiate basketball athletes. 49 players served as subjects. Results indicated a low standard error of the estimate for the Sloan (.0073 gm-ml-1) and Jackson (.0085 gm-ml-1) equations; however, both equations yielded large total error (.014 and .016 gm-ml-1).
LEVEL: A LANG: Eng SIRC ARTICLE NO: 101109

BIOGRAPHY AND AUTOBIOGRAPHY

Baden, L. U.S. banks on Jordan: North Carolina star wants gold. (Michael Jordan) *Olympian (Colorado Springs, Colo.) 10(8), Mar 1984, 8-10.*
LEVEL: B LANG: Eng SIRC ARTICLE NO: 099403

Diaz, J. Small colleges: he picks up the pointers. Guard Terry Porter is Sweetness to his teammates at Wisconsin - Steven Point. *Sports illustrated (Los Angeles, Calif.) 61(24), 26 Nov 1984, 104;107.*
LEVEL: B LANG: Eng SIRC ARTICLE NO: 101077

Kirkpatrick, C. He may have saved the best for last. In his 42nd and final season at DePaul, coach Ray Meyer was 16-0 with a team that refuses to quit. *Sports illustrated 60(5), 6 Feb 1984, 22-25.*
LEVEL: B LANG: Eng SIRC ARTICLE NO: 090497

Kirkpatrick, C. Just a guy from da naybuhhood. St. John's hoopaholic Chris Mullin may be the King of Queen's but he belongs (pale) body and soul to his beloved borough of Brooklyn. *Sports illustrated (Los Angeles, Calif.) 61(24), 26 Nov 1984, 42-44;49-50;52;57.*
LEVEL: B LANG: Eng SIRC ARTICLE NO: 101089

Lundgren, L. Reggie Theus: refugee from Chicago's 'twilight zone'. *Inside sports (Evanston, III.) 6, Oct 1984, 18-22.*
LEVEL: B LANG: Eng SIRC ARTICLE NO: 104576

Newman, B. From Russia with love. (Max Lazorovich Blank) *Sports illustrated (Chicago, III.) 60(18), 30 Apr 1984, 74-78;80;83;86;88.*
LEVEL: B LANG: Eng SIRC ARTICLE NO: 094880

Robson, B. A secret told: he's good as gold. Quite simply, he's the best college point guard in America. Plus, he's polite, hard working and loves his mother. You say you've never har of Leon Wood? Just wait till the Olympics. *Sport (New York) 75(3), Mar 1984, 55-59.*
LEVEL: B LANG: Eng SIRC ARTICLE NO: 094883

Wolff, A. Two bits, four bits, six bits, a Deutsche Mark. Basketball with a Teutonic twist has sent the Washington Huskies t the top of the Pac-10, and that's just the tip of the Eisberg in the U.S. *Sports illustrated 60(11), 12 Mar 1984, 40-42;47-48.*
LEVEL: B LANG: Eng SIRC ARTICLE NO: 091953

Wolff, A. In the driver's seat. Rookie Michael Jordan has quickly become Chicago's big wheel and the NBA's big deal at the box office. *Sports illustrated (Los Angeles, Calif.) 61(26), 10 Dec 1984, 36-38;41;44-45.*
LEVEL: B LANG: Eng SIRC ARTICLE NO: 103056

BASKETBALL (continued)

BIOMECHANICS

Saunders, H.L. A cinematographical study of the relationship between speed of movement and available force. Eugene, Ore.: Microform Publications, University of Oregon, 1984. 3 microfiches : negative, ill. ; 11 x 15 cm.
NOTES: Thesis (Ph.D.) - Texas A & M University, 1980; (xvi, 204 leaves); vita; includes bibliography.
LEVEL: A LANG: Eng UO84 5-7

CHILDREN

Robin, M. Adolescence et basket. *Basketball (Paris) 492, fevr/mars/avr 1984, 6-8.*
LEVEL: B LANG: Fr SIRC ARTICLE NO: 0979

CLUBS AND TEAMS

Kort, M. A tale of two cities. *Women's sports (Palo Alto, Calif.) 6(3), Mar 1984, 18-21;54.*
LEVEL: B LANG: Eng SIRC ARTICLE NO: 097950

MacDonald, F. Cleveland Cavaliers. (Mankato, Minn.?): Creative Education, (c1984). 48 p. : ill.
LEVEL: B LANG: Eng ISBN: 0871919737 LC CARD: 83-073291

Martin, M. New York Knicks. (Mankato, Min.): Creative Education, (c1984). 48 p. : ill.
LEVEL: B LANG: Eng ISBN: 0871919842 LC CARD: 83-073304

Martin, M. Portland Trail Blazers. (Mankato, Minn.): Creative Education, (c1984). 48 p. : ill.
LEVEL: B LANG: Eng ISBN: 0871919877 LC CARD: 83-073306

Moore, J. New Jersey Nets. (Mankato, Minn.): Creative Education, (c1984). 48 p.
LEVEL: B LANG: Eng ISBN: 0871919834 LC CARD 83-073300

Moore, J. Los Angeles Lakers. (Mankato, Minn.): Creative Education, c1984. 48 p. : ill.
LEVEL: B LANG: Eng ISBN: 0871919818 LC CARD: 83-073297

Moore, J. Washington Bullets. (Mankato, Minn.): Creative Education, (c1984). 48 p. : ill.
LEVEL: B LANG: Eng ISBN: 08719199 LC CARD: 83-073294

Moore, J. San Diego Clippers. (Mankato, Minn.): Creative Education, (c1984). 48 p. : ill.
LEVEL: B LANG: Eng ISBN: 0871919893 LC CARD: 83-073299

Moore, J. Houston Rockets. (Mankato, Minn.): Creative Education, (c1984). 48 p. : ill.
LEVEL: B LANG: Eng ISBN: 0871919788 LC CARD: 83-073288

Moore, J. Utah Jazz. (Mankato, Minn.): Creative Education, (c1984). 48 p. : ill.
LEVEL: B LANG: Eng ISBN: 0871919915 LC CARD: 83-073301

Moore, J. Phoenix Suns. (Mankato, Minn.): Creative Education, (c1984). 48 p. : ill.
LEVEL: B LANG: Eng ISBN: 0871919869 LC CARD: 83-073289

Moore, J. Milwaukee Bucks. (Mankato, Minn.): Creative Education, (c1984). 48 p. : ill.
LEVEL: B LANG: Eng ISBN: 0871919826 LC CARD: 83-073287

Moore, J. Dallas Mavericks. (Mankato, Minn.): Creative Education, (c1984). 48 p. : ports. ; 25 cm.

LEVEL: B LANG: Eng ISBN: 0871919745 LC CARD: 83-073303

Nelli, H.S. The winning tradition: a history of Kentucky Wildcat Basketball. Lexington, Ky.: University Press of Kentucky, c1984. 1v.
NOTES: Includes index.
LEVEL: B LANG: Eng ISBN: 0813115191 LC CARD: 84-007306

Ward, D. Seattle Supersonics. (Mankato, Minn.): Creative Education, c1984. 48 p. : ill.
LEVEL: B LANG: Eng ISBN: 0871919907 LC CARD: 83-073295

COACHING

Barringer, R.D. Theories of coaching junior varsity basketball. *Coaching clinic 22(6), Feb 1984, 6-7.*
LEVEL: B LANG: Eng SIRC ARTICLE NO: 090481

Bilger, L.E. Manchester basketball program. *Basketball clinic (Princeton, N.J.) 16(8), Apr 1984, 13-15.*
LEVEL: B LANG: En SIRC ARTICLE NO: 094855

Bill Foster: man to man against stress. 'You have to get to know the enemy, and sometimes it's YOU.' *Scholastic coach 53(7), Feb 1984, 38-40;42;75.*
LEVEL: B LANG: Eng SIRC ARTICLE NO: 093299

Bradshaw, D. Motivation through basketball statistics. (Refs: 5)*Coaching review (Ottawa, Ont.) 7, May/Jun 1984, 52-54.*
LEVEL: B LANG: Eng SIRC ARTICLE NO: 094856

Brennan, S. Coaching preparations for an all-star game. *Basketball clinic (Princeton, N.J.) 16(6), Feb 1984, 4-5.*
LEVEL: LANG: Eng SIRC ARTICLE NO: 094857

Brubaker, B. Dear Chris: when you're Chris Washburn - 6' 11' with a can't miss jumper - you can expect to have hundreds of pen pals, and sacks, cartons and drawers full of mail. *Sports illustrated (Los Angeles, Calif.) 61(24), 26 Nov 1984, 120-124;126-128;130;132;134;136.*
LEVEL: B LANG: Eng SIRC ARTICLE NO: 100512

Crevecoeur, G. Smets, A. Noteboom, Th. Jouer au basket: enseignement et pratique. Paris: Amphora, c1984. (208) p. : ill. (Sports & loisirs.)
NOTES: Bibliographie: p. 207-(208).
LEVEL: I LANG: Eng ISBN: 2-85180-076-0 GV885.3 17832

Dickie, D. The coaches: Debbie Muir, Jack Donohue, Ken Maeda, and Marina van der Merwe. Les entraineurs: Debbie Muir, Jack Donohue, Ken Maeda, et Marina van der Merwe. *Champion (Ottawa) 8(3), Aug 1984, 61-65.*
LEVEL: B LANG: Eng Fr SIRC ARTICLE NO: 095750

Douglas, D. Winning basketball: four ingredients. *Women's coaching clinic (Princeton, N.J.) 8(2), Oct 1984, 4-5.*
LEVEL: B LANG: Eng SIRC ARTICLE NO: 099411

Field, C.A. Coach's desk... Scouting procedures and ethics. *Basketball clinic (Princeton, N.J.) 16(10), Jun 1984, 10-11.*
LEVEL: B LANG: Eng SIRC ARTICLE NO: 096514

Galvan, P. Paul Galvan: major college basketball referee and supervisor. *Referee (Franksville, Wis.) 9(2), Feb 1984, 16-19.*
LEVEL: B LANG: Eng SIRC ARTICLE NO: 097943

Hart, W.B. Presenting the written game plan. *Basketball clinic (Princeton, N.J.) 16(9), May 1984, 13-14.*
LEVEL: B LANG: E SIRC ARTICLE NO: 094867

Hurley, J. The science of shot discipline. *Juco review (Hutchinson, Kan.) 35(3), Nov 1983, 4;6.*
LEVEL: B LANG: Eng SIRC ARTICLE NO: 096518

Hynson, M. A winning basketball program. *Basketball clinic (Princeton, N.J.) 16(8), Apr 1984, 15-16.*
LEVEL: B LANG: Eng SIRC ARTICLE NO: 094870

Interview with potential summer olympic coaches: Don McCrae. *Coaching review 7, Mar/Apr 1984, 8-12.*
LEVEL: B LANG: Eng SIRC ARTICLE NO: 093303

Johnston, B. The hornette draft system. *Women's coaching clinic (Princeton, N.J.) 8(2), Oct 1984, 7-8.*
LEVEL: B LANG: Eng SIRC ARTICLE NO: 099417

Kontor, K. Head sets - set. *National Strength & Conditioning Association journal 6(1), Feb/Mar 1984, 42.*
LEVEL: B LANG: E SIRC ARTICLE NO: 093432

Krause, J. Better basketball basics: before the X's and O's. 2nd ed. New York: Leisure Press, 1984. 1v.
LEVEL: B LANG: Eng ISBN: 088011259X LC CARD: 84-014387

Ladner, J.L. Basketball drills and their relationship to winning. *Basketball clinic (Princeton, N.J.) 17(3), Nov 1984, 1-4.*
LEVEL: B LANG: Eng SIRC ARTICLE NO: 103035

Le statut de l'entraineur. *Basketball (Paris) 491, supplement 3, 25 mars 1984, 145-152.*
LEVEL: B LANG: Fr SIRC ARTICLE NO: 101107

Lehane, J. When is more important than how. *Basketball monthly (Lincoln, Eng.) 23(8), Apr/May 1984, 20-21.*
LEVEL: B LANG: Eng SIRC ARTICLE NO: 094874

McCallum, J. The march of the wooden soldiers. Walt Hazzard becomes the fifth coach in a decade to try to reestablish John Wooden's championship tradition at UCLA. *Sports illustrated 60(16), 16 Apr 1984, 26-28;33.*
LEVEL: B LANG: Eng SIRC ARTICLE NO: 093304

Nack, W. I made my own bed, I've got to lie in it. What's a guy who has come within one game of the NBA title and two of the NCAA championship doing coaching a high school team in Picayune, Mississippi? Ask Butch van Breda Kolff. *Sports illustrated 60(8), 20 Feb 1984, 60-65;67-68;70;72;74;76.*
LEVEL: B LANG: Eng SIRC ARTICLE NO: 090502

Newmann, S. Tasks for the assistant. *Coaching review (Ottawa, Ont.) Jan/Feb 1985, 28-32.*
LEVEL: B LANG: Eng SIRC ARTICLE NO: 102352

O'Rourke, B. Coach's desk... The coach as teacher. *Basketball clinic (Princeton, N.J.) 16(7), Mar 1984, 14-15.*
LEVEL: B LANG: Eng SIRC ARTICLE NO: 096529

Olson, W.A. 'What's the difference? Coaching is coaching' or is it. *Juco review (Hutchison, Kan.) 36(4), Dec 1984, 16-17.*
LEVEL: B LANG: Eng SIRC ARTICLE NO: 103043

Paye, B. Basketball's zone presses: a complete coaching guide. West Nyack, N.Y.: Parker Pub. Co., c1984. 204 p.

NOTES: Includes index.
LEVEL: B LANG: Eng ISBN: 0130692379 LC
CARD: 83-013186 GV888 15737

Phillips, B. A big vote for urban re-newell: the Hall
of Fame basketball coach (he coached an N.I.T.
winner in 1949, an NCAA winner in 1959, and an
Olympic gold medalist in 1960) touches on his
legendary career in the college and professional
games as well as changes in techniques and
strategy. (Pete Newell) *Scholastic coach (New
York) 54(5), Dec 1984, 28-31;61.*
LEVEL: B LANG: Eng SIRC ARTICLE NO: 103045

Rosen, C. Nobody coaches like Gene Shue: he's
different from the other 22 coaches in the NBA.
He's lost more games than any of them. But he's
lasted longer than all of them. *Sport (New York)
75(12), Dec 1984, 67-70;72.*
LEVEL: B LANG: ENG SIRC ARTICLE NO: 108692

Rozek, M. What does a coach do, anyways? Some
say basketball coaches are mostly just for show.
Some say in college they coach, in the pros they
don't. Some say quite the opposite. Here's what
the coaches say. *Sport (New York) 75(3), Mar
1984, 34-36;38-39;41.*
LEVEL: B LANG: Eng SIRC ARTICLE NO: 094885

Samaras, B. A treasury of winning basketball tips.
West Nyack, N.Y.: Parker Pub. Co., c1984. xiii, 247
p. : ill.
NOTES: Includes index.
LEVEL: B LANG: Eng ISBN: 0139301992 LC
CARD: 83-022104 GV885.3 18112

Santos, R.D. Ingredients to winning. (Refs:
3)*Basketball clinic (Princeton, N.J.) 17(1), Sept
1984, 15-16.*
LEVEL: B LANG: Eng SIRC ARTICLE NO: 101103

Schmidt, D.R. Involve the entire team. *Women's
coaching clinic (Princeton, N.J.) 8(1) Sept 1984,
1-3.*
LEVEL: B LANG: Eng SIRC ARTICLE NO: 099426

Smith, G. Where you gonna be next year, Larry?
(Larry Brown) *Sports illustrated (Los Angeles, Calif.)
61(22), 12 Nov 1984, 106-110;112;114-120.*
LEVEL: B LANG: Eng SIRC ARTICLE NO: 101105

The power & the glory & the coach's art. (Jack
Ramsay) *Scholastic coach (New York) 54(2), Sept
1984, 38-40;84-85.*
LEVEL: B LANG: Eng SIRC ARTICLE NO: 099423

Wideman, J. Listen to the drum. A celebrated
author indulges an obsession to separate the facts
from the fictions he has heard about Georgetown
coach John Thompson. *Sports illustrated (Los
Angeles) 61(24), 26 Nov 1984, 58-60;67-69.*
LEVEL: B LANG: Eng SIRC ARTICLE NO: 101111

Wolff, A. The son has also risen. Two notable
Tarkanians, Jerry the coach and Danny the
playmaker, have UNLV's Rebels runnin again.
*Sports illustrated 60(8), 20 Feb 1984, 30;32;35-
36;40.*
LEVEL: B LANG: Eng SIRC ARTICLE NO: 090513

COUNTRIES AND REGIONS

Genevois, B. Le principe de libre acces aux
activites sportives: conclusions sur Conseil d'Etat
16 mars 1984. *Recueil Dallo Sirey (Paris) 22, 1984,
317-320.*
LEVEL: B LANG: Fr

Olin, K. International exchange in terms of the
recruitment of star foreign players: the reactions of

sports clubs in Finnis Basketball. (Refs: 10)*In,
Ilmarinen, M. (ed.) et al., Sport and International
Understanding: proceedings of the congress held in
Helsinki, Finland, July 7-10, 1982, Berlin, Springer-
Verlag, 1984, p. 335-338.*
CONF: Congress on Sport and International
Understanding (1982 : Helsinki).
LEVEL: I LANG: Eng GV706.8 18979

DISABLED

Brasile, F.M. A wheelchair basketball skill test.
(Refs: 3)*Sports 'n stokes (Phoenix, Ariz.) 10(1),
May/Jun 1984, 36-39.*
LEVEL: B LANG: Eng SIRC ARTICLE NO: 094311

Desjardins, D.M. A study of physiologic
parameters before and after a season of wheelchair
basketball competition. (Refs: 18
NOTES: In, Cantu, R.C. (ed.), Clinical sports
medicine, Lexington, Mass. ; Toronto, Collamore
Press : D.C. Heath, c1984, p. 45-52.
LEVEL: A LANG: Eng RC1201 15964

Druvert, J.C. Basketball... en fauteuil roulant.
Basketball (Paris) 495, oct/nov/dec 1984, 36-38.
LEVEL: B LANG: Fr SIRC ARTICLE NO: 109122

Heer, M. A new generation of athletes learn the
ropes. *Sports 'n spokes (Phoenix, Ariz.) 9(5), Jan/
Feb 1984, 34-36.*
LEVEL B LANG: Eng SIRC ARTICLE NO: 094316

Hoeberigs, J.H. Verstappen, F.T.J. Muscle
soreness in wheelchair basketballers. (Refs:
11)*International journal of sports medicine
(Stuttgart) Suppl. 5, Nov 1984, 177-179.*
CONF: International Congress on Sports and Health
(1983 : Maastricht, Netherlands).
LEVEL: A LANG: Eng SIRC ARTICLE NO: 103964

ECONOMICS

Culverhouse, J. Chasing the million pound dream.
*Basketball monthly (Leeds, Eng.) 24(3), Nov 1984,
10-13.*
NOTES: Special report.
LEVEL: B LANG: Eng SIRC ARTICLE NO: 104567

HISTORY

History of the Olympics. *International basketball
(Budapest, Hungary) 24, 1984, 4-9.*
LEVEL: B LANG: Eng SIRC ARTICLE NO: 105676

Hobson, H. Shooting ducks: a history of University
of Oregon basketball. Portland, Ore.: Western
Imprints, (1984). 1v.
NOTES: Includes index.
LEVEL: B LANG: Eng ISBN: 0875951414 LC
CARD: 84-003564

Robert, C. International basketball celebrates half a
century of progress. *Olympian (Colorado Springs,
Colo.) 9(2), Jul/Aug 1984, 14-16.*
LEVEL: B LANG: Eng SIRC ARTICLE NO: 104581

Young, S.B. The history of professional basketball:
1946-1979. Eugene, Ore.: Microform Publications,
University of Oregon, 1984. 2 microfiches : negative
; 11 x 15 cm.
NOTES: Thesis (M.S.) - Western Illinois University,
1981; (vi, 103 leaves); includes bibliography.
LEVEL: A LANG: Eng UO84 25-26

INJURIES AND ACCIDENTS

Ahuja, A. Injuries in basketball. (Refs: 7)*Snipes
journal (Patiala, India) 7(3), Jul 1984, 40-44.*
LEVEL: I LANG: Eng SIRC ARTICLE NO: 099402

Blanc, J. Grunberg, C. Problemes de rotule chez
la basketteuse. *Basketball (Paris) 492, fevr/mars/
avr 1984, 10-20.*
LEVEL: LANG: Fr SIRC ARTICLE NO: 097935

Chow, A.Y. Goldberg, M.F. Frenkel, M. Evulsion
of the optic nerve in association with basketball
injuries. *Annals of ophthalmology (New York) 16(1),
Jan 1984, 35-37.*
LEVEL: I LANG: Eng SIRC ARTICLE NO: 099410

Christopher, J. Basketball. *In, Adams, S.H. (ed.),
et al., Catastrophic injuries in sports: avoidance
strategies, Salinas, Calif., Cayote Press, c1984, p.
83-86.*
LEVEL: B LANG: Eng RD97 19088

Mackie, J. Custom-made harness answer to
recurring dislocations. *First aider (Gardner, Kans.)
54(3), Nov 1984, 8-9.*
LEVEL B LANG: Eng SIRC ARTICLE NO: 108461

Michigan - girls' basketball player sues for
'premises liability' for locker room assault. *Sports
and the courts (Winston-Salem, N.C.) 5(1), Winter
1984, 6.*
LEVEL: B LANG: Eng SIRC ARTICLE NO: 094878

Tehranzadeh, J. Labosky, D.A. Detection of
intraarticular loose osteochondral fragments by
double-contrast wrist arthrography. A case report of
a basketball injury. (Refs: 17)*American journal of
sports medicine (Baltimore, Md.) 12(1), Jan/Feb
1984, 77-79.*
ABST: A basketball injury to the wrist went
undetected by plain radiographs. A double-contrast
arthrogram, involving injection of renographin and
air revealed calcified bone fragments. Gravity
assisted in the detection; the wrist was moved
upside down causing movement of the calcified
bodies. The fragments were removed surgically.
LEVEL: A LANG: Eng SIRC ARTICLE NO: 094889

JUVENILE LITERATURE

Aaseng, N. College basketball: you are the coach.
Minneapolis: Lerner Pub. Co., c1984. 1v.
LEVEL: B LANG: Eng ISBN: 0822515 LC CARD:
83-019996

MacDonald, F. Chicago Bulls. (Mankato, Minn.):
Creative Education, (c1984). 48 p. : ill.
LEVEL: B LANG: Eng ISBN: 087191972 LC CARD:
83-073285

LAW AND LEGISLATION

Alabama - court upholds 'clean shaven' policy for
high school athletes. *Sports and the courts
(Winston-Salem, N.C.) 5(4), Fal 1984, 1-2.*
LEVEL: B LANG: Eng SIRC ARTICLE NO: 102553

Appenzeller, H. Ross, C.T. Utah - can a student
trainer be held to the same standard of care as a
physician or surgeon? *Sports and the courts
(Winston-Salem, N.C.) 5(3), Summer 1984, 11-13.*
LEVEL: B LANG: Eng SIRC ARTICLE NO: 097933

Pennsylvania - athlete association's transfer rule
upheld. *Sports and the courts (Winston-Salem,
N.C.) 5(4), Fall 1984, 7.*
LEVEL: B LANG: Eng SIRC ARTICLE NO: 103044

BASKETBALL (continued)

MASS MEDIA

Newman, B. From high above the western sideline: painting world pictures that have made him the Michelangelo of basketball broadcasters, Chick Hearn is the enduring voice of the Lakers. *Sports illustrated 60(15), 9 Apr 1984, 78-82;84;86-88;90.*
LEVEL: B LANG: Eng SIRC ARTICLE NO: 093305

MEDICINE

Duda, M. Basketball coaches guard against cardiovascular stress. *Physician and sportsmedicine 12(3), Mar 1984, 193-194.*
LEVEL: B LANG: Eng SIRC ARTICLE NO: 091934

Duda, M. Hovik monitor aids in Cummings's diagnosis. *Physician and sportsmedicine 12(4), Apr 1984, 35.*
LEVEL: B LANG: Eng SIRC ARTICLE NO: 093302

Musante, R. Preziuso, M. Cupelli, V. Attina, D.A. The Marfan syndrome. M-mode and two dimensional echocardiography study of two basket-ball players. (Refs: 11)*International journal of sports cardiology (Torino, Italy) 1(2), Jul/Dec 1984, 88-95.*
LEVEL: A LANG: Eng SIRC ARTICLE NO: 179173

Vegso, J.J. Mandibular position in upper body strength. *Sportsmedicine digest (Van Nuys, Calif.) 6(2), Feb 1984, 4-5.*
LEVEL: I LANG: Eng SIRC ARTICLE NO: 099429

OFFICIATING

Fremon, D. Chicago's heavyweights: The Central Officials' Association. *Referee (Franksville, Wis.) 9(5), May 1984, 24-28.*
LEVEL: B LANG: Eng SIRC ARTICLE NO: 097631

Hammill, T. Rocky mountain low: Denver area high school referee Rich Puter wanted some answers. *Referee (Franksville, Wis.) 9(1), Jan 1984, 16-20;24.*
LEVEL: B LANG: Eng SIRC ARTICLE NO: 097944

Hansen, J. About face: to players, coaches and NBA officials, chief of staff Drell Garretson is an enigma. A former union leader, recently he defected to management. *Referee (Franksville, Wis.) 9(3), Mar 1984, 24-29.*
LEVEL: B LANG: Eng SIRC ARTICLE NO: 097945

Harris, P.A. Blum, D.S. AOA Sports Vision Section screening of basketball officials. *Journal of the American Optometric Association (St. Louis) 55(2), Feb 1984, 130-134;141.*
ABST: 60 basketball officials were tested on their vision. Results indicated that officials' vision was at a very high level.
LEVEL: A LANG: Eng SIRC ARTICLE NO: 101082

Interview: Billy Packer. A former player and coach in the Atlantic Coast Conference, Packer is considered the top college basketball analyst for CBS Sports. *Referee (Franksville, Wis.) 9(12), Dec 1984, 16-19.*
LEVEL: B LANG: Eng SIRC ARTICLE NO: 109337

Interview: David Turner. *Referee (Franksville, Wis.) 9(7), Jul 1984, 16-19.*
LEVEL: B LANG: Eng SIRC ARTICLE NO: 101087

Ives, D. Doing it: off-the-court problems. *Referee (Franksville, Wis.) 9(1), Jan 1984, 35;61.*
LEVEL: B LANG: Eng SIRC ARTICLE NO: 097946

Ives, D. A practical guide to in-between calls. *Referee (Franksville, Wis.) 9(11), Nov 1984, 36-37.*
LEVEL: B LANG: Eng SIRC ARTICLE NO: 108615

Ives, D. Doing it: how to judge an intentional foul. *Referee (Franksville, Wis.) 9(12), Dec 1984, 37;61.*
LEVEL: B LANG: E SIRC ARTICLE NO: 109342

Jim Drucker: Commissioner of the CBA, he is former four-sport official whose father (Norm) was a long-time pro basketball referee supervisor. *Referee (Franksville, Wis.) 9(8), Aug 1984, 16-19.*
LEVEL: B LANG: Eng SIRC ARTICLE NO: 097947

Lucas, B. The Americanization of Davit. A world-class referee while living in Russia, Davit Davitian emigrated to the U.S. where he found his services were rarely desired. Effectively sidelined, Davitian and his wife retain elements of their heritage while enjoying the American way of life. *Referee (Franksville, Wis.) 9(12), Dec 1984, 48-52.*
LEVEL: B LANG: Eng SIRC ARTICLE NO: 109340

Pennsylvania - basketball referee improperly disciplined by official's union. *Sports and the courts (Winston-Salem, N.C.) 5(1), Winter 1984, 7.*
LEVEL: B LANG: Eng SIRC ARTICLE NO: 094881

Purdy, D.A. Snyder, E.E. A profile of high school basketball officials. *Ohio high school athletic (Columbus, Ohio) 44(1), Oct 1984, 2-3.*
LEVEL: I LANG: Eng SIRC ARTICLE NO: 108779

Qualifications of an official. *Sportorials (West Hartford, Conn.) 34(260), Jan 1984, 3;6.*
LEVEL: B LANG: Eng SIRC ARTICLE NO: 106289

Schuler, J. 'Come on in', pull up a chair. Erv Delman has something to say, but that's nothing new. *Referee (Franksville, Wis.) 9(5), May 1984, 48-52.*
LEVEL: B LANG: Eng SIRC ARTICLE NO: 097956

Staneff, S. Rituals, habits, and mandates. *Sportorials (West Hartford, Conn.) 34(262), Apr/May 1984, 2.*
LEVEL: B LANG: En SIRC ARTICLE NO: 104587

Steitz, E. By the rules: player-control and airborne-shooter fouls. *Referee (Franksville, Wis.) 9(12), Dec 1984, 36-37.*
LEVEL: B LANG: Eng SIRC ARTICLE NO: 109341

Tapp, J. Grand rapids blues. *Referee (Franksville, Wis.) 9(12), Dec 1984, 24-28.*
LEVEL: B LANG: Eng SIRC ARTICLE NO: 1093

Toliver, G. Training the basketball official for intramurals, and beyond. (Refs: 2)*NIRSA journal (Mt. Pleasant, Mich.) 8(2) Winter 1984, 42-43.*
LEVEL: B LANG: Eng SIRC ARTICLE NO: 097958

PHILOSOPHY

Bredemeier, B.J. Shields, D.L. Divergence in moral reasoning about sport and everyday life. (Refs: 23)*Sociology of sport journal (Champaign, Ill.) 1(4), Dec 1984, 348-357.*
ABST: The observation that sport represents a unique context has been widely discussed, but social scientists have done little to empirically examine the moral adaptations of sport participants. In the present study, the divergence between levels of moral reasoning used to discuss hypothetical dilemmas set in sport and in everyday life contexts was investigated among 120 high school and collegiate basketball players, swimmers, and nonathletes. Protocols were scored according to Haan's interactional model of moral development. It was found that levels of moral reasoning used to

discuss sport dilemmas were lower than levels characterizing reasoning about issues within an everyday life context. Findings were discussed in terms of the specific social and moral context of sport experience.
LEVEL: A LANG: Eng SIRC ARTICLE NO: 104214

PHYSIOLOGY

Calsamiglia, G. Ross, A. Testa, M. Achilli, M.P. Ricciardi, L. La componente periferica nel corso dell'esercizio muscolare dinamico: studio su un gruppo di cestisti. (The peripheral component during dynamic muscular exertion: study of a group of basketball players.) *Bollettino - Societa italiana biologia sperimentale (Napoli) 60(3), 30 Mar 1984, 589-593.*
LEVEL: A LANG: It

Rossi, A. Calsamigli, G. Riccardi, L. Bartoletti, S. Orlandi, M. Sardi, C. Galli, N. Minelli, R. Stima dell'impegno energetico e cardiovascolare del giocatore di basket nel corso di una gara. (The cost of energy and cardiovascular expenditure in basketball players during a game.) *Bollettino - Societa italiana biologia sperimentale (Napoli) 60(3), 30 Mar 1984, 581-587.*
ABST: The authors evaluated the energy expenditure of 6 basketball players exercising in a cyclergometer. Data was obtained for oxygen consumption, pulmonary ventilation, heart rate, respiratory quotient, and other parameters at various levels of exercise load. Heart rate and arterial blood pressure of subjects were also monitored during a regular game. Energy expenditure cost was evaluated at 0.1339 Kcal x kg-1 xmin - 1.
LEVEL: A LANG: It

PSYCHOLOGY

Banks, B. The choke. *Sports now (St. Louis, Mo.) 2(9), Sept 1984, 20-23.*
LEVEL: B LANG: Eng SIRC ARTICLE NO: 099405

Bar-Eli, M. Zur Diagnostik individueller psychischer Krisen im sportlichen Wettkampf: eine wahrscheinlichkeitsorientierte, theoretische und empirische Studie unter besonderer Beruecksichtigung des Basketballspiels. Koeln: Deutsche Sporthochschule, Psychologisches Institut, 1984. viii, 366 p.
NOTES: Thesis (Ph.D.) - Deutsche Sporthochschule Koeln, 1984. Bibliography: p. 306-343.
LEVEL: A LANG: Ger GV706.4 17550

Bredemeier, B.J. Shields, D.L. The utility of moral stage analysis in the investigation of athletic aggression. (Refs: 21) *Sociology of sport journal (Champaign, Ill.) 1(2), 1984, 138-149.*
ABST: The purpose of this study was to demonstrate the theoretical and empirical relationship between stages of moral reasoning and athletic aggression, and thus to offer a new model for the investigation of aggression in sport. In this pilot work, 22 female and 24 male basketball players' moral reasoning levels were determined through the administration of Rest's Defining Issues Test (DIT); athletic aggression measures included coaches' ranking and ratings of player aggressiveness, and statistics pertaining to players' fouls per season game. Significant judgment-action results were congruent with hypothesized relationships. The results are discussed within a

cognitive-developmental framework.
LEVEL: A LANG: Eng SIRC ARTICLE NO: 103023

Crossman, J. The effects of directing attentional focus on varsity basketball performance. (Refs: 10)*CAHPER journal (Ottawa 51(2), Nov/Dec 1984, 17-20.*
ABST: 10 female varsity basketball players are divided into two equal groups: 1) an experimental group that is taught the focusing technique and 2) a control group. Both groups are tested before and after intervention on the following variables: subject's field goal percentage, free throw percentage, average number of points per game, offensive and defensive rebounds, and turnovers. The control group obtains better results for free throw percentage only. Overall, the experimental group performs better than the control group.
LEVEL: A LANG: Eng SIRC ARTICLE NO: 103027

DeKalb, S.E. Expectancies, causal attributions, and anxiety in collegiate women basketball players. Eugene, Ore.: Microform Publications, University of Oregon, 1984. 1 microfiche : negative ; 11 x 15 cm.
NOTES: Thesis (M.S.) - Pennsylvania State University, 1981; (ix, 86 leaves); includes bibliography.
LEVEL: A LANG: Eng UO84 118

Donohue, J. Part 2: the crowd, the referee and bending the rules a little. *Sport-talk (Toronto) 13(1), Mar 1984, 2-3.*
LEVEL: B LANG: Eng SIRC ARTICLE NO: 094860

Hawkinson, N.J. Motivating a female college basketball team. *Women's varsity sports (Kalispell, Mont.) 5(3), Jan/Feb 1984, 6-7;9.*
LEVEL: B LANG: Eng SIRC ARTICLE NO: 101083

Kieffer, R. Pregame emotional stress in intramural basketball players. (Refs: 5)*In, Vendl, B.C. (ed.) et al., Interpretive aspects of intramural-recreational sports: selected proceedings from the Thirty-fifth Annual National Intramural-Recreational Sports Association Conference, Corvallis, Or., Oregon State University, c1984, p. 93-102.*
CONF: National Intramural-Recreational Sports Association Conference (35th : 1984 : Fort Worth, Tex.).
LEVEL: A LANG: Eng GV710 18914

Kimiecik, J.C. Children's perceptions of success and failure in a competitive sports activity. Eugene, Ore.: Microform Publications, University of Oregon, 1984. 2 microfiches : negative ; 11 x 15 cm.
NOTES: Thesis (M.S.) - Purdue University, 1983; (ix, 94 leaves); includes bibliography.
LEVEL: A LANG: Eng UO84 304-305

Lidstone, J.E. The relationships of selected psycho-social variables associated with achievement to the performance of male and female intercollegiate basketball players. Eugene, Ore.: Microform Publications, University of Oregon, 1984. 2 microfiches : negative ; 11 x 15 cm.
NOTES: Thesis (Ed.D.) - University of North Carolina at Greensboro, 1982; (vii, 130 leaves); appendix E omitted; includes bibliography.
LEVEL: A LANG: Eng UO84 172-173

Mathison, T. Sit down coach, maybe the spectators are right. *Texas coach (Austin, Tex.) 28(3), Oct 1984, 31.*
LEVEL: B LANG: Eng SIRC ARTICLE NO: 173204

Paxton, B. Setting goals. *Texas coach 27(4), Jan 1984, 44-46.*
LEVEL: B LANG: Eng SIRC ARTICLE NO: 093306

Siegel, D. Newhof, C. The sports orientation of female collegiate basketball players at different competitive levels. (Refs: 16)*Perceptual and motor skills (Missoula, Mont.) 59(1), Aug 1984, 79-87.*
ABST: Female basketball players participating in Division I (n, 76), Division II (n, 90), and Division III (n, 92) university programs were surveyed on various sport-related concepts such as self improvement, social experience, winning, aggression, external rewards and power. The authors tested the hypothesis than Division I athletes would be more favorably disposed toward concepts dealing with winning and dominating others while those in Division III would favour concepts related to personal values and involvement. Division I athletes had mariginally more positive attitudes toward mastering opponents than Division III athletes. The second prediction was contradicted since no difference across divisions was found.
LEVEL: A LANG: Eng SIRC ARTICLE NO: 099427

Weinberg, R. Reveles, M. Jackson, A. Attitudes of male and female athletes toward male and female coaches. (Refs: 13)*Journa of sport psychology (Champaign, Ill.) 6(4), Dec 1984, 448-453.*
ABST: This investigation was done to gather some exploratory data concerning the attitudes and feelings of male and female college, high school, and junior high school varsity basketball players toward having a female coach versus a male coach. Subjects (N, 85) were instructed to complete a questionnaire consisting of 11 items that tapped their attitudes and feelings toward a new coach. Identical background information was provided to subjects concerning the qualifications of the coach, the only difference being that for one group of subjects the coach was said to be female whereas for the other group of subjects the coach was said to be a male. Results were analyzed by a MANOVA and indicated significant interactions on seven questions, with simple main effects consistently indicating that males displayed more negative attitudes toward female coaches than did females while males and females did not differ in their view of male coaches. Results are discussed in terms of sex-role socialization patterns for males and females.
LEVEL: A LANG: Eng SIRC ARTICLE NO: 104590

RACE RELATIONS

Nogawa, H. Suttie, S.J. A Japanese-American Basketball League and the assimilation of its members into mainstream of United States Society. (Refs: 31)*International review for the sociology of sport (Warszawa, Poland) 19(3/4), 1984, 259-271.*
ABST: This study investigated the effects of participation in a Japanese-American youth basketball league on the assimilation of its members into the dominant American culture. Two groups of Japanese-Americans were compared: participants (players) and non-participants (non-members). The data were collected by a written questionnaire, formal and informal interviews, and direct observation. Significant differences were found between the groups in the dimensions of structural, marital and identificational assimilation. Participation in the ethnic basketball league did not appear to promote overall assimilation into the mainstream of American life.
LEVEL: A LANG: Eng SIRC ARTICLE NO: 105693

RULES AND REGULATIONS

Explanatory brochure... (parts) (basketball) *International basketball (Budapest, Hungary) 24, 1984, 10-13.*
LEVEL: B LANG: E SIRC ARTICLE NO: 105671

Ferrigno, E. The front of the torso. *Sportorials (West Hartford, Conn.) 34(262), Apr/May 1984, 5-6.*
LEVEL: B LANG: Eng SIRC ARTICLE NO: 104570

Hutchison, J. History of smaller basketball rule change. *Juco review (Hutchinson, Kans.) 36(2), Oct 1984, 20-21.*
LEVEL: B LANG: Eng SIRC ARTICLE NO: 101086

Official basketball rules for men and women. As adopted by the International Amateur Basketball Federation (F.I.B.A.). Ottawa: Basketball Canada, 1984?. 90 p.
CORP: Basketball Canada.
NOTES: Cover title.
LEVEL: B LANG: Eng GV885.45 20336

Perez, F.V. Creating a positive atmosphere for intramural basketball through rules modifications. *NIRSA journal (Mt. Pleasant, Mich.) 8(2), Winter 1984, 53.*
LEVEL: B LANG: Eng SIRC ARTICLE NO: 097953

Shaper, R. New rules - a new game? *International basketball (Budapest, Hungary) 4(25), 1984, 22-23.*
LEVEL: B LANG: Eng SIRC ARTICLE NO: 108653

Stanton, M. Inside Ed Steitz. *Eastern basketball (West Hempstead, N.Y.) 9(50, 1 Feb 1984, 21-24.*
LEVEL: B LANG: Eng SIRC ARTICLE NO: 094887

Steitz, E. Dribbling misconceptions. *Referee (Franksville, Wis.) 9(1), Jan 1984, 33-35.*
LEVEL: B LANG: Eng SIRC ARTICLE NO: 097957

Taylor, P. Basketball rules - major differences - NAGWS/High School Federation 1984-85. *Sportorials (West Hartford, Conn.) 35(265), Nov 1984, 4-6.*
LEVEL: B LANG: Eng SIRC ARTICLE NO: 104588

SOCIAL PSYCHOLOGY

Baumeister, R.F. Steinhilber, A. Paradoxical effects of supportive audiences on performance under pressure: the home field disadvantages in sports championships. (Refs: 30)*Journal of personality and social psychology (Washington, D.C.) 47(1), Jul 1984, 85-93.*
ABST: Results from baseball's World Series from 1924 to 1982 and from National Basketball Association (NBA) championship and semifinal series from 1967 to 1982 are used in this study. The authors set up to test the following hypothesis: the presence of supportive audiences is detrimental to performance in decisive contests. Findings corroborate the hypothesis. Results from both World Series and NBA series games show that home teams tend to win early games but lose final ones.
LEVEL: A LANG: Eng SIRC ARTICLE NO: 096496

Smith, M.E. Attributional control processes in the coach-player interaction. Eugene, Ore.: Microform Publications, Universit of Oregon, 1984. 2 microfiches : negative ; 11 x 15 cm.
NOTES: Thesis (Ed.D.) - Virginia Polytechnic Institute and State University, 1982; (vi, 95 leaves); vita; includes bibliography.
LEVEL: A LANG: Eng UO84 174-175

BASKETBALL (continued)

Wright, W.T. The effect of ability and gender on the rating of team cohesion within successful intercollegiate basketball teams. Eugene, Ore.: Microform Publications, University of Oregon, 1984. 1 microfiche : negative ; 11 x 15 cm.
NOTES: Thesis (M.S.) - Pennsylvania State University, 1981; (vii, 57 leaves); includes bibliography.
LEVEL: A LANG: Eng UO84 107

Yukelson, D. Weinberg, R. Jackson, A. A multidimensional group cohesion instrument for intercollegiate basketball teams. (Refs: 45)*Sport psychology (Champaign, Ill.) 6(1), 1984, 103-117.* ABST: The purpose of the present study was to develop a valid and reliable group cohesion instrument that measures both task-related and social-related forces that are presumed to exist in interacting sport groups. Male and female intercollegiate basketball players (N, 196) completed a 41-item sport cohesion instrument. Results from two different factor analytical techniques revealed four robust common factors which accounted for greater than 80 percent of the variance of the total common factor structure. The four derived common factors were labeled Attraction to the Group, Unity of Purpose, Quality of Teamwork, and Valued Roles. The findings suggest that group cohesion in intercollegiate basketball teams is multidimensional in nature, consisting of common goals, valued roles, team-word that is complimentary to the goals the group is striving to achieve, and feelings of satisfaction and/or identification with group membership.
LEVEL: A LANG: Eng SIRC ARTICLE NO: 108488

Yukelson, D.P. Group cohesion in sport: a multidimensional approach. Eugene, Ore.: Microform Publications, University of Oregon, 1984. 1 microfiche : negative ; 11 x 15 cm.
NOTES: Thesis (Ph.D.) - North Texas State University, 1982; (vi, 70 leaves); includes bibliography.
LEVEL: A LANG: Eng UO84 222

STATISTICS AND RECORDS

Dirsa, T. Charting your team's success. *Basketball clinic (Princeton, N.J.) 16(8), Apr 1984, 12-13.*
LEVEL: B LANG: Eng SIRC ARTICLE NO: 094859

Jones, D. A complete statistics sheet. *Basketball clinic (Princeton, N.J.) 16(10), Jun 1984, 8-9.*
LEVEL: B LANG: Eng SIRC ARTICLE NO: 096519

MacAdam, M. Taking stats with good purpose. *Coaching review (Ottawa, Ont.) 7, Nov/Dec 1984, 55-56;58.*
LEVEL: B LANG: Eng SIRC ARTICLE NO: 099418

Stein, J.U. Basketball statistics the mirocomputer way. *Athletic journal 64(7), Feb 1984, 52;68-69.*
LEVEL: B LANG: Eng SIRC ARTICLE NO: 091952

Stein, J.U. Basketball statistics the microcomputer way. *Physical education newsletter (Old Saybrook, Conn.) 157, Mar 1984, 2-3.*
LEVEL: B LANG: Eng SIRC ARTICLE NO: 096532

Sutton, M. Basketball & baseball computer programs at John C. Calhoun State Community College. *Juco review (Hutchinson, Kans.) 36(3), Nov 1984, 4;6;8.*
LEVEL: B LANG: Eng SIRC ARTICLE NO: 173371

STRATEGY

Congres international des entraineurs de basketball. Paris/Bercy 21/22/23 et 24 mai 1984. *Basketball (Paris) 495, oct/nov/dec 1984, 4-14.*
LEVEL: B LANG: Fr SIRC ARTICLE NO: 109121

Krahling, L. Practice everything. *Women's coaching clinic 7(7), Mar 1984, 7-8.*
LEVEL: B LANG: Eng SIRC ARTICLE NO: 091943

Lynch, D. Playing championship basketball. *Women's coaching clinic (Princeton, N.J.) 8(4), Dec 1984, 1-4.*
LEVEL: B LANG: Eng SIRC ARTICLE NO: 103037

Quelques points techniques a l'intention des equipes masculines. *Basketball (Paris) 491, dec 1983/janv 1984, 6-14.*
LEVEL: B LANG: Fr SIRC ARTICLE NO: 099424

Ray, H. Cardette offense and defense. *Women's coaching clinic (Princeton, N.J.) 8(4), Dec 1984, 4-6.*
LEVEL: B LANG: Eng SIRC ARTICLE NO: 103046

Rozak, P. The platoon system. *Basketball clinic (Princeton, N.J.) 16(9), May 1984, 9-13.*
LEVEL: B LANG: Eng SIRC ARTICLE NO: 094884

White, K. Off the ball movement: for maximum offensive scoring. *Women's coaching clinic (Princeton, N.J.) 8(2), Oct 1984, 5-6.*
LEVEL: B LANG: Eng SIRC ARTICLE NO: 099431

STRATEGY - DEFENSIVE

Abraham, S. The 1-2-1-1 press. *Women's coaching clinic (Princeton, N.J.) 7(9), May 1984, 8.*
LEVEL: B LANG: Eng SIRC ARTICLE NO: 094849

Butcher, A. Hints for success: man to man defense. *Women's coaching clinic (Princeton, N.J.) 8(2), Oct 1984, 1-3.*
LEVEL: LANG: Eng SIRC ARTICLE NO: 099406

Byrnes, J. Face the shooter: by facing the offensive player and boxing out, the defensive players should be able to control rebounds. *Athletic journal (Evanston, Ill.) 65(3), Oct 1984, 20;48.*
LEVEL: B LANG: Eng SIRC ARTICLE NO: 099407

Danik, D. Sequencing alternating defenses. *Basketball clinic (Princeton, N.J.) 17(4), Dec 1984, 9-10.*
LEVEL: B LANG: Eng SIRC ARTICLE NO: 104568

Davis, J. Roanne State's 'gut' zone defense. *Juco review (Hutchison, Ka.) 36(4), Dec 1984, 8-9.*
LEVEL: B LANG: Eng SIRC ARTICLE NO: 103028

Drake, L. Beating the 4-corner delay game. *Scholastic coach (New York) 54(4), Nov 1984, 20;16.*
LEVEL: B LANG: Eng SIRC ARTICLE NO: 103029

English, J. Building the press. *Texas coach (Austin, Tex.) 28(3), Oct 1984, 50-55.*
LEVEL: B LANG: Eng SIRC ARTICLE NO: 173211

Fearing, D. A proven 1-3-1 defense. *Basketball clinic (Princeton, N.J.) 17(2), Oct 1984, 9-11.*
LEVEL: B LANG: Eng SIRC ARTICLE NO: 101080

Field , C.A. Defensive play... Speaking of man to man defense and team defense. *Basketball clinic (Princeton, N.J.) 16(7), Mar 1984, 9-11.*
LEVEL: B LANG: Eng SIRC ARTICLE NO: 096513

Field, C. Zone defenses. *Basketball clinic (Princeton, N.J.) 17(1), Sept 1984, 7-10.*
LEVEL: B LANG: Eng SIRC ARTICLE NO: 101081

Field, C.A. Team defense: a player's guide. *Basketball clinic (Princeton, N.J.) 16(6), Feb 1984, 8-9.*
LEVEL: B LANG: Eng SIRC ARTICLE NO: 094861

Galbraith, D. Attaque pour battre une defense zone trappe. *Basketball (Paris) 491, dec 1983/janv 1984, 48-49.*
LEVEL: B LANG: Fr SIRC ARTICLE NO: 099412

Gamble J. Defensive, pride and discipline. *Basketball clinic (Princeton, N.J.) 16(7), Mar 1984, 11-12.*
LEVEL: B LANG: Eng SIRC ARTICLE NO: 096515

Hudson, S. Zone 1-2-2 en trappe sur demi-terrain. *Basketball (Paris) 491, dec 1983/janv 1984, 46-47.*
LEVEL: B LANG: Fr SIRC ARTICLE NO: 099415

Jarrett, R. Color-coded systems for changing defenses on the run. *Scholastic coach (New York) 54(2), Sept 1984, 69-70;82.*
LEVEL: B LANG: Eng SIRC ARTICLE NO: 099416

Kitchens, R. Progressive man-to-man defensive 'help' drills. Each drill is given a name and, once explained, is never allowe to run over six minutes. *Scholastic coach (New York) 54(3), Oct 1984, 56-58;78-79;83.*
LEVEL: B LANG: Eng SIRC ARTICLE NO: 101090

Littrell, G. A 'poor man's' 1-2-1-1 zone press. *Basketball clinic (Princeton, N.J.) 16(7), Mar 1984, 4-6.*
LEVEL: B LANG: Eng SIRC ARTICLE NO: 096521

Martin, T. A press for any situation. *Athletic journal (Evanston, Ill.) 65(1), Aug 1984, 18-19;62-64.*
LEVEL: B LANG: Eng SIRC ARTICLE NO: 096524

May, J. Improve your zone defense. *Athletic journal (Evanston, Ill.) 65(4), Nov 1984, 10-11;46.*
LEVEL: B LANG: Eng SIRC ARTICLE NO: 101093

Menesplier, P. Une defense tout terrain: la zone-press 1-2-2 et ses variantes. (Refs: 1)*Pivot (France) 22, 1984, 14-19.*
LEVEL: B LANG: Fr

Parkinson, W. Why press? *Athletic journal 64(7), Feb 1984, 66-67.*
LEVEL: B LANG: Eng SIRC ARTICLE NO: 091945

Robinson, R. Cornering the 'four-corners'. *Scholastic coach (New York) 54(2), Sept 1984, 46.*
LEVEL: B LANG: Eng SIRC ARTICLE NO: 099425

Savage, D.E. Basic strategy in women's basketball. *Basketball clinic (Princeton, N.J.) 17(2), Oct 1984, 11-13.*
LEVEL: B LANG: Eng SIRC ARTICLE NO: 101104

Tolkes, R. Good defense wins games. *Women's coaching clinic 7(8), Apr 1984, 1-2.*
LEVEL: B LANG: Eng SIRC ARTICLE NO: 0933

Warkentien, D.D. Continuous trapping defense. *Athletic journal 64(6), Jan 1984, 40-41.*
LEVEL: B LANG: Eng SIRC ARTICLE NO 090512

Webster, F. Basketball's amoeba defense: complete multiple system. West Nyack, N.Y.: Parker Pub. Co., c1984. 264 p. : ill.
NOTES: Includes index.
LEVEL: I LANG: Eng ISBN: 0130691399 LC CARD: 83-023654 GV888 18164

Williams, L.C. Switching. (man-to-man defence) *Juco review (Hutchinson, Kans.) 36(2), Oct 1984,*

8;11.
LEVEL: B LANG: Eng SIRC ARTICLE NO: 101112

Winston, L.K. Variations on the basic 2-3 zone theme. *Scholastic coach (New York) 54(5), Dec 1984, 24-26;58-59.*
LEVEL: B LANG: Eng SIRC ARTICLE NO: 103055

STRATEGY - OFFENSIVE

Adams, S. Stack zone offense with a rover. *Athletic journal (Evanston, Ill.) 65(2), Sept 1984, 50-51.*
LEVEL: B LANG: Eng SIRC ARTICLE NO: 099400

Affleck, J. Beating full-court pressure defense. *Athletic journal (Evanston, Ill.) 65(2), Sept 1984, 20;40.*
LEVEL: B LANG Eng SIRC ARTICLE NO: 099401

Allocco, J. The triple stack offense. *Basketball clinic (Princeton, N.J.) 16(8), Apr 1984, 9-12.*
LEVEL: B LANG: Eng SIRC ARTICLE NO: 094850

Begly, G. Fast break basics. (Refs: 2)*Journal of physical education, recreation and dance (Reston, Va.) 55(8), Oct 1984, 22-23.*
LEVEL: B LANG: Eng SIRC ARTICLE NO: 101074

Bender, S. Smile when you see a zone. *Athletic journal (Evanston, Ill.) 65(5), Dec 1984, 40-41.*
LEVEL: B LANG: Eng SIRC ARTICLE NO: 104560

Bentley, D. An inside game for high school basketball. *Women's coaching clinic (Princeton, N.J.) 7(9), May 1984, 1-4.*
LEVEL: B LANG: Eng SIRC ARTICLE NO: 094854

Bonham, A.R. Paye, B. Secrets of winning fast break basketball. West Nyack, N.Y.: Parker Pub. Co., c1984. 211 p.
NOTES: Includes index.
LEVEL: B LANG: Eng ISBN: 0137987455 LC CARD: 84-006997 GV889 18674

Brace, T. Attacking zones with the passing game. *Coaching clinic (Princeton, N.J.) 23(4), Dec 1984, 4-6.*
LEVEL: B LANG: E SIRC ARTICLE NO: 103021

Braun, B. Side out-of-bounds: an offensive weapon. An effective side out-of-bounds series should be a part of every team's offense. *Athletic journal 64(7), Feb 1984, 32-33.*
LEVEL: B LANG: Eng SIRC ARTICLE NO: 091929

Cameron, D.J. Score from the sideline: the Owens Tech basketball team believes in pressuring the defense in as many situations as possible throughout the game. *Scholastic coach (New York) 54(5), Dec 1984, 44-45.*
LEVEL: B LANG: Eng SIRC ARTICLE NO: 103024

Clodfelter, R. The fast offense vs. the full court press. *Basketball clinic (Princeton, N.J.) 16(7), Mar 1984, 8.*
LEVEL: LANG: Eng SIRC ARTICLE NO: 096510

Corbett, J. A simple and effective offense. *Basketball clinic (Princeton, N.J.) 16(7), Mar 1984, 6-8.*
LEVEL: B LANG: Eng SIRC ARTICLE NO: 096511

Cox, T. Made free throw into pressure offense. Use your imagination to create your own 'free throw frolics' that take advantage of every situation and increase your chances for success. *Athletic journal (Evanston, Ill.) 65(1), Aug 1984, 44-48.*
LEVEL: B LANG: Eng SIRC ARTICLE NO: 096512

Cox, T. Stack & rover inbound series vs. a zone. *Scholastic coach (New York) 54(4), Nov 1984, 22-24;68.*
LEVEL: B LANG: En SIRC ARTICLE NO: 103026

Darnall, D. Eureka. A versatile zone offense. *Athletic journal 64(7), Feb 1984, 16;25.*
LEVEL: B LANG: Eng SIRC ARTICLE NO 091932

Darnall, D. Eureka's fast break down the side. *Scholastic coach (New York) 54(3), Oct 1984, 24-26;84.*
LEVEL: B LANG: Eng SIRC ARTICLE NO: 101076

Edinger, D. A simple screening continuity of the passing game. *Scholastic coach (New York) 54(5), Dec 1984, 38-40;55.*
LEVEL: B LANG: Eng SIRC ARTICLE NO: 103030

Fowler, N. Tulane's high post offense. *Texas coach (Austin, Tex.) 28(3), Oct 1984, 36-41.*
LEVEL: B LANG: Eng SIRC ARTICLE NO: 173206

Garrard, P. Five player offense against player to player defense. *Women's coaching clinic 7(6), Feb 1984, 1-2.*
LEVEL: B LANG: Eng SIRC ARTICLE NO: 090489

Gess, R. Four to score offense. *Basketball clinic (Princeton, N.J.) 16(7), Mar 1984, 3-4.*
LEVEL: B LANG: Eng SIRC ARTICLE NO: 096516

Gonzalez, B.G. Double high post offence with baseline movement. (Refs: 9)*Coaching review 7, Jan/Feb 1984, 47-49.*
LEVEL: B LANG: Eng SIRC ARTICLE NO: 091938

Green, G. An all-purpose 1-3-1 offense. *Basketball clinic (Princeton, N.J.) 16(9), May 1984, 1-3.*
LEVEL: B LANG: Eng SIRC ARTICLE NO: 094864

Harkins, H.L. Basketball's stack offense. West Nyack, N.Y.: Parker Pub. Co., c1984. 180 p. : ill.
NOTES: Includes index.
LEVEL: B LANG: Eng ISBN: 0130694517 LC CARD: 84-003194 GV889 18163

Harless, R.V. Basketball's T.D. offense. *Basketball clinic 16(4/5), Dec 1983/Jan 1984, 6-7.*
LEVEL: B LANG: Eng SIRC ARTICLE NO: 091939

Hayes, D. Individual offense - outside moves. *Basketball clinic (Princeton, N.J.) 16(6), Feb 1984, 5-8.*
LEVEL: B LANG: En SIRC ARTICLE NO: 094868

Hoch, D. Attack the gaps: penetration of an even zone can provide an effective attack. *Athletic journal (Evanston, Ill.) 65(3), Oct 1984, 42-43;55.*
LEVEL: B LANG: Eng SIRC ARTICLE NO: 099414

Horyza, L. The pick-and-screen offense for winning basketball. West Nyack, N.Y.: Parker Pub. Co., c1984. 1v.
NOTES: Include index.
LEVEL: B LANG: Eng ISBN: 0136761313 LC CARD: 83-026346

Jones, D. McKeown, S. Sideline fast break. *Basketball clinic (Princeton, N.J.) 17(2), Oct 1984, 6-7.*
LEVEL: B LANG: Eng SIRC ARTICLE NO: 101088

Knight, B. WABC: offence *International basketball (Budapest, Hungary) 24, 1984, 43-47.*
LEVEL: B LANG: Eng SIRC ARTICLE NO 105682

Larson, M.A. Triple post offense vs. 2-1-2 (2-3) zone defense. *Basketball clinic (Princeton, N.J.) 16(9), May 1984, 4-6.*
LEVEL: B LANG: Eng SIRC ARTICLE NO: 094873

Lee, P. Kiss - the phoebus philosophy. *Women's coaching clinic 7(6), Feb 1984, 2-3.*
LEVEL: B LANG: Eng SIRC ARTICLE NO: 090498

Lewis, G.K. Teaching the full-court press. *Basketball clinic (Princeton, N.J.) 16(10), Jun 1984, 5-8.*
LEVEL: B LANG: Eng SIRC ARTICLE NO: 096520

Loftin, J. Offensive play... The 'X' offense. *Basketball clinic (Princeton, N.S.) 16(10), Jun 1984, 1-3.*
LEVEL: B LANG: E SIRC ARTICLE NO: 096522

Margaritis, J. The '2-3 high' offense: giving food passing, cutting and screening, it's highly effective against a tight, aggressive defense. *Athletic journal (Evanston, Ill.) 65(4), Nov 1984, 36-37.*
LEVEL: B LANG: Eng SIRC ARTICLE NO: 101092

Mathes, M. Organization is the key to your press offense. *Basketball clinic (Princeton, N.J.) 16(9), May 1984, 3-4.*
LEVEL: B LANG: Eng SIRC ARTICLE NO: 094875

McClary, T. Full court offenses. *Basketball clinic (Princeton, N.J.) 17(3), Nov 1984, 4-6.*
LEVEL: B LANG: Eng SIRC ARTICL NO: 103039

McKiernan, D. The spots offense vs. man to man defense. *Basketball clinic 16(4/5), Dec 1983/Jan 1984, 1-4.*
LEVEL: B LANG: Eng SIRC ARTICL NO: 091944

Meek, J. Screen away to beat the man-for-man. *Athletic journal (Evanston, Ill.) 65(3), Oct 1984, 40-41.*
LEVEL: B LANG: En SIRC ARTICLE NO: 099420

Miller, D. Offensive play... Concentrate on the outlet pass. *Basketball clinic (Princeton, N.J.) 16(7), Mar 1984, 1-3.*
LEVEL: B LANG: Eng SIRC ARTICLE NO: 096526

Neill, M. The full and half court zone press offense. *Women's coaching clinic (Princeton, N.J.) 8(1), Sept 1984, 4-7.*
LEVEL: B LANG: Eng SIRC ARTICLE NO: 099421

Nichols, G. Beating the half court pass. (half-court offence) *Texas coach (Austin, Tex.) 28(1), Aug 1984, 53-55.*
LEVEL: B LANG: Eng SIRC ARTICLE NO: 103042

Nitchman, N. Beating the zone and the full-court press: a review of '83 offenses. *Athletic journal (Evanston, Ill.) 65(2), Sept 1984, 28-31.*
LEVEL: B LANG: Eng SIRC ARTICLE NO: 099422

Nolan, M. A 2-3 offense that 'keeps it simple'. *Scholastic coach (New York) 54(3), Oct 1984, 32-35.*
LEVEL: B LANG: Eng SIRC ARTICLE NO: 101095

Olson, J.R. The use of similar offenses to attack zone and man to man pressure. *Basketball clinic (Princeton, N.J.) 17(2), Oct 1984, 1-5.*
LEVEL: B LANG: Eng SIRC ARTICLE NO: 101097

Pim, R. The 'swinging overload'. With multiple zones increasing, here's a continuity offense designed to find the high-percentage shot. *Athletic journal (Evanston, Ill.) 65(5), Dec 1984, 12-13;38.*
LEVEL: B LANG: Eng SIRC ARTICLE NO: 104579

Pollock, F. Getting into a half-court offense from the transition game. *Basketball clinic (Princeton, N.J.) 17(1), Sept 1984, 5-7.*
LEVEL: B LANG: Eng SIRC ARTICLE NO: 101099

Potter, G. Designing assessing, and employing set pattern offenses effectively. *Basketball clinic*

BASKETBALL (continued)

(Princeton, N.J.) 17(1), Sept 1984, 1-3.
LEVEL: B LANG: Eng SIRC ARTICLE NO: 101100

Reilly, T. The expanded pick & roll. *Scholastic coach (New York)* 54(4), Nov 1984, 26-28.
LEVEL: B LANG: Eng SIRC ARTICLE NO: 103047

Reisman, L. Southeastern's reverse-lob half-court press offense. *Scholastic coach (New York)* 54(3), Oct 1984, 72-74.
LEVEL: B LANG: Eng SIRC ARTICLE NO: 101101

Renkens, J.H. Out of bounds - sideline. *Basketball clinic (Princeton, N.J.)* 17(4), Dec 1984, 8.
LEVEL: B LANG: Eng SIRC ARTICLE NO: 104580

Ropes, G. End of game plays. *Basketball clinic (Princeton, N.J.)* 17(1), Sept 1984, 10-12.
LEVEL: B LANG: Eng SIRC ARTICLE NO: 101102

Russell, B. Winning with a positive and simplified approach. *Women's coaching clinic* 7(7), Mar 1984, 3-5.
LEVEL: B LANG: Eng SIRC ARTICLE NO: 091948

Shea, T. The Viking fast break. *Basketball clinic (Princeton, N.J.)* 16(10), Jun 1984, 3-5.
LEVEL: B LANG: Eng SIRC ARTICL NO: 096531

Shelton, P. Developing an offensive system in a small school. *Texas coach (Austin, Tex.)* 28(1), Aug 1984, 42-44.
LEVEL: B LANG: Eng SIRC ARTICLE NO: 103050

Singleton, T.F. A planned attack against the full court man to man press. *Basketball clinic (Princeton, N.J.)* 17(3), Nov 1984, 7-14.
LEVEL: B LANG: Eng SIRC ARTICLE NO: 103051

Singleton, T.F. 1-3-1 screening offense vs. the 2-3 zone. *Basketball clinic (Princeton, N.J.)* 17(4), Dec 1984, 1-5.
LEVEL B LANG: Eng SIRC ARTICLE NO: 104584

Singleton, T.F. The 2-2-1 baseline offense vs. odd-front zones. *Basketball clinic (Princeton, N.J.)* 17(4), Dec 1984, 5-7.
LEVEL: B LANG: Eng SIRC ARTICLE NO: 104585

Smith, J. University of South Alabama motion offense. *Basketball clinic* 16(4/5), Dec 1983/Jan 1984, 8-12.
LEVEL: B LANG: Eng SIRC ARTICLE NO: 091950

Snyder, J. The 'Headhunter II'. It's an update of a successful offense which simply requires setting a good pick to free the cutter. *Athletic journal (Evanston, Ill.)* 65(5), Dec 1984, 14-15;39.
LEVEL: B LANG: Eng SIRC ARTICLE NO: 104586

Southworth, M. 'Shadow & slide' breaking full court traps. *Basketball clinic* 16(4/5), Dec 1983/Jan 1984, 4-6.
LEVEL: B LANG: Eng SIRC ARTICLE NO: 091951

Southworth, M. Big guard oriented team offense. *Scholastic coach (New York)* 54(2), Sept 1984, 32-34;74.
LEVEL: B LANG: En SIRC ARTICLE NO: 099428

Southworth, M. Multiple fastbreak system. *Athletic journal (Evanston, Ill.)* 65(4), Nov 1984, 38-39.
LEVEL: B LANG: Eng SIRC ARTICLE NO: 101106

Swanson, D. Free throw fastbreak. *Basketball clinic (Princeton, N.J.)* 17(1), Sept 1984, 3-5.
LEVEL: B LANG: Eng SIRC ARTICLE NO: 101108

Taylor, D. 10 basic principles in beating a 'help' type man-to-man. (man-to-man offence) *Scholastic coach (New York)* 54(5), Dec 1984, 20-23.
LEVEL: B LANG: Eng SIRC ARTICLE NO: 103052

Traywick, J. Fastbreak: the ultimate weapon. *Athletic journal (Evanston, Ill.)* 65(1), Aug 1984, 34;53-55.
LEVEL: B LANG: Eng SIRC ARTICLE NO: 096533

Van Harless, R. Basketball's 1-4 press offense. *Basketball clinic (Princeton, N.J.)* 16(6), Feb 1984, 1-2.
LEVEL: B LANG: Eng SIRC ARTICLE NO: 094891

Vore, E.D. Basic offense at Forgan High School. *Basketball clinic (Princeton, N.J.)* 16(6), Feb 1984, 2-3.
LEVEL: B LANG: Eng SIRC ARTICLE NO: 094892

Walker, F. 3-point offense: try the 'cherry picker' for a three-point play. *Athletic journal (Evanston, Ill.)* 65(3), Oct 1984, 16;53.
LEVEL: B LANG: Eng SIRC ARTICLE NO: 099430

Wallis, J. A five-man movement offense. *Basketball clinic (Princeton, N.J.)* 16(8), Apr 1984, 1-5.
LEVEL: B LANG: Eng SIR ARTICLE NO: 094894

Wellenreiter, D. The passing game. *Scholastic coach (New York)* 54(3), Oct 1984, 41-42.
LEVEL: B LANG: Eng SIRC ARTICLE NO 101110

TEACHING

Chappell, R. The first in a series on the teaching of basketball: basketball - setting the scene. (Refs: 5)*British journal of physical education (London)* 15(1), Jan/Feb 1984, 10-11.
LEVEL: B LANG: Eng SIRC ARTICLE NO: 099409

TECHNIQUES AND SKILLS

Maugh, T.H. In search of the perfect jump shot. *In, Schrier, E.W. and Allman, W.F. (eds.), Newton at the bat: the science i sports, New York, Scribner, c1984, p. 25-28.*
LEVEL: B LANG: Eng RC1235 18609

Thomas, H. Feeding the ball for the double play. *Scholastic coach* 53(7), Feb 1984, 26-30;59.
LEVEL: B LANG: Eng SIRC ARTICLE NO: 093293

TECHNIQUES AND SKILLS - REBOUNDING

May, J.A. Offensive rebounding. *Basketball clinic (Princeton, N.J.)* 16(8), Apr 1984, 5-9.
LEVEL: B LANG: Eng SIRC ARTICLE NO: 094876

TECHNIQUES AND SKILLS - SHOOTING

Hurley, J. The science of shot discipline. *Women's varsity sports (Kalispell, Mont.)* 5(3), Jan/Feb 1984, 16.
LEVEL: B LANG: Eng SIRC ARTICLE NO: 101085

Ladner, J.L. Psychological and sociological factors that may affect shooting. *Basketball clinic (Princeton, N.J.)* 17(4), De 1984, 11-16.
LEVEL: I LANG: Eng SIRC ARTICLE NO: 104574

Meschery, T. Free throw shooting. No possibility, however slight, should be overlooked when trying to improve players' free throw shooting acccuracy. *Athletic journal (Evanston, Ill.)* 64(10), May 1984, 14;67-69.
LEVEL: B LANG: Eng SIRC ARTICLE NO: 094877

TESTING AND EVALUATION

Bosc, G. Brenot, J. Contribution a la recherche et a l'evaluation des talents en basketball. *Basketball (Paris)* 492, fevr/mars/avr 1984, 38-52.
LEVEL: B LANG: Fr SIRC ARTICLE NO: 097936

Brooks, C. A basketball player's real worth. *Basketball clinic (Princeton, N.J.)* 16(7), Mar 1984, 15-16.
LEVEL: B LANG: E SIRC ARTICLE NO: 096509

Gallois, A. Un exemple d'evaluation. *EPS: Education physique et sport (Paris, France)* 186, mars/avr 1984, 33-38.
NOTES: A suivre.
LEVEL: B LANG: Fr SIRC ARTICLE NO: 094863

Hopkins, D.R. Shick, J. Plack, J.J. Basketball for boys and girls: skills test manual. Reston, Va.: American Alliance for Health, Physical Education, Recreation and Dance, c1984. vii, 39 p. : ill.
LEVEL: B LANG: Eng ISBN: 0-88314-265-1 GV885.35 18106

Johns, E.J. The basketball season in retrospect: a foundation for the future. *Women's coaching clinic* 7(7), Mar 1984, 1-3.
LEVEL: B LANG: Eng SIRC ARTICLE NO: 091941

Kirschenbaum, D.S. Wittrock, D.A. Smith, R.J. Monson, W. Criticism inoculation training: concept in search of strategy. (Refs: 39)*Sport psychology (Champaign, Ill.)* 6(1), 1984, 77-93.
ABST: This experiment evaluated the efficacy of one potential (criticism inoculation training) strategy, positive self-monitoring (systematically oobserving and recording instances of success). A laboratory paradigm was used in which 60 male college students attempted to learn the underhand free throw basketball technique from one of four undergraduate pseudocoaches. Subjects were randomly assigned to four groups determined by a 2 (negative vs. no feedback) by 2 (positive vs. no self-monitoring) factorial design. Negative feedback was expected to debilitate, while positive self-monitoring was expected to facilitate performance, substained self-observation of videotapes of performance, and subjective evaluations of the 'coach' and the technique. Negative feedback clearly produced extensive adverse effects, but surprisingly, positive self-monitoring also decreased performance.
LEVEL: A LANG: Eng SIRC ARTICLE NO: 108486

Sapin, J. Une fiche d'observation facile a utiliser. *Pivot (France)* 22, 1984, 11-14.
LEVEL: B LANG: Fr

TRAINING AND CONDITIONING

Balestro, W. Preparation physique des centres de formation: developpement de l'endurance. *Basketball (Paris)* 491, dec 1983/janv 1984, 50-52.
LEVEL: B LANG: Fr SIRC ARTICLE NO: 099404

Evans, F. How to win on the road. *Scholastic coach (New York)* 54(3), Oct 1984, 36;38;75.
LEVEL: B LANG: Eng SIRC ARTICLE NO: 101079

Foley, J. Tips for coaches: youth basketball effective conditioning. *Spotlight on youth sports (East Lansing, Mich.)* 7(4), Winter 1984, 4.
LEVEL: B LANG: Eng SIRC ARTICLE NO: 108878

Goebel, R. Eleven-week jump training for women's basketball. *National Strength & Conditioning Association journal (Lincoln, Neb.)* 6(4), Aug/Sept

1984, 59-61.
LEVEL: B LANG: Eng SIRC ARTICLE NO: 099413

Lum, J.R. Organizing a sure-fire conditioning program for high school basketball. *Basketball clinic (Princeton, N.J.) 17(3) Nov 1984, 14-16.*
LEVEL: B LANG: Eng SIRC ARTICLE NO: 103036

Norris, J. Chenango forks' basketball self-improvement plan. *Basketball clinic (Princeton, N.J.) 17(1), Sept 1984, 12-15.*
LEVEL: B LANG: Eng SIRC ARTICLE NO: 101096

TRAINING AND CONDITIONING - CIRCUIT TRAINING

Chitwood, A.A. Basketball circuit drill. *Texas coach (Austin, Tex.) 28(3), Oct 1984, 48-49.*
LEVEL: B LANG: Eng SIRC ARTICLE NO: 173210

Mrozinski, M. Circuit training for basketball. *Basketball clinic (Princeton, N.J.) 16(9), May 1984, 6-9.*
ABST: This article details a circuit training program for high school basketball players which incorporates fundamental skills, quickness and agility. The program offers a wide variety of stations with the players spending only 30 seconds at each station. Over 40 possible stations are listed but a training session should only use 15 to 25 stations covering the major elements of the game.
LEVEL: B LANG: Eng SIRC ARTICLE NO: 094879

Pappas, A. Pre-practice routines: a well organized program, using six stations over 12 minutes, is bound to improve each participant's offensive skills. *Athletic journal (Evanston, Ill.) 65(4), Nov 1984, 22;45.*
LEVEL: B LANG: Eng SIRC ARTICLE NO: 101098

TRAINING AND CONDITIONING - DRILLS

Anderson, C. Using the eleven man fast break drill with the controlled break. *JUCO review (Hutchinson, Kans.) 35(5), Jan 1984, 4.*
LEVEL: B LANG: Eng SIRC ARTICLE NO: 108651

Carey, J. Weight vest training at Garden City Community College. *Juco review (Hutchison, Kan.) 36(4), Dec 1984, 4;6.*
LEVEL: B LANG: Eng SIRC ARTICLE NO: 103025

Chappell, B. Introducing basketball. (Refs: 3)*British journal of physical education (London) 15(1), Mar/Apr 1984, 60-61.*
LEVEL: B LANG: Eng SIRC ARTICLE NO: 099408

Cleveland, K. Practice organization for the entire year. *Texas coach (Austin, Tex.) 28(4), Nov 1984, 30-37.*
LEVEL: B LANG Eng SIRC ARTICLE NO: 173436

Coleman, K. Winning in the final seconds. *Athletic journal (Evanston, Ill.) 65(4), Nov 1984, 8-9;32.*
LEVEL: B LANG: Eng SIRC ARTICLE NO: 101075

Diehl, T. Shoot to kill. *Women's varsity sports (Kalispell, Mont.) 5(3), Jan/Feb 1984, 6-7.*
LEVEL: B LANG: Eng SIRC ARTICLE NO: 101078

Edmonston, D. Lehane, J. Progressive basketball drills: a coach's guide. Boston ; Toronto: Allyn and Bacon, c1984. vii, 256 p. : ill.
LEVEL: I LANG: Eng ISBN: 0205080642 LC CARD: 83-019666 GV885.35 17751

English, J. Fast break. *Texas coach (Austin, Tex.) 28(4), Nov 1984, 48-50.*
LEVEL: B LANG: Eng SIRC ARTICLE NO: 173444

Hill, K. Fundamentals can be fun. *Athletic journal (Evanston, Ill.) 65(1), Aug 1984, 38.*
LEVEL: B LANG: Eng SIRC ARTICLE NO: 096517

Hoch, D. Face guarding: use it in your press. These drills will be helpful in incorporating face guarding into your press. *Athletic journal (Evanston, Ill.) 64(10), May 1984, 44-45.*
LEVEL: B LANG: Eng SIRC ARTICLE NO: 094869

Hughes, W. Phenis, J. On-the-ball defense: in the long run good defense prevails, and every team needs a scrappy 'stopper.' *Athletics journal (Evanston, Ill.) 65(4), Nov 1984, 30;47.*
LEVEL: B LANG: Eng SIRC ARTICLE NO: 101084

Ladner, J.L. Fundamentals of shooting free-throws. *Basketball clinic (Princeton, N.J.) 16(9), May 1984, 14-16.*
LEVEL: B LANG: Eng SIRC ARTICLE NO: 094872

Lail, S. Practice organization. *Basketball clinic (Princeton, N.J.) 17(2), Oct 1984, 13-16.*
LEVEL: B LANG: Eng SIRC ARTICLE NO: 101091

Lawson, B. Basketball at John Tyler High School. *Texas coach (Austin, Tex.) 28(4), Nov 1984, 42-44.*
LEVEL: B LANG: Eng SIRC ARTICLE NO: 173440

McCauley, M. Building a championship team. *Women's coaching clinic (Princeton, N.J.) 8(3), Nov 1984, 1-4.*
LEVEL: B LANG: Eng SIRC ARTICLE NO: 103038

McClary, T. Defensive rebounding drills. *Basketball clinic (Princeton, N.J.) 17(2), Oct 1984, 8-9.*
LEVEL: B LANG: Eng SIR ARTICLE NO: 101094

Mrazek, C. Les geants du basket. *Macolin (Suisse) 9, sept 1984, 7-9.*
LEVEL: B LANG: Fr SIRC ARTICLE NO: 103040

Randow, G. Pre-season conditioning program. *Basketball clinic 16(4/5), Dec 1983/Jan 1984, 14-16.*
LEVEL: B LANG: Eng SIRC ARTICLE NO: 091947

Renkens, J.H. Woodstock drill game. *Basketball clinic (Princeton, N.J.) 16(6), Feb 1984, 9-11.*
LEVEL: B LANG: Eng SIRC ARTICLE NO: 094882

Ribble, L. Off-season work-out program. *Athletic journal 64(8), Mar 1984, 16;25-26.*
LEVEL: B LANG: Eng SIRC ARTICLE NO: 093307

Rusch, K. Teaching the controlled fast break. *Women's coaching clinic 7(8), Apr 1984, 9-12.*
LEVEL: B LANG: Eng SIRC ARTICLE NO: 093308

Simmons, K. Herrington, J. Selecting drills for intensity. *Women's coaching clinic (Princeton, N.J.) 7(9), May 1984, 4-7.*
LEVEL: B LANG: Eng SIRC ARTICLE NO: 094886

Steenhoek, C.F. Small-school basketball. *Women's coaching clinic 7(8), Apr 1984, 3-5.*
LEVEL: B LANG: Eng SIRC ARTICLE NO: 093311

Williams, L.C. Practice organization. *JUCO review (Hutchinson, Kans.) 35(7), Mar 1984, 5-6.*
LEVEL: B LANG: Eng SIRC ARTICLE NO: 108655

Zigler, T. Volunteer one-on one drills. *Scholastic coach 53(7), Feb 1984, 7C-72.*
LEVEL: B LANG: Eng SIRC ARTICLE NO: 0933

TRAINING AND CONDITIONING - TRAINING CAMPS

McCallum, J. The world according to Garf...and others. *Sports illustrated (Chicago, Ill.) 61(10), 27 Aug 1984, 70-74;76-77;80-82;84.*
LEVEL: B LANG: Eng SIRC ARTICLE NO: 097951

TRAINING AND CONDITIONING - WARM-UPS, WARM-DOWNS, LEAD-UP GAMES

Hammer, R.L. The effects of selected warm-up procedures on internal core temperature. Eugene, Ore.: Microform Publication, University of Oregon, 1984. 1 microfiche : negative, ill. ; 11 x 15 cm.
NOTES: Thesis (M.S.) - Brigham Young University, 1982; (ix, 55 leaves); includes bibliography.
LEVEL: A LANG: Eng UO84 404

TRAINING AND CONDITIONING - WEIGHT AND STRENGTH TRAINING

Dunn, W.H. Soudek, E.H. Gieck, J. Strength training and conditioning for basketball: featuring Ralph Sampson's training program. Chicago: Contemporary, c1984. 106 p. : ill.
NOTES: Includes index.
LEVEL: B LANG: Eng ISBN: 0-8092-5375-5 LC CARD: 84-019903 GV885.35 20440

Lynch, D.F. Conditioning... Weight training. *Basketball clinic (Princeton, N.J.) 16(7), Mar 1984, 12-13.*
LEVEL: B LANG: E SIRC ARTICLE NO: 096523

McCormick, M. Developing the big center. *Athletic journal (Evanston, Ill.) 65(3), Oct 1984, 8;51-52.*
LEVEL: B LANG: Eng SIRC ARTICLE NO: 099419

O'Bryant, H.S. Programs for basketball, wrestling, football. (Refs: 5)*National Strength & Conditioning Association journal 5(6), Jan 1984, 41;66-67.*
ABST: Weight training is an important training method for pre-season strength-power development in athletes. The role of circuit and non-circuit weight training programs are discussed for basketball, wrestling and football. Ten week programs are outlined with specific phases of development being used to attain specific physical goals. This article is extremely useful in planning the progression of a pre-season circuit training program.
LEVEL: B LANG: Eng SIRC ARTICLE NO: 090414

VARIATIONS

Herschlag, J. Halfcourt basketball: the official book of three-on-three basketball. Englewood Cliffs, N.J.: Prentice-Hall, c1984. xi, 131 p. : ill. (A Reward book: pbk.)
NOTES: Includes index.
LEVEL: B LANG: Eng ISBN: 0133720799 LC CARD: 83-027238 GV887 17503

Le baby-basket: entre le jeu et le sport. *Sante et sport (Paris) 224, dec 1984, 20-21.*
LEVEL: B LANG: Fr SIRC ARTICLE NO: 173512

WOMEN

Combs, D.G. Interesting facts about scheduling women's basketball. *Athletic administration (Cleveland, Oh.) 19(6), Dec 1984 17-19.*
LEVEL: B LANG: Eng SIRC ARTICLE NO: 105670

BASKETBALL (continued)

Delachet, J. Horvath, S. Preparation de la force specifique de l'equipe de basket feminine de l'INSEP pour les Championnats d'Europe de 1983.
NOTES: Dans, Renforcement musculaire, Paris, Institut national du sport et de l'education physique, c1984, p. 44-54.
LEVEL: I LANG: Fr GV711.5 18233

Schmidt, L. Basketball odyssey: playing the game in Europe. *Women's sports (Palo Alto, Calif.) 6(1), Jan 1984, 44-45.*
LEVEL: B LANG: Eng SIRC ARTICLE NO: 097955

Smith, R.A. The rise of basketball for women in colleges. (Refs: 66)
NOTES: In, Riess, S.A. (ed.), The American sporting experience: a historical anthology of sport in America, New York, Leisure Press, c1984, p. 239-254. Originally published in, Canadian journal of history of sport and physical education 1, December 1970, p. 18-36.
LEVEL: A LANG: Eng GV583 17631

Strike, M.S. Role models and females in athletics: selected case studies. Eugene, Ore.: Microform Publications, University o Oregon, 1984. 2 microfiches : negative ; 11 x 15 cm.
NOTES: Thesis (M.S.) - University of Oregon, 1983; (vii, 150 leaves); vita; includes bibliography.
LEVEL: A LANG: Eng UO84 57-58

Williams, S.B. Official 1984 media guide. Columbus, Ohio: Women's American Basketball Association, c1984. 26 p. : ill.
CORP Women's American Basketball Association.
LEVEL: B LANG: Eng GV886 18284

BELLY DANCING

DeBarra, M. Bellydancing: give it a fair shake. *Fit (Mountain View, Calif.) 3(11), Apr 1984, 26-29;84.*
LEVEL: B LANG: Eng SIRC ARTICLE NO: 099516

BIATHLON

BIOGRAPHY AND AUTOBIOGRAPHY

Hobson, A. Yves Rousseau, tremplin vers l'avenir. Yves Rousseau, breaking trail. *Champion 8(1), Feb 1984, 40-41.*
LEVEL: B LANG: Eng Fr SIRC ARTICLE NO: 090899

BICYCLE TOURING

Dickerson, S. Touring times two. *Bike report (Missoula, Mont.) 8(9), Jun/Jul 1984, 21-23.*
LEVEL: B LANG: Eng SIRC ARTICLE NO: 099465

Ferguson, G. Cleeland, A. James, B. Freewheeling: bicycling the open road. Seattle, Wash.: Mountaineers, c1984. 1v.
NOTES: Includes index.
LEVEL: I LANG: Eng ISBN: 0898860474 LC CARD: 84-016643

Kranzley, G. Ten tips for mountain touring. *Bicycling (Emmaus, Pa.) 25(4), May 1984, 84;94;100-101.*
LEVEL: B LANG: Eng SIRC ARTICLE NO: 094947

Leaden, B.W. Bicycle camping in Canada. Winnipeg, Man.: Queenston House Publishing Co., c1984. 170 p. : ill.
NOTES: Bibliography: p. 168-170.
LEVEL: B LANG: Eng ISBN: 0-919866-95-6 LC CARD: C84-091332-X GV1046.C3 20189

Levy, M. Two-wheeled travels. *Women's sports (Palo Alto, Calif.) 6(9), Sept 1984, 18-22;24-26;28-29.*
LEVEL: B LANG: Eng SIRC ARTICLE NO: 173591

Nesbitt, H. Preparing for a tour. *Freewheeling (Sydney, Aust.) 27, Sept 1984, 12-15.*
LEVEL: B LANG: Eng SIRC ARTICLE NO: 109353

Woodward, B. Breaking away: bikepacking is really just backpacking in the fast lane. So, if you want to cover more than the usual ground between campsites, maybe you should get into high gear. *Backpacker (New York) 12(4), Jul 1984, 44-50;52;54-55;58.*
LEVEL: I LANG: Eng SIRC ARTICLE NO: 102164

ADMINISTRATION

Nash, D. Group touring...how to choose the best one for you. *Bicycling 25(3), Apr 1984, 86-87.*
LEVEL: B LANG: Eng SIRC ARTICLE NO: 093367

BIOGRAPHY AND AUTOBIOGRAPHY

D'Ambrosio, D. High-wheeling into history: the story of the first trans America journey by bicycle. *Freewheeling (Sydney, Aust.) 27, Sept 1984, 50-53.*
LEVEL: B LANG: Eng SIRC ARTICLE NO: 109352

CHILDREN

King, T. King, L. Taking the kids along: with a thoughtful choice of equipment, your children can tour with you at all ages. *Bicycle USA (Baltimore, Md.) 20(8), Aug 1984, 21-22.*
LEVEL: B LANG: Eng SIRC ARTICLE NO: 099479

COUNTRIES AND REGIONS

Butwin, D. Summertime in Vermont. *Physician and sportsmedicine 12(3), Mar 1984, 155;158;160.*
LEVEL: B LANG: Eng SIRC ARTICLE NO: 091985

Jackson, K. Keith's incredible journey. Winston-Salem, N.C.: Mr. Binkley's Printery, 1984. xv, 152 p. 1 leaf of plates ; ill., maps ; 24 cm.
LEVEL: B LANG: Eng LC CARD: 84-231157

Kirkendall, T. Spring, V. Bicycling the Pacific Coast. Seattle: Mountaineers, c1984. 1 v.
LEVEL: B LANG: Eng ISBN: 08988608 LC CARD: 84-006787

McRae, M. The essential weekender: fast and easy two-day breakaways. *Outside (Chicago, Ill.) 9(5), Jun 1984, 48-49.*
LEVEL B LANG: Eng SIRC ARTICLE NO: 101182

Stone, H. Short bike rides in Rhode Island. 2nd ed. Chester, Conn.: Globe Pequot Press, c1984. 244 p. : ill.
NOTES: Bibliography: p. 24-25.
LEVEL: B LANG: Eng ISBN: 0871069482 LC CARD: 84-182552

Woods, E. Woods, B. Bicycling the backroads of Northwest Washington. 2nd ed. Seattle, Wash.: Mountaineers, 1984. 1v.
NOTES: Includes indexes.

LEVEL: B LANG: Eng ISBN: 0898860806 LC CARD: 84-001262

DIRECTORIES

Adams, D. Speicher, D. Twenty-five bicycle tours in Eastern Pennsylvania: day trips and overnights from Philadelphia to the Highlands. Woodstock, Vt.: Backcountry Pub., 1984. 1v.
LEVEL: B LANG: Eng ISBN: 0942440196 LC CARD: 84-006288

Freidin, J.S. 25 bicycle tours in Vermont. Rev. & expanded ed. Woodstock, Vt.: Backcountry Publications, c1984. 1v.
NOTES: Rev. ed. of: 20 bicycle tours in Vermont, c1979.
LEVEL: B LANG: Eng ISBN: 0942440188 LC CARD: 84-070168

Helgason, G. Dodd, J. Bicycle Alberta - 60 tours: mountains, cities, country. Edmonton: Lone Pine Publishing, c1984. 240 p. ill.
NOTES: Includes index.
LEVEL: B LANG: Eng ISBN: 0-919433-18-9 LC CARD: C84-91282-X GV1046.C3 17799

Jones, P.N. Bicycling the backroads of Northwest Oregon. Seattle, Wash.: Mountaineers, c1984. 1v.
NOTES: Includes bibliographical references and index.
LEVEL: B LANG: Eng ISBN: 0898860768 LC CARD: 84-006786

Lieb, T. Bikepacking American style. *Backpacker (New York) 12(4), Jul 1984, 62-69.*
LEVEL: B LANG: Eng SIRC ARTICLE NO: 102165

Priest, S. Klint, K. Bicycling Vancouver Island and the Gulf Islands. Vancouver: Douglas & McIntyre, c1984. 256 p. : ill.
NOTES: Bibliography: p. 255.
LEVEL: B LANG: Eng ISBN: 0-88894-420-9 LC CARD: C84-91056-8 GV1046.C3 17594

The cyclists' yellow pages. 5th ed. Missoula, Mont.: Bikecentennial, c1984. 86 p.
CORP: Bicycle Travel Association.
LEVEL: B LANG: Eng GV1044 12137

EQUIPMENT

Berto, F. Rear derailleurs for touring. *Bicycling (Emmaus, Pa.) 25(4), May 1984, 126-128;131-133;136-141.*
NOTES: Last article in a series of three.
LEVEL: B LANG: Eng SIRC ARTICLE NO: 094932

Berto, F. All about loaded touring bikes. Three Prairie schooners for your next world tour. *Bicycling (Emmaus, Pa.) 25(6) Jul 1984, 128-130;132;134-135;136-144.*
LEVEL: B LANG: Eng SIRC ARTICLE NO: 096566

Bicycle road test. *Freewheeling (Sydney, Aust.) 28, Summer 1984/1985, 62-67.*
LEVEL: B LANG: Eng SIRC ARTICLE NO: 173116

Burlace, M. A tent for touring. Equipment review. The Flashlight tent by Sierra Designs. *Freewheeling (Haymarket, N.S.W.) 25, May/Jun 1984, 53-54.*
LEVEL: B LANG: Eng SIRC ARTICLE NO: 101164

Costantino, T. Four light touring bikes. Pack up and go - for less than $400. *Bicycling (Emmaus, Pa.) 25(5), Jun 1984, 124-132;134-138.*
LEVEL: B LANG: Eng SIRC ARTICLE NO: 096572

Lieb, T. New shelter: how to feel at home when you roam. *Bicycling 25(2), Mar 1984, 195-197;199.* LEVEL: B LANG: Eng SIRC ARTICLE NO: 092012

EQUIPMENT - RETAILING

Quinn, R. Touring: your biggest potential market? *Bicycle business journal (Fort Worth, Tex.) 38(6), Jun 1984, 14;16.* LEVEL: B LANG: Eng SIRC ARTICLE NO: 101185

HISTORY

Graves, C. Journey into the unknown: the story of how Thomas Stevens made the first round-the-world bicycle tour. *Bicycle U.S.A. (Baltimore, Md.) 20(3), Mar 1984, 4-7.* LEVEL: B LANG: Eng SIRC ARTICLE NO: 098013

INJURIES AND ACCIDENTS

Goossens, T. Recommandations medicales en matiere de cyclisme. *Tempo medical (Paris) 155, 1984, 63-70.* LEVEL: I LANG: Fr

Rothschild, A. Avoiding injury: on your next long tour, don't forget to take along your base mileage. (Refs: 7)*Bike report (Missoula, Mont.) 8(10), Aug/Sept 1984, 12-14.* LEVEL: B LANG: Eng SIRC ARTICLE NO: 103115

MEDICINE

Burnand, M. Plaidoyer en faveur du sport-sante: une histoire de selle(s) et de boyaux. *Macolin (Macolin, Suisse) 41(12), de 1984, 16-17.* LEVEL: B LANG: Fr SIRC ARTICLE NO: 108767

BICYCLING

Di Cyan, A. Piggyback bicycle: or how to carry a bike on your bike. *Bicycling (Emmaus, Pa.) 25(5), Jun 1984, 200-201.* LEVEL: B LANG: Eng SIRC ARTICLE NO: 096579

COUNTRIES AND REGIONS

Watkins, S. The new opportunities for cycling. (Refs: 11)*ILAM: Institute of Leisure & Amenity Management (London, Eng.) 2(9), Sept 1984, 17-19.* LEVEL: I LANG: Eng SIRC ARTICLE NO: 101191

White, R. The classic country tour: a week in Ireland-and beyond. *Outside (Chicago, Ill.) 9(5), Jun 1984, 50-52.* LEVEL: B LANG: Eng SIRC ARTICLE NO: 101192

EQUIPMENT

Are you missing a sales bet? The total reliability market. *American bicyclist and motorcyclist (New York) 105(9), Sept 1984, 71.* LEVEL: B LANG: Eng SIRC ARTICLE NO: 103080

Brand, Sommerville, P. Bicycle pannier bags: tried and true and a look at what's new. *Freewheeling (Haymarket, N.S.W.) 23, Jan/Feb 1984, 42-48.* LEVEL: B LANG: Eng SIRC ARTICLE NO: 099458

Brown, S. Allen, J.S. Five new folding bicycles. *Bicycling (Emmaus, Pa.) 25(4), May 1984,103-107;111;113-114;118;121-123;125.* LEVEL: B LANG: Eng SIRC ARTICLE NO: 094936

Ezell, W.K. Counterpoint tandem: you can harmonize and switch off on this jive new machine. *Bicycle U.S.A. (Baltimore, Md.) 20(3), Mar 1984, 11;34.* LEVEL: B LANG: Eng SIRC ARTICLE NO: 098008

Farren, C. Puck Free Spirit. Bicycle road test. *Freewheeling (Haymarket, N.S.W.) 25, May/Jun 1984, 35-36.* LEVEL: B LANG: Eng SIRC ARTICLE NO: 101167

Farren, P. How to choose a tandem. *Freewheeling (Haymarket, N.S.W.) 23, Jan/Feb 1984, 51.* LEVEL: B LANG: Eng SIRC ARTICLE NO: 099468

Graecross constellation: at last, positive gear shifting. *Freewheeling (Haymarket, N.S.W.) 23, Jan/Feb 1984, 55-56..* LEVEL: LANG: Eng SIRC ARTICLE NO: 099472

Immler, R. Child stoker conversions: another approach to tandeming. *Bicycling 25(3), Apr 1984, 136;142;144.* LEVEL: B LANG Eng SIRC ARTICLE NO: 093357

Krausz, J. The 3-speed makeover: the once-favored clubman is long out of production. Here's how to have the next best thing. *Bicycle USA (Baltimore, Md.) 20(5), May 1984, 8-9.* LEVEL: B LANG: Eng SIRC ARTICLE NO: 099480

Mitchell Lightweight: an unusual blend. *Freewheeling (Haymarket, N.S.W.) 24, Mar/Apr 1984, 37-38.* LEVEL: B LANG: Eng SIRC ARTICLE NO: 099489

Ricardo Commuter: click go the gears on this easy to ride six-speed. Bicyle road test. *Freewheeling (Haymarket, N.S.W.) 25, May/Jun 1984, 39-40.* LEVEL: B LANG: Eng SIRC ARTICLE NO: 101188

Rosman, A. Allen, J.S. Better lighting at night: beefed-up Berec. *Bicycling (Emmaus, Pa.) 25(5), Jun 1984, 176-177.* LEVEL B LANG: Eng SIRC ARTICLE NO: 096602

Salomon, W. Buying a bike: Freewheeling helps you avoid the pitfalls. *Freewheeling (Haymarket, N.S.W.) 24, Mar/Apr 1984, 23-26.* LEVEL: B LANG: Eng SIRC ARTICLE NO: 099504

Thompson, D. A slide mount system for panniers. *Freewheeling (Sydney) 26, Jul/Aug 1984, 51-52.* LEVEL: B LANG: Eng SIRC ARTICLE NO: 105778

EQUIPMENT - MAINTENANCE

Farren, P. Tandem drive systems. *Freewheeling (Haymarket, N.S.W.) 25, May/Jun 1984, 44-45.* LEVEL: B LANG: Eng SIRC ARTICL NO: 101168

EQUIPMENT - RETAILING

Quinn, R. How are your doing on carrier sales? *Bicycle business journal (Fort Worth, Tex.) 38(7), Jul 1984, 16.* LEVEL: B LANG: Eng SIRC ARTICLE NO: 102410

FACILITIES

Peace, R. The cycleways of Melbourne. *Freewheeling (Haymarket, N.S.W.) 23, Jan/Feb 1984, 32-33.37-38.* LEVEL: B LANG: Eng SIRC ARTICLE NO: 099496

INJURIES AND ACCIDENTS

Bouvier, R. Bicycle accidents in childhood. Social and preventive aspects. *Australian family physician (Sydney) 13(4), Apr 1984, 287-289.* LEVEL: B LANG: Eng

Gunn, A. Cycle accidents. (letter) *New Zealand medical journal (Dunedin) 97(768), 28 Nov 1984, 832.* LEVEL: B LANG: Eng

Subrahmanyam, M. Bicycle injury pattern among children in rural India. *Tropical and geographical medicine (Amsterdam) 36(3) Sept 1984, 243-247.* LEVEL: A LANG: Eng

Westman, J.A. Morrow, G. Moped injuries in children. *Pediatrics (Evanston, Ill.) 74(5), Nov 1984, 820-822.* LEVEL: I LANG: Eng

NUTRITION

Navarro, J.L. Jund, M. Riviere, D. Garrigues, M. A propos d'une randonnee cyclotouriste de 24 heures. *Medecine du sport (Paris) 58(6), nov 1984, 12-15.* RESUME: L'alimentation et les repercussions physiologiques au cours d'une randonnee cyclotouriste longue de 350 km en 24 heures font l'objet de cette etude. Une femme et trois hommes, ages entre 30 et 36 ans, servent de sujets. Les resultats indiquent: 1) qu'une ration alimentaire de 6 000 calories est suffisante; et 2) que les taux de glycemie, de lactatemie, de cortisolemie, et de testosteronomie ne sont pas affectes de facon significative. LEVEL: A LANG: Fr SIRC ARTICLE NO: 103109

PHYSICAL FITNESS

Poirier, L. Pour etre en forme cet ete: le velo. *Marathon, la revue de la bonne forme (Montreal) 16, mai 1984, 39-41.* LEVEL: B LANG: Fr SIRC ARTICLE NO: 108714

PHYSIOLOGY

Navarro, J.L. Jund, M. Riviere, D. Garrigues, M. A propos d'une randonnee cyclotouriste de 24 heures. *Medecine du sport (Paris) 58(6), nov 1984, 12-15.* RESUME: L'alimentation et les repercussions physiologiques au cours d'une randonnee cyclotouriste longue de 350 km en 24 heures font l'objet de cette etude. Une femme et trois hommes, ages entre 30 et 36 ans, servent de sujets. Les resultats indiquent: 1) qu'une ration alimentaire de 6 000 calories est suffisante; et 2) que les taux de glycemie, de lactatemie, de cortisolemie, et de testosteronomie ne sont pas affectes de facon significative. LEVEL: A LANG: Fr SIRC ARTICLE NO: 103109

BICYCLING (continued)

RULES AND REGULATIONS

Allen, J.S. Lanes and laws. Part II: intersections. *Bicycling 25(1), Jan/Feb 1984, 20-22;175.*
LEVEL: B LANG: Eng SIRC ARTICLE NO: 090544

SAFETY

Watts, G.R. Pedal cycle lamps and reflectors - some visibility tests and surveys. Crowthorne, Berkshire: Transport and Road Research Laboratory, 1984. 19 p.
NOTES: Report no. LR-1108.
LEVEL: A LANG: Eng

Watts, G.R. Evaluation of conspicuity aids for pedal cyclists. Crowthorne, Berkshire: Transport and Road Research Laboratory 1984. 11 p.
NOTES: Report no. LR-1103.
LEVEL: A LANG: Eng

Watts, G.R. Evaluation of pedal cycle spacers. Crowthorne, Berkshire: Transport and Road Research Laboratory, 1984. 8 p.
NOTES: Report NO. SR-820.
LEVEL: I LANG: Eng

TRAINING AND CONDITIONING - WARM-UPS, WARM-DOWNS, LEAD-UP GAMES

Prevot L'entrainement. *Cyclotourisme (Paris) 317, juin 1984, 54-55.*
LEVEL: B LANG: Fr SIRC ARTICLE NO: 099498

VARIATIONS - UNICYCLING

Kucera, J. Building a regular unicycle. *On one wheel (Redford, Mich.) 11(1), Winter 1984, 10-11.*
LEVEL: B LANG: Eng SIRC ARTICLE NO: 099482

BICYCLING AND CYCLING

Forester, J. Effective cycling. 5th ed. 1st MIT ed. Cambridge, Mass.: MIT Press, c1984. xv, 344 p. : ill.
LEVEL: I LANG: En ISBN: 0-262-56026-7 LC CARD: 83-43021 GV1041 18121

Hosler, R. The Runner's world bike book. Mountain View, Calif.: Runner's World Books, c1984. 224 p. : ill.
LEVEL: B LANG: E ISBN: 089037287X LC CARD: 84-003281 GV1041 18170

Howard, J. The cyclist's companion. 1st ed. Brattleboro, Vt.: Stephen Greene Press, c1984. xii, 286 p.
NOTES: Bibliography: p. 275-278.
LEVEL: I LANG: Eng ISBN: 0-8289-0529-0 LC CARD: 84-1648 GV1041 17651

Hoyt, C.S. Hoyt, J. Cycling. 2nd ed. Dubuque, Iowa: W.C. Brown, c1984. xi, 78 p. : ill. (Exploring sports series.)
NOTES: Bibliography: p. 64-66.
LEVEL: B LANG: Eng ISBN: 0-697-00292-6 LC CARD: 84-070346 GV1041 6350

Martini, S. Blanton, B. Two wheeling: the bicycle and recreational sports. (Refs: 10)*NIRSA journal (Mt. Pleasant, Mich.) 8(2), Winter 1984, 35-38.*
LEVEL: B LANG: Eng SIRC ARTICLE NO: 098022

Salomon, W. Human powered vehicle feature: into a new era - the human powered vehicle challenge.

Freewheeling (Haymarket, N.S.W.) 25, May/Jun 1984, 9-13;15.
LEVEL: B LANG: Eng SIRC ARTICLE NO: 101189

Visser, K. American bike month: make it a big one. *Bicycle U.S.A. (Baltimore, Md.) 20(3), Mar 1984, 14-17.*
LEVEL: B LANG: Eng SIRC ARTICLE NO: 098034

AERODYNAMICS

Isvan, O. The effect of winds on a bicyclist's speed. *Bike tech (Emmaus, Pa.) 3(3), Jun 1984, 1-6.*
LEVEL: I LANG: Eng SIR ARTICLE NO: 101173

Jow, R. All about aero, part II: practical implications. *Bicycling 25(2), Mar 1984, 189-190.*
LEVEL: B LANG: Eng SIRC ARTICLE NO: 092008

Perlman, E. Building better bikes. *In, Schrier, E.W. and Allman, W.F. (eds.), Newton at the bat: the science in sports, New York, Scribner, c1984, p. 79-82.*
LEVEL: B LANG: Eng RC1235 18609

ASSOCIATIONS

Ezell, W.K. Changing magazines titles: an L.A.W. tradition. *Bicycle USA (Baltimore, Md.) 20(4), Apr 1984, 6-7.*
LEVEL: B LANG: Eng SIRC ARTICLE NO: 094940

BIOMECHANICS

Haushalter, G. Lang, G. Biomecanique du pied du cycliste appliquee au positionnement de la chaussure. (Refs: 4)*Medecine du sport (Paris) 58(3), 25 mai 1984, 22-25.*
LEVEL: I LANG: Fr SIRC ARTICLE NO: 096586

CLOTHING

Cycling: geared for profit. *Fitness industry (Miami, Fla.) 2(2), Mar/Apr 1984, 16-17;19-20;22;27-29.*
LEVEL: B LANG: Eng SIR ARTICLE NO: 098003

Feingold, M.L. Fancy footwork: selecting cleated shoes. *Bicycling 25(1), Jan/Feb 1984, 164-170;172.*
LEVEL: B LANG: Eng SIRC ARTICLE NO: 090552

Feingold, M.L. Footloose and fancy: shoes for riding and walking. *Bicycling (Emmaus, Pa.) 25(8), Sept/Oct 1984, 120-126;129-133.*
LEVEL: B LANG: Eng SIRC ARTICLE NO: 098941

Keeping out of the rain: a look at wet weather cycling gear. *Freewheeling (Haymarket, N.S.W.) 25, May/Jun 1984, 60-61.*
LEVEL: B LANG: Eng SIRC ARTICLE NO: 100558

Walz, T. Cycling clothing care. How to protect those expensive togs. *Bicycling (Emmaus, Pa.) 25(6), Jul 1984, 26;29-31.*
LEVEL: B LANG: Eng SIRC ARTICLE NO: 096608

DIRECTORIES

1984 buyers' guide. *Bicycling 25(1), Jan/Feb 1984, 113-118;120;122;124-126;128;131-132;134;136;138;140;142-143;146;148-151;154-155.*
LEVEL: B LANG: Eng SIRC ARTICLE NO: 090543

Fermont, J. The 1985 bicycle information guide. *Bicycle USA (Baltimore, Md.) 21(12), Dec 1984,*

6-15.
LEVEL: B LANG: Eng SIRC ARTICLE NO: 107099

Fremont, J. State-by-state: guide for cyclists. *Bicycle USA (Baltimore, Md.) 21(12), Dec 1984, 20-81.*
LEVEL: B LANG: Eng SIRC ARTICLE NO: 107101

DISABLED

Human powered vehicles open new doors for handicapped . *HPV news (Seal Beach, Calif.) 2(2), Sept 1984, 1;5-6.*
LEVEL: B LANG Eng SIRC ARTICLE NO: 099006

DOCUMENTATION

Ezell, W. Cycling mags are sprouting like weeds. *Bicycle USA (Baltimore, Md.) 20(9), Sept 1984, 29-30.*
LEVEL: B LANG: Eng SIRC ARTICLE NO: 099467

EQUIPMENT

3Rensho: Yoshi Konno builds bikes Japanese-style. *American bicyclist and motorcyclist (New York) 105(10), Oct 1984, 21-22.*
LEVEL: B LANG: Eng SIRC ARTICLE NO: 107083

Berto, F. Mid-range rear derailleurs. Thirty-six models go on the test stand. *Bicycling 25(3), Apr 1984, 146-147;152-159.*
LEVEL: B LANG: Eng SIRC ARTICLE NO: 093346

Bicycle security devices. *Bicycle dealer showcase (Santa Ana, Calif.) 13(8), Aug 1984, 8-10;12.*
LEVEL: B LANG: Eng SIRC ARTICLE NO: 104623

Bicycle-seat covers: pampering your posterior. *Executive fitness newsletter (Emmaus, Pa.) 15(14), 7 Jul 1984, 4.*
LEVEL: B LANG: Eng SIRC ARTICLE NO: 104624

Burne, J. Make your bike collapsible: the Pingel conversion kit really works. *Bicycling (Emmaus, Pa.) 25(7), Aug 1984, 143-144.*
LEVEL: B LANG: Eng SIRC ARTICLE NO: 099461

Burnesn, R. Part: Counterpart - saddles. *Bike report (Missoula, Mont.) 8(10), Aug/Sept 1984, 24-26.*
LEVEL: B LANG: Eng SIRC ARTICLE NO: 103084

Buttars, K. Kent's diamond chart: gearing at a glance. *Bicycling (Emmaus, Pa.) 25(5), Jun 1984, 204-205.*
LEVEL: B LANG: E SIRC ARTICLE NO: 096568

Champlin, C. HPVS at the races: inciting evolution in Indiana. *Bicycling 25(2), Mar 1984, 74-77;79-80.*
LEVEL: B LANG: Eng SIRC ARTICLE NO: 091986

City bikes now appearing in a town near you. *Bicycling (Emmaus, Pa.) 25(8), Sept/Oct 1984, 80-82;86-87;90;92;94;97-100;102;104-106;108;110-113.*
LEVEL: B LANG: Eng SIRC ARTICLE NO: 099463

DeLong, F. Out of round throughout the years: 45 years of experience with elliptical and non-circular chainrings. *Bicycling 25(2), Mar 1984, 146;152-153.*
LEVEL: B LANG: Eng SIRC ARTICLE NO: 091997

DeLong, F. Tires: what's coming in tire and tube developments. *American bicyclist and motorcyclist (New York) 105(9), Sept 1984, 43;45-46;64.*
LEVEL: B LANG: Eng SIRC ARTICLE NO: 103092

DeLong, F. Rims: performance of aluminum alloy rims has continued to improve. These rims are now made from a variety of aluminum alloys with a great range of strength and resiliency. *American bicyclist and motorcyclist (New York) 105(9), Sept 1984, 47-49.*
LEVEL: B LANG: Eng SIRC ARTICLE NO: 103093

DeLong, F. Spokes. *American bicyclist and motorcyclist (New York) 105(9), Sept 1984, 51;53.*
LEVEL: B LANG: Eng SIRC ARTICLE NO: 103094

DeLong, F. Saddles & seat posts: an intimate point of contact. *American bicyclist and motorcyclist (New York) 105(11), Nov 1984, 15-17.*
LEVEL: B LANG: Eng SIRC ARTICLE NO: 107095

Di Cyan, A. Inflate Schraeder tubes with a Presta pump: an adapter from junked parts. *Bicycling (Emmaus, Pa.) 25(5), Jun 1984, 208.*
LEVEL: B LANG: Eng SIRC ARTICLE NO: 096580

Emiliani, M. Can surface finish affect the strength of your frame? Particle blasting, part II. *Bike tech (Emmaus, Pa.) 3(1) Feb 1984, 1-6.*
NOTES: To be continued in June issue.
LEVEL: I LANG: Eng SIRC ARTICLE NO: 094939

Emiliani, M. Can surface finish affect the strength of your frame? Part 111: chrome plating. *Bike tech (Emmaus, Pa.) 3(3), Jun 1984, 10-16.*
LEVEL: I LANG: Eng SIRC ARTICLE NO: 101166

Essentials of fitting. *American bicyclist and motorcyclist (New York) 105(11), Jan 1985, 18-19.*
LEVEL: B LANG: Eng SIRC ARTICLE NO: 107097

Flower, R.G. Cranksets and cycling efficiency, the final word. *Bicycling (Emmaus, Pa.) 25(8), Sept/Oct 1984, 180-184;186-188.*
LEVEL: B LANG: Eng SIRC ARTICLE NO: 099470

Gilmore, J. Hayes, M. Sealed bearing components. *Bicycle business journal (Fort Worth, Tex.) 38(11), Nov 1984, 36-37.*
LEVEL: B LANG: Eng SIRC ARTICLE NO: 103097

Hjertberg, E. Wood rims... nowhere else has 'Nature's composite' made such a valuable and enduring contribution to the bicycle as with wood rims. *American bicyclist and motorcyclist (New York) 105(9), Sept 1984, 37-38.*
LEVEL: B LANG: Eng SIRC ARTICLE NO: 103099

Hjertberg, E. Wheel futures: a revolution is occurring in the style and design of the wheel. *American bicyclist and motorcyclist (New York) 105(9), Sept 1984, 66.*
LEVEL: B LANG: Eng SIRC ARTICLE NO: 103100

Hreno, T. Partially faired HPVs. *Human power (Long Beach, Calif.) 3(1), Spring 1984, 15-17.*
LEVEL: I LANG: Eng SIRC ARTICLE NO: 099473

Hubs: a review of hubs: types, construction and attachment methods. *American bicyclist and motorcyclist (New York) 105(9), Sept 1984, 59-60.*
LEVEL: B LANG: Eng SIRC ARTICLE NO: 103101

Hulbert, H. Technical tirade: try a tricycle. *Bicycling news Canada (West Vancouver, B.C.) 5(4), Spring 1984, 30-31.*
LEVEL: B LANG: Eng SIRC ARTICLE NO: 099474

ISO tire markings. *American bicyclist and motorcyclist (New York) 105(9), Sept 1984, 62-63.*
LEVEL: B LANG: Eng SIRC ARTICLE NO: 103102

Jenkins, N. Centurion Turbo 12: a sleek swift all-Japanese bike to take your breath away. Bicycle road test. *Freewheeling (Haymarket, N.S.W.) 25,*

May/Jun 1984, 37-38.
LEVEL: B LANG: Eng SIRC ARTICLE NO: 101176

Jow, R. The Roto component group: Tutti Italiani for a lot less lire. *Bicycling 25(3), Apr 1984, 160-165.*
LEVEL: B LANG: Eng SIRC ARTICLE NO: 093359

Jow, R. Cuevas Custom and Super Corsa. Two framesets from a Spanish master. *Bicycling (Emmaus, Pa.) 25(6), Jul 1984, 158;162-166;168-169.*
LEVEL: B LANG: Eng SIRC ARTICLE NO: 096589

Jow, R. The Shimano 105 group: conservative design at a low price. *Bicycling (Emmaus, Pa.) 25(7), Aug 1984, 124-130.*
LEVEL: B LANG: Eng SIRC ARTICLE NO: 099475

Juden, C. The aluminum rim: design and function. *Bike tech (Emmaus, Pa.) 3(2), Apr 1984, 1-5.*
LEVEL: I LANG: Eng SIRC ARTICLE NO: 099476

La fin du cale-pied? 1 - la pedale Manolo. *Cyclotourisme (Paris) 321, dec 1984, 29-30;35-37.*
LEVEL: B LANG: Fr SIRC ARTICLE NO: 173396

Langley, J. Building a bike: is your frame worth reconditioning? *Bicycling (Emmaus, Pa.) 25(9), Nov/Dec 1984, 158;160;162.*
LEVEL: B LANG: Eng SIRC ARTICLE NO: 101179

Lighting up the night: a look at what's new in bicycle lighting. *Freewheeling (Sydney) 26, Jul/Aug 1984, 59-62.*
LEVEL: B LANG: Eng SIRC ARTICLE NO: 105761

Lunas, L. Painting with imron, part 1: corrosion of metals. (Refs: 5)*Bike tech (Emmaus, Pa.) 3(3), Jun 1984, 6-10.*
LEVEL: I LANG: Eng SIRC ARTICLE NO: 101180

Lunas, L. Painting with Imron, Part II. *Bike tech (Emmaus, Penn.) 3(4), Aug 1984, 6-7.*
LEVEL: I LANG: Eng SIRC ARTICLE NO 105762

Milkie, T. HPV scientific symposium. *Human power (Long Beach, Calif.) 3(1), Spring 1984, 18-20.*
LEVEL: B LANG: Eng SIRC ARTICLE NO: 099487

Milkie, T. A note on rear-wheel steering. *HPV news (Seal Beach, Calif.) 1(11), Jun 1984, 6-7.*
LEVEL: B LANG: Eng SIRC ARTICLE NO: 099488

Miller, C. Chain behavior in front derailleurs. *Bike tech (Emmaus, Pa.) 3(1), Feb 1984, 6-8.*
LEVEL: B LANG: Eng SIRC ARTICLE NO: 094949

Perkins, R.D. Tricycles: front and rear steered. *HPV news (Seal Beach, Calif.) 2(3), Oct 1984, 4-5.*
LEVEL: B LANG: Eng SIRC ARTICLE NO: 107134

Pipkin, R. Ideas & opinions. *Bike tech (Emmaus, Pa.) 3(1), Feb 1984, 15-16.*
LEVEL: I LANG: Eng SIRC ARTICLE NO: 094951

Repco Superlite: new directions from Taiwan. *Freewheeling (Haymarket, N.S.W.) 24, Mar/Apr 1984, 39-40.*
LEVEL: B LANG: Eng SIRC ARTICLE NO: 099500

Schubert, J. Berto, F. How to buy a bike: here's what to look for. *Bicycling 25(1), Jan/Feb 1984, 110-111;162.*
LEVEL: B LANG: Eng SIRC ARTICLE NO: 090562

Schubert, J. Walz, T. The Tandems of 1984: faster and smoother than solo bikes, and the choice has improved. *Bicycling 25(2), Mar 1984, 108-110;112-118;120-123;126.*
LEVEL: B LANG: Eng SIRC ARTICLE NO: 092019

Schubert, J. Trek is going strong: handbuilt bikes are still in Wisconsin. *Bicycling 25(2), Mar 1984, 137-140.*
LEVEL: B LANG: Eng SIRC ARTICLE NO: 092020

Seat posts. *American bicyclist and motorcyclist (New York) 105(11), Nov 1984, 17-18.*
LEVEL: B LANG: Eng SIRC ARTICLE NO: 107140

Sellers, D. Touring racks: your foundation for a home on the road. *Bicycling (Emmaus, Pa.) 25(6), Jul 1984, 172-176;189;191.*
LEVEL: B LANG: Eng SIRC ARTICLE NO: 096604

Talbot, R.P. Designing and building your own frameset: an illustrated guide for the amateur bicycle builder. 2nd ed. (Babson Park, Mass.): The Manet Guild, c1984. v, 161 p. : ill.
LEVEL: I LANG: Eng ISBN: 0-9602418-3-3 LC CARD: 83-51801 GV1041 20110

The Ricardo Bushbike: entry level all terrain biking. Fat-tyre road test. *Freewheeling (Haymarket, N.S.W.) 25, May/Jun 1984, 49-50.*
LEVEL: B LANG: Eng SIRC ARTICLE NO: 101187

Wachter, E. Choice seating: no if's, ands, or sore butts. *Bicycling (Emmaus, Pa.) 25(7), Aug 1984, 104;107-108;110;112;114;116.*
LEVEL: B LANG: Eng SIRC ARTICLE NO: 099513

Walz, T. Shimano's biopace: not just another elliptical chainring. *Bicycling 25(2), Mar 1984, 142;144.*
LEVEL: B LANG: Eng SIRC ARTICLE NO: 092024

Walz, T. The kit bike: making fantasy into reality. *Bicycling (Emmaus, Pa.) 25(5), Jun 1984, 180;182;185;186;188.*
LEVEL: LANG: Eng SIRC ARTICLE NO: 096609

Walz, T. Extension levers and stem shifters: convenience or hazzard? *Bicycling (Emmaus, Pa.) 25(5), Jun 1984, 26;28-29.*
LEVEL: B LANG: Eng SIRC ARTICLE NO: 096610

Weaver, S. Powercam: some folks claim it's out of this world. *Bicycling (Emmaus, Pa.) 25(8), Sept/Oct 1984, 38-40;42;44;138-141.*
LEVEL: B LANG: Eng SIRC ARTICLE NO: 099514

Zahradnik, F. Travel light: panniers are being built better than ever. *Bicycling (Emmaus, Pa.) 25(5), Jun 1984, 148-149;151-156.*
LEVEL: B LANG: Eng SIRC ARTICLE NO: 096613

EQUIPMENT - MAINTENANCE

Brown, S. Tool tips: fixed wrenches. The workshop choice for precision and strength. *Bicycling 25(1), Jan/Feb 1984, 99-101.*
LEVEL: B LANG: Eng SIRC ARTICLE NO: 090546

Brown, S. Tool tips: hammers. The care and feeding of our oldest tool. *Bicycling 25(2), Mar 1984, 154;157;159.*
LEVEL: B LANG: Eng SIRC ARTICLE NO: 091983

Brown, S. Tool tips: chain tools. These tools do a unique job. *Bicycling (Emmaus, Pa.) 25(8), Sept/Oct 1984, 177-179.*
LEVEL: B LANG: Eng SIRC ARTICLE NO: 099459

Cantilever brake adjustment: roll, pitch, yaw, and spin dynamics. *Bicycling (Emmaus, Pa.) 25(7), Aug 1984, 148-149;152.*
LEVEL: B LANG: Eng SIRC ARTICLE NO: 099462

Costantino, T. Front derailleur adjustment: seven steps to perfect chainwheel shifts. *Bicycling 25(1),*

BICYCLING AND CYCLING (continued)

Jan/Feb 1984, 108-109.
LEVEL: B LANG: Eng SIRC ARTICLE NO: 090548

Costantino, T. Rear derailleur adjustment: seven steps to shifting nirvana. *Bicycling 25(2), Mar 1984, 176-177.*
LEVEL: B LANG: Eng SIRC ARTICLE NO: 091989

Costantino, T. Derailleur cable replacement: a change for the better. *Bicycling (Emmaus, Pa.) 25(4), May 1984, 146-148.*
LEVEL: B LANG: Eng SIRC ARTICLE NO: 094937

Costantino, T. Brake adjustment: smooth stops for sidepulls and centerpulls. *Bicycling (Emmaus, Pa.) 25(6), Jul 1984, 151-154.*
LEVEL: B LANG: Eng SIRC ARTICLE NO: 096571

Costantino, T. Tool tips: freewheel removers. How to make these tools work for you. *Bicycling (Emmaus, Pa, 25(5), Jun 1984 160-163.*
LEVEL: B LANG: Eng SIRC ARTICLE NO: 096573

Costantino, T. Cable housing replacement: new shelter for your direct connections. *Bicycling (Emmaus, Pa.) 25(5), Jun 1984, 178-179.*
LEVEL: B LANG: Eng SIRC ARTICLE NO: 096574

Cuthbertson, T. Quick fixes - part 1: don't let flats get you down. *Bicycling (Emmaus, Pa.) 25(9), Nov/Dec 1984, 141-142;144-147;150-151.*
LEVEL: B LANG: Eng SIRC ARTICLE NO: 101165

Davis, H.J. An introduction to frame repair: when should you consider it? *Bicycling (Emmaus, Pa.) 25(7), Aug 1984, 140-142.*
LEVEL: B LANG: Eng SIRC ARTICLE NO: 099464

Di Cyan, A. Tool tips: tools to do double duty. Or, how to travel light and fix anything. *Bicycling 25(3), Apr 1984, 130;132;135.*
LEVEL: B LANG: Eng SIRC ARTICLE NO: 093353

Di Cyan, A. Cotter pin removal and installation: the piranha method. *Bicycling (Emmaus, Pa.) 25(5), Jun 1984, 168-169.*
LEVEL: B LANG: Eng SIRC ARTICLE NO: 096578

Gilmore, J. Hayes, M. Headsets. Part 2: replacement & repair. *Bicycle business journal (Fort Worth, Tex.) 38(10), Oct 1984, 34-36.*
LEVEL: B LANG: Eng SIRC ARTICLE NO: 107104

Gilmore, J. Hayes, M. Headsets. Part 1: Frame preparation. *Bicycle business journal (Fort Worth, Tex.) Sept 1984, 32-34.*
LEVEL: B LANG: Eng SIRC ARTICLE NO: 109087

Girardot, P. Le cyclisme. *Revue du jeune medecin (Paris) Supp(130), 1984, 4-5.*
LEVEL: B LANG: Fr

Grove, D. Bicycling: how to achieve a proper fit. *Ohio runner (Columbus, Ohio) 6(5), Nov 1984, 8.*
LEVEL: B LANG: Eng SIRC ARTICLE NO: 173408

Norcross, P. Brake maintenance. *Bike report (Missoula, Mont.) 8(10), Aug/Sept 1984, 22-23.*
LEVEL: B LANG: Eng SIRC ARTICL NO: 103110

Rhea, K. Bike maintenance. *Ohio runner (Columbus, Oh.) 6(3), Sept 1984, 16-17.*
LEVEL: B LANG: Eng SIRC ARTICLE NO: 101186

Rogers, N. Save that wheel. A crash course in rim straightening. *Bicycling (Emmaus, Pa.) 25(5), Jun 1984, 202-203.*
LEVEL: LANG: Eng SIRC ARTICLE NO: 096601

The art and business of frame restoration. *American bicyclist and motorcyclist (New York) 105(10), Oct 1984, 12-14.*
LEVEL: LANG: Eng SIRC ARTICLE NO: 107085

Tool tips: freewheel sprocket removers, the painless way to a multi-speed future. *Bicycling (Emmaus, Pa.) 25(7), Aug 1984, 118;120;122-123.*
LEVEL: B LANG: Eng SIRC ARTICLE NO: 099512

Weems, D. Murphy, M. The repair that can save your tour: ingenuity for a quick fix. *Bicycling (Emmaus, Pa.) 25(5) Jun 1984, 144;146.*
LEVEL: B LANG: Eng SIRC ARTICLE NO: 096612

EQUIPMENT - RETAILING

Berst, J. Understanding technical terms can help when you talk to a computer salesman. *Bicycle business journal (Texas), 38(2), Feb 1984, 29-30;32;34.*
LEVEL: B LANG: Eng SIRC ARTICLE NO: 099452

Bicycle Business Journal dealer survey. *Bicycle business journal (Fort Worth, Tex.) Sept 1984, 26;28;30.*
LEVEL: B LANG: Eng SIRC ARTICLE NO: 109084

Cuff, J.H. Big wheels in biking: the Kent family has propelled Bloor Cycle to success. *Financial post magazine (Toronto) 1 Sept 1984, 44-46;48.*
LEVEL: B LANG: Eng SIRC ARTICLE NO: 098002

Jarvis, W. Bicycle carriers: cartop, bumper, trunklid. *Bicycle dealer showcase (Irvine, Calif.) 13(3), Mar 1984, 24;26-28;30;32-33.*
LEVEL: B LANG: Eng SIRC ARTICLE NO: 101174

Jarvis, W. Tires: refinement in the rubber market. *Bicycle dealer showcase (Irvine, Calif.) 13(6), Jun 1984, 6;8;11-12;14-15.*
LEVEL: B LANG: Eng SIRC ARTICLE NO: 101175

Knight, T. Peddling bicycles: if you are going to sell bicycles, you must jump in all the way, according to this retailer. *Sports retailer (Mt. Prospect, Ill.) 37(1), Jan 1984, 22-23.*
LEVEL: B LANG: Eng SIRC ARTICLE NO: 098020

Looking good on a bicycle: today's bikers like the new look, but the quality, comfort and price are also important. *American bicyclist and motorcyclist (New York) 105(2), Feb 1984, 103-105;127;131;138.*
LEVEL: B LANG: Eng SIRC ARTICLE NO: 098021

Quinn, R. How to become a big wheel in the tire and tube game. *Bicycle business journal (Fort Worth, Tex.) 38(5), May 1984, 16-18.*
LEVEL: B LANG: Eng SIRC ARTICLE NO: 101184

San Diego dealer shows...How to double apparel sales: 1. Create distinctive department. 2. Display imaginatively. 3. Keep current. *American bicyclist and motorcyclist (New York) 105(1), Jan 1984, 58-59;80-82.*
LEVEL: B LANG: Eng SIRC ARTICLE NO: 098029

The 1983 bicycle market in review. *American bicyclist and motorcyclist (New York) 105(6), Jun 1984, 15-17.*
LEVEL: B LANG: E SIRC ARTICLE NO: 101161

Twentieth century miracle: a computer program designed especially for the bicycle dealer. *American bicyclist and motorcyclist (New York) 105(3), Mar 1984, 33-36;78-79.*
LEVEL: B LANG: Eng SIRC ARTICLE NO: 098032

Wares, B.R. Sales. *American bicyclist and motorcyclist (New York) 105(9), Sept 1984, 78;80.*
LEVEL: B LANG: Eng SIRC ARTICLE NO: 103120

HISTORY

Stewart, J. The two-wheeled miracle. *Ilam: institute of leisure & amenity management (London) 2(6), Jun 1984, 18-19.*
LEVEL: B LANG: Eng SIRC ARTICLE NO: 099510

INJURIES AND ACCIDENTS

Bjoernstig, U. Naeslund, K. Pedal cycling accidents - mechanisms and consequences. A study from northern Sweden. *Acta chirurgica scandinavica (Stockholm) 150(5), 1984, 353-359.*
LEVEL: A LANG: Eng

Bracken, S. Neck pain. *Bicycle Ontario (Willowdale) 7(1), Feb 1984, 18-19.*
LEVEL: B LANG: Eng SIRC ARTICLE NO: 098000

Dickson, T. Treating road rash: an expert tells how to handle abrasions. *Bicycling 25(2), Mar 1984, 56;201.*
LEVEL: B LANG Eng SIRC ARTICLE NO: 091998

Gross, A. Pains in the butt. Some tips on the prevention and treatment of health problems associated with the saddle. *American bicyclist and motorcyclist (New York) 105(11), Nov 1984, 31-32.*
LEVEL: B LANG: Eng SIRC ARTICLE NO: 107106

Johannessen, A.C. Frandsen, P. Myocarditis acuta. Arsag til pludselig dod i forbindelse med fysisk anstrengelse. (Acute myocarditis. Cause of sudden death in connection with physical exertion.) *Ugeskrift for laeger (Copenhagen) 147(1), 31 Dec 1984, 26-27.*
LEVEL: I LANG: Dan

McKenna, S. Borman, B. Fleming, H. Pedal cycle accidents. (letter) *New Zealand medical journal (Dunedin) 97(764), 26 Sept 1984, 657-658.*
LEVEL: B LANG: Eng SIRC ARTICLE NO: 104644

Mogensen, H. Krogh, A. Kruse, T. Peulicke, E. Wengler, K. Cykelhjulslaesioner i odense-omradet. En kombineret registrerings- observations- og interviewstudie. (Bicycle-wheel injuries in the Odense district. A combined registration, observation and interview study.) *Ugeskrift for laeger (Copenhagen) 146(3), 16 Jan 1984, 222-225.*
LEVEL: A LANG: Dan

Nichols, T.W. Bicycle-seat hematuria. (letter) *New England journal of medicine (Boston) 311(17), 25 Oct 1984, 1128.*
LEVEL I LANG: Eng

Off your bike: CTC publishes accident report. *Cycletouring (Surrey, Eng.) Oct/Nov 1984, 281-283.*
LEVEL: B LANG: Eng SIRC ARTICLE NO: 109358

JUVENILE LITERATURE

Chlad, D. Halverson, L. Bicycles are fun to ride. Chicago, Ill.: Childrens Press, 1984. 1v.
LEVEL: B LANG: Eng ISBN: 0516019759 LC CARD: 83-023234

MASS MEDIA

Fremont, J. Rating the cycling films. *Cyclist's almanac (Baltimore, Md.) 19(12), Dec 1983, 46-51.* LEVEL: B LANG: Eng SIRC ARTICLE NO: 099471

MATHEMATICS

Hammaker, A. Perspectives on gearing. *Bicycling (Emmaus, Pa.) 25(4), May 1984, 154-160;164.* LEVEL: I LANG: Eng SIRC ARTICLE NO: 094941

Pipkin, R. An analysis of front fork flexibility. *Bike tech (Emmaus, Penn.) 3(4), Aug 1984, 8-13.* LEVEL: I LANG: Eng SIRC ARTICLE NO: 105770

Singh, D. The importance of gear ratios in cycling. *Snipes journal (Patiala, India) 7(3), Jul 1984, 19-20.* LEVEL: I LANG: Eng SIRC ARTICLE NO: 099505

MEDICINE

Smith, D.L. First aid kits. *Bicycling (Emmaus, Pa.) 25(4), May 1984, 44;47-49.* LEVEL: B LANG: Eng SIRC ARTICLE NO: 094437

NUTRITION

Kail, K. Spring shape-up: the best way to shed your spare tire. *Bicycling 25(3), Apr 1984, 35-36;38.* LEVEL: B LANG: Eng SIRC ARTICLE NO: 093360

PHYSICAL FITNESS

Get fit fast. *New body (New York) 3(4), Jul 1984, 56-59.* LEVEL: B LANG: Eng SIRC ARTICLE NO: 100858

McCullagh, J.C. The complete bicycle fitness book. New York: Warner Books, c1984. 286 p. NOTES: Includes index. Bibliography: p. 278-280. LEVEL: I LANG: Eng ISBN: 0446378941 LC CARD: 83-025904 GV1043.7 18321

PHYSICS

Allen, J.S. A musical test for correct spoke tension. *Bike tech (Emmaus, Penn.) 3(4), Aug 1984, 14-16.* LEVEL: I LANG: Eng SIRC ARTICLE NO: 105740

Emiliani, M. Anodized rims are more rigid. *Bike tech (Emmaus, Pa.) 3(2), Apr 1984, 5.* LEVEL: I LANG: Eng SIRC ARTICLE NO: 177557

Erard, H.R. Les braquets. (Refs: 30)*Cyclotourisme (Paris) 317, juin 1984, 28-29;31-33.* LEVEL: I LANG: Fr SIRC ARTICLE NO: 099466

Roosa, D. Updike, D. Flower, B. Relating rim rigidity and strength. *Bike tech (Emmaus, Pa.) 3(2), Apr 1984, 6-9.* LEVEL: I LANG: Eng SIRC ARTICLE NO: 099502

PHYSIOLOGY

de Mondenard, J.P. Les bases de l'alimentation du cycliste: le fonctionnement du moteur humain: du carburant pour le corps; les besoins en calories du cycliste. (Refs: 1)*Cycle (Paris) 103, 1984, 60-63.* NOTES: A suivre. LEVEL: I LANG: Fr

de Mondenard, J.P. Les bases de l'alimentation du cycliste: le fonctionnement du moteur humain: du carburant pour le corps; les besoins en calories du cycliste. *Cycle (Paris) 104, 1984, 70-73.*

NOTES: A suivre. LEVEL: I LANG: Fr

de Mondenard, J.P. Les bases de l'alimentation du cycliste: le fonctionnement du moteur humain: du carburant pour le corps; les besoins en calories du cycliste. *Cycle (Paris) 105, 1984, 120-125.* NOTES: Suite et fin. LEVEL: I LANG: Fr

PHYSIOLOGY - MUSCLE

Davies, C.T. Wemyss-Holden, J. Young, K. Measurement of short term power output: comparison between cycling and jumping. *Ergonomics (London) 27(3), Mar 1984, 285-296.* LEVEL: A LANG: Eng SIRC ARTICLE NO: 103091

PROTECTIVE DEVICES

A consumer's guide to bicycle helmets. Washington, D.C.: Washington Area Bicyclist Association, 1984. 1 pamphlet CORP: Washington Area Bicyclist Association. LEVEL: B LANG: Eng GV1041 18949

Beames, D. The get smart head shop or how to choose a helmet intelligently. *Bicycling news Canada (West Vancouver, B.C.) 5(4), Spring 1984, 16-17.* LEVEL: B LANG: Eng SIRC ARTICLE NO: 099451

Bicycle helmets: safety first, but comfort, too. *Executive fitness newsletter (Emmaus, Pa.) 15(6), 17 Mar 1984, 4.* LEVEL: B LANG: Eng SIRC ARTICLE NO: 094933

Bishop, P. Briard, B. Helmets put to the test. *Bicycling news Canada (West Vancouver, B.C.) 5(4), Spring 1984, 12-13.* LEVEL: I LANG: Eng SIRC ARTICLE NO: 099453

Bishop, P.J. Briard, B.D. Impact performance of bicycle helmets. (Refs: 21)*Canadian journal of applied sport sciences/Journal canadien des sciences appliquees au sport (Windsor, Ont.) 9(2), Jun 1984, 94-101.* ABST: This study compared seven brands of bicycle helmets by means of a drop test, at various locations on the helmet and at various heights. The results indicate that helmets with crushable polystyrene liners are much superior to helmets with soft foam liners. However, the superiority of these helmets disappeared when they were subjected to two consecutive drops at the same location. Despite this disadvantage helmets with polystyrene liners appear to offer the best protection against brain injury to the cyclist. LEVEL: A LANG: Eng SIRC ARTICLE NO: 095806

McDermott, F.T. Why pedal cyclists should wear safety helmets. *Australian family physician (Sydney) 13(4), Apr 1984, 284-285.* LEVEL: B LANG: Eng

Montgomery, R.K. Helmets; voice of dissent. *Bicycling news Canada (West Vancouver, B.C.) 5(4), Spring 1984, 14-15.* LEVEL: LANG: Eng SIRC ARTICLE NO: 099490

Swart, R. Part: counterpart helmets. *Bike report (Missoula, Mont.) 8(9), Jun/Jul 1984, 15-17.* LEVEL: B LANG: Eng SIRC ARTICLE NO: 099511

PSYCHOLOGY

deVoss, G. High anxiety: coping with cycling related fear. *Bicycling (Emmaus, Pa.) 25(5), Jun 1984, 79-80.* LEVEL: B LANG: Eng SIRC ARTICLE NO: 096577

SAFETY

Anti-theft product directory. *American bicyclist and motorcyclist (New York) 105(6), Jun 1984, 25-29.* LEVEL: B LANG: Eng SIRC ARTICLE NO: 101163

Bicycle security devices. *Bicycle dealer showcase (Irvine, Calif.) 13(8), Aug 1984, 8-10;12.* LEVEL: B LANG: Eng SIRC ARTICL NO: 105744

STATISTICS AND RECORDS

Van Doren, C.S. Bicycles. In, Clawson, M. and Van Doren, C.S. (eds.), Statistics on outdoor recreation, Washington, Resources for the Future, c1984, p. 267-271. LEVEL: B LANG: Eng GV191.4 20254

STATISTICS AND RECORDS - PARTICIPATION

Bicycling -- not just a fair weather activity. Le cyclisme -- l'activite d'ete par excellence. *Highlights/Faits saillants (Ottawa) 27, May 1984, 1-2.* CORP: Canada Fitness Survey. CORP: Enquete condition physique Canada. LEVEL: B LANG: Eng Fr SIRC ARTICLE NO: 094934

TESTING AND EVALUATION

Boston, B. Knox, D. Taking the bicyclist's measure. Data from Gear Up show why most women have trouble with fit. *Bicycle US (Baltimore, Md.) 20(9), Sept 1984, 27.* LEVEL: B LANG: Eng SIRC ARTICLE NO: 099457

TRANSPORTATION

Macklin, J. Transporting your bicycle by plane. *Pedal power (Queen Victoria Terrace, Aust.) 62, Nov/Dec 1984, 10-11.* LEVEL: B LANG: Eng SIRC ARTICLE NO: 173495

BILLIARDS AND POOL

BIOGRAPHY AND AUTOBIOGRAPHY

Gammon, C. The great snooker graze: as a pastime to pull heartstrings it seems most unlikely, but on TV in Britain its emotional appeal is such that it surpasses even Wimbledon. *Sports illustrated (Chicago, Ill.) 60(19), 7 May 1984, 42-44;46;48;73.* LEVEL: B LANG: Eng SIRC ARTICLE NO: 094896

PHYSICS

Allman, W.F. Pool hall physics. *Science 84, Mar 1984, 100-102.* LEVEL: B LANG: Eng SIRC ARTICLE NO: 093316

Allman, W.F. Pool-hall science. In, Schrier, E.W. and Allman, W.F. (eds.), Newton at the bat: the science in sports, New York, Scribner, c1984, p.

38-43.
LEVEL: I LANG: Eng RC1235 18609

BIOGRAPHY AND AUTOBIOGRAPHY

BIOGRAPHY

Ackermann-Blount, J. Great feats on foot: from humble beginnings walking for 18 straight hours on a high school track, Jesse Castaneda, here before Red Rock Cliff in New Mexico, has set world records and gained renown as a formidable perambulator. *Sports illustrated 60(13), 26 Mar 1984, 58-62;64;66;68-72.*
LEVEL: B LANG: Eng SIRC ARTICLE NO: 093866

Bengston, B. Prince of sport. (Prince Bertil of Sweden) *Olympic review (Lausanne) 198, Apr 1984, 267-268.*
LEVEL: B LANG: Eng SIRC ARTICLE NO: 096405

Bengston, B. Un prince du sport. (Prince Bertil de Suede) *Revue olympique (Lausanne) 198, avr 1984, 267-268.*
LEVEL: B LANG: Fr SIRC ARTICLE NO: 096406

Collins, W. Mixing work and play: these full-time businessmen are also full-fledged athletes. *Financial post magazine 1 Feb 1984, 24-26;28-29;32;34.*
LEVEL: B LANG: Eng SIRC ARTICLE NO: 091865

Dickey, G. The professor of protest: Harry Edwards speaks truth, but it's too painful for whites - and many blacks. *Inside sports (Evanston, Ill.) 6, Nov 1984, 78-84;86-87.*
LEVEL: B LANG: Eng SIRC ARTICLE NO: 102916

Dolan, G.K. Athletes and athletics: sports almanac, USA. 1st ed. Loma Linda, Calif.: Footprint Pub. Co., c1984. 397 p. ; 23 cm.
NOTES: Bibliography: p. 396-397.
LEVEL: B LANG: Eng LC CARD: 84-090369

Hawley, G.H. Champions. Grand Rapids, Mich.: Zondervan Pub. House, c1984. 1v.
LEVEL: B LANG: Eng ISBN: 031070331X LC CARD: 84-019502

Juli, R.B. A sportsman named Pau Casals. *Olympic review (Lausanne, Switzerland) 195/196, Jan/Feb 1984, 47-49.*
LEVEL: B LANG: Eng SIRC ARTICLE NO: 094755

Juli, R.B. Un sportif nomme Pau Casals. *Revue olympique (Lausanne) 195/196, janv/fevr 1984, 47-49.*
LEVEL: B LANG: Fr SIRC ARTICLE NO: 096422

Marcil, F. Ferragne, Poulet et Lacourse. *Revue de l'entraineur (Montreal) juil/sept 1984, 26-27.*
LEVEL: B LANG: Fr SIRC ARTICLE NO: 102924

Szubra, T. In memoriam Prof. Zygmunt Majewski: 1894-1984. *International bulletin of sports information (The Hague, Neth.) 6(4), 1984, 2-4.*
LEVEL: B LANG: Eng SIRC ARTICLE NO: 104496

Tassin, M. Bob Mathias: the life of the Olympic champion. New York: St. Martin's Press, 1984. 1v.
LEVEL: B LANG: Eng ISBN: 0312087306 LC CARD: 83-021194

BIOMECHANICS

Adrian, M. Biomechanics of female athletes. *ICSSPE/CIEPSS review (Berlin, GDR) 7, 1984, 24-29.*
ABST: This review of the literature focuses on biomechanical research on women participating in the following sports: swimming, running, jumping and gymnastics.
LEVEL: A LANG: Eng SIRC ARTICLE NO: 096464

Ariel, G. The 'mechanics' in modern 'biomechanics'. *Scholastic coach 53(7), Feb 1984, 46;49.*
LEVEL: B LANG: Eng SIRC ARTICLE NO: 092688

Ariel, G. Biomechanics and athletic achievement. *Scholastic coach (New York) 53(9), Apr 1984, 70-72;74-75.*
LEVEL: B LANG: Eng SIRC ARTICLE NO: 094190

Ekholm, J. Svensson, O. Arborelius, U.P. Nemeth, G. Ankle joint load and leg muscle activity during lifting. (Refs: 54)*Foot & ankle (Baltimore) 4(6), May/Jun 1984, 292-300.*
ABST: The authors tested healthy subjects lifting a 12.8 kg box from floor to table level with bent and straight knees. The bent knee lift was also performed with the load between the knees. The load on the talocrucal joint during all three lifts was compared and analyzed biomechanically and ergonomically. The lowest loading stress was obtained from lifting the burden between bent knees and close to the pelvis.
LEVEL: A LANG: Eng SIRC ARTICLE NO: 097421

Hochmuth, G. Biomechanics of athletic movement. Berlin: Sportverlag Berlin, 1984. 171 p. : ill.
NOTES: Bibliography: p. 154
LEVEL: A LANG: Eng QP302 18665

Jeannerod, M. The timing of natural prehension movements. (Refs: 28)*Journal of motor behavior (Washington) 16(3), Sept 1984 235-254.*
ABST: Prehension movements were studied by film in 7 adult subjects. Transportation of the hand to the target-object location had features very similar to any aiming arm movement, that is, it involved a fast-velocity initial phase and a low-velocity final phase. The low-velocity phase consistently began after about 75 per cent of movement time had elapsed. This ratio was maintained for different movement amplitudes. Formation of the finger grip occurred during hand transportation. The onset of the closure phase was highly correlated to the beginning of the low velocity phase of transportation. This pattern for both transportation and finger grip formation was maintained in conditions whether visual feedback from the moving limb was present or not.
LEVEL: A LANG: Eng SIRC ARTICLE NO: 103828

Preiss, R. The theory of models describing the two-dimensional movements of airborne systems consisting of N rigid segments. (Refs: 4)*Journal of human movement studies (London) 10(4), 1984, 231-238.*
ABST: It was shown, that the orientation of a planar airborne system consisting of an arbitrary number of rigid segments can be found by solving three equations, provided that the initial values of the motion and the time histories of all the joint angles through the motion are known. The three required equations are: 1. vertical motion of the center of gravity of the system; 2. horizontal motion of the center of gravity of the system; 3. angular velocity

of the orientation angle of an arbitrary selected segment.
LEVEL: A LANG: Eng SIRC ARTICLE NO: 103830

Saziorski, W.M. Aruin, A.S. Selujanow, W.N. Biomechanik des menschlichen Bewegungsapparates. Berlin: Sportverlag, 1984. 144 p. : ill.
NOTES: Translated from Russian. Bibliography: p. 141-144.
LEVEL: A LANG: Ger QP302 18149

Shapiro, R. Marett, J.R. Proceedings: Second National Symposium on Teaching Kinesiology and Biomechanics in Sports, Colorado Springs, Colorado, January 12-14, 1984. Dekalb, Ill.: AAHPERD, 1984. x, 274 p.
CONF: National Symposium on Teaching Kinesiology and Biomechanics in Sports (2nd : 1984 : Colorado Springs).
NOTES: Includes bibliographies.
LEVEL: A LANG: Eng QP302 18223

Terauds, J. Barthels, K. Kreighbaum, E. Mann, R. Crakes, J. Sports biomechanics. Proceedings of ISBS 1984. Del Mar, Calif.: Research Center for Sports, c1984. x, 317 p.
CONF: International Symposium of Biomechanics in Sports (2nd : 1984 : Colorado Springs, Colo).
NOTES: Includes bibliographies.
LEVEL: A LANG: Eng QP302 20774

EQUIPMENT EVALUATION

Frederick, E.C. Sport shoes and playing surfaces: biomechanical properties. Champaign, Ill.: Human Kinetics Publishers, c1984. x, 198 p. : ill.
LEVEL: A LANG: Eng ISBN: 0-931250-51-X LC CARD: 83-083166 QP302 17870

MacLellan, G.E. Skeletal heel strike transients, measurement, implications, and modification by footwear. (Refs: 25)
NOTES: In, Frederick, E.C. (ed.), Sport shoes and playing surfaces: biomechanical properties, Champaign, Ill., Human Kinetics Publishers, c1984, p. 76-86.
LEVEL: A LANG: Eng QP302 17870

Nigg, B.M. Denoth, J. Kerr, B. Luethi, S. Smith, D. Stacoff, A. Load sport shoes and playing surfaces. (Refs: 12)
NOTES: In, Frederick, E.C. (ed.), Sport shoes and playing surfaces: biomechanical properties, Champaign, Ill., Human Kinetics Publishers, c1984, p. 1-23.
LEVEL: A LANG: Eng QP302 17870

Njus, G.O. Liu, Y.K. Nye, T.A. The inertial and geometrical properties of helmets. (Refs: 5)*Medicine and science in sports and exercise (Indianapolis) 16(5), Oct 1984, 498-505.*
ABST: The center of gravity (CG) and the principal mass moments of inertia about the CG of Army aviator, American football, and bicycle helmets were experimentally determined by a variation of the classic differential weighing and torsional pendulum techniques. An electronic caliper, which measured length, was used with a computer algorithm to achieve 3D digitization. The results of the above measurements show that the weight of the helmet and the distances from the CG to the orthogonal coordinate axes intercepts with the outer shell surface were highly correlated with its principal mass moments of inertia. Our results indicate that the principal mass moments of inertia of helmets vary linearly with its mass but

nonlinearly with size and shape.
LEVEL: A LANG: Eng SIRC ARTICLE NO: 102407

Stockholm, A.J. Practical experiences with the biomechanics of projectiles and ball impacts.
CONF: National Symposium on Teaching Kinesiology and Biomechanics in Sports (2nd : 1984 : Colorado Springs).
NOTES: In, Shapiro, R. and Marett, J.R. (eds.), Proceedings: Second National Symposium on Teaching Kinesiology and Biomechanics in Sports, Colorado Springs, Colorado, January 12-14, Dekalb, Ill., AAHPERD, 1984, p. 191-194.
ABST: This paper details two laboratory exercises that require common physical education devices and equipment in the study of projectile behaviour and ball impacts.
LEVEL: I LANG: Eng SIRC ARTICLE NO: 100498

ERGONOMICS

Boudrifa, H. Davies, B.T. The effect of backrest inclination, lumbar support and thoracic support on the intra-abdominal pressure while lifting. *Ergonomics (London) 27(4), Apr 1984, 379-387.*
LEVEL: A LANG: Eng

Fleishman, E.A. Gebhardt, D.L. Hogan, J.C. The measurement of effort. *Ergonomics (London) 27(9), Sept 1984, 947-954.*
LEVEL: I LANG: Eng

Kumar, S. The physiological cost of three different methods of lifting in sagittal and lateral planes. *Ergonomics (London) 27(4), Apr 1984, 425-433.*
LEVEL: A LANG: Eng

Mairiaux, P. Davis, P.R. Stubbs, D.A. Baty, D. Relation between intra-abdominal pressure and lumbar moments when lifting weights in the erect posture. *Ergonomics (London) 27(8), Aug 1984, 883-894.*
LEVEL: A LANG: Eng

Reilly, T. Lees, A. Exercise and sports equipment: some ergonomics aspects. *Applied ergonomics (Surrey, Eng.) 15(4), 1984, 259-279.*
LEVEL: A LANG: Eng SIRC ARTICLE NO: 103915

Reilly, T. Ergonomics in sport: an overview. (Refs: 2)*Applied ergonomics (Surrey, Eng.) 15(4), 1984, 243-244.*
LEVEL: I LANG: Eng SIRC ARTICLE NO: 103831

Reilly, T. Ergonomics in sport: an overview. *Applied ergonomics (Surrey, Eng.) 15(4), 1984, 243-244.*
ABST: The performanc related effects of shoe design on traction and on the economy of locomotion are reviewed in this paper. Traction measurements in various types of running shoes and on various surfaces appear adequate for all but running shoes and on various surfaces appear adequate for all but running on wet asphalt roads. Effects on the economy of locomotion as small as 1 percent can be determined using conventional oxygen uptake measurements. The effect of carrying extra weight on the foot during running has been measured at 1 percent per 100 g per foot.
LEVEL: I LANG: Eng

FACILITIES

Stucke, H. Baudzus, W. Baumann, W. On friction characteristics of playing surfaces. (Refs: 13)
NOTES: In, Frederick, E.C. (ed.), Sport shoes and playing surfaces: biomechanical properties, Champaign, Ill., Human Kinetics Publishers, c1984,

p. 87-97.
LEVEL: A LANG: Eng QP302 17870

GAIT

Boissonnault, W. Donatelli, R. The influence of hallux extension on the foot during ambulation. (Refs: 13)*Journal of orthopaedic and sports physical therapy (Baltimore, Md.) 5(5), Mar/Apr 1984, 240-242.*
ABST: This review article discusses the functional anatomy of the components of the foot/ankle complex. During normal ambulation, relative hallux extension of between 60-65 degrees is necessary. For this reason, normal hallux extension is an important goal when treating patients with foot dysfunction.
LEVEL: I LANG: Eng SIRC ARTICLE NO: 094192

Cappozzo, A. Gait analysis methodology. *Human movement science (Netherlands) 3(1/2), 1984, 27-50.*
ABST: This paper report a discussion on the objectives of gait analysis and on the experimental and analytical methods used in this context. In particular, the use of an effective method of description of joint kinematics and kinetics i.e. joint function, as applied to the lower limb joints during normal walking is reported. A methodological hypothesis for the evaluation of gait, as an integrated phenomenon is presented and supported by experimental data concerning normal and pathological walking and sportive gaits.
LEVEL: A LANG: Eng

Carey, P.B. Wolf, S.L. Binder-Macleod, S.A. Bain, R.L. Assessing the reliability of measurements from the Krusen limb load monitor to analyze temporal and loading characteristics of normal gait. (Refs: 11)*Physical therapy (Alexandria, Va.) 64(2), Feb 1984, 199-203.*
ABST: The purpose of this study was to assess the Krusen limb load monitor (LLM) as a clinical gait assessment tool by determining the interrater and intrarater reliability of four physical therapists' computations of eleven step and gait variables from data on ten healthy subjects. The LLM consists of a pressure transducer that may be worn within a shoe and a control box worn on the patient's waist. Intraclass correlation coefficients for the five step components (stance time, time up, time to second peak, and force at the first and second peaks) and three of the gait measures (ambulation time, velocity, and cadence) showed high measurement reliability. It was thus concluded that the LLM provides a rapid, easily operated, objective, qualitative impression of these variables in healthy subjects.
LEVEL: A LANG: Eng SIRC ARTICLE NO: 094193

Cerny, K. Pathomechanics of stance: clinical concepts for analysis. (Refs: 29)*Physical therapy (Alexandria, Va.) 64(12), De 1984, 1851-1859.*
LEVEL: A LANG: Eng SIRC ARTICLE NO: 102313

Corcoran, P.J. Peszczynski, M. Gait and gait retraining. (Refs: 66)
NOTES: In, Basmajian, J.V. (ed.), Therapeutic exercise, 4th ed., Baltimore, Md., Williams & Wilkins, c1984, p. 285-302.
LEVEL: A LANG: Eng RM719 17505

Cromwell-Stabrawa, R. A quantitative analysis of loads imposed on the spine during normal level walking at slow and fast speeds. Eugene, Ore.: Microform Publications, University of Oregon, 1984. 1 microfiche : negative, ill. ; 11 x 15 cm.

NOTES: Thesis (M.S.) - University of Illinois at Chicago, 1983; (vii, 52 leaves); includes bibliography.
LEVEL: A LANG: Eng UO84 263

Eke-Okoro, S.T. Sandlund, B. The effects of load, shoes, sex and direction on the gait characteristics of street pedestrians (Refs: 10)*Journal of human movement studies (Edinburgh, Eng.) 10(2), 1984, 107-114.*
ABST: This study investigated the relations between velocity, stride length and stride frequency with respect to sex, heel height (shoe type), load and direction of gait. Five hundred twenty seven pedestrians were observed. Male and female subjects walked at the same velocity. Velocity was not altered by heel height. Load decreased the velocity of travel.
LEVEL: A LANG: Eng SIRC ARTICLE NO: 095714

Gollhofer, A. Schmidtbleicher, D. Dietz, V. Regulation of muscle stiffness in human locomotion. (Refs: 28)*International journal of sports medicine 5(1), Feb 1984, 19-22.*
ABST: Force-time curves, angular displacements, film analyses, innervation patterns and Achilles tendon tensions were taken from 10 subjects as they walked or ran at various speeds. The main finding of this study was the temporal coincidence of maximal dorsiflexion, maximal Achilles tendon tension, transition from amortization to acceleration phase, and projection of the center of gravity to the supporting leg. During running, the gastrocnemius was slightly preactivated before impact with the ground. The authors suggest two functions for the preactivation of the triceps surae muscle: 1) to buffer high initial force peaks and 2) to trigger an adequate segmental reflex activity for producing a corresponding muscle stiffness to support and push off the body.
LEVEL: A LANG: Eng SIRC ARTICLE NO: 093092

Gronley, J.K. Perry, J. Gait analysis techniques. (Refs: 18)*Physical therapy (Alexandria, Va.) 64(12), Dec 1984, 1831-1838.*
LEVEL: A LANG: Eng SIRC ARTICLE NO: 102318

Hoberman, M. Basmajian, J.V. Crutch and cane exercises and use. (Refs: 14)
NOTES: In, Basmajian, J.V. (ed.), Therapeutic exercise, 4th ed., Baltimore, Md., Williams & Wilkins, c1984, p. 267-284.
LEVEL: A LANG: Eng RM719 17505

Kinoshita, H. Effects of different loads and carrying systems on selected biomechanical parameters describing walking gait. Eugene, Ore.: Microform Publications, University of Oregon, 1984. 2 microfiches : negative, ill. ; 11 x 15 cm.
NOTES: Thesis (Ph.D.) - University of Oregon, 1982; (xi, 153 leaves); vita; includes bibliography.
LEVEL: A LANG: Eng UO84 39-40

Laughman, R.K. Askew, L.J. Bleimeyer, R.R. Chao, E.Y. Objective clinical evaluation of function: gait analysis. (Refs: 11) *Physical therapy (Alexandria, Va.) 64(12), Dec 1984, 1839-1845.*
LEVEL: A LANG: Eng SIRC ARTICLE NO: 102321

Nigg, B.M. Luethi, S. Stacoff, A. Segesser, B. Biomechanical effects of pain and sportshoe corrections. (Refs: 11)*Australia journal of science & medicine in sport (Kingston, Aust.) 16(1), Jun 1984, 10-16.*
ABST: The goal of this study was to understand the biomechanical effects of sport shoes and sport shoe corrections. It was considered especially important to determine the differences in the

BIOMECHANICS (continued)

characteristics of the pattern of human gait in walking and running for subjects with and without pain. 84 subjects were used in the study which included a medical examination, cinematography and force plate measurements. The results are subdivided into two groups, the effects of pain and the effects of shoes and shoe corrections.
LEVEL: A LANG: Eng SIRC ARTICLE NO: 103829

Vilensky, J.A. Gehlsen, G. Temporal gait parameters in humans and quadrupeds: how do they change with speed? (Refs: 11) *Journal of human movement studies (Edinburgh, Eng.) 10, 1984, 175-188.*
ABST: Temporal gait parameters for 10 human, 6 cat and 1 monkey subject are presented and compared. All three species exhibited good negative relationships between total stride and absolute and relative stance durations, and speed. For relative swing duration all the subjects exhibited good positive relationships with speed. In contrast to the noted parameters, absolute swing duration varied in its relationships with speed among the human subjects, increasing in four of them and showing no relationship in the others. In our quadrupedal subjects, 2 cats showed good negative relationships between absolute swing duration and speed, while no relationship was apparent for the remaining animals. These findings indicate that despite human bipedality the relationship between temporal gait parameters and speed in humans is similar to that found in quadrupeds (except for absolute swing).
LEVEL: A LANG: Eng SIRC ARTICLE NO: 108762

KINEMATICS

Calhoun, R. Klatt, L.A. Koetke, D. Computer projectile project: moving object through viscous medium.
CONF: National Symposium on Teaching Kinesiology and Biomechanics in Sports (2nd : 1984 : Colorado Springs).
NOTES: In, Shapiro, R. and Marett, J.R. (eds.), Proceedings: Second National Symposium on Teaching Kinesiology and Biomechanics in Sports, Colorado Springs, Colorado, January 12-14, Dekalb, Ill., AAHPERD, 1984, p. 201-203.
LEVEL: I LANG: Eng SIRC ARTICLE NO: 100464

Rodrigue, D. Gagnon, M. Validation of Weinbach's and Hanavan's models for computation of physical properties of the forearm. (Refs: 15)*Research quarterly for exercise & sport (Reston, Va.) 55(3), Sept 1984, 272-277.*
ABST: The purpose of the present study was to validate the Weinbach and the Hanavan models for the determinations of the forearm volume and center of mass. The study was conducted using 20 forearms from six male and four female cadavers. Results from the present investigation indicate that Weinbach's model is more accurate than Hanavan's model. The Hanavan model should be used only in the cases where the shape of the forearm closely resembles that of a truncated cone.
LEVEL: A LANG: Eng SIRC ARTICLE NO: 102324

KINETICS

Farrell, M. Richards, J.G. Use of microcomputers in a laboratory environment for teaching kinetic parameters of gait and skill activities.
CONF: National Symposium on Teaching Kinesiology and Biomechanics in Sports (2nd : 1984 : Colorado Springs).

NOTES: In, Shapiro, R. and Marett, J.R. (eds.), Proceedings: Second National Symposium on Teaching Kinesiology and Biomechanics in Sports, Colorado Springs, Colorado, January 12-14, Dekalb, Ill., AAHPERD, 1984, p. 221-226.
LEVEL: I LANG: Eng SIRC ARTICLE NO: 100471

Hamill, J. Bates, B.T. Knutzen, K.M. Ground reaction force symmetry during walking and running. (Refs: 15)*Research quarterl for exercise & sport (Reston, Va.) 55(3), Sept 1984, 289-293.*
LEVEL: I LANG: Eng SIRC ARTICLE NO: 102320

LOCOMOTION

Dickinson, J. Bawa, P. Corlett, J.T. Properties of locomotor generators in man. (Refs: 13)*Canadian journal of applied sport sciences/Journal canadien des sciences appliquees au sport (Windsor, Ont.) 9(2), Jun 1984, 102-106.*
ABST: This study compared maximal stepping rate during standing or sitting, with one leg or two legs and with auditory cue-paced or self-paced action. The sitting condition produced a higher maximum stepping rate than the standing condition. The authors interpret this as a gravitational load effect or mechanical advantage effect on the locomotion generators. There were no significant differences in the other conditions. Training did not alter the responses of the locomotor generators.
LEVEL: A LANG: Eng SIRC ARTICLE NO: 095713

Klinger, A.K. Adrian, M.J. Application of biomechanical principles to movement patterns of pregnant women. (Refs: 2)
CONF: National Symposium on Teaching Kinesiology and Biomechanics in Sports (2nd : 1984 : Colorado Springs).
NOTES: In, Shapiro, R. and Marett, J.R. (eds.), Proceedings: Second National Symposium on Teaching Kinesiology and Biomechanics in Sports, Colorado Springs, Colorado, January 12-14, Dekalb, Ill., AAHPERD, 1984, p. 211-213.
LEVEL: I LANG: Eng SIRC ARTICLE NO: 100484

Raley, B.F. The effects of shoe type on foot functioning and contact pressures during walking performances. Eugene, Ore.: Microform Publications, University of Oregon, 1984. 1 microfiche : negative, ill. ; 11 x 15 cm.
NOTES: Thesis (M.S.) - North Texas State University, 1982; (vi, 49 leaves); includes bibliography.
LEVEL: A LANG: Eng UO84 206

RESEARCH

Legwold, G. Can biomechanics produce Olympic medals? *Physician and sportsmedicine 12(1), Jan 1984, 187-188;191.*
LEVEL: I LANG: Eng SIRC ARTICLE NO: 091282

Middleton, C. The secrets of success: Chris Middleton meets a team of sports scientists who have the knowledge to turn the mediocre into medal-winners. *Sport and leisure (London) 25(5), Nov/Dec 1984, 32-33.*
LEVEL: B LANG: Eng SIRC ARTICLE NO: 108964

SKILLS ANALYSIS

Brown, E.W. Kinesiological analysis of motor skills via visual evaluation techniques. (Refs: 4)
CONF: National Symposium on Teaching Kinesiology and Biomechanics in Sports (2nd : 1984 : Colorado Springs).

NOTES: In, Shapiro, R. and Marett, J.R. (eds.), Proceedings: Second National Symposium on Teaching Kinesiology and Biomechanics in Sports, Colorado Springs, Colorado, January 12-14, Dekalb, Ill., AAHPERD, 1984, p. 95-96.
LEVEL: I LANG: Eng SIRC ARTICLE NO: 100462

Daniels, D.B. Basic movements and modeling: an approach to teaching skill analysis in the undergraduate biomechanics course. (Refs: 5)
CONF: National Symposium on Teaching Kinesiology and Biomechanics in Sports (2nd : 1984 : Colorado Springs).
NOTES: In, Shapiro, R. and Marett, J.R. (eds.), Proceedings: Second National Symposium on Teaching Kinesiology and Biomechanics in Sports, Colorado Springs, Colorado, January 12-14, Dekalb, Ill., AAHPERD, 1984, p. 243-246.
LEVEL: I LANG: Eng SIRC ARTICLE NO: 100467

Hay, J.G. The development of deterministic models for qualitative analysis.
CONF: National Symposium on Teaching Kinesiolog and Biomechanics in Sports (2nd : 1984 : Colorado Springs).
NOTES: In, Shapiro, R. and Marett, J.R. (eds.), Proceedings: Second National Symposium on Teaching Kinesiology and Biomechanics in Sports, Colorado Springs, Colorado, January 12-14, Dekalb, Ill., AAHPERD, 1984, p. 71-83.
ABST: This paper details current relationships that have been found to be useful in the development of deterministic models for the qualitative analysis of human movements. It is an attempt of present a catalog of such relationships.
LEVEL: A LANG: Eng SIRC ARTICLE NO: 100475

Hoshizaki, T.B. The application of models to understanding the biomechanical aspects of performance. (Refs: 12)
CONF: National Symposium on Teaching Kinesiology and Biomechanics in Sports (2nd : 1984 : Colorado Springs).
NOTES: In, Shapiro, R. and Marett, J.R. (eds.), Proceedings: Second National Symposium on Teaching Kinesiology and Biomechanics in Sports, Colorado Springs, Colorado, January 12-14, Dekalb, Ill., AAHPERD, 1984, p. 85-93.
ABST: This paper presents two models which are designed to identify biomechanical elements and illustrate their interaction. These are the Muscular Force-Control Model and the Model of the Biomechanical Factors which Influence Motor Skill Acquisition.
LEVEL: A LANG: Eng SIRC ARTICLE NO: 100477

Kindig, L.E. Windell, E.J. Analysis of filmed sports skills.
CONF: National Symposium on Teaching Kinesiology and Biomechanics in Sports (2nd : 1984 : Colorado Springs).
NOTES: In, Shapiro, R. and Marett, J.R. (eds.), Proceedings: Second National Symposium on Teaching Kinesiology and Biomechanics in Sports, Colorado Springs, Colorado, January 12-14, Dekalb, Ill., AAHPERD, 1984, p. 231-232.
LEVEL: I LANG: Eng SIRC ARTICLE NO: 100482

Stoner, L.J. Is the performer skilled or unskilled?
CONF: National Symposium on Teaching Kinesiology and Biomechanics in Sports (2nd : 1984 : Colorado Springs).
NOTES: In, Shapiro, R. and Marett, J.R. (eds.), Proceedings: Second National Symposium on Teaching Kinesiology and Biomechanics in Sports, Colorado Springs, Colorado, January 12-14,

Dekalb, Ill., AAHPERD, 1984, p. 233-234.
LEVEL: I LANG: Eng SIRC ARTICLE NO: 100499

Straub, W.F. The oral report: kinematic and kinetic analyses of a selected motor skill.
CONF: National Symposium on Teachin Kinesiology and Biomechanics in Sports (2nd : 1984 : Colorado Springs).
NOTES: In, Shapiro, R. and Marett, J.R. (eds.), Proceedings: Second National Symposium on Teaching Kinesiology and Biomechanics in Sports, Colorado Springs, Colorado, January 12-14, Dekalb, Ill., AAHPERD, 1984, p. 247-257.
LEVEL: I LANG: Eng SIRC ARTICLE NO: 100771

Tolotchek, V.A. (Structure and form of the individual style in sporting activities.) (Refs: 22)*Voprosy psikhologii (Moscow) 5, 1984, 137-141.*
LEVEL: I LANG: Rus

TEACHING

Coleman, J. Adrian, M.J. Yamamoto, H. The teaching of the mechanics of jump landing.
CONF: National Symposium on Teaching Kinesiology and Biomechanics in Sports (2nd : 1984 : Colorado Springs).
NOTES: In, Shapiro, R. and Marett, J.R. (eds.), Proceedings: Second National Symposium on Teaching Kinesiology and Biomechanics in Sports, Colorado Springs, Colorado, January 12-14, Dekalb, Ill., AAHPERD, 1984, p. 195-198.
LEVEL: I LANG: Eng SIRC ARTICLE NO: 100465

Davis, K. Biomaximechanics or biominimechanics - a pedagogical dilemma. (Refs: 6)*Journal of human movement studies (Edinburgh, Eng.) 10(2), 1984, 115-122.*
ABST: This paper provides guidelines for the planning and implementation of courses in sport biomechanics at the undergraduate level. Biominimechanics describes a teaching approach which emphasizes application of a bare minimum of theory to problems encountered in practise. Biomaximechanics describes a teaching approach which emphasizes mathematics and physical sciences to better prepare students for advanced study. The author favours a biominimechanics approach to undergraduate biomechanics.
LEVEL: A LANG: Eng SIRC ARTICLE NO: 095710

Francis, P.R. Interactive computer programs for teaching and research in biomechanics. (Refs: 4)
CONF: National Symposium on Teaching Kinesiology and Biomechanics in Sports (2nd : 1984 : Colorado Springs).
NOTES: In, Shapiro, R. and Marett, J.R. (eds.), Proceedings: Second National Symposium on Teaching Kinesiology and Biomechanics in Sports, Colorado Springs, Colorado, January 12-14, Dekalb, Ill., AAHPERD, 1984, p. 109-115.
LEVEL: I LANG: Eng SIRC ARTICLE NO: 100472

Hoffman, S.J. The contributions of biomechanics to clinical competence: a view from the gymnasium. (Refs: 2)
CONF: National Symposium on Teaching Kinesiology and Biomechanics in Sports (2nd : 1984 : Colorado Springs).
NOTES: In, Shapiro, R. and Marett, J.R. (eds.), Proceedings: Second National Symposium on Teaching Kinesiology and Biomechanics in Sports, Colorado Springs, Colorado, January 12-14, Dekalb, Ill., AAHPERD, 1984, p. 67-70.
LEVEL: I LANG: Eng SIRC ARTICLE NO: 100476

Knapp, R.F. Garrett, G.E. Interactive computer assisted instruction for undergraduate biomechanics. (Refs: 11)
CONF: Nationa Symposium on Teaching Kinesiology and Biomechanics in Sports (2nd : 1984 : Colorado Springs).
NOTES: In, Shapiro, R. and Marett, J.R. (eds.), Proceedings: Second National Symposium on Teaching Kinesiology and Biomechanics in Sports, Colorado Springs, Colorado, January 12-14, Dekalb, Ill., AAHPERD, 1984, p. 123-127.
LEVEL: I LANG: Eng SIRC ARTICLE NO: 100485

Kreighbaum, E. Dillon, C. Instructional design in the teaching of kinesiology/biomechanics.
CONF: National Symposium on Teaching Kinesiology and Biomechanics in Sports (2nd : 1984 : Colorado Springs).
NOTES: In, Shapiro, R. and Marett, J.R. (eds.), Proceedings: Second National Symposium on Teaching Kinesiology and Biomechanics in Sports, Colorado Springs, Colorado, January 12-14, Dekalb, Ill., AAHPERD, 1984, p. 185-189.
ABST: Instructional design is the solving of instructional problems by the application of learning research to the development of instructional system components. The learning environment, the capabilities of available resources, characteristics of the learner, and the types of learning required must all be analyzed in order to apply instructional design information.
LEVEL: A LANG: Eng SIRC ARTICLE NO: 100486

Liu, Z.C. Fortney, V.L. Use of an Apple II computer in undergraduate sport biomechanics laboratory experiments.
CONF: National Symposium on Teaching Kinesiology and Biomechanics in Sports (2nd : 1984 : Colorado Springs).
NOTES: In, Shapiro, R. and Marett, J.R. (eds.), Proceedings: Second National Symposium on Teaching Kinesiology and Biomechanics in Sports, Colorado Springs, Colorado, January 12-14, Dekalb, Ill., AAHPERD, 1984, p. 141-145.
ABST: This study evaluated the utilization of the computer by undergraduates performing 2 different experiments. It was found to be an effective teaching tool.
LEVEL: A LANG: Eng SIRC ARTICLE NO: 100487

Miller, D.I. Le, T. Scheirman, G.L. Teaching data smoothing and differentiation using microcomputers. (Refs: 6)
CONF: National Symposium on Teaching Kinesiology and Biomechanics in Sports (2nd : 1984 : Colorado Springs).
NOTES: In, Shapiro, R. and Marett, J.R. (eds.), Proceedings: Second National Symposium on Teaching Kinesiology and Biomechanics in Sports, Colorado Springs, Colorado, January 12-14, Dekalb, Ill., AAHPERD, 1984, p. 137-140.
LEVEL: I LANG: Eng SIRC ARTICLE NO: 100490

Morgan, W.R. Garrett, G.E. A developmental biomechanics instructional approach - learning basic track & field skills (ages 5-12). (Refs: 17)
CONF: National Symposium on Teaching Kinesiology and Biomechanics in Sports (2nd : 1984 : Colorado Springs).
NOTES: In, Shapiro, R. and Marett, J.R. (eds.), Proceedings: Second National Symposium on Teaching Kinesiology and Biomechanics in Sports, Colorado Springs, Colorado, January 12-14, Dekalb, Ill., AAHPERD, 1984, p. 97-104.
LEVEL: I LANG: Eng SIRC ARTICLE NO: 100491

Nelson, R.C. Teaching kinesiology and sport biomechanics: an international perspective.
CONF: National Symposium on Teachin Kinesiology and Biomechanics in Sports (2nd : 1984 : Colorado Springs).
NOTES: In, Shapiro, R. and Marett, J.R. (eds.), Proceedings: Second National Symposium on Teaching Kinesiology and Biomechanics in Sports, Colorado Springs, Colorado, January 12-14, Dekalb, Ill., AAHPERD, 1984, p. 3-5.
LEVEL: I LANG: Eng SIRC ARTICLE NO: 100492

Richards, J. Wilkerson, J. The use of microcomputers for facilitating the teaching of kinesiology through film analysis. (Refs: 3)
CONF: National Symposium on Teaching Kinesiology and Biomechanics in Sports (2nd : 1984 : Colorado Springs).
NOTES: In, Shapiro, R. and Marett, J.R. (eds.), Proceedings: Second National Symposium on Teaching Kinesiology and Biomechanics in Sports, Colorado Springs, Colorado, January 12-14, Dekalb, Ill., AAHPERD, 1984, p. 147-150.
ABST: This paper illustrates the use of a microcomputer based film analysis system in teaching the kinematic aspects of biomechanical analyses. An inexpensive system for digitizing and data reduction using a microcomputer is described.
LEVEL: I LANG: Eng SIRC ARTICLE NO: 100495

Stoner, L.J. Injury is basically a biomechanical problem.
CONF: National Symposium on Teaching Kinesiology and Biomechanics in Sports (2nd : 1984 : Colorado Springs).
NOTES: In, Shapiro, R. and Marett, J.R. (eds.), Proceedings: Second National Symposium on Teaching Kinesiology and Biomechanics in Sports, Colorado Springs, Colorado, January 12-14, Dekalb, Ill., AAHPERD, 1984, p. 47-48.
LEVEL: I LANG: Eng SIRC ARTICLE NO: 100700

TECHNIQUE

Atha, J. Current techniques for measuring motion. *Applied ergonomics (Surrey, Eng.) 15(4), 1984, 245-257.*
ABST: In measuring motion in sport, cinematography has played a dominant role. The method has obvious advantages; but analysing film is a slow, pedestrian task, and subject to human error. Where an investigator is experienced, he can adopt automatic and specific techniques of acquiring information. Such methods include alternative photographic techniques, but also invovle the specialised transducers and automatic analysers that are not burgeoning in the field. Some of these techniques are discussed.
LEVEL: A LANG: Eng

Elliott, B. Biomechanics and teaching/coaching: the state of the art. (Refs: 13)*Sports coach (Wembley, Aust.) 8(1), 1984, 45-47;50.*
LEVEL: I LANG: Eng SIRC ARTICLE NO: 095715

Kaylor, K.K. Application of high speed videography to kinesiology and biomechanics.
CONF: National Symposium on Teaching Kinesiology and Biomechanics in Sports (2nd : 1984 : Colorado Springs).
NOTES: In, Shapiro, R. and Marett, J.R. (eds.), Proceedings: Second National Symposium on Teaching Kinesiology and Biomechanics in Sports, Colorado Springs, Colorado, January 12-14, Dekalb, Ill., AAHPERD, 1984, p. 51-52.
LEVEL: I LANG: Eng SIRC ARTICLE NO: 100479

BIOMECHANICS (continued)

McGrain, P. Videography: an inexpensive alternative to film analysis in kinesiology and biomechanics. (Refs: 14)
CONF: National Symposium on Teaching Kinesiology and Biomechanics in Sports (2nd : 1984 : Colorado Springs).
NOTES: In, Shapiro, R. and Marett, J.R. (eds.), Proceedings: Second National Symposium on Teaching Kinesiology and Biomechanics in Sports, Colorado Springs, Colorado, January 12-14, Dekalb, Ill., AAHPERD, 1984, p. 59-63.
LEVEL: I LANG: Eng SIRC ARTICLE NO: 100489

Yack, H.J. Techniques for clinical assessment of human movement. (Refs: 78)*Physical therapy (Alexandria, Va.) 64(12), Dec 1984, 1821-1830.*
LEVEL: A LANG: Eng SIRC ARTICLE NO: 102326

Zollman, D. Fuller, R.G. Interactive videodiscs: new technology for the analysis of human motion. (Refs: 13)
CONF: National Symposium on Teaching Kinesiology and Biomechanics in Sports (2nd : 1984 : Colorado Springs).
NOTES: In, Shapiro, R. and Marett, J.R. (eds.), Proceedings: Second National Symposium on Teaching Kinesiology and Biomechanics in Sports, Colorado Springs, Colorado, January 12-14, Dekalb, Ill., AAHPERD, 1984, p. 53-56.
LEVEL: I LANG: Eng SIRC ARTICLE NO: 100501

TECHNIQUE - CINEMATOGRAPHY

Elliot, B. Video systems as a biomechanical resource tool. *Sports coach (Wembley, W. Aust.) 8(2), Oct 1984, 20.*
LEVEL: B LANG: Eng SIRC ARTICLE NO: 103824

Mason, B.R. The use of still photography in biomechanical analysis. *Sports coach (Wembley, Aust.) 8(1), 1984, 48-50.*
LEVEL: I LANG: Eng SIRC ARTICLE NO: 095716

Phillips, S.J. Kelly, D.L. Prassas, S.G. Accuracy of a perspective control lens. (Refs: 2)*Research quarterly for exercise & sport (Reston, Va.) 55(2), Jun 1984, 197-200.*
ABST: This study assessed the accuracy of a perspective control (PC) lens prior to its adoption for the quantitative study of human motion. Specifically, the Nikon 35 mm PC)Nikkor lens was tested. It was tested at distances of 6 and 10m using a grid target of known dimensions. This lens gives rise to very little error. It is therefore suitable for the quantitative study of human motion.
LEVEL: A LANG: Eng SIRC ARTICLE NO: 095718

Rasmussen, S.A. Goslow, G.E. Hannon, P.R. Mirrored three-view cinematography in small animal locomotion studies. (Refs: 13) *Research quarterly for exercise & sport (Reston, Va.) 55(2), Jun 1984, 201-205.*
ABST: This paper presents a technique which allows the recording and analysis of an extended number of kinematic variables. A validating model to establish the accuracy of the measurements is included. In this paper the mirrored cinematographic technique was used to study cat locomotion in three dimensions.
LEVEL: A LANG: Eng SIRC ARTICLE NO: 095720

TECHNIQUE - COMPUTER ANALYSIS

Dillman, C.J. High-tech performance: the computer can make you a better athlete. *Bicycling (Emmaus, Pa.) 25(8), Sept/Oct 1984, 46-47;142.*
LEVEL: B LANG: Eng SIRC ARTICLE NO: 098881

Stevenson, J.M. A computer system for the student and the professor.
CONF: National Symposium on Teaching Kinesiology and Biomechanics in Sports (2nd : 1984 : Colorado Springs).
NOTES: In, Shapiro, R. and Marett, J.R. (eds.), Proceedings: Second National Symposium on Teaching Kinesiology and Biomechanics in Sports, Colorado Springs, Colorado, January 12-14, Dekalb, Ill., AAHPERD, 1984, p. 131-135.
ABST: Detailed discussion of the BIOM computer system used by undergraduate students studying biomechanics at Queen's University.
LEVEL: I LANG: Eng SIRC ARTICLE NO: 100497

TECHNIQUE - COMPUTER SIMULATION

Smith, G.A. Adrian, M.J. Enhancement of biomechanics instruction through computer simulation. (Refs: 5)
CONF: National Symposium on Teaching Kinesiology and Biomechanics in Sports (2nd : 1984 : Colorado Springs).
NOTES: In, Shapiro, R. and Marett, J.R. (eds.), Proceedings: Second National Symposium on Teaching Kinesiology and Biomechanics in Sports, Colorado Springs, Colorado, January 12-14, Dekalb, Ill., AAHPERD, 1984, p. 117-122.
LEVEL: A LANG: Eng SIRC ARTICLE NO: 100496

Vaughan, C.L. Computer simulation of human motion in sports biomechanics. (Refs: 101)*Exercise and sport sciences reviews (Lexington, Mass.) 12, 1984, 373-416.*
ABST: This review begins with definitions of computer simulation and computer modeling. Computer modeling refers to the formation of a computer program to describe a system while a computer simulation uses a valid computer model to carry out 'experiments' on the system which has been modeled. The advantages and disadvantages of computer simulation are discussed. Finally, contemporary papers in this area are reviewed.
LEVEL: A LANG: Eng SIRC ARTICLE NO: 095722

TECHNIQUE - ELECTROMYOGRAPHY

Grabiner, M.D. The role of electromyography in the biomechanics curriculum. (Refs: 8)
CONF: National Symposium on Teaching Kinesiology and Biomechanics in Sports (2nd : 1984 : Colorado Springs).
NOTES: In, Shapiro, R. and Marett, J.R. (eds.), Proceedings: Second National Symposium on Teaching Kinesiology and Biomechanics in Sports, Colorado Springs, Colorado, January 12-14, Dekalb, Ill., AAHPERD, 1984, p. 153-154.
LEVEL: I LANG: Eng SIRC ARTICLE NO: 100474

Hannaford, B. Lakminarayanan, V. Stark, L. Nam, M.-H. Electromyographic evidence of neurological controller signals with viscous load. (Refs: 51)*Journal of motor behavior (Washington) 16(3), Sept 1984, 255-274.*
ABST: Ensemble averaging after pre-editing of surface EMG potentials has enabled construction of underlying controller signals from sterotyped head movements. Carefully controlled, intended time-optimal movements by trained, actively participating human subjects have been found to yield repeatable, multipulse controller signals. Also, adaptive changes in these horizontal head movements in response to added viscous loads

showed further causal relationships between movement dynamics and EMG signals from left and right splenius muscles.
LEVEL: A LANG: Eng SIRC ARTICLE NO: 103826

Soderberg, G.L. Cook, T.M. Electromyography in biomechanics. (Refs: 46)*Physical therapy (Alexandria, Va.) 64(12), Dec 1984, 1813-1820.*
LEVEL: A LANG: Eng SIRC ARTICLE NO: 102325

TECHNIQUE - FORCE MEASUREMENT

Brooke, J.D. Chapman, A. Fischer, L. Rosenrot, P. A note on stability in force applied to control a repetitive task with the legs. (Refs: 13)*Journal of motor behavior (Washington) 16(3), Sept 1984, 313-319.*
ABST: The forces applied to pedals during cycling were collected every 40 ms from approximately 29,000 movement repetitions. Intra-cycle mean values of force and its variability were significantly correlated, supporting Schmidt's impulse variability theroy of within-movement activities of the legs. In addition, as mean forces approached peak values, coefficients of variation decreased. From averages taken minute by minute, intra-cycle forces were seen to rise or fall in concert, implying that the pattern as a whole constituted a significant neuro-muscular unit of control.
LEVEL: A LANG: Eng SIRC ARTICLE NO: 103823

Poty, P. Roattino, J.P. Chabanne, G. Le dynamometre isokinetique. Interets et limites. (Refs: 4)*Cinesiologie (Paris) 94, mars/avr 1984, 155-159.*
LEVEL: I LANG: Fr SIRC ARTICLE NO: 095719

TECHNIQUE - GONIOMETRY

Moore, M.L. Clinical assessment of joint motion. (Refs: 68)
NOTES: In, Basmajian, J.V. (ed.), Therapeutic exercise, 4th ed., Baltimore, Md., Williams & Wilkins, c1984, p. 192-224.
LEVEL: A LANG: Eng RM719 17505

BOARDSAILING

Aguera, A. Learn the ropes. *WindRider (Winter Park, Fla.) 3(4), Jul/Aug 1984, 31.*
LEVEL: B LANG: Eng SIRC ARTICLE NO: 106263

Bleakley, B. You oughta regatta: how to prepare for your first event. *Wind rider (Winter Park, Fla.) 3(1), Feb/Mar 1984, 52-55;76-77.*
LEVEL: B LANG: Eng SIRC ARTICLE NO: 100218

Boden, C. Chater, A. The windsurfing funboard handbook. Toronto: Thomas Allen & Son, c1984. 176 p. : ill.
LEVEL: B LANG: En ISBN: 0-919028-69-1 LC CARD: C84-098419-7 GV811.63.W56 17610

Broze, J. Flying high on a competitive edge. *Sail (Boston, Mass.) 15(7), Jul 1984, 50-57.*
LEVEL: B LANG: Eng SIRC ARTICLE NO: 103694

Evans, J. Antoine, M.P. La planche a voile: guide complet. Paris: Arthaud, 1984. 191 p. : ill.
NOTES: Traduit de l'anglais.
LEVEL: B LANG: Fr ISBN: 2-7003-0452-7

Farke, U. Moehle, V. Schroeder, D. This is boardsailing. London: Nautical Books, c1984. 120 p. : ill.

LEVEL: B LANG: Eng ISBN: 0-333-366948
GV811.63.W56 17599

Hall, M. Boardsailing and the sailor. *Yacht racing & cruising (Philadelphia, Pa.) 23(4), Apr 1984, 40.*
LEVEL: B LANG: Eng SIRC ARTICLE NO: 098843

Hall, M. You too can learn to boardsail. *Yacht racing & cruising (Philadelphia, Pa.) 23(5), May 1984, 30;32.*
NOTES: Excerpted from, Hall, M., Sports illustrated boardsailing.
LEVEL: B LANG: Eng SIRC ARTICLE NO: 101846

Kamphorst, T.J. Giljam, M. Windsurfing in Holland; results of a pilot study for the proposed international research project of the Research Committee on the Sociology of Leisure (RC. 13) of ISA. *Leisure newsletter (The Netherlands) 11(1), Summer 1984, 24-28.*
LEVEL: I LANG: Eng SIRC ARTICLE NO: 098844

Lelarge, P. Six questions sur la planche. *Marathon, la revue de la bonne forme (Montreal) 16, mai 1984, 8-11.*
LEVEL: B LANG: Fr SIRC ARTICLE NO: 108699

Simmer, K. So you want to be a rock star. (professional boardsailing) *Sail boarder (San Juan Capistrano, Calif.) 4(4), Jun 1984, 96-97.*
LEVEL: B LANG: Eng SIRC ARTICLE NO: 105134

ADMINISTRATION

Washburn, J. The flipside: how to run a regatta. *Wind Rider (Winter Park, Fla.) 3(5), Oct 1984, 30-36.*
LEVEL: B LANG: Eng SIRC ARTICLE NO: 098849

Wendell, K. Getting organized: start at the grass roots. *Wind Rider (Winter Park, Fla.) 3(5), Oct 1984, 58-59;61-62;64.*
LEVEL: B LANG: Eng SIRC ARTICLE NO: 098850

BIOGRAPHY AND AUTOBIOGRAPHY

Alan Cadiz. *Sail boarder (San Juan Capistrano, Calif.) 4(4), Jun 1984, 90-93.*
LEVEL: B LANG: Eng SIRC ARTICLE NO: 105110

Feeter, C. Peter Cabrinha: carving up the crossroads. *Wind surf (Dana Point, Calif.) 14(6), Oct 1984, 28;30;32;34;36;38;40.*
NOTES: Interview.
LEVEL: B LANG: Eng SIRC ARTICLE NO: 173609

Feeter, C. Anne Gardner Nelson: endless reach. *Wind surf (Dana Point, Calif.) 14(8), Dec 1984, 24;26;28;30;32;69.*
LEVEL: LANG: Eng SIRC ARTICLE NO: 173615

Fort, C. The Baron's strait act. (Arnaud de Rosnay) *Outside 9(4), May 1984, 58-60.*
LEVEL: B LANG: Eng SIRC ARTICLE NO: 094087

Fort, C. The baron's strait act. (Arnaud de Rosnay) *Outside (Chicago, Ill.) 9(4), May 1984, 58-60.*
LEVEL: B LANG: Eng SIR ARTICLE NO: 101841

Heenan, B. Up front with Karen Morch. *Windsport (Oakville, Ont.) 3(2), Apr 1984, 31;33-35.*
LEVEL: B LANG: Eng ARTICL NO: 100222

Kampion, D. Philip Pudenz: sailing professions. *Wind surf (Dana Point, Calif.) 14(7), Nov 1984, 26;28;30;32;71.*
LEVEL: B LANG: Eng SIRC ARTICLE NO: 173603

Pileggi, S. A candidate for chairman of the board. After losing 20 pounds, former heavyweight boardsailor Klaus Maran is almost thin as the air

that may propel him to a gold medal in one of the new Olympic sports. *Sports illustrated (Chicago, Ill.) 61(4), 18 Jul 1984, 444-446;450;454;456;459.*
NOTES: Special preview: the 1984 Olympics.
LEVEL: B LANG: Eng SIRC ARTICLE NO: 097095

Robberson, K. Interview: Nancy Johnson. On and off the road again. *Wind surf (Dana Point, Calif.) 14(2), Jun 1984, 28;30;32;34;36.*
LEVEL: B LANG: Eng SIRC ARTICLE NO: 097096

Up front with Stephan Van Den Berg. *Windsport (Oakville, Ont.) 3(3), May 1984, 26-29.*
LEVEL: B LANG: Eng SIRC ARTICLE NO: 101864

CHILDREN

Cathelineau, J. Target, C. La planche a voile: un jeu d'enfant. *EPS: Revue education physique et sport (Paris) 188, juil/aout 1984, 37-42.*
LEVEL: B LANG: Fr SIRC ARTICLE NO: 098839

CLOTHING

1984 preview: wetsuits: a boardsailor's second skin. *Windsport (Oakville, Ont.) 3(2), Apr 1984, 48-51.*
LEVEL: B LANG: Eng SIRC ARTICLE NO: 100217

Linskey, T. Drysuits and wetsuits: the new cold remedies. *Sail (Boston, Mass.) 15(5), May 1984, 8-13.*
LEVEL: B LANG: Eng SIRC ARTICLE NO: 100562

ENVIRONMENT

Powell, M. Instant weather: how to nowcast the current conditions for boardsailing. *Windrider (Winter Park, Fla.) 3(2), Apr/May 1984, 68-73.*
LEVEL: B LANG: Eng SIRC ARTICLE NO: 101858

Powell, M. Breezy business: nowcasting in Regatta competition. *Windrider (Winter Park, Fla.) 3(3), Jun 1984, 36-38;40;42;44.*
LEVEL: B LANG: Eng SIRC ARTICLE NO: 101859

EQUIPMENT

Alpha 'inspiration'. *Windsport (Oakville, Ont.) 3(5), Jul 1984, 44-45.*
LEVEL: B LANG: Eng SIRC ARTICLE NO: 102173

AMF Mares 'Prima Deluxe'. *Windsport (Oakville, Ont.) 3(5), Jul 1984, 47-48.*
LEVEL: B LANG: Eng SIRC ARTICLE NO: 102174

Angulo, E. Tech: wave board basics. *Wind surf (Dana Point, Calif.) 14(5), Sept 1984, 76-77.*
LEVEL: B LANG: Eng SIRC ARTICLE NO: 173584

Beaudry, M. Boom test. *Windsport (Oakville, Ont.) 3(6), Aug 1984, 28-31.*
LEVEL: B LANG: Eng SIRC ARTICLE NO: 101836

Beaudry, M. Mast test. *Windsport (Oakville, Ont.) 3(5), Jul 1984, 30-33.*
LEVEL: I LANG: Eng SIRC ARTICLE NO: 102171

Blanchard, M. Acheter une planche d'occasion... en connaisseur. *Velimag (Dorval, Que.) 1(4), juin 1984, 36-38.*
LEVEL: B LANG: Fr SIRC ARTICLE NO: 173435

Bleasby, J. Les voiles (1ere partie). Objectif: controle. *Becois volants (Montreal) 5(19), automne 1984, 17-19.*
NOTES: Extrait de, Velimag, mai 1984.
LEVEL: B LANG: Fr SIRC ARTICLE NO: 103692

Bleasby, J. Les voiles (2e partie). Les coupes verticales. *Velimag (Dorval, que.) 1(4), juin 1984, 18-22.*
LEVEL: B LANG: SIRC ARTICLE NO: 173432

Bleasby, J. Le profil de la voile. *Velimag (Dorval, Que.) 1(5), aout 1984, 12-14.*
LEVEL: B LANG: Fr SIRC ARTICLE NO: 1734

Board chart - all the specs. *Windsport (Oakville, Ont.) 3(1), Mar 1984, 44-45.*
LEVEL: B LANG: Eng SIRC ARTICLE NO: 108790

Board Windsport test: BIC 210S. *Windsport (Oakville, Ont.) 3(3), May 1984, 51-52.*
LEVEL: B LANG: Eng SIRC ARTICLE NO: 10183

Board Windsport test: Surf Partner P.A.L. *Windsport (Oakville, Ont.) 3(3), May 1984, 41-42.*
LEVEL: B LANG: Eng SIRC ARTICLE NO: 101838

Board Windsport test: Tiga Fun Cup. *Windsport (Oakville, Ont.) 3(3), May 1984, 44-45;47-48.*
LEVEL: B LANG: Eng SIRC ARTICLE NO: 101839

Boards. *Windsport (Oakville, Ont.) 3(1), Mar 1984, 36;38;40-42;69.*
LEVEL: B LANG: Eng SIRC ARTICLE NO: 108789

Buying a board: what you should know. *Windsport (Oakville, Ont.) 3(1), Mar 1984, 34.*
LEVEL: B LANG: Eng SIRC ARTICLE NO: 108787

Crowell, N.K. Sailboards: a landlubber's guide to boards, sails, masts, and booms. *Outside (Chicago) 9(6), Jul 1984, 85-87.*
LEVEL: B LANG: Eng SIRC ARTICLE NO: 105113

Design forum: big wave guns. The new breed of board. *Sail boarder (San Juan Capistrano, Calif.) 4(5), Summer 1984, 78-81;101.*
LEVEL: B LANG: Eng SIRC ARTICLE NO: 105114

England, H. Boom story. *Sail boarder international (Dana Point, Calif.) 4(3), May 1984, 50-57.*
LEVEL: B LANG: Eng SIRC ARTICLE NO: 095571

England, H. Boom straps and harness lines. *Sail boarder (San Juan Capistrano, Calif.) 4(5), Summer 1984, 84-85.*
LEVEL: B LANG: Eng SIRC ARTICLE NO: 105115

Enquete Voile libre. (planche a voile) *Voile libre (Montreal) 3(4), juil 1984, 15-19.*
LEVEL: B LANG: Fr SIRC ARTICLE NO: 105117

Entrevue: Craig Straetzel, 'shaper' de planches de coupe du monde. *Voile libre (Montreal) 3(4), juil 1984, 39;41-43.*
LEVEL: LANG: Fr SIRC ARTICLE NO: 105118

Equipment & accessories summary. *Windsport (Oakville, Ont.) 3(1), Mar 1984, 46-49.*
LEVEL: B LANG: Eng SIRC ARTICLE NO: 1087

F2 'lightning II fun line'. *Windsport (Oakville, Ont.) 3(4), Jun 1984, 40;42.*
LEVEL: B LANG: Eng SIRC ARTICLE NO: 103695

Farneti, M. Calculating board flotation. *Wind surf (Dana Point, Calif.) 14(5), Sept 1984, 40.*
LEVEL: B LANG: Eng SIRC ARTICLE NO: 173583

Gadd, M. Safety leashes. *Windsport (Oakville, Ont.) 3(6), Aug 1984, 19.*
LEVEL: B LANG: Eng SIRC ARTICLE NO: 101843

Goss, T. Boardsailing: choosing a mast. *Yacht racing & cruising (Philadelphia, Pa.) 23(8), Sept 1984, 34;38.*
LEVEL: B LANG: Eng SIRC ARTICLE NO: 103697

BOARDSAILING (continued)

Hall, H. Installing your own footstraps. *Windsport (Oakville, Ont.) 3(5), Jul 1984, 28-29.*
LEVEL: B LANG: Eng SIRC ARTICL NO: 102170

Hansen, J. Jarrett, S. Sail selection: what you should know. *Windsport (Oakville, Ont.) 3(4), Jun 1984, 35-39.*
LEVEL: B LANG: Eng SIRC ARTICLE NO: 103700

HiFly '500CS'. *Windsport (Oakville, Ont.) 3(4), Jun 1984, 44-45.*
LEVEL: B LANG: Eng SIRC ARTICLE NO: 103701

Industry interview. (Cees Nater and Eckart Wagner) *Sail boarder (San Juan Capistrano, Calif.) 4(5), Summer 1984, 110-111.*
LEVEL: B LANG: Eng SIRC ARTICLE NO: 105119

Jarrett, S. Rigging up. *Windsport (Oakville, Ont.) 3(3), May 1984, 23.*
LEVEL: B LANG: Eng SIRC ARTICLE NO: 101849

Johnson, P. Light air handling and board speed. *Sail boarder (San Juan Capistrano, Calif.) 4(4), Jun 1984, 21;45.*
LEVEL: LANG: Eng SIRC ARTICLE NO: 105121

Koby, R. Boom height. *Windsport (Oakville, Ont.) 3(2), Apr 1984, 23.*
LEVEL: B LANG: Eng SIRC ARTICLE NO: 100226

Koby, R. Using a mast track. *Windsport (Oakville, Ont.) 3(6), Aug 1984, 17.*
LEVEL: B LANG: Eng SIRC ARTICLE NO: 101851

Le guide bleu. (planches a voile) *Voile libre (Montreal) 3(1), mars/avr 1984, 39-60.*
LEVEL: B LANG: Fr SIRC ARTICLE NO: 098842

Leroux, G. Tech: wings & things. *Wind surf (Dana Point, Calif.) 14(2), Jun 1984, 56-57.*
LEVEL: B LANG: Eng SIRC ARTICLE NO: 097090

Lewis, J. Speed hulls: fooling the water. *Wind surf (Dana Point, Calif.) 14(8), Dec 1984, 56-57.*
LEVEL: B LANG: Eng SIRC ARTICLE NO: 173618

Lockhart, R. Rigging. *Sail boarder (San Juan Capistrano, Calif.) 4(5), Summer 1984, 58-61.*
LEVEL: B LANG: Eng SIRC ARTICL NO: 105122

Lockhart, R. How to buy a sail. *Sail boarder (San Juan Capistrano, Calif.) 4(4), Jun 1984, 68-71.*
LEVEL: B LANG: Eng SIRC ARTICLE NO: 105123

Magnan, J. The hi-tension wing sail. *Wind surf (Dana Point, Calif.) 14(2), Jun 1984, 58-59.*
LEVEL: B LANG: Eng SIRC ARTICLE NO: 097092

Mistral 'Malibu'. *Windsport (Oakville, Ont.) 3(4), Jun 1984, 51-52.*
LEVEL: B LANG: Eng SIRC ARTICLE NO: 103703

Myerscough, R. Footstrap sailing. *Windsport (Oakville, Ont.) 3(3), May 1984, 21-22.*
LEVEL: B LANG: Eng SIRC ARTICLE NO: 101856

Naish, R. Fins: the outline and rake of a fin make a huge difference in how your board handles. *Sail boarder international (Dana Point, Calif.) 4(3), May 1984, 74-77.*
LEVEL: B LANG: Eng SIRC ARTICLE NO: 095572

O'Brien 'Sensation'. *Windsport (Oakville, Ont.) 3(5), Jul 1984, 49-50.*
LEVEL: B LANG: Eng SIRC ARTICLE NO: 102175

Parlee, J. Daggerboards: vital statistics. *Windrider (Winter Park, Fla.) 3(2), Apr/May 1984, 58-60;63-66.*
LEVEL: B LANG: Eng SIRC ARTICLE NO: 101857

Perry, C. Board construction - 1984. *Sail boarder (San Juan Capistrano, Calif.) 4(4), Jun 1984, 30.*
LEVEL: B LANG: Eng SIRC ARTICLE NO: 105126

Quand on aime on a toujours vingt planches. *Planche a voile (Cedex, France) 22, juil/aout 1984, 51-63.*
LEVEL: B LANG: Fr SIRC ARTICLE NO: 173193

Ratcliffe, K. Techniques et materiaux: les secrets de la fabrication d'une voile. *Voile libre (Montreal) 3(2), mai 1984, 17;19-20;69.*
LEVEL: B LANG: Fr SIRC ARTICLE NO: 102095

Robichaud, R. Masts: updating your rig. *Windrider (Winter Park, Fla.) 3(3), Jun 1984, 60-66.*
LEVEL: B LANG: Eng SIRC ARTICLE NO: 101860

Silvia, L. Fins: facts and theory. *Wind rider (Winter Park, Fla.) 3(1), Feb/Mar 1984, 20-24.*
LEVEL: B LANG: Eng SIRC ARTICLE NO: 100230

Simmer, M. Le greement et la nagivation dans les vagues. *Voile libre (Montreal) 3(4), juil 1984, 21-22.*
LEVEL: B LANG: Fr SIRC ARTICLE NO: 105135

Spanier, B. Bourne, G. Foils - present & future: the leading edge. *Sail boarder international (Dana Point, Calif.) 4(3), Ma 1984, 22.*
LEVEL: B LANG: Eng SIRC ARTICLE NO: 095575

Spindler, M. Expanding our awareness of the encounter. *Sail boarder (San Juan Capistrano, Calif.) 4(4), Jun 1984, 24;29;46-47;100.*
LEVEL: B LANG: Eng SIRC ARTICLE NO: 105136

Star, S. Concaves and slalom boards: the new all-arounders. *Sail boarder international (San Juan Capistrano, Calif.) 4(6), Fall 1984, 66-67;94.*
LEVEL: B LANG: Eng SIRC ARTICLE NO: 108861

Stroetzel, C. Tech: World Cup race boards. *Wind surf (Dana Point, Calif.) 14(7), Nov 1984, 66-67.*
LEVEL: B LANG: Eng SIRC ARTICLE NO: 173605

Ten Cate Runner: Board Windsport test. *Windsport (Oakville, Ont.) 3(3), May 1984, 47-48.*
LEVEL: B LANG: Eng SIRC ARTICLE NO 101862

The Rotating Asymmetrical Foil. *Sail boarder (San Juan Capistrano, Calif.) 4(4), Jun 1984, 48.*
LEVEL: B LANG: Eng SIRC ARTICLE NO: 105128

Treu, E. L'ABC du fun... laquelle choisir? *Velimag (Dorval, Que.) 1(4), juin 1984, 32-34.*
LEVEL: B LANG: Fr SIRC ARTICLE NO: 173433

Vigneau, A. Mats. *Voile libre (Montreal) 3(3), juin 1984, 12-15.*
LEVEL: B LANG: Fr SIRC ARTICLE NO: 109083

Wayler 'YPSI'. *Windsport (Oakville, Ont.) 3(5), Jul 1984, 51-52.*
LEVEL: B LANG: Eng SIRC ARTICLE NO: 102176

Wilbur, H.B.. The essential race board: division II boards. *Wind surf (Dana Point, Calif.) 14(7), Nov 1984, 52-53.*
LEVEL: LANG: Eng SIRC ARTICLE NO: 173604

Wind rider board review. *Wind Rider (Winter Park, Fla.) 3(5), Oct 1984, 68-70;72-74;76-78.*
LEVEL: B LANG: Eng SIRC ARTICLE NO: 098853

Wind rider: board review. *Windrider (Winter Park, Fla.) 3(3), Jun 1984, 75-76;78-80;82-84.*
LEVEL: B LANG: Eng SIRC ARTICLE NO: 101866

WindRider board review. *WindRider (Winter Park, Fla.) 3(4), Jul/Aug 1984, 78-80;82-84;86-88.*
LEVEL: B LANG: Eng SIRC ARTICL NO: 106269

Windsurfer 'One-Design'. *Windsport (Oakville, Ont.) 3(4), Jun 1984, 47;49.*
LEVEL: B LANG: Eng SIRC ARTICLE NO: 103704

Wings - new horizons. (sails) *Sail boarder (San Juan Capistrano, Calif.) 4(5), Summer 1984, 22.*
LEVEL: B LANG: Eng SIRC ARTICLE NO: 105137

Winner, K. Talking mast tracks. *Wind surf (Dana Point, Calif.) 14(2), Jun 1984, 74-75.*
LEVEL: B LANG: Eng SIRC ARTICLE NO 097097

Wyn-Edwards, R. Jarrett, S. Sail selection. Part 2. *Windsport (Oakville, Ont.) 3(5), Jul 1984, 37-41.*
LEVEL: B LANG: Eng SIRC ARTICLE NO: 102172

EQUIPMENT - MAINTENANCE

England, H. Boom grip installation. *Sail boarder (San Juan Capistrano, Calif.) 4(4), Jun 1984, 94-95.*
LEVEL: B LANG: Eng SIRC ARTICLE NO: 105116

Hall, H. Do your own board repair. *Windsport (Oakville, Ont.) 3(6), Aug 1984, 26-27.*
LEVEL: B LANG: Eng SIRC ARTICLE NO: 101844

Hall, H. Mast repair. *Windsport (Oakville, Ont.) 3(4), Jun 1984, 20-21.*
LEVEL: B LANG: Eng SIRC ARTICLE NO: 103699

Perry, M. Tips: ding repair. *Wind surf (Dana Point, Calif.) 14(2), Jun 1984, 38;40.*
LEVEL: B LANG: Eng SIRC ARTICLE NO: 097094

Smyth, S. Sail repair: what to do with rip and tear. *Windrider (Winter Park, Fla.) 3(2), Apr/May 1984, 26.*
LEVEL: B LANG: Eng SIRC ARTICLE NO: 101861

EQUIPMENT - RETAILING

The sailboard 'grey market' examined. David Jones of Leslee Sport Imports. *Sports marketing magazine suppl (Mississauga) Jan 1985, 3-4.*
NOTES: Sailboard business supplement, Dec 1984, 3-4.
LEVEL: B LANG: Eng SIRC ARTICLE NO: 105132

HUMOUR

Westfield, J. Ten commandments of boardsailing. *Wind rider (Winter Park, Fla.) 3(1), Feb/Mar 1984, 36-39.*
LEVEL: B LANG: Eng SIRC ARTICLE NO: 100231

INJURIES AND ACCIDENTS

Colin, J. Fily, J. Bonissent, J.F. Accidents oculaires de la planche a voile. (lettre) (Eye injuries in windsurfing (letter) (Refs: 2)*Presse medicale (Paris) 13(4), 4 fevr 1984, 224.*
LEVEL: I LANG: Fr SIRC ARTICLE NO: 100219

Dibben, A. Mills, J. Sea stings & remedies. *Wind surf (Dana Point, Calif.) 14(6), Oct 1984, 24.*
LEVEL: B LANG: Eng SIRC ARTICLE NO: 173607

Dutoit, M. Guerrin, F. Planche a voile, saut de vague, style libre: pathologie. (Windsurfing, free-style wave jumping: pathology.) (Refs: 5)*LARC medical (Lille, France) 4(2), fevr 1984, 115-116.*
LEVEL: B LANG: Fr SIRC ARTICLE NO: 101840

Dutoit, M. Guerrin, F. Planche a voile, saut de vague, style libre: pathologie. (Refs: 5)*Larc medical (France) 4(2), 1984, 115-116.*
LEVEL: B LANG: Fr

Lappan, B. Hypothermia. *Windsport (Oakville, Ont.) 3(2), Apr 1984, 44-45.*
LEVEL: B LANG: Eng SIRC ARTICLE NO: 100227

Paskowitz, D. My aching back. *Wind surf (Dana Point, Calif.) 14(7), Nov 1984, 20.*
LEVEL: B LANG: Eng SIRC ARTICLE NO: 173600

Pedailles, S. Charbonneau, P. Lechevalier, B. Bazin, C. Fabre, J. Electrocution sur une planche a voile: a propos d'un cas. (Refs: 6)*Medecine du sport 58(1), 25 janv 1984, 23-24.*
LEVEL: I LANG: Fr SIRC ARTICLE NO: 092647

Re, G. Borgogna, E. Fogliano, F. Scotto, G. Patologia e traumatologia dento-maxillo-facciale nella pratica del nuoto subacqueo e del wind-surf. (Maxillodentofacial pathology and traumatology in skin diving and wind surfing.) *Minerva stomatologia (Turin) 33(2), Mar/Apr 1984, 375-376.*
LEVEL: I LANG: It

Rudelic, I. Rudelic, E. Jedrenje na dasci i turisticka medicna. (Windsurfing and travel medicine.) *Lijecnicki vjesnik (Zagreb) 106(11/12), Nov/Dec 1984, 463-465.*
LEVEL: I LANG: Scr

Ullis, K.C. Anno, K. Injuries of competitive board sailors. (Refs: 8)*Physician and sportsmedicine (Minneapolis, Minn.) 12(6), Jun 1984, 86-93.*
ABST: This retrospective study of 43 male and 14 female elite boardsailing injuries found skin, feet, shins, back and forearms to be the most commonly injuried areas. The authors feel that the advanced techniques of wave jumping and wave sailing with the use of footstraps may lead to significantly more knee and ankle injuries.
LEVEL: A LANG: Eng SIRC ARTICLE NO: 095576

MEDICINE

Labadie, J.C. Medecine et planche a voile. (Medicine and windsurfing.) *Union medicale du Canada (Montreal) 113(8), aout 198 640-643.*
LEVEL: I LANG: Fr

Medved, R. Sportskomedicinski aspekti jedrenja na dasci. (Sports medicine aspects of windsurfing.) (Refs: 5)*Lijecnicki vjesnik (Zabreb) 106(6), June 1984, 254-256.*
LEVEL: B LANG: Scr SIRC ARTICLE NO: 109741

PHYSIOLOGY

Loquet, H. Guilbert, J. Jacquesson, J.M. Milbled, G. Etude electromyographique sur simulateur de la pratique de la planche a voile. (Electromyographic study on a simulator of the practice of windsurfing.) *LARC medical (Lille) 4(5), mai 1984, 306;309-310;312.*
LEVEL: I LANG: Fr SIRC ARTICLE NO: 105124

Medved, R. Oreb, G. Blood lactic acid values in boardsailors. (Refs: 3)*Journal of sports medicine and physical fitness (Torino, Italy) 24(3), Sept 1984, 234-237.*
ABST: In the two studies with 7 and 11 board-sailers respectively, the blood lactate values obtained in the first study in 1982 were: the mean value 5.48 mmol/l, standard deviation 1.67, and the range from 2.51 to 4.98; in the second study in 1983 the mean value was 3.14 mmol/l, standard deviation 0.81, and the range from 2.06 to 4.98, with the correlation coefficient of .29.
LEVEL: A LANG: Eng SIRC ARTICLE NO: 106268

RULES AND REGULATIONS

Hart, D. Racing tactics: handling ye old protest, facing up to the inevitable. *Wind rider (Winter Park, Fla.) 3(1), Feb/Mar 1984, 25.*
LEVEL: B LANG: Eng SIRC ARTICLE NO: 100221

Hart, D. Protests, part 11: dazzle the committee. *Windrider (Winter Park, Fla.) 3(2), Apr/May 1984, 31;34.*
LEVEL: B LANG: Eng SIRC ARTICLE NO: 101847

Yoakum, J. Racing rules: pumping the butterfly syndrome. *Wind Rider (Winter Park, Fla.) 3(5), Oct 1984, 20-21;25.*
LEVEL: B LANG: Eng SIRC ARTICLE NO: 098835

Yoakum, J. Racing rules: windward/leeward, not as simple as you think. *Windrider (Winter Park, Fla.) 3(2), Apr/May 1984, 16;18.*
LEVEL: B LANG: Eng SIRC ARTICLE NO: 101868

SAFETY

Dibben, A. Contest safety. *Wind surf (Dana Point, Calif.) 14(8), Dec 1984, 22.*
LEVEL: B LANG: Eng SIRC ARTICLE NO: 173614

Morch, K. Self-rescue. *Windsport (Oakville, Ont.) 3(3), May 1984, 15.*
LEVEL: B LANG: Eng SIRC ARTICLE NO: 101854

Simmer, K. Safety: or how to avoid dangerous situations while boardsailing or, if it can't be avoided, how to deal with thos situations. *Sail boarder international (Dana Point, Calif.) 4(3), May 1984, 94-99;101.*
LEVEL: B LANG: Eng SIRC ARTICLE NO: 095574

SPORTING EVENTS

Funboard competition: fast becoming a regatta favourite, funboard competition is an exciting combination of high wind fun and fast-paced racing action. *Windsport (Oakville, Ont.) 3(4), Jun 1984, 30-31.*
LEVEL: B LANG: Eng SIRC ARTICLE NO: 103696

Iden, P. Is triangle racing dying? *Windsport (Oakville, Ont.) 3(2), Apr 1984, 36-39.*
LEVEL: B LANG: Eng SIRC ARTICLE NO: 100223

Iden, P. Le triangle est-il mort? *Velimag (Dorval, Que.) 1(5), aout 1984, 36-41.*
LEVEL: B LANG: Fr SIRC ARTICLE NO: 17343

Winner, K. Why the world cup? A history and justification of the Windsurfing World Cup by one of the top three Americans on the circuit. *Sail boarder international (Dana Point, Calif.) 4(3), May 1984, 62-63.*
LEVEL: B LANG: Eng SIRC ARTICLE NO: 095577

STRATEGY

Baird, E. Defining tactics. *Sail boarder (San Juan Capistrano, Calif.) 4(4), Jun 1984, 32;37.*
LEVEL: B LANG: Eng SIRC ARTICLE NO: 105111

Graveline, A. Competition. Les slaloms. Comment gagner. *Voile libre (Montreal) 3(2), mai 1984, 56.*
LEVEL: B LANG: Fr SIRC ARTICLE NO: 102093

Hart, D. Racing tactics: covering, staying ahead to win. *Windrider (Winter Park, Fla.) 3(3), Jun 1984, 16-17.*
LEVEL: B LANG: Eng SIRC ARTICLE NO: 101848

Hart, D. Fast reach tactics: staying competitive on all legs. *WindRider (Winter Park, Fla.) 3(4), Jul/Aug 1984, 23-24.*
LEVEL: B LANG: Eng SIRC ARTICLE NO: 106266

LeRoux, G. The windward leg: tactics and strategies. *Wind surf (Dana Point, Calif.) 14(8), Dec 1984, 16.*
LEVEL: B LANG: E SIRC ARTICLE NO: 173611

TEACHING

Bates, M. Simulate a simulator and teach a friend to sail. *Wind surf (Dana Point, Calif.) 14(6), Oct 1984, 26.*
LEVEL: B LANG: Eng SIRC ARTICLE NO: 173608

TECHNIQUES AND SKILLS

Anno, K. Splits on the rail: stretching to the limits in freestyle. *WindRider (Winter Park, Fla.) 3(4), Jul/Aug 1984, 74-75*
LEVEL: B LANG: Eng SIRC ARTICLE NO: 106264

Begley, W. Larkin, R. Launching from piers. Avoiding the obstructions. *Wind Rider (Winter Park, Fla.) 3(5), Oct 1984, 18-19.*
LEVEL: B LANG: Eng SIRC ARTICLE NO: 098838

Blum, T. How to obtain maximum downhill purchase without a block system. *Wind rider (Winter Park, Fla.) 3(6), Nov/Dec 1984, 26-27.*
LEVEL: B LANG: Eng SIRC ARTICLE NO: 173006

Borgmeyer, J. Duck gybe. *Windsport (Oakville, Ont.) 3(5), Jul 1984, 21.*
LEVEL: B LANG: Eng SIRC ARTICLE NO: 102179

Boyd, I. The helicopter tack. *Sail boarder international (San Juan Capistrano, Calif.) 4(6), Fall 1984, 22-23.*
LEVEL: B LANG: Eng SIRC ARTICLE NO: 108863

Brown, P. Sail trim. *Windsport (Oakville, Ont.) 3(4), Jun 1984, 17.*
LEVEL: B LANG: Eng SIRC ARTICLE NO: 103693

Cadiz, A. Helicopter tack: on the merry-go-round. *WindRider (Winter Park, Fla.) 3(4), Jul/Aug 1984, 32-33.*
LEVEL: B LANG: Eng SIRC ARTICLE NO: 106265

Chater, A. Wave sailing relative to wind direction: an illustrated guide to wave sailing - how, when, where and why waves should be sailed. *Sail boarder (San Juan Capistrano, Calif.) 4(5), Summer 1984, 82-83.*
LEVEL: B LANG: Eng SIRC ARTICLE NO: 105112

Feeter, C. Rolling it up for the paddle back. *Wind surf (Dana Point, Calif.) 14(7), Nov 1984, 22.*
LEVEL: B LANG: Eng SIRC ARTICLE NO: 173601

Frylund, R. Boardsailing: try learning with two. *Sail (Boston, Mass.) 15(1), Jan 1984, 63-64;66;68.*
LEVEL: B LANG: Eng SIRC ARTICLE NO: 098840

Frylund, R. Handling the heavy stuff. *Sail (Boston, Mass.) 15(6), Jun 1984, 19-20;22;24;26.*
LEVEL: B LANG: Eng SIRC ARTICLE NO: 101842

Graveline, E. Board 360. *Windsport (Oakville, Ont.) 3(4), Jun 1984, 18.*
LEVEL: B LANG: Eng SIRC ARTICLE NO: 103698

Guay, S. Il etait une fois un debutant. *Velimag (Dorval, Que.) 1(4), juin 1984, 10-14.*
LEVEL: B LANG: Fr SIRC ARTICLE NO: 173428

Hanselmann, E. La planche a voile: fascination d'un sport audacieux. *Macolin (Macolin, Suisse)*

BOARDSAILING (continued)

41(5), mai 1984, 6-9.
NOTES: Traduction de, Francoise Huguenin.
LEVEL: B LANG: Fr SIRC ARTICLE NO: 108768

Hawley, R. Regatta sail adjustment and tuning.
Wind surf (Dana Point, Calif.) 14(7), Nov 1984, 24.
LEVEL: B LANG: Eng SIR ARTICLE NO: 173602

Jajam, J. Relaxing freestyle: Let your feet do the work. *Wind rider (Winter Park, Fla.) 3(6)*, Nov/Dec 1984, 54-55.
LEVEL: LANG: Eng SIRC ARTICLE NO: 173007

Jarrett, S. Carved gybe. *Windsport (Oakville, Ont.) 3(4)*, Jun 1984, 23.
LEVEL: B LANG: Eng SIRC ARTICLE NO: 103702

Jeangirard, P. Pulling the daggerboard: how to handle this tricky essential. *Windrider (Winter Park, Fla.) 3(2)*, Apr/May 1984, 32-33.
LEVEL: B LANG: Eng SIRC ARTICLE NO: 101850

Johnson, N. Water starts: how to practice this essential maneuver. *Wind rider (Winter Park, Fla.) 3(1)*, Feb/Mar 1984, 70-71.
LEVEL: B LANG: Eng SIRC ARTICLE NO: 100224

Johnson, P. Light air performance - II. Board handling. *Sail boarder (San Juan Capistrano, Calif.) 4(5)*, Summer 1984, 32;37;40.
LEVEL: B LANG: Eng SIRC ARTICLE NO: 105120

Johnson, P. Moderate winds, marginal days. *Sail boarder international (San Juan Capistrano, Calif.) 4(6)*, Fall 1984, 12;16.
LEVEL: B LANG: Eng SIRC ARTICLE NO: 108862

Kniskern, R. Short board jibe: how to stay in control. *Wind rider (Winter Park, Fla.) 3(1)*, Feb/Mar 1984, 48-49.
LEVEL: B LANG: Eng SIRC ARTICLE NO: 100225

Laporte, J. Perfectionnement: l'empannage en puissance. *Voile libre (Montreal) 3(2)*, mai 1984, 34-35.
LEVEL: B LANG: Fr SIRC ARTICLE NO: 102094

Leroux, G. Tackling: sail to win. *Wind surf (Dana Point, Calif.) 14(2)*, Jun 1984, 24.
LEVEL: B LANG: Eng SIRC ARTICLE NO: 097091

LeRoux, G. Downwind: an inner look. *Wind surf (Dana Point, Calif.) 14(6)*, Oct 1984, 20.
LEVEL: B LANG: Eng SIRC ARTICLE NO: 173606

Marrullier, A. The mast grip: good practice for upwind technique. *Wind rider (Winter Park, Fla.) 3(1)*, Feb/Mar 1984, 26-27.
LEVEL: B LANG: Eng SIRC ARTICLE NO: 100228

Marrullier, A. Grabbing the uphaul: the first step. *Windrider (Winter Park, Fla.) 3(2)*, Apr/May 1984, 24-25.
LEVEL: B LANG: Eng SIRC ARTICLE NO: 101853

Marrullier, A. Tacking and jibing: back to basics. *WindRider (Winter Park, Fla.) 3(4)*, Jul/Aug 1984, 26-27.
LEVEL: B LANG Eng SIRC ARTICLE NO: 106267

Matelotage de planche: comment eviter les noeuds de viperes. *Voile libre (Montreal) 3(4)*, juil 1984, 44-45.
LEVEL: B LANG: SIRC ARTICLE NO: 105125

McArron, G. Basic form: Common beginning errors. *Wind rider (Winter Park, Fla.) 3(6)*, Nov/Dec 1984, 18-19.
LEVEL: B LANG: Eng SIRC ARTICLE NO: 173005

Morch, K. Gripping the boom. *Windsport (Oakville, Ont.) 3(2)*, Apr 1984, 17.
LEVEL: B LANG: Eng SIRC ARTICLE NO: 100229

Morch, K. Harness basics. *Windsport (Oakville, Ont.) 3(6)*, Aug 1984, 14.
LEVEL: B LANG: Eng SIRC ARTICLE NO: 101855

Morch, K. Fast tacks. *Windsport (Oakville, Ont.) 3(5)*, Jul 1984, 17.
LEVEL: B LANG: Eng SIRC ARTICLE NO: 102177

Naish, R. Closing the gap: the end-plate effect. *Wind surf (Dana Point, Calif.) 14(8)*, Dec 1984, 20.
LEVEL: B LANG: Eng SIRC ARTICLE NO: 173613

Pudenz, P. Duck jibe. *Sail boarder international (Dana Point, Calif.) 4(3)*, May 1984, 34-35.
LEVEL: B LANG: Eng SIRC ARTICLE NO: 095573

Rouleau, R. Le vent arriere. *Voile libre (Montreal) 3(4)*, juil 1984, 12-13.
LEVEL: B LANG: Fr SIRC ARTICLE NO: 105129

Rouleau, R. L'hirondelle. *Voile libre (Montreal) 3(4)*, juil 1984, 35.
LEVEL: B LANG: Fr SIRC ARTICLE NO: 105130

Rouleau, R. L'empannage. *Voile libre (Montreal) 3(4)*, juil 1984, 24.
LEVEL: B LANG: Fr SIRC ARTICLE NO: 105131

Schweitzer, M. Using the force: a short-board guide to high wind sailing. *Sail boarder (San Juan Capistrano, Calif.) 4(5)*, Summer 1984, 50-53.
LEVEL: B LANG: Eng SIRC ARTICLE NO: 105133

Seaman, G. Ways to speed. *Wind surf (Dana Point, Calif.) 14(8)*, Dec 1984, 36-43.
LEVEL: B LANG: Eng SIRC ARTICLE NO: 1736

Technique. *Planche a voile (Cedex, France) 22*, juil/aout 1984, 36-47.
LEVEL: B LANG: Fr SIRC ARTICLE NO: 173192

Vachon, R. Le 360o par la planche. *Voile libre (Montreal) 3(3)*, juin 1984, 29.
LEVEL: B LANG: Fr SIRC ARTICLE NO: 109086

Vachon, R. Le virement sous la voile. *Voile libre (Montreal) 3(3)*, juin 1984, 44.
LEVEL: B LANG: Fr SIRC ARTICLE NO: 1090

Weber, K. Bottoms up: how to carry your short board. *Windrider (Winter Park, Fla.) 3(2)*, Apr/May 1984, 86-87.
LEVEL: B LANG: Eng SIRC ARTICLE NO: 101865

Winans, C. Greenwood, M. Furlow, J.
Boardsailing made easy: teaching and techniques. Harwichport, Mass.: C. Winans Productions, 1984. 188 p. : ill.
NOTES: Includes index.
LEVEL: B LANG: Eng ISBN: 096132340X LC CARD: 84-223834

Wulff, D. Morch, K. Basic boardsailing skills: the CYA learn to boardsail manual. Ottawa: Canadian Yachting Association, c1984. 142 p. : ill.
CORP: Canadian Yachting Association.
NOTES: Produced with the assistance of Fitness Canada.
LEVEL: B LANG: Eng ISBN: 0-920232-06-X LC CARD: C84-90096-1 GV811.63.W56 17605

Wulff, D. Learning to railride. *Windsport (Oakville, Ont.) 3(2)*, Apr 1984, 21.
LEVEL: B LANG: Eng SIRC ARTICLE NO: 100232

Wulff, D. Freestyle tips: back to sail. *Windsport (Oakville, Ont.) 3(3)*, May 1984, 17-18.
LEVEL: B LANG: Eng SIRC ARTICLE NO: 101867

Wulff, D. Clew first sailing. *Windsport (Oakville, Ont.) 3(5)*, Jul 1984, 19.
LEVEL: B LANG: Eng SIRC ARTICLE NO: 102178

Wulff, D. Freestyle tips. *Windsport (Oakville, Ont.) 3(1)*, Mar 1984, 22.
LEVEL: B LANG: Eng SIRC ARTICLE NO: 108797

TECHNIQUES AND SKILLS - GRIP

Hall, M. Boardsailing, rig control: hands and arms. *Yacht racing & cruising (Philadelphia, Pa.) 23(7)*, Aug 1984, 24-26.
LEVEL: B LANG: Eng SIRC ARTICLE NO: 101845

TECHNIQUES AND SKILLS - STANCE

Hall, M. Boardsailing: proper stance. *Yacht racing & cruising (Philadelphia) 23(6)*, Jun 1984, 28;30.
LEVEL: B LANG: Eng SIRC ARTICLE NO: 097089

Hall, M. Boardsailing: putting your body into it. *Yacht racing & cruising (Philadelphia, Pa.) 23(9)*, Oct 1984, 30-31.
LEVEL: B LANG: Eng SIRC ARTICLE NO: 107920

Morch, K. The proper stance. *Windsport (Oakville, Ont.) 3(1)*, Mar 1984, 18.
LEVEL: B LANG: Eng SIRC ARTICLE NO: 108793

TECHNIQUES AND SKILLS - START

Graveline, E. Waterstarts. *Windsport (Oakville, Ont.) 3(2)*, Apr 1984, 19.
LEVEL: B LANG: Eng SIRC ARTICLE NO: 100220

Leroux, G. Starting: techniques and tactics. *Wind surf (Dana Point, Calif.) 14(7)*, Nov 1984, 18;69.
LEVEL: B LANG: Eng SIRC ARTICLE NO: 173599

Perry, M. The beach start. *Wind surf (Dana Point, Calif.) 14(5)*, Sept 1984, 38.
LEVEL: B LANG: Eng SIRC ARTICLE NO: 17358

Pudenz, P. The water start. *Sail boarder (San Juan Capistrano, Calif.) 4(4)*, Jun 1984, 22-23.
LEVEL: B LANG: Eng SIRC ARTICLE NO: 105127

TRAINING AND CONDITIONING

Koby, R. Conditioning tips. *Windsport (Oakville, Ont.) 3(1)*, Mar 1984, 20.
LEVEL: B LANG: Eng SIRC ARTICLE NO: 108795

Paskowitz, D. Muscle in: Dr. wind. *Wind surf (Dana Point, Calif.) 14(2)*, Jun 1984, 26.
LEVEL: B LANG: Eng SIRC ARTICLE NO 097093

VARIATIONS

Mindnich, P. Mohler, C. O'Neill, R. Winter alternatives. *Wind surf (Dana Point, Calif.) 14(8)*, Dec 1984, 50-55.
LEVEL: B LANG: Eng SIRC ARTICLE NO: 173617

BOATING

BIOGRAPHY AND AUTOBIOGRAPHY

Merkel, J.A. Nine boats & nine kids. 1st ed. Bernard, Me.: Ledge Books, 1984. 1v.
LEVEL: B LANG: Eng LC CARD: 84-019422

COUNTRIES AND REGIONS

Brazer, M.C. The sweet water sea: a guide to Lake Huron's Georgian Bay. Charlevoix, Mich.: Peach Mountain Press, c1984. 1v.
NOTES: Includes index.

LEVEL: B LANG: Eng ISBN: 0931850037 LC
CARD: 84-000992

EQUIPMENT

Adams, A. Buying a boat: a checklist of items to consider when you're looking for that new boat. *Canadian boating (Mississauga, Ont.) Jan 1984, 21-24.*
LEVEL: B LANG: Eng SIRC ARTICLE NO: 097959

Boatpox: scratching the surface of a perplexing problem. (blistering) *Practical sailor (Riverside, Conn.) 10(15), 1 Aug 1984, 1;4-6.*
LEVEL: B LANG: Eng SIRC ARTICLE NO: 104593

Brooks, A.N. The flying fish hydrofoil. *Human power (Cambridge, Mass.) 3(2), Winter 1984, 1;7-8.*
LEVEL: B LANG: Eng SIRC ARTICLE NO: 105711

Jones, C. Riding on air. (inflatable boats) *Diver (London) 29(12), Dec 1984, 14-15.*
NOTES: First in a series.
LEVEL: B LANG: Eng SIRC ARTICLE NO: 108464

Knapp, J. Human-powered boating: four years' experience. *Human power (Cambridge, Mass.) 3(2), Winter 1984, 12-13.*
LEVEL: LANG: Eng SIRC ARTICLE NO: 105712

Larrabee, E.E. Propellers for human-powered vehicles. (Refs: 4)*Human power (Cambridge, Mass.) 3(2), Winter 1984, 9-11.*
LEVEL: A LANG: Eng SIRC ARTICLE NO: 105713

Rennicke, J. The dory story: evolution of a classic watercraft. *River runner (Vista, Calif.) 4(4), Jul/Aug 1984, 10-15.*
LEVEL: B LANG: Eng SIRC ARTICLE NO: 101113

Reynolds, J. Davidson, J.W. Miller, P. McCourtney, D. Boats for backpackers. *Backpacker (New York) 12(2), Mar 1984, 100-105.*
LEVEL: B LANG: Eng SIRC ARTICLE NO: 097961

Roy, M. Electric outboard motors: if you don't expect a lot of power, they are a peaceful way to travel and great for fishin *Protect yourself (Montreal) Jun 1984, 52-55.*
LEVEL: B LANG: Eng SIRC ARTICLE NO: 096534

Sowden, E. Fabric design factors in the production of inflatable craft. *Journal of coated fabrics (Lancaster, Penn.) 13(4), Apr 1984, 250-257.*
LEVEL: I LANG: Eng SIRC ARTICLE NO: 099432

Thiel, P. The dorycycle, pedal power and screw propulsion in a traditional watercraft. (Refs: 4)*Human power (Cambridge, Mass.) 3(2), Winter 1984, 4-6.*
LEVEL: I LANG: Eng SIRC ARTICLE NO: 105714

What you always wanted to know about inflatable boat fabric but were afraid to ask. *New Zealand canoeing & rafting (Auckland, N.Z.) 32, Autumn 1984, 19-23.*
CORP: Lancer Industries.
LEVEL: B LANG: Eng SIRC ARTICLE NO: 097963

EQUIPMENT - MAINTENANCE

Groene, G. Groene, J. How to plug a hole in a fiberglass boat. *Outdoor Canada 12(1), Dec/Jan 1984, 22.*
LEVEL: B LANG: Eng SIRC ARTICLE NO: 090514

EQUIPMENT - RETAILING

Fletcher, J.E. Sales of boats, motors, and trailers as an index to water-based recreation. *In, Clawson, M. and Van Doren, C.S. (eds.), Statistics on outdoor recreation, Washington, Resources for the Future, c1984, p. 258-262.*
LEVEL: B LANG: Eng GV191.4 20254

Sales of outboard motors, boats, and trailers as an index to outdoor recreation. *In, Clawson, M. and Van Doren, C.S. (eds.), Statistics on outdoor recreation, Washington, Resources for the Future, c1984, p. 59-61.*
LEVEL: I LANG: Eng GV191.4 20254

SAFETY

Anglin, B. Horseshoe buoys or life rings? *Gam on yachting (Toronto, Ont.) 28(1), Jan 1984, 34.*
LEVEL: B LANG: Eng SIRC ARTICLE NO: 094897

Camping (and even some waterfront) safety. *Your health & fitness (Highland Park, Ill.) 6(3), Jun/Jul 1984, 19-20.*
LEVEL: B LANG: Eng SIRC ARTICLE NO: 096555

Man overboard: a retrieval system that works. *Practical sailor (Riverside, Conn.) 10(23), 1 Dec 1984, 12-14.*
LEVEL: B LANG: Eng SIRC ARTICLE NO: 103683

Sabel, J. Overboard rescue: it's mind over muscle. *Sea & Pacific skipper (Los Angeles, Calif.) 76(1), Jan 1984, 64-66.*
LEVEL: B LANG: Eng SIRC ARTICLE NO: 097962

BOATING SPORTS

COUNTRIES AND REGIONS

Pratt-Johnson, B. Whitewater trips for kayakers, canoeists annd rafters on Vancouver Island. Vancouver: Soules Book Pub., c1984. 127 p. : ill.
NOTES: 'The first in a series of five guidebooks covering 157 whitewater trips in British Columbia and Washington.' Bibliography: p. 110-111.
LEVEL: B LANG: Eng ISBN: 0-919574-67-X LC CARD: 83-026190 GV776.15.V36 17439

FACILITIES - DESIGN, CONSTRUCTION AND PLANNING

Architecture of docks, harbor buildings, harbors and marinas: a bibliography. Monticello, Ill.: Vance Bibliographies, 1984. 10 p. (Architecture series: bibliography; A-1190.)
CORP: Coppa and Avery Consultants.
NOTES: ISSN: 0194-1356.
LEVEL: I LANG: Eng ISBN: 0-88066-980-2 GV770.7 17745

INJURIES AND ACCIDENTS

Pikkarainen, J. Penttilae, A. Vesiliikenne, hukkuminen ja alkoholi. (Water traffic, drowning and alcohol.) *Duodecim (Helsinki) 100(19), 1984, 1277-1284.*
LEVEL: A LANG: Fin

BOBSLEDDING

BIOGRAPHY AND AUTOBIOGRAPHY

Dickie, D. Alan MacLachlan, un peu d'air frais. Alan MacLachlan, intrepid driver. *Champion 8(1), Feb 1984, 38-39.*
LEVEL: LANG: Eng Fr SIRC ARTICLE NO: 090517

Wulf, S. Bobsledding: he's real trouble on the run. Brent Rushlaw is the best - and brashest - U.S. two-man bobsled driver. *Sports illustrated 60(1), 9 Jan 1984, 46-47.*
LEVEL: B LANG: Eng SIRC ARTICLE NO: 090518

BOCCIE

SOCIOLOGY

Pierini, B. 'Morti, Morti, Morti': the death of a bocce ball club. (Refs: 8)
NOTES: In, Sutton-Smith, B. and Kelly-Byrne, D. (eds.), The masks of play, New York, Leisure Press, c1984, p. 98-105.
LEVEL: I LANG: Eng HQ782 17029

BODYBUILDING

Hatfield, F.C. Bodybuilding: a scientific approach. Chicago: Contemporary Books, c1984. xxviii, 276 p. : ill.
LEVEL: I LANG Eng ISBN: 0-8092-54581 LC CARD: 84-5817 GV546.5 18280

Kennedy, R. Mason, V. Hardcore bodybuilder's source book. New York: Sterling, c1984. 256 p. : ill.
NOTES: Bibliography: p. 245-250.
LEVEL: I LANG: Eng ISBN: 0-8069-7894-5 LC CARD: 84-8821 GV546.5 18198

Kennedy, R. Gironda, V. Unleashing the wild physique. New York: Sterling Pub. Co., c1984. 1v.
NOTES: Includes index.
LEVEL B LANG: Eng ISBN: 0806941804 LC CARD: 84-008451

S'Jongers, J.J. Vogelaere, P. Approche medico-sportive du culturisme. (Refs: 16)*Sport: Communaute francaise de belgique (Bruxelles) 108, 1984, 209-217.*
LEVEL: B LANG: Fr SIRC ARTICLE NO: 103059

Weider, J. Reynolds, B. Competitive bodybuilding. Chicago, Ill.: Contemporary Books, c1984. 172 p. : ill.
NOTES: Includes index. Bibliography: p. 167-168.
LEVEL: I LANG: Eng ISBN: 0809254662 LC CARD: 83-026209 GV546.5 18216

ADMINISTRATION

Duchaine, D. So you want to be a promoter. There are good promoters and there are bad promoters, and to help you understand why, FLEX interviewed Dave Zelon, a young entrepreneur who seems to have promotion down to a science. *Flex (Woodland Hills, Calif.) 2(10), Jan 1985, 84-86.*
LEVEL: B LANG: Eng SIRC ARTICLE NO: 107046

BIOGRAPHY AND AUTOBIOGRAPHY

Dardenne, G. Marcel Rouet (1910-1982). *Sante et sport (Paris) 214, janv 1984, 12-14.*
LEVEL: B LANG: Fr SIRC ARTICLE NO: 097965

Dunbar, I. Some more early training days. *Health & strength (Sunbury, Middlesex) Sept 1984, 11-16.*
LEVEL: B LANG: Eng SIR ARTICLE NO: 109014

Foster, J. Legend in his own time. Mentor for Joe Weider and one of the strongest men to walk the planet, George Jowett continues to inspire long after going to the gym in the sky. *Flex (Woodland Hills, Calif.) 2(8), Nov 1984, 46-48;96;98.*
LEVEL: B LANG: Eng SIRC ARTICLE NO: 105718

Klein, S. Sandow the magnificent: the dramatic story of Sandow's defeat of cyclops and of Samson, and the glamorous career that followed. (Eugene Sandow) *Muscle training illustrated (New York) 18(7), Oct 1984, 54-56;70-71.*
NOTES: Part II.
LEVEL: B LANG: Eng SIRC ARTICLE NO: 109106

CLOTHING

Malone, J. Shoes that fit bodybuilding. *Joe Weider's muscle & fitness (Woodland Hills, Calif.) 45(8), Aug 1984, 76-79;198;200;202;204.*
LEVEL: B LANG: Eng SIRC ARTICLE NO: 096542

DRUGS, DOPING AND ERGOGENIC AIDS

Burkett, L.N. Falduto, M.T. Steroid use by athletes in a Metropolitan area. (Refs: 9)*Physician and sportsmedicine (Minneapolis, Minn.) 12(8), Aug 1984, 69-70;73-74.*
ABST: This article explores the use of anabolic steroid of 24 weight training athletes. Nineteen bodybuilders, two powerlifters, two football players, and one discus thrower were administered an oral questionnaire. Results showed that athletes took a combined steroid dose of four to eight times the recommended medical dose, stacked an injectable steroid with an oral steroid, and used the drugs for more than one cycle.
LEVEL: A LANG: Eng SIRC ARTICLE NO: 097964

Hurley, B.F. Seals, D.R. Hagberg, J.M. Goldberg, A.C. Ostrove, S.M. Holloszy, J.O. Wiest, W.G. Goldberg, A.P. High-density-lipoprotein cholesterol in bodybuilders v powerlifters. Negative effects of androgen use. (Refs: 21)*JAMA: Journal of the American Medical Association (Chicago) 252(4), 27 Jul 1984, 507-513.*
ABST: 8 bodybuilders and 4 powerlifters were tested before and after androgen use to evaluate the effects of anabolic-androgenic steroids on lipids and the relationship to type of weight training. Androgen use by the bodybuilders and powerlifters lowered values of both HDL-Cholesterol and HDL2-C by 55 percent and raised values of LDL-C 61 percent and LDL-C/HDL-C ratios 280 percent. The training regimen of bodybuilders is associated with a more favorable lipid profile than the training use by powerlifters.
LEVEL: A LANG: Eng SIRC ARTICLE NO: 103058

Pardee, R. Is there a steroid alternative? *Muscle and fitness (Woodland Hills, Calif.) 45(2), Feb 1984, 94;206;246.*
LEVEL B LANG: Eng SIRC ARTICLE NO: 096543

Pardee, R. Shocking report: dietary problems of the steroid user. *Muscle & fitness (Woodland Hills, Calif.) 45(11), Nov 1984, 72-73;144-145.*
LEVEL: B LANG: Eng SIRC ARTICLE NO: 101118

Price, R. Weighing the biological risks. (Refs: 4)*Muscle and fitness (Woodland Hills, Calif.) 45(2), Feb 1984, 91;199-200;202.*
LEVEL: B LANG: Eng SIRC ARTICLE NO: 095800

Starr, B. Jack King - drugs almost killed him. *Iron man (Alliance, Neb.) 44(1), Nov 1984, 46-47;88-89.*
NOTES: Continued from last issue.
LEVEL: B LANG: Eng SIRC ARTICLE NO: 105723

Starr, B. Jack King - drugs almost killed him. *Iron man (Alliance, Neb.) 43(6), Sept 1984, 46-47.*
NOTES: Continued next issue.
LEVEL: B LANG: Eng SIRC ARTICLE NO: 105724

EQUIPMENT

Darden, E. Lund, C. High-intensity bodybuilding: for massive muscles fast: Nautilus training principles applied to free weights and conventional equipment. New York: Perigee Books, c1984. 1v.
LEVEL: B LANG: Eng ISBN: 0399511032 LC CARD: 84-019010

Stone, R. A guide to heavy-duty hi-tech. How to spot first-rate equipment. *Flex (Woodland Hills, Calif.) 2(5), Sept 1984, 37-38;40;42;107-108.*
LEVEL: B LANG: Eng SIRC ARTICLE NO: 105725

HISTORY

Chapman, D. Bodybuilding's first contest. *Muscle and fitness (Woodland Hills, Calif.) 45(2), Feb 1984, 82-83;220;222-224.*
LEVEL: B LANG: Eng SIRC ARTICLE NO: 096536

INJURIES AND ACCIDENTS

Hamilton, H.K. Stress fracture of the diaphysis of the ulna in a body builder. *American journal of sports medicine (Baltimore, Md.) 12(5), Sept/Oct 1984, 405-406.*
LEVEL: I LANG: Eng SIRC ARTICLE NO: 104600

Sherman, O.H. Snyder, S.J. Fox, J.M. Triceps tendon avulsion in a professional body builder. (Refs: 18)*American journal of sports medicine (Baltimore, Md.) 12(4), Jul/Aug 1984, 328-329.*
ABST: There are only 14 reported cases of avulsion or rupture of the triceps tendon from the olecranon in the American and English literature. We are reporting a case of tricps tendon avulsion in a professional body builder with successful repair of the tendon 6 months after injury, allowing the patient to successfully return to body building competition.
LEVEL: A LANG: Eng SIRC ARTICLE NO: 108541

JUDGING

Manion, J. Parees, L. What the hell are the judges looking for? *Flex (Woodland Hills, Calif.) 2(6), Oct 1984, 26-28;82-83.*
LEVEL: B LANG: Eng SIRC ARTICLE NO: 105720

MEDICINE

Hoffman, B. Affecting physical recovery. *Muscular development (York, Pa.) 21(3), May/Jun 1984, 20-21;69.*
LEVEL: B LANG: E SIRC ARTICLE NO: 101117

Zulak, G. In the training torture chamber. *Muscle mag international (Brampton, Ont.) 43, May 1984, 69-71;80.*
LEVEL: B LANG: Eng SIRC ARTICLE NO: 099433

NUTRITION

Beverley, B. Fairhurst, A. The role of nutrition in bodybuilding. *Health & strength (Sunbury, Middlesex) Sept 1984, 57-58;60-61.*
LEVEL: B LANG: Eng SIRC ARTICLE NO: 109017

Duchaine, D. Newest developments in precontest: carbing up. *Flex (Woodland Hills, Calif.) 2(9), Dec 1984, 48-50;110;112;114-115.*
LEVEL: B LANG: Eng SIRC ARTICLE NO: 105717

Pardee, R. Is there a steroid alternative? *Muscle and fitness (Woodland Hills, Calif.) 45(2), Feb 1984, 94;206;246.*
LEVEL B LANG: Eng SIRC ARTICLE NO: 096543

The case for multivitamin and multimineral supplementation. *Health & strength (London) Aug 1984, 24-25.*
LEVEL: B LANG: Eng SIRC ARTICLE NO: 104596

PHYSIOLOGY

Lhomme, R. Le souffle c'est la vie: apprenez a bien respirer. *Sante et sport (Paris) 217, avr 1984, 31-34.*
LEVEL: B LANG: Fr SIRC ARTICLE NO: 097968

Miller, G.H. Enzymes: bodybuilding through body chemistry. *Muscular development (York, Pa.) 21(5), Spet/Oct 1984, 49;64-65.*
LEVEL: I LANG: Eng SIRC ARTICLE NO: 173297

Mollica, M. Naturally big: four free-from amino acids to boost anabolic conditions. *Flex (Woodland Hills, Calif.) 2(5), Sep 1984, 51.*
LEVEL: B LANG: Eng SIRC ARTICLE NO: 105721

Yessis, M. Sports medicine: aerobic (running) for bodybuilders, part II. *Muscle & fitness (Woodland Hills, Calif.) 45(12), Dec 1984, 13;176-177.*
LEVEL: B LANG: Eng SIRC ARTICLE NO: 109034

Yki-Jaervinen, H. Koivisto, V.A. Taskinen, M.-R. Nikkilae, E.A. Glucose tolerance, plasma lipoproteins and tissue lipoprotei lipase activities in body builders. (Refs: 34)*European journal of applied physiology and occupational physiology (Berlin) 53(3), Dec 1984, 253-259.*
ABST: Oral glucose tolerance, insulin binding to erythrocyte receptors, serum lipids, and lipoproteins, and lipoprotein lipase activities of adipose tissue and skeletal muscle were measured in nine body builders, eight weight-matched and seven normal-weight controls. In the oral glucose tolerance test, blood glucose levels, and plasma insulin levels were lower in the body builders than in weight-matched controls. Plasma total cholesterol, low-density lipoprotein cholesterol, and very low-density lipoprotein triglyceride concentrations were significantly lower in the body builders than in weight-matched controls. In comparison with the normal-weight group, the body builders had a lower total cholesterol level.
LEVEL: A LANG: Eng SIRC ARTICLE NO: 104603

Zale, N. Metabolism: the key to weight control. *Muscle & fitness (Woodland Hills, Calif.) 45(12), Dec 1984, 114-116;170-172*
LEVEL: B LANG: Eng SIRC ARTICLE NO: 109031

PHYSIOLOGY - MUSCLE

Hatfield, F.C. The killer troll: a demon lurking under the bridge to stardom, the sodium troll will drown your chances for success. *Flex (Woodland Hills, Calif.) 2(6),* Oct 1984, 46-47;85;117-118.
LEVEL: B LANG: Eng SIRC ARTICLE NO: 105719

Lamb, L. Energy for muscle work. *Muscle & fitness (Woodland Hills, Calif.) 45(12),* Dec 1984, 25;193-194;196.
LEVEL: B LANG: Eng SIRC ARTICLE NO: 109039

MacDougall, J.D. Sale, D.G. Alway, S.E. Sutton, J.R. Muscle fiber number in biceps brachii in bodybuilders and control subjects. (Refs: 20)*Journal of applied physiology: respiratory, environmental and exercise physiology (Bethesda, Md.) 57(5),* Nov 1984, 1399-1403.
ABST: Muscle fiber quantities were estimated in biceps brachii in 5 elite bodybuilders, 7 intermediate bodybuilders and 13 age matched controls. These was a wide range in individual fiber numbers but despite these and muscle size differences the two bodybuilding groups and the controls had the same number of muscle fibres. The authors conclude that heavy resistance training performed for maximizing muscle size does not increase muscle fiber numbers. Differences in muscle fiber numbers are more likely due to genetic factors.
LEVEL: A LANG: Eng SIRC ARTICLE NO: 108915

Yessis, M. Sports medicine: work the muscle from both ends. *Muscle and fitness (Woodland Hills, Calif.) 45(2),* Feb 1984, 13;240.
LEVEL: B LANG: Eng SIRC ARTICLE NO: 096544

PSYCHOLOGY

Dielens, S. Narcissisme et activites physiques a la mode. Profil psychologique des pratiquants d'aerobic, de jogging et de bodybuilding. (Refs: 13)*Revue de l'education physique (Liege, Belgique) 24(1),* 1984, 21-24.
LEVEL: I LANG: Fr SIRC ARTICLE NO: 096321

Kubistant, T. The psychology of peaking. *Joe Weider's muscle & fitness (Woodland Hills, Calif.) 45(8),* Aug 1984, 110-111;211;213-214;216;219.
LEVEL: B LANG: Eng SIRC ARTICLE NO: 096541

Siegel, P. The psych-out game. Don't get caught in powerplays. *Flex (Woodland Hills, Calif.) 2(5),* Sept 1984, 26-28.
LEVEL: B LANG: Eng SIRC ARTICLE NO: 105722

Zulak, G. Power thinking, concentration in bodybuilding. *Muscle mag international (Brampton, Ont.) 42,* Mar 1984, 22-25;64.
LEVEL: B LANG: Eng SIRC ARTICLE NO: 101122

TECHNIQUES AND SKILLS

Grymkowski, P. Kimber, T. Reynolds, B. The Gold's gym training encyclopedia. Chicago, Ill.: Contemporary Books, c1984. 255 p : ill.
NOTES: Includes index.
LEVEL: B LANG: Eng ISBN: 0809254468 LC CARD: 84-009611 GV546.5 18339

Manion, J. Denie Bodybuilding for amateurs. South Bend, Ind.: Icarus Press, 1984. 1v.
NOTES: Includes index.
LEVEL: B LANG Eng ISBN: 0896510581 LC CARD: 84-003803

Ross, D. Building strong arms. Mountain View, Calif.: Anderson World Books, 1984. 1v. (The

Getting strong book series: bk. 2.)
LEVEL: B LANG: Eng ISBN: 0890373051 LC CARD: 84-012403

Yessis, M. Kinesiology: straight-arm pullover. *Muscle and fitness (Woodland Hills, Calif.) 45(2),* Feb 1984, 22-23.
LEVEL: LANG: Eng SIRC ARTICLE NO: 096545

Yessis, M. Kinesiology: front arm raises. *Muscle & fitness (Woodland Hills, Calif.) 45(7),* Jul 1984, 22-23.
LEVEL: B LANG Eng SIRC ARTICLE NO: 096547

Yessis, M. Kinesiology: lateral prone raise. *Muscle & fitness (Woodland Hills, Calif.) 45(1),* Jan 1984, 24-25.
LEVEL: B LANG: Eng SIRC ARTICLE NO: 096548

Yessis, M. The best way to do exercise. *Muscle & fitness (Woodland Hills, Calif.) 4(9),* Sept 1984, 13;158-159.
LEVEL: B LANG: Eng SIRC ARTICLE NO: 101121

TESTING AND EVALUATION

Sale, D.G. MacDougall, J.D. Isokinetic strength in weight-trainers. (Refs: 18)*European journal of applied physiology and occupational physiology (Berlin, W.G.) 53(2),* 1984, 128-132.
ABST: Isokinetic strength of ankle plantarflexion (APF), knee extension (KE) and elbow extension (EE) was measured in male weight-trainers (6 power-lifters and 7 bodybuilders) and 25 untrained men of similar age and height. The weight-trainers exceeded control subjects by 21 per cent, 25 per cent and 73 per cent in APF, KE and EE strength respectively. The relatively greater enhancement of upper versus lower limb strength and muscle mass in the weight-trainers was considered in respect to training habits, trainability of different muscle groups and the state of training of muscle groups in untrained men.
LEVEL: A LANG: Eng SIRC ARTICLE NO: 104602

TRAINING AND CONDITIONING

Christensen, V. To the ladies. *Strength & health (York, Pa.) 52(6),* Oct/Nov 1984, 42-44.
LEVEL: B LANG: Eng SIRC ARTICLE NO: 103057

Fagot, H. Le confort du bodybuilder. *Sante et sport (Paris) 214,* janv 1984, 3-6.
LEVEL: B LANG: Fr SIRC ARTICLE NO: 09796

Fagot, H. Dix exercices pour le volume. *Sante et sport (Paris) 217,* avr 1984, 3-5.
LEVEL: B LANG: Fr SIRC ARTICLE NO: 097967

Fagot, H. Le cours du mois: pour des proportions ideales corrigez vos faiblesses. *Sante et sport (Paris) 224,* dec 1984, 3-5
LEVEL: B LANG: Fr SIRC ARTICLE NO: 173511

Herman, S. Couples body building: the hot new sport of the '80s. *Shape (Woodland Hills, Calif.) 3(7),* Mar 1984, 76-80;115.
LEVEL: B LANG: Eng SIRC ARTICLE NO: 100167

Koebel, G.F. Can fitness be programmed? *Sport & fitness (Sunbury, Middlesex) Dec 1984,* 16-17.
LEVEL: B LANG: Eng SIRC ARTICLE NO: 108871

Tanny, A. Breaking away for bodybuilders. *Muscle & fitness (Woodland Hills, Calif.) 45(10),* Oct 1984, 98-100;177;179-180;183;186.
LEVEL: B LANG: Eng SIRC ARTICLE NO: 108999

Weider, J. The best of Joe Weider's Muscle and Fitness: chest and shoulders. Chicago:

Contemporary Books, c1984. 122, (1) p. : ill.
LEVEL: B LANG: Eng ISBN: 0809254670 LC CARD: 83-026310 GV546.5 17307

Yessis, M. Sports medicine: high-intensity training and flexibility. *Muscle & fitness (Woodland Hills, Calif.) 45(7),* Jul 1984, 13;181-182;184.
LEVEL: B LANG: Eng SIRC ARTICLE NO: 096546

Yessis, M. The many faces of overload. *Muscle & fitness (Woodland Hills, Calif.) 45(10),* Oct 1984, 13;200;203-204.
LEVEL: LANG: Eng SIRC ARTICLE NO: 109000

TRAINING AND CONDITIONING - AEROBIC TRAINING

Taylor, W.N. Aerobics & bodybuilding underlying advantages. Are the two exercise approaches counterproductive, or can you combine them for maximum gains? Here's how to get the best of both. *Muscle & fitness (Woodland Hills, Calif.) 45(6),* Jun 1984, 76-77;202.
LEVEL: B LANG: Eng SIRC ARTICLE NO: 101780

Yessis, M. Aerobics (running) for bodybuilding, part 1. *Muscle & fitness (Woodland Hills, Calif.) 45(11),* Nov 1984, 13;168;171-172.
LEVEL: B LANG: Eng SIRC ARTICLE NO: 101120

TRAINING AND CONDITIONING - WEIGHT AND STRENGTH TRAINING

Bernstein, L. Follow the basics for success. *Health & strength (Sunbury, Middlesex) Sept 1984,* 50-52.
LEVEL: B LANG: Eng SIRC ARTICLE NO: 109015

Centrella, B.A. The essence of bodybuilding: building muscle. *Muscle mag international (Brampton, Ont.) 42,* Mar 1984, 37-40.
LEVEL: B LANG: Eng SIRC ARTICLE NO: 101115

Fagot, H. Intensifiez vos efforts. *Sante et sport (Paris) 219,* juin 1984, 3-5.
LEVEL: B LANG: Fr SIRC ARTICLE NO: 101116

Intermediate course: split training. How to make it work for you. *Health & strength (London) Aug 1984,* 7-8.
LEVEL: B LANG: Eng SIRC ARTICLE NO: 104601

Mather, D. Make a muscle. Want bigger arms? *Muscle training illustrated (New York) 18(7),* Oct 1984, 14-16;24.
LEVEL: B LANG: Eng SIRC ARTICLE NO: 109105

Yessis, M. Aerobics & strength build a muscular foundation. For injury avoidance and complete fitness development, you need strong muscular foundation for successful aerobics. *Muscle & fitness (Woodland Hills, Calif.) 45(6),* Jun 1984, 80-81;207-209.
LEVEL: B LANG: Eng SIRC ARTICLE NO: 101781

WOMEN

Bowen, L. A general workout: getting started. *Muscle & fitness (Woodland Hills, Calif.) 45(7),* Jul 1984, 70-75.
LEVEL: B LANG: Eng SIRC ARTICLE NO: 096535

Csencsits, C. Bodybuilding for women: body composition, body type and the female physique. *Muscle & fitness (Woodland Hills Calif.) 45(7),* Jul 1984, 62-63;191-192.
LEVEL: B LANG: Eng SIRC ARTICLE NO: 096537

Duff, R.W. Hong, L.K. Self-images of women bodybuilders. (Refs: 8)*Sociology of sport journal*

(Champaign, Ill.) 1(4), Dec 1984, 374-380.
ABST: In analyzing the data from a questionnaire survey of 205 competitive women bodybuilders conducted by the International Federation of Body-Builders, the authors attempt to find out how these women define their roles. What emerges from the analysis is a new concept of femininity that combines aspects of the traditional definitions with added dimensions of muscularity and body symmetry. They see muscularity, fitness, strength, and health as increasing their femininity, adding to their attractiveness as women, and increasing their sex appeal to men. They do not see themselves as emulating men. Relatively few see themselves as feminists or androgynists.
LEVEL: A LANG: Eng SIRC ARTICLE NO: 104597

Everson, C. Exploding the myths: separating facts from fiction. *Muscle & fitness (Woodland Hills, Calif.) 45(7), Jul 1984, 64-65;192;195-196.*
LEVEL: B LANG: Eng SIRC ARTICLE NO: 096538

Franck, L. Are women bodybuilders feminine? *Muscle digest (San Gabriel, Calif.) 8(4), Aug 1984, 20;44;54.*
LEVEL: B LANG: Eng SIRC ARTICLE NO: 104598

Franck, L. Exposure and gender effects in the social perception of women bodybuilders. (Refs: 24)*Journal of sport psycholog (Champaign, Ill.) 6(2), 1984, 239-245.*
ABST: A 3 by 4 factorial design was used to test the effects of gender, frequency of exposure, and magnitude of exposure on subjects' ratings of women bodybuilders. Dependent variables were subjects' ratings of the bodybuilders' femininity, physical attractiveness, dominance, and aggressiveness. Subjects were 76 introductory psychology students (45 female, 31 male) at a large Utah university who completed a 10-item rating scale after viewing 20 color slides of some of the world's leading women bodybuilders. A multivariate analysis of covariance showed that males rated the women bodybuilders as more attractive than did females and that the longer they had been exposed to women bodybuilders, the higher were their attractiveness ratings for women bodybuilders. Gender-frequency of exposure interaction effects were also statistically significant. Males with low frequency of exposure rated the women bodybuilders as less dominant than did low-frequency females. However, high frequency-of-exposure males rated the women bodybuilders as more dominant than did high-frequency females.
LEVEL: A LANG: Eng SIRC ARTICLE NO: 108496

Gruwell, S. Sizing up the sexes. Can women train like men? *Muscle & fitness (Woodland Hills, Calif.) 45(7), Jul 1984, 66;196;199.*
LEVEL: B LANG: Eng SIRC ARTICLE NO: 096539

Hendrikx, R. La femme et la musculation ou la peur du 'muscle'. *Sante et sport (Paris) 223, nov 1984, 23-26.*
LEVEL: B LANG: Fr SIRC ARTICLE NO: 173516

Herman, S. Training for shape and fitness: some basic guidelines. *Muscle & fitness (Woodland Hills, Calif.) 45(7), Jul 1984 68-69;205.*
LEVEL: B LANG: Eng SIRC ARTICLE NO: 096540

Koch, S. Body dynamics: the body shape-up book for women. New York: Leisure Press, c1984. 160 p. : ill.
LEVEL: B LANG: Eng ISBN: 0880111151 LC CARD: 82-83947 GV546.6.W64 17999

Nutrition and training for women bodybuilders. Chicago: Contemporary Books, c1984. 108 p. : ill. (The best of Joe Weider's Muscle & Fitness.)
LEVEL: I LANG: Eng ISBN: 0-8092-54689 LC CARD: 84-3140 GV546.6.W64 18094

Pirie, L. Getting built. New York: Warner Books, 1984. 1v.
LEVEL: B LANG: Eng ISBN: 0446378577 LC CARD: 83-026002

Pollard, T. Women's body composition testing update. *Muscle & fitness (Woodland Hills, Calif.) 45(11), Nov 1984, 118-119;152-153.*
LEVEL: I LANG: Eng SIRC ARTICLE NO: 101119

Weider, B. Weider, J. The Weider body book. Chicago: Contemporary Books, 1984. 1v.
NOTES: Includes index.
LEVEL: I LANG: E ISBN: 0809254298 LC CARD: 84-012724

Zwingle, E. Iron maidens. Competitive women's bodybuilding is locked in controversy over defining the ideal female physique. But there is no question about the sport's growing popular appeal. *Ultrasport (Boston, Mass.) 1(3), May/Jun 1984, 34-39;42-43.*
LEVEL: B LANG: Eng SIRC ARTICLE NO: 096549

BOOMERANGING

Georget, A. Le monde magique du boomerang. Le championnat de France open de boomerang aura lieu aujourd'hui et demain a Bagatelle, au bois de Boulogne. L'occasion de decouvrir un monde etrange et fascinant. *Equipe magazine (Paris) 222, 8 dec 1984, 54-55.*
LEVEL: B LANG: Fr SIRC ARTICLE NO: 103060

SPORTING EVENTS

Segell, M. Sideline: the Aussies had many happy returns in the Boomerang Challenge Cup II. *Sports illustrated (Chicago, Ill.) 61(10), 27 Aug 1984, 6-7.*
LEVEL: B LANG: Eng SIRC ARTICLE NO: 097969

BOWLING SPORTS

VARIATIONS

Pedersen, E. The games corner: battle ball - Europe. *MAHPERD journal (Ypsilanti, Mich.) Winter 1984, 14.*
LEVEL: B LANG: E SIRC ARTICLE NO: 098601

BOXING

Rouet, J.M. Un univers impitoyable. (boxe) *Equipe magazine (Paris) 218, 10 nov 1984, 28-33.*
LEVEL: B LANG: Fr SIRC ARTICL NO: 101132

Sion, D. La boxe. *Larc medical (France) 4(7), 1984, 443-447.*
LEVEL: I LANG: Fr

Sion, D. La boxe. (Refs: 22)*Larc Medical (France) 4(8), 1984, 498-505.*
LEVEL: I LANG: Fr

ADMINISTRATION

Underwood, J. 'Look up and he's got your money': gambler Billy Baxter, who won big when Miami toppled Nebraska, is also a fight manager who does work - in his car. *Sports illustrated (Chicago, Ill.) 60(21), 28 May 1984, 80-84;86;88;90;92;94.*
LEVEL: B LANG: Eng SIRC ARTICLE NO: 094910

ART

Ardolino, F.R. Christian symbolism in Serling's Requiem for a heavyweight. (Refs: 12)*Arete: the journal of sport literature (San Diego, Calif.) 2(1), Fall 1984, 159-168.*
LEVEL: A LANG: Eng SIRC ARTICLE NO: 108410

BIOGRAPHY AND AUTOBIOGRAPHY

Barra, A. Boxing's Futch factor. *Inside sports (Evanston, Ill.) 6, Jun 1984, 76-84;86-87.*
LEVEL: B LANG: Eng SIRC ARTICLE NO: 094900

Barra, A. The opponent Larry Holmes can't beat. *Inside sports (Evanston, Ill.) 6, Dec 1984, 68-74;76-79.*
LEVEL: B LANG: E SIRC ARTICLE NO: 101123

Beaudin, M. Willie de Wit: the lord of the ring. Scarborough, Ont.: Avon Books of Canada, c1984. 223 p. : ill.
LEVEL: B LANG: Eng ISBN: 0-380-89485-8 LC CARD: C84-98995-4 GV1132.D42 18186

Boxe: Willie DeWit. Boxing: Willie DeWit. *Champion (Ottawa) 8(3), Aug 1984, 46-47.*
LEVEL: B LANG: Fr Eng SIRC ARTICLE NO: 096550

Cieszkowski, K.Z. Bendigo the boxer. (William Thompson) *History today (London) 34, Feb 1984, 25-30.*
ABST: William Thompson, known as Bendigo was one of early Victoria England's most popular sportsmen. This article details his life and provides useful descriptions of boxing prior to the introduction of the Marquess of Queensbury rules in 1867.
LEVEL: A LANG: Eng

Darling, L. A case of pride and prejudice. Gerrie Coetzee is driven by a need to succeed and, as WBA heavyweight champ, haunted by his homeland of South Africa. *Sports illustrated (Chicago, Ill.) 60(25), 18 Jun 1984, 64-68;70;72;74-76;78.*
LEVEL: B LANG: Eng SIRC ARTICLE NO: 094903

Diaz, J. He doesn't make any bones about it. To Larry Holmes, Marciano's mark is gravy. He keeps fighting for bread. *Sports illustrated (Los Angeles, Calif.) 61(23), 19 Nov 1984, 50-51.*
LEVEL: B LANG: Eng SIRC ARTICLE NO: 101125

Duhatschek, E. Champion interview: 'I think I'll be a much better pro'. (Willie deWit) Entrevue de Champion: 'Je serais probablement meilleur en tant que professionnel.' (Willie deWit) *Champion (Vanier, Ont.) 8(2), May/mai 1984, 36-41.*
LEVEL: B LANG: Eng Fr SIRC ARTICLE NO: 094904

Encinosa, E.G. Kaplan, H. Boxing -- this is it. Palm Springs, Calif.: ETC Pub., c1984. 1v.
LEVEL: B LANG: Eng ISBN: 0882801058 LC CARD: 84-001649

Gilmore, A.T. Jack Johnson: a magnificent black anachronism of the early twentieth century. (Refs: 45)
NOTES: In, Riess, S.A (ed.), The American sporting experience: a historical anthology of sport in America, New York, Leisure Press, c1984, p. 306-315. Previously published in, Journal of social and behavioural sciences 19, Winter 1973, p. 35-42.
LEVEL: I LANG: Eng GV583 17631

Goldman, H.G. Henry Armstrong's whirlwind month: 5 title defenses in 22 days for the triple-crown champion. Ring (New York) 63(3), Apr 1984, 82-85.
LEVEL: B LANG: Eng SIRC ARTICLE NO: 099437

Hanrahan, T. The education of Mark Breland. Ring (New York) 63(7), Aug 1984, 18-23.
LEVEL: B LANG: Eng SIRC ARTICLE NO: 101126

Lidz, F. The Ivy's Irish pug. Princeton grad Henry Milligan, the amateur heavyweight champ of the U.S., has Olympic hopes. Sports illustrated 60(12), 19 Mar 1984, 46-48;50.
LEVEL: B LANG: Eng SIRC ARTICLE NO: 091966

Montgomery, R.N. Cut'n shoot. Austin, Tex.: Eakin Press, 1984. 1v.
LEVEL: B LANG: Eng ISBN: 0890154295 LC CARD: 83-020822

Nack, W. The writing is on the wall. That Mark Breland, a five-time Golden Gloves champion, will win an Olympic gold medal i as plain as the graffiti on the buildings in Bed-Stuy. Sports illustrated (Chicago, Ill.) 61(2), 9 Jul 1984, 32-34;36-37;40.
LEVEL: B LANG: Eng SIRC ARTICLE NO: 094908

Nicolaisen, S.R. Those unforgettable Olympians: if at first you don't succeed...gold medal winners who failed the first time around. Ring (New York) 63(7), Aug 1984, 82-87.
LEVEL: B LANG: Eng SIRC ARTICLE NO: 101130

Putnam, P. A road least traveled. No Canadian has gone to the victory stand for an Olympic boxing gold medal since '32, but Toronto's Shawn O'Sullivan and Willie deWit, a son of the plains, should alter that. Sports illustrated (Chicago, Ill.) 61(4), 18 Jul 1984, 378-382;385-386;388;391;394;397;399.
NOTES: Special preview the 1984 Olympics.
LEVEL: B LANG: Eng SIRC ARTICLE NO: 096553

Smith, G. After the fall. (George Foreman) Sports illustrated (Chicago, Ill.) 61(17), 8 Oct 1984, 62-70;72;74;76;78-80.
LEVEL: B LANG: Eng SIRC ARTICLE NO: 099438

Sugar, B.R. The 100 greatest boxers of all time. New York: Bonanza Books, 1984. 1v.
LEVEL: B LANG: Eng ISBN: 0517448262 LC CARD: 84-018224

Wright, R. Defender of the faith. Boxer Shawn O'Sullivan's not just out to win an Olympic gold. He intends to restore the public image of his sport. Saturday night (Toronto) 99(8), Aug 1984, 47-50.
LEVEL: B LANG: Eng SIRC ARTICLE NO: 096554

BIOMECHANICS

Roy, B. Bernier-Cardou, M. Cardou, A. Plamondon, A. Influence des bandages sur la force d'impact des coups de poing a la box (Refs: 32)Canadian journal of applied sport sciences/ Journal canadien des sciences appliquees au sport (Windsor, Ont.) 9(4), dec 1984, 181-187.
RESUME: L'objectif de ce travail consistait a comparer les forces d'impact atteintes avec la main nue a celles obtenues avec differents types de bandages constitues de gaze et de diachylon. Pour les fins de cette etude, 22 boxeurs furent selectionnes. La force d'impact etait mesuree a l'aide d'une plate forme de force Kistler, recoverte d'un matelas synthetique. Un systeme de cellules photoelectriques permettait de mesurer la velocite du poing a l'impact. Chaque sujet devait donner 10 coups de poing sur la cible alors que sa main etait recouverte de l'un ou l'autre des quatre bandages experimentaux, de meme que main nue. Cette etude a demontre que le bandage de la main augmente significativement la force d'impact du coup de poing.
LEVEL: A LANG: Fr SIRC ARTICLE NO: 103066

CHILDREN

Harman, A. Surkein, R.J. Junior boxers: how old should they be. Amateur boxer (Portland, Conn.) 7(6), Nov/Dec 1984, 8-12.
LEVEL: B LANG: Eng SIRC ARTICLE NO: 103063

Palango, P. The myth of amateur boxing. In, Barnes, J. (ed.), Sports Violence and Law Reform. Proceedings of a consultation organized by the Institute for Studies in Policy, Ethics & Law (I.S.P.E.L.) and the Law Reform Commission of Canada..., Ottawa, Carleton University, 1984?, p. 37-41.
CONF: Sports Violence and Law Reform (1984 : Ottawa).
LEVEL: B LANG: Eng GV706.7 20192

COACHING

Gordon, R. The fighters' manager: enjoying his most successful year in 1984, Lou Duva manages to stay hungry. Ring (New York) 63(5), Jun 1984, 14-20.
LEVEL: B LANG: Eng SIRC ARTICLE NO: 103062

INJURIES AND ACCIDENTS

Borgogna, E. Re, F. Re, G. Torreri, S. I traumatismi maxillo-facciali nelle pratiche sportive: il pugilato. (Maxillofacial injuries in sports: boxing.) Minerva stomatologica (Torino) 33(1), Jan/Feb 1984, 203-207.
LEVEL: A LANG: It

Boxing in the army. Journal of the Royal Army Medical Corps (London) 130(3), Oct 1984, 141-143.
LEVEL: A LANG: Eng

Bregeat, P. Dangers encours par la pratique de la boxe. (Dangers related to the practice of boxing.) Bulletin de l'Academi nationale de medecine (Paris) 168(1/2), janv/fevr 1984, 112-119.
LEVEL: I LANG: Fr

Bregeat, P. Gounelle de Pontanel, H. La boxe professionnelle devrait etre interdite. Bulletin de l'academie nationale de medecine (France) 168(5/6), 1984, 580-581.
LEVEL: B LANG: Fr

Casson, I.R. Siegel, O. Sham, R. Campbell, E.A. Tarlau, M. DiDomenico, A. Brain damage in modern boxers. JAMA: Journal of the American Medical Association (Chicago) 251(20), 25 May 1984, 2663-2667.
ABST: 18 former and active boxers were examined in this study. 87% had brain damage. All the boxers had abnormal results on at least one of the neuropsychological tests.
LEVEL: A LANG: Eng SIRC ARTICLE NO: 101124

Dabkowski, M. nastepstwa psychiatryczne boksu na marginesie przypadku encefalopatii u boksera. (Psychiatric consequences of boxing in light of the case of encephalopathy in a boxer.) Psychiatria polska (Warsaw) 18(1), Jan/Feb 1984, 69-72.
LEVEL: I LANG: Pol

Estwanik, J.J. Boitano, M. Ari, N. Amateur boxing injuries at the 1981 and 1982 USA/ABF National Championships. (Refs: 11) Physician and sportsmedicine (Minneapolis, Minn.) 12(10), Oct 1984, 123-124;127-128.
LEVEL: I LANG: Eng SIRC ARTICLE NO: 099435

Falletta, J. Don't ban amateur boxing in Canada. (Refs: 3)Canadian Medical Association journal/ Journal de l'Association medicale canadienne (Ottawa) 131(5), 1 Sept 1984, 500-501.
LEVEL: B LANG: Eng SIRC ARTICLE NO: 099436

Ioannou, S. Should boxing be banned? (letter) Canadian Medical Association journal/Journal de l'Association medicale canadienne (Ottawa) 131(1), 1 Jul 1984, 10.
LEVEL: B LANG: Eng SIRC ARTICLE NO: 096551

Jensen, J. Intraorale mundbeskyttere hos en gruppe idraetsfolk (boksere). (Intraorale mouth guards in a group of athletes (boxers).) Tandlaegebladet/Danish dental journal (Copenhagen) 88(19), Nov 1984, 681-686.
LEVEL: A LANG: Dan

Kidd, B. Boxing and the law of assault. (Refs: 15)In, Barnes, J. (ed.), Sports Violence and Law Reform. Proceedings of a consultation organized by the Institute for Studies in Policy, Ethics & Law (I.S.P.E.L.) and the Law Reform Commission of Canada..., Ottawa, Carleton University, 1984?, p. 31-36.
CONF: Sports Violence and Law Reform (1984 : Ottawa).
LEVEL: I LANG: Eng GV706.7 20192

La Cava, G. Why padded gloves are dangerous. Olympic review (Lausanne) 204, Oct 1984, 749-751.
LEVEL: B LANG: Eng SIRC ARTICLE NO: 101127

La Cava, G. Pourquoi les gants rembourres sont dangereux. Revue olympique (Lausanne) 204, oct 1984, 749-751.
LEVEL: B LANG: Fr SIRC ARTICLE NO: 101128

Lampert, P.W. Hardman, J.M. Morphological changes in brains of boxers. JAMA: Journal of the American Medical Association (Chicago) 251(20), 25 May 1984, 2676-2679.
LEVEL: A LANG: Eng SIRC ARTICLE NO: 101129

McCunney, R.J. Russo, P.K. Brain injuries in boxers. (Refs: 53)Physician and sportsmedicine (Minneapolis, Minn.) 12(5), May 1984, 52-54;57-59;62-64;67.
LEVEL: I LANG: Eng SIRC ARTICLE NO: 094906

Millar, A.P. Boxing - time for fresh action. (editorial) Medical journal of Australia (Sydney) 141(10), 10 Nov 1984, 624-626.
LEVEL: I LANG: Eng

Pearce, J.M. Boxers' brains. (letter) British medical journal (clinical research) (London) 288(6421), 24 Mar 1984, 933-934.
LEVEL: B LANG: Eng SIRC ARTICLE NO: 101131

Richards, N.G. Ban boxing. *Neurology (New York)* 34(11), Nov 1984, 1485-1486.
LEVEL: I LANG: Eng

Simon, A. Boxe et medecine. Avant toute blessure. *France boxe (France)* 54, 1984, 7-9.
LEVEL: B LANG: Fr

Simon, A. Boxe et medecine, traitement des lesions cutanees. *France boxe (France)* 55, 1984, 24-25.
LEVEL: I LANG: Fr

LAW AND LEGISLATION

Morin, J. Les sports de combat et le droit criminel. (Refs: 1)*Dans, Barnes, J. (ed.), La violence dans les sports et la reforme du droit. Proces-verbal d'une consultation organisee par l'Institute for Studies in Policy, Ethics & Law (I.S.P.E.L.) et la Commission de reforme de droit du Canada..., Ottawa, Carleton University, 1984?, p. 42-46.*
CONF: La violence dans les sports et la reforme du droit (1984 : Ottawa).
LEVEL: I LANG: Fr GV706.7 20192

MASS MEDIA

McCormack, T. Hollywood's prizefight films: violence or 'Jock' appeal? (Refs: 10)*Journal of sport and social issues (Boston Mass.)* 8(2), Summer/Fall 1984, 19-29.
ABST: Many psychological experiments on aggression use prizefight films as their stimuli. This paper questions the use of such films for studies of media agression. Examining prizefight films from 1939 to 1982, it is suggested that they are primarily about 'jock' appeal rather than violence. Jock appeal is defined as male narcissism, and the 'jock' is contrasted with the professional athlete who must be a thinker and organizer as well as a doer. Hollywood, however, prefers the less holistic model of the 'jock' which is easier to comprehend by mass audiences. To the extent that the films deal with violence, it is the contrast between the instrumental violence of the ring and the expressive violence of the fans. The paper concludes with a brief discussion of the value of 'jock' appeal in discussions of media experiences, and the relevance of the 'jock' concept in some of the newer films about women athletes.
LEVEL: A LANG: Eng SIRC ARTICLE NO: 104606

MEDICINE

Cohen, L. Should the sport of boxing be banned in Canada? *Canadian Medical Association journal/ Journal de l'Association medicale canadienne (Ottawa, Ont.)* 130(6), 15 Mar 1984, 767-768.
LEVEL: I LANG: Eng SIRC ARTICLE NO: 094902

Murphy, P. Medical groups take positions on boxing. *Physician and sportsmedicine (Minneapolis, Minn.)* 12(12), Dec 1984, 23.
LEVEL: B LANG: Eng SIRC ARTICLE NO: 103064

Nguyen, M. La medecine sur le ring. *Impact medecin (Puteaux, France)* 99, 1984, 75-78.
LEVEL: B LANG: Fr

Participation in boxing among children and young adults. (Refs: 10)*Pediatrics (Evanston, Ill.)* 74(2), Aug 1984, 311-312.
CORP: American Academy of Pediatrics. Committee on Sports Medicine.
LEVEL: I LANG: Eng SIRC ARTICLE NO: 104608

Ryan, A.J. The fight continues. (editorial) *Physician and sportsmedicine* 12(3), Mar 1984, 37.
LEVEL: B LANG: Eng SIRC ARTICLE NO: 091967

Sion, D. La boxe. 2eme partie. (Boxing. 2.) *LARC medical (Lille)* 4(8), oct 1984, 498-505.
LEVEL: I LANG: Fr

Vega, A. Les medecins et le monde de la boxe. *Impact medecin (Puteaux, France)* 104, 1984, 35-39.
LEVEL: B LANG: Fr

OFFICIATING

Connell, B.R. Interview Davey Pearl: one of the top boxing referees in the world. *Referee (Franksville, Wis.)* 9(1), Jan 1984, 8-11.
LEVEL: B LANG: Eng SIRC ARTICLE NO: 097970

PHILOSOPHY

Corruption in boxing: the Ike Williams testimony.
NOTES: In, Riess, S.A. (ed.), The American sporting experience: a historica anthology of sport in America, New York, Leisure Press, c1984, p. 348-364. Reprinted from, U.S. Congress, Senate, Judiciary Committee, professional boxing: hearings before Subcommittee on Antitrust and Monopoly, 86th Cong., 2nd sess., pursuant to S. Res. 238, December 5-14, 1960, Washington, D.C., Government Printing Office, 1961, p. 664-677.
LEVEL: I LANG: Eng GV583 17631

PHYSIOLOGY

Jako, P. Szabo, G. Bodnar, L. Hajos, M. Ifjusagi labdarugok es oekoelvivok nehany fizikai karakterisztikumanak vizsgalata. (Some physical characteristics of junior football players and boxers.) (Refs: 13)*Sportorvosi szemle/Hungarian review of sports medicine (Budapest)* 25(1), 1984, 43-51.
ABST: The purpose of the present paper was to study and compare the physical abilities in two events which though technically different, both require an alternation between aerobic and anaerobic energy sources. Anthropometry, spiroergometry, dynamometry, body composition, and reaction time was studied in soccer players and boxers of the national junior teams, each group consisting of 30 subjects. The obtained results were compared to the respective means of the senior national teams. No characteristic differences were found between the two events, and junior competitors did not differ significantly from the adult ones either.
LEVEL: A LANG: Hun SIRC ARTICLE NO: 095679

Jako, P. Birkozok es oekoelvivok sulyszabalyozasanak nehany kerdese. (The weight control of wrestlers and boxers.) (Refs: 20 *Sportorvosi szemle/Hungarian review of sports medicine (Budapest)* 25(1), 1984, 53-58.
ABST: Wrestlers and boxers usually reduce their body weight before weighing in by forced dehydration. The need for that arises in part from the existing system of weight categories, and in part from the inadequacy of conditioning. Dehydration obviously will reduce the athlete's performance capacity, primarily by affecting his blood composition and circulation. The right answer to this problem is to help competitors maintain their optimum - individually assessed - weight by bringing their physical activity in harmony with a suitably diet. In this way, only a minimum weight

reduction is necessary before weighing in. Diuretics should be avoided, and after weighing in care should be taken to supply the necessary kind and amount of fluids and food.
LEVEL: A LANG: Hun SIRC ARTICLE NO: 095680

PSYCHOLOGY - MENTAL TRAINING

Landis, D. Five training ingredients. *National Strength & Conditioning Association journal (Lincoln, Neb.)* 6(2), Apr/May 1984, 26-35.
LEVEL: I LANG: Eng SIRC ARTICLE NO: 094905

TRAINING AND CONDITIONING

Bastian, M. On the purpose, contents and efficiency of training in young boxers. *CABA news bulletin (Ottawa, Ont.)* 4(1), 20 Jan 1984, 7.
NOTES: Reprinted from, European Boxing Magazine.
LEVEL: B LANG: Eng SIRC ARTICLE NO: 094901

Landis, D. Five training ingredients. *National Strength & Conditioning Association journal (Lincoln, Neb.)* 6(2), Apr/May 1984, 26-35.
LEVEL: I LANG: Eng SIRC ARTICLE NO: 094905

TRAINING AND CONDITIONIONING - WEIGHT AND STRENGTH TRAINING

Mizerski, M. Developing dynamic strength. *Coaching review (Ottawa, Ont.)* 7, May/Jun 1984, 43-44.
LEVEL: B LANG: Eng SIRC ARTICLE NO: 094907

BRAZIL

Diem, L. Report of a longitudinal project in sport promotion in Brazil as a means of fostering international understanding. *In, Ilmarinen, M. (ed.) et al., Sport and International Understanding: proceedings of the congress held in Helsinki, Finland, July 7-10, 1982, Berlin, Springer-Verlag, 1984, p. 307-309.*
CONF: Congress on Sport and International Understanding (1982 : Helsinki).
LEVEL: B LANG: Eng GV706.8 18979

BROOMBALL

OFFICIATING

Programme de formation des officiels. Theorique et technique: niveau 1. (Montreal): Federation provinciale des clubs de ballon sur glace, (1984). 119 feuillets
CORP: Federation provinciale des clubs de ballon sur glace.
NOTES: Titre de la couverture. Bibliographie: p. 119.
LEVEL: B LANG: Fr GV857.B7 17980

BULGARIA

HISTORY

Martinski, T. Sports in the People's Republic of Bulgaria. Sofia: Sofia Press, 1984. 86 p., (32) p. of plates : ill.
NOTES: Title in colophon: Sportut v narodna republika Bulgariia.
LEVEL: B LANG: Eng LC CARD: 85-206648

CAMPING

Henderson, K.A. Bialeschki, M.D. What's new in camping Research? Abstracts of the Proceedings of the American Camping Association National Convention, San Diego, Calif., February 27-March 3, 1984. Alexandria, Va.: Computer Microfilm International, 1984. 1 microfiche (47 fr.)
CONF: American Camping Association National Convention (1984 : San Diego).
LEVEL: A LANG: Eng EDRS: ED245852

Riviere, B. Biggar, J. Camper's bible. 3rd ed. Garden City, N.Y.: Doubleday, 1984. 178 (1) p. : ill. (Sports & recreation.)
LEVEL: B LANG: Eng ISBN: 0385170505 LC CARD: 82-045267 GV191.7 17323

ADMINISTRATION

Blackstock, J.B. Latimer, J. Camp counsellor's handbook. 2nd ed. Toronto: Methuen, c1984. 124 p. : ill.
LEVEL: B LANG: Eng ISBN: 0-458-97620-2 LC CARD: 84-98381-6 GV198.C6 17643

Gallup, T.P. The effectiveness of a cartoon illustrated interpretive brochure on the enhancement of campers' knowledge of rules and the decrease in rates of rule violation per campsite. Eugene, Ore.: Microform Publications, University of Oregon, 1984. 1 microfiche : negative, ill. ; 11 x 15 cm.
NOTES: Thesis (M.S.) - Pennsylvania State University, 1981; (vii, 56 12 leaves); includes bibliography.
LEVEL: A LANG: Eng UO84 91

Glick, J. Brand, C.P. Shared responsibility. (Refs: 1)Camping magazine (Martinsville, Ind.) 56(6), Apr 1984, 18-20.
LEVEL B LANG: Eng SIRC ARTICLE NO: 101137

Horn, G. Horn, J. Staff training your next move: board game focuses on problem-solving skills and provides instant feedback. Camping magazine (Martinsville, Ind.) 56(6), Apr 1984, 13-14.
LEVEL: B LANG: Eng SIRC ARTICLE NO: 101138

Howe, C.Z. Change, computers, and the camp administration. (Refs: 6)Camping magazine (Martinsville, Ind.) 57(1), Sept/Oct 1984, 14-18.
LEVEL: I LANG: Eng SIRC ARTICLE NO: 173549

Knapp, C.E. Staff education: balancing people and activity skills. Interpersonal skills training improves staff education. (Refs: 6)Camping magazine (Martinsville, Ind.) 56(6), Apr 1984, 22-24.
LEVEL: B LANG: Eng SIRC ARTICLE NO: 101139

Rodney, L.S. Ford, P.M. Camp administration: schools, communities, organizations. Malabar, Fla.: Krieger, 1984, c1971. 1v.
NOTES: Reprint. Originally published: New York :

Wiley, 1971. Includes index.
LEVEL: I LANG: Eng ISBN: 0898747058 LC CARD: 83-019986

Rotman, C.B. Crisis at camp: a crisis management plan will not prevent a crisis situation from occuring, but it will prepare staff to deal with the problem in a constructive manner. Camping magazine (Martinsville, Ind.) 57(2), Nov/Dec 1984, 27-29.
LEVEL: B LANG: Eng SIRC ARTICLE NO: 108457

Winslow, B.B. The seed and the harvest: leadership training program is an opportunity for camps to 'grow their own counselors.' Camping magazine (Martinsville, Ill.) 57(2), Nov/Dec 1984, 12-15.
LEVEL: B LANG: Eng SIRC ARTICLE NO: 108453

AGED

Lathen, C.W. Senior citizens: a new market. Elderly camping programs open new doors for seniors and camps. (Refs: 4)Camping magazine (Martinsville, Ind.) 56(5), Mar 1984, 44-45.
LEVEL: B LANG: Eng SIRC ARTICLE NO: 097974

CERTIFICATION

Camp standards without interpretations. Martinsville, Ind.: American Camping Association, c1984. 1v.
CORP: American Camping Association.
LEVEL: B LANG: Eng ISBN: 0876030738 LC CARD: 84-012468

CHILDREN

Blue lake and rocky shore. A history of children's camping in Ontario. Toronto: Natural Heritage/ Natural History Inc., c1984. xviii, 90 p. : ill.
NOTES: Bibliography: p. 88-90.
LEVEL: B LANG: Eng ISBN: 0-920474-32-2 LC CARD: C84-098297-6 GV191.46.O5 17782

Ferguson, D.D. Microcomputers: an exciting addition for camp programs. (Refs: 22)Camping magazine (Martinsville, Ind.) 57(1 Sept/Oct 1984, 32-36.
LEVEL: I LANG: Eng SIRC ARTICLE NO: 173552

Grant, S.N. The one minute counselor: helping children feel good about themselves is one key to effecting good behavior. Camping magazine (Martinsville, Ind.) 57(2), Nov/Dec 1984, 16-17;24.
LEVEL: B LANG: Eng SIRC ARTICLE NO: 108454

Rhodes, R.I. Computer craze: implications for camping. Camping magazine (Martinsville, Ind.) 57(1), Sept/Oct 1984, 19-20;29-31.
LEVEL: I LANG: Eng SIRC ARTICLE NO: 173550

COUNTRIES AND REGIONS

Market survey indicates enrollment held even. (United States) Camping update (Martinsville, Ind.) Fall 1984, 2-3.
LEVEL: B LANG: Eng SIRC ARTICLE NO: 104610

DIRECTORIES

Bourgeois, P. Le guide de l'Ontario: du Manitoba et de la Saskatchewan. Montreal: La Presse, c1984. 339 p. : ill. (Collectio tourisme.)
LEVEL: B LANG: Fr ISBN: 2-89043-127-4 GV56.O5 17793

Lawton, P. 75 super summer camps. Ottawa magazine 3(12), Mar 1984
LEVEL: B LANG: Eng SIRC ARTICLE NO: 093331

Miller, G.O. Tull, D. Texas parks and campgrounds: a vacation guide to North, East, and the Gulf Coast. Austin, Tex.: Texas Monthly Press, c1984. 1v.
NOTES: Includes index.
LEVEL: B LANG: Eng ISBN: 0932012701 LC CARD: 84-000035

DISABLED

Lutfiyya, Z. Schaefer, N. A unique camping trip to the Rockies. Journal of leisurability (Waterloo, Ont.) 11(2), Spring 1984, 16-19.
NOTES: Reprinted from, Mental retardation Winter 1984,
LEVEL: B LANG: Eng SIRC ARTICLE NO: 095865

Sanders, R. New Hampshire Y Camp serves asthmatic children. Journal of physical education and program (Columbus, Oh.) 81(4) Apr 1984, D18-D19.
LEVEL: B LANG: Eng SIRC ARTICLE NO: 094326

ECONOMICS

Camping's national economic estimate: study discloses U.S. has 11,200 camps; industry is $2.5 billion annually. Camping magazine (Martinsville, Ind.) 56(7), May 1984, 10-11.
LEVEL: B LANG: Eng SIRC ARTICLE NO: 101134

ENVIRONMENT

Christy, W.R. An assessment of the effects of two residential camp settings on environmental attitude development. Eugene, Ore.: Microform Publications, University of Oregon, 1984. 2 microfiches : negative ; 11 x 15 cm.
NOTES: Thesis (Ed.D.) - Virginia Polytechnic Institute and State University, 1982; (vii, 122 leaves); vita; includes bibliography.
LEVEL: A LANG: Eng UO84 157-158

Reading, J. Acid rain: understanding the problem at camp. Canadian camping 35(4), Winter 1984, 13-16.
LEVEL: B LANG: Eng SIRC ARTICLE NO: 093334

EQUIPMENT

Andreen, M. Materiel tent poles: not what they used to be. Backpacker (New York) 12(2), Mar 1984, 35-36.
LEVEL: B LANG: E SIRC ARTICLE NO: 097470

EQUIPMENT - RETAILING

McElroy, P.E. Combine fishing and camping for more retail sales. Sports retailer (Mt. Prospect, Ill.) 37(5), May 1984, 20-22.
LEVEL: B LANG: Eng SIRC ARTICLE NO: 100570

INJURIES AND ACCIDENTS

Davies, J.S. Crisis management: case studies suggest ways to deal with serious problems. Camping magazine (Martinsville, Ind.) 56(7), May 1984, 27-31.
LEVEL: B LANG: Eng SIRC ARTICLE NO: 101135

CAMPING (continued)

JUVENILE LITERATURE

Marsoli, L.A. Things to know before going to camp. Morristown, N.J.: Silver Burdett Co., c1984. 1v.
NOTES: Includes index.
LEVEL: B LANG: Eng ISBN: 0382067878 LC CARD: 84-050446

PHILOSOPHY

Chenery, M.F. Nurturing the human spirit in camping. (Refs: 5)*Camping magazine (Martinsville, Ind.) 57(1), Sept/Oct 1984, 21-27.*
LEVEL: I LANG: Eng SIRC ARTICLE NO: 173551

PSYCHOLOGY

Becker, W.A. The key to staff motivation. (Refs: 8)*Camping magazine (Martinsville, Ind.) 56(7), May 1984, 32-35.*
LEVEL: I LANG: Eng SIRC ARTICLE NO: 101133

SAFETY

Camping (and even some waterfront) safety. *Your health & fitness (Highland Park, Ill.) 6(3), Jun/Jul 1984, 19-20.*
LEVEL: B LANG: Eng SIRC ARTICLE NO: 096555

Reamon, T.A. Accidents are preventable: New York's camp program stresses safety education. *Camping magazine (Martinsville, Ind.) 56(4), Feb 1984, 12-13.*
LEVEL: B LANG: Eng SIRC ARTICLE NO: 097975

SOCIAL PSYCHOLOGY

Farrell, P. Campers and free choice: a camper must be given chances to explore behavior boundaries and develop positive patterns. (Refs: 1)*Camping magazine (Martinsville, Ind.) 57(2), Nov/Dec 1984, 18-21.*
LEVEL: B LANG: Eng SIRC ARTICLE NO: 108455

Freeman, D. Power of positive modeling: camp leaders are in a unique position to help youth develop positive attitudes about themselves and others. *Camping magazine (Martinsville, Ind.) 56(6), Apr 1984, 16-17;28.*
LEVEL: B LANG: Eng SIRC ARTICLE NO: 101136

Latimer, J. Group dynamics exercise. The counsellor's perception vs. the camper's perception. *Canadian camping (Toronto) 36(1), Spring 1984, 12.*
LEVEL: B LANG: Eng SIRC ARTICLE NO: 099439

SOCIOLOGY

Fenton, H. The value of it all: it's time for all of us in camping to reach out to others. *Camping magazine (Martinsville, Ind.) 57(2), Nov/Dec 1984, 22-24.*
LEVEL: B LANG: Eng SIRC ARTICLE NO: 108456

Henderson, K.A. Bialeschki, M.D. Organized camping and the future research on major trends. (Refs: 8)*Camping magazine (Martinsville, Ind.) 56(3), Jan 1984, 19-25.*
LEVEL: I LANG: Eng SIRC ARTICLE NO: 097973

Packer, M.E. The computer generation: how much exposure to computers is beneficial to camps and campers? *Camping magazine (Martinsville, Ind.)*
57(1), Sept/Oct 1984, 12-13.
LEVEL: B LANG: Eng SIRC ARTICLE NO: 173548

STATISTICS AND RECORDS - PARTICIPATION

ACA's 1983 market survey: enrollment trends studied. *Camping magazine (Martinsville, Ind.) 56(5), Mar 1984, 12-13.*
LEVEL: I LANG: Eng SIRC ARTICLE NO: 097972

CANADA

Bedecki, T. International sport relations. (Refs: 14)*In, Ilmarinen, M. (ed.) et al., Sport and International Understanding: proceedings of the congress held in Helsinki, Finland, July 7-10, 1982, Berlin, Springer-Verlag, 1984, p. 312-315.*
CONF: Congress on Sport and International Understanding (1982 : Helsinki).
LEVEL: I LANG: Eng GV706.8 18979

New Minister of sport: Jacques Olivier. Nouveau ministre du sport: Jacques Olivier. *Champion (Vanier, Ont.) 8(2), May/mai 1984, 27.*
LEVEL: B LANG: Eng Fr SIRC ARTICLE NO: 094183

New Minister of sport: Otto Jelinek. Nouveau ministre du sport: Otto Jelinek. *Champion (Ottawa) 8(4), Nov 1984, 15-16.*
LEVEL: B LANG: Eng Fr SIRC ARTICLE NO: 100458

Otto Jelinek: new sports minister skates into cabinet. *Ringette review/Revue ringuette (Vanier) 6(4), Dec 1984, 14-17.*
LEVEL: B LANG: Eng SIRC ARTICLE NO: 108854

Rennie, J. Market trends 1984. *Jim Rennie's sports letter (Collingwood, Ont.) 8(23), 4 Jun 1984, 1-6.*
LEVEL: I LANG: Eng SIRC ARTICLE NO: 094762

Sport Canada applied sport research program: policy and guidelines 1984-1985. Sport Canada programme de recherche appliquee dans le sport: politique et lignes directrices 1984-1985. Ottawa: Supply and Services Canada, c1984. 12, 12 p. (Cat. no. H93-85/1984.)
CORP: Canada. Fitness and Amateur Sport.
CORP: Canada. Condition physique et sport amateur.
NOTES: French and English texts on inverted pages with separate paging. Textes francais et anglais disposes tete-beche avec pagination separee. Includes Application form for the Sport Canada applied Sport Research Program 1984-85. Comprend le Formulaire de demande de contribution du Programme de recherche appliquee dans le sport de Sport Canada 1984-1985.
LEVEL: B LANG: Eng Fr ISBN: 0-662-52887-5 GV585 17021

Sport Canada contributions program 1985-1986. Sport Canada programme de contributions 1985-1986. (Ottawa): Minister of Supply and Services, c1984. 42, 46 p.
CORP: Canada. Fitness and Amateur Sport.
CORP: Canada. Condition physique et Sport amateur.
NOTES: French and English texts on inverted pages with separate paging. Textes francais et anglais disposes tete-beche avec pagination separee.

LEVEL: B LANG: Eng Fr ISBN: 0-662-53376-3 GV716 18851

Tremblay, N. Sport Canada: un support vital pour les athletes. *Marathon, la revue de la bonne forme (Montreal) 16, mai 1984 56-57.*
LEVEL: B LANG: Fr SIRC ARTICLE NO: 108716

ALBERTA

Newton, D.M. Canada fitness survey: how active are Albertans? (Refs: 4)*Runner (Edmonton) 21(4), Winter 1983/1984, 5-7.*
LEVEL: I LANG: Eng SIRC ARTICLE NO: 096427

HISTORY

Brown, D.W. Imperialism and games on the playing fields of Canada's private schools. (Refs: 23)*Unpublished Olympic Congress paper 1984, 1-8.*
CONF: Olympic Scientific Congress (1984 : Eugene, Oregon).
ABST: The author examines the use of such sports as cricket to extol British imperial values in nineteenth century Canadian private schools. Upper Canada College and Bishop Ridley College are two schools examined in this paper.
LEVEL: A LANG: Eng SIRC ARTICLE NO: 095891

Cowan, W. Papers of the fifteenth Algonquian Conference. Ottawa: Carleton University, 1984. viii, 467 p.
CONF: Algonquian Conference (15th : 1983 : Cambridge, Mass.).
LEVEL: A LANG: Eng ISBN: 0-7709-0165-4 GV585 18629

Franks, C.E.S. Macintosh, D. The evolution of federal government policies toward sport and culture in Canada: a comparison. (Refs: 12)
CONF: North American Society for the Sociology of Sport. Conference (3rd : 1982 : Toronto, Ont.).
NOTES: In, Theberge, N. and Donnelly, P. (eds.), Sport and the sociological imagination: refereed proceedings of the 3rd Annual Conference of the North American Society for the Sociology of Sport, Toronto, Canada, November 1982, Fort Worth, Tex., Texas Christian University Press, c1984, p. 193-209.
ABST: This paper compares and contrasts the development and initiatives of Canadian federal government policies in the areas of culture and sport since the early 1950s to the late 1970s.
LEVEL: A LANG: Eng SIRC ARTICLE NO: 097560

Howell, M.L. Howell, R.A. Massicotte, J.P. Salter, M.A. Developments prior to 1800. (Refs: 52)
NOTES: In, Howell, M.L. and Howell, R.A. (eds.), History of sport in Canada, Champaign, Ill., Stipes Publishing Company, c1981, p. 1-50.
LEVEL: A LANG: Eng GV585 18153

Lappage, R.S. The physical feats of the voyageur. (Refs: 39)*Canadian journal of history of sport/ Revue canadienne de l'histoire des sports (Windsor) 15(1), May 1984, 30-37.*
ABST: This paper gives an account of the extraordinary feats of physical strength and endurance characteristic of the Canadian voyageurs between the years 1763 and 1840. The size of the canoes limited the height of voyageurs to under 5'11' tall (avg. 5'6'). They paddled from 12-15 hrs/day at a pace of 40 strokes/min., resting spells 10-15 minutes apart. Distances of 80 miles/ day were not uncommon. During portages at a trotting pace. These weights often induced

strangulated hernias. Approximately 7,200 cal./day was consumed by the voyageur. The author argues that the main motivation for the voyageur was the lifestyle itself: pride, competition, adventure, and freedom. Background information about the voyageurs and the fur trade is also given.
LEVEL: A LANG: Eng SIRC ARTICLE NO: 108314

Massicotte, J.P. L'activite physique en Nouvelle-France: jeux et sports. (Refs: 35)*Dans, Massicotte, J.P. et Lessard, C. (eds.), Histoire du sport de l'antiquite au XIXe siecle, Sillery, Que., Presses de l'Universite du Quebec, 1984, p. 185-194.*
LEVEL: A LANG: Fr GV571 18971

Metcalfe, A. L'evolution de la recreation physique organisee a Montreal 1840-1895. *Dans, Massicotte, J.P. et Lessard, C. (eds.), Histoire du sport de l'antiquite au XIXe siecle, Sillery, Que., Presses de l'Universite du Quebec, 1984, p. 271-297.*
LEVEL: A LANG: Fr GV571 18971

Wiggins, D.K. Smith, R.A. North American Society for Sport History proceedings and newsletter 1984. s.l.: North American Society for Sport History, c1984. 76 p. : ill.
CONF: North American Society for Sport History Conference (12th : 1984 : Louisville, Ky.).
CORP: North American Society for Sport History.
NOTES: ISSN: 0093-6235.
LEVEL: I LANG: Eng LC CARD: 74-642308 GV571 18383

OLYMPIC GAMES

Canada at the Olympics. Canada au Jeux olympiques. *Canada's sports hall of fame/Temple de la renommee des sports du Canada (Toronto) 7(2), Spring/printemps 1984, 6-7.*
LEVEL: B LANG: Eng Fr SIRC ARTICLE NO: 097637

La selection des athletes pour les Jeux olympiques. *Canada aux Jeux olympiques: un bulletin du service d'information de l'Association olympique canadienne (Montreal) 1984, 1-4.*
LEVEL: B LANG: Fr SIRC ARTICLE NO: 094186

The selection of Canadian athletes for the Olympic Games. *Canada at the Olympics: an information service bulletin of the Canadian Olympic Association (Montreal) 1984, 1-4.*
LEVEL: B LANG: Eng SIRC ARTICLE NO: 094187

ONTARIO

Dean, P.J. Physical activity patterns in Ontario - winter patterns. Based on the February 1981, 1983, and 1984 surveys. Toronto: Sports & Fitness Ontario, 1984. iii, 15 p.
LEVEL: I LANG: Eng GV585.3.O5 18923

Recreation services for youth in Ontario. Toronto: Ministry of Tourism and Recreation, 1984. ix, 48 p.
CORP: Ontario. Ministr of Tourism and Recreation.
NOTES: Cover title. Bibliography: p. 47-48.
LEVEL: B LANG: Eng GV56.O5 17875

PHYSICAL FITNESS

A guide to Fitness Canada contributions program 1985-1986. Un guide au programme de contributions de Condition physique Canada 1985-1986. Ottawa: Fitness Canada : Condition physique Canada, 1984?. 31, 33 p.
CORP: Canada. Fitness and Amateur Sport.
CORP: Canada. Condition physique et Sport

amateur.
NOTES: French and English texts on inverted pages with separate paging. Textes francais et anglais disposes tete-beche avec pagination separee.
LEVEL: B LANG: Eng Fr GV716 18852

Allocution presentee par Michel Bedard, directeur a Condtion physique Canada. An address by Michel Bedard, Director, Fitness Canada. *CAHPER journal (Ottawa) 51(1), Sept/Oct 1984, 28-35.*
LEVEL: B LANG: Fr Eng SIRC ARTICLE NO: 100848

Canada's runners and joggers: a massive movement. Les coureurs et les joggers du Canada: un mouvement de masse. *Highlights/Faits saillants (Ottawa) 33, Aug/aout 1984, 1-2.*
LEVEL: B LANG: Eng Fr SIRC ARTICLE NO: 099183

Curtis, J.E. White, P.G. Age and sport participation: decline in participation or increased specialization with age? (Refs: 22)
CONF: North American Society for the Sociology of Sport. Conference (3rd : 1982 : Toronto, Ont.).
NOTES: In, Theberge, N. and Donnelly, P. (eds.), Sport and the sociological imagination: refereed proceedings of the 3rd Annual Conference of the North American Society for the Sociology of Sport, Toronto, Canada, November 1982, Fort Worth, Tex., Texas Christian University Press, c1984, p. 273-293.
ABST: This paper discusses results from a national sample of adult Canadians dealing with patterns of sport participation for various age groups. The findings support both the disengagement theory (which hypothesizes that as age increases so does withdrawal from sport and physical activity) and the continuity and activity theory (which hypothesizes that sport or fitness roles once acquired will be maintained).
LEVEL: A LANG: Eng SIRC ARTICLE NO: 097841

Dean, P.J. Physical activity patterns in Ontario - IIa. A research report from the Ministry of Tourism and Recreation. 1982-83 update. Toronto: Ministry of Tourism and Recreation, 1984?. 7 leaves
CORP: Ontario. Ministry of Tourism and Recreation.
CORP: Fitness Ontario.
NOTES: Cover title.
LEVEL: B LANG: Eng GV481 17878

Exercise classes: popularity signalled by Canada Fitness survey. Les cours d'exercices sont tres populaires selon l'ECPC. *Highlights/Faits saillants (Ottawa) 34, Aug/aout 1984, 1-2.*
LEVEL: B LANG: Eng Fr SIRC ARTICLE NO: 099186

Guide to Fitness Canada Professional Development Practicum - 1984-1985. Guide du stage de formation professionnelle de Condition physique Canada 1984-1985. Ottawa: Fitness and Amateur Sport, 1984?. (8, 9) p.
CORP: Canada. Fitness and Amateur Sport.
CORP: Canada. Condition physique et sport amateur.
NOTES: French and English texts on inverted pages with separate paging. Textes francais et anglais disposes tete-beche avec pagination separee.
LEVEL: B LANG: Eng Fr GV733 14335

How hard do Canadians play? *CPHA health digest/ ACHP selection sante (Ottawa) Apr/avr 1984, 12.*
LEVEL: B LANG: Eng SIRC ARTICLE NO: 100862

Lignes directrices sur les adaptations au programme Jeunesse en forme Canada: enfants aux capacites physiques diminuees. Guidelines for adaptations to the Canada Fitness Award: youth with limited physical abilities. Ottawa: Condition physique et Sport amateur : Fitness and Amateur Sport, c1984. 17, 18 p. : ill. (Cat. no. H93-87/ 1984.)
CORP: Canada. Condition physique et Sport amateur.
CORP: Canada. Fitness and Amateur Sport.
NOTES: Cover title. Titre de la couverture. French and English texts on inverted pages with separate paging. Textes francais et anglais disposes tete-beche avec pagination separee.
LEVEL: B LANG: Fr Eng ISBN: 0-662-52989-8 GV709.3 17258

Newton, D.M. Canada fitness survey: how active are Albertans? (Refs: 4)*Runner (Edmonton) 21(4), Winter 1983/1984, 5-7.*
LEVEL: I LANG: Eng SIRC ARTICLE NO: 096427

Newton, D.M. Canada fitness survey findings: adolescent girls are different. Resultats de l'enquete condition physique Canada: les adolescentes sont, en effet, differentes. (Refs: 5)*CAHPER journal/Revue de l'ACSEPR (Ottawa) 50(4), Mar/Apr 1984, 25-30*
LEVEL: I LANG: Eng Fr SIRC ARTICLE NO: 096197

Newton, D.N. Towards a more active lifestyle. A la recherche d'une vie plus active. (Refs: 5)*CAHPER journal/Revue de l'ACSEPR (Vanier, Ont.) 50(3), Jan-Feb/janv-fevr 1984, 24-29.*
LEVEL: I LANG: Eng Fr SIRC ARTICLE NO: 094568

O'Seen, M. Bell, D. Faulkner, B. Evaluation de la condition physique des femmes du milieu rural en Saskatchewan. Fitness evaluation in rural Saskatchewan females. (Refs: 7)*Recreation Canada (Ottawa) 42(4), Sept/sept 1984, 30-32.*
LEVEL: I LANG: Fr Eng SIRC ARTICLE NO: 099203

Peepre, M. Toward a fitter Canada. Pour un Canada plus en forme. *CPHA health digest/ACHP selection sante (Ottawa) Apr/avr 1984, 10-11;10-12.*
LEVEL: B LANG: Eng Fr SIRC ARTICLE NO: 100873

Pfeiffer, S. Graham, T.E. Webb, R.D.G. Wilson, B.A. Rivington-Moss, E.G. Fisher-Ingram, L.M. Aspects of physical fitness and health in Ontario dairy farmers. *Canadian journal of public health/ Revue canadienne de sante publique (Ottawa) 75(3), May/Jun 1984, 204-211.*
ABST: The purpose of this study was to assess the fitness and health states of farmers compared to urban males. Anthropometric, physiological and psychosensory variables were recorded for 106 male dairy farmers, aged 32-67 years, from Wellington County, Ontario. Farmers showed lower estimated percent body fat, very high grip strength values, reduced back flexibility, hearing loss due to occupational noise exposure, certain low pulmonary function values, high energy intake and low HDL: total cholesterol ratio.
LEVEL: A LANG: Eng SIRC ARTICLE NO: 099204

Physical fitness of Canadians: norms at a glance. Condition physique des canadiens: les normes en bref. *Highlights/Faits saillants (Ottawa) 40, Nov 1984, 1-2.*
LEVEL: B LANG: Eng Fr SIRC ARTICLE NO: 102736

Recreation Canada. Selected articles on: fitness. Recreation Canada. Collection d'articles: conditionnement physique. Ottawa: Canadian Parks/Recreation Association
Association canadienne des loisirs/parcs, 1984. 94 p. : ill.
CORP: Canadian Parks/Recreation Association.
CORP: Association canadienne des loisirs/parcs.
NOTES: Cover title. Titre de la couverture.
LEVEL: B LANG: Eng Fr ISBN: 0-919963-11-0
GV481 17448

Revised Canada Fitness Award Program (CFA) 1984. Programme modifie de Jeunesse en forme Canada (JFC) 1984. *CAHPER journal (Ottawa) 51(2), Nov/Dec 1984, 24-27.*
LEVEL: B LANG: Eng Fr SIRC ARTICLE NO: 102741

Rode, A. Shephard, R.J. Ten years of 'civilization': fitness of Canadian Inuit. (Refs: 16)*Journal of applied physiology: respiratory, environmental and exercise physiology (Bethesda, Md.) 56(6), Jun 1984, 1472-1477.*
ABST: This cross-sectional study compared the fitness of 74 men and 44 women tested in 1970-71 with the fitness of 107 men and 74 women tested in 1980-81. All subjects lived in the remote northern settlement of Igloolik. The results indicate that there has been a 15% decrease in predicted VO2 max, accompanied by a 2- to 4-kg increase in body mass, accumulation of subcutaneous fat and a decrease in leg extension strength from 1970 to 1980. The authors suggest that the subjects' adoption of a more sedentary lifestyle is responsible for the dramatic decrease in fitness.
LEVEL: A LANG: Eng SIRC ARTICLE NO: 097699

Schrodt, B. Federal programmes of physical recreation and fitness: the contributions of Ian Eisenhardt and BC's Pro-Rec. (Refs: 71)*Canadian journal of history of sport/Revue canadienne de l'histoire des sports (Windsor, Ont.) 15(2), Dec 1984, 45-61.*
LEVEL: A LANG: Eng SIRC ARTICLE NO: 104449

Seasons affect activity levels. *Fitnews (Toronto, Ont.) 17, Dec 1984, 1-2.*
LEVEL: I LANG: Eng SIRC ARTICLE NO: 173015

QUEBEC

Brassard, A. L'athlete d'elite: son encadrement. *Coup d'oeil sur l'halterophilie (Montreal) 17(2), avr/mai 1984, 33-35.*
LEVEL: B LANG: Fr SIRC ARTICLE NO: 109108

Jurtschyschyn, P. L'entrevue du mois avec Paul Ohl. *Marathon (Montreal) 17, 1984, 27-28.*
LEVEL: B LANG: Fr SIRC ARTICLE NO: 103808

Le temps de l'excellence: un defi quebecois. La politique quebecoise de developpement de l'excellence sportive. (Quebec): Ministere du loisir, de la chasse et de la peche, 1984. 112 p. : ill.
CORP: Quebec. Ministere du loisir, de la chasse et de la peche.
LEVEL: B LANG: Fr ISBN: 2-550-10754-3
GV585.3.Q7 17557

Marcotte, G. Un retour a la tour d'ivoire. *Revue de l'entraineur janv/mars 1984, 30.*
LEVEL: B LANG: Fr SIRC ARTICLE NO: 091871

Six questions a Paul Ohl. *Revue de l'entraineur (Montreal) oct/dec 1984, 25.*
LEVEL: B LANG: Fr SIRC ARTICLE NO: 105600

Vers l'excellence. *Revue de l'entraineur janv/mars 1984, 16-17.*
LEVEL: B LANG: Fr SIRC ARTICLE NO: 091874

CANADIAN FOOTBALL

ADMINISTRATION

Hickey, P. Jake's legacy: in his 17-year reign as commissioner Jake Gaudaur united the CFL under one banner - he also got players to tuck in their shirts. *CFL illustrated (Toronto) 15(1), 1984, 13-14.*
LEVEL: B LANG: Eng SIRC ARTICLE NO: 098088

BIOGRAPHY AND AUTOBIOGRAPHY

Quinn, D. Ontario Amateur Football: alive, and growing. *Ontario sportscene (Toronto) 6(3), May/Jun 1984, 8-10.*
NOTES: Interview with Dennis Laverty, director of the Ontario Amateur Football Association.
LEVEL: B LANG: Eng SIRC ARTICLE NO: 095017

CLUBS AND TEAMS

Calder, B. Andrews, G. Rider pride: the story of Canada's best-loved football team. Saskatoon: Western Producer Prairie Books, c1984. 215 p. : ill.
NOTES: Bibliography: p. 208.
LEVEL: B LANG: Eng ISBN: 0-88833-128-2 LC CARD: C84-091238-2 GV948 17538

COACHING

Interview with John Hier. John Hier: personal background. *Audible (Willowdale, Ont.) Summer 1984, 5-8.*
LEVEL: B LANG: Eng SIRC ARTICLE NO: 099578

Owen, D. The team concept in a coaching staff. *Audible (Willowdale, Ont.) Fall 1984, 4-5.*
LEVEL: B LANG: Eng SIRC ARTICLE NO: 108654

HISTORY

Roberts, L. The forward pass is here. *P.F.R.A. annual (Canton, Oh.) 1984, 51-57.*
NOTES: Reprinted from, the Canadian magazine, Sept 1931.
LEVEL: B LANG: Eng SIRC ARTICLE NO: 104732

Sproule, B. Snap back vs. scrimmage. *P.F.R.A. annual (Canton, Oh.) 1984, 25-28.*
LEVEL: B LANG: Eng SIRC ARTICLE NO: 10473

RULES AND REGULATIONS

Casey, T. Should the CFL eliminate the single point on a wide field-goal attempt? Yes, No. *CFL illustrated (Toronto) 15(3), 1984, 17-20.*
LEVEL: B LANG: Eng SIRC ARTICLE NO: 098084

Green, K. The retreat block: a clarification of the rule. *Audible (Willowdale, Ont.) Fall 1984, 11-12.*
LEVEL: B LANG: Eng SIRC ARTICLE NO: 108659

Hickey, P. Rules made to be kept. With Norm Kimball leading the charge the CFL quashed a proposed rule change that attacked the roots of Canadian football. *CFL illustrated (Toronto) 15(2), 1984, 13-14.*
LEVEL: B LANG: Eng SIRC ARTICLE NO: 098089

STRATEGY - DEFENSIVE

Laycoe, R. Defending against the forward pass. *Coaching review (Ottawa) 7, Sept/Oct 1984, 53-55.*
LEVEL: B LANG: Eng SIRC ARTICLE NO: 098091

Riley, M. Defensive backfield play. *Audible (Toronto) Spring 1984, 9-12.*
LEVEL: B LANG: Eng SIRC ARTICLE NO: 096669

Vespaziani, B. Techniques and tactics for blocking punts. *Audible (Willowdale, Ont.) Summer 1984, 12-15.*
LEVEL: B LANG: E SIRC ARTICLE NO: 099611

STRATEGY - OFFENSIVE

Wolfe, S. McGill's call blocking system. *Audible (Toronto) Spring 1984, 14-15.*
LEVEL: B LANG: Eng SIRC ARTICLE NO: 096675

TECHNIQUES AND SKILLS - QUARTERBACK

Ponzi, J. The quarterback-centre exchange. *Audible (Willowdale, Ont.) Fall 1984, 5-8.*
NOTES: Excerpt from, Ponzi, J. and Workowski, N., Handbook of offensive liveplay.
LEVEL: B LANG: Eng SIRC ARTICLE NO: 108656

TRAINING AND CONDITIONING - DRILLS

Robinson, P. Drilling the offensive backs and receivers. *Audible (Willowdale, Ont.) Fall 1984, 8-10.*
LEVEL: B LANG: Eng SIRC ARTICLE NO: 108658

CANOEING

Combs, R. Gillen, S. Runoff rivers: they only run when it rains. Here's how to predict the time to paddle them. *Canoe (Camden, Me.) 12(4), Jul/Aug 1984, 58-59;61.*
LEVEL: B LANG: Eng SIRC ARTICLE NO: 103067

Riviere, B. Biggar, J. Camper's bible. 3rd ed. Garden City, N.Y.: Doubleday, 1984. 178 (1) p. : ill. (Sports & recreation.)
LEVEL: B LANG: Eng ISBN: 0385170505 LC CARD: 82-045267 GV191.7 17323

ANTHROPOMETRY

Vaccaro, P. Gray, P.R. Clarke, D.H. Morris, A.F. Physiological characteristics of world class white-water slalom paddlers. (Refs: 37)*Research quarterly for exercise & sport (Reston, Va.) 55(2), Jun 1984, 206-210.*
ABST: This descriptive study reports the physiological characteristics of 13 members of the United States White-Water Slalom Team. Data on body composition and somatotype as well as maximal exercise measurements are given.
LEVEL: A LANG: Eng SIRC ARTICLE NO: 096558

BIBLIOGRAPHIES

Shortley, R. Hittin' the books: an annotated guide to some paddling literature. *Canoe (Camden, Me.) 12(5), Sept/Oct 1984, 20;87.*
LEVEL: B LANG: Eng SIRC ARTICLE NO: 173542

BIOGRAPHY AND AUTOBIOGRAPHY

Canoeing: Alwyn Morris. Canotage: Alwyn Morris. *Champion (Ottawa) 8(3), Aug 1984, 48-49.* LEVEL: B LANG: Eng Fr SIRC ARTICLE NO: 096557

Marathon canoeists: Gilverson & Kirby. (Pam Gilverson and Sandi Kirby) *Paddles up (Ottawa) 2(1), May 1984, 6-7.* LEVEL: B LANG: Eng SIRC ARTICLE NO: 099443

Stuller, S. Body and soul: Serge Corbin. *Ultrasport (Boston, Mass.) 1(6), Nov/Dec 1984, 16;18-19.* LEVEL: B LANG: Eng SIRC ARTICLE NO: 172953

CERTIFICATION

Sprint racing canoeing. Level 1 coaching certification. Ottawa: Canadian Canoe Association, c1984. iii, 66 p. : ill. (National Coaching Certification Program.) CORP: Canadian Canoe Association. NOTES: Cover title. LEVEL: B LANG: Eng GV786 18728

Sprint racing canoeing. Level 2 coaching certification. Ottawa: Canadian Canoe Association, c1984. vi, 68 p. : ill. (National Coaching Certification Program.) CORP: Canadian Canoe Association. NOTES: Cover title. LEVEL: B LANG: Eng GV786 18727

CLOTHING

Vickery, J.D. Singin' in the rain: a canoe paddler's quest for the ultimate raingear. *Canoe (Camden, Me.) 12(2), Apr 1984, 22-30.* LEVEL: B LANG: Eng SIRC ARTICLE NO: 099444

COUNTRIES AND REGIONS

Dohnal, K. Yukon solo. 1st ed. Portland, Or.: Binford & Mort Pub., 1984. xv, 215 p., (1) leaf of plates : ill. LEVEL: B LANG: Eng ISBN: 0832304212 LC CARD: 83-070953

Proskine, A.C. Berry, J. Adirondack canoe waters: south and west flow. Glen Falls, N.Y.: Adirondack Mountain Club, c1984. 1v NOTES: Including the 3 main watersheds of the Southern Adirondacks - the Black, the Mohawk, and the Upper Hudson - plus the 2 major streams of the Tug Hill Plateau. Includes index. LEVEL: B LANG: Eng ISBN: 0935272232 LC CARD: 84-018516

Wirth, B. Open boat canoeing. West Nyack, N.Y.: Parker Pub. Co., c1984. 1v. NOTES: Includes index. LEVEL: B LANG: Eng ISBN 0136375960 LC CARD: 84-014907

DISABLED

Frith, G.H. Warren, L.D. Adapted canoeing for the handicapped. *Teaching exceptional children (Reston, Va.) 16(3), Spring 1984, 213-218.* ABST: Safety and instructional recommendations are presented. LEVEL: I LANG: Eng SIRC ARTICLE NO: 099005

ENVIRONMENT

Dale Vickery, J. Eyes to the sky. *Canoe (Camden, Me.) 12(3), May/Jun 1984, 60-65.* LEVEL: B LANG: Eng SIRC ARTICLE NO: 101140

EQUIPMENT

Au lieu du traditionnel sac a dos pourquoi pas une simple boite? *Courant (Montreal) aout/sept 1984, 5.* LEVEL: B LANG: Fr SIRC ARTICLE NO: 099440

Buying guide. *Canoeing (London, Eng.) 73, Feb 1984, 16-18.* LEVEL: B LANG: Eng SIRC ARTICLE NO: 097476

Carden, G. CLASS-C (5m). *Downeast sailor (Concord, Ma.) 19, Apr 1984, 2-4.* LEVEL: B LANG: Eng SIRC ARTICLE NO: 103675

Evans, E. Gene Jensen: when it comes to canoes, those two words spell f-a-s-t and f-a-s-t-e-r. *Canoe (Camden, Me.) 12(4), Jul/Aug 1984, 26-27;29-33.* LEVEL: B LANG: Eng SIRC ARTICLE NO: 103068

Finding your canoe: how to get the most out of the buyer's guide listings. *Canoe (Camden, Me.) 12(6), Nov/Dec 1984, 26-34;37;39-44;46-48;50-51;54-58;62;64-66.* LEVEL: B LANG: Eng SIRC ARTICLE NO: 108621

Kattel, E. Swan: 5 meter sailing canoe. *Downeast sailor (Concord, Mass.) 18, Feb 1984, 3.* LEVEL: B LANG: Eng SIRC ARTICLE NO: 094914

McCurdy, P. He waka tete hou: a new canoe for Maori canoe racing. *New Zealand canoeing & rafting (Auckland, N.Z.) 33, Winte 1984, 21-24.* NOTES: Reprinted from, The Journal of the Traditional Small Craft Society. LEVEL: B LANG: Eng SIRC ARTICLE NO: 097981

Rock, H. Getchell, D.R. Viehman, J. Fully-equipped: some notes on gear. *Canoe (Camden, Me.) 12(1), Feb/Mar 1984, 28-29;60;62-63.* LEVEL: B LANG: Eng SIRC ARTICLE NO: 097983

Sebring, T. We-no-nah Odyssey: user-friendly. *Canoe (Camden, Me.) 12(1), Feb/Mar 1984, 74;76.* LEVEL: B LANG: Eng SIRC ARTICLE NO: 097985

Sebring, T. Tricking it out: personalizing your canoe for performance. *Canoe (Camden, Me.) 12(3), May/Jun 1984, 18-21;23.* LEVEL: B LANG: Eng SIRC ARTICLE NO: 100577

Sebring, T. Sawyer Summersong: a comfortably fast solo cruiser. *Canoe (Camden, Me.) 12(3), May/Jun 1984, 92-94.* LEVEL: B LANG: Eng SIRC ARTICLE NO: 101145

Sebring, T. Boat cores: toward stronger, lighter layups. *Canoe (Camden, Me.) 12(4), Jul/Aug 1984, 22;24;78.* LEVEL: B LANG Eng SIRC ARTICLE NO: 103070

Sebring, T. Trends '85: design, construction and gear: our predictions for the coming year. *Canoe (Camden, Me.) 12(6), ov/Dec 1984, 23-25.* LEVEL: B LANG: Eng SIRC ARTICLE NO: 108620

EQUIPMENT - MAINTENANCE

Boulanger, F. Reparer son canot. *Courant (Montreal) aout/sept 1984, 11.* LEVEL: B LANG: Fr SIRC ARTICLE NO: 099441

HISTORY

Lessard, C. Massicotte, J.P. Histoire du canotage en Mauricie. (Refs: 7)*Dans, Massicotte, J.P. et Lessard, C. (eds.), Histoire du sport de l'antiquite au XIXe siecle, Sillery, Que., Presses de l'Universite du Quebec, 1984, p. 217-227.* NOTES: Presente au VIeme Seminaire HISPA, Trois-Rivieres, 1976. LEVEL: A LANG: Fr GV571 18971

Massicotte, J.P. Histoire du canot. *Dans, Massicotte, J.P. et Lessard, C. (eds.), Histoire du sport de l'antiquite au XIXe siecle, Sillery, Que., Presses de l'Universite du Quebec, 1984, p. 229-241.* LEVEL: A LANG: Fr GV571 18971

INJURIES AND ACCIDENTS

Hunt, S. First aid for paddlers. Accidents will happen. *Canoe (Camden, Me.) 12(3), May/Jun 1984, 42-44.* LEVEL: B LANG: En SIRC ARTICLE NO: 101141

Miller, P. Tendinitis: over-enthusiastic boaters, beware... *Canoe (Canden, Me.) 12(6), Nov/Dec 1984, 102-103.* LEVEL: B LANG: Eng SIRC ARTICLE NO: 108619

MEDICINE

Csanady, M. Gruber, N. Comparative echocardiographic studies in leading canoe-kayak and handball sportsmen. (Refs: 15)*Cor et vasa (Prague) 26(1), 1984, 32-37.* ABST: The purpose of this study was to compare echocardiographic data of 21 elite kayak-canoeists and 16 elite handball players. A thicker posterior wall and interventricular system as well as a greater left ventricular mass were observed in the kayak-canoeists. LEVEL: A LANG: Eng SIRC ARTICLE NO: 103507

PHOTOGRAPHY

Ray, S. Cameras and the water. Simple ways to protect your investment. *Canoe (Camden, Me.) 12(3), May/Jun 1984, 37;39-40.* LEVEL: B LANG: Eng SIRC ARTICLE NO: 101144

PHYSIOLOGY

Bennett, A. Thought for fuel: the problems of energy supply for the marathon canoeist. *Canoeing (London, Eng.) 74, Mar 1984 8-9.* LEVEL: I LANG: Eng SIRC ARTICLE NO: 097976

Csanady, M. Forster, T. Gruber, N. Hogye, M. Moczo, I. A kajakozast vagy kenuzast versenyszeruleg elkezdo fiuk echokardiografias oesszahasonlitasa azonos koru, nem sportolo tarsaikkal. (Comparison of echocardiographic data on beginner kayakcanoeists and non-sporting boys of the same age.) (Refs: 26)*Sportorvosi szemle/ Hungarian review of sports medicine (Budapest) 25(3), 1984, 197-207.* ABST: A series of examinations is planned for years, to follow the changes in the

echocardiographic parameters of kayak-canoeist competitors in comparison with the data on non-trained boys of the same age. The present publication reports the starting data at the end of the first season. Significant differences were found between the groups: the left ventricular cavity of kayak-canoeists was larger, while the left ventricular posterior wall and especially the interventricular septum were thicker, than in non-trained boys.
LEVEL: A LANG: Hun SIRC ARTICLE NO: 100236

Vaccaro, P. Gray, P.R. Clarke, D.H. Morris, A.F. Physiological characteristics of world class white-water slalom paddlers. (Refs: 37)*Research quarterly for exercise & sport (Reston, Va.) 55(2), Jun 1984, 206-210.*
ABST: This descriptive study reports the physiological characteristics of 13 members of the United States White-Water Slalom Team. Data on body composition and somatotype as well as maximal exercise measurements are given.
LEVEL: A LANG: Eng SIRC ARTICLE NO: 096558

PSYCHOLOGY

Paulk, K.E. The effects of canoe tripping on the self-concepts of campers in a long-term therapeutic wilderness camp. Eugene Ore.: Microform Publications, University of Oregon, 1984. 1 microfiche : negative, 11 x 15 cm.
NOTES: Thesis (M.S.) - Pennsylvania State University, 1982; (vi, 63 leaves); includes bibliography.
LEVEL: A LANG: Eng UO84 357

SAFETY

Bechdel, L. River rescue systems. *American whitewater (Hagerstown, Md.) 29(5), Sept/Oct 1984, 26-27.*
NOTES: Reprinted from, Nantahala Outdoor Center.
LEVEL: B LANG: Eng SIRC ARTICLE NO: 108852

Green slime throw bag. *Canoeing (London) 77, Jun 1984, 18.*
LEVEL: B LANG: Eng SIRC ARTICLE NO: 098944

Miller, D. Close calls on the river. Learning from someone else's mistakes. *Canoe (Camden, Me.) 12(3), May/Jun 1984, 26-27;78.*
LEVEL: B LANG: Eng SIRC ARTICLE NO: 101143

SPORTSMANSHIP

Kohler, S. Code of the wet: peaceful coexistence on the river. *Canoe (Camden, Me.) 12(3), May/Jun 1984, 24-25.*
LEVEL: B LANG: Eng SIRC ARTICLE NO: 101142

TECHNIQUES AND SKILLS

Colby, C. Solo clinics. *American whitewater (Hagerstown, Md.) 29(5), Sept/Oct 1984, 28-30.*
CORP: Lower Columbia Canoe Club.
LEVEL: B LANG: Eng SIRC ARTICLE NO: 108853

Scarborough, S. Canoe techniques: inside solo wave surfing. *River runner (Vista, Calif.) 4(2), Mar/Apr 1984, 37-38.*
LEVEL B LANG: Eng SIRC ARTICLE NO: 097984

Shelander, J. A whitewater primer: how to roll an open canoe. *Canoe (Camden, Me.) 12(1), Feb/Mar 1984, 26-27.*
LEVEL: B LANG: Eng SIRC ARTICLE NO: 097986

Walbridge, C. Power paddling in a solo canoe. *River runner (Vista, Calif.) 4(3), May/Jun 1984, 22-23.*
LEVEL: B LANG: Eng SIRC ARTICLE NO: 099445

TRAINING AND CONDITIONING

McCormick, M. Swomley, B. Training plan of Luc Verger. *ACA competitor's newsletter (Lorton, Va.) 10, Dec 1984, 5.*
NOTES: section from Bill Endicott's forthcoming book, 'Danger Zone, Downriver Canoeing at the Highest Levels'. The Athlete's exchange 3(9), Oct 1984.
LEVEL: B LANG: Eng SIRC ARTICLE NO: 103069

Preece, J. Guidelines for a practice. *Paddles up (Ottawa) 2(2), Jul/Aug 1984, 5-6.*
LEVEL: B LANG: Eng SIRC ARTICLE NO: 097982

TRAINING AND CONDITIONING - DRYLAND TRAINING

Campagna, P. Garner, F. Cardiovascular conditioning during the general preparation cycle. (Refs: 12)*Paddles up (Ottawa) 2(1), May 1984, 4-5.*
LEVEL: I LANG: Eng SIRC ARTICLE NO: 099442

TRAINING AND CONDITIONING - WEIGHT AND STRENGTH TRAINING

Cezard, J.P. Reflexion sur le renforcement musculaire en canoe-kayak.
NOTES: Dans, Renforcement musculaire, Paris, Institut national du sport et de l'education physique, c1984, p. 99-124.
LEVEL: A LANG: Fr GV711.5 18233

McCormick, M. Strength, power and weights. *ACA competitor's newsletter (Lorton, Va.) Sept/Oct 1984, 9-10.*
NOTES: The Athlete's exchange 3(7), Oct 1984.
LEVEL: B LANG: Eng SIRC ARTICLE NO: 103276

TRANSPORTATION

Dutton, V.L.S. Build yourself a canoe trailer. *Leader (Ottawa, Ont.) 14(5), Jan 1984, 12-14.*
LEVEL: B LANG: Eng SIRC ARTICLE NO: 097977

WOMEN

Miller, P. Women on water. *Canoe (Camden, Me.) 12(5), Sept/Oct 1984, 22-29.*
LEVEL: B LANG: Eng SIRC ARTICLE NO: 173543

CHEERLEADING

Cheerleading: Memphis State Tigers win 1984 NCA National Championships and $5,000. *International gymnast (Santa Monica, Calif.) 26(3), Mar 1984, 61-65.*
LEVEL: B LANG: Eng SIRC ARTICLE NO: 099652

Webb, G. Cheerleaders - spirit leaders and then some. *Interscholastic athletic administration (Kansas City) 11(1), Fall 198 18-19.*
LEVEL: B LANG: Eng SIRC ARTICLE NO: 105893

Webb, G. Maximizing you home field advantage. *Interscholastic athletic administration (Kansas City) 11(2), Winter 1984, 20-21;23.*
LEVEL: B LANG: Eng SIRC ARTICLE NO: 108263

TRAINING AND CONDITIONING - WEIGHT AND STRENGTH TRAINING

Bostian, L.C. Nolte, W. Cheerleading conditioning tips... Conditioning programs for selected cheerleading activities. (Refs: 21)*Women's coaching clinic (Princeton, N.J.) 8(3), Nov 1984, 4-8.*
LEVEL: B LANG: Eng SIRC ARTICLE NO: 103216

CHILDREN AND ADOLESCENTS

Affleck, J.A. Kid sports - the emerging youth sport snowball. *Spotlight on youth sports (East Lansing, Mich.) 7(4), Winter 1984, 5.*
LEVEL: B LANG: Eng SIRC ARTICLE NO: 108879

Bean, D. Young children really are different. (Refs: 7)*Runner (Edmonton) 21(4), Winter 1983/1984, 22-25.*
LEVEL: B LANG: E SIRC ARTICLE NO: 095725

Blair, S. Youth sport review. (Refs: 31)*Foil (Indianapolis) Spring 1984, 11-13.*
LEVEL: B LANG: Eng SIRC ARTICLE NO: 10904

Blann, M.E. Developing a cooperative relationship between physical education and agency sponsored youth sports. *Physical education newsletter (Old Saybrook, Conn.) 161, Aug 1984, 2-4.*
LEVEL: B LANG: Eng SIRC ARTICLE NO: 100502

Children in sport. *ACHPER national journal 103, Mar 1984, 62-66.*
CORP: Confederation of Australian Sport.
CORP: Australian Council for Health, Physical Education and Recreation.
CORP: Australian Sports Medicine Federation.
ABST: A policy statement prepared jointly by the Confederation of Australian Sport (CAS), The Australian Council for Health, Physical Education and Recreation (ACHPER) and the Australian Sports Medicine Federation (ASMF). The statement defines and discusses: (1) children's sport; (2) physical education; (3) girls sport; (4) sport in the school and community; (5) Bill of Rights for children's sport, children in competitive sport; (6) parent involvement; (7) coaching; (8) modified sport; (9) medical and psychological aspects of sport for children.
LEVEL: I LANG: Eng SIRC ARTICLE NO: 097423

Engstroem, L.M. Reactions to and conclusions from the papers. *In, Idrett for barn. Sport for Children. Sport pour les enfants 27.9.-1.10.1982 Tonsberg, Norway. Report. Oslo, Norway, Ministry of Cultural and Scientific Affairs: Norwegian Confederation of Sport, 1984, p. (44)-(45).*
CONF: Idrett for barn. Sport for Children. Sport pour les enfants (1982 : Tonsberg, Norway).
LEVEL: A LANG: Eng GV709.2 20111

Engstroem, L.M. Reactions faisant suite aux document et conclusions. *Dans, Idrett for barn. Sport for Children. Sport pour les enfants 27.9.-1.10.1982 Tonsberg, Norway. Rapport. Oslo, Norvege, Ministere de la culture et de la science : Confederation norvegienne des sports, 1984, p. (46)-(47).*
CONF: Idrett for barn. Sport for Children. Sport pour les enfants (1982 : Tonsberg, Norway).
LEVEL: A LANG: Fr GV709.2 20112

Fontaine, G. Le sport et l'enfant. (Sports and the child.) *LARC medical (Lille, France) 4(1), janv 1984, 45-46;49;51-52.*
LEVEL: A LANG: Fr SIRC ARTICLE NO: 100504

Garrick, J.G. Sportsmedicine for the pediatrician. Chicago: Teach'em Inc., 1984?. 2 sound cassettes : study guide (Audio cassette series on sports medicine, AAP-35.)
NOTES: Cassettes recorded and produced by Teach'em Inc. in cooperation with the Physician and Sportsmedicine.
LEVEL: I LANG: Eng

Hahn, E. Psychological aspects of children in sports. Psychologically-oriented studies on the problem of performance sport with children. (Refs: 56)*In, Idrett for barn. Sport for Children. Sport pour les enfants 27.9.-1.10.1982 Tonsberg, Norway. Report. Oslo, Norway, Ministry of Cultural and Scientific Affairs: Norwegian Confederation of Sport, 1984, p. (25)-(33).*
CONF: Idrett for barn. Sport for Children. Sport pour les enfants (1982 : Tonsberg, Norway).
LEVEL: A LANG: Eng GV709.2 20111

Hahn, E. La psychologie enfantine et le sport. Etudes psychologiques relatives au sport de performance pour les enfants. (Refs: 56)*Dans, Idrett for barn. Sport for Children. Sport pour les enfants 27.9.-1.10.1982 Tonsberg, Norway. Rapport. Oslo, Norvege, Ministere de la culture et de la science : Confederation norvegienne des sports, 1984, p. (26)-(34).*
CONF: Idrett for barn. Sport for Children. Sport pour les enfants (1982 : Tonsberg, Norway).
LEVEL: A LANG: Fr GV709.2 20112

Idrett for barn. Sport for Children. Sport pour les enfants 27. 9. - 1. 10. 1982 Tonsberg, Norway. Report. Oslo, Norway: Ministry of Cultural and Scientific Affairs : Norwegian Confederation of Sport, 1984. (56) p. : ill. (CDDS (82) 66)
CONF: Idrett for barn. Sport for Children. Sport pour les enfants (1982 : Tonsberg, Norway).
CORP: Council of Europe.
CORP: Norwegian Confederation of Sport.
NOTES: Cover title. Includes bibliographies.
LEVEL: A LANG: Eng GV709.2 20111

Lacour, J.P. Enfant. Choisissez bien son sport. *Psychologies (France) 7, 1984, 55-59.*
LEVEL: B LANG: Fr

Le sport pour les enfants. *Revue de l'education physique (Liege, Belgique) 24(1), 1984, 45-47.*
LEVEL: B LANG: Fr SIRC ARTICLE NO: 095742

Leglise, H. Le debutant: prospection, detection. *Revue de l'Amicale des entraineurs francais d'athletisme (Paris) 86, janv/fevr/mars 1984, 55-58.*
NOTES: Extrait de l'amicale des entraineurs aquitains d'athletisme.
LEVEL: B LANG: Fr SIRC ARTICLE NO: 094205

Nettleton, B. Children in sport: some perspectives on the policy statement 'Children in Sport'. *ACHPER national journal (Kingswood, Aust.) 105, Spring 1984, 11-15.*
LEVEL: B LANG: Eng SIRC ARTICLE NO: 102337

Nguyen, M. L'enfant et le sport. *Impact medecin (Puteaux, France) 121, 1984, 39-42.*
LEVEL: B LANG: Fr

Robertson, I. Sport in the lives of South Australian children. *Sports coach (Wembley, Australia) 7(4),*

Mar 1984, 3-6.
LEVEL: I LANG: Eng SIRC ARTICLE NO: 094210

Seefeldt, V. Branta, C.F. Patterns of participation in children's sport. (Refs: 33)*In, Thomas, J.R. (ed.), Motor developmen during childhood and adolescence, Minneapolis, Minn., Burgess Publishing Co., 1984, p. 190-211.*
LEVEL: A LANG: Eng BF1 20187

Van Lierde, A. Sport pour tous - groupe cible: les enfants. Etude de quelques recommandations existantes sur le sport pour les enfants (6 a 12 ans). (Refs: 18)*Dans, Idrett for barn. Sport for Children. Sport pour les enfants 27.9.-1.10.1982 Tonsberg, Norway. Rapport. Oslo, Norvege, Ministere de la culture et de la science : Confederation norvegienne des sports, 1984, p. (48)-(51).*
CONF: Idrett for barn. Sport for Children. Sport pour les enfants (1982 : Tonsberg, Norway).
LEVEL: A LANG: Fr GV709.2 20112

Wafelbakker, F. Advising on sports, A task for the Youth Health Services. *International journal of sports medicine (Stuttgart) Suppl. 5, Nov 1984, 3-4.*
CONF: International Congress on Sports and Health (1983 : Maastricht, Netherlands).
LEVEL: B LANG: Eng SIRC ARTICLE NO: 103841

Wood, D.D. Childhood sporting injury. *Modern athlete and coach (Athelstone, Aust.) 22(3), Jul 1984, 20-22.*
LEVEL: B LANG: Eng SIRC ARTICLE NO: 100511

ADMINISTRATION

Knight, D. Target Gold: an inner city initiative. *ILAM: Institute of Leisure & Amenity Management (London, Eng.) 2(7), Jul 1984, 8;10.*
LEVEL: B LANG: Eng SIRC ARTICLE NO: 100454

Valeriote, T. Children's sport programs: the administrator. Ottawa: New Traditions, c1984. v, 32, A10 p. : ill.
NOTES: Includes bibliography.
LEVEL: B LANG: Eng ISBN: 0-9691563-1-6 LC CARD: C84-90050-3 GV709.2 17662

CHILD DEVELOPMENT

Bredemeier, B.J. Sport, gender, and moral growth.
NOTES: In, Silva, J.M. and Weinberg, R.S. (eds.), Psychological foundations of sport, Champaign, Ill., Human Kinetics Publishers, c1984, p. 400-413.
LEVEL: A LANG: Eng GV706.4 17779

Exercise and skeletal development. *Health letter (San Antonio, Tex.) 24(8), 26 Oct 1984, 1-2.*
LEVEL: I LANG: Eng SIRC ARTICLE NO: 102575

Hill, P. Role of play in child development. *IPA: International Association for the Child's Right to Play newsletter (Sheffield) 8(8), Apr 1984, 14-19.*
LEVEL: I LANG: Eng SIRC ARTICLE NO: 103835

Johnsen, E.P. Christie, J.F. Play and social cognition. (Refs: 18)
NOTES: In, Sutton-Smith, B. and Kelly-Byrne, D. (eds.), The masks of play, New York, Leisure Press, c1984, p. 109-118.
LEVEL: A LANG: Eng HQ782 17029

Khosla, R.P. Inaugural address - play and child development. *IPA: International Association for the Child's Right to Play newsletter (Sheffield) 8(8), Apr 1984, 3-7.*
LEVEL: B LANG: Eng SIRC ARTICLE NO: 103837

Krassner, L.S. Maturation in sports. *Wrestling USA (Bozeman, Mont.) 20(5), 15 Dec 1984, 13-14.*
LEVEL: B LANG: Eng SIRC ARTICLE NO: 173869

Rieu, M. Les jeunes sportifs et sportives et les relations medecins-entraineurs. *Dans, Mandel, C. (ed.), Le medecin, l'enfant et le sport, Paris, (Vigot), c1984, p. 25-29.*
LEVEL: B LANG: Fr RC1218.C45 18886

Rogol, A. Endurance and pubertal development. *Running & fitness (Washington, D.C.) 16(4), Jul/Aug 1984, 8-9.*
LEVEL: B LANG: Eng SIRC ARTICLE NO: 105169

Ulrich, B.D. The effects of stimulation programs on the development of high risk infants: a review of research. (Refs: 69) *Adapted physical activity quarterly 1(1), 1984, 68-80.*
ABST: This paper has reviewed the effects of auditory, tactile, vestibular, kinesthetic and multimodal stimulation programs on the development of preterm infants. These types of programs have been instituted in neonatal intensive care units. Although research in this area is very diverse the author suggests that there is overwhelming evidence that indicates these programs are beneficial for the preterm infant.
LEVEL: A LANG: Eng SIRC ARTICLE NO: 092831

COMPETITION

Children in competitive sport. *Athletic Asia (Patiala, India) 13(2), Sept 1984, 5-9.*
NOTES: Extract from the statement of principles of the German Sports Federation (DBS).
LEVEL: B LANG: Eng SIRC ARTICLE NO: 105165

Passer, M.W. Competitive trait anxiety in children and adolescents.
NOTES: In, Silva, J.M. and Weinberg, R.S. (eds.), Psychological foundations of sport, Champaign, Ill., Human Kinetics Publishers, c1984, p. 130-144.
LEVEL: A LANG: Eng GV706.4 17779

Ramage, B. Competitive sport for children: a look into the future. (Refs: 9)
CONF: Physical Education Graduating Seminar Conference (1984 : Footscray Institute Of Technology).
NOTES: In, Physical education in Australia: past, present and future directions, s.l., Footscray Institute of Technology, 1984, Suppl. p. 7-12.
LEVEL: I LANG: Eng SIRC ARTICLE NO: 095739

Scanlan, T.K. Competitive stress and the child athlete.
NOTES: In, Silva, J.M. and Weinberg, R.S. (eds.), Psychological foundations of sport, Champaign, Ill., Human Kinetics Publishers, c1984, p. 118-129.
LEVEL: A LANG: Eng GV706.4 17779

Watson, G.G. Competition and intrinsic motivation in children's sport and games: a conceptual analysis. (Refs: 43) *International journal of sport psychology (Rome) 15(3), 1984, 205-218.*
LEVEL: A LANG: Eng SIRC ARTICLE NO: 103842

Weiss, G. Child's play: competitive sports programs should be approached with sensitivity for the camper's needs and interests. *Camping magazine (Martinsville, Ind.) 56(3), Jan 1984, 11-13.*
LEVEL: B LANG: Eng SIRC ARTICLE NO: 097426

CHILDREN AND ADOLESCENTS (continued)

DROP-OUT

Gould, D. Horn, T. Participation motivation in young athletes.
NOTES: In, Silva, J.M. and Weinberg, R.S. (eds.), Psychological foundations of sport, Champaign, Ill., Human Kinetics Publishers, c1984, p. 359-370.
LEVEL: A LANG: Eng GV706.4 17779

Rasmussen, O.C. Tidligere frafald end forventet. (Earlier drop-out than expected.) *Dansk ungdom og idraet 87(43), 1984, 16.*
ABST: Discusses the droping out from sport of 10-11 year old children.
LEVEL: I LANG: Dan

INJURIES AND ACCIDENTS

Birrer, R.B. Special considerations in the injured child. (Refs: 8)
NOTES: In, Birrer, R.B. (ed.), Sports medicine for the primary care physician, Norwalk, Conn., Appleton-Century-Crofts, c1984, p. 249-251.
LEVEL: B LANG: Eng RC1210 17030

Conrad, N.L. Juvenile sports programmes - viewpoint. *Canadian Podiatric Sports Medicine Academy newsletter (Toronto) Fall/Winter 1984, 7-8.*
LEVEL: B LANG: Eng SIRC ARTICLE NO: 102329

Du Boullay, C.T. Bardier, M. Cheneau, J. Bortolasso, J. Gaubert, J. Les traumatismes sportifs de l'enfant. Etude epidemiologique. (Sports injuries in children. Epidemiologic study.) *Chirurgie pediatrique (Paris) 25(3), 1984, 125-135.*
LEVEL: A LANG: Fr SIRC ARTICLE NO: 104032

Dubousset, J. Enfant, l'adolescent, le rachis et l'activite sportive. (Refs: 6)*Dans, Mandel, C. (ed.), Le medecin, l'enfant et le sport, Paris, (Vigot), c1984, p. 163-181.*
LEVEL: I LANG: Fr RC1218.C45 18886

Emans, J.B. Upper extremity injuries in sports. (Refs: 15)
NOTES: In, Micheli, L.J. (ed.), Pediatric and adolescent sports medicine, Boston ; Toronto, Little, Brown, c1984, p. 49-79.
LEVEL: I LANG: Eng RC1210 17791

Goldberg, B. Les traumatismes dus au sort: sont-ils evitables? *Dans, Mandel, C. (ed.), Le medecin, l'enfant et le sport, Paris, (Vigot), c1984, p. 245-251.*
LEVEL: I LANG: Fr RC1218.C45 18886

Hayes, J.M. Masear, V.R. Avulsion fracture of the tibial eminence associated with severe medial ligamentous injury in an adolescent. (Refs: 18)*American journal of sports medicine (Baltimore, Md.) 12(4), Jul/Aug 1984, 330-333.*
ABST: In the presence of open physes, tibial eminence fratures are usually isolated injuries. However, adults sustaining a fracture of the tibial eminence are more likely to have other associated injuries, most commonly a tear of the medial collateral ligament. A case of an adolescent with a tibial eminence fracture and a complete tear of the medial collateral ligament is reported. Review of the literature revealed two similar cases in adolescents. If medial instability is demonstrated on valgus stress of the knee in an adolescent with tibial eminence fracture, we believe stress roentgenograms of the knee should be obtained to distinguish between physeal injury and collateral

ligament tear.
LEVEL: A LANG: Eng SIRC ARTICLE NO: 108542

Jackson, D.W. Spinal injuries in children's sports. (Refs: 12)
NOTES: In, Micheli, L.J. (ed.), Pediatric and adolescent sports medicine, Boston ; Toronto, Little, Brown, c1984, p. 107-123.
LEVEL: I LANG: Eng RC1210 17791

Kay, N.R. Traumatic and orthopaedic conditions in adolescents. *Practitioner (London) 228(1391), May 1984, 473-477.*
LEVEL: LANG: Eng SIRC ARTICLE NO: 104046

Klimt, F. Kinderunfaelle bei Spiel und Sport. (Childhood accidents in play and sport.) *Monatsschrift Kinderheilkunde (Berlin) 132(6), Jun 1984, 341-344.*
LEVEL: B LANG: Ger

Lereim, I. Sahlin, Y. Barneulykker. En studie av ulykkes- og skademonstre hos barn som er behandlet ved Regionsykehuset i Trondheim. (Child accidents. A study of the pattern of accidents and injuries in children treated at the Trondheim County Hospital.) *Tidsskrift for de norske laegeforening (Oslo) 104(31), 10 Nov 1984, 2155-2158.*
LEVEL: A LANG: Nor

Mayer, P.J. Lower limb injuries in childhood and adolescence. (Refs: 42)
NOTES: In, Micheli, L.J. (ed.), Pediatric and adolescent sports medicine, Boston ; Toronto, Little, Brown, c1984, p. 80-106.
LEVEL: I LANG: Eng RC1210 17791

Micheli, L.J. Sports injuries in the young athlete: questions and controversies. (Refs: 28)
NOTES: In, Micheli, L.J. (ed.), Pediatric and adolescent sports medicine, Boston ; Toronto, Little, Brown, c1984, p. 1-8.
LEVEL: I LANG: Eng RC1210 17791

Micheli, L.J. LaChabrier, L. The young female athlete. (Refs: 33)
NOTES: In, Micheli, L.J. (ed.), Pediatric and adolescent sports medicine, Boston ; Toronto, Little, Brown, c1984, p. 167-178.
LEVEL: I LANG: Eng RC1210 17791

Personne, J. L'entrainement sportif intensif precoce. *EPS: Revue education physique et sport (Paris) 188, juil/aout 1984, 52-53.*
LEVEL: B LANG: Fr SIRC ARTICLE NO: 097424

Petit, M. Raveno, M. Pilardeau, P. Vaysse, J. Garnier, M. Influence de la preparation physique et du suivi dietetique sur la traumatologie observee lors des classes de neige. (Refs: 15)*Medecine du sport (Paris) 58(2), 25 mars 1984, 4-8*
RESUME: Les auteurs proposent un programme d'entrainement physique pour les enfants participant aux classes de neige. Ils soulignent l'importance d'une bonne alimentation lors de la duree des activites. L'etude de 4,300 enfants en 1979-1980 et 4,330 enfants en 1980-1981 dont l'age varie de 9 a 11 ans, indique une diminution de la frequence des accidents suite a la mise en place du programme de prevention.
LEVEL: A LANG: Fr SIRC ARTICLE NO: 094207

Schneider, V. Todesfaelle beim Sport im jugendlichen Alter. (Fatalities in sports in the young.) *Unfallheilkunde (Berlin) 8 (12), Dec 1984, 495-505.*
LEVEL: A LANG: Ger

Stanish, W.D. Reardon, G.P. Emergencies in children's sports. (Refs: 29)

NOTES: In, Micheli, L.J. (ed.), Pediatric and adolescent sports medicine, Boston ; Toronto, Little, Brown, c1984, p. 9-29.
LEVEL: I LANG: Eng RC1210 17791

Stark, E. Growing pains for the young athlete. *In, Schrier, E.W. and Allman, W.F. (eds.), Newton at the bat: the science in sports, New York, Scribner, c1984, p. 119-122.*
LEVEL: B LANG: Eng RC1235 18609

Thillaye du Boullay, C. Bardier, M. Cherneau, J. Bortolasso, J. Gaubert, J. Les traumatismes sportifs de l'enfant. Etude epidemiologique. *Chirurgie pediatrique (Paris) 25(3), 1984, 125-135.*
LEVEL: A LANG: Fr

Watson, A.W.S. Sports injuries during one academic year in 6799 Irish school children. (Refs: 17)*American journal of sports medicine (Baltimore, Md.) 12(1), Jan/Feb 1984, 65-71.*
ABST: 116 injuries were noted in 6799 children aged 10 to 18 during the course of one academic year in Irish schools. Injuries occurred more often in boys over the age of fourteen compared to younger boys or girls of any age. The injuries were most often caused through unsafe play by the injured player or another player. It was felt that this could be improved through stricter enforcement of the rules.
LEVEL: A LANG: Eng SIRC ARTICLE NO: 094396

Wright, G. Know your children. (Refs: 10)*Sports coach (Wembley, Australia) 7(4), Mar 1984, 7-10.*
LEVEL: B LANG: Eng SIRC ARTICLE NO: 094218

Youth sports injuries: Is the risk acceptable? *Athletic purchasing and facilities (Madison, Wis.) 8(1), Jan 1984, 14;16;18;20.*
LEVEL: B LANG: Eng SIRC ARTICLE NO: 094402

JUVENILE DELINQUENCY

Malmisur, M.C. Schempp, P.G. Sport participation: its influence on juvenile delinquency. (Refs: 8)*International journal of physical education (Schorndorf, W. Germany) 21(3), 1984, 14-16.*
LEVEL: I LANG: Eng SIRC ARTICLE NO: 102335

Middleton, C. Settled out of court: Chris Middleton visits a scheme aimed at channelling young offenders into sport. *Sport and leisure (London) 25(2), May/Jun 1984, 54-55.*
LEVEL: B LANG: Eng SIRC ARTICLE NO: 103839

Munson, W.W. The separate and combined effects of systematic strength training and structured leisure counseling on selected psychological and physical attributes of institutionalized juvenile delinquents. Eugene, Ore.: Microform Publications, University of Oregon, 1984. 2 microfiches : negative, ill. ; 11 x 15 cm.
NOTES: Thesis (Ph.D.) - Pennsylvania State University, 1983; ((11), 176 leaves); vita; includes bibliography.
LEVEL: A LANG: Eng UO84 355-356

Segrave, J.O. Hastad, D.N. Future directions in sport and juvenile delinquency research. (Refs: 65)*Quest (Champaign, Ill.) 36(1), 1984, 37-47.*
LEVEL: I LANG: Eng SIRC ARTICLE NO: 098886

Segrave, J.O. Hastad, D.N. Interscholastic athletic participation and delinquent behavior: an empirical assessment of relevant variables. (Refs: 53)*Sociology of sport journal (Champaign, Ill.) 1(2), 1984, 117-137.*
ABST: The purpose of this study was to analyze the dynamic processes underlying the relationship

between participation in interscholastic athletics and delinquent behavior. The study evaluated the relative contribution of 12 socio-psychological variables in the etiology of delinquent behavior among male and female athletes and nonathletes. Of the total sample of 1,693 high school students, 788 (442 males and 346 females) were classified as athletes. Overall, the results indicated that a similar pattern persists in the etiology of delinquent behavior among male and female athletes and nonathletes. Several differences were also found in the etiology of delinquent behavior among male athletes and nonathletes, female athletes and nonathletes, and male and female athletes.
LEVEL: A LANG: Eng SIRC ARTICLE NO: 102339

MINI-SPORT

Cuthbertson, T. A justification for modifying adult sport for children. (Refs: 11)
CONF: Physical Education Graduating Seminar Conference (1984 : Footscray Institute of Technology).
NOTES: In, Physical education in Australia: past, present and future directions, s.l., Footscray Institute of Technology, 1984, p. 45-49.
LEVEL: I LANG: Eng SIRC ARTICLE NO: 095732

NUTRITION

Akerblom, H.K. Viikari, J. Uhari, M. Rasanen, L. Dahl, M. Lahde, P-L. Pesonen, E. Pietikainen, M. Suoninen, P. Dahlstrom, S. Nikkari, T. Moilanen, T. Ahola, M. Byckling, T. Seppanen, A. Aromaa, A. Pyorala, K. Multicenter study of atherosclerosis precursors in Finnish children: report of two pilot studies. (Refs: 15)
CONF: Symposium of Paediatric Work Physiology (10th : 1981 : Joutsa, Finland).
NOTES: In, Ilmarinen, J. and Vaelimaeki, I. (eds.), Children and sport: paediatric work physiology, Berlin, Springer-Verlag, 1984, p. 219-230.
LEVEL: A LANG: Eng SIRC ARTICLE NO: 102327

Deudon, J. Rouaud, C. Grimault, M.L. Albrecht, R. Dupin, H. Consommation alimentaire d'enfants et d'adolescents en periode d'activite sportive intense. (Refs: 22)*Cahiers de nutrition et de dietetique (Paris) 1, 1984, 15-23.*
LEVEL: A LANG: Fr

Douglas, P.D. Douglas, J.G. Nutrition knowledge and food practices of high school athletes. *Journal of the American Dietiti Association (Chicago) 84(10), Oct 1984, 1198-1202.*
LEVEL: A LANG: Eng

Giovannini, M. Galluzzo, C.R. Bisson, G. Ortisi, M.T. Riva, E. Attivita sportiva e alimentazione nel bambino. (Sports and child nutrition.) *Minerva pediatrica (Torino) 36(22), 30 Nov 1984, 1141-1146.*
LEVEL: I LANG: It

Harvey, J.S. Nutritional management of the adolescent athlete. *Clinics in sports medicine (Philadelphia) 3(3), Jul 1984, 671-678.*
NOTES: Symposium on nutritional aspects of exercise.
ABST: This article discusses the additional concerns that athletics place on the teenager's diet. Adolescent food habits are taken into consideration. Education of parents, coaches, and trainers to provide sound nutritional information to adolescent athletes is stressed.
LEVEL: I LANG: Eng SIRC ARTICLE NO: 100781

Klepping, J. Moreau, D. Guilland, J.C. Pratique du sport chez l'enfant et problemes alimentaires. (Refs: 15)*Dans, Mandel, C (ed.), Le medecin, l'enfant et le sport, Paris, (Vigot), c1984, p. 55-66.*
LEVEL: I LANG: Fr RC1218.C45 18886

Morgan, B.L. Nutritional needs of the female adolescent. (Refs: 27)*Woman & health (New York) 9(2/3), Summer/Fall 1984, 15-28.*
LEVEL: I LANG: Eng SIRC ARTICLE NO: 104183

Smith, N.J. Nutrition in children's sports. (Refs: 12)
NOTES: In, Micheli, L.J. (ed.), Pediatric and adolescent sports medicine, Boston ; Toronto, Little, Brown, c1984, p. 134-143.
LEVEL: I LANG: Eng RC1210 17791

PARENT-CHILD RELATIONS

Griffiths, A. L'effet de sublimation des parents sur les athletes. The sport parent. *Champion (Ottawa) 8(4), Nov 1984, 2-5.*
LEVEL: B LANG: Fr Eng SIRC ARTICLE NO: 100505

Myers, R. How to handle pushy parents. *Sports now (St. Louis, Mo.) 2(9), Sept 1984, 26.*
LEVEL: B LANG: Eng SIRC ARTICLE NO: 098885

Ogilvie, B. Psychology: the ties that bind. *Women's sports (Palo Alto, Calif.) 6(2), Feb 1984, 12.*
LEVEL: B LANG: Eng SIR ARTICLE NO: 099293

Sutton, W. Family involvement in youth sports: an examination of the YMCA Y-winners philosophy. (Refs: 2)*Journal of physica education, recreation and dance (Reston, Va.) 55(8), Oct 1984, 59-60.*
LEVEL: B LANG: Eng SIRC ARTICLE NO: 100990

Valeriote, T. Children's sport programs: the parent. Ottawa: New Traditions, c1984. v, 26, A10 p. : ill.
NOTES: Includes bibliography.
LEVEL: B LANG: Eng ISBN: 0-9691563-2-4 LC CARD: C84-90052-X GV709.2 17663

PHILOSOPHY

Coaching corner: not set of rules...code for living *Soccer news (Willowdale, Ont.) 2(3), Apr/May 1984, 22.*
LEVEL: B LANG: Eng SIRC ARTICLE NO: 094202

L'ecole et le fair play. *Macolin (Suisse) 8, aout 1984, 16-17.*
LEVEL: B LANG: Fr SIRC ARTICLE NO: 100503

Strenbrenner, G.M. Program responsibilities: a commitment to youth - America's greatest resource. *Interscholastic athletic administration 10(3), Spring 1984, 18-19;21.*
LEVEL: B LANG: Eng SIRC ARTICLE NO: 092700

PHYSICAL FITNESS

Armstrong, N. Children and exercise. (Refs: 10)*Bulletin of physical education (London) 20(2), Summer 1984, 79-85.*
CONF: British Association of Advisers and Lecturers in Physical Education. Congress (64th : 1984 : Cardiff).
LEVEL: I LANG: Eng SIRC ARTICLE NO: 104241

Carne, P. Aptitudes physiques au sport de l'adolescent. (Refs: 8)*Gazette medicale (Paris) 91(9), 1984, 31-35.*
LEVEL: I LANG: Fr

Elnashar, A.N. Mayhew, J.L. Physical fitness status of Egyptian children aged 9-18 years. (Refs: 11)*British journal of sports medicine (Loughborough, Leicestershire) 18(1), Mar 1984, 26-29.*
ABST: This study examined the performance of 710 Egyptian schoolchildren (399 males, 311 females) on the 6-item AAHPER. The Egyptian sample was substantially below the average fitness level of the AAHPER norms. After eight weeks of twice weekly intensified physical education the Egyptian schoolchildren exhibited significant improvement on all 6 items of the AAHPER test.
LEVEL: A LANG: Eng SIRC ARTICLE NO: 096184

Fares, M. Physical fitness and motor agility among 10 to 14 years old German and Egyptian pupils - a comparative study. *International journal of physical education (Schorndorf, W. Germany) 21(2), 19-26 Jul 1984, 27-31.*
ABST: This study found German 10 to 14 year old students to be ahead of their Egyptian counterparts in physical fitness and agility. This can be in part attributed to the fact that the German students have larger gymnasia and sport facilities, better equipment and better sport and physical education programs. The study also established a relationship between social class and sport motor performance.
LEVEL: A LANG: Eng SIRC ARTICLE NO: 097686

Fitness facts - understanding the basics. (Canada Fitness Award) La condition physique: comprendre les principes fondamentaux. (Jeunesse en forme Canada) *Canadian Intramural Recreation Association/Association canadienne de loisirs-intramuros bulletin (Ottawa) 9(5), Feb/fevr 1984, 4-5.*
LEVEL: B LANG: Eng Fr SIRC ARTICLE NO: 099188

Geubelle, F. De quelques aspects de la tolerance a l'effort physique. (Refs: 113)*Dans, Mandel, C. (ed.), Le medecin, l'enfant et le sport, Paris, (Vigot), c1984, p. 209-243.*
LEVEL: A LANG: Fr RC1218.C45 18886

Ghesquiere, J. Eeckels, R. Health, physical development and fitness of primary school children in Kinshasa. (Refs: 10)
CONF: Symposium of Paediatric Work Physiology (10th : 1981 : Joutsa, Finland).
NOTES: In, Ilmarinen, J. and Vaelimaeki, I. (eds.), Children and sport: paediatric work physiology, Berlin, Springer-Verlag, 1984, p. 18-30.
ABST: This study collects some basic information on the health status of 670 primary school children in Kinshasa, and evaluates to what degree it is influenced by their socioeconomic background.
LEVEL: A LANG: Eng SIRC ARTICLE NO: 102331

Gorman, C.P. The effect of health education upon the lifestyle of the elementary child. Eugene, Ore.: Microform Publications University of Oregon, 1984. 3 microfiches : negative, ill, ; 11 x 15 cm.
NOTES: Thesis (M.A.) - Texas Woman's University, 1982; (xi, 233 leaves); includes bibliography.
LEVEL: A LANG: Eng UO84 243-245

Griffith, L.L. Fit kids: start your child down the path to good health. *Fit (Mountain View, Calif.) 4(3), Aug 1984, 62-64;76.*
LEVEL: B LANG: Eng SIRC ARTICLE NO: 102720

Hayes, A. Youth Physical Fitness Hearings: an interim report from the President's Council on Physical Fitness and Sports. *Journal of physical education, recreation & dance (Reston, Va.) 55(9),*

Nov/Dec 1984, 29-32;40.
LEVEL: B LANG: Eng SIRC ARTICLE NO: 102722

Imre, M. Ovodasok alkalmassagi vizsgalata sporttagozatos osztalyba valo felvetelhez. (Screening kindergarten children if the are fit for attending special sport classes in primary education.) (Refs: 3)*Sportorvosi szemle/Hungarian review of sports medicine (Budapest) 25(2), 1984, 109-115.*
ABST: The authors describe their experiences in screening 500 children of kindergarten age concerning the children's fitness for attending classes with a special physical education curriculum when they enter primary schooling. It was observed that 28.2% of these children showed such deficiencies of either physique or functional capacity that contraindicated their admittance to theses classes in view of their prospective health status and future successful performance or training work.
LEVEL: A LANG: Hun SIRC ARTICLE NO: 097265

Jenner, B. Dobbins, B. Bruce Jenner's the athletic body: a complete fitness guide for teenagers - sports, strength, health, agility. New York: Simon and Schuster, c1984. 190 p. : ill.
LEVEL: B LANG: Eng ISBN: 067146549X LC CARD: 84-010529 GV481 18091

Jette, M. Ashton, N.J. Sharratt, M.T. Development of a cardiorespiratory step-test of fitness for children 7-14 years of age (Refs: 23)*Canadian journal of public health/Revue canadienne de sante publique (Ottawa) 75(3), May/Jun 1984, 212-217.*
ABST: A modified version of the Canadian Home Fitness Test was used to estimate the cardiorespiratory fitness of 59 children aged between 7 and 14 years. Measurements were recorded during and after a progressive three-stage step test and a treadmill run. Findings indicated that stage 3 of the step-test induced a mean exercise heart rate response of 81 and 87% of maximal heart rate for the 7-10 year old boys and girls and 84 and 95% for the 11-14 year old boys and girls respectively.
LEVEL: A LANG: Eng SIRC ARTICLE NO: 099194

Kerr, M. The effects of a circuit training/slow stretching program on the fitness development of selected fifth and sixth grade students. Eugene, Ore.: Microform Publications, University of Oregon, 1984. 1 microfiche : negative ; 11 x 15 cm.
NOTES: Thesis (M.S.) - Western Illinois University, 1982; (iv, 84 leaves); includes bibliography.
LEVEL: A LANG: Eng UO84 204

Kondakova-Varlamova, L.P. Zakalivanie doshkolnikov (material dlia besed). (Physical fitness training of preschoolers (material for talks).) *Feldsher i akusherka (Moscow) 49(4), Apr 1984, 43-48.*
LEVEL: B LANG: Rus

Leard, J.S. Flexibility and conditioning in the young athlete. (Refs: 29)
NOTES: In, Micheli, L.J. (ed.), Pediatric and adolescent sports medicine, Boston ; Toronto, Little, Brown, c1984, p. 194-210.
LEVEL: I LANG: Eng RC1210 17791

Pangrazi, R. Slaughter, M. National Youth Fitness Conference. *Journal of physical education, recreation & dance (Reston, Va.) 55(9), Nov/Dec 1984, 44-46.*
LEVEL: B LANG: Eng SIRC ARTICLE NO: 102735

Powers, S.K. Children and exercise. (Refs: 37)*In, Thomas, J.R. (ed.), Motor development during childhood and adolescence, Minneapolis, Minn., Burgess Publishing Co., 1984, p. 27-47.*
LEVEL: A LANG: Eng BF1 20187

Renfrow, N.E. The effects of a twelve minute aerobic training program on second and fourth grade students. Eugene, Ore.: Microform Publications, University of Oregon, 1984. 2 microfiches : negative, ill. ; 11 x 15 cm.
NOTES: Thesis (Ed.D.) - University of Arkansas, 1981; (vii, 113 leaves); includes bibliography.
LEVEL: A LANG: Eng UO84 141-142

Ross, J.G. Gilbert, G.G. Dotson, C.O. Youth fitness revisited: part I. *Parks & recreation (Alexandria, Va.) 19(12), Dec 198 41-45;66-67.*
LEVEL: B LANG: Eng SIRC ARTICLE NO: 173251

Ruminski, S. Hartowanie dziecka. (Child physical fitness training.) *Pielegniarka i polozna (Warsaw) 6, 1984, 6-7.*
LEVEL: LANG: Pol

Sakamaki, T. Kato, N. Morimoto, M. Hayashi, T. Uzuki, H. (CMI and physical fitness of girls in a newly-established high school.) *Nippon Ika Daigaku Zasshi/Journal of the Nippon Medical School (Tokyo) 51(1), Feb 1984, 119-123.*
LEVEL: A LANG: Jpn

Saris, W.H.M. de Koning, F. Elvers, J.W.H. deBoo, T. Binkhorst, R.A. Estimation of W170 and maximal oxygen consumption in young children by different treadmill tests. (Refs: 14)
CONF: Symposium of Paediatric Work Physiology (10th : 1981 : Joutsa, Finland).
NOTES: In, Ilmarinen, J. and Vaelimaeki, I. (eds.), Children and sport: paediatric work physiology, Berlin, Springer-Verlag, 1984, p. 86-92.
ABST: Directly measured maximal oxygen uptake is the most precise index of physical performance capacity. However, this method requires the full cooperation and motivation of the subjects, but young children are difficult to motivate. The treadmill is generally used for children under 10 years of age and this study tested 5 year olds using a variety of treadmill procedures in order to establish a suitable nonmaximal treadmill procedure for predicting performance capacity.
LEVEL: A LANG: Eng SIRC ARTICLE NO: 102824

Seefeldt, V. Physical fitness in preschool and elementary school-aged children. (Refs: 41)*Journal of physical education, recreation & dance (Reston, Va.) 55(9), Nov/Dec 1984, 33-37;40.*
LEVEL: I LANG: Eng SIRC ARTICLE NO: 102744

Shephard, R.J. Physical activity and child health. (Refs: 377)*Sports medicine (Auckland, N.Z.) 1(3), May/Jun 1984, 205-233.*
ABST: This review discusses the advantages and disadvantages of physical activity for children. Overall, the benefits of physical activity far outweigh the risks of physical activity. Indeed, a good exercise/education program will enable the child to make important lifestyle decisions as he/she grows older. The author believes that clinicians should direct greater attention to positive health, with particular reference to the role of physical activity, in optimising the well-being of the child.
LEVEL: A LANG: Eng SIRC ARTICLE NO: 095741

Shephard, R.J. Physical activity and 'wellness' of the child. (Refs: 153)*In, Boileau, R.A. (ed.), Advances in pediatric sport sciences. Volume 1: biological issues, Champaign, Ill., Human Kinetics*

Publishers, c1984, p. 1-27.
LEVEL: A LANG: Eng RJ125 20044

Siegel, J.A. Manfredi, T.G. Effects of a ten-month fitness program on children. (Refs: 29)*Physician and sportsmedicine (Minneapolis, Minn.) 12(5), May 1984, 91-94;96-97.*
LEVEL: I LANG: Eng SIRC ARTICLE NO: 094212

Stephenson, J. Tot to teen fitness: how to meet the teen challenge. *Shape (Woodland Hills, Calif.) 4(4), Dec 1984, 51;122.*
LEVEL: B LANG: Eng SIRC ARTICLE NO: 173234

Stewart, G. How fit are you kids? Test them for strength stamina and suppleness...and help them improve. *Canadian living (Toronto) 9(6), Jan 1984, 140-146.*
LEVEL: B LANG: Eng SIRC ARTICLE NO: 094580

Sturbois, X. Epreuves fonctionnelles d'effort: indications et limites. (Refs: 12)*Dans, Mandel, C. (ed.), Le medecin, l'enfant et le sport, Paris, (Vigot), c1984, p. 67-77.*
LEVEL: I LANG: Fr RC1218.C45 18886

Symonette, P.L. Assessment of the physical fitness of Bahamian youths age 13 thru 17 years, and their attitudes toward physical education. Eugene, Ore.: Microform Publications, University of Oregon, 1984. 1 microfiche : negative ; 11 x 15 cm.
NOTES: Thesis (M.S.) - Howard University, 1983; (x, 52 leaves); vita; includes bibliography.
LEVEL: A LANG: Eng UO84 330

Tacha, K.K. Edwards, V. Miller, S. Sports fitness school for children. *Journal of physical education, recreation and dance (Reston, Va.) 55(7), Sept 1984, 61-63.*
LEVEL: B LANG: Eng SIRC ARTICLE NO: 100508

Tucker, L.A. Cigarette smoking intentions and physical fitness: a multivariate study of high school males. *Adolescence (Roselyn Heights, N.Y.) 19(74), Summer 1984, 313-321.*
ABST: 381 high school males were administered the Physical Performance Test for California to measure sex traits of physical fitness, and a written questionnaire to assess smoking intentions. Findings indicated that males who reported no intentions of smoking were significantly more fit than mild and strong intenders.
LEVEL: A LANG: Eng SIRC ARTICLE NO: 104267

Van Gerven, D. Vanden Eynde, B. Peerlinck, G. Influence of activity and age on the working capacity of boys and girls aged 8 - 12 years. (Refs: 6)
CONF: Symposium of Paediatric Work Physiology (10th : 1981 : Joutsa, Finland).
NOTES: In, Ilmarinen, J. and Vaelimaeki, I. (eds.), Children and sport: paediatric work physiology, Berlin, Springer-Verlag, 1984, p. 106-110.
ABST: This study presents data collected on 266 normal Belgian schoolchildren of both sexes aged 8-12 years. The effect of active sport participation as well as sex are considered.
LEVEL: A LANG: Eng SIRC ARTICLE NO: 102345

Vanden Eynde, B. Ghesquiere, J. van Gerven, D. Vuylsteke-Wauters, M. Vande Perre, H. Follow-up study of physical fitness in boys aged 10 - 14 years. (Refs: 25)
CONF: Symposium of Paediatric Work Physiology (10th : 1981 : Joutsa, Finland).
NOTES: In, Ilmarinen, J. and Vaelimaeki, I. (eds.), Children and sport: paediatric work physiology, Berlin, Springer-Verlag, 1984, p. 111-118.
ABST: 21 boys were studied over a period of three

years in order to investigate differences in growth and maturation and cardiorespiratory endurance levels. This study assesses the submaximal working capacity of these children in relation to their increasing body height, weight, and age.
LEVEL: A LANG: Eng SIRC ARTICLE NO: 102346

Verschuur, R. Kemper, H.C.G. Besseling, C.W.M. Habitual physical activity and health in 13- and 14-year-old teenagers. (Refs 26)
CONF: Symposium of Paediatric Work Physiology (10th : 1981 : Joutsa, Finland).
NOTES: In, Ilmarinen, J. and Vaelimaeki, I. (eds.), Children and sport: paediatric work physiology, Berlin, Springer-Verlag, 1984, p. 255-261.
LEVEL: A LANG: Eng SIRC ARTICLE NO: 102749

Viikari, J. Valimaki, I. Telama, R. Siren-Tiusanen, H. Akerblom, H.K. Dahl, M. Lahde, P.L. Pesonen, E. Pietikainen, M. Suoninen, P. Uhari, M. Atherosclerosis precursors in Finnish children: physical activity and plasma lipids in 3-and 12 year-old children. (Refs: 13)
CONF: Symposium of Paediatric Work Physiology (10th : 1981 : Joutsa, Finland).
NOTES: In, Ilmarinen, J. and Vaelimaeki, I. (eds.), Children and sport: paediatric work physiology, Berlin, Springer-Verlag, 1984, p. 231-240
LEVEL: A LANG: Eng SIRC ARTICLE NO: 102347

Vogelaere, P. Duquet, W. CT 170: validation en fonction du VO2 max pour une population agee de 6 a 12 ans. (Refs: 29) *Medecine du sport (Paris) 58(5), 25 sept 1984, 6-12.*
RESUME: Cette etude vise a verifier la validite d'une procedure experimentale du CT170 a divers paliers d'intensite sur la base du VO2 max derive du test cyclergometrique (Vita max). 93 enfants ages de 6 a 12 ans classes selon le sexe en trois groupes d'age participent a l'etude. Les variables suivantes sont mesurees: la capacite de travail, le niveau maximal de la charge imposee et VO2 max. Pour l'ensemble de l'echantillon les auteurs observent une forte correlation du CT170 et de la Vita max.
LEVEL: A LANG: Fr SIRC ARTICLE NO: 100882

Vrijens, J. Hebbellinck, M. Somatic characteristics and physical fitness of primary school children aged 6 to 12 year. (Refs 3) *In, Idrett for barn. Sport for Children. Sport pour les enfants 27.9.-1.10.1982 Tonsberg, Norway. Report. Oslo, Norway, Ministry of Cultural and Scientific Affairs: Norwegian Confederation of Sport, 1984, p. (3)-(9).*
CONF: Idrett for barn. Sport for Children. Sport pour les enfants (1982 : Tonsberg, Norway).
LEVEL: A LANG: Eng GV709.2 20111

Vrijens, J. Hebbelinck, M. Caracteristiques somatiques et valeur physique des eleves de l'enseignement primaire ages de 6 a 12 ans. (Refs: 3) *Dans, Idrett for barn. Sport for Children. Sport pour les enfants 27.9.-1.10.1982 Tonsberg, Norway. Rapport. Oslo, Norvege, Ministere de la culture et de la science : Confederation norvegienne des sports, 1984, p. (3)-(9).*
CONF: Idrett for barn. Sport for Children. Sport pour les enfants (1982 : Tonsberg, Norway).
LEVEL: A LANG: Fr GV709.2 20112

Wanne, O. Viikari, J. Valimaki, I. Physical performance and serum lipids in 14 - 16-year-old trained, normally active, and inactive children. (Refs: 16)
CONF: Symposium of Paediatric Work Physiology (10th : 1981 : Joutsa, Finland).
NOTES: In, Ilmarinen, J. and Vaelimaeki, I. (eds.),

Children and sport: paediatric work physiology, Berlin, Springer-Verlag, 1984, p. 241-246.
LEVEL: A LANG: Eng SIRC ARTICLE NO: 102839

Ylitalo, V.M. Exercise performance and serum lipids in obese schoolchildren before and after reconditioning program. (Refs: 29)
CONF: Symposium of Paediatric Work Physiology (10th : 1981 : Joutsa, Finland).
NOTES: In, Ilmarinen, J. and Vaelimaeki, I. (eds.), Children and sport: paediatric work physiology, Berlin, Springer-Verlag, 1984, p. 247-254.
ABST: This study investigated the effects of obesity and a 2-year reconditioning program on the ergometric capacity and the serum lipids and insulin of 61 obese schoolchildren aged 7-15 years at the beginning of the study.
LEVEL: A LANG: Eng SIRC ARTICLE NO: 102841

PLAY

Lindsay, P.L. The physical characteristics of playground games in public elementary schools in Edmonton. *CAHPER journal (Ottawa) 51(2), Nov/ Dec 1984, 8-11.*
LEVEL: I LANG: Eng SIRC ARTICLE NO: 102334

Silva, K. Nurturing play in a cold economic climate. (Refs: 5) *IPA: International Association for the Child's Right to Play newsletter (Sheffield) 8(8), Apr 1984, 8-13.*
LEVEL: I LANG: Eng SIRC ARTICLE NO: 103840

Walsh, E.R. Let's give young players a sporting chance. (Refs: 10) *Leisure information (New York) 10(4), Spring 1984, 10-12.*
LEVEL: B LANG: Eng SIRC ARTICLE NO: 100510

PSYCHOLOGY

Brown, J.G. Burger, C. Playground designs and preschool childrens behaviors. (Refs: 38) *Environment and behavior (Beverly Hills, Calif.) 16(5), 1984, 599-626.*
LEVEL: I LANG: Eng SIRC ARTICLE NO: 098962

Dickmeyer, L.A. Humphreys, M. Winning and losing. New York: F. Watts, 1984. 1v. (An easy-read sports book.)
NOTES: Includes index.
LEVEL: B LANG: Eng ISBN: 0531047148 LC CARD: 83-021626

McCabe, N. Burnout has experts questioning training setup. *Globe and mail (Toronto) 4 May 1984, 18.*
LEVEL: B LANG: Eng SIRC ARTICLE NO: 094656

Missoum, G. Laforesterie, R. Psychologie du sport: approche des mecanismes psychologiques lies a la detection des sportifs e a l'optimisation des performances. (Refs: 15) *Bulletin de psychologie (Paris) 37(364), jan/fevr 1984, 347-357.*
RESUME: Le but de cette etude etait d'analyser les facteurs psychologiques lies a la realisation de la performance sportive de haut niveau. 92 sportifs de haut niveau (16 ans), 62 sportifs 'en devenir' (16 ans), et 66 non sportifs (17 ans) sont soumis a l'echelle d'auto-evaluation du comportement de Bortner, a l'inventaire de personalite d'Eysenck, a un test de performance sous stress, a la 'Matrix of intra and inter-individual processes in group'. Les resultats indiquent que les athletes demontrent une plus grande maitrise emotionnelle, une plus grande ambition et competitivite ainsi qu'un plus grand dynamisme et engagement par rapport aux non

sportifs.
LEVEL: A LANG: Fr SIRC ARTICLE NO: 102862

Silvennoinen, M. Relations between different kinds of physical activity and motive types among Finnish comprehensive and upper secondary school pupils. (Refs: 20) *Scandinavian journal of sports sciences (Helsinki, Finland) 6(2), Dec 1984, 77-82.*
ABST: The purpose of this study was to reveal the relations between physical activity and disposition or motives for physical activity among Finnish school children of different ages. The sample consisted of 3,106 pupils from 73 schools. The results showed that a highly differentiated and many-sided sports motivation is typical of boys and of younger comprehensive school pupils (11-13 years) and a highly differentiated but relatively more narrow motivation is typical of girls and of older age groups (14-19 years). The relations between the activity and the motive groups showed remarkable and logical connections.
LEVEL: A LANG: Eng SIRC ARTICLE NO: 106340

Vaughan, L.K. Psychological impact of organized sports on children. (Refs: 105)
NOTES: In, Micheli, L.J. (ed.), Pediatric an adolescent sports medicine, Boston ; Toronto, Little, Brown, c1984, p. 144-166.
LEVEL: I LANG: Eng RC1210 17791

Walsh, E.R. Let's give young players a sporting chance. (Refs: 10) *Leisure information (New York) 10(4), Spring 1984, 10-12.*
LEVEL: B LANG: Eng SIRC ARTICLE NO: 100510

Watson, G.G. Henry, F.J. Motivating children to motivate themselves. (Refs: 22) *Sports coach (Wembley, Australia) 7(4), Mar 1984, 11-15.*
LEVEL: B LANG: Eng SIRC ARTICLE NO: 094216

Watson, G.G. Social motivation in children's games: a comparison of sex, class and formality of setting. (Refs: 40) *Australian journal of science & medicine in sport (Kingston, Aust.) 16(3), Oct 1984, 20-31.*
ABST: A sample of 240 children involved in informal playground activities or formalised sporting activities were first observed using naturalistic observation procedures, followed by focussed interviews to derive statements for subsequent content analysis and validation of a game attraction inventory. The procedure was designed to test a conceptual framework of social motivation in games. The framework suggests that games are able to motivate through three central elements of instrinsic reward or self-expression, co-operation or social reciprocity, and thirdly, task mastery. The major findings were that games differ markedly in their form of attraction when degree of formality and sex are considered.
LEVEL: A LANG: Eng SIRC ARTICLE NO: 105171

West, H.P. Responding with dance. (Refs: 11) *Momentum (Edinburgh, Scotland) 9(3), Autumn 1984, 14-24.*
LEVEL: I LANG: Eng SIRC ARTICLE NO: 105172

Wilson, V.J. Help children deal with the stress factors found in competition. (Refs: 4) *Momentum: a journal of human movemen studies (Edinburgh) 9(1), Spring 1984, 26-28.*
LEVEL: I LANG: Eng SIRC ARTICLE NO: 098888

Worsley, A. Coonan, W. Ten year old's attributions towards common physical activities. (Refs: 18) *Australian journal of science & medicine in sport (Kingston, Aust.) 16(4), Dec 1984, 24-30.*
ABST: Four hundred and forty five children rated

seven common physical activities on nine attributes before and after their participation in one of five physical education programs. Results of multivariate analyses indicated that there were major differences in the ways boys and girls perceived the activities. Boys positively evaluated activities which they regarded as dangerous and difficult (e.g. football): girls on the other hand, rated dangerous, difficult activities negatively.
LEVEL: A LANG: Eng SIRC ARTICLE NO: 105523

SAFETY

Charvet, D. Guillon, F. Proteau, J. La securite des materiels de jeux de plein air pour enfants, apport de la demarche ergonomique pour un probleme de sante publique. (The safety of outdoor games equipment for children. Contribution of the ergonomic approach for a public health problem.) *Archives des maladies professionelles de medecine du travail et de securite sociale (Paris) 45(1), 1984, 48-49.*
LEVEL: I LANG: Fr

SOCIAL PSYCHOLOGY

Gould, D. Psychosocial development and children's sport. (Refs: 55)*In, Thomas, J.R. (ed.), Motor development during childhood and adolescence, Minneapolis, Minn., Burgess Publishing Co., 1984, p. 212-236.*
LEVEL: A LANG: Eng BF1 20187

Ogilvie, B.C. The child and adolescent in sports: a psychosocial profile. (Refs: 19)
NOTES: In, Birrer, R.B. (ed.), Sports medicine for the primary care physician, Norwalk, Conn., Appleton-Century-Crofts, c1984, p. 305-312.
LEVEL: I LANG: Eng RC1210 17030

Railo, W.S. La relation entre le sport et la sante mentale et sociale chez les enfants et les adolescents. (Refs: 32)
NOTES: Dans, Lagarde, F. (ed.), Sante et activite physique, Longueuil, Que., College Edouard-Montpetit, c1984, p. 67-82.
LEVEL: A LANG: Fr GV481 17104

Telama, R. Psychosocial problems of physical activity in childhood. (Refs: 62)
CONF: Symposium of Paediatric Work Physiology (10th : 1981 : Joutsa, Finland).
NOTES: In, Ilmarinen, J. and Vaelimaeki, I. (eds.), Children and sport: paediatric work physiology, Berlin, Springer-Verlag, 1984, p. 145-155.
ABST: The author reviews relevant social psychological literature and discusses some of the interesting correlations that have been established.
LEVEL: A LANG: Eng SIRC ARTICLE NO: 102344

SOCIOLOGY

Givi, M. The role of the family in the socialization of children into sport. Eugene, Ore.: Microform Publications, Universit of Oregon, 1984. 3 microfiches : negative, ill. ; 11 x 15 cm.
NOTES: Thesis (Ph.D.) - University of Oregon, 1982; (xvii, 231 leaves); vita; includes bibliography.
LEVEL: A LANG: Eng UO84 121-123

Godin, G. Shephard, R.J. Normative beliefs of school children concerning regular exercise. (Refs: 18)*Journal of school health (Kent, Oh.) 54(11), Dec 1984, 443-445.*
LEVEL: A LANG: Eng SIRC ARTICLE NO: 174302

Okihiro, N.R. Extracurricular participation, educational destinies and early job outcomes. (Refs: 19)
CONF: North American Society for the Sociology of Sport. Conference (3rd : 1982 : Toronto, Ont.).
NOTES: In, Theberge, N. and Donnelly, P. (eds.), Sport and the sociological imagination: refereed proceedings of the 3rd Annual Conference of the North American Society for the Sociology of Sport, Toronto, Canada, November 1982, Fort Worth, Tex., Texas Christian University Press, c1984, p. 334-349.
ABST: This study assesses the effects of high school athletic and social activities participation on eventual occupational outcomes. 2555 Ontario Grade 12 students contacted in 1973 as a part of an educational intention survey were re-contacted in 1979. 69 per cent were successfully contacted and responded for this survey. The survey considered a number of factors which largely indicated in the results that athletic and social involvement in extracurricular activities play an important role in the process of education and early job attainment.
LEVEL: A LANG: Eng SIRC ARTICLE NO: 097847

Perie, H. Du jeu spontane de l'enfant a l'equipe sportive. *Dans, Mandel, C. (ed.), Le medecin, l'enfant et le sport, Paris, (Vigot), c1984, p. 131-139.*
LEVEL: B LANG: Fr RC1218.C45 18886

Ryan, S. The Fritz Duras Memorial Lecture. *ACHPER national journal 103, Mar 1984, 12-14.*
ABST: A speech by the Federal Minister for Education and Youth Affairs.
LEVEL: I LANG: Eng SIRC ARTICLE NO: 097425

William, G. Sport should become a fundamental right in education. *Olympic review (Lausanne, Switzerland) 195/196, Jan/Feb 1984, 42-43.*
NOTES: Extracted from, Frankfurter Allgemeine Zeitung, 21 Sept 1983.
LEVEL: B LANG: Eng SIRC ARTICLE NO: 094217

William, G. Le sport doit devenir un droit fondamental dans l'education. *Revue olympique (Lausanne) 195/196, janv/fevr 1984 42-43.*
NOTES: Extraits ci-dessus, a ete publie dans le Frankfurter Allgemeine Zeitung, 21 Sept 1983.
LEVEL: B LANG: Fr SIRC ARTICLE NO: 095744

TESTING

Bjornaraa, B. Apple Valley high school pentathlon. *National Strength & Conditioning Association journal 6(1), Feb/Mar 1984, 21;54-58.*
LEVEL: B LANG: Eng SIRC ARTICLE NO: 093188

Goldberg, B. Boiardo, R. Profiling children for sports participation. (Refs: 94)*Clinics in sports medicine (Philadelphia) 3(1), Jan 1984, 153-169.*
NOTES: Symposium on profiling.
ABST: The intent of profiling children is to prevent injury and improve fitness and performance in their chosen sport. Care should be taken to use the profile for these intents and not to push the child into a sport he has not chosen nor eliminate him from the chosen sport unless there is a risk. The profile includes a careful medical evaluation, a musculoskeletal assessment for possible orthopedic problems and a fitness evaluation.
LEVEL: A LANG: Eng SIRC ARTICLE NO: 092695

Imre, M. Ovodasok alkalmassagi vizsgalata sporttagozatos osztalyba valo felvetelhez. (Screening kindergarten children if the are fit for attending special sport classes in primary education.) (Refs: 3)*Sportorvosi szemle/Hungarian review of sports medicine (Budapest) 25(2), 1984, 109-115.*
ABST: The authors describe their experiences in screening 500 children of kindergarten age concerning the children's fitness for attending classes with a special physical education curriculum when they enter primary schooling. It was observed that 28.2% of these children showed such deficiencies of either physique or functional capacity that contraindicated their admittance to theses classes in view of their prospective health status and future successful performance or training work.
LEVEL: A LANG: Hun SIRC ARTICLE NO: 097265

Leduc, M. La detection du talent sportif chez les jeunes. *Loisirs presse (Montreal) 3(12), 1 mars 1984, 7.*
LEVEL: B LANG: Fr SIRC ARTICLE NO: 095736

TRAINING AND CONDITIONING

Baumgartner, T.A. Wood, S.S. Development of shoulder-girdle strength-endurance in elementary children. (Refs: 7)*Research quarterly for exercise & sport (Reston, Va.) 55(2), Jun 1984, 169-171.*
ABST: This study investigated the effect of training on a modified pull-up test apparatus on the shoulder-girdle strength endurance of 91 elementary school children. Ninety-two children served as control subjects. The experimental subjects performed one set of as many repetitions as possible of modified pull-ups 3 times/week for 12 weeks. The experimental group improved to a significantly greater degree in their ability to perform modified pull-ups than did the control group. Thus, this device is an effective training device for elementary children.
LEVEL: A LANG: Eng SIRC ARTICLE NO: 095724

Brown, E.W. Should young athletes lift weights as part of sport training? (Refs: 1)*Spotlight (East Lansing, Mich.) 7(3), Fall 1984, 1-2;4.*
LEVEL: I LANG: Eng SIRC ARTICLE NO: 103834

Cazorla, G. Bigrel, F. Le sport et l'enfant. *Science et vie (Paris) HS147, 1984, 128-136.*
LEVEL: I LANG: Fr

Hunt, R. An inexpensive but effective method for conditioning young athletes. *National Strength & Conditioning Association journal 5(6), Jan 1984, 48-49.*
ABST: This article outlines the benefits and objectives of a circuit training program for children under 14 years of age. The 20 stations are divided into sections for arms; shoulders and chest; legs; hips and buttocks; stomach and lower back; and running or walking. Hand and ankle weights are added to students with a higher level of ability. The program is a general conditioning program and does not focus on any particular sport.
LEVEL: B LANG: Eng SIRC ARTICLE NO: 089884

Lemaire, A. Entrainement sportif intensif et precoce. (Refs: 5)*Loisirs sante (Paris) 10, juin/juil/aout 1984, 14-16.*
NOTES: Tire de, Education Hebdo 33, 9 juin 1983.
LEVEL: B LANG: Fr SIRC ARTICLE NO: 103838

Smith, T.K. Preadolescent strength training: some considerations. (Refs: 14)*Journal of physical education, recreation & dance 55(1), Jan 1984, 43-44;80.*
LEVEL: B LANG: Eng SIRC ARTICLE NO: 091292

Topchiyan, V.S. Kadachkova, P.I. Komarova, A.D. Training young athletes in the yearly cycle in speed-strength and cyclical type sports. *Soviet sports review (Escondido, Calif.)* 19(4), Dec 1984, 157-160.
NOTES: Condensed translation from, Teoriya i praktika fizicheskoi kultury 11, 1983, 47-50.
LEVEL: I LANG: Eng SIRC ARTICLE NO: 104509

Tschiene, P. L'entrainement de la force chez les jeunes. Approche d'un systeme d'entrainement. *Revue de l'entraineur (Montreal)* oct/dec 1984, 13-17.
NOTES: Tire de, Scuola dello Sport Rivista di cultura sportiva, aout 1983.
LEVEL: I LANG: Fr SIRC ARTICLE NO: 105628

CHILE

von Vriessen, C.L. Some recreational and social sporting activities of the Mapuche Indians in the South of Chile. (Refs: 10) *In, Ilmarinen, M. (ed.) et al., Sport and International Understanding: proceedings of the congress held in Helsinki, Finland, July 7-10, 1982, Berlin, Springer-Verlag, 1984, p. 339-344.*
CONF: Congress on Sport and International Understanding (1982 : Helsinki).
LEVEL: A LANG: Eng GV706.8 18979

CLOTHING

Brin, C. Textiles et technologie. *Mousqueton (Montreal)* 13(4), 1984, 7.
LEVEL: B LANG: Fr SIRC ARTICLE NO: 097472

Hansen, D.S. There is nothing wrong with gore-tex. *Summit (Big Bear Lake, Calif.)* 30(4), Jul/Aug 1984, 24-25.
LEVEL: B LANG: Eng SIRC ARTICLE NO: 102403

Holzel, T. Gore-tex clothing: is it any good? *Summit (Big Bear City, Calif.)* 30(3), May/Jun 1984, 6-8.
LEVEL: B LANG: Eng SIRC ARTICLE NO: 098949

Holzel, T. Comment on gore-tex article. *Summit (Big Bear Lake, Calif.)* 30(4), Jul/Aug 1984, 26-27.
LEVEL: B LANG: Eng SIR ARTICLE NO: 102404

Loesel, H. Important medical aspects on sport referring to the Olympic Games in Summer 1984. (Part 3) Sportmedizinisch relevante Aspekte bezueglich der Olympischen Spiele im Sommer 1984. (3. Teil) Aspects importants du point de vue de la medecine et du sport pour les Jeux olympiques d'ete 1984. (3ieme partie) Aspectos importantes de punto de vista de la medicina y del deporte para los Juegos Olimpicos de 1984. (3a parte) *UIT shooting sport journal (Muenchen, FRG)* 24(1), Jan/Feb 1984, 15-19;35-38.
NOTES: A source
LEVEL: B LANG: Eng Ger Fr Spa SIRC ARTICLE NO: 098450

Moffatt, T. Foul-weather fabrics: product evolution coming. *Sport style (New York)* 6(4), 20 Feb 1984, 46;48.
LEVEL: B LANG: Eng SIRC ARTICLE NO: 092752

The sports/fitness/leisure markets. New York: Fairchild Publications, c1984. 50 p. (Fairchild fact files.)
CORP: Fairchild Market Research Division.

LEVEL: B LANG: Eng ISBN: 0-87005-482-1 GV706.8 18797

Walzer, E. Insulations: improved batting technology. *Sport style (New York)* 6(4), 20 Feb 1984, 40;44.
LEVEL: B LANG: Eng SIRC ARTICLE NO: 092759

Walzer, E. Fibers: synthesizing nature is top priority. *Sport style (New York)* 6(4), 20 Feb 1984, 50.
LEVEL: B LANG: Eng SIRC ARTICLE NO: 092760

Watkins, S.M. Clothing: the portable environment. Anes, Iowa: Iowa State University Press, c1984. xviii, 254 p. : ill.
NOTES: Includes bibliographical references.
LEVEL: I LANG: Eng ISBN: 0-8138-0316-0 LC CARD: 83-7902

DESIGN

Watkins, S.M. Clothing systems for thermal protection. (Refs: 7)*In, Watkins, S.M., Clothing: the portable environment, Anes Iowa, Iowa State University Press, c1984, p. 35-37.*
LEVEL: I LANG: Eng SIRC ARTICLE NO: 107989

Watkins, S.M. Providing mobility in clothing. (Refs: 19)*In, Watkins, S.M., Clothing: the portable environment, Anes, Iowa, Iowa State University Press, c1984, p. 144-184.*
LEVEL: I LANG: Eng SIRC ARTICLE NO: 107987

Watkins, S.M. Fastening systems. (Refs: 1)*In, Watkins, S.M., Clothing: the portable environment, Anes, Iowa, Iowa State University Press, c1984, p. 185-210.*
LEVEL: I LANG: Eng SIRC ARTICLE NO: 107986

MANUFACTURING

Tourtet, J.F. Tourny-Eteve, S. Les armes legeres des industries sportives. *Science et vie (Paris)* HS147, 1984, 30-43.
LEVEL: I LANG: Fr

RETAILING

Mills, J. Head-to-toe bodywear: selling the fashion collection. *Action sports retailer (South Laguna, Calif.)* 5(6), Jun 1984, 52-54;57-59.
LEVEL: B LANG: Eng SIRC ARTICLE NO: 103913

Sturdy, R. Buying it right... *Sports trade Canada (Downsview, Ont.)* 12(4), May/Jun 1984, 24-25.
LEVEL: B LANG: Eng SIRC ARTICLE NO: 103917

Warm-up sales? No sweat. *Fitness industry (Miami, Fl.)* 2(7), Nov/Dec 1984, 8-10;12-13.
LEVEL: B LANG: Eng SIRC ARTICLE NO: 102414

SHOES

Adi Dassler - a man and his dream. *Canadian runner (Toronto, Ont.)* Jun 1984, 26.
LEVEL: B LANG: Eng SIRC ARTICLE NO: 094282

Cahlin, M. Eliminate agony in your feet. (shock absorber) *National racquetball (Glenview, Ill.)* 13(10), Oct 1984, 10-11.
LEVEL: B LANG: Eng SIRC ARTICLE NO: 105201

Edwards, S. Footwear merchandising: footwear for emerging sports. *Sporting retailer (Mt. Prospect, Ill.)* 37(1), Jan 1984, 18-19.
LEVEL: B LANG: Eng SIRC ARTICLE NO: 097482

Tips for buying athletic shoes. *First serve (Vanier, Ont.)* 2(2), Sept 1984, 9-10.
NOTES: Reprinted from the Canadian Podiatric Sport Medicine Academy publication 'Tips on buying athletic shoes'.
LEVEL: B LANG: Eng SIRC ARTICLE NO: 173017

What's new in athletic shoes? High tech and the modern shoe. *Scholastic coach (New York)* 53(10), May/Jun 1984, 57-58;60;62-63;65-66;68;100-101.
NOTES: Scholastic coach special survey.
LEVEL: B LANG: Eng SIRC ARTICLE NO: 094291

CLUBS

Hobson, A. The best we've got: an inside look at four of Canada's most successful sports clubs. *Coaching review (Ottawa, Ont.)* 7, Nov/Dec 1984, 27-34.
LEVEL: B LANG: Eng SIRC ARTICLE NO: 099340

Membership: who goes where and why. *Recreation, sports & leisure (Minneapolis)* 4(6), Aug 1984, 35-36.
NOTES: Special issue: Managed recreation research report.
LEVEL: B LANG: Eng SIRC ARTICLE NO: 104439

ADMINISTRATION

How to take the worry out of fund-raising. Some money-spinning advice from the Sports Council's Sports Development Unit. *Gras (Leicestershire, Eng.)* 3(10), 1984, 130-131.
LEVEL: B LANG: Eng SIRC ARTICLE NO: 173131

Joachim, G. Guinot, R. Quand une philosophie engendre une technique. Le sport au Club mediterranee. (Refs: 5)*Dans, Culture technique no. 13, Neuilly-sur-Seine, France, Centre de Recherche sur la Culture Technique, c1984, p. 86-91.*
LEVEL: I LANG: Fr RC1235 20096

ECONOMICS

Heinemann, K. Socioeconomic problems of sports clubs. (Refs: 20)*International review for the sociology of sport (Warszawa, Poland)* 19(3/4), 1984, 201-214.
ABST: There are many characteristics which distinguish the economic situation of a sports club from that of a profit oriented business. They include the constitutional organization of a sports clubs, voluntary membership, orientation towards the interests of members, democratic decision-making and voluntary work. Similarities can be seen in the structures of resources and kinds of financing, the types of goods produced, the optimization of goods production, the use of control mechanisms through which various demands and expectations are connected to each other, goals of the executive board and decision-making according to majority vote. These factors affect the social structure of the club and form the basis for an economic theory of sports clubs.
LEVEL: A LANG: Eng SIRC ARTICLE NO: 105592

Francis, A. Sports science and the coach. (Refs: 8)*Scottish journal of physical education (Glasgow, Scotland) 12(2), Apr 1984, 41-46.*
LEVEL: I LANG: Eng SIRC ARTICLE NO: 094226

Franks, R. Zulauf, G. The ol' coach on the banquet circuit. Amarillo, Tex.: Ray Franks Publishing Ranch, c1984. 80 p. : ill.
LEVEL: B LANG: Eng ISBN: 0-943976-01-4 GV711 18956

Hoehn, R.G. Nagging problem. Here's how you might solve eight coaching headaches. *Coaching review 7, Mar/Apr 1984, 39-40.*
LEVEL: B LANG: Eng SIRC ARTICLE NO: 092705

Hotz, A. L'entraineur et ses taches de dirigeant. *Macolin (Suisse) 9, sept 1984, 10-11.*
LEVEL: B LANG: Fr SIRC ARTICLE NO 102350

Lyle, J. Towards a concept of coaching. (Refs: 1)*Scottish journal of physical education (Glasgow, Scotland) 12(1), Jan 1984 27-31.*
LEVEL: I LANG: Eng SIRC ARTICLE NO: 094232

Metrailler, D. L'entraineur au centre du monde. *Macolin (Suisse) 9, sept 1984, 19.*
NOTES: Adaptation de, Yves Jeannotat.
LEVEL: B LANG: Fr SIRC ARTICLE NO: 102351

Scott, M.D. Pelliccioni, L. Understanding coaching style and performance. *Women's varsity sports (Kalispell, Mont.) 5(3), Jan/Feb 1984, 28-30.*
LEVEL: B LANG: Eng SIRC ARTICLE NO: 100515

Tindall, R. Coaches and instructors: their roles and responsibilities. Wembley, W.A.: Department for Youth, Sport and Recreation, 1984. 26 p.
CORP: Western Australia. Department for Youth, Sport and Recreation.
NOTES: Cover title.
ABST: A workbook for coaches considering the types of coach; skill learning and coaching; the aim of the coach and target setting; roles and relationships; and the particular demands of coaching junior sport.
LEVEL: B LANG: Eng GV711 18661

ADMINISTRATION

Fabianic, D. Organization effectiveness and managerial succession: an update of an old problem. (Refs: 18)*Journal of sport behavior (Mobile, Ala.) 7(4), Dec 1984, 139-152.*
ABST: An examination of midseason managerial successions in professional baseball between 1951-80 reveals that managerial replacements usually occur during a team slump, and team performance ordinarily improves in the period immediately following the managerial change. This finding is consistent with the common sense theory which suggests that team performance will improve following managerial replacement. However, when the effects of the prereplacement slump and recovery period are removed, the data are consistent with the ritual scapegoating explanation of succession which posits that managers have little effect on team performance. When team performances under new and old managers are compared in general, with no consideration of other variables, there is weak support for the common sense theory. The results of this study indicate that the relationship of organizational effectiveness and managerial succession is one that is dependent upon the time periods considered to discern team performance, and the character of the replacement process and origin of successor.
LEVEL: A LANG: Eng SIRC ARTICLE NO: 101069

Kozoll, C.E. No time for wasting time. Developing good habits is essential to practical time management for coaches. *Coaching review (Ottawa, Ont.) 7, May/Jun 1984, 30-32.*
LEVEL: B LANG: Eng SIRC ARTICLE NO: 094230

Virgilio, S.J. Krebs, P.S. Smith, J. How to play (and win) the game of time management. (Refs: 4)*Women's coaching clinic (Princeton, N.J.) 8(2), Oct 1984, 14-16.*
LEVEL: I LANG: Eng SIRC ARTICLE NO: 098893

ADMINISTRATION - ECONOMICS

Martin, D. Tax tips for coaches. *Athletic journal 64(8), Mar 1984, 30;73-74.*
LEVEL: B LANG: Eng SIRC ARTICLE NO: 092707

ADMINISTRATION - PLANNING

Coackburn, J. Systematic application of common sense. *Coaching review 7, Jan/Feb 1984, 38-39.*
LEVEL: B LANG: Eng SIRC ARTICLE NO: 091298

ADMINISTRATION - RECRUITMENT

Brubaker, B. Dear Chris: when you're Chris Washburn - 6' 11' with a can't miss jumper - you can expect to have hundreds of pen pals, and sacks, cartons and drawers full of mail. *Sports illustrated (Los Angeles, Calif.) 61(24), 26 Nov 1984, 120-124;126-128;130;132;134;136.*
LEVEL: B LANG: Eng SIRC ARTICLE NO: 100512

Cassidy, T.P. Guidelines for recruiting high school athletes. *Texas coach 27(4), Jan 1984, 58-61.*
LEVEL: B LANG: Eng SIRC ARTICLE NO: 093190

ADMINISTRATION - SCHOLARSHIPS

Seriously considering a career in coaching? Those wishing to participate in the CAC program of coaching scholarships for university study have a deadline. *Coaching review 7, Jan/Feb 1984, 24.*
LEVEL: B LANG: Eng SIRC ARTICLE NO: 091305

ADMINISTRATION - TRAVEL

Drager, N. Body physic: travel bugs. Un corps sain: votre corps en voyage. *Champion 8(1), Feb 1984, 6;13.*
LEVEL: B LANG: Eng Fr SIRC ARTICLE NO: 090071

Hobson, A. Le sud: journees ensoleillees sans plaisir. The southern sweat. *Champion 8(1), Feb 1984, 62-65.*
LEVEL: B LANG: Eng Fr SIRC ARTICLE NO: 089862

ASSOCIATIONS

Programs, services & policies. Ottawa: Coaching Association of Canada, c1984. 99 p. (loose-leaf)
CORP: Coaching Association o Canada.
NOTES: Cover title. Aussi publie en francais sous le titre: Programmes, services & directives.
LEVEL: B LANG: Eng GV711 20068

AUDIO VISUAL AIDS

Lovece, F. The case for video recording. *Scholastic coach 53(8), Mar 1984, 56-57.*
LEVEL: B LANG: Eng SIRC ARTICLE NO: 092706

Sutherland, J. Motion picture film technology. *Scholastic coach 53(8), Mar 1984, 60;62.*
LEVEL: B LANG: Eng SIRC ARTICLE NO: 092711

BIOGRAPHY AND AUTOBIOGRAPHY

Coaches with a future. The recipients of CAC coaching scholarships for 1983-84. *Coaching review (Ottawa, Ont.) 7, May/Jun 1984, 22-25.*
LEVEL: B LANG: Eng SIRC ARTICLE NO: 094223

McKinzie, P. Following in family footsteps. Family members are following in the footsteps of honorable coaching examples. *Coaching review (Ottawa, Ont.) 7, May/Jun 1984, 25-26.*
LEVEL: B LANG: Eng SIRC ARTICLE NO: 094235

The medal makers: a few of Canada's unsung Olympic heroes. *Coaching review (Ottawa, Ont.) 7, Nov/Dec 1984, 17-26.*
LEVEL: B LANG: Eng SIRC ARTICLE NO: 098890

BIOMECHANICS

Mahr, J. Biomechanics made simpler for the coach. *Women's coaching clinic (Princeton, N.J.) 8(2), Oct 1984, 12-14.*
LEVEL: LANG: Eng SIRC ARTICLE NO: 098889

CAREERS

Clark, S. Coaches overseas: finding a coaching job isn't necessarily like trying to find a needle in a haystack. *Coaching review 7, Mar/Apr 1984, 29-31.*
LEVEL: B LANG: Eng SIRC ARTICLE NO: 092704

Rog, J.A. Teaching and coaching: the ultimate challenge. (Refs: 6)*Journal of physical education, recreation & dance (Reston Va.) 55(6), Aug 1984, 48-49.*
ABST: In the author's opinion, the teaching of physical education and the coaching of a sport are two distinct activities. In a school situation, it is very rare that an individual will only be involved in one or the other - more usual is the hybrid teacher-coach. The author outlines the context differences between teaching physical education and coaching as well as offers suggestions on how best to insure quality performance in both activities.
LEVEL: B LANG: Eng SIRC ARTICLE NO: 097430

CERTIFICATION

Beran, J.A. Coaches should they be teachers? IAHPERD takes a stand. (Refs: 9)*Journal of teaching in physical education (Backsburg, Va.) 3(3), Spring 1984,*
NOTES: The JTPE forum: a brewing controversy: should interscholastic coaches be certified?
LEVEL: I LANG: Eng SIRC ARTICLE NO: 095747

Corcoran, P. Review of the National Coaching Accreditation Scheme. *Sports coach (Wembley, Aust.) 8(1), 1984, 43-44.*
NOTES A presented paper in Sports Administration Section - Biennial Annual Conference, January 1984.
LEVEL: B LANG: Eng SIRC ARTICLE NO: 095749

Johnson, C. U.K. coach education scheme - 1980 and beyond. *Athletic coach (London) 18(2), Jun 1984, 27-28.*
LEVEL: B LANG: Eng SIRC ARTICLE NO: 094229

Massengak, J.D. The certification of coaches: considering the lack thereof. (Refs: 13)*Journal of teaching in physical education (Backsburg, Va.) 3(3), Spring 1984, 6-9.*
NOTES: The JTPE forum: a brewing controversy: should interscholastic coaches be certified?
LEVEL: I LANG: Eng SIRC ARTICLE NO: 095757

McKie, D. Planting the right seeds. Winning redefined. *Coaching review (Ottawa, Ont.) 7, Jul/ Aug 1984, 31-32.*
LEVEL: B LANG: Eng SIRC ARTICLE NO: 094234

Pyke, F.S. Some considerations in the education of sports coaches. *New Zealand journal of health, physical education & recreation (Wellington, N.Z.) 17(3), Nov 1984, 3-5.*
CONF: New Zealand Association of Health, Physical Education and Recreation. Conference (1984 : Wellington).
LEVEL: B LANG: Eng SIRC ARTICLE NO: 103847

Sisley, B. Coaching specialization: the Oregon program. (Refs: 5)*Physical educator (Indianapolis, Ind.) 3(41), Oct 1984, 149-152.*
LEVEL: B LANG: Eng SIRC ARTICLE NO: 100516

Stier, W. One university's answer to the professional preparation of athletic coaches. *Journal of teaching in physical education (Blacksburg, Va.) 3(3), Spring 1984,*
NOTES: The JTPE forum: a brewing controversy: should interscholastic coaches be certified?
LEVEL: I LANG: Eng SIRC ARTICLE NO: 095759

Svoboda, B. Coaches and physical education teachers training in socialist countries. Prague: Olympia, 1984. 103 p. (A collection of studies in the international scientific cooperation (task no. 6); v. 2.)
CORP: Charles University, Prague. Faculty of Physical Education and Sport.
CORP: Czechoslovak Union of Physical Education. Central Committee.
NOTES: Includes bibliographies.
LEVEL: I LANG: Eng GV361 20849

Theorie de l'entrainement. Niveau 3. Supplement. Vanier, Ont.: Association canadienne des entraineurs, c1984. 1v. en paginatio multiple (Programme national de certification des entraineurs.)
CORP: Association canadienne des entraineurs.
NOTES: Titre de la couverture. Contenu: A. Questions et reponses - physiologie. B. Procedures de testing-psychologie. Also published in English under the title: Coaching theory. Level 3. Supplement.
LEVEL: I LANG: Fr GV711 18359

Valeriote, T. Publishing a manual. Ottawa: New Traditions, c1984. 67 p. : ill.
NOTES: Bibliography: p. 65.
LEVEL: B LANG: Eng ISBN: 0-9691563-3-2 LC CARD: 84-90049-X GV713 17607

CHILDREN AND YOUTH

Smoll, F.L. Smith, R.E. Leadership research in youth sports.
NOTES: In, Silva, J.M. and Weinberg, R.S. (eds.), Psychologica foundations of sport, Champaign, Ill.,

Human Kinetics Publishers, c1984, p. 371-386.
LEVEL: A LANG: Eng SIRC ARTICLE NO: 109690

Valeriote, T. Children's sport programs: the coach. Ottawa: New Traditions, c1984. v, 66, A11 p. : ill.
NOTES: Includes bibliography.
LEVEL: B LANG: Eng ISBN: 0-9691563-0-8 LC CARD: C84-90051-1 GV709.2 17661

Vogel, P. Feltz, D. Your role as a youth sports coach. *Spotlight on youth sports (East Lansing, Mich.) 7(4), Winter 1984, 1;3.*
LEVEL: B LANG: Eng SIRC ARTICLE NO: 108876

DOCUMENTATION

Blundell, N. Superior coaching: the ingredients are identical, the blend may vary, but the key is INNOVATION. (Refs: 7) *Sports coach (Wembley, Australia) 7(4), Mar 1984, 49-53.*
LEVEL: I LANG: Eng SIRC ARTICLE NO: 094220

INJURIES AND ACCIDENTS

Aris, H. The role and responsibilities of the coach in the diagnosis and the treatment of sport injuries. *Pan athlete (San Juan, Puerto Rico) 2(7), 1984, 50-51.*
LEVEL: B LANG: Eng SIRC ARTICLE NO: 097563

Stapleton, K.L. Tomlinson, C.M. Shepard, K.F. Coon, V.A. High school coaches' perceptions of their responsibilities in managing their athletes' injuries. (Refs: 17)*Journal of orthopaedic and sports physical therapy (Baltimore, Md.) 5(5), Mar/Apr 1984, 253-260.*
ABST: Thirty coaches were asked six open-ended questions regarding their responsibilities and abilities for athletic health care and opinions about certification and liability. The results indicate that coaches currently assume the major responsibility of athletic health care although the coaches felt that they lacked the knowledge to manage athletic injuries. The authors conclude that more involvement by health care professionals is needed to assist coaches in carrying out the responsibilities of athletic injury management. The coaches were in favour of coaching certification.
LEVEL: A LANG: Eng SIRC ARTICLE NO: 094240

LAW AND LEGISLATION

Adams, S.H. Liability and negligence. *In, Adams, S.H. (ed.), et al., Catastrophic injuries in sports: avoidance strategies, Salinas, Calif., Coyote Press, c1984, p. 1-4.*
LEVEL: B LANG: Eng RD97 19088

Borkowski, R.P. A mini-course for the youth sport coach on legal responsibilities. *Spotlight (East Lansing, Mich.) 7(2), Summer 1984, 1-2;5.*
LEVEL: B LANG: Eng SIRC ARTICLE NO: 097585

Cotten, D.J. Staying out of court. A coach has no legal liability unless negligent. (Refs: 5)*Scholastic coach (New York) 53(10), May/Jun 1984, 84;102.*
LEVEL: B LANG: Eng SIRC ARTICLE NO: 094224

Farrell, C.S. Nevada judge rejects Tarkanian's suspension: issues scathing opinion on NCAA's behavior. *Chronicle of higher education (Washington) 28(19), 5 Jul 1984, 19;21.*
LEVEL: B LANG: Eng SIRC ARTICLE NO: 103852

Frank, N.L. Knowledge tests covering selected liabilities of physical educators and coaches. Eugene, Ore.: Microform Publications, University of Oregon, 1984. 2 microfiches : negative ; 11 x 15

cm.
NOTES: Thesis (M.S.) - University of North Carolina at Greensboro, 1982; (vi, 105 leaves); includes bibliography.
LEVEL: A LANG: Eng UO84 198-199

Goldman, P.S. Text of Nevada judge's opinion invalidating NCAA action against coach. *Chronicle of higher education (Washington) 28(19), 5 Jul 1984, 20-21.*
LEVEL: B LANG: Eng SIRC ARTICLE NO: 103855

Mallios, H.G. In defense of athletic administrators facing litigation. *Athletic administration 19(1), Feb 1984, 17-19.*
LEVEL: B LANG: Eng SIRC ARTICLE NO: 092912

McDonald, M. Wilton, D. Coaching and the laws of liability. (Refs: 27)
NOTES: In, Brown, R. (ed.) et al., Sport, physical activity and the law, Ottawa, Canadian Association for Health, Physical Education, Recreation and Dance, c1984, p. 26-38.
LEVEL: I LANG: Eng GV705 18324

Missouri - can a coach write a letter to a newspaper without the fear of losing his/her job? *Sports and the courts (Winston-Salem, N.C.) 5(1), Winter 1984, 4-5.*
LEVEL: B LANG: Eng SIRC ARTICLE NO: 094236

Simpson, W.K. Some legal concerns for coaches. (Refs: 8)*Texas coach (Austin, Tex.) 28(3), Oct 1984, 22-23.*
LEVEL: B LANG: Eng SIRC ARTICLE NO: 173201

Wendt, J.T. Coaches in court - be prepared. *Sideline view (Minneapolis, Minn.) 6(2), Sept 1984, 1-4.*
LEVEL: B LANG: Eng SIRC ARTICLE NO: 099078

MEDICINE

Kelley, E.J. Inservice on athletic training: a safeguard for student athletes. *NASSP bulletin (Reston, Va.) 68(471), Apr 1984, 131-133.*
ABST: Details a program in Pennsylvania to provide the school coach with minimum knowledge in athletic training and sports medicine.
LEVEL: B LANG: Eng SIRC ARTICLE NO: 097428

Lyle, J. The coach and sports medicine. *Sports coach (Wembley, Australia) 7(4), Mar 1984, 39-46.*
LEVEL: B LANG: Eng SIRC ARTICLE NO: 094428

Wathen, D. Athletic trainer/conditioning coach relations - communication is the key. (Refs: 7)*National Strength & Conditioning Association journal (Lincoln, Neb.) 6(5), Oct/Nov 1984, 32-33.*
LEVEL: B LANG: Eng SIRC ARTICLE NO: 102962

OFFICIALS AND COACHES

Staffo, D.F. The coach-referee relationship: from an objective viewpoint. *Sportorials (West Hartford, Conn.) 34(261), Feb/Mar 1984, 2.*
LEVEL: B LANG: Eng SIRC ARTICLE NO: 106291

PHILOSOPHY

Parsons, T.W. Gamesmanship and sport ethics. Exposing young people to the rights and wrongs in sport could help us establish a more acceptable moral code. *Coaching review (Ottawa, Ont.) 7, Jul/ Aug 1984, 28-30.*
LEVEL: B LANG: Eng SIRC ARTICLE NO: 094237

Pearlstein, M B. Coaches win both sainthood and slaps. *Soccer journal (Philadelphia, Pa.) 29(2),*

COACHING (continued)

Mar/Apr 1984, 11-12.
LEVEL: B LANG: Eng SIRC ARTICLE NO: 094238

PHYSIOLOGY

Pate, R.R. McClenaghan, B. Rotella, R. Scientific foundations of coaching. Philadelphia ; Montreal: Saunders College Pub., c1984. xii, 344 p. : ill.
NOTES: Includes bibliographies and index.
LEVEL: I LANG: Eng ISBN: 0030579619 LC CARD: 83-020117 GV711 17143

PSYCHOLOGY

Chappell, A.J. When coaching is not enough. Counselling your athletes. *Coaching review 7,* Jan/Feb 1984, 26-28.
LEVEL: B LANG: Eng SIRC ARTICLE NO: 091297

Edwards, S.W. Huston, S.A. The clinical aspects of sport psychology. (Refs: 8)*Physical educator (Indianapolis, Ind.) 3(41),* Oct 1984, 142-148.
LEVEL: I LANG: Eng SIRC ARTICLE NO: 100937

Silva, J.M. The status of sport psychology: a national survey of coaches. (Refs: 3)*Journal of physical education, recreatio and dance (Reston, Va.) 55(7),* Sept 1984, 46-49.
LEVEL: I LANG: Eng SIRC ARTICLE NO: 100948

PSYCHOLOGY - BEHAVIOUR

Lombardo, B.J. The coach in action: a descriptive analysis. (Refs: 13)*Bulletin of the Federation international d'education physique (Toulouse, France) 54(3/4),* Jul/Dec 1984, 9-15.
LEVEL: I LANG: Eng SIRC ARTICLE NO: 105176

Terry, P.C. Howe, B.L. Coaching preferences of athletes. (Refs: 18)*Canadian journal of applied sport sciences/Journal canadien des sciences appliquees au sport (Windsor, Ont.) 9(4),* Dec 1984, 188-193.
ABST: The study examined the coaching preferences of 80 male and 80 female athletes, as measured by the Leadership Scale for Sports (Chelladurai and Saleh, 1978, 1980). In addition, it attempted to assess the applicability to sport of the Life-cycle and Path-goal theories of leadership. Comparisons between groups were made on the basis of sex, age, and type of sport. A MANOVA indicated that athletes in independent sports preferred more democratic behaviour and less autocratic behaviour than athletes in interdependent sports. No differences in coaching preferences were found which could be attributed to the age or sex of the athlete, or the variability of the sports task. These results partially supported the Path-goal theory, but did not support the Life-cycle theory.
LEVEL: A LANG: Eng SIRC ARTICLE NO: 102356

Terry, P.C. The coaching preferences of elite athletes competing at Universiade '83. (Refs: 18)*Canadian journal of applied sport sciences/Journal canadien des sciences appliquees au sport (Windsor, Ont.) 9(4),* Dec 1984, 201-208.
ABST: The study investigated the coaching preferences of 95 male and 65 female elite athletes competing at Universiade '83 (Edmonton, Canada). Preferred coaching behavior (PCB) was measured using a version of the Leadership Scale for Sports (Chelladurai and Saleh, 1978, 1980). Preference scores were analyzed on the basis of sex, age, nationality, and type of sport. A MANOVA indicated that males prefer significantly more Autocratic behaviour than females. Also, athletes in team

sports prefer significantly more Training behaviour, Autocratic behaviour, and Rewarding behaviour, and significantly less Democratic behaviour and Social Support behaviour than athletes in individual sports. No significant differences in PCB attributable to the age or nationality of the athlete were found.
LEVEL: A LANG: Eng SIRC ARTICLE NO: 102357

PSYCHOLOGY - MENTAL TRAINING

Griffiths, A. La preparation psychologique des athletes. Preparing athletes' minds. *Champion 8(1),* Feb 1984, 2-5.
ABST: People are beginning to realize today that one of the limiting factors in sports performance is psychological. Avoiding distractions during performance is one important factor of this. Achieving self-control through mental training is another important factor. This details monitoring one's state of arousal and reacting positively to any problem situations that may occur rather than increasing levels of frustration and seeking aid from a coach. There are many mental training techniques being used to help athletes, but mental imagery is one of the oldest and most favoured. Essentially it involves mentally rehearsing performances so as to eliminate actual errors during competition. Many feel that the advantage of a winning athlete can be seen in his or her mental preparation.
LEVEL: B LANG: Eng Fr SIRC ARTICLE NO: 090327

Grove, J.R. Motivation and mental preparation for sport. Wembley, W.A.: Department for Youth, Sport and Recreation, 1984. 19 p.
CORP: Western Australia. Department for Youth, Sport and Recreation.
NOTES: Cover title.
LEVEL: I LANG: Eng GV706.4 18662

Regnier, G. La pratique mentale. (Refs: 2)*Revue de l'entraineur (Montreal)* avr/juin 1984, 23.
LEVEL: B LANG: Fr SIRC ARTICLE NO: 094659

Surgent, F.C. An approach to reaching peak performance. (Refs: 16)*Coaching clinic 22(6),* Feb 1984, 8-10.
ABST: A workable outline is presented for mental rehearsal through which coaches and their athletes can formulate their own visualization training programs to achieve peak performance. Practical procedures for mental rehearsal are presented in a question and answer format which allows for easy comprehension of the various techniques and how best to utilize them.
LEVEL: I LANG: Eng SIRC ARTICLE NO: 090336

PSYCHOLOGY - MOTIVATION

Blair, S. Dressing room slogans: as this review clearly shows, dressing room slogans can serve to stimulate and motivate athletes. (Refs: 2)*Athletic journal 64(6),* Jan 1984, 48;54;56.
LEVEL: B LANG: Eng SIRC ARTICLE NO: 089892

Carron, A.V. Motivation: implications for coaching and teaching. London, Ont.: Sports Dynamics, c1984. vi, 191 p.
NOTES: Includes bibliographies.
LEVEL: B LANG: Eng ISBN: 0-9691619-0-5 LC CARD: C84-098180-5 GV706.4 17217

DeFazio, J. Motivation...through consistency of philosophy. *Women's coaching clinic (Princeton,*

N.J.) 7(9), May 1984, 8-9.
LEVEL: B LANG: Eng SIRC ARTICLE NO: 094225

Hrycaiko, D.W. Motivation: the importance of psychology in sport. (Refs: 5)*Coaching science update (Ottawa, Ont.)* 1984, 46-48.
LEVEL: B LANG: Eng SIRC ARTICLE NO: 094649

Hrycaiko, D.W. La motivation: l'importance de la psychologie dans le sport. (Refs: 5)*Nouveautes en science de l'entrainemen (Ottawa)* 1984, 40-42.
LEVEL: I LANG: Fr SIRC ARTICLE NO: 096328

Krause, K. Motivation. *Coaching clinic (Princeton, N.J.) 22(8),* Apr 1984, 15-16.
LEVEL: B LANG: Eng SIRC ARTICLE NO: 0946

Singer, R.N. Persistence at training over time. (Refs: 7)*Coaching science update (Ottawa, Ont.)* 1984, 49-53.
NOTES: Adapted from a presentation given at the fourth annual National Coaches Seminar, Mont Ste. Marie, Que. Oct 1982.
LEVEL: I LANG: Eng SIRC ARTICLE NO: 094665

Singer, R.N. La perseverance dans l'entrainement: maintenir la motivation. (Refs: 7)*Nouveautes en science de l'entrainement (Ottawa)* 1984, 44-48.
NOTES: Cet article est adapte d'un expose donne au 4e Seminaire annuel national des entraineurs tenu au Mont Ste-Marie (Quebec) en octobre 1982.
LEVEL: I LANG: Fr SIRC ARTICLE NO: 096344

PSYCHOLOGY - PERSONALITY

Krebs, P. Hoffpauir, D. Mind and body as one in athletic performance. (Refs: 8)*Coaching clinic 22(7),* Mar 1984, 12-14.
LEVEL: B LANG: Eng SIRC ARTICLE NO: 093151

Malhotra, M.S. Khan, H.A. Personality traits of experienced coaches. (Refs: 23)*SNIPES journal (Patiala, India) 7(4),* Oct 1984, 32-37.
ABST: The purpose of this study was to assess the personality traits of experienced Indian coaches. 30 soccer and cricket coaches were surveyed. The 8 personality traits assessed were: activity, cyclothymia, super-ego, dominance, paranoid tendencies, depressive tendencies, emotional instability and introversion. Results indicated that: 1) experienced coaches tend to be suspicious and doubtful, 2) a few of these coaches suffer from fluctuations of mood, 3) some of the coaches have tendencies toward introversion and 4) most of the coaches are normally active, emotionally stable, with no depressive tendencies.
LEVEL: A LANG: Eng SIRC ARTICLE NO: 171613

PSYCHOLOGY - SELF-CONCEPT

Poole, R.C. Peck, J. Alanzo, S. Bills, R. Gregory, J. Mathis, G. Improving performance through improving self-esteem. *Women's coaching clinic (Princeton, N.J.) 8(4),* Dec 1984, 12-16.
LEVEL: B LANG: Eng SIRC ARTICLE NO: 102353

PSYCHOLOGY - STRESS

Alderson, J. The stress of umpiring, and its management. *Netball (London) 3(4),* Dec 1984, 14;27.
LEVEL: B LANG: Eng SIRC ARTICLE NO: 102638

Caccese, T.M. Mayerberg, C.K. Gender differences in perceived burnout of college coaches. (Refs: 12)*Journal of sport psychology (Champaign, Ill.) 6(3),* 1984, 279-288.
ABST: A study was undertaken to assess the level

of perceived burnout in college athletic coaches, and to determine whether male coaches differed from female coaches in level of burnout. Burnout was measured with the Maslach Burnout Inventory, a self-report rating scale that provides three subscores: Emotional Exhaustion, Depersonalization, and Personal Accomplishment. Subjects were NCAA and AIAW Division I college head coaches (138 male and 93 female coaches). The sexes differed on both the emotional exhaustion and the personal accomplishment subscales, in terms of both frequency of response and intensity of response. Female coaches reported significantly higher levels of emotional exhaustion and significantly lower levels of personal accomplishment than male coaches.
LEVEL: A LANG: Eng SIRC ARTICLE NO: 102844

RESEARCH

Blundell, N.L. Coaches - don't be intimidated. *Sports coach (Wembley, Aust.)* 8(1), 1984, 56-57.
NOTES: A presented paper in Sports Administration Section - ACHPER Biennial Conference, January 1984.
LEVEL: B LANG: Eng SIRC ARTICLE NO: 095748

Lacey, A.C. Darst, P.W. Evolution of a systematic observation system: the ASU coaching observation instrument. (Refs: 12) *Journal of teaching in physical education (Blacksburg, Va.)* 3(3), Spring 1984, 59-66.
ABST: This article introduces the Arizona State University (ASU) Observation Instrument. This instrument was designed to observe the behaviors of coaches but can also be used to observe physical education teachers during lessons. The authors hope this instrument will stimulate discussion and find use within the physical education teaching spectrum.
LEVEL: A LANG: Eng SIRC ARTICLE NO: 095755

What coaches really think. The answers to the 25 vital questions in Scholastic Coach's readership survey in the May/June issue *Scholastic coach (New York)* 54(3), Oct 1984, 66;68-70.
LEVEL: B LANG: Eng SIRC ARTICLE NO: 100517

SOCIAL PSYCHOLOGY

Shaver, L. Dealing with irresponsibility. *Sports 'n spokes (Phoenix, Ariz.)* 9(5), Jan/Feb 1984, 19-20.
LEVEL: B LANG: Eng SIRC ARTICLE NO: 094239

Weiss, M.R. Sisley, R.L. Where have all the coaches gone. (Refs: 12) *Sociology of sport journal (Champaign, Ill.)* 1(4), Dec 1984, 332-347.
ABST: The present study examined the problem of coaching attrition in youth sports by asking former coaches why they quit. Also, dropout and current coaches were compared on demographic characteristics, coaching orientations, self-ratings of coaching abilities, and attitudes toward program politics. Current (n, 159) and dropout (n, 97) coaches associated with a youth sports agency responded to a background questionnaire and a coaching orientations and preferred outcomes questionnaire. Dropout coaches also completed a questionnaire to assess the reasons why they quit coaching. Multiple reasons were cited: time involvement, conflicts with job, child no longer participating, loss of motivation, problems with unqualified officiating, and dissatisfaction with program philosophy.
LEVEL: A LANG: Eng SIRC ARTICLE NO: 103849

SOCIAL PSYCHOLOGY - ATHLETE-COACH RELATIONSHIP

McCready, G. L'entraineur: agent de perfectionnement des ressources humaines. (Refs: 14) *Science du sport: Documents de recherche et de technologie P-1, janv 1984, 1-6.*
LEVEL: I LANG: Fr SIRC ARTICLE NO: 091299

McCready, G. The coach as a developer of human resources. (Refs: 14) *Sports: Science periodical on research and technology i sport P-1, Jan 1984, 1-6.*
LEVEL: I LANG: Eng SIRC ARTICLE NO: 091300

Smoll, F.L. Smith, R.E. Improving the quality of coach-player interaction. (Refs: 32) *In, Thomas, J.R. (ed.), Motor development during childhood and adolescence, Minneapolis, Minn., Burgess Publishing Co., 1984, p. 237-257.*
LEVEL: A LANG: Eng BF1 20187

Taylor, J. Negative over-coaching. *Sport-talk (Toronto)* 13(1), Mar 1984, 4.
LEVEL: B LANG: Eng SIRC ARTICLE NO: 094241

SOCIAL PSYCHOLOGY - COMMUNICATION

Ende, H. Through the mind's eye: there's another way to get through to players when yelling and shouting fails. *Sports coac (Wembley, W. Aust.)* 8(2), Oct 1984, 18-19.
LEVEL: B LANG: Eng SIRC ARTICLE NO: 103844

Leathers, J. The pencil and paper practice. How a coach dramatically improved communication with her players. *Coaching review (Ottawa, Ont.)* 7, Jul/Aug 1984, 27.
LEVEL: B LANG: Eng SIRC ARTICLE NO: 094231

SOCIAL PSYCHOLOGY - LEADERSHIP

Boucher, R. A la recherche du leadership. (Refs: 12) *Science du sport: documents de recherche et de technologie (Ottawa) BU-2, nov 1984, 1-5.*
LEVEL: I LANG: Fr SIRC ARTICLE NO: 102348

Boucher, R.L. In search of leadership. (Refs: 12) *Sports: Science periodical on research and technology in sport (Ottawa) BU-2, Nov 1984, 1-5.*
LEVEL: I LANG: Eng SIRC ARTICLE NO: 102349

Case, R.W. Leadership in sport: the situational leadership theory. (Refs: 3) *Journal of physical education, recreation & dance* 55(1), Jan 1984, 15-16.
LEVEL: B LANG: Eng SIRC ARTICLE NO: 091296

Rice, H.C. Leadership for leaders: part 4, management. *Scholastic coach (New York)* 54(5), Dec 1984, 42-43.
LEVEL: B LANG: Eng SIRC ARTICLE NO: 102354

SOCIAL PSYCHOLOGY - PARENT-COACH RELATIONSHIP

Woog, D. Coaching parents to success. How to keep the parents, of the children you coach, on your side. *Coaching review* 7, Jan/Feb 1984, 29-30.
LEVEL: B LANG: Eng SIRC ARTICLE NO: 091306

SOCIOLOGY

Bette, K.H. Die Trainerrolle im Hochleistungssport: system- und rollentheoretische Ueberlegungen zur Sozialfigur des Trainer Sankt Augustin: Verlag Hans Richarz, c1984. 128 p. (Schriften der Deutschen Sporthochschule Koeln, Bd. 14.)
NOTES: Bibliography: p. 124-128.
LEVEL: A LANG: Ger ISBN: 3-88345-313-7 GV709.14 18384

STATISTICS

Wolfe, W.T. Computerized stats, the ultimate state-of-the-art coaching tool. *Scholastic coach (New York)* 54(5), Dec 1984, 18;56-57.
LEVEL: B LANG: Eng SIRC ARTICLE NO: 102358

TEACHING

Dooey, D. Teaching tips for the inexperienced. Inexperienced coaches can do simple but important things when teaching. *Coaching review (Ottawa)* 7, Sept/Oct 1984, 38.
LEVEL: B LANG: Eng SIRC ARTICLE NO: 097427

Porto, B.L. When coaches are teachers, athletes will be students. *Liberal education (Washington)* 70(3), 1984, 231-233.
LEVEL: B LANG: Eng SIRC ARTICLE NO: 103845

TEACHING METHODS

Byra, M. Putting reality back into the repetition. (skill development) *Coaching review (Ottawa, Ont.)* 7, Jul/Aug 1984, 54-55.
LEVEL: B LANG: Eng SIRC ARTICLE NO: 094221

TESTING

Franks, I.M. Goodman, D. Une approche hierarchique a l'evaluation de la performance. (Refs: 20) *Science du sport: documents de recherche et de technologie (Ottawa, Ont.) GY-1, juin 1984, 1-4.*
LEVEL: I LANG: Fr SIRC ARTICLE NO: 094227

Franks, I.M. Goodman, D. A hierarchical approach to performance analysis. (Refs: 20) *Sports: science periodical on research and technology in sport (Ottawa, Ont.) GY-1, Jun 1984, 1-4.*
LEVEL: I LANG: Eng SIRC ARTICLE NO: 094228

Macdonald, N. Avoiding the pitfalls in player selection. (Refs: 9) *Coaching science update (Ottawa, Ont.)* 1984, 41-45.
LEVEL: I LANG: Eng SIRC ARTICLE NO: 094233

Macdonald, N. Comment eviter les pieges de la selection des joueurs. (Refs: 9) *Nouveautes en science de l'entrainement (Ottawa)* 1984, 36-39;42.
LEVEL: I LANG: Fr SIRC ARTICLE NO: 095756

TESTING - PHYSICAL

Cerny, E. Assessing performance...an evaluation-goal check-off system. *Coaching clinic (Princeton, N.J.)* 23(2), Oct 1984, 15-16.
LEVEL: B LANG: Eng SIRC ARTICLE NO: 100513

WOMEN

Kindig, L.E. Soares, P.L. Wisenbaker, J.M. Mrvos, S.R. Standard scores for women's weight training. (Refs: 9) *Physician and sportsmedicine (Minneapolis, Minn.)* 12(10), Oct 1984, 67-74.

COACHING (continued)

ABST: This report focuses on the standard scores for women on the bench press, bent-arm pullover, dead lift, half squat, and military press following a ten week beginning weight-training course. 221 young (20.4 plus or minus 2.12 years) females divided in seven body-weight classifications served as subjects.
LEVEL: A LANG: Eng SIRC ARTICLE NO: 099369

WOMEN COACHES

Women coaches: an endangered species? *Athletic director & coach (Madison, Wisc.) 1984, 1-2.*
LEVEL: B LANG: Eng SIRC ARTICLE NO: 102982

COLLEGE AND UNIVERSITY SPORTS

Figler, S.K. Figler, H. The athlete's game plan for college and career. Princeton, N.J.: Peterson's Guide, 1984. 1v.
LEVEL: LANG: Eng LC CARD: 83-022112

Schulke, H.J. Recherche dans le sport universitaire: passe, present et futur. Research into University sport: past, present and future. *Bulletin of the International University Sports Federation/ Bulletin de la Federation internationale du sport universitaire (Bruxelles, Belgique) Jun/juin 1984, 6-7;22.*
LEVEL: B LANG: Fr Eng SIRC ARTICLE NO: 102361

Stier, B. Study determines present status of junior colleges. *Athletic administration (Cleveland, Oh.) 19(6), Dec 1984, 14-16.*
LEVEL: B LANG: Eng SIRC ARTICLE NO: 105183

ACADEMIC ACHIEVEMENT

Berlowe, J.A. Athletic and academic involvement: institutional responsibility for the 80's. (Refs: 2)*MAHPERD journal (Ypsilanti, Mich.) Winter 1984, 2.*
LEVEL: B LANG: Eng SIRC ARTICLE NO: 097433

Figler, S.K. Measuring academic exploitation of college athletes and a suggestion for sharing data. (Refs: 6)*Sociology of sport journal (Champaign, Ill.) 1(4), Dec 1984, 381-388.*
ABST: College athletes are exploited when some aspect of their athletic involvement mitigates against their receiving a full and useful education toward a postcollegiate career. Two specific means for assessing academic performace and progress of athletes are suggested here. These measures provide a timely assessment of progress of athletes that more acutely measures their academic performance than traditional means. Further, these measures may become a base of data that can be used to assess academic performance of athletes between teams on a given campus or between schools. Privacy regulations prohibit researchers from obtaining raw data from academic records at institutions other than their own. A method for pooling and sharing this individual obtained data is suggested.
LEVEL: A LANG: Eng SIRC ARTICLE NO: 103853

Henschen, K.P. Fry, D. An archival study of the relationship of intercollegiate athletic participation and graduation. (Refs 4)*Sociology of sport journal (Champaign, Ill.) 1(1), 1984, 52-56.*
ABST: This study was undertaken for the purpose of investigating the relationship of athletic participation and graduation rates of both male and female athletes at the University of Utah over the span of nearly a decade (1973-1982). Athletic participants, male and female, graduate at a higher rate than the nonathletic student body. In addition, as emphasis in a particular sport increases and that sport becomes nationally competitive, prospects for graduation of those athletes involved greatly diminishes. A final deduction from the results of this study is that a professional athletic career is a definite detriment to obtaining a college degree.
LEVEL: A LANG: Eng SIRC ARTICLE NO: 108346

Moriarty, F.J. End zone: pros in academic drag. *Women's sports (Palo Alto, Calif.) 6(9), Sept 1984, 60;58.*
LEVEL: B LANG: Eng SIRC ARTICLE NO: 173595

Shapiro, B.J. Intercollegiate athletic participation and academic achievement: a case study of Michigan State University student-athletes, 1950-1980. (Refs: 4)*Sociology of sport journal (Champaign, Ill.) 1(1), 1984, 46-51.*
ABST: The present study examines the graduation rates of male student athletes at Michigan State University (M.S.U.) during a 25-year time period. Graduation rates are compared by sport, by decade of matriculation, by race, and by athletic success (e.g., whether or not the athlete earned a varsity letter) to determine whether or not there are differences in the educational experiences of these subcategories of student athletes. The graduation rate of athletes and nonathletes at M.S.U. are also compared. In addition, the data collected at M.S.U. are compared with national data on student athletes to determine the relative academic success of M.S.U. athletes. A total of 1,642 letterwinners and nonletterwinners for football, men's basketball, baseball, and hockey, who were freshmen between the fall of 1950 and the fall of 1974, were included in this study. The graduation rate for athletes in this study enrolled from 1950 through 1978 was 7170. For the 1953 cohort, athletes graduated at a much higher rate than nonathletes (80 percent for athletes and 45 percent for nonathletes). But the differences between both groups have declined sharply in time. By 1973, graduation rates were pratically the same for athletes and nonathletes (61 percent and 62 percent).
LEVEL: A LANG: Eng SIRC ARTICLE NO: 108345

Vickrey, J. Enhancing the image of intercollegiate athletics with academic credibility. *NAIA news (Kansas, Mo.) 33(5), Apr/May 1984, 30-31.*
CONF: National Association of Intercollegiate Athletics. Annual national convention (44th: 1984: Kansas City).
LEVEL: B LANG: Eng SIRC ARTICLE NO: 097439

Warfield, J.L. NCAA rule 48, black leaders, and collegiate student-athletes' bill of rights: a critique. Alexandria, Va.: Computer Microfilm International, 1984. 1 microfiche (25 fr.) (African and Afro-American studies and research center papers: series 2. number 6.)
LEVEL: A LANG: Eng EDRS: ED246151

ADMINISTRATION

Audette, D.N. The effects of Title IX legislation and regulations on the administration of intercollegiate athletic programs for schools in Divisions I, II, and III of the NCAA. Eugene, Ore.: Microform Publications, University of Oregon, 1984. 2 microfiches : negative ; 11 x 15 cm.
NOTES: Thesis (Ed.D.) - West Virginia University, 1982; (viii, 179 leaves); vita; includes bibliography.
LEVEL: A LANG: Eng UO84 178-179

Barger, D. Athletic promotions: trial and error. *NAIA news (Kansas City, Mo.) 34(2), Oct/Nov 1984, 10-11.*
LEVEL: B LANG: Eng SIRC ARTICLE NO: 173328

Carey, D.M. A survey of weight room operations in selected U.S. colleges and universities. *In, Vendl, B.C. (ed.) et al., Interpretive aspects of intramural-recreational sports: selected proceedings from the Thirty-fifth Annual National Intramural-Recreational Sports Association Conference, Corvallis, Or., Oregon State University, c1984, p. 81-85.*
CONF: National Intramural-Recreational Sports Association Conference (35th : 1984 : Fort Worth, Tex.).
LEVEL: I LANG: Eng GV710 18914

Chelladurai, P. Danylchuk, K.E. Operative goals of intercollegiate athletics: perceptions of athletic administrators. (Refs: 15)*Canadian journal of applied sport sciences/Journal canadien des sciences appliquees au sport 9(1), Mar 1984, 33-41.*
ABST: Ninety athletic administrators answered a questionnaire designed to elucidate the operative goals of intercollegiate athletics. All sub-groups of administration (based on size of institution, sex of administrator, conference membership) rated transmission of culture, athletes' personal growth, public relations, prestige as the operative goals belonging to the most important category. Administrators from the Maritimes and Western provinces favoured athletic scholarships more than administrators from Ontario and Quebec. The authors suggest that this is a logical result considering the death of athletic talent, owing to sparsely populated areas, in the Maritimes and Western provinces.
LEVEL: A LANG: Eng SIRC ARTICLE NO: 092713

Chelladurai, P. Inglis, S.E. Danylchuk, K.E. Priorities in intercollegiate athletics: development of a scale. (Refs: 15) *Research quarterly for exercise & sports (Reston, Va.) 55(1), Mar 1984, 74-79.*
ABST: The purpose of this study was to develop a psychometrically sound scale that could be used by administrators of intercollegiate athletics to assess and articulate the goal orientations of their constituents. The development of the Scale of Athletic Priorities and the assessment of its psychometric properties was carried out through the selection of 74 items to reflect 11 objectives, and administering the scale to a total of 939 students from two Canadian universities. After analysis, the revised version of the scale was administered to 90 administrators of intercollegiate athletic programs in Canada, and to a new sample of 141 students. Thus, the Scale of Athletic Priorities consists of 36 items to assess the importance attached by respondents to nine distinct operative goals of intercollegiate athletics.
LEVEL: A LANG: Eng SIRC ARTICLE NO: 095761

Greene, L.S. The new NCAA rules of the game: academic integrity or racism? Alexandria, Va.: Computer Microfilm International 1984. 1 microfiche (53 fr.); 10 x 15 cm.
LEVEL: I LANG: Eng EDRS: ED242690 ERIC 242690

Haggerty, T.R. The use of computers in sport administration. (Refs: 10)*CAHPER journal/Revue de l'ACSEPR (Vanier, Ont.) 50(3), Jan/Feb 1984,*

20-23.
LEVEL: I LANG: Eng SIRC ARTICLE NO: 094179

Hart, D. 'Ain't it great to tailgate' *Athletic administration (Cleveland, Ohio.) 19(2), Apr 1984, 13-14.*
LEVEL: B LANG: E SIRC ARTICLE NO: 094242

Jenkins, G. NCAA rule no. 48: a national study of the academic implications for U.S. secondary schools. Alexandria, Va.: Computer Microfilms International, 1984. 2 microfiches (108 fr.); 10 x 15 cm.
NOTES: Bibliography: l. 82-83.
LEVEL: A LANG: Eng EDRS: ED240692 ERIC 240692

McGee, M. Management approach: training athletic directors. *Athletic administration 19(1), Feb 1984, 20-21.*
LEVEL: B LANG Eng SIRC ARTICLE NO: 092717

NCAA regulations on recruiting and eligibility. *American hockey magazine (Colorado Springs, Colo.) 5(7), Dec 1984, 10C-11C.*
LEVEL: B LANG: Eng SIRC ARTICLE NO: 106351

Ostro, H. The new, tough eligibility rules: good points and 'red flags'. *Scholastic coach (New York) 53(9), Apr 1984, 10;12;14;16;88.*
LEVEL: B LANG: Eng SIRC ARTICLE NO: 094244

Parsons, T.W. Risk-management: sport administrators' assessment of reality. (Refs: 1)*NIRSA journal (Corvallis, Ore.) 9(1), Fall 1984, 8;10-13.*
LEVEL: I LANG: Eng SIRC ARTICLE NO: 105574

Remington, F.J. NCAA enforcement procedures including the role of the committee on infractions. *Journal of college and university law (Washington) 10(2), Fall 1983/1984, 181-196.*
LEVEL: B LANG: Eng SIRC ARTICLE NO: 095764

Sekkal, B.A. Le developpement du sport universitaire. The progress of university sport. *Bulletin of the International University Sports Federation/Bulletin de la Federation internationale du sport universitaire (Bruxelles, Belgique) Jun/juin 1984, 28-30.*
LEVEL: B LANG: Fr Eng SIRC ARTICLE NO: 102362

Watkins, D.L. Leader behavior of directors of athletics at eight liberal arts colleges. Eugene, Ore.: Microform Publications University of Oregon, 1984. 2 microfiches : negative, ill. ; 11 x 15 cm.
NOTES: Thesis (D.Ed.) - Pennsylvania State University, 1983; (xiv, 135, (1) leaves); vita; includes bibliography.
LEVEL: A LANG: Eng UO84 348-349

Zimmer, C. Success in intercollegiate athletics: what is it? *Athletic administration (Cleveland, Ohio.) 19(2), Apr 1984, 15-17.*
LEVEL: I LANG: Eng SIRC ARTICLE NO: 094247

ASSOCIATIONS

13 universities on NCAA probation. *Chronicle of higher education (Washington) 29(2), 5 Sept 1984, 33.*
LEVEL: B LANG: Eng SIRC ARTICLE NO: 103850

Ervin, L. The right direction but short of the mark. *College board review (New York) 131, Spring 1984, 15-19.*
LEVEL: B LANG: Eng SIRC ARTICLE NO: 103851

Farrell, C.S. Nevada judge rejects Tarkanian's suspension: issues scathing opinion on NCAA's behavior. *Chronicle of higher education (Washington) 28(19), 5 Jul 1984, 19;21.*
LEVEL: B LANG: Eng SIRC ARTICLE NO: 103852

Goldman, P.S. Text of Nevada judge's opinion invalidating NCAA action against coach. *Chronicle of higher education (Washington) 28(19), 5 Jul 1984, 20-21.*
LEVEL: B LANG: Eng SIRC ARTICLE NO: 103855

Maeki-Reinikka, H. The Finnish Student Sports Federation as a promoter of international understanding. *In, Ilmarinen, M. (ed.) et al., Sport and International Understanding: proceedings of the congress held in Helsinki, Finland, July 7-10, 1982, Berlin, Springer-Verlag, 1984, 193-195.*
CONF: Congress on Sport and International Understanding (1982 : Helsinki).
LEVEL: B LANG: Eng GV706.8 18979

Monaghan, P. Lawyers ensure whether court's eligibility ruling will hamper NCAA in enforcing its regulations. *Chronicle of higher education (Washington) 28(20), 11 Jul 1984, 27.*
LEVEL: B LANG: Eng SIRC ARTICLE NO: 103858

Operations manual. s.l.: Canadian Interuniversity Athletic Union : Union sportive interuniversitaire canadienne, 1984. 1v. (loose-leaf)
CORP: Canadian Interuniversity Athletic Union.
CORP: Union sportive interuniversitaire canadienne.
LEVEL: B LANG: Eng GV347 18405

Proceedings of the seventh General Assembly Meeting, June 17-20, 1984, Brudenell Resort, P.E.I. Vanier, Ont.: Canadian Interuniversity Athletic Union, 1984. ca. 120 p. in various pagings
CONF: Canadian Interuniversity Athletic Union. General Assembly Meeting (7th : 1984 : Brudenell Resort, P.E.I.).
CORP: Canadian Interuniversity Athletic Union.
NOTES: Cover title.
LEVEL: I LANG: Eng GV347 18501

Toner, J.L. A statement of NCAA policy and intentions regarding proposal 48. *College board review (New York) 131, Spring 1984, 13-15.*
LEVEL: B LANG: Eng SIRC ARTICLE NO: 103861

Vickers, J.N. Gosling, B.J. The changing participation of men and women in the Canadian Interuniversity Athletic Union 1978-1982. Ottawa: Women's Representative Committee, Canadian Interuniversity Athletic Union, 1984. v, 41 p. : ill.
CORP: Canadian Interuniversity Athletic Union. Women's Representative Committee.
NOTES: Bibliography; p. 36.
LEVEL: A LANG: Eng GV347 18726

DIRECTORIES

Blue book of college athletics for 1984. Akron, Ohio: Rohrich Corporation, 1984. 511 p. : ill.
LEVEL: B LANG: Eng ISBN: 0-9611500-0-9 GV347 17665

ECONOMICS

Coughlin, C.C. Erekson, O.H. An examination of contributions to support intercollegiate athletics. (Refs: 26)*Southern economic journal (Chapel Hill, N.C.) 51(1), 1984, 180-195.*
LEVEL: A LANG: Eng SIRC ARTICLE NO: 097435

Gaski, J.F. Etzel, M.J. Collegiate athletic success and alumni generosity: dispelling the myth. (Refs:

4)*Social behavior an personality (Sudbury) 12(1), 1984, 29-38.*
LEVEL: I LANG: Eng SIRC ARTICLE NO: 103854

Hart-Nibbrig, N. Corporate athleticism: an inquiry into political economy of college sports. (Refs: 9)*NAPEHE proceedings (Champaign, Ill.) 5, 1984, 11-20.*
CONF: National Association for Physical Education in Higher Education. Annual Conference (1984 : College Park, Md.).
NOTES: Conference theme: Current challenge: revitalization or obsolescence?
LEVEL: I LANG: Eng SIRC ARTICLE NO: 102360

Koch, J.V. The economics of 'Big-Time' intercollegiate athletics. (Refs: 22)
NOTES: In, Riess, S.A. (ed.), The American sporting experience: a historical anthology of sport in America, New York, Leisure Press, c1984, p. 371-385. Previously published in, Social science quarterly 52, September 1971, p. 248-260.
LEVEL: I LANG: Eng GV583 17631

Lumpkin, A. The Graham plan: an early attempt to achieve sanity in sport. Alexandria, Va.: Computer Microfilm International, 1984. 1 microfiche (12 fr.)
CONF: American Alliance for Health, Physical Education, Recreation and Dance. Convention (1984 : Anaheim, Calif.).
LEVEL: A LANG: Eng EDRS: ED243877

Nader, S.J. Financing intercollegiate athletics in the Southeastern Conference: 1970-1979. Eugene, Ore.: Microform Publications, University of Oregon, 1984. 2 microfiches : negative, ill. ; 11 x 15 cm.
NOTES: Thesis (Ph.D.) - Louisiana State University, 1982; (xi, 167 leaves); vita; includes bibliography.
LEVEL: A LANG: Eng UO84 229-230

HISTORY

Chu, D. Sport and the charter of American higher education: a case study of Skidmore College 1960-1980. (Refs: 20)*NAPEHE proceedings (Champaign, Ill.) 5, 1984, 128-137.*
CONF: National Association for Physcial Education in Higher Education. Annual Conference (1984 : College Park, Md.).
NOTES: Conference theme: Current challenge: revitalization or obsolescence?
LEVEL: I LANG: Eng SIRC ARTICLE NO: 102359

Jones, J.C. The history of physical activities at an emerging Christian liberal arts college. Eugene, Ore.: Microform Publications, University of Oregon, 1984. 3 microfiches : negative ; 11 x 15 cm.
NOTES: Thesis (M.Ed.) - University of North Carolina at Greensboro, 1982; (vi, 244 leaves); includes bibliography.
LEVEL: A LANG: Eng UO84 323-325

Lipping, A. Harvard University and the emergence of international collegiate athletics, 1869-1874. (Refs: 15)*Physical educator (Indianapolis) 41(4), Dec 1984, 176-178.*
LEVEL: B LANG: Eng SIRC ARTICLE NO: 103857

Mangan, J.A. Oars and the man: pleasure and purpose in Victorian and Edwardian Cambridge. (Refs: 143)*British journal of sports history (London) 1(3), Dec 1984, 245-271.*
ABST: This article focuses on athleticism in Jesus College, Cambridge, during the Victorian and Edwardian eras (1875-1914). The author also discusses athleticism in the ancient Universities of Oxford and Cambridge in the same period.
LEVEL: A LANG: Eng SIRC ARTICLE NO: 105180

COLLEGE AND UNIVERSITY SPORTS (continued)

Paul, J. McGhee, R.V. Fant, H. The arrival and ascendance of black athletes in the Southeastern Conference 1966-1980. (Refs: 14)*Phylon (Atlanta) 45(4), 1984, 284-297.*
LEVEL: A LANG: Eng

LAW AND LEGISLATION

Appenzeller, H. Ross, C.T. Indiana - does a university have a duty to protect its patrons from the acts of third persons? *Sports and the courts (Winston-Salem, N.C.) 5(3), Summer 1984, 10.*
LEVEL: B LANG: Eng SIRC ARTICLE NO: 097432

Atkinson, M.A. Worker's compensation and college athletics: should universities be responsible for athletes who incur seriou injuries? *Journal of college and university (Washington) 10(2), Fall 1983/1984, 197-208.*
LEVEL: I LANG: Eng SIRC ARTICLE NO: 095980

Farrell, C.S. Colleges free to negotiate own contracts. *Chronicle of higher education (Washington) 28(19), 5 Jul 1984, 1;24.*
LEVEL: B LANG: Eng SIRC ARTICLE NO: 104709

Fields, C.M. Appeals court rejects charge that NCAA forced women's group out of business. *Chronicle of higher education (Washington) 28(14), 30 May 1984, 27-28.*
LEVEL: B LANG: Eng SIRC ARTICLE NO: 098894

Gullard, E.D. Byrne, J.P. Steinback, S.E. Intercollegiate athletics and television contracts - beyond economic justification in antitrust analysis of agreements among colleges. (Refs: 9)*Fordham law review (New York) 52(5), 1984, 717-731.*
LEVEL: I LANG: Eng SIRC ARTICLE NO: 098895

Mallios, H.G. In defense of athletic administrators facing litigation. *Athletic administration 19(1), Feb 1984, 17-19.*
LEVEL: B LANG: Eng SIRC ARTICLE NO: 092912

Michigan - court rules that an athletic scholarship constitutes 'wages' but the athlete is not an 'employee' entitled to workers compensation. *Sports and the courts (Winston-Salem, N.C.) 5(2), Spring 1984, 5-7.*
ABST: Few athletes ever consider what may happen to their scholarship funding after a serious injury impairs further competition. A football player at Western Michigan University sustained an injury in his third year of college and did not play the season though he was still on full scholarship. In his fourth year he was unable to contribute to the team and there were cuts in the scholarship program so his grant was reduced. He sought compensation under the Workers Disability Compensation Act. Though the court ruled that an athletic scholarship could be viewed as 'wages' it did not view the football player as an employee since he was a student first and an athlete second.
LEVEL: B LANG: Eng SIRC ARTICLE NO: 094407

New York - is there legal duty to recommend students for college scholarships? *Sports and the courts (Winston-Salem, N.C.) 5(1), Winter 1984, 1-2.*
LEVEL: B LANG: Eng SIRC ARTICLE NO: 094243

Pennsylvania - college not liable for bill incurred by bankrupt alumni association. *Sports and the courts (Winston-Salem, N.C.) 5(2), Spring 1984, 1-2.*
LEVEL: B LANG: Eng SIRC ARTICLE NO: 094409

Pennsylvania - top ranked tennis player challenges bylaws of the NCAA and ECAC in court. *Sports and the courts (Winston-Salem N.C.) 5(1), Winter 1984, 2-4.*
LEVEL: B LANG: Eng SIRC ARTICLE NO: 094245

Related documents from counsel from university of Richard V. Bell. *Journal of college and university law (Washington) 10(1), 1983/1984, 34-62.*
LEVEL: I LANG: Eng SIRC ARTICLE NO: 095763

Staton, R. Recent cases concerning the rights of student athletes. *Journal of college and university law (Washington) 10(2) Fall 1983/1984, 209-224.*
LEVEL: I LANG: Eng SIRC ARTICLE NO: 095992

Weistart, J.C. Legal accountability and the NCAA. *Journal of college and university law (Washington) 10(2), Fall 1983-84, 167-180.*
LEVEL: B LANG: Eng SIRC ARTICLE NO: 095995

White, B.R. Justice White's dissent from court's ruling on NCAA control of football telecasts. *Chronicle of higher educatio (Washington) 28(19), 5 Jul 1984, 25-26;28.*
LEVEL: B LANG: Eng SIRC ARTICLE NO: 104745

MEDICINE

Gillespie, C.A. Student trainers: essential link between athletes and coaches. *First aider (Gardner, Kan.) 53(6), Mar 1984, 11.*
LEVEL: B LANG: Eng SIRC ARTICLE NO: 094419

Splain, S.H. Rolnick, A. Sports injuries at a nonscholarship university. (Refs: 9)*Physician and sportsmedicine (Minneapolis Minn.) 12(7), Jul 1984, 55-56;58-59;62.*
LEVEL: I LANG: Eng SIRC ARTICLE NO: 095967

PSYCHOLOGY

Basow, S.A. Spinner, J. Social acceptability of college athletes: effects of sport sex-typing athlete sex, and rater sex. (Refs: 8)*International journal of sport psychology (Rome, Itlay) 15(2), 1984, 79-87.*
ABST: 226 male and female college students evaluated the social acceptability of either a male or female college athlete who was an active participant in either football (masculine sport), tennis (less masculine), or figure skating (least masculine) via a written questionnaire. Results showed no differential evaluation of athletes as a function of athlete sex and sport sex-typing. Rather, all athletes were rated as generally socially acceptable, although football players were viewed as significantly less acceptable than tennis players or figure skaters. There was a significant relationship between raters' own athletic status and amount of sports participation, and their ratings of the hypothetical athlete. When these variables were controlled for, male raters found all athletes less socially acceptable than did female raters.
LEVEL: A LANG: Eng SIRC ARTICLE NO: 099280

Chalip, L. Csikszentmihalyi, M. Kleiber, D. Larson, R. Variations of experience in formal and informal sport. (Refs: 30) *Research quarterly for exercise & sport (Reston Va.) 55(2), Jun 1984, 109-116.*
ABST: This paper examines the psychological effects of participating in organized sport, informal sport and physical education classes. The experiences of 75 high school students were monitored through the use of the Experience Sampling Method (ESM). Sport, as a whole, was perceived as a more positive experience than the rest of everyday life. The students perceived their skills as being at their highest when engaged in informal sport. During organized sport and physical education classes the students perceived the challenges as being greater than their skills. These results are consistent with earlier research showing perceived ability to be related to the attractiveness of an activity.
LEVEL: A LANG: Eng SIRC ARTICLE NO: 095728

Cooker, P.G. Caffey, C.A. Addressing the cognitive and affective needs of college athletes: effects of group counseling on self-esteem, reading skills, and coaches' perceptions of attitude. (Refs: 19)*Journal of sport psychology (Champaign, Ill.) 6(4), Dec 1984, 377-384.*
ABST: The purpose of this study was to determine the effects of group counseling on the self-esteem, athletic attitude, and reading skills of freshman, sophomore, and junior male athletes at the University of Mississippi. The study focused on the personal growth of athletes through the affective domain as well as the cognitive domain; it particularly examined group counseling in relation to the self-esteem of athletes and their attitude on the playing field as perceived by the coaches. The secondary focus of the study was to determine the effects of group counseling on reading rate, reading comprehension, and reading efficiency of athletes. The rationale for the study was based on the recent emphasis in sport psychology of treating athletes from a developmental and humanistic base. Group counseling was chosen as the mode of treatment, based on potential interactive effects of peer perception with facilitation by trained leaders.
LEVEL: A LANG: Eng SIRC ARTICLE NO: 104403

Leet, D.R. James, T.F. Rushall, B.S. Intercollegiate teams in competition. A field study to examine variables influencing contest results. (Refs: 23)*International journal of sport psychology (Rome) 15(3), 1984, 193-204.*
ABST: Observations of 510 male and female athletes in interactional and coacting team contests were made on the variables of: sex, team type, team record, experience on the team, success expectancy, performance evaluations and contest outcomes. Regression analyses yielded several significant relationships. The athletes' perception of their chances of winning the contest was an important indicator of contest outcomes for male and female athletes regardless of team type.
LEVEL: A LANG: Eng SIRC ARTICLE NO: 103856

Progen, J.L. An exploration of the flow experience among selected collegiate athletes. Eugene, Ore.: Microform Publications, University of Oregon, 1984. 3 microfiches : negative, ill. ; 11 x 15 cm. NOTES: Thesis (Ed.D.) - University of North Carolina at Greensboro, 1981; (x, 200 leaves); includes bibliography.
LEVEL: A LANG: Eng UO84 50-52

SOCIAL PSYCHOLOGY

Chelladurai, P. Discrepancy between preferences and perceptions of leadership behavior and satisfaction of athletes in varying sports. (Refs: 34)*Sport psychology (Champaign, Ill.) 6(1), 1984, 27-41.*
ABST: This study examined the relationship between the discrepancy between preferred and perceived leadership and athletes' satisfaction. The five preferred and perceived leadership behaviors assessed were training and instruction, democratic behavior, autocratic behavior, social support, and positive feedback. Four facets of satisfaction were measured: satisfaction with individual performance, satisfaction with team performance, satisfaction

with leadership, and satisfaction with overall involvement. The athletes were selected from sports differentiated on the basis of task variability and/or task dependance. Discrepancy in leadership was computed by subtracting the perception of a specific dimension of leader behavior from preference for such behavior. The results showed that discrepancy in leadership for athletes in the various sports was associated with three measures of satisfaction: satisfaction with team performance, with leadership, and with overall involvement. Further, training and instruction, and positive feedback were the most common dimensions of leader behavior affecting the athletes' satisfaction.
LANG: Eng SIRC ARTICLE NO: 108483

Pawlowski, T.F. The proposal of a communication design leading to a proactive counseling program for athletes. (Refs: 13) *Juco review (Hutchinson, Kans.) 36(2), Oct 1984, 16-17.*
LEVEL: B LANG: Eng SIRC ARTICLE NO: 100519

SOCIOLOGY

No laughing matter: character-building in college athletics. *NAIA news (Roeland Park, Kans.) 33(6), Jun/Jul 1984, 4-5.*
LEVEL: B LANG: Eng SIRC ARTICLE NO: 103859

WOMEN

Abbott, A. Smith, D.R. Governmental constraints and labor market mobility, turnover a Mong College athletic personnel. *Work and occupations: an international sociological journal (Beverly Hills, Calif.) 11(1), Feb 1984, 29-53.*
LEVEL: I LANG: Eng SIRC ARTICLE NO: 096462

Ames, N.R. Women and sports. *Journal of the National Association of Women Deans, Administrators, and counselors (Washington 47(2), Winter 1984, 3-39.*
ABST: Reviews issues relating to the participation and socialization of women in college sport.
LEVEL: I LANG: Eng SIRC ARTICLE NO: 097431

Coakely, J.J. Pacey, P.L. The distribution of athletic scholarships among women in intercollegiate sport.
CONF: North American Society for the Sociology of Sport. Conference (3rd : 1982 : Toronto, Ont.).
NOTES: In, Theberge, N. and Donnelly, P. (eds.), Sport and the sociological imagination: refereed proceedings of the 3rd Annual Conference of the North American Society for the Sociology of Sport, Toronto, Canada, November 1982, Fort Worth, Tex., Texas Christian University Press, c1984, p. 228-241.
ABST: This paper details the results of a survey of women participating in intercollegiate sports. 2272 questionnaires were returned from an extensive mailing to NCAA Divisions I and II schools. The results found that the majority of female athletes do not receive any sport scholarship aid. Of the respondents who do, over 80 per cent of these women had fathers with relatively high status income occupations. Black athletes made up less than 5% of the total sample and received about 5% of the total scholarships. Black female athletes tended to participate largely in basketball and track and field. The overall findings were similar to those found previously in men's programs.
LEVEL: A LANG: Eng SIRC ARTICLE NO: 097434

Jones, D.E. A history of women's intercollegiate athletics at the University of North Carolina at Greensboro. Eugene, Ore.: Microform Publications, University of Oregon, 1984. 2 microfiches : negative ; 11 x 15 cm.
NOTES: Thesis (M.Ed.) - University of North Carolina at Greensboro, 1981; (v, 172 leaves); includes bibliography.
LEVEL: A LANG: Eng UO84 202-203

Lopiano, D.A. A political analysis of the possibility of impact alternatives for the accomplishment of feminist objectives within American intercollegiate sport. *Arena review (Boston, Ma.) 8(2), Jul 1984, 49-61.*
NOTES: Edited version of a paper presented at the 'Feminism and sport: connections and directions' workshop, the 1982 Women as Leaders in Physical Education Workshop, sponsored by the Department of Physical Education and Dance, University of Iowa.
LEVEL: I LANG: Eng SIRC ARTICLE NO: 101050

Lubking, S.W. Athletic scholarships: effects on expectations, motivation, and player attitudes of college women athletes. Eugene, Ore.: Microform Publications, University of Oregon, 1984. 2 microfiches : negative ; 11 x 15 cm.
NOTES: Thesis (M.Ed.) - Temple University, 1980; ((5), 129 leaves); includes bibliography.
LEVEL: A LANG: Eng UO84 266-267

COMBAT SPORTS

BIOGRAPHY AND AUTOBIOGRAPHY

Chapman, M. The toughest men in sports: looking for the mental edge. New York: Leisure Press, c1984. 144 p. : ill.
LEVEL: B LANG: Eng ISBN: 0-88011-187-9 LC CARD: 83-80730 GV1111 17652

COMMONWEALTH GAMES, BRISBANE AUSTRALIA 1982

CANADA

Canada's part in the 12th Commonwealth Games, Brisbane, Australia, September 30th to October 9th, 1982. Official report of the Commonwealth Games Association of Canada 1979-1982. s.l.: Commonwealth Games Association of Canada, 1984?. 209 p. : ill.
CORP: Commonwealth Games Association of Canada.
LEVEL: B LANG: Eng GV722.5.B7 1982 17107

MEDICINE

Jull, G.A. Cupit, R.L. Physiotherapy at the XII Commonwealth Games: part 2: injuries and management. (Refs: 1)*Australian journal of physiotherapy 30(1), Feb 1984, 10-14.*
ABST: At the XII Commonwealth Games, Australian physiotherapists treated the injuries of competitors from the 10 sports contested. A high incidence of vertebrogenic pain and knee joint injuries were noted. Percentage of types of injuries treated in each sport is tabulated.
LEVEL: I LANG: Eng SIRC ARTICLE NO: 097573

Jull, G.A. Cupit, R.L. Physiotherapy at the XII Commonwealth Games: part 1: organization and utilization of services. *Australian journal of physiotherapy 30(1), Feb 1984, 3-9.*
ABST: A report on the organizational and administrative aspects of the physiotherapy service provided by 60 Australian physiotherapists at the Commonwealth Games in Brisbane in 1982. A total of 988 individuals were treated over a 5 week period, 80% of whom were competitors. Of 4,427 consultations, 3,536 were for treatment of pain or injury, 891 were for rub downs only.
LEVEL: I LANG: Eng SIRC ARTICLE NO: 097601

COTSWOLD GAMES

Charlton, B. The English Olympics: an alternative games which very few people know about. *Sport and leisure (London) 25(3), Jul/Aug 1984, 43.*
LEVEL: B LANG: Eng SIRC ARTICLE NO: 101006

CRICKET

Bright-Holmes, J. The joy of cricket. s.l.: Secker and Warburg, (1984?). 1v.
LEVEL: B LANG: Eng

Dexter, T. Lemmon, D. A walk to the wicket. s.l.: George Allen and Unwin, (1984?). 1v.
LEVEL: B LANG: Eng

Freeman, G. Cricket. s.l.: Cambridge Educational, (1984?). 1v.
LEVEL: B LANG: Eng

Murray, S. Micky Stewart on the modern game. *Cricketer international (Kent, Eng.) 65(12), Dec 1984, 28-29.*
LEVEL: B LANG: Eng SIRC ARTICLE NO: 101154

BIBLIOGRAPHIES

Padwick, E.W. A bibliography of cricket. 2nd ed., rev. and enl. London: Library Association, 1984. xxxiii, 877 p. : ill.
LEVEL: I LANG: Eng ISBN: 0-85365-902-8 GV917 18631

BIOGRAPHY AND AUTOBIOGRAPHY

Benaud, R. Keith Miller - the captain who never did the obvious. *Cricketer international (Kent, Eng.) 65(6), Jun 1984, 20-21.*
NOTES: Taken from, Benaud on reflection by Richie Benaud, Collins Willow, 1984.
LEVEL: B LANG: Eng SIRC ARTICLE NO: 094916

Brearley, M. Bob Willis: unique character and technique. *Cricketer international (Kent, Eng.) 65(11), Nov 1984, 34.*
LEVEL B LANG: Eng SIRC ARTICLE NO: 101146

Coldham, J.D. Jacker and his background. (Frank Stanley Jackson) *Cricketer international (Kent, Eng.) 65(8), Aug 1984, 42-43.*
LEVEL: B LANG: Eng SIRC ARTICLE NO: 096559

Cozier, T. The noblest West Indian of them all. (George Headley) *Cricketer international 65(2), Feb 1984, 19.*
LEVEL: B LANG: Eng SIRC ARTICLE NO: 090534

Evans, G. Godfrey Evans in conversation with Leslie Ames. *Cricketer international (Kent, Eng.)*

CRICKET (continued)

65(7), July 1984, 30-31.
NOTES: An extract from, Wicket-keepers of the World by Godfrey Evans, New English Library, 1984.
LEVEL: B LANG: Eng SIRC ARTICLE NO: 094920

Gavaskar, S. Idols. s.l.: George Allen & Unwin, (1984?). 1v.
LEVEL: B LANG: Eng

Gavaskar, S. Runs 'n ruins. Calcutta: Rupa & Co., 1984?. 1v.
LEVEL: B LANG: Eng

Gibson, A. A properly adventurous captain. Cricketers remembered: Peter Cranmer (Warwickshire). *Cricketer international* 65(2), Feb 1984, 31.
LEVEL: B LANG: Eng SIRC ARTICLE NO: 090535

Gibson, A. The cheerful man from Swansea. (Alan Jones) *Cricketer international* 65(3), Mar 1984, 37.
LEVEL: B LANG: Eng SIRC ARTICLE NO: 093338

Gibson, A. Cricketers remembered: G.R. Langdale (Somerset). Good old 'gogs'. *Cricketer international (Kent, Eng.)* 65(12), Dec 1984, 39.
LEVEL: B LANG: Eng SIRC ARTICLE NO: 101148

Gibson, A. Fine 'keeper and funny man. Cricketers remembered: Arthur Wood (Yorks and England). *Cricketer international (Kent, Eng.)* 65(11), Nov 1984, 37.
LEVEL: B LANG: Eng SIRC ARTICLE NO: 101149

Grahame Booker remembers... Fred Barratt: big man, bit hitter. *Cricketer international* 65(4), Apr 1984, 73.
LEVEL: B LANG: Eng SIRC ARTICLE NO: 093341

Hughes, S. Enry and Ernie. (John Emburey and Phil Edmonds) *Cricketer international (Kent, Eng.)* 65(6), Jun 1984, 14-15.
LEVEL: B LANG: Eng SIRC ARTICLE NO: 094925

Lemmon, D. The great wicket-keepers. London: Stanley Paul, 1984. 175 p., (12) p. of plates : ill. ; 23 cm.
LEVEL: B LANG: E ISBN: 0091552109 LC CARD: 84-179739

MacDonald, T. Viv Richards - the authorised story. *Cricketer international (Kent, Eng.)* 65(7), July 1984, 16-17.
NOTES: A extract from, Viv Richards: the authorised biography, published by Pelham Books.
LEVEL: B LANG: Eng SIRC ARTICLE NO: 094927

Murphy, P. Richard Hadlee: man of the season. *Cricketer international (Kent, Eng.)* 65(11), Nov 1984, 40-41.
LEVEL: B LANG Eng SIRC ARTICLE NO: 101153

Patil, S. Sandy storm. Calcutta: Rupa & Co., 1984?. 1v.
LEVEL: B LANG: Eng

Pawson, G. An invitation from Yorkshire. *Cricketer international* 65(1), Jan 1984, 28.
NOTES: Last in a series of articles on Guy Pawson's early cricketing days.
LEVEL: B LANG: Eng SIRC ARTICLE NO: 090538

Ramchand, P. Great feats of Indian cricket. Calcutta: Rupa & Co., 1984?. 1v.
LEVEL: B LANG: Eng

Reese, M. Max Reese remembers Harry Storer...a man for both seasons. *Cricketer international (Kent, Eng.)* 65(12), Dec 1984, 38.
LEVEL: B LANG: Eng SIRC ARTICLE NO: 101155

Richards, H. Alfred Lyttelton - the happy warrior. *Cricketer international (Kent, Eng.)* 65(10), Oct 1984, 34-35.
LEVEL: B LANG: Eng SIRC ARTICLE NO: 099448

Rochford, P. Connie - the great entertainer. Peter Rockford reassesses the legend of Sir Learie Constantine. *Cricketer international (Kent, Eng.)* 65(11), Nov 1984, 45.
LEVEL: B LANG: Eng SIRC ARTICLE NO: 101156

Smith, J. Sir Frank Worrell: the apostle of non-violence. *Cricketer international (Kent, Eng.)* 65(8), Aug 1984, 18-19.
LEVEL: B LANG: Eng SIRC ARTICLE NO: 096565

The legacy of the 'little wonder' Alan Hill pays a centenary tribute to John Wisden. *Cricketer international* 65(4), Apr 1984, 77.
LEVEL: B LANG: Eng SIRC ARTICLE NO: 093342

Turner, K. Ken Turner: financier, lawyer, team-builder and talent scout. *Cricketer international (Kent, Eng.)* 65(10, Oct 1984, 16.
LEVEL: B LANG: Eng SIRC ARTICLE NO: 099449

Van der Bijl, V. Bishop, J. Cricket in the shadows. Surrey, Eng.: Shuter and Shooter, 1984. 1v.
LEVEL: B LANG: Eng

West, D. Cricket spotlight. Squinting Jemmy. *Cricketer international (Kent, Eng.)* 65(7), July 1984, 41.
LEVEL: B LANG: En SIRC ARTICLE NO: 094931

Woodall, R.D. The 'demon bowler' of Notts. (John 'Foghorn' Jackson) *Cricket international* 65(2), Feb 1984, 33.
LEVEL: B LANG: Eng SIRC ARTICLE NO: 090541

BIOMECHANICS

Elliott, B.C. Foster, D.H. A biomechanical analysis of the front-on and side-on fast bowling techniques. (Refs: 17)*Journal of human movement studies (Edinburgh, Eng.) 10(2), 1984, 83-94.*
ABST: Four elite cricket bowlers were filmed both laterally and from directly above while bowling such that their front foot landed on a force platform during the delivery stride. There were no significant differences in force production between the front-on side-on techniques. Kinematic analysis indicates that the side-on technique may enable the bowler to summate body forces in a more efficient manner and thus allow production of maximal bowling velocity with minimum of effort.
LEVEL: A LANG: Eng SIRC ARTICLE NO: 096560

CERTIFICATION

Cricket, course conductor manual: levels 1 & 2. Ottawa: Canadian Cricket Association, 1984. 60 leaves (National Coaching Certification Program.)
CORP: Canadian Cricket Association. National Coaching Committee.
CORP: Coaching Association of Canada.
LEVEL: B LANG: Eng GV926 17897

Cricket, level 1 technical, coaching manual. Ottawa: Canadian Cricket Association : Coaching Association of Canada, 1984. iii, 35 p. : ill. (National Coaching Certification Program.)
CORP: Canadian Cricket Association. National Coaching Committee.
CORP: Coaching Association of Canada.
NOTES: Cover title.
LEVEL: B LANG: Eng GV926 17929

CHILDREN

Spence, P. Kanga Cricket For Kids - designed to suit the expressed needs of children and teachers. (Refs: 8)*ACHPER national journal (Kingswood, Aust.) 105, Spring 1984, 4-7.*
LEVEL: B LANG: Eng SIRC ARTICLE NO: 103075

Spence, P. Kanga cricket: Australia's new junior development program. (Refs: 12)*Sports coach (Wembley, W. Aust.) 8(2), Oct 1984, 21-25.*
LEVEL: B LANG: Eng SIRC ARTICLE NO: 104617

Tyson, F. Harris, J. Sobers, G. Cricket skills. Lane Cove, N.S.W.: Doubleday, 1984. viii, 151 p. : ill.
ABST: Basic cricket skills in batting, bowling, wicketkeeping and fielding for boys and girls are presented through a series of sequential steps. Each sequence is clearly illustrated and follow up activities are designed to increase enjoyment of the game. The simple language and illustrations allow use by the young player, as well as by parents, youth leaders and teachers.
LEVEL: B LANG: Eng ISBN: 0-86824-084-2 GV929.3 17522

COUNTRIES AND REGIONS

Mullins, P. Derriman. P. Bat and pad: writings on Australian cricket, 1804-1984. England: Oxford University Press, 1984. 1v.
LEVEL: I LANG: Eng

Neely, D. DB cricket annual 1984. Auckland, N.Z.: MOA Pub., 1984. 1v.
LEVEL: B LANG: Eng

Partridge, T. Sichel, P. The 1984 Protea cricket annual of South Africa, vol. 31. Greenmarket Square, Cape Town: Protea Assurance, 1984. 1v.
LEVEL: B LANG: Eng

Payne, F. Smith, I. The 1984 Shell Cricket Almanack of New Zealand. Auckland, N.Z.: MOA Pub., 1984. 1v.
LEVEL: B LANG: Eng

The Bermuda cricket annual. Southampton, Bermuda: Barrier Reefs, (1984?). 112 p.
LEVEL: B LANG: Eng

Thyagarajan, S. Indian cricket 1984. Cumbria: Appleby's Books, 1984. 1v.
LEVEL: B LANG: Eng

DISABLED

Hargreaves, P.S. Derbyshire's dane. Chesterfield, Derbyshire: Ian Buxton, (1984?). 1v.
NOTES: More information about Mortensen.
LEVEL: B LANG: Eng

EQUIPMENT

Bazalgette, C. Indoor cricket - a new season. *Cricketer international (Kent, Eng.)* 65(10), Oct 1984, 45;47.
NOTES: The author reviews the products available for the indoors.
LEVEL: B LANG: Eng SIRC ARTICLE NO: 099446

FACILITIES

Arundell, P.A. Baker, S.W. Photomicrographic examination of soil conditions of problem pitches at two county grounds in England. (Refs: 4)*Journal of the Sports Turf Research Institute (Bingley, West*

Yorkshire) 60, June 1984, 54-60.
ABST: A number of pitches at Old Trafford and Headingley cricket grounds have recently had to be re-constructed because of unfavourable playing characteristics. Structural and physical properties of the soils from the discarded pitches are examined by photomicrography and particle size analysis and explanations for the poor performance are suggested.
LEVEL: A LANG: Eng SIRC ARTICLE NO: 108514

FACILITIES - MAINTENANCE

Dury, P. Water your way to a good wicket. *Cricketer international (Kent, Eng.) 65(8), Aug 1984, 50.*
LEVEL: B LANG: Eng SIRC ARTICLE NO: 095839

Dury, P. What is a non-turf cricket pitch? *Turf management (Surrey, Eng.) 3(7), Jul 1984, 20-22.*
LEVEL: B LANG: Eng SIRC ARTICLE NO: 102148

Dury, P. How to repair non-turf cricket pitches. *Turf management (Surrey, Eng.) 3(7), Jul 1984, 21.*
LEVEL: B LANG: Eng SIRC ARTICLE NO: 102149

Fairbrothers, J. Moore, R. Testing the wicket: from Trent bridge to Lord's. s.l.: Pelham Books, (1984?). 1v.
LEVEL: B LANG: Eng

Parkes, K. Cricket wickets: spare a thought for the groundsman. *Parks, golf courses & sports grounds (Middlesex, Eng.) 49(11), Aug 1984, 106-107.*
LEVEL: B LANG: Eng SIRC ARTICLE NO: 102432

Parkes, K. Get rid of the hump on your wickets. *Parks, golf courses & sports grounds (Staines, Middlesex) 50(2), Nov 1984, 30.*
LEVEL: B LANG: Eng SIRC ARTICLE NO: 108870

Tyson, F. Ground management from a player's viewpoint. *Australian parks & recreation (Campbell, Aust.) May 1984, 16-20.*
LEVEL: B LANG: Eng SIRC ARTICLE NO: 100635

HISTORY

Kirsch, G.B. American cricket: players and clubs before the Civil War. *Journal of sports history (Seattle, Wash.) 11(1), Spring 1984, 28-50.*
ABST: The purpose of this study was to assess demographic, social, and cultural characteristics of American cricketers and clubs before the Civil War. The author especially focused his attention on those Eastern States where cricket was very popular.
LEVEL: A LANG: Eng SIRC ARTICLE NO: 096562

Martin-Jenkins, C. Twenty years on. Cricket's years of change, 1963-83. s.l.: Collins Willow, 1984. 1v.
LEVEL: B LANG: Eng

Ross, G. 100 years of tests at Old Trafford. *Cricketer international (Kent, Eng.) 65(7), July 1984, 24.*
LEVEL: B LANG: En SIRC ARTICLE NO: 094930

Sandiford, K.A.P. Victorian cricket technique and industrial technology. (Refs: 61)*British journal of sports history (London) 1(3), Dec 1984, 272-285.*
LEVEL: I LANG: Eng SIRC ARTICLE NO: 105735

INJURIES AND ACCIDENTS

Corrigan, A.B. Cricket injuries. *Australian family physician (Sydney) 13(8), Aug 1984, 558-559;562.*
LEVEL: A LANG: Eng

JUVENILE LITERATURE

Phipson, J. The grannie season. United Kingdom?: Hamish Hamilton, 1984?. 1v. : ill.
LEVEL: B LANG: Eng

MASS MEDIA

Cardus, N. Neville Cardus: autobiography. s.l.: Hamish Hamilton, (1984?). 1v.
NOTES: First published in 1947.
LEVEL: B LANG: Eng

PERCEPTUAL MOTOR PROCESSES

Abernethy, B. Russell, D.G. Advanced cue utilisation by skilled cricket batsmen. (Refs: 40)*Australian journal of science & medicine in sport (Kingston, Aust.) 16(2), Aug 1984, 2-10.*
ABST: The importance of advance cue sources to decision-making in cricket batting was examined in two experiments. Eighteen batsmen from three skill groups were required to make response selection decisions to filmed sequences of the run-up and delivery action of two medium-pace bowlers. In the first experiment, in which ball flight information was available, first grade batsmen produced more accurate stroke-selection than lower grade batsmen. In the second experiment, in which ball flight was occluded and the viewing time was held constant for all subjects, there was a trend towards greater extraction of advance information by the highly skilled batsmen.
LEVEL: A LANG: Eng SIRC ARTICLE NO: 104614

PROTECTIVE DEVICES

Pringle, D. But what about common sense? *Cricketer international (Kent, Eng.) 65(8), Aug 1984, 5.*
LEVEL: B LANG: Eng SIRC ARTICLE NO: 096564

SOCIAL PSYCHOLOGY

Pawson, T. The mystique of captaincy. *Cricketer international 65(1), Jan 1984, 11.*
LEVEL: B LANG: Eng SIRC ARTICLE NO: 090539

SOCIOLOGY

James, C.L.R. Lipsyte, R. Beyond a boundary. New York: Pantheon Boks, 1984, c1963. 1v.
NOTES: Originally published: London Stanley Paul & Co., 1963. Includes index.
LEVEL: I LANG: Eng ISBN: 0394722833 LC CARD: 83-043148

SPECTATORS

Crofts, M. Crowd behaviour: Bay 13 at the world series one-day internationals, Melbourne. (Refs: 22)*Pelops 5, Feb 1984, 17-21.*
ABST: Outlines some of the sociological aspects of spectator behaviour and attempts to relate them to the sporting audience in Bay 13 at the one-day international cricket matches held at the Melbourne Cricket Ground. Bay 13 is the stadium area where the most vocal and least inhibited spectators tend

to congregate.
LEVEL: I LANG: Eng SIRC ARTICLE NO: 097987

Where have the crowds gone? *Cricketer Pakistan (Karachi) 13(4), Jul 1984, 39;41.*
LEVEL: B LANG: Eng SIRC ARTICLE NO: 101158

SPORTING EVENTS

The Asda cricket challenge. London: Counsel Ltd., (1984?). 1v.
NOTES: Souvenir program.
LEVEL: B LANG: Eng

Woodhouse, R. Shrewsbury at Lord's. Shropshire, Eng.: Camels, Annscroft, (1984?). 104 p.
LEVEL: B LANG: Eng

SPORTSMANSHIP

Cheating. *Cricketer Pakistan (Karachi) 13(4), Aug 1984, 44-46.*
LEVEL: B LANG: Eng SIRC ARTICLE NO: 101147

STATISTICS AND RECORDS

Irish Cricket Union yearbook 1984. Dublin: Derek Scott, 1984. 1v.
CORP: Irish Cricket Union.
LEVEL: B LANG: Eng

Pakistan one-day internationals. Kent, Eng.: Martin Wood, (1984?). 1v.
LEVEL: B LANG: Eng

Pakistan test cricket, 1983-84. Kent, Eng.: Martin Wood, 1984. 1v.
LEVEL: B LANG: Eng

Saulez, G. Career records. *Cricketer quarterly facts and figures (Tunbridge Wells, Eng.) 11(3), Winter 1983-1984, 60-69.*
LEVEL: B LANG: Eng SIRC ARTICLE NO: 097990

TECHNIQUES AND SKILLS

Gover, A. Keeping to the spinners. *Cricketer international 65(3), Mar 1984, 46.*
LEVEL: B LANG: Eng SIRC ARTICLE NO: 09333

Gover, A. Wrong 'un for the leg spinner. *Cricketer international 65(4), Apr 1984, 80.*
LEVEL: B LANG: Eng SIRC ARTICLE NO: 093340

Larkins, W. Shots of the month. *Cricketer international (Kent, Eng.) 65(8), Aug 1984, 37.*
NOTES: Second part of a series.
LEVEL: B LANG: Eng SIRC ARTICLE NO: 096563

TECHNIQUES AND SKILLS - BATTER AND BATTING

Gover, A. Off-diving for the left-hander. *Cricketer international 65(1), Jan 1984, 31.*
LEVEL: B LANG: Eng SIRC ARTICLE NO 090536

Gover, A. Back foot shots and spotting the googly. *Cricketer international 65(2), Feb 1984, 41.*
LEVEL: B LANG: Eng SIRC ARTICLE NO: 090537

Gover, A. Getting out of a bad 'trot'. *Cricketer international (Kent, Eng.) 65(9), Sept 1984, 54.*
LEVEL: B LANG: Eng SIRC ARTICLE NO: 097988

Gover, A. Front foot shots. *Cricketer international (Kent, Eng.) 65(10), Oct 1984, 52.*
LEVEL: B LANG: Eng SIRC ARTICLE NO 099447

CRICKET (continued)

Gover, A. Alf Gover's cricket manual. *Cricketer Pakistan (Karachi) 13(4),* Aug 1984, 111-112.
LEVEL: B LANG: Eng SIRC ARTICLE NO: 101150

Gover, A. Alf Gover's cricket manual. *Cricketer Pakistan (Karachi) 13(4),* Jul 1984, 95;97.
LEVEL: B LANG: Eng SIRC ARTICL NO: 101151

Gover, A. Eye-line for a left-hander. *Cricketer international (Kent, Eng.) 65(12),* Dec 1984, 42.
LEVEL: B LANG: Eng SIRC ARTICLE NO: 101152

Larkins, W. Shots of the month: the off-drive. *Cricketer international (Kent, Eng.) 65(7),* Jul 1984, 39.
LEVEL: B LANG: E SIRC ARTICLE NO: 094926

Larkins, W. Shots of the month. *Cricketer international (Kent, Eng.) 65(9),* Sept 1984, 37.
LEVEL: B LANG: Eng SIRC ARTICL NO: 097989

TECHNIQUES AND SKILLS - BOWLER AND BOWLING

Foster, D. Elliot, B. Gray, S. Herzberg, L. Guidelines for the fast bowler. *Sports coach (Wembley, Australia) 7(4),* Mar 1984, 47-48.
LEVEL: B LANG: Eng SIRC ARTICLE NO: 094921

Gover, A. Straightening the bowling arm. *Cricketer international (Kent, Eng.) 65(6),* Jun 1984, 36-37.
LEVEL: B LANG: Eng SIRC ARTICLE NO: 094923

Gover, A. The art of flight. *Cricketer international (Kent, Eng.) 65(7),* Jul 1984, 59.
LEVEL: B LANG: Eng SIRC ARTICLE NO 094924

Roebuck, P. Intimidation: the name of the modern test game? *Cricketer international 65(2),* Feb 1984, 23;26.
LEVEL: B LANG Eng SIRC ARTICLE NO: 090540

Samdani, Z. Bouncers: manly... or intimidatory? *Cricketer Pakistan (Karachi) 13(4),* Jul 1984, 46-47.
LEVEL: B LANG: Eng SIRC ARTICLE NO: 101157

TRAINING AND CONDITIONING - DRILLS

Gover, A. Organising practice. *Cricketer international (Kent, Eng.) 65(8),* Aug 1984, 52.
LEVEL: B LANG: Eng SIRC ARTICLE NO: 096561

VARIATIONS

Pedersen, E. The games corner. *MAHPERD: Michigan journal for Health, Physical Education, Recreation, Dance (Ypsilanti, Mich.)* Spring 1984, 13.
LEVEL: B LANG: Eng SIRC ARTICLE NO: 094929

CROSS-COUNTRY CYCLING

Abramson, D.M. Conquering the century: one hundred miles of calculated energy. *Outside (Chicago, Ill.) 9(5),* Jun 1984, 46-47.
LEVEL: B LANG: Eng SIRC ARTICLE NO: 101162

BIOGRAPHY AND AUTOBIOGRAPHY

Laurence, R.P. The man who made history: meet the cyclist who started the cross-country craze. (Paul Cornish) *Bicycling (Emmaus, Pa.) 25(7),* Aug 1984, 83-85.
LEVEL: B LANG: Eng SIRC ARTICLE NO: 099484

EQUIPMENT

At last a bicycle for Australian conditions. *Freewheeling (Sydney) 26,* Jul/Aug 1984, 8-9;11.
LEVEL: B LANG: Eng SIRC ARTICL NO: 105741

How good is the all-terrain bike: a look at how the current designs perform off-road and on-road. *Freewheeling (Sydney) 26,* Jul/Aug 1984, 13;15.
LEVEL: B LANG: Eng SIRC ARTICLE NO: 105755

Kelly, C.R. Mountain bike tires: the tire's the thing... *American bicyclist and motorcyclist (New York) 105(9),* Sept 1984, 75;85.
LEVEL: B LANG: Eng SIRC ARTICLE NO: 103103

Malvern Star Highwayman: the all-purpose bike joins the Malvern Star range. *Freewheeling (Sydney) 26,* Jul/Aug 1984, 34.
LEVEL: B LANG: Eng SIRC ARTICLE NO: 105763

Olsen, J. Frame geometry for rough trail riding. *Bike tech (Emmaus, Pa.) 3(2),* Apr 1984, 9-12;14.
LEVEL: I LANG: Eng SIRC ARTICLE NO: 099494

Raleigh Trek. The Raleigh Trek fifteen-speed all-purpose bike. *Freewheeling (Sydney) 26,* Jul/Aug 1984, 33.
LEVEL: B LANG: E SIRC ARTICLE NO: 105772

Raleigh Yukon: the Raleigh Yukon ten-speed all-purpose bike. *Freewheeling (Sydney) 26,* Jul/Aug 1984, 35.
LEVEL: B LANG: Eng SIRC ARTICLE NO: 105773

Ross, A. Ross, B. Springing the question: improving the all-terrain bicycle. *Bicycling (Emmaus, Pa.) 25(8),* Sept/Oct 1984, 152;154;156-158.
LEVEL: B LANG: Eng SIRC ARTICLE NO: 099503

The fat tyre fanatic: Hillman Alpine. *Freewheeling (Haymarket, N.S.W.) 24,* Mar/Apr 1984, 41-42.
LEVEL: B LANG: Eng SIRC ARTICLE NO: 099469

The market takes shape from the top down. The first Freewheeling fat tyre bike survey. *Freewheeling (Sydney) 26,* Jul/Aug 1984 25-28;30-31.
LEVEL: B LANG: Eng SIRC ARTICLE NO: 105766

Woodward, B. Rock and roll: this unique brand of cycling blends European racing, motocross and delivery boy chic. *Ultraspor (Boston) 1(4),* Jul/Aug 1984, 20-25.
LEVEL: B LANG: Eng SIRC ARTICLE NO: 098035

MASS MEDIA

Lampley, J. Behind the cameras. *Bicycling (Emmaus, Pa.) 25(7),* Aug 1984, 91-94.
LEVEL: B LANG: Eng SIRC ARTICLE NO: 09948

SPORTING EVENTS

Olivier, H. A new sport: observed trials for mountain bikes. *Bicycle USA (Baltimore, Md.) 20(5),* May 1984, 6-7.
LEVEL: B LANG: Eng SIRC ARTICLE NO: 099493

Van Daele, M. The Monster Race of 1933. *Bicycle Ontario (Willowdale) 7(1),* Feb 1984, 27-28.
LEVEL: B LANG: Eng SIRC ARTICLE NO: 098033

TECHNIQUES AND SKILLS

Climb every mountain... All-terrain bike enthusiast Warren Salomon a conservative rider at heart (not wishing to relive the agonies of his youth) gives a few hints on the best techniques for all terrain biking. *Freewheeling (Sydney) 26,* Jul/Aug 1984, 16.
LEVEL: B LANG: Eng SIRC ARTICLE NO: 105748

Kelly, C. Riding styles for the wilds: off-road technique. *Bicycling (Emmaus, Pa.) 25(8),* Sept/Oct 1984, 96.
LEVEL: B LANG: Eng SIRC ARTICLE NO: 099477

Olsen, J. Hill climbing for trail riders. *Bicycling (Emmaus, Pa.) 25(4),* May 1984, 24;27.
LEVEL: B LANG: Eng SIRC ARTICLE NO: 094950

Olsen, J. Log jumping for trail riders. It's easy and fun to ride over large obstacles. *Bicycling (Emmaus, Pa,) 25(5),* Jun 1984, 30;32;34.
LEVEL: B LANG: Eng SIRC ARTICLE NO: 096598

CROSS-COUNTRY RIDING

Drummond, M. Try team chasing - if you're brave. *Riding (London) 49(11),* Nov 1984, 40-41.
LEVEL: B LANG: Eng SIRC ARTICLE NO: 107281

TECHNIQUES AND SKILLS

Holden, A. Bruce Davidson on jumping into water: how to properly school for, and ride water obstacles. *USCTA news (Hamilton Mass.) 13(4),* Aug 1984, 13-16.
NOTES: From an interview with Fifi Coles.
LEVEL: B LANG: Eng SIRC ARTICLE NO: 101349

TRAINING AND CONDITIONING - WARM-UPS, WARM-DOWNS, LEAD-UP GAMES

Fleischmann, T. The warm-up: preparing the novice/training horse for cross-country and show jumping at a one-day-event. *USCTA news (South Hamilton, Mass.) 13(3),* Jun 1984, 14-15;48.
LEVEL: B LANG: Eng SIRC ARTICLE NO: 098197

CROSS-COUNTRY RUNNING

Temple, C. Getting the X-C bug. *Track and field quarterly review (Kalamazoo, Mich.) 84(3),* Fall 1984, 9-11.
LEVEL: B LANG Eng SIRC ARTICLE NO: 097005

ADMINISTRATION

King, L.T. Improved record-keeping for track & cross-country. *Scholastic coach (New York) 53(9),* Apr 1984, 68-69.
LEVEL: LANG: Eng SIRC ARTICLE NO: 095428

BIOGRAPHY AND AUTOBIOGRAPHY

Butler, M. Spotlight on youth: Steven Fury - no longer an unknown. *Athletics weekly (Rochester, Kent, Eng.) 38(41),* 13 Oct 1984, 34-38.
LEVEL: B LANG: Eng SIRC ARTICLE NO: 101661

Christie, J. The flying Scotsman is still steaming. (Gordon James Porteous) *Athletics weekly*

(Rochester, Kent, Eng.) 38(41) 13 Oct 1984, 21-23.
LEVEL: B LANG: Eng SIRC ARTICLE NO: 101665

Downes, S. Profile: Basil Heatley, a man for all seasons. *Running magazine (London) 35, Mar 1984, 50-53.*
LEVEL: B LANG: E SIRC ARTICLE NO: 098626

Enda Fitzpatrick: interview. *Marathon magazine (Charleville, Ireland) 22(3), May 1984, 8-9.*
NOTES: Continued next month.
LEVEL: B LANG: Eng SIRC ARTICLE NO: 108675

Interview with Robert Costello. *Marathon magazine (Charleville, Ireland)) 22(2), Mar 1984, 4-7.*
LEVEL: B LANG: Eng SIRC ARTICLE NO: 108679

Ireland rejoice - you have Monica and Regina Joyce. *Marathon magazine (Charleville, Ireland) 22(3), May 1984, 12-14.*
LEVEL: LANG: Eng SIRC ARTICLE NO: 108677

Kelleher, L. Enda Fitzpatrick: interview. *Marathon (Charleville, Co. Cork, Ireland) 22(4), June 1984, 38-39.*
NOTES: Continued from last month.
LEVEL: B LANG: Eng SIRC ARTICLE NO: 109116

Profile: Lynn Williams. *Track and field journal (Ottawa, Ont.) 27, Aug 1984, 17-18.*
LEVEL: B LANG: Eng SIRC ARTICLE NO: 100082

Whitefield, N. Julian Goater - still looking for a big win. *Athletics weekly (Kent, Eng.) 38(51), 22 Dec 1984, 30-35;37.*
LEVEL: B LANG: Eng SIRC ARTICLE NO: 103620

Wickers, D. The rugged Joss Naylor: at 47, this Lake District native is unsurpassed in the strenuous British sport of fell running. *Runner (New York) 7(2), Nov 1984, 60-62;64;81.*
LEVEL: B LANG: Eng SIRC ARTICLE NO: 108626

COACHING

Baycock, C. Motivation is the key. Cross country tips. *Coaching clinic (Princeton, N.J.) 23(1), Sept 1984, 3-5.*
LEVEL: B LANG: Eng SIRC ARTICLE NO: 100039

HISTORY

Ingham, R. A guide to the guides: concluding our review of the history and tradition of open fell racing. Part III: beyond the war. *Compass sport: the orienteer (Middlesex, Eng.) 5(3), Jun/Jul 1984, 32-33.*
LEVEL: B LANG: Eng SIRC ARTICLE NO: 104984

MEDICINE

Court, C.A. Anorexic behavior among female intercollegiate distance runners. Eugene, Ore.: Microform Publications, Universit of Oregon, 1984. 1 microfiche : negative, ill, ; 11 x 15 cm.
NOTES: Thesis (M.S.) - Pennsylvania State University, 1983; ((9)), 74 leaves); includes bibliography.
LEVEL: A LANG: Eng UO84 331

PHYSIOLOGY

Friden, J. Sjoestreom, M. Ekblom, B. Muscle fibre type characteristics in endurance trained and untrained individuals. (Refs 15)*European journal of applied physiology and occupational physiology (Heidelberg) 52(3), Apr 1984, 266-271.*
ABST: Muscle biopsies were obtained from six trained and four untrained males. The main fibre types were quantitatively determined according to the M-band appearance. The volume of mitochondria (Vmit) was higher in Type 1 fibres than in Type 2 fibres; although results indicate that this is not a satisfactory criterion to distinguish between fibre types. Z band width was larger in Type 1 fibres than in Type 2 fibres. The classification of fibres based on ultrastructural criteria (Vmit, Zband width, lipid droplets) was found to be useful but not entirely specific.
LEVEL: A LANG: Eng SIRC ARTICLE NO: 097724

Hughson, R.L. Orok, C.J. Staudt, L.E. A high velocity treadmill running test to assess endurance running potential. (Refs: 1 *International journal of sports medicine 5(1), Feb 1984, 23-25.*
ABST: This study investigated whether or not it is appropriate to express the results from a high velocity running test with a hyperbolic relationship between velocity and endurance time. Six cross-country runners ran to exhaustion with the treadmill set at 6 different velocities between 19.2 km/h and 22.4 km/h. The results indicate that treadmill runs of 2-12 min duration conform to a similar hyperbolic function as that described for cycle ergometry. The authors feel that components of this function may provide valuable indices of training efficacy in competitive runners.
LEVEL: A LANG: Eng SIRC ARTICLE NO: 093897

Reilly, T. Foreman, T.K. Multiple regression of selected fitness measures on performance in cross-country running. (Refs: 19 *SNIPES journal (Patiala, India) 7(4), Oct 1984, 3-10.*
ABST: Physiological and anthropometric measurements of 19 male cross-country runners were recorded. Correlations were established between these variables and race performance time. Multiple regression equations were derived to predict performance from the variables studies.
LEVEL: A LANG: Eng SIRC ARTICLE NO: 171610

Thoren, C.A.R. Asano, K. Functional capacity and cardiac function in 10-year-old-boys and girls with high and low running performance. (Refs: 6)
CONF: Symposium of Paediatric Work Physiology (10th : 1981 : Joutsa, Finland).
NOTES: In, Ilmarinen, J. and Vaelimaeki, I. (eds.), Children and sport: paediatric work physiology, Berlin, Springer-Verlag, 1984, p. 182-188.
ABST: The first five girls and first five boys of 481 boys and girls who participated in a 1700 m run for 10 year olds were tested. This paper focused upon the cardiac function at rest and during exercise, studying systolic time intervals, stroke volume by impedance cardiography.
LEVEL: A LANG: Eng SIRC ARTICLE NO: 103613

Wilcox, A.R. Bulbulian, R. Changes in running economy relative to VO2max during a cross-country season. (Refs: 8)*Journal of sports medicine and physical fitness (Torino, Italy) 24(4), Dec 1984, 321-326.*
ABST: The present investigation studied the effects of a cross-country season on these measures as well as the relationship of running economy (RE) and percent VO2 max to race performance at the beginning and the end of the season. The subjects were 7 female, university cross-country runners. It was found that an 8 week period of training for cross-country resulted in an increase in VO2 max and an improvement of percent VO2 max at 215 and 241 m.min-1, but was not sufficient for improving RE.
LEVEL: A LANG: Eng SIRC ARTICLE NO: 107774

SPORTING EVENTS

Van Schoore, A. Le cross des nations devenue au fil du temps championnat du monde. (1e partie) *Sport: Communaute francaise de Belgique (Bruxelles) 27(3), 1984, 131-155.*
NOTES: A suivre.
LEVEL: B LANG: Fr SIRC ARTICLE NO: 100101

Van Schoore, A. Le Cross des Nations devenu au fil du temps Championnat du monde. (Refs: 12)*Sport: Communaute francaise de belgique (Bruxelles) 108, 1984, 222-239.*
NOTES: Deuxieme partie.
LEVEL: B LANG: Fr SIRC ARTICLE NO: 103616

TRAINING AND CONDITIONING

Berg, E. The neglected 110 in cross-country. *Coaching clinic 22(6), Feb 1984, 10-11.*
LEVEL: B LANG: Eng SIRC ARTICLE NO: 091069

Dooley, J. Traininng for juveniles (under 14s). *Marathon magazine (Charleville, Ireland) 22(2), Mar 1984, 20-21.*
LEVEL: B LANG: Eng SIRC ARTICLE NO: 108680

VARIATIONS

Ingram, R. A guide to the guides. Part II: the stars begin to shine. *Compass sport orienteer (Middlesex, Eng.) 5(1), Feb/Ma 1984, 38-39.*
LEVEL: B LANG: Eng SIRC ARTICLE NO: 096972

Smoot, S. Cross-country express. As an added feature to a cross-country meet, a 'cross-country express' can generate team spirit, morale, and excitement. *Athletic journal 64(8), Mar 1984, 28;59.*
LEVEL: B LANG: Eng SIRC ARTICLE NO: 093944

CROSS-COUNTRY SKIING

Caldwell, J. The cross-country ski book. 7th rev. ed. Brattleboro, Vt.: Stephen Greene Press, c1984. x, 180 p. : ill.
NOTES Bibliography: p. 173-174.
LEVEL: I LANG: Eng ISBN: 0-8289-0544-4 LC CARD: 84-13588 GV855.3 18539

Exercise is the main reason people cross-country ski. *Employee services management (Westchester, Ill.) 26(10), Dec/Jan 1983/1984, 28.*
LEVEL: B LANG: Eng SIRC ARTICLE NO: 098485

Formo, I. My Olympic experience. (Ivar Formo) *Olympic review (Lausanne, Switzerland) 195/196, Jan/Feb 1984, 30-35.*
LEVEL: LANG: Eng SIRC ARTICLE NO: 095243

Formo, I. Mon experience olympique. *Revue olympique (Lausanne) 195-196, janv/fevr 1984, 30-35.*
LEVEL: B LANG: Fr SIRC ARTICLE NO: 096822

Sheahan, C. Jaspersohn, B. Sports Illustrated cross-country skiing. 1st ed. New York: Harper & Row, c1984. 186 p. : ill. (Sports Illustrated library.)
LEVEL: B LANG: Eng ISBN: 0060910429 LC CARD: 83-047543 GV855.3 15865

Slade, A. How to ski cross-country. Vancouver: Special Interest Publications, c1984. 30 p. : ill. (B.C. outdoors discovery series; v.3.)
LEVEL: B LANG: Eng ISBN: 0-88896-149-9 LC CARD: C84-91537-3 GV855.3 18988

CROSS-COUNTRY SKIING (continued)

BIOGRAPHY AND AUTOBIOGRAPHY

Hobson, A. Pierre Harvey, la chasse a l'argent. Pierre Harvey, struggle for the bucks. *Champion 8(1), Feb 1984, 36-37.* .
LEVEL: B LANG: Eng Fr SIRC ARTICLE NO: 090903

Hobson, A. Jon Servold, quelques annees trop tot. Jon Servold, four years too soon. *Champion 8(1), Feb 1984, 42-43.*
LEVEL B LANG: Eng Fr SIRC ARTICLE NO: 090918

Krakauer, J. Waxing poetic. *Ultrasport (San Diego, Calif.) 1(1), Jan/Feb 1984, 57-59;64.*
LEVEL: B LANG: Eng SIRC ARTICLE NO: 095244

Moore, K. A fire burns fiercely within him. Bill Koch, the one U.S. hope for an Olympic cross-country skiing medal, drives himself in hot pursuit of perfection. *Sports illustrated 60(5), 6 Feb 1984, 38-40;45-46;48;50.*
LEVEL: B LANG: Eng SIRC ARTICLE NO: 090904

Ottum, B. A man of many parts. Kerry Lynch, impressionist, drummer and double-duty skier, is a favorite to win the Nordic combined at Sarajevo. *Sports illustrated 60(5), 6 Feb 1984, 52-54;56;61.*
LEVEL: B LANG: Eng SIRC ARTICLE NO: 090919

Robbins, P. Bill Koch: there's so much more than winning, especially in cross-country, where there is so much beauty to the sport. *Inside sports (Evanston, Ill.) 6, Mar 1984, 38-44.*
LEVEL: B LANG: Eng SIRC ARTICLE NO: 108803

BIOMECHANICS

Vikander, N. A model for the qualitative biomechanical analysis of double poling. (Refs: 9)*Journal of professional ski coaching and instruction (Boulder, Colo.) May 1984, 20-22.*
LEVEL: I LANG: Eng SIRC ARTICLE NO: 096823

CERTIFICATION

Exall, M. New certification in cross country ski facility, management and design. *Tour leader (Ottawa, Ont.) 4(1), 1984, 23-28.*
LEVEL: B LANG: Eng SIRC ARTICLE NO: 098484

CHILDREN

Ilmarinen, J. Nygard, C-H. Komi, P.V. Karlsson, J. Heart rate and blood lactate level of 8 - 12 years-old boys and girls during cross-country ski-competitions.
CONF: Symposium of Paediatric Work Physiology (10th : 1981 : Joutsa, Finland).
NOTES: In, Ilmarinen, J. and Vaelimaeki, I. (eds.), Children and sport: paediatric work physiology, Berlin, Springer-Verlag, 1984, p. 189-195.
LEVEL: A LANG: Eng SIRC ARTICLE NO: 103442

Tiainen, J. Telama, R. Children and parents in skiing competitions. (Refs: 3)
CONF: Symposium of Paediatric Work Physiology (10th : 1981 : Joutsa, Finland).
NOTES: In, Ilmarinen, J. and Vaelimaeki, I. (eds.), Children and sport: paediatric work physiology, Berlin, Springer-Verlag, 1984, p. 196-200.
ABST: This study examined competitive cross-country skiing among 8 to 12 year old children. The authors investigated the quantity and quality of training among children, parents' participation in the training, parents' attitudes towards their children's

interest in competitive skiing and anxiety in children caused by competition.
LEVEL: A LANG: Eng SIRC ARTICLE NO: 103448

COUNTRIES AND REGIONS

Cogbill, T. Zdrastvuitye: going cross country in the USSR. *Powder (Dana Points, Calif.) 12(5), Jan 1984, 46-50.*
LEVEL: B LANG: Eng SIRC ARTICLE NO: 093738

EQUIPMENT

Goldsworthy, D. Testing with the Telemark Kids. *Powder (San Juan Capistrano, Calif.) 13(1), Fall 1984, 114-119.*
LEVEL: B LANG: Eng SIRC ARTICLE NO: 098943

Kerasote, T. Telemark skis: the most versatile metal edges you can take to the slopes. *Outside (Chicago, Ill.) 9(11), Dec 1984, 91-94.*
LEVEL: B LANG: Eng SIRC ARTICLE NO: 108747

Poles: technology hits the trail. *Outdoor Canada 12(1), Dec/Jan 1984, 49-51;53.*
LEVEL: B LANG: Eng SIRC ARTICLE NO: 090912

Reynolds, J. Skiing with a pack. *Powder (Dana Points, Calif.) 12(5), Jan 1984, 64.*
LEVEL: B LANG: Eng SIRC ARTICLE NO: 093747

Saint-Hilaire, A. Cross-country skis: starting on the right foot. *Protect yourself (Montreal) Nov 1984, 37-43.*
LEVEL: B LANG: Eng SIRC ARTICLE NO: 103445

Ski de fond: nouveautes, ameliorations et perfectionnements. *Ski Quebec (Montreal) 10(2), nov 1984, 67-68;70-71;74.*
LEVEL: LANG: Fr SIRC ARTICLE NO: 179529

Turville, D. A soft snow primer: skis for the backcountry. *Powder (Dana Points, Calif.) 12(5), Jan 1984, 67-70.*
LEVEL: B LANG: Eng SIRC ARTICLE NO: 093750

Wiltsie, G. Packing it in. *Powder (Dana Points, Calif.) 12(5), Jan 1984, 59-63.*
LEVEL: B LANG: Eng SIRC ARTICLE NO: 09375

Woodward, B. Skiing in your living room. Would you trade in your skis for a bunch of pulleys and flywheels? Never. Good thin that's not what Nordic exercisers are for. *Backpacker (Los Angeles) 12(6), Nov 1984, 24-25.*
LEVEL: B LANG: Eng SIRC ARTICLE NO: 104882

EQUIPMENT - MAINTENANCE

Chase, A. Cross-country skiing: the hows of wax. In, Schrier, E.W. and Allman, W.F. (eds.), Newton at the bat: the science in sports, New York, Scribner, c1984, p. 76-78.
LEVEL: B LANG: Eng RC1235 18609

Stetson, E. What about grooming your cross-country skis? *Ski racing (Poultney, Vt.) 17(70, Dec 1984, 19.*
LEVEL: B LANG: E SIRC ARTICLE NO: 103447

EQUIPMENT - RETAILING

Report on cross country skiing: consumers move up-market. *Sports trade Canada (Downsview, Ont.) 12(2), Apr 1984, 14-15.*
LEVEL: B LANG: Eng SIRC ARTICLE NO: 103444

FACILITIES - DESIGN, CONSTRUCTION AND PLANNING

Wiesel, J. X-country connection: implementation of federal regulations. *Ski area management (North Salem, N.Y.) 23(1), Jan 1984, 42-43.*
LEVEL: B LANG: Eng SIRC ARTICLE NO: 096824

FACILITIES - MAINTENANCE

Buchen, R.T. Hilperts, J. For courses with snow: tracks without tears. *Golf course management (Lawrence, Kans.) 52(12), Dec 1984, 20-22;26.*
LEVEL: B LANG: Eng SIRC ARTICLE NO: 106047

INJURIES AND ACCIDENTS

Demenois, Y. La traumatologie du ski de fond. *Generaliste (Paris) 615, 1984, 20-21.*
LEVEL: B LANG: Fr

Hannoun, M. Que risque le skieur de fond? *Pratique medicale: le journal (Paris) 92, 1984, 1-2.*
LEVEL: B LANG: Fr

La securite en ski de randonnee: dossier Alpirando pratique. *Alpirando (Paris) 71, 1984, 41-48.*
LEVEL: I LANG: Fr

Mathieu, M. Baehrel, M. Le ski de fond: sport a risques. *Generaliste (Paris) 625, 1984, 57-68.*
LEVEL: B LANG: Fr

Mathieu, R. Le sauvetage des victimes d'avalanche. 1re partie: les moyens techniques. (Refs: 11)*Montagne & alpinisme (Paris 137, 1984, 456-461.*
LEVEL: B LANG: Fr SIRC ARTICLE NO: 099918

PHYSICAL FITNESS

Bigard, A.X. Surveillance de skieurs de fond par un test de recuperation cardiaque: le test de Chanon. (Refs: 9)*Medecine du sport 58(1), 25 janv 1984, 33-36.*
RESUME: Le but de cette etude etait d'appliquer un test de recuperation cardiaque, le test de Chanon, au ski de fond. Onze skieurs ont ete suivis. L'auteur souligne la simplicite du test et son utilite pour la conduite de l'entrainement.
LEVEL: A LANG: Fr SIRC ARTICLE NO: 092382

Lie, H. Erikssen, J. Five-year follow-up of ECG aberrations, latent coronary heart disease and cardiopulmonary fitness in various age groups of Norwegian cross-country skiers. *Acta medica scandinavica (Stockholm) 216(4), 1984, 377-383.*
LEVEL: I LANG: Eng

PHYSIOLOGY

Conconi, F. Borsetto, C. D'Incal, D. Droghetti, P. Ferrari, M. Paolini, A. Ziglio, P.G. Le seuil anaerobie en ski de fond. *Macolin (Macolin, Suisse) 41(11), nov 1984, 4-9.*
NOTES: Tire de, Rivista di cultura sportiva 2(1), 1983. Traduction de, Fabio Gilardi.
LEVEL: I LANG: Fr SIRC ARTICLE NO: 108753

Karlsson, J. Profiles of cross-country and alpine skiers. (Refs: 30)*Clinics in sports medicine (Philadelphia) 3(1), Jan 1984, 245-271.*
NOTES: Symposium on profiling.
ABST: The profile of cross-country skiers shows an emphasis on endurance; whereas, the alpine profile shows an emphasis on leg muscle strength. The skiing profile can determine the potential for injury

which can be partly prevented by training programs.
LEVEL: A LANG: Eng SIRC ARTICLE NO: 093694

Milner, E.G. The influence of conditioned reflex sleep on the heart cycle after heavy loads in ski racers. *Soviet sports review (Escondido, Calif.) 19(1), Mar 1984, 18-19.*
NOTES: Translated from, Teoriya i praktika fizicheskoi kultury 3, 1980, 21.
LEVEL: I LANG: Eng SIRC ARTICLE NO: 095245

Schmid, P. Gleispach, H. Wolf, W. Pessenhofer, H. Schwaberger, G. Influence sur la performance et modifications du metabolisme au cours d'un effort physique de longue duree sous l'action de l'aspartate d'arginine. (Refs: 51)*Cinesiologie (Paris) 96, juil/aout 1984, 329-337.*
RESUME: Les auteurs etudient l'action de l'aspartate d'arginine (Sargenor) sur l'effort physique de 10 skieurs de fond (age 23 + - 3 ans). Une etude en double aveugle est aussi realisee aupres de 24 skieurs de fond (age 34 + - 4 ans). Les modifications biologiques metaboliques (glucose, lactate, creatinine, uree, acide urique) et hormonales (insuline et hormone somatotrope) sont analysees avant, pendant et apres une course de ski de fond, et ce, avant et apres traitement par Sargenor. Une amelioration significative (9,59%) de l'endurance est observee apres traitement chez le groupe des 10 skieurs.
LEVEL: A LANG: Fr SIRC ARTICLE NO: 099919

Zuliani, U. Novarini, A. Bonetti, A. Astorri, E. Montani, G. Simoni, I. Zappavigna, A. Endocrine modifications caused by sport activity: effect in leisure-time cross-country skiers. (Refs: 38)*Journal of sports medicine and physical fitness (Torino, Italy) 24(3), Sept 1984, 263-269.*
ABST: A number of hormonal measurements were studied in a group of so-called leisure-time sportsmen before, during and after severe psycho-physical exertion ('24 ore di Pinzolo, Trento, Italy' - a cross-country skiing relay race). However strenuous and stressful, the effort appeared to induce no significant changes in the circadian rhythms of plasma cortisol, GH and insulin in the subjects observed.
LEVEL: A LANG: Eng SIRC ARTICLE NO: 106049

PSYCHOLOGY

Lie, H. Erikssen, G. Psycho-social behavior of long-time active Norwegian male cross-country competition skiers. (Refs: 37) *Scandinavian journal of sports science (Helsinki, Finland) 6(1), Jul 1984, 27-30.*
ABST: The present study examines some psychosocial aspects in a group of middle-aged and elderly Norwegian cross-country competition skiers, compared to the adult Norwegian male population. In a cross-sectional study 117 skiers out of 122 (95.9%) took part in 1981 in a five year follow-up study of latent coronary heart disease. In addition to the test program dealing with coronary heart disease, a detailed verbal pre-arranged questionnaire on some selected aspects of psycho-social behavior was added. Out of 112 marriages there were five divorces. The mean annual absence from work was 17.9% in the upper social classes and 13.1% in the lower social classes, of the registered absence from work in the adult Norwegian male population. The study indicates that long-time active training subjects may demonstrate psycho-social behavior above the mean of the population.
LEVEL: A LANG: Eng SIRC ARTICLE NO: 103443

SPORTING EVENTS

Stott, G. Recipe for winter fun. Join the king of cross-country races. *Canadian living 9(2), Feb 1984, 01-03;05-06.*
LEVEL B LANG: Eng SIRC ARTICLE NO: 090914

STATISTICS AND RECORDS - PARTICIPATION

Echelberger, H. Monitor's measure: cross-country business was erratic according to reports received by the Industry Monitor. *Ski area management (North Salem, N.Y.) 23(1), Jan 1984, 26-28;30;70;73-74.*
LEVEL: I LANG: Eng SIRC ARTICLE NO: 096821

Echelberger, H.E. Skier visits up: final report shows increases nationally. *Ski area management (North Salem, N.Y.) 23(4), Jul 1984, 28-30.*
LEVEL: B LANG: Eng SIRC ARTICLE NO: 099917

TEACHING

Adams, S. Nature appreciation and the ski tour leader. (Refs: 4)*Tour leader (Ottawa, Ont.) 4(1), 1984, 14-19.*
LEVEL: I LANG: Eng SIRC ARTICLE NO: 098483

Le ski de fond: les activites physiques de pleine nature a l'ecole elementaire. (Paris): Revue EPS, (1984). 55 p. : ill. (Essa de reponses.)
CORP: France. Education nationale.
NOTES: Bibliographie.
LEVEL: B LANG: Fr ISBN: 2-86713-006-9

Nelson, J.E. Teaching cross-country skiing. (Refs: 3)*Journal of physical education, recreation & dance 55(3), Mar 1984, 58-64.*
LEVEL: B LANG: Eng SIRC ARTICLE NO: 093744

TECHNIQUES AND SKILLS

English, B. Total telemarking. Crested Butte, Colo.: East River Pub. Co., c1984. 120 p. : ill.
NOTES: Bibliography: p. 118-119.
LEVEL: B LANG: Eng ISBN: 0-915789-00-0 LC CARD: 83-083417 GV854.9.T44 18904

Shelton, P. Natural techniques: the three keys to superior skiing. *Outside (Chicago, Ill.) 9(11), Dec 1984, 50-52.*
LEVEL: LANG: Eng SIRC ARTICLE NO: 108745

Slade, A. How to ski telemark. Vancouver: Special Interest Publications, c1984. 30 p. : ill. (B.C. outdoors discovery series v.4.)
LEVEL: B LANG: Eng ISBN: 0-88896-150-2 LC CARD: C84-91538-1 GV855.3 18987

TESTING AND EVALUATION

Saar, P. Scheier, A. Testing of elite cross country skiers. s.l.: Cross Country Canada, 1984. iii, 98 p. : ill.
NOTES: Bibliography: p. (87).
LEVEL: A LANG: Eng RC1220.S5 18387

Wolfe, J.E. Anthropometric, physiologic, and psychological measures to predict performance in cross-country skiing. (Refs: 1
NOTES: In, Cantu, R.C. (ed.), Clinical sports medicine, Lexington, Mass. ; Toronto, Collamore Press : D.C. Heath, c1984, p. 15-23.
LEVEL: A LANG: Eng RC1201 15964

TRAINING AND CONDITIONING

NordicTrack: the inside track on cross-country skiing. *Executive fitness newsletter 15(2), 21 Jan 1984, 4.*
LEVEL: B LANG: E SIRC ARTICLE NO: 090906

Sharkey, B.J. Training for cross-country ski racing: a physiological guide for athletes and coaches. Champaign, Ill.: Human Kinetics Publishers, c1984. x, 210 p. : ill. (U.S. Ski Team sports medicine series.)
NOTES: Bibliography: p. 206-210.
LEVEL: I LANG: Eng ISBN: 0-931250-46-3 LC CARD: 83-082292 GV855.R33 17443

TRAINING AND CONDITIONING - DRYLAND TRAINING

Terraz, C. Macadam'ski pour preparer votre saison d'hiver. *Ski magazine (Neuilly, Cedex) 65, nov 1984, 103-107.*
LEVEL: B LANG: Fr SIRC ARTICLE NO: 173517

VARIATIONS

Shimek, S. The telemark trend: this cross-breed alpine/nordic skier may be a new lucrative profit center. *Ski area management (New York) 23(2), Mar 1984, 60;78.*
LEVEL: B LANG: Eng SIRC ARTICLE NO: 098486

Woodward, B. Topheavy touring. A simple guide to skiing with a pack on your back. *Backpacker (Los Angeles) 12(6), Nov 1984, 36;38-39;43.*
LEVEL: B LANG: Eng SIRC ARTICLE NO: 104881

CUBA

Moya Vasquez, L.F. Solutions for physical education in developing countries: the Cuban experience. *Bulletin of the Federation internationale d'education physique (Cheltenham, Eng.) 54(2), Apr/Jun 1984, 19-27.*
LEVEL: B LANG: Eng SIRC ARTICLE NO: 102686

CURLING

Howe, R. Ryan, J. So this is curling. (Bemidji, Minn.): (Howe, R.), c1984. ix, 123 p. : ill.
NOTES: Bibliography: p. 116-11
LEVEL: B LANG: Eng GV845 19091

ADMINISTRATION

Thompson, K. The OCR takes you behind the broom skirmish: Hexagon grounds Air Canada. *Ontario curling report (Toronto, Ont. 11(1), Nov 1984, 1;4.*
LEVEL: B LANG: Eng SIRC ARTICLE NO: 103077

BIOGRAPHY AND AUTOBIOGRAPHY

Gibson, A. Soldier, keeper and England captain. (R.T. Stanyforth) *Cricketer international (Kent, Eng.) 65(5), May 1984, 31.*
LEVEL: B LANG: Eng SIRC ARTICLE NO: 094922

Normandale, B. Cecil Parkin and the Rochdale affair. *Cricketer international (Kent, Eng.) 65(5), May 1984, 57-58.*
LEVEL: LANG: Eng SIRC ARTICLE NO: 094928

O'Malley, M. The life of Riley. In a curling-mad city in a curling-mad province, Mike Riley - the 1984 Canadian men's champion - is a star. *Saturday night (Toronto) 99(11), Nov 1984, 61-62;64.* LEVEL: B LANG: Eng SIRC ARTICLE NO: 104619

Ward, J. Ed Werenich: Canadian and world curling champion. *Sports people (Toronto) 4(1), Jan 1984, 7.* LEVEL: B LANG: Eng SIRC ARTICLE NO: 097992

FACILITIES

Dury, P.L.K. Look at the base, not the surface. *Cricketer international (Kent, Eng.) 65(5), May 1984, 53;55.* LEVEL: B LANG: Eng SIRC ARTICLE NO: 094919

HISTORY

Weather ruled oldtime curling: the curling history corner. *North American curling news (Portage, Wis.) 41(1), Nov 1984, 12;15.* LEVEL: B LANG: Eng SIRC ARTICLE NO: 101160

RULES AND REGULATIONS

Burky, P. Les cousins d'Olympe. The cousins of Olympe. *Message olympique/Olympic message (Lausanne) 7, juin/Jun 1984, 67-72.* LEVEL: B LANG: Fr Eng SIRC ARTICLE NO: 104618

SPORTING EVENTS

Browning, R. Duguid, D. Championship curling 1984. Montreal: CBC Enterprises, c1984. 128 p. : ill. LEVEL: B LANG: Eng ISBN: 0-88794-140-0 GV845 18374

Cricket - the Pennie way: David Shimwell ends his cricketing journey along the Pennie Way at Preston... *Cricketer international (Kent, Eng.) 65(5), May 1984, 32-33.* LEVEL: B LANG: Eng SIRC ARTICLE NO: 094918

STRATEGY

Blanking can point to zero gain. *North American curling news (Portage, Wis.) 41(1), Nov 1984, 8-9;11.* LEVEL: B LANG: Eng SIRC ARTICLE NO: 101159

Strategy tips. *North American curling news (Portage, Wis.) 40(5), Apr 1984, 16.* LEVEL: B LANG: Eng SIRC ARTICLE NO: 097991

CYCLING

Grove, D. Basics of bicycle racing. *Ohio runner (Columbus, Oh.) 6(1), Jul 1984, 8.* LEVEL: B LANG: Eng SIRC ARTICLE NO: 101171

Messenger, C. Our struggle with a sporting conscience. *Cycling (Sussex, Eng.) 4842, 16 Jun 1984, 28.* NOTES: Four-part series. LEVEL: B LANG: Eng SIRC ARTICLE NO: 098023

ADMINISTRATION

Blanchard, L. La veloution de Quebec: extraits de la constitution de Velo Quebec. *CAAW&S newsletter 3(1), Winter 1984, 11.* LEVEL: B LANG: Fr

AERODYNAMICS

Brown, G. Spoke drag. *Bike tech (Emmaus, Penn.) 3(4), Aug 1984, 4-5.* LEVEL: I LANG: Eng SIRC ARTICLE NO: 105746

Kyle, C.R. Burke, E. Improving the racing bicycle. (Refs: 7)*Mechanical engineering (New York) 106(9), 1984, 34-45.* ABST: This paper details studies performed over two years on the U.S. National Cycling team leading up to the 1984 Olympics. Over 600 wind tunnel experiments were conducted to evaluate the influence of body position, drafting locations, types of uniforms and helmets, tire size and pressure, and numerous bicycle design features. The main focus was on reducing drag without increasing the weight of the material. This paper contains the results of these experiments and their implications for practice. LEVEL: A LANG: Eng SIRC ARTICLE NO: 105758

Malewicki, D.J. Aerodynamics: who will win the DuPont prize? Drag vs. Power at 65 Mi/hr. (Refs: 15)*Bike tech (Emmaus, Pa.) 3(5), Oct 1984, 1-8.* ABST: This article looks at the factors to consider in making an attempt to win the $15,000 DuPont prize for reaching 65 m.p.h. in a single human powered vehicle. Factors include training, air drag, rolling resistance, road selection, wind, altitude, and temperature. LEVEL: I LANG: Eng SIRC ARTICLE NO: 103108

Spina, M. Changements d'air. *Miroir du cyclisme (Paris) 360, oct/nov 1984, 10-13.* LEVEL: B LANG: Fr SIRC ARTICLE NO: 1031

AGED

Wollein, W. Bachl, N. Prokop, L. Endurance capacity of trained older aged athletes. (Refs: 15)*European heart journal (Londo 5(Suppl E), Nov 1984, 21-25.* LEVEL: A LANG: Eng SIRC ARTICLE NO: 109717

ASSOCIATIONS

Syssoev, V. Cycling and Olympism. *Olympic review (Lausanne) 201/202, Jul/Aug 1984, 531-566.* LEVEL: B LANG: Eng SIRC ARTICLE NO: 096605

Syssoev, V. Le cyclisme et l'olympisme. *Revue olympique (Lausanne) 201/202, juil/aout 1984, 531-566.* LEVEL: B LANG: Fr SIRC ARTICLE NO: 104655

AUDIO VISUAL MATERIAL

Matlack, F. Get the picture: using video to train. *Bicycling (Emmaus, Pa.) 25(8), Sept/Oct 1984, 48;50.* LEVEL: B LANG: En SIRC ARTICLE NO: 099486

BIOGRAPHY AND AUTOBIOGRAPHY

Long, B. Oppy at eighty: Bill Long looks at the life and times of Australia's greatest cyclist - Sir Hubert Opperman. *Freewheeling (Sydney, Aust.) 27, Sept 1984, 33-36.* LEVEL: B LANG: Eng SIRC ARTICLE NO: 109351

BIOMECHANICS

Costantino, T. The complete athlete: the human component of the technical race. *Bicycling 25(2), Mar 1984, 34-38.* LEVEL: LANG: Eng SIRC ARTICLE NO: 091988

CLOTHING

DeCosta, T. Radical chic: designs for the future. *Bicycling 25(2), Mar 1984, 50-52;54.* LEVEL: B LANG: Eng SIRC ARTICLE NO 091992

Ingram, M. Women's cycling apparel. *Bicycle dealer showcase (Irvine, Calif.) 13(2), Feb 1984, 28;30-34.* LEVEL: B LANG: En SIRC ARTICLE NO: 098950

COUNTRIES AND REGIONS

Gordis, K.K. Loustalot, G. Le cyclisme americain. Enquete: le meilleur coureur du monde est americain. Il s'appelle Greg Le Mond. Celebre en Europe, il est pratiquement inconnu dans son pays. *Miroir du cyclisme (Paris) 349, avr 1984, 62-68.* LEVEL: B LANG: Fr SIRC ARTICLE NO: 098011

Smith, K. 1936 Canadian Olympic Team. *Bicycle Ontario (Willowdale, Ont.) 7(4), Sept 1984, 19.* LEVEL: B LANG: Eng SIRC ARTICLE NO: 099506

White, R. Professionalism - the way forward. *International cycle sport (Keighley, Eng.) 198, Nov 1984, 14-15.* LEVEL: B LANG: Eng SIRC ARTICLE NO: 104657

DRUGS, DOPING AND ERGOGENIC AIDS

Delbeke, F.T. Debackere, M. Caffeine: use and abuse in sports. (Refs: 21)*International journal of sports medicine (Stuttgart) 5(4), Aug 1984, 179-182.* ABST: The urinary caffeine content was compared between a control group and 775 cyclists checked for doping during the 1982 season. The data for sportsmen demonstrate that the (mis)use of caffeine is more pronounced in both professional and amateur classes than in the younger categories (debutant and junior). Caffeine was also monitored during a 60-h period in the urine of several coffee drinkers. Based on all results, a 'maximum level of caffeine' of 15 ug.ml-1 in urine for sporting competitions is proposed. LEVEL: A LANG: Eng SIRC ARTICLE NO: 103889

McCullagh, J.C. The caffeine controversy: what you need to succeed. *Bicycling (Emmaus, Pa.) 25(8), Sept/Oct 1984, 56-59.* LEVEL: B LANG: Eng SIRC ARTICLE NO: 098926

Porte, G. Le dopage des cyclistes professionels: une realite. *Generaliste (Paris) 659, 1984, 21-22.* LEVEL: B LANG: Fr

Safra, J.M. Vous avez dit dopage? *Nouvelle revue de medecine de Toulouse (France) 2(6), 1984, 302-309.* LEVEL: I LANG: Fr

ECONOMICS

BMX clubs or teams? The benefits and the aggravations. *American bicyclist and motorcyclist (New York) 105(2), Feb 1984, 95-97;126.*
LEVEL: B LANG: Eng SIRC ARTICLE NO: 097999

Ritter, A. Sponsorship growing with athlete participation. *Sport style (New York) 6(19), 22 Oct 1984, 80.*
LEVEL: B LANG: Eng SIRC ARTICLE NO: 099501

EQUIPMENT

Anderson, I. Technological warfare on the cycle track. *New scientist (London) 1415, 2 Aug 1984, 30-31.*
NOTES: The Americans plan to make a killing in the Olympics with their new aerodynamic bikes, helmets, shoes and clothing.
LEVEL: I LANG: Eng SIRC ARTICLE NO: 099450

Burlace, M. Salomon, W. Did technology win olympic gold for the Americans? *Freewheeling (Sydney, Aust.) 27, Sept 1984, 19;21.*
LEVEL: B LANG: Eng SIRC ARTICLE NO: 109348

Costantino, T. More for your money: five sport tourers prove that more is more. *Bicycling 25(3), Apr 1984, 116-124;127-128.*
LEVEL: B LANG: Eng SIRC ARTICLE NO: 093349

DeCosta, T. Radical chic: designs for the future. *Bicycling 25(2), Mar 1984, 50-52;54.*
LEVEL: B LANG: Eng SIRC ARTICLE NO 091992

Emilian, M. Steel frame tubing. *Bicycle guide (Redondo Beach, Calif.) 1(1), Autumn 1984, 83-88.*
LEVEL: I LANG: Eng SIRC ARTICLE NO: 178854

Jow, R. All about aero. Part I: equipment and effects. *Bicycling 25(1), Jan/Feb 1984, 96-98.*
LEVEL: B LANG: Eng SIRC ARTICLE NO: 090557

Kita, J. The dream machines: an affordable reality. *Bicycling (Emmaus, Pa.) 25(9), Nov/Dec 1984, 122-133.*
LEVEL: B LANG: Eng SIRC ARTICLE NO: 101177

Koch, C. The technical edge: what we're taking to the Olympics. *Bicycling 25(2), Mar 1984, 42-45;55.*
LEVEL: B LANG: Eng SIRC ARTICLE NO: 092010

Krygowski, F. Anodized rim stiffness: bending vs. compression vs. spray paint. (letter) *Bike tech (Emmaus, Pa.) 3(5), Oct 1984, 15.*
LEVEL: I LANG: Eng SIRC ARTICLE NO: 103104

Matheny, F. New tricks: high-tech equipment breaks old habits. *Bicycling (Emmaus, Pa.) 25(6), Jul 1984, 72-74.*
LEVEL: B LANG: Eng SIRC ARTICLE NO: 096596

Olympic wheels: some called the new look in racing cycles 'funny bikes'... but they stopped laughing when the results came in. Disk wheels were the most striking innovation. Here are the secrets of their construction. *American bicyclist and motorcyclist (New York) 105(9), Sept 1984, 33-34.*
LEVEL: B LANG: Eng SIRC ARTICLE NO: 103111

Racing bikes anyone can afford: for another month's rent, you can buy a competitive machine. *Bicycling (Emmaus, Pa.) 25(7), Aug 1984, 50-56;58-62;158-160;162.*
LEVEL: B LANG: Eng SIRC ARTICLE NO: 099499

Schubert, J. Bike flight: framebuilder Mike Melton makes them go faster. *Bicycling 25(2), Mar 1984,* 39-42.
LEVEL: B LANG: Eng SIRC ARTICLE NO: 092018

Sherman, P. Sizing up your cycle. *Triathlon (Santa Monica, Calif.) 2(3), Jun/Jul 1984, 23.*
LEVEL: B LANG: Eng SIRC ARTICL NO: 101190

Snowling, S. Choose the right wheels for the job. *Cycling (Essex, Eng.) 4832, 7 Apr 1984, 26-28.*
LEVEL: B LANG: Eng SIRC ARTICLE NO: 099507

Soens, B. Bike test: the Peugeot avance. *International cycle sport (West Yorkshire, Eng.) 191, Apr 1984, 25-26.*
LEVEL: B LANG: Eng SIRC ARTICLE NO: 093373

Soens, B. Bike test: Coventry Eagle 'Kermesse'. *International cycle sport (West Yorkshire, Eng.) 190, Mar 1984, 21-22.*
LEVEL: B LANG: Eng SIRC ARTICLE NO: 095818

Soens, B. Bike test: Dave Lloyds's 1984 road bike. *International cycle sport (West Yorkshire, Eng.) 189, Feb 1984, 15-17.*
LEVEL: B LANG: Eng SIRC ARTICLE NO: 095819

Soens, B. Bike test: Harry Hall Elan 600. *International cycle sport (West Yorkshire, Eng.) 188, Jan 1984, 20-21.*
LEVEL: B LANG: Eng SIRC ARTICLE NO: 095820

Soens, B. Bike test: Frontiera competition. *International cycle sport (West Yorkshire, Eng.) 194, Jul 1984, 20-21.*
LEVEL: B LANG: Eng SIRC ARTICLE NO: 099508

Soens, B. Bike test: Dawes Imperial. *International cycle sport (West Yorkshire, Eng.) 197, Oct 1984, 9-10.*
LEVEL: B LANG: Eng SIRC ARTICLE NO: 103117

Soens, B. Bike test: OLMO 'Super Gentleman'. *International cycle sport (West Yorkshire, Eng.) 195, Aug 1984, 9-11.*
LEVEL: B LANG: Eng SIRC ARTICLE NO: 103118

Soens, B. Bike test: Peugeot Professional. *International cycle sport (Keighley, Eng.) 198, Nov 1984, 24-25.*
LEVEL: B LANG Eng SIRC ARTICLE NO: 104654

Spokesman No. 1 sports. *Freewheeling (Haymarket, N.S.W.) 23, Jan/Feb 1984, 57-58.*
LEVEL: B LANG: Eng SIRC ARTICLE NO: 09950

Sunderland, T.A. Champion's saddles: a look at what sits well with America's Olympic cyclists. *American bicyclist and motorcyclist (New York) 105(11), Nov 1984, 25-26.*
LEVEL: B LANG: Eng SIRC ARTICLE NO: 107143

EQUIPMENT - MAINTENANCE

Delorme, D. Velo. *Marathon, la revue de la bonne forme (Montreal) 15, avr 1984, 27;29.*
LEVEL: B LANG: Fr SIRC ARTICLE NO: 108697

Prehn, T. The trials of an Olympic team mechanic; hard work and good judgement are critical. (Steve Bishop) *Bicycling (Emmaus, Pa.) 25(7), Aug 1984, 96-97;99;102.*
LEVEL: B LANG: Eng SIRC ARTICLE NO: 099497

EQUIPMENT - RETAILING

Is the BMX market changing? Has it peaked? *American bicyclist and motorcyclist (New York) 105(3), Mar 1984, 50;52-53.*
LEVEL: B LANG: Eng SIRC ARTICLE NO: 098018

HISTORY

Maynard, D.N. The divergent evolution of competitive cycling in the United States and Europe: a materialist perspective. (Refs: 27)
NOTES: In, Sutton-Smith, B. and Kelly-Byrne, D. (eds.), The masks of play, New York, Leisure Press, c1984, p. 78-87.
LEVEL: I LANG: Eng HQ782 17029

INJURIES AND ACCIDENTS

Apple, D. Heal thyself: at-home treatment for injuries. *Bicycling (Emmaus, Pa.) 25(9), Nov/Dec 1984, 34-37.*
LEVEL: B LANG Eng SIRC ARTICLE NO: 100672

Borysewicz, E. How to treat and recover from crash injuries. *Velo-news (Brattleboro, Ver.) 13(18), 14 Dec 1984, 12-13.*
LEVEL: B LANG: Eng SIRC ARTICLE NO: 103081

Kesting, C. Off the saddle. (chondromalacia patella and tendinitis) *Freewheeling (Haymarket, N.S.W.) 23, Jan/Feb 1984, 53.*
LEVEL: B LANG: Eng SIRC ARTICLE NO: 099478

Kranzley, G. Treating olympic injuries. *Bicycling (Emmaus, Pa.) 25(4), May 1984, 35-36;39-41.*
LEVEL: B LANG: Eng SIRC ARTICLE NO: 094946

Newman, J.A. Letting safety go to your head. *Bicycles today (Flemington, N.J.) 6(5), Jul 1984, 6;18.*
NOTES: Reprinted from, the May issue of Kart-tech.
LEVEL: B LANG: Eng SIRC ARTICLE NO: 099491

MEDICINE

Monti, M. Jaeger, M. Guisan, Y. Payot, M. Mazzoni, S. Diagnostic de l'insuffisance arterielle peripherique chez le sportif amateur claudicant et depistage du 'syndrome de la stenose arterielle iliaque isolee chez le jeune cycliste sans facteur de risque' par examen Doppler et test sur tapis roulant. (Refs: 19)*Revue medicale de la Suisse romande (Lausanne) 104(10), oct1984, 823-830.*
RESUME: Cette etude rapporte les resultats d'un examen cardio-angiologique pratique chez 11 cyclistes professionels et quatre sportifs amateurs souffrant de claudication intermittente. Quatre cas de sportifs insuffisants arteriels (dont 2 jeunes cyclistes) opere (1 cas) ou dilates (3 cas) pour insuffisance arterielle consecutive a une stenose iliaque furent observes. Des anomalies electrocardiographiques furent enregistrees chez les professionels: 7 ont un bloc de branche droit et 7 presentent des signes electrocardiographiques d'hypertrophie ventriculaire gauche; 3 ont un bi-bloc cardiaque et 1 presente un QT allonge.
LEVEL: A LANG: Fr SIRC ARTICLE NO: 174102

Virot, P. Cheipe, A. Blanc, P. Doumeix, J.J. Delhoume, B. Tardieu, A. Chassain, A.P. Surveillance medico-sportive de cyclistes par l'ECG et les tests dynamiques. (Refs: 14)*Mises a jour cardiologiques (Nantes) 13(4), 1984, 137-144.*
LEVEL: I LANG: Fr

NUTRITION

de Mondenard, J.P. L'eau du Tour de France. (Refs: 5)*Science et vie (Paris) HS147, 1984, 110-118.*
LEVEL: I LANG: Fr

CYCLING (continued)

Kail, K. Food for touring. You are what you eat. *Bicycling (Emmaus, Pa.) 25(6), Jul 1984, 60;62.* LEVEL: B LANG: Eng SIRC ARTICLE NO: 096590

McCullagh, J.C. The lowdown on carbo-loading: how to use food for fuel. *Bicycling (Emmaus, Pa.) 25(8), Sept/Oct 1984, 54-55;144.* LEVEL: B LANG: Eng SIRC ARTICLE NO: 099126

Perry, P. Jump start: getting out of the blocks with good nutrition. *Bicycling (Emmaus, Pa.) 25(9), Nov/Dec 1984, 28-32.* LEVEL: I LANG: Eng SIRC ARTICLE NO: 101183

Reiser, R. Comments on plasma lipid response of cyclists to diet lipids. (letter) *American journal of clinical nutrition (Bethesda, Md.) 40(2), Aug 1984, 360-361.* LEVEL: I LANG: Eng SIRC ARTICLE NO: 104649

OFFICIATING

Hansen, J. Cycling: overview. There's a lot more to officiating cycling than meets the eye. Even becoming certified takes some real doing. *Referee (Franksville, Wis.) 9(7), Jul 1984, 56-58.* LEVEL: B LANG: Eng SIRC ARTICLE NO: 101172

PHYSIOLOGY

Anjuere, J. Collin, J.P. Pillet, J. Etude comparative, sur trois mois, de 8 intervalles de temps systoliques, chez les sportifs. Proposition d'un 'indice de forme cardiaque' fiable. (Refs: 16)*Medecine du sport (Paris) 58(6), nov 1984, 22-25.* LEVEL: I LANG: Fr SIRC ARTICLE NO: 103079

Boysen, R.L. Finding your own 'optimum aerobic cadence'. *Bike tech (Emmaus, Pa.) 3(5), Oct 1984, 10-13.* LEVEL: I LANG: En SIRC ARTICLE NO: 103082

Boysen, R.L. Hammaker, A. High-cadence data questioned. (letter) *Bike tech (Emmaus, Pa.) 3(5), Oct 1984, 13-15.* LEVEL: I LANG: Eng SIRC ARTICLE NO: 103083

Dawson, B. Pyke, F. The effects of heat stress on anaerobic threshold. (Refs: 28)*Australian journal of science & medicine i sport (Kingston, Aust.) 16(1), Jun 1984, 3-9.* ABST: This study examined the possibility of the anaerobic threshold (AT) being decreased during prolonged constant load exercise in hot conditions and the effect of training status on any such observed decrement. Nine trained cyclists of State-Level ability and nine active men with no significant cycling experience performed a maximal capacity bicycle ergometer test during which VO2 max, aerobic threshold (AerT) and AT were all found to be significantly greater in the trained group. In both a controlled hot and cool environment, the subjects then performed a constant load bicycle ergometer exercise test for 30 minutes. There were no significant differences in oxygen uptake between the hot and cool climates in either group. LEVEL: A LANG: Eng SIRC ARTICLE NO: 104632

Faria, I.E. Applied physiology of cycling. (Refs: 76)*Sports medicine (Auckland, N.Z.) 1(3), May/Jun 1984, 187-204.* ABST: The purpose of this review is to discuss research related to cycling and in so doing bridge the gap between the exercise scientist and the practitioner. The author discusses the physiology of cycling from an exercise physiologist's viewpoint in order to make valuable suggestions concerning the training of cyclists. Methods of injury prevention are briefly discussed. These methods include the mechanical set-up of the bike, proper selection of gears, and protecting the head and lungs. LEVEL: A LANG: Eng SIRC ARTICLE NO: 096583

Hoppeler, H. Lindstedt, S. Quality in your training: a revolution in endurance. That marvelous machine, part II. *Bicycling 25(3), Apr 1984, 40-41;43-44;46.* LEVEL: I LANG: Eng SIRC ARTICLE NO: 093356

Katz, A. Sharp, Armstrong, L.E. King, D.S. Oxygen tension in antecubital blood of trained and untrained males after maximal leg exercise. (Refs: 18)*Canadian journal of applied sport sciences/ Journal canadien des sciences appliquees au sport 9(1), Mar 1984, 11-15.* ABST: Six untrained (UT) and six endurance trained cyclists (ET) males performed graded leg ergometer exercise to exhaustion. The values for oxygen tension (pO2) and percent oxygen saturation (SO2) at rest and at exhaustion were not significantly different between the two groups. During recovery the ET subjects demonstrated significantly higher pO2 and SO2 levels than UT subjects at each post-exercise measurement period. The authors suggest that ET athletes have a greater arterialization of the antecubital venous blood during recovery from maximal leg exercise than that of UT subjects. LEVEL: A LANG: Eng SIRC ARTICLE NO: 093361

Kuenstlinger, U. Ludwig, H.-G. Stegemann, J. Force kinetics and oxygen consumption during bicycle ergometer work in racing cyclists and reference-group. (Refs: 9)*International journal of sports medicine (Stuttgart) Suppl. 5, Nov 1984, 118-119.* CONF: International Congress on Sports and Health (1983 : Maastricht, Netherlands). LEVEL: A LANG: Eng SIRC ARTICLE NO: 104639

Martin, W.H. Coyle, E.F. Joyner, M. Santeusanio, D. Ehsani, A.A. Holloszy, J.O. Effects of stopping exercise training on epinephrine-induced lipolysis in humans. (Refs: 28)*Journal of applied physiology: respiratory, environmental and exercise physiology 56(4), Apr 1984, 845-848.* ABST: Six highly trained male athletes stopped exercise training for two months. Four days after the cessation of training there was a significantly smaller increase in serum free fatty acids and blood glycerol and a greater rise in blood lactate in response to a constant infusion of epinephrine. These parameters did not exhibit further change in the two months study period. The authors suggest that epinephrine-induced lipolysis is enhanced in endurance-exercise-trained individuals but that this adaptation is lost very rapidly after cessation of exercise training. LEVEL: A LANG: Eng SIRC ARTICLE NO: 096983

Pilardeau, P.A. Garnier, M. Fischer, F. Desbleds, M. Vaysse, J. Lesenechal, M. Margo, J.N. Origin of the increase in H.D.L. cholesterol on sportsmen. (Refs: 28)*Journal of sports medicine and physical fitness (Torino, Italy) 24(4), Dec 1984, 311-314.* ABST: In this study, the authors suggest two experiments on a group of 10 trained cyclists after giving the present facts in specialised works dealing with the increase in H.D.L.c on trained sportsmen. This work puts into light a significant increase of circulating V.L.D.L. and triglycerides at the beginning of the exercise. Using the arguments mispelled by Schefer on the regulation of the synthesis of H.D.L.c they try to explain the two most frequent variations usually noticed in trained sportsmen: an increase in H.D.L.c and a decrease in triglycerides. They give the hypothesis that the repeated increase in triglycerides during heavy exercises could provoke the increase in the synthesis of H.D.L.c and a decrease in the synthesis of V.L.D.L. after several weeks. LEVEL: A LANG: Eng SIRC ARTICLE NO: 106803

Veicsteinas, A. Samaja, M. Gussoni, M. Cerretelli, P. Blood O2 affinity and maximal O2 consumption in elite bicycle racers. (Refs: 31)*Journal of applied physiology: respiratory, environmental and exercise physiology (Bethesda, Md.) 57(1), Jul 1984, 52-58.* ABST: The following values were determined in eleven elite cyclists in pre-season, competitive season and off-season: the P02 at which hemoglobin is half-saturated with 02 (P50) at 37C, PC02 equal 42 Torr, measured pH and 2,3-diphosphoglycerate-to-hemoglobin concentration ratio, Hill's coefficient at rest, and maximal oxygen consumption (V02 max). The 02 equilibrium curve was hardly effected by training (OEC), so that the increase in V02 max cannot be explained with adaptive changes in the OEC. Furthermore, V02 max predicted according to computer simulation does not rise significantly as a consequence of the measured rise in 2,3-DPG. LEVEL: A LANG: Eng SIRC ARTICLE NO: 108363

Vrielink, H.H.E.O. Vissers, A.C.A. Binkhorst, R.A. Oxygen consumption and speed of cycling using an air-resistance simulator on a hometrainer roller. (Refs: 9)*International journal of sports medicine (Stuttgart, FRG) 5(2), Apr 1984, 98-101.* ABST: Oxygen consumption was determined for subjects cycling on a hometrainer roller with a racing bicycle. In part of the experiments the bicycle was supplied with an air-resistance simulator. The relation between oxygen consumption and velocity of cycling on the roller is linear: similar to that during bicycle ergometry. The relation is almost the same as during bicycling outdoors on a touring bicycle when the simulator is used while cycling on the roller. Cycling with the simulator only on the bicycle on a support is comparable to cycling outdoors on a racing bicycle. It is concluded that the use of a roller and an air-resistance simulator can be used for ergometry and training. LEVEL: A LANG: Eng SIRC ARTICLE NO: 108525

White, J.A. Ward, C. Nelson, H. Ergogenic demands of a 24 hour cycling event. (Refs: 22)*British journal of sports medicine (Loughborough, Eng.) 18(3), Sept 1984, 165-171.* ABST: The maximal aerobic performance (VO2 max) and energy costs of cycling at various power outputs and equivalent road speeds of a highly trained endurance cyclist (age 23.4 yrs), were measured in the laboratory on an eddy-current cycle ergometer, and the physiological responses related to determinations made during a 24 h cycling time trial event. The cyclist covered a distance of 694 km during the event at an average speed of 28.9 km.h-1 which corresponded to an equivalent oxygen cost of 38.5 ml.kg-1 min-1 and represented approximately 55% of his VO2 max. During the event, the cyclist expended an estimated 82,680 kJ of energy, of which approximately 44,278 kJ (54%) were supplied by repeated feedings of liquids, solids and semi-solids and some 38,402 kJ (46%) came from the stored energy reserves which resulted in a 1.19 kg loss of body weight during the event. LEVEL: A LANG: Eng SIRC ARTICLE NO: 103123

PHYSIOLOGY - MUSCLE

Lindstedt, S. That marvellous machine: what you need to know about muscles. *Bicycling 25(1), Jan/Feb 1984, 28;31.*
LEVEL: LANG: Eng SIRC ARTICLE NO: 090265

PROTECTIVE DEVICES

DeCrosta, T. Making headway: a new helmet to cheat the wind. *Bicycling 25(2), Mar 1984, 46-47;49.*
LEVEL: B LANG: Eng SIRC ARTICLE NO: 091993

Newman, J.A. Letting safety go to your head. *Bicycles today (Flemington, N.J.) 6(5), Jul 1984, 6;18.*
NOTES: Reprinted from, the May issue of Kart-tech.
LEVEL: B LANG: Eng SIRC ARTICLE NO: 099491

PSYCHOLOGY

deVoss, G. Giving up guilt: how to break that vicious cycle. *Bicycling 25(1), Jan/Feb 1984, 38-39.*
LEVEL: B LANG: Eng SIR ARTICLE NO: 090551

deVoss, G. After the crash: how to take a break from cycling. *Bicycling (Emmaus, Pa.) 25(4), May 1984, 58-59.*
LEVEL: B LANG: Eng SIRC ARTICLE NO: 094938

deVoss, G. Every person a winner: beating the cycling blahs. *Bicycling (Emmaus, Pa.) 25(6), Jul 1984, 54;56;58.*
LEVEL: B LANG: Eng SIRC ARTICLE NO: 096576

Koch, C. The pressure to perform. One Olympian's solution to the problem. *Bicycling (Emmaus, Pa.) 25(6), Jul 1984, 75-76;78;80.*
LEVEL: B LANG: Eng SIRC ARTICLE NO: 096591

PSYCHOLOGY - MENTAL TRAINING

de Voss, G. Coping with pain: how to overcome it. *Bicycling 25(3), Apr 1984, 64-66.*
LEVEL: B LANG: Eng SIRC ARTICLE NO: 093350

SOCIOLOGY

Albert, E. Equipment as a feature of social control in the sport of bicycle racing. (Refs: 11)
CONF: North American Society for the Sociology of Sport. Conference (3rd : 1982 : Toronto, Ont.).
NOTES: In, Theberge, N. and Donnelly, P. (eds.), Sport and the sociological imagination: refereed proceedings of the 3rd Annual Conference of the North American Society for the Sociology of Sport, Toronto, Canada, November 1982, Fort Worth, Tex., Texas Christian University Press, c1984, p. 318-333.
ABST: This paper examines the relationship of bike racers to their bicycle. Three specific areas are explored: the manner in which the equipment provides a rider with a means for claiming acceptance into the sport; the relationship of the bicycle to the competitor's perception of the sport; and a discussion on the role of equipment in maintaining an elitist cast in North American cycling.
LEVEL: A LANG: Eng SIRC ARTICLE NO: 097994

SPORTING EVENTS

Bernhardt, L. Atkinson, L. Davies, J. Robinson, M. 'Let us speak of famous men': the 1932 Canadian Olympic Team. *Bicycling news Canada (West Vancouver, B.C.) 24(5), Summer 1984, 20-22.*
LEVEL: B LANG: Eng SIRC ARTICLE NO: 097997

Bonura, L.S. Cycling at the 1896 Olympics. *Bicycle USA (Baltimore, Md.) 20(6), Jun 1984, 7.*
LEVEL: B LANG: Eng SIRC ARTICLE NO: 099456

Donovan, D. The two Olympic medals we didn't bother to mention. *Cycling (Sussex, Eng.) 4847, 21 Jul 1984, 18-19.*
LEVEL: B LANG: Eng SIRC ARTICLE NO: 098005

Le cyclisme et l'olympisme. *Revue olympique (Lausanne) 201/202, juil/aout 1984, 531-566.*
LEVEL: B LANG: Fr SIRC ARTICLE NO: 102134

Syssoev, V. Cycling and Olympism. *Olympic review (Lausanne) 201/202, Jul/Aug 1984, 531-566.*
LEVEL: B LANG: Eng SIRC ARTICLE NO: 096605

Syssoev, V. Le cyclisme et l'olympique. *Revue olympique (Lausanne) 201/202, juil/aout 1984, 531-566.*
LEVEL: B LANG: Fr SIRC ARTICLE NO: 104655

TESTING AND EVALUATION

Ennis, P. The test Conconi. *Velo-news (Brattleboro, Vt.) 13(18), 14 Dec 1984, 4-6.*
LEVEL: I LANG: Eng SIRC ARTICLE NO: 103095

Loosen up. Part 1: the flexibility standards of the elite athlete program. *Bicycling (Emmaus, Pa.) 25(5), Jun 1984, 38-41.*
LEVEL: B LANG: Eng SIRC ARTICLE NO: 096592

TRAINING AND CONDITIONING

Betmanis, J. Winter training: building your own racermate. *Bicycle Ontario (Willowdale) 7(1), Feb 1984, 20.*
LEVEL: B LANG Eng SIRC ARTICLE NO: 097998

Gilchrist, R. Training methods: the pre-junior cyclist. *Coaching review 7, Mar/Apr 1984, 50-51.*
LEVEL: B LANG: Eng SIRC ARTICLE NO: 093355

Hochart, G. Roussel, A. Tusseau, G. Cyclisme moderne. Les secrets d'un entrainement methodique. Paris: Chiron, 1984. 135 p. ill.
LEVEL: B LANG: Fr

Kruse, B. Speedwork and play: for racers and tourists. *Bicycling (Emmaus, Pa.) 25(7), Aug 1984, 44-47;153;156-157.*
LEVEL: LANG: Eng SIRC ARTICLE NO: 099481

Matheny, F. Surviving a slump: how to feel good about training...again. *Bicycling 25(3), Apr 1984, 68;71-73.*
LEVEL: B LANG: Eng SIRC ARTICLE NO: 093365

Matheny, F. Secrets for the Soviets: lessons for 1988. *Bicycling (Emmaus, Pa.) 25(6), Jul 1984, 64-66.*
LEVEL: B LANG: Eng SIRC ARTICLE NO: 096594

Matheny, F. The empire emerges. America develops the strongest cyclists ever. *Bicycling (Emmaus, Pa.) 25(6), Jul 1984, 67-71.*
LEVEL: B LANG: Eng SIRC ARTICLE NO: 096595

Schubert, J. Learning from a group: a true story about Bicycling's riding technique school. *Bicycling 25(3), Apr 1984, 54;57-58.*
LEVEL: B LANG: Eng SIRC ARTICLE NO: 093370

Singleton, G. A coach of your own: tips on keeping a training diary. *Bicycling 25(1), Jan/Feb 1984, 32-33;35-36.*
LEVEL: B LANG: Eng SIRC ARTICLE NO: 090563

Stultz, J. Basic training: how to make a beginner into an enthusiast. *Bicycling 25(3), Apr 1984, 56.*
LEVEL: B LANG: Eng SIRC ARTICLE NO: 093374

TRAINING AND CONDITIONING - STRETCHING AND FLEXIBILITY EXERCISES

Bracken, S. Stretching. *Bicycle Ontario (Willowdale, Ont.) 7(5), Nov 1984, 15-17.*
LEVEL: B LANG: Eng SIRC ARTICLE NO: 104625

Loosen up. Part II: extending range of motion. *Bicycling (Emmaus, Pa.) 25(6), Jul 1984, 50-53.*
LEVEL: B LANG: Eng SIRC ARTICLE NO: 096593

TRAINING AND CONDITIONING - WARM-UPS, WARM-DOWNS, LEAD-UP GAMES

Prehn, T, A good warm-up: one key to win. *Bicycling (Emmaus, Pa.) 25(5), Jun 1984, 22;25.*
LEVEL: B LANG: Eng SIRC ARTICLE NO: 096599

TRAINING AND CONDITIONING - WEIGHT AND STRENGTH TRAINING

DeCrosta, T. In praise of weight training: how to build strength and endurance this winter. *Bicycling 25(1), Jan/Feb 1984, 24-27.*
LEVEL: B LANG: Eng SIRC ARTICLE NO: 090549

DeCrosta, T. Getting started: your own circuit training program. *Bicycling 25(1), Jan/Feb 1984, 27.*
LEVEL: B LANG: Eng SIRC ARTICLE NO: 090550

VARIATIONS

Brown, G. Directions for HPV drag reduction *Bike tech (Emmaus, Pa.) 3(1), Feb 1984, 14-15.*
LEVEL: B LANG: Eng SIRC ARTICL NO: 094935

Healy, T. New technology from Indianapolis. *Bike tech (Emmaus, Pa.) 3(1), Feb 1984, 9-12.*
LEVEL: B LANG: Eng SIRC ARTICLE NO: 094942

CYCLING - ROAD RACING

Prehn, T. A varied menu: there are many kinds of races - the choice is yours. *Bicycling 25(2), Mar 1984, 24;27.*
LEVEL: B LANG: Eng SIRC ARTICLE NO: 092016

Prehn, T. Getting to the starting line. *Bicycling (Emmaus, Pa.) 25(4), May 1984, 30;32.*
LEVEL: B LANG: Eng SIRC ARTICLE NO: 094953

Stuller, J. Beyond tough: it's time to end the bickering. What's really the hardest, sickest ultra-endurance event of them all? *Outside 9(1), Jan/Feb 1984, 39-43;76-77.*
LEVEL: B LANG: Eng SIRC ARTICLE NO: 093237

CYCLING - ROAD RACING (continued)

BIOGRAPHY AND AUTOBIOGRAPHY

Blumenthal, T. The Twigg technique; it's all in the pedals. *Bicycling (Emmaus, Pa.)* 25(7), Aug 1984, 48-49.
LEVEL: B LANG: Eng SIRC ARTICLE NO: 099454

Carpenter, C. Phinney, D. Life on the road: a week in our racing lives. *Bicycling (Emmaus, Pa.)* 25(5), Jun 1984, 66;68;70-72;74.
LEVEL: B LANG: Eng SIRC ARTICLE NO: 096569

Ciccodicola, A. L'enigmatique vicomte. Le Vicomte Jean de Gribaldy est une enigme. On le dit matois, comedien, faussaire, genereux, createur, fin spychologue. Avec Kelly, il collectionne les plus belles victoires. Nous avons voulu percer le mystere de cette etonnante personalite. *Miroir du cyclisme (Paris)* 351, mai 1984, 16-19.
LEVEL: B LANG: Fr SIRC ARTICLE NO: 103085

Cyclisme: Karen Strong Hearth. Cycling: Karen Strong Hearth. *Champion (Ottawa)* 8(3), Aug 1984, 50-51.
LEVEL: B LANG: Fr Eng SIRC ARTICLE NO: 096575

Driver, W.E. Gerrit Schulte: the pedalling fool? *International cycle sport (West Yorkshire, Eng.)* 199, Dec 1984, 19-23.
LEVEL: B LANG: Eng SIRC ARTICLE NO: 108992

Lindstrom, C. The women to watch. Cooperation is the key to a U.S. Gold Medal. *Bicycling* 25(3), Apr 1984, 75-77;79;82-83.
LEVEL: B LANG: Eng SIRC ARTICLE NO: 093364

Ottum, B. Climbing clear up to the heights: Greg LeMond, a Huck Finn with steel tights, is the first American to pedal his way to the top ranks of European bike racing royalty. *Sports illustrated (Chicago)* 61(11), 3 Sept 1984, 50-54;56-60;62-64.
LEVEL: B LANG: Eng SIRC ARTICLE NO: 098026

Weck, L. Reluctant hero. Connie Carpenter is everybody's favorite to romp in cycling's first-ever Olympic women's road race. *Ultrasport (Boston, Mass.)* 1(3), May/Jun 1984, 20-25.
LEVEL: B LANG: Eng SIRC ARTICLE NO: 096611

White, R. Coventry ladies - the record breakers. *International cycle sport (West Yorkshire, Eng.)* 199, Dec 1984, 24-25.
LEVEL: B LANG: Eng SIRC ARTICLE NO: 108993

Yerkey, G. Greg LeMond, Superstar: this American was the pro rider of the year for '83. *Bicycling* 25(2), Mar 1984, 101-102;104-105.
LEVEL: B LANG: Eng SIRC ARTICLE NO: 092026

EQUIPMENT

Berto, F. Rear derailleurs for racing: the country's leading expert on gearing tests 37 models. *Bicycling* 25(2), Mar 1984, 160-161;165;167;170-172;178.
LEVEL: B LANG: Eng SIRC ARTICLE NO: 091975

FACILITIES

Jacobs, C. The making of an Olympic road course. Mission: challenging the world's best. *Bicycling (Emmaus, Pa.)* 25(5), Jun 1984, 106;108.
LEVEL: B LANG: Eng SIRC ARTICLE NO: 096588

HISTORY

1949 la revolution Coppi. *Miroir du cyclisme (Paris)* 349, avr 1984, 58-61.
LEVEL: B LANG: Fr SIRC ARTICLE NO: 097993

1955 Louison Bobet plus fort que la douleur. *Miroir du cyclisme (Paris)* 351, mai 1984, 50-53.
LEVEL: B LANG: Fr SIRC ARTICL NO: 103078

MEDICINE

Bourdon, A. Potiron-Josse, M. Megret, A. Paruit-Portes, M.C. Ginet, J.D. Atypies de la repolarisation a propos de l'ECG quotidien de 10 coureurs pendant le Tour de France 1982. (Refs: 29)*Mises a jour cardiologiques (Nantes)* 13(4), 1984, 145-154.
LEVEL: A LANG: Fr

Vega, A. Tour de France 1984: le coeur a l'epreuve. *Impact medecin (Puteaux, France)* 108, 1984, 31-34.
LEVEL: B LANG: Fr

NUTRITION

Blumenthal, T. Beverage of champions: a key factor to victory in Los Angeles. *Bicycling (Emmaus. Pa.)* 25(5), Jun 1984, 42-44;47-48;52-54.
LEVEL: B LANG: Eng SIRC ARTICLE NO: 096567

White, J.A. Ford, M.A. The carbohydrate maintenance properties of an experimental sports drink. (Refs: 23)*British journal o sports medicine (Loughborough, Eng.)* 18(2), Jun 1984, 64-69.
ABST: The effects of an experimental sports drink (Q) were compared with a commercial sports drink (D) of proven ergogenic efficacy. Seven highly trained subjects performed two hours of cycle ergometry exercise at approximately 65% maximal aerobic power (VO2 max) while receiving levels of Q and D in quantities designed to supply approximately 28% of the total energy requirement of the exercise task. Q was equally as effective as D in terms of the maintenance of plasma glucose concentrations during exercise, while selected physiological indices of work performance favoured Q. However, the time course of plasma glucose concentration changes during and after exercise indicated a trend towards more rapid uptake and assimilation of carbohydrate in the case of Q. The findings suggest that Q may provide a more readily available carbohydrate source during exercise and may enhance work performance through its ergogenic properties.
LEVEL: A LANG: Eng SIRC ARTICLE NO: 103122

PHYSIOLOGY

Boening, D. Goenen, Y. Maassen, N. Relationship between work load, pedal frequency, and physical fitness. (Refs: 23) *International journal of sports medicine (Stuttgart, FRG)* 5(2), Apr 1984, 92-97.
ABST: The aim of this investigation was to study how the known dependence of working efficiency on pedaling frequency is influenced by the work load as well as by physical fitness. Oxygen uptake, CO2 output, ventilation, heart rate, and lactate concentration in capillary blood from the ear-lobe were determined at varying combinations of work loads and pedaling rates in road-racing cyclists and medical students. Respiratory exchange ratio, consumption of energy, gross efficiency, net efficiency, and delta efficiency were calculated. All parameters showed a nonlinear dependence on pedaling frequency. The lowest oxygen uptake and the highest efficiency shifted to higher frequencies with increasing work load. Delta efficiency increased with rising pedaling frequency. Differences of VO2 and efficiencies between trained and untrained subjects were only small. Most effects can be explained by variations in leg movement frequency and recruitment of muscle fibers. There is evidence that racing cyclists chose pedaling rates yielding optimal efficiency at any load.
LEVEL: A LANG: Eng SIRC ARTICLE NO: 108524

Garrigues, M. Navarro, J.L. Riviere, D. Interet des tests de laboratoire dans le controle de l'entrainement des cyclistes de haut-niveau. *Medecine du sport (Paris)* 58(5), 25 sept 1984, 3-5.
RESUME: Les auteurs ont teste l'aptitude et la condition physique des cyclistes de l'equipe colombienne du Tour de France 1983. La consommation maximale d'oxygene, le taux des lactates: sanguins, la consommation d'oxygene, la concentration en hemoglobine et la frequence cardiaque des athletes sont mesures. L'equipe est en excellente condition physique. Une tres bonne correlation existe entre les resultats des tests et les performances sur le Tour de France.
LEVEL: A LANG: Fr SIRC ARTICLE NO: 101170

SPORTING EVENTS

1947 Jean Robic fait battre les coeurs. *Miroir du cyclisme (Paris)* 355, juil 1984, 14-17.
LEVEL: B LANG: Fr SIRC ARTICLE NO 104620

American classic: it began as a regional event - a bicycle festival sponsored by an herbal team company. It quickly became the premier American bike race. In 1984, only its tenth year, it is a race of international renown, attracting the best in the world, rivaling the Olympics in depth and drama. *Ultrasport (Boston)* 1(4), Jul/Aug 1984, 34-39.
LEVEL: B LANG: Eng SIRC ARTICLE NO: 097995

Prehn, T. A decade to be proud of: the Red Zinger/Coors Classic. *Bicycling (Emmaus, Pa.)* 25(4), May 1984, 75-76.
LEVEL: B LANG: Eng SIRC ARTICLE NO: 094952

STRATEGY

Breaking away. Think a slipstream is what you'd find in the mountains of Colorado? That a mass start is when church begins? Here's help. *Health magazine (New York)* 16(2), Feb 1984, 28;30.
LEVEL: B LANG: Eng SIRC ARTICLE NO: 098001

Prehn, T. Strategy: the right moment to attack. *Bicycling (Emmaus, Pa.)* 25(6), Jul 1984, 32;34;36.
LEVEL: B LANG: Eng SIR ARTICLE NO: 096600

TECHNIQUES AND SKILLS

Genzling, C. Bernard Hinault: la bonne position. *Miroir du cyclisme (Paris)* 362, dec 1984, 16-18.
LEVEL: B LANG: Fr SIRC ARTICLE NO: 107103

Pavelka, E. Making it to the top; Giovanni Battaglin's hill-climbing techniques. *Bicycling (Emmaus, Pa.)* 25(8), Sept/Oct 1984, 52-53;60-61.
LEVEL: B LANG: Eng SIRC ARTICLE NO: 099495

TESTING AND EVALUATION

Malhotra, M.S. Verma, S.K. Gupta, R.K. Khanna, G.L. Physiological basis for selection of competitive road cyclists. (Refs: 1 *Journal of sports medicine and physical fitness (Torino) 24(1), Mar 1984, 49-57.*
ABST: 14 Indian road cyclists were tested to correlate their physiological parameters with their performance in 84km road races. There was significant correlation between performance and VO2 max and EVCO2 max. A regression equation was computed for predicting road racing performance on the basis of these two variables.
LEVEL: A LANG: Eng SIRC ARTICLE NO: 099485

TRAINING AND CONDITIONING

Eastman, S. Training for Los Angeles. Three Olympic prospects describe their workouts. *Bicycling (Emmaus, Pa.) 25(5). Jun 1984, 56;58;62;64.*
LEVEL: B LANG: Eng SIRC ARTICLE NO: 096582

McKinney, B. Life in the next century: learning the discipline of the double. *Bicycling 25(3), Apr 1984, 48-49;51;53.*
LEVEL: B LANG: Eng SIRC ARTICLE NO: 093366

CYCLING - TRACK RACING

Prehn, T. A varied menu: there are many kinds of races - the choice is yours. *Bicycling 25(2), Mar 1984, 24;27.*
LEVEL: B LANG: Eng SIRC ARTICLE NO: 092016

BIOGRAPHY AND AUTOBIOGRAPHY

Chauner, D. The infernal grind: among the most famous athletes of an era that included Babe Ruth and Jack Dempsey were six-day bike racers - tough pros who made their fortunes grinding out laps in smoke-filled arenas. *Ultrasport (Boston, Mass.) 1(5), Sept/Oct 1984, 57-59;61-63.*
LEVEL: B LANG: Eng SIRC ARTICLE NO: 173304

EQUIPMENT

Berto, F. Rear derailleurs for racing: the country's leading expert on gearing tests 37 models. *Bicycling 25(2), Mar 1984, 160-161;165;167;170-172;178.*
LEVEL: B LANG: Eng SIRC ARTICLE NO: 091975

FACILITIES

Brunel, P. Paris sur scene. (Vel'd'Hiv') *Equipe magazine (Paris) 180, 4 fevr 1984, 32-41;57.*
LEVEL: B LANG: Fr SIRC ARTICLE NO: 099460

FACILITIES - DESIGN, CONSTRUCTION AND PLANNING

Wittwer, E. Sportstaetten Beleuchtung: Offene Radrennbahn Zuerich Oerlikon im fernsehgerechten Licht. (Stadium illumination: Zuerich-Oerlikon bicycle course in TV suitable light.) *Licht (Munich) 36(4), Jun 1984, 288-291.*
LEVEL: I LANG: Ger

HISTORY

Nicolini, M. Record de l'heure: de Desgranges a Moser. *Miroir du cyclisme (Paris) 347, fevr 1984, 38-41.*
LEVEL: B LANG: F SIRC ARTICLE NO: 099492

STATISTICS AND RECORDS

His finest hour. Many had considered cycling's hour record unbreakable. No rider had even approached it in the past twelve years. Then, on an innovative, controversial machine, Francesco Moser broke it - twice in one week. *Ultrasport (Boston, Mass.) 1(3), May/Jun 1984, 53-55.*
LEVEL: B LANG: Eng SIRC ARTICLE NO: 096587

Sanders, W. The longest hour. *Ultrasport (San Diego, Calif.) 1(1), Jan/Feb 1984, 47-51.*
LEVEL: B LANG: Eng SIRC ARTICLE NO: 094954

Schneider, S. Duniecq, J. Henderson, N. Magnificent Moser massacres Merckx. *International cycle sport (West Yorkshire, Eng. 189, Feb 1984, 19-24.*
LEVEL: B LANG: Eng SIRC ARTICLE NO: 096603

TRAINING AND CONDITIONING

Eastman, S. Training for Los Angeles. Three Olympic prospects describe their workouts. *Bicycling (Emmaus, Pa.) 25(5). Jun 1984, 56;58;62;64.*
LEVEL: B LANG: Eng SIRC ARTICLE NO: 096582

Prehn, T. Spin is in: learning your way around cadence. *Bicycling 25(3), Apr 1984, 60-61;63-65.*
LEVEL: B LANG: Eng SIRC ARTICLE NO: 093369

CYCLO-CROSS AND BICYCLE MOTO-CROSS

Fisher, M. Le 'bicross', nouveaute americaine a la conquete de la Suisse. *Macolin (Suisse) 4, avr 1984, 2-3.*
LEVEL: B LANG: Fr SIRC ARTICLE NO: 101169

Ruffell, A. Evans, K. BMX from start to finish. London: A & C Black, c1984. 125 p. : ill.
LEVEL: B LANG: Eng ISBN: 0-7136-2471-X GV1049.3 20821

Thomsen, S. Hadley, B. Stu Thomsen's book of BMX: the world champ's tips on racing, freestyling, equipment, conditioning and more. Chicago, Ill.: Contemporary Books, c1984. 104 p. : ill.
NOTES: Includes index. Bibliography: p. 100.
LEVEL: B LANG: Eng ISBN: 0809254492 LC CARD: 84-005869 GV1049.3 18093

CLOTHING

Jarvis, W. BMX jersey's and leathers. *Bicycle dealer showcase (Irvine, Calif.) 16(5), May 1984, 14;16-23.*
LEVEL: B LANG: Eng SIRC ARTICLE NO: 100557

EQUIPMENT

Cuerdon, D. Cyclocross equipment: you can spend $45 or go for state of the art. *Velo-news (Brattleboro, Vt.) 13(18), 14 Dec 1984, 8-9.*
LEVEL: B LANG: Eng SIRC ARTICLE NO: 103087

Kundig, C. BMX saddles & posts: an update on what's hot in the motocross marketplace. *American bicyclist and motorcyclist (New York) 105(11), Nov 1984, 21-22;26.*
LEVEL: B LANG: Eng SIRC ARTICLE NO: 107124

Making it happen. A California frame building firm has some unique approaches to BMX and freestyle bicycles. *American bicyclist and motorcyclist (New York) 105(10), Oct 1984, 25-27.*
LEVEL: B LANG: Eng SIRC ARTICLE NO: 107128

EQUIPMENT - RETAILING

Jarvis, W. Freestyle leading edge in motocross? A new dimension in the BMX market. *Bicycle dealer showcase (Irvine, Calif.) 13(9), Sept 1984, 7;11-12;14.*
LEVEL: B LANG: Eng SIRC ARTICLE NO: 108433

Lyte, S. BMX spotlight on industry: getting the business holeshot. *Bicycle dealer showcase (Irvine, Calif.) 13(6), Jun 1984 68-71.*
LEVEL: B LANG: Eng SIRC ARTICLE NO: 101181

FACILITIES - DESIGN, CONSTRUCTION AND PLANNING

Dreusche, D.V. BMX - Eine neue Radsportsparte benoetigt eigene Anlagen. *Sportstaettenbau und Baederanlagen (Cologne, W. Germany) 18(6), Nov/Dec 1984, 313-314;316-318.*
LEVEL: B LANG: Ger SIRC ARTICLE NO: 173528

Gornall, A. Wright, N. Gateshead BMX is 'Dyno-Ryno'. *Ilam: Institute of leisure & amenity management (London) 2(1), Jan 1984, 15;18-19.*
LEVEL: B LANG: Eng SIRC ARTICLE NO: 098012

Postle, F. BMX moto-cross starting gate. *Design (Arlington, Va.) Spring 1984, 3-12.*
LEVEL: I LANG: Eng SIRC ARTICLE NO: 102096

INJURIES AND ACCIDENTS

Adlam, D.M. Mandibular condyle fractures and the BMX bicycle. (letter) *British dental journal (London) 156(12), 23 Jun 1984 430.*
LEVEL: B LANG: Eng SIRC ARTICLE NO: 104621

BMX bike injuries. (letter) *British medical journal (Clinical Research Ed.) (London) 289(6453), 3 Nov 1984, 1226-1227.*
LEVEL: I LANG: Eng

Illingworth, C.M. Injuries to children riding BMX bikes. *British medical journal (Clinical Research ed.) (London) 289(6450) 13 Oct 1984, 956-957.*
LEVEL: A LANG: Eng

Soysa, S.M. Grover, M.L. McDonald, P.J. BMX bike injuries: the latest epidemic. *British medical journal (Clinical Research ed.) (London) 289(6450), 13 Oct 1984, 960-961.*
LEVEL: A LANG: Eng

PROTECTIVE DEVICES

McNamura, D. Mouthguard or full face: which is better? *Bicycle today (Flemington, N.J.) 6(11), Nov 1984, 8.*
LEVEL: B LANG Eng SIRC ARTICLE NO: 108788

CZECHOSLOVAKIA

Kostkova, J. Koerpererziehung der Frauen in der CSSR. (The physical education of women in the CSSR.) *ICSSPE/CIEPSS review (Berlin, GDR) 7, 1984, 61-65.*
LEVEL: I LANG: Ger SIRC ARTICLE NO: 095658

DANCE

Middleton, C. Spreading wings: a dance centre business that's taking off. *Sport and leisure (London) 25(2), May/Jun 1984, 26-27.*
LEVEL: B LANG: Eng SIRC ARTICLE NO: 104666

Yetman, W. Aerobics: sport of the '80s. *Canadian runner (Toronto) Sept/Oct 1984, 19-23.*
LEVEL: B LANG: Eng SIRC ARTICLE NO: 099527

ADMINISTRATION

Solomon, R. Field notes on summer dance. *Journal of physical education, recreation & dance 55(1), Jan 1984, 56-59.*
LEVEL: LANG: Eng SIRC ARTICLE NO: 092034

ANTHROPOMETRY

Bogart, S.K. Nutrition status and body composition of female dancers. How lean can a woman's body be? (Refs: 2)*New Zealand journal of health, physical education & recreation (Wellington, N.Z.) 17(3), Nov 1984, 11-12.*
CONF: New Zealand Association of Health, Physical Education and Recreation. Conference (1984 : Wellington).
LEVEL: I LANG: Eng SIRC ARTICLE NO: 104659

BIBLIOGRAPHIES

Ruyter, N.C. Annual international bibliography of dance history: the Western tradition. Works published in 1978. Part II. *Dance research journal (New York) 16(1), Spring 1984, 41-49.*
LEVEL: B LANG: Eng SIRC ARTICLE NO: 103133

BIOMECHANICS

Laws, K. Swope, M. The physics of dance. New York: Schirmer Books, c1984. xv, 160 p. : ill.
LEVEL: I LANG: Eng ISBN: 0-02-872030-X LC CARD: 83-20462 RC1220.D35 18156

Laws, K. Dance kinesiology - difficulties and directions. (Refs: 6)*Kinesiology for dance (Carlisle, Pa.) 7(1), Oct 1984, 6-7.*
LEVEL: B LANG: Eng SIRC ARTICLE NO: 108794

Stephens, R. Biomechanics of dance and dance injuries. Chicago: Teach'em Inc., 1984?. 1 sound cassette : 36 35mm slides (Audio cassette series on sports medicine: New dance medicine programs, SM-46.)
NOTES: Cassettes recorded and produced by Teach'em Inc. in cooperation with the Physician and Sportsmedicine.
LEVEL: I LANG: Eng

CAREERS

Glazer, S. Performing opportunities in regional dance companies. *Journal of physical education, recreation & dance (Reston, Va.) 55(5), May/Jun 1984, 78-81.*
LEVEL: B LANG: Eng SIRC ARTICLE NO: 094958

Lappe, M.M. Dance careers for the next decade. (Refs: 3)*Journal of physical education, recreation & dance. (Reston Va.) 55(5), May/Jun 1984, 76-77.*
LEVEL: B LANG: Eng SIRC ARTICLE NO: 094960

Lee, S. Dance administrative opportunities. (Refs: 3)*Journal of physical education, recreation & dance (Reston Va.) 55(5), May/Jun 1984, 74-75;81.*
LEVEL: B LANG: Eng SIRC ARTICLE NO: 094961

Weeks, S. Dance careers in the 80s. *Journal of physical education, recreation & dance (Reston, Va.) 55(5), May/Jun 1984, 73.*
LEVEL: B LANG: Eng SIRC ARTICLE NO: 094967

CHILDREN

Lamouroux, N. Pesquie, S. Rencontres: 15 danses collectives. *EPS: Education physique et sport (Paris) 187, mai/juin 1984, 37-42.*
LEVEL: B LANG: Fr SIRC ARTICLE NO: 096621

Soren, B. Integrating dance with other arts. Integrer la danse aux autres arts. *CAHPER journal/ Revue de l'ACSEPR (Ottawa) 50(4), Mar/Apr 1984, 33-34.*
NOTES: Part of a series prepared by the Dance Committee of CAHPER. Provient de la serie preparee par le comite de la danse ACSEPR.
LEVEL: B LANG: Eng SIRC ARTICLE NO: 096633

CHOREOGRAPHY AND MUSIC

Hankin, T. Laban movement analysis in dance education. (Refs: 4)*Journal of physical education, recreation & dance (Reston, Va.) 55(9), Nov/Dec 1984, 65-66.*
LEVEL: B LANG: Eng SIRC ARTICLE NO: 103130

Ryman, R. Singh, B. Beatty, J.C. Booth, K.S. A computerized editor of Benesh movement notation. (Refs: 58)*Dance research journal (New York) 16(1), Spring 1984, 27-34.*
LEVEL: I LANG: Eng SIRC ARTICLE NO: 103134

COUNTRIES AND REGIONS

Sussmann, L. Anatomy of the dance company boom, 1958-1980. (United States) (Refs: 8)*Dance research journal (New York) 16(2) Fall 1984, 23-28.*
LEVEL: I LANG: Eng SIRC ARTICLE NO: 104669

DISABLED

Lagomarcino, A. Reid, D.H. Ivancic, M.T. Faw, G.D. Leisure dance instruction for severely and profoundly retarded persons - teaching an intermediate community living skill. (Refs: 18)*Journal of applied behavior analysis (Lawrence, Kan.) 17(1), 1984, 71-84.*
LEVEL: I LANG: Eng SIRC ARTICLE NO: 095864

Lagomarcino, A. Reid, D.H. Ivancic, M.T. Faw, G.D. Leisure-dance instruction for severely and profoundly retarded persons: teaching an intermediate community-living skill. (Refs: 18)*Journal of applied behavior analysis (Lawrence,*

Kan.) 17(1), Spring 1984, 71-84.
LEVEL: I LANG: Eng SIRC ARTICLE NO: 104663

Schneider, F.J. Die Auswirkungen einer Unterrichtseinheit 'Schoepferische Bewegung und Pantomime' und einer Unterrichtseinheit 'Badminton' auf die Gesamt-koerperkoordination aelterer legasthener Jungen. (Effects of classes in 'creative movement and pantomime' and 'badminton' on total-body coordination in older dyslexic boys.) *Rehabilitation (Stuttgart) 23(4), Nov 1984, 148-154.*
NOTES: English abstract.
LEVEL: A LANG: Ger

FACILITIES

Seals, J.G. Considerations of dance surfaces. Chicago: Teach'em Inc., 1984?. 1 sound cassette : 11 35mm slides (Audio cassette series on sports medicine: New dance medicine programs, SM-45.)
NOTES: Cassettes recorded and produced by Teach'em Inc. in cooperation with the Physician and Sportsmedicine.
LEVEL: I LANG: Eng

FACILITIES - DESIGN, CONSTRUCTION AND PLANNING

Fitness & fittings: everything you need to know about building a dance or health studio. *Sport and leisure (London) 25(2), May/Jun 1984, 36-37.*
LEVEL: B LANG: Eng SIRC ARTICLE NO: 103919

HISTORY

Forbes, J.M. Early American dance instruction. (Refs: 11)*Journal of physical education, recreation and dance (Reston, Va.) 55(7), Sept 1984, 34-36.*
LEVEL: B LANG: Eng SIRC ARTICLE NO: 101195

Lockman, E. The development of American contemporary dance. (Refs: 6)*Asian journal of physical education (Taipei, Taiwan) 7(3), Oct 1984, 45-54.*
LEVEL: B LANG: Eng Chi SIRC ARTICLE NO: 103132

Massicotte, J.P. Lessard, C. L'activite physique et le loisir en Nouvelle-France: la danse aux XVIIe et XVIIIe siecles. Dans, Massicotte, J.P. et Lessard, C. (eds.), *Histoire du sport de l'antiquite au XIXe siecle, Sillery, Que., Presses de l'Universite du Quebec, 1984, p. 255-262.*
LEVEL: A LANG: Fr GV571 18971

INJURIES AND ACCIDENTS

Fond, D. Flexor hallucis longus tendinitis - a case of mistaken identity and posterior impingement syndrome in dancers: evaluation and management. (Refs: 4)*Journal of orthopaedic and sports physical therapy (Baltimore) 5(4), Jan/Feb 1984, 204-206.*
ABST: This paper discusses the mechanisms of flexor hallucis longus tendinitis and posterior impingement syndrome in ballet dancers. A conservative treatment approach involves deep friction massage, ice application and range of motion exercises in the nonweightbearing position. If this treatment is unsuccessful, surgery may be indicated and a longer rehabilitation plan, which is described, may be consequently required.
LEVEL: I LANG: Eng SIRC ARTICLE NO: 093378

Howse, J. Injuries due to poor technique and their correction. Chicago: Teach'em Inc., 1984?. 2

sound cassettes : 38 35mm slides (Audio cassette series on sports medicine: New dance medicine programs, SM-43.)
NOTES: Cassettes recorded and produced by Teach'em Inc. in cooperation with the Physician and Sportsmedicine.
LEVEL: I LANG: Eng

Milhan, D. Rohan, J. Limitation of movement due to hip ligaments and implications for teaching exercise and dance. (Refs: 6) *Florida journal of health, physical education, recreation and dance (Gainsville, Fla.) 22(2), May 1984, 5-6.*
LEVEL: I LANG: Eng SIRC ARTICLE NO: 095946

Sammarco, G.J. Forefoot conditions in dancers. Chicago: Teach'em Inc., 1984?. 1 sound cassette : 31 35mm slides (Audio cassette series on sports medicine: New dance medicine programs, SM-44.)
NOTES: Cassettes recorded and produced by Teach'em Inc. in cooperation with the Physician and Sportsmedicine.
LEVEL: I LANG: Eng

MEDICINE

Garner, D.M. Maloney, M.J. The dancer and anorexia nervosa. Chicago: Teach'em Inc., 1984?. 1 sound cassette : 10 p. of print (Audio cassette series on sports medicine: New dance medicine programs, SM-42.)
NOTES: Cassettes recorded and produced by Teach'em Inc. in cooperation with the Physician and Sportsmedicine.
LEVEL: I LANG: Eng

NUTRITION

Novick, A. Mackey, K. The dancer's body: dieting and sound nutrition. (Refs: 2) *Kinesiology for dance (Carlisle, Pa.) 7(1), Oct 1984, 10.*
LEVEL: B LANG: Eng SIRC ARTICLE NO: 108798

PHYSICAL FITNESS

Moore, D. Search, G. Roper, D. The pineapple dance book: an insider's guide to all that's best in dance and exercise today. New York: Delilah Communications : Putnam Pub. Group, 1984, c1983. 157 p. : ill. (A Delilah book.)
NOTES: Includes bibliographies.
LEVEL: B LANG: Eng ISBN: 0933328923 LC CARD: 84-207624

PHYSIOLOGY

Cohen, A. Dance - aerobic and anaerobic. (Refs: 10) *Journal of physical education, recreation & dance 55(3), Mar 1984, 51-53.*
LEVEL: I LANG: Eng SIRC ARTICLE NO: 093377

Schantz, P.G. Astrand, P.-O. Physiological characteristics of classical ballet. (Refs: 7) *Medicine and science in sports and exercise (Indianapolis) 16(5), Oct 1984, 472-476.*
ABST: The aerobic and anaerobic energy yield during professional training sessions ('classes') of classical ballet as well as during rehearsed and performed ballets has been studied by means of oxygen uptake, heart rate, and blood lactate concentration determinations on professional ballet dancers. The measured oxygen uptake during six different normal classes at the theatre averaged about 35-45% of the maximal oxygen uptake, and the blood lactate concentration averaged 3 mM. During 10 different solo parts of choreographed

dance representative for moderately to very strenuous dance, an average oxygen uptake (measured during the last minute) of 80% of maximum and blood lactate concentration of 10 mM was measured. In addition, heart rate registrations from soloists in different ballets during performance and final rehearsals frequently indicated a high oxygen uptake relative to maximum and an average blood lactate concentration of 11 mM.
LEVEL: A LANG: Eng SIRC ARTICLE NO: 103135

PSYCHOLOGY

Gay, J.A. A catalog of dance teacher behaviors. (Refs: 16) *Journal of teaching in physical education (Blacksburg, Va.) 3(2), Winter 1984, 71-80.*
ABST: The goal for the use of this catalog is to better understand the dance teaching process. This catalog allows specific dance teacher behaviors to be objectively and precisely identified, recorded and subsequently analyzed.
LEVEL: A LANG: Eng SIRC ARTICLE NO: 093379

Gurley, V. Neuringer, A. Massee, J. Dance and sports compared: effects on psychological well-being. (Refs: 30) *Journal of sports medicine and physical fitness (Torino) 24(1), Mar 1984, 58-68.*
ABST: 133 college students in dance, sports and academic classes filled out a 20 scale semantic differential inventory before and after a 90 minute class. Dance and sports classes had decreased anxiety and depression compared to the academic. The dance class also produced more positive evaluations of psychological well-being than did the sports class.
LEVEL: A LANG: Eng SIRC ARTICLE NO: 099518

Smyth, M.M. Kinesthetic communication in dance. (Refs: 11) *Dance research journal (New York) 16(2), Fall 1984, 19-22.*
LEVEL: I LANG: Eng SIRC ARTICLE NO: 104668

Zakrajsek, D.B. Johnson, R.L. Walker, D.B. Comparison of learning styles between physical education and dance majors. (Refs: 6) *Perceptual and motor skills (Missoula, Mont.) 58(2), Apr 1984, 583-588.*
ABST: This paper investigates the learning styles of 80 dance and 87 physical education majors. Kolb's Learning Style Inventory, which assesses the level of abstractness or concreteness and the level of activity or reflectivity, was used in the assessment. Findings indicate no significant differences between the two majors or between female and male students.
LEVEL: A LANG: Eng SIRC ARTICLE NO: 094540

RELIGION

Hume, J.B. Dancing for God: a clarification of the distinguishing characteristics of Christian dance worship. Eugene, Ore.: Microform Publications, University of Oregon, 1984. 2 microfiches : negative ; 11 x 15 cm.
NOTES: Thesis (M.A.) - University of Oregon, 1982; (vii, 113 leaves); vita; includes bibliography.
LEVEL: A LANG: Eng UO84 132-133

Novak, E.G.M. A ceremony of carols: a program of liturgical dance. Eugene, Ore.: Microform Publications, University of Oregon, 1984. 1 microfiche : negative, ill. ; 11 x 15 cm.
NOTES: Thesis (M.S.) - Louisiana State University, 1982; (iv, 78 leaves); vita; includes bibliography.
LEVEL: A LANG: Eng UO84 205

TEACHING

Andrews, M. Strategies for dance education in a multicultural society. Strategies d'enseignement de la danse dans une societ multiculturelle. (Refs: 4) *CAHPER journal (Ottawa) 51(2), Nov/Dec 1984, 40-42.*
NOTES: Part of a series prepared by the Dance Committee of CAHPER. Ces conseils en administration proviennent de la serie preparee par le comite de danse de l'ACSEPL.
LEVEL: B LANG: Eng Fr SIRC ARTICLE NO: 103127

Gray, J.A. A conceptual framework for the study of dance teaching. (Refs: 20) *Quest (Champaign, Ill.) 36(2), 1984, 153-163.*
ABST: In order to understand and improve the dance teaching-learning process it is first necessary to design a conceptual framework which will contain and sequence the relevant elements. The framework presented here meets certain key criteria and provides the infrastructure for an instructional theory for dance. It is patterned on the Presage-Process-Product model, yet is sufficiently comprehensive to be applied to a variety of dance teaching settings. So long as the dance teaching role is critical to the evolution and preservation of dance in society, research based on this framework is needed to generate practical and theoretical pedagogical guidelines.
LEVEL: I LANG: Eng SIRC ARTICLE NO: 103129

Lord, M. La danse, une discipline scolaire motrice et artistique. (Refs: 11) *CAHPER journal/Revue de l'ACSEPR (Vanier, Ont.) 50(3), janv/fevr 1984, 9-12.*
LEVEL: I LANG: Fr SIRC ARTICLE NO: 094962

Lord, M. Creative teaching in dance. L'enseignement creatif de la danse. *CAHPER journal/Revue de l'ACSEPR (Ottawa) 50(5), May/Jun 1984, 32-34.*
LEVEL: B LANG: Eng Fr SIRC ARTICLE NO: 096623

Matsumoto, C. Teaching method of creative dance (thirty years in Japan). *Asian journal of physical education (Taiwan, China 7(2), Jul 1984, 17-22.*
NOTES: Abstract in Chinese.
LEVEL: B LANG: Eng SIRC ARTICLE NO: 099519

McCutcheon, G. The effect of the Paideia proposal on dance. *Tennessee education (Nashville) 13(3), Winter 1984, 25-29.*
LEVEL: I LANG: Eng SIRC ARTICLE NO: 099520

Moyle, J. The continuing merchandising of dance - a package of bright ideas for the new school year. Promouvoir la danse - u ensemble d'idees geniales pour la nouvelle annee scolaire. *CAHPER journal (Ottawa) 51(1), Sept/Oct 1984, 42-43.*
NOTES: Part of series prepared by the Dance Committee of CAHPER. Ces conseils en administration proviennent de la serie preparee par le Comite de danse de l'ACSEPL.
LEVEL: B LANG: Eng Fr SIRC ARTICLE NO: 101204

Murray, N.R. Selecting music for educational dance. Le choix de la musique pour la danse educative. *CAHPER journal/Revue de l'ACSEPR (Vanier, Ont.) 50(3), Jan-Feb/janv-fevr 1984, 34-35.*
NOTES: Part of a series prepared by the Dance Committee of CAHPER. Provient de la serie preparee par le Comite de la danse ACSEPR.

DANCE (continued)

LEVEL: B LANG: Eng Fr SIRC ARTICLE NO: 094964

Sanderson, P. Reflections on British and Soviet dance education. (Refs: 29)*Physical education review (Manchester) 7(1), Spring 1984, 47-55.* LEVEL: I LANG: Eng SIRC ARTICLE NO: 099524

TECHNIQUES AND SKILLS

Lamouroux, N. Pesquie, S. Rencontres: 15 danses collectives. *EPS: Education physique et sport (Paris) 189, sept/oct 1984, 15-18.* LEVEL: B LANG: Fr SIRC ARTICLE NO: 101202

TESTING AND EVALUATION

Bartenieff, I. Hackney, P. Jones, B.T. van Zile, J. Wolz, C. The potential of movement analysis as a research tool: a preliminary analysis. (Refs: 18)*Dance research journal (New York) 16(1), Spring 1984, 3-26.* LEVEL: I LANG: Eng SIRC ARTICLE NO: 103128

Hellerman, A. Skrinar, M.H. Relationship of technical skill rank to age, gender, and number of years in dance training. (Refs: 12)*Research quarterly for exercise & sport (Reston, Va.) 55(2), Jun 1984, 188-190.* ABST: This study examined the extent to which age, gender, and number of years in training contributed to the technical skill level of 56 dance students (43 female, 13 males). The results indicate that women have more years in training than men but do not possess a higher technical skill level than men. This suggests that men may be either beginning at technically higher levels, or progressing at faster rates than females. The results also suggest that the more technically proficient dancers are leaving college dance programs before completing a given program. LEVEL: A LANG: Eng SIRC ARTICLE NO: 096618

DARTS

Brackin, I.L. Fitzgerald, W. Darts. 1st Fireside ed. New York: Simon & Schuster, 1984. 1v. NOTES: Originally published: All about darts, 1975. Includes index. LEVEL: B LANG: Eng ISBN: 0671532391 LC CARD: 84-014163

Tierney, J. The finer points of darts. *In, Schrier, E.W. and Allman, W.F. (eds.), Newton at the bat: the science in sports, New York, Scribner, c1984, p. 167-172.* LEVEL: I LANG: Eng RC1235 18609

EQUIPMENT

Buckland, R. Good darts. *Darts world (Croydon, Eng.) 137, Apr 1984, 8.* LEVEL: B LANG: Eng SIRC ARTICLE NO: 099528

TECHNIQUES AND SKILLS

Buckland, R. The science of darts: nice throwing. *Darts world (Surrey, Eng.) 143, Oct 1984, 8.* LEVEL: B LANG: Eng SIRC ARTICLE NO: 107155

TECHNIQUES AND SKILLS - STANCE

Buckland, R. The science of darts: stand fast. *Darts world (Croydon, Eng.) 141, Aug 1984, 14.* NOTES: First of a three-par series. LEVEL: B LANG: Eng SIRC ARTICLE NO: 098043

DECATHLON

BIOGRAPHY AND AUTOBIOGRAPHY

Decathlon's eternal challenge: Daley Thompson interview in California by Jon Hendershott. *Athletics weekly (Rochester, Kent, Eng.) 38(17), 28 Apr 1984, 20-22;24-29.* LEVEL: B LANG: Eng SIRC ARTICLE NO: 095370

Hendershott, J. T & F N interview: Daley Thompson. *Track & field news (Los Altos, Calif.) 37(3), Apr 1984, 40-42.* LEVEL: LANG: Eng SIRC ARTICLE NO: 093843

Moore, K. He's a perfect 10: to world champion Daley Thompson of England, the decathlon is an event of such beauty that he gladly gives all his considerable speed, strength and fervor in trying to conquer it. *Sports illustrated (Chicago, Ill.) 61(4), 18 Jul 1984, 194-198;201-202;204-206;210-211;214;216-218.* NOTES: Special preview: the 1984 Olympics. LEVEL: B LANG: Eng SIRC ARTICLE NO: 096934

Prokop, D. Runner's World gold medal exclusive. Daley Thompson puts his distinctive mark on the decathlon with wit, irreverence and incredible athletic ability. *Runner's world (Mountain View, Calif.) 19(7), Jul 1984, 25-26;28;31;34;37;40.* LEVEL: B LANG: Eng SIRC ARTICLE NO: 095382

Rafer Johnson: his decathlon win was highlight of '60 games. *Sporting news (St. Louis) 198(4), 23 Jul 1984, Olympic special insert, 14;18.* LEVEL: B LANG: Eng SIRC ARTICLE NO: 096935

Who's who in British athletics. Brad McStravick. *Athletics weekly (Kent, Eng.) 38(50), 15 Dec 1984, 38-39.* LEVEL: B LANG: E SIRC ARTICLE NO: 103541

SPORTING EVENTS

Multi-events. *Athletics coach (London) 18(4), Dec 1984, 60-66.* LEVEL: B LANG: Eng SIRC ARTICLE NO: 104941

TESTING AND EVALUATION

Gambetta, V. Decathlon. (Helsinki observations) *Modern athlete and coach (Athelstone, Aust.) 22(2), Apr 1984, 5-8.* LEVEL: LANG: Eng SIRC ARTICLE NO: 096926

TRAINING AND CONDITIONING

Talbot, J. Decathlon training for the novice. *Athletics coach (Halesowen, England) 18(1), Mar 1984, 22-23.* LEVEL: B LANG: Eng SIRC ARTICLE NO: 093850

DENMARK

HISTORY

Moller, J. Sports and old village games in Denmark. (Refs: 41)*Canadian journal of history of sport/Revue canadienne de l'histoire des sports (Windsor, Ont.) 15(2), Dec 1984, 19-29.* LEVEL: A LANG: Eng SIRC ARTICLE NO: 104008

DISABLED

Achieving excellence - quality research in adapted physical activity. (Refs: 4)*Adapted physical activity quarterly (Champaign Ill.) 1(2), 1984, 95-96.* LEVEL: B LANG: Eng SIRC ARTICLE NO: 102438

Ball, D. Chariots of fire. *Nursing times (London) 80(34), 22-28 Aug 1984, 16-18.* LEVEL: B LANG: Eng

Cantu, R.C. Fitness for the handicapped: an overview. (Refs: 55) NOTES: In, Cantu, R.C. (ed.), Clinical sports medicine, Lexington, Mass. ; Toronto, Collamore Press : D.C. Heath, c1984, p. 27-43. LEVEL: B LANG: Eng RC1201 15964

Danigelis, N.L. Sport and the disabled elderly. (Refs: 27)*Arena review 8(1), Mar 1984, 68-79.* NOTES: Special issue: spor and disability. LEVEL: I LANG: Eng SIRC ARTICLE NO: 103712

Davis, G.M. Jackson, R.W. Shephard, R.J. Sports and recreation for the physically disabled. (Refs: 129) NOTES: In, Strauss, R.H. (ed.), Sports medicine, Philadelphia ; Toronto, Saunders, 1984, p. 286-304. LEVEL: I LANG: Eng RC1210 17196

DePauw, K.P. Commitment and challenges: sport opportunities for athletes with disabilities. *Journal of physical education, recreation & dance 55(2), Feb 1984, 34-35.* LEVEL: B LANG: Eng SIRC ARTICLE NO: 091410

Holmes, P. A sporting chance. *Nursing times (London) 80(9), 29 Feb/6 Mar 1984, 16-18.* LEVEL: B LANG: Eng SIRC ARTICLE NO: 100653

Lebarbe, M. Menard, D. Touzin, L. Valois, P. Sport pour les adultes physiquement handicapes: la clientele, les techniques, les reglements, l'equipement, les ressources. Montreal: Association quebecoise de loisirs pour personnes handicapees, 1984. 419 p. CORP: Association quebecoise de loisirs pour personnes handicapees. NOTES: Document realise dans le cadre du Programme canadien de relance de l'aide a l'emploi (RELAIS). Bibliographie: p. 418-419. LEVEL: I LANG: Fr GV709.3 16094

Ohry, A. (Sports for the disabled and the rehabilitation physician.) *Harefuah (Tel Aviv) 107(3/4), Aug 1984, 95-97.*
LEVEL: B LANG: Heb

Olympic Scientific Congress, July 1984 - Sports and disabled athletes. (Refs: 6)*Adapted physical activity quarterly (Champaign, Ill.) 1(3), 1984, 181-184.*
LEVEL: B LANG: Eng SIRC ARTICLE NO: 102464

Schilling, M.L. Familiar sports and activities adapted for multiply impaired persons. Alexandria, Va.: Computer Microfilm International, 1984. 1 microfiche (11 fr.); 10 x 15 cm.
LEVEL: B LANG: Eng EDRS: ED242189 ERIC 242189

Stein, J.U. Using the microcomputer to promote the physical proficiency and motor development of handicapped students. *Physical education newsletter (Old Saybrook, Conn.) 156, Feb 1984, 2-4.*
LEVEL: B LANG: Eng SIRC ARTICLE NO: 097550

Verbeek, A.L.M. Prevalence of some motoric handicaps in community. (Refs: 4)*International journal of sports medicine (Stuttgart) Suppl. 5, Nov 1984, 165-166.*
CONF: International Congress on Sports and Health (1983 : Maastricht, Netherlands).
LEVEL: A LANG: Eng SIRC ARTICLE NO: 103984

Williams, S. Sport and the paraplegic patient. (Refs: 2)*Remedial gymnastics and recreational therapy (Manchester, Eng.) 112 May 1984, 11-13.*
LEVEL: B LANG: Eng SIRC ARTICLE NO: 100663

Winnick, J.P. Recent advances related to special physical education and sport. (Refs: 47)*Adapted physical activity quarterl (Champaign, Ill.) 1(3), 1984, 197-206.*
ABST: This article synthesizes advances related to special physical education and sport from 1975 to the present. Generic advances are presented within the categories of legislation, sport programs and activities, testing and assessment, certification, and instructional and curricular materials. Subsequently, additional advances particularly relevant to individuals with orthopedic, educational, auditory, or visual handicapping conditions are presented.
LEVEL: B LANG: Eng SIRC ARTICLE NO: 102474

Yes you can: a review of a cross-section of the projects sponsored by Fitness and Amateur Sport Canada in celebration of the International Year of Disabled Persons. Oui, vous le pouvez: un survol de l'eventail des projets commandites par Condition physique et Sport amateur Canada pour marquer l'Annee internationale des personnes handicapees. Ottawa: C.F.S.O.D. : F.C.O.S.H., 1984?. 40, (2), 39, (2) p.
CORP: Canadian Federation of Sport Organizations for the Disabled.
CORP: Federation canadienne des organisations de sport pour handicapes.
CORP: Canada. Fitness and Amateur Sport.
CORP: Canada. Condition physique et Sport amateur.
NOTES: French and English texts on inverted pages with separate paging. Textes francais et anglais disposes tete-beche avec pagination separee. Cover title: Yes you can: integrate the mentally and physically disabled into your fitness programs. Titre de la couverture: Oui, vous le pouvez: introduire les services aux handicapes physiques ou mentaux dans vos programmes de conditionnement physique.
LEVEL: B LANG: Eng Fr GV709.3 17106

ADMINISTRATION

Clarke, K.S. The Amateur Sports Act of 1978 and the athlete with disability. *Palaestra (Macomb, Ill.) 1(1), Fall 1984, 11-12;42.*
LEVEL: B LANG: Eng SIRC ARTICLE NO: 171811

Drowatzky, J. Marcal, H. Volunteers in sport for the disabled: a case study. *In, Ilmarinen, M. (ed.) et al., Sport and International Understanding: proceedings of the congress held in Helsinki, Finland, July 7-10, 1982, Berlin, Springer-Verlag, 1984, p. 271-274.*
CONF: Congress on Sport and International Understanding (1982 : Helsinki).
LEVEL: B LANG: Eng GV706.8 18979

Hedrick, B. Community sports programs for disabled residents. *Parks & recreation 19(3), Mar 1984, 38-42.*
LEVEL: I LANG: E SIRC ARTICLE NO: 091418

Jaeaeskelaeinen, M. Heikkinen, E. Koivumaeki, K. Lahtinen, U. Puputti, V. The improvement of international co-operation and exchange of information in relation to sports for the disabled and other special groups. (Refs: 1)*In, Ilmarinen, M. (ed.) et al., Sport and International Understanding: proceedings of the congress held in Helsinki, Finland, July 7-10, 1982, Berlin, Springer-Verlag, 1984, p. 267-270.*
CONF: Congress on Sport and International Understanding (1982 : Helsinki).
LEVEL: B LANG: Eng GV706.8 18979

AMPUTEE SPORTS

Bernhard, K.F. Amputee athletes. *Journal of rehabilitation (Washington) 50(3), 1984, 70-71.*
LEVEL: B LANG: Eng SIRC ARTICLE NO: 097530

ASSOCIATIONS

Adams, C. Ammons, D.K. The National Association of Sports for Cerebral Palsy. American Athletic Association for the Deaf. *Journal of physical education, recreation & dance 55(2), Feb 1984, 36-37.*
LEVEL: B LANG: Eng SIRC ARTICLE NO: 091401

Bryant, D. Beaver, D.P. United States Amputee Athletic Association. United States Association for Blind Athletes. *Journal o physical education, recreation & dance 55(2), Feb 1984, 40-41.*
LEVEL: B LANG: Eng SIRC ARTICLE NO: 091406

Hernley, R. Fleming, A. National Handicapped Sports and Recreation Association. The National Wheelchair Athletic Association *Journal of physical education, recreation & dance 55(2), Feb 1984, 38-39.*
LEVEL: B LANG: Eng SIRC ARTICLE NO: 091419

Jochheim, K.-A. The extent, content and organisation of international sport for the disabled in the past, present and future (Refs: 7)*In, Ilmarinen, M. (ed.) et al., Sport and International Understanding: proceedings of the congress held in Helsinki, Finland, July 7-10, 1982, Berlin, Springer-Verlag, 1984, p. 262-266.*
CONF: Congress on Sport and International Understanding (1982 : Helsinki).
LEVEL: I LANG: Eng GV706.8 18979

Steele, D. Gildner, K.E. Report on CFSOD planning session, February 3-5, 1984. Ottawa: Canadian Federation of Sport Organizations for the Disabled, 1984. iv, 19, (29) leaves
CORP: Canadian Federation of Sport Organizations for the Disabled.
CORP: Federation canadienne des organisations de sport pour handicapes.
NOTES: Bibliography: leaf 19. Cover title: 1984 Planning Conference.
LEVEL: B LANG: Eng GV709.3 17036

BIBLIOGRAPHIES

Kelly, S. Stark, R. Sport and recreation for the disabled: an index of resource materials. Sport et loisirs pour handicapes: un repertoire de la litterature. Ottawa: Sport Information Resource Centre, 1984. xxxi, 186 p.
CORP: Centre de documentation pour le sport.
CORP: Sport Information Resource Centre.
NOTES: Produit avec l'appui de la Direction generale de la Sante et du Sport amateur Canada. A Fitness and Amateur Sport supported publication.
LEVEL: I LANG: Eng Fr ISBN: 0-920678-38-6 LC CARD: C85-090023 GV709.3 15486

BIOGRAPHY AND AUTOBIOGRAPHY

S.J. Picariello: basketball's best man. *Paraplegia news (Phoenix, Ariz.) 38(1), Jan 1984, 65.*
LEVEL: B LANG: Eng SIRC ARTICLE NO: 092825

BLINDNESS

Bachelart, E. Activites physiques pour les handicapes visuels. *Loisirs sante (Paris) 8, janv 1984, 6-7.*
LEVEL: B LANG: Fr SIRC ARTICLE NO: 095844

Chinn, A. Turner, W. Designing an exercise program for the visually impaired. *RCDNS focus (Halifax) Sept 1984, 18-19.*
LEVEL: B LANG: Eng SIRC ARTICLE NO: 100648

Copeland, A.E. Progress in sports for the blind, U.S.A. *Asian journal of physical education (Taiwan, China) 7(2), Jul 1984, 45-48.*
NOTES: Abstract in Chinese.
LEVEL: B LANG: Eng SIRC ARTICLE NO: 099002

Deschamps, G. Le Moing Ben Larbie, F. L'education psycho-motrice des aveugles. (2e partie) *EPS: Education physique et sport 185, janv/fevr 1984, 16-19.*
LEVEL: B LANG: Fr SIRC ARTICLE NO: 092810

Goalball growing in Canada. *RCDNS newsletter (Halifax, N.S.) Apr 1984, 3-6.*
LEVEL: B LANG: Eng SIRC ARTICLE NO: 097536

Sherrill, C. Rainbolt, W. Ervin, S. Attitudes of blind persons toward physical education and recreation. (Refs: 19)*Adapted physical activity quarterly 1(1), 1984, 3-11.*
ABST: This study investigated the attitudes of 30 blind adults towards physical education and the factors which contributed to the development of these feelings. The respondents indicated that school-based physical education experiences were positive experiences whereas neighborhood, community, church, and family physical education experiences were negative experiences. Males had a more positive attitude towards physical education than females.
LEVEL: A LANG: Eng SIRC ARTICLE NO: 092826

Showdown coaching manual level 1. Ottawa: Canadian Blind Sports Association, c1984. 49 p. : ill. (loose-leaf) (National Coaching Certification

Program.)
CORP: Canadian Blind Sports Association.
LEVEL: B LANG: Eng GV709.3 18848

CEREBRAL PALSY

Anderson, N.E. Golden opportunities. *Palaestra (Macomb, Ill.) 1(1), Fall 1984, 40-41;48.*
LEVEL: B LANG: Eng SIRC ARTICLE NO: 171818

Hartley, E. Rushton, C. The therapeutic use of a trampoline in inhibiting abnormal reflex reactions and facilitating normal patterns of movements in some cerebral palsied children. (Refs: 6)*Journal of the society of remedial gymnastics and recreational therapy (Manchester) 113, Aug 1984, 6-11.*
LEVEL: I SIRC ARTICLE NO: 108555

CHILDREN AND ADOLESCENTS

Cantu, R.C. Sports and the handicapped child.
NOTES: In, Micheli, L.J. (ed.), Pediatric and adolescent sports medicine, Boston ; Toronto, Little, Brown, c1984, p. 179-193.
LEVEL: I LANG: Eng RC1210 17791

Hunter, I.R. Reynolds, R.P. Williams, M.L. The elaboration model in adapted activity research: increasing the programmatic value of program evaluations. (Refs: 9)*Adapted physical activity quarterly 1(1), 1984, 12-18.*
ABST: The elaboration model enables a researcher to interpret or explain the relationship between two variables via the introduction of other variables into the analysis. The authors believe that the elaboration model can be used effectively by adapted activity specialists who do not have extensive training in statistics. An example using the elaboration model is included in the paper in which the impact of a child-life program on the regressive behaviour of hospitalized children is studied. An inverse relationship was found between regressive behaviour and participation in the program's recreational activities.
LEVEL: A LANG: Eng SIRC ARTICLE NO: 092816

Kennell, J.H. Sports participation for the child with a chronic health problem. (Refs: 22)
NOTES: In, Strauss, R.H. (ed.), Sports medicine, Philadelphia ; Toronto, Saunders, 1984, p. 218-236.
LEVEL: A LANG: Eng RC1210 17196

CLASSIFICATION

McCann, B.C. Classification of the locomotor disabled for competitive sports: theory and practice. (Refs: 4)*International journal of sports medicine (Stuttgart) Suppl. 5, Nov 1984, 167-170.*
CONF: International Congress on Sports and Health (1983 : Maastricht, Netherlands).
LEVEL: A LANG: Eng SIRC ARTICLE NO: 103970

DEAFNESS

Brunt, D. Layne, C.S. Cook, M. Rowe, L. Automatic postural responses of deaf children from dynamic and static positions. (Refs: 11)*Adapted physical activity quarterly (Champaign, Ill.) 1(3), 1984, 247-252.*
ABST: This paper describes automatic postural responses of deaf children during anterior body sway. Subjects were placed in a vestibular dysfunction (VDD) or vestibular nondysfunction (VNDD) group based on postrotary nystagmus response. They stood on an electrically driven platform, and brief support surface movement (12 cm/sec) elicited automatic postural responses under both static and dynamic conditions. Subjects underwent trials with and without vision, and electromyographical (EMG) data was recorded from posterior leg muscles. Both groups displayed some response characteristics found in previous reports (Nashner & Cordo, 1981), and under dynamic conditions the response latencies significantly decreased. However, the major finding was the response delay of some 40 msec by VDD subjects. It was proposed that this delay could in part be responsible for balance and movement problems exhibited by many deaf children.
LEVEL: A LANG: Eng SIRC ARTICLE NO: 102445

Stewart, D.A. The hearing impaired student in physical education. *Palaestra (Macomb, Ill.) 1(1), Fall 1984, 35-37.*
LEVEL: LANG: Eng SIRC ARTICLE NO: 171816

DOCUMENTATION

Surmounting obstacles. Third report of the Government of Canada response to recommendations arising from the International Yea of Disabled Persons. Franchir les obstacles. Troisieme rapport sur la reaction du gouvernement du Canada aux recommandations issues de l'Annee internationale des personnes handicapees. Ottawa: Minister of Supply and Services Canada, c1984. 176, 188 p.
CORP: Canada. Dept. of the Secretary of State. Communications Branch.
NOTES: French and English texts on inverted pages with separate paging. Textes francais et anglais disposes tete-beche avec pagination separee.
LEVEL: I LANG: Eng Fr ISBN: 0-662-52501-9 GV183.5 18809

EQUIPMENT

Crase, N. 1984 survey of sport wheelchair manufacturers. *Sports 'n spokes (Phoenix, Ariz.) 9(6), Mar/Apr 1984, 12-14;16-19;22;24.*
LEVEL: B LANG: Eng SIRC ARTICLE NO: 094312

EXERCISE THERAPY

Berrol, C. The effects of 2 movement therapy approaches on selected academic, physical and socio-behavioral measures of 1st grade children with learning and perceptual motor problems. (Refs: 19)*American journal of dance therapy (Columbia, Md.) 7, 1984, 32-48.*
LEVEL: A LANG: Eng SIRC ARTICLE NO: 103956

Manfredi, T.G. DiPietro, L. Gavin, M. Pulmonary and cardiac adjustments of orthopedic patients to a mask-flippers-snorkel aquatic therapeutic exercise program. (Refs: 11)
NOTES: In, Cantu, R.C. (ed.), Clinical sports medicine, Lexington, Mass. ; Toronto, Collamore Press : D.C. Heath, c1984, p. 53-61.
LEVEL: A LANG: Eng RC1201 15964

FACILITIES

Bullock, C.C. McGuire, F. Access (and safety) for all. *Grounds maintenance (Overland Park, Kans.) 19(3), Mar 1984, 40;42;47;135.*
LEVEL: B LANG: Eng SIRC ARTICLE NO: 098999

Dardick, G. Independence Trail: John Olmsted is carving an accessible path through the wilderness. *Paraplegia news (Phoenix Ariz.) 38(4), Apr 1984, 49-50.*
LEVEL: B LANG: Eng SIRC ARTICLE NO: 099003

John, G. Indoor dry sports centres.
NOTES: In, Thomson, N. (ed.) et al., Sports and recreation provision for disabled people, London, Architectural Press, c1984, p. 41-49.
LEVEL: I LANG: Eng GV433.G7 17991

John, G. Soames, P. Ward, J. Edgcumbe, J. Felgate, P. Sturges, H. Outdoor sports.
NOTES: In, Thomson, N. (ed.) et al., Sports and recreation provision for disabled people, London, Architectural Press, c1984, p. 51-59.
LEVEL: I LANG: Eng GV433.G7 17991

Rowan, E. Sports report: LAOOC ensuring access to Olympics. *Paraplegia news (Phoenix, Ariz.) 38(5), May 1984, 71-72.*
LEVEL: B LANG: Eng SIRC ARTICLE NO: 095877

Thomson, N. Dendy, E. de Deney, D. Sports and recreation provision for disabled people. London: Architectural Press, c1984. (x), 86 p. : ill.
CORP: Disabled Living Foundation.
CORP: Sports Council.
NOTES: Bibliography: p. 79-80.
LEVEL: I LANG: Eng ISBN: 0-85139-620-8 GV433.G7 17991

Thomson, N. The general needs of different disability groups.
NOTES: In, Thomson, N. (ed.) et al., Sports and recreation provision for disabled people, London, Architectural Press, c1984, p. 5-20.
LEVEL: I LANG: Eng GV433.G7 17991

Thomson, N. Improvements and adaptations to enable disabled people to use existing facilities.
NOTES: In, Thomson, N. (ed.) et al., Sports and recreation provision for disabled people, London, Architectural Press, c1984, p. 21-24.
LEVEL: B LANG: Eng GV433.G7 17991

HISTORY

John, G. Introduction.
NOTES: In, Thomson, N. (ed.) et al., Sports and recreation provision for disabled people, London, Architectural Press, c1984, p. 1-4.
LEVEL: B LANG: Eng GV433.G7 17991

LaMere, T. Labanowich, S. The history of sport wheelchairs - part II: the racing wheelchair 1956-1975. *Sports 'n spokes (Phoenix, Ariz.) 10(1), May/Jun 1984, 12-15.*
NOTES: Second of three part series.
LEVEL: I LANG: Eng SIRC ARTICLE NO: 094320

INTEGRATION

French, R. Henderson, H. Teacher attitudes toward mainstreaming. (Refs: 7)*Journal of physical education, recreation and dance (Reston, VA.) 55(8), Oct 1984, 69-71.*
LEVEL: B LANG: Eng SIRC ARTICLE NO: 100651

Jansma, P. Gayle, G.W. Mainstreaming the handicapped into sports: prerequisites and benefits. (Refs: 17)*Arena review 8(1), Mar 1984, 27-34.*
NOTES: Special issue: sport and disability.
ABST: This article discusses how lobbying, literature, litigation, and legislation are major catalysts which have led to increased sports participation for disabled people. The authors present a stepwise education and training model which show how disabled people can become more

involved in school and community programs.
LEVEL: I LANG: Eng SIRC ARTICLE NO: 103707

Nixon, H.L. The creation of appropriate integration opportunities in sport for disabled and nondisabled people: a guide for research and action. (Refs: 14)*Sociology of sport journal (Champaign, Ill.) 1(2), 1984, 184-192.*
ABST: This paper focuses on the appropriate integration of disabled and nondisabled people in sport. It considers some potentially salient personal attribute and background parameters (i.e., type and severity of disability and amount of sports background) and sports structure parameters (i.e., type of sport, amount of disability adaptation, and degree of competition) that could affect the extent to which integration efforts in sport result in genuine integration and a reduction in the stigmatization and handicapped minority status of disabled people.
LEVEL: B LANG: Eng SIRC ARTICLE NO: 102461

Storrs, N. Mainstreaming through sport. (Refs: 12)*Utah journal of health, physical education, recreation and dance (Provo, Utah) 16, Autumn 1984, 13-15.*
LEVEL: B LANG: Eng SIRC ARTICLE NO: 102472

INTRAMURAL SPORTS

Byrne, D. Grant writing and special populations. *In, Vendl, B.C. (ed.) et al., Interpretive aspects of intramural-recreational sports: selected proceedings from the Thirty-fifth Annual National Intramural-Recreational Sports Association Conference, Corvallis, Or., Oregon State University, c1984, p. 241-253.*
CONF: National Intramural-Recreational Sports Association Conference (35th : 1984 : Fort Worth, Tex.).
LEVEL: I LANG: Eng GV710 18914

Gutierrez, T.E. Baldizan, R.A. Special populations: beep ball over-the-line (visually impaired). *In, Vendl, B.C. (ed.) et al., Interpretive aspects of intramural-recreational sports: selected proceedings from the Thirty-fifth Annual National Intramural-Recreational Sports Association Conference, Corvallis, Or., Oregon State University, c1984, p. 254-257.*
CONF: National Intramural-Recreational Sports Association Conference (35th : 1984 : Fort Worth, Tex.).
LEVEL: B LANG: Eng GV710 18914

LAW AND LEGISLATION

Cowden, J.E. Wright, J. Gant, S.A. Gary W., et al. v. the State of Louisiana - Implications for adapted physical education, recreation, and leisure education. (Refs: 8)*Adapted physical activity quarterly (Champaign, Ill.) 1(2), 1984, 97-104.*
ABST: Litigation has been a major reason for the expansion of services in physical education and recreation for handicapped individuals. Public Law 94-142, the Education for All Handicapped Children Act, 1975, mandated that physical education was an instructional service to be included in the child's individual education program. This recent class action suit has major implications for the rights of handicapped individuals and improvement of service delivery systems. The purpose of this article is to review the civil suit and to describe the changes which have occurred in services for the handicapped with specific emphasis on adapted physical education recreation and leisure.
LEVEL: I LANG: Eng SIRC ARTICLE NO: 102448

MEDICINE

Barnes, L. The computer: a new twist on a 'walking program'. *Physician and sportsmedicine 12(1), Jan 1984, 163-166;170.*
LEVEL: I LANG: Eng SIRC ARTICLE NO: 091403

Maxwell, B. The nursing role in the Special Olympic program. (Refs: 4)*Journal of school health (Kent, Oh.) 54(3), Mar 1984, 131-133.*
LEVEL: B LANG: Eng SIRC ARTICLE NO: 099010

Maxwell, B.M. The nursing role in the Special Olympic program. *Journal of school health (Kent, Ohio) 54(3), Mar 1984, 131-133.*
LEVEL: B LANG: Eng SIRC ARTICLE NO: 100655

Moreau, S. Gymnastique preventive de l'affaissement des voutes plantaires. *Revue de l'education physique (Liege, Belgique) 24(1), 1984, 31-34.*
LEVEL: I LANG: Fr SIRC ARTICLE NO: 095870

Ryan, A.J. The physician and the disabled athlete. *Palestra (Macomb, Ill.) 1(1), Fall 1984, 28-29.*
LEVEL: B LANG: Eng SIR ARTICLE NO: 171815

PHYSICAL EDUCATION

Adams, G. Younger, T. Personal perspectives on counseling in adapted physical education. (Refs: 8)*Adapted physical activity quarterly (Champaign, Ill.) 1(3), 1984, 185-193.*
ABST: Adapted physical education teachers usually work in a setting in which the instruction of handicapped students is highly individualized. Thus, they need to have skills that focus on personal as well as movement characteristics. It is suggested that an understanding of the role of counselor, and of the specific means of counseling, would enable the teachers to work more effectively with their students and their other colleagues.
LEVEL: B LANG: Eng SIRC ARTICLE NO: 102439

Aharoni, H. The role of the adapted physical education teachers in the school and community. (Refs: 2)*Physical educator (Indianapolis, Ind.) 41(1), Mar 1984, 30-34.*
LEVEL: B LANG: Eng SIRC ARTICLE NO: 095842

Cain, E.J. The challenge of technology: educating the exceptional child for the world of tomorrow. *Teaching exceptional children (Reston, Va.) 16(4), Summer 1984, 239-241.*
LEVEL: I LANG: Eng SIRC ARTICLE NO: 103957

Canabal, M.Y. Itinerant adapted physical education teachers. (Refs: 10)*TAHPERD journal (Austin, Tex.) 53(1), Oct 1984, 12-13;67.*
LEVEL: B LANG: Eng SIRC ARTICLE NO: 109091

Cutforth, N.J. Policies and provisions for adapted physical education in the ordinary school: a cross-cultural comparison between the United States of America and England and Wales. *Bulletin of the Federation international d'education physique (Toulouse, France) 54(3/4), Jul/Dec 1984, 21-32.*
LEVEL: I LANG: Eng SIRC ARTICLE NO: 105256

DePaepe, J. Mainstream malpractice. (Refs: 23)*Physical educator (Indianapolis, Ind.) 41(1), Mar 1984, 51-56.*
LEVEL: I LANG: Eng SIRC ARTICLE NO: 095851

Deschamps, G. Le Moing Ben Larbie, F. L'education psycho-motrice des aveugles. (2e partie) *EPS: Education physique et sport 185, janv/ fevr 1984, 16-19.*
LEVEL: B LANG: Fr SIRC ARTICLE NO: 092810

Ellis, L. The role of the physical educator in rehabilitation. *Pelops 5, Feb 1984, 23-25.*
ABST: Physical education is now far more than a vague extension of physiotherapy in the area of rehabilitation. The physical educator's most effective role is in the areas of development of personal fitness, recreational skills, and extending basic principles of movement, balance, co-ordination and spatial awareness in a group setting.
LEVEL: I LANG: Eng SIRC ARTICLE NO: 097535

Fait, H.F. Dunn, J.M. Fait, G. Special physical education: adapted, individualized, and developmental. 5th ed. Philadelphia: Saunders College Pub., c1984. xiii, 576 p.
NOTES: Includes bibliographies and index.
LEVEL: I LANG: Eng ISBN: 0030585465 LC CARD: 82-024021 GV445 15602

Folsom-Meek, S.L. Parents: forgotten teacher aides in adapted physical education. (Refs: 15)*Adapted physical activity quarterly (Champaign, Ill.) 1(4), 1984, 275-281.*
ABST: The use of parents of handicapped children as support personnel to augment adapted physical education instruction is discussed. Reports in the literature support supplementary instruction by parents to enhance children's physical and motor development gains. Possible benefits include improvement of students' motor abilities and fitness levels, enrichment of parent-child relationships, and strengthening of adapted physical education programs.
LEVEL: A LANG: Eng SIRC ARTICLE NO: 103960

Huber, J.H. Smith, J. Comeau, C.E. The children's physical developmental clinic: an overview of philosophy and program. *MAHPERD journal (Northboro, Mass.) 31(3), Spring 1984, 8-9.*
LEVEL: B LANG: Eng SIRC ARTICLE NO: 094317

Jackson, T.Y. The effects of an inservice model for regular physical educators working with handicapped students in the mainstream setting. Eugene, Ore.: Microform Publications, University of Oregon, 1984. 2 microfiches : negative, ill. ; 11 x 15 cm.
NOTES: Thesis (Ed.D.) - University of Georgia, 1982; (xi, 146 leaves); includes bibliography.
LEVEL: A LANG: Eng UO84 264-265

Jennings, M.M. The importance of physical education for the intellectually handicapped within Australia. (Refs: 6)
CONF: Physical Education Graduating Seminar Conference (1984 : Footscray Institute of Technology).
NOTES: In, Physical education in Australia: past, present and future directions, s.l., Footscray Institute of Technology, 1984, p. 71-77.
LEVEL: I LANG: Eng SIRC ARTICLE NO: 095861

Jerome, C. Outdoor education and the disabled: implications for physical education. (Refs: 10)
CONF: Physical Education Graduating Seminar Conference (1984 : Footscray Institute of Technology).
NOTES: In, Physical education in Australia: past, present and future directions, s.l., Footscray Institute of Technology, 1984, p. 78-83.
LEVEL: I LANG: Eng SIRC ARTICLE NO: 095862

Jones, S. Physical education and the disabled: a new measure of responsibility. (Refs: 8)
CONF: Physical Education Graduatin Seminar Conference (1984 : Footscray Institute of Technology).
NOTES: In, Physical education in Australia: past,

present and future directions, s.l., Footscray Institute of Technology, 1984, p. 84-87.
LEVEL: I LANG: Eng SIRC ARTICLE NO: 095863

Lavey, B. Physical activity as a reinforcer in physical education. (Refs: 23)*Adapted physical activity quarterly (Champaign Ill.) 1(4), 1984, 315-321.*
ABST: A systematic management program is often needed to control student behavior or elicit their optimum level of performance. One management system that is beginning to receive attention in physical education is the application of physical activity reinforcement (McKenzie, 1979; Siedentop, 1983). This system of reinforcement is defined as a systematic procedure in which a structured time to choose among various physical education activities is contingent on the individual's meeting a predetermined criterion of behavior. The following discussion of the research conducted on program strategies and benefits utilizing physical activity reinforcement will enable practitioners to incorporate such a management system into their physical education program.
LEVEL: A LANG: Eng SIRC ARTICLE NO: 103968

Lockwood, R. Waters, C. UNIGYM: the University of Western Australia's remedial physical education clinic. (Refs: 9)*ACHPER national journal 103, Mar 1984, 7-9.*
ABST: A program of special physical education for children with minimal cerebral dysfunction, or developmental clumsiness, was established at the University of Western Australia, Dept. of Human Movement and Recreation Studies in 1980 in conjunction with Nedlands Teachers' College. Called Unigym, the program offers compensatory programs to offset motor skill deficiencies which are assessed on referral by use of Stott, Henderson and Moyes 'Test of Motor Impairment' (1972). A typical session involves warm up, group activity, individual remedial activity and pool session. The program now caters for 90 children attending 1 session per week. Future developments will include greater cooperation with the Education Dept. of Western Australia and teaching and program materials for parents and teachers.
LEVEL: I LANG: Eng SIRC ARTICLE NO: 097544

Megginson, N.L. Adapted physical education needs assessment: a cooperative manpower planning model for the local school district. Eugene, Ore.: Microform Publications, University of Oregon, 1984. 3 microfiches : negative, ill. ; 11 x 15 cm.
NOTES: Thesis (Ph.D.) - Texas Women's University, 1982; (ix, 244 leaves); includes bibliography.
LEVEL: A LANG: Eng UO84 226-228

Minner, S. Prater, G. Beane, A. Provision of adapted physical education: a dilemma for special educators. (Refs: 5)*Adapted physical activity quarterly (Champaign, Ill.) 1(4), 1984, 282-286.*
ABST: Preservice teachers from a special education undergraduate training program and inservice teachers working in special education classrooms read a descriptive vignette of a hypothetical placement meeting. All subjects were asked to assume that they felt the child being discussed needed adapted physical education, but that no person in their local school district was trained to provide such services. In short, a 'professional dilemma' was devised. After reading the vignette, subjects responded to several questions that assessed their willingness to recommend that the student be provided with the necessary service and

the potential impact of this recommendation. Results indicated that both groups were willing to recommend the service but that the inservice group was more fearful of negative repercussions.
LEVEL: A LANG: Eng SIRC ARTICLE NO: 103971

Okunrotifa, E.B. Rationale for physical education programmes for the handicapped. (Refs: 20)*Scottish journal of physical education (Glasgow, Scotland) 12(4), Nov 1984, 8-10.*
LEVEL: B LANG: Eng SIRC ARTICLE NO: 102463

Reid, G. O'Neill, K. Love is not enough. (adapted physical education) L'amour ne suffit pas. (education physique adaptee) (Refs: 4)*CAHPER journal/Revue de l'ACSEPR (Ottawa) 50(6), Jul/Aug-juil/aout 1984, 23-25..*
NOTES: Part of a series prepared by the Adaptive Committee of CAHPER. Provient de la serie preparee par le Comite des programmes adaptes.
LEVEL: B LANG: Eng Fr SIRC ARTICLE NO: 099014

Rizzo, T.L. Attitudes of physical educators toward teaching handicapped pupils. (Refs: 20)*Adapted physical activity quarterly (Champaign, Ill.) 1(4), 1984, 267-274.*
ABST: This study assessed the attitudes of 194 physical educators toward teaching handicapped pupils in the regular class. The survey instrument used was the Physical Educators Attitude Toward Teaching the Handicapped (PEATH), which assesses teacher attitudes according to the type of handicapping condition (learning and physical) and grade level (K-3, 4-6, 7-8). A2 x 3 randomized block factorial design and the Tukey (HSD) post hoc analysis were applied to the data. Results indicated that physical educators held more favorable attitudes toward teaching pupils with learning handicaps than those with physical handicaps. Furthermore, as grade level advanced from primary (K-3) to intermediate (4-6) and upper (7-8) grades, teacher attitudes became progressively less favorable.
LEVEL: A LANG: Eng SIRC ARTICLE NO: 103975

Sherrill, C. Megginson, N. A needs assessment instrument for local school district use in adapted physical education. (Refs: 22)*Adapted physical activity quarterly (Champaign, Ill.) 1(2), 1984, 147-157.*
ABST: The purpose was to develop and field test a comprehensive needs assessment instrument for use in determining and prioritizing local school district adapted physical education needs. The resulting Survey of Adapted Physical Education Needs (SAPEN) was comprised of 50 items, encompassing five areas: (a) significance of physical education, (b) assessment, placement, and individualized educational programming, (c) instruction and programming, (d) personnel, and (e) other. Items were to be rated on two, 6-point Likert-type scales, relating respectively to the extent to which each adapted physical education condition now exists and should exist in one's school district. Data analysis and cooperative planning follow-up procedures were field tested in a selected school district with SAPENs returned by 37 administrators, 48 physical educators, 55 special educators, and 12 parents.
LEVEL: A LANG: Eng SIRC ARTICLE NO: 102469

Shoval, E. An integrated program of movement education for children with learning disabilities. *In, Simri, U. (ed.), et al. Preschool and elementary school children and physical activity. Proceedings of the 26th ICHPER World Congress 1983, Wingate*

Institute, Israel, vol. III, Jerusalem, Israel, 1984, p. 143-148.
CONF: ICHPER World Congress (26th : 1983 : Wingate Institute, Israel).
LEVEL: I LANG: Eng GV443 20093

Vogler, E.W. Bishop, P. Brief considerations in physical education programming for the severely and multiple handicapped. *Colorado journal of health, physical education, recreation, and dance (Denver, Colo.) 11(1), Fall 1984, 10-12.*
LEVEL: B LANG: Eng SIRC ARTICLE NO: 100662

Williams, D. Children with special needs. *Bulletin of physical education (London) 20(2), Summer 1984, 43-45.*
CONF: Britis Association of Advisers and Lecturers in Physical Education. Congress (64th : 1984 : Cardiff).
LEVEL: B LANG: Eng SIRC ARTICLE NO: 103989

Winnick, J.P. Recent advances related to special physical education and sport. (Refs: 47)*Adapted physical activity quarterl (Champaign, Ill.) 1(3), 1984, 197-206.*
ABST: This article synthesizes advances related to special physical education and sport from 1975 to the present. Generic advances are presented within the categories of legislation, sport programs and activities, testing and assessment, certification, and instructional and curricular materials. Subsequently, additional advances particularly relevant to individuals with orthopedic, educational, auditory, or visual handicapping conditions are presented.
LEVEL: B LANG: Eng SIRC ARTICLE NO: 102474

PHYSICAL FITNESS

Anderson, B. Bornell, D.G. Stretch and strengthen for rehabilitation and development. Willowdale, Ont.: Stretching Inc., c1984. 91 p. : ill.
NOTES: Bibliography: p. 86-87.
LEVEL: B LANG: Eng GV482.7 20104

Canada fitness award: level of achievement. Adapted for use by trainable mentally handicapped youth. Jeunesse en forme Canada: niveau de performance. Adapte a l'intention des jeunes deficients profonds educables. Ottawa: Fitness and Amateur Sport, 1984?. (7), (7) p.
CORP: Canada. Fitness and Amateur Sport.
CORP: Canada. Condition physique et Sport amateur.
NOTES: French and English texts on inverted pages with separate paging. Textes francais et anglais disposes tete-beche avec pagination separee. Cover title. Titre de la couverture.
LEVEL: B LANG: Eng Fr GV445 17736

Lafreniere-Joannette, L. Sante et loisir pour les personnes handicapees. (Refs: 15)
NOTES: Dans, Lagarde, F. (ed.), Sante et activite physique, Longueuil, Que., College Edouard-Montpetit, c1984, p. 107-118.
LEVEL: I LANG: Fr GV481 17104

Lignes directrices sur les adaptations au programme Jeunesse en forme Canada: enfants aux capacites physiques diminuees. Guidelines for adaptations to the Canada Fitness Award: youth with limited physical abilities. Ottawa: Condition physique et Sport amateur : Fitness and Amateur Sport, c1984. 17, 18 p. : ill. (Cat. no. H93-87/ 1984.)
CORP: Canada. Condition physique et Sport amateur.
CORP: Canada. Fitness and Amateur Sport.

NOTES: Cover title. Titre de la couverture. French and English texts on inverted pages with separate paging. Textes francais et anglais disposes tete-beche avec pagination separee.
LEVEL: B LANG: Fr Eng ISBN: 0-662-52989-8
GV709.3 17258

Marwick, C. Wheelchair calisthenics keep patients fit. (news) *JAMA: Journal of the American Medical Association (Chicago)* 251(3), 20 Jan 1984, 303.
LEVEL: B LANG: Eng SIRC ARTICLE NO: 097545

Stein, J.U. Fitness and disability: inclusive programming. *Parks & recreation (Alexandria, Va.)* 19(12), Dec 1984, 50-56;68.
LEVEL: B LANG: Eng SIRC ARTICLE NO: 173254

Sullivan, J.V. Stein, J.U. Fitness for the handicapped: an instructional approach. Springfield, Ill.: Charles C. Thomas, c1984. xvi, 194 p. : ill.
NOTES: Includes index. Bibliography: p. 181-187.
LEVEL: I LANG: Eng ISBN: 0398050341 LC CARD: 84-008490 GV482.7 18313

Walsh, C.M. Steadward, R.D. Get fit. Muscular fitness exercises for the wheelchair user. Edmonton, Alta.: University of Alberta, Research and Training Centre for the Physically Disabled, 1984. 29, (1) p. : ill.
NOTES: Bibliography: p. (30).
LEVEL: B LANG: Eng GV482.7 18505

Winnick, J.P. Short, F.X. The physical fitness of youngsters with spinal neuromuscular conditions. (Refs: 16)*Adapted physical activity quarterly 1(1), 1984, 37-51.
ABST: This study examined the influence of sex, age, and severity of condition on the physical fitness performance of paraplegic spinal neuromuscular (PSN) youngsters and compared some of these performance measurements with the performance measurements of normal children of the same sex and age. The scores of normal subjects for grip strength and arm hang were significantly superior to those of PSN subjects. The results also indicate that PSN subjects do not increase their physical fitness throughout the developmental years whereas normal subjects do increase their physical fitness throughout the developmental years. Finally, the results indicate that site of lesion occurring at thoracic 6 (T6) or below does not discriminate performance on the physical fitness test items.
LEVEL: A LANG: Eng SIRC ARTICLE NO: 092836

Winnick, J.P. Short, F.X. Test item selection: for the project UNIQUE physical fitness test. (Refs: 29)*Adapted physical activity quarterly (Champaign, Ill.) 1(4), 1984, 296-314.
ABST: In order to enhance the physical fitness development of individuals with selected handicapping conditions, Winnick and Short (1984b) published a manual which presented the Project UNIQUE Physical Fitness Test and training program. This article presents criteria and supporting technical information pertaining to the selection of test items.
LEVEL: A LANG: Eng SIRC ARTICLE NO: 103991

PHYSIOLOGY

Asayama, K. Nakamura, Y. Ogata, H. Morita, H. Kodama, S. Hatada, K. Energy expenditure of paraplegic marathon runners measured during a wheelchair marathon. *Sangyo ika daigaku zasshi (Kitakyushu) 6(2), 1 June 1984, 121-130.
LEVEL: A LANG: Eng

Coutts, K. Relation between oxygen uptake & power output during wheelchair ergometry in tetraplegics and paraplegics. (Refs: 6)*Canadian journal of applied sport sciences/Journal canadien des sciences appliquees au sport 9(1), Mar 1984, 17-19.
ABST: Twenty-one disabled subjects performed work on a wheelchair ergometer using a progressive protocol until volitional fatigue. Both high lesion and low lesion paraplegics exhibited a significant relationship between power output and oxygen uptake. Tetraplegics exhibited a non-significant correlation between power output and oxygen uptake. The author has developed an equation to predict oxygen uptake from power output during wheelchair ergometry in high and low lesion paraplegics.
LEVEL: A LANG: Eng SIRC ARTICLE NO: 092806

de Bruin, M.I. Binkhorst, R.A. Cardiac output of paraplegics during exercise. (Refs: 4)*International journal of sports medicine (Stuttgart) Suppl. 5, Nov 1984, 175-176.
CONF: International Congress on Sports and Health (1983 : Maastricht, Netherlands).
LEVEL: A LANG: Eng SIRC ARTICLE NO: 103958

Druvert, J.C. Les problemes poses par l'entrainement des handicapes physiques. (Refs: 7)*Cinesiologie (Paris) 96, juil/aout 1984, 320-328.
LEVEL: I LANG: Fr SIRC ARTICLE NO: 099004

Gass, G.C. Camp, E.M. The maximum physiological responses during incremental wheelchair and arm cranking exercise in male paraplegics. (Refs: 17)*Medicine and science in sports and exercise (Indianapolis) 16(4), Aug 1984, 355-359.
ABST: Ten physically active male paraplegics (29-31 years old) underwent two incremental exercise tests to exhaustion. The exercise tests were arm cranking, utilizing an electronically-braked arm cranker, and wheelchair propulsion on a motor-driven treadmill. The subjects were randomly assigned to group. For the first six subjects, during both modes of exercise, VO2, Vco2, R, Ve, and heart rates were recorded throughout; for the remaining four subjects the same variables were recorded after the heart rate reached 160 b.min-1. The VO2 (l.min-1 and ml.min-1.kg-1), Vco2 (l.min-1), HR, and Ve BTPS (l.min-1) were significantly higher at the termination of the wheelchair exercise than at the termination of the arm cranking exercise. The minute ventilation showed a relatively linear phase at first, followed by a culvilinear phase.
LEVEL: A LANG: Eng SIRC ARTICLE NO: 102453

Gorman, D. Brown, B. Marty, P.J. The role of aerobic exercise in fat loss. *Paraplegia news (Phoenix, Ariz.) 38(2), Feb 1984 25-26;28.
LEVEL: B LANG: Eng SIRC ARTICLE NO: 097537

Goswami, A. Ghosh, A.K. Ganguli, S. Banerjee, A. Aerobic capacity of severely disabled Indians. *Ergonomics (London) 27(12), Dec 1984, 1267-1269.
LEVEL: I LANG: Eng

Hjeltnes, N. Control of medical rehabilitation of para- and tetraplegics by repeated evaluation of endurance capacity. (Refs 10)*International journal of sports medicine (Stuttgart) Suppl. 5, Nov 1984, 171-174.
CONF: International Congress on Sports and Health (1983 : Maastricht, Netherlands).
LEVEL: A LANG: Eng SIRC ARTICLE NO: 103963

Sandrini, G. Aquilani, R. Nappi, G. Ventilatory response to passive limb movement; effect of hemiplegia. (Refs: 18)*Annals o sports medicine (North Hollywood, Calif.) 2(1), 1984, 11-15.
ABST: The effect of passive limb movement (PLM) was studied in five patients with flaccid hemiplegia and in five normal subjects. Hyperventilation induced by PLM was abolished in hemiplegic patients on the affected side. It was observed, though less than in normals, during PLM of the unaffected side. End-tidal CO2 pressure (PET co2) diminished significantly in normal, but not in hemiplegic subjects. Since no change in VO2 was observed, while VA/Vo2 and VA/Vco2 had increased, this reflex ventilatory response is probably not due to chemical, but rather to neurogenic drive. All patients presented evident motor disturbance due to cortical or capsular lesions.
LEVEL: A LANG: Eng SIRC ARTICLE NO: 103976

Whiting, R.B. Dreisinger, T.E. Hayden, C.R. Wheelchair exercise testing: comparison of continuous and discontinuous exercise (Refs: 13)*Paraplegia (Edinburgh) 22(2), Apr 1984, 92-98.
ABST: This study compared wheelchair exercise performed at submaximal levels in a continuous versus discontinuous format. There was a positive linear relationship between heart rate, systolic blood pressure, and VO2 with increasing workload. This was true for both modes of testing with no significant difference in heart rate, systolic blood pressure, VO2, Ve, or Ve/VO2. The authors conclude that clinical wheelchair exercise testing can be performed in a continuous format without sacrificing physiological data.
LEVEL: A LANG: Eng SIRC ARTICLE NO: 103988

PLAYGROUNDS

Fitch, G. Play-for-integrated playground: a case study. *Recreation reporter (Vancouver, B.C.) Jun/Jul 1984, 14-15.
LEVEL: LANG: Eng SIRC ARTICLE NO: 098964

Storage, T.W. Bowen, L.E. Playgrounds of the future. *Recreation reporter (Vancouver) Jan/Feb 1984, 4-5.
LEVEL: B LANG: En SIRC ARTICLE NO: 095823

Wyatt, J. Water wonderland 'a group activity for the profoundly handicapped'. *Florida journal of health, physical education recreation and dance (Gainsville, Fla.) 22(1), Feb 1984, 7.
LEVEL: B LANG: Eng SIRC ARTICLE NO: 095885

PSYCHOLOGY

Henschen, K. Horvat, M. French, R. A visual comparison of psychological profiles between able-bodied and wheelchair athletes (Refs: 22)*Adapted physical activity quarterly (Champaign, Ill.) 1(2), 1984, 118-124.
ABST: The purpose of this study was to visually compare the psychological profile of 33 male wheelchair athletes who competed in track and field events, with previous results of able-bodied athletes. Based on the data gathered using the Profile of Mood States and the State-Trait Anxiety Inventory the wheelchair athletes demonstrated a profile similar to that of able-bodied athletes. This finding was discussed in terms of mental skills that may be developed by wheelchair athletes because of their injuries, possible influence of medication, and higher level of demonstrated anger.
LEVEL: A LANG: Eng SIRC ARTICLE NO: 102454

DISABLED (continued)

Lehmann, R. Motivations des sportifs handicapes, aspects educatifs et pedagogiques, incidences psychologiques de l'arret du sport. *Cinesiologie (Paris) 95, mai/juin 1984, 225-228.*
LEVEL: I LANG: Fr SIRC ARTICLE NO: 097543

Patrick, G.D. Comparison of novice and veteran wheelchair athletes self-concept and acceptance of disability. (Refs: 9) *Rehabilitation counseling bulletin (Alexandria, Va.) 27(3), 1984, 186-188.*
LEVEL: I LANG: Eng SIRC ARTICLE NO: 095874

Patrick, G.D. Comparison of novice and veteran wheelchair athletes' self-concept and acceptance of disability. *Rehabilitation counseling bulletin (Alexandria, Va.) 27(3), Jan 1984, 186-188.*
ABST: This study compared 10 novice and 12 veteran wheelchair athletes on measures of self-concept and acceptance of disability. The novice disabled athletes were found to be significantly different with lower acceptance of disability lower perceived social adequacy and lower consistency of self-perception.
LEVEL: A LANG: Eng SIRC ARTICLE NO: 097548

Roswal, G. Frith, G. Dunleavy, A.O. The effect of a developmental play program on the concept, risk-taking behaviors, and motoric proficiency of mildly handicapped children. (Refs: 36) *Physical educator (Indianapolis, Ind.) 41(1), Mar 1984, 43-50.*
ABST: The purpose of this study was to evaluate the effect of the Children's Developmental Play Program (CDPP) in the behavioral and neuromotor functioning of developmentally disabled children. 32 children between the ages of 5 and 13 years enrolled in educable mentally retarted classed, served as subjects. Data was collected on self concept, risk taking behaviors and motor proficiency of the students. Half of the children were enrolled in the CDPP. Overall improvements were observed in the experimental group, and this especially in both self concept and motor proficiency.
LEVEL: A LANG: Eng SIRC ARTICLE NO: 095876

Snyder, E.E. Sport involvement for the handicapped: some analytic and sensitizing concepts. (Refs: 26) *Arena review 8(1), Mar 1984, 16-26.*
NOTES: Special issue: sport and disabilily.
ABST: This article examines a number of analytic and sensitizing concepts about stigma, serious leisure, self-efficacy, sport, and role commitment that are important in understanding social, social psychological, and psychological dimensions of the participation of disabled people in sport and related leisure activities.
LEVEL: A LANG: Eng SIRC ARTICLE NO: 103706

SCHOOL SPORT

Carmichael, D.L. Sport, leisure and recreation skills for the handicapped: a broader perspective. (Refs: 5) *Arena review 8(1 Mar 1984, 35-40.*
NOTES: Special issue: Sport and disability.
ABST: This article examines some important deficiencies and problems in program development for disabled participants. School programs are often incomplete and poorly integrated with community programs organized to serve the disabled. The ultimate integration implications of highly popular and praised programs such as the Special Olympic are questioned. The author consequently details the basic characteristics of a systematically organized core program for the integration of disabled and non-disabled children in school

activities and sports.
LEVEL: A LANG: Eng SIRC ARTICLE NO: 103708

Stein, J.U. A challenge to change. *Journal of physical education, recreation & dance 55(2), Feb 1984, 44-46.*
LEVEL: B LANG: Eng SIRC ARTICLE NO: 091430

SOCIOLOGY

Hahn, H. Sports and the political movement of disabled persons: examining nondisabled social values. (Refs: 34) *Area review (1), Mar 1984, 1-15.*
NOTES: Special issue: sport and disability.
ABST: This article provides a broad conceptual frame-work concerning sport and the political movement of disabled persons which examines the connections among inequalities, prejudice, and discrimination in sport and the larger society. A number of key issues are raised regarding integration, the emulation of nondisabled values, the risks of sports participation for disabled people, and the role of physical competition in modern society.
LEVEL: A LANG: Eng SIRC ARTICLE NO: 103705

Hamilton, R. Education for life: assessment of the role of a recreational programme in the rehabilitation of day patients in a psychiatric hospital. *International journal of lifelong education (London) 3(3), Apr/Jun 1984, 223-232.*
LEVEL: A LANG: Eng SIRC ARTICLE NO: 103962

Kinkead, H. Opening closed doors. National Hospital's Capital Wheelchair Invitational Games build self-confidence through sport activities. *Paraplegia news (Phoenix, Ariz.) 38(1), Jan 1984, 62-63.*
LEVEL: B LANG: Eng SIRC ARTICLE NO: 092818

Nixon, H.L. Handicapism and sport: new directions for sport sociology research. (Refs: 42)
CONF: North American Society for the Sociology of Sport. Conference (3rd : 1982 : Toronto, Ont.).
NOTES: In, Theberge, N. and Donnelly, P. (eds.), Sport and the sociological imagination: refereed proceedings of the 3rd Annual Conference of the North American Society for the Sociology of Sport, Toronto, Canada, November 1982, Fort Worth, Tex., Texas Christian University Press, c1984, p. 162-176.
ABST: This paper serves as an introduction to sport sociologists of the nature of handicapism and sport through the examination of labeling and stigmatization of the handicapped, the minority status of the handicapped, and the role of sport participation in creating and overcoming a handicap. The paper concludes by identifying areas for further research.
LEVEL: I LANG: Eng SIRC ARTICLE NO: 097547

SPORTING EVENTS

Monroche, A. Les 7mes 'Jeux olympiques' de New York pour handicapes physiques. (I.M.C. et amputes) *Cinesiologie: medecine d sport (Paris) 98, nov/dec 1984, 489-491.*
LEVEL: B LANG: Fr SIRC ARTICLE NO: 103972

Perkins, V. Paralympics. *ACHPER national journal 103, Mar 1984, 6.*
LEVEL: B LANG: Eng SIRC ARTICLE NO: 097549

Ryan, A.J. Competition needed for disabled athletes. *Physician and sportsmedicine (Minneapolis, Minn.) 12(5), May 1984, 49.*
LEVEL: B LANG: Eng SIRC ARTICLE NO: 094325

TRAINING AND CONDITIONING

Druvert, J.C. Les problemes poses par l'entrainement des handicapes physiques. (Refs: 7) *Cinesiologie (Paris) 96, juil/aout 1984, 320-328.*
LEVEL: I LANG: Fr SIRC ARTICLE NO: 099004

Kaiser, D.S. Kaiser, K.P. A conditioning program for physically impaired individuals. *NIRSA journal (Corvallis, Ore.) 8(3), Spring 1984, 34-37.*
LEVEL: B LANG: Eng SIRC ARTICLE NO: 097541

Skuldt, A. Exercise limitations for quadriplegics. (Refs: 8) *Sports 'n spokes (Phoenix, Ariz.) 10(1), May/Jun 1984, 19-20.*
LEVEL: B LANG: Eng SIRC ARTICLE NO: 094327

WHEELCHAIR SPORTS

Ceccotti, F.S. Wheelchair sport injuries: an athletic training approach. (Refs: 6) *Paraplegia news (Phoenix, Ariz.) 38(2), Feb 1984, 29-30.*
LEVEL: B LANG: Eng SIRC ARTICLE NO: 097532

Denson, P. Extended wheels: a report. (Refs: 7) *Pelops 5, Feb 1984, 31-37.*
ABST: Outlines the stages involved in formulating the final design for an ergometer to be used in the evaluation and specific training of wheelchair athletes. A brief discussion of the problems encountered and their solutions which led to the various design changes is included.
LEVEL: I LANG: Eng SIRC ARTICLE NO: 097534

Druvert, J.C. Les problemes poses par l'entrainement des handicapes physiques. (Refs: 7) *Cinesiologie (Paris) 96, juil/aout 1984, 320-328.*
LEVEL: I LANG: Fr SIRC ARTICLE NO: 099004

Horvat, M.A. Golding, L.A. Beutel-Horvat, T. McConnell, T.J. A treadmill modification for wheelchairs. (Refs: 18) *Research quarterly for exercise & sport (Reston, Va.) 55(3), Sept 1984, 297-301.*
LEVEL: I LANG: Eng SIRC ARTICLE NO: 102455

Kinkead, H. Opening closed doors. National Hospital's Capital Wheelchair Invitational Games build self-confidence through sport activities. *Paraplegia news (Phoenix, Ariz.) 38(1), Jan 1984, 62-63.*
LEVEL: B LANG: Eng SIRC ARTICLE NO: 092818

Labanowich, S. Karman, P. Veal, L.E. Wiley, B.D. Wheelchair sports: a paper on organization. The principles and foundations for the organization of wheelchair sports. *Sports 'n spokes (Phoenix, Ariz.) 9(6), Mar/Apr 1984, 25-32.*
LEVEL: B LANG: Eng SIRC ARTICLE NO: 094319

LaMere, T.J. Labanowich, S. The history of sport wheelchairs - part 1: the development of the basketball wheelchair. *Sports 'n spokes (Phoenix, Ariz.) 9(6), Mar/Apr 1984, 6-8;10-11.*
LEVEL: B LANG: Eng SIRC ARTICLE NO: 094321

LaMere, T.J. Labanowich, S. The history of sport wheelchairs - Part III: the racing wheelchair 1976-1983. *Sports 'n spokes (Phoenix, Ariz.) 10(2), Jul/Aug 1984, 12-16.*
LEVEL: B LANG: Eng SIRC ARTICLE NO: 097542

Madorsky, J.G.B. Curtis, K.A. Wheelchair sports medicine. (Refs: 9) *American journal of sports medicine (Baltimore, Md.) 12(2), Mar/Apr 1984, 128-132.*
ABST: This article describes the advent of the wheelchair sports movement and focuses on the field of wheelchair sports medicine. Wheelchair

sports medicine classifies individuals so that people with a similar degree of disability can compete against each other. The common injuries of wheelchair athletes are discussed and described.
LEVEL: A LANG: Eng SIRC ARTICLE NO: 094322

Marshall, T. Wheelchairs and marathon road racing. *British journal of sports medicine (Loughborough, Eng.) 18(4), Dec 1984, 301-304.*
CONF: London Marathon Conference (1984 : London).
LEVEL: I LANG: Eng SIRC ARTICLE NO: 104997

Mason, B. Gunther, S. van der Waarde, T. Fisher, R. Postural positioning in wheelchair sports. Ottawa: Royal Ottawa Regional Rehabilitation Centre, 1984. (iv), 19, (2) p.
NOTES: Report financially supported by Fitness Canada, Fitness and Amateur Sport Canada (Project No. 425-0060-83/84). Bibliography: p. (1-2).
LEVEL: A LANG: Eng GV709.3 17429

Murray, G. Parke, J.K. Joining the race. *Palaestra (Macomb, Ill.) 1(1), Fall 1984, 17.*
LEVEL: B LANG: Eng SIRC ARTICLE NO 171813

Ward, S. Murderball/quad rugby. *RCDNS newsletter (Halifax, N.S.) Feb 1984, 5-6.*
LEVEL: B LANG: Eng SIRC ARTICLE NO: 09755

DISABLED - MENTAL RETARDATION

Garrigues, R. Sport adapte aux handicapes mentaux. *Loisirs sante (Paris) 12, nov/dec 1984, 14-16.*
LEVEL: B LANG: Fr SIRC ARTICLE NO: 106464

DOWN'S SYNDROME

Cook, A.S. Developmental aspects of postural control in normal and Down's Syndrome children. Eugene, Ore.: Microform Publications, University of Oregon, 1984. 3 microfiches : negative, ill. ; 11 x 15 cm.
NOTES: Thesis (Ph.D.) - University of Oregon, 1983; (xv, 198 leaves); vita; includes bibliography.
LEVEL: A LANG: Eng UO84 438-440

Cooke, R. Atlantoaxial instability in individuals with Down syndrome. *Mental retardation (Washington) 22(4), Aug 1984, 193-194.*
LEVEL: I LANG: Eng

Cooke, R.E. Atlantoaxial instability in individuals with Down's syndrome. (Refs: 8)*Adapted physical activity quarterly (Champaign, Ill.) 1(3), 1984, 194-196.*
ABST: Atlantoaxial Instability occurs in approximately 17% of all persons with Down's syndrome. Such persons are susceptible to serious spinal cord injury if marked flexion of the neck occurs. Every person with Down's syndrome should have cervical spine x-rays before performing in certain sports even though the frequency of sports-induced neurological damage is low.
LEVEL: I LANG: Eng SIRC ARTICLE NO: 102447

DePauw, K.P. Total body mass centroid and segmental mass centroid locations found in Down's syndrome individuals. (Refs: 42) *Adapted physical activity quarterly (Champaign, Ill.) 1(3), 1984, 221-229.*
ABST: This study was undertaken to investigate the

total body and segmental centers of mass of individuals with Down's syndrome. The 40 subjects were divided equally by gender into the following age groups: (a) ages 6 to 10, (b) ages 11 to 18, (c) adult females, and (d) adult males. A computer program calculated the segmental mass centroid locations and total body center of mass. Differences in total body and segmental center of mass location were found between individuals with Down's syndrome (DS) and nonhandicapped individuals. Analysis of the data on the DS children indicated that the mean center of mass location for the total body was within the range reported for nonhandicapped children. The adult DS male and female subjects were found to have a lower total body center when compared to existing data on nonhandicapped adults.
LEVEL: A LANG: Eng SIRC ARTICLE NO: 102452

EXERCISE THERAPY

Crain, C. Eisenhart, M. McLaughlin, J. The application of a multiple measurement approach to investigate the effects of a dance program on educable mentally retarded adolescents. (Refs: 10)*Research quarterly for exercise & sport (Reston, Va.) 55(3), Sept 1984, 231-236.*
ABST: The present study is an example of a multiple measurement approach that uses eight measurements, in combination, to answer four research questions regarding the physical and social effects that occur when a group of educable mentally retarded adolescents is exposed to a 10-week dance program. The findings revealed that four students showed improvement in both social and physical behaviors, seven students showed improvement in either social or physical behaviors, and two students showed no improvement. There was no evidence of a 'transfer effect' due to participation in the program, and some students' behaviors were affected by external factors.
LEVEL: A LANG: Eng SIRC ARTICLE NO: 102449

Tseo, C. The effect of an aerobic dance program on the self-concepts and physical fitness levels of young adult institutionalized female mental patients. Eugene, Ore.: Microform Publications, University of Oregon, 1984. 2 microfiches : negative, ill. ; 11 x 15 cm.
NOTES: Thesis (M.S.) - Pennsylvania State University, 1981; (viii, 124 leaves); includes bibliography.
LEVEL: A LANG: Eng UO84 105-106

MEDICINE

Atlantoaxial instability in Down Syndrome. *Pediatrics (Evanston, Ill.) 74(1), Jul 1984, 152-154.*
CORP: American Academy of Pediatrics. Committee on Sports Medicine.
LEVEL: I LANG: Eng SIRC ARTICLE NO: 102441

Moreau, S. Gymnastique preventive de l'affaissement des voutes plantaires. *Revue de l'education physique (Liege, Belgique) 24(1), 1984, 31-34.*
LEVEL: I LANG: Fr SIRC ARTICLE NO: 095870

PERCEPTUAL MOTOR PROCESSES

Broadhead, G.D. Church, G.E. Influence of test selection on physical education placement of mentally retarded children. (Refs: 15)*Adapted physical activity quarterly (Champaign, Ill.) 1(2), 1984, 112-117.*

ABST: Intact classes of mentally retarded and nonhandicapped children were administered the Physical Dexterity scales of the System of Multicultural Pluralistic Assessment and the short form of the Bruininks-Oseretsky Test of Motor Proficiency. Separate discriminant analyses of each data set revealed that the subjects comprised four distinct levels of motor performance. Although overall predicted correct classification was above 65% misclassifications occurred in each class. Differences resulting from the separate analyses suggest differential program placement for physical education. There is a tendency for the Physical Dexterity data to predict higher levels of motor functioning than the Motor Proficiency data for half of the mentally retarded children.
LEVEL: A LANG: Eng SIRC ARTICLE NO: 102444

Byde, R. McClenaghan, A. Effects of selected types of feedback on an anticipation timing task with moderately mentally retarded children. (Refs: 18)*Adapted physical activity quarterly (Champaign, Ill.) 1(2), 1984, 141-146.*
ABST: The purpose of this study was to examine the effects of selected types of feedback on the performance of an anticipation timing task by moderately mentally retarded children. Seventeen children, aged 10 to 16 years and classified as moderately mentally retarded participated as subjects for this investigation. Subjects were required to perform a key press response in anticipation to the arrival of a stimulus light. No significant main or interactive effects were found. Several possible explanations may account for these results included, (a) age range of the subjects may have biased the results, (b) the moderately retarded child may have had insufficient motor skills to successfully perform the tasks, (c) the personality characteristics of the subjects prevented them from perceiving their impact on performance, and/or (d) the type of feedback provided may not have been appropriately interpreted by the subjects.
LEVEL: A LANG: Eng SIRC ARTICLE NO: 102446

Heitman, R.J. Cronis, T.G. Gilley, W.F. Effects of pretask speed training on the transfer performance of trainable mentally retarded subjects on pursuit rotor tasks. (Refs: 18)*American corrective therapy journal (San Diego, Calif.) 38(1), Jan/Feb 1984, 19-23.*
ABST: This study investigated the effects of preliminary training at various speeds of the pursuit rotor on the transfer performance of trainable mentally retarded subjects (T.M.R.). Thirty T.M.R. subjects were randomly assigned to one of three treatment conditions: 1) 15-15-30 rpm 2) 30-30-30 rpm 3) 45-45-30 rpm. After 3 days of practise the subjects were tested on the pursuit rotor which was set at 30 rpm. The 30-30-30 rpm group had better results than the 15-15-30 rpm group and the 45-45-30 rpm group. These results concur with previous research using normal subjects.
LEVEL: A LANG: Eng SIRC ARTICLE NO: 094458

Hsu, P.-Y. Dunn, J.M. Comparing reverse and forward chaining instructional methods on a motor task with moderately mentally retarded individuals. (Refs: 11)*Adapted physical activity quarterly (Champaign, Ill.) 1(3), 1984, 240-246.*
ABST: The purpose of this study was to compare reverse chaining and forward chaining instructional methods in teaching task to moderately mentally retarded individuals. The motor task employed was a modified bowling skill using a four-step approach. Thirty moderately mentally retarded individuals were randomly assigned to either the reverse

chaining or the forward chaining group. Results showed that the subjects in the reverse chaining group required significantly fewer trails and physical assists to learn the given motor task than the subjects in the forward chaining group. No significant differences in retention scores were found between the two groups.
LEVEL: A LANG: Eng SIRC ARTICLE NO: 102456

Porretta, D.L. Formation of a motor schema in educable mentally retarded and intellecturally normal males. Eugene, Ore.: Microform Publications, University of Oregon, 1984. 2 microfiches : negative, ill. ; 11 x 15 cm.
NOTES: Thesis (Ph.D.) - Temple University, 1981; (viii, 96 leaves); includes bibliography.
LEVEL: A LANG: Eng UO84 286-287

Sim, L.J. Stewart, C. The effects of videotape feedback on the standing broad jump performances of mildly and moderately mentally retarded adults. (Refs: 34)*Physical educator (Indianapolis, Ind.) 41(1), Mar 1984, 21-29.*
ABST: The authors review the literature on feedback and motor skill acquisition. Ten male and six female mildly and moderately mentally retarded adults served as subjects. They were divided in three treatment groups. The control group, the verbal feedback group, and the video/verbal feedback group. The standing broad jump performances of subjects were assessed. Findings indicated that videotape and extrinsic verbal feedback did not positively affect the aquisition of the standing broad jump by the mentally retarded subjects. The authors recommended further research in the area.
LEVEL: A LANG: Eng SIRC ARTICLE NO: 095878

Thomas, K.T. Applying knowledge of motor development to mentally retarded children. (Refs: 34)*In, Thomas, J.R. (ed.), Motor development during childhood and adolescence, Minneapolis, Minn., Burgess Publishing Co., 1984, p. 174-184.*
LEVEL: A LANG: Eng BF1 20187

Tomporowski, P.D. Ellis, N.R. Preparing severely and profoundly mentally retarded adults for tests of motor fitness. (Refs: 11)*Adapted physical activity quarterly (Champaign, Ill.) 1(2), 1984, 158-163.*
ABST: The effectiveness of using behavior shaping techniques to prepare nine institutionalized severely and profoundly mentally retarded adults for tests of motor fitness was assessed. Three severely mentally retarded subjects served as the executive subjects in a yoked-control study. Each executive subject was paired randomly with two profoundly mentally retarded subjects. A three-phase baseline experiment was then conducted with executive subjects; yoked subjects received the same intervention as their executive partner. The training program consisted of a verbal instruction baseline phase, a modeling phase, and a graduated guidance phase. Tasks used for training were the shuttle run and standing long jump. Modeling instruction produced minimal improvement in subject performance; however, graduated guidance instruction produced marked, immediate improvement in the performance of six of nine subjects on both tasks.
LEVEL: A LANG: Eng SIRC ARTICLE NO: 102473

Ulrich, D.A. The reliability of classification decisions made with the objectives-based motor skill assessment instrument. (Refs: 30)*Adapted physical activity quarterly 1(1), 1984, 52-60.*
ABST: This study examined the reliability of

classification decisions made with the Objectives-Based Motor Skill Assessment Instrument based on two different cut-off scores. Eighty nonhandicapped and forty mentally retarded students, aged 3 to 10, were assessed on two separate days. The results indicate that this criterion-referenced test consistently classifies students as masters or non-masters of fundamental motor skills using either cut-off score.
LEVEL: A LANG: Eng SIRC ARTICLE NO: 092832

PHYSICAL EDUCATION

Fox, R. Burkhart, J.E. Rotatori, A.F. Physical fitness and personality characteristics of obese and nonobese retarded adults *International journal of obesity (London) 8(1), 1984, 61-67.*
ABST: In this article, the cardiovascular endurance, self-concept and anxiety levels of 22 obese and 20 nonobese mentally retarded adults were compared. Differences were observed in the cardiovascular endurance of both groups.
LEVEL: A LANG: Eng SIRC ARTICLE NO: 100650

PHYSICAL FITNESS

Findlay, H.A. Watkinson, E.J. Dahlgren, W.J. Evans, J. Lafreniere-Joannette, L. Bothwell-Meyers, C. Jeunesse en Forme Canada guide d'emploi: guide d'adaptation. Canada Fitness Award: how to use it: how to change it. (Refs: 3)*CAHPER journal/Revue de l'ACSEPR (Ottawa) 50(5), May/Jun 1984, 8-16;23-25.*
LEVEL: B LANG: Fr Eng SIRC ARTICLE NO: 095855

Pizarro, D.C. Health related fitness of mainstreamed EMR/TMR children. Eugene, Ore.: Microform Publications, University of Oregon, 1984. 2 microfiches : negative, ill. ; 11 x 15 cm.
NOTES: Thesis (Ed.D.) - University of Georgia, 1982; (xi, 153 leaves); includes bibliography.
LEVEL: A LANG: Eng UO84 270-271

Reid, G. Montgomery, D.L. The effects of an exercise program conducted by workshop employees on the physical fitness and absenteeism of mentally retarded workers. Final report to Fitness Canada. Montreal: McGill University, 1984. 26 leaves
NOTES: Report financially assisted by Fitness and Amateur Sport. Bibliography: I. 25-26.
LEVEL: A LANG: Eng GV183.7 18401

Tomporowski, P.D. Ellis, N.R. Effects of exercise on the physical fitness, intelligence, and adaptive behavior of institutionalized mentally retarded adults. (Refs: 17)*Applied research in mental retardation (Elmsford, N.Y.) 5(3), 1984, 329-337.*
LEVEL: A LANG: Eng SIRC ARTICLE NO: 103981

Tomporowski, P.D. Ellis, N.R. Effects of exercise on the physical fitness, intelligence, and adaptive behavior of institutionalized mentally retarded adults. *Applied research in mental retardation (Elmsford, N.Y.) 5(3), 1984, 329-337.*
LEVEL: A LANG: Eng

PLAY

McGill, J. Bailey, B. Play for play's sake: cooperative games as a strategy for integration. Toronto: National Institute on Mental Retardation, 1984?. v, 45 p.
NOTES: Bibliography: p. 45.

LEVEL: B LANG: Eng ISBN: 0-920121-05-5 LC CARD: C84-98788-9 GV183.7 18046

PROGRAMS

McClements, J. Integration '84: access to generic sports competition. *Journal of leisurability (Waterloo, Mich.) 11(2), Spring 1984, 20-23.*
LEVEL: B LANG: Eng SIRC ARTICLE NO: 095867

Smith, D. Tobin, P. Altering attitudes: a workshop. (Refs: 2)*Journal of leisurability (Waterloo, Ont.) 11(2), Spring 1984, 27-29.*
LEVEL: B LANG: Eng SIRC ARTICLE NO: 095879

PSYCHOLOGY

Fox, R. Burkhart, J.E. Rotatori, A.F. Physical fitness and personality characteristics of obese and nonobese retarded adults *International journal of obesity (London) 8(1), 1984, 61-67.*
ABST: In this article, the cardiovascular endurance, self-concept and anxiety levels of 22 obese and 20 nonobese mentally retarded adults were compared. Differences were observed in the cardiovascular endurance of both groups.
LEVEL: A LANG: Eng SIRC ARTICLE NO: 100650

Nearingburg, P.C. The effects of three outdoor programs on the self-concept of selected disabled participants. Eugene, Ore.: Microform Publications, University of Oregon, 1984. 2 microfiches : negative ; 11 x 15 cm.
NOTES: Thesis (M.S.) - University of Oregon, 1982; (x, 123 leaves); vita; includes bibliography.
LEVEL: A LANG: Eng UO84 100-101

RESEARCH

Watkinson, E.J. Wasson, D.L. The use of single-subject time-series designs in adapted physical activity. (Refs: 32)*Adapted physical activity quarterly 1(1), 1984, 19-29.*
ABST: The purpose of this paper is to describe single-subject time series designs that are appropriate for use in the field of adapted physical education and to point out some of the issues that arise when using them. These designs allow researchers and practitioners to monitor behavior changes in an individual under treatment and non-treatment conditions. The authors encourage adapted physical educators to use these designs to examine the acquisition, maintenance, and generalization of motor skills in instructional programs.
LEVEL: A LANG: Eng SIRC ARTICLE NO: 092834

DISCUS THROW

Steinbach, V. Discus talk. *Thrower (West Midlands, Eng.) 31, Dec 1984, 62.*
LEVEL: B LANG: Eng SIRC ARTICLE NO: 173503

BIOGRAPHY AND AUTOBIOGRAPHY

50m next stop for ambitious thrower. Catherine Bradley. *Athletics weekly (Kent, Eng.) 28(50), 15 Dec 1984, 59-60.*
LEVEL: B LANG: Eng SIRC ARTICLE NO: 103624

Bauer, S. Face to face: Al Oerter. *Ultrasport (Boston, Mass.) 1(3), May/Jun 1984, 6-8;10-13.*
LEVEL: B LANG: Eng SIRC ARTICLE NO: 097022

Caulfield, B. Al Oerter: the four-time Olympic Champion tries again-at age 47. *Running news (New York) 29(5), Jun/Jul 1984, 52-54;75;80.* LEVEL: B LANG: Eng SIRC ARTICLE NO: 098704

Hendershott, J. T & FN interview: Ben Plucknett. *Track and field news (Los Angeles, Calif.) 37(4), May 1984, 56-57.* LEVEL B LANG: Eng SIRC ARTICLE NO: 095488

Profile: Rosemarie Hauch. *Track and field journal (Ottawa) 26, May 1984, 17-18.* LEVEL: B LANG: Eng Fr SIRC ARTICLE NO: 0987

Vilara, R. Lia Manoliu: six times in the O.G. *Sports in Romania (Bucharest, Romania) 1, 1984, 26-29.* LEVEL: B LANG: Eng SIRC ARTICLE NO: 100113

Wilman, H. T & FN interview: John Powell. *Track & field news (Los Altos) 37(11), Dec 1984, 46-47.* LEVEL: B LANG: Eng SIRC ARTICLE NO: 103632

BIOMECHANICS

Duginyets, I. Discus analysis: Igor Duginyets. *Thrower (West Midlands, Eng.) 28, Feb 1984, 38-39.* LEVEL: I LANG: Eng SIRC ARTICLE NO: 095486

Steben, R.E. The discus technique of an elite prep athlete. CONF: National Symposium on Teaching Kinesiology and Biomechanics in Sports (2nd : 1984 : Colorado Springs). NOTES: In, Shapiro, R. and Marett, J.R. (eds.), Proceedings: Second National Symposium on Teaching Kinesiology and Biomechanics in Sports, Colorado Springs, Colorado, January 12-14, Dekalb, Ill., AAHPERD, 1984, p. 215-218. LEVEL: I LANG: Eng SIRC ARTICLE NO: 101724

COACHING

Interview: cycling success despite the system. (Walsh, C.) *Sports coach (Wembley, Australia) 7(4), Mar 1984, 54-57.* LEVEL: LANG: Eng SIRC ARTICLE NO: 094944

PERCEPTUAL MOTOR PROCESSES

Calvi, F. Essai d'analyse du role et de l'utilisation des informations visuelles dans le lancer du disque. (Refs: 8)*Revue de l'Amicale des entraineurs francais d'athletisme (Paris) 86, janv/fevr/mars 1984, 35-45.* LEVEL: A LANG: Fr SIRC ARTICLE NO: 095482

PSYCHOLOGY

Powell, J. The training philosophy of John Powell. *Thrower (West Midlands, Eng.) 31, Dec 1984, 31-34.* NOTES: Text taken from a lecture given at Lilleshall Recreation Centre. LEVEL: B LANG: Eng SIRC ARTICLE NO: 173497

STATISTICS AND RECORDS

Matthews, P. Discus - world records. *Thrower (West Midlands, Eng.) 29, May 1984, 27-29.* LEVEL: B LANG: Eng SIRC ARTICLE NO: 098715

TECHNIQUES AND SKILLS

Mardle, P. Powell throwing - an American experience. *Thrower (West Midlands, Eng.) 31, Dec 1984, 35-37.* LEVEL: B LANG: EN SIRC ARTICLE NO: 173498

Powell, J. Seminar with John Powell at Crystal Palace on 19th November 1983. *Thrower (West Midlands, Eng.) 29, May 1984, 4-23.* LEVEL: B LANG: Eng SIRC ARTICLE NO: 098716

Soudek, E.H. John Powell's classic discus style: the thrower gets acceleration across the circle by continuously pivoting th feet, knees, and hips. *Scholastic coach 53(8), Mar 1984, 38-40;67.* LEVEL: B LANG: Eng SIRC ARTICLE NO: 093973

Stenlund, G.M. The discus throw. Part II. *Sports (Kallang, Singapore) 12(8), Sept 1984, 30-31.* LEVEL: B LANG: Eng SIRC ARTICLE NO: 101726

TRAINING AND CONDITIONING

Ceronie, R. Torok, D. Pre-season training for shot put & discus throwers. Movement and medicine ball routines provide an effective method of preseason training for throwers. (Refs: 1)*Athletic journal 64(7), Feb 1984, 48;68.* LEVEL: B LANG: Eng SIRC ARTICLE NO: 092548

Marks, R. Specialized strength & technique training for shot put and discus. *Thrower (West Midlands, Eng.) 30, Aug 1984, 26-28.* LEVEL: B LANG: Eng SIRC ARTICLE NO: 098714

Tancred, B. The discus - training and competition hints. *Modern athlete and coach (Athelstone, Aust.) 22(1), Jan 1984, 39-40.* LEVEL: B LANG: Eng SIRC ARTICLE NO: 097029

Vanni, M. The discus. (Helsinki observations). *Modern athlete and coach (Athelstone, Aust.) 22(2), Apr 1984, 10.* LEVEL: B LANG: Eng SIRC ARTICLE NO: 097030

Vanni, M. Observing the discus throwers in world championships. *Track and field journal (Ottawa) 26, May 1984, 21;28.* LEVEL: B LANG: Eng SIRC ARTICLE NO: 098722

TRAINING AND CONDITIONING - DRILLS

Shannon, K. Shot put and discus drills. *Track & field quarterly review (Kalamazoo, Mich.) 84(1), Spring 1984, 25-26.* LEVEL: B LANG: Eng SIRC ARTICLE NO: 095503

Stenlund, G.M. The discus throw. Part I. *Sports (Kallang, Singapore) 12(7), Aug 1984, 30-31.* LEVEL: B LANG: Eng SIRC ARTICLE NO: 101725

DISEASES AND DISORDERS

Birrer, R.B. Common skin problems of athletes. NOTES: In, Birrer, R.B. (ed.), Sports medicine for the primary care physician, Norwalk, Conn., Appleton-Century-Crofts, c1984, p. 239-248. LEVEL: I LANG: Eng RC1210 17030

Blanc, J. Jusserand, J. Comment tenter d'eviter une chondropathie. *Basketball (Paris) 492, fevr/mars/avr 1984, 21.* LEVEL: LANG: Fr SIRC ARTICLE NO: 097588

Burke, E.J. Germain, M.J. Braden, G.L. Fitzgibbons, J.P. Mild steady-state exercise during hemodialysis treatment. (Refs: 17 *Physician and sportsmedicine (Minneapolis, Minn.) 12(6), Jun 1984, 153-157.* ABST: 3 men and 3 women pedaled a bicycle ergometer for 5 minutes during the first hour of hemodialysis treatment. Heart rate, blood pressure, hydrogen-ion concentration and respiratory and blood gases were measured before hemodialysis treatment, before exercise, during exercise and at selected post-exercise times. The physiological responses were typical of a deconditioned person performing low level exercise. The authors feel these results have positive implications for hemodialysis treatment. LEVEL: A LANG: Eng SIRC ARTICLE NO: 094589

Creff, A.F. Mouton, A. Nathan, P. Le syndrome de Shulman (fasciite avec eosinophiles) est-il une hypothyroidie masquee? *Medecine du sport (Paris) 58(6), nov 1984, 8-10.* LEVEL: I LANG: Fr SIRC ARTICLE NO: 102566

Fielding, J.E. Health promotion and disease prevention at the worksite. *Annual review of public health 5, 1984, 237-265.* LEVEL: I LANG: Eng SIRC ARTICLE NO: 102578

Hanson, P. Illness among athletes: an overview. (Refs: 22) NOTES: In, Strauss, R.H. (ed.), Sports medicine, Philadelphia ; Toronto, Saunders, 1984, p. 79-90. LEVEL: A LANG: Eng RC1210 17196

Kettner, A. Goldberg, A. Harter, H. Endurance exercise in hemodialysis patients. Effects on the sympathetic nervous system and serum glucose regulation. *Contributions to nephrology (Basel) 41, 1984, 269-271.* LEVEL: A LANG: Eng

Kottke, T.E. Caspersen, C.J. Hill, C.S. Exercise in the management and rehabilitation of selected chronic diseases. (Refs: 7 *Preventive medicine (New York) 13(1), Jan 1984, 47-65.* ABST: The role of exercise in the management and rehabilitation of eight chronic diseases or medical conditions is reviewed. Some of the diseases investigated: cardiovascular disease, rheumatoid arthritis, cystic fibrosis, kidney disease and oseteoporosis. LEVEL: A LANG: Eng SIRC ARTICLE NO: 100731

Layne, T.N. Life-threatening illnesses: the commom and not-so-common. *First aider (Gardner, Kan.) 53(5), Feb 1984, 8-10.* NOTES: Last of a three-part series. LEVEL: B LANG: Eng SIRC ARTICLE NO: 096030

Legwold, G. Aortic graft gives hope to Marfan's athletes. *Physician and sportsmedicine 12(2), Feb 1984, 19-20.* LEVEL: I LANG: Eng SIRC ARTICLE NO: 091519

Lewis, S.F. Haller, R.G. Cook, J.D. Blomqvist, C.G. Metabolic control of cardiac output response to exercise in McArdle's disease. (Refs: 25)*Journal of applied physiology: respiratory, environmental and exercise physiology (Bethesda, Md.) 57(6), Dec 1984, 1749-1753.* LEVEL: A LANG: Eng SIRC ARTICLE NO: 108564

DISEASES AND DISORDERS (continued)

McCray, R.E. Patton, N.J. Pain relief at trigger points: a comparaison of moist head and shortwave diathermy. (Refs: 15) *Journal of orthopaedic and sports physical therapy (Baltimore) 5(4), Jan/Feb 1984, 175-178.*
ABST: This study was undertaken to determine if pain measurement can be objectively used to determine the relative effectiveness of moist heat and shortwave diathermy treatments. Pain trigger points on the neck or back were measured with a pressure algometer. The results indicate that shortwave diathermy is more effective at relieving pain at trigger points than moist heat (P0.0581). **It was also shown that the use of a pressure algometer to determine trigger point sensitivity may aid in the selection of a treatment modality.** LEVEL: A LANG: Eng SIRC ARTICLE NO: 092942

Schaberg, J.E. Harper, M.C. Allen, W.C. The snapping hip syndrome. (Refs: 12)*American journal of sports medicine (Baltimore Md.) 12(5), Sept/Oct 1984, 361-365.*
ABST: A clinical, radiographic, and anatomical study of eight patients with the snapping hip syndrome, secondary to an internal etiology, was undertaken to aid in the diagnosis and surgical treatment. Iliopsoas bursography with cineradiography revealed subluxation of the iliopsoas tendon to be an apparent cause of the snapping hip. The anatomy of the hip in relationship to the iliopsoas tendon is defined with the anterior inferior iliac spine, iliopectineal eminence, and lesser trochanter assuming a significant role in the syndrome. An operative approach involving a partial release and lengthening of the iliopsoas tendon, with minimal resection of a lesser trochanteric bony ridge, if involved, is described.
LEVEL: A LANG: Eng SIRC ARTICLE NO: 104076

Schindler, R.J. Infectious diseases affecting athletes. (Refs: 7)*Sideline view 5(7), Feb 1984, 1-4.*
LEVEL: B LANG: Eng SIRC ARTICLE NO: 091530

Sherman, M.F. Reilly, J.P. Bonamo, J.R. Birrer, R.B. Athletic participation in the presence of chronic disorders: asthma, obesity, diabetes, and seizure disorders. (Refs: 20)
NOTES: In, Birrer, R.B. (ed.), Sports medicine for the primary care physician, Norwalk, Conn., Appleton-Century-Crofts, c1984, p. 252-258.
LEVEL: I LANG: Eng RC1210 17030

ALLERGY

Erffmeyer, J.E. Holman, J. Exercise-induced 'allergic' syndromes. *Texas medicine (Austin, Tex.) 80(3), Mar 1984, 48-50.*
LEVEL: I LANG: Eng SIRC ARTICLE NO: 102574

International symposium on special problems and management of allergic athletes. January 13-14, 1984, Palm Springs, California *Journal of allergy and clinical immunology (St. Louis) 73(5 Pt 2), May 1984, 629-748.*
LEVEL: A LANG: Eng SIRC ARTICLE NO: 100726

Kaplan, A.P. Exercise-induced hives. (Refs: 19)*Journal of allergy and clinical immunology (St. Louis) 73(5 Pt 2), May 1984, 704-707.*
LEVEL: I LANG: Eng SIRC ARTICLE NO: 100727

Mahan, L.K. Nutrition and the allergic athlete. (Refs: 51)*Journal of allergy and clinical immunology (St. Louis) 72(5 Pt 2) May 1984, 728-734.*
LEVEL: I LANG: Eng SIRC ARTICLE NO: 100737

Mijailovic, B. Stefanovic, Z. Arneric, S. Karadlaglic, D. Ninkovic, M. Lazarevic, T. Holinergicna urtikarija sa anafilakticnom reakcijom na fizicki napor. (Cholinergic urticaria with an anaphylactic reaction to physical stress.) *Vojnosanitetski pregled (Belgrad) 41(2), Mar/Apr 1984, 127-129.*
LEVEL: I LANG: Scr

ANAPHYLAXIS

Baadsgaard, O. Lindskov, R. Cholinergic urticaria with anaphylaxis induced by exercise or heating. *Acta dermato-venereologica (Stockholm) 64(4), 1984, 344-346.*
LEVEL: A LANG: Eng

Eisenstadt, W.S. Nicholas, S.S. Velick, G. Enright, T. Allergic reactions to exercise. (Refs: 23)*Physician and sportsmedicine (Minneapolis, Minn.) 12(12), Dec 1984, 94-98;100;102;104.*
LEVEL: I LANG: Eng SIRC ARTICLE NO: 102572

El-Dieb, M.R. Food-dependent, exercise-induced anaphylaxis. (letter) *JAMA: Journal of the American Medical Association (Chicago) 251(24), 22-29 Jun 1984, 3224.*
LEVEL: B LANG: Eng SIRC ARTICLE NO: 102573

Erffmeyer, J.E. Holman, J. Exercise-induced 'allergic' syndromes. (Refs: 21)*Texas medicine Mar 1984, 48-50.*
LEVEL: I LANG Eng SIRC ARTICLE NO: 092928

Sabbah, A. Drouet, M. Anaphylaxie induite par l'exercice et liee a l'allergie alimentaire. (Anaphylaxis induced by exertion and related to dietary allergy. (letter)) *Presse medicale (Paris) 13(39), 3 nov 1984, 2390-2391.*
LEVEL: I LANG: Fr

Sheffer, A.L. Austen, K.F. Exercise-induced anaphylaxis. *Journal of allergy and clinical immunology (St. Louis) 73(5 Pt 2), May 1984, 699-703.*
LEVEL: I LANG: Eng SIRC ARTICLE NO: 100754

ANEMIA

Aronow, W.S. Schlueter, W.J. Williams, M.A. Petratis, M. Sketch, M.H. Aggravation of exercise performance in patients with anemia by 3 per cent carboxyhemoglobin. (Refs: 19)*Environmental research (New York) 35(2), Dec 1984, 394-398.*
LEVEL: A LANG: Eng SIRC ARTICLE NO: 174264

Feinstein, R.A. Daniel, W.A. Anemia and 'anemia' in adolescents: value in screening examinations for sports. (Refs: 8) *Physician and sportsmedicine 12(1), Jan 1984, 140-143;146.*
LEVEL: I LANG: Eng SIRC ARTICLE NO: 091506

McDonald, R. Hegenauer, J. Sucec, A. Saltman, P. Effects of iron deficiency and exercise on myoglobin in rats. (Refs: 29) *European journal of applied physiology and occupational physiology (Berlin, FRG) 52(4), Jun 1984, 414-419.*
ABST: This study examined the effects of iron-deficiency anemia and endurance training on myoblogin (Mb) in order to define its role in oxidative metabolism. Forty female Sprague-Dawley rats were divided into the following four groups: 1) training with normal diet (NT), training with low-iron diet (AT), sedentary with normal diet (NS), and sedentary with low-iron diet (AS). The training rats ran 3 days per week for 6 weeks at speeds and grades which were progressively increased until the rats could run for 90 min at a grade of 10 degrees

and a speed of 0.55 m.5 1. The anemic animals showed an inability to perform at maximal work rates compared to the normal group's performance. The trained anemic rats showed an increase in skeletal muscle Mb. The authors suggest that this increase is a compensatory mechanism to offset the decrease in hemoglobin concentration.
LEVEL: A LANG: Eng SIRC ARTICLE NO: 097604

Pate, R.R. Anemia in female athletes. Chicago: Teach'em Inc., 1984?. 1 sound cassette (Audio cassette series on sports medicine: Sportsmedicine for female athletes, SM-38.)
NOTES: Cassettes recorded and produced by Teach'em Inc. in cooperation with the Physician and Sportsmedicine.
LEVEL: I LANG: Eng

Seshadri, S. Malhotra, S. The effect of hematinics on the physical work capacity in anemics. *Indian pediatrics (Bombay) 21 (7), Jul 1984, 529-533.*
LEVEL: A LANG: Eng

Woodson, R.D. Hemoglobin concentration and exercise capacity. (Refs: 18)*American review of respiratory disease (New York) 129(2 Pt 2), Feb 1984, S72-S75.*
CONF: Exercise Testing in the Dyspneic Patient Workshop (1982 : Bethesda).
ABST: This paper reviews research on the effects of mild to moderate anemia on exercise capacity and hemodynamics. The close relationship between hemoglobin and VO2 max is believed to be part of the reason for sex differences in VO2 max in age matched subjects. Anemia is compensated for in submaximal exercise by relative increases in cardiac output, heart rate and ventilation. Reduced hemoglobin levels result in an almost proportional reduction in maximal exercise capacity.
LEVEL: I LANG: Eng SIRC ARTICLE NO: 099278

ARTERIOSCLEROSIS

Boyd, C.E. Bird, P.J. Teates, C.D. Wellons, H.A. MacDougall, M.A. Wolfe, L.A. Pain free physical training in intermittent claudication. (Refs: 37)*Journal of sports medicine and physical fitness (Torino, Italy) 24(2), Jun 1984, 112-122.*
ABST: Following a program of physical training, eight patients suffering from vascular intermittent claudication significantly improved their exercise performance. Four diabetics and four non-diabetics participated in 25 to 40 minutes of submaximal, pain free, endurance exercise three times per week for twelve weeks. Significant increases were found for all exercise tolerance measures. No significant changes were found in body weight or resting and exercise heart rate and blood pressures. There were no significant differences between the diabetics and the non-diabetics for all variables studied.
LEVEL: A LANG: Eng SIRC ARTICLE NO: 102364

Bridges, F.S. The effects of vasectomy and exercise upon arterial extensibility and the extent and severity of atherosclerosis. Eugene, Ore.: Microform Publications, University of Oregon, 1984. 2 microfiches : negative, ill. ; 11 x 15 cm.
NOTES: Thesis (Ed.D.) - University of Alabama, 1982; (vii, 139 leaves); includes bibliography.
LEVEL: A LANG: Eng UO84 409-410

Markiewicz, K. Cholewa, M. Jazdzewski, B. Gawor, Z. Wplyw submaksymalnego wysilku fizycznego na stezenie lipidow surowicy oraz na uklad krzepniecia krwi i fibrynolizy u chorych z miazdzyca. (Effect of submaximal physical exertion

on serum lipid levels and the blood coagulation and fibrinolysis sytems in patients with arteriosclerosis.) *Polski tygodnik lekarski (Warsaw) 39(25/26), 12-25 June 1984, 857-861.*
LEVEL: A LANG: Pol

Paulev, P.E. Exercise and risk factors for arteriosclerosis in 42 married couples followed over four years. (Refs: 28) *Journal of chronic diseases (Elmsford) 37(7), 1984, 545-553.*
ABST: 42 married couples were measured yearly with respect to risk factors for arteriosclerosis. Advice was provided on relaxed, enjoyable exercise. At the end of the four year period both men and women had improved their well being and their health profile as evaluated with respect to arteriosclerosis risk factors. Exhaustive exercise was not necessary for these benefits.
LEVEL: A LANG: Eng SIRC ARTICLE NO: 104354

Reggiani, E. Bertolini, S. Chiodini, G. Elicio, N. Montanari, D. Valice, S. Zannini, G. Baruzzo, D. Montagna, G. Pistocchi, G Lassa, G. Croce, S. Effects of physical activity and diet on lipemic risk factors for atherosclerosis in women. (Refs: 41) *International journal of sports medicine (Stuttgart) 5(4), Aug 1984, 183-186.*
ABST: Serum lipoproteins were studied in active and sedentary young women. A quantitative and qualitative evaluation of the diet was performed. In spite of a higher intake of saturated fat and cholesterol, serum concentrations of triglyceride, total cholesterol, and low-density lipoprotein cholesterol in the active group were not significantly different from the controls. Nevertheless, high-density lipoprotein cholesterol levels were significantly higher in the active subjects even after covariance adjustment for nutrient intake.
LEVEL: A LANG: Eng SIRC ARTICLE NO: 104141

Ruell, P.A. Imperial, E.S. Bonar, F.J. Thursby, P.F. Gass, G.C. Intermittent claudication: the effect of physical training o walking tolerance and venous lactate concentration. (Refs: 16)*European journal of applied physiology and occupational physiology (Berlin, FRG) 52(4), Jun 1984, 420-425.*
ABST: This study evaluated the effect of physical training on the exercise capacity and venous lactate concentration in patients with intermittent claudication. Twenty-one patients were divided into three groups of equal size based on initial maximal walking tolerance. All groups exercised on a bicycle ergometer 30 min/day, 3 days/week for 8 weeks. At the end of the training period all three groups showed a significant improvement to pain and stress test capacity. The authors conclude that a physical training program increases walking tolerance in different categories of claudication. Possible mechanisms for the improvement are discussed.
LEVEL: A LANG: Eng SIRC ARTICLE NO: 097611

Slezkina, L.A. Proiavleniia ateroskleroza mozgovykh i koronarnykh arterii u bol'nykh, perenesshikh infarkt miokarda. (Manifestations of arteriosclerosis of the cerebral and coronary arteries in patients with a history of myocardial infarct.) *Klinicheskaia meditsina (Moskva) 62(3), Mar 1984, 46-49.*
LEVEL: A LANG: Rus

ARTHRITIS

Blake, B. Exercise and arthropathy. (Refs: 25)*American Academy of Physical Education papers (Champaign, Ill.) 17, 1984, 49-58.*
CONF: American Academy of Physical Education. Annual Meeting (54th : 1983 : Minneapolis). NOTES: Conference theme: Exercise and health.
LEVEL: I LANG: Eng SIRC ARTICLE NO: 104107

Croce, P. Vanett, B.B. The arthritic's guide to sports and fitness. New York: Leisure Press, 1984. 256 p. : ill.
LEVEL: I LANG: Eng ISBN: 0-88011-230-1

Lewis, C. Arthritis and exercise. (Refs: 8) NOTES: In, Biegel, L. (ed.), Physical fitness and the older person: a guide to exercise for health care professionals, Rockville, Md., Aspen Systems Corp., 1984, p. 129-149.
LEVEL: I LANG: Eng GV482.6 17754

Siegel, A.J. How I manage gout in athletes. (Refs: 4)*Physician and sportsmedicine 12(2), Feb 1984, 62-64;72-73.*
LEVEL: I LANG: Eng SIRC ARTICLE NO: 091532

Sullivan, K. The asthmatic athlete. *Starting line (Reseda, Calif.) 13(72), Spring 1984, 12.*
LEVEL: B LANG: Eng SIRC ARTICLE NO: 103979

Wilson, C.H. Exercise for arthritis. (Refs: 29) NOTES: In, Basmajian, J.V. (ed.), Therapeutic exercise, 4th ed., Baltimore, Md., Williams & Wilkins, c1984, p. 529-545.
LEVEL: A LANG: Eng RM719 17505

ASTHMA

Arborelius, M. Svenonius, E. Decrease of exercise-induced asthma after physical training. (Refs: 16)*European journal of respiratory diseases. Supplement (Copenhagen) 136, 1984, 25-31.*
ABST: Training with high load interval exercise after premedication with beta 2-aerosol significantly increased the anaerobic threshold in three groups of children and a significant decrease in exercise-induced asthma was recorded.
LEVEL: A LANG: Eng SIRC ARTICLE NO: 102754

Athletes and anti-asthma/exercise-induced bronchospasm medications. *Sports mediscope (Colorado Springs) 4(2), Summer 1984, 12.*
NOTES: USOC sports medicine info sheet 11-2, July 1984.
LEVEL: B LANG: Eng SIRC ARTICLE NO: 095784

Bhagat, R.G. Grunstein, M.M. Comparison of responsiveness to methacholine, histamine, and exercise in subgroups of asthmatic children. *American review of respiratory disease (New York) 129(2), Feb 1984, 221-224.*
ABST: 2 groups of steroid requiring asthmatic children, 9 to 15 years of age, had their nonspecific bronchial reactivity tested with methacoline, histamine and treadmill exercise.
LEVEL: A LANG: Eng SIRC ARTICLE NO: 098998

Cundell, D. Danks, J. Phillips, M.J. Davies, R.J. Effect of exercise on isoprenaline-induced lymphocyte cAMP production in atopic asthmatics and atopic and non-atopic, non-asthmatic subjects. *Clinical allergy (Oxford) 14(5), Sept 1984, 433-442.*
LEVEL: A LANG: Eng

Deal, E.C. McFadden, E.R. Ingram, R.H. Jaeger, J.J. Role of respiratory heat exchange in asthma. (Refs: 3)*Journal of applie physiology: respiratory,*

environmental and exercise physiology (Bethesda, Md.) 57(2), Aug 1984, 608-609.
LEVEL: A LANG: Eng SIRC ARTICLE NO: 108360

Eggleston, P.A. Methods of exercise challenge. *Journal of allergy and clinical immunology (St. Louis) 73(5 Pt 2), May 1984, 666-669.*
LEVEL: I LANG: Eng SIRC ARTICLE NO: 100716

EIB and the Olympic athlete. *Sports mediscope (Colorado Springs) 4(2), Summer 1984, 11.*
NOTES: USOC sports medicine info sheet 10-1, May 1984.
LEVEL: B LANG: Eng SIRC ARTICLE NO: 096013

Eisenstadt, W.S. Nicholas, S.S. Velick, G. Enright, T. Allergic reactions to exercise. (Refs: 23)*Physician and sportsmedicine (Minneapolis, Minn.) 12(12), Dec 1984, 94-98;100;102;104.*
LEVEL: I LANG: Eng SIRC ARTICLE NO: 102572

Epstein, S. Allergies and the developing athlete. *Starting line (Reseda, Calif.) 13(75), Fall 1984, 7.*
LEVEL: B LANG: Eng SIRC ARTICLE NO: 173507

Exercise and asthma: a round table. (Refs: 4)*Physician and sportsmedicine 12(1), Jan 1984, 58-66;71-73;76-77.*
LEVEL: I LANG Eng SIRC ARTICLE NO: 091413

Fitch, K.D. Management of allergic Olympic athletes. *Journal of allergy and clinical immunology (St. Louis) 73(5 Pt 2), May 1984, 722-727.*
LEVEL: B LANG: Eng SIRC ARTICLE NO: 100717

Godfrey, S. Symposium on special problems and management of allergic athletes. Introduction. *Journal of allergy and clinica immunology (St. Louis) 73(5 Pt 2), May 1984, 630-633.*
LEVEL: I LANG: Eng SIRC ARTICLE NO: 100719

Holzer, F.J. Schnall, R. Landau, L.I. The effect of a home exercise programme in children with cystic fibrosis and asthma. *Australian paediatric journal (Melbourne) 20(4), Nov 1984, 297-301.*
LEVEL: I LANG: Eng

International symposium on special problems and management of allergic athletes. January 13-14, 1984, Palm Springs, California *Journal of allergy and clinical immunology (St. Louis) 73(5 Pt 2), May 1984, 629-748.*
LEVEL: A LANG: Eng SIRC ARTICLE NO: 100726

Katz, R.M. Sports and asthma. *Sportsmedicine digest (Van Nuys, Calif.) 6(3), Mar 1984, 3.*
LEVEL: B LANG: Eng SIRC ARTICLE NO: 097603

Kennedy, S.L. Comparing the effects of the PRECEDE model on an asthma education program. Eugene, Ore.: Microform Publications, University of Oregon, 1984. 3 microfiches : negative, ill, ; 11 x 15 cm.
NOTES: Thesis (Ph.D.) - Pennsylvania State University, 1983; (xi, 248, (1) leaves); vita; includes bibliography.
LEVEL: A LANG: Eng UO84 375-377

King, J.T. Bye, M.R. Demopoulos, J.T. Exercise programs for asthmatic children. *Comprehensive therapy (Harvard, Mass.) 10 (11), Nov 1984, 67-71.*
LEVEL: B LANG: Eng

Legwold, G. Program offers aid to Olympics with EIB. (Exercise-induced bronchospasm) *Physician and sportsmedicine (Minneapolis, Minn.) 12(7), Jul 1984, 117-121;124;126.*
NOTES: Olympic update: the relationship between drugs and the Olympics.
LEVEL: B LANG: Eng SIRC ARTICLE NO: 095797

DISEASES AND DISORDERS (continued)

Linn, W.S. Shamoo, D.A. Venet, T.G. Bailey, R.M. Wightman, L.H. Hackney, J.D. Comparative effects of sulfur dioxide exposure at 5 degrees C and 22 degrees C in exercising asthmatics. *American review of respiratory disease (New York) 129(2), Feb 1984, 234-239.*
ABST: Eight young adult asthmatic volunteers were exposed to various sulfur dioxide (SO2) concentrations, during 5 min heavy exercise at 5 degrees C, both with high and low relative humidity. Physiologic response increased with increasing SO2 concentration but did not vary significantly with humidity. Twenty-four asthmatics were exposed similarly to clean air and to a SO2 concentration at 5 degrees C and also at 22 degrees C. For this group, physiologic and clinical responses to SO2 (in excess of responses to clean air) were highly significant, regardless of temperature. Moderate cold stress exacerbated the response to SO2 only slightly and inconsistently in these asthmatic subjects.
LEVEL: A LANG: Eng SIRC ARTICLE NO: 099009

McFadden, E.R. Exercise performance in the asthmatic. (Refs: 33)*American review of respiratory disease (New York) 129(2 Pt 2), Feb 1984, S84-S87.*
CONF: Exercise Testing in the Dyspneic Patient Workshop (1982 : Bethesda).
ABST: Factors that modify the bronchospastic responses to exercise in asthmatics include patterns of breathing, intensity/duration of work load, air temperature and humidity, medication, and possible training effects. Data is presented to demonstrate these factors.
LEVEL: I LANG: Eng SIRC ARTICLE NO: 099011

Metivier, G. The asthmatic child and physical exercise. (Refs: 88)*Journal of human movement studies (Edinburgh) 10(1), 1984 21-33.*
ABST: This review discusses possible mechanisms by which exercise causes asthma, physiological parameters of asthmatic children, physical assessment of asthmatic patients and methods to prevent exercise-induced asthma.
LEVEL: A LANG: Eng SIRC ARTICLE NO: 094611

Mitsubayashi, T. (Effect of physical training on exercise-induced bronchospasm of institutionalized asthmatic children.) *Arerugi. Japanese journal of allergology (Tokyo) 33(6), Jun 1984, 318-327.*
LEVEL: A LANG: Jpn

Murphy, S. Exercise-induced immunological responses. Part I: exercise-induced asthma. *Cutis (New York) 34(4), Oct 1984, 332;334-336.*
LEVEL: A LANG: Eng

Orenstein, D.M. Competitive sports for children with chronic pulmonary diseases. (Refs: 3)*Sports medicine digest (Van Nuys, Calif.) 6(5), May 1984, 1-3.*
LEVEL: I LANG: Eng SIRC ARTICLE NO: 100657

Popper, E. Dobiasova, L. Vyskyt ponamanoveho bronchospasmu a funkcni zdatnost detskych astmatiku. (Incidence of post-exertional bronchospasm and the functional fitness of asthmatic children.) *Ceskoslovenska pediatrie (Prague) 39(1), Jan 1984, 15-20.*
LEVEL: A LANG: Cze

Prescott, L.M. Air pollutants might aggravate athletes' asthma, allergies. (news) *JAMA: Journal of the American Medical Association (Chicago) 251(19), 18 May 1984, 2496.*
LEVEL: B LANG: Eng SIRC ARTICLE NO: 100658

Shturman, R. Management of asthma: understanding, communication, and health maintenance. *Journal of asthma (Ossining, N.Y.) 21(4), 1984, 279-280.*
LEVEL: B LANG: Eng SIRC ARTICLE NO: 103978

Sly, R.M. Beta-adrenergic drugs in the management of asthma in athletes. *Journal of allergy and clinical immunology (St. Louis) 73(5 Pt 2), May 1984, 680-685.*
LEVEL: A LANG: Eng SIRC ARTICLE NO: 100759

Spack, N.P. Medical problems of the exercising child: asthma, diabetes, and epilepsy. (Refs: 18)
NOTES: In, Micheli, L.J. (ed.), Pediatric and adolescent sports medicine, Boston ; Toronto, Little, Brown, c1984, p. 124-133.
LEVEL: I LANG: Eng RC1210 17791

Terral, C. L'asthme et le sport. *Pratique medicale (Paris) 8, 1984, 11-32.*
LEVEL: I LANG: Fr

The asthmatic child's participation in sports and physical education. *Pediatrics (Evanston, Ill.) 74(1), Jul 1984, 155-156.*
CORP: American Academy of Pediatrics. Committee on Children with Disabilities.
CORP: American Academy of Pediatrics. Committee on Sports Medicine.
LEVEL: B LANG: Eng SIRC ARTICLE NO: 102440

Todaro, A. Berlutti, G. Caldarone, G. Dal Monte, A. Bronchial asthma in top athletes. (Refs: 18)*Journal of sports medicine and physical fitness (Torino, Italy) 24(3), Sept 1984, 246-251.*
ABST: Over the last ten years, 39 athletes affected with bronchial asthma who practice high level sports activity were observed. In all subjects spirographic measurements were obtained at rest; 20 also underwent spirographic examination after bronchodilator aerosol. Finally 15 of the athletes underwent a maximal effort test. Serious bronchial obstruction limited neither the maximum ventilation nor the oxygen intake in these subjects.
LEVEL: A LANG: Eng SIRC ARTICLE NO: 105264

Vadheim, L. Breathing pitfalls: respiratory snow snakes Part 1. *Journal of professional ski coaching and instruction (Boulder, Colo.) May 1984, 15-16.*
LEVEL: B LANG: Eng SIRC ARTICLE NO: 096059

van Herwaarden, C.L.A. Exercise and training in chronic non-specific lung disease (CSNLD). (Refs: 18)*International journal of sports medicine (Stuttgart) Suppl. 5, Nov 1984, 54-58.*
CONF: International Congress on Sports and Health (1983 : Maastricht, Netherlands).
LEVEL: A LANG: Eng SIRC ARTICLE NO: 104153

Weiner, P. Greif, J. Fireman, E. Kivity, S. Topilsky, M. Bronchodilating effect of cromolyn sodium in asthmatic patients at rest and following exercise. *Annals of allergy (Bloomington, Minn.) 53(2), Aug 1984, 186-188.*
LEVEL: A LANG: Eng SIRC ARTICLE NO: 103987

Witts, R.C. The differing effects of continuous and intermittent exercise in initiating exercise-induced asthma. (abstract) *Carnegie research papers (Beckett Park, Leeds) 1(6), Dec 1984, 33-34.*
CONF: Carnegie Undergraduate Research Symposium (1984 : Leeds, Eng.).
LEVEL: I LANG: Eng SIRC ARTICLE NO: 172510

BACTERIAL INFECTIONS

Gove, S. Slutkin, G. Infections acquired in the fields and forests of the United States. *Emergency medical clinics of North America 2(3), Aug 1984, 623-633.*
LEVEL: I LANG: Eng

BONE DISEASES

Andersen, L.A. Gotzsche, P.C. Naproxen and aspirin in acute musculoskelatal disorders: a double-blind, parallel study in patients with sports injuries. *Pharmatherapeutica (London) 3(8), 1984, 531-537.*
ABST: This study evaluates the efficacy of either 750 mg naproxen or 2 g acetylsalicyclic acid administered to 75 patients with sport injuries. Significant improvement is observed in both treatment groups. The authors note better results when treatment starts as early as possible after the injury.
LEVEL: A LANG: Eng SIRC ARTICLE NO: 099031

Caldwell, F. Walking maintains bone, says NIH panel. *Physician and sportsmedicine (Minneapolis, Minn.) 12(9), Sept 1984, 31.*
LEVEL: B LANG: Eng SIRC ARTICLE NO: 099082

Harrison, J.E. Neutron activation studies and the effect of exercise on osteoporosis. *Journal of medicine: clinical, experimental and theoretical (Westbury, N.Y.) 15(4), 1984, 285-294.*
LEVEL: A LANG: Eng

Howse, A.J.G. Problems of the adolescent knee and their treatment. *Physiotherapy (London) 70(4), 10 Apr 1984, 150-153.*
LEVEL: I LANG: Eng SIRC ARTICLE NO: 095931

Larson, K.A. Shannon, S.C. Decreasing the incidence of osteoporosis related injuries through diet and exercise. (Refs: 19) *Public health reports (Hyattsville, Md.) 99(6), 1984, 609-613.*
LEVEL: A LANG: Eng SIRC ARTICLE NO: 104050

Montoye, H.J. Exercise and osteoporosis. (Refs: 90)*American Academy of Physical Education papers (Champaign, Ill.) 17, 1984 59-75.*
CONF: American Academy of Physical Education. Annual Meeting (54th : 1983 : Minneapolis).
NOTES: Conference theme: Exercise and health.
LEVEL: I LANG: Eng SIRC ARTICLE NO: 104127

Musante, R. Preziuso, M. Cupelli, V. Attina, D.A. The Marfan syndrome. M-mode and two dimensional echocardiography study of two basket-ball players. (Refs: 11)*International journal of sports cardiology (Torino, Italy) 1(2), Jul/Dec 1984, 88-95.*
LEVEL: A LANG: Eng SIRC ARTICLE NO: 179173

Oyster, N. Morton, M. Linnell, S. Physical activity and osteoporosis in post-menopausal women. (Refs: 53)*Medicine and science in sports and exercise 16(1), 1984, 44-50.*
ABST: Osteoporosis has been found to occur in post menopausal women for various reasons, one of which is the lack of estrogen. This study of 40 post-menopausal women aged 60 to 69 years indicates that osteoporosis can be retarded with regular physical activity. The latent effects of estrogen are considered, but it is felt that additional research on estrogen and other supplements is needed.
LEVEL: A LANG: Eng SIRC ARTICLE NO: 091906

Palmason, D. Managing POP. (osteoporosis) *Fitness leader (Ottawa) 3(3)*, Nov 1984, 9-12. LEVEL: B LANG: Eng SIRC ARTICLE NO: 105314

Palmason, D. Postmenopausal osteoporosis. *Fitness leader (Ottawa) 3(2)*, Oct 1984, 5-8. LEVEL: B LANG: Eng SIRC ARTICLE NO 105315

Palmason, D. The POP risk profile. (osteoporosis) *Fitness leader (Ottawa) 3(2)*, Oct 1984, 3-4. LEVEL: B LANG: Eng SIRC ARTICLE NO: 105316

Pritikin, N. There's more to strong bones than calcium: they need exercise. *Runner's world (Mountain View, Calif.) 19(10)*, Oct 1984, 145. LEVEL: B LANG: Eng SIRC ARTICLE NO: 178853

Rundgre, A. Aniansson, A. Ljungberg, P. Wetterqvist, H. Effects of a training programme for elderly people on mineral conten of the heel bone. *Archives of gerontology and geriatrics (Amsterdam) 3(3)*, Oct 1984, 243-248. ABST: Fifteen women (mean age, 72 yr) participated in a 9 mth training program in order to study the effects of exercise on bone mineral content. Inactive patients from the same age group served as controls. Results indicated that exercise diminished bone loss due to age and that physical training influenced positively bone mineral content. LEVEL: A LANG: Eng

Smith, E.L. Smith, P.E. Ensign, C.J. Shea, M.M. Bone involution decrease in exercising middle-aged women. *Calcified tissue international (New York) 36(Suppl. 1)*, 1984, S129-S138. ABST: Bilateral bone mineral mass and width of the radius, ulna, and humerus were measured by single photon absorptiometry on 200 women between the ages of 35 and 65 over a 3-4 year period. Two groups were formed: 80 in a control group and 120 in a physical activity group exercising 3 days/week. During the first year of the program, a decrease by 3.77 per cent in bone mineral mass of the left radius while during the second and third years, bone mineral mass of the left radius increased by 1.39 per cent per year, and the rate of change was significantly different from that of the control group. There were similar increases in the other bones measured. The data from this study support the importance of physical activity in the prevention of bone mineral loss in the aging female. LEVEL: A LANG: Eng SIRC ARTICLE NO: 104148

Thatcher, P.C. The effects of running on the density and breaking strength of the femora of male rats with induced experimental osteoporosis. Eugene, Ore.: Microform Publications, University of Oregon, 1984. 1 microfiche : negative, ill. ; 11 x 15 cm. NOTES: Thesis (M.S.) - University of Oregon, 1982; (xi, 59 leaves); vita; includes bibliography. LEVEL: A LANG: Eng UO84 59

Woerman, A.L. Binder-Macleod, S.A. Leg length discrepancy assessment: accuracy and precision in five clinical methods of evaluation. (Refs: 27)*Journal of orthopaedic and sports physical therapy (Baltimore, Md.) 5(5)*, Mar/Apr 1984, 230-239. ABST: Twenty physical therapists employed one indirect and four direct methods to evaluate the leg length discrepancy (LLD) of five subjects. Of all methods tested, the indirect method, which employed lift blocks under a foot with the subject in the standing position, was the most accurate and precise method of LLD assessment. Of the direct methods tested, a measurement of the distance from the anterior superior iliac spine to the lateral

malleolus gave the most accurate and precise assessment of LLD. LEVEL: A LANG: Eng SIRC ARTICLE NO: 094449

Yeater, R.A. Martin, R.B. Senile osteoporosis. The effects of exercise. (Refs: 80)*Postgraduate medicine (Minneapolis) 75(2)* 1 Feb 1984, 147-159;163. ABST: This review of osteoporosis research literature finds that a high level of physical activity throughout life can result in increased skeletal mass during one's forties. Studies of animals and humans have found that physical activity retards or prevents bone loss in both recently postmenopausal and very elderly women. LEVEL: I LANG: Eng SIRC ARTICLE NO: 099112

CANCER

Dusinberre, R.H. How I can manage pilonidal disease. *Physician and sportsmedicine (Minneapolis, Minn.) 12(11)*, Nov 1984, 55-57;61. LEVEL: I LANG: Eng SIRC ARTICLE NO: 100715

Hausman, P. Fighting cancer with nutrition: can you use your diet as the first line of defense in the fight for health? *Runner's world (Mountain View, Calif.) 19(6)*, Jun 1984, 58-62;78. LEVEL: B LANG: Eng SIRC ARTICLE NO: 094421

Hinton, A.J. Risks of fishermen's dyes. (letter) *Lancet (London) 1(8387)*, 26 May 1984, 1179. LEVEL: I LANG: Eng SIRC ARTICLE NO: 102591

Maggots dyed with chrysoidine. (letter) *British medical journal (Clinical Research Ed.) (London) 289(6456)*, 24 Nov 1984, 1451-1452. LEVEL: I LANG: Eng

Sole, G.M. Maggots dyed with chrysoidine: a possible risk to anglers. *British medical journal (Clinical Research ed.) (London) 289(6451)*, 20 Oct 1984, 1043-1044. LEVEL: A LANG: Eng

Vigorita, V.J. Jones, J.K. Ghelman, B. Marcove, R.C. Intracortical osteosarcoma. *American journal of surgical pathology (Ne York) 8(1)*, Jan 1984, 65-71. ABST: The case of a 15 year old boy having osteosarcoma arising in the tibia is reported. It had a benign roentgenographic appearance and the tumor was confined within the cortex of the bone. LEVEL: A LANG: Eng SIRC ARTICLE NO: 099110

CARDIOVASCULAR DISEASE

Abdon, N.J. Landin, K. Johansson, B.W. Athlete's bradycardia as an embolising disorder? Symptomatic arrhythmias in patients aged less than 50 years. *British heart journal (London) 52(6)*, Dec 1984, 660-666. LEVEL: A LANG: Eng

Becquemin, J.P. Melliere, D. Lamour, A. Kenesi, C. The popliteal entrapment syndrome. *Anatomica clinica (New York) 6(3)*, 1984, 203-207. ABST: The causes of 5 occurrences of the popliteal entrapment syndrome in 4 patients aged between 17 and 41 are identified in this paper: 1) abnormally high insertion of the inner genellus muscle tendon (3 cases), 2) hypertrophic muscular plantaris (1 case), and 3) abnormal fibrous bands (1 case). 111 additional cases reported from 1970 to 1983 are also reviewed. LEVEL: A LANG: Eng

Bradycardia, ventricular pauses, syncope, and sports. (Letter) *Lancet (London) 2(8409)*, 27 Oct 1984, 990-991. LEVEL: I LANG Eng

Bylund-Fellenius, A.C. Walker, P.M. Elander, A. Schersten, T. Peripheral vascular disease. (Refs: 9)*American review of respiratory disease (New York) 129(2 Pt 2)*, Feb 1984, S65-S67. CONF: Exercise Testing in the Dyspneic Patient Workshop (1982 : Bethesda). ABST: Peripheral vascular disease was examined in four studies (2 with humans and 2 with rats) in order to evaluate the effects of reduced blood flow on skeletal muscle metabolism. Compensatory mechanisms in the ischemic skeletal muscle were found to include increased activity of oxidative enzymes and increased capillary and/or mitochondrial density. Gastrocnemius muscle oxygen tension decreased and muscle lactate increased in patients with claudication compared to normal subjects performing the same level of work. LEVEL: A LANG: Eng SIRC ARTICLE NO: 098905

Colle, J.P. Legoff, G. Bonnet, J. Aouizerate, E. Ohayon, J. Besse, P. Bricaud, H. Etude de la fonction ventriculaire gauche globale et segmentaire dans le prolapsus valvulaire mitral pur avec mauvaise tolerance a l'effort. (Left ventricular global and segmental function in pure mitral valve prolapse with poor tolerance for exertion.) *Archives des maladies du coeur et des vaisseaux (Paris) 77(6)*, juin 1984, 616-624. ABST: Left ventricular function and segmental wall motion were studied retrospectively in a group of 17 patients with idiopathic mitral valve prolapse (IMVP). The patients, average age 53 plus or minus 12 years, had poor effort tolerance justifying catheter and angiographic studies. All patients had IMVP confirmed on RAO left ventriculography. There was no associated mitral regurgitation or coronary artery disease. Left ventricular funtion was studied by parameters of global function (systolic and diastolic parameters, volume measurements) and by a quantitative study of segmental wall contraction. LEVEL: A LANG: Fr SIRC ARTICLE NO: 104109

Cousteau, J.P. Fabiani, F. Le coeur du sportif. (Refs: 2)*Concours medical (Paris) 106(35)*, 1984, 3357-3360. LEVEL: I LANG Fr

Fecteau, D. Athletic heart syndrome: differentiating normal physiologic changes from pathologic changes. (Refs: 12) *Dimensions of critical care nursing (Philadelphia) 3(3)*, May/Jun 1984, 134-139. LEVEL: A LANG: Eng SIRC ARTICLE NO: 100520

Fleg, J.L. Lakatta, E.G. Prevalence and prognosis of exercise-induced nonsustained ventricular tachycardia in apparently healthy volunteers. *American journal of cardiology (New York) 54(7)*, 1 Oct 1984, 762-764. LEVEL: A LANG: Eng

Fraciosa, J.A. Leddy, C.L. Wilen, M. Schwartz, D.E. Relation between hemodynamic and ventilatory responses in determining exercise capacity in severe congestive heart failure. *American journal of cardiology (New York) 53(1)*, 1 Jan 1984, 127-134. ABST: The testing of 28 patients with severe left ventricular failure found exercise intolerance to be associated with marked elevation of pulmonary capillary wedge pressure and anaerobic metabolism

without hypoxemia or altered carbon dioxide tension. This leads the authors to suggest that exercise ability in congestive heart failure is more dependent on cardiac output rather than pulmonary congestion factors.
LEVEL: A LANG: Eng SIRC ARTICLE NO: 097442

Furlanello, F. Bettini, R. Vergara, G. Cozzi, F. Visona, L. Disertori, M. Thiene, G. Problematica delle cardiopatie aritmogene a rischio dello sportivo con particolare riguardo alla pre-eccitazione cardiaca. (Problem of arrhythmogenic cardiopathies at risk in athletes with special reference to cardiac preexcitation.) *Giornale italiano di cardiologia (Roma) 14(12), Dec 1984, 1062-1068.*
LEVEL: A LANG: It

Furlanello, F. Vergara, G. Bettini, R. Disertori, M. Inama, G. Guarnerio, M. Visona, L. Progress in the study of Wolff-Parkinson-White Syndrome of the athletes. The transesophageal atrial pacing during bicycle exercise. (Refs: 83)*International journal of sports cardiology (Torino, Italy) 1(2), Jul/Dec 1984, 102-110.*
ABST: The prognostic arrhythmologic evaluation of athletes must include the study of the arrhythmias in a situation as similar as possible to that of the athletic effort of the subject. The authors have developed a method which can be adapted for the athletes, for the electrophysiological study of the W.P.W. This method involves inducing atrial fibrillation by means of transesophageal pacing during bicycle ergometer tests. With this method it is possible to see immediately the electrophysiological and clinical consequences of the atrial fibrillation in each athlete with W.P.W. during physical effort, even though asymptomatic. The advantage of this simple and rapid method, which does not require X-ray control for positioning of the catheter, is that it does not require 'hospitalisation', thus permitting frequent check-ups of electrophysiological characteristics of arrhythmias both for subjects at risk and for ones who appear to be fit.
LEVEL: A LANG: Eng SIRC ARTICLE NO: 179175

Goforth, D. James, F.W. Kaplan, S. Donner, R. Mays, W. Maximal exercise in children with aortic regurgitation: an adjunct to noninvasive assessment of disease severity. *American heart journal (St. Louis) 108(5), Nov 1984, 1306-1311.*
LEVEL: A LANG: Eng

Iskandrian, A.S. Hakki, A.H. Amenta, A. Mandler, J. Kane, S. Regulation of cardiac output during upright exercise in patient with aortic regurgitation. *Catheterization and cardiovascular diagnosis (New York) 10(6), 1984, 573-582.*
LEVEL: A LANG: Eng

Janicki, J.S. Weber, K.T. Likoff, M.J. Fishman, A.P. Exercise testing to evaluate patients with pulmonary vascular disease. (Refs: 13)*American review of respiratory disease (New York) 129(2 Pt 2), Feb 1984, S93-S95.*
CONF: Exercise Testing in the Dyspneic Patient Workshop (1982 : Bethesda).
ABST: This paper examines the need for earlier detection of pulmonary vascular disease and the usefulness of exercise testing with gas exchange to accomplish this. The testing of a study group of 9 patients found maximal oxygen use correlated directly with the maximal level of cardiac output and was inversely proportional to the pulmonary vascular resistance and level of pulmonary artery pressure. This determination then can become a practical screening technique for detecting and

predicting the severity of pulmonary vascular disease. The appearance of the anaerobic threshold at earlier work loads than normal was another observation that is associated with pulmonary vascular disease.
LEVEL: A LANG: Eng SIRC ARTICLE NO: 098911

Kraus, F. Rudolph, W. Symptoms, exercise capacity and exercise hemodynamics: interrelationships and their role in quantification of the valvular lesion. *Herz (Munich) 9(4), Aug 1984, 187-199.*
LEVEL: A LANG: Eng

Lepaentalo, M. Sundberg, S. Gordin, A. The effects of physical training and flunarizine on walking capacity in intermittent claudication. *Scandinavian journal of rehabilitation medicine (Stockholm) 16(4), 1984, 159-162.*
LEVEL: A LANG: Eng

Lobanchikov, A. The doctor answers. (varicose veins in young athletes) *Soviet sports review (Escondido, Calif.) 19(2), Jun 1984, 83-84.*
NOTES: Translated from, Legkaya atletika, 2: 15, 1983.
LEVEL: I LANG: Eng SIRC ARTICLE NO: 099094

Manz, H.J. Gomes, M.N. Sports injury as cause of traumatic pseudoaneurysm of superficial temporal artery. (letter) *Archives of pathology and laboratory medicine (Chicago) 108(10), Oct 1984, 775-776.*
LEVEL: I LANG: Eng SIRC ARTICLE NO: 104056

Matsen, F.A. Wyss, C.R. Simmons, C.W. Robertson, C.L. Burgess, E.M. The effect of exercise upon cutaneous oxygen delivery in the extremities of patients with claudication and in a human laboratory model of claudication. *Surgery gynecology & obstetrics (Chicago) 158(6), Jun 1984, 522-528.*
LEVEL: I LANG: Eng SIRC ARTICLE NO: 102603

Opasich, C. Assandri, J. Calsamiglia, G. Febo, O. Pozzoli, M. Tramarin, R. Traversi, E. Cobelli, F. Specchia, G. Exertional hypotension after myocardial infarction. *Giornale italiano di cardiologia (Roma) 14(8), Aug 1984, 614-617.*
LEVEL: A LANG: Eng

Pillet, J. Wullaert, P. Chevalier, J.M. Enon, B. Moreau, P. Lescalie, F. Les phlebites d'effort. (Refs: 8)*Cinesiologie: medecine du sport (Paris) 98, nov/dec 1984, 451-455.*
RESUME: La phlebite dite d'effort est maintenant consideree comme appartenant aux syndromes de compression de la traversee thoraco-cervico-brachiale. Elle est souvent precedee d'une periode de 'claudication veineuse' pendant laquelle une intervention chirurgicale simple (resection de la 1re cote par voie axillaire) est efficace. Au stade de phlebite constituee, les interventions de thrombectomie sont le plus souvent vouees a l'echec, la resection de la 1re cote peut ameliorer la situation mais partiellement. Quant aux interventions de derivation veineuse, leurs indications sont rares et reservees aux cas les plus invalidants.
LEVEL: A LANG: Fr SIRC ARTICLE NO: 104135

Podrid, P.J. Graboys, T.B. Exercise stress testing in the management of cardiac rhythm disorders. *Medical clinic of North America (Philadelphia) 68(5), Sept 1984, 1139-1152.*
LEVEL: A LANG: Eng

Santi, C. Pugliese, P. Bernabei, M. Eufrate, S. Rottura traumatica dell'arco aortico. Presentazione di un caso clinico trattato con successo. Rottura

aortica - Caso clinico. Traumatic rupture of the aortic arch. Presentation of a successfully treated clinical case. Ruptured aorta - clinical case. (Refs: 9)*Italian journal of sports traumatology (Milano, Italy) 6(2), Apr/Jun 1984, 159-163.*
CONF: Italian Society of Sports Traumatology. Congress (1st : 1983 : Rome).
ABST: This paper describes the case of a young soccer player with undiagnosed aortic coarctation. He ruptured his aortic isthmus during a soccer match and underwent surgery to repair it. There were no postoperative complications. The incidence of such disorders among athletes is discussed.
LEVEL: A LANG: It Eng SIRC ARTICLE NO: 099101

Snape, L. Traumatic temporal aneurysm. *British journal of oral and maxillofacial surgery (Edinburgh) 22(3), Jun 1984, 208-211.*
ABST: The case of a sportsman is described of a traumatic aneurysm of the superficial, temporal artery and the differential diagnosis is discussed.
LEVEL: A LANG: Eng SIRC ARTICLE NO: 104078

Vinogradov, A.V. Lobzeva, V.I. Rylova, A.K. Sposob differentsial'noi diagnostiki stenokardii i neirotsirkuliatornoi distonii (Means of differential diagnosis between angina pectoris and neurocirculatory dystonia.) *Kardiologiia (Moscow) 24(5), May 1984, 73-77.*
ABST: Plasma somatotropic hormone and cortisol were measured at rest, at the peak of physical stress and 2 hours after the discontinuation of exercise in 15 normal male subjects, 18 male patients with neurocirculatory dystonia and 69 with angina pectoris. The determination of one-dimensional hyperplanes of plasma STH and cortisol during and after exercise allows one to distinguish anginal patients from those with neurocirculatory dystonia and make a diagnosis in patients with nonspecified chest pains.
LEVEL: A LANG: Rus

Weber, K.T. Wilson, J.R. Janicki, J.S. Likoff, M.J. Exercise testing in the evaluation of the patient with chronic cardiac failure. (Refs: 14)*American review of respiratory disease (New York) 129(2 Pt 2), Feb 1984, S60-S62.*
CONF: Exercise Testing in the Dyspneic Patient Workshop (1982 : Bethesda).
ABST: As the overall cardiovascular function of a heart disease patient deteriorates there is a quantifiable progressive deterioration in aerobic capacity. Oxygen must be delivered to the skeletal muscle to meet its aerobic needs. In heart disease patients increased oxygen required during exercise by the skeletal muscle may not be accomplished by a sufficient increase in oxygen flow. The severity of this can be determined through monitoring respiratory gas exchange which will measure the VO2 max and the anaerobic threshold.
LEVEL: A LANG: Eng SIRC ARTICLE NO: 098919

Young, D.Z. Lampert, S. Graboys, T.B. Lown, B. Safety of maximal exercise testing in patients at high risk for ventricular arrhythmia. *Circulation (Dallas) 70(2), Aug 1984, 184-191.*
ABST: The authors reviewed the complications of symptom limited exercise in 263 patients with malignant ventricular arrhythmias. These patients underwent a total of 1377 maximal treadmill tests.
LEVEL: A LANG: Eng

CARDIOVASCULAR DISEASE - EXERCISE REHABILITATION AND THERAPY

Bergan, J.J. There is no second. Presidential address. Society for vascular surgery. *Journal of vascular surgery (St. Louis Mo.) 1(6), Nov 1984, 723-726.*
LEVEL: I LANG: Eng

Casasoprana, A. L'exercice physique et sportif: conseils a l'enfant cardiaque. *Pratique medicale (Paris) 40, 1984, 36-40.*
LEVEL: B LANG: Fr

Conradson, T.B. Ryden, L. Improved cardiac performance during exercise following hydralazine treatment in chronic heart failure. *Acta medica scandinavica (Stockholm) 216(1), 1984, 41-45.*
LEVEL: A LANG: Eng

Dancy, M. Leech, G. Leatham, A. Changes in ecochardiographic left ventricular minor axis dimensions during exercise in patients with aortic stenosis. *British heart journal (London) 52(4), Oct 1984, 446-450.*
LEVEL: A LANG: Eng

Diehm, C. Kohlenhydrat- und Fettstoffwechsel bei Normalpersonen und Patienten mit peripherer arterieller Verschlusskrankheit Auswirkungen eines Ausdauertrainings. (Carbohydrate and lipid metabolism in normal subjects and patients with peripheral arterial occlusive diseases. Effect of stamina training.) *Vasa (Bern) Suppl. 13, 1984, 1-61.*
LEVEL: A LANG: Ger

Dirner, O. Arato, O. Guha, M. Vad, M. Group rehabilitation of students exempted from physical education due to cardiac and circulatory disease 1972 to 1976.
CONF: Sports Cardiology International Conference (1978 : Rome).
NOTES: In, Lubich, T. and Venerando, A. (eds.), Sports Cardiology International Conference, Rome - April 1978, Bologna, Aulo Gaggi Publisher, 1980, p. 919-928.
LEVEL: A LANG: Eng

Francis, K.T. Maynard, E.H. Exercise and uric acid: implication in cardiovascular disease. (Refs: 32)*Journal of orthopaedic and sports physical therapy (Baltimore, Md.) 6(1), Jul/Aug 1984, 34-38.*
ABST: The association of elevated serum uric acid (SUA) concentration (hyperuricemia) with gout has been known for many years, but more recently hyperuricemia has been observed to be associated with many of the known major risk factors for coronary heart disease (hypertension, stress, hypercholesterolemia) with much greater frequency than in the general population. Several epidemiological studies have indicated a beneficial relationship between physical activity, risk factor modification, and susceptibility to coronary heart disease. Physical activity has been shown to modify not only the major identified risk factors but SUA levels as well. Whereas acute exercise lasting between one-half and three hours elevates SUA in proportion to intensity of exercise, chronic exercise lowers SUA levels. Mechanisms for these changes are discussed as well as implications in relation to coronary disease.
LEVEL: A LANG: Eng SIRC ARTICLE NO: 100521

Hanson, P. Exercise prescription. Part II: Clinical guidelines for exercise training. (Refs: 29)

NOTES: In, Strauss, R.H. (ed.), Sports medicine, Philadelphia ; Toronto, Saunders, 1984, p. 45-56.
LEVEL: A LANG: Eng RC1210 17196

Hellerstein, H.K. Franklin, B.A. Evaluating the cardiac patient for exercise therapy: role of exercise testing. (Refs: 33) *Clinics in sports medicine (Philadelphia) 3(2), Apr 1984, 371-393.*
ABST: This article reviews the utilization of several types of exercise tests. The authors suggest some modifications to the tests in order to better meet the varied needs of normal individuals and patients with cardiac problems. Guidelines for the stopping of exercise tests are given as are methods for evaluating the patients' responses to the exercise stress. Borg's Rating of Perceived Exertion Scale is seen as a useful addition to cardiac exercise testing but it should not be the sole basis for an exercise prescription.
LEVEL: A LANG: Eng SIRC ARTICLE NO: 094252

Kostis, J.B. Lacy, C.R. Krieger, S.D. Cosgrove, N.M. Atenolol, nadolol, and pindolol in angina pectoris on effort: effect of pharmacokinetics. *American heart journal (St. Louis) 108(4 Pt 2), Oct 1984, 1131-1136.*
LEVEL: A LANG: Eng

Landry, F. Habel, C. Desaulniers, D. Dagenais, G.R. Moisan, A. Cote, L. Vigorous physical training after aortic valve replacement: analysis of 10 patients. *American journal of cardiology (New York) 53(4), 1 Feb 1984, 562-566.*
ABST: 10 men who had undergone aortic valve replacement participated in a training program on a bicycle ergometer 3 times per week for 8 weeks. 10 other men who had undergone AVR were used as controls. Significant improvements were registered in the exercise group in maximum tolerated workload, aerobic capacity and in double product at submaximal work load. Pre and post training echocardiograms did not show any alterations.
LEVEL: A LANG: Eng SIRC ARTICLE NO: 098912

Leach, C.N. Shannon, L.M. New Britain cardiac rehabilitation: thirteen years' experience. *Connecticut medicine (New Haven, Conn.) 48(10), Oct 1984, 625-629;633.*
LEVEL: A LANG: Eng

Magorien, R.D. Leier, C.V. Kolibash, A.J. Barbush, T.J. Unverferth, D.V. Beneficial effects of nifedipine on rest and exercise myocardial energetics in patients with congestive heart failure. *Circulation (Dallas, Tex.) 70(5), Nov 1984, 884-890.*
LEVEL: A LANG: Eng

Malval, G. L'activite physique et les maladies cardio-vasculaires. (Physical activity and cardiovascular diseases.) *Soins. Cardiologie (Paris) 15, mai 1984, 39-48.*
LEVEL: I LANG: Fr SIRC ARTICLE NO: 103873

Molajo, A.O. Coupe, M.O. Bennett, D.H. Effect of Corwin (ICI 118587) on resting and exercise heart rate and exercise tolerance and digitalised patients with chronic atrial fibrillation. *British heart journal (London) 52(4), Oct 1984, 392-395.*
LEVEL: A LANG: Eng

Quyyumi, A.A. Wagstaff, D. Evans, T.R. Long-term beneficial effects of endralazine, a new arteriolar vasodilator at rest and during exercise capacity in chronic congestive heart failure. *American journal of cardiology (New York) 54(8), 1 Nov 1984, 1020-1024.*
LEVEL: A LANG: Eng

Wayne, V.S. Exercise-induced atrioventricular block. (letter) *Journal of the American College of Cardiology (New York) 4(5) Nov 1984, 1068-1069.*
LEVEL: A LANG: Eng

Wu, D.K. Bissett, J.K. Watson, J.I. Baker, J. Effect of exercise on repolarisation abnormalities in patients with asymptomatic QT prolongation. *Cardiovascular research (London) 18(1), Jan 1984, 60-65.*
ABST: Patients with congenital QT prolongation have an increased incidence of ventricular arrhythmias and sudden death. The purpose of this study was to determine the pattern of QT change with exercise in patients with QT prolongation without exercise-induced arrhythmias. Treadmill exercise testing was performed in 10 patients with a QTc greater than 0.44 s, the results were compared with 14 patients with a normal QTc.
LEVEL: A LANG: Eng SIRC ARTICLE NO: 098920

CARDIOVASCULAR DISEASE - PREVENTION

Blackburn, H. Luepker, R. Kline, F.G. Bracht, N. Carlaw, R. Jacobs, D. Mittelmark, M. Stauffer, L. Taylor, H.L. The Minnesot Heart Health Program: a research and demonstration project in cardiovascular disease prevention. (Refs: 6)*In, Matarazzo, J.D. (ed.) et al., Behavioral health: a handbook of health enhancement and disease prevention, New York, Wiley, c1984, p. 1171-1178.*
LEVEL: I LANG: Eng

France, K. Body conditioning: a thinking person's guide to aerobic fitness. Atlanta, Ga.: Humanics, c1984. 1v.
NOTES: Includes index and bibliography.
LEVEL: I LANG: Eng ISBN: 0893340804 LC CARD: 84-019801

Kattus, A.A. On exercise and cardiovascular health. *Executive health (Sante Fe, Calif.) 20(7), Apr 1984, 1-5.*
LEVEL: I LANG: Eng SIRC ARTICLE NO: 092730

LaPorte, R.E. Adams, L.L. Savage, D.D. Brenes, G. Dearwater, S. Cook, T. The spectrum of physical activity, cardiovascular disease and health: an epidemiologic perspective. (Refs: 56)*American journal of epidemiology (Baltimore) 120(4), Oct 1984, 507-517.*
LEVEL: I LANG: Eng SIRC ARTICLE NO: 103870

Lasater, T. Abrams, D. Artz, L. Beaudin, P. Cabrera, L. Elder, J. Ferreira, A. Knisley, P. Peterson, G. Rodrigues, A. Rosenberg, P. Snow, R. Carleton, R. Lay volunteer delivery of a community-based cardiovascular risk factor change program: the Pawtucket experiment. (Refs: 7)*In, Matarazzo, J.D. (ed.) et al., Behavioral health: a handbook of health enhancement and disease prevention, New York, Wiley, c1984, p. 1166-1170.*
LEVEL: B LANG: Eng

Milhorn, H.T. Prescribing a cardiovascular fitness program. *Comprehensive therapy (Harvard, Ma.) 10(2), Feb 1984, 46-53.*
LEVEL: I LANG: Eng SIRC ARTICLE NO: 100743

Prokop, D. A diet for life. Marathoner Rolet de Castella, whose son is no slouch, swears by the Pritikin plan. *Runners worl (Mountain View, Calif.) 19(12), Dec 1984, 60-66;68;90.*
LEVEL: I LANG: Eng SIRC ARTICLE NO: 100788

Puska, P. Community-based prevention of cardiovascular disease: the North Karelia Project.

(Refs: 10)*In, Matarazzo, J.D. (ed.) et al., Behavioral health: a handbook of health enhancement and disease prevention, New York, Wiley, c1984, p. 1140-1147.*
LEVEL: A LANG: Eng

Sidorenko, G.I. Aktual'nye voprosy tselenapravlennoi profilaktiki cerdechno-sosudistykh zabolevanii. (Urgent problems in the effective prevention of cardiovascular diseases.) *Kardiologiia (Moscow) 24(11), Nov 1984, 5-10.*
LEVEL: A LANG: Rus

Verschuur, R. Kemper, H.C.G. Besseling, C.W.M. Habitual physical activity and health in 13- and 14-year-old teenagers. (Refs 26)
CONF: Symposium of Paediatric Work Physiology (10th : 1981 : Joutsa, Finland).
NOTES: In, Ilmarinen, J. and Vaelimaeki, I. (eds.), Children and sport: paediatric work physiology, Berlin, Springer-Verlag, 1984, p. 255-261.
LEVEL: A LANG: Eng SIRC ARTICLE NO: 102749

CARDIOVASCULAR DISEASE - RISK FACTORS

Vuori, I. Kardiovasculaera risker i samband med motion. (Cardiovascular risks in connection with exercise.) *Nordisk medicin (Halsingberg, Sweden) 99(6/7), 1984, 174-176.*
LEVEL: I LANG: Swe

CEREBRAL PALSY

Beuter, A. Describing multijoint coordination: preliminary investigation with nonhandicapped, cerebral palsied, and elderly individuals. (Refs: 14)*Adapted physical activity quarterly (Champaign, Ill.) 1(2), 1984, 105-111.*
ABST: This paper proposes a computer graphics approach to represent the kinematics of the lower limb during a multijoint coordinated motor task. The methodology is based on automatic digitization by a microprocessor of reflective markers placed on anatomical landmarks and videotaped using a videomotion analyzer and camera. With joint angles, or the first or second derivative of the angles serving as the coordinates for the three mutually perpendicular axes in R3, the technique gives a point in space corresponding to each time increment as the movement sequence progresses. Using this method a graphical representation of the position, velocity, or acceleration can be generated in movement space, velocity space, or acceleration space, respectively. A sample of the results of this technique is presented using the movement space of elderly, nonhandicapped, and cerebral palsied individuals as each steps over a low obstacle.
LEVEL: A LANG: Eng SIRC ARTICLE NO: 102442

Halpern, D. Therapeutic exercises for cerebral palsy. (Refs: 31)
NOTES: In, Basmajian, J.V. (ed.), Therapeutic exercise, 4th ed., Baltimore, Md., Williams & Wilkins, c1984, p. 309-338.
LEVEL: A LANG: Eng RM719 17505

Hartley, E. Rushton, C. The therapeutic use of a trampoline in inhibiting abnormal reflex reactions and facilitating normal patterns of movements in some cerebral palsied children. (Refs: 6)*Journal of the society of remedial gymnastics and recreational therapy (Manchester) 113, Aug 1984, 6-11.*
LEVEL: I SIRC ARTICLE NO: 108555

COMMON COLD

Low, T. A cold or flu could mean sudden death. *Gymnast (London) Feb 1984, 17-19.*
LEVEL: B LANG: Eng SIRC ARTICLE NO: 0990

Shevtsov, V.V. Zakalivanie organizma v protsesse zaniatii po fizicheskomu vospitaniiu. (Increasing bodily resistance during physical training.) *Gigiena i sanitariia (Moskva) 3, Mar 1984, 35-37.*
LEVEL: I LANG: Rus

CONGENITAL HEART DEFECT

Frazee, R. Brunt, D. Castle, R.F. Exercise tolerance level of a young child with congenital heart disease associated with asplenia syndrome. (Refs: 7)*Adapted physical activity quarterly (Champaign, Ill.) 1(4), 1984, 322-326.*
ABST: This paper describes the exercise tolerance of a young girl with a congenital heart defect associated with asplenia syndrome. The child was exercised minimally on a treadmill for a period of 10 minutes, during which time heart rate, blood pressure, ECG, and transcutaneous PO2 values were monitored. Due to a small increase in heart rate and a very low PO2 during exercise, it was suggested that some adaptive mechanism had been developed to counteract her cyanotic condition. An optimal increase in hematocrit and hemoglobin levels supported this. No ECG abnormalities were noted. It was concluded that this child should have some, but minimal involvement in physical education programs despite the severity of her condition.
LEVEL: A LANG: Eng SIRC ARTICLE NO: 103961

Freed, M.D. Recreational and sports recommendations for the child with heart disease. *Pediatric clinics of North America (Philadelphia) 31(6), Dec 1984, 1307-1320.*
LEVEL: I LANG: Eng

Pernot, C. Le sport chez l'enfant cardiaque. (Refs: 10)*Dans, Mandel, C. (ed.), Le medecin, l'enfant et le sport, Paris, (Vigot), c1984, p. 183-197.*
LEVEL: I LANG: Fr RC1218.C45 18886

Vaccaro, P. Gallioto, F.M. Bradley, L.M. Hansen, D.A. Vaccaro, J. Development of a cardiac rehabilitation programme for children. (Refs: 26)*Sports medicine (Auckland, N.Z.) 1(4), Jul/Aug 1984, 259-262.*
LEVEL: I LANG: Eng SIRC ARTICLE NO: 102379

CORONARY HEART DISEASE

Adamian, K.G. Oganesian, N.M. Oganesian, L.S. Babaian, A.S. Asatrian, M.A. Znachenie radiokardiograficheskikh issledovanii s nagruzkoi v izuchenii funktsionalnogo sostoianiia serdechno-sosudistoi sistemy pri khronicheskoi ishemicheskoi bolezni serdtsa. (Value of radiocardiographic studies during exertion in the study of the functional state of the cardiovascular system in chronic ischemic heart disease.) *Kardiologiia (Moscow) 24(3), Mar 1984, 39-42.*
LEVEL: A LANG: Rus

Allen, C.J. Craven, M.A. Rosenbloom, D. Sutton, J.R. Beta-blockade and exercise in normal subjects and patients with coronar artery disease. (Refs: 48)*Physician and sportsmedicine (Minneapolis, Minn.) 12(10), Oct 1984, 51-54;56;59-60.*
LEVEL: I LANG: Eng SIRC ARTICLE NO: 098896

Anderson, J.L. Wagner, J.M. Datz, F.L. Christian, P.E. Bray, B.E. Taylor, A.T. Comparative effects of diltiazem, propranolol and placebo on exercise performance using radionuclide ventriculography in patients with symptomatic coronary artery disease: results of a double-blind, randomized, crossover study. *American heart journal (St. Louis) 107(4), Apr 1984, 698-706.*
ABST: The authors compared the effects of oral diltiazem (120 mg), propranolol (100 mg), and placebo in exercise performance, and left ventricular function before and during bicycle exercise in 12 coronary artery disease patients. Exercise performance increased significantly after diltiazem (plus 27%, P less than 0.01) but not after propranolol (plus 16%, P
NS) Ejection fraction (EF) was increased by diltiazem at both submaximal exercise, and maximal exercise. Propranolol had no effect on exercise EF at any stage.
LEVEL: A LANG: Eng SIRC ARTICLE NO: 098897

Attina, D.A. Cupelli, V. Giuliano, G. Galanti, A. Musante, R. Bucchino, G. Frosini, F. Maximal exercise stress testing in evaluation of premature beats in children with normal hearts. (Refs: 20)*International journal of sports cardiology (Torino, Italy) 1(1), Jan/June 1984, 25-30.*
ABST: The authors tested on a bicycle ergometer 97 children aged 10 to 15 years with premature beats (PBs) at rest and 50 control ones without PBs. Heart rate, blood pressure, maximum tolerated work, and total work were monitored. No significant differences were observed between children: 1) with and without PBs; 2) with supraventricular and ventricular PBs; 3) with simple and complex PBs; 4) with suppressed and still present PBs at heart rate greater than 150 beats/min.
LEVEL: A LANG: Eng SIRC ARTICLE NO: 171821

Balu, V. Hook, N. Dean, D.C. Naughton, J. Effect of left ventricular aneurysmectomy on exercise performance. *International journal of cardiology (Amsterdam) 5(2), Feb 1984, 210-213.*
ABST: Twelve patients received coronary artery bypass surgery and ventricular aneurysmectomy and two patients ventricular aneurysmectomy alone. Patients improved their exercise performance and tolerance, their double product and their work capacity.
LEVEL: A LANG: Eng SIRC ARTICLE NO: 098898

Barlow, J.B. Pocock, W.A. Mitral valve prolapse, the athlete's heart, physical activity and sudden death. (Refs: 68) *International journal of sports cardiology (Torino, Italy) 1(1), Jan/June 1984, 9-24.*
CONF: Italian Society of Sports cardiology. Congress (1st : 1983 : Rome).
ABST: The authors discuss the primary mitral valve prolapse (MVP) syndrome. With prolonged strenuous exercise, highly trained athletes develop electrocardiographic alterations, arrhythmias and conduction defects. The term 'athlete's heart' is used to describe these physiological changes. Coronary artery disease or anomalies, hypertrophic cardiomyopathy, acute myopericarditis, aortic stenosis, the congenital prolonged QT syndrome, and the primary MVP syndrome are the commonest cardiac causes of sudden death during exercise. The general management of asymptomatic and symptomatic primary MVP is outlined.
LEVEL: A LANG: Eng SIRC ARTICLE NO: 171820

Berberich, S.N. Zager, J.R.S. Plotnick, G.D. Fisher, M.L. A practical approach to exercise echocardiography: immediate postexercise echocardiography. (Refs: 24)*Journal of the American College of Cardiology 3(2 Pt 1), Feb 1984, 284-290.*
ABST: Echocardiographic measurements were compared in normal and coronary artery disease patients. The results found post exercise echocardiography to be a practical and valuable method in the detection of coronary artery disease during exercise testing.
LEVEL: A LANG: Eng SIRC ARTICLE NO: 098899

Blank, A. Wolf, E. Magora, A. Ferber, I. Gonen, B. The electrophysiological pattern of sustained muscular contraction in ischemic heart disease (IHD). *Electromyography and clinical neurophysiology (Louvain) 24(1/2), Jan/Feb 1984, 39-46.*
LEVEL: A LANG: Eng SIRC ARTICLE NO: 098900

Bonow, R.O. Green, M.V. Bacharach, S.L. Radionuclide angiography during exercise in patients with coronary artery disease: diagnostic, prognostic and therapeutic implications. *International journal of cardiology (Amsterdam) 5(2), Feb 1984, 229-233.*
LEVEL: A LANG: Eng SIRC ARTICLE NO: 098901

Bouhour, J.B. Lefevre, M. Soulard, M. Potiron-Josse, M. Louvet, S. Grossetete, R. Reynaud, J.P. Evaluation a long terme et activites physiques et sportives apres corrections de tetralogie de Fallot. (Long-term evaluation, physical and sports activities after correction of Fallot's tetralogy.) *Archives des maladies du coeur et des vaisseaux (Paris) 77(5), May 1984, 543-549.*
ABST: This study focused on the follow-up study of 32 patients (20 boys and 12 girls) after correction of Fallot's tetralogy. The patients were assessed on average 7.5 years postoperatively (range 4 to 13 years). 28 patients underwent treadmill exercise testing. Significant decreases in aerobic capacity, of CO_2 excretion, of ventilation, of heart rate, of work developed and total work were observed.
LEVEL: A LANG: Fr SIRC ARTICLE NO: 102363

Brodan, V. Janota, M. Lexa, J. Stupka, J. Izopotencialove mapovani EKG v klid a po zatezi u kontrolni skupiny, vrcholovych bezcu a u nemocnych s ischemickou chorobou srdecni. (Isopotential ECG mapping at rest and after loading in a control group, in leading runners and in patients with ischemic heart disease.) *Casopis lekaru ceskych (Praha) 123(29), 20 Jul 1984, 893-898.*
LEVEL: A LANG: Cze

Broustet, J.P. Guern, P. Mora, B. Douard, H. Saliou, B. Surveillance electrocardiographique des sportifs: electrocardiogramm et aptitude au sport. (Refs: 3)*Revue medicale de la Suisse romande (Lausanne) 104(10), oct 1984, 807-814.*
RESUME: Les auteurs passent en revue les diverses pathologies enregistrees sur electrocardiogramme chez le sportif: anomalies de conduction, infarctus du myocarde, arythmies, syndrome de Wolff Parkinson White, myocardiopathie obstructive et extrasystoles ventriculaires.
LEVEL: A LANG: Fr SIRC ARTICLE NO: 174100

Bruce, R.A. Value and limitations of the electrocardiogram in progressive exercise testing. (Refs: 30)*American review of respiratory disease (New York) 129(2 Pt 2), Feb 1984, S28-S30.*

CONF: Exercise Testing in the Dyspneic Patient Workshop (1982 : Bethesda).
ABST: This review of the values of the electrocardiogram during exercise discusses its pathophysiologic significance, standards, and diagnostic and prognostic values.
LEVEL: I LANG: Eng SIRC ARTICLE NO: 098902

Burke, J.F. Morganroth, J. Soffer, J. Panidis, I. Chen, C.C. David, D. The cardiokymography exercise test compared to the thallium-201 perfusion exercise test in the diagnosis of coronary artery disease. *American heart journal (St. Louis) 107(4), Apr 1984, 718-725.*
ABST: The authors examined the value of the cardiokymography exercise test (CKG) in the diagnosis of coronary artery disease. 179 patients (averaging 54 years) served as subjects. Results indicated that when CKG and treadmill exercise tests results are concordant (both positive or both negative), the sensitivity and specificity of the test are equal to or better than thallium-201 perfusion scanning.
LEVEL: A LANG: Eng SIRC ARTICLE NO: 098904

Cantwell, J.D. Hypertrophic cardiomyopathy and the athlete. (Refs: 53)*Physician and sportsmedicine (Minneapolis, Minn.) 12(9), Sept 1984, 110-116;118-121.*
LEVEL: I LANG: Eng SIRC ARTICLE NO: 098906

Carey, J. Ablow, K. Keeping fit for life. In the aftermath of a famous runner's death while jogging, experts debate the many merits of exercise. *Newsweek (New York) 104(6), 6 Aug 1984, 63-64.*
LEVEL: B LANG: Eng SIRC ARTICLE NO: 102366

Catapano, F. Teagno, P.S. Giuliani, G.C. Verdun Di Cantogno, L. Rottura di corda tendinea e prolasso mitralico. Considerazioni generali e descrizione di un caso. (Rupture of the chordae tendinae and mitral prolapse. General considerations and description of a case.) *Minerva medica (Torino) 75(5), 11 Feb 1984, 185-190.*
LEVEL: A LANG: It

Cecconi, M. Colonna, P.L. Manfrin, M. Pierantozzi, A. Cesari, G.P. Cuccaroni, G. Cecchetti, P. Budini, A. Bettuzzi, M.G. Massini, C. The role of exercise test in the assessment of sport fitness in 164 subjects after surgical correction of congenital heart diseases with right ventricular overload. (Refs: 11)*International journal of sports cardiology (Torino, Italy) 1(1), Jan/June 1984, 31-33.*
ABST: The sporting fitness of 48 patients (pts) with secundum atrial septal defect (ASD), 54 pts with pulmonary stenosis (PS) and 62 pts with tetralogy of Fallot (TOF) was assessed 6 months to 14 years following corrective surgery. 67 per cent of the ASD patients, 55 per cent of the PS patients and 35 per cent of the TOF patients achieved an endurance time greater than 90 per cent of the normal value for the same age and sex groups.
LEVEL: A LANG: Eng SIRC ARTICLE NO: 171822

Cerri, B. Grasso, F. Cefis, M. Pollavini, G. Comparative evaluation of the effect of two doses of Nitroderm TTS on exercise-related parameters in patients with angina pectoris. *European heart journal (London) 5(9), Sept 1984, 710-715.*
LEVEL: A LANG: Eng

Crea, F. Davies, G. Romeo, F. Chierchia, S. Bugiardini, R. Kaski, J.C. Freedman, B. Maseri, A. Myocardial ischemia during ergonovine testing: different susceptibility to coronary vasoconstriction in patients with exertional and variant angina.

Circulation (New York) 69(4), Apr 1984, 690-695.
LEVEL: A LANG: Eng SIRC ARTICLE NO: 098908

Danko, I.I. Kuznetsov, I.I. Loginov, V.G. Vliianie polozhitel'nykh emotsii na amplitudu zubtsa t EGK sportsmenov s distrofie miokarda vsledstvie khronicheskogo fizicheskogo perenapriazheniia. (Effect of positive emotions on T-wave amplitude of ECG in sportsmen with myocardial dystrophy caused by chronic physical overstrain.) *Kardiologiia (Moscow) 24(10), Oct 1984, 106-108.*
LEVEL: A LANG: Rus

Douste-Blazy, P. Sie, P. Boneu, B. Marco, J. Eche, N. Bernadet, P. Exercise-induced platelet activation in myocardial infarction survivors with normal coronary arteriogram. *Thrombosis and haemostasis (Stuttgart) 52(3), 29 Dec 1984, 297-300.*
LEVEL: A LANG: Eng

Driscoll, D.J. Staats, B.A. Heise, C.T. Rice, M.J. Puga, F.J. Danielson, G.K. Ritter, D.G. Functional single ventricle: cardiorespiratory response to exercise. *Journal of the American College of Cardiology (New York) 4(2), Aug 1984, 337-342.*
ABST: This study documented the precise level of exercise intolerance in 27 patients with functional single ventricle. All 27 patients had a significant reduction in exercise time, work performed, maximal exercise heart rate, maximal oxygen uptake and systemic arterial blood oxygen saturation. The reduction in exercise performance increased with increasing age of the patients.
LEVEL: A LANG: Eng SIRC ARTICLE NO: 102367

Duda, M. Exercising MI patients smoke less or quit. *Physician and sportsmedicine (Minneapolis, Minn.) 12(10), Oct 1984, 23.*
LEVEL: I LANG: Eng SIRC ARTICLE NO: 098909

Dymond, D.S. Foster, C. Grenier, R.P. Carpenter, J. Schmidt, D.H. Peak exercise and immediate postexercise imaging for the detection of left ventricular functional abnormalities in coronary artery disease. *American journal of cardiology (New York) 53(11), 1 Jun 1984, 1532-1537.*
ABST: Rest, peak exercise and immediate postexercise imaging were performed on 11 patients without significant coronary artery disease (CAD) (group A), 22 patients with significant CAD and no prior myocardial infarction (MI) (group B), and 10 patients with CAD and a previous MI (group C). No significant changes, of mean left ventricular (LV), ejection fraction (EF) in group A or group C were observed at peak exercise while significant decreases occurred in group B. However, mean LVEF increased significantly in all groups after exercise. 47% of the patients with CAD showed a normal response after exercise.
LEVEL: A LANG: Eng SIRC ARTICLE NO: 102368

Dzizinskii, A.A. Cherniak, B.A. Tolerantnost' k fizicheskoi nagruzke u bol'nykh ishemicheskoi bolezn'iu serdtsa s soputstvuiushchim tserebral'nym. (Physical exertion tolerance in patients with ischemic heart disease associated with cerebral arteriosclerosis.) *Terpevticheskii arkhiv (Moscow) 56(12), 1984, 28-32.*
ABST: The authors provide the results of a comparative study of exercise tolerance (bicycle ergometry test) in 64 patients with coronary heart disease (CHD) and in 68 patients with associated CHD and cerebral atherosclerosis. During the latter syndrome the working capacity was lowered as a result of less economical work of the circulatory

apparatus. In particular, physical loading in such patients was accompanied by marked increment of the heart rate and blood pressure elevation. Increased heart oxygen requirement in the second group patients during exercise was accompanied by more frequent ischemic alterations in the myocardium attended by ST segment depression on the ECG.
LEVEL: A LANG: Rus

Ector, H. Bourgois, J. Verlinden, M. Hermans, L. Vanden Eynde, E. Fagard, R. De Geest, H. Bradycardia, ventricular pauses, syncope, and sports. *Lancet (London) 2(8403), 15 Sept 1984, 591-594.*
ABST: 16 athletic patients were examined because of syncope, Stokes-Adams attacks, or both. The life-threatening condition required pacemaker implantation in 7 patients. 8 of the 9 other subjects became symptom-free after stopping heavy physical training. 37 top-ranking athletes underwent 24 h Holter monitoring. Pauses longer than 2 s occurred in 19 per cent and resulted from sinus arrest. The longest pause lasted 2.5 s. Second-degree atrioventricular block was noted in 13 per cent.
LEVEL: A LANG: Eng SIRC ARTICLE NO: 103863

Ehsani, A.A. Biello, D. Seals, D.R. Austin, M.B. Schultz, J. The effect of left ventricular systolic function on maximal aerobic exercise capacity in asymptomatic patients with coronary artery disease. *Circulation (Dallas) 70(4), Oct 1984, 552-560.*
LEVEL: A LANG: Eng

Erdman, R.A. Duivenvoorden, H.J. Verhage, F. Kazemier, M. Hugenholtz, P.G. Hartrevalidatie: een vervolgonderzoek over 5 jaar naar psychisch functioneren, werkhervatting, rookgewoonten en sportieve activiteiten. (Cardiac rehabilitation: a 5-year follow-up study of mental functioning, work resumption, smoking habits and sports activities.) *Nederlands tijdschrift voor geneeskunde (Amsterdam) 128(18), 5 May 1984, 846-851.*
LEVEL: A LANG: Dut

Fagard, R. Reybrouck, T. Vanhees, L. Cattaert, A. Vanmeenen, T. Grauwels, R. Amery, A. The effects of beta blockers on exercise capacity and on training response in elderly subjects. (Refs: 21)*European heart journal (London) 5(Suppl E), Nov 1984, 117-120.*
ABST: The effects of atenolol and labetalol on exercise performance were assessed in 8 hypertensive elderly subjects and 15 elderly patients with ischaemic heart disease. Both beta blockers did not alter patients' response.
LEVEL: A LANG: Eng SIRC ARTICLE NO: 109714

Fox, R.M. Hakki, A.H. Iskandrian, A.S. Relation between electrocardiographic and scintigraphic location of myocardial ischemia during exercise in one-vessel coronary artery disease. *American journal of cardiology (New York) 53(11), 1 Jun 1984, 1529-1531.*
ABST: This paper investigates the usefulness of exercise electrocardiography in predicting the site of myocardial ischemia. Fifty-two patients with 1-vessel coronary artery disease (CAD) are divided in two groups: group I (28 patients) with left anterior descending CAD and group II with left circumflex or right CAD. Some findings: a) the size of the perfusion defect is larger in group I than II; b) ST depression occurs in 16 patients (57%), in group I and 11 patients (46%) in group II; and c) the site of ST depression during exercise is not a good predictor of the site of exercise-induced perfusion

defect or anatomic site of CAD.
LEVEL: A LANG: Eng SIRC ARTICLE NO: 102369

Furkalo, N.K. Rishko, N.V. Kislorodnoe i gemodinamicheskoe obespechenie dozirovannykh fizicheskikh nagruzok u bol'nykh ishemicheskoi bolezniu serdtsa s poraxhennymi aterosklerozom i intaktnymi venechnymi arteriiami. (Oxygen and hemodynamic provisions for measured physical exertion in ischemic heart disease patients with intact and atherosclerotic coronary arteries.) *Kardiologiia (Moscow) 24(1), Jan 1984, 48-51.*
ABST: Cardiorespiratory responses to exercise was studied in 111 coronary patients. Resting oxygen and hemodynamic support was not affected in either the patients with atherosclerosed coronary arteries, or those with intact ones. Three types of cardiorespiratory response to exercise were identified--normal, compensated and subcompensated. A possibility of predicting the extent of coronary reserve in coronary patients, without exercise intensified to threshold values, was explored. The pattern of cardiorespiratory response to exercise in coronary patients with intact coronary arteries is described.
LEVEL: A LANG: Rus

Furkalo, N.K. Lutai, M.I. Tolerantnost' k fizicheskoi nagruzke u bol'nykh s koronarnoi nedostatochnot'iu v zavisimosti ot nalichiia zon asinergii. (Physical exertion tolerance in patients with coronary insufficiency in relation to the presence of asynergic areas.) *Kardiologiia (Moskva) 24(2), Feb 1984, 52-56.*
ABST: A comparative study of coronarographic, ventriculographic and bicycle ergometry results in 81 coronary patients demonstrated that myocardial contractility disorders (extensive asynergic areas, elevated ultimate diastolic pressure) combined with considerable coronary arterial lesion could result in reduced physical stress tolerance.
LEVEL: A LANG: Rus

Golikov, A.P. Charchoglian, R.A. Zingerman, L.S. Levshunov, S.P. Esin, N.N. Tolerantnost' k nagruzke u bol'nykh s anevrizmoi levogo zheludochka. (Loading tolerance in patients with left ventricular aneurysm.) *Klinicheskaia meditsina (Moskva) 62(3), Mar 1984, 55-60.*
LEVEL: A LANG: Rus

Gonzalez Juanatey, J.R. Amaro Cendon, A. Rublio Alvarez, J. Gil de la Pena, M. Esfuerzo y espasmo coronario: asociacion infrecuente. (Exertion and coronary spasm: an uncommon association. (letter) *Medicine clinica (Barcelona) 82(3), 28 Jan 1984, 134-135.*
LEVEL: I LANG: Spa

Gorbachenkov, A.A. Kholodova, O.E. Khlobystova, G.O. Pochkhua, T.G. Singhk, K.S. Primenenie nitroglitserina vo vremia trenirovok bolnykh so stenokardiei napriazheniia. (Use of nitroglycerin during the training of patients with exertion angina.) *Kardiologiia (Moscow) 24(9), Sept 1984, 73-76.*
LEVEL: A LANG: Rus

Greenfield, K. The dilemma of the abnormal exercise electrocardiogram. *Aerobics (Dallas, Tex.) 5(2), Feb 1984, 4;8.*
LEVEL B LANG: Eng SIRC ARTICLE NO: 097443

Grossman, M. Baker, B.E. Current cardiology problems in sports medicine. (Refs: 27)*American journal of sports medicine (Baltimore, Md.) 12(4), Jul/Aug 1984, 262-267.*
LEVEL: I LANG: Eng SIRC ARTICLE NO: 108531

Hakki, A.H. Iskandrian, A.S. Colby, J. Similarity between women and men in manifestation of myocardial ischemia during exercise. *International journal of cardiology (Amsterdam) 5(6), Jun 1984, 721-729.*
ABST: This retrospective study assessed the electrocardiographic response to exercise of 29 women and 60 men with coronary artery disease. Exercise tolerance was insignificantly lower in women compared to men. Exercise heart rate, double product, and the electrocardiographic response to exercise were similar for both genders.
LEVEL: A LANG: Eng SIRC ARTICLE NO: 103866

Hare, T.W. Lowenthal, D.T. Hakki, H. Goodwin, M.J. Training effect in elderly patients with coronary artery disease on beta adrenergic blocking drugs. (Refs: 23)*Annals of sports medicine (North Hollywood, Calif.) 2(1), 1984, 36-40.*
ABST: The authors examined 27 patients with cardiac disease, who underwent symptom-limited exercise testing prior to and at the completion of an eight week aerobic activities training program. A training effect was demonstrated for workload and total duration in each of four groups. A: 54 years or younger on beta adrenergic blocking drugs (BABD) (n, 6); B: 54 years or younger off BABD (n, 7): C: older than 54 years on BABD (n, 9); D: older than 54 years off BABD (n, 5). The results demonstrate the neither age (54 years or younger), (older than 54 years) nor drug (off BABD) (on BABD) interfere with benefits derived from an eight week training program.
LEVEL: A LANG: Eng SIRC ARTICLE NO: 103868

Heart attacks during exercise. *Health letter (San Antonio, Tex.) 24(9), 9 Nov 1984, 1-2.*
LEVEL: I LANG: Eng SIRC ARTICLE NO 102371

Higginbotham, M.B. Coleman, R.E. Jones, R.H. Cobb, F.R. Mechanism and significance of a decrease in ejection fraction during exercise in patients with coronary artery disease and left ventricular dysfunction at rest. *Journal of the American College of Cardiology 3(1), Jan 1984, 88-97.*
ABST: This study evaluated the ejection fraction response of 246 patients with coronary artery disease and compared them with a control group of 48 patients. The results indicate that a decrease in ejection fraction during exercise is more likely to indicate ischemia than a nonspecific response to exercise stress in patients with coronary artery disease and left ventricular dysfunction at rest.
LEVEL: A LANG: Eng SIRC ARTICLE NO: 097444

Hinshelwood, R.A. Prevalence and reproducibility of ECG-documented premature contractions with exercise in young adults. Eugene, Ore.: Microform Publications, University of Oregon, 1984. 1 microfiche : negative ; 11 x 15 cm.
NOTES: Thesis (M.S.) - University of Wisconsin-La Crosse, 1982; (vi, 49 leaves); includes bibliography.
LEVEL: A LANG: Eng UO84 298

Hossack, K.F. Bruce, R.A. Ivey, T.D. Kusumi, F. Kannagi, T. Improvement in aerobic and hemodynamic responses to exercise following aorta-coronary bypass grafting. *Journal of thoracic and cardiovascular surgery (St. Louis) 87(6), Jun 1984, 901-907.*
LEVEL: A LANG: Eng SIRC ARTICLE NO: 102372

Jokl, E. Olympic medicine and sports cardiology. (Refs: 201)*Annals of sports medicine (Hollywood, Calif.) 1(4), 1984, 127-169.*
LEVEL: I LANG: Eng SIRC ARTICLE NO: 095770

Kalischer, A.L. Johnson, L.L. Johnson, Y.E. Stone, J. Feder, J.L. Escala, E. Cannon, P.J. Effects of propranolol and timolol on left ventricular volumes during exercise in patients with coronary artery disease. *Journal of the American College of Cardiology 3(1), Jan 1984, 210-218.*
ABST: Left ventricular volumes and peak systolic pressure/end-systolic volume (PSP/ESV) were measured in 18 coronary artery disease patients in the control state and after 2 weeks of daily maintenance therapy with either propranolol or timolol. Values at rest and during symptom-limited upright exercise were compared. No difference was found between the propranolol and timolol groups. The value for PSP/ESV at rest was lower after treatment. The exercise ejection fraction was greater after treatment due to an increase in end-diastolic volume and unchanged end-systolic volume.
LEVEL: A LANG: Eng SIRC ARTICLE NO: 097445

Kamikawa, T. Suzuki, Y. Kobayashi, A. Hayashi, H. Masumura, Y. Nishihara, K. Abe, M. Yamazaki, N. Effects of L-carnitine on exercise tolerance in patients with stable angina pectoris. *Japanese heart journal (Tokyo) 25(4), Jul 1984, 587-597.*
LEVEL: A LANG: Eng

Karlsson, J. Astroem, H. Holmgren, A. Kaijser, C. Orinius, E. Angina pectoris and blood lactate concentration during graded exercise. (Refs: 15)*International journal of sports medicine (Stuttgart) 5(6), Dec 1984, 348-351.*
ABST: Nineteen patients with angina pectoris were studied by psychophysical scaling of the chest pain according to Borg and blood lactate determination at rest and during a graded exercise test. Anginal pain, systolic blood pressure, heart rate (HR), and blood lactate concentration were determined at the end of each work load. The exercise test was interrupted at a rated anginal pain level (RAP) of 5-6/9 (Wmax). The patients were divided into three groups: A with a Wmax or over 74 W; B 75-124 W, and C over 125 W. The heart rate at Wmax averaged 98 (A), 118 (B), and 136 (C), respectively. Corresponding peak values for RAP were 3.8, 4.5, and 4.8. Blood lactate at rest ranged from 1.0-1.6 mmol and increased curvilinearly with intensity, which was also the case for RAP.
LEVEL: A LANG: Eng SIRC ARTICLE NO: 103869

Kawamura, M. Komatsu, C. Suzuki, Y. Takayama, K. Takahashi, I. Tokuhisa, Y. Ishinaga T. Sanada, T. Morita, H. Yoshimura, S. (Two cases of exercise-induced ventricular tachycardia -- catecholamine-induced ventricular tachycardia.) *Kokyu to junkan/Respiration and circulation (Tokyo) 32(10), Oct 1984, 1071-1077.*
LEVEL: A LANG: Jpn

Kirlin, P.C. Das, S. Zijnen, P. Wijns, W. Domenicucci, S. Roelandt, J. Pitt, B. The exercise response in idiopathic dilated cardiomyopathy. *Clinical cardiology (New York) 7(4), Apr 1984, 205-210.*
LEVEL: A LANG: Eng

Koga, Y. Itaie, K. Takahashi, K. Utsu, N. Yamaguchi, R. (Plasma norepinephrine levels in patients with heart diseases during exercise.) *Kokyu to junkan/Respiration and circulation (Tokyo) 32(11), Nov 1984, 1155-1157.*
LEVEL: A LANG: Jpn

Kozlowski, J.H. Ellestad, M.H. The exercise test as a guide to management and prognosis. (Refs:

143)*Clinics in sports medicine (Philadelphia) 3(2), Apr 1984, 395-416.*
ABST: The efficacy of physical stress testing in the diagnosis of ischemic heart disease is reviewed. Furthermore, the prognostic capability of exercise testing is discussed. The exercise stress test is a very useful procedure in the management of ischemic heart disease as it yields a large amount of diagnostic and prognostic information.
LEVEL: A LANG: Eng SIRC ARTICLE NO: 094253

Lamb, L.E. Exercise and heart attacks - part I. *Muscle & fitness (Woodland Hills, Calif.) 45(6), Jun 1984, 13;172-173.*
LEVEL: B LANG: Eng SIRC ARTICLE NO: 100523

Levine, S.P. Suarez, A.J. Sorenson, R.R. Raymond, N.M. Knieriem, L.K. Platelet factor 4 release during exercise in patients with coronary artery disease. *American journal of hematology (New York) 17(2), Aug 1984, 117-127.*
LEVEL: A LANG: Eng SIRC ARTICLE NO: 103872

Matangi, M.F. Woodhouse, S.P. Amarasingham, R. Isometric exercise following myocardial infarction. *New Zealand medical journal (Dunedin) 97(761), 8 Aug 1984, 518-519.*
ABST: Twenty-six consecutive patients had measurement of ejection fraction by gated blood-pool imaging at rest and during isometric exercise, following recovery from an uncomplicated myocardial infarction. We found there was a highly significant fall in ejection fraction at rest from 56 plus or minus 3 per cent to 43 plus or minus 3 per cent during isometric exercise. There was a dramatic fall in ejection fraction during isometric exercise in some patients with a normal resting value. Our preliminary findings suggest these latter patients are at risk for future cardiac events such as, unstable angina, further myocardial infarction and future coronary bypass surgery.
LEVEL: A LANG: Eng SIRC ARTICLE NO: 103874

McGuigan, P.A. Diagnostic implications of graded exercise testing in an elderly population. Eugene, Ore.: Microform Publications, University of Oregon, 1984. 1 microfiche : negative, ill. ; 11 x 15 cm.
NOTES: Thesis (M.S.) - Pennsylvania State University, 1983); (ix, 50 leaves) includes bibliography.
LEVEL: A LANG: Eng UO84 341

McKirnan, M.D. Sullivan, M. Jensen, D. Froelicher, V.F. Treadmill performance and cardiac function in selected patients with coronary heart disease. *Journal of the American College of Cardiology (New York) 3(2 Pt 1), Feb 1984, 253-261.*
ABST: Treadmill testing was performed by 88 patients with coronary heart disease, free of angina pectoris. The results found myocardial damage predicted ejection fraction at rest and the ability to increase heart rate with treadmill exercise appeared to be an important component of exercise capacity. Exercise capacity was minimally affected by asymptomatic ischemia and was relatively independent of ventricular function.
LEVEL: A LANG: Eng SIRC ARTICLE NO: 098915

Meyer-Myklestad, L. Koronar bypass-operasjon og effekt pa funksjonsniva. En litteraturgjennomgang. (Coronary bypass operatio and its effect on the level of function. A review of the literature.) *Tiddskrift for den norske laegeforening (Oslo) 104(30), 30 Oct 1984, 2078-2082.*
LEVEL: A LANG: Nor

Millit, H.D. Gaglani, R. Antalis, J.P. Exertional angina pectoris associated with post-exercise ST segment elevation and nearly normal coronary arteries. *Cleveland clinic quarterly (Cleveland) 51(1), Spring 1984, 71-75.*
LEVEL: A LANG: Eng SIRC ARTICLE NO: 100525

Mizutani, Y. Nakano, S. Ote, N. Iwase, T. Fujinami, T. Evaluation of effects of aging, training and myocardial ischemia on cardiac reserve by exercise echocardiography. (Refs: 25)*Japanese circulation journal (Kyoto) 48(9), Sept 1984, 969-979.*
LEVEL: A LANG: Eng SIRC ARTICLE NO: 109745

Moore, R.B. Shapiro, L.M. Gibson, D.G. Relation between electrocardiographic repolarisation changes and mechanical events in left ventricular hypertrophy. *British heart journal (London) 52(5), Nov 1984, 516-523.*
LEVEL: A LANG: Eng

Naafs, M.A. de Boer, A.C. Koster, R.W. Klazen, C.W. Dunning, A.J. Exercise capacity with transdermal nitroglycerin in patients with stable angina pectoris. *European heart journal (London) 5(9), Sept 1984, 705-709.*
LEVEL: A LANG: Eng

Nelson, G.I. Silke, B. Ahuja, R.C. Verma, S.P. Hussain, M. Taylor, S.H. Hemodynamic effects of nifedipine during upright exercise in stable angina pectoris and either normal or severely impaired left ventricular function. *American journal of cardiology (New York) 53(4), 1 Feb 1984, 451-455.*
LEVEL: A LANG: Eng

Newsholme, E. Leech, T. The elixir of life: it keeps you young, it keeps you healthier, and it reduces the risk of heart attacks. What is it? *Sport and leisure (London) 25(2), May/Jun 1984, 18-19.*
LEVEL: B LANG: Eng SIRC ARTICLE NO: 103876

Noreau, L. Theriault, G. La fonction ventriculaire chez le sujet normal et coronarien suite a l'entrainement. (Refs: 49) *Canadian journal of applied sport sciences/Journal canadien des sciences appliquees au sport (Windsor, Ont.) 9(3), sept 1984, 133-140.*
RESUME: Le but de cette revue est de faire etat des connaissances et des donnees recentes sur les adaptations et les modifications de la pompe cardiaque suite a l'entrainement physique chez les sujets normaux et cardiaques.
LEVEL: A LANG: Fr SIRC ARTICLE NO: 102808

O'Hara, M.J. Subramanian, V.B. Davies, A.B. Raftery, E.B. Changes of Q wave amplitude during exercise for the prediction of coronary artery disease. *International journal of cardiology (Amsterdam) 6(1), Jul 1984, 35-45.*
LEVEL: A LANG: Eng SIRC ARTICLE NO: 103877

Poyatos, M.E. Lerman, J. Estrada, A. Chiozza, M. Perosio, A. Predictive value of changes in R-wave amplitude after exercise in coronary heart disease. *American journal of cardiology (New York) 54(10), 1 Dec 1984, 1212-1215.*
LEVEL: A LANG: Eng

Puri, V.K. Agarwal, S.K. Mehrotra, A. Hasan, M. Effect of oxyfedrine on exercise performance and systolic time intervals in patients of angina pectoris. *Indian heart journal (Bombay) 36(4), Jul/Aug 1984, 226-230.*
LEVEL: A LANG: Eng

Riviere, A. Denolin, H. Contre-indications cardiologiques a la pratique du sport. (Refs:

DISEASES AND DISORDERS (continued)

12)*Revue medicale de la Suisse romande (Lausanne) 104(10), oct 1984, 815-821.*
LEVEL: I LANG: Fr SIRC ARTICLE NO: 174101

Romakov, A.I. Sagirov, A.M. Sumarokov, A.B. Mazur, N.A. Sravnitel'naia effektivnost' propranolola, nifedipina i ikh sochetaniia u bol'nykh stenokardiei napriazheniia. (Comparative effectiveness of propranolol, nifedipine and their combination in exertion stenocardia patients.) *Klinicheskaia meditsina (Moskva) 62(3), Mar 1984, 71-75.*
LEVEL: A LANG: Rus

Rosing, D.R. Van Raden, M.J. Mincemoyer, R.M. Bonow, R.O. Bourassa, M.G. David, P.R. Ewels, C.J. Detre, K.M. Kent, K.M. Exercise, electrocardiographic and functional responses after percutaneous transluminal coronary angioplasty. *American journal of cardiology (New York) 53(12), 15 Jun 1984, 36C-41C.*
ABST: Sixty-six coronary disease patients were surveyed before and after percutaneous transluminal coronary angioplasty (PTCA). Exercise testing an average of 8 months after PTCA showed improved cardiac functional status, symptomatic responses, myocardial perfusion and global and regional left ventricular function.
LEVEL: A LANG: Eng SIRC ARTICLE NO: 102377

Roskamm, H. Gohlke, H. Stuerzenhofecker, P. Samek, L. Betz, P. Myocardial infarction at a young age (under 40 years). (Refs: 80)*International journal of sports medicine 5(1), Feb 1984, 1-10.*
ABST: This study presents the coronary morphology, risk factors, long-term prognosis and progression of coronary arteriosclerosis of 679 (649 men and 30 women) post-infarction patients under 40 years of age. A second coronary angiogram was performed approximately 3.8 years after the first angiogram, which was done an average of 3 months after the initial infarction. The results of this second angiogram indicated that progression of arteriosclerosis is rare in patients who exhibited zero-vessel disease or unilocular disease in the first angiogram. However, if multilocular disease was present in the first angiogram there was a high tendency for the coronary arteriosclerosis to proceed in the year between angiograms. Smoking was associated with the progression of arteriosclerosis.
LEVEL: A LANG: Eng SIRC ARTICLE NO: 092734

Rost, R. Clinical significance of echocardiographic findings in athletes. (Refs: 6)*International journal of sports cardiology (Torino, Italy) 1(1), Jan/June 1984, 34-40.*
LEVEL: I LANG: Eng SIRC ARTICLE NO: 171823

Sakakibara, T. Hirose, H. Nakano, S. Matsuda, H. Shirakura, R. Sato, S. Shimazaki, Y. Kawachi, K. Kitamura, S. Kawashima, Y. (Evaluation of left ventricular function and coronary sinus blood flow during exercise after aortocoronary bypass surgery - influence of previous myocardial infarction.) *Nippon kyobu geka gakkai zasshi/Journal of the Japanese Association for Thoracic Surgery (Tokyo) 32(9), Sept 1984, 1354-1361.*
LEVEL: A LANG: Jpn

Sami, M. Chaitman, B. Fisher, L. Holmes, D. Fray, D. Alderman, E. Significance of exercise-induced ventricular arrhythmia in stable coronary artery disease: a coronary artery surgery study project. *American journal of cardiology (New York) 54(10), 1 Dec 1984, 1182-1188.*
LEVEL: A LANG: Eng

Sato, H. Matsuyama, T. Ozaki, H. Fukushima, M. Matsumoto, M. (Effect of beta 1-partial agonist (ICI 118-587) on plasma catecholamines level and hemodynamics during exercise in congestive heart failure.) *Kokyu to junkan/Respiration and circulation (Tokyo) 32(11), Nov 1984, 1159-1162.*
LEVEL: A LANG: Jpn

Sennels, F. Rasmussen, K. Bagger, J.P. Anstrengelsessynkope ved aortastenose. (Exertion syncope in aortic stenosis.) *Ugeskrift for laeger (Copenhagen) 146(50), 10 Dec 1984, 3910-3913.*
LEVEL: A LANG: Dan

Shephard, R.J. Applications of exercise and training coronary heart disease. (Refs: 46)*International journal of sports medicine (Stuttgart) Suppl. 5, Nov 1984, 49-53.*
CONF: International Congress on Sports and Health (1983 : Maastricht, Netherlands).
LEVEL: I LANG: Eng SIRC ARTICLE NO: 103879

Siconolfi, S.F. Garber, C.E. Baptist, G.D. Cooper, F.S. Carleton, R.A. Circulatory effects of mental stress during exercise in coronary artery disease patients. *Clinical cardiology (New York) 7(8), Aug 1984, 441-444.*
ABST: The effects of mental stress during steady-state exercise on heart rate, blood pressure, pressure-rate product, and oxygen uptake in 10 coronary artery disease patients were analysed. A computerized Stroop-Color-Word Test (mental stress) was added one minute after the subject reached steady-state exercise. When mental stress was added to steady-state exercise it significantly increased the heart rate (101 plus or minus 15 to 108 plus or minus 19 beats per min), systolic (154 plus or minus 26 to 170 plus or minus 26 mmHg) and diastolic (86 plus or minus 10 to 92 plus or minus 13 mmHg) blood pressure, and pressure-rate product (158 plus or minus 42 to 179 plus or minus 48 x 10 (-2)). This increase in the mean response during exercise and mental stress was not observed for oxygen uptake (17 plus or minus 6 to 18 plus or minus 5 ml/kg/min).
LEVEL: A LANG: Eng SIRC ARTICLE NO: 103880

Sledzevskaia, I.K. Golovkov, I.Z. Chmir, V.P. Viatchenko-Karpinskaia, E.V. Arterial'naia gipertenziia i gemodinamicheskoe obespechenie fizicheskoi nagruzki u bol'nykh, perenesshikh infarkt miokarda. (Arterial hypertension and hemodynamic support through physical load in patients with a history of myocardial infarct.) *Vrachebnoe delo (Kiev) 2, Feb 1984, 30-33.*
LEVEL: A LANG: Rus

Slezkina, L.A. Proiavleniia ateroskleroza mozgovykh i koronarnykh arterii u bol'nykh, perenesshikh infarkt miokarda. (Manifestations of arteriosclerosis of the cerebral and coronary arteries in patients with a history of myocardial infarct.) *Klinicheskaia meditsina (Moskva) 62(3), Mar 1984, 46-49.*
LEVEL: A LANG: Rus

Steingart, R.M. Wexler, J. Slagle, S. Scheuer, J. Radionuclide ventriculographic responses to graded supine and upright exercise: critical role of the Frank-Starling mechanism at submaximal exercise. *American journal of cardiology (New York) 53(11), 1 Jun 1984, 1671-1677.*
ABST: 25 coronary artery disease patients and 17 normal subjects were examined during graded supine and upright exercise. End-diastolic counts increase in both groups with supine exercise while

ejection fraction and peak systolic pressure-end-systolic volume relation increased in normal subjects only. At upright rest, end-diastolic counts decreased in both groups and then increased with exercise. No significant changes in ejection fraction or peak systolic pressure-end-systolic volume relation were observed.
LEVEL: A LANG: Eng SIRC ARTICLE NO: 102378

Strauzenberg, S.E. Recommendations for physical activity and sports in children with heart disease. (Refs: 7)*International journal of sports cardiology (Torino, Italy) 1(1), Jan/June 1984, 1-8.*
ABST: The author classifies the type of activities in which children with heart disease may participate without risk. The degree of exertion which safely can be tolerated is also defined. Congenital and acquired defects, arrhythmias and ECG abnormalities are all discussed in detail.
LEVEL: A LANG: Eng SIRC ARTICLE NO: 171819

Strong, W.B. Steed, D. Cardiovascular evaluation of the young athlete. (Refs: 14)*Primary care: clinics in office practice (Philadelphia) 11(1), Mar 1984, 61-75.*
LEVEL: I LANG: Eng SIRC ARTICLE NO: 100528

Sugishita, Y. Koseki, S. Matsuda, M. Ogawa, T. Ajisaka, R. Iida, K. Ito, I. Oshima, M. Takeda, T. Akisada, M. Functional significance of coronary collateral vessels during exercise evaluated by radionuclide angiocardiography: the importance of supplying arteries. *Acta cardiologica (Brussels) 39(4), 1984, 273-283.*
LEVEL: A LANG: Eng

Sumarokov, A.B. Romakov, A.I. Sagirov, A.M. Iurkova, V.B. Mazur, N.A. Farmakodinamicheskoe sravnenie propranolola i verapamila pri stenokardii napriazheniia. (Pharmacodynamic comparison of propranolol and verapamil in exertion stenocardia.) *Klineskaia meditsina (Moskva) 62(3), Mar 1984, 42-46.*
LEVEL: A LANG: Rus

Superko, H.R. Adams, W.C. Daly, P.W. Effects of ozone inhalation during exercise in selected patients with heart disease. *American journal of medicine (New York) 77(3), Sept 1984, 463-470.*
LEVEL: A LANG: Eng

Tavazzi, L. Giordano, A. Exercise haemodynamics in patients over 65 years of age with recent myocardial infarction. (Refs: 5 *European heart journal (London) 5(Suppl E), Nov 1984, 85-87.*
ABST: Hemodynamic changes during exercise testing were compared in myocardial infarction patients in three age groups: 136 patients 45 or less years of age (group A), 323 patients 46-64 years of age (group B) and 41 patients over 64 years of age (group C). At rest, lower stroke volume and cardiac output (CO) were observed in group C. During exercise, the same group experimented more frequent ST depression, an higher pulmonary artery end-diastolic pressure at a lower work load and a higher incidence of patients with inappropriate increments of CO.
LEVEL: A LANG: Eng SIRC ARTICLE NO: 109721

Tellier, P. Bedig, G. Marcadet, D. Laffay, N. Aubry, P. Vulpillat, M. Contribution de la scintigraphie myocardique a l'effor au diagnostic positif et topographique de la maladie coronarienne. Etude chez 115 patients sans antecedents d'infarctus du myocarde. (Exercise myocardial scintigraphy for the positive and topographic diagnosis of coronary disease. Study in 115

patients without antecedents of myocardial infarction.) *Annales de cardiologie et d'angeiologie (Paris) 33(2), fevr/mars 1984, 87-92.*
LEVEL: I LANG: Fr SIRC ARTICLE NO: 100529

The Jim Fixx lesson. (coronary artery disease) *Health letter (San Antonio, Tex.) 24(3), 10 Aug 1984, 1-2.*
LEVEL: B LANG: En SIRC ARTICLE NO: 102373

Vanhees, L. Fagard, R. Lijnen, P. Moerman, E. de Geest, H. Amery, A. Influence of physical training on blood pressure, plasm renin, angiotensin and catecholamines in patients with ischaemic heart disease. (Refs: 36)*European journal of applied physiology and occupational physiology (Berlin) 53(3), Dec 1984, 219-224.*
ABST: Eighteen patients with ischaemic heart disease were trained for 3 months, three times a week. Blood pressure was not significantly affected during the training period. At rest and at submaximal exercise plasma renin activity (PRA) was lower after training. Plasma angiotensin I concentration (PA I) and angiotensin II concentration (PA II) were not significantly affected. Plasma aldosterone concentration (PAC), only measured at rest, was not significantly changed after the training period, while plasma norepinephrine (PNE) and epinephrine (PE) concentrations were significantly decreased, but only at high levels of exercise.
LEVEL: A LANG: Eng SIRC ARTICLE NO: 103883

Volkov, V.S. Nikolskaia, E.A. Ramdzhutun, U.S. Kardialgii, tolerantnost' kfizicheskoi nagruzke i osobennosti lichnosti u bol'nykh klimaktericheskoi kardiopatiei. (Cardialgia, physical exertion tolerance and personality characteristics in patients with climacteric cardiopathy.) *Klinicheskaia meditsina (Moscow) 62(8), Aug 1984, 34-38.*
LEVEL: A LANG: Rus

Wasir, H.S. Mittal, R.B. Subramanyan, K. Rajani, M. Mukerjee, S. Manchanda, S.C. Kaul, U. Talwar, K.K. Reddy, K.S. Bhatia, M.L. Correlation of exercise induced 'R' wave changes and systolic blood pressure response with coronary angiographic findings. *Indian heart journal (Bombay) 36(1), Jan/Feb 1984, 50-55.*
LEVEL: A LANG: Eng SIRC ARTICLE NO: 100530

Willens, H.J. Advances in cardiac diagnosis: nuclear cardiology. (Refs: 22)*Clinics in sports medicine (Philadelphia) 3(2), Apr 1984, 417-424.*
ABST: The noninvasive techniques of nuclear cardiology have complemented and sometimes replaced the invasive diagnostic techniques. The thallium perfusion scan, the isotope angiocardiogram, and myocardial infarct scan are discussed. The thallium perfusion scan is very useful in evaluating patients suspected of having coronary artery disease. The isotope angiogram is useful in evaluating ventricular ejection fraction. The myocardial infarct scan visualizes recent myocardial infarctions.
LEVEL: A LANG: Eng SIRC ARTICLE NO: 094265

Wilson, J.R. Martin, J.L. Schwartz, D. Ferraro, N. Exercise intolerance in patients with chronic heart failure: role of impaired nutritive flow to skeletal muscle. *Circulation (Dallas, Tex.) 69(6), Jun 1984, 1079-1087.*
ABST: The authors researched whether exercise intolerance in patients with chronic heart failure was due to inadequate nutritive flow to skeletal muscle. Measurements of cardiac outputs, leg blood flow and leg metabolism were obtained during maximal

bicycle exercise for 7 patients with normal maximal oxygen uptake (vo2), 8 patients with heart failure and moderately reduced maximal v02. Findings indicated exercise intolerance of patients was clearly caused by impaired nutritive flow to skeletal muscle.
LEVEL: A LANG: Eng SIRC ARTICLE NO: 100531

Yamabe, H. Kobayashi, K. Fujitani, K. Fukuzaki, H. (Clinical significance of ST changes on exercise electrocardiogram in old myocardial infarction.) *Nippon Naika Gakkai Zasshi/Journal of the Japanese Society of Internal Medicine (Tokyo) 73(1), Jan 1984, 1-6.*
LEVEL: A LANG: Jpn

Yamabe, H. Kobayashi, K. Fukuzaki, H. The effect of nitrate on the oxygen availability during exercise in effort angina pectoris. *Japanese heart journal (Tokyo) 25(6), Nov 1984, 1019-1028.*
LEVEL: A LANG: Eng

Zeppilli, P. Pelliccia, A. Pirrami, M.M. Cecchetti, F. Sassara, M. Venerando, A. Etiopathogenetic and clinical spectrum of ventricular repolarisation disturbances in athletes. (Refs: 33)*International journal of sports cardiology (Torino, Italy) 1(1), Jan/June 1984, 41-51.*
ABST: 98 athletes with ventricular repolarisation disturbances at rest and/or during exercise were investigated in this study. 52 out of the 98 athletes (53 per cent) were free of heart diseases. 37 out of the 98 (37.7 per cent) had mitral valve prolapse; 3 (3.1 per cent) had hyperkinetic heart syndrome; 3 (3.1 per cent) had hypertrophic cardiomyopathy; and 1 (1 per cent) had aortic stenosis. 2 other athletes (2 per cent) were suspected of having hypertrophic cardiomyopathy. 61 out of the 88 athletes who were allowed to continue their sports were followed for 2 to 264 months during activity and after retirement.
LEVEL: A LANG: Eng SIRC ARTICLE NO: 171824

CORONARY HEART DISEASE - EXERCISE REHABILITATION AND THERAPY

Aleshin, I.A. Fizicheskie trenirovki u bolnykh s I-IIa stadiei serdechnoi nedostatochnosti posle infarkta miokarda. (Physica training of patients with stage I and II cardiac insufficiency after myocardial infarction.) *Voprosy kurortologii, Fizioterapii i lechebnoi fizicheskoi kultury (Moscow) 2, Mar/Apr 1984, 60-61.*
LEVEL: I LANG: Rus

Bestetti, R.B. dos Santos, J.E. Influencia do exercicio fisico aerobico na prevencao da doenca coronariana. (Influence of aerobic physical exercise on the prevention of coronary disease.) *Revista de saude publica (Sao Paulo) 18(4), Aug 1984, 333-336.*
LEVEL: I LANG: Por

Cantwell, J.D. Exercise and coronary heart disease: role in primary prevention. *Heart and lung (St. Louis) 13(1), Jan 1984, 6-13.*
LEVEL: I LANG: Eng SIRC ARTICLE NO: 098907

Dugmore, D. The role of exercise in the rehabilitation of the post myocardial infarct patient. (Refs: 14)*Carnegie research papers (Beckett Park, Leeds) 1(6), Dec 1984, 16-18.*
ABST: The author considers practical guidelines to be followed when planning and implementing an exercise programme for the post myocardial infarction subject. Subjects should undergo

exercise testing (sub-maximal treadmill, bicycle ergometer or bench stepping tests) to evaluate their physical work capacity before entering a conditioning programme. Contra-indications to participation are enumerated.
LEVEL: A LANG: Eng SIRC ARTICLE NO: 172500

Fletcher, G.F. Long-term exercise in coronary artery disease and other chronic disease states. *Heart and lung (St. Louis) 13(1), Jan 1984, 28-46.*
LEVEL: I LANG: Eng SIRC ARTICLE NO: 098910

Fletcher, G.F. Chiaramida, A.J. LeMay, M.R. Johnston, B.L. Thiel, J.E. Spratlin, M.C. Telephonically-monitored home exercise early after coronary artery bypass surgery. *Chest (Chicago) 86(2), Aug 1984, 198-202.*
ABST: To evaluate the usefulness of telephonically-monitored home exercise in patients within two weeks postcoronary bypass surgery, we randomly enrolled 46 male patients in a 12-week home program of either short walks or bicycle ergometry. Home exercise was done five times weekly and monitored both before and immediately after three times weekly. New arrhythmias or conduction disturbances were detected in 18 of 23 of the bicycle group and in 20 of 23 of the short walk patients. New symptoms developed in three patients, two from the short walk group and one from the bicycle group.
LEVEL: A LANG: Eng SIRC ARTICLE NO: 103865

Franklin, B.A. Wrisley, D. Johnson, S. Mitchell, M. Rubenfire, M. Chronic adaptations to physical conditioning in cardiac patients. Implications regarding exercise trainability. (Refs: 168)*Clinics in sports medicine (Philadelphia) 3(2), Apr 1984, 471-512.*
ABST: This article reviews the physiologic basis and rationale for exercise therapy in patients with coronary heart disease with specific reference to potential variables affecting exercise trainability. Regular exercise increases functional capacity, promotes relief of angina pectoris, reduces the 'risk factor' profile, enhances psychologic status and generally improves the quality of the patient's life. The mechanisms underlying these changes are not well understood.
LEVEL: A LANG: Eng SIRC ARTICLE NO: 094249

Fuchs, P. Sevic, D. Fuchs, N. Carson, W. Walter, J. The influence of coronary sport group training on the flexibility of joints, heart rate and blood pressure of coronary patients. (Refs: 29)*Journal of sports medicine and physical fitness (Torino, Italy) 24(4), Dec 1984, 280-285.*
ABST: We were able to show that in just a three months period during coronary sport training there is an increase in the flexibility of the shoulder, pelvic girdles and lumbar spine. Such an improvement in flexibility, together with improvements in coordination, aids in increasing condition of the patient, thus improving his capacity for exercise. The 'battery of tests' we devised to judge the flexibility of joints of coronary patients is a method easy to reproduce, and one which, using proper breathing techniques, presents no risk to the patients.
LEVEL: A LANG: Eng SIRC ARTICLE NO: 106361

Gori, P. Pivotti, F. Mase, N. Zucconi, V. Scardi, S. Compliance with cardiac rehabilitation in the elderly. (Refs: 10) *European heart journal (London) 5(Suppl E), Nov 1984, 109-111.*
ABST: This longitudinal study evaluated the compliance of elderly myocardial patients with cardiac rehabilitation (CR). Out of 259 patients

DISEASES AND DISORDERS (continued)

investigated, 43 began the CR program and 39 completed it. Factors associated with lack of participation in a sample of 83 patients were as follows: associated diseases and low exercise tolerance (41 percent), socioeconomic problems (9.5 percent), lack of motivation (52.3 percent) and inadequate information (38.1 percent).
LEVEL: A LANG: Eng SIRC ARTICLE NO: 109712

Hartley, L.H. Exercise prescription. Part I: General principles of exercise prescription.
NOTES: In, Strauss, R.H. (ed.), Sports medicine, Philadelphia ; Toronto, Saunders, 1984, p. 41-45.
LEVEL: A LANG: Eng RC1210 17196

Haskell, W.L. Cardiovascular benefits and risks of exercise: the scientific evidence. (Refs: 58)
NOTES: In, Strauss, R.H. (ed.), Sports medicine, Philadelphia ; Toronto, Saunders, 1984, p. 57-75.
LEVEL: A LANG: Eng RC1210 17196

Haskell, W.L. Safety of outpatient cardiac exercise programs. Issues regarding medical supervision. (Refs: 37)*Clinics in sports medicine (Philadelphia) 3(2), Apr 1984, 455-469.*
ABST: This article promotes the concept that the medical supervision of cardiac exercise programs should be individualized to suit the patient's needs. Those patients who are at high risk should receive intense supervision for as long as required. Low risk patients should be immediately cleared for programs without on-site medical supervision. This approach should make appropriate exercise training accessible to a greater number of patients, reduce the costs and increase the safety of patients who are now without adequate guidance and supervision.
LEVEL: A LANG: Eng SIRC ARTICLE NO: 094251

Jaeger, M. Coeur et exercice physique. (Refs: 5)*Revue medicale de la Suisse romande (Lausanne) 104(10), oct 1984, 801-806.*
LEVEL: I LANG: Fr SIRC ARTICLE NO: 174099

Jaggi, C.P. Readaptation cardio-vasculaire institutionnalisee. (Refs: 14)*Revue medicale de la Suisse romande (Lausanne) 104 (10), oct 1984, 831-839.*
LEVEL: I LANG: Fr SIRC ARTICLE NO: 174103

Kambara, H. Kinoshita, M. Hirota, Y. Kadota, K. Sawamura, M. Saito, T. Kawai, C. Effect on exercise tolerance and pharmacokinetics of conventional and sustained release preparations of propranolol in patients with angina pectoris - a double-blind cross-over study. *Japanese circulation journal (Kyoto) 48(10), Oct 1984, 1066-1073.*
LEVEL: A LANG: Eng

Kappagoda, C.T. Greenwood, P.V. Physical training with minimal hospital supervision of patients after coronary artery bypass surgery. (Refs: 18)*Archives of physical medicine and rehabilitation 65(2), Feb 1984, 57-60.*
ABST: This paper investigates the effect of a physical training program with minimal hospital supervision of patients after coronary artery bypass surgery. 15 patients were selected for training while the remainder were assigned to self-administered activity. Improvements in both the effort tolerance and the highest rate pressure products were observed in all patients. In the group that trained, 9 months postoperatively there were significant increases in work capacity as well as in the highest rate pressure products.
LEVEL: A LANG: Eng SIRC ARTICLE NO: 092729

Kavanagh, T. Distance running and cardiac rehabilitation: physiologic and psychosocial considerations. (Refs: 81)*Clinics in sports medicine (Philadelphia) 3(2), Apr 1984, 513-526.*
ABST: Research to date supports the contention that regular endurance exercise such as distance running has mental and physical benefits. From this research it could be extrapolated that distance running will improve the prognosis in ischemic heart disease. Although there have not been any well constructed studies which have conclusively proven such a relationship there also have not been any studies which show that exercise is hazardous for patients with ischemic heart disease. For this reason it seems sensible to advocate and support the use of distance running in the management of ischemic heart disease.
LEVEL: A LANG: Eng SIRC ARTICLE NO: 095426

Kavanagh, T. Exercise and coronary artery disease. (Refs: 90)
NOTES: In, Basmajian, J.V. (ed.), Therapeutic exercise, 4th ed., Baltimore, Md., Williams & Wilkins, c1984, p. 565-586.
LEVEL: A LANG: Eng RM719 17505

Lehmann, M. Berg, A. Keul, J. Anderung der sympathischen Aktivitaet bei 18 Postinfarktpatienten nach 1 Jahr Bewegungstherapi (Changes in sympathetic activity in 18 postinfarct patients following a year of exercise therapy.) *Zeitschrift fuer Kardiologie (Darmstadt) 73(12), Dec 1984, 756-759.*
ABST: Hormonal and hemodynamic changes in 18 postinfarct patients (47-65 years) following 1 year of physical therapy were examined in this study. Maximal heart rate responses were similar at rest both before and after physical therapy. Following therapy, significant reductions in noradrenaline responses (16 per cent), adrenaline responses (25 per cent), and mean arterial blood pressure (14 mm Hg) were observed. At a 50 watt work-load, reductions after physical therapy were 25 per cent for noradrenaline, 41 per cent for adrenaline, 16 per cent in heart rate, and a 21 mm Hg reduction of mean arterial blood pressure.
LEVEL: A LANG: Ger

Maranto, G. Exercise: how much is too much? *Discover (Los Angeles) 5(10), Oct 1984, 18-22.*
LEVEL: B LANG: Eng SIRC ARTICL NO: 098913

Martin, W.H. Heath, G. Coyle, E.F. Bloomfield, S.A. Holloszy, J.O. Ehsani, A.A. Effect of prolonged intense endurance training on systolic time intervals in patients with coronary artery disease. *American heart journal (St. Louis) 107(1), Jan 1984, 75-81.*
ABST: The effect of exercise training on systolic time intervals was studied in 13 coronary artery disease patients who trained 3 times per week for 3 months followed by 4 times per week for a further 7 months. Significant training effects were seen in increased aerobic capacity, lower resting heart rate and lower blood pressure and heart rate during submaximal exercise. Total electromechanical systole and left ventricular ejection time did not change significantly while pre-ejection period index did decrease. Post training increases were found in the left ventricular end-diastolic dimension and posterior wall thickness.
LEVEL: A LANG: Eng SIRC ARTICLE NO: 097447

May, G.A. Nagle, F.J. Changes in rate-pressure product with physical training of individuals with coronary artery disease. (Refs: 35)*Physical therapy (Alexandria, Va.) 64(9), Sept 1984, 1361-1366.*

ABST: The effects of progression of coronary disease and exercise on rate-pressure product (RRP) is determined in this study. One hundred twenty-one subjects aged between 40 and 70 years old are tested. Subjects are divided in one experimental and two control groups. The maximal aerobic capacity of the experimental group increases (p.01), the rate-pressure product increases (p.01) in maximal exercise while it decreases (p.01) in submaximal exercise. No significant changes are observed in the control groups.
LEVEL: A LANG: Eng SIRC ARTICLE NO: 098914

Moes, D.M. Comparison of the hemodynamic responses of phase I cardiac rehabilitation to the DiGXT in the post-surgical population. Eugene, Ore.: Microform Publications, University of Oregon, 1984. 1 microfiche : negative, ill. ; 11 x 15 cm.
NOTES: Thesis (M.S.) - University of Wisconsin-La Crosse, 1982; (vii, 83 leaves); includes bibliography.
LEVEL: A LANG: Eng UO84 299

Myers, J. Ahnve, S. Froelicher, V. Livingston, M. Jensen, D. Abramson, I. Sullivan, M. Mortara, D. A randomized trial of the effects of 1 year of exercise training on computer-measured ST segment displacement in patients with coronary artery disease. *Journal of the American College of Cardiology (New York) 4(6), Dec 1984, 1094-1102.*
LEVEL: A LANG: Eng

Naughton, J. Contributions of exercise clinical trials to cardiac rehabilitation. (Refs: 17)*Clinics in sports medicine (Philadelphia) 3(2), Apr 1984, 545-557.*
ABST: Clinical investigations on the efficacy of exercise in cardiac rehabilitation have shown that regularly performed physical activity can benefit properly selected, motivated patients with coronary heart disease. Further clinical studies are needed to clarify the unanswered questions regarding the use and applicability of exercise training in the process of cardiac rehabilitation.
LEVEL: A LANG: Eng SIRC ARTICLE NO: 094256

Nicklas, K. Auswirkungen massiver Gesundheitsschaeden auf die Lebenssituation der Betroffenen und Formen der Kompensation: aufgezeigt am Beispiel von Querschnittgelaehmten und Herzinfarktpatienten... Koeln: Deutsche Sporthochschule, Institut fuer Rehabilitation und Behindertensport, 1984. 283 p.
NOTES: Thesis (Ph.D.) - Deutsche Sporthochschule Koeln, 1984. Bibliography: p. 250-280.
LEVEL: A LANG: Ger RD795 17682

O'Callaghan, W.G. Teo, K.K. O'Riordan, J. Webb, H. Dolphin, T. Horgan, J.H. Comparative response of male and female patients with coronary artery disease to exercise rehabilitation. *European heart journal (London) 5(8), Aug 1984, 649-651.*
LEVEL: A LANG: Eng

Obma, R.T. Keritzinsky, G. Anderson, R. Exercise for pacemaker patients. (Refs: 7)*Physician and sportsmedicine 12(4), Apr 1984, 127-130.*
LEVEL: I LANG: Eng SIRC ARTICLE NO: 092732

Oldridge, N.B. Stoedefalke, K.G. Compliance and motivation in cardiac exercise programs. (Refs: 25)*Clinics in sports medicine (Philadelphia) 3(2), Apr 1984, 443-454.*
ABST: This paper discusses methods of getting and keeping patients involved in cardiac rehabilitation

programs. Although the basic format of most cardiac rehabilitation programs is similar, truly successful programs provide an optimal social environment in order to stimulate patient compliance. In the final analysis it is the ability of the exercise specialists to motivate the patients which ensures the success of the program.
LEVEL: A LANG: Eng SIRC ARTICLE NO: 094257

Payne, F.E. The role of the primary care physician in cardiac rehabilitation. (Refs: 20)
NOTES: In, Birrer, R.B. (ed.), Sports medicine for the primary care physician, Norwalk, Conn., Appleton-Century-Crofts, c1984, p. 297-304.
LEVEL: I LANG: Eng RC1210 17030

Physical conditioning for patients with coronary artery disease. (editorial) *Lancet (London) 2(8403), 15 Sept 1984, 615-616.*
LEVEL: B LANG: Eng SIRC ARTICLE NO: 103878

Pollock, M.L. Pels, A.E. Exercise prescription for the cardiac patient: an update. (Refs: 72)*Clinics in sports medicine (Philadelphia) 3(2), Apr 1984, 425-442.*
ABST: This article discusses the application of the basic training principles of exercise physiology and modifications thereof to post-myocardial infarction and post-coronary artery bypass graft patient programs. The use of Borg's Rating of Perceived Exertion scale in cardiac rehabilitation is discussed. The framework of exercise programs is given commencing with an in-patient program, followed by an outpatient program, and a community-based program. Special considerations such as beta adrenergic blocking drugs, assessing risk for cardiac rehabilitation patients, and medical problems during inpatient and outpatient programs are briefly discussed.
LEVEL: A LANG: Eng SIRC ARTICLE NO: 094259

Puleo, P. Verani, M.S. Wyndham, C.R. Hixson, J. Raizner, A.E. Exercise-induced left bundle branch block: resolution after coronary angioplasty. *American heart journal (St. Louis) 108(5), Nov 1984, 1373-1374.*
LEVEL: A LANG: Eng

Raineri, A. Assennato, P. Candela, B. Traina, M. Effetto training e parametri e modinamici in pazienti con infarto del miocardio sottoposti a riabilitazione. (Training effect and hemodynamic parameters in myocardial infarct patients undergoing rehabilitation.) *Giornale italiano di cardiologia (Rome) 14(2), Feb 1984, 85-90.*
ABST: Thirty-five myocardial infarct patients were subjected to a physical rehabilitation program. A training effect (TE) was observed in 22 patients after rehabilitation. In patients with TE, the ejection fraction (EF) was 52-62% at rest, and 55-73% during exercise; in patients without TE, the EF was 44-60% at rest and 36-56% during exercise.
LEVEL: A LANG: It

Sakakibara, T. Hirose, H. Nakano, S. Matsuda, H. Shimazaki, Y. Satho, S. Taniguchi, K. Matsumura, R. Kobayashi, J. Kawashima, Y. (Correlation between grade or revascularization and the left ventricular function during exercise after aortocoronary bypass.) *Nippon kyobu geka gakkai zasshi/Japanese Association for Thoracic Surgery (Tokyo) 32(6), June 1984, 879-884.*
LEVEL: A LANG: Jpn

Sivarajan, E.S. Newton, K.M. Exercise, education, and counseling for patients with coronary artery disease. (Refs: 104) *Clinics in sports medicine (Philadelphia) 3(2), Apr 1984, 349-369.*

ABST: The components of a multifactorial approach to cardiac rehabilitation are outlined. These components are exercise, education and counseling. Although unsupervised multifactorial programs for the individual are beneficial, supervised multifactorial programs for groups tend to have greater compliance and therefore a greater chance of success.
LEVEL: A LANG: Eng SIRC ARTICLE NO: 094263

Thomas, K.R. Development of a phase II cardiac rehabilitation patient education program. Eugene, Ore.: Microform Publications, University of Oregon, 1984. 2 microfiches : negative, ill. ; 11 x 15 cm.
NOTES: Thesis (M.S.) - University of Wisconsin-La Crosse, 1982; (v, 150 leaves); includes bibliography.
LEVEL: A LANG: Eng UO84 302-303

Vanhess, L. Fagard, R. Grauwels, R. De Geest, H. Amery, A. Changes in systolic time intervals during physicla training in patients with ischemic heart disease. Effect of beta-blockade. *Cardiology (Basel) 71(4), 1984, 207-214.*
LEVEL: A LANG: Eng

Vitruk, S.K. Kuklia, I.I. Effektivnost razlichnykh rezhemov fizicheskoi reabilitatsii u bolnykh melkoochagovym infarktom miokarda. (Effetiveness of different regimens of physical rehabilitation with patients with microfocal myocardial infarct.) *Vrachebnoe delo (Kiev) 8, Aug 1984, 10-13.*
LEVEL: A LANG: Rus

Volkov, V.S. Vinogradov, V.F. Ob adaptatsii k fizicheskoi nagruzke bol'nykh ishemicheskoi bolez'iu serdtsa. (Adaptation of patients with ischemic heart disease to physical exertion.) *Kardiologiia (Moskva) 24(2), Feb 1984, 116-117.*
LEVEL: A LANG: Rus

Walenting, C. Roethle, J. Damken, M.A. Rowing study yields data for an upper body rehabilitation and training method. *CardioGram (La Crosse, Wis.) 11(5), Oct/Nov 1984, 10.*
LEVEL: B LANG: Eng SIRC ARTICLE NO: 173569

Wiliams, M.A. Esterbrooks, D.J. Sketch, M.H. Guidelines for exercise therapy of the elderly after myocardial infarct. (Refs: 1)*European heart journal (London) 5(Suppl E), Nov 1984, 121-123.*
LEVEL: I LANG: Eng SIRC ARTICLE NO: 109715

Williams, M.A. Prognosis for post-myocardial infarction patients entering cardiac rehabilitation. Eugene, Ore.: Microform Publications, University of Oregon, 1984. 1 microfiche : negative, ill. ; 11 x 15 cm.
NOTES: Thesis (Ph.D.) - Texas A & M University, 1980; (xi, 85 leaves); vita; includes bibliography.
LEVEL: A LANG: Eng UO84 17

Williams, M.A. Maresh, C.M. Aronow, W.S. Esterbrooks, D.J. Mohiuddin, S.M. Sketch, M.H. The value of early out-patient cardiac exercise programmes for the elderly in comparison with other selected age groups. (Refs: 2)*European heart journal (London) 5(Suppl E), Nov 1984, 113-115.*
ABST: The benefits of an early exercise program in elderly cardiac patients (over 65 years) were investiaged in this study. 76 patients participated in an exercise program over a 12 week period within 6 weeks of myocardial infarct or cardiac surgery. Impovements in both elderly and younger patients were comparable.
LEVEL: A LANG: Eng SIRC ARTICLE NO: 109713

Williams, R.S. McKinnis, R.A. Cobb, F.R. Higginbotham, M.B. Wallace, A.G. Coleman,

R.E. Califf, R.M. Effects of physical conditioning on left ventricular ejection fraction in patients with coronary artery disease. *Circulation (Dallas, Tex.) 70(1), Jul 1984, 69-75.*
ABST: 53 coronary artery disease patients were tested at rest and during upright bicycle exercise before and after 6 to 12 months of exercise training. The peak bicycle workload achieved before fatigue, dyspnea, or angina increased by an average of 22% after training, and the mean heart rate at maximum workload decreased by 10 beats/min after training.
LEVEL: A LANG: Eng SIRC ARTICLE NO: 102380

Wilson, P.K. Hall, L.K. Industrial fitness, adult fitness, and cardiac rehabilitation: graduate programs specific to trainin exercise specialists. *Journal of physical education, recreation & dance 55(3), Mar 1984, 40-44.*
LEVEL: B LANG: Eng SIRC ARTICLE NO: 093063

CORONARY HEART DISEASE - PREVENTION

Akerblom, H.K. Viikari, J. Uhari, J. Rasanen, L. Dahl, M. Lahde, P-L. Pesonen, E. Pietikainen, M. Suoninen, P. Dahlstrom, S. Nikkari, T. Moilanen, T. Ahola, M. Byckling, T. Seppanen, A. Aromaa, A. Pyorala, K. Multicenter study of atherosclerosis precursors in Finnish children: report of two pilot studies. (Refs: 15)
CONF: Symposium of Paediatric Work Physiology (10th : 1981 : Joutsa, Finland).
NOTES: In, Ilmarinen, J. and Vaelimaeki, I. (eds.), Children and sport: paediatric work physiology, Berlin, Springer-Verlag, 1984, p. 219-230.
LEVEL: A LANG: Eng SIRC ARTICLE NO: 102327

Bryant, J.G. Garett, H.L. Dean, M.S. Coronary heart disease: the beneficial effects of exercise to children. (Refs: 12) *Journal of the Louisiana State Medical Society (New Orleans) 136(5), May 1984, 15-17.*
LEVEL: A LANG: Eng SIRC ARTICLE NO: 102365

Bryant, J.G. Garrett, H.L. Mostafa, M.S.D. The effects of an exercise program on selected risk factors to coronary heart disease in children. *Social science & medicine (Oxford) 19(7), 1984, 765-766.*
LEVEL: I LANG: Eng SIRC ARTICLE NO: 103862

Eichner, E.R. The exercise hypothesis - an updated analysis. (Refs: 20)*In, Krakauer, L.J. (ed.) et al., 1984 year book of sports medicine, Chicago, Ill., Year Book Medical Publishers, Inc., 1984, p. 9-19.*
LEVEL: I LANG: Eng RC1210 18955

Exercise, alcohol and good cholesterol. *Health letter (San Antonio, Tex.) 23(10), 25 May 1984, 3-4.*
LEVEL: B LANG: Eng SIRC ARTICLE NO: 094248

Goldberg, A.P. A potential role for exercise training in modulating coronary risk factors in uremia. *American journal of nephrology (Basel) 4(2), Mar/Apr 1984, 132-133.*
LEVEL: I LANG: Eng SIRC ARTICLE NO: 100522

Hartung, G.H. Diet and exercise in the regulation of plasma lipids and lipoproteins in patients at risk of coronary disease. (Refs: 22)*Sports medicine (Auckland, N.Z.) 1(6), Nov/Dec 1984, 413-418.*
LEVEL: I LANG: Eng SIRC ARTICLE NO: 102370

Leon, A.S. Forum: exercise and health. Introduction. *Preventive medicine (New York) 13(1),*

Jan 1984, 1-2.
LEVEL: B LANG: Eng SIRC ARTICLE NO: 100524

Morrison, J.F. van Malsen, S. Noakes, T.D.
Leisure-time physical activity levels, cardiovascular fitness and coronary risk factors in 1015 white Zimbabweans. (Refs: 34)*South African medical journal (Cape Town) 65(7), 18 Feb 1984, 250-256.*
ABST: To determine a 'threshold' level of habitual physical activity for the reduction of coronary risk factors, a cross-sectional study of 646 male and 369 female White Zimbabweans aged 20-70 years was undertaken. The data shows that a 'threshold' level of exercise might exist above which there is a reduction in the percentage of body fat, the incidence of smoking and abnormal ST-segment depression during exercise, increased VO2MAX values and a reduced rate of fall of VO2MAX with age. Whereas participation in only light exercises had little effect, more strenuous exercise was associated with beneficial alterations in all these parameters.
LEVEL: A LANG: Eng SIRC ARTICLE NO: 098916

Noakes, T.D. Opie, L.H. Rose, A.G. Marathon running and immunity to coronary heart disease: fact versus fiction. (Refs: 61) *Clinics in sports medicine (Philadelphia) 3(2), Apr 1984, 527-543.*
ABST: This prospective study was designed to determine if coronary heart disease could be found in marathon runner's. The results indicate that coronary atherosclerosis and sudden cardiac death do occur in marathon runners. Thus, marathon running does not confer complete immunity from heart disease on its participants. However, this form of endurance training may provide partial protection from coronary heart disease.
LEVEL: A LANG: Eng SIRC ARTICLE NO: 095445

Paffenbarger, R.S. Hyde, R.T. Jung, D.L. Wing, A.L. Epidemiology of exercise and coronary heart disease. (Refs: 78)*Clinics in sports medicine (Philadelphia) 3(2), Apr 1984, 297-318.*
ABST: This paper reviews studies concerned with the effect of exercise on the incidence of coronary heart disease. All of the studies reviewed show that adequate exercise reduces the risk of coronary heart disease and its associated risk factors.
LEVEL: A LANG: Eng SIRC ARTICLE NO: 094258

Paffenbarger, R.S. Hyde, R.T. Exercise in the prevention of coronary heart disease. (Refs: 55)*Preventive medicine (New York 13(1), Jan 1984, 3-22.*
ABST: The authors review the literature on the relationship between exercise and coronary heart disease risk. Studies indicate a strong inverse relationship between these two factors.
LEVEL: A LANG: Eng SIRC ARTICLE NO: 100526

Patsch, J.R. Patsch, W. Exercise, high density lipoproteins, and fat tolerance. *Comprehensive therapy (Harvard, Ma.) 10(2), Feb 1984, 29-37.*
LEVEL: A LANG: Eng SIRC ARTICLE NO: 100917

Viikari, J. Valimaki, I. Telama, R. Siren-Tiusanen, H. Akerblom, H.K. Dahl, M. Lahde, P.L. Pesonen, E. Pietikainen, M. Suoninen, P. Uhari, M. Atherosclerosis precursors in Finnish children: physical activity and plasma lipids in 3-and 12 year-old children. (Refs: 13)
CONF: Symposium of Paediatric Work Physiology (10th : 1981 : Joutsa, Finland).
NOTES: In, Ilmarinen, J. and Vaelimaeki, I. (eds.), Children and sport: paediatric work physiology, Berlin, Springer-Verlag, 1984, p. 231-240
LEVEL: A LANG: Eng SIRC ARTICLE NO: 102347

CORONARY HEART DISEASE - RISK FACTORS

Appels, A. Mulder, P. Imminent myocardial infarction: a psychological study. *Journal of human stress (Shelburne Falls, Mass 10(3), Fall 1984, 129-134.*
ABST: A survey of 3,571 males indicated that the prevalence of 'imminent myocardial infarction' was more than four times higher among exhausted and depressive persons than healthy persons.
LEVEL: A LANG: Eng

Armstrong, N. Children and exercise. (Refs: 10)*Bulletin of physical education (London) 20(2), Summer 1984, 79-85.*
CONF: British Association of Advisers and Lecturers in Physical Education. Congress (64th : 1984 : Cardiff).
LEVEL: I LANG: Eng SIRC ARTICLE NO: 104241

Etchells, A. Exercise: the benefits and the risks. *Running (London) 43, Nov 1984, 36-37.*
LEVEL: B LANG: Eng SIRC ARTICLE NO: 103864

Fernhall, B. Manfredi, T.G. Rierson, H. Effects of ten weeks of cardiac rehabilitation on blood clotting and risk factors. (Refs: 37)*Physician and sportsmedicine 12(2), Feb 1984, 85-91;93;96.*
ABST: The authors researched the effects of a ten-week cardiac rehabilitation program on selected coronary heart disease (CHD) and blood-clotting factors in eleven male and three female cardiac patients. Selected physical, physiological and blood lipid parameters were compated before and after the program. This study concludes that some CHD risk factors can be increased while others can be decreased by following the program. A longer period of rehabilitation seems necessary to effectively reduce risk factors.
LEVEL: A LANG: Eng SIRC ARTICLE NO: 091323

Gilliam, T.B. MacConnie, S.E. Coronary heart disease risk in children and their physical activity patterns. (Refs: 42)*In, Boileau, R.A. (ed.), Advances in pediatric sport sciences. Volume 1: biological issues, Champaign, Ill., Human Kinetics Publishers, c1984, p. 171-187.*
LEVEL: A LANG: Eng RJ125 20044

Hammermeister, K.E. Is exertional hypotension a useful indicator of high risk coronary artery disease? *International journa of cardiology (Amsterdam) 5(6), Jun 1984, 757-761.*
LEVEL: I LANG: Eng SIRC ARTICLE NO: 103867

Leon, A.S. Exercise and risk of coronary heart disease. (Refs: 67)*American Academy of Physical Education papers (Champaign, Ill.) 17, 1984, 14-31.*
CONF: American Academy of Physical Education. Annual Meeting (54th : 1983 : Minneapolis).
NOTES: Conference theme: Exercise and health.
LEVEL: A LANG: Eng SIRC ARTICLE NO: 103871

Mathur, D.N. Toriola, A.L. Twelve weeks jogging effects on selected cardiovascular risk factors in untrained healthy males. (Refs: 20)*Journal of sports medicine and physical fitness (Torino, Italy) 24(3), Sept 1984, 259-262.*
ABST: The purpose of the study was to investigate the effectiveness of 12 weeks of different jogging programmes on selected cardiac risk factors such as blood pressure, blood glucose and serum uric acid. 40 untrained, healthy male undergraduates were randomly assigned to 1.6 km, 3.2 km, 4.8 km jogging and nonjogging groups. Insignificant reductions in blood pressure and serum uric acid

levels were observed among the joggers. Subjects of 4.8 km jogging group had a significant lowering in blood glucose values. It was concluded that level of reduction of blood glucose value is related to distance of jogging.
LEVEL: A LANG: Eng SIRC ARTICLE NO: 105188

Mikes, Z. Kristufek, J. Petrovicova, J. Strelkova, V. Viskupicova, A. Gavornik, P. Relativene riziko ischemickej choroby srdca, telesna vykonnost a prognoza 40-55-rocnych Bratislavskych muzov. (The relative risk of ischemic heart disease, physical performance and prognosis in 40-to-55-year-old males in Bratislava.) *Bratislavske lekarske listy (Bratislava) 82(3), Sept 1984, 1069-1076.*
LEVEL: A LANG: Slo

Paffenbarger, R.S. Hyde, R.T. Wing, A.L. Steinmetz, C.H. A natural history of athleticism and cardiovascular health. (Refs: 27)*JAMA: Journal of the American Medical Association (Chicago) 252(4), 27 Jul 1984, 491-495.*
ABST: This study reports on the analysis of 572 first attacks among 16,936 Harvard alumni, 1962 to 1972, and 1,413 total deaths, 1962 to 1978. These show that habitual postcollege exercise, not student sports play, predicts low coronary heart disease risk. Sedentary alumni, even ex-varsity athletes, have high risk. Exercise benefit is independent of contrary life-style elements in affecting coronary heart disease incidence. Hypertension was found to be the strongest predictor of coronary attack.
LEVEL: A LANG: Eng SIRC ARTICLE NO: 102374

Pavela, S.L. Gabster, A.A. DeVoll, C. Runners' myths must be measured against the reality of risk factors, La Crosse authorities say. *CardioGram (La Crosse, Wis.) 11(5), Oct/Nov 1984, 4-5;12.*
LEVEL: B LANG: Eng SIRC ARTICLE NO: 173568

Poole, G.W. Exercise, coronary heart disease and risk factors: a brief report. (Refs: 48)*Sports medicine (Auckland, N.Z.) 1(5), Sept/Oct 1984, 341-349.*
ABST: This article focuses on the link between exercise and coronary heart disease, with special attention given to the relationship of aerobic fitness levels to coronary heart disease factors.
LEVEL: A LANG: Eng SIRC ARTICLE NO: 102375

Rauramaa, R. Salonen, J.T. Kukkonen-Harjula, K. Seppaenen, K. Seppaelae, E. Vapaatalo, H. Huttunen, J.K. Effects of mild physical exercise on serum lipoproteins and metabolites of arachidonic acid: a controlled randomised trial in middle aged men. *British medical journal (clinical research) (London) 288(6417), 25 Feb 1984, 603-606.*
ABST: This paper explores the effect of exercise on biochemic risk factors for coronary disease in 31 middle aged men. The authors observe that in the exercising patients serum cholesterol concentrations increase 26% more in the high density lipoprotein susfraction two (HDL2) and decrease 31% more in the susfraction three (HDL3) and 9% more in the low density lipoprotein fraction than in the controls.
LEVEL: A LANG: Eng SIRC ARTICLE NO: 099260

Riales, R. Cholesterol: re-tarnishing a bad reputation. *Running & fitness (Washington, D.C.) 16(3), May/Jun 1984, 1;20-21.*
LEVEL: I LANG: Eng SIRC ARTICLE NO: 100527

Riviere, A. Denolin, H. Contre-indications a la pratique du sport chez le cardiaque. (Contra-indications to sports activitie in cardiac patients.) *Annales de cardiologie et d'angeiologie (Paris)*

33(3), Apr 1984, 145-151.
LEVEL: I LANG: Fr SIRC ARTICLE NO: 102376

Sedgwick, A.W. Davidson, A.H. Taplin, R.E. Thomas, D.W. Relationships between physical fitness and risk factors for coronary heart disease in men and women. *Australian and New Zealand journal of medicine (Sydney) 14(3), June 1984, 208-214.*
LEVEL: A LANG: Eng

Shephard, R.J. Can we identify those for whom exercise is hazardous? (Refs: 43)*Sports medicine (Auckland) 1(1), Jan/Feb 1984, 75-86.*
ABST: The prime objective of this article was to suggest ways in which an identification of individuals who are at an increased risk of cardiac emergency, due to vigorous physical activity, might be made. Discussed are screening options which range from self-administered questionnaires and clinical examination to the use of an exercise electrocardiogram (ECG) and other quite sophisticated laboratory tests. The sensitivities and specificities of such methods are reported from other studies to illustrate their advantages. The author suggests seeking an optimum combination of variables and a stratified plan of pre-exercise evaluation that will best distinguish between those who are at risk and those who are not.
LEVEL: A LANG: Eng SIRC ARTICLE NO: 094262

Siscovick, D.S. Weiss, N.S. Fletcher, R.H. Schoenbach, V.J. Wagner, E.H. Habitual vigorous exercise and primary cardiac arrest: effect of other risk factors on the relationship. (Refs: 14)*Journal of chronic diseases (Elmsford, N.Y.) 37(8), 1984, 625-631.*
ABST: The authors investigated if the relationship between habitual vigorous exercise and primary cardiac arrest (PCA) is modified by other risk factors. 133 male cases of PCA, 25-75 years of age, and 133 controls served as subjects. Subjects involved in high-intensity exercise for less than 20 min per week were classified as non-vigorous. The risk of PCA was more than doubled for non-vigorous males independently of other risk factors, i.e. hypertension, smoking, obesity and family history.
LEVEL: A LANG: Eng SIRC ARTICLE NO: 103881

Siscovick, D.S. Weiss, N.S. Fletcher, R.H. Lasky, T. The incidence of primary cardiac arrest during vigorous exercise. *New England journal of medicine (Boston) 311(14), 4 Oct 1984, 874-877.*
ABST: The authors interviewed the wives of 133 men without known prior heart disease who had had primary cardiac arrest. Cases were classified according to their activity at the time of cardiac arrest and the amount of their habitual vigorous activity. Among men with low levels of habitual activity, the relative risk of cardiac arrest during exercise compared with that at other times was 56. The risk during exercise among men at the highest level of habitual activity was also elevated, but only by a factor of 5. However, among the habitually vigorous men, the overall risk of cardiac arrest -- i.e., during and not during vigourous activity -- was only 40 per cent that of the sedentary men.
LEVEL: A LANG: Eng SIRC ARTICLE NO: 103882

CYSTIC FIBROSIS

Benson, L.N. Newth, C.J. DeSouza, M. Lobraico, R. Kartodihardjo, W. Corkey, C. Gilday, D. Olley, P.M. Radionuclide assessment of right and left ventricular function during bicycle exercise in young patients with cystic fibrosis. *American review or respiratory disease (New York) 130(6), Dec 1984, 987-992.*
LEVEL: A LANG: Eng

Cerny, F.J. Cropp, G.J. Bye, M.R. Hospital therapy improves exercise tolerance and lung function in cystic fibrosis. *American journal of diseases of children (Chicago) 138(3), Mar 1984, 261-265.*
ABST: This study focuses on the improvement of lung function and exercise tolerance in 17 cystic fibrosis patients following in-hospital therapy. Significant improvements are observed in all patients.
LEVEL: A LANG: Eng SIRC ARTICLE NO: 099001

Henke, K.G. Orenstein, D.M. Oxygen saturation during exercise in cystic fibrosis. *American review of respiratory disease (New York) 129(5), May 1984, 708-711.*
ABST: Oxygen saturation (Sa 02) of 91 cystic fibrosis patients during exercise to exhaustion was assessed in this study. Changes of Sa O2 by 5% or more were observed in only 13 patients: 4 patients increased Sa 02 by 5 % or more, whereas 9 decreased by 5% or more. Larger decreases in Sa 02 were more common in patients with forced expiratory volume in one second less than 50% of vital capacity.
LEVEL: A LANG: Eng SIRC ARTICLE NO: 100652

Holzer, F.J. Schnall, R. Landau, L.I. The effect of a home exercise programme in children with cystic fibrosis and asthma. *Australian paediatric journal (Melbourne) 20(4), Nov 1984, 297-301.*
LEVEL: I LANG: Eng

Orenstein, D.M. Competitive sports for children with chronic pulmonary diseases. (Refs: 3)*Sports medicine digest (Van Nuys, Calif.) 6(5), May 1984, 1-3.*
LEVEL: I LANG: Eng SIRC ARTICLE NO: 100657

DIABETES

Bogardus, C. Ravussin, E. Robbins, D.C. Wolfe, R.R. Horton, E.S. Sims, E.A. Effects of physical training and diet therapy on carbohydrate metabolism in patients with glucose intolerance and non-insulin-dependent diabetes mellitus. *Diabetes (New York) 33(4), Apr 1984, 311-318.*
ABST: The purpose of this study was to investigate the effects of 12 weeks of a training program and diet therapy (DPT group, 10) on body composition, carbohydrate (CHO) tolerance and insulin secretion compared with the effects of diet therapy alone (D group, 8) in CHO-intolerant and non-insulin-dependent diabetic subjects. Decreases in fat mass, fat-free mass, mean fasting plasma glucose, serum C-peptide, and insulin concentrations were observed in both groups.
LEVEL: A LANG: Eng SIRC ARTICLE NO: 100645

Campaigne, B.N. Gilliam, T.B. Spencer, M.L. Lampman, R.M. Schork, M.A. Effects of a physical activity program on metabolic control and cardiovascular fitness in children with insulin-dependent diabetes mellitus. *Diabetes care (New York) 7(1), Jan/Feb 1984, 57-62.*
ABST: The authors researched the effects of exercise on children aged 5-11 years with insulin-dependent diabetes mellitus. 9 subjects participated in a 30-min exercise program three times a week for 12 wk while 10 others served as controls. Metabolic control was assessed by measuring hemoglobin A1 (HbA1), and fasting blood glucose (FBG). Significant decreases of HbA1 and FBG and increase in aerobic capacity (45.20 to 49.08 versus 49.39 to 51.99) were observed in the experimental group.
LEVEL: A LANG: Eng SIRC ARTICLE NO: 100647

Compaigne, B.N. Gilliam. T.B. Spencer, M.L. Gold, E.R. Heart rate Holter monitoring of 6- and 7- year old children with insulin dependent diabetics mellitus cardiovascular and short term metabolic response to exercise: a pilot story. (Refs: 14) *Research quarterly for exercise & sport (Reston, Va.) 55(1), Mar 1984, 69-73.*
ABST: The purpose of this study was to examine the heart rate of four children with insulin dependent diabetics mellitus during a normal day at camp, and to compare this to a day that included special vigorous physical exercise programs. A heart rate monitoring device was worn by each child from 9:00 AM to 7:00 PM on each day of study. Insulin usage and urine glucose (Clinitest) were also monitored and recorded three times daily. The results showed that the exercise day resulted in 26.3 minutes during which the heart rate was greater than 160 beats per minute in comparison to 1.0 minutes for the normal activity day. Thus, the authors conclude that the children did not participate in vigorous activity on a voluntary basis. However, it is possible to increase physical activity, measured by heart rate, to increase cardiovascular fitness and to establish short-term metabolic control of urine glucose and hypoglycemia.
LEVEL: A LANG: Eng SIRC ARTICLE NO: 096006

Exercise and the heart: diabetics should take special care with their exercise programs. *Cardiac alert (Bethesda, Md.) 6(13), Nov 1984, 6-7.*
LEVEL: B LANG: Eng SIRC ARTICLE NO: 173570

Ferrante, M.R. Annuzzi, G. Caso, P. Rivellese, A. Santangelo, L. Vaccaro, O. Risposta cardiovascolare allo sforzo in soggett con ridotta tolleranza al glucosio. (Cardiovascular response to exercise in subjects with reduced glucose tolerance.) *Cardiologia 29(12), Dec 1984, 661-669.*
LEVEL: A LANG: It

Gaztambide Saenz, S. Merodio Vigiola, M.L. Garcia Sanchez-Gabriel, J.A. Vazquez Garcia, J.A. Influencia del ejercicio sobre el metabolismo lipidico en la diabetes mellitus tipo I. (Influence of exercise on lipid metabolism in type 1 diabetes mellitus.) *Medicine clinica (Barcelona) 83(10), 6 Oct 1984, 411-413.*
LEVEL: A LANG: Spa

Huttunen, N.P. Kaeaer, M.L. Knip, M. Mustonen, A. Puukka, R. Akerblom, H.K. Physical fitness of children and adolescents wit insulin-dependent diabetes mellitus. *Annals of clinical research (Helsinki) 16(1), 1984, 1-5.*
LEVEL: A LANG: Eng

Jette, D.U. Physiological effects of exercise in the diabetic. (Refs: 26)*Physical therapy (Alexandria, Va.) 64(3), Mar 1984,339-342.*
ABST: This review article discusses the physiological effects of exercise and training in the diabetic. Exercise treatment can improve glucose tolerance and cardiovascular disease in the diabetic if it is correctly administered.
LEVEL: A LANG: Eng SIRC ARTICLE NO: 094425

Kemmer, F.W. Berger, M. Exercise in therapy and the life of diabetic patients. *Clinical science (London) 67(3), Sept 1984, 279-283.*
LEVEL: I LANG: Eng SIRC ARTICLE NO: 103965

Koivisto, V.A. Pelkonen, R. Nikkilae, E.A. Heding, L.G. Human and procine insulins are equally effective in the regulation o glucose kinetics of diabetic patients during exercise. *Acta endocrinologica (Copenhagen) 107(4), Dec 1984, 500-505.*
LEVEL: A LANG: Eng

Larsson, Y. Physical performance and the young diabetic. (Refs: 55)*In, Boileau, R.A. (ed.), Advances in pediatric sport sciences. Volume 1: biological issues, Champaign, Ill., Human Kinetics Publishers, c1984, p. 131-156.*
LEVEL: A LANG: Eng RJ125 20044

Maehlum, S. Clinical application of exercise and training in diabetes mellitus. (Refs: 21)*International journal of sports medicine (Stuttgart) Suppl. 5, Nov 1984, 47-48.*
CONF: International Congress on Sports and Health (1983 : Maastricht, Netherlands).
LEVEL: I LANG: Eng SIRC ARTICLE NO: 103969

Mohamed, A. Wilkin. T. Leatherdale, B.A. Rowe, D. Response of urinary albumin to submaximal exercise in newly diagnosed non-insulin dependent diabetes. *British medical journal (clinical research) (London) 288(6427), 5 May 1984, 1342-1343.*
LEVEL: A LANG: Eng SIRC ARTICLE NO: 100656

O'Dea, K. Marked improvement in carbohydrate and lipid metabolism in diabetic Australian aborigines after temporary reversio to traditional lifestyle. *Diabetes (New York) 33(6), Jun 1984, 596-603.*
LEVEL: I LANG: Eng SIRC ARTICLE NO: 102462

Rauramaa, R. Relationship of physical activity, glucose tolerance, and weight management. (Refs: 58)*Preventive medicine (Ne York) 13(1), Jan 1984, 37-46.*
LEVEL: A LANG: Eng SIRC ARTICLE NO: 100749

Reitman, J.S. Vasquez, B. Klimes, I. Nagulesparan, M. Improvement of glucose homeostasis after exercise training in non-insulin-dependent diabetes. *Diabetes care (New York) 7(5), Sept/Oct 1984, 434-441.*
LEVEL: A LANG: Eng

Robertson, C. Clear the exercise hurdles for your diabetic patient (continuing education credit). *Nursing (Springhouse, Pa. 14(10), Oct 1984, 58-64.*
LEVEL: I LANG: Eng

Schiffrin, A. Parikh, S. Marliss, E.B. Desrosiers, M.M. Metabolic response to fasting exercise in adolescent insulin-dependent diabetic subjects treated with continuous subcutaneous insulin infusion and intensive conventional therapy. *Diabetes care (New York) 7(3), May/Jun 1984, 255-260.*
LEVEL: A LANG: Eng SIRC ARTICLE NO: 102467

Schneider, S.H. Amorosa, L.F. Khachadurian, A.K. Ruderman, N.B. Studies on the mechanism of improved glucose control during regular exercise in Type 2 (non-insulin-dependent) diabetes. (Refs: 41)*Diabetologia (Berlin) 26(5), May 1984, 355-360.*
ABST: The effects of 6 weeks of training 3 times per week on glycaemic control were assessed in 20 sedentary Type 2 (non-insulin-dependent) diabetic patients and 11 control subjects. The results indicate that an exercise program can produce a significant decrease in glycosylated haemoglobin levels in Type 2 diabetic males probably due to the cumulative effect of transient improvements in glucose tolerance following individual periods of exercise.
LEVEL: A LANG: Eng SIRC ARTICLE NO: 102468

Simonson, D.C. Koivisto, V. Sherwin, R.S. Ferrannini, E. Hendler, R. Juhlin-Dannfelt, A. DeFronzo, R.A. Adrenergic blockade alters glucose kinetics during exercise in insulin-dependent diabetics. *Journal of clinical investigation (New York) 73(6), Jun 1984, 1648-1658.*
ABST: The authors compared the effects of phentolamine and/or propranolol on glucose homeostasis during exercise in 6 normal subjects and 7 Type 1 diabetic subjects. No change was observed in normal subjects following the administration of either phentolamine or propranolol, or combined phentolamine and propranolol. In diabetics, a decline in glucose concentration occurred during exercise. This decline was accentuated with propranolol administration. On the other hand, glucose concentration rose in diabetics during exercise with phentolamine.
LEVEL: A LANG: Eng SIRC ARTICLE NO: 102470

Spack, N.P. Medical problems of the exercising child: asthma, diabetes, and epilepsy. (Refs: 18) NOTES: In, Micheli, L.J. (ed.), Pediatric and adolescent sports medicine, Boston ; Toronto, Little, Brown, c1984, p. 124-133.
LEVEL: I LANG: Eng RC1210 17791

Stein, R. Goldberg, N. Kalman, F. Chesler, R. Exercise and the patient with Type I diabetes mellitus. *Pediatric clinics of North America (Philadelphia) 31(3), Jun 1984, 665-673.*
LEVEL: A LANG: Eng SIRC ARTICLE NO: 102471

Summers, S. Exercise: a vital component for patients on the Biostator. *Diabetes educator (Chicago) 10(2), Summer 1984, 22-24.*
LEVEL: I LANG: Eng SIRC ARTICLE NO: 103980

Sundkvist, G. Almer, L.O. Lilja, B. Pandolfi, M. Growth hormone and endothelial function during exercise in diabetics with and without retinopathy. *Acta medica scandinavica (Stockholm) 215(1), 1984, 55-61.*
ABST: 50 insulin dependent diabetics were evaluated for changes in plasma growth hormone, factor VIII related antigen, and plasminogen activator activity during exercise. In patients having had diabetes for 5 to 19 years growth hormone only increased in those with retinopathy while the other 2 functions increased most pronouncedly in retinopathy subjects as well. No significant difference was noted between retinopathy and non-retinopathy subjects who had had diabetes for over 20 years.
LEVEL: A LANG: Eng SIRC ARTICLE NO: 099018

Sutton, J.R. Metabolic responses to exercise in normal and diabetic individuals. (Refs: 45) NOTES: In, Strauss, R.H. (ed.), Sports medicine, Philadelphia ; Toronto, Saunders, 1984, p. 190-204.
LEVEL: A LANG: Eng RC1210 17196

Taylor, R. Ram, P. Zimmet, P. Raper, L.R. Ringrose, H. Physical activity and prevalence of diabetes in Melanesian and Indian men in Fiji. *Diabetologia (Berlin) 27(6), Dec 1984, 578-582.*
ABST: A survey of Fiji Melanesian and Indian men indicated that diabetes prevailed twice as much in non or light exercisers than in moderate or heavy exercisers. Ethnicity, age factor, obesity and urban/rural status did not influenced this finding.
LEVEL: A LANG: Eng

Trovati, M. Carta, Q. Cavalot, F. Vitali, S. Passarino, G. Rocca, G. Emanuelli, G. Lenti, G. Continuous subcutaneous insulin infusion and postprandial exercise in tightly controlled type I (insulin-dependent) diabetic patients. *Diabetes care (New York) 7(4), Jul/Aug 1984, 327-330.*
ABST: The aim of this study was to investigate the influence of short-term submaximal postprandial exercise on plasma glucose concentrations in tightly controlled insulin-dependent diabetic patients treated by means of continuous subcutaneous insulin infusion. Two hours after breakfast, five diabetic patients and five healthy control subjects followed this protocol: 30 min of mild exercise, 30 min rest, 30 min of moderate exercise, 150 min rest. Serial determinations of plasma glucose, free insulin, and growth hormone (GH) were made. A significant GH increase was observed after the exercise periods. Plasma glucose and insulin concentrations throughout the exercise study were not significantly different from the control study concentrations. Plasma free insulin concentrations of the diabetic patients were higher than the concentrations of healthy subjects.
LEVEL: A LANG: Eng SIRC ARTICLE NO: 103982

Trovati, M. Carta, Q. Cavalot, F. Vitali, S. Banaudi, C. Lucchina, P.G. Fiocchi, F. Emanuelli, G. Lenti, G. Influence of physical training on blood glucose control, glucose tolerance, insulin secretion, and insulin action in non-insulin-dependent diabetic patients. *Diabetes care (New York) 7(5), Sept/Oct 1984, 416-420.*
LEVEL: A LANG: Eng

van der Beek, E.J. Wedel, M. van de Zedde, A. Bovens, M. Leep, B.J. Hermus, R.J.J. Schouten, J.A. van der Veen, E.A. The relationship of diet, body composition, physical activity and quality of metabolic control to blood lipid levels in type-I-diabetic men. (Refs: 67)*International journal of sports medicine (Stuttgart) Suppl. 5, Nov 1984, 59-63.*
CONF: International Congress on Sports and Health (1983 : Maastricht, Netherlands).
LEVEL: A LANG: Eng SIRC ARTICLE NO: 103983

Viberti, G.C. Home, P.D. Bilous, R.W. Alberti, K.G. Dalton, N. Keen, H. Pickup, J.C. Metabolic effects of physical exercise in insulin-dependent diabetics controlled by continuous subcutaneous insulin infusion or conventional injection therapy. *Acta endocrinologica (Copenhagen) 105(4), Apr 1984, 515-520.*
ABST: The authors researched the metabolic and hormonal effects of exercise in 8 diabetics during insulin injection therapy and following three weeks of continuous subcutaneous insulin infusion. Blood glucose decreased from 12.1 to 4.4 mmol/l in injection therapy while free insulin increased to 57 mU/l. On infusion therapy, a decrease from 7.7 mmol/l to 3.6 mmol/l following exercise was observed, while free insulin level remained the same (31 mU/l).
LEVEL: A LANG: Eng SIRC ARTICLE NO: 101401

Vicari, A.M. Margonato, A. Petrelli, P. Vicedomini, G.G. Pozza, G. Plasma beta-thromboglobulin concentration at rest and after physical exercise in complicated and uncomplicated diabetes mellitus. *Diabete et metabolisme (Paris) 10(4), oct 1984, 235-238.*
LEVEL: A LANG: Eng

Wallberg-Henriksson, H. Gunnarsson, R. Henriksson, J. Ostman, J. Wahren, J. Influence of physical training on formation of muscle

capillaries in type I diabetes. *Diabetes (New York) 33(9), Sept 1984, 851-857.*
ABST: The effects of physical training on skeletal muscle morphology and enzyme activities were compared in 10 male, type I diabetic subjects and 10 healthy, male, control subjects. The training program consisted of running for 45 min, three times per week for 8 wk. Muscle biopsies were obtained before and after the training period from the lateral portion of the gastrocnemius muscle. Muscle capillarization (number of capillaries per muscle fiber) increased on the average in the control group, but was unchanged in the diabetic group. Capillary density, also increased on the average in controls but failed to do so in the diabetic patients. The activities of the mitochondrial enzymes citrate synthase and succinate dehydrogenase increased significantly and similarly in the two groups, whereas training did not result in significant changes in the activities of the glycolytic enzymes 6-phosphofructokinase and glyceraldehyde-phosphate dehydrogenase.
LEVEL: A LANG: Eng SIRC ARTICLE NO: 103985

Williams, J.G. Morris, A.I. Hayter, R.C. Ogilvie, C.M. Respiratory responses of diabetics to hypoxia, hypercapnia, and exercise. *Thorax (London) 39(7), Jul 1984, 529-534.*
ABST: The respiratory responses of 52 diabetics and 65 non-diabetic controls to hypoxia, hypercapnia, and exercise were studied. Twenty five per cent of the diabetics showed evidence of impaired sensitivity to hypoxia or decreased ventilatory response to hypercapnia, while 7 per cent of the diabetics who performed the exercise tests had an abnormal pattern of respiration during exercise; 33 per cent of the diabetics who performed all three tests of respiratory reflex action had at least one abnormal test response.
LEVEL: A LANG: Eng SIRC ARTICLE NO: 103990

Winter, J The diabetics' get fit book. New York: Arco Publishing, c1984. 108 p. : ill. (Positive health guide.)
LEVEL: B LANG: Eng ISBN: 0-668-06149-9 LC CARD: 84-2850 RA781 18950

Yki-Jaervinen, H. DeFronzo, R.A. Koivisto, V.A. Normalization of insulin sensitivity in type I diabetic subjects by physical training during insulin pump therapy. *Diabetes care (New York) 7(6), Nov/Dec 1984, 520-527.*
LEVEL: A LANG: Eng

Zinman, B. Zuniga-Guajardo, S. Kelly, D. Comparison of the acute and long-term effects of exercise on glucose control in typ I diabetes. *Diabetes care (New York) 7(6), Nov/Dec 1984, 515-519.*
ABST: 13 subjects with type I diabetes and 7 control subjects performed 45 minutes of bicycle exercise 3 times per week for 12 weeks. Physical fitness levels (V02 max) increased significantly in both groups while body weight remained unchanged. The diabetic subjects experienced an acute glucose-lowering effect with each exercise session throughout the 12 weeks of training. Fasting plasma glucose and glycosylated hemoglobin had insignificant changes in both groups. Caloric intake increased significantly on exercising days and neutralized significant decreases in plasma glucose levels experienced on exercising days. The authors recommend the formulation of more precise guidelines and recommendations as to the timing of exercise and

nutrient intake for diabetes.
LEVEL: A LANG: Eng

EPILEPSY

Berman, W. Sports and the child with epilepsy. (letter) *Pediatrics (Evanston, Ill.) 74(2), Aug 1984, 320-321.*
LEVEL: B LANG: Eng SIRC ARTICLE NO: 103955

Dubinsky, B.L. The use of therapeutic recreation for intervention in epileptic psychosocial problems in youth. *Epilepsia (New York) 25(5), 1984, 646.*
LEVEL: I LANG: Eng SIRC ARTICLE NO: 103959

Spack, N.P. Medical problems of the exercising child: asthma, diabetes, and epilepsy. (Refs: 18)
NOTES: In, Micheli, L.J. (ed.), Pediatric and adolescent sports medicine, Boston ; Toronto, Little, Brown, c1984, p. 124-133.
LEVEL: I LANG: Eng RC1210 17791

Sports activity and the child with epilepsy. *Sports medicine digest (Van Nuys, Calif.) 6(5), May 1984, 1.*
LEVEL: B LANG: En SIRC ARTICLE NO: 100659

GASTROINTESTINAL DISEASES

Gullmo, A. Broome, A. Smedberg, S. Herniography. *Surgical clinics of North America (Philadelphia) 64(2), Apr 1984, 229-244.*
LEVEL: I LANG: Eng SIRC ARTICLE NO: 102586

Henderson, D.E. Shaffer, T.E. The gastrointestinal system. (Refs: 6)
NOTES: In, Strauss, R.H. (ed.), Sports medicine, Philadelphia ; Toronto, Saunders, 1984, p. 140-148.
LEVEL: A LANG: Eng RC1210 17196

HEMATOLOGIC DISEASES

Adner, M.M. Hematology. (Refs: 35)
NOTES: In, Strauss, R.H. (ed.), Sports medicine, Philadelphia ; Toronto, Saunders, 1984, p. 120-129.
LEVEL: A LANG: Eng RC1210 17196

Koch, B. Galioto, F.M. Kelleher, J. Goldstein, D. Physical fitness in children with hemophilia. (Refs: 30)*Archives of physical medicine and rehabilitation (Chicago, Ill.) 65(6), Jun 1984, 324-326.*
ABST: Eleven hemophilic boys ranging in age from 8 to 15 years old were tested on a bicycle ergometer to determine their level of physical fitness. Compared to results for normal children these boys demonstrated poor exercise performance believed to be due to a lack of physical conditioning. Exercise prescription recommendations are made.
LEVEL: A LANG: Eng SIRC ARTICLE NO: 094564

Koch, B. Luban, N.L.C. Galioto, F.M. Rick, M.E. Goldstein, D. Kelleher, J.F. Changes in coagulation parameters with exercise in patients with classic hemophilia. (Refs: 29)*American journal of hematology (New York) 16(3), Apr 1984, 227-233.*
ABST: This paper investigates the changes in coagulation parameters in 11 hemophiliacs exercising on a bicycle ergometer. A decrease in mean prothrombin time (11.7 to 11.2 sec) is observed in all patients. An increase in mean VIII: C (14.5% to 17.3%) and VIII: CAg (12% to 17.8%) is noted in the four mild hemophiliacs. Changes in fibrinogen, factor II and factor VII occur in all

patients.
LEVEL: A LANG: Eng SIRC ARTICLE NO: 100654

HYPERTENSION

Balfour, I.C. Strong, W.B. Chez l'enfant: hypertension et sports. (Refs: 10)*Dans, Mandel, C. (ed.), Le medecin, l'enfant et le sport, Paris, (Vigot), c1984, p. 199-207.*
LEVEL: I LANG: Fr RC1218.C45 18886

Bennett, T. Wilcox, R.G. Macdonald, I.A. Post-exercise reduction in blood pressure in hypertensive men is not due to acute impairment of baroreflex function. *Clinical science (London) 67(1), Jul 1984, 97-103.*
LEVEL: A LANG: Eng SIRC ARTICLE NO: 102758

Blair, S.N. Goodyear, N.N. Gibbons, L.W. Cooper, K.H. Physical fitness and incidence of hypertension in healthy normotensive men and women. (Refs: 26)*JAMA: Journal of the American Medical Association (Chicago) 252(4), 27 Jul 1984, 487-490.*
ABST: The physical fitness measures of 4,820 men and 1,219 women aged 20 to 65 were evaluated by maximal treadmill testing. These people were followed for one to twelve years for the development of hypertension. After adjustment for sex, age, follow-up interval, baseline blood pressure, and baseline body-mass index, persons with low levels of physical fitness (72 percent of the group) had a relative risk of 1.52 for the development of hypertension when compared with highly fit persons. Risk of hypertension developing also increased substantially with increased baseline blood pressure.
LEVEL: A LANG: Eng SIRC ARTICLE NO: 102706

Block, L.H. Luetold, B.E. Bolli, P. Kiowski, W. Buehler, F.R. High salt intake blunts plasma catecholamine and renin responses to exercise: less suppressive epinephrine in borderline essential hypertension. *Journal of cardiovascular pharmacology (New York) 6(Suppl. 1), 1984, S95-S100.*
LEVEL: A LANG: Eng

Boyer, J. Bruns, B. Eating away at hypertension: the epidemic of the '80s can be controlled. *Runner's world 19(5), May 1984 77-82.*
LEVEL: B LANG: Eng SIRC ARTICLE NO: 092918

Costa, F.V. Borghi, C. Boschi, S. Ambrosioni, E. Cardiovascular response to mental stress: dynamic and isometric exercise in hypertensive patients treated with prizidilol hydrochloride (SK&F 92657). *International journal of clinical pharmacology research (Geneva) 4(5), 1984, 373-379.*
ABST: 13 hypertensive patients treated with prizidilol hydrochloride were tested at rest and during mental stress and isometric or dynamic exercise. Following 6 weeks of therapy, the blood pressure of patients was significantly reduced in all testing conditions while heart rate was only slightly affected.
LEVEL: A LANG: Eng

Cronin, C.J. Owens, C.W. Prichard, B.N. Exercise testing in hypertensive patients. (letter) *JAMA: Journal of the American Medical Association (Chicago) 251(3), 20 Jan 1984, 343.*
LEVEL: B LANG: Eng SIRC ARTICLE NO: 097592

Cupelli, V. Attina, D.A. Giuliano, G. Brettoni, M. Musante, R. Bini, G. Cupelli, G. Abnormal blood pressure response to the bicycle ergometer maximal stress test in apparently healthy and

normotensive middle-aged subjects practising aerobic physical activity in leisure-time. (Refs: 19)*International journal of sports cardiology (Torino, Italy) 1(2), Jul/Dec 1984, 80-83.*
ABST: A bicycle ergometer maximal stress test carried out on 133 middle-aged, apparently healthy and normotensive male subjects was characterized by an abnormal blood response in 38 cases (28.6 percent). Statistically significant differences between these subjects and the ones with normal blood pressure response were found, as to the mean values of baseline systolic and diastolic pressure (tendentially higher, event if still within normal limits) and intensity of physical training (lower). The usefulness of the maximal stress test in sports practising people and the favourable effect of aerobic physical exercise of adequate intensity in possibly preventing arterial hypertension in emphasized.
LEVEL: A LANG: Eng SIRC ARTICLE NO: 179171

Dantzker, D.R. D'Alonzo, G.E. Bower, J.S. Popat, K. Crevey, B.J. Pulmonary gas exchange during exercise in patients with chronic obliterative pulmonary hypertension. *American review of respiratory disease (New York) 130(3), Sept 1984, 412-416.*
LEVEL: A LANG: Eng

Die Hypertonie als staendige Herausforderung unserer Zeit. (Hypertension as a standing challenge in our time.) *Verhandlungen der deutschen gesellschaft fur innere medizin (Munchen) 90(Pt 1), 1984, 45-98.*
LEVEL: A LANG: Ger

Diuretics: powerful medicines. *Your health & fitness (Highland Park, Ill.) 6(3), Jun/Jul 1984, 12-13.*
LEVEL: B LANG: Eng SIRC ARTICLE NO: 096011

Dodek, A. Hypertension in the runner. (Refs: 32)*Canadian journal of applied sport sciences/ Journal canadien des sciences appliquees au sport (Windsor, Ont.) 9(4), Dec 1984, 169-175.*
ABST: A therapeutic game plan is important for the management of hypertension in the runner. Participation in physical training programs may result in lower resting blood pressure in mild hypertension. Maximal exercise tests can be used to identify those hypertensive patients with a dangerously high exercise blood pressure. Most antihypertensive drugs can be used for the treatment of hypertension which is refractory to exercise training. Atenolol, a cardioselective beta blocker has minimal side effects and the least risk of impairing performance. Calcium channel blockers effectively lower exercise blood pressure and should be used when side effects of beta blockers contraindicate their use in patients.
LEVEL: A LANG: Eng SIRC ARTICLE NO: 102571

Dubbert, P.M. Martin, J.E. Zimering, R.T. Burkett, P.A. Lake, M. Cushman, W.C. Behavioral-control of mild hypertension with aerobic exercise - 2 case studies. (Refs: 17)*Behavior therapy (New York) 15(4), 1984, 373-380.*
LEVEL: A LANG: Eng SIRC ARTICLE NO: 099087

Evdokimova, T.A. Bershadskii, B.G. Fizicheskie nagruzki v diagnostike i otsenke effektivnosti lecheniia gipertonicheskoi bolezni. (Physical loading in the diagnosis and evaluation of the efficacy of treatment of hypertension.) *Kardiologiia (Moscow) 24(3), Mar 1984, 75-78.*
ABST: On the basis of the study into the parameters of systemic hemodynamics during bicycle ergometric exercise, and their processing

with the help of the programme of multiple step-wise regression in computer CM-3, an algorithm was derived whose employment makes it possible to determine very reliably the severity of the disease, and which also facilitates an early diagnosis of essential hypertension and reflects the effectiveness of the therapy.
LEVEL: A LANG: Rus

Fagard, R. Reybrouck, T. Vanhees, L. Cattaert, A. Vanmeenen, T. Grauwels, R. Amery, A. The effects of beta blockers on exercise capacity and on training response in elderly subjects. (Refs: 21)*European heart journal (London) 5(Suppl E), Nov 1984, 117-120.*
ABST: The effects of atenolol and labetalol on exercise performance were assessed in 8 hypertensive elderly subjects and 15 elderly patients with ischaemic heart disease. Both beta blockers did not alter patients' response.
LEVEL: A LANG: Eng SIRC ARTICLE NO: 109714

Francois, B. Cahen, R. Gravejat, M.F. Estrade, M. Do beta blockers prevent pressor responses to mental stress and physical exercise? *European heart journal (London) 5(5), May 1984, 348-353.*
ABST: 15 hypertensive patients and 16 controls were measured before and after treatment with atenolol for variations in blood pressure and pulse rate observed with dynamic effort and during tests of mental calculation, colour stress, and grip strength. The tests of mental stress and static physical effort caused a rise in blood pressure, significantly greater in the untreated patients than in the control subjects. Atenolol diminished the rise in systolic blood presure and pulse rate secondary to a dynamic effort, but did not significantly alter the blood pressure variations induced by static physical effort and mental stress.
LEVEL: A LANG: Eng

Franz, I.W. Wiewel, D. Antihypertensive effects on blood pressure at rest and during exercise of calcium antagonists, beta-receptor blockers, and their combination in hypertensive patients. *Journal of cardiovascular pharmacology (New York) 6(Suppl 7), 1984, S1037-S1042.*
LEVEL: A LANG: Eng

Greenwood, R.D. Exertional chest pain in a five-year-old boy. *Hospital practice (New York) 19(11), Nov 1984, 216;219.*
LEVEL: A LANG: Eng

Hagberg, J.M. Ehsani, A.A. Goldring, D. Hernandez, A. Sinacore, D.R. Holloszy, J.O. Effect of weight training on blood pressure and hemodynamics in hypertensive adolescents. *Journal of pediatrics (St. Louis) 104(1), Jan 1984, 147-151.*
ABST: Six adolescents with persistent essential hypertension were evaluated before and after an average of 5 months of weight training after which they ceased training and were evaluated an average of 12 months later. The results indicate that weight training in this group of subjects appears to maintain reductions in blood pressure achieved by prior endurance training and may even further reduce blood pressure. The only significant hemodynamic change was a reduction in systemic vascular resistance during weight training.
LEVEL: A LANG: Eng SIRC ARTICLE NO: 097728

Hagberg, J.M. Goldring, D. Heath, G.W. Ehsani, A.A. Hernandez, A. Holloszy, J.O. Effect of exercise training on plasma catecholamines and haemodynamics of adolescent hypertensives during

rest, submaximal exercise and orthostatic stress. *Clinical physiology (Oxford) 4(2), Apr 1984, 117-124.*
ABST: The authors investigate the effects of exercise training on plasma catecholamine concentrations, blood pressure and cardiovascular hemodynamics of 12 adolescent hypertensives during rest, submaximal exercise and orthostatic stress. Training induces increases of maximal oxygen consumption and decreases of systolic and diastolic blood pressure, heart rates, plasma norepinephrine and epinephrine levels.
LEVEL: A LANG: Eng SIRC ARTICLE NO: 102588

Herd, J.A. Hartley, L.H. Hypertension and exercise: the role of physical conditioning in treatment and prevention. (Refs: 67 *In*, Matarazzo, J.D. (ed.) et al., Behavioral health: a handbook of health enhancement and disease prevention, New York, Wiley, c1984, p. 836-845.*
LEVEL: I LANG: Eng

Kenney, W.L. Kamon, E. Comparative physiological responses of normotensive and essentially hypertensive men to exercise in the heat. (Refs: 34)*European journal of applied physiology and occupational physiology (Heidelberg) 52(2), Jan 1984, 196-201.*
ABST: In this study several physiological responses were examined and compared between normotensive and hypertensive subjects as the additional stress of exercise, within a heated environment, was applied. Thermoregulatory and sudomotor responses were examined; however, comparisons of cardiovascular responses were emphasized. Physiological differences between the groups were maintained, but under the given experimental conditions, the essential hypertensives were still able to tolerate the heat and workload as well as their normotensive counterparts.
LEVEL: A LANG: Eng SIRC ARTICLE NO: 096262

Kenney, W.L. Kamon, E. Buskirk, E.R. Effect of mild essential hypertension on control of forearm blood flow during exercise in the heat. (Refs: 35)*Journal of applied physiology: respiratory, environmental and exercise physiology 56(4), Apr 1984, 930-935.*
ABST: The purpose of this study was to examine the extent to which chronically elevated resting arterial blood pressure affects the cutaneous vascular response to exercise in a warm environment. Six hypertensive men and eight normotensive men performed 1 hour of cycle ergometer work at 40% VO2 max in an environment with a 38oC dry-bulb temperature and a 28oC wet-bulb temperature. Forearm blood flow increased in both groups, but the increase was significantly less in the hypertensive group. The magnitude of forearm blood flow increase was inversely proportional to resting mean arterial blood pressure (0.89).
LEVEL: A LANG: Eng SIRC ARTICLE NO: 096027

Kenney, W.L. Zambraski, E.J. Physical activity in human hypertension: a mechanisms approach. (Refs: 108)*Sports medicine (Auckland, N.Z.) 1(6), Nov/Dec 1984, 459-473.*
ABST: The concept of treating hypertension without medication is seen as an attractive alternative to the problems that can arise with the use of drug therapy. Weight loss, salt restriction, relaxation therapy, and exercise have been the non-pharmacological treatments for hypertension. The role of long term exercise in lowering resting arterial pressure in hypertension, and its use as a non-drug

therapy have been studied. Epidemiological studies of athletic ability, occupation, and leisure-time activities have provided equivocal findings and the effect of training on chronic high blood pressure of hypertensives is still unclear. Further well-controlled studies (with respect to training intensities, weight loss, concurrent hypotensive medication, salt restriction, and hypertensive classification), with an emphasis on elucidating the physiological mechanisms involved, are required so that the contribution of exercise to hypertensive therapy can be determined.
LEVEL: A LANG: Eng SIRC ARTICLE NO: 102592

Klein, A.A. McCrory, W.W. Engle, M.A. Rosenthal, R. Ehlers, K.H. Sympathetic nervous system and exercise tolerance response in normotensive and hypertensive adolescents. *Journal of the American College of Cardiology 3(2 Pt 1), Feb 1984, 381-386.*
ABST: Normotensive, borderline hypertensive and hypertensive adolescents were compared during isometric and dynamic exercise. The results indicate that modifications in hemodynamic response to peak dynamic exercise appears to exist in adolescents with borderline and significant hypertension and is partly due to altered activity of the sympathetic nervous system.
LEVEL: A LANG: Eng SIRC ARTICLE NO: 099249

Knight, J.A. Evaluation of the role of the sympathetic nervous system in primary hypertension through measurement of plasma catecholamines during rest and exercise. Eugene, Ore.: Microform Publications, University of Oregon, 1984. 1 microfiche : negative, ill. ; 11 x 15 cm.
NOTES: Thesis (Ph.D.) - Pennsylvania State University, 1981; (viii, 80, 1 leaves); vita; includes bibliography.
LEVEL: A LANG: Eng UO84 85

Lund-Johansen, P. Hemodynamic effects of verapamil in essential hypertension at rest and during exercise. *Acta medica scandinavica. Supplementum (Stockholm) 681, 1984, 109-115.*
ABST: Ten males, aged 35-55 years, suffering from hypertension were administered verapamil 120-140 mg daily for one year. Oxygen consumption, heart rate, cardiac output and intra-arterial brachial pressure were recorded at rest and during exercise. The main findings were: a) a statistically significant reduction in arterial pressure at rest as well as during exercise; b) a statistically significant reduction in total peripheral resistance and; c) a decrease of about 8% of the heart rate.
LEVEL: A LANG: Eng SIRC ARTICLE NO: 102601

Lund-Johansen, P. Omvik, P. Long-term haemodynamic effects of enalapril at rest and during exercise in essential hypertensio *Scandinavian journal of urology and nephrology (Stockholm) (Suppl), 1984, 79;87-91.*
ABST: Twelve males with moderately severe essential hypertension were studied at rest supine and sitting and during bicycle exercise (50, 100 and 150 W). Intraarterial blood pressure (BP), and heart rate (HR) were recorded continuously. Cardiac output (CO) was measured by dye dilution (Cardiogreen). After 6-8 months (enalapril dose 10-40 mg daily) patients were restudied. BP fell in all patients, at rest sitting from 184/107 mmHg to 150/87 and during 100 W from 223/117 to 194/98 mmHg. No significant changes were seen in CO, HR or stroke volume.
LEVEL: A LANG: Eng SIRC ARTICLE NO: 103895

Macdonald, I.A. Bennett, T. Brown, A.M. Wilcox, R.G. Skene, A.M. The effects of acute or chronic ingestion of propranolol or metoprolol on the metabolic and hormonal responses to prolonged, submaximal exercise in hypertensive men. *British journal of clinical pharmacology (London) 17(3), Mar 1984, 283-293.*
LEVEL: A LANG: Eng SIRC ARTICLE NO: 100736

Melloni, G.F. Brera, V. Signorelli, G. Melloni, R. Scarazatti, E. Analisi delle correlazioni tra parametri cardiodinamici e sistema adrenergico nella ipertensione arteriosa essenziale a riposo e dopo sforzo. (Correlations of cardiodynamic parameters and the adrenergic system in essential arterial hypertension at rest and during exertion.) *Bollettino - Societa italiana biologia sperimentale (Napoli) 60(2), 28 Feb 1984, 237-243.*
LEVEL: A LANG: It

Middeke, M. Remien, J. Holzgreve, H. The influence of sex, age, blood pressure and physical stress on beta 2-adrenoceptor density of mononuclear cells. *Journal of hypertension (London) 2(3), June 1984, 261-264.*
LEVEL: A LANG: Eng

Nannan, M.E. Melin, J.A. Vanbutsele, R.J. Lavenne, F. Detry, J.M. Acute and long-term effects of nitrendipine on resting and exercise hemodynamics in essential hypertension. *Journal of cardiovascular pharmacology (New York) 6(Suppl 7), 1984, S1043-S1048.*
LEVEL: A LANG: Eng

Nelson, G.I. Silke, B. Hussain, M. Verma, S.P. Taylor, S.H. Rest and exercise hemodynamic effects of sequential alpha-1-adrenoceptor (trimazosin) and beta-adrenoceptor (propranolol) antagonism in essential hypertension. *American heart journal (St. Louis) 108(1), Jul 1984, 124-131.*
ABST: This study reports on the hemodynamic effects of sequential alpha-1 (trimazosin)- and beta (propanolol)- adrenoceptor blockade in 10 men (34 to 58 years) with hypertension. Measurements are taken at rest and during exercise. The authors conclude that alpha-1-adrenoceptor blockade modifies the adverse effects of acute beta blockade at rest but not during exercise.
LEVEL: A LANG: Eng SIRC ARTICLE NO: 102604

Patel, C. A relaxation-centered behavioral package for reducing hypertension. (Refs: 100)*In, Matarazzo, J.D. (ed.) et al., Behavioral health: a handbook of health enhancement and disease prevention, New York, Wiley, c1984, p. 846-861.*
LEVEL: I LANG: Eng

Paulev, P.-E. Jordal, R. Kristensen, O. Ladelfoged, J. Therapeutic effect of exercise on hypertension. (Refs: 34)*European journal of applied physiology and occupational physiology (Berlin, W.G.) 53(2), 1984, 180-185.*
ABST: Arterial blood pressure, total peripheral resistance (TPR), plasma catecholamine and other hormone concentrations were measured or estimated during, and 4 h following, a 20-min exercise test on the bicycle ergometer in 10 women with marginal hypertension. Compared with the control, the exercise reduced the driving blood pressure from 103 (94-110) to 95 (80-100) mm Hg and the TPR from 1.13 (0.96-1.40) to 0.91 (0.79-1.11) PRUs - both reductions being statistically significant.
LEVEL: A LANG: Eng SIRC ARTICLE NO: 104132

Peden, N.R. Dow, R.J. Isles, T.E. Martin, B.T. Beta adrenoceptor blockade and responses of

serum lipids to a meal and to exercise. *British medical journal (Clinical research) (London) 288(6433), 16 Jun 1984, 1788-1790.*
ABST: During a randomised placebo controlled trial of the effects of nadolol in hypertensive patients serum lipid profiles were obtained while the patients were fasting and during and after a meal and an exercise test. Treatment with nadolol was associated with a significant reduction in high density lipoprotein cholesterol at all time points. The changes in high density lipoprotein cholesterol and triglyceride concentrations during beta adrenoceptor blockade may be secondary to a reduction in lipoprotein lipase activity.
LEVEL: A LANG: Eng

Radice, M. Alberti, D. Alli, C. Avanzini, F. Di Tullio, M. Mariotti, G. Taioli, E. Zussino, A. Folli, G. Comportamento della pressione arteriosa durante esercizio in adolescenti con diverso rischio di sviluppare ipertensione. (Behavior of blood pressure during exercise in adolescents at various risks of developing hypertension.) *Bollettino della societa italiana di cardiologia (Rome) 29(11), Nov 1984, 519-522.*
NOTES: English abstract.
LEVEL: A LANG: It

Seals, D.R. Hagberg, J.M. The effect of exercise training on human hypertension: a review. (Refs: 68)*Medicine and science i sports and exercise (Indianapolis) 16(3), June 1984, 207-215.*
ABST: Numerous sources of information in both the medical and exercise physiology areas state that exercise training lowers blood pressure at rest and during submaximal exercise in normotensive and hypertensive individuals. Based on these statements, the medical community is currently recommending regular exercise as a non-pharmacological therapy for reducing blood pressure in hypertensive patients. The purpose of this review was to assess the existing literature in this area to determine whether a basis exists for this recommendation. Our findings indicate that most of the studies reviewed reported modest reductions in blood pressure at rest and during submaximal exercise after training. However, even the modest reductions in blood pressure reported in these studies must be interpreted with caution because of numerous methodological shortcomings and inadequate study design, most notably the omission of non-exercising hypertensive control groups.
LEVEL: A LANG: Eng SIRC ARTICLE NO: 108586

Shapiro, L.M. McKenna, W.J. Left ventricular hypertrophy. Relation of structure to diastolic function in hypertension. *British heart journal (London) 51(6), Jun 1984, 637-642.*
ABST: Digitised M mode echocardiography was used to determine the relation between the degree of left ventricular hypertrophy and abnormalities of isovolumic relaxation and diastolic function. Fifty six patients with varying severity of non-malignant systemic hypertension were studied. In addition, 10 athletes with hypertrophy and 20 normal subjects were studied. Athletes and patients with moderate and severe hypertension had a significant increase in left ventricular mass. Cavity dimensions were normal in hypertensive patients and increased in athletes. Systolic function was normal in all groups. Athletes who had an equivalent degree of hypertrophy to patients with moderate or severe hypertension had entirely normal function. Measurements of diastolic function were significantly correlated with wall thickness and left

DISEASES AND DISORDERS (continued)

ventricular mass. Thus in hypertensive patients with non-dilated left ventricular hypertrophy there appears to be a relation between the degree of wall thickening and abnormalities of diastolic function.
LEVEL: A LANG: Eng SIRC ARTICLE NO: 102608

Svishchenko, E.P. Gomazkov, O.A. Zanozdra, N.S. Iakovlev, A.A. Chornoguz, L.S. Sootnoshenie renin-angiotenzinnoi i kallikrein-kininovoi sistem krovi pri fizicheskoi nagruzke u bolnykh gipertonicheskoi bolezniu. (Relation between the renin-angiotensin and kallikrein-kinin systems of the blood during physical loading of hypertension patients.) *Kardiologiia (Moscow) 24(3), Mar 1984, 79-83.*
ABST: Blood angiotensin-converting enzyme, renin, kallikrein and prekallikrein ratios were investigated in 61 essentially hypertensive patients at rest and during rationed exercise. Biochemical findings were compared with major parameters of systemic hemodynamics measured under the same conditions. Grouping of patients on the basis of renin activity was mirrored in different levels of the angiotensin-converting enzyme and kallikrein: increased renin activity was accompanied by the activation of the said enzymes, and reduced activity, by their suppression. Rationed exercise did not produce noticeable kallikrein-kinin shifts in hypertensive patients, their renin-angiotensin response depending on the baseline.
LEVEL: A LANG: Rus

Taylor, W.C. Falkner, B. Lowenthal, D.T. Hemodynamic response to isometric exercise in normotensive and hypertensive adolescent females. (Refs: 16)*Annals of sports medicine (North Hollywood, Calif.) 2(1), 1984, 26-29.*
ABST: The hemodynamic response to sub-maximal sustained handgrip exercise of hypertensive female adolescents (n, 10) was compared with that of normotensive females (n, 7). Heart rate and blood pressure were measured during rest, 50 per cent of maximal voluntary contraction, and recovery. The hypertensive female adolescents had significantly higher mean baseline blood pressure levels and mean peak blood pressure values in response to isometric handgrip exercise. The change from baseline systolic blood pressure (SBP) to peak or maximum SBP was approximately the same for both groups. However, the change from baseline diastolic blood pressure (DBP) to maximum DBP was greater in the normotensive females. There was no difference between the two groups in heart rate response.
LEVEL: A LANG: Eng SIRC ARTICLE NO: 104380

Tipton, C.M. Exercise, training, and hypertension. (Refs: 233)*Exercise and sport sciences reviews (Lexington, Mass.) 12, 1984, 245-306.*
ABST: This review discusses the effects of acute and chronic exercise on hypertension. Exercise training to decrease blood pressure is recommended for a) hypertension-prone individuals, regardless of their age; and b) individuals whose resting blood pressures are approximately 140/90 mmhg. The literature indicates that training is associated with decreased resting blood pressure. The author makes recommendations for future human investigations concerned with exercise and hypertension.
LEVEL: A LANG: Eng SIRC ARTICLE NO: 096056

Tipton, C.M. Exercise and resting blood pressure. (Refs: 29)*American Academy of Physical Education papers (Champaign, Ill.) 17, 1984, 32-41.*
CONF: American Academy of Physical Education.

Annual Meeting (54th : 1983 : Minneapolis).
NOTES: Conference theme: Exercise and health.
LEVEL: A LANG: Eng SIRC ARTICLE NO: 104151

Tsikulin, A.E. Volkov, D.V. Tolerantnost' k dinamicheskoi i statischeskoi fizicheskoi nagruzke u bol'nykh gipertonicheskoi bolezniu. (Dynamic and static physical exertion tolerance in patients with hypertension.) *Kardiologiia (Moskva) 24(2), Feb 1984, 113-114.*
LEVEL: A LANG: Rus

van Hooff, M.E.J. Rahn, K.H. van Baak, M.A. Effects of acute and chronic administration of propranolol during submaximal exercise in essential hypertension. (Refs: 17)*International journal of sports medicine (Stuttgart) Suppl. 5, Nov 1984, 186-188.*
CONF: International Congress on Sports and Health (1983 : Maastricht, Netherlands).
LEVEL: A LANG: Eng SIRC ARTICLE NO: 103905

Wilcox, R.G. Bennett, T. Macdonald, I.A. Herbert, M. Skene, A.M. The effects of acute or chronic ingestion of propranolol or metoprolol on the physiological responses to prolonged, submaximal exercise in hypertensive men. *British journal of clinical pharmacology (London) 17(3), Mar 1984, 273-281.*
ABST: The authors discuss the physiological responses to moderate exercise in hypertensive men following treatment with placebo, propranolol or metoprolol. Findings indicate a significant decrease in heart rate and blood pressure of patients in the two experimental groups, while perceived exertion scores increase.
LEVEL: A LANG: Eng SIRC ARTICLE NO: 100766

Zabetakis, P.M. Profiling the hypertensive patient in sports. (Refs: 59)*Clinics in sports medicine (Philadelphia) 3(1), Jan 1984, 137-152.*
NOTES: Symposium on profiling.
ABST: Profiling for hypertension must consider the patient's history and the current medication he is using. Conditioning of the cardiovascular system has a positive impact on blood pressure while isometric or static exercise has a negative impact. Medication for hypertension can adversely effect the response to exercise as in the case of beta-adrenergic blocking agents.
LEVEL: A LANG: Eng SIRC ARTICLE NO: 092957

Zanozdra, N.S. Krishchuk, A.A. Mozgovoe krovoobrashchenie u bol'nykh gipertonicheskoi bolezn'iu pri fizicheskoi nagruzke. (Cerebral circulation in hypertensive patients during physical exertion.) *Vrachebnoe delo (Kiev) 1, Jan 1984, 71-75.*
LEVEL: A LANG: Rus

JOCK ITCH

Webster, S.B. How I manage jock itch. *Physician and sportsmedicine (Minneapolis, Minn.) 12(5), May 1984, 109-110;113.*
LEVEL: I LANG: Eng SIRC ARTICLE NO: 094447

LIVER DISEASES

Chang, K. Akaike, M. Thuyuki, K. Nomura, M. Hase, H. Ebine, K. Yabuki, S. Ukai, K. (The effects of exercise training by cardiac rehabilitation program in chronic hemodialysis patients.) *Nippon Jinzo Gakkai Shi/Japanese journal of nephrology (Tokyo) 26(2), Feb 1984, 203-211.*
LEVEL: A LANG: Jpn

LUNG DISEASE

Atkins, C.J. Kaplan, R.M. Timms, R.M. Reinsch, S. Lofback, K. Behavioral exercise programs in the management of chronic obstructive pulmonary disease. *Journal of consulting and clinical psychology (Washington) 52(4), Aug 1984, 591-603.*
LEVEL: I LANG: Eng

Barnes, L. Jogging the lungs good for patients with COLD. (chronic obstructive lung disease) *Physician and sportsmedicine 12(2), Feb 1984, 22.*
LEVEL: B LANG: Eng SIRC ARTICLE NO: 091500

Brown, S.E. King, R.R. Temerlin, S.M. Stansbury, D.W. Mahutte, C.K. Light, R.W. Exercise performance with added dead space i chronic airflow obstruction. (Refs: 30)*Journal of applied physiology: respiratory, environmental and exercise physiology 56(4), Apr 1984, 1020-1026.*
ABST: Twenty-two subjects with moderate to severe chronic airflow obstruction (CAO) performed symptom-limited incremental cycle ergometry with and without added dead space. The VO3 max and maximum CO_2 production decreased with dead space while Ve max and tidal volume increased with dead space. The authors conclude that exercise performance is limited primarily by impaired ventilatory mechanics in CAO.
LEVEL: A LANG: Eng SIRC ARTICLE NO: 096002

Brown, S.E. Pakron, F.J. Milne, N. Linden, G.S. Stansbury, D.W. Fischer, D.W. Light, C.E. R.W. Effects of digoxin on exercise capacity and right ventricular function during exercise in chronic airflow obstruction. *Chest (Chicago) 85(2), Feb 1984, 187-191.*
ABST: 12 patients were studied with stable chronic airflow obstruction and no clinical evidence of left ventricular disease to determine the effects of oral digoxin on exercise capacity (VO2 max) and on right ventricular pump function during exercise. In this randomized, double blind, placebo controlled, cross-over study, patients performed bicycle exercise tests and underwent measurement of ejection fractions after two weeks of therapy with oral digoxin (0.25 mg/day) and after two weeks of placebo. The results lead the authors to conclude that digoxin does not significantly improve exercise capacity in severe chronic airflow obstruction with impaired right ventricular function, nor does it improve right ventricle ejection fraction either at rest or during supine submaximal exercise.
LEVEL: A LANG: Eng SIRC ARTICLE NO: 099081

Bundgaard, A. Ingemann-Hansen, T. Halkjaer-Kristensen, J. Physical training in bronchial asthma. *International rehabilitation medicine (Basel) 6(4), 1984, 179-182.*
LEVEL: I LANG: Eng

Dodd, D.S. Brancatisano, T. Engel, L.A. Chest wall mechanics during exercise in patients with severe chronic air-flow obstruction. *American review of respiratory disease (New York) 129(1), Jan 1984, 33-38.*
LEVEL: A LANG: Eng SIRC ARTICLE NO: 099084

Evans, T.W. Howard, P. Whistle for your wind. (editorial) *British medical journal (clinical research) (London) 289(6443), 2 Aug 1984, 449-450.*
LEVEL: B LANG: Eng SIRC ARTICLE NO: 104115

Gimenez, M. Servera, E. Candina, R. Mohan Kumar, T. Bonnassis, J.B. Hypercapnia during maximal exercise in patients with chronic airflow

obstruction. *Bulletin europeen de physiopathologie respiratoire* (Oxford) 20(2), Mar/Apr 1984, 113-119.
LEVEL: A LANG: Eng SIRC ARTICLE NO: 102584

Jederlinic, P. Muspratt, J.A. Miller, M.J. Inspiratory muscle training in clinical practice. Physiologic conditioning or habituation to suffocation? (Refs: 13)*Chest (Chicago)* 86(6), Dec 1984, 870-873.
LEVEL: A LANG: Eng SIRC ARTICLE NO: 174134

Jones, N.L. Berman, L.B. Gas exchange in chronic air-flow obstruction. (Refs: 15)*American review of respiratory disease* (Ne York) 129(2 Pt 2), Feb 1984, S81-S83.
CONF: Exercise Testing in the Dyspneic Patient Workshop (1982 : Bethesda).
ABST: This paper reviews exercise capacity limitations in patients with lung disease. The major limitations to exercise in patients with chronic air-flow obstruction are related to abnormal mechanical characteristics of the respiratory system. Altered cardiac function may however also contribute to the disability through the adverse effects of lung mechanics on cardiac performance.
LEVEL: A LANG: Eng SIRC ARTICLE NO: 099243

Keogh, B.A. Lakatos, E. Price, D. Crystal, R.G. Importance of the lower respiratory tract in oxygen transfer. Exercise testing in patients with interstitial and destructive lung disease. (Refs: 33)*American review of respiratory disease* (New York) 129(2 Pt 2), Feb 1984, S76-S80.
CONF: Exercise Testing in the Dyspneic Patient Workshop (1982 : Bethesda).
ABST: 176 patients with four different alveolar disorders were evaluated during steady state treadmill exercise. Idiopathic pulmonary fibrosis (107 patients) and sarcoidosis (42) were the most common disorders among this study group. The results found that patients with interstitial lung disease may have no evidence of a ventilatory or cardiac limitation by traditional analysis even though severe exercise limitations exist.The evaluation of gas exchange revealed significant abnormality of oxygen transfer in these patients which can be measured and related to exercise intolerance. These results reaffirmed previous findings which indicate that resting parameters of gas exchange cannot predict the magnitude of gas exchange abnormality induced by exercise.
LEVEL: A LANG: Eng SIRC ARTICLE NO: 099247

Lee, H.Y. Lai, j.S. Lien, I.N. Exercise performance in male patients with chronic obstructive pulmonary disease. *Taiwan i hsueh hui tsa chih* (Taipei) 83(5), May 1984, 444-451.
LEVEL: A LANG: Eng

Light, R.W. Mintz, H.M. Linden, G.S. Brown, S.E. Hemodynamics of patients with severe chronic obstructive pulmonary disease during progressive upright exercise. (Refs: 34)*American review of respiratory disease* (New York) 130(3), Sept 1984, 391-395.
LEVEL: A LANG: Eng SIRC ARTICLE NO: 109765

Loke, J. Mahler, D.A. Man, S.F. Wiedemann, H.P. Matthay, R.A. Exercise impairment in chronic obstructive pulmonary disease. *Clinics in chest medicine* (Philadelphia) 5(1), Mar 1984, 121-143.
ABST: The authors review the factors that may affect exercise performance in patients with chronic obstructive pulmonary mechanics, respiratory muscle fatigue, impairment in pulmonary gas exchange, and poor nutritional status.
LEVEL: A LANG: Eng SIRC ARTICLE NO: 102600

Mahler, D.A. Brent, B.N. Loke, J. Zaret, B.L. Matthay, R.A. Right ventricular performance and central circulatory hemodynamics during upright exercise in patients with chronic obstructive pulmonary disease. *American review of respiratory disease* (New York) 130(5), Nov 1984, 722-729.
LEVEL: A LANG: Eng

Mohan-Kumar, T. Gimenez, M. Maximal ventilation at rest and exercise in patients with chronic pulmonary disease. *Respiratio (Basel)* 46(3), 1984, 291-302.
LEVEL: A LANG: Eng

Novo, S. Davi, G. Caimi, G. Castello, F. Valdes, L. Marino, S. Romano, A. Fazio, M. La Menza, B. Mazzola, A. et al. Platelet activity in relation to smoke and exercise in patients with chronic obstructive lung disease: effects of platelet antiaggregating drugs. *Advances in experimental medicine and biology* (New York) 164, 1984, 339-357.
LEVEL: A LANG: Eng

Pardy, R.L. Hussain, S.N. Macklem, P.T. The ventilatory pump in exercise. *Clinics in chest medicine* (Philadelphia) 5(1), Ma 1984, 35-49.
ABST: The authors review the response of the ventilatory pump during exercise in healthy and obstructive lung disease patients.
LEVEL: A LANG: Eng SIRC ARTICLE NO: 102810

Pineda, H. Haas, F. Axen, K. Haas, A. Accuracy of pulmonary function tests in predicting exercise tolerance in chronic obstructive pulmonary disease. *Chest (Chicago)* 86(4), Oct 1984, 564-567.
LEVEL: A LANG: Eng

Risk, C. Epler, G.R. Gaensler, E.A. Exercise alveolar-arterial oxygen pressure difference in interstitial lung disease. *Chest (Chicago)* 85(1), Jan 1984, 69-74.
LEVEL: A LANG: Eng

Saito, G. (A study on pulmonary gas exchange during muscular exercise by patients with idiopathic interstitial pneumonia.) *Nippon kyobu shikkan gakkai zasshi/Japanese journal of thoracic diseases* (Tokyo) 22(9), Sept 1984, 733-741.
LEVEL: A LANG: Jpn

Schrijen, F. Ravez, P. Candina-Villar, R. Respiratory and circulatory adaptation to isometric and dynamic exercise in chroni lung disease. *Clinical physiology* (Oxford) 4(5), Oct 1984, 371-378.
LEVEL: A LANG: Eng

Sinclair, J.D. Exercise in pulmonary disease. (Refs: 50)
NOTES: In, Basmajian, J.V. (ed.), Therapeutic exercise, 4th ed., Baltimore, Md., Williams & Wilkins, c1984, p. 587-612.
LEVEL: A LANG: Eng RM719 17505

Smith, T.P. Kinasewitz, G.T. Tucker, W.Y. Spillers, W.P. George, R.B. Exercise capacity as a predictor of post-thoracotomy morbidity. *American review of respiratory disease* (New York) 129(5), May 1984, 730-734.
LEVEL: A LANG: Eng SIRC ARTICLE NO: 100760

Sonne, L.J. Respiratory muscle training. (letter) *Chest (Chicago)* 86(6), Dec 1984, 939-940.
LEVEL: I LANG: Eng

Steyer, B.J. Exercise training in chronic obstructive lung disease. *Arizona medicine* (Phoenix) 41(1), Jan 1984, 11-14.
LEVEL: A LANG: Eng SIRC ARTICLE NO: 099107

Swinburn, C.R. Wakefield, J.M. Jones, P.W. Relationship between ventilation and breathlessness during exercise in chronic obstructive airways disease is not altered by prevention of hypoxaemia. *Clinical science* (London) 67(5), Nov 1984, 515-519.
LEVEL: A LANG: Eng

van Herwaarden, C.L.A. Exercise and training in chronic non-specific lung disease (CSNLD). (Refs: 18)*International journal of sports medicine* (Stuttgart) Suppl. 5, Nov 1984, 54-58.
CONF: International Congress on Sports and Health (1983 : Maastricht, Netherlands).
LEVEL: A LANG: Eng SIRC ARTICLE NO: 104153

Wilson, S.H. Cooke, N.T. Moxham, J. Spiro, S.G. Sternomastoid muscle function and fatigue in normal subjects and in patients with chronic obstructive pulmonary disease. *American review of respiratory disease* (New York) 129(3), Mar 1984, 460-464.
ABST: This report focuses on the study of the frequency: force curves of the sternomastoid muscle of four normal subjects, and five patients with chronic obstructive pulmonary disease. Subjects are tested before and 5 min after a 12-min treadmill walk, a progressive exercise test (normal subjects only) and 10-min of sustained maximal voluntary ventilation (SMVV). During SMVV, all the subjects achieved minute ventilation greater than 70% of predicted maximal breathing capacity (MBC). During the 12-min walk, all patients exceeded 70% MBC, and 4 showed low frequency fatigue (LFF). Subjects performing progressive exercise also exceeded 70% MBC, and all had LFF.
LEVEL: A LANG: Eng SIRC ARTICLE NO: 099111

Zadai, C.C. Kigin, C.M. Rehabilitation of the pulmonary patient. (Refs: 63)
NOTES: In, Cantu, R.C. (ed.), Clinical sports medicine, Lexington, Mass. ; Toronto, Collamore Press : D.C. Heath, c1984, p. 139-160.
LEVEL: A LANG: Eng RC1201 15964

MOVEMENT DISORDERS

Michelsen, N. Jansen, J. Grusgaard, H. Ibsen, K.K. Klebak, S. Lykkegaard, E. Merrick, J. Niclasen, B. Pahlsson, I. Skoleborn motoriske udvikling. Hvornar er der behov for behandling? (Motor development in schoolchidren. When is treatment required?) *Ugeskrift for laeger* (Copenhagen) 146(20), 14 May 1984, 1507-1511.
NOTES: Includes English abstract.
LEVEL: A LANG: Dan

MULTIPLE SCLEROSIS

Cailliet, R. Exercise in multiple sclerosis. (Refs: 32)
NOTES: In, Basmajian, J.V. (ed.), Therapeutic exercise, 4th ed., Baltimore, Md., Williams & Wilkins, c1984, p. 407-420.
LEVEL: A LANG: Eng RM719 17505

Gehlsen, G.M. Grigsby, S.A. Winant, D.M. Effects of an aquatic fitness program on the muscular strength and endurance of patients with multiple sclerosis. (Refs: 19)*Physical therapy* (Alexandria, Va.) 64(5), May 1984, 653-657.
ABST: The authors determined the effects of a 10-week aquatic exercise program on muscular strength, endurance, work, and power of 10 multiple sclerosis patients. Overall, the program had a beneficial effect on the variables studied.
LEVEL: A LANG: Eng SIRC ARTICLE NO: 094314

DISEASES AND DISORDERS (continued)

Pacer, R. Woo, G.C. Contrast sensitivity function for vision testing in suspected demyelinating disease. (Letter) *Lancet (London) 1(8373), 18 Feb 1984, 405-406.*
LEVEL: I LANG: Eng

MUSCULAR DYSTROPHY

Danko, Y.I. Kuznetsov, Y.I. Loginov, V.G. (Positive emotions and the T-wave amplitude on the ECG in sportsmen with myocardia dystrophy as a result of chronic physical overstrain.) (Refs: 17)*Kardiologiya (Moscow) 24(10), 1984, 106-108.*
LEVEL: A LANG: Rus

MUSCULOSKELETAL DISEASE

Arciero, R.A. Shishido, N.S. Parr, T.J. Acute anterolateral compartment syndrome secondary to rupture of the peroneus longus muscle. (Refs: 8)*American journal of sports medicine (Baltimore, Md.) 12(5), Sept/Oct 1984, 366-367.*
LEVEL: I LANG: Eng SIRC ARTICLE NO: 104103

Davey, J.R. Rorabeck, C.H. Fowler, P.J. The tibialis posterior muscle compartment: an unrecognized cause of exertional compartment syndrome. (Refs: 21)*American journal of sports medicine (Baltimore, Md.) 12(5), Sept/Oct 1984, 391-397.*
ABST: This paper reports investigations which were performed to prove that the tibialis posterior muscle is contained in its own osseofascial compartment, separate from the rest of the deep posterior compartment. Radiographs following the injection of radio-opaque dye into the tibialis posterior muscle demonstrated the fluid-impermeable, osseofascial boundaries surrounding this muscle. Compartment syndromes created in cadaver legs reveal that traditional techniques of fasciotomy of the deep posterior compartment are inadequate in decompressing the tibialis posterior muscle.
LEVEL: A LANG: Eng SIRC ARTICLE NO: 104113

Florence, J.M. Hagberg, J.M. Effect of training on the exercise responses of neuromuscular disease patients. (Refs: 17) *Medicine and science in sports and exercise (Indianapolis) 16(5), Oct 1984, 460-465.*
CONF: American College of Sports Medicine. Meeting (30th : 1983 : Montreal).
ABST: The purpose of this investigation was to determine whether patients with slowly-progressive or non-progressive neuromuscular diseases could complete a 12-wk training program without untoward responses, and develop cardiovascular training adaptations. All eight patients completed the training program with better than 90% compliance. Resting creatine kinase and myoglobin in the group as a whole showed no change with training, though two patients did have definite elevations after training. Their VO2 max increased by 25 plus or minus 5% with training and their relative increase in VO2 max was not different from that of healthy subjects undergoing the same training. Heart rate reductions during submaximal exercise were somewhat delayed or non-existent in the two patients with Charcot-Marie-Tooth disease, a hereditary neuropathy. However, the six patients with myopathies had heart rate adaptations similar to those in healthy subjects.
LEVEL: A LANG: Eng SIRC ARTICLE NO: 102579

Fourneyron, V. Boyer, C. Pasquis, P. Une methode simple de mesure de pression dans le syndrome chronique de la loge tibiale anterieure.

(Refs: 11)*Medecine du sport (Paris) 58(6), nov 1984, 16-18.*
LEVEL: I LANG: Fr SIRC ARTICLE NO: 102581

Haller, R.G. Lewis, S.F. Pathophysiology of exercise performance in muscle disease. (Refs: 31)*Medicine and science in sport and exercise (Indianapolis) 16(5), Oct 1984, 456-459.*
CONF: American College of Sports Medicine. Meeting (30th : 1983 : Montreal).
ABST: Diseases of skeletal muscles (myopathies) produce two major patterns of exercise intolerance. In muscular dystrophies, there is a progressive loss of muscle fibers which results in increasing muscle weakness and reduced VO2 max due to the loss of functional muscle mass. In disorders of muscle energy metabolism, muscle bulk and resting strength are preserved, but an imbalance in muscle energy production and utilization in exercise results in exertional muscle pain, cramping, weakness, or fatigue. Isometric exercise is impaired by disorders of anaerobic glycolysis. Dynamic exercise is limited by disorders of oxidative metabolism.
LEVEL: A LANG: Eng SIRC ARTICLE NO: 102589

Lewis, S.F. Exercise and human neuromuscular diseases: a symposium overview. (Refs: 22)*Medicine and science in sports and exercise (Indianapolis) 16(5), Oct 1984, 449-450.*
CONF: American College of Sports Medicine. Meeting (30th : 1983 : Montreal).
LEVEL: B LANG: Eng SIRC ARTICLE NO: 102598

Lewis, S.F. Haller, R.G. Blomqvist, C.G. Neuromuscular diseases as models of cardiovascular regulation during exercise. (Refs: 49)*Medicine and science in sports and exercise (Indianapolis) 16(5), Oct 1984, 466-471.*
CONF: American College of Sports Medicine. Meeting (30th : 1983 : Montreal).
ABST: This article reviews the research performed to date on the cardiovascular responses to exercise in patients with neuromuscular diseases and lesions affecting the transmission of afferent impulses from skeletal muscle. These studies have provided important information about the roles of central command and reflexes from skeletal muscle afferents in circulatory control. Few animal models of neuromuscular diseases are available. Studies of patients with specific defects in skeletal muscle energy metabolism are particularly valuable because the local metabolic state participates in both systemic and local cardiovascular regulation.
LEVEL: A LANG: Eng SIRC ARTICLE NO: 102599

Lyager, S. Naeraa, N. Pedersen, O.F. Cardiopulmonary response to exercise in patients with neuromuscular diseases. *Respiration (Basel) 45(2), 1984, 89-99.*
ABST: This study compared the cardiopulmonary response to exercise in 13 patients suffering from neuromuscular disease and 17 healthy controls. No significant differences were observed between both groups' results.
LEVEL: A LANG: Eng SIRC ARTICLE NO: 102602

Riggs, J.E. Gutmann, L. McComas, C.F. Morehad, M.A. Louden, M.B. Martin, J.D. Exercise-induced weakness in paramyotonia congenita: exacerbation with thyrotoxicosis. *Neurology (New York) 34(2), Feb 1984, 233-235.*
ABST: This article details the case of a patient with classic paramyotonia congenita who developed thyrotoxicosis and severe weakness after exercise. The thyrotoxicosis was treated and the symptom was resolved.
LEVEL: A LANG: Eng SIRC ARTICLE NO: 099099

Wallensten, R. Eriksson, E. Intramuscular pressures in exercise-induced lower leg pain. (Refs: 27)*International journal of sports medicine 5(1), Feb 1984, 31-35.*
ABST: This investigation measured intramuscular pressures in the deep posterior as well as in the anterior tibial muscle compartments in 12 athletes with lower leg pain diagnosed as medial tibial syndrome. These values were then compared with the corresponding values found in 12 patients with clinical signs of chronic anterior compartment syndrome. There was no change in pressure in the deep posterior compartment in either group during or after exercise. However, exercise induced a significant increase in the anterior tibial muscle compartment of patients with chronic anterior compartment syndrome. The athletes with medial tibial syndrome exhibited anterior tibial muscle compartment pressures between control values and values obtained from the patients with chronic anterior compartment syndrome. The authors conclude that intramuscular pressure measurement after exercise is a valuable diagnostic tool.
LEVEL: A LANG: Eng SIRC ARTICLE NO: 092954

Wallensten, R. Karlsson, J. Histochemical and metabolic changes in lower leg muscles in exercise-induced pain. (Refs: 45) *International journal of sports medicine (Stuttgart) 5(4), Aug 1984, 202-208.*
ABST: Intramuscular pressure, fiber type distribution, relative cross-sectional area of slow-twitch muscle fibers, muscle lactate, and water content were studied in eight patients with medial tibial syndrome and in eight patients with chronic anterior compartment syndrome. The variables were determined before and after standardized exercise that provoked lower leg pain. The findings indicate that the chronic anterior compartment syndrome is related to changes on the muscle fiber level and to a subsequently changed anaerobic metabolism and fluid infiltration. The medial tibial syndrome may be caused by abnormal biomechanics during running that by means of local adaptation causes changes in fiber types and local metabolic and microcirculatory capacities.
LEVEL: A LANG: Eng SIRC ARTICLE NO: 104089

MYOCARDIAL INFARCTION

Akhmedzhanov, M.I. Afanaseva, M.S. Arkhangelskii, V.V. Latyshev, G.D. Ziablov, V.D. Reaktsiia bol'nykh, perenesshikh infarkt miokarda, na kupaniia s dozirovannym plavaniem v basseine i more. (Reaction of patients with a history of myocardial infarct to bathing under controlled swimming in swimming pools and in the sea.) *Voprosy kurortologii, fizioterapii i lechebnoi fizicheskoi kultury (Moscow) 3, May/Jun 1984, 27-29.*
LEVEL: I LANG: Rus

Carson, P. Activity after myocardial infarction. (editorial) *British medical journal (clinical research) (London) 288(6410) 7 Jan 1984, 1-2.*
LEVEL: B LANG: Eng SIRC ARTICLE NO: 097440

Ehsani, A.A. Heath, G.W. Martin, W.H. Hagberg, J.M. Holloszy, J.O. Effects of intense exercise training on plasma catecholamines in coronary patients. (Refs: 22)*Journal of applied physiology: respiratory, environmental and exercise physiology (Bethesda, Md.) 57(1), Jul 1984, 154-159.*
ABST: Eleven male coronary patients participated in a 12-mo-long exercise program. Oxygen consumption increased by 42 percent and resting

heart rate was lower after the program, but there was no effect on resting blood pressure and plasma catecholamines. Ischemic S-T segment depression was unchanged after training, while plasma norepinephrine concentration, rate-pressure product and sytolic blood pressure at maximal exercise were significantly higher.
LEVEL: A LANG: Eng SIRC ARTICLE NO: 108365

Eisenberg, J.H.N. Moore, N.A. Wilcockson, A. Elevated cardiac enzymes after contact sport. (Refs: 8)*International journal o sports cardiology (Torino, Italy) 1(2), Jul/Dec 1984, 76-79.*
ABST: Serial measurements were made of creatine kinase and its MB isoenzyme, lactate dehydrogenase and aspartate aminotransferase before and after exercise in a soccer match (6 subjects) a rugby match (6 subjects) and rigorous rugby training (6 subjects). Estimates were made at 16 and 40 hours after exercise. Total creatine kinase was significantly elevated above the normal range in all three groups at 16 hours. Although the creatine kinase MB isoenzyme was elevated, above the normal range in some subjects, in no case was it more than 5 percent of the total creatine kinase i.e. into the range considered highly specific and sensitive for myocardial infarction. Modest elevation of lactate dehydrogenase and asparate aminotransferase after exercise was noticed. It is suggested that measurements of serum creatine kinase MB isoenzyme after contact sports will not lead to false positive diagnosis of myocardial infarction. A theoretical situation in which a false negative diagnosis for myocardial infarction after contact sport can occur is given.
LEVEL: A LANG: Eng SIRC ARTICLE NO: 179170

Fukui, S. Satoh, K. Tanaka, T. Inoue, H. Hamano, Y. Katoh, O. Minamino, T. Fujii, K. Satoh, H. Inoue, M. Effects of sublingual isosorbide dinitrate on left ventricular performance during exercise in patients with mycoardial infarction. *Japanese circulation journal (Kyoto) 48(10), Oct 1984, 1057-1065.*
LEVEL: A LANG: Eng

Miller, N.H. Haskell, W.L. Berra, K. DeBusk, R.F. Home versus group exercise training for increasing functional capacity after myocardial infarction. *Circulation (Dallas) 70(4), Oct 1984, 645-649.*
LEVEL: A LANG: Eng

Perna, G.P. Fanelli, R. Villella, A. Lanna, P. Russo, A. Zeppilli, P. Hypertrophic cardiomyopathy and inadequate septal hypertrophy in athletes. A report on two cases. (Refs: 8)*International journal of sports cardiology (Torino, Italy) 1(2), Jul/Dec 1984, 96-101.*
ABST: Two athletes with uncommon aspects of hypertrophic cardiomyopathy (HCM) and inadequate asymmetric septal hypertrophy (ASH) respectively are reported. The first case had an apical HCM with giant negative T-wave in precordial leads and a family history of HCM. The second case had inadequate ASH for which a close causal relationship with sports activity was unequivocally proved by the complete normalization of echocardiographic and electrocardiographic pictures after 12 months without exercise.
LEVEL: A LANG: Eng SIRC ARTICLE NO: 179174

Rubin, S.A. Brown, H.V. Ventilation and gas exchange during exercise in severe chronic heart failure. (Refs: 9)*American review of respiratory disease (New York) 129(2 Pt 2), Feb 1984, S63-S64.*
CONF: Exercise Testing in the Dyspneic Patient

Workshop (1982 : Bethesda).
ABST: This study evaluated 28 patients (mean age 61 yr.) at upright rest and during cycle ergometry. 19 patients had prior myocardial infarct and 9 patients had idiopathic cardiomyopathy. Arterial oxygen tension and saturation were normal at rest and exercise. Ventilation was increased at rest and exercise because of increased dead space to tidal volume and alveolar hyperventilation. The authors concluded that when considering the symptoms of dyspnea and exercise limitation, arterial oxygenation is probably not important, but excessive ventilation may be a contributing factor.
LEVEL: A LANG: Eng SIRC ARTICLE NO: 098918

Shah, S.J. Karnadikar, N.G. Vaidya, S.V. Pathak, L. Cardiac rehabilitation after myocardial infarction. *Journal of the Association of Physicians of India (Bombay) 32(6), June 1984, 517-519.*
LEVEL: I LANG: Eng

Wenger, N.K. Early ambulation after myocardial infarction: the in-patient exercise program. (Refs: 53)*Clinics in sports medicine (Philadelphia) 3(2), Apr 1984, 333-348.*
ABST: The author discusses the trend towards early ambulation of the post-myocardial infarction patients. Early ambulation is presently thought to offset the deleterious physiologic responses which accompany prolonged immobilization. Early ambulation is also thought to improve the patients' self-confidence. A program for early ambulation is outlined.
LEVEL: A LANG: Eng SIRC ARTICLE NO: 094264

OBESITY

Abrosimova, L.I. Baibikova, L.S. Simonova, L.A. Malova, N.A. Fetisov, G.V. Vliianie dvigatel'noi aktivnosti na fizicheskuiu rabotosposobnost' shkol'nikov s izbytochnoi massoi tela. (Effect of motor activity on the physical work capacity of schoolchildren with excessive body weight.) *Gigiena i sanitariia (Moscow) 8, Aug 1984, 29-32.*
LEVEL: A LANG: Rus

Atomi, Y. Miyashita, M. Maximal oxygen uptake of obese middle-aged women related to body composition and total body potassiu (Refs: 35)*Journal of sports medicine and physical fitness (Torino, Italy) 24(3), Sept 1984, 212-218.*
ABST: The effect of obesity on maximal oxygen uptake (V02max) related to lean body mass (LBM) and total body potassium was determined by means of comparisons between 15 non-obese and 22 obese middle-aged women (30 to 50 years of age). Between the non-obese and obese groups a significant difference was found in the following three areas: mean body weight(51.40 vs 60.25 kg, non-obese and obese, respectively), mean body density (1.0409 vs 1.0125 g/ml), and mean % body fat (25.7 vs 33.4%). There was no significant difference in the means of LBM (38.51 vs 40.04 kg) and V02max1 1.487 vs 1.5181/min) between the two groups. Total body potassium per body weight and V02max per body weight of the obese women was significantly lower than the non-obese ones.
LEVEL: A LANG: Eng SIRC ARTICLE NO: 105458

Binkhorst, R.A. Heevel, J. Noordeloos, A.M. Energy expenditure of (severe) obese subjects during submaximal and maximal exercise. (Refs: 18)*International journal of sports medicine (Stuttgart) Suppl. 5, Nov 1984, 71-73.*
CONF: International Congress on Sports and Health

(1983 : Maastricht, Netherlands).
LEVEL: A LANG: Eng SIRC ARTICLE NO: 104281

Blundell, J.E. Behaviour modification and exercise in the treatment of obesity. *Postgraduate medicine (Minneapolis, Minn.) (Suppl. 3), 1984, 37-49.*
LEVEL: I LANG: Eng

Brownell, K.D. Behavioral and psychological aspects of motivation to exercise. (Refs: 12)*International journal of sports medicine (Stuttgart) Suppl. 5, Nov 1984, 69-70.*
CONF: International Congress on Sports and Health (1983 : Maastricht, Netherlands).
LEVEL: I LANG: Eng SIRC ARTICLE NO: 104400

Chen, W. Lafferty, J. Biofeedback training as an adjunct to a behavioral modification weight reduction program. (Refs: 16) *Florida JOHPERD (Gainesville, Fla.) 22(4), Nov 1984, 5-8.*
ABST: In this study the effect of biofeedback training was tested with the help of 24 volunteers whose average body weight was 49% above ideal weight. While there was no significant difference of weight loss with the addition of biofeedback training, the authors point out that subjects with an extended history of being overweight may require a longer training period. Further studies with a larger sample size and restricted criteria in selecting experimental subjects are recommended.
LEVEL: A LANG: Eng SIRC ARTICLE NO: 105334

Epstein, L.H. McGowan, C. Woodall, K. A behavioral observation system for free play activity in young overweight female children. (Refs: 6)*Research quarterly for exercise & sport (Reston, Va.) 55(2), Jun 1984, 180-183.*
ABST: This pilot study report presents a reliable behavioral observation system that has been validated by heart rate and metabolic data. This system enables the intensity as well as the frequency and duration of activity to be recorded for later use. The system was validated on 19 overweight female children between 5 and 8 years of age. Further research is needed to validate this system for use with non-obese children.
LEVEL: A LANG: Eng SIRC ARTICLE NO: 096014

Garrow, J.S. Physiological aspects of exercise in relation to obesity. (Refs: 21)*International journal of sports medicine (Stuttgart) Suppl. 5, Nov 1984, 66-68.*
CONF: International Congress on Sports and Health (1983 : Maastricht, Netherlands).
LEVEL: I LANG: Eng SIRC ARTICLE NO: 104310

Grunberg, C. Le sport fait-il maigrir? *Science et vie (Paris) HS147, 1984, 142-145.*
LEVEL: I LANG: Fr

Hansen, J.E. Sue, D.Y. Wasserman, K. Predicted values for clinical exercise testing. (Refs: 47)*American review of respiratory disease (New York) 129(2 Pt 2), Feb 1984, S49-S55.*
CONF: Exercise Testing in the Dyspneic Patient Workshop (1982 : Bethesda).
ABST: 265 current or ex-shipguard workers were thoroughly evaluated at rest and then exercised on a bicycle ergometer with equal work increments each minute to exhaustion while continuous multiple noninvasive cardiorespiratory and intermittent blood pressure and blood gas measures were made. Seventy-seven men, with a mean age of 54 were judged to have normal cardiorespiratory systems. The statistical results are detailed and analyzed. The authors found that for predicting maximal oxygen uptake and oxygen pulse in an overweight man, the use of age and

height were preferred to age and weight.
LEVEL: A LANG: Eng SIRC ARTICLE NO: 099239

Kaminska, K. Woynaroska, B. Ocena poziomu i dynamiki zmian wydolnosci fizycznej dzieci i mlodziezy z otyloscia prosta. (Evaluation of the degree and dynamics of changes in the physical fitness of children and adolescents with simple obesity.) *Pediatria polska (Warsaw) 59(4), Apr 1984, 279-285.*
LEVEL: A LANG: Pol

Kaufman, D.A. Lynch, R.O. Effect of weight loss products on body composition and body weight. (Refs: 4)*Florida JOHPERD (Gainesville, Fla.) 22(4), Nov 1984, 9-10.*
ABST: In this study the effects of two diet aids and a placebo were tested on 29 overweight volunteers aged 18-33. After two weeks there were no statistically significant differences in the cardiovascular and body composition variables for the three treatments. Significant weight loss through time is probably attributable to psychological factors.
LEVEL: A LANG: Eng SIRC ARTICLE NO: 105343

Krotkiewski, M. Bjoerntorp, P. Holm, G. Marks, V. Morgan, L. Smith, U. Feurle, G.E. Effects of physical training on insulin, connecting peptide (C-peptide), gastric inhibitory polypeptide (GIP) and pancreatic polypeptide (PP) levels in obese subjects. *International journal of obesity (London) 8(3), 1984, 193-199.*
ABST: Ten severely obese women were subjected to physical training for three months on ad libitum diet. Under metabolic ward condition oral glucose tolerance test was performed before and after the training period with the same energy intake quantitatively and qualitatively, and glucose, insulin, connecting (C)-peptide, gastric inhibitory polypeptide and pancreatic polypeptide were determined. In confirmation of previous work, physical training caused no decrease in body fat in these severely obese subjects, and no change in body cell mass or glucose tolerance, while insulin and blood pressure decreased. C-peptide concentrations decreased also, indicating effects of physical training in obesity on insulin production.
LEVEL: A LANG: Eng SIRC ARTICLE NO: 104121

Krotkiewski, M. Sjoestroem, L. Sullivan, L. Lundberg, P.A. Lindstedt, G. Wetterqvist, H. Bjoerntorp, P. The effect of acute and chronic exercise on thyroid hormones in obesity. *Acta medica scandinavica (Stockholm) 216(3), 1984, 269-275.*
LEVEL: A LANG: Eng

Mandroukas, K. Krotkiewski, M. Hedberg, M. Wroblewski, Z. Bjorntorp, P. Grimby, G. Physical training in obese women. Effects of muscle morphology, biochemistry and function. (Refs: 37)*European journal of applied physiology and occupational physiology (Berlin, FRG) 52(4), Jun 1984, 355-361.*
ABST: The effects of three months of physical endurance training without food restrictions were studied in 14, middle aged, physically untrained, obese women. The subjects trained 50 min/day, 3 days/week. A training session consisted of a 10-15 min warm-up followed by alternating heavy and light intervals. The heavy intervals lasted 4 min. each and were performed at 80-85% of VO2 max while the light intervals lasted 8-10 min each. VO2 max increased 20% as a result of training but body weight, body fat and the number and weight of fat cells did not change as a result of the training.

Glucose tolerance was improved after training.
LEVEL: A LANG: Eng SIRC ARTICLE NO: 097741

McKenzie, T.L. Buono, M. Nelson, J. Modification of coronary heart disease (CHD) risk factors in obese boys through diet and exercise. (Refs: 8)*American corrective therapy journal (San Diego, Calif.) 38(2), Mar/Apr 1984, 35-37.*
ABST: This study examined the effect of a 7-week diet and exercise program on selected coronary heart disease (CHD) risk factors in 35 obese boys. The subjects were maintained on approximately 1170 kcal/day and participated in extensive physical education/recreation activities. The results indicated significant changes in body weight, skinfold thickness, resting systolic and diastolic pressures, and predicted maximum aerobic power had occurred. The authors suggest that an intense program combining exercise and diet can favourably reduce the CHD risks of obese children.
LEVEL: A LANG: Eng SIRC ARTICLE NO: 095771

Oscai, L.B. Recent progress in understanding obesity. (Refs: 33)*American Academy of Physical Education papers (Champaign, Ill.) 17, 1984, 42-48.*
CONF: American Academy of Physical Education. Annual Meeting (54th : 1983 : Minneapolis).
NOTES: Conference theme: Exercise and health.
LEVEL: I LANG: Eng SIRC ARTICLE NO: 104130

Petroiu, A. Schneider, F. Lungu, G. Mihalas, G. Varadeanu, A. Man, I. Lipodogram structure and the exercise capacity in obesity. *Physiologie (Bucarest) 21(2), Apr/Jun 1984, 117-120.*
ABST: 30 women between 21 and 52 years of age were studied while exercising on a bicycle ergometer at a submaximal exercise intensity. No statistically significant correlations were found between plasma lipid fraction and the exercise adaptability coefficient.
LEVEL: A LANG: Eng SIRC ARTICLE NO: 102813

Porikos, K.P. Pi-Sunyer, F.X. Regulation of food intake in human obesity: studies with caloric dilution and exercise. *Clinics in endocrinology and metabolism (London) 13(3), Nov 1984, 547-561.*
LEVEL: I LANG: Eng

Segal, K.R. Presta, E. Gutin, B. Thermic effect of food during graded exercise in normal weight and obese men. *American journal of clinical nutrition (Bethesda, Md.) 40(5), Nov 1984, 995-1000.*
LEVEL: A LANG: Eng

Short, M.A. DiCarlo, S. Steffee, W.P. Pavlov, K. Effects of physical conditioning on self-concept of adult obese males. *Physical therapy (Alexandria, Va.) 64(2), Feb 1984, 194-198.*
ABST: The purpose of this study was to investigate the possible effects of a supervised physical conditioning program on psychological measures in 45 obese police men. For an eight-week program of instruction regarding physical conditioning and nutrition, 22 randomly selected subjects also participated in an aerobic conditioning program. The remaining 23 subjects were asked to maintain activity habits similar to those before the study. At the end of eight weeks, the exercising group displayed significantly higher measures of maximal oxygen consumption, an index of physical fitness, and higher scores on the Physical Self and Self-satisfaction subscales of the Tennessee Self-concept Scale. These results reinforce the interrelationship between physical exercise and self-concept, as conditioning and diet were associated with greater improvements in obese

police men.
LEVEL: A LANG: Eng SIRC ARTICLE NO: 094661

Southam, M.A. Kirkley, B.G. Murchison, A. Berkowitz, R.I. A summer day camp approach to adolescent weight loss. *Adolescence (Roslyn Heights, N.Y.) 19(76), Winter 1984, 855-868.*
LEVEL: A LANG: Eng

Stern, J.S. Is obesity a disease of inactivity? *Research publications - Association for Research in Nervous and Mental Disease (Baltimore) 62, 1984, 131-139.*
LEVEL: I LANG: Eng SIRC ARTICLE NO: 099106

Supplement: Exercise testing in the dyspneic patient. New York: American Thoracic Society, 1984. 102 p. (American review of respiratory disease (New York) 129(2 Pt 2), Feb 1984.)
CONF: Exercise Testing in the Dyspneic Patient Workshop (1982 : Bethesda).
NOTES: From a Workshop held September 1-3, 1982, Bethesda, Md.
LEVEL: A LANG: Eng RC90 15485

Whipp, B.J. Davis, J.A. The ventilatory stress of exercise in obesity. (Refs: 22)*American review of respiratory disease (Ne York) 129(2 Pt 2), Feb 1984, S90-S92.*
CONF: Exercise Testing in the Dyspneic Patient Workshop (1982 : Bethesda).
ABST: The effect of obesity on the exercise performance test is discussed with respect to the influences of the state of obesity on metabolic cost at a given work load.
LEVEL: I LANG: Eng SIRC ARTICLE NO: 099275

Worsley, A. Coonan, W. Leitch, D. Crawford, D. Slim and obese children's perceptions of physical activities. *International journal of obesity (London) 8(3), 1984, 201-211.*
ABST: The authors compared the perceptions of physical activities of slim and obese children. Two samples were used: 1) 600 ten-year-olds from seven regions in Australia and 2) 528 ten-year-olds from South Australia. Endurance activities were perceived more negatively by obese children while the same group perceived flexibility-coordination activities more positively than the slim children.
LEVEL: A LANG: Eng SIRC ARTICLE NO: 104425

Ylitalo, V.M. Exercise performance and serum lipids in obese schoolchildren before and after reconditioning program. (Refs: 29)
CONF: Symposium of Paediatric Work Physiology (10th : 1981 : Joutsa, Finland).
NOTES: In, Ilmarinen, J. and Vaelimaeki, I. (eds.), Children and sport: paediatric work physiology, Berlin, Springer-Verlag, 1984, p. 247-254.
ABST: This study investigated the effects of obesity and a 2-year reconditioning program on the ergometric capacity and the serum lipids and insulin of 61 obese schoolchildren aged 7-15 years at the beginning of the study.
LEVEL: A LANG: Eng SIRC ARTICLE NO: 102841

Zuliani, U. Novarini, A. Bonetti, A. Borghi, L. Borghetti, A. Physical activity in obesity: a study of some biohumoral parameters. (Refs: 19)*International journal of sports medicine (Stuttgart) Suppl. 5, Nov 1984, 76-78.*
CONF: International Congress on Sports and Health (1983 : Maastricht, Netherlands).
LEVEL: A LANG: Eng SIRC ARTICLE NO: 104158

OSGOOD-SCHLATTER'S DISEASE

Imbert, J.C. Demonteil, G. Osteochondrite dissequante des condyles femoraux chez le sportif. *Cinesiologie (Paris) 94, mars/avr 1984, 183-185.*
LEVEL: I LANG: Fr SIRC ARTICLE NO: 096025

Kvist, M. Kujala, U. Heinonen, O. Kolu, T. Osgood-Schlatterin ja severin taudit urheilevilla nuorilla. (Osgood-Schlatter and Sever's disease in young athletes.) *Duodecim (Helsinki) 100(3), 1984, 142-150.*
LEVEL: A LANG: Fin

Skrabal, J. Sobora, J. Durda, D. Naspristup k operativnimu leceni juvenilni asepticke osteochondronekrozy hlavice 2. metatarzu u sportujici mladeze. (Our approach to the surgical treatment of juvenile aseptic osteochondronecrosis in the head of the 2d metatarsus in young athletes.) *Acta chirurgiae orthopaedicae et traumatologiae ceshoslovaca (Prague) 51(2), Apr 1984, 133-137.*
LEVEL: A LANG: Cze

Soos, A. Balogh, E. A tuber ossis ischii asepticus osteochondronecrosisa mint a sportserueleseketek egyik formaja. (Aseptic osteochondronecrosis of the Tuber O. Ischii as a form of sports injuries.) (Refs: 16)*Sportorvosi szemle/Hungarian review of sports medicine (Budapest) 25(2), 1984, 129-132.*
ABST: The authors describe cases of aseptic osteochondronecroses of the tuber of the ischial bone which could be attributed to overstrain conditions developed in the course of sport training.
LEVEL: A LANG: Hun SIRC ARTICLE NO: 097262

von Gumppenberg, S. Jakob, R.P. Engelhardt, P. Beeinflusst der M. Osgood-Schlatter die Position der Patella? (Does Osgood-Schlatter disease modify the position of the patella?) *Zeitschrift fuer Orthopaedie und ihre Grenzgebiete (Stuttgart) 122 (6), Nov/Dec 1984, 798-802.*
LEVEL: I LANG: Ger

RESPIRATORY TRACT DISEASE

Aversa, C. Camassa, A. Giurgola, S. Guercia, S. Paiano, L. Approccio epidemiologico alle malattie respiratorie croniche e recidivanti dell'adolescente. (Epidemiologic approach to chronic and recurrent respiratory diseases in adolescents.) *Archivio monaldi per la tisiologia e le malattie dell apparato respiratorio (Naples) 39(1/2), Jan/Apr 1984, 61-74.*
LANG: It

Baumgartl, P. Sport bei banalen Infekten? (Sports during commonplace infections? (letter).) *Deutsche Medizinische Wochenschrift (Stuttgart) 109(37), 14 Sept 1984, 1423.*
LEVEL: B LANG: Ger

Becklake, M.R. Organic or functional impairment. Overall perspective. (Refs: 32)*American review of respiratory disease (New York) 129(2 Pt 2), Feb 1984, S96-S100.*
CONF: Exercise Testing in the Dyspneic Patient Workshop (1982 : Bethesda).
ABST: Disability can be evaluated by measuring maximal exercise performance and relating it to the metabolic needs required by the patient's usual functions. Anaerobic threshold provides an assessment of oxygen delivery, respiratory pattern, and total level of ventilation for a given work load as an evaluation on respiratory muscle fatigue, and Vo2 max serves as an assessment of overall exercise capacity. These tests, coupled with conventional assessment of pulmonary and cardiac function, provide tools for objective evaluation of dysfunction and evaluation of disability.
LEVEL: A LANG: Eng SIRC ARTICLE NO: 098997

Hansen, J.E. Exercise instruments, schemes, and protocols for evaluating the dyspneic patient. (Refs: 42)*American review of respiratory disease (New York) 129(2 Pt 2), Feb 1984, S25-S27.*
CONF: Exercise Testing in the Dyspneic Patient Workshop (1982 : Bethesda).
ABST: This paper describes and evaluates several exercise instruments, schemes and protocols for testing dyspneic patients. The exercise bicycle is safe and allows for measurement of external work and work efficiency with a minimum of measuring devices, while the treadmill provides a higher maximum oxygen uptake. The ideal protocol consists of repeated measurement of cardiorespiratory function at rest, during warmup, and during work at one minute increments to a symptom assessed limit in approximately ten minutes.
LEVEL: A LANG: Eng SIRC ARTICLE NO: 099238

Jones, N.L. Dyspnea in exercise. (Refs: 25)*Medicine and science in sports and exercise 16(1), 1984, 14-19.*
ABST: The author reviews recent studies in respiratory physiology and the effects of exercise on dyspnea. To this end he analyzes the factors which influence the sense of respiratory effort. These included the ventilatory demands of exercise, impedance to breathing, the pattern and timing of breathing, the inspired volume and flow during exercise, and the strength of respiratory muscles. Through the measurement of these factors the relative causes of dyspnea can be determined and appropriate management methods can be established.
LEVEL: A LANG: Eng SIRC ARTICLE NO: 091515

Katz, R.M. Rhinitis in the athlete. *Journal of allergy and clinical immunology (St. Louis) 73(5 Pt 2), May 1984, 708-711.*
LEVEL: I LANG: Eng SIRC ARTICLE NO: 100728

Kim, M.J. Respiratory muscle training: implications for patient care. *Heart and lung (St. Louis) 13(4), Jul 1984, 333-340.*
LEVEL: I LANG: Eng SIRC ARTICLE NO: 102593

Moore, S. Management of a pneumothorax in a football player. Case report. (Refs: 1)*Athletic training (Greenville, N.C.) 19(2), Summer 1984, 129-130.*
LEVEL: I LANG: Eng SIRC ARTICLE NO: 094430

Sasaki, T. Index for evaluation of walking-training of patients with chronic severe respiratory failure. *Japanese journal o medicine (Tokyo) 23(2), May 1984, 171-173.*
LEVEL: I LANG: Eng SIRC ARTICLE NO: 102607

Scharf, S. Bye, P. Pardy, R. Macklem, P.T. Dyspnea, fatigue, and second wind. (Refs: 3)*American review of respiratory disease (New York) 129(2 Pt 2), Feb 1984, S88-S89.*
CONF: Exercise Testing in the Dyspneic Patient Workshop (1982 : Bethesda).
ABST: This paper addresses the question of different testing dyspnea from fatigue by examining the concept of 'second wind' Diaphragmatic fatigue has been associated with the sensation of dyspnea when fatigue was expressed by Diaphragmatic EMG. This sensation of dyspnea disappeared with the appearance of 'second wind' and a change in the EMG spectrum to normal. This provides an important tool for the evaluation of respiratory muscle fatigue.
LEVEL: A LANG: Eng SIRC ARTICLE NO: 099264

Shapiro, G.G. Methacholine challenge - relevance for the allergic athlete. *Journal of allergy and clinical immunology (St. Louis) 73(5 Pt 2), May 1984, 670-675.*
LEVEL: I LANG: Eng SIRC ARTICLE NO: 100753

Slavin, R.G. Sinusitis. *Journal of allergy and clinical immunology (St. Louis) 73(5 Pt 2), May 1984, 712-716.*
LEVEL: I LANG: Eng SIRC ARTICLE NO: 100758

Zejda, J. Ocena zdolnosci do wysilku fizycznego chorych na przewlekle zapalenie oskrzeli. (Work capacity evaluation in patients with chronic bronchitis.) *Polski tygodnik lekarski (Warsaw) 39(38), 17 Sept 1984, 1253-1256.*
LEVEL: A LANG: Pol

RHEUMATISM

Demarais, Y. Activites sportives et rhumatismes. *Science et vie (Paris) HS147, 1984, 150-155.*
LEVEL: I LANG: Fr

SCOLIOSIS

Cailliet, R. Exercises for scoliosis. (Refs: 15)
NOTES: In, Basmajian, J.V. (ed.), Therapeutic exercise, 4th ed., Baltimore, Md., Williams & Wilkins, c1984, p. 464-484.
LEVEL: A LANG: Eng RM719 17505

SICKLE CELL TRAIT

Alcorn, R. Bowser, B. Henley, E.J. Holloway, V. Fluidotherapy and exercise in the management of sickle cell anemia. (Refs: 6 *Physical therapy (Alexandria, Va.) 64(10), Oct 1984 , 1520-1522.*
LEVEL: I LANG: Eng SIRC ARTICLE NO: 099079

Alpert, B.S. Dover, E.V. Strong, W.B. Covitz, W. Longitudinal exercise hemodynamics in children with sickle cell anemia. *American journal of diseases of children (Chicago) 138(11), Nov 1984, 1021-1024.*
LEVEL: A LANG: Eng

Diggs, L.W. The sickle cell trait in relation to the training and assignment of duties in the armed forces: III. Hyposthenuria, hematuria, sudden death, rhabdomyolysis, and acute tubular necrosis. *Aviation space and environmental medicine (Washington) 55(5), May 1984, 358-364.*
LEVEL: I LANG: Eng SIRC ARTICLE NO: 102570

SPINAL DISORDERS

Brunt, D. Apraxic tendencies in children with meningomyelocele. (Refs: 18)*Adapted physical activity quarterly 1(1), 1984, 61-67.*
ABST: Seven children with meningomyelocele (MM) and associated hydrocephalus were compared to seven children with MM on motor tasks performed first to verbal commands and then to imitation. The children with MM and associated hydrocephalus were unable to assemble an appropriate motor plan to trigger the desired movements when verbal cues were given. Both groups performed better when they were cued for the movement by imitation. Although aproxia may be the cause of hydrocephalus group's inability to respond to verbal cues it is not the only possibility; thus further research is called for.
LEVEL: A LANG: Eng SIRC ARTICLE NO: 092804

DISEASES AND DISORDERS (continued)

Lechowski, S. Urbaniak, J. Stypula, J.
Przepukliny jadra miazdzystego krazkow
miedzykregowych ledzwiowego odcinka kregoslupa
w wieku mlodzienczym. (Lumbar intervertebral disk
herniation in adolescents.) *Neurologia i
neurochirurgica polska (Warsaw) 18(1), Jan/Feb
1984, 37-41.*
LEVEL: I LANG: Pol

Miltenyi, M. Elvonalbeli atletak mozgatorendszeri
problemairol. (Health care of the locomotor system
in top athletes.) (Refs 17)*Sportorvosi szemle/
Hungarian review of sports medicine (Budapest)
25(3), 1984, 209-217.*
ABST: Comparatively less attention is devoted to a
regular screening for locomotor system disorders in
sportsmedicine than is usual for other system
disorders in top level athletes. Accordingly,
overstrain problems manifest mainly in the motor
apparatus. Especially before allowing participation
in regular high intensity training such screening is
indispensable with particular regard to the spine.
Experience has shown that morpho-functional
disorders in spine construction play a part in the
pathogenesis of lower extremity injuries. By
strengthening the deep back muscles adequately,
one may obtain protection not only against injuries
of the lumbar region, but also against those
affecting the lower limb muscles. As an illustration,
three cases are reported. These top level athletes
could continued their successful sports career
despite their x-ray evidenced spine deformity.
Sports physicians should be aware of the
techniques employed in the sport event they care
for. Examples are given in track and field athletics
(javelin throwing, high jump, pole vaulting).
LEVEL: A LANG: Hun SIRC ARTICLE NO: 100237

THROMBOSIS

Steingard, P.M. How I manage varicose veins and
venous thrombosis in athletes. (Refs: 4)*Physician
and sportsmedicine (Minneapolis, Minn.) 12(6), Jun
1984, 97-101.*
LEVEL: I LANG: Eng SIRC ARTICLE NO: 094441

VARICOSE VEINS

Steingard, P.M. How I manage varicose veins and
venous thrombosis in athletes. (Refs: 4)*Physician
and sportsmedicine (Minneapolis, Minn.) 12(6), Jun
1984, 97-101.*
LEVEL: I LANG: Eng SIRC ARTICLE NO: 094441

VENEREAL DISEASE

Howe, W.B. How I manage genital herpes. (Refs:
6)*Physican and sportsmedicine 12(1), Jan 1984,
46-48;51;53.*
LEVEL: I LANG: Eng SIRC ARTICLE NO: 091511

VIRUS DISEASES

**Hoofnagle, J.H. Hanson, R.G. Minuk, G.Y.
Pappas, S.C. Schafer, D.F. Dusheiko, G.M.
Straus, S.E. Popper, H. Jones, E.A.** Randomized
controlled trial of adenine arabinoside
monophosphate for chronic type B hepatitis.
*Gastroenterology (Baltimore) 86(1), Jan 1984, 150-
157.*
ABST: This paper investigated the effects of
arabinofuranozyladenine monophosphate on ten
patients with chronic type B hepatitis. Ten other
patients served as controls. From 2 to 9 months
following 4 weeks of therapy, 4 of the 10 treated

patients became hepatitis B e antigen or hepatitis B
virus-deorxyribonucleic acid polymenase negative,
or both. 2 of these patients relapsed later on.
Overall results indicated long-term improvements in
only 20% of the subjects.
LEVEL: A LANG: Eng SIRC ARTICLE NO: 096024

DISTANCE SWIMMING

Stuller, J. Beyond tough: it's time to end the
bickering. What's really the hardest, sickest ultra-
endurance event of them all? *Outside 9(1), Jan/
Feb 1984, 39-43;76-77.*
LEVEL: B LANG: Eng SIRC ARTICLE NO: 093237

BIOGRAPHY AND AUTOBIOGRAPHY

Smith, G. From stillness comes swiftness. (Vladimir
Salnikov) *Sports illustrated (Chicago, Ill.) 60(20), 21
May 1984, 72-76;78;80;82;84-86.*
LEVEL: B LANG: Eng SIRC ARTICLE NO: 095321

Weck, L. Taming the waters. Suzanne Heim has
braved riptides, cross-currents, hypothermia - even
an early brush with death - to claim nearly every
open water swimming record in San Francisco Bay.
*Ultrasport (Boston, Mass.) 1(3), May/Jun 1984, 60-
66.*
LEVEL: B LANG: Eng SIRC ARTICLE NO: 096906

HISTORY

Underwood, T. Water & will: the history of open
water swimming is filled with romanticism and
legend, hucksterism and whimsy and, at times,
tragedy. It has been fraught with controversies over
esoteric matters of style and substance. But always
the two essential elements have remained.
Ultrasport (Boston) 1(4), Jul/Aug 1984, 26-33.
LEVEL: B LANG: Eng SIRC ARTICLE NO: 098544

PHYSIOLOGY

**Brisson, G.R. Quirion, A. Ledoux, M. Rajotte, D.
Pellerin-Massicotte, J.** Influence of long-distance
swimming on serum androgens in males. *Hormone
and metabolic research (Stuttgart) 16(3), Mar 1984,
160.*
LEVEL: I LANG: Eng SIRC ARTICLE NO: 101543

TECHNIQUES AND SKILLS -
BUTTERFLY

Thornton, K.M. Learning from the Olympians:
sprint and distance butterfly. *Swimming world and
junior swimmer (Los Angeles, Calif.) 25(4), Apr
1984, 28-30.*
LEVEL: B LANG: Eng SIRC ARTICLE NO: 095326

DIVING

A great summer job: dive-for-pay ranks. *Diver
(Portland, Conn.) 5(1), Feb/Mar 1984, 3-5.*
LEVEL: B LANG: Eng SIRC ARTICLE NO 098046

ASSOCIATIONS

1984 Canadian Amateur Diving Association
constitution and policy guidelines. s.l.: Canadian
Amateur Diving Association, 1984. 1v. (loose-leaf)
CORP: Canadian Amateur Diving Association.

NOTES: Aussi publie en francais sous le titre:
Charte et directives generales de l'Association
canadienne de plongeon amateur 1984.
LEVEL: B LANG: Eng GV838.63.C3 18585

Charte et directives generales de l'Association
canadienne de plongeon amateur 1984. s.l.:
Association canadienne de plongeon amateur,
1984. 1v. (feuilles mobiles)
CORP: Association canadienne de plongeon
amateur.
NOTES: Also published in English under the title:
1984 Canadian Amateur Diving Association
constitution and policy guidelines.
LEVEL: B LANG: Fr GV838.63.C3 18586

BIOGRAPHY AND AUTOBIOGRAPHY

Allen, S.B. She took a dive for U.S. and won
medal. (Velma Dunn) *Foil (Indianapolis) Spring
1984, 4-5.*
LEVEL: B LANG: Eng SIRC ARTICLE NO: 109040

Ewald, R. Platform princess. (Wendy Wyland)
*Swimming world and junior swimmer (Inglewood,
Calif.) 25(8), Aug 1984, 41-45.*
LEVEL: B LANG: Eng SIRC ARTICLE NO: 099530

Ewald, R. Duffy, T. Diving's superstar can finally
relax. (Greg Louganis) *Swimming world and junior
swimmer (Inglewood, Calif.) 25(10), Oct 1984, 31-
36.*
LEVEL: B LANG: Eng SIRC ARTICLE NO: 107158

Mother, daughter eschew comparisons: Kelly seeks
her own glory. (Kelly McCormick) *Diver 4(6), Dec
1983/Jan 1984, 2-3.*
LEVEL B LANG: Eng SIRC ARTICLE NO: 093393

Nightingale, D. The comeback kid: a near-fatal
auto accident hasn't kept Bruce Kimball from
becoming one of the world's premier platform
divers. *Sporting news (St. Louis) 198(4), 23 Jul
1984, Olympic special insert, 8;10.*
LEVEL: B LANG: Eng SIRC ARTICLE NO: 096638

Scott, B.T. No rest for the best: though this diving
star has no equal, he won't rest at the top of his
sport. (Greg Lougani *Sports now (St. Louis, Mo.)
2(5), May 1984, 18.*
LEVEL: B LANG: Eng SIRC ARTICLE NO: 098047

Stathoplos, D. No one does it better. There's no
surer bet for a gold medal than Greg Louganis of
the U.S., a diver who is s skilled in his complex
sport that he soars far above his rivals. Here's why.
*Sports illustrated (Chicago, Ill.) 61(4), 18 Jul 1984,
480-484;487;490;493.*
NOTES: Special preview: the 1984 Olympics.
LEVEL: B LANG: Eng SIRC ARTICLE NO: 096639

Tymn, M. A pioneer in women's sports. (Aileen
Niggin) *National masters news (Van Ruys, Calif.)
72, Aug 1984, 6-7;9.*
LEVEL B LANG: Eng SIRC ARTICLE NO: 098049

BIOMECHANICS

Brown, J.G. Abraham, L.D. Bertin, J.J.
Descriptive analysis of the rip entry in competitive
diving. (Refs: 19)*Research quarterly for exercise &
sport (Reston, Va.) 55(2), Jun 1984, 93-102.*
ABST: The purpose of this study was to identify the
factors which enable certain highly skilled divers to
enter the water without apparent splash. Twelve
elite male divers performed four dives each, all of
which were filmed for later analysis. The main

difference between rip entries (no splash) and non-rip entries (splash) appears to be that divers performing a rip entry move their arms ventrally just prior to impact whereas divers performing a non-rip entry move their arms dorsally just prior to impact. There were no anthropometric differences between rip and non-rip entry divers.
LEVEL: A LANG: Eng SIRC ARTICLE NO: 096635

Miller, D.I. Biomechanical characteristics of the final approach step, hurdle and take-off of elite American springboard divers. (Refs: 9)*Journal of human movement studies (London) 10(4), 1984, 189-212.*
ABST: Temporal, displacement and velocity characteristics of the final approach step, hurdle and take-off of 6 male and 10 female elite American divers were analysed cinematographically. The length of their final approach steps and hurdles averaged 59 and 36 per cent of their heights, respectively. The men had higher average vertical velocities than the women at the beginning of hurdle flight (3.4 m/s vs 2.8 m/s). Consequently, they spent a longer time in the air (0.77 sec vs 0.66 sec for the women) resulting in a greater downward velocity at the beginning of the take-off (minus 4.2 m/s vs minus 3.6 m/s). By the end of the take-off, the men's upward velocity for a given dive was approximately 1 m/s greater than that for women.
LEVEL: A LANG: Eng SIRC ARTICLE NO: 104671

Miller, D.I. Munro, C.F. Body segment contributions to height achieved during the flight of a springboard dive. (Refs: 8) *Medicine and science in sports and exercise (Indianapolis) 16(3), June 1984, 234-242.*
ABST: The way in which athletes achieve the necessary height to accomplish the rotational requirements of springboard dives was investigated by focusing upon the take-offs of dives from the forward and reverse groups. Films of eight women and of five men provided data for the analysis. The vertical acceleration of the diver's center of gravity was expressed relative to that of the metatarsals, which represented the point on the board directly beneath the feet. The divers were only able to accelerate upward relative to the metatarsals for approximately the first half of springboard depression. This period of positive relative acceleration was considered to be a key factor in effective deflection of the springboard. The lower extremities were responsible for about three-quarters of the diver's vertical acceleration during this period. Two-thirds of their contribution was attributed to their role in accelerating the large mass of the trunk upward. The upper extremities accounted for about 10 per cent of the diver's vertical acceleration during the initial half of springboard depression.
LEVEL: A LANG: Eng SIRC ARTICLE NO: 108591

CHILDREN

Jones, D. Je plonge pour le plaisir. Ottawa: Association canadienne de plongeon amateur, c1984. 24 p. : ill.
CORP: Association canadienne du plongeon amateur.
NOTES: Titre de la couverture: Sylvie Bernier dit 'Je plonge pour le plaisir'. Also published in English under the title: I dive for fun.
LEVEL: B LANG: Fr GV838.62.C45 18790

Jones, D. I dive for fun. Ottawa: Canadian Amateur Diving Association, c1984. 24 p. : ill.
CORP: Canadian Amateur Diving Association.

NOTES: Cover title: Sylvie Bernier says 'I dive for fun'. Aussi publie en francais sous le titre: Je plonge pour le plaisir.
LEVEL: B LANG: Eng GV838.62.C45 18789

COACHING

Kimball, D. Dick Kimball's advice. *Diver (Portland, Conn.) 5(2), Apr/May 1984, 8-9;19.*
LEVEL: B LANG: Eng SIRC ARTICLE NO 093392

Newman, S. Jellyfish, springboards and Ron O'Brien; a look at one of the World's leading diving coaches. *Coaching review 7, Mar/Apr 1984, 35-38.*
LEVEL: B LANG: Eng SIRC ARTICLE NO: 093394

DIRECTORIES

1984 United States diving directory. Indianapolis, Ind.: United States Diving, 1984. 46 p.
CORP: United States Diving.
LEVEL B LANG: Eng GV838.63.U5 15781

FACILITIES

Desmarais, H. Les tremplins. *Alerte (Montreal) 17, mars 1984, 21-25.*
LEVEL: B LANG: Fr SIRC ARTICLE NO: 098045

INJURIES AND ACCIDENTS

Brown, M.L. Boegli, C. Design of swimming pool liners to reduce spinal cord injuries. *In, Proceedings of the 1st Mid-Centra Ergonomics/Human-Factors Conference, Cincinnati, Ohio, April 12-13, 1984, Edited by A. Mital, p. 298-303.*
LEVEL: I LANG: Eng

DeMers, G. Competitive diving and swimming. *In, Adams, S.H. (ed.), et al., Catastrophic injuries in sports: avoidance strategies, Salinas, Calif., Cayote Press, c1984, p. 22-37.*
LEVEL: I LANG: Eng RD97 19088

Scarfi, G. Mariani, D. Calabrese, C. Incidenza delle fratture vertebrali mieliche nei traumi sportivi. Occurrence of sport traumas in vertebral fractures with neurologic involvement. (Refs: 7)*Italian journal of sports traumatology (Milano, Italy) 6(4), Oct/Dec 1984, 297-301.*
CONF: S.I.O.T. Congress (68th : 1983 : Rome)
ABST: In this paper the statistical occurrence of sport traumas within a very large case-study of vertebral fractures involving neurologic damage is reported. Following a careful analysis of the causes and mechanism of the lesion according to the particular sport in question, the authors conclude by pointing out that all too often carelessness and inadequate technical and athletic preparation represent determining factors in the cause of these lesions.
LEVEL: A LANG: It Eng SIRC ARTICLE NO: 105795

NUTRITION

Taylor, T. Nutrition scene: water, a diver's friend in more ways than one. *Diver (Portland, Conn.) 5(1), Feb/Mar 1984, 18-19.*
LEVEL: B LANG: Eng SIRC ARTICLE NO: 098048

PHYSICS

Cooke, P. Physics on the high dive. *In, Schrier, E.W. and Allman, W.F. (eds.), Newton at the bat: the science in sports, Ne York, Scribner, c1984, p. 145-149.*
LEVEL: I LANG: Eng RC1235 18609

PROTECTIVE DEVICES

DeMarie, J. Wrestling earguards solve diving problem. *Diver 4(6), Dec 1983/Jan 1984, 13-14.*
LEVEL: B LANG: Eng SIRC ARTICLE NO: 093391

RULES AND REGULATIONS

How the game is played. *Women's sports (Palo Alto, Calif.) 6(4), Apr 1984, 48.*
LEVEL: B LANG: Eng SIRC ARTICLE NO: 101211

SAFETY

Harlan, B. Vosler, K. Tower diving safety. *Florida journal of health, physical education, recreation and dance (Gainsville, Fla.) 22(1), Feb 1984, 18.*
LEVEL: B LANG: Eng SIRC ARTICLE NO: 096636

TEACHING

Atkinson, D. Edgeworth, M.A. Jones, T. McCune, E. Music, G. I teach for fun. Ottawa: Canadian Amateur Diving Association, c1984. 38 p. : ill.
CORP: Canadian Amateur Diving Association Inc..
LEVEL: B LANG: Eng GV838.67.T4 18787

TECHNIQUES AND SKILLS

Billingsley, H. Forward 1-1/2 somersaults-layout (3 meter). *Diver 4(6), Dec 1983/Jan 1984, 18-19.*
LEVEL: B LANG: Eng SIRC ARTICLE NO: 093389

Billingsley, H. Hobie's illustrated dives: flying forward 1-1/2 somersaults - pike. (3 meter) *Diver (Portland, Conn.) 5(2), Apr/May 1984, 10-11.*
LEVEL: B LANG: Eng SIRC ARTICLE NO: 093390

Billingsley, H. Hobie's illustrated dives: flying forward 1-1/2 somersaults - tuck (1 meter). *Diver (Portland, Conn.) 5(1), Feb/Mar 1984, 16-17.*
LEVEL: B LANG: Eng SIRC ARTICLE NO: 098044

Billingsley, H. Forward double somersault - pike (1 meter). *Diver (Portland, Conn.) 5(4), Aug/Sept 1984, 12-13.*
LEVEL: B LANG: Eng SIRC ARTICLE NO: 099529

Coaches' corner. (Full twisting forward one and one-half somersault) *USA diving (Indianapolis, Ind.) 6(8), Nov 1984, 6-7.*
LEVEL: B LANG: Eng SIRC ARTICLE NO: 101210

Jerome, J. Diving: the art of aerial mathematics. *Science digest (New York) 92(8), Aug 1984, 38-39;88-89.*
LEVEL: B LANG: Eng SIRC ARTICLE NO: 096637

TRAINING AND CONDITIONING - DRILLS

Katchuk, R.L. Improving straight-position required dives via T-set drills: a training technique that greatly enhanced rotational control and entry consistency. *Scholastic coach (New York) 54(5), Dec 1984, 32-35;47.*
LEVEL: B LANG: Eng SIRC ARTICLE NO: 103136

DIVING (continued)

TRAINING AND CONDITIONING - WEIGHT AND STRENGTH TRAINING

Vosler, K.D. Diving strength program at the University of Florida. *National Strength & Conditioning Association journal 5(6), Jan 1984, 27-28.*
LEVEL: B LANG: Eng SIRC ARTICLE NO: 090589

DOWNHILL SKIING

Bilodeau, D. Are you ready for your first downhill? Probably not. But by following these pointers and getting yourself race ready you can enjoy the ride of your life. *Ski Canada 12(5), Jan 1984, 38-42.*
LEVEL: B LANG: Eng SIRC ARTICLE NO: 092360

Kidd, B. Grout, B. Billy Kidd's ski racing book. Chicago, Ill.: Contemporary Books, c1984. ix, 262 p. : ill.
NOTES: Include index.
LEVEL: I LANG: Eng ISBN: 0809254123 LC CARD: 84-016989 GV854.9.R3 18322

Sevack, M. Full bore on their boards. (speed skiing) *Ski Canada (Toronto) 12(6), Spring 1984, 18;20-21.*
LEVEL: B LANG: En SIRC ARTICLE NO: 098478

BIOGRAPHY AND AUTOBIOGRAPHY

Fisher, M. Podborski won't spell it out, but he's probably millionaire. Trust fund earnings only tip of iceberg for skiers. *Globe and mail 141(41,913), 6 Apr 1984, 17.*
LEVEL: B LANG: Eng SIRC ARTICLE NO: 092366

Hobson, A. Laurie Graham, l'avenir est a portee de la main. Laurie Graham, the future is now. *Champion 8(1), Feb 1984, 34-35.*
LEVEL: B LANG: Eng Fr SIRC ARTICLE NO: 090883

Kramon, G. On top of the world: Tamara McKinney is the U.S. team's best hope for a gold in Alpine skiing. *Women's sports (Palo Alto, Calif.) 6(2), Feb 1984, 40-43.*
LEVEL: B LANG: Eng SIRC ARTICLE NO: 099904

Lewis, G. Bill Johnson: skiing's Lone Ranger. *Skiing (Boulder, Colo.) 37(1), Sept 1984, 170;172-173;175;177;179;202.*
LEVEL: B LANG: Eng SIRC ARTICLE NO: 099906

Miller, P. Being Bill 'there is basically nothing I can't do right or at any other time'. (Billy Johnson) *Ski (New York) 49(3), Nov 1984, 46-48;50;52;56;58;63.*
LEVEL: B LANG: Eng SIRC ARTICLE NO: 099912

Perlman, E. Ballistics of speed skiing. *In, Schrier, E.W. and Allman, W.F. (eds.), Newton at the bat: the science in sports New York, Scribner, c1984, p. 131-133.*
LEVEL: B LANG: Eng RC1235 18609

Sevack, M. Klammer: the other side. Self-portrait of a comeback champ - with a little help from his friend. (Franz Klammer) *Ski 48(6), Feb 1984, 72;74;76.*
LEVEL: B LANG: Eng SIRC ARTICLE NO: 093732

Shames, L. Reckless: Bill Johnson is unsafe at any speed. *Outside (Chicago, Ill.) 9(10), Nov 1984, 46-50;86-87.*
LEVEL: B LANG: Eng SIRC ARTICLE NO: 173264

CHILDREN

Lucas, J. Lucas, J. Teaching children to ski. (Refs: 4)*Journal of professional ski coaching and instruction (Boulder, Colo. May 1984, 31-40.*
LEVEL: B LANG: Eng SIRC ARTICLE NO: 096811

COACHING

Best ever. Calgary '88. The team behind the team. *Ski Canada magazine (Toronto) 13(4), Dec 1984, 67;69;71-73.*
NOTES: The fourth in a six-part series.
LEVEL: B LANG: Eng SIRC ARTICLE NO: 106043

Yugoslavs test young racers. *Ski racing (Poultney, Vt.) 17(5), Nov 1984, 16.*
LEVEL: B LANG: Eng SIRC ARTICLE NO: 107522

COUNTRIES AND REGIONS

Best ever. Calgary '88. What does it take to make a ski racer? *Ski Canada magazine (Toronto) 13(2), Oct 1984, 67;69;71;73.*
NOTES: The second of a six-part series.
LEVEL: B LANG: Eng SIRC ARTICLE NO: 106044

Lennie, I. Making the team. The success of Steve Podborski, Todd Brooker, and the rest of the Canadian men's downhill team i the result of a concerted effort begun twelve years ago. *Saturday night Jan 1984, 59-61.*
LEVEL: B LANG: Eng SIRC ARTICLE NO: 092370

Meyers, E.J. Skiers: a closer look. *Journal of professional ski coaching and instruction (Boulder, Colo.) May 1984, 42-44.*
LEVEL: B LANG: Eng SIRC ARTICLE NO: 096812

Robbins, P. Japan studies U.S. ski racing. *Ski racing (Poultney, Vt.) 17(5), Nov 1984, 8.*
LEVEL: B LANG: Eng SIRC ARTICLE NO: 107514

DISABLED

Neff, F. Les sportifs handicapes connaissent-ils aussi l'angoisse et le stress? *Macolin (Macolin, Suisse) 41(11), nov 1984, 16.*
NOTES: Traduction de, Marianne Weber.
LEVEL: B LANG: Fr SIRC ARTICLE NO: 108756

ECONOMICS

Read, K. Racers could decide the future of downhill. *Ski Canada magazine (Toronto) 13(3), Nov 1984, 86-88.*
LEVEL: B LANG: Eng SIRC ARTICLE NO: 099915

EQUIPMENT

Grout, W. The super G's: the new World Cup even has spawned a new generation of high-speed cruisers. Here are reports on ten notable models, with slop- and bench-test results. *Skiing 36(6), Feb 1984, 94;96-98.*
LEVEL: B LANG: Eng SIRC ARTICLE NO: 093711

FACILITIES

Fry, J. Calgary 1988: will the thrill be gone? *Ski (New York) 49(3), Nov 1984, 32.*
LEVEL: B LANG: Eng SIRC ARTICLE NO: 099896

INJURIES AND ACCIDENTS

Injury-related trauma overcoming your fears. *Slimmer (Santa Monica, Calif.) 5(7), Dec 1984, 63-64.*
LEVEL: B LANG: Eng SIRC ARTICLE NO: 173237

SPORTING EVENTS

Kidd, B. The Aspen Winternational: with an outstanding GS course and a technically difficult downhill that challenges the world's best, Aspen, Colo., has become a key stop on the World Cup circuit. *Skiing 36(5), Jan 1984, 67-68;70.*
LEVEL: B LANG: Eng SIRC ARTICLE NO: 093722

Sevack, M. Downhillers come out of the closet: finally, an event for skiers who have no business on a race course. Whether you're fast, fat or forty, recreational downhills are for you, and everyone else. *Ski Canada 12(5), Jan 1984, 34-36;47-48.*
LEVEL: B LANG: Eng SIRC ARTICLE NO: 092378

Sevack, M. Whistler: now a race to be reckoned with. *Ski Canada (Toronto) 12(6), Spring 1984, 22-28.*
LEVEL: B LANG: Eng SIRC ARTICLE NO: 098477

TECHNIQUES AND SKILLS

Joubert, G. How Bill Johnson won the gold. *Skiing (Boulder, Colo.) 37(1), Sept 1984, 199-202.*
LEVEL: B LANG: Eng SIRC ARTICLE NO: 099903

Joubert, G. What makes a great downhill racer? It's not just courage, says the author, a top analyst of ski technique, in assessing the personal and technical elements essential to a modern world-class downhiller. *Skiing (Los Angeles) 37(2), Oct 1984, 218-219;223-224;226;228.*
LEVEL: B LANG: Eng SIRC ARTICLE NO: 103435

DRESSAGE

CHOREOGRAPHY AND MUSIC

Grimes, N. Riding to music: part 2 - rhythm and paces. *Equi (Cheshire, Eng.) 23, Aug/Sept 1984, 13-14.*
NOTES: To be continued.
LEVEL: B LANG: Eng SIRC ARTICLE NO: 101346

Grimes, N. Music in riding. Part 3 - music to help 'difficult' horses. *Equi (Cheshire, Eng.) 24, Oct/Nov 1984, 27-28.*
LEVEL: B LANG: Eng SIRC ARTICLE NO: 109658

Musto, J. Movements with music. *Horse & driving (Macclesfield, Eng.) Nov/Dec 1984, 44-45.*
LEVEL: B LANG: Eng SIRC ARTICLE NO: 105947

COACHING

di Craiker, P. George Theodorescu-USET dressage coach. *Horses (Beverley Hills, Calif.) 22(2), Winter 1984, 33-34.*
LEVEL: LANG: Eng SIRC ARTICLE NO: 099715

COUNTRIES AND REGIONS

de Szinay, A. Thinking aloud. US dressage 1983 - the state of the states. *Dressage & CT (Cleveland, Ohio) 21(2), Feb 1984, 25;39.*
LEVEL: B LANG: Eng SIRC ARTICLE NO: 098192

DIRECTORIES

USDF dressage directory: instructors, clinicians, trainers, judges, technical delegates. 4th ed. Lincoln, Nebr.: United States Dressage Federation, 1984. 94 p. : ill.
CORP: United States Dressage Federation.
LEVEL: I LANG: Eng SF309.5 18459

HISTORY

Froissard, J. Froissard, L. Dressage at the Olympics in 1932: passage, piaffe and pirouette were introduced for the first time. *Horse & driving (West Yorkshire, Eng.) 36, Mar/Apr 1984, 30-31.*
LEVEL: B LANG: Eng SIRC ARTICLE NO: 099720

Henriquet, M. Savoir lire... Baucher par exemple. *Cheval-magazine (Paris) 153, 1984, 44-47.*
LEVEL: B LANG: Fr

Powell, L. Francois Baucher the creative genius. *Equi (Cheshire, Eng.) 22, Jun/Jul 1984, 11-13;15.*
NOTES: History of equitation, part 10.
LEVEL: B LANG: Eng SIRC ARTICLE NO: 099748

HORSES

Boesche, J. What does the dressage rider want from the breeder? *Dressage & CT (Cleveland, Ohio) 21(1), Jan 1984, 30;32.*
NOTES: Speech given on April 7, 1983, at the Annual Membership Meeting of the Association of Breeders of the Hanoverian Warmblood, in Verden, FRG.
LEVEL: B LANG: Eng SIRC ARTICLE NO: 095098

JUDGING

Valko, C. The philosophy of judging & judging in general. *Dressage & CT (Cleveland Heights, Ohio) 21(3), Mar 1984, 5;23.*
LEVEL: B LANG: Eng SIRC ARTICLE NO: 171487

SPORTING EVENTS

Bezugloff, I.I. Equestrian Olympic Games in retrospect: part 1. Stockholm 1912 - Los Angeles 1932. *Dressage & CT (Cleveland Heights, Ohio) 21(3), Mar 1984, 6-9.*
LEVEL: B LANG: Eng SIRC ARTICLE NO: 171488

STRATEGY

Ostergaard, G. Dressage arena strategy: the international-caliber trainer demonstrates the techniques that make a winning ride. *Practical horseman (Unionville, Pa.) 12(11), Nov 1984, 6-9;12;14-A-14-B;14-D;14-F.*
LEVEL: B LANG: Eng SIRC ARTICLE NO: 105948

TEACHING

Preketes, A. Sawyer, T. Teaching the teachers: the USDF/Violet M. Hopkins National Seminar for dressage instructors. *USDF bulletin (Lincoln, Nebr.) 11(3), Fall 1984, 12-16;18.*
LEVEL: B LANG: Eng SIRC ARTICLE NO: 103261

TECHNIQUES AND SKILLS

Fabre, L. La position du cavalier a cheval dans les transitions de deux pistes. *Plaisirs equestres (Paris) 137, 1984, 65-69*
NOTES: Suite du no. 134 et 136.
LEVEL: B LANG: Eng

Francis, V. Val Francis discusses travers and demi-pirouette. *Horse and rider (Surrey, Eng.) 38(382), Feb 1984, 38-39.*
LEVEL: B LANG: Eng SIRC ARTICLE NO: 099719

Meredith, K. Half-halt: as elusive as a unicorn. *Dressage & CT (Cleveland, Ohio) 21(1), Jan 1984, 4-5.*
LEVEL: B LANG: Eng SIRC ARTICLE NO: 095115

Wagschal, J.L. Walk, trot and halt. *Canadian Arabian news (Bowden, Alta.) 24(4), Apr 1984, 25-26.*
LEVEL: B LANG: Eng SIRC ARTICLE NO: 098256

TESTING AND EVALUATION

Wagschal, J.L. Arabian dressage: actual riding in a dressage performance. *Canadian Arabian news (Bowden, Alta.) 24(8), Aug 1984, 4;8;10.*
LEVEL: B LANG: Eng SIRC ARTICLE NO: 099760

Wagschal, J.L. Arabian dressage: the canter & walk on a loose rein. *Canadian Arabian news (Bowden, Alta.) 24(7), Jul 1984, 7-8;12.*
LEVEL: B LANG: Eng SIRC ARTICLE NO: 099761

TRAINING AND CONDITIONING

Froissard, J. Schooling from A to Z: lateral suppling. Part 9. *Equi (Warrington, Eng.) 20, Jan/Feb 1984, 3-4.*
NOTES: To b continued.
LEVEL: B LANG: Eng SIRC ARTICLE NO: 095104

Froissard, J. Schooling from A-Z; part 10. Longitudinal suppling. *Equi (Cheshire, Eng.) 21, Apr/May 1984, 7-8.*
NOTES: To be continued.
LEVEL: B LANG: Eng SIRC ARTICLE NO: 098200

Palm, L. Training your horse for the hunt seat futurities. Lesson five: the finishing touches. *Performance horseman (Unionville, Pa.) 3(10), Sept 1984, 47-53;56.*
LEVEL: B LANG: Eng SIRC ARTICLE NO: 098224

Palm, L. Lynn Palm training your horse for the hunt seat futurities. Lesson one: getting started. *Performance horseman (Unionville, Pa.) 3(6), May 1984, 50-57.*
LEVEL: B LANG: Eng SIRC ARTICLE NO: 099747

Step-by-step: Lynn Palm. Training your horse for the hunt seat futurities: whether your horse is a futurity prospect or a candidate for regular hunt-seat classes, this easy-to-use 'building blocks' approach from a famous hunt-seat trainer will help you make the most of his natural talents. *Performance horseman (Unionville, Pa.) 3(9), Aug 1984, 49-55;58-59.*
NOTES: Lesson four: Beginning mounted work.
LEVEL: B LANG: Eng SIRC ARTICLE NO: 103269

Step-by-step: Lynn Palm. Training your horse for the hunt seat futurities: whether your horse is a futurity prospect or a candidate for regular hunt-seat classes, this easy-to-use 'building blocks' approach from a famous hunt-seat trainer will help you make the most of his natural talents.

Performance horseman (Unionville Pa.) 3(7), Jun 1984, 50-58.
NOTES: Lesson two: Groundwork.
LEVEL: B LANG: Eng SIRC ARTICLE NO: 103271

DRIVING

Bloom, L. Pleasure driving: harnessing, dress, and show ring etiquette. *Western horseman (Colorado Springs, Colo.) 49(1), Nov 1984, 34-36.*
LEVEL: B LANG: Eng SIRC ARTICLE NO: 108809

EQUIPMENT

Cantle, G. Basic measurement for gigs: achieving the maximum efficiency of the horse with comfort and convience. *Horse & driving (West Yorkshire, Eng.) 37, May/Jun 1984, 46-49.*
LEVEL: I LANG: Eng SIRC ARTICLE NO: 101338

Hansen, K. Collection: bits and bitting. *Carriage journal (Salem, N.J.) 22(3), Winter 1984, 133-134.*
LEVEL: B LANG: Eng SIRC ARTICLE NO: 173021

HISTORY

American driving methods. *Carriage journal (Salem, N.J.) 22(3), Winter 1984, 129-132.*
LEVEL: B LANG: Eng SIRC ARTICLE NO: 173020

Ryder, T. The Governess cart. *Carriage journal (Salem, N.J.) 22(3), Winter 1984, 122-125.*
LEVEL: B LANG: Eng SIRC ARTICLE NO: 173019

Ryder, T. The suspension of American carriages. (Refs: 2)*Carriage journal (Salem, N.J.) 22(3), Winter 1984, 145-149.*
LEVEL: B LANG: Eng SIRC ARTICLE NO: 173022

SPORTING EVENTS

Kellogg, J. Competitive trail driving: Something new on the driving scene. *Carriage journal (Salem, N.J.) 22(3), Winter 198 155-156.*
LEVEL: B LANG: Eng SIRC ARTICLE NO: 173023

TECHNIQUES AND SKILLS

Hansen, K. The education of the driving horse: Achenbach's safe, sane driving grips. *Carriage journal (Salem, N.J.) 22(2), Fall 1984, 66-68.*
LEVEL: B LANG: Eng SIRC ARTICLE NO: 101347

TRAINING AND CONDITIONING

Hansen, K. Trots and more trots. *Carriage journal (Salem, N.J.) 22(1), Summer 1984, 9-11.*
LEVEL: B LANG: Eng SIRC ARTICLE NO: 098205

Roth, C.D. Driving the light horse: training for pleasure and competition. New York: Arco, 1984. 1v.
NOTES: Includes index.
LEVEL: B LANG: Eng ISBN: 0668056525 LC CARD: 83-025667

Step-by-step: Lynn Palm. Training your horse for the hunt seat futurities: whether your horse is a futurity prospect or a candidate for regular hunt-seat classes, this easy-to-use 'building blocks' approach from a famous hunt-seat trainer will help you make the most of his natural talents. *Performance horseman (Unionville Pa.) 3(8), Jul 1984, 47-53.*

NOTES: Lesson three: Ground-driving and the cart.
LEVEL: B LANG: Eng SIRC ARTICLE NO: 103270

Von Blixen-Fincke, H. The Swedish way: part 4: communication. *Horse & driving (West Yorkshire, Eng.) 37, May/Jun 1984, 39-40.*
LEVEL: B LANG: Eng SIRC ARTICLE NO: 101365

VETERINARY MEDICINE

Grenside, F.C. The horses's mouth. *Carriage journal (Salem, N.J.) 22(2), Fall 1984, 91-93.*
NOTES: Excerpt from, Grenside, F.C., Essays on horse subjects, New York, 1907.
LEVEL: B LANG: Eng SIRC ARTICLE NO: 101345

DRUGS AND DOPING

Beckett, A.H. Drugs in sport. *Sportsmedicine digest (Van Nuys, Calif.) 6(3), Mar 1984, 2-3.*
LEVEL: B LANG: Eng SIRC ARTICLE NO: 097453

Bergman, R.T. Drug abuse: an ever-growing problem. *First aider (Gardner, Kans.) 54(3), Nov 1984, 1;4-5.*
LEVEL: B LANG: En SIRC ARTICLE NO: 108458

Brown, T.C. Benner, C. The nonmedical use of drugs in sports. (Refs: 55)
NOTES: In, Scott, W.N. (ed.) et al., Principles of sports medicine, Baltimore, Williams & Wilkins, c1984, p. 32-39.
LEVEL: I LANG: Eng RC1210 18016

Buzzeo, R.W. Kaverman, D. A commentary on the national scope of drug problems. *Athletic training 19(1), Spring 1984, 11-13.*
LEVEL: B LANG: Eng SIRC ARTICLE NO: 091341

Dugal, R. Information for athletes, coaches and medical practioners on the safe, restricted and banned use of drugs in amateur sport. Renseignements sur les medicaments acceptables, declarables et proscrits dans le Sport Amateur a l'intention des athletes, des entraineurs et des medecins. *Sport med info (Ottawa, Ont.) 4(2), 1984, 1-7.*
LEVEL: B LANG: Eng SIRC ARTICLE NO: 102386

Dymen, P.G. Drugs and the adolescent athlete. *Pediatric annals (New York) 13(8), Aug 1984, 602-604.*
LEVEL: I LANG: Eng

Findlay, S.F. Common drugs can be abused, too. The next time you swallow that painkiller or pour that nighttime cold medicine, stop and think: does it do what you want it to - or more than you expected it to? *Runner's world (Mountain View, Calif.) 19(7), Jul 1984, 56-60;123-124.*
LEVEL: I LANG: Eng SIRC ARTICLE NO: 094271

Harichaux, P. Why do sportsmen use dopes? Why should they not use them? The two questions in the title comprise the entire problem. *World gymnastics (Budapest, Hungary) 2(19), 1984, 26-27.*
LEVEL: B LANG: Eng SIRC ARTICLE NO: 097458

Les drogues interdites. (Refs: 21)*Revue de l'entraineur janv/mars 1984, 11-13.*
LEVEL: B LANG: Fr SIRC ARTICLE NO: 091345

Mallejac, J. Drogue et fric discreditent le sport. *Revue de l'entraineur (Montreal) oct/dec 1984, 24.*
LEVEL: B LANG: Fr SIRC ARTICLE NO: 105195

Poulet, D. Dopage: l'enigme des steroides. *Marathon, la revue de la bonne forme (Montreal) 15, avr 1984, 20-22.*
LEVEL: B LANG: Fr SIRC ARTICLE NO: 108694

Prieser, U. Doping: the use of drugs. It deceives the opponent, the spectator and the athlete himself. *Sport & fitness (Sunbury, Middlesex) Nov 1984, 24-25;66.*
LEVEL: B LANG: Eng SIRC ARTICLE NO: 109019

Rooney, R.F. Sports and clean living: a useful myth? *Drug and alcohol dependence (Lausanne) 13(1), Jan 1984, 75-87.*
ABST: The effects of school athletics upon participants' concern for health and community norms were investigated through a correlational analysis of sports participation and use of mood-altering drugs among high school seniors. The results of this study indicate that participation in all types of sports has very little effect on the use of mood-altering drugs.
LEVEL: A LANG: Eng

Ryan, A.J. More hormone abuse. *Physician and sportsmedicine (Minneapolis, Minn.) 12(8), Aug 1984, 31.*
LEVEL: B LANG: Eng SIRC ARTICLE NO: 097466

Ryan, A.J. Causes and remedies for drug misuse and abuse by athletes. *JAMA: Journal of the American Medical Association (Chicago) 252(4), 27 Jul 1984, 517-519.*
LEVEL: B LANG: Eng SIRC ARTICLE NO: 102396

Strauss, R.H. Drugs in sports. (Refs: 37)
NOTES: In, Strauss, R.H. (ed.), Sports medicine, Philadelphia ; Toronto, Saunders, 1984, p. 481-491.
LEVEL: I LANG: Eng RC1210 17196

Zipes S.J. Recreational mood altering chemicals. *Athletic training (Greenville, N.C.) 19(2), Summer 1984, 84-87.*
NOTES: Schering Symposium.
LEVEL: I LANG: Eng SIRC ARTICLE NO: 094281

ALCOHOL

Crawford, A. Alcohol and expectancy--II. Perceived sex differences in the role of alcohol as a source of aggression. *Alcoho and alcoholism (Oxford) 19(1), 1984, 71-75.*
LEVEL: A LANG: Eng

Exercise, alcohol and good cholesterol. *Health letter (San Antonio, Tex.) 23(10), 25 May 1984, 3-4.*
LEVEL: B LANG: Eng SIRC ARTICLE NO: 094248

Hollinshead, K. Liquor licensing: for leisure and recreation. A workshop on liquor licensing, legislation and facility provision for recreation centres, community complexes, sports bodies, leisure organisations and other concerned practitioners and individuals. Victoria, Australia: The Institute of Recreation (Vic.), 1984. 106 p.
CONF: Liquor Licensing: for Leisure and Recreation (1983 : City of Moorabbin).
CORP: Institute of Recreation (Vic.).
NOTES: Cover title: Proceedings for liquor licensing: for leisure and recreation. Statewide seminar, March 1983.
LEVEL: I LANG: Eng ISBN: 0 949376 00 0 GV182 17877

Ledoux, M. L'alcool: un risque calcule? *Marathon (Montreal) 17, 1984, 12-13;53.*
LEVEL: B LANG: Fr SIRC ARTICLE NO: 103893

AMPHETAMINES

Ivy, J.L. Amphetamines in sports: are they worth the risk? (Refs: 4)*Sportsmedicine digest (Van Nuys, Calif.) 6(3), Mar 1984 1-2.*
LEVEL: B LANG: Eng SIRC ARTICLE NO: 097461

ANABOLIC STEROIDS

Alen, M. Suominen, J. Effect of androgenic and anabolic steroids on supermatogensis in power athletes. (Refs: 15) *International journal of sports medicine (Stuttgart) Suppl. 5, Nov 1984, 189-192.*
CONF: International Congress on Sports and Health (1983 : Maastricht, Netherlands).
LEVEL: A LANG: Eng SIRC ARTICLE NO: 103884

Alen, M. Haekkinen, K. Komi, P.V. Lihaksiston voimantuottokyvyn muutokset androgeenisia steroideja kaeyttaeneillae voimailijoila. (Changes in muscle power production capacity in power athletes self-administering androgenic anabolic steroids.) *Duodecim (Helsinki) 100(17), 1984, 1096-1104.*
LEVEL: A LANG: Fin

Appell, H.J. Heller-Umpfenbach, B. Feraudi, M. Weicker, H. Ultrastructural and morphometric investigations on the effects of training and administration of anabolic steroids on the myocardium of guinea pigs. (Refs: 31)*International journal of sports medicine (Stuttgart, FRG) 4(4), Dec 1983, 268-274.*
ABST: Twenty male mature guinea pigs were tested in this study for the purpose of demonstrating the effect of a training program, of anabolic steroids, and of both combined on the myocardium. The results show that both anabolic steroids and training have a similar effect on the cellular components but have different influences on mitochondrial proliferation. The combination of the two produces pathological alterations of the cells, a consequence of drug abuse that athletes should be aware of.
LEVEL: A LANG: Eng SIRC ARTICLE NO: 097452

Athletes and androgens: what's wrong with steroids? A panel discussion. *Pharos of Alpha Onega Alpha Honor Medical Society (Menlo Park, Calif.) 47(3), Summer 1984, 32-37.*
LEVEL: I LANG: Eng

Burkett, L.N. Falduto, M.T. Steroid use by athletes in a Metropolitan area. (Refs: 9)*Physician and sportsmedicine (Minneapolis, Minn.) 12(8), Aug 1984, 69-70;73-74.*
ABST: This article explores the use of anabolic steroid of 24 weight training athletes. Nineteen bodybuilders, two powerlifters, two football players, and one discus thrower were administered an oral questionnaire. Results showed that athletes took a combined steroid dose of four to eight times the recommended medical dose, stacked an injectable steroid with an oral steroid, and used the drugs for more than one cycle.
LEVEL: A LANG: Eng SIRC ARTICLE NO: 097964

Costill, D.L. Pearson, D.R. Fink, W.J. Anabolic steroid use among athletes: changes in HDL-C levels. (Refs: 12)*Physician an sportsmedicine (Minneapolis, Minn.) 12(6), Jun 1984, 112-117.*
ABST: Testing of nine strength trained men using anabolic steroids found their mean HDL-cholesterol levels to be significantly lower than that for untrained men and strength trained men who were

non-users. Research has linked low levels of HDL-C with a high incidence of coronary artery disease.
LEVEL: A LANG: Eng SIRC ARTICLE NO: 094269

Forsyth, A. Strong medicine. In the controversy over anabolic steroids, little attention has been paid to their damaging, long-term effects. *Saturday night 99(5), May 1984, 15-17.*
LEVEL: B LANG: Eng SIRC ARTICLE NO: 092739

Frankle, M.A. Cecero, G.J. Payne, J. Use of androgenic anabolic steroids by athletes. (letter) (Refs: 3)*JAMA: Journal of th American Medical Association (Chicago) 252(4), 27 Jul 1984, 482.*
LEVEL: B LANG: Eng SIRC ARTICLE NO: 102387

Geringer, D. The final word on steroids. *Runner's world (Mountain View, Calif.) 19(8), Aug 1984, 144-146;148;150-152;154.*
LEVEL: B LANG: Eng SIRC ARTICLE NO: 095789

Goldman, B. Bush, P. Klatz, R. Death in the locker room: steroids and sports. South Bend, Ind.: Icarus Press, 1984. xviii, 370 p. : ill.
NOTES: Includes index. Bibliography: p. 316-359.
LEVEL: A LANG: Eng ISBN: 0896511553 LC CARD: 84-006638 RC1230 17718

Goldman, B. Bush, P. Klatz, R. Drug merry-go-round an upper-downer trip. *Globe and Mail (Toronto) 141(42,005), 23 Jul 1984, 53.*
NOTES: Second in a three part series, titled Death in the locker room.
LEVEL: B LANG: Eng SIRC ARTICLE NO: 095790

Goldman, B. Bush, P. Klaty, R. Steroids for women, a reversal of nature. *Globe and mail (Toronto) 141(42,006), 24 Jul 1984, 54.*
NOTES: Third in a three part series, titled Death in the locker room.
LEVEL: B LANG: Eng SIRC ARTICLE NO: 095791

Goldman, B. The death of a friend - and anabolic steroids. *Globe and mail (Toronto) 141(42,004), 21 Jul 1984, S5.*
NOTES: First of a three part series.
LEVEL: B LANG: Eng SIRC ARTICLE NO: 095792

Goldman, B. Roids - the slow suicide. (anabolic steroids) *Flex (Woodland Hills, Calif.) 2(9), Dec 1984, 56-57;92-95.*
LEVEL: B LANG: Eng SIRC ARTICLE NO: 105189

Goldman, B. Drug queens: Death in the locker room, the book the native's press is raving about, takes a hard look at steroid use by women. What follows is a red-hot excerpt. *Muscle & fitness (Woodland Hills, Calif.) 45(12), Dec 1984, 74-75;140-141;145-146;147-149.*
NOTES: Excerpt from, Goldman, B., Death in the locker room, South Bend, Indianna, Icarus Press, 1984.
LEVEL: B LANG: Eng SIRC ARTICLE NO: 109032

Hatfield, F.C. The last words on steroids. *Muscle and fitness (Woodland Hills, Calif) 45(2), Feb 1984, 86-87;181;185;187.*
LEVEL: B LANG: Eng SIRC ARTICLE NO: 095794

Haupt, H.A. Rovere, G.D. Anabolic steroids: a review of the literature. (Refs: 112)*American journal of sports medicine (Baltimore) 12(6), Nov/Dec 1984, 469-484.*
ABST: This detailed review provides a concise summary of the research literature on anabolic steroids. The review also assesses the side effects of anabolic steroids found in both athletes and non-athletes.
LEVEL: A LANG: Eng SIRC ARTICLE NO: 103890

Johnson, D.A. Use of anabolic steroids by athletes. (letter) *JAMA: Journal of the American Medical Association (Chicago) 251(11), 16 Mar 1984, 1430-1431.*
LEVEL: B LANG: Eng SIRC ARTICLE NO: 098925

Krakauer, J. Endocrine roulette: this introduces a new column which will examine how athletes of all types, ar all levels, attempt to alter their physiologies to gain a competitive edge. This first installment: steroids and growth hormones. *Ultrasport (Boston, Mass.) 1(5), Sept/Oct 1984, 22-26;28.*
LEVEL: I LANG: Eng SIRC ARTICLE NO: 173310

Kuc, J. For a drug-free sport. *Muscle and fitness (Woodland Hills, Calif.) 45(2), Feb 1984, 89;195.*
LEVEL: B LANG: Eng SIRC ARTICLE NO: 095796

Lamb, D.R. Anabolic steroids in athletics: how well do they work and how dangerous are they? (Refs: 84)*American journal of sports medicine (Baltimore, Md.) 12(1), Jan/Feb 1984, 31-38.*
ABST: This review of studies on the use of anabolic steroids shows that an increase of lean body weight generally results from the use of these drugs. Aerobic capacity does not appear to improve with the use of anabolic steroids. The side effects of anabolic steroid use have involved the secondary sex characteristics, such as testicular atrophy in men and masculization in women and liver function impairment.
LEVEL: I LANG: Eng SIRC ARTICLE NO: 094276

Lamb, D.R. Anabolic steroids and athletic performance. (Refs: 6)*Sports medicine digest (Van Nuys, Calif.) 6(7), Jul 1984, 1-3.*
LEVEL: B LANG: Eng SIRC ARTICLE NO: 100540

Lambert, M. Sports medicine review. *Powerlifting USA (Camarillo, Calif.) 8(3), Oct 1984, 7.*
LEVEL: I LANG: Eng SIRC ARTICLE NO: 173184

Les steroides anabolisants. *Revue de l'entraineur janv/mars 1984, 9-10.*
LEVEL: B LANG: Fr SIRC ARTICLE NO: 091354

Letter to the editor: are anabolic steroids for the long distance runner? *Annals of sports medicine (North Hollywood, Calif.) 2(1), 1984, 51-52.*
LEVEL: I LANG: Eng SIRC ARTICLE NO: 103894

Mellion, M.B. Anabolic steroids in athletics. (Refs: 19)*American family physician (Kansas) 30(1), Jul 1984, 113-119.*
LEVEL: I LANG: Eng SIRC ARTICLE NO: 103896

Meltzer, A. Steroids for athletes. (letter) *Pharos of Alpha Omego Alpha Honor Medical Society (Menlo Park, Calif.) 47(4), Fall 1984, 36-37.*
LEVEL: I LANG: Eng

Morgan, J.D. The athlete and anabolic steroids: effectiveness versus effects. *World water skiing (Winter Park, Fla.) 6(3), Jun 1984, 18.*
LEVEL: B LANG: Eng SIRC ARTICLE NO: 100541

Nassif, D. Steroid underground. *Muscle and fitness (Woodland Hills, Calif.) 45(2), Feb 1984, 92-93;202-204;206.*
LEVEL: B LANG: Eng SIRC ARTICLE NO: 095799

Peterson, G.E. Fahey, T.D. HDL-C in five elite athletes using anabolic-androgenic steroids. (Refs: 14)*Physician and sportsmedicine (Minneapolis, Minn.) 12(6), Jun 1984, 120-123;126;130.*
ABST: This study of five elite weight trained athletes measured HDL cholesterol levels during steroid use and while off steroids. The athletes had significantly lower HDL-C levels while using

steroids. These levels were also significantly lower than levels found in 28 healthy men of a similar age. Low HDL-C levels represent an elevated risk of heart disease.
LEVEL: A LANG: Eng SIRC ARTICLE NO: 094277

Research continues on steroids, growth hormone. *First aider (Gardner, Kans.) 54(3), Nov 1984, 1;12.*
LEVEL: B LANG: Eng SIRC ARTICLE NO: 108459

Riley, D.B. Danger. Athletics who are dying to win. Steroids are potential killers; doctors who prescribe them should be prosecuted. *Scholastic coach (New York) 54(4), Nov 1984, 48-50;66-67.*
LEVEL: B LANG: Eng SIRC ARTICLE NO: 102394

Sex hormones and athletes. *Health letter (San Antonio, Tex.) 23(9), 11 May 1984, 1-2.*
LEVEL: B LANG: Eng SIRC ARTICLE NO: 094279

Steroids '84. *Your health & fitness (Highland Park, Ill.) 6(3), Jun/Jul 1984, 26-27.*
LEVEL: B LANG: Eng SIRC ARTICLE NO: 095803

Strauss, R.H. Anabolic steroids. (Refs: 24)*Clinics in sports medicine (Philadelphia) 3(3), Jul 1984, 743-748.*
NOTES: Symposium on nutritional aspects of exercise.
ABST: Anabolic-androgenic steroid hormones are used by athletes in an attempt to improve performance. Side effects include decreased testosterone and sperm production, acne, balding, and increased aggression. The long-term effects are not known.
LEVEL: I LANG: Eng SIRC ARTICLE NO: 100544

Taylor, E. Steroids: over the competitive edge. can the rewards of taking steroids possibly be worth the risk? *New body (Ne York) 3(5), Sept 1984, 20;65-66;68.*
LEVEL: B LANG: Eng SIRC ARTICLE NO: 173282

Taylor, W. Severe liver diseases possibly associated with anabolic steroids. *Muscle digest (San Gabriel, Calif.) 8(4), Aug 1984, 8;34;41;43.*
LEVEL: B LANG: Eng SIRC ARTICLE NO: 103901

Taylor, W.N. Medicine: can't ignore the issue. *Muscle and fitness (Woodland Hills, Calif.) 45(2), Feb 1984, 88;187-188.*
LEVEL: B LANG: Eng SIRC ARTICLE NO: 095804

Taylor, W.N. Are anabolics atherogenic? *Strength & health (York, Pa.) 52(6), Oct/Nov 1984, 60-61.*
LEVEL: B LANG: Eng SIRC ARTICLE NO: 098929

Taylor, W.N. Anabolic steroid use by women athletes. *Powerlifting USA (Camarillo, Calif.) 8(3), Oct 1984, 20-21.*
LEVEL: I LANG: Eng SIRC ARTICLE NO: 173185

Taylor, W.N. Are anabolics atherogenic? *Powerlifting USA (Camarillo, Calif.) 8(2), Sept 1984, 18.*
LEVEL: I LANG: Eng SIRC ARTICLE NO: 173485

Wells, J. Biron, S. Androgens and anabolic steroids. (Refs: 19)*Athletic training (Greenville, N.C.) 19(3), Fall 1984, 175-177.*
LEVEL: I LANG: Eng SIRC ARTICLE NO: 098931

ANTI-INFLAMMATORY AGENTS

Zale, N. The risks and dangers of anti-arthritis drugs. *Iron man (Alliance, Neb.) 43(4), Apr/May 1984, 31;95-97.*
LEVEL: B LANG: Eng SIRC ARTICLE NO: 100546

DRUGS AND DOPING (continued)

BIBLIOGRAPHIES

Sport bibliography. *Track and field journal 25, Feb 1984, 14-15;22-23.*
LEVEL: B LANG: Eng SIRC ARTICLE NO: 092745

BLOOD DOPING

Glenhill, N. Blood doping. *Sportsmedicine digest (Van Nuys, Calif.) 6(3), Mar 1984, 4.*
LEVEL: B LANG: Eng SIRC ARTICLE NO 097457

Krakauer, J. Blood doping. *Ultrasport (Boston, Mass.) 1(6), Nov/Dec 1984, 20;22;24.*
LEVEL: B LANG: Eng SIRC ARTICLE NO: 172954

Robertson, R.J. Gilcher, R. Metz, K.F. Caspersen, C.J. Allison, T.G. Abbot, R.A. Skrinar, G.S. Krause, J.R. Nixon, P.A. Hemoglobin concentration and aerobic work capacity in women following induced erythrocythemia. (Refs: 31)*Journal of applied physiology: respiratory, environmental and exercise physiology (Bethesda, Md.) 57(2), Aug 1984, 568-575.*
ABST: This study investigates the effect of induced erythrocythemia on hemoglobin concentration (Hb) and work capacity. Nine women performed cycle tests at prereinfusion (T1), 2 days after a placebo infusion (T2), 2 days postreinfusion of 334 ml of red blood cells (T3), 8 days postreinfusion (T4), and 14 days postreinfusion (T5). The placebo did not have any effect. Hb increased at T3 and then remained constant. Physical work capacity was greater at T3, T4 and T5 than at T1.
LEVEL: A LANG: Eng SIRC ARTICLE NO: 108358

CAFFEINE

Delbeke, F.T. Debackere, M. Caffeine: use and abuse in sports. (Refs: 21)*International journal of sports medicine (Stuttgart) 5(4), Aug 1984, 179-182.*
ABST: The urinary caffeine content was compared between a control group and 775 cyclists checked for doping during the 1982 season. The data for sportsmen demonstrate that the (mis)use of caffeine is more pronounced in both professional and amateur classes than in the younger categories (debutant and junior). Caffeine was also monitored during a 60-h period in the urine of several coffee drinkers. Based on all results, a 'maximum level of caffeine' of 15 ug.ml-1 in urine for sporting competitions is proposed.
LEVEL: A LANG: Eng SIRC ARTICLE NO: 103889

Jerome, J. A cup of ambition: the caffeine kick - and its cost. *Outside (Chicago, Ill.) 9(5), Jun 1984, 29-31.*
LEVEL: B LANG: Eng SIRC ARTICLE NO: 100539

DIMETHYL SULFOXIDE

DMSO: American Academy of Pediatrics policy statement. *Physician and sportsmedicine 12(1), Jan 1984, 192.*
NOTES: Reprinted from, News and comment 33, Aug 1982, 13.
LEVEL: B LANG: Eng SIRC ARTICLE NO: 091344

Fried, T. The DMSO dilemma: some facts. (Refs: 23)*Sports: science periodical on research and technology in sport (Ottawa) O-2, Jul 1984, 1-5.*
LEVEL: I LANG: Eng SIRC ARTICLE NO: 095787

Fried, T. Le dilemme du DMSO. *Science du sport: documents de recherche et de technologie (Ottawa) O-2, juil 1984, 1-5.*
LEVEL: I LANG: Fr SIRC ARTICLE NO: 095788

DOPING

Actualite du dopage des sportifs. (Refs: 5)*Concours medical (Paris) 106(39), 1984, 3849-3850.*
LEVEL: I LANG: Fr

Barrault, D. Kubacsi, A. Le dopage des sportifs n'est pas l'affaire des medecins. *Generaliste (Paris) 626, 1984, 38-39.*
LEVEL: B LANG: Fr

Cugurra, F. Il doping: evoluzione, trasformazione. (Doping: development, transformation.) *Clinica terapeutica (Rome) 109(5) 15 June 1984, 397-403.*
LEVEL: I LANG: It

Dardik, I.I. Breaking the 'breakthrough' myth. *Physician and sportsmedicine 12(3), Mar 1984, 183.*
NOTES: Olympic update, part 2.
LEVEL: B LANG: Eng SIRC ARTICLE NO: 091342

de Mondenard, J.P. Une perversion du sport: le dopage. *Dans, Culture technique no. 13, Neuilly-sur-Seine, France, Centre de Recherche sur la Culture Technique, c1984, p. 184-193.*
LEVEL: I LANG: Fr RC1235 20096

Des questions morales surtout. *Revue de l'entraineur janv/mars 1984, 10-11.*
LEVEL: B LANG: Fr SIRC ARTICLE NO: 091343

Drug use and doping control in sport: a Sport Canada policy. L'usage de drogues et le controle du dopage dans le sport: une politique de Sport Canada. Ottawa: Fitness and Amateur Sport / Condition physique et sport amateur, 1984. 4, 4 p.
CORP: Canada. Fitness and Amateur Sport.
CORP: Canada. Condition physique et sport amateur.
NOTES: French and English texts on inverted pages with separate paging. Textes francais et anglais disposes tete-beche avec pagination separee.
LEVEL: B LANG: Eng Fr ISBN: 0-662-52847-6 RC1230 16074

How certain drugs can be used to aid competitors. *Weightlifters newsletter (West Newton, Mass.) 110, 5 May 1984, 17.*
LEVEL: LANG: Eng SIRC ARTICLE NO: 097460

Pepin, R. Des muscles en pilules: combien d'athletes revent, pour gagner les Jeux, de trouver la potion magique qui leur assurera la victoire? *Quebec science 22(6), fevr 1984, 18-25.*
LEVEL: B LANG: Fr SIRC ARTICLE NO: 091351

Peterson, D.M. Doping in sports: a primer for nurses. *Orthopedic nursing (Pitman, N.J.) 3(4), Jul/Aug 1984, 10-15.*
LEVEL: LANG: Eng SIRC ARTICLE NO: 103897

Sperryn, P. Drugged and victorious: doping in sport. *New scientist (London) 1415, 2 Aug 1984, 16-19.*
NOTES: We spend larg sums of money testing athletes for drugs, yet doping is still commonplace. An international revolt against the present system of drugs control is gathering momentum.
LEVEL: B LANG: Eng SIRC ARTICLE NO: 098928

DRUG CONTROL AND DETECTION

Beckett, A. Philosophy, chemistry and the athlete. *New scientist (London) 1415, 2 Aug 1984, 18.*
LEVEL: B LANG: Eng SIRC ARTICLE NO: 098921

Bilan d'un atelier 'ergogene'. *Revue de l'entraineur (Montreal) avr/juin 1984, 9-10.*
LEVEL: B LANG: Fr SIRC ARTICLE NO: 094267

Clarke, K.S. USOC drug control program. *Journal of physical education, recreation & dance (Reston, Va.) 55(4), Apr 1984, 23-24.*
LEVEL: B LANG: Eng SIRC ARTICLE NO: 094268

Connolly, H. Fair play through drug tests? *Muscle and fitness (Woodland, Hills, Calif) 45(2), Feb 1984, 90;195-196;199.*
LEVEL: B LANG: Eng SIRC ARTICLE NO: 095785

Di Pasquale, M.G. Drug use and detection in amateur sports. Warkworth, Ont.: M.G.D. Press, c1984. 123 p.
NOTES: Bibliography: p. 111-115.
LEVEL: I LANG: Eng RC1230 18908

Dickie, D. Surbir le test olympique. Passing the Olympic test. *Champion (Ottawa) 8(3), Aug 1984, 6-11.*
LEVEL: B LANG: Fr Eng SIRC ARTICLE NO: 095786

Duda, M. Drug testing challenges college and pro athletes. *Physician and sportsmedicine (Minneapolis, Minn.) 12(11), Nov 1984, 109-113;117-118.*
LEVEL: B LANG: Eng SIRC ARTICLE NO: 100537

Georges, C. Banned, but not forgotten: steroids won't just go away, but maybe their use can be made less pervasive in the Olympic sports. *Swimming technique (Los Angeles, Calif.) 20(3), Nov 1983/Jan 1984, 15-20.*
LEVEL: I LANG: Eng SIRC ARTICLE NO: 094272

Gulyas, H. Kemeny, G. Hollosi, I. Pucsok, J. Determination of some doping agents by overpressured thin-layer chromatography. *Journal of chromatography (Amsterdam) 291, 18 May 1984, 471-475.*
LEVEL: A LANG: Eng SIRC ARTICLE NO: 102388

Gunby, P. Olympics drug testing: basis for future study. *JAMA: Journal of the American Medical Association (Chicago) 252(4) 27 Jul 1984, 454-455;459-460.*
LEVEL: B LANG: Eng SIRC ARTICLE NO: 102389

Leach, R.E. Drug testing and the games. *Skiing 36(6), Feb 1984, 30-31;132.*
LEVEL: B LANG: Eng SIRC ARTICLE NO: 092740

Legwold, G. Have we learned a lesson about drugs in sports? *Physician and sportsmedicine 12(3), Mar 1984, 175-178;180.*
NOTES: Olympic update, part 2.
LEVEL: B LANG: Eng SIRC ARTICLE NO: 091349

Nightingale, D. Steroid Wars: the crackdown on drug use intensifies as the 1984 Summer Games draw near. *Sporting news (New York) 197(19), 7 May 1984, 2;12.*
LEVEL: B LANG: Eng SIRC ARTICLE NO: 092742

Oseid, S. Doping and athletes - prevention and counseling. (Refs: 2)*Journal of allergy and clinical immunology (St. Louis) 73(5 Pt 2), May 1984, 735-739.*
LEVEL: I LANG: Eng SIRC ARTICLE NO: 100542

Pepin, R. Des muscles en pilules: combien d'athletes revent, pour gagner les Jeux, de trouver la potion magique qui leur assurera la victoire? *Quebec science 22(6), fevr 1984, 18-25.*
LEVEL: B LANG: Fr SIRC ARTICLE NO: 091351

Prescott, L. Drug testing stricter in Norway than US. *Physician and sportsmedicine (Minneapolis, Minn.) 12(6), Jun 1984, 61.*
LEVEL: B LANG: Eng SIRC ARTICLE NO: 094278

Schaenzer, W. Untersuchungen zum Nachweis und Metabolismus von Hormonen und Dopingmitteln, insbesondere mit Hilfe der Hochdruckfluessigkeitschromatographie. Koeln: Deutsche Sporthochschule, Institut fuer Biochemie, 1984. 440 p.
NOTES: Thesis (Ph.D.) - Deutsche Sporthochschule Koeln, 1984. Bibliography: p. 415-440.
LEVEL: A LANG: Ger RC1230 19007

Taylor, W.N. We can not afford to falsely accuse our Olympic athletes. *Powerlifting U.S.A. (Camarillo, Calif.) 7(8), Mar 1984, 30.*
LEVEL: B LANG: Eng SIRC ARTICLE NO: 097469

USOC's war on drugs. *Swimming world and junior swimmer (Los Angeles, Calif.) 25(2), Feb 1984, 60-63.*
LEVEL: B LANG: Eng SIR ARTICLE NO: 094280

Vodickova, I. Haris, I.M. Hampl, R. Hanus, V. Derivaty nortestosteronovych metabolitu vhodne k priprave imunogenu pro radioimunologickou kontrolu dopingu. (Derivatives of nortestosterone metabolites useful in the preparation of immunogens for the radioimmunologic control of doping.) *Ceskoslovenska famarcie (Prague) 33(6), Jul 1984, 221-229.*
LEVEL: A LANG: Cze

DRUG POLICIES AND REGULATIONS

Athletes and anti-asthma/exercise-induced bronchospasm medications. *Sports mediscope (Colorado Springs) 4(2), Summer 1984, 12.*
NOTES: USOC sports medicine info sheet 11-2, July 1984.
LEVEL: B LANG: Eng SIRC ARTICLE NO: 095784

Dickie, D. Le controle du dopage. Doping crackdown. *Champion (Vanier, Ont.) 8(2), May/mai 1984, 52-57.*
LEVEL: B LANG: Fr Eng SIRC ARTICLE NO: 094270

Drug use and doping control in sport: a Sport Canada policy. L'usage de drogues et le controle du dopage dans le sport: une politique de Sport Canada. *Track and field journal 25, Feb 1984, 4-7.*
LEVEL: B LANG: Eng Fr SIRC ARTICLE NO: 092738

Gowan, G. Taking a stand. The CAC president lauds Sport Canada's recent stand on drug taking. *Coaching review 7, Jan/Feb 1984, 16.*
LEVEL: B LANG: Eng SIRC ARTICLE NO: 091347

Guidelines for the control of drug abuse. *ARA: Amateur Rowing Association Club news (Bedford, Eng.) 7(5), May 1984, 10.*
CORP: Sports Council.
LEVEL: B LANG: Eng SIRC ARTICLE NO: 108691

Legwold, G. Program offers aid to Olympics with EIB. (Exercise-induced bronchospasm) *Physician and sportsmedicine (Minneapolis, Minn.) 12(7), Jul 1984, 117-121;124;126.*

NOTES: Olympic update: the relationship between drugs and the Olympics.
LEVEL: B LANG: Eng SIRC ARTICLE NO: 095797

Mallejac, J. Drogues: le leadership du Canada. *Revue de l'entraineur janv/mars 1984, 33.*
LEVEL: B LANG: Fr SIRC ARTICLE NO: 091350

Oseid, S. Dopingmidler i idretten. Idrettsmyndighetenes regler og kontrolltiltak. (Doping in sports. The sports authorities' rules and control measures.) *Tidsskrift for den norske laegeforening (Oslo) 104(19/21), 30 Jun 1984, 1327-1329.*
LEVEL: B LANG: Nor

Policy on doping and drug usage. Politique sur le doping et l'usage des drogues. *Track and field journal (Ottawa) 26, May 1984, 4;6.*
CORP: Canadian Olympic Association.
CORP: Association olympique canadienne.
NOTES: As published by Sport Canada in January 1984. Publie par Sport Canada en janvier 1984.
LEVEL: B LANG: Eng Fr SIRC ARTICLE NO: 097464

Politiques de l'A.O.C. sur le doping et l'usage des drogues. Canadian Olympic Association policy on doping and drug usage. *Track and field journal 25, Feb 1984, 7-9.*
LEVEL: B LANG: Eng Fr SIRC ARTICLE NO: 092743

Recommendation no. R(84)19 of the Committee of ministers to member states on the 'European anti-doping charter for sport'. *Council of Europe Committee of Ministers Recommendation R(84)19, Sept 1984, 1-2.*
CORP: Council of Europe. Committee of Ministers.
LEVEL: I LANG: Eng SIRC ARTICLE NO: 105197

Teff, J. Administrating drug and alcohol codes. *Interscholastic athletic administration (Kansas City) 11(2), Winter 1984, 23;25.*
LEVEL: B LANG: Eng SIRC ARTICLE NO: 108264

DRUG THERAPY

Boel, J. Andersen, L.B. Rasmussen, B. Hansen, S.H. Dossing, M. Hepatic drug metabolism and physical fitness. *Clinical pharmacology and therapeutics (St. Louis) 36(1), Jul 1984, 121-126.*
ABST: Maximal oxygen uptake was measured in 14 subjects before and during 3 months of 4 to 8 hr of daily physical training. There was only a moderately significant correlation between the extent of change in VO2 max and the corresponding relative change in antipyrine metabolism during the 3-month period of this investigation. The correlation between oxygen uptake and aminopyrine metabolism was not significant. Improved physical fitness associated with enhanced drug metabolism may lead to changes in drug efficacy and drug toxicity that may be clinically important in the case of drugs with low therapeutic indices.
LEVEL: A LANG: Eng SIRC ARTICLE NO: 102382

Marechal, R. Utilisation du Reparil Gel dans les phenomenes inflammatoires d'origine sportive. (Refs: 14)*Medecine du sport (Paris) 58(2), 25 mars 1984, 41-44.*
RESUME: Le but de cette etude etait d'analyser l'impact therapeutique du Reparil Gel sur les lesions inflammatoires d'origine sportive. 111 patients presentant des lesions achilleennes (39 cas), ligamentaire laterale du genou (42 cas) ou rotuliennes (30 cas) furent traites par ionisation au Reparil-Gel et par 2 application cutanees

journalieres de ce meme produit. Dans 70% des cas, une rehabilitation complete fut observee moins de 2 semaines apres le debut du traitement.
LEVEL: A LANG: Fr SIRC ARTICLE NO: 094374

Sherman, M.F. Bonamo, J.R. Birrer, R.B. Injection therapy. (Refs: 8)
NOTES: In, Birrer, R.B. (ed.), Sports medicine for the primary care physician, Norwalk, Conn., Appleton-Century-Crofts, c1984, p. 269-272.
LEVEL: I LANG: Eng RC1210 17030

van Baak, M. The influence of drugs on physical performance. (Refs: 24)*International journal of sports medicine (Stuttgart) Suppl. 5, Nov 1984, 180-182.*
CONF: International Congress on Sports and Health (1983 : Maastricht, Netherlands).
LEVEL: A LANG: Eng SIRC ARTICLE NO: 103904

Youcha, G. The use and abuse of cortisone. Feeling the pressure to perform, athletes are paying the price for meddling with nature. *Runner's world 19(3), Mar 1984, 92-96;100-101.*
LEVEL: I LANG: Eng SIRC ARTICLE NO: 091356

ELECTRIC STIMULATION

Houston, M.E. La stimulation electrique des muscles. (Refs: 21)*Nouveautes en science de l'entrainement (Ottawa) 1984, 20-22.*
NOTES: Traduction d'un article redige par Michael E. Houston, qui a paru dans le Canadian journal of applied sport sciences, mars 1983, 8(2), 49-51.
LEVEL: I LANG: Fr SIRC ARTICLE NO: 096254

Kaada, B. Improvement of physical performance by transcutaneous nerve stimulation in athletes. (Refs: 26)*Acupuncture and electro-therapeutics research (Oxford) 9(3), 1984, 165-180.*
ABST: The effects of transcutaneous nerve stimulation (TNS) on the performance of 21 competitive athletes were assessed in this study. Average improvements were as follows: 4.3 sec (2.2 per cent) in 1000 m road racing, 2.3 sec (1.8 per cent) in 800 m track racing, 0.9 sec (1.4 per cent) in 100 m swimming, 1.3 sec (0.8 per cent) in 200 m swimming, and 2.5 sec (0.9 per cent) in 400 m swimming. During a bicycle ergometer test, the maximal capacity was increased by 9 per cent with TNS.
LEVEL: A LANG: Eng SIRC ARTICLE NO: 109742

Mouchot, P. L'electro-stimulation musculaire au secours du sportif. *Marathon plus (Laval, Que.) 2(1), dec 1984/janv 1985, 29.*
LEVEL: B LANG: Fr SIRC ARTICLE NO: 173454

Passive exercise: there's nothing to it. *Your health & fitness (Highland Park, Ill.) 6(4), Aug/Sept 1984, 12-13.*
LEVEL: B LANG: Eng SIRC ARTICLE NO: 100872

MARIJUANA

Biron, S. Wells, J. Marijuana and athletics. *Sports medicine digest (Van Nuys, Calif.) 6(7), Jul 1984, 3-4.*
LEVEL: B LANG Eng SIRC ARTICLE NO: 100533

NICOTINE

ACHPER position statment: the association of tobacco products with sport. *ACHPER national journal (Kingswood, Aust.) 106, Summer 1984, 3.*
LEVEL: B LANG: Eng SIRC ARTICLE NO: 105138

DRUGS AND DOPING (continued)

Blakeney, M. McKeough, J. The cigarette debate. *ACHPER national journal (Kingswood, Aust.) 106, Summer 1984, 11.*
NOTES: Reprinted from, Media information Australia 31, Feb 1984.
LEVEL: B LANG: Eng SIRC ARTICLE NO: 105143

Brown, H. Carroll, A. Clark, K. Fisher, D. What teachers think about smoking education in schools. (Refs: 2)*ACHPER national journal (Kingswood, Aust.) 106, Summer 1984, 12-13.*
LEVEL: B LANG: Eng SIRC ARTICLE NO: 105144

Chapman, S. The lung goodbye. *ACHPER national journal (Kingswood, Aust.) 106, Summer 1984, 9-10.*
NOTES: Exerpts from a paper delivered at the 5th World Conference on Smoking and Health, Winnipeg, Canada, Jul 1983.
LEVEL: B LANG: Eng SIRC ARTICLE NO: 105142

Gingrich, V.F. The effects of advertising on cigarette smoking. Eugene, Ore.: Microform Publications, University of Oregon, 1984. 1 microfiche : negative ; 11 x 15 cm.
NOTES: Thesis (M.Ed.) - Pennsylvania State University, 1983; ((3), 59 leaves); includes bibliography.
LEVEL: A LANG: Eng UO84 374

Gray, N. Daube, M. The case against the promotion of cigarettes. *ACHPER national journal (Kingswood, Aust.) 106, Summer 198 7-8.*
NOTES: Excerpts from, Gray, N., Daube, M., Guidelines for smoking control, International Union Against Cancer, Technical Report Series, Volume 52, 1980.
LEVEL: B LANG: Eng SIRC ARTICLE NO: 105141

Hart, G. Physical activity: occupation and smoking in South Australia. (Refs: 13)*ACHPER national journal (Kingswood, Aust.) 106, Summer 1984, 14-16.*
LEVEL: I LANG: Eng SIRC ARTICLE NO: 109704

Lamendin, H. Experimentation en milieu sportif d'un soutien therapeutique pour se liberer de la sujetion tabagique: le valerbe. (Refs: 3)*Gazette medicale (Paris) 91(7), 1984, 85-86.*
LEVEL: I LANG: Fr

Landau, C. No smoking: the good news is that you're not a smoker. You find it difficult to tolerate those who are. The bad news is the extent of the risk you run just by being in the same room with a smoker. The evidence will shock and suprise you. *Runner's world (Mountain View, Calif.) 19(9), Sept 1984, 50-53;94;96;98;100;102;104.*
LEVEL: B LANG: Eng SIRC ARTICLE NO: 097462

Magnus, P. The addictiveness of cigarette smoking. (Refs: 12)*ACHPER national journal (Kingswood, Aust.) 106, Summer 1984, 6*
LEVEL: B LANG: Eng SIRC ARTICLE NO: 105140

Quit. Quit. For life. Smoking and the workplace: a resource manual. *ACHPER national journal (Kingswood, Aust.) 106, Summer 1984, 23-24.*
LEVEL: B LANG: Eng SIRC ARTICLE NO: 105149

Smoking and heart disease. *ACHPER national journal (Kingswood, Aust.) 106, Summer 1984, 21.*
NOTES: Reprinted with the permission of the National Heart Foundation.
LEVEL: B LANG: Eng SIRC ARTICLE NO: 105147

Smoking statistics and smoking control strategies in Australia. (Refs: 15)*ACHPER national journal (Kingswood, Aust.) 106, Summer 1984, 18-19.*
NOTES: Reproduced with the permission of the

Australia Council on Smoking and Health (ACOSH), WA.
LEVEL: B LANG: Eng SIRC ARTICLE NO: 105145

Tobacco sponsorship of sport. *ACHPER national journal (Kingswood, Aust.) 106, Summer 1984, 26-27.*
NOTES: Excerpt from, The way we p(l)ay, a report of the House of Representatives Standing Committee on Expenditure, Nov 1983.
LEVEL: B LANG: Eng SIRC ARTICLE NO: 105150

What does tobacco promotion do? *ACHPER national journal (Kingswood, Aust.) 106, Summer 1984, 20.*
LEVEL: B LANG: Eng SIRC ARTICLE NO: 105146

What does tobacco smoking do? It contributes to 16,000 deaths each year. *ACHPER national journal (Kingswood, Aust.) 106, Summer 1984, 22.*
NOTES: Excerpt from, Not so much a hobby, more a revolution...Freedom from tobacco multinationals, a manual produced by Health Promotion Services of the South Australian Health Commission.
LEVEL: I LANG: Eng SIRC ARTICLE NO: 105148

Woodward, S. Smoking control activities in Australia. *ACHPER national journal (Kingswood, Aust.) 106, Summer 1984, 4-5.*
LEVEL: B LANG: Eng SIRC ARTICLE NO: 105139

ECONOMICS AND FINANCE

Bretagne, T. Les milliardaires du sport. *Equipe magazine (Paris) 212, 29 sept 1984, 33-36.*
LEVEL: B LANG: Fr SIRC ARTICLE NO: 099336

Dixon, D.M. The finance of sport: a talk to the British Academy of Forensic Sciences. *Medicine, science and the law (Brentford, Eng.) 24(4), 1984, 294-298.*
LEVEL: I LANG: Eng SIRC ARTICLE NO: 103803

McCarthy, C. Australia's highest paid sports stars. *Australian business 4(5), 4 Jan 1984, 38-41.*
ABST: At least 13 Australian athletes earn over $100,000 per year with contracts managed by the International Management Group (IMG) or PBL. John Newcombe is the highest earner with estimated annual earnings of $500,000 through IMG and net worth of $15 million.
LEVEL: B LANG: Eng SIRC ARTICLE NO: 092684

Nightingale, D. Just how much is a gold medal worth? The stars of the 1984 summer games enter the arena of financial opportunity. *Sporting news (St. Louis, Mo.) 198(11), 10 Sept 1984, 13.*
LEVEL: B LANG: Eng SIRC ARTICLE NO: 097870

Rosen, M. The sport 100: our annual salary report. *Sport (New York) 75(3), Mar 1984, 25-28;30-32.*
LEVEL: B LANG: Eng SIRC ARTICLE NO: 094763

Victor, F. Les enjeux economiques du developpement des pratiques sportives. (Refs: 5)*Dans, Culture technique no. 13, Neuilly-sur-Seine, France, Centre de Recherche sur la Culture Technique, c1984, p. 62-69.*
LEVEL: I LANG: Fr RC1235 20096

AGENTS

Bott, R. Corpsport goes for gold in managing athletes. Willie deWit, Gretzky among stars in Edmonton firm's impressive lineu *Financial times (Toronto) 73(13), 17 Sept 1984, 28-29;34.*
LEVEL: B LANG: Eng SIRC ARTICLE NO: 099335

Interview John Manton: former official who currently acts as an attorney/representative for about 20 pro athletes. *Referee (Franksville, Wis.) 9(5), May 1984, 16-19.*
LEVEL: B LANG: Eng SIRC ARTICLE NO: 097406

FINANCIAL MANAGEMENT

Dixon, D.M. The finance of sport--a talk to the British Academy of Forensic Sciences. *Medicine, science and the law (Brentford, Eng.) 24(4), Oct 1984, 294-298.*
LEVEL: B LANG: Eng

Meyer, D. Norman, R. Saunders, S. Financial management for sports and recreation organizations. A guide to managing your group's finances. North Bay, Ont.: Northeastern Ontario Regional Sports Committee : Ministry of Tourism and Recreation, 1984. ii, 56 p. (Sport and recreation resource series for community groups; v.3.)
CORP: Northeastern Ontario Regional Sports Committee.
CORP: Ontario. Ministry of Tourism and Recreation. Field Services Office.
LEVEL: B LANG: Eng GV181.5 19016

FUND RAISING

Alsop, W.J. What does academe need from business/agencies? $Money$. (Refs: 5)*In, Zanger, B.K. and Parks, J.B. (eds.), Sport management curricula: the business and education nexus, Bowling Green, Ohio, Bowling Green State University, 1984, p. 33-35.*
CONF: Bowling Green State University Sport Management Curriculum Symposium (1983 : Bowling Green, Ohio).
LEVEL: I LANG: Eng GV713 20087

Aufsesser, P.M. Mechikoff, R. Grantsmanship and external funding: the paper chase. (Refs: 8)*Journal of physical education, recreation & dance (Reston, Va.) 55(6), Aug 1984, 69;76.*
LEVEL: B LANG: Eng SIRC ARTICLE NO: 097400

Fundraising: here is a listing of products and professional consultants for fundraising projects. *Athletic purchasing and facilities (Madison, Wis.) 8(2), Feb 1984, 71.*
NOTES: 1984 buyers guide.
LEVEL: B LANG: Eng SIRC ARTICLE NO: 108278

Kontor, K. LiftAmerica - athletes giving athletes a lift. *National Strength & Conditioning Association journal (Lincoln, Neb.) 6(3), Jun/Jul 1984, 42.*
LEVEL: B LANG: Eng SIRC ARTICLE NO: 096423

Leith, L.M. La sollicitation directe et indirecte de fonds. (Refs: 8)*Science du sport: documents de recherche et de technologie (Ottawa) P-1, dec 1984, 1-7.*
LEVEL: B LANG: Fr SIRC ARTICLE NO: 102302

Leith, L.M. Direct and indirect fund raising. (Refs: 8)*Sports science periodical on research and technology in sport (Ottawa) P-1, Dec 1984, 1-7.*
LEVEL: B LANG: Eng SIRC ARTICLE NO: 102303

Mitchelson, B. Fund raising strategies. Compagne de financement. *CAHPER journal/Revue de l'ACSEPR (Vanier, Ont.) 50(3), Jan-Feb/janv-fevr 1984, 32-33;8.*
NOTES: Part of a series of administration tips prepared by the Administration Committee of CAHPER. Ces conseils en administration proviennent de la serie preparee par le Comite

d'administration ACSEPR.
LEVEL: B LANG: Eng Fr SIRC ARTICLE NO:
094182

Strain drain: how to take the worry out of fund-
raising. Some money-spinning advice from the
Sports Council's Development Unit *Sport and
leisure (London) 24(6), Jan/Feb 1984, 20-21.*
LEVEL: B LANG: Eng SIRC ARTICLE NO: 097416

Waters, J.V. Big Foot's big event: a LiftAmerica
success story. (Refs: 2)*National Strength &
Conditioning Association journal (Lincoln, Neb.)
6(3), Jun/Jul 1984, 46-48.*
LEVEL: B LANG: Eng SIRC ARTICLE NO: 096439

FUNDING

Gratton, C. Efficiency and equity aspects of public
subsidies to sport and recreation. (Refs: 21)*Local
government studies (Birmingham, Eng.) 10(2),
1984, 53-74.*
LEVEL: A LANG: Eng SIRC ARTICLE NO: 099338

Saint-Hilaire, J. Olympisme et $. *Revue de
l'entraineur janv/mars 1984, 34.*
LEVEL: B LANG: Fr SIRC ARTICLE NO: 091576

HISTORY

Bilsborough, P. The commercialisation of sport:
Glasgow 1870-1914. (Refs: 29)*Momentum: a
journal of human movement studies (Edinburgh)
9(2), Summer 1984, 7-16.*
LEVEL: I LANG: Eng SIRC ARTICLE NO: 099027

LABOUR ECONOMICS

Marple, D.P. Professional sports and labor market
theories. (Refs: 70)*Arena review (Boston) 8(3), Nov
1984, 30-44.*
LEVEL: LANG: Eng SIRC ARTICLE NO: 104490

LOTTERIES

Paillou, N. Un loto pour le sport? *Temps libre,
jeunesse an 2000 (France) 131, 1984, 2.*
LEVEL: B LANG: Fr

Scammell, R. Les paris collectifs sportifs. Sports
pool. *Champion (Vanier, Ont.) 8(2), May/mai 1984,
2-5.*
LEVEL: B LANG: Fr Eng SIRC ARTICLE NO:
094764

POLITICAL ECONOMY

Johnson, A. The uneasy partnership of cities and
professional sport: public policy considerations.
(Refs: 25)
CONF: North American Society for the Sociology of
Sport. Conference (3rd : 1982 : Toronto, Ont.).
NOTES: In, Theberge, N. and Donnelly, P. (eds.),
Sport and the sociological imagination: refereed
proceedings of the 3rd Annual Conference of the
North American Society for the Sociology of Sport,
Toronto, Canada, November 1982, Fort Worth,
Tex., Texas Christian University Press, c1984, p.
210-227.
ABST: This review of sport franchises since 1950
identifies trends related to professional franchise
instability and analyzes the franchise-city
relationship in the political context. Public policy
options are examined which have been proposed to
resolve the problems of franchise instability.
LEVEL: A LANG: Eng SIRC ARTICLE NO: 097407

SCHOLARSHIPS

1984 Camp guide and scholarship program by the
Women's Sports Foundation. *Women's sports (Palo
Alto, Calif.) 6(4), Apr 1984, 57;59-63;66-71.*
LEVEL: B LANG: Eng SIRC ARTICLE NO: 101037

1984 scholarship guide. *Women's sports (Palo Alto,
Calif.) 6(2), Feb 1984, 77;79-90.*
CORP: Women's Sports Foundation.
ABST: Women's sports magazine publishes one of
the best athletic scholarship guides for universities
in the United States. This guide lists colleges and
universities alphabetically by state. Each institution
has the name of a contact person, the kinds of
scholarships available, their value and the
numbered offered. This is a useful guide for any
female high school athlete considering applying for
collegiate athletic scholarships available in the
United States.
LEVEL: B LANG: Eng SIRC ARTICLE NO: 099361

Newman, S. Making the right choice. Should
Canadian athletes accept athletic scholarships in
the United States, and if so, where? Coaches,
administrators and athletes give their advice on
how athletes (and coaches) can make these
important decisions. *Coaching review (Ottawa) 7,
Sept/Oct 1984, 28-37.*
LEVEL: B LANG: Eng SIRC ARTICLE NO: 097869

Sport Canada. The Athlete Assistance Program ...a
guide 1984-1985. Sport Canada. Le programme
d'aide aux athletes ...un guide 1984-1985. Ottawa:
Fitness and Amateur Sport : Condition physique et
Sport amateur, c1984. 25 p.
CORP: Canada. Fitness and Amateur Sport.
CORP: Canada. Condition physique et Sport
amateur.
NOTES: French and English texts on inverted
pages with separate paging. Textes francais et
anglais disposes tete-beche avec pagination
separee.
LEVEL: B LANG: Eng Fr ISBN: 0-662-53040-3
GV716 18461

SPONSORSHIP

Howell, D. The Howell report. (Sponsorship). *Sport
and leisure (London) 24(6), Jan/Feb 1984, 14-17.*
LEVEL: B LANG: Eng SIRC ARTICLE NO: 097405

Lang, E.J. The sponsorship dilemma. *Chimo
magazine 7(2), Apr 1984, 6-7.*
LEVEL: B LANG: Eng SIRC ARTICLE NO: 092682

Lemaire, P. Le sponsoring. Sport media et sport
business. *Dans, Culture technique no. 13, Neuilly-
sur-Seine, France, Centre de Recherche sur la
Culture Technique, c1984, p. 70-77.*
LEVEL: I LANG: Fr RC1235 20096

Noble, K. Firms making the team to make money.
*Globe and mail (Toronto) 5369, 11 Aug 1984,
B1;B4.*
LEVEL: B LANG: Eng SIRC ARTICLE NO: 095705

Perry, P. Selling the olympians: there's a system
for cashing in on gold medals, and both the buyers
and the sellers are using it. *Runner (New York)
6(12), Sept 1984, 46-47;51-52.*
LEVEL: B LANG: Eng SIRC ARTICLE NO: 102928

Tobacco sponsorship of sport. *ACHPER national
journal (Kingswood, Aust.) 106, Summer 1984, 26-
27.*
NOTES: Excerpt trom, The way we p(l)ay, a report
of the House of Representatives Standing

Committee on Expenditure, Nov 1983.
LEVEL: B LANG: Eng SIRC ARTICLE NO: 105150

Townley, S. Grayson, E. Sponsorship of sport,
arts and leisure: law, tax and business
relationships. London: Sweet and Maxwell, 1984.
xiii, 333 p.
LEVEL: I LANG: Eng ISBN: 0-421-30410-3 GV716
18023

Wayne, J. More corporations ready to jump into
amateur sports sponsorships arena. *Financial post
78(2), 14 Jan 1984, 28.*
LEVEL: B LANG: Eng SIRC ARTICLE NO: 089872

What does tobacco promotion do? *ACHPER
national journal (Kingswood, Aust.) 106, Summer
1984, 20.*
LEVEL: B LANG: Eng SIRC ARTICLE NO: 105146

Wigle, D.T. Morgan, P.P. The tobacco industry:
still resourceful in recruiting smokers. (Refs:
6)*Canadian Medical Association journal (Ottawa,
Ont.) 130(12), 15 Jun 1984, 1537-1539.*
LEVEL: B LANG: Eng SIRC ARTICLE NO: 094189

EGYPT

Ibrahim, H.M. Asker, N.F. Ideology politics and
sport in Egypt. (Refs: 10)*Leisure studies (London)
3(1), Jan 1984, 97-106.*
ABST: A brief historical background of the ideology
and politics of sport in Egypt is provided. In the last
two decades three factors may have led to growth
of sport in Egypt: industrialization, urbanization and
democracy. Presently, sport in Egypt is highly
bureaucratized and directed toward participation
rather than elitism.
LEVEL: A LANG: Eng SIRC ARTICLE NO: 094754

ENDURANCE RIDING

Greasley, C. Distance riding. *Horse and rider
(Surrey, Eng.) 34(385), May 1984, 25.*
NOTES: Last in a series.
LEVEL: B LANG: Eng SIRC ARTICLE NO: 099723

Hyland, A. Endurance riding. Part 4: pre-ride
vetting and first events. *Equi (Warrington, Eng.) 20,
Jan/Feb 1984, 14-16.*
LEVEL: B LANG: Eng SIRC ARTICLE NO: 095108

HORSES

Hyland, A. Hundred miling. *Equi (Cheshire, Eng.)
24, Oct/Nov 1984, 6-8;10.*
LEVEL: B LANG: Eng SIRC ARTICLE NO: 109652

TRAINING AND CONDITIONING

Greasley, C. Distance riding: Part three. *Horse and
rider (Surrey, Eng.) 38(382), Feb 1984, 21-22.*
LEVEL: B LANG: Eng SIR ARTICLE NO: 099722

Lieberman, B. A month in the life... Three horses,
three sports, three programs. *Equus (Farmingdale,
N.Y.) 79, May 1984, 28-29;33.*
LEVEL: B LANG: Eng SIRC ARTICLE NO: 099734

VETERINARY MEDICINE

Essen-Gustavsson, B. Karlstroem, K. Lindholm, A. Fibre types, enzyme activities and substrate utilisation in skeletal muscle of horses competing in endurance rides. (Refs: 19)*Equine veterinary journal (London) 16(3), May 1984, 197-202.* ABST: Venous blood samples and middle gluteal muscle biopsies were obtained from 21 horses taking part in 100 km or 50 km endurance rides. The results of this study show that intramuscular carbohydrate and lipid stores are both important fuels during endurance rides.
LEVEL: A LANG: Eng SIRC ARTICLE NO: 103251

Hyland, A. Endurance riding - Part 5. After-ride care and feeding of the long-distance horse. *Equi (Cheshire, Eng.) 21, Apr/May 1984, 10-12.*
LEVEL: B LANG: Eng SIRC ARTICLE NO: 098215

ENGLAND

Middleton, C. Sweeping up: we visit a team trying to rebuild people's lives after an economic tornado. *Sport and leisure (London) 25(3), Jul/Aug 1984, 22-24.*
LEVEL: B LANG: Eng SIRC ARTICLE NO: 101012

EQUESTRIAN SPORT

Chambry, P. Equitation. Ed. rev. et augm. Paris: Editions Amphora, 1984. 301 p. : ill. (Sports et loisirs.)
LEVEL: I LANG: ISBN: 2-85180-011-6 SF309 17975

Rotella, R. Jones, C. Sloanaker, J. Riding out of your mind: a series on applied sport psychology for riders: part nine: making the most of lessons. *Practical horseman (Unionville, Pa.) 12(2), Feb 1984, 41-43;46-A.*
LEVEL: B LANG: Eng SIRC ARTICLE NO: 098236

ADMINISTRATION

Wood, M. The judged horse show: show management. *Western horseman (Colorado Springs, Colo.) 49(6), Jun 1984, 12;14.*
LEVEL B LANG: Eng SIRC ARTICLE NO: 099762

BIOGRAPHY AND AUTOBIOGRAPHY

Herbert, L. O'Brien, J. Vincent O'Brien's great horses. s.l.: Pelham, (1984?). 1v.
LEVEL: B LANG: Eng ISBN: 0-7207-1547-4

EQUIPMENT

Kaplan, J.K. Emergency halters: what will work in a pinch? *Polo (Gaithersburg, Md.) 9(8), Apr 1984, 50-51.*
LEVEL: B LANG: Eng SIRC ARTICLE NO: 101351

Norman, P.W. Young entry: spurs. *Chronicle of the horse (Middleburg, Va.) 47(48), 30 Nov 1984, 16-17.*
LEVEL: B LANG: Eng SIRC ARTICLE NO: 173572

FACILITIES

Hardin, J. Santa Anita's Olympics. As host for the Olympic equestrian events, Santa Anita has expanded its staff and built a temporary arena across the homestretch. *Thoroughbred record (Lexington, Ky.) 218(29), 18 Jul 1984, 3496-3497.*
LEVEL: B LANG: Eng SIRC ARTICLE NO: 098206

FACILITIES - DESIGN, CONSTRUCTION AND PLANNING

Weston, J. Make your own manege. *Riding (London) 49(7), Jul 1984, 28-29.*
LEVEL: B LANG: Eng SIRC ARTICLE NO: 097522

HORSES

Jung, E.-B. Evaluating the sport horse for purchase. *USCTA news (Hamilton, Mass.) 13(6), Dec 1984, 10;12-13.*
LEVEL: B LANG: Eng SIRC ARTICLE NO: 173393

McCarthy, G. Forbidden fruits. Prohibited substances in feeds for competitive horses. What they are, what they do and how to avoid them. *Equi (Warrington, Eng.) 23, Aug/Sept 1984, 22;24.*
NOTES: To be continued.
LEVEL: B LANG: Eng SIRC ARTICLE NO: 181882

PROTECTIVE DEVICES

Seaber, A.V. Safety helmet research: studies support use of head protection for equestrians. (Refs: 18)*Camping magazine (Martinsville, Ind.) 56(4), Feb 1984, 10-11;21.*
LEVEL: I LANG: Eng SIRC ARTICLE NO: 098240

PSYCHOLOGY

Rotella, R. Jones, C. Sloanaker, J. Riding out of your mind: a series on applied sport psychology for riders: part eight: goal-setting. *Practical horseman (Unionville, Pa.) 12(1), Jan 1984, 40-42.*
LEVEL: B LANG: Eng SIRC ARTICLE NO: 098235

Rotella, R. Jones, C. Sloanaker, J. Riding out of your mind: a series of applied sport psychology for riders: the joys of competition. *Practical horseman (Unionville, Pa.) 12(3), Mar 1984, 38-39.*
LEVEL: B LANG: Eng SIRC ARTICLE NO: 098237

RULES AND REGULATIONS

How the game is played. *Women's sports (Palo Alto, Calif.) 6(3), Mar 1984, 34-36.*
LEVEL: B LANG: Eng SIRC ARTICLE NO: 09821

SPORTING EVENTS

Past glory. (Olympic Games) *Riding (London) 49(8), Aug 1984, 60-61.*
LEVEL: B LANG: Eng SIRC ARTICLE NO: 103260

Roll of honour. (Olympic Games) *Riding (London) 49(8), Aug 1984, 62-63.*
LEVEL: B LANG: Eng SIRC ARTICLE NO: 103263

Strassburger, J. Equestrian. *Women's sports (Palo Alto, Calif.) 6(3), Mar 1984, 25-26.*
LEVEL: B LANG: Eng SIRC ARTICLE NO 098246

STATISTICS AND RECORDS

Medal winners and United States participants in Olympic equestrian events 1912-1980. *Chronicle of the horse (Middleburg, Va.) 47(29), 20 Jul 1984, 4-8.*
LEVEL: B LANG: Eng SIRC ARTICLE NO: 099742

TEACHING

Cooney, B. Madden, F. The Cooney-Madden school of rider education. *Practical horseman (Unionville, Pa.) 12(3), Mar 1984, 6-13;14-E.*
LEVEL: B LANG: Eng SIRC ARTICLE NO: 098188

TRAINING AND CONDITIONING

Churchill, P. Guidance from the ground: it's what every rider - and horse - needs. *Riding (London) 49(11), Nov 1984, 44-45.*
LEVEL: B LANG: Eng SIRC ARTICLE NO: 107279

Doulier, R. Le basket-ball a cheval ou le pato-komdu. *Sport: Communaute francaise de belgique (Bruxelles) 108, 1984, 201-207.*
LEVEL: B LANG: Fr SIRC ARTICLE NO: 103249

Green, C. The right approach. *Horse and rider (Surrey, Eng.) 34(387), Jul 1984, 42-43.*
LEVEL: B LANG: Eng SIRC ARTICLE NO 101344

Trauig, B. Training your horse to jump his best. The famous trainer of hunters and jumpers shares his unique system for maximizing jumping performance, in a series of lessons you can apply to your own horse: lesson one: single-aid control. *Practical horseman (Unionville, Pa.) 12(1), Jan 1984, 48-53;56-57.*
LEVEL: B LANG: Eng SIRC ARTICLE NO: 098249

Wagschal, J.L. Arabian dressage: mounting the green horse. *Canadian Arabian news (Calgary, Alta.) 24(3), Mar 1984, 24-25.*
LEVEL: B LANG: Eng SIRC ARTICLE NO: 098255

VETERINARY MEDICINE

Ogilvie, T.W.B. Heat stroke and exhaustion in competing horses. *Equi (Cheshire, Eng.) 22, Jun/Jul 1984, 7-9.*
LEVEL: B LANG: Eng SIRC ARTICLE NO: 099745

EQUIPMENT

Kay, L. Serving the coach. *Sports retailer (Mt. Prospect, Calif.) 37(2), Feb 1984, 54-55.*
LEVEL: B LANG: Eng SIRC ARTICLE NO: 098951

Maxey, B. Equipment inventory: a systematic approach. *Interscholastic athletic administration (Kansas City) 11(1), Fall 198 20-21.*
LEVEL: B LANG: Eng SIRC ARTICLE NO: 105203

Oliver, P. A buyer's guide to non-inflatable balls: surprise, the old horsehide is really made out of cowhide. *Scholastic coach (New York) 54(5), Dec 1984, 48-51;63.*
LEVEL: B LANG: Eng SIRC ARTICLE NO: 102409

Reilly, T. Lees, A. Exercise and sports equipment: some ergonomics aspects. *Applied ergonomics (Surrey, Eng.) 15(4), 1984, 259-279.*
LEVEL: A LANG: Eng

The sports/fitness/leisure markets. New York: Fairchild Publications, c1984. 50 p. (Fairchild fact

files.)
CORP: Fairchild Market Research Division.
LEVEL: B LANG: Eng ISBN: 0-87005-482-1
GV706.8 18797

Walzer, E. Insulations: improved batting technology. *Sport style (New York) 6(4), 20 Feb 1984, 40;44.*
LEVEL: B LANG: Eng SIRC ARTICLE NO: 092759

DESIGN

Anderson, I. Design for winning. Equipment threatens to become a source of controversy at international sporting events. The US is hunting systematically for technologies that will give its athletes an advantage over competitors from less advanced countries. *New scientist (London) 26 Jul 1984, 12-13.*
LEVEL: B LANG: Eng SIRC ARTICLE NO: 095805

Andreff, W. Le muscle et la machine. Le dialogue entre le sport et l'innovation. (Refs: 103)*Dans, Culture technique no. 13, Neuilly-sur-Seine, France, Centre de Recherche sur la Culture Technique, c1984, p. 38-61.*
LEVEL: A LANG: Fr RC1235 20096

Reilly, T. Lees, A. Exercise and sports equipment: some ergonomics aspects. *Applied ergonomics (Surrey, Eng.) 15(4), 1984, 259-279.*
LEVEL: A LANG: Eng SIRC ARTICLE NO: 103915

DIRECTORIES

84 8th annual buyers guide. Madison, Wis.: Athletic Purchasing and Facilities, 1984. 174 p. : ill (Athletic purchasing and facilities (Madison, Wis.) 8(2), Feb 1984.)
LEVEL: I LANG: Eng

Action sports retailer: manufacturer/distributor alphabetical directory. *Action sports retailer (South Laguna, Calif.) 5(12), Dec 1984, 94;96;98;100;102-120.*
LEVEL: B LANG: Eng SIRC ARTICLE NO: 105200

Athletic equipment: products needed for individual sports are listed here. The manufacturers and suppliers of each products ar listed alphabetically following the heading. *Athletic purchasing and facilities (Madison, Wis.) 8(2), Feb 1984, 35-36;38;40;42;44;46;48;50-52;54;56;58;60;62.*
NOTES: 1984 buyers guide.
LEVEL: B LANG: Eng SIRC ARTICLE NO: 108276

Manufacturers and suppliers directory: here is the alphabetical listing of the manufacturers and suppliers of the products and services listed in this guide. *Athletic purchasing and facilities (Madison, Wis.) 8(2), Feb 1984, 73-74;76;78;80-82;84-99.*
NOTES: 1984 buyers guide.
LEVEL: B LANG: Eng SIRC ARTICLE NO: 108279

Product directory. *Action sports retailer (South Laguna, Calif.) 5(12), Dec 1984, 24;26;28;30;32;34;40;42;44;46;48-71.*
LEVEL: B LANG: Eng SIRC ARTICLE NO: 105205

MANUFACTURING

Materiaux composites. *Dans, Culture technique no. 13, Neuilly-sur-Seine, France, Centre de Recherche sur la Culture Technique c1984, p. 250-251.*
LEVEL: B LANG: Fr RC1235 20096

Sleeping bags. *Camping Canada (Montreal) 13(6), Aug 1984, 20-22.*
LEVEL: B LANG: Eng SIRC ARTICLE NO: 102412

Sporting goods and toy industries 1982: annual census of manufactures. Fabrication d'articles de sport et de jouets 1982: recensement annuel des manufactures. Ottawa: Supply and Services Canada / Approvisionnements et services Canada, 1984. 28 p. (Cat. 47-204.)
CORP: Statistics Canada.
CORP: Statistique Canada.
NOTES: ISSN: 0575-979X.
LEVEL: B LANG: Eng Fr GV745 17714

Tourtet, J.F. Tourny-Eteve, S. Les armes legeres des industries sportives. *Science et vie (Paris) HS147, 1984, 30-43.*
LEVEL: I LANG: Fr

PROTECTIVE DEVICES

Bishop, P.J. Helmets for sport: use and misuse. *Coaching science update (Ottawa, Ont.) 1984, 4-6.*
LEVEL: I LANG: Eng SIRC ARTICLE NO: 094283

Bishop, P.J. Le casque protecteur. (Refs: 5)*Nouveautes en science de l'entrainement (Ottawa) 1984, 4-6.*
LEVEL: I LANG: Fr SIRC ARTICLE NO: 095807

Doran, G.A. Allwood, C. Towards preventing reinjury in contact sport. (Refs: 3)*Journal of sports medicine and physical fitness (Torino, Italy) 24(2), Jun 1984, 90-93.*
ABST: This short paper presents two case reports illustrating the use of dental mouthguard plastic in the fabrication of protective sporting guards. Anatomical and orthopaedic factors involved include: pliable moulding to body contour, absorption of traumatic forces by the guard, no protruding or sharp edges. The psychological advantages of wearing the guards is increased confidence due to reduction of the fear of reinjury.
LEVEL: I LANG: Eng SIRC ARTICLE NO: 102401

Helmets. *Sports physiotherapy division (Victoria, B.C.) 9(3), May/Jun 1984, 30-33.*
LEVEL: B LANG: Eng SIRC ARTICLE NO: 0974

Marron, J.T. Tucker, J.B. Protective equipment in high-risk sports. (Refs: 32)
NOTES: In, Birrer, R.B. (ed.), Sports medicin for the primary care physician, Norwalk, Conn., Appleton-Century-Crofts, c1984, p. 85-90.
LEVEL: I LANG: Eng RC1210 17030

Mattison, R. Protective equipment. *Sports physiotherapy division (Victoria, B.C.) 9(2), Mar/Apr 1984, 20-22.*
LEVEL: B LANG: Eng SIRC ARTICLE NO: 097495

Shimojo, M. Ban, K. Study on shock absorb properties of protective helmet. (Refs: 18)*Japan Society of Mechanical Engineers bulletin (Tokyo) 27(225), Mar 1984, 553-560.*
LEVEL: A LANG: Eng SIRC ARTICLE NO: 095817

Watkins, S.M. Designing impact-protective clothing. (Refs: 2)*In, Watkins, S.M., Clothing: the portable environment, Anes, Iowa, Iowa State University Press, c1984, p. 91-107.*
LEVEL: I LANG: Eng SIRC ARTICLE NO: 107988

PROTECTIVE DEVICES - MOUTH PROTECTION

Lamendin, H. A propos des relations entre etat bucco-dentaire et pratique sportive. Protection et prevention. (Relation between orodental status and sports performance. Protection and prevention.) *Chirurgien-dentiste de France (Paris) 54(267), 25 oct 1984, 27-32.*
LEVEL: I LANG: Fr

Mouthpieces. *Sports physiotherapy division (Victoria, B.C.) 9(3), May/Jun 1984, 35-37.*
LEVEL: B LANG: Eng SIRC ARTICLE NO: 097497

Powers, J.M. Godwin, W.C. Heintz, W.D. Mouth protectors and sports team dentists. *Journal of the American Dental Associatio (Chicago) 109(1), Jul 1984, 84-87.*
CORP: Council on Dental Materials, Instruments, and Equipment. Bureau of Health Educational and Audiovisual Services.
LEVEL: I LANG: Eng SIRC ARTICLE NO: 104138

Seals, R.R. Dorrough, B.C. Custom mouth protectors: a review of their applications. *Journal of prosthetic dentistry (St. Louis) 51(2), Feb 1984, 238-242.*
LEVEL: I LANG: Eng SIRC ARTICLE NO: 099102

The issues of foot and mouth. *Fitness & health newsletter (Wembley, W.A.) 15, 1984?, 1-4.*
LEVEL: B LANG: Eng SIRC ARTICLE NO: 177412

RETAILING

'83 sporting goods places-of-purchase study. *Sports retailer (Mt.Prospect, Ill.) 37(5), May 1984, 25-40.*
LEVEL: B LANG: Eng SIRC ARTICLE NO: 100547

Brodsky, A.B. Health equipment. *Pool & spa news (Los Angeles, Calif.) 23(4), 27 Feb 1984, 30-32;55.*
LEVEL: B LANG: Eng SIRC ARTICLE NO: 097473

Computers: are they for sports retailers? *Sports trader (London) 145(1011), 17 May 1984, 16-18;20;22-23.*
LEVEL: B LANG: Eng SIRC ARTICLE NO: 102400

Finland prospers through exports. *Sports trade Canada (Downsview, Ont.) 12(1), Feb 1984, 114-115.*
LEVEL: B LANG: Eng SIRC ARTICLE NO: 092749

Friedman, H.J. Sales management for sports retailers: Part I. A look at store management's responsibility for increasing sales productivity. *Sports retailer (Mt. Prospect, Ill.) 37(7), Jul 1984, 20-21;66.*
LEVEL: B LANG: Eng SIRC ARTICLE NO: 105202

Hennessey, F. Setting up a retail co-op action plan. *Sports retailer (Mt.Prospect, Ill.) 37(2), Feb 1984, 24-26;28;30-31.*
LEVEL: B LANG: Eng SIRC ARTICLE NO: 098948

Knight, T. Utilizing co-op ads. *Sports retailer (Mt. Prospect, Ill.) 37(2), Feb 1984, 34-35;66.*
LEVEL: B LANG: Eng SIRC ARTICLE NO: 098952

Quinton, J. The check's in the mail. *Sports retailer (Mt. Prospect, Ill.) 37(2), Feb 1984, 36-38.*
LEVEL: B LANG: Eng SIRC ARTICLE NO: 098957

Sturdy, R. Buying it right... *Sports trade Canada (Downsview, Ont.) 12(4), May/Jun 1984, 24-25.*
LEVEL: B LANG: Eng SIRC ARTICLE NO: 103917

EQUIPMENT (continued)

Where consumers buy exercise/fitness equipment: a graphic analysis of their purchase places and prices. *Sports retailer (Mt. Prospect, Ill.) 37(8), Aug 1984, 22.*
LEVEL: B LANG: Eng SIRC ARTICLE NO: 102416

Youth sports '84. *Sports retailer (Mt. Prospect, Ill.) 37(7), Jul 1984, 32-35.*
LEVEL: B LANG: Eng SIRC ARTICLE NO: 105211

SCOREBOARDS

More features offered a lower prices. Special report: timing & scoreboards. *Athletic business (Madison, Wis.) 8(3), Mar 1984, 38.*
LEVEL: B LANG: Eng SIRC ARTICLE NO: 178381

STANDARDS

Rosenthal, P.P. Sports equipment standards. (Refs: 13)
NOTES: In, Scott, W.N. (ed.) et al., Principles of sports medicine, Baltimore, Williams & Wilkins, c1984, p. 363-366.
LEVEL: I LANG: Eng RC1210 18016

STATISTICS

Rennie, J. The early 1984 summer goods market. *Jim Rennie's sports letter (Collingwood, Ont.) 8(22), 28 May 1984, 1-6.*
LEVEL: I LANG: Eng SIRC ARTICLE NO: 094185

Rennie, J. Special report. The 1984 spring/summer market. *Jim Rennie's sports letter (Collingwood, Ont.) 8(31), Jul 1984, 1-6.*
LEVEL: I LANG: Eng SIRC ARTICLE NO: 095816

STOPWATCHES AND TIMERS

Bovay, J.P. Le chronometrage sportif. *Dans, Culture technique no. 13, Neuilly-sur-Seine, France, Centre de Recherche sur la Culture Technique, c1984, p. 200-217.*
LEVEL: A LANG: Fr RC1235 20096

Chronographs: the latest in high-tech wristware can put time at your fingertips, time after time. *Runner's world 19(1), Jan 1984, 58-60.*
LEVEL: B LANG: Eng SIRC ARTICLE NO: 089921

Lieb, T. Time changes: computer chronographs are small but mighty. *Bicycling (Emmaus, Pa.) 25(9), Nov/Dec 1984, 20-23.*
LEVEL: B LANG: Eng SIRC ARTICLE NO: 100561

ERGOGENIC AIDS

Coyle, E.F. Ergogenic aids. (Refs: 26)*Clinics in sports medicine (Philadelphia) 3(3), Jul 1984, 731-742.*
NOTES: Symposium on nutritional aspects of exercise.
ABST: The effectiveness of various ergogenic aids for improving physical performance is discussed. Specific topics include carbohydrate supplementation during exercise and fat utilization, as well as methods of reducing the accumulation of metabolic by-products (that is, heat and acid) and increasing muscular strength.
LEVEL: I LANG: Eng SIRC ARTICLE NO: 100534

Flynn, P.M. More on MORA. (letter) *Journal of the American Dental Association (Chicago) 108(5), May*

1984, 728;730.
LEVEL: LANG: Eng SIRC ARTICLE NO: 102580

Frenkl, R. Richtofit krem es spray sportorvosi alkalmazasanak tapasztalatai. (Observations with Richtofit cream and spray in sports medicine.) (Refs: 2)*Sportorvosi szemle/Hungarian review of sports medicine (Budapest) 25(2), 1984, 125-128.*
ABST: The effect of Richtofit cream and spray has been studied in healthy male and female athletes and in sports medicine. 87% of the persons participating in the study applied the preparations readily and found their effect beneficial. The beneficial effect was manifested mainly in the elimination of fatigue after exertion (games, race, training) and in the shortening of regeneration period. Similarly good effect was observed in the elimination of 'muscles stiffness' and in the curing of muscle strain associated with minor pain and restricted motion. In more extensive dermal injurie, haematomas, and severe muscle sprains, Richtofit treatment proved to be inferior to traditional preparations. In the final stage of healing, however, Richtofit may have a beneficial effect.
LEVEL: LANG: Hun SIRC ARTICLE NO: 097263

Houtkooper, L. Nutritional ergogenic aids. *Swimming world and junior swimmer (Englewood, Calif.) 25(11), Nov 1984, 26-31.*
NOTES: Fifth in a series.
LEVEL: B LANG: Eng SIRC ARTICLE NO: 102390

Houtkooper, L. Nutritional ergogenic aids: performance boosters? A nutrition expert sorts out the fact and fiction of the benefits and risks of vitamins and minerals for athletes. *Swimming world and junior swimmer (Inglewood, Calif.) 25(10), Oct 1984, 14-20.*
NOTES: Fourth in a series.
LEVEL: I LANG: Eng SIRC ARTICLE NO: 106371

Krakauer, J. Endocrine roulette: this introduces a new column which will examine how athletes of all types, ar all levels, attempt to alter their physiologies to gain a competitive edge. This first installment: steroids and growth hormones. *Ultrasport (Boston, Mass.) 1(5), Sept/Oct 1984, 22-26;28.*
LEVEL: I LANG: Eng SIRC ARTICLE NO: 173310

Ledoux, M. Le bicarbonate de sodium: une substance au pouvoir inconnu. *Revue de l'entraineur (Montreal) juil/sept 1984, 23.*
LEVEL: B LANG: Fr SIRC ARTICLE NO: 102393

Todd, T. The use of human growth hormone poses a grave dilemma for sport. *Sports illustrated (Chicago, Ill) 61(18), 15 Oct 1984, 6;8;10-11;13-15.*
LEVEL: I LANG: Eng SIRC ARTICLE NO: 098930

EUROPE

Recommendations, publications, reports and other results of CDDS work 1975-1984, set out with reference to the European Sport for All Charter. Strasbourg: Council of Europe, Committee for the Development of Sport, 1984. 7 p. (loose-leaf)
CORP: Council of Europe. Committee for the Development of Sport.
LEVEL: B LANG: Eng GV603 20879

Schilling, G. Le Conseil de l'Europe et le sport. *Macolin (Suisse) 6, juin 1984, 12-13.*
NOTES: Traduction de, Marianne Weber.
LEVEL: B LANG: Fr SIRC ARTICLE NO: 102930

Textes adoptes aux reunions precedentes des ministres europeens responsables du sport. Pour information. Strasbourg: Conseil d l'Europe, 1984. 44 p.
CONF: Conference des ministres europeens responsables du sport (4e : 1984 : Malte).
NOTES: Also published in English under the title: Texts adopted at previous meetings of European ministers responsible for sport. For information.
LEVEL: B LANG: Fr GV701 18479

Texts adopted at previous meetings of European ministers responsible for sport. For information. Strasbourg: Council of Europe 1984. 41 p.
CONF: Conference of European Ministers Responsible for Sport (4th : 1984 : Malta).
NOTES: Aussi publie en francais sous le titre: Textes adoptes aux reunions precedentes des ministres europeens responsables du sport.
LEVEL: B LANG: Eng GV701 18478

FACILITIES

Fachwoerterbuch Sport- und Freizeitanlagen. Special dictionary sports and leisure facilities. Dictionnaire speciale equipement de sport et de loisirs. Diccionario tecnico instalaciones deportivas y recreativas. Cologne: Internationaler Arbeitskreis Sport- und Freizeiteinrichtungen e.V., 1984. 69 p.
CORP: Internationaler Arbeitskreis Sport-und Freizeiteinrichtungen e.V..
CORP: Groupe international de travail pour les equipements de sport et de loisirs.
CORP: International Working Group for the Construction of Sports and Leisure Facilities.
CORP: Grupo Intercional de Trabajo para Instalaciones Deportivas y Recreatives.
NOTES: Cover title. Titre de la couverture.
LEVEL: B LANG: Ger Eng Fr Spa GV401 18623

Jacobs, B. Use closed schools to develop extension sites. *Journal of physical education and program (Columbus, Oh.) 81(4), Apr 1984, D14-D15.*
LEVEL: B LANG: Eng SIRC ARTICLE NO: 094296

Keeping ahead of the game at Normandale Racquet Clubs. *Recreation, sports & leisure (Minneapolis) 4(6), Aug 1984, 99-101.*
NOTES: Special issue: Managed recreation research report.
LEVEL: B LANG: Eng SIRC ARTICLE NO: 103920

Single, D. Northwestern sees renaissance of McGaw Hall. *Athletic administration (Cleveland, Oh.) 19(6), Dec 1984, 10;12-13.*
LEVEL: B LANG: Eng SIRC ARTICLE NO: 105224

Vining, B. New gym Bolsters Ouachita athletics. *Athletic administration 19(1), Feb 1984, 12-16.*
LEVEL: B LANG: Eng SIRC ARTICLE NO: 092776

ADMINISTRATION

Breckner, S. Opportunities in facility management for sport management graduates. *In, Zanger, B.K. and Parks, J.B. (eds.), Sport management curricula: the business and education nexus, Bowling Green, Ohio, Bowling Green State University, 1984, p. 67-70.*
CONF: Bowling Green State University Sport Management Curriculum Symposium (1983 : Bowling Green, Ohio).
LEVEL: B LANG: Eng GV713 20087

Galipault, S.M. Tips on marketing Y weight training centers. *Journal of physical education and program (Columbus, Ohio)* 81 (8), Dec 1984, H9-H11.
LEVEL: B LANG: Eng SIRC ARTICLE NO: 108251

Jackson, J.J. Leisure and sports center management. Springfield, Ill.: Charles C. Thomas, c1984. xii, 200 p.
NOTES: Include bibliographical references and index.
LEVEL: I LANG: Eng ISBN: 0398049440 LC CARD: 83-018311 GV182 17478

Kozlowski, J.C. Negligence liability for third party assaults during recreational activities. *Parks & recreation* 19(2), Feb 1984, 34-37.
LEVEL: B LANG: Eng SIRC ARTICLE NO: 091491

The Management and Use of Artificial Outdoor Surfaces for Sport: report of a seminar held at Bisham Abbey National Sport Centre, 20 October 1983. Reading, England: Sports Council, 1984?. 37 p.
CONF: Management and Use of Artificial Outdoor Surfaces for Sport (1983 : Bisham Abbey National Sport Centre).
CORP: Sports Council.
LEVEL: I LANG: Eng GV411 20399

Watkins, D.L. Computers can streamline your program operations. *Athletic purchasing and facilities (Madison, Wis.)* 8(1), Ja 1984, 26-27.
LEVEL: B LANG: Eng SIRC ARTICLE NO: 094301

ARCHITECTURE

Palais omnisports de Paris. *Recherche et architecture (Paris)* 58, 1984, 15-26.
LEVEL: B LANG: Fr

ARENAS

Carbon monoxide intoxication associated with use of a gasoline-powered resurfacing machine at an ice-skating rink -- Pennsylvania. (Refs: 3)*Morbidity and mortality weekly report: MMWR/Center for disease control (Atlanta, Ga.)* 33(4), 3 Feb 1984, 49-51.
LEVEL: I LANG: Eng SIRC ARTICLE NO: 097519

Modhorat, J. Ice castles: a unique look at rinks and arenas across the United States. *American hockey & arena (Colorado Springs)* 5(3), Spring 1984, 30-35;45.
LEVEL: B LANG: Eng SIRC ARTICLE NO: 095832

BIBLIOGRAPHIES

Literature documentation sports and leisure facilities from: Sport Documentation. Koeln: International Working Group for the Construction of Sports and Leisure Facilities, 1984. 25 leaves
CORP: International Working Group for the Construction of Sports and Leisure Facilities.
CORP: Federal Insitute of Sports Science.
NOTES: Cover title.
LEVEL: I LANG: Eng Ger GV401 18404

CONSTRUCTION AND RENOVATION

IAKS-Planungsgrundlagen fuer Sporthallen - Hallen fuer Turnen und Spiele. Empfehlungen fuer Planung und Bau. IAKS-Planning guidelines for sporthalls - halls for gymnastics and games. Recommendations for planning and building. Principe de base de l'AKS pour le planning des salles de sport - salles de gymnastique et de jeu. Recommandations concernant le planning et la construction. *Sportstaettenbau + Baederanlagen (Cologne, W. Germany)* 18(2), Mar/Apr 1984, M1-M15.
LEVEL: B LANG: Ger Eng Fr SIRC ARTICLE NO: 095830

Locker rooms: home away from home. *Fitness industry (Miami, Fla.)* 2(6), Oct 1984, 34-36.
LEVEL: B LANG: Eng SIRC ARTICLE NO 106432

DESIGN

Calvert, J.S. Taylor, N. Clarement sports hall: the university background. *Ilam: Institute of leisure & amenity management (London)* 2(10), Oct 1984, 12-14.
LEVEL: B LANG: Eng SIRC ARTICLE NO: 102422

Geraint, J. The design desert: the shape of things. *Sports and leisure (London)* 25(1), Mar/Apr 1984, 16-17.
LEVEL: B LANG Eng SIRC ARTICLE NO: 102424

Kellas, I. The comprehensive guide to sports centres in England. *Sports and leisure (London)* 25(1), Mar/Apr 1984, 33-52.
LEVEL: B LANG: Eng SIRC ARTICLE NO: 102426

Kent Commons becomes a community focal point. The 1983 AP&F facility of merit. *Athletic purchasing and facilities (Madison, Wis.)* 8(1), Jan 1984, 28;30-31.
LEVEL: B LANG: Eng SIRC ARTICLE NO: 094298

Wilson, R. Saluting the standard. (standardized approach for sports hall) *Sports and leisure (London)* 25(1), Mar/Apr 1984, 19-21.
LEVEL: B LANG: Eng SIRC ARTICLE NO: 102427

DIRECTORIES

84 8th annual buyers guide. Madison, Wis.: Athletic Purchasing and Facilities, 1984. 174 p. : ill (Athletic purchasing and facilities (Madison, Wis.) 8(2), Feb 1984.)
LEVEL: I LANG: Eng

Building and facility components: products used in constructing and operating an athletic facility are listed here. Manufacturers and suppliers of each product are listed alphabetically following each heading. *Athletic purchasing and facilities (Madison, Wis.)* 8(2), Feb 1984, 131-134;136;138;140;142;144.
NOTES: 1984 buyers guide.
LEVEL: B LANG: Eng SIRC ARTICLE NO: 108282

Directory of professionals: sports and recreation facility architects, builders and consultants are listed here. *Athletic purchasing and facilities (Madison, Wis.)* 8(2), Feb 1984, 125-126;128.
NOTES: 1984 buyers guide.
LEVEL: B LANG: Eng SIRC ARTICLE NO: 108281

Indoor sports and recreation buildings to visit. *Sports and leisure (London)* 25(1), Mar/Apr 1984, 28-32.
LEVEL: B LANG: Eng SIRC ARTICLE NO: 102425

Outdoor recreational components: products used in building and operating outdoor recreation facilities are listed here. Manufacturers and suppliers of each product are listed alphabetically after each heading. *Athletic purchasing and facilities (Madison, Wis.)* 8(2), Feb 1984, 161-162;164;166;168;170;172.
NOTES: 1984 buyers guide.
LEVEL: B LANG: Eng SIRC ARTICLE NO: 108284

ECONOMICS

Bronzan, R.T. Student fees: a new source for funding facilities. *Athletic business (Madison, Wis.)* 8(3), Mar 1984, 18-20;22
LEVEL: B LANG: Eng SIRC ARTICLE NO: 175921

Construire des equipements sportifs ou de loisirs? Les elus raisonnent de plus en plus en terme de rentabilite des installations. *Moniteur des travaux publics et du batiment (Paris)* 51, 1984, 19.
LEVEL: B LANG: Fr

Delforge, M. Remans, A. Infrastructure sportive et crise economique: quelques reflexions sur les tendances actuelles dans le pays du Conseil de l'Europe. (Refs: 77)*Sport: Communaute francaise de Belgique (Bruxelles)* 27(3), 1984, 170-183.
LEVEL: B LANG: Fr SIRC ARTICLE NO: 098967

ENERGY CONSERVATION

New game at Yankee Stadium strikes out rising energy costs. *Energy management technology (Willow Grove, Penn.)* 8(4), May/Jun 1984, 32-33.
ABST: This article describes a new computer monitoring system that has been installed at Yankee Stadium to more efficiently administer the energy needs of this facility.
LEVEL: I LANG: Eng SIRC ARTICLE NO: 098973

FLOORING

Artifical surfaces. *Sports turf bulletin (Bingley, England)* 144, Jan/Mar 1984, 3-5.
LEVEL: B LANG: Eng SIRC ARTICLE NO: 092765

Junqua, A. Lacouture, P. Sols sportifs. Confort et performance. (Refs: 17)*Dans, Culture technique no. 13, Neuilly-sur-Seine France, Centre de Recherche sur la Culture Technique, c1984, p. 226-233.
LEVEL: A LANG: Fr RC1235 20096

GYMNASIUMS

Chauvel, P. Eclairage naturel et eclairage electrique dans les gymnases et les piscines couvertes. *Temps libre equipements (France)* 11(17/23), 1984, 6 p..
LEVEL: B LANG: Fr

JOINT-USE

Public support pays off. *American school and university (Philadelphia)* 56(6), Feb 1984, 44;46.
ABST: This article outlines guidelines and policies for the use of school physical education facilities by nonschool groups.
LEVEL: B LANG: Eng SIRC ARTICLE NO: 095706

Swanson, V. Twardus, B. Facilities management: cooperative efforts benefiting school and recreational interests. *Interscholastic athletic administration* 10(3), Spring 1984, 4-7;9.
LEVEL: B LANG: Eng SIRC ARTICLE NO: 092762

LIGHTING

Bieri, J. Lighting: let it shine on your employee services program. *Employee services management (Westchester, Ill.)* 27(9), Nov 1984, 19-22.
LEVEL: B LANG: Eng SIRC ARTICLE NO: 108423

Gregory, S. Lewis, A. Stewart, J. Maw, R. Sports hall lighting: a guide to visibility and lighting in small multipurpose sports halls. London: Sports Council,

FACILITIES (continued)

1984. 13 p. : ill. (TUS design note 10.)
LEVEL: I LANG: Eng GV401 20000

La preparation des terrains de football et de tennis pour les nocturnes. *Lettre des techniques municipales (France)* 118, 1984 6-7.
LEVEL: B LANG: Fr

Meyers, A. Bring night to life... (lighting) *Grounds maintenance (Overland Park, Kans.)* 19(8), Aug 1984, 30;32-34;52;54.
LEVEL: B LANG: Eng SIRC ARTICLE NO: 103921

Virginia tech's tv level lighting. *Park maintenance and grounds management (Appleton, Wis.)* 37(4), Apr 1984, 14-15.
LEVEL: LANG: Eng SIRC ARTICLE NO: 100590

PLANNING

To get the facility you want, decide what you want and then spell it out. *Athletic purchasing and facilities (Madison, Wis.)* 8(1), Jan 1984, 22;24.
LEVEL: B LANG: Eng SIRC ARTICLE NO: 094300

PLAYGROUNDS

Brown, J.G. Burger, C. Playground designs and preschool childrens behaviors. (Refs: 38)*Environment and behavior (Beverly Hills, Calif.)* 16(5), 1984, 599-626.
LEVEL: I LANG: Eng SIRC ARTICLE NO: 098962

Good playground equipment lets kids be kids-safely. *Executive educator (Washington)* 6(2), Feb 1984, 43.
LEVEL: B LANG: Eng SIRC ARTICLE NO: 095821

Hadley, F. Planning is key to playgound management. *Park maintenance (Appleton, Wis.)* 37(10), Oct 1984, 34-36;38.
LEVEL: LANG: Eng SIRC ARTICLE NO: 109098

Storage, T.W. Bowen, L.E. Playgrounds of the future. *Recreation reporter (Vancouver)* Jan/Feb 1984, 4-5.
LEVEL: B LANG: En SIRC ARTICLE NO: 095823

PLAYGROUNDS - EQUIPMENT

Playground equipment: brighten up your play areas safely. This month's product focus centres on some of the items and surfaces available to equip today's playgrounds. *Parks, golf courses & sports grounds (Middlesex, Eng.)* 49(4), Jan 1984, 10;13;15.
LEVEL: B LANG: Eng SIRC ARTICLE NO: 097508

Roy, M. Playground equipment: the equipment manufactured for home use is not as solid as the local school or park equipment. *Protect yourself (Montreal)* Jun 1984, 42-44.
LEVEL: B LANG: Eng SIRC ARTICLE NO: 095822

Smith, C. Play - not just kids' stuff. *Groundsman (London)* 37(7), Jul 1984, 11-14.
LEVEL: B LANG: Eng SIRC ARTICLE NO: 103925

STADIUMS

B.C. place stadium. *Journal of the Prestressed Concrete Institute (Chicago)* 29(2), Mar/Apr 1984, 132-143.
LEVEL: B LANG: En SIRC ARTICLE NO: 095824

Brancatelli, D. Saddledome: the Olympic ice stadium in Calgary (Canada). Il Saddledome: stadio olimpico del ghiaccio a Calgary (Canada). *Industria*

Italiana del cemento (Rome) 54(5), May 1984, 280-313.
LEVEL: I LANG: It Eng SIRC ARTICLE NO: 103935

Marcum, B. South Carolina's Williams-Brice Stadium: a touch of class. *Athletic administration (Cleveland, Oh.)* 19(3), May 1984, 21-22.
LEVEL: B LANG: Eng SIRC ARTICLE NO: 094299

Schmidt, T. Die Stadionanlagen der Olympischen Sommerspiele von 1896 bis 1936. (Refs: 19)*Sport und Baeder und Freizeit-Bauten (Duesseldorf)* 2, Apr 1984, 71-88.
LEVEL: I LANG: Ger SIRC ARTICLE NO: 094097

STANDARDS

Kolitzus, H.J. Functional standards for playing surfaces. (Refs: 10)
NOTES: In, Frederick, E.C. (ed.), Sport shoes and playing surfaces: biomechanical properties, Champaign, Ill., Human Kinetics Publishers, c1984, p. 98-118.
LEVEL: A LANG: Eng QP302 17870

Specification for artificial sports surfaces: draft for development. London: Sports Council, c1984. 3v.
CORP: Sports Council.
CORP: Rubber and Plastics Research Association of Great Britain.
NOTES: Contents: Part 1: General principles and classification. - Part 2: Surfaces for general use. - Part 3: Surfaces for individual sports/section 1: cricket.
LEVEL: I LANG: Eng ISBN: 0-906577-30-6 0-906577-31-4 0-906577-32-2 GV401 20829

STATISTICS

The shape of an industry: present facilities, predictions for tommorrow. *Recreation, sports & leisure (Minneapolis)* 4(6), Aug 1984, 39-43.
NOTES: Special issue: Managed recreation research report.
LEVEL: B LANG: Eng SIRC ARTICLE NO: 103931

TURF

Beard, J.B. Grasses for the transition zone. *Grounds maintenance (Overland Park, Kans.)* 19(11), Jan 1984, 60;62.
LEVEL: I LANG: Eng SIRC ARTICLE NO: 100593

Christians, N. How a turfgrass plant uses nitrogen. *Grounds maintenance (Overland Park, Kans.)* 19(2), Feb 1984, 80.
LEVEL: I LANG: Eng SIRC ARTICLE NO: 098982

Engelke, M. Zoysia - the golden species. *Grounds maintenance (Overland Park, Kans.)* 19(11), Jan 1984, 22;26;30;99.
LEVEL: LANG: Eng SIRC ARTICLE NO: 100603

Establishment of new areas from seed. *Sports turf bulletin (West Yorkshire, Eng.)* 146, Jul/Sept 1984, 2-5.
LEVEL: B LANG: E SIRC ARTICLE NO: 102430

Hayes, P. The turfgrass industry, past, present, future. *Parks, golf courses & sports grounds (Middlesex, Eng.)* 50(1), Oct 1984, 8;10;13.
LEVEL: B LANG: Eng SIRC ARTICLE NO: 173194

Pepper, I.L. Kneebone, W.R. Growth of bentgrass as affected by nitrogen, soil pH and age of stand. *USGA Green Section Recor (Far Hills, N.J.)* 22(3), May/Jun 1984, 10-12.
LEVEL: I LANG: Eng SIRC ARTICLE NO: 100617

Sheard, R.W. Mineral nutrition of bentgrass on sand rooting systems. *Greenmaster (Toronto)* 20(8), Nov/Dec 1984, 19.
LEVEL I LANG: Eng SIRC ARTICLE NO: 173145

Shildrick, J. Turf species: choosing cultivars for low maintenance. *Parks, golf courses and sports grounds (Middlesex, Eng. 49(5)*, Feb 1984, 30-32.
LEVEL: B LANG: Eng SIRC ARTICLE NO: 100629

Top dressing for greens, wickets and pitches. *Sports turf bulletin (West Yorkshire, Eng.)* 146, Jul/Sept 1984, 5-8.
LEVEL: B LANG: Eng SIRC ARTICLE NO: 102436

TURF - ADMINISTRATION

Addresses of manufacturers, growers and suppliers. *Grounds maintenance (Overland Park, Kans.)* 19(12), Dec 1984, 52;54;58;60;62;66-69.
LEVEL: B LANG: Eng SIRC ARTICLE NO: 105225

Directory of associations. *Grounds maintenance (Overland Park, Kans.)* 19(12), Dec 1984, 2;83-88.
LEVEL: B LANG: Eng SIRC ARTICLE NO: 105229

Grimwood, J. Back to basics: the living plant. *Groundsman (London)* 37(6), Jun 1984, 11-12.
LEVEL: B LANG: Eng SIRC ARTICL NO: 100608

TURF - ARTIFICIAL

Artifical surfaces. *Sports turf bulletin (Bingley, England)* 144, Jan/Mar 1984, 3-5.
LEVEL: B LANG: Eng SIRC ARTICLE NO: 092765

Dereix, A.J. Elle se fume pas, elle se broute pas...c'est l'herbe synthetique. *Tennis de France (Paris)* 371, mars 1984, 36-37.
LEVEL: B LANG: Fr SIRC ARTICLE NO: 094303

Dury, P. How to make sports facilities more profitable. *Turf management (Surrey, Eng.)* 3(5), May 1984, 16-19.
LEVEL: B LANG: Eng SIRC ARTICLE NO: 102154

Fleischmann, T. Commission d'experts elargie pour les installations de sport CFGS/ASS. Conference annuelle (1983) des conseillers cantonaux en installations sportives. *Macolin (Suisse)* 1, janv 1984, 12-14.
NOTES: Traduction et adaptation de, Marianne Weber et Yves Jeannotat.
LEVEL: B LANG: Fr SIRC ARTICLE NO: 095840

Hawkins, P. Developments in synthetic grasses. *Turf management (Surrey, Eng.)* 3(7), Jul 1984, 2325.
LEVEL: B LANG: Eng SIRC ARTICLE NO: 102150

Rapoport, R. Artificial turf: is the grass greener? *In, Schrier, E.W. and Allman, W.F. (eds.), Newton at the bat: the science in sports*, New York, Scribner, c1984, p. 63-66.
LEVEL: B LANG: Eng RC1235 18609

Roberts, J. Performance tests in need of development. (Refs: 6)*Turf management (Surrey, Eng.)* 3(7), Jul 1984, 26-27;29.
LEVEL: B LANG: Eng SIRC ARTICLE NO: 102151

Robin, M. Grassard, P. Une premiere: un terrain avec revetement gazon synthetique et sable. *Temps libre equipements (France 10(33/37)*, 1984, 4 p..
LEVEL: B LANG: Fr

Squires, T. The alternative: synthetic turf. *Park maintenance and grounds management (Appleton,*

Wisc.) 37(8), Aug 1984, 8-9.
LEVEL: B LANG: Eng SIRC ARTICLE NO: 105246

Stobbs, J. What role for synthetic golf greens? *Turf management (Great Bookham, Surrey) 3(9), Sept 1984, 33-35.*
LEVEL: B LANG: Eng SIRC ARTICLE NO: 105248

Van Ness, R. Trenton State is first with 'sports field'. *Athletic administration (Cleveland, Ohio) 19(4), Sept 1984, 9-11.*
LEVEL: B LANG: Eng SIRC ARTICLE NO: 108232

TURF - CONSTRUCTION

Mills, W. Turf and turfing. *Groundsman (London) 37(6), Jun 1984, 13-14;16.*
LEVEL: B LANG: Eng SIRC ARTICLE NO: 100614

Parr, T. Are recommended seed rates too high? *Parks, golf courses & sports grounds (Middlesex, Eng.) 49(12), Sept 1984, 6-8*
LEVEL: I LANG: Eng SIRC ARTICLE NO: 106453

Schmidt, R.E. Better sports fields - part 1: construction. *Grounds maintenance (Overland Park, Kans.) 19(4), Apr 1984, 26;30;34;40;112.*
NOTES: Part 1 of a three-part series.
LEVEL: B LANG: Eng SIRC ARTICLE NO: 100624

Shiels, G. The growing medium: solving the riddle of the sands. *Parks, golf courses and sports grounds (Middlesex, Eng.) 49(5), Feb 1984, 6;8;10.*
LEVEL: I LANG: Eng SIRC ARTICLE NO: 100627

Swan, H. Keeping sports grounds in our urban areas. *Parks, golf courses & sports grounds (Middlesex, Eng.) 50(1), Oct 1984, 58;60.*
LEVEL: B LANG: Eng SIRC ARTICLE NO: 173195

Szy, Z. Construction of playing fields in British Columbia. *Australian parks & recreation (Victoria, Aust.) Feb 1984, 38-40.*
LEVEL: B LANG: Eng SIRC ARTICLE NO: 095841

Templeton, M. The principles behind sports field construction: sports field construction is a considerable undertaking and requires a good deal of long-term planning. Matt Templeton, managing director of Nickerson Turfmaster Ltd., describes why thought should be given now if a pitch is to be built next spring. *Parks, golf courses & sports grounds (Middlesex, Eng.) 49(11), Aug 1984, 74;77.*
LEVEL: B LANG: Eng SIRC ARTICLE NO: 102435

Zehren, R. You can renovate on a low budget. *Park maintenance and grounds management (Appleton, Wis.) 37(4), Apr 1984, 12-14.*
LEVEL: B LANG: Eng SIRC ARTICLE NO: 100642

TURF - DISEASE

Beard, J.B. Herbicide update. *Grounds maintenance (Overland Park, Kans.) 19(11), Jan 1984, 54;56;58.*
LEVEL: B LANG: Eng SIRC ARTICLE NO: 100592

Burpee, L. Goutty, L. Evaluation of fungicides for control of pink snow mold on creeping bentgrass. *Greenmaster (Toronto) 2 (7), Sept/Oct 1984, 14-15.*
LEVEL: B LANG: Eng SIRC ARTICLE NO: 105228

Couch, H.B. Garber, J.M. Jones, D. Turfgrass fungicides: application methods and effectiveness, part 1. *Golf course management (Lawrence, Kans.) 52(7), Jul 1984, 40;42-43;46;48;50-52.*
LEVEL: I LANG: Eng SIRC ARTICLE NO: 100599

Couch, H.B. Turfgrass fungicides: part II. Dilution rates, nozzle size, nozzle pressure and disease control: here's a detailed look at a combination of factors that help determine spraying effectiveness. *Golf course management (Lawrence, Kans.) Aug 1984, 73-76;78;80.*
LEVEL: I LANG: Eng SIRC ARTICLE NO: 103947

Hurley, R. Pompei, M. The turf managers' friendly fungus: endophyte. *Grounds maintenance (Overland Park, Kans.) 19(8), Aug 1984, 18;20;62.*
LEVEL: B LANG: Eng SIRC ARTICLE NO: 103949

Niemczyk, H. The bluegrass billbug: frequently misdiagnosed. *Park maintenance (Appleton, Wis.) 37(3), Mar 1984, 19;22;24-25.*
NOTES: Reprinted from, American Lawn Applicator 4(3).
LEVEL: B LANG: Eng SIRC ARTICLE NO: 098991

Sanders, P. Infrared photography: fairways stand exposed. *Golf course management (Kansas) 52(5), May 1984, 28;32.*
LEVEL: LANG: Eng SIRC ARTICLE NO: 100622

Woolhouse, A.R. Wright, A.J. Technical notes: an investigation of the effectiveness of various systemic fungicides in suppressing worm-casting. (Refs: 2)*Journal of the Sports Turf Research Institute (Bingley, West Yorkshire) 60, June 1984, 96-97.*
ABST: Four commercially available turf fungicides (benomyl, carbendazim, thiabendazole, thiophanate-methyl) were tested, each at two rates of application, for their ability to suppress worm cast production in amenity grassland. All had some effect although none achieved complete control.
LEVEL: A LANG: Eng SIRC ARTICLE NO: 108518

TURF - DRAINAGE AND IRRIGATION

Barson, W. Equipment for irrigation. *Groundsman (London) 37(5), May 1984, 17-18;20.*
LEVEL: B LANG: Eng SIRC ARTICLE NO: 103942

Correctly calculating your irrigation levels... *Parks, golf course & sports grounds (Middlesex, Eng.) 49(9), Jun 1984, 32;34-35.*
LEVEL: I LANG: Eng SIRC ARTICLE NO: 103946

Drainage options on winter pitches. *Sports turf bulletin (Bingley, Eng.) 147, Oct/Dec 1984, 7-9.*
LEVEL: B LANG: Eng SIRC ARTICLE NO: 100600

Harbridge, M. Maintenance problems of sand slit systems. *Turf management (Surrey, Eng.) 3(3), Mar 1984, 25-27.*
LEVEL: B LANG: Eng SIRC ARTICLE NO: 108684

How drainage helps fight compaction. *Turf management (Great Bookham, Surrey) 3(8), Aug 1984, 24-25.*
LEVEL: B LANG: Eng SIRC ARTICLE NO: 105236

Kuhn, C.H. Use your heads for better athletic fields. (irrigation) *Grounds maintenance (Overland Park, Kans.) 19(4), Apr 1984, 42;46;48;52.*
NOTES: Adapted from a talk presented to the 30th Northwest Turfgrass Conference at Yakina, Wash., in September 1982.
LEVEL: B LANG: Eng SIRC ARTICLE NO: 100612

Mills, W. Not too little not too much: why irrigation and drainage are necessary. *Groundsman (London) 37(4), Apr 1984, 20-25.*
LEVEL: B LANG: Eng SIRC ARTICLE NO: 100615

Mills, W. Drainage in action. *Groundsman (London) 37(5), May 1984, 22-25;27-28.*
LEVEL: B LANG: Eng SIRC ARTICLE NO: 10395

Mills, W. Drainage in action. *Groundsman (London, Eng.) 37(5), May 1984, 22-25;27-28.*
LEVEL: B LANG: Eng SIRC ARTICLE NO: 102125

Sarsfield, A.C. Irrigation problems? Should you... repair or replace? *Grounds maintenance (Overland Park, Kans.) 19(10), Oc 1984, 26;30;32;34;36;52.*
LEVEL: B LANG: Eng SIRC ARTICLE NO: 173299

Schmidt, R.E. Water quality testing. *Grounds maintenance (Overland Park, Kans.), 19(2), Feb 1984, 72;74;78.*
LEVEL: I LANG: Eng SIRC ARTICLE NO: 098994

Sheard, R.W. A water budget for irrigation scheduling. *Greenmaster (Toronto) 20(3), Apr 1984, 11-13.*
LEVEL: I LANG: Eng SIRC ARTICLE NO: 100626

Templeton, M. Why good drainage is essential for turf. *Parks, golf courses & sports grounds (Staines, Middlesex) 49(8), May 1984, 8;10.*
LEVEL: B LANG: Eng SIRC ARTICLE NO: 109179

Truttmann, D. Your irrigation system: preparation for winter. *Greenmaster (Toronto) 20(7), Sept/Oct 1984, 12-13.*
LEVEL: B LANG: Eng SIRC ARTICLE NO: 105251

Watson, J. Irrigation: a pre-construction evaluation. *Greenmaster (Toronto) 20(3), Apr 1984, 5;7.*
NOTES: Transcribed from a talk at the Atlantic Golf Superintendents Fall Field Day, 1983.
LEVEL: B LANG: Eng SIRC ARTICLE NO: 100637

TURF - ENVIRONMENT

Gurney, M. Polyester provides protection. *Greenmaster (Toronto) 20(7), Sept/Oct 1984, 19-21.*
LEVEL: B LANG: Eng SIRC ARTICLE NO: 105234

Winter is... wet, windy, wild, wonderful,...? *Greenmaster (Toronto) 20(7), Sept/Oct 1984, 9-10.*
LEVEL: B LANG: Eng SIRC ARTICLE NO: 105253

TURF - EVALUATION

Bamford, K. Cattani, D. Clark, K.W. Cultivar trials at the University of Manitoba. *Greenmaster (Toronto) 20(8), Nov/Dec 198 9-10.*
LEVEL: I LANG: Eng SIRC ARTICLE NO: 173140

Daniels, R.W. Competitiveness of perennial ryegrass and annual bluegrass (Poa Annua L). *Greenmaster (Toronto) 20(8), Nov/De 1984, 17.*
LEVEL: I LANG: Eng SIRC ARTICLE NO: 173143

TURF - FERTILIZER

Beard, J.B. Insecticide update. *Grounds maintenance (Overland Park, Kans.) 19(2), Feb 1984, 16;18.*
LEVEL: B LANG: Eng SIR ARTICLE NO: 098978

Beard, J.B. Fungicide update. *Grounds maintenance (Overland Park, Kans.) 19(3), Mar 1984, 48;50.*
LEVEL: B LANG: Eng SIRC ARTICLE NO: 098980

Canaway, P.M. The response of Lolium perenne (perennial ryegrass) turf grown on sand and soil to fertilizer nitrogen I. Ground cover response as affected by football-type wear. (Refs: 22)*Journal of the Sports Turf Research Institute (Bingley, West Yorkshire) 60, Jun 1984, 8-18.*
ABST: The response of Lolium prenne L. to fertilizer nitrogen was studied on a sand rootzone and on the local topsoil. The trials were sown in August

FACILITIES (continued)

1981, and during 1982 the following nitrogen treatments were applied: 0.25, 100, 225, 400, 625 kg ha minus 1 N. Ground cover was measured before, during and after artificial football-type wear treatments applied during the 1982-83 football season. The results showed that before wear ground cover increased rapidly with increasing nitrogen, Mitscherlich curves being fitted to these responses. However, once the wear treatment started the plots which had received high levels of nitrogen deteriorated at a faster rate than those receiving intermediate levels, so that an optimum level became evident. These responses were fitted by inverse polynomial curves and the optimum nitrogen levels were calculated at each sampling date. Disregarding the early stages of wear and the last date of sampling on the soil, where little ground cover remained, the average optimum nitrogen input for the best wear tolerance of turf in its first season of use was 289 kg ha minus 1 N per year.
LEVEL: A LANG: Eng SIRC ARTICLE NO: 108509

Canaway, P.M. The response of Lolium perenne (perennial ryegrass) turf grown on sand and soil to fertilizer nitrogen II. Above-ground biomass, tiller numbers and root biomass. (Refs: 16)*Journal of the Sports Turf Research Institute (Bingley, West Yorkshire) 60, June 1984, 19-26.*
ABST: The response of Lolium perenne L. to fertilizer nitrogen in terms of above-ground biomass, tiller numbers and root biomass was studied. Above-ground biomass and tiller numbers were recorded on both sand and soil rootzones, and root biomass was recorded at three sampling depths (0-5 cm, 5-10 cm and 10-15 cm) on sand only. The measurements were made on unworn turf in September 1982, just over one year after sowing. The results showed that above-ground increased rapidly with increasing nitrogen but at the highest level a decline was evident, particularly in the case of the turf grown on soil. Inverse polynomial curves were fitted to these data from which the nitrogen level yielded the maximum biomass was calculated. The values were 462 and 445 kg ha minus 1 N for the sand and soil areas respectively. Tiller numbers showed a continuous increase over the whole range of treatments, an upper limit of tiller density not being reached. Mean dry weight per tiller declined with incresing nitrogen. Root biomass decreased with increasing nitrogen and with sampling depth, the majority of the roots being found in the 0-5 cm depth.
LEVEL: A LANG: Eng SIRC ARTICLE NO: 108510

Canaway, P.M. The response of Lolium perenne (perennial ryegrass) turf grown on sand and soil to fertilizer nitrogen III. Aspects of playability - ball bounce resilience and shear strength. (Refs: 12)*Journal of the Sports Turf Research Institute (Bingley, West Yorkshire) 60, June 1984, 27-36.*
ABST: Measurements were made of ball bounce resilience and shear strength of Lolium perenne L. turf grown on sand and soil subjected to a range of fertilizer nitrogen treatments (0 to 625 kg ha minus 1), and receiving artificial football-type wear during the winter months. The results showed that before wear, ball bounce resilience decreased with increasing nitrogen but shear strength did not show consistent results. During and after wear ball bounce was dependent more on the type of rootzone than on the nitrogen treatments, the sand construction retaining much higher values of ball bounce throughout the winter months, in contrast to the soil area which deteriorated to a muddy condition, with a consequent reduction in ball

bounce resilience, Shear strength showed similar results but these were less conclusive. There was some evidence of an optimum annual nitrogen input for turf shear strength, during and after wear, of 225 kg ha minus 1 when data sets of similar moisture content were compared.
LEVEL: A LANG: Eng SIRC ARTICLE NO: 108511

Hull, R. Nutrition of athletic turf. *Park maintenance and grounds management (Appleton, Wis.) 37(4), Apr 1984, 27-29.*
LEVEL: B LANG: Eng SIRC ARTICLE NO: 100611

Nelson, S.H. Nitrogen fertilizing of Kentucky bluegrass. *Greenmaster (Waterloo, Ont.) 20(4), May 1984, 9.*
LEVEL: I LANG: Eng SIRC ARTICLE NO: 100616

Sears, M.K. Bowhey, C. Thompson, D. Stephenson, G.R. Braun, H. Dislodgeable residues and persistence of diazinon following application to turfgrass. *Greenmaster (Waterloo, Ont.) 20(5), Jun 1984, 14-15.*
LEVEL: I LANG: Eng SIRC ARTICLE NO: 100625

Smith, E. Sprayer nozzle selection & calibration. *Grounds maintenance (Overland Park, Kans.) 19(11), Jan 1984, 46;48;50.*
LEVEL: B LANG: Eng SIRC ARTICLE NO: 100630

Some principles for use of fertilizers on sports turf. *Sports turf bulletin (West Yorkshire, Eng.) 146, Jul/ Sept 1984, 8-10.*
LEVEL: B LANG: Eng SIRC ARTICLE NO: 102434

TURF - INJURY

Beard, J.B. Diagnosing & repairing winterkill on turf. *Grounds maintenance (Overland Park, Kans.) 19(3), Mar 1984, 18;24;26.*
LEVEL: B LANG: Eng SIRC ARTICLE NO: 098979

TURF - MAINTENANCE

All you ever wanted to know about turf tyres. *Parks, golf courses & sports grounds (Staines, Middlesex) 50(2), Nov 1984, 22-24.*
LEVEL: B LANG: Eng SIRC ARTICLE NO: 108869

Bennett, R. How mowing dictates turf quality. *Turf management (Great Bookham, Surrey) 3(9), Sept 1984, 27-28;30.*
LEVEL: B LANG: Eng SIRC ARTICLE NO: 105227

Copley, K. Safe equipment operation. *Grounds maintenance (Overland Park, Kans.) 19(8), Aug 1984, 36;40;44.*
LEVEL: B LANG: Eng SIRC ARTICLE NO: 103945

Dernoeden, P.H. The turf management. *Grounds management forum (Pikesville, Md.) 8(5), Jun 1984, 7-8.*
LEVEL: B LANG: Eng SIRC ARTICLE NO: 098983

Hall, J.R. Timing: the key to good turf. *Grounds maintenance (Overland Park, Kans.) 19(3), Mar 1984, 30;32;35;139-140.*
LEVEL: B LANG: Eng SIRC ARTICLE NO: 098988

Hermitage, R. Herbicides. *Greenmaster (Toronto) 20(6), Jul/Aug 1984, 18.*
LEVEL: B LANG: Eng SIRC ARTICLE NO: 102431

Hull, R. Weed control on athletic areas. *Park maintenance and grounds management (Appleton, Wis.) 37(4), Apr 1984, 9-10.*
LEVEL: B LANG: Eng SIRC ARTICLE NO: 100610

Jones, B. Turf management by computer is here for athletic areas. *Park maintenance (Appleton,*

Wis.) 37(1), Jan 1984, 17-18.
LEVEL: B LANG: Eng SIRC ARTICLE NO: 098990

Jones, M. The perennial problem of fine turf areas. *Parks, golf courses & sports grounds (Middlesex) 49(10), Jul 1984, 30;33-34.*
LEVEL: B LANG: Eng SIRC ARTICLE NO: 105240

Luba, T. The biggest athletic area problems. *Park maintenance and grounds management (Appleton, Wis.) 37(4), Apr 1984, 23-24.*
LEVEL: B LANG: Eng SIRC ARTICLE NO: 100613

Mann, I. Changing patterns for turf-tyres. *Turf management (Surrey, Eng.) 3(7), Jul 1984, 15-16.*
LEVEL: B LANG: Eng SIRC ARTICLE NO: 102147

Martin, G. Solving problems on local authority budgets. *Turf management (Surrey, Eng.) 3(12), Dec 1984, 21.*
LEVEL: B LANG Eng SIRC ARTICLE NO: 105241

Nesbitt, S. Maintaining spray equipment. *Grounds maintenance (Overland Park, Kans.) 19(7), Jul 1984, 26;28;72;74.*
LEVEL: B LANG: Eng SIRC ARTICLE NO: 105242

Parr, T.W. Cox, R. Plant, R.A. The effects of cutting height on root distribution and water use of ryegrass (Lolium perenne L. S23) turf. (Refs: 29)*Journal of the Sports Turf Research Institute (Bingley, West Yorkshire) 60, June 1984, 45-53.*
ABST: The effects of 3 cutting heights (20 mm, 44mm and uncut) shoot growth, root growth and water use during the establishment of a spring turf of Lolium perenne were compared. The 44 mm cut only reduced root biomass at soil depths below 15 cm whereas the 20 mm cut reduced roots at all depths and resulted in a 35 percent reduction in total root biomass. Total water use over the summer period was greatest in the uncut plots (2.8 mm day minus 1) and least in the low cut plots (2.2 mm day minus 1). Cutting also reduced the depth at which water was used from 90 cm to 65 cm. Although cutting reduced the total gras biomass, the root: total shoot (including cuttings) ratio remained constant indicating a direct relationship between root and shoot production. The pattern of soil water use within the soil profile was positively correlated with the distribution of root biomass.
LEVEL: A LANG: Eng SIRC ARTICLE NO: 108513

Roberts, E.C. St. Augustinegrass: a profile for Southern turf. *Southern golf(Clearwater, Fla.) 15(5), Nov/Dec 1984, 32;23.*
LEVEL: B LANG: Eng SIRC ARTICLE NO: 105244

Roberts, E.C. Wintergrasses: a profile for Southern turf. *Southern golf (Clearwater, Fla.) 15(4), Sept/ Oct 1984, 29;23;46.*
LEVEL: B LANG: Eng SIRC ARTICLE NO: 105245

Rollers and rolling. *Sports turf bulletin (Bringley, England) 144, Jan/Mar 1984, 10-12.*
LEVEL: B LANG: Eng SIRC ARTICLE NO: 092773

Salettel, D. Don't be afraid to use wetting agents. *Grounds maintenance (Overland Park, Kans.) 19(8), Aug 1984, 14;70.*
LEVEL: B LANG: Eng SIRC ARTICLE NO: 103953

Sands for sports turf construction and maintenance. *Sports turf bulletin (Bingley, Eng.) 147, Oct/Dec 1984, 3-5.*
LEVEL: B LANG: Eng SIRC ARTICLE NO: 100623

Shildrick, J.P. Peel, C.H. Preliminary trials of perennial ryegrass cultivars (trials A1, B2 and B3), 1980-3. (Refs: 12) *Journal of the Sports Turf Research Institute (Bingley, West Yorkshire) 60,*

June 1984, 73-95.
ABST: Information is given on 33 cultivars and selections of perennial ryegrass, with ten control cultivars for comparison. They were sown at Bingley in August-September 1980 and assessed for nearly three years under three management regimes: 1) high nitrogen level (280 kg ha minus 1 N per annum) with artificial football wear starting in autumn 1981; 2) low nitrogen level (75 kg ha minus 1 N in spring 1981 only) with wear identical to (a); and 3) a low maintenance no-wear regime, with no fertilizer after sowing, and one cut a year in early July. The main features of turf performance are summarized in two tables and in brief notes on each cultivar. Data for shoot number and biomass from 40 cultivars are examined in more detail, and compared with similar data from an earlier trial, leading to the conclusion that above-ground biomass is more useful than shoot number for predicting end-of-wear cover. Correlations between shoot size and cover indicate that, before wear, cultivars with numerous small shoots had the best ground cover but that after a period of wear cultivars with fewer more robust shoots had better cover.
LEVEL: A LANG: Eng SIRC ARTICLE NO: 108517

Stansfield, D. Restoring grass cover and maintaining it. *Parks, golf courses & sports grounds (Middlesex) 49(10), Jul 1984, 12-13.*
LEVEL: B LANG: Eng SIRC ARTICLE NO: 105247

Synnestvedt, D.O. Training key employees. *Grounds maintenance (Overland Park, Kans.) 19(4), Apr 1984, 100-102;104.*
LEVEL: LANG: Eng SIRC ARTICLE NO: 100632

Taylor, R. Renewed interest in chemical growth control. *Turf management (Surrey, Eng.) 3(5), May 1984, 23-24;26.*
LEVEL: B LANG: Eng SIRC ARTICLE NO: 102155

Toma, G. George Toma tells how to get green grass in a hurry. *Grounds maintenance (Overland Park, Kans.) 19(2), Feb 1984, 29;33-34;126-127.*
LEVEL: B LANG: Eng SIRC ARTICLE NO: 098995

Watson, J. Cost conscious mowing. *Park maintenance (Appleton, Wis.) 37(1), Jan 1984, 6-8.*
LEVEL: B LANG: Eng SIRC ARTICLE NO: 098996

Weed control guide: effective control depends on identification. *Turf management (Great Bookham, Surrey) 3(10), Oct 1984, 15-17.*
LEVEL: B LANG: Eng SIRC ARTICLE NO: 105252

TURF - RESEARCH

Bhowmik, P. Turf research: the Northeast. *Park maintenance and grounds management (Appleton, Mich.) 37(7), Jul 1984, 9-12.*
LEVEL: I LANG: Eng SIRC ARTICLE NO: 103943

Cook, T. Turf research: the West. *Park maintenance and grounds management (Appleton, Mich.) 37(7), Jul 1984, 6-8.*
LEVEL: LANG: Eng SIRC ARTICLE NO: 103944

Danneberger, K. Turf research: the Midwest. *Park maintenance and grounds management (Appleton, Mich.) 37(7), Jul 1984, 16-17.*
LEVEL: B LANG: Eng SIRC ARTICLE NO: 103948

Lettner, R.G. Turfgrass research at Fairview College. *Greenmaster (Toronto) 20(8), Nov/dec 1984, 15.*
LEVEL: B LANG: Eng SIRC ARTICLE NO: 173142

Peacock, C. Turf research: the South. *Park maintenance and grounds management (Appleton, Mich.) 37(7), Jul 1984, 12-14;16.*
LEVEL: I LANG: Eng SIRC ARTICLE NO: 103952

TURF - SOIL

Baker, S.W. Long-term effects of three amendment materials on the moisture retention characteristics of a sand-soil mix. (Refs: 5)*Journal of the Sports Turf Research Institute (Bingley, West Yorkshire) 60, June 1984, 61-65.*
ABST: The moisture retention characteristics of a sand-soil mix and similar material amended by additions of peat, perlite and Forest Bark were studied six years after each material was sown with a fescue-bent seeds mix. All three products improved moisture retention and gave better turf quality at times of drought stress, with the peat amendment having the greatest effect. However, significant differences in visual assessment between the materials only became apparent after 5.5 weeks without watering by which time the quality of the sward was well below that which would be regarded as acceptable for a fine turf playing surface.
LEVEL: A LANG: Eng SIRC ARTICLE NO: 108515

Grimwood, J. Back to basics. *Groundsman (London) 37(1), Jan 1984, 36-37.*
LEVEL: B LANG: Eng SIRC ARTICLE NO: 098987

Grimwood, J. Back to basics. *Groundsman (London) 37(4), Apr 1984, 16-18.*
LEVEL: I LANG: Eng SIRC ARTICLE NO: 100609

Waddington, D.V. Learning about soil texture. *Grounds maintenance (Overland Park, Kans.) 19(4), Apr 1984, 58;61-62;65-66.*
LEVEL: I LANG: Eng SIRC ARTICLE NO: 100636

TURF - WEAR TOLERANCE

Shildrick, J. Natural surfaces: the grass roots of wear tolerance. (Refs: 4)*Parks, golf courses and sports grounds (Middlesex, Eng.) 49(7), Apr 1984, 6-8.*
LEVEL: I LANG: Eng SIRC ARTICLE NO: 100628

Shildrick, J.P. Peel, C.H. Shoot numbers, biomass and shear strength in smooth-stalked meadow-grass (Poa pratensis). (Refs: *Journal of the Sports Turf Research Institute (Bingley, West Yorkshire) 60, June 1984, 66-72.*
ABST: The evaluation of cultivars under winter wear treatment is particularly difficult with smooth-stalked meadow-grass because of the build-up of thatch before wear and the dormancy of some cultivars during winter. For these reasons, the conventional expression of 'wear tolerance' in terms of ground cover seems inadequate for this species. Data are presented here from cores taken before wear (to assess shoot number and above-ground biomass) and shear strength values obtained near the end of the wear season, to show that important cultivar differences were not being made clear by conventional assessment, and to underline the importance of shear strength as a character relevant to the 'wear tolerance' of cultivars.
LEVEL: A LANG: Eng SIRC ARTICLE NO: 108516

FEDERAL REPUBLIC OF GERMANY

Bentz, G. Frauensport in der Bundesrepublik Deutschland - eine positive und negative Bilanz. (Women's sport in the German Democratic Republic - positive and negative aspects.) (Refs: 17)*ICSSPE/CIEPSS review (Berlin, GDR) 7, 1984, 57-61.*
LEVEL: I LANG: Ger SIRC ARTICLE NO: 095657

Bette, K.H. Strukturelle Aspekte des Hochleistungssports in der Bundesrepublik: Ansatzpunkte fuer eine System-Umwelt-Theorie des Hochleistungssports. Sankt Augustin: Verlag Hans Richarz, c1984. 239 p. (Schriften der Deutschen Sporthochschule Koeln; Bd. 13.)
NOTES: Bibliography: p. 225-238.
LEVEL: A LANG: Ger ISBN: 3-888345-312-9 GV611 18386

Booth, B. Sport and political autonomy. *OPHEA: Ontario Physical and Health Education Association (London, Ont.) 10(2), Spring 1984, 57-75.*
LEVEL: I LANG: Eng SIRC ARTICLE NO: 099332

International development program. Report. May 5 - May 16, 1984. Vanier, Ont.: National Sport and Recreation Centre, 1984. 29 leaves : ill.
CORP: National Sport and Recreation Centre.
NOTES: Cover title. Bibliography: p. 29.
LEVEL: I LANG: Eng GV611 20053

Jahrbuch des Sports 1984. (Niedernhausen/ Taunus): Schors-Verlag, 1984. 416 p. : ill.
CORP: Deutscher Sportbund.
LEVEL: B LANG: Ger GV611 18271

COACHING

Knecht, W.P. Die Wegbereiter. 10 Jahre Trainerakademie des Deutschen Sportbundes. Koeln: Trainerakademie, c1984. 108 p. : il
LEVEL: B LANG: Ger GV711 20643

FENCING

Curry, N.L. Fencing book: a comprehensive manual for developing fencing skills and fundamentals. New York: Leisure Press, 1984. 149 p. : ill.
NOTES: Bibliography: p. 147.
LEVEL: B LANG: Eng ISBN: 0918438993 LC CARD: 82-83919 GV1147 15869

Czajkowski, Z. The main types of fencers from the point of view of tactics and psychology. *Fencing (Surrey, Eng.) 16(4), Ma 1984, 18-19.*
NOTES: Part one of two parts.
LEVEL: B LANG: Eng SIRC ARTICLE NO: 098050

Kovacs, P. L'escrime au sabre: stage d'arbitrage international au sabre. *Escrime (Paris) 51, janv/fevr 1984, 16-18;23-24.*
LEVEL: I LANG: Fr SIRC ARTICLE NO: 094969

FENCING (continued)

ADMINISTRATION

Interview with Jan Romary. *American fencing (Colorado Springs) 35(4), Mar/Apr 1984, 26-28.*
LEVEL: B LANG: Eng SIRC ARTICLE NO: 101217

BIOGRAPHY AND AUTOBIOGRAPHY

De Capriles, M. Helene Mayer (1910-1953). *American fencing (Albany, Calif.) 35(3), Jan/Feb 1984, 14-15.*
LEVEL: B LANG: En SIRC ARTICLE NO: 099532

Keenan, S. On the scene: so Michael Lofton isn't fencing's Jackie Robinson: he's in the games. *Sports illustrated (Chicago, Ill.) 61(5), 23 Jul 1984, 78.*
LEVEL: B LANG: Eng SIRC ARTICLE NO: 096642

COACHING

Tutton, M. Amateur coaches: molding muscle and mind. (Duane Jones, John Fitzgerald and John ApSimon) *Ottawa magazine 4(1), Apr 1984, 12-13;45-50;52-53.*
LEVEL: B LANG: Eng SIRC ARTICLE NO: 092712

COUNTRIES AND REGIONS

Evered, D. The Hungarian contribution to modern competitive sabre fencing. *Fencing (Surrey, Eng.) 16(4), Mar 1984, 8-9.*
LEVEL: B LANG: Eng SIRC ARTICLE NO: 098051

EQUIPMENT

BYRNES, J. CFCI. (ground circuit interruptor) *American fencing (Albany, Calif.) 35(3), Jan/Feb 1984, 29-30.*
LEVEL: B LANG Eng SIRC ARTICLE NO: 099531

Byrnes, J. Technical talks. *American fencing (Colorado Springs) 36(1), Sept/Oct 1984, 21-22.*
LEVEL: B LANG: Eng SIRC ARTICLE NO: 101212

EQUIPMENT - MAINTENANCE

Byrnes, J. Technical talks. *American fencing (Colorado Springs) 35(4), Mar/Apr 1984, 29-30.*
LEVEL: B LANG: Eng SIRC ARTICLE NO: 101213

HISTORY

Lacaze, P. Si le fleuret m'etait conte: les pointes voltigent. *Escrime (Paris) 53, mai/juin 1984, 17-19.*
LEVEL: B LANG: F SIRC ARTICLE NO: 098053

INJURIES AND ACCIDENTS

Crawfurd, A.R. Death of a fencer. (Refs: 1)*British journal of sports medicine (Loughborough, Eng.) 18(3), Sept 1984, 220-222.*
LEVEL: I LANG: Eng SIRC ARTICLE NO: 103137

Klinger, A.K. Fencing. *In, Adams, S.H. (ed.), et al., Catastrophic injuries in sports: avoidance strategies, Salinas, Calif., Cayote Press, c1984, p. 120-124.*
LEVEL: B LANG: Eng RD97 19088

OFFICIATING

Bowlsby, C. The tribulations of a fencing official. Trial by combat. *Referee (Franksville, Wisc.) 9(10), Oct 1984, 47.*
LEVEL: B LANG: Eng SIRC ARTICLE NO: 105796

Clery, R. L'escrime au sabre (suite). Rome, 17, 18 & 19 novembre 1983. Stage d'arbitrage international. *Escrime (Paris) 52, mars/avr 1984, 26-28.*
LEVEL: B LANG: Fr SIRC ARTICLE NO: 101214

Kolombatovitch, G. Annuling a touch. *American fencing (Colorado Springs, Colo) 35(5), May/Jun 1984, 22-23.*
LEVEL: B LANG: Eng SIRC ARTICLE NO: 104672

Mitchell, J. President de Jury notes - Part fourteen: the crimes and punishments of fencing. *Ontario fencer (Toronto) May 1984, 7-8.*
LEVEL: B LANG: Eng SIRC ARTICLE NO: 098054

PERCEPTUAL MOTOR PROCESSES

Papin, J.P. Condon, A. Guezennec, Y. Evolution de la strategie d'exploration visuelle d'enfants apprenant l'escrime. (Refs: *Medecine du sport (Paris) 58(5), 25 sept 1984, 27-35.*
RESUME: Les comportement visuel de quatre escrimeurs, ages de 10 a 12 ans, est evalue au cours d'une annee scolaire d'entrainement. La direction du regard des sujets est enregistree a l'aide du photo-oculographe 'NAC Eye Mark Recorder' une fois par trimestre trois trimestres consecutifs. Les auteurs constatent une variation du comportement visuel au cours des trois trimestres.
LEVEL: A LANG: Fr SIRC ARTICLE NO: 101221

PHYSICAL FITNESS

Elliott, M. Creating sport-specific fitness tests. (Refs: 10)*Coaching review 7, Jan/Feb 1984, 57-59;61.*
LEVEL: I LANG: En SIRC ARTICLE NO: 092040

PHYSIOLOGY

Sapega, A.A. Minkoff, J. Valsamis, M. Nicholas, J.A. Musculoskeletal performance testing and profiling of elite competitive fencers. (Refs: 9)*Clinics in sports medicine (Philadelphia) 3(1), Jan 1984, 231-244.*
NOTES: Symposium on profiling.
ABST: The authors studied 24 members of the U.S. Olympic team. The muscular development of fencers is such that both upper and lower body develop assymmetrical. Upon collection of biographical information and anthropometric data, a physiological profile was constructed which involved measures of flexibility, muscular strength, endurance and power. The correlations between the profile and success in competition were not always accurate. However, the profiles of the 1976 U.S. Olympic team members were able to generally predict their assignment to the team.
LEVEL: A LANG: Eng SIRC ARTICLE NO: 093401

Vander, L.B. Franklin, B.A. Wrisley, D. Scherf, J. Kogler, A.A. Rubenfire, M. Physiological profile of national-class National Collegiate Athletic Association fencers. (Refs: 39)*JAMA: Journal of the American Medical Association (Chicago) 252(4), 27 Jul 1984, 500-503.*
ABST: Selected physiological characteristics of

seven elite level fencers were studied and the results compared with those for normal persons and athletes of similar age. Maximal oxygen uptake during arm and leg ergometry, serum lipids, body composition, and standard spirometry were evaluated in these athletes. The results suggest that success in fencing may depend more on technique, speed, and agility as opposed to a high aerobic capacity and low percent body fatness.
LEVEL: A LANG: Eng SIRC ARTICLE NO: 103138

PROTECTIVE DEVICES

Resistance test of protection masks for fencing. *Fencing (Surrey, Eng.) 17(1), Jul 1984, 22.*
CORP: Commission on electrical signalling of material and installations..
LEVEL: B LANG: Eng SIRC ARTICLE NO: 097294

RULES AND REGULATIONS

Oles, D. A look at the rating system. *American fencing (Colorado Springs, Colo.) 35(5), May/Jun 1984, 16-17.*
LEVEL: B LANG: Eng SIRC ARTICLE NO: 104673

STRATEGY

Czajkowski, Z. The main types of fencers from the point of view of tactics and psychology. *Fencing (Surrey, Eng.) 17(1), Ju 1984, 9-10.*
NOTES: Part two of a two part article.
LEVEL: B LANG: Eng SIRC ARTICLE NO: 097292

Morgareidge, K. Image matching: part 11. *American fencing (Colorado Springs,) 36(1), Sept/Oct 1984, 14-15.*
LEVEL: B LANG: Eng SIRC ARTICLE NO: 101219

Morgareidge, K.R. Image matching. *American fencing (Colorado Springs) 35(6), Jul/Aug 1984, 25-27.*
NOTES: To be continued.
LEVEL: B LANG: Eng SIRC ARTICLE NO: 101220

TEACHING

McKenzie, E.K. McKenzie, R. McKenzie, T.L. Instructional strategies: influence on teacher and student behavior. (Refs: 21) *Journal of teaching in physical education (Blacksburg, Va.) 3(2), Winter 1984, 20-28.*
ABST: A fencing instructor used two different teaching strategies for two separate fencing classes. Data was collected for students and for the instructor. The results indicate that the different teaching strategies placed different requirements on student behavior and on instructor behavior. These requirements resulted in different opportunities for the students to learn. The authors conclude that teachers should examine their teaching strategies to determine how successful they are in reaching instructional goals.
LEVEL: A LANG: Eng SIRC ARTICLE NO: 093014

TECHNIQUES AND SKILLS

Smith, J. Aspects of the lunge - some observations. *Fencing (Surrey, Eng.) 17(1), Jul 1984, 12-13.*
LEVEL: B LANG: Eng SIR ARTICLE NO: 097293

Smith, J. Basic footwork. *Fencing (Kingswood, Surrey) 17(2), Dec 1984, 12-13.*
LEVEL: B LANG: Eng SIRC ARTICLE NO: 173556

TRAINING AND CONDITIONING

Greening, P. Northam, P. Honved training system. *Fencing (Kingswood, Surrey) 17(2), Dec 1984, 9-11.*
LEVEL: B LANG: Eng SIRC ARTICLE NO: 173555

FESTIVALS

HISTORY

Powell, J.T. Ancient Greek athletic festivals. *Olympic review (Lausanne, Switzerland) 198, Apr 1984, 259-264.*
NOTES: To b continued.
LEVEL: I LANG: Eng SIRC ARTICLE NO: 094343

Powell, J.T. Celebrations athletiques dans la Grece antique. *Revue olympique (Lausanne) 198, avr 1984, 259-264.*
NOTES: A suivre.
LEVEL: I LANG: Fr SIRC ARTICLE NO: 095898

FIELD ARCHERY

PHYSICS

Siatkowski, S. The ups and downs of field archery. *Canadian archer (Norbert, Man.) Mar/Apr 1984, 13-16.*
LEVEL: I LANG: En SIRC ARTICLE NO: 099384

FIELD HOCKEY

Lee, M.J. Team structure and captaincy. (Refs: 3)*Hockey field (Truro, Eng.) 71(7), 31 Mar 1984, 175-176.*
LEVEL: B LANG: E SIRC ARTICLE NO: 099538

ANTHROPOMETRY

Sidhu, L.S. Grewal, R. Verma, S.K. Positional differences in physique and body composition among top level indian (sic) wome hockey players. (Refs: 25)*Journal of sports medicine and physical fitness (Torino, Italy) 24(4), Dec 1984, 337-342.*
ABST: Thirty Indian women hockey players, selected to participate in the world cup competition to be held at Spain (Madrid), have been studied for stature, weight, three skinfolds, percentage of body fat and anaerobic power. The results show that players differ in physique and body composition according to the field positions, in which the players specialize. Forwards are the lightest whereas backs are heaviest among all. Amount of fat is minimum in forwards and maximum in goalkeepers. Distribution of fat at the sites of biceps, triceps and subscapular also show the same trend.
LEVEL: A LANG: Eng SIRC ARTICLE NO: 107166

ASSOCIATIONS

Hockey and Olympism. *Olympic review (Lausanne) 204, Oct 1984, 807-838.*
LEVEL: B LANG: Eng SIRC ARTICLE NO: 101228

Le hockey et l'olympisme. *Revue olympique (Lausanne) 204, oct 1984, 807-838.*
LEVEL: B LANG: Fr SIRC ARTICLE NO: 101229

CHILDREN

Cavill, G. What primary children can bring to the secondary school. *Hockey field (Truro, Eng.) 71(9), 31 May 1984, 234-236.*
LEVEL: B LANG: Eng SIRC ARTICLE NO: 099535

CHILDREN - MINI-SPORT

Aewha, C.P. Equipment for schools. (mini-field hockey) *Hockey field (Truro, Eng.) 71(8), 28 Apr 1984, 203-204.*
LEVEL: B LANG: Eng SIRC ARTICLE NO: 099534

Bell, J. Let's try it - Minkey. *Sports coach (Wembley, Australia) 7(4), Mar 1984, 62-63.*
LEVEL: B LANG: Eng SIRC ARTICLE NO: 094970

COACHING

Bleck, C. Hobbs, N. Vonnie Gros: taking USA field hockey places. *Olympian (Colorado Springs, Colo.) 9(2), Jul/Aug 1984, 18-19.*
LEVEL: B LANG: Eng SIRC ARTICLE NO: 104674

Dickie, D. The coaches: Debbie Muir, Jack Donohue, Ken Maeda, and Marina van der Merwe. Les entraineurs: Debbie Muir, Jack Donohue, Ken Maeda, et Marina van der Merwe. *Champion (Ottawa) 8(3), Aug 1984, 61-65.*
LEVEL: B LANG: Eng Fr SIRC ARTICLE NO: 095750

Read, B. Corinthians X111 2. Corinthians X111 2. *Counter attack (Vanier, Ont.) 4(1), Apr 1984, 24-27.*
LEVEL: B LANG: Eng SIRC ARTICLE NO: 098057

COUNTRIES AND REGIONS

Wulf, S. Who are these guys? And why aren't they wearing skirts? After all, everyone knows field hockey in the U.S. is a girls' sport. Well, now some American boys have taken up the game for the Games. *Sports illustrated (Chicago, Ill.) 61(4), Jul 1984, 402-404;406;410;412;415;418.*
NOTES: Special preview: the 1984 Olympics.
LEVEL: B LANG: Eng SIRC ARTICLE NO: 096646

FACILITIES - DESIGN, CONSTRUCTION AND PLANNING

Zadorozhnaya, L.S. Zolotavin, S.V. Shcherbakov, A.V. Ovseshchenie khabarovskogo stadiona im. V.I. Lenina. (Lighting the V.I. Lenin stadium in Khabarovsk.) (Refs: 5)*Svetotekhnika 5, May 1984, 7-8.*
ABST: The authors describe the lighting system installed in 1981 for the 12th world hockey championship in Khabarovsk. The system allows for colour TV transmission.
LEVEL: I LANG: Rus

HISTORY

Donegani, E. A brief history of hockey in Canada. *Canadian field and hockey news (Ottawa) 20(2), Jul 1984, 31-34.*
LEVEL: LANG: Eng SIRC ARTICLE NO: 096644

Miroy, N. The history of hockey - volume 11; chapter XXV1 1912 to 1919. *Hockey digest (Laleham-on-Thames, Eng.) 11(6), Summer 1984, 30-31.*
NOTES: To be continued.
LEVEL: B LANG: Eng SIRC ARTICLE NO: 099540

Miroy, N. The history of hockey - volume III. Chapter 1. India. *Hockey digest (London) 12(1), Sept 1984, 54-55.*
LEVEL: B LANG: Eng SIRC ARTICLE NO: 101230

Miroy, N. The history of hockey - volume III. *Hockey digest (Laleham-on-Thames, Eng.) 12(3), Dec 1984, 46-49.*
LEVEL: B LANG: Eng SIRC ARTICLE NO: 107163

INJURIES AND ACCIDENTS

Elliott, A.J. Jones, D. Major ocular trauma: a disturbing trend in field hockey injuries. *British medical journal (Clinical research) (London) 289(6436), 7 Jul 1984, 21-22.*
LEVEL: I LANG: Eng SIRC ARTICLE NO: 103139

Moore, S. Field hockey. In, Adams, S.H. (ed.), et al., *Catastrophic injuries in sports: avoidance strategies, Salinas, Calif., Cayote Press, c1984, p. 76-82.*
LEVEL: B LANG: Eng RD97 19088

Taunton, J. National team medical report. *Counter attack (Ottawa) 4(2), Aug 1984, 8-12.*
LEVEL: B LANG: Eng SIRC ARTICLE NO: 101232

OFFICIATING

McClintock, J. Game preparation. *CounterATTACK (Vanier, Ont.) 4(3), Dec 1984, 7-11.*
LEVEL: B LANG: Eng SIRC ARTICLE NO: 173574

van Rossum, J.H.A. van der Togt, C.R. Gootjes, H.A. The acceptance of referee's decisions in field hockey. (Refs: 4) *International journal of sports medicine (Stuttgart) Suppl. 5, Nov 1984, 212-213.*
CONF: International Congress on Sports and Health (1983 : Maastricht, Netherlands).
LEVEL: A LANG: Eng SIRC ARTICLE NO: 104675

PERCEPTUAL MOTOR PROCESSES

Lyle, J. Cook, M. Non-verbal cues and decision making in games. (Refs: 9)*Momentum: a journal of human movement studies (Edinburgh) 9(1), Spring 1984, 20-25.*
ABST: This paper examines specific sport cues and the decision making they produce in the behaviour of the opponent. A video taped recording was made from a field hockey goaltender's view of penalty flicks taken by a number of hockey players. 40 flicks in all were evaluated by goaltenders, players, physical education students and non-participants. Subjects were asked to anticipate the eventual direction of the ball. The differences between the four groups were found to be inconclusive in this exploratory investigation.
LEVEL: A LANG: Eng SIRC ARTICLE NO: 099539

Starkes, J.L. Perceptual training in field hockey. (Refs: 6)*Counter attack (Ottawa) 4(2), Aug 1984, 25-28.*
LEVEL: B LANG: Eng SIRC ARTICLE NO: 101231

PHYSIOLOGY

DeMeersman, R.E. Schiltz, J.H. Decreased training frequency and pulmonary function retention in the female athlete. *Journal of sports medicine and physical fitness (Torino, Italy) 24(2), Jun 1984, 155-158.*
ABST: Pulmonary function and body composition retention were observed in 18 female collegiate athletes exposed to a decrease in training frequency while participating in consecutive field

FIELD HOCKEY (continued)

hockey and lacrosse competitive seasons. Although one sport season represented 31% fewer workouts than the other, no significant differences were noted in body density, body fat, closing volume, nitrogen delta, closing capacity, residual volumes, functional residual volume, expiratory reserve volume, total lung capacity and vital capacity post-season scores. Results were noted as being in agreement with previous investigations in that the degree of fitness achieved can be maintained despite a substantial decrease in training frequency.
LEVEL: A LANG: Eng SIRC ARTICLE NO: 102768

Mathur, D.N. Morphological and physiological differences among Nigerian hockey players in relation to their field positions. *Asian journal of physical education (Taipei, Taiwan) 7(3), Oct 1984, 64-71.*
ABST: 40 highly skilled Nigerian hockey players were tested and compared for morphological, anthropometric and physiologic differences. Significant differences were seen between goalkeepers, backs, halves and forwards.
LEVEL: A LANG: Eng SIRC ARTICLE NO: 103141

Sidhu, L.S. Grewal, R. Effect of hard physical training on the cardio-vascular system of the Indian women hockey players. (Refs: 11)*Journal of sports medicine and physical fitness (Torino) 24(1), Mar 1984, 37-40.*
ABST: 15 World Cup field hockey players were studied before and after 25 days of training. After training the resting heart rate, maximum exercise heart rate and recovery heart rate all showed significant improvement. No changes were seen in body weight.
LEVEL: A LANG: Eng SIRC ARTICLE NO: 099541

PROTECTIVE DEVICES

Rocher, J. Quelques propos concernant l'utilisation des protections dento-maxillaires en hockey sur gazon. (The use of orodental protectors in field hockey.) *Chirurgien-dentiste de France (Paris) 54(274/275), 13-20 dec 1984, 59-60.*
LEVEL: I LANG: Fr

PSYCHOLOGY

Miller, S. The mental side of winning hockey. *Sportimes (Lahore, Pakistan) 29(6/7), Jun/Jul 1984, 18.*
LEVEL: B LANG: Eng SIRC ARTICLE NO: 103142

Miller, S. The mental side of winning hockey. *World hockey (Brussels) 48, Apr/May 1984, 28.*
LEVEL: B LANG: Eng SIRC ARTICLE NO: 108657

Whitehead, J. Potts, P. Sport psychology: what to do first? (Refs: 3)*Hockey field (Truro, Eng.) 71(9), 31 May 1984, 237;239.*
LEVEL: B LANG: Eng SIRC ARTICLE NO: 099542

RULES AND REGULATIONS

O'Connor, K. The penalty corner: a field hockey problem. *CounterATTACK (Vanier, Ont.) 4(3), Dec 1984, 14-16.*
LEVEL: B LANG: Eng SIRC ARTICLE NO: 173576

SOCIAL PSYCHOLOGY

Greenawalt, N.J. The application of polyhedral dynamics to the examination of team structure in field hockey. Eugene, Ore.: Microform Publications, University of Oregon, 1984. 2 microfiches :

negative, ill. ; 11 x 15 cm.
NOTES: Thesis (M.S.) - Pennsylvania State University, 1981; (x, 104 leaves); includes bibliography.
LEVEL: A LANG: Eng UO84 124-125

White, A. Towards a theory of dyadic interaction in team play. Eugene, Ore.: Microform Publications, University of Oregon, 1984. 2 microfiches : negative, ill. ; 11 x 15 cm.
NOTES: Thesis (Ed.D.) - University of Northern Colorado, 1982; (viii, 111, 1 leaves); vita; includes bibliography.
LEVEL: A LANG: Eng UO84 189-190

SPORTING EVENTS

Hockey and Olympism. *Olympic review (Lausanne) 204, Oct 1984, 807-838.*
LEVEL: B LANG: Eng SIRC ARTICLE NO: 101228

Le hockey et l'olympisme. *Revue olympique (Lausanne) 204, oct 1984, 807-838.*
LEVEL: B LANG: Fr SIRC ARTICLE NO: 101229

The history of the Olympics. *Hockey digest (London, Eng.) 12(1), Sept 1984, 14-15.*
LEVEL: B LANG: Eng SIRC ARTICLE NO: 1012

STRATEGY

Jagday, S. Coaches corner: aerial hockey. *Canadian field hockey news (Ottawa) 20(2), Jul 1984, 37-40.*
LEVEL: B LANG: Eng SIRC ARTICLE NO: 096645

Plant, S. Depth and recovery for the job in hand. *Hockey field (Cornwall, U.K.) 72(4), 22 Dec 1984, 88-91.*
LEVEL: B LANG: Eng SIRC ARTICLE NO: 173373

STRATEGY - OFFENSIVE

Slipp, J. Penalty corners in attack. *CounterATTACK (Vanier, Ont.) 4(3), Dec 1984, 2-6.*
LEVEL: B LANG: Eng SIRC ARTICLE NO 173573

TEACHING

John, J. Hockey sur gazon: modele de perfectionnement. Ottawa: Association canadienne feminine de hockey sur gazon : Association canadienne de hockey sur gazon, c1984. 32 p.
CORP: Association canadienne feminine de hockey sur gazon.
CORP: Association canadienne de hockey sur gazon.
NOTES: Bibliographie: p. 32. Also published in English under the title: Field hockey development model.
LEVEL: B LANG: Fr ISBN: 0-920193-01-3 GV1017.H7 18134

TECHNIQUES AND SKILLS

Burrows, P. Beating the goalkeeper. *Counter attack (Ottawa) 4(2), Aug 1984, 20-23.*
LEVEL: B LANG: Eng SIRC ARTICLE NO: 101225

Cardwell, J. Slocombe, S. The developing game of field hockey on artificial surfaces. *Hockey field (Truro, Eng.) 72(1), 29 Sept 1984, 16-17.*
LEVEL: B LANG: Eng SIRC ARTICLE NO: 101226

Charlton, N. The chip shot. *CounterATTACK (Vanier, Ont.) 4(3), Dec 1984, 12-13.*
LEVEL: B LANG: Eng SIRC ARTICLE NO: 17357

Guignet, B. Hockey sur terre. *Macolin (Suisse) 10, oct 1984, 7-9.*
LEVEL: B LANG: Fr SIRC ARTICLE NO: 103140

TECHNIQUES AND SKILLS - GOALTENDER AND GOALTENDING

New advances in goalkeeping equipment. *CounterATTACK (Vanier, Ont.) 4(3), Dec 1984, 36-39.*
LEVEL: B LANG: Eng SIRC ARTICLE NO: 173578

TECHNIQUES AND SKILLS - PASSING

Jones, C. The art of passing. *Hockey field (Truro, Eng.) 71(8), 28 Apr 1984, 205-206.*
LEVEL: B LANG: Eng SIRC ARTICLE NO: 099536

White, A. The art of the perfect pass: an interactionist perspective. *Hockey field (Cornwall, Eng.) 71(6), 25 Feb 1984, 152-154.*
LEVEL: B LANG: Eng SIRC ARTICLE NO: 094975

TESTING AND EVALUATION

Alexander, M. The Zelenka test: a test of field hockey skill. (Refs: 8)*CounterATTACK (Vanier, Ont.) 4(3), Dec 1984, 22-32.*
LEVEL: I LANG: Eng SIRC ARTICLE NO: 173577

Broderick, K. Eye on the goalkeeper. *Counter attack (Vanier, Ont.) 4(1), Apr 1984, 28-32.*
ABST: This article provides a good overview of the evaluation of a field hockey goalkeeper. His physical conditioning should be tested for agility, endurance, and strength levels. A goalkeeper's skills includes effective positioning, ability to perform first time saves, slide tackling, and defence of penalty corners or penalty strokes. Methods for testing in these skills in practice situations are outlined. Suggestions are made on how to improve any deficiencies in the goalkeeper's skills.
LEVEL: B LANG: Eng SIRC ARTICLE NO: 098056

Kostrinsky, D. A player-improvement analysis sheet for field hockey. *Scholastic coach (New York) 54(2), Sept 1984, 80-81;88.*
LEVEL: B LANG: Eng SIRC ARTICLE NO: 099537

Wilson, G. Crofts, A. Feature: bits, bytes and balls. (Refs: 3)*Counter attack (Vanier, Ont.) 4(1), Apr 1984, 9-21.*
LEVEL: LANG: Eng SIRC ARTICLE NO: 098058

VARIATIONS

Miroy, N. Indoor hockey: its origin. *Hockey digest (Laleham-on-Thames, Eng.) 12(3), Dec 1984, 40.*
NOTES: Excerpted from: Miroy, N., A history of hockey, to be published in 1986.
LEVEL: B LANG: Eng SIRC ARTICLE NO: 107162

Wiedmer, R. Le unihoc. *Macolin (Berne) 2, fevr 1984, 14-15.*
LEVEL: B LANG: Fr SIRC ARTICLE NO: 101233

Wiedmer, R. Lecon d'entrainement pour joueurs de unihoc debutants et avances. *Macolin (Berne) 2, fevr 1984, 16-17.*
LEVEL: LANG: Fr SIRC ARTICLE NO: 101234

FIGURE SKATING

Mason, A. Canfigure-skate program stroking skills. *Canadian skater (Ottawa) Spring 1984, 33-36.*
LEVEL: B LANG: Eng SIRC ARTICLE NO: 098064

Petkevich, J.M. The skater's handbook. New York: Charles Scribner's Sons, c1984. xii, 210 p. : ill.
NOTES: Includes index. Bibliography: p. 199-204.
LEVEL: I LANG: Eng ISBN: 0684180162 LC CARD: 83-016514 GV850.4 17064

ADMINISTRATION

Bafo, T.S. Sundae's review. *Skating (Boston, Mass.) 61(4), Apr 1984, 13;23.*
LEVEL: B LANG: Eng SIRC ARTICLE NO: 094977

Bafo, T.S. How to organize a precision team. *Skating magazine (Colorado Springs) 61(3), Mar 1984, 54.*
LEVEL: B LANG: Eng SIRC ARTICLE NO: 099543

Mason, A. Sher, H. You and your club. Ottawa: Canadian Figure Skating Association, c1984. vi, 175 p. : ill.
CORP: Canadian Figure Skating Association.
NOTES: Cover title. Aussi publie en francais sous le titre: Votre club et vous.
LEVEL: B LANG: Eng ISBN: 0-9690110-9-1 GV850.4 20119

Wright, B.T. The Hall of Fame: George H. Browne (1857-1931) United States. *Skating magazine (Colorado Springs) 61(3), Mar 1984, 21-23.*
LEVEL: B LANG: Eng SIRC ARTICLE NO: 099553

BIOGRAPHY AND AUTOBIOGRAPHY

Cummings, A. Sonja Henie's last hurrah. *Skating magazine (Colorado Springs, Colo.) 61(6), Jun 1984, 19-20;31.*
LEVEL: B LANG: Eng SIRC ARTICLE NO: 103143

Dickie, D. Tracy Wilson et Robert McCall, couple sans pareil. Tracy Wilson and Robert McCall, dazzling duo. *Champion 8(1), Feb 1984, 44-45.*
LEVEL: B LANG: Eng Fr SIRC ARTICLE NO: 090605

Martin, K. Tiffany & Co.: it hasn't always been smooth skating. *Women's sports (Palo Alto, Calif.) 6(11), Nov 1984, 26-30.*
LEVEL: B LANG: Eng SIRC ARTICLE NO: 173596

Ottum, B. Wow. Power. A sure bet for Olympic gold is Scott Hamilton, the U.S. and world figure skating champion, who has a knockout program for Sarajevo. *Sports illustrated 60(5), 6 Feb 1984, 88-92;94;96-99;101-102.*
LEVEL: B LANG: Eng SIRC ARTICLE NO: 090607

Slate, L. JoJo Starbuck & Ken Shelley: the silver anniversary of a golden partnership. *Skating magazine (Colorado Springs, Colo.) Oct 1984, 18-19;36-37;53-54.*
LEVEL: B LANG: Eng SIRC ARTICLE NO: 099550

Stafford, C. The Ivaniches. *Skater 2(1), Winter 1984, 27-28.*
LEVEL: B LANG: Eng SIRC ARTICLE NO: 092063

Steere, M. Skating for gold: the intimate life story of Scott Hamilton. New York: St. Martin's Press, 1984. 1v.
LEVEL: B LANG: Eng ISBN: 0312727607 LC CARD: 83-021193

Stensrude, C. The path to excellence. (Brian Orser) *Skating (Colorado Springs, Colo.) 61(9), Nov 1984, 14-15;28.*
LEVEL: B LANG: Eng SIRC ARTICLE NO: 173244

Wark, J. Ice dream. (Torvill and Dean) *Gymnast (London, Eng.) Apr 1984, 22-25.*
LEVEL: B LANG: Eng SIRC ARTICLE NO: 101235

Welch, P. Sonja Henie. (Refs: 28)*Journal of physical education, recreation & dance 55(1), Jan 1984, 23-24;30.*
LEVEL: B LANG: Eng SIRC ARTICLE NO: 092065

West, T. Looking back: skater gets perfect marks. (Don Jackson) Il etait une fois: Don Jackson, pointage parfait. *Champion 8(1), Feb 1984, 51;52.*
LEVEL: B LANG: Eng Fr SIRC ARTICLE NO: 090611

Williams, G. Tiffany Chin: the world joins San Diego's fan club. *Skating magazine (Colorado Springs, Colo.) 61(6), Jun 1984 24-26.*
LEVEL: B LANG: Eng SIRC ARTICLE NO: 103145

Wright, B.T. The Hall of Fame: Eugene Turner: United States. *Skating magazine (Colorado Springs, Colo.) 61(2), Feb 1984, 34-35.*
LEVEL: B LANG: Eng SIRC ARTICLE NO: 099552

Young, D. The golden age of Canadian figure skating. Toronto: Summerhill Press, c1984. 200 p. : ill.
LEVEL: B LANG: Eng ISBN: 0-920197-04-3 LC CARD: C84-099434-6 GV850.A2 18246

COACHING

Davies, V. 7 steps to effective instruction. (Refs: 9)*Coaching review 7, Jan/Feb 1984, 50-52.*
LEVEL: B LANG: Eng SIRC ARTICLE NO: 092055

West, T. Il etait une fois: Sheldon Galbraith. Looking back: Sheldon Galbraith. *Champion (Ottawa) 8(4), Nov 1984, 7;18.*
LEVEL: B LANG: Fr Eng SIRC ARTICLE NO: 101236

EQUIPMENT - MAINTENANCE

Koehnlein, K.W. More on skate sharpening: blades have more than one dimension. *Skating magazine (Colorado Springs, Colo.) 61(5), May 1984, 40-41.*
LEVEL: B LANG: Eng SIRC ARTICLE NO: 098061

HISTORY

Martin, K. Figure skating. *Women's sports (Palo Alto, Calif.) 6(1), Jan 1984, 21-23.*
LEVEL: B LANG: Eng SIRC ARTICLE NO: 098063

Stevenson, S. BBC book of skating. London: British Broadcasting Corporation, c1984. 160 p. : ill.
LEVEL: B LANG: Eng ISBN: 0-563-20223-8 GV850.4 17316

INJURIES AND ACCIDENTS

Berthet, J.C. Danowski, R. Patinage sur glace: bilans d'un stage. Lesions de l'appareil locomoteur. Etude. Traitement. (Refs 10)*Medecine du sport 58(1), 25 janv 1984, 46-50.*
LEVEL: I LANG: Fr SIRC ARTICLE NO: 092054

Bradley, M. First responder techniques. (Refs: 2)*Skating magazine (Colorado Springs) 61(3), Mar 1984, 49-51.*
LEVEL: B LANG: Eng SIRC ARTICLE NO: 099545

Davies, M.W. Litman, T. The figure skater's foot. *Skating magazine (Colorado Springs, Colo.) 61(2), Feb 1984, 13;16-17.*
LEVEL: I LANG: Eng SIRC ARTICLE NO: 099546

Stanish, W.D. Vincent, N. Recurrent dislocation of the tibialis posterior tendon - a case report with a new surgical approac (Refs: 5)*Canadian journal of applied sport sciences/Journal canadien des sciences appliquees au sport (Windsor, Ont.) 9(4), Dec 1984, 220-222.*
ABST: Recurrent dislocation of the tibialis posterior tendon of the ankle is a rare problem, but may result in considerable disability, particularly in the athlete. The description of a simple surgical technique which provides immediate stabilization of the tendon is discussed. This technique is simple and allows early mobilization, resulting in prompt return to athletics.
LEVEL: A LANG: Eng SIRC ARTICLE NO: 102548

JUDGING

Hanson, M.S. The failure figure test. *Skating (Boston, Mass.) 61(4), Apr 1984, 47;50.*
LEVEL: B LANG: Eng SIRC ARTICLE NO: 094979

JUVENILE LITERATURE

Young, S. Curtis, B. Peggy Fleming: portrait of an ice skater. New York: Avon, 1984. 1v.
LEVEL: B LANG: Eng ISBN: 038085720 LC CARD: 83-045914

MEDICINE

Nelson, F.S. Medical tips for travelers. *Skating (Colorado Springs, Colo.) 61(9), Nov 1984, 13;18;32.*
LEVEL: B LANG: Eng SIRC ARTICLE NO: 173243

NUTRITION

Denton, A.E. Khoo, C.S. Nutritional guide for the skater: skater survey. *Skating magazine (Colorado Springs, Colo.) 61(2), Feb 1984, 9-10.*
LEVEL: B LANG: Eng SIRC ARTICLE NO: 099547

Denton, A.E. Khoo, C.-S. Getting a balanced diet. *Skating (Colorado Springs, Colo.) 61(9), Nov 1984, 9-10;28.*
LEVEL: B LANG: Eng SIRC ARTICLE NO: 173242

PHYSIOLOGY

Guisewite, C. The recognition and prevention of overtraining. *Skating magazine (Colorado Springs) 61(1), Jan 1984, 12-13;70;81.*
LEVEL: B LANG: Eng SIRC ARTICLE NO: 098059

Hahn, C.K.G. Pre-adaptive circadian rhythm programming for International Canadian Athletes.
NOTES: In: Proceedings of the 1984 International Conference on Occupational Ergonomics, Toronto, Ontario, 7-9th May 1984, Edited by D.A. Attwood and C. McCann, Volume 1, p. 210-214.
ABST: This paper examines the methods and results of the application of a circadian rhythm pre-flight synchronization programme for competitive figure-skaters changing time zones prior to international competition and discusses some possibilities of an appropriate scheduling programme in other fields.
LEVEL: A LANG: Eng SIRC ARTICLE NO: 103144

FIGURE SKATING (continued)

PSYCHOLOGY

Berenson, C.K. Sports medicine brief: the toughest competition. *Skating (Boston, Mass.) 61(4), Apr 1984, 19-20;49.*
LEVEL: LANG: Eng SIRC ARTICLE NO: 094978

Huck, B. The psychology of winning. *Canadian skater (Ottawa, Ont.) 11(3), Summer 1984, 27-28.*
LEVEL: B LANG: Eng SIRC ARTICLE NO: 099549

MacDonald, N. Psychology of precision skating. *Canadian skater (Ottawa) Spring 1984, 13-15.*
LEVEL: B LANG: Eng SIRC ARTICLE NO: 098062

Stafford, C. Coping with the pressure. *Canadian skater (Ottawa, Ont.) 11(3), Summer 1984, 29-30.*
LEVEL: B LANG: Eng SIRC ARTICLE NO: 099551

RULES AND REGULATIONS

How the game is played. *Women's sports (Palo Alto, Calif.) 6(1), Jan 1984, 32-33.*
LEVEL: B LANG: Eng SIRC ARTICLE NO: 09806

Official rulebook 1984 rev. ed. Letters patent: general by-laws; official rules. Ottawa: Canadian Figure Skating Association, c1984. xvi, 332 p.
CORP: Canadian Figure Skating Association.
NOTES: Looseleaf binder.
LEVEL: I LANG: Eng ISBN: 0-920507-00-X
GV850.4.Z9 18380

SPORTING EVENTS

Le patinage et l'olympisme. *Revue olympique (Lausanne) 199, mai 1984, 345-387.*
LEVEL: B LANG: Fr SIRC ARTICLE NO: 102132

Poulsen, O. Le patinage, des origines a nos jours. Skating from its origins to the present day. *Message olympique/Olympic message (Lausanne) 7, juin/ Jun 1984, 33-44.*
LEVEL: B LANG: Fr Eng SIRC ARTICLE NO: 104678

Sher, H. Precision line-up. *Skater 2(1), Winter 1984, 29-31.*
LEVEL: B LANG: Eng SIRC ARTICLE NO: 092061

Stevenson, A. Olympics past. *Ice and roller skate (Surrey, Eng.) 135, Jan 1984, 19-21;14.*
LEVEL: B LANG: Eng SIRC ARTICLE NO: 096649

STATISTICS AND RECORDS

Poulsen, O. Skating and Olympism. *Olympic review (Lausanne) 199, May 1984, 345-348.*
LEVEL: B LANG: Eng SIRC ARTICLE NO: 096648

Poulsen, O. Le patinage et l'olympisme. *Revue olympique (Lausanne) 199, mai 1984, 345-348.*
LEVEL: B LANG: Fr SIRC ARTICLE NO: 104679

TECHNIQUES AND SKILLS

Dyer, L. Tracking in ice dancing. *Skating magazine (Colorado Springs, Colo.) Oct 1984, 30-31.*
NOTES: First in a series. Excerpts from, Dyer, L., Ice dancing illustrated.
LEVEL: B LANG: Eng SIRC ARTICLE NO: 099548

Dyer, L. Tracking in ice dancing. *Skating magazine (Colorado Springs, Colo.) 61(10), Dec 1984, 15;30.*
NOTES: Second in a series excerpted from, Dyer, L., Ice dancing illustrated, Redmond WA, Moore Publications.
LEVEL: B LANG: Eng SIRC ARTICLE NO: 105801

TRAINING AND CONDITIONING - DRILLS

Bafo, T.S. First practice. *Skating magazine (Colorado Springs, Colo.) Oct 1984, 10-11.*
LEVEL: B LANG: Eng SIRC ARTICLE NO 099544

FINLAND

Finland: memorandum on the dissemination of information on physical education and sport. Helsinki: Ministry of Education, 1984 106 p.
LEVEL: I LANG: Eng

Klemola, H. The state as sponsor of international sports. *In, Ilmarinen, M. (ed.) et al., Sport and International Understanding: proceedings of the congress held in Helsinki, Finland, July 7-10, 1982, Berlin, Springer-Verlag, 1984, p. 323-326.*
CONF: Congress on Sport and International Understanding (1982 : Helsinki).
LEVEL: B LANG: Eng GV706.8 18979

Uunila, J. The meaning of international sporting events to a small country (from the viewpoint of a sports leader). *In, Ilmarinen, M. (ed.) et al., Sport and International Understanding: proceedings of the congress held in Helsinki, Finland, July 7-10, 1982, Berlin, Springer-Verlag, 1984, p. 327-329.*
CONF: Congress on Sport and International Understanding (1982 : Helsinki).
LEVEL: B LANG: Eng GV706.8 18979

PHYSICAL FITNESS

Oja, P. Vuori, I. Urponen, H. Physical activity and use of health services in early adulthood. (Refs: 4)
CONF: Symposium of Paediatric Work Physiology (10th : 1981 : Joutsa, Finland).
NOTES: In, Ilmarinen, J. and Vaelimaeki, I. (eds.), Children and sport: paediatric work physiology, Berlin, Springer-Verlag, 1984, p. 262-271.
ABST: This paper focuses on the younger portion of the Kainuu, Finland study population with the purpose of describing the changes in physical activity habits during early adulthood and the patterns of and reasons for the use of health services during this phase of life.
LEVEL: A LANG: Eng RC1235 17600

FLAG FOOTBALL

TEACHING

Flanigan, M. Flag football with the Navajos. A teacher's coaching experience in the Arizona desert. *Coaching review (Ottawa Ont.) 7, Jul/Aug 1984, 24-26.*
LEVEL: B LANG: Eng SIRC ARTICLE NO: 094996

FLOOR HOCKEY

INJURIES AND ACCIDENTS

Kozlowski, J.C. Floor hockey risk factors evident in school games. *Parks & recreation 19(3), Mar 1984, 20;22;24-26;70.*
LEVEL: I LANG: Eng SIRC ARTICLE NO: 092066

FLYING

AGED

Mohler, S.R. Age and sport flying. *Sport aviation (Oshkosh, Wisc.) 33(8), Aug 1984, 53.*
LEVEL: B LANG: Eng SIRC ARTICLE NO: 103147

BIOGRAPHY AND AUTOBIOGRAPHY

Jones, M.R. Above and beyond: eight great American aerobic champions. Blue Ridge Summit, Pa.: Tab Books, 1984. 1 v.
LEVEL: LANG: Eng ISBN: 0830623531 LC CARD: 84-008531

EQUIPMENT

MacFarlane, M.G. Airspeed & airspeed indicators. *Glider rider 8(11), Jan 1984, 29;31;33;35;56.*
LEVEL: B LANG: Eng SIRC ARTICLE NO: 090622

INJURIES AND ACCIDENTS

Delahaye, R.P. Auffret, R. Leger, A. Le parachutisme moyen de secours. *Dans, Pathologie du parachutisme, Paris, Maloine, 1984, p. 67-78.*
LEVEL: I LANG: Fr RC1220.P37 19033

MEDICINE

Johnson, L.F. Aviation medicine part 2: fitness to fly and the role of doctor travellers. *New Zealand medical journal (Dunedin) 97(763), 12 Sept 1984, 602-605.*
LEVEL: I LANG: Eng SIRC ARTICLE NO: 104684

L'oreille humaine. *Aeroscope (Montreal) 1, nov 1984, 8-9.*
NOTES: Tire de, Aviation medical bulletin, novembre 1983.
LEVEL: LANG: Fr SIRC ARTICLE NO: 109173

PHYSICS

Balldin, U.I. Physical training and plus Gz tolerance. *Aviation space and environmental medicine (Washington) 55(11), Nov 1984, 991-992.*
LEVEL: I LANG: Eng

TECHNIQUES AND SKILLS

Beggs, G. Aerobatics with Beggs: a universal spin recovery method. *Sport aviation (Oshkosh, Wisc.) 33(8), Aug 1984, 15-18.*
NOTES: Reprinted from, Sport Aerobatics, Feb 1984.
LEVEL: B LANG: Eng SIRC ARTICLE NO: 103146

FOLK DANCE

Ramsay, J.M. Folk dancing is for everyone. *Journal of physical education, recreation and dance (Reston, Va.) 55(7), Sept 1984, 37-38.*
LEVEL: B LANG: Eng SIRC ARTICLE NO: 101207

TEACHING

Withers, A.F. Teaching clogging in the elementary physical education program. (Refs: 1)*Journal of physical education, recreation and dance (Reston, Va.) 55(7), Sept 1984, 43-45.*
LEVEL: B LANG: Eng SIRC ARTICLE NO: 101208

FOOTBALL

Attner, P. Dear Pete: here are a few suggestions from one of your NFL friends on how to improve your game. *Sporting news (St. Louis) 198(26), 31 Dec 1984, 13.*
LEVEL: B LANG: Eng SIRC ARTICLE NO: 104694

Blaudschun, M. The Bowl Game: decision$, decision$. *Sporting news (St. Louis) 198(26), 31 Dec 1984, 39.*
LEVEL: B LANG: En SIRC ARTICLE NO: 104697

Donaldson, J. The official fantasy football league manual: how to own your own football team, coach your players, outsmart your friends, and win big. Chicago, Ill.: Contemporary Books, c1984. 1v.
LEVEL: B LANG: Eng ISBN: 0809253887 LC CARD: 84-009546

Fischler, S. LaPlace, M. Duff, B. Green, T. Waltzman, R. Amazing trivia from the world of football. Markham, Ont.: Penguin Books, c1984. 175 p. : ill.
LEVEL: B LANG: Eng ISBN: 0-14-007388-4 LC CARD: C84-98295-X GV950.5 17797

Isaak, O. Football -- and then some. 1st ed. Denver, Colo.: Planners Workshop, c1984. vii, 106, 6 p., (21) leaves of plates ill.
NOTES: Includes index.
LEVEL: B LANG: Eng ISBN: 0961246405 LC CARD: 83-090487

Janssen, C.T.L. Daniel, T.E. A decision-theory example in football. (Refs: 3)*Decision sciences (Atlanta) 15(2), 1984, 253-259.*
LEVEL: B LANG: Eng SIRC ARTICLE NO: 096661

Johnson, J.L. How to watch football. New York: Tribeca Communications, 1984. 1v.
LEVEL: B LANG: Eng ISBN: 0943392543 LC CARD: 84-008562

Lamb, K. Quarterbacks, nickelbacks, and other loose change: a fan's guide to the changing game of pro football. Chicago: Contemporary Books, c1984. 1 v.
NOTES: Includes index.
LEVEL: B LANG: Eng ISBN: 0809253992 LC CARD: 84-011414

Lawton, J. The All American war game. Oxford, Eng.: B. Blackwell, 1984. ix, 153 p., (16) p. of plates : ill.
NOTES: Include index.
LEVEL: B LANG: Eng ISBN: 0631134735 LC CARD: 84-147183

Riggins, J. Gameplan: the language & strategy of pro football. 2nd ed., completely rev., updated, and expanded. Santa Barbara, Calif.: Santa Barbara Press, 1984. 237 p. : ill.
NOTES: Rev. ed. of: The language of pro football, by Kyle Rote and Jack Winter, 1966.
LEVEL: I LANG: Eng ISBN: 0915643081 LC CARD: 84-040402

Zimmerman, P. Dr. Z's RX to revive the NFL. *Sports illustrated (Los Angeles, Calif.) 61(22), 12 Nov 1984, 24-25;28-31.*
LEVEL: B LANG: Eng SIRC ARTICLE NO: 101258

Zimmerman, P.L. The new thinking man's guide to pro football. New York: Simon and Schuster, c1984. 1v.
NOTES: Rev. ed. of: thinking man's guide to pro football. Rev. ed. 1971. Includes index.
LEVEL: B LANG: Eng ISBN: 0671453947 LC CARD: 84-010688

ADMINISTRATION

Fiffer, S. Puttin' on the Blitz - without cash. *Inside sports (Evanston, Ill.) 6, Jul 1984, 70-72;74-75.*
LEVEL: B LANG: E SIRC ARTICLE NO: 094995

Hitzges, N. Whitford, D. Wake up, college football: your playoffs are here. No more selling of bowls. No more final pools. Here's how to find the true national champion. *Sport (New York) 75(1), Jan 1984, 56-61.*
LEVEL: B LANG: Eng SIRC ARTICLE NO: 095001

Holtz, R. Injured reserve: the NFL's player stash. The league is putting up roadblocks to put a halt to creative and inspire abusers. *Football digest 13(6), Feb 1984, 44-47;49.*
LEVEL: B LANG: Eng SIRC ARTICLE NO: 093429

Ratliff, J.C. Marketing radio rights in division I-AA: Georgia southern style. *Athletic administration (Cleveland, Ohio) 19 (4), Sept 1984, 12-13.*
LEVEL: B LANG: Eng SIRC ARTICLE NO: 108233

AERODYNAMICS

Newman, S. Learning to fly. Wind tunnel research by the National Research Council is being used to help Canadian athletes an coaches. *Coaching review 7, Jan/Feb 1984, 17-19.*
LEVEL: I LANG: Eng SIRC ARTICLE NO: 092387

ANTHROPOMETRY

Daniel, M.L. Brown, B.S. Gorman, D. Strength and anthropometric characteristics of selected offensive and defensive university level football players. (Refs: 10)*Perceptual and motor skills (Missoula, Mont.) 59(1), Aug 1984, 127-130.*
ABST: The purpose of this study is to compare body composition and explosive power of defensive linemen, offensive linemen defensive backs, and linebackers. Forty-three university football players are tested. The major findings are that 1) both defensive and offensive linemen have greater lean-body weight than either defensive backs on linebackers and 2) offensive linemen lack explosive power and speed due to excess body fat. The authors develop equations for predicting football playing ability. Both body fat and skinfolds (important variables of all prediction equations) can be accurately assessed from two sites, iliac crest and cheek.
LEVEL: A LANG: Eng SIRC ARTICLE NO: 099567

Smith, J.F. Mansfield, E.R. Body composition prediction in university football players. (Refs: 33)*Medicine and science in sports and exercise (Indianapolis) 16(4), Aug 1984, 398-405.*
ABST: This study was intended to determine if previously-developed body composition prediction equations were valid for use with a Division I university football team. A sample of 68 Division I football players with a mean age of 19.7 yr, was assessed for body density (BD) by underwater weighing (UWW), residual volume by helium dilution, and 26 selected anthropometric measures. A predicted BD was obtained by using two sets of equations developed from college football players and from three generalized equations. The differences between predicted and observed body densities were analyzed. Seven of the nine models examined failed to accurately predict the BD for this population of university football players.
LEVEL: A LANG: Eng SIRC ARTICLE NO: 103176

ASSOCIATIONS

Farrell, C.A. College football powers reject plan for national championship game. *Chronicle of higher education (Washington 28(20), 11 Jul 1984, 27.*
LEVEL: B LANG: Eng SIRC ARTICLE NO: 104708

BIOGRAPHY AND AUTOBIOGRAPHY

Barnett, B. Carroll, B. Frank Gatski. *Coffin corner (N. Huntingdon, Pa.) 6(11/12), Nov/Dec 1984, 10-11.*
LEVEL: B LANG: En SIRC ARTICLE NO: 105804

Boyle, R.H. The USFL's Trump card. Builder Donald Trump, owner of the New Jersey Generals, has bid big bucks to make his league a winner. *Sports illustrated 60(7), 13 Feb 1984, 53;55-56;58;60;63.*
LEVEL: B LANG: Eng SIRC ARTICLE NO: 090633

Brady, J.T. Walsh, J.A. The Heisman: a symbol of excellence. 1st ed. New York: Atheneum, 1984. 218 p. : ill.
LEVEL: B LANG: Eng ISBN: 0-689-11497-4 LC CARD: 84-045033 GV939.A1 18307

Buck, R. Million dollar moon: Warren Moon, who has been labeled a 'black Joe Montana,' lit up the Canadian Football League for six years. Now he's ready to do the same for the Oilers, who have been wandering in football darkness. *Inside sports (Evanston, Ill.) 6, Oct 1984, 32-36.*
LEVEL: B LANG: Eng SIRC ARTICLE NO: 104701

Chandler, B. Fox, N.C. Violent Sundays. New York: Simon & Schuster, c1984. 1v. (A Fireside book.)
LEVEL: B LANG: Eng ISBN: 067147460X LC CARD: 84-005316

Dye, J. Al Mahrt: wonder athlete. *Coffin corner (N. Huntingdon, Pa.) 6(3), Mar 1984, 5-6.*
NOTES: Reprinted from, Dayton daily news 10 Jan 1965.
LEVEL: B LANG: Eng SIRC ARTICLE NO: 094993

Fiffer, S. Sweetness keeps running to light: Walter Payton wants that shining ring - more than anything. *Inside sports (Evanston, Ill.) 6, Oct 1984, 24-28;30.*
LEVEL: B LANG: Eng SIRC ARTICLE NO: 104714

George Preston Marshall. *Coffin corner (N. Huntingdon, Pa.) 6(11/12), Nov/Dec 1984, 12-13.*
LEVEL: B LANG: Eng SIRC ARTICLE NO: 105819

Jenkins, W. Effective scouting can provide the competitive edge. *Athletic journal (Evanston, Ill.) 65(4), Nov 1984, 28-29;58-59.*
LEVEL: B LANG: Eng SIRC ARTICLE NO: 101245

Jim Otto. *Coffin corner (N. Huntingdon, Pa.) 6(11/12), Nov/Dec 1984, 13-14.*
LEVEL: B LANG: Eng SIRC ARTICLE NO: 105822

Keyes, R. Tiny Maxwell cut a wide swath as a football player, ref and writer. (Robert W. Maxwell) *Sports illustrated (Los Angeles, Calif.)* 61(22), 12 Nov 1984, 10;12-14.
LEVEL: B LANG: Eng SIRC ARTICLE NO: 101247

Lamb, K. The second coming. On the first day, God created Jim Brown. On the second, he created Walter Payton. *Sport (New York)* 75(10), Oct 1984, 30-32;34;37-38.
LEVEL: B LANG: Eng SIRC ARTICLE NO: 099583

Looney, D.S. He came out picture perfect: a 'can't miss kid' in high school, Stefan Humphries didn't disappoint any profs or coaches at Michigan. *Sports illustrated (Chicago, Ill.)* 60(22), 4 Jun 1984, 44-46;48;50.
LEVEL: B LANG: Eng SIRC ARTICLE NO: 095007

Looney, D.S. I know I'm different. (Bill Fralic) *Sports illustrated (Chicago, Ill.)* 61(13), 10 Sept 1984, 30-32;36;38.
LEVEL: B LANG: Eng SIRC ARTICLE NO: 098092

Madden, J. Anderson, D. Hey, wait a minute, I did a book. 1st ed. New York: Villard Books, 1984. 1 v.
LEVEL: B LANG: Eng ISBN: 0394531094 LC CARD: 84-040175

Mara, T. Mr. Mara. *Coffin corner (N. Huntingdon, Pa.)* 6(11/12), Nov/Dec 1984, 7-8.
LEVEL: B LANG: Eng SIRC ARTICLE NO: 105831

McCallum, J. The man with the golden arm. The Los Angeles Express came up with a 43-year, $36 million package to lure Steve Young to the USFL. *Sports illustrated* 60(11), 12 Mar 1984, 28-31.
LEVEL: B LANG: Eng SIRC ARTICLE NO: 092082

Neff, C. A man with deep roots and deep routes. Miami's Mark Duper has strong ties to his native Louisiana and a passing for pulling in passes. *Sports illustrated (Los Angeles, Calif.)* 61(23), 19 Nov 1984, 52;54;59;62;67.
LEVEL: B LANG: Eng SIRC ARTICLE NO: 101249

Newman, B. No. No. No. Gastineau. The NFL outlawed his sack dance but the Jets' Mark Gastineau still plans to make his presence felt, particularly by opposing quarterbacks. *Sports illustrated (Chicago)* 61(12), 5 Sept 1984, 46-50.
LEVEL: B LANG: Eng SIRC ARTICLE NO: 098094

Paige, D. Whittingham, R. What a game they played: stories of the early days of pro football by those who were there. 1st ed New York: Harper & Row, c1984. 1v.
LEVEL: B LANG: Eng ISBN: 0060153555 LC CARD: 84-047610

Raissman, R. Now just wait a minute. Networks in Madden scramble. *Advertising age (Chicago)* 55(61), 17 Sept 1984, 1;90.
LEVEL: B LANG: Eng SIRC ARTICLE NO: 099598

Schwartz, H. Wild Bill Kelly: short biography of a sports legend. (William Carl Kelly) *P.F.R.A. annual (Canton, Oh.)* 1984, 29-49.
LEVEL: B LANG: Eng SIRC ARTICLE NO: 104735

Schwartz, L. Sport interview: Herschel Walker. Football's forgotten star doesn't want to be a superman, just a good FBI agen *Sport (New York)* 75(3), Mar 1984, 15;17;20;22.
LEVEL: B LANG: Eng SIRC ARTICLE NO: 095019

Smith, D. Roosevelt Brown. *Coffin corner (N. Huntingdon, Pa.)* 6(4), Apr 1984, 5-6.
LEVEL: B LANG: Eng SIRC ARTICLE NO: 099605

Telander, R. He can really dish it out: Michigan Panther strong safety David Greenwood, a superior athlete, is a 'lumberjack who loves to cut down opponents. *Sports illustrated (Chicago, Ill.)* 60(17), 23 Apr 1984, 28-31.
LEVEL: B LANG: Eng SIRC ARTICLE NO: 095022

Telander, R. He's aiming to make history. Walter Payton of the Chicago Bears is on target to become pro football's alltime leading rusher this season. *Sports illustrated (Chicago)* 61(12), 5 Sept 1984, 26-28;32;34;36-37;40-41.
LEVEL: B LANG: Eng SIRC ARTICLE NO: 098099

Telander, R. He's got 'em cornered. (Mike Haynes) *Sports illustrated (Chicago, Ill.)* 61(15), 24 Sept 1984, 38-40;42;44.
LEVEL: B LANG: Eng SIRC ARTICLE NO: 099608

Telander, R. Idol of the Marino Corps: Is Miami's remarkable Dan Marino a celebrity hunk? A ham-and-egger? *Sports illustrated (Los Angeles, Calif.)* 61(28), 34-31 Dec 1984, 86-88;90-91.
LEVEL: B LANG: Eng SIRC ARTICLE NO: 103179

Underwood, J. Miami's set of sparkling studs. Dan Marino of the Dolphins may be the best young pro quarterback, but is he better than the Hurricanes' Bernie Kosar? *Sports illustrated (Chicago)* 61(12), 5 Sept 1984, 104-108;113-114;116;118.
LEVEL: B LANG: Eng SIRC ARTICLE NO: 098100

Underwood, J. He'll tackle anything. (Randy White) *Sports illustrated (Chicago, Ill.)* 61(19), 22 Oct 1984, 106-110;112;114;116;118;120.
LEVEL: B LANG: Eng SIRC ARTICLE NO: 099609

Wolff, A. Bo on the go. The straw that stirs the drink at Auburn, Bo Jackson is a legend in Alabama and this season's hottes Heisman candidate. *Sports illustrated (Chicago)* 61(12), 5 Sept 1984, 134-138;140;142;144.
LEVEL: B LANG: Eng SIRC ARTICLE NO: 098101

Zimmerman, P. This raider's a real riot. Off the field, L.A. linebacker Matt Miller can be a funny man, but on it he has a well-deserved reputation for being a bowler and a smartmouth. *Sports illustrated* 60(16), 16 Apr 1984, 34-36;38;40;43-44;46;48;52;54.
LEVEL: B LANG: Eng SIRC ARTICLE NO: 093452

Zimmerman, P. A rose by any other name. Steeler linebacker Jack Lambert is known as a sweetie, but he sure knows the sweet smell of success. *Sports illustrated (Chicago, Ill.)* 61(6), 30 Jul 1984, 26-30;32-32;40.
LEVEL: B LANG: Eng SIRC ARTICLE NO: 096676

Zimmerman, P. The last in a long line. (Jeff Kemp) *Sports illustrated (Chicago, Ill.)* 61(19), 22 Oct 1984, 64;77-78.
LEVEL: B LANG: Eng SIRC ARTICLE NO: 099616

Zimmerman, P. He's catching up to the catching record. (Charlie Joiner) *Sports illustrated (Chicago, Ill.)* 61(17), 8 Oct 1984, 36-38;42-43.
LEVEL: B LANG: Eng SIRC ARTICLE NO: 099617

BIOMECHANICS

Morrison, W.E. Calibration and utilization of an instrumented football helmet for the monitoring of impact accelerations. Eugene, Ore.: Microform Publications, University of Oregon, 1984. 2 microfiches : negative, ill. ; 11 x 15 cm.
NOTES: Thesis (Ph.D.) - Pennsylvania State University, 1983; (x, 143, (1) leaves); vita; includes bibliography.
LEVEL: A LANG: Eng UO84 345-346

Yessis, M. Throwing the football. *National Strength & Conditioning Association journal* 6(1), Feb/Mar 1984, 6-8;71-73.
LEVEL: I LANG: Eng SIRC ARTICLE NO: 093451

CHILDREN

Torba, E.M. Boys club guide to youth football. New York: Leisure Press, c1984. 207 p.
LEVEL: B LANG: Eng ISBN: 0-88011-178- LC CARD: 83-80714 GV950.7 17632

CLUBS AND TEAMS

Brennan, C. The miracle of Miami: the inside story of the Hurricanes' championship season. Miami, Fla.: Miami Herald Pub. Co., c1984. ix, 116 p. : ill. ; 21 cm.
LEVEL: B LANG: Eng LC CARD: 84-050048

Chamberlain, D. Praise the lord, pass the ball: at BYU, they don't smoke or drink and they don't like sex. So how come they win so many damn football games? *Sport (New York)* 75(12), Dec 1984, 55-58;64.
LEVEL: B LANG: Eng SIRC ARTICLE NO: 108689

Eckhouse, M. Day by day in Cleveland Brown history. New York: Leisure Press, 1984. 1v.
LEVEL: B LANG: Eng ISBN: 0880111895 LC CARD: 84-010012

Gill, B. The Bulldogs: L.A. hits the big time. (Refs: 7)*P.F.R.A. annual (Canton, Oh.)* 1984, 1-24.
LEVEL: B LANG: Eng SIRC ARTICLE NO: 104716

Johnson, W.O. New deal in gopherland. With a new coach and new hope, an alum recalls when Minnesota's football players seeme godlike. *Sports illustrated (Los Angeles, Calif.)* 61(21), 5 Nov 1984, 44-46;48;50;59.
LEVEL: B LANG: Eng SIRC ARTICLE NO: 101246

Keith, H. Forty-seven straight: the surge of Sooner football under Bud. Norman: University of Oklahoma Press, c1984. 1v.
NOTES: Includes bibliographical references and index.
LEVEL: B LANG: Eng ISBN: 0806118989 LC CARD: 84-040274

Kravitz, B. The AFL: 'The other league' is no more but its legends go on and on. *Coffin corner (N. Huntingdon, Pa.)* 6(11/12), Nov/Dec 1984, 15-16.
LEVEL: B LANG: Eng SIRC ARTICLE NO: 105826

LeRose, P. The Racine legion. *Coffin corner (N. Huntingdon, Pa.)* 6(11/12), Nov/Dec 1984, 8-9.
NOTES: Originally published in: The Journal times, Racine, Wis., August 5, 1979.
LEVEL: B LANG: Eng SIRC ARTICLE NO: 105828

Lieber, J. Telander, R. And one to grow on. (Scouting reports) *Sports illustrated* 60(9), 27 Feb 1984, 32-35.
LEVEL: B LANG: Eng SIRC ARTICLE NO: 092080

Miller, T. Pac-10 football guide. New York: Leisure Press, 1984. 1v.
LEVEL: B LANG: Eng ISBN: 088011228X LC CARD: 84-012258

Stowers, C. The Cowboy chronicles: a sportswriter's view of America's most celebrated team. Austin, Tex.: Eakin Press, 1984. 1v.
LEVEL: B LANG: Eng ISBN: 0890154724 LC CARD: 84-013832

Stowers, C. Dallas Cowboys: the first twenty-five years. Dallas, Tex.: Taylor Pub., c1984. 1v.
LEVEL: B LANG: Eng ISBN: 0878334483 LC CARD: 84-016152

Wetsteon, R. What became of the New York Giants? The tragedy of a broken dynasty. The comedy of losing in remarkable ways. The high drama of a family feud. The pathos of a frustrated fanhood. This production has it all. *Sport (New York) 75(12), Dec 1984, 75-76;78-81.*
LEVEL: B LANG: Eng SIRC ARTICLE NO: 108696

COACHING

Anderson, H.D. Developing a sophomore football program to supplement the varsity. *Coaching clinic (Princeton, N.J.) 23(1), Sept 1984, 6-8.*
LEVEL: B LANG: Eng SIRC ARTICLE NO: 099561

Borges, R. Scouting combines reap pro talent. *Football digest (Evanston, Ill.) 14(3), Nov 1984, 36-41.*
LEVEL: B LANG: Eng SIRC ARTICLE NO: 099565

Buck, R. New image in the Bayou. Ever since Bum Phillips and Ken Stabler hit town, the Saints ain't been all that bad. *Inside sports 6, Jan 1984, 27-30;32.*
LEVEL: B LANG: Eng SIRC ARTICLE NO: 092069

Deford, F. The toughest coach there ever was. (Robert Victor Sullivan) *Sports illustrated (Chicago, Ill.) 60(18), 30 Apr 1984, 44-61.*
LEVEL: B LANG: Eng SIRC ARTICLE NO: 094991

Fuoss, D.E. Complete handbook of winning football drills. Boston ; Toronto: Allyn and Bacon, c1984. xxix, 362 p. : ill.
LEVEL: I LANG: Eng ISBN: 0205080715 LC CARD: 83-015706 GV956.6 17506

Fussman, C. Who the hell is Jim Hanifan? He's perhaps the least-known head coach in the NFL. And his St. Louis Cardinals are among the least feared. This season should change all that. *Sport (New York) 75(9), Sept 1984, 71-72;74;77-78.*
LEVEL: B LANG: Eng SIRC ARTICLE NO: 103156

Garrity, J. He's a one-man gang. Producing the nation's No. 1 junior-college team and a bevy of future stars had made Dick Foster almost as legendary in Coffeyville, Kansas as the Dalton gang. *Sports illustrated (Chicago) 61(12), 5 Sept 1984, 196-198;200-201.*
LEVEL: B LANG: Eng SIRC ARTICLE NO: 098085

Gleason, M. Computerized football scouting: a time-saver, a game-saver. *Scholastic coach (New York) 54(4), Nov 1984, 44-46;67.*
LEVEL: B LANG: Eng SIRC ARTICLE NO: 103157

Gordon Wood: Texas' living legend. *Scholastic coach 53(8), Mar 1984, 44-46;48;8;10;12.*
LEVEL: B LANG: Eng SIRC ARTICLE NO: 093427

Henning, L. Bo Schembechler: he's a winner, honestly. *Inside sports (Evanston, Ill.) 6, Dec 1984, 18;20-22.*
LEVEL: B LANG Eng SIRC ARTICLE NO: 101243

Homer Rice: 'I believe'. The Tech A.D. sounds off on the folly of the TV war, the latest trends in football, and the way to stop the cheaters. *Scholastic coach (New York) 54(3), Oct 1984, 48-50;54;71.*
LEVEL: B LANG: Eng SIRC ARTICLE NO: 101244

Keith, H. Forty-seven straight: the surge of Sooner football under Bud. Norman: University of

Oklahoma Press, c1984. 1v.
NOTES: Includes bibliographical references and index.
LEVEL: B LANG: Eng ISBN: 0806118989 LC CARD: 84-040274

Klein, J. The last roundup? It's been 25 years since Tom Landry rode into Dallas and unsmilingly and unfailingly built a miserable expansion team into a national institution. But now, time are changing... *Sport (New York) 75(12), Dec 1984, 46-48;50;52.*
LEVEL: B LANG: Eng SIRC ARTICLE NO: 108686

Kontor, K. Head sets - set. *National Strength & Conditioning Association journal 6(1), Feb/Mar 1984, 42.*
LEVEL: B LANG: E SIRC ARTICLE NO: 093432

Mudra, D. Freedom in the huddle. West Point, N.Y.: Leisure Press, 1984. 1v.
LEVEL: I LANG: Eng ISBN: 0880112611 LC CARD: 84-020182

Nuwer, H. Fred Akers: hooked on horns. The Texas coach has gotten the point of Longhorn tradition, which is always win. *Inside sports (Evanston, Ill.) 6, Oct 1984, 74-85.*
LEVEL: B LANG: Eng SIRC ARTICLE NO: 104727

Oates, B. Tom Flores: moving upfield in the land of opportunity. *Inside sports (Harlan, Iowa) 6, May 1984, 18-22.*
LEVEL: LANG: Eng SIRC ARTICLE NO: 093439

Puggelli, J. Motivation: the secret of getting kids to commit themselves. *Scholastic coach (New York) 54(1), Aug 1984, 23-24;71.*
LEVEL: B LANG: Eng SIRC ARTICLE NO: 099597

Schnellenberger, H. Be organized, work hard, sleep nights... & throw the ball. (Howard Schnellenberger) *Scholastic coach (New York) 54(1), Aug 1984, 30-32;67-68.*
LEVEL: B LANG: Eng SIRC ARTICLE NO: 099602

Wolff, A. A new kick on the boot. (Alfredo Primavera) *Sports illustrated (Los Angeles, Calif.) 61(22), 12 Nov 1984, 54-56;58;63.*
LEVEL: B LANG: Eng SIRC ARTICLE NO: 101256

Zimmerman, P. Al to world: get out of our way. On the field and off, Al Davis and his L.A. Raiders keep rolling over the NFL establishment in their own inimitable way. *Sports illustrated (Chicago) 61(12), 5 Sept 1984, 86-90;92;94;98;100;102.*
LEVEL: B LANG: Eng SIRC ARTICLE NO: 098102

DICTIONARIES AND TERMINOLOGY

Pincus, A. Jones, T. How to talk football. New York: Dembner Books, c1984. 143 p. : ill.
LEVEL: B LANG: Eng ISBN: 0-934878-41-2 LC CARD: 84-011337 GV959 18980

DOCUMENTATION

Ours, R.M. College football almanac. 1st ed. New York: Barnes & Noble Books, c1984. 1v.
LEVEL: B LANG: Eng ISBN: 0064640914 LC CARD: 84-047660

DRUGS, DOPING AND ERGOGENIC AIDS

Bond, V. Gresham, K.E. Balkissoon, B. Clearwater, H.E. Effects of small and moderate doses of alcohol on peak torque and average

torque in an isokinetic contraction. (Refs: 10)*Scandinavian journal of sports science (Helsinki, Finland) 6(1), Jul 1984, 1-5.*
ABST: Twelve college male athletes were evaluated isokinetically for their elbow flexor, extensor, and knee extensor torque generating capabilities after the ingestion of alcohol. Each subject was tested on a Cybex II dynamometer at the following speeds to evaluate peak and average peak torque: (1) dominant arm flexor, 0, 60, 90, 120 and 150o .s-1, (2) dominant arm extensor, 60, 90, 120 and 150o .s-1, and (3) dominant leg extensor, 0, 30, 102, 210 and 300o .s-1. Prior to each experimental test the subject consumed either a placebo (.0g.Kg-1), small (.34g.Kg-1), or a moderate (.69g.Kg-1) dose of pure ethanol. Analysis of the results by a one-way ANOVA indicated that the ingestion of a small or moderate amount of alcohol had no significant effect on the peak and average torque generating capabilities during elbow flexion, extension and knee extension.
LEVEL: A LANG: Eng SIRC ARTICLE NO: 102383

Collins, G.B. Janesz, J.W. Pippenger, C.E. Links in the chain: an approach to the treatment of drug abuse on a professional football team. (Refs: 9)*Cleveland clinic quarterly (Cleveland) 51(3), 1984, 485-492.*
LEVEL: I LANG: Eng SIRC ARTICLE NO: 104702

ECONOMICS

Cromwell, R.L. Klages, W.J. Super Bowl XXIII: economic impact on the Tampa Bay area: a survey of the attending public. (Winter Park, Fla.): Research Data Services, c1984. viii, 34 p.
CORP: Research Data Services.
LEVEL: I LANG: Eng LC CARD: 84-166637

Felser, L. Can the USFL survive on its own? *Sporting news (St. Louis, Mo.) 197(23), 4 Jun 1984, 2-3;11.*
LEVEL: B LANG: En SIRC ARTICLE NO: 094994

Fierman, J. Advertisers show designs of football fatigue. *Fortune (Chicago) 110(8), 1984, 141.*
LEVEL: B LANG: Eng SIRC ARTICLE NO: 099573

Tryfos, P. Casey, S. Cook, S. Leger, G. Pylypiak, B. The profitability of wagering on NFL games. (Refs: 2)*Management scienc (Providence, R.I.) 30(1), 1984, 123-132.*
LEVEL: I LANG: Eng SIRC ARTICLE NO: 096674

FACILITIES

Marcum, B. South Carolina's Williams-Brice Stadium: a touch of class. *Athletic administration (Cleveland, Oh.) 19(3), May 1984, 21-22.*
LEVEL: B LANG: Eng SIRC ARTICLE NO: 094299

GAMBLING

Merwin, J. Whitford, D. Betting football: you could call it the great American pastime - 20$ billion worth. And it's against the law. But not for long. *Sport (New York) 75(11), Nov 1984, 26-28;30.*
LEVEL: B LANG: Eng SIRC ARTICLE NO: 103168

HALLS OF FAME AND MUSEUMS

Rathet, M. Smith, D. The pro football hall of fame presents their deeds and dogged faith. New York: Balsam Press, c1984. 1 v
LEVEL: B LANG: Eng ISBN: 0917439023 LC CARD: 84-011188

FOOTBALL (continued)

HISTORY

Andrews, D.S. The G.I. Bill and college football: the birth of a spectator sport. (Refs: 17)*Journal of physical education, recreation and dance (Reston, Va.) 55(7), Sept 1984, 23-26.*
LEVEL: B LANG: Eng SIRC ARTICLE NO: 101237

Bergin, T.G. The game: the Harvard-Yale football rivalry, 1875-1983. New Haven: Yale University Press, c1984. 1v.
NOTES: Includes index.
LEVEL: B LANG: Eng ISBN: 0300032676 LC CARD: 84-040189

Braunwart, B. Carroll, B. Blondy Wallace and the biggest football scandal ever. (Canton A.C. and Masillon Tigers) *P.F.R.A. annual (Canton, Oh.) 1984, 59-88.*
LEVEL: I LANG: Eng SIRC ARTICLE NO: 104698

Eldridge, L. America's game: 25 years of NFL history. New York: New American Library, c1984. 1v.
NOTES: Includes index.
LEVEL: B LANG: Eng ISBN: 0453004717 LC CARD: 84-014799

Gill, W. Uncommon valor: the army-navy rivalry. New York: Leisure Press, 1984. 1v.
LEVEL: B LANG: Eng ISBN: 088011245X LC CARD: 84-012256

Park, R.J. From football to rugby - and back, 1906-1919: the University of California-Stanford University response to the 'football crisis of 1905'. (Refs: 101)*Journal of sport history (Pennsylvania) 11(3), Winter 1984, 5-40.*
LEVEL: I LANG: Eng SIRC ARTICLE NO: 106032

Steele, M.R. The fighting Irish football encyclopedia. New York: Leisure Press, 1984. 1v.
LEVEL: B LANG: Eng ISBN: 08801122 LC CARD: 84-012622

INJURIES AND ACCIDENTS

Allman, W.F. Architecture of the knee. *In, Schrier, E.W. and Allman, W.F. (eds.), Newton at the bat: the science in sports,* New York, Scribner, c1984, p. 114-118.
LEVEL: B LANG: Eng RC1235 18609

Bandy, W.D. Shaw, D.K. Injury profile of Northeastern Ohio high school football officials. (Refs: 8)*Physician and sportsmedicine (Minneapolis, Minn.) 12(10), Oct 1984, 77-78;80;83.*
ABST: This study reports on the type, location, and mechanism of injuries sustained by football officials. 81 high school football officials are surveyed. Findings indicate that 67.4% of the injuries occurred in the lower extremity, 48.8% during the third quarter of the game, and that 51.2% resulted from a collision with a player.
LEVEL: A LANG: Eng SIRC ARTICLE NO: 099562

Cahill, B.R. Griffith, E.H. Sunderlin, J. Madden T. Weltman, A. Effect of preseason conditioning: high school football knee injuries. *Illinois medical journal (Chicago) 166(5), Nov 1984, 356-358.*
ABST: The effect of preseason conditioning on knee injuries of senior high school football players was evaluated retrospectively in three groups of players. One group did not condition before the season, another participated in a closely supervised preseason conditioning program, and a third participated in a preseason program but with

decreased supervision. The results indicate that preseason conditioning lessens the incidence and severity of knee injuries and that these benefits are not affected by the amount of supervision used in preseason training.
LEVEL: I LANG: Eng

deShazo, W.F. Hematoma of the rectus abdominis in football. *Physician and sportsmedicine (Minneapolis, Minn.) 12(9), Sept 1984, 73-75.*
LEVEL: I LANG: Eng SIRC ARTICLE NO: 099568

Fleck, S.J. Dudley, G.A. A life-threatening situation. (Refs: 33)*National Strength & Conditioning Association journal 5(6), Jan 1984, 22-26.*
LEVEL: I LANG: Eng SIRC ARTICLE NO: 090022

Foley, J. The use of the vitabounder as a component in the rehabilitation of lower leg injuries in football. *Athletic training 19(1), Spring 1984, 55-56.*
LEVEL: I LANG: Eng SIRC ARTICLE NO: 092074

Forti, D.S. The study of off-season football strength and conditioning programs at selected major colleges. Eugene, Ore.: Microform Publications, University of Oregon, 1984. 1 microfiche ; negative ; 11 x 15 cm.
NOTES: Thesis (M.S.) - Springfield College, 1982; (vi, 84 leaves); includes bibliography.
LEVEL: A LANG: Eng UO84 225

Goldberg, B. Rosenthal, P.P. Nicholas, J.A. Injuries in youth football. (Refs: 13)*Physician and sportsmedicine (Minneapolis Minn.) 12(8), Aug 1984, 122-124;127-129;132.*
LEVEL: I LANG: Eng SIRC ARTICLE NO: 098086

Grace, T.G. Sweetser, E.R. Nelson, M.A. Ydens, L.R. Skipper, B.J. Isokinetic muscle imbalance and knee-joint injuries. A prospective blind study. *Journal of bone and joint surgery (Boston) 66(5), Jun 1984, 734-740.*
ABST: The purpose of this prospective blind study is to assess if any relationship between an imbalance in thigh-muscle function and the occurrence of knee injuries exists. Pre-season isokinetic muscle-testing was performed on 172 high-school football players. Findings indicate that there is no relationship between the two variables studied.
LEVEL: A LANG: Eng SIRC ARTICLE NO: 103159

Heiser, T.M. Weber, J. Sullivan, G. Clare, P. Jacobs, R.R. Prophylaxis and management of hamstring muscle injuries in intercollegiate football players. (Refs: 15)*American journal of sports medicine (Baltimore, Md.) 12(5), Sept/Oct 1984, 368-370.*
ABST: Hamstring muscle strains were responsible for the loss of playing time of a significant number of football players at the University of Nebraska in the early 1970s. After the acquisition of a Cybex II isokinetic dynamometer, the number of injuries was noted to decrease. A retrospective study was performed over the period 1973 to 1982. Group I (from 1973 to 1977) consisted of 534 player-years. There were 41 primary hamstring injuries with 13 recurrences. Group II (from 1978 to 1982) consisted of 564 player-years. There were six primary hamstring injuries with no recurrences. It is concluded that isokinetic testing and rehabilitation of muscle imbalances can prevent hamstring strains. Also, isokinetic testing of hamstring muscle injuries can prevent recurrences by ensuring the athlete has regained near-normal muscle strength

before returning to action.
LEVEL: A LANG: Eng SIRC ARTICLE NO: 104718

Howe, D. Serious neck injuries: a story of facts and advice, so coaches can help prevent the crippling injury of quadriplegi *Coaching review 7, Mar/Apr 1984, 23-28.*
LEVEL: B LANG: Eng SIRC ARTICLE NO: 093430

Kaufman, R.S. Kaufman, A. An experimental study on the effects of the MORA on football players. *Basal facts (Chicago) 6(4), 1984, 119-126.*
LEVEL: A LANG: Eng SIRC ARTICLE NO: 107180

Kulwin, D.R. Leadbetter, M.G. Orbital rim trauma causing a blowout fracture. *Plastic and reconstructive surgery (Baltimore) 73(6), Jun 1984, 969-971.*
LEVEL: I LANG: Eng SIRC ARTICLE NO: 103165

Marks, M.W. Argenta, L.C. Dingman, R.O. Traumatic arteriovenous malformation of the external carotid arterial system. *Head neck surgery (Boston) 6(6), Jul/Aug 1984, 1054-1058.*
LEVEL: I LANG: Eng SIRC ARTICLE NO: 104057

Micheli, L.J. Injuries in the football sports. (Refs: 25)
NOTES: In, Cantu, R.C. (ed.), Clinical sports medicine, Lexington, Mass. ; Toronto, Collamore Press : D.C. Heath, c1984, p. 203-210.
LEVEL: I LANG: Eng RC1201 15964

Moretz, J.A. Harlan, S.D. Goodrich, J. Walters, R. Long-term followup of knee injuries in high school football players. (Refs: 13)*American journal of sports medicine (Baltimore, Md.) 12(4), Jul/Aug 1984, 298-300.*
ABST: Twenty-three American football participants were studied 20 years after high school competition, as well as 11 age-matched controls, to assess the development of knee osteoarthritis. No statistically significant increase in osteoarthritis could be demonstrated ratiographically, subjectively, or objectively. A significant subgroup of football players who had sustained a knee injury.
LEVEL: A LANG: Eng SIRC ARTICLE NO: 108536

Morton, S. Football. *In, Adams, S.H. (ed.), et al., Catastrophic injuries in sports: avoidance strategies,* Salinas, Calif., Cayote Press, c1984, p. 91-95.
LEVEL: B LANG: Eng RD97 19088

Mueller, F.O. Blyth, C.S. Can we continue to improve injury statistics in football? (Refs: 3)*Physician and sportsmedicine (Minneapolis, Minn.) 12(9), Sept 1984, 79-81;84.*
LEVEL: I LANG: Eng SIRC ARTICLE NO: 099587

Mueller, F.O. Schindler, R.D. Annual survey of football injury research 1931-1983. (Refs: 16)*Athletic training (Greenville, N.C.) 19(3), Fall 1984, 189-192;208.*
ABST: The authors provide statistics from 1931-1983 on deaths directly and indirectly due to football in United States high schools and universities. Case reports from 1983 are discussed.
LEVEL: A LANG: Eng SIRC ARTICLE NO: 099588

Mueller, F.O. Blyth, C.S. Annual survey of catastrophic football injuries, 1977-1983. Alexandria, Va.: Computer Microfilm International, 1984. 1 microfiche (16 fr.)
LEVEL: A LANG: Eng EDRS: ED243861

Murphy, P. Football injuries: any kind, any time. *Physician and sportsmedicine (Minneapolis, Minn.) 12(10), Oct 1984, 21-22.*
LEVEL: B LANG: Eng SIRC ARTICLE NO: 099589

Olerud, C. Molander, H. Atypical pronation-aversion ankle joint fractures. *Archives of orthopaedic and traumatic surgery (Munchen)* 102(3), 1984, 201-202.
LEVEL: I LANG: Eng SIRC ARTICLE NO: 099592

Oregon - quadriplegic entitled to recover $980,000 from athletic association. *Sports and the courts (Winston-Salem, N.C.)* 5(2), Spring 1984, 2-3.
LEVEL: B LANG: Eng SIRC ARTICLE NO: 095016

Poindexter, D.P. Johnson, E.W. Football shoulder and neck injury: a study of the 'stinger'. (Refs: 9)*Archives of physical medicine and rehabilitation (Chicago, Ill.)* 65(10), Oct 1984, 601-602.
LEVEL: I LANG: Eng SIRC ARTICLE NO: 099596

Saunders, R.L. Harbaugh, R.E. The second impact in catastrophic contact-sports head trauma. (Refs: 8)*JAMA: Journal of the American Medical Association (Chicago)* 252(4), 27 Jul 1984, 538-539.
LEVEL: I LANG: Eng SIRC ARTICLE NO: 103174

Schor, S.S. Relation of football injuries to exposure time. (letter) *American journal of public health (Washington)* 74(10), Oct 1984, 1169-1171.
LEVEL: I LANG: Eng SIRC ARTICLE NO: 104734

Seals, R.R. Morrow, R.M. Kuebker, W.A. The dentist's role in Texas high school mouthguard programs. *Texas dental journal (Austin)* 101(10), Oct 1984, 6-9.
LEVEL: I LANG: Eng

Shankman, G.A. Conditioning and injury prevention in semi-professional football. *National Strength & Conditioning Association journal (Lincoln, Neb.)* 6(5), Oct/Nov 1984, 48-49.
LEVEL: B LANG: Eng SIRC ARTICLE NO: 103175

Ziccardi, N. Coffman, M.B. Rehabilitation of the knee: a combination of diet, training and medical care had this injury victim back on the field in three weeks. *Athletic journal (Evanston, Ill.)* 65(2), Sept 1984, 22-23.
LEVEL: B LANG: Eng SIRC ARTICLE NO: 099615

JUVENILE LITERATURE

Lerner, A. Boehm, R. Fantasy football: the greatest football game since real football. Minneapolis: Lerner Pub. Co., c1984. 1v.
LEVEL: B LANG: Eng ISBN: 0822515016 LC CARD: 84-015489

Quill, R. Greene, C. I can be a football player. Chicago: Childrens Press, 1984. 1v.
LEVEL: B LANG: Eng ISBN: 0516018396 LC CARD: 84-009609

LAW AND LEGISLATION

Alabama - court upholds 'clean shaven' policy for high school athletes. *Sports and the courts (Winston-Salem, N.C.)* 5(4), Fal 1984, 1-2.
LEVEL: B LANG: Eng SIRC ARTICLE NO: 102553

Appenzeller, H. Ross, C.T. NCAA TV update. *Sports and the courts (Winston-Salem, N.C.)* 5(3), Summer 1984, 3-5.
LEVEL: B LANG: Eng SIRC ARTICLE NO: 098082

Arkansas - first amendment rights of assistant football coaches upheld in corporal punishment case. *Sports and the courts (Winston-Salem, N.C.)* 5(4), Fall 1984, 2-4.
LEVEL: B LANG: Eng SIRC ARTICLE NO: 102555

Illinois - football coach granted immunity in injury case. *Sports and the courts (Winston-Salem, N.C.)* 5(4), Fall 1984, 8.
LEVEL: B LANG: Eng SIRC ARTICLE NO: 103162

Kozlowski, J.C. Jungle act featured in RPLR road show. *Parks & recreation (Alexandria, Va.)* 19(6), Jun 1984, 28-31.
LEVEL B LANG: Eng SIRC ARTICLE NO: 094404

MASS MEDIA

Celizic, M. NFL films: football as cinematic art. *Football digest (Evanston, Ill.)* 13(10), Jul/Aug 1984, 40-43.
LEVEL: B LANG: Eng SIRC ARTICLE NO: 096653

Farrell, C.S. Colleges free to negotiate own contracts. *Chronicle of higher education (Washington)* 28(19), 5 Jul 1984, 1;24.
LEVEL: B LANG: Eng SIRC ARTICLE NO: 104709

Farrell, C.S. NCAA tries to please football powers and Federal judge with new TV plan. *Chronicle of higher education (Washington)* 28(20), 11 Jul 1984, 1;30.
LEVEL: B LANG: Eng SIRC ARTICLE NO: 104710

Farrell, C.S. Supreme Court strikes down NCAA control of football on television. *Chronicle of higher education (Washington)* 28(19), 5 Jul 1984, 1;22.
LEVEL: B LANG: Eng SIRC ARTICLE NO: 104711

Flygare, T.J. The end of NCAA control over college football television rights. *Phi Delta Kappan (Dayton)* 66(2), 1984, 148-150.
LEVEL: B LANG: Eng SIRC ARTICLE NO: 099574

Monaghan, P. Some tentative plans for football on TV. *Chronicle of higher education (Washington)* 28(20), 11 Jul 1984, 30.
LEVEL: B LANG: Eng SIRC ARTICLE NO: 104726

Patton, P. Razzle-dazzle: the curious marriage of television and professional football. Garden City, N.Y.: Dial Press: Doubleday, 1984. viii, 230 p. NOTES: Includes index.
LEVEL: B LANG: Eng ISBN: 0-385-27879-9 LC CARD: 83-027207 GV742.3 17649

Stevens, J.P. Text of Supreme Court's majority opinion striking down NCAA's control of college football telecasts. *Chronicl of higher education (Washington)* 28(19), 5 Jul 1984, 22-25.
LEVEL: B LANG: Eng SIRC ARTICLE NO: 104739

Taaffe, W. Footage that can go to your head. NFL films, a family-run business, is a house organ that has made sweet music, reeling in 33 Emmy Awards. *Sports illustrated (Chicago)* 61(12), 5 Sept 1984, 84-85.
LEVEL: B LANG: Eng SIRC ARTICLE NO: 098097

Taaffe, W. A supremely unsettling smorgasbord. Thanks to the high court we'll get a rich menu of games, but most schools wil get less bread. *Sports illustrated (Chicago)* 61(12), 5 Sept 1984, 150-151.
LEVEL: B LANG: Eng SIRC ARTICLE NO: 098098

The expanding role of television in college football: a chronology. *Chronicle of higher education (Washington)* 28(19), 5 Jul 1984, 26.
LEVEL: B LANG: Eng SIRC ARTICLE NO: 104707

White, B.R. Justice White's dissent from court's ruling on NCAA control of football telecasts. *Chronicle of higher educatio (Washington)* 28(19), 5 Jul 1984, 25-26;28.
LEVEL: B LANG: Eng SIRC ARTICLE NO: 104745

MEDICINE

Johnson, P.R. Krafcik, J. Greene, J.W. Massive pulmonary embolism in a varsity athlete. *Physician and sportsmedicine (Minneapolis, Minn.)* 12(12), Dec 1984, 61-63.
LEVEL: I LANG: Eng SIRC ARTICLE NO: 103163

Krebs, B. Gron, L.K. Simultaneous dorsal dislocation of both interphalangeal joints in a finger. (Refs: 10)*British journal of sports medicine (Loughborough, Eng.)* 18(3), Sept 1984, 217-219. ABST: Following simultaneous dorsal dislocation of both interphalangeal joints of a finger, attention must be paid to the risk of a long period of recovery because of the severity of the lesion. Approximately one year after such an accident to a footballer arthrodesis was performed on the proximal interphalangeal joint, as the patient was still suffering from constant pain in the finger.
LEVEL: A LANG: Eng SIRC ARTICLE NO: 103164

Mosteller, J.H. The Stallions' dentist. *Journal of the Alabama Dental Association (Birmingham)* 68(2), Spring 1984, 15-18.
LEVEL: B LANG: Eng SIRC ARTICLE NO: 103169

Rovere, G.D. Adair, D.A. Yates, C.S. Miller, R. Malek, S.T. A survey of team physician and trainer availability and participation in intercollegiate football. (Refs: 4)*Physician and sportsmedicine (Minneapolis, Minn.)* 12(11), Nov 1984, 90-94;97-100;103-104.
LEVEL: I LANG: Eng SIRC ARTICLE NO: 101253

Tucker, M.E. Team dentist. The New York Jets. *New York State dental journal (New York)* 50(5), May 1984, 304-305.
LEVEL: B LANG: Eng SIRC ARTICLE NO: 101255

Vetter, E. Nursing care study: a child with tetanus. *Nursing times (London)* 80(3), 18-24 Jan 1984, 59-61.
LEVEL: I LANG: Eng SIRC ARTICLE NO: 099612

OFFICIATING

Calhoun, G. Pass coverage in a five-official crew. *Referee (Franksville, Wis.)* 9(8), Aug 1984, 36-37.
LEVEL: B LANG: Eng SIRC ARTICLE NO: 098083

Calhoun, G. Running and kicking plays in a five-official crew. *Referee (Franksville, Wis.)* 9(9), Sept 1984, 37;61.
LEVEL: LANG: Eng SIRC ARTICLE NO: 101238

Calhoun, G. Working with off-field officials. *Referee (Franksville, Wis.)* 9(10), Oct 1984, 37;61.
LEVEL: B LANG: Eng SIRC ARTICLE NO: 105811

Fremon, D. Chicago's heavyweights: The Central Officials' Association. *Referee (Franksville, Wis.)* 9(5), May 1984, 24-28.
LEVEL: B LANG: Eng SIRC ARTICLE NO: 097631

Interview Norm Lamb: state senator, attorney and football official. *Referee (Franksville, Wis.)* 9(4), Apr 1984, 16-19.
LEVEL: B LANG: Eng SIRC ARTICLE NO: 098090

Interview: John Adams. *Referee (Franksville, Wis.)* 9(10), Oct 1984, 16-19.
LEVEL: B LANG: Eng SIRC ARTICLE NO: 105821

Narol, M. Recent cases: player injuries and the official. *Referee (Franksville, Wis.)* 9(9), Sept 1984, 14.
LEVEL: B LANG: Eng SIRC ARTICLE NO: 101525

FOOTBALL (continued)

Pemberton, J. Penalty enforcements. *Referee (Franksville, Wis.) 9(8), Aug 1984, 35-36.*
LEVEL: B LANG: Eng SIRC ARTICLE NO 098095

Pemberton, J. Goal-line and scoring situations. *Referee (Franksville, Wis.) 9(10), Oct 1984, 36.*
LEVEL: B LANG: Eng SIRC ARTICLE NO: 105840

PHILOSOPHY

Meredith, L. Of Super Bowls and Sisyphus: why do we care who wins any contest? *Arete: the journal of sport literature (San Diego, Calif.) 1(2), Spring 1984, 9-21.*
NOTES: The author establishes a parallel between the Super Bowl and two myths: the myth of Sisyphus and the myth of Armageddon.
LEVEL: A LANG: Eng SIRC ARTICLE NO: 098093

PHYSICAL FITNESS

'Scouting' your team by computer: football conditioning program analyzes fitness of players. *First aider (Gardner, Kans.) 54 (3), Nov 1984, 14-15.*
LEVEL: B LANG: Eng SIRC ARTICLE NO: 108463

PHYSIOLOGY

Cohen, A. O'Shea, M. Behrens, J. Is exercise physiology reaching professional football? (Refs: 7)*Athletic training (Greenville, N.C.) 19(3), Fall 1984, 185-188.*
ABST: The athletic trainers of 28 professional football teams from the National Footbal Leage are surveyed on the administration of supplements before and after practice, on the administration of fluids during and after practice, on the administration of vitamin and protein supplements, and on the preferred equipment used for strength training and rehabilitation. Results indicate that 1) salt tablets, K-Lyte, and Fosfree are used heavily before and after practice, 2) players are encouraged to drink during and after practice, 3) 62% of the teams give vitamins to all players, while 48% give out protein supplements, and 4) free weights are more frequently used for strength training and the Cybex and Orthotron machines for rehabilitation.
LEVEL: A LANG: Eng SIRC ARTICLE NO: 099566

Glein, G.W. The profiling of professional football players. (Refs: 20)*Clinics in sports medicine (Philadelphia) 3(1), Jan 1984, 185-197.*
NOTES: Symposium on profiling.
ABST: The author examined one professional football team over the course of the 1979 season. Using tests of strength, flexibility, performance, oxygen consumption as well as anthropometric data playing time and history of injury, four football position categories were defined. The linemen, tight ends and linebackers, offensive running backs and quarterback and defensive backs and wide receivers all showed different profiles. Using the statistical treatment of discriminant analysis the players could be placed into positional categories with a high degree of accuracy.
LEVEL: A LANG: Eng SIRC ARTICLE NO: 093426

Jaffe, A.S. Garfinkel, B.T. Ritter, C.S. Sobel, B.E. Plasma MB creatine kinase after vigorous exercise in professional athletes. *American journal of cardiology (New York) 53(6), 1 Mar 1984, 856-858.*
ABST: This study examined the plasma MB creatine kinase activity of nine professional football athletes following competition. Total plasmac activity increased in seven athletes while four of these athletes also had elevated MB-CK.
LEVEL: A LANG: Eng SIRC ARTICLE NO: 099579

PHYSIOLOGY - MUSCLE

Schlinkman, B. Norms for high school football players derived from cybex data reduction computer. (Refs: 10)*Journal of orthopaedic and sports physical therapy (Baltimore, Md.) 5(5), Mar/Apr 1984, 243-245.*
ABST: Three hundred forty-two male high school football players were tested for muscular imbalances and joint abnormalities using a Cybex II Isokinetic Dynamometer and Cybex Data Reduction Computer. Through the use of the Data Reduction Computer and by weighing the lower limb for its effect against gravity in extension and with gravity in flexion, the hamstring-quadriceps ratio was re-set at 50-55% at 60 degrees per second. The author suggests that preseason screening will prevent injuries and aid in designing strength-training programs.
LEVEL: A LANG: Eng SIRC ARTICLE NO: 095018

Schubert, M.M. Guttu, R.L. Hunter, L.H. Hall, R. Thomas, R. Changes in shoulder and leg strength in athletes wearing mandibular orthopedic repositioning appliances. *Journal of the American Dental Association (Chicago) 108(3), Mar 1984, 334-337.*
LEVEL: A LANG: Eng SIRC ARTICLE NO: 101254

Stafford, M.G. Grana, W.A. Hamstring/quadriceps ratios in college football players: a high velocity evaluation. (Refs: 21) *American journal of sports medicine (Baltimore) 12(3), May/Jun 1984, 209-211.*
ABST: The purpose of this study was to determine the hamstring/quadriceps torque ratios, at three functional speeds (90, 180 and 300 deg/sec), for the dominant and nondominant knees of 60 varsity intercollegiate football players. Two Cybex II isokinetic dynamometers were used to measure the power outputs of the quadriceps and hamstrings during reciprocol contractions. The results indicated that the hamstring/quadricep torque ratios rose significantly bilaterally as the test speed increased. Also, the hamstring/quadricep torque ratio differed significantly bilaterally at all speeds, with the ratio lower for the dominant knee. The authors suggest that the results help establish normative data for football players, at functional speeds, through which one could determine functional ability and readiness to return to competition.
LEVEL: A LANG: Eng SIRC ARTICLE NO: 103177

Yates, J.W. Koen, T.J. Semenick, D.M. Kuftinec, M.M. Effects of a mandibular orthopedic repositioning appliance on muscular strength. *Journal of the American Dental Association (Chicago) 108(3), Mar 1984, 331-333.*
ABST: The authors performed strength tests on 14 football players wearing no mouthpiece, wearing a placebo mouthpiece, and wearing a MORA mouthpiece. No significant differences between the three tests were observed.
LEVEL: A LANG: Eng SIRC ARTICLE NO: 101257

PHYSIOLOGY - TEMPERATURE

Wailgum, T.D. Paolone, A.M. Heat tolerance of college football linemen and backs. (Refs: 18)*Physician and sportsmedicine (Minneapolis, Minn.) 12(5), May 1984, 81-85;88.*
LEVEL: I LANG: Eng SIRC ARTICLE NO: 095024

PICTORIAL WORKS

Riffenburgh, B. Boss, D. Running wild: a pictorial tribute to the NFL's greatest runners. Los Angeles: NFL Properties, Inc., 1984. 1v.
LEVEL: B LANG: Eng LC CARD: 84-016673

PROTECTIVE DEVICES

Bishop, P.J. Norman, R.W. Kozey, J.W. An evaluation of football helmets under impact conditons. (Refs: 8)*American journal o sports medicine (Baltimore) 12(3), May/Jun 1984, 233-236.*
ABST: The purpose of this study was to evaluate the impact attenuating characteristics of 81 football helmets used previously in competitive high school programs. The helmets were grouped according to liner type: suspension, padded-suspension, and padded liner. Each helmet was then measured on a Gadd Severity Index (GSI) scale, after being given two consecutive right rear boss impacts. Using a criterion of GSI/500, the failure rate for suspension helmets was 19 per cent, in comparison to a 2 per cent failure rate for the padded helmets. Resultant acceleration-time curves were also done on computer plots and indicated that the effect of padding was to slow the headform at a fairly uniform rate upon impact. The authors thus found suspension helmets inferior to the padded and padded-suspension helmets.
LEVEL: A LANG: Eng SIRC ARTICLE NO: 103149

Bryce, G.R. Barker, R.M. Variability and sampling inspection in the NOCSAE standards for football helmets. (Refs: 10) *Research quarterly for exercise & sport (Reston, Va.) 55(2), Jun 1984, 103-108.*
ABST: Among the purposes of the National Operating Committee on Standards for Athletic Equipment (NOCSAE) is a drive to improve football safety through the development of impact resistance standards for new and refinished football helmets. This study examines the various sources of variability in the helmet testing procedure. This study reveals that NOCSAE standards are inadequate. In turn this result causes an unacceptably high probability of returning unsafe helmets to the playing field.
LEVEL: A LANG: Eng SIRC ARTICLE NO: 095808

Ellfeldt, H.J. Football equipment. (Refs: 25)
NOTES: In, Scott, W.N. (ed.) et al., Principles of sports medicine, Baltimore, Williams & Wilkins, c1984, p. 375-392.
LEVEL: I LANG: Eng RC1210 18016

Fong, N. Football equipment. *Audible (Toronto) Winter 1984, 9.*
LEVEL: B LANG: Eng SIRC ARTICLE NO: 093423

Gibbs, R.W. A protective collar for cervical radiculopathy. (Refs: 7)*Physician and sportsmedicine (Minneapolis, Minn.) 12(5), May 1984, 139-140;142-143.*
LEVEL: I LANG: Eng SIRC ARTICLE NO: 094998

Morrow, R.M. Kuebker, W.A. Golden, L. Walters, F.E. Day, E.A. Quarterback mouth

guards: speech intelligibility and player preference. (Refs: 3)*Physician and sportsmedicine 12(4)*, Apr 1984, 71-73;76.
ABST: Five mouth guard designs were tested by eighteen quarterbacks from two universities and three high schools. Speech intelligibility and player preference were evaluated. The findings show that speech intelligibility was better with custom mouth guards than with self-adapted ones. All quarterbacks favoured the custom mouth guard with occlusion and reduced palatal extensions.
LEVEL: A LANG: Eng SIRC ARTICLE NO: 093437

Roberts, J. A program for fitting football shoulder pads. *Audible (Toronto) Winter 1984, 12-14.*
LEVEL: B LANG: Eng SIRC ARTICLE NO: 093443

Ryan, A.J. What price protection? *Physician and sportsmedicine 12(1), Jan 1984, 32.*
LEVEL: B LANG: Eng SIRC ARTICLE NO: 092090

Schubert, M.M. Guttu, R.L. Hunter, L.H. Hall, R. Thomas, R. Changes in shoulder and leg strength in athletes wearing mandibular orthopedic repositioning appliances. *Journal of the American Dental Association (Chicago) 108(3), Mar 1984, 334-337.*
LEVEL: A LANG: Eng SIRC ARTICLE NO: 101254

Sparks, B. Getting equipped: even the toughest players use body-gard. *Sports now (St. Louis, Mo.) 2(8), Aug 1984, 28.*
LEVEL: B LANG: Eng SIRC ARTICLE NO: 098096

Wilkerson, G.B. The fine art of helmet fitting: a proper fit is crucial to the safety of every player. *Audible (Toronto) Winter 1984, 14;16-17.*
LEVEL: B LANG: Eng SIRC ARTICLE NO: 093448

Yates, J.W. Koen, T.J. Semenick, D.M. Kuftinec, M.M. Effects of a mandibular orthopedic repositioning appliance on muscular strength. *Journal of the American Dental Association (Chicago) 108(3), Mar 1984, 331-333.*
ABST: The authors performed strength tests on 14 football players wearing no mouthpiece, wearing a placebo mouthpiece, and wearing a MORA mouthpiece. No significant differences between the three tests was observed.
LEVEL: A LANG: Eng SIRC ARTICLE NO: 101257

PSYCHOLOGY

Pilkington, R. Pilkington, M. Positive psychology for the kicker. *Scholastic coach (New York) 54(2), Sept 1984, 58;60.*
LEVEL: B LANG: Eng SIRC ARTICLE NO: 099595

Schurr, K.T. Ruble, V.E. Nisbet, J. Wallace, D. Myers-Briggs type inventory characteristics of more and less successful players on an American football team. (Refs: 22)*Journal of sport behavior (Mobile, Ala.) 7(2), Jun 1984, 47-57.*
ABST: The relationship between the personality characteristics of 182 American football players and the positions they played on the team as well as their relative success were investigated using the Myers-Briggs type Indicator (MBTI). The data were analyzed using MULTIQUAL, a computer program for the log-linear analysis of complex contingency tables. In addition to the classification resulting from the MBTI scoring, the players were classified according to whether they played offense or defense, the line or backfield, and on either the first or second string or at some other level. Odds ratios were also computed for single MBTI scales and combinations of scales. The results indicated that for all positions the preferences tended to be the

Thinking mode for the most successful player. Also, the successful linemen tended to prefer the Sensing mode, the successful offensive backs preferred the Intuition mode, and the successful defensive backs tended to be Introverted. The odds ratios suggested that the observed results might be of practical value.
LEVEL: A LANG: Eng SIRC ARTICLE NO: 099603

RACE RELATIONS

Button, S.M. A test of the stacking hypothesis in Big Ten football. Eugene, Ore.: Microform Publications, University of Oregon, 1984. 1 mirofiche : negative, ill. ; 11 x 15 cm.
NOTES: Thesis (M.S.) - Western Illinois University, 1981; (5, v, 52 leaves); includes bibliography.
LEVEL: A LANG: Eng UO84 24

RULES AND REGULATIONS

Pemberton, J. Pass interference. *Referee (Franksville, Wis.) 9(9), Sept 1984, 35-36.*
LEVEL: B LANG: Eng SIRC ARTICLE NO: 101250

Safety is stressed in new football rules. *First aider (Gardner, Kan.) 53(5), Feb 1984, 3.*
LEVEL: B LANG: Eng SIRC ARTICLE NO: 096670

SOCIAL PSYCHOLOGY

Rees, C.R. Segal, M.W. Role differentiation in groups: the relationship between instrumental and expressive leadership. *Small group behavior (Beverley Hills, Calif.) 15, 1984, 109-123.*
ABST: Leadership role differentiation was examined in two Division I NCAA college football teams. The results found a high degree of leadership role integration in that several members of each team fulfilled both instrumental and expressive leadership roles. These players were either task or social leaders. Task leaders had high formal status within the team while social specialists had high or medium formal status.
LEVEL: A LANG: Eng SIRC ARTICLE NO: 099599

Rees, C.R. Segal, M.W. Role differentiation in groups: the relationship between instrumental and expressive leadership. *Small group behavior (Beverly Hills, Calif.) 15(1), Feb 1984, 109-123.*
LEVEL: A LANG: Eng

SPECTATORS

Lewis, V.F. Powder puff: appreciation of the man's game football: a digest of information for the female spectator. s.l.: Wm L. Pettiford, c1984. 184 p. : ill.
NOTES: Cover title. Bibliography: p. 181.
LEVEL: B LANG: Eng LC CARD: 85-243057

STATISTICS AND RECORDS

Greunke, L.R. Football rankings: college teams in the Associated Press poll, 1936-1984. Jefferson, N.C.: McFarland, 1984. 1v
CORP: Associated Press.
NOTES: Includes index.
LEVEL: I LANG: Eng ISBN: 0899501087 LC CARD: 83-025595

Walsh, J.A. Inside football 1984. 1st Ballantine Books ed. New York: Fawcett Columbine, c1984. 169 p. ; 28 cm.
CORP: Massillon Society.
LEVEL: B LANG: Eng ISBN: 0449901297 LC CARD: 84-090835

STRATEGY

Swanson, K. Football goals that work. *Athletic journal (Evanston, Ill.) 65(3), Oct 1984, 44-45.*
LEVEL: B LANG: Eng SIRC ARTICLE NO: 099607

STRATEGY - DEFENSIVE

Beam, R. The 5-3 run-pass defense. *Athletic journal (Evanston, Ill.) 65(3), Oct 1984, 18-19.*
LEVEL: B LANG: Eng SIRC ARTICLE NO: 099563

Blateri, F. Put a twist in your rush. *Athletic journal (Evanston, Ill.) 65(5), Dec 1984, 22-23;42.*
LEVEL: B LANG: Eng SIR ARTICLE NO: 104696

Curran, D. Play 'bingo' & win on defense. *Scholastic coach (New York) 53(9), Apr 1984, 48-49;67.*
LEVEL: B LANG: Eng SIRC ARTICLE NO: 094990

Ervin, M. Attacking from a multiple 50. *Coaching clinic (Princeton, N.J.) 23(3), Nov 1984, 11-13.*
LEVEL: B LANG: Eng SIRC ARTICLE NO: 103155

Fico, D. Defending two tight ends with teams that run away from the monster. *Football clinic (Princeton, N.J.) 2(8), Apr 1984, 5-6.*
LEVEL: B LANG: Eng SIRC ARTICLE NO: 096656

Garcia, E. Bang & scarpe technique for inside linebackers. *Football clinic (Princeton, N.J.) 2(10), Jun 1984, 2-3.*
LEVEL: LANG: Eng SIRC ARTICLE NO: 094997

Giampalmi, J. Complete book of linebacker play. West Nyack, N.Y.: Parker, c1984. 156 p.
LEVEL: B LANG: Eng ISBN: 0131575112 LC CARD: 83-013437 GV951.18 15864

Gigantino, A. You, too, can use the Southern Cal nickel defense. *Scholastic coach (New York) 54(3), Oct 1984, 28-30;80.*
LEVEL: B LANG: Eng SIRC ARTICLE NO: 101241

Goehl, C. The nickel defense. *Athletic journal 64(6), Jan 1984, 16;25.*
LEVEL: B LANG: Eng SIRC ARTICLE NO: 090646

Griggs, D. Overlap concept to pass defense. *Coaching clinic (Princeton, N.J.) 23(3), Nov 1984, 2-5.*
LEVEL: B LANG: Eng SIRC ARTICLE NO: 103160

Harris, E. The gap control defense: the gap control defense seeks to move defensive orientation from player control to a gap control keying ideology. *Athletic journal (Evanston, Ill.) 65(4), Nov 1984, 48-51.*
LEVEL: B LANG: Eng SIRC ARTICLE NO: 101242

Hennings, D. A 'cowboy' look to the stacked 44. *Scholastic coach (New York) 54(2), Sept 1984, 42;44.*
LEVEL: B LANG: Eng SIRC ARTICLE NO: 099577

Kaminsky, H. Unscramble your secondary coverages with the 'scramble'. *Football clinic (Princeton, N.J.) 2(10), Jun 1984, 4-6.*
LEVEL: B LANG: Eng SIRC ARTICLE NO: 095002

Karlov, R.E. Curie's flexible '5' secondary. *Scholastic coach (New York) 54(1), Aug 1984, 55-58.*
LEVEL: B LANG: Eng SIRC ARTICLE NO: 099580

Kramer, L. Be prepared... defensing the veer at Austin College. *Football clinic (Princeton, N.J.) 2(9), May 1984, 6-8.*
LEVEL: B LANG: Eng SIRC ARTICLE NO: 096662

FOOTBALL (continued)

Mannie, K. Playing reckless man with a free safety. *Scholastic coach (New York) 53(10), May/Jun 1984, 22;24.*
LEVEL: B LANG: Eng SIRC ARTICLE NO: 095009

Mannie, K. Pro 3-4: outside linebacker play vs. I backs. *Texas coach (Austin, Tex.) 28(3), Oct 1984, 28-30.*
LEVEL: B LANG Eng SIRC ARTICLE NO: 173203

Mannion, M. A multiple look defense. The 6-2-3's multiple-look interior defensive line alignments are sure to confuse the opponent. *Athletic journal (Evanston, Ill.) 64(10), May 1984, 48-49;63.*
LEVEL: B LANG: Eng SIRC ARTICLE NO: 095010

McDaniels, M. Putting more flexibility into the 5-2. *Athletic journal (Evanston, Ill.) 65(1), Aug 1984, 36-37;55-56.*
LEVEL: B LANG: Eng SIRC ARTICLE NO: 096664

McWilliams, D.L. Texas linebacker play. *Texas coach (Austin, Tex.) 28(3), Oct 1984, 9-11.*
LEVEL: B LANG: Eng SIRC ARTICLE NO: 173197

Mehlbrech, D. An effective defense... a slanting multiple 4-4 defense. *Football clinic (Princeton, N.J.) 2(9), May 1984, 4-6.*
LEVEL: B LANG: Eng SIRC ARTICLE NO: 096666

Newman, D. Hashmark rules. *Coaching clinic (Princeton, N.J.) 22(9), May 1984, 11-13.*
LEVEL: B LANG: Eng SIRC ARTICLE NO: 095012

Olivadotti, T. Defensive analysis of pass offense. *Scholastic coach (New York) 54(1), Aug 1984, 48-49;69.*
LEVEL: B LANG: Eng SIRC ARTICLE NO: 099593

Pergolizzi, F. No return kickoff. The no-return kickoff provides a simple, but effective method of kickoff coverage. *Athletic journal 64(7), Feb 1984, 56;80-81.*
LEVEL: B LANG: Eng SIRC ARTICLE NO: 092088

Peterson, B. Secondary play. *Texas coach (Austin, Tex.) 28(4), Nov 1984, 28-29.*
LEVEL: B LANG: Eng SIRC ARTICLE NO: 17343

Petricca, J. Blue slant defense. *Athletic journal (Evanston, Ill.) 65(3), Oct 1984, 22-24.*
LEVEL: B LANG: Eng SIRC ARTICL NO: 099594

Proctor, B. Oklahoma secondary play coverage calls and coverages. *Texas coach 27(5), Feb 1984, 37-62.*
LEVEL: B LANG: Eng SIRC ARTICLE NO: 092089

Raffey, K. Pass rushing skills for defensive linemen. *Audible (Toronto) Winter 1984, 10-12.*
LEVEL: B LANG: Eng SIRC ARTICLE NO: 093442

Richter, N. Defensive end play from the 4-3 defense. *Athletic journal (Evanston, Ill.) 65(2), Sept 1984, 42-44.*
LEVEL: B LANG: Eng SIRC ARTICLE NO: 099600

Schuster, M.A. Coaching the defensive secondary. West Nyack, N.Y.: Parker Pub. Co., c1984. 1v.
NOTES: Includes index.
LEVEL: B LANG: Eng ISBN: 0131389424 LC CARD: 84-007770

STRATEGY - OFFENSIVE

Alexander, N. The U. of California-Davis running game. *Athletic journal (Evanston, Ill.) 65(3), Oct 1984, 12-14.*
LEVEL: B LANG: Eng SIRC ARTICLE NO: 099559

Arakelian, G. A simplified pass read package for the high school level. *Coaching clinic (Princeton,*

N.J.) 22(8), Apr 1984, 7-9.
LEVEL: B LANG: Eng SIRC ARTICLE NO: 094982

Arakelian, G. Sight adjusted patterns. *Football clinic (Princeton, N.J.) 2(10), Jun 1984, 1-2.*
LEVEL: B LANG: Eng SIRC ARTICLE NO: 094983

Arakelian, G. Guideline for a short passing attack. *Texas coach (Austin, Tex.) 28(1), Aug 1984, 40-41.*
LEVEL: B LANG: Eng SIRC ARTICLE NO: 103148

Arnold, F. Judson multiple sets from the I offense. *Texas coach (Austin, Tex.) 28(4), Nov 1984, 20-23.*
LEVEL: B LANG: Eng SIRC ARTICLE NO: 173429

Baxter, J.S. Stunting from the secondary. *Athletic journal (Evanston, Ill.) 64(10), May 1984, 12;55-56.*
LEVEL: B LANG: En SIRC ARTICLE NO: 094985

Bluth, D. How to develop the option quarterback. The option quarterback must be coached individually with particular emphasi placed on cognitive skills and their relation to functional techniques. *Athletic journal 64(7), Feb 1984, 34-35;38-39;76-77.*
LEVEL: B LANG: Eng SIRC ARTICLE NO: 092068

Bluth, D. Football's twin-I: a complete multiple option attack. West Nyack, N.Y.: Parker Pub., c1984. 1v.
NOTES: Includes index.
LEVEL: B LANG: Eng ISBN: 0133243028 LC CARD: 84-003138

Brock, J. Using the veer option from the wishbone set. These plays add another dimension to your outside attack, while takin pressure off the quarterback in the option. *Athletic journal (Evanston, Ill.) 64(10), May 1984, 26-28.*
LEVEL: B LANG: Eng SIRC ARTICLE NO: 094987

Cardone, D. The tight end as a decoy: try using the tight end as a decoy versus a read 50 defense and look forward to a happ 'ending' to your game. *Athletic journal (Evanston, Ill.) 65(4), Nov 1984, 16-18.*
LEVEL: B LANG: Eng SIRC ARTICLE NO: 101239

Clark, R. Option adjustment from the 'I'. *Coaching clinic (Princeton, N.J.) 23(4), Dec 1984, 9-11.*
LEVEL: B LANG: Eng SIR ARTICLE NO: 103152

Coffman, B. Offense execution: key to consistent winning. *Coaching clinic (Princeton, N.J.) 23(3), Nov 1984, 8-10.*
LEVEL: B LANG: Eng SIRC ARTICLE NO: 103153

Colby, G. Schlarman's flexible passing system. *Football clinic (Princeton, N.J.) 2(10), Jun 1984, 6-8.*
LEVEL: B LANG: Eng SIRC ARTICLE NO: 094988

DeMeo, T. Tempo control football. *Scholastic coach 53(8), Mar 1984, 32;68-69.*
LEVEL: B LANG: Eng SIRC ARTICLE NO: 093422

Dolezal, G. The 'power' pass. *Coaching clinic (Princeton, N.J.) 23(3), Nov 1984, 6-7.*
LEVEL: B LANG: Eng SIRC ARTICLE NO: 103154

Donahue, T. Smith, H. UCLA's passing attack: successful patterns and adjustable routes. *Athletic journal (Evanston, Ill.) 65(2), Sept 1984, 8-13.*
LEVEL: B LANG: Eng SIRC ARTICLE NO: 099570

Dulgarian, D. Set the tailback in motion. *Athletic journal (Evanston, Ill.) 65(2), Sept 1984, 54;58-59.*
LEVEL: B LANG: En SIRC ARTICLE NO: 099571

Durham, J.W. Football's modular offense: a flexible system of attack. West Nycak, N.Y.: Parker Pub. Co., c1984. xiv, 166 p.

NOTES: Includes index.
LEVEL: B LANG: Eng ISBN: 0133241602 LC CARD: 83-010532 GV951.8 15736

Dyer, P. Keep an 'I' on the Delaware Wing-T. *Scholastic coach (New York) 54(1), Aug 1984, 36-38;40-41.*
LEVEL: B LANG: Eng SIRC ARTICLE NO: 099572

Ellison, G. Run-and-shoot football: the now attack. West Nyack, N.Y.: Parker Pub. Co., 1984, c1982. 1v.
NOTES: Includes index.
LEVEL: B LANG: Eng ISBN: 0137838794 LC CARD: 84-014786

Hand, L. Attacking football defenses with radar blocking. West Nyack, N.Y.: Parker Pub., c1984. 1v.
NOTES: Includes index.
LEVEL: B LANG: Eng ISBN: 0130502200 LC CARD: 84-022643

Hannaman, K. Misdirection from multiple offensive sets. *Athletic journal (Evanston, Ill.) 65(3), Oct 1984, 46-47.*
LEVEL: LANG: Eng SIRC ARTICLE NO: 099575

Harris, W. Tennessee's quick-game package. *Scholastic coach (New York) 54(2), Sept 1984, 28-31;77.*
LEVEL: B LANG: Eng SIR ARTICLE NO: 099576

Haubrich, B. Breaking the big play. *Scholastic coach (New York) 53(9), Apr 1984, 22;24;88.*
LEVEL: B LANG: Eng SIRC ARTICL NO: 095000

Hendrickson, B. A new approach: stand-up offensive line play. This unique new technique can improve your offensive line play *Athletic journal (Evanston, Ill.) 65(1), Aug 1984, 26-29.*
LEVEL: B LANG: Eng SIRC ARTICLE NO: 096660

Jacklin, E. The wishbone from the I formation: running the wishbone out of the I formation can really help a team's passing game. *Athletic journal 64(6), Jan 1984, 52-53.*
LEVEL: B LANG: Eng SIRC ARTICLE NO: 090649

Jones, J. Simplified triple option techniques. *Athletic journal 64(6), Jan 1984, 42-43;70-71.*
LEVEL: B LANG: Eng SIRC ARTICLE NO: 090651

Kelly, M. Pass cuts made easy with a tree. *Coaching clinic (Princeton, N.J.) 23(1), Sept 1984, 5-6.*
LEVEL: B LANG: Eng SIRC ARTICLE NO: 099581

Klos, D. Counter plays from the wishbone. *Athletic journal (Evanston, Ill.) 65(3), Oct 1984, 30-31.*
LEVEL: B LANG: Eng SIRC ARTICLE NO: 099582

Knight, D. Veer offense... TLC style. *Coaching clinic (Englewood Cliffs, N.J.) 22(10), Jun 1984, 4-6.*
LEVEL: B LANG: Eng SIRC ARTICLE NO: 095004

Koehler, M. Revitalize the screen pass. *Athletic journal (Evanston, Ill.) 65(5), Dec 1984, 36-37.*
LEVEL: B LANG: Eng SIRC ARTICLE NO: 104719

Langord, R. Perryton offensive. *Texas coach (Austin, Tex.) 28(1), Aug 1984, 50-51.*
LEVEL: B LANG: Eng SIRC ARTICLE NO: 103166

Lockhart, H. A simple one-step drop-back short passing game. *Scholastic coach (New York) 53(10), May/Jun 1984, 28-30;106.*
LEVEL: B LANG: Eng SIRC ARTICLE NO: 095006

Long, J. Scoring from deep with only seconds to go. *Athletic journal (Evanston, Ill.) 65(4), Nov 1984,*

40-41.
LEVEL: B LANG: Eng SIRC ARTICLE NO: 101248

Luke, B.J. The sprint draw. *Athletic journal 64(9),* Apr 1984, 8;10;72.
LEVEL: B LANG: Eng SIRC ARTICLE NO: 093435

Luke, B.J. Reading the outside veer. *Athletic journal (Evanston, Ill.) 65(5), Dec 1984, 44-46;57.*
LEVEL: B LANG: Eng SIRC ARTICLE NO: 104720

Manley, D. Misdirection passing: throw against the flow. *Athletic journal (Evanston, Ill.) 65(5), Dec 1984, 52-53.*
LEVEL: LANG: Eng SIRC ARTICLE NO: 104721

Mariani, F. Delay passing game. This passing series is structured for any level of football - and it doesn't require a quarterback with a rifle for an arm. *Athletic journal (Evanston, Ill.) 65(5), Dec 1984, 16-17;62-63.*
LEVEL: B LANG: Eng SIRC ARTICLE NO: 104722

Marmie, L. Tennessee's slant defense: a closely integrated four-stunt package that upsets the blocking. *Scholastic coach (New York) 54(1), Aug 1984, 26-27.*
LEVEL: B LANG: Eng SIRC ARTICLE NO: 099585

Martin, J. The wing T at Denton High school. *Texas coach 27(5), Feb 1984, 32-35.*
LEVEL: B LANG: Eng SIRC ARTICLE NO: 0920

McCann, M. A simple and successful passing attack. *Coaching clinic (Princeton, N.J.) 23(4), Dec 1984, 6-9.*
LEVEL: B LANG: Eng SIRC ARTICLE NO: 103167

McDaniels, M. The pro-T offense: winning football with a modern passing attack. West Nyack, N.Y.: Parker Pub. Co., c1984. 21 p. : ill.
NOTES: Includes index.
LEVEL: B LANG: Eng ISBN: 0137312253 LC CARD: 84-009414 GV951.8 18113

McKee, R.M. An exciting play...sprint out, read pass or run. *Football clinic (Princeton, N.J.) 2(9), May 1984, 1-4.*
LEVEL: B LANG: Eng SIRC ARTICLE NO: 096665

Murray, B. Silver offense. *Coaching clinic 22(7), Mar 1984, 7-9.*
LEVEL: B LANG: Eng SIRC ARTICLE NO: 093438

Nitchman, N. The double wing...no passing fancy in '83. *Athletic journal (Evanston, Ill.) 64(10), May 1984, 18-21;62.*
LEVEL: B LANG: Eng SIRC ARTICLE NO: 095013

O'Hara, J. Protecting the quarterback. *Texas coach (Austin, Tex.) 28(2), Sept 1984, 16-19.*
LEVEL: B LANG: Eng SIRC ARTICL NO: 105836

O'Hara, J. Southwest Texas' split-back offense. *Texas coach (Austin, Tex.) 28(3), Oct 1984, 32-35.*
LEVEL: B LANG: Eng SIR ARTICLE NO: 173205

O'Neal, B. A multiple blocking scheme. *Athletic journal (Evanston, Ill.) 65(3), Oct 1984, 34-35.*
LEVEL: B LANG: Eng SIRC ARTICLE NO: 099591

Pergolizzi, F. Delaware Wing-T passing game: how to get the ball to the tight end. *Athletic journal (Evanston, Ill.) 65(5), Dec 1984, 26-27;55-56.*
LEVEL: B LANG: Eng SIRC ARTICLE NO: 104729

Perry, G.A. Sabol, R.F. Attacking the split-6 8-man front. *Athletic journal (Evanston, Ill.) 65(4), Nov 1984, 24-27.*
LEVEL: B LANG: Eng SIRC ARTICLE NO: 101251

Plaga, G. The shovel pass: the shovel pass will leave the defense wondering where the ballcarrier

came from, and the opposin coaches wondering how to stop the play. *Athletic journal 64(6), Jan 1984, 36;58-60.*
LEVEL: B LANG: Eng SIRC ARTICLE NO: 090656

Ross, B.T. The 'whirlybird' catches the worm. (wishbone) *Scholastic coach (New York) 54(2), Sept 1984, 56-57;82.*
LEVEL: B LANG: Eng SIRC ARTICLE NO: 099601

Rowen, K. Beat the blitz. *Athletic journal 64(9), Apr 1984, 52;70-71.*
LEVEL: B LANG: Eng SIRC ARTICLE NO: 093444

Schnellenberger, H. Stevens, G. Miami's 50 series: 3-step dropback pass. The 50 series has played an important part in the success of the 1983 national champions. *Athletic journal (Evanston, Ill.) 65(1), Aug 1984, 8-13.*
LEVEL: B LANG: Eng SIRC ARTICLE NO: 096671

Shipp, D. Rose, G. A simple two-minute no-huddle offense. *Scholastic coach (New York) 53(10), May/Jun 1984, 88-89;92.*
LEVEL: B LANG: Eng SIRC ARTICLE NO: 095020

Skinner, C. The case for multiple offensive sets. *Scholastic coach (New York) 54(2), Sept 1984, 22;24.*
LEVEL: B LANG: Eng SIRC ARTICLE NO: 099604

Smith, J.R. Lozano, J. The I-bone: the ulitmate concept in option football. *Texas coach (Austin, Tex.) 28(4), Nov 1984, 25-27.*
LEVEL: B LANG: Eng SIRC ARTICLE NO: 173431

Strickland, S. Zone blocking for the option offense. Once the techniques of zone blocking are learned and used with your other blocking schemes, you will have a complete blocking package for your option attack. *Athletic journal (Evanston, Ill.) 65(1), Aug 1984, 30-31;52-53.*
LEVEL: B LANG: Eng SIRC ARTICLE NO: 096672

Taylor, J. Hereford offense. *Texas coach (Austin, Tex.) 28(1), Aug 1984, 39.*
LEVEL: B LANG: Eng SIRC ARTICLE NO: 103178

Thompson, S. The smash series. With the Smash Series, a coach does not have to depend upon well-developed and experienced linemen in order to run the ball effectively. *Athletic journal (Evanston, Ill.) 65(5), Dec 1984, 30-33.*
LEVEL: B LANG: Eng SIRC ARTICLE NO: 104743

Venuto, J. Put a little 'fruit' into your offense. *Scholastic coach (New York) 53(9), Apr 1984, 32-34;83.*
LEVEL: B LANG: Eng SIRC ARTICLE NO: 095023

Welch, J. Basic blocking techniques vs. man coverage. *Texas coach (Austin, Tex.) 28(2), Sept 1984, 28-29.*
LEVEL: B LANG: Eng SIRC ARTICLE NO: 105845

White, R. Crane football. *Texas coach (Austin, Tex.) 28(1), Aug 1984, 32-33;62.*
LEVEL: B LANG: Eng SIRC ARTICLE NO: 10318

Willis, F. The Blanchard sprint-out package. *Coaching clinic 22(7), Mar 1984, 9-10.*
LEVEL: B LANG: Eng SIRC ARTICLE NO: 093450

TEACHING

Downing, F.M. Heimer, R.T. Teaching football via the computer. *Scholastic coach (New York) 53(9), Apr 1984, 62-64.*
LEVEL: LANG: Eng SIRC ARTICLE NO: 094992

TECHNIQUES AND SKILLS

Bouche, J. The cross-buck kick-return package. *Scholastic coach (New York) 54(5), Dec 1984, 36-37;57.*
LEVEL: B LANG: Eng SIRC ARTICLE NO: 103150

Storey, E.J. You can develop your own placekicker. *Athletic journal (Evanston, Ill.) 65(2), Sept 1984, 16-19;24-25;64-65.*
LEVEL: B LANG: Eng SIRC ARTICLE NO: 099606

TECHNIQUES AND SKILLS - BLOCKING

Aiken, R. Pocket pass protection. *Athletic journal (Evanston, Ill.) 65(1), Aug 1984, 40-41;58.*
LEVEL: B LANG: Eng SIRC ARTICLE NO: 096650

Lemonick, S. Ginenthal, D. Teaching the drive block. *Athletic journal 64(8), Mar 1984, 32-33;62-63.*
LEVEL: B LANG: Eng SIRC ARTICLE NO: 093433

Mannie, K. Principals and techniques for offensive linemen. *Football clinic (Princeton, N.J.) 2(8), Apr 1984, 1-5.*
LEVEL: B LANG: Eng SIRC ARTICLE NO: 096663

TECHNIQUES AND SKILLS - KICKING

Phillips, B. Mark Mosley, alive & kicking...straight on. *Scholastic coach (New York) 54(4), Nov 1984, 34-36;38.*
LEVEL: B LANG: Eng SIRC ARTICLE NO: 103171

TECHNIQUES AND SKILLS - LINEMAN

Altemus, C. Training the offensive 'horses'. (offensive lineman) *Scholastic coach (New York) 54(2), Sept 1984, 54-55;66.*
LEVEL: B LANG: Eng SIRC ARTICLE NO: 099560

Mannie, K. Pass protection basics. There are several key coaching points involved in teaching high school linemen pass protection techniques. *Athletic journal (Evanston, Ill.) 64(10), May 1984, 50-52.*
LEVEL: B LANG: Eng SIRC ARTICLE NO: 095008

TECHNIQUES AND SKILLS - PASS RECEPTION

Noppenberger, F. Put a little square-out into your life. Can be executed at any depth with no change in technique. *Scholastic coach (New York) 53(10), May/Jun 1984, 44-45.*
LEVEL: B LANG: Eng SIRC ARTICLE NO: 095014

Stinchcomb, B. The picture perfect pass pattern. *Scholastic coach (New York) 53(10), May/Jun 1984, 32;34;103.*
LEVEL: B LANG: Eng SIRC ARTICLE NO: 095021

TECHNIQUES AND SKILLS - PASSING

Koehler, M. Perfecting play-action passing in football. West Nyack, N.Y.: Parker Pub. Co., c1984. 1v.
NOTES: Includes index
LEVEL: B LANG: Eng ISBN: 0136566464 LC CARD: 83-027122

FOOTBALL (continued)

Zwiefel, S. The trips passing attack. *Football clinic (Princeton, N.J.) 2(8), Apr 1984, 6-8.*
LEVEL: B LANG: Eng SIRC ARTICLE NO: 096677

TECHNIQUES AND SKILLS - QUARTERBACK

Anderson, K. Clary, J. Brown, P.E. The art of quarterbacking. New York: Linden Press, c1984. 220 p. : ill. (A mountain lion book.)
NOTES: Includes index.
LEVEL: I LANG: Eng ISBN: 0671507249 LC CARD: 84-007193 GV951.3 18090

Bicknell, J. Training the 'little' QB to play 'big'. *Scholastic coach (New York) 54(1), Aug 1984, 50-54.*
LEVEL: B LANG: E SIRC ARTICLE NO: 099564

TECHNIQUES AND SKILLS - TACKLE

Bilovecky, D. Defense. Tackling guide. *Coaching clinic 22(6), Feb 1984, 11-13.*
LEVEL: B LANG: Eng SIRC ARTICLE NO: 090631

Morris, B. Feld, F. Junko, B. Sports performance series: proper tackling technique. *National Strength & Conditioning Association journal (Lincoln, Neb.) 6(3), Jun/Jul 1984, 4;71;73.*
LEVEL: B LANG: Eng SIRC ARTICLE NO: 096667

TESTING AND EVALUATION

Shields, C.L. Whitney, F.E. Zomar, V.D. Exercise performance of professional football players. (Refs: 8)*American journal of sports medicine (Baltimore) 12(6), Nov/Dec 1984, 455-459.*
ABST: With the likely hypothesis that the degree to which a football player is physically suited to his position will determine his value as a player, the authors attempted to describe the characteristics of a given player and position and, from that, to determine the characteristics that make up a first class player in that position. Over a 4-year period 167 football players were examined and grouped according to playing position and class. Classes were: I, rookies (nonstarters); II, veterans (nonstarters); and III, starters. Testing was in two phases, body characteristics and direct measurement of body function. All testing was done in connection with the preseason physical exam. Significant differences were found when data were analyzed by position. While few differences were seen when data were analyzed by class, one interesting finding was that Class III players (starters) were not only the oldest, but also had the highest level of cardiovascular fitness.
LEVEL: A LANG: Eng SIRC ARTICLE NO: 104736

TRAINING AND CONDITIONING

Forti, D.S. The study of off-season football strength and conditioning programs at selected major colleges. Eugene, Ore.: Microform Publications, University of Oregon, 1984. 1 microfiche : negative ; 11 x 15 cm.
NOTES: Thesis (M.S.) - Springfield College, 1982; (vi, 84 leaves); includes bibliography.
LEVEL: A LANG: Eng UO84 225

Grosse, S.J. Dorow, K.M. Krueger, R.J. Aerobic-dance your team into condition. *Scholastic coach (New York) 54(4), Nov 1984, 64-65;71.*
LEVEL: B LANG: Eng SIRC ARTICLE NO: 102944

Special issues in the high school strength and conditioning football program. *National Strength & Conditioning Association journal 6(1), Feb/Mar 1984, 12-20;62-65.*
LEVEL: B LANG: Eng SIRC ARTICLE NO: 093446

Streety, J. Build your team in the off season. *Texas coach (Austin, Tex.) 28(4), Nov 1984, 38-41.*
LEVEL: B LANG: Eng SIRC ARTICLE NO: 173438

TRAINING AND CONDITIONING - CIRCUIT TRAINING

Walderzak, P.E. Super circuit training. *National Strength & Conditioning Association journal (Lincoln, Neb.) 6(4), Aug/Sept 1984, 38-40.*
LEVEL: B LANG: Eng SIRC ARTICLE NO: 099613

TRAINING AND CONDITIONING - DRILLS

Beltran, J.D. Training the veer quarterback. *Texas coach (Austin, Tex.) 28(4), Nov 1984, 52-55.*
LEVEL: B LANG: Eng SIRC ARTICLE NO: 173447

Connolly, J. Get the offensive line going. *Athletic journal 64(9), Apr 1984, 60;66-67.*
LEVEL: B LANG: Eng SIRC ARTICLE NO 093421

Harms, D. Diving for the football - in a fascinating way. Poolside drill improves concentration and tuckaway of pass receivers; water is the 'tackler'. *Athletic journal (Evanston, Ill.) 65(5), Dec 1984, 54.*
LEVEL: B LANG: Eng SIRC ARTICLE NO: 104717

Proctor, B. Oklahoma secondary play and drills. *Texas coach 27(4), Jan 1984, 26-31;34-39.*
LEVEL: B LANG: Eng SIRC ARTICLE NO: 093441

Tolley, J.R. The American football coaches guide book to championship football drills. Elon College, NC: Jerry R. Tolley, c1984. x, 291 p. : ill.
CORP: American Football Coaches Association.
LEVEL: B LANG: Eng ISBN: 0-9614191-0-5 LC CARD: 84-091397 GV951.15 19072

TRAINING AND CONDITIONING - STRETCHING AND FLEXIBILITY EXERCISES

Marble, J. A flexibility program for football. A well-conditioned athlete is less injury-prone and will give the best performance - and that's the only type of athlete to have on the field. (Refs: 11)*Athletic journal (Evanston, Ill.) 64(10), May 1984, 36-37;40-43.*
LEVEL: B LANG: Eng SIRC ARTICLE NO: 095011

TRAINING AND CONDITIONING - WARM-UPS, WARM-DOWNS, LEAD-UP GAMES

Howell, J. Run-the-line. Warming up. *Coaching clinic 22(6), Feb 1984, 13-15.*
LEVEL: B LANG: Eng SIRC ARTICLE NO: 090648

TRAINING AND CONDITIONING - WEIGHT AND STRENGTH TRAINING

Apple Valley training program. *National Strength & Conditioning Association journal 6(1), Feb/Mar 1984, 58-61.*
LEVEL: B LANG: Eng SIRC ARTICLE NO: 093418

Asselta, A. Strengthening the quarterback's throwing action. (Refs: 2)*Audible (Toronto) Spring 1984, 7-8.*
LEVEL: B LANG: Eng SIRC ARTICLE NO: 096652

Briles, A. Strength training. *Texas coach (Austin, Tex.) 28(2), Sept 1984, 58-59.*
LEVEL: B LANG: Eng SIRC ARTICLE NO: 105809

Burk, D. Football in-season weight training. *Texas coach (Austin, Tex.) 28(3), Oct 1984, 47.*
LEVEL: B LANG: Eng SIRC ARTICLE NO: 173209

Clark, M. Conditioning the shoulder. *National Strength & Conditioning Association journal (Lincoln, Neb.) 6(3), Jun/Jul 1984, 58.*
LEVEL: B LANG: Eng SIRC ARTICLE NO: 096654

Costello, F. Using weight training and plyometrics to increase explosive power for football. *National Strength & Conditioning Association journal (Lincoln, Neb.) 6(2), Apr/May 1984, 22-25.*
LEVEL: B LANG: Eng SIRC ARTICLE NO: 094989

Diange, J. Strengthening the neck for football. *Athletic journal (Evanston, Ill.) 65(2), Sept 1984, 46-48.*
LEVEL: B LANG: Eng SIRC ARTICLE NO: 099569

Ganong, R. University of Miami approach to a successful football strength program. *National Strength & Conditioning Association journal (Lincoln, Neb.) 6(3), Jun/Jul 1984, 24-25.*
LEVEL: B LANG: Eng SIRC ARTICLE NO: 096657

Ganong, R. Miami's in-season strength training program. The Miami Hurricanes' in-season conditioning program for football emphasizes effectiveness and organization. *Athletic journal (Evanston, Ill.) 65(1), Aug 1984, 16-17;48.*
LEVEL: B LANG: Eng SIRC ARTICLE NO: 096658

Ganong, R. Ziccardi, N. 15 minutes of manual high intensity strength training for in-season high school football. *Coaching clinic (Princeton, N.J.) 23(2), Oct 1984, 7-11.*
LEVEL: B LANG: Eng SIRC ARTICLE NO: 101240

Laycoe, R. Strengthening the thunderbirds. (Refs: 7)*Coaching review 7, Jan/Feb 1984, 54-56.*
LEVEL: B LANG: Eng SIRC ARTICLE NO: 092079

Mannie, K. Strengthening the neck for football. *Scholastic coach (New York) 54(1), Aug 1984, 62-66;69.*
LEVEL: B LANG: Eng SIRC ARTICLE NO: 099584

Martinelli, P. Juraszek, J. Football: University of Oklahoma off-season strength program. *National Strength & Conditioning Association journal (Lincoln, Neb.) 6(4), Aug/Sept 1984, 24-26.*
LEVEL: B LANG: Eng SIRC ARTICLE NO: 099586

Newell, G. Durant High School's weight lifting & offseason conditioning program. *Scholastic coach (New York) 54(2), Sept 1984, 49-50.*
LEVEL: B LANG: Eng SIRC ARTICLE NO: 099590

O'Bryant, H.S. Programs for basketball, wrestling, football. (Refs: 5)*National Strength & Conditioning Association journal 5(6), Jan 1984, 41;66-67.*
ABST: Weight training is an important training method for pre-season strength-power development in athletes. The role of circuit and non-circuit weight training programs are discussed for basketball, wrestling and football. Ten week programs are outlined with specific phases of development being used to attain specific physical goals. This article is extremely useful in planning the progression of a pre-season circuit training program.
LEVEL: B LANG: Eng SIRC ARTICLE NO: 090414

Pearson, D.R. Wallace, D.D. Winter strength conditioning program at Ball State University. *National Strength & Conditioning Association journal 6(1), Feb/Mar 1984, 28-30.*
LEVEL: B LANG: Eng SIRC ARTICLE NO: 093440

Riley, D.B. Building strength the Redskin way. *Scholastic coach (New York) 54(3), Oct 1984, 64-65;70.*
LEVEL: B LANG: Eng SIRC ARTICLE NO: 101252

Riley, D.B. Check your program for inconsistencies. *Scholastic coach (New York) 54(5), Dec 1984, 52-55.*
LEVEL: B LANG: En SIRC ARTICLE NO: 103173

Tkach, J. Rudisill, F. Specific weight training at Lehigh University. *National Strength & Conditioning Association journal 5(6), Jan 1984, 32-33.*
LEVEL: B LANG: Eng SIRC ARTICLE NO: 090663

Williams, D. Training football linemen - practical applications. *National Strength & Conditioning Association journal (Lincoln, Neb.) 6(4), Aug/Sept 1984, 45;67-70.*
LEVEL: B LANG: Eng SIRC ARTICLE NO: 099614

Yessis, M. Throwing the football. *National Strength & Conditioning Association journal 6(1), Feb/Mar 1984, 6-8;71-73.*
LEVEL: I LANG: Eng SIRC ARTICLE NO: 093451

FRANCE

Charles, L. Leaute, S. L'ANVAR, les industries du sport et l'innovation technologique. *Dans, Culture technique no. 13, Neuilly-sur-Seine, France, Centre de Recherche sur la Culture Technique, c1984, p. 324-325.*
LEVEL: B LANG: Fr RC1235 20096

Izel, M. Le loto et le tierce conduisent au fonds national de developpement du sport. *Temps libre equipements (France) 9, 1984, 45-51.*
LEVEL: B LANG: Fr

Joffrion, E. Apres l'ecole... le temps libre. Pour apprendre? pour jouer? *Temps libre equipements (France) 11, 1984, 43-47.*
LEVEL: I LANG: Fr

Le sport en France. *Monde, dossiers et documents (Nantes) 112, 1984, 1-4.*
LEVEL: B LANG: Fr

Malenfant, C. Le sport et le temps libre. (Refs: 4)*Science et vie (Paris) 147, 1984, 8-15.*
LEVEL: I LANG: Fr

Malenfant, C. L'economie du sport. *Science et vie (Paris) HS147, 1984, 16-24.*
LEVEL: B LANG: Fr

Malenfant, C. Croissance et qualite. Les pratiques sportives du temps libre evoluent. *Temps libre equipements (France) 10, 1984, 45-49.*
LEVEL: I LANG: Fr

Malenfant, C. Dimensions commerciales du loisir. (Refs: 28)*Loisir & societe/Society and leisure (Trois-Rivieres, Que.) 7(2) automne 1984, 371-394.*
RESUME: Le developpement technologique reduit le temps de travail et cree de temps de temps libere qui lui-meme est la condition de l'extension de la pratique corporelle volontaire de la plupart des praticiens amateurs. Aujourd'hui le temps libre a permis le developpement de valeurs nouvelles qui ont entraine des pratiques corporelles autres, meme

dans les sports de competition. Les industries du sport (dans leur perspective d'action pour le futur) doivent s'interroger sur les caracteristiques principales de la transformation des activites sportives. Elles doivent s'orienter vers la recherche des technologies appropriees sur le plan des sports de competition, axer la production et la commercialisation en vue d'echanges sur le plan international; le marche des articles de sport etant devenu un lieu ou la concurrence est vive. Le sponsoring et la publicite sont deux moyens de la technique de communication qui se developpent rapidement dans le secteur sport, meme si le sponsoring apparait encore comme un phenomene relativement recent en France.
LEVEL: A LANG: Fr SIRC ARTICLE NO: 171330

Mas, L. Le suivi medical de l'equipe de France. (Medical follow-up of the French team.) *Union medical du Canada (Montreal) 113(8), aout 1984, 634-636.*
LEVEL: I LANG: Fr

Paillet, P. Activites corporelles et animation: ambiguites et enjeux. *Cahiers de l'animation (Marly-le-Roi, France) 46, 198 77-91.*
LEVEL: I LANG: Fr

Trottein, R. Incitations du Ministere de la jeunesse et des sports a l'innovation. *Dans, Culture technique no. 13, Neuilly-sur-Seine, France, Centre de Recherche sur la Culture Technique, c1984, p. 78-85.*
LEVEL: I LANG: Fr RC1235 20096

HISTORY

Adam, P. Barres, M. Bergerat, E. Bernard, T. Le sport a la une. Paris: S. Messinger, 1984. 184 p. : ill. (Les Reporters de l'histoire.)
NOTES: Bibliographie.
LEVEL: I LANG: Fr ISBN: 2-86746-007-7

Braun, D. Le sport francais entre les deux guerres et les Jeux olympiques en France en 1924. *Relations internationales (Paris) 38, 1984, 193-211.*
LEVEL: I LANG: Fr

FREESTYLE SKIING

CERTIFICATION

Association canadienne de ski: programme de certification des entraineurs de ski acrobatique. Manuel de l'examinateur. Ottawa: Association canadienne de ski, 1984?. ca. 30 feuillets
CORP: Association canadienne de ski.
NOTES: Titre de la couverture. Also published in English under the title: Canadian Ski Association freestyle coaching certification manual. Examiners handbook.
LEVEL: B LANG: Fr GV854.9.A25 17892

Canadian Ski Association freestyle coaching certification manual. Examiners handbook. Ottawa: Canadian Ski Association, 1984?. 29 leaves
CORP: Canadian Ski Association.
NOTES: Cover title. Aussi publie en francais sous le titre: Association canadienne de ski: programme de certification des entraineurs de ski acrobatique. Manuel de l'examinateur.
LEVEL: B LANG: Eng GV854.9.A25 17891

Certification des entraineurs de ski acrobatique niveau I. Ottawa: Association canadienne de ski,

c1984. v, 100 p. : ill. (Programme national de certification des entraineurs.)
CORP: Association canadienne de ski.
NOTES: Titre de la couverture: Certification des entraineurs de ski acrobatique. Niveau 1, manuel technique.
LEVEL: B LANG: Fr GV854.9.A25 17939

Freestyle coaching certification level II. Vanier, Ont.: Canadian Ski Association Freestyle Discipline, c1984. v, 152 p. : ill
CORP: Canadian Ski Association. Freestyle Discipline.
LEVEL: I LANG: Eng GV854.89.A25 13175

COACHING

Fitzgerald, J. Know what you know and know what you don't know. *Coaching review 7, Jan/Feb 1984, 40-42.*
LEVEL: B LANG: En SIRC ARTICLE NO: 092386

TECHNIQUES AND SKILLS

Courtier, J.L. La vrille disco. *Ski flash magazine (Paris) 64, mars/avr 1984, 90-91.*
LEVEL: B LANG: Fr SIRC ARTICLE NO: 099920

L'enchainement des virages en slalom. *Ski (Paris) 62, janv 1984, 30-33.*
LEVEL: B LANG: Fr SIRC ARTICLE NO: 099894

FRISBEE THROWING

Osborn, R.L. Lewis, J.A. Flying disc sports and games: the intramural-recreational sports alternative. (Refs: 6)*In, Vendl, B.C. (ed.) et al., Interpretive aspects of intramural-recreational sports: selected proceedings from the Thirty-fifth Annual National Intramural-Recreational Sports Association Conference, Corvallis, Or., Oregon State University, c1984, p. 68-75.*
CONF: National Intramural-Recreational Sports Association Conference (35th : 1984 : Fort Worth, Tex.).
LEVEL: B LANG: Eng GV710 18914

GAELIC FOOTBALL

HISTORY

Reynolds, T. The men from the Mournes: not satisfied to choose his top team Tom goes on to pick his best fifteen of that era *Gaelic sport (Dublin, Ireland) 27(5), Spring 1984, 22-23;25.*
LEVEL: B LANG: Eng SIRC ARTICLE NO: 095255

Young, E. How has gaelic football changed? *Gaelic sport (Dublin, Ireland) 27(5), Spring 1984, 8-11.*
LEVEL: B LANG: Eng SIRC ARTICLE NO: 095266

GAMBLING

Abt, V. Mcgurrin, M.C. Smith, J.F. Gambling: the misunderstood sport - a problem in social definition. (Refs: 17)*Leisure sciences (New York) 6(2), 1984, 205-220.*
ABST: The paper presents gambling as a sport instead of a socially deviant behavior. Gambling

has many of the attributes of sport including conventional rules, regulatory commissions, standardized equipment, and an element of sociability. It also promotes a collective validation of the basic values of society. The authors believe that the perceived gambling problem may be better understood as an ideological conflict between gamblers and the moral judges of the proprietary limits and functions of sports.
LEVEL: A LANG: Eng SIRC ARTICLE NO: 096402

Ignatin, G. Sports betting. (Refs: 13)*Annals of the American Academy of Political and Social Science 474, Jul 1984, 168-177*
LEVEL: A LANG: Eng

McGurrin, M. Abt, V. Smith, J. Play or pathology: a new look at the gambler and his world. (Refs: 11)
NOTES: In, Sutton-Smith, B. and Kelly-Byrne, D. (eds.), The masks of play, New York, Leisure Press, c1984, p. 88-97.
LEVEL: I LANG: Eng HQ782 17029

Salter, M. Les jeux, les biens et les dieux: une analyse du jeu chez les Iroquois et les Hurons. (Refs: 15)*Dans, Massicotte J.P. et Lessard, C. (eds.), Histoire du sport de l'antiquite au XIXe siecle, Sillery, Que., Presses de l'Universite du Quebec, 1984, p. 263-270.*
LEVEL: A LANG: Fr GV571 18971

Underwood, J. 'Look up and he's got your money': gambler Billy Baxter, who won big when Miami toppled Nebraska, is also a fight manager who does work - in his car. *Sports illustrated (Chicago, Ill.) 60(21), 28 May 1984, 80-84;86;88;90;92;94.*
LEVEL: B LANG: Eng SIRC ARTICLE NO: 094910

GAMES

Chang, C.H. Hu, C.C. Yeh-jen, H.T. Tui li yu hsi. Tai-Pei Shih: Shui fu jung chu pan she, Min Kuo 73-, (1984). v. (1-2) : il
NOTES: Juvenile literature.
LEVEL: B LANG: Chi LC CARD: 84-173924

Gomme, A.B. Webb, D. The traditional games of England, Scotland, and Ireland. London: Thames and Hudson, c1984. 433, xv, 531 p.
NOTES: First published in Great Britain in two volumes, 1894-98.
LEVEL: I LANG: Eng ISBN: 0-500-27316-2 GV1204.43 18100

Lambert, P. Treadwell, T.W. Kumar, V.K. Popular games, where did they originate. (Refs: 1)*International journal of sport psychology (Rome) 15(1), 1984, 35-39.*
LEVEL: I LANG: Eng SIRC ARTICLE NO: 094758

Lao, X. Weiqi in China: past and present. *China sports (Beijing, China) 16(4), Apr 1984, 37-40.*
LEVEL: B LANG: Eng SIRC ARTICLE NO: 100668

Lidz, F. If brick carrying is your thing, get a load of these olde village games. *Sports illustrated (Chicago, Ill.) 61(19) 22 Oct 1984, 122;126.*
LEVEL: B LANG: Eng SIRC ARTICLE NO: 099344

GAMES - COOPERATIVE

Driessen, T.S.H. Tijs, S.H. Extensions and modifications of the tau-value for cooperative games. (Refs: 11)*Lecture notes in economics and mathematical systems (New York) 226, 1984, 252-261.*
LEVEL: I LANG: Eng

McGill, J. Bailey, B. Play for play's sake: cooperative games as a strategy for integration. Toronto: National Institute on Mental Retardation, 1984?. v, 45 p.
NOTES: Bibliography: p. 45.
LEVEL: B LANG: Eng ISBN: 0-920121-05-5 LC CARD: C84-98788-9 GV183.7 18046

GERMAN DEMOCRATIC REPUBLIC

Berenyi, I. Nichols, R. Cracking the secrets of the Eastern Bloc: are the Eastern European athletes supermen or do they just know something we don't? *Runner's world (Mountain View, Calif.) 19(6), Jun 1984, 72-74;76.*
LEVEL: B LANG: Eng SIRC ARTICLE NO: 095393

Fisher, M. The children's crusade: GDR geared to sports prodigies. *Globe and mail (Toronto) 12 Jun 1984, 57.*
LEVEL: B LANG: Eng SIRC ARTICLE NO: 094750

From the history of the German sports and gymnastics union of the GDR. *Sports in the GDR (Berlin, GDR) 3, 1984, 12-13.*
LEVEL: B LANG: Eng SIRC ARTICLE NO: 108720

Gehrisch, H. Zur Nutzung der Sportinformationen der DDR durch Jugendliche. (The utilisation by young people of sports information in the DDR.) (Refs: 2)*In: Internationales Symposium Sportpaedagogik - Koerpererziehung - Persoenlichkeit: Protokoll, Potsdam, Deutsche Demokratische Republik, ICSSPE/CIEPSS, 1984?, p. 193-197.*
CONF: Internationales Symposium Sportpaedagogik - Koerpererziehung - Persoenlichkeit (1983 : Potsdam).
LEVEL: I LANG: Ger GV205 20231

Sport for all. *Sports in the GDR (Berlin, GDR) 3, 1984, 9-11.*
LEVEL: B LANG: Eng SIRC ARTICLE NO: 108717

Sports for children and young people in the GDR. *ACHPER national journal (Kingswood, Aust.) 105, Spring 1984, 62.*
LEVEL: B LANG: Eng SIRC ARTICLE NO: 102341

Wonneberger, I. Frau und Sport in der DDR. (Women and sport in the GDR.) (Refs: 19)*ICSSPE/ CIEPSS review (Berlin, GDR) 7, 1984, 43-48.*
LEVEL: I LANG: Ger SIRC ARTICLE NO: 095655

GERMANY

HISTORY

Van Dalen, D.B. Bennett, B.L. L'education physique et le nationalisme educatif allemand. (Refs: 27)*Dans, Massicotte, J.P. e Lessard, C. (eds.), Histoire du sport de l'antiquite au XIXe siecle, Sillery, Que., Presses de l'Universite du Quebec, 1984, p. 127-153.*
LEVEL: A LANG: Fr GV571 18971

GLIDING AND SOARING

Eley, H. A X-C primer. *Free flight/Vol libre (Ottawa) 3, May/Jun 1984, 16.*
LEVEL: B LANG: Eng SIRC ARTICLE NO: 101260

Georgeson, D. Flying the wave in New Zealand. *New Zealand gliding kiwi (Tauranga, N.Z.) 16(4), Aug/Sept 1984, 2-13.*
LEVEL: I LANG: Eng SIRC ARTICLE NO: 103190

Hindman, W. Anatomy of a wave flight. *Soaring & motorgliding (Los Angeles) 48(11), Nov 1984, 44-49.*
LEVEL: I LANG: Eng SIRC ARTICLE NO: 104748

Robertson, I. On pilot education and opportunity. *Australian gliding (Adelaide, South Australia) 33(9), Sept 1984, 14-16.*
LEVEL: B LANG: Eng SIRC ARTICLE NO: 108441

Sklarewitz, N. Soaring. *Ultrasport (Boston, Mass.) 1(6), Nov/Dec 1984, 77-81.*
LEVEL: B LANG: Eng SIRC ARTICLE NO: 172951

Valentine, M. Aerobatics. *Australian gliding (Adelaide, Aust.) 33(1), Jan 1984, 4-7.*
LEVEL: I LANG: Eng SIRC ARTICLE NO: 098119

ADMINISTRATION

Adams, R.C. Bob Mainwood and Sir Sydney Camm. (Refs: 6)*Sailplane and gliding (Leicester, Eng.) 35(1), Feb/Mar 1984, 24-25.*
LEVEL: B LANG: Eng SIRC ARTICLE NO: 099618

Alway, J. Gliding - a marketing approach. *Sailplane and gliding (Leicester, Eng.) 35(5), Oct/Nov 1984, 214-215.*
LEVEL: B LANG: Eng SIRC ARTICLE NO: 103182

AERODYNAMICS

Drebler, U. Aerodynamic design of winglets for a standard-class glider. *Technical soaring (Los Angeles, Calif.) 8(4), Jul 1984, 118-126.*
ABST: At the 1981 World Championships in Paderborn, the members of the French National team surprised their competitors with winglets mounted on their gliders. There was a lot of discussion about the effectiveness of this wing arrangement for high-performance gliders. This report describes the theoretical effect of different geometrical winglet parameters on the flight performance of an AS-W 19 glider. A promising winglet version was selected, built and measured in flight by the Akaflieg Braunschweig.
LEVEL: A LANG: Eng SIRC ARTICLE NO: 103187

Hunter, L. Art and physics of soaring. *Physics today (New York) 37(4), Apr 1984, 34-41.*
LEVEL: I LANG: Eng SIRC ARTICLE NO: 098107

Kroo, I. Trim drag, tail sizing, and soaring performance. (Refs: 16)*Technical soaring (Los Angeles, Calif.) 8(4), Jul 1984, 127-137.*
ABST: In this paper, the increments in 'trim drag' due to induced drag, increased wing profile drag, and wetted area changes are evaluated for standard-class sailplanes. Airfoil section data, combined with a simple method for computing trimmed induced drag of wing/tail systems, are

used to compute total trim drag over the entire flight regime, illustrating the effects of circling flight, airfoil pitching moment, and static margin changes. An investigation of the effects of tail size, aspect ratio, position, and wing lift distribution shape, suggests methods by which trim drag may be reduced. Finally, the paper considers the potential of unconventional configurations for reducing trimmed drag.
LEVEL: A LANG: Eng SIRC ARTICLE NO: 103195

NASA explores controlled flight in the deep stall: that sinking sensation. *Soaring (Los Angeles, Calif)* 48(3), Mar 1984, 36-38.
LEVEL: B LANG: Eng SIRC ARTICLE NO: 098110

Nicks, O. W. Drag awareness in simple English: the comedown on slowdown.. (Refs: 9)*Soaring (Los Angeles, Calif.)* 48(2), Feb 1984, 20-21;23-24;27.
LEVEL: I LANG: Eng SIRC ARTICLE NO: 095031

Payne, J. Question - Low, skidding turns: why the fuss? Answer - Because they tend to cause sailplanes to bore holes in the ground. (Refs: 3)*Soaring (Santa Monica, Calif.)* 48(12), Dec 1984, 38-41.
LEVEL: I LANG: Eng SIRC ARTICLE NO: 173357

Payne, J.M. Spins: some clear talk about how, why, and what to do. (Refs: 3)*Soaring (Los Angeles, Calif.)* 48(5), May 1984, 27-28;30-31.
LEVEL: I LANG: Eng SIRC ARTICLE NO: 103201

Said, B. Stalls: the deeper, the worst. *Soaring (Los Angeles, Calif)* 48(3), Mar 1984, 32-35.
LEVEL: I LANG: Eng SIRC ARTICLE NO: 098113

Smith, A.M.O. The possibilities of laminar flow control. *Soaring (Santa Monica, Calif.)* 48(12), Dec 1984, 18-23.
LEVEL: B LANG: Eng SIRC ARTICLE NO: 173352

Stovkovic, B. Sad, N. Computer-aider research of different ways leaving a thermal. (Refs: 6)*Technical soaring (Los Angeles, Calif.)* 8(4), Jul 1984, 142-150.
ABST: A dynamic computer study of various ways of leaving a thermal has been made. The principal goal was to evaluate different thermal-outs, considering cross-country flights tactics. Therefore, a few thousand flight simulations have been made. The research shows the possibility of practical utilization of vertical wind speed gradient through 'dynamic' thermal-outs.
LEVEL: A LANG: Eng SIRC ARTICLE NO: 103207

ASSOCIATIONS

Strojnik, A. Improving the constant-chord wing: the simplest and easiest-to-build wing planform can be made to fly better than you think. (Refs: 3)*Soaring (Santa Monica, Calif.)* 48(10), Oct 1984, 36-40.
LEVEL: I LANG: Eng SIRC ARTICLE NO: 173347

BIOGRAPHY AND AUTOBIOGRAPHY

Bange, T. Doughton, J. 30 years old primary glider flies again. (John Bange) *New Zealand gliding kiwi (Tauranga, N.Z.)* 16(3), Jun/Jul 1984, 2-4.
LEVEL: B LANG: Eng SIRC ARTICLE NO: 103183

CLUBS

Holland, J. Scull, B. Club development and performance: an assessment based on BGA annual statistics. *Sailplane and gliding (Leicester, Eng.)* 35(2), Apr/May 1984, 66-67.
LEVEL: I LANG: Eng SIRC ARTICLE NO: 103194

Prelgauskas, E. Survival of gliding clubs. *Australian gliding (Adelaide, Aust.)* 33(8), Aug 1984, 20-25.
LEVEL: B LANG: En SIRC ARTICLE NO: 103203

COUNTRIES AND REGIONS

Mander, P. Reviewing Rieti. *Australian gliding (Adelaide, Aust.)* 33(12), Dec 1984, 20-21.
LEVEL: B LANG: Eng SIRC ARTICLE NO: 173150

DISABLED

Frazier, T. Soarathon. *Soaring (Los Angeles, Calif.)* 48(2), Feb 1984, 14-15.
LEVEL: B LANG: Eng SIRC ARTICLE NO: 095026

DRUGS, DOPING AND ERGOGENIC AIDS

Voge, V.M. Are you a flying druggie? *Free flight/Vol libre (Ottawa)* 5, Sept/Oct 1984, 12.
LEVEL: B LANG: Eng SIRC ARTICLE NO: 102397

ENVIRONMENT

Bradbury, T.A.M. Wave soaring over the British Isles: some theoretical aspects and practical observations. (Refs: 1) *Sailplane and gliding (Leicester, Eng.)* 35(4), Aug/Sept 1984, 166-169.
LEVEL: I LANG: Eng SIRC ARTICLE NO: 098104

Bradbury, T.A.M. Wave soaring over the British Isles. Some theoretical aspects and practical observations. (Refs: 2) *Sailplane and gliding (Leicester, Eng.)* 35(3), Jun/Jul 1984, 118-121.
NOTES: First of a two-part series.
LEVEL: I LANG: Eng SIRC ARTICLE NO: 099620

Dorning, R. A meteorological diagram for gliding purposes. (Refs: 4)*Australian gliding (Adelaide, Aust.)* 33(8), Aug 1984, 28-34.
LEVEL: I LANG: Eng SIRC ARTICLE NO: 103186

Kuettner, J.P. The 2000 kilometer wave flight. From the Pacific to Oklahoma? Kansas? The Mississippi Valley? Go for it. Says this expert. *Soaring (Los Angeles, Calif.)* 48(5), May 1984, 14-19.
LEVEL: B LANG: Eng SIRC ARTICLE NO: 103196

Seibels, G. Turnpoints: thermals. *Soaring (Los Angeles, Calif.)* 48(2), Feb 1984, 37-38;42.
LEVEL: B LANG: Eng SIRC ARTICL NO: 095033

Wrenford, B. The magic carpet ride: inversion waves for cross country flying. *Australian gliding (Adelaide, Aust.)* 33(4), Apr 1984, 22-28.
LEVEL: I LANG: Eng SIRC ARTICLE NO: 101261

EQUIPMENT

Benbough, R.H. The convertible Albatross: today's trend toward powered gliders has deep roots: Hawley Bowlus built his first one more than 50 years ago. *Soaring (Los Angeles, Calif.)* 48(5), May 1984, 36-38.
LEVEL: B LANG: Eng SIRC ARTICLE NO: 103184

Eggen, G. Power steering systems. *Whole air (Lookout Mtn., Tenn.)* 7(6), Dec 1984/Jan 1985, 16-18.
LEVEL: B LANG: Eng SIRC ARTICLE NO: 173581

Enevoldson, E. Bohn-Meyer, M. Pilot report: the Rutan Solitaire. A flight evaluation of the homebuilt sailplane design contest winner. (Refs: 3)*Soaring (Los Angeles, Calif)* 48(3), Mar 1984, 24-25;27-31.
LEVEL: B LANG: Eng SIRC ARTICLE NO: 098105

Enevoldson, E.K. Bohn-Meyer, M.R. Flight test measurements of the longitudinal stability and performance of the Canard sailplane Solitaire. *Technical soaring (Los Angeles, Calif.)* 8(4), Jul 1984, 138-141.
ABST: This paper presents measurements of the longitudinal trim and static stability of the Solitaire, an analysis of the aircraft drag in steady gliding flight, and compares the performance of the Solitaire to the performance of an hypothetical aft-tail alternative of similar size.
LEVEL: A LANG: Eng SIRC ARTICLE NO: 103188

Gross, F.R. The Cadet glider: a look at one of the nation's earliest club gliders. *Soaring (Los Angeles, Calif.)* 48(6), Jun 1984, 28-31.
LEVEL: B LANG: Eng SIRC ARTICLE NO: 103191

Hall, S. Judging the homebuilt sailplane design competition. *Soaring & motorgliding (Los Angeles)* 48(11), Nov 1984, 30-32.
LEVEL: B LANG: Eng SIRC ARTICLE NO: 104747

Jacobs, D. First impressions: a contest pilot reports on flying the Discus. *Soaring & motorgliding (Los Angeles)* 48(11), No 1984, 14-16.
LEVEL: B LANG: Eng SIRC ARTICLE NO: 104749

Jeffries, J. Flying the K-23. *Sailplane and gliding (Leicester, Eng.)* 35(1), Feb/Mar 1984, 12-14.
LEVEL: B LANG: Eng SIRC ARTICLE NO: 099623

Johnson, R.H. A flight test evaluation of the Grob G-102 Club IIIB. (Refs: 3)*Soaring (Los Angeles, Calif.)* 48(1), Jan 1984, 18-23.
LEVEL: B LANG: Eng SIRC ARTICLE NO: 093455

Johnson, R.H. A flight test evaluation of an LS-4a. *Soaring (Los Angeles, Calif.)* 48(9), Sept 1984, 14-19.
LEVEL: B LANG: Eng SIRC ARTICLE NO: 099624

le Cheminant, A.N. C-FZCS, the Harbinger saga: how a post-war glider design finally transformed itself into the real thing a quarter century later. (Refs: 3)*Free flight/Vol libre (Ottawa)* 4, Jul/Aug 1984, 8-9.
LEVEL: B LANG: Eng SIRC ARTICLE NO: 099625

Newgard, P. Total energy: problems and solutions. *Soaring (Los Angeles, Calif.)* 48(4), Apr 1984, 31-34;37.
LEVEL: I LANG: Eng SIRC ARTICLE NO: 095030

Paggen, V. Build & fly Monerai. *Soaring (Los Angeles, Calif.)* 48(6), Jun 1984, 14-19.
LEVEL: B LANG: Eng SIRC ARTICLE NO: 103200

Prelgauskas, E. The minimum sailplane. AG index compilation. *Australian gliding (Adelaide, Aust.)* 33(3), Mar 1984, 38-41.
LEVEL: B LANG: Eng SIRC ARTICLE NO: 096683

Roediger, N. Flight evaluation. (Schneider ES 65 Platypus) *Australian gliding (Adelaide, Aust.)* 33(10), Oct 1984, 5-9.
LEVEL: B LANG: Eng SIRC ARTICLE NO: 107209

Said, B. First impressions: A pilot reports on flying Windrose. *Soaring (Santa Monica, Calif.)* 48(12),

GLIDING AND SOARING (continued)

Dec 1984, 24-25;27-29.
LEVEL: B LANG: Eng SIRC ARTICLE NO: 173354

Schuemann, W. Water, water everywhere: a serious look at one side of a very weighty issue... *Soaring (Los Angeles, Calif.) 48(6), Jun 1984, 20-24.*
LEVEL: B LANG: Eng SIRC ARTICLE NO: 103204

Seaman, A. Tow ropes & splices. A discouse on the nature of polypropylene. *Free flight/Vol libre (Ottawa) 6, Nov/Dec 1984, 10-11.*
LEVEL: B LANG: Eng SIRC ARTICLE NO: 173406

Sebald, L. Cooper, T. Beating the high cost of speed rings. *Soaring (Los Angeles, Calif.) 48(3), Mar 1984, 53-54.*
LEVEL: LANG: Eng SIRC ARTICLE NO: 098114

Sebald, L. A radio field strength meter. *Soaring (Los Angeles, Calif.) 48(6), Jun 1984, 43.*
LEVEL: I LANG: Eng SIRC ARTICLE NO: 103205

Smith, S. A look inside the mechanical variometer. *New Zealand gliding kiwi (Tauranga, N.Z.) 15(10), Dec 1983/Jan 1984, 9;11-13.*
LEVEL: I LANG: Eng SIRC ARTICLE NO: 098115

Sunderland, G. High speed testing. *Australian gliding (Adelaide, Aust.) 33(8), Aug 1984, 16-18.*
LEVEL: B LANG: Eng SIRC ARTICLE NO: 103208

Thelin, G. Something new in masks 'medical oxygen tubes'. *New Zealand gliding kiwi (Wellington, N.Z.) 16(1), Feb/Mar 1984, 9-10.*
LEVEL: B LANG: Eng SIRC ARTICLE NO: 098118

Williams, P. Are we giving people what they want? *Sailplane and gliding (Leicester, Eng.) 35(2), Apr/May 1984, 68.*
LEVEL: LANG: Eng SIRC ARTICLE NO: 103211

Wrenford, B. Oxygen systems for the higher flier. *Australian gliding (Adelaide, Aust.) 33(6), Jun 1984, 6-9.*
LEVEL: I LANG: Eng SIRC ARTICLE NO: 098121

EQUIPMENT - MAINTENANCE

Carter, D. Leaky statics. *New Zealand gliding kiwi (Tauranga, N.Z.) 16(4), Aug/Sept 1984, 17.*
LEVEL: B LANG: Eng SIRC ARTICLE NO: 103185

Druce, R. Clark, B. Exfoliation corrosion. *Australian gliding (Adelaide, Aust.) 33(12), Dec 1984, 10-16.*
LEVEL: I LANG: E SIRC ARTICLE NO: 173149

Sebald, L. Maintenance and projects: tips on the use of Dacron covering. *Soaring (Los Angeles, Calif.) 48(1), Jan 1984, 42-43.*
NOTES: First of a two part series.
LEVEL: B LANG: Eng SIRC ARTICLE NO: 093461

Sebald, L. Maintenance and projects. *Soaring (Los Angeles, Calif.) 48(2), Feb 1984, 46-47.*
LEVEL: B LANG: Eng SIRC ARTICL NO: 095032

Sebald, L. Maintenance and projects. (control system friction) *Soaring (Los Angeles, Calif.) 48(5), May 1984, 41-44.*
LEVEL: B LANG: Eng SIRC ARTICLE NO: 103206

Sunderland, G. Welded joints. *Australian gliding (Adelaide, Aust.) 33(2), Feb 1984, 34-36.*
LEVEL: B LANG: Eng SIRC ARTICL NO: 096685

Valdata, P. Pasquier, M.-C. Two close calls: an assembly goof and a weight problem which could have upped the statistics. *Soaring (Los Angeles, Calif.) 48(4), Apr 1984, 38-40.*
LEVEL: I LANG: Eng SIRC ARTICLE NO: 095034

HISTORY

A cavalcade of glider winches. *Australian gliding (Adelaide, Aust.) 33(2), Feb 1984, 16-19.*
LEVEL: B LANG: Eng SIRC ARTICLE NO: 096680

INJURIES AND ACCIDENTS

Combs, H. That beautiful mountain and her sinister trap. *Soaring (Los Angeles, Calif.) 48(9), Sept 1984, 20-23.*
LEVEL: B LANG: Eng SIRC ARTICLE NO: 099621

Gaines, R. Anatomy of an accident. *Soaring (Santa Monica, Calif.) 48(12), Dec 1984, 34;37.*
LEVEL: B LANG: Eng SIRC ARTICL NO: 173359

Mitchell, K. BGA accident summary. *Sailplane and gliding (Leicester, Eng.) 34(6), Dec/Jan 1984, 272-273;275.*
LEVEL: B LANG: Eng SIRC ARTICLE NO: 098109

Mitchell, K. BGA accident summary. *Sailplane and gliding (Leicester, Eng.) 35(1), Feb/Mar 1984, 30-31.*
LEVEL: B LANG: Eng SIRC ARTICLE NO: 099626

Mitchell, K. BGA accident summary. *Sailplane and gliding (Leicester, Eng.) 35(2), Apr/May 1984, 79;81.*
LEVEL: B LANG: Eng SIRC ARTICLE NO: 103198

Muller, B. Accident concern. *Australian gliding (Adelaide, Aust.) 33(11), Nov 1984, 16-20.*
LEVEL: B LANG: Eng SIRC ARTICL NO: 107207

Spiekhout, D.J. de Rijk, P. Picking up cables. *Australian gliding (Adelaide, Aust.) 33(1), Jan 1984, 26-29.*
LEVEL: B LANG Eng SIRC ARTICLE NO: 098117

The no excuse dept.: sailplance accident briefs. (New Zealand) *New Zealand gliding kiwi (Tauranga, N.Z.) 16(3), Jun/Jul 1984, 29-32.*
LEVEL: B LANG: Eng SIRC ARTICLE NO: 103199

MATHEMATICS

de Jong, J.L. The 'convex-combination approach', a geometric approach to the optimization of sailplane trajectories. (Refs: 17)*Technical soaring (Santa Monica, Calif.) 8(3), Feb 1984, 98-117.*
NOTES: An abridged version of Eindhoven Technical University paper COSOR 80-10. It covers an update of material presented at the XVI OSTIV Congress, Chateauroux, France (1978) and new material presented at the XVII OSTIV Congress, Paderborn, Germany, 1981.
ABST: This paper discusses three different problems encountered in the sport of soaring. Firstly, the classical 'MacCready problem' is reviewed. This review is concerned with the determination of the best cruise speed between columns of rising air under cumulus clouds. Secondly, a new solution concept is presented for the 'optimal dolphin soaring problems'. Finally, new ideas are discussed in relation to the 'optimal zigzagging problem'.
LEVEL: A LANG: Eng SIRC ARTICLE NO: 096681

MEDICINE

Textes reglementaires concernant l'aptitude au parachutisme (et a l'aile volante). *Dans, Pathologie du parachutisme, Paris, Maloine, 1984, p. 131-156.*
LEVEL: I LANG: Fr RC1220.P37 19033

Valentine, M. Dehydration and gliding. *Australian gliding (Adelaide, Aust.) 33(3), Mar 1984, 17.*
LEVEL: B LANG: Eng SIRC ARTICLE NO: 096686

NAVIGATION

James, P.W. An airborne computer and area navigation system. *Sailplane and gliding (Leicester, Eng.) 34(6), Dec/Jan 1984, 248-249.*
LEVEL: I LANG: Eng SIRC ARTICLE NO: 098108

PHILATELY, NUMISMATICS AND COLLECTING

Averill, G. The history of gliding stamps. *Sailplane and gliding (Leicester, Eng.) 35(4), Aug/Sept 1984, 164-165.*
LEVEL: LANG: Eng SIRC ARTICLE NO: 098103

PHYSICS

Valdata, P. Pasquier, M.-C. Two close calls: an assembly goof and a weight problem which could have upped the statistics. *Soaring (Los Angeles, Calif.) 48(4), Apr 1984, 38-40.*
LEVEL: I LANG: Eng SIRC ARTICLE NO: 095034

PSYCHOLOGY - MENTAL TRAINING

Dale, H. Remembering check-lists. *Sailplane and gliding (Leicester, Eng.) 35(3), Jun/Jul 1984, 110-111.*
LEVEL: B LANG: En SIRC ARTICLE NO: 099622

RULES AND REGULATIONS

Waibel, G. On the future of the racing class. *New Zealand gliding kiwi (Tauranga, N.Z.) 15(10), Dec 1983/Jan 1984, 15-17.*
LEVEL: I LANG: Eng SIRC ARTICLE NO: 098120

SAFETY

Bungey, L. Climbing the busy thermal. *Free flight/Vol libre (Ottawa) 3, May/Jun 1984, 17.*
LEVEL: B LANG: Eng SIRC ARTICLE NO: 101259

Gaines, R. Safety corner: flying safety is more attitude than altitude. *Soaring (Los Angeles, Calif) 48(3), Mar 1984, 49.*
LEVEL: B LANG: Eng SIRC ARTICLE NO: 098106

Gaines, R. See and be seen, part 1--see. *Soaring (Los Angeles, Calif.) 48(6), Jun 1984, 33-34.*
LEVEL: B LANG: Eng SIRC ARTICLE NO: 103189

Knauff, T. Pt 3: premature termination of the tow. *Soaring (Los Angeles, Calif.) 48(1), Jan 1984, 34-35;37-38;41.*
NOTES: Adapted from, Knauff, T., Glider basics from Solo to license.
LEVEL: B LANG: Eng SIRC ARTICLE NO: 093456

Meyer, A. Oxygen system safety. *Free flight/Vol libre (Ottawa) 5, Sept/Oct 1984, 13;19.*
LEVEL: B LANG: Eng SIRC ARTICLE NO: 103197

Parachute saves aircraft. *Australian gliding (Adelaide, Aust.) 33(2), Feb 1984, 32-33.*
LEVEL: B LANG: Eng SIRC ARTICLE NO: 096682

Piggott, D. See and be seen. *Sailplane and gliding (Leicester, Eng.) 35(4), Aug/Sept 1984, 156-157.*
LEVEL: B LANG: Eng SIRC ARTICLE NO: 098111

Radius, M. Getting out in time: what to do with a parachute. *Free flight/Vol libre (Claresholm, Alta.)*

2, Mar/Apr 1984, 10-11.
LEVEL: B LANG: Eng SIRC ARTICLE NO: 098112

Ramsden, P. Don't camouflage your sailplane. *Soaring (Los Angeles, Calif.)* 48(1), Jan 1984, 47.
LEVEL: B LANG: Eng SIRC ARTICLE NO: 093459

Valentine, M. Aerotow operation: GFA directive follows fatal accident. *Australian gliding (Adelaide, Aust.)* 33(10), Oct 198 44-45.
LEVEL: B LANG: Eng SIRC ARTICLE NO: 107212

STATISTICS AND RECORDS

Annual statistics - October 1, 1982 to September 30, 1983. *Sailplane and gliding (Leicester, Eng.)* 35(1), Feb/Mar 1984, 22-23.
LEVEL: B LANG: Eng SIRC ARTICLE NO: 099619

Harwood, R. Annual records. *Sailplane and gliding (Leicester, Eng.)* 35(2), Apr/May 1984, 76-77.
LEVEL: B LANG: Eng SIRC ARTICLE NO: 103192

TEACHING

Hayes, T. Low loss instructing: one of the tasks of an instructor is to stimulate motivation for learning in a pupil. *Australian gliding (Adelaide, Aust.)* 33(8), Aug 1984, 8-10.
LEVEL: B LANG: Eng SIRC ARTICLE NO: 103193

Hayes, T. Low loss instructing. Part 3: environment. *Australian gliding (Adelaide, Aust.)* 33(10), Oct 1984, 33-37.
LEVEL: LANG: Eng SIRC ARTICLE NO: 107201

Hayes, T. Low loss instructing. Part 4: stalling and spinning. *Australian gliding (Adelaide, Aust.)* 33(11), Nov 1984, 22-25
LEVEL: B LANG: Eng SIRC ARTICLE NO: 107202

Hayes, T. Low loss instructing. Part 2: reducing the losses. *Australian gliding (Adelaide, South Australia)* 33(9), Sept 198 6-10.
LEVEL: B LANG: Eng SIRC ARTICLE NO: 108440

TECHNIQUES AND SKILLS

Gaines, R. Johnson, D. Safety corner: approach to land (not by the numbers). *Soaring (Los Angeles, Calif.)* 48(2), Feb 1984, 41-42.
LEVEL: B LANG: Eng SIRC ARTICLE NO: 095027

Hayes, T. Low loss instructing. Part 4 - stalling and spinning (concluded.) *Australian gliding (Adelaide, Aust.)* 33(12), De 1984, 26-28.
LEVEL: B LANG: Eng SIRC ARTICLE NO: 173152

Knauff, T. Transition to gliders: a flight training handbook for power pilots. 1st ed. Julian, Pa.: Ridge Soaring Gliderport c1984. vi, 160 p. : ill.
NOTES: Bibliography: p. 160.
LEVEL: B LANG: Eng ISBN: 0-9605676-2-3 LC CARD: 83-83439 GV764 17710

Piggott, D. Back to basics - part I. *Sailplane and gliding (Leicester, Eng.)* 35(5), Oct/Nov 1984, 204-205.
LEVEL: B LANG: Eng SIRC ARTICLE NO: 103202

Speight, G. Rules for leaving thermals. *Sailplane and gliding (Leicester, Eng.)* 35(4), Aug/Sept 1984, 176-177.
LEVEL: B LANG: Eng SIRC ARTICLE NO: 098116

TESTING AND EVALUATION

A Renner-version Libelle. *Australian gliding (Adelaide, Aust.)* 33(2), Feb 1984, 28-29.
LEVEL: B LANG: Eng SIRC ARTICLE NO: 096684

Boermans, L.M.M. Terleth, D.C. Wind tunnel tests of eight sailplane wing-fuselage combinations. (Refs: 19)*Technical soaring (Santa Monica, Calif.)* 8(3), Feb 1984, 70-85.
CONF: OSTIV Congress (18th : 1983 : Hobbs, New Mexico).
ABST: This investigation studied wing-fuselage interference effects in a wind tunnel. Three different fuselages were combined with a wing at various positions to obtain eight wing-fuselage combinations. The results indicate that crossflow effects can be minimized and separation in the rear part of the junction postponed if the fuselage shape is fitted to the streamlines of the wing produced at high lift coefficients. The flow at the junction is not laminar so that great care must be taken when laminar wing air-foils are applied.
LEVEL: A LANG: Eng SIRC ARTICLE NO: 096678

Boermans, L.M.M. Oolbekkink, B. Wind tunnel tests on an outer wing segment of the ASW-19X sailplane. (Refs: 6)*Technical soaring (Santa Monica, Calif.)* 8(3), Feb 1984, 86-97.
CONF: OSTIV Congress (18th : 1983 : Hobbs, New Mexico).
ABST: This investigation studied the aerodynamic characteristics of an outer wing segment of the ASW-19X sailplane. The authors observed that at a typical lift coefficient of 1.2 and an angle of bank of 35 degrees, the aileron deflection needed to compensate for the spanwise variation in dynamic pressure is about 5 degrees. Such a deflection created a large drag which is probably in evidence in every wing with the FX60-126 airfoil in the tip. The authors suggest that the development of a new tip airfoil is justified.
LEVEL: A LANG: Eng SIRC ARTICLE NO: 096679

Buchanan, J. Choosing contest pilots. *Australian gliding (Adelaide, Aust.)* 33(12), Dec 1984, 30-33.
LEVEL: B LANG: Eng SIRC ARTICLE NO: 173153

Evans, J.M. Selection of Australian pilots for internationals by formula. *Australian gliding (Adelaide, Aust.)* 33(12), Dec 1984, 24a-24h.
LEVEL: I LANG: Eng SIRC ARTICLE NO: 173154

Johnson, R.H. A flight test evaluation of the 16.6-Meter Ventus. *Soaring (Los Angeles, Calif.)* 48(4), Apr 1984, 20-24.
LEVEL: B LANG: Eng SIRC ARTICLE NO: 095028

Schindler, J. Possible adverse reactions between epoxy, resorcinol and aerolite adhesives. *Australian gliding (Adelaide, Aust.)* 33(12), Dec 1984, 22-24.
LEVEL: I LANG: Eng SIRC ARTICLE NO: 173151

Suderland, G. More on testing requirements. *Australian gliding (Adelaide, Aust.)* 33(10), Oct 1984, 49-51.
LEVEL: B LANG: Eng SIRC ARTICLE NO: 107210

Suderland, G. Spin testing. *Australian gliding (Adelaide, Aust.)* 33(11), Nov 1984, 28-30.
LEVEL: B LANG: Eng SIRC ARTICLE NO: 107211

Sunderland, G. Static calibration system. *Australian gliding (Adelaide, Aust.)* 33(7), Jul 1984, 18-21.
LEVEL: I LANG: Eng SIRC ARTICLE NO: 103209

TRAINING AND CONDITIONING

Stewart, K. Exercises for field landings. *Sailplane and gliding (Leicester, Eng.)* 35(1), Feb/Mar 1984, 35.
LEVEL: B LANG: Eng SIRC ARTICLE NO: 099627

WOMEN

Watson, T. What do women think about themselves and gliding? *Sailplane and gliding (Leicester, Eng.)* 35(2), Apr/May 1984, 62-64.
LEVEL: B LANG: Eng SIRC ARTICLE NO: 103210

GO-KARTING

ADMINISTRATION

Lugo, A. Mestizo Production Associates promote karting: Part 2. *Karter news (Montclair, Calif.)* 24(4), Apr 1984, 10;32.
LEVEL: B LANG: Eng SIRC ARTICLE NO: 098122

Schupack, A. Sponsorship: we all want it...here's where to start...preparing a proper proposal. *Karter news (Montclair, Calif.)* 24(4), Apr 1984, 15;35.
NOTES: Part 1.
LEVEL: B LANG: Eng SIRC ARTICLE NO: 098123

EQUIPMENT

Dunlop information. (go-kart tire) *Karting magazine (Chislehurst, Eng.)* 341, Aug 1984, 132-133.
LEVEL: I LANG: Eng SIRC ARTICLE NO: 101262

FACILITIES - DESIGN, CONSTRUCTION AND PLANNING

Weir, F. Sprint kart track design. *Karter news (Montclair, Calif.)* 24(4), Apr 1984, 16;36.
LEVEL: B LANG: Eng SIRC ARTICL NO: 098124

GOLF

Bunker, L.K. Owens, D. Golf, better practice for better play. New York: Leisure Press, c1984. 272 p. : ill.
NOTES: Bibliography: p. 272.
LEVEL: I LANG: Eng ISBN: 088011181X LC CARD: 83-080712

Lofi, A. Frayssineau, H. Bar-Garapon, C. Helal, H. Leveque, M. Golf: comment progresser du debutant au champion. Paris: Amphora, c1984. 165 p. : ill. (Sport et connaissance.)
NOTES: Bibliographie: p. 161-164.
LEVEL: B LANG: Fr ISBN: 2-85180-073-6 GV965 17480

What you told us about the game. *Golf digest (Norwalk, Conn.)* 35(3), Mar 1984, 76-80.
LEVEL: B LANG: Eng SIRC ARTICLE NO: 099647

ADMINISTRATION

Berst, J. What computers can do for a country club and pro shop. *Golf industry (N. Miami, Fla.)* 9(3), Apr/May 1984, 8-11.
ABST: Computers can be a definite aid in the administrative functions of golf club operations. The right combination of equipment can allow club administration to automate many of the routine

functions, such as maintaining membership and automating accounting functions. Computers can assist in cash management, word processing, as well as the scheduling of not only equipment maintenance but also lessons. Special software can be added to assist the club pro in the biomechanical analysis of student's golf swings.
LEVEL: B LANG: Eng SIRC ARTICLE NO: 100450

Bissell, K. Special report: golf in the computer age. The future is now. *PGA magazine (Palm Beach Gardens, Fla.) 65(7), Jul 1984, 22-33.*
LEVEL: B LANG: Eng SIRC ARTICLE NO: 101265

Green, R. Mark McCormack: McCormack - the man, his men and his methods. *Golf world (London) 23(10), Oct 1984, 48-55.*
LEVEL: B LANG: Eng SIRC ARTICLE NO: 105868

ART

Les artistes et le golf: Philippe Le Tellier. *Golf europeen (Paris) 170, oct (1) 1984, 164-173.*
LEVEL: B LANG: Fr SIRC ARTICLE NO: 107213

AUDIO VISUAL MATERIAL

Dupouey, P. Golf et video. *Golf europeen (Paris) 171, oct (2) 1984, 70-71.*
LEVEL: B LANG: Fr SIRC ARTICLE NO: 107218

BIOGRAPHY AND AUTOBIOGRAPHY

Dunne, P. My mother, the golf Olympian. (Margaret Abbott) *Golf digest (Norwalk, Conn.) 35(8), Aug 1984, 92-95.*
LEVEL: B LANG: Eng SIRC ARTICLE NO: 101271

Fox, W.P. The not-so-mad bomber. (Andy Bean) *Golf digest (Norwalk, Conn.) 35(12), Dec 1984, 92-94;96;98;100.*
LEVEL: B LANG: Eng SIRC ARTICLE NO: 172919

Kanterman, C.B. A dentist's landmark contribution to golf. (Dr. William Lowell) *TIC (Alabany) 43(8), Aug 1984, 12-13.*
LEVEL: B LANG: Eng

McDermott, B. Nothing pitty-pot about Patty. Patty Sheehar, LPGA Player of the Year for '83 and contender for '84, is long off the tee and long on the heart. *Sports illustrated 60(12), 19 Mar 1984, 36-38;42-44.*
LEVEL: B LANG: Eng SIRC ARTICLE NO: 092122

McDermott, B. The extra-ordinary Mr. X. (Miller Barber) *Sports illustrated (Chicago, Ill.) 61(14), 17 Sept 1984, 64-68;70;72-73;74-78.*
LEVEL: B LANG: Eng SIRC ARTICLE NO: 098127

Nelford, J. Rubenstein, L. Seasons in a golfer's life. Toronto: Methuen, c1984. 151 p. : ill.
LEVEL: B LANG: Eng ISBN: 0-458-97910-4 LC CARD: C84-98355-7 GV964.N44 17642

Seitz, N. The two worlds of Tom Watson. An intimate profile of the complex man behind the Huck Finn smile, as he sucks his sixth British Open Title and his third in a row. *Golf digest (Norwalk, Conn.) 35(7), Jul 1984, 44-51.*
LEVEL: B LANG: Eng SIRC ARTICLE NO: 101290

Wulf, S. Searching for a sea of tranquility. Life had become one big unpayable lie for Phil McGleno, so he changed his name to Mac O'Grady, found love and fulfillment and, best of all, on his 17th attempt finally qualified to play on the PGA Tour. *Sports illustrated 60(16), 16 Apr 1984, 74-78;80-81;84-86;88.*
LEVEL: B LANG: Eng SIRC ARTICLE NO: 093480

BIOMECHANICS

Van Hoeck, J. Frayssineau, H. Lofi, A. La dynamique du golf. (Refs: 1)*Science et vie (Paris) HS147, 1984, 76-79.*
LEVEL: I LANG: Fr

CAREERS

Les metiers du golf. *Golf europeen (Paris) 162, mars 1984, 36-45.*
LEVEL: B LANG: Fr SIRC ARTICLE NO: 099638

CHILDREN

Sutton, H. How to push your junior golfer - the right way. The defending PGA champion tells how parents can help their youngsters reach their potential. *Golf digest (Norwalk, Conn.) 35(8), Aug 1984, 82-83.*
LEVEL: B LANG: Eng SIRC ARTICLE NO: 101292

CLOTHING

1984 golf shoe market report. *Golf industry (N. Miami, Fla.) 9(3), Apr/May 1984, 12-13;15-18.*
LEVEL: B LANG: Eng SIRC ARTICLE NO: 100548

Golf shoe marketplace. *Golf industry (N. Miami, Fla.) 9(3), Apr/May 1984, 24-25;28-29.*
LEVEL: B LANG: Eng SIRC ARTICLE NO: 100555

CLUBS

Leishman, R. The Royal Montreal Golf Club. *Greenmaster (Toronto) 20(6), Jul/Aug 1984, 7.*
LEVEL: B LANG: Eng SIRC ARTICLE NO: 103213

COACHING

Moriarty, J. College preview 1984: golf grows in football country. (David Yates) *Golf world (London) 37(32), 2 Mar 1984, 16-18;20.*
LEVEL: B LANG: Eng SIRC ARTICLE NO: 099640

COUNTRIES AND REGIONS

Callander, C. Where Asia wears a smile. A guide to golf in the Philippines. *Golf monthly (Glasgow, Scotland) 74(6), Jun 1984, 53-58.*
LEVEL: B LANG: Eng SIRC ARTICLE NO: 101268

Green, R. Golf on the other side of the world: South Africa. *Golf world (London, Eng.) 23(1), Jan 1984, 94-98;100.*
LEVEL: LANG: Eng SIRC ARTICLE NO: 095040

Hamilton, D. Golf in Scotland. *Golf monthly (Glasgow) 74(1), Jan 1984, 51;54-55;58-59;62-64.*
LEVEL: B LANG: Eng SIRC ARTICLE NO: 098126

Hamilton, D. The good golf guide to Scotland. Gretna, La.: Pelican Pub. Co., 1984. 1v.
NOTES: Reprint. Originally published Edinburgh : Canongate, 1982. Includes index.
LEVEL: B LANG: Eng ISBN: 0882894463 LC CARD: 84-003141

Mosca, J.D. Experiencing golf in Scotland: a guide to Scottish courses. Mankato, Minn.: Golfing Scotland, c1984. 1v.
NOTES: Includes index.

LEVEL: B LANG: Eng ISBN: 0914867113 LC CARD: 84-002979

Parlons peu mais comptons bien. Le golf francais va-t-il bien? En regardant les chiffres, oui, En regardant les resultats, euh *Golf europeen (Paris) 164, mai 1984, 68-70.*
LEVEL: B LANG: Fr SIRC ARTICLE NO: 101285

DIRECTORIES

1985 Official Florida golf guide. *Golf magazine (Los Angeles) 26(12), Dec 1984, 57;59-60;62-76;78-83.*
LEVEL: B LANG: Eng SIRC ARTICLE NO: 173157

America's 75 best public courses: Golf digest ranks the greatest courses, from coast to coast, that everyone can play. *Golf digest (Norwalk, Conn.) 35(11), Nov 1984, 40-53.*
LEVEL: B LANG: Eng SIRC ARTICLE NO: 105858

Fore: 1985 guide to desert golf. *Fore (North Hollywood, Calif.) 17(4), Winter 1984, 31;33-34;38-40;42-45.*
LEVEL: B LANG: En SIRC ARTICLE NO: 105867

Golf magazine's guide to jr. camps and schools. *Golf magazine (Boulder, Colo.) 26(5), May 1984, 125;127.*
LEVEL: B LANG: Eng SIRC ARTICLE NO: 099634

DISABLED

Owens, D. Teaching golf to special populations. New York: Leisure Press, 1984. 160 p. : ill.
NOTES: Bibliography: p. 154.
LEVEL: I LANG: Eng ISBN: 0880110368 LC CARD: 84-005772 GV965 18005

Owens, D. Assessing present skills and capabilities.
NOTES: In, Owens, D. (ed.), Teaching golf to special populations, New York, Leisure Press, 1984, p. 74-83.
LEVEL: B LANG: Eng GV965 18005

Owens, D. Golf instruction for the mentally retarded.
NOTES: In, Owens, D. (ed.), Teaching golf to special populations, New York, Leisure Press, 1984, p. 99-103.
LEVEL: B LANG: Eng GV965 18005

Owens, D. Golf instruction for the visually and hearing impaired.
NOTES: In, Owens, D. (ed.), Teaching golf to special populations, New York, Leisure Press, 1984, p. 112-118.
LEVEL: B LANG: Eng GV965 18005

Owens, D. Golf instruction for the physically impaired.
NOTES: In, Owens, D. (ed.), Teaching golf to special populations, New York, Leisure Press, 1984, p. 119-133.
LEVEL: B LANG: Eng GV965 18005

Rotella, R. Psychological considerations and pleasure of teaching golf to special populations. (Refs: 12)
NOTES: In, Owens, D. (ed.), Teaching golf to special populations, New York, Leisure Press, 1984, p. 136-153.
LEVEL: I LANG: Eng GV965 18005

Shasby, G. Communicating with the golfer.
NOTES: In, Owens, D. (ed.), Teaching golf to special populations, New York, Leisure Press,

1984, p. 84-93.
LEVEL: B LANG: Eng GV965 18005

Shasby, G. Mental retardation.
NOTES: In, Owens, D. (ed.), Teaching golf to special populations, New York, Leisure Press, 1984, p. 94-98.
LEVEL: B LANG: Eng GV965 18005

Shasby, G. Visually and hearing impaired.
NOTES: In, Owens, D. (ed.), Teaching golf to special populations, New York, Leisure Press, 1984, p. 104-111.
LEVEL: B LANG: Eng GV965 18005

ECONOMICS

Green, R. The taxing problems of European golf. *Golf world (London) 23(8), Aug 1984, 109-112.*
LEVEL: B LANG: Eng SIRC ARTICLE NO: 101278

Rottenberg, D. The richest men in golf: a first-ever look at the 10 largest fortunes in the game. *Golf magazine (Los Angele 26(10), Oct 1984, 38-41;56;71.*
LEVEL: B LANG: Eng SIRC ARTICLE NO: 105878

Rubenstein, L. Golf is big business no matter how you slice it. *Financial post magazine (Toronto, Ont.) 1 Jun 1984, 49-52.*
LEVEL: B LANG: Eng SIRC ARTICLE NO: 095046

ENVIRONMENT

Williams, B.R. Lighting protection and avoidance: lightning and golf courses are destined to rendezvous. Don't let anyone ge caught between. *Golf course management (Lawrence, Kans.) Aug 1984, 34;36;38.*
LEVEL: B LANG: Eng SIRC ARTICLE NO: 104751

EQUIPMENT

1984 guide to golf cars. *Golf industry (N. Miami, Fla.) 9(4), Jun/Jul 1984, 16-17.*
LEVEL: B LANG: Eng SIRC ARTICLE NO: 1012

Broadbent, P. Getting to grips with wet weather. *Golf world (London, Eng.) 23(3), Mar 1984, 51-52.*
LEVEL: B LANG: Eng SIR ARTICLE NO: 099630

Brown, B. Finishing custom made woods. *Golf clubmaker newsletter (Dunedin, Fla.) 7(2), 1984, 4;6.*
LEVEL: B LANG: Eng SIRC ARTICLE NO: 101266

Carney, R. Is there really a longest ball? *Golf digest (Norwalk, Conn.) 35(12), Dec 1984, 40-45.*
LEVEL: B LANG: Eng SIRC ARTICLE NO: 172910

Carney, R. How to pick the longest ball for you. *Golf digest (Norwalk, Conn.) 35(12), Dec 1984, 46-47.*
LEVEL: B LANG: Eng SIRC ARTICLE NO: 172911

Chase, A. A slice of golf. *In, Schrier, E.W. and Allman, W.F. (eds.), Newton at the bat: the science in sports, New York, Scribner, c1984, p. 29-32.*
LEVEL: B LANG: Eng RC1235 18609

Duclos, D. Should putters be swing-weighted? *Golf monthly (Glasgow, Scotland) 74(7), Jul 1984, 41;43-44.*
LEVEL: B LANG: E SIRC ARTICLE NO: 101270

Elsey, N. Dennis, L. The feather weight clubs controversy: are they for you? *Golf world (London) 23(10), Oct 1984, 78-79;81;83.*
LEVEL: B LANG: Eng SIRC ARTICLE NO: 105862

Fishman, L. Which light is right? The barrage of lightweight clubs are not all birds of a 'feather'. *Golf magazine (Los Angeles) 26(10), Oct 1984, 46-49;71.*
LEVEL: B LANG: Eng SIRC ARTICLE NO: 105865

Hains, L. It'll be a vintage year for putters. *Golf digest (Norwalk, Conn.) 35(12), Dec 1984, 66-67.*
LEVEL: B LANG: Eng SIRC ARTICLE NO: 172914

Le centre de la cible: messieurs les fabricants, on vous en supplie: (harmonisez le centre de vos clubs). *Golf europeen (Pari 173, dec 1984, 74-75.*
LEVEL: B LANG: Fr SIRC ARTICLE NO: 108827

Les clubs poids-plume sont-ils fait pour vous? Les fameux clubs ultra-legers ont leurs defenseurs acharnes et leurs adversaire resolus. Sont-ils des gadgets ou une revolution? Faites votre opinion. *Golf europeen (Paris) 170, oct (1) 1984, 56-58;60.*
LEVEL: B LANG: Fr SIRC ARTICLE NO: 107216

Love, D. The only way to buy new clubs. *Golf digest (Norwalk, Conn.) 35(12), Dec 1984, 48;65.*
LEVEL: B LANG: Eng SIRC ARTICLE NO: 172912

McCleery, P. Are you ready for hollow irons? *Golf digest (Norwalk, Conn.) 35(12), Dec 1984, 68-69.*
LEVEL: B LANG: Eng SIR ARTICLE NO: 172915

Mccleery, P. One year later: Heavier feathers. *Golf digest (Norwalk, Conn.) 35(12), Dec 1984, 70-71.*
LEVEL: B LANG: Eng SIRC ARTICLE NO: 172916

Standard and custom clubs '85: Golf digest's complete listing of the new club lines. *Golf digest (Norwalk, Conn.) 35(12), Dec 1984, 1-15.*
NOTES: Special pullout section.
LEVEL: B LANG: Eng SIRC ARTICLE NO: 172913

The pull cart. *Golf industry (N.Miami, Fla.) 9(4), Jun/Jul 1984, 50-53.*
LEVEL: B LANG: Eng SIRC ARTICLE NO: 101287

EQUIPMENT - MAINTENANCE

Brown, B. Reshafting woods with steel shafts. *Golf clubmaker newsletter (Dunedin, Fla.) 6(4), 1984, 6-7;11.*
LEVEL: B LANG Eng SIRC ARTICLE NO: 098936

Harvey, J.C. Golfer's repair and maintenance handbook. Chicago: Contemporary Books, c1984. viii, 126 p. : ill.
NOTES: Includes index.
LEVEL: B LANG: Eng ISBN: 0-8092-5448-4 LC CARD: 84-005802 GV976 17593

Lancaster, J. Club repair. *Golf industry (N. Miami, Fla.) 9(1), Dec/Jan 1984, 27-28;32;34.*
LEVEL: B LANG: Eng SIRC ARTICL NO: 098953

FACILITIES

A.C.G. systemes nationaux de handicap et d'evaluation des parcours. En vigueur le 1er janvier 1984. Vanier, Ont.: Association canadienne des golfeuses, 1984. 54 p.
CORP: Association canadienne des golfeuses.
NOTES: Titre de la couverture. Published also in English under the title: C.L.G.A. National handicap and course rating systems. Effective January 1, 1984.
LEVEL: B LANG: Fr GV966 11457

Beard, J.B. The contributing of research to quality playing conditions. *Greenmaster (Toronto) 20(8), Nov/Dec 1984, 23;25;27-28.*
LEVEL: I LANG: Eng SIRC ARTICLE NO: 173148

Burpee, L. Summer survival of annual blue-grass in golf course fairways. *Greenmaster (Waterloo, Ont.) 20(4), May 1984, 5;7.*
LEVEL: I LANG: Eng SIRC ARTICLE NO: 100595

Burpee, L. Fungus vs. fungus on the golf green. *Greenmaster (Waterloo, Ont.) 20(5), Jun 1984, 7-8.*
LEVEL: I LANG: Eng SIR ARTICLE NO: 100596

C.L.G.A. national handicap and course rating systems. Effective January 1, 1984. Vanier, Ont.: Canadian Ladies' Golf Association, 1984. 45 p.
CORP: Canadian Ladies' Golf Association.
NOTES: Publie aussi en francais sous le titre: A.C.G. systemes nationaux de handicap et d'evaluation des parcours. En vigueur le 1er janvier 1984. Cover title.
LEVEL: B LANG: Eng GV966 11458

Eggens, J.L. Do fairways really need sand topdressing? (Refs: 5)*Greenmaster (Waterloo, Ont.) 20(4), May 1984, 11;13.*
LEVEL: I LANG: Eng SIRC ARTICLE NO: 100602

Eggens, J.L. Wright, C.P.M. Effect of clipping removal and mower injury on fairway turf quality. *Greenmaster (Toronto) 20(8 Nov/Dec 1984, 19.*
LEVEL: I LANG: Eng SIRC ARTICLE NO: 173146

Fiander, K. Perennial ryegrass in Canada. *Greenmaster (Waterloo, Ont.) 20(4), May 1984, 15-16.*
LEVEL: B LANG: Eng SIRC ARTICLE NO: 100605

Gallup, D. Gallup, J. Golf courses of Colorado: a guide to public and resort courses. 1984 ed. Estes Park, Colo.: Colorado Leisure Sports, c1984. 320 p. : ill.
LEVEL: B LANG: Eng ISBN: 0961345802 LC CARD: 84-070834

Irwin, H. Different strokes for different grass: how to identify the major types and how to play on them more effectively. *Golf digest (Norwalk, Conn.) 35(3), Mar 1984, 52-57.*
LEVEL: B LANG: Eng SIRC ARTICLE NO: 099635

Kavanagh, T. Is there a case for annual meadow-grass? *Turf management (Surrey, Eng.) 3(4), Apr 1984, 19-20.*
LEVEL: B LANG Eng SIRC ARTICLE NO: 102103

Les 50 meilleurs parcours du monde. Pour la premiere fois, un Comite mondial d'experts a juge et classe les 50 meilleurs parcours du monde. *Golf europeen (Paris) 160, janv 1984, 43-49.*
LEVEL: B LANG: Fr SIRC ARTICLE NO: 098977

Not (only) for profit - the 'social' golf and athletic club. (Athens Country Club) *Recreation, sports & leisure (Minneapolis) 4(6), Aug 1984, 75-77.*
NOTES: Special issue: Managed recreation research report.
LEVEL: B LANG: Eng SIRC ARTICLE NO: 103937

Osterman, R.W. Who sets the standards for play on your golf course? *USGA Green Section Record (Far Hills, N.J.) 22(2), Mar/Apr 1984, 12-14.*
LEVEL: B LANG: Eng SIRC ARTICLE NO: 100587

Pileggi, S. Playing ancient games: golf's best-kept secret, these six spectacular Irish links represent the essence of the game, and there are no six-hour waiting times. *Sports illustrated (Chicago, Ill.) 60(22), 4 Jun 1984, 54-69.*
LEVEL: B LANG: Eng SIRC ARTICLE NO: 095045

Rothwell, J.D. A cost effective approach to turfgrass disease management. *Greenmaster (Waterloo, Ont.) 20(5), Jun 1984, 11;13.*
LEVEL: I LANG: Eng SIRC ARTICLE NO: 100620

Sanders, P. Infrared photography: fairways stand exposed. *Golf course management (Kansas) 52(5), May 1984, 28;32.*
LEVEL: LANG: Eng SIRC ARTICLE NO: 100622

Shiels, G. Using synthetics: could this finish golf as we know it? *Parks, golf courses & sports grounds (Middlesex, Eng.) 49(4), Jan 1984, 8-9.*
LEVEL: B LANG: Eng SIRC ARTICLE NO: 097525

Shildrick, J.P. Grasses for the golf course. *Turf management (Surrey, Eng.) 3(3), Mar 1984, 20-23.*
LEVEL: B LANG: Eng SIR ARTICLE NO: 108682

Superintendents report on: turfgrass disease management practices. *Greenmaster (Waterloo, Ont.) 20(5), Jun 1984, 16-17.*
LEVEL: I LANG: Eng SIRC ARTICLE NO: 100631

Traffic of golf turf. *Sports turf bulletin (Bingley, Eng.) 145, Apr/Jun 1984, 8-10.*
LEVEL: B LANG: Eng SIRC ARTICLE NO: 100634

Zontek, S.J. Perennial ryegrasses are getting better. *USGA Green Section Record (Far Hills, N.J.) 22(3), May/Jun 1984, 1-6.*
LEVEL: B LANG: Eng SIRC ARTICLE NO: 100643

FACILITIES - DESIGN, CONSTRUCTION AND PLANNING

Bad design adds to compaction problems. *Turf management (Surrey, Eng.) 3(6), Jun 1984, 12-13.*
LEVEL: B LANG: Eng SIRC ARTICLE NO: 102158

Construction of a sand ameliorated golf green. *Sports turf bulletin (Bingley, Eng.) 145, Apr/Jun 1984, 10-12.*
LEVEL: B LANG Eng SIRC ARTICLE NO: 100597

Eberl, G. Building a golf course. There's more to your favorite golf course than meets the eye, and as you prepare to tee off, not all the butterflies are in your stomach. *Golf journal (Far Hills, N.J.) 37(8), Nov/Dec 1984, 9-13.*
LEVEL: B LANG: Eng SIRC ARTICLE NO: 105230

From sponge to stability. *Golf course management (Lawrence, Kans.) 52(11), Nov 1984, 46-47.*
LEVEL: B LANG: Eng SIRC ARTICLE NO: 173003

Goodner, R. Golf's great land rush. *Golf digest (Norwalk, Conn.) 35(3), Mar 1984, 134-142;145-146;148.*
LEVEL: B LANG: Eng SIRC ARTICLE NO: 098986

Hurdzan, M.J. A look at dams today. *Golf course management (Lawrence, Kans.) 52(11), Nov 1984, 20;22;26;28.*
LEVEL: B LANG Eng SIRC ARTICLE NO: 172999

Stevens, P. Californian landfill site allows for golf course expansion. *Turf management (Great Bookham, Eng.) 3(1), Jan 198 34-35.*
LEVEL: B LANG: Eng SIRC ARTICLE NO: 178664

Stobbs, J. What role for synthetic golf greens? *Turf management (Great Bookham, Surrey) 3(9), Sept 1984, 33-35.*
LEVEL: B LANG: Eng SIRC ARTICLE NO: 105248

Tee construction and enlargement. *Sports turf bulletin (Bingley, Eng.) 145, Apr/Jun 1984, 6-8.*
LEVEL: B LANG: Eng SIRC ARTICLE NO: 100633

Toucher a l'intouchable? On peut toujours faire mieux. Meme le parcours du Masters a Augusta, considere comme parfait. En voic deux exemples revelateurs. *Golf europeen (Paris) 166, juin 1984, 88-89.*
LEVEL: B LANG: Fr SIRC ARTICLE NO: 101294

Trees add beauty to a course. *Turf management (Surrey, Eng.) 3(5), May 1984, 45-48.*
LEVEL: B LANG: Eng SIRC ARTICLE NO: 102156

Watson, J. Irrigation: a pre-construction evaluation. *Greenmaster (Toronto) 20(3), Apr 1984, 5;7.*
NOTES: Transcribed from a talk at the Atlantic Golf Superintendents Fall Field Day, 1983.
LEVEL: B LANG: Eng SIRC ARTICLE NO: 100637

Whitten, R. New bunkers: Back to the auld sod. *Golf digest (Norwalk, Conn.) 35(12), Dec 1984, 72-74.*
LEVEL: B LANG: Eng SIRC ARTICLE NO: 172918

FACILITIES - MAINTENANCE

Baskin, C. Chemical usages and controversies. *Golf course management (Kansas) 52(3), Mar 1984, 29;31;33;37.*
LEVEL: B LANG Eng SIRC ARTICLE NO: 100591

Batten, S.M. Those irrepressible, incredible, impossible grassy weeds. *Green section record (Far Hills, N.J.) 22(5), Sept/Oct 1984, 1-4.*
LEVEL: B LANG: Eng SIRC ARTICLE NO: 105226

Before the snow begins to fall... *Golf course management (Lawrence, Kans.) 52(11), Nov 1984, 52-53.*
LEVEL: B LANG: Eng SIRC ARTICLE NO: 173004

Brown, D. Can drip and subsurface irrigation replace sprinkler systems in golf courses? *Greenmaster (Toronto) 20(3), Apr 1984, 27.*
LEVEL: B LANG: Eng SIRC ARTICLE NO: 100594

Buchanan, W.G. Why don't the greens hold? *USGA Green Section Record (Far Hill, N.J.) 22(4), Jul/Aug 1984, 1-5.*
LEVEL: B LANG: Eng SIRC ARTICLE NO: 102429

Burpee, L. Goutty, L. Evaluation of fungicides for control of pink snow mold on creeping bentgrass. *Greenmaster (Toronto) 2 (7), Sept/Oct 1984, 14-15.*
LEVEL: B LANG: Eng SIRC ARTICLE NO: 105228

Burpee, L.L. Goulty, L.G. The influence of fairway cultivation practices on the incidence and management of anthracnose. *Greenmaster (Toronto) 20(8), Nov/Dec 1984, 21.*
LEVEL: I LANG: Eng SIRC ARTICLE NO: 173147

Campbell, J. The effects of rolling. *Groundsman (London) 37(1), Jan 1984, 15.*
LEVEL: B LANG: Eng SIRC ARTICLE NO: 098981

Certification: restructuring the route to professionalism. *Golf course management (Lawrence, Kans.) 52(9), Sept 1984, 68-70;72-74;76;78.*
LEVEL: B LANG: Eng SIRC ARTICLE NO: 108829

Cooper, R.J. Henderlong, P.R. Street, J.R. Annual bluegrass management: getting to the root of the problem. (Refs: 6)*Golf course management (Kansas) 52(3), Mar 1984, 39;41;43.*
LEVEL: B LANG: Eng SIRC ARTICLE NO: 100598

Drainage problems on the golf course. *Sports turf bulletin (Bingley, Eng.) 145, Apr/Jun 1984, 3-5.*
LEVEL: B LANG: Eng SIRC ARTICLE NO: 100601

Eggens, J.L. Fairway overseeding with embark. *Greenmaster (Toronto) 20(8), Nov/Dec 1984, 17.*
LEVEL: I LANG: Eng SIRC ARTICLE NO: 173144

Engel, R.E. Some (more) thoughts on putting green speed. *Green section record (Far Hills, N.J.)*

22(6), Nov/Dec 1984, 5-6.
LEVEL: B LANG: Eng SIRC ARTICLE NO: 105863

Fowler, W.R. The scene at Hope Valley: bringing bunkers back to life. *Golf course management (Lawrence, Kan.) 52(2), Feb 1984, 33;35;37.*
LEVEL: B LANG: Eng SIRC ARTICLE NO: 098984

Fuchs, M. Bringing back a bonnie course. *Golf course management (Lawrence, Kans.) 52(11), Nov 1984, 34;36;38.*
LEVEL: B LANG: Eng SIRC ARTICLE NO: 173001

Gihuly, L.W. Heesen, R. The assistant superintendent: two complimentary views. *Golf course management (Lawrence, Kan.) 52(2), Feb 1984, 77;80;82-83.*
LEVEL: B LANG: Eng SIRC ARTICLE NO: 098985

Golden, B. The master plan concept. *Greenmaster (Toronto) 20(3), Apr 1984, 9.*
LEVEL: B LANG: Eng SIRC ARTICLE NO: 100606

Goss, R.L. Sulfur, the fourth major plant nutrient. *Green section record (Far Hills, N.J.) 22(5), Sept/Oct 1984, 5-7.*
LEVEL: B LANG: Eng SIRC ARTICLE NO: 105231

Greenfield, I. Budgets and records are essential. *Turf management (Surrey, Eng.) 3(12), Dec 1984, 16-17.*
LEVEL: B LANG: E SIRC ARTICLE NO: 105232

Gurney, M. Polyester provides protection. *Greenmaster (Toronto) 20(7), Sept/Oct 1984, 19-21.*
LEVEL: B LANG: Eng SIRC ARTICLE NO: 105234

Hand, J.R. Some qualities of great golf course superintendents. *USGA Green Section Record (Far Hills, N.J.) 22(2), Mar/Apr 1984, 26-29.*
LEVEL: B LANG: Eng SIRC ARTICLE NO: 100584

Harivandi, M.A. Irrigation efficiency. (Refs: 7)*Golf course management (Lawrence, Kans.) 52(4), Apr 1984, 49;51;53.*
LEVEL B LANG: Eng SIRC ARTICLE NO: 098989

Harris, R.Q. After a hurricane, who you gonna call? *Golf course management (Lawrence, Kans.) 52(11), Nov 1984, 30;32.*
LEVEL: B LANG: Eng SIRC ARTICLE NO: 173000

Hawes, D.T. The secrets of championship greens revealed. *Green section record (Far Hills, N.J.) 22(6), Nov/Dec 1984, 1-4.*
LEVEL: B LANG: Eng SIRC ARTICLE NO: 105235

Hogevoll, J. Improved ryegrasses: overcoming overseeding problems *Golf course management (Lawrence, Kan.) 52(1), Jan 1984, 13;17.*
LEVEL: B LANG: Eng SIRC ARTICLE NO: 095041

How compaction destroys good teeing areas. *Turf management (Surrey, Eng.) 3(7), Jul 1984, 45-46.*
LEVEL: B LANG: Eng SIRC ARTICLE NO: 102152

How drainage helps fight compaction. *Turf management (Great Bookham, Surrey) 3(8), Aug 1984, 24-25.*
LEVEL: B LANG: Eng SIRC ARTICLE NO: 105236

Major, D.P. Another dimension in golf course grooming, part 11. *Golf course management (Lawrence, Kans.) 52(11), Nov 1984, 42;44-45.*
LEVEL: B LANG: Eng SIRC ARTICLE NO: 173002

Mooney, W.P. Winterizing a golf course by straw mulching and burning: modern management revitalizes a time-proven approach t winterizing established grasses. *Golf course management*

(Lawrence, Kans.) Aug 1984, 31-32.
LEVEL: B LANG: Eng SIRC ARTICLE NO: 103951

Nelson, S.H. Schroeder, W.R. Sand rootzones for bentgrass. *Greenmaster (Toronto) 20(8), Nov/Dec 1984, 12-13;15.*
LEVEL: I LANG: Eng SIRC ARTICLE NO: 173141

Park, N. The danger of following American trends. (course maintenance) *Golf monthly (Glasgow, Scotland) 74(6), Jun 1984, 48-51.*
LEVEL: B LANG: Eng SIRC ARTICLE NO: 101283

Petrovic, A.M. What about liming? *Grounds maintenance (Overland Park, Kans.) 19(9), Sept 1984, 10;16;18;65;.*
LEVEL: B LANG: Eng SIRC ARTICLE NO: 105243

Plan now to pursue poa. *Golf course management (Kansas) 52(6), Jun 1984, 48;50.*
LEVEL: B LANG: Eng SIRC ARTICLE NO: 100618

Prusa, J.G. Golf course maintenance costs: surging or stable? *Golf course management (Lawrence, Kan.) 52(2), Feb 1984, 45;51;53;55-56.*
LEVEL: B LANG: Eng SIRC ARTICLE NO: 098992

Radko, A.M. The stimpmeter - a perspective. *Green section record (Far Hills, N.J.) 22(5), Sept/Oct 1984, 12-13.*
LEVEL: B LANG: Eng SIRC ARTICLE NO: 105876

Results from fairway maintenance questionnaire. *Greenmaster (Waterloo, Ont.) 20(4), May 1984, 20.*
LEVEL: B LANG: Eng SIRC ARTICLE NO: 100619

Shoulders, J.F. Couch, H.B. Schmidt, R.E. Overseeding for improved winter turf: twenty-five years of studies help identify key principles for successful overseeding. (Refs: 9)*Golf course management (Lawrence, Kans.) 52(9), Sept 1984, 50-52;54;106..*
LEVEL: I LANG: Eng SIRC ARTICLE NO: 108828

Stobbs, J. White line control for good fringes. *Turf management (Great Bookham, Surrey) 3(8), Aug 1984, 13-15.*
LEVEL: B LANG: Eng SIRC ARTICLE NO: 105249

Stobbs, J. Five year plan is vital for all courses. *Turf management (Surrey, Eng.) 3(12), Dec 1984, 12-14.*
LEVEL: B LANG: Eng SIRC ARTICLE NO: 105250

Truttmann, D. Your irrigation system: preparation for winter. *Greenmaster (Toronto) 20(7), Sept/Oct 1984, 12-13.*
LEVEL: B LANG: Eng SIRC ARTICLE NO: 105251

Walsh, E. Golf cars: Economic boom - agronomic disaster? *Golf course management (Lawrence, Kans.) 52(11), Nov 1984, 72-74.*
LEVEL: B LANG: Eng SIRC ARTICLE NO: 172997

White, C.B. Playing par with Jack Frost. *Green section record (Far Hills, N.J) 22(5), Sept/Oct 1984, 8-11.*
LEVEL: B LANG Eng SIRC ARTICLE NO: 105881

Whitten, R.E. Misting bentgrass greens: the pause that refreshes. *Golf course management (Lawrence, Kans.) Aug 1984, 6-7;10;12-14;16.*
LEVEL: B LANG: Eng SIRC ARTICLE NO: 103954

Williams, B.R. Meeting today's demands: fairway maintenance and improvement. *Golf course management (Kansas) 52(5), May 1984, 46;48;51.*
LEVEL: B LANG: Eng SIRC ARTICLE NO: 100638

Winter fairway maintenance. *Sports turf bulletin (Bingley, Eng.) 147, Oct/Dec 1984, 10-12.*
LEVEL: B LANG: Eng SIRC ARTICLE NO: 100639

Zontek, S.J. Turf management in England and Scotland: so similar, yet so different. *USGA Green Section Record (Far Hills, N.J.) 22(4), Jul/Aug 1984, 12-13.*
LEVEL: B LANG: Eng SIRC ARTICLE NO: 102437

HANDICAPPING

A.C.G. systemes nationaux de handicap et d'evaluation des parcours. En vigueur le 1er janvier 1984. Vanier, Ont.: Association canadienne des golfeuses, 1984. 54 p.
CORP: Association canadienne des golfeuses.
NOTES: Titre de la couverture. Published also in English under the title: C.L.G.A. National handicap and course rating systems. Effective January 1, 1984.
LEVEL: B LANG: Fr GV966 11457

C.L.G.A. national handicap and course rating systems. Effective January 1, 1984. Vanier, Ont.: Canadian Ladies' Golf Association, 1984. 45 p.
CORP: Canadian Ladies' Golf Association.
NOTES: Publie aussi en francais sous le titre: A.C.G. systemes nationaux de handicap et d'evaluation des parcours. En vigueur le 1er janvier 1984. Cover title.
LEVEL: B LANG: Eng GV966 11458

Tarde, J. How your handicap stacks up: the largest computer survey ever lets you measure yours against the country. *Golf digest (Norwalk, Conn) 35(3), Mar 1984, 50-51.*
LEVEL: B LANG: Eng SIRC ARTICLE NO: 099645

HISTORY

Elliott, C.N. Bisher, F. East Lake Country Club history: home course of Bobby Jones. Atlanta, Ga.: Cherokee Pub. Co., 1984. 1v.
NOTES: Includes index.
LEVEL: B LANG: Eng ISBN: 0877970920 LC CARD: 84-022991

Nelson, J. The St. Andrews champions. *Golf monthly (Glasgow, Scotland) 74(6), Jun 1984, 89-91;93-94;97-100;102-107.*
LEVEL B LANG: Eng SIRC ARTICLE NO: 101280

Sarazen, G. Oh, how it has changed. All about how a 'mediocre' Augusta National course has become a great one - and other tricks of time. *Golf magazine (Boulder, Colo.) 25(4), Apr 1984, 58-63.*
LEVEL: B LANG: Eng SIRC ARTICLE NO: 099644

Stanley, L. Characters of St. Andrews. *Golf world (London) 23(7), Jul 1984, 67-68.*
LEVEL: B LANG: Eng SIRC ARTICLE NO: 101291

Taylor, D. The golden years at Augusta. It's not like it was 50 years ago. *Golf world (Southern Pines, N.C.) 37(37), 6 Apr 1984, 17-20;22;24.*
LEVEL: B LANG: Eng SIRC ARTICLE NO: 095047

Towne, R. Sideline. Brentwood Country Club's history is probably Greek to marathoner. *Sports illustrated (Los Angeles, Calif.) 60(26), 25 Jun 1984, 10;13-14.*
LEVEL: B LANG: Eng SIRC ARTICLE NO: 095048

HUMOUR

Dobereiner, P. The book of golf disasters. 1st American ed. New York: Atheneum, 1984, c1983. 1 v.
LEVEL: B LANG: Eng ISBN: 0689114532 LC CARD: 83-045491

Oman, M. Portrait of a golfaholic. Chicago: Contemporary Books, 1984. 1v.
LEVEL: B LANG: Eng ISBN: 0809253356 LC CARD: 84-015593

INJURIES AND ACCIDENTS

Berry, W. Enemy number one: everyone has a bad back - and more and more of us are discovering it on the golf course. *Golf magazine (Boulder, Colo.) 25(3), Mar 1984, 34-39.*
LEVEL: B LANG: Eng SIRC ARTICLE NO: 093465

Chaouat, D. Golf. Pathologie rhumatologique. (Refs: 5)*Medecine du sport (Paris) 58(4), 25 juil 1984, 22-25.*
LEVEL: I LANG Fr SIRC ARTICLE NO: 098125

Christopher, J. Golf. *In, Adams, S.H. (ed.), et al., Catastrophic injuries in sports: avoidance strategies, Salinas, Calif. Cayote Press, c1984, p. 73-75.*
LEVEL: B LANG: Eng RD97 19088

Koutchinsky, F. Comment eviter le mal au dos? La 'maladie du golfeur' peut etre vaincue. *Golf europeen (Paris) 165(2), mai 1984, 52-54.*
LEVEL: B LANG: Fr SIRC ARTICLE NO: 101279

McCleery, P. Bad back: how to avoid an old hang-up. *Golf digest (Norwalk, Conn.) 35(3), Mar 1984, 58-60;62;64-65.*
LEVEL: LANG: Eng SIRC ARTICLE NO: 099637

MASS MEDIA

Etcheverry, E. Un magazine de golf a la television. Mais cela se passe - pour l'instant - aux Etats-Unis. Voici comment ESPN la chaine des sports en Amerique, traite le golf. *Golf (Bruxelles, Belgique) 4, mai 1984, 44-45.*
LEVEL: B LANG: Fr SIRC ARTICLE NO: 101272

Van Der Gucht, G. Golf et television. *Golf europeen (Paris) 171, oct (2) 1984, 68-69.*
LEVEL: B LANG: Fr SIRC ARTICLE NO: 107225

PHILATELY, NUMISMATICS AND COLLECTIONS

Watt, A.A. Woods 1820 to 1920. *Golf monthly (Glasgow, Scotland) 74(3), Mar 1984, 66-68.*
NOTES: Collecting: part 2.
LEVEL B LANG: Eng SIRC ARTICLE NO: 098960

Watt, A.A. Collecting: part 4. The first generation of iron clubs. *Golf monthly (Glasgow, Scotland) 74(5), May 1984, 71-74.*
LEVEL: B LANG: Eng SIRC ARTICLE NO: 101295

Watt, A.A. Collecting: part 5. The second generation of clubs. *Golf monthly (Glasgow, Scotland) 74(6), Jun 1984, 61-64.*
LEVEL: B LANG: Eng SIRC ARTICLE NO: 101296

Watt, A.A. Collecting: part 6. Some specialist clubs. *Golf monthly (Glasgow, Scotland) 74(7), Jul 1984, 144-145;147-148.*
LEVEL: B LANG: Eng SIRC ARTICLE NO: 101297

Watt, A.A. Vigilance is the key. Collecting, part 9. *Golf monthly (Glasgow, Scotland) 7(10), Oct 1984, 37-39;41.*
LEVEL: B LANG: Eng SIRC ARTICLE NO: 108823

GOLF (continued)

PHYSICAL FITNESS

Fitness and golf. *Golf industry (N.Miami, Fla.) 9(4), Jun/Jul 1984, 46-49.*
LEVEL: B LANG: Eng SIRC ARTICLE NO: 101275

PHYSICS

Park, N. The impact between ball and turf. *Golf monthly (Glasgow, Scotland) 74(7), Jul 1984, 135-136;139-140.*
LEVEL: I LANG: Eng SIRC ARTICLE NO: 101284

PHYSIOLOGY

Crews, D. Thomas, G. Shirreffs, J.H. Helfrich, H.M. A physiological profile of Ladies Professional Golf Association Tour players. (Refs: 11)*Physician and sportsmedicine (Minneapolis, Minn.) 12(5), May 1984, 69-70;72-73;76.*
LEVEL: I LANG: Eng SIRC ARTICLE NO: 095038

PHYSIOLOGY - MUSCLE

Friedman, M.H. Weisberg, J. Nelson, A. Jond, J. Reduction of neuromuscular hypertension for improvement of athletic performance. (Refs: 9)*Journal of orthopaedic and sports physical therapy (Baltimore) 5(6), May/Jun 1984, 384-390.*
ABST: This study investigates the inhibition of neuromuscular tension in specific key muscles, for the purpose of increasing athletic efficiency. Four golfers were studied electromyographically during the backswing. Integrated EMG findings from the right wrist flexors showed a significant decrease following application of passive stretch. The theoretical and practical aspects of this technique are discussed.
LEVEL: A LANG: Eng SIRC ARTICLE NO: 101276

PSYCHOLOGY

Ballingall, P. Mind control. *Golf monthly (Glasgow, Scotland) 74(5), May 1984, 50-52.*
LEVEL: B LANG: Eng SIRC ARTICLE NO: 101264

Bryan, M. The undriven: in the case of some players, the fire doesn't burn quite as hot. *Golf magazine (Boulder, Colo.) 26(8), Aug 1984, 58-60;69.*
LEVEL: B LANG: Eng SIRC ARTICLE NO: 101267

Johnson, R.T. Bjorkland, R. Krotee, M.L. The effects of cooperative, competition and individualistic student interaction patterns on the achievements and attitudes of students learning the golf skill of putting. (Refs: 10)*Research quarterly for exercise & sport (Reston, Va.) 55(2), Jun 1984, 129-134.*
ABST: One hundred fifteen university students were randomly assigned to either a cooperative, competitive or individualistic group. The students learned the golf skill of putting within the interaction pattern of these groups. The feelings of the students with regards to the instructor, their peers, themselves, and the interaction patterns were monitored as was their putting ability. The results indicate that cooperative interaction tends to promote putting skill and positive attitudes towards self and instructor. The students had the least positive feelings for the individualistic condition.
LEVEL: A LANG: Eng SIRC ARTICLE NO: 096688

Nuhn, G. Temper, temper. Does an excitable temper help or hurt your game? Yes. *Golf magazine 26(2), Feb 1984, 34-37.*
LEVEL: B LANG: Eng SIRC ARTICLE NO: 093475

Rotella, R.J. You, too, can be your own best friend. A leading sports psychologist tells you how to stop punishing yourself and, like Fuzzy, play up to your potential. *Golf digest (Norwalk, Conn.) 35(9), Sept 1984, 47-49.*
LEVEL: B LANG: Eng SIRC ARTICLE NO: 108822

Toski, B. Flick, J. How to control yourself on the course: keep your emotions in check so you can keep your scores down. *Golf digest (Norwalk, Conn.) 35(6), Jun 1984, 135-136;138;140;142;146;149;151.*
LEVEL: B LANG: Eng SIRC ARTICLE NO: 099646

PSYCHOLOGY - MENTAL TRAINING

Gallwey, T. Lafaurie, A.J. Golf: le jeu interieur. (Paris): R. Laffont, 1984. 227 p. : ill. (Sports pour tous.)
NOTES: Traduit de l'anglais.
LEVEL: B LANG: Fr ISBN: 2-221-04410-X

Hogan, C.A. Your mind hits the shots: your game is only as good as your images. *Golf magazine (Los Angeles) 26(12), Dec 198 50.*
LEVEL: B LANG: Eng SIRC ARTICLE NO: 173156

Nuhn, G. Mind games: some tour pros have decided that improved play depends largely on the mental side of the game. *Golf magazine (Los Angeles) 26(12), Dec 1984, 46-48;90-91.*
LEVEL: B LANG: Eng SIRC ARTICLE NO: 173155

RULES AND REGULATIONS

Decisions on the rules of golf. Far Hills, N.J.: United States Golf Association, c1984. 1v. (loose-leaf)
CORP: United States Golf Association.
CORP: Royal and Ancient Golf Club of St. Andrews.
NOTES: Includes indexes.
LEVEL: B LANG: Eng LC CARD: 82-202441 GV971 17656

Golf rules in pictures. New and rev. ed. New York: Perigee Books, c1984. 1v.
CORP: United States Golf Association.
LEVEL: B LANG: Eng ISBN: 0399509844 LC CARD: 83-026345

USGA golf handicap system; and, golf committee manual: with USGA course rating system for men and women. (Far Hills, N.J.): United States Golf Association, c1984. 72 p.
CORP: United States Golf Association.
NOTES: Rev. ed. of: Golf committee manual; and, USGA golf handicap system, c1982, 'Effective April 1, 1984'.
LEVEL: B LANG: Eng LC CARD: 84-159962

Watson, T. Hannigan, F. The new rules of golf. New York: Random House, c1984. viii, 181 p. : ill.
NOTES: Includes index.
LEVEL: B LANG: Eng ISBN: 0394721810 LC CARD: 83-042781 GV971 18079

SPORTING EVENTS

Bryan, M. Open market: dozens of courses would love to host the National Championship-but it's tough to get an open invitation. *Golf magazine (Boulder, Colo.) 26(6), Jun 1984, 68-70;72.*
LEVEL: B LANG: Eng SIRC ARTICLE NO: 099631

Ryde, P. The Halford Hewitt: a festival of foursomes. Banbury, Oxon: Hyde's, 1984?. 1v.
LEVEL: B LANG: Eng

STATISTICS AND RECORDS

Van Doren, C.S. Golf. In, Clawson, M. and Van Doren, C.S. (eds.), Statistics on outdoor recreation, Washington, Resources for the Future, c1984, p. 274-276.
LEVEL: B LANG: Eng GV191.4 20254

STATISTICS AND RECORDS - PARTICIPATION

Golf -- almost for(e) men only. Le golf - ou sont les femmes? (Refs: 1)*Highlights/Faits saillants (Ottawa) 32, Jul/juil 1984, 1-2.*
LEVEL: B LANG: Eng Fr SIRC ARTICLE NO: 096687

TEACHING

Mackey, R.T. Teach golf with a self-correcting club. *Journal of physical education, recreation & dance 55(1), Jan 1984, 54.*
LEVEL: B LANG: Eng SIRC ARTICLE NO: 092120

Meacci, W.G. Golf - instilling confidence: a successful technique. *Journal of physical education, recreation & dance (Reston, Va.) 55(4), Apr 1984, 76-77.*
LEVEL: B LANG: Eng SIRC ARTICLE NO: 095043

TECHNIQUES AND SKILLS

Adwick, K. Ken Adwick's 'Dirty dozen': part 4: three causes of shanking - and how to prevent them. *Golf world (London) 23(2), Feb 1984, 56-59.*
LEVEL: B LANG: Eng SIRC ARTICLE NO: 099628

Corrigez votre slice: la revue complete des causes du slice et une douzaine de conseils pour le corriger. *Golf europeen (Paris) 163, avr 1984, 28-29;31-34;37.*
LEVEL: B LANG: Fr SIRC ARTICLE NO: 099632

Johnson, C. Johnstone, A. Techniques of golf instruction: the short shot and putting. (Refs: 4)
NOTES: In, Owens, D. (ed.), Teaching golf to special populations, New York, Leisure Press, 1984, p. 60-72.
LEVEL: B LANG: Eng GV965 18005

Miller, J. Ne jouez pas au plus fin. Vous devez pitcher un drapeau dans une position difficile, n'hesitez pas a assurer, jouez 3 metres derriere le trou. *Golf europeen (Paris) 161, fevr 1984, 18-19.*
LEVEL: B LANG: Fr SIRC ARTICLE NO: 099639

Sable et sensation: une lecon de stabilite donnee par trois professionnels. *Golf europeen (Paris) 161, fevr 1984, 28-29.*
LEVEL: B LANG: Fr SIRC ARTICLE NO: 099643

Saunders, V. The mystery of spin. *Golf world (London) 23(7), Jul 1984, 145-146.*
LEVEL: B LANG: Eng SIRC ARTICLE NO: 10128

Une affaire de centimetres. Prendre peu ou beaucoup de sable? Cela depend du coup a jouer. *Golf europeen (Paris) 163, avr 1984, 48-49.*
LEVEL: B LANG: Fr SIRC ARTICLE NO: 099629

Wiren, G. Taylor, D. Super-power golf. Chicago: Contemporary Books, c1984. 1v.
NOTES: Includes index.

LEVEL: B LANG: Eng ISBN: 0809254654 LC CARD: 84-005025

TECHNIQUES AND SKILLS - PUTTING

Boutcher, S.H. Crews, D.J. Focus of attention and putting performance. Alexandria, Va.: Computer Microfilm International, 1984. 1 microfiche (10 fr.) CONF: American Alliance for Health, Physical Education, Recreation and Dance. Convention (1984 : Anaheim, Calif.).
LEVEL: A LANG: Eng EDRS: ED244940

TECHNIQUES AND SKILLS - SWING

Ballard, J. Compact power. *Golf magazine (Boulder, Co.) 26(1), Jan 1984, 24-29.*
LEVEL: B LANG: Eng SIRC ARTICLE NO: 09503

Ballingall, P. Only two things can go wrong. *Golf monthly (Glasgow, Scotland) 7(10), Oct 1984, 61-63.*
LEVEL: B LANG: Eng SIRC ARTICLE NO: 108824

Crenshaw, B. Toujours plus haut. Apprenez ces techniques simples pour monter tres haut la balle. *Golf europeen (Paris) 167, juil 1984, 46-51.*
NOTES: Traduit de Golf magazine Jun 1984.
LEVEL: B LANG: Fr SIRC ARTICLE NO: 101269

Dennis, L. Pourquoi Greg Norman tape si fort... et si droit. *Golf europeen (Paris) 173, dec 1984, 54-59.*
LEVEL: B LANG: F SIRC ARTICLE NO: 108825

Etes-vous un lanceur ou un frappeur? Jouez-vous plutot comme Nicklaus ou comme Palmer? Testez votre swing, car la reponse explique un grand nombre de vos fautes. *Golf europeen (Paris) 166, juin 1984, 76-81.*
NOTES: Traduit de Golf magazine Feb 1984.
LEVEL: B LANG: Fr SIRC ARTICLE NO: 101273

Graham, D. Augmenter la distance et diminuer les scores. En suivant les pas du double vainqueur du Trophee Lancome. *Golf europeen (Paris) 171, oct (2) 1984, 36-41.*
LEVEL: B LANG: Fr SIRC ARTICLE NO: 107220

Johnson, C. Johnstone, A. Techniques of golf instruction: full swing.
NOTES: In, Owens, D. (ed.), Teaching golf to special populations, New York, Leisure Press, 1984, p. 53-59.
LEVEL: B LANG: Eng GV965 18005

Nicklaus, J. Tout sur le sommet. *Golf europeen (Paris) 168, aout 1984, 40-49.*
NOTES: Traduit de Golf digest Jan, Feb, Mar 1984.
LEVEL: B LANG: Fr SIRC ARTICLE NO: 101281

Owens, D. Johnson, C. Model for golf instruction.
NOTES: In, Owens, D. (ed.), Teaching golf to special populations, New York, Leisure Press, 1984, p. 18-42.
LEVEL: B LANG: Eng GV965 18005

Owens, D. Evolution of the modern golf swing. (Refs: 8)
NOTES: In, Owens, D. (ed.), Teaching golf to special populations, Ne York, Leisure Press, 1984, p. 43-52.
LEVEL: I LANG: Eng GV965 18005

Qui a un swing compact? Etre long et precis? Oui, si l'on monte le club tres loin tout en restant tres compact. Les meilleurs joueurs du monde vous montrent comment. *Golf europeen (Paris) 165(2),*

mai 1984, 84-89.
LEVEL: B LANG: Fr SIRC ARTICLE NO: 101288

Swinguez votre age: juniors, adultes, seniors: chacun devrait avoir un type de swing different. *Golf europeen (Paris) 173, de 1984, 68-73.*
LEVEL: B LANG: Fr SIRC ARTICLE NO: 108826

The no-strain swing. *Golf magazine (Boulder, Colo.) 25(3), Mar 1984, 40-43.*
LEVEL: B LANG: Eng SIRC ARTICLE NO: 093474

Toski, B. Ces swings bizarres ont tout gagne. *Golf europeen (Paris) 165(2), mai 1984, 70-75.*
LEVEL: B LANG: Fr SIRC ARTICLE NO: 101293

TESTING AND EVALUATION

Bissell, K. Special report: golf in the computer age. The future is now. *PGA magazine (Palm Beach Gardens, Fla.) 65(7), Jul 1984, 22-33.*
LEVEL: B LANG: Eng SIRC ARTICLE NO: 101265

Etes-vous fait pour le golf? 20 questions simples pour connaitre le fond de votre vie golfique. *Golf europeen (Paris) 170, oc (1) 1984, 25-26;193.*
LEVEL: B LANG: Fr SIRC ARTICLE NO: 107219

Owens, D. Bunker, L. Gansneder, B. Validation of electronic golf swing analyzer in terms of distance and accuracy measures from field test data. (Refs: 7)*Research quarterly for exercise & sport (Reston, Va.) 55(3), Sept 1984, 305-307.*
LEVEL: I LANG: Eng SIRC ARTICLE NO: 103214

TRAINING AND CONDITIONING

Faits d'hiver. Peut-on jouer chez soi? en principe, non. Mais... *Golf europeen (Paris) 160, janv 1984, 52-54.*
LEVEL: B LANG Fr SIRC ARTICLE NO: 099633

TRAINING AND CONDITIONING - DRILLS

Exercice concentre pour joueur presse. Vous n'avez que trois minutes avant votre depart? Voici cinq exercices-express qui vaudront une seance entiere de practice. *Golf europeen (Paris) 167, juil 1984, 44-45.*
NOTES: Traduit de Golf magazine May 1984.
LEVEL: B LANG: Fr SIRC ARTICLE NO: 101274

Jouez en 'couleurs'. Apprenez a varier vos coups grace aux zones rouge et jaune. *Golf europeen (Paris) 163, avr 1984, 63-64;66-67.*
LEVEL: B LANG: Fr SIRC ARTICLE NO: 099636

Nicklaus, J. The full swing in photos: 14. Try these tips to keep tension out of your body before you swing. *Golf world (London) 23(7), Jul 1984, 134-135.*
LEVEL: B LANG: Eng SIRC ARTICLE NO: 101282

Pelz, D. My 3-minute drill: make the most of your pre-tee-off warmup with this 'scramble' drill. *Golf magazine (Boulder, Colo.) 26(7), Jul 1984, 50-51.*
LEVEL: B LANG: Eng SIRC ARTICLE NO: 101286

TRAINING AND CONDITIONING - STRETCHING AND FLEXIBILITY EXERCISES

La petite revolution du stretching dans le golf. *Golf europeen (Paris) 160, janv 1984, 54-55.*
LEVEL: B LANG: Fr SIRC ARTICL NO: 099641

TRAINING AND CONDITIONING - WEIGHT AND STRENGTH TRAINING

Caporusso, D. Fitness conditioning for golf: strength and endurance of the muscles contributes to your functional ability in golf. *Athletic journal 64(9), Apr 1984, 34-35;80.*
LEVEL: B LANG: Eng SIRC ARTICLE NO: 093466

Get yourself in shape for the new season. *Golf world (London, Eng.) 23(5), May 1984, 146-148;151.*
LEVEL: B LANG: Eng SIRC ARTICLE NO: 101277

WOMEN

Richardson, P.A. Norton, D.J. A stress inventory for women's golf. *Scholastic coach (New York) 54(1), Aug 1984, 60-61;72.*
LEVEL: I LANG: Eng SIRC ARTICLE NO: 099642

GREAT BRITAIN

Burch, E. Community participation: opportunities and provision II. (Refs: 5)*Bulletin of phsycial education (London) 20(2), Summer 1984, 61-67.*
CONF: British Association of Advisers and Lecturers in Physical Education. Congress (64th : 1984 : Cardiff).
LEVEL: I LANG: Eng SIRC ARTICLE NO: 104460

Burnup, C. Community participation - opportunity and provision - I action sport - West Midlands. (Refs: 6)*Bulletin of physical education (London) 20(2), Summer 1984, 54-60.*
CONF: British Association of Advisers and Lecturers in Physical Education. Congress (64th : 1984 : Cardiff).
LEVEL: I LANG: Eng SIRC ARTICLE NO: 104461

State of the sport: we visit the House of Commons to heart MP's debate the subject of health and recreation in Britain. *Sport & leisure (London, Eng.) Sept/Oct 1984, 44-45.*
LEVEL: B LANG: Eng SIRC ARTICLE NO: 108898

Whitehead, N. Spreading the cream. *Sport & leisure (London, Eng.) Sept/Oct 1984, 18-20.*
LEVEL: B LANG: Eng SIRC ARTICLE NO: 108895

HISTORY

Bilsborough, P. The commercialisation of sport: Glasgow 1870-1914. (Refs: 29)*Momentum: a journal of human movement studies (Edinburgh) 9(2), Summer 1984, 7-16.*
LEVEL: I LANG: Eng SIRC ARTICLE NO: 099027

Brailsford, D. 1787: an eighteenth century sporting year. (Refs: 61)*Research quarterly for exercise & sport (Reston, Va.) 55(3), Sept 1984, 217-230.*
ABST: The review of 1787 shows regular contests, particularly in pugilism, cock fighting, horse racing, and cricket, through the summer season. The systematic and popular nature of much sport in 1787 suggests a questioning of any motion that organized sport was a product of nineteeth century industrialization.
LEVEL: A LANG: Eng SIRC ARTICLE NO: 102481

Brailsford, D. Religion and sport in Eighteenth-Century England: 'for the encouragement of piety and virtue, and for the preventing or punishing of vice, profaneness and immorality'. (Refs: 53)*British journal of sports history (London) 1(2), Sept 1984,*

166-183.
LEVEL: A LANG: Eng SIRC ARTICLE NO: 104002

Caron, F. Les sports en Angleterre durant l'epoque contemporaine. (Refs: 7)*Dans, Massicotte, J.P. et Lessard, C. (eds.), Histoire du sport de l'antiquite au XIXe siecle, Sillery, Que., Presses de l'Universite du Quebec, 1984, p. 161-169.*
LEVEL: I LANG: Fr GV571 18971

Cox, R.W. Annual bibliography of publications on the history of sport in Britain, 1982/83. *British journal of sports histor (London) 1(3), Dec 1984, 318-334.*
LEVEL: B LANG: Eng SIRC ARTICLE NO: 105276

Cox, R.W. A survey of literature on the history of sport in Britain. *British journal of sports history (London) 1(1), May 1984, 41-59.*
ABST: This is the first in a series of surveys in which the author reviews articles, anthologies and conference proceedings on the history of sport in Britain. The abstracts are non-evaluative. A list of publications to be surveyed in this series is included. Books are not reviewed.
LEVEL: A LANG: Eng SIRC ARTICLE NO: 108506

James I The Kinges Majesties declaration concerning lawfull sports.
NOTES: In, Riess, S.A. (ed.), The American sporting experience: a historical anthrology of sport in America, New York, Leisure Press, c1984, p. 12-14.
LEVEL: B LANG: Eng GV583 17631

Lidz, F. If brick carrying is your thing, get a load of these olde village games. *Sports illustrated (Chicago, Ill.) 61(19) 22 Oct 1984, 122;126.*
LEVEL: B LANG: Eng SIRC ARTICLE NO: 099344

Lowerson, J. Sport and the Victorian Sunday: the beginnings of middle-class apostasy. (Refs: 80)*British journal of sports history (London) 1(2), Sept 1984, 202-220.*
LEVEL: A LANG: Eng SIRC ARTICLE NO: 104006

Malcolmson, R.W. Sports in society: a historical perspective. (Refs: 32)*British journal of sports history (London) 1(1), Ma 1984, 60-72.*
ABST: This article surveys the changing attitude to sport and recreation in British society. The main focus is on the 17th and 18th century: the Puritan misgivings about sport giving way to a more relaxed post-Restauration attitude, and traditional popular recreations being undermined by people in authority towards the end of the 18th century. The author underlines the importance of always looking at sport and recreation in the context of society as a whole.
LEVEL: A LANG: Eng SIRC ARTICLE NO: 108507

Mangan, J.A. Oars and the man: pleasure and purpose in Victorian and Edwardian Cambridge. (Refs: 143)*British journal of sports history (London) 1(3), Dec 1984, 245-271.*
ABST: This article focuses on athleticism in Jesus College, Cambridge, during the Victorian and Edwardian eras (1875-1914). The author also discusses athleticism in the ancient Universities of Oxford and Cambridge in the same period.
LEVEL: A LANG: Eng SIRC ARTICLE NO: 105180

Park, R.J. British sports and pastimes in San Francisco, 1848-1900. (Refs: 54)*British journal of sports history (London) 1(3), Dec 1984, 300-317.*
ABST: This study focuses on the recreational and sporting activities from 1848 to 1900 of English, Scottish and Irish immigrants living in San

Francisco.
LEVEL: A LANG: Eng SIRC ARTICLE NO: 105277

Rubinstein, D. Sport and the sociologist 1890-1914. (Refs: 53)*British journal of sports history (London) 1(1), May 1984, 14-24.*
ABST: The author examines the work of sociologists in Britain prior to World War I. Mass spectator sports were largely a new phenomena and were not yet being examined by social observers. The sociological studies of this time witnessed the great expansion in spectator sport and recreation activities. However, the brevity in which such topics were treated indicates that the sociologist of the day had little interest in such matters.
LEVEL: A LANG: Eng SIRC ARTICLE NO: 108504

Ruehl, J.K. Religion and amusement in Sixteenth- and Seventeenth-Century England: 'time might be better bestowed, and beside wee see sin acted'. (Refs: 322)*British journal of sports history (London) 1(2), Sept 1984, 125-165.*
LEVEL: A LANG: Eng SIRC ARTICLE NO: 104010

Vamplew, W. Close of play: career termination in English professional sport 1870-1914. (Refs: 54)*Canadian journal of histor of sport/Revue canadienne de l'histoire des sports (Windsor) 15(1), May 1984, 64-79.*
ABST: This paper is a study of the causes of career cessation, the career lengths, and the post-playing problems of English professional athletes in horse racing, football, soccer, and cricket for the years 1870-1914. Athletes had very little job security because their contracts were usually only one year in length or, as in the case of jockeys, were nonexistent. There were three main causes for a career to end: injury, usurpation by competing athletes, and misbehaviour of the athlete, such as drunkeness, breaking club rules, and criticizing superiors. Football players had the shortest careers, half lasting only one year, while nearly half of the rugby players lasted over three seasons. Cricket was comparable to rugby in that approximately 50 percent of players played for over 3 years. But the upper limit of a career for cricket was 20 years or more, while rugby players rarely lasted over 12 years. Only 40 percent of jockeys became licensed and of these only about 30 percent lasted for over 3 years of a licensed career, although 8 percent lasted for over 20 years. Little is known of the post-play lives of the athletes except that most were forgotten, many went broke and with poor chances of employment, particularly if injured, and only a few remained in the sport as coaches, trainers and assistants.
LEVEL: A LANG: Eng SIRC ARTICLE NO: 108316

GROWTH AND DEVELOPMENT

Berenshtein, G.F. Nurbaeva, M.N. Medvedev, P.A. Karavaev, A.G. K otsenke uspevaemosti i fizicheskogo razvitiia selskikh shkolnikov. (Evaluation of the educational achievement and pysical development of rural schoolchildren.) *Gigiena i sanitariia (Moscow) 10, Oct 1984, 72-73.*
LEVEL: I LANG: Rus

Sodhi, H.S. Saini, K. Physical growth and performance of Punjabi males aged 13 to 16 years. (Refs: 5)*SNIPES journal (Patiala, India) 7(4), Oct 1984, 11-21.*

ABST: The purpose of this study was to assess the role of maturity and physical growth in performance. The anthropometric measurements, performance and jumping ability, and maturity status of 234 Punjabi males, age 13 to 16 years, were recorded. The horizontal and vertical jumps constituted the jumping ability tests. The maturity was recorded with the help of pubic hair rating. Findings indicated that the maturity status of the children influenced their performance and physical growth. The early maturers performed better than the late maturers.
LEVEL: A LANG: Eng SIRC ARTICLE NO: 171611

Taylor, W.N. Sports medicine forum: the perils of HGH. *Strength & health (York, Pa.) 52(5), Aug/Sept 1984, 62-64.*
LEVEL: LANG: Eng SIRC ARTICLE NO: 173479

GYMNASTICS

Eckert, S. Computers in the gym. *International gymnast (Santa Monica, Calif.) 26(2), Feb 1984, 84.*
LEVEL: B LANG: Eng SIR ARTICLE NO: 095049

Freifeld, K. Engelmayer, S. How to watch 'another perfect 10': here's all you need to know to stay one step ahead of the wraps, giants, layouts and somies. *Health (New York) 16(3), Mar 1984, 52;55;57-58.*
LEVEL: B LANG: Eng SIRC ARTICLE NO: 099660

Gerber, E. Gymnastique et sport - similitudes et dissemblances. *Macolin (Suisse) 8, aout 1984, 14-15.*
NOTES: Traduction de, Michel Burnand.
LEVEL: B LANG: Fr SIRC ARTICLE NO: 101302

Gillot, L. Galceran, R. Lutte et gymnastique. Paris: Hachette, 1984. 95 p.
LEVEL: B LANG: Fr

Hassan, P. Pan Am clinic. *Australian gymnast (Melbourne, Aust.) 10(19), Oct/Nov 1984, Coaches suppl. 7-8.*
LEVEL: B LANG: Eng SIRC ARTICLE NO: 173115

Magakian, A. Aspects historiques et structurels dans le monde. *Revue de l'education physique (Liege) 24(3), 1984, 9-11.*
LEVEL: B LANG: Fr SIRC ARTICLE NO: 104768

Magakian, A. Synthese sur le symposium. *Revue de l'education physique (Liege) 24(3), 1984, 61-62.*
LEVEL: B LANG: Fr SIRC ARTICLE NO: 104769

Sands, B. Conklin, M. Everybody's gymnastics book. New York: Charles Scribner's Sons, c1984. 211 p. : ill.
LEVEL: I LANG: E ISBN: 0-684-18091-X LC CARD: 84-1276 GV461 18116

ADMINISTRAITON

Ellis, P.M. Corn, R.W. Using bivalent integer programming to select teams for intercollegiate women's gymnastics competition (Refs: 3)*Interfaces (Providence, R.I.) 14(3), 1984, 41-46.*
LEVEL: B LANG: Eng SIRC ARTICLE NO: 096691

Jost-Relyveld, A. Sempe, M. Morphologie comparee de jeunes gymnastes et skieurs de haut niveau. (Refs: 4)*Cinesiologie (Paris) 95, mai/juin 1984, 241-247.*
RESUME: Le but de cette etude consiste a comparer les mensurations de 45 filles gymnastes, 11 etudiantes de gymnastique rythmique sportive, 9

skieuses alpines juniors, 35 garcons gymnastes et 8 skieurs de fond juniors. Les resultats indiquent: 1) des retards pubertaires chez les gymnastes comparativement aux autres groupes et 2) un developpement normal chez les sujets pratiquant la gymnastique rythmique sportive en classe.
LEVEL: A LANG: Fr SIRC ARTICLE NO: 098141

Malmberg, E. Implementing the systems approach: (the key to our gymnastics future?). (Refs: 1)*International gymnast (Santa Monica) 26(8), Aug 1984, 30.*
LEVEL: B LANG: Eng SIRC ARTICLE NO: 098145

Saunders, C. A team that refused to die. A team program ends because someone doesn't consider it worthwhile, not because it doesn't have enough financial backing. *Coaching review 7, Jan/Feb 1984, 31-32.*
LEVEL: B LANG: Eng SIRC ARTICLE NO: 092162

Sjursen, H. End of an era: William Buffa retires from YMCA. Bill always felt strongly about the philosophy of amateur sports and the voluntary time and effort contributed to gymnastics by former gymnasts and other participants. *International gymnast (Santa Monica) 26(8), Aug 1984, 48-49;55.*
LEVEL: B LANG: Eng SIRC ARTICLE NO: 098152

Success in gymnastics - a leap in the right direction. *Australian gymnast: coaches supplement (Victoria, Aust.) 10(16), Dec 1983/Jan 1984, 3-8.*
LEVEL: B LANG: Eng SIRC ARTICLE NO: 096697

ANTHROPOMETRY

Auberge, T. Zenny, J.C. Duvallet, A. Godefroy, D. Horreard, P. Chevrot, A. Etude de la maturation osseuse et des lesions osteo-articulaires des sportifs de haut niveau. A propos de 105 cas. (Bone maturation and osteoarticular lesions in top level sportsmen. Apropos of 105 cases.) *Journal de radiologie (Paris) 65(8/9), aout/sept 1984, 555-561.*
LEVEL: A LANG: Fr SIRC ARTICLE NO: 107228

Barlett, H.L. Mance, M.J. Buskirk, E.R. Body composition and expiratory reserve volume in female gymnasts and runners. (Refs 20)*Medicine and science in sports and exercise (Indianapolis) 16(3), June 1984, 311-315.*
ABST: Previous research in this laboratory demonstrated a reduction in expiratory reserve volume of the lungs (ERV) with increasing body fatness (percent F, by densitometry). The present study was done to determine if smaller ERV values could be demonstrated in lean female athletes with greater than normal upperbody muscle development. Expiratory reserve volume, vital capacity (VC), and segmental body volumes by densitometry were measured in members of two collegiate women's teams - gymnastics (G) (N, 10) and track (R) (N, 10). The runners provided a control group by being similar to gymnasts in age, weight, and body fatness, but they did not engage in upper-body weight training or gymnastic exercises. The two groups were not significantly different in body weight or percent F, but R subjects were taller. Expiratory reserve volume was significantly less in the gymnats as compared to the runners. All other lung capacities as volumes were comparable in both groups.
LEVEL: A LANG: Eng SIRC ARTICLE NO: 108604

Leglise, M. Quelques propos sur la croissance du gymnaste de haut niveau. *Revue de l'education physique (Liege) 24(3), 1984 47-48.*
LEVEL: I LANG: Fr SIRC ARTICLE NO: 104767

Moffat, R.J. Surina, B. Golden, B. Ayres, N. Body composition and physiological characteristics of female high school gymnasts. (Refs: 24)*Research quarterly for exercise & sport (Reston, Va.) 55(1), Mar 1984, 80-84.*
ABST: The purpose of this investigation was to compare the body composition, physical dimensions and maximal physiological responses of 13 female high school gymnasts to 13 non-athletic female control subjects from the same school. The gymnasts had similar skeletal structure when compared to the non-athletic controls. However the non-athletic females had less lean tissue and more body fat indicated by densiometry and anthropometry. Two female gymnasts exhibited higher VO2 max. values and performed better on tests to estimate anaerobic capacity power output than the controls. Some comparisons to other studies on female gymnasts are also made.
LEVEL: A LANG: Eng SIRC ARTICLE NO: 096693

Peltenburg, A.L. Erich, W.B.M. Bernink, M.J.E. Zonderland, M.L. Huisveld, I.A. Biological maturation, body composition, and growth of female gymnasts and control groups of schoolgirls and girl swimmers, aged 8 to 14 years: a cross-sectional survey of 1064 girls. (Refs: 21)*International journal of sports medicine 5(1), Feb 1984, 36-42.*
ABST: The results of this study indicate that the onset of puberty and menarche was delayed in the gymnasts by about 1 or 2 years compared to schoolgirls and girl swimmers. Gymnasts were observed to be smaller than the schoolgirls and swimmers; this observation became more pronounced after the age of 10 years. The gymnasts were leaner than the schoolgirl and swimmers. The relationships between body composition and biological maturation are discussed.
LEVEL: A LANG: Eng SIRC ARTICLE NO: 093499

Peltenburg, A.L. Erich, W.B.M. Zonderland, M.L. Bernink, M.J.E. VanDenBrande, J.L. Huisveld, I.A. A retrospective growth study of female gymnasts and girl swimmers. (Refs: 13)*International journal of sports medicine (Stuttgart) 5(5), Oct 1984, 262-267.*
ABST: The aim of this investigation was to retrospectively evaluate growth patterns of different groups of gymnasts as compared to schoolgirls and girl swimmers from 1 until 11 years of age. The differences in body height between the groups of sports participants and schoolgirls in the prepubertal period appeared to be mainly based on the genetic growth regulation and seemed to be largely dependent in the gymnastic groups on inheritance of the mothers' height. Significant differences existed in weight as percentage of normal weight for height between the gymnasts and the swimmers.
LEVEL: A LANG: Eng SIRC ARTICLE NO: 104774

Satwanti Kapoor, A.K. Bhalla, R. Singh, I.P. Study of the distribution pattern of fat in male gymnasts. (Refs: 8) *Anthropologischer Anzieger (Stuttgart) 42(2), Jun 1984, 131-136.*
LEVEL: A LANG: Eng SIRC ARTICLE NO: 104776

BIOGRAPHY AND AUTOBIOGRAPHY

Deford, F. Rising to great heights: sportsman and sportswoman of the year. (Edwin Moses and Mary Lou Retton) *Sports illustrated (Los Angeles, Calif.) 61(28), 24-31 Dec 1984, 32-34;36;38;43;44.*
LEVEL: B LANG: Eng SIRC ARTICLE NO: 103218

Freifeld, K. Engelmayer, S. Who to watch, the next Nadia? (Mary Lou Retton) *Health (New York) 16(3), Mar 1984, 48-49;52.*
NOTES: Second in a six-part series: 'Health's Olympic watch'.
LEVEL: B LANG: Eng SIRC ARTICLE NO: 099659

Nikolaidis, Z. Natalia Yurchenko: 'my way to the top'. *International gymnast (Santa Monica, Calif.) 26(4), Apr 1984, 74-75.*
LEVEL: B LANG: Eng SIRC ARTICLE NO: 099670

Nikolaidis, Z. Meet Bulgaria's best. (Boriana Stoyanova, Zoya Grantcharova) *International gymnast (Santa Monica, Calif.) 26(6), Jun 1984, 72-73.*
LEVEL: B LANG: Eng SIRC ARTICLE NO: 099671

Ottum, B. It's up to you, Mary Lou. Little Mary Lou Retton has vaulted so high that she may well do what no U.S. woman gymnast has ever done, win an Olympic medal - perhaps even a gold. *Sports illustrated (Chicago, Ill.) 61(4), 18 Jul 1984, 462-466;468;471-472;475-476.*
NOTES: Special preview: the 1984 Olympics.
LEVEL: B LANG: Eng SIRC ARTICLE NO: 096695

Wilson, S. West Virginia pixie: a possible '10' at 16. (Mary Lou Retton) *Olympian (Colorado Springs, Colo.) 11(1), Jun 1984 4-5.*
LEVEL: B LANG: Eng SIRC ARTICLE NO: 101315

BIOMECHANICS

Bollen, J. Effets des contractions musculaires executees pendant le vol libre et leur utilisation dans l'execution des salto et des vrilles. *Revue de l'education physique (Liege) 24(3), 1984, 29-35.*
LEVEL: I LANG: Fr SIRC ARTICLE NO: 104757

Hery, G. Parabolas. *International gymnast (Santa Monica) 26(8), Aug 1984, 56.*
LEVEL: I LANG: Eng SIRC ARTICLE NO: 098139

Hery, G. Movement (initiation, control, efficiency). *International gymnast (Santa Monica) 26(7), Jul 1984, 58-59.*
LEVEL: LANG: Eng SIRC ARTICLE NO: 098140

Hery, G. Principals of movement. *International gymnast (Santa Monica, Calif.) 26(6), Jun 1984, 70-71.*
LEVEL: I LANG: Eng SIRC ARTICLE NO: 099663

Hery, G. What makes us somersault? *International gymnast (Santa Monica, Calif.) 26(9), Sept 1984, 58.*
LEVEL: I LANG: Eng SIRC ARTICLE NO: 101304

Hery, G. Twisting. *International gymnast (Santa Monica, Calif.) 26(10), Oct 1984, 52-53.*
LEVEL: I LANG: Eng SIRC ARTICLE NO: 101305

Hery, G. Movement (initiation, control, efficiency). *New Zealand gymnast (New Plymouth, N.Z.) 9(6), Nov 1984, 10-12.*
LEVEL: I LANG: Eng SIRC ARTICLE NO: 103219

GYMNASTICS (continued)

CERTIFICATION

Kinsman, T. Coaching certification manual. Level 3 women. Vanier, Ont.: Canadian Gymnastics Federation, c1984. 335 p. : ill. (National Coaching Certification Program.)
CORP: Canadian Gymnastics Federation.
NOTES: Includes bibliographies.
LEVEL: I LANG: Eng ISBN: 0-920611-00-1 GV464 19001

CLUBS AND TEAMS

Dorrington, J. Dite, W. Some impressions of gymnastics in the United States of America. *Pelops 5, Feb 1984, 27-30.*
ABST: brief analysis of gymnastics programs in the United States and Australia. The programs, coaching education, and resources of the National Academy of Gymnastics at Eugene, and the Southern California Acrobatic Team at Huntington Beach in California are outlined. Recommendations are made for future developments in Australia.
LEVEL: I LANG: Eng SIRC ARTICLE NO: 098132

Going with what you've got: cramped facilities won't stand in the way of progress for this small New Brunswick gymnastics club *Coaching review (Ottawa, Ont.) 7, Nov/Dec 1984, 37.*
LEVEL: B LANG: Eng SIRC ARTICLE NO: 099662

COACHING

Fenwick, J. Bela Karolyi: 'This sport deserves to be respected'. *International gymnast (Santa Monica, Calif.) 26(2), Feb 1984, 46-47;73;80.*
LEVEL: B LANG: Eng SIRC ARTICLE NO: 095051

Handling the team. *Grasp (Leicestershire, Eng.) 3(12), 1984, 149-151.*
LEVEL: B LANG: Eng SIRC ARTICLE NO: 173123

Sands, B. Coaching women's gymnastics. Champaign, Ill.: Human Kinetics Publishers, c1984. xvi, 264 p. : ill.
NOTES: Bibliography: p. 260-264.
LEVEL: I LANG: Eng ISBN: 0-931250-58-7 LC CARD: 83-083163 GV464 18995

Weiss, G. Marketing: reference point tumbling. *International gymnast (Santa Monica, Calif.) 26(1), Jan 1984, 29.*
LEVEL: B LANG: Eng SIRC ARTICLE NO: 095066

COUNTRIES AND REGIONS

Forbes, W. A look into Bulgarian gymnastics. *Australian gymnast (Melbourne, Aust.) 10(19), Oct/Nov 1984, Coaches suppl. 1-3*
LEVEL: B LANG: Eng SIRC ARTICLE NO: 173113

Jarvis, F.G. Profile of an 'overnight' success: fifty years of struggle and dedication lay the groundwork for gymnastics Olympic gold. *Winged foot (New York) 95(9), Sept 1984, 25-28.*
LEVEL: B LANG: Eng SIRC ARTICLE NO: 099666

Kaplan, R.D. Ceausescu looks West but acts East: Romanian gymnastics. *New republic (Washington) 191(25), 1984, 10-12.*
LEVEL: B LANG: Eng SIRC ARTICLE NO: 104765

Parker, D. 'Organizational discipline': gymnastics, Chinese-style. *International gymnast magazine (Santa Monica, Calif.) 26 (12), Dec 1984, 56-57.*
LEVEL: B LANG: Eng SIRC ARTICLE NO: 109314

ECONOMICS

Raissman, R. U.S. gymnastics face endorsement flap. *Advertising age (Chicago, Ill.) 55(54), 27 Aug 1984, 1;66.*
LEVEL: B LANG: Eng SIRC ARTICLE NO: 099673

EQUIPMENT

Charles, L. Siskova, B. Gymnastique sportive feminine et innovation technologique. *Dans, Culture technique no. 13, Neuilly-sur-Seine, France, Centre de Recherche sur la Culture Technique, c1984, p. 274-283.*
LEVEL: A LANG: Fr RC1235 20096

EQUIPMENT - MAINTENANCE

Care of your equipment. *New Zealand gymnast (New Plymouth, N.Z.) 9(2), May 1984, 6-7.*
LEVEL: B LANG: Eng SIRC ARTICLE NO: 108916

HISTORY

Barney, R.K. Notes, documents, and queries: America's first Turnverein: commentary in favor of Louisville, Kentucky. *Journa of sport history (Seattle, Wash.) 11(1), Spring 1984, 134-137.*
LEVEL: I LANG: Eng SIRC ARTICLE NO: 096689

Koivusalo, I. Gymnastics as a subject in Finnish secondary schools between 1843 and 1917. (Refs: 15)*In, Ilmarinen, M. (ed.) et al., Sport and International Understanding: proceedings of the congress held in Helsinki, Finland, July 7-10, 1982, Berlin, Springer-Verlag, 1984, p. 330-334.*
CONF: Congress on Sport and International Understanding (1982 : Helsinki).
LEVEL: I LANG: Eng GV706.8 18979

INJURIES AND ACCIDENTS

Auberge, T. Zenny, J.C. Duvallet, A. Godefroy, D. Horreard, P. Chevrot, A. Etude de la maturation osseuse et des lesions osteo-articulaires des sportifs de haut niveau. A propos de 105 cas. (Bone maturation and osteoarticular lesions in top level sportsmen. Apropos of 105 cases.) *Journal de radiologie (Paris) 65(8/9), aout/sept 1984, 555-561.*
LEVEL: A LANG: Fr SIRC ARTICLE NO: 107228

Colby, J. Fricker, P. Can we prevent back injuries to elite women gymnasts? (Refs: 3)*Sports science & medicine quarterly 1(1), Jun 1984, 13-16.*
ABST: Describes a two year study of women's artistic gymnasts at the Australian Institute of Sport, which analysed injuries and in particular back injuries. The most common back injuries were identified as spondylolysis (fracture or stress fracture of the back) spondylolisthesis (shifting of one vertebra on another producing malalignment of the spine), Scheuermanns disease, ligament sprains and muscle sprains. In order to prevent back injuries, a back exercise program was introduced into the Institute during the second year. The authors conclude that this program had a positive effect in preventing back injuries.
LEVEL: I LANG: Eng SIRC ARTICLE NO: 098131

Colby, J. Fricker, P. Can we prevent back injuries to elite women gymnasts? (Refs: 3)*Australian gymnast (Melbourne, Aust.) (19), Oct/Nov 1984, Coaches suppl. 4-5.*
NOTES: Reprinted from, Sports Science and

Medicine Quarterly.
LEVEL: I LANG: Eng SIRC ARTICLE NO: 173114

Deroanne, R. Delhez, L. Loverius, J.P. Hypotheses concernant l'origine des lombalgies chez les gymnastes sportifs. (Refs: 7) *Revue de l'education physique (Liege) 24(3), 1984, 37-46.*
LEVEL: I LANG: Fr SIRC ARTICLE NO: 104762

Franchimont, P. Crielaard, J.-M. Le poignet douloureux du gymnaste. *Revue de l'education physique (Liege) 24(3), 1984, 49-50.*
LEVEL: B LANG: Fr SIRC ARTICLE NO: 104763

Hooper, J. Gymnastic injuries. *Australian family physician (Sydney) 13(7), Jul 1984, 508-509.*
LEVEL: B LANG: Eng

Huurman, W.W. Shelton, G.L. Walsh, W.M. Overuse injuries of the knee and spine in girls' gymnastics. (Refs: 13)*Clinics in sports medicine (Philadelphia) 3(4), Oct 1984, 829-850.*
NOTES: Symposium on the athletic woman.
ABST: Overuse injuries of the extensor mechanism of the knee and the spine continue to plague those caring for the young female gymnast. Patellofemoral disorders can frequently be controlled by rehabilitative exercises and bracing. Spine injuries may require rest, casting, or, occasionally, surgery.
LEVEL: A LANG: Eng SIRC ARTICLE NO: 101307

Milhan, D. Rohan, J. Limitation of movement due to hip ligaments and implications for teaching exercise and dance. (Refs: 6) *Florida journal of health, physical education, recreation and dance (Gainsville, Fla.) 22(2), May 1984, 5-6.*
LEVEL: I LANG: Eng SIRC ARTICLE NO: 095946

Minnesota - student injured on vaulting horse sues for damages. *Sports and the courts (Winston-Salem, N.C.) 5(1), Winter 1984 2.*
LEVEL: B LANG: Eng SIRC ARTICLE NO: 095063

Peavy, B. Gymnastics. *In, Adams, S.H. (ed.), et al., Catastrophic injuries in sports: avoidance strategies, Salinas, Calif. Coyote Press, c1984, p. 109-111.*
LEVEL: B LANG: Eng RD97 19088

Pica, R. Injury prevention through dance training. *International gymnast (Santa Monica, Calif.) 26(3), Mar 1984, 58;83.*
LEVEL: B LANG: Eng SIRC ARTICLE NO: 099672

Ryan, A.J. Gymnasts require full recovery after injury. *Physician and sportsmedicine (Minneapolis, Minn.) 12(9), Sept 1984, 32.*
LEVEL: B LANG: Eng SIRC ARTICLE NO: 185095

Whiteside, J.A. Kalenak, A. Gymnasts' injuries of the hip and leg. (Refs: 3)*Sports medicine digest (Van Nuys, Calif.) 6(8), Aug 1984, 1-3.*
LEVEL: B LANG: Eng SIRC ARTICLE NO: 105895

JUDGING

An aid for the referee judge? *Australian gymnast (Victoria, Aust.) 10(17), Apr 1984, 22;21.*
LEVEL: B LANG: Eng SIRC ARTICLE NO: 098129

Criley, D. Where do we go from here? *International gymnast (Santa Monica, Calif.) 26(9), Sept 1984, 62.*
LEVEL: B LANG: En SIRC ARTICLE NO: 101300

From the F.I.G. - OV/RV bonus points. *Australian gymnast (Victoria, Aust.) 10(17), Apr 1984, 14-19.*
NOTES: Reprinted courtesy of the Federation

internationale de gymnastique.
LEVEL: B LANG: Eng SIRC ARTICLE NO: 098135

Hardy, L. Assessing the efficiency of gymnastics judging. (Refs: 8)*Gymnast (Bicester, Oxford) Jan 1984, 18-20.*
LEVEL: I LANG: Eng SIRC ARTICLE NO: 095057

Pflughoeft, M. Gymnastics judging: fatigue, frustration, confusion. *International gymnast magazine (Santa Monica, Calif.) 2 (12), Dec 1984, 40.*
LEVEL: B LANG: Eng SIRC ARTICLE NO: 109318

Wanvig, S. Judging gymnastics: the subjective nature of the sport makes it one of the most difficult to judge. *Referee (Franksville, Wis.) 9(7), Jul 1984, 29-31.*
LEVEL: B LANG: Eng SIRC ARTICLE NO: 101314

JUVENILE LITERATURE

Prestidge, J. Prestidge, P. Warren, M.
Gymnastics. Vero Beach, Fl.: Rourke Corp., 1984. 1v.
NOTES: Includes index.
LEVEL: LANG: Eng ISBN: 0865927685 LC CARD: 83-024652

MEDICINE

Ankle taping. *International gymnast (Santa Monica, Calif.) 26(6), Jun 1984, 55.*
LEVEL: B LANG: Eng SIRC ARTICLE NO: 099649

Calabrese, L.H. Weight control in dance and gymnastics. Chicago: Teach'em Inc., 1984?. 1 sound cassette (Audio cassette series on sports medicine: Sportsmedicine for female athletes, SM-40.)
NOTES: Cassettes recorded and produced by Teach'em Inc. in cooperation with the Physician and Sportsmedicine.
LEVEL: I LANG: Eng

First aid guide. *Gymnast (Slough, Eng.) Jul/Aug 1984, 12-14.*
LEVEL: B LANG: Eng SIRC ARTICLE NO: 101301

Singer, K.M. Roy, S.P. Osteochondrosis of the humeral capitellum. (Refs: 29)*American journal of sports medicine (Baltimore, Md.) 12(5), Sept/Oct 1984, 351-360.*
ABST: Seven cases of osteochondrosis of the capitellum occurring in five high performance female gymnasts between the ages of 11 and 13 are presented. Two of the patients were treated by surgical excision of the loose osteochondral fragment in three elbows. Four of the five gymnasts, including the two who underwent surgical treatment, were able to return to full workouts without recurrence of symptoms within the 3 year followup. A survey of 37 actively competing gymnasts at a nationally known gymnastics academy was performed, including a detailed history and physical examination and radiographic examination. No other cases of osteochondrosis were detected.
LEVEL: A LANG: Eng SIRC ARTICLE NO: 104777

Sonneville, F. Niquet, G. Gymnastique aerobic. Aspects medico-sportifs. (Aerobic gymnastics. Medico-athletic aspects.) *LARC medical (Lille) 4(6), juin/juil 1984, 384-387.*
LEVEL: I LANG: Fr SIRC ARTICLE NO: 104779

NUTRITION

Moffatt, R.J. Dietary status of elite female high school gymnasts: inadequacy of vitamin and mineral intake. *Journal of the American Dietetic Association (Chicago) 84(11), Nov 1984, 1361-1363.*
LEVEL: A LANG: Eng

Ottaway, P.B. Nutrition for gymnasts. (Refs: 8)*Gymnast (Slough, Eng.) Jun 1984, 18-19.*
LEVEL: I LANG: Eng SIRC ARTICLE NO 101311

Ottaway, P.B. Nutrition for gymnasts. *Gymnast (London) May 1984, 18-19.*
LEVEL: B LANG: Eng SIRC ARTICLE NO: 104773

PERCEPTUAL MOTOR PROCESSES

Baiverlin, A. Olislagers, P. Apprentissage moteur et amenagement du milieu. Exemple de l'acquisition d'une habilete motrice en gymnastique sportive. (Refs: 20)*Revue de l'education physique (Liege) 24(3), 1984, 13-22.*
LEVEL: A LANG: Fr SIRC ARTICLE NO: 104755

PHYSICAL FITNESS

Gymnastique avec ballon gonflable. *Frauenturnen/Gymnastique feminine (Magglingen) 21, 1 Nov 1984, 13.*
LEVEL: B LANG: Fr SIR ARTICLE NO: 173405

PHYSIOLOGY

Sinyakov, A.F. Restoration of work capacity of gymnasts. *Soviet sports review (Escondido, Calif.) 19(3), Sept 1984, 105-109.*
NOTES: Translated from, Gymnastika 1, 1982, 48-51.
LEVEL: I LANG: Eng SIRC ARTICLE NO: 103226

Zonderland, M.L. Erich, W.B.M. Peltenburg, A.L. Havekes, L. Bernink, M.J.E. Huisveld, I.A.
Apolipoprotein and lipid profiles in young female athletes. (Refs: 34)*International journal of sports medicine (Stuttgart, FRG) 5(2), Apr 1984, 78-82.*
ABST: The apolipoprotein and lipid profiles were investigated in 22 female gymnasts, 20 girl swimmers, and 12 controls. The average age of all groups was about 12 years, and the girls were matched for sexual development. The gymnasts appeared to have the highest level of HDL cholesterol and the highest HDL cholesterol / total cholesterol, HDL cholesterol / LDL cholesterol and HDL cholesterol/apo A-I ratios in comparison to both the swimmers and the control group. The swimmers had the highest level of apo A-I, but a lipid profile similar to that of the controls. It is concluded that in children, as in adults, regular physical activity affect the lipid and apolipoprotein profiles. In addition, it appears that the apolipoproteins discriminate between trained and nontrained subjects as well as (apo B) or better (apo A-I) than the lipid components of the corresponding lipoproteins (LDL cholesterol or HDL cholesterol).
LEVEL: A LANG: Eng SIRC ARTICLE NO: 108522

PSYCHOLOGY

Arnold, E. Patience is a virtue. *Gymnast (Slough, Eng.) Jul/Aug 1984, 26.*
LEVEL: B LANG: Eng SIRC ARTICLE NO: 101298

Hamilton, T. The right brain for gymnastics. *International gymnast (Santa Monica, Calif.) 26(2), Feb 1984, 78-79.*
LEVEL: LANG: Eng SIRC ARTICLE NO: 095056

Massimo, J. Fear. *International gymnast (Santa Monica) 26(5), May 1984, 50;56.*
LEVEL: B LANG: Eng SIRC ARTICLE NO: 098146

Massimo, J. A coach's guide to: non-verbal communication. *International gymnast (Santa Monica, Calif.) 26(10), Oct 1984, 56-57.*
LEVEL: B LANG: Eng SIRC ARTICLE NO: 101309

Weiss, M.S. Parent burnout...(Mom and Dad have given up). *International gymnast (Santa Monica) 26(7), Jul 1984, 44-45;56.*
LEVEL: B LANG: Eng SIRC ARTICLE NO: 098158

PSYCHOLOGY - MENTAL TRAINING

Makarova, V.I. Dmitrieva, E. The use of ideo-motor preparation of gymnasts 10-12 years of age. *Soviet sports review (Escondido, Calif.) 19(4), Dec 1984, 176-178.*
NOTES: Translated from, Gymnastika 1, 1983, 38-39.
LEVEL: I LANG: Eng SIRC ARTICLE NO: 104770

PSYCHOPHYSIOLOGY

Olislagers, P. Lateralite du gymnaste et sens preferentiel individuel de rotation longitudinale. (Refs: 21)*Revue de l'education physique (Liege) 24(3), 1984, 23-28.*
LEVEL: A LANG: Fr SIRC ARTICLE NO: 104772

SOCIAL PSYCHOLOGY

Massimo, J. The decision to quit. *International gymnast (Santa Monica, Calif.) 26(1), Jan 1984, 56-57;77.*
LEVEL: B LANG: Eng SIRC ARTICLE NO: 095061

SOCIOLOGY

Edwards, S.W. Gordin, R.D. Henschen, K.P.
Sex-role orientations of female NCAA championship gymnasts. (Refs: 6)*Perceptual and motor skills (Missoula, Mont.) 58(2), Apr 1984, 625-626.*
LEVEL: I LANG: Eng SIRC ARTICLE NO: 095050

Sequera, S. A comparison of female Venezuelan and United States gymnasts in anthropometric measures, forward flexibility, an upper body strength. Eugene, Ore.: Microform Publications, University of Oregon, 1984. 1 microfiche : negative, ill. ; 11 x 15 cm.
NOTES: Thesis (M.S.) - Springfield College, 1982; (vi, 45 leaves); includes bibliography.
LEVEL: A LANG: Eng UO84 232

Wasterlain, M. La gymnastique sportive dans les societes occidentales. *Revue de l'education physique (Liege) 24(3), 1984, 4-7.*
LEVEL: B LANG: Fr SIRC ARTICLE NO: 104782

GYMNASTICS (continued)

SPORTING EVENTS

Creagh, T.L. Junior gymnastic competitions. *New Zealand gymnast (New Plymouth, N.Z.) 9(2)*, May 1984, 8-9.
LEVEL: B LANG: Eng SIRC ARTICLE NO: 108917

Cumiskey, F.J. A history of gymnastics: the Olympiads and the intervening years: chapter XV. *International gymnast (Santa Monica, Calif.) 26(3)*, Mar 1984, 17-28.
LEVEL: B LANG: Eng SIRC ARTICLE NO: 099655

Cumiskey, F.J. A history of gymnastics: the Olympiads and the intervening years: chapter XVI. *International gymnast (Santa Monica, Calif.) 26(4)*, Apr 1984, 17-28.
LEVEL: B LANG: Eng SIRC ARTICLE NO: 099656

Gaehler, J. Gymnastics at the Olympic Games. Part IX. *World gymnastics (Milan) 3(20)*, 1984, 48.
LEVEL: B LANG: Eng SIRC ARTICLE NO: 102099

Goehler, J. Gymnastics at the Olympic Games. Part VII. *World gymnastics (Budapest, Hungary) 18*, 1984, 45.
LEVEL: B LANG: Eng SIRC ARTICLE NO: 099661

Goehler, J. Gymnastics at the Olympic Games. Part X. *World gymnastics (Budapest, Hungary) 21*, 1984, 33.
LEVEL: B LANG: En SIRC ARTICLE NO: 172569

Gohler, J. Gymnastics at the Olympic Games: Part VIII. *World gymnastics (Budapest, Hungary) 2(19)*, 1984, 48.
LEVEL: B LANG: Eng SIRC ARTICLE NO: 098137

TEACHING

Bean, D. Themes and variations: essentials for planning. (Refs: 2)*Runner (Edmonton) 22(3)*, Fall/Winter 1984, 18-20.
LEVEL B LANG: Eng SIRC ARTICLE NO: 104756

Branda, A.H. Vickers, J.N. The implementation of the Canadian Gymnastics Development Program by direct and indirect teaching methodologies. *CAHPER journal/Revue de l'ACSEPR (Ottawa) 50(5)*, May/Jun 1984, 20-22;25.
LEVEL: I LANG: Eng SIRC ARTICLE NO: 096690

Carroll, M.E. Garner, D.R. Gymnastics 7-11: a lesson-by-lesson approach. London: Falmer Press, c1984. 183 p. : ill.
LEVEL: LANG: Eng ISBN: 0-905273-43-5 GV461 18003

Johns, D. A teaching guide to gymnastic skills for women. El Cerrito, Calif.: Leisure Press, 1984. 1v.
LEVEL: B LANG: Eng ISBN: 0880110899 LC CARD: 84-012597

Robe, J. Comparaison entre trois methodes d'apprentissage pour le pique poirier, le kip nuque et le kip tete. (Refs: 11) *Sport: Communaute francaise de Belgique (Bruxelles) 106*, 1984, 91-102.
RESUME: Au cours de cette etude, les auteurs comparent l'efficacite de trois methodes d'enseignement pour le pique, poirier, le kip nuque et le kip tete. 53 etudiants en education physique sont divises en trois groupes d'apprentissage: selon la methode Carrasco (base sur le travail en atelier), la methode Inspection (base sur les progressions) et la methode Individualisation (apprentissage global-analytique-global). Les resultats indiquent qu'au plan pratique, la methode Inspection semble plus appropriee etant donne que tous les eleves

travaillent les memes progressions en meme temps.
LEVEL: A LANG: Fr SIRC ARTICLE NO: 098151

Tollich, H. Die Aufgaben der Leibeserziehung im Hinblick auf die Persoenlichkeitsbildung im oesterreichischen Schulturnen. (The tasks of physical education regarding personality development in Austrian gymnastic lessons.) (Refs: 22)In: *Internationales Symposium Sportpaedagogik - Koerpererziehung - Persoenlichkeit: Protokoll, Potsdam, Deutsche Demokratische Republik, ICSSPE/CIEPSS, 1984?, p. 150-160.*
CONF: Internationales Symposium Sportpaedagogik - Koerpererziehung - Persoenlichkeit (1983 : Potsdam).
LEVEL: I LANG: Ger GV205 20231

Wedmann, W. Bonesky, C. Johnston, N. Gymnastics: instructor's resource manual. (Vancouver): British Columbia Recreation and Sport, 1984. vii, 91 p. : ill.
CORP: British Columbia. Recreation and Sport.
NOTES: At head of title: Premier's Sport Awards Program.
LEVEL: B LANG: Eng ISBN: 0-7726-0035-X LC CARD: C84-092096-2 GV464.5 18935

TECHNIQUES AND SKILLS

A cartwheel... and its use. *Grasp (Leicestershire, Eng.) 3(9)*, 1984, 108-109.
LEVEL: B LANG: Eng SIRC ARTICLE NO: 173134

Coca cola award scheme: the backward roll to handstand. *Grasp (New Plymouth, N.Z.) 3(3)*, 1984, 40-43.
LEVEL: B LANG: Eng SIRC ARTICLE NO: 099654

Jump with a half turn. *Grasp (Leicestershire, Eng.) 3(10)*, 1984, 124-125.
LEVEL: B LANG: Eng SIRC ARTICLE NO: 173130

Margueritat, C. Gymnastique: le salto avant groupe. *EPS: Education physique et sport 185*, janv/fevr 1984, 30-33.
LEVEL: B LANG: Fr SIRC ARTICLE NO: 093494

Teaching the half in half out. *Grasp (Bruntingthorpe, Eng.) 3(2)*, 1984, 25-27.
LEVEL: B LANG: Eng SIRC ARTICLE NO: 098153

The backward roll tree. *Grasp (Leicestershire, Eng.) 3(11)*, 1984, 139-142.
NOTES: Reprinted from, Abeceda cvicitele.
LEVEL B LANG: Eng SIRC ARTICLE NO: 173126

Witten, C. Witten, W. Connecting round-offs and back handsprings. *MAHPERD: Michigan journal for Health, Physical Education, Recreation, Dance (Ypsilanti, Mich.)* Spring 1984, 8-9.
LEVEL: B LANG: Eng SIRC ARTICLE NO: 095068

Witten, C. Witten, W. The round off. *MAHPERD journal (Ypsilanti, Mich.)* Winter 1984, 12-13.
LEVEL: B LANG: Eng SIRC ARTICLE NO: 098159

TESTING AND EVALUATION

Bollen, J. Le probleme du sens de rotation en vrille dans des enchainements de figures vrillees. (Refs: 4)*Revue de l'education physique (Liege) 24(2)*, 1984, 19-23.
LEVEL: I LANG: Fr SIRC ARTICLE NO: 101299

Bollen, J. Appellation du sens des rotations longitudinales. *Revue de l'education physique (Liege, Belgique) 24(4)*, 1984, 45-56.
LEVEL: I LANG: Fr SIRC ARTICLE NO: 104758

Brueggermann, P. Nissinen, M. Kibicka, V. Gymnastic competition of friendship. *Australian gymnast (Highett, Melbourne) 10(18)*, Jul/Aug 1984, Coaches Supple. 1-2.
NOTES: Translated from, Kunstturnen aktuel 5, Sept 1983.
LEVEL: B LANG: Eng SIRC ARTICLE NO: 103217

Toth, J. The basic criteria of sport-giftedness in gymnastics. *World gymnastics (Budapest, Hungary) 2(19)*, 1984, 44-45.
LEVEL: B LANG: Eng SIRC ARTICLE NO: 098156

TRAINING AND CONDITIONING

Davis, J. Conditioning for gymnastics: a handbook of conditioning for gymnastics. *Grasp (Leicestershire, Eng.) 3(4/5)*, Mar/Apr 1984, 1-11.
NOTES: Special insert.
LEVEL: B LANG: Eng SIRC ARTICLE NO: 173119

Malmberg, E. Shaping: an effective learning aid for the young gymnast. *International gymnast magazine (Santa Monica, Calif. 26(12)*, Dec 1984, 42.
LEVEL: B LANG: Eng SIRC ARTICLE NO: 109319

Saint-Genies, M. L'entrainement en gymnastique feminine sportive.
NOTES: Dans, Renforcement musculaire, Paris, Institut national du sport et de l'education physique, c1984, p. 137-148.
LEVEL: I LANG: Fr GV711.5 18233

TRAINING AND CONDITIONING - STRETCHING AND FLEXIBILITY EXERCISES

Weiss, M. Weiss, G. The importance of flexibility. *International gymnast (Santa Monica) 26(7)*, Jul 1984, 53.
LEVEL: B LANG: Eng SIRC ARTICLE NO: 098157

TRAINING AND CONDITIONING - WEIGHT AND STRENGTH TRAINING

Hesson, J. Shoulder joint flexion (progressive resistance strength training exercise). *International gymnast (Santa Monica, Calif.) 26(1)*, Jan 1984, 58-59;78-79.
LEVEL: B LANG: Eng SIRC ARTICLE NO: 095058

Hesson, J. Shoulder joint extension (Progressive resistance strength straining exercise). *International gymnast (Santa Monica, Calif.) 26(2)*, Feb 1984, 58-59.
LEVEL: B LANG: Eng SIRC ARTICLE NO: 095059

Hesson, J. Shoulder joint hyperextension (Progressive resistance strength training exercise). *International gymnast (Santa Monica, Calif.) 26(4)*, Apr 1984, 58-59.
LEVEL: B LANG: Eng SIRC ARTICLE NO: 099664

Warren, M. The straddle lever. *Gymnast (Slaugh, Eng.)* Sept 1984, 11.
LEVEL: B LANG: Eng SIRC ARTICLE NO: 103228

WOMEN

Gladders, C. An investigation of the potential career problems of female olympic gymnasts. (abstract) *Carnegie research papers (Beckett Park, Leeds) 1(6)*, Dec 1984, 35-36.
CONF: Carnegie Undergraduate Research Symposium (1984 : Leeds, Eng.).
LEVEL: I LANG: Eng SIRC ARTICLE NO: 172513

Peltenburg, A.L. Erich, W.B.M. Thijssen, J.J.H. Zonderland, M.L. Veeman, W. Jansen, M. Bernink, M.J.E. van den Brande, J.L. Huisveld, I.A. Sex hormones profiles of premenarcheal athletes. (Refs: 34)*European journal of applied physiology and occupational physiology (Berlin, FRG) 52(4), Jun 1984, 385-392.*
ABST: This study tested the hypothesis that the delay in onset of puberty in gymnasts as compared to girl swimmers is modulated by a lower estrone level due to a smaller amount of body fat. Sex-hormone and gonadotropin levels were measured in 46 gymnasts and 37 swimmers. The subjects were at a similar stage of biological maturation. There is a clear relationship between estrone levels and the levels of testosterone and androstenedione but not between estrone levels and fat mass. The authors conclude that the testosterone and androstenedione levels are responsible for differences in estrone levels between the two groups rather than the amount of body fat.
LEVEL: A LANG: Eng SIRC ARTICLE NO: 097895

Yabuuchi, F. Ichikawa, Y. Arakawa, M. Chiba, G. The influence of strenuous muscle stimulation on the menarche. (Refs: 6) *Sangyo ika daigaku zasshi (Tokyo) 6(1), 1 Mar 1984, 47-55.*
ABST: A small number of gymnasts participating in competitions were surveyed. Findings indicated that, at the age of 14, the percentage of women who had menstruated is almost 100 per cent among women in general, but only 24 per cent among World Cup Championship gymnasts. At the age of 16, the percentage of women who had menstruated is 100 per cent among women in general, but on the other hand, it is only 60 per cent among World Cup Championship gymnasts. Finally in our study, we established that the age at menarche of gymnasts is three or five years later than that of women in general.
LEVEL: A LANG: Eng SIRC ARTICLE NO: 104786

GYMNASTICS - BALANCE BEAM

Goewey, J. Confidence of the beam. *International gymnast magazine (Santa Monica, Calif.) 26(12), Dec 1984, 36-37.*
LEVEL: LANG: Eng SIRC ARTICLE NO: 109316

HISTORY

Frederick, A.B. Gymnastics: then, now & what next? Balance beam. *International gymnast (Santa Monica, Calif.) 26(2), Feb 1984, 55-57.*
LEVEL: B LANG: Eng SIRC ARTICLE NO: 095054

TECHNIQUES AND SKILLS

Beam... the forward roll. *Grasp (Leicestershire, Eng.) 3(12), 1984, 152-153.*
LEVEL: B LANG: Eng SIRC ARTICLE NO: 173120

GYMNASTICS - FLOOR EXERCISES

Floor exercise: using the space effectively. *Grasp (Bruntingthorpe, Eng.) 3(2), 1984, 18-19.*
LEVEL: B LANG: Eng SIRC ARTICL NO: 098133

CHOREOGRAPHY AND MUSIC

Pica, R. Gardzina, R. Choosing your music. Part II. *International gymnast (Santa Monica) 26(8), Aug 1984, 46.*
LEVEL: B LANG: Eng SIRC ARTICLE NO: 098149

Pica, R. Gardzina, R. Choosing your music. Part I. *International gymnast (Santa Monica) 26(7), Jul 1984, 52-53.*
LEVEL: B LANG: Eng SIRC ARTICLE NO: 098150

FACILITIES

Spomer, A. Principles of mixing soils for golf greens. *Southern golf (Clearwater, Fla.) 15(1), Winter 1983/1984, 24-26.*
LEVEL: B LANG: Eng SIRC ARTICLE NO: 097526

TECHNIQUES AND SKILLS

Back flip with full twist. *Grasp (Leicestershire, Eng.) 3(12), 1984, 154-155.*
LEVEL: B LANG: Eng SIRC ARTICLE NO: 173121

GYMNASTICS - HORIZONTAL BAR

TEACHING

Teaching aids for giant swings. *Gymnast (Slough, Eng.) Jul/Aug 1984, 14.*
LEVEL: B LANG: Eng SIRC ARTICLE NO: 101313

TECHNIQUES AND SKILLS

Extending the forward seat circle. *Grasp (Leicestershire, Eng.) 3(9), 1984, 102-103.*
LEVEL: B LANG: Eng SIRC ARTICLE NO: 173132

Olympic set skills. (horizontal bar) *Grasp (Leicestershire, Eng.) 3(9), 1984, 104-105.*
LEVEL: B LANG: Eng SIRC ARTICLE NO: 173133

The Gienger turn. *Grasp (Leicestershire, Eng.) 3(10), 1984, 118-123.*
LEVEL: B LANG: Eng SIRC ARTICLE NO: 173129

GYMNASTICS - PARALLEL BARS

HISTORY

Frederick, A.B. Gymnastics: then, now & what next? Parallel bars. *International gymnast (Santa Monica, Calif.) 26(1), Jan 1984, 82-84.*
LEVEL: B LANG: Eng SIRC ARTICLE NO: 095053

TECHNIQUES AND SKILLS

Advanced upstart skills for parallel bars. *Grasp (New Plymouth, N.Z.) 3(6), 1984, 58-59.*
LEVEL: B LANG: Eng SIRC ARTICLE NO 099648

Basic parallel bar combinations. *Grasp (Bruntingthorpe, Eng.) 3(2), 1984, 30-31.*
LEVEL: B LANG: Eng SIRC ARTICLE NO: 098130

Coaching parallel bar: under bar somersaults. *New Zealand gymnast (New Plymouth, N.Z.) 9(4), Aug 1984, 19-20.*
LEVEL: B LANG Eng SIRC ARTICLE NO: 099653

Olympic set skills. *Grasp (Leicestershire, Eng.) 3(10), 1984, 126-129.*
LEVEL: B LANG: Eng SIRC ARTICLE NO: 173128

Parallel bars... back uprise to handstand. *New Zealand gymnast (New Plymouth, N.Z.) 9(5), Oct 1984, 13.*
LEVEL: B LANG: Eng SIRC ARTICLE NO: 109011

GYMNASTICS - POMMEL HORSE

BIOMECHANICS

Ricard, M.D. A biomechanical analysis of side horse vaulting. Eugene, Ore.: Microform Publications, University of Oregon, 1984. 1 microfiche : negative, ill. ; 11 x 15 cm.
NOTES: Thesis (M.A.) - Southeast Missouri State University, 1982; (vii, 69 leaves); vita; includes bibliography.
LEVEL: A LANG: Eng UO84 231

TECHNIQUES AND SKILLS

Development of modern pommel horse skills. *Grasp (New Plymouth, N.Z.) 3(6), 1984, 62-67.*
LEVEL: B LANG: Eng SIRC ARTICLE NO 099657

Frederick, A.B. Gymnastics: then, now & what next? Pommel horse. *International gymnast (Santa Monica) 26(5), May 1984, 54-55.*
LEVEL: B LANG: Eng SIRC ARTICLE NO: 098134

Kormann, P. Training tips, PH: the Moore. *International gymnast (Santa Monica, Calif.) 26(3), Mar 1984, 81.*
LEVEL: B LANG Eng SIRC ARTICLE NO: 099668

The single leg circles. *Grasp (Leicestershire, Eng.) 3(11), 1984, 134-138.*
LEVEL: B LANG: Eng SIRC ARTICLE NO: 173125

GYMNASTICS - RINGS

TECHNIQUES AND SKILLS

Jian, Z. Guangying, Z. Front uprise - rearways hanging swing-L-support. *China sports (Beijing, China) 16(7), Jul 1984, 36-38.*
LEVEL: B LANG: Eng SIRC ARTICLE NO: 102180

Kormann, P. Rings: backward giant swing. *International gymnast (Santa Monica, Calif.) 26(4), Apr 1984, 81.*
LEVEL: B LANG: Eng SIRC ARTICLE NO: 099669

The back uprise. *Grasp (Leicestershire, Eng.) 3(12), 1984, 156-157.*
LEVEL: B LANG: Eng SIRC ARTICLE NO: 173124

The Honma. *Grasp (New Plymouth, N.Z.) 3(7), 1984, 79-83.*
LEVEL: B LANG: Eng SIRC ARTICLE NO: 099665

BIOMECHANICS

Jones, W.A. The front-shoot front somersault dismount from assymetric bars - a cinematographical investigation. (abstract) *Carnegie research papers (Beckett Park, Leeds) 1(6), Dec 1984, 27.*
CONF: Carnegie Undergraduate Research Symposium (1984 : Leeds, Eng.).
LEVEL: I LANG: Eng SIRC ARTICLE NO: 172503

TEACHING

Teaching aids for giant swings. *Gymnast (Slough, Eng.) Jul/Aug 1984, 14.*
LEVEL: B LANG: Eng SIRC ARTICLE NO: 101313

TECHNIQUES AND SKILLS

Asymmetric bars: forward somersault mounts. *Grasp (New Plymouth, N.Z.) 3(3), 1984, 44-45.*
LEVEL: B LANG: Eng SIRC ARTICLE NO: 099650

Forward somersault dismounts. *Grasp (New Plymouth, N.Z.) 3(3), 1984, 34-39.*
LEVEL: B LANG: Eng SIRC ARTICLE NO: 099658

The back away: asymmetric bars and horizontal bar. *Grasp (New Plymouth, N.Z.) 3(7), 1984, 70-78.*
LEVEL: B LANG: Eng SIRC ARTICLE NO: 099651

The Gienger turn. *Grasp (Leicestershire, Eng.) 3(10), 1984, 118-123.*
LEVEL: B LANG: Eng SIRC ARTICLE NO: 173129

The Korbut flip and the Moukina. *Grasp (New Plymouth, N.Z.) 3(6), 1984, 54-56.*
LEVEL: B LANG: Eng SIRC ARTICLE NO: 099667

The leg acting upstart. *Gymnast (Slaugh, Eng.) Sept 1984, 17.*
LEVEL: B LANG: Eng SIRC ARTICLE NO: 103221

The Retton somersault. *Grasp (Leicestershire, Eng.) 3(11), 1984, 143.*
LEVEL: B LANG: Eng SIRC ARTICLE NO: 173127

Tonry, D. Uneven parallel bars. *New Zealand gymnast (New Plymouth, N.Z.) 9(3), Jun 1984, 15.*
LEVEL: B LANG: Eng SIRC ARTICLE NO: 098155

Tonry, D. Uneven parallel bars. *New Zealand gymnat (New Plymouth, N.Z.) 9(5), Oct 1984, 11-12.*
LEVEL: B LANG: Eng SIRC ARTICLE NO: 109010

GYMNASTICS - VAULTING

COACHING

Stevens, N. The measure of success. *AVA vaulting news (Paicines, Calif.) Sept/Oct 1984, 3-4.*
LEVEL: B LANG: Eng SIRC ARTICLE NO: 103227

TEACHING

Moore, J.A. Thoughts on teaching. *AVA vaulting news (Paicines, Calif.) Sept/Oct 1984, 7-8.*
LEVEL: B LANG: Eng SIRC ARTICL NO: 103222

TECHNIQUES AND SKILLS

Ming, Y.M. Chinese Lou Yun presents 2 new vaults. *International gymnast (Santa Monica) 26(8), Aug 1984, 40-41.*
LEVEL: B LANG: Eng SIRC ARTICLE NO: 098147

Mingming, Y. Lou Yun's vaulting stunt: handspring tuck, front 1 1/2 turns. *World gymnastics (Budapest, Hungary) 2(19), 1984 47.*
LEVEL: B LANG: Eng SIRC ARTICLE NO: 098148

Overswing with full twist. *Grasp (Leicestershire, Eng.) 3(12), 1984, 146-148.*
LEVEL: B LANG: Eng SIRC ARTICLE NO: 173122

Turnbow, D. V: handspring, full twist. *International gymnast (Santa Monica, Calif.) 26(6), Jun 1984, 65.*
LEVEL: B LANG: E SIRC ARTICLE NO: 099674

Vaulting...height, rotation and distance. *Grasp (New Plymouth, N.Z.) 3(6), 1984, 60-61.*
LEVEL: B LANG: Eng SIRC ARTICLE NO: 099675

Wild, S. Factors controlling success in vaulting. *Gymnast (London) Mar 1984, 19-20.*
LEVEL: B LANG: Eng SIRC ARTICLE NO: 099676

TRAINING AND CONDITIONING - DRILLS

Rastouil, M. Le saut de cheval. Premiere partie. *EPS: Education physique et sport (Paris) 189, sept/oct 1984, 45-49.*
LEVEL: B LANG: Fr SIRC ARTICLE NO: 101312

Rastouil, M. Le saut de cheval. Progression pour le saut par renversement: la lune. Deuxieme partie. *EPS: Education physiqu et sport (Paris) 190, nov/dec 1984, 13-16.*
NOTES: A suivre.
LEVEL: B LANG: Fr SIRC ARTICLE NO: 103224

HALLS OF FAME AND MUSEUMS

Bonkowski, J. The best sports museum, and you can bank on it. *Sporting news (St. Louis) 198(26), 31 Dec 1984, 74.*
LEVEL: LANG: Eng SIRC ARTICLE NO: 104485

Tivy, M. The museum and archive of games. Un musee consacre aux jeux. *Recreation Canada (Ottawa) 42(3), Jul/juil 1984, 16-20.*
LEVEL: B LANG: Eng Fr SIRC ARTICLE NO: 096436

HAMMER THROW

BIOMECHANICS

Bosen, K.O. A comparison in the duration of acceleration of the hammer path in the single & double support phases. *Snipes journal (Patiala, India) 7(3), Jul 1984, 3-11.*
LEVEL: I LANG: Eng SIRC ARTICLE NO: 100108

Goldhammer, J. Post 1976 hammer technique changes. *Track & field quarterly review (Kalamazoo, Mich.) 84(1), Spring 1984, 38-40.*
LEVEL: I LANG: Eng SIRC ARTICLE NO: 095487

Johnson, C. The modern technique of hammer throwing (part 2). *Athletics coach (Halesowen, England) 18(1), Mar 1984, 10-11.*
LEVEL: I LANG: Eng SIRC ARTICLE NO: 093970

Johnson, C. The acceleration path of the hammer. *Athletics coach (London) 18(3), Sept 1984, 15-16.*
LEVEL: I LANG: Eng SIR ARTICLE NO: 100110

STATISTICS AND RECORDS

Jones, M. 1983 hammer statistics. *Track & field quarterly review (Kalamazoo, Mich.) 84(1), Spring 1984, 37.*
NOTES: Reprinted from, Thrower Nov 1983.
LEVEL: B LANG: Eng SIRC ARTICLE NO: 095490

TEACHING

McGill, K. Teaching the hammer. *Track & field quarterly review (Kalamazoo, Mich.) 84(1), Spring 1984, 41-42.*
LEVEL: I LANG: Eng SIRC ARTICLE NO: 095495

TECHNIQUES AND SKILLS

Bakarinov, Y. Fantalis, A. Chebotarev, V. Hammer throwing. *Thrower (West Midlands, Eng.) 31, Dec 1984, 38-48.*
NOTES: Reprinted from: Legkaya Athletika.
LEVEL: I LANG: Eng SIRC ARTICLE NO: 173499

Bowden, R.J. Rhythm & hammer throwing, rhythm & delivery. *Thrower (West Midlands, Eng.) 29, May 1984, 31-33.*
LEVEL: B LANG: Eng SIRC ARTICLE NO: 098703

Johnson, C. Introducing the modern technique of hammer throwing to beginners. *Athletics coach (London) 18(2), Jun 1984, 6-8.*
LEVEL: B LANG: Eng SIRC ARTICLE NO: 095489

Johnson, C. The modern technique of hammer throwing. *Thrower (West Midlands, Eng.) 30, Aug 1984, 19-21.*
LEVEL: B LANG: En SIRC ARTICLE NO: 098709

Klement, E. Analysis of the hammer throw. *Modern athlete and coach (Athelstone, Aust.) 22(4), Oct 1984, 36-39.*
LEVEL: B LANG: Eng SIRC ARTICLE NO: 105045

McGill, K. Hammer clinic. *Track & field quarterly review (Kalamazoo, Mich.) 84(1), Spring 1984, 42-49.*
NOTES: This brief discussion of Russian hammer technique was given by the author at the October 16th, 1983 throwing clinic at the Naval Academy.
LEVEL: I LANG: Eng SIRC ARTICLE NO: 095496

HANDBALL

Lesmeister, R.A. Help beginners prepare for that first game. *Handball (Tucson, Ariz.)* 34(1), Jan/Feb 1984, 44.
LEVEL: B LANG: Eng SIRC ARTICLE NO: 095069

HISTORY

McElligott, T. The story of handball: the game, the players, the history. Dublin: Wolfhound Press, c1984. 176 p. : ill.
NOTES: Bibliography: p. 176.
LEVEL: B LANG: Eng ISBN: 0863270182 LC CARD: 84-116761 GV1017.H2 18675

INJURIES AND ACCIDENTS

Aronen, J. Shoulder injuries and their rehabilitation. *Handball (Tucson, Ariz.)* 34(5), Sept/Oct 1984, 56-58.
LEVEL: B LANG: Eng SIRC ARTICLE NO: 105896

Aronen, J. Answering the sore shoulder questions. *Handball (Tucson, Ariz.)* 34(6), Nov/Dec 1984, 64-65.
LEVEL: B LANG: Eng SIRC ARTICLE NO: 173376

OFFICIATING

Metz, D. Why not the referee in the court? *Handball (Tuscon, Ariz.)* 34(5), Sept/Oct 1984, 70-71.
LEVEL: B LANG: Eng SIRC ARTICLE NO: 101317

Metz, D. Why not the referee in the court? *Handball (Tucson, Ariz.)* 34(5), Sept/Oct 1984, 70-71.
LEVEL: B LANG: Eng SIRC ARTICLE NO: 105897

STRATEGY - DEFENSIVE

Tyson, P. Shot anticipation for making great gets. *Handball (Tuscon, Ariz.)* 34(5), Sept/Oct 1984, 16-18.
LEVEL: B LANG: E SIRC ARTICLE NO: 101319

TECHNIQUES AND SKILLS

Dau, M. Finding your 'strike zone'. *Handball (Tucson, Ariz.)* 34(6), Nov/Dec 1984, 46-47.
LEVEL: B LANG: Eng SIRC ARTICLE NO: 173375

Lewis, F. The ceiling shot. *Handball (Tucson, Ariz.)* 34(4), Jul/Aug 1984, 60-61.
LEVEL: B LANG: Eng SIRC ARTICLE NO: 0996

Lewis, F. The ceiling shot. *Handball (Tucson, Ariz.)* 34(4), Jul/Aug 1984, 60-61.
LEVEL: B LANG: Eng SIRC ARTICLE NO: 1021

Muck, T. The fly shot. *Handball (Tuscon, Ariz.)* 34(5), Sept/Oct 1984, 46-48.
LEVEL: B LANG: Eng SIRC ARTICLE NO: 101318

Muck, T. The fly shot. *Handball (Tuscon, Ariz.)* 34(5), Sept/Oct 1984, 46-48.
LEVEL: B LANG: Eng SIRC ARTICLE NO: 105898

Muck, T. The pass shot. *Handball (Tucson, Ariz.)* 34(6), Nov/Dec 1984, 26-28.
LEVEL: B LANG: Eng SIRC ARTICLE NO: 173374

Tyson, P. Shot anticipation: for making great gets. *Handball (Tucson, Ariz.)* 34(5), Sept/Oct 1984, 16-18.
LEVEL: B LANG: Eng SIRC ARTICLE NO: 105899

TECHNIQUES AND SKILLS - SERVING

Tyson, P. Serving, the percentage way. *Handball (Tucson, Ariz.)* 34(4), Jul/Aug 1984, 32-33.
LEVEL: B LANG: Eng SIRC ARTICLE NO: 099678

Tyson, P. Serving, the percentage way. *Handball (Tucson, Ariz.)* 34(4), Jul/Aug 1984, 32-33.
LEVEL: B LANG: Eng SIRC ARTICLE NO: 102138

HANG GLIDING

Hewett, D. Skyting update. *Hang gliding (Los Angeles, Calif.)* 14(1), Jan 1984, 34-37;39.
LEVEL: I LANG: Eng SIRC ARTICLE NO: 095076

ADMINISTRATION

Fair, E. Hang gliding interviews: Steve Hawxhurst. *Hang gliding (Los Angeles, Calif.)* 14(4), Apr 1984, 14-17;33;43.
LEVEL B LANG: Eng SIRC ARTICLE NO: 099682

Hansler, J. Boot strap success. (marketing) *Hang gliding (Los Angeles)* 14(11), Nov 1984, 4-5.
LEVEL: B LANG: Eng SIRC ARTICLE NO: 173467

AERODYNAMICS

Kurtz, F. New harness design. *Flypaper (Calgary)* 10(2), 1984, 29.
NOTES: Translated from, Drachenflieger May 1984. Translated by, Jean-Claude Hauchecorne.
LEVEL: I LANG: Eng SIRC ARTICLE NO: 103230

Meier, M. The answer man. (mechanics of a turn) *Hang gliding (Los Angeles, Calif.)* 14(3), Mar 1984, 26-27.
LEVEL: I LANG: Eng SIRC ARTICLE NO: 099687

Midwinter, S. Les zones d'ombre de vent (windshadows). *Becois volants (Montreal)* 5(18), hiver 1984, 21-22.
NOTES: Traduit de, The Flypaper 9(4).
LEVEL: B LANG: Fr SIRC ARTICLE NO: 095080

Pagen, D. Preventing stalls - a primer. *Hang gliding (Los Angeles, Calif.)* 14(3), Mar 1984, 34-36.
LEVEL: B LANG: Eng SIR ARTICLE NO: 099690

Salmun, M. What a drag. (and what can be done about it): an exploration of the benefits of streamlining. *Hang gliding (Los Angeles, Calif.)* 14(7), Jul 1984, 32-37.
LEVEL: I LANG: Eng SIRC ARTICLE NO: 098162

AUDIO VISUAL MATERIAL

Sanders, T. Hang gliding with video. *Hang gliding (Los Angeles, Calif.)* 14(4), Apr 1984, 24-25;28.
LEVEL: B LANG: Eng SIR ARTICLE NO: 099692

BIOGRAPHY AND AUTOBIOGRAPHY

Lockwood, R. Hang gliding interviews. Wendy Kamm. *Hang gliding (Los Angeles, Calif.)* 14(5) May 1984, 20-21.
LEVEL: B LANG Eng ARTICLE NO: 095079

Warrender, L.M. Hang gliding interviews, Dick Boone. *Hang gliding (Los Angeles, Calif.)* 14(3), Mar 1984, 16-20.
LEVEL: B LANG: Eng SIRC ARTICLE NO: 099696

COUNTRIES AND REGIONS

Powell, V. The next decade. *Hang gliding (Los Angeles)* 14(9), Sept 1984, 14-15;33.
LEVEL: B LANG: Eng SIRC ARTICLE NO: 108800

Wolfe, B. Pilot demographics. *Whole air (Lookout Mtn., Tenn.)* 7(5), Oct 1984, 24-25.
LEVEL: I LANG: Eng SIRC ARTICLE NO: 109102

ENVIRONMENT

Pfeiffer, R. Rowe, M. Soaring in thermal lift. *Hang gliding (Los Angeles, Calif.)* 14(7), Jul 1984, 10-15.
NOTES: Continue next month. Reprinted from, Hang gliding according to Pfeiffer: skills for the advancing pilot, by Rich Pfeiffer.
LEVEL: I LANG: Eng SIRC ARTICLE NO: 098161

Pfeiffer, R. Rowe, M. Ridge soaring principles. *Hang gliding (Los Angeles, Calif.)* 14(6), Jun 1984, 12-17;46.
NOTES: From Hang gliding according to Pfeiffer-skills for the advancing pilot.
LEVEL: I LANG: Eng SIRC ARTICLE NO: 099691

Pfeiffer, R. Rowe, M. Soaring in thermal lift. *Hang gliding (Los Angeles, Calif.)* 14(8), Aug 1984, 26-27;29-32;42.
NOTES: From, Hang gliding according to Pfeiffer - skills for the advancing pilot.
LEVEL: I LANG: Eng SIRC ARTICLE NO: 101323

Williams, D.G. Remote thermal detection. (Refs: 11)*Hang gliding (Los Angeles, Calif.)* 14(3), Mar 1984, 37-39.
LEVEL: I LANG: Eng SIRC ARTICLE NO: 099697

EQUIPMENT

Abbott, S. A look back at 1983: hang gliding in Great Britain. *Glider rider magazine 9(2)*, Apr 1984, 61-62;64-65.
LEVEL: LANG: Eng SIRC ARTICLE NO: 093503

Allard, J. He. Jo, t'as-tu vu les gars de Quebec, y'ont des C.B. *Becois volants (Montreal)* 5(18), hiver 1984, 8-9.
LEVEL: LANG: Fr SIRC ARTICLE NO: 095070

Burns, P. The Breez. *Whole air (Lookout Mountain, Tenn.)* 7(2), May 1984, 32-33.
LEVEL: B LANG: Eng SIRC ARTICLE NO: 09967

Burns, P. Wills Wing Skyhawk. *Whole air (Lookout Mtn., Tenn.)* 7(4), Aug 1984, 13-15.
LEVEL: B LANG: Eng SIRC ARTICLE NO: 104787

Burns, P. Gemini: our second PiRep (pilot report) takes us up in the air with Ultralite Products' Gemini: series. *Whole air (Lookout Mtn., Tenn.)* 7(3), Jun/Jul 1984, 26-28.
LEVEL: B LANG: Eng SIRC ARTICLE NO: 105900

Burns, P. Moyes Mars. *Whole air (Lookout Mtn., Tenn.)* 7(5), Oct 1984, 26-28.
LEVEL: B LANG: Eng SIRC ARTICLE NO: 109103

Burns, P. Dawn. *Whole air (Lookout Mtn., Tenn.)* 7(6), Dec 1984/Jan 1985, 13-15.
LEVEL: B LANG: Eng SIRC ARTICLE NO: 17358

Dodgen, G. Wills wing skyhawk. *Hang gliding (Los Angeles, Calif.)* 14(2), Feb 1984, 12-14.
LEVEL: B LANG: Eng SIRC ARTICLE NO: 095071

Eggen, G. 'Minimum' motorglider. *Whole air (Lookout Mtn., Tenn.)* 7(4), Aug 1984, 20-25.
LEVEL: B LANG: Eng SIRC ARTICLE NO: 104788

HANG GLIDING (continued)

Eggen, G. Power steering systems. *Whole air (Lookout Mtn., Tenn.) 7(6), Dec 1984/Jan 1985, 16-18.*
LEVEL: B LANG: Eng SIRC ARTICLE NO: 173581

Heiney, J. Point-of-view: Mounting a camera (safely) on your glider. *Hang gliding (Los Angeles, Calif,) 14(1), Jan 1984, 22-25.*
LEVEL: I LANG: Eng SIRC ARTICLE NO: 095075

Johnson, D. The Dawn. *Whole air (Lookout Mountain, Tenn.) 7(2), May 1984, 14-18.*
LEVEL: B LANG: Eng SIRC ARTICLE NO: 0996

Johnson, D. Phillips, T. Aero test I. *Whole air (Lookout Mtn., Tenn.) 7(4), Aug 1984, 17-19;31.*
LEVEL: B LANG: Eng SIRC ARTICLE NO: 104789

Litek ... of variometers and talking weather stations. *Whole air (Lookout Mtn., Tenn.) 7(5), Oct 1984, 10.*
LEVEL: B LANG: E SIRC ARTICLE NO: 109099

Pagen, D. Hang glider design considerations. *Hang gliding (Los Angeles, Calif.) 14(2), Feb 1984, 38-39.*
LEVEL: B LANG: En SIRC ARTICLE NO: 095082

Pagen, D. Hang glider design considerations. *Hang gliding (Los Angeles, Calif.) 14(1), Jan 1984, 20-21.*
LEVEL: B LANG: En SIRC ARTICLE NO: 095083

Pagen, D. Flying the French connection. *Hang gliding (Los Angeles, Calif.) 14(5), May 1984, 17-19.*
LEVEL: I LANG: Eng SIR ARTICLE NO: 095084

Pagen, D. Flying the line: the ins and outs of variable geometry gliders. *Hang gliding (Los Angeles, Calif.) 14(6), Jun 1984, 38-40.*
LEVEL: I LANG: Eng SIRC ARTICLE NO: 099688

Pagen, D. Pilot report - the Systek II Vario. *Hang gliding magazine (Los Angeles) 14(10), Oct 1984, 14-16.*
LEVEL: B LANG: Eng SIRC ARTICLE NO: 108419

Pagen, D. French connections and speed rails - take two. *Hang gliding (Los Angeles) 14(11), Nov 1984, 15-18.*
LEVEL: I LANG: Eng SIRC ARTICLE NO: 173468

Perlman, E. Hang gliding: science in the clouds. *In, Schrier, E.W. and Allman, W.F. (eds.), Newton at the bat: the science in sports, New York, Scribner, c1984, p. 91-93.*
LEVEL: B LANG: Eng RC1235 18609

Roberts, C. Taras Kiceniuk: the Icarus II was one of the great landmarks in hang gliding. It's concept served as a precursor for modern day ultralights... *Air progress ultralights (Canoga Park, Calif.) 2(3), Apr 1984, 74-79.*
LEVEL: B LANG: Eng SIRC ARTICLE NO: 104692

Shaw, G. Owner survey: up Comet. *Whole air (Lookout Mountain, Tenn.) 7(1), Mar 1984, 14-17.*
LEVEL: B LANG: Eng SIRC ARTICLE NO: 099693

Siecinski, K. Sailcloth and sailcloth care. *Hang gliding (Los Angeles, Calif.) 14(2), Feb 1984, 16-18;20.*
LEVEL: B LANG: Eng SIRC ARTICLE NO: 095085

The flying wings of Reimar Horten. *Whole air (Lookout Mtn., Tenn.) 7(3), Jun/Jul 1984, 16-20.*
NOTES: Reprinted from: Drachenflieger Magazine.
LEVEL: I LANG: Eng SIRC ARTICLE NO: 105901

The Nomad. *Whole air (Lookout Mtn., Tenn.) 7(3), Jun/Jul 1984, 24-25.*
LEVEL: B LANG: Eng SIRC ARTICLE NO: 105903

Wolfe, B. Owners survey 3: Sensor. *Whole air (Lookout Mountain, Tenn.) 7(2), May 1984, 35-38.*
LEVEL: B LANG: Eng SIRC ARTICLE NO: 099698

Wolfe, B. Owner survey...Harrier. *Whole air (Lookout Mountain, Tenn.) 7(1), Mar 1984, 32-35.*
LEVEL: B LANG: Eng SIRC ARTICLE NO: 099699

Wolfe, B. Owners survey: Prostar. *Whole air (Lookout Mtn., Tenn.) 7(4), Aug 1984, 32-33.*
LEVEL: B LANG: Eng SIRC ARTICLE NO: 104790

Wolfe, B. Owners survey/Gemini. *Whole air (Lookout Mtn., Tenn.) 7(3), Jun/Jul 1984, 31-33.*
LEVEL: B LANG: Eng SIRC ARTICL NO: 105904

EQUIPMENT - MAINTENANCE

Pagen, D. Sail repair. Can you repair your own sail? The answer is a qualified yes, if you have: (1) the right materials; (2 an understanding of what you are doing; and (3) patience. *Glider rider magazine 9(3), May 1984, 61-63.*
LEVEL: B LANG: Eng SIRC ARTICLE NO: 093414

FACILITIES

Hawxhurst, S. Site procurement. *Hang gliding (Los Angeles, Calif.) 14(3), Mar 1984, 32-33.*
NOTES: Excerpt from, The USHGA Site Manual, by Steve Hawxhurst.
LEVEL: B LANG: Eng SIRC ARTICLE NO: 099683

FACILITIES - DESIGN, CONSTRUCTION AND PLANNING

Fabrication d'un monte-aile motorise. *Becois volants (Montreal) 5(18), hiver 1984, 15-17.*
LEVEL: I LANG: Fr SIRC ARTICLE NO 095072

INJURIES AND ACCIDENTS

Hildreth, D. 1983 accident review. *Hang gliding (Los Angeles, Calif.) 14(4), Apr 1984, 34-36.*
LEVEL: B LANG: Eng SIRC ARTICLE NO: 099684

Karadzos, G. Polytraumatismus pri novem sportovnim odvetvi-letani deltaplanem (Rogallem). (Multiple injuries in a new sports activity--flying with delta planes (Rogallos).) *Rozhledy v chirurgii (Prague) 63(10), Oct 1984, 693-696.*
NOTES: English abstract.
LEVEL: I LANG: Cze

MASS MEDIA

Fisher, B. A simple efficient cb aerial. *Hang gliding (Los Angeles, Calif,) 14(5) May 1984, 24;8.*
LEVEL: B LANG: Eng SIRC ARTICLE NO: 095074

MATHEMATICS

Speed to fly ring for hang gliders. *Flypaper (Calgary) 10(2), 1984, 35-41.*
LEVEL: I LANG: Eng SIRC ARTICLE NO: 103231

MEDICINE

Leonard, F. How to stay healthy through hang gliding. *Hang gliding (Los Angeles, Calif.) 14(6), Jun 1984, 44-45.*
LEVEL: B LANG: Eng SIRC ARTICLE NO: 099686

PHYSICAL FITNESS

Leonard, F. How to stay healthy through hang gliding. *Hang gliding (Los Angeles, Calif.) 14(5) May 1984, 45-46;37.*
LEVEL: LANG: Eng SIRC ARTICLE NO: 095078

PHYSICS

Caldwell, K. PAFs and PIF-PAFs. *Flypaper (Calgary) 10(2), 1984, 15-18.*
LEVEL: I LANG: Eng SIRC ARTICLE NO: 103229

PSYCHOLOGY

Leonard, F. How to stay healthy through hang gliding. *Hang gliding (Los Angeles, Calif.) 14(8), Aug 1984, 33;42.*
LEVEL: B LANG: Eng SIRC ARTICLE NO: 101320

RULES AND REGULATIONS

Higdon, D. FAA update. *Whole air (Lookout Mtn., Tenn.) 7(3), Jun/Jul 1984, 34-35.*
LEVEL: B LANG: Eng SIRC ARTICLE NO: 105902

SAFETY

Locke, R. Safety forum. (surf landing) *Hang gliding (Los Angeles, Calif.) 14(8), Aug 1984, 17.*
LEVEL: B LANG: Eng SIRC ARTICLE NO: 101321

Pagen, D. Harness update - Part 1. *Hang gliding (Los Angeles, Calif.) 14(7), Jul 1984, 44-46.*
LEVEL: B LANG: Eng SIRC ARTICLE NO: 098160

STRATEGY

Nicholson, R. Approche d'atterrissage...suicidaire? *Becois volants (Montreal) 5(18), hiver 1984, 12-14.*
LEVEL: B LANG: Fr SIRC ARTICLE NO: 095081

TEACHING

Phillips, T. The crystal simulator. *Hang gliding (Los Angeles) 14(12), Dec 1984, 40-42.*
LEVEL: B LANG: Eng SIRC ARTICLE NO: 108421

TECHNIQUES AND SKILLS

Cassetta, D. Aero towing a la France. *Whole air (Lookout Mountain, Tenn.) 7(1), Mar 1984, 18-20.*
LEVEL: B LANG: Eng SIRC ARTICLE NO: 099680

Eggen, G. Stuffenschlepp/step towing. *Whole air (Lookout Mtn., Tenn.) 7(5), Oct 1984, 19-22.*
LEVEL: B LANG: Eng SIRC ARTICLE NO: 109101

Fair, E. Going prone. *Hang gliding (Los Angeles, Calif.) 14(1), Jan 1984, 14-17.*
LEVEL: B LANG: Eng SIRC ARTICLE NO: 0950

Fair, E. Launch characteristics: angle of attack. *Hang gliding (Los Angeles, Calif.) 14(6), Jun 1984, 8-10;37.*
LEVEL: B LANG: Eng SIRC ARTICLE NO: 099681

Nicholson, R. What's your approach. (landing) *Whole air (Lookout Mtn., Tenn.) 7(5), Oct 1984, 15-18.*
LEVEL: B LANG: Eng SIRC ARTICLE NO: 109100

Pagen, D. Alighting lightly: the art and essence of landing properly. *Hang gliding (Los Angeles, Calif.) 14(4), Apr 1984, 32-33;43.*
LEVEL: B LANG: Eng SIRC ARTICLE NO: 099689

Pagen, D. Getting treed: the art of tree landing revisited. *Hang gliding (Los Angeles, Calif.) 14(8), Aug 1984, 10-12.*
LEVEL: B LANG: Eng SIRC ARTICLE NO: 101322

Pagen, D. Cliff launches, lurches, lunches and lunges. *Hang gliding (Los Angeles) 14(9), Sept 1984, 10-13.*
LEVEL: B LANG: Eng SIRC ARTICLE NO: 108799

Pfeiffer, R. Rowe, M. Stafford, R. Hang gliding according to Pfeiffer: skills for the advancing pilot. Laguna Beach, Calif.: Publitec Editions, c1984. 1v.
NOTES: Includes index.
LEVEL: I LANG: Eng ISBN: 091358102X LC CARD: 84-015037

Pfeiffer, R. Rowe, M. Soaring in other types of lift. *Hang gliding (Los Angeles) 14(10), Oct 1984, 18-22.*
NOTES: Extraced from, Hang gliding according to Pferffer - skills for the advancing pilot.
LEVEL: I LANG: Eng SIRC ARTICLE NO: 108420

Thompson, B. Supine: a lost (almost) art. *Hang gliding (Los Angeles, Calif.) 14(4), Apr 1984, 18-21;46-47.*
LEVEL: B LANG: Eng SIRC ARTICLE NO: 099694

Thompson, B. Tow lines. *Hang gliding (Los Angeles, Calif.) 14(3), Mar 1984, 30-31.*
LEVEL: B LANG: Eng SIRC ARTICLE NO: 099695

TRAINING AND CONDITIONING

Ladouceur, G. Operation: preparation saison '84. *Becois volants (Montreal) 5(18), hiver 1984, 22-23.*
LEVEL: B LANG: Fr SIRC ARTICLE NO: 095077

HARNESS RACING

ADMINISTRATION

Bergstein, S. Changes needed for progress likely to transcend borders. Que nous reserve l'avenir?? *Trot (Toronto) 11(11), Dec 1984, 63-64;66-67.*
LEVEL: B LANG: Eng Fr SIRC ARTICLE NO: 103246

BIOGRAPHY AND AUTOBIOGRAPHY

Pearce, R.M. Karen's cooking: her 1:57.3 trip with Bets Sparky makes her fastest woman driver in history on a half-mile track. (Karen Rose Fekete) *Trot (Toronto) 11(2), Feb 1984, 12;60.*
LEVEL: B LANG: Eng SIRC ARTICLE NO: 098227

Smith, R.M. Looking back. (J. Russell Miller) *Standardbred (Acton, Ont.) 13(9), 1984, 34-36;38;57.*
LEVEL: B LANG: Eng SIR ARTICLE NO: 098243

Smith, R.M. Looking back: Dr.W.H. Riddell - Ontario's Dean of racing. *Standardbred (Acton, Ont.) 13(10), 9 May 1984, 14-15.*
LEVEL: B LANG: Eng SIRC ARTICLE NO: 098245

Smith, R.M. The legend lives on: Lindsay Fraser and Dr. Stanton. *Standardbred (Acton, Ont.) 12(22), 15 Aug 1984, 60-64.*
LEVEL: B LANG: Eng SIRC ARTICLE NO: 103265

Smith, R.S. Marshall Moore - a young oldtimer. *Standardbred (Acton, Ont.) 12(12), 6 Jun 1984, 12-14.*
LEVEL: B LANG: Eng SIRC ARTICLE NO: 101361

ECONOMICS

McGillivray, T. To insure or not to insure: that's the name of the game. *Trot (Toronto) 11(7), Jul 1984, 12;42.*
LEVEL: B LANG: Eng SIRC ARTICLE NO: 101353

FACILITIES

Smith, R.M. Looking back: early days at Windsor. (Windsor Raceway) *Standardbred (Acton, Ont.) 12(28), 26 Sept 1984, 35-37;52.*
LEVEL: B LANG: Eng SIRC ARTICLE NO: 099753

HISTORY

Smith, R.M. Looking back: under the Northern Lights. *Standardbred (Acton, Ont.) 12(18), 18 Jul 1984, 36-38.*
LEVEL: B LANG Eng SIRC ARTICLE NO: 098244

HORSES

Bray, M. Importance of balance. *Trot (Toronto) 11(10), Oct 1984, 22;36-37.*
NOTES: Reprinted from, Anvil newspaper.
LEVEL I LANG: Eng SIRC ARTICLE NO: 101336

MASS MEDIA

Bridgland, R. Horsemen concur: Harry belongs in winner's circle. (Harry Eisen) *Trot (Toronto) 11(3), Mar 1984, 16;20;72.*
LEVEL: B LANG: Eng SIRC ARTICLE NO: 098183

PROTECTIVE DEVICES

Abraham, D. Western drivers experiment with bell helmets. *Standardbred (Acton, Ont.) 13(6), 4 Jul 1984, 17;30.*
LEVEL: B LANG: Eng SIRC ARTICLE NO: 098182

Ethier, R. Introducing the new safety helmet. Effort of Ron Dancer committee paying off in bid for safer racing following several track tragedies. *Trot (Toronto) 11(7), Jul 1984, 8-10;48.*
LEVEL: B LANG: Eng SIRC ARTICLE NO: 101341

SAFETY

Abraham, D. Stampede Park first Canadian track to install Fontana safety rail. *Standardbred 13(1), 4 Jan 1984, 19.*
LEVEL: LANG: Eng SIRC ARTICLE NO: 092214

SPORTING EVENTS

Smith, R.M. Derby days at New Hamburg: part II of III. (Canadian Pacing Derby) *Standardbred (Acton, Ont.) 12(21), 8 Aug 1984, 18-20.*
LEVEL: B LANG: Eng SIRC ARTICLE NO: 103266

Smith, R.M. Derby days at New Hamburg: part III. (Canadian Pacing Derby) *Standardbred (Acton, Ont.) 12(23), 22 Aug 1984, 15-16.*
LEVEL: B LANG: Eng SIRC ARTICLE NO: 103267

The breeders crown: changing the face of harness racing. *Hoofbeats (Columbus, Ohio) 52(8), Oct 1984, 22;24;26.*
LEVEL: B LANG: Eng SIRC ARTICLE NO: 105919

TRAINING AND CONDITIONING

Lieberman, B. A month in the life... Three horses, three sports, three programs. *Equus (Farmingdale, N.Y.) 79, May 1984, 28-29;33.*
LEVEL: B LANG: Eng SIRC ARTICLE NO: 099734

HEALTH AND HYGIENE

Carter, G.F. Health is a status. (Refs: 15)*Health education (Reston, Va.) 15(1), Jan/Feb 1984, 33-35.*
LEVEL: B LANG: Eng SIRC ARTICLE NO: 097554

Furney, S.R. Reducing health care costs. (Refs: 8)*TAHPERD journal (Austin, Tex.) 53(1), Oct 1984, 8-9;67.*
LEVEL: B LANG: Eng SIRC ARTICLE NO: 109089

Laptev, A.P. Polievskii, S.A. Pereshivko, N.S. Malysheva, I.N. El-Din, A.G. Vopros gigienicheskogo normirovaniia mikroklimat krytykh sportivnykh sooruzhenii. (Hygienic standardization of the microclimate of indoor sport facilities.) *Gigiena i sanitariia (Moscow) 12, Dec 1984, 12-15.*
LEVEL: A LANG: Rus

Palmer, D.L. Wellness, it goes way beyond fitness. *Journal of physical education and program (Columbus, Oh.) 81(5), Jun 1984, 7-8.*
LEVEL: B LANG: Eng SIRC ARTICLE NO: 095886

Pierce, E.E. The effect of a health promotion program on the wellness behavior and self-esteem upon behavior change. Eugene, Ore.: Microform Publications, University of Oregon, 1984. 2 microfiches: negative, ill. ; 11 x 15 cm.
NOTES: Thesis (M.S.) - University of Wisconsin-La Crosse, 1982; (viii, 170 leaves); includes bibliography.
LEVEL: A LANG: Eng UO84 300-301

Ryan, A.J. Exercise and health: lessons from the past. (Refs: 42)*American Academy of Physical Education papers (Champaign, Ill.) 17, 1984, 3-13.*
CONF: American Academy of Physical Education. Annual Meeting (54th : 1983 : Minneapolis).
NOTES: Conference theme: Exercise and health.
LEVEL: I LANG: Eng SIRC ARTICLE NO: 103993

Weiss, U. Le sport et la sante. *Macolin (Suisse) 1, janv 1984, 9-11.*
NOTES: Traduction de, Yves Jeannotat.
LEVEL: B LANG Fr SIRC ARTICLE NO: 095888

ENVIRONMENTAL HEALTH - AIR POLLUTION

Kleinman, M.T. Sulfur dioxide and exercise: relationships between response and absorption in upper airways. *Journal of the Air Pollution Control Association (Pittsburgh) 34(1), Jan 1984, 32-37.*
LEVEL: A LANG: Eng SIRC ARTICLE NO: 099250

Raven, P.B. When should air pollution restrict physical activity? (Refs: 2)*Sports medicine digest (Van Nuys, Calif.) 6(6), Jun 1984, 1-3.*
LEVEL: I LANG: Eng SIRC ARTICLE NO: 102142

Reading, J. Acid rain: understanding the problem at camp. *Canadian camping 35(4), Winter 1984, 13-16.*
LEVEL: B LANG: Eng SIRC ARTICLE NO: 093334

Shephard, R.J. Athletic performance and urban air pollution. (Refs: 19)*Canadian Medical Association journal/Journal de l'Association medicale*

canadienne (Ottawa) 131(2), 15 Jul 1984, 105-109.
LEVEL: I LANG: Eng SIRC ARTICLE NO: 096297

HEALTH SURVEYS

Blair, S.N. Collingwood, T.R. Reynolds, R. Smith, M. Hagan, R.D. Sterling, C.L. Health promotion for educators: impact on health behaviors, satisfaction, and general well-being. *American journal of public health (Washington) 74(2), Feb 1984, 147-149.*
ABST: 117 teachers in three treatment schools and one control school responded to a health survey before and after a 10 week health promotion program in the treatment schools. This program focused on exercise, stress management and nutrition. The results found that the treatment group reported increased exercise participation, improved physical fitness, lost weight, lower blood pressure, higher levels of well-being and better stress management.
LEVEL: A LANG: Eng SIRC ARTICLE NO: 097553

Malinskii, D.M. Kuderkov, S.M. Kompleksnyi pokazatel' fizicheskoi podgotovlennosti voennosluzhashchikh. (Physical readiness for military service based on health status indicators.) *Voenno-meditsinskii zhurnal (Moscow) 12, Dec 1984, 41-46.*
LEVEL: I LANG: Rus

OCCUPATIONAL HEALTH

Daniel, W.H. Freeborg, R.P. Konopinski, V.J. Results from one special study: an on-course look at pesticide exposure. *Golf course management (Kansas) 52(3), Mar 1984, 71;75;79;81;83;84-85.*
LEVEL: I LANG: Eng SIRC ARTICLE NO: 100665

HEALTH EDUCATION

Ballard, D.J.R. A comparison of direct and indirect health instruction and its effect on students' acquisition of health knowledge. Eugene, Ore.: Microform Publication, Univeristy of Oregon, 1984. 2 microfiches : negative, ill, ; 11 x 15 cm.
NOTES: Thesis (Ed.D.) - Oklahoma State University, 1982; (vii, 106, (1) leaves); vita; includes bibliography.
LEVEL: A LANG: Eng UO84 321-322

Buckellew, W. The role of colleges and universities in providing educational programs in health, physical education, and recreation. *Asian journal of physical education (Taipei, Taiwan) 7(3), Oct 1984, 41-42.*
LEVEL: B LANG: Eng Chi SIRC ARTICLE NO: 102654

Carlton, B. The role of the health educator in interdisciplinary health team development: an organizational development strategy. (Refs: 9)*Health education (Reston, Va.) 15(6), Oct/Nov 1984, 13-15.*
LEVEL: B LANG: Eng SIRC ARTICLE NO: 105266

Davis, J.H. A study of the high school principal's role in health education. (Refs: 19)*Journal of school health (Kent, Ohio 53(10), Dec 1984, 610-612.*
LEVEL: I LANG: Eng SIRC ARTICLE NO: 095889

Folio, S.B. Elliott, G.D. Baker, S. Hott, S. A survey of elementary school health education in West Virginia. (Refs: 11) *Journal of school health*

(Kent, Ohio) 54(10), Nov 1984, 401-402.
LEVEL: I LANG: Eng SIRC ARTICLE NO: 108221

Glover, E.D. Health education in Texas. (Refs: 4)*Journal of school health (Kent, Oh.) 54(8), Sept 1984, 310-311.*
LEVEL: I LANG: Eng SIRC ARTICLE NO: 105269

Hosokawa, M.C. Roberts, C.R. Hansen, P.L. Health education in rural Missouri: phase II. *Health education (Reston, Va.) 15(2), Mar/Apr 1984, 18-21.*
LEVEL: B LANG: Eng SIRC ARTICLE NO: 099022

Hosokawa, M.C. Insurance incentives for health promotion. (Refs: 14)*Health education (Reston, Va.) 15(6), Oct/Nov 1984, 9-12.*
LEVEL: B LANG: Eng SIRC ARTICLE NO: 105271

Howat, P. Fisher, J. Health education for self responsibility or health education for structural perspectives. (Refs: 48) *ACHPER national journal (Kingswood, Aust.) 104, Winter 1984, 5-9.*
LEVEL: B LANG: Eng SIRC ARTICLE NO: 100667

Kolbe, L.J. Newman, I.M. The role of school health education in preventing heart, lung, and blood diseases. (Refs: 210) *Proceedings of the National Conference on School Health Education Research in the Heart, Lung and Blood Areas (Washington) 1984, 15-26.*
CONF: National Conference on School Health Education Research in the Heart, Lung, and Blood Areas (1983 : Bethesda, Md.).
NOTES: Joint issue of Health Education (Reston, Va.) 15(4), 1984 and Journal of School Health (Washington) 54(6), 1984.
LEVEL: I LANG: Eng SIRC ARTICLE NO: 103997

Leviton, D. Campanelli, L.C. Have we avoided the frail aged and dying older person in HPERD? (Refs: 23)*Health education (Reston, Va.) 15(6), Oct/Nov 1984, 43-47.*
LEVEL: B LANG: Eng SIRC ARTICLE NO: 105273

O'Donnell, N.L. An investigation of the impact of a nutrition mini-grant on nutrition awareness of elementary school childre Eugene, Ore.: Microform Publications, University of Oregon, 1984. 1 microfiche : negative ; 11 x 15 cm.
NOTES: Thesis (M.S.) - Pennsylvania State University, 1981; (viii, 70 leaves); includes bibliography.
LEVEL: A LANG: Eng UO84 117

Perry, C.L. A conceptual approach to school-based health promotion. (Refs: 14)*Proceedings of the National Conference on School Health Education Research in the Heart, Lung and Blood Areas (Washington) 1984, 33-38.*
CONF: National Conference on School Health Education Research in the Heart, Lung, and Blood Areas (1983 : Bethesda, Md.).
NOTES: Joint issue of Health education (Reston, Va.) 15(4), 1984 and Journal of school health (Washington) 54(6), 1984.
LEVEL: I LANG: Eng SIRC ARTICLE NO: 104001

Simonds, S.K. Health education. (Refs: 27)*In, Matarazzo, J.D. (ed.) et al., Behavioral health: a handbook of health enhancement and disease prevention, New York, Wiley, c1984, p. 1223-1229.*
LEVEL: I LANG: Eng

The limitations to excellence in education: a response by the coalition of National Health Education Organizations to the Report by the National Commission on Excellence in Education, A Nation at Risk. (Refs: 11)*Journal of school health*

(Kent, Oh.) 54(7), Aug 1984, 256-257.
LEVEL: B LANG: Eng SIRC ARTICLE NO: 103999

ADMINISTRATION

Daly, N. European Health Tour 1984 - promoting health through sport and international co-operation. *In, Ilmarinen, M. (ed.) et al., Sport and International Understanding: proceedings of the congress held in Helsinki, Finland, July 7-10, 1982, Berlin, Springer-Verlag, 1984, p. 241-247.*
CONF: Congress on Sport and International Understanding (1982 : Helsinki).
LEVEL: I LANG: Eng GV706.8 18979

Smith, R.P.P. Promotion of school health education through state-level health systems planning. (Refs: 7)*Health education (Reston, Va.) 15(5), Aug/Sept 1984, 20-23.*
LEVEL: B LANG: Eng SIRC ARTICLE NO: 173135

CERTIFICATION

Drolet, J.C. Evaluation of the Seaside Health Education Conferences and nutrition education training programs in the Oregon school systems. Eugene, Ore.: Microform Publications, University of Oregon, 1984. 3 microfiches : negative, ill. ; 11 x 15 cm.
NOTES: Thesis (Ph.D.) - University of Oregon, 1982; (xiii, 229 leaves); vita; includes bibliography.
LEVEL: A LANG: Eng UO84 159-161

DIRECTORIES

Moore, L.M. AAHE directory of institutions offering specialization in undergraduate and graduate professional preparation programs in health education. 1985 edition. *Health education (Reston, Va.) 15(5), Aug/Sept 1984, 80-88.*
LEVEL: B LANG: Eng SIRC ARTICLE NO: 173137

EVALUATION

DuShaw, M.L. A comparative study of three model comprehensive elementary school health education programs. (Refs: 5)*Journal of school health (Kent, Ohio) 54(10), Nov 1984, 397-400.*
LEVEL: I LANG: Eng SIRC ARTICLE NO: 108220

HISTORY

Thomson, I. Almond of Loretto: origins and development of his system of health education. (Refs: 26)*Scottish journal of physical education (Glasgow, Scotland) 12(1), Jan 1984, 32-36.*
LEVEL: I LANG: Eng SIRC ARTICLE NO: 094344

LAW AND LEGISLATION

Alexander, B.L. The reasonable prudent physical and health educator. *OPHEA: Ontario Physical and Health Education Association 10(3), Fall 1984, 42-50.*
LEVEL: B LANG: Eng SIRC ARTICLE NO: 102648

PHILOSOPHY

Thomas, S.B. The holistic philosophy and perspective of selected health educators. (Refs: 13)*Health education (Reston, Va.) 15(1), Jan/Feb 1984, 16-20.*
LEVEL: I LANG: Eng SIRC ARTICLE NO: 097558

PROGRAMS

Birch, D.A. Nybo, V. Promoting school health education in Maine: the Maine School Health Education Program. *Health educatio (Reston, V)* 15(5), Aug/Sept 1984, 67-68.
LEVEL: B LANG: Eng SIRC ARTICLE NO: 173136

Brunson, M.L. Concepts of health promotion for the occupational setting. Eugene, Ore.: Microform Publications, University of Oregon, 1984. 2 microfiches : negative ; 11 x 15 cm.
NOTES: Thesis (M.S.) - Pennsylvania State University, 1981; (vii, 97 leaves); includes bibliography.
LEVEL: A LANG: Eng UO84 110-111

Comprehensive school health education. *Journal of school health (Kent, Oh.)* 54(8), Sept 1984, 312-315.
LEVEL: B LANG: Eng SIRC ARTICLE NO: 105267

Comprehensive school health education. (Refs: 14)*Health education (Reston, Va.)* 15(6), Oct/Nov 1984, 4-7.
LEVEL: B LANG: En SIRC ARTICLE NO: 105268

Davis, M.F. Worksite health promotion: an overview of programs and practices. *Personnel administrator (Berea, Oh.)* 29(12), Dec 1984, 45;47-50.
LEVEL: B LANG: Eng SIRC ARTICLE NO: 102478

Fisher, J. Gay, J. Howart, P. Health education for behavioural or structural perspectives? (Refs: 14)*ACHPER national journa (Kingswood, Aust.)* 105, Spring 1984, 8-10.
LEVEL: B LANG: Eng SIRC ARTICLE NO: 102479

Fleming, J.H. Hospital organization, administration and wellness programming. (Refs: 24)*Physical educator (Indianapolis, Ind.)* 3(41), Oct 1984, 157-164.
LEVEL: B LANG: Eng SIRC ARTICLE NO: 100666

Frandsen, B.R. A needs assessment of selected corporations for health education programs. Eugene, Ore.: Microform Publications, University of Oregon, 1984. 1 microfiche : negative ; 11 x 15 cm.
NOTES: Thesis (M.S.) - Western Illinois University, 1981; (4, vi, 69 leaves); includes bibliography.
LEVEL: A LANG: Eng UO84 28

Gray, S.W. Status of church-related health promotion programs. (Refs: 9)*Florida JOHPERD (Gainesville, Fla.)* 22(4), Nov 1984 17-18;26.
LEVEL: I LANG: Eng SIRC ARTICLE NO: 105270

Hendricks, C.M. Development of a comprehensive health curriculum for Head Start. (Refs: 7)*Health education (Reston, Va.)* 15(2), Mar/Apr 1984, 28-31.
LEVEL: B LANG: Eng SIRC ARTICLE NO: 099021

Insurance companies offer employee wellness programs. *Employee health & fitness (Atlanta, Ga.)* 6(10), Oct 1984, 121-123.
LEVEL: B LANG: Eng SIRC ARTICLE NO: 102475

Kendall, P.C. Turk, D.C. Cognitive-behavioral strategies and health enhancement. (Refs: 73)*In, Matarazzo, J.D. (ed.) et al. Behavioral health: a handbook of health enhancement and disease prevention, New York, Wiley, c1984, p. 393-405.*
LEVEL: A LANG: Eng

Kittleson, M.J. Ragon, B.M. A survey of health education requirements in American universities. *Journal of school health (Kent, Oh.)* 54(2), Feb 1984, 91-92.
LEVEL: I LANG: Eng SIRC ARTICLE NO: 097555

Kolbe, L.J. Iverson, D.C. Comprehensive school health education programs. (Refs: 132)*In, Matarazzo, J.D. (ed.) et al., Behavioral health: a handbook of health enhancement and disease prevention, New York, Wiley, c1984, p. 1094-1116.*
LEVEL: I LANG: Eng

Livingood, W.C. The School Health Curriculum Project: its theory, practice, and measurement experience as a health education curriculum. (Refs: 18)*Health education (Reston, Va.)* 15(2), Mar/Apr 1984, 9-13.
LEVEL: B LANG: Eng SIRC ARTICLE NO: 099024

Livingwood, W.C. Backwards and not very humanistic: the Pennsylvania health curriculum progression chart. (Refs: 9)*Health education (Reston, Va.)* 15(6), Oct/Nov 1984, 49-52.
LEVEL: B LANG: Eng SIRC ARTICLE NO: 105274

Mehne, P.R. Garton, P.T. Barnes, R.C. Experience with competency-based curriculum design: a school and community health mode *Health education (Reston, Va.)* 15(3), May/Jun 1984, 14-18.
LEVEL: B LANG: Eng SIRC ARTICLE NO: 102480

Merwin, D.J. Northrop, B.A. Les programmes de sante en milieu de travail: des problemes complexes sans solutions simples. (Refs: 43)
NOTES: Dans, Lagarde F. (ed.), Sante et activite physique, Longueuil, Que., College Edouard-Montpetit, c1984, p. 97-105.
LEVEL: I LANG: Fr GV481 17104

Noble, K.A. A directory of Canadian Universities offering baccalaureate degree programmes with health education related courses. Ottawa: Canadian Health Education Society, 1984. 16 leaves (CHES technical publications; no. 5.)
LEVEL: B LANG: Eng RA440 18635

Okerlund, K. Launching the corporate health fair. (Refs: 3)*Employee services management (Westchester, Ill.)* 27(1), Feb 1984 34-35.
LEVEL: B LANG: Eng SIRC ARTICLE NO: 092837

Petosa, R. Wellness: an emerging opportunity for health education. (Refs: 23)*Health education (Reston, Va.)* 15(6), Oct/Nov 1984, 37-39.
LEVEL: B LANG: Eng SIRC ARTICLE NO: 105275

Pigg, R.M. Emerging trends in professional preparation: implications for the future of health education. (Refs: 11)*Journal of school health (Kent, Oh.)* 54(3), Mar 1984, 110-111.
LEVEL: I LANG: Eng SIRC ARTICLE NO: 099025

Preiffer, G. Build program support through involvement, communication. *Employee health & fitness (Atlanta, Ga.)* 6(10), Oct 1984, 117-120.
LEVEL: B LANG: Eng SIRC ARTICLE NO: 102739

Stevens, N.H. School health promotion: a study of exemplar districts. Eugene, Ore.: Miroform Publications, University of Oregon, 1984. 2 microfiches : negative, ill. ; 11 x 15 cm.
NOTES: Thesis (Ph.D.) - University of Oregon, 1984; (xi, 143 leaves); vita; includes bibliography.
LEVEL: A LANG: Eng UO84 432-433

Wallace, H. Cooke, G. The California statewide family health education and training program 1981-1982. (Refs: 19)*Journal of school health (Kent, Oh.)* 54(3), Mar 1984, 118-121.
LEVEL: B LANG: Eng SIRC ARTICLE NO: 099026

Weiss, S.M. Community health promotion demonstration programs: introduction. (Refs: 2)*In, Matarazzo, J.D. (ed.) et al., Behavioral health: a handbook of health enhancement and disease prevention, New York, Wiley, c1984, p. 1137-1139.*
LEVEL: B LANG: Eng

PSYCHOLOGY

Miller, N.E. Learning: some facts and needed research relevant to maintaining health. (Refs: 28)*In, Matarazzo, J.D. (ed.) e al., Behavioral health: a handbook of health enhancement and disease prevention, New York, Wiley, c1984, p. 199-208.*
LEVEL: I LANG: Eng

Richardson, G.E. Wylie, W.E. The effects of educational imagery on university students' creativity levels and locus of control. (Refs: 15)*Health education (Reston, Va.)* 15(1), Jan/Feb 1984, 42-47.
ABST: This report focuses on the effects of decision-making imagery and imagery geared toward the internalization of control on university students' creativity levels and locus of control. Two health education classes served as experimental groups while two others were the control groups. Both variables studied were positively influenced by educational imagery.
LEVEL: A LANG: Eng SIRC ARTICLE NO: 097556

RESEARCH AND RESEARCH METHODS

Basch, C.E. Research on disseminating and implementing health education programs in schools. (Refs: 109)*Proceedings of the National Conference on School Health Education Research in the Heart, Lung and Blood Areas (Washington) 1984, 57-66.*
CONF: National Conference on School Health Education Research in the Heart, Lung, and Blood Areas (1983 : Bethesda, Md.).
NOTES: Joint issue of Health Education (Reston, Va.) 15(4), 1984 and Journal of School Health (Washington) 54(6), 1984.
LEVEL: I LANG: Eng SIRC ARTICLE NO: 103994

Iverson, D.C. Issues related to designing and conducting school health education research. (Refs: 59)*Proceedings of the National Conference on School Health Education Research in the Heart, Lung and Blood Areas (Washington) 1984, 50-56.*
CONF: National Conference on School Health Education Research in the Heart, Lung, and Blood Areas (1983 : Bethesda, Md.).
NOTES: Joint issue of Health education (Reston, Va.) 15(4), 1984 and Journal of school health (Washington) 54(6), 1984.
LEVEL: I LANG: Eng SIRC ARTICLE NO: 103996

Jackson, V.D. Theoretical constructs underlaying the process of content validation in health education research. (Refs: 8) *Health education (Reston, Va.)* 15(2), Mar/Apr 1984, 37-39.
LEVEL: B LANG: Eng SIRC ARTICLE NO: 099023

Kreuter, M.W. Christenson, G.M. Davis, R. School health education research: future issues and challenges. (Refs: 18) *Proceedings of the National Conference on School Health Education Research in the Heart, Lung and Blood Areas (Washington) 1984, 27-32.*
CONF: National Conference on School Health Education Research in the Heart, Lung, and Blood Areas (1983 : Bethesda, Md.).

HEALTH EDUCATION (continued)

NOTES: Joint issue of Health Education (Reston, Va.) 15(4), 1984 and Journal of School Health (Washington) 54(6), 1984.
LEVEL: I LANG: Eng SIRC ARTICLE NO: 103998

Levenson, P.M. Morrow, J.R. Gregory, E.K. Pfefferbaum, B.J. A comparison of views of school nurses, teachers and middle-school students regarding health information interests and concerns. *Public health nursing (Boston) 1(3), Sept 1984, 141-151.*
LEVEL: A LANG: Eng

Parcel, G.S. Theoretical models for application in school health education research. (Refs: 121)*Proceedings of the National Conference on School Health Education Research in the Heart, Lung and Blood Areas (Washington) 1984, 39-49.*
CONF: National Conference on School Health Education Research in the Heart, Lung, and Blood Areas (1983 : Bethesda, Md.).
NOTES: Joint issue of Health education (Reston, Va.) 15(4), 1984 and Journal of school health (Washington) 54(6), 1984.
LEVEL: I LANG: Eng SIRC ARTICLE NO: 104000

SOCIOLOGY

Gross, R. A preliminary evaluation of a health promotion program for the reduction of health-risk behaviors of college students. Eugene, Ore.: Microform Publications, University of Oregon, 1984. 1 microfiche : negative, ill. ; 11 x 15 cm.
NOTES: Thesis (M.S.) - University of Oregon, 1984; (viii, 88 leaves); vita; includes bibliography.
LEVEL: A LANG: Eng UO84 428

Papenfuss, R. Developing, implementing, and evaluating a wellness education program. (Refs: 5)*Journal of school health (Kent, Ohio) 54(9), Oct 1984, 360-362.*
LEVEL: I LANG: Eng SIRC ARTICLE NO: 108224

TEACHER TRAINING

Gold, R. Gilbert, G.G. Levine, D.M. Training needs in school health education research. (Refs: 103)*Proceedings of the National Conference on School Health Education Research in the Heart, Lung and Blood Areas (Washington) 1984, 67-74.*
CONF: National Conference on School Health Education Research in the Heart, Lung, and Blood Areas (1983 : Bethesda, Md.).
NOTES: Joint issue of Health Education (Reston, Va.) 15(4), 1984 and Journal of School Health (Washington) 54(6), 1984.
LEVEL: I LANG: Eng SIRC ARTICLE NO: 103995

Lawrenz, F. A new approach to health education inservice training. (Refs: 12)*Journal of school health (Kent, Ohio) 54(9), Oct 1984, 353-354.*
LEVEL: B LANG: Eng SIRC ARTICLE NO: 108223

TEACHING

Scalzi, J. Health education in the elementary school. *WVAHPERD journal (Morgantown, W. Va.) 2(1), Winter/Spring 1984, 9-10.*
LEVEL: B LANG: Eng SIRC ARTICLE NO: 097557

TEACHING METHODS

Petosa, R. Gillespie, T. Microcomputers in health education: characteristics of quality instructional software. (Refs: 6) *Journal of school health (Kent, Ohio) 54(10), Nov 1984, 394-396.*
LEVEL: B LANG: Eng SIRC ARTICLE NO: 108219

WOMEN

Lechich, M.L. Health education in a women's prison. (Refs: 7)*Health education (Reston, Va.) 15(6), Oct/Nov 1984, 34-36.*
LEVEL: B LANG: Eng SIRC ARTICLE NO: 105272

HEPTATHLON

TRAINING AND CONDITIONING

Daly, J.A. How Glynis Nunn trains. *Modern athlete and coach (Athelstone, Aust.) 22(1), Jan 1984, 28-30.*
LEVEL: B LANG: En SIRC ARTICLE NO: 096924

HIGH JUMP

Dragan Tancic a l'I.N.S.E.P. *Revue de l'Amicale des entraineurs francais d'athletisme (Paris) 87, avr/mai/juin 1984, 33-37.*
LEVEL: B LANG: Fr SIRC ARTICLE NO: 096939

BIOGRAPHY AND AUTOBIOGRAPHY

Berenyi, I. Ludmila Andonova's quantum jump. *Athletics weekly (Kent, Eng.) 38(45), 10 Nov 1984, 52-54.*
LEVEL: B LANG: Eng SIRC ARTICLE NO: 103542

Fisher, M. Brill jumping for joy of it. Veteran track athlete isn't ready to retire. (Debbie Brill) *Globe and mail 140(41,932), 28 Apr 1984, S3.*
LEVEL: B LANG: Eng SIRC ARTICLE NO: 093857

Knight, K.T. High hopes for gold. (Louise Ritler) *Olympian (Colorado Springs, Colo.) 11(1), Jun 1984, 16-17.*
LEVEL: B LANG: Eng SIRC ARTICLE NO: 101640

Neff, C. He feels a bit constricted. Tyke Peacock longs for the NBA even as he sets high-jump marks. *Sports illustrated 60(7), 13 Feb 1984, 89;91.*
LEVEL: B LANG: Eng SIRC ARTICLE NO: 091055

Smith, G. The great leap upward. Appropriately, Zhu Jianhua of China was born in the Year of the Rabbit, for no man has jumped higher than he and only a very few are as skittish. *Sports illustrated (Chicago, Ill.) 61(4), 18 Jul 1984, 522-531;533.*
NOTES: Special preview: the 1984 Olympics.
LEVEL: B LANG: Eng SIRC ARTICLE NO: 096946

Willman, H. T&FN interview: Louise Ritter. *Track & field news (Los Altos, Calif.) 37(2), Mar 1984, 66-67.*
LEVEL: B LANG: Eng SIRC ARTICLE NO: 093864

Zhou, H. Zhu Jianhua - China's standard-bearer at the Los Angeles Olympics. *Sports (Kallang, Singapore) 12(6), Jul 1984, 8;30.*
LEVEL: B LANG: Eng SIRC ARTICLE NO: 101651

BIOMECHANICS

Reid, P. Speed floppers and power floppers. *Athletics coach (London) 18(3), Sept 1984, 18-20.*
NOTES: First presented at the Old Bushmills International Sports Academy for Coaches at the New University of Ulster, Corelaine, Northern Ireland on April, 1984.
LEVEL: I LANG: Eng SIRC ARTICLE NO: 100034

DISABLED

Alexander, M.J.L. Analysis of the high jump technique of an amputee. (Refs: 23)*Palaestra (Macomb, Ill.) 1(1), Fall 1984, 18-23;44-48.*
LEVEL: I LANG: Eng SIRC ARTICLE NO: 171814

HISTORY

Macleod, I. Women's high jump - no longer a Cinderella event. Jain Macleod traces the event from Iolanda Balas to Lyudmila Andonava. *Athletics weekly (Kent, Eng.) 38(51), 22 Dec 1984, 40-42;44-46;48-49.*
LEVEL: B LANG: Eng SIRC ARTICLE NO: 103545

INJURIES AND ACCIDENTS

Israeli, A. Ganel, A. Blankstein, A. Horoszowski, H. Stress fracture of the tibial tuberosity in a high jumper: case report. (Refs: 6)*International journal of sports medicine (Stuttgart) 5(6), Dec 1984, 299-300.*
ABST: A 16-year-old male high jumper sustained a stress fracture of the tibial tuberosity. Continued activity resulted in a type III fracture of the tibial tuberosity necessitating treatment via open reduction and internal fixation.
LEVEL: I LANG: Eng SIRC ARTICLE NO: 104947

PSYCHOLOGY

Hongfei, H. Zhu Jianhua's psycho-training. *China sports (Beijing, China) 16(3), Mar 1984, 10-13.*
LEVEL: B LANG: Eng SIRC ARTICLE NO: 100032

Reid, P. The psychological side of jumping high. *Modern athlete and coach (Athelstone, Aust.) 22(3), Jul 1984, 7-10.*
LEVEL: B LANG: Eng SIRC ARTICLE NO: 101645

STATISTICS AND RECORDS

Hongfei, H. From 2.37m to 2.38m. (high jump) *Track and field quarterly review (Kalamazoo, Mich.) 84(4), Winter 1984, 22-23.*
LEVEL: B LANG: Eng SIRC ARTICLE NO: 101639

Reid, P. World championships technical reports: women's and men's high jump. *Track and field journal (Ottawa) 28, Nov 1984, 20-31.*
LEVEL: B LANG: Eng SIRC ARTICLE NO: 103549

TEACHING

Keller, J. Saut en hauteur: une demarche pedagogique. (Refs: 5)*EPS: Education physique et sport (Paris, France) 186, mars/avr 1984, 17-19.*
NOTES: A suivre.
LEVEL: B LANG: Fr SIRC ARTICLE NO: 095384

Keller, J. Une demarche pedagogique. 2e partie. Saut en hauteur. (Refs: 6)*EPS: Education physique et sport (Paris) 187, mai/juin 1984, 23-27.*
LEVEL: B LANG: Fr SIRC ARTICLE NO: 096943

Portmann, M. L'enseignement du saut en hauteur dorsal en six etapes. *Track & field journal (Ottawa)* 28, Nov 1984, 9-13.
LEVEL: B LANG: Fr SIRC ARTICLE NO: 103547

TECHNIQUES AND SKILLS

Chu, D.A. The approach pattern in the Fosbury flop. *Track and field quarterly review (Kalamazoo, Mich.)* 84(4), Winter 1984, 15-16.
LEVEL: B LANG: Eng SIRC ARTICLE NO: 101629

Couling, D. Jumping above yourself. *Athletics coach (Halesowen, England)* 18(1), Mar 1984, 15-17.
LEVEL: B LANG: Eng SIRC ARTICLE NO: 093855

Crissey, J. Developing the flop approach run. *Athletic journal* 64(9), Apr 1984, 14;75.
LEVEL: B LANG: Eng SIRC ARTICLE NO 093856

Dursenev, L.I. Papanov, V. Gennady Avdeenko in the high jump. *Soviet sports review (Escondido, Calif.)* 19(4), Dec 1984, 178-181.
NOTES: Translated from, Legkaya atletika 9, 1984, 16-17.
LEVEL: B LANG: Eng SIRC ARTICLE NO: 104946

Hongfei, H. Fast approach and quick take-off: the technique of Zhu Jianhua. *Athletic Asia (Patiala, India)* 13(2), Sept 1984 23-28.
LEVEL: I LANG: Eng SIRC ARTICLE NO: 106126

Muthiah, C.M. High jump. *Athletic Asia (Patiala, India)* 13(2), Sept 1984, 29-40.
NOTES: Presented during the IOC Solidarity Asian Regional Track and Field Course, New Delhi 1984.
LEVEL: B LANG: Eng SIRC ARTICLE NO: 106130

Sloan, R. Factors influencing the development of the flop high jumper. *Track and field quarterly review (Kalamazoo, Mich.)* 84(4), Winter 1984, 12-14.
LEVEL: B LANG: Eng SIRC ARTICLE NO: 101647

Wang, F. Zhu's salient features. (Zhu Jianhua) *China sports (Beijing, China)* 16(6), Jun 1984, 34-36.
LEVEL: B LANG: Eng SIRC ARTICLE NO: 102187

Webb, D.G. Effective high jumping. *Coaching clinic* 22(6), Feb 1984, 15-16.
LEVEL: B LANG: Eng SIRC ARTICLE NO: 091060

TESTING AND EVALUATION

Goss, M. Pole vaulter's movie analysis. *Track and field quarterly review (Kalamazoo, Mich.)* 84(4), Winter 1984, 34-35.
LEVEL: B LANG: Eng SIRC ARTICLE NO: 101635

Reid, P. Helsinki observations: high jump - men. *Modern athlete and coach (Athelstone, Aust.)* 22(2), Apr 1984, 3-5.
LEVEL B LANG: Eng SIRC ARTICLE NO: 096945

Viitasalo, J.T. Aura, O. Seasonal fluctuations of force production in high jumpers. (Refs: 24)*Canadian journal of applied sport sciences/ Journal canadien des sciences appliquees au sport (Windsor, Ont.)* 9(4), Dec 1984, 209-213.
ABST: To investigate the influence of training on the isometric force-time (f-t) characteristics and on dynamic force production, eight Finnish male high jumpers were tested six to seven times during a twelve month period. The variations in the isometric maximal force, in the rate of isometric force development (RFD) as well as in the vertical jumping height during the follow-up period were

compared to the respective changes in the high jump results. The RFD and vertical jumping heights were found to show their highest values relative to the other seasons during the competitive seasons in January and July-August. The changes in the maximal isometric strengths did not coincide with the changes in the high jump results.
LEVEL: A LANG: Eng SIRC ARTICLE NO: 103552

Xinwang, F. An analysis of Zhu Jianhua's run-up technique. *China sports (Beijing, China)* 16(10), Oct 1984, 15-18.
LEVEL: LANG: Eng SIRC ARTICLE NO: 109051

TRAINING AND CONDITIONING

Dyatchkov, V.M. Kutsar, K. The preparation training phase of top level high jumpers. *Modern athlete and coach (Athelstone, Aust.)* 22(2), Apr 1984, 33-35.
NOTES: Based on information collected from Dyatchkov's last published works.
LEVEL: B LANG: Eng SIRC ARTICLE NO: 096940

Gainey, L. High jumping. *Track and field quarterly review (Kalamazoo, Mich.)* 84(4), Winter 1984, 10-11.
NOTES: Presented at the 1979 Medalist Track Coaches' Clinic, Atlanta, Georgia.
LEVEL: B LANG: Eng SIRC ARTICLE NO: 101633

Hongfei, H. How I trained Zhu Jianhua. *China sports (Beijing, China)* 16(2), Feb 1984, 12-13.
LEVEL: B LANG: Eng SIRC ARTICLE NO: 098608

Reid, P. Preparing to peak when it counts. How one coach is planning for a personal best in a 1984 Olympic final. *Coaching review (Ottawa, Ont.)* 7, May/Jun 1984, 19-21.
LEVEL: B LANG: Eng SIRC ARTICLE NO: 095387

Reid, P. Technique and training of speed and power floppers. *Modern athlete and coach (Athelstone, Aust.)* 22(4), Oct 1984, 3-6.
LEVEL: B LANG: Eng SIRC ARTICLE NO: 104951

TRAINING AND CONDITIONING - DRILLS

Goss, M. The beginning pole vaulter's start and problem solving. *Track and field quarterly review (Kalamazoo, Mich.)* 84(4), Winter 1984, 33-34.
LEVEL: B LANG: Eng SIRC ARTICLE NO: 101634

Goss, M. Pole vault - drills. *Track and field quarterly review (Kalamazoo, Mich.)* 84(4), Winter 1984, 35.
LEVEL: B LANG: Eng SIRC ARTICLE NO: 101636

HIGHLAND GAMES

HISTORY

Crawford, S.A.G.M. The origins of Scottish Highland Games. (Refs: 16)*Scottish journal of physical education (Glasgow, Scotland)* 12(4), Nov 1984, 44-47.
LEVEL: B LANG: Eng SIRC ARTICLE NO: 102482

Jarvie, G. Sport, social class and the Highland landlords. (Refs: 12)*Carnegie research papers (Beckett Park, Leeds)* 1(6), Dec 1984, 12-15.
ABST: The author briefly discusses the social organisation and reorganisation of Highland Society from the 12th century to the end of the 19th

century. He underlines the significance of sport to the Highland landlords and the influence of the aristocracy upon the development of the Highland Games.
LEVEL: A LANG: Eng SIRC ARTICLE NO: 172499

HISTORICAL RESEARCH AND HISTORIOGRAPHY

DIRECTORIES

Morrow, D. Directory of scholars identifying with the history of sport 1984. 3rd ed. s.l.: North American Society for Sport History, 1984. v, 70 leaves
CORP: North American Society for Sport History.
LEVEL: B LANG: Eng GV571 9040

TEACHING

Jebsen, H. Integrating sports history into American history courses. *Social studies (Washington)* 75(2), Mar/Apr 1984, 62-67.
LEVEL: I LANG: Eng SIRC ARTICLE NO: 097561

Jebsen, H. Integrating sports history into American history courses. (Refs: 75)*Social studies (Washington)* Mar/Apr 1984, 62-67.
LEVEL: I LANG: Eng

HISTORY

Bale, J. International sports history as innovation diffusion. (Refs: 59)*Canadian journal of history of sport/Revue canadienne de l'histoire des sports (Windsor)* 15(1), May 1984, 38-63.
ABST: Modeling in sports history has been unpopular because of the unpredictable and uneven nature in the development of sports. Hierarchical diffusion is one model that has gained recognition for the explanation of growth trends in modern sports. Innovation diffusion - the diffusion of sports to neighboring areas where the sport is perceived as new - is offered as another process affecting the spread of sports. Evidence is given in support of both models. Sports growth curves show a faster rate of adoption of sports in industrialized nations, predicted by hierarchical diffusion, yet the typical S-shape of the curves indicate an important temporal factor, supported by innovation diffusion. As well, figures show the spacial radiation of sports over time from its place of origin. These models are used only to depict the patterns of events, leaving the manner by which sports may spread open for discussion.
LEVEL: A LANG: Eng SIRC ARTICLE NO: 108315

Eyler, M.H. Massicotte, J.P. Les origines de divers sports contemporains. *Dans, Massicotte, J.P. et Lessard, C. (eds.), Histoire du sport de l'antiquite au XIXe siecle, Sillery, Que., Presses de l'Universite du Quebec*, 1984, p. 171-179.
NOTES: Traduit par, Jean-Paul Massicotte.
LEVEL: A LANG: Fr GV571 18971

Mandell, R.D. Sport - a cultural history. New York: Colombia University Press, c1984. xx, 340 p.
NOTES: Includes bibliographical essays.
LEVEL: A LANG: Eng ISBN: 0-231-05470-X LC CARD: 83-20017 GV706.5 21001

Massicotte, J.P. Lessard, C. Histoire du sport de l'antiquite au XIXe siecle. Sillery, Que.: Presses de l'Universite du Quebec, 1984. xii, 311 p. : ill.
NOTES: Comprend des bibliographies.
LEVEL: A LANG: Fr ISBN: 2-7605-0344-5 GV571 18971

Redmond, G. Sport history in academe: reflections on a half-century of peculiar progress. (Refs: 75)*British journal of sports history (London) 1(1), May 1984, 24-40.*
ABST: The author surveys the relatively new discipline of sport history. Particular attention is paid to the kind of research being done and to the kind of people attracted to the new specialization, e.g. physical educators, historians, classicists etc. Status within the academic community varies considerably according to the subject and the department involved.
LEVEL: A LANG: Eng SIRC ARTICLE NO: 108505

Walvin, J. Sport, social history and the historian. *British journal of sports history (London) 1(1), May 1984, 5-13.*
LEVEL: I LANG: Eng SIRC ARTICLE NO: 108503

Wonneberger, G. Liebold, K. International compilation of sports historical documents. V. Recueil international de documents sportifs historiques. V. Coleccion internacional de documentos historicos de deporte. V. Mezhdynarodnuj sbornik sportivnoistoricheskikh dokumentov. V. Internationale Sammlung sporthistorischer Dokumente. V. Leipzig, G.D.R.: German College for Physical Culture, 1984. 272 p. : ill.
CORP: International Committee for the History of Sports and Physical Education.
LEVEL: A LANG: Eng Fr Spa Rus Ger GV571 18466

Wynne, B.A. Wynne, J.C. Book of sports trophies. New York: Cornwall Books, c1984. 185 p. : ill.
NOTES: Includes index. Bibliography: p. 179-182.
LEVEL: B LANG: Eng ISBN: 0845347462 LC CARD: 82-071438 GV576 18226

ANCIENT HISTORY

Howell, M.L. Reflexions sur la place des sports, des jeux et des activites physiques durant l'Antiquite. *Dans, Massicotte, J.P. et Lessard, C. (eds.), Histoire du sport de l'antiquite au XIXe siecle, Sillery, Que., Presses de l'Universite du Quebec, 1984, p. 9-19.*
LEVEL: I LANG: Fr GV571 18971

Howell, M.L. Les sceaux de pierre de musee Ashmolean illustrant les activites physiques de la periode minoenne. *Dans, Massicotte, J.P. et Lessard, C. (eds.), Histoire du sport de l'antiquite au XIXe siecle, Sillery, Que., Presses de l'Universite du Quebec, 1984, p. 21-30.*
LEVEL: A LANG: Fr GV571 18971

Howell, M.L. Les sports et les jeux chez les Etrusques. (Refs: 34)*Dans, Massicotte, J.P. et Lessard, C. (eds.), Histoire du sport de l'antiquite au XIXe siecle, Sillery, Que., Presses de l'Universite du Quebec, 1984, p. 51-64.*
LEVEL: A LANG: Fr GV571 18971

Olivova, V. Sports and games in the ancient world. London: Orbis Publishing Limited, 1984. 207, (1) p. : ill.
NOTES: Bibliography: p. 199-203.
LEVEL: I LANG: Eng ISBN: 0-85613-273-X GV17 18223

ANCIENT HISTORY - EGYPT

Abdou, K.S. Les sports et les jeux de l'ancienne Egypte. (Refs: 22)*Dans, Massicotte, J.P. et Lessard, C. (eds.), Histoire d sport de l'antiquite au XIXe siecle, Sillery, Que., Presses de l'Universite du Quebec, 1984, p. 31-40.*
LEVEL: A LANG: Fr GV571 18971

Frank, R. Olympic myths and realities. *Arete: the journal of sport literature (San Diego, Calif.) 1(2), Spring 1984, 155-161.*
LEVEL: I LANG: Eng SIRC ARTICLE NO: 097559

ANCIENT HISTORY - GREECE

Dickie, M.W. Fair and foul play in the funeral games in the Iliad. (Refs: 9)*Journal of sport history (University Park, Pa.) 11(2), Summer 1984, 8-17.*
LEVEL: I LANG: Eng SIRC ARTICLE NO: 099028

Forbes, C. L'education physique a Athenes au Ve siecle avant Jesus-Christ. (Refs: 11)*Dans, Massicotte, J.P. et Lessard, C. (eds.), Histoire du sport de l'antiquite au XIXe siecle, Sillery, Que., Presses de l'Universite du Quebec, 1984, p. 41-50.*
LEVEL: A LANG: Fr GV571 18971

Lefkowitz, M.R. The poet as athlete. (Refs: 19)*Journal of sport history (University Park, Pa.) 11(2), Summer 1984, 18-24.*
LEVEL: I LANG: Eng SIRC ARTICLE NO: 099343

Poliakoff, C. Poliakoff, M. Jacob, Job, and other wrestlers: reception of Greek athletics by Jews and Christians in Antiquit (Refs: 31)*Journal of sport history (University Park, Pa.) 11(2), Summer 1984, 48-65.*
LEVEL: I LANG: Eng SIRC ARTICLE NO: 099029

Powell, J.T. Ancient Greek athletic festivals. *Olympic review (Lausanne, Switzerland) 198, Apr 1984, 259-264.*
NOTES: To b continued.
LEVEL: I LANG: Eng SIRC ARTICLE NO: 094343

Powell, J.T. Ancient Greek athletic festivals. *Olympic review (Lausanne) 199, May 1984, 329-332;340.*
NOTES: Continuation and end.
LEVEL: B LANG: Eng SIRC ARTICLE NO: 095897

Powell, J.T. Celebrations athletiques dans la Grece antique. *Revue olympique (Lausanne) 198, avr 1984, 259-264.*
NOTES: A suivre.
LEVEL: I LANG: Fr SIRC ARTICLE NO: 095898

Powell, J.T. Celebrations athletiques dans la Grece antique. *Revue olympique (Lausanne) 199, mai 1984, 329-332;340.*
NOTES Suite et fin.
LEVEL: B LANG: Fr SIRC ARTICLE NO: 104009

Scanlon, T.F. Greek and Roman athletics: a bibliography. 1st ed. Chicago, Ill.: Ares, 1984. 142 p.
LEVEL: I LANG: Eng ISBN: 0-89005-522-X GV17 17988

ANCIENT HISTORY - ROME

Howell, M.L. L'activite physique et le sport a Rome. (Refs: 4)*Dans, Massicotte, J.P. et Lessard, C. (eds.), Histoire du sport de l'antiquite au XIXe siecle, Sillery, Que., Presses de l'Universite du Quebec, 1984, p. 65-70.*
LEVEL: I LANG: Fr GV571 18971

Scanlon, T.F. Greek and Roman athletics: a bibliography. 1st ed. Chicago, Ill.: Ares, 1984. 142 p.
LEVEL: I LANG: Eng ISBN: 0-89005-522-X GV17 17988

MIDDLE AGES

Broekhoff, J. L'education physique, le sport et les ideaux de la chevalerie. (Refs: 36)*Dans, Massicotte, J.P. et Lessard, C (eds.), Histoire du sport de l'antiquite au XIXe siecle, Sillery, Que., Presses de l'Universite du Quebec, 1984, p. 75-91.*
LEVEL: A LANG: Fr GV571 18971

Carter, J.M. Muscular Christianity and its makers: sporting monks and churchmen in Anglo-Norman Society, 1000-1300. (Refs: 201)*British journal of sports history (London) 1(2), Sept 1984, 109-124.*
LEVEL: A LANG: Eng SIRC ARTICLE NO: 104003

MODERN HISTORY - NINETEENTH CENTURY

Mangan, J.A. Christ and the Imperial Games Fields: Evangelical athletes of the Empire. (Refs: 85)*British journal of sports history (London) 1(2), Sept 1984, 184-201.*
LEVEL: A LANG: Eng SIRC ARTICLE NO: 104007

RENAISSANCE

McIntosh, P.C. L'education phsyique en Italie durant la Renaissance et en Angleterre a l'epoque des Tudors. (Refs: 19)*Dans, Massicotte, J.P. et Lessard, C. (eds.), Histoire du sport de l'antiquite au XIXe siecle, Sillery, Que., Presses de l'Universite du Quebec, 1984, p. 93-108.*
LEVEL: A LANG: Fr GV571 18971

HOCKEY

Chouinard, N. Proulx, R. Survey on university ice hockey players. (Refs: 5)*CAHPER journal (Ottawa) 51(2), Nov/Dec 1984, 12-16.*
ABST: 487 ice hockey players from 30 Canadian university teams participated in this study. Results were analysed as a whole and also by conference. Subjects were asked about their past and present hockey experiences as well as about their reasons for selecting their particular university. 72.% of the athletes played junior hockey, 30.2% played at high school level and 28.1% played with a major junior club. Academic program (27.2%), hockey program (26.1%) and geographical proximity (18%) were the major reasons for choosing present university.
LEVEL: A LANG: Eng SIRC ARTICLE NO: 103233

Cooper, B. Hart, G. The hockey trivia book. New York: Leisure Press, c1984. 141 p. : ill.
LEVEL: B LANG: Eng ISBN: 08801123 LC CARD: 84-000757 GV847 18172

Hull, B. Nelson, R.G. Bereswill, P.J. Deslauriers, N. La methode de hockey Bobby Hull. Montreal: Accent sport, (1984). 90 p. : ill.
NOTES: Traduit de: Bobby Hull's hockey made easy.
LEVEL: B LANG: Fr ISBN: 2-89066-089-3 LC CARD: C84-9666-6 GV847 18899

Parrish, W. TV game book. The new hockey action digest. Montreal: CBC Enterprises, c1984. 128 p. : ill.

LEVEL: B LANG: Eng ISBN: 0-88794-144-3 GV847 18345

ADMINISTRATION

McKenzie, B. Agents: love 'em or loathe 'em, they're as much a part of the game today as the players. *Hockey news 37(26)*, 3 Mar 1984, 16;18.
LEVEL: B LANG: Eng SIRC ARTICLE NO: 093521

Milbert, N. The Goal interview: William Wirtz. *Goal (New York) 12*, Dec 1984, 26-28.
LEVEL: B LANG: Eng SIRC ARTICLE NO: 108704

Proudfoot, J. The goal interview: Harold Ballard. *Goal (New York) 11*, Mar 1984, 26-28.
LEVEL: B LANG: Eng SIRC ARTICLE NO 099703

Strachan, A. Managing quite nicely, thank you. *Goal (New York) 11*, Jan 1984, 56-59.
LEVEL: B LANG: Eng SIRC ARTICLE NO: 095097

ASSOCIATIONS

Constitution, by-laws, history: as adopted at Ottawa, December 4th, 1914 and amended to May, 1984. Vanier, Ont.: Canadian Amateur Hockey Association, 1984. 83 p.
CORP: Canadian Amateur Hockey Association.
LEVEL: B LANG: Eng GV848.4.C3 18305

Constitution, statuts, historique tel qu'adopte a Ottawa, le 4 decembre, 1914 et amende jusqu'a mai 1984. Ottawa: Association canadienne de hockey amateur, 1984. 86 p.
CORP: Association canadienne de hockey amateur.
LEVEL: B LANG: Fr GV848.4.C3 18646

BIOGRAPHY AND AUTOBIOGRAPHY

Capouya, J. Gretzkymania: the man who owns Canada. Canada is spread over 4 million square miles. Its people speak two different languages. But all Canadians have two things in common: their flag and Wayne Gretzky. *Sport (New York) 75(5)*, May 1984, 28-29;31-32;34.
LEVEL: B LANG: Eng SIRC ARTICLE NO: 093509

Dickie, D. Pat Flatley, en attendant de passer professionnel. Pat Flatley, putting the pros on hold. *Champion 8(1)*, Feb 1984, 32-33.
LEVEL: B LANG: Eng Fr SIRC ARTICLE NO: 090735

Fischler, S. Hall, G. Hockey's 100: a personal ranking of the best players in hockey history. Toronto: Stoddart, c1984. xii, 366 p. : ill.
NOTES: Includes index
LEVEL: B LANG: Eng ISBN: 0-7737-5014-2 LC CARD: C84-099051-0 GV848.5.A1 18320

Fischler, S. Who is (was) hockey's greatest superstar? *Goal (New York) 11*, Feb 1984, 62;64;66.
LEVEL: B LANG: Eng SIRC ARTICLE NO: 098167

Fischler, S. And a child shall lead them. (Mario Lemieux) *Inside sports (Evanston, Ill.) 6*, Dec 1984, 62;64-66.
LEVEL: B LANG: Eng SIRC ARTICLE NO: 101326

Friedman, R. Courage and hope: a salute to Normand Leveille. *Goal (New York) 12*, Nov 1984, 57.
LEVEL: B LANG: Eng SIRC ARTICLE NO: 173379

Glauber, B. Family man: as much as the Islanders' superstar Bryan Trottier loves the fame he plays so well, family is his number one priority. *Goal (New*

York) 12, Dec 1984, 2;4;6;8.
LEVEL: B LANG: Eng SIRC ARTICLE NO: 108700

Gretzky, W. Taylor, J. Gretzky: from the back yard rink to the Stanley Cup. (Toronto): McClelland & Stewart, c1984. 281 p. : ill.
LEVEL: B LANG: Eng ISBN: 0-7710-8438-2 LC CARD: C84-099172-X GV848.5.G73 17963

Hirdt, P. Gretzkyology: going by the numbers. At age 23, Gretzky ranks with the titans of team sports. But the GREAT ONE IS NOT THE GREATEST ONE. Not yet. *Sport (New York) 75(5)*, May 1984, 36-37.
LEVEL: B LANG: Eng SIRC ARTICLE NO: 093513

Jackson, T. The secretary of defense: Norris Trophy winner Rod Langway is teaching his Capitals that even after they lose some battles, if they keep coming back, they'll probably win the war. *Inside sports (Evanston, Ill.) 6*, Mar 1984, 46-48;52;54.
LEVEL: B LANG: Eng SIRC ARTICLE NO: 108804

Levine, D. Gretskyism: way ahead of the game. He towers over his game like no one else today on any team in any other sport. The list of NHL scoring leaders reads: Gretzky, then the rest. How does he do it? *Sport (New York) 75(5)*, May 1984, 39-41.
LEVEL: B LANG: Eng SIRC ARTICLE NO: 093518

McFarlane, B. Brian McFarlane's NHL hockey. (Toronto): McClelland and Stewart Limited, c1984. 128 p. : ill.
NOTES: On cover The young fan's indispensable guide to the 1984-85 season.
LEVEL: B LANG: Eng ISBN: 0-7710-5431-9 LC CARD: C84-099320-X GV847.8.N3 18194

Mordhorst, J. Thayer Tutt: hockey's in his system. What started out as a passive interest has turned out ot be a full-time friendship. *American hockey magazine (Colorado Springs, Colo.) 5(6)*, Nov 1984, 20-24.
LEVEL: B LANG: Eng SIRC ARTICLE NO: 107268

Norville, D. Bobby Clarke: he loves to play the old-fashioned way. *Inside sports (Evanston, Ill.) 6*, Apr 1984, 18-24.
LEVEL: B LANG: Eng SIRC ARTICLE NO: 095093

Papanek, J. Brubaker, B. The man who rules hockey. Alan Eagleson, union boss, friend of management, players' agent and international negotiator, has used his many conflicting roles to take control of the sport in the NHL and beyond. *Sports illustrated (Chicago, Ill.) 61(1)*, 2 Jul 1984, 60-64;66;68-72;74.
LEVEL: B LANG: Eng SIRC ARTICLE NO: 095095

Phillips, B. The Goal interview: Emile Francis. *Goal (New York) 12*, Nov 1984, 54-56.
LEVEL: B LANG: Eng SIRC ARTICLE NO: 173378

Proudfoot, J. The goal interview: Alan Eagleson. *Goal (New York) 11*, Apr 1984, 17-19.
LEVEL: B LANG: Eng SIRC ARTICLE NO: 101329

Sport interview: Mike Milbury. You may not have heard of him, but his ideas have everyone in hockey listening. *Sport (New Yor 75(12)*, Dec 1984, 17-20;22-23.
LEVEL: B LANG: Eng SIRC ARTICLE NO: 108683

Swift, E.M. Pat these Pats on the back: Olympic star Pat LaFontaine and Pat Flatley are lighting up the NHL. *Sports illustrated 60(13)*, 26 Mar 1984, 22-24;27.
LEVEL: B LANG: Eng SIRC ARTICLE NO: 093525

Swift, E.M. Rough chips off the old block. The NHL's Hunter brothers, Dave, Dale and Mark, learned to play hockey the old-fashioned way, from their old-fashioned father, Dick. *Sports illustrated (Los Angeles, Calif.) 61(26)*, 10 Dec 1984, 46-48;55;58;63.
LEVEL: B LANG: Eng SIRC ARTICLE NO: 103243

Williams, T. Lawton, J. Tiger: a hockey story. Vancouver: Douglas & McIntyre, c1984. 172 p. : ill.
LEVEL: B LANG: Eng ISBN: 0-88894-448-9 LC CARD: C84-091225-0 GV848.5.W54 17885

Wolff, C.T. Curtis, B. Bennett, B. Subrahmanyam, A. Wayne Gretzky: profil d'un joueur de hockey. Scarborough, Ont.: Avon Books, c1984. (70) p. : ill. (Un livre Avon/Camelot.)
NOTES: Traduit de, Wayne Gretzky: portrait of a hockey player, Scarborough, Ont., Avon, c1983.
LEVEL: B LANG: Fr ISBN: 0-380-85753-7 LC CARD: 82-20570 GV848.5.G73 17510

BIOMECHANICS

Emmert, W. The slap shot - strength and conditioning program for hockey at Boston College. (Refs: 8)*National Strength & Conditioning Association journal (Lincoln, Neb.) 6(2)*, Apr/May 1984, 4-6;68;71;73.
LEVEL: I LANG: Eng SIRC ARTICLE NO: 095087

Greer, N.L. Application of biomechanics to ice hockey. *American hockey magazine (Colorado Springs, Colo.) 5(7)*, Dec 1984, 21-23.
LEVEL: B LANG: Eng SIRC ARTICLE NO: 107265

Marino, G.W. Analysis of selected factors in the ice skating strides of adolescents. (Refs: 5)*CAHPER journal/Revue de l'ACSEPR (Vanier, Ont.) 50(3)*, Jan/Feb 1984, 4-8.
LEVEL: I LANG: Eng SIRC ARTICLE NO: 095089

CHILDREN

Robertson, H. Minor hockey: who's really playing, parents or kids? *Chatelaine 57(3)*, Mar 1984, 78-79;202;204;206-207.
LEVEL: B LANG: Eng SIRC ARTICLE NO: 090739

CLUBS AND TEAMS

Chamberlain, D. The strangest team under the sun. Blue skies, wavering palms, sandy beaches. How can anyone play hockey unde these conditions? *Sport (New York) 75(4)*, Apr 1984, 91-94;96;98.
LEVEL: B LANG: Eng SIRC ARTICLE NO: 093510

Powers, J. Kaminsky, A.C. One goal: a chronicle of the 1980 U.S. Olympic Hockey Team. 1st ed. New York: Harper & Row, c1984. x, (259) p. : ill.
NOTES: Bibliography: p. (259).
LEVEL: I LANG: Eng ISBN: 0060152001 LC CARD: 83-047540 GV848.4.U6 15939

COACHING

Bergeron, M. Donnelly, B. Behind the bench with: Michel Bergeron. *Goal (New York) 11*, Feb 1984, 8;10.
LEVEL: B LANG: Eng SIRC ARTICLE NO: 098166

Demers, J. Csolak, G. Behind the bench with: Jacques Demers. *Goal (New York) 12*, Dec 1984, 20-21.
LEVEL: B LANG: Eng SIRC ARTICLE NO: 108703

HOCKEY (continued)

Evans, J. Lantier, J. Behind the bench with: Jack Evans. *Goal (New York) 11, Mar 1984, 8;10.*
LEVEL: B LANG: Eng SIRC ARTICLE NO: 099700

Fischler, S. The goal interview: Scotty Bowman. *Goal (New York) 11, May/Jun 1984, 22-24.*
LEVEL: B LANG: Eng SIRC ARTICLE NO: 099701

Garvie, G. Coach you're worth a million bucks: a nostalgic piece about a coach who cared. *Coaching review 7, Mar/Apr 1984, 42-44.*
LEVEL: B LANG: Eng SIRC ARTICLE NO: 093511

Greenberg, J. The cutting edge of Scotty Bowman. Buffalo's belligerent coach is the conscience of his young team: demanding the best, ridiculing excuses, and kicking out the crutches. *Inside sports (Harlan, Iowa) 6, May 1984, 42-44;46;48.*
LEVEL: B LANG: Eng SIRC ARTICLE NO: 093512

Howland, C. A thorough approach: Canadian-born coach Terry Martin and his hockey team keep rolling along. *Coaching review 7 Mar/Apr 1984, 19-22.*
LEVEL: B LANG: Eng SIRC ARTICLE NO: 093515

Jacques Lemaire: the man with one of the toughest jobs in professional hockey talks about his coaching experiences in Europe, in the college and junior ranks, and with the Montreal Canadiens. *Coaching review (Ottawa) 7, Sept/Oct 1984, 8-16.*
LEVEL: B LANG: Eng SIRC ARTICLE NO: 098171

Mehr, M. The puck starts here. *Financial post magazine (Toronto, Ont.) 1 Apr 1984, 108-109;113-114.*
LEVEL: B LANG: Eng SIRC ARTICLE NO: 095091

Milbert, N. Cheevers, G. Behind the bench with: Gerry Cheevers. *Goal (New York) 11, Jan 1984, 8;10.*
LEVEL: B LANG: Eng SIRC ARTICLE NO: 095092

Newman, S. Coaching in Europe. *Coaching review 7, Mar/Apr 1984, 32-38.*
LEVEL: B LANG: Eng SIRC ARTICLE NO: 093522

Orr, F. Four years in Sweden opened my eyes. (Tom Martin) *Sport-talk (Toronto) 13(1), Mar 1984, 1;4.*
LEVEL: B LANG: Eng SIRC ARTICLE NO: 095094

Orr, F. Pep talks: do's and don'ts. *Sport-talk (Toronto) 13(2), May 1984, 1-2.*
LEVEL: B LANG: Eng SIRC ARTICLE NO: 098176

Orr, F. Why NHL teams haven't copied the Oilers' style. *Sport-talk (Toronto) 13(4), Dec 1984, 6.*
LEVEL: B LANG: Eng SIRC ARTICLE NO: 104799

Simmons, S. The goal interview: Dave King. *Goal (New York) 11, Jan 1984, 17-19.*
LEVEL: B LANG: Eng SIRC ARTICLE NO: 09509

Swift, E.M. At least he hasn't lost his voice: coach Tom McVie of the Devils has one more hellish team to holler at. *Sports illustrated 60(1), 9 Jan 1984, 40-43.*
LEVEL: B LANG: Eng SIRC ARTICLE NO: 090740

Taylor, J. A new season, a new team a new set of programs: coach weaknesses play strengths. *Sport-talk (Toronto) 13(2), May 1984, 3.*
LEVEL: B LANG: Eng SIRC ARTICLE NO: 098180

Tessier, O. Behind the bench with: Orval Tessier. *Goal (New York) 11, May/Jun 1984, 14;16.*
LEVEL: B LANG: Eng SIRC ARTICL NO: 099705

The interview: Bill LaForge. *Hockey news (Toronto, Ont.) 38(11), 7 Dec 1984, M1;M3;M6.*
LEVEL: B LANG: Eng SIRC ARTICLE NO: 103236

DIRECTORIES

1984-85 College Hockey directory. *American hockey magazine (Colorado Springs, Colo.) 5(7), Dec 1984, 6C-9C.*
LEVEL: B LANG: Eng SIRC ARTICLE NO: 107261

Griffin, M. Halligan, J. National Hockey League official guide and record book 1984-85. (Toronto): National Hockey League, c1984. 352 p. : ill.
LEVEL: B LANG: Eng ISBN: 0-920445-00-4
GV847.8.N3 18189

Jepson, G. 1984 annual summer camp guide. *American hockey & arena (Colorado Springs, Colo.) 5(2), Feb 1984, G-1/G-15.*
LEVEL: B LANG: Eng SIRC ARTICLE NO: 098173

ECONOMICS

Marsh, J.S. The economic impact of a small city annual sporting event: an initial case study of the Peterborough Church League Atom Hockey Tournament. (Refs: 5)*Recreation research review (Concord, Ont.) 11(1), Mar 1984, 48-55.*
ABST: A survey was conducted during the 1982 Peterborough Church League Atom Tournament to determine overall expenditures of tournament participants and organizers in the Peterborough area. Finding indicated expenditure of some $165,165 in Peterborough.
LEVEL: A LANG: Eng SIRC ARTICLE NO: 105912

Mordhorst, J. Division I: who's getting the aid? *American hockey magazine (Colorado Springs, Colo.) 5(7), Dec 1984, 15C-16C*
LEVEL: B LANG: Eng SIRC ARTICLE NO: 107269

Wayne, J. Carling tries to lure TV hockey fans in $25-million face-off. *Financial post 78(7), 18 Feb 1984, 24.*
LEVEL: B LANG: Eng SIRC ARTICLE NO: 090741

Wayne, J. Canada Cup full of profits for many. *Financial post (Toronto) 78(35), 1 Sept 1984, 1;2.*
LEVEL: B LANG: Eng SIRC ARTICLE NO: 096702

ENCYCLOPEDIAS

Ronberg, G. Stayer, R.A. The illustrated hockey encyclopedia. New York: Balsam Press, 1984. 1v.
NOTES: Rev. ed. of: The hockey encyclopedia, 1974.
LEVEL: I LANG: Eng ISBN: 0917439031 LC CARD: 84-011169

EQUIPMENT

Roy, B. Delisle, G. Caracteristiques geometriques et dynamiques des batons de hockey en regard de leur performance. (Refs: 1 *Canadian journal of applied sport sciences/Journal canadien des sciences appliquees au sport (Windsor, Ont.) 9(4), dec 1984, 214-219.*
RESUME: Les caracteristiques de 14 modeles de batons furent mesurees selon le protocole decrit anterieurement par Roy et Dore (1975). Pour verifier la longevite du baton, 45 joueurs de niveau Midget AA furent selectionies. A chacun d'eux, on remit deux echantillons de batons choisis aleatoirement et qu'ils devaient utiliser au cours des pratiques et parties. Pour la durabilite, 15 joueurs adultes furent selectionnes. Ce travail confirme l'etude anterieure de Roy et Dore (1975) en ce qui a trait a l'homogeneite des mesures geometriques et la grande heterogeneite des

mesures dynamiques. Une analyse de regression multiple a permis d'etablir que la largeur et l'epaisseur du manche, de meme que la charge a la rupture et le module de rigidite du manche (dans un plan parallele a la lame) etaient des variables contribuant significativement a la longevite du baton.
LEVEL: A LANG: Fr SIRC ARTICLE NO: 103242

Savoir choisir un equipement de hockey. *Marathon plus (Laval, Que.) 2(1), dec 1984/janv 1985, 5-6.*
LEVEL: B LANG: Fr SIRC ARTICLE NO: 173451

EQUIPMENT - RETAILING

Hockey stick market: an industry in transition. *Sports trade Canada (Downsview, Ont.) 12(2), Apr 1984, 17;20.*
LEVEL: B LANG Eng SIRC ARTICLE NO: 103235

Know by hockey alone. *Sports trade Canada (Downsview, Ont.) 12(1), Feb 1984, 42-43.*
LEVEL: B LANG: Eng SIRC ARTICLE NO: 093517

HISTORY

Dorr, D. Hockey town USA: on the American hockey scene, when you say 'Warroad, Minn.,' you've said it all. *Sporting news 197(6), 6 Feb 1984, 15-17.*
LEVEL: B LANG: Eng SIRC ARTICLE NO: 090736

Dorr, D. Hockey town USA: '80 dream: 'I do believe in miracles'. *Sporting news 197(7), 13 Feb 1984, 13-15.*
NOTES: Second of two part article.
LEVEL: B LANG: Eng SIRC ARTICLE NO: 092193

Histoire du hockey a Drummondville. Drummondville, Que.: Societe historique du centre du Quebec, 1984. vi, 112 p. : ill. (Les grands du sport: v.16.)
CORP: Societe historique du centre du Quebec.
NOTES: ISSN: 0707-350X.
LEVEL: B LANG: Fr LC CARD: C84-8766-7
GV846.5 18890

Ice hockey and Olympism. *Olympic review (Lausanne, Switzerland) 197, Mar 1984, 181-203.*
LEVEL: B LANG: Eng SIRC ARTICLE NO: 095088

Le hockey sur glace et l'olympisme. *Revue olympique (Lausanne) 197, mars 1984, 181-203.*
LEVEL: B LANG: Fr SIRC ARTICLE NO: 096699

Sabetzki, G. L'histoire mouvementee du hockey sur glace. The eventful history of ice-hockey. *Message olympique/Olympic message (Lausanne) 7, juin/Jun 1984, 45-49.*
LEVEL: B LANG: Fr Eng SIRC ARTICLE NO: 104801

INJURIES AND ACCIDENTS

Carbon monoxide exposure at indoor ice hockey rinks. *Sports medicine digest (Van Nuys, Calif.) 6(6), Jun 1984, 3.*
LEVEL: B LANG: Eng SIRC ARTICLE NO: 102143

Castaldi, C. Ice hockey. In, Adams, S.H. (ed.), et al., Catastrophic injuries in sports: avoidance strategies, Salinas, Calif., Cayote Press, c1984, p. 38-52.
LEVEL: I LANG: Eng RD97 19088

Hunter, J. Hockey takes a heavy injury toll. *Globe and mail (Toronto) 141(42,094) 3 Nov 1984, 51;54.*
LEVEL: B LANG: Eng SIRC ARTICLE NO: 099702

Lemire, L. Rosman, M. Sternoclavicular epiphyseal separation with adjacent clavicular fracture. *Journal of pediatric orthopaedics (New York) 4(1), Jan 1984, 118-120.*
ABST: This case report details the diagnosis and treatment of an unusual double fracture of the medial left clavicle in a 15 year old male hockey player.
LEVEL: A LANG: Eng SIRC ARTICLE NO: 099046

Mackesy, D. A case report: ligamentous failure in a hockey goaltender. (Refs: 3)*Canadian Academy of Sport Medicine newsletter (Ottawa) 5(4), 1984, 24-25.*
LEVEL: I LANG: Eng SIRC ARTICLE NO: 105911

McGrail, J.S. How to recognize a serious injury...and what to do about it. *Sport-talk (Toronto) 13(1), Mar 1984, 5.*
LEVEL B LANG: Eng SIRC ARTICLE NO: 095090

McGrail, J.S. Hidden dangers in head injuries. *Sport-talk (Toronto) 13(3), Oct 1984, 4.*
LEVEL: B LANG: Eng SIRC ARTICLE NO: 103237

Peterson, L. Pitman, M.I. Gold, J. The active pivot shift: the role of the popliteus muscle. (Refs: 25)*American journal of sports medicine (Baltimore, Md.) 12(4), Jul/Aug 1984, 313-317.*
ABST: Ligament insufficiency due to athletic injury is widely recognized and reported as an etiological factor in knee joint instability. It was recognized that a patient presenting with knee joint instability due to past hockey injury to the anterior cruciate liagment, subsequently verified surgically, was able to voluntarily and actively perform the pivot shift maneuver with his knee as a result of his anterolateral rotatory instability. During a subsequent 6 month period, three other patients with similar anterior cruciate deficiencies presented with this same active pivot shift maneuver phenomenon. A study was designed to determine the active muscle or muscles involved in this abnormal active motion in the knee joint with anterolateral rotatory instability. Electromyogrphic studies with needle electrodes were conducted on a variety of muscles in four subjects presenting with the instability. Results indicated that the popliteus muscle plays a major role in the active performance of the pivot shift maneuver.
LEVEL: A LANG: Eng SIRC ARTICLE NO: 108538

Tator, C.H. Edmonds, V.E. National survey of spinal injuries in hockey players. (Refs: 28)*Canadian Medical Association journal/Journal de l'Association medical canadienne (Ottawa) 130(7), 1 Apr 1984, 875-880.*
ABST: The purpose of this study was to determine the incidence of hockey-related and neurologic injuries. Between 1976 and 1983, 42 injuries were reported. The median age of the players injured was 17 and the average age 20 years. Most injuries (26) cccurred in Ontario. Of the 42 players, 28 had spinal cord injuries and 17 of them were paralysed below the vertebral level of the injury. Checks from behind and collisions with the boards were common mechanisms of injury.
LEVEL: A LANG: Eng SIRC ARTICLE NO: 099704

Tator, C.H. Ekong, C.E. Rowed, D.W. Schwartz, M.L. Edmonds, V.E. Cooper, P.W. Spinal injuries due to hockey. (Refs: 17) *Canadian journal of neurological sciences (Winnipeg) 11(1), Feb 1984, 34-41.*
ABST: The authors report the case of 6 hockey players suffering from cervical spinal injury, five of whom were seen during a 13 month period from

September, 1980 to October, 1981. They are aged between 15 and 26 years. A burst fracture of C5 or C6 is the most common bony injury.
LEVEL: A LANG: Eng SIRC ARTICLE NO: 101332

MEDICINE

Ferstle, J. Nagobads: hockey's 'half-and-half' physician. (George Nagobads) *Physician and sportsmedicine 12(1), Jan 1984, 183;186.*
LEVEL: B LANG: Eng SIRC ARTICLE NO: 092195

van der Wurff, P. Hagmeyer, R.H.M. Rijnders, W. Case study: isolated anterior interosseous nerve paralysis: the Kiloh-Nevin syndrome. (Refs: 13)*Journal of orthopaedic and sports physical therapy (Baltimore, Md.) 6(3), Nov/Dec 1984, 178-180.*
ABST: A new case of isolated paralysis of the anterior interosseous nerve of a 24-year-old man is described. It is thought that this was caused by a fall on the left arm. This paralysis has a typical clinical picture with a characteristic disturbance of the pinch grip. The patient recovered spontaneously. A review of the findings previously reported in the literature is presented.
LEVEL: A LANG: Eng SIRC ARTICLE NO: 102612

NUTRITION

Hockey demands lots of energy. Nobody can perform at 100 percent if he or she isn't in good health. *Hockey today 1983/1984, 95-96.*
LEVEL: B LANG: Eng SIRC ARTICLE NO: 093514

OFFICIATING

Rains, P. The production of fairness: officiating in the National Hockey League. *Sociology of sport journal (Champaign, Ill.) 1(2), 1984, 150-162.*
ABST: Using the work of National Hockey League linesmen and referees as examples, this article describes three methods used by professional sports leagues to produce fairness on the part of officials and, more importantly, to prove that fairness has been accomplished. The author has characterized these methods as the procedural production of consistency, the substantive production of consistency, and the supervision of officials' work. The failure of these methods to produce compelling and objective evidence of fairness supplies a persistent and essentially unresolvable problem for those who man the social control apparatus. Ironically, the tension that this problem generates, and the attention therefore paid to the issue of fairness, is probably the best guarantee that fairness is produced.
LEVEL: A LANG: Eng SIRC ARTICLE NO: 103241

Rudolph, M. Officiating etiquette. *American hockey & arena (Colorado Springs, Colo.) 5(2), Feb 1984, 31;41.*
LEVEL: B LANG Eng SIRC ARTICLE NO: 098177

van Deelen, W. The right stuff. *American hockey & arena (Colorado Springs) 5(4), Summer 1984, 35-36.*
LEVEL: B LANG: Eng SIRC ARTICLE NO: 101333

Walker, D.K. Fading light: Bob Kennedy was just doing his job. Then... *Referee (Franksville, Wis.) 9(8), Aug 1984, 24-28.*
LEVEL: B LANG: Eng SIRC ARTICLE NO: 098181

PROTECTIVE DEVICES

Honeyman, D. Considerations for prevention of hockey injuries. (Refs: 11)*Sports physiotherapy division (Victoria, B.C.) 9(2), Mar/Apr 1984, 24-25.*
LEVEL: B LANG: Fr SIRC ARTICLE NO: 098170

Jepson, G. Staying ahead of the equipment game. *American hockey & arena (Colorado Springs, Colo.) 5(1), Jan 1984, 7-8.*
LEVEL: B LANG: Eng SIRC ARTICLE NO: 098172

New head form developed to test smaller helmets. *Consumer Winter 1984, 8.*
LEVEL: B LANG: Eng SIRC ARTICLE NO: 089188

PSYCHOLOGY

Chouinard, N. L'etablissement d'objectifs pour hockeyeurs: une strategie de motivation pour l'entraineur. (Refs: 6)*Revue de l'entraineur (Montreal) oct/dec 1984, 8-9.*
LEVEL: B LANG: Fr SIRC ARTICLE NO: 105907

Harris, W. Psychological skills: the invisible foundation of athletic performance. *American hockey & arena (Colorado Springs) 5(4), Summer 1984, 17-19.*
NOTES: First of a two-part series.
LEVEL: B LANG: Eng SIRC ARTICLE NO: 101328

Harris, W. Psychological skills: the invisible foundation of athletic performance. *American hockey magazine (Colorado Springs, Colo.) 5(5), Fall 1984, 22-23;39.*
NOTES: Second of a two-part series.
LEVEL: B LANG: Eng SIRC ARTICLE NO: 108442

Talbot, S. Godin, G. Drouin, D. Goulet, C. Cognitive styles of young ice hockey players. (Refs: 12)*Perceptual and motor skills (Missoula, Mont.) 59(3), Dec 1984, 692-694.*
ABST: 60 young French Canadian hockey players with a median age of 8 years were tested for field dependency using the Children's Embedded Figures Test. Variance analysis showed significant age group differences with the older children scoring more field-independence.
LEVEL: A LANG: Eng SIRC ARTICLE NO: 103245

Widmeyer, W.N. Birch, J.S. Aggression in professional ice hockey - a strategy for success or a reaction to failure. (Refs: 1 *Journal of psychology (Provincetown) 117(1), 1984, 77-84.*
LEVEL: A LANG: Eng SIRC ARTICLE NO: 096703

RULES AND REGULATIONS

C.A.H.A. regulations 1984/85. Vanier: Canadian Amateur Hockey Association, 1984. iii, 98 p.
CORP: Canadian Amateur Hockey Association.
LEVEL: B LANG: Eng GV847.5 18304

Gilbert, J. Registering a complaint. *American hockey magazine (Colorado Springs, Colo.) 5(5), Fall 1984, 29-31.*
LEVEL: B LANG: Eng SIRC ARTICLE NO: 108443

Reglements de l'A.C.H.A. 1984-85. Vanier, Ont.: Association canadienne de hockey amateur, 1984. iv, 113 p.
CORP: Association canadienne de hockey amateur.
LEVEL: B LANG: Fr GV847.5 18640

Rudolph, M. Throwing the stick. *American hockey magazine (Colorado Springs, Colo.) 5(7), Dec 1984, 26-27.*
LEVEL: B LANG: Eng SIRC ARTICLE NO: 107271

SOCIAL PSYCHOLOGY

Taylor, J. Aggression: how much is too macho? *Sport-talk (Toronto) 13(4), Dec 1984, 1;5.*
LEVEL: B LANG: Eng SIRC ARTICLE NO: 104802

SPORTING EVENTS

Falconnet, G. Ski - XIVe JO, Sarajevo 84. *EPS: Education physique et sport (Paris, France) 186, mars/avr 1984, 26-29.*
LEVEL: B LANG: Fr SIRC ARTICLE NO: 095236

Ogrean, D. Olympic ice hockey in review. *American hockey & arena (Colorado Springs, Colo.) 5(1), Jan 1984, 13-15;30.*
LEVEL: B LANG: Eng SIRC ARTICLE NO: 098175

STRATEGY

Smith, M. Executing the 2/3 system. *American hockey magazine (Colorado Springs, Colo.) 5(6), Nov 1984, 29-30.*
LEVEL: B LANG: Eng SIRC ARTICLE NO: 107272

STRATEGY - OFFENSIVE

Smith, M. Coach's playbook: the extra attacker. *American hockey & arena (Colorado Springs, Colo.) 593), Spring 1984, 43.*
LEVEL: B LANG: Eng SIRC ARTICLE NO: 096701

Smith, M. Getting defensemen into the offense. *American hockey magazine (Colorado Springs, Colo.) 5(7), Dec 1984, 29-30.*
LEVEL: B LANG: Eng SIRC ARTICLE NO: 107273

TEACHING

Drouin, D. Talbot, S. Indice de conformite de l'application du programme debutant III de la Federation quebecoise de hockey sur glace. (Refs: 7)*CAHPER journal (Ottawa) 51(1), sept/oct 1984, 18-22.*
LEVEL: I LANG: Fr SIRC ARTICLE NO: 101325

TECHNIQUES AND SKILLS

Blatherwick, J. Quickness: how important is it? *American hockey & arena (Colorado Springs, Colo.) 5(3), Spring 1984, 13-14.*
LEVEL: B LANG: Eng SIRC ARTICLE NO: 096698

McDonald, D. Skating: the quickest way to become a better hockey player is to improve your skating. That means working on th basics - starting, stopping, and turning - everytime you get on the ice. *Hockey today 1983/1984, 24-25;27;30.*
LEVEL: B LANG: Eng SIRC ARTICLE NO: 093520

TECHNIQUES AND SKILLS - GOALTENDER AND GOALTENDING

Carlyle, J. Patience is a virtue. The backup goaltender... He has to keep his skills sharp, be ready at all times and just wait for his chance to play. *Goal (New York) 11, Apr 1984, 62;64;66.*
LEVEL: B LANG: Eng SIRC ARTICLE NO: 101324

Doucet, A. Ouelette, G. Give back-up goaltenders a valuable task. *Coaching review (Ottawa, Ont.) 7, May/Jun 1984, 51.*
LEVEL: B LANG: Eng SIRC ARTICLE NO: 095086

Doucet, A. Ouelette, G. Give back-up goaltenders a valuable task. *Spotlight (East Lansing, Mich.)*

7(3), Fall 1984, 5.
LEVEL: B LANG: Eng SIRC ARTICLE NO: 104792

Simmons, S. The state of goaltending. *Goal (New York) 12, Dec 1984, 62;64;66.*
LEVEL: B LANG: Eng SIRC ARTICLE NO: 108715

TESTING AND EVALUATION

LaChappelle, F. Hockey statistics made simple. *Women's coaching clinic 7(6), Feb 1984, 4-8.*
LEVEL: B LANG: Eng SIRC ARTICLE NO: 090738

Quinney, H.A. Smith, D.J. Wenger, H.A. A field test for the assessment of abdominal muscular endurance in professional ice hockey players. (Refs: 11)*Journal of orthopaedic and sports physical therapy (Baltimore, Md.) 6(1), Jul/Aug 1984, 30-33.*
ABST: The purpose of this study was to develop a test protocol and produce normative data for measuring abdominal muscular endurance in professional ice hockey players. The protocol was developed using elite speed skaters and professional ice hockey players. The test involves the measurement of total number of curl-ups that can be completed at a prescribed rate of 25 repetitions per minute. The test protocol maximizes the isolation of the abdominal muscle group and the control of the movement. Normative data is presented from tests on 117 professional hockey players. This protocol provides discriminatory power and has high face validity in its application.
LEVEL: A LANG: Eng SIRC ARTICLE NO: 101330

TRAINING AND CONDITIONING

Neck and spine conditioning for hockey players. *Sport-talk (Toronto) 13(4), Dec 1984, 2-4.*
LEVEL: B LANG: Eng SIRC ARTICLE NO: 104798

TRAINING AND CONDITIONING - AEROBIC TRAINING

Orr, F. Aerobics: the message is beginning to get through. *Sport-talk (Toronto) 13(3), Oct 1984, 2-3.*
LEVEL: B LANG: Eng SIRC ARTICLE NO: 103239

TRAINING AND CONDITIONING - DRILLS

Fun & functional. (hockey drills) *American hockey & arena (Colorado Springs) 5(4), Summer 1984, 29-31.*
LEVEL: B LANG: Eng SIRC ARTICLE NO: 101327

Norton, M.D. Innovative games for youth hockey players. *American hockey & arena (Colorado Springs, Colo.) 5(2), Feb 1984, 30.*
LEVEL: B LANG: Eng SIRC ARTICLE NO: 098174

Palmer, G. The hockey drill book. New York: Leisure Press, c1984. 360 p. : ill.
NOTES: Bibliography: p. 359-360.
LEVEL: I LANG: Eng ISBN: 0-918438-76-4 LC CARD: 81-81390 GV848.3 18442

TRAINING AND CONDITIONING - WEIGHT AND STRENGTH TRAINING

Emmert, W. The slap shot - strength and conditioning program for hockey at Boston College. (Refs: 8)*National Strength & Conditioning Association journal (Lincoln, Neb.) 6(2), Apr/May 1984, 4-6;68;71;73.*
LEVEL: I LANG: Eng SIRC ARTICLE NO: 095087

WOMEN

Lenskyj, H. Can I play? No, not in Ontario. *CAAWS newsletter/Bulletin de l'ACAFs (Ottawa) 3(4), Fall/automne 1984, 10-11.*
NOTES: Part of a longer article appearing in a forthcoming issue of Broadside.
LEVEL: B LANG: Eng SIRC ARTICLE NO: 173414

Lenskyj, H. Girls caught offside. *Broadside: a feminist review (Toronto) 6, Nov 1984, 6.*
LEVEL: B LANG: Eng SIRC ARTICLE NO: 183327

HORSE RACING

Callaham, D.M. Educating new fans: race tracks around the country are experimenting with a variety of programs which seek to introduce new fans to details of the sport. *Thoroughbred record (Lexington, Ky.) 218(40), 3 Oct 1984, 4987-4988;4990.*
LEVEL: B LANG: Eng SIRC ARTICLE NO: 101337

Kellman, J. A body unsupported. *Blood-horse (Lexington, Ky.) 110(28), 14 Jul 1984, 4804;4808-4809;4820;4822-4824;4828;4830.*
LEVEL: B LANG: Eng SIRC ARTICLE NO: 098218

ADMINISTRATION

'Nick' Nicholson. George 'Nick' Nicholson, executive vice-president of the Kentucky Thoroughbred Association, discusses some o the problems and opportunities facing him and the industry as a whole. *Thoroughbred record (Lexington, Ky.) 218(1), 4 Jan 1984, 65-67;70;76.*
LEVEL: B LANG: Eng SIRC ARTICLE NO: 093527

Heckerman, D.L. Perspective on regulation. Warren Schweder has worked 14 years with racing's rule-makers, and the experience has given him some mixed views on the sport's regulation. *Thoroughbred record (Lexington, Ky.) 218(35), 29 Aug 1984, 4302-4304.*
LEVEL: B LANG: Eng SIRC ARTICLE NO: 099726

Heckerman, D.L. Joseph Kellman: a member of the Illinois Racing Board for six years, Joe Kellman has developed some strong opinions about the integrity of the sport. *Thoroughbred record (Lexington, Ky.) 218(39), 26 Sept 1984, 4880;4882.*
LEVEL: B LANG: Eng SIRC ARTICLE NO: 099727

Hollingsworth, K. Sales, and accountability. *Blood-horse (Lexington, Ky.) 110(5), 4 Feb 1984, 943-946.*
LEVEL: B LANG: Eng SIRC ARTICLE NO: 095107

Mooney, B. It all starts with them: dealing with fractious horses for eight or nine races a day is part of the routine for gate crews at race tracks everywhere. *Thoroughbred record (Lexington, Ky.) 218(27), 4 Jul 1984, 3145-3146;3148;3150;3152.*
LEVEL: B LANG: Eng SIRC ARTICLE NO: 098222

Mooney, B. A shot in the arm. *Thoroughbred record (Lexington, Ky.) 218(26), 5 Sept 1984, 4448;4450;4452;4454;4456.*
NOTES: The Thoroughbred Record continues to examine corporate underwriting of Throughbred racing. Part two of three-part series looks at Phillip Morris, Inc. and Anheuser-Busch Companies, Inc. and the history and growth of the Malboro Cup and the Budweiser-Arlington Million.
LEVEL: B LANG: Eng SIRC ARTICLE NO: 099743

Race track promotions. Faced with increasing competition for the entertainment dollar, what are race tracks across the country doing to draw fans? *Thoroughbred record (Lexington, Ky.) 218(4), 25 Jan 1984, 522-523;526;528;532.*
LEVEL: B LANG: Eng SIRC ARTICLE NO: 093554

ANIMAL HUSBANDRY

Dink, D. After the classics: a study of the post-classic racing records of six decades of American and English classic winners indicates that early retirement of leading colts is not a new phenomenon. *Thoroughbred record (Lexington, Ky.) 218(49), 5 Dec 1984, 6420;6422;6424;6426;6428;6430.*
LEVEL: I LANG: Eng SIRC ARTICLE NO: 105923

Herbert, K.S. Training in foal: breeding a filly and returning her to the races can be economical, and sometime's helps the runner's attitude. *Blood-horse (Lexington, Ky.) 110(28), 14 Jul 1984, 4790-4792.*
LEVEL: B LANG: Eng SIRC ARTICLE NO: 098209

Thomas, S. Have groom, will travel. *Blood-horse (New York) 110(41), 13 Oct 1984, 7232-7234.*
LEVEL: B LANG: Eng SIRC ARTICLE NO: 101363

ART

Carrell, R.A. We must meditate pleasure, Dufy is pleasure. (Raoul Dufy) *Blood-horse (New York) 110(42), 20 Oct 1984, 7436-7437;7439-7441.*
LEVEL: B LANG: Eng SIRC ARTICLE NO: 101339

BIOGRAPHY AND AUTOBIOGRAPHY

Deford, F. 'Riding horses is the pleasure of his life': so says the wife of Angel Cordero, probably the best - certainly the most controversial - jockey currently riding. *Sports illustrated (Chicago, Ill.) 60(17), 23 Apr 1984, 68-72;74-78;80;82.*
LEVEL: B LANG: Eng SIRC ARTICLE NO: 095102

Dizikes, J. Tod Sloan: fairy tales and nightmares. *Arete: the journal of sport literature (San Diego, Calif.) 1(2), Spring 1984, 95-112.*
LEVEL: I LANG: Eng SIRC ARTICLE NO: 098193

Interview: Angel Cordero Jr., who in 1983 won his second consecutive Eclipse Award as the nation's leading jockey, has gained reputation as one of the most talented and controversial riders in American Turf history during his immensely successful career. *Thoroughbred record (Lexington, Ky.) 218(11), 14 Mar 1984, 1497-1498;1500;1502.*
LEVEL: B LANG: Eng SIRC ARTICLE NO: 095109

Seth-Smith, M. The head waiter. s.l.: Michael Joseph, 1984. 1v.
NOTES: Biography of Harry Wragg, one of England's greatest pre-war jockeys.
LEVEL: B LANG: Eng ISBN: 0-7181-2248-X

COACHING

Emery, D. Straight from the coach's mouth. *Running (London) 43, Nov 1984, 58-59;89.*
LEVEL: B LANG: Eng SIRC ARTICLE NO: 104967

COUNTRIES AND REGIONS

Marshall, C.B. The good life at Baden-Baden. Baden-Baden racecourse in Germany is in operation less than three weeks out of every year, but it provides visitors with international-class racing, yearling sales, and a taste of luxury.

Thoroughbred record (Lexington, Ky.) 218(5), 1 Feb 1984, 760-763.
LEVEL: B LANG: Eng SIRC ARTICLE NO: 093547

McCormack, B. Provincial promise. (Canada) *Spur (Middleburg, Va.) Nov/Dec 1984, 44-50;52.*
LEVEL: B LANG: Eng SIRC ARTICLE NO: 103256

Racing in Japan. *Canadian horse (Markham, Ont.) Mar/Apr 1984, 18-20.*
LEVEL: B LANG: Eng SIRC ARTICLE NO: 098232

Sampson, A.A. Courses of action: the homes of horse racing. London: R. Hale, 1984. 207 p. : ill., 1 map ; 24 x 17 cm.
NOTES Companion to: Grounds of appeal. Includes index. Bibliography: p. 204-205.
LEVEL: B LANG: Eng ISBN: 0709014376 LC CARD: 84-181223

DOCUMENTATION

Mooney, B. The Palmer method. Joe Palmer, who died in 1952 at the age of 48, left behind a legendary reputation and is still considered by many to be the finest turf writer in the history of thoroughbred racing. *Thoroughbred record (Lexington, Ky.) 218(17), 25 Apr 1984, 2086-2090;2092;2094.*
LEVEL: B LANG: Eng SIRC ARTICLE NO: 095117

Morris, T. Reading habits of an English racing gentleman. *Thoroughbred record (Lexington, Ky.) 218(37), 12 Sept 1984, 4578;4580;4582.*
LEVEL: B LANG: Eng SIRC ARTICLE NO: 101356

Rhodemyre, S. The thoroughbred publisher. (Joseph Allen) *Thoroughbred record (Lexington, Ky.) 218(37), 12 Sept 1984, 4584;4586.*
LEVEL: B LANG: Eng SIRC ARTICLE NO: 101358

DRUGS, DOPING AND ERGOGENIC AIDS

Drug research centre makes racing safer. Jerseyville complex carries out full-time testing of horses under actual training, racing conditions. *Trot (Toronto) 11(8), Aug 1984, 10-11;71.*
LEVEL: B LANG: Eng SIRC ARTICLE NO: 101340

Moss, M.S. Survey of positive results from racecourse antidoping samples received at Racecourse Security Services' Laboratories. *Equine veterinary journal (London) 16(1), Jan 1984, 39-42.*
ABST: This study examines positive drug tests obtained during 12 years, from 1970 to 1981 inclusively, in the United States and compared the results with certain overseas racing authorities between 1975 and 1981.
LEVEL: A LANG: Eng SIRC ARTICLE NO: 101357

Scott, A. The search for improved drug testing procedures. Researchers at Cornell and Ohio State are monitoring racing labs around the country in efforts to improve tests for illegal drugs. *Thoroughbred record (Lexington, Ky.) 218(45), 7 Nov 1984, 5832;5836;5842.*
LEVEL: I LANG: Eng SIRC ARTICLE NO: 099750

Thomas, S. Sport and drugs: abuse of alcohol and drugs has become a problem in professional sports, and racing is among thos grappling with methods of control and rehabilitation. *Blood-horse (Lexington, Ky.) 60(51), 22 Dec 1984, 9481-9483.*
LEVEL: B LANG: Eng SIRC ARTICLE NO: 107313

ECONOMICS

Hecherman, D.L. Fashion and performance: a study of the racing records of three crops of Keeneland select yearlings provides basic data on how they fared in competition. *Thoroughbred record (Lexington, Ky.) 218(28), 11 Jul 1984, 3312-3314;3316.*
LEVEL: I LANG: Eng SIRC ARTICLE NO: 098208

Lawrence, R.G. All about purses. An examination of the economics of racing from the standpoint of purse distribution in 1983 *Thoroughbred record (Lexington, Ky.) 218(18), 2 May 1984, 2182-2184;2186;2188;2190;2192;2194;2196;2198.*
LEVEL: B LANG: Eng SIRC ARTICLE NO: 095112

Mearns, D. A mixed recovery. While the national economy continued to improve last year, business fluctuated at major tracks. *Blood-horse (Lexington, Ky.) 110(4), 28 Jan 1984, 707-709.*
NOTES: To be continued.
LEVEL: B LANG: Eng SIRC ARTICLE NO: 095113

Mearns, D. Another hit show. (pari-mutuel betting) *Blood-horse (Lexington, Ky.) 110(36), 8 Sept 1984, 6340-6341.*
LEVEL: B LANG: Eng SIRC ARTICLE NO: 099741

Milbert, N. Simulcasting in Illinois. A look at the status of the simulcasting arrangement involving three Chicago-area tracks: Arlington Park, Sportman's Park, and Maywood Park harness track. *Thoroughbred record (Lexington, Ky.) 218(11), 14 Mar 1984, 1503.*
LEVEL: B LANG: Eng SIRC ARTICLE NO: 095116

Mooney, B. Deep in the heart...of Texas lies a belief that pari-mutuel horse racing, which flourished from 1933-'37 and has been banned ever since, might someday return. Part one of a two-part series examines the heritage, issues, hopes, dreams, and schemes that enter into the situation. *Thoroughbred record (Lexington, Ky.) 218(8), 22 Feb 1984, 1133-1134;1136;1138;1140;1142.*
LEVEL: B LANG: Eng SIRC ARTICLE NO: 093549

Mooney, B. Deep in the heart...The conclusion of a two-part series on the efforts to bring pari-mutuel racing to Texas looks at some of the key individuals and issues involved in the current situation in the Lone Star State. *Thoroughbred record (Lexington, Ky.) 218(9), 29 Feb 1984, 1290-1295.*
LEVEL: B LANG: Eng SIRC ARTICLE NO: 093550

Mooney, B. A shot in the arm. *Thoroughbred record (Lexington, Ky.) 218(21), 23 May 1984, 2500-2504.*
NOTES: Part one of a three-part series.
LEVEL: B LANG: Eng SIRC ARTICLE NO: 098223

Shull, S.L. Jockey Club Foundation: for more than 40 years, The Jockey Club Foundation has provided financial assistance to racetrackers in need. *Thoroughbred record (Lexington, Ky.) 218(40) 3 Oct 1984, 4991-4992.*
LEVEL: B LANG: Eng SIRC ARTICLE NO: 101360

Syndication: owning a piece of a great horse. *Performance horseman (Unionville, Pa.) 3(10), Sept 1984, 33-36.*
LEVEL: B LANG Eng SIRC ARTICLE NO: 098247

Wayne, J. Financial hurdles for those chasing Queen's Plate dream. *Financial post (Toronto) 78(29), 21 Jul 1984, 23.*
LEVEL: B LANG: Eng SIRC ARTICLE NO: 098258

EQUIPMENT

Mearns, D. Purely gates: getting races underway has been Clay Puett's concern for most of his 85 years, the former cowboy having been a pioneer in the development of the modern starting gate. *Blood-horse (Lexington, Ky.) 110(48), 1 Dec 1984, 8910-8915.*
LEVEL: B LANG: Eng SIRC ARTICLE NO: 103257

FACILITIES

Racetrack, A. Tall fescue to the rescue. *Grounds maintenance (Overland Park, Kans.) 19(2), Feb 1984, 88.*
LEVEL: B LANG: E SIRC ARTICLE NO: 098993

Ryval, M. The inside track on Woodbine. *Financial post magazine (Toronto, Ont.) 1 Mar 1984, 50-51;54;56;58.*
LEVEL: I LANG Eng SIRC ARTICLE NO: 095123

FACILITIES - DESIGN, CONSTRUCTION AND PLANNING

Crawford, B. Importance of racetrack design. *Canadian rider (Ancaster, Ont.) 14(6), Feb/Mar 1984, 30-31.*
NOTES: Reprinted from, Horse Health Lines.
LEVEL: B LANG: Eng SIRC ARTICLE NO: 097520

GAMBLING

Quirin, W.L. Thoroughbred handicapping: state of the art. 1st ed. New York: William Morrow, 1984. 329 p.
NOTES: Bibliography: p. 328-329.
LEVEL: I LANG: Eng ISBN: 0-688-03064-5 LC CARD: 84-60211 SF331 17611

Ziemba, W.T. Hausch, D.B. Thorp, E.O. Beat the racetrack. 1st ed. San Diego: Harcourt Brace Jovanovich, c1984. 1v.
NOTES: Includes index.
LEVEL: I LANG: Eng ISBN: 0151112754 LC CARD: 83-022849

HALLS OF FAME AND MUSEUMS

Morton, L. The stuff of memories. *Blood-horse 110(2), 14 Jan 1984, 265-269.*
LEVEL: B LANG: Eng SIRC ARTICLE NO: 093551

HISTORY

Bongianni, M. Cozzaglio, P. Champion horses. New York: Bonanza Books, 1984. 1v.
NOTES: Translation of: I grandi cavalli. Includes index.
LEVEL: B LANG: Eng ISBN: 0517439336 LC CARD: 84-011012

Breen, T.H. Horses and gentlemen: the cultural significance of gambling among the gentry of Virginia. (Refs: 70)
NOTES: In, Riess, S.A. (ed.), The American sporting experience: a historical anthology of sport in America, New York, Leisure Press, c1984, p. 35-54. Reprinted from, William & Mary quarterly 34, April 1977, p. 329-347.
LEVEL: A LANG: Eng GV583 17631

Bryant, B. Williams, J. Portraits in roses: 109 years of Kentucky Derby winners. New York: McGraw-Hill, c1984. x, 146 p. : ill.

LEVEL: B LANG: Eng ISBN: 0070086028 LC CARD: 83-023872 SF357.K4 17309

The great contest: Fashion v. Peytona (1845). NOTES: In, Riess, S.A. (ed.), The American sporting experience: a historical anthology of sport in America, New York, Leisure Press, c1984, p. 91-103. Reprinted from, New York herald, 5 May 1845.
LEVEL: B LANG: Eng GV583 17631

HORSES

Labrunie, S. Chevaux de course. Paris: Richer-Vilo, 1984. 127 p. : ill.
LEVEL: B LANG: Fr

Ross, D.M. Work horses of the track: selected by trainers, outsiders, and riders for different reasons, ponies at the race track fill a variety of roles, and their character complements their function. *Blood-horse (Lexington, Ky.) 110(34), 25 Aug 1984, 5934-5935.*
LEVEL: B LANG: Eng SIRC ARTICLE NO: 098234

LAW AND LEGISLATION

Mandel, S.J. Greenspun, J.S. Buyers and sellers beware: legal pitfalls at the sales. *Hoof beats (Columbus, Ohio) 52(7), Sep 1984, 84;86;124.*
LEVEL: B LANG: Eng SIRC ARTICLE NO: 099737

MASS MEDIA

Interview: Fred Capossela. Fred Capossela, a race track announcer for 37 years, reflects on his career, which earned him the reputation as the 'dean of American race callers'. *Thoroughbred record (Lexington, Ky.) 218(14), 4 Apr 1984, 1784;1786;1788.*
LEVEL: B LANG: Eng SIRC ARTICLE NO: 095110

Mooney, B. A future with cable? Thoroughbred racing provides an attractive entertainment commodity and, in recent years, the cable television industry has been looked to as a new means of exposure. But how marketable is racing? *Thoroughbred record (Lexington, Ky.) 218(15), 11 Apr 1984, 1880-1882;1884;1886.*
NOTES: Part two of a two-part series.
LEVEL: B LANG: Eng SIRC ARTICLE NO: 095118

Mooney, B. A future with cable? Cable television in the United States is a huge, rapidly expanding industry, and many see th future of thoroughbred racing as having integral ties with this broadcast medium. But if that is to be the case, cable's needs, goals, and aspirations must be understood. *Thoroughbred record (Lexington, Ky.) 218(14), 4 Apr 1984, 1778-1780;1782.*
NOTES: Part one of a two-part series.
LEVEL: B LANG: Eng SIRC ARTICLE NO: 095119

PROTECTIVE DEVICES

Thomas, S. Toward a safer sport. Since the manufacture of jockey helmets in this country is unregulated as to material and design, improvement would require institution of voluntary standards. *Blood-horse (Lexington, Ky.) 110(18), 5 May 1984, 3266-3269.*
LEVEL: B LANG: Eng SIRC ARTICLE NO: 095125

RULES AND REGULATIONS

Ballenger, W.S. Open claiming rule boon to new owners. *Hoof beats (Columbus, Ohio) 52(7), Sept 1984, 90;92.*
LEVEL: B LANG Eng SIRC ARTICLE NO: 099707

SPORTING EVENTS

A history of the Kentucky Derby: from past to present. *Thoroughbred record (Lexington, Ky.) 218(17), 25 Apr 1984, 2082-2083.*
LEVEL: B LANG: Eng SIRC ARTICLE NO: 095106

Cauz, L.E. The Plate: a royal tradition. Toronto: Deneau, (1984). 301 p. : ill.
LEVEL: I LANG: Eng ISBN: 0-88879-104-6 LC CARD: C84-90174-7 SF357.Q4 18903

Dink, D. Charting the Derby trail. *Thoroughbred record (Lexington, Ky.) 218(17), 25 Apr 1984, 2074;2076;2079-2080.*
LEVEL: LANG: Eng SIRC ARTICLE NO: 095103

STATISTICS AND RECORDS

Mearns, D. Drawing a crowd. Attendance at U.S. tracks. Part II. *Blood-horse (Lexington, Ky.) 110(5), 4 Feb 1984, 934-936.*
LEVEL: B LANG: Eng SIRC ARTICLE NO: 095114

Race Track Division, 1983 annual review. Division des hippodromes, 1983 revue annuelle. Ottawa: Agriculture Canada, c1984. 41 p. : ill. (Cat. no. A61-11/1983.)
CORP: Canada. Dept. of Agriculture. Race Track Division.
LEVEL: B LANG: Eng Fr ISBN: 0-662-52946-4 SF334 17715

TEACHING

Hardin, J. Learning horsemanship the British way. *Thoroughbred record (Lexington, Ky.) 218(37), 12 Sept 1984, 4588;4590.*
LEVEL: B LANG: Eng SIRC ARTICLE NO: 101348

Virgets, R. Learning in Louisiana: Louisiana Tech University's equine education program is preparing students to be trainers and race track officials. *Thoroughbred record (Lexington, Ky.) 218(32), 8 Aug 1984, 3886-3887.*
LEVEL: B LANG: Eng SIRC ARTICLE NO: 098254

TESTING AND EVALUATION

Roman, S.A. An analysis of dosage. An explanation of the author's concept of dosage, a method for attempting to evaluate a horse's racing potential based on the influences of speed and stamina in its pedigree. *Thoroughbred record (Lexington, Ky.) 218(16), 18 Apr 1984, 1979-1980;1982-1984.*
LEVEL: I LANG: Eng SIRC ARTICLE NO: 095122

TRAINING AND CONDITIONING

Ivers, T. Tapering: tactics and techniques. *Equus (Farmingdale, N.Y.) 80, Jun 1984, 31;33-36.*
LEVEL: B LANG: Eng SIRC ARTICLE NO: 099728

O'Leary, E. Doug Arthur is becoming a king of conditioners. *Hoof beats (Columbus, Ohio) 52(6), Aug 1984, 100;102;104.*
LEVEL: B LANG: Eng SIRC ARTICLE NO: 099744

Turner, P. The transformation. (training of race horses) *Blood-horse (Lexington, Ky.)* 110(37), 15 Sept 1984, 6526-6528.
LEVEL: B LANG: Eng SIRC ARTICLE NO: 099757

TRAINING AND CONDITIONING - INTERVAL TRAINING

Toby, M.C. Intervals and condition. Under the heading of interval training is a program of equine conditioning whose impact is yet to be determined, but is based on human successes. *Blood-horse (Lexington, Ky.)* 110(7), 18 Feb 1984, 1342-1344;1346-1347.
LEVEL: B LANG: Eng SIRC ARTICLE NO: 095126

VETERINARY MEDICINE

Mason, D.K. Collins, E.A. Watkins, K.L. Effect of bedding on the incidence of exercise induced pulmonary haemorrhage in racehorses in Hong Kong. *Veterinary record (London)* 115(11), 15 Sept 1984, 268-269.
LEVEL: A LANG: Eng

Sweeney, C.R. Soma, L.R. Bucan, C.A. Ray, S.G. Exercise-induced pulmonary hemorrhage in exercising Thoroughbreds: preliminar results with pre-exercise medication. *Cornell veterinarian (Ithaca, N.Y.)* 74(3), Jul 1984, 263-268.
LEVEL: A LANG: Eng SIRC ARTICLE NO: 103272

Sweeney, C.R. Soma, L.R. Exercise-induced pulmonary hemorrhage in thoroughbred horses: response to furosemide or hesperidin-citrus bioflavinoids. *Journal of the American Veterinary Medical Association (Chicago)* 185(2), 15 Jul 1984, 195-197.
LEVEL: A LANG: Eng SIRC ARTICLE NO: 104808

Trottere, C. Soundings on soundness. The non-invasive bone scan, also known as diagnostic ultrasound, gives trainers information on bone strength of horses in training. *Blood-horse (Lexington, Ky.)* 110(4), 28 Jan 1984, 704-706.
LEVEL: I LANG: Eng SIRC ARTICLE NO: 095127

HORSE RACING - STEEPLECHASE

Shull, S.L. Characteristics of the steeplechase runner. Conformation, pedigree, and training all contribute to the making of the successful steeplechaser who can run fast and jump well. *Thoroughbred record (Lexington, Ky.)* 218(44), 31 Oct 1984, 5620-5622;5624;5626.
LEVEL: B LANG: Eng SIRC ARTICLE NO: 099752

ASSOCIATIONS

Shull, S.L. Organizing the jumpers. The National and Steeplechase and Hunt Association carries the primary responsibility fo perpetuation of North America's jump racing. *Thoroughbred record (Lexington, Ky.)* 218(28), 11 Jul 1984, 3326-3328;3329.
LEVEL: B LANG: Eng SIRC ARTICLE NO: 098241

HISTORY

Bongianni, M. Cozzaglio, P. Champion horses. New York: Bonanza Books, 1984. 1v.
NOTES: Translation of: I grandi cavalli. Includes index.
LEVEL: B LANG: Eng ISBN: 0517439336 LC CARD: 84-011012

HORSEBACK RIDING AND HORSEMANSHIP

Cahill, T. Return of the chariot: from the circus maximus to Rexburg, Idaho. *Outside (Chicago, Ill.)* 9(3), Apr 1984, 33-34;36.
LEVEL: B LANG: Eng SIRC ARTICLE NO: 099711

Clarke, S. The habit and the horse. Mt. Holly, N.J.: International Side-Saddle Organization, 1984. 220 p.
NOTES: Originally published in 1857. 500 numbered copies.
LEVEL: B LANG: Eng

D'Orgeix, J. Equitation/2: angles et rythmes. Paris: Robert Laffont, c1984. 157 p. : ill. (Sport pour tous.)
LEVEL: B LANG: Fr ISBN: 2-221-04480-0 SF309 17795

Godson, W.D. The natural aid for horse-related problems. Caledon, Ont.: Godson Publishing, c1984. 236 p. : ill.
LEVEL: I LANG: Eng ISBN: 0-9691435-1-6 LC CARD: C84-099639-X SF285.3 20311

Pervier, E. Hughes, M. Horsemanship: basics for beginners. New York: Arco Pub., c1984. 95 p. : ill.
NOTES: Includes index. Bibliography: p. 92.
LEVEL: B LANG: Eng ISBN: 0668059354 LC CARD: 83-010004 SF309 17132

Pervier, E. Hughes, M. Horsemanship: basics for intermediate riders. New York: Arco Pub., c1984. 94 p. : ill.
NOTES: Includes index. Bibliography: p. 91.
LEVEL: B LANG: Eng ISBN: 0668059427 LC CARD: 83-010003 SF309 17134

Pervier, E. Hughes, M. Horsemanship: basics for more advanced riders. New York: Arco Pub., c1984. 94 p. : ill.
NOTES: Includes index. Bibliography: p. 90.
LEVEL: I LANG: Eng ISBN: 0668059508 LC CARD: 83-010002 SF295.2 17133

ADMINISTRATION

Lefaive, M. Riding the computer wave. *Horse sense (Elora, Ont.)* 3(6), Oct/Nov 1984, 23-26.
LEVEL: B LANG: Eng SIRC ARTICL NO: 105938.

ANATOMY

Bennett, D. Choosing a riding horse: more on the 'motor'. *Dressage & CT (Cleveland Heights, Ohio)* 21(3), Mar 1984, 16-19.
LEVEL: I LANG: Eng SIRC ARTICLE NO: 171490

ANIMAL HUSBANDRY

Barton, J. Quest for the perfectly shod horse. *Horse sense (Elora, Ont.)* 3(6), Oct/Nov 1984, 31-33.
NOTES: Second in a series.
LEVEL: B LANG: Eng SIRC ARTICLE NO: 105918

Choosing a ferrier (?). *Canadian Arabian news (Bowden, Alta.)* 24(4), Apr 1984, 47-50.
NOTES: Reprinted with permission of American Farrier's Association.
LEVEL: B LANG: Eng SIRC ARTICLE NO: 098186

The art and science of cooling out: what's the right way to do it... in terms of the events taking place inside your horse? *Practical horseman (Unionville, Pa.)* 12(12), Dec 1984, 15-22.
LEVEL: B LANG: Eng SIRC ARTICLE NO: 108098

Waltman, L. Grooming: taking care of your horse's needs. This installment deals with a few basic rules and the use of common sense in bandaging so you help your horse rather than hinder or even hurt him. *Dressage & CT (Cleveland, Ohio)* 21(2), Feb 1984, 28-33.
LEVEL: B LANG: Eng SIRC ARTICLE NO: 098257

BIOGRAPHY AND AUTOBIOGRAPHY

Irvine, J.L. Attention to detail: by never settling for less than perfection, Joan Santos has shaped her career as a halter trainer. *Appaloosa news (Moscow, Idaho)* 41(12), Dec 1984, 132-138.
LEVEL: B LANG: Eng SIRC ARTICLE NO: 107291

BIOMECHANICS

Boese, A. Linkages and leverages: the horse's motion mechanism. (Refs: 5)*Equus (Gaithersburg, Md.)* 81, Jul 1984, 26-28;30-31;33.
LEVEL: I LANG: Eng SIRC ARTICLE NO: 101335

COUNTRIES AND REGIONS

Cooper, C. Amateur: status of the non pro horseman. *Horseman (Houston, Tex.)* 28(11), Jun 1984, 48-49.
LEVEL: B LANG: Eng SIRC ARTICLE NO: 103248

DISABLED

Dismuke, R. Handicapped riding. *Quarter horse journal (Amarillo, Tex.)* 36(11), Aug 1984, 34-37.
LEVEL: B LANG: Eng SIRC ARTICLE NO: 095852

Fox, V.M. Lawlor, V.A. Luttges, M.W. Pilot study of novel test instrumentation to evaluate therapeutic horseback riding. (Refs: 10)*Adapted physical activity quarterly 1(1), 1984, 30-36.
ABST: A test devide designed and built by the Department of Aerospace Engineering Sciences was used to assess changes in balance, coordination and strength in a group of nineteen subjects involved in a therapeutic horseback riding course. Results indicate that the therapeutic horseback riding course improved balance, coordination and strength as measured by the test device. The authors conclude that this instrument can aid in both diagnosis and measurement of motor system characteristics.
LEVEL: A LANG: Eng SIRC ARTICLE NO: 092812

HORSEBACK RIDING AND HORSEMANSHIP (continued)

Worrall, M. Program for special riders successful in Talbot County. *Maryland horse (Lutherville-Timonium, Md.) 50(9), Aug 1984, 76-81.*
LEVEL: B LANG: Eng SIRC ARTICLE NO: 099020

DRUGS, DOPING AND ERGOGENIC AIDS

Vogel, C. Drug prescription and equine events. *Veterinary record (London) 115(18), 3 Nov 1984, 452.*
LEVEL: I LANG: Eng

Vogel, C. Drug prescription and equine events. *Veterinary record (London) 115(18), 3 Nov 1984, 452.*
LEVEL: I LANG: Eng

ENVIRONMENT

Boese, A. Pollution: the unseen and unclear. *Equus (Gaithersburg, Md.) Aug 1984, 67-68;70.*
LEVEL: B LANG: Eng SIRC ARTICL NO: 103247

EQUIPMENT

Darnall, G. The science of bits: the shanks. *Horseman (Marion, Ohio) 29(2), Sept 1984, 134-136;138;140.*
NOTES: Fifth in a series.
LEVEL: B LANG: Eng SIRC ARTICLE NO: 098191

Darnall, G. The science of bits: balance. *Horseman (Houston, Tex.) 29(3), Oct 1984, 64-65;69.*
NOTES: Sixth in a series.
LEVEL: B LANG: Eng SIRC ARTICLE NO: 105922

Darnell, G. The science of bits: the snaffle. *Horseman (Houston, Tex.) 28(12), Jul 1984, 40-42;44-45.*
NOTES: Third in a series.
LEVEL: B LANG: Eng SIRC ARTICLE NO: 099713

Darnell, G. The science of bits: the mouthpiece. *Horseman (Houston, Tex.) 29(1), Aug 1984, 70-72;74;77.*
NOTES: Fourth in series.
LEVEL: B LANG: Eng SIRC ARTICLE NO: 099714

Emerson, R.L. 100 years of artillery curb bits: a survey of the regulation curb bits used by the U.S. Artillary from the 1840's to the beginning of World War 11. *Western horseman (Colorado Springs, Colo.) 49(2), Feb 1984, 21-24.*
LEVEL: B LANG: Eng SIRC ARTICLE NO: 098194

Floyd, J. Correct saddle fit - what to look for. *Side-saddle news (Mount Holly, N.J.) 11(6), Summer 1984, 22-23.*
LEVEL: B LANG: Eng SIRC ARTICLE NO: 099717

Gordon-Watson, M. The snaffle bit: the second part of a review bits and bitting. *Horse & driving (West Yorkshire, Eng.) 35, Jan/Feb 1984, 44-45.*
LEVEL: B LANG: Eng SIRC ARTICLE NO: 099721

Stockho, C. Coming to grips with ground grippers. Ways to eliminate slipups in your horse's stride. *Equus (Farmingdale, N.Y.) 75, Jan 1984, 36;38-40.*
LEVEL: B LANG: Eng SIRC ARTICLE NO: 096713

Stuska, S. Selection and care of tack and equipment. *Quarter horse journal (Amarillo, Tex.) 36(12), Sept 1984, 160-163.*
LEVEL: B LANG: Eng SIRC ARTICLE NO: 099755

Torrey, T. Taking the mystery out of shoe studs. *USCTA news (Hamilton, Mass.) 13(4), Aug 1984,*

8-10.
LEVEL: B LANG: Eng SIRC ARTICLE NO: 101364

EQUIPMENT - MAINTENANCE

Kneeland, C. An interview with Smokey Everhart: side -saddle repair & restoration specialist. *Side-saddle news (Mount Holly N.J.) 11(6), Summer 1984, 12-15;27-28.*
LEVEL: B LANG: Eng SIRC ARTICLE NO: 099730

FACILITIES - DESIGN, CONSTRUCTION AND PLANNING

Affordable outdoor arenas. *Practical horseman (Unionville, Pa.) 12(3), Mar 1984, 19-23;46-A-46-C.*
LEVEL: B LANG: Eng SIRC ARTICLE NO: 097516

Horse housing facilities. *Canadian Arabian news (Bowden, Alta.) 24(4), Apr 1984, 53-56.*
LEVEL: B LANG: Eng SIRC ARTICLE NO: 098210

HISTORY

Maar, N.T. Rediscovering the sidesaddle. *Equus (Farmingdale, N.Y.) 80, Jun 1984, 70-71;73-74;76;79.*
LEVEL: B LANG: Eng SIRC ARTICLE NO: 099736

Powell, L. The age of splendour. A history of equitation: part IX. *Equi (Warrington, Eng.) 20, Jan/Feb 1984, 24-26.*
NOTES To be continued.
LEVEL: B LANG: Eng SIRC ARTICLE NO: 095121

Powell, L. A history of equitation - Part 9. The age of splendour. *Equi (Cheshire, Eng.) 21, Apr/May 1984, 24-26.*
LEVEL: LANG: Eng SIRC ARTICLE NO: 098230

HORSES

The stress factor. *Horse and rider (Surrey, Eng.) 34(386), Jun 1984, 24-25.*
LEVEL: B LANG: Eng SIRC ARTICLE NO: 101362

INJURIES AND ACCIDENTS

Boese, A. Tactical errors: solving the riddle of rider-induced pain. *Equus (Gaithersburg, Md.) Oct 1984, 42-45;48-49;106.*
LEVEL: B LANG: Eng SIRC ARTICLE NO: 109588

Bromiley, M. The effect of machines in injury. Part 2: mechanical aids to tissue healing. *Horse & driving (West Yorkshire, Eng.) 35, Jan/Feb 1984, 48-49.*
LEVEL: B LANG: Eng SIRC ARTICLE NO: 099710

Hurtig, M. Bailey, J. Horsehealthlines: Equine arthroscopy: working towards a better understanding of joint disorders and their treatment. *Canadian Arabian news 24(1), Jan 1984, 9-11.*
LEVEL: B LANG: Eng SIRC ARTICLE NO: 092224

Ilgren, E.B. Teddy, P.J. Vafadis, J. Briggs, M. Gardiner, N.G. Clinical and pathological studies of brain injuries in horse-riding accidents: a description of case and review with a warning to the unhelmeted. *Clinical neuropathology (Deisenhofen, W. Ger.) 3(6), Nov/Dec 1984, 253-259.*
ABST: The authors report cases of brain injuries following horse-riding accidents. They underline the inedequacy of the present types of riding helmets and the dangers that unhelmeted riders expose themselves to.
LEVEL: A LANG: Eng

Pounder, D.J. The grave yawns for the horseman. Equestrian deaths in South Australia 1973-1983. *Medical journal of Australi (Sydney) 141(10), 10 Nov 1984, 632-635.*
LEVEL: A LANG: Eng

MEDICINE

Greiss, F.C. Equestrian dyspareunia. *American journal of obstetrics and gynecology (St. Louis) 150(2), 15 Sept 1984, 168.*
LEVEL: I LANG: Eng SIRC ARTICLE NO: 104806

NUTRITION

Feeding the super athlete: feeding the high-performance horse has long posed hazards... but now it's an ordinary household substance to the rescue. *Practical horseman (Unionville, Pa.) 12(12), Dec 1984, 38-40;42.*
LEVEL: B LANG: Eng SIRC ARTICLE NO: 109453

Kronfeld, D. Donohue, S. Feeding the super athlete: feeding the high-performance horse has long posed hazards... but now it' an ordinary household substance to the rescue. *Performance horseman (Unionville, Pa.) 4(1), Dec 1984, 38-40;42.*
LEVEL: I LANG: Eng SIRC ARTICLE NO: 105937

Lieberman, B. Feeding for performance: it's energy, not protein, that counts. *Equus (Farmingdale, N.Y.) 77, Mar 1984, 24-28.*
LEVEL: B LANG: Eng SIRC ARTICLE NO: 098220

PHYSICAL FITNESS

Reynolds, C.S. Stay fit to ride. *Horseman (Houston, Tex.) 28(9), Apr 1984, 71-72;74.*
LEVEL: B LANG: Eng SIRC ARTICLE NO: 099749

PHYSIOLOGY

Piston, pendulums and swings: integrating equine biomechanics and respiration. *Equus (Gaithersburg, Md.) Sept 1984, 20;22;24.*
LEVEL: B LANG: Eng SIRC ARTICLE NO: 108095

PSYCHOLOGY

Hamilton, S. Do they feel what we feel? Five experts explore equine emotion. *Equus (Gaithersburg, Md.) Oct 1984, 56-58;60-62;64;100-101.*
LEVEL: B LANG: Eng SIRC ARTICLE NO: 109589

TECHNIQUES AND SKILLS

Boese, A. The four-beat formula: gaited horses on the move. *Equus (Farmingdale, N.Y.) 80, Jun 1984, 38-39;41-42;44-45;102-103.*
LEVEL: B LANG: Eng SIRC ARTICLE NO: 099709

Floyd, J. Riding side-saddle. *Side-Saddle news (Mount Holly, N.J.) 11(6), Summer 1984, 18-19.*
LEVEL: B LANG: Eng SIRC ARTICLE NO: 099716

Francis, V. Back to school. *Horse and rider (Surrey, Eng.) 34(386), Jun 1984, 22-23.*
NOTES: First of a two-part series.
LEVEL: B LANG: Eng SIRC ARTICLE NO: 101342

Francis, V. Back to school. *Horse and rider (Surrey, Eng.) 34(387), Jul 1984, 24-25.*
NOTES: Part two of a series on introducing your horse to side-saddle.
LEVEL: B LANG: Eng SIRC ARTICLE NO: 101343

Fregin, F. The art and science of cooling out: what's the right way to do it... in terms of the events taking place inside your horse? *Performance horseman (Unionville, Pa.) 4(1), Dec 1984, 15-22.*
LEVEL: I LANG: Eng SIRC ARTICLE NO: 105924

Hill, C. Lynch, B. Turnaround: accomplishment in degrees - the goal. *Horseman (Houston, Tex.) 29(3), Oct 1984, 26-27;29-32.*
NOTES: First in a series.
LEVEL: B LANG: Eng SIRC ARTICLE NO: 105930

Hill, C. Turnaround: accomplishment in degrees - groundwork. *Horseman (Houston, Tex.) 29(4), Nov 1984, 34-39.*
NOTES: Second in a series.
LEVEL: B LANG: Eng SIRC ARTICLE NO: 105931

Johnson, C. Power behind the please: put that shoulder precisely where you want it. Part 2. *Horseman (Marion, Ohio) 29(5), Dec 1984, 36-39;41.*
LEVEL: B LANG: Eng SIRC ARTICLE NO: 109310

Kilby, E. Controlling the flow: aim your aids at harmonious motion. *Equus (Gaithersburg, Md.) Sept 1984, 66-68;70;72;75-76;78.*
LEVEL: B LANG: Eng SIRC ARTICLE NO: 109590

Stewart, S. Mounting from the right, or why do you think it's called the 'Off' side? *Side-saddle news (Mount Holly, N.J.) 11(6), Summer 1984, 9.*
LEVEL: B LANG: Eng SIRC ARTICLE NO: 099754

Wells, C. The first ninety days. Lesson three: introducing the bit. *Performance horseman (Unionville, Pa.) 4(1), Dec 1984, 47-57.*
LEVEL: B LANG: Eng SIRC ARTICLE NO: 105955

Young, J.R. Head-shy. *Horseman (Houston, Tex.) 29(3), Oct 1984, 70-72;74.*
LEVEL: B LANG: Eng SIRC ARTICLE NO: 105957

TECHNIQUES AND SKILLS - STANCE

Von Blixen-Finecke, H. The Swedish way. Part 3: the rider and the saddle. *Horse & driving (West Yorkshire, Eng.) 36, Mar/Ap 1984, 62-64.*
LEVEL: B LANG: Eng SIRC ARTICLE NO: 099759

TRAINING AND CONDITIONING

Dunn, D. Cutting in the cold: Dave Batty of Alberta trains cutting horses under sometimes frigid conditions. *Western horseman (Colorado Springs, Colo.) 49(11), Nov 1984, 24-26.*
LEVEL: B LANG: Eng SIRC ARTICLE NO: 108808

Houpt, K.A. Timetables for learning: a behavioral view of nature's educational schedule. *Equus (Gaithersburg, Md.) Nov 1984 42-46;48;50;120-121.*
LEVEL: B LANG: Eng SIRC ARTICLE NO: 108896

Individualized instruction: how seven successful trainers spot potential and plot progress. *Equus (Gaithersburg, Md.) Nov 198 68-72;74-77;80;83.*
LEVEL: B LANG: Eng SIRC ARTICLE NO: 108901

Kilby, E. Get even: overcoming riding imbalances brought on by sidedness. *Equus (Farmingdale, N.Y.) 75, Jan 1984, 30-34;78-79;109.*
LEVEL: B LANG: Eng SIRC ARTICLE NO: 096706

Kilby, E. 'Blank slates' and 'old dogs': accommodating the age-related aspects of trainability. *Equus (Gaithersburg, Md.) Nov 1984, 54-58;60;62;65;122-123.*
LEVEL: B LANG: Eng SIRC ARTICLE NO: 108899

Pflueger-Clarke, S. Morris, G. Johnson, C. What does it mean to train by a 'system'? *Practical horseman (Unionville, Pa.) 12(9), Sept 1984, 24-25.*
LEVEL: B LANG: Eng SIRC ARTICLE NO: 105949

Shape up. *Horse and rider (Surrey, Eng.) 34(385), May 1984, 40-41.*
LEVEL: B LANG: Eng SIRC ARTICLE NO: 099751

Young, J.R. Bag full of training tricks. *Horseman (Houston, Tex.) 28(9), Apr 1984, 45-48.*
LEVEL: B LANG: Eng SIRC ARTICLE NO: 099763

TRANSPORTATION

First time traveller. *Riding (London) 49(10), Oct 1984, 34-37.*
LEVEL: B LANG: Eng SIRC ARTICLE NO: 107283

Laws, K. Safety in tow: before you hit the road, weave a security blanket of control. *Equus (Farmingdale, N.Y.) 78, Apr 1984, 62-64;66;68;70;72;120-121.*
LEVEL: B LANG: Eng SIRC ARTICLE NO: 099732

VARIATIONS - FOX HUNTING

Carroll, T. Diary of a fox-hunting man. s.l.: Hamish Hamilton, (1984?). 1v.
NOTES: Survey of fox-hunting in Britain today.
LEVEL: B LANG: Eng ISBN: 0-241-11361-X

Harrison, C.S. Fox hunting injuries in North America. (Refs: 7)*Physician and sportsmedicine (Minneapolis, Minn.) 12(10), Oc 1984, 130-134;136-137.*
LEVEL: I LANG: Eng SIRC ARTICLE NO: 099725

Simpson, A. English drag-hunting. *Chronicle of the horse (Middleburg, Va.) 47(20), 11 May 1984, 40.*
LEVEL: B LANG: Eng SIRC ARTICLE NO: 098242

VETERINARY MEDICINE

Acupuncture for aching backs: an age-old technique is providing relief where modern treatment often fails. *Practical horseman (Unionville, Pa.) 12(11), Nov 1984, 21-25.*
LEVEL: B LANG: Eng SIRC ARTICLE NO: 105916

Alternative therapy. *Horse and rider (Surrey, Eng.) 34(385), May 1984, 16-18.*
LEVEL: B LANG: Eng SIRC ARTICLE NO: 099706

Anemia mania, does your horse have iron-poor blood? *Equus (Gaithersburg, Md.) 81, Jul 1984, 58-59;61-63.*
LEVEL: B LANG: Eng SIRC ARTICLE NO: 101334

Bayly, W.M. Grant, B.D. Breeze, R.G. Arterial blood gas tension and acid base balance during exercise in horses with pharyngeal lymphoid hyperplasia. *Equine veterinary journal (London) 16(5), Sept 1984, 435-438.*
LEVEL: A LANG: Eng

Blair, J. Good food guide. *Horse and rider (Surrey, Eng.) 34(388), Aug 1984, 29-31.*
NOTES: Part two of a four part specia
LEVEL: B LANG: Eng SIRC ARTICLE NO: 099708

Dahl, A. Magnetic magic: healing process aids racehorses. *Canadian Arabian news (Calgary, Alta.) 24(3), Mar 1984, 41-42.*
LEVEL: B LANG: Eng SIRC ARTICLE NO: 098190

Edwards, R.H. Exercise physiology in horses - lessons from human physiology. *Equine veterinary journal (London) 16(3), May 1984, 154-155.*
LEVEL: I LANG: Eng SIRC ARTICLE NO: 103250

Evans, R. Is your horse hot stuff? (Thermotherapy) *Canadian Arabian news (Calgary, Alta.) 24(3), Mar 1984, 29-30.*
LEVEL: LANG: Eng SIRC ARTICLE NO: 098195

Fisher, R. Riding's vets: to fire or not to fire. *Riding (London) 49(4), Apr 1984, 28-29.*
LEVEL: B LANG: Eng SIRC ARTICLE NO: 098196

Focus on fitness:. How does exercise affect the horse's body systems? *Horse and rider (Surrey, Eng.) 38(382), Feb 1984, 43-44.*
LEVEL: B LANG: Eng SIRC ARTICLE NO: 099718

Hamilton, S. The equine thermostat. How your horse keeps his cool - and his warmth. *Equus (Farmingdale, N.Y.) 75, Jan 1984, 49-52;54.*
LEVEL: I LANG: Eng SIRC ARTICLE NO: 096704

Hardman, H.J. Magnetic therapy - the new wave. *Canadian Arabian news (Bowden, Alta.) 24(5), May 1984, 47-48.*
LEVEL: B LANG: Eng SIRC ARTICLE NO: 099724

Hi-tech medicine. *Horse sense (Elora, Ont.) 3(6), Oct/Nov 1984, 16-17.*
LEVEL: B LANG: Eng SIRC ARTICLE NO: 105928

Jackson, S.G. Feeding for optimum growth, reproduction, and performance. *Standardbred (Acton, Ont.) 13(2), 18 Jan 1984, 25;28;30;32-34;36-37.*
LEVEL: I LANG: Eng SIRC ARTICLE NO: 098217

Jefferies, R. Hydro therapy. *Canadian horse (Rexdale, Ont.) Jun 1984, 25-26.*
LEVEL: B LANG: Eng SIRC ARTICLE NO: 096705

Lakin, R. Getting to know the nose. The structural secrets of that touchable muzzle. *Equus (Farmingdale, N.Y.) 75, Jan 1984 42;44-46.*
LEVEL: B LANG: Eng SIRC ARTICLE NO: 096707

Lanyon, L. Conditioning your horse's bone. *Practical horsemen (Unionville, Pa.) 12(5), May 1984, 22-23;25-26;28.*
LEVEL: I LANG: Eng SIRC ARTICLE NO: 099731

Lieberman, B. A heart you can count on: on-board monitoring adds new dimension to training. *Equus (Farmingdale, N.Y.) 78, Apr 1984, 24-28.*
LEVEL: B LANG: Eng SIRC ARTICLE NO: 099735

McKibbin, L.S. The standardbred interview: Dr. McKibbin on cryosurgery. *Standardbred (Acton, Ont.) 12(26), 12 Sept 1984, 12-17.*
LEVEL: B LANG: Eng SIRC ARTICLE NO: 099740

McSparren, C. How to make a good horse last. *Canadian Arabian news (Bowden, Alta.) 24(4), Apr 1984, 11;14-16;18-19.*
LEVEL B LANG: Eng SIRC ARTICLE NO: 098221

Mearns, D. Park place. (Cornell's Equine Research Park) *Blood-horse (New York) 110(39), 29 Sept 1984, 6870-6873.*
LEVEL: B LANG: Eng SIRC ARTICLE NO: 101354

Ogilvie, T.W.B. Testing for health and fitness. *Equi (Cheshire, Eng.) 24, Oct/Nov 1984, 20-21;23.*
LEVEL: B LANG: Eng SIRC ARTICLE NO: 109654

Osborne, R. Making memories: how the brain selects the lessons horses learn. *Equus (Gaithersburg, Md.) Nov 1984, 28-33;36;38-39.*
LEVEL: I LANG: Eng SIRC ARTICLE NO: 108893

Owen, R.A. Marsh, J.A. Hallett, F.R. Lumsden, J.H. Johnson, J. Intra-articular corticosteroid- and exercise-induced arthropathy in a horse. *Journal of the American Veterinary Medical Association*

(Chicago) 184(3), 1 Feb 1984, 302-308.
LEVEL: I LANG: Eng SIRC ARTICLE NO: 099746

Pain: how your horse perceives it. (Refs: 2)*Practical horseman (Unionville, Pa.) 12(8), Aug 1984, 32-35.*
LEVEL: I LANG: Eng SIRC ARTICLE NO: 103259

Paulo, K.R. Wrapping legs: step by step instructions for applying a standing bandage and also a spider wrap. *Western horseman (Colorado Springs, Colo.) 49(3), Mar 1984, 84;86;88.*
LEVEL: B LANG: Eng SIRC ARTICLE NO: 098226

Perceived exertion vs. real fatigue: a question of matter over mind. *Equus (Farmingdale, N.Y.) 76, Feb 1984, 23;25-28.*
LEVEL: B LANG: Eng SIRC ARTICLE NO: 095120

Sellnow, L. Solving a tall problem: research has alleviated a problem with tall fescue, developing a strain free of the fungus which has caused problems both for horses and cattle. *Blood-horse (Lexington, Ky.) 110(47), 24 Nov 1984, 8676-8677.*
LEVEL: B LANG: Eng SIRC ARTICLE NO: 103264

Smalley, A. Mackay-Smith, M. The bad back: all it asks is a little respect. (Refs: 13)*Equus (Farmingdale, N.Y.) 76, Feb 1984, 46-50.*
LEVEL: I LANG: Eng SIRC ARTICLE NO: 095124

Sportscience: calling all recruits. *Equus (Farmingdale, N.Y.) 75, Jan 1984, 22;25-27.*
LEVEL: I LANG: Eng SIRC ARTICLE NO: 096712

The truth about bute. *Practical horseman (Unionville, Pa.) 12(10), Oct 1984, 15-16;18;20.*
LEVEL: I LANG: Eng SIRC ARTICLE NO: 105953

The vet's arrived at your barn in response to your call. You watch her perform her silent ritual of examination, and you wonder: what's the vet thinking? Session nine: endoscopic examination. *Practical horseman (Unionville, Pa.) 12(12), Dec 1984, 24-25.*
LEVEL: B LANG: Eng SIRC ARTICLE NO: 108099

Von Blixen-Finecke, H. The Swedish way. Part 2: how the horse moves and the effects of training. *Horse & driving (West Yorkshire, Eng.) 35, Jan/Feb 1984, 38-39.*
LEVEL: I LANG: Eng SIRC ARTICLE NO: 099758

WOMEN

Holcomb, K.E. Is there trouble in riding double? *Equus (Gaithersburg, Md.) Sept 1984, 84-85;89.*
LEVEL: B LANG: Eng SIRC ARTICLE NO: 109591

HORSESHOE PITCHING

Berman, S. Horseshoe film, facts, and fun. New York: Cornwall Books, 1984. 1v.
LEVEL: B LANG: Eng ISBN: 0845347705 LC
CARD: 82-046092

Gilbert, B. Pitchin' shoes. *Sports illustrated (Chicago, Ill.) 61(15), 24 Sept 1984, 66-70;72-75;78-79.*
LEVEL: B LANG: En SIRC ARTICLE NO: 099764

HUMOUR AND SATIRE

Fink, J. The average athlete. *Running & fitness (Washington, D.C.) 16(4), Jul/Aug 1984, 22.*
LEVEL: B LANG: Eng SIRC ARTICLE NO: 105590

Green, L. Sportswit. 1st ed. New York: Harper & Row, c1984. xiv, 270 p.
NOTES: Includes indexes.
LEVEL: B LANG: Eng ISBN: 0060911336 LC
CARD: 83-048840 GV706.8 18119

HURDLE RACE

Brejzer, V. Brublevzkij, E. The 400 metres hurdles - a summary of information-. *Modern athlete and coach (Athelstone, Aust. 22(3), Jul 1984, 32-34.*
NOTES: Translated from, Legkaya Atletika (Moscow) 11, 1982.
LEVEL: B LANG: Eng SIRC ARTICLE NO: 101628

Ross, W.L. How to teach the hurdling action. *Track & field quarterly review (Kalamazoo, Mich.) 84(2), Summer 1984, 26-31.*
LEVEL: I LANG: Eng SIRC ARTICLE NO: 095453

BIBLIOGRAPHIES

Dates, G.G. Theses and dissertations in track & field. *Track & field quarterly review (Kalamazoo, Mich.) 84(2), Summer 1984 60-62.*
LEVEL: B LANG: Eng SIRC ARTICLE NO: 095402

Sport bibliography. *Track and field journal 25, Feb 1984, 33-35.*
LEVEL: B LANG: Eng SIRC ARTICLE NO: 093947

BIOGRAPHY AND AUTOBIOGRAPHY

Aitken, A. Getting to grips with the event. Alastair Atken interviews Gladys Taylor, following her victory in the WAAA 400 hurdles, and her coach, Ron Bowden. *Athletics weekly (Rochester, Kent, Eng.) 38(26), 30 Jun 1984, 56-58.*
LEVEL: B LANG: Eng SIRC ARTICLE NO: 096922

Deford, F. Rising to great heights: sportsman and sportswoman of the year. (Edwin Moses and Mary Lou Retton) *Sports illustrated (Los Angeles, Calif.) 61(28), 24-31 Dec 1984, 32-34;36;38;43;44.*
LEVEL: B LANG: Eng SIRC ARTICLE NO: 103218

Dobbs, G. Runner's world gold medal exclusive. *Runner's world (Mountain View, Calif.) 19(8), Aug 1984, 174;177-178;180.*
LEVEL: B LANG: Eng SIRC ARTICLE NO: 096959

Kirkpatrick, C. The man who never loses. Edwin Moses, the winner of 89 straight races in the 400 hurdles, is a gold-pipe cinch to get number 90 in the Olympics. *Sports illustrated (Chicago, Ill.) 61(6), 30 Jul 1984, 52-58;60-65.*
LEVEL: B LANG: Eng SIRC ARTICLE NO: 096931

Olsen, E. A man for all seasons: as an athlete and role model of uncompromising integrity, Edwin Moses is unsurpassed. *Runner (New York) 6(12), Sept 1984, 26-30;32;34.*
LEVEL: B LANG: Eng SIRC ARTICLE NO: 103599

Riding a long winning streak, Greg Foster enters the Olympic season short on publicity and long on confidence. *Runner's world 19(3), Mar 1984, 23-24;26;30;32;34;36;38.*
LEVEL: B LANG: Eng SIRC ARTICLE NO: 092522

Ward, F. Paul Brice - 110m hurdles bronze medallist, Vienna, 1983. *Athletics coach (London) 18(2), Jun 1984 15-16.*
LEVEL: LANG: Eng SIRC ARTICLE NO: 095474

BIOMECHANICS

Breizer, V. On the track with Ekaterina Fesenko. *Soviet sports review (Escondido, Calif.) 20(2), June 1985, 75-78.*
NOTES: Translated from, Legkaya atletika 7, 1984, 16-17.
LEVEL: B LANG: Eng SIRC ARTICLE NO: 182400

Mero, A, Luhtanen, P. A biomechanical analysis of top hurdling. (Refs: 9)*Modern athlete and coach (Athelstone, Aust.) 22(3) Jul 1984, 3-6.*
LEVEL: I LANG: Eng SIRC ARTICLE NO: 101643

Nickson, T.R. A logical approach to improve hurdling technique. *Track & field quarterly review (Kalamazoo, Mich.) 84(2), Summer 1984, 32-33.*
LEVEL: I LANG: Eng SIRC ARTICLE NO: 095444

SPORTING EVENTS

Knight, G. Sprint hurdles... competition and specifications. *Athletics coach (Halesowen, England), Mar 1984, 19.*
LEVEL: B LANG: Eng SIRC ARTICLE NO: 093908

Saplin, S. Olympic replay; skimming the years. (hurdle race) *Runner (New York) 6(8), May 1984, 95.*
LEVEL: B LANG: Eng SIR ARTICLE NO: 101646

TEACHING

Aubert, F. Courses de haies hautes: situations de perfectionnement. Premiere partie. *EPS: Education physique et sport (Paris) 190, nov/dec 1984, 29-32.*
LEVEL: B LANG: Fr SIRC ARTICLE NO: 103557

TECHNIQUES AND SKILLS

Behm, J.J. Klaus Eidam entraineur national de haies en RDA a Karl Marx Stadt. *Revue de l'Amicale des entraineurs francais d'athletisme (Paris) 89, oct/nov/dec 1984, 35-39.*
LEVEL: B LANG: Fr SIRC ARTICLE NO: 103561

Engelbrecht, R. The 8,50m distance in the room hurdles. *Athletics coach (Halesowen, England) 18(1), Mar 1984, 31-32.*
LEVEL: B LANG: Eng SIRC ARTICLE NO: 093886

Engelbrecht, R. The 8.50m distance in the 100m hurdles. (Refs: 8)*Track & field quarterly review (Kalamazoo, Mich.) 84(2), Summer 1984, 38-39.*
LEVEL: I LANG: Eng SIRC ARTICLE NO: 095406

Olsen, E. Training & technique: the hurdles. *Runner (New York) 6(8), May 1984, 92.*
LEVEL: B LANG: Eng SIRC ARTICLE NO: 101644

Stastny, O. Technique and rhythm development for women's 400m hurdlers. *Modern athlete and coach (Athelstone, Aust.) 22(4), Oct 1984, 32-34.*
NOTES: Translated and condensed from: Die Lehre der Leichtathletik.
LEVEL: B LANG: Eng SIRC ARTICLE NO: 105026

Steben, R.E. Steve Kerho over the highs. *Scholastic coach 53(7), Feb 1984, 34-36.*
LEVEL: B LANG: Eng SIRC ARTICLE NO: 093948

Steben, R.E. Over the intermediates. *Scholastic coach 53(8), Mar 1984, 42-43;65-67.*
LEVEL: B LANG: Eng SIRC ARTICLE NO: 093949

Ulin, A. Papanov, V. On the track with Anna Ambrazene. *Soviet sports review (Escondido, Calif.) 19(1), Mar 1984, 23-25.*
NOTES: Translated from, Legkaya atletika 11, 1983, 16-17.
LEVEL: I LANG: Eng SIRC ARTICLE NO: 095472

TECHNIQUES AND SKILLS - START

Glover, D. Stand-up starts. For younger or less powerful sprinters and hurdlers, the stand-up start may be of great benefit. *Athletic journal (Evanston, Ill.) 64(10), May 1984, 16;69;71.*
LEVEL: B LANG: Eng SIRC ARTICLE NO: 095409

TESTING AND EVALUATION

Knoke, G. The hurdles. (Helsinki observation) *Modern athlete and coach (Athelstone, Aust.) 22(2), Apr 1984, 8-9.*
LEVEL: B LANG: Eng SIRC ARTICLE NO: 096978

Ross, W.L. A 400m formula for the 110m high hurdler. *Track & field quarterly review (Kalamazoo, Mich.) 84(2), Summer 1984, 42.*
LEVEL: I LANG: Eng SIRC ARTICLE NO: 095454

TRAINING AND CONDITIONING

Arnold, M. Training activities for the 400 metres hurdles. *Athletics coach (London) 18(3), Sept 1984, 7-8.*
LEVEL: B LANG: Eng SIRC ARTICLE NO: 100036

Groves, H. Intermediate hurdles 'an event for competitors'. *Track & field quarterly review (Kalamazoo, Mich.) 84(2), Summer 1984, 43-45.*
LEVEL: B LANG: Eng SIRC ARTICLE NO: 095412

McFarlane, B. Sequencing speed - a basic pattern. *Track and field journal 25, Feb 1984, 28-29.*
LEVEL: B LANG: Eng SIRC ARTICLE NO: 093917

McFarlane, B. Speed endurance...rhythm...sequencing. *Track & field quarterly review (Kalamazoo, Mich.) 84(2), Summer 1984, 31.*
LEVEL: I LANG: Eng SIRC ARTICLE NO: 095435

McFarlane, B. Special strength...horizontal and/or vertical? (Refs: 6)*Track & field quarterly review (Kalamazoo, Mich.) 84(2), Summer 1984, 51-54.*
LEVEL: B LANG: Eng SIRC ARTICLE NO: 095439

Szczepanki, T. The 100 metres hurdles. *Modern athlete and coach (Athelstone, Aust.) 22(4), Oct 1984, 15-18.*
NOTES: Based on author's address to XI European Track and Field Coaches Congress.
LEVEL: I LANG: Eng SIRC ARTICLE NO: 105029

TRAINING AND CONDITIONING - STRETCHING AND FLEXIBILITY EXERCISES

McFarlane, B. 25 steps to a continuous warm-up. *OPHEA: Ontario Physical and Health Education Association 10(3), Fall 1984, 24-26.*
LEVEL: B LANG: Eng SIRC ARTICLE NO: 103592

TRAINING AND CONDITIONING - WARM-UPS, WARM-DOWNS, LEAD-UP GAMES

McFarlane, B. The first World Track and Field Championships, Helsinki, 1983: a report on the women's sprint hurdle. *Track & field quarterly review (Kalamazoo, Mich.) 84(2), Summer 1984, 40-41.*
LEVEL: B LANG: Eng SIRC ARTICLE NO: 095436

McFarlane, B. 25 steps to a continuous warm up. *Track & field quarterly review (Kalamazoo, Mich.) 84(2), Summer 1984, 49-50.*
LEVEL: B LANG: Eng SIRC ARTICLE NO: 095438

McFarlane, B. No static stretching eh? (warm-up methods) *Coaching review (Ottawa, Ont.) 7, May/Jun 1984, 47-48.*
NOTES: Reprinted from, Canadian track and field journal.
LEVEL: B LANG: Eng SIRC ARTICLE NO: 095440

McFarlane, B. Women's 100m hurdles. *Modern athlete and coach (Athelstone, Aust.) 22(1), Jan 1984, 7-9.*
LEVEL: B LANG: Eng SIRC ARTICLE NO: 096985

TRAINING AND CONDITIONING - WEIGHT AND STRENGTH TRAINING

Crossley, G. Special strength: a link with hurdling. (Refs: 5)*Modern athlete and coach (Athelstone, Aust.) 22(2), Apr 1984, 24-26.*
LEVEL: I LANG: Eng SIRC ARTICLE NO: 096938

Szczepanski, T. The women's 100m hurdles. *Track & field quarterly review (Kalamazoo, Mich.) 84(2), Summer 1984, 34-37.*
CONF: ELLV Conference (11th : 1981 : Venice, Italy).
NOTES: Translated by, Herald Mach. Edited by, Brent McFarlane.
LEVEL: I LANG: Eng SIRC ARTICLE NO: 095469

ICE SAILING

Lewis, G.A. Iceboat racing: faster than the wind. *New Jersey outdoors (Trenton, N.J.) 11(1), Jan/Feb 1984, 24-25.*
LEVEL: LANG: Eng SIRC ARTICLE NO: 098271

Wood, P.S. Iceboating; fraternity and the race against the wind. *Outside 9(1), Jan/Feb 1984, 63-64.*
LEVEL: B LANG: Eng SIRC ARTICLE NO: 093570

EQUIPMENT

Carucci, M. The amphibious scooter: truly a unique craft, the scooter can sail on both ice and water - without the aid of a rudder. *Yacht racing & cruising (Philadelphia, Pa.) 23(3), Mar 1984, 64-66.*
LEVEL: B LANG: Eng SIRC ARTICLE NO: 098269

Durand, J.C. Patin de glisse et de glace. *Cahiers du yachting (Paris) 255, mars 1984, 68-73.*
LEVEL: Fr SIRC ARTICLE NO: 099765

Mindnich, P. Mohler, C. O'Neill, R. Winter alternatives. *Wind surf (Dana Point, Calif.) 14(8), Dec 1984, 50-55.*
LEVEL: B LANG: Eng SIRC ARTICLE NO: 173617

HISTORY

Didillon, H. La voile d'hiver: retrospective. *Ecoute (Montreal) 38, hiver 1984, 13-15.*
LEVEL: B LANG: Fr SIRC ARTICLE NO: 098270

SAFETY

La voile d'hiver: quelques conseils. *Ecoute (Montreal) 38, hiver 1984, 15.*
LEVEL: B LANG: Fr SIRC ARTICLE NO: 098272

STRATEGY

Bossett, H. Iceboat strategy & tactics: racing the fastest boats in the world requires planning ahead for strategic and tactical moves. *Yacht racing & cruising (Philadelphia, Pa.) 23(2), Feb 1984, 39-41.*
LEVEL: B LANG: Eng SIRC ARTICLE NO: 098268

de Cotret, P.R. Les voiliers sur glace. *Quebec yachting (Montreal) 6(8), dec 1983/janv 1984, 27-31.*
LEVEL: B LANG: Fr SIR ARTICLE NO: 095129

ICE SPORTS

ENVIRONMENT

Carbon monoxide intoxication associated with use of a gasoline-powered resurfacing machine at an ice-skating rink -- Pennsylvania. (Refs: 3)*Morbidity and mortality weekly report: MMWR/Center for disease control (Atlanta, Ga.) 33(4), 3 Feb 1984, 49-51.*
LEVEL: I LANG: Eng SIRC ARTICLE NO: 097519

FACILITIES

Johnson, A. Gilchrist, J. The ice-rink in contemporary society - a critical appraisal. (Refs: 187)*Momentum: a journal of human movement studies (Edinburgh) 9(2), Summer 1984, 26-70.*
LEVEL: I LANG: Eng SIRC ARTICLE NO: 098970

FACILITIES - DESIGN, CONSTRUCTION AND PLANNING

Ice rink buying and specifying. Guide and check list. St. Paul, Minn.: Holmsten Ice Rinks, Inc., c1984. 27 p. : ill.
NOTES: Cover title.
LEVEL: B LANG: Eng GV850.7 20874

INDIA

HISTORY

Pearson, M.N. Recreation in Mughal India. (Refs: 75)*British journal of sports history (London) 1(3), Dec 1984, 335-350.*
ABST: The author discusses the recreational and sporting activities in Mughal India during the period of 1550-1650.
LEVEL: A LANG: Eng SIRC ARTICLE NO: 105553

Gondowidjojo, M. The development of sport and physical education in Indonesia. *Asian journal of physical education (Taiwan, China) 7(1), Apr 1984, 46-54.*
NOTES: Abstract in Chinese.
LEVEL: B LANG: Eng Chi SIRC ARTICLE NO: 096244

INJURIES AND ACCIDENTS

Bedford, P.J. Macauley, D.C. Attendances at a casual department for sport related injuries. (Refs: 19)*British journal of sports medicine (Loughborough, Eng.) 18(2), Jun 1984, 116-121.*
ABST: In a prospective study over a period of 5 months (July-November, 1982), 506 patients were treated at a District General Hospital for a sports related injury. All the patients were seen initially in the Casualty Department and the majority of attendances (58%) were due to injuries caused by the two principal contact sports - Association and Rugby football. There were 294 patients (58%) aged 21 or less and 45 (9%) were aged 15.
LEVEL: A LANG: Eng SIRC ARTICLE NO: 102494

CAIRS-1 recorder's handbook. Ottawa: University of Ottawa, 1984?. vi, 59 p., (35) leaves
NOTES: Cover title.
LEVEL: I LANG: Eng RD97 18868

Camus, G. Lecomte, J. Manifestations pathologiques associees, chez le sportif amateur, a l'entrainement mal conduit: apercu general. *Revue de l'education physique (Liege, Belgique) 24(4), 1984, 25-28.*
LEVEL: B LANG: Fr SIRC ARTICLE NO: 104017

Chan, K.M. Leung, L. Sports injuries survey on university students in Hong Kong. (Refs: 10)*British journal of sports medicine (Loughborough, Eng.) 18(3), Sept 1984, 195-202.*
ABST: A sports injuries survey was conducted among 1714 students of the Chinese University of Hong Kong. The common sports involved in injuries were Soccer (26%), Basketball (18%), Cycling (11%), Track and field athletics (11%) and Swimming (10%). The lower limb usually took the brunt of the injuries (67%) followed by the upper limb (28%) and spinal injuries were relatively uncommon (3%). The majority of the injuries were mild to moderate and the commonest ones were abrasion (37%), contusion (21%), cramp (20%), sprains (9%), and strains (7%). Of the injuries 80% recovered in less than 10 days and 50% of them were self-treated. However, a significant group of more severe injuries was recorded: fracture, concussion and heat stroke. The preventive aspects of sports injuries was not well recognised with only 40% of the students regularly practising warm-up exercises, 18% stretching exercises and 4% using protective aids.
LEVEL: A LANG: Eng SIRC ARTICLE NO: 102501

Denton, A.E. Diet for the injured athlete. *Skating magazine (Colorado Springs, Colo.) 61(10), Dec 1984, 4;14.*
LEVEL: B LANG: Eng SIRC ARTICLE NO: 105369

Dmitriev, S.L. Prichiny, profilaktika i okazanie pervoi meditsinskoi pomoshchi pri travmakh v sporte. (Causes, prevention an the rendering of medical first aid in injuries in sports.) *Fel'dsher i akusherka (Moscow) 49(12), Dec 1984, 12-15.*
LEVEL: I LANG: Rus

Grisogono, V. Sports injuries: a self-help guide. London: John Murray, c1984. 294 p. : ill.
LEVEL: I LANG: Eng ISBN: 0-7195-4111-5 RD97 18243

Hawkins, J.D. Sports medicine: a guide for youth sports. Greensboro, N.C.: Sport Studies Foundation, c1984. 72 p. : ill.
LEVEL: B LANG: Eng RD97 17750

Helal, B. Physical risks in modern sport. *Medicine, science and the law (Brentford, Eng.) 24(4), 1984, 247-248.*
LEVEL: I LANG: Eng SIRC ARTICLE NO: 104038

Hunter, L.Y. Women's athletics: the orthopedic surgeon's viewpoint. (Refs: 39)*Clinics in sports medicine (Philadelphia) 3(4), Oct 1984, 809-827.*
NOTES: Symposium on the athletic woman.
ABST: Generally, athletic injuries are more sports-specific than sex-specific. Nevertheless, there are some injuries that occur with a slightly greater frequency in one sex than the other. The particular problems discussed in this article include overuse syndromes of the knee and other conditions of the knee, shoulder, ankle, and foot. Stress fractures are also considered.
LEVEL: I LANG: Eng SIRC ARTICLE NO: 100680

Kamuti, J. Medical aspects of violence at sports events. *Olympic review (Lausanne, Switzerland) 195/196, Jan/Feb 1984, 36-41.*
LEVEL: B LANG: Eng SIRC ARTICLE NO: 094370

Kamuti, J. Aspects medicaux de la violence dans les manifestations sportives. *Revue olympique (Lausanne) 195/196, janv/fevr 1984, 36-41.*
LEVEL: B LANG: Fr SIRC ARTICLE NO: 095935

Knortz, K.A. Reinhart, R.S. Women's athletics: the athletic trainer's viewpoint. (Refs: 17)*Clinics in sports medicine (Philadelphia) 3(4), Oct 1984, 851-868.*
NOTES: Symposium on the athletic woman.
ABST: Five disorders common to female athletes are discussed. These include anorexia nervosa, thoracic outlet syndrome, patellofemoral joint dysfunction, lower leg syndromes, and anterior shoulder subluxation. Since most of these problems result from overuse, careful attention to technique, conditioning, and training environment in women's sports is warranted.
LEVEL: I LANG: Eng SIRC ARTICLE NO: 100681

Les athletes attendent trop longtemps avant de rapporter leurs blessures. (Refs: 4)*Revue de l'entraineur janv/mars 1984, 14-15.*
LEVEL: B LANG: Fr SIRC ARTICLE NO: 091448

Lombardo, J.A. Symposium on sports medicine. Philadelphia: W.B. Saunders, ix, 198 p. : ill. (Primary care (Philadelphia) 11 (1), Mar 1984.)
NOTES: ISSN 0095-4543.
LEVEL: I LANG: Eng 18901

Lysens, R. van den Auweele, Y. Claessens, A. Steverlynck, A. Lefevre, J. Renson, L. Ostyn, M. The predictability of sports injuries. (Refs: 21)*Sports medicine (Auckland) 1(1), Jan/Feb 1984, 6-10.*
ABST: This study was undertaken in order to determine whether or not sport injuries are predictable from intrinsic risk factors, which are individual physical and psychosocial characteristics. A group of 138 physical education students, trained in similar extreme risk factors, were used in this investigation. Among the results it was indicated that students with a history of previous injury were generally at high risk of recurrence. Also, increases in flexibility and ligaments laxity seemed to predispose athletes to sprains and dislocations. These results, and those of other studies, point to the possibility of predicting sports injuries. However, the authors indicate some of the limitations involved in injury statistics.
LEVEL: A LANG: Eng SIRC ARTICLE NO: 094372

Lysens, R. Lefevre, J. Renson, L. Ostyn, M. The predictability of sports injuries: a preliminary report. (Refs: 18) *International journal of sports medicine (Stuttgart) Suppl. 5, Nov 1984, 153-155.*
CONF: International Congress on Sports and Health (1983 : Maastricht, Netherlands).
LEVEL: A LANG: Eng SIRC ARTICLE NO: 104054

Maehlum, S. Daljord, O.A. Acute sports injuries in Oslo: a one-year study. (Refs: 19)*British journal of sports medicine (Loughborough, Eng.) 18(3), Sept 1984, 181-185.*
ABST: All sport injuries treated at the Emergency Department, Ulleval Hospital in Oslo (OKL) were registered for one year. 4673 patients were seen; 3292 males and 1381 females. Most of the men (64%) were injured in connection with competitive sports, but 52% of the women sustained their injury pursuing recreational sports. Football and skiing accounted for 49% of the total number of injuries. In males football caused most injuries - 35%. In females handball accounted for most injuries - 18%. Nearly 3/4 of the injuries affected the extremities; the most common injury being the ankle sprain (16%). Almost 1/4 of the patients had a fracture, and 218 patients (4.7%) were admitted to hospital. In all, the sports injuries required 7658 consultations.
LEVEL: A LANG: Eng SIRC ARTICLE NO: 102527

McLatchie, G. Sport injuries, treatment and prevention. *Scottish journal of physical education (Glasgow, Scotland) 12(2), Apr 1984, 50-54.*
LEVEL: B LANG: Eng SIRC ARTICLE NO: 094376

Nadori, L. Az edzeselmelet ervenyessege a rehabilitacio, a prevencio es a kompenzacio terueleten. (The validity of the training theory on the field of the rehabilitation, the prevention and the compensation.) *Sportorvosi szemle/Hungarian review of sports medicine (Budapest) 25(2), 1984, 137-146.*
LEVEL: I LANG: Hun SIRC ARTICLE NO: 097260

Reiser, M. Rupp, N. Computertomographie bei Sportverletzungen. (Computer tomography of sports injuries.) *Radiologe (Berlin) 24(1), Jan 1984, 40-45.*
LEVEL: I LANG: Ger

Renstroem, P. Swedish research in sports traumatology. *Clinical orthopaedics and related research (Philadelphia) 191, Dec 1984, 144-158.*
LEVEL: A LANG: Eng

Shankman, G.A. Training related injuries in progressive resistive exercise programs. *National Strength & Conditioning Association journal (Lincoln, Neb.) 6(4), Aug/Sept 1984, 36-37.*
LEVEL: B LANG: Eng SIRC ARTICLE NO: 099069

Sports injury manual. Adelaide, S. Aust.?: Dept. of Recreation and Sport, 1984?. 151 p. : ill.
CORP: S. Aust. Department of Recreation and Sport.
NOTES: Bibliography: p. 139-140.
LEVEL: B LANG: Eng ISBN: 0-7243-4592-2 RD97 20837

Stockland, L. Scintigraphy in trauma and the 'limping syndrome'. *Clinical nuclear medicine (Philadelphia) 9(1), Jan 1984, 39-40.*
LEVEL: I LANG: Eng SIRC ARTICLE NO: 099072

Sullivan, J.A. Recurring pain in the pediatric athlete. *Pediatric clinics of North America (Philadelphia) 31(5), Oct 1984, 1097-1112.*
LEVEL: I LANG: Eng

Wassel, A.C. Sports medicine: acute and overuse injuries. *Orthopedic nursing (Pitman, N.J.) 3(2), Mar/Apr 1984, 29-33.*
LEVEL: I LANG: Eng

Weight training and injury. *Wrestling USA (Bozeman, Mont.) 20(4), 15 Nov 1984, 15.*
LEVEL: B LANG: Eng SIRC ARTICLE NO: 1738

ABDOMINAL INJURIES

Birrer, R.B. Common injuries of the chest and abdomen. (Refs: 5)
NOTES: In, Birrer, R.B. (ed.), Sports medicine for the primary care physician, Norwalk, Conn., Appleton-Century-Crofts, c1984, p. 178-184.
LEVEL: I LANG: Eng RC1210 17030

Blair, D. Trainers' corner: intra-abdominal injuries in athletics. *NAIA news (Kansas, Mo.) 33(3), Dec 1983-Jan 1984, 30.*
LEVEL: B LANG: Eng SIRC ARTICLE NO: 097564

Horsky, I. Huraj, E. Operacna liecba bolestiveho triesla. (Surgical treatment of the painful groin.) *Acta chirurgiae orthopaedicae et traumatologiae cechoslovaca (Prague) 51(4), Jul 1984, 350-353.*
LEVEL: A LANG: Slo

Mustalish, A.C. Quash, E.T. Sports injuries to the chest and abdomen. (Refs: 57)
NOTES: In, Scott, W.N. (ed.) et al., Principles of sports medicine, Baltimore, Williams & Wilkins, c1984, p. 226-241.
LEVEL: A LANG: Eng RC1210 18016

ACHILLES TENDON INJURIES

Baruah, D.R. Case report: Bilateral spontaneous rupture of the Achilles tendons in a patient on long-term systemic steroid therapy. (Refs: 10)*British journal of sports medicine (Loughborough, Eng.) 18(2), Jun 1984, 128-129.*
LEVEL: I LANG: Eng SIRC ARTICLE NO: 102491

Boularan, C. Savoir traiter une tendinite d'Achille chez le sportif. *Impact medecin (Puteaux, France) 118, 1984, 59-61.*
LEVEL: B LANG: Fr

Chamot, A.M. Gobelet, C. Tendinite d'Achille: une pathologie de confins. (Refs: 13)*Revue medicale de la Suisse romande (Lausanne) 104(10), oct 1984, 783-787.*
LEVEL: I LANG: Fr SIRC ARTICLE NO: 174096

Clement, D. Padmore, T. A complete guide to the achilles tendon: how to make sure your achilles tendon doesn't turn out to b your achilles heel. *Runner's world 19(4), Apr 1984, 64-70.*
LEVEL: B LANG: Eng SIRC ARTICLE NO: 092851

Clement, D.B. Taunton, J.E. Smart, G.W. Achilles tendinitis and peritendinitis: etiology and treatment. (Refs: 15)*American journal of sports medicine (Baltimore) 12(3), May/Jun 1984, 179-184.*
ABST: This paper presents the results of conservative treatment of 109 runners with overuse injury to the Achilles tendon and discusses the implications of functional overpronation as an etiological factor in this condition. After a diagnosis of Achilles tendinitis with peritendinitis, each subject was given an appropriate treatment strategy. This involved a daily program of gastrocnemius/soleus strength and flexibility training, control of inflammation and pain, and control of biomechanical parameters (ie. functional overpronation). 73 of the cases were again training symptom-free, at preinjury levels, in a mean recovery time of 5 weeks. The authors believe that virtually all cases of Achilles tendinitis with peritendinitis result from structural or dynamic disturbances in lower leg function, which can be managed conservatively with excellent results in most patients.
LEVEL: A LANG: Eng SIRC ARTICLE NO: 102502

Hosey, T. Wettheimer, S. A retrospective study on surgical repair of the Achilles tendon. *Journal of foot surgery (Baltimore) 23(2), Mar/Apr 1984, 112-115;184.*
LEVEL: I LANG: Eng SIRC ARTICLE NO: 102513

Kouvalchouk, J.F. Rodineau, J. Watin Augouard, L. Les ruptures du tendon d'Achille. Comparaison des resultats du traitement operatoire et non operatoire. (Ruptures du tendon d'Achille. Comparison of the results of surgical and nonsurgical treatment.) *Revue de chirurgie orthopedique et reparatrice de l'appareil moteur (Paris) 70(6), 1984, 473-478.*
LEVEL: A LANG: Fr

Kuwada, G.T. Schuberth, J. Evaluation of Achilles tendon rerupture. *Journal of foot surgery (Baltimore) 23(4), Jul/Aug 1984 340-343.*
ABST: The authors found that after either surgical or conservative treatment ankle dorsiflexion played a significant role in patients with reruptures and also in those who did not rerupture. They believe that patients who are either casted or treated by surgical repair with their foot in equinus may have a greater chance of rerupture.
LEVEL: A LANG: Eng SIRC ARTICLE NO: 104048

Le Saout, J. Kerboul, B. Riot, O. Courtois, B. Tendinite d'Achille du sportif. (Refs: 4)*Ouest medical (Paris) 37(13), 1984, 703-709.*
LEVEL: I LANG: Fr

Leach, R.E. Achilles tendinitis. *Sportsmedicine digest (Van Nuys, Calif.) 6(3), Mar 1984, 6-7.*
LEVEL: B LANG: Eng SIRC ARTICLE NO: 098646

Lowdon, A. Bader, D.L. Mowat, A.G. The effect of heel pads on the treatment of Achilles tendinitis: a double blind trial. (Refs: 14)*American journal of sports medicine (Baltimore) 12(6), Nov/Dec 1984, 431-435.*
ABST: Thirty-three subjects entered a blind-observer, random, prospective study of three forms of conservative treatment of sports-induced Achilles tendinitis, results being assessed by clinical and biomechanical parameters. Two patient groups received heel pads, ultrasound, and exercises, while the third received only ultrasound and exercises. All three groups showed some improvement at both 10 day and 2 month assessment, but the claimed benefit of viscoelastic pads widely used by athletes was not substantiated. The more striking benefit from ultrasound and exercises alone occurred in patients with a shorter history; a comparison of duration of injury in all three groups suggested this was an important factor influencing outcome.
LEVEL: A LANG: Eng SIRC ARTICLE NO: 104052

Mironova, Z.S. Cherkasova, T.I. Arkhipov, S.V. Otdalennye rezul'taty operativnogo lecheniia podkozhnogo razryva Akhillova sukhozhiliia. (Remote results of the surgical treatment of subcutaneous rupture of the Achilles tendon.) *Vestnik khirurgii imeni I.I. Grekova (Leningrad) 132(3), Mar 1984, 117-118.*
LEVEL: I LANG: Rus

Paar, O. Bernett, P. Therapie der Achillessehnen-Ruptur beim Sportler. Vorteile der Fibrinklebung. (Therapy of Achilles tendon rupture in athletes. Advantages of fibrin gluing.) *Fortschritte der Medizin (Leipzig) 102(43), 22 Nov 1984, 1106-1108.*
ABST: Fibrin gluing of the ruptured Achilles tendon represents an alternative to tenorrhaphy. A report is presented on 17 cases, with particular emphasis on the surgical technique, the results of follow-up, and the findings of CT scanning.
LEVEL: A LANG: Ger

Parsons, J.R. Rosario, A. Weiss, A.B. Alexander, H. Achilles tendon repair with an absorbable polymer-carbon fiber composite (Refs: 23)*Foot & ankle (Baltimore, Md.) 5(2), Sept/Oct 1984, 49-53.*
ABST: Fourteen patients of an original group of twenty-seven patients treated for Achilles tendon rupture were evaluated post-operatively. The average follow-up was 14.4 month and the maximum was over 2.5 years. Patients were operated using a flexible carbon absorbable polymer ligament/tendon repair material. Results indicated 90% return of function at 18 months.
LEVEL: A LANG: Eng SIRC ARTICLE NO: 099056

ALTITUDE SICKNESS

Acute mountain sickness. *Sports medicine digest (Van Nuys, Calif.) 6(8), Aug 1984, 5.*
LEVEL: B LANG: Eng SIRC ARTICLE NO: 105278

Houston, C.S. Man at altitude. (Refs: 7)
NOTES: In, Strauss, R.H. (ed.), Sports medicine, Philadelphia ; Toronto, Saunders, 1984, p. 344-360.
LEVEL: A LANG: Eng RC1210 17196

ANKLE INJURIES

Black, H.M. Brand, R.L. Injuries of the foot and ankle. (Refs: 23)
NOTES: In, Scott, W.N. (ed.) et al., Principles of sports medicine, Baltimore, Williams & Wilkins, c1984, p. 348-362.
LEVEL: A LANG: Eng RC1210 18016

Bruffeman, A. Bruggeman, J.H. Modifications in the treatment-programme of the inversion sprain of the ankle. (Refs: 11) *International journal of sports medicine (Stuttgart) Suppl. 5, Nov 1984, 42-44.*
CONF: International Congress on Sports and Health (1983 : Maastricht, Netherlands).
LEVEL: I LANG: Eng SIRC ARTICLE NO: 104016

Burkus, J.K. Sella, E.J. Southwick, W.O. Occult injuries of the talus diagnosed by bone scan and tomography. (Refs: 17)*Foot & ankle (Baltimore) 4(6), May/Jun 1984, 316-324.*
ABST: This paper details the diagnosis of an osteochondral lesion which was not first diagnosed with normal plain radiographs in 5 patients. Bone scans of the tali demonstrated the specific talar joint

that was injured, while tomography confirmed the osteochondral lesion injury.
LEVEL: A LANG: Eng SIRC ARTICLE NO: 097566

Canale, S.T. Beaty, J.H. Injuries of the talus. (Refs: 46)*In, Hamilton, W.C. (ed.), Traumatic disorders of the ankle, New York, Springer-Verlag, c1984, p. 227-254.*
LEVEL: A LANG: Eng RD97 18981

Cetti, R. Christensen, S.-E. Corfitzen, M.T. Ruptured fibular ankle ligament: plaster or pliton brace? (Refs: 14)*British journal of sports medicine (Loughborough, Eng.) 18(2), Jun 1984, 104-109.*
ABST: A prospective randomised study was performed in order to compare plaster cast with Pliton-80 cast brace with a mobile plastic shoe insert in the treatment of ruptured fibular ankle ligaments. The two treatment groups consisted of 65 patients in each and all were participating in the follow-up sixth months after the accident. There were no statistically significant differences in the overall results between the two treatment groups. Because 1) the mobile Pliton-80 bandage subjectively is more acceptable to the patients and - 2) the disability time in the Pliton-80 group was considerably shorter than in the plaster group - it was concluded that the mobile Pliton-80 bandage can be recommended as the treatment of ruptures of the fibular ankle ligaments.
LEVEL: A LANG: Eng SIRC ARTICLE NO: 102500

Cotler, J.M. Lateral ligamentous injuries of the ankle. (Refs: 29)*In, Hamilton, W.C. (ed.), Traumatic disorders of the ankle, New York, Springer-Verlag, c1984, p. 113-123.*
LEVEL: A LANG: Eng RD97 18981

Good, R.P. Arthrodesis and arthroplasty. (Refs: 75)*In, Hamilton, W.C. (ed.), Traumatic disorders of the ankle, New York, Springer-Verlag, c1984, p. 254-267.*
LEVEL: A LANG: Eng RD97 18981

Hamilton, W.C. Traumatic disorders of the ankle. New York: Springer-Verlag, c1984. x, 293 p. : ill. NOTES: Includes bibliographies.
LEVEL: A LANG: Eng ISBN: 0-387-90831-5 LC CARD: 83-10610 RD97 18981

Hamilton, W.C. Anatomy. (Refs: 31)*In, Hamilton, W.C. (ed.), Traumatic disorders of the ankle, New York, Springer-Verlag, c1984, p. 1-12.*
LEVEL: I LANG: Eng RD97 18981

Hamilton, W.C. Surgical anatomy. (Refs: 25)*In, Hamilton, W.C. (ed.), Traumatic disorders of the ankle, New York, Springer-Verlag, c1984, p. 23-27.*
LEVEL: I LANG: Eng RD97 18981

Hamilton, W.C. Malleolar fractures and dislocations of the ankle. (Refs: 104)*In, Hamilton, W.C. (ed.), Traumatic disorders of the ankle, New York, Springer-Verlag, c1984, p. 67-80.*
LEVEL: I LANG: Eng RD97 18981

Hamilton, W.C. Malleolar fractures and dislocations of the ankle: treatment. (Refs: 138)*In, Hamilton, W.C. (ed.), Traumatic disorders of the ankle, New York, Springer-Verlag, c1984, p. 81-99.*
LEVEL: A LANG: Eng RD97 18981

Hamilton, W.C. Supination-adduction injuries. (Refs: 25)*In, Hamilton, W.C. (ed.), Traumatic disorders of the ankle, New York, Springer-Verlag, c1984, p. 101-112.*
LEVEL: A LANG: Eng RD97 18981

Hamilton, W.C. External rotation injuries. (Refs: 94)*In, Hamilton, W.C. (ed.), Traumatic disorders of*

the ankle, New York, Springer-Verlag, c1984, p. 125-153.
LEVEL: A LANG: Eng RD97 18981

Hamilton, W.C. Pronation-external rotation injuries. (Refs: 57)*In, Hamilton, W.C. (ed.), Traumatic disorders of the ankle, New York, Springer-Verlag, c1984, p. 155-173.*
LEVEL: A LANG: Eng RD97 18981

Hamilton, W.C. Pronation-abduction injuries. (Refs: 19)*In, Hamilton, W.C. (ed.), Traumatic disorders of the ankle, New York Springer-Verlag, c1984, p. 175-185.*
LEVEL: A LANG: Eng RD97 18981

Hamilton, W.C. Fractures of the posterior and anterior tibial margins. (Refs: 52)*In, Hamilton, W.C. (ed.), Traumatic disorders of the ankle, New York, Springer-Verlag, c1984, p. 187-196.*
LEVEL: A LANG: Eng RD97 18981

Hamilton, W.C. Comminuted fractures of the tibial plafond. (Refs: 40)*In, Hamilton, W.C. (ed.), Traumatic disorders of the ankle, New York, Springer-Verlag, c1984, p. 197-212.*
LEVEL: A LANG: Eng RD97 18981

Hamilton, W.C. Good, R.P. Malleolar injuries: aftercare, prognosis, and complications. (Refs: 110)*In, Hamilton, W.C. (ed.), Traumatic disorders of the ankle, New York, Springer-Verlag, c1984, p. 213-226.*
LEVEL: A LANG: Eng RD97 18981

Hoffman, J.D. Radiography of the ankle. (Refs: 170)*In, Hamilton, W.C. (ed.), Traumatic disorders of the ankle, New York, Springer-Verlag, c1984, p. 29-54.*
LEVEL: I LANG: Eng RD97 18981

Hume, E.L. Overuse syndromes. (Refs: 40)*In, Hamilton, W.C. (ed.), Traumatic disorders of the ankle, New York, Springer-Verlag, c1984, p. 55-66.*
LEVEL: I LANG: Eng RD97 18981

Incorvaia, T.I. Reducing recovery time: the evolution and concept of the 'sponge splint-compression dressing'. *Journal of the Canadian Athletic Therapists Association (Oakville, Ont.) 11(2), Fall 1984, 19-20.*
LEVEL: B LANG: Eng SIRC ARTICLE NO: 104043

Jenoure, P.J. Feinstein, R. Segesser, B. Au sujet de la plus frequente lesion en traumatologie du sport: l'entorse de la cheville. *Revue medicale de la Suisse romande (Lausanne) 104(10), oct 1984, 789-794.*
LEVEL: I LANG: Fr SIRC ARTICLE NO: 174097

Larsen, E. Taping the ankle for chronic instability. *Acta orthopaedica scandinavica (Copenhagen) 55(5), Oct 1984, 551-553.*
LEVEL: A LANG: Eng

Lepp, T.M. Trainer's corner: when can I...? *NAIA news (Kansas, Mo.) 34(1), Aug/Sept 1984, 22-23.*
ABST: The injured athlete's most frequent concern is when can he return to competition. This can only be accomplished after a rehabilitation or reconditioning program has achieved its two main goals. First to restore the injured part of the body to the same level of condition it had prior to the injury, and second to prevent deconditioning of the whole body. This article follows these two main principles in detailing a rehabilitation program for an ankle injury. Three distinct phases in the rehabilitation process are identified along with the various methods employed by athletic trainers to maintain muscle strength and flexibility and encourage the

healing process. The author stresses the fact that an athlete should only gradually return to training and competition as well as maintain muscle strength in the ankle region in order to prevent reinjury.
LEVEL: B LANG: Eng SIRC ARTICLE NO: 100684

Meani, E. Merlo, M. Indagine radiografica funzionale nella traumatologia della caviglia. Functional radiographic investigations in ankle traumatology. (Refs: 11)*Italian journal of sports traumatology (Milano, Italy) 6(3), Jul/Sept 1984, 241-247.*
ABST: Lesions of ankle lateral compartment are increasingly frequent in sports traumatology. In order to make possible an exact diagnosis and an appropriate treatment, an exact insight of the anatomical damage is necessary. The present paper deals with the use of functional ankle radiography to evidence and quantitatively evaluate the 'drawer' and the lateral displacements of the tibio-talar joint as well as distal tibio-fibular diastase. The employed apparatus is shown. By this way is possible to exactly define type and severity of lesions.
LEVEL: A LANG: Eng It SIRC ARTICLE NO: 102528

Myburgh, K.H. Vaughan, C.L. Isaacs, S.K. The effects of ankle guards and taping on joint motion before, during, and after a squash match. (Refs: 12)*American journal of sports medicine (Baltimore) 12(6), Nov/Dec 1984, 441-446.*
ABST: The effects of ankle guards and taping on joint motion before, during, and after exercise were studied. Twelve league squash players played two matches, each lasting 1 hour. Two different ankle guards, and two types of tape applied by the same method, served as supports. A specially designed goniometer with electronic digital display was used to determine joint range of motion: plantar-flexion and dorsiflexion, neutral inversion and eversion, plantar-flexed inversion and eversion. The results were statistically analyzed to determine the significance of the restriction provided by the supports. This revealed that the two ankle guards provided no significant support. The two tapes, however, provided significant support before exercise and after 10 minutes but not after 1 hour of exercise.
LEVEL: A LANG: Eng SIRC ARTICLE NO: 104907

Nakajima, K. (Injury of ankle joint ligaments.) *Nippon seikeigeka gakkai zasshi/Journal of the Japanese Orthopaedic Association (Tokyo) 58(13), Dec 1984, 1303-1314.*
LEVEL: A LANG: Jpn

Pizzutillo, P.D. Ankle injuries in the child. (Refs: 54)*In, Hamilton, W.C. (ed.), Traumatic disorders of the ankle, New York, Springer-Verlag, c1984, p. 269-278.*
LEVEL: I LANG: Eng RD97 18981

Riegler, H.F. Reconstruction for lateral instability of the ankle. *Journal of bone and joint surgery (Boston) 66(3), Mar 1984, 336-339.*
LEVEL: A LANG: Eng SIRC ARTICLE NO: 099063

Samuelson, K.M. Functional anatomy. (Refs: 57)*In, Hamilton, W.C. (ed.), Traumatic disorders of the ankle, New York, Springer-Verlag, c1984, p. 13-22.*
LEVEL: I LANG: Eng RD97 18981

Sando, B. Injuries to the ankle. *Australian family physician (Sydney) 13(8), Aug 1984, 581-584.*
LEVEL: A LANG: Eng

Seitz, C.J. Goldfuss, A.J. The effect of taping and exercise on passive foot inversion and ankle plantarflexion. (Refs: 9) *Athletic training (Greenville, N.C.) 19(3), Fall 1984, 178-182.*
LEVEL: I LANG: Eng SIRC ARTICLE NO: 099068

Southmayd, W. Hoffman, M. The ankle. *National racquetball (Skokie, Ill.) 13(4), Apr 1984, 26-29.*
ABST: This examination o ankle sprains begins by describing the various bones and ligaments that make up the anatomy of the ankle joint. From there it is easy to understand the causes of grades I, II and III ankle sprains. The greater part of this article deals with the treatment of single and two-ligament sprains. The various stages of rehabilitation are clearly outlined and presented in an orderly fashion. This article is written by a physician and can be easily understood by the layman and the athlete searching for information on this common athletic ailment.
LEVEL: B LANG: Eng SIRC ARTICLE NO: 094392

Thompson, J.P. Loomer, R.L. Osteochondral lesions of the talus in a sports medicine clinic. (Refs: 16) *American journal of sports medicine (Baltimore) 12(6), Nov/Dec 1984, 460-463.*
ABST: A retrospective review of 11 patients with osteochondral lesions of the talus was undertaken. There was a predominance of posteromedial talar dome lesions. A flexion-inversion ankle injury could be documented in the majority of cases. There was frequently a long delay in diagnosing these ankle sprain mimics. Historical details which should raise one's index of suspicion include: (1) history of flexion-inversion injury; (2) exercise-related ankle pain; (3) sensations of 'clicking and catching'; and (4) persistent swelling. Surgery produced consistently good early results in these active patients without osteotomizing the medial malleolus. The optimal radiographic technique for identifying the posteromedial osteochondral lesion consists of an anteroposterior view of the ankle in maximum plantar flexion with the kilovoltage set at 70.
LEVEL: A LANG: Eng SIRC ARTICLE NO: 104080

Tropp, H. Ekstrand, J. Gillquist, J. Stabilometry in functional instability of the ankle and its value in predicting injury. (Refs: 17) *Medicine and science in sports and exercise 16(1), 1984, 64-66.*
ABST: Stabilometry was used to determine whether the incidence of ankle injuries affected postural sway and whether ankle injuries were affected by postural sway. This study tested 127 soccer players and found that those who showed poor stabilometry scores ran a higher risk of ankle injury. This suggests that these players may have underlying balance problems. Players with a previous ankle injury did not run a higher risk of injury than the other players.
LEVEL: A LANG: Eng SIRC ARTICLE NO: 092398

Tropp, H. Ekstrand, J. Gillquist, J. Factors affecting stabilometry recordings of single limb stance. (Refs: 23) *American journal of sports medicine (Baltimore) 12(3), May/Jun 1984, 185-188.*
ABST: The authors sought to determine whether an acute ankle sprain resulted in a defective ability to maintain postural equilibrium and whether the postural control could be improved by coordination training or by ankle taping. Stabilometric recordings of 25 male soccer players, during single leg support, were made on a force platform. Comparisons were made between the injured and non-injured sides of the same subject one to three weeks after injury. No significant differences in the mean stabilometric values were found. Similarly, in a group of 38 players, ankle taping had no effect upon postural control. Coordination training in 10 players successfully treated functional instability. Thus, the existing theory that an ankle joint injury itself produces functional instability was not demonstrated in this study.
LEVEL: A LANG: Eng SIRC ARTICLE NO: 102611

van den Hoogenband, C.R. van Moppes, F.I. Coumans, P.F. Stapert, J.W.J.L. Greep, J.M. Study on clinical diagnosis and treatment of lateral ligament lesion of the ankle joint: a prospective clinical randomized trial. (Refs: 4) *International journal of sports medicine (Stuttgart) Suppl. 5, Nov 1984, 159-161.*
CONF: International Congress on Sports and Health (1983 : Maastricht, Netherlands).
LEVEL: A LANG: Eng SIRC ARTICLE NO: 104083

van der Ent, F.W. Surgical treatment of lateral ankle ligament ruptures. (Refs: 6) *International journal of sports medicine (Stuttgart) Suppl. 5, Nov 1984, 149-150.*
CONF: International Congress on Sports and Health (1983 : Maastricht, Netherlands).
LEVEL: A LANG: Eng SIRC ARTICLE NO: 104084

Voight, M.L. Reduction of post traumatic ankle edema with high voltage pulsed galvanic stimulation. (Refs: 12) *Athletic training (Greenville, N.C.) 19(4), Winter 1984, 278-279;311.*
LEVEL: I LANG: Eng SIRC ARTICLE NO: 104087

Weiker, G.G. Ankle injuries in the athlete. (Refs: 9) *Primary care: clinics in office practice (Philadelphia) 11(1), Mar 1984, 101-108.*
LEVEL: I LANG: Eng SIRC ARTICLE NO: 100703

BACK INJURIES

Birrer, R.B. Common injuries of the back. (Refs: 5) NOTES: In, Birrer, R.B. (ed.), Sports medicine for the primary care physician, Norwalk, Conn., Appleton-Century-Crofts, c1984, p. 172-177.
LEVEL: I LANG: Eng RC1210 17030

Milon, C. Les lombalgies du sportif. (Refs: 6) *Revue du jeune medecin (Paris) Supp(130), 1984, 6-8.*
LEVEL: I LANG: Fr

Prevention des blessures au dos. *Revue de l'entraineur (Montreal) avr/juin 1984, 35.*
NOTES: 1ere partie.
LEVEL: B LANG: Fr SIRC ARTICLE NO: 094383

Sports injuries *Netball (London) 3(4), Dec 1984, 8;5.*
LEVEL: B LANG: Eng SIRC ARTICLE NO: 102546

BACK PAIN

Back owner's manual. Toronto: PARTICIPaction, c1984. 16 p. ; ill.
CORP: PARTICIPaction.
NOTES: Cover title.
LEVEL: B LANG: Eng RA781.5 20863

Back to backs. (Refs: 3) *Your health & fitness (Highland Park, Ill.) 6(3), Jun/Jul 1984, 3-7.*
LEVEL: B LANG: Eng SIRC ARTICL NO: 095903

Cannon, S.R. James, S.E. Back pain in athletes. (Refs: 25) *British journal of sports medicine (Loughborough, Eng.) 18(3), Sept 1984, 159-164.*
ABST: There were one hundred and ninety seven patients who came with back pain to an Athletes Clinic over four years. Their mode of presentation, investigations, diagnoses and treatments are analysed. The majority of patients were male and below 30 years of age. The average duration of symptoms prior to presentation, despite an easy access policy, was 42 weeks. Injury was usually related to six popular sports. Radiological examination was a rewarding investigation in these patients and included an A-P view of the pelvis. The diagnostic label of prolapsed intervertebral disc appears to have been used too frequently. Physiotherapy was the most useful treatment modality regardless of age, mode of onset and duration of symptoms.
LEVEL: A LANG: Eng SIRC ARTICLE NO: 102496

Fonstad, P. Low back pain. (Refs: 10) *Runner (Edmonton) 21(4), Winter 1983/1984, 34-35.*
NOTES: This paper was presented at the 'Fitness Round Up' Conference, June 1983.
LEVEL: B LANG: Eng SIRC ARTICLE NO: 095919

Gerasimov, A.A. Kipper, S.N. Atanova, S.A. Oksigenatsiia tkanei pri klinicheskikh variantakh poiasnichnykh vertebrogennykh boeli. (Tissue oxygenation in clinical variants of lumbar vertebrogenic pain.) *Orthopediia travamatologiia i protezirovanie (Moskva) 3, Mar 1984, 17-20.*
LEVEL: A LANG: Rus

How to cope with low back pain. Douleurs au bas du dos. *Sport med info (Ottawa) 4(3), 1984, 1-6.*
LEVEL: B LANG: Eng Fr SIRC ARTICLE NO: 105302

Hsieh, C.Y. Yeung, B.W. Bed transfer for unilateral sacroiliac pain. (Refs: 1) *Journal of orthopaedic and sports physical therapy (Baltimore, Md.) 6(2), Sept/Oct 1984, 140-141.*
ABST: A nontraditional transfer technique is found to be pain-free for a patient with unilateral sacroliac joint pain. This method emphasizes constant contact of both buttocks to the bed during the entire transfer process.
LEVEL: I LANG: Eng SIRC ARTICLE NO: 100724

La prevention des maux de dos. (Refs: 6) *Revue de l'entraineur (Montreal) oct/dec 1984, 30-31.*
LEVEL: B LANG: Fr SIRC ARTICL NO: 105319

Mal de dos, mal du siecle. *Marathon plus (Laval, Que.) 2(1), dec 1984/janv 1985, 36-38.*
LEVEL: B LANG: Fr SIRC ARTICLE NO: 173453

McKee, P. Effects of using enjoyable imagery with biofeedback induced relaxation for chronic pain patients. (Refs: 22) *Therapeutic recreation journal (Alexandria, Va.) 18(1), 1984, 50-61.*
ABST: Twenty patients with chronic back pain took part in a nine week treatment program using biofeedback - assisted deep relaxation and enjoyable or play imagery. The subjects were assigned to one of the following groups: 1) imagery with biofeedback, 2) biofeedback 3) day treatment only, and 4) a no-treatment waiting list control. The imagery-biofeedback and biofeedback groups reported less pain and showed greater increases in amount of daily activity enjoyed than the other groups. Patients in the biofeedback groups showed a greater ability to relax as indicated by EMG ratings.
LEVEL: A LANG: Eng SIRC ARTICLE NO: 094711

Mette, F. Role de la ceinture de maintien lombaire dans le traitement des lombalgies. (Refs: 5) *Cinesiologie: medecine du sport (Paris) 98, nov/dec 1984, 483-486;488.*
RESUME: Le ceinture de maintien lombaire a un role determine et temporaire dans le traitement des

lombalgiques: confort lors de la phase douloureuse, reconstitution du caisson abdominal et rappel de la bonne position pendant la periode de readaptation. Sa prescription doit etre associee a celle d'une reeducation specifique.
LEVEL: A LANG: Fr SIRC ARTICLE NO: 104061

Murtagh, J. Doran, R.J. Lum-Doran, P.A. Back pain. Toronto: Copp Clark Pitman, c1984. viii, 71 p. (Pitman health information series.)
NOTES: Bibliography: p. 71.
LEVEL: B LANG: Eng ISBN: 0-7730-4055-2 RA440 17545

Ponte, D.J. Jensen, G.J. Kent, B.E. A preliminary report on the use of the McKenzie protocol versus Williams protocol in the treatment of low back pain. (Refs: 30)*Journal of orthopaedic and sports physical therapy (Baltimore, Md.) 6(2), Sept/Oct 1984, 130-139.*
ABST: The purpose of this study was to determine whether the Williams or McKenzie protocol of treatment was more effective in both decreasing pain and hastening the return of pain-free range of lumbar spine movement. Twenty-two subjects underwent an initial evaluation which involved six measurements: subjective pain, comfortable sitting time, forward flexion, right and left lateral flexion, and straight leg raise. Subjects required to perform Williams' protocol were assigned accordingly, while those referred as 'evaluate and treat' were placed in the McKenzie group. Following the completion of treatment, a second evaluation was performed taking the same six measurements. A comparison of the improvement scores of the two groups indicated that those receiving the McKenzie protocol improved to a significantly greater extent than did the subjects in the Williams group, and that these changes came about in a significantly shorter period of time.
LEVEL: A LANG: Eng SIRC ARTICLE NO: 100748

Sarno, J.E. Therapeutic exercise for back pain. (Refs: 21)
NOTES: In, Basmajian, J.V. (ed.), Therapeutic exercise, 4th ed., Baltimore, Md., Williams & Wilkins, c1984, p. 441-463.
LEVEL: A LANG: Eng RM719 17505

Smith, D. Nursing your lower back. Part 2. *Nursing success today (London) 1(3), Nov 1984, 30-31.*
LEVEL: B LANG: Eng

Temple, C. Hanging around: it's not a case of bats in the belfry, but athletes in Cliff Temple's garage, as he discovers a new method of avoiding backache. *Running (London) 44, Dec 1984, 56-58.*
LEVEL: B LANG: Eng SIRC ARTICLE NO: 104079

Your back is always working. Toronto: PARTICIPaction, c1984. 16 p.
CORP: PARTICIPaction.
LEVEL: B LANG: Eng RA781.5 20858

CARDIAC ARREST

Maranto, G. Exercise: how much is too much? *Discover (Los Angeles) 5(10), Oct 1984, 18-22.*
LEVEL: B LANG: Eng SIRC ARTICL NO: 098913

Pool, J. Medical examination of cardiovascular and pulmonary patients in relation to sporting activities. *International journal of sports medicine (Stuttgart) Suppl. 5, Nov 1984, 5-6.*
CONF: International Congress on Sports and Health (1983 : Maastricht, Netherlands).
LEVEL: I LANG: Eng SIRC ARTICLE NO: 104137

CHEST INJURIES

Birrer, R.B. Common injuries of the chest and abdomen. (Refs: 5)
NOTES: In, Birrer, R.B. (ed.), Sports medicine for the primary care physician, Norwalk, Conn., Appleton-Century-Crofts, c1984, p. 178-184.
LEVEL: I LANG: Eng RC1210 17030

Blasiak, M. Pankiewicz, B. Przypadek czestoskurczu komorowego po tepym urazie klatki piersiowej u sportowca. (Case of ventricular tachycardia after blunt chest injury in a sportsman.) *Wiadomosci lekarskie (Warsaw) 37(11), 1 June 1984, 861-865.*
LEVEL: A LANG: Pol

Mustalish, A.C. Quash, E.T. Sports injuries to the chest and abdomen. (Refs: 57)
NOTES: In, Scott, W.N. (ed.) et al., Principles of sports medicine, Baltimore, Williams & Wilkins, c1984, p. 226-241.
LEVEL: A LANG: Eng RC1210 18016

Petel, B. Thillaye du Boullay, C. Petel, H. Lombard, F. Gaubert, J. L'evisceration pulmonaire traumatique chez l'enfant. A propos de 2 cas. (Traumatic pulmonary evisceration in a child. Apropos of 2 cases.) *Chirurgie pediatrique (Paris) 25(2), 1984, 79-82.*
LEVEL: I LANG: Fr SIRC ARTICLE NO: 104073

CONCUSSION

Aronyk, K. Neurological injuries in sport. *Canadian Academy of Sport Medicine newsletter (Ottawa) 5(4), 1984, 35-36.*
NOTES: Presented at the Grey Cup Symposium.
LEVEL: B LANG: Eng SIRC ARTICLE NO: 105281

Smythe, S. Use your head: prevent serious brain damage. *Audible (Toronto) Winter 1984, 4-5.*
LEVEL: B LANG: Eng SIRC ARTICLE NO: 092892

DEATH

Kirshenbaum, J. About the deaths of those Soviet athletes. *Sports illustrated (Chicago, Ill.) 61(17), 8 Oct 1984, 11.*
LEVEL: B LANG: Eng SIRC ARTICLE NO: 099045

DENTAL INJURIES

Comer, R.W. Caughman, W.F. Caswell, C.W. Oral appliances in injury prevention and performance modification in athletics. *Missouri dental journal (Jefferson City, Mo.) 40(2), Fall 1984, 15-16.*
LEVEL: I LANG: Eng

Dental injuries can be serious business. *First aider (Gardner, Kans.) 54(1), Sept 1984, 8-9.*
LEVEL: B LANG: Eng SIRC ARTICL NO: 105291

Mayet, A. Lamendin, H. Reconstitution par collage du fragment d'une incisive centrale superieure fracturee. Application en odontostomatologie du sport. *Chirurgie dentiste de Paris (Paris) 54(269), 1984, 25-27.*
LEVEL: B LANG: Fr

Mayet, A. Lamendin, H. Reconstitution par collage du fragment d'une incisive centrale superieure fracturee. Application en odonto-stomatologie du sport. (Reconstruction by bonding of a fragment of a fractured upper central incisor. Applications in sports dentistry.) *Chirurgien-dentiste de France*

(Paris) 54(269), 8 nov 1984, 25-27.
LEVEL: A LANG: Fr

DISLOCATIONS

Miller, L.S. Donahue, J.R. Good, R.P. Staerk, A.J. The Magnuson-Stack procedure for treatment of recurrent glenohumeral dislocations. (Refs: 11)*American journal of sports medicine (Baltimore, Md.) 12(2), Mar/Apr 1984, 133-137.*
ABST: This study evaluated the efficacy of the Magnuson-Stack procedure in preventing further dislocations of the shoulder and introduced the Cybex Isokinetic Dynamometer as a quantitative tool in evaluating shoulder function. The Cybex system showed that patients had a 25o lack of external rotation postoperatively. When external rotation was tested by a hand-held goniometer a 10o loss of external rotation was noted. The Cybex system also showed that the patients had decreased force values in external rotation. The authors conclude that the Magnuson-Stack procedure was effective in the treatment of recurrent glenohumeral dislocations and that the Cybex system provides accurate, reproducible shoulder function evaluations.
LEVEL: A LANG: Eng SIRC ARTICLE NO: 094378

Pedersen, C.B. Luksationer i det proksimale tibio-fibulare led. (Luxation of the proximal tibio-fibular joint.) *Ugeskrift for laeger (Copenhagen) 146(31), 30 Jul 1984, 2293-2295.*
NOTES: Includes English abstract.
LEVEL: I LANG: Dan

DROWNING

Juniere, J. Rousseau, J.M. Noto, R. Les accidents de noyade en piscine. Aspects epidemiologiques a propos de 141 cas. *Revue des samu (Paris) 7(5), 1984, 156-160.*
LEVEL: B LANG: Fr

Lemenager, J. Fabre, J. Sesboue, B. Laryngospasme et noyade. (Refs: 8)*Medecine du sport 58(1), 25 janv 1984, 25-27.*
LEVEL I LANG: Fr SIRC ARTICLE NO: 092426

MacLachlan, J. Drownings, other aquatic injuries and young Canadians. *Canadian journal of public health/Revue canadienne de sante publique (Ottawa) 75(3), May/Jun 1984, 218-222.*
ABST: This study focuses on the extent of drownings or other aquatic injuries, on the age groups most affected, and on the circumstances surrounding these accidents. Ontario coroners' reports, from 1979 to 1981, and Statistics Canada data were analysed. The author makes some recommendations regarding the prevention of these aquatic injuries.
LEVEL: A LANG: Eng SIRC ARTICLE NO: 099048

Pia, F. The rid factor, as a cause for drowning. *Recreation reporter (Vancouver, B.C.) Aug/Sept 1984, 7-9.*
LEVEL: B LANG: Eng SIRC ARTICLE NO: 100693

Ryan, A.J. Avoiding the tragedy of drowning. *Physician and sportsmedicine (Minneapolis, Minn.) 12(7), Jul 1984, 29.*
LEVEL B LANG: Eng SIRC ARTICLE NO: 096046

Smith, D.S. Notes on drowning: the misunderstood, preventable tragedy. (Refs: 31)*Physician and sportsmedicine (Minneapolis, Minn.) 12(7), Jul 1984, 66-73.*
LEVEL: I LANG: Eng SIRC ARTICLE NO: 095964

When is a drowning not a drowning? Answer: when it's a near drowning. *Diver (London) 29(10), Oct 1984, 22-23.*
LEVEL: I LANG Eng SIRC ARTICLE NO: 108469

DRUG THERAPY

Andersen, L.A. Gotzsche, P.C. Naproxen and aspirin in acute musculoskelatal disorders: a double-blind, parallel study in patients with sports injuries. *Pharmatherapeutica (London) 3(8), 1984, 531-537.*
ABST: This study evaluates the efficacy of either 750 mg naproxen or 2 g acetylsalicylic acid administered to 75 patients with sport injuries. Significant improvement is observed in both treatment groups. The authors note better results when treatment starts as early as possible after the injury.
LEVEL: A LANG: Eng SIRC ARTICLE NO: 099031

Barrau, J. Molinie, J. Porte, G. Manifestations inflammatoires aigues en traumatologie du sport: leur traitement par l'alminoprofene. *Medecine du sport (Paris) 58(6), nov 1984, 38-42.*
RESUME: Les auteurs evaluent l'activite anti-inflammatoire de l'Alminoprofene chez 60 patients atteints de traumatismes osteo-articulaires. La douleur diminue tres rapidement chez les sujets et l'oedeme regresse egalement tres vite. Une deuxieme etude compare en double insu l'activite anti-inflammatoire et surtout anti-oedemateuse de l'Alminoprofene a celle de l'acide Tiaprofenique chez 40 jeunes adultes ayant une entorse de la cheville. Il n'existe aucune difference significative entre les resultats des deux traitements. Cependant, les resultats concernant l'oedeme favorisent l'utilisation de l'Alminoprofene.
LEVEL: A LANG: Fr SIRC ARTICLE NO: 102489

Bernas, P. Experimentation de trois remedes homeopathiques en medecine sportive: arnica, gelsemium, rhus, toxicodendron. *Homeopathie francaise (Paris) 72(5), 1984, 331-333.*
LEVEL: I LANG: Fr

Boghemans, J. The efficacy of depo-medrone in sports injuries. *Acta Belgica. Medica physica (Bruxelles) 7(2), Apr/Jun 1984, 47-50.*
LEVEL: I LANG: Eng SIRC ARTICLE NO: 104014

Capitani, D. Nannini, G. Considerazioni sulluso del piroxicam in pazienti affetti da patologia da sovraccarico. (Considerations on the use of piroxicam in patients with pathology caused by strain.) *Clinica Terapeutica (Rome) 109(2), 30 Apr 1984, 149-153.*
LEVEL: I LANG: It

Cox, J. Current concepts in the role of steroids in the treatment of sprains and strains. (Refs: 29)*Medicine and science in sports and exercise (Indianapolis) 16(3), June 1984, 216-218.*
ABST: With the development of nonsteroidal anti-inflammatory drugs, the use of corticosteroids in the treatment of sprains and strains has greatly diminished. They are used occasionnally in the treatment of tendinitis in various areas of the body, but they are not used for ligamentous sprains and muscle strains. Injection of corticosteroids into ligaments, tendons and joints is often quite controversial and most clinicians have abandoned their use in the treatment of common athletic injuries.
LEVEL: I LANG: Eng SIRC ARTICLE NO: 108587

Coz, L. Mesotheraphy celebrates its 30th birthday. *Olympic review (Lausanne) 199, May 1984, 338-340.*
LEVEL: B LANG: Eng SIRC ARTICLE NO: 095910

Coz, L. Les trente ans de la mesotherapie. *Revue olympique (Lausanne) 199, mai 1984, 338-340.*
LEVEL: B LANG: Fr SIRC ARTICLE NO: 104024

Edwards, V. Wilson, A.A. Harwood, H.F. Manning, S.I. Brabbin, W. Walker, J.W. Jones, D.G. Thomas, D.V. Rimmer, R. Berry, W.H. A multicentre comparison of piroxicam and indomethacin in acute soft tissue sports injuries. *Journal of international medical research (North Hampton, Eng.) 12(1), 1984, 46-50.*
ABST: 105 patients suffering from soft tissue sport injuries participated in a randomized controlled trial comparing the efficiency and side-effects of piroxicam and indomethacin. Patients were treated for 7 days. 88 per cent of patients on piroxicam showed a marked or moderate improvement in their injury at the end of the trial and 79 per cent of the indomethacin-treated patients. Approximately 50 per cent of patients in both groups resumed full activity within 7 days.
LEVEL: A LANG: Eng SIRC ARTICLE NO: 098924

Frenkl, R. Richtofit krem es spray sportorvosi alkalmazasanak tapasztalatai. (Observations with Richtofit cream and spray in sports medicine.) (Refs: 2)*Sportorvosi szemle/Hungarian review of sports medicine (Budapest) 25(2), 1984, 125-128.*
ABST: The effect of Richtofit cream and spray has been studied in healthy male and female athletes and in sports medicine. 87% of the persons participating in the study applied the preparations readily and found their effect beneficial. The beneficial effect was manifested mainly in the elimination of fatigue after exertion (games, race, training) and in the shortening of regeneration period. Similarly good effect was observed in the elimination of 'muscles stiffness' and in the curing of muscle strain associated with minor pain and restricted motion. In more extensive dermal injurie, haematomas, and severe muscle sprains, Richtofit treatment proved to be inferior to traditional preparations. In the final stage of healing, however, Richtofit may have a beneficial effect.
LEVEL: A LANG: Hun SIRC ARTICLE NO: 097263

Hayes, T.B. Fyvie, A. Janke, P.G. Vandenburg, M.J. Currie, W.J.C. Sulindac versus Ibuprofen in sprains and strains. (Refs: 2 *British journal of sports medicine (Loughborough, Leicestershire) 18(1), Mar 1984, 30-33.*
ABST: This study compared the efficacy of the relatively new non-steroidal anti-inflammatory drug (NSAID) Sulindac with the efficacy of the NSAID Ibuprofen, in treating acute sprains and strains. Ninety-three patients with acute sprains or strains received 200 mg of Sulindac twice daily for 4 day while eighty-three patients with acute sprains or strains received 400 mg Ibuprofen three times daily for 4 days. The study was conducted using a double-blind design. The results indicate that Sulindac and Ibuprofen are equally beneficial in the management of acute soft tissue injuries.
LEVEL: A LANG: Eng SIRC ARTICLE NO: 095795

Le Coz Les trente ans de la mesotherapie. *Revue olympique (Lausanne) 199, mai 1984, 338-340.*
LEVEL: B LANG: Fr SIRC ARTICLE NO: 102130

Marechal, R. Utilisation du Reparil Gel dans les phenomenes inflammatoires d'origine sportive. (Refs: 14)*Medecine du sport (Paris) 58(2), 25 mars 1984, 41-44.*
RESUME: Le but de cette etude etait d'analyser l'impact therapeutique du Reparil Gel sur les lesions inflammatoires d'origine sportive. 111 patients presentant des lesions achilleennes (39 cas), ligamentaire laterale du genou (42 cas) ou rotuliennes (30 cas) furent traites par ionisation au Reparil-Gel et par 2 application cutanees journalieres de ce meme produit. Dans 70% des cas, une rehabilitation complete fut observee moins de 2 semaines apres le debut du traitement.
LEVEL: A LANG: Fr SIRC ARTICLE NO: 094374

Subotnick, S.I. On cortisone. *California track & running news (Fresno, Calif.) 90, Apr 1984, 21.*
LEVEL: B LANG: Eng SIRC ARTICLE NO: 099073

Torma, Z. Gyulladasgatlo gyogyszerek: V. Pelsonin es Indomethacin oesszehasonlito vizsgalata kueloenboezo sulyossagu sportserueleseekben. (Anti-inflammation pharacotherapy. Part V. A comparative study of pelsonin and indomethacin in sports injuries.) (Refs: 15)*Sportorvosi szemle/ Hungarian review of sports medicine (Budapest) 25(3), 1984, 187-195.*
ABST: In a double-blind random design three treatments (Pelsonin, Indomethacin, and placebo) were compared in altogether 120 patients. In athletes with a severe injury Pelsonin was found to reduce mean recovery time more effectively than Indomethacin. The same difference was observed in athletes suffering from injuries of medium severity, while the two active treatments did not differ in their effects on slighter sports, injuries. As shown by dynamometry, functions related to the injured area improved faster under Pelsonin treatment than under Indomethacin treatment. The two active treatments reduced malonic dialdehyde activity to the same extent. Relying on these results the authors believe that certain differences exist between the biochemical mechanicms of the exudative and non-exudative forms of inflammation. Side effects were more often observed under Indomethacin treatment. With Pelsonin, the side effects when present at all, were very mild. Accordingly, the authors recommend the use of Pelsonin for the sports medical practice in the treatment of acute and subacute sports injuries.
LEVEL: A LANG: Hun SIRC ARTICLE NO: 100235

EAR INJURIES

Davis, J.A. Nason, J.E. Racquet ear. (letter) *JAMA: Journal of the American Medical Association (Chicago) 251(23), 15 Jun 1984, 3081.*
LEVEL: B LANG: Eng SIRC ARTICLE NO: 102504

ELBOW INJURIES

Kohn, H.S. Current status and treatment of tennis elbow. *Wisconsin medical journal (Milwaukee, Wisc.) 83(3), Mar 1984, 18-19.*
LEVEL: B LANG: Eng SIRC ARTICLE NO: 102519

Parkes, J.C. Common injuries about the elbow in sports. (Refs: 56)
NOTES: In, Scott, W.N. (ed.) et al., Principles of sports medicine, Baltimore, Williams & Wilkins, c1984, p. 140-155.
LEVEL: A LANG: Eng RC1210 18016

Pizzetti, M. Fredella, D. Allegro, A. La laserterapia nell'epicondilite. Controllo mediante teletermografia. (Telethermograph in the follow-up of tennis elbow after laser treatment. (Refs: 46)*Italian journal of sports traumatology (Milano, Italy) 6(2),*

INJURIES AND ACCIDENTS (continued)

Apr/Jun 1984, 133-141.
CONF: Italian Society of Sports Traumatology.
Congress (1st : 1983 : Rome).
ABST: Laser biostimulation in the treatment of
uncomplicated tennis elbow in 31 individuals was
found to provide satisfactory outcome in 90 per
cent of the cases.
LEVEL: A LANG: It Eng SIRC ARTICLE NO: 099059

Priest, J.D. Elbow injuries in sports. (Refs:
5)*Sideline view (Minneapolis, Minn.) 6(4), Nov
1984, 1-4.*
LEVEL: I LANG: En SIRC ARTICLE NO: 100694

Stamford, B. Treatment and prevention of tennis
elbow. *Physician and sportsmedicine (Minneapolis,
Minn.) 12(5), May 1984, 194.*
LEVEL: B LANG: Eng SIRC ARTICLE NO: 094394

Wilkerson, G.B. Preventing epicondylitis. (Refs:
3)*Physician and sportsmedicine (Minneapolis,
Minn.) 12(6), 194;197.*
LEVEL: B LANG: Eng SIRC ARTICLE NO: 094397

EYE INJURIES

Barascu, D. Traumatismele oculare in sport.
(Ocular injuries in sports.) *Revista de chirurgie,
oncologie, radiologie, orl, oftalmologie,
somatologie, Seria: Oftalmologie (Bucharest) 28(2),
Apr/Jun 1984, 153-157.*
LEVEL: I LANG: Rum

Bovino, J.A. Marcus, D.F. Physical activity after
retinal detachment surgery. *American journal of
ophtalmology (Chicago) 98(2), 15 Aug 1984, 171-
179.*
ABST: 108 patients were divided into two groups
with the first group being encouraged to be
physically active while the second group was
strictly forbidden to perform physical activities for
six weeks. No statistically significant difference was
found between the two groups six months and one
year after surgery.
LEVEL: A LANG: Eng SIRC ARTICLE NO: 104015

**Diamond, G.R. Quinn, G.E. Pashby, T.J.
Easterbrook, M.** Ophthalmologic injuries. (Refs:
15)*Primary care: clinics in office practice
(Philadelphia) 11(1), Mar 1984, 161-174.*
LEVEL: I LANG: Eng SIRC ARTICLE NO: 100678

Gorman, B.D. Ophthalmology and sports medicine.
(Refs: 14)
NOTES: In, Scott, W.N. (ed.) et al., Principles of
sports medicine, Baltimore, Williams & Wilkins,
c1984, p. 87-96.
LEVEL: A LANG: Eng RC1210 18016

Le Buisson, D.A. Jeux de raquette et
traumatismes oculaires. *Concours medical (Paris)
106(41), 1984, 4059-4061.*
LEVEL: B LANG: Fr

Leleux, D. Poletti, J. Emphyseme retro-bulbaire
isole post-traumatique. (Post-traumatic isolated
retrobulbar emphysema.) *Bulletin des Societes
d'opthalmologie de France (Paris) 84(5), mai 1985,
655-656.*
LEVEL: I LANG: Fr

Les blessures occulaires dans le sport. Bilan des
donnees recueillies sur une periode de 2 ans et
demi. Trois-Rivieres: Regie de la securite dans les
sports, 1984. (8) feuillets
CORP: Regie de la securite dans les sports.
CORP: Association des ophtalmologistes du
Quebec.
LEVEL: I LANG: Fr RD97 20603

Moran, M. Rozsahle sitnicove krvaceni po
pretahovani lanem (Valsalvova hemorrhagicka
retinopatie). (Extensive retinal hemorrhage after a
game of tug-of-war (Valsalva's hemorrhagic
retinopathy).) *Ceskoslovenska oftalmologie
(Prague) 40(6), Nov 1984, 375-380.*
LEVEL: A LANG: Cze

Pavisic, Z. Vaznost vida i zdravstvenog stanja oka
za sport i fizicki odgoj. (The importance of vision
and the health status of the eye in sports and
physical education.) *Lijecnicki vjesnik (Zagreb)
106(6), Jun 1984, 264-266.*
LEVEL: B LANG: Scr

The athlete's eye: proper eye safety measures and
knowledge of effective care of injuries should be the
concern of every coach *Athletic journal 64(9), Apr
1984, 38-40.*
LEVEL: B LANG: Eng SIRC ARTICLE NO: 092847

What's your game. New York: National Society to
Prevent Blindness, c1984. 1 pamphlet
CORP: National Society to Prevent Blindness.
LEVEL: B LANG: Eng RD97 18948

FIRST AID AND EMERGENCY PROCEDURES

Berson, B.L. Cherney, S. Field management of
athletic injuries. (Refs: 9)
NOTES: In, Birrer, R.B. (ed.), Sports medicine for
the primary care physician, Norwalk, Conn.,
Appleton-Century-Crofts, c1984, p. 122-139.
LEVEL: I LANG: Eng RC1210 17030

Collins, T.L. How to speed emergency treatment.
*Physician and sportsmedicine (Minneapolis, Minn.)
12(11), Nov 1984, 142.*
LEVEL: B LANG: Eng SIRC ARTICLE NO: 100677

Hollinshead, R.M. Olympic medicine: emergency
treatment of the injured in sports. *Canadian
Academy of Sport Medicine newsletter (Ottawa)
5(4), 1984, 30-32.*
NOTES: Abstract from the Calgary Winter Sports
Symposium.
LEVEL: B LANG: Eng SIRC ARTICLE NO: 105300

**Miles, D.S. Underwood, P.D. Nolan, D.J. Frey,
M.A.B. Gotshall, R.W.** Metabolic, hemodynamic,
and respiratory responses to performing
cardiopulmonary resuscitation. *Canadian journal of
applied sport sciences/Journal canadien des
sciences appliquees au sport (Windsor, Ont.) 9(3),
Sept 1984, 141-147.*
ABST: The purpose of this study was to evaluate
the cardiorespiratory demands inherent to the
maintenance of continuous one- and two-man
cardiopulmonary resuscitation (CPR) for 10 min.
Ten male paramedics certified to perform CPR
participated. Each subject assumed the three
possible roles for administering CPR: ventilator,
compressor, and one-man technique. All three roles
elicited an increase in oxygen uptake compared to
kneeling rest, with the roles of one-man and
compressor being the most demanding. There were
moderate increases in cardiac output and heart rate
during the exercise roles, but stroke volume
remained similar to resting values. Pulmonary
ventilation increased during exercise, with the
greatest increase occurring for the one-man role.
Properly trained ane experienced individuals can
perform CPR efficiently for at least 10 min while
eliciting only moderate physiological stress.
LEVEL: A LANG: Eng SIRC ARTICLE NO: 102805

Otten, R.D. A comfortability level scale for
performance of cardiopulmonary resuscitation
(CPR). Eugene, Ore.: Microform Publications,
University of Oregon, 1984. 1 microfiche : negative
; 11 x 15 cm.
NOTES: Thesis (M.S.) - Purdue University, 1982;
(viii, 41 leaves); includes bibliography.
LEVEL: A LANG: Eng UO84 326

Serra, J.B. Management of trauma in the
wilderness environment. *Emergency medical clinics
of North America 2(3), Aug 1984, 635-647.*
LEVEL: I LANG: Eng

Smith, D.L. First aid kits. *Bicycling (Emmaus, Pa.)
25(4), May 1984, 44;47-49.*
LEVEL: B LANG: Eng SIRC ARTICLE NO: 094437

Thomas, D.R. Amos, W.L. Medical services
provided at the 1982 Southern Open Golf
Tournament. (Refs: 8)*American journal of sports
medicine (Baltimore, Md.) 12(2), Mar/Apr 1984,
155-158*
ABST: The author provides lists of equipment,
supplies and medications that are needed to
operate first aid centers at this event and other
events of similar size and character. The medical
needs of the population described were wide in
nature which underlines the importance of adequate
medical service preparation.
LEVEL: A LANG: Eng SIRC ARTICLE NO: 094443

Voss, M.W. When an athlete's life is in danger.
(Refs: 31)
NOTES: In, Birrer, R.B. (ed.), Sports medicine for
the primary care physician, Norwalk, Conn.,
Appleton-Century-Crofts, c1984, p. 140-150.
LEVEL: I LANG: Eng RC1210 17030

FOOT INJURIES

Baxter, D.E. Thigpen, C.M. Heel pain-operative
results. (Refs: 28)*Foot & ankle (Baltimore, Md.)
5(1), Jul/Aug 1984, 16-25.*
ABST: The authors discuss the anatomy of the heel
and the biomechanical pathogenesis of heel pain.
The cases of 34 operated heels in 26 patients are
reported. Follow-up studies show that 32
operations were successfull while 2 were not.
LEVEL: A LANG: Eng SIRC ARTICLE NO: 099032

Black, H.M. Brand, R.L. Injuries of the foot and
ankle. (Refs: 23)
NOTES: In, Scott, W.N. (ed.), Principles of
sports medicine, Baltimore, Williams & Wilkins,
c1984, p. 348-362.
LEVEL: A LANG: Eng RC1210 18016

Claustre, J. Benezis, C. Simon, L. Le pied en
pratique sportive. Paris: Masson, 1984. xii, 263 p.
(Monographies de podologie no 5.)
NOTES: ISSN: 0246-4896. Comprend des
bibliographies.
LEVEL: A LANG: Fr ISBN: 2-225-80423-0 RD97
20781

de Palma, L. Tamburrelli, F. La lussazione
sottoastragalica nella pratica sportiva.
Subastragalar luxation and sport. (Refs: 17)*Italian
journal of sports traumatology (Milano, Italy) 6(2),
Apr/Jun 1984, 149-157.*
CONF: Italian Society of Sports Traumatology.
Congress (1st : 1983 : Rome).
ABST: This study presents 5 cases of subastragalar
luxation which occurred as a result of sports
activities. Possible pathogenetic mechanisms for
the injury are described along with
anatomicopathological considerations. All patients

studied were forced to give up their sport though they were able to lead normal working lives.
LEVEL: A LANG: It Eng SIRC ARTICLE NO: 099037

Garfinkel, D. Rothenberger, L.A. Foot problems in athletes. (Refs: 34)*Journal of family practice (New York)* 19(2), Aug 1984 239-250.
LEVEL: I LANG: Eng SIRC ARTICLE NO: 104033

Gordon, J.C. Stress of running, other activities can lead to heel injuries. 'Bruised heel' could turn out to be any one of several conditions common to athletes. *First aider (Gardner, Kan.)* 53(4), Dec 1983/Jan 1984, 16-17.
LEVEL: B LANG: Eng SIRC ARTICLE NO: 094361

Goulet, M.J. Role of soft orthosis in treating plantar fasciitis: suggestion from the field. (Refs: 1)*Physical therapy (Alexandria, Va.)* 64(10), Oct 1984, 1544.
LEVEL: I LANG: Eng SIRC ARTICLE NO: 099040

Henricson, A.S. Westlin, N.E. Chronic calcaneal pain in athletes: entrapment of the calcaneal nerve? (Refs: 16)*American journal of sports medicine (Baltimore, Md.)* 12(2), Mar/Apr 1984, 152-154.
ABST: Ten elite athletes were surgically treated for chronic calcaneal pain after conservative treatment failed to alleviate the condition. The calcaneal branches of the tibial nerve were surgically decompressed. Nine of the ten athletes were asymptomatic at a 58 month follow-up. The patients were able to resume athletic participation 5 weeks after surgery.
LEVEL: A LANG: Eng SIRC ARTICLE NO: 094364

The issues of foot and mouth. *Fitness & health newsletter (Wembley, W.A.)* 15, 1984?, 1-4.
LEVEL: B LANG: Eng SIRC ARTICLE NO: 177412

Vachaud, M. Costagliola, M. Micheau, P. Chavoin, J.P. Delannes, B. Accidents par rayons de roue. Interet du lambeau cutaneo-aponevrotique. (Injuries caused by wheel spokes. Value of the cutaneo-aponeurotic flap.) *Acta orthopaedica belgica (Bruxelles)* 50(6), 1984, 864-872.
LEVEL: A LANG: Fr

Vasavada, P.J. DeVries, D.F. Nishiyama, H. Plantar fascitis - early blood pool images in diagnosis of inflammatory process. (Refs: 8)*Foot & ankle (Baltimore, Md.)* 5(2), Sept/Oct 1984, 74-76.
LEVEL: I LANG: Eng SIRC ARTICLE NO: 099075

FRACTURES

Andrew, T.A. Brooks, S. Case report: Bullworker fracture. (Refs: 4)*British journal of sports medicine (Loughborough, Eng.)* 18(2), Jun 1984, 126-127.
LEVEL: I LANG: Eng SIRC ARTICLE NO: 102485

Bergmann, L. Ermuedungsfrakturen der ersten Rippe und ihre Kombination mit einem Spontanpneumothorax. (Fatigue fractures of the 1st rib and their combination with spontaneous pneumothorax.) *Zeitschrift fuer Erkrankungen der Atmungsorgane, mit folia Bronchologica (Leipzig)* 163(1), 1984, 75-79.
LEVEL: A LANG: Ger

Daffner, R.H. Anterior tibial striations. *AJR: American journal of roentgenology (Baltimore, Md.)* 143(3), Sept 1984, 651-653.
ABST: The cases of seven basketball players, two professional dancers, and one hurdler suffering from anterior tibial striations are reported in this study.
LEVEL: A LANG: Eng SIRC ARTICLE NO: 104025

Gangitano, Bonfiglio, G. Longo, G. Il trattamento con 'gessi funzionali' delle fratture di gamba negli sportivi. Treatment of sports-incurred leg fractures with functional casts. (Refs: 5)*Italian journal of sports traumatology (Milan)* 6(1), Jan/Mar 1984, 21-33.
ABST: This paper presents the technique for the use of a functional cast in the treatment of a leg fracture. The use of such treatment was evaluated over a four year period at the University of Catania Orthopaedic Clinic. 87 fractures were treated from 1979 to the end of 1982. Only among the medium stable fractures, in each of which there was some displacement and partial mobility, were 7% of the results poor. The treatment of more stable fractures yielded 100% results were very good. The authors conclude that excellent results and shorter recovery times, when compared with conventional orthopaedic treatment, can be found with this treatment. This method would be extremely useful for most athletes.
LEVEL: A LANG: Eng It SIRC ARTICLE NO: 097352

Greiss, M.E. Khincha, H.P. Adult Monteggia lesion with ipsilateral wrist fracture. *Journal of the Royal Society of Medicine (London)* 77(12), Dec 1984, 1050-1052.
LEVEL: B LANG: Eng

Haines, J.F. Williams, E.A. Hargadon, E.J. Davies, D.R. Is conservative treatment of displaced tibial shaft fractures justified? *Journal of bone joint surgery. British volume (London)* 66(1), Jan 1984, 84-88.
ABST: This prospective study examined all tibial shaft fractures (91) treated at one hospital during a five year period. Conservative treatment was employed including bone grafting when indicated. This conservative policy of treatment is concluded to be satisfactory since bony union of all displaced tibial fractures was achieved in a reasonable period of time.
LEVEL: A LANG: Eng SIRC ARTICLE NO: 099041

Leyshon, A. Ireland, J. Trickey, E.L. The treatment of delayed union and non-union of the carpal scaphoid by screw fixation. *Journal of bone joint surgery. British volume (London)* 66(1), Jan 1984, 124-127.
ABST: This paper describes a simple technique for screw fixation of the carpal scaphoid in delayed union and non-union. 32 patients were treated by this method and observed in a follow-up study averaging 3 years. Successful union was obtained in 28 patients. The advantages of this treatment technique are discussed.
LEVEL: A LANG: Eng SIRC ARTICLE NO: 099047

Lipscomb, A.B. Gilbert, P.P. Johnston, R.K. Anderson, A.F. Snyder, R.B. Fracture of the tibial tuberosity with associated ligamentous and meniscal tears. A case report. *Journal of bone and joint surgery (Boston)* 66(5), Jun 1984, 790-792.
LEVEL: I LANG: Eng SIRC ARTICLE NO: 102525

McGuigan, J.A. O'Reilly, M.J. Nixon, J.R. Popliteal arterial thrombosis resulting from disruption of the upper tibial epiphysis. *Injury: British journal of accident surgery (Bristol)* 16(1), Jul 1984, 49-50.
ABST: As a result of a fall, a young athlete sustained a type 2 epiphyseal fracture of the proximal tibia. Three days later it became apparent that the popliteal artery had thrombosed and a successful arterial reconstruction was carried out.
LEVEL: I LANG: Eng SIRC ARTICLE NO: 104059

Morgan, D.A. Walters, J.W. A prospective study of 100 consecutive carpal scaphoid fractures. *Australia and New Zealand journal of surgery (Melbourne)* 54(3), Jun 1984, 233-241.
LEVEL: A LANG: Eng SIRC ARTICLE NO: 104064

Robert, M. Longis, B. Gouault, E. Alain, J.L. Les fractures du tubercule antero-externe de l'extremite inferieure du tibia chez l'enfant. *Medecine du sport (Paris)* 58(6), nov 1984, 19-21.
RESUME: Les auteurs rapportent 10 cas de traumatisme de la cheville avec fracture decollement epiphysaire du tubercule ontero-externe de l'extremite inferieure du tibia. 6 filles et 4 garcons (age moyen de 14,4 ans) sont observes apres une periode minimum de 2 ans. Le traitement orthopedique est utilise 5 fois, lorsque le deplacement etait nul, et le traitement chirurgicale est utilise dans les cinq autres cas, deplaces. Les resultats indiquent une restitution anatomique et une fonction normale de la cheville.
LEVEL: A LANG: Fr SIRC ARTICLE NO: 102537

Schmit-Neuerburg, K.P. Die Plattenosteosynthese geschlossener Tibia-Schaftfrakturen. (Plate osteosynthesis of closed tibial shaft fractures.) *Orthopade* 13(4), Sept 1984, 271-286.
LEVEL: A LANG: Ger

Sebold, D. Tape support for the fractured distal fibula. *Athletic training (Greenville, N.C.)* 19(2), Summer 1984, 121-123.
LEVEL: B LANG: Eng SIRC ARTICLE NO: 094435

FROSTBITE

Massol, P. Steinschneider, R. Gelures et pathologie de haute montagne. *Revue du jeune medecin (Paris)* 148, 1984, 12-13.
LEVEL: B LANG: Fr

HAND INJURIES

Brunet, M.E. Haddad, R.J. Sanchez, J. Leonard, E. How I manage sprained finger in athletes. (Refs: 1)*Physician and sportsmedicine (Minneapolis, Minn.)* 12(8), Aug 1984, 99-105;108.
LEVEL: I LANG: Eng SIRC ARTICLE NO: 097565

Call, W.H. Injuries to the hand and wrist in athletics. (Refs: 2)*Sideline view 5(6), Jan 1984, 1-4.
LEVEL: B LANG: Eng SIRC ARTICLE NO: 091453

Carlier, A. Leclercq, D. Khuc, T. Depierreux, L. Lejeune, G. Quelques traumatismes frequents de la main chez le sportif. (Frequent injuries of the hand in athletes.) *Revue medicale de Liege (Liege)* 39(9), 1 mai 1984, 385-401.
LEVEL: A LANG: Fr SIRC ARTICLE NO: 102497

Cugola, L. Una tecnica per il trattamento della deformita cronica a bottoniera. A technique for chronic boutonniere deformit repair. (Refs: 9)*Italian journal of sports traumatology (Milano, Italy)* 6(3), Jul/Sept 1984, 207-211.
ABST: A technique for surgical correction of the chronic boutonniere deformity is presented using a free palmaris longus tendon graft.
LEVEL: A LANG: Eng It SIRC ARTICLE NO: 102503

Ireland, D. Common hand injuries in sport. *Australian family physician (Sydney)* 13(11), Nov 1984, 797-800.
LEVEL: I LANG: Eng SIRC ARTICLE NO: 106520

Lunn, P.G. Lamb, D.W. Rugby finger -- avulsion of profundus of ring finger. *Journal of hand surgery*

(British volume) (Edinburgh) 9(1), Feb 1984, 69-71.
LEVEL: I LANG: Eng SIRC ARTICLE NO: 100687

Matthews, R.N. Walton, J.N. Spontaneous rupture of both flexor tendons in a single digit. *Journal of hand surgery: British volume (Edinburgh) 9(2), Jun 1984, 134-136.*
ABST: This case report describes and discusses the rare event of a simultaneous, spontaneous rupture of both flexor tendons in the mid-segment of one finger of an athlete.
LEVEL: I LANG: Eng SIRC ARTICLE NO: 104058

Peimer, C.A. Sullivan, D.J. Wild, D.R. Palmar dislocation of the proximal interphalangeal joint. *Journal of hand surgery (St. Louis) 9A(1), Jan 1984, 39-48.*
ABST: 15 patients with palmar dislocations of the proximal interphalangeal joint (PIP) were reviewed with a follow-up study averaging 17.8 months after treatment. The serious nature of the injuries from this dislocation was initially unrecognized. Twelve of the 15 required surgery while three treated earlier were managed by closed reduction and percutaneous pinning. All returned to full activities including heavy labor. However, a full range of PIP motion was not recovered in any case.
LEVEL: A LANG: Eng SIRC ARTICLE NO: 099057

Posner, M.A. Hand and digit injuries. (Refs: 26)
NOTES: In, Scott, W.N. (ed.) et al., Principles of sports medicine, Baltimore, Williams & Wilkins, c1984, p. 178-211.
LEVEL: A LANG: Eng RC1210 18016

Rao, V.K. Feins, R.S. Fishing for a thumb - an unusual replantation. *Wisconsin medical journal (Madison) 83(9), Sept 1984, 22-23.*
LEVEL: I LANG: Eng

Schroeder, J.A. Suggestions for the clinic: alphabet spelling exercises for the wrist and hand. *Journal of orthopaedic and sports physical therapy (Baltimore) 5(6), May/Jun 1984, 382-383.*
ABST: This article presents a relatively simple active range-of-motion program for the wrist and hand which can be utilized by a variety of patients.
LEVEL: I LANG: Eng SIRC ARTICLE NO: 100751

Wray, R.C. Young, V.L. Holtman, B. Proximal interphalangeal joint sprains. *Plastic and reconstructive surgery (Baltimore) 74(1), Jul 1984, 101-107.*
ABST: 50 sprains in 48 patients are reviewed in detail by the authors.
LEVEL: A LANG: Eng SIRC ARTICLE NO: 102551

HEAD INJURIES

Albright, J.P. Van Gilder, J. El Khoury, G. Crowley, E. Foster, D. Head and neck injuries in sports. (Refs: 30)
NOTES: In, Scott, W.N. (ed.) et al., Principles of sports medicine, Baltimore, Williams & Wilkins, c1984, p. 40-86.
LEVEL: A LANG: Eng RC1210 18016

Birrer, R.B. Common injuries of the head and neck. (Refs: 43)
NOTES: In, Birrer, R.B. (ed.), Sports medicine for the primary care physician, Norwalk, Conn., Appleton-Century-Crofts, c1984, p. 151-171.
LEVEL: I LANG: Eng RC1210 17030

Bruce, D.A. Schut, L. Sutton, L.N. Brain and cervical spine injuries occurring during organized sports activities in childre and adolescents. (Refs: 75) *Primary care: clinics in office practice*

(Philadelphia) 11(1), Mar 1984, 175-194.
LEVEL: I LANG: Eng SIRC ARTICLE NO: 100674

Chrzavzez, G. Chrzavzez, J.P. Erceville, T. Kharrat, N. Barbillon, C. Pilz, F. Les traumas sportifs de la face. *Revue de stomatologie et de chirurgie maxillo-faciale (Paris) 85(5), 1984, 411-413.*
LEVEL: B LANG: Fr

Chrzavzez, G. Chrzavzez, J.P. D'Erceville, T. Kharrat, N. Barbillon, C. Pilz, F. Les traumas sportifs de la face. (Sports injuries of the face.) *Revue de stomatologie et de chirurgie maxillo-faciale (Paris) 85(5), 1984, 411-413.*
LEVEL: A LANG: Fr

Head first: reduction of disabling and fatal injuries is the aim of an Easter Seal public information program. *Coaching revie 7, Mar/Apr 1984, 45-46.*
LEVEL: B LANG: Eng SIRC ARTICLE NO: 092863

Head injuries in athletics. *First aider (Gardner, Kans.) 54(2), Oct 1984, 1;4-7.*
LEVEL: B LANG: Eng SIRC ARTICLE NO: 105297

Kirshner, B.J. Headaches: oh, your aching head. What causes that dreadful pounding, and what besides two aspirin will bring you relief? *Fit (Mountain View, Calif.) 4(7), Dec 1984, 32-35;67-69.*
LEVEL: B LANG: Eng SIRC ARTICLE NO: 173557

Lamendin, H. A propos des relations entre etat bucco-dentaire et pratique sportive. Protection et prevention. (Relation between orodental status and sports performance. Protection and prevention.) *Chirurgien-dentiste de France (Paris) 54(267), 25 oct 1984, 27-32.*
LEVEL: I LANG: Fr

Nelson, W.E. Jane, J.A. Gieck, J.H. Minor head injury in sports: a new system of classification and management. (Refs: 9) *Physician and sportsmedicine 12(3), Mar 1984, 103-107.*
LEVEL: I LANG: Eng SIRC ARTICLE NO: 091477

Nelson, W.E. Gieck, J.H. Jane, J.A. Hawthorne, P. Athletic head injuries. (Refs: 13) *Athletic training (Greenville, N.C.) 19(2), Summer 1984, 95-102.*
LEVEL: I LANG: Eng SIRC ARTICLE NO: 094381

Re, G. Borgogna, E. Fogliano, F. Re, F. Scotto, G. Lesioni traumatiche maxillo-facciali nella pratica del rugby, del calcio, della equitazione. (Traumatic maxillofacial lesions in rugby, soccer and horseback riding.) *Minerva stomatologica (Torino) 33(3), May/Jun 1984, 533-535.*
LEVEL: I LANG: It

Reid, S.E. Head and neck injuries in sports. Springfield, Ill.: C.C. Thomas, c1984. xi, 200 p. : ill.
NOTES: Includes bibliographies.
LEVEL: I LANG: Eng ISBN: 0-398-04974-2 LC CARD: 83-24294 RD97 19085

Rolland, A. Les malaires du sportif. (Refs: 4) *Medecine du sport 58(1), 25 janv 1984, 9-11.*
LEVEL: I LANG: Fr SIRC ARTICLE NO: 091483

Schultz, R.C. de Camara, D.L. Athletic facial injuries. *JAMA: Journal of the American Medical Association (Chicago) 252(24) 28 Dec 1984, 3395-3398.*
LEVEL: I LANG: Eng

Solon, R.C. Maxillofacial trauma.
NOTES: In, Scott, W.N. (ed.) et al., Principles of sports medicine, Baltimore, Williams & Wilkins, c1984, p. 97-109.
LEVEL: I LANG: Eng RC1210 18016

Young, R. Head and neck injuries primary assessment and treatment. *Journal of the Canadian Athletic Therapists Association (Oakville, Ont.) 11(2), Fall 1984, 9-12.*
LEVEL: B LANG: Eng SIRC ARTICLE NO: 104093

HEAT EXHAUSTION

Beyer, C.B. Heat stress and the young athlete. Recognizing and reducing the risks. *Postgraduate medicine (Minneapolis) 76(1), Jul 1984, 109-112.*
LEVEL: I LANG: Eng SIRC ARTICLE NO: 102564

Cabanac, M. Hyperthermie maligne ou coup de chaleur? (Malignant hyperthermia or heat stroke? (letter)) *Nouvelle presse medicale (Paris) 13(8), 25 fevr 1984, 506.*
LEVEL: I LANG: Fr SIRC ARTICLE NO: 099034

Chase, J.L. Hot weather: dangerous to your health. *Rugby (New York) 10(4), Jul 1984, 28.*
LEVEL: B LANG: Eng SIRC ARTICLE NO: 097567

de Mondenard, J.P. Un dossier brulant: la chaleur. Il fait trop chaud pour...courir. *Revue de l'Amicale des entraineurs francais d'athletisme (Paris) 87, avr/mai/juin 1984, 5-7;9-10.*
LEVEL: I LANG: Fr SIRC ARTICLE NO: 095911

Duncan, J. Hyperthermia during exercise. *Aerobics (Dallas, Tex.) 5(8), Aug 1984, 5.*
LEVEL: B LANG: Eng SIRC ARTICLE NO: 100679

Hankins, D. Heat stress a danger during fall, spring. *First aider (Gardner, Kan.) 53(7), Summer 1984, 11.*
LEVEL: B LANG: Eng SIRC ARTICLE NO: 095926

Haymes, E.M. Heat precautions for female athletes. Chicago: Teach'em Inc., 1984?. 1 sound cassette : 14 35mm slides (Audio cassette series on sports medicine: Sportsmedicine for female athletes, SM-37.)
NOTES: Cassettes recorded and produced by Teach'em Inc. in cooperation with the Physician and Sportsmedicine.
LEVEL: I LANG: Eng

Henry, C. Heat illness: on-field emergencies. (Refs: 8) *Texas coach (Austin, Tex.) 28(2), Sept 1984, 49-53.*
LEVEL: B LANG: Eng SIRC ARTICLE NO: 105298

Layne, T.N. Life-threatening illnesses: the commom and not-so-common. *First aider (Gardner, Kan.) 53(5), Feb 1984, 8-10.*
NOTES: Last of a three-part series.
LEVEL: B LANG: Eng SIRC ARTICLE NO: 096030

Lyles, B.D. Heat exhaustion and heat stroke. *Aerobics (Dallas, Tex.) 5(7), Jul 1984, 4;8.*
LEVEL: B LANG: Eng SIRC ARTICLE NO: 095944

Mad dogs and Englishmen. *Nursing times (London) 80(32), 8-14 Aug 1984, 16-19.*
ABST: Examines the diagnosis and prevention o heat exhaustion in sports.
LEVEL: B LANG: Eng SIRC ARTICLE NO: 104055

Murphy, R.J. Heat illness in the athlete. (Refs: 7) *Athletic training (Greenville, N.C.) 19(3), Fall 1984, 166-170.*
LEVEL: I LANG: Eng SIRC ARTICLE NO: 099053

Murphy, R.J. Heat illness in the athlete. (Refs: 7) *American journal of sports medicine (Baltimore, Md.) 12(4), Jul/Aug 1984 258-261.*
ABST: Heat illness is one of the most common causes of disability in American football and there are frequent deaths caused by heatstroke. A better

understanding of the physiology of heatstroke has changed the manner of the approach to heat problems in the past 25 years. Sweating is the way the body dissipates the internal heat produced by muscular exercise. Since sweat is hypotonic, the result of excessive loss of weight through sweating is a water deficit in the body. The clinical disorders resulting from exercise in hot and humid environment are heat cramps, heat syncope, heat exhaustion, and heatstroke. Ways to prevent problems from heat illness include conditioning for the exercise, identifying the individuals who are most susceptible to heat problems, wearing proper clothing with as much skin as possible exposed to the air, evaluating the environmental conditions on the field, and providing adequate amounts of water on the field.
LEVEL: A LANG: Eng SIRC ARTICLE NO: 108530

Schiltz, J. Heat: the athlete killer. Coaches must understand the dangers involved in playing in hot weather and be prepared to cope with heat stress in their athletes. *Athletic journal 64(8), Mar 1984, 14;60-62.*
LEVEL: B LANG: Eng SIRC ARTICLE NO: 093127

Sebold, D. Heat illnesses. *In, Adams, S.H. (ed.), et al., Catastrophic injuries in sports: avoidance strategies, Salinas, Calif., Cayote Press, c1984, p. 7-15.*
LEVEL: I LANG: Eng RD97 19088

Smith, N.J. The prevention of heat disorders in sports. *American journal of diseases of children (Chicago) 138(8), Aug 1984 786-790.*
LEVEL: I LANG: Eng SIRC ARTICLE NO: 102544

Sutton, J.R. Heat illness. (Refs: 57)
NOTES: In, Strauss, R.H. (ed.), Sports medicine, Philadelphia ; Toronto, Saunders, 1984, p. 307-322.
LEVEL: A LANG: Eng RC1210 17196

HEMORRHAGE

Eichel, B.S. Kaplan, H.J. How I manage nosebleeds in athletes. *Physician and sportsmedicine 12(4), Apr 1984, 67-68.*
LEVEL I LANG: Eng SIRC ARTICLE NO: 092855

HIP INJURIES

Grisogono, V. The running body: 26. The hip abductors. *Running (London, Eng.) 36, Apr 1984, 73.*
LEVEL: B LANG: Eng SIRC ARTICLE NO: 095924

Henry, J.H. The hip. (Refs: 55)
NOTES: In, Scott, W.N. (ed.) et al., Principles of sports medicine, Baltimore, Williams & Wilkins, c1984, p. 242-269.
LEVEL: A LANG: Eng RC1210 18016

Hoekstra, H.J. Binnendijk, B. Restrictions in sports activities after a hipfracture in a child or adolescent criteria for th medical examination. (Refs: 8)*International journal of sports medicine (Stuttgart) Suppl. 5, Nov 1984, 10-12.*
CONF: International Congress on Sports and Health (1983 : Maastricht, Netherlands).
LEVEL : A LANG: Eng SIRC ARTICLE NO: 104041

HYPOTHERMIA

Bangs, C.C. Cold injuries. (Refs: 6)
NOTES: In, Strauss, R.H. (ed.), Sports medicine, Philadelphia ; Toronto, Saunders, 1984 p. 323-343.
LEVEL: A LANG: Eng RC1210 17196

Connors, G.P. Winter exercise calls for caution. Extended exposure to cold, wind can lead to hypothermia. *First aider (Gardner, Kan.) 53(4), Dec 1983/Jan 1984, 1;4.*
LEVEL: B LANG: Eng SIRC ARTICLE NO: 094353

de Mondenard, J.P. Un dossier brulant: la chaleur. Il fait trop chaud pour...courir. *Revue de l'Amicale des entraineurs francais d'athletisme (Paris) 87, avr/mai/juin 1984, 5-7;9-10.*
LEVEL: I LANG: Fr SIRC ARTICLE NO: 095911

Hayward, J.S. Matthews, B.R. Hay, C. Overweel, C.H. Radford, D.D. Temperature effect on the human dive response in relation to cold water near-drowning. (Refs: 34)*Journal of applied physiology: respiratory, environmental and exercise physiology (Bethesda, Md.) 56(1), Jan 1984, 202-206.*
ABST: In the dive response there appears to be a conservation of oxygen for the brain and heart. At water temperatures 15o C, breath hold durations were found to be approximately 30% of nonimmersed values in 160 humans who were tested. No significant changes in heart rate were found with immersion in cold water. The authors conclude that the dive response would be reduced in cold water temperatures and would not improve resuscitability with near-drowning.
LEVEL: A LANG: Eng SIRC ARTICLE NO: 096249

INTERNAL ORGAN INJURIES

de Vries, J. Eeftinck Schattenkerk, M. Eggink, W.F. Bruining, H.A. Obertop, H. Van der Slikke, W. Van Houten, H. Treatment o pancreatic injuries. *Netherlands journal of surgery (Utrecht) 36(1), Feb 1984, 13-16.*
ABST: The authors reported the cases of 14 patients with pancreatic injuries. Various treatment methods were used i.e. whipple pancreatoduo, denectomy, drainage, pancreatectomy and splenectomy. Six patients died (43%).
LEVEL: A LANG: Eng SIRC ARTICLE NO: 099038

Hunter, R.A. Kiroff, G.K. Jamieson, G.G. The injured spleen: should consideration be given to conservative management? (Refs 26)*Australian and New Zealand journal of surgery (Melbourne) 54(2), Apr 1984, 129-135.*
ABST: This retrospective study over a 13 year period studied patients who underwent splenectomy. The incidence of associated major abdominal injuries following blunt trauma in these subjects. Patients who suffered splenic injuries whilst playing sport or who were conscious and did not have major extra-abdominal injuries or clear evidence of other intra-abdominal injury could possibly have been managed expectantly. Such a policy might have avoided splenectomy in a substantial number of cases and thus have eliminated the risk of post-splenectomy infection in these patients.
LEVEL: A LANG: Eng SIRC ARTICLE NO: 109760

Kidder, R.E. Doherty, P.W. Pseudo-obstruction of the biliary tract associated with a traumatic biliary fistula. *Clinical nuclear medicine (Philadelphia) 9(5), May 1984, 259-261.*
ABST: Documentation of a biliary fistula as a complication of hepatic trauma may be made simply and noninvasively using radionuclide cholescintigraphy. This report describes the utility of this approach in the evaluation of the pathophysiology underlying apparent biliary obstruction in a patient with a large traumatic biliary fistula.
LEVEL: A LANG: Eng

Layne, T.N. Internal injuries. Athletic injuries that are truly life-threatening often involve damage to the internal organs It's essential to recognize such injuries and obtain prompt medical care. Part II. *First aider (Gardner, Kan.) 53(4), Dec 1983/Jan 1984, 12-14.*
LEVEL: I LANG: Eng SIRC ARTICLE NO: 094371

JOINT INJURIES

Faye, L.J. Joint dysfunction: its significance in athletic performance. (Refs: 6)*Ontario judoka (Willowdale, Ont.) 9(3), May/Sept 1984, 16-17.*
LEVEL: I LANG: Eng SIRC ARTICLE NO: 108892

Gerber, C. Differentialdiagnostische Aspekte posttraumatischer Schulterschmerzen. (Differential diagnostic aspects of posttraumatic shoulder pain.) *Unfallheilkunde (Berlin) 87(9), Sept 1984, 357-362.*
LEVEL: A LANG: Ger

Gray, S. Strapping of joints. *Australian family physician (Sydney) 13(8), Aug 1984, 610;612-614.*
LEVEL: A LANG: Eng

Hepburn, G.R. Crivelli, K.J. Use of elbow dynasplint for reduction of elbow flexion contractures: a case study. (Refs: 11) *Journal of orthopaedic and sports physical therapy (Baltimore, Md.) 5(5), Mar/Apr 1984, 269-274.*
ABST: This study describes the use of the elbow Dynasplint in remediating a case of severe elbow flexion contracture. The severe elbow flexion contracture was present following a supracondylar fracture in a 13-year-old male. The Dynasplint was applied primarily at night. The Dynasplint, along with other active and resistive exercises, was successful in bringing elbow extension to 0 degrees over a period of 5 months.
LEVEL: A LANG: Eng SIRC ARTICLE NO: 094365

Jones, R.N. Rotatory dislocation of both atlanto-axial joints. *Journal of bone joint surgery. British volume (London) 66(1) Jan 1984, 6-7.*
ABST: A case of rotatory dislocation of both atlanto-axial joints is presented. A review of the literature reveals two other cases, both in children. This would appear to be the first report in an adult, who made a full recovery.
LEVEL: I LANG: Eng SIRC ARTICLE NO: 099044

Selivanov, V.P. K voprosu o gipermobil'nosti kistevykh sustavov v sportsmenov. (Hypermobility of the wrist joint in athletes *Ortopediia travmatologiia i protezirovanie (Moscow) 8, Aug 1984, 44-48.*
LEVEL: A LANG: Rus

KNEE INJURIES

Aglietti, P. Buzzi, R. Bassi, P.B. Saggini, R. Meniscectomie artroscopiche. Tecnica e risultati iniziali. Arthroscopic meniscectomy. Description of a technique and initial results. (Refs: 69)*Italian journal of sports traumatology (Milan) 6(1), Jan/Mar 1984, 35-50.*
ABST: This paper describes the evaluation and method of partial arthroscopic meniscectomy which

was performed on 47 males and 10 females between October, 1981, and December, 1982. In the follow up evaluations, there were 29 excellent results (51%), 21 good results (37%), 7 fair results (12%), and no poor results. Meniscectomy is probably the most suitable fo the many fields in which surgical arthroscopy can be applied. The authors state that although its clinical results are not remarkably different from those offered by arthrotomy, a brief hospitalization period, ambulatorial operability, low morbidity, and short recovery periods are advantages of this method.
LEVEL: A LANG: Eng It SIRC ARTICLE NO: 097353

Allman, W.F. Architecture of the knee. *In, Schrier, E.W. and Allman, W.F. (eds.), Newton at the bat: the science in sports, New York, Scribner, c1984, p. 114-118.*
LEVEL: B LANG: Eng RC1235 18609

Andrish, J.T. Ligamentous injuries of the knee. (Refs: 11)*Primary care: clinics in office practice (Philadelphia) 11(1), Ma 1984, 77-88.*
LEVEL: I LANG: Eng SIRC ARTICLE NO: 100671

Ariees, R.P. van Loon, P.J. van Akkerveeken, P.F. van den Berg, A.F. Arthroscopische bevindingen bij traumatische haemarthro van de knie. (Arthroscopic findings in traumatic hemarthrosis of the knee.) *Nederlands tijdschrift voor geneeskunde (Amsterdam) 128 (47), 24 Nov 1984, 2214-2217.*
LEVEL: A LANG: Dut

Baugher, W.H. Warren, R.F. Marshall, J.L. Joseph, A. Quadriceps atrophy in the anterior cruciate insufficient knee. (Refs: 2 *American journal of sports medicine (Baltimore) 12(3), May/Jun 1984, 192-195.*
ABST: The purpose of this study was to test the hypothesis that the apparent muscle atrophy, which appears in symptomatic patients lacking an anterior cruciate ligament (ACL), is due to the impaired function of the fast twitch fibres in the quadriceps. Fourteen males who underwent surgery for an acute disruption of the ACL or reconstruction of the ACL, with a minimal interval to surgery of one year, were used as subjects. The group was divided into subjects with and without clinical atrophy, and at the time of operation a biopsy was taken from the vastus medialus in each subject. Histochemical staining techniques revealed that the FT/ST area ratio was significantly lower in the group with clinical atrophy. The authors suggest that the atrophy seen in chronically unstable ACL insufficient knees correlates with a decrease in the area of fast twitch muscle fibres.
LEVEL: A LANG: Eng SIRC ARTICLE NO: 102492

Beguin, J. Locker, B. Sabatier, J.P. Vielpeau, C. Interets de l'arthroscopie du genou chez le sportif. *Medecine du sport 58(1), 25 janv 1984, 4-5.*
LEVEL: B LANG: Fr SIRC ARTICLE NO: 091450

Bell, D. Reliability of knee examinations. *Canadian Academy of Sport Medicine newsletter (Ottawa) 5(4), 1984, 33-34.*
NOTES: Abstract from the Winter Sports Conference, University of Calgary, October 26-27, 1984.
LEVEL: B LANG: Eng SIRC ARTICLE NO: 105284

Biaggi, J. Scheidegger, A. Bandlaesionen am Knie--auch typische Arbeitsverletzungen. (Ligament lesions of the knee--also a typical occupational injury.) *Chirurg (Berlin) 55(11), Nov 1984, 717-720.*
LEVEL: A LANG: Ger

Black, J.E. Alten, S.R. How I manage infrapatellar tendinitis. (Refs: 10)*Physician and sportsmedicine (Minneapolis, Minn.) 12(10), Oct 1984, 86-90;92.*
LEVEL: I LANG: Eng SIRC ARTICLE NO: 099033

Brown, D. E. Alexander, A.H. Lichtman, D.M. The Elmslie-Trillat procedure: evaluation in patellar dislocation and subluxatio (Refs: 19)*American journal of sports medicine (Baltimore, Md.) 12(2), Mar/Apr 1984, 104-109.*
ABST: The Elmslie-Trillat procedure was performed on 27 knees. The results were evaluated an average of 42 months post-surgery. Good or excellent results were obtained in 81% overall and in 91% of those knees with patella alta. All patients with a fair or poor result had Q-angles of 15o or greater. The authors conclude that inadequate menial displacement of the anterior tibial tuberosity may lead to unsatisfactory results and that this may be avoided by intraoperative measurement of the Q-angle.
LEVEL: A LANG: Eng SIRC ARTICLE NO: 094350

Cabaud, H.E. Nonligamentous problems of the athlete's knee. (Refs: 3)*Primary care: clinics in office practice (Philadelphia 11(1), Mar 1984, 89-100.*
LEVEL: I LANG: Eng SIRC ARTICLE NO: 100675

Clancy, W.G. Keene, J.S. Goletz, T.H. Symptomatic dislocation of the anterior horn of the medial meniscus. (Refs: 12) *American journal of sports medicine (Baltimore, Md.) 12(1), Jan/Feb 1984, 57-64.*
CONF: American Orthopedic Society for Sports Medicine (1980: Big Sky, Mon.).
ABST: Repair of anterior horn dislocation of the medial meniscus was performed using three surgical methods. In three patients an arthrotomy was performed removing the medial meniscus. In six other patients an arthrotomy was performed with repair of the anterior horn. In four patients athroscopy was performed resecting the anterior horn. Although no method was more successful, treatment with the arthroscope was preferred.
LEVEL: A LANG: Eng SIRC ARTICLE NO: 094351

Colon, V.F. Stephens, W.K. Graman, P. Kues, J. The pogo stick as an adjunct in the knee rehabilitation of athletes. (Refs: 5 *Physician and sportsmedicine (Minneapolis, Minn.) 12(8), Aug 1984, 59-62;64.*
ABST: This paper investigates the efficacy of a pogo stick program for rehabilitation of athletes with injured knees. The effect of this program and a standard Orthotron knee rehabilitation program were compared on a group of ten uninjured female athletes. Strength, power, and endurance in the quadriceps and hamstring muscles were measured prior and following the study. The two program provided equal benefits.
LEVEL: A LANG: Eng SIRC ARTICLE NO: 097568

de Keizer, G. Acute diagnosis and treatment in the injured knee joint. (Refs: 5)*International journal of sports medicine (Stuttgart) Suppl. 5, Nov 1984, 151-152.*
CONF: International Congress on Sports and Health (1983 : Maastricht, Netherlands).
LEVEL: A LANG: Eng SIRC ARTICLE NO: 104027

Delacerda, F.G. A biomechanical analysis of the knee joint undergoing rehabilitation: a case study. (Refs: 9)*Journal of orthopaedic and sports physical therapy (Baltimore, Md.) 5(5), Mar/Apr 1984, 261-264.*
ABST: This study describes the biomechanical analysis of the knee joint of a 20-year-old female athlete undergoing rehabilitation following extensive ligament repair surgery. Fifteen weeks after surgery a nine week progressive resistive exercise program was initiated. During this nine week program biomechanical analyses of the time percentage of each gait cyclephase, velocity profiles of knee joint motion, and dynamic force determinations were carried out. These parameters changed significantly throughout the nine week program.
LEVEL: A LANG: Eng SIRC ARTICLE NO: 094356

Devereaux, M.D. Lachmann, S.M. Patello-femoral arthralgia in athletes attending a sports injury clinic. (Refs: 18)*British journal of sports medicine (Loughborough, Leicestershire) 18(1), Mar 1984, 18-21.*
ABST: Over a five year period, patello-femoral arthralgia was diagnosed in 137 athletes who presented themselves to a Sports Injury Clinic. Conservative treatment was successful in 28.6% of the athletes at a mean follow up of 13.1 months. The authors discuss the symptoms and treatment of patello-femoral arthralgia. Currently, there exists a need to determine the relationship between patello-femoral arthralgia, extensor mechanism dysfunction and chondromalacia patellae.
LEVEL: A LANG: Eng SIRC ARTICLE NO: 095913

Dubs, L. Bandlaxitaet und Sport. Ein aetiologischer Beitrag zum femoropatellaeren Schmerzsyndrom. (Joint instability and sports. Etiologic aspects of the femoro-patellar pain syndrome.) *Orthopade (Berlin) 13(1), Jan 1984, 46-51.*
LEVEL: A LANG: Ger

Ducloux, M. Les etats d'ame d'un chirurgien orthopedique face aux modes chirurgicales actuelles. *Cinesiologie (Paris) 94, mars/avr 1984, 173-176.*
LEVEL: I LANG: Fr SIRC ARTICLE NO: 095915

Eriksson, E. Akuta ledbandsskador i knaeleden - diagnostik och behandling. (Acute ligament injuries of the knee--diagnosis and treatment.) *Lakartidningen (Stockholm) 81(13), 28 Mar 1984, 1261-1263.*
LEVEL: A LANG: Swe

Fairbank, J.C. Pynsent, P.B. van Poortvliet, J.A. Phillips, H. Mechanical factors in the incidence of knee pain in adolescents and young adults. *Journal of bone and joint surgery (Boston) 66(5), Nov 1984, 685-693.*
LEVEL: A LANG: Eng

Gustafson, P. Contributing factors to knee injury. (Refs: 10)*Texas coach 27(4), Jan 1984, 50.*
LEVEL: B LANG: Eng SIRC ARTICLE NO: 092862

Halpern, A.A. The Runner's World knee book: what every athlete needs to know about the prevention and treatment of knee problems. New York: Collier Books, c1984. 160 p. : ill.
LEVEL: B LANG: Eng ISBN: 0-02-014010-X LC CARD: 84-15526 RD97 20088

Heckman, J.D. Alkire, C.C. Distal patellar pole fractures: a proposed common mechanism of injury. (Refs: 19)*American journa of sports medicine (Baltimore) 12(6), Nov/Dec 1984, 424-428.*
ABST: A variety of names has been given to disorders of the inferior pole of the patella occurring in young athletic individuals and several different causes have been proposed for these disorders. Occasionally a direct blow will cause fracture of the inferior pole of the patella, but the only other mechanism which seems to be responsible is

subluxation or dislocation. Ten cases of distal patellar pole fracture secondary to dislocation or subluxation of the patella are reported. From these cases and an extensive review of the literature it is concluded that patellar subluxation or dislocation is the usual common mechanism of distal patellar pole fractures in young, active individuals and that adequate treatment of this problem must address the patellar instability as well as the fracture.
LEVEL: A LANG: Eng SIRC ARTICLE NO: 104037

Heisel, J. Schwarz, B. Meniskusschaeden im Kindes- und Jugendalter. Ursachen--Behandlung--Ergebnisse. (Meniscus injuries in childhood and adolescence. Causes--treatment--results.) *Aktuelle Traumatologie (Stuttgart) 14(3), Jun 1984, 108-114.*
ABST: A brief outline of special morphological features of meniscus structure during growth is followed by an analysis of meniscus lesions during this age period. Between 1964 and 1981, the authors performed 3,579 meniscectomies with only 19 patients between 3 and 12 years old, and 223 cases between 13 and 18 years. Whereas dysplastic changes of menisci were the main causes for meniscectomy in childhood, traumatic lesions of the menisci were prominent in adolescence. A causal relationship to regular activity in sports is assumed. 77.7 per cent of the cases could be controlled clinically after an average postoperative period of 8.5 and 10.0 years, respectively.
LEVEL: A LANG: Ger

Hermann, G. Berson, B.L. Directed medial meniscus: two cases of tears presenting as lacked knee due to athletic trauma. (Refs: 15)*American journal of sports medicine (Baltimore, Md.) 12(1), Jan/Feb 1984, 74-76.*
ABST: The arthrogram and arthroscope were useful in diagnosing the massive type of discoid medial meniscus in the 2 cases reported here. The discoid menisci became problematic after trauma. Partial meniscectomy in one case and total meniscectomy in the other case relieved the problems with uneventful recovery.
LEVEL: A LANG: Eng SIRC ARTICLE NO: 094366

Hester, J.T. Falkel, J.E. Isokinetic evaluation of tibial rotation: assessment of a stabilization technique. (Refs: 15) *Journal of orthopaedic and sports physical therapy (Baltimore, Md.) 6(1), Jul/Aug 1984, 46-51.*
ABST: The purpose of this study was to present a wide range of normative data on maximum active tibial rotation utilizing isokinetic resistance and a relatively new stabilization technique. Both legs of 25 healthy adult male subjects were tested at 30, 60, 120, and 180 degrees per second of angular velocity. Data were collected on total range of motion, component internal/external range of motion (via two different methods), joint position at peak torque production, peak torque production, and torque production as a percentage of body weight. The effect of weight and leg length on peak torque production and total range of motion was also determined. In light of recent studies which have shown the need for specific rotational rehabilitation for rotatory knee instabilities, this study serves to present normative data for practical use in either the clinical or research setting.
LEVEL: A LANG: Eng SIRC ARTICLE NO: 100723

Howse, A.J.G. Problems of the adolescent knee and their treatment. *Physiotherapy (London) 70(4),* 10 Apr 1984, 150-153.
LEVEL: I LANG: Eng SIRC ARTICLE NO: 095931

Jokl, P. Kaplan, N. Stovell, P. Keggi, K. Non-operative treatment of severe injuries to the medial and anterior cruciate ligaments of the knee. *Journal of bone and joint surgery (Boston) 66(5), Jun 1984, 741-744.*
ABST: This follow-up study reports on the results of non-operative treatment given to 28 patients (average age, 28 years) suffering from injuries to the medial and anterior cruciate ligaments of the knee. 22 patients obtained good or excellent results. Older and non-athlete patients scored the lowest.
LEVEL: A LANG: Eng SIRC ARTICLE NO: 102515

Judet, H. Bernard, P. Chirurgie reparatrice des ligaments du genou et reeducation post-operatoire en pratique sportive. *Cinesiologie 92/93, nov/dec 1983-janv/fevr 1984, 59-63.*
NOTES: Numero special: Medecine du sport et thermalisme.
RESUME: Les auteurs discutent du diagnostic et du traitement chirurgical des ruptures fraiches et anciennes des ligaments du genou. Ils decrivent les trois phases de la reeducation post-operative: la periode platree, la periode de recuperation, et la periode de readaptation a l'effort.
LEVEL: A LANG: Fr SIRC ARTICLE NO: 092870

King, J.B. Knee injuries: their nature, cause and consequence. *Medicine, science and the law (Brentford, Eng.) 24(4), Oct 1984, 243-246.*
LEVEL: I LANG: Eng

Knutzen, K.M. Bates, B.T. Hamill, J. Knee brace influences on the tibial rotation and torque patterns of the surgical limb. (Refs: 12)*Journal of orthopaedic and sports physical therapy (Baltimore, Md.) 6(2), Sept/Oct 1984, 116-122.*
ABST: Tibial rotation and torque were evaluated using a specifically designed device to assess the effects of two different knee braces on the performance of the surgically repaired knee. Six subjects, aged 21 to 28, were tested while seated in an adjustable chair which allowed the torso, pelvis, thigh, and femoral condyles to be stabilized utilizing a series of straps and brackets. The foot was immobilized by a special boot which was connected to the input shaft of a Cybex isokinetic dynamometer. Subjects were asked to maximally externally or internally rotate the tibia on the femur during two brace conditions: the surgical limb condition and the healthy limb conditon. The results indicated that there were differences across all conditions of tibial range of motion and torque with external direction values being significantly greater. Comparison between conditions yielded no significant differences; however, a consistent trend characteristic of a knee brace reduction in internal rotation and torque parameters was present.
LEVEL: A LANG: Eng SIRC ARTICLE NO: 100682

Legwold, G. Bovine xenograft fails in knee study. (Refs: 2)*Physician and sportsmedicine (Minneapolis, Minn.) 12(7), Jul 1984, 23-25.*
LEVEL: I LANG: Eng SIRC ARTICLE NO: 095941

Levine, J. Chondromalacia of the patella in female athletes. Chicago: Teach'em Inc., 1984?. 1 sound cassette : 23 35mm slide (Audio cassette series on sports medicine: Sportsmedicine for female athletes, SM-41.)
NOTES: Cassettes recorded and produced by Teach'em Inc. in cooperation with the Physician and Sportsmedicine.
LEVEL: I LANG: Eng

Lucie, R.S. Wiedel, J.D. Messner, D.G. The acute pivot shift: clinical correlation. (Refs: 11)*American journal of sports medicine (Baltimore) 12(3), May/Jun 1984, 189-191.*
CONF: American Orthopaedic Society for Sports Medicine. Interim Meeting (1982 : New Orleans).
ABST: In this study, 50 knees with acute traumatic hemarthrosis were examined under general anesthesia to assess the reliability of the pivot shift test. After arthrotomy or arthroscopy was performed, it was revealed that there were 38 knees with positive shifts, 35 with complete anterior cruciate tears, and 3 with significant partial tears of the ligament. Among their conclusions, the authors stated that the pivot shift is a direct test of anterior cruciate competence, and when performed under general anesthesia, is a very reliable test for significant tears of the ligament.
LEVEL: A LANG: Eng SIRC ARTICLE NO: 102526

Ludolph, E. Roesgen, M. Patellaluxation und femoro-patellare Dysplasie--Kausalitaet in der gesetzlichen Unfallversicherung. (Patella luxation and femoro-patellar dysplasia--causality and statutory accident insurance.) *Unfallheilkunde (Berlin) 87(6), Jun 1984, 273-276.*
LEVEL: A LANG: Ger

Lysholm, J. Nordin, M. Ekstrand, J. Gillquist, J. The effect of a patella brace on performance in a knee extension strength test in patients with patellar pain. (Refs: 16)*American journal of sports medicine (Baltimore, Md.) 12(2), Mar/Apr 1984, 110-112.*
ABST: Twenty-four patients performed knee extension exercise with and without a knee brace. Twenty-one patients (88%) improved their force development when they used the brace. These results support the assumption that the major pathology in patients with patellofemoral pain is a lateral slipping of the patella which, in the present study, was eliminated by the use of the knee brace with a lateral pad.
LEVEL: A LANG: Eng SIRC ARTICLE NO: 094429

Mariani, P.P. Serrecchia, S. Riabilitazione dopo intervento di meniscectomia artroscopica. Rehabilitation after arthroscopic meniscectomy. (Refs: 3)*Italian journal of sports traumatology (Milano, Italy) 6(2), Apr/Jun 1984, 87-92.*
ABST: A rehabilitation program after arthroscopic meniscectomy is detailed in this paper.
LEVEL: I LANG: It Eng SIRC ARTICLE NO: 099096

Mattison, R. Comment on knee basketweave. *Sports physiotherapy division (Victoria, B.C.) 9(1), Jan/Feb 1984, 24-30.*
LEVEL I LANG: Eng SIRC ARTICLE NO: 099050

Michaux, M. L'examen des affections traumatiques du genou: les 'trucs' et les 'pieges'. *Annales de kinesitherapie (Paris) 11(6), 1984, 271-278.*
LEVEL: I LANG: Fr SIRC ARTICLE NO: 099051

Murray, J. Chronic knee pain in the athlete. *Pediatric annals (New York) 13(8), Aug 1984, 613-615;618-619;621.*
LEVEL: I LANG: Eng

Nisonson, B. Hershman, E. Scott, W.N. Yost, J. The knee. (Refs: 209)
NOTES: In, Scott, W.N. (ed.) et al., Principles of sports medicine, Baltimore, Williams & Wilkins, c1984, p. 270-341.
LEVEL: A LANG: Eng RC1210 18016

INJURIES AND ACCIDENTS (continued)

Noyes, F.R. McGinniss, G.H. Mooar, L.A.
Functional disability in the anterior cruciate insufficient knee syndrome. Review of knee rating systems and projected risk factors in determining treatment. (Refs: 32)*Sports medicine (Auckland, N.Z.) 1(4), Jul/Aug 1984, 278-302.*
ABST: The complete tear of the anterior cruciate ligament initiates the clinical syndrome represented by continued functional disability. An historical review and analysis of functional and subjective rating systems is reported. A subjective and functional rating system is proposed in which 6 activity levels are related to pain, swelling, giving-way and overall activity. In addition, we propose the utilisation of a risk factor checklist, based on the statistics drawn from our previous articles, to identify those patients at significant risk for future joint arthrosis. Thirdly, we examine controversial aspects of the anterior cruciate ligament syndrome existing in the literature today. Finally we propose our treatment guidelines for management of the acute and chronic anterior cruciate ligament insufficient knee.
LEVEL: A LANG: Eng SIRC ARTICLE NO: 102530

Noyes, F.R. Keller, C.S. Grood, E.S. Butler, D.L.
Advances in the understanding of knee ligament injury, repair, and rehabilitation. (Refs: 70)*Medicine and science in sports and exercise (Indianapolis) 16(5), Oct 1984, 427-443.*
CONF: American College of Sports Medicine. Meeting (30th : 1983 : Montreal).
NOTES: Presented at the twelfth Joseph B. Wolfe Memorial Lecture, May 18-21, 1983.
ABST: This manuscript reviews contributions which the Giannestras Biomechanics Laboratory has made to the understanding of knee injury, highlighting those research findings which form the basis for their clinical treatment of knee ligament injuries. High strain-rate techniques for studying knee ligament failure have replaced the previous low strain-rate methods and distinguish the failure mechanism of ligaments from that of bone. The development of the 6-degrees-of-freedom concept and the instrumented kinematic chain now permit precise analysis of joint position, motion, and laxity.
LEVEL: A LANG: Eng SIRC ARTICLE NO: 102531

Pritsch, M. Comba, D. Frank, G. Horoszowski, H. Articular cartilage fractures of the knee. (Refs: 7)*Journal of sports medicine and physical fitness (Torino, Italy) 24(4), Dec 1984, 299-302.*
ABST: Articular cartilage fractures should be distinguished from the more frequently recognized osteochondral fractures concerning diagnostic, therapeutic and prognostic aspects. Clinically they mimic a torn meniscus and may frequently be accompanied by meniscal tears. The best way of diagnosis is by arthroscopy. Injured knees that have had traumatic hemarthrosis or persistent knee symptoms such as recurrent swelling, pain with activity or loose body symptoms after a blunt or shearing trauma of the knee should raise the suspicion of articular cartilage fractures and arthroscopy should be considered.
LEVEL: A LANG: Eng SIRC ARTICLE NO: 106532

Puddu, G. Ferretti, A. Mariani, P. La Spesa, F.
Meniscal tears and associated anterior cruciate ligament tears in athletes: course of treatment. (Refs: 4)*American journal of sports medicine (Baltimore) 12(3), May/Jun 1984, 196-198.*
ABST: The purpose of this study was to develop a rating system to determine if reconstruction of the anterior cruciate ligament (ACL) should be done if a

lesion is found during a meniscectomy. In a post-operative follow-up on 51 of 62 patients (54 men and 8 women), during a period of 2 1/2 to 7 years, 24 patients had excellent or good diagnoses as opposed to 27 with fair or poor results. On the basis of more detailed examinations, it was found that there are three variables on which the surgeon may base the indication for reconstruction of the ACL. These are: i) an objective evaluation post-meniscectomy with the jerk test, ii) the type of meniscal tear, and iii) the type of sport involved. These were given values on a point system to aid in the evaluation of need for ACL reconstruction.
LEVEL: A LANG: Eng SIRC ARTICLE NO: 102534

Puddu, G. Il caso clinico. Clinical cases. *Italian journal of sports traumatology (Milan) 6(1), Jan/Mar 1984, 79-81.*
ABST A quiz was distributed to the participatns of the Third Congress of the International Society of the Knee, outlining a clinical case which had many possible treatments. Participants were asked what they would have done and with which techniques. The author has found that particularly important standpoints emerged from this investigation. Arthroscopy has assumed a fundamental role in the identification of types of tears and has become a necessary aid in planning the intraarticular surgical treatment. Also, many respondents favoured reconstruction of the anterior cruciate ligament and/or an anterolateral peripheral reconstruction, as opposed to other techniques which would have been more common a few years ago.
LEVEL: I LANG: Eng It SIRC ARTICLE NO: 097357

Rand, J.A. The role of arthroscopy in the management of knee injuries in the athlete. *Mayo clinic proceedings (Rochester, Minn.) 59(2), Feb 1984, 77-82.*
LEVEL: I LANG: Eng SIRC ARTICLE NO: 099062

Riddell, A.J. Physiotherapy for sports injuries of the knee. *Physiotherapy (London) 70(4), 10 Apr 1984, 157-159.*
LEVEL: I LANG: Eng SIRC ARTICLE NO: 095953

Riddell, A.J. Physiotherapy for sports injuries of the knee. *Physiotherapy (London) 70(4), Apr 1984, 157-160.*
LEVEL: I LANG: Eng

Riddell, A.J. Examination of the knee. *Physiotherapy in sport (Dymchurch, Kent) 7(2), Autumn 1984, 6.*
LEVEL: B LANG: Eng SIRC ARTICLE NO: 105320

Rideout, W. Two-hinged brace protects injuried knee. *First aider (Gardner, Kan.) 53(4), Dec 1983/ Jan 1984, 23.*
LEVEL: B LANG: Eng SIRC ARTICLE NO: 094385

Roncalli-Benedetti, L. Scaraglio, C. Marchini, M.
Recent and long-established lesions of the capsular ligaments of the knee. (Refs: 12)*Italian journal of orthopaedics and traumatology (Bologna) 10(1), Mar 1984, 39-47.*
ABST: Twenty-two cases of capsulo-ligamentous lesions of the knee are discussed.
LEVEL: A LANG: Eng SIRC ARTICLE NO: 109762

Saillant, G. Benazet, J.P. Gagna, G. Roy-Camille, R. Les ruptures ligamentaires recentes du genou. (Refs: 5)*Vie medicale (Paris) 65(17/18), 1984, 665-672.*
LEVEL: I LANG: Fr

Selivanov, V.P. Sindrom lateral'noi giperpressii nadkolennika. (Lateral hyperpressive syndrome of the patella.) *Ortopediia travmatologiia i*

protezirovanie (Moscow) 7, Jul 1984, 23-28.
LEVEL: I LANG: Rus

Simonet, W.T. Lim, F.H. Repair and reconstruction of rotatory instability of the knee. (Refs: 29)*American journal of sports medicine (Baltimore, Md.) 12(2), Mar/Apr 1984, 89-97.*
ABST: This study reviews the results of treatment in 110 patients who underwent reconstruction of the knee ligaments. Patients who underwent intraarticular reconstruction of the anterior cruciate ligament combined with extraarticular repair of secondary stabilizers had significantly better treatment results compared to patients who underwent only extraarticular reconstruction. In addition acute instabilities of the knee have a better prognosis if dealt with in the acute phase rather than the chronic phase.
LEVEL: A LANG: Eng SIRC ARTICLE NO: 094390

Simonet, W.T. Sim, F.H. Symposium on sports medicine: Part I. Current concepts in the treatment of ligamentous instability o the knee. *Mayo clinic proceedings (Rochester, Minn.) 59(2), Feb 1984, 67-76.*
LEVEL: A LANG: Eng SIRC ARTICLE NO: 099070

Smidt, G.L. Albright, J.P. Deusinger, R.H. Pre- and postoperative functional changes in total knee patients. (Refs: 13) *Journal of orthopaedic and sports physical therapy (Baltimore, Md.) 6(1), Jul/ Aug 1984, 25-29.*
ABST: Objective laboratory measurements were obtained preoperatively and up to 24 months postoperatively for 102 patients (140 knees). This longitudinal study was an effort to determine changes in functional status as a result of surgery and rehabilitation. In the main, the function improved in arthritic patients who received a geometric knee implant and subsequent physical therapy in a manner described in this study. Function improved in terms of joint motion, muscle strength, standing posture, and gait in both rheumatoid and osteoarthritic groups. Some functional abnormalities which seemed to persist were deficits in knee extension motion and knee extensor strength, and that the subjects stand with the knee in a flexed position. Time asymmetries of foot placement were present during gait, patient's stance phase time and body accelerations were excessive, and body acclerations were arrhythmic in the forward-backward directions.
LEVEL: A LANG: Eng SIRC ARTICLE NO: 100697

Stebbins, F. Injury-free knees. *Fun runner 5(6), Feb/Mar 1984, 39.*
LEVEL: B LANG: Eng

Stickland, A. Examination of the knee joint. (Refs: 6)*Physiotherapy (London) 70(4), 10 Apr 1984, 144-150.*
LEVEL: I LANG: Eng SIRC ARTICLE NO: 095969

Strand, T. Engesaeter, L.B. Molster, A.O. Raugstad, T.S. Stangeland, L. Stray, O. Alho, A.
Knee function following suture of fresh tear of the anterior cruciate ligament. *Acta orthopaedica scandinavica (Copenhagen) 55(2), Apr 1984, 181-184.*
ABST: 60 patients are treated with suture of knee ligament injuries. All patients have an anterior ligament tear. A four year follow-up study shows that 11 patients are suffering from joint instability; 30 of 47 patients with negative Slocum tests have excellent function, compared with 4 of 13 patients with positive tests.
LEVEL: A LANG: Eng SIRC ARTICLE NO: 100761

Stuller, J. The Achilles' knee. Recovery from a serious injury to 'the most poorly constructed joint in the body' is never complete. Once damaged, the knee is always vulnerable. *Inside sports (Harlan, Iowa) 6, May 1984, 88-92.*
LEVEL: B LANG: Eng SIRC ARTICLE NO: 092895

Sullivan, D. Levey, I.M. Sheskier, S. Torzilli, P.A. Warren, R.F. Medical restrains to anterior-posterior motion of the knee *Journal of bone and joint surgery (Boston) 66(6), Jul 1984, 930-936.*
ABST: The authors tested cadaver knees before and after cuts to the medial structures and the anterior cruciate ligament. Load tests were performed to determine the effect of such injuries on knee joint motion.
LEVEL: A LANG: Eng SIRC ARTICLE NO: 102549

Tippett, S.R. A case study: Lennox Hill bracing for postoperative total knee replacement. (Refs: 6)*Journal of orthopaedic and sports physical therapy (Baltimore, Md.) 5(5), Mar/Apr 1984, 265-268.*
ABST: This study describes the use of the Lennox Hill brace in the management of post total knee replacement pain and instability in a 75-year-old obese female. Quadriceps strength using the Lennox Hill brace was noticeably improved as compared to quadriceps strength with no brace and with a hinge brace.
LEVEL: A LANG: Eng SIRC ARTICLE NO: 094444

Venturi, R. Chiggio, P. Prozzo, F. Sindesmoplastica dei ligamenti collaterali del ginocchio in traumatologia sportiva. Syndesmoplasty of the collateral ligaments of the knee in sports traumatology. (Refs: 22)*Italian journal of sports traumatology (Milano, Italy) 6(2), Apr/Jun 1984, 93-103.*
ABST: This paper describes injury to the collateral ligaments of the knee and presents the anatomapathological clinical and radiographic depiction of such injuries. A method of surgery is detailed in which a pedicled biceps tendon flap is used as a replacement for the lateral and gracilis tendon for the medical ligament. A follow-up study of 35 athletes who had undergone such an operation as met with excellent or good results in 25 of the subjects.
LEVEL: A LANG: It Eng SIRC ARTICLE NO: 099076

Veth, R.P.H. Jansen, H.W.B. Nielson, H.K.L. Hartel, R.M. Natural repair and reconstructive procedures in artificially made lesions of the meniscus in rabbits. (Refs: 9)*International journal of sports medicine (Stuttgart) Suppl. 5, Nov 1984, 96-97.*
CONF: International Congress on Sports and Health (1983 : Maastricht, Netherlands).
LEVEL: A LANG: Eng SIRC ARTICLE NO: 104086

Wise, H.H. Fiebert, I.M. Kates, J.L. EMG biofeedback as treatment for patellofemoral pain syndrome. (Refs: 18)*Journal of orthopaedic and sports physical therapy (Baltimore, Md.) 6(2), Sept/Oct 1984, 95-103.*
ABST: Patellofemoral pain syndrome may be classified as a dysfunction of the patella's ability to track in the femoral groove. This study integrates the concept of improved patellar tracking through selective enhancement of the vastus medialis oblique muscle with conventional exercise regimens for patellofemoral pain syndrome. Six patellofemoral pain syndrome patients were enrolled in a three-phase electromyographic biofeedback and exercise program. All six patients learned to alter their vastus medialis oblique activity

through the use of this treatment approach. The alteration of vastus medialis oblique activity resulted in an apparent change in the patellofemoral forces and a concomitant decrease in the patients' complaints of pain. These patients were able to return to pain-free functional activities in only six to nine treatment sessions within a 4- to 6-week period. The use of electromyographic biofeedback coupled with a graded exercise program is an efficient and effective treatment approach for patellofemoral pain syndrome patients.
LEVEL: A LANG: Eng SIRC ARTICLE NO: 100704

Zeman, S.C. Acute knee injury. How to determine if the knee is stable. *Postgraduate medicine (Minneapolis, Minn.) 76(8), De 1984, 38-46.*
LEVEL: A LANG: Eng

LIGAMENT INJURIES

Arms, S.W. Pope, M.H. Johnson, R.J. Fischer, R.A. Arvidsson, I. Eriksson, E. The biomechanics of anterior cruciate ligament rehabilitation and reconstruction. (Refs: 39)*American journal of sports medicine (Baltimore, Md.) 12(1), Jan/Feb 1984, 8-18.*
CONF: American Orthopaedic Society for Sports Medicine. Annual Meeting (1983: Williamsburg, Va.).
ABST: A reconstructed anterior cruciate ligament can irrate the normal ligament when inserted in a position close to the original attachment sites. It was recommended that the attachment be made at a flexion angle of 35o. Quadriceps activity did appear to strain the repair, but at knee flexion angles greater than 60o the quadriceps activity appeared to be safe.
LEVEL: A LANG: Eng SIRC ARTICLE NO: 094347

Bahbout, S. Analisi dei metodi di misura della sezione retta dei legamenti dell' articolazione del ginocchio e proposta di u nuovo metodo di misura. An analysis of methods for measuring the cross-section of knee ligaments and a proposed new method. (Refs: 19)*Italian journal of sports traumatology (Mialn) 6(1), Jan/Mar 1984, 73-78.*
ABST: A number of methods for the measurement of physical properties of knee ligaments is reviewed and critiqued in this paper. In particular, two destructive methods (i.e. afterwhich the specimens cannot be used for mechanical tests) and three non-destructive methods, for the measurement of the cross-section of a ligament, were briefly examined. The authors feel that the shortcomings of these methods are overcome by a described electrical method, by which the electrical resistance of the ligament is measured.
LEVEL: A LANG: Eng It SIRC ARTICLE NO: 097356

Baker, C.L. Norwood, L.A. Hughston, J.C. Acute combined posterior cruciate and posterolateral instability of the knee. (Refs 15)*American journal of sports medicine (Baltimore) 12(3), May/Jun 1984, 204-208.*
CONF: American Orthopaedic Society for Sports Medicine. Interim Meeting (1981 : Las Vegas).
ABST: 13 patients averaging 26 years of age underwent surgical treatment for acute combined posterior cruciate and posterolateral instability. The methods of diagnosis and the results of these patients are examined.
LEVEL: A LANG: Eng SIRC ARTICLE NO: 102488

Barton, T.M. Torg, J.S. Das, M. Posterior cruciate ligament insufficiency: a review of the literature. (Refs: 51)*Sports medicine (Auckland, N.Z.) 1(6),*

Nov/Dec 1984, 419-430.
ABST: A review of the English language literature establishes athletic mishaps as a major cause of posterior cruciate ligament injury. However, diversity of opinion exists regarding the functional significance of the lesion, its occurrence as an isolated entity, and the roles of conservative and surgical management.
LEVEL: A LANG: Eng SIRC ARTICLE NO: 102490

Burks, R. Daniel, D. Losse, G. The effect of continuous passive motion on anterior cruciate ligament reconstruction stabilit (Refs: 10)*American journal of sports medicine (Baltimore, Md.) 12(4), Jul/Aug 1984, 323-327.*
CONF: American Orthopaedic Society for Sports Medicine. Meeting (1983 : Williamsburg, Va.)
ABST: This study was undertaken to examine the immediate effect of continuous passive motion (CPM) on anterior cruciate ligament (ACL) reconstruction stability. Cadaver knees were tested with a knee arthrometer with the anterior cruciate intact and then with the anterior cruciate sectioned. One of three anterior cruciate reconstructions wa then performed and stability was restored to the knee and it was again tested with the knee arthrometer. The three operations selected where the Marshall-MacIntosh 'over-the-top,' (OTT) a patellar bone-patellar tendon-tubercle bone specimens were placed on a CPM device in a cooler at 38oF and put through a range of motion of 20 to 70o than a 2 mm increase in the post-CPM. All three bone-tendon-bone operations failed. The semitendinosis operation was successful in only three out of eight speciments. The OTT operation was successful in eight out of nine specimens.
LEVEL: A LANG: Eng SIRC ARTICLE NO: 108540

Chambat, P. Walch, G. Deschamps, G. Dejour, H. Les lesions aigues du ligament croise anterieur du genou. A propos de 71 malades revus. (Acute lesions of the anterior cruciate ligament of the knee. Apropos of 71 follow-up cases.) *Revue de chirurgie orthopedique et reparatrice de l'appareil moteur (Paris) 70(Suppl. 2), 1984, 152-155.*
LEVEL: A LANG: Fr SIRC ARTICLE NO: 104018

Chiapuzzo, A. Chiapuzzo, E. La ricostruzione del ramo anteriore del legamento talo-curural esterno nelle lesioni inveterate Surgical repair of inveterate anterior talofibular ligament lesions. (Refs: 7)*Italian journal of sports traumatology (Milano, Italy) 6(4), Oct/Dec 1984, 265-269.*
CONF: International Meeting on the Pathology of the Locomotor System (2nd: 1981: Cogoleto)
ABST: Inveterate lesions of the fascicles reinforcing the lateral side of the ankle are nearly always confined to the anterior talofibular ligament. Its reconstruction is thus sufficient to restore stability. An account is given of a personal technique in which a periosteal flap from the lateral malleolus is turned over forwards and downwards, and then sutured to the neck of the talus.
LEVEL: A LANG: It Eng SIRC ARTICLE NO: 105287

Cornwall, M.W. Leveau, B. The effect of physical activity on ligamentous strength: an overview. (Refs: 18)*Journal of orthopaedic and sports physical therapy (Baltimore, Md.) 5(5), Mar/Apr 1984, 275-277.*
ABST: The authors note that there have not been any studies regarding this topic which have adequately controlled all variables. However, despite methodological flaws, most studies seem to indicate that systematic exercise strengthens the

bone-ligament-bone complex. The actual mechanism of this increase in strength remains to be elucidated.
LEVEL: I LANG: Eng SIRC ARTICLE NO: 094592

Cross, M.J. Powell, J.F. Long-term followup of posterior cruciate ligament rupture: a study of 116 cases. (Refs: 20)*America journal of sports medicine (Baltimore, Md.) 12(4), Jul/Aug 1984, 292-297.*
CONF: International Society of the knee. Meeting (3rd : 1981 : New Orleans)
ABST: With adequate quadriceps exercises, the prognosis of a ruptured posterior cruciate ligament can be greatly improved. Of the 116 cases followed in this report, 55 were sports injuries while most of the remainder were traffic accidents. An excellent or good result was obtained in 47 sports-injured patients, while only 5 involved in road trauma obtained this result. Surgery was used to improve the eventual result and this was successful in nine cases. Early repair is still the treatment of choice. Eighty percent of ruptures can have a good or excellent result with effective management.
LEVEL: A LANG: Eng SIRC ARTICLE NO: 108535

Crova, M. Lazzarone, C. Brach del Prever, E. Botto, Micca, F. La sostituzione del legamento crociato mediante bioprotesi Xenograft. Cruciate ligament replacement by Xenograft bioprosthesis. (Refs: 21)*Italian journal of sports traumatology (Milan) 6(1), Jan/Mar 1984, 1-20.*
ABST: This investigation followed up nine cases of complete lesion of the anterior cruciate ligament, replaced surgically by a bovine tendon graft, fixed in glutaraldehyde. Six patients were males and three were females. In four of these cases, there was a failure of the bioprosthesis, which indicated another operation. Analyses of these particular cases were made on a macroscopic and microscopic level and descriptions of particular areas of the knee are made. These contradict the findings by other studies in that the prostheses showed poor resistance to weak forces upon the joint in the first months after surgery. In spite of the small number of cases, the authors suggest that care be taken in the use of these bioprostheses.
LEVEL: A LANG: Eng It SIRC ARTICLE NO: 097351

Fullerton, L.R. Andrews, J.R. Mechanical block to extension following augmentation of the anterior cruciate ligament. *American journal of sports medicine (Baltimore, Md.) 12(2), Mar/Apr 1984, 166-168.*
ABST: This case report describes some of the problems inherent in the augmentation of the anterior cruciate ligament with the medial one third of the patellar ligament. In this case full extension was limited by a calcified module in the transposed tissue and an impingement of the transposed tissue on the intercondylar notch. Surgery corrected these problems. The authors conclude that inexact placement of the transposed ligaments can cause a mechanical blockage through future hypertrophy of the transposed tissue. The authors suggest that enlargement of the intercondylar notch should be considered at the initial surgery.
LEVEL: A LANG: Eng SIRC ARTICLE NO: 094358

Gamble, J.G. Edwards, C.C. Max, S.R. Enzymatic adaptation in ligaments during immobilization. (Refs: 31)*American journal of sports medicine (Baltimore) 12(3), May/Jun 1984, 221-228.*
ABST: The purpose of this study was to describe the morphological and enzymatic changes which took place in the medial collateral ligaments, during

immobilization, in 20 experimental rabbits. After 8 weeks of immobilization, a connective tissue mat had formed over the ligament, and an atrophy of the ligament resulted in a 20 per cent reduction in its weight. LDH and MDH enzyme activities decreased significantly during this period, while some of the lysosomal hydrolase activities increased to up to 50 per cent above control levels. This indicates that a shift from an anabolic, synthetic state to a catabolic, degradative state occurs, during immobility, in the cell. From a clinical viewpoint, cast-bracing and functional splints would thus be preferred to rigid plasters in many ligamentous injuries.
LEVEL: A LANG: Eng SIRC ARTICLE NO: 102509

Gomes, J.L.E. Marczyk, L.R.S. Anterior cruciate ligament reconstruction with a loop or double thickness of smitendinosus tendon. (Refs: 30)*American journal of sports medicine (Baltimore) 12(3), May/Jun 1984, 199-203.*
ABST: This study reports the use of double loops of semitendinosus tendons in the reconstruction of 39 cases of anterior cruciate ligament damage. Candidates for surgery were those with knee instability as determined by the Anterior Drawer test, Lachman's test, and the Pivot Shift test. In each case, a portion of the semitendinosus tendon was surgically dissected and the looped free tendon was fixed tightly, in holes in the femur and tibia, by means of a bone plug, used to cat these holes. In the 26 cases, which were followed for at least two years, functional tests revealed 23 good results and 3 fair results. Based on these findings, the authors concluded that this is a good choice for surgical reconstruction of the anterior cruciate ligament.
LEVEL: A LANG: Eng SIRC ARTICLE NO: 102511

Johansson, J.E. Barrington, T.W. Coracoacromial ligament division. (Refs: 4)*American journal of sports medicine (Baltimore, Md.) 12(2), Mar/Apr 1984, 138-141.*
ABST: This paper reports the results of treatment for 40 patients who underwent simple coracoacromial ligament division for coracoacromial ligament impingement. The follow-up ranged from 8 to 76 months with an average of 36.3 months. The results were satisfactory to excellent for 95% of the shoulders. The authors conclude that the described technique is a simple and effective method of treatment for persistent painful arc syndrome secondary to coracoacromial ligament inflammation.
LEVEL: A LANG: Eng SIRC ARTICLE NO: 094368

Kieffer, D.A. Curnow, R.J. Southwell, R.B. Tucker, W.F. Kendrick, K.K. Anterior cruciate ligament arthroplasty. (Refs: 61) *American journal of sports medicine (Baltimore, Md.) 12(4), Jul/Aug 1984, 301-312.*
CONF: American Orthopaedic Society for Sports Medicine. Meeting (1981 : Lake Tahoe, CA)
ABST: From 1976 to 1983, 544 cases with known ACL insufficiency were selected for study. In 397 subsequent anterior cruciate stabilizations arthroplasties were performed. One hundred nine arthroplasties are reported: 80 isolated ACL tears and 29 multiple ligament injuries. Statistically significant relationships between elapsed time from ACL tear to surgery and meniscal tears, and elapsed time and degenerative changes in the articular surfaces were seen. No patient had failed to return to his or her original sport or occupational demands. Pivot shift, disengagement, or spontaneous rupture of the arthroplasty has not occurred postoperatively. Full participation has occurred with bilateral ACL arthroplasties and

artroplasty performed for pervious intraarticular augmentation failure. The operative success in the preliminary follow-up period was based on: ligamentous substitution, anatomical placement, femoral intercondylar notch compliance in full range of motion, revascularization of the ligament substitute, and histologic support of the procedure.
LEVEL: A LANG: Eng SIRC ARTICLE NO: 108537

Lepp, T.M. The relationship between extent of time and type of rehabilitation and present function in anterior cruciate ligament reconstruction patients. Eugene, Ore.: Microform Publications, University of Oregon, 1984. 2 microfiches : negative, ill. ; 11 x 15 cm.
NOTES: Thesis (M.S.) - University of Oregon, 1982; (ix, 119 leaves); vita; includes bibliography.
LEVEL: A LANG: Eng UO84 44-45

Lettere al direttore. (ricostruzione de crociato) Letters to the editor. (cruciate reconstruction surgery) *Italian journal of sports traumatology (Milano, Italy) 6(3), Jul/Sept 1984, 249-253.*
LEVEL: I LANG: Eng It SIRC ARTICLE NO: 102524

Lynch, J.K. Jokl, P. Regular review: sports injuries. (Refs: 2)*Annals of sports medicine (North Hollywood, Calif.) 2(1), 1984, 9-11.*
LEVEL: I LANG: Eng SIRC ARTICLE NO: 104053

Matter, P. Holzach, P. Rekonstruktion und Nachbehandlung frischer ligamentaerer Knieverletzungen. (Reconstruction and after care in recent ligamentous knee injuries.) *Helvetica chirurgica (Basel) 51(5), Nov 1984, 539-550.*
LEVEL: B LANG: Ger

Murray, S.M. Warren, R.F. Otis, J.C. Kroll, M. Wickiewicz, T.L. Torque-velocity relationships of the knee extensor and flexo muscles in individuals sustaining injuries of the anterior cruciate ligament. (Refs: 5)*American journal of sports medicine (Baltimore) 12(6), Nov/Dec 1984, 436-440.*
ABST: Muscle deficits in 58 patients with chronic anterior cruciate ligament (ACL) insufficiency were evaluated after completion of a 6 month rehabilitation program. Quadriceps and hamstring torques were measured on a modified Cybex II isokinetic dynamometer. Twenty-nine of our patients were tested just prior to undergoing ACL reconstruction, and patients who were continuing to tolerate their conditions served as controls. Of interest was the observation that the hamstring: quadriceps (H:Q) ratio was found to be both speed-position dependent. Overall, no correlation was found between the presence of strength deficits following a rehabilitation program and the need for surgery.
LEVEL: A LANG: Eng SIRC ARTICLE NO: 104067

Reider, B. Clancy, W. Langer, L.O. Diagnosis of cruciate ligament injury using single contrast arthrography. (Refs: 8) *American journal of sports medicine (Baltimore) 12(6), Nov/Dec 1984, 451-454.*
CONF: American Orthopaedic Society for Sports Medicine. Meeting (9th : 1983 : Williamsburg, Va.).
ABST: To evaluate the accuracy of arthrography for assessing the status of the anterior cruciate ligament (ACL), 212 arthrograms from 212 knees in 205 consecutive patients undergoing single contrast arthrography and subsequent arthroscopy or arthrotomy were reviewed. Criteria for evaluation of the ACL included the clarity of its radiographic appearance as well as the anterior laxity of the knee as seen on manual stress views. On the 111 knees having intact ACLs at surgery, 98 (88 per

cent) were evaluated correctly by arthrography. Of the 101 knees having a damaged ACL, 85 were read as torn or attenuated on the arthrogram. When the torn and attenuated ligaments were considered separately, accuracy was decreased. Single contrast arthrography is, therefore, highly accurate in distinguishing intact from damaged ACLs. The distinction between torn and attenuated ligaments, however, is not valuable.
LEVEL: A LANG: Eng SIRC ARTICLE NO: 104074

Rosenberg, T.D. Rasmussen, G.L. The function of the anterior cruciate ligament during anterior drawer and Lachmen's testing. (Refs: 22)*American journal of sports medicine (Baltimore, Md.) 12(4), Jul/Aug 1984, 318-322.*
CONF: American Orthopaedic Society for Sports Medicine. Meeting (1983 : Anaheim, CA)
ABST: In order to clarify the function of the anterior cruciate ligament (ACL) during clinical testing an in vivo arthroscopic method of assessing the tension of ACL was developed. Twenty young adult patients with normal knee ligaments and menisci were selected. A spring mechanism in the handle of the specially designed probe allowed the surgeon to apply a known perpendicularly directed force to the ligament while the amount of displacement was observed and recorded. Tension was determined in the anteromedial central and posterolateral portions of ACL before and during an anterior drawer test (knee flexed 90o) and before and during a Lachman's test (knee flexed 15o). The results were consistent in all 20 knees. Baseline tension was greater at 15o of flexion than at 90o. A Lachman's test produced maximal tension in the majority of the ligaments. The anterior drawer did not produce maximal tension in any portion of the ligament. Tension within the anteromedial and central portion of the ligament predominated during both uses.
LEVEL: A LANG: Eng SIRC ARTICLE NO: 108539

St. Pierre, R.K. Andrews, L. Allman, F. Fleming, L.L. The Cybex II evaluation of lateral ankle ligamentous reconstructions. (Refs: 17)*American journal of sports medicine (Baltimore, Md.) 12(1), Jan/Feb 1984, 52-56.*
CONF: American Orthopaedic Society for Sports Medicine. Anual Meeting (1983: Williamsburg, Va.).
ABST: Lateral ankle instability is corrected using the Chisman-Snook method or the Evans method. In the former procedure half of the peroneus brevis tendon is used to replace ankle ligaments; whereas, in the latter procedure the entire tendon is transected. Using the Cybex Isokinetic Dynamometer it was found that the loss of the peroneus brevis tendon did not affect the loss and power of the ankle. However both techniques left the ankles insignificantly weaker than normal ankles in a follow-up study.
LEVEL: A LANG: Eng SIRC ARTICLE NO: 094393

Stanish, W.D. Kirkpatrick, J. Rubinovich, R.M. Reconstruction of the anterior cruciate ligament with a quadricep patellar tendon graft preliminary results. (Refs: 20)*Canadian journal of applied sport sciences/Journal canadien des sciences appliquees au sport 9(1), Mar 1984, 21-24.*
ABST: This study presents the results of 50 patients who underwent reconstructive surgery of the anterior cruciate ligament using a quadricep patellar tendon graft. The surgical technique is also presented. The results indicate that this procedure can be expected to enable the majority of patients to return to sports. The authors caution that proper patient selection and adequate rehabilitation are key

factors in the success of this treatment.
LEVEL: A LANG: Eng SIRC ARTICLE NO: 092894

Trecco, F. De Paulis, F. Bonanni, G. Beomonte Zobel, B. Romanini, L. Passariello, R. Pappalardo, S. Calvisi, V. The use of computerized tomography in the study of the cruciate ligaments of the knee. *Italian journal of orthopaedics and traumatology (Bologna) 10(1), Mar 1984, 109-120.*
LEVEL: A LANG: Eng

Walker, J.M. Deep transverse frictions in ligament healing. (Refs: 16)*Journal of orthopaedic and sports physical therapy (Baltimore, Md.) 6(2), Sept/Oct 1984, 89-94.*
ABST: The purpose of this study was to examine the effect of deep transverse frictions on the healing of a minor sprain of the knee medial collateral ligament in rabbits, using histological observations. Right knees of 18 animals were manually sprained; left knees served as controls. Deep transverse frictions were given five times to six animals; ten times to six animals. It was not possible on stained tissue sections to distinguish either between sprained or unsprained ligaments, or between treated and untreated sprained ligaments. The hypothesis that deep transverse frictions promote repair of sprained ligaments is not supported by the results of this study.
LEVEL: A LANG: Eng SIRC ARTICLE NO: 100702

Wirth, C.J. Jager, M. Dynamic double tendon replacement of the posterior ligament. (Refs: 29)*American journal of sports medicine (Baltimore, Md.) 12(1), Jan/Feb 1984, 39-43.*
ABST: Replacement of a torn posterior cruciate ligament was done using the tendons of the gracilis and semitendinous muscle. The tendons were joined to the tibia via holes drilled in the femur and then in the head of the tibia. To improve the laxity in the capsule other reconstructive procedures were also performed. The dynamic surgical method to replace the posterior cruciate was felt to be successful as all 12 patients who underwent surgery returned to athletics.
LEVEL: A LANG: Eng SIRC ARTICLE NO: 094398

Woods, G.W. Chapman, D.R. Repairable posterior menisco-capsular disruption in anterior cruciate ligament injuries. (Refs: 6) *American journal of sports medicine (Baltimore, Md.) 12(5), Sept/Oct 1984, 381-385.*
ABST: Two hundred thirty-four consecutive patients with a positive Lachman test underwent examination under anesthesia and diagnostic arthroscopy to include complete evaluation of both posterior menisco-capsular attachments. Complete repairable posterior menisco-capsular disruptions occurred in 31 of 112 (27.7 per cent) acute cases and 36 of 122 (29.5 per cent) knees in the chronic group. These lesions are not predictable by physical examination or by routine clinical grading of instability.
LEVEL: A LANG: Eng SIRC ARTICLE NO: 104092

LOWER EXTREMITY INJURIES

Andrish, J.T. Overuse syndromes of the lower extremity in youth sports. (Refs: 44)*In, Boileau, R.A. (ed.), Advances in pediatric sport sciences. Volume 1: biological issues, Champaign, Ill., Human Kinetics Publishers, c1984, p. 189-202.*
LEVEL: A LANG: Eng RJ125 20044

Birrer, R.B. Common injuries of the lower extremity. (Refs: 21)

NOTES: In, Birrer, R.B. (ed.), Sports medicine for the primary care physician, Norwalk, Conn., Appleton-Century-Crofts, c1984, p. 208-238.
LEVEL: I LANG: Eng RC1210 17030

Bolz, S. Davies, G.J. Leg length differences and correlation with total leg strength. (Refs: 21)*Journal of orthopaedic and sports physical therapy (Baltimore, Md.) 6(2), Sept/Oct 1984, 123-129.*
ABST: The evaluation of leg length differences is a significant point in the examination of a patient. Many problems can result from or underlie a leg length discrepancy. These problems occur in both the average population and may be even more pronounced in a more athletic group. One problem which is hypothesized is that the leg strength of a person with leg length difference is unequal bilaterally. This paper discusses the examination, types of leg length differences, the resulting problems of a leg length difference, some basic treatments, and then report the results of a study performed to compare leg length differences with total leg strength as measured isokinetically.
LEVEL: A LANG: Eng SIRC ARTICLE NO: 100709

Durey, A. Lesions musculaires aigues des membres inferieurs du sportif. *Vie medicale (Paris) 65(17/18), 1984, 657-662.*
LEVEL: I LANG: Fr

Garrett, J.C. The lower leg. (Refs: 18)
NOTES: In, Scott, W.N. (ed.) et al., Principles of sports medicine, Baltimore, Williams & Wilkins, c1984, p. 342-347.
LEVEL: A LANG: Eng RC1210 18016

Martens, M.A. Backaert, M. Vermaut, G. Mulier, J.C. Chronic leg pain in athletes due to a recurrent compartment syndrome. (Refs: 10)*American journal of sports medicine (Baltimore, Md.) 12(2), Mar/Apr 1984, 148-151.*
ABST: This study describes the use of the wick catheter technique to determine which compartments were involved in the chronic leg pain of 29 athletic patients. Twenty-six patients had involvement of the deep posterior compartment. There were also a predominance of multiple compartment involvement as there were 43 involved compartments in the 29 patients. Fasciotomy yielded favorable results in all cases whereas conservative treatment was unsuccessful in every patient.
LEVEL: A LANG: Eng SIRC ARTICLE NO: 094375

Mayer, P.J. Lower limb injuries in childhood and adolescence. (Refs: 42)
NOTES: In, Micheli, L.J. (ed.), Pediatric and adolescent sports medicine, Boston ; Toronto, Little, Brown, c1984, p. 80-106.
LEVEL: I LANG: Eng RC1210 17791

Pedersen, J.J. Gronfeldt, W. Traeningsskader pa underekstremiteterne hos vaernepligtige. (Training injuries of the lower limbs in recruits.) *Ugeskrift for laeger (Copenhagen) 146(15), 9 Apr 1984, 1168-1171.*
LEVEL: I LANG: Dan

MUSCLE CRAMPS AND SORENESS

Armstrong, R.B. Mechanisms of exercise-induced delayed onset muscular soreness: a brief review. (Refs: 148)*Medicine and science in sports and exercise (Indianapolis) 16(6), Dec 1984, 529-538.*
ABST: Delayed-onset muscular soreness (DOMS) can adversely affect muscular performance, both from voluntary reduction of effort and from inherent

loss of capacity of the muscles to produce force. A number of clinical correlates are associated with DOMS, including elevations in plasma enzymes, myoglobinemia, and abnormal muscle histology and ultrastructure; exertional rhabdomyolysis appears to be the extreme form of DOMS. Presently, the best treatment for DOMS appears to be muscular activity, although the sensation again returns following the exercise. Training for the specific contractile activity that causes DOMS reduces the soreness response.
LEVEL: A LANG: Eng SIRC ARTICLE NO: 104275

Bonnet, P. Moline, J. A quel type de perturbations correspondent les crampes chez un sportif qui fait des competitions de tennis? (Refs: 4)*Revue de medecine de Tours (France) 18(8-1), 1984, 973-974.*
LEVEL: B LANG: Fr

Francis, K.T. Delayed muscle soreness. *Sports medicine digest (Van Nuys, Calif.) 6(10), Oct 1984, 6.*
LEVEL: B LANG: Eng SIRC ARTICLE NO: 102507

Friden, J. Kjoerell, U. Thornell, L.E. Delayed muscle soreness and cytoskeletal alterations: an immunocytological study in man. (Refs: 18)*International journal of sports medicine 5(1), Feb 1984, 15-18.*
ABST: The purpose of this study was to investigate whether the intermediate filament system is affected in delayed muscle soreness caused by eccentric work. Biopsies taken from six males suffering from severe post-exercise muscle soreness showed abundant longitudinal 'desmin' extensions. Normally desmin is thought to act as a structural protein; the disruption of desmin indicates that the intermediate filament system as well as the myofibrils themselves are disrupted in a delayed muscle soreness. The authors also observed that there was increased lysosomal activity present in the muscles subjected to intense, eccentric exercise.
LEVEL: A LANG: Eng SIRC ARTICLE NO: 093089

Friden, J. Muskelsmaerta efter fysisk traening. (Muscular pain after physical training.) *Lakartidningen (Stockholm) 81(18), 2 May 1984, 1825-1826.*
LEVEL: B LANG: Swe

Friden, J. Muscle soreness after exercise: implications of morphological changes. (Refs: 76)*International journal of sports medicine (Stuttgart, FRG) 5(2), Apr 1984, 57-66.*
ABST: The author reviews the literature on techniques used to study muscle soreness: ergographic techniques, biochemical techniques, EMG techniques, rating scale techniques, and morphological techniques. Etiological factors are also considered.
LEVEL: A LANG: Eng SIRC ARTICLE NO: 108519

Leigh, D. Strrrrretch the distance between you and your next sore muscle by knowing causes and cures. (Refs: 4)*CardioGram (La Crosse, Wis.) 11(2), Feb/Mar 1984, 2-3.*
LEVEL: B LANG: Eng SIRC ARTICLE NO: 097576

Morgan, J.D. Leg cramps: night or day - they hurt. *World water skiing (Winter Park, Fla.) 6(5), Aug 1984, 12.*
LEVEL: B LANG: Eng SIRC ARTICLE NO: 104065

Physiology of muscle soreness - cause and relief. (Refs: 1)*Grasp (New Plymouth, N.Z.) 3(3), 1984,*

46-47.
LEVEL: I LANG: Eng SIRC ARTICLE NO: 099058

Sjoestroem, M. Friden, J. Muscle soreness and muscle structure. (Refs: 28)
CONF: International Course on Physiology and Biochemistry of Exercise and Detraining (2nd : 1982 : Nice).
NOTES: In, Marconnet, P. (ed.) et al., Physiological chemistry of training and detraining, New York, Karger, c1984, p. 169-186.
LEVEL: A LANG: Eng RC1235 17596

Stamford, B. Why do your muscles get sore? *Physician and sportsmedicine (Minneapolis, Minn.) 12(11), Nov 1984, 147.*
LEVEL B LANG: Eng SIRC ARTICLE NO: 100698

MUSCLE INJURIES

Aso, K. Torisu, T. Muscle belly tear of the triceps. (Refs: 6)*American journal of sports medicine (Baltimore) 12(6), Nov/De 1984, 485-487.*
ABST: Triceps injury at the tendo-osseous junction of the olecranon is not uncommon, but a muscle belly tear of the triceps is extremely rare. Two cases of muscle belly tears of triceps are reported. One case was treated surgically and the other conservatively.
LEVEL: A LANG: Eng SIRC ARTICLE NO: 104012

Baker, B.E. Current concepts in the diagnosis and treatment of musculotendinous injuries. (Refs: 26)*Medicine and science in sports and exercise (Indianapolis) 16(4), Aug 1984, 323-327.*
ABST: A strain, by definition, is a stretching or tearing of a musculotendinous unit. The degree of disability associated with this injury is dietated by the location and severity of the injury and the specific needs of the patient. Swelling, bleeding, and localized discomfort accompany the injury which may produce temporary disability. Initial treatment following an acute strain should consist of the use of ice, immobilization of the musculotendinous unit, and subsequent rehabilitation. Depending on the degree of disability and the specific structure injured, surgery may be indicated. Rehabilitation to a normal state following the initial healing phase is required prior to return to athletic competition.
LEVEL: I LANG: Eng SIRC ARTICLE NO: 102487

Carcy, J.B. Barbut, J.P. Granier, J.L. Turblin, J. L'elongation musculaire: une micro-dechirure precisee par l'echographie. Applications pratiques. (Refs: 9)*Cinesiologie (Paris) 96, juil/aout 1984, 314-318.*
LEVEL: I LANG: Fr SIRC ARTICLE NO: 099035

Carlson, W.O. Klassen, R.A. Myositis ossificans of the upper extremity: a long-term follow-up. *Journal of pediatric orthopedics (New York) 4(6), Nov 1984, 693-696.*
LEVEL: A LANG: Eng

Cooperman, J.M. Case studies: isolated strain of the tensor fasciae latae. (Refs: 7)*Journal of orthopaedic and sports physical therapy (Baltimore) 5(4), Jan/Feb 1984, 201-203.*
ABST: This paper reviews three isolated cases of isolated strains of the tensor fasciae latae (TFL) muscle. Some differentiation between the iliotibial band and the TFL seems to be indicated, since isolated strains of the TFL may occur with or without iliotibial band involvement. Effective treatment usually consists of rest, heat, and

flexibility exercises.
LEVEL: I LANG: Eng SIRC ARTICLE NO: 092853

Garrett, W.E. Califf, J.C. Bassett, F.H. Histochemical correlates of hamstring injuries. (Refs: 51)*American journal of sports medicine (Baltimore, Md.) 12(2), Mar/Apr 1984, 98-103.*
ABST: This study determined the fibre distribution in the hamstring muscles of ten autopsy specimens. The data indicate that the hamstrings contain a relatively high proportion of Type II fibres. All ten specimens had more than 50% Type II fibres in all seven of the hamstrings biopsy sites. Thus, in order to ensure adequate injury prevention and rehabilitation, the hamstrings must be trained at an intensity using the overload principle.
LEVEL: A LANG: Eng SIRC ARTICLE NO: 094359

Henry, C. Muscle injuries: prevention and treatment. (Refs: 4)*Texas coach (Austin, Tex.) 28(3), Oct 1984, 24-27.*
LEVEL: B LANG: Eng SIRC ARTICLE NO: 173202

Imbriglia, J.E. Boland, D.M. An exercise-induced compartment syndrome of the dorsal forearm--a case report. *Journal of hand surgery (St. Louis) 9A(1), Jan 1984, 142-143.*
LEVEL: I LANG: Eng SIRC ARTICLE NO: 099043

Kihlstroem, M. Salminen, A. Vihko, V. Prednisolone decreases exercise-induced acid hydrolase response in mouse skeletal muscle. (Refs: 23)*European journal of applied physiology and occupational physiology (Berlin, W.G.) 53(1), 1984, 53-56.*
ABST: Male mice were subjected to exhaustive treadmill exercise. 3 and 6 days after the exertion, quadriceps femoris muscles were examined histologically and analyzed for acid hydrolases in order to follow the degree and progress of injuries. Prednisolone (PRED), an anti-inflammatory corticosteroid, was given to some of the animals. The activities of both arylsulphatase and B-glycuronidase increased significantly in the exercise control group after 3 and 6 days. The increase in activity correlated with fibre necrosis and an abundant infiltration of inflammatory cells, and was greatest after 3 days. After 6 days the inflammatory response decreased and regenerating muscle fibres were seen. PRED decreased the exercise-induced acid hydrolase response. PRED also diminished degeneration and inflammation.
LEVEL: A LANG: Eng SIRC ARTICLE NO: 104328

Krummel, J. Muscle injuries and their treatment. *NAIA news (Kansas, Mo.) 33(5), Apr/May 1984, 32.*
LEVEL: B LANG: Eng SIRC ARTICLE NO: 097574

Oakes, B.W. Hamstring muscle injuries. *Australian family physician (Sydney) 13(8), Aug 1984, 587-591.*
LEVEL: A LANG: Eng

Oraval, S. Sorasto, A. Aalto, K. Kvist, H. Total rupture of pectoralis major muscle in athletes. (Refs: 8)*International journal of sports medicine (Stuttgart) 5(5), Oct 1984, 272-274.*
ABST: Five cases of total rupture of the pectoralis major muscle treated in athletes are reported. Two of them had made an extremely exerted effort in weight lifting, one was ice hockey match, and one injured his pectoralis major muscle while pushing himself up from a swimming pool. In two cases the diagnosis was made early and in three cases 2-4 months after the injury. All of the patients were male and were treated successfully with surgery.
LEVEL: A LANG: Eng SIRC ARTICLE NO: 104071

Percy, E.C. Telep, G.N. Anomalous muscle in the leg: soleus accessorium. (Refs: 19)*American journal of sports medicine (Baltimore) 12(6), Nov/ Dec 1984, 447-450.*
ABST: In the last 4 years the authors have had the opportunity to investigate an anomalous muscle mass on the medial aspect of the distal leg of three young athletes. A review of the clinical literature had revealed only nine reported cases of a similar muscle mass in this area. Surgical exploration was carried out in three cases with relief of symptoms in two of the cases following decompression of the overlying fascial sheath. The authors believe this muscle to represent the soleus accessorius and its presence, which may be rare. The presence of this muscle should be considered in the differential diagnosis of a symptomatic or asymptomatic mass of the posteromedial aspect of the distal leg. Surgical exploration and fascial release is recommended.
LEVEL: A LANG: Eng SIRC ARTICLE NO: 104072

Pillet, J. Delaby, J. Legroux, P. Wullaert, P. Cronier, P. La desinsertion du jumeau interne. (Chef medical ou gastroctemien (Refs: 6)*Medecine du sport (Paris) 58(3), 25 mai 1984, 33-35.*
LEVEL: I LANG: Fr SIRC ARTICLE NO: 095950

Saillant, G. La place de la chirurgie dans le traitement des accidents musculaires. *Revue de l'Amicale des entraineurs francais d'athletisme (Paris) 89, oct/nov/dec 1984, 5-6.*
LEVEL: B LANG: Fr SIRC ARTICLE NO: 102538

Saint-Blanquat, C. Les accidents du muscle vus par le kinesitherapeute. (Refs: 3)*Revue de l'Amicale des entraineurs francai d'athletisme (Paris) 89, oct/nov/dec 1984, 7-8.*
LEVEL: B LANG: Fr SIRC ARTICLE NO: 102539

Senecail, B. Courgeon, P. Quelques aspects echographiques de la pathologie musculaire traumatique du sportif. (Refs: 4) *Cinesiologie (Paris) 94, mars/avr 1984, 161-165.*
LEVEL: B LANG: Fr SIRC ARTICLE NO: 095962

Sutton, G. Hamstrung by hamstring strains: a review of the literature. (Refs: 40)*Journal of orthopaedic and sports physical therapy (Baltimore) 5(4), Jan/Feb 1984, 184-195.*
ABST: This paper reviews many of the studies which deal with aspects of hamstring muscle strains. Areas of review include: the anatomy of the hamstring muscle group; the biomechanics of the hamstring muscles; the mechanisms of hamstring strain; and the etiologies of hamstring strain. The evaluation of the hamstring muscles through various tests of strength and flexibility is also considered and several recommendations are made for hamstring strain prevention and care.
LEVEL: A LANG: Eng SIRC ARTICLE NO: 092896

Valk, P. Muscle localization of Tc-99m MDP after exertion. *Clinical nuclear medicine (Philadelphia) 9(9), Sept 1984, 493-494.*
LEVEL: A LANG: Eng

Wilson, F.R. Repetitive strain injuries. (letter) *Medical journal of Australia (Sydney) 140(5), 3 Mar 1984, 307-308.*
LEVEL: B LANG: Eng SIRC ARTICLE NO: 099077

MUSCULOSKELETAL INJURIES

Bouchier-Hayes, T.A.I. Naproxen sodium and piroxicam in acute musculo-skeletal disorders. (Refs: 6)*British journal of sport medicine (Loughborough, Eng.) 18(2), Jun 1984, 80-83.*

ABST: Of one hundred patients originally entered for this trial eighty-three with acute musculo-skeletal disorders were treated with either naproxen sodium (SYNFLEX, Syntex), 550 mg initially followed by 275 mg four times daily, or piroxicam (FELDENE, Pfizer), 20 mg twice daily for two days then 20 mg once daily. No statistically significant differences were detected between the treatment groups for any of the efficacy measurements. Of the eighty-three patients analysed, twenty-four patients withdrew from treatment twenty of whom did not need further analgesia (13 in the naproxen sodium group and 7 in the piroxicam group). Three patients experienced side-effects; all were in the piroxicam group, and one patient withdrew from the study because of epigastric pain. Both naproxen sodium and piroxicam proved effective in the treatment of musculo-skeletal disorders. Naproxen sodium did not give rise to any side-effects.
LEVEL: A LANG: Eng SIRC ARTICLE NO: 102495

Commandre, F. Gagnerie, F. Lesions radiologiques chroniques du sport. Incidences thermales et hydrotherapiques. (Refs: 13) *Cinesiologie 92/93, nov/dec 1983-janv/fevr 1984, 51-57.*
NOTES: Numero special: Medecine du sport et thermalisme.
LEVEL: I LANG: Fr SIRC ARTICLE NO: 092852

Fuller, P.J. Musculotendinous leg injuries. *Australian family physician (Sydney) 13(7), Jul 1984, 495-498.*
LEVEL: I LANG: Eng

Geesink, R.G.T. Drukker, J. van der Linden, A.J. Stress response of articular cartilage. (Refs: 4)*International journal of sports medicine (Stuttgart) Suppl. 5, Nov 1984, 100-101.*
CONF: International Congress on Sports and Health (1983 : Maastricht, Netherlands).
LEVEL: A LANG: Eng SIRC ARTICLE NO: 104116

Helbing, G. Transplantation of chondrocytes in cartilage defects. (Refs: 3)*International journal of sports medicine (Stuttgart) Suppl. 5, Nov 1984, 136-139.*
CONF: International Congress on Sports and Health (1983 : Maastricht, Netherlands).
LEVEL: A LANG: Eng SIRC ARTICLE NO: 104039

Keats, T.E. The spectrum of musculoskeletal stress injury. *Current problems in diagnostic radiology (Chicago) 13(2), Mar/Ap 1984, 7-51.*
LEVEL: A LANG: Eng SIRC ARTICLE NO: 102517

Picard, H. Valton, C. Sport, thermalisme et oligo-elements en pathologie osteo-articulaire et O.R.L. (Refs: 10)*Cinesiologie 92/93, nov/dec 1983-janv/fevr 1984, 75-80;83-84.*
NOTES: Numero special: Medecine du sport et thermalisme.
RESUME: Les auteurs discutent de l'utilisation des oligo-elements dans le traitements des pathologies osteo-articulaires et musculo-tendineuses. Ils expliquent le role joue par quelques uns de ces elements. La crenotherapie est percue comme le moyen privilegie, simple et facile de la cure par les oligo-elements.
LEVEL: A LANG: Fr SIRC ARTICLE NO: 092884

Rios, J.C. Preventing exercise-related injuries. *Cardiac alert (Bethesda, Md.) 6(2), Feb 1984, 8.*
LEVEL: B LANG: Eng SIRC ARTICLE NO: 097579

Stanish, W. Sports medicine: the state of restoration, enhancement, and rehabilitation. *Canadian Academy of Sports Medicine newsletter*

(Ottawa) 5(3), 1984, 30-32.
LEVEL: I LANG: Eng SIRC ARTICLE NO: 100699

van Mameren, H. Drukker, J. A functional anatomical basis of injuries to the ligamentum and other soft tissues around the elbow joint: transmission of tensile and compressive loads. (Refs: 16)*International journal of sports medicine (Stuttgart) Suppl. 5, Nov 1984, 88-92.*
CONF: International Congress on Sports and Health (1983 : Maastricht, Netherlands).
LEVEL: A LANG: Eng SIRC ARTICLE NO: 104085

NECK INJURIES

Commandre, F. Osteo-articular rheumatism and sport. (Refs: 7)*Olympic review (Lausanne, Switzerland) 198, Apr 1984, 255-258.*
LEVEL: I LANG: Eng SIRC ARTICLE NO: 094352

Commandre, F. Rhumatismes osteo-articularies et sport. *Revue olympique (Lausanne) 198, avr 1984, 255-258.*
LEVEL: I LANG: SIRC ARTICLE NO: 095909

Shankman, G.A. Prevention of cervical spine injuries in high school athletics: physiological aspects. (Refs: 17)*National Strength & Conditioning Association journal (Lincoln, Neb.) 6(2), Apr/May 1984, 40;65-67.*
LEVEL: I LANG: Eng SIRC ARTICLE NO: 094388

Shankman, G.A. Prevention of cervical spine injuries in high school athletics: practical aspects. *National Strength & Conditioning Association journal (Lincoln, Neb.) 6(2), Apr/May 1984, 41;63-64.*
LEVEL: B LANG: Eng SIRC ARTICLE NO: 094389

Young, R. Head and neck injuries primary assessment and treatment. *Journal of the Canadian Athletic Therapists Association (Oakville, Ont.) 11(2), Fall 1984, 9-12.*
LEVEL: B LANG: Eng SIRC ARTICLE NO: 104093

NERVE INJURIES

Crielaard, J.M. Franchimont, P. Chronique en pathologie osteo-articulaire. L'attente isolee du nerf sus-scapulaire en medecine du sport. A propos de deux cas. (Chronicles in osteoarticular pathology. Isolated involvement of the suprascapular nerve in sports medicine. Apropos of 2 cases.) *Revue medicale de Liege: journal du practicien (Liege) 39(24), 15 dec 1984, 886-888.*
LEVEL: A LANG: Fr

Kushner, S. Reid, D.C. Medial tarsal tunnel syndrome: a review. (Refs: 29)*Journal of orthopaedic and sports physical therap (Baltimore, Md.) 6(1), Jul/Aug 1984, 39-45.*
ABST: The medial tarsal tunnel syndrome is a compression neuropathy involving the tibial nerve or its branches as they pass through the tarsal tunnel under the flexor retinaculum. This syndrome can lead to a painful burning sensation in the medial border of the foot and into the great toe. In its fullest extent medial tarsal tunnel syndrome can involve sensory changes in the heel and the lateral part of the sole of the foot as well as the remaining toes. In addition, it may lead to weakness of the intrinsic muscles of the foot. This syndrome often goes unrecognized or misdiagnosed particularly in the athlete. While medial tarsal tunnel syndrome may respond initially to nonoperative techniques of ultrasound and modification of footwear, as it progresses surgical release of the nerve in the

tunnel will be required for optimal results. This paper reviews the anatomy, etiology, pathology, clinical presentation, and treatment of the medial tarsal tunnel syndrome.
LEVEL: A LANG: Eng SIRC ARTICLE NO: 100683

Mendell, J.R. The nervous system. (Refs: 100) NOTES: In, Strauss, R.H. (ed.), Sports medicine, Philadelphia ; Toronto, Saunders, 1984, p. 149-174.
LEVEL: A LANG: Eng RC1210 17196

Worth, R.M. Kettelkamp, D.B. Delalque, R.J. Duane, K.V. Saphenous nerve entrapment: a cause of medical knee pain. (Refs: 2) *American journal of sports medicine (Baltimore, Md.) 12(1), Jan/Feb 1984, 80-81.*
ABST: Saphenous knee entrapment involves medical knee pain. In the cases sited in this study 10 out of 14 occurred following knee surgery. Treatment by neurectomy, ligation of the nerve and resection distal to the ligation, provided pain relief more consistantly than neurolysis, splitting the fascia to free the nerve. A numbness in the area innervated by the saphenous nerve also occurred, but did not seem to bother the patients.
LEVEL: A LANG: Eng SIRC ARTICLE NO: 094401

NOSE INJURIES

Mazzetta, F. Venturino, G. Stellatelli, M. Nuova metodica nella contenzione delle fratture delle ossa nasali negli sportivi. A new technique for the containment of nasal fractures in sportsmen. (Refs: 22)*Italian journal of sports traumatology (Milano, Italy) 6(4), Oct/Dec 1984, 283-291.*
ABST: Several techniques are available for the containment of nasal bone fractures after reduction. It is particularly valuable where the patient is a sportsman needing quickly to recover physically and psychologically in order to return to the practice of his sport, but also offers full protection of the nasal pyramid and complete immobilisation of the reset bone fragments. The cast in question consists of a piece of gauze impregnated with an anallergic stiffening substance which is modelled on the patients and secured with adhesive tape.
LEVEL: A LANG: It Eng SIRC ARTICLE NO: 105308

OCCURRENCE

Dowey, K.E. Preliminary report - sports injury clinic. *Ulster medical journal (Belfast) 53(1), 1984, 88-92.*
LEVEL: I LANG Eng SIRC ARTICLE NO: 104031

Ediriweera, S.A. Accidental trauma. *Ceylon medical journal (Colombo) 29(1), Mar 1984, 3-22.*
LEVEL: A LANG: Eng

Helal, B. Physical risks in modern sport. *Medicine, science and the law (Brentford, Eng.) 24(4), Oct 1984, 247-248.*
LEVEL I LANG: Eng

Kraus, J.F. Conroy, C. Mortality and morbidity from injuries in sports and recreation. (Refs: 97)*Annual review of public health (Palo Alto, Calif.) 5, 1984, 163-192.*
LEVEL: A LANG: Eng SIRC ARTICLE NO: 102520

Lorentzon, R. Johnasson, C. Bjoernstig, U. Analys av idrottsskador och samhaellskostnad i ett nordligt sjukvardsdistrikt. Fotbollen orsakar flest skador men badmintonskadan aer dyrast. (Analysis of athletic injuries and the cost to society at a northern health care region. Soccer is the cause of most of the injuries but badminton is the most expensive.) *Lakartidningen (Stockholm) 81(5), 1 Feb 1984, 340-343.*
LEVEL: A LANG: Swe

Tointon, J.A. Sports injuries in the Services 1969-1980. *Journal of the Royal Army Medical Corps (London) 130(3), Oct 1984, 193-197.*
ABST: The incidence of sport injuries in the Armed Services was recorded between 1969 and 1980. There were on average 2135 injuries annually with the trend falling over time until 1979 and then rising. Soccer accounted for 43 percent of the injuries. 85 percent of the injuries occurred in soldiers under 30.
LEVEL: A LANG: Eng

OVERUSE SYNDROME

McKeag, D.B. The concept of overuse. The primary care aspects of overuse syndromes in sports. (Refs: 17)*Primary care: clinics in office practice (Philadelphia) 11(1), Mar 1984, 43-59.*
LEVEL: I LANG: Eng SIRC ARTICLE NO: 100688

Segesser, B. L'etiologie des blessures et des lesions de surcharge dues a la pratique sportive. *Revue medicale de la Suisse romande (Lausanne) 104(10), oct 1984, 779-782.*
LEVEL: I LANG: Fr SIRC ARTICLE NO: 174095

Sperryn, P. Injury stops play. *New scientist (London) 1415, 2 Aug 1984, 27-29.*
NOTES: The performance of elite athletes today is limited largely by how much punishment their bodies can take before they break down.
LEVEL: B LANG: Eng SIRC ARTICLE NO: 099071

Staeheli, J.W. Lehn, T.A. Sim, F.H. Overuse injuries of the shoulder. (Refs: 5)*Sideline view (Minneapolis, Minn.) 5(9), Apr 1984, 1-4.*
LEVEL: I LANG: Eng SIRC ARTICLE NO: 092893

Stanish, W.D. Overuse injuries in athletes: a perspective. (Refs: 23)*Medicine and science in sports and exercise 16(1), 1984, 1-7.*
ABST: Overuse injuries have become far more frequent in recent years as a result of increased sport participation. The etiological factors of various types of overuse injuries are discussed with respect to genetic and environment causes. Total rest is no longer seen as the best method of treatment due to muscle atrophy. Analysis and correction of underlying mechanical problems appear to be fundamental to successful treatment.
LEVEL: A LANG: Eng SIRC ARTICLE NO: 091487

PAIN

Abstracts: pain. *Sports physiotherapy division (Victoria, B.C.) 9(1), Jan/Feb 1984, 18-23.*
LEVEL: I LANG: Eng SIRC ARTICLE NO: 099030

Davis, J.C. Analgesic and psychoactive drugs in the chronic pain patient. (Refs: 7)*Journal of orthopaedic and sports physical therapy (Baltimore, Md.) 5(6), May/Jun 1984, 315-317.*
LEVEL: I LANG: Eng SIRC ARTICLE NO: 100535

Drummond, P.D. Extracranial vascular changes during headache, exercise and stress. (Refs: 13)*Journal of psychosomatic research (Oxford) 28(2), 1984, 133-138.*
LEVEL: A LANG: Eng SIRC ARTICLE NO: 109695

Ducloux, M. Les etats d'ame d'un chirurgien orthopedique face aux modes chirurgicales actuelles. *Cinesiologie (Paris) 94, mars/avr 1984, 173-176.*
LEVEL: I LANG: Fr SIRC ARTICLE NO: 095915

Guck, T.P. Stress management for chronic pain patients. (Refs: 10)*Journal of orthopaedic and sports physical therapy (Baltimore, Md.) 6(1), Jul/Aug 1984, 5-7.*
LEVEL: I LANG: Eng SIRC ARTICLE NO: 100721

Le Jeune, J.J. Rochcongar, P. Vazelle, F. Bernard, A.M. Herry, J.Y. Ramee, A. Pubic pain syndrome in sportsmen: comparison o radiographic and scintigraphic findings. *European journal of nuclear medicine (Heidelberg) 9(6), 1984, 250-253.*
LEVEL: I LANG: Eng SIRC ARTICLE NO: 104051

Meilman, P.W. Chronic pain: the nature of the problem. (Refs: 4)*Journal of orthopaedic and sports physical therapy (Baltimore, Md.) 5(6), May/Jun 1984, 307-308.*
LEVEL: I LANG: Eng SIRC ARTICLE NO: 100738

Meilman, P.W. Chronic pain: basic assumptions regarding treatment. (Refs: 6)*Journal of orthopaedic and sports physical therapy (Baltimore, Md.) 5(6), May/Jun 1984, 308-310.*
LEVEL: I LANG: Eng SIRC ARTICLE NO: 100739

Meilman, P.W. Choices for dealing with chronic pain. (Refs: 8)*Journal of orthopaedic and sports physical therapy (Baltimore Md.) 5(6), May/Jun 1984, 310-312.*
LEVEL: I LANG: Eng SIRC ARTICLE NO: 100740

Meilman, P.W. Legitimizing chronic pain. (Refs: 7)*Journal of orthopaedic and sports physical therapy (Baltimore, Md.) 5(6), May/Jun 1984, 312-315.*
LEVEL: I LANG: Eng SIRC ARTICLE NO: 100741

Meilman, P.W. Chronic pain: the benefits of being sick. (Refs: 9)*Journal of orthopaedic and sports physical therapy (Baltimore, Md.) 6(1), Jul/Aug 1984, 7-9.*
LEVEL: I LANG: Eng SIRC ARTICLE NO: 100742

Schaefer, C.A. Letter to the editor. *Journal of orthopaedic and sports physical therapy (Baltimore, Md.) 6(3), Nov/Dec 1984 208.*
LEVEL: B LANG: Eng SIRC ARTICLE NO: 102542

Siracusano, G. The physical therapist's use of exercise in the treatment of chronic pain. (Refs: 13)*Journal of orthopaedic and sports physical therapy (Baltimore, Md.) 6(2), Sept/Oct 1984, 73-88.*
LEVEL: I LANG: Eng SIRC ARTICLE NO: 100755

Siracusano, G. Problems faced by the physical therapist in the treatment of chronic pain. (Refs: 14)*Journal of orthopaedic and sports physical therapy (Baltimore, Md.) 6(1), Jul/Aug 1984, 3-5.*
LEVEL: I LANG: Eng SIRC ARTICLE NO: 100756

Skultety, F.M. The management of the chronic pain patient: clinical considerations. (Refs: 6)*Journal of orthopaedic and sports physical therapy (Baltimore, Md.) 5(6), May/Jun 1984, 305-307.*
LEVEL: I LANG: Eng SIRC ARTICLE NO: 100757

Vecchiet, L. Marini, I. Colozzi, A. Feroldi, P. Effects of aerobic exercise on muscular pain sensitivity. *Clinical therapeutics (Princeton, N.J.) 6(3), 1984, 354-363.*
LEVEL: A LANG: Eng SIRC ARTICLE NO: 102550

PARALYSIS

Abramson, A.S. Exercise in paraplegia. (Refs: 17)
NOTES: In, Basmajian, J.V. (ed.), Therapeutic
exercise, 4th ed., Baltimore Md., Williams &
Wilkins, c1984, p. 339-356.
LEVEL: A LANG: Eng RM719 17505

Lemaire Prevention des complications
orthopediques. (Prevention of orthopedic
complications.) *Revue de l'infirmiere (Paris) 34(9),
May 1984, 39-44.*
LEVEL: I LANG: Fr SIRC ARTICLE NO: 102459

Nicklas, K. Auswirkungen massiver
Gesundheitsschaeden auf die Lebenssituation der
Betroffenen und Formen der Kompensation:
aufgezeigt am Beispiel von Querschnittgelaehmten
und Herzinfarktpatienten... Koeln: Deutsche
Sporthochschule, Institut fuer Rehabilitation und
Behindertensport, 1984. 283 p.
NOTES: Thesis (Ph.D.) - Deutsche
Sporthochschule Koeln, 1984. Bibliography: p. 250-
280.
LEVEL: A LANG: Ger RD795 17682

Swenson, J.R. Therapeutic exercise in hemiplegia.
(Refs: 91)
NOTES: In, Basmajian, J.V. (ed.), Therapeutic
exercise, 4th ed. Baltimore, Md., Williams &
Wilkins, c1984, p. 357-380.
LEVEL: A LANG: Eng RM719 17505

Wynn Parry, C.B. Vicarious motions (trick
movements). (Refs: 5)
NOTES: In, Basmajian, J.V. (ed.), Therapeutic
exercise, 4th ed., Baltimore, Md., Williams &
Wilkins, c1984, p. 179-191.
LEVEL: A LANG: Eng RM719 17505

PELVIC INJURIES

Goldman, M.S. Repair of shattered solitary testicle.
*Urology (Ridgewood, N.J.) 24(3), Sept 1984, 229-
231.*
ABST: A shattered testicle with complete
eventration of the semin ferous tubules was
surgically repaired with resultant satisfactory
function. Principles of management in testicular
trauma are reviewed briefly.
LEVEL: I LANG: Eng SIRC ARTICLE NO: 104034

PREVENTION

Adams, S.H. Adrian, M. Bayless, M.A.
Catastrophic injuries in sports: avoidance
strategies. Salinas, Calif.: Coyote Press, c1984. v,
139 p. : ill.
NOTES: Bibliography: p. 137-139.
LEVEL: I LANG: Eng RD97 19088

Adrian, M. Action model to evaluate and reduce
risk of catastrophic injuries. In, Adams, S.H. (ed.),
et al., Catastrophic injuries in sports: avoidance
strategies, Salinas, Calif., Coyote Press, c1984, p.
125-130.
LEVEL: B LANG: Eng RD97 19088

Carlson, R. Spalding, C. KeHogg, D. Coping with
exercise injuries: exercising doesn't have to be a
pain if you take some simple precautions that will
help you avoid the hurt and enjoy your workouts to
the fullest. *Fit (Mountain View, Calif.) 4(3), Aug
1984, 28-32.*
LEVEL: B LANG: Eng SIRC ARTICLE NO: 102498

Deloupy, H. Reflexions sur la pratique des sports.
*Homeopathie francaise (Paris) 72(5), 1984, 321-
324.*
LEVEL: B LANG: Fr

Durst, L. Athletes discover weaknesses with aid of
computer. *First aider (Gardner, Kans.) 54(1), Sept
1984, 1;4.*
LEVEL: B LANG: Eng SIRC ARTICLE NO: 105292

Greensher, J. Prevention of childhood injuries.
*Pediatrics (Evanston, Ill.) 74(5 Pt 2), Nov 1984,
970-975.*
LEVEL: A LANG: Eng

Haines, A. Sports injuries - a shared responsibility:
administrators, coaches and trainers face moral,
legal obligations of proper injury care. *First aider
(Gardner, Kans.) 54(1), Sept 1984, 1;14-15.*
NOTES: Adapted from: Athletic journal, January
1984. First of a series.
LEVEL: B LANG: Eng SIRC ARTICLE NO: 105296

Hemstrom, C. Why, when and how to use exercise
to warm-up for game preparation. (Refs: 16)*Sports
coach (Wembley, Aust.) 8(1), 1984, 16-19.*
LEVEL: I LANG: Eng SIRC ARTICLE NO: 096450

Hershman, E. The profile for prevention of
musculoskeletal injury. (Refs: 28)*Clinics in sports
medicine (Philadelphia) 3(1) Jan 1984, 65-84.*
NOTES: Symposium on profiling.
ABST: To compile a profile for the prevention of
musculoskeletal injury three main components are
studied. These are the specific demands of the
sport, the risk factors for injury in that sport and the
state of the individual's musculoskeletal system.
Abnormalities such as in the athlete's strength and/
or flexibility are important considerations for the
prevention of injuries in his sport.
LEVEL: A LANG: Eng SIRC ARTICLE NO: 092864

Penman, K.A. Safe sports equipment and facilities.
In, Adams, S.H. (ed.), et al., Catastrophic injuries in
sports: avoidanc strategies, Salinas, Calif., Cayote
Press, c1984, p. 5-6.
LEVEL: B LANG: Eng RD97 19088

Stoner, L.J. Injury is basically a biomechanical
problem.
CONF: National Symposium on Teaching
Kinesiology and Biomechanics in Sports (2nd :
1984 : Colorado Springs).
NOTES: In, Shapiro, R. and Marett, J.R. (eds.),
Proceedings: Second National Symposium on
Teaching Kinesiology and Biomechanics in Sports,
Colorado Springs, Colorado, January 12-14,
Dekalb, Ill., AAHPERD, 1984, p. 47-48.
LEVEL: I LANG: Eng SIRC ARTICLE NO: 100700

PROTECTIVE DEVICES

The little piece of protection that does a big job.
*First aider (Gardner, Kans.) 54(1), Sept 1984, 10-
11.*
LEVEL: B LANG: En SIRC ARTICLE NO: 105305

PSYCHOLOGY

Caruso, I. Montesarchio, G. L'intervento
psicologico nell'atleta costretto a un lungo periodo
di riabilitazione: contributo per una riflessione.
Psychological effects on athletes under long term
rehabilitation: food for thought. *Italian journal of
sports traumatology (Milano, Italy) 6(3), Jul/Sept
1984, 183-185.*
CONF: Italian Society of Sports Traumatology.

Congress (1st : 1983 : Rome).
LEVEL: B LANG: Eng It SIRC ARTICLE NO: 102499

Reactions psychologiques aux blessures. *Revue de
l'entraineur (Montreal) juil/sept 1984, 10-11.*
CORP: Regie de la securite dans les sports.
LEVEL: B LANG: Fr SIRC ARTICLE NO: 102536

Salisbury, N. The comeback trail. *New body (New
York) 3(6), Nov 1984, 56-58.*
LEVEL: B LANG: Eng SIRC ARTICLE NO: 173281

REHABILITATION

Bloom, M. Electric stimulation may speed healing.
*Physician and sportsmedicine (Minneapolis, Minn.)
12(6), Jun 1984, 40-41.*
LEVEL: B LANG: Eng SIRC ARTICLE NO: 094349

Johnson, B.C. Exercise minimizes muscle atrophy.
*Physician and sportsmedicine (Minneapolis, Minn.)
12(5), May 1984, 191-192.*
LEVEL: B LANG: Eng SIRC ARTICLE NO: 094369

Kegerreis, S. Malone, T. McCarroll, J. Functional
progressions:an aid to athletic rehabilitation. (Refs:
11)*Physician and sportsmedicine (Minneapolis,
Minn.) 12(12), Dec 1984, 67-71.*
LEVEL: I LANG: Eng SIRC ARTICLE NO: 102518

Long, J.P. Rehabilitation and return to activity after
sports injuries. (Refs: 22)*Primary care: clinics in
office practice (Philadelphia) 11(1), Mar 1984, 137-
150.*
LEVEL: I LANG: Eng SIRC ARTICLE NO: 100686

McClements, J. Harrison, L. Armstrong, C.
Planning, management by objectives and self
evaluation in the sport physiotherapy clinic. (Refs:
10)*Journal of the Canadian Athletic Therapists
Association (Oakville, Ont.) 11(2), Fall 1984, 5-7.*
LEVEL: B LANG: Eng SIRC ARTICLE NO: 104126

Norman, D. A strengthening program without
weights. Exercises done using elastic bands or
surgical tubing can be a valuable part of
conditioning or rehab programs. *First aider
(Gardner, Kans.) 54(2), Oct 1984, 8-9.*
LEVEL: B LANG: Eng SIRC ARTICLE NO: 105313

Scott, S.G. Current concepts in the rehabilitation of
the injured athlete. *Mayo clinic proceedings
(Rochester, Minn.) 59(2) Feb 1984, 83-90.*
LEVEL: I LANG: Eng SIRC ARTICLE NO: 099067

Silbuit, D. The shock that heals. *Maclean's
(Toronto) 30 Apr 1984, 64.*
LEVEL: B LANG: Eng SIRC ARTICLE NO: 092890

SHIN SPLINTS

Clark, L. Trainer's room. (shin splints) *Athletic
journal (Evanston, Ill.) 65(5), Dec 1984, 6;56.*
LEVEL: B LANG: Eng SIRC ARTICLE NO: 104022

Holder, L.E. Michael, R.H. The specific
scintigraphic pattern of 'shin splints in the lower
leg': concise communication. *Journal of nuclear
medicine, JNM (New York) 25(8), Aug 1984, 865-
869.*
ABST: In this prospective study, ten patients with
this syndrome were evaluated using three-phase
bone scintigrams, and a specific scintigraphic
pattern was determined. On delayed images, tibial
lesions involved the posterior cortex, were
longitudinally oriented, were long, involving one
third of the length of the bone, and often showed
varying tracer uptake along that length. Obtaining
both lateral and medial views was crucial. The

location of activity suggested that this entity is related to the soleus muscle. These scintigraphic findings can be used to differentiate shin splints from stress fractures or other conditions causing pain in the lower leg in athletes.
LEVEL: A LANG: Eng SIRC ARTICLE NO: 104042

Scheuch, P.A. Tibialis posterior shin splint: diagnosis and treatment. (Refs: 11)*Athletic training (Greenville, N.C.) 19(4) Winter 1984, 271-274.*
LEVEL: I LANG: Eng SIRC ARTICLE NO: 104077

Wallensten, R. Karlsson, J. Histochemical and metabolic changes in lower leg muscles in exercise-induced pain. (Refs: 45) *International journal of sports medicine (Stuttgart) 5(4), Aug 1984, 202-208.*
ABST: Intramuscular pressure, fiber type distribution, relative cross-sectional area of slow-twitch muscle fibers, muscle lactate, and water content were studied in eight patients with medial tibial syndrome and in eight patients with chronic anterior compartment syndrome. The variables were determined before and after standardized exercise that provoked lower leg pain. The findings indicate that the chronic anterior compartment syndrome is related to changes in the muscle fiber level and to a subsequently changed anaerobic metabolism and fluid infiltration. The medial tibial syndrome may be caused by abnormal biomechanics during running that by means of local adaptation causes changes in fiber types and local metabolic and microcirculatory capacities.
LEVEL: A LANG: Eng SIRC ARTICLE NO: 104089

SHOULDER AN UPPER LIMB INJURIES

Anderson, T.E. Shoulder injuries in the athlete. (Refs: 9)*Primary care: clinics in office practice (Philadelphia) 11(1), Ma 1984, 129-136.*
LEVEL: I LANG: Eng SIRC ARTICLE NO: 100670

Andrews, J.R. Carson, W.G. Ortega, K. Arthroscopy of the shoulder: technique and normal anatomy. (Refs: 28)*American journal of sports medicine (Baltimore, Md.) 12(1), Jan/Feb 1984, 1-7.*
ABST: Arthroscopy of the shoulder involves passing the instruments through layers of fat and muscle and a thick capsule. The anterior instruments are placed on either side of the biceps tendon while the arthroscope enters the capsule posteriorly. Some variation of the glenohumeral ligaments makes it important to examine the anatomy of the shoulder sequentially. The authors detail the technique they use in examining the shoulder and its related structure. Systematic and consistent technique make arthroscopy of the shoulder an effective diagnostic practise.
LEVEL: A LANG: Eng SIRC ARTICLE NO: 094411

Aronen, J. Shoulder injuries and their rehabilitation. *Handball (Tuscon, Ariz.) 34(5), Sept/Oct 1984, 56-58.*
LEVEL: B LANG: Eng SIRC ARTICLE NO: 100673

Aronen, J.G. Regan, K. Decreasing the incidence of recurrence of first time anterior shoulder dislocations with rehabilitation. (Refs: 6) *American journal of sports medicine (Baltimore, Md.) 12(4), Jul/Aug 1984, 283-291.*
ABST: Studies of adolescent and young adult males sustaining primary anterior shoulder dislocations reveal the likelihood of recurrence to be virtually always about 50 percent and as high as 79 percent

to 94 percent. Common among these investigations is the lack of a specific, rigidly adhered to rehabilitation program. During a 3 1/2 year period, 20 midshipmen at the United States Naval Academy sustained primary anterior shoulder dislocations. All participated in an identical treatment regimen which included a restrengthening program emphasizing the muscles of internal rotation and adduction, plus rigid restrictions of activities until the goals of their rehabilitation program were satisfied. Patients were followed for an average of 35.8 months (with a rnage of 17 to 45 months). During the period of study there were five recurrences (25 percent).
LEVEL: A LANG: Eng SIRC ARTICLE NO: 108534

Birrer, R.B. Common injuries of the upper extremity. (Refs: 16)
NOTES: In, Birrer, R.B. (ed.), Sports medicine for the primary care physician, Norwalk, Conn., Appleton-Century-Crofts, c1984, p. 185-207.
LEVEL: I LANG: Eng RC1210 17030

Bracker, M.D. New treatment for dislocated shoulders. *Physician and sportsmedicine (Minneapolis, Minn.) 12(7), Jul 1984, 155.*
LEVEL: B LANG: Eng SIRC ARTICLE NO: 095907

Chen, S.K. Perry, J. Jobe, F.W. Healy, B.S. Moynes, D.R. Elbow flexion analysis in Bristow patients: a preliminary report. (Refs: 9)*American journal of sports medicine (Baltimore, Md.) 12(5), Sept/Oct 1984, 347-350.*
ABST: Seven male nonathletes who had Bristow procedures for shoulder dislocation were analyzed by dynamic electromyography (EMG) and Cybex strength measurement to evaluate the function of elbow flexion. Bilateral strength of elbow flexion also was measured in the 10 controlled subjects to compare the dominant and non-dominant arms. The EMG data showed the operated short head of biceps function at low constant intensity, compared with the nonoperated side, while the long head of biceps and brachialis increased their activity. The strength measured by the Cybex demonstrated the elbow flexion on the operated side was not significantly different from the normal group.
LEVEL: A LANG: Eng SIRC ARTICLE NO: 104019

Cofield, R.H. Simonet, W.T. The shoulder in sports. *Mayo Clinic proceedings (Rochester, Minn.) 59(3), Mar 1984, 157-164.*
LEVEL: I LANG: Eng SIRC ARTICLE NO: 100676

Cooney, W.P. Sports injuries to the upper extremity. How to recognize and deal with some common problems. (Refs: 14) *Postgraduate medicine (Minneapolis) 76(4), 15 Sept 1984, 45-50.*
LEVEL: I LANG: Eng SIRC ARTICLE NO: 104023

Crielaard, J.M. Franchimont, P. Rodineau, J. Le syndrome du bourrelet glenoidien en medecine du sport. (Syndrome of the glenoid ridge in sports medicine.) *Acta Belgica. Medica physica (Bruxelles) 7(4), Oct/Dec 1984, 117-120.*
LEVEL: A LANG: Fr

Differential diagnosis of athletic shoulder injuries. *Sportsmedicine digest (Van Nuys, Calif.) 6(2), Feb 1984, 8.*
LEVEL: B LANG: Eng SIRC ARTICLE NO: 099039

Emans, J.B. Upper extremity injuries in sports. (Refs: 15)
NOTES: In, Micheli, L.J. (ed.), Pediatric and adolescent sports medicine, Boston ; Toronto, Little, Brown, c1984, p. 49-79.
LEVEL: I LANG: Eng RC1210 17791

Henry, J.H. How I manage dislocated shoulder. (Refs: 6)*Physician and sportsmedicine (Minneapolis, Minn.) 12(9), Sept 1984, 65-69.*
LEVEL: I LANG: Eng SIRC ARTICLE NO: 099042

Johnston, G.H. Hawkins, R.J. Haddad, R. Fowler, P.J. A complication of posterior glenoid osteotomy for recurrent posterior shoulder instability. *Clinical orthopaedics and related research (Philadelphia) 187, Jul/Aug 1984, 147-149.*
ABST: Posterior glenoid osteotomy (posterior glenoplasty) is a standard surgical reconstructive operation for recurrent posterior instability of the shoulder. A 34-year-old football player was treated by glenoid osteotomy and subsequently developed significant glenohumeral arthritis. Following several surgical procedures, only total shoulder arthroplasty gave substantial pain relief and restored stability. Inadvertent penetration of the glenohumeral joint at the time of osteotomy may have predisposed the patient to glenohumeral arthritis. Extreme care should be exercised not to damage the shoulder joint during this procedure.
LEVEL: A LANG: Eng SIRC ARTICLE NO: 104045

Lacroix, H. Quartero, H.W. De gemodificeerde Bristow-plastiek bij recidief van de voorste schouderluxatie als gevolg van trauma. (Modified Bristow procedure in recurrent anterior shoulder dislocation caused by trauma.) *Nederlands tijdschrift voor geneeskunde (Amsterdam) 128(28), 14 Jul 1984, 1318-1321.*
LEVEL: A LANG: Dut

Lemire, L. Rosman, M. Sternoclavicular epiphyseal separation with adjacent clavicular fracture. *Journal of pediatric orthopaedics (New York) 4(1), Jan 1984, 118-120.*
ABST: This case report details the diagnosis and treatment of an unusual double fracture of the medial left clavicle in a 15 year old male hockey player.
LEVEL: A LANG: Eng SIRC ARTICLE NO: 099046

McCue, F.C. Throwing injuries of the shoulder. Alexandria, Va.: Computer Microfilm International, 1984. 1 microfiche (30 fr.); 10 x 15 cm.
LEVEL: I LANG: Eng EDRS: ED246047 ERIC 246047

Nieminen, S. Aho, A.J. Anterior dislocation of the acromioclavicular joint. *Annales chirurgiae et gynaecologiae (Helsinki) 73(1), 1984, 21-24.*
LEVEL: I LANG: Eng SIRC ARTICLE NO: 102529

Norwood, L.A. Terry, G.C. Shoulder posterior subluxation. (Refs: 17)*American journal of sports medicine (Baltimore, Md.) 12(1), Jan/Feb 1984, 25-30.*
ABST: A follow-up study of 21 patients who had chronic recurrent posterior subluxation was conducted at an average of 39.9 months after surgery. The results suggest that opening osteotomy is indicated for posterior instability in cases of instability which resulted from direct trauma or muscular contracts, and also for anterior-posterior instability instability. A classification system is detailed which allows for better preoperative prediction of subsequent recovery and joint stability.
LEVEL: A LANG: Eng SIRC ARTICLE NO: 094382

Norwood, L.A. Treatment of acute shoulder dislocations. *Alabama medicine (Montgomery, Ala.) 54(6), Dec 1984, 30;32;36 passim.*
LEVEL: I LANG: Eng

Oliver J. Soins des blessures communes a l'epaule. Don't shoulder the pain: help for common shoulder injuries. (Refs: 1) *Sport Med Info (Ottawa)* 4(1), 1984, 1-6.
LEVEL: I LANG: Fr Eng SIRC ARTICLE NO: 099054

Oliver, J. Harris, L. Un corps sain: soin des blessures communes a l'epaule. Body physic: common shoulder injuries. *Champio (Ottawa)* 8(4), Nov 1984, 6;8;17;19;21.
LEVEL: I LANG: Fr Eng SIRC ARTICLE NO: 100691

Orava, S. Virtanen, K. Holopainen, Y.V. Posttraumatic osteolysis of the distal ends of the clavicle. Report of three cases. *Annales chirurgiae et gynaecoligiae (Helsinki)* 73(2), 1984, 83-86.
ABST: Two judo participants and a cyclist were treated for acromioclavicular joint dislocations. Osteolysis developed slowly and the joint line was typically widened in the radiographs. The disorder settled within one year.
LEVEL: A LANG: Eng SIRC ARTICLE NO: 104070

Rodineau, J. L'epaule douloureuse du sportif. *Vie medicale (Paris)* 65(17/18), 1984, 649-655.
LEVEL: I LANG: Fr

Rowe, C.R. Zarins, B. Ciullo, J.V. Recurrent anterior dislocation of the shoulder after surgical repair. Apparent causes of failure and treatment. *Journal of bone joint surgery. American volume (Boston)* 66(2), Feb 1984, 159-168.
ABST: Unsuccessful surgical repair of recurrent anterior dislocation of the shoulder was evaluated in 39 patients. Thirty-two shoulders were treated by reoperation. These were followed for 2 years or longer and recurrent instability after the second operation was 8 per cent.
LEVEL: A LANG: Eng SIRC ARTICLE NO: 099065

Simonet, W.T. Cofield, R.H. Prognosis in anterior shoulder dislocation. (Refs: 22)*American journal of sports medicine (Baltimore, Md.)* 12(1), Jan/Feb 1984, 19-24.
CONF: American Orthopedic Society for Sports Medicine. Interim Meeting (1983: Anaheim, Calif.).
ABST: This follow-up study of 116 first time glenohumeral dislocations indicates that there is a high degree of recurrent shoulder dislocations after the first one. Young athletes are significantly more susceptible to recurrence. A period of three to six weeks of immobilization followed by intensive rehabilitation is recommended for the prevention of future shoulder dislocations.
LEVEL: A LANG: Eng SIRC ARTICLE NO: 094391

Tullos, H.S. Bennett, J.B. The shoulder in sports. (Refs: 84)
NOTES: In, Scott, W.N. (ed.) et al., Principles of sports medicine, Baltimore, Williams & Wilkins, c1984, p. 110-139.
LEVEL: A LANG: Eng RC1210 18016

Zarins, B. Rowe, C.R. Current concepts in the diagnosis and treatment of shoulder instability in athletes. (Refs: 48) *Medicine and science in sports and exercise (Indianapolis)* 16(5), Oct 1984, 444-448.
ABST: Glenohumeral joint instability is a fairly common clinical disorder in athletes, especially in sports that involve the throwing motion. The direction of shoulder instability can be anterior, inferior posterior or multidirectional. The cause can be trauma, congenital laxity, or voluntary muscle action. A common condition encountered in the shoulder of a throwing arm is anterior subluxation, which can be diagnosed by the positive apprehension sign and confirmed by arthroscopy. A

torn glenoid labrum is a common injury also. Improvement in the diagnosis and treatment of shoulder disorders has been made recently by arthroscopy which allows direct visualization of the joint; many conditions can now be corrected by means of arthroscopic surgery.
LEVEL: A LANG: Eng SIRC ARTICLE NO: 102552

SOFT TISSUE INJURIES

Bergfeld, W.F. The skin. (Refs: 27)
NOTES: In, Strauss, R.H. (ed.), Sports medicine, Philadelphia ; Toronto, Saunders, 1984, p. 91-104.
LEVEL: A LANG: Eng RC1210 17196

de Bruijn, R. Deep transverse friction; its analgesic effect. (Refs: 22)*International journal of sports medicine (Stuttgart Suppl 5, Nov 1984, 35-36.
CONF: International Congress on Sports and Health (1983 : Maastricht, Netherlands).
LEVEL: A LANG: Eng SIRC ARTICLE NO: 104026

Edwards, V. Wilson, A.A. Harwood, H.F. Manning, S.I. Brabbin, W. Walker, J.W. Jones, D.G. Thomas, D.V. Rimmer, R. Berry, W.H. A multicentre comparison of piroxicam and indomethacin in acute soft tissue sports injuries. *Journal of international medical research (North Hampton, Eng.)* 12(1), 1984, 46-50.
ABST: 105 patients suffering from soft tissue sport injuries participated in a randomized controlled trial comparing the efficiency and side-effects of piroxicam and indomethacin. Patients were treated for 7 days. 88 per cent of patients on piroxicam showed a marked or moderate improvement in their injury at the end of the trial and 79 per cent of the indomethacin-treated patients. Approximately 50 per cent of patients in both groups resumed full activity within 7 days.
LEVEL: A LANG: Eng SIRC ARTICLE NO: 098924

Laine, H. Harjula, A. Peltokallio, P. Varstela, E. Real time sonography to diagnose soft-tissue sports injuries. (letter) *Lancet (London)* 1(8367), 7 Jan 1984, 55.
LEVEL: B LANG: Eng SIRC ARTICLE NO: 097575

SPINAL INJURIES

Bruce, D.A. Schut, L. Sutton, L.N. Brain and cervical spine injuries occurring during organized sports activities in childre and adolescents. (Refs: 75)*Primary care: clinics in office practice (Philadelphia)* 11(1), Mar 1984, 175-194.
LEVEL: I LANG: Eng SIRC ARTICLE NO: 100674

Drevet, J.G. Plawesky, S. Mont, J.L. Phelip, X. Le rachis du skieur alpin de competition. *Pratique medicale (Paris)* 38, 198 41-44.
LEVEL: I LANG: Fr

Dubousset, J. Enfant, l'adolescent, le rachis et l'activite sportive. (Refs: 6)*Dans, Mandel, C. (ed.), Le medecin, l'enfant et le sport, Paris, (Vigot), c1984, p. 163-181.
LEVEL: I LANG: Fr RC1218.C45 18886

Figoni, S.F. Spinal cord injury and maximal aerobic power. (Refs: 52)*American corrective therapy journal (San Diego, Calif. 38(2), Mar/Apr 1984, 44-52.
ABST: This paper reviews the limitations and abilities of spinal cord injury (SCI) patients as related to maximal aerobic power. Specifically, the author presents a rationale for including cardiovascular endurance exercise in rehabilitation and physical fitness programs for the SCI

population. The main aim of this rationale is to increase the fitness of the SCI population thereby hopefully avoiding potential hypokinetic diseases.
LEVEL: A LANG: Eng SIRC ARTICLE NO: 095917

Giovanni, C.D. Santis, E.D. Esposito, L. Il distacco della spina iliaca antero-superiore (S.I.A.S.). Avulsion of the anterosuperior iliac spine (ASIS). (Refs: 17)*Italian journal of sports traumatology (Milano, Italy)* 6(3), Jul/Sept 1984, 221-227.
ABST: The clinical and anatomico-radiological aspects of ASIS avulsion-fracture are discussed on the basis of 9 cases treated over some 14 years. After a discussion of the pathogenetic mechanisms involved (uncoordinated movement associated with brusque muscle contraction in sportsmen), various treatment strategies are considered.
LEVEL: A LANG: Eng It SIRC ARTICLE NO: 102510

Grisogono, V. The running body: 27. The lumbar spine. Many runners' injury problems can be traced to the lower back or lumba spine region. This month we look at the structure and functions of the five lumbar vertebrae, and what can go wrong. *Running (London)* 37, May 1984, 112-113.
LEVEL: B LANG: Eng SIRC ARTICLE NO: 095922

Grisogono, V. The running body: 28. The spine. *Running (London, Eng.)* 38, Jun 1984, 62-63.
LEVEL: B LANG: Eng SIRC ARTICL NO: 095923

Jackson, D.W. Spinal injuries in children's sports. (Refs: 12)
NOTES: In, Micheli, L.J. (ed.), Pediatric and adolescent sports medicine, Boston ; Toronto, Little, Brown, c1984, p. 107-123.
LEVEL: I LANG: Eng RC1210 17791

Jackson, D.W. Mannarino, F. Lumbar spine injuries in athletes. (Refs: 29)
NOTES: In, Scott, W.N. (ed.) et al., Principles of sports medicine, Baltimore, Williams & Wilkins, c1984, p. 212-225.
LEVEL: A LANG: Eng RC1210 18016

Kiwerski, J. Urazy kregoslupa w nastepst wie uprawiania sportu. (Spinal injuries in sports.) *Polski tygodnik lekarski (Warsaw)* 39(17), 23 Apr 1984, 569-572.
LEVEL: I LANG: Pol

McGuire, E.J. Savastano, J.A. Research review: spinal cord injury and the bladder and urethral sphincter mechanisms. *Paraplegia news (Phoenix, Ariz.)* 38(5), May 1984, 43-46.
LEVEL: I LANG: Eng SIRC ARTICLE NO: 095869

Miltenyi, M. Elvonalbeli atletak mozgatorendszeri problemairol. (Health care of the locomotor system in top athletes.) (Refs 17)*Sportorvosi szemle/ Hungarian review of sports medicine (Budapest)* 25(3), 1984, 209-217.
ABST: Comparatively less attention is devoted to a regular screening for locomotor system disorders in sportsmedicine than is usual for other system disorders in top level athletes. Accordingly, overstrain problems manifest mainly in the motor apparatus. Especially before allowing participation in regular high intensity training such screening is indispensable with particular regard to the spine. Experience has shown that morpho-functional disorders in spine construction play a part in the pathogenesis of lower extremity injuries. By strengthening the deep back muscles adequately, one may obtain protection not only against injuries of the lumbar region, but also against those affecting the lower limb muscles. As an illustration,

three cases are reported. These top level athletes could continued their successful sports career despite their x-ray evidenced spine deformity. Sports physicians should be aware of the techniques employed in the sport event they care for. Examples are given in track and field athletics (javelin throwing, high jump, pole vaulting).
LEVEL: A LANG: Hun SIRC ARTICLE NO: 100237

Petrushenko, N.I. Povrezhdeniia pozvonochnika u detei. (Spinal injuries in children.) *Feldsher i akusherka (Moscow) 49(8), Aug 1984, 33-38.*
LEVEL: A LANG: Rus

Sances, A. Myklebust, J.B. Joel, B. Maiman, D.J. Larson, S.J. Cusick, J.F. Jobat, R.W. Biomechanics of spinal injuries. (Refs: 244)*CRC critical reviews in biomedical engineering (Boca Raton, Fla.) 11(1), 1984, 78.*
LEVEL: A LANG: Eng SIRC ARTICLE NO: 095959

Sances, A. Myklebust, J.B. Maiman, D.J. Larson, S.J. Cusick, J.F. Jodat, R.W. The biomechanics of spinal injuries. (Refs: 24 *Critical reviews in biomedical engineering (Boca Raton, Fla.) 11(1), 1984, 1-76.*
ABST: The authors review the epidemiology of spinal trauma, the anatomy of the vertebral column, spinal ligaments, muscles, motion of the spine and spinal cord.
LEVEL: A LANG: Eng SIRC ARTICLE NO: 102541

Spinelli, M. D'Elia, L. Marcacci, M. Pagano, G. Raffaeta, G. Il distacco della spina iliaca anteriore superiore nei giovani atleti. Avulsion of the anterosuperior iliac spine in young sportsmen. (Refs: 17)*Italian journal of sports traumatology (Milano, Italy) 6(3), Jul/Sept 1984, 213-219.*
ABST: Avulsions of the anterosuperior iliac spine in young sportsmen treated at Pisa University Orthopaedic Clinic are described. The condition was treated by surgical reduction and osteosynthesis sometimes in association with spica cast. The pathogenetic mechanism symptoms and treatment results of the 9 cases observed are described in detail.
LEVEL: A LANG: Eng It SIRC ARTICLE NO: 102545

Wise, D. Un corps sain. Traumatismes vertebraux: catastrophes evitables? Body physic. Spinal injuries: catastrophes? *Champion (Vanier, Ont.) 8(2), May/mai 1984, 44-49.*
LEVEL: I LANG: Fr Eng SIRC ARTICLE NO: 094399

STATISTICS

Accidental injuries report: consumer products April/May 1984. Rapport sur les blessures accidentelles: produits de consommatio avril/mai 1984. Ottawa: Consumer and Corporate Affairs / Consommation et Corporations Canada, 1984. 4, 4 p.
CORP: Canada. Consumer and Corporate Affairs.
CORP: Canada. Consommation et corporations.
NOTES: French and English texts on inverted pages with separate paging. Textes francais et anglais disposes tete-beche avec pagination separee. Cover title. Titre de la couverture.
LEVEL: B LANG: Eng Fr RD97 17726

Accidental injuries report: consumer products October/November 1984. Rapport sur les blessures accidentelles: produits de consommation. Ottawa: Consumer and Corporate Affairs / Consommation et Corporations, 1984. 4, 4 p.
CORP: Canada. Consumer and Corporate Affairs.
CORP: Canada. Consommation et corporations.
NOTES: Titre de la couverture. Cover title. French

and English texts on inverted pages with separate paging. Textes francais et anglais disposes tete-beche avec pagination separee.
LEVEL: B LANG: Eng Fr RD97 18838

Adrian, M. Catastrophic injury surveillance and reporting. *In, Adams, S.H. (ed.), et al., Catastrophic injuries in sports: avoidance strategies, Salinas, Calif., Cayote Press, c1984, p. 131-135.*
CORP: United States Gymnastics Safety Association.
NOTES: Reprinted from: Fourth annual national gymnastic catastrophic injury report, 1981-1982, Vienna, Va., United States Gymnastics Safety Association, c1983.
LEVEL: B LANG: Eng RD97 19088

Boyce, W.T. Playground equipment injuries in a large, urban school district. *American journal of public health (Washington) 74(9), Sept 1984, 984-986.*
LEVEL: I LANG: Eng SIRC ARTICLE NO: 103833

Kraus, J.F. Conroy, C. Mortality and morbidity from injuries in sports and recreation. (Refs: 97)*Annual review of public health 5, 1984, 163-192.*
LEVEL: A LANG: Eng SIRC ARTICLE NO: 095939

Nicholson, R. Accident statistics. *Hang gliding (Los Angeles, Calif.) 14(8), Aug 1984, 4-5.*
LEVEL: B LANG: Eng SIRC ARTICLE NO: 100690

Prince, P. Releve des blessures survenues au Championnat sportif quebecois Rouyn Noranda, ete 1983. Trois-Rivieres: Regie de la securite dans les sports, 1984. 1v.
CORP: Regie de la securite dans les sports. Service de la recherche.
LEVEL: I LANG: Fr RD97 20595

Prince, P. Releve des blessures survenues sur le territoire de la Regie des installations olympiques 1981-1982. Trois-Rivieres: Regie de la securite dans les sports, 1984. 1v.
CORP: Regie de la securite dans les sports. Service de la recheche.
LEVEL: I LANG: Fr RD97 20595

STRESS FRACTURES

Collier, B.D. Johnson, R.P. Carrera, G.F. Akhtar, K. Isitman, A.T. Scintigraphic diagnosis of stress-induced incomplete fractures of the proximal tibia. *Journal of trauma (Baltimore) 24(2), Feb 1984, 156-160.*
ABST: Bone scintigraphy can be successfully used to diagnose incomplete stress fractures of the proximal tibial diaphysis. This injury heals completely in 4 to 6 weeks with the restriction of activity.
LEVEL: A LANG: Eng SIRC ARTICLE NO: 099036

Devereaux, M.D. Parr, G.R. Lachmann, S.M. Page-Thomas, P. Hazelman, B.L. The diagnosis of stress fractures in athletes. (Refs: 10)*JAMA: Journal of the American Medical Association (Chicago) 252(4), 27 Jul 1984, 531-533.*
ABST: Eighteen patients believed to have stress fractures underwent radiological, thermographic and scintigraphic studies and a test of ultrasound induced pain. The efficiency of these various diagnostic procedures is evaluated.
LEVEL: A LANG: Eng SIRC ARTICLE NO: 102505

Doury, P. Pattin, S. Granier, R. Eulry, F. Metges, P.J. Gaillard, F. Flageat, J. Marcelli, C. Donnees nouvelles sur les 'fractures de fatigue'. A propos

d'une observation de fracture de fatigue bilaterale de l'astragale. Interet de la scintigraphie osseuse dans le diagnostic des fractures de fatigue. (New data on stress fractures. Apropos of a case of a bilateral talus stress fracture. Value of bone scintigraphy in the diagnosis of stress fractures.) *Revue du rhumatisme et des maladies osteo-articulaires (Paris) 51(9), oct 1984, 483-486.*
LEVEL: A LANG: Fr

Furuta, A. Tanohata, K. Itake, T. Hashizume, T. Kobayashi, Y. Nakazima, H. (Clinical evaluation of stress fractures using bone scintigraphy.) *Kaku igaku. Japanese journal of nuclear medicine (Tokyo) 21(5), May 1984, 435-443.*
LEVEL: A LANG: Jpn

Kirshberger, R. Henning, A. Graff, K.H. Ermuedungbrueche beit Hochleistungssportlern. Stellenwert und Indikation der Skeletiszintigraphie. (Fatigue fractures in top athletes. Value of and indications for skeletal scintigraphy.) *Nuklearmedizin. Nuclear medicine (Stuttgart) 23(6), Dec 1984, 305-309.*
LEVEL: A LANG: Ger

Kuusela, T.V. Incidence of bone lesions in the lower extremities during endurance training. *Annals of clinical research (Helsinki) 16(Suppl 40), 1984, 17-19.*
ABST: The author reported on the occurrence of stress fracture in 120 recruits following a 10 weeks training period. 63% of the parachutists, 35% of the infantrymen, and 15% of the light infantrymen had stress fractures.
LEVEL: A LANG: Eng SIRC ARTICLE NO: 102522

Michael, J. Fatigue fractures in athletes. Clinical signs and treatment. (Refs: 2)*International journal of sports medicine (Stuttgart) Suppl. 5, Nov 1984, 164.*
CONF: International Congress on Sports and Health (1983 : Maastricht, Netherlands).
LEVEL: I LANG: Eng SIRC ARTICLE NO: 104062

Milgrom, C. Chisin, R. Giladi, M. Stein, M. Kashtan, H. Margulies, J. Atlan, H. Negative bone scans in impending tibial stress fractures. (Refs: 6)*American journal of sports medicine (Baltimore) 12(6), Nov/Dec 1984, 488-491.*
ABST: Three highly motivated military recruits who presented with tibial pain on exertion are reported. Their initial bone scan assessments to rule out stress fracture were normal, and the recruits were returned to demanding training. One month later, because of persistent and increasing tibial pain, they were rescanned and focal activity representative of tibial stress fractures was found in each case. Until now it has been assumed that a negative bone scan ruled out a stress fracture unequivocally. These reported cases show that bone pain may in fact precede scintigraphic evidence of a stress fracture. Persistent and increasing bone pain during demanding physical activity, even in the presence of a prior normal bone scan, may represent stress fracture and repeat bone scan may be indicated.
LEVEL: A LANG: Eng SIRC ARTICLE NO: 104063

Oosterhuis, K.J. Stapert, J.W.J.L. van den Hoogenband, C.R. Greep, J.M. Diagnosis and treatment of stress fractures. (Refs: 11)*International journal of sports medicine (Stuttgart) Suppl. 5, Nov 1984, 162-163.*
CONF: International Congress on Sports and Health (1983 : Maastricht, Netherlands).
LEVEL: A LANG: Eng SIRC ARTICLE NO: 104069

Orava, S. Hulkko, A. Stress fracture of the mid-tibial shaft. *Acta orthopaedica scandinavica (Copenhagen) 55(1), Feb 1984, 35-37.*
LEVEL: I LANG: Eng SIRC ARTICLE NO: 099055

Sebold, D. Tape support for the fractured distal fibula. *Athletic training (Greenville, N.C.) 19(2), Summer 1984, 121-123.*
LEVEL: B LANG: Eng SIRC ARTICLE NO: 094435

SUDDEN DEATH

Banta, G.R. Fleg, J.L. Hartley, L.H. Dimsdde, J.E. Zucker, M.I. Postexercise peril. (letter) (Refs: 15)*JAMA: Journal of the American Medical Association (Chicago) 252(4), 27 Jul 1984, 480-481.*
LEVEL: B LANG: Eng SIRC ARTICLE NO: 102533

Cousergue, C. Peut-on prevenir la mort subite du sportif? *Generaliste (Paris) 620, 1984, 36.*
LEVEL: B LANG: Fr

Dolmans, A.J. Pool, J. Erdman-Trip J.F. Smit, B. Lubsen, J. Het risico van overlijden bij sport. (The risk of dying during sports activities.) *Nederlands tijdschrift voor geneeskunde (Amsterdam) 128(13), 31 Mar 1984, 595-598.*
LEVEL: A LANG: Dut

Furlanello, F. Bettini, R. Cozzi, F. Del Favero, A. Disertori, M. Vergara, G. Durante, G.B. Guarnerio, M. Inama, G. Thiene, G Ventricular arrhythmias and sudden death in athletes. *Annals of the New York Academy of Sciences (New York) 427, 1984, 253-279.*
LEVEL: A LANG: Eng SIRC ARTICLE NO: 102508

Haiat, R. Eiferman, C. La mort subite du sportif. (Refs: 7)*Information cardiologique (France) 8(6), 1984, 583-585.*
LEVEL: LANG: Fr

Johannessen, A.C. Frandsen, P. Dod i forbindelse med sportsudovelse. (Death in connection with active sports.) *Ugeskrift fo laeger (Copenhagen) 147(1), 31 Dec 1984, 1-4.*
LEVEL: I LANG: Dan

Nguyen, M. Sports: d'abord etre en forme. *Impact medecin (Puteaux, France) 102, 1984, 41-43.*
LEVEL: B LANG: Fr

Northcote, R.J. Ballantyne, D. Sudden death and sport. (Refs: 34)*Sports medicine (Auckland, N.Z.) 1(3), May/Jun 1984, 181-186.*
ABST: The authors discuss the relationship between sport and death occurring during the activity or in the first hour after cessation of exercise. The risk of sudden death during sport is small but is greater in those with asymptomatic cardiovascular disease. Unfortunately, contemporary screening procedures fail to reveal the underlying disease in the asymptomatic population. The author provides some useful suggestions to reduce sudden death in sport. These include: admission criteria to unsupervised programs, paying heed to prodromal symptoms and proper warming-up and cooling down procedures.
LEVEL: A LANG: Eng SIRC ARTICLE NO: 095949

Northcote, R.J. Ballantyne, D. Sudden death and sport. (letter) *Lancet (London) 1(8368), 14 Jan 1984, 113.*
LEVEL: B LANG: Eng SIRC ARTICLE NO: 097578

Northcote, R.J. Ballantyne, D. Reducing the prevalence of exercise related cardiac death. (Refs: 29)*British journal of sports medicine (Loughborough, Eng.) 18(4), Dec 1984, 288-292.*
CONF: London Marathon Conference (1984 : London).
LEVEL: I LANG: Eng SIRC ARTICLE NO: 104129

Oakley, D. Cardiac hypertrophy in athletes. (editorial) *British heart journal (London) 52(2), Aug 1984, 121-123.*
LEVEL: I LANG: Eng SIRC ARTICLE NO: 104068

Pedoe, D.T. Sudden death and sport - preventable or inevitable. (Refs: 1)*British journal of sports medicine (Loughborough, Eng.) 18(4), Dec 1984, 293-294.*
CONF: London Marathon Conference (1984 : London).
LEVEL: I LANG: Eng SIRC ARTICLE NO: 104133

Ragosta, M. Crabtree, J. Sturner, W.Q. Thompson, P.D. Death during recreational exercise in the state of Rhode Island. (Refs 16)*Medicine and science in sports and exercise (Indianapolis) 16(4), Aug 1984, 339-342.*
ABST: From January 1, 1975 to May 1, 1982, 81 individuals died during or immediately after recreational exercise in the State of Rhode Island. Deaths occurred during a variety of activities, but the majority of deaths occurred during golf (23%), jogging (20%), and swimming (11%). Atherosclerotic coronary heart disease (ASHD) was the presumed cause of 88% of the deaths, primarily in subjects over age 29 with known cardiac abnormalities. In contrast, deaths in young subjects were rarely associated with ASHD or prior knowledge of cardiovascular disease. Only six deaths in individuals aged 29 or younger occurred during the study period. These deaths were associated with congenital cardiovascular disease (2), valvular heart disease (1), hemorrhagic gastritis (1), idiopathic myocardial hypertrophy (1), and hypertrophic cardiomyopathy with ASHD (1).
LEVEL: A LANG: Eng SIRC ARTICLE NO: 102535

Sudden cardiac death in sport. (letter) *British medical journal (clinical research) (London) 288(6410), 7 Jan 1984, 63-64.*
LEVEL: B LANG: Eng SIRC ARTICLE NO: 097583

Thompson, P.D. Mitchell, J.H. Exercise and sudden cardiac death: protection or provocation. (editorial) *New England journal of medicine (Boston) 311(14), 4 Oct 1984, 914-915.*
LEVEL: B LANG: Eng SIRC ARTICLE NO: 104081

SUNBURN

Smith, D.L. Sunscreens: you could call them 'skin insurance'. *Bicycling (Emmaus, Pa.) 25(5), Jun 1984, 76-78.*
LEVEL: B LANG: Eng SIRC ARTICLE NO: 095963

TENDINITIS

Curwin, S. Stanish, W.D. Tendinitis: its etiology and treatment. Lexington, Mass. ; Toronto: Collamore Press : D.C. Heath an Co., c1984. viii, 189 p. : ill.
NOTES: Bibliography: p. 167-181.
LEVEL: I LANG: Eng ISBN: 0-669-07394-6 LC CARD: 83-72496 RD97 17259

Demarais Houles Parier Poux Echoscannographie dans les tendinites achilleennes et rotuliennes specialement chez le sportif. (Refs: 19)*Cinesiologie (Paris) 95, mai/juin 1984, 249-256.*
LEVEL: I LANG: Fr SIRC ARTICLE NO: 097569

Lowdon, A. Bader, D.L. Mowat, A.G. The effect of heel pads on the treatment of Achilles tendinitis: a double blind trial. (Refs: 14)*American journal of sports medicine (Baltimore) 12(6), Nov/Dec 1984, 431-435.*
ABST: Thirty-three subjects entered a blind-observer, random, prospective study of three forms of conservative treatment of sports-induced Achilles tendinitis, results being assessed by clinical and biomechanical parameters. Two patient groups received heel pads, ultrasound, and exercises, while the third received only ultrasound and exercises. All three groups showed some improvement at both 10 day and 2 month assessment, but the claimed benefit of viscoelastic pads widely used by athletes was not substantiated. The more striking benefit from ultrasound and exercises alone occurred in patients with a shorter history; a comparison of duration of injury in all three groups suggested this was an important factor influencing outcome.
LEVEL: A LANG: Eng SIRC ARTICLE NO: 104052

Other tendinitis syndromes of the hindfoot. *Sports medicine digest (Van Nuys, Calif.) 6(5), May 1984, 7-8.*
LEVEL: B LANG: E SIRC ARTICLE NO: 100692

TENDON INJURIES

Fornage, B.D. Rifkin, M.D. Touche, D.H. Segal, P.M. Sonography of the patellar tendon: preliminary observations. *AJR: American journal of roentgenology (Baltimore, Md.) 143(1), Jul 1984, 179-182.*
LEVEL: A LANG: Eng SIRC ARTICLE NO: 102506

Kelly, D.W. Carter, V.S. Jobe, F.W. Kerlan, R.K. Patellar and quadriceps tendon ruptures - jumper's knee. (Refs: 11)*America journal of sports medicine (Baltimore, Md.) 12(5), Sept/Oct 1984, 375-380.*
ABST: We reviewed 13 patients with end stage jumper's knee, 10 with patellar tendon ruptures, and 3 with ruptures of the quadriceps tendon to evaluate our long-term results in treating these tendon ruptures in an athletic population. The focus was on the natural history, the time until return, and the level of return, to athletic activity. At followup, averaging 4 1/2 years, patients underwent functional and clinical, as well as Cybex and roentgenographic, evaluations. Results indicated patellar tendon ruptures, where the ruptures are complete, have a more favorable prognosis than those of the quadriceps tendon which are incomplete. All of the latter patients continued to have quadriceps tendinitis following repair.
LEVEL: A LANG: Eng SIRC ARTICLE NO: 104047

Larsen, E. Lauridsen, F. Dislocation of the tibialis posterior tendon in two athletes. (Refs: 5)*American journal of sports medicine (Baltimore) 12(6), Nov/Dec 1984, 429-430.*
ABST: Dislocation of the tibialis posterior tendon occurred in an 18-year-old man and in a 36-year-old woman during running activities. Several years earlier both patients had suffered minor injuries to the affected ankle. The mechanism of the current injury was dorsal flexion and inversion of the foot. Suturing the flexor retinaculum to the posterior margin of the medial malleolus obtained good results in both cases. Dislocation of the tibialis posterior tendon is rare, but should be considered in athletes with even minor traumas to the foot accompanied by pain on the inside of the ankle.
LEVEL: I LANG: Eng SIRC ARTICLE NO: 104049

Poell, R.G. Duijfjes, F. The treatment of recurrent dislocation of the peroneal tendons. *Journal of bone joint surgery. British volume (London) 66(1), Jan 1984, 98-100.*
ABST: Ten cases of recurrent dislocation of the peroneal tendons were operated on between 1974 and 1982. The disturbed superior peroneal retinaculum was reconstructed by transposition of the calcaneofibular ligament to the lateral side of the peroneal tendons. An average follow-up of four years found that all the results were satisfactory.
LEVEL: A LANG: Eng SIRC ARTICLE NO: 099060

Pozo, J.L. Jackson, A.M. A rerouting operation for dislocation of peroneal tendons: operative technique and case report. (Refs: 12)*Foot & ankle (Baltimore, Md.) 5(1), Jul/Aug 1984, 42-44.*
LEVEL: I LANG: Eng SIRC ARTICLE NO: 099061

TREATMENT

Barham, F.L. Aspirin: dangers behind the benefits. Prolonged bleeding following injuries is focus of concern. *First aider (Gardner, Kan.) 53(6), Mar 1984, 1;4-5.*
NOTES: Adapted from a speech given at the Garden State Sports Medicine Symposium, April 1983.
LEVEL: B LANG: Eng SIRC ARTICLE NO: 094348

Coulter, B. Guidelines for care of injured players. *CAPHERD journal times (Danville, Calif.) 46(8), May 1984, 12-13.*
LEVEL: B LANG: Eng SIRC ARTICLE NO: 094354

Dine, G. Colas, M. Zemzami, A. Lallement, J.J. Utilisation d'un appareil laser en medecine du sport. Resultats de l'etude preliminaire. (Refs: 7)*Medecine du sport (Paris) 58(2), 25 mars 1984, 30;32-33.*
LEVEL: I LANG: Fr SIRC ARTICLE NO: 094357

Grunberg, C. Prevoir et guerir les bobos. *Science et vie (Paris) HS147, 1984, 156-160.*
LEVEL: B LANG: Fr

Haines, A. Principles of emergency care: it is essential that coaches be prepared for any emergency situation that might arise. (Refs: 12)*Athletic journal 64(6), Jan 1984, 8-10;65-67.*
LEVEL: I LANG: Eng SIRC ARTICLE NO: 090076

Le Coz, J. Mesotherapie et traumatologie du sport. *Vie medicale, aide visuelle du praticien (France) 78, 1984, 5-6.*
LEVEL B LANG: Fr

Massalsky, C. La medecine du sport et l'homeopathie. *Homeopathie francaise (Paris) 72(5), 1984, 319-321.*
LEVEL: B LANG: F

O'Donoghue, D.H. Frank, G.R. Allman, F.L. Rutledge, B.J. Wilkinson, C.P. Treatment of injuries to athletes. 4th ed. Philadelphia ; Toronto: W.B. Saunders, 1984. xxi, 714 p. : ill.
NOTES: Includes bibliograhical references.
LEVEL: A LANG: Eng ISBN: 0-7216-6928-X LC CARD: 83-4501 RD97 17813

Olupitan, S.B. Evaluation of piroxicam (Feldene) as an anti-inflammatory analgesic. A 3-part multicentre study in Nigeria. Part II. Study in sports injuries. *Current therapeutic research (Tenafly, N.J.) 36, 1984, 826-832.*
ABST: For this study 174 patients with minor sports injuries underwent 10 days of piroxicam therapy. The results confirmed piroxicam's efficacy and tolerability. Only 12 patients reported side effects,

none of which warranted withdrawal of treatment.
LEVEL: A LANG: Eng

Parienti, I.J. Parienti-Amsellem, J. Creme rap en traumatologie sportive. Etude en double aveugle contre placebo sur 54 sujets. *Lyon Mediterranee medical (Lyon) 20(14), 1984, 9353-9355.*
LEVEL: I LANG: Fr

UNCONCIOUSNESS

van Assendelft, A.H. Rasituksesta johtuva kolinerginen anafylaksia ja metakoliinin aiheuttama tajuttomuus. (Syncope caused b methacholine exercise-induced cholinergic analphylaxis.) *Duodecim (Helsinki) 100(10), 1984, 623-626.*
LEVEL: I LANG: Fin

UROGENITAL INJURIES

Albertazzi, A. Del Rosso, G. Cappelli, P. Acute renal failure after repeated physical stress. (letter) *Lancet (London) 1(8391), 23 Jun 1984, 1418-1419.*
LEVEL: I LANG: Eng SIRC ARTICLE NO: 102484

Avrillon, A.M. Les pubalgies. *Revue du jeune medecin (Paris) 131, 1984, 27-28.*
LEVEL: I LANG: Fr

Brunet, B. Brunet-Guedj, E. Genety, J. Imbert, J.C. Moyen, B. Comtet, J.J. La pubalgie: syndrome 'fourre-tout' pour une plus grande rigueur diagnostique et therapeutique. (Refs: 22)*Intantanes medicaux (France) 55(1), 1984, 25-30.*
LEVEL: A LANG: Fr

Enderli, J.B. Studer, U.E. Terrier, F. Un cas de pseudopriapisme: hematome pericaverneux du penis. (A case of pseudopriapism pericavernous hematoma of the penis.) *Journal d'urologie (Paris) 90(2), 1984, 139-140.*
LEVEL: A LANG: Fr

Krieger, J.N. Algood, C.B. Mason, J.T. Copass, M.K. Ansell, J.S. Urological trauma in the Pacific Northwest: etiology, distribution, management and outcome. *Journal of urology (Baltimore) 132(1), Jul 1984, 70-73.*
LEVEL: I LANG: Eng SIRC ARTICLE NO: 102521

Montgomery, J.H. Moinuddin, M. Buchignani, J.S. Rockett, J.F. Callison, M.K. Renal infarction after aerobics. *Clinical nuclear medicine (Philadelphia) 9(11), Nov 1984, 664-665.*
LEVEL: A LANG: Eng

Mustalish, A.C. Quash, E.T. Sports injuries to the chest and abdomen. (Refs: 57)
NOTES: In, Scott, W.N. (ed.) et al., Principles of sports medicine, Baltimore, Williams & Wilkins, c1984, p. 226-241.
LEVEL: A LANG: Eng RC1210 18016

Turblin, J. Symphysite et perisymphysite pubienne chez le sportif. *Nouvelle revue de medecine de Toulouse. Supp (France) 2 (3), 1984, 133-134.*
LEVEL: B LANG: Fr

WOUNDS

Kahn, J. Case reports: open wound management with the HeNe (6328 AU) Cold Laser. (Refs: 1)*Journal of orthopaedic and sports physical therapy (Baltimore, Md.) 6(3), Nov/Dec 1984, 203-206.*
ABST: The cold laser, HeNe, 6328 AU, was used in an attempt to enhance open lesion healing. In both

cases cited, planned surgery was cancelled because of the effectiveness of the lasings. Suggested techniques and procedures are outlined.
LEVEL: I LANG: Eng SIRC ARTICLE NO: 102516

WRIST INJURIES

Call, W.H. Injuries to the hand and wrist in athletics. (Refs: 2)*Sideline view 5(6), Jan 1984, 1-4.*
LEVEL: B LANG: Eng SIRC ARTICLE NO: 091453

O'Brien, E.T. Acute fractures and dislocations of the carpus. *Orthopedic clinics of North America (Philadelphia) 15(2), Apr 1984, 237-258.*
LEVEL: A LANG: Eng SIRC ARTICLE NO: 102532

Parier, J. Poux, D. Houles, J.P. Demarais, Y. Le poignet douloureux chronique du sportif adulte. *Tempo medical (Paris) 165, 1984, 85-88.*
LEVEL: B LANG: Fr

Posner, M.A. Wrist injuries. (Refs: 41)
NOTES: In, Scott, W.N. (ed.) et al., Principles of sports medicine, Baltimore, Williams & Wilkins, c1984, p. 156-177.
LEVEL: A LANG: Eng RC1210 18016

INTRAMURAL SPORTS

Loveland, D. Mara, J. Sports day spectacular. *British Columbia Intramural Recreation Association newsletter (Vancouver) 5(4 Apr 1984, 4-5.*
LEVEL: B LANG: Eng SIRC ARTICLE NO: 108751

Spindt, G.B. Athletics for everyone. *Journal of physical education, recreation & dance (Reston, Va.) 55(6), Aug 1984, 46-47.*
LEVEL: B LANG: Eng SIRC ARTICLE NO: 097837

Vendl, B.C. Dutler, D.C. Holsberry, W.M. Jones, T.C. Ross, M. Interpretive aspects of intramural-recreational sports: selected proceedings from the Thirty-fifth Annual National Intramural-Recreational Sports Association Conference. Corvallis, Or.: Oregon State University, c1984. 285 p.
CONF: National Intramural-Recreational Sports Association Conference (35th : 1984 : Fort Worth, Tex.).
CORP: National Intramural-Recreational Sports Association.
LEVEL: A LANG: Eng GV710 18914

ADMINISTRATION

Gartenberg, M. Intramurals in the athletic department: an approach for survival. *In, Vendl, B.C. (ed.) et al., Interpretive aspects of intramural-recreational sports: selected proceedings from the Thirty-fifth Annual National Intramural-Recreational Sports Association Conference, Corvallis, Or., Oregon State University, c1984, p. 25-30.*
CONF: National Intramural-Recreational Sports Association Conference (35th : 1984 : Fort Worth, Tex.).
LEVEL: B LANG: Eng GV710 18914

Gray, S. Brown, G.M. The M & M's of recreational sports: don't let them melt in you hand. (Refs: 5)*In, Vendl, B.C. (ed.) et al., Interpretive aspects of intramural-recreational sports: selected proceedings from the Thirty-fifth Annual National Intramural-Recreational Sports Association Conference, Corvallis, Or., Oregon State University, c1984, p. 40-48.*
CONF: National Intramural-Recreational Sports

Association Conference (35th : 1984 : Fort Worth, Tex.).
LEVEL: I LANG: Eng GV710 18914

Hirt, S.W. Organization and administration for new sport clubs directors. *In, Vendl, B.C. (ed.) et al., Interpretive aspect of intramural-recreational sports: selected proceedings from the Thirty-fifth Annual National Intramural-Recreational Sports Association Conference, Corvallis, Or., Oregon State University, c1984, p. 212-218.*
CONF: National Intramural-Recreational Sports Association Conference (35th : 1984 : Fort Worth, Tex.).
LEVEL: B LANG: Eng GV710 18914

Hoyles, H. Getting the best use out of all your golf clubs - cooperation between intercollegiates and intramurals - the key to survival in the 80's and 90's. *In, Western Canadian Intramural Workshop, Fifteenth Annual Proceedings, (Banff, Alta.), Alberta Intramural Recreation Association, 1984, p. 11-13.*
CONF: Western Canadian Intramural Workshop (15th : 1984 : Banff, Alta.).
ABST: This paper identifies the ways in which cooperation between intramurals and intercollegiate activities can ultimately benefit the total education process of the student.
LEVEL: B LANG: Eng SIRC ARTICLE NO: 107964

Imergoot, L.S. A tragedy of intramurals: major and minor sports classifications. *NIRSA journal (Corvallis, Ore.) 8(3), Spring 1984, 40-41.*
LEVEL: B LANG: Eng SIRC ARTICLE NO: 097436

Kovalakides, N. Ejections, forfeits and protests. *In, Vendl, B.C. (ed.) et al., Interpretive aspects of intramural-recreational sports: selected proceedings from the Thirty-fifth Annual National Intramural-Recreational Sports Association Conference, Corvallis, Or., Oregon State University, c1984, p. 30-40.*
CONF: National Intramural-Recreational Sports Association Conference (35th : 1984 : Fort Worth, Tex.).
LEVEL: B LANG: Eng GV710 18914

Lamke, G.G. Identifying inservice training needs for recreational sports professionals. (Refs: 5)*NIRSA journal (Corvallis, Ore.) 8(3), Spring 1984, 24-26.*
LEVEL: I LANG: Eng SIRC ARTICLE NO: 097409

Maas, G.M. Leadership and/or management in intramural-recreational sports. (Refs: 11)*NIRSA journal (Corvallis, Ore.) 8(3), Spring 1984, 10;12-13.*
LEVEL: B LANG: Eng SIRC ARTICLE NO: 097410

Maas, G.M. The happy intramural programmer - a modern day fable. *NIRSA journal (Corvallis, Ore.) 8(3), Spring 1984, 42-44.*
NOTES: Based on a similar story found in the following: Ward, William J. The happy worker. Management review. 71(7), 1982, 52-54.
LEVEL: B LANG: Eng SIRC ARTICLE NO: 097437

Maas, G.M. Selected considerations regarding microcomputer hardware and software in intramural-recreational sports applications. (Refs: 18)*NIRSA journal (Corvallis, Ore.) 9(1), Fall 1984, 37-40;53.*
LEVEL: B LANG: Eng SIRC ARTICLE NO: 105153

MacTaggart, B.E. An effective round robin schedule. *Journal of physical education, recreation & dance (Reston, Va.) 55(4), Apr 1984, 74-75.*
LEVEL: B LANG: Eng SIRC ARTICLE NO: 094759

McLellan, R.W. Pope, J.R. Intramural-recreational programs: selecting qualified coordinators. (Refs: 8)*Journal of physical education, recreation & dance (Reston, Va.) 55(6), Aug 1984, 57-58;83.*
LEVEL: I LANG: Eng SIRC ARTICLE NO: 097411

McMinn, W.P. Dunn, J.M. The Mock interview program - an important part of professional development. *NIRSA journal (Corvallis, Ore.) 8(3), Spring 1984, 7-9.*
LEVEL: B LANG: Eng SIRC ARTICLE NO: 097412

Reznik, J.W. The delicate art of terminating staff. *NIRSA journal (Corvallis, Ore.) 8(3), Spring 1984, 28-30.*
LEVEL: B LANG: Eng SIRC ARTICLE NO: 097438

van Snellenberg, J. What's so great about intramurals? Part five - equality. *BC newsletter (Vancouver) 5(5), Jun 1984, 1-3.*
LEVEL: B LANG: Eng SIRC ARTICLE NO: 102933

Wells, J. Renewing facility memberships by mail - efficient/effective. *In, Vendl, B.C. (ed.) et al., Interpretive aspects o intramural-recreational sports: selected proceedings from the Thirty-fifth Annual National Intramural-Recreational Sports Association Conference, Corvallis, Or., Oregon State University, c1984, p. 206-212.*
CONF: National Intramural-Recreational Sports Association Conference (35th : 1984 : Fort Worth, Tex.).
LEVEL: B LANG: Eng GV710 18914

DISABLED

Ducharme, M. Integration and intramurals. *British Columbia Intramural Recreation Association newsletter (Vancouver) 5(4), Apr 1984, 1-2.*
LEVEL: B LANG: Eng SIRC ARTICLE NO: 108750

ECONOMICS

Cargill, T. Morich, J. Taylor, H. McLean, J. Sweeney, J. Closing the income-generation gap. (Refs: 3)*In, Vendl, B.C. (ed.) et al., Interpretive aspects of intramural-recreational sports: selected proceedings from the Thirty-fifth Annual National Intramural-Recreational Sports Association Conference, Corvallis, Or., Oregon State University, c1984, p. 9-19.*
CONF: National Intramural-Recreational Sports Association Conference (35th : 1984 : Fort Worth, Tex.).
LEVEL: I LANG: Eng GV710 18914

Hardy, C. Carswell, B.P. Commercialism in the intramural program - is it worth it? *In, Vendl, B.C. (ed.) et al., Interpretive aspects of intramural-recreational sports: selected proceedings from the Thirty-fifth Annual National Intramural-Recreational Sports Association Conference, Corvallis, Or., Oregon State University, c1984, p. 19-25.*
CONF: National Intramural-Recreational Sports Association Conference (35th : 1984 : Fort Worth, Tex.).
LEVEL: B LANG: Eng GV710 18914

Stinson, R. Green fee sources to keep your programs on par. *In, Western Canadian Intramural Workshop, Fifteenth Annual Proceedings, (Banff, Alta.), Alberta Intramural Recreation Association, 1984, p. 1-7.*
CONF: Western Canadian Intramural Workshop (15th : 1984 : Banff, Alta.).
ABST: Funding sources to help you program

survive and thrive are identified and detailed.
LEVEL: B LANG: Eng SIRC ARTICLE NO: 107961

LAW AND LEGISLATION

House, M.J. McMurray, P.A. Sport club liability - 'who is responsible?' (Refs: 7)*In, Vendl, B.C. (ed.) et al., Interpretive aspects of intramural-recreational sports: selected proceedings from the Thirty-fifth Annual National Intramural-Recreational Sports Association Conference, Corvallis, Or., Oregon State University, c1984, p. 230-234.*
CONF: National Intramural-Recreational Sports Association Conference (35th : 1984 : Fort Worth, Tex.).
LEVEL: I LANG: Eng GV710 18914

OFFICIATING

Craven, J. Hollister, K. McMinn, W. Are your officials going to cope or cop-out? (Refs: 7)*In, Vendl, B.C. (ed.) et al., Interpretive aspects of intramural-recreational sports: selected proceedings from the Thirty-fifth Annual National Intramural-Recreational Sports Association Conference, Corvallis, Or., Oregon State University, c1984, p. 147-156.*
CONF: National Intramural-Recreational Sports Association Conference (35th : 1984 : Fort Worth, Tex.).
LEVEL: I LANG: Eng GV710 18914

Fox, R.L. Officiating: recruiting, training, scheduling, evaluating and paying: a total package. *In, Vendl, B.C. (ed.) et al., Interpretive aspects of intramural-recreational sports: selected proceedings from the Thirty-fifth Annual National Intramural-Recreational Sports Association Conference, Corvallis, Or., Oregon State University, c1984, p. 164-168.*
CONF: National Intramural-Recreational Sports Association Conference (35th : 1984 : Fort Worth, Tex.).
LEVEL: B LANG: Eng GV710 18914

McIntosh, M. The POTACT Evaluation System. (Refs: 9)*In, Vendl, B.C. (ed.) et al., Interpretive aspects of intramural-recreational sports: selected proceedings from the Thirty-fifth Annual National Intramural-Recreational Sports Association Conference, Corvallis, Or., Oregon State University, c1984, p. 157-163.*
CONF: National Intramural-Recreational Sports Association Conference (35th : 1984 : Fort Worth, Tex.).
LEVEL: I LANG: Eng GV710 18914

Seger, J.A. Thesis abstract: an analysis of training methods of selected universities. *NIRSA journal (Corvallis, Ore.) 8(3) Spring 1984, 31.*
LEVEL: B LANG: Eng SIRC ARTICLE NO: 097884

Van Snellenberg, J. Intramural officials. *In, Western Canadian Intramural Workshop, Fifteenth Annual Proceedings, (Banff, Alta.), Alberta Intramural Recreation Association, 1984, p. 1-12.*
CONF: Western Canadian Intramural Workshop (15th : 1984 : Banff, Alta.).
ABST: Provides an overview of the qualities that officials need, such as self-image, fitness and concentration.
LEVEL: B LANG: Eng SIRC ARTICLE NO: 107963

INTRAMURAL SPORTS (continued)

PHYSICAL FITNESS

Bradley, B. Fitness anywhere, for anyone. (Refs: 4)*In, Vendl, B.C. (ed.) et al., Interpretive aspects of intramural-recreational sports: selected proceedings from the Thirty-fifth Annual National Intramural-Recreational Sports Association Conference, Corvallis, Or., Oregon State University, c1984, p. 262-266.*
CONF: National Intramural-Recreational Sports Association Conference (35th : 1984 : Fort Worth, Tex.).
LEVEL: B LANG: Eng GV710 18914

PROGRAMS

Carlton, P. Stinson, R. Achieving the goals of education through intramurals. *Canadian Intramural Recreation Association/Association canadienne de loisirs-intramuros (Ottawa) 9(4), Jan/janv 1984, 12-13.*
LEVEL: B LANG: Eng SIRC ARTICLE NO: 097854

Carter, R. Midday intramurals. *Journal of physical education, recreation & dance (Reston, Va.) 55(4), Apr 1984, 80-81.*
LEVEL: B LANG: Eng SIRC ARTICLE NO: 094747

Cleave, S. Student leaders: dealing with catch 22. (Refs: 10)*In, Canadian Intramural Recreation Association, Sixth National Conference Proceedings, (Geneva Park, Ont.), C.I.R.A., 1984, p. 25-34.*
CONF: Canadian Intramural Recreation Association. National Conference (6th : 1984 : Geneve Park, Ont.).
ABST: Identifies the advantages of student leaders and provides practical suggestions on working with and developing leadership skills in them.
LEVEL: B LANG: Eng SIRC ARTICLE NO: 107947

Fearon, R. Intramurals in the north - a success story to be shared. *In, Canadian Intramural Recreation Association, Sixth National Conference Proceedings, (Geneva Park, Ont.), C.I.R.A., 1984, p. 1-3.*
CONF: Canadian Intramural Recreation Association. National Conference (6th : 1984 : Geneva Park, Ont.).
ABST: Identifies methods and factors used to achieve success in a small intramural program.
LEVEL: B LANG: Eng SIRC ARTICLE NO: 107952

Hatten, T. The fitness educators. *In, Canadian Intramural Recreation Association, Sixth National Conference Proceedings, (Geneva Park, Ont.), C.I.R.A., 1984, p. 35-46.*
CONF: Canadian Intramural Recreation Association. National Conference (6th : 1984 : Geneva Park, Ont.).
ABST: Outlines fundamental principles of physical fitness and approaches to use in implementing a fitness recreation program.
LEVEL: B LANG: Eng SIRC ARTICLE NO: 107953

PROGRAMS - SECONDARY SCHOOL

Costa, M. Specialty events you can offer in your intramural program. *In, Western Canadian Intramural Workshop, Fifteenth Annual Proceedings, (Banff, Alta.), Alberta Intramural Recreation Association, 1984, p. 1-6.*
CONF: Western Canadian Intramural Workshop (15th : 1984 : Banff, Alta.).
ABST: Numerous specific examples of special days

are provided.
LEVEL: B LANG: Eng SIRC ARTICLE NO: 107960

Groves, B. Schiltz, J. Intramurals: a program in trouble. *Virginia journal (Harrisonburg, Va.) 6(2), Apr 1984, 23.*
LEVEL: LANG: Eng SIRC ARTICLE NO: 099329

PROGRAMS - UNIVERSITY AND COLLEGE

Chesnutt, J.T. Haney, R.L. Psychological motivations for participation in recreational sports activities. (Refs: 15)*In, Vendl, B.C. (ed.) et al., Interpretive aspects of intramural-recreational sports: selected proceedings from the Thirty-fifth Annual National Intramural-Recreational Sports Association Conference, Corvallis, Or., Oregon State University, c1984, p. 86-93.*
CONF: National Intramural-Recreational Sports Association Conference (35th : 1984 : Fort Worth, Tex.).
LEVEL: I LANG: Eng GV710 18914

Colgate, J. Sport clubs - self governance and the future. *In, Vendl, B.C. (ed.) et al., Interpretive aspects of intramural-recreational sports: selected proceedings from the Thirty-fifth Annual National Intramural-Recreational Sports Association Conference, Corvallis, Or., Oregon State University, c1984, p. 218-225.*
CONF: National Intramural-Recreational Sports Association Conference (35th : 1984 : Fort Worth, Tex.).
LEVEL: B LANG: Eng GV710 18914

Colline, D.L. Van Whitley, A. Non-credit instruction: a look at two existing programs. *In, Vendl, B.C. (ed.) et al., Interpretive aspects of intramural-recreational sports: selected proceedings from the Thirty-fifth Annual National Intramural-Recreational Sports Association Conference, Corvallis, Or., Oregon State University, c1984, p. 235-241.*
CONF: National Intramural-Recreational Sports Association Conference (35th : 1984 : Fort Worth, Tex.).
LEVEL: B LANG: Eng GV710 18914

Dunn, J.M. Lewis, J. Lore, R. Hawkins, J. Anthony, B. Wysocki, R. Lukes, B. Future shock: campus recreation's odyssey. (Refs 8)*In, Vendl, B.C. (ed.) et al., Interpretive aspects of intramural-recreational sports: selected proceedings from the Thirty-fifth Annual National Intramural-Recreational Sports Association Conference, Corvallis, Or., Oregon State University, c1984, p. 103-107.*
CONF: National Intramural-Recreational Sports Association Conference (35th : 1984 : Fort Worth, Tex.).
LEVEL: I LANG: Eng GV710 18914

Dutler, D.C. Brown, S.C. Intramural 'superstars' competition the easy way operation and financing. (Refs: 4)*In, Vendl, B.C. (ed.) et al., Interpretive aspects of intramural-recreational sports: selected proceedings from the Thirty-fifth Annual National Intramural-Recreational Sports Association Conference, Corvallis, Or., Oregon State University, c1984, p. 57-63.*
CONF: National Intramural-Recreational Sports Association Conference (35th : 1984 : Fort Worth, Tex.).
LEVEL: B LANG: Eng GV710 18914

Goldammer, B. Edmonston, C. Comparison of university sport club programs in the Big 8, Big 10,

Pac 10, Southeastern, and Southwest Athletic Conferences. *In, Vendl, B.C. (ed.) et al., Interpretive aspects of intramural-recreational sports: selected proceedings from the Thirty-fifth Annual National Intramural-Recreational Sports Association Conference, Corvallis, Or., Oregon State University, c1984, p. 225-230.*
CONF: National Intramural-Recreational Sports Association Conference (35th : 1984 : Fort Worth, Tex.).
LEVEL: B LANG: Eng GV710 18914

Hunter, E.D. Give a lift to your weightroom facilities. (Refs: 3)*In, Vendl, B.C. (ed.) et al., Interpretive aspects of intramural-recreational sports: selected proceedings from the Thirty-fifth Annual National Intramural-Recreational Sports Association Conference, Corvallis, Or., Oregon State University, c1984, p. 191-206.*
CONF: National Intramural-Recreational Sports Association Conference (35th : 1984 : Fort Worth, Tex.).
LEVEL: I LANG: Eng GV710 18914

Kintigh, S. Pascuzzi, A. Breaking down the dorm doors. *In, Vendl, B.C. (ed.) et al., Interpretive aspects of intramural-recreational sports: selected proceedings from the Thirty-fifth Annual National Intramural-Recreational Sports Association Conference, Corvallis, Or., Oregon State University, c1984, p. 75-80.*
CONF: National Intramural-Recreational Sports Association Conference (35th : 1984 : Fort Worth, Tex.).
LEVEL: B LANG: Eng GV710 18914

Krasevec, J. Hydrorobics. *In, Vendl, B.C. (ed.) et al., Interpretive aspects of intramural-recreational sports: selected proceedings from the Thirty-fifth Annual National Intramural-Recreational Sports Association Conference, Corvallis, Or., Oregon State University, c1984, p. 53-57.*
CONF: National Intramural-Recreational Sports Association Conference (35th : 1984 : Fort Worth, Tex.).
LEVEL: B LANG: Eng GV710 18914

Osborn, R.L. Lewis, J.A. Flying disc sports and games: the intramural-recreational sports alternative. (Refs: 6)*In, Vendl, B.C. (ed.) et al., Interpretive aspects of intramural-recreational sports: selected proceedings from the Thirty-fifth Annual National Intramural-Recreational Sports Association Conference, Corvallis, Or., Oregon State University, c1984, p. 68-75.*
CONF: National Intramural-Recreational Sports Association Conference (35th : 1984 : Fort Worth, Tex.).
LEVEL: B LANG: Eng GV710 18914

Smyth, J.P. How to get rich in the summer months. *In, Vendl, B.C. (ed.) et al., Interpretive aspects of intramural-recreational sports: selected proceedings from the Thirty-fifth Annual National Intramural-Recreational Sports Association Conference, Corvallis, Or., Oregon State University, c1984, p. 63-68.*
CONF: National Intramural-Recreational Sports Association Conference (35th : 1984 : Fort Worth, Tex.).
LEVEL: B LANG: Eng GV710 18914

Stewart, R.E. Intramural-recreational sports trends. (Refs: 4)*NIRSA journal (Corvallis, Ore.) 9(1), Fall 1984, 15-17.*
LEVEL: B LANG: Eng SIRC ARTICLE NO: 105602

PROMOTION

Bradley, B. How to slice into the intramural market. *In, Western Canadian Intramural Workshop, Fifteenth Annual Proceedings (Banff, Alta.), Alberta Intramural Recreation Association, 1984, p. 1-2.* CONF: Western Canadian Intramural Workshop (15th : 1984 : Banff, Alta.). ABST: Presents a summary of advertising techniques used at one post-secondary institution. LEVEL: B LANG: Eng SIRC ARTICLE NO: 107962

Grimard, A. Publicite et promotion. *Canadian Intramural Recreation Assoc./Assoc. canadienne de loisirs-intramuros bulletin (Ottawa) 10(3), nov/dec 1984, 5-6.* LEVEL: B LANG: Fr SIRC ARTICLE NO: 173403

IRAQ

Sabie, M. Sports of the Desert Arabs of Iraq. (Refs: 8)*KAHPERD journal (Richmond, Ky.) 20(2), Summer 1984, 4-7.* LEVEL: I LANG: Eng SIRC ARTICLE NO: 097871

IVORY COAST

Tano, B. Lassina Diarra. *Revue de l'entraineur janv/mars 1984, 31-32.* LEVEL: B LANG: Fr SIRC ARTICLE NO: 091275

JAI ALAI

ANTHROPOMETRY

Laporte, G. Etude du somatotype du pilotari. Interet prospectif. (Refs: 2)*Medecine du sport (Paris) 58(3), 25 mai 1984, 19-21.* RESUME: L'auteur etudie le somatotype de 44 joueurs de pelote basque. La methode anthropometrique de Heath-Carter est utilise. Les observations suivantes sont faites: 1) le somatotype moyen du pilotari se situe dans la zone endo-mesomorphe, 2) le pilotari arriere doit etre de grande taille et muscle, 3) le pilotari avant doit surtout avoir un 'temperament'. LEVEL: A LANG: Fr SIRC ARTICLE NO: 096716

JAPAN

Leiske, C. Japan advances leisure service. *WLRA journal (New York) 26(2), Mar/Apr 1984, 14-19.* LEVEL: B LANG: Eng SIRC ARTICLE NO: 097865

Niwa, T. The prerequisites for the improvement of international understanding by sports organisations. (Refs: 8)*In, Ilmarinen, M. (ed.) et al., Sport and International Understanding: proceedings of the congress held in Helsinki, Finland, July 7-10, 1982, Berlin, Springer-Verlag, 1984, p. 196-206.* CONF: Congress on Sport and International Understanding (1982 : Helsinki). LEVEL: A LANG: Eng GV706.8 18979

Wilson, L.R. Leisure and recreation in Singapore and Japan. *WLRA journal (New York) 26(2), Mar/Apr 1984, 12-13.* NOTES: Excerpt from presentation at the 1982

United States Mediterranean Sports Congress in Monte Carlo. LEVEL: B LANG: Eng SIRC ARTICLE NO: 097877

JAVELIN THROW

BIOGRAPHY AND AUTOBIOGRAPHY

Berenyi, I. Hundred metre barrier breaker: javelin ace Uwe Hohn profiled by Ivan Berenyi. *Athletics weekly (London) 38(44), 3 Nov 1984, 24-25.* LEVEL: B LANG: Eng SIRC ARTICLE NO: 103625

Moore, K. The latest in a long line. Finland, known for its male javelin throwers, now has a female champion in Tiina Lillak who brings to her event a balance of strength and beauty. *Sports illustrated (Chicago, Ill.) 61(4), 18 Jul 1984, 310-312;314;317;320;323;327;330;332.* NOTES: Special preview: the 1984 Olympics. LEVEL: B LANG: Eng SIRC ARTICLE NO: 097027

Profile: Laslo Babits. *Track and field journal (Ottawa) 26, May 1984, 19-20.* LEVEL: B LANG: Eng Fr SIRC ARTICLE NO: 098717

Willman, H. Lillak a national treasure to Finns. (Ilse Kristiina Lillak) *Track and field news (Los Altos, Calif.) 37(4), Ma 1984, 66.* LEVEL: B LANG: Eng SIRC ARTICLE NO: 095508

BIOMECHANICS

Koltai, J. Problems and techniques in the javelin throw. *Track & field quarterly review (Kalamazoo, Mich.) 84(1), Spring 1984, 32-35.* CONF: International Track & Field Coaches' Congress (8th : 1981 : Olympia). NOTES: Translated by, Marie Cole. LEVEL: I LANG: Eng SIRC ARTICLE NO: 095493

Koltai, J. 8e Congres mondial de l'Association internationale des entraineurs d'athletisme: 'les problemes et la technique d lancer du javelot' ou tout l'art de lacher le javelot au bon moment. *Revue de l'Amicale des entraineurs francais d'athletisme (Paris) 87, avr/mai/juin 1984, 49-52.* LEVEL: I LANG: Fr SIRC ARTICLE NO: 097025

Paish, W. Sequence analysis of Tiina Lillak. *Thrower (West Midlands, Eng.) 28, Feb 1984, 21-24.* LEVEL: I LANG: Eng SIRC ARTICLE NO: 095497

Terauds, J. Biomechanics of Tom Petranoff's javelin throw. (Refs: 5)*Thrower (West Midlands, Eng.) 28, Feb 1984, 10-13.* LEVEL: I LANG: Eng SIRC ARTICLE NO: 095504

Whitbread, M. Bio-mechanics of javelin throwing. *Athletics coach (London) 18(2), Jun 1984, 31-32.* LEVEL: I LANG: Eng SIRC ARTICLE NO: 095507

COACHING

Berenyi, I. As the spear flies. The boycott of the 1984 Olympic Games was a second Olympic disappointment for East Germany javelin coach Karl Hellmann. But he has had many international success stories, among them Ruth Fuchs, Petra Felke and Antje Kempe. *Coaching review (Ottawa) 7, Sept/Oct 1984, 17-21.* LEVEL: B LANG: Eng SIRC ARTICLE NO: 098701

INJURIES AND ACCIDENTS

Francois, M. Ledoyen, C. Khayata, B. Lancer de javelot. Un accident original. *Medecine du sport (Paris) 58(3), 25 mai 1984, 32.* LEVEL: B LANG: Fr SIRC ARTICLE NO: 097023

Sing, R.F. Shoulder injuries in the javelin thrower. (Refs: 23)*Journal of the American Osteopathic Association (Chicago) 83(9), May 1984, 680-684.* LEVEL: I LANG: Eng SIRC ARTICLE NO: 103629

STATISTICS AND RECORDS

Salmenkyla, M. Javelin throw in Finland. *Track & field quarterly review (Kalamazoo, Mich.) 84(1), Spring 1984, 27-28.* NOTES: Reprinted from, The Official Press Guide of the 1st World Track & Field Championships, Helsinki, Finland, 1983. LEVEL: B LANG: Eng SIRC ARTICLE NO: 095502

TECHNIQUES AND SKILLS

Borgstrom, A. Javelin throwing - the Swedish way. *Thrower (West Midlands, Eng.) 29, May 1984, 24-26.* LEVEL: B LANG: Eng SIRC ARTICLE NO: 098702

Geinitz, R. Tasks of the javelin run-up. *Modern athlete and coach (Athelstone, Aust.) 22(3), Jul 1984, 23.* NOTES: From, Der Leichtathlet (East Germany) 37, Sept 1984. LEVEL: B LANG: Eng SIRC ARTICLE NO: 101722

Lawler, P. The javelin - a unique throw. *Modern athlete and coach (Athelstone, Aust.) 22(4), Oct 1984, 19-22.* LEVEL: B LANG: Eng SIRC ARTICLE NO: 105046

Piasenta, J. Technique javelot. *Revue de l'Amicale des entraineurs francais d'athletisme (Paris) 89, oct/nov/dec 1984, 32-33.* LEVEL: B LANG: Fr SIRC ARTICLE NO: 103628

Stenlund, G.M. Javelin throwing for beginners. *Sports (Kallang, Singapore) 12(6), Jul 1984, 28-29.* NOTES: First of a series of six articles. LEVEL: B LANG: Eng SIRC ARTICLE NO: 101727

White, S.C. Introducing the essentials of javelin throwing to beginners. *Technical bulletin - Ontario Track and Field Association (Willowdale, Ont.) 43, Fall 1984, 8-17.* LEVEL: B LANG: Eng SIRC ARTICLE NO: 103631

TRAINING AND CONDITIONING

Digeorgio, G. Javelin training - the dynamic approach. *Track and field journal (Ottawa) 26, May 1984, 25-28.* LEVEL: B LANG: Eng SIRC ARTICLE NO: 098705

Paish, W. The use of the basketball as a training aid for the javelin thrower. *Carnegie research papers (Beckett Park, Leed 1(6), Dec 1984, 19-21.* LEVEL: B LANG: Eng SIRC ARTICLE NO: 172501

Paraanen, A. Pusa, L. Javelin throwers in Helsinki. *Modern athlete and coach (Athelstone, Aust.) 22(3), Jul 1984, 38-40.* NOTES: Summary of the men's javelin observations at the 1st world track and field championships in Helsinki, translated from the throwing section of the final report by the Finnish Athletic Federation. LEVEL: B LANG: Eng SIRC ARTICLE NO: 101723

Pedemonte, J. Specific conditioning for javelin throwers. *Modern athlete and coach (Athelstone, Aust.)* 22(1), Jan 1984, 12-14.
LEVEL: B LANG: Eng SIRC ARTICLE NO: 097028

Tina Lillak (Finland) - her training programme 1981-2. *Thrower (West Midlands, Eng.)* 28, Feb 1984, 25-27.
LEVEL: B LANG: En SIRC ARTICLE NO: 095506

JAZZ DANCE

HISTORY

Midol, N. Pissard, H. La danse jazz 'de la tradition a la modernite'. Paris: Amphora, 1984. 142 p. : ill.
LEVEL: B LANG: Fr

JEUX DU QUEBEC

MEDICINE

Lavallee, H. Goulet, M.P. Prevalence des blessures et des maladies lors des Jeux du Quebec. (Prevalence of wounds and diseas during the Quebec Games.) *Union medicale du Canada (Montreal)* 113(3), mar 1984, 209-210;212-216.
LEVEL: A LANG: Fr SIRC ARTICLE NO: 102523

Prince, P. Releve des blessures survenues aux Jeux du Quebec Sept-Iles - ete 1983. Trois-Rivieres: Regie de la securite dans les sports, 1984. 1v.
CORP: Regie de la securite dans les sports. Service de la recherche.
LEVEL: I LANG: Fr RD97 20599

JU-JUTSU

COUNTRIES AND REGIONS

Kirby, G. Jujitsu in Europe: the French connection. *Black belt (Burbank, Calif.)* 22(3), Mar 1984, 73-75.
LEVEL: B LANG: E SIRC ARTICLE NO: 101392

HISTORY

Le ju-jitsu a-t-il ete decouvert par un Hollandais? *Judo (Paris)* 63, juin 1984, 38-39.
LEVEL: B LANG: Fr SIRC ARTICLE NO: 096742

TECHNIQUES AND SKILLS

Shuper, M. Hakko ryu jujutsu: with power to spare your opponent. *Inside kung-fu (Hollywood, Calif.)* 11(3), Mar 1984, 44-48.
LEVEL: B LANG: Eng SIRC ARTICLE NO: 098327

JUDO

Barrault, D. Le judoka et son poids. *Science et vie (Paris)* HS147, 1984, 98-103.
LEVEL: B LANG: Fr

Parulski, G.R. The complete book of judo. Endorsed by: the American Society of Classical Judoka; the All-Japan Seibukan Martial Arts and Ways Association. Chicago: Contemporary Books,

c1984. ix, 182 p. : ill.
NOTES: Includes index. Bibliography: p. 178.
LEVEL: B LANG: Eng ISBN: 0-8092-5450-6 LC
CARD: 84-004319 GV1114 17591

BIOGRAPHY AND AUTOBIOGRAPHY

Smith, G. There's gold on his menu. For Yasuhiro Yamashita of Japan, an eater of Olympian proportions and possibly the best judo player in history, the competition in the Los Angeles Games should prove to be a real feast. *Sports illustrated (Chicago, Ill.)* 61(4), 18 Jul 1984, 422-426;428;431;434;438;441.
NOTES: Special preview: the 1984 Olympics.
LEVEL: B LANG: Eng SIRC ARTICLE NO: 096722

Un maitre du judo: Sakujiro Yokoyama. *Judo (Paris)* 63, juin 1984, 44-45.
LEVEL: B LANG: Fr SIRC ARTICLE NO: 096717

HISTORY

Aux sources du judo: le Japon. *Judo (Paris)* 61, mars/avr 1984, 19.
NOTES: A suivre.
LEVEL: B LANG: Fr SIRC ARTICLE NO: 099767

Parulski, G.R. Dr. Jigoro Kano and the evolution of judo. *Inside karate (Burbank, Calif.)* 5(8), Aug 1984, 43-49.
LEVEL: B LANG: Eng SIRC ARTICLE NO: 103275

Un siecle de judo. *Judo (Paris)* 60, janv/fevr 1984, 20-21.
NOTES: A suivre.
LEVEL: B LANG: Fr SIRC ARTICLE NO: 096720

Un siecle de judo. *Judo (Paris)* 63, juin 1984, 28.
NOTES: A suivre.
LEVEL: B LANG: Fr SIRC ARTICLE NO: 096721

Un siecle de judo. *Judo (Paris)* 61, mars/avr 1984, 28-29.
NOTES: A suivre.
LEVEL: B LANG: Fr SIRC ARTICLE NO: 099768

Un siecle de judo. Voice de nouvelles pages d'histoire sur les debuts de notre sport. Avec des evenements impressionnants, fantastiques et pleins d'emotions. *Judo (Paris)* 62, mai 1984, 20-21.
NOTES: Voir 'Judo' depuis le no. 55. A suivre.
LEVEL: B LANG: Fr SIRC ARTICLE NO: 099769

INJURIES AND ACCIDENTS

Lelong, D. Prevention des accidents majeurs inherents a l'instabilite chronique de la cheville chez le judoka. (Refs: 19) *Kinesitherapie scientifique (Paris)* 223, 1984, 34-64.
LEVEL: I LANG: Fr

Purcell, M. Judo. *In, Adams, S.H. (ed.), et al., Catastrophic injuries in sports: avoidance strategies, Salinas, Calif., Cayote Press, c1984, p. 117-119.*
LEVEL: B LANG: Eng RD97 19088

Rabenseifner, L. Sportverletzungen und Sportschaeden im Judosport. (Sports injuries and sports damage in judo.) *Unfallheilkunde (Berlin)* 87(12), Dec 1984, 512-516.
LEVEL: I LANG: Ger

Schroeder, E. Injuries to the neck or cervical spine. *Ontario judoka (Willowdale, Ont.)* 9(2), Mar/Apr 1984, 5-6.
LEVEL: B LANG: Eng SIRC ARTICLE NO: 096719

MEDICINE

Barrault, D. Jourdan-Lemoine, M. Badillet, G. Puissant, A. Judo et mycoses interdigitoplantaires. (Refs: 11)*Cinesiologie (Paris)* 95, mai/juin 1984, 235-238.
LEVEL: I LANG: Fr SIRC ARTICLE NO: 098275

PHYSIOLOGY

Ohyabu, Y. Yoshida, A. Hayashi, F. Nishibayashi, Y. Sakakibara, Y. Sato, N. Honda, Y. Ventilatory and heart rate responses t hypoxia in well-trained judo athletes. (Refs: 11)*European journal of applied physiology and occupational physiology (Berlin, FRG)* 52(4), Jun 1984, 451-456.
ABST: This study sought to determine if heavyweight judo athletes have an enhanced ventilatory sensitivity during progressive isocapnic hypoxia. Twenty-four judo athletes breathed steadily decreasing concentrations of O2 in air until the PET O2 (infinite endtidal concentration of O2) was 40 mm Hg. The results indicate that ventilatory sensitivity is enhanced with increasing body weight. There is no such relationship between ventilatory sensitivity and heart rate.
LEVEL: A LANG: Eng SIRC ARTICLE NO: 098276

PSYCHOLOGY

Bacherius, C. Etude de la relation personalite/accidents chez les judokas. (Refs: 27)*Sport: Communaute francaise de Belgiqu (Bruxelles)* 106, 1984, 74-80.
RESUME: Un groupe de 10 judokas ceinture bleue (ages entre 17 et 24 ans), et 10 judokas ceinture noire (ages entre 19 et 26 ans), furent soumis aux tests suivants: le test de reaction a la frustration de Rosenzweig, le psychodiagnostic myokinetique du professeur Mira y Lopez, et le test d'anxiete manifeste de Taylor. Les judokas repondirent egalement a un questionnaire relatifs aux types d'accidents ainsi qu'aux moments ou ces accidents se produisent. Quelques resultats: 1) le judoka est extremement extrapunitif, 2) il presente une forte aggressivite dirigee vers l'exterieure, 3) une relation significative existe entre son autograssivite et les accidents.
LEVEL: A LANG: Fr SIRC ARTICLE NO: 098274

TEACHING

Albertini, P. Pour une pratique et une pedagogie de l'opposition codifiee. *Judo (Paris)* 61, mars/avr 1984, 41-44.
LEVEL: LANG: Fr SIRC ARTICLE NO: 099766

Bresciani, R. Un cycle de judo au college. *EPS: Education physique et sport (Paris, France)* 186, mars/avr 1984, 46-49.
LEVEL: B LANG: Fr SIRC ARTICLE NO: 095130

Hallander, J. Hitting stride: the U.S. judo effort. A former US National Judo Team Coach surveys the improvements made in th United States' Judo program. *Inside karate (Burbank, Calif.)* 5(8), Aug 1984, 37-40.
LEVEL: B LANG: Eng SIRC ARTICLE NO: 103274

KARATE

Dillon, R.W. The myth of the perfected technique. *Inside karate (Burbank, Calif.) 5(12), Dec 1984, 10-11.*
LEVEL: B LANG: Eng SIRC ARTICLE NO: 108137

Habersetzer, R. Karate de la tradition 'Maitres et ecoles de l'Okinawa-te'. Paris: Amphora, c1984. 133 p. : ill. (Sports & loisirs.)
NOTES: Bibliographie: p. 133.
LEVEL: B LANG: Fr ISBN: 2-85180-074-4 GV1114.3 17625

Horsey, T. The scientific search for Ki: karate and behavioral kinesiology. *Inside karate (Burbank, Calif.) 5(7), Jul 1984, 30-35.*
LEVEL: B LANG: Eng SIRC ARTICLE NO: 103306

Joerg, T. The American style: can it ever be called traditional? *Karate illustrated (Burbank, Calif.) 15(12), Dec 1984, 24-27.*
LEVEL: B LANG: Eng SIRC ARTICLE NO: 107359

King, F. Brooks, V. Traditional vs. eclectic free style: who's the best? Part II. *Karate illustrated (Burbank, Calif.) 15(6), Jun 1984, 32-35.*
LEVEL: B LANG: Eng SIRC ARTICLE NO: 103313

Kozuki, R. Winning karate. New York: Sterling Pub. Co., c1984. 1v.
NOTES: Includes index.
LEVEL: B LANG: Eng ISBN: 0806978589 LC CARD: 83-020387

Segal, S. Karate vs kung-fu: which is better? Art does not make the man, the man makes the art. *Inside kung-fu (Hollywood, Calif.) 11(1), Jan 1984, 24-25;30-32.*
LEVEL: B LANG: Eng SIRC ARTICLE NO: 098325

Stone, M. Mike Stone's book of American eclectic karate. Chicago, Ill.: Contemporary Books, c1984. xv, 176 p. : ill.
NOTES: Includes index.
LEVEL: B LANG: Eng ISBN: 0809255065 LC CARD: 83-026291 GV1114.3 18279

Webb, D.A. Karate: challenges and benefits. *NIRSA journal (Corvallis, Ore.) 9(1), Fall 1984, 18-19.*
LEVEL: B LANG: Eng SIRC ARTICLE NO: 105976

ADMINISTRATION

Carnahan, L. Tournament promotion tips. *Karate illustrated (Burbank, Calif.) 15(3), Mar 1984, 24.*
LEVEL: B LANG: Eng SIRC ARTICLE NO: 096731

Ivan, D. Ivan, D. Martial arts in Japan: part seven. Fusajiro Takagi: world karate leader. *Inside karate (Burbank, Calif.) 5(7), Jul 1984, 37-39.*
LEVEL: B LANG: Eng SIRC ARTICLE NO: 103308

BIOGRAPHY AND AUTOBIOGRAPHY

Baker, T. Frank Smith: America's greatest JKA fighter. *Black belt (Burbank, Calif.) 22(1), Jan 1984, 20-25;80.*
LEVEL: B LANG: Eng SIRC ARTICLE NO: 108608

Burke, M. Jean Frenette: Canada's king of kata. *Official karate (Derby, Conn.) 16(125), Nov 1984, 34-36.*
LEVEL: B LANG: E SIRC ARTICLE NO: 108131

Buttitta, B. Dwain Magett: coming back to have some fun. *Karate illustrated (Burbank, Calif.) 15(6),*

Jun 1984, 28-31.
LEVEL: B LANG: Eng SIRC ARTICLE NO: 103287

Crompton, P. Dervan, S. Victor Kan wing chun master: a direct pupil of Yip Man. *Karate and oriental arts (London) 106, Feb/Mar 1984, 6-10.*
LEVEL: B LANG: Eng SIRC ARTICLE NO: 098299

Franck, L. Female full-contact: Cheryl Wheeler's 'leg up' on the competition. *Inside karate (Burbank, Calif.) 5(6), Jun 1984, 56-59.*
LEVEL: B LANG: Eng SIRC ARTICLE NO: 103293

Hoag, D. The quiet ambition of Lori Lantrip. *Karate illustrated (Burbank, Calif.) 15(7), Jul 1984, 16-21;77.*
LEVEL: B LANG: Eng SIRC ARTICLE NO: 103302

Hobbs, R.J. Shian Toma and the legacy of Okinawan karate. *Official karate (Derby, Conn.) 16(120), Apr 1984, 18-20;54.*
LEVEL: B LANG: Eng SIRC ARTICLE NO: 098310

Hosey, T. Percival, B. The 'American' Oyama: a disciple of no-pad, full-contact traditional karate. *Inside karate (Burbank, Calif.) 5(9), Sept 1984, 19-27.*
LEVEL: B LANG: Eng SIRC ARTICLE NO: 107358

Ivan, D. Ivan, D. Master Kunehiko Tosa Gensei-ryu: karate training the 'hard way'. (Kinehiko Tosa) *Kick illustrated (Hollywood, Calif.) 5(1), Jan 1984, 32-36.*
LEVEL: B LANG: Eng SIRC ARTICLE NO: 096740

Ivan, D. Ivan, D. Master Hironori Ohtsuka: heir to Japan's Wado-ryu karate dynasty. *Kick illustrated (Hollywood, Calif.) 5(1), Jan 1984, 38-42.*
LEVEL: B LANG: Eng SIRC ARTICLE NO: 096741

Ivan, D. Ivan, D. The gentle master. *Kick illustrated (Hollywood, Calif.) 5(2), Feb 1984, 40-47.*
LEVEL: B LANG: Eng SIRC ARTICLE NO: 098313

Ivan, D. Ivan, D. Teruo Yamaguchi & the spiritual power of karate. Believe or die. *Kick illustrated (Burbank, Calif.) 5(3), Mar 1984, 44-45.*
NOTES: Martial arts in Japan, part 3.
LEVEL: B LANG: Eng SIRC ARTICLE NO: 098314

Lindsey, R. The last Samurai: the saga of Okinawa's last karate warrior. *Inside karate (Burbank, Calif.) 5(7), Jul 1984, 46-50.*
LEVEL: B LANG: Eng SIRC ARTICLE NO: 103314

Mintale, S. Larry Carnahan: karate's quiet Renaissance man. *Karate illustrated (Burbank, Calif.) 15(3), Mar 1984, 18-24;77.*
LEVEL: B LANG: Eng SIRC ARTICLE NO: 096744

Parulski, G. Kichiro Shimabuku: isshinryu karate's living legend. In this exclusive interview, Kichiro Shimabuku, one of Isshin-ryu's founders, provides keen insight into the style and what it means to be a martial artist. *Official karate (Derby, Conn.) 16(124), Oct 1984, 18-22;24-25.*
LEVEL: B LANG: Eng SIRC ARTICLE NO: 106288

Shuper, M. Ernie Reyes: tradition & the individual talent. *Kick illustrated (Burbank, Calif.) 5(5), May 1984, 24-28.*
LEVEL: B LANG: Eng SIRC ARTICLE NO: 101396

Shuper, M. Hirokazu Kanazawa: Shotokan's ultimate master? *Inside karate (Burbank, Calif.) 5(6), Jun 1984, 18-23.*
LEVEL: B LANG: Eng SIRC ARTICLE NO: 103320

Stevens, C. The legendary Richard Kim: karate's guiding light. *Black belt (Burbank, Calif.) 22(4), Apr 1984, 20-24;106.*
LEVEL: B LANG: Eng SIRC ARTICLE NO: 099811

Takatsuno, S. A modern-day Funakoshi: keeping traditional karate's flame alive. *Black belt (Burbank, Calif.) 22(8), Aug 1984, 45-48;96.*
LEVEL: B LANG: Eng SIRC ARTICLE NO: 105975

BIOMECHANICS

Muzila, T. Biomechanics and karate. *Karate illustrated (Burbank, Calif.) 15, Yearbook 1984, 20;23-24.*
LEVEL: B LANG: Eng SIRC ARTICLE NO: 099804

Muzila, T. Biomechanics and the power line of the traditional karate punch. *Karate illustrated (Burbank, Calif.) 15(10), Oc 1984, 38-43.*
LEVEL: B LANG: Eng SIRC ARTICLE NO: 108116

Nistico, V.P. A kinematic investigation of two performance conditions of the karate counter-punch technique. Eugene, Ore.: Microform Publications, University of Oregon, 1984. 1 microfiche : negative, ill. ; 11 x 15 cm.
NOTES: Thesis (M.S.) - University of Oregon, 1982; (viii, 50 leaves); vita; includes bibliography.
LEVEL: A LANG: Eng UO84 46

CHILDREN

Cho, S.H. Better karate for boys. New York: Dodd, Mead, (1984), c1970. 61 p. : ill. (A better sports book.)
LEVEL: B LANG: Eng ISBN: 039608477X LC CARD: 84-008089

Habersetzer, R. Karate pour les jeunes: technique et pedagogie. Paris: Amphora, 1984. 254 p. : ill. (Sports & loisirs.)
NOTES: Includes index.
LEVEL: B LANG: Fr ISBN: 2851800094 LC CARD: 82-163688 GV1114.32 17482

Hoag, D. A modest proposal: has the time arrived for nationalized children's rules? *Karate illustrated (Burbank, Calif.) 15(4), Apr 1984, 54-58.*
LEVEL: B LANG: Eng SIRC ARTICLE NO: 098308

COUNTRIES AND REGIONS

Strandberg, K.W. Kumite over China: karate in Taiwan. *Inside karate (Burbank, Calif.) 5(7), Jul 1984, 62-65.*
LEVEL: B LANG: Eng SIRC ARTICLE NO: 103322

EQUIPMENT

Demura, F. Kama: karate weapon of self-defense. Burbank, Calif.: Ohara Publications, c1984. 159 p. : ill. ; 23 cm.
LEVEL: B LANG: Eng ISBN: 0897501012 LC CARD: 84-061149

Parulski, G.R. The art of karate weapons: a complete manual of traditional and modern applications. Chicago: Contemporary Books, 1984. 1v.
NOTES: Includes index.
LEVEL: I LANG: Eng ISBN: 0809254409 LC CARD: 84-007021

FACILITIES

Haog, D. The Dojo/Health Club: new-wave instruction may be traditional karate's downfall. *Black belt (Burbank, Calif.) 22(2), Feb 1984, 66-70;95.*
LEVEL: B LANG: Eng SIRC ARTICLE NO: 096739

KARATE (continued)

HISTORY

Shuper, M. Present: at the creation. A personal memoir of shotokan karate. *Inside karate (Burbank, Calif.) 5(11), Nov 1984, 20-25.*
NOTES: Part 1 (1942-1955).
LEVEL: B LANG: Eng SIRC ARTICLE NO: 107369

INJURIES AND ACCIDENTS

Bjerrum, L. Scapula alata opstaet ved karatetraening. (Scapula alata induced by karate.) *Ugeskrift for laeger (Copenhagen) 146(27), 2 Jul 1984, 2022.*
NOTES: Includes English abstract.
LEVEL: I LANG: Dan

Vayssairat, M. Priollet, P. Capron, L. Hagege, A. Housset, E. Does karate injure blood vessels of the hand? (letter) *Lancet (London) 2(8401), 1 Sept 1984, 529.*
LEVEL: I LANG: Eng SIRC ARTICLE NO: 104826

MEDICINE

Delaunay, M. Vu-Dinh, S. Homeopathie et preparation de sportifs: deux ans de recul. *Homeopathie francaise (Paris) 72(5), 1984, 328-330.*
LEVEL: I LANG: Fr

OFFICIATING

The best referees and judges in tournament karate (as selected by the best competitors). *Karate illustrated (Burbank, Calif.) 15(1), Jan 1984, 52-55.*
LEVEL: B LANG: Eng SIRC ARTICLE NO: 108124

PHYSICAL FITNESS

Nardi, T.J. Roadwork: running for martial arts success. *Black belt (Burbank, Calif.) 22(4), Apr 1984, 54-57;107-108;112.*
LEVEL: B LANG: Eng SIRC ARTICLE NO: 099806

Stricevic, M.V. Patel, M.R. Kanamura, S. Kerner, M.S. Stricevic, B. Non-contact vs. semi-contact karate: which is a better cardiovascular workout? *Black belt (Burbank, Calif.) 22(8), Aug 1984, 58-62;104.*
LEVEL: I LANG: Eng SIRC ARTICLE NO: 105974

PHYSIOLOGY

Allard, Y.E. Kickboxers vs karate fighters: who's in better shape? *Black belt (Burbank, Calif.) 22(2), Feb 1984, 44-48;107.*
LEVEL: I LANG: Eng SIRC ARTICLE NO: 096730

Allard, Y.E. Kickboxers vs. karate fighters: part 11. Who trains harder? *Black belt (Burbank, Calif.) 22(3), Mar 1984, 62-66;101-102.*
LEVEL: I LANG: Eng SIRC ARTICLE NO: 099789

Sticevic, M.V. Tanner, A.J. Okazaki, T. Michielli, D.W. Kerner, M.S. High-tech karate: monitering cardiovascular and metabolic responses to selected techniques. *Black belt (Burbank, Calif.) 22 (Yearbook), 1984, 48-52.*
LEVEL: I LANG: Eng SIRC ARTICLE NO: 101399

PSYCHOLOGY

Seabourne, T. Weinberg, R. Jackson, A. Effect of individualized practice and training of visuo-motor behavior rehearsal in enhancing karate performance. (Refs: 18)*Journal of sport behavior (Mobile, Ala.) 7(2), Jun 1984, 58-67.*
ABST: The purpose of the present investigation was to determine whether individualized practice and training in visuo-motor behavior rehearsal (VMBR) is more effective in improving karate performance than a placebo control practice and training condition (memorizing Chinese proverbs and writings). Subjects were composed of 18 male and 26 female students from two karate classes with one class serving as the VMBR training group and the other as the placebo control training group. During the first session of the class (which met twice a week for 16 weeks) each subject was individually provided with a detailed description of their specific cognitive strategy including handouts and manipulation checks to use for practice at home. In addition to their home practice, subjects were provided with individual training during each karate class period with modifications made in their strategy when appropriate. Results for the state anxiety and high activation scales showed that the VMBR group exhibited significantly greater decreases in both state anxiety and activation over time than the placebo group. Performance results indicated that the VMBR group displayed greater levels of improvement over time than the placebo control group for three measures of karate performance (i.e., skill, combinations and sparring).
LEVEL: A LANG: Eng SIRC ARTICLE NO: 099810

PSYCHOLOGY - MENTAL TRAINING

Schreck, T. Control the beast within: relaxation, concentration and something called VMBR to improve technique. *Karate illustrated (Burbank, Calif.) 15(4), Apr 1984, 38-41.*
LEVEL: B LANG: Eng SIRC ARTICLE NO: 098324

RULES AND REGULATIONS

Hoag, D. The problems of an unregulated sport. *Karate illustrated (Burbank, Calif.) 15, Yearbook 1984, 65-69.*
LEVEL: B LANG: Eng SIRC ARTICLE NO: 099799

SPORTING EVENTS

Hoag, D. Richard Plowden and a manifesto for the future of tournament karate. *Karate illustrated (Burbank, Calif.) 15(10), Oct 1984, 16-17;20-22;43.*
LEVEL: B LANG: Eng SIRC ARTICLE NO: 108111

Lowry, D. Whither thou goest, Olympic karate? *Karate illustrated (Burbank, Calif.) 15(10), Oct 1984, 60-63.*
LEVEL: B LANG Eng SIRC ARTICLE NO: 108118

STRATEGY

Baker, T. Competing at traditional tournaments: how to play the game - and win. *Black belt (Burbank, Calif.) 22(8), Aug 1984, 36-40.*
LEVEL: B LANG: Eng SIRC ARTICLE NO: 105965

Buttitta, B. The rated tournament game: can you beat the system? *Karate illustrated (Burbank, Calif.) 15(7), Jul 1984, 48-53;82.*
LEVEL: B LANG: Eng SIRC ARTICLE NO: 103288

Know thy opponent. *Karate illustrated (Burbank, Calif.) 15(10), Oct 1984, 18-19.*
LEVEL: B LANG: Eng SIRC ARTICLE NO: 108112

Sternberg, A. Body shifting: the secret to fighting success. *Black belt (Burbank, Calif.) 22(8), Aug 1984, 64-67.*
LEVEL: LANG: Eng SIRC ARTICLE NO: 105973

TEACHING

Hassell, R.G. In the hornets' nest: a look at traditional instruction for instructors. *Karate illustrated (Burbank, Calif.) 15(8), Aug 1984, 47-51.*
LEVEL: B LANG: Eng SIRC ARTICLE NO: 104823

Hassell, R.G. Keep training: the Okazaki prescription for success. *Black belt magazine (Burbank, Calif.) 22(10), Oct 1984, 20-24;26.*
LEVEL: B LANG: Eng SIRC ARTICLE NO: 107355

Melton, J.R. Learning and practice: where to start learning to teach. *Karate illustrated (Burbank, Calif.) 15(10), Oct 1984 24-27;76-77.*
LEVEL: B LANG: Eng SIRC ARTICLE NO: 108113

Soller, D.S. Teaching in the College Dojo. *Black belt (Burbank, Calif.) 22(1), Jan 1984, 8;97-98.*
LEVEL: B LANG: Eng SIRC ARTICLE NO: 108614

Sylvia, R. So you want to be a sensei? *Inside karate (Burbank, Calif.) 5(9), Sept 1984, 54-56.*
LEVEL: B LANG: Eng SIRC ARTICLE NO: 107377

TECHNIQUES AND SKILLS

Annesi, T. Kicking for depth. *Inside karate (Burbank, Calif.) 5(10), Oct 1984, 52-57.*
LEVEL: B LANG: Eng SIRC ARTICLE NO: 107334

Buttitta, B. Yoskukai karate: not for the weak of heart. *Black belt magazine (Burbank, Calif.) 22(5), May 1984, 54-57;106;108.*
LEVEL: B LANG: Eng SIRC ARTICLE NO: 103286

Carrabis, J.-D. Japanese Goju vs. Okinawan Goju. *Black belt (Burbank, Calif.) 22(7), Jul 1984, 64-67;100-101.*
LEVEL: B LANG: Eng SIRC ARTICLE NO: 103289

Christensen, L.W. Block and you might have to block all day. Counter and you're likely to get hit. The solution? Blockcounte *Karate illustrated (Burbank, Calif.) 15(6), Jun 1984, 24-27;76-77.*
LEVEL: B LANG: Eng SIRC ARTICLE NO: 103290

Comparative systems. *Kick illustrated (Hollywood, Calif.) 5(1), Jan 1984, 66-69.*
LEVEL: B LANG: Eng SIRC ARTICLE NO: 096734

Franck, L. Deadly spinning kicks. *Black belt magazine (Burbank, Calif.) 22(10), Oct 1984, 28-32.*
LEVEL: B LANG: Eng SIRC ARTICLE NO: 107346

Ganci, M.T. Traditional karate: components for a school program. *Journal of physical education, recreation & dance (Reston, Va.) 55(9), Nov/Dec 1984, 68-69.*
LEVEL: B LANG: Eng SIRC ARTICLE NO: 103294

Gilbert, G. Wadokikai: the 'complete' karate system. Master Johnny Pereria's incorporation of old and new is the basis for the production of a balanced, powerful, effective karate system. *Official karate (Derby, Conn.) 16(125), Nov 1984, 29-33;52.*
LEVEL: B LANG: Eng SIRC ARTICLE NO: 108130

Hausman, C. Dakas, C. Common sense self defense. Wauwatosa, Wisc. : Aurora, Ill.: Leather

Stocking Books ; Caroline House, c1984. 208 p. : ill.
LEVEL: B LANG: Eng ISBN: 089769080X LC CARD: 84-225517

Hoag, D. Hara and traditional karate: a lesson with shotokan's Hirokazu Kanazawa. *Karate illustrated (Burbank, Calif.) 15(9), Sept 1984, 16-22.*
LEVEL: B LANG: Eng SIRC ARTICLE NO: 103303

Hoag, D. Sanchin kata: Hidy Ochiai explains it all for you. *Karate illustrated (Burbank, Calif.) 15(1), Jan 1984, 21-24;76.*
LEVEL: B LANG: Eng SIRC ARTICLE NO: 108119

Hosey, T. No free kicks. 'Never give a kicker an even break'. *Official karate (Derby, Conn.) 16(125), Nov 1984, 37-41.*
LEVEL: B LANG: Eng SIRC ARTICLE NO: 108132

Kamhi, N. Pinan Shodan: the beginner's kata of self-defense. *Karate illustrated (Burbank, Calif.) 15(4), Apr 1984, 46-49.*
LEVEL: B LANG: Eng SIRC ARTICLE NO: 098316

Kearney, G. Leg techniques: the key to developing powerful punching efficiency. *Inside karate (Burbank, Calif.) 5(6), Jun 1984, 33-37;39.*
LEVEL: B LANG: Eng SIRC ARTICLE NO: 103311

Lenzi, S. The blocking & striking arsenal of Okinawan Goju-Ryu. *Black belt magazine (Burbank, Calif.) 22(12), Dec 1984, 28-32.*
LEVEL: B LANG: Eng SIRC ARTICLE NO: 107360

Maberry, J.E. Karate and jujitsu: working harmony? *Karate illustrated (Burbank, Calif.) 15(7), Jul 1984, 26-30.*
LEVEL: B LANG: Eng SIRC ARTICLE NO: 103315

Naito, I. Lenzi, S. The history and evolution of Shorei-Kan Goju-Ryu karate. *Black belt (Burbank, Calif.) 22(4), Apr 1984, 50-53.*
LEVEL: B LANG: Eng SIRC ARTICLE NO: 099805

Nardi, T.J. Tensho and Sil Lim Tao: the Goju-Wing Chun connection. *Black belt (Burbank, Calif.) 22(2), Feb 1984, 38-42;112.*
LEVEL: B LANG: Eng SIRC ARTICLE NO: 096745

Shuper, M. Bassai kata: karate's living history. *Kick illustrated (Hollywood, Calif.) 5(2), Feb 1984, 20-29.*
LEVEL: B LANG: Eng SIRC ARTICLE NO: 098326

Sullivan, D. The winning kumite theory of Kanzen Goju. The first in our exclusive three-part series covering Shihan Harry Rosenstein's comprehensive guide for the tournament karate fighter. *Official karate (Derby, Conn.) 16(125), Nov 1984, 18-22;24-25.*
LEVEL: B LANG: Eng SIRC ARTICLE NO: 108128

Turshiary, M. Straight from the heart: an Okinawan teacher of teachers looks backward and forward from 30 years in the art. *Karate illustrated (Burbank, Calif.) 15(2), Feb 1984, 21-24;38.*
LEVEL: B LANG: Eng SIRC ARTICLE NO: 108213

Vitali, K. Mitchell, K. Keith Vitali's winning karate techniques. Chicago: Contemporary Books, c1984. 1v.
NOTES: Includes index.
LEVEL: B LANG: Eng ISBN: 0809254921 LC CARD: 84-001814

Westerlin, D. Empty hand, loaded gun: the ultimate system for close combat. Boulder, Colo.: Paladin Press, c1984. iii, 116 p : ill.
LEVEL: B LANG: Eng ISBN: 0873642910 LC CARD: 84-226138

TECHNIQUES AND SKILLS - BLOCKING

Maberry, J.E. Grabbing the kick: an alternative to blocking. *Karate illustrated (Burbank, Calif.) 15(12), Dec 1984, 34-38.*
LEVEL: B LANG: Eng SIRC ARTICLE NO: 107362

TRAINING AND CONDITIONING

Annesi, T. Creating free-sparring combinations: building a foundation for freestyle sparring. *Inside karate (Burbank, Calif.) 5(7), Jul 1984, 55-60.*
LEVEL: B LANG: Eng SIRC ARTICLE NO: 103282

Birrer, R.B. Training to break safely: it's one thing to know how to break... but it's another to know how to do it without being injured. *Karate illustrated (Burbank, Calif.) 15(8), Aug 1984, 22-26.*
LEVEL: B LANG: Eng SIRC ARTICLE NO: 104820

Christensen, L.W. Solo training: walking the path alone. *Karate illustrated (Burbank, Calif.) 15(8), Aug 1984, 39-42;82.*
LEVEL: B LANG: Eng SIRC ARTICLE NO: 104821

Rabesa, A. Kumite: the complete fighting text. Plymouth, N.H.: Peabody Pub. Co., 1984. 1v.
NOTES: Includes index.
LEVEL: B LANG: Eng ISBN: 0930559002 LC CARD: 84-016609

Siverio, M. The training partner: how to enhance your training program and improve performance. *Kick illustrated (Hollywood Calif.) 5(2), Feb 1984, 30-35.*
LEVEL: B LANG: Eng SIRC ARTICLE NO: 098328

Wilson, R. The makiwara: karate's silent training partner. *Black belt magazine (Burbank, Calif.) 22(11), Nov 1984, 59-61.*
LEVEL: B LANG: Eng SIRC ARTICLE NO: 107380

TRAINING AND CONDITIONING - DRILLS

Christensen, L. Reps reps reps: once is not enough for the martial artist training to be a champion. *Karate illustrated (Burbank, Calif.) 15(3), Mar 1984, 44-49.*
LEVEL: B LANG: Eng SIRC ARTICLE NO: 096732

TRAINING AND CONDITIONING - WEIGHT AND STRENGTH TRAINING

Siverio, M. Abdominal training: everybody trains for a stronger punch and a higher kick, but are you neglecting that far mor vulnerable midsection? *Karate illustrated (Burbank, Calif.) 15(12), Dec 1984, 40-43;82.*
LEVEL: B LANG: Eng SIRC ARTICLE NO: 107372

Wheeler, C. The great weight training debate: part II. Should a female fighter lift? *Black belt magazine (Burbank, Calif.) (11), Nov 1984, 44-48;110.*
LEVEL: B LANG: Eng SIRC ARTICLE NO: 107379

WOMEN

Parulski, G.R. Confessions of a woman black belt. An instructor of isshin ryu karate (and a former AAU National Champion) expounds on training, tradition and Americanization. *Kick illustrated (Hollywood, Calif.) 5(2), Feb 1984, 50-52.*
LEVEL: B LANG: Eng SIRC ARTICLE NO: 098323

KAYAKING

Beaudou, A. Les bassins de slalom en canoe-kayak. (Refs: 17)*Dans, Culture technique no. 13, Neuilly-sur-Seine, France, Centre de Recherche sur la Culture Technique, c1984, p. 314-323.*
LEVEL: I LANG: Fr RC1235 20096

Freifeld, K. Sprinting on water: kayakers paddle at a wicked 105 strokes per minute - and that's when they're really relaxin *Health (New York) 16(6), Jun 1984, 27;30-32.*
LEVEL: B LANG: Eng SIRC ARTICLE NO: 101372

Sanders, W. Kayak touring. Harrisburg, Pa.: Stackpole Books, c1984. vii, 247 p. : ill.
NOTES: Bibliography: p. 235-239.
LEVEL: I LANG: Eng ISBN: 0-8117-2193-0 LC CARD: 83-18145 GV789 17511

Welhouse, M. Downriver racing: part II. *American whitewater (Hagerstown, Md.) 29(4), Jul/Aug 1984, 12-14.*
LEVEL: B LANG: Eng SIRC ARTICLE NO: 103278

BIOGRAPHY AND AUTOBIOGRAPHY

Craven, S. A kayak winner who's born to luge. (David Gilman) *Olympian (Colorado Springs, Colo.) 11(1), Jun 1984, 10-12.*
LEVEL: B LANG: Eng SIRC ARTICLE NO: 101382

Evans, E. The old ways will not do: Lugbill. *Canoe (Camden, Me.) 12(2), Apr 1984, 32-38;40-41;92-93.*
LEVEL: B LANG: Eng SIRC ARTICLE NO: 099772

Freifeld, K. The kayak kid. Cathy Marino and her sport just might make it to the big time together. *Health (New York) 16(6) Jun 1984, 24-26.*
LEVEL: B LANG: Eng SIRC ARTICLE NO: 101373

CHILDREN

Leurson, G. La kayak a l'ecole elementaire. *EPS: Revue education physique et sport (Paris) 188, juil/aout 1984, 30-33.*
LEVEL: B LANG: Fr SIRC ARTICLE NO: 098280

CLUBS AND TEAMS

Jackson, B. The making of a club: the how & why of gettin' it all together. *American whitewater (Hagerstown, Md.) 29(1), Jan/Feb 1984, 31-35.*
ABST: This article offers excellent advice on how to transform an informal group of whitewater enthusiasts into an active club organization. Initial concerns will focus on administering the club, conducting club meetings, scheduling trips, establishing policies, and controlling money. The newsletter is touted as an important source of information for both members and prospective members and can often be the lifeline of a club. Finally, useful tips on how to attract more members are outlined so that the member support base can be broadened.
LEVEL: B LANG: Eng SIRC ARTICLE NO: 108885

COACHING

Beaudou, A. Championnats du monde de canoe-kayak 1983. Interview de Bill Endicott, entraineur des slalomeurs americains. *EPS: Education physique et sport (Paris, France) 186, mars/avr 1984, 50-53.*
LEVEL: B LANG: Fr SIRC ARTICLE NO: 095132

KAYAKING (continued)

COUNTRIES AND REGIONS

Walbridge, C. River classification: a new look at an old problem. *American whitewater (Hagerstown, Md.) 29(1), Jan/Feb 1984 17-23.*
LEVEL: B LANG: Eng SIRC ARTICLE NO: 108883

DISABLED

Hugon, E. Sports a risques et nouveaux sports: canoe-kayak. *Handisport magazine (Paris) 33, sept/oct 1984, 14-15.*
LEVEL: LANG: Fr SIRC ARTICLE NO: 173377

Jacobs, S. Saltwater kayaking for the marine enthusiast. *Sports 'n spokes (Phoenix, Ariz.) 9(5), Jan/Feb 1984, 24-26.*
LEVEL: B LANG: Eng SIRC ARTICLE NO: 094318

EQUIPMENT

Allan, M. Sportyaks: small boats big thrills. *River runner (Vista, Calif.) 4(4), Jul/Aug 1984, 16-18.*
LEVEL: B LANG: Eng SIRC ARTICLE NO: 101369

Anderson, F. Hydra P-51 Mustang: short in length, long on performance. *Canoe (Camden, Me.) 12(1), Feb/Mar 1984, 71-73.*
LEVEL: B LANG: Eng SIRC ARTICLE NO: 098278

Arnold, G.E. The $100 kayak. (Refs: 1)*NIRSA journal (Mt. Pleasant, Mich.) 8(2), Winter 1984, 32-34.*
LEVEL: B LANG: Eng SIRC ARTICLE NO: 098279

Buying guide. *Canoeing (London, Eng.) 73, Feb 1984, 16-18.*
LEVEL: B LANG: Eng SIRC ARTICLE NO: 097476

Chute, J. Perception Gyramax. Finally a plastic decked canoe for REAL paddlers. *Canoe (Camden, Me.) 12(3), May/Jun 1984, 96-98.*
LEVEL: B LANG: Eng SIRC ARTICLE NO: 101370

Finding your kayak: how to get the most out of the buyer's guide listings. *Canoe (Camden, Me.) 12(6), Nov/Dec 1984, 74-82;84-90;92-98.*
LEVEL: B LANG: Eng SIRC ARTICLE NO: 108622

Rock, H. Getchell, D.R. Viehman, J. Fully-equipped: some notes on gear. *Canoe (Camden, Me.) 12(1), Feb/Mar 1984, 28-29;60;62-63.*
LEVEL: B LANG: Eng SIRC ARTICLE NO: 097983

Woodward, B. Prijon's new T-Slalom Kayak: a fresh, foreign approach. *River runner (Vista, Calif.) 4(6), Nov/Dec 1984, 21-22*
LEVEL: B LANG: Eng SIRC ARTICLE NO: 173162

PHYSIOLOGY

Csanady, M. Forster, T. Gruber, N. Hogye, M. Moczo, I. A kajakozast vagy kenuzast versenyszeruleg elkezdo fiuk echokardiografias oesszahasonlitasa azonos koru, nem sportolo tarsaikkal. (Comparison of echocardiographic data on beginner kayakcanoeists and non-sporting boys of the same age.) (Refs: 26)*Sportorvosi szemle/ Hungarian review of sports medicine (Budapest) 25(3), 1984, 197-207.*
ABST: A series of examinations is planned for years, to follow the changes in the echocardiographic parameters of kayak-canoeist competitors in comparison with the data on non-trained boys of the same age. The present publication reports the starting data at the end of the first season. Significant differences were found between the groups: the left ventricular cavity of kayak-canoeists was larger, while the left ventricular posterior wall and especially the interventricular septum were thicker, than in non-trained boys.
LEVEL: A LANG: Hun SIRC ARTICLE NO: 100236

Melchionda, A.M. Clarkson, P.M. Denko, C. Freedson, P. Graves, J. Katch, F. The effect of local isometric exercise in serum levels of beta-endorphin/beta-lipotropin. (Refs: 17)*Physician and sportsmedicine (Minneapolis, Minn.) 12(9), Sept 1984, 102-105;108-109.*
ABST: The purpose of this study was to compare serum levels of beta-endorphin and beta-lipotropin before and after an isometric knee-extension exercise regimen. Six elite kayak paddlers and fourteen untrained subjects participated in the study. No significant differences in resting beta-endorphin and beta-lipotropin was observed between the two groups. Subjects experimented a strength loss of approximatively 34% and severe muscle exertion and discomfort.
LEVEL: A LANG: Eng SIRC ARTICLE NO: 099773

Tesch, P.A. Lindeberg, S. Blood lactate accumulation during arm exercise in world class kayak paddlers and strength trained athletes. (Refs: 28)*European journal of applied physiology and occupational physiology (Berlin, FRG) 52(4), Jun 1984, 441-445.*
ABST: Blood lactate accumulation during continuous arm cranking of progressively increasing intensity was compared in 11 elite flat water kayakers, 6 elite weight-/power-lifters, 8 body-builders and 6 physically active non-athletes. Blood lactate concentrations were significantly lower in the kayakers compared to the other groups at low submaximal exercise intensities. At higher work outputs the differences between male kayakers and non-kayakers increased while the differences between female kayakers and non-kayakers decreased. The results suggest that factors other than muscle mass per se are responsible for the blood lactate response during progressive arm-cranking exercise.
LEVEL: A LANG: Eng SIRC ARTICLE NO: 098769

PHYSIOLOGY - MUSCLE

Tesch, P.A. Karlsson, J. Muscle metabolite accumulation following maximal exercise: a comparison between short-term and prolonged kayak performance. (Refs: 30)*European journal of applied physiology and occupational physiology (Heidelberg) 52(2), Jan 1984, 243-246.*
ABST: Muscle metabolites were measured in five elite flatwater kayak paddlers before and after short-term arm work, which simulated competitive kayak racing, varying in intensity and duration. Lactate, glycogen, ATP, CP, glucose and G-6-P were determined from muscle biopsy samples. This study demonstrates some of the distinguishable metabolic responses to a specific athletic performance task. The implications are discussed and related to other studies.
LEVEL: A LANG: Eng SIRC ARTICLE NO: 096724

SAFETY

Derrer, T. Sea kayak flotation: some buoyant ideas. *River runner (Vista, Calif.) 4(3), May/Jun 1984, 46-51.*
NOTES: First in a series of three.
LEVEL: B LANG: Eng SIRC ARTICLE NO: 099771

Derrer, T. A practical guide to keeping the capsized sea kayak afloat. *River runner (Vista, Calif.) 4(4), Jul/Aug 1984, 41-42.*
NOTES: Second in a series of three articles.
LEVEL: B LANG: Eng SIRC ARTICLE NO: 101371

Moyer, L. Coastal kayaking is a matter of seamanship. *River runner (Vista, Calif.) 4(2), Mar/ Apr 1984, 47-49.*
LEVEL: B LANG: Eng SIRC ARTICLE NO: 098281

Skinner, P. Considerations of mortality. *American whitewater (Hagerstown, Md.) 29(4), Jul/Aug 1984, 27-29.*
LEVEL: B LANG: Eng SIRC ARTICLE NO: 103277

TECHNIQUES AND SKILLS

Banducci, D. Surfing river waves: making time (and a kayak) stand still. *Canoe (Camden, Me.) 12(2), Apr 1984, 18-21;70-71.*
LEVEL: B LANG: Eng SIRC ARTICLE NO: 099770

Chute, J. Kayak touring: how to paddle in open water - all day long. *Canoe (Camden, Me.) 12(5), Sept/Oct 1984, 30-34;59.*
LEVEL: B LANG: Eng SIRC ARTICLE NO: 173544

Endicott, B. The ideal upstream. *American whitewater (Hagerstown, Md.) 29(1), Jan/Feb 1984, 26-30.*
LEVEL: B LANG: Eng SIR ARTICLE NO: 108884

Ray, R. Secrets of the Eskimo roll. *River runner (Vista, Calif.) 4(2), Mar/Apr 1984, 39-40;53.*
LEVEL: B LANG: Eng SIRC ARTICLE NO: 098282

West Virginia squirt boaters: blasting into the third dimension. *River runner (Vista, Calif.) 4(6), Nov/ Dec 1984, 25-26.*
LEVEL: B LANG: Eng SIRC ARTICLE NO: 173163

TRAINING AND CONDITIONING - DRILLS

Wall, C. Mastering the downstream lean makes hands-off boating easy. *River runner (Vista, Calif.) 4(3), May/Jun 1984, 28-29.*
LEVEL: B LANG: Eng SIRC ARTICLE NO: 099775

TRAINING AND CONDITIONING - WEIGHT AND STRENGTH TRAINING

Cezard, J.P. Reflexion sur le renforcement musculaire en canoe-kayak.
NOTES: Dans, Renforcement musculaire, Paris, Institut national du sport et de l'education physique, c1984, p. 99-124.
LEVEL: A LANG: Fr GV711.5 18233

McCormick, M. Strength, power and weights. *ACA competitor's newsletter (Lorton, Va.) Sept/Oct 1984, 9-10.*
NOTES: The Athlete's exchange 3(7), Oct 1984.
LEVEL: B LANG: Eng SIRC ARTICLE NO: 103276

VARIATIONS

Nordby, L. Kayak kite sailing: gone with the wind. *River runner (Vista, Calif.) 4(4), Jul/Aug 1984, 40.*
LEVEL: B LANG: En SIRC ARTICLE NO: 101374

KENDO

MEDICINE

Mineoka, K. Yamamoto, K. Isemura, T. Fujii, H. Wada, S. Masaki, K. (A case of march hemoglobinuria following 'kendo' (Japanese fencing) exercise.) *Rinsho Ketsueki (Tokyo) 25(10), Oct 1984, 1680-1685.*
LEVEL: A LANG: Jpn

TECHNIQUES AND SKILLS

Raick, J.P. Iai do: l'art de degainer le sabre. *Voix du kendo (France) 12, 1984, 7-8.*
NOTES: A suivre.
LEVEL: B LANG: Fr

Raick, J.P. Iai do: l'art de degainer le sabre. (Refs: 2)*Voix du kendo (France) 13, 1984, 12-13.*
NOTES: Suite du no. 12.
LEVEL: B LANG: Fr

Raick, J.P. Planche technique kendo no. 11. *Voix du kendo (France) 12, 1984, 6-7.*
LEVEL: B LANG: Fr

Raick, J.P. Kiri Gaeshi. (Exercices de frappe successives). *Voix du kendo (France) 13, 1984, 9;11.*
LEVEL: B LANG: Eng

KICK BOXING

Sion, D. La boxe. *Larc medical (France) 4(7), 1984, 443-447.*
LEVEL: I LANG: Fr

Sion, D. La boxe. (Refs: 22)*Larc Medical (France) 4(8), 1984, 498-505.*
LEVEL: I LANG: Fr

BIOGRAPHY AND AUTOBIOGRAPHY

Buttitta, B. Detroit's newest model. (Richard Plowden) *Karate illustrated (Burbank, Calif.) 15(2), Feb 1984, 44-47.*
LEVEL B LANG: Eng SIRC ARTICLE NO: 108216

Royers, F. Maslak, P. An exclusive interview with Rob 'The Adonis' Kaman: Europe's new world middleweight champion. *Officia karate (Derby, Conn.) 16(121), May 1984, 18-22.*
LEVEL: B LANG: Eng SIRC ARTICLE NO: 099809

INJURIES AND ACCIDENTS

Burke, M. Full contact gets the green light in Canada. The medical investigators' view of kickboxing was that its only purpose was to inflict brain damage, discounting the fact that a match can be won by points or body blows. *Official karate (Derby, Conn.) 16(123), Aug 1984, 35-37;50;56.*
LEVEL: B LANG: Eng SIRC ARTICLE NO: 106287

PHYSIOLOGY

Allard, Y.E. Kickboxers vs karate fighters: who's in better shape? *Black belt (Burbank, Calif.) 22(2), Feb 1984, 44-48;107.*
LEVEL: I LANG: Eng SIRC ARTICLE NO: 096730

Allard, Y.E. Kickboxers vs. karate fighters: part 11. Who trains harder? *Black belt (Burbank, Calif.)* 22(3), Mar 1984, 62-66;101-102.
LEVEL: I LANG: Eng SIRC ARTICLE NO: 099789

TECHNIQUES AND SKILLS

Buttitta, B. The spinning back kick: the technique to put boxing out for the count. *Karate illustrated (Burbank, Calif.) 15(4), Apr 1984, 18-24.*
LEVEL: B LANG: Eng SIRC ARTICLE NO: 098297

Gauvin, G. Le nouveau visage de la boxe francaise et la self-defense feminine. Paris: Editions Amphora, c1984. 127 p. : ill. (Sports & loisirs.)
LEVEL: B LANG: Fr ISBN: 2-85180-077-9 GV1115 17974

KINESIOLOGY

Cooper, J.M. Future directions. (Refs: 14)
CONF: National Symposium on Teaching Kinesiology and Biomechanics in Sports (2nd 1984 : Colorado Springs).
NOTES: In, Shapiro, R. and Marett, J.R. (eds.), Proceedings: Second National Symposium on Teaching Kinesiology and Biomechanics in Sports, Colorado Springs, Colorado, January 12-14, Dekalb, Ill., AAHPERD, 1984, p. 269-274.
LEVEL: I LANG: Eng SIRC ARTICLE NO: 100466

Torrey, L. How science creates winners. *Science digest (New York) 92(8), Aug 1984, 33-37;40;91.*
LEVEL: B LANG: Eng SIRC ARTICLE NO: 096437

DICTIONARIES AND TERMINOLOGY

Rodgers, M.M. Cavanagh, P.R. Glossary of biomechanical terms, concepts, and units. *Physical therapy (Alexandria, va.) 64(12), Dec 1984, 1886-1902.*
LEVEL: B LANG: Eng SIRC ARTICLE NO: 102323

TEACHING

Kindig, L.E. Undergraduate kinesiology: the challenge of change. (Refs: 6)
CONF: National Symposium on Teaching Kinesiology and Biomechanics in Sports (2nd : 1984 : Colorado Springs).
NOTES: In, Shapiro, R. and Marett, J.R. (eds.), Proceedings: Second National Symposium on Teaching Kinesiology and Biomechanics in Sports, Colorado Springs, Colorado, January 12-14, Dekalb, Ill., AAHPERD, 1984, p. 43-46.
LEVEL: I LANG: Eng SIRC ARTICLE NO: 100481

Marett, J.R. Pavlacka, J.A. Siler, W.L. Shapiro, R. Kinesiology status update: a national survey.
CONF: National Symposium on Teaching Kinesiology and Biomechanics in Sports (2nd : 1984 : Colorado Springs).
NOTES: In, Shapiro, R. and Marett, J.R. (eds.), Proceedings: Second National Symposium on Teaching Kinesiology and Biomechanics in Sports, Colorado Springs, Colorado, January 12-14, Dekalb, Ill., AAHPERD, 1984, p. 7-15.
ABST: This survey updates information relative to the status of teaching kinesiology. The survey instrument developed by Deutsch et al was modified and mailed to 436 four year colleges and/ or universities which offered BA or BS degrees in Physical Education. Ninety-nine percent of the responding institutions offer at least one undergraduate course in kinesiology. Institutional and departmental composites have undergone a few changes. Enrollment of students majoring and minoring in physical education has decreased, most likely to do with the job market. Most of the responding institutions were familiar with the 'Guidelines and Standards' for teaching undergraduate kinesiology, which were published in 1980. The impact of these guidelines and standards has been the greatest (71%) on course revision and supplementation. Content-wise, the emphasis of the kinesiology course is on the anatomical, the mechanical, and application aspects with greater attention given to the mechanical and application.
LEVEL: A LANG: Eng SIRC ARTICLE NO: 100488

Phillips, S.J. Clark, J.E. An integrative approach to teaching kinesiology: a lifespan approach. (Refs: 22)
CONF: National Symposium on Teaching Kinesiology and Biomechanics in Sports (2nd : 1984 : Colorado Springs).
NOTES: In, Shapiro, R. and Marett, J.R. (eds.), Proceedings: Second National Symposium on Teaching Kinesiology and Biomechanics in Sports, Colorado Springs, Colorado, January 12-14, Dekalb, Ill., AAHPERD, 1984, p. 19-23.
LEVEL: I LANG: Eng SIRC ARTICLE NO: 100494

TEACHING METHODS

Dowell, L.J. Research results - experimental replication - inquiry method of teaching principles of kinesiology.
CONF: National Symposium on Teaching Kinesiology and Biomechanics in Sports (2nd : 1984 : Colorado Springs).
NOTES: In, Shapiro, R. and Marett, J.R. (eds.), Proceedings: Second National Symposium on Teaching Kinesiology and Biomechanics in Sports, Colorado Springs, Colorado, January 12-14, Dekalb, Ill., AAHPERD, 1984, p. 25-33.
ABST: Mechanical kinesiology teaching principles using the research results - experimental replication - inquiry method offer more student involvement and help them to remember these principles longer and make them more meaningful.
LEVEL: A LANG: Eng SIRC ARTICLE NO: 100469

Kindig, L.E. Mrvos, S.R. Kinesiology laboratory for undergraduates: exercise for wellness. (Refs: 6)
CONF: National Symposiu on Teaching Kinesiology and Biomechanics in Sports (2nd : 1984 : Colorado Springs).
NOTES: In, Shapiro, R. and Marett, J.R. (eds.), Proceedings: Second National Symposium on Teaching Kinesiology and Biomechanics in Sports, Colorado Springs, Colorado, January 12-14, Dekalb, Ill., AAHPERD, 1984, p. 205-209.
LEVEL: I LANG: Eng SIRC ARTICLE NO: 100865

Noble, L. Eck, J. Piagetian learning paradigm for teaching mechanical concepts. (Refs: 2)
CONF: National Symposium on Teaching Kinesiology and Biomechanics in Sports (2nd : 1984 : Colorado Springs).
NOTES: In, Shapiro, R. and Marett, J.R. (eds.), Proceedings: Second National Symposium on Teaching Kinesiology and Biomechanics in Sports, Colorado Springs, Colorado, January 12-14, Dekalb, Ill., AAHPERD, 1984, p. 35-42.
ABST: This paper demonstrates the application of a learning paradigm to teach mechanical concepts that is based on the learning theories of Piaget. A 5-step model was designed to bridge the gap between presentation of a mechanical principle and in-depth understanding. This model was fully illustrated using the principles of center-of-mass,

stability, and projectile motion of a multi-segmented body.
LEVEL: A LANG: Eng SIRC ARTICLE NO: 100493

Zebas, C.J. Brody, P. The use of visual information in the teaching of kinesiology. (Refs: 3) CONF: National Symposium on Teaching Kinesiology and Biomechanics in Sports (2nd : 1984 : Colorado Springs).
NOTES: In, Shapiro, R. and Marett, J.R. (eds.), Proceedings: Second National Symposium on Teaching Kinesiology and Biomechanics in Sports, Colorado Springs, Colorado, January 12-14, Dekalb, Ill., AAHPERD, 1984, p. 219-220.
LEVEL: I LANG: Eng SIRC ARTICLE NO: 100500

KINESIOLOGY - FUNCTIONAL ANATOMY

GROWTH AND DEVELOPMENT

LeVeau, B.F. Bernhardt, D.B. Developmental biomechanics: effect of forces on the growth, development, and maintenance of the human body. (Refs: 95)*Physical therapy (Alexandria, Va.) 64(12), Dec 1984, 1874-1882.*
LEVEL: A LANG: Eng SIRC ARTICLE NO: 102322

MUSCULAR ACTION

Ariel, G. Basic laws of force. Good athletes summate the forces exerted on joints. *Scholastic coach (New York) 53(10), May/Jun 1984, 94-96.*
LEVEL: B LANG: Eng SIRC ARTICLE NO: 094191

Aruin, A.S. Zatsiosky, V.M. Biomechanical characteristics of human ankle-joint muscles. (Refs: 18)*European journal of applied physiology and occupational physiology (Berlin, FRG) 52(4), Jun 1984, 400-406.*
ABST: This study measured the stiffness and damping of the ankle-joint muscles by methods based on impact and vibration actions. Stiffness coefficients for impact and vibration actions were found to be (2.67 plus or minus 0.48) x 10 4 N.m-1 and (1.49 plus or minus 0.35) x 10 4 N.m-1 respectively. Damping coefficients for impact and vibration actions were found to be (811.58 plus or minus 201.3) N.s.m-1 and (430.1 plus or minus 36.1) N.s.m-1 respectively. Furthermore, the stiffness and damping coefficients of the ankle-joint muscles of representatives of different kinds of sports are different.
LEVEL: A LANG: Eng SIRC ARTICLE NO: 097419

Bobet, J. Norman, R.W. Effects of load placement on back muscle activity in load carriage. (Refs: 8)*European journal of applied physiology and occupational physiology (Berlin, W.G.) 53(1), 1984, 71-75.*
ABST: The effect of two different load placements (just below mid-back or just above shoulder level) on erector spinae EMG, trapezius EMG, and heart rate were investigated during load carriage. The EMG and heart rates were telemetered from 11 subjects while they walked on a smooth level surface carrying a load of 19.5 kg in a specially designed backpack. The high load placement resulted in significantly higher levels of muscle activity than did the lower placement. Heart rate was not significantly different between the two placements. A qualitative biomechanical analysis suggests that the EMG differences are primarily due

to differences in the moments and forces arising from the angular and linear accelerations of the load and trunk.
LEVEL: A LANG: Eng SIRC ARTICLE NO: 104282

Brown, E.W. Larkins, C. Laboratory experiment: measurement and interaction of muscle force vectors, net muscle moments, and power. (Refs: 2) CONF: National Symposium on Teaching Kinesiology and Biomechanics in Sports (2nd : 1984 : Colorado Springs).
NOTES: In, Shapiro, R. and Marett, J.R. (eds.), Proceedings: Second National Symposium on Teaching Kinesiology and Biomechanics in Sports, Colorado Springs, Colorado, January 12-14, Dekalb, Ill., AAHPERD, 1984, p. 227-229.
LEVEL: I LANG: Eng SIRC ARTICLE NO: 100463

Chuan-Show, C. Tetsuo, K. The relationship among load, performance, and maximum muscle strength of two throwing patterns. *Asian journal of physical education (Taipei, Taiwan) 7(3), Oct 1984, 26-40.*
LEVEL: A LANG: Eng Chi SIRC ARTICLE NO: 102314

Crosman, L.J. Chateauvert, S.R. Weisberg, J. The effects of massage to the hamstring muscle group on range of motion. (Refs: 14)*Journal of orthopaedic and sports physical therapy (Baltimore, Md.) 6(3), Nov/Dec 1984, 168-172.*
ABST: This study was designed to measure the effect on range of motion of a single massage treatment to the hamstring muscle group. Thirty-four normal female subjects between 18 and 35 years of age were given a 9-12 minute massage treatment to the posterior aspect of one randomly assigned lower extremity. Passive range of motion of both lower extremities was measured. Measurements were taken pre-, and post-, and 7-days postmassage treatment. Immediate postmassage increases in range of motion were noted in the test group (massaged) legs with significance at the 0.05 level.
LEVEL: A LANG: Eng SIRC ARTICLE NO: 102567

Cummings, G.S. Comparison of muscle to other soft tissue in limiting elbow extension. (Refs: 8)*Journal of orthopaedic and sports physical therapy (Baltimore) 5(4), Jan/Feb 1984, 170-174.*
ABST: The purpose of this investigation was to determine whether it is muscle or dense connective tissue which primarily limits the extension of the elbow in normal individuals. The terminal range of elbow extension was measured under two conditions in 9 middle aged female subjects; a) when the subject was normally relaxed, and b) under conditions of paralysis, induced by a myoneural blocking agent. Since paralysis resulted in increased elbow extension in all subjects, it was concluded that elbow extension is limited primarily by muscle.
LEVEL: A LANG: Eng SIRC ARTICLE NO: 092924

Ditson, L. Maximizing efficiency through IKFs *Utah journal of health, physical education, recreation and dance (Provo, Utah 16, Autumn 1984, 15-17.*
LEVEL: I LANG: Eng SIRC ARTICLE NO: 102316

Ekholm, J. Nisell, R. Arborelius, U.P. Hammerberg, C. Nemeth, G. Load on knee joint structures and muscular activity during lifting. (Refs: 33)*Scandinavian journal of rehabilitation medicine (Stockholm) 16(1), 1984, 1-9.*
LEVEL: I LANG: Eng SIRC ARTICLE NO: 100470

Grood, E.S. Suntay, W.J. Noyes, F.R. Butler, D.L. Biomechanics of the knee-extension exercise.

Effect of cutting the anterio cruciate ligament. *Journal of bone and joint surgery (Boston) 66(5), Jun 1984, 725-734.*
LEVEL: A LANG: Eng SIRC ARTICLE NO: 102319

Nemeth, G. Ekholm, J. Arborelius, U.P. Schueldt, K. Harms-Ringdahl, K. Hip joint load and muscular activation during rising exercises. *Scandinavian journal of rehabilitation medicine (Stockholm) 16(3), 1984, 93-102.*
LEVEL: A LANG: Eng

MUSCULO-SKELETAL ANATOMY

Cornwall, M.W. Biomechanics of noncontractile tissue. (bone, articular cartilage, and collagenous tissues) (Refs: 65) *Physical therapy (Alexandria, Va.) 64(12), Dec 1984, 1869-1873.*
LEVEL: A LANG: Eng SIRC ARTICLE NO: 102315

Ericson, M.O. Nisell, R. Ekholm, J. Varus and valgus loads on the knee joint during ergometer cycling. (Refs: 41) *Scandinavian journal of sports sciences (Helsinki, Finland) 6(2), Dec 1984, 39-45.*
ABST: The varus and valgus knee load moments obtained during cycling on a bicycle ergometer were calculated using measurements from a quartz force-measuring transducer mounted on the pedal. Six healthy subjects rode in three different ways at two different pedal foot positions and in one position with the knee joints moving close to the midline of the bicycle. The mean knee load moment acting in the coronal plane during standardized ergometer cycling measured up to 24.5 Nm varus and 2.9 Nm valgus load moment. There was no significant difference in varus or valgus knee load between the anterior and posterior foot positions. Cycling with the knees close decreased the mean maximum varus load from 24.5 Nm to 11.2 Nm.
LEVEL: A LANG: Eng SIRC ARTICLE NO: 106319

Fabbriciani, C. Delcogliano, A. Panni, A.S. Lorini, G. La distribuzione delle sollecitazioni nel sistema osteo-muscolo-tendineo-legamentoso in riferimento al 'gesto atletico'. Stress distribution within the bone-muscle-tendon-ligament system in athletes. (Refs: 20)*Italian journal of sports traumatology (Milano, Italy) 6(3), Jul/Sept 1984, 229-239.*
ABST: The authors present an hypothesis regarding the patterns of stress and strain relief into the bone-muscle-tendon complex considered as a variable-geometry system. The analysis is done by measuring the in vivo changes of the leg diameter consequent to the quadriceps contractions against increasing and known resistance. The results are critically discussed and finally considered qualitatively significant.
LEVEL: A LANG: Eng It SIRC ARTICLE NO: 102317

Huson, A. Mechanics of joints. (Refs: 36)*International journal of sports medicine (Stuttgart) Suppl. 5, Nov 1984, 83-87.*
CONF: International Congress on Sports and Health (1983 : Maastricht, Netherlands).
LEVEL: A LANG: Eng SIRC ARTICLE NO: 103827

Sauren, A.A.H.J. Huson, A. Schouten, R.Y. An axisymmetric finite element analysis of the mechanical function of the meniscus (Refs: 7)*International journal of sports medicine (Stuttgart) Suppl. 5, Nov 1984, 93-95.*
CONF: International Congress on Sports and Health (1983 : Maastricht, Netherlands).
LEVEL: A LANG: Eng SIRC ARTICLE NO: 103832

Stucke, H. Zu dynamischen Belastungen des oberen Sprunggelenkes und seines Sehnen- und Bandapparates. Koeln: Deutsche Sporthochschule, Institut fuer Biomechanik, 1984. 200 p.
NOTES: Bibliography: p. 189-200. Thesis (Ph.D.) - Deutsche Sporthochschule Koeln, 1984.
LEVEL: A LANG: Ger QP302 18377

POSTURE

Ayub, E. Glasheen-Wray, M. Kraus, S. Head posture: a case study of the effects on the rest position of the mandible. (Refs: 30)*Journal of orthopaedic and sports physical therapy (Baltimore) 5(4), Jan/Feb 1984, 179-183.*
ABST: The purpose of this study was to investigate the changes in the resting vertical dimension of the mandible with a correction of a forward head posture in an edentulous patient. After ten treatments of manual physical therapy, a plumb line test demonstrated an improvement in forward head posture. Also, the resting vertical dimension of the mandible increased by an average of 8 millimeters. This indicates that correct head posture may be required to accurately measure the resting vertical dimension of the mandible.
LEVEL: A LANG: Eng SIRC ARTICLE NO: 092689

Powell, G.M. Dzendolet, E. Power spectral density analysis of lateral human standing sway. (Refs: 23)*Journal of motor behavior (Washington) 16(4), Dec 1984, 424-441.*
ABST: Using PSD analysis, over a frequency range from 0.02-2.5 Hz, the present study examined two trials of lateral sway in each of 80 men. The results showed that little change occurred in PSD values between the first and second trials. The values of the parameter estimates obtained from the curve-fitting were regressed on the values of various direct, and derived anthropometric variables to try to explain the variance of the parameter estimates in terms of the anthropometrics. The subject's center of gravity location accounted for no more than 15.8 per cent of the parameter variance, whereas the remaining anthropometrics explained even less. The overall averaged data suggest that three functions (related to visual, vestibular, and proprioceptive processes) may underlie the sway pattern over this frequency range.
LEVEL: A LANG: Eng SIRC ARTICLE NO: 105160

STRUCTURAL INTERACTIONS

Scull, E.R. Joint biomechanics and therapy: contribution or confusion? (Refs: 12)*In, Glasgow, E.F. et al., Aspects of manipulative therapy, 2nd., Melbourne, Churchill Livingstone, 1984, p. 3-14.*
LEVEL: I LANG: Eng SIRC ARTICLE NO: 102289

Viel, E. Gautier, R. Dusautois, J.L. Examen differentiel de la force prehensile du pouce des doigts externes et des doigts internes. (Refs: 10)*Medecine du sport (Paris) 58(2), 25 mars 1984, 22-26.*
LEVEL: I LANG: Fr SIRC ARTICLE NO: 094445

TEACHING

Donnelly, J.E. The Living Anatomy Technique. CONF: National Symposium on Teaching Kinesiology and Biomechanics in Sports (2nd : 1984 : Colorado Springs).
NOTES: In, Shapiro, R. and Marett, J.R. (eds.), Proceedings: Second National Symposium on Teaching Kinesiology and Biomechanics in Sports, Colorado Springs, Colorado, January 12-14, Dekalb, Ill., AAHPERD, 1984, p. 155-157.
ABST: Detailed description of the Living Anatomy Technique, a 'hands on' practitioner oriented method of study.
LEVEL: I LANG: Eng SIRC ARTICLE NO: 100468

Frishberg, B.A. Practical anatomy laboratory experiences. (Refs: 34)
CONF: National Symposium on Teaching Kinesiology and Biomechanics in Sports (2nd : 1984 : Colorado Springs).
NOTES: In, Shapiro, R. and Marett, J.R. (eds.), Proceedings: Second National Symposium on Teaching Kinesiology and Biomechanics in Sports, Colorado Springs, Colorado, January 12-14, Dekalb, Ill., AAHPERD, 1984, p. 165-171.
ABST: This detailed examination of anatomy laboratories discusses student roles, objectives and organization, different types of anatomy laboratories and muscular torque laboratories.
LEVEL: I LANG: Eng SIRC ARTICLE NO: 100473

JiChun, J. Determination of the anatomical mover of human movement. (Refs: 3)
CONF: National Symposium on Teaching Kinesiology and Biomechanics in Sports (2nd : 1984 : Colorado Springs).
NOTES: In, Shapiro, R. and Marett, J.R. (eds.), Proceedings: Second National Symposium on Teaching Kinesiology and Biomechanics in Sports, Colorado Springs, Colorado, January 12-14, Dekalb, Ill., AAHPERD, 1984, p. 173-181.
ABST: The determination of the mover of human movement at the point of performance can be greatly improved by teaching the method of analyzing forces applied upon various body segments. The methods of analysis and of teaching them are detailed.
LEVEL: A LANG: Eng SIRC ARTICLE NO: 100478

Kelley, D.L. Phillips, S.J. Prosection laboratory to support kinesiology/biomechanics teaching. (Refs: 5)
CONF: National Symposium on Teaching Kinesiology and Biomechanics in Sports (2nd : 1984 : Colorado Springs).
NOTES: In, Shapiro, R. and Marett, J.R. (eds.), Proceedings: Second National Symposium on Teaching Kinesiology and Biomechanics in Sports, Colorado Springs, Colorado, January 12-14, Dekalb, Ill., AAHPERD, 1984, p. 159-163.
LEVEL: I LANG: Eng SIRC ARTICLE NO: 100480

Kiyoguchi, J. York, S.L. Flatten, E.K. Perkins, D.R. Giampino, L.A. Using videotape Chromakey to teach the shoulder girdle. (Refs: 3)
CONF: National Symposium on Teaching Kinesiology and Biomechanics in Sports (2nd : 1984 : Colorado Springs).
NOTES: In, Shapiro, R. and Marett, J.R. (eds.), Proceedings: Second National Symposium on Teaching Kinesiology and Biomechanics in Sports, Colorado Springs, Colorado, January 12-14, Dekalb, Ill., AAHPERD, 1984, p. 57-58.
LEVEL: I LANG: Eng SIRC ARTICLE NO: 100483

KITE FLYING

Barnhart, T.C. A high flying festival with kites of many colors. *Parks and recreation (Alexandria, Va.) 19(7), Jul 1984, 50-52.*
LEVEL: B LANG: Eng SIRC ARTICLE NO: 096350

EQUIPMENT

Gregor, G. No wind kite thermal lifting. *AKA news (Baltimore, Md.) 6(4), Aug/Sept 1984, 21-22.*
LEVEL: B LANG: Eng SIRC ARTICLE NO: 102402

How Ohashi makes the expansible box kite. *Kitelines (Baltimore, Md.) 5(2), Summer/Fall 1984, 28-29.*
LEVEL: B LANG: Eng SIRC ARTICLE NO: 172907

Leigh, D. Alick Pearson's Roller and the Round Pond Fliers. *Kitelines (Baltimore, Md.) 5(1), Spring 1984, 30-31.*
LEVEL: B LANG: Eng SIRC ARTICLE NO: 172905

Sasaki, M.S. The culprit is the knot: naughty, naughty knots. *AKA news (Baltimore, Md.) 6(2), Apr/May 1984, 16-17.*
NOTES: Reprinted from, Aydlett, G., Piney Mountain Air Force Data Letter.
LEVEL: B LANG: Eng SIRC ARTICLE NO: 101015

van Glider, J. How come my kite won't fly? *AKA news (Baltimore, Md.) 6(4), Aug/Sept 1984, 23.*
LEVEL: B LANG: Eng SIRC ARTICLE NO: 102413

HISTORY

Ye, S. The story of kites. With a history of over 2,000 years, Chinese kites are second to none in the world. *China sports (Beijing, China) 16(8), Aug 1984, 27-32.*
LEVEL: B LANG: Eng SIRC ARTICLE NO: 101018

KUNG FU

Bennett, R. Korea's kung-fu: they call it sib pal gee. *Inside kung-fu (Hollywood, Calif.) 11(2), Feb 1984, 76-78.*
LEVEL: LANG: Eng SIRC ARTICLE NO: 098295

Carrabis, J.-D. The Wah Lum performance troupe of Boston: paving the way to a new martial arts. *Black belt magazine (Burbank, Calif.) 22(11), Nov 1984, 20-24;26;78;80.*
LEVEL: B LANG: Eng SIRC ARTICLE NO: 107336

Funk, J. The complete guide to Northern praying mantis kung-fu. *Inside kung-fu (Hollywood, Calif.) 11(2), Feb 1984, 64-73.*
LEVEL: B LANG: Eng SIRC ARTICLE NO: 098302

Parulski, G.R. The secrets of kung-fu: a complete guide to the fundamentals of Shaolin kung-fu and the principles of inner power (ch'i). Chicago: Contemporary Boks, 1984. 1v.
NOTES: Includes index.
LEVEL: I LANG: Eng ISBN: 0809254387 LC CARD: 84-011383

Secret animals of Hsing-I Chuan: 'The combat art of hsing-i is famous for exploding power and the effectiveness of its element techniques, but do the animal techniques also live up to that reputation?' *Karate illustrated (Burbank, Calif.) 15(9), Sept 1984, 24-27.*
LEVEL: B LANG: Eng SIRC ARTICLE NO: 103319

Segal, S. Karate vs kung-fu: which is better? Art does not make the man, the man makes the art. *Inside kung-fu (Hollywood, Calif.) 11(1), Jan 1984, 24-25;30-32.*
LEVEL: B LANG: Eng SIRC ARTICLE NO: 098325

KUNG FU (continued)

BIOGRAPHY AND AUTOBIOGRAPHY

Holzer, J.W. White tiger steps hard: triumph of a kung-fu heretic... (David German) *Inside kung-fu (Hollywood, Calif.) 11(6), Jun 1984, 75-80.*
LEVEL: B LANG: Eng SIRC ARTICLE NO: 103304

Illar, L. Master Chiang Ken: legend of a tiger. *Inside kung-fu (Hollywood, Calif.) 11(3), Mar 1984, 57-59.*
LEVEL: B LANG: Eng SIRC ARTICLE NO: 098311

King, F. Olrech, D. Al Dacascos' wun hop kuen do: the truly complete martial art. *Black belt magazine (Burbank, Calif.) 22(5), May 1984, 20-25;75;98;100.*
LEVEL: B LANG: Eng SIRC ARTICLE NO: 103312

HISTORY

Yong Fa, C. Chan Heung: the legendary creator of choy li fut. *Inside kung-fu (Burbank, Calif.) 11(12), Dec 1984, 75-78;80.*
NOTES: Translated from the Chinese.
LEVEL: I LANG: Eng SIRC ARTICLE NO: 107382

TECHNIQUES AND SKILLS

Co, A.L. Tam tui: Northern shaolin's 'snapping legs'. *Inside kung-fu (Burbank, Calif.) 11(12), Dec 1984, 53-56;58.*
LEVEL: LANG: Eng SIRC ARTICLE NO: 107340

Fong, A. McDonald, N. Bil jee: the power of a shooting arrow. (wing shun) *Inside kung-fu (Burbank, Calif.) 11(10), Oct 1984 86-93.*
LEVEL: B LANG: Eng SIRC ARTICLE NO: 105967

Gonzales, M.J. Pek Kwar: China's rare 'axe-fist' kung-fu. *Kick illustrated (Burbank, Calif.) 5(5), May 1984, 41-43.*
LEVEL: B LANG: Eng SIRC ARTICLE NO: 101386

Gonzalez, M.J. Monkey style kung fu: rare and unusual, but deadly effective. *Black belt magazine (Burbank, Calif.) 22(11), Nov 1984, 40-43.*
LEVEL: B LANG: Eng SIRC ARTICLE NO: 107348

Hallander, J. Short kung fu: fighting tight. *Karate illustrated (Burbank, Calif.) 15(3), Mar 1984, 50-53;75.*
LEVEL: B LANG: Eng SIRC ARTICLE NO: 096738

Hallander, J. Choy li fut kung-fu: self-defense from the basics. *Official karate (Derby, Conn.) 16(120), Apr 1984, 3337.*
LEVEL: B LANG: Eng SIRC ARTICLE NO: 098307

Hallander, J. The secret theories of praying mantis kung-fu. *Black belt (Burbank, Calif.) 22(3), Mar 1984, 20-24;85.*
LEVEL: B LANG: Eng SIRC ARTICLE NO: 099798

Hallander, J. Kung fu vs. Tae kwon do: which approach to kicking strategy and tactics is really more effective? *Inside karate (Burbank, Calif.) 5(9), Sept 1984, 48-51.*
LEVEL: B LANG: Eng SIRC ARTICLE NO: 107353

Hallander, J. The five animals and elements of Hung Gar Kung Fu. *Black belt (Burbank, Calif.) 22(1), Jan 1984, 29-32;82;85.*
LEVEL: B LANG: Eng SIRC ARTICLE NO: 108609

Hoag, D. Bruce Lee's jeet kune do: what it is what it isn't. *Black belt (Burbank, Calif.) 22(3), Mar 1984, 34-38;112.*
LEVEL: B LANG: Eng SIRC ARTICLE NO: 099800

Johnson, J.A. Pa Kua Chang: step by step to mastery. *Inside kung-fu (Hollywood, Calif.) 11(6),*

Jun 1984, 68-72.
LEVEL: B LANG: Eng SIRC ARTICLE NO: 103309

Lamb, A. Bruce Lee and modified wing chun. *Karate illustrated (Burbank, Calif.) 15(10), Oct 1984, 34-37;82.*
LEVEL: B LANG Eng SIRC ARTICLE NO: 108115

LaRue, S. John Leong: the moral power of Hung Gar. *Inside kung-fu (Los Angeles, Calif.) 11(5), May 1984, 36-42.*
LEVEL: B LANG: Eng SIRC ARTICLE NO: 101393

Maberry, J.E. Exotic hand techniques of kung fu. *Karate illustrated (Burbank, Calif.) 15(4), Apr 1984, 50-53.*
LEVEL: B LANG: Eng SIRC ARTICLE NO: 098318

Nardi, T.J. Tensho and Sil Lim Tao: the Goju-Wing Chun connection. *Black belt (Burbank, Calif.) 22(2), Feb 1984, 38-42;112.*
LEVEL: B LANG: Eng SIRC ARTICLE NO: 096745

Segal, S. Jeet Kune do: ten years later. *Inside kung-fu (Hollywood, Calif.) 11(4), Apr 1984, 32-37.*
LEVEL: B LANG: Eng SIRC ARTICLE NO: 096746

Wong, D.F. Shaolin's dragon style: kung fu that breathes fire. *Karate illustrated (Burbank, Calif.) 15(7), Jul 1984, 32-37;76.*
LEVEL: B LANG: Eng SIRC ARTICLE NO: 103323

TRAINING AND CONDITIONING

Knoble, K. Lama kung fu: an overview of a fighting only art. *Karate illustrated (Burbank, Calif.) 15(8), Aug 1984, 28-33.*
LEVEL: B LANG: Eng SIRC ARTICLE NO: 104825

LACROSSE

COACHING

Lidz, F. 'My teams are collages': sculptor Roy Simmons Jr. followed his dad as Syracuse lacrosse coach and last year won the national title. *Sports illustrated 60(13), 26 Mar 1984, 43-44;46;48-49.*
LEVEL: B LANG: Eng SIRC ARTICLE NO: 093571

INJURIES AND ACCIDENTS

Black, J.E. Two cervical spine fractures in lacrosse. (Refs: 6)*Physician and sportsmedicine (Minneapolis, Minn.) 12(9), Sep 1984, 128-130;133-134.*
LEVEL: I LANG: Eng SIRC ARTICLE NO: 099776

JUVENILE LITERATURE

Reynolds, R.E. Olney, R.R. Lacrosse is for me. Minneapolis: Lerner Pub. Co., c1984. 1v.
LEVEL: B LANG: Eng ISBN: 0822511452 LC CARD: 84-010079

PHYSIOLOGY

DeMeersman, R.E. Schiltz, J.H. Decreased training frequency and pulmonary function retention in the female athlete. *Journal of sports medicine and physical fitness (Torino, Italy) 24(2), Jun 1984, 155-158.*
ABST: Pulmonary function and body composition retention were observed in 18 female collegiate athletes exposed to a decrease in training frequency while participating in consecutive field

hockey and lacrosse competitive seasons. Although one sport season represented 31% fewer workouts than the other, no significant differences were noted in body density, body fat, closing volume, nitrogen delta, closing capacity, residual volumes, functional residual volume, expiratory reserve volume, total lung capacity and vital capacity post-season scores. Results were noted as being in agreement with previous investigations in that the degree of fitness achieved can be maintained despite a substantial decrease in training frequency.
LEVEL: A LANG: Eng SIRC ARTICLE NO: 102768

STRATEGY - DEFENSIVE

Smith, J. Player-to-player defense at Delaware. *Crosse checks (Havertown, Pa.) 8(1), Spring 1984, 13-14;16-17.*
LEVEL: B LANG: Eng SIRC ARTICLE NO: 096726

TEACHING

Howarth, K. The teaching of lacrosse - an example for debate. *Lacrosse (London) 37(1), Spring 1984, 4.*
NOTES: To be continued.
LEVEL: B LANG: Eng SIRC ARTICLE NO: 098284

TRAINING AND CONDITIONING - DRILLS

Cockerton, S. Shooting for success. *Coaching review (Ottawa) 7, Sept/Oct 1984, 56-57.*
LEVEL: B LANG: Eng SIRC ARTICLE NO: 098283

VARIATIONS

It's fast...it's skilful...it's exciting...it's sof-crosse. *Sports coach (Wembley, Aust.) 8(1), 1984, 58.*
LEVEL: B LANG: En SIRC ARTICLE NO: 096725

LAW AND LEGISLATION

Alaphilippe, F. Karaquillo, J.P. Lenclos, J.L. Marty, J.P. Mouly, J. Wagner, E. Droit du sport. *Recueil Dalloz Sirey (Paris 17, 1984, 177-182.*
NOTES: A suivre.
LEVEL: I LANG: Fr

Alaphilippe, F. Karaquillo, J.P. Lenclos, J.L. Marty, J.P. Mouly, J. Wagner, E. Droit du sport. *Recueil Dalloz Sirey (Paris 18, 1984, 185-190.*
NOTES: Suite du no. 17.
LEVEL: I LANG: Fr

Appenzeller, H. Engler, T. Mathews, N.N. Riekes, L. Ross, C.T. Sports and law. St. Paul, Minn.: West Publishing, c1984. x, 174 p. : ill.
NOTES: Bibliography: p. 171-174.
LEVEL: I LANG: Eng ISBN: 0-314-79386-0 LC CARD: 83-24296 GV705 18866

Brown, R. Moriarty, D. Prpich, M. Sport, physical activity and the law. Ottawa: Canadian Association for Health, Physical Education, Recreation and Dance, c1984. xii, 127 p.
CORP: Canadian Association for Health, Physical Education and Recreation.
NOTES: Bibliography: p. 97-105.
LEVEL: I LANG: Eng ISBN: 0-919068-18-9 GV705 18324

Brown, R.E. The law of torts. (Refs: 37)
NOTES: In, Brown, R. (ed.) et al., Sport, physical

activity and the law, Ottawa, Canadian Association for Health, Physical Education, Recreation and Dance, c1984, p. 83-96.
LEVEL: I LANG: Eng GV705 18324

Galasso, P.J. Sport and the law: intersections. (Refs: 6)
NOTES: In, Brown, R. (ed.) et al., Sport, physical activity and th law, Ottawa, Canadian Association for Health, Physical Education, Recreation and Dance, c1984, p. 1-7.
LEVEL: B LANG: Eng GV705 18324

Garrett, R.A. Hochberg, P.R. Sports broadcasting and the law. (Refs: 58)*Indiana law journal (Bloomington, Ind.) 59(2), 1984 155-193.*
LEVEL: I LANG: Eng SIRC ARTICLE NO: 095984

Les problemes juridiques du sport. Responsabilite et assurance, Universite de Nice, L.A.R.J.E.P.T.A.E., Centre de Droit du Sport, Colloque 17-18 mars 1983. Paris: Economica, 1984. 211 p.
CONF: Colloque sur les problemes juridiques du sport: responsabilite et assurance (2e : 1983 : Universite de Nice).
NOTES: Includes bibliographical references.
LEVEL: A LANG: Fr ISBN: 2-7178-0727-6 GV705 20746

Williams, J.S. Legislation, common law and sport in Canada. (Refs: 2)
NOTES: In, Brown, R. (ed.) et al., Sport, physical activity and the law, Ottawa, Canadian Association for Health, Physical Education, Recreation and Dance, c1984, p. 8-15.
LEVEL: B LANG: Eng GV705 18324

BIBLIOGRAPHIES

Schwarz, J. Bibliographie zum Sportrecht. Deutschsprachige Literatur. Muenchen: Alkos Verlag, c1984. xi, 212 p. (Bibliothek des Sports; Bd. 3.)
LEVEL: A LANG: Ger ISBN: 3-920902-15-7 GV705 18166

CRIMINAL LAW - VIOLENCE

Urie, J.J. Athletic violence and the courts. (Refs: 5)
NOTES: In, Brown, R. (ed.) et al., Sport, physical activity and the law, Ottawa, Canadian Association for Health, Physical Education, Recreation and Dance, c1984, p. 75-82.
LEVEL: B LANG: Eng GV705 18324

HUMAN RIGHTS

Illinois - 'Your rights end where my nose begins'. *Sports and the courts (Winston-Salem, N.C.) 5(4), Fall 1984, 13.*
LEVEL: LANG: Eng SIRC ARTICLE NO: 102556

LEGISLATION

Bouquin, C. La loi pour 'l'organisation et la promotion des activites physiques et sportives'. *EPS: Education physique et sport (Paris) 187, mai/ juin 1984, 2-3.*
LEVEL: B LANG: Fr SIRC ARTICLE NO: 095981

Juckett, R. Athletic Safety Bill substitute Senate Bill No. 4484. *Washington coach (Seattle, Wash.) Fall 1984, 13.*
LEVEL: LANG: Eng SIRC ARTICLE NO: 100705

Loi relative a l'organisation et a la promotion des activites physiques et sportives. *Aviron (Paris) 499, dec 1984, 4-5.*
NOTES: A suivre.
LEVEL: B LANG: Fr SIRC ARTICLE NO: 106553

Statute law amendment, 1984. Fitness and Amateur Sport Act. Loi corrective de 1984. Loi sur la sante et le sport amateur. *Canada gazette, part III/ Gazette du Canada, partie III (Ottawa) 7(6), 1984, 1552-1557.*
CORP: Canada. Parliament.
LEVEL: B LANG: Eng Fr SIRC ARTICLE NO: 181606

LIABILITY

Appenzeller, H. Liability issues in athletics program management: risk management. *In, Della-Guistina, D. and Moore, L.M. (eds.), Proceedings of the National Conference on Liability in the Schools, Reston, Va., American School and Community Safety Association, c1984, p. 29-38.*
CONF: National Conference on Liability in the Schools (1984 : Morgantown, West Virginia).
LEVEL: I LANG: Eng GV705 18960

Assurances. Sports d'ete: accidents et responsabilites. *Particulier (France) 673, 1984, 21-24.*
LEVEL: B LANG: Fr

Bullock, L. Norwood, D. Liability in the physical education classroom. (Refs: 45)
NOTES: In, Brown, R. (ed.) et al., Sport, physical activity and the law, Ottawa, Canadian Association for Health, Physical Education, Recreation and Dance, c1984, p. 16-25.
LEVEL: I LANG: Eng GV705 18324

Clarke, K.S. Sport liability and the expert witness from associated professions. *In, Della-Guistina, D. and Moore, L.M. (eds.), Proceedings of the National Conference on Liability in the Schools, Reston, Va., American School and Community Safety Association, c1984, p. 15-21.*
CONF: National Conference on Liability in the Schools (1984 : Morgantown, West Virginia).
LEVEL: B LANG: Eng GV705 18960

Daniels, M.A. Liability for injuries in sports activities. (Refs: 12)*In, Vendl, B.C. (ed.) et al., Interpretive aspects of intramural-recreational sports: selected proceedings from the Thirty-fifth Annual National Intramural-Recreational Sports Association Conference, Corvallis, Or., Oregon State University, c1984, p. 1-9.*
CONF: National Intramural-Recreational Sports Association Conference (35th : 1984 : Fort Worth, Tex.).
LEVEL: I LANG: Eng GV710 18914

District of Columbia - teacher not liable for playground injury. *Sports and the courts (Winston-Salem, N.C.) 5(2), Spring 1984, 7-8.*
LEVEL: B LANG: Eng SIRC ARTICLE NO: 094403

Hales, C. Legal liability of Physical Therapists and Athletic Trainers. (Refs: 12)
NOTES: In, Brown, R. (ed.) et al., Sport, physical activity and the law, Ottawa, Canadian Association for Health, Physical Education, Recreation and Dance, c1984, p. 48-55.
LEVEL: I LANG: Eng GV705 18324

Kaiser, R.A. Program liability waivers: do they protect the agency and staff? (Refs: 9)*Journal of physical education, recreation & dance (Reston,*

Va.) 55(6), Aug 1984, 54-56.
LEVEL: I LANG: Eng SIRC ARTICLE NO: 097586

Kozlowski, J.C. Negligence liability for third party assaults during recreational activities. *Parks & recreation 19(2), Feb 1984, 34-37.*
LEVEL: B LANG: Eng SIRC ARTICLE NO: 091491

Kozlowski, J.C. Let's get physical with fitting RPLR exercise suits. *Parks & recreation (Alexandria, Va.) 19(12), Dec 1984, 20-23;66.*
LEVEL: B LANG: Eng SIRC ARTICLE NO: 173262

Louisiana - inadequate supervision on playground blamed for injury to student. *Sports and the courts (Winston-Salem, N.C.) 5(1), Winter 1984, 7-8.*
LEVEL: B LANG: Eng SIRC ARTICLE NO: 094405

Louisiana - it was not unreasonable for a coach to wrestle a student. *Sports and the courts (Winston-Salem, N.C.) 5(1), Winte 1984, 5.*
LEVEL: B LANG: Eng SIRC ARTICLE NO: 094406

McDonald, M. Wilton, D. Coaching and the laws of liability. (Refs: 27)
NOTES: In, Brown, R. (ed.) et al., Sport, physical activity and the law, Ottawa, Canadian Association for Health, Physical Education, Recreation and Dance, c1984, p. 26-38.
LEVEL: I LANG: Eng GV705 18324

McNamara, S. Moriarty, D. Liability: ensure you're insured. (Refs: 23)
NOTES: In, Brown, R. (ed.) et al., Sport, physical activity and the law, Ottawa, Canadian Association for Health, Physical Education, Recreation and Dance, c1984, p. 63-74.
LEVEL: I LANG: Eng GV705 18324

Michigan - girls' basketball player sues for 'premises liability' for locker room assault. *Sports and the courts (Winston-Salem, N.C.) 5(1), Winter 1984, 6.*
LEVEL: B LANG: Eng SIRC ARTICLE NO: 094878

Pennsylvania - college not liable for bill incurred by bankrupt alumni association. *Sports and the courts (Winston-Salem, N.C.) 5(2), Spring 1984, 1-2.*
LEVEL: B LANG: Eng SIRC ARTICLE NO: 094409

Preventing liability. *Audible (Toronto) Winter 1984, 22.*
LEVEL: B LANG: Eng SIRC ARTICLE NO: 092914

West, C. Facilities and equipment: who's liable? (Refs: 10)
NOTES: In, Brown, R. (ed.) et al., Sport, physical activity and the law, Ottawa, Canadian Association for Health, Physical Education, Recreation and Dance, c1984, p. 56-62.
LEVEL: I LANG: Eng GV705 18324

LITIGATION

Appenzeller, H. Ross, C.T. Louisiana - nursing school found negligent for failing to provide qualified driver for field trip *Sports and the courts (Winston-Salem, N.C.) 5(3), Summer 1984, 1-3.*
LEVEL: B LANG: Eng SIRC ARTICLE NO: 097584

Experts say prevention best remedy for sports injury lawsuits. *Employee health & fitness (Atlanta, Ga.) 6(1), Jan 1984, 7-9.*
LEVEL: B LANG: Eng SIRC ARTICLE NO: 092907

New York - is there legal duty to recommend students for college scholarships? *Sports and the courts (Winston-Salem, N.C.) 5(1), Winter 1984, 1-2.*
LEVEL: B LANG: Eng SIRC ARTICLE NO: 094243

LAW AND LEGISLATION (continued)

Silverman, G. Athletic injuries: a road to litigation. (Refs: 12)
NOTES: In, Brown, R. (ed.) et al., Sport, physical activit and the law, Ottawa, Canadian Association for Health, Physical Education, Recreation and Dance, c1984, p. 39-47.
LEVEL: I LANG: Eng GV705 18324

MEDICINE

Samuels, A. Sport injury and the law. *Medicine, science and the law (Brentford, Eng.) 24(4), 1984, 254-260.*
LEVEL: I LANG Eng SIRC ARTICLE NO: 104100

NEGLIGENCE

Cotten, D.J. Staying out of court. A coach has no legal liability unless negligent. (Refs: 5)*Scholastic coach (New York) 53(10), May/Jun 1984, 84;102.*
LEVEL: B LANG: Eng SIRC ARTICLE NO: 094224

New York - question of negligence was for the jury to decide. *Sports and the courts (Winston-Salem, N.C.) 5(2), Spring 1984, 8.*
LEVEL: B LANG: Eng SIRC ARTICLE NO: 094408

Oregon - quadriplegic entitled to recover $980,000 from athletic association. *Sports and the courts (Winston-Salem, N.C.) 5(2), Spring 1984, 2-3.*
LEVEL: B LANG: Eng SIRC ARTICLE NO: 095016

LAWN BOWLING

Bell, B. An alternative and instructive method of playing a pairs game of bowls... *Bowls (Cape Town, South Africa) 16(5), Nov 1984, 6-7.*
LEVEL: B LANG: Eng SIRC ARTICLE NO: 105961

COACHING

de Kock, J.J. Coaching the beginner. *Bowls (Cape Town, S.A.) 16(4), Oct 1984, 8-10.*
NOTES: Reprinted from, de Kock, J.J., Bowls in South Africa, Cape Town, HAUM, 1984.
LEVEL: B LANG: Eng SIRC ARTICLE NO: 104814

DICTIONARIES AND TERMINOLOGY

De Kock, J.J. Bowls in South Africa: getting the right terminology. *Bowls magazine (Capetown, S.A.) 15(9), Mar 1984, 7-9.*
NOTES: Reprinted from, Bowls in South Africa, by J.J. de Kock, Cape Town, HAUM, 1984.
LEVEL: B LANG: Eng SIRC ARTICLE NO: 095137

DISABLED

Bell, B. Ivor, and his bowling independence. *Bowls magazine (Cape Town, S.A.) 15(10), Apr 1984, 6-7.*
LEVEL: B LANG: Eng SIRC ARTICLE NO: 095846

Holesh, R. Bowls for the blind. *Green (Ottawa) Jul 1984, 5.*
LEVEL: B LANG: Eng SIRC ARTICLE NO: 101379

EQUIPMENT

Bell, B. Magic mats. *Bowls magazine (Cape Town, South Africa) 16(1), Jul 1984, 12-13.*
LEVEL: B LANG: Eng SIRC ARTICLE NO: 101375

de Kock, J.J. More facts about equipment. *Bowls (Capetown, South Africa) 15(12), Jun 1984, 8-9.*

NOTES: Reprinted from, de Kock, J.J., Bowls in South Africia, Capetown, HAUM, C1984.
LEVEL: B LANG: Eng SIRC ARTICLE NO: 099778

FACILITIES

de Kock, J.J. Playing area and equipment. *Bowls (Capetown, South Africa) 15(11), May 1984, 8-9.*
NOTES: Reprinted from, de Kock, J.J., Bowls in South Africia, Capetown, HAUM, C1984.
LEVEL: B LANG: Eng SIRC ARTICLE NO: 099777

Evans, P.S. The use of cotula for bowling greens in New Zealand. (Refs: 17)*Journal of the Sports Turf Research Institute (Bingley, West Yorkshire) 60, June 1984, 37-44.*
ABST: Cotula first occurred in a Dunedin green. When players found that it produced a superior surface to grass, its presence was encouraged. Use has increased with time until it is now the predominant bowling surface in New Zealand. Two species, Cotula dioica and C. maniototo are used, either separately or in combination. A good early season running speed (14-18 sec.) is more easily achieved on cotula than on grass and winter play is practical. Rain has little effect on playing speed. Establishment is more rpaid, end wear less common, a very uniform surface can be achieved and renovation costs are low. Establishment and renovation use vegetative material with the risk of introducing weeds and pests. Weed control is difficult compared with grass and a high degree of greenkeeping skill is necessary to establish and maintain high quality greens. Mowing and fertilising practices are different to those for grass. Particular attention has to be paid to renovation and irrigation.
LEVEL: A LANG: Eng SIRC ARTICLE NO: 108512

FACILITIES - DESIGN, CONSTRUCTION AND PLANNING

Greenfield, I. Penncross for Spain's new bowling greens. *Turf management (Surrey, Eng.) 3(12), Dec 1984, 18-20.*
LEVEL: B LANG: Eng SIRC ARTICLE NO: 105233

Hennigar, M. Notes on green construction. *Green (Montreal, Que.) May 1984, 16-17.*
LEVEL: B LANG: Eng SIRC ARTICLE NO: 098968

FACILITIES - MAINTENANCE

Campbell, J. The effects of rolling. *Groundsman (London) 37(1), Jan 1984, 15.*
LEVEL: B LANG: Eng SIRC ARTICLE NO: 098981

Evans, R. Turf maintenance: spring work on the bowling green. *Parks, golf courses and sports grounds (Middlesex, Eng.) 49(6), Mar 1984, 22-23.*
LEVEL: B LANG: Eng SIRC ARTICLE NO: 100604

Harris, D. Abrasive soils. *SA bowler (Adelaide, S.A.) 18(9), May 1984, 8-9.*
NOTES: Part III of three articles.
LEVEL: B LANG: Eng SIRC ARTICLE NO: 097523

Harris, J. Follow the bouncing bowl. *S.A. bowler (Adelaide, S.A.) 18(6), Feb 1984, 20-21.*
LEVEL: B LANG: Eng SIRC ARTICL NO: 094306

Harris, J. Turf roughness. *SA bowler (Adelaide, S.A.) 18(8), Apr 1984, 8-9.*
NOTES: Part II of three articles.
LEVEL: B LANG: Eng SIRC ARTICLE NO: 097524

Woods, L. Greens guide: irrigation. *Green (Ottawa) Jul 1984, 16.*
LEVEL: B LANG: Eng SIRC ARTICLE NO: 100640

Woods, L. Greens guide: producing faster greens. (Refs: 1)*Green (Ottawa) Aug 1984, 18.*
LEVEL: B LANG: Eng SIRC ARTICLE NO 100641

Woods, L. Greens guide: fall aerating and topdressing. *Green (Ottawa) 1984, 15.*
LEVEL: B LANG: Eng SIRC ARTICLE NO: 17338

HISTORY

Lyne, J. First Empire Games held in Canada. *Bowls magazine (Capetown, S.A.) 15(9), Mar 1984, 16.*
LEVEL: B LANG: Eng SIRC ARTICLE NO: 095139

Lyne, J. First women's club in UK. *Bowls magazine (Cape Town, S.A.) 15(10), Apr 1984, 11.*
LEVEL: B LANG: Eng SIRC ARTICLE NO: 096727

Lyne, J. Travel levy for South Africans. (1935-1936) *Bowls (Capetown, South Africa) 15(11), May 1984, 13.*
LEVEL: B LANG: Eng SIRC ARTICLE NO: 099782

Lyne, J. The way of the bowl. 1937, 1938 *Bowls (Capetown, South Africa) 15(12), Jun 1984, 7.*
LEVEL: B LANG: Eng SIRC ARTICLE NO: 099783

Lyne, J. Old bowlers never die... *Bowls (Capetown, South Africa) 15(7), Jan 1984, 11.*
LEVEL: B LANG: Eng SIRC ARTICLE NO: 099784

Lyne, J. Break - for Sterner stuff. *Bowls magazine (Cape Town, South Africa) 16(1), Jul 1984, 13.*
LEVEL: B LANG: Eng SIRC ARTICLE NO: 101380

Lyne, J. Rhodesians move in. *Bowls magazine (Cape Town, South Africa) 16(2), Aug 1984, 7.*
LEVEL: B LANG: Eng SIRC ARTICLE NO: 101381

Lyne, J. Boks win fours... *Bowls (Capetown, South Africa) 16(3), Sept 1984, 3;11.*
LEVEL: B LANG: Eng SIRC ARTICLE NO: 103281

Lyne, J. Super guy is Aussie champ four years running. (1953, 1954) *Bowls (Cape Town) 16(6), Dec 1984, 7.*
LEVEL: B LANG: Eng SIRC ARTICLE NO: 104817

MASS MEDIA

Feeny, P. How to make it with the media. *World bowls (London) Sept 1984, 33.*
LEVEL: B LANG: Eng SIRC ARTICLE NO: 099779

RULES AND REGULATIONS

de Kock, J.J. Modern approach to the game. *Bowls magazine (Cape Town, South Africa) 16(1), Jul 1984, 8-9.*
NOTES: Reprinte from, de Kock, J.J., Bowls in South Africa, 1984.
LEVEL: B LANG: Eng SIRC ARTICLE NO: 101377

SOCIOLOGY

Bell, B. Etiquette: for beginners of the game bowls. *Bowls (Capetown, S.A.) 15(8), Feb 1984, 10.*
LEVEL: B LANG: Eng SIRC ARTICLE NO: 098285

STATISTICS AND RECORDS

Medlycott, J. Analysis: ten years of Middleton Cup performances. *World bowls (London) Aug 1984, 16.*
LEVEL: B LANG: Eng SIRC ARTICLE NO: 098287

STRATEGY

Sergay, J. The tactics of bowls, and how to protect your shots. *Bowls magazine (Cape Town, S.A.) 15(10), Apr 1984, 12-13.*
LEVEL: B LANG: Eng SIRC ARTICLE NO: 096728

Sergay, J. Tactics in the fours game... *Bowls (Capetown, South Africa) 15(7), Jan 1984, 2-4.*
LEVEL: B LANG: Eng SIRC ARTICLE NO: 099787

TECHNIQUES AND SKILLS

de Kock, J.J. The mechanics of bowls. *Bowls magazine (Cape Town, South Africa) 16(2), Aug 1984, 8-9.*
NOTES: Reprinted from, de Kock, J.J., Bowls in South Africa, 1984.
LEVEL: B LANG: Eng SIRC ARTICLE NO: 101378

de Kock, J.J. Starting to play... *Bowls (Cape Town) 16(6), Dec 1984, 10-11.*
NOTES: Reprinted from, de Kock, J.J., Bowls i South Africa, Cape Town, HAUM.
LEVEL: B LANG: Eng SIRC ARTICLE NO: 104813

Faults that creep in and their self cure. *World bowls (London) Jul 1984, 31.*
NOTES: Reproduced from, Lawn bowls: winning techniques, by Jock Jepson, published by Lansdowne Press.
LEVEL: B LANG: Eng SIRC ARTICLE NO: 098286

Jepson, J. Guide to better bowling: weight or pace. *World bowls (London) Oct 1984, 29.*
NOTES: Reprinted from, Jepson, J., Lawn bowls: winning techniques, Lansdowne Press.
LEVEL: B LANG: Eng SIRC ARTICLE NO: 099780

Jepson, J. Guide to better bowling: the meaning of shots. *World bowls (London) Nov 1984, 11.*
NOTES: Reproduced from, Jepon, J., Lawn bowls: winning techniques, Lansdowne Press.
LEVEL: B LANG: Eng SIRC ARTICLE NO: 103280

Jepson, J. Guide to better bowling: playing the shots. *World bowls (London) Dec 1984, 18-19.*
NOTES: Reprinted from Jepson J., Lawn bowls: winning techniques, Landsowne Press.
LEVEL: B LANG: Eng SIRC ARTICLE NO: 104816

Sergay, J. Don't rush your game. *Bowls (Capetown, South Africa) 15(11), May 1984, 10.*
LEVEL: B LANG: Eng SIRC ARTICLE NO: 099785

Sergay, J. The draw shot. *Bowls (Capetown, South Africa) 15(12), Jun 1984, 5-6.*
LEVEL: B LANG: Eng SIRC ARTICLE NO: 09978

Wyeth, E. Coaching confusion. *World bowls (London) Aug 1984, 15-16.*
LEVEL: B LANG: Eng SIRC ARTICLE NO: 098291

TECHNIQUES AND SKILLS - AIMING

Jepson, J. Guide to better bowling: centre line bowling. *World bowls (London) Sept 1984, 29.*
NOTES: Reprinted from, Jepson, J., Lawn bowls: winning techniques, Lansdowne Press.
LEVEL: B LANG: Eng SIRC ARTICLE NO: 099781

TECHNIQUES AND SKILLS - GRIP

Sergay, J. Why the clinic style? *Bowls (Capetown, S.A.) 15(8), Feb 1984, 2-3.*
LEVEL: B LANG: Eng SIRC ARTICLE NO: 098290

TECHNIQUES AND SKILLS - STANCE

de Kock, J.J. Never aim for the Jack. *Bowls (Capetown, South Africa) 16(3), Sept 1984, 8-9.*
NOTES: Reprinted from, de Kock, J.J., Bowls in South Africa, 1984.
LEVEL: B LANG: Eng SIRC ARTICLE NO: 103279

TESTING AND EVALUATION

Medlycott, J. Analysis: does it pay to have the Jack? *World bowls (London) Jul 1984, 20.*
LEVEL: B LANG: Eng SIRC ARTICLE NO: 098288

VARIATIONS

Bell, B. How about a R100 000 prize for top score in the game of discs. *Bowls magazine (Cape Town, South Africa) 16(2), Aug 1984, 10-11.*
LEVEL: B LANG: Eng SIRC ARTICLE NO: 101376

Newby, D. Growth of indoor bowls. *World bowls (Halesworth, Eng.) Feb 1984, 15-16.*
NOTES: Extracted from a series publishe in, Sports Industry.
LEVEL: B LANG: Eng SIRC ARTICLE NO: 095141

Newby, D. Setting up an indoor bowls centre. *World bowls (Halesworth, Eng.) Mar 1984, 10-11.*
NOTES: Extracted from a series published in, Sports Industry.
LEVEL: B LANG: Eng SIRC ARTICLE NO: 095142

LIFESAVING

Anderson, S. Le bon samaritain (sauveteur) et le surveillant-sauveteur... Quelle differences? *Alerte (Montreal) 19, dec 198 9-11.*
LEVEL: B LANG: Fr SIRC ARTICLE NO: 107567

Montminy, A. Techniques de base en surveillance. *Alerte (Montreal) 18, sept 1984, 26-29.*
LEVEL: B LANG: Fr SIRC ARTICLE NO: 107591

Palm, J. Pour une juste simulation de victimes. *Alerte (Montreal) 17, mars 1984, 10-12.*
LEVEL: B LANG: Fr SIRC ARTICLE NO 098540

Pia, F. The rid factor: as a cause of drowning. *Parks & recreation (Alexandria, Va.) 19(6), Jun 1984, 52-55;67.*
LEVEL: B LANG: Eng SIRC ARTICLE NO: 095317

ADMINISTRATION

Enfin devenu une realite: 'Sauvetage-Quebec'. *Alerte (Montreal) 18, sept 1984, 5-7.*
LEVEL: B LANG: Fr SIRC ARTICLE NO: 1075

HISTORY

Huint, R. Lost and found: the search continues... *Alerte (Montreal) 19, Dec 1984, 15-17.*
LEVEL: B LANG: Eng SIRC ARTICLE NO: 107584

TEACHING

Chevalier, N. Les principes d'enseignement & leurs applications. *Alerte (Montreal) 19, dec 1984, 18-20.*
NOTES: Premier article d'une conference prononcee par l'auteur, avec la collaboration de M. Leo Morissette, dans le cadre du Symposium annuel de la Societe Royale de sauvetage du Canada, Sherbrooke, mai 1984.
LEVEL: B LANG: Fr SIRC ARTICLE NO: 107572

Dubois, C. Robin, J.P. Le parcours de sauvetage. *EPS: Education physique et sport 185, janv/fevr 1984, 43-45.*
LEVEL: B LANG: Fr SIRC ARTICLE NO: 093774

Neneman, J. Adults in lifesaving classes are 'Gold Mine'. *Journal of physical education and program (Columbus, Oh.) Sept 1984, F-11-F-12.*
LEVEL: B LANG: Eng SIRC ARTICLE NO: 103496

TECHNIQUES AND SKILLS

Angers, N. Portage et remorquage a vos frais. *Alerte (Montreal) 17, juin 1984, 8-9.*
LEVEL: B LANG: Fr SIRC ARTICLE NO: 109092

Scott, R. An alternative method for deep water resuscitation. *Journal of physical education and program (Columbus, Oh.) 81(4), Apr 1984, D22.*
LEVEL: B LANG: Eng SIRC ARTICLE NO: 095320

LITERATURE AND SPORT

Boe, F. Olsen, L. Navigating Huck Finn's river. (Refs: 4)*Arete: the journal of sport literature (San Diego, Calif.) 2(1), Fall 1984, 1-8.*
LEVEL: I LANG: Eng SIRC ARTICLE NO: 108403

Keller, R.D. The man in charge: coaches in modern literature. *Arete: the journal of sport literature (San Diego, Calif.) 1(2), Spring 1984, 139-150.*
ABST: This essay focuses on the perception of coaches by American writers. Some of the works studied are Bernard Malamud's The Natural (1952), Joseph Heller's Something Happened (1975) and a poem by James Dickey, 'The Bee'.
LEVEL: A LANG: Eng SIRC ARTICLE NO: 097864

Olsen, L. Sport and literature: the best of both worlds. *College board review (New York) 131, Spring 1984, 20-24.*
LEVEL: LANG: Eng SIRC ARTICLE NO: 104492

Siner, H. Sports classics: American writers choose their best. 1st McGraw-Hill pbk. ed. New York: McGraw-Hill, 1984, c1983. 1v.
LEVEL: B LANG: Eng ISBN: 0070572984 LC CARD: 84-010046

LITERATURE AND SPORT (continued)

FICTION

Burton, R.J. Ernest Hemingway: the artist as athlete. *Inside sports (Evanston, Ill.) 6, Oct 1984, 46-48.*
LEVEL: B LANG: E SIRC ARTICLE NO: 104486

Hollands, R.G. Images of women in Canadian sports fiction. (Refs: 41)
CONF: North American Society for the Sociology of Sport. Conference (3rd : 1982 : Toronto, Ont.).
NOTES: In, Theberge, N. and Donnelly, P. (eds.), Sport and the sociological imagination: refereed proceedings of the 3rd Annual Conference of the North American Society for the Sociology of Sport, Toronto, Canada, November 1982, Fort Worth, Tex., Texas Christian University Press, c1984, p. 40-56.
ABST: This paper discusses the notion that there are some basic similarities between recent developments in Marxist and feminist literary analyses. This is applied to the characterization of women in three contemporary Canadian sports novels.
LEVEL: A LANG: Eng SIRC ARTICLE NO: 097845

Lessa, R. Our nervous, sporadic games: sports in The Great Gatsby. *Arete: the journal of sport literature (San Diego, Calif.) 1(2), Spring 1984, 69-79.*
ABST: The author discusses the role of sports in The Great Gatsby, a novel written by F. Scott Fitzgerald in 1925. The main characters, Tom Buchanan, Jordan Baker, Nick Carraway and Gatsby, are analysed.
LEVEL: A LANG: Eng SIRC ARTICLE NO: 097866

Sherrill, A. The male athlete in young adult sport fiction. (Refs: 14)*Arete: the journal of sport literature (San Diego, Calif.) 2(1), Fall 1984, 111-130.*
LEVEL: A LANG: Eng SIRC ARTICLE NO: 108408

Talentino, A. Alienation and the super-jock: Sometimes a great notion. (Refs: 8)*Arete: the journal of sport literature (San Diego, Calif.) 2(1), Fall 1984, 63-73.*
LEVEL: A LANG: Eng SIRC ARTICLE NO: 108406

JUVENILE LITERATURE

Lipsyte, R. Assignment, sports. Rev. ed. New York: Harper & Row, 1984. 1v.
NOTES: Revised and expanded by Robert Lipsyte.
LEVEL: B LANG: Eng ISBN: 0060239085 LC CARD: 83-048436

Sobol, D.J. Encyclopedia Brown's book of wacky sports. New York: Morrow, 1984. 1v.
LEVEL: B LANG: Eng ISBN: 0688038840 LC CARD: 82-084250

POETRY

Folsom, E. The manly and healthy game: Walt Whitman and the development of American baseball. (Refs: 45)*Arete: the journal of sport literature (San Diego, Calif.) 2(1), Fall 1984, 43-62.*
LEVEL: A LANG: Eng SIRC ARTICLE NO: 108405

Lefkowitz, M.R. The poet as athlete. (Refs: 19)*Journal of sport history (University Park, Pa.) 11(2), Summer 1984, 18-24.*
LEVEL: I LANG: Eng SIRC ARTICLE NO: 099343

Scanlon, T.F. Olympic dust, the Delphic Laurel, and Isthmian Toil: Horace and Greek athletics.

Arete: the journal of sport literature (San Diego, Calif.) 1(2), Spring 1984, 163-175.
ABST: This essay focuses on the discussion of Greek athletics in the poetry of Horace.
LEVEL: A LANG: Eng SIRC ARTICLE NO: 097872

LONG JUMP

BIOGRAPHY AND AUTOBIOGRAPHY

Herdershott, J. Athlete of the year. Carl Lewis: more in '84. *Track & field news 36(12), Jan 1984, 9-10.*
LEVEL: B LANG: E SIRC ARTICLE NO: 092467

Smith, G. 'I do what I want to do' (Carl Lewis) *Sports illustrated (Chicago, Ill.) 61(4), 18 Jul 1984, 22-26;29-30;32;34;36-39.*
LEVEL: B LANG: Eng SIRC ARTICLE NO: 097000

With an eye on multiple medals in Los Angeles, Carl Lewis' glorious past might be only prologue. *Runner's world 19(1), Jan 1984, 21-22;24;26;29-30.*
LEVEL: B LANG: Eng SIRC ARTICLE NO: 091125

BIOMECHANICS

Lindeman, R. Dynamics of the long jump. *Athletic journal 64(9), Apr 1984, 6-7.*
LEVEL: B LANG: Eng SIRC ARTICLE NO: 093859

Wai, J.P. A kinematic analysis of an elite long jumper's take-off. *Asian journal of physical education (Taipei, Taiwan) 7(3), Oct 1984, 58-59.*
LEVEL: I LANG: Eng Chi SIRC ARTICLE NO: 103553

COACHING

Groseclose, B. Track and field coaching hints. *Texas coach (Austin, Tex.) 28(3), Oct 1984, 44-46.*
LEVEL: B LANG: Eng SIRC ARTICLE NO: 173208

TECHNIQUES AND SKILLS

Hayes, D. The long jump. *Track and field quarterly review (Kalamazoo, Mich.) 84(4), Winter 1984, 8.*
LEVEL: B LANG: Eng SIRC ARTICLE NO: 101637

Jarver, J. Boase, G. Helsinki observations - horizontal jumps. *Modern athlete and coach (Athelstone, Aust.) 22(1), Jan 1984 3-7.*
LEVEL: B LANG: Eng SIRC ARTICLE NO: 096942

Javer, J. Boase, G. Helsinki observations - horizontal jumps. *Track and field journal (Ottawa) 28, Nov 1984, 31-33.*
LEVEL B LANG: Eng SIRC ARTICLE NO: 109769

Sidorenko, S. The sprint and the jump. *Soviet sports review (Escondido, Calif.) 19(4), Dec 1984, 182-184.*
NOTES: Translated from, Legkaya atletika 7, 1984, 18.
LEVEL: I LANG: Eng SIRC ARTICLE NO: 104952

Zotko, R. Papanov, V. Heike Daute in the long jump. *Soviet sports review (Escondido, Calif.) 19(3), Sept 1984, 127-129.*
NOTES: Translated from, Legkaya atletika 5, 1984, 16-17.
LEVEL: I LANG: Eng SIRC ARTICLE NO: 103554

TRAINING AND CONDITIONING

Prost, R. L'entrainement des sauteurs en longueur et des triple-sauteurs en altitude. *Revue de l'Amicale des entraineurs francais d'athletisme (Paris) 89, oct/nov/dec 1984, 19-21.*
LEVEL: B LANG: Fr SIRC ARTICLE NO: 103548

Tenke, Z. Preparation of long and triple-jumpers. (Refs: 2)*Track and field journal (Ottawa) 28, Nov 1984, 15-19.*
LEVEL: B LANG: Eng SIRC ARTICLE NO: 103551

Yuchkevitsh, T. Training suggestions for young horizontal jumpers. *Modern athlete and coach (Athelstone, Aust.) 2(3), Jul 1984, 18-20.*
NOTES: Translated and condensed from Legkaja Atletika (Moscow) 3, Mar 1983.
LEVEL: B LANG: Eng SIRC ARTICLE NO: 101650

LUGE

BIOGRAPHY AND AUTOBIOGRAPHY

Chaffie, N. What's California Girl doing on that sled? Bonny Warner plans for success in luge. *Olympian (Colorado Springs, Colo.) 9(2), Jul/Aug 1984, 10-11.*
LEVEL: B LANG: Eng SIRC ARTICLE NO: 104818

Craven, S. A kayak winner who's born to luge. (David Gilman) *Olympian (Colorado Springs, Colo.) 11(1), Jun 1984, 10-12.*
LEVEL: B LANG: Eng SIRC ARTICLE NO: 101382

Dickie, D. Marie-Claude Doyon, la vie de casse-cou. Marie-Claude Doyon, leading the crazy life. *Champion 8(1), Feb 1984, 30-31.*
LEVEL: B LANG: Eng Fr SIRC ARTICLE NO: 090779

Scammell, R. Miroslav Zajonc - victime des tracasseries administratives. Miroslav Zajonc - luger sidelined by red tape. *Champion 8(1), Feb 1984, 14-17.*
LEVEL: B LANG: Eng Fr SIRC ARTICLE NO: 090780

Sullivan, R. Sliding into the big picture. Out of tiny Kiens in the Sudtirol comes Paul Hildgartner to take aim at an Olympi singles luge victory. *Sports illustrated 60(5), 6 Feb 1984, 64-66.*
LEVEL: B LANG: Eng SIRC ARTICLE NO: 090781

HISTORY

Kunkel, K. An old/new sport - luge. *Journal of physical education, recreation & dance 55(1), Jan 1984, 26.*
LEVEL: B LANG: Eng SIRC ARTICLE NO: 092254

SPORTING EVENTS

Isatitsch, B. Le flocon de neige olympique. The Olympic snowflake. *Message olympique/Olympic message (Lausanne) 7, juin/Jun 1984, 55-58.*
LEVEL: B LANG: Fr Eng SIRC ARTICLE NO: 104819

MARATHON AND ULTRAMARATHON

Brannen, D. Dubious and dastardly deeds. *Running times (Woodbridge, Va.) 86, Mar 1984, 10-13.*
LEVEL: B LANG: Eng SIRC ARTICLE NO: 096953

Burfoot, A. 10 little things that make a difference: here are 10 tips that can add up to better training and racing. *Runner's world 19(2), Feb 1984, 66-69.*
LEVEL: B LANG: Eng SIRC ARTICLE NO: 091073

Gynn, R.R.W. Guinness book on the marathon. Enfield, Middlesex: Guinness Superlatives Ltd., c1984. 168 p. : ill.
NOTES: Includes index.
LEVEL: B LANG: Eng ISBN: 0-85112-410-0 LC CARD: 84-670145 GV1065 18391

Henderson, J. Your first race: if you get your first race correct, you'll be setting yourself up for a long career of enjoyment. *Runner's world 19(5), May 1984, 52-55;126.*
LEVEL: B LANG: Eng SIRC ARTICLE NO: 093893

Ryan, A.J. How much is enough? *Physician and sportsmedicine (Minneapolis, Minn.) 12(10), Oct 1984, 33.*
LEVEL: B LANG: Eng SIRC ARTICLE NO: 100086

Smith, G. Burfoot, A. Things I should have known about running the marathon: Geoff Smith ran the fastest debut marathon in history at NYC '83. The only problem was he didn't win. If he only knew then what he knows now. *Runner's world 19(4), Apr 1984, 72-75;114;117.*
LEVEL: B LANG: Eng SIRC ARTICLE NO: 093943

Stuller, J. Beyond tough: it's time to end the bickering. What's really the hardest, sickest ultra-endurance event of them all? *Outside 9(1), Jan/Feb 1984, 39-43;76-77.*
LEVEL: B LANG: Eng SIRC ARTICLE NO: 093237

Youngman, M. Ten types of marathoner. *Running (London) 41, Sept 1984, 30-31.*
LEVEL: B LANG: Eng SIRC ARTICLE NO: 105041

ADMINISTRATION

Foster, J. Police action: a race director who doesn't cooperate with the local authorities is courting disaster. *Runner's world 19(2), Feb 1984, 62-65;113.*
LEVEL: B LANG: Eng SIRC ARTICLE NO: 091087

Merhar, G. Computerizing a race: the 1983 New York City Marathon. *Running & fitness (Washington, D.C.) 16(2), Apr 1984, 17-18.*
LEVEL: B LANG: Eng SIRC ARTICLE NO: 098660

Shonebarger, M. Curren, M. What makes a good road race? *Ohio runner (Columbus, Oh.) 5(8), Apr/May 1984, 12-13.*
LEVEL: B LANG: Eng SIRC ARTICLE NO: 095461

Ward, T. The marathon double act. Whatever you think of its organization, the London Marathon wouldn't exist without the combined talents of Chris Brasher and John Disley. *Running (London) 37, May 1984, 107-111.*
LEVEL: B LANG: Eng SIRC ARTICLE NO: 097014

AGED

Hogan, D.B. Cape, R.D. Marathoners over sixty years of age: results of a survey. (Refs: 6)*Journal of the American Geriatric Society (New York) 32(2), Feb 1984, 121-123.*
ABST: 32 marathoners over the age of 60 were surveyed. They were predominantly male, well educated and health conscious with six runners claiming addiction to running. The injury rate was comparable to that of younger runners.
LEVEL: A LANG: Eng SIRC ARTICLE NO: 100055

BIOGRAPHY AND AUTOBIOGRAPHY

A short interview with Jacqueline Gareau. *Canadian runner Jan/Feb 1984, 26-27.*
LEVEL: B LANG: Eng SIRC ARTICLE NO: 091115

Albom, M. Marianne Dickerson: her silver medal in Helsinki was the Cinderella story of the year. *Running times (Woodbridge, Va.) 85, Feb 1984, 24;26.*
LEVEL: B LANG: Eng SIRC ARTICLE NO: 098609

Albom, M. Carlos Lopes. *Running times (Woodbridge, Va.) 94, Nov 1984, 21-23.*
LEVEL: B LANG: Eng SIRC ARTICLE NO: 101652

Baxter, K. Mary Decker: up front and at home. In Helsinki, America's premier woman middle-distance runner gained overdue respect around the world, but she still seems more at home in small-town Eugene. *Runner's world 19(2), Feb 1984, 92-96;98-99.*
LEVEL: B LANG: Eng SIRC ARTICLE NO: 091068

Bentsen, C. Simeon Kigen, Kenya. *Runner (Boulder, Colo.) 6(10), Jul 1984, 84-85.*
LEVEL: B LANG: Eng SIRC ARTICLE NO: 1016

Bentsen, C. Juma Ikangaa, Tanzania. *Runner (Boulder, Colo.) 6(10), Jul 1984, 90-96.*
LEVEL: B LANG: Eng SIRC ARTICLE NO: 101656

Berenyi, I. Waldemar Cierpinski, East Germany. *Runner (Boulder, Colo.) 6(10), Jul 1984, 74-75.*
LEVEL: B LANG: Eng SIRC ARTICLE NO: 101657

Blaikie, D. Jack Caffery (1900, 1901).
NOTES: In, Blaikie, D., Boston: the Canadian story, Ottawa, Seneca House Books, 1984 p. 19-32.
LEVEL: B LANG: Eng GV1065.22.B6 17078

Blaikie, D. Tom Longboat (1907).
NOTES: In, Blaikie, D., Boston: the Canadian story, Ottawa, Seneca House Books, 1984, p. 33-52.
LEVEL: B LANG: Eng GV1065.22.B6 17078

Blaikie, D. Fred Cameron (1910).
NOTES: In, Blaikie, D., Boston: the Canadian story, Ottawa, Seneca House Books, 1984, p. 53-65.
LEVEL: B LANG: Eng GV1065.22.B6 17078

Blaikie, D. James Duffy (1914).
NOTES: In, Blaikie, D., Boston: the Canadian story, Ottawa, Seneca House Books, 1984, p. 71-82.
LEVEL: B LANG: Eng GV1065.22.B6 17078

Blaikie, D. Edouard Fabre (1915).
NOTES: In, Blaikie, D., Boston: the Canadian story, Ottawa, Seneca House Books, 1984, p. 83-96.
LEVEL: B LANG: Eng GV1065.22.B6 17078

Blaikie, D. Johnny Miles (1926, 1929).
NOTES: In, Blaikie, D., Boston: the Canadian story, Ottawa, Seneca House Books, 1984 p. 97-110.
LEVEL: B LANG: Eng GV1065.22.B6 17078

Blaikie, D. Dave Komonen (1934).
NOTES: In, Blaikie, D., Boston: the Canadian story, Ottawa, Seneca House Books, 1984, p. 115-124.
LEVEL: B LANG: Eng GV1065.22.B6 17078

Blaikie, D. Walter Young (1937).
NOTES: In, Blaikie, D., Boston: the Canadian story, Ottawa, Seneca House Books, 1984, p. 125-134.
LEVEL: B LANG: Eng GV1065.22.B6 17078

Blaikie, D. Gerard Cote (1940, 1943, 1944, 1948).
NOTES: In, Blaikie, D., Boston: the Canadian story, Ottawa, Seneca House Books, 1984, p. 135-149.
LEVEL: B LANG: Eng GV1065.22.B6 17078

Blaikie, D. Jerome Drayton (1977).
NOTES: In, Blaikie, D., Boston: the Canadian story, Ottawa, Seneca House Books, 1984, p. 151-175.
LEVEL: B LANG: Eng GV1065.22.B6 17078

Blaikie, D. Jacqueline Gareau (1980).
NOTES: In, Blaikie, D., Boston: the Canadian story, Ottawa, Seneca House Books, 1984, p. 177-193.
LEVEL: B LANG: Eng GV1065.22.B6 17078

Blaikie, D. Boston: the Canadian story. (Jerome Drayton) *Canadian runner (Toronto) May 1984, 15-17.*
NOTES: Third in a series of excerpts from, Blaikie, D., Boston: The Canadian story, 1984.
LEVEL: B LANG: Eng SIRC ARTICLE NO: 095394

Bloom, M. Robert De Castella: Australia. *Runner (Boulder, Colo.) 6(10), Jul 1984, 62-65;97.*
LEVEL: B LANG: Eng SIRC ARTICLE NO: 101658

Brant, J. A workingman's marathoner. There's a lot more to the Pete Pfitzinger story than his Olympic trials marathon win. *Runners world (Mountain View, Calif.) 19(12), Dec 1984, 74-79.*
LEVEL: B LANG: Eng SIRC ARTICLE NO: 101659

Brooks, J.R. Jacqueline Gareau, Canada. *Runner (New York) 6(9), Jun 1984, 68-69.*
LEVEL: B LANG: Eng SIRC ARTICLE NO: 1016

Burfoot, A. Simple values keep Joan Benoit's life under control. The marathon world-record holder runs in the Maine winter t toughen up for the Los Angeles summer. *Runner's world 19(3), Mar 1984, 82-87;110.*
LEVEL: B LANG: Eng SIRC ARTICLE NO: 092475

Burfoot, A. Brant, J. A century of excellence; two outstanding masters runners follow parallel paths; in running and in life (Norm Green; Marion Irvine) *Runner's world (Mountain View, Calif.) 19(6), Jun 1984, 50-53.*
LEVEL: B LANG: Eng SIRC ARTICLE NO: 095396

Castro, R. Interview: Carlos Lopes. *Track and field news (Los Angeles, Calif.) 37(10), Nov 1984, 8-9.*
LEVEL: B LANG: Eng SIRC ARTICLE NO: 101663

Caulfield, B. Robert De Castella: he's the working man's runner. He harbors no secrets, no surprises, yet he has methodicall established himself as the Olympic Marathon favorite. *Ultrasport (Boston) 1(4), Jul/Aug 1984, 8-12;14.*
LEVEL: B LANG: Eng SIRC ARTICLE NO: 098618

Chacour, M. La petite fille qui jouait au marathon. (Mary Etta Boitano) *Spiridon (Salvan, Suisse) 71, janv 1984, 18-22.*
LEVEL: B LANG: Fr SIRC ARTICLE NO: 098620

Downes, S. Profile: Basil Heatley, a man for all seasons. *Running magazine (London) 35, Mar 1984, 50-53.*
LEVEL: B LANG: E SIRC ARTICLE NO: 098626

Elliott, L. Interview with Noel and Karina Nequin. *Running & fitness (Washington, D.C.) 16(3), May/Jun 1984, 1;15-17.*
LEVEL: B LANG: Eng SIRC ARTICLE NO: 101670

Flippin, R. Joan Benoit, United States. *Runner (New York) 6(9), Jun 1984, 64-66.*
LEVEL: B LANG: Eng SIRC ARTICLE NO: 1016

Gains, P. Carlos Lopes: a profile of the 37 year old Olympic marathon champion. *Athletics (Willowdale, Ont.) Nov/Dec 1984, 6-8.*
LEVEL: B LANG: Eng SIRC ARTICLE NO: 177568

Having stood marathoning on its ear for the third time, Joan Benoit turns to ordering her post-Olympic life. *Runner's world (Mountain View, Calif.) 19(11), Nov 1984, 23-24;26;30;32;34;36.*
LEVEL: B LANG: Eng SIRC ARTICLE NO: 100053

Hidgon, D. Carlos Lopes, Portugal. *Runner (Boulder, Colo.) 6(10), Jul 1984, 82-83.*
LEVEL: B LANG: Eng SIRC ARTICLE NO: 101680

Higdon, H. She outruns everyone-including the press: the elusive Joan Benoit. *Women's sports (Palo Alto, Calif.) 6(3), Mar 1984, 39-42;56.*
LEVEL: B LANG: Eng SIRC ARTICLE NO: 098640

Higdon, H. Grete Waitz, Norway. *Runner (New York) 6(9), Jun 1984, 60-63.*
LEVEL: B LANG: Eng SIRC ARTICLE NO: 101681

Higdon, H. Anatomy of a marathoner: professor, Bill Hall, a 43-year-old student of the brain, has the long distances down to a science. *Runner (New York) 7(2), Nov 1984, 82-86;88-89.*
LEVEL: B LANG: Eng SIRC ARTICLE NO: 108636

Joyce, G. Kanchan Stott becomes first woman to run across Canada. *Canadian runner Jan/Feb 1984, 14-15.*
LEVEL: B LANG: Eng SIRC ARTICLE NO: 091095

Lebow, F. Woodley, R. Inside the world of big-time marathoning. 1st ed. New York: Rawson Associates, c1984. 230 p. : ill.
LEVEL: B LANG: Eng ISBN: 0-89256-262-5 LC CARD: 83-43110 GV1065.22.N49 18052

Maddaford, T. Rod Dixon, New Zealand. *Runner (Boulder, Colo.) 6(10), Jul 1984, 80-81.*
LEVEL: B LANG: Eng SIRC ARTICLE NO: 101687

Maddaford, T. Anne Audain, New Zealand. *Runner (New York) 6(9), Jun 1984, 70-72.*
LEVEL: B LANG: Eng SIRC ARTICLE NO: 1016

McCrea, M. Entrevue de Champion: 'j'ai merite une place au sein de l'equipe'. (Jacqueline Gareau) Champion interview: 'I earned a spot on the Canadian team'. (Jacqueline Gareau) *Champion (Ottawa) 8(3), Aug 1984, 12-17.*
LEVEL: B LANG: Fr Eng SIRC ARTICLE NO: 096984

Merhar, G. Mr. Boston Marathon: Jock Semple. *Running & fitness (Washington, D.C.) 16(4), Jul/Aug 1984, 1;17-18.*
LEVEL: B LANG: Eng SIRC ARTICLE NO: 106175

Mills, A.R. Peters the great. It is 30 years since Jim Peters was picked up Dorando-style from the track at the end of his last ever race. *Running (London, Eng.) 36, Apr 1984, 58-61.*
LEVEL: B LANG: Eng SIRC ARTICLE NO: 096986

Moore, K. A man wreathed in glory. Rob de Castella of Australia became the top marathoner by being impervious to injury, unvarying in his training and unswerving in his goals. *Sports illustrated (Chicago, Ill.) 61(4), 18 Jul 1984, 356-360;363;366;369-370;375.*
NOTES: Special preview: the 1984 Olympics.
LEVEL: B LANG: Eng SIRC ARTICLE NO: 096987

Newman, S. Diane Palmason: Canada's top female master runner is a proponent of women's rights on and off the track. *Athletics (Willowdale, Ont.) Jun 1984, 25-27.*
LEVEL: B LANG: Eng SIRC ARTICLE NO: 098665

Olsen, E. Alive and still kicking. (Bell Rodgers) *Runner (Boulder, Colo,) 6(5), Feb 1984, 26-32.*
LEVEL: B LANG: Eng SIRC ARTICLE NO: 095446

Olsen, E. Alberto Salazar, United States. *Runner (Boulder, Colo.) 6(10), Jul 1984, 70-72.*
LEVEL: B LANG: Eng SIRC ARTICLE NO: 101696

Olsen, E. Rodolfo Gomez, Mexico. *Runner (Boulder, Colo.) 6(10), Jul 1984, 76-78.*
LEVEL: B LANG: Eng SIRC ARTICLE NO: 1016

Olsen, E. Bound for glory. (Sister Marion Irvine) *Runner (New York) 6(9), Jun 1984, 28-33.*
LEVEL: B LANG: Eng SIRC ARTICL NO: 101698

Popham, P. Glorious redemption. That is what a marathon victory in Los Angeles would be for stoic Toshihiko Seko, his controversial samurai coach, and the country whose values they embody. *Ultrasport (Boston) 1(4), Jul/Aug 1984, 48;50-52.*
LEVEL: B LANG: Eng SIRC ARTICLE NO: 098676

Profile: David Edge. *Track and field journal (Ottawa, Ont.) 27, Aug 1984, 19-20.*
LEVEL: B LANG: Eng SIRC ARTICLE NO: 100081

Robert de Castella: en forme toute l'annee. *Spiridon (Salvan, Suisse) 75, sept/oct 1984, 51-53;55.*
LEVEL: B LANG: Eng SIRC ARTICLE NO: 108865

Runner's world gold medal exclusive: the first lady of marathoning speaks up on times, troubles and the Los Angeles Olympics. (Grete Waitz) *Runner's world (Mountain View, Calif.) 19(6), Jun 1984, 21-22;25;27-28;32;34;37-38.*
LEVEL: B LANG: Eng SIRC ARTICLE NO: 095456

Schlesinger, D. Toshihiko Seko, Japan. *Runner (Boulder, Colo.) 6(10), Jul 1984, 66-68.*
LEVEL: B LANG: Eng SIRC ARTICLE NO 101708

Schlesinger, D. Akemi Masuda, Japan. *Runner (New York) 6(9), Jun 1984, 74-76.*
LEVEL: B LANG: Eng SIRC ARTICLE NO: 101709

Sheehy, L. George Gallant - 36 years of New Brunswick running history. *Canadian runner (Toronto) Sept/Oct 1984, 28-29.*
NOTES: Part one of a two-part series.
LEVEL: B LANG: Eng SIRC ARTICLE NO: 100089

Shorter, F. Bloom, M. Olympic gold: a runner's life and times. Boston: Houghton Mifflin, 1984. x, 258 p. : ill.
LEVEL: B LANG: Eng ISBN: 0-395-35403-X LC CARD: 83-49180 GV1061.15.S48 17633

Smith, C. Backtracking: Ron Wallingford. Born: Sept. 13, 1933 in Ottawa, 1m72/68kg. *Athletics (Willowdale, Ont.) Jul 1984, 40.*
LEVEL: B LANG: Eng SIRC ARTICLE NO: 098682

Sport interview: Alberto Salazar. He's been outspoken and heartbroken. Now he's ready for the toughest marathon of all. *Sport (New York) 75(1), Jan 1984, 17;19;21;24.*
LEVEL: B LANG: Eng SIRC ARTICLE NO: 095465

Stu Mittleman: the Bruce Springsteen of distance thinks running is only rock'n roll - but he likes it. *Ultrasport (San Diego, Calif.) 1(1), Jan/Feb 1984, 6-8;11.*
LEVEL: B LANG: Eng SIRC ARTICLE NO: 095466

Temple, C. Hugh Jones, Great Britain. *Runner (Boulder, Colo.) 6(10), Jul 1984, 86-88.*
LEVEL: B LANG: Eng SIRC ARTICLE NO: 101719

Temple, C. 'When I started racing, they just didn't come'. (Steve Jones) *Running (London) 44, Dec 1984, 54-55.*
LEVEL: B LANG: Eng SIRC ARTICLE NO: 105031

Thatcher, P. T & FN interview: Alberto Salazar. *Track & field news 36(12), Jan 1984, 78-80.*
LEVEL: B LANG: Eng SIRC ARTICLE NO: 092539

Turnbull, A. Coming in from the cold-at age 39. (Priscilla Welch) *Running magazine (London) 33, Jan 1984, 50-53.*
LEVEL: B LANG: Eng SIRC ARTICLE NO: 098693

Watman, M. It's not the end of the road yet. Mel Watman profiles Olympic marathon champion Carlos Lopes. *Athletics weekly (Rochester, Kent, Eng.) 38(37), 15 Sept 1984, 58-60.*
LEVEL: B LANG: Eng SIRC ARTICLE NO: 100103

Watman, M. Triumph over adversity: a marathon drama in twelve acts - starring the one ad only Joan Benoit. *Athletics weekly (Kent, Eng.) 38(38), 22 Sept 1984, 8-10;12-15.*
LEVEL: B LANG: Eng SIRC ARTICLE NO: 103618

Weck, L. Bjorg Austrheim-Smith: the four-time winner of the Western States 100-mile enduracne run thrives on a regimen of 250-mile weeks, ballet and a sense of humor. *Ultrasport (Boston, Mass.) 1(5), Sept/Oct 1984, 16;18;20.*
LEVEL: B LANG: Eng SIRC ARTICLE NO: 173308

Wischnia, B. Burfoot, A. Post, M. Making it to the trials: for some marathoners - America's second wave - merely making it t the trials is victory. *Runner's world 19(2), Feb 1984, 36-42;110.*
LEVEL: B LANG: Eng SIRC ARTICLE NO: 091124

Wischnia, B. Rob de Castella: a world-champion marathoner is on his way up from down under, and it's doubtful anyone will stop him. *Runner's world 19(4), Apr 1984, 58-63;105;108;112.*
LEVEL: B LANG: Eng SIRC ARTICLE NO: 093967

Wischnia, B. The pride of Portugal. (Carlos Lopes, Rosa Mota) *Runner's world (Mountain View, Calif.) 19(11), Nov 1984, 60-65.*
LEVEL: B LANG: Eng SIRC ARTICLE NO: 100106

Wyatt, D. Higdon, H. Profile: Joan Benoit. Laid back lady in the fast lane. Last April Joan Benoit sliced nearly three minutes from the women's world marathon best. *Running magazine (London) 34, Feb 1984, 72-75.*
LEVEL: B LANG: Eng SIRC ARTICLE NO: 098698

COACHING

Meier, H. Running with eastern promise. Japan's top marathoners were out in force for December's Fukuoka Marathon - their Olympic trials. *Running magazine (London) 34, Feb 1984, 66-71.*
LEVEL: B LANG: Eng SIRC ARTICLE NO: 098657

DISABLED

Asayama, K. Nakamura, Y. Ogata, H. Morita, H. Kodama, S. Hatada, K. Energy expenditure of paraplegic marathon runners measured during a wheelchair marathon. *Sangyo ika daigaku zasshi*

(Kitakyushu) 6(2), 1 June 1984, 121-130.
LEVEL: A LANG: Eng

Burfoot, A. The long run of Linda Down. Once you see this marathoner run, you'll never forget her. Her best time for the event -8:45- is the least of her concerns, because she's overcome a handicap that for most would be insurmountable: cerebral palsy. *Runner's world (Mountain View, Calif.) 19(10), Oct 1984, 72-76.*
LEVEL: B LANG: Eng SIRC ARTICLE NO: 099000

Marshall, T. Wheelchairs and marathon road racing. *British journal of sports medicine (Loughborough, Eng.) 18(4), Dec 1984, 301-304.*
CONF: London Marathon Conference (1984 : London).
LEVEL: I LANG: Eng SIRC ARTICLE NO: 104997

ECONOMICS

Burfoot, A. The high cost of racing. Entry fees are racing, too-but are we getting less for our money? *Runner's world 19(3) Mar 1984, 40-43;106;109.*
LEVEL: B LANG: Eng SIRC ARTICLE NO: 092474

Donaldson, G. Fast bucks: marathoners are going the distance for dollars. *Financial post magazine (Toronto, Ont.) 1 Jul 1984, 28-30;32;34.*
LEVEL: B LANG: Eng SIRC ARTICLE NO: 095403

McCarthy, C. Running for fame and fortune. Robert de Castella is singleminded in his quest for Olympic gold. But he also knows that a win in Los Angeles will more than quadruple his present $150,000 a year income. *Australian business 4(5), 4 Jan 1984, 36-38.*
LEVEL: B LANG: Eng SIRC ARTICLE NO: 093916

Turnbull, A. The fund runners: Hyde Park or Himalayas, two miles or 2,000 - still the sponsorship money rolls in. *Running magazine (London) 33, Jan 1984, 59;61.*
LEVEL: B LANG: Eng SIRC ARTICLE NO: 098694

ENVIRONMENT

NYC Marathon: should it have been stopped? *Physician and sportsmedicine (Minneapolis, Minn.) 12(12), Dec 1984, 23;26.*
LEVEL B LANG: Eng SIRC ARTICLE NO: 103598

Porter, A.M.W. Marathon running and adverse weather conditions: a miscellany. (Refs: 22)*British journal of sports medicine (Loughborough, Eng.) 18(4), Dec 1984, 261-264.*
CONF: London Marathon Conference (1984 : London).
ABST: This paper considers various predisposing and corrective factors for hypothermia and hyperthermia in marathon runners. It is concluded that a race should be cancelled or deferred if the forecast suggests that certain climatic thresholds are likely to be met or crossed.
LEVEL: I LANG: Eng SIRC ARTICLE NO: 105015

HISTORY

The Olympic marathon saga. *Athletics weekly (Kent, Eng.) 38(19), 12 May 1984, 41-42;44-46;48.*
LEVEL: B LANG: Eng SIRC ARTICLE NO: 095447

INJURIES AND ACCIDENTS

Adno, J. Jogger's testicles in marathon runners. (letter) *South African medical journal (Cape Town) 65(26), 30 Jun 1984, 1036.*
LEVEL: B LANG: Eng SIRC ARTICLE NO: 103555

Baer, S. Shakespeare, D. Stress fracture of the femoral neck in a marathon runner. (Refs: 4)*British journal of sports medicine (Loughborough, Leicestershire) 18(1), Mar 1984, 42-43.*
LEVEL: I LANG: Eng SIRC ARTICLE NO: 096949

Brotherwood, R.W. Marathons and St. John. *British journal of sports medicine (Loughborough, Eng.) 18(4), Dec 1984, 281.*
CONF: London Marathon Conference (1984 : London).
LEVEL: B LANG: Eng SIRC ARTICLE NO: 104957

Caine, D.J. Lindner, K.J. Growth plate injury: a threat to young distance runners? (Refs: 31)*Physician and sportsmedicine 12(4), Apr 1984, 118-122;124.*
LEVEL: I LANG: Eng SIRC ARTICLE NO: 093879

Catalano, P. Burfoot, A. The come back trail. Injuries can seem like eternal punishment to the laid-up runner, but take hear from the story of a world-class runner who's been to hell-and back. *Runner's world (Mountain View, Calif.) 19(7), Jul 1984, 70-72;118;120;122.*
LEVEL: B LANG: Eng SIRC ARTICLE NO: 095399

Graham, R. Podiatrist's advice for marathon casualty management. (Refs: 4)*British journal of sports medicine (Loughborough, Eng.) 18(4), 286-287.*
CONF: London Marathon Conference (1984 : London).
LEVEL: B LANG: Eng SIRC ARTICLE NO: 104976

Helpful hints for the marathon runner. *Marathon magazine (Charleville, Ireland) 22(3), May 1984, 18-19.*
LEVEL: B LANG: Eng SIRC ARTICLE NO: 108805

Hutson, M.A. Medical implications of ultra marathon running: observations on a six day track race. *British journal of sport medicine (Loughborough, Leicestershire) 18(1), Mar 1984, 44-45.*
ABST: This paper describes the medical aspect of a six day track race. There were 25 competitors in this race, 15 of whom eventually sustained injuries severe enough to impair their performance.
LEVEL: I LANG: Eng SIRC ARTICLE NO: 096971

Kuipers, H. De marathon; een verantwoorde uitdaging? (The marathon; a justified challenge?) *Nederlands tijdschrift voor geneeskunde (Amsterdam) 128(32), 11 Aug 1984, 1528-1530.*
LEVEL: I LANG: Dut

MacDonald, R. Physiotherapy management of marathon musculo-skeletal casualties. *British journal of sports medicine (Loughborough, Eng.) 18(4), Dec 1984, 283-285.*
CONF: London Marathon Conference (1984 : London).
LEVEL: I LANG: Eng SIRC ARTICLE NO: 104993

Meisler, K. How to stop hurting during a race. The trick is to recognize the dangerous problems and learn some simple remedies for the others, where you'll find that discretion is the better part of running. *Runner's world 19(3), Mar 1984, 70-75;108;110.*
LEVEL: B LANG: Eng SIRC ARTICLE NO: 092503

Parsons, M.A. Anderson, P.B. Williams, B.T. An 'unavoidable' death in a people's marathon. *British journal of sports medicine (Loughborough, Leicestershire) 18(1), Mar 1984, 38-39.*
ABST: This paper reports a death which occurred 3 1/2 miles after the start of a marathon race. The 45 year-old male had previously completed a marathon. The subject had been on medication for sarcoidosis for 3 years. The authors concluded that 3 years of prednisolone therapy led to adrenal atrophy which combined with the stress of running and insufficient prednisolone the day of the race led to acute adrenal insufficiency with hypotension. The authors feel that this death was unavoidable as the runner knew he was taking a calculated risk before he started the marathon.
LEVEL: I LANG: Eng SIRC ARTICLE NO: 096991

Porter, K. Benoit: from hospital bed to victory stand in 17 days. (Joan Benoit) *Physician and sportsmedicine (Minneapolis, Minn.) 12(10), Oct 1984, 167-168;170.*
LEVEL: B LANG: Eng SIRC ARTICLE NO: 100080

Prevention of thermal injuries during distance running. (Refs: 48)*Physician and sportsmedicine (Minneapolis, Minn.) 12(7), Ju 1984, 43-47;50-51.*
LEVEL: B LANG: Eng SIRC ARTICLE NO: 095951

Richards, R. Richards, D. Exertion-induced heat exhaustion and other medical aspects of the City-of-Surf fun runs, 1978-1984 *Medical journal of Australia (Sydney) 141(12/13), 8-22 Dec 1984, 799-805.*
LEVEL: A LANG: Eng

MASTERS COMPETITION

Christie, J. The flying Scotsman is still steaming. (Gordon James Porteous) *Athletics weekly (Rochester, Kent, Eng.) 38(41) 13 Oct 1984, 21-23.*
LEVEL: B LANG: Eng SIRC ARTICLE NO: 101665

MEDICINE

Burfoot, A. Coming back from a marathon. Whether your performance was your best or worst, keep in mind that 26.2 miles exact quite a toll, and afterward it's in your best interest to take things one step at a time. *Runner's world (Mountain View, Calif.) 19(10), Oct 1984, 46-49;112.*
LEVEL: B LANG: Eng SIRC ARTICLE NO: 100042

Costill, D.L. How to run a faster marathon. The ABCs of training and racing, from the research expert who's best probed the body under stress. *Runner (Boulder, Colo.) 6(4), Jan 1984, 58-63.*
LEVEL: B LANG: Eng SIRC ARTICLE NO: 093882

Isaacs, P. Marathon without a colon: salt and water balance in endurance running ileostomates. *British journal of sports medicine (Loughborough, Eng.) 18(4), Dec 1984, 295-300.*
CONF: London Marathon Conference (1984 : London).
ABST: Five trained ileostomates completed a marathon in a cool environment without ill effect. During the race, the ileostomy losses of sodium (1.0-2.7 mmol.-1) and of water (9.2-19 ml.h-1) were

small, but urinary excretion of sodium was very low (0.2-0.75 mmol.h-1) despite drinking a combination of water and lucose-electrolyte solution. The concentration of potassium in the ileostomy discharge tended to increase, also suggesting a sodium retaining state. Healthy ileostomates after suitable training are successful marathon runners, but the prevalence of mild salt depletion in ileostomates generally suggests that it may be advisable for them to take only glucose-electrolyte solutions when competing at any ambient temperature or when preparing for a marathon which is to take place in a warm environment.
LEVEL: A LANG: Eng SIRC ARTICLE NO: 104985

Kardong, D. The fatal flaw. Every runner has a weakness, and nothing can bring it out quite like the marathon. *Runner (Boulder, Colo.) 6(4), Jan 1984, 70-73.*
LEVEL: B LANG: Eng SIRC ARTICLE NO: 093903

Kretsch, A. Grogan, R. Duras, P. Allen, F. Sumner, J. Gillam, I. 1980 Melbourne marathon study. *Medical journal of Australi (Sydney) 141(12/13), 8-22 Dec 1984, 809-814.*
LEVEL: A LANG: Eng

Kuoppasalmi, K. Effects of side stress on human plasma hormone levels. *Track and field quarterly review (Kalamazoo, Mich.) 84(3), Fall 1984, 56-58.*
NOTES: Abstracted from the Academic Dissertation presented at the XIth European Track & Field Coaches Association Congress, Venice, Italy, March 17-20, 1981.
LEVEL: I LANG: Eng SIRC ARTICLE NO: 096980

Lamb, L.E. Lean runners and fatal heart irregularities. *Health letter (San Antonio, Tex.) 24(5), 14 Sept 1984, 1.*
LEVEL: LANG: Eng SIRC ARTICLE NO: 100064

Maughan, R. Drink: we've all seen dramatic pictures of dehydrated runners collapsing at marathon finishes - perhaps we've al suffered a little ourselves. What is dehydration, and what can you do to avoid it? *Running (London) 44, Dec 1984, 42-43.*
LEVEL: B LANG: Eng SIRC ARTICLE NO: 104999

Murphy, P. Olympic marathon fury heats up. (Refs: 5)*Physician and sportsmedicine (Minneapolis, Minn.) 12(10), Oct 1984, 161-163.*
LEVEL: B LANG: Eng SIRC ARTICLE NO: 100071

Noakes, T.D. Opie, L.H. Rose, A.G. Marathon running and immunity to coronary heart disease: fact versus fiction. (Refs: 61) *Clinics in sports medicine (Philadelphia) 3(2), Apr 1984, 527-543.*
ABST: This prospective study was designed to determine if coronary heart disease could be found in marathon runner's. The results indicate that coronary atherosclerosis and sudden cardiac death do occur in marathon runners. Thus, marathon running does not confer complete immunity from heart disease on its participants. However, this form of endurance training may provide partial protection from coronary heart disease.
LEVEL: A LANG: Eng SIRC ARTICLE NO: 095445

Palatini, P. Maraglino, G. Sperti, G. Casale, G. Pessina, A.C. Dal Palu, C. Prevalence of hyperkinetic arrhythmias in traine runners. (Refs: 13)*International journal of sports cardiology (Torino, Italy) 1(2), Jul/Dec 1984, 84-87.*
ABST: Twenty highly trained endurance runners aged between 13 and 33 and twenty sedentary age matched control subjects were studied. In all the subjects the existence of cardiovascular disease

was excluded through physical examination, laboratory routine tests, plain chest film, EKG, echocardiography and stress test. Standard twelve lead EKG showed in the athletes a longer Q-Tc interval (mean 404 msec) than in sedentary subjects (mean 383 msec). This difference was statistically significant. We evaluated in these forty subjects the incidence of hyperkinetic ventricular arrhythmias with 24 hours Holter EKG monitoring. Ventricular ectopic beats were recorded in 13 (65 percent) athletes, while more complex types of ventricular arrhythmias in 5 (25 percent) (2 cases belonged to the third class according to Lown, 1 to the fourth a) and 2 to the fourth b). Among controls ventricular ectopic beats were recorded in 11 cases (55 percent) and only 1 case of complex ventricular ectopy was discovered (third class according to Lown). The highly trained athletes seem to have an high incidence of ventricular hyperkinetic arrhythmias: this could be due to modification in sympathetic activity as it is suggested by the prolonged Q-T interval.
LEVEL: A LANG: Eng SIRC ARTICLE NO: 179172

Pedoe, D.T. Marathon medicine and introduction. *British journal of sports medicine (Loughborough, Eng.) 18(4), Dec 1984, 238-240.*
CONF: London Marathon Conference (1984 : London).
LEVEL: I LANG: Eng SIRC ARTICLE NO: 105013

Popular marathons, half marathons, and other long distance runs: recommendations for medical support. *British medical journal (clinical research) (London) 288(6427), 5 May 1984, 1355-1359.*
LEVEL: I LANG: Eng SIRC ARTICLE NO: 101703

Porter, A.M.W. How do marathon runners fare? (Refs: 4)*British journal of sports medicine (Loughborough, Leicestershire) 18(1), Mar 1984, 46.*
ABST: This paper describes the results of a questionnaire completed by 299 of the 415 entrants in a provincial marathon race. The marathon proved to be a relatively benign experience for the majority of runners. However, the authors acknowledge that the climatic conditions were ideal for this race (temperature 9.1-10.1 oC, relative humidity 80%, moderate wind 12-16 kts and the onset of drizzle in the second hour) and that adverse climatic conditions could have changed the results considerably.
LEVEL: I LANG: Eng SIRC ARTICLE NO: 096993

Sullivan, S.N. Champion, M.C. Christofides, N.D. Adrian, T.E. Bloom, S.R. Gastrointestinal regulatory peptide responses in long-distance runners. (Refs: 54)*Physician and sportsmedicine (Minneapolis, Minn.) 12(7), Jul 1984, 77-82.*
ABST: Plasma concentrations of gastrointestinal regulatory peptides were analysed during a 30-km run by seven male marathon runners. Throughout the run increases in plasma concentrations of gastrin, motilin, somatostatin, pancreatic glucagon, pancreatic polypeptide, and vasoactive intestinal polypeptide were observed. Plasma epinephine and norepinephine also increased.
LEVEL: A LANG: Eng SIRC ARTICLE NO: 097002

Williams, J.A. Wagner, J. Wasnich, R. Heilbrun, L. The effect of long-distance running upon appendicular bone mineral conten (Refs: 16)*Medicine and science in sports and exercise (Indianapolis) 16(3), June 1984, 223-227.*
ABST: The bone mineral content (BMC) of the os calcis was measured for a group of 20 male runners at the beginning and end of a 9-month

marathon training program. The participants had no previous running experience. The percent change in bone mineral in the runners was compared with that of a control group of male subjects of the same age range (38-68 yr). The consistent runners showed a significant increase in bone mineral over that of the controls: the increase was not significant for inconsistent runners. The data suggest that those runners with longer, more consistent distances gained more bone mineral than those with shorter, more inconsistent distances.
LEVEL: A LANG: Eng SIRC ARTICLE NO: 108589

Young, A. Plasma creatine kinase after the marathon - a diagnostic dilemma. (Refs: 34)*British journal of sports medicine (Loughborough, Eng.) 18(4), Dec 1984, 269-272.*
CONF: London Marathon Conference (1984 : London).
ABST: The mechanism of the protein leak from exercised muscle remains obscure, but may be related to depletion of intracellular high-energy phosphate and/or to mechanical disruption. The high levels of creatine kinease (CK) and other muscle proteins found in plasma for several days after marathon running, especially downhill running, are due to protein efflux from skeletal muscle. There is no evidence that marathon running damages the healthy, well-perfused myocardium, despite the fact that the plasma levels of total creatine kinase (CK), the isoenzyme CK-MB, CK-MB/total CK (percent), myoglobin, aspartate transaminase, lactate dehydrogenase and tropomyosin may be the same as after myocardial infarction. These indices must be interpreted with greater caution when found in anyone who habitually undertakes strenuous exercise, especially if they have done so within the previous week.
LEVEL: A LANG: Eng SIRC ARTICLE NO: 105040

NUTRITION

Burke, L. Read, R.S.D. Food to keep marathon men on the run. (Refs: 7)*Sports coach (Wembley, Australia) 7(4), Mar 1984, 23-26.*
LEVEL: I LANG: Eng SIRC ARTICLE NO: 095398

PHILOSOPHY

Lee, L.L. Running the toads off the road. *Running times (Woodbridge, Va.) 89, June 1984, 32;34-*
LEVEL: B LANG: Eng SIRC ARTICLE NO: 095431

PHYSIOLOGIE - TEMPERATURE

Maughan, R.J. Temperature regulation during marathon competition. (Refs: 11)*British journal of sports medicine (Loughborough, Eng.) 18(4), Dec 1984, 257-260.*
CONF: London Marathon Conference (1984 : London).
ABST: This article describes the mechanism which produces heat injuries in marathon running, particularly at high ambient temperatures. The author advises runners on appropriate precautions such as proper clothing, adequate fluid intake etc.
LEVEL: A LANG: Eng SIRC ARTICLE NO: 105000

PHYSIOLOGY

Appenzeller, O. Appenzeller, J. Standefer, J. Skipper, B. Atkinson, R. Opioids and endurance training: longitudinal study. (Refs: 9)*Annals of sports medicine (North Hollywood, Calif.) 2(1), 1984, 22-26.*

ABST: Beta-endorphin, beta-lipotropin (i-BE-BL), and myoglobin were assessed in participants of the annual Sandia Wilderness Crossing Research Run. This 45.9 K run beginning and finishing at an altitude of 1,890 m and reaching a zenith at 3,232 m produced a marked increase in plasma beta-endorphin at the finish in 1979. The results of samples drawn for three consecutive hours after finishing in 1980 and at 5 K into the race at an altitude of 2,300 m, at the summit at 30 K, and at the finish in 1981 were compared. Longitudinal comparisons for three consecutive years in the same runners were reported. No significant increase in plasma i-BE-BL at 5 K, or at 30 K occurred. A significant increase occurred at the finish, but a return two hours later of i-BE-Bl to baseline levels was found. A significant reduction in the run-induced elevation of i-BE-BL was evident at the finish in runners participating in three consecutive races.
LEVEL: A LANG: Eng SIRC ARTICLE NO: 104955

Bueno, M. Les conceptions actuelles sur l'endurance du coureur de fond et de demi-fond. (Refs: 29)Revue de l'Amicale des entraineurs francais d'athletisme (Paris) 87, avr/mai/juin 1984, 45-47.
LEVEL: I LANG: Fr SIRC ARTICLE NO: 096954

Dessypris, A. Adlercreutz, H. Serum, total/free testosterone and sex hormone binding globulin binding capacity (SHBG) in a non-competitive marathon run. Acta endocrinologica (suppl.) (Copenhagen) 265, 1984, 18-19.
LEVEL: A LANG: Eng

Guglielmini, C. Paolini, A.R. Conconi, F. Variations of serum testosterone concentrations after physical exercises of different duration. (Refs: 20)International journal of sports medicine (Stuttgart) 5(5), Oct 1984, 246-249.
ABST: Serum testosterone concentration was determined before and after physical activities of different duration. The subjects under study were: (1) 7 competitive walkers before and after a 20-km race; (2) 9 middle-distance runners before and after 1-h training; (3) 16 marathon runners before and after a marathon run; (4) 30 ultramarathon runners before and after a 107-km race. Serum testosterone increased by 51.8 per cent in competitive walkers, by 38.2 per cent in middle-distance runners, and by 44.9 per cent marathon runners: it decreased by 31.9 per cent in the ultramarathon runners.
LEVEL: A LANG: Eng SIRC ARTICLE NO: 104978

Hermansen, L. Metabolic acidosis and changes in water and electrolyte balance in relation to fatigue during maximal exercise of short duration. (Refs: 24)International journal of sports medicine (Stuttgart) Suppl. 5, Nov 1984, 110-115.
CONF: International Congress on Sports and Health (1983 : Maastricht, Netherlands).
LEVEL: A LANG: Eng SIRC ARTICLE NO: 104980

Janssen, E. Kuipers, H. Keizer, H. Verstappen, F. Plasma enzyme activities and running performance in a maximal treadmill test before and after a 30 km race or a marathon. (Refs: 4)International journal of sports medicine (Stuttgart) Suppl. 5, Nov 1984, 98-99.
LEVEL: A LANG: Eng SIRC ARTICLE NO: 104987

Jobin, J. Tremblay, A. Samson, P. Effect of a 6,400-km run on a 60-year-old man. (Refs: 14)Physician and sportsmedicine (Minneapolis, Minn.) 12(9), Sept 1984, 53-55;58;61.

ABST: The authors measured the percent body fat, VO2 max, anaerobic threshold, hemoglobin, hematocrit, and the blood glucose of a well-trained 60-year-old man prior and following a four month, 6,400-km run. No negative physiological effects were observed. The subject's body weight decreased while its anaerobic threshold improved.
LEVEL: A LANG: Eng SIRC ARTICLE NO: 100057

Kantor, M.A. Cullinane, E.M. Herbert, P.N. Thompson, P.D. Acute increase in lipoprotein lipase following prolonged exercise. Metabolism, clinical and experimental (New York) 33(5), May 1984, 454-457.
ABST: The serum lipid and lipoprotein concentrations and plasma postheparin lipolytic activity of 10 men (ages 21 to 39) were measured prior to and following a marathon. A decrease of LDL cholesterol by 10% and an increase of HDL-cholesterol by 9% were observed the day after the race. The level of lipoprotein lipase activity nearly doubled after the race.
LEVEL: A LANG: Eng SIRC ARTICLE NO: 100902

Kuusi, T. Kostiainen, E. Vartiainen, E. Pitkaenen, L. Ehnholm, C. Korhonen, H.J. Nissinen, A. Puska, P. Acute effects of marathon running on levels of serum lipoproteins and androgenic hormones in healthy males. Metabolism, clinical and experimental (New York) 33(6), Jun 1984, 527-531.
ABST: The serum lipid and lipoprotein levels, and the levels of serum androgenic hormones were assessed in 20 healthy marathon runners during and following competition. Both very-low-density lipoprotein triglyceride and cholesterol levels decreased significantly, whereas low-density lipoprotein triglyceride but not cholesterol levels increased. High-density lipoprotein cholesterol (HDL-C) and HDL2-C levels increased but HDL3-C remained the same. Serum levels of luteinizing hormone, testosterone, and sex-hormone-binding globulin all decreased during the marathon.
LEVEL: A LANG: Eng SIRC ARTICLE NO: 103581

Lehmann, M. Dickhuth, H.H. Schmid, P. Porzig, H. Keul, J. Plasma catecholamines, B-adrenergic reception, and isoproterenol sensitivity in endurance trained and non-endurance trained volunteers. (Refs: 33)European journal of applied physiology and occupational physiology (Berlin, FRG) 52(4), Jun 1984, 362-369.
ABST: Six male non-endurance trained subjects and six male marathon runners performed a graded treadmill test. Blood samples were taken to determine the beta-adrenergic receptor density on intact polymorphonuclear leucocytes. Some days after the test the subjects underwent an isoproterenol stimulation experiment. The trained group exhibited superior work performance on the treadmill test and a greater beta-adrenergic receptor density than the untrained group. Isoproterenol administration induced a significant increase in stroke volume in the endurance trained group but not in the untrained endurance group. This result may indicate a more economic regulation of heart work in trained subjects as compared to untrained subjects.
LEVEL: A LANG: Eng SIRC ARTICLE NO: 098648

Mahler, D.A. Loke, J. The physiology of endurance exercise. The marathon. Clinics in chest medicine (Philadelphia) 5(1), Ma 1984, 63-76.
LEVEL: I LANG: Eng SIRC ARTICLE NO: 103589

Mercier, D. Leger, L. Desjardins, M. Prediction de la performance, du VO2 max et de l'endurance

relative du coureur de fond. (Refs: 6)Revue de l'entraineur janv/mars 1984, 21-25.
LEVEL: I LANG: Fr SIRC ARTICLE NO: 092504

Niemelae, K. Palatsi, I. Linnaluoto, M. Competitive ultra-marathon: too much even for a well-trained athlete? (Refs: 16) Scandinavian journal of sports science (Helsinki, Finland) 6(1), Jul 1984, 7-10.
ABST: We report a case of a 35-year-old experienced ultra-marathon runner who attained a new national record (227 km) in a 24-hour race. The energy cost of running appeared to be 50-60% of the subject's maximal O2 uptake. The heart rates on the Holter monitor were 130-140 beats/min during running. A nearly 135-fold increase was observed in the total creatine kinase (447 to 60060 U/l). Although the MB fraction was also markedly elevated (11 to 1680 U/l), the MB percentage of total creatine kinase was within normal limits (or equal 4%) during the race. The T waves on the anterior chest leads were clearly higher after the race. M-mode echocardiography, however, revealed markedly reduced left ventricular performance after the 24 hours of running.
LEVEL: A LANG: Eng SIRC ARTICLE NO: 103597

Ohman, E.M. Teo, K.K. Johnson, A.H. Collins, P.B. Dowsett, D.P. Ennis, J.T. Horgan, J.H. Cardiospecific creatine kinase afte strenuous exercise in female athletes. (Refs: 9)Journal of sports medicine and physical fitness (Torino, Italy) 24(3), Sept 1984, 270-272.
ABST: Serial estimations of creatine kinase (CK) CK-MB and alpha-acid glycoprotein together with Technetium-99m pyrophosphate myocardial scintigrams were performed in 12 female runners before and after a marathon race. None of the subjects developed cardiac symptoms. Activities of CK and CK-MB became maximal 24 hours after the race. Alpha-acid glycoprotein was normal throughout and technetium-99m pyrophosphate scintigraphy was normal, thus indicating that none of the subjects suffered any myocardial damage.
LEVEL: A LANG: Eng SIRC ARTICLE NO: 106178

Rhodes, E.C. McKenzie, D.C. Predicting marathon time from anaerobic threshold measurements. (Refs: 9)Physician and sportsmedicine 12(1), Jan 1984, 95-98.
LEVEL: I LANG: Eng SIRC ARTICLE NO: 092521

Rieu, M. Le cout energetique du marathon. (Refs: 29)Dans, Culture technique no. 13, Neuilly-sur-Seine, France, Centre de Recherche sur la Culture Technique, c1984, p. 118-125.
LEVEL: A LANG: Fr RC1235 20096

Rogol, A.D. Veldhuis, J.D. Williams, F.A. Johnson, M.L. Pulsatile secretion of gonadotropins and prolactin in male marathon runners. Relation to the endogenous opiate system. Journal of andrology (Philadelphia) 5(1), Jan/Feb 1984, 21-27.
LEVEL: A LANG: Eng SIRC ARTICLE NO: 101705

Schriewer, H. Jung, K. Emke, F. Assmann, G. Changes in HDL composition in female subjects following a 100-km run. (Refs: 19) International journal of sports medicine (Stuttgart) 5(4), Aug 1984, 209-212.
ABST: In 12 female subjects participating in a 100-km run, the concentrations of cholesterol and triglycerides as well as those of HDL components were measured before and after the run. The concentration of HDL unesterified cholesterol, HDL

phosphatidylcholine, and HDL apolipoprotein A-I of the participants of the 100-km run were higher than the corresponding values of a control group of female company employees, whereas there was no difference in triglycerides, total cholesterol, HDL cholesterol, and HDL apolipoprotein A-II.
LEVEL: A LANG: Eng SIRC ARTICLE NO: 105021

Schuermeyer, T. Jung, K. Nieschlag, E. The effect of an 1100 km run on testicular, adrenal and thyroid hormones. *International journal of andrology (Copenhagen) 7(4), Aug 1984, 276-282.*
LEVEL: A LANG: Eng

Sherman, W.M. Costill, D.L. The marathon: dietary manipulation to optimize performance. (Refs: 44)*American journal of sport medicine (Baltimore, Md.) 12(1), Jan/Feb 1984, 44-51.*
ABST: The limiting factor in a marathon is the fuel supplies, specifically muscle glycogen. Several dietary manipulations have been attempted to improve performance in the marathon. Studies manipulating the type of carbohydrate ingested are being done to assist food selection for training as well as for race day. Many other manipulations are reviewed in this article also, such as muscle glycogen supercompensation and fat oxidation to spare muscle glycogen.
LEVEL: I LANG: Eng SIRC ARTICLE NO: 095460

Sutherland, W.H. Woodhouse, S.P. Nye, E.R. Gerard, D.F. Post-heparin hepatic lipase activity and plasma high density lipoprotein levels in men during physical training. *Biochemical medicine (New York) 3191), Feb 1984, 31-35.*
ABST: Plasma post-heparin hepatic lipase (PHHL) activity, plasma lipids, and high density lipoprotein cholesterol (HDL-C) levels, pulse rate at submaximal workload, and body weight were measured in 12 men during 18 weeks of physical training for their first marathon run. Reduced pulse rate at submaximal workload indicated that the men increased their physical fitness during the training period. Plasma HDL-C levels and PHHL activity also increased significantly after the 18 weeks of training. These changes were not in accord with the inverse correlation between plasma HDL-C levels and PHHL activity which was observed before training. The results of this study do not support the concept that reduced PHHL activity is mainly responsible for increased levels of plasma HDL-C with training.
LEVEL: A LANG: Eng

Tanaka, B. Matsuura, Y. Marathon performance, anaerobic threshold, and onset of blood lactate accumulation. (Refs: 20) *Journal of applied physiology: respiratory, environmental and exercise physiology (Bethesda, Md.) 57(3), Sept 1984, 640-643.*
ABST: This study of twelve highly trained male marathoners or distance runners found that anaerobic threshold is closely associated with marathon running performance. Useful equations are presented to demonstrate this.
LEVEL: A LANG: Eng SIRC ARTICLE NO: 108929

Whiting, P.H. Maughan, R.J. Miller, J.D.B. Dehydration and serum biochemical changes in marathon runners. (Refs: 23)*Europea journal of applied physiology and occupational physiology (Heidelberg) 52(2), Jan 1984, 183-187.*
ABST: The aim of this investigation was to study fluid balance in a group of marathon runners of widely varying levels of ability and to compare the effects of the administration of either water or a dilute glucose electrolyte solution on the

physiological and biochemical responses to a marathon race. The results indicate that several haematological and serum biochemical parameters changed significantly during the race and these are discussed. All subjects suffered from a net loss of fluid amounting to 1-5% of body weight during the race. Plasma glucose levels did not decrease, when measured after the race, suggesting that hypoglycemia was not a significant factor in this marathon.
LEVEL: A LANG: Eng SIRC ARTICLE NO: 097017

Williams, C. Brewer, J. Patton, A. The metabolic challenge of the marathon. (Refs: 42)*British journal of sports medicine (Loughborough, Eng.) 18(4), Dec 1984, 245-252.*
CONF: London Marathon Conference (1984 : London).
LEVEL: I LANG: Eng SIRC ARTICLE NO: 105036

PHYSIOLOGY - ALTITUDE

Lenzi, G. Conconi, F. Ameliorations des capacites aerobiques chez un groupe de coureurs et de marcheurs apres un mois d'entrainement en altitude. *Revue de l'Amicale des entraineurs francais d'athletisme (Paris) 89, oct/nov/dec 1984, 15-17.*
LEVEL: I LANG: Fr SIRC ARTICLE NO: 103586

PHYSIOLOGY - MUSCLE

Corbucci, G.G. Montanari, G. Cooper, M.B. Jones, D.A. Edwards, R.H.T. The effect of exertion on mitochondrial oxidative capacity and on some antioxidant mechanisms in muscle from marathon runners. (Refs: 12)*International journal of sports medicine (Stuttgart) Suppl. 5, Nov 1984, 135.*
CONF: International Congress on Sports and Health (1983 : Maastricht, Netherlands).
LEVEL: A LANG: Eng SIRC ARTICLE NO: 104964

Hagerman, F.C. Hikida, R.S. Staron, R.S. Sherman, W.M. Costill, D.L. Muscle damage in marathon runners. (Refs: 37)*Physician and sportsmedicine (Minneapolis, Minn.) 12(11), Nov 1984, 39-40;43-44;46;48.*
LEVEL: I LANG: Eng SIRC ARTICLE NO: 101678

Sherman, W.M. Armstrong, L.E. Murray, T.M. Hagerman, F.C. Costill, D.L. Staron, R.C. Ivy, J.L. Effect of a 42.2-km footrace and subsequent rest or exercise on muscular strength and work capacity. (Refs: 23)*Journal of applied physiology: respiratory, environmental and exercise physiology (Bethesda, Md.) 57(6), Dec 1984, 1668-1673.*
ABST: This paper investigated the effect of a 42.2-km footrace on leg extensor strength (maximal peak torque, MPT) and work capacity (WC) total work produced during a 50-contraction leg extensor fatigue test). Ten male runners were tested premarathon and 15-20 min, 1,3,5, and 7 days postmarathon. Subjects participated either in a rest or exercise-recovery regimen. After 1 week, neither group had recovered to the premarathon MPT. The WC of the exercise group was still lower on day 7 (90 percent of premarathon level), whereas the rest group had recovered 3 days postmarathon.
LEVEL: A LANG: Eng SIRC ARTICLE NO: 108561

PSYCHOLOGY

Durtschi, S.K. Psychological characteristics of elite and non-elite marathon runners. Eugene, Ore.: Microform Publications, University of Oregon, 1984. 2 microfiches : negative, ill. ; 11 x 15 cm.
NOTES: Thesis (M.S.) - University of Oregon, 1983; (xii, 109 leaves); vita; includes bibliography.
LEVEL: A LANG: Eng UO84 402-403

Morgan, W.P. Mind over matter. One of the nation's leading sport psychologists suggests you may be able to think yourself to a faster, and less painful, marathon. *Runner (Boulder, Colo.) 6(4), Jan 1984, 64-66;68.*
LEVEL: B LANG: Eng SIRC ARTICLE NO: 093921

RULES AND REGULATIONS

Cimons, M. The leaders of the pack: we all need a little help from our friends. And if two women run together, they call it camaraderie, but if a man runs with a woman, they call it pacing - and they call that illegal. *Runner's world 19(2), Feb 1984, 56-59.*
LEVEL: B LANG: Eng SIRC ARTICLE NO: 091078

SOCIOLOGY

McTeer, W. Curtis, J. Sociological profiles of marathoners. (Refs: 9)
CONF: North American Society for the Sociology of Sport. Conference (3rd : 1982 : Toronto, Ont.).
NOTES: In, Theberge, N. and Donnelly, P. (eds.), Sport and the sociological imagination: refereed proceedings of the 3rd Annual Conference of the North American Society for the Sociology of Sport, Toronto, Canada, November 1982, Fort Worth, Tex., Texas Christian University Press, c1984, p. 368-384.
ABST: This paper supplies a profile on marathoners based on a survey of finishers and entrants in the Canadian National Capital Marathon. The results indicated that marathoners are predominantly young unmarried males who have been highly educated and who earn higher incomes than the general population.
LEVEL: A LANG: Eng SIRC ARTICLE NO: 098656

SPORTING EVENTS

Blaikie, D. Boston: the Canadian story. Ottawa: Seneca House Books, c1984. v, 222 p. : ill.
NOTES: Bibliography: p. 201-204
LEVEL: B LANG: Eng ISBN: 0-920598-04-8 GV1065.22.B6 17078

Blaikie, D. The Labatt's National Capital Marathon. Ten years later and the Olympic Trials. *Canadian runner Mar 1984, 16-18.*
LEVEL: B LANG: Eng SIRC ARTICLE NO: 093873

Blaikie, D. Boston: the Canadian story. *Canadian runner Mar 1984, 27-28;30.*
NOTES: Excerpt from, Blankie, D. Boston: The Canadian story, 1984. First of three excerpts.
LEVEL: B LANG: Eng SIRC ARTICLE NO: 093874

Blaikie, D. Boston: the Canadian story. *Canadian runner Apr 1984, 16;18;22.*
NOTES: Second of three excerpts from, Blaikie D., Boston: the Canadian story.
LEVEL: B LANG: Eng SIRC ARTICLE NO: 093876

Burfoot, A. Can the Boston marathon be saved? *Runner's world (Mountain View, Calif.) 19(11), Nov*

1984, 48-52;85-87;90.
LEVEL: B LANG: Eng SIRC ARTICLE NO: 100043

Pardivala, J. The saga of the marathon. (Part I)
Olympic review (Lausanne) 206, Dec 1984, 974-980.
NOTES: To be continued
LEVEL: B LANG: Eng SIRC ARTICLE NO: 106180

Pardivala, J. L'epopee du marathon. (1re partie)
Revue olympique (Lausanne) 206, dec 1984, 974-980.
LEVEL: B LANG: Fr SIR ARTICLE NO: 106181

Post, M. Wischnia, B. The marathon: here's the good news: women can finally run an Olympic marathon. The bad news? They will have to battle the same sun and smog facing their male counterparts in LA. *Runner's world 19(5), May 1984, 84-88;140;143.*
LEVEL: B LANG: Eng SIRC ARTICLE NO: 093932

Reavis, T. What is going to happen to Boston: is the Boston marathon on its last legs? New leadership and a new focus might yet save the revered race. *Runner's world 19(4), Apr 1984, 76-78.*
LEVEL: B LANG: Eng SIRC ARTICLE NO: 093937

Ward, T. The Boston: death of a tradition. *Running (London, Eng) 36, Apr 1984, 48-51;99.*
LEVEL: B LANG: Eng SIRC ARTICLE NO: 097015

STATISTICS AND RECORDS

1984 humanathon results book. Huntsville, Ala.: Huntsville Track Club, (1984). 39 p. : ill.
CORP: Huntsville Track Club.
NOTES: Cover title.
LEVEL: B LANG: Eng GV1065.22.H8 20222

Post, M. Off the record: all records are not created equal - just ask Ken and Jennifer Young of the NRDC. *Runner's world 19(5), May 1984, 56-58;130.*
LEVEL: B LANG: Eng SIRC ARTICLE NO: 093931

STRATEGY

Salazar, A. Wischnia, B. How to use surging like a world-class runner. Alberto Salazar instructs in the gentle art of completely demoralizing the competition. *Runner's world (Mountain View, Calif.) 19(7), Jul 1984, 48-49;116.*
LEVEL: B LANG: Eng SIRC ARTICLE NO: 095457

TECHNIQUES AND SKILLS - PACING

Cimons, M. The leaders of the pack: we all need a little help from our friends. And if two women run together, they call it camaraderie, but if a man runs with a woman, they call it pacing - and they call that illegal. *Runner's world 19(2), Feb 1984, 56-59.*
LEVEL: B LANG: Eng SIRC ARTICLE NO: 091078

TESTING AND EVALUATION

Daniels, J. Tymn, M. How fast can you run? Science has the answer for some, but others learn on the roads. *Runner's world 19(5), May 1984, 75-76;132;136-138.*
LEVEL: I LANG: Eng SIRC ARTICLE NO: 093884

Kaslanskas, V. Looking for potential marathoners. *Modern athlete and coach (Athelstone, Aust.) 22(2), Apr 1984, 36-38.*
NOTES: Slightly condensed translation from

Legkaya atletika (Moscow) 2, 1983.
LEVEL: I LANG: Eng SIRC ARTICLE NO: 096977

Mercier, D. Leger, M. Desjardins, M. Prediction de la performance VO2 Max et de l'endurance relative du coureur de fond. (Refs: 6) *Track and field journal (Ottawa, Ont.) 27, Aug 1984, 27-31.*
LEVEL: I LANG: Fr SIRC ARTICLE NO: 100069

TRAINING AND CONDITIONING

'Marathon's' sub. 3 training program. *Marathon magazine (Charleville, Ireland) 22(3), May 1984, 22-23.*
LEVEL: B LANG: Eng SIRC ARTICLE NO: 108806

Costill, D.L. How to run a faster marathon. The ABCs of training and racing, from the research expert who's best probed the body under stress. *Runner (Boulder, Colo.) 6(4), Jan 1984, 58-63.*
LEVEL: B LANG: Eng SIRC ARTICLE NO: 093882

Dixon, R. Reaching your peak: consistency is the key to better performance. *Runner (New York) 6(6), Mar 1984, 22.*
LEVEL: LANG: Eng SIRC ARTICLE NO: 100047

Edwards, S. Bicycling and synergistic fitness. *Running & fitness (Washington, D.C.) 16(4), Jul/Aug 1984, 1;24.*
LEVEL: B LANG: Eng SIRC ARTICLE NO: 106156

Grant, S.J.Y. Sharp, R.H. Aitchison, T.C. First time marathoners and distance training. (Refs: 10) *British journal of sports medicine (Loughborough, Eng.) 18(4), Dec 1984, 241-243.*
CONF: London Marathon Conference (1984 : London).
ABST: This study contradicts the popular theory that marathon training involves running exceptionally long distances each week. 72 first-time marathoners from the 1982 Glasgow Marathon provided information on their training schedules. The average training distance turned out to be 37.2 miles per week during the last 12 weeks before the race. In addition, there was no relationship between training distances and race time.
LEVEL: A LANG: Eng SIRC ARTICLE NO: 104977

Henderson, J. Improving your marathon: planning, pacing and purpose are the keys to being the best you can be. *Runner's world 19(1), Jan 1984, 42-43;66.*
LEVEL: B LANG: Eng SIRC ARTICLE NO: 091091

Henderson, J. LSD flashback: where did all those (slow) miles get the foundling fathers of LSD? Here's an update on what became of that old gang of ours. *Runner's world 19(4), Apr 1984, 48-50;112.*
LEVEL: B LANG: Eng SIRC ARTICLE NO: 093894

Johnson, B. Speed builds: sprinting your way to endurance. *Runner (New York) 6(9), Jun 1984, 16.*
LEVEL: B LANG: Eng SIRC ARTICLE NO: 101682

Klecker, B. Fedo, M. Running on snow. How snowshoes can help your springtime speed. *Runner (Boulder, Colo.) 6(4), Jan 1984, 20;22.*
LEVEL: B LANG: Eng SIRC ARTICLE NO: 093907

Markowitz, D. Are you running too much? Unbridled enthusiasm, manifested in workouts on a herculean scale, may be doing you more harm than good. *Runner's world (Mountain View, Calif.) 19(9), Sept 1984, 45-49;90.*
LEVEL: B LANG: Eng SIRC ARTICLE NO: 098653

Nisenbaum, J. Core training for the marathon. *California track & running news (Fresno, Calif.) 90,*

Apr 1984, 24.
LEVEL: B LANG: Eng SIRC ARTICLE NO: 100073

Tulloh, B. Marathon training: the vital weeks. *Running (London, Eng.) 36, Apr 1984, 70-71.*
LEVEL: B LANG: Eng SIRC ARTICL NO: 097009

Tulloh, B. Marathon training: down to work. *Running magazine (London) 35, Mar 1984, 64-65.*
LEVEL: B LANG: Eng SIRC ARTICL NO: 098691

Tulloh, B. Marathon training. *Running magazine (London) 34, Feb 1984, 54-55.*
LEVEL: B LANG: Eng SIRC ARTICLE NO: 098692

You too can run a marathon. Belfast: The Sports Council for Northern Ireland, 1984. 27 p. (Sports Council for Northern Ireland advisory leaflet no. 19.)
CORP: Sports Council for Northern Ireland.
NOTES: Cover title.
LEVEL: B LANG: Eng GV1065.17.T73 18300

WOMEN

Dash and distance: in a sprint, the bottom line is speed. In a marathon, it's hunger. *Health (New York) 16(4), Apr 1984, 37-38;40;62.*
LEVEL: B LANG: Eng SIRC ARTICLE NO: 100046

MARTIAL ARTS

Allard, J.P. What is Ki or Chi? Part 3 of our enquiry. *Karate and oriental arts (London) 106, Feb/Mar 1984, 30.*
LEVEL: B LANG: Eng SIRC ARTICLE NO: 098293

Almeida, B. Capoeira: a dance, a song, a fight. *Inside kung-fu (Burbank, Calif.) 11(10), Oct 1984, 32-37.*
NOTES: Excerpte from, Almeida, B., Capoeira: a Brazilian art form, Berkeley, North Atlantic Books.
LEVEL: B LANG: Eng SIRC ARTICLE NO: 105964

Aranha, J.D. Kalarippayat: India's ancient art of war. *Inside kung-fu (Hollywood, Calif.) 11(3), Mar 1984, 76-79.*
LEVEL: LANG: Eng SIRC ARTICLE NO: 098294

Back, A. Kim, D. The future course of the Eastern martial arts. (Refs: 9) *Quest (Champaign, Ill.) 36(1), 1984, 7-14.*
LEVEL I LANG: Eng SIRC ARTICLE NO: 099790

Cater, D. Ninjamania: America goes wild over art of invisibility. *Black belt magazine (Burbank, Calif.) 22(12), Dec 1984, 20-24;26;112.*
LEVEL: B LANG: Eng SIRC ARTICLE NO: 107338

Gilbey, J.F. The skeptical warrior. *Inside kung-fu (Los Angeles, Calif.) 11(5), May 1984, 70-73.*
NOTES: Excerpted from, Gilbey, J.F., The way of a warrior.
LEVEL: B LANG: Eng SIRC ARTICLE NO: 101385

Guide to the masters. Renown masters of the martial arts speak out about their philosophy of fighting...the competing values o tradition and innovation...their personal training regimens...and more. *Inside kung-fu (Hollywood, Calif.) 11(1), Jan 1984, 35-39;42-44;46-49;52-56;58-60;62;64;66-72;74-75;79-80;82-84;86-92;94-95.*
NOTES: Special bonus feature.
LEVEL: B LANG: Eng SIRC ARTICLE NO: 098303

Ivan, D. Ivan, D. Mysteries of ju-kenpo: a mysterious art from Japan's feudal past. *Inside karate (Burbank, Calif.) 5(6), Jun 1984, 42-45.*
LEVEL: B LANG: Eng SIRC ARTICLE NO: 103307

MARTIAL ARTS (continued)

Kosho shorei kenpo: a style of Heresy and insight. *Karate illustrated (Burbank, Calif.) 15(2), Feb 1984, 28-33;52.*
LEVEL: B LANG: Eng SIRC ARTICLE NO: 108214

Lowry, D. Budo no nangyodo (budo and the way of hardship). *Karate illustrated (Burbank, Calif.) 15(12), Dec 1984, 60-63.*
LEVEL: B LANG: Eng SIRC ARTICLE NO: 107361

Mainstorm, B. Ninjutsu: a fighting system, a life system. *Black belt (Burbank, Calif.) 22(2), Feb 1984, 20-24;85.*
LEVEL: LANG: Eng SIRC ARTICLE NO: 096743

Malterer, J.L. Be calm, but deadly: the Poekoelan fighting arts of Indonesia. *Inside kung-fu (Hollywood, Calif.) 11(6), Jun 1984, 61-66.*
NOTES: Part 1 of a two-part series.
LEVEL: B LANG: Eng SIRC ARTICLE NO: 103316

Marinas, M.P. The lost hand. *Kick illustrated (Burbank, Calif.) 5(4), Apr 1984, 44-46.*
LEVEL: B LANG: Eng SIRC ARTICLE NO 099802

Martial arts: go ju. *Karate illustrated (Burbank, Calif.) 15, Yearbook 1984, 33-39.*
LEVEL: B LANG: Eng SIRC ARTICLE NO: 099803

Pillot, P.L. In search of Ki Power. *Black belt magazine (Burbank, Calif.) 22(12), Dec 1984, 56-60;114.*
LEVEL: B LANG: Eng SIRC ARTICLE NO: 107368

Seegmuller, J. Arts martiaux et therapie orientale. *Impact medecin (Puteaux, France) 100, 1984, 83-86.*
LEVEL: B LANG: Fr

Van Clief, R. The Ron van Clief white belt guidebook. 1st ed. New York: Crown, c1984. 1v.
NOTES: Includes index.
LEVEL: B LANG: Eng ISBN: 0517551802 LC CARD: 84-001927

Van Clief, R. The Ron van Clief green and purple belt guide book. New York: Crown, Publishers, c1984. 1v.
NOTES: Includes index.
LEVEL: B LANG: Eng ISBN: 0517551837 LC CARD: 84-001926

Vitali, K. Tournament fighting, the techniques, training drills and strategy of open competition. Hollywood, Calif.: Unique Publications, c1984. 168 p. : ill.
LEVEL: B LANG: Eng ISBN: 0-86568-049-3 LC CARD: 83-50973 GV1112 18209

Yates, K.D. Another black belt: when studying one style isn't enough. *Inside karate (Burbank, Calif.) 5(10), Oct 1984, 31-35.*
LEVEL: B LANG: Eng SIRC ARTICLE NO: 107381

ASSOCIATIONS

Buttitta, B. The World Tang Soo Do Association: the last bastion for traditional Korean martial arts? *Black belt (Burbank, Calif.) 22(3), Mar 1984, 28-32.*
LEVEL: B LANG: Eng SIRC ARTICLE NO: 099793

Ivan, D. Ivan, D. The International Martial Arts Federation: once Japan's secret society of martial arts. *Kick illustrated (Hollywood, Calif.) 5(2), Feb 1984, 38-39.*
LEVEL: B LANG: Eng SIRC ARTICLE NO: 098312

BIOGRAPHY AND AUTOBIOGRAPHY

Chapman, M. The toughest men in sports: looking for the mental edge. New York: Leisure Press, c1984. 144 p. : ill.
LEVEL: B LANG: Eng ISBN: 0-88011-187-9 LC CARD: 83-80730 GV1111 17652

Coleman, J. Tang Soo. The evolution of Tae Kwon Do's bitter rival. (Hwang Kee) *Black belt (Burbank, Calif.) 22(9), Sept 1984, 20-24;120-121.*
LEVEL: B LANG: Eng SIRC ARTICLE NO: 103291

Culvert, M. Hardly soft: Keith Hirabayashi's individualized training program. Will it help him become the first number-one male forms competitor who is also a soft stylist? *Karate illustrated (Burbank, Calif.) 15(11), Nov 1984, 16-21.*
LEVEL: B LANG: Eng SIRC ARTICLE NO: 107342

Forbach, G. Professor Adriano D. Emperado: for the first ever in print - an exclusive interview with the formidable founder of Kajukenbo. *Inside kung-fu (Hollywood, Calif.) 11(2), Feb 1984, 30-36.*
LEVEL: B LANG: Eng SIRC ARTICLE NO: 098301

Ivan, D. Ivan, D. Dr. Yoshio Sugino, master of the seven samurai. *Kick illustrated (Burbank, Calif.) 5(3), Mar 1984, 40-43.*
NOTES: Martial arts in Japan, part 3.
LEVEL: B LANG: Eng SIRC ARTICLE NO: 098315

Ivan, D. Ivan, D. The legacy: one man is heir to the legacies left by Jigoro Kano and Morihei Ueshiba - a man who wove those legacies into his own unique vision of martial art. (M. Noru Mochizuki) *Kick illustrated (Burbank, Calif.) 5(5), May 1984, 30-33.*
LEVEL: B LANG: Eng SIRC ARTICLE NO: 101390

O'Connor, R. J.C. Shin: Tang Soo Do luminary legend - and Chuck Norris' first instructor. (Jae Chul Shin) *Kick illustrated (Burbank, Calif.) 5(4), Apr 1984, 28-32.*
LEVEL: B LANG: Eng SIRC ARTICLE NO: 099807

This is Frank Dux: a koga ninja. *Karate and oriental arts (London) 110, Oct/Nov 1984, 30-32.*
LEVEL: B LANG: Eng SIRC ARTICL NO: 108985

CHILDREN

Buttitta, B. The young masters. The real karate kids. *Inside karate (Burbank, Calif.) 5(12), Dec 1984, 18-30.*
LEVEL: B LANG: Eng SIRC ARTICLE NO: 108133

Depasquale, M. Martial arts for young athletes. New York: Wanderer Books, c1984. 1v.
LEVEL: B LANG: Eng ISBN: 0671507338 LC CARD: 84-007435

Hallander, J. Teach your children well. *Kick illustrated (Burbank, Calif.) 5(4), Apr 1984, 39-42.*
LEVEL: B LANG: Eng SIRC ARTICLE NO: 099797

Watson, K.J. The value of martial arts training for children. *Karate and oriental arts (London) 107, Apr/May 1984, 34.*
LEVEL: B LANG: Eng SIRC ARTICLE NO: 108665

COUNTRIES AND REGIONS

Wilson, R. The making of China's modern martial arts: from revolution to Wushu. *Inside kung-fu (Burbank, Calif.) 11(10), Oc 1984, 62-66.*
LEVEL: B LANG: Eng SIRC ARTICLE NO: 105977

DICTIONARIES AND TERMINOLOGY

Parulski, G.R. The dictionary of the martial arts experience. Part II. The traditions, history and philosophy of Japanese an Chinese martial arts. *Inside karate (Burbank, Calif.) 5(11), Nov 1984, 56-59.*
LEVEL: B LANG: Eng SIRC ARTICLE NO: 107366

Parulski, G.R. The dictionary of the martial arts experience. Part I. The traditions, history and philosophy of Japanese and Chinese martial arts. *Inside karate (Burbank, Calif.) 5(10), Oct 1984, 48-51.*
LEVEL: B LANG: Eng SIRC ARTICLE NO: 107367

Standberg, K.W. Martial arts language: where to start. *Black belt (Burbank, Calif.) 22 (Yearbook), 1984, 40-43.*
LEVEL: B LANG: Eng SIRC ARTICLE NO: 101398

DIRECTORIES

Directory. (Martial arts schools.) *Inside kung-fu (Hollywood, Calif.) 11(1), Jan 1984, 106-114.*
LEVEL: B LANG: Eng SIRC ARTICLE NO: 098300

HEALTH AND HYGIENE

Cahn, L. Total fitness the five animal way: a Chinese doctor's 2,000-year-old prescription for health and harmony. *Inside kung-fu (Burbank, Calif.) 11(8), Aug 1984, 52-56;58.*
LEVEL: B LANG: Eng SIRC ARTICLE NO: 105966

HISTORY

Guo, B. Leitai: boxing on the platform. *China sports (Beijing, China) 16(1), Jan 1984, 23.*
LEVEL: B LANG: Eng SIRC ARTICL NO: 098304

Van Horne, W.W. The flower blooms: a history of Zen & the martial arts. *Kick illustrated (Hollywood, Calif.) 5(1), Jan 1984 43-44;46.*
LEVEL: B LANG: Eng SIRC ARTICLE NO: 096747

INJURIES AND ACCIDENTS

Birrer, R.B. Martial arts injuries: their spectrum and management. (Refs: 4)*Sports medicine digest (Van Nuys, Calif.) 6(1), Jan 1984, 1-3.*
LEVEL: I LANG: Eng SIRC ARTICLE NO: 099791

Blum, M. Schloss, M.F. Martial-arts thyroiditis. (letter) *New England journal of medicine (Boston) 311(3), 19 Jul 1984, 199-200.*
LEVEL: I LANG: Eng SIRC ARTICLE NO: 103285

Borgogna, E. Re, F. Re, G. Viterbo, S. Fogliano, F. I traumatismi maxillo-facciali nelle pratiche sportive: le arti marziali (Maxillofacial injuries in sports practice: the martial arts.) *Minerva stomatologica (Torino) 33(4), Jul/Aug 1984, 743-745.*
LEVEL: A LANG: It

Marinas, M.P. Arnis elbow. *Inside kung-fu (Burbank, Calif.) 11(10), Oct 1984, 22;24.*
LEVEL: B LANG: Eng SIRC ARTICLE NO: 105970

Odsen, D. The alarming rise in martial arts injuries, are teachers to blame? *Black belt (Burbank, Calif.) 22(3), Mar 1984, 52-56;106.*
LEVEL: B LANG: Eng SIRC ARTICLE NO: 099808

Ryan, J. Ever been hurt? If not, don't read this. But at some time or other every martial artist has. Injuries to joints & related structures in martial arts.

(Refs: 11)*Karate and oriental arts (London, Eng.)* 108, Jun/Jul 1984, 34-35.
LEVEL: B LANG: Eng SIRC ARTICLE NO: 100695

LAW AND LEGISLATION

Kimball, R. Kojasho, the copyrighted martial art. *Karate illustrated (Burbank, Calif.) 15(1), Jan 1984, 36-37.*
LEVEL: B LANG: Eng SIRC ARTICLE NO: 108122

Venable, G. Kata copyright: the whys and wherefores. *Karate illustrated (Burbank, Calif.) 15(1), Jan 1984, 34-39.*
LEVEL: LANG: Eng SIRC ARTICLE NO: 108121

MASS MEDIA

Buttitta, B. Martial arts TV shows: bringing instruction into the living room. *Black belt (Burbank, Calif.) 22(1), Jan 1984 72-75.*
LEVEL: B LANG: Eng SIRC ARTICLE NO: 108613

MEDICINE

Jorgenson, K.P. CPR and the martial arts: it could mean the difference between life and death. *Black belt (Burbank, Calif.) 22(7), Jul 1984, 60-62.*
LEVEL: B LANG: Eng SIRC ARTICLE NO: 103310

Parulski, G. OK's guide to martial arts folk medicine: Part III therapeutic breathing. *Official karate (Derby, Conn.) 16(120), Apr 1984, 27-29.*
LEVEL: B LANG: Eng SIRC ARTICLE NO: 098322

NUTRITION

Staff, R. The martial artist's diet: part IV. *Black belt (Burbank, Calif.) 22(1), Jan 1984, 58-62.*
LEVEL: B LANG: Eng SIR ARTICLE NO: 108611

PHILOSOPHY

Hassell, R.G. The sun source: traditional karate's link to China. *Black belt (Burbank, Calif.) 22(9), Sept 1984, 62-67;84;86-87.*
LEVEL: B LANG: Eng SIRC ARTICLE NO: 103301

Le Nedic, J. Les voies du KI pour atteindre la sagesse. *Psychologies (France) 13, 1984, 51-53.*
LEVEL: B LANG: Fr

PHYSICAL FITNESS

Block, B.H. Martial arts for fitness. *Running & fitness (Washington, D.C.) 16(2), Apr 1984, 16.*
LEVEL: B LANG: Eng SIRC ARTICLE NO: 098296

PSYCHOLOGY

King, F. Psyching you opponent out: an insider's look. *Karate illustrated (Burbank, Calif.) 15(1), Jan 1984, 41-44.*
LEVEL B LANG: Eng SIRC ARTICLE NO: 108123

PSYCHOLOGY - MENTAL TRAINING

Melton, J.R. Mental discipline: a movable skill. *Karate illustrated (Burbank, Calif.) 15(6), Jun 1984, 58-61.*
LEVEL: B LANG: Eng SIRC ARTICLE NO: 103318

Wynne, M. The mental training of Chuck Norris: an American approach to developing a strong mind. *Black belt magazine (Burbank, Calif.) 22(5), May 1984, 68-72.*
LEVEL: B LANG: Eng SIRC ARTICLE NO: 103324

TEACHING

Byrne, R. DeMarco, V. Tomorrow's martial artists are the kids of today: teach your children well. *Black belt (Burbank, Calif.) 22(3), Mar 1984, 68-71;92.*
LEVEL: B LANG: Eng SIRC ARTICLE NO: 099794

Gulick, C. The discipline of respect: does it have a place in the American Dojo? *Black belt (Burbank, Calif.) 22(9), Sept 1984, 26-33;82.*
LEVEL: B LANG: Eng SIRC ARTICLE NO: 103295

Holzer, J.W. Running a martial arts school: you need more than just a black belt. *Black belt (Burbank, Calif.) 22(9), Sept 1984, 50-54;118-119.*
LEVEL: B LANG: Eng SIRC ARTICLE NO: 103305

TECHNIQUES AND SKILLS

Buttitta, B. Developing the ultimate knockout punch: it's all in your mind. *Black belt (Burbank, Calif.) 22(4), Apr 1984, 62-65.*
LEVEL: B LANG: Eng SIRC ARTICLE NO: 099792

Christensen, L. Leg attacks: no frills, just results. *Black belt magazine (Burbank, Calif.) 22(12), Dec 1984, 68-72;128.*
LEVEL: B LANG: Eng SIRC ARTICLE NO: 107339

Daniel, C. Taijutsu: unarmed combat of the Ninja. *Black belt magazine (Burbank, Calif.) 22(11), Nov 1984, 50-53;118-119.*
LEVEL: B LANG: Eng SIRC ARTICLE NO: 107343

Dowd, S.K. Sweep your opponent the kuntaw way. *Inside kung-fu (Los Angeles, Calif.) 11(5), May 1984, 65-69.*
LEVEL: B LANG Eng SIRC ARTICLE NO: 101384

Fitch, D. Getting close to your attacker: Kenpo's simple way to victory. *Inside kung-fu (Hollywood, Calif.) 11(4), Apr 1984 77-79.*
LEVEL: B LANG: Eng SIRC ARTICLE NO: 096735

Franck, L. Six ways to sweep your opponent. *Karate illustrated (Burbank, Calif.) 15(7), Jul 1984, 38-43.*
LEVEL: B LANG: E SIRC ARTICLE NO: 103292

Gilbert, G. Shaolin Kenpo: the best of two martial art worlds. *Black belt (Burbank, Calif.) 22(6), Jun 1984, 20-24;94-97;112.*
LEVEL: B LANG: Eng SIRC ARTICLE NO: 096737

Gray, E. White, M. Reeling silk energy: the essential power of body and mind. (chan si jin) *Inside kung-fu (Los Angeles, Calif.) 11(5), May 1984, 51-55.*
LEVEL: B LANG: Eng SIRC ARTICLE NO: 101388

Hallander, J. Shintai-do: from sword to empty hands. *Karate illustrated (Burbank, Calif.) 15(6), Jun 1984, 36-40.*
LEVEL: LANG: Eng SIRC ARTICLE NO: 103296

Hallander, J. Maek Cha Ki: Korean kicks to painful pressure points. *Karate illustrated (Burbank, Calif.) 15(7), Jul 1984, 44-46.*
LEVEL: B LANG: Eng SIRC ARTICLE NO: 103297

Hallander, J. Martial arts & olympic wrestling: how the Korean Martial Art of Kuk Sool Won promises to revolutionize Western Amateur Wrestling. *Inside karate (Burbank, Calif.) 5(8), Aug 1984, 62-66.*
LEVEL: B LANG: Eng SIRC ARTICLE NO: 103298

Hallander, J. Combining acrobatics with self-defense: Korean stylists are flipping over it. *Black belt (Burbank, Calif.) 22(8), Aug 1984, 54-56;69;71.*
LEVEL: B LANG: Eng SIRC ARTICLE NO: 105969

Hallander, J. The fighting animals of Korean martial arts. The use of animal fighting tactics is not unique to Chinese martial arts. *Karate illustrated (Burbank, Calif.) 15(10), Oct 1984, 28-33.*
LEVEL: B LANG: Eng SIRC ARTICLE NO: 108114

Holub, A.S. The classical Chinese quarter-staff. *Karate illustrated (Burbank, Calif.) 15(2), Feb 1984, 40-43;76-77.*
LEVEL B LANG: Eng SIRC ARTICLE NO: 108215

Jinshen, Z. Tongbeiquan. *China sports (Beijing, China) 16(8), Aug 1984, 57-60.*
NOTES: To be continued in next issue.
LEVEL: B LANG: Eng SIRC ARTICLE NO: 101391

Michaels, D. American arnis: the evolution of an art. *Black belt (Burbank, Calif.) 22(1), Jan 1984, 66-70.*
LEVEL: B LANG: Eng SIRC ARTICLE NO: 108612

Odsen, D. Shintaido: a new martial art struggles for recognition. *Black belt (Burbank, Calif.) 22 (Yearbook), 1984, 44-47.*
LEVEL: B LANG: Eng SIRC ARTICLE NO: 101395

Shaw, B. Strategies of holds and escapes. Part II. Types of escapes. *Karate illustrated (Burbank, Calif.) 15(10), Oct 1984, 44-48.*
LEVEL: B LANG: Eng SIRC ARTICLE NO: 108117

Snyder, J.J. The sources and applications of Bruce Lee's techniques. *Fencing (Surrey, Eng.) 17(1), Jul 1984, 14-15.*
LEVEL B LANG: Eng SIRC ARTICLE NO: 101397

Tongbeiquan. (cont'd) *China sports (Beijing, China) 16(9), Sept 1984, 55-59.*
LEVEL: B LANG: Eng SIRC ARTICLE NO: 108874

Za shadow boxing (2). *China sports (Beijing, China) 16(5), May 1984, 57-59.*
NOTES: To be continued in next issue.
LEVEL: B LANG: Eng SIRC ARTICLE NO: 101402

Zha-style shadow boxing (2). *China sports (Beijing, China) 16(6), Jun 1984, 56-59.*
NOTES: To be continued in next issue.
LEVEL: B LANG: Eng SIRC ARTICLE NO: 102189

Zha-style shadow boxing (4). *China sports (Beijing, China) 16(7), Jul 1984, 56-59.*
LEVEL: B LANG: Eng SIRC ARTICLE NO: 1021

Zha-style shadow boxing. *China sports (Beijing, China) 16(4), Apr 1984, 54-59.*
NOTES: To be continued in next issue.
LEVEL B LANG: Eng SIRC ARTICLE NO: 101403

TESTING AND EVALUATION

A glimpse of the Coto de Caza research center. *Karate illustrated (Burbank, Calif.) 15, Yearbook 1984, 22.*
LEVEL: B LANG: E SIRC ARTICLE NO: 099796

TRAINING AND CONDITIONING

Hallander, J. White belt training: the first step to black belt. *Black belt magazine (Burbank, Calif.) 22(12), Dec 1984, 62-64.*
LEVEL: B LANG: Eng SIRC ARTICLE NO: 107350

MARTIAL ARTS (continued)

Hallander, J. Chinese iron hand training. *Karate illustrated (Burbank, Calif.) 15(11), Nov 1984, 34-38.*
LEVEL: B LANG: En SIRC ARTICLE NO: 107351

Holzer, J.W. The last word on training equipment. *Inside kung-fu (Los Angeles, Calif.) 11(5), May 1984, 58-62.*
LEVEL: B LANG: Eng SIRC ARTICLE NO: 101389

McKay, R.S. Arvanitis, J. Steiner, B.J. LaTourrette, J. The great debate: sparring. Fighting to win...will it help you or hurt you when you're fighting to survive? *Inside kung-fu (Hollywood, Calif.) 11(2), Feb 1984, 59-62.*
NOTES: Part 11.
LEVEL: B LANG: Eng SIRC ARTICLE NO: 098320

Siverio, M. Elbow and knee strikes: make your next sparring session a smashing affair. *Inside karate (Burbank, Calif.) 5(11 Nov 1984, 27-30.*
LEVEL: B LANG: Eng SIRC ARTICLE NO: 107373

Wedlake, L. The (sparring) games martial artists play. *Inside kung-fu (Hollywood, Calif.) 11(3), Mar 1984, 72-75.*
LEVEL: LANG: Eng SIRC ARTICLE NO: 098331

TRAINING AND CONDITIONING - DRILLS

Siverio, M. MCIA kicking drills: developing a martial artist's most potent weapon. *Inside karate (Burbank, Calif.) 5(12), Dec 1984, 32-37.*
LEVEL: B LANG: Eng SIRC ARTICLE NO: 108134

TRAINING AND CONDITIONING - MASSAGE

Hallander, J. Shiatsu and the modern martial artist. *Kick illustrated (Burbank, Calif.) 5(3), Mar 1984, 52-54.*
LEVEL: B LANG: Eng SIRC ARTICLE NO: 098305

TRAINING AND CONDITIONING - STRETCHING AND FLEXIBILITY EXERCISES

Strandberg, K.W. Stretching for the heights of execution. *Karate illustrated (Burbank, Calif.) 15(11), Nov 1984, 44-47.*
LEVEL: B LANG: Eng SIRC ARTICLE NO: 107375

TRAINING AND CONDITIONING - TRAINING CAMPS

Loya, P. So...you want to open a martial arts school: owning your own studio might be your lifelong dream, but if you don't take the proper precautions, it could turn into a nightmare. *Inside karate (Burbank, Calif.) 5(12), Dec 1984, 60-64.*
LEVEL: B LANG: Eng SIRC ARTICLE NO: 108136

TRAINING AND CONDITIONING - WEIGHT AND STRENGTH TRAINING

Byrne, R. The great weight training debate; part 1. To lift or not to lift? *Black belt magazine (Burbank, Calif.) 22(10), Oct 1984, 80-83.*
LEVEL: B LANG: Eng SIRC ARTICLE NO: 107335

Siverio, M. Isometrics: the road to stronger fighting skills or a route to inefficiency? *Karate illustrated (Burbank, Calif.) 15(9), Sept 1984, 34-37.*
LEVEL: B LANG: Eng SIRC ARTICLE NO: 103321

Siverio, M. Barbells 101: an introduction to high-intensity weight training for the martial artist. *Karate illustrated (Burbank, Calif.) 15(11), Nov 1984, 39-43;76-77.*
LEVEL: B LANG: Eng SIRC ARTICLE NO: 107370

Siverio, M. Excellent weapons and vulnerable targets, the three most important elements of self-defense are arms and the man Your muscles protect your joints, bones and tendons. Your arms protect you. What do you do for them? *Karate illustrated (Burbank, Calif.) 15(2), Feb 1984, 48-51.*
LEVEL: B LANG: Eng SIRC ARTICLE NO: 108217

WOMEN

Birrer, R.B. Birrer, C.D. Safety for women: a doctor's notes on treatment and prevention of injuries. *Karate illustrated (Burbank, Calif.) 15(6), Jun 1984, 52-57.*
LEVEL: B LANG: Eng SIRC ARTICLE NO: 103284

Gonzalez, M.J. Women instructors: teaching is no longer just a man's domain. *Black belt (Burbank, Calif.) 22(8), Aug 1984, 50-53;101-103.*
LEVEL: B LANG: Eng SIRC ARTICLE NO: 105968

Yates, K.D. Kick forum; from a woman's perspective. *Kick illustrated (Hollywood, Calif.) 5(1), Jan 1984, 59-61.*
LEVEL: B LANG: Eng SIRC ARTICLE NO: 096750

MASS MEDIA

Gitter, W. Mass media, sport and international understanding. (Refs: 5)*In, Ilmarinen, M. (ed.) et al., Sport and International Understanding: proceedings of the congress held in Helsinki, Finland, July 7-10, 1982, Berlin, Springer-Verlag, 1984, p. 292-296.*
CONF: Congress on Sport and International Understanding (1982 : Helsinki).
LEVEL: I LANG: Eng GV706.8 18979

Kirsch, A. Preising, W. Sport in the mass media and international understanding. (Refs: 24)*In, Ilmarinen, M. (ed.) et al., Sport and International Understanding: proceedings of the congress held in Helsinki, Finland, July 7-10, 1982, Berlin, Springer-Verlag, 1984, p. 285-291.*
CONF: Congress on Sport and International Understanding (1982 : Helsinki).
LEVEL: I LANG: Eng GV706.8 18979

BIOGRAPHY AND AUTOBIOGRAPHY

Brant, J. The games according to Greenspan. Bud Greenspan has spent 32 years capturing on film the spirit of the Olympic flame. *Runner's world (Mountain View, Calif.) 19(7), Jul 1984, 50-54.*
LEVEL: B LANG: Eng SIRC ARTICLE NO: 094476

Taaffe, W. You can't keep him down on the farm. (Jim McKay) *Sports illustrated (Chicago, Ill.) 61(4), 18 Jul 1984, 286-289;291-292;294;297-298.*
NOTES: Special preview the 1984 Olympics.
LEVEL: B LANG: Eng SIRC ARTICLE NO: 096434

BROADCASTING

Garrett, R.A. Hochberg, P.R. Sports broadcasting and the law. (Refs: 58)*Indiana law journal (Bloomington, Ind.) 59(2), 1984 155-193.*
LEVEL: I LANG: Eng SIRC ARTICLE NO: 095984

Scharf, A. Creer une ethique. To create an ethic. *Message olympique/Olympic message (Lausanne) 8, Dec 1984, 42-47.*
CONF: International Symposium of Sport, Media and Olympism (1984 : Lausanne).
LEVEL: B LANG: Fr Eng SIRC ARTICLE NO: 104494

Schuermann, L. L'universalite du sport tributaire des medias. The universality of sport depends upon the media. *Message olympique/Olympic message (Lausanne) 8, Dec 1984, 33-37.*
CONF: International Symposium of Sport, Media and Olympism (1984 : Lausanne).
LEVEL: B LANG: Fr Eng SIRC ARTICLE NO: 104495

BROADCASTING - TELEVISION

Forkan, J.P. Can sports TV and marketing come back? *Advertising age (Chicago, Ill.) 55(86), 17 Dec 1984, 50.*
LEVEL: B LANG: Eng SIRC ARTICLE NO: 102919

Joyce, P. Television payante: le sport amateur aux heures d'ecoute maximum. Pay TV: prime time for amateurs. *Champion (Ottawa) 8(3), Aug 1984, 20-23.*
LEVEL: B LANG: Fr Eng SIRC ARTICLE NO: 096421

Maes, J. Regional sports networks boast strong lineups. *Advertising age (Chicago, Ill.) 55(86), 6 Dec 1984, 34.*
LEVEL: B LANG: Eng SIRC ARTICLE NO: 102923

Meier, K.V. Much ado about nothing: the television broadcast packaging of team sport championship games. (Refs: 8)*Sociology of sport journal (Champaign, Ill.) 1(3), 1984, 263-279.*
ABST: This study provided a detailed, descriptive content analysis of the television broadcast packaging of the 1982-83 championship games, both professional and university, of the four most popular North American team sports - baseball, football, hockey, and basketball. Videotape recordings of the entire broadcast packages centered upon these games were analyzed. The program content was divided into four specific and distinct components: advertisements, pre- and postgame programs, between-play time, and live-play time. The ensuing discussion addressed the basic structure of each broadcast package, the absolute and relative data for each of the four components of the various games and, finally, the intriguing relationship between the derived data and concomitant levels of viewer ratings.
LEVEL: A LANG: Eng SIRC ARTICLE NO: 102925

Nash, H.L. Sports medicine on television: airway to fitness or injury. *Physician and sportsmedicine (Minneapolis, Minn.) 12(11), Nov 1984, 122-126;128.*
LEVEL: B LANG: Eng SIRC ARTICLE NO: 101013

Powers, R. Supertube: the rise of television sports. New York: Coward-McCann, c1984. 288 p.
NOTES: Includes index. Bibliography: p. 276.
LEVEL: I LANG: Eng ISBN: 0698112539 LC CARD: 83-007425 GV742.3 15883

Rader, B.G. In its own image: how television has transformed sports. New York: Free Press, c1984. ix, 228 p.
NOTES: Include index. Bibliography: p. 211-215.
LEVEL: I LANG: Eng ISBN: 002925700X LC CARD: 84-047856 GV742.3 18034

Unravelling cable: our research unit explains what cable TV means for sport. *Sport & leisure (London, Eng.) Sept/Oct 1984*, 46-47.
LEVEL: B LANG: Eng SIRC ARTICLE NO: 108900

White, A.G. Public administration, policy, and sports - television and professional sports: a selected bibliography. Monticello, Ill.: Vance Bibliographies, 1984. 9 p. (Pub. admin. series; bibliography P1523.)
NOTES: ISSN: 0193-970X.
LEVEL: B LANG: Eng ISBN: 0-89028-103-3 GV713 18432

CINEMA

Crawford, S.A.G.M. The celluloid athlete: sports movies as teaching tools. (Refs: 10)*Journal of physical education, recreation and dance (Reston, Va.) 55(8), Oct 1984*, 24-27.
LEVEL: B LANG: Eng SIRC ARTICLE NO: 101002

Umphlett, W.L. The dynamics of fiction on the aesthetics of the sport film. *Arete: the journal of sport literature (San Diego, Calif.) 1(2), Spring 1984*, 113-121.
ABST: The authors review the sport films produced by Hollywood from the 1920's to today. Some of the films discussed are Jim Thorpe - All American (1951) Raging Bull (1980) and Chariots of Fire (1981).
LEVEL: A LANG: Eng SIRC ARTICLE NO: 097876

JOURNALISM

Elliott, S.J. Rodale Press getting in shape for the '80s. *Advertising age (Chicago, Ill.) 55(88), 24 Dec 1984*, 4;31.
LEVEL: B LANG: Eng SIRC ARTICLE NO: 102917

Lever, J. Wheeler, S. The Chicago Tribune sports page, 1900 - 1975. (Refs: 6)*Sociology of sport journal (Champaign, Ill.) 1(4), Dec 1984*, 299-313.
ABST: A content analysis of the Chicago Tribune's sports page from 1900 to 1975 provides an empirical base for assessing the changing nature of organized sport in American life. The findings show that there has been an expansion of the sports page relative to the rest of the newspaper; there has been remarkable stability in the coverage of the dominant sports of baseball and football; and there has been a progressive shift from amateur to professional, from local or regional events to national ones, and from individual to team sporting activity. This expanded role for sport is part of a more general trend to be expected in a leisure oriented society.
LEVEL: A LANG: Eng SIRC ARTICLE NO: 104489

Mallejac, J. La presse sportive: fiasco. *Revue de l'entraineur (Montreal) avr/juin 1984*, 24.
LEVEL: B LANG: Fr SIRC ARTICLE NO: 094760

Telander, R. The written word: player-press relationships in American sports. *Sociology of sport journal (Champaign, Ill.) (1), 1984*, 3-14.
ABST: This paper provides an overview of the role relationship between professional athletes and sports journalists. After a brief historical review it discusses (a) the current conflicts between players and sports writers in light of changing role definitions for both athletes and journalists, (b) ethical guidelines for writers covering athletes as personalities, and (c) how the emergence of superstar athletes has intensified the potential for conflict in player-press relations. The major conclusion is that conflict in player-press relations

is likely to continue. Its intensity will vary with the players' understanding of the role of the press in professional sport, the knowledge and empathy of the sports writers themselves, and the sophistication of the consumers of sport publications.
LEVEL: A LANG: Eng SIRC ARTICLE NO: 108341

RACE RELATIONS

Condor, R. Anderson, D.F. Longitudinal analysis of coverage accorded black and white athletes in feature articles of Sports Illustrated (1960-1980). *Journal of sport behavior (Mobile, Ala.) 7(1), Feb 1984*, 39-43.
ABST: The authors have taken a sample of Sports Illustrated feature articles drawn from the years 1960, 1967, 1974 and 1981 in order to examine the extent of coverage given to blacks and whites. There was a marked increase in the number of articles featuring blacks in 1981 compared to 1960, 1967 and 1974. The authors feel this increase is due to an increased coverage of baseball and football. The authors conclude that Sports Illustrated personnel have accepted that black athletes are of interest to the general population.
LEVEL: A LANG: Eng SIRC ARTICLE NO: 096391

MASTERS SPORT

SPORTING EVENTS

Yetman, W. Jeux des maitres. Masters of the game. *Champion (Ottawa) 8(3), Aug 1984*, 86-89.
LEVEL: B LANG: Fr Eng SIRC ARTICLE NO: 096440

MEDICINE

1984 American College of Sports Medicine Annual Meeting abstracts. Indianapolis: American College of Sports Medicine, 1984. xx 109 p. (Medicine and science in sports and exercise 16(2), 1984.)
CONF: American College of Sports Medicine. Annual Meeting (1984 : San Diego).
CORP: American College of sports Medicine.
LEVEL: A LANG: Eng

29th Meeting of the German Society of Sports Medicine. (abstracts) *International journal of sports medicine (Stuttgart) 5(5), Oct 1984*, 275-298.
LEVEL: A LANG: Eng SIRC ARTICLE NO: 104101

Biomechanics - kinanthropometry and sports medicine, exercise science. Scientific program abstracts: 1984 Olympic Scientific Congress, July 19-26, University of Oregon, Eugene, Oregon. Eugene, Or.: University of Oregon, Microform Publications, 1984. 179 p.
CONF: Olympic Scientific Congress (1984 : Eugene, Or.).
NOTES: Cover title.
LEVEL: A LANG: Eng RC1201 17867

Birrer, R.B. Sports medicine for the primary care physician. Norwalk, Conn.: Appleton-Century-Crofts, c1984. xv, 347 p.
NOTES: Includes index and bibliographies.
LEVEL: A LANG: Eng ISBN: 0838586511 LC CARD: 83-011870 RC1210 17030

Brodiagin, N.A. Petrova, E.A. Otsenka donozologicheskikh sostoianii v razlichnykh professionalnykh gruppakh po dannym aktivnosti reguliatornykh sistem. (Evaluation of the health status of various professional groups based on the activity of the regulatory systems.) *Gigiena truda i professionalnye zabolevaniia (Moscow) 12, Dec 1984*, 33-37.
LEVEL: I LANG: Rus

Cantu, R.C. Clinical sports medicine. Lexington, Mass. ; Toronto: Collamore Press : D.C. Heath, c1984. xii, 219 p.
NOTES: Includes bibliographical references and index. Papers presented at the Annual meeting of the New England Chapter of the American College of Sports Medicine, Nov. 19-20, 1982.
LEVEL: A LANG: Eng ISBN: 066906842X LC CARD: 83-071035 RC1201 15964

Dan, B.B. Citius, altius, fortius. (editorial) *JAMA: Journal of the American Medical Association (Chicago) 252(4), 27 Jul 1984*, 527.
LEVEL: B LANG: Eng SIRC ARTICLE NO: 102568

Facts of life and death... a new sports council publications examines the medical reasons why exercise actually improves our health - and mood. *Sport and leisure (London) 25(5), Nov/Dec 1984*, 34-35.
LEVEL: B LANG: Eng SIRC ARTICLE NO: 108965

Hamilton, I. Physician heal thyself? Final-year medical students averaged only six out of 10 in a vital test paper on sports medicine. *Running (London) 39, Jul 1984*, 66-67;69.
LEVEL: B LANG: Eng SIRC ARTICLE NO: 102590

Henderson, E.D. Symposium on sports medicine. (editorial) *Mayo clinic proceedings (Rochester, Minn.) 59(2), Feb 1984*, 126.
LEVEL: B LANG: Eng SIRC ARTICLE NO: 099090

Hillman, R.S. Travel. (Refs: 4)
NOTES: In, Strauss, R.H. (ed.), Sports medicine, Philadelphia ; Toronto, Saunders, 1984, p. 492-500.
LEVEL: I LANG: Eng RC1210 17196

Krakauer, L.J. Anderson, J.L. George, F. Shephard, R.J. Torg, J.S. 1984 year book of sports medicine. Chicago, Ill.: Year Book Medical Publishers, Inc., 1984. 459 p. : ill.
NOTES: ISSN: 0162-0908.
LEVEL: A LANG: Eng ISBN: 0-8151-5158-6 RC1210 18955

Larkin, T. Herbs are often more toxic than magical. *Sports mediscope (Colorado Springs, Colo.) 4(3), Fall 1984*, 15-20.
NOTES: HHS Publication No. (FDA) 84-1105. Reprinted from, FDA Consumer, Oct 1983.
LEVEL: B LANG: Eng SIRC ARTICLE NO: 100734

Morris, A.F. Sports medicine: prevention of athletic injuries. Dubuque, Iowa: Wm.C. Brown, c1984. xviii, 377 p. : ill.
NOTES: Includes bibliographies.
LEVEL: I LANG: Eng ISBN: 0-697-00087-7 LC CARD: 83-071289 RC1210 18568

Olympic issue. Chicago: American Medical Association, 1984. 136 p. : ill. (JAMA: Journal of the American Medical Association (Chicago) 252(4), 27 Jul 1984.)
LEVEL: A LANG: Eng RC1210 20686

Scott, W.N. Nisonson, B. Nicholas, J.A. Principles of sports medicine. Baltimore: Williams & Wilkins, c1984. xiv, 433 p. : ill.

NOTES: Includes index. Includes bibliographical references.
LEVEL: A LANG: Eng ISBN: 0683076159 LC CARD: 83-003538 RC1210 18016

Southwest Chapter - American College of Sports Medicine: Las Vegas, Nevada, November 18-19, 1983. (abstracts) *International journal of sports medicine (Stuttgart) 5(3), Jun 1984, 156-164.*
LEVEL: A LANG: Eng SIRC ARTICLE NO: 104149

Sports science and sports medicine units at the AIS. *Sports science & medicine quarterly 1(1), Jun 1984, 9-10.*
LEVEL: B LANG: Eng SIRC ARTICLE NO: 097613

Strauss, R.H. Sports medicine. Philadelphia ; Toronto: Saunders, 1984. xv, 560 p. : ill.
NOTES: Includes bibliographical references.
LEVEL: A LANG: Eng ISBN: 0721686117 LC CARD: 83-004456 RC1210 17196

Wullaert, P. Pillet, J. Guide pratique de medecine du sport. Paris: Masson, 1984. xii, 247 p.
NOTES: Reedition du Guide pratique de medecine du sport, Editions medicales et universitaires, 1980. Bibliographie: p. 241.
LEVEL: I LANG: Fr ISBN: 2-225-80168-1 RC1210 17774

ACCUPUNCTURE

Mitchell, I.C. Remedial gymnastics and acupuncture - a combined aproach. *Journal of the society of remedial gymnastics and recreational therapy (Manchester) 113, Aug 1984, 14-17.*
LEVEL: I LANG: Eng SIRC ARTICLE NO: 108557

Nguyen, A. Acupuncture et medecine sportive. *Revue francaise de medecine traditionnelle chinoise (France) 105, 1984, 609-611.*
LEVEL: B LANG: Fr

ADMINISTRATION

Legwold, G. When sports medicine groups speak, who listens? *Physician and sportsmedicine 12(3), Mar 1984, 162-166.*
LEVEL: LANG: Eng SIRC ARTICLE NO: 091520

Suver, J.D. Miller, J.A. Control of the marketing effort in health care organizations. (Refs: 10)*Health marketing quarterly (New York) 1(4), Summer 1984, 83-100.*
LEVEL: I LANG: Eng SIRC ARTICLE NO: 100461

ANATOMY

Bouillerot, J.M. Le genou: approche anatomique et physiologique. *Cyclotourisme (Paris) 316, mai 1984, 48-49.*
LEVEL: B LANG: Fr SIRC ARTICLE NO: 097590

Fecher, K. The spinal column - the body's support. *Sport & fitness (Sunbury, Middlesex) Dec 1984, 56-57.*
LEVEL: B LANG: E SIRC ARTICLE NO: 108872

Geesink, R.G.T. Drukker, J. van der Linden, A.J. Stress response of articular cartilage. (Refs: 4)*International journal of sports medicine (Stuttgart) Suppl. 5, Nov 1984, 100-101.*
CONF: International Congress on Sports and Health (1983 : Maastricht, Netherlands).
LEVEL: A LANG: Eng SIRC ARTICLE NO: 104116

Grisogono, V. The running body: 23 the pelvis. *Running magazine (London) 33, Jan 1984, 67;69.*
LEVEL: B LANG: Eng SIRC ARTICLE NO: 097598

Kuusela, T. Kurri, J. Virtama, P. Stress response of the tibial cortex: a longitudinal radiographic study. *Annals of clinical research (Helsinki) 16(Suppl 40), 1984, 14-16.*
ABST: The authors evaluate the effects of exercise on bone tissue in a sample of 30 conscripts. Roentgenographic examinations were performed on the lower legs after 10, 20 and 40 weeks' service. After the first 10 weeks, the cortical bone was longitudinally striated; after 40 weeks, the bone structure was quite homogenous and solid. 73% of the diagnosed stress lesions were developed during the first 10 weeks.
LEVEL: A LANG: Eng SIRC ARTICLE NO: 102595

Levy, I.M. Landmarks and surface anatomy. (Refs: 3)
NOTES: In, Birrer, R.B. (ed.), Sports medicine for the primary care physician, Norwalk, Conn., Appleton-Century-Crofts, c1984, p. 14-26.
LEVEL: I LANG: Eng RC1210 17030

Palmoski, M.J. Brandt, K.D. Effects of altered load on canine articular cartilage in vivo and in vitro. (Refs: 12) *International journal of sports medicine (Stuttgart) Suppl. 5, Nov 1984, 79-82.*
CONF: International Congress on Sports and Health (1983 : Maastricht, Netherlands).
LEVEL: A LANG: Eng SIRC ARTICLE NO: 104131

Videman, T. Eronen, I. Effects of treadmill running on glycosaminoglycans in articular cartilage of rabbits. (Refs: 26) *International journal of sports medicine (Stuttgart) 5(6), Dec 1984, 320-324.*
ABST: In a study of the effects of motion load on weight-bearing articular cartilage, rabbits were made to run on a treadmill for 1-, 5-, and 30-day periods. One group ran on a level surface, and another ran uphill. In vivo 35 S-sulfate bound in glycosaminoglycans (GAG) after running was used as an indicator of the synthesis rate of GAGs. After 30 days of running the glucosamine content was markedly reduced in GAGs of both tibial and femoral cartilage. The possible role of different factors affecting the cartilage metabolism is discussed.
LEVEL: A LANG: Eng SIRC ARTICLE NO: 104388

Yates, J.W. Jackson, D.W. Current status of meniscus surgery. (Refs: 19)*Physician and sportsmedicine 12(2), Feb 1984, 51-56;59.*
LEVEL: I LANG: Eng SIRC ARTICLE NO: 091536

ANESTHESIA

Ringrose, N.H. Cross, M.J. Femoral nerve block in knee joint surgery. (Refs: 1)*American journal of sports medicine (Baltimore, Md.) 12(5), Sept/Oct 1984, 398-402.*
ABST: Assessment is made of the effectiveness of femoral nerve block, administered either before or after surgery, in supplementing postoperative analgesia for knee joint (anterior cruciate) reconstruction surgery. Femoral nerve block, performed before surgery, with Bupivacaine 0.5 per cent, reduced intramuscular opiate administration by 80 per cent in the recovery room and 40 per cent in the first 24 postoperative hours. An effective and rapidly performed technique for femoral nerve block is described.
LEVEL: A LANG: Eng SIRC ARTICLE NO: 104142

BIOCHEMISTRY

Golf, S.W. Happel, O. Graef, V. Seim, K.E. Plasma aldosterone, cortisol and electrolyte concentrations in physical exercise after magnesium supplementation. *Journal of clinical chemistry and clinical biochemistry (Berlin) 22(11), Nov 1984, 717-721.*
LEVEL: A LANG: Eng

Picard, H. Valton, C. Sport, thermalisme et oligo-elements en pathologie osteo-articulaire et O.R.L. (Refs: 10)*Cinesiologie 92/93, nov/dec 1983-janv/fevr 1984, 75-80;83-84.*
NOTES: Numero special: Medecine du sport et thermalisme.
RESUME: Les auteurs discutent de l'utilisation des oligo-elements dans le traitements des pathologies osteo-articulaires et musculo-tendineuses. Ils expliquent le role joue par quelques uns de ces elements. La crenotherapie est percue comme le moyen privilegie, simple et facile de la cure par les oligo-elements.
LEVEL: A LANG: Fr SIRC ARTICLE NO: 092884

BIOGRAPHY AND AUTOBIOGRAPHY

Hage, P. Jack Wilmore: he can't say no. *Physician and sportsmedicine 12(2), Feb 1984, 145-147;150.*
LEVEL: B LANG: Eng SIR ARTICLE NO: 091509

Jokl, E. Personalia: mind and energy: John C. Eccles and William C. Gibson on 'Sherrington, his life and thought'. (Charles Scott Sherrington) (Refs: 15)*Annals of sports medicine (North Hollywood, Calif.) 2(1), 1984, 2-8.*
NOTES: Reprinted from, Transactions and Studies of the College of Physicians of Philadelphia Ser. 5, 2: 223-235, 1980.
LEVEL: I LANG: Eng SIRC ARTICLE NO: 104119

CARDIOLOGY

Chamoux, A. Catilina, P. Le systeme Holter en pratique. (Refs: 6)*Medecine du sport (Paris) 58(5), 25 sept 1984, 43-54.*
RESUME: Les auteurs exposent les modalites d'utilisation du systeme Holter et ses applications pratiques en cardiologique et en physiologie de l'exercice physique sportif. Ils proposent des exemples d'application dans le domaine sportif (kayak, cyclisme, course a pied, ski de fond et halterophilie).
LEVEL: A LANG: Fr SIRC ARTICLE NO: 100711

Cumming, G.R. Langford, S. Maximal treadmill tests five years apart in asymptomatic men aged 45-72 years. (Refs: 26)*Canadia journal of applied sport sciences/Journal canadien des sciences appliquees au sport (Windsor, Ont.) 9(2), Jun 1984, 80-86.*
ABST: One hundred sixty-nine men performed two maximal treadmill tests (Bruce protocol) spaced five years apart. Time to exhaustion and ECG responses to exercise were obtained at both tests. Treadmill endurance time declined 4 to 8 seconds per year and maximal heart rate declined about 1 beat/min per year. There was a high frequency of exercise-induced ventricular extrasystoles and ST depressions in this population. It is not known if there is a need for intervention.
LEVEL: A LANG: Eng SIRC ARTICLE NO: 096007

Fainting from fitness. *Health letter (San Antonio, Tex.) 24(9), 9 Nov 1984, 2-3.*
LEVEL: B LANG: Eng SIRC ARTICLE NO: 102576

Ferst, J.A. Chaitman, B.R. The electrocardiogram and the athlete. (Refs: 52)*Sports medicine (Auckland, N.Z.) 1(5), Sept/Oct 1984, 390-403.*
ABST: Physiological adaptations of the heart to prolonged, intense physical training produce electrocardiographic changes considered abnormal in untrained persons. Increased vagal tone, anatomical changes in the heart, and other less understood mechanisms are thought to cause a spectrum of surface ECG changes characteristic of trained athletes. Arrhythmias frequently seen include sinus bradycardia, sinus pauses, and supraventricular ectopic beats. Conduction abnormalities such as prolonged P-R interval, first degree AV heart block, Wenckebch type I AV heart block, non-sinus escape rhythms, and intraventricular conduction delays of right bundle branch type are also found. Changes in ECG parameters with exercise include a shortening of the P-R interval with a concomitant increase in P wave/P-R interval ratio, improved AV conduction with cessation of Weckebach phenomenon, and normalisation of ST segment and other T wave changes.
LEVEL: A LANG: Eng SIRC ARTICLE NO: 102577

Jaeger, M. Coeur et exercice physique. (Refs: 5)*Revue medicale de la Suisse romande (Lausanne) 104(10), oct 1984, 801-806.*
LEVEL: I LANG: Fr SIRC ARTICLE NO: 174099

Jokl, E. Olympic medicine and sports cardiology. (Refs: 201)*Annals of sports medicine (Hollywood, Calif.) 1(4), 1984, 127-169.*
LEVEL: I LANG: Eng SIRC ARTICLE NO: 095770

Kavtaradze, V.G. Areshidze, T.K. Iosava, K.V. Kurashvili, R.B. Lezhava, M.G. Kompiuternyi analiz EKG pri fizicheskoi nagruzk (Computer analysis of the ECG during physical exercise.) *Kardiologiia (Moscow) 24(3), Mar 1984, 70-75.*
ABST: Treadmill tests were performed in one hundred men below 60, with computerized assessment of their ECG data. Reduced R wave amplitude from lead V5 at maximum exercise was only noted in subjects showing no electrocardiographic evidence of ischemia. Increased R wave from lead V5 was regarded as cardiac dysfunction in response to exercise, which, in the presence of ischemic ECG changes, preceded the development of pathologic ST depression. A negative T wave from leads III and aVF on resting ECG did not correlate with abnormal exercise test results. Ventricular arrhythmias were more common in subjects with non-ischemic ECG changes during exercise.
LEVEL: A LANG: Rus

Kuan, P. Ellestad, M.H. Cardiokymography during exercise testing. (letter) *American journal of cardiology (New York) 53(9), 1 May 1984, 1413.*
LEVEL: B LANG: Eng SIRC ARTICLE NO: 100732

Lake, B. Cardiac exercise testing. (letter) *Medical journal of Australia (Sydney) 140(8), 14 Apr 1984, 505-506.*
LEVEL: I LANG: Eng SIRC ARTICLE NO: 100733

CERTIFICATION

Chantraine, A. De la necessite d'un enseignement de la medecine du sport. *Revue medicale de la Suisse romande (Lausanne) 10 (10), oct 1984, 747-749.*
LEVEL: B LANG: Fr SIRC ARTICLE NO: 174091

de Fallois, A. Formation des medecins du sport dans differents pays de l'Europe. *Cinesiologie: medecine du sport (Paris) 98 nov/dec 1984, 499-500.*
LEVEL: B LANG: Fr SIRC ARTICLE NO: 104114

Hocutt, J.E. Moody, K. The volunteer physician program of the Lake Placid Olympic Training Center. *Delaware medical journal (Wilmington) 56(11), Nov 1984, 681-683.*
LEVEL: B LANG: Eng

Projet d'enseignement de la medecine du sport (janvier 1984). *Cinesiologie: medecine du sport (Paris) 98, nov/dec 1984, 492-498.*
LEVEL: B LANG: Fr SIRC ARTICLE NO: 104139

COUNTRIES AND REGIONS

Barrault, D. La medecine du sport. *Science et vie (Paris) HS147, 1984, 146-149.*
LEVEL: B LANG: Fr

Caldwell, J.E. Sports medicine training in Kuopio - international co-operation. *In, Ilmarinen, M. (ed.) et al., Sport and International Understanding: proceedings of the congress held in Helsinki, Finland, July 7-10, 1982, Berlin, Springer-Verlag, 1984, p. 346-351.*
CONF: Congress on Sport and International Understanding (1982 : Helsinki).
LEVEL: I LANG: Eng GV706.8 18979

Dirner, O. Toerekvesek testneveleseges zeguegyuenk tovabbi javitasara. (Efforts to improve health care and medical service in physical education and sports.) *Sportorvosi szemle/Hungarian review of sports medicine (Budapest) 25(2), 1984, 97-107.*
LEVEL: A LANG: Hun SIRC ARTICLE NO: 097266

Erbach, E. Successful development of sports medicine. *Sports in the GDR (Berlin, GDR) 3, 1984, I-III.*
LEVEL: B LANG: Eng SIRC ARTICLE NO: 108722

Fazey, H. The injury debate. Teaching sports medicine - who pays? *Running (London, Eng.) 36, Apr 1984, 74-75;77.*
NOTES: Third in a series.
LEVEL: B LANG: Eng SIRC ARTICLE NO: 096017

Heluwaert, A. La consultation d'aptitude a un sport. (Refs: 4)*Revue du jeune medecin (Paris) Supp(130), 1984, 1-2.*
LEVEL: LANG: Fr

Knuttgen, H.G. A personal view of Chinese sports medicine. *Physician and sportsmedicine 12(2), Feb 1984, 134-137;141-142.*
LEVEL: B LANG: Eng SIRC ARTICLE NO: 091517

Shaw, D. Inside athletics. Remarkably there is no official medical provision for our international athletes. *Running (London) 37, May 1984, 159.*
LEVEL: B LANG: Eng SIRC ARTICLE NO: 096051

DEHYDRATION

De Mondenard, J.P. Place des eaux minerales dans l'hydratation des sportifs. (Refs: 8)*Cinesiologie 92/93, nov/dec 1983-janv/fevr 1984, 65-74.*
NOTES: Numero special: Medecine du sport et thermalisme.
LEVEL: I LANG: Fr SIRC ARTICLE NO: 092926

Loesel, H. Important medical aspects on sport referring to the Olympic Games in Summer 1984.

(Part 5) Sportmedizinisch relevante Aspekte bezueglich der Olympischen Spiele im Sommer 1984. (5. Teil) Aspects importants du point de vue de la medecine du sport pour les Jeux olympiques d'ete 1984. (5ieme partie) Aspectos importantes de la medicina y del deporte para los Juegos Olimpicos de verano de 1984. (5a parte) *UIT shooting sport journal (Muenchen, FRG) 24(3), May/Jun 1984, 13-14;16-19;40-43.*
LEVEL: I LANG: Eng Ger Fr Spa SIRC ARTICLE NO: 098447

Schiltz, J. Heat: the athlete killer. Coaches must understand the dangers involved in playing in hot weather and be prepared to cope with heat stress in their athletes. *Athletic journal 64(8), Mar 1984, 14;60-62.*
LEVEL: B LANG: Eng SIRC ARTICLE NO: 093127

DENTISTRY

Allen, M.E. Walter, P. McKay, C. Elmajian, A. Occlusal splints (MORA) vs. placebos show no difference in strength in symptomatic subjects: double blind/cross-over study. (Refs: 22)*Canadian journal of applied sport sciences/Journal canadien des sciences appliquees au sport (Windsor, Ont.) 9(3), Sept 1984, 148-152.*
ABST: Eight subjects with TMJ disorders were tested for strength changes in 4 muscle groups with a custom MORA and placebo splint in a tightly controlled double-blind cross-over protocol using a Cybex II dynamometer. A two-way analysis of variance (ANOVA) did not show significant differences in strength change between the two splints. Neither were there any trends that would suggest strength benefits from the MORA.
LEVEL: A LANG: Eng SIRC ARTICLE NO: 102562

Birkhed, D. Sugar content, acidity and effect on plaque pH of fruit juices, fruit drinks, carbonated beverages and sport drinks. *Caries research (Basel) 18(2), 1984, 120-127.*
LEVEL: A LANG: Eng SIRC ARTICLE NO: 099080

Dental community's role in the Olympic movement. *Dental student/dental practice (Waco, Tex.) 62(4), Jan 1984, 20-22.*
LEVEL: LANG: Eng SIRC ARTICLE NO: 099083

Donnelly, B. Incorporating sports into private practice. (interview) *Dental student/dental practice (Waco, Tex.) 62(4), Jan 1984, 18-19.*
LEVEL: B LANG: Eng SIRC ARTICLE NO: 099085

Dreyer, R. Mouth protectors, trauma care top sports dentistry agenda. *Dental student/dental practice (Waco, Tex.) 62(4), Ja 1984, 12-15.*
LEVEL: I LANG: Eng SIRC ARTICLE NO: 099086

Kerr, I.L. Going for the gold. Dentistry's role in the Olympics. *Journal of the American College of Dentists (Cherry Hill, N.J.) 51(2), Summer 1984, 12-14.*
LEVEL: B LANG: Eng

Klemons, I.M. Chronic head and facial pain and dysfunction: their interrelationships, diagnosis and treatment by mandibular orthopedic repositioning. Eugene, Ore.: Microform Publications, University of Oregon, 1984. 3 microfiches : negative, ill. ; 11 x 15 cm.
NOTES: Thesis (Ph.D.) - Pennsylvania States University, 1981; (ix, 238, 1 leaves); vita; includes bibliography.
LEVEL: A LANG: Eng UO84 114-115

MEDICINE (continued)

Seals, R.R. Dorrough, B.C. Custom mouth protectors: a review of their applications. *Journal of prosthetic dentistry (St. Louis) 51(2), Feb 1984, 238-242.*
LEVEL: I LANG: Eng SIRC ARTICLE NO: 099102

DERMATOLOGY

Baadsgaard, O. Lindskov, R. Cholinergic urticaria with anaphylaxis induced by exercise or heating. *Acta dermato-venereologica (Stockholm) 64(4), 1984, 344-346.*
LEVEL: A LANG: Eng

Bergfeld, W.F. Dermatologic problems in athletes. (Refs: 29)*Primary care: clinics in office practice (Philadelphia) 11(1), Mar 1984, 151-160.*
LEVEL: I LANG: Eng SIRC ARTICLE NO: 100708

Black, M. Germs you can catch at the gym: just when you thought it was safe to go back in the locker room... *New body (New York) 3(5), Sept 1984, 44-45.*
LEVEL: B LANG: Eng SIRC ARTICLE NO: 173288

Clement, M. Pembroke, A.C. Greaves, M.W. Exertional angio-oedema. *Journal of the Royal Society of Medicine (London) 77(11), Nov 1984, 961-962.*
LEVEL: I LANG: Eng

Del Campo, D.V. Strenuous exercise with isotretinoin. (letter) *Journal of the American Academy of Dermatology (St. Louis) 1 (2 Pt 1), Aug 1984, 301.*
LEVEL: I LANG: Eng

Karstorp, A. Prevention of schistosomiasis. (letter) *JAMA. Journal of the American Medical Association (Chicago) 252(22), 1 Dec 1984, 3129-3130.*
LEVEL: I LANG: Eng

Rogers, E. The dangers of sun-worship. *Gam on yachting (Toronto), 28(5), May 1984, 26-27.*
LEVEL: B LANG: Eng SIRC ARTICLE NO: 099100

DICTIONARIES AND TERMINOLOGY

Garfinkel, D. Glossary. (Refs: 19)
NOTES: In, Birrer, R.B. (ed.), Sports medicine for the primary care physician, Norwalk, Conn., Appleton-Century-Crofts, c1984, p. 335-339.
LEVEL: B LANG: Eng RC1210 17030

DIRECTORIES

AR&FA's 1984 survey of sportsmedicine clinics. *Running & fitness (Washington, D.C.) 16(4), Jul/Aug 1984, 13-14;19-21.*
LEVEL B LANG: Eng SIRC ARTICLE NO: 105328

Tally, J. Will sports medicine become more than just a sideline? (sports medicine program) *Physician and sportsmedicine (Minneapolis, Minn.) 12(11), Nov 1984, 133-136.*
LEVEL: B LANG: Eng SIRC ARTICLE NO: 100762

Trainers' supplies: training and first aid products are listed here. The manufacturers and suppliers of each product are liste alphabetically following the heading. *Athletic purchasing and facilities (Madison, Wis.) 8(2), Feb 1984, 65-66;68.*
NOTES: 1984 buyers guide.
LEVEL: B LANG: Eng SIRC ARTICLE NO: 108277

DOCUMENTATION

Marron, J.T. Tucker, J.B. The preparticipation health inventory. (Refs: 18)
NOTES: In, Birrer, R.B. (ed.), Sports medicine for the primary care physician, Norwalk, Conn., Appleton-Century-Crofts, c1984, p. 27-41.
LEVEL: I LANG: Eng RC1210 17030

ENDOCRINOLOGY

Christensen, S.E. Jorgensen, O.L. Moller, N. Orskov, H. Characterization of growth hormone release in response to external heating. Comparison to exercise induced release. *Acta endocrinologica (Copenhagen) 107(3), Nov 1984, 295-301.*
LEVEL: A LANG: Eng

Lamb, L. How sex hormones influence your fitness, part 1. *Muscle & fitness (Woodland Hills, Calif.) 45(10), Oct 1984, 17;190-191.*
LEVEL: B LANG: Eng SIRC ARTICLE NO: 109001

O'Shea, P. The endocrine system and physical activity. (Refs: 29)*National Strength & Conditioning Association journal 6(1), Feb/Mar 1984, 31-35.*
LEVEL: I LANG: Eng SIRC ARTICLE NO: 092946

Stone, M.H. Byrd, R. Johnson, C. Observations on serum androgen response to short term resistive training in middle age sedentary males. (Refs: 27)*National Strength & Conditioning Association journal 5(6), 1984, 30-31;71;73.*
ABST: The serum testosterone concentration levels of the following three groups of middle age males were compared: a weight training group, an aerobic training group, and a sedentary control group. Significant increases were observed in the first two groups while no significant changes were found in the control group.
LEVEL: A LANG: Eng SIRC ARTICLE NO: 090098

EQUIPMENT

Blair, D. Crutch use in athletics. (Refs: 5)*Athletic training (Greenville, N.C.) 19(4), Winter 1984, 275-277.*
LEVEL: B LANG: Eng SIRC ARTICLE NO: 104106

Filsinger, L. Knee bracing. (Refs: 18)*Sports physiotherapy division (Victoria, B.C.) 9(3), May/Jun 1984, 26-30.*
LEVEL: I LANG: Eng SIRC ARTICLE NO: 097595

Hofmann, A.A. Wyatt, R.W.B. Bourne, M.H. Daniels, A.U. Knee stability in orthotic knee braces. (Refs: 4)*American journal of sports medicine (Baltimore, Md.) 12(5), Sept/Oct 1984, 371-374.*
ABST: The ability of six commercially available orthotic knee braces to stabilize ligamentous injuries of the knee was evaluated using fresh cadaver specimens. Anterior, valgus, and rotational forces were applied to the intact knee, after the anterior cruciate and medial collateral ligaments were cut, and after application of the knee braces. Bony displacement was measured using half pins and an external fixator applied to the tibia and femur. There was a significant difference in brace performance, most likely due to differences in brace design. Of the six braces tested, the 3D 3-way brace provided the greatest knee stability.
LEVEL: A LANG: Eng SIRC ARTICLE NO: 104117

Orthotic and padding materials in sports. (Refs: 15)*Sports physiotherapy division (Victoria, B.C.)*
9(2), Mar/Apr 1984, 26-28.
LEVEL: B LANG: Eng SIRC ARTICLE NO: 097607

Tank, R. Letter to the editor. (Lenox Hill knee brace cost) *Journal of orthopaedic and sports physical therapy (Baltimore, Md.) 6(1), Jul/Aug 1984, 54.*
LEVEL: B LANG: Eng SIRC ARTICLE NO: 100763

FACILITIES

Bourbonne-les-Bains ou la renovation exemplaire d'une station. *Cinesiologie 92/93, nov/dec 1983-janv/fevr 1984, 89-95.*
NOTES: Numero special: Medecine du sport et thermalisme.
LEVEL: B LANG: Fr SIRC ARTICLE NO: 092917

Goux, R. Rostan, A. Un centre medico-sportif: sa raison d'etre, sa conception, son utilisation. (Refs: 4)*Revue medicale de la Suisse romande (Lausanne) 104(10), oct 1984, 751-755.*
LEVEL: B LANG: Fr SIRC ARTICLE NO: 174092

Hutson, M.A. The Nottingham Sports Injury Clinic . *British journal of sports medicine (Loughborough, Eng.) 18(2), Jun 1984, 122-123.*
LEVEL: B LANG: Eng SIRC ARTICLE NO: 102514

Jillimore, M. L'Institut de conditionnement physique - centre de tests officiel. The Fitness Institute - official testing centre. *Champion (Ottawa) 8(3), Aug 1984, 80-83.*
LEVEL: B LANG: Fr Eng SIRC ARTICLE NO: 096026

Sports medicine directory 1984. *Physician and sportsmedicine (Minneapolis, Minn.) 12(9), Sept 1984, 169-175;179-180.*
LEVEL: LANG: Eng SIRC ARTICLE NO: 099105

GERIATRICS

Steinberg, F.U. Education in geriatrics in physical medicine residency training programs. (Refs: 7)*Archives of physical medicine and rehabilitation (Chicago) 65(1), Jan 1984, 8-10.*
ABST: The authors emphasize the need to keep the aged independent for as long a time as possible and to either prevent or postpone confinement to custodial institutions. The reasons cited are both humanitarian and economic. In order to fulfill this need medical students, young physicians and members of the medical community must be taught to satisfactorily deal with the problems of older patients.
LEVEL: A LANG: Eng SIRC ARTICLE NO: 094440

HEMATOLOGY

Brodde, O.E. Daul, A. O'Hara, N. Beta-adrenoceptor changes in human lymphocytes, induced by dynamic exercise. *Naunyn-Schmiedebergs archives of pharmacology (Berlin) 325(2), Feb 1984, 190-192.*
LEVEL: A LANG: Eng SIRC ARTICLE NO: 100710

Edwards, A.J. Bacon, T.H. Elms, C.A. Verardi, R. Felder, M. Knight, S.C. Changes in the populations of lymphoid cells in human peripheral blood following physical exercise. *Clinical and experimental immunology (Oxford) 58(2), Nov 1984, 420-427.*
LEVEL: A LANG: Eng

Ross, J.H. Attwood, E.C. Severe repetitive exercise and haematological status. *Postgraduate*

medical journal (Oxford) 60(705), Jul 1984, 454-457.
LEVEL: I LANG: Eng SIRC ARTICLE NO: 104144

Singhal, P. Bansal, I.J.S. A comparison of values for osmotic fragility of R.B.C.s and persistence test of athletes. (Refs: *Journal of sports medicine and physical fitness (Torino, Italy) 24(3), Sept 1984, 230-233.*
ABST: The present study has been undertaken to see the relation between the persistence test and the osmotic fragility of the athletes. 98 male athletes were tested for osmotic fragility test. Out of these athletes, 55 athletes underwent persistence tests with the help of grip dynamometer. The results reveal that in the majority (41.84 per cent) of athletes initial hemolysis started in 0.45 per cent NaC1 and it reached 100 per cent lysis in 48.98 per cent cases at 0.20 per cent concentration of NaC1. The median corpuscular fragility (MCF) in 48.98 per cent of the athletes was caused by 0.35 per cent NaC1. The persistence power ranged between 5 seconds to 85 seconds and most of them (30.91 per cent) had a range between 20 seconds to 50 seconds.
LEVEL: A LANG: Eng SIRC ARTICLE NO: 105351

Vicente, V. Alberca, I. Mannucci, P.M. Reduced effect of exercise and DDAVP on factor VIII-von Willebrad Factor and plasminogen activator after sequential application of both the stimuli. *Thrombosis and haemostasis (Stuttgart) 51(1), 28 Feb 1984, 129-130.*
LEVEL: A LANG: Eng SIRC ARTICLE NO: 100929

HISTORY

Jackson, D.W. The history of sports medicine. Part 2. *American journal of sports medicine (Baltimore, Md.) 12(4), Jul/Aug 1984, 255-257.*
LEVEL: I LANG: Eng SIRC ARTICLE NO: 108529

Snook, G.A. The history of sports medicine. Part 1. (Refs: 11)*American journal of sports medicine (Baltimore, Md.) 12(4), Jul/Aug 1984, 252-254.*
LEVEL: I LANG: Eng SIRC ARTICLE NO: 108528

The history of sports medicine. (Refs: 6)
NOTES: In, Birrer, R.B. (ed.), Sports medicine for the primary care physician, Norwalk, Conn., Appleton-Century-Crofts, c1984, p. 1-4.
LEVEL: B LANG: Eng RC1210 17030

IMMUNOLOGY

Kassil, G.N. Levando, V.A. Suzdalnitskii, R.S. Pershin, B.B. Kuzmin, S.N. Neiro-gumoralnaia reguliatsiia immunnogo gomeostaz v protsesse prisposobleniia k ekstremalnym nagruzkam na modeli sovremennogo sporta. (Neurohumoral regulation of immune homeostasis during adaptation to extreme loads in a modern sports model.) *Academiia nauk SSSR. Doklady (Leningrad) 275(2), 1984, 506-509.*
LEVEL: A LANG: Rus

Simon, H.B. The immunology of exercise. A brief review. *JAMA: Journal of the American Medical Association (Chicago) 252(19) 16 Nov 1984, 2735-2738.*
LEVEL: I LANG: Eng

LAW AND LEGISLATION

Journees nationales d'etudes de la FNOMS Lyon 12 et 13 novembre 1983; le controle medico-sportif, dans le cadre de la decentralisation et la loi relative a l'organisation et a la promotion des APS. *Sport dans la cite (France) 98, 1984, 14-25.*
CONF: Journees nationales d'etudes de la FNOMS (1983 : Lyon).
LEVEL: A LANG: Fr

Samuels, A. Sport injury and the law. *Medicine, science and the law (Brentford, Eng.) 24(4), Oct 1984, 254-260.*
LEVEL: I LANG: Eng

Walker, E.J. Bianco, E.A. Hartmann, P.M. Legal aspects of sports medicine. (Refs: 23)
NOTES: In, Birrer, R.B. (ed.), Sports medicine for the primary care physician, Norwalk, Conn., Appleton-Century-Crofts, c1984, p. 326-333.
LEVEL: I LANG: Eng RC1210 17030

Wood, L.M. Wood, C.B. Victory in Brighton County Court. *Colorado medicine (Denver) 81(10), Oct 1984, 157-158.*
LEVEL: I LANG: Eng

LONGEVITY AND LIFESPAN

Stephens, K.E. Van Huss, W.D. Olson, H.W. Montoye, H.J. The longevity, morbidity, and physical fitness of former athletes - an update. (Refs: 53)*American Academy of Physical Education papers (Champaign, Ill.) 17, 1984, 101-119.*
CONF: American Academy of Physical Education. Annual Meeting (54th : 1983 : Minneapolis).
NOTES: Conference theme: Exercise and health.
LEVEL: A LANG: Eng SIRC ARTICLE NO: 104150

NEUROLOGY

Bellande, S. Neurological examination. *NAIA news (Roeland Park, Kans.) 33(6), Jun/Jul 1984, 30-31.*
LEVEL: B LANG: Eng SIR ARTICLE NO: 104105

Gavrilenko, P. Allary, B. La cure a Bourbonne-les-Bains et ses resultats sur 63 cas d'algodystrophie. *Cinesiologie 92/93, nov/dec 1983-janv/fevr 1984, 13-17.*
NOTES: Numero special: Medecine du sport et thermalisme.
LEVEL: A LANG: Fr SIRC ARTICLE NO: 092931

Jokl, E. Personalia: mind and energy: John C. Eccles and William C. Gibson on 'Sherrington, his life and thought'. (Charles Scott Sherrington) (Refs: 15)*Annals of sports medicine (North Hollywood, Calif.) 2(1), 1984, 2-8.*
NOTES: Reprinted from, Transactions and Studies of the College of Physicians of Philadelphia Ser. 5, 2: 223-235, 1980.
LEVEL: I LANG: Eng SIRC ARTICLE NO: 104119

NURSING

Jahre, T. Portraettet: Tuulikki Jahre. (Portrait: Tuulikki Jahre (interview by Inger Lernevall).) *Vardfacket (Stockholm) 8 (17), 28 Sept 1984, 16-17.*
LEVEL: B LANG: Swe

Leone, R. Sports medicine for nurses? *Canadian nurse (Montreal) 80(6), Jun 1984, 44-46.*
LEVEL: B LANG: Eng SIRC ARTICLE NO: 102597

OPHTHALMOLOGY

Dobromyslov, A.N. Maimulov, V.G. Morfo-funktsional'noe sostoianie organizma doshkol'nikov, stradaiushchikh kosoglaziem i slabovideniia. (Morphofunctional body status of preschoolers suffering from strabismus and asthenopia.) *Oftalmologicheskii zhurnal (Odessa) 3, 1984, 130-133.*
LEVEL: I LANG: Rus

Horvath, L. Matyiko, F. Vass, J. A szemeszeti vizsgalatok jelentoesege a sportorvosi gyakorlatban. (The importance of ophthalmologic examination in the practice of sport medicine.) *Orvosi hetilap (Budapest) 125(11), 11 Mar 1984, 649-651.*
LEVEL: I LANG: Hun

OPTOMETRY

Verma, S. Vision screening of specialized populations. *American journal of optometry and physiological optics (Baltimore) 61(6), Jun 1984, 367-370.*
ABST: This paper describes the vision screening tests for specialized populations as used by the Community Eye Care Services Program of the Pennsylvania College of Optometry. Referral criteria have been elaborated. This paper is designed to help those who are interested in organizing such a screening.
LEVEL: I LANG: Eng SIRC ARTICLE NO: 102613

OPTOMETRY - CONTACT LENSES

Blau, M. The ultimate guide to contact lens. *Referee (Franksville, Wis.) 9(1), Jan 1984, 48-52.*
LEVEL: B LANG: Eng SIRC ARTICLE NO: 097589

Herold, J. The active person's guide to contact lenses: how to choose the right lens for your lifestyle. *New body (New York 3(5), Sept 1984, 62-64;72.*
LEVEL: B LANG: Eng SIRC ARTICLE NO: 173290

ORTHOPEDICS

Bouche, R.T. Kuwada, G.T. Equinus deformity in the athlete. (Refs: 15)*Physician and sportsmedicine 12(1), Jan 1984, 81-86;91.*
ABST: The authors describe the types of equinus: the ankle equinus, the gastrocnemius and/or soleus equinus, the metatarsal equinus and the forefoot equinus. These types are subsequently divided in 3 classes: acquired, congenital and transitional equinus. The effects of equinus on the biomechanics of sprinting, running, and walking are evaluated. Currently available treatment methods are presented.
LEVEL: A LANG: Eng SIRC ARTICLE NO: 091503

Davenport, M.P. Jackson, E.A. Use of a sports medicine clinic in a family practice residency. (Refs: 17)*Journal of family practice (New York) 19(2), Aug 1984, 225-228.*
LEVEL: I LANG: Eng SIRC ARTICLE NO: 104112

Leach, R.E. Presidential address of the American Orthopaedic Society for sports medicine. *American journal of sports medicine (Baltimore) 12(6), Nov/Dec 1984, 413-416.*
CONF: American Orthopaedic Society for Sports Medicine. Meeting (1984 : Anaheim, Cal.).
LEVEL: B LANG: Eng SIRC ARTICLE NO: 104005

Lysholm, J. Nordin, M. Ekstrand, J. Gillquist, J. The effect of a patella brace on performance in a knee extension strength test in patients with patellar pain. (Refs: 16)*American journal of sports medicine (Baltimore, Md.) 12(2), Mar/Apr 1984, 110-112.* ABST: Twenty-four patients performed knee extension exercise with and without a knee brace. Twenty-one patients (88%) improved their force development when they used the brace. These results support the assumption that the major pathology in patients with patellofemoral pain is a lateral slipping of the patella which, in the present study, was eliminated by the use of the knee brace with a lateral pad.
LEVEL: A LANG: Eng SIRC ARTICLE NO: 094429

McArdle, W.D. Goldstein, L.B. Last, F.C. Spina, R. Lichtman, S. Meyer, J.E. Berger, A.I. Temporomandibular joint repositioning and exercise performance: a double-blind study. (Refs: 20)*Medicine and science in sports and exercise (Indianapolis) 16(3), June 1984, 228-233.* ABST: In the present study, the effects of temporomandibular joint (TM) repositioning by use of an acrylic appliance on maximum and submaximum physiologic and performance measures were evaluated in seven male and four female volunteers with documented TMJ malalignment. Subjects were randomly assigned to each of four conditions: 1) normal, without a bite splint, 2) with a placebo splint with no occlusal contact so as to maintain normal jaw position, 3) with a splint that optimized jaw position, and 4) with a splint that magnified the subjects normal degree of malocclusion. Measurements were taken of visual reaction time and movement time, muscular strength of the grip, elbow flexors, and leg extensors, submaximal and maximal oxygen uptake, perceived exertion, anaerobic power output, and all-out working capacity in both arm and leg exercise on a cycle ergometer. Analysis of variance for repeated measures indicated that in no instance were the differences in mean scores on physiologic and performance measures with TMJ repositioning or placebo statistically significant when compared with the normal condition.
LEVEL: A LANG: Eng SIRC ARTICLE NO: 108590

Reasoner, A.E. A western states survey of certified athletic trainers' use of joint mobilization in treatment programs. Eugene, Ore.: Microform Publications, University of Oregon, 1984. 2 microfiches : negative, ill. ; 11 x 15 cm.
NOTES: Thesis (M.S.) - University of Oregon, 1982; (xiii, 112 leaves); vita; includes bibliography.
LEVEL: A LANG: Eng UO84 139-140

OTORHINOLARYNGOLOGY

Juto, J.E. Lundberg, C. Nasal mucosa reaction, catecholamines and lactate during physical exercise. *Acta otolaryngologica (Stockholm) 98(5/6), Nov/Dec 1984, 533-542.* ABST: This study examined the effects of exercise on mucosal congestion and blood concentrations of lactate, epinephrine and nor-epinephrine. Of 7 subjects, 6 showed mucosal decongestion during exercise. An increase of nor-epinephrine concentration was observed when half of the mucosal decongestion ability was utilized, while concentration of both lactate and epinephrine did not rise until almost maximal decongestion was established.
LEVEL: A LANG: Eng SIRC ARTICLE NO: 106578

L'oreille humaine. *Aeroscope (Montreal) 1, nov 1984, 8-9.*
NOTES: Tire de, Aviation medical bulletin, novembre 1983.
LEVEL: LANG: Fr SIRC ARTICLE NO: 109173

Pichanic, M. Mudrak, J. Preventivny vyznam vysetrenia vestibularnej reaktivity a adaptability. (Preventive significancy of studying vestibular reactivity and adaptability.) *Ceskoslovenska otolaryngologie (Prague) 33(3), June 1984, 179-184.*
LEVEL: A LANG: Slo

Schuller, D.E. Bruce, R.A. Ear, nose, throat, and eye. (Refs: 2)
NOTES: In, Strauss, R.H. (ed.), Sports medicine, Philadelphia ; Toronto, Saunders, 1984, p. 175-189.
LEVEL: A LANG: Eng RC1210 17196

Shevtsov, V.V. Tselenapravlennaia trenirovka vestibuliarnoi ustoichivosti studentov v protsesse zaniatii po fizicheskomu vospitaniiu. (Targeted training of vestibular resistance in students during physical education classes.) *Fiziologiya cheloveka (Moscow) 10(4), Jul/Aug 1984, 589-593.*
LEVEL: A LANG: Rus

Wahbeh-Foster, E. A comparison of selected muscle strength tests and endurance in children with vestibular deficits and children with normal vestibular functions. Eugene, Ore.: Microform Publications, University of Oregon, 1984. 2 microfiches : negative, ill. ; 11 x 15 cm.
NOTES: Thesis (M.S.) - University of Kansas, 1981; (ix, 148 leaves); includes bibliography.
LEVEL: A LANG: Eng UO84 413-414

PEDIATRICS

Boileau, R.A. Advances in pediatric sport sciences. Volume 1: biological issues. Champaign, Ill.: Human Kinetics Publishers, c1984. viii, 211 p. (Advances in pediatric sport sciences; v.1.)
NOTES: Includes bibliographies. ISSN: 0748-6375.
LEVEL: A LANG: Eng ISBN: 0-931250-71-4 RJ125 20044

Goldberg, B. Pediatric sports medicine. (Refs: 412)
NOTES: In, Scott, W.N. (ed.) et al., Principles of sports medicine, Baltimore, Williams & Wilkins, c1984, p. 403-426.
LEVEL: A LANG: Eng RC1210 18016

Goldberg, B. The pediatrician and athletic injuries. *Pediatric annals (New York) 13(8), Aug 1984, 596-600.*
LEVEL: I LANG: Eng

Mandel, C. Hennequet, A. Une enquete nationale sur les pediatres et le sport. (Refs: 13)*Dans, Mandel, C. (ed.), Le medecin, l'enfant et le sport, Paris, (Vigot), c1984, p. 15-23.*
LEVEL: I LANG: Fr RC1218.C45 18886

Mandel, C. Contenus et objectifs d'une consultation pediatrique hospitaliere. (Refs: 10)*Dans, Mandel, C. (ed.), Le medecin, l'enfant et le sport, Paris, (Vigot), c1984, p. 97-105.*
LEVEL: I LANG: Fr RC1218.C45 18886

Micheli, L.J. Pediatric and adolescent sports medicine. Boston ; Toronto: Little, Brown, c1984. xv, 218 p. : ill.
NOTES: Includes bibliographies.
LEVEL: I LANG: Eng ISBN: 0-316-56949-6 LC CARD: 83-81536 RC1210 17791

PHILOSOPHY

Cmich, D.E. Theoretical perspectives of holistic health. (Refs: 14)*Journal of school health 54(1), Jan 1984, 30-32.*
LEVEL I LANG: Eng SIRC ARTICLE NO: 090064

PHYSICAL EXAMINATION

Jokl, P. The medical evaluation of the athlete patient. Part II. (Refs: 2)*AMJA newsletter Feb 1984, 4.*
LEVEL: B LANG: Eng SIRC ARTICLE NO: 092936

Lombardo, J.A. Pre-participation physical evaluation. (Refs: 21)*Primary care: clinics in office practice (Philadelphia) 11(1), Mar 1984, 3-21.*
LEVEL: B LANG: Eng SIRC ARTICLE NO: 100735

Martini, G. Delli Colli, G. Aspetti medico-legali dell'attivita di indagine sulla idoneita alla pratica sportiva. The medicolegal aspects of assessment of fitness for sport. (Refs: 9)*Italian journal of sports traumatology (Milano, Italy) 6(2), Apr/Jun 1984, 105-111.*
CONF: Italian Society of Sports Traumatology. Congress (1st : 1983 : Rome).
ABST: This paper examines the concepts of ability, physical fitness, aptitude, and sport ability with respect to the examination of individuals wanting to participate in competitive sports. The completeness of health examinations is becoming more important with the emergence of professional liability on the part of the physician. The authors propose the introduction of a standard examination form to be completed by both the physician and the patient.
LEVEL: A LANG: It Eng SIRC ARTICLE NO: 099097

Myers, G.C. Garrick, J.G. The preseason examination of school and college athletes. (Refs: 12)
NOTES: In, Strauss, R.H. (ed.), Sports medicine, Philadelphia ; Toronto, Saunders, 1984, p. 237-249.
LEVEL: A LANG: Eng RC1210 17196

Poole, S.R. Schmitt, B.D. Sophocles, A. Cullen, J. Kharas, A. Updike, J. The family physician's role in school health. *Journal of family practice (New York) 18(6), Jun 1984, 843-848;851;854-856.*
LEVEL: B LANG: Eng SIRC ARTICLE NO: 102476

Preparticipation exams: when to give them, what to include. *First aider (Gardner, Kan.) 53(7), Summer 1984, 1;4-5.*
LEVEL: B LANG: Eng SIRC ARTICLE NO: 096043

Runyan, D.K. Essentials of sports physicals for young athletes. *Sports medicine digest (Van Nuys, Calif.) 6(5), May 1984, 3-4.*
LEVEL: B LANG: Eng SIRC ARTICLE NO: 100750

Tucker, J.B. Marron, J.T. The qualification/disqualification process in athletics. *American family physician (Kansas City, Mo.) 29(2), Feb 1984, 149-154.*
LEVEL: B LANG: Eng SIRC ARTICLE NO: 099108

Verstappen, F.T.J. Effectivity and efficiency of medical examination in sports. *International journal of sports medicine (Stuttgart) Suppl. 5, Nov 1984, 7-9.*
CONF: International Congress on Sports and Health (1983 : Maastricht, Netherlands).
LEVEL: B LANG: Eng SIRC ARTICLE NO: 104154

PHYSICIAN - ROLE AND RESPONSIBILITY

Brukner, P. The role of the team doctor: a report from the World University Games, Edmonton, Canada. (Refs: 6)*Sport health (Pennant Hills, Aust.) 2(1), 1984, 21-22.*
ABST: A report from the World University Games, Edmonton, Canada 1983, by the doctor for the Australian team. The following are included: preparation on arrival, training, competition, femininity testing, drug testing, injuries, illness, professional contact, conference, the games, the doctor. Includes a list of equipment and medications required by the team doctor.
LEVEL: B LANG: Eng SIRC ARTICLE NO: 094415

Garfinkel, D. The role of the team physician. (Refs: 19)
NOTES: In, Birrer, R.B. (ed.), Sports medicine for the primary care physician, Norwalk, Conn., Appleton-Century-Crofts, c1984, p. 5-13.
LEVEL: I LANG: Eng RC1210 17030

McKeag, D.B. Brody, H. Hough, D.O. Medical ethics in sport. (Refs: 13)*Physician and sportsmedicine (Minneapolis, Minn.) 12(8), Aug 1984, 145-148;150.*
LEVEL: B LANG: Eng SIRC ARTICLE NO: 097605

Moore, M. Doc shock: how to find a good practitioner. *Bicycling (Emmaus, Pa.) 25(9), Nov/ Dec 1984, 38-39;48.*
LEVEL: B LANG: Eng SIRC ARTICLE NO: 100744

Murray, T.H. Divided loyalties in sports medicine. (Refs: 10)*Physician and sportsmedicine (Minneapolis, Minn.) 12(8), Aug 1984, 134-138;140.*
LEVEL: B LANG: Eng SIRC ARTICLE NO: 097606

Shaffer, T.E. Duties of the team physician. *Sports medicine digest (Van Nuys, Calif.) 6(5), May 1984, 4.*
LEVEL: B LANG: E SIRC ARTICLE NO: 100752

Sherman, M.F. The team doctor in the computer age. *Scholastic coach (New York) 54(1), Aug 1984, 46-47;68.*
LEVEL: B LANG: Eng SIRC ARTICLE NO: 099103

Stackpole, J.W. The team physician. *Pediatric annals (New York) 13(8), Aug 1984, 592-594.*
LEVEL: I LANG: Eng

Taunton, J.E. The role of the chief medical officer. *Canadian Academy of Sport Medicine newsletter (Ottawa) 5(3), 1984, 26-29.*
LEVEL: B LANG: Eng SIRC ARTICLE NO: 100764

Wallace, P.G. Haines, A.P. General practitioner and health promotion: what patients think. *British medical journal (clinica research) (London) 289(6444), 1 Sept 1984, 534-536.*
LEVEL: I LANG: Eng SIRC ARTICLE NO: 104155

PODIATRY

Goulart, F.S. Feet first: a guide to healthy feet. *National racquetball (Glenview, Ill.) 13(10), Oct 1984, 42-43.*
LEVEL: LANG: Eng SIRC ARTICLE NO: 105339

Smith, R.W. Reynolds, J.C. Stewart, M.J. Hallux valgus assessment: report of research committee of American Orthopaedic Foot and Ankle Society. (Refs: 38)*Foot & ankle (Baltimore, Md.) 5(2), Sept/ Oct 1984, 92-103.*
LEVEL: I LANG: Eng SIRC ARTICLE NO: 099104

SLEEP

Bunnell, D.E. Bevier, W.C. Horvath, S.M. Sleep interruption and exercise. *Sleep (New York) 7(3), 1984, 261-271.*
LEVEL: A LANG: Eng

Horne, J.A. Pettitt, A.N. Sleep deprivation and the physiological response to exercise under steady-state conditions in untrained subjects. *Sleep (New York) 7(2), 1984, 168-179.*
ABST: This study tested seven subjects who underwent 72 hours of total sleep deprivation daily at 04:00 and 16:00 on a bicycle ergometer at 40, 60 and 80 per cent of maximum oxygen consumption. The physiological ability to do work of the type and duration here was not adversely affected by the sleep deprivation.
LEVEL: A LANG: Eng SIRC ARTICLE NO: 102786

Legg, S.J. Haslam, D.R. Effect of sleep deprivation on self-selected workload. *Ergonomics (London) 27(4), Apr 1984, 389-396.*
LEVEL: A LANG: Eng

Martin, B.J. Chen, H.I. Sleep loss and the sympathoadrenal response to exercise. (Refs: 26)*Medicine and science in sports and exercise 16(1), 1984, 56-59.*
ABST: Comparisons were made between 2 groups of subjects exercising on a treadmill after a normal sleep and after fifty hours of sleep deprivation. The physiological sympathetic responses to exercise were similar for both groups. However, the sleep-deprived group reduced their time to exhaustion by 20%. Other factors may have contributed to this reduction.
LEVEL: A LANG: Eng SIRC ARTICLE NO: 091750

McMurray, R.G. Brown, C.F. The effect of sleep loss on high intensity exercise and recovery. *Aviation space and environmental medicine (Washington) 55(11), Nov 1984, 1031-1035.*
LEVEL: A LANG: Eng

Nowak, S. Blaszczyk, B. Zespol Kleine-Levina (opis przypadku). (Klein-Levin syndrome (case report).) *Neurologia i neurochirurgia polska (Warsaw) 18(2), Mar/Apr 1984, 179-181.*
ABST: The authors observed this syndrome in a 17-year-old boy weighing 86 kg and training in weight-lifting. Between 10 and 20 months he had periods of physiological sleep lasting on the average 7 days, with voracious appetite and dysphoris. EDP in the cerebrospinal fluid was raised - 0.4 micrograms/ml. The results of other laboratory investigations were normal. Since about 3 months the patient has been completely healthy and his scholastic progress is good. The authors suspect that excessive exertion may be a causative factor for this syndrome when it occurs at the time of adolescence.
LEVEL: I LANG: Pol

Paxton, S.J. Trinder, J. Shapiro, C.M. Adam, K. Oswald, I. Graef, K.J. Effect of physical fitness and body composition on sleep and sleep-related hormone concentrations. *Sleep (New York) 7(4), 1984, 339-346.*
LEVEL: A LANG: Eng

Sawka, M.N. Gonzalez, R.R. Pandolf, K.B. Effects of sleep deprivation on thermoregulation during exercise. *American journal of physiology (Bethesda, Md.) 246(1 Pt 2), Jan 1984, R72-R77.*
ABST: Five physically fit men completed a practice, a control and a sleep deprivation exercise test. The results indicate that sleep deprivation decreases evaporative and dry heat loss during moderate intensity exercise.
LEVEL: A LANG: Eng SIRC ARTICLE NO: 099263

Shapiro, C.M. Warren, P.M. Trinder, J. Paxton, S.J. Oswald, I. Flenley, D.C. Catterall, J.R. Fitness facilitates sleep. (Refs: 24)*European journal of applied physiology and occupational physiology (Berlin, W.G.) 53(1), 1984, 1-4.*
ABST: Eight army recruits were studied at the start, middle, and end of their initial 18-week training programme. At each point the subjects were studied for four consecutive nights in the sleep laboratory. Within 2 days of the sleep recordings (but never on the same day) each subject spent 2 non-consecutive days in the exercise laboratory. On the 1st day a maximum oxygen consumption measurement was performed on a treadmill and on the 2nd day a 24-min progressive exercise bicycle ergometer test was carried out. Slow wave sleep (SWS) as a percentage of total sleep time increased significantly between the start and the measurements at 9 and 18 weeks, being 21.9 per cent, 29.9 per cent, and 28.5 per cent respectively. Anaerobic threshold increased significantly over the first 9 weeks and continued to increase to the end of the training period. With increase in fitness, sleep onset latency and wake time improved.
LEVEL: A LANG: Eng SIRC ARTICLE NO: 104147

Torsvall, L. Akerstedt, T. Lindbeck, G. Effects on sleep stages and EEG power density of different degrees of exercise in fi subjects. (Refs: 28)*Electroencephalography and clinical neurophysiology (Limerick) 57(4), Apr 1984, 347-353.*
ABST: The effects of exercise on the sleep of 6 men aged between 30 and 35 years were investigated in this study. Subjects were exposed to four conditions: 1) sleep after a day with no running; 2) sleep after a day with a moderate training run (15-20 km); 3) the first night after an extremely exacting race (30 or 43 km); 4) the second night after the race. The race produced a delay and decrease of REM sleep, an increase of stage 2 sleep and a weak decrease of SWS latency. An increase of EEG power density was observed after physical activity.
LEVEL: A LANG: Eng SIRC ARTICLE NO: 100927

Walsh, B.T. Puig-Antich, J. Goetz, R. Gladis, M. Novacenko, H. Glassman, A.H. Sleep and growth hormone secretion in women athletes. *Electromyography and clinical neurophysiology (Louvain) 57(6), Jun 1984, 528-531.*
ABST: Assessments of growth hormone secretion and sleep pattern of six women athletes were performed in this study. More stage 4 sleep, less REM activity and a similar REM density were observed in athletes when compared with 5 normal women. The nocturnal secretion of growth hormone was higher in the first hour following sleep onset in the athletes.
LEVEL: A LANG: Eng SIRC ARTICLE NO: 102980

SURGERY

Bergan, J.J. There is no second. Presidential address. Society for vascular surgery. *Journal of vascular surgery (St. Louis Mo.) 1(6), Nov 1984, 723-726.*
LEVEL: I LANG: Eng

Courroy, J.B. Daubinet, G. La meniscectomie arthroscopique. *Cinesiologie: medecine du sport*

(Paris) 98, nov/dec 1984, 477-482.
RESUME: La technique de meniscectomie sous arthroscopie est decrite ainsi que les suites post-operatoires et le materiel utilise. Si toute meniscectomie est techniquement possible sous arthroscopie, un bilan soigneux du genou est un prealable indispensable pour ne pas meconnaitre une lesion ligamentaire associee. Cette methode offre de nombreux avantages: diagnostic fiable, hospitalisation courte (24 h), marche normale en quelques jours, reprise du sport a 1 mois sans aucun probleme dans 70 pour cent des cas.
LEVEL: A LANG: Fr SIRC ARTICLE NO: 104110

Mariani, P.P. Ferretti, A. Puddu, G.C. Rimozione artroscopica di corpi liberi endoarticolari del ginocchio. Tecnica e risultati. The removal of loose bodies from the knee under arthroscopic control. Technique and results. (Refs: 3)*Italian journal of sports traumatology (Milano, Italy) 6(4), Oct/Dec 1984, 271-281.*
ABST: Our technique is described and the results reported at 40 arthroscopic operations for the removal of loose bodies from the knee. Apart from its well-known advantages, the closed technique permits detection of transradiant loose bodies which are not detectable at pre-operative radiography, and the removal of loose bodies from areas of difficult access by arthrotomy.
LEVEL: A LANG: It Eng SIRC ARTICLE NO: 105347

McClelland, C.J. Arthroscopy and arthroscopic surgery of the knee. *Physiotherapy (London) 70(4), 10 Apr 1984, 154-156.*
LEVEL: I LANG: Eng SIRC ARTICLE NO: 096034

Peek, R.D. Haynes, D.W. Compartment syndrome as a complication of arthroscopy: a case report and a study of interstitial pressures. (Refs: 8)*American journal of sports medicine (Baltimore) 12(6), Nov/Dec 1984, 464-468.*
LEVEL: A LANG: Eng SIRC ARTICLE NO: 104134

Yates, J.W. Jackson, D.W. Current status of meniscus surgery. (Refs: 19)*Physician and sportsmedicine 12(2), Feb 1984, 51-56;59.*
LEVEL: I LANG: Eng SIRC ARTICLE NO: 091536

TESTING

All about the test Jim Fixx refused to take. (exercise stress test) *Executive fitness newsletter (Emmaus, Pa.) 15(20), 29 Sep 1984, 1-2.*
LEVEL: B LANG: Eng SIRC ARTICLE NO: 102561

Francis, K.T. Microcomputers in sports medicine. (Refs: 9)*Journal of orthopaedic and sports physical therapy (Baltimore, Md.) 6(3), Nov/Dec 1984, 198-202.*
LEVEL: I LANG: Eng SIRC ARTICLE NO: 102582

Lavoie, C. Leger, L. Exactitude de la vitesse de deroulement des electrocardiographes. *Canadian journal of applied sport sciences/Journal canadien des sciences appliquees au sport (Windsor, Ont.) 9(2), Jun 1984, 79.*
RESUME: Les auteurs verifient l'exactitude de la vitesse de deroulement d'electrocardiographes de differents marques (n 13) et modeles (n 22) en usage dans les hopitaux et universites. En general, tous les electrocardiographes semblent tres exacts et fiables pour mesurer la frequence cardiaque.
LEVEL: A LANG: Fr SIRC ARTICLE NO: 096029

UROLOGY AND UROGENITAL SYSTEM

Heaton, A. Amer, H. Bullock, R.E. Ward, M.K. Hall, R.J. Kerr, D.N. Importance of impaired exercise tolerance in patients on renal replacement therapy. *Contributions to nephrology (Basel) 41, 1984, 272-275.*
LEVEL: A LANG: Eng

Iunusov, F.A. Vliianie lechebnoi fizkul'tury na obshchee fizickeskoe sostaoianie zhenshchin s nederzhaniem mochi pri napriazhenii. (Effect of therapeutic physical exercise on the overall physical status of women with stress urinary incontinence.) *Voproso kurortologii, fizioterapii i lechebnoi fizicheskoi kultury (Moscow) 1, Jan/Feb 1984, 50.*
LEVEL: I LANG: Rus

Jones, R.L. Exercise-induced hermaturia, or bloody urine. *Running & fitness (Washington, D.C.) 16(2), Apr 1984, 8.*
LEVEL: LANG: Eng SIRC ARTICLE NO: 097600

Kettner, A. Goldberg, A. Harter, H. Endurance exercise in hemodialysis patients. Effects on the sympathetic nervous system and serum glucose regulation. *Contributions to nephrology (Basel) 41, 1984, 269-271.*
LEVEL: A LANG: Eng

Kettner, A. Goldberg, A. Hagberg, J. Delmez, J. Harter, H. Cardiovascular and metabolic responses to submaximal exercise in hemodialysis patients. *Kidney international (New York) 26(1), Jul 1984, 66-71.*
LEVEL: A LANG: Eng

Shalom, R. Blumenthal, J.A. Williams, R.S. McMurray, R.G. Dennis, V.W. Feasibility and benefits of exercise training in patients on maintenance dialysis. *Kidney international (New York) 25(6), Jun 1984, 958-963.*
ABST: Fourteen of 174 patients receiving maintenance dialysis volunteered to participate in a 12-week exercise conditioning program. Seven patients attended more than 50 per cent of the sessions held three times each week. These seven patients achieved a 42 per cent improvement in work capacity. No changes occurred in psychologic functioning, blood pressure control, hematocrit, or left ventricular ejection fraction. Seven patients attended fewer than half of the sessions and did not demonstrate improved exercise capacity. Psychologic testing at entry revealed that those who did not attend regularly had higher scores for hostility, anxiety, and depression as compared to those patients who completed the program.
LEVEL: A LANG: Eng SIRC ARTICLE NO: 104146

Wisemann, V. Kramer, W. Thormann, J. Kindler, M. Schlepper, M. Schuetterle, G. Rest and exercise response of left ventricula functions of patients on maintenance hemodialysis with and without coronary artery disease. *Contributions to nephrology (Basel) 41, 1984, 276-279.*
LEVEL: A LANG: Eng

MEMORABILIA

Ketchum, W.C. Sports collectibles for fun & profit. Toronto: HP Books, 1984?. 96 p.
LEVEL: B LANG: Eng ISBN: 0-89586-249-2

MIDDLE DISTANCE AND LONG DISTANCE RUNNING

Brannen, D. Dubious and dastardly deeds. *Running times (Woodbridge, Va.) 86, Mar 1984, 10-13.*
LEVEL: B LANG: Eng SIRC ARTICLE NO: 096953

Cottereau, S. L'art de reussir dans la course de fond. St. Affrique, France: Serge Cottereau, 1984. 228 p.
LEVEL: I LANG: F

Henderson, J. Your first race: if you get your first race correct, you'll be setting yourself up for a long career of enjoyment. *Runner's world 19(5), May 1984, 52-55;126.*
LEVEL: B LANG: Eng SIRC ARTICLE NO: 093893

Marathons, half marathons, and long distance runs: medical advice to runners. *British journal of sports medicine (Loughborough, Eng.) 18(4), Dec 1984, 275.*
CONF: London Marathon Conference (1984 : London).
NOTES: Guidelines produced by a consensus conference, convenor Dr. D. Tunstall Pedoe, Cardiac Department, St. Bartholomew's Hospital, London.
LEVEL: B LANG: Eng SIRC ARTICLE NO: 104995

ADMINISTRATION

Chriss, A. The future lies ahead: ('Everything you've always wanted to know about big time road racing but didn't know whom to ask.'). *Ohio runner (Columbus, Ohio) 6(5), Nov 1984, 9-10.*
LEVEL: B LANG: Eng SIRC ARTICLE NO: 173271

Shonebarger, M. Curren, M. What makes a good road race? *Ohio runner (Columbus, Oh.) 5(8), Apr/May 1984, 12-13.*
LEVEL: B LANG: Eng SIRC ARTICLE NO: 095461

ANTHROPOMETRY

Barlett, H.L. Mance, M.J. Buskirk, E.R. Body composition and expiratory reserve volume in female gymnasts and runners. (Refs 20)*Medicine and science in sports and exercise (Indianapolis) 16(3), June 1984, 311-315.*
ABST: Previous research in this laboratory demonstrated a reduction in expiratory reserve volume of the lungs (ERV) with increasing body fatness (percent F, by densitometry). The present study was done to determine if smaller ERV values could be demonstrated in lean female athletes with greater than normal upperbody muscle development. Expiratory reserve volume, vital capacity (VC), and segmental body volumes by densitometry were measured in members of two collegiate women's teams - gymnastics (G) (N, 10) and track (R) (N, 10). The runners provided a control group by being similar to gymnasts in age, weight, and body fatness, but they did not engage in upper-body weight training or gymnastic exercises. The two groups were not significantly different in body weight or percent F, but R subjects were taller. Expiratory reserve volume was significantly less in the gymnasts as compared to the runners. All other lung capacities as volumes were comparable in both groups.
LEVEL: A LANG: Eng SIRC ARTICLE NO: 108604

Sakajev, V. Athropometric economy. *Modern athlete and coach (Athelstone, Aust.) 22(3), Jul 1984, 24.*
NOTES: From, Legkaja Atletika (Moscow) 7, July 1982.
LEVEL: I LANG: Eng SIRC ARTICLE NO: 101707

Tremblay, A. Despres, J.P. Bouchard, C. Adipose tissue characteristics of ex-obese long-distance runners. *International journal of obesity (London) 8(6), 1984, 641-648.*
LEVEL: A LANG: Eng

BIBLIOGRAPHIES

Sport bibliography. *Track and field journal (Ottawa, Ont.) 27, Aug 1984, 33-36.*
LEVEL: B LANG: Eng SIRC ARTICLE NO: 100091

BIOGRAPHY AND AUTOBIOGRAPHY

Aitken, A. The unique partnership. (Mel Batty, Eamonn Martin) *Athletics weekly (Rochester, Kent, Eng.) 38(20), 19 May 1984, 37-39;41-43.*
LEVEL: B LANG: Eng SIRC ARTICLE NO: 096947

Aouita: master of many distances. (Said Aouita) *Track & field news (Los Altos, Calif.) 37(9), Oct 1984, 41.*
LEVEL: B LANG: Eng SIRC ARTICLE NO: 103556

Burfoot, A. The world's best at 5000: barred from the LA Olympics. (Zola Budd) *Runner's world 19(5), May 1984, 42-50;112;116;118;120;124-126.*
LEVEL: B LANG: Eng SIRC ARTICLE NO: 093877

Butler, M. Spotlight on youth: Steven Fury - no longer an unknown. *Athletics weekly (Rochester, Kent, Eng.) 38(41), 13 Oct 1984, 34-38.*
LEVEL: B LANG: Eng SIRC ARTICLE NO: 101661

Ferstle, J. A star is born: an interview with Mark Nenow, who's fast becoming America's best in the 10,000 meters. *Runner (New York) 6(9), Jun 1984, 77;96.*
LEVEL: B LANG: Eng SIRC ARTICLE NO: 101672

Goodbody, J. LA Olympians thirties style. (Jerry Cornes) *Running (London) 40, Aug 1984, 60-61.*
LEVEL: B LANG: Eng SIRC ARTICLE NO: 100050

Hawthorne, P. Moore, K. A flight to a stormy heaven. *Sports illustrated 60(15), 9 Apr 1984, 24-28;33.*
LEVEL: B LANG: Eng SIRC ARTICLE NO: 093892

Hlus, C. Alberta report: Karen Chorney. *Canadian runner (Toronto, Ont.) Jun 1984, 22-23.*
LEVEL: B LANG: Eng SIRC ARTICLE NO: 095419

Johnson, L. Steve Ovett interviewed 'down under' *Athletics weekly (Rochester, Kent, Eng.) 38(21), 26 May 1984, 34-38.*
NOTES: Reprinted from, Australian runner 1984.
LEVEL: B LANG: Eng SIRC ARTICLE NO: 095421

Jordan, T. T & FN interview: Joaquim Cruz. *Track & field news (Los Altos, Calif.) 37(9), Oct 1984, 48-49.*
LEVEL: B LANG: Eng SIRC ARTICLE NO: 103577

Joyce, G. Crothers: twenty years later. (Bill Crothers) *Canadian runner Mar 1984, 22-25.*
LEVEL: B LANG: Eng SIRC ARTICLE NO: 093902

Kardong, D. Mike Manley's not looking back. *Running times (Woodbridge, Va.) 85, Feb 1984, 18;20-21.*
LEVEL: B LANG: Eng SIRC ARTICLE NO: 098645

Kelleher, L. Roisin Smith: a quality performer. *Marathon (Charleville, Co. Cork, Ireland) 22(4), June 1984, 4-6.*
LEVEL: B LANG: Eng SIRC ARTICLE NO: 109114

Leglise, H. Andre Lavie valeur sure de 800 m. *Revue de l'Amicale des entraineurs francais d'athletisme (Paris) 89, oct/nov/dec 1984, 43-45.*
LEVEL: B LANG: Fr SIRC ARTICLE NO: 103584

Lenton, B. Steve Scott, vous connaissez? *Spiridon (Salvan, Suisse) 72, fevr/mars 1984, 25-27;29.*
LEVEL: B LANG: Fr SIRC ARTICLE NO: 100066

Macintyre, E. I enjoyed racing 42 times this year: Eric Macintyre interviews Ikem Billy on his return to Loughborough this autumn after a hectic summer. *Athletics weekly (Kent, Eng.) 38(49), 8 Dec 1984, 34-39.*
LEVEL: B LANG: Eng SIRC ARTICLE NO: 103588

Miller, D. Sebastian Coe - coming back. s.l.: Sidgwick & Jackson Ltd., 1984?. 1v.
LEVEL: B LANG: Eng

Moore, K. Strength is her strength. Jarmila Kratochvilova was an easy winner in her U.S. debut, but only in practice was her full power evident. *Sports illustrated 60(4), 30 Jan 1984, 30-31.*
LEVEL: B LANG: Eng SIRC ARTICLE NO: 091106

Moore, K. Spinning straw into gold: raised in poverty, Joaquim Cruz of Brazil became a prince in his sport after his impressive Olympic 800. *Sports illustrated (Los Angeles, Calif.) 61(28), 24-31 Dec 1984, 48-54;59.*
LEVEL: B LANG: Eng SIRC ARTICLE NO: 103595

Namkoong, S. Profile of Karen McQuilkin: long distance runner finds teamwork successful. *Ohio runner (Columbus, Ohio) 5(7), Feb/Mar 1984, 62-63.*
LEVEL: B LANG: Eng SIRC ARTICLE NO: 108669

Naudin, P. Ah la belle chose que le record. (Jules Ladoumegue) *Spiridon (Salvan, Suisse) 75, sept/oct 1984, 26-31.*
LEVEL: LANG: Fr SIRC ARTICLE NO: 108864

Needham, K. Women on the move: Anne Morie Malone. *Athletics (Willowdale, Ont.) Nov/Dec 1984, 24-25.*
LEVEL: B LANG: Eng SIRC ARTICLE NO: 177579

Neff, C. No nipping this Budd. Zola Budd won a brave, barefoot 3,000 to acquire an Olympic berth. *Sports illustrated (Chicago, Ill.) 60(25), 18 Jun 1984, 54;56.*
LEVEL: B LANG: Eng SIRC ARTICLE NO: 095443

Olympic victory inspired by love: the Tom Hampson story (part 2). *Athletics weekly (Rochester, Kent, Eng.) 38(16), 21 Apr 1984, 46;48-50.*
LEVEL: B LANG: Eng SIRC ARTICLE NO: 095448

Ovett, S. Rodda, J. Ovett - an autobiography. s.l.: Collins Willow, 1984?. 1v.
LEVEL: B LANG: Eng

Ovett: an autobiography. *Running (London) 44, Dec 1984, 50-53;75.*
NOTES: Extracted from, Ovett, S., Ovett, Collins Willow, 1984.
LEVEL: B LANG: Eng SIRC ARTICLE NO: 105010

Ovett: an autobiography: he is known throughout the world, but Steve Ovett remains the most inscrutable of men. But now his private face is revealed for the first time in Ovett extracted exclusively by Running... *Running (London) 43,*

Nov 1984, 16-22.
NOTES: Extracted from, Ovett, S., Ovett, Collins W., 1984.
LEVEL: B LANG: Eng SIRC ARTICLE NO: 105011

Profile: Lynn Williams. *Track and field journal (Ottawa, Ont.) 27, Aug 1984, 17-18.*
LEVEL: B LANG: Eng SIRC ARTICLE NO: 100082

Runner's world gold medal exclusive. Great Scott. Not since the days of Ryun has America had a miler of Steve Scott's mettle going for a medal. *Runner's world 19(2), Feb 1984, 25.*
LEVEL: B LANG: Eng SIRC ARTICLE NO: 091111

Ryun, J. Phillips, M. In quest of gold: the Jim Ryun story. 1st ed. San Francisco: Harper & Row, c1984. 1v.
NOTES: Includes index.
LEVEL: B LANG: Eng ISBN: 0060670215 LC CARD: 84-047735

Srebnitsky, A. Tatyana Kazankina - Olympic champion. *Canadian runner (Toronto) Sept/Oct 1984, 8-9.*
LEVEL: B LANG: Eng SIR ARTICLE NO: 100092

Temple, C. Zola's mixed welcome. A studious bespectacled waif named Zola Budd became 'the hottest property in athletics' on her dramatic arrival in Britain. *Running (London, Eng.) 38, Jun 1984, 42-47.*
LEVEL: B LANG: Eng SIRC ARTICLE NO: 097006

Turnbull, S. The Charlie Spedding story. *Athletics weekly (Rochester, Kent, Eng.) 38(22), 2 Jun 1984, 25-30;32.*
LEVEL: B LANG: Eng SIRC ARTICLE NO: 097011

Ward, T. A new bloom for Zola? A look at the past and the future for the controversial runner. *Athletics (Willowdale, Ont.) Nov/Dec 1984, 16-17.*
LEVEL: B LANG: Eng SIRC ARTICLE NO: 177574

Watman, M. The shy hero who won for Britain in Los Angeles...52 years ago. *Athletics weekly (Rochester, Kent) 38(15), 14 Ap 1984, 14;16-22;24-25.*
NOTES: The Tom Hampson story (Part I).
LEVEL: B LANG: Eng SIRC ARTICLE NO: 093961

Watman, M. The supermilers: the four minute barrier... and beyond. *Athletics weekly (Rochester, Kent, Eng.) 38(18), 5 May 1984, 38-39;41-42;44-46;48-50.*
LEVEL: B LANG: Eng SIRC ARTICLE NO: 095475

Watman, M. The Zola Budd phenomenon. *Athletics weekly (Rochester, Kent, Eng.) 38(17), 28 Apr 1984, 52-54.*
LEVEL: B LANG: Eng SIRC ARTICLE NO: 095476

Watman, M. The rise of 'Jones the record'. *Athletics weekly (Kent, Eng.) 38(44), 3 Nov 1984, 44-46;48-49.*
LEVEL: B LANG: Eng SIRC ARTICLE NO: 173963

Whitefield, N. The man behind the Turner Report. Nigel Whitefield profiles and interviews Dr. Mike Turner. *Athletics weekly 38(9), 3 Mar 1984, 46-47;49-51;53-54.*
LEVEL: B LANG: Eng SIRC ARTICLE NO: 093963

Whitefield, N. The man who revolutionised the course of distance running: Dave Bedford. *Athletics weekly (Rochester, Kent, Eng.) 38(28), 14 Jul 1984, 42-46;48-49.*
LEVEL: B LANG: Eng SIRC ARTICLE NO: 098697

Whitefield, N. Jack Buckner - almost a star. *Athletics weekly (Rochester, Kent, Eng.) 38(39), 29*

Sept 1984, 49-50;52-54.
LEVEL: B LANG: Eng SIRC ARTICLE NO: 101720

Whitefield. N. John Whetton - 'king of the boards'. *Athletics weekly (Rochester, Kent, Eng.) 38(36), 8 Sept 1984, 64-66;68-70.*
LEVEL: B LANG: Eng SIRC ARTICLE NO: 100104

Williams, S. Jack Tait: a grandson profiles one of Canada's forgotten running heroes. *Athletics (Willowdale, Ont.) Nov/Dec 1984, 10-12.*
LEVEL: B LANG: Eng SIRC ARTICLE NO: 177571

Zola Budd: the 17 year old former South African running prodigy is at the centre of a raging controversy in England after gaining British citizenship less than ten days after applying. *Athletics (Willowdale, Ont.) Jun 1984, 14-17.*
LEVEL: B LANG: Eng SIRC ARTICLE NO: 098699

Zola, ou la rage de vaincre. *Spiridon (Salvan, Suisse) 74, juil/aout 1984, 14-19.*
LEVEL: B LANG: Fr SIRC ARTICLE NO: 105042

BIOMECHANICS

Lui, M.L. The kinematic analysis of male and female distance runners in treadmill running. Eugene, Ore.: Microform Publications, University of Oregon, 1984. 2 microfiches : negative ; 11 x 15 cm.
NOTES: Thesis (M.S.) - University of Wisconsin-La Crosse, 1981; (vii, 105 leaves); includes bibliography.
LEVEL: A LANG: Eng UO84 293-294

Steinberg, M.C. Variability of selected ground reaction force parameters during running. Eugene, Ore.: Microform Publications, University of Oregon, 1984. 2 microfiches : negative, ill. ; 11 x 15 cm.
NOTES: Thesis (M.S.) - University of Oregon, 1982; (x, 110 leaves); vita; includes bibliography.
LEVEL: A LANG: Eng UO84 55-56

White, C.A. The effects of selected running shoes and orthotic devices on ground reaction force parameters. Eugene, Ore.: Microform Publications, University of Oregon, 1984. 2 microfiches : negative, ill. ; 11 x 15 cm.
NOTES: Thesis (M.S.) - University of Oregon, 1982; (x, 120 leaves); vita; includes bibliography.
LEVEL: A LANG: Eng UO84 76-77

CHILDREN

Cawden, J.E. The child and running: theoretical implications for developmental research. (Refs: 16)*TAHPERD journal (Austin, Tex.) 52(3), May 1984, 6-7;32.*
LEVEL: I LANG: Eng SIRC ARTICLE NO: 109094

Gras, R. Des 'aleas' dans la saison d'un jeune athlete de demi-fond aux aleas du demi-fond francais. *Revue de l'Amicale des entraineurs francais d'athletisme (Paris) 86, janv/fevr/mars 1984, 47-48.*
LEVEL: B LANG: Fr SIRC ARTICLE NO: 095410

Harvey, H. 'The young endurance runner'. (Refs: 5)*Athletics coach (London) 18(3), Sept 1984, 3-7.*
LEVEL: B LANG: Eng SIRC ARTICLE NO: 100052

COACHING

Emery, D. Straight from the coach's mouth. *Running (London) 43, Nov 1984, 58-59;89.*
LEVEL: B LANG: Eng SIRC ARTICLE NO: 104967

Jugan, A. Coaching middle distance runners. *Track and field quarterly review (Kalamazoo, Mich.) 84(3), Fall 1984, 13-18.*
NOTES: Reprinted from, the Twentieth Annual Clinic Notes, Michigan Interscholastic Track Coaches' Association, Jan 1978.
LEVEL: B LANG: Eng SIRC ARTICLE NO: 096974

Lenton, B. New Zealand runner interview: Franz Stampfl. *New Zealand runner (Auckland, N.Z.) 32, May/Jun 1984, 54-56;59-63.*
LEVEL: B LANG: Eng SIRC ARTICLE NO: 098651

Parker, J.L. Patience for the distance. (Bob Sevene) *Runner (New York) 6(6), Mar 1984, 68-73.*
LEVEL: B LANG: Eng SIRC ARTICLE NO: 100076

Wilson, N. From shipbuilder to champion-maker: some people think Jimmy Hedley is a fool to let 1,500m World Champion Steve Cram play soccer, but Neil Wilson finds that 'Hotfoot Hedley' knows what he's doing. *Running (London) 44, Dec 1984, 36-39.*
LEVEL: B LANG: Eng SIRC ARTICLE NO: 105037

COUNTRIES AND REGIONS

Stapleton, P. The Asian runner: a look at the obstacles hindering the emergence of world class runners from Asia. *Athletics (Willowdale, Ont.) Nov/Dec 1984, 18-19.*
LEVEL: B LANG: Eng SIRC ARTICLE NO: 177576

DISABLED

O'Malley, A.E. I have multiple sclerosis: the victim of a crippling disease won't let illness hold her back, and running keeps her on the road to health and a full life. (Anne O'Malley) *Runner's world 19(5), May 1984, 70-74.*
LEVEL: B LANG: Eng SIRC ARTICLE NO: 092824

DRUGS, DOPING AND ERGOGENIC AIDS

Gledhill, N. Bicarbonate ingestion and anaerobic performance. (Refs: 11)*Sports medicine (Auckland, N.Z.) 1(3), May/Jun 1984 177-180.*
ABST: This review discusses the research pertaining to 'soda loading' (bicarbonate ingestion) as a method of increasing running performance in middle distance events. The implications for sport and doping controls are also reviewed. The author provides a general mechanism for the observation that soda loading improves running performance. The correct dosage to achieve this effect is given. The author concludes by noting that soda loading contravenes the doping policy of athletic organizations and will be quite easy to detect should the need arise.
LEVEL: A LANG: Eng SIRC ARTICLE NO: 096965

Stephan, H. Jousselin, E. Questel, R. Lecomte, A. Experimentation de l'eleutherocoque en athletisme au cours d'un cycle d'entrainement a dominante aerobie. (Refs: 21)*Cinesiologie 92/93, nov/dec 1983-janv/fevr 1984, 97-103.*
NOTES: Numero special: Medecine du sport et thermalisme.
RESUME: Cette etude visait a evaluer les effets de la poudre d'Eleutherocoque sur un groupe de 8 coureurs de demi-fond au cours d'un entrainement anaerobique. 12 athletes servirent de groupe temoin. Une amelioration sensible du VO2 max, des seuils aerobie et anaerobie, et de la puissance maximale aerobie fut constatee chez les deux groupes. Les auteurs notent une amelioration plus importante chez les athletes ayant pris de l'Eleutherocoque.
LEVEL: A LANG: Fr SIRC ARTICLE NO: 093950

Virtanen, R. Burfoot, A. The Olympic drug bust. A test for banned substances cost Finnish star Martti Vainio his medal in th 10,000 and cast his homeland into mourning. He admitted to B-12 injections, but not to the knowledge that they contained steroids. *Runners world (Mountain View, Calif.) 19(12), Dec 1984, 80-83;85-86.*
LEVEL: B LANG: Eng SIRC ARTICLE NO: 100545

INJURIES AND ACCIDENTS

American College Sports Medicine position stand on prevention of thermal injuries during distance running. (Refs: 48)*Sports medicine bulletin (Indianapolis) 19(3), Jul 1984, 8-12.*
CORP: American College of Sports Medicine.
LEVEL: I LANG: Eng SIRC ARTICLE NO: 098610

Bienfaits et mefaits de la course a pied. *Athletisme et course sur route 4(62), janv 1984, 15;37.*
NOTES: Extrait de, Courir juin 1983.
LEVEL: I LANG: Fr SIRC ARTICLE NO: 093872

Caine, D.J. Lindner, K.J. Growth plate injury: a threat to young distance runners? (Refs: 31)*Physician and sportsmedicine 12(4), Apr 1984, 118-122;124.*
LEVEL: I LANG: Eng SIRC ARTICLE NO: 093879

Fink-Bennett, D.M. Benson, M.T. Unusual exercise-related stress fractures. Two case reports. *Clinical nuclear medicine (Philadelphia) 9(8), Aug 1984, 430-434.*
LEVEL: A LANG: Eng

Klein, K.K. Biomechanical problems of distance runners and joggers. (Refs: 15)
CONF: National Symposium on Teaching Kinesiology and Biomechanics in Sports (2nd : 1984 : Colorado Springs).
NOTES: In, Shapiro, R. and Marett, J.R. (eds.), Proceedings: Second National Symposium on Teaching Kinesiology and Biomechanics in Sports, Colorado Springs, Colorado, January 12-14, Dekalb, Ill., AAHPERD, 1984, p. 235-242.
LEVEL: I LANG: Eng SIRC ARTICLE NO: 101684

Lindenberg, G. Pinshaw, R. Noakes, T.D. Iliotibial band friction syndrome in runners. (Refs: 16)*Physician and sportsmedicin (Minneapolis, Minn.) 12(5), May 1984, 118-121;124;127-128;130.*
ABST: The authors describe the processes involved in a one-year study of iliotibial friction syndrome in 36 long-distance runners. A brief overview of diagnostic tests as well as conservative treatment for the syndrome is given. The authors concluded that road camber and the hardness of the running shoe appear also to be etiological factors. Conventional treatment aimed at relieving symptoms should also be accompanied by a change to softer running shoes, stretching of the iliotibial band, running on soft surfaces and avoidance of downhill or sidehill running
LEVEL: I LANG: Eng SIRC ARTICLE NO: 095432

Marathons, half marathons, and long distance runs: first aid and casualty management. *British journal of*

sports medicine (Loughborough, Eng.) 18(4), Dec 1984, 277.
CONF: London Marathon Conference (1984 : London).
NOTES: Guidelines produced by a consensus conference, convenor Dr. D. Tunstall Pedoe, Cardiac Department, St. Bartholomew's Hospital, London.
LEVEL: B LANG: Eng SIRC ARTICLE NO: 104996

Prevention of thermal injuries during distance running. (Refs: 48)Physician and sportsmedicine (Minneapolis, Minn.) 12(7), Ju 1984, 43-47;50-51.
LEVEL: B LANG: Eng SIRC ARTICLE NO: 095951

Richards, R. Richards, D. Exertion induced heat exhaustion and other medical aspects of the City-to-Surf Fun Runs, 1978-1984 (Refs: 14)Medical journal of Australia (Sydney) 141(12), 1984, 799-805.
LEVEL: I LANG: Eng SIRC ARTICLE NO: 105018

Rozycki, T.J. Oral and rectal temperatures in runners. (Refs: 7)Physician and sportsmedicine (Minneapolis, Minn.) 12(6), Ju 1984, 105-107;110.
ABST: 16 men and 7 women had their body temperature measured orally and rectally 3, 15 and 30 minutes after completing a 14 mile race in a tropical climate. The mean rectal temperature at 3 minutes after the race was 103.5 F while the mean oral temperature was 98 F. These results indicate the importance of using rectal temperature measurement in accurately assessing and diagnosing heat injury.
LEVEL: A LANG: Eng SIRC ARTICLE NO: 095455

Sainsbury, R. Medical experience of the Great North Run. British journal of sports medicine (Loughborough, Eng.) 18(4), Dec 1984, 265-267.
CONF: London Marathon Conference (1984 : London).
LEVEL: I LANG: Eng SIRC ARTICLE NO: 105020

Stebbins, F. Injury-free knees. Fun runner 5(6), Feb/Mar 1984, 39.
LEVEL: B LANG: Eng

MEDICINE

Buckman, M.T. Gastrointestinal bleeding in long-distance runners. (editorial) Annals of internal medicine (Philadelphia) 101(1), Jul 1984, 127-128.
LEVEL: B LANG: Eng SIRC ARTICLE NO: 103563

Byrd, S.A.K. The effects of iron supplementation on serum ferritin levels in male runners. Eugene, Ore.: Microform Publications, University of Oregon, 1984. 1 microfiche : negative, ill. ; 11 x 15 cm.
NOTES: Thesis (M.S.) - University of Oregon, 1983; (ix, 45 leaves); vita; includes bibliography.
LEVEL: A LANG: Eng UO84 425

Goldfarb, L.A. Plante, T.G. Fear of fat in runners. An examination of the connection between anorexia nervosa and distance running. (Refs: 4)Psychological reports (Missoula, Mont.) 55(1), 1984, 296.
LEVEL: I LANG: Eng SIRC ARTICLE NO: 099089

Jerome, J. Cooling the core: how water can help you win the race. Outside (Chicago) 9(8), Sept 1984, 23-24;26.
LEVEL: B LANG: Eng SIRC ARTICLE NO: 108866

Kavanagh, T. Distance running and cardiac rehabilitation: physiologic and psychosocial considerations. (Refs: 81)Clinics in sports medicine (Philadelphia) 3(2), Apr 1984, 513-526.
ABST: Research to date supports the contention that regular endurance exercise such as distance running has mental and physical benefits. From this research it could be extrapolated that distance running will improve the prognosis in ischemic heart disease. Although there have not been any well constructed studies which have conclusively proven such a relationship there also have not been any studies which show that exercise is hazardous for patients with ischemic heart disease. For this reason it seems sensible to advocate and support the use of distance running in the management of ischemic heart disease.
LEVEL: A LANG: Eng SIRC ARTICLE NO: 095426

Kuoppasalmi, K. Effects of side stress on human plasma hormone levels. Track and field quarterly review (Kalamazoo, Mich.) 84(3), Fall 1984, 56-58.
NOTES: Abstracted from the Academic Dissertation presented at the XIth European Track & Field Coaches Association Congress, Venice, Italy, March 17-20, 1981.
LEVEL: I LANG: Eng SIRC ARTICLE NO: 096980

Pagliano, J. Chemico surgical treatment: a chemical surgical treatment for permanent correction of ingrown nails on the long distance runner. AMJA newsletter (Hollywood, Calif.) Apr 1984, 5;7.
LEVEL: I LANG: Eng SIRC ARTICLE NO: 100075

Potera, C. GI bleeding found in long-distance runners. Physician and sportsmedicine (Minneapolis, Minn.) 12(12), Dec 1984, 29.
LEVEL: I LANG: Eng SIRC ARTICLE NO: 103603

Tripp, A.D. Nickerson, J. Maurer, W.J. Iron deficiency anemia in adolescent girls. Women's varsity sports (Kalispell, Mont. 5(3), Jan/Feb 1984, 17.
LEVEL: B LANG: Eng SIRC ARTICLE NO: 100792

Warren, B.L. Anatomical factors associated with predicting plantar fasciitis in long-distance runners. (Refs: 18)Medicine and science in sports and exercise 16(1), 1984, 60-63.
ABST: The following variables were studied in a group of subjects as to whether or not they could predict plantar fasciitis: leg length, pronation of the subtalar joint, plantar and dorsiflexion ability, arch height, body height, weight, age and miles run per week. Running over thirty miles per week appears to have a correlation with plantar fasciitis, but is not a good predictor. Other variables which correlated with the condition were also found to be poor predictors of the injury, but some factors could predict the non-sufferers.
LEVEL: A LANG: Eng SIRC ARTICLE NO: 092541

NUTRITION

Mahurin, J. Fructose facilitation: fact or fiction? (Refs: 2)Racing south (Nashville) 7(3), Sept 1984, 24-25.
LEVEL: B LANG: Eng SIRC ARTICLE NO: 104994

PERCEPTUAL MOTOR PROCESSES

Dirks, S.J. Hutton, R.S. Endurance training and short latency reflexes in man. (Refs: 33)Scandinavian journal of sports science (Helsinki, Finland) 6(1), Jul 1984, 21-26.
ABST: The influence of exercise training on reflex excitability was assessed by tendon tap (T-) and Hoffmann (H-) reflex responses in 8 long distance runners and 8 sedentary control subjects. Recordings were made from soleus and tibialis anterior muscles. There were no significant differences found between the percent gain in reflex responses of athletes vs. those of controls. However, the probability of the appearance of an M-wave, caused by direct activation of efferents, was found to be significantly greater in controls than in athletes (p.025 level) at 1.1 x Th.
LEVEL: A LANG: Eng SIRC ARTICLE NO: 103567

Montgomery, W.A. Jones, G.E. Hollandsworth, J.G. The effects of physical fitness and exercise on cardiac awareness. Biological psychology (Amsterdam) 18(1), Feb 1984, 11-22.
ABST: This experiment evaluated the role of individual difference factors in perception of heart beats (cardiac awareness). 24 male subjects who showed high and moderate levels of physical fitness were examined. Subjects differentiated between numerous trials of standing quietly on a treadmill, walking briskly on a motorized treadmill, and recovering from exercise. Results indicated that only the moderate fitness group showed heightened awareness during exercise, while both groups showed greater than chance awareness during recovery from exercise. These results fail to support notions that high fitness distance runners are highly aware of cardiac function during exercise.
LEVEL: A LANG: Eng

PHYSICAL FITNESS

de Mondenard, J.P. Les reponses du specialiste: tome 4, le jogging en 'questions', du footing a la course de fond. Paris: Editions Amphora, c1984. 228 p. : ill. (Sports & loisirs.)
NOTES: Bibliographie: p. 215-217.
LEVEL: I LANG: Fr ISBN: 2-85180-081-7 GV494 17977

Dielens, S. Pour un jogging reflechi. Bruxelles: ADEPS, 1984. 128 p. : ill.
NOTES: Bibliograhie: p. 124-127.
LEVEL: B LANG Fr GV494 17997

PHYSIOLOGY

Agnew, J.W. The relationship of LDH isoenzyme subunit ratio, muscle fiber composition, and ventilatory and lactate threshold in middle distance and long distance runners. Eugene, Ore.: Microform Publications, University of Oregon, 1984. 2 microfiches : negative, ill. ; 11 x 15 cm.
NOTES: Thesis (Ph.D.) - University of Oregon, 1983; (xi, 109 leaves); vita; includes bibliography.
LEVEL: A LANG: Eng UO84 398-399

Cade, R. Conte, M. Zauner, C. Mars, D. Peterson, J. Lunne, D. Hommen, N. Packer, D. Effects of phosphate loading on 2,3-diphosphoglycerate and maximal oxygen uptake. (Refs: 26)Medicine and science in sports and exercise (Indianapolis) 16(3), June 1984, 263-268.
ABST: The authors investigated the effects of oral phosphate loading on several parameters including plasma phosphate concentration, RBC 2,3-DPG, hematocrit and hemoglobin concentration, maximal oxygen uptake (VO2 max), and degree of lactic acidemia in 10 well-trained distance runners. After control determinations were made, either a phosphate load or a placebo was given for 3 d before the athlete was restudied. Blood samples for control value were drawn before and after a standard warm-up period after treadmill exercise at a 10 per cent grade, and at the completion of the VO2 determination. After oral phosphate loading

MIDDLE DISTANCE AND LONG DISTANCE RUNNING (continued)

there was a significant increase in serum phosphate and RBC 2,3-DPG. Maximal oxygen uptake was significantly increased and correlated with the rise in RBC 2,3-DPG.
LEVEL: A LANG: Eng SIRC ARTICLE NO: 108595

Conley, D.L. Krahenbuhl, G.S. Burkett, L.N. Millar, A.L. Following Steve Scott: physiological changes accompanying training. (Refs: 9)*Physician and sportsmedicine 12(1), Jan 1984, 103-106.*
LEVEL: I LANG: Eng SIRC ARTICLE NO: 092478

Crielaard, J.M. Pirnay, F. Qualites physiques des coureurs de fond. *Sport: Communaute francaise de Belgique (Bruxelles) 106 1984, 103-105.*
LEVEL: I LANG: Fr SIRC ARTICLE NO: 098622

Crielaard, J.M. Mouton, G. Boudart, J. Pirnay, F. Etude longitudinale de l'aptitude physique en athletisme. (Refs: 10)*Sport Communaute francaise de belgique (Bruxelles) 108, 1984, 218-221.*
LEVEL: I LANG: Fr SIRC ARTICLE NO: 103565

Garshnek, V. The effect of long-distance training on orthostatic efficiency in young adult females. Eugene, Ore.: Microform Publications, University of Oregon, 1984. 1 microfiche : negative, ill. ; 11 x 15 cm.
NOTES: Thesis (M.S.) - University of Oregon, 1982; (xii, 86 leaves); vita; includes bibliography.
LEVEL: A LANG: Eng UO84 60

Gilli, P. Vitali, E. Tataranni, G. Farinelli, A. Exercise-induced urinary abnormalities in long-distance runners. (Refs: 19) *International journal of sports medicine (Stuttgart) 5(5), Oct 1984, 237-240.*
ABST: The post-exercise urine samples from 122 long-distance runners showed evident abnormalities upon microscopic examination in 95 percent of all subjects. Proteinuria, alone or with microscopic hematuria, was frequently found. Macroscopic hematuria was a rare occurrence. The urine samples collected in 30 runners before, immediately after the race, and 6, 12, 24, 36, and 48 h later showed a significant post-race decrease in the osmolarity and a significant increase in gamma-glutamyl transferase and N-acetyl-beta-glucosaminidase enzyme activity.
LEVEL: A LANG: Eng SIRC ARTICLE NO: 104975

Heazlewood, I. Pay attention to anaerobic training. (Refs: 10)*Modern athlete and coach (Athelstone, Aust.) 22(3), Jul 1984, 29-31.*
LEVEL: I LANG: Eng SIRC ARTICLE NO: 101027

Hove, A.G. Anaerobic threshold as predictor of middle distance running performance. Eugene, Ore.: Microform Publications, University of Oregon, 1984. 2 microfiches : negative, ill. ; 11 x 15 cm.
NOTES: Thesis (M.S.) - University of Kansas, 1981; (v, 102 leaves); includes bibliography.
LEVEL: A LANG: Eng UO84 411-412

Hughson, R.L. The energy continuum - laboratory tests as predictors of endurance in long-term high intensity exercise. (Refs 15)*Track and field quarterly review (Kalamazoo, Mich.) 84(3), Fall 1984, 51-55.*
NOTES: Proceedings of the FISU Conference - Universiade '83, The University's Role in the Development of Modern Sport: Past, Present, and Future (Sanda Kereliuk, Editor), Edmonton, Alberta, July 2-4, 1983.
LEVEL: I LANG: Eng SIRC ARTICLE NO: 096970

Humphreys, J.H.L. The application of physiological measurements to training. (Refs: 25)*Carnegie research papers (Beckett Park, Leeds)*

1(6), Dec 1984, 4-7.
ABST: This brief review of the literature focuses in maximum oxygen uptake (VO2 max) during physical work, VO2 max and distance running performance, and methods of training VO2 max for distance running.
LEVEL: A LANG: Eng SIRC ARTICLE NO: 172497

Israel, S. Rational breathing. *Modern athlete and coach (Athelstone, Aust.) 22(4), Oct 1984, 39-41.*
NOTES: Translated and condensed from: Der Leichtathlet, no. 11, 1984.
LEVEL: B LANG: Eng SIRC ARTICLE NO: 104986

Janal, M.N. Colt, E.W. Clark, W.C. Glusman, M. Pain sensitivity, mood and plasma endocrine levels in man following long-distance running: effects of naloxone. *Pain (Amsterdam) 19(1), May 1984, 13-25.*
ABST: Twelve long-distance runners were evaluated on thermal ischemic, and cold pressor pain tests and on mood visual analogue scales under naloxone and saline conditions before and after a 6.3 mile run. The results show that long-distance running produces hypoalgesia and mood elevation in man. The effects of naloxone implicate endogenous opioid neural systems as mechanisms of some but not all of the run-induced alterations in mood and pain perception.
LEVEL: A LANG: Eng SIRC ARTICLE NO: 103576

Jousselin, E. Stephan, H. Le suivi medico-physiologique des coureurs de demi-fond. *Revue de l'Amicale des entraineurs francais d'athletisme (Paris) 86, janv/fevr/mars 1984, 13-16.*
LEVEL: I LANG: Fr SIRC ARTICLE NO: 095424

Jousselin, E. Handschuh, R. Stephan, H. Etude de la transition aerobie-anaerobie chez les coureurs de demi-fond francais (hommes et femmes). (Refs: 17)*Cinesiologie (Paris) 96, juil/aout 1984, 305-313.*
RESUME: Au cours de cette etude, 73 coureurs de demi-fond et de fond (hommes et femmes) sont testes sur un tapis roulant a des paliers d'intensite croissantes. Les valeurs mesurees, a chaque palier sont: l'intensite de l'exercice, la frequence cardiaque, la lactemie, et la consommation d'oxygene. L'etude demontre que l'athlete de haut niveau utilise un fort pourcentage de sa puissance maximale aerobie et de sa frequence cardiaque au niveau du seuil anaerobie.
LEVEL: A LANG: Fr SIRC ARTICLE NO: 100058

Kelly, A.E. An assessment of physiological profiles of middle-distance athletes and rugby players. (abstract) *Carnegie research papers (Beckett Park, Leeds) 1(6), Dec 1984, 35.*
CONF: Carnegie Undergraduate Research Symposium (1984 : Leeds, Eng.).
LEVEL: I LANG: Eng SIRC ARTICLE NO: 172512

Mercier, D. Leger, L. Desjardins, M. Prediction de la performance, du VO2 max et de l'endurance relative du coureur de fond. (Refs: 6)*Revue de l'entraineur janv/mars 1984, 21-25.*
LEVEL: I LANG: Fr SIRC ARTICLE NO: 092504

Mikesell, K.A. Dudley, G.A. Influence of intense endurance training on aerobic power of competitive distance runners. (Refs: 25)*Medicine and science in sports and exercise (Indianapolis) 16(4), Aug 1984, 371-375.*
ABST: This study examined the time course of the aerobic response to strenuous training in well-conditioned distance runners when intensity was held fairly constant relative to maximal aerobic power, and the effect of this training on 10-km run time. Seven runners trained 6 d/wk for 6 wk. On 3

d/wk they ran as far as possible in 40 min. with the intention of running a greater distance each run. On alternate days the subjects performed five 5-min rides on a cycle ergometer (CE) separated by 5-min intervals of jogging, with the resistance adjusted to induced peak-CE VO2 during minutes 4 and 5 of each ride. Peak-CE VO2 increased (56.1 to 65.0 ml.min-1.kg-1, P0.050 in a linear manner during the firs 5 wk. The average weekly increase was 0.11 l.min-1. Unexpectedly, peak-CE VO2 decreased significantly after week six. Treadmill VO2 max was not significantly different after training. The mean decrease (P0.05) in 10-km run time was approximately 81 s.
LEVEL: A LANG: Eng SIRC ARTICLE NO: 103593

Nice, C. Reeves, A.G. Brinck-Johnsen, T. Noll, W. The effects of pantothenic acid on human exercise capacity. (Refs: 14) *Journal of sports medicine and physical fitness (Torino) 24(1), Mar 1984, 26-29.*
ABST: 9 highly trained distance runners consumed one gram of panthothenic acid per day for two weeks while 9 others took a placebo in this double blind study. Both groups were exercised to exhaustion on a treadmill before and after the two week period. No significant effects on human exercise capacity were observed.
LEVEL: A LANG: Eng SIRC ARTICLE NO: 099256

Ohkuwa, T. Kato, Y. Katsumata, K. Nakao, T. Miyamura, M. Blood lactate and glycerol after 400-m and 3,000-m runs in sprint and long distance runners. (Refs: 27)*European journal of applied physiology and occupational physiology (Berlin) 53(3), Dec 1984, 213-218.*
ABST: Lactate, glycerol, and catecholamine in the venous blood after 400-m and 3,000-m runs were determined in eight sprint runners, eight long distance runners, and seven untrained students. In 400-m sprinting, average values of velocity, peak blood lactate, and adrenaline were significantly higher in the sprint group than in the long distance and untrained groups. In the 3,000-m run, on the other hand, average values of velocity and glycerol were significantly higher in the long distance group than in the sprint and untrained groups, but there are no significant differences in lactate levels between the three groups.
LEVEL: A LANG: Eng SIRC ARTICLE NO: 105008

Peronnet, F. Thibault, G. Consommation maximale d'oxygene, endurance et performance en course a pied. *Macolin (Suisse) 7, juil 1984, 14-17.*
LEVEL: I LANG: Fr SIRC ARTICLE NO: 101701

Peronnet, F. Thibault, G. Consommation maximale d'oxygene endurance et performance. *Revue de l'entraineur (Montreal) oct/de 1984, 20-22.*
LEVEL: I LANG: Fr SIRC ARTICLE NO: 105489

Rea, A.M. Physiological responses to repeated bouts of prolonged running. Eugene, Ore.: Microform Publications, University o Oregon, 1984. 1 microfiche : negative, ill. ; 11 x 15 cm.
NOTES: Thesis (M.S.) - Western Illinois University, 1981; (4, vii, 56 leaves); includes bibliography.
LEVEL: A LANG: Eng UO84 27

Ready, A.E. Physiological characteristics of male and female middle distance runners. (Refs: 30)*Canadian journal of applied sport sciences/Journal canadien des sciences appliquees au sport (Windsor, Ont.) 9(2), Jun 1984, 70-77.*
ABST: This study describes the physiological

characteristics of seven male and five female provincial-class middle distance runners. The author provides data on VO2 max, percent fat, power, anthropometric, and hematological measurements.
LEVEL: A LANG: Eng SIRC ARTICLE NO: 096994

Sady, S.P. Cullinane, E.M. Herbert, P.N. Kantor, M.A. Thompson, P.D. Training, diet and physical characteristics of distance runners with low or high concentrations of high density lipoprotein cholesterol. *Atherosclerosis (Amsterdam) 53(3), Dec 1984, 273-281.*
LEVEL: A LANG: Eng

Schrader, T.A. Fluid ingestion and long-distance running. Eugene, ore.: Microform Publications, University of Oregon, 1984. microfiche : negative, ill. ; 11 x 15 cm.
NOTES: Thesis (M.S.) - Arizona State University, 1982; (viii, 82, (1) leaves); vita; includes bibliography.
LEVEL: A LANG: Eng UO84 328

Sparling, P.B. Physiological determinants of distance running performance. (Refs: 30)*Physician and sportsmedicine 12(3), Ma 1984, 68-69;72;75-77.*
ABST: A model of the physiological determinants of distance running performance is presented in this paper. The three main factors considered are: aerobic capacity relative to body weight, running economy, and the percentage of aerobic capacity used during the race.
LEVEL: A LANG: Eng SIRC ARTICLE NO: 092531

Surbery, G.D. Andrew, G.M. Cervenko, F.W. Hamilton, P.P. Effects of naloxone on exercise performance. (Refs: 40)*Journal of applied physiology: respiratory, environmental and exercise physiology (Bethesda, Md.) 57(3), Sept 1984, 674-679.*
ABST: Two groups of elite middle distance runners performed an exercise protocol after double-blind injection of either naloxone or saline. No significant differences between placebo and naloxone were found in the perception of pain as assessed by a questionnaire. No physiological differences were found.
LEVEL: A LANG: Eng SIRC ARTICLE NO: 108930

Svedenhag, J. Sjoedin, B. Maximal and submaximal oxygen uptakes and blood lactate levels in elite male middle- and long-distance runners. (Refs: 26)*International journal of sports medicine (Stuttgart) 5(5), Oct 1984, 255-261.*
ABST: Twenty-seven middle- and long-distance runners and two 400-m runners were divided into six groups from 400 m up to the marathon. The maximal oxygen uptake on the treadmill was higher the longer the main distance except for the marathon runners. Running economy evaluated from oxygen uptake measurements at 15 km/h and 20 km/h did not differ significantly between the groups. The running velocity corresponding to a blood lactate concentration of 4 mmol/l (vHla 4.0) differed markedly between the groups with the highest value in the 5000-10,000-m group. The oxygen uptake (VO2) at vHla 4.0 in percentage of VO2 max did not differ significantly between the groups.
LEVEL: A LANG: Eng SIRC ARTICLE NO: 105028

Tanaka, K. Matsuura, Y. Matsuzaka, A. Hirakoba, K. Kumagai, S. Sun, S.O. Asano, K. A longitudinal assessment of anaerobic threshold and distance-running performance. (Refs: 18)*Medicine and science in sports and exercise (Indianapolis) 16(3), June 1984, 278-282.*
ABST: Longitudinal changes in the anaerobic threshold (AT) and distance-running performances (DRP) were assessed with a 4.5-month interval between the pre-, mid-, and post-tests in a relatively homogenous trained, endurance runners (mean age, 18.5 yr). Higher relationships between the DRP and AT-related attributes help up consistently over the 9-month training period. Anaerobic threshold showed a correlation higher than 0.80 with 10,000-m race time in every set of tests. When the relationships between the absolute amount of change in the VO2 at AT and the absolute amount of change in DRP were evaluated, significant correlations were found in several different time periods, Running velocity at AT also improved significantly, and was closely related to DRP changes.
LEVEL: A LANG: Eng SIRC ARTICLE NO: 108598

Thompson, P.D. Cullinane, E. Eshleman, R. Herbert, P.N. Lipoprotein changes when a reported diet is tested in distance runners. *American journal of clinical nutrition (Bethesda, Md.) 39(3), Mar 1984, 368-374.*
ABST: Ten male runners who ran 16 km per day consumed a diet for 21 days which consisted of 3354 to 3800 Kcal per day which was composed of 53 per cent carbohydrates, 15 per cent protein and 32 per cent fat. Serum was studied before and during the diet. Low density lipoprotein fell before and during the diet period while high density lipoprotein decreased during the diet period. No additional serum lipid changes were seen after 14 days on the diet. The magnitude of the lipoprotein changes were expected and the authors suggest either the diet diaries were unreliable or unaccounted for factors produced these significant effects.
LEVEL: A LANG: Eng SIRC ARTICLE NO: 100096

Thompson, P.D. Cullinane, E.M. Eshleman, R. Kantor, M.A. Herbert, P.N. The effects of high-carbohydrate and high-fat diets o the serum lipid and lipoprotein concentrations of endurance athletes. *Metabolism, clinical and experimental (New York) 33(11), Nov 1984, 1003-1010.*
LEVEL: A LANG: Eng

Upton, S.J. Hagan, R.D. Lease, B. Rosentswieg, J. Gettman, L.R. Duncan, J.J. Comparative physiological profiles among young and middle-aged female distance runners. (Refs: 24)*Medicine and science in sports and exercise 16(1), 1984, 67-71.*
ABST: Young marathoners, middle-aged marathoners, middle-aged ten kilometre runners and middle aged sedentary women were compared using physiological parameters. Both marathon groups and ten kilometre runners had similar values on the criteria measured except for resting heart rate which was higher in the ten kilometre runners. Distance running appears to increase aerobic capacity, but lipid levels seem to be unaffected by physical activity levels.
LEVEL: A LANG: Eng SIRC ARTICLE NO: 092540

Vinikka, L. Vuori, J. Ylikorkala, O. Lipid peroxides, prostacyclin, and thromboxane A2 in runners during acute exercise. (Refs: 25)*Medicine and science in sports and exercise (Indianapolis) 16(3), June 1984, 275-277.*
ABST: We studied the effect of physical activity on lipid peroxidation and on the production of antiaggregatory, vasodilatory prostacyclin

(epoprostenol, PGI2) and its endogenous antagonist, thromboxane A2 (TxA2) in 10 well-trained long-distance runners before, during, and after maximal exercise on a cycle ergometer. Pre-exercise levels of lipid peroxides plasma immunoreactive 6-keto-prostaglandin F1a (i 6-keto-PGF1a) and serum immunoreactive thromboxane B2 (i TxB2) did not differ from those of 10 non-athletic controls. Plasma i 6-keto-PGF1a was increased at the seventh minute of the exercise test, but not any more at the end of the exercise or 30 min later. Lipid peroxides or i TxB2 did not change.
LEVEL: A LANG: Eng SIRC ARTICLE NO: 108597

Ward, G.R. Basic physiology of middle distance running. *Track and field quarterly review (Kalamazoo, Mich.) 84(3), 1984, 35-39.*
LEVEL: I LANG: Eng SIRC ARTICLE NO: 097013

PHYSIOLOGY - ALTITUDE

Lenzi, G. Conconi, F. Ameliorations des capacites aerobiques chez un groupe de coureurs et de marcheurs apres un mois d'entrainement en altitude. *Revue de l'Amicale des entraineurs francais d'athletisme (Paris) 89, oct/nov/dec 1984, 15-17.*
LEVEL: I LANG: Fr SIRC ARTICLE NO: 103586

PHYSIOLOGY - MUSCLE

de Koning, F.L. Vos, J.A. Binkhorst, R.A. Vissers, A.C.A. Influence of training on the force-velocity relationship of the ar flexors of active sportsmen. (Refs: 12)*International journal of sports medicine 5(1), Feb 1984, 43-46.*
ABST: The force-velocity curve of the arm flexors of four rowers, five athletes competing in the tug-of-war, and six runners was established and periodically re-assessed throughout a year of training and competition. The results showed very few changes in the force-velocity curve of these athletes. The authors conclude that variation in type, intensity, and volume of arm training throughout a year hardly affected the course of the force-velocity curve of the arm flexors of well-trained athletes.
LEVEL: A LANG: Eng SIRC ARTICLE NO: 093670

Ready, A.E. Physiological characteristics of male and female middle distance runners. (Refs: 30)*Canadian journal of applied sport sciences/ Journal canadien des sciences appliquees au sport (Windsor, Ont.) 9(2), Jun 1984, 70-77.*
ABST: This study describes the physiological characteristics of seven male and five female provincial-class middle distance runners. The author provides data on VO2 max, percent fat, power, anthropometric, and hematological measurements.
LEVEL: A LANG: Eng SIRC ARTICLE NO: 096994

Staron, R.S. Hikida, R.S. Hagerman, F.C. Dudley, G.A. Murray, T.F. Human skeletal muscle fiber type adaptability to various workloads. *Journal of histochemistry and cytochemistry (Baltimore) 32(2), Feb 1984, 146-152.*
ABST: Muscle biopsy specimens were removed from the vastus lateralis muscles of controls, weight lifters, and distance runners. A histochemical analysis of the biopsy specimens revealed that the runners had a significantly higher percentage of fiber types I and IIC than either the controls or the weight lifters. The results of volume-percent mitochondria analysis demonstrated a strong

relationship between the ATPase activity and oxidative potential of the fiber types for all three groups. Irrespective of fiber type, there were significant differences between the groups with regard to muscle-fiber mitochondrial (runners greater than lifters greater than controls) and lipid content (runners greater than controls greater than lifters). The lifters had a significantly greater content of mitochondria than the controls, which may suggest that inactivity rather than the lifting exercise contributes to a low volume-percent mitochondria and a high percentage of type IIB fibers.
LEVEL: A LANG: Eng SIRC ARTICLE NO: 099269

PHYSIOLOGY - TEMPERATURE

Gregory, W.B. Thermoregulatory boundaries to exercise in hot, humid environments. Eugene, Ore.: Microform Publications, University of Oregon, 1984. 2 microfiches : negative, ill.; 11 x 15 cm.
NOTES: Thesis (Ph.D.) - Texas A & M University, 1979; (x, 102 leaves); vita; includes bibliography.
LEVEL: A LANG: Eng UO84 9-10

Nethery, V.M. The effect of heat stress and work on total plasma protein concentration, albumin concentration and hematocrit in endurance trained and sedentary adult females. Eugene, Ore.: Microform Publications, University of Oregon, 1984. 1 microfiche : negative, ill. ; 11 x 15 cm.
NOTES: Thesis (M.S.) - University of Oregon, 1982; (x, 69 leaves); vita; includes bibliography.
LEVEL: A LANG: Eng UO84 61

SOCIOLOGY

Carrell, C. How marathon running affects family life: peaceful co-existence? *New Zealand runner (Auckland, N.Z.)* 31, Mar/Ap 1984, 46-48.
LEVEL: B LANG: Eng SIRC ARTICLE NO: 101662

SPORTING EVENTS

Ayres, E. America's Olympic distance runners: who made it, who didn't and why. *Running times (Woodbridge, Va.)* 92, Sept 1984, 20-23;25.
LEVEL: B LANG: Eng SIRC ARTICLE NO: 101654

Coe, S. Mason, N. The nearly men. *Running (London)* 41, Sept 1984, 38-40;109.
LEVEL: B LANG: Eng SIRC ARTICLE NO: 104962

Endurance. *Athletics coach (London)* 18(4), Dec 1984, 35-44.
LEVEL: B LANG: Eng SIRC ARTICLE NO: 104968

Pennington, G. Kay, C. Round the Bays. Christchurch, N.Z.: Whitcoulls Publishers, c1984. 79 p. : ill.
LEVEL: B LANG: Eng ISBN: 0-7233-0694-X GV1062.5.R6 18412

Wischnia, B. The long distances: will the Yanks get kicked again in the steeple, 5000 and 10,000? *Runner's world* 19(4), Apr 1984, 40-47.
LEVEL: B LANG: Eng SIRC ARTICLE NO: 093966

STATISTICS AND RECORDS

Kitson, T. The ultimate mile. *New scientist (London)* 1415, 2 Aug 1984, 34.
NOTES: A mathematical analysis of the record-breaking runs of the past suggests we may already be within one second of the fastest mile possible.
LEVEL: I LANG: Eng SIRC ARTICLE NO: 100059

STRATEGY

Anderson-Jordan, T. Racing tactics in the middle distances. *Scholastic coach 53(7)*, Feb 1984, 50-51;72.
LEVEL: B LANG: En SIRC ARTICLE NO: 093868

TECHNIQUES AND SKILLS

Falcke, C. Skills in middle distance running. (Refs: 7)*Modern athlete and coach (Athelstone, Aust.)* 22(3), Jul 1984, 11-14.
NOTES: Based on extracts from the author's paper presented as, part of the level 11 coaching qualifications requirements under the National Coaching Accreditation Scheme.
LEVEL: B LANG: Eng SIRC ARTICLE NO: 101671

TESTING AND EVALUATION

Daniels, J. Tymn, M. How fast can you run? Science has the answer for some, but others learn on the roads. *Runner's world 19(5)*, May 1984, 75-76;132;136-138.
LEVEL: I LANG: Eng SIRC ARTICLE NO: 093884

Horwill, F. BMC fitness testing for middle distance. *Athletics weekly (Kent, Eng.)* 38(48), 1 Dec 1984, 39-41.
NOTES: A report on the Southern BMC Fitness Testing Project.
LEVEL: B LANG: Eng SIRC ARTICLE NO: 103575

Joussellin, E. Le suivi medical des coureurs de demi-fond. *Revue de l'Amicale des entraineurs francais d'athletisme (Paris)* 86, janv/fevr/mars 1984, 11-12.
LEVEL: B LANG: Fr SIRC ARTICLE NO: 095425

Mercier, D. Leger, L. Desjardins, M. Nomogramme pour predire la performance, le VO2 max. et l'endurance relative en course d fond. (Refs: 4)*Medecine du sport (Paris)* 58(4), 25 juil 1984, 15-21.
LEVEL: I LANG: Fr SIRC ARTICLE NO: 098658

Mercier, D. Leger, M. Desjardins, M. Prediction de la performance VO2 Max et de l'endurance relative du coureur de fond. (Refs: 6)*Track and field journal (Ottawa, Ont.)* 27, Aug 1984, 27-31.
LEVEL: I LANG: Fr SIRC ARTICLE NO: 100069

Peronnet, F. Thibault, G. Hermann: the running computer. (training methods) *Coaching review (Ottawa, Ont.)* 7, Jul/Aug 1984, 56-58.
NOTES: Translated from, La revue de l'entraineur oct/dec 1983.
LEVEL: B LANG: Eng SIRC ARTICLE NO: 095450

TRAINING AND CONDITIONING

Beyer, J. A six-minute mile: a beginning runner tells how at age 40 she tackled a six-minute mile and how you can too. McLean, Va.: EPM Pub., c1984. 1v.
LEVEL: B LANG: Eng ISBN: 0914440764 LC CARD: 84-006031

Cannon, J. Eight-week program for high school distance runners. *Fun runner (Rose Bay, Aust.)* 6(3), Aug/Sept 1984, 63-64.
NOTES: Reprinted from, Birubi Track Club Newsletter, April 1981.
LEVEL: B LANG: Eng SIRC ARTICLE NO: 106147

Christensen, S. The 800 meter runner. Training for the 800-meter run must involve concepts specific to

that event. *Athletic journal 64(7)*, Feb 1984, 26-28.
LEVEL: B LANG: Eng SIRC ARTICLE NO: 092477

Fedo, M. Big shots. Heavyweight runners can go the distance, too. *Runner (New York)* 6(11), Aug 1984, 18.
LEVEL: B LANG: E SIRC ARTICLE NO: 106157

Fix, D. Distance training basics. *Athletic journal (Evanston, Ill.)* 65(1), Aug 1984, 22-23;57.
LEVEL: B LANG: Eng SIRC ARTICLE NO: 096961

Henderson, J. Training for the half-marathon. The half-marathon is no longer just a fraction of another race. Now it stands on its own as a worthy event - maybe the perfect one for you. *Runner's world* 19(3), Mar 1984, 66-67;104.
LEVEL: B LANG: Eng SIRC ARTICLE NO: 092487

Henderson, J. LSD flashback: where did all those (slow) miles get the foundling fathers of LSD? Here's an update on what became of that old gang of ours. *Runner's world* 19(4), Apr 1984, 48-50;112.
LEVEL: B LANG: Eng SIRC ARTICLE NO: 093894

Hessel, D.G. Middle - distance running. *Track and field quarterly review (Kalamazoo, Mich.)* 84(3), Fall 1984, 18-21.
LEVEL: B LANG: Eng SIRC ARTICLE NO: 096967

Karikosk, O. Training volume in distance running. *Modern athlete and coach (Athelstone, Aust.)* 22(2), Apr 1984, 18-20.
NOTES: Based on a condensed translation from Kehakultuur (Estonia) 44(9), 1983.
LEVEL: B LANG: Eng SIRC ARTICLE NO: 096975

Knudson, L. The dilemma - cross country, track, or the roads. *Track and field journal (Ottawa, Ont.)* 27, Aug 1984, 4-5.
LEVEL: B LANG: Eng SIRC ARTICLE NO: 100061

Korobov, A. Volkov, N. Planning of middle distance training. *Modern athlete and coach (Athelstone, Aust.)* 22(4), Oct 1984, 7-10.
NOTES: Condensed translation of the original published in Legkaya Atletika, Moscow, no. 12, 1983.
LEVEL: I LANG: Eng SIRC ARTICLE NO: 104991

Krusmann, R. Schmidt, P. Stepping up to 800 metres. *Modern athlete and coach (Athelstone, Aust.)* 22(1), Jan 1984, 20-22.
NOTES: Based on a condensed translation from, Die Lehre der Leichtathletik 40/41, 1979.
LEVEL: B LANG: Eng SIRC ARTICLE NO: 096979

Lawrence, A. Scheid, M. Cohessy, P. The self-coached runner. 1st ed. Boston ; Toronto: Little, Brown & Co., c1984. xiv, 223 p. : ill.
LEVEL: B LANG: Eng ISBN: 0-316-516716 LC CARD: 84-7934 GV1062 17744

Liquori, M. Training & technique: getting on track. *Runner (New York)* 6(6), Mar 1984, 80.
LEVEL: B LANG: Eng SIRC ARTICLE NO: 100067

Paish, W. Training for the middle distance events - a successful formula. *Athletics coach (London)* 18(2), Jun 1984, 28.
LEVEL: B LANG: Eng SIRC ARTICLE NO: 095449

Pereira, M. The Portuguese school of middle and long distance running. *Track and field (Ottawa, Ont.)* 27, Aug 1984, 23-25.
LEVEL: B LANG: Eng SIRC ARTICLE NO: 100077

Pisuke, A. Planning of endurance training. *Modern athlete and coach (Athelstone, Aust.)* 22(1), Jan 1984, 15-17.

NOTES: Based on a condensed translation from the Track and Field Supplement No. 1, 1982 of Kehakultuur.
LEVEL: B LANG: Eng SIRC ARTICLE NO: 096992

Rotondaro, L.P. An all-purpose workout for middle distance girls. *Women's coaching clinic 7(6), Feb 1984, 12.*
LEVEL: B LANG: Eng SIRC ARTICLE NO: 091109

Schmidt, P. Le 800 m: generalites. Approches d'une saison. *Revue de l'Amicale des entraineurs francais d'athletisme (Paris) 86, janv/fevr/mars 1984, 20-27.*
LEVEL: B LANG: Fr SIRC ARTICLE NO: 095458

Schmidt, P. 800 m: evolution et entrainement de Ferner et de Wuelbeck. *Revue de l'Amicale des entraineurs francais d'athletisme (Paris) 87, avr/mai/juin 1984, 23-26.*
LEVEL: B LANG: Fr SIRC ARTICLE NO: 096997

Shatohin, A. Smirnov, U. The 'express' method. (for correcting training loads) *Soviet sports review (Escondido, Calif.) 19(2), Jun 1984, 102-104.*
NOTES: Translated from, Legkaya atletika, 9:5, 1983.
LEVEL: I LANG: Eng SIRC ARTICLE NO: 100088

Sparks, K. Bjorklund, G. Long-distance runner's guide to training and racing: build your endurance, strength and efficiency. Englewood Cliffs, N.J.: Prentice-Hall, c1984. xi, 242 p. : ill. (Spectrum book.)
NOTES: Includes bibliographies and index.
LEVEL: I LANG: Eng ISBN: 0135402115 LC CARD: 83-024711 GV1062 17465

Surtees, G. Preparation of a European junior champion. *Athletics coach (Halesowen, England) 18(1), Mar 1984, 12-14.*
LEVEL B LANG: Eng SIRC ARTICLE NO: 093953

Tiurin, Y. A report on the preparation of Ulmasova - 3,000 m champion of Europe 1982. *Athletics coach (Halesowen, England) 18(1), Mar 1984, 25-30.*
LEVEL: B LANG: Eng SIRC ARTICLE NO: 093955

Tulloh, B. Teens on the track. *Running (London) 39, Jul 1984, 74-75;77.*
NOTES: Extract from, Tulloh, B., The Teenage Runner.
LEVEL: B LANG: Eng SIRC ARTICLE NO: 103615

Van Praagh, E. La musclation specifique en demi-fond et en fond.
NOTES: Dans, Renforcement musculaire, Paris, Institut national du sport et de l'education physique, c1984, p. 149-156.
LEVEL: I LANG: Fr GV711.5 18233

Verhoshansky, U. Sirenko, V. Strength preparation of middle distance runners. *Soviet sports review (Escondido, Calif.) 19(4), Dec 1984, 185-190.*
NOTES: Translated from, Legkaya atletika 12, 1983, 9-10.
LEVEL: I LANG: Eng SIRC ARTICLE NO: 105033

Walker, G. Distance training in Australia - the last 25 years. *Fun runner (Rose Bay, NSW) 6(5), Dec 1984/Jan 1985, 59-60.*
NOTES: Reprinted from, Queensland Marathon and Road Runners Club Newsletter.
LEVEL: B LANG: Eng SIRC ARTICLE NO: 173030

Ward, G.R. Factors to consider when planning a training programme for middle & longer distances. *Track and field quarterly review (Kalamazoo, Mich.)*

84(3), Fall 1984, 6-8.
NOTES: Presented at Ontario Track Association Clinic, Toronto.
LEVEL: B LANG: Eng SIRC ARTICLE NO: 097012

Warhurst, R. Training for the mile. *Track and field quarterly review (Kalamazoo, Mich.) 84(3), Fall 1984, 31-34.*
NOTES: Presented at the Michigan Interscholastic Track Coaches Clinic, Oakland University, January 9-10, 1976.
LEVEL: B LANG: Eng SIRC ARTICLE NO: 097016

Wilson, H. Speed in enduruce events. *Technical bulletin - Ontario Track and Field Association (Willowdale, Ont.) 43, Fall 1984, 27-28.*
NOTES: Reprinted from, Technical Bulletin no. 5 (Nov 1982) (taken from South African Athlete).
LEVEL: B LANG: Eng SIRC ARTICLE NO: 103623

WOMEN

Boyden, T.W. Pamenter, R.W. Stanforth, P.R. Rotkis, T.C. Wilmore, J.H. Impaired gonadotropin responses to gonadotropin-releasing hormone stimulation in endurance-trained women. *Fertility and sterility (Birmingham, Ala.) 41(3), Mar 1984, 359-363.*
ABST: Changes in body composition, menstrual cycles, and gonadotropins were examined in 19 female endurance runners. Midfollicular plasma concentrations of unstimulated and gonadotropin-releasing hormone, (GNRH)-stimulated luteinizing hormone and follicle-stimulating hormone were determined at baseline, at 30 miles/week and at 50 miles/week. GNRH-stimulated luteinizing hormone decreased from an average of 76.3 micrograms/min/ml at baseline to an average of 20.2 micrograms/min/ml at 30 miles/week. GNRH-stimulated follicle-stimulating hormone decreased from an average of 28.4 at baseline to an average of 9.6 at 50 miles/week.
LEVEL: A LANG: Eng SIRC ARTICLE NO: 099362

Rainville, S. Vaccaro, P. The effects of menopause and training on serum lipids. (Refs: 39)*International journal of sports medicine (Stuttgart) 5(3), Jun 1984, 137-141.*
ABST: Forty women were studied to determine the effect of training and menopause on serum levels of total cholesterol (Tc), HDL cholesterol (HDL-C), LDL cholesterol (LDL-C), and the ratio of HDL-C/LDL-C. Subjects were assigned to one of four groups: (a) 10 premenopausal trained runners (25-75 miles per week); (b) 10 premenopausal untrained who took part in no regular aerobic exercise; (c) 10 postmenopausal trained runners (25-65 miles per week); (d) 10 postmenopausal untrained who took part in no regular aerobic exercise. It was concluded that training prior to menopause had a positive effect on LDL-C levels and the HDL-C/LDL-C ratio. This positive effect continued with training following menopause and in addition HDL-C levels were also elevated. It was further suggested that menopause causes adverse changes in serum lipid levels that may be offset, at least in part, by endurance training.
LEVEL: A LANG: Eng SIRC ARTICLE NO: 105016

Travin, U. Belina, O. Chernov, S. Training of women middle-distance runners. *Soviet sports review (Escondido, Calif.) 19(3) Sept 1984, 153-155.*
NOTES: Translated from, Legkaya atletika 3, 1983.
LEVEL: I LANG: Eng SIRC ARTICLE NO: 103614

Vincent, T. Pioneer women. *Footnotes (Reston, Va.) 12(2), Summer 1984, 14-16.*
LEVEL: B LANG: Eng SIRC ARTICLE NO: 109177

MINI-TRAMPOLINING

PHYSICAL FITNESS

White, J.R. Barnes, L. Jump for joy: the rebounding exercise book. New York: Arco Pub., c1984. viii, 200 p. : ill.
LEVEL: I LANG: Eng ISBN: 0668058366 LC CARD: 83-012211 GV555 15968

MODERN DANCE

Pilobolus. Deux etudiants americains s'ennuyent a l'Universite et decident de suivre un cours de choregraphie. 'Pilobolus' es ne... *EPS: Education physique et sport (Paris) 189, sept/oct 1984, 11-14.*
LEVEL: B LANG: Fr SIRC ARTICLE NO: 101206

BIOMECHANICS

Gray, M. Skinar, M.H. Support base use in two dance idioms. (Refs: 10)*Research quarterly for exercise & sport (Reston, Va.) 55(2), Jun 1984, 184-187.*
ABST: This study investigated the size of the bases of support used in ballet and modern dance classes. The authors indicate that dance literature suggests that ballet utilizes a narrow and non-supported base while modern dance utilizes wider and grounded bases of support. This study confirms this hypothesis for the warm-up phase of the two types of dance. Thus, the results indicate that there exist inherent similarities along with fundamental differences between ballet and modern dance.
LEVEL: A LANG: Eng SIRC ARTICLE NO: 096617

CHILDREN

Sutlive, J.L. A description of children's verbal responses to a modern dance work in grades kindergarten through six. Eugene Ore.: Microform Publications, University of Oregon, 1984. 2 microfiches : negative, ill. ; 11 x 15 cm.
NOTES: Thesis (Ed.D.) - University of North Carolina at Greensboro, 1982; (x, 154 leaves); includes bibliography.
LEVEL: A LANG: Eng UO84 146-147

MEDICINE

Stoller, S.M. Hekmat, F. Kleiger, B. A comparative study of the frequency of anterior impingement exostoses of the ankle in dancers and nondancers. (Refs: 13)*Foot & ankle 4(4), Jan/Feb 1984, 201-203.*
ABST: This study compared the incidence of anterior impingement exostoses of the ankle in 100 nondancers and 32 professional or preprofessional (students) classical and modern ballet dancers. Findings show that 4% of the nondancers suffered from talar exostoses while 59.3% of the dancers had talar exostoses.
LEVEL: A LANG: Eng SIRC ARTICLE NO: 093387

MODERN DANCE (continued)

PSYCHOLOGY

Leste, A. Rust, J. Effects of dance on anxiety. (Refs: 10)*Perceptual and motor skills (Missoula, Mont.) 58(3), Jun 1984, 767-772.*
ABST: In this paper, the authors determine the effects of modern dance on anxiety before and after 3 months of an education program. 29 undergraduate students from modern dance classes serve as subjects while 21 physical education students, 12 music students and 55 mathematics students serve as controls. The Spielberger State-Trait Anxiety Inventory is administered. Age, sex, attitude towards dance, and previous experience in sport, dance and relaxation of subjects are considered. A significant reduction of anxiety is observed following modern dance course.
LEVEL: A LANG: Eng SIRC ARTICLE NO: 096622

Simon, J.L. The choreography and audience analysis of 'Episodes,' a dance based on non-verbal communication. Eugene, Ore.: Microform Publications, University of Oregon, 1984. 2 microfiches : negative, ill. ; 11 x 15 cm.
NOTES: Thesis (M.S.) - Illinois State University, 1982; (vi, 120 leaves); includes bibliography.
LEVEL: A LANG: Eng UO84 143-144

TECHNIQUES AND SKILLS

Leray, Cl. Hip, Hop. Sport? Danse? Un entretien avec Sydney. *EPS: Revue education physique et sport (Paris) 188, juil/aout 1984, 7-13.*
LEVEL: B LANG: Fr SIRC ARTICLE NO: 098040

MODERN PENTATHLON

Glenesk, N. Modern pentathlon. *Journal of physical education, recreation & dance (Reston, Va.) 55(4), Apr 1984, 27-28.*
LEVEL: B LANG: Eng SIRC ARTICLE NO: 094751

MODERN RHYTHMIC GYMNASTICS

Ottum, B. Getting into the swirl. *Sports illustrated (Chicago, Ill.) 61(4), 18 Jul 1984, 236-239.*
NOTES: Special preview: the 1984 Olympics.
LEVEL: B LANG: Eng SIRC ARTICLE NO: 096694

CERTIFICATION

Modern rhythmic gymnastics: syllabus of coaching awards. (Slough, Berks, England): British Amateur Gymnastics Association, (1984). 11, (1) p.
CORP: British Amateur Gymnastics Association.
NOTES: Cover title.
LEVEL: B LANG: Eng GV464 18286

CHILDREN

Loquet, M. L'enfant a la decouverte de l'autre...partenaire, public, adversaire. 2e partie. *EPS: Education physique et spor (Paris) 187, mai/juin 1984, 43-47.*
NOTES: A suivre.
LEVEL: B LANG: Fr SIRC ARTICLE NO: 096692

Loquet, M. L'enfant a la decouverte de l'autre...partenaire, public, adversaire. 3e partie.

EPS: Revue education physique e sport (Paris) 188, juil/aout 1984, 67-72.
NOTES: A suivre.
LEVEL: B LANG: Fr SIRC ARTICLE NO: 098144

Loquet, M. GRS l'enfant a la decouverte de l'autre... partenaire, public, adversaire. (Refs: 12)*EPS: Education physique et sport (Paris) 189, sept/oct 1984, 50-52.*
LEVEL: B LANG: Fr SIRC ARTICLE NO: 101308

CHOREOGRAPHY AND MUSIC

Bott, J. Modern rhythmic gymnastics: duets for modern rhythmic gymnastics. *Gymnast (London) May 1984, 19.*
LEVEL: B LANG: Eng SIRC ARTICLE NO: 104759

Honeyman, J. Modern rhythmic gymnastics. Choreography - some helpful guidelines. *Gymnast (Slough, Eng.) Jul/Aug 1984, 11-12.*
LEVEL: B LANG: Eng SIRC ARTICLE NO: 101306

COUNTRIES AND REGIONS

Langsley, E. Rhythmic royalty: the Bulgarians will be sadly missed at L.A. '84. *International gymnast (Santa Monica) 26(8), Aug 1984, 26-29.*
LEVEL: B LANG: Eng SIRC ARTICLE NO: 098142

MEDICINE

Lindboe, C.F. Slettebo, M. Are young female gymnasts malnourished? An anthropometric, electrophysiological, and histological study. (Refs: 13)*European journal of applied physiology and occupational physiology (Berlin, FRG) 52(4), Jun 1984, 457-462.*
ABST: This study sought to determine if there were any signs of latent or incipient malnutrition among eight young women who represented Norway in rhythmic gymnastics in 1982. The gymnasts were compared to ten normal girls who were matched for age and height to the gymnasts. The mean body weight of the gymnasts did not differ from the control group. The authors conclude that the gymnasts were not generally malnourished. There were electrophysiological and histological differences between the groups but the relationship of these differences to nutrition is not clear.
LEVEL: A LANG: Eng SIRC ARTICLE NO: 098143

SPORTING EVENTS

GRS XIe Championnats du monde, Strasbourg - 10-13 novembre 1983. *EPS: Education physique et sport (Paris, France) 186, mars/avr 1984, 61-72.*
LEVEL: B LANG: Fr SIRC ARTICLE NO: 095055

Schmid, A.B. Rhythmic gymnastics: new Olympic sport. *Journal of physical education, recreation & dance (Reston, Va.) 55(5), May/Jun 1984, 70-71.*
LEVEL: B LANG: Eng SIRC ARTICLE NO: 095065

TEACHING

Bennett, J.P. Rhythmic gymnastics: a challenge with balls and ropes. Alexandria, Va.: Computer Microfilm International, 1984 1 microfiche (19 fr.) 10 x 15 cm.
NOTES: Bibliography. I. 5.
LEVEL: B LANG: Eng EDRS: 244915 ERIC 244915

Loquet, M. GRS: l'enfant a la decouverte de l'autre...partenaire, public, adversaire. 1re partie. (Refs: 2)*EPS: Education physique et sport 185, janv/fevr 1984, 65-68.*
NOTES: A suivre.
LEVEL: B LANG: Fr SIRC ARTICLE NO: 093493

TECHNIQUES AND SKILLS

Abad, H. Hoop technique. *World gymnastics (Budapest, Hungary) 2(19), 1984, 43.*
LEVEL: B LANG: Eng SIRC ARTICLE NO: 098128

Abad, H. Improve your ball handling. *World gymnastics (Milan) 3(20), 1984, 47.*
LEVEL: B LANG: Eng SIRC ARTICLE NO: 102100

Audenaerde, C. Gymnastique rythmique sportive: etude de l'evolution des exercices avec ruban et cerceau de 1975 a 1981. *Sport: Communaute francaise de belgique (Bruxelles) 108, 1984, 195-200.*
NOTES: D'apres un memoire redige sous la direction de Madame L. Willems, professeur a l'Universite catholique de Louvain.
LEVEL: B LANG: Fr SIRC ARTICLE NO: 103215

MOTO-CROSS

Osborn, B. Esparza, A. The complete book of BMX. 1st ed. New York: Harper & Row, c1984. 248 p. : ill.
LEVEL: B LANG: Eng ISBN: 0060911352 LC CARD: 83-048937 GV1049.3 17992

ADMINISTRATION

McDermott, B. Flying bikes and wealthy tykes. *Sports illustrated (Los Angeles, Calif.) 61(22), 12 Nov 1984, 32-34;39.*
LEVEL: B LANG: Eng SIRC ARTICLE NO: 101421

CHILDREN

Sullivan, G. Better BMX riding and racing for boys and girls. New York: Dodd, Mead & Co., c1984. 64 p. : ill.
LEVEL: B LANG Eng ISBN: 0-396-08331-5 LC CARD: 83-25440 GV1049.3 17990

DIRECTORIES

Who, what & where. How to get started, here is what you need to know. *Motorcross action magazine (Mission Hills, Calif.) 12(3), Mar 1984, 26.*
LEVEL: B LANG: Eng SIRC ARTICLE NO: 096766

ECONOMICS

Bucher, D. How to get sponsored: confessions of a sponsor. *Motocross action magazine (Mission Hills, Calif.) 12(8), Aug 1984, 66;68-69;96-97.*
LEVEL: B LANG: Eng SIRC ARTICLE NO: 104834

EQUIPMENT

125 motocross comparison. Magnificent seven shoot it out: Cagiva, Honda, Husqvarna, Kawasaki, KTM, Suzuki & Yamaha go for thei guns. *Motocross action magazine (Mission Hills, Calif.) 12(7), Jul 1984, 58-60;62-64;67.*
LEVEL: B LANG: Eng SIRC ARTICLE NO: 104829

125 MX shootout. RM vs. CR vs. YZ vs. KX. *Motorcross action magazine (Mission Hills, Calif.)* 12(4), Apr 1984, 74-75;77-78;80;82;84.
LEVEL: B LANG: Eng SIRC ARTICLE NO: 096753

1985 guided tour: Kawasakis exposed. Still green, but with a touch of silver. *Motocross action magazine (Mission Hills, Calif 12(11), Nov 1984, 38.*
LEVEL: B LANG: Eng SIRC ARTICLE NO: 108979

1985 Honda CR250R: riding with big Mo & the Red tide. *Motocross action magazine (Mission Hills, Calif.) 12(12), Dec 1984, 34-35;37-38.*
LEVEL: B LANG: Eng SIRC ARTICLE NO: 108982

1985 RM250 prototype. Suzuki: men at work. Sneak peek at next year's RM. *Motocross action magazine (Mission Hills, Calif.) 12 (11), Nov 1984, 42;45.*
LEVEL: B LANG: Eng SIRC ARTICLE NO: 108980

A handy guide to the best & worst used bikes: 1983's good & bad buys. *Motocross action magazine (Mission Hills, Calif.) 12(4), Apr 1984, 88-89.*
LEVEL: B LANG: Eng SIRC ARTICLE NO: 096760

Attack of the mini missiles. *Motocross action magazine (Mission Hills, Calif.) 12(8), Aug 1984, 22-24;29.*
LEVEL: B LANG: En SIRC ARTICLE NO: 104831

Battle of the titans: Yamaha vs. Honda vs. Suzuki vs. Husqvarna vs. M-Star vs. KTM: 500 CC shootout. *Dirt bike (Mission Hills Calif.) 14(10), Oct 1984, 44-49;70.*
LEVEL: B LANG: Eng SIRC ARTICLE NO: 109071

Breaking the stodgy old-world traditions KTM 125. Race test. *Motocross action magazine (Mission Hills, Calif.) 12(3), Mar 1984, 68-69;71-72;74.*
LEVEL: B LANG: Eng SIRC ARTICLE NO: 096755

But is it better than the KDX? An impromptu shootout of the 200cc giants. (KDX200 and IT200) *Dirt bike (Mission Hills, Calif. 14(5), May 1984, 49.*
LEVEL: B LANG: Eng SIRC ARTICLE NO: 101410

Cagiva WMX 250: an orphaned waif from Italy. *Motocross action magazine (Mission Hills, Calif.) 12(11), Nov 1984, 55-56.*
LEVEL: B LANG: Eng SIRC ARTICLE NO: 108981

Cagiva, Honda, Kawasaki, KTM, Suzuki & Yamaha comparison: no-holds-barred 125 MX shootout. *Dirt bike (Mission Hills, Calif.) (10), Oct 1984, 20-25.*
NOTES: Cagiva, Honda, Kawasaki, KTM, Suzuki & Yamaha comparison.
LEVEL: B LANG: Eng SIRC ARTICLE NO: 109067

Cycle world test: Suzuki RM125. Dynamite comes in small packages. *Cycle world (New York) 23(2), Feb 1984, 56-58.*
LEVEL: B LANG: Eng SIRC ARTICLE NO: 098342

Deuce-and-a-half weapons: Kawasaki, Honda, Suzuki & Yamaha take on the MXA wrecking crew. *Motocross action magazine (Mission Hills, Calif.) 12(6), Jun 1984, 72-73;75-78;80-83.*
LEVEL: B LANG: Eng SIRC ARTICLE NO: 103327

Dirt bike owner's survey: the bikes you love & hate. *Dirt bike (Mission Hills, Calif.) 14(5), May 1984, 50-52;54;72.*
LEVEL: LANG: Eng SIRC ARTICLE NO: 101413

Enough to make those red and yellow 125s green with envy. (Kawasaki KX125) *Cycle world (Los Angeles) 23(8), Aug 1984, 38-41.*
LEVEL: B LANG: Eng SIRC ARTICLE NO: 105984

Going to Honda heaven: the complete guide to the '84 CR250R. *Motocross action magazine (Mission Hills, Calif.) 12(12), Dec 1984, 40-42;47.*
LEVEL: B LANG: Eng SIRC ARTICLE NO: 108986

Honda CR125R motocrosser: rocket roulette: it handles & might be fast. *Dirt bike (Mission Hills, Calif.) 14(4), Apr 1984, 22;27-29.*
LEVEL: B LANG: Eng SIRC ARTICLE NO: 101416

Honda CR500R: what are the three little things? Race test. *Motocross action magazine (Mission Hills, Calif.) 12(3), Mar 1984 36;39-40;42.*
LEVEL: B LANG: Eng SIRC ARTICLE NO: 096761

Honda XR5OOR: the target: it's big, it's plush, it's under fire. *Dirt bike (Mission Hills, Calif.) 14(10), Oct 1984, 32-34.*
NOTES: Honda XR500R.
LEVEL: B LANG: Eng SIRC ARTICLE NO: 109070

If you're digging for motocross horsepower, you've just struck the mother lode. (Yamaha YZ490) *Cycle world (Los Angeles) 23(7), Jul 1984, 32-36.*
LEVEL: B LANG: Eng SIRC ARTICLE NO: 103329

Inside the Honda Mark I: look, but don't touch. *Motocross action magazine (Mission Hills, Calif.) 12(8), Aug 1984, 20.*
LEVEL: B LANG: Eng SIRC ARTICLE NO: 104842

Kawasaki KX125: could this be the king of the hill? Race test. *Motocross action magazine (Mission Hills, Calif.) 12(4), Apr 1984, 36-37;39-40.*
LEVEL: B LANG: Eng SIRC ARTICLE NO: 096762

Kawasaki KX250: grabbing for the brass ring. *Motocross action magazine (Mission Hills, Calif.) 12(6), Jun 1984, 26-28;30;112.*
LEVEL: B LANG: Eng SIRC ARTICLE NO: 103332

Kawasaki KX60A2: turn it loose. Leading the pack, for now. *Dirk bike (Mission Hills, Calif.) 14(4), Apr 1984, 68-69.*
LEVEL: LANG: Eng SIRC ARTICLE NO: 101420

Monsters of the midway: Suzuki RM500E versus Yamaha YZ490L versus Honda CR500R. *Motocross action magazine (Mission Hills, Calif.) 12(9), Sept 1984, 52-55;57-58.*
LEVEL: B LANG: Eng SIRC ARTICLE NO: 108776

Once again new and improved; but is it once again the best? (Honda CR250R) *Cycle world (Los Angeles) 23(7), Jul 1984, 54-58.*
LEVEL: B LANG: Eng SIRC ARTICLE NO: 103336

Race test: 1985 KTM 250. Balancing the scales with the Austrian handler. *Motocross action magazine (Mission Hills, Calif.) 12 (12), Dec 1984, 60-61;65.*
LEVEL: B LANG: Eng SIRC ARTICLE NO: 108983

Race test: Suzuki RM500E. Mighty Casey comes to bat. *Motocross action magazine (Mission Hills, Calif.) 12(7), Jul 1984, 42-43;45-46.*
LEVEL: B LANG: Eng SIRC ARTICLE NO: 104845

Suzuki RM125E motocrosser: rev it till it melts...and keep it there. *Dirt bike (Mission Hills, Calif.) 14(5), May 1984, 20-21;23-24.*
LEVEL: B LANG: Eng SIRC ARTICLE NO: 101423

Suzuki RM500E motocrosser. Just enough: something old, something new, something borrowed & a bit blue. *Dirt bike (Mission Hills, Calif.) 14(7), Jul 1984, 62-63;70.*
LEVEL: B LANG: Eng SIRC ARTICLE NO: 104848

The motor's, the thing. (Can-Am 250ASE) *Cycle world (Los Angeles, Calif.) 23(5), May 1984, 46-51.*
LEVEL: B LANG: Eng SIRC ARTICLE NO: 101422

Think of it as miss congeniality. (Susuki RM250) *Cycle world (Los Angeles, Calif.) 23(5), May 1984, 74-79.*
LEVEL: B LANG: E SIRC ARTICLE NO: 101424

Tire choices of the pros: what tires work where... & why. *Dirt bike (Mission Hills, Calif.) 14(10), Oct 1984, 54-55;72.*
LEVEL: B LANG: Eng SIRC ARTICLE NO: 109072

Yamaha IT200L: breaking away. *Dirt bike (Mission Hills, Calif.) 14(5), May 1984, 44-45;47-49.*
LEVEL: B LANG: Eng SIRC ARTICLE NO: 101426

Yamaha YZ490L: altered states: looks can be deceiving. *Dirt bike (Mission Hills, Calif.) 14(4), Apr 1984, 60-61;63-65.*
LEVEL: B LANG: Eng SIRC ARTICLE NO: 101427

Yamaha YZ490L: the open class bill of particulars. *Motocross action magazine (Mission Hills, Calif.) 12(8), Aug 1984, 38-40;43.*
LEVEL: B LANG: Eng SIRC ARTICLE NO: 104852

EQUIPMENT - MAINTENANCE

Clipper, M. 12 tips to keep your bike alive: little things that make a huge difference. *Dirt bike (Mission Hills, Calif.) 14(5), May 1984, 56-57.*
LEVEL: B LANG: Eng SIRC ARTICLE NO: 101411

INJURIES AND ACCIDENTS

Husson, J.L. Marquer, Y. Jourdain, R. Rebaud, C. Blouet, J.M. Masse, A. Duval, J.M. Anatomical relationship between the medial head of the gastrocnemius and the occurrence of a dystrophic bony lacuna. *Anatomia clinica (New York) 6(1), 1984, 37-43.*
ABST: A bony lesion with identical radiological features was seen in the medial part of the distal femoral methaphysis in five patients who practised cross-country motorcycling. These findings suggested that the cause of the lesions was of muscular origin. This study shows that the bone-tendon-muslce complex forms a veritable biomechanical unit.
LEVEL: A LANG: Eng

SAFETY

End knee problems forever: helping solve the puzzle of the weak link. (C.T.: knee brace) *Motocross action magazine (Mission Hills, Calif) 12(3), Mar 1984, 83-84.*
LEVEL: B LANG: Eng SIRC ARTICLE NO: 096758

STRATEGY

Fontanes, L. The o'show's 125 tactics: how to ride a 125 & make the most of it. *Motocross action magazine (Mission Hills, Calif.) 12(12), Dec 1984, 76.*
LEVEL: B LANG: Eng SIRC ARTICLE NO: 108990

Van Camp, M. First-turn basics. Guaranteed hole shots: how to get there first, anywhere, anytime, anyplace. *Motocross action magazine (Mission Hills, Calif.) 12(3), Mar 1984, 92-93;102.*
LEVEL: B LANG: Eng SIRC ARTICLE NO: 096763

TECHNIQUES AND SKILLS

Bailey, G. Gary & David Bailey's riding tips: saving energy. How to keep going when you're exhausted. *Dirt bike (Mission Hills, Calif.) 14(5), May 1984, 40-42.*
LEVEL: B LANG: Eng SIRC ARTICLE NO: 101409

Bailey, G. Berms: the major mistakes. Why you do them wrong & how to do them right. *Dirt bike (Mission Hills, Calif.) 14(12 Dec 1984, 36-37.*
LEVEL: B LANG: Eng SIRC ARTICLE NO: 108976

Bailey, G. How to pass... and make it stick. *Dirt bike (Mission Hills, Calif.) 14(10), Oct 1984, 60-61;63.*
LEVEL: B LANG: Eng SIRC ARTICLE NO: 109073

Fontanes, L. The art of passing: the best way to pass is to do it, says the Hurricane. *Motocross action magazine (Mission Hills, Calif.) 12(12), Dec 1984, 30.*
LEVEL: B LANG: Eng SIRC ARTICLE NO: 108984

How to ride swell. Trail tips for twits. *Dirt bike (Mission Hills, Calif.) 14(4), Apr 1984, 30-32.*
LEVEL: B LANG: Eng SIRC ARTICLE NO: 101419

Weisel, J. New techniques: inside the riding tricks that made America the best. *Motorcross action magazine (Mission Hills, Calif.) 12(3), Mar 1984, 76-78.*
LEVEL: B LANG: Eng SIRC ARTICLE NO: 096765

MOTOR BOATING

BIOGRAPHY AND AUTOBIOGRAPHY

Schoen, V. The Kiekhaefer legacy: the Reed Value makes outboards run better. Kiekhaefer considered it his most important invention. *Lakeland boating (Los Angeles, Calif.) 39(2), Feb 1984, 42-44.*
LEVEL: B LANG: Eng SIRC ARTICLE NO: 098335

SPORTING EVENTS

Morris, J. Supertest: unlimited nerve and 2,000 horsepower propelled Canada's legendary challenge. *Canadian yachting power sail (Toronto) 9(4), Apr 1984, 28-32;53;55.*
LEVEL: B LANG: Eng SIRC ARTICLE NO: 101404

Ryder, T. Gold Cup Race. *Journal of sports philately (Berwyn, Ill.) 22(6), Jul/Aug 1984, 189-191;193.*
LEVEL: B LANG: Eng SIRC ARTICLE NO: 101405

TESTING AND EVALUATION

Elsey, D. Set-up: how to set-up your performance boat to reach its full potential. *Canadian boating (Missauga, Ont.) 60(5), May 1984, 12-14.*
LEVEL: B LANG: Eng SIRC ARTICLE NO: 104828

VARIATIONS

Maki, M. Many snowmobilers think it should be relegated to Ripley's 'Believe-it-or-not' world of the bizzare. A closer look at... Water skipping. *Snowmobiler's race & ralley (Alexandria, Minn.) 17(2), Nov/Dec 1984, 40-41.*
LEVEL: B LANG: Eng SIRC ARTICLE NO: 173241

MOTORCYCLING

10 ways to get wild in the dirt. The official racer's guide to getting loose. *Dirt bike (Mission Hills, Calif.) 14(12), Dec 1984, 32-34.*
LEVEL: B LANG: Eng SIRC ARTICLE NO: 108978

Anderson, B. Wood, B. Fill 'er up - maybe. *American motorcyclist (Westerville, Ohio) 38(9), Sept 1984, 17-19.*
LEVEL: B LANG: Eng SIRC ARTICLE NO: 108444

Wood, B. Speedway's sideways spectacular. *American motorcyclist (Westerville, Ohio) 38(12), Dec 1984, 26;28;30.*
LEVEL: B LANG: Eng SIRC ARTICLE NO: 107383

ASSOCIATIONS

The first 60 years: an illustrated history of the American Motorcyclist Association: administration. *AM American motorcyclist (Westerville, Oh.) 38(1), Jan 1984, 55-58.*
LEVEL: B LANG: Eng SIRC ARTICLE NO: 098347

BIOGRAPHY AND AUTOBIOGRAPHY

Lawson, E. Worldbeater. (Eddie Lawson) *Motorcyclist (Los Angeles) 1050, Dec 1984, 50-52.*
LEVEL: B LANG: Eng SIRC ARTICLE NO: 172909

CLOTHING

Malcolm Smith ISDE professional jacket. *Cycle world (Los Angeles) 23(8), Aug 1984, 22-23.*
LEVEL: B LANG: Eng SIRC ARTICLE NO: 105985

EQUIPMENT

A dirty trickster. Shaft drive, electric start and a smooth, torquey engine make the YTM225 a friendly tearabout. Cycle Canada test, Yamaha YTM 225. *Cycle Canada (Toronto, Ont.) 14(2), Feb 1984, 53-54.*
LEVEL: I LANG: Eng SIRC ARTICLE NO: 096757

A great, big bike. (Honda V65 Sabre) *Cycle world (Los Angeles, Calif.) 23(5), May 1984, 38-44.*
LEVEL: B LANG: Eng SIRC ARTICLE NO: 101414

Altab, Harris sport fairings: two fairing from England for RD350's delay hibernation for street squirrels who want to drive in the cold and wet. Cycle Canada product test. *Cycle Canada (Toronto, Ont.) 14(2), Feb 1984, 36;38.*
LEVEL: B LANG: Eng SIRC ARTICLE NO: 096754

Anderson, S. How motorcycles work. 3: the friction clutch. *Cycle world (Los Angeles, Calif.) 23(5), May 1984, 83-87.*
LEVEL: B LANG: Eng SIRC ARTICLE NO: 101408

Anderson, S. The gearbox. *Cycle world (Los Angeles) 23(8), Aug 1984, 55-57;60-61.*
NOTES: How motorcycles work. 4.
LEVEL: LANG: Eng SIRC ARTICLE NO: 105981

Anderson, S. Final drives: how motorcycles work. 5. *Cycle world (Los Angeles) 23(10), Oct 1984, 57-62;64.*
LEVEL: I LANG: Eng SIRC ARTICLE NO: 108721

ATC vs. KXT: the fight of the year. A small advantage is all it takes. *Dirt bike (Mission Hills, Calif.) 14(8), Aug 1984, 60-61;63-64;72.*
LEVEL: B LANG: Eng SIRC ARTICLE NO: 104830

Berger, R.K. Adams, S.K. Motorcycle helmet design. *In, Proceedings of the Human Factors Society 28th Annual Meeting 'New Frontiers for Science and Technology', San Antonio, Texas, 22-26 October 1984, edited by M.J. Alluisi, S. De Groot and E.A. Alluisi. The Human Factors Society, Santa Monica, California, 1984, Vol. 1, p. 433-437.*
LEVEL: I LANG: Eng

BMW's way ahead. *Engineering (London) 224(3), Mar 1984, 178-180.*
LEVEL: I LANG: Eng

Brute force. Is bigger better? (Honda CR500R) *Dirt bike (Mission Hills, Calif.) 14(2), Feb 1984, 34-37;72.*
LEVEL: B LANG: E SIRC ARTICLE NO: 098337

Cagiva WMX125. Fasta pasta: deep-dish delight. *Dirt bike (Mission Hills, Calif.) 14(8), Aug 1984, 26-27.*
LEVEL: B LANG: Eng SIRC ARTICLE NO: 104835

Cameron, K. Anatomy of a hybrid: a technical analysis of the OW69, a bike built for one specific purpose: to win the Daytona 200. (Yamaha W69) *Cycle world (Los Angeles) 23(7), Jul 1984, 40-42;44.*
LEVEL: B LANG: Eng SIRC ARTICLE NO: 103326

Can-Am ASE 250: Can-Am's return to form. Cycle Canada test. *Cycle Canada (Toronto, Ont.) 14(2), Feb 1984, 64-67.*
LEVEL: I LANG: Eng SIRC ARTICLE NO: 096756

Cathcart, A. Aboard Honda's RS500 V3. Join us for a ride on the privateer's choice: the RS500 Honda. It's a close replica of Spencer's machine. *Cycle Canada (Toronto) 14(1), Jan 1984, 54-57.*
LEVEL: B LANG: Eng SIRC ARTICLE NO: 098338

Cloned from the XR200: Honda rewrites the book on 250cc four-strokes. (Honda XR250R). *Dirt bike (Mission Hills, Calif.) 14(2) Feb 1984, 20-24.*
LEVEL: B LANG: Eng SIRC ARTICLE NO: 098339

Cross-country cruiser: six speeds, four strokes & two shocks. 1985 Husqvarna 510TX. *Dirt bike (Mission Hills, Calif.) 14(11), Nov 1984, 44-48.*
LEVEL: B LANG: Eng SIRC ARTICLE NO: 108775

Cycle world test: Harley-Davidson XLX. A human touch for a high-tech world. *Cycle world (New York) 23(2), Feb 1984, 60-64.*
LEVEL: B LANG: Eng SIRC ARTICLE NO: 098340

Cycle world test: Honda CB700SC Nighthawks. *Cycle world (New York) 23(2), Feb 1984, 32-37.*
LEVEL: B LANG: Eng SIRC ARTICLE NO: 098341

Cycle world's ninth annual ten best motorcycles of the year celebration. *Cycle world (Los Angeles) 23(10), Oct 1984, 35-42.*
LEVEL: B LANG: Eng SIRC ARTICLE NO: 108718

Dragstrip. (motorcycling) *Motorcyclist (Los Angeles) 1045, Jul 1984, 27-28.*
LEVEL: B LANG: Eng SIRC ARTICLE NO: 105983

Fire's in the iron: the soul of a dirt tracker finds rebirth on the street in the shape of Harley's smoking hot XR1000 production racer. *Cycle Canada (Toronto) 14(1), Jan 1984, 46-49.*
LEVEL: B LANG: Eng SIRC ARTICLE NO: 098343

Ford, D. Motorcycle radials. *Motorcyclist (Los Angeles) 1050, Dec 1984, 40-41;44-45.*
LEVEL: B LANG: Eng SIRC ARTICLE NO: 172908

Going for broke: good overall power with decent suspension for the off-roader make the XT a nice play bike. Roosting through the mud should be

done with caution, as the bike is only meant to go so far. *Dirt bike (Mission Hills, Calif.)* 14(6), Jun 1984, 62-63.
LEVEL: B LANG: Eng SIRC ARTICLE NO: 103328

Gordon, P. Riding impression: Kawasaki GPz900R Ninja. Second generation superbike assassin. *Motorcyclist (Los Angeles, Calif.)* 1041, Mar 1984, 86-88.
LEVEL: B LANG: Eng SIRC ARTICLE NO: 096759

Grace under pressure. Turbocharging's reputation receives a boost from the Kawasaki 750 Turbo. *Cycle Canada (Toronto)* 14(1), Jan 1984, 28-35.
LEVEL: B LANG: Eng SIRC ARTICLE NO: 098348

Griewe, R. Honda XR500R Lite: everything I ever wanted in a four-stroke dirt bike-and less. *Cycle world (Los Angeles)* 23(10 Oct 1984, 50-53;55-56.
LEVEL: B LANG: Eng SIRC ARTICLE NO: 108719

Griewe, R. Yamaha comparison: YZ250 vs. YZ250 vs. YZ250. Ever wonder how a factory-modified YZ250 works bike stacks up against a stocker and a support-ride YZ? So did we. *Cycle world (Los Angeles)* 23(11), Nov 1984, 54-58.
LEVEL: B LANG: Eng SIRC ARTICLE NO: 109359

Harley-Davidson FLTC Tour Glide Enduro Bike: revolutionary new four-stroke: cat quick & grizzly tough. *Dirk bike (Mission Hills, Calif.)* 14(4), Apr 1984, 34-36;38;69.
LEVEL: B LANG: Eng SIRC ARTICLE NO: 101415

Honda V65 Sabre: the motorcyclist's Mercedes. *Motor cyclist (Los Angeles, Calif.)* 1043, May 1984, 30-31;33-36;38.
LEVEL: B LANG: Eng SIRC ARTICLE NO: 101417

Honda VF1000F Interceptor: superbike in the middle. *Motor cyclist (Los Angeles, Calif.)* 1043, May 1984, 40-41;43-49;52.
LEVEL: B LANG: Eng SIRC ARTICLE NO: 101418

Honda vs. Kawasaki vs. Suzuki vs. Yamaha. The maximum minicrossers: 80cc shootout. *Dirt bike (Mission Hills, Calif.)* 14(8), Aug 1984, 54-57.
LEVEL: B LANG: Eng SIRC ARTICLE NO: 104836

Honda XL250R. When the pavement stops, the fun begins: not just a foo-foo bike. *Dirt bike (Mission Hills, Calif.)* 14(7), Jul 1984, 35.
LEVEL: B LANG: Eng SIRC ARTICLE NO: 104837

Honda XL350R. Moving violation: remember that the asphalt trails have speed limits. *Dirt bike (Mission Hills, Calif.)* 14(8), Aug 1984, 48-49.
LEVEL: B LANG: Eng SIRC ARTICLE NO: 104838

Honda XR200R. The fun actor: serious improvements to the king of the play bikes. *Dirt bike (Mission Hills, Calif.)* 14(8), Aug 1984, 44-47;72.
LEVEL: B LANG: Eng SIRC ARTICLE NO: 104839

Husqvarna 500CR motocrosser. Six-speed thunder wagon: testing the MX/Baja/GP/desert/trail bike special. *Dirt bike (Mission Hills, Calif.)* 14(7), Jul 1984, 24-25;27.
LEVEL: B LANG: Eng SIRC ARTICLE NO: 104841

Just enough to dominate: the world's first open class, water-cooled enduro bike. Husqvarna 400Wr Enduro. *Dirt bike (Mission Hills, Calif.)* 14(6), Jun 1984, 56-57;59;72.
LEVEL: B LANG: Eng SIRC ARTICLE NO: 103331

Kawasaki KLR600. Is it a dirt, street or total technoid monster? No holds barred. *Dirt bike (Mission Hills, Calif.)* 14(8), Au 1984, 30-31.
LEVEL: B LANG: Eng SIRC ARTICLE NO: 104843

Konan the barbarian: kross-kountry killer. KTM 495MXC. *Dirt bike (Mission Hills, Calif.)* 14(6), Jun 1984, 46-47;70.
LEVEL: LANG: Eng SIRC ARTICLE NO: 103333

KTM 125MXC. Ferocious feather: you have to be crazy to ride one. *Dirt bike (Mission Hills, Calif.)* 14(7), Jul 1984, 56-57;59;72.
LEVEL: B LANG: Eng SIRC ARTICLE NO: 104844

Move over KX? Big improvements for the littlest CR. Honda CR60R. *Dirt bike (Mission Hills, Calif.)* 14(6), Jun 1984, 35.
LEVEL: B LANG: Eng SIRC ARTICLE NO: 103334

No rest for the wicked: armed for battle. Honda ATC250R. *Dirt bike (Mission Hills, Calif.)* 14(6), Jun 1984, 52-53;70.
LEVEL B LANG: Eng SIRC ARTICLE NO: 103335

Racetrack. (motorcycling) *Motorcyclist (Los Angeles)* 1045, Jul 1984, 18-19;21-24.
LEVEL: B LANG: Eng SIRC ARTICLE NO: 10598

Reborn pocket-rocket. (Yamaha RZ350) *Cycle world (Los Angeles)* 23(7), Jul 1984, 26-30.
LEVEL: B LANG: Eng SIRC ARTICLE NO: 103337

Rev it past the limit: 22 hp at 12,000 rpm equals fire. (Kawasaki KX80E) *Dirt bike (Mission Hills, Calif.)* 14(2), Feb 1984, 40-42.
LEVEL: B LANG: Eng SIRC ARTICLE NO: 098350

Riding the tires off the: KTM 250MXC, Kawasaki KDX250, Honda XR250R, Can-Am 250ASE and Husqvarna WR250. *Cycle world (Los Angeles)* 23(6), Jun 1984, 36-47.
LEVEL: B LANG: Eng SIRC ARTICLE NO: 103338

Run for the money: a production racer for the factory boys. (Yamaha YZ250L) *Dirt bike (Mission Hills, Calif.)* 14(2), Feb 1984 60-61;63-65.
LEVEL: B LANG: Eng SIRC ARTICLE NO: 098351

Son of the spider: liquid-cooling for a familiar face. Exclusive. 1984 M-STAR 250 supercross. *Dirt bike (Mission Hills, Calif.)* 14(6), Jun 1984, 48-49;51.
LEVEL: B LANG: Eng SIRC ARTICLE NO: 103339

Sudden Suzuki works replica: Ross Pederson wins on one. How about you? The Full Floater chassis can do it, but the powerband's a puzzle. *Cycle Canada (Toronto)* 14(7), Jul 1984, 50-52.
NOTES: Suzuki RM250.
LEVEL: B LANG: Eng SIRC ARTICLE NO: 102145

Suzuki DR100 & DR125. Trail twins: trouble-free mini thumpers. *Dirt bike (Mission Hills, Calif.)* 14(7), Jul 1984, 46-47.
LEVEL: B LANG: Eng SIRC ARTICLE NO: 104846

Suzuki PE175. The last of the 175s: could a bigger piston be waiting in the wings? *Dirt bike (Mission Hills, Calif.)* 14(7), Jul 1984, 20-22.
LEVEL: B LANG: Eng SIRC ARTICLE NO: 104847

Swallow off road tires. *Cycle world (New York)* 23(2), Feb 1984, 52.
LEVEL: B LANG: Eng SIRC ARTICLE NO: 098352

The cutting edge: 1985 KTM 250MXC. *Dirt bike (Mission Hills, Calif.)* 14(11), Nov 1984, 20-21;23-24.
LEVEL: B LANG: Eng SIRC ARTICLE NO: 108774

The Italian stallion: is it a fast 200 or a peaky 250? Cagiva WRX250. *Dirt bike (Mission Hills, Calif.)* 14(6), Jun 1984, 64-65.
LEVEL: B LANG: Eng SIRC ARTICLE NO: 103330

The leader in soft saddle bags. Skookum-Paks are expensive and have a complicated system, but

they're well worth the money and effort. *Cycle Canada (Toronto)* 14(1), Jan 1984, 58.
LEVEL: B LANG: Eng SIRC ARTICLE NO: 098349

Tree torquer: is no news good news? Kawasaki KDX250B4. *Dirt bike (Mission Hills, Calif.)* 14(6), Jun 1984, 20-22.
LEVEL: B LANG: Eng SIRC ARTICLE NO: 103341

Trick trak: lean, green & mean. (Kawasaki KX250C2) *Dirt bike (Mission Hills, Calif.)* 14(2), Feb 1984, 50-53.
LEVEL: B LANG: Eng SIRC ARTICLE NO: 098353

Underdog. (Honda XL350R) *Cycle world (Los Angeles, Calif.)* 23(5), May 1984, 52-56.
LEVEL: B LANG: Eng SIRC ARTICLE NO: 1014

Vreeke, K. Honda RS500 GP roadracer: ticket to ride. *Motorcyclist (Los Angeles, Calif.)* 1041, Mar 1984, 46;49-52.
LEVEL: LANG: Eng SIRC ARTICLE NO: 096764

Where's the beef? Last year's rocket is this year's rockette. Yamaha YZ125L motocrosser. *Dirt bike (Mission Hills, Calif.)* 14(6), Jun 1984, 24-25;27-29.
LEVEL: B LANG: Eng SIRC ARTICLE NO: 103342

Wind it up let it go: rev high and swing low, Honda's smallest interceptor is fearless of flying. *Cycle Canada (Toronto)* 14(9), Sept 1984, 18-24.
LEVEL: B LANG: Eng SIRC ARTICLE NO: 098354

Yamaha FJ1100: brand Y's superbike entry goes to the front of the pack. *Motorcyclist (Los Angeles)* 1044, Jun 1984, 26-28;30-33.
LEVEL: B LANG: Eng SIRC ARTICLE NO: 103343

Yamaha IT490. Big blue is still a threat: sole survivor. *Dirt bike (Mission Hills, Calif.)* 14(7), Jul 1984, 36-39.
LEVEL: B LANG: Eng SIRC ARTICLE NO: 104849

Yamaha TT600L. Workhorse: heavy-duty hauler. *Dirt bike (Mission Hills, Calif.)* 14(8), Aug 1984, 20-21;23.
LEVEL: B LANG: En SIRC ARTICLE NO: 104850

Yamaha vs. Honda: FJ600 meets VF500F. *Motorcyclist (Los Angeles)* 1044, Jun 1984, 50-57;82.
LEVEL: B LANG: Eng SIRC ARTICLE NO: 103344

Yamaha XT250. Works hard for the money: mellow fellow. *Dirt bike (Mission Hills, Calif.)* 14(8), Aug 1984, 40-41.
LEVEL: B LANG: Eng SIRC ARTICLE NO: 104851

Yamaha's lightweight enduro goes bionic: it's bigger, faster, stronger than ever. (Yamaha IT200) *Cycle world (Los Angeles)* 23(8), Aug 1984, 50-54.
LEVEL: B LANG: Eng SIRC ARTICLE NO: 105987

EQUIPMENT - MAINTENANCE

Booth, D. The how to of valve adjustment. *Cycle Canada (Toronto)* 14(7), Jul 1984, 39-40.
LEVEL: B LANG: Eng SIRC ARTICLE NO: 102146

Clipper, P. Mike Melton's national-winning husky secrets. This is what the boys in the back room do. *Dirt bike (Mission Hills, Calif.)* 14(4), Apr 1984, 52-54.
LEVEL: B LANG: Eng SIRC ARTICLE NO: 101412

MOTORCYCLING (continued)

HISTORY

The first 60 years: an illustrated history of the American Motorcyclist Association: competition. *AM American motorcyclist (Westerville, Oh.) 38(1), Jan 1984, 27-28;30-34;36-38.*
LEVEL: B LANG: Eng SIRC ARTICLE NO: 098344

The first 60 years: an illustrated history of the American Motorcyclist Association: road riding. *AM American motorcyclist (Westerville, Oh.) 38(1), Jan 1984, 40;43-46.*
LEVEL: B LANG: Eng SIRC ARTICLE NO: 098345

The first 60 years: an illustrated history of the American Motorcyclist Association: government. *AM American motorcyclist (Westerville, Oh.) 38(1), Jan 1984, 48;50-54.*
LEVEL: B LANG: Eng SIRC ARTICLE NO: 098346

INJURIES AND ACCIDENTS

Hubens, A. van Thielen, F. Wyffels, G. Isolated unilateral adrenal hemorrhage after a motorcycle race. *Journal of trauma (Baltimore) 24(8), Aug 1984, 765-767.*
ABST: The authors report the case of a 19 year-old girl with an isolated unilateral adrenal hemorrhage following a motorcycle cross-country race. The patient was treated surgically by thoracolaparotomy.
LEVEL: I LANG: Eng SIRC ARTICLE NO: 104840

McInerney, P.D. Case report: helmets and haematomas. (Refs: 4)*British journal of sports medicine (Loughborough, Eng.) 18(2) Jun 1984, 124-125.*
ABST: This report discusses two cases referred on the same day to the Mersey Regional Neurosurgical Unit. Both patients bore positions of responsibility and each developed an extradural haematoma as a result of neglecting to wear the appropriate safety helmet for their respective sports. The two survived, without detectable morbidity, to learn the relevant lesson.
LEVEL: I LANG: Eng SIRC ARTICLE NO: 103350

Westman, J.A. Morrow, G. Moped injuries in children. *Pediatrics (Evanston, Ill.) 74(5), Nov 1984, 820-822.*
LEVEL: I LANG: Eng

PROTECTIVE DEVICES

Cycle World evaluation: Bell Moto-4 helmet. *Cycle world (Los Angeles) 23(10), Oct 1984, 16-17;19.*
LEVEL: B LANG: Eng SIRC ARTICLE NO: 108723

Gordon, P. Helmet guide: part 2: crucial choice: living with 53 helmets. *Motorcyclist (Los Angeles, Calif.) 1039, Jan 1984, 41-56.*
LEVEL: B LANG: Eng SIRC ARTICLE NO: 097487

PSYCHOLOGY

Sieman, R. How to beat fear: there's one proven way to get back on the track. *Dirt bike (Mission Hills, Calif.) 14(10), Oct 1984, 66.*
LEVEL: B LANG: Eng SIRC ARTICLE NO: 109074

RULES AND REGULATIONS

AM special supplement: official 1984 AMA road rider rule book. *AM: American motorcyclist (Westerville, Oh.) 38(4), Apr 1984, 29-36.*
LEVEL: B LANG: Eng SIRC ARTICLE NO: 101407

SPORTING EVENTS

The ABC's of road riding: getting involved in organized riding is a snap. *AM: American motorcyclist (Westerville, Oh.) 38(6), Jun 1984, 36-37.*
LEVEL: B LANG: Eng SIRC ARTICLE NO: 101406

STATISTICS AND RECORDS

Van Doren, C.S. Motorcycles. *In, Clawson, M. and Van Doren, C.S. (eds.), Statistics on outdoor recreation, Washington, Resources for the Future, c1984, p. 266.*
LEVEL: B LANG: Eng GV191.4 20254

TECHNIQUES AND SKILLS

Bailey, G. Riding muddy, rutted corners. Stay loose on the bike; it knows what to do. *Dirt bike (Mission Hills, Calif.) 14(6), Jun 1984, 32-33.*
LEVEL: B LANG: Eng SIRC ARTICLE NO: 103325

Bailey, G. How to climb hills: not only is it great training, it's fun too. *Dirt bike (Mission Hills, Calif.) 14(8), Aug 1984, 38-39.*
LEVEL: B LANG: Eng SIRC ARTICLE NO: 104832

Bailey, G. Mastering double jumps: double the pressure & double your fun. *Dirt bike (Mission Hills, Calif.) 14(7), Jul 1984 30-31.*
LEVEL: B LANG: Eng SIRC ARTICLE NO: 104833

Baily, G. Clutch slipping: the key to control. Ride a gear higher & go faster. *Dirt bike (Mission Hills, Calif.) 14(2), Feb 1984, 26-28.*
LEVEL: B LANG: Eng SIRC ARTICLE NO: 098336

MOUNTAINEERING

Gicquel, M. Les differents aspects de l'alpinisme. (Refs: 4)
NOTES: Dans, Richalet, J.P. (ed.) et al., Medecine de l'alpinisme, Paris, Masson, 1984, p. 5-13.
LEVEL: I LANG: Fr RC1220.M6 17787

Muir, J. Fleck, R.F. Mountaineering essays. Salt Lake City: G.M. Smith, 1984. 1v. (Literature of the American Wilderness.)
LEVEL: B LANG: Eng ISBN: 0879051698 LC CARD: 84-013950

Roper, S. Steck, A. Ascent, the mountaineering experience in word and image. San Francisco: Sierra Club Books, 1984. 1v.
LEVEL: B LANG: Eng ISBN: 0871568268 LC CARD: 84-005379

Scott, D.K. MacIntyre, A. The Shishapangma expedition. Seattle, Wa.: Mountaineers Books, c1984. 1v.
NOTES: Includes index.
LEVEL: B LANG: Eng ISBN: 0898860989 LC CARD: 84-016516

Thorn, J. Reuther, D. Carroll, B. The armchair mountaineer. New York: Scribner, 1984. 1v.
LEVEL: B LANG: Eng ISBN: 06841819 LC CARD: 84-014095

ADMINISTRATION

Eugenis, T.P. Anatomy of an expedition: how the Canadians really conquered Everest. *Backpacker (New York) 12(1), Jan 1984, 76-80.*
LEVEL: B LANG: Eng SIRC ARTICLE NO: 095155

BIOGRAPHY AND AUTOBIOGRAPHY

Blanchard, S. Robinson, D. Walking up and down in the world: the life and adventures of a mountain wanderer. San Francisco: Sierra Club Books, 1984. 1v.
LEVEL: B LANG: Eng ISBN: 0871568276 LC CARD: 84-005380

Blaurock, C. Euser, B.J. Lavender, D. A climber's climber: on the trail with Carl Blaurock. 1st ed. Louisville, Co.: Cordillera Press, c1984. 1v.
NOTES: Includes index.
LEVEL: B LANG: Eng LC CARD: 84-009539

Ferbos, H. Henry Russell (1834-1909). (Refs: 20)*Montagne & alpinisme (Paris) 138, 1984, 528-529.*
LEVEL: B LANG: Fr SIRC ARTICLE NO: 103349

Speer, G. High ambition: in the world of super-alpinism, altitude is a matter of attitude. *Ultrasport (Boston, Mass.) 1(5), Sept/Oct 1984, 46-52;54.*
LEVEL: B LANG: Eng SIRC ARTICLE NO: 173303

Vetter, C. Lucky Yvon. How a starving Yosemite ironmonger became the King of Patagonia. *Outside (Chicago) 9(2), Mar 1984, 38-42;44;77.*
LEVEL: B LANG: Eng SIRC ARTICLE NO: 098363

CLOTHING

Sellers, G. Introducing John Keighley. *Climber & rambler (Glasgow) 23(3), Mar 1984, 58-59.*
LEVEL: B LANG: Eng SIRC ARTICL NO: 096774

Sellers, G. The boot revolution. *Climber & rambler (Glasgow) 23(4), Apr 1984, 70-72;75.*
LEVEL: B LANG: Eng SIRC ARTICLE NO: 098359

COUNTRIES AND REGIONS

Murray, B. Scotland: the 1930's. *Mountain (Sheffield, Eng.) 98, Jul/Aug 1984, 18-23.*
LEVEL: B LANG: Eng SIRC ARTICLE NO: 101430

Randall, G. Breaking point. Denver, Colo.: Chockstone Press, c1984. 1v.
LEVEL: B LANG: Eng ISBN: 0960945237 LC CARD: 84-021391

DIRECTORIES

Borneman, W. Colorado's other mountains: a climbing guide to selected peaks under 13,000 feet. *Louisville? Colo.*: Cordillera Press, 1984. 1v.
NOTES: Includes index.
LEVEL: B LANG: Eng LC CARD: 84-007623

Garratt, M. Martin, B. Borneman, W.R. Colorado's high thirteeners: a climbing & hiking guide. 1st ed. (Louisville, Colo.): Cordillera Press, c1984. 1v.
NOTES: Includes index.
LEVEL: B LANG: Eng ISBN: 0917895037 LC CARD: 84-027436

DISABLED

Botvin Madorsky, J.G. Kiley, D.P. Wheelchair mountaineering. (Refs: 10)*Archives of physical medicine and rehabilitation (Chicago) 65(8), Aug 1984, 490-492.*
LEVEL: B LANG: Eng SIRC ARTICLE NO: 097531

DOCUMENTATION

Perrin, J. The great historical Mountain review. *Mountain (Sheffield, Eng.) 100, Nov/Dec 1984, 20-25.*
LEVEL: B LANG: Eng SIRC ARTICLE NO: 109218

ENVIRONMENT

Rivolier, J. L'environnement de montagne. (Refs: 22)
NOTES: Dans, Richalet, J.P. (ed.) et al., Medecine de l'alpinisme, Paris, Masson, 1984, p. 14-26.
LEVEL: I LANG: Fr RC1220.M6 17787

EQUIPMENT

Ashton, S. Gear special report: choosing a tent. *Climber & rambler (Glasgow, Scotland) 23(6), Jun 1984, 34-35;38-39.*
LEVEL: B LANG: Eng SIRC ARTICLE NO: 098934

Ashton, S. Gear special: ice-axes. *Climber & rambler (Edinburgh, Eng.) 23(11), Nov 1984, 41-43;45.*
LEVEL: B LANG: Eng SIR ARTICLE NO: 173562

Bourdon, C. Aspects techniques du materiel et des methodes d'assurage. *Montagne & alpinisme (Paris) 138, 1984, 551-553.*
LEVEL: B LANG: Fr SIRC ARTICLE NO: 103346

Cinnamon, J. A versatile leash for hard-water ice tools. *Summit (Big Bear City, Calif.) 30(5), Sept/Oct 1984, 16-17.*
LEVEL: B LANG: Eng SIRC ARTICLE NO: 173474

Ice screw/ice piton tests - report from the Deutscher Alpenverein. *B.C. mountaineering club newsletter (Vancouver, B.C.) 61(7), Aug/Sept 1984, 8-11.*
LEVEL: I LANG: Eng SIRC ARTICLE NO: 099812

O'Connell, K. Choosing a climbing rope: some points to consider. *Summit (Big Bear City, Calif.) 30(5), Sept/Oct 1984, 12-13*
LEVEL: B LANG: Eng SIRC ARTICLE NO: 173473

Perlman, E. A mountaineer's best friends. *In, Schrier, E.W. and Allman, W.F. (eds.), Newton at the bat: the science in sports, New York, Scribner, c1984, p. 71-75.*
LEVEL: B LANG: Eng RC1235 18609

Sellers, G. Introducing John Keighley. *Climber & rambler (Glasgow) 23(3), Mar 1984, 58-59.*
LEVEL: B LANG: Eng SIRC ARTICL NO: 096774

Taupin, D. Essais a la rupture de pitons et anneaux de scellement. *Montagne & alpinisme (Paris) 135, 1984, 309-311.*
LEVEL: B LANG: Fr SIRC ARTICLE NO: 096775

Toft, M. Brearley, A. How strong are used rappel slings? *Climber & rambler (Glasgow) 23(4), Apr 1984, 69.*
LEVEL: B LANG: Eng SIRC ARTICLE NO: 098361

Turville, D. A short course in rope physics. *Climbing (Aspen, Colo.) 84, Apr 1984, 56-59.*
LEVEL: I LANG: Eng SIRC ARTICLE NO: 098362

HISTORY

Echevarria, E. Early mountaineering in Ecuador, 1582-1870. (Refs: 12)*Appalachia (Boston, Mass.) 178, Summer 1984, 107-114.*
LEVEL: B LANG: Eng SIRC ARTICLE NO: 103348

Jouty, S. L'histoire de l'alpinisme est une enigme. *Dans, Culture technique no. 13, Neuilly-sur-Seine, France, Centre de Recherche sur la Culture Technique, c1984, p. 308-313.*
LEVEL: B LANG: Fr RC1235 20096

Logan, H. Mount Cook: Part one of a history of New Zealand Alpinism. *Mountain (Sheffield, Eng.) 96, Mar/Apr 1984, 16-23.*
LEVEL: B LANG: Eng SIRC ARTICLE NO: 098356

Roberts, D. The K2 Mystery. *Outside (Chicago, Ill.) 9(9), Oct 1984, 39-44;79-82.*
LEVEL: B LANG: Eng SIRC ARTICLE NO: 1087

Sames, M. Czech climbing history: a short account. *Mountain (Sheffield, Eng.) 94, Dec/Jan 1983-1984, 22-25.*
LEVEL: B LANG Eng SIRC ARTICLE NO: 098358

Scott, D. Himalayan climbing. Part one of a personal review. *Moutnain (Sheffield, Eng.) 100, Nov/Dec 1984, 26-35.*
LEVEL: LANG: Eng SIRC ARTICLE NO: 109219

INJURIES AND ACCIDENTS

Accidents. *Appalachia (Boston, Mass.) 178, Summer 1984, 141-151.*
LEVEL: B LANG: Eng SIRC ARTICLE NO: 103345

Bourdon, C. Les accidents de montagne en France du 1er octobre 1982 au 30 septembre 1983. *Montagne & alpinisme (Paris) 138, 1984, 554-555.*
LEVEL: I LANG: Fr SIRC ARTICLE NO: 103347

Carroll, S. Climb till it hurts. *Backpacker (New York) 12(1), Jan 1984, 53-54;57.*
LEVEL: I LANG: Eng SIRC ARTICLE NO: 095154

Foray, J. Les accidents de montagne. (Refs: 3)
NOTES: Dans, Richalet, J.P. (ed.) et al., Medecine de l'alpinisme, Paris, Masson, 1984, p. 71-75.
LEVEL: I LANG: Fr RC1220.M6 17787

Foray, J. Pathologie liee au froid. (Refs: 6)
NOTES: Dans, Richalet, J.P. (ed.) et al., Medecine de l'alpinisme, Paris, Masson, 1984, p. 108-120.
LEVEL: I LANG: Fr RC1220.M6 17787

Foray, J. Cahen, C. Darnaud, B. Pathologie diverse. (Refs: 4)
NOTES: Dans, Richalet, J.P. (ed.) et al., Medecine de l'alpinisme, Paris, Masson, 1984, p. 124-133.
LEVEL: I LANG: Fr RC1220.M6 17787

Genevey, A. Montagne et medecine. (Refs: 6)*Tempo medical (Paris) 168, 1984, 75-77.*
LEVEL: B LANG: Fr

Gicquel, M. Le secours en montagne et son organisation. (Refs: 3)
NOTES: Dans, Richalet, J.P. (ed.) et al., Medecine de l'alpinisme, Paris, Masson, 1984, p. 176-180.
LEVEL: B LANG: Fr RC1220.M6 17787

Mazeaud, J.F. La prevention des accidents. (Refs: 8)
NOTES: Dans, Richalet, J.P. (ed.) et al., Medecine de l'alpinisme, Paris, Masson, 1984, p. 167-175.
LEVEL: I LANG: Fr RC1220.M6 17787

McInerney, P.D. Case report: helmets and haematomas. (Refs: 4)*British journal of sports medicine (Loughborough, Eng.) 18(2) Jun 1984, 124-125.*
ABST: This report discusses two cases referred on the same day to the Mersey Regional Neurosurgical Unit. Both patients bore positions of responsibility and each developed an extradural haematoma as a result of neglecting to wear the appropriate safety helmet for their respective sports. The two survived, without detectable morbidity, to learn the relevant lesson.
LEVEL: I LANG: Eng SIRC ARTICLE NO: 103350

Menthonnex, P. Le polytraumatise.
NOTES: Dans, Richalet, J.P. (ed.) et al., Medecine de l'alpinisme, Paris, Masson, 1984, p 78-82.
LEVEL: B LANG: Fr RC1220.M6 17787

Olland, P.L. Haute altitude: comment eviter les accidents. *Generaliste (Paris) 651, 1984, 20-25.*
LEVEL: B LANG: Fr

Smart, J. Hunter, D. Alpine travel. Mountain sickness, the unwelcome companion. *Medical journal of Australia (Sydney) 141 (12/13), 8-22 Dec 1984, 792-795.*
LEVEL: I LANG: Eng

MEDICINE

Ajasse, D. Le mal des montagnes: un essai therapeutique a double insu a 7700 metres. (Refs: 11)*Vie medicale (Paris) 65(19), 1984, 749-750.*
LEVEL: B LANG: Fr

Battestini, R. Medicina y montana. (Medicine and mountains.) *Medicina clinica (Barcelona) 83(12), 20 Oct 1984, 497-499.*
LEVEL: B LANG: Spa

Villar, R.N. So you want to climb Everest...? *British medical journal (clinical research) (London) 289(6460), 22-29 Dec 198 1773-1775.*
LEVEL: I LANG: Eng SIRC ARTICLE NO: 107388

NUTRITION

Richalet, J.P. Les aspects dietetiques. (Refs: 9)
NOTES: Dans, Richalet, J.P. (ed.) et al., Medecine de l'alpinisme, Paris, Masson, 1984, p. 162-166.
LEVEL: I LANG: Fr RC1220.M6 17787

PHYSICAL FITNESS

Mathieu, D. Pour l'escalade etes-vous pret? *Mousqueton (Montreal) 13(2), 1984, 2-3.*
LEVEL: B LANG: Fr SIRC ARTICLE NO: 096770

PHYSIOLOGY

Herry, J.P. La visite medicale d'aptitude. (Refs: 9)
NOTES: Dans, Richalet, J.P. (ed.) et al., Medecine de l'alpinisme, Paris, Masson, 1984, p. 157-161.
LEVEL: I LANG: Fr RC1220.M6 17787

Richalet, J.P. Darnaud, B. Cohen, C. Foray, J. Carette, G. Medecine de l'alpinisme. Paris: Masson, 1984. x, 203 p. (Collection de monographies de medecine du sport.)
NOTES: ISSN: 0338-9383. Comprend des bibliographies.
LEVEL: I LANG: Fr ISBN: 2-225-80092-8 RC1220.M6 17787

PHYSIOLOGY - ALTITUDE

Guilland, J.C. Mareau, D. Malval, M. Morville, R. Klepping, J. Evaluation of sympathoadrenal activity adrenocortical functions and androgenic status in five men during a Himalayan mountaineering expedition (ascent of Mt. Pabil, 7, 102 m, 23, 294 ft). (Refs: 37)*European journal of applied physiology and occupational physiology (Heidelberg) 52(2), Jan 1984, 156-162.*

MOUNTAINEERING (continued)

ABST: In this descriptive investigation, levels of urinary catecholamines adrenal steroids and androgens were examined in five mountain climbers, during different phases of an ascent of Mount Pabil (7,102 m). The results clearly demonstrated that well-trained climbers undergo major neuro-endocrine changes during Himalayan mountain expeditions, as sympathetic hyperactivity, adrenocratical hyperfunction and hypogonadisn were evident from the measurements taken.
LEVEL: A LANG: Eng SIRC ARTICLE NO: 096768

Hughson, R.L. The limit to man's performance. *Canadian runner Mar 1984, 20.*
LEVEL: B LANG: Eng SIRC ARTICLE NO: 093628

Hultgren, H.N. Pathologie en altitude. *Tempo medical (Paris) 153, 1984, 13-24.*
LEVEL: I LANG: Fr

Rathat, C. Darnaud, B. Pathologie liee a l'hypoxie d'altitude. (Refs: 35)
NOTES: Dans, Richalet, J.P. (ed.) et al., Medecine de l'alpinisme, Paris, Masson, 1984, p. 83-107.
LEVEL: A LANG: Fr RC1220.M6 17787

Richalet, J.P. Les reactions de l'organisme a l'altitude. (Refs: 53)
NOTES: Dans, Richalet, J.P. (ed.) et al., Medecine de l'alpinisme, Paris, Masson, 1984, p. 30-55.
LEVEL: A LANG: Fr RC1220.M6 17787

Schoene, R.B. Lahiri, S. Hackett, P.H. Peters, R.M. Milledge, J.S. Pizzo, C.J. Sarnquist, F.H. Boyer, S.J. Graber, D.J. Maret K.H. West, J.B. Relationship of hypoxic ventilatory response to exercise performance on Mount Everest. (Refs: 41)*Journal of applied physiology: respiratory, environmental and exercise physiology (Bethesda, Md.) 56(6), Jun 1984, 1478-1483.*
ABST: This study investigated the relationship of hypoxic ventilatory response (HVR) to exercise performance at high altitude. HVR and exercise ventilation were measured at sea level and 5,400m in nine subjects. The subjects had either a low or a high ventilation response to the altitude end-tidal PO2 of 40 Torr; based on this finding subjects were grouped into high (H) and low (L) HVR responders. The H group ventilated more during low and moderate exercise than the L group. The authors suggest that the H group may be better suited for high-altitude work as their ventilation response maintains a higher oxygen saturation than the ventilation response of the L group.
LEVEL: A LANG: Eng SIRC ARTICLE NO: 097761

Winslow, R.M. Samaja, M. West, J.B. Red cell function at extreme altitude on Mount Everest. (Refs: 29)*Journal of applied physiology: respiratory, environmental and exercise physiology (Bethesda, Md.) 56(1), Jan 1984, 109-116.*
ABST: Red cell 2,3-diphosphoglycerate (2,3-DPG) has a profound effect on hemoglobin oxygen affinity. This compound causes the oxygen equilibrium curve to be shifted to the right . However the American Medical Research Expedition to Everest in 1981 found that at altitudes above 6,300 meters extreme alkalasis causes the oxygen equilibrium curve to shift to the left overriding the effects of 2,3-DPG.
LEVEL: A LANG: Eng SIRC ARTICLE NO: 096776

PHYSIOLOGY - TEMPERATURE

Houdas, Y. Carette, G. L'organisme au froid: echanges thermiques, reactions physiologiques et protection vestimentaire. (Refs: 15)
NOTES: Dans, Richalet, J.P. (ed.) et al., Medecine de l'alpinisme, Paris, Masson, 1984, p. 56-69.
LEVEL: I LANG: Fr RC1220.M6 17787

PSYCHOLOGY

McMartin, L. Endurance: a nurse's hike in the Rockies helped her survive her father's illness. *Journal of Christian nursing (Downers Grove, Ill.) 1(1), Spring 1984, 21-22.*
LEVEL: I LANG: Eng SIRC ARTICLE NO: 101429

Rivolier, J. Les aspects psychologiques de la pratique de l'alpinisme. (Refs: 58)
NOTES: Dans, Richalet, J.P. (ed.) et al., Medecine de l'alpinisme, Paris, Masson, 1984, p. 134-155.
LEVEL: A LANG: Fr RC1220.M6 17787

SAFETY

Josi, W. Securite en montagne. *Macolin (Macolin, Suisse) 41(5), mai 1984, 12-13.*
NOTES: Traduction de, Marianne Weber.
LEVEL: B LANG: Fr SIRC ARTICLE NO: 108769

Mathieu, R. Zuanon, J.P. Ski alpinisme: la prevention du risque d'avalanche et le sauvetage des victimes (2e partie). (Refs: 8)*Montagne & alpinisme (Paris) 135, 1984, 278-284.*
LEVEL: I LANG: Fr SIRC ARTICLE NO: 096771

Smutek, R. The plain truth about avalanche rescue beacons. *Summit (Big Bear Lake, Calif.) 30(1), Jan/Feb 1984, 28-31.*
NOTES: To be continued.
LEVEL: B LANG: Eng SIRC ARTICLE NO: 098360

Smutek, R. A comparison of rescue beacons. (Refs: 4)*Summit (Big Bear City, Calif.) 30(3), May/Jun 1984, 26-29.*
LEVEL: I LANG: Eng SIRC ARTICLE NO: 099813

TEACHING

Alberti, T. Comment creer une A.S. de pleine nature? *EPS: Revue education physique et sport (Paris) 188, juil/aout 1984, 57-59.*
LEVEL: B LANG: Fr SIRC ARTICLE NO: 098355

TECHNIQUES AND SKILLS

Walker, J.A. A manual for basic mountaineering and technical climbing. 1st ed. Laramie, Wysc. : Markleeville, Calif.: Jelm Mountain Press ; Dist. by Green Mountain Book Co., 1984. 1v.
LEVEL: B LANG: Eng ISBN: 0936204512 LC CARD: 84-015471

TRAINING AND CONDITIONING

Chisnall, R. McKay, I. Buildering at Queen's University. *Canadian alpine journal/Journal alpin canadien (Alberta) 67, 1984, 33-35.*
LEVEL: B LANG: Eng SIRC ARTICLE NO: 101428

VARIATIONS

Ferguson, D. Climbing on thin ice. *Climbing (Aspen, Colo.) 87, Dec 1984, 55-56.*
LEVEL: B LANG: Eng SIRC ARTICLE NO: 10844

Krakauer, J. Choosing tools for snow and ice climbing. *Climbing (Aspen, Colo.) 87, Dec 1984, 50-54.*
LEVEL: B LANG: Eng SIRC ARTICLE NO: 108445

Mazerolle, C. Les outils de glacieristes. *Mousqueton (Montreal) 13(2), 1984, 3-6.*
LEVEL: B LANG: Fr SIRC ARTICLE NO: 0967

Pettifer, T. Ski mountaineering. *Climber & rambler (Glasgow) 23(1), Jan 1984, 39;41.*
LEVEL: B LANG: Eng SIRC ARTICLE NO: 098357

Vetter, C. Ice climbing: just for the hell of it. *Outside 9(1), Jan/Feb 1984, 65-66.*
LEVEL: B LANG: Eng SIRC ARTICLE NO: 093633

WOMEN

De Colombel, C. Belden, D. Voix de femmes au K2: une expedition franco-polonaise sur le deuxieme sommet du monde. Paris: Denoel, c1984. 121 p. : ill.
LEVEL: B LANG: Fr ISBN: 2207230821 LC CARD: 84-247779

Moore, M.H. Petticoats on the mountains: a look at the early history of female mountaineering. *Mountain (Sheffield, Eng.) 95, Jan/Feb 1984, 42-45.*
LEVEL: B LANG: Eng SIRC ARTICLE NO: 096773

NETBALL

INJURIES AND ACCIDENTS

Skinner, L. Back care and posture. (Refs: 2)*Netball (London) 3(3), Sept 1984, 18-19.*
LEVEL: B LANG: Eng SIRC ARTICLE NO: 101432

SOCIAL PSYCHOLOGY

Reynolds, S. A study of player communication in netball. *Carnegie research papers (Beckett Park, Leeds) 1(6), Dec 1984, 28-29.*
CONF: Carnegie Undergraduate Research Symposium (1984 : Leeds, Eng.).
LEVEL: I LANG: Eng SIRC ARTICLE NO: 172504

TECHNIQUES AND SKILLS - GOALTENDER AND GOALTENDING

Galsworthy, B. Improve your game. Goal keeper - the 'reject' position? *Netball (London) 3(2), Jun 1984, 6;20.*
ABST: After listing the qualities a good netball goalkeeper should have the author points out that all of these skills are trainable. Coaches can improve their goaltender's play by insuring such skills are practiced regularly. The remainder of this article focuses on intercepting or deflecting either lob or forward passes. Proper tactical positioning is important to accomplish this and a series of drills are outlined to improve the goalkeeper's skills in this area.
LEVEL: B LANG: Eng SIRC ARTICLE NO: 098364

Galsworthy, B. Improve your game: goal keeper - positional play and spacial awareness. *Netball*

(London) 3(3), Sept 1984, 12-13.
LEVEL: B LANG: Eng SIRC ARTICLE NO: 101431

TECHNIQUES AND SKILLS - STANCE

Perry, J. Improve your game:'you need feet..'
Netball (London) 3(1), Mar 1984, 6;10.
LEVEL: B LANG: Eng SIRC ARTICLE NO: 098365

NETHERLANDS

Kok, F. Matroos, A. Van den Ban, A. Hautvast,
J. Regular exercise. A profile of the inactives. Hygie
(Paris) 3(1), Mar 1984 51-56.
LEVEL: A LANG: Eng SIRC ARTICLE NO: 101011

NEUROENDOCRINOLOGY

Goldszer, R.C. Siegel, A.J. Renal abnormalities
during exercise. (Refs: 73)
NOTES: In, Strauss, R.H. (ed.), Sports medicine,
Philadelphia ; Toronto, Saunders, 1984, p. 130-
139.
LEVEL: A LANG: Eng RC1210 17196

Keusch, G. Jenni, T. Tartini, R. Fechter, P.
Steinbrunn, W. Binswanger, U. Ergometrisch
bestimmte Arbeitskapazitaet bei chronischer
Haemodialysebehandlung. (Ergometrically
determined work capacity in chronic hemodialysis
treatment.) Schweizerische Medizinische
Wochenschrift/Journal suisse de medicine (Basel)
114(39), 29 Sept 1984, 1326-1330.
LEVEL: A LANG: Ger

Lagrue, G. Les troubles renaux de l'effort. Science
et vie (Paris) HS147, 1984, 120-122.
LEVEL: I LANG: Fr

Poortmans, J.R. Exercise and renal function.
(Refs: 121)Sports medicine (Auckland) 1(2), Mar/
Apr 1984, 125-153.
ABST: The purpose of this paper was to review the
previous literature, to relate some observations
from the author's work, to explain the mechanisms
underlying this postexercise proteinuria and to draw
from this information some implications relevant to
researchers and partitioners of physical activities.
Post-exercise proteinuria seems to be directly
related to the intensity of exercise not the duration
of the exercise. Training does not eliminate the
transient renal disturbances which occur with heavy
work.
LEVEL: A LANG: Eng SIRC ARTICLE NO: 094620

Tatar, P. Kozlowski, S. Vigas, M. Nazar, K.
Kvetnansky, R. Jezova, D. Kaciuba-Uscilko, H.
Endocrine response to physical efforts with
equivalent total work loads but different intensities
in man. Endocrinologi experimentalis (Bratislava)
18(4), Dec 1984, 233-239.
ABST: The purpose of this study was to determine
relationships between some exercise-induced
neurohormonal changes and either exercise
intensity, or its duration, or the total work output.
Plasma catecholamine, cortisol, growth hormone
and insulin concentrations were measured in male
subjects performing three bicycle-ergometer
exercise tests of the same total work output but
differing in intensity and duration. No relationship
was demonstrated between the exercise-induced
increases in plasma growth hormone concentration
and work intensity or its duration, while the plasma
insulin concentration was more decreased during
the effort of lower intensity, but longer duration than
during a short exercise of high intensity.
LEVEL: A LANG: Eng SIRC ARTICLE NO: 106810

Vanhelder, W.P. Goode, R.C. Radomski, M.W.
Effect of anaerobic and aerobic exercise of equal
duration and work expenditure o plasma growth
hormone levels. (Refs: 9)European journal of
applied physiology and occupational physiology
(Heidelberg) 52(3), Apr 1984, 255-257.
ABST: Five subjects performed approximately 120
kJ of external work in two separate cycling
protocols, one aerobic and the other anaerobic.
Plasma lactic acid and growth hormone levels were
significantly elevated at the end of exercise in the
anaerobic protocol as compared to the aerobic
protocol. Furthermore, growth hormone levels after
anaerobic work were increased at the 30 min
recovery measurement after which the levels slowly
decreased throughout the 60 and 90 min recovery
measurements.
LEVEL: A LANG: Eng SIRC ARTICLE NO: 097772

Vanhelder, W.P. Radomski, M.W. Goode, R.C.
Growth hormone responses during intermittent
weight lifting exercise in men. (Refs: 16)European
journal of applied physiology and occupational
physiology (Berlin, W.G.) 53(1), 1984, 31-34.
ABST: Five normal male volunteers performed two
intermittent weight lifting exercises of equal total
external work output and duration (20 min).
Exercise I consisted of seven sets of seven vertical
leg lifts at 85 per cent of the subject's repetition
maximum and, 5 days later, seven sets of 21
vertical leg lifts with one-third of the previously used
load (Exercise II). Growth hormone increased after
20 min of Exercise I to a peak during the recovery
period. Significantly elevated growth hormone (GH)
levels were found after 5,10, and 15 min of
recovery after Exercise I. No significant elevations
of GH occurred in Exercise II.
LEVEL: A LANG: Eng SIRC ARTICLE NO: 104387

Wade, C.E. Response, regulation, and actions of
vasopressin during exercise: a review. (Refs:
76)Medicine and science in sports and exercise
(Indianapolis) 16(5), Oct 1984, 506-511.
ABST: Plasma concentration of vasopressin
(antidiuretic hormone), a powerful pressor agent
and primary regulator of body fluid homeostasis,
are elevated in a dose-related fashion to increases
in exercise intensity. The response of plasma
vasopressin levels to exercise is not modified by
gender, but is reduced with training at absolute
submaximal exercise intensities. The increase in
plasma vasopressin concentrations during exercise
may be mediated by a variety of factors: plasma
osmolality, blood pressure, blood volume, plasma
concentrations of angiotensin II, psychological
variables, and peripheral nerve stimulation.
LEVEL: A LANG: Eng SIRC ARTICLE NO: 102838

ADRENAL FUNCTION

Warren, J.B. Dalton, N. Turner, C. Clark, T.J.
Toseland, P.A. Adrenaline secretion during
exercise. Clinical science (London) 66(1), Jan
1984, 87-90.
ABST: Six normal subjects were infused
intravenously with adrenaline both during rest and
after they had started moderate exercise on a
bicycle. Adrenaline levels were monitored
throughout the study. No significant rises in plasma
adrenaline were recorded. The clearance rate of
adrenaline from plasma was found to be reduced
during exercise. There was no significant increase
in secretion by the adrenal medulla in response to
mild or moderate exercise.
LEVEL: A LANG: Eng SIRC ARTICLE NO: 097777

THYROID FUNCTION

Acheson, K. Jequier, E. Burger, A. Danforth, E.
Thyroid hormones and thermogenesis: the
metabolic cost of food and exercise. Metabolism,
clinical and experimental (New York) 33(3), Mar
1984, 262-265.
ABST: Six lean healthy men received replacement
amounts of L-thyroxine (T4) to block endogenous
thyroid hormone production while consuming their
habitual diet. After 4 weeks equilibration on T4,
L-triiodothyronine (T3) was given in addition to T4,
to produce mild T3-thyrotoxicosis, for another 2
weeks. At the end of this period T3 was
discontinued but the subjects continued to receive
T4 for another 2 weeks. There was a significant
increase in the resting metabolic rate of 6% while
the subjects were mildly T3-thyrotoxic. Bicycle
ergometry exercise testing found that mild T3-
toxicosis does not alter the efficiency of exercise or
the thermic effect of food. These results suggest
that the increased plasma T3 levels, observed in
overfeeding, could explain corresponding increases
in resting metabolic rate but not changes in the
efficiency of exercise or the utilization of food.
LEVEL: A LANG: Eng SIRC ARTICLE NO: 099219

Boyden, T.W. Pamenter, R.W. Rotkis, T.C.
Stanforth, P. Wilmore, J.H. Thyroidal changes
associated with endurance training in women.
(Refs: 20)Medicine and science in sports and
exercise (Indianapolis) 16(3), June 1984, 243-246.
ABST: The associations between endurance
training, body composition, and the pituitary-thyroid
axis were studied in 17 healthy, young women.
Body composition and plasma concentrations of T4,
T3, rT3, resin T3 uptake, TSH, and TRH-stimulated
TSH were examined at baseline and after each
subject's weekly distance had increased 48 km and
80 km above baseline. Mean lean weight in kg
increased from 42.9 plus or minus 1.2 baseline to
44.8 plus or minus 1.2 at 80 km. We have reported
previously that at 48 km the subjects had evidence
of mild thyroidal impairment, which consisted of
decreased T3 and rT3, and an exaggerated TSH
response to TRH. With more prolonged training (48
km to 80 km) there were significant increases in T4,
rT3, and unstimulated TSH, while the ratios of T4/
rT3 and T3/rT3, and the TSH response to TRH
decreased significantly.
LEVEL: A LANG: Eng SIRC ARTICLE NO: 108592

Licata, G. Scaglione, R. Nov, S. Dichiara, M.A.
Di Vincenzo, D. Behaviour of serum T3, rT3, TT4,
FT4 and TSH levels after exercise on a bicycle
ergometer in healthy euthyroid male young
subjects. Bollettino - Societa italiana biologia
sperimental (Napoli) 60(4), 30 Apr 1984, 753-759.
ABST: In order to know thyroid function during
physical activity, the authors have submitted 10
young subjects, non athletes, aged 22-25 years
(mean age 23) to a biologically maximal exercise
on a bicycle ergometer. They have also examined
the change of TSH serum levels during exercise.
The data shows evident increase of T4, an
increment of FT4, and no relevant change of T3
and rT3 serum levels. Moreover TSH values show
a reduction in comparison with the basal level.
These findings confirm the known increment of T4
and FT4 serum level after physical activity. It can

NEUROENDOCRINOLOGY (continued)

be due, more than an hemoconcentration supported by others, to a real rise of thyroid incretion as in our opinion TSH levels reduction suggests. The authors believe that the increase of T4 and decrease of TSH could be due to a direct influence of the physical activity on the system interested in their production.
LEVEL: A LANG: Eng

Opstad, P.K. Falch, D. Oktedalen, O. Fonnum, F. Wergeland, R. The thyroid function in young men during prolonged exercise an the effect of energy and sleep deprivation. *Clinical endocrinology (Oxford) 20(6), Jun 1984, 657-669.*
ABST: Thyroid function has been investigated in 24 young military cadets participating in a 5 d ranger training course with heavy physical exercise, calorie deficiency and deprivation of sleep. The cadets were divided into three groups, each differing in the amount of sleep and food consumption. The serum levels of thyroid hormones (T4, FT4, T3, rT3) and TBG showed a biphasic pattern during the course. Initially there was an increased secretion concomitant with an increased deiodination of T4 to T3 and rT3 mainly due to physical exercise. When the activities lasted for several days without sufficient food supply the thyroid secretion decreased simultaneously with an alteration of the peripheral conversion of T4 to rT3 instead of T3.
LEVEL: A LANG: Eng SIRC ARTICLE NO: 104351

Sawhney, R.C. Malhotra, A.S. Gupta, R.B. Rai, R.M. A study of pituitary-thyroid function during exercise in man. *Indian journal of physiology and pharmacology (New Delhi) 28(2), Apr/June 1984, 153-158.*
LEVEL: A LANG: Eng

NEW ZEALAND

Stothart, B. Recreation and sport: the New Zealand experience. *WLRA journal (New York) 26(2), Mar/Apr 1984, 5-8.*
LEVEL: B LANG: Eng SIRC ARTICLE NO: 097873

HISTORY

Crawford, S.A.G.M. The consolidation of sport and the expansion of recreation in Colonial New Zealand: the case study of Dunedin in the 1870s and 1880s. (Refs: 84)*New Zealand journal of health, physical education & recreation (Wellington, N.Z.) 17(3), Nov 1984, 5-11.*
LEVEL: I LANG: Eng SIRC ARTICLE NO: 104004

PHYSICAL FITNESS

Russell, D.G. Health and fitness: our professional responsibility. (Refs: 2)*New Zealand journal of health, physical education & recreation (Dunedin, New Zealand) 17(2), Aug 1984, 9-11.*
LEVEL: I LANG: Eng SIRC ARTICLE NO: 099205

NIGER

OLYMPIC GAMES

Le Niger et l'olympisme. *Revue olympique (Lausanne) 204, oct 1984, 842-843.*
LEVEL: B LANG: Fr SIRC ARTICLE NO: 100809

Niger and Olympism. *Olympic review (Lausanne) 204, Oct 1984, 842-843.*
LEVEL: B LANG: Eng SIRC ARTICLE NO: 100808

NUTRITION

Addleman, F.G. Winning edge: nutrition for athletic fitness and performance. Englewood Cliffs, N.J.: Prentice-Hall, c1984. viii, 220 p. (A reward book.)
NOTES: Includes index.
LEVEL: B LANG: Eng ISBN: 0139611371 LC CARD: 83-013785 RA784 16088

Addleman, F.G. Landau, C. Do you really need a balanced diet? When planning your meals, be sure to get good foods, the whole good foods and nothing but the good foods - it's your health that hangs in the balance. *Runner's world (Mountain View, Calif.) 19(7), Jul 1984, 42-47.*
LEVEL: B LANG: Eng SIRC ARTICLE NO: 094463

Angel, J.B. Nutrition and athletes. *Virginia journal (Harrisonburg, Va.) 7(1), Nov 1984, 7;10;20.*
LEVEL: I LANG: Eng SIRC ARTICLE NO: 100772

Aronson, V. Stare, F.J. Going on a binge. Athletes' tendency to starve, then stuff themselves signals a dangerous dietary trend. *First aider (Gardner, Kans.) 54(2), Oct 1984, 12-13.*
LEVEL: B LANG: Eng SIRC ARTICLE NO: 105367

Biegel, L. Food for fitness. (Refs: 1)
NOTES: In, Biegel, L. (ed.), Physical fitness and the older person: a guide to exercise for health care professionals, Rockville, Md., Aspen Systems Corp., 1984, p. 151-156.
LEVEL: I LANG: Eng GV482.6 17754

Brotherhood, J.R. Nutrition and sports performance. (Refs: 268)*Sports medicine (Auckland, N.Z.) 1(5), Sept/Oct 1984, 350-389.*
ABST: The author reviews the published information on the dietary habits and attitudes of athletes, then examines the specific nutritional stresses associated with sports activity and, finally, states practical recommandations for nutrition and optimal physical performance.
LEVEL: A LANG: Eng SIRC ARTICLE NO: 102625

Clark, N. How I manage athletes' food obsessions. (Refs: 5)*Physician and sportsmedicine (Minneapolis, Minn.) 12(7), Jul 1984, 96-100;102-103.*
LEVEL: B LANG: Eng SIRC ARTICLE NO: 096081

Cumming, C. Nutrition: smog alert. *Women's sports (San Francisco) 6(6), Jun 1984, 60.*
LEVEL: B LANG: Eng SIRC ARTICLE NO: 104172

de Mondenard, J.P. Mise a jour sur l'alimentation du sportif. (Refs: 7)*Dans, Culture technique no. 13, Neuilly-sur-Seine, France, Centre de Recherche sur la Culture Technique, c1984, p. 180-183.*
LEVEL: I LANG: Fr RC1235 20096

Devison, J. The fundamentals of food. Basic food knowledge for the coach who is advising athletes on their nutritional requirements. *Coaching review*

(Ottawa, Ont.) 7, Jul/Aug 1984, 16-18.
LEVEL: B LANG: Eng SIRC ARTICLE NO: 094468

Douglas, P.D. Douglas, J.G. Nutrition knowledges and food practices of high-school athletes. (Refs: 13)*Journal of the American Dietetic Association (Chicago) 84(10), 1984, 1198-1202.*
LEVEL: I LANG: Eng SIRC ARTICLE NO: 099120

Dwyer, T. Brotherhood, J. What to eat and when to eat it on the big day. (Refs: 2)*Sports coach (Wembley, Aust.) 8(1), 1984, 8-11.*
NOTES: Presented at an 'Update your coaching knowledge' seminar held by the New South Wales Department of Leisure, Sport and Tourism in July, 1983.
LEVEL: I LANG: Eng SIRC ARTICLE NO: 096083

Good nutrition: the extra edge for executive exercises. *Executive fitness newsletter (Emmaus, Pa.) 15(10), 12 May 1984, 1-2.*
LEVEL: B LANG: Eng SIRC ARTICLE NO: 100779

Goulart, F.S. Vitality through vegetable oils: helping your health with the polysaturates. *National racquetball (Glenview, Ill.) 13(2), Feb 1984, 36-37.*
LEVEL: B LANG: Eng SIRC ARTICLE NO: 099121

Goulart, F.S. 10 day diet for a healthy heart. *National racquetball (Glenview, Ill.) 13(9), Sept 1984, 32-33.*
LEVEL: B LANG: Eng SIRC ARTICLE NO: 105370

Goulart, S. Supplements for sports. *Kick illustrated (Burbank, Calif.) 5(4), Apr 1984, 55-57.*
LEVEL: B LANG: Eng SIRC ARTICLE NO: 099122

Haas, R. Kids eat the darndest things. *World tennis (Los Angeles, Calif.) 31(10), Mar 1984, 38-40.*
LEVEL: B LANG: Eng SIR ARTICLE NO: 099123

Haas, R. Quick bites: are you so busy you can't sit down to eat? Here is a fast-food primer for those who have to munch on the run. *World tennis (Los Angeles, Calif.) 32(1), Jun 1984, 52-54.*
LEVEL: B LANG: Eng SIRC ARTICLE NO: 100780

Hartmann, P.M. Bell, E.H. Nutrition for the athlete. (Refs: 23)
NOTES: In, Birrer, R.B. (ed.), Sports medicine for the primary care physician, Norwalk, Conn., Appleton-Century-Crofts, c1984, p. 105-121.
LEVEL: I LANG: Eng RC1210 17030

Hecker, A.L. Nutritional conditioning for athletic competition. (Refs: 37)*Clinics in sports medicine (Philadelphia) 3(3), Jul 1984, 567-582.*
NOTES: Symposium on nutritional aspects of exercise.
ABST: Diet in itself cannot provide fitness or championship form, but a poor diet can ruin both. Optimal nutrition is a basic component of training that is necessary for the development and maintenance of top physical performance. Appropriate application of recent research findings can have a beneficial impact on exercise performance.
LEVEL: I LANG: Eng SIRC ARTICLE NO: 100782

Herrmann, E. The importance of breakfast. If you find the thought of bacon and eggs first thing in the morning hard to stomach, your body may be trying to tell you something. *Runner's world (Mountain View, Calif.) 19(10), Oct 1984, 53-54;112.*
LEVEL: B LANG: Eng SIRC ARTICLE NO: 099124

Katch, F.I. Katch, V.L. How dieting affects muscle tissue. *Muscle & fitness (Woodland Hills, Calif.) 45(10), Oct 1984, 19;186.*
LEVEL: B LANG: Eng SIRC ARTICLE NO: 109002

Klepping, J. Boggio, V. Marcer, I. Resultats d'enquetes alimentaires realisees chez des sportifs francais. (Results of a nutritional survey among French athletes.) *Schweizerische Zeitschrift fuer Sportmedizin (Geneva) 32(1), Mar 1984, 15-19.*
LEVEL: A LANG: Fr SIRC ARTICLE NO: 100783

Krueger, K.A. Practical sports psychology: nutrition. (Refs: 24)*SNIPES journal (Patiala, India) 7(4), Oct 1984, 54-59.*
LEVEL: I LANG: Eng SIRC ARTICLE NO: 171617

Layman, D.K. Quig, D.W. Keys to health and performance: exercise and proper nutrition. *Illinois teacher of home economics (Champaign, Ill.) 27(3), Jan/Feb 1984, 82-84.*
LEVEL: B LANG: Eng SIRC ARTICLE NO: 099125

Ledoux, M. Sel et performance. *Revue de l'entraineur janv/mars 1984, 20.*
LEVEL: B LANG: Fr SIRC ARTICLE NO: 091554

Ledoux, M. Prendre du poids... une bataille perdue d'avance? *Revue de l'entraineur (Montreal) oct/dec 1984, 27.*
LEVEL: B LANG: Fr SIRC ARTICLE NO: 105371

Lineback, D.R. Chem I supplement: nutrition (diet) and athletics. *Journal of chemical education (Easton, Penn.) 61(6), Jun 1984, 536-539.*
LEVEL: I LANG: Eng SIRC ARTICLE NO: 104179

McCutcheon, M.L. Nutritional preparation of athletes: what makes sense? (Refs: 18)*Journal of the American College Health Association (Washington) 32(6), Jun 1984, 247-251.*
LEVEL: I LANG: Eng SIRC ARTICLE NO: 104181

McLatchie, G. Prevention of injury in sport - Part II. *Scottish journal of physical education (Glasgow, Scotland) 12(3), Au 1984, 45-47.*
LEVEL: B LANG: Eng SIRC ARTICLE NO: 099127

Michael, J.W. Breakfast, lunch, and dinner of champions: star athletes' diet programs for maximum energy and performance. 1s Quill ed. New York: Quill, 1984. 263 p.
LEVEL: B LANG: Eng ISBN: 0-688-031951 LC CARD: 84-60451 RA784 17584

Mirkin, G. Milk and milk products. *Running & fitness (Washington, D.C.) 16(2), Apr 1984, 27.*
LEVEL: B LANG: Eng SIRC ARTICLE NO: 097627

Morton, C. Can we live without additives? Lists of ingredients read like the national debt these days, with additives galore *Runner's world (Mountain View, Calif.) 19(10), Oct 1984, 58-63;120;122.*
LEVEL: B LANG: Eng SIRC ARTICLE NO: 099128

Mouton, A. Alimentation courante d'un sportif. *Tempo medical (Paris) 165, 1984, 81-82.*
LEVEL: B LANG: Fr

Nutrition for sport success. Reston, Va.: American Alliance for Health, Physical Education, Recreation and Dance, c1984. ix, 3 p. : ill.
CORP: National Association for Sport and Physical Education.
CORP: Nutrition Foundation, Inc..
CORP: Swanson Center for Nutrition, Inc..
CORP: United States Olympic Committee.
NOTES: Bibliography: p. 38.
LEVEL: B LANG: Eng ISBN: 0-88314-279-1 RA784 19050

Pardee, R. Aerobic nutrition for high energy and fat loss. Establishing the right dietary patterns and food combinations is essential to your aerobics program. *Muscle & fitness (Woodland Hills, Calif.) 45(6), Jun* 1984, 78-79;205-207.
LEVEL: B LANG: Eng SIRC ARTICLE NO: 100786

Parr, R.B. Porter, M.A. Hodgson, S.C. Nutrition knowledge and practice of coaches, trainers, and athletes. (Refs: 11) *Physician and sportsmedicine 12(3), Mar 1984, 126-128;133-134;137-138.*
ABST: The authors surveyed a total of 348 coaches, 179 athletic trainers, and 2,977 athletes at high school and college levels on their nutrition knowledge and practices. Results indicate that: 1) athletic trainers had the best nutrition background of the three groups questioned and 2) fluid intake is of a great concern to coaches and athletic trainers while weight is an important factor for athletes.
LEVEL: A LANG: Eng SIRC ARTICLE NO: 091556

Perkin, J.E. Kelly, J. A nutrition update for the athlete. (Refs: 16)*Florida journal of health, physical education, recreation and dance (Gainsville, Fla.) 22(2), May 1984, 3-4.*
LEVEL: B LANG: Eng SIRC ARTICLE NO: 096085

Porche, J. Know your nutrition. *Wrestling USA (Bozeman, Mont.) 20(3), 15 Oct 1984, 10-11.*
LEVEL: B LANG: Eng SIRC ARTICLE NO: 173409

Prokop, D. A diet for life. Marathoner Rolet de Castella, whose son is no slouch, swears by the Pritikin plan. *Runners worl (Mountain View, Calif.) 19(12), Dec 1984, 60-66;68;90.*
LEVEL: I LANG: Eng SIRC ARTICLE NO: 100788

Schoene, R.B. Nutrition for ultra-endurance: several hours to several months. (Refs: 27)*Clinics in sports medicine (Philadelphia) 3(3), Jul 1984, 679-692.*
NOTES: Symposium on nutritional aspects of exercise.
ABST: The nutritional needs of three types of ultra-endurance athletes are reviewed, including those whose events last several hours, those engaged in day-after-day competition, and those involved in expeditions lasting months. Several requirements are common to all three - an adequate supply of fuel already available, judicious repletion of fuel and fluid losses during the event, and postcompetition repletion.
LEVEL: I LANG: Eng SIRC ARTICLE NO: 100789

Shatemikov, V.A. Korovnikov, K.A. Russian nutrition: the power of food. *Muscle and fitness (Woodland Hills, Calif.) 45(2), Feb 1984, 64-67.*
NOTES: Excerpted from the IFBB report 'Nutrition and Sport'.
LEVEL: B LANG: Eng SIRC ARTICLE NO: 096087

Smith, N.J. Nutrition. (Refs: 7)
NOTES: In, Strauss, R.H. (ed.), Sports medicine, Philadelphia ; Toronto, Saunders, 1984, p. 468-480.
LEVEL: I LANG: Eng RC1210 17196

Smith, N.J. Nutrition and athletic performance. (Refs: 11)
NOTES: In, Scott, W.N. (ed.) et al., Principles of sports medicine, Baltimore, Williams & Wilkins, c1984, p. 27-31.
LEVEL: A LANG: Eng RC1210 18016

Smith, N.J. Nutrition and athletic performance. (Refs: 13)*Primary care: clinics in office practice (Philadelphia) 11(1), Ma 1984, 33-42.*
LEVEL: I LANG: Eng SIRC ARTICLE NO: 100790

Stein, M.D. The calcium connection. *Bicycling (Emmaus, Pa.) 25(4), May 1984, 55;57-58.*
LEVEL: B LANG: Eng SIRC ARTICLE NO 094471

The executive's guide to exercise and fat loss. *Executive fitness newsletter (Emmaus, Pa.) 15(13), 23 Jun 1984, 1 Suppl.*
LEVEL: B LANG: Eng SIRC ARTICLE NO: 102630

van Swearingen, J.M. Nutrition and the growing athlete. (Refs: 14)*Journal of orthopaedic and sports physical therapy (Baltimore, Md.) 6(3), Nov/Dec 1984, 173-177.*
ABST: A review and synthesis of the recent literature concerning characteristics of adolescent athletes and the nutritional requirements of growth and performance are provided. Common nutritional deficiencies of the young athlete and dietary inadequacies resulting in disturbances of growth are identified. Maximal athletic performance and the promotion of the present and future good health of young people challenges health and fitness professionals to provide adolescents with accurate nutritional information and caution against widespread nutritional frauds.
LEVEL: I LANG: Eng SIRC ARTICLE NO: 102635

Wooton, S. How do you rate your diet? *Running (London) 43, Nov 1984, 60-61.*
LEVEL: B LANG: Eng SIRC ARTICLE NO: 104187

BEE POLLEN

Bee pollen insignificant, studies show. *First aider (Gardner, Kan.) 53(5), Feb 1984, 7.*
LEVEL: B LANG: Eng SIRC ARTICLE NO: 096080

BEVERAGES

Digangi, J. Nature's most perfect food --- MILK. *Powerlifting USA (Camarillo, Calif.) 8(3), Oct 1984, 28-29.*
LEVEL: B LANG: Eng SIRC ARTICLE NO: 173186

Hecker, A.L. Wheeler, K.B. Impact of hydration and energy intake on performance. (Refs: 26)*Athletic training (Greenville, N.C.) 19(4), Winter 1984, 260-264;311.*
LEVEL: I LANG: Eng SIRC ARTICLE NO: 104177

CARBOHYDRATE LOADING

Coleman, E. Carbohydrate loading - new and improved methods. *Sports medicine digest (Van Nuys, Calif.) 6(8), Aug 1984, 4.*
LEVEL: B LANG: Eng SIRC ARTICLE NO: 105368

Cumming, C. Nutrition: carbo-loafing. *Women's sports (Palo Alto, Calif.) 6(9), Sept 1984, 50.*
LEVEL: B LANG: Eng SIRC ARTICLE NO: 173594

Denton, A.E. Khoo, C.S. Carbohydrate loading. *Skating magazine (Colorado Springs) 61(1), Jan 1984, 9.*
LEVEL: B LANG: Eng SIRC ARTICLE NO: 097623

Hargreaves, M. Costill, D.L. Carbohydrate feedings and exercise performance. (Refs: 20)*Sports coach (Wembley, W. Aust.) 8(2), Oct 1984, 47-49.*
LEVEL: I LANG: Eng SIRC ARTICLE NO: 104175

Stamford, B. Does carbohydrate loading work? *Physician and sportsmedicine (Minneapolis, Minn.) 12(9), Sept 1984, 196.*
LEVEL: B LANG: Eng SIRC ARTICLE NO: 099130

Wooton, S. The low-down on loading. Loughborough nutritionist Steve Wootton uncovers some of the latest thinking on carbo-loading, and recommends some delicious high-carbo dishes.

Running (London) 37, May 1984, 96-99.
LEVEL: B LANG: Eng SIRC ARTICLE NO: 096089

CARBOHYDRATES

Berntorp, K. Lindgaerde, F. Malmquist, J. High and low insulin responders: relations to oral glucose tolerance, insulin secretion and physical fitness. *Acta medica scandinavica (Stockholm) 216(1), 1984, 111-117.*
LEVEL: A LANG: Eng

Coyle, E.F. Coggan, A.R. Effectiveness of carbohydrate feeding in delaying fatigue during prolonged exercise. (Refs: 49) *Sports medicine (Auckland, N.Z.) 1(6), Nov/Dec 1984, 446-458.*
ABST: Carbohydrate feeding during moderate intensity exercise postpones the development of fatigue by approximately 15 to 30 minutes, yet it does not prevent fatigue. This observation agrees with data suggesting that carbohydrate supplementation reduces muscle glycogen depletion. In contrast to moderate intensity exercise, carbohydrate feeding during low intensity exercise results in hyperinsulinaemia. Consequently, muscle glucose uptake and total carbohydrate oxidation are increased by approximately the same amount. The amount of ingested glucose which is oxidised is greater than the increase in total carbohydrate oxidation and therefore endogenous carbohydrate is spared. The majority of sparing appears to occur in the liver, which is reasonable since muscle glycogen is not utilised to a large extent during mild exercise.
LEVEL: A LANG: Eng SIRC ARTICLE NO: 102628

Gollnick, P.D. Matoba, H. Role of carbohydrate in exercise. (Refs: 31)*Clinics in sports medicine (Philadelphia) 3(3), Jul 1984, 583-593.*
NOTES: Symposium on nutritional aspects of exercise.
ABST: Carbohydrate is an important source of energy during exercise. During short, heavy exercise, it may be the only energy source for the working muscle and may be derived solely from the glycogen stored within the muscle fibers themselves. During prolonged, submaximal exercise, the extent of the contribution that carbohydrate makes to the total fuel consumed depends upon several factors, which are discussed in detail in this article.
LEVEL: I LANG: Eng SIRC ARTICLE NO: 100778

What you burn up you have to replace. *Sport-talk (Toronto) 13(1), Mar 1984, 3.*
LEVEL: B LANG: Eng SIRC ARTICLE NO: 094473

FOODS

Aronson, V. Are there really diet foods? *Runner's world 19(4), Apr 1984, 51-55;102-104.*
LEVEL: B LANG: Eng SIRC ARTICLE NO: 092972

Barnett, R. A run on rice. *Runner (Boulder, Colo.) 6(5), Feb 1984, 36-39.*
LEVEL: B LANG: Eng SIRC ARTICLE NO: 094465

Barnett, R. Hooked on fish: even carbo-loaders need protein, and there's no better place to get it than the sea. *Runner (Ne York) 7(2), Nov 1984, 90-92.*
LEVEL: B LANG: Eng SIRC ARTICLE NO: 108627

GLUCOSE

Ledoux, M. Dextrose, sorbitol, mannitol... lequel choisir? *Revue de l'entraineur (Montreal) avr/juin 1984, 14.*
LEVEL: B LANG: Fr SIRC ARTICLE NO: 094469

GLYCOGEN

Angel, J.B. Nutrition and athletes. *Virginia journal (Harrisonburg, Va.) 7(1), Nov 1984, 7;10;20.*
LEVEL: I LANG: Eng SIRC ARTICLE NO: 100772

Drew, D.L. Effects of a prolonged low carbohydrate diet on liver glycogen and endurance in rats. Eugene, Ore.: Microform Publications, University of Oregon, 1984. 1 microfiche : negative ; 11 x 15 cm.
NOTES: Thesis (M.S.) - Brigham young University, 1982; (vi, 54 leaves); includes bibliography.
LEVEL: A LANG: Eng UO84 319

What you burn up you have to replace. *Sport-talk (Toronto) 13(1), Mar 1984, 3.*
LEVEL: B LANG: Eng SIRC ARTICLE NO: 094473

IRON

Clement, D.B. Sawchuk, L.L. Iron status and sports performance. (Refs: 68)*Sports medicine (Auckland) 1(1), Jan/Feb 1984, 65-74.*
ABST: This review summarises the present knowledge of the relationship between iron status and exercise. The areas of concern include: the metabolic role of iron in exercise, the factors influencing iron deficiency, the effects of iron deficiency in exercise, sport specificity and the frequency of iron deficiency, the diagnosis of iron deficiency and the treatment of iron deficiency. The authors conclude by stating that iron deficiency, with or without anemia, appears to be a relatively common occurrence in athletes. A proper monitoring of serum ferritin and nutrition counselling, with oral iron supplementation, will maintain iron stores to enable maximal physical performance.
LEVEL: A LANG: Eng SIRC ARTICLE NO: 094466

Colt, E. Heyman, B. Low ferritin levels in runners. (Refs: 17)*Journal of sports medicine and physical fitness (Torino) 24(1), Mar 1984, 13-17.*
ABST: This survey of 86 male and 32 female runners found 3 males and 9 females who had iron deficiency. The distribution of serum ferritin concentrations in this group of runners indicates lower levels than those found in control populations. This is attributed to increased iron losses through sweating and hemolysis, and possibly decreased absorption of iron due to binding in the intestine of high fiber foods.
LEVEL: A LANG: Eng SIRC ARTICLE NO: 100045

Female athletes low in iron. *Health letter (San Antonio, Tex.) 23(11), 8 Jun 1984, 3-4.*
LEVEL: B LANG: Eng SIRC ARTICLE NO: 094791

MINERALS

Coleman, E. Nutritional supplements vs. adequate, balanced diets. *Sports medicine digest (Van Nuys, Calif.) 6(5), May 1984, 6-7.*
LEVEL: B LANG: Eng SIRC ARTICLE NO: 100774

Crouse, S.F. Hooper, P.L. Atterbom, H.A. Papenfuss, R.L. Zinc ingestion and lipoprotein values in sedentary and endurance-trained men. *JAMA. Journal of the American Medical Association (Chicago) 252(6), 10 Aug 1984, 785-787.*
ABST: Twenty-one endurance-trained and 23 sedentary men received either placebo or 50 mg of zinc sulfate daily for eight weeks. Despite the fact that plasma zinc increased 15 per cent, fasting plasma high-density-lipoprotein cholesterol, total cholesterol, low-density-lipoprotein cholesterol, and triglyceride levels did not change in response to zinc ingestion. The authors conclude that low-dose zinc supplementation does not affect lipid or lipoprotein values in either endurance-trained or sedentary men.
LEVEL: A LANG: Eng SIRC ARTICLE NO: 104171

Golf, S.W. Happel, O. Graef, V. Seim, K.E. Plasma aldosterone, cortisol and electrolyte concentrations in physical exercise after magnesium supplementation. *Journal of clinical chemistry and clinical biochemistry (Berlin) 22(11), Nov 1984, 717-721.*
LEVEL: A LANG: Eng

Lukaski, H.C. Bolonchuk, W.W. Klevay, L.M. Milne, D.B. Sandstead, H.H. Changes in plasma zinc content after exercise in men fed a low-zinc diet. *American journal of physiology (Bethesda, Md.) 247(1 Pt 1), Jul 1984, E88-E93.*
ABST: For 30 days five healthy men aged 23-57 yr consumed a diet adequate in zinc (8.6 mg/day); they ate a low-zinc diet (3.6 mg/day) for the next 120 days and then received a zinc-supplemented (33.6 mg/day) diet for 30 days. Aerobic capacity was determined periodically during each diet period. Relative zinc balance declined during depletion. Pre- and postexercise zinc concentrations decreased when dietary zinc was restricted and increased with supplementation. Both plasma zinc and hematocrit increased after maximal exercise. To minimize the effect of hemoconcentration during exercise, the van Beaumont quotient was calculated using pre- and postexercise hematocrit and plasma zinc. The initial quotient declined during depletion. With zinc repletion, the quotient increased to levels greater than the quotient in depletion but similar to the initial quotient. The quotient was a strong predictor of the change in relative zinc balance during zinc depletion.
LEVEL: A LANG: Eng SIRC ARTICLE NO: 102633

Nasolodin, V.V. Opredelenie balansa nekotorykh mikro'elementov u sportsmenov. (Determination of the balance of various trace elements in athletes.) *Gigiena i sanitariia (Moscow) 11, Nov 1984, 78-80.*
LEVEL: I LANG: Rus

Niquet, G. Milbled, G. Guerrin, F. Choquel, D. Hequet, B. Lipka, E. Magnesium et sport. (Magnesium and sports.) *LARC medica (Lille, France) 4(3), mar 1984, 165-172.*
LEVEL: A LANG: Fr SIRC ARTICLE NO: 100785

Sharman, I.M. Need for micro-nutrient supplementation with regard to physical performance. (Refs: 23)*International journal of sports medicine (Stuttgart) Suppl. 5, Nov 1984, 22-24.*
CONF: International Congress on Sports and Health (1983 : Maastricht, Netherlands).
LEVEL: A LANG: Eng SIRC ARTICLE NO: 104184

Sodium and potassium. *Sport & fitness (Sunbury, Middlesex) Nov 1984, 32-33.*
LEVEL: B LANG: Eng SIRC ARTICLE NO: 109022

PRE-COMPETITION MEALS

Allman, W.F. Winning recipes in the athlete's kitchen. *In, Schrier, E.W. and Allman, W.F. (eds.), Newton at the bat: the science in sports, New York, Scribner, c1984, p. 101-104.*
LEVEL: B LANG: Eng RC1235 18609

Courson, R. The pre-game meal: how can it harm or help you? Besides following some basic nutritional guidelines, the 'ideal' meal contains foods the athlete likes to eat. *First aider (Gardner, Kan.) 53(4), Dec 1983/Jan 1984, 8-9.*
LEVEL: B LANG: Eng SIRC ARTICLE NO: 094467

Newman, S. Eating to win. A coach's guide to pre-training and pre-competition eating. *Coaching review (Ottawa, Ont.) 7, Jul/Aug 1984, 19-23.*
NOTES: Originally published in, New Zealand runner magazine.
LEVEL: B LANG: Eng SIRC ARTICLE NO: 094470

PROTEINS

Butterfield, G.E. Calloway, D.H. Physical activity improves protein utilization in young men. *British journal of nutrition (London) 51(2), Mar 1984, 171-184.*
ABST: This study concludes that physical activity affects protein utilization negatively by increasing sweat and faecal N losses, and positively by supporting increased energy intake.
LEVEL: A LANG: Eng SIRC ARTICLE NO: 100773

Dohm, G.L. Protein nutrition for the athlete. (Refs: 28)*Clinics in sports medicine (Philadelphia) 3(3), Jul 1984, 595-604.*
NOTES: Symposium on nutritional aspects of exercise.
ABST: Owing the changes in protein metabolism, there is an increased dietary requirement for protein in both endurance exercise and strength exercise. However, the normal dietary intake of protein is adequate for athletes as long as the energy intake is sufficient to maintain body weight. There is little scientific evidence that consumption of large protein supplements will have any beneficial effect on muscle hypertrophy, muscular strength, or physical performance.
LEVEL: I LANG: Eng SIRC ARTICLE NO: 100776

Frenkl, R. Gyoere, A. Use of Hungarian milk-protein products in sport. *Acta medica hungarica (Budapest) 41(2/3), 1984, 171-173.*
ABST: Protein-based food products intended for athletes - (Hamomid powder and tablets, Amino-acid Capsules) - were studied for absorption, elimination and excretion. On the evidence of the findings all were readily absorbed, the serum amino-acid levels attained their peaks 60 to 90 min after ingestion of the daily dose. At the end of 10 day periods which the products in question had been administered a minor increase was found in the urinary excretion of alpha-aminonitrogen.
LEVEL: A LANG: Eng SIRC ARTICLE NO: 104173

Fuller, P. The protein myth. *Spray's water ski magazine (Holmes, Penn.) 8(5), Jul 1984, 33-35.*
LEVEL: B LANG: Eng SIRC ARTICLE NO: 100777

Lemon, P.W.R. Yarasheski, K.E. Dolny, D.G. The importance of protein for athletes. (Refs: 53)*Sports medicine (Auckland, N.Z.) 1(6), Nov/Dec 1984, 474-484.*
ABST: Generally, exercise promotes: (a) a decrease in protein synthesis (production) unless the exercise duration is prolonged when increases occur; (b) either an increase or no change in protein catabolism (breakdown); and (c) an increase in amino acid oxidation. In addition, significant subcellular damage to skeletal muscle has been shown following exercise. Taken together, these observations suggest that the protein requirements of active individuals are greater than those of inactive individuals. At present, it is not possible to precisely determine protein requirements. However, because deficiencies in total protein or in specific amino acids may occur, the authors suggest that athletes consume 1.8 to 2.0g of protein/kg of bodyweight/day. This is approximately twice the recommended requirements for sedentary individuals.
LEVEL: A LANG: Eng SIRC ARTICLE NO: 102632

Protein, exercise and muscles. *Health letter (San Antonio, Tex.) 23(5), 9 Mar 1984, 2-3.*
LEVEL: B LANG: Eng SIRC ARTICLE NO 092975

Riales, R. Protein: losing its sex appeal. *Running & fitness (Washington, D.C.) 16(2), Apr 1984, 12.*
LEVEL: B LANG: Eng SIRC ARTICLE NO: 097629

REDUCING DIETS

Aronson, V. Effective weight control. Pay attention to details: a few calories here and there can bring your weight under control or send scales soaring. *Runner's world 19(3), Mar 1984, 58-65.*
NOTES: Second of two parts.
LEVEL: B LANG: Eng SIRC ARTICLE NO: 091550

Dintiman, G. Exercise and weight control: the road to lasting fitness. St. Paul: West Pub. Col., c1984. 1v.
NOTES: Includes index.
LEVEL: B LANG: Eng ISBN: 0314696466 LC CARD: 83-023550

Morel, S. Reducing diets and weight-loss products: people who want to lose weight are faced with a veritable cornucopia of reducing plans, weight-loss products and diet books. But many find that only their pocketbook grows thinner and they are lucky if their health does not suffer as well. *Protect yourself (Montreal) Jul 1984, 45-53;55-56.*
LEVEL: B LANG: Eng SIRC ARTICLE NO: 102863

Porcello, L.A. A practical guide to fad diets. (Refs: 15)*Clinics in sports medicine (Philadelphia) 3(3), Jul 1984, 723-729.*
NOTES: Symposium on nutritional aspects of exercise.
ABST: Weight control is an issue of great interest to many athletes. Unfortunately, misconceptions regarding nutrition and weight control lead to poor dietary practice and consequently to poor athletic performance. Fourteen popular fad diets are reviewed to assist the health professional in providing safe weight control counseling for athletes.
LEVEL: I LANG: Eng SIRC ARTICLE NO: 100787

SUGAR

Findlay, S. The real saccharin story: choose a substitute for sugar and you may end up picking your own poison. *Runner's world 19(2), Feb 1984, 43-47.*
LEVEL: B LANG: Eng SIRC ARTICLE NO: 090120

VEGETARIANISM

Slavin, J. Lutter, J. Cushman, S. Amenorrhoea in vegetarian athletes. (letter) *Lancet (London) 1(8392), 30 Jun 1984, 1474-1475.*
LEVEL: B LANG: Eng SIRC ARTICLE NO: 102977

VITAMINS

Applegate, E. Vitamin overdose: vitamin megadosing is the latest rage in nutrition, but you might end up with more than you bargained for. *Runner's world 19(1), Jan 1984, 61-63;69-70.*
LEVEL: B LANG: Eng SIRC ARTICLE NO: 090112

Aronson, V. Vitamins: uses & abuses. Supplementing your diet with extra, unnecessary nutrients can do your body more harm than good. *Fit (Mountain View, Calif.) 4(3), Aug 1984, 24-27;77;79;81.*
LEVEL: B LANG: ENG SIRC ARTICLE NO: 102624

Belko, A.Z. Obarzanek, E. Roach, R. Rotter, M. Urban, G. Weinberg, S. Roe, D.A. Effects of aerobic exercise and weight loss on riboflavin requirements of moderately obese, marginally deficient young women. *American journal of clinical nutrition (Bethesda, Md.) 40(3), Sept 1984, 553-561.*
ABST: This study examined the effect of exercise and weight loss on riboflavin status of moderately overweight women. The experiment was designed as a two-period cross-over with an initial base-line period and two 5-wk metabolic periods. The basic diet contained 1200 kcal with a riboflavin concentration of 0.8 mg/1000 kcal. Exercise consisted of a program of aerobic dance exercise. Riboflavin depletion was not related to the rate or composition of weight loss or to change in aerobic capacity.
LEVEL: A LANG: Eng SIRC ARTICLE NO: 104169

Coleman, E. The truth about vitamin C. *Fit (Mountain View, Calif.) 3(9), Feb 1984, 52-53;56.*
LEVEL: B LANG: Eng SIRC ARTICLE NO: 099117

Denton, A.E. Khoo, C.S. Water-soluble vitamins essential to mankind. *Skating magazine (Colorado Springs) 61(3), Mar 1984, 13;26.*
LEVEL: B LANG: Eng SIRC ARTICLE NO: 099118

Denton, A.E. Khoo, C.S. Food for thought: vitamin supplements good or bad? *Skating magazine (Colorado Springs, Colo.) Oct 1984, 5;28-29.*
LEVEL: B LANG: Eng SIRC ARTICLE NO: 099119

Goulart, S. Supplements for sports. *Kick illustrated (Burbank, Calif.) 5(4), Apr 1984, 55-57.*
LEVEL: B LANG: Eng SIRC ARTICLE NO: 099122

Haynes, S.P. The facts about vitamins. (Refs: 15)*Sports coach (Wembley, W. Aust.) 8(2), Oct 1984, 33-35.*
LEVEL: B LANG: E SIRC ARTICLE NO: 104176

Horwitt, M.K. Comments on methods for estimating riboflavin requirements. (letter) *American journal of clinical nutrition (Bethesda, Md.) 39(1), Jan 1984, 159-163.*
LEVEL: I LANG: Eng SIRC ARTICLE NO: 097624

Sharman, I.M. Need for micro-nutrient supplementation with regard to physical performance. (Refs: 23)*International journal of sports medicine (Stuttgart) Suppl. 5, Nov 1984, 22-24.*
CONF: International Congress on Sports and Health

NUTRITION (continued)

(1983 : Maastricht, Netherlands).
LEVEL: A LANG: Eng SIRC ARTICLE NO: 104184

The case for multivutamin and multimineral supplementation. (vitamin E) *Health & strength (Sunbury, Middlesex) Sept 1984, 8-9*
LEVEL: B LANG: Eng SIRC ARTICLE NO: 109013

Williams, M.H. Vitamin and mineral supplements to athletes: do they help? (Refs: 85)*Clinics in sports medicine (Philadelphia) 3(3), Jul 1984, 623-637.*
NOTES: Symposium on nutritional aspects of exercise.
ABST: Vitamins and minerals are essential for the regulation of many metabolic processes involved in exercise. Consequently, vitamin and mineral supplements have been utilized by a number of athletes in attempts to increase physical performance. However, research has, in general, revealed that such supplementation will not be effective if given to an athlete who is already receiving an adequate supply of nutrients.
LEVEL: I LANG: Eng SIRC ARTICLE NO: 100793

WATER

Joublin, M. Pilardeau, P. Garnier, M. Sport, hydratation et poids. (Refs: 7)*Vie medicale (Paris) 65(11/12), 1984, 468.*
LEVEL: B LANG: Fr

Sandick, B.L. Engell, D.B. Maller, O. Perception of drinking water temperature and effects for humans after exercise. *Physiology and behavior (Elmsford, N.Y.) 32(5), May 1984, 851-855.*
LEVEL: A LANG: Eng

OCCUPATIONS IN SPORT

Baletka, M. Paper lion or paper mouse: your resume. (Refs: 6)*In, Vendl, B.C. (ed.) et al., Interpretive aspects of intramural-recreational sports: selected proceedings from the Thirty-fifth Annual National Intramural-Recreational Sports Association Conference, Corvallis, Or., Oregon State University, c1984, p. 108-112.*
CONF: National Intramural-Recreational Sports Association Conference (35th : 1984 : Fort Worth, Tex.).
LEVEL: B LANG: Eng GV710 18914

Breckner, S. Opportunities in facility management for sport management graduates. *In, Zanger, B.K. and Parks, J.B. (eds.), Sport management curricula: the business and education nexus, Bowling Green, Ohio, Bowling Green State University, 1984, p. 67-70.*
CONF: Bowling Green State University Sport Management Curriculum Symposium (1983 : Bowling Green, Ohio).
LEVEL: B LANG: Eng GV713 20087

Clayton, R.D. Clayton, J.A. Careers and professional preparation programs. (Refs: 8)*Journal of physical education, recreation & dance (Reston, Va.) 55(5), May/Jun 1984, 44-45.*
LEVEL: B LANG: Eng SIRC ARTICLE NO: 094748

Figler, S.K. Figler, H. The athlete's game plan for college and career. Princeton, N.J.: Peterson's Guide, 1984. 1v.
LEVEL: LANG: Eng LC CARD: 83-022112

Guide to Fitness Canada Professional Development Practicum - 1984-1985. Guide du stage de formation professionnelle de Condition physique

Canada 1984-1985. Ottawa: Fitness and Amateur Sport, 1984?. (8, 9) p.
CORP: Canada. Fitness and Amateur Sport.
CORP: Canada. Condition physique et sport amateur.
NOTES: French and English texts on inverted pages with separate paging. Textes francais et anglais disposes tete-beche avec pagination separee.
LEVEL: B LANG: Eng Fr GV733 14335

Hamilton, A.B. Polansky, J. A legal basis for the interview process: the implications for intramural-recreational sports professionals and potential job applicants. (Refs: 16)*In, Vendl, B.C. (ed.) et al., Interpretive aspects of intramural-recreational sports: selected proceedings from the Thirty-fifth Annual National Intramural-Recreational Sports Association Conference, Corvallis, Or., Oregon State University, c1984, p. 125-134.*
CONF: National Intramural-Recreational Sports Association Conference (35th : 1984 : Fort Worth, Tex.).
LEVEL: I LANG: Eng GV710 18914

Koontz, J.L. Sport management - a profession. *In, Zanger, B.K. and Parks, J.B. (eds.), Sport management curricula: the business and education nexus, Bowling Green, Ohio, Bowling Green State University, 1984, p. 29-32.*
CONF: Bowling Green State University Sport Management Curriculum Symposium (1983 : Bowling Green, Ohio).
LEVEL: I LANG: Eng GV713 20087

Lindsey, C. For fun and profit: self-employment opportunities in recreation, sports and travel. Boulder, Colo.: Live Oak Publications, c1984. 179 p.
NOTES: Bibliography: p. 171-174.
LEVEL: B LANG: Eng ISBN: 0911781013 LC CARD: 84-047761 GV160 17577

Lopiano, D.A. How to pursue a sport management career. (Refs: 1)*Journal of physical education, recreation and dance (Reston Va.) 55(7), Sept 1984, 15-19.*
LEVEL: B LANG: Eng SIRC ARTICLE NO: 100455

Lynch, D.J. Opportunities in the fitness industry for sport management graduates. *In, Zanger, B.K. and Parks, J.B. (eds.), Sport management curricula: the business and education nexus, Bowling Green, Ohio, Bowling Green State University, 1984, p. 58-62.*
CONF: Bowling Green State University Sport Management Curriculum Symposium (1983 : Bowling Green, Ohio).
LEVEL: B LANG: Eng GV713 20087

McCarthy, J. Opportunities in the sports industry for sport management graduates. *In, Zanger, B.K. and Parks, J.B. (eds.), Sport management curricula: the business and education nexus, Bowling Green, Ohio, Bowling Green State University, 1984, p. 63-66.*
CONF: Bowling Green State University Sport Management Curriculum Symposium (1983 : Bowling Green, Ohio).
LEVEL: B LANG: Eng GV713 20087

Smith, K. Fitness careers and services. Carrieres et services en conditionnement physique. (Refs: 3)*CAHPER journal (Ottawa) 51(2), Nov/Dec 1984, 32;34-35.*
NOTES: Part of a series of Fitness Tips prepared by the Fitness Committee of CAHPER. Ces conseils en conditionnement physique proviennent de la

serie preparee par le comite de la condition physique ACSEPL.
LEVEL: B LANG: Eng Fr SIRC ARTICLE NO: 102746

CAREER COUNSELING

Dickie, D. Le defi d'une carriere. Meeting the employment challenge. *Champion (Ottawa) 8(4), Nov 1984, 46-49.*
LEVEL: B LANG: Fr Eng SIRC ARTICLE NO: 101008

Dunn, D.R. Economics and equity: critical choices. (Refs: 3)*Journal of physical education, recreation & dance (Reston, Va.) 55(5), May/Jun 1984, 23-26.*
LEVEL: B LANG: Eng SIRC ARTICLE NO: 094749

Lambert, C. Career directions. (Refs: 7)*Journal of physical education, recreation & dance (Reston, Va.) 55(5), May/Jun 1984 40-43;53.*
LEVEL: B LANG: Eng SIRC ARTICLE NO: 094757

OFFICIATING

Green, L. Allen, L. Judgement day. (judging) *Women's sports and fitness (Palo Alto, Calif.) 6(8), Aug 1984, 47-50;52-53.*
LEVEL: B LANG: Eng SIRC ARTICLE NO: 100794

Interview: Paul Anger. *Referee (Franksville, Wis.) 9(9), Sept 1984, 16-19.*
LEVEL: B LANG: Eng SIRC ARTICLE NO: 100795

McVay, R. What is a qualified official? *Ohio high school athlete (Columbus, Oh.) 43(6), Sept 1984, 3-4.*
LEVEL: B LANG: En SIRC ARTICLE NO: 100796

Shaw, A. Le jugement humain. A judgement call. *Champion (Ottawa) 8(3), Aug 1984, 92-95.*
LEVEL: B LANG: Fr Eng SIRC ARTICL NO: 096090

Tapp, J. Reading between the lines. Are the officials a factor when it comes to handicapping sporting events? *Referee (Franksville, Wis.) 9(9), Sept 1984, 48.*
LEVEL: B LANG: Eng SIRC ARTICLE NO: 100798

The Miller Lite sports officials' survey. *Referee (Franksville, Wis.) 9(11), Nov 1984, 56-58.*
LEVEL: B LANG: Eng SIRC ARTICLE NO: 108618

ADMINISTRATION

Hammill, T. Hill, M.B. Herm: characterized as 'The Godfather of Officials,' former Big Ten Supervisor Herm Rohrig has just about done it all. *Referee (Franksville, Wis.) 9(4), Apr 1984, 24-28;58.*
LEVEL: B LANG: Eng SIRC ARTICLE NO: 097632

Interview; Doug Ruedlinger. One of the country's pioneers in providing insurance coverage to officials, schools, teams, etc. offers an overview of the insurance business as it pertains to referees. *Referee (Franksville, Wis.) 9(11), Nov 1984, 16-19.*
LEVEL: B LANG: Eng SIRC ARTICLE NO: 108616

BIOGRAPHY AND AUTOBIOGRAPHY

Bob Morris: a multi-sport official who feels refereeing at the high school level is what the avocation is all about. *Referee (Franksville, Wis.) 9(3), Mar 1984, 16-19.*
LEVEL: B LANG: Eng SIRC ARTICLE NO: 097630

INJURIES AND ACCIDENTS

Lawrence, G.J. The common ankle sprain. *Sportorials (West Hartford, Conn.) 34(261), Feb/Mar 1984, 3.*
LEVEL: B LANG: Eng SIRC ARTICLE NO: 106290

LAW AND LEGISLATION

Goldberger, A.S. Sports officiating: a legal guide. West Point, N.Y.: Leisure Press, c1984. 160 p. : ill. NOTES: Bibliography: p. 142-144.
LEVEL: I LANG: Eng ISBN: 0-88011-092-9 LC CARD: 82-83925 GV735 18929

Texas - volunteer injured by shot-put entitled to trial against University of Texas. *Sports and the courts (Winston-Salem, N.C.) 5(4), Fall 1984, 7-8.*
LEVEL: B LANG: Eng SIRC ARTICLE NO: 102560

PHILOSOPHY

Laws, J.R. Ethical sports officiating. (Refs: 8)*In, Vendl, B.C. (ed.) et al., Interpretive aspects of intramural-recreational sports: selected proceedings from the Thirty-fifth Annual National Intramural-Recreational Sports Association Conference, Corvallis, Or., Oregon State University, c1984, p. 141-147.*
CONF: National Intramural-Recreational Sports Association Conference (35th : 1984 : Fort Worth, Tex.).
LEVEL: B LANG: Eng GV710 18914

PHYSICAL FITNESS

Kohn, H. Conditioning: how much is too much? *Referee (Franksville, Wis.) 9(3), Mar 1984, 53.*
LEVEL: B LANG: Eng SIRC ARTICLE NO: 097694

PSYCHOLOGY

Nelson, B. The secrets of success. *Referee (Franksville, Wis.) 9(11), Nov 1984, 49-53.*
LEVEL: B LANG: Eng SIRC ARTICLE NO 108617

Ross, C. Emotions can hinder logical thinking. *Referee (Franksville, Wis.) 9(4), Apr 1984, 29.*
LEVEL: B LANG: Eng SIRC ARTICLE NO: 097633

Sawyer, T.H. How mature are you? *Referee (Franksville, Wis.) 9(4), Apr 1984, 56-57.*
LEVEL: B LANG: Eng SIRC ARTICLE NO: 097635

RULES AND REGULATIONS

Metric conversion of sport rule books: phase III. Claremont, Ont.: Leisure and Recreation Consultants Limited, 1984. 64 leaves (loose-leaf) CORP: Leisure and Recreation Consultants Limited. NOTES: Cover title.
LEVEL: B LANG: Eng GV731 18630

SAFETY

Narol, M. Pre-game responsibilities. *Referee (Franksville, Wisc.) 9(10), Oct 1984, 14.*
LEVEL: B LANG: Eng SIRC ARTICLE NO 105374

SOCIAL PSYCHOLOGY

Gavitt, D. Some thoughts on officiating. *Sportorials (West Hartford, Conn.) 35(266), Dec 1984, 4-6.*
NOTES: Reprinted from Sportorials, Nov 1979.
LEVEL: B LANG: Eng SIRC ARTICLE NO: 104189

Tapp, J. What's the beef: arguing can be constructive. *Referee (Franksville, Wis.) 9(9), Sept 1984, 56-57.*
LEVEL: B LANG: Eng SIRC ARTICLE NO: 100799

SOCIOLOGY

Staneff, S. Why haven't you quit? *Sportorials (West Hartford, Conn.) 35(266), Dec 1984, 3;4;8.*
LEVEL: B LANG: Eng SIRC ARTICLE NO: 104191

TEACHING

Rowbottom, S. Schools of the trade. *Referee (Franksville, Wis.) 9(3), Mar 1984, 48-52.*
LEVEL: B LANG: Eng SIRC ARTICLE NO 097634

OLYMPIC GAMES

Fleuridas, C. Thomas, R. Les Jeux Olympiques: aspects historiques, institutionnels, sociologiques. Paris: Revue EPS, 1984. 142 p.
NOTES: Bibliographie: p. 135-136.
LEVEL: I LANG: Fr ISBN: 2-86713-007-7 GV721.5 18159

Leathes, R. The Olympic aims 1985. *Olympic review (Lausanne) 205, Nov 1984, 863-869.*
LEVEL: B LANG: Eng SIRC ARTICLE NO: 105378

Leathes, R. Les objectifs olympiques pour 1985. *Revue olympique (Lausanne) 205, nov 1984, 863-869.*
LEVEL: B LANG: Fr SIRC ARTICLE NO: 105379

Tomlinson, A. Whannel, G. Five-ring circus. Money, power and politics at the Olympic Games. London: Pluto Press, c1984. x, 116 p.
LEVEL: I LANG: Eng ISBN: 0-86104-769-9 GV721.5 18892

Toomey, W.A. King, B. The olympic challenge. Reston, Va.: Reston Pub. Co., c1984. xii, 332, 28, (5) p. : ill.
LEVEL: B LANG Eng ISBN: 0835952223 LC CARD: 83-024605 GV721.5984 17303

ADMINISTRATION

Gardiner, G. Problems with Olympic team selection. The dubious use of statistics may be robbing Canadians of berths on Olympic teams. But there may be a solution. *Coaching review (Ottawa) 7, Sept/Oct 1984, 40-42.*
LEVEL: B LANG: Eng SIRC ARTICLE NO: 097638

Valste, A. The classical Olympic games. Les jeux classiques d'Olympie. *Track and field journal (Ottawa, Ont.) 27, Aug 1984 2-3.*
LEVEL: B LANG: Eng Fr SIRC ARTICLE NO: 099143

ADMINISTRATION - PROMOTION

Krasevec, J.A. The Olympics: an educational opportunity. *Journal of physical education, recreation & dance 55(2), Feb 1984, 24-26.*
LEVEL: B LANG: Eng SIRC ARTICLE NO: 091569

ADMINISTRATION - STANDARDS AND GUIDELINES

Jurtschyschyn, P. Selection olympique: une question de standards. *Marathon, la revue de la bonne forme (Montreal) 15, avr 1984, 10-13.*
LEVEL: B LANG: Fr SIRC ARTICLE NO: 108693

AMATEURISM

Lovo, D. Professionalism in Olympic amateur sport? *Canadian archer (Norbert, Man.) Mar/Apr 1984, 8-10.*
LEVEL: B LANG: Eng SIRC ARTICLE NO: 099135

Messenger, C. Olympic sham. Where are the true-blue amateurs? They're chasing the fast buck. *Cycling (Sussex, Eng.) 4840, 2 Jun 1984, 24.*
LEVEL: B LANG: Eng SIRC ARTICLE NO: 097644

ASSOCIATIONS AND COMMITTEES - INTERNATIONAL OLYMPIC ACADEMY

Szymiczek, O. Beyond the games. (National Olympic Academies) *Olympic review (Lausanne) 204, Oct 1984, 764-769.*
LEVEL: B LANG: Eng SIRC ARTICLE NO: 100815

Szymiczek, O. Au dela des jeux. (Academies nationales olympiques) *Revue olympique (Lausanne) 204, oct 1984, 764-769.*
LEVEL: B LANG: Fr SIRC ARTICLE NO: 100816

ASSOCIATIONS AND COMMITTEES - INTERNATIONAL OLYMPIC COMMITTEE

Gammon, O. Still carrying the torch. (Juan Antonio Samaranch) *Sports illustrated (Chicago, Ill.) 61(3), 16 Jul 1984, 54-58;60-67.*
LEVEL: B LANG: Eng SIRC ARTICLE NO: 096093

Marshall, R. Delessert, E. Gallaz, C. Dix questions sur les Jeux olympiques. Lausanne: Comite International Olympique, c1984 24 p. : ill.
CORP: Centre d'etudes olympiques.
LEVEL: B LANG: Fr GV721.3 20564

Repertoire 1984. Directory 1984. Lausanne: Comite international olympique, c1984. 108 p.
LEVEL: B LANG: Fr Eng GV721.3 6999

ASSOCIATIONS AND COMMITTEES - NATIONAL OLYMPIC COMMITTEES

$75 million boost for U.S.O.C. *Olympian (Colorado Springs, Colo.) 11(4), Oct/Nov 1984, 14-15.*
LEVEL: B LANG: Eng SIRC ARTICLE NO: 108777

Davenport, J. The American Alliance/U.S. Olympic Committee relationship. *Journal of physical education, recreation & dance 55(3), Mar 1984, 18-19;30.*
LEVEL: B LANG: Eng SIRC ARTICLE NO: 092978

Friermood, H.T. The USOC Education Council: a commitment to the Olympic movement. *Journal of physical education, recreation & dance 55(3), Mar 1984, 21-22;30.*
LEVEL: B LANG: Eng SIRC ARTICLE NO: 092980

OLYMPIC GAMES (continued)

BIBLIOGRAPHIES

Ghent, G. Olympic bibliography: guide to sources of information on the Olympic Games with special emphasis on the Winter Games (includes the holdings of the University of Calgary Libraries). 2nd ed. Calgary: University of Calgary, Social Sciences Library, 1984. 1v. in various pagings
LEVEL: A LANG: Eng GV721.5 17274

Mallon, B. The Olympics: a bibliography. New York: Garland Pub., 1984. xviii, 258 p. (Garland reference library of social science: v. 246.)
LEVEL: A LANG: Eng ISBN: 082408926X LC CARD: 84-004072 GV721.5 18245

Meyers, E.S. The Olympic Games and world politics - a select annotated bibliography. (Refs: 80)*Reference quarterly (Chicago 23(3), 1984, 297-305.*
LEVEL: B LANG: Eng SIRC ARTICLE NO: 096105

The Olympics: a social science perspective. Waterloo, Ont.: SIRLS, University of Waterloo, 1984. 92 leaves
CORP: SIRLS.
LEVEL: A LANG: Eng GV721.5 20733

BIOGRAPHY AND AUTOBIOGRAPHY

Guttmann, A. Games must go on: Avery Brundage and the Olympic movement. New York: Columbia University Press, 1984. xiv, 317 p. : ill.
NOTES: Includes bibliographical references and index.
LEVEL: I LANG: Eng ISBN: 0231054440 LC CARD: 83-005360 GV721.2.B78 15849

Mallon, B. Buchanan, I. Tishman, J. Quest for gold: the encyclopedia of American olympians. New York: Leisure Press, c1984. 495 p. : ill.
LEVEL: B LANG: Eng ISBN: 0880112174 LC CARD: 84-000966 GV697.A1 17445

Piper, T. Crook, F. Anderson, D. Champions of gold. Blue Earth, Minn.: Pipier Pub., c1984. 1v.
LEVEL: B LANG: Eng ISBN: 0878320504 LC CARD: 84-042760

COUBERTIN, PIERRE DE

Petrov, R. Pierre de Coubertin and World Peace. (Refs: 8)*In, Ilmarinen, M. (ed.), Sport and International Understanding: proceedings of the congress held in Helsinki, Finland, July 7-10, 1982, Berlin, Springer-Verlag, 1984, p. 121-124.*
CONF: Congress on Sport and International Understanding (1982 : Helsinki).
LEVEL: I LANG: Eng GV706.8 18979

Tomlinson, A. De Coubertin and the modern Olympics. *In, Tomlinson, A. and Whannel, G. (eds.), Five-ring circus. Money, powe and politics at the Olympic Games, London, Pluto Press, c1984, p. 84-97.*
LEVEL: B LANG: Eng GV721.5 18892

DRUGS AND DOPING

Adams, B. Doping control and the Olympics. (Refs: 2)*Washington coach (Seattle, Wash.) Fall 1984, 12.*
LEVEL: B LANG: Eng SIRC ARTICLE NO: 100532

Black, T. Doping - l'ideal de Thomas Back du C.I.O. *Coup d'oeil sur l'halterophilie (Montreal) 17(1), mars 1984, 16.*
LEVEL: B LANG: Fr SIRC ARTICLE NO: 098922

Connolly, H. Fair play through drug tests? *Muscle and fitness (Woodland, Hills, Calif) 45(2), Feb 1984, 90;195-196;199.*
LEVEL: B LANG: Eng SIRC ARTICLE NO: 095785

Drugs in the Olympics. *Medical letter on drugs and therapeutics (New York) 26(665), 6 Jul 1984, 65-66.*
LEVEL: B LANG: Eng SIRC ARTICLE NO: 102385

Georges, C. Banned, but not forgotten: steroids won't just go away, but maybe their use can be made less pervasive in the Olympic sports. *Swimming technique (Los Angeles, Calif.) 20(3), Nov 1983/Jan 1984, 15-20.*
LEVEL: I LANG: Eng SIRC ARTICLE NO: 094272

Poulet, D. L'olympisme a l'heure du dopage. *Revue de l'entraineur janv/mars 1984, 5-9.*
LEVEL: B LANG: Fr SIRC ARTICLE NO: 091352

Radford, T. Doping control and the Olympics. *Canpara (Ottawa) 16(5), Sept/Oct 1984, 18-19.*
NOTES: Reprinted from the Canadian pharmaceutical journal.
LEVEL: B LANG: Eng SIRC ARTICLE NO: 098927

Ryan, A.J. Drug problem building since 1952 Olympics. *Physician and sportsmedicine (Minneapolis, Minn.) 12(7), Jul 1984, 119-121;124.*
NOTES: Olympic update: the relationship between drugs and the Olympics.
LEVEL: B LANG: Eng SIRC ARTICLE NO: 095801

Substances banned by the International Olympic Committee, 1983. *Powerlifting USA (Camarillo, Calif.) 7(6), Jan 1984, 18-19.*
LEVEL: B LANG: Eng SIRC ARTICLE NO: 092746

USOC's war on drugs. *Swimming world and junior swimmer (Los Angeles, Calif.) 25(2), Feb 1984, 60-63.*
LEVEL: B LANG: Eng SIR ARTICLE NO: 094280

ECONOMICS

Gruneau, R. Commercialism and the modern Olympics. *In, Tomlinson, A. and Whannel, G. (eds.), Five-ring circus. Money, power and politics at the Olympic Games, London, Pluto Press, c1984, p. 1-15.*
LEVEL: B LANG: Eng GV721.5 18892

ECONOMICS - SPONSORSHIP

Wayne, J. More corporations ready to jump into amateur sports sponsorships arena. *Financial post 78(2), 14 Jan 1984, 28.*
LEVEL: B LANG: Eng SIRC ARTICLE NO: 089872

FACILITIES

Schmidt, T. Die Stadionanlagen der Olympischen Sommerspiele von 1896 bis 1936. (Refs: 19)*Sport und Baeder und Freizeit-Bauten (Duesseldorf) 2, Apr 1984, 71-88.*
LEVEL: I LANG: Ger SIRC ARTICLE NO: 094097

HISTORY

In the beginning the ancient Olympic Games differed greatly from the modern version. *Sporting news (St. Louis) 198(4), 23 Jul 1984, Olympic special insert, 4;6.*
LEVEL: B LANG: Eng SIRC ARTICLE NO: 096094

Jarvis, F.G. Muddles and myths: a history of the modern Olympic Games. *Winged foot (New York)*

95(6), Jun 1984, 39-41;43-44;46;48-54;56-64.
NOTES: Continued in next issue.
LEVEL: B LANG: Eng SIRC ARTICLE NO: 094483

Mathys, F.K. La fete de Zeus: les jeux olympiques, de l'antiquite a nos jours. *Macolin (Macolin, Suisse) 41(5), mai 1984, 17-19.*
LEVEL: B LANG: Fr SIRC ARTICLE NO: 108771

Svahn, A. The Olympic Games at Ramloesa in 1834 and 1836. *Olympic review (Lausanne) 204, Oct 1984, 753-758.*
LEVEL: B LANG Eng SIRC ARTICLE NO: 100813

Svahn, A. Les jeux olympiques a Ramloesa en 1834 et 1836. *Revue olympique (Lausanne) 204, oct 1984, 753-758.*
LEVEL: B LANG: Fr SIRC ARTICLE NO: 100814

Zimmerman, P.B. The story of the Olympics - B.C. to A.D. *California history 63(1), Winter 1984, 8-21.*
LEVEL: A LANG: Eng SIRC ARTICLE NO: 105389

HISTORY - ANCIENT OLYMPICS

Kidd, B. The myth of the ancient Games. *In, Tomlinson, A. and Whannel, G. (eds.), Five-ring circus. Money, power and politics at the Olympic Games, London, Pluto Press, c1984, p. 71-83.*
LEVEL: B LANG: Eng GV721.5 18892

Mouratidis, J. Heracles at Olympia and the exclusion of women from the Ancient Olympic Games. (Refs: 124)*Journal of sport history (Pennsylvania) 11(3), Winter 1984, 41-55.*
LEVEL: I LANG: Eng SIRC ARTICLE NO: 105380

Nightingale, D. Conquering adversity: an Olympic ideal through the ages. *Sporting news (St. Louis) 198(4), 23 Jul 1984, Olympic special insert, 3.*
LEVEL: B LANG: Eng SIRC ARTICLE NO: 096106

Powell, J.T. Celebrations athletiques de la Grece antique. (suite et fin) *Revue olympique (Lausanne) 199, mai 1984, 329-332;340.*
LEVEL: B LANG: Fr SIRC ARTICLE NO: 102128

Stutts, A. Our Greek heritage. (Refs: 3)*Journal of physical education, recreation & dance 55(1), Jan 1984, 27-28.*
LEVEL: LANG: Eng SIRC ARTICLE NO: 091577

Swaddling, J. The ancient Olympic Games. Austin, Tex.: University of Texas Press : British Museum, (1984). 80 p. : ill.
NOTES: Bibliography: p. 80.
LEVEL: B LANG: Eng ISBN: 0-292-70373-2 LC CARD: 83-051502 GV721.1 18794

The Olympic Games: history of the Ancient Olympic Games 776 BC-393 AD. *Wrestling USA (Missoula, Tenn.) 19(6), 15 Jan 1984, 8;10.*
LEVEL: B LANG: Eng SIRC ARTICLE NO: 099140

HISTORY - MODERN OLYMPICS

Leigh, M.H. The renaissance of the Olympic Games. (Refs: 9)*Journal of physical education, recreation & dance 55(2), Feb 1984, 20-21.*
LEVEL: B LANG: Eng SIRC ARTICLE NO: 091570

Ullrich, K. La fondation du mouvement olympique - victoire du rapprochement. The founding of the Olympic movement was a victory for understanding. *Comite national olympique de la Republique democratique allemande bulletin (Berlin, GDR) 29(2), 1984, 19-22.*
LEVEL: B LANG: Fr Eng SIRC ARTICLE NO: 108724

Wallechinsky, D. The complete book of the Olympics. New York: Viking Press, 1984. xxvi, 628 p. : ill.
LEVEL: I LANG: Eng ISBN: 0670234036 LC CARD: 83-047920 GV721.5 17469

MASS MEDIA

Bader, M. Les couteuses obligations d'un hote. The expensive obligations of a host. *Message olympique/Olympic message (Lausanne) 8, Dec 1984, 15-19.*
CONF: International Symposium of Sport, Media and Olympism (1984 : Lausanne).
LEVEL: B LANG: Fr Eng SIRC ARTICLE NO: 104193

Berlioux, M. Un mariage de raison. A marriage of reason. *Message olympique/Olympic message (Lausanne) 8, Dec 1984, 25-29.*
CONF: International Symposium of Sport, Media and Olympism (1984 : Lausanne).
LEVEL: B LANG: Fr Eng SIRC ARTICLE NO: 104194

Coe, S. L'olympisme face au defi des medias. Olympism facing the challenge of the media. *Message olympique/Olympic message (Lausanne) 8, Dec 1984, 30-32.*
CONF: International Symposium of Sport, Media and Olympism (1984 : Lausanne).
LEVEL: B LANG: Fr Eng SIRC ARTICLE NO: 104196

Daume, W. Un spectacle a sa juste valeur. Every spectacle has its price. *Message olympique/ Olympic message (Lausanne) 8, De 1984, 9-13.*
CONF: International Symposium of Sport, Media and Olympism (1984 : Lausanne).
LEVEL: B LANG: Fr Eng SIRC ARTICLE NO: 104197

Fox, B. Olympic TV: from Baird to computer animation. *New scientist (London) 1415, 2 Aug 1984, 19-21.*
NOTES: An equal number of live and television viewers watched the Berlin Olympics in 1936. At Los Angeles, broadcast technology has eclipsed the games as a live event.
LEVEL: B LANG: Eng SIRC ARTICLE NO: 099133

Samaranch, J.A. Perspectives et tendances. Perspectives and tendencies. *Message olympique/ Olympic message (Lausanne) 8, Dec 1984, 38-41.*
CONF: International Symposium of Sport, Media and Olympism (1984 : Lausanne).
LEVEL: B LANG: Fr Eng SIRC ARTICLE NO: 104210

Whannel, G. The television spectacular. *In, Tomlinson, A. and Whannel, G. (eds.), Five-ring circus. Money, power and politics at the Olympic Games, London, Pluto Press, c1984, p. 30-43.*
LEVEL: B LANG: Eng GV721.5 18892

OFFICIATING

Tapp, J. Controversy: in the annuals of the games, officials have been the focus of a number of major brouhahas. *Referee (Franksville, Wis.) 9(7), Jul 1984, 48-52.*
LEVEL: B LANG: Eng SIRC ARTICLE NO: 100797

OLYMPIC EVENTS

Condron, B. All dressed up but nowhere to go. *Olympian (Colorado Springs, Colo.) 11(3), Sept 1984, 4-5.*
LEVEL: B LANG: En SIRC ARTICLE NO: 108606

Killian, G.E. Adding sports to the Olympic program. (Refs: 6)*Journal of physical education, recreation & dance (Reston, Va. 55(5), May/Jun 1984, 66-67.*
LEVEL: B LANG: Eng SIRC ARTICLE NO: 094485

Meyer, G. Should the Olympic programme be revised? *Olympic review (Lausanne, Switzerland) 195/196, Jan/Feb 1984, 29.*
LEVEL: B LANG: Eng SIRC ARTICLE NO: 094488

Meyer, G. Faut-il reviser le programme olympique? *Revue olympique (Lausanne) 195/196, janv/fevr 1984, 29.*
LEVEL: B LANG: SIRC ARTICLE NO: 096104

OPENING CEREMONY

Mallon, B. Independent views: the history of the opening ceremonies. *Olympic review (Lausanne) 200, Jun 1984, 449-450.*
NOTES: Continuation and end.
LEVEL: B LANG: Eng SIRC ARTICLE NO: 096099

Mallon, B. The history of the opening ceremonies. *Olympic review (Lausanne) 199, May 1984, 333-337.*
NOTES: To be continue
LEVEL: B LANG: Eng SIRC ARTICLE NO: 096100

Mallon, B. Les ceremonies d'ouverture. *Revue olympique (Lausanne) 199, mai 1984, 333-337.*
NOTES: Premiere partie.
LEVEL: LANG: Fr SIRC ARTICLE NO: 104205

Mallon, B. Les ceremonies d'ouverture. *Revue olympique (Lausanne) 199, mai 1984, 333-337.*
NOTES: A suivre.
LEVEL: B LANG Fr SIRC ARTICLE NO: 102129

PHILATELY

Bergman, M. An outline of a thematic Olympic collection. *Journal of sports philately (Berwyn, Ill.) 22(6), Jul/Aug 1984, 197-198.*
LEVEL: B LANG: Eng SIRC ARTICLE NO: 100801

Vidal Torrens, J.M. Olympism and philately. *Olympic review (Lausanne, Switzerland) 198, Apr 1984, 292-293.*
LEVEL: B LANG: Eng SIRC ARTICLE NO: 094496

Vidal Torrens, J.M. L'olympisme et la philatelie. *Revue olympique (Lausanne) 198, avr 1984, 292-293.*
LEVEL: B LANG: Fr SIRC ARTICLE NO: 096114

PHILOSOPHY

Drapeau, J. Une mission partagee. A shared mission. *Message olympique/Olympic message (Lausanne) 8, Dec 1984, 21-23.*
CONF International Symposium of Sport, Media and Olympism (1984 : Lausanne).
LEVEL: B LANG: Fr Eng SIRC ARTICLE NO: 104198

Krueger, A. The notions of peace of selected leaders of the olympic movement and their realisation in the Olympic Games. (Refs: 31)*In, Ilmarinen, M. (ed.) et al., Sport and International Understanding: proceedings of the congress held in*

Helsinki, Finland, July 7-10, 1982, Berlin, Springer-Verlag, 1984, p. 116-120.
CONF: Congress on Sport and International Understanding (1982 : Helsinki).
LEVEL: I LANG: Eng GV706.8 18979

Leathes, R. Les objectifs olympiques pour 1985. *Revue olympique (Lausanne) 205, nov 1984, 863-869.*
LEVEL: B LANG: Fr SIRC ARTICLE NO: 104203

Leathes, R. The Olympic aims 1985. *Olympic review (Lausanne) 205, Nov 1984, 863-869.*
LEVEL: B LANG: Eng SIRC ARTICLE NO: 104204

Lenk, H. The essence of Olympic man: toward an Olympic philosophy and anthropology. *International journal of physical education (Schorndorf, W. Germany) 21(2), 19-26 Jul 1984, 9-10;12-14.*
LEVEL: I LANG: Eng SIRC ARTICLE NO: 097643

Lucas, J. The survival of the Olympic idea. *Journal of physical education, recreation & dance 55(1), Jan 1984, 29;32.*
LEVEL: B LANG: Eng SIRC ARTICLE NO: 091572

McIntyre, M. Marketing olympism in the schools. (Refs: 4)*TAHPERD journal (Austin, Tex.) 52(2), Feb 1984, 8;45.*
LEVEL: B LANG: Eng SIRC ARTICLE NO: 093013

Mzali, M. L'olympisme aujourd'hui. Paris: Jeune Afrique, 1984. 127 p. : ill.
LEVEL: B LANG: Fr ISBN: 2-85258-330-5 GV721.6 18162

Paulin, G. Jimenez, R. The role of the Olympic Games in international understanding. (Refs: 3)*In, Ilmarinen, M. (ed.) et al., Sport and International Understanding: proceedings of the congress held in Helsinki, Finland, July 7-10, 1982, Berlin, Springer-Verlag, 1984, p. 125-127.*
CONF: Congress on Sport and International Understanding (1982 : Helsinki).
LEVEL: I LANG: Eng GV706.8 18979

Seurin, P. To save the Olympic Games: tomorrow's sport. *Momentum: a journal of human movement studies (Edinburgh) 9(2), Summer 1984, 1-6.*
NOTES: Translated by, J.R. Gilchrist.
LEVEL: B LANG: Eng SIRC ARTICLE NO: 099141

Tallberg, P. Challenges facing the Olympic Movement - the outcome of the XIth Olympic Congress. *In, Ilmarinen, M. (ed.) et al., Sport and International Understanding: proceedings of the congress held in Helsinki, Finland, July 7-10, 1982, Berlin, Springer-Verlag, 1984, p. 128-132.*
CONF: Congress on Sport and International Understanding (1982 : Helsinki).
LEVEL: I LANG: Eng GV706.8 18979

Wright, J.J. Teaching Olympism in the schools. (Refs: 5)*WAHPERD, journal (Milwaukee, Wis.) 13(1), May 1984, 6;27.*
LEVEL: LANG: Eng SIRC ARTICLE NO: 100847

POLITICS AND GOVERNMENT

Durry, J. Les jeux olympiques: chance de comprehension internationale ou terrain d'affrontement? *Relations internationales (Paris) 38, 1984, 213-225.*
LEVEL: I LANG: Fr

Johnson, W.O. Is there life after Los Angeles? *Sports illustrated (Chicago, Ill.) 60(20), 21 May 1984, 32-34;36.*
LEVEL: B LANG: Eng SIRC ARTICLE NO: 094484

Kanfer, S. How politics and profits have corrupted the Olympics. The great sports swindle. (Refs: 6)*New Republic (Washington) 190(7), 1984, 27-32.*
LEVEL: B LANG: Eng SIRC ARTICLE NO: 099134

Koppett, L. End zone: overhaul the Olympics. *Women's sports and fitness (Palo Alto, Calif.) 6(7), Jul 1984, 132;130.*
LEVEL: B LANG: Eng SIRC ARTICLE NO: 100806

Mechikoff, R.A. The Olympic Games: sport as international politics. *Journal of physical education, recreation & dance 55(3) Mar 1984, 23-25;30.*
LEVEL: B LANG: Eng SIRC ARTICLE NO: 092985

Meyers, E.S. The Olympic Games and world politics - a select annotated bibliography. (Refs: 80)*Reference quarterly (Chicago 23(3), 1984, 297-305.*
LEVEL: B LANG: Eng SIRC ARTICLE NO: 096105

Read, K. Conseil consultatif des athletes. Athletes' advisory council: boycott lesson unlearned. *Champion (Ottawa) 8(3), Au 1984, 84;91.*
LEVEL: B LANG: Fr Eng SIRC ARTICLE NO: 096429

Riordan, J. Do western leaders want to play with communists? *Washington journal of health, physical education, recreation and dance (Bellingham, Wash.) 40(2), Fall 1984, 5;10.*
LEVEL: B LANG: Eng SIRC ARTICLE NO: 102644

Thomas, R. La reussite olympique. (Refs: 4)*Revue de l'Amicale des entraineurs francais d'athletisme (Paris) 89, oct/nov/dec 1984, 57-59.*
LEVEL: B LANG: Fr SIRC ARTICLE NO: 102647

Triesman, D. The Olympic Games as a political forum. *In, Tomlinson, A. and Whannel, G. (eds.), Five-ring circus. Money, power and politics at the Olympic Games, London, Pluto Press, c1984, p. 16-29.*
LEVEL: B LANG: Eng GV721.5 18892

POLITICS AND GOVERNMENT - BOYCOTT

Ward, T. De Coubertin's dream: our nightmare. *Running (London) 40, Aug 1984, 57-59;86.*
LEVEL: B LANG: Eng SIRC ARTICLE NO 099144

RACE RELATIONS

Cowan, W. The Indian from Olympus. (Refs: 10)*In, Cowan, W. (ed.), Papers of the fifteenth Algonquian Conference, Ottawa, Carleton University, 1984, p. 125-134.*
CONF: Algonquian Conference (15th : 1983 : Cambridge, Mass.).
LEVEL: I LANG: Eng GV585 18629

Kjeldsen, E.K.M. Integration of minorities into Olympic sport in Canada and the USA. (Refs: 23)*Journal of sport and social issues (Boston, Mass.) 8(2), Summer/Fall 1984, 30-44.*
ABST: This paper examines the pattern and degree of integration of black athletes from the USA and French/Canadian athletes from Canada into the Olympic teams of their respective countries. A number of theoretical propositions regarding integration are examined for their 'fit' with the actual pattern of Olympic team participation manifested in these two countries. Changes over time are examined by analyzing the composition of teams chosen by their countries for the 1936, 1960 and 1980 Games. Minorities are identified through photographs in Olympic year books (USA) and

through name/ethnic derivation (Canada). The findings lead to some interesting speculations regarding the root causes of the disproportionate representation of minorities on the teams of these nations.
LEVEL: A LANG: Eng SIRC ARTICLE NO: 104200

Ramsamy, S. Apartheid, boycotts and the games. *In, Tomlinson, A. and Whannel, G. (eds.), Five-ring circus. Money, power and politics at the Olympic Games, London, Pluto Press, c1984, p. 44-52.*
LEVEL: B LANG: Eng GV721.5 18892

RULES AND REGULATIONS

Lucas, J. No more amateurs - only nonprofessional athletes at the Olympic Games. *Journal of physical education, recreation dance 55(2), Feb 1984, 22-23.*
LEVEL: B LANG: Eng SIRC ARTICLE NO: 091571

SOCIOLOGY

Cagigal, J.M. The educational values of Olympism. *Bulletin of the Federation internationale d'education physique (Cheltenham, Eng.) 54(1), Jan/Mar 1984, 31-36.*
LEVEL: I LANG: Eng SIRC ARTICLE NO: 094478

Seppaenen, P. The Olympics: a sociological perspective. (Refs: 22)*International review for the sociology of sport (Munich) 19(2), 1984, 113-127.*
CONF: Olympic Scientific Congress (1984 : Eugene, Ore.).
ABST: The modern Olympic Games have grown into a social and cultural spectacle without parallel in kind or scope. In spite of its goals of mutual understanding, the Olympic movement has been quite powerless in promoting peace and understanding. Rather, it has become an institution whose primary function is the consolidation of the existing order. Not the individual athlete but the nation-state is the primary unit of the Olympic system. Olympics are misused for political purposes. They depend on the world power balance and on business and are best described by the trinity of Nationalism, Commercialism and Athletism.
LEVEL: A LANG: Eng SIRC ARTICLE NO: 104211

STATISTICS AND RECORDS

Roll of honour. (Olympic Games) *Riding (London) 49(8), Aug 1984, 62-63.*
LEVEL: B LANG: Eng SIRC ARTICLE NO: 103263

Zinkewych, O. Ukrainian Olympic champions. 3rd rev. ed. Baltimore, Md.: V.S. Smoloskyp Publishers, 1984. 157 p. : ill. ; 24 cm.
NOTES: Includes index. Bibliography: p. 143-147.
LEVEL: B LANG: Eng LC CARD: 84-051196

WOMEN

Emery, L. Women's participation in the Olympic Games: a historical perspective. (Refs: 4)*Journal of physical education, recreation & dance (Reston, Va.) 55(5), May/Jun 1984, 62-63;72.*
LEVEL: B LANG: Eng SIRC ARTICLE NO: 094482

Hargreaves, J. Women and the Olympic phenomenon. *In, Tomlinson, A. and Whannel, G. (eds.), Five-ring circus. Money, power and politics at the Olympic Games, London, Pluto Press, c1984, p. 53-70.*
LEVEL: B LANG: Eng GV721.5 18892

Lenskyj, H. Women in the Olympics: media myth-making. *CAAWS newsletter/Bulletin de l'ACAFS (Ottawa) 3(4), Fall/automne 1984 2-3.*
LEVEL: B LANG: Eng SIRC ARTICLE NO: 173412

Les femmes aux olympiques. Women at the Olympics. *Champion (Ottawa) 8(3), Aug 1984, 70-71.*
LEVEL: B LANG: Fr Eng SIRC ARTICLE NO: 096472

Levy, M. 3,000 years in the making: the story of women at the summer Olympics. *Women's sports and fitness (Palo Alto, Calif.) 6(7), Jul 1984, 32-37.*
LEVEL: B LANG: Eng SIRC ARTICLE NO: 101049

Programme olympique: progression feminine. *Revue olympique (Lausanne) 195/196, janv/fevr 1984, 26-28.*
LEVEL: B LANG: Fr SIR ARTICLE NO: 096110

Sheafer, S.A. Olympic women, the best in the world. Mariposa, Calif.: Journal Publications, c1984. 1v.
LEVEL: B LANG: Eng L CARD: 84-012187

The Olympic programme: women's progression. *Olympic review (Lausanne, Switzerland) 195/196, Jan/Feb 1984, 26-28.*
LEVEL: B LANG: Eng SIRC ARTICLE NO: 094491

OLYMPIC GAMES (SUMMER)

FILM

Brant, J. The games according to Greenspan. Bud Greenspan has spent 32 years capturing on film the spirit of the Olympic flame. *Runner's world (Mountain View, Calif.) 19(7), Jul 1984, 50-54.*
LEVEL: B LANG: Eng SIRC ARTICLE NO: 094476

GREAT BRITAIN

Past glory. (Olympic Games) *Riding (London) 49(8), Aug 1984, 60-61.*
LEVEL: B LANG: Eng SIRC ARTICLE NO: 103260

HISTORY

Jarvis, F.G. Olympic saga: Reds sneak into Helsinki certain of gold ambush. *Winged foot (New York) 95(7), Jul 1984, 43-48;50.*
LEVEL: B LANG: Eng SIRC ARTICLE NO: 096095

Jarvis, F.G. Olympic saga (cont'd). Japanese juggle room service and rain dates. *Winged foot (New York) 95(8), Aug 1984, 41-46;56.*
LEVEL: B LANG: Eng SIRC ARTICLE NO: 096096

Life magazine. Chicago: Time Inc., 1984. 118 p. : ill.
NOTES: Special issue 'Olympics' of Life Magazine, volume 7 , number 7, Summer 1984.
LEVEL: B LANG: Eng GV721.18 17644

zur Megede, E. Die Olympische Liechtathletik, Band III. Darmstadt (FRG): Justus von Liebig Verlag, 1984. 452 p.
LEVEL: I LANG: Ger

WOMEN

Kort, M. Preview '84: track and field, part 1. *Women's sports (Palo Alto, Calif.)* 6(5), May 1984, 27;29-31 .
LEVEL: B LANG: Eng SIRC ARTICLE NO: 100062

Levy, M. All-time greats. *Women's sports (San Francisco)* 6(6), Jun 1984, 37-40.
LEVEL: B LANG: Eng SIRC ARTICLE NO: 10451

Pahud, J.F. La femme et les Jeux olympiques d'ete. *Macolin (Suisse)* 1, janv 1984, 15-17.
LEVEL: B LANG: Fr SIRC ARTICLE NO: 096478

OLYMPIC GAMES (SUMMER), AMSTERDAM 1928

CANADA

McDonald, D. Le jour ou le Canada menaca de boycotter les Jeux de Los Angeles. The day Canada threatened to boycott L.A. *Champion (Ottawa)* 8(3), Aug 1984, 66-69.
LEVEL: B LANG: Fr Eng SIRC ARTICLE NO: 096103

McLean, J. The golden age of women's sport. (Fanny Rosenfeld; Ethel Catherwood) *Canadian runner (Toronto)* May 1984, 26;29;38.
LEVEL: B LANG: Eng SIRC ARTICLE NO: 094798

OLYMPIC GAMES (SUMMER), BERLIN 1936

POLITICS AND GOVERNMENT

Eisen, G. The Nazi Olympiad. (Refs: 1)*Journal of physical education, recreation & dance (Reston, Va.)* 55(4), Apr 1984, 25-26;28.
LEVEL: B LANG: Eng SIRC ARTICLE NO: 094481

OLYMPIC GAMES (SUMMER), HELSINKI 1952

PEOPLE'S REPUBLIC OF CHINA

Qi, H. China at the 1952 Olympics. *China sports (Beijing, China)* 16(5), May 1984, 6-8.
LEVEL: B LANG: Eng SIRC ARTICLE NO 100812

OLYMPIC GAMES (SUMMER), LOS ANGELES 1932

Zimmerman, P.B. Watson, D. Los Angeles, the Olympic City, 1932, 1984. (Hollywood, Calif.): D. Watson, (c1984). 59 p. : ill.
NOTES: Cover title.
LEVEL: B LANG: Eng LC CARD: 84-168324

BIOGRAPHY AND AUTOBIOGRAPHY

Lanker, B. The rich patina of old gold. *Sports illustrated (Chicago, Ill.)* 61(4), 18 Jul 1984, 109-135.
NOTES: Special preview the 1984 Olympics.
LEVEL: B LANG: Eng SIRC ARTICLE NO: 096097

CANADA

Bernhardt, L. Atkinson, L. Davies, J. Robinson, M. 'Let us speak of famous men': the 1932 Canadian Olympic Team. *Bicycling news Canada (West Vancouver, B.C.)* 24(5), Summer 1984, 20-22.
LEVEL: B LANG: Eng SIRC ARTICLE NO: 097997

HISTORY

Halphen, A. Los Angeles 1932. Premiere seance...105 000 spectateurs remplissent le Memorial Coliseum lorsque la flamme olympique embrase la vasque. Le 31 juillet 1932. *Equipe magazine (Paris)* 204, 21 juil 1984, 48-51.
LEVEL: B LANG: Fr SIRC ARTICLE NO: 097640

Toohey, D.M. The Xth Olympiad: Los Angeles 1932. *Journal of physical education, recreation & dance 55(3),* Mar 1984, 26-27.
LEVEL: B LANG: Eng SIRC ARTICLE NO: 092990

OLYMPIC GAMES (SUMMER), LOS ANGELES 1984

Deschatres, D. Essais d'etude comparative entre les performances des J.O. de Moscou en 1980, et celles de Los Angeles en 198 *Revue de l'Amicale des entraineurs francais d'athletisme (Paris)* 89, oct/nov/dec 1984, 56.
LEVEL: B LANG: Fr SIRC ARTICLE NO: 102639

Edwards, H. The free enterprise olympics. *Journal of sport and social issues (Boston, Mass.)* 8(2), Summer/Fall 1984, 1-iv.
LEVEL: B LANG: Eng SIRC ARTICLE NO: 104199

Hedges, D. Wigley, J.V. Robinson, J. Los Angeles 1984. Salt Lake City: Commemorative Publications, c1984. 275 p. : ill.
LEVEL: B LANG: Eng ISBN: 0-918883-00-3 LC CARD: 84-071760 GV721.5984 18541

LAOOC Pres. Peter Ueberroth on the L.A. Olympics. *International gymnast (Santa Monica)* 26(5), May 1984, 6;32;66-67;76.
LEVEL: B LANG: Eng SIRC ARTICLE NO: 097642

Le relais de la flamme olympique. *Revue olympique (Lausanne)* 195/196, janv/fevr 1984, 44-45.
LEVEL: B LANG: Fr SIRC ARTICLE NO: 096112

Olympic torch relay. *Olympic review (Lausanne, Switzerland)* 195/196, Jan/Feb 1984, 44-45.
LEVEL: B LANG: Eng SIRC ARTICLE NO: 094492

Perelman, R.B. Baker, L.L. Olympic countdown: 200 days to go. Games of the XXIIIrd Olympiad, Los Angeles 1984, July 28 - August 12. January 9, 1984 edition. Los Angeles, Calif.: Los Angeles Olympic Organizing Committee, c1984. 173 p. : ill.
CORP: Los Angeles Olympic Organizing Committee.
NOTES: Cover title.
LEVEL: B LANG: Eng GV721.5984 18581

Prokop, D. Los Angeles '84: the games people will have to play. *Runner's world (Mountain View, Calif.)* 19(8), Aug 1984, 131;133-134.
LEVEL: B LANG: Eng SIRC ARTICLE NO: 096111

Reich, K. Dragnet: is L.A. safe for the games? *Runner (New York)* 6(11), Aug 1984, 28-30;32-33.
LEVEL: B LANG: Eng SIRC ARTICLE NO: 105384

The Los Angeles Times book of the 1984 Olympic Games. New York: Harry W. Abrams, c1984. 191 p. : ill.
CORP: Los Angeles Times
LEVEL: B LANG: Eng ISBN: 0-8109-1284-8 LC CARD: 84-70392 GV721.5984 18447

Toomey, W.A. King, B. The olympic challenge. Reston, Va.: Reston Pub. Co., c1984. xii, 332, 28, (5) p. : ill.
LEVEL: B LANG Eng ISBN: 0835952223 LC CARD: 83-024605 GV721.5984 17303

Ziffren, P. Sharing the dream. *Olympic review (Lausanne, Switzerland)* 197, Mar 1984, 167-169.
LEVEL: B LANG: Eng SIRC ARTICLE NO: 094499

Ziffren, P. Le partage d'un reve. *Revue olympique (Lausanne)* 197, mar 1984, 167-169.
LEVEL: B LANG: Fr SIRC ARTICLE NO: 096115

ADMINISTRATION

Freifeld, K. Personal computers at the Olympics. The personal computer is at the Olympic starting gate, waiting for the opening gun in the race for the gold. *Personal computing (Rochelle Park, N.J.)* 8(7), Jul 1984, 116-117;119;122-123;127;128.
LEVEL: I LANG: Eng SIRC ARTICLE NO: 096092

How an obscure businessman overcame adversity and presented the L.A. Games on time and under budget. *Runner's world (Mountain View, Calif.)* 19(9), Sept 1984, 27;29-30;32;34.
LEVEL: B LANG: Eng SIRC ARTICLE NO: 097641

Reich, K. Ready to play, Sam? From the eagle mascot to the prospects for its success, everything about the L.A. Olympics looks bright and cheery, except for the mood of the organizers. *Sports illustrated 60(10),* 15 Mar 1984, 64-68;70;72-74;76-78.
LEVEL: B LANG: Eng SIRC ARTICLE NO: 091575

ADMINISTRATION - PLANNING

Tatarchuk, W.E. Organization and management: reflections of XXIII Olympic experience. Organisation et administration: reflections sur l'experience de la XXIII Olympiade. *Periscope (Ottawa)* 16, 1984, 72-80.
LEVEL: B LANG: Eng Fr SIRC ARTICLE NO: 179919

ART

Toohey, D.M. Olympic innovation and artistry. *Journal of physical education, recreation & dance 55(3),* Mar 1984, 28.
LEVEL: B LANG: Eng SIRC ARTICLE NO: 092991

ASSOCIATIONS AND COMMITTEES

Toohey, D.M. The return of the Olympic Flame to Los Angeles. *Journal of physical education, recreation & dance 55(1),* Jan 1984, 31.
LEVEL: B LANG: Eng SIRC ARTICLE NO: 091580

CANADA

Canadian medalists of the 1984 Olympics. Medailles canadiens des Jeux olympiques de 1984. *Champion (Ottawa) 8(4), Nov 1984, 32-33.* LEVEL: B LANG: Eng Fr SIRC ARTICLE NO: 100802

The medal makers: a few of Canada's unsung Olympic heroes. *Coaching review (Ottawa, Ont.) 7, Nov/Dec 1984, 17-26.* LEVEL: B LANG: Eng SIRC ARTICLE NO: 098890

DRUGS AND DOPING

Gunby, P. Olympics drug testing: basis for future study. *JAMA: Journal of the American Medical Association (Chicago) 252(4) 27 Jul 1984, 454-455;459-460.* LEVEL: B LANG: Eng SIRC ARTICLE NO: 102389

Hansen, J. Drug testing: the athletes will be tested, but what about the officials? *Referee (Franksville, Wis.) 9(7), Jul 1984, 24.* LEVEL: B LANG: Eng SIRC ARTICLE NO: 100538

Kardong, D. Tests that can't be beat. How Olympic drug testing will work, and what the athletes found guilty have to lose. *Runner (New York) 6(11), Aug 1984, 38-44.* LEVEL: B LANG: Eng SIRC ARTICLE NO: 105190

Measuring up for the trials. *Runner's world 18(13), 1984 Annual, 90.* LEVEL: B LANG: Eng SIRC ARTICLE NO: 092501

Noret, A. Le dopage des sportifs. *Recherche (Paris) 157, 1984, 1022-1033.* LEVEL: I LANG: Fr

ECONOMICS

Doerner, W.R. Blaylock, W. Cate, B.W. Auditing the capitalist games. Though Moscow's move will hurt, the mood is still upbea *Time (Chicago) 123(21), 21 May 1984, 20-21.* LEVEL: B LANG: Eng SIRC ARTICLE NO: 094480

Hluchy, P. The first corporate Olympic Games. *Maclean's (Toronto) 97(21), 21 May 1984, 45.* LEVEL: B LANG: Eng SIRC ARTICL NO: 092982

Saint-Hilaire, J. Olympisme et $. *Revue de l'entraineur janv/mars 1984, 34.* LEVEL: B LANG: Fr SIRC ARTICLE NO: 091576

ECONOMICS - SPONSORSHIP

Hume, S. Olympic links prove bargains. *Advertising age (Chicago, Ill.) 55(61), 17 Sept 1984, 3;80.* LEVEL: B LANG: Eng SIR ARTICLE NO: 099341

Wheeler, M. Our team of Olympic sponsors. *Inside sports (Evanston, Ill.) 6, Jun 1984, 58;60.* LEVEL: B LANG: Eng SIRC ARTICLE NO: 094497

ENVIRONMENT

Marwick, C. Olympic athletes may face extra challenge - pollution. (news) *JAMA: Journal of the American Medical Association (Chicago) 251(19), 18 May 1984, 2495-2497.* LEVEL: B LANG: Eng SIRC ARTICLE NO: 101689

Olsen, E. In the heat of the day. Will searing, smoggy air confront the athletes? It depends which way the wind blows. *Runner (New York) 6(11), Aug*

1984, 34-37. LEVEL: B LANG: Eng SIRC ARTICLE NO: 105381

Pyke, F. Morton, A.R. Air pollution at Los Angeles Olympics. *Sports coach (Wembley, Aust.) 8(1), 1984, 12-15.* LEVEL: B LANG: Eng SIRC ARTICLE NO: 095887

Stulrajter, V. L'adaptation aux conditions climatiques de Los Angeles. *Macolin (Suisse) 7, juil 1984, 2-3.* NOTES: Traduction de, Jaroslav Pivoda et Laurent Ballif. LEVEL: B LANG: Fr SIRC ARTICLE NO: 100924

The Los Angeles Olympic Games: effects of pollution unclear. *Physician and sportsmedicine (Minneapolis, Minn.) 12(5), May 1984, 172-174;177-178;181-183.* LEVEL: B LANG: Eng SIRC ARTICLE NO: 094487

FACILITIES

Ayer, N.R. A preview of the Olympic three day event course: an informative description of the 34 obstacles, the terrain and climate. *USCTA news (South Hamilton, Mass.) 13(1), Feb 1984, 12-13.* LEVEL: B LANG: Eng SIRC ARTICLE NO: 097518

Jacobs, C. The making of an Olympic road course. Mission: challenging the world's best. *Bicycling (Emmaus, Pa.) 25(5), Jun 1984, 106;108.* LEVEL: B LANG: Eng SIRC ARTICLE NO: 096588

Rowan, E. Sports report: LAOOC ensuring access to Olympics. *Paraplegia news (Phoenix, Ariz.) 38(5), May 1984, 71-72.* LEVEL: B LANG: Eng SIRC ARTICLE NO: 095877

Toohey, D.M. Mecca for Olympic sports: Southern California. *Journal of physical education, recreation & dance 55(2), Feb 1984, 29.* LEVEL: B LANG: Eng SIRC ARTICLE NO: 091579

LAW AND LEGISLATION

Usher, H.L. The law and the 1984 Olympics: crucial partners. *Olympic review (Lausanne) 198, Apr 1984, 245-246.* LEVEL: B LANG: Eng SIRC ARTICLE NO: 095993

Usher, H.L. La loi et les Jeux olympiques de 1984: des partenaires inseparables. *Revue olympique (Lausanne) 198, avr 1984, 245-246.* LEVEL: B LANG: Fr SIRC ARTICLE NO: 095994

MASS MEDIA

Arledge, R. The role of television. *Olympic review (Lausanne) 199, May 1984, 327-328.* LEVEL: B LANG: Eng SIRC ARTICLE NO: 096091

Arledge, R. Le role de la television. *Revue olympique (Lausanne) 199, mai 1984, 327-328.* LEVEL: B LANG: Fr SIRC ARTICLE NO: 104192

Arledge, R. Le role de la television. *Revue olympique (Lausanne) 199, mai 1984, 327-328.* LEVEL: B LANG: Fr SIRC ARTICLE NO: 102127

Pavelec, B.J. Editorial. (TV and the Olympics) *Sports media news (Princeton, N.J.) 5(6), 18 Jun 1984, 3.* LEVEL: B LANG: E SIRC ARTICLE NO: 096108

Portmann, M. Les jeux olympiques. *Revue de l'entraineur (Montreal) juil/sept 1984, 6-8.* LEVEL: B LANG: Fr SIRC ARTICLE NO 102643

Seifart, H. Sport and economy: the commercialization of olympic sport by the media. (Refs: 19)*International review for the sociology of sport (Warszawa, Poland) 19(3/4), 1984, 305-316.* NOTES: Revised version of a paper originally presented at the Conference of the Deutscher Hochschulausschuss fuer Leibeserziehung, Sept 10-13, 1984. ABST: The Los Angeles Olympics 1984 showed a culmination in the interrelationship of sport and economy. The 'commodity' sport was marketed and exploited. American enterprises spent almost US $900 million on sponsoring and television advertising. The private organizers made a surplus of $162 million. The American Broadcasting Company (ABC) received about &650 million from advertising. LEVEL: A LANG: Eng SIRC ARTICLE NO: 105386

Short, C.D. Bud Greenspan's Olympic challenge. Making the official film of the L.A. Games is an awesome task, but America's premier producer of sports documentaries is ready for action. *Runner (New York) 6(11), Aug 1984, 49-53.* LEVEL: B LANG: Eng SIRC ARTICLE NO: 105387

MEDICINE

Frank, I.C. Medical coverage of the 1984 Olympic Games in Los Angeles. *JEN: Journal of emergency nursing (Chicago) 10(3), May/Jun 1984, 22A-25A.* LEVEL: B LANG: Eng SIRC ARTICLE NO: 102583

Gunby, P. A medical team goes to Olympics. *JAMA: Journal of the American Medical Association (Chicago) 252(4), 27 Jul 1984 453-454.* LEVEL: B LANG: Eng SIRC ARTICLE NO: 102587

Kerr, I.L. Going for the gold. Dentistry's role in the Olympics. *Journal of the American College of Dentists (Cherry Hill, N.J.) 51(2), Summer 1984, 12-14.* LEVEL: B LANG: Eng

Koplan, J.P. Powell, K.E. Physicians and the Olympics. (editorial) (Refs: 17)*JAMA: Journal of the American Medical Association (Chicago) 252(4), 27 Jul 1984, 529-530.* LEVEL: B LANG: Eng SIRC ARTICLE NO: 102594

Rickard, C. The Summer Games. *California nurse (San Francisco) 80(8), Oct 1984, 12.* LEVEL: B LANG: Eng

OFFICIATING

Hansen, J. Cycling: overview. There's a lot more to officiating cycling than meets the eye. Even becoming certified takes some real doing. *Referee (Franksville, Wis.) 9(7), Jul 1984, 56-58.* LEVEL: B LANG: Eng SIRC ARTICLE NO: 101172

Hansen, L. Profile: Larry Houston. If it can be accomplished by a track and field arbiter, Larry Houston has probably done i *Referee (Franksville, Wis.) 9(7), Jul 1984, 25-28.* LEVEL: B LANG: Eng SIRC ARTICLE NO: 101625

OLYMPIC EVENTS

Golla, J. The CBC guide to the Summer Olympics. Montreal: CBC Enterprises, c1984. 160 p. : ill. LEVEL: B LANG: Eng ISBN: 0-88794-138-9 LC CARD: C84-98513-4 GV721.5984 17496

Jenner, B. Abraham, M. Bruce Jenner's viewers' guide to the 1984 Summer Olympics. Fairway, Kan.: Andrews, McMeel & Parker, c1984. x, 182 p.

: ill.
LEVEL: B LANG: Eng ISBN: 0-8362-67052 LC
CARD: 84-2821 GV721.5984 17498

Official Olympic souvenir program. (Los Angeles):
Los Angeles Olympic Organizing Committee,
c1984. 322 p. : ill.
LEVEL: B LANG: Eng ISBN: 0-8094-5600-1
GV721.5984 18263

PHILATELY

Podolsky, S. XXXIIIrd Olympiad: the postmark
panic. *Journal of sports philately (Berwyn, Ill.)*
23(1), Sept/Oct 1984, 19-24.
LEVEL: B LANG: Eng SIRC ARTICLE NO: 100811

Podolsky, S.D. Les obliterations postales de la
XXIIIe Olympiade. *Revue olympique (Lausanne)*
205, nov 1984, 894-899.
LEVEL: B LANG: Fr SIRC ARTICLE NO: 104207

Podolsky, S.D. The postal meters of the XXIIIrd
Olympiad. *Olympic review (Lausanne)* 205, Nov
1984, 894-899.
LEVEL: B LANG Eng SIRC ARTICLE NO: 104208

Podolsky, S.D. The postal meters of the XXIIIrd
Olympiad. *Olympic review (Lausanne)* 205, Nov
1984, 894-899.
LEVEL: B LANG Eng SIRC ARTICLE NO: 105382

Podolsky, S.D. Les obliterations postales de la
XXIIIe olympiade. *Revue olympique (Lausanne)*
205, nov 1984, 894-899.
LEVEL: B LANG: Fr SIRC ARTICLE NO: 105383

PICTORIAL WORKS

Games of the XXIIIrd Olympiad Los Angeles 1984.
Salt Lake City: International Sport Publications,
1984. 287 p. : ill.
LEVEL: LANG: Eng ISBN: 0-913927-02-3 LC
CARD: 84-80729 GV721.5984 18281

POLITICS AND GOVERNMENT - BOYCOTT

**Church, G.J. Arnfitheratrof, E. Barrett, L.Z.
Holmes, S.** A Soviet nyet to the games. Anger and
vengefulness spur an Olympic pullout. *Time
(Chicago)* 123(21), 21 May 1984, 8-13.
LEVEL: B LANG: Eng SIRC ARTICLE NO: 094479

Hersh, B. A track fan's lament. Once again a
boycott has denied us something precious. *Runner
(New York)* 6(11), Aug 1984, 60-63.
LEVEL: B LANG: Eng SIRC ARTICLE NO: 106166

Moore, K. Oh, for the days of a county fair. *Sports
illustrated (Chicago, Ill.)* 60(20), 21 May 1984,
26;31-34;36.
LEVEL: LANG: Eng SIRC ARTICLE NO: 094489

Nichols, P. Mourning absent friends. (Los Angeles
Olympic Games) *Running (London)* 40, Aug 1984,
40-41.
LEVEL: B LANG: Eng SIRC ARTICLE NO: 099136

O'Hara, J. The tarnished Olympics. *Maclean's
(Toronto)* 97(21), 21 May 1984, 38-42.
LEVEL: B LANG: Eng SIRC ARTICLE NO: 092986

Reich, K. Doleful days for the games. *Sports
illustrated (Chicago, Ill.)* 60(20), 21 May 1984, 16-
22.
LEVEL: B LANG: Eng SIRC ARTICLE NO: 094493

STATISTICS AND RECORDS

JO XXIIIe Los Angeles 1984. *EPS: Education
physique et sport (Paris)* 190, nov/dec 1984, 37-
84.
LEVEL: B LANG: Fr SIRC ARTICLE NO: 102641

Olympic medal winners. *Sports illustrated (Chicago,
Ill.)* 61(9), 20 Aug 1984, 100;102;104;106.
LEVEL: B LANG: Eng SIRC ARTICLE NO: 096107

Tableau d'honneur. Roll of honour. Cuadro de
honor. *Revue olympique (Lausanne)* 203, sept
1984, 629-714.
LEVEL: B LANG: Fr Eng Spa SIRC ARTICLE NO:
105388

The official results of the 1984 Olympic Games.
Olympic record. Los Angeles, Calif.: L.A. Olympic
Committee, c1984. 384 p. : ill.
CORP: L.A. Olympic Committee.
LEVEL: B LANG: Eng GV721.5984 18376

TRANSPORTATION

Toohey, D.M. Los Angeles 1984: problems and
concerns. *Journal of physical education, recreation
& dance (Reston, Va.)* 55(4) Apr 1984, 29.
LEVEL: B LANG: Eng SIRC ARTICLE NO: 094494

VIOLENCE

Nightingale, D. Olympic terrorism: because of the
1972 Legacy of Munich, security is a hugh chore at
any major international sports event. *Sporting news
(St. Louis, Mo.)*, 21 May 1984, 12-13.
LEVEL: B LANG: Eng SIRC ARTICLE NO: 094490

Toohey, D.M. Los Angeles 1984: problems and
concerns. *Journal of physical education, recreation
& dance (Reston, Va.)* 55(4) Apr 1984, 29.
LEVEL: B LANG: Eng SIRC ARTICLE NO: 094494

WOMEN

Biles, F.R. Women and the 1984 Olympics. (Refs:
8)*Journal of physical education, recreation & dance
(Reston, Va.)* 55(5), May/Jun 1984, 64-65;72.
LEVEL: B LANG: Eng SIRC ARTICLE NO: 094475

Fleming, L. Women at the Summer Olympics.
CAAWS newsletter/Bulletin de l'ACAFS (Ottawa)
3(4), Fall/automne 1984, 11.
LEVEL: B LANG: Eng SIRC ARTICLE NO: 173416

Les femmes aux olympiques. Women at the
Olympics. *Champion (Ottawa)* 8(3), Aug 1984, 70-
71.
LEVEL: B LANG: Fr Eng SIRC ARTICLE NO:
096472

OLYMPIC GAMES (SUMMER), MEXICO 1968

STATISTICS AND RECORDS

Gohler, J. Gymnastics at the Olympic Games: Part
VIII. *World gymnastics (Budapest, Hungary)* 2(19),
1984, 48.
LEVEL: B LANG: Eng SIRC ARTICLE NO: 098137

OLYMPIC GAMES (SUMMER), MONTREAL 1976

OLYMPIC EVENTS

Kemp, N. Looking back at the Montreal Games.
Swim Canada (Toronto) 11(7), Jul 1984, 14.
LEVEL: B LANG: Eng SIRC ARTICLE NO: 100805

OLYMPIC GAMES (SUMMER), MOSCOW 1980

Deschatres, D. Essais d'etude comparative entre
les performances des J.O. de Moscou en 1980, et
celles de Los Angeles en 198 *Revue de l'Amicale
des entraineurs francais d'athletisme (Paris)* 89,
oct/nov/dec 1984, 56.
LEVEL: B LANG: Fr SIRC ARTICLE NO: 102639

CANADA

Cantelon, H. The Canadian absence from the
XXIInd Olympiad - some plausible explanations.
(Refs: 37)*In, Ilmarinen, M. (ed.) et al., Sport and
International Understanding: proceedings of the
congress held in Helsinki, Finland, July 7-10, 1982,
Berlin, Springer-Verlag, 1984, p. 145-151.
CONF: Congress on Sport and International
Understanding (1982 : Helsinki).
LEVEL: I LANG: Eng GV706.8 18979

GREAT BRITAIN

Riordan, J. Great Britain and the 1980 Olympics: a
victory for olympism. (Refs: 2)*In, Ilmarinen, M. (ed.)
et al., Sport and International Understanding:
proceedings of the congress held in Helsinki,
Finland, July 7-10, 1982, Berlin, Springer-Verlag,
1984, p. 138-144.
CONF: Congress on Sport and International
Understanding (1982 : Helsinki).
LEVEL: I LANG: Eng GV706.8 18979

PEOPLE'S REPUBLIC OF CHINA

Epstein, E.B. Misha the Moscow Mascot. *Journal
of sports philately (Berwyn, Ill.)* 23(1), Sept/Oct
1984, 1;3;5;6-9.
LEVEL: LANG: Eng SIRC ARTICLE NO: 100803

Wilcock, B. The stamps and postal history of the
Moscow Olympics. *Journal of sports philately
(Berwyn, Ill.)* 22(3), Jan/Feb 1984, 81-82;85;87-93.
LEVEL: B LANG: Eng SIRC ARTICLE NO: 094498

POLITICS AND GOVERNMENT - BOYCOTT

Frey, J.H. The United States and Great Britain:
responses to the 1980 boycott of the Olympic
Games. Alexandria, Va.: Compute Microfilm
International, 1984. 1 microfiche (18 fr.)
CONF: American Alliance for Health, Physical
Education, Recreation and Dance. Convention
(1984 : Anaheim, Calif.).
LEVEL: I LANG: Eng EDRS: ED243862

OLYMPIC GAMES (SUMMER), MUNICH 1972

POLITICS AND GOVERNMENT

Denbeck, D.J. A comparison of the opinions of the United States Olympic athletes concerning political involvement in the Olympic Games. Eugene, Ore.: Microform Publications, University of Oregon, 1984. 1 microfiche : negative ; 11 x 15 cm.
NOTES: Thesis (M.S.) - Western Illinois University, 1982; (v, 83 leaves); includes bibliography.
LEVEL: A LANG: Eng UO84 197

Jonas, G. Vengeance: the true story of an Israeli counter-terrorist team. Toronto: Lester & Orpen Dennep : Collins, c1984. 376 p. : ill.
NOTES: Bibliography: p. 375-376.
LEVEL: I LANG: Eng ISBN: 0-00-217269-0 LC
CARD: C84-98361-1 GV721.5972 17700

OLYMPIC GAMES (SUMMER), PARIS 1924

BIOGRAPHY AND AUTOBIOGRAPHY

Lazarus, H. Yesterday: in 1924 an American boxer was put to the test of his olympic pledge. (Joe Lazarus) Sports illustrate (Chicago, Ill.) 60(19), 7 May 1984, 108;110.
LEVEL: B LANG: Eng SIRC ARTICLE NO: 094486

HISTORY

Halphen, A. Paris J.O./24. Les Jeux de la VIIIe Olympiade se sont deroules a Paris du 3 mai au 27 juillet 1924. 44 nations. 3075 concurrents. Coup de retro soixante ans plus tard: les coulisses, les exploits et les problemes de ces Jeux. Equipe magazine (Paris) 203, 14 juil 1984, 32-37.
LEVEL: B LANG: Fr SIRC ARTICLE NO: 097639

OLYMPIC GAMES (SUMMER), SEOUL 1988

Lines, P. Seoul Olympics: will all the guests arrive? Sport and leisure (London) 25(5), Nov/Dec 1984, 16-17.
LEVEL: B LANG: Eng SIRC ARTICLE NO: 108961

McCrea, M. Seoul se prepare a accueillir les Jeux de 1988. Seoul readies for 1988. Champion (Ottawa) 8(3), Aug 1984, 72-73.
LEVEL: B LANG: Fr Eng SIRC ARTICLE NO: 096102

KOREA

Johnson, W.O. A rich harvest from a sea of trouble: South Korea, the host nation of the 1988 Summer Olympics in Seoul, is reaping the rewards of three decades dedicated in recovering from centuries of war and foreign oppression. Sports illustrated (Los Angeles, Calif.) 61(28), 24-31 Dec 1984, 60-66;71-78;81-85.
LEVEL: B LANG: Eng SIRC ARTICLE NO: 102642

MASS MEDIA

Nightingale, D. South Korea has its sights set on 1988: construction is 60 percent complete...now for the tv arrangements. Sporting news (St.Louis, Mont.) 19 Nov 1984, 60.
LEVEL: B LANG: Eng SIRC ARTICLE NO: 100810

OLYMPIC GAMES (SUMMER), ST. LOUIS 1904

HISTORY

Becht, J.W. America's premier Olympics. (Olympic Games, St. Louis 1904) Olympian (Colorado Springs, Colo.) 10(8), Mar 1984, 12-13;19.
LEVEL: B LANG: Eng SIRC ARTICLE NO: 099131

Dobor, D. History of the Olympic Games, part III: St. Louis 1904. Histoire des Jeux olympiques, IIIe partie: St. Louis 1904. International sport (Milano, Italy) 1, 1984, 18-19;40-41.
LEVEL: B LANG: Eng Fr SIRC ARTICLE NO: 099132

OLYMPIC GAMES (WINTER)

CANADA

Resume des performances olympiques. Canadian team status report. Champion 8(1), Feb 1984, 22-25.
LEVEL: B LANG: Eng Fr SIRC ARTICLE NO: 090153

HISTORY

Jarvis, F.G. Olympic saga: Reds sneak into Helsinki certain of gold ambush. Winged foot (New York) 95(7), Jul 1984, 43-48;50.
LEVEL: B LANG: Eng SIRC ARTICLE NO: 096095

Jarvis, F.G. Olympic saga (cont'd). Japanese juggle room service and rain dates. Winged foot (New York) 95(8), Aug 1984, 41-46;56.
LEVEL: B LANG: Eng SIRC ARTICLE NO: 096096

Jeannotat, Y. Origines des Jeux olympiques d'hiver. Macolin (Berne) 2, fevr 1984, 18-19.
LEVEL: B LANG: Fr SIRC ARTICLE NO: 100804

Lang, S. Jeux d'hiver, cote cour, cote jardin. The Winter Games: from both sides. Message olympique/Olympic message (Lausanne) 7, juin/Jun 1984, 21-26.
LEVEL: B LANG: Fr Eng SIRC ARTICLE NO: 104202

OLYMPIC EVENTS

Ice hockey and Olympism. Olympic review (Lausanne, Switzerland) 197, Mar 1984, 181-203.
LEVEL: B LANG: Eng SIRC ARTICLE NO: 095088

Le hockey sur glace et l'olympisme. Revue olympique (Lausanne) 197, mars 1984, 181-203.
LEVEL: B LANG: Fr SIRC ARTICLE NO: 096699

Le ski et l'Olympisme. Revue olympique (Lausanne) 195/196, janv/fevr 1984, 51-98.
LEVEL: I LANG: Fr SIRC ARTICLE NO: 096814

Ski-ing and Olympism. Olympic review (Lausanne, Switzerland) 195/196, Jan/Feb 1984, 51-98.
LEVEL: I LANG: Eng SIRC ARTICLE NO: 095231

PHILATELY

Nikolchev, S. The Winter Olympics on Bulgarian stamps. Timbres-poste Bulgares consacres aux Jeux olympiques d'hiver. Bulletin - Comite olympique Bulgare/Bulgarian Olympic Committee bulletin (Sofia, Bulgaria) 184/185, 1984, 61-62;63-64.
LEVEL: B LANG: Eng Fr SIRC ARTICLE NO: 099137

WOMEN

Levy, M. From stepchild to heiress: the story of women in Winter Olympics. Women's sports (Palo Alto, Calif.) 6(2), Feb 1984, 36-39.
LEVEL: B LANG: Eng SIRC ARTICLE NO: 099370

OLYMPIC GAMES (WINTER), CALGARY 1988

Pratt, B. Rendez-vous a Calgary. Come together in Calgary. Message olympique/Olympic message (Lausanne) 7, juin/Jun 1984, 73-76.
LEVEL: B LANG: Fr Eng SIRC ARTICLE NO: 104209

FACILITIES - DESIGN, CONSTRUCTION AND PLANNING

Brancatelli, D. Saddledome: the Olympic ice stadium in Calgary (Canada). Il Saddledome: stadio olimpico del ghiaccio a Calgary (Canada). Industria Italiana del cemento (Rome) 54(5), May 1984, 280-313.
LEVEL: I LANG: It Eng SIRC ARTICLE NO: 103935

Thomas, A. The spirit of '76? Calgary, site of the 1988 Winter Games, is showing symptoms of 'Montreal disease' - the scanda and debt that followed in the wake of the Montreal Olympics. Saturday night Mar 1984, 67-68.
LEVEL: B LANG: Eng SIRC ARTICLE NO: 091578

OLYMPIC GAMES (WINTER), SARAJEVO 1984

ADMINISTRATION

Skow, J. Moody, J. Rolling out the red carpet. Time 123(5), 30 Jan 1984, 32-35.
LEVEL: B LANG: Eng SIRC ARTICLE NO: 09015

CANADA

Brooks, J.R. Analyse des Jeux olympiques d'hiver 1984. 1984 Winter Olympics analysis. Champion (Vanier, Ont.) 8(2), May/mai 1984, 28-33.
LEVEL: B LANG: Fr Eng SIRC ARTICLE NO: 094477

ECONOMICS - SPONSORSHIP

Hume, S. Olympic links prove bargains. *Advertising age (Chicago, Ill.) 55(61), 17 Sept 1984, 3;80.*
LEVEL: B LANG: Eng SIR ARTICLE NO: 099341

MEDICINE

Hage, P. The Olympic Winter Games medical team. *Physician and sportsmedicine 12(1), Jan 1984, 182.*
LEVEL: B LANG: Eng SIR ARTICLE NO: 091567

Strovas, J. The medical side of the Sarajevo game. *Physician and sportsmedicine 12(1), Jan 1984, 180-181;183.*
LEVEL: B LANG: Eng SIRC ARTICLE NO: 091488

UNITES STATES OF AMERICA

Paul, C.R. Outlook for 1984 at Sarajevo. *Journal of physical education, recreation & dance 55(1), Jan 1984, 25;30.*
LEVEL: LANG: Eng SIRC ARTICLE NO: 091574

ORIENTEERING

Collet, W. La course d'orientation. *Loisirs sante (Paris) 10, juin/juil/aout 1984, 28-30.*
LEVEL: B LANG: Fr SIRC ARTICLE NO: 104854

Nilsson, K. Technique and tactics at night. *Compass sport orienteer (Middlesex, Eng.) 5(5), Oct/Nov 1984, 15.*
LEVEL: B LANG: Eng SIRC ARTICLE NO: 173566

ADMINISTRATION

Beck, H. The age group tragedy. *Compass sport: the orienteer (Ashford, Eng.) 5(2), Apr/May 1984, 10-11.*
LEVEL: B LANG: En SIRC ARTICLE NO: 101434

Beck, H. Bring back the vetter: controllers of big orienteering events are overworked and responsible for too many aspects o the competition. The role of the controller is nowhere clearly defined. We should simplify things and get back to basics... *Compass sport orienteer (Middlesex, Eng.) 5(4), Aug/Sept 1984, 12-13.*
LEVEL: B LANG: Eng SIRC ARTICLE NO: 173571

BIBLIOGRAPHIES

OL-Bibliographie 1984. 0 - Bibliography 1984. Vienna, Austria: International Orienteering Federation, 1984. 57 p.
CORP: International Orienteering Federation.
NOTES: Cover title: IOF Bibliographie.
LEVEL: I LANG: Eng Ger GV200.4 18786

CHILDREN

Lee, J. Masses of kids and orienteering. *Orienteering Canada (Ottawa) 12(4), Dec 1984, 6-8.*
LEVEL: B LANG: Eng SIRC ARTICLE NO: 173333

Linthicum, D. Orienteering for the young. *Orienteering Canada (Vanier, Ont.) 12(1), Apr 1984, 43-44.*
NOTES: Reprinted fro O-USA Oct 1983.
LEVEL: B LANG: Eng SIRC ARTICLE NO: 101437

COACHING

Palmer, P. Orienteering coaching: the why, where and how? *Compass sport: the orienteer (Ashford, Eng.) 5(2), Apr/May 1984, 20.*
LEVEL: B LANG: Eng SIRC ARTICLE NO: 101439

COUNTRIES AND REGIONS

Baechtold, E. La course d'orientation sera-t-elle encore possible en l'an 2000? *Macolin (Suisse) 4, avr 1984, 18-19.*
NOTES: Traduction de, Marianne Weber.
LEVEL: B LANG: Fr SIRC ARTICLE NO: 101433

ENVIRONMENT

Farfan, F. Orienteering and the law: the natural environment in Ontario. (Refs: 5)*Orienteering Ontario (Willowdale, Ont.) 16(1), Spring 1984, 24-31.*
LEVEL: B LANG: Eng SIRC ARTICLE NO: 099814

EQUIPMENT

A million compasses a year. *Compass sport: the orienteer (Ashford, Eng.) 5(2), Apr/May 1984, 14-15.*
LEVEL: B LANG: Eng SIRC ARTICLE NO: 101438

Robinson, L. Marathoning with maps. *In, Schrier, E.W. and Allman, W.F. (eds.), Newton at the bat: the science in sports, Ne York, Scribner, c1984, p. 163-166.*
LEVEL: B LANG: Eng RC1235 18609

MEDICINE

Gravelle, A. On seeing orange: learning to slow down and look for certain colours. *IOF report (Doune, Scotland) 1984, 22.*
LEVEL: B LANG: Eng SIRC ARTICLE NO: 107393

NAVIGATION

Kingsford, N. What price base maps? part II. *Compass sport orienteer (Middlesex, Eng.) 5(1), Feb/Mar 1984, 16-17.*
LEVEL: LANG: Eng SIRC ARTICLE NO: 096777

TEACHING

De Pass, J. Hands on: methods for teaching contours. *IOF report (Doune, Scotland) 1984, 21.*
LEVEL: B LANG: Eng SIRC ARTICLE NO: 107391

de Pass, J. Hands on: methods for teaching contours. *IOF report (Doune, Scotland) 1984, 21.*
LEVEL: B LANG: Eng SIRC ARTICLE NO: 109212

Gilchrist, J. Lee, J. Orienteering. Instructor's manual. (Ontario?): Orienteering Ontario, c1984. ix, 89 p. : ill.
LEVEL: B LANG: Eng ISBN: 0-920285-00-7 GV200.4 18677

Teneschok, M. A new direction for your program: orienteering. (Refs: 7)*GAHPER journal (Smyrna, Ga.) 17(2), Winter 1984, 9-10.*
LEVEL: B LANG: Eng SIRC ARTICLE NO: 099815

TECHNIQUES AND SKILLS

Belmas, G. Vous avez dit... psychique? *Ligne d'arret (France) 19, 1984, additif.*
LEVEL: I LANG: Fr

Paul, N. The techniques of distance estimation... pace counting. (Refs: 2)*Compass sport orienteer (Middlesex, Eng.) 5(1), Feb/Mar 1984, 14-15.*
LEVEL: B LANG: Eng SIRC ARTICLE NO: 096778

TESTING AND EVALUATION

De Pass, J. Methods for teaching contours. *Orienteering Canada (Ottawa) 12(2), Jun 1984, 17-18.*
LEVEL: B LANG: Eng SIRC ARTICLE NO: 101435

Sidney, K. Learning from the world's best. (performance analysis) *Coaching review (Ottawa, Ont.) 7, Jul/Aug 1984, 47-49.*
LEVEL: B LANG: Eng SIRC ARTICLE NO: 095166

TRAINING AND CONDITIONING

Hooker, J. Keep to the lines: don't let your next event become an away-day, do as Sture Bjoerk, former Swedish international and World Championship relay gold medalist recommends and go by handrail. *Compass sport: the orienteer (Middlesex, Eng.) 5(3), Jun/Jul 1984, 13.*
LEVEL: B LANG: Eng SIRC ARTICLE NO: 104855

TRAINING AND CONDITIONING - WEIGHT AND STRENGTH TRAINING

Hintermann, B. Hintermann, M. Le musculation au service du coureur d'orientation. *Macolin (Suisse) 9, sept 1984, 4-6.*
LEVEL: B LANG: Fr SIRC ARTICLE NO: 103353

VARIATIONS

Hunter, G. Where goes Canada in the ski orienteering? *Orienteering Canada (Vanier, Ont.) 12(1), Apr 1984, 39.*
LEVEL: B LANG: Eng SIRC ARTICLE NO: 101436

OUTDOOR EDUCATION

Adams, S. Nature appreciation and the ski tour leader. (Refs: 4)*Tour leader (Ottawa, Ont.) 4(1), 1984, 14-19.*
LEVEL: I LANG: Eng SIRC ARTICLE NO: 098483

Henderson, B. A cultural imperative. Essentielle a la culture. (Refs: 3)*CAHPER journal/Revue de l'ACSEPR (Ottawa) 50(6), Jul/Aug-juil/aout 1984, 28-29;31-32.*
NOTES: Part of series prepared by the Outdoor Education Committee of CAHPER. Provient de la serie preparee par le Comite de l'education en plein air.
LEVEL: B LANG: Eng Fr SIRC ARTICLE NO: 099816

March, B. Where do outdoor pursuits graduates go? *Runner (Edmonton, Alb.) 22(2), Summer 1984, 27-29.*
LEVEL: I LANG: Eng SIRC ARTICLE NO: 101442

Ongena, J. Should our schools offer adventure education? (Refs: 23)*CAHPER journal/Revue de l'ACSEPR (Ottawa) 50(5), May/Jun 1984, 4-7.*
LEVEL: B LANG: Eng SIRC ARTICLE NO: 096780

OUTDOOR EDUCATION (continued)

ADMINISTRATION

Raiola, E. Sugarman, D. Bits/bytes and outdoor wilderness recreation. *Journal of physical education, recreation & dance (Reston, Va.) 55(4), Apr 1984, 59.*
LEVEL: B LANG: Eng SIRC ARTICLE NO: 095171

Yerkes, R. Staffing 'adventure' programs: staff selection is the key to successful adventure programming. (Refs: 2)*Camping magazine (Martinsville, Ind.) 56(5), Mar 1984, 16-19.*
LEVEL: B LANG: Eng SIRC ARTICLE NO: 098369

CERTIFICATION

Wilkinson, K. Certification schemes or accepted peer practices? *Tour leader (Ottawa, Ont.) 4(1), 1984, 19-21.*
ABST: Certification has been a controversial issue for outdoor/adventure-oriented professionals during recent years. For the Association of Experiential Education this has been particularly true. At their 1983 annual conference a working document was finally presented after 8 years of work, entitled 'Accepted Peer Practices'. It provides member institutions with a reference guide of accepted standards for a wide range of outdoor activities and sports Its contents are outlined in this paper. Surprisingly, this document combines the common aspects of many existing certification programmes in its documentation. With the emotive nature of the word 'certification' forgotten the conference participants almost universally accepted this document.
LEVEL: B LANG: Eng SIRC ARTICLE NO: 097671

CHILDREN

Clothier, G.M. Clothier, P.A. Begin again: Deer Creek camp offers opportunities for troubled youth. (Refs: 3)*Camping magazine (Martinsville, Ind.) 56(7), May 1984, 16-20.*
LEVEL: B LANG: Eng SIRC ARTICLE NO: 101440

Weidman, S. Discovery trails. Environmental concepts spring to life for hiking campers. *Camping magazine (Martinsville, Ind.) 56(3), Jan 1984, 34-37.*
LEVEL: B LANG: Eng SIRC ARTICLE NO: 098368

DISABLED

Stearn, S. Accessible programs: research addresses accessibility for special populations in outdoor education programs. (Refs: 3)*Camping magazine (Martinsville, Ind.) 56(7), May 1984, 12-15.*
LEVEL: B LANG: Eng SIRC ARTICLE NO: 100660

INJURIES AND ACCIDENTS

Udall, J.R. Thinking about safety. Let the 'accident dynamic' help you take a look at safety awareness. *Camping magazine (Martinsville, Ind.) 56(3), Jan 1984, 38-41.*
LEVEL: B LANG: Eng SIRC ARTICLE NO: 098367

PSYCHOLOGY

Ewert, A.W. A study of the effects of participation in an Outward Bound short course upon the reported self-concepts of selected participants. Eugene, Ore.: Microform Publications, University of Oregon, 1984. 3 microfiches : negative, ill. ; 11 x

15 cm.
NOTES: Thesis (Ph.D.) - University of Oregon, 1982; (xiii, 221 leaves); vita; includes bibliography.
LEVEL: A LANG: Eng UO84 64-66

TEACHING

Drommeter, B. Integrating safety and education. *North Carolina journal of outdoor education 3(1), Spring 1984, 46-51.*
LEVEL: I LANG: Eng SIRC ARTICLE NO: 097651

Hammerman, D.R. Hammerman, E.L. Hammerman, W.M. Packaged programs: they make teaching environmental education as easy as 1, 2, 3. *Camping magazine (Martinsville, Ind.) 56(3), Jan 1984, 15-16.*
LEVEL: B LANG: Eng SIRC ARTICLE NO: 098366

Kudlas, J. Environmental awareness: an interdisciplinary approach. *Journal of physical education, recreation & dance (Reston, Va.) 55(4), Apr 1984, 10-12.*
LEVEL: B LANG: Eng SIRC ARTICLE NO: 095170

Malsam, M. Nelson, L. Integrating curriculum objectives into your outdoor education program. *Journal of physical education, recreation and dance (Reston, Va.) 55(7), Sept 1984, 52-54.*
LEVEL: B LANG: Eng SIRC ARTICLE NO: 101441

McGuckian, A. The nature of outdoor education and the role of the physical educator in outdoor education. (Refs: 10)
CONF: Physical Education Graduating Seminar Conference (1984 : Footscray Institute of Technology).
NOTES: In, Physical education in Australia: past, present and future directions, s.l., Footscray Institute of Technology, 1984, p. 135-140.
LEVEL: I LANG: Eng SIRC ARTICLE NO: 096154

WOMEN

Parkhurst, M.J. A study of the perceived influence of a Minnesota Outward Bound course on the lives of selected women graduates. Eugene, Ore.: Microform Publications, University of Oregon, 1984. 2 microfiches : negative, ill. ; 11 x 15 cm.
NOTES: Thesis (Ph.D.) - University of Oregon, 1983; (xiii, 125 leaves); vita; includes bibliography.
LEVEL: A LANG: Eng UO84 415

OUTDOOR SPORTS AND ACTIVITIES

Angier, B. The master backwoodsman. 1st Ballantine Books ed. New York: Fawcett Columbine, 1984, c1978. 224 p. : ill.
NOTES: Reprint. Originally published: Harrisburg, Pa. : Stackpole Books, c1978. Includes index.
LEVEL: B LANG: Eng ISBN: 0449901262 LC CARD: 84-167498

Peccard, A. Pour une determination du concept 'Plein Air'. *Animateur (Paris) 6, 1984, 13-16;21-22.*
LEVEL: B LANG: Fr SIRC ARTICLE NO: 099319

BIOGRAPHY AND AUTOBIOGRAPHY

With an eye on multiple medals in Los Angeles, Carl Lewis' glorious past might be only prologue. *Runner's world 19(1), Jan 1984, 21-22;24;26;29-30.*
LEVEL: B LANG: Eng SIRC ARTICLE NO: 091125

CHILDREN

Huot, F. Portmann, M. Guide des jeux scouts. Montreal: Editions de l'homme, c1984. 154 p. : ill.
CORP: Association des scouts du Canada.
LEVEL: B LANG: Fr ISBN: 2-7619-0350-1 GV1217 18678

Leiser, V. L'idee gymnique - a mettre en pratique. *Frauenturnen/Gymnastique feminine 18, 15 Sept 1984, 10-11.*
LEVEL: B LANG: Fr SIRC ARTICLE NO: 100507

COUNTRIES AND REGIONS

Butwin, D. Steamboat without skis and other summer tales. *Physician and sportsmedicine (Minneapolis, Minn.) 12(7), Jul 1984 143-146.*
LEVEL: B LANG: Eng SIRC ARTICLE NO: 096411

DISABLED

Hage, P. Wilderness inquiry II: new challenge for the disabled. *Physician and sportsmedicine 12(1), Jan 1984, 173-174;178.*
LEVEL: B LANG: Eng SIRC ARTICLE NO: 091417

Walshe, P. Informal outdoor recreation.
NOTES: In, Thomson, N. (ed.) et al., Sports and recreation provision for disabled people, London, Architectural Press, c1984, p. 63-73.
LEVEL: I LANG: Eng GV433.G7 17991

ENVIRONMENT

March, B. Lightning: wilderness hazard. *Summit (Big Bear Lake, Calif.) 30(2), Mar/Apr 1984, 6-9.*
LEVEL: B LANG: Eng SIRC ARTICLE NO: 103355

EQUIPMENT

Masia, S. Sleeping bags: the latest in enduring loft, heat shields, and other warm matters. *Outside (Chicago) 9(8), Sept 1984, 77-80.*
LEVEL: B LANG: Eng SIRC ARTICLE NO: 108867

Norman, G. The fundamental tool: can anyone get along without a good, sharp knife? *Outside (Chicago, Ill.) 9(7), Aug 1984, 49-52;62.*
LEVEL: B LANG: Eng SIRC ARTICLE NO: 103914

MASS MEDIA

Spadoni, M. Outdoors man maps strategy for Outside. *Advertising age (Chicago, Ill.) 55(70), 18 Oct 1984, 36.*
LEVEL: B LANG: Eng SIRC ARTICLE NO: 101443

PSYCHOLOGY

Kaplan, R. Wilderness perception and psychological benefits: an analysis of a continuing program. (Refs: 23)*Leisure science (New York) 6(3), 1984, 271-290.*
ABST: For over a decade, a wilderness outing program in Michigan's Upper Peninsula has been the object of continuing research focusing on the

impact of an intense nature experience on people's lives. The results discussed here are based on the questionnaires completed by 49 participants in the last two years of the Program. A consistently striking finding of this ongoing research program has been the richness of the psychological benefits obtained. Based on familiarity and preference ratings of photographs, reactions to the solo experience, and ratings of moods and feelings both before and at the conclusion of the program, the results speak to the pervasive power of the wilderness environment experience.
LEVEL: A LANG: Eng SIRC ARTICLE NO: 103354

SAFETY

Peccard, A. Le risque en plein air? oui. Mais pas n'importe quoi... et pas n'importe quand. *Animateur (Paris) 7, 1984, 8-9.*
LEVEL: B LANG: Fr SIRC ARTICLE NO: 104857

WOMEN

The ranger programme. Toronto: Girl Guides of Canada, 1984. 44 p.
NOTES: Cover title.
LEVEL: B LANG: Eng GV183 17257

PADDLEBALL

Pitcher, D. Paddleball: making a comeback at 55. *NIRSA journal (Corvallis, Ore.) 9(1), Fall 1984, 14;45.*
LEVEL: B LANG: E SIRC ARTICLE NO: 105988

PARACHUTING

Dwyer, N. The tandem revolution. *Parachutist (Alexandria, Va.) 25(8), Aug 1984, 25-31.*
LEVEL: B LANG: Eng SIRC ARTICLE NO 101445

May, J.M. Guest comment: understanding each other. *Skydiving (Deltona, Fla.) 5(5), Nov 1984, 13.*
LEVEL: B LANG: Eng SIRC ARTICLE NO: 103361

Ottley, W.H. USPA and FAA start joint program for professional exhibition jumps. *Parachutist (Alexandria, Va.) 25(1), Jan 1984, 37-40.*
LEVEL: B LANG: Eng SIRC ARTICLE NO: 096784

Rode, J. Sauvage, G. Parachutisme. Paris: R. Laffont, 1984. 221 p. : ill. (Sport pour tous.)
LEVEL: B LANG: Fr ISBN: 2.221-04423-1

ADMINISTRATION

Dawson, D. Computers and skydiving? Micro gear? Now micro computers. *Canpara (Vanier, Ont.) 17(1), Jan/Feb 1984, 9-10.*
LEVEL: B LANG: Eng SIRC ARTICLE NO: 093644

Worth, B.J. Diving into the future: the new block RW system. *Parachutist (Alexandria, Va.) 25(4), Apr 1984, 13;15-18;20;22-24.*
LEVEL: B LANG: Eng SIRC ARTICLE NO: 098393

ASSOCIATIONS

Jacir, D. L'Association nationale des anciens parachutistes. *Dans, Pathologie du parachutisme, Paris, Maloine, 1984, p. 13-14.*
LEVEL: B LANG: Fr RC1220.P37 19033

COACHING

Bradley, E. How I made the national team (and the people who helped me). *Canpara (Ottawa) 16(4), Jul/Aug 1984, 12-14.*
LEVEL: B LANG: Eng SIRC ARTICLE NO: 098376

COUNTRIES AND REGIONS

Jacir, F. Preparation militaire parachutiste et Service national ou comment avoir le plus de chances de faire son Service national dans un regiment parachutiste. *Dans, Pathologie du parachutisme, Paris, Maloine, 1984, p. 181-183.*
LEVEL: B LANG: Fr RC1220.P37 19033

ECONOMICS

Ogershok, J.J. Wilt, W.D. Helping your demo sponsor help himself. *Parachutist (Alexandria, Va.) 25(10), Oct 1984, 20;22.*
LEVEL: B LANG: Eng SIRC ARTICLE NO: 109583

EQUIPMENT

Auerbach, I. Mead, J.W. Mead, K.E. Ericksen, R.H. Burns, F.B. Renschler, C.L. Effect of material aging on parachute pack life: a synopsis of Sandia national laboratories studies. (Refs: 5)
CONF: Aerodynamic Decelerator and Balloon Technology Conference (8th : 1984 : Hyannis, Mass.).
NOTES: In, A collection of technical papers: AIAA 8th Aerodynamic Decelerator and Balloon Technology Conference, New York, American Institute of Aeronautics and Astronautics, 1984, p. 1-8.
ABST: This study of the effects of environmental factors on nylon 66 and Kevlar 29 has found that air, humidity and smog contribute to the strength degradation of these parachute components.
LEVEL: A LANG: Eng SIRC ARTICLE NO: 098373

Booth, W.R. 3 ring, inc. safety bulletin 3: rings stamped RW-1-82 or RW-1-83 may be defective; replace or test before jumping, says manufacturer. *Parachutist (Alexandria, Va.) 25(4), Apr 1984, 7.*
LEVEL: B LANG: Eng SIRC ARTICLE NO: 098374

Booth, W.R. The development and function of the three ring release and hand deployed pilot chute.
CONF: Aerodynamic Decelerator and Balloon Technology Conference (8th : 1984 : Hyannis, Mass.).
NOTES: In, A collection of technical papers: AIAA 8th Aerodynamic Decelerator and Balloon Technology Conference, New York, American Institute of Aeronautics and Astronautics, 1984, p. 260-263.
LEVEL: I LANG: Eng SIRC ARTICLE NO: 098375

Butler, M.C. How to get an FAA TSO for parachutes. Georgetown, Tex.: Technical Information Publication Service, 1984. 112 p.
LEVEL: I LANG: Eng

Canopy badly damaged during tandem jump. *Skydiving (Deltona, Fla.) 5(1), Jul 1984, 5.*
LEVEL: B LANG: Eng SIRC ARTICLE NO: 102168

Dubourg, J. Parachutes d'hier et d'aujourd'hui. *Dans, Pathologie du parachutisme, Paris, Maloine, 1984, p. 35-43.*
LEVEL: LANG: Fr RC1220.P37 19033

Ericksen, R.H. Pepper, W.B. Whinery, L.D. Preliminary results of the effects of sewing, packing

and parachute deployment on material strength. (Refs: 14)
CONF: Aerodynamic Decelerator and Balloon Technology Conference (8th : 1984 : Hyannis, Mass.).
NOTES: In, A collection of technical papers: AIAA 8th Aerodynamic Decelerator and Balloon Technology Conference, New York, American Institute of Aeronautics and Astronautics, 1984, p. 170-176.
ABST: Ribbon parachute fabrics were tested during development and production of a 24 ft. parachute and after 2.5 years storage on several sites. The effects of sewing, packing and parachute deployment on material strength were obtained in the 1000 lb Kevlar ribbon fabric. There do not appear to be any uncontrollable changes in material strength which would limit the use of Kevlar in parachute applications.
LEVEL: A LANG: Eng SIRC ARTICLE NO: 098382

First look: National Parachute Industries Warp III. *Skydiving (Deltona, Fla.) 5(5), Nov 1984, 12;14.*
LEVEL: B LANG: Eng SIRC ARTICLE NO: 103356

Gibson, K. Truffer, M. First look: GQ Security's Mariah and Sirocco. (canopies) *Skydiving (Deltona, Fla) 5(6), Oct 1984, 11;15.*
LEVEL: B LANG: Eng SIRC ARTICLE NO: 103357

Jaffe, L. USPA survey shows first class equipment, personal attention increase student retention. *Parachutist (Alexandria, Va.) 25(10), Oct 1984, 16;18.*
LEVEL: B LANG: Eng SIRC ARTICLE NO: 109582

Khudaiberdiev, R. Teoriya parashyuta s uchetom struktury tkani kupola. (Parachute theory taking account of the canopy fabric structure.) (Refs: 10)*Problemy prochnosti (Kiev) 9(183), Sept 1984, 90-94.*
LEVEL: A LANG: Rus

Poynter, D. Parachute manual: a technical treatise on aerodynamic decelerators. 3rd rev. ed. Santa Barbara, Calif.: Para Publications, c1984. 1v. (various pagings)
LEVEL: A LANG: Eng ISBN: 0-915516-35-7 LC CARD: 83-13350 GV770 18196

Puskas, E. The history of ram air design. *Sport parachutist (Leicester, Eng.) 20(1), Feb 1984, 17.*
LEVEL: B LANG: Eng SIR ARTICLE NO: 098384

Puskas, E. Ram Air parachute design considerations and applications.
CONF: Aerodynamic Decelerator and Balloon Technology Conference (8th : 1984 : Hyannis, Mass.).
NOTES: In, A collection of technical papers: AIAA 8th Aerodynamic Decelerator and Balloon Technology Conference, New York, American Institute of Aeronautics and Astronautics, 1984, p. 255-259.
ABST: This paper examines similarities, overlaps, and differences between ram air parachute design and conventional design as well as details ram air parachute applications.
LEVEL: I LANG: Eng SIRC ARTICLE NO: 098385

Roe, R.C. What's wrong with good ol' ripcords? *Parachutist (Alexandria, Va.) 25(7), Jul 1984, 17-18;20.*
LEVEL: I LANG: En SIRC ARTICLE NO: 101449

Strong, T. Thomas, D. Two for the price of one? *Sport parachutist (Leicester, Eng.) 20(1), Feb 1984, 24.*
LEVEL: B LANG: E SIRC ARTICLE NO: 098390

PARACHUTING (continued)

Warner, R. Dead centre machines. (ram air parachutes) *Canpara (Ottawa)* 16(6), Nov/Dec 1984, 19-21.
LEVEL: B LANG: Eng SIR ARTICLE NO: 108581

West, S. Square parachute construction. *Paravoice (Willowdale, Ont.)* Jun/Jul 1984, 8-9.
LEVEL: B LANG: Eng SIRC ARTICLE NO: 099824

Woodward, J. Back to basics: diapers for students. *Parachutist (Alexandria, Va.)* 25(1), Jan 1984, 25-28.
LEVEL: B LANG: E SIRC ARTICLE NO: 096786

EQUIPMENT - MAINTENANCE

Gibson, K. Care of the 3-ring release. *Skydiving (Deltona, Fla.)* 5(4), Oct 1984, 14;19.
LEVEL: B LANG: Eng SIRC ARTICLE NO: 103358

HISTORY

Chaney, R. Airborne: a brief history of the parachuting in the U.S. Armed Forces. *Parachutist (Alexandria, Va.)* 25(5), May 1984, 19;22-23.
LEVEL: B LANG: Eng SIRC ARTICLE NO: 098377

History and present status of Canadian Sport Parachuting Association. *Canpara (Ottawa)* 16(5), Sept/Oct 1984, 26-27.
LEVEL: LANG: Eng SIRC ARTICLE NO: 099820

Horan, M. Smoke ballooning. The original method of parachuting that is almost an extinct folk art. *Let's talk parachute (Middlesex, Eng.)* Jun 1984, 9-16.
NOTES: Brief edited version of 'Earning one's smoke', from the book 'Parachuting folklore, the evolution of freefall' by Michael Horan.
LEVEL: B LANG: Eng SIRC ARTICLE NO: 099821

Horan, M. On wings of wood and canvas. *Parachutist (Alexandria, Va.)* 25(12), Dec 1984, 19-22.
LEVEL: B LANG: Eng SIRC ARTICLE NO: 109586

Vitte, B. Histoire de la voltige: l'ere sovietique. *Hommes volants (Paris)* 28, avr/mai 1984, 11-13.
NOTES: A suivre.
LEVEL: B LANG: Fr SIRC ARTICLE NO: 095172

Worth, B.J. History and evolution of competitive body flight.
CONF: Aerodynamic Decelerator and Balloon Technology Conference (8th : 1984 : Hyannis, Mass.).
NOTES: In, A collection of technical papers: AIAA 8th Aerodynamic Decelerator and Balloon Technology Conference, New York, American Institute of Aeronautics and Astronautics, 1984, p. 264-266.
LEVEL: B LANG: Eng SIRC ARTICLE NO: 098394

INJURIES AND ACCIDENTS

Accident reports. *Parachutist (Alexandria, Va.)* 25(4), Apr 1984, 50.
LEVEL: B LANG: Eng SIRC ARTICLE NO: 098372

Accident reports. *Parachutist (Alexandria, Va.)* 25(2), Feb 1984, 34.
LEVEL: B LANG: Eng SIRC ARTICLE NO: 099817

Accident reports. *Parachutist (Alexandria, Va.)* 25(9), Sept 1984, 48.
LEVEL: B LANG: Eng SIRC ARTICLE NO: 101444

Accident reports. *Parachutist (Alexandria, Va.)* 25(10), Oct 1984, 36.
LEVEL: B LANG: Eng SIRC ARTICLE NO: 109584

Delahaye, R.P. Auffret, R. Leger, A. Le parachutisme moyen de secours. *Dans, Pathologie du parachutisme, Paris, Maloine, 1984, p. 67-78.*
LEVEL: I LANG: Fr RC1220.P37 19033

Dwyer, N. 10-way speed star competition (or the red badge of courage). *Canpara (Ottawa)* 16(4), Jul/Aug 1984, 24-25.
LEVEL B LANG: Eng SIRC ARTICLE NO: 098381

King, A. Johnston, M. Minimizing student accidents: an ounce of prevention. *Parachutist (Alexandria, Va.)* 25(2), Feb 1984, 23.
LEVEL: B LANG: Eng SIRC ARTICLE NO: 099822

Marchal, A. Rondy, J.L. Berger, Ch. La traumatologie chez le parachutiste. *Dans, Pathologie du parachutisme, Paris, Maloine 1984, p. 98-106.*
LEVEL: I LANG: Fr RC1220.P37 19033

Marchal, A. Rondy, J.L. Berger, Ch. Evaluation des invalidites consecutives aux affections des parachutistes dans les differents baremes en usage en France. *Dans, Pathologie du parachutisme, Paris, Maloine, 1984, p. 173-176.*
LEVEL: B LANG: Fr RC1220.P37 19033

Poussiere, B. Le vol libre et sa pathologie. *Dans, Pathologie du parachutisme, Paris, Maloine, 1984, p. 161-172.*
LEVEL: I LANG: Fr RC1220.P37 19033

Schmitt, B. Neuropathologie du parachutiste. *Dans, Pathologie du parachutisme, Paris, Maloine, 1984, p. 114-119.*
LEVEL: B LANG: Fr RC1220.P37 19033

Sitter, P. Fatalities '83: focus on students. *Parachutist (Alexandria, Va.)* 25(8), Aug 1984, 19;21-22;32.
LEVEL: B LANG: Eng SIRC ARTICLE NO: 101450

Vanuxem, P. Sequelles ORL en pathologie parachutiste. *Dans, Pathologie du parachutisme, Paris, Maloine, 1984, p. 109-111.*
LEVEL: B LANG: Fr RC1220.P37 19033

Vanuxem, P. Sequelles opthalmologiques en pathologie parachutiste. *Dans, Pathologie du parachutisme, Paris, Maloine, 1984, p. 112-113.*
LEVEL: B LANG: Fr RC1220.P37 19033

JUDGING

Bennett, B. Free-style: a new concept for individual freefall competition. *Canpara (Ottawa)* 16(6), Nov/Dec 1984, 16-18.
LEVEL: B LANG: Eng SIRC ARTICLE NO: 108580

LAW AND LEGISLATION

Jaffe, L. Justice weighs in favor of Steve Snyder; Django ordered to cease production. *Parachutist (Alexandria, Va.)* 25(1), Jan 1984, 17-21.
LEVEL: B LANG: Eng SIRC ARTICLE NO: 096783

Legal barriers to tandem jumping nearly cleared. *Skydiving (Deltona, Fla.)* 5(1), Jul 1984, 6.
LEVEL: B LANG: Eng SIRC ARTICLE NO: 102169

Liability, insurance problems worry DZ operators. *Skydiving (Deltona, Fla.)* 5(6), Dec 1984, 8-9;14;16.
LEVEL: B LANG: Eng SIRC ARTICLE NO: 103360

Towner, D. Who's to blame? *Parachutist (Alexandria, Va.)* 25(9), Sept 1984, 34-36;38.
LEVEL: I LANG: Eng SIRC ARTICLE NO: 101451

USPA wins decisive judgement against injured student jumper. *Parachutist (Alexandria, Va.)* 25(2), Feb 1984, 22-23.
LEVEL: B LANG: Eng SIRC ARTICLE NO: 099823

MEDICINE

Heid, R. Got bad ankles? *Canpara (Vanier, Ont.)* 17(1), Jan/Feb 1984, 20.
LEVEL: B LANG: Eng SIRC ARTICLE NO: 093645

Rondy, J.L. Apercu sur les moyens sanitaires dont disposent les unites aeroportees. *Dans, Pathologie du parachutisme, Paris Maloine, 1984, p. 45-48.*
LEVEL: B LANG: Fr RC1220.P37 19033

Schmitt, B. Psychopathologie du parachutiste. *Dans, Pathologie du parachutisme, Paris, Maloine, 1984, p. 120-125.*
LEVEL: LANG: Fr RC1220.P37 19033

Schmitt, B. L'asthenie des anciens combattants parachutistes. *Dans, Pathologie du parachutisme, Paris, Maloine, 1984, p. 177-180.*
LEVEL: B LANG: Fr RC1220.P37 19033

Textes reglementaires concernant l'aptitude au parachutisme (et a l'aile volante). *Dans, Pathologie du parachutisme, Paris, Maloine, 1984, p. 131-156.*
LEVEL: I LANG: Fr RC1220.P37 19033

Vanuxem, P. Sequelles cardio-vasculaires en pathologie parachutiste. *Dans, Pathologie du parachutisme, Paris, Maloine, 1984 p. 107-108.*
LEVEL: B LANG: Fr RC1220.P37 19033

PHYSICS

Cockrell, D.J. Doherr, K.F. Polpitiye, S.J. Further experimental determination of parachute virtual mass coefficients. (Refs 10)
CONF: Aerodynamic Decelerator and Balloon Technology Conference (8th : 1984 : Hyannis, Mass.).
NOTES: In, A collection of technical papers: AIAA 8th Aerodynamic Decelerator and Balloon Technology Conference, New York, American Institute of Aeronautics and Astronautics, 1984, p. 82-88.
ABST: The authors performed experiments in a ship tank in arriving at a mathematical model which determines the virtual mass coefficient of steady parachute descent.
LEVEL: A LANG: Eng SIRC ARTICLE NO: 098378

Jorgensen, D.S. Experimental determination of the input parameters to the parachute equations of motion. (Refs: 10)
CONF: Aerodynamic Decelerator and Balloon Technology Conference (8th : 1984 : Hyannis, Mass.).
NOTES: In, A collection of technical papers: AIAA 8th Aerodynamic Decelerator and Balloon Technology Conference, New York, American Institute of Aeronautics and Astronautics, 1984, p. 89-97.
ABST: From research with fabric canopies towed under water in a ship tank the author investigated the equations of motion of a parachute system. The results indicate that the value of the first angle of attack derivative of the normal force component function is most significant in determining a parachute system's dynamic characteristics.
LEVEL: A LANG: Eng SIRC ARTICLE NO: 098383

Khudaiberdiev, R. Teoriya osesimmetrichnogo parashyuta s uchetom deformiruemosti tkani. (Theory of an axisymmetric parachute with allowance for fabric deformability.) (Refs: 5)*Problemy prochnosti (Kiev) 3(177), Mar 1984, 94-96.*
ABST: The authors present a method of calculating the state of stress of an axisymmetrical parachute canopy with allowance for fabric deformability. Principles and some results of the study are given.
LEVEL: A LANG: Rus

PHYSIOLOGY

Lewis, D. Ray, W.J. Wilkinson, M.O. Doyle, L. Ricketts, R. Self-report and heart rate responses to a stressful task. *International journal of psychophysiology (Amsterdam) 2(1), Aug 1984, 33-37.*
LEVEL: A LANG: Eng

Vanuxem, P. Physiopathologie de la pratique du parachutisme. *Dans, Pathologie du parachutisme, Paris, Maloine, 1984, p. 88-97.*
LEVEL: I LANG: Fr RC1220.P37 19033

PSYCHOLOGY

Bibliographie litteraire concernant les motivations du parachutisme civil et militaire. *Dans, Pathologie du parachutisme, Paris, Maloine, 1984, p. 32-34.*
LEVEL: B LANG: Fr RC1220.P37 19033

Boccadoro, P.C. Motivations du parachutisme militaire. *Dans, Pathologie du parachutisme, Paris, Maloine, 1984, p. 15-24.*
LEVEL: I LANG: Fr RC1220.P37 19033

Dubourg, J. Motivations du parachutisme civil. *Dans, Pathologie du parachutisme, Paris, Maloine, 1984, p. 25-31.*
LEVEL: B LANG: Fr RC1220.P37 19033

Schmitt, B. Psychologie du parachutiste. *Dans, Pathologie du parachutisme, Paris, Maloine, 1984, p. 83-87.*
LEVEL: B LANG: Fr RC1220.P37 19033

Social support and coping: the buffer against loss of students. *Canpara (Ottawa) 16(4), Jul/Aug 1984, 26-27.*
NOTES: Reprinted from, Skydiver magazine.
LEVEL: B LANG: Eng SIRC ARTICLE NO: 098389

Vanuxem, P. Le stress du parachutiste. *Dans, Pathologie du parachutisme, Paris, Maloine, 1984, p. 79-82.*
LEVEL: B LANG: F RC1220.P37 19033

SAFETY

Gath, P. New York DZ experiences student in tow: the importance of being prepared. *Parachutist (Alexandria, Va.) 25(6), Jun 1984, 19-21.*
LEVEL: B LANG: Eng SIRC ARTICLE NO: 099819

Leaper, B. Jump plane radio procedures: let locals know. *Skydiving (Deltona, Fla.) 5(4), Oct 1984, 12.*
LEVEL: B LANG: Eng SIRC ARTICLE NO: 103359

Poynter, D. Landing in, atop and around obstacles. *Parachutist (Alexandria, Va.) 25(7), Jul 1984, 31;33.*
LEVEL: B LANG: E SIRC ARTICLE NO: 101448

TEACHING

Wright, B. State-of-the-art in student training. *Canpara (Vanier, Ont.) 16(2), Mar/Apr 1984, 9-1;12.*
LEVEL: B LANG: Eng SIRC ARTICLE NO: 093653

TECHNIQUES AND SKILLS

Colpus, R. Exit together. *Parachutist (Alexandria, Va.) 25(1), Jan 1984, 22-23.*
LEVEL: B LANG: Eng SIRC ARTICLE NO: 09678

Connolly, G. Hand deployment: ripcord with a difference. *Canpara (Ottawa) 16(4), Jul/Aug 1984, 20-22.*
LEVEL: B LANG: Eng SIRC ARTICLE NO: 098379

Dause, B. Beginning relative work (R.W.) . *Sport parachutist (Leicester, Eng.) 20(1), Feb 1984, 28-30.*
LEVEL: B LANG: Eng SIRC ARTICLE NO: 098380

Ellis, R. Demanding demo jumps: how to handle them. *Parachutist (Alexandria, Va.) 25(8), Aug 1984, 13-16.*
NOTES: Reprinte from, Sport parachutist.
LEVEL: B LANG: Eng SIRC ARTICLE NO: 101446

King, S. Tri-bi-side. *Canpara (Vanier, Ont.) 17(1), Jan/Feb 1984, 15.*
LEVEL: B LANG: Eng SIRC ARTICLE NO: 093648

Robertson, D. CRW - the downplane. *Canpara (Vanier, Ont.) 16(2), Mar/Apr 1984, 13-14.*
LEVEL: B LANG: Eng SIRC ARTICLE NO: 093651

Waterman, D. 4-Way CRW rotations skill or stupidity. *Sport parachutist (Leicester, Eng.) 20(1), Feb 1984, 18-20.*
LEVEL: B LANG: Eng SIRC ARTICLE NO: 098391

TESTING AND EVALUATION

Wright, B. Do-it-yourself test chamber. *Canpara (Vanier, Ont.) 16(3), May/Jun 1984, 18-19.*
LEVEL: B LANG: Eng SIRC ARTICL NO: 096787

TRAINING AND CONDITIONING

Bradley, E. Beginning - team training. *Canpara (Ottawa) 16(5), Sept/Oct 1984, 20-22.*
LEVEL: B LANG: Eng SIRC ARTICLE NO: 099818

VARIATIONS

Chevalier, J. Gasser, J.G. Le parachutisme ascensionnel. *Dans, Pathologie du parachutisme, Paris, Maloine, 1984, p. 157-160*
LEVEL: B LANG: Fr RC1220.P37 19033

Gardiner, S. Canopy soaring. *Parachutist (Alexandria, Va.) 25(7), Jul 1984, 35-36.*
LEVEL: B LANG: Eng SIRC ARTICLE NO: 101447

Para ski: the combined art of gate crashing and hill hammering. *Canpara (Vanier, Ont.) 16(2), Mar/Apr 1984, 19.*
LEVEL: B LANG: Eng SIRC ARTICLE NO: 093650

WOMEN

de la Besse, R.M. La femme parachutiste. *Dans, Pathologie du parachutisme, Paris, Maloine, 1984, p. 126-130.*
LEVEL: B LANG: Fr RC1220.P37 19033

PARTICIPATION

STATISTICS

Sports participation, high school sports attract five million. Football remains most popular boys sport; basketball draws most girls. *Washington coach (Seattle, Wash.) Winter 1984, 42.*
NOTES: Excerpts from, The National Federation news, Dec 1984.
LEVEL: B LANG: Eng SIRC ARTICLE NO: 102906

PENTATHLON

BIOGRAPHY AND AUTOBIOGRAPHY

Battersby, E. Mary P - the meeting of an Olympic champion. (Mary Peters) *Athletics weekly (Rochester, Kent, Eng.) 38(40), 6 Oct 1984, 56-58.*
LEVEL: B LANG: Eng SIRC ARTICLE NO: 101621

PEOPLE'S REPUBLIC OF CHINA

A nos lecteurs... La Chine aujourd'hui. *Basketball (Paris) Supp. 493, 5 juil 1984, 241-242.*
NOTES: Suite et fin du preceden numero.
LEVEL: B LANG: Fr SIRC ARTICLE NO: 102140

Baohai, L. Here sports thrive as a tradition. *China sports (Beijing, China) 16(11), 1984, 25-26.*
LEVEL: B LANG: Eng SIRC ARTICLE NO: 108447

Baoyan, H. The Jingwu Sports Society. *China sports (Beijing, China) 16(11), 1984, 42-44.*
LEVEL: B LANG: Eng SIRC ARTICLE NO: 108451

La Chine aujourd'hui: les sports. *Basketball (Paris) supplement, 493, mai/juin 1984, 225-227.*
NOTES: A suivre.
LEVEL: B LANG: Fr SIRC ARTICLE NO: 097855

Ren, H. Moriarty, D. The awakening and promotion of physical activity in the media: People's Republic of China (P.R.C.). Les medias et l'activite physique en Republique populaire de Chine (R.P.C.). *CAHPER journal (Ottawa) 51(2), Nov/Dec 1984, 22-23.*
LEVEL: B LANG: Eng Fr SIRC ARTICLE NO: 102929

Zhou, H. Birthplace of China's champions. *Sportimes (Lahore, Pakistan) 29(3), Mar 1984, 25-26.*
LEVEL: B LANG: Eng SIRC ARTICLE NO: 097878

Zhou, H. Sparetime sports school: birth place of China's champions. *Sports (Kallang, Singapore) 12(2), Feb 1984, 10-11.*
LEVEL: B LANG: Eng SIRC ARTICLE NO: 101019

HISTORY

Bian, Z. Qigong: its origin and development. *China sports (Beijing, China) 16(7), Jul 1984, 46-47;53.*
LEVEL: B LANG: Eng SIRC ARTICLE NO: 102183

Lao, X. Weiqi in China: past and present. *China sports (Beijing, China) 16(4), Apr 1984, 37-40.*
LEVEL: B LANG: Eng SIRC ARTICLE NO: 100668

PERCEPTUAL MOTOR PROCESSES

Buechele, W. Knaup, H. Brandt, T. Time course of training effects on balancing on one foot. *Acta oto-laryngologica. Supplement (Stockholm) 406, 1984, 140-142.*
LEVEL: I LANG: Eng SIRC ARTICLE NO: 104160

Jeannerod, M. Erratum. *Journal of motor behavior (Washington) 16(4), Dec 1984, 469-470.*
NOTES: Correct figures of M. Jeannerod article, The timing of natural prehension movements, printed in the JMB September 1984 issue, 242-244.
LEVEL: A LANG: Eng SIRC ARTICLE NO: 105361

Navon, D. Gopher, D. Chillag, N. Spitz, G. On separability of and interference between tracking dimensions in dual-axis tracking. (Refs: 12)*Journal of motor behavior (Washington) 16(4), Dec 1984, 364-391.*
ABST: Practiced subjects performed tracking on one or two axes, with or without feedback indicators and with or without a requirement to allocate resources unevenly between axes. They also performed with or without a concurrent binary classification of visually presented digits which were presented within a moving square that served as the target for tracking. Small deficits were found in the performance of both tracking and digit classification when performed together. However, the conditions of tracking did not have a discernible effect on either tracking or digit classification. Hence, the introduction of a second tracking axis probably does not have harmful consequences either on tracking itself or on any other task time-shared with tracking.
LEVEL: A LANG: Eng SIRC ARTICLE NO: 105363

Newell, K.M. Hancock, P.A. Robertson, R.N. A note on the speed-amplitude function in movement control. (Refs: 15)*Journal of motor behavior (Washington) 16(4), Dec 1984, 460-468.*
ABST: An experiment is reported that documents the maximum average speed-amplitude relationship across the full range of motion for elbow flexion. Minimum movement time increased as a negative exponential within the movement range up to 94-97 per cent of the maximum range of motion. At this point a discontinuity occurred with movement time increasing at an increasing rate probably due to anatomical and morphological constraints. Kinematic analysis of the movements as a function of range of motion suggests that a simple pulse-step model of movement control cannot account for the present findings.
LEVEL: A LANG: Eng SIRC ARTICLE NO: 105364

Sullivan, M.P. The accuracy of aiming movements as a function of starting point and terminal location. Eugene, Ore.: Microform Publications, University of Oregon, 1984. 1 microfiche : negative, ill. ; 11 x 15 cm.
NOTES: Thesis (M.S.) - Pennsylvania State University, 1981; (viii, 68 leaves); includes bibliography.
LEVEL: A LANG: Eng UO84 131

Weeks, D.L. Motor-output variability in a ballistic task. Eugene, Ore.: Microform Publications, University of Oregon, 1984. microfiche : negative, ill. ; 11 x 15 cm.
NOTES: Thesis (M.S.) - Texas A & M University, 1981; (x, 71 leaves); vita; includes bibliography.
LEVEL: A LANG: Eng UO84 29

AGING AND AGED

Johnson, S.K. Time-series analysis of individual performances of older women on a serial gross motor task. Eugene, Ore.: Microform Publications, University of Oregon, 1984. 4 microfiches : negative, ill. ; 11 x 15 cm.
NOTES: Thesis (Ed.D.) - University of North Carolina at Greensboro, 1982; (xiii, 295 leaves); includes bibliography.
LEVEL: A LANG: Eng UO84 213-216

Lange, E.W. The relationship between reaction time, movement time, and anticipation time in the performance of older female adults. Eugene, Ore.: Microform Publications, University of Oregon, 1984. 1 microfiche : negative ; 11 x 15 cm.
NOTES: Thesis (M.S.) - University of Illinois at Chicago, 1983; (xi, 58 leaves); includes bibliography.
LEVEL: A LANG: Eng UO84 220

Mowatt, M. Evans, G.G. Adrian, M. Assessment of perceptual - motor abilities of healthy rural elderly men and women. (Refs: 16)*Physical educator (Indianapolis, Ind.) 3(41), Oct 1984, 114-120.*
ABST: The authors measure hand steadiness, finger dexterity, accuracy of anticipation timing, and reaction time of 8 rural men and 11 rural women aged between 60 and 76 years. Younger subjects are tested on hand steadiness and finger dexterity: 13 women and 10 men on dexterity and 12 women and 8 men on steadiness. Results indicate differences due to visual impairment, age, sex, number of trials, manner of test, and attribute tested. The authors suggest guidelines for performance evaluation of the elderly.
LEVEL: A LANG: Eng SIRC ARTICLE NO: 100769

ATTENTION

Furst, D.M. Individual differences in attentional flexibility in the performance of tasks requiring changes in attentional set. Eugene, Ore.: Microform Publications, University of Oregon, 1984. 2 microfiches : negative, ill. ; 11 x 15 cm.
NOTES: Thesis (Ph.D.) - Pennsylvania State University, 1981; (x, 124, 1); vita; includes bibliography.
LEVEL: A LANG: Eng UO84 119-120

Girouard, Y. Laurencelle, L. Proteau, L. On the nature of the probe reaction-time task to uncover the attentional demands of movement. (Refs: 17)*Journal of motor behavior (Washington) 16(4), Dec 1984, 442-459.*
ABST: McLeod (1980) reported some findings which showed that no phase of a movement was more attention-demanding than the other phases, contrary to all the results previously reported. In order to try to replicate McLeod's findings, two experiments were conducted. The hypothesis was that time certainty associated with a constant interval would facilitate the allocation of time and would thus artificially reduce the interference between tasks. In Experiment I, manual responses were used for the RT task; in Experiment II, they were vocal. Manipulation of the response-signal interval does not change one of the conclusions reached by McLeod: when the RT task involves vocal responses and the results on the RT task are analyzed in terms of response rather than stimulus arrival during the movement, then there is no phase

of the movement which is more attention-demanding than the other phases.
LEVEL: A LANG: Eng SIRC ARTICLE NO: 105359

Rose, D.J. A study of selective attention as it relates to age and physical activity level. Eugene, Ore.: Microform Publications, University of Oregon, 1984. 2 microfiches : negative ; 11 x 15 cm.
NOTES: Thesis (M.S.) - University of Oregon, 1982; (ix, 127 leaves); vita; includes bibliography.
LEVEL: A LANG: Eng UO84 69-70

Theulen, M.D. The effects of arousal and task complexity on the range of cue utilization. Eugene, Ore.: Microform Publications, University of Oregon, 1984. 2 microfiches : negative, ill. ; 11 x 15 cm.
NOTES: Thesis (D.P.E.) - Springfield College, 1983; (ix, 137 leaves); includes bibliography.
LEVEL: A LANG: Eng UO84 443-444

BIOFEEDBACK

Cummings, M.S. Wilson, V.E. Bird, E.I. Flexibility development in sprinters using EMG biofeedback and relaxation training. (Refs: 20)*Biofeedback and self regulation (New York) 9(3), 1984, 395-405.*
LEVEL: A LANG: Eng SIRC ARTICLE NO: 174381

CHILDREN AND ADOLESCENCE

Branta, C. Haukenstricker, J. Seefeldt, V. Age changes in motor skills during childhood and adolescence. (Refs: 118)*Exercis and sport sciences reviews (Lexington, Mass.) 12, 1984, 467-520.*
ABST: This review discusses the developmental movement skills and the controversy surrounding the qualitative description of movement via total body configuration versus components analysis. This is followed by a compilation of longitudinal and cross-sectional studies of age changes in motor skills and motor achievements by children and youth from various areas around the world. The paper concludes with a review of the stability of selected movement skills in the development years.
LEVEL: A LANG: Eng SIRC ARTICLE NO: 096065

Erbaugh, S.J. Clifton, M.A. Sibling relationships of preschool-aged children in gross motor environments. (Refs: 27)*Researc quarterly for exercise and sport (Reston, Va.) 55(4), Dec 1984, 323-331.*
ABST: This research describes the behaviors and interactions of preschool-aged siblings in two conditions: object-oriented and body-oriented. The hypothesis was that a child's social network, and more specifically, the child's siblings significantly influence motor skill development. Thirty-five pairs of same-sex (20), and mixed-sex (15) siblings individually performed motor tasks for seven minutes in each condition, and a Sony video camera recorded all behaviors. Two major categories of sibling behaviors and interactions - moving (five items) and observing (four items) - were coded using standard procedures from social-developmental psychology (Lamb, Suomi, & Stephenson, 1979). Two of the major findings for the movement items were (1) in the body-oriented conditon, the older siblings ususally initiated task performance while the younger siblings watched them, and (2) in the object-oriented conditon, the older siblings repeated or practiced the same task more frequently than their younger siblings.
LEVEL: A LANG: Eng SIRC ARTICLE NO: 104163

Keshner, E.A. Organization of equilibrium reactions in children under varying conditions of

temporal and spatial certainty. Eugene, Ore.: Microform Publications, University of Oregon, 1984. 3 microfiches : negative, ill. ; 11 x 15 cm.
NOTES: Thesis (Ed.D.) - Columbia University, 1983; (x, 203 leaves); includes bibliography.
LEVEL: A LANG: Eng UO84 217-219

Kisabeth, K.L. A child's movement performance using Labanotation and referenced to the Laban framework: a case study. Eugene Ore.: Microform Publications, University of Oregon, 1984. 3 microfiches : negative, ill. ; 11 x 15 cm.
NOTES: Thesis (Ed.D.) - University of North Carolina at Greensboro, 1980; (xi, 223 leaves); includes bibliography.
LEVEL: A LANG: Eng UO84 41-43

Shasby, G.B. Goal-Ball-Find: a teaching learning game. *Virginia journal (Harrisonburg, Va.)* 6(2), Apr 1984, 5;19.
LEVEL: LANG: Eng SIRC ARTICLE NO: 099116

Thomas, J.R. Planning 'Kiddie' research: little 'Kids' but big problems. (Refs: 23)*In, Thomas, J.R. (ed.), Motor developmen during childhood and adolescence, Minneapolis, Minn., Burgess Publishing Co., 1984, p. 260-273.*
NOTES: Developed from a paper presented at the Physical Education Measurement Symposium, Houston, October 1980.
LEVEL: A LANG: Eng BF1 20187

DISABLED

Cratty, B.J. Sport international: motor development for special populations: issues, problems, and operations. (Refs: 24) *International journal of physical education (Schorndorf, W. Germany)* 21(3), 1984, 27-35.
LEVEL: I LANG: Eng SIRC ARTICLE NO: 102450

Davis, W.E. Motor ability assessment of populations with handicapping conditions: challenging basic assumptions. (Refs: 85) *Adapted physical activity quarterly (Champaign, Ill.)* 1(2), 1984, 125-140.
ABST: Several problems of current motor assessment practices and instruments used for populations with handicapping conditions, are identified from recent surveys and a literature review. Such problems are the basis for an examination of some of the theoretical assumptions underlying current instrumentation and practice. These assumptions are challenged from the perspective of emerging theories of motor control, development, and perception. The traditional standardized approach, the diagnostic approach, and the criterion-referenced approach are considered. Although the criterion-referenced approach is believed to hold the most promise, it has serious shortcomings. Substantial and radical changes in constructing assessment instruments are suggested.
LEVEL: A LANG: Eng SIRC ARTICLE NO: 102451

Deschamps, G. Le Moing Ben Larbie, F. L'education psycho-motrice des aveugles. (2e partie) *EPS: Education physique et sport* 185, janv/fevr 1984, 16-19.
LEVEL: B LANG: Fr SIRC ARTICLE NO: 092810

Liemohn, W. Knapczyk, D.R. An analysis of the Southern California Perceptual Motor Tests. (Refs: 31)*Research quarterly for exercise & sport (Reston, Va.)* 55(3), Sept 1984, 248-253.
ABST: The purpose of this study was to examine the Southern California Perceptual Motor Tests

(SCPMT). The subjects were 386 children characterized as having learning and/or perceptual problems. A factor analysis was made based on the subjects' performances on the 42 individual items. The results indicated that the test items generally have good discriminative ability. However, the distribution of items of some of the individual tests across more than one factor suggests that, at least in children with learning disorders, the tests are sampling a wider number of constructs than was intended in their design.
LEVEL: A LANG: Eng SIRC ARTICLE NO: 102620

Stein, J. Microcomputer uses to promote physical proficiency and motor development of students with handicapped conditions. *Physical educator (Indianapolis, Ind.)* 41(1), Mar 1984, 40-42.
NOTES: Part 11 to be in October, 1984 issue.
LEVEL: B LANG: Eng SIRC ARTICLE NO: 095882

Stein, J. Part 11: microcomputer uses to promote physical proficiency and motor development of students with handicapped conditions. *Physical educator (Indianapolis, Ind.)* 3(41), Oct 1984, 153-156.
NOTES: Second of a two part series.
LEVEL: B LANG: Eng SIRC ARTICLE NO: 100661

GROWTH AND DEVELOPMENT

Casciani, J. Developmental relationships between logical or operational schemes, motor schemes, and scheme coordinating ability. Eugene, Ore.: Microform Publications, University of Oregon, 1984. 2 microfiches : negative ; 11 x 15 cm.
NOTES: Thesis (Ed.D.) - West Virginia University, 1980; (149 leaves); includes bibliography.
LEVEL: A LANG: Eng UO84 185-186

Holopainen, S. Lumiaho-Haekkinen, P. Telama, R. Level and rate of development of motor fitness, motor abilities and skills b somatotype. (Refs: 14)*Scandinavian journal of sports sciences (Helsinki, Finland)* 6(2), Dec 1984, 67-75.
ABST: This paper describes the somatotype of girls and boys and the relationship between the motor performances of school-aged children (7-16 years) and their somatotypes. 919 children served as subjects. The following tests were used: motor abilities (6 tests); motor fitness (7 tests); basic skills (8 tests) and apparatus gymnastics (using a large test battery). Somatotype explained 0-4 per cent of the variability in motor abilities, 1-12 per cent of that in motor fitness, and 1-2 per cent of that in basic skills; except in standing five jump, basic and apparatus gymnastics, in which the variability explained was 11 per cent for girls and 14 for boys. Centrals and ecto-mesomorphs were the most favorable somatotypes in girls for motor fitness, motor abilities, and basic skills. For boys the performances do not differ so clearly by somatotype.
LEVEL: A LANG: Eng SIRC ARTICLE NO: 106603

Jolibois, R.P. Effets de l'activite physique et developpement psychomoteur des tout-petits. (Refs: 11)*Dans, Mandel, C. (ed.), Le medecin, l'enfant et le sport, Paris, (Vigot), c1984, p. 107-115.*
LEVEL: A LANG: Fr RC1218.C45 18886

Newell, K.M. Physical constraints to development of motor skills. (Refs: 60)*In, Thomas, J.R. (ed.), Motor development durin childhood and adolescence, Minneapolis, Minn., Burgess Publishing Co., 1984, p. 105-120.*
LEVEL: A LANG: Eng BF1 20187

Roberton, M.A. Changing motor patterns during childhood. (Refs: 67)*In, Thomas, J.R. (ed.), Motor development during childhood and adolescence, Minneapolis, Minn., Burgess Publishing Co., 1984, p. 48-90.*
LEVEL: A LANG: Eng BF1 20187

Saunders, J.E. The motor activity of children in preschool. (Refs: 32)*In, Simri, U. (ed.), et al., Preschool and elementary school children and physical activity. Proceedings of the 26th ICHPER World Congress 1983, Wingate Institute, Israel, vol. III, Jerusalem, Israel, 1984, p. 122-136.*
CONF: ICHPER World Congress (26th : 1983 : Wingate Institute, Israel).
LEVEL: A LANG: Eng GV443 20093

Silva, P.A. Birkbeck, J. Russell, D.G. Wilson, J. Some biological, developmental, and social correlates of gross and fine motor performance in Dunedin seven year olds. A report from the Dunedin multidisciplinary health and development research unit. (Refs: 25)*Journal of human involvement studies (Edinburgh)* 10(1), 1984 35-51.
ABST: This longitudinal study represents the latest phase in the motor performance assessment of a sample of Dunedin babies. Motor performance of 835 of the 1139 eligible children was assessed with the Basic Motor Ability Test. The results give support to the premise that gross and fine motor performance are influenced by the sex of the child, are built on earlier motor development, reflect the anthropometric characteristics of the child and are related to cognitive ability. The authors conclude that gross and fine motor performance reflect the complex interaction of varying biological, development and to a lesser extent social and experiential factors which together explain a substantial proportion of the variance of these aspects of human development.
LEVEL: A LANG: Eng SIRC ARTICLE NO: 094461

Thomas, J.R. Children's motor skill development. (Refs: 31)*In, Thomas, J.R. (ed.), Motor development during childhood and adolescence, Minneapolis, Minn., Burgess Publishing Co., 1984, p. 91-104.*
LEVEL: A LANG: Eng BF1 20187

Thomas, J.R. Thomas, K.T. Kids and numbers: assessing children's motor development. *In, Thomas, J.R. (ed.), Motor development during childhood and adolescence, Minneapolis, Minn., Burgess Publishing Co., 1984, p. 185-188.*
LEVEL: B LANG: Eng BF1 20187

Thomas, J.R. Laboratory experiences in motor development. (Refs: 13)*In, Thomas, J.R. (ed.), Motor development during childhood and adolescence, Minneapolis, Minn., Burgess Publishing Co., 1984, p. 274-286.*
LEVEL: A LANG: Eng BF1 20187

Tiainen, J. Tiainen, A. Physical education and its significance on personality development at the sensorimotor period. (Refs 8)*In: Internationales Symposium Sportpaedagogik - Koerpererziehung - Persoenlichkeit: Protokoll, Potsdam, Deutsche Demokratische Republik, ICSSPE/CIEPSS, 1984?, p. 143-149.*
CONF: Internationales Symposium Sportpaedagogik - Koerpererziehung - Persoenlichkeit (1983 : Potsdam).
LEVEL: I LANG: Eng GV205 20231

PERCEPTUAL MOTOR PROCESSES (continued)

KINESTHESIS

Barrack, R.L. Skinner, H.B. Brunet, M.E. Cook, S.D. Joint kinesthesia in the highly trained knee. (Refs: 10)*Journal of sports medicine and physical fitness (Torino) 24(1), Mar 1984, 18-20.*
ABST: 5 male and 7 female members of a professional ballet company were tested for their ability to small position changes in their knee joint. An age-matched group of healthy active controls were also tested. The dancers were found to be more sensitive to the detection of the onset of motion at the knee joint. It is concluded that this sense of joint motion and position can be attributed to extensive athletic training.
LEVEL: A LANG: Eng SIRC ARTICLE NO: 099515

Craske, B. Kenny, F.T. Keith, D. Modifying an underlying component of perceived arm length: adaptation of tactile location induced by spatial discordance. *Journal of experimental psychology: human perception and performance (Washington) 10(2), Apr 1984, 307-317.*
LEVEL: A LANG: Eng SIRC ARTICLE NO: 101007

LATERALITY

Azemar, G. Activite sportive chez l'enfant et lateralite. (Refs: 12)*Dans, Mandel, C. (ed.), Le medecin, l'enfant et le sport, Paris, (Vigot), c1984, p. 117-129.*
LEVEL: I LANG: Fr RC1218.C45 18886

Dummer, S.M. The nondominant hand as a determinant for performance in large and small motor tasks. Eugene, Ore.: Microform Publications, University of Oregon, 1984. 1 microfiche : negative, ill. ; 11 x 15 cm.
NOTES: Thesis (M.S.) - University of Wisconsin-La Crosse, 1982; (vii, 63 leaves); includes bibliography.
LEVEL: A LANG: Eng UO84 289

Solin, J. La lateralisation du schema corporel de l'enfant sportif. La lateralite du tronc dans le programme moteur. *Medecine du sport (Paris) 58(2), 25 mars 1984, 34-38.*
LEVEL: I LANG: Fr SIRC ARTICLE NO: 094214

MEMORY

Dowell, M.N. The serial-position curve in kinesthetic short-term memory. Eugene, Ore.: Microform Publications, University of Oregon, 1984. 2 microfiches : negative, ill. ; 11 x 15 cm.
NOTES: Thesis (Ph.D.) - Texas A & M University, 1979; (xii, 115 leaves); vita; includes bibliography.
LEVEL: A LANG: Eng UO84 18-19

Gallagher, J.D. Thomas, J.R. Rehearsal strategy effects on development differences for recall of a movement series. (Refs: 2 *Research quarterly for exercise & sport (Reston, Va.) 55(2), Jun 1984, 123-128.*
ABST: This investigation studied the effects of passive (instance-by instance practise) and active (practise using several items together) rehearsal on the developmental processing differences for movement reproduction. The authors hypothesized that the use of the mature active rehearsal would facilitate the movement reproduction of young children whereas the use of the immature passive rehearsal would decrease the movement reproduction of adults. The authors tested this hypothesis in a group of 120 subjects, who were divided into four equal groups by ages (5, 7, 11, 19

years). The results confirm the hypothesis and demonstrate the importance of active rehearsal for the younger children.
LEVEL: A LANG: Eng SIRC ARTICLE NO: 096069

Housner, L.D. The role of visual imagery in recall of modeled motoric stimuli. (Refs: 35)*Sport psychology (Champaign, Ill.) (2), 1984, 148-158.*
ABST: Subjects (N, 29) classified as high or low visual imagers (highs and lows, respectively) viewed and reproduced six filmed examples of motoric stimuli constructed by combining a variety of leg, trunk, arm, and head movements. The motor stimuli represented three levels of complexity (4, 7, and 10 components) and two levels of orientation (model facing subject or facing away). Highs and lows were randomly assigned to one of two experimental groups: (a) one viewing of the stimuli, or (b) two viewings of the stimuli. Analysis of the data revealed significant main effects for imagery ability, $F(1,25)$ equals 6.41, where highs reproduced the stimuli with less error than lows, and viewings, $F(1,25)$ equals 6.41 where two viewings resulted in less recall error than one viewing. Also, the orientation by complexity interaction was found to be significant, $F(2,50)$ equals 25.51 , and indicated that recall accuracy was best when the model was facing away, but only for movement sequences of seven components.
LEVEL: A LANG: Eng SIRC ARTICLE NO: 108490

Magill, R.A. Influences on remembering movement information. (Refs: 50)*In, Straub, W.F. and Williams, J.M. (eds.), Cognitiv sport psychology, Lansing, N.Y., Sport Science Associates, c1984, p. 175-188.*
LEVEL: A LANG: Eng GV706.4 20099

Pigatt, R.E. Shapiro, D.C. Motor schema: the structure of the variability session. (Refs: 10)*Research quarterly for exercis & sport (Reston, Va.) 55(1), Mar 1984, 41-45.*
ABST: The purpose of this study was to examine the effects of the structure of the variability session and its subsequent influence on transfer performance to a novel variation of the task. Thirty-two male and thirty-two female children were given the task of throwing weighted bean bags at a fixed target. Between the practice sessions, the number of task variations and trials was kept constant while the trial-to-trial presentation of each variation was manipulated (ie. different weights). The results indicated that the group practising with blocks of three trials at each variation led to superior performance at transfer to novel variations of the task. The authors conclude that there appears to be an optimal way to structure the variable practice session for children to strengthen the formation of the recall schema.
LEVEL: A LANG: Eng SIRC ARTICLE NO: 096075

Stelmach, G.E. Hughes, B. Memory, cognition and motor behavior. (Refs: 37)*In, Straub, W.F. and Williams, J.M. (eds.), Cognitive sport psychology, Lansing, N.Y., Sport Science Associates, c1984, p. 163-174.*
LEVEL: A LANG: Eng GV706.4 20099

MENTAL IMAGERY

Heil, J. Imagery for sport: theory, research and practice. (Refs: 35)*In, Straub, W.F. and Williams, J.M. (eds.), Cognitive sport psychology, Lansing, N.Y., Sport Science Associates, c1984, p. 245-252.*
LEVEL: A LANG: Eng GV706.4 20099

Suinn, R.M. Imagery and sports. (Refs: 49)*In, Straub, W.F. and Williams, J.M. (eds.), Cognitive sport psychology, Lansing, N.Y., Sport Science Associates, c1984, p. 253-271.*
LEVEL: A LANG: Eng GV706.4 20099

MOTIVATION

Vallerand, R.J. Reid, G. On the causal effects of perceived competence on intrinsic motivation: a test of cognitive evaluation theory. (Refs: 33)*Sport psychology (Champaign, Ill.) 6(1), 1984, 94-102.*
ABST: The purpose of this study was to test the validity of the psychological processes proposed by cognitive evaluation theory when the informational aspect of the situation is salient. More specifically, it was the purpose of this study to determine whether the effects of verbal feedback on intrinsic motivation are mediated by perceived competence. Male undergraduate students (N, 115) participated in a first phase wherein their intrinsic motivation and perceived competence toward an interesting motor task, the stabilometer, was assessed. Subjects (N, 84) who reported at least a moderate level of intrinsic motivation toward the task returned for the second phase of the study in which they were subjected to conditions of either positive, negative, or no verbal feedback of performance. Intrinsic motivation and perceived competence were again assessed. One-way analyses of variance with dependent variables, intrinsic motivation and perceived competence change scores from the first to the second phase, showed that positive feedback increased while negative feedback decreased both intrinsic motivation and perceived competence.
LEVEL: A LANG: Eng SIRC ARTICLE NO: 108487

MOTOR ABILITY

Ashy, M.H. Lee, A.M. Applying the mastery learning model to motor skill instruction for children. (Refs: 18)*Physical educator (Bloomington, Ind.) 41(2), May 1984, 60-63.*
LEVEL: I LANG: Eng SIRC ARTICLE NO: 099113

Battinelli, T. From motor ability to motor learning: the generality specificity connection. (Refs: 48)*Physical educator (Indianapolis, Ind.) 3(41), Oct 1984, 108-113.*
LEVEL: I LANG: Eng SIRC ARTICLE NO: 100767

Bird, A.M. Ross, D. Current methodological problems and future directions for theory development in the psychology of sport and motor behavior. (Refs: 19)*Quest (Champaign, Ill.) 36(1), 1984, 1-6.*
LEVEL: I LANG: Eng SIRC ARTICLE NO: 099282

Butterly, R. The effect of different levels of verbalisation on a concurrent unimanual tapping task. (Refs: 21)*Carnegie research papers (Beckett Park, Leeds) 1(6), Dec 1984, 8-11.*
ABST: The purposes of this study were 1) to evaluate the effect of a verbal task with two levels of difficulty on tapping task performance; and 2) to compare the results of 15 boys aged 12-13 and 15 first year university undergraduates. Results indicated impaired performance of both right and left hand for university students and schoolboys with the onset of the verbal task. Right hand and schoolboy performances were more affected. The deterioration of performance was less pronounced when increasing the difficulty of the verbal task compared to its onset.
LEVEL: A LANG: Eng SIRC ARTICLE NO: 172498

Cook, C.F. Broadhead, J.D. Motor performance of pre-school twins and singletons. (Refs: 21)*Physical educator (Indianapolis, Ind.) 41(1), Mar 1984, 16-20.*
ABST: The purpose of this study was to assess motor performance within pairs of twins, and between twins and singletons. 12 male and 12 female pairs aged 2 1/2 to 5 1/2 years, participated in the study. In addition, 275 male and 207 female singletons in the same age range were evaluated. Results indicated higher level performance of older twins and/or singletons as well as higher performance for singletons in general.
LEVEL: A LANG: Eng SIRC ARTICLE NO: 096068

Dix, C.L. Time-series analysis of intraindividual performances of a complex serial gross motor task. Eugene, Ore.: Microform Publications, University of Oregon, 1984. 3 microfiches : negative, ill. ; 11 x 15 cm.
NOTES: Thesis (Ed.D.) - University of North Carolina at Greensboro, 1982; (ix, 216 leaves); includes bibliography.
LEVEL: A LANG: Eng UO84 168-170

Dwyer, J. Influence of physical fatigue on motor performance and learning. (Refs: 25)*Physical educator (Indianapolis, Ind.) 3(41), Oct 1984, 130-136.*
LEVEL: A LANG: Eng SIRC ARTICLE NO: 100768

Gabbard, C. Teaching motor skills to children: theory into practice. (Refs: 7)*Physical educator (Bloomington, Ind.) 41(2), May 1984, 69-71.*
LEVEL: B LANG: Eng SIRC ARTICLE NO: 099114

Golby, J. The effects of temazepam, a 1,4 - Benzodiazepine, on a battery of tests of perceptual-motor performance. (Refs: 22 *Carnegie research papers (Beckett Park, Leeds) 1(6), Dec 1984, 37-44.*
ABST: This study reports on the effect of temazepam on a battery of seven perceptual motor skill tests: 1) reaction/recognition time; 2) movement time; 3) total time i.e. the sum of 1) and 2); 4) catching; 5) aiming (darts); 6) hand steadiness; and 7) body control. Eight females participated in the study.
LEVEL: A LANG: Eng SIRC ARTICLE NO: 172515

Hughes, J.R. South Auckland perceptual motor dysfunction survey. (Refs: 13)*New Zealand journal of health, physical educatio & recreation (Wellington, N.Z.) 17(1), May 1984, 4-7.*
LEVEL: I LANG: Eng SIRC ARTICLE NO: 097617

Lichtman, B. Motor schema: putting theory into action. (Refs: 23)*Journal of physical education, recreation & dance 55(3), Mar 1984, 54-56.*
LEVEL: I LANG: Eng SIRC ARTICLE NO: 092965

Logan, D.A. The effectiveness of a sensory-motor program with academically handicapped and normal first grade children. Eugene, Ore.: Microform Publications, University of Oregon, 1984. 4 microfiches : negative, ill. ; 11 x 15 cm.
NOTES: Thesis (Ph.D.) - Texas Woman's University, 1982; (viii, 297 leaves); includes bibliography.
LEVEL: A LANG: Eng UO84 253-256

Mechling, H. Is the concept of 'motor fitness' still or again all right? (Refs: 34)*International journal of physical education (Schorndorf, W. Germany) 21(1), 1984, 18-24;29.*
LEVEL: I LANG: Eng SIRC ARTICLE NO: 092967

Schmuecker, B. Rigauer, B. Hinrichs, W. Trawinski, J. Motor abilities and habitual physical activity in children. (Refs: 17)
CONF: Symposium of Paediatric Work Physiology (10th : 1981 : Joutsa, Finland).
NOTES: In, Ilmarinen, J. and Vaelimaeki, I. (eds.), Children and sport: paediatric work physiology, Berlin, Springer-Verlag, 1984, p. 46-52.
ABST: This study compared observations employing different criteria in the motor area by using standardized tests and defined assignments and situations. The physiologic, coordinative, and communicative criteria were subjected to a correlation analysis so that their relationships with one another could be established. Habitual physical activity was assessed to study its importance in motor performance.
LEVEL: A LANG: Eng SIRC ARTICLE NO: 102621

Servais, A. Treffer, J. Une collaboration entre le professeur d'education physique et le professeur de pratique professionnelle: le travail en hauteur. *Revue de l'education physique (Liege, Belgique) 24(1), 1984, 41-44.*
LEVEL: I LANG: Fr SIRC ARTICLE NO: 096076

Ulrich, D.A. Wise, S.L. Reliability of scores obtained with the Objectives-Based Motor Skill Assessment Instrument. (Refs: 1 *Adapted physical activity quarterly (Champaign, Ill.) 1(3), 1984, 230-239.*
ABST: This study was designed to investigate the reliability of individual and composite scores obtained with the Objectives-Based Motor Skill Assessment Instrument. Generalizability theory was used to determine if the test scores were reliable across raters and occasions. Two D studies were conducted to ascertain whether an increase in the number of raters from 10 to 20 would increase the reliability. Twenty raters were required to evaluate the fundamental motor skills of 10 subjects across two occasions from videotapes. In 92% of the individual skill scores, the between-subject variance component contributed the most to total variance.The test is extremely reliable across raters and occasions and the reliability is not largely affected by increasing the number of raters.
LEVEL: A LANG: Eng SIRC ARTICLE NO: 102622

Vankersschaver, J. (Information-processing capacities in a sensorimotor skill - a sport skill example). (Refs: 16)*Travail humain (Paris) 47(3), 1984, 281-286.*
LEVEL: A LANG: Fr

MOTOR COORDINATION

Abbs, J.H. Gracco, V.L. Cole, K.J. Control of multimovement coordination: sensorimotor mechanisms in speech motor programmin (Refs: 128)*Journal of motor behavior (Washington) 16(2), Jun 1984, 195-232.*
ABST: The present paper provides some hypotheses concerning the role of sensorimotor mechanisms in the coordination and programming of multimovement behaviors. The primary database is from experiments on the control of speech, a motor behavior that inherently requires multimovement coordination. From these data, it appears that coordination may be implemented by calibrated, sensorimotor actions which couple multiple movements for the accomplishment of common functional goals. The data from speech and select observations in other motor systems also reveal that these sensorimotor linkages are task-dependent and may underlie the

intermovement motor equivalence that characterizes many natural motor behaviors. In this context, it is hypothesized also that motor learning may involve the calibration of these intermovement sensorimotor actions.
LEVEL: A LANG: Eng SIRC ARTICLE NO: 102614

Beuter, A. Describing multijoint coordination: preliminary investigation with nonhandicapped, cerebral palsied, and elderly individuals. (Refs: 14)*Adapted physical activity quarterly (Champaign, Ill.) 1(2), 1984, 105-111.*
ABST: This paper proposes a computer graphics approach to represent the kinematics of the lower limb during a multijoint coordinated motor task. The methodology is based on automatic digitization by a microprocessor of reflective markers placed on anatomical landmarks and videotaped using a videomotion analyzer and camera. With joint angles, or the first or second derivative of the angles serving as the coordinates for the three mutually perpendicular axes in R3, the technique gives a point in space corresponding to each time increment as the movement sequence progresses. Using this method a graphical representation of the position, velocity, or acceleration can be generated in movement space, velocity space, or acceleration space, respectively. A sample of the results of this technique is presented using the movement space of elderly, nonhandicapped, and cerebral palsied individuals as each steps over a low obstacle.
LEVEL: A LANG: Eng SIRC ARTICLE NO: 102442

Carcos, D.M. Two - handed movement control. (Refs: 9)*Research quarterly for exercise & sport (Reston, Va.) 55(2), Jun 1984, 117-122.*
ABST: This study investigated the discrepancy between the finding that when hands make movements to targets of different distances, they have the same movement time and conversely, the finding that they have different movement times. Twelve subjects performed two-handed movements in four experimental situations. The results indicate that when the ratio of the distance traveled by the hands is 4:1, they do not take the same time. This occurs because the hand moving the shorter distance takes less time than the hand moving the longer distance; although the hand moving the shorter distance takes more time than when it is moving alone or moving the same distance as the other hand.
LEVEL: A LANG: Eng SIRC ARTICLE NO: 096066

Fentress, J.C. The development of coordination. (Refs: 124)*Journal of motor behavior (Washington) 16(2), Jun 1984, 99-134.*
ABST: This paper provides a framework for analyzing the development of coordinated action systems. By emphasizing the general theme of pattern formation in coordinated action, attention is drawn to dual problems of establishing separable dimensions of action that are in turn combined into higher-order configurations. During development processes differentiation and integration are combined to make coordinated action possible. The rules by which this is accomplished, however, are still poorly understood. The perspective offered here is that to understand the development of coordinated action it is valuable to seek relative degrees of continuity-discontinuity and change-stability from several complementary perspectives.
LEVEL: A LANG: Eng SIRC ARTICLE NO: 102616

Hinton, G. Parallel computations for controlling an arm. (Refs: 22)*Journal of motor behavior (Washington) 16(2), Jun 1984, 171-194.*

ABST: In order to control a reaching movement of the arm and body, several different computational problems must be solved. Some parallel methods that could be implemented in networks of neuron-like processors are described. First, a method is described for finding the torques necessary to follow a desired trajectory. The method is more economical and more versatile than table look-up and requires very few sequential steps. Then a way of generating an internal representation of a desired trajectory is described. This method shows the trajectory one piece at a time by applying a large set of heuristic rules to a 'motion blackboard' that represents the static and dynamic parameters of the state of the body at the current point in the trajectory. The computations are simplified by expressing the positions, orientations, and motions of parts of the body in terms of a single, non-accelerating, world-based frame of reference.
LEVEL: A LANG: Eng SIRC ARTICLE NO: 102618

Lee, W.A. Neuromotor synergies as a basis for coordinated intentional action. (Refs: 127)*Journal of motor behavior (Washington) 16(2), Jun 1984, 135-170.*
NOTES: Part of this paper was presented at the 1981 Meeting of the North American Society for the Psychology of Sport and Physical Activity, May 1981.
ABST: Although neurally based units of action (neuromotor synergies) have often been proposed as a possible basis for coordinated intentional as well as automatic actions, the idea has rarely been translated into sets of testable hypotheses. This essay examines four issues which should facilitate the development of such hypotheses: (a) definitions of neuromotor synergies, (b) criteria for recognizing and comparing synergies in automatic and intentional actions, (c) problems in representing systems of synergies, and (d) models for generating intentional actions from sets of neuromotor synergies. Limitations of, and support for the neuromotor synergy hypothesis are discussed, both in general and for the specific cases of postural synergies and cervico-spinal reflexes. Although current data do not provide conclusive support for or against the neuromotor synergy hypothesis, the problem can be formulated in ways open to experimental investigation.
LEVEL: A LANG: Eng SIRC ARTICLE NO: 102619

Williams, L.R.T. Sissons, A.C. Performance, learning and transfer of balance skill in relation to achievement level in sport (Refs: 17)*Australian journal of science & medicine in sport (Kingston, Aust.) 16(4), Dec 1984, 21-23.*
ABST: The relationship of sporting ability to balancing ability was examined using a proactive transfer design and two versions of the stabilometer balance task. Highly skilled sportsmen and non-sportsmen (n, 48) were sub-divided into experimental and control groups. The hypothesis that the high skill group would perform better than the low skill group on both tasks was supported as was the prediction that the highly skilled subjects would demonstrate more ability to transfer to the second task. The prediction that the rate of learning would be faster for the high skill group was not supported.
LEVEL: A LANG: Eng SIRC ARTICLE NO: 105366

MOTOR PROGRAMS

Cooke, J.D. Diggles, V.A. Rapid error correction during human arm movements: evidence for central monitoring. (Refs: 24) *Journal of motor behaviour (Washington) 16(4), Dec 1984, 348-363.*
ABST: Studies were made of rapid error correction movements in eight subjects performing a visually guided tracking task involving flexion-extension movements about the elbow. Subjects were required to minimize reaction times in this two-choice task. Errors in initial movement direction occurred in about 3 per cent of the trials. Error correction times (time from initiation to reversal of movement in incorrect direction) ranged from 30-150 ms. The first sign of correction of the error movement was a suppression of the electromyographic (EMG) activity in the muscle producing the error movement. The correction of the error movement was also accompanied by an increase in the drive to the muscle which moved the arm in the correct direction.
LEVEL: A LANG: Eng SIRC ARTICLE NO: 105355

Stanforth, D.J. Focus: the perceptual-motor development clinic in the kinesiotherapy center of the University of Toledo. (Refs: 12)*American corrective therapy journal (San Diego, Calif.) 38(2), Mar/Apr 1984, 30-34.*
ABST: This paper describes the services offered by a particular perceptual-motor development clinic. The clinic provides perceptual-motor development activities for children and adults and provides instruction to school teachers, parents and guardians in perceptual-motor development. The activities range from traditional perceptual-motor development activities to kinesiotherapy and cardiorespiratory fitness activities.
LEVEL: A LANG: Eng SIRC ARTICLE NO: 095881

MOVEMENT EDUCATION

Guezille, G. Le mouvement: fonctionnement et renforcement. *Revue de l'Amicale des entraineurs francais d'athletisme (Paris) 86, janv/fevr/mars 1984, 29-33.*
LEVEL: B LANG: Fr SIRC ARTICLE NO: 094455

PERCEIVED EXERTION

Collins, M.L. Rating of perceived exertion, ergometer specificity and sex differences as functions of work intensity. Eugene Ore.: Microform Publications, University of Oregon, 1984. 2 microfiches : negative, ill. ; 11 x 15 cm.
NOTES: Thesis (M.S.) - Springfield College, 1982; (viii, 119 leaves); includes bibliography.
LEVEL: A LANG: Eng UO84 235-236

Hage, P. Full-bodied fitness: monitor your training progress at home. (perceived exertion) *Bicycling (Emmaus, Pa.) 25(9), Nov/Dec 1984, 6-10.*
LEVEL: I LANG: Eng SIRC ARTICLE NO: 100897

Kircher, M.A. Motivation as a factor of perceived exertion in purposeful versus nonpurposeful activity. (Refs: 32)*American journal of occupational therapy (Rockville, Md.) 38(3), Mar 1984, 165-170.*
ABST: Perceived exertion of 26 women was evaluated during jumping rope, a purposeful activity, and when jumping in place without a rope, a nonpurposeful activity. Results indicated that the increase of heart rate at a given rate of perceived exertion was higher (.001) for jumping rope. It was shown that purposeful activity is an intrinsic

motivator to the performer.
LEVEL: A LANG: Eng SIRC ARTICLE NO: 100939

Loverin, J. 'Perceived level of exertion' chart used to monitor heart rates. *Journal of physical education and program (Columbus, Oh.) 81(5), Jun 1984, 12-14.*
LEVEL: I LANG: Eng SIRC ARTICLE NO: 096274

Pandolf, K.B. Billings, D.S. Drolet, L.L. Pimental, N.A. Sawka, M.N. Differentiated ratings of perceived exertion and variou physiological responses during prolonged upper and lower body exercise. (Refs: 28)*European journal of applied physiology and occupational physiology (Berlin, W.G.) 53(1), 1984, 5-11.*
ABST: This study examined whether prolonged exercise employing upper or lower body muscle groups led to significant alterations in three differentiated ratings of perceived exertion (RPE). Nine volunteer males performed 60min of arm crank and cycle exercise at similar absolute and at similar relative exercise intensities. The RPE included local RPE (muscle and joint exertion), central RPE (ventilatory and circulatory exertion), and overall RPE. During the absolute tests, the final means for all three RPE were lower for leg than arm exercise. No differences between arm and leg exercise for any of the three RPE. Local RPE was generally higher than central RPE. The various physiological responses accounted for more (total) variance in all three RPE for arm than leg exercise.
LEVEL: A LANG: Eng SIRC ARTICLE NO: 104352

Plato, P.A. The influence of fitness level and suggestion on ratings of perceived exertion by college-aged women. Eugene, Ore.: Microform Publications, University of Oregon, 1984. 2 microfiches : negative, ill. ; 11 x 15 cm.
NOTES: Thesis (M.S.) - University of Arizona, 1981; (ix, 120 leaves); includes bibliography.
LEVEL: A LANG: Eng UO84 364-365

Rejeski, W.J. Sanford, B. Feminine-typed females: the role of affective schema in the perception of exercise intensity. (Refs: 25)*Sport psychology (Champaign, Ill.) 6(2), 1984, 197-207.*
ABST: The purpose of this research was to examine the hypothesis that feminine-typed females who process exercie-related physiological changes via affective schema overreact to the actual intensity of work. The design involved two groups of women, 20 in each group, who were feminine-typed on the personal attributes questionnaire. One group was shown an intolerant model prior to a bicycle ergometer ride, whereas the second group viewed a tolerant model. Results revealed that those female in the intolerant condition experienced negative affect prior to the task, a set that resulted in higher RPEs during ergometry performance when compared to those in the tolerant condition. The data are discussed from the perspective of a parallel processing model of pain and their practical implications for exercise and sport.
LEVEL: A LANG: Eng SIRC ARTICLE NO: 108493

Siegel, D. Johnson, J. Kline, G. Attentional load and the reproduction of physical work. (Refs: 28)*Research quartely for exercise & sport (Reston, Va.) 55(2), Jun 1984, 146-152.*
ABST: Forty-four subjects performed a fixed interval of work at either 50 or 75% of their predicted VO2 max. during which they were required to solve a continuous flow of arithmetic problems or to perform in an unfilled control condition. The authors hypothesized that subjects required to perform an attentional demanding task during work would tend

to underestimate the extent of that work when asked to reproduce it. It was also hypothesized that control subjects would be more accurate in their reproduction. During reproduction of the work it was found that individuals in the control condition produced more work than they had done in the original trial while those in the attentional focus performed about the same amount of work.
LEVEL: A LANG: Eng SIRC ARTICLE NO: 096077

Stamford, B. What's your exertostat? *Physician and sportsmedicine 12(1), Jan 1984, 203.*
LEVEL: I LANG: Eng SIRC ARTICLE NO: 091780

PERCEPTUAL MOTOR LEARNING

Bishop, P. Horvat, M.A. Effects of home instruction on the physical and motor performance of a clumsy child. (Refs: 10) *American corrective therapy journal (San Diego, Calif.) 38(1), Jan/Feb 1984, 6-10.*
ABST: This paper describes the case study of an 8-year-old male who underwent home instruction designed to increase his motor proficiency. The parents implemented the instructional activities, which were designed by the authors, three times weekly for 30 minutes at a time over a period of 7 weeks. The results indicate that the home instruction method brought about beneficial changes with the gross motor skills exhibiting a greater change than the fine motor skills.
LEVEL: A LANG: Eng SIRC ARTICLE NO: 094453

Cox, R.H. Consolidation of pursuit rotor learning under condition of threat of electrical shock. (Refs: 15)*International journal of sport psychology (Rome) 15(1), 1984, 1-10.*
ABST: This paper investigates the relationship between stress and the performance and learning of a pursuit rotor task. 60 male and 60 female undergraduate students were given 21 20-second acquisition trials under the threat of shock, followed 24 or 48 hours later by nine additional trials in the absence of stress. The analysis of performance shows that stress does not elicit a facilitative effect as predicted by perserverative consolidation theory.
LEVEL: A LANG: Eng SIRC ARTICLE NO: 094454

Crocket, P.R.E. Dickinson, J. Incidental psychomotor learning: the effects of number of movements, practice, and rehearsal. (Refs: 22)*Journal of motor behavior (Washington, D.C.) 16(1), Mar 1984, 61-75.*
ABST: Three experiments were conducted to investigate the effects of the number of movements, practice, and rehearsal on incidental and intentional psychomotor learning. Incidental learners received no formal instructions to learn the central task to which they were exposed in a choice reaction-time task. The movements to the targets in this task comprised a movement sequence. Intentional learners also performed the choice reaction-time task but were additionally instructed to remember the order of the movements. Intentional learning was superior to incidental learning, unless rehearsal was disrupted; all three independent variables demonstrated similar functional effects under both learning conditions. It was concluded that incidental and intentional learning are not distinct types of learning; and that 'intent to learn' per se is a significant factor in psychomotor learning only when it elicits beneficial cognitive processes such as rehearsal.
LEVEL: A LANG: Eng SIRC ARTICLE NO: 108338

Day, R.E. The development of motor skills in children. *Momentum (Edinburgh, Scotland) 9(3), Autumn 1984, 2-6.*
LEVEL: I LANG: Eng SIRC ARTICLE NO: 105356

Frohlich, D.M. Elliott, J.M. The schematic representation of effector function underlying perceptual-motor skill. (Refs: 54) *Journal of motor behavior (Washington, D.C.) 16(1), Mar 1984, 40-60.*
ABST: Conceptual and methodological problems related to Schmidt's (1975) motor schema theory are discussed.In particular, the motor schema is interpreted as representing the dynamics of the system being controlled, which may or may not be associated with a referent movement pattern. Furthermore, it is suggested that prior familarity with a control system's dynamics is a critical but uncontrolled factor in tests of the theory, and largely accounts for their equivocal findings. These ideas are examined by two experiments in which subjects had to bimanually control the movement of a computer-displayed cursor along a track on a CRT screen. Different track orientations required different patterns of movement not entailing a singly generalized motor program. Experiment 1 shows that variable track performance with a given control system, results in better transfer to novel tracks than does fixed practice. Experiment 2 demonstrates that altering the control system disrupts performance whether or not the the required movements remain the same.
LEVEL: A LANG: Eng SIRC ARTICLE NO: 108337

Gallagher, J.D. Influence of developmental information processing abilities on children's motor performance. (Refs: 61)*In, Straub, W.F. and Williams, J.M. (eds.), Cognitive sport psychology, Lansing, N.Y., Sport Science Associates, c1984, p. 153-162.*
LEVEL: A LANG: Eng GV706.4 20099

Gioux, M. Arne, P. Paty, J. Bensch, C. Cognitive potentials and skill acquisition in sports. *Annals of the New York Academy of Sciences (New York) 425, 1984, 465-469.*
LEVEL: I LANG: Eng SIRC ARTICLE NO: 102617

Graydon, J.K. Townsend, J. Proprioceptive and visual feedback in the learning of two gross motor skills. (Refs: 11) *International journal of sport psychology (Rome, Italy) 15(4), 1984, 227-235.*
ABST: Two groups of ten schoolgirl novices, aged 12-13 years, were each given 20 instructional sessions in the skills of the badminton short serve, and the trampoline forward somersault. One group was blindfolded in order to maximise attention to proprioceptive feedback, and was given information relating to the 'feel' of the movements they were performing. The other group were not blindfolded and were given feedback of a visuo-spatial nature. The results showed a significantly higher final score for the blindfolded group in the trampoline skill. The group given visuo-spatial feedback had a higher final score than the blindfolded group in the badminton serve, but this result failed to reach significance.
LEVEL: A LANG: Eng SIRC ARTICLE NO: 106601

Herkowitz, J. Developmentally engineered equipment and playgrounds. (Refs: 56)*In, Thomas, J.R. (ed.), Motor development during childhood and adolescence, Minneapolis, Minn., Burgess Publishing Co., 1984, p. 139-173.*
LEVEL: A LANG: Eng BF1 20187

Hodges, D.L. How to teach yourself physical skills: an audio tape for college students with some introductory comments and a detailed outline. Eugene, Or.: Lane Community College, Testing Office, 1984. 1 microfiche (35 fr.)
LEVEL: I LANG: Eng EDRS: ED245757

Housner, L.D. The role of imaginal processing in the retention of visually-presented sequential motoric stimuli. (Refs: 17) *Research quarterly for exercise & sport (Reston, Va.) 55(1), Mar 1984, 24-31.*
ABST: The purpose of the present investigation was to compare 28 subjects classified as 'high' and 29 subjects classified as 'low' in visual imagery ability on the short term retention of complex sequences of visually-presented movement sequences. After viewing a film of movement sequences done by a male dancer, subjects were asked to reproduce six such sequences after a rehearsal and also after a distraction condition. The data indicated that 'high' imagers exhibited significantly higher free recall scores than the 'low' imagers. The author concluded that visual imagery marginally facilitated the short term retention of visually presented sequences of movement. It is suggested that visual imagery may have a functional role in the free recall of movement information, but not in the rehearsal and recall of the temporal order of body positions within a sequence.
LEVEL: A LANG: Eng SIRC ARTICLE NO: 096071

Langley, D.J. Zelaznik, H.N. The acquisition of time properties associated with a sequential motor skill. (Refs: 39)*Journal of motor behavior (Washington, D.C.) 16(3), Sept 1984, 275-301.*
ABST: Three experiments are reported that examined the relative importance of phasing and duration training in the motor learning of a sequential task. The phasing task required the subject to contact each of the barriers in a particular goal time interval. The duration task required the subject to contact the final barrier in a total elapsed-time goal defined by the experimenter. Following training, half of the subjects in each training condition transferred to either a novel duration or a novel phasing task. Phasing-trained subjects, compared to duration-trained subjects, produced equivalent transfer performance on the duration transfer task but superior performance on the phasing transfer task.
LEVEL: A LANG: Eng SIRC ARTICLE NO: 104164

Lee, T.D. On the locus of contextual interference in motor skill acquisition. Eugene, Ore.: Microform Publications, University of Oregon, 1984. 1 microfiche : negative, ill. ; 11 x 15 cm.
NOTES: Thesis (Ph.D.) - Louisiana State University, 1982; (vii, 83 leaves); vita; includes bibliography.
LEVEL: A LANG: Eng UO84 252

Mertens, C. A program for training of perception through movement. (Refs: 29)*In, Simri, U. (ed.), et al., Preschool and elementary school children and physical activity. Proceedings of the 26th ICHPER World Congress 1983, Wingate Institute, Israel, vol. III, Jerusalem, Israel, 1984, p. 99-108.*
CONF: ICHPER World Congress (26th : 1983 : Wingate Institute, Israel).
LEVEL: A LANG: Eng GV443 20093

Motor development - sport psychology and motor learning/motor control. Scientific program abstracts: 1984 Olympic Scientific Congress, July 19-26, University of Oregon, Eugene, Oregon. Eugene, Or.: University of Oregon, Microform

Publications, 1984. 113 p.
CONF: Olympic Scientific Congress (1984 : Eugene, Or.).
NOTES: Cover title.
LEVEL: A LANG: Eng RC1201 17866

Murdoch, E.B. Motor learning - progression, differentiation and assessment in the teaching of young children. (Refs: 23) *Momentum (Edinburgh, Scotland) 9(3), Autumn 1984, 25-35.*
LEVEL: I LANG: Eng SIRC ARTICLE NO: 105362

Roswal, G. Frith, G. Dunleavy, A.O. The effect of a developmental play program on the concept, risk-taking behaviors, and motoric proficiency of mildly handicapped children. (Refs: 36)*Physical educator (Indianapolis, Ind.) 41(1), Mar 1984, 43-50.*
ABST: The purpose of this study was to evaluate the effect of the Children's Developmental Play Program (CDPP) in the behavioral and neuromotor functioning of developmentally disabled children. 32 children between the ages of 5 and 13 years enrolled in educable mentally retarted classed, served as subjects. Data was collected on self concept, risk taking behaviors and motor proficiency of the students. Half of the children were enrolled in the CDPP. Overall improvements were observed in the experimental group, and this especially in both self concept and motor proficiency.
LEVEL: A LANG: Eng SIRC ARTICLE NO: 095876

Shea, J.B. Hunt, J.P. Motor control. (Refs: 81)*Clinics in sports medicine (Philadelphia) 3(1), Jan 1984, 171-183.*
NOTES: Symposium on profiling.
ABST: Conditions of practice, knowledge of results and assessment are the important components of learning a skill. To determine the prerequisites necessary to obtain a high level of skill an assessment is used. The task is analysed and the abilities needed to perform the task are determined. A test battery is devised that will hopefully predict the success of the individual in the sport.
LEVEL: A LANG: Eng SIRC ARTICLE NO: 092970

Simonnet, P. Feed-back par video et apprentissage des habiletes motrices. (Refs: 20)*Dans, Culture technique no. 13, Neuilly-sur-Seine, France, Centre de Recherche sur la Culture Technique, c1984, p. 220-225.*
LEVEL: A LANG: Fr RC1235 20096

Singer, R.N. The learning of athletic skills and the use of strategies. (Refs: 33)*International journal of sport psychology (Rome, Italy) 15(4), 1984, 271-282.*
LEVEL: I LANG: Eng SIRC ARTICLE NO: 106612

Starkes, J.L. Deakin, J. Perception in sport: a cognitive approach to skilled performance. (Refs: 68)*In, Straub, W.F. and Williams, J.M. (eds.), Cognitive sport psychology, Lansing, N.Y., Sport Science Associates, c1984, p. 115-128.*
LEVEL: A LANG: Eng GV706.4 20099

Sugden, D.A. The learning of motor skills by children of different intellectual abilities. (Refs: 21)*In, Simri, U. (ed.), e al., Preschool and elementary school children and physical activity. Proceedings of the 26th ICHPER World Congress 1983, Wingate Institute, Israel, vol. III, Jerusalem, Israel, 1984, p. 149-153.*
CONF: ICHPER World Congress (26th : 1983 : Wingate Institute, Israel).
LEVEL: A LANG: Eng GV443 20093

Swinnen, S. Field dependence independence as a factor in learning complex motor skills and underlying sex differences. (Refs 40)*International journal of sport psychology (Rome, Italy) 15(4), 1984, 236-249.*
ABST: The purpose of this study was to determine the relationship between field dependence-independence as measured by paper-and-pencil tests and the acquisition of a gymnastic skill in an unstructured learning environment. Subjects (39 boys and 45 girls) were 15-years old senior high school students. The hypothesis that field dependent subjects would perform less well than field independent subjects in an unstructured learning situation was upheld for boys only. Significant positive correlations were found between visual perceptual test scores and improvement in the skill. For girls no significant relationships were found.
LEVEL: A LANG: Eng SIRC ARTICLE NO: 106613

Vigarello, G. Vives, J. Technique corporelle et discours technique. *Dans, Culture technique no. 13, Neuilly-sur-Seine, France, Centre de Recherche sur la Culture Technique, c1984, p. 264-273.*
LEVEL: A LANG: Fr RC1235 20096

Weeks, D.L. Shea, C.H. Assimilation effects in coincident timing responses. (Refs: 4)*Research quarterly for exercise & sports (Reston, Va.) 55(1), Mar 1984, 89-92.*
ABST: The purpose of the present investigation was to determine the influence of the preceding movement/stimulus velocity, of the hand and arm, on the response structure and accuracy of the slowest (67 cm/sec) and fastest (201cm/sec) components of a movement/stimulus velocity continuum. Six right handed subjects were told to make a continuous, horizontal, right to left arm movement in an attempt to displace a switch at the precise moment the last light, on a stimulus runway of lights, was illuminated. Analysis of the results indicated that the preceding stimulus velocity in this coincident timing task had little or no reliable effect on the constant error of response either to the 67 or to the 201 cm/sec stimulus velocity. It was suggested that coincident timing response in an open environment is controlled in a closed-loop manner and that movement initiation is biased by the preceding stimulus velocity.
LEVEL: A LANG: Eng SIRC ARTICLE NO: 096078

PROPRIOCEPTION

Montgomery, W.A. Jones, G.E. Hollandsworth, J.G. The effects of physical fitness and exercise on cardiac awareness. *Biological psychology (Amsterdam) 18(1), Feb 1984, 11-22.*
ABST: This experiment evaluated the role of individual difference factors in perception of heart beats (cardiac awareness). 24 male subjects who showed high and moderate levels of physical fitness were examined. Subjects differentiated between numerous trials of standing quietly on a treadmill, walking briskly on a motorized treadmill, and recovering from exercise. Results indicated that only the moderate fitness group showed heightened awareness during exercise, while both groups showed greater than chance awareness during recovery from exercise. These results fail to support notions that high fitness distance runners are highly aware of cardiac function during exercise.
LEVEL: A LANG: Eng

REACTION TIME

Carlton, L.G. Carlton, M.J. A note on constant error shifts in post-perturbation responses. (Refs: 20)*Journal of motor behavior (Washington, D.C.) 16(1), Mar 1984, 84-96.*
ABST: Response biasing was examined in the production of well-learned discrete timing responses. Interpolated movements consisted of trials which were briefly perturbed by an accelerating or decelerating force with subjects requested to amend the response in order to complete the trial successfully. Movement time analysis indicated that the response immediately following the perturbation trial demonstrated large biasing effects with the direction of the constant error shift a function of the direction of the perturbation. Responses following deceleration perturbations were produced too rapidly and those following acceleration pertubations were produced too slowly. Analysis of kinematic variables associated with these responses showed that post perturbation trials were characterized by systematic changes in peak acceleration and peak deceleration as well as the timing of these parameters. The biasing effects were temporary and showed other similarities to fingings from short-term motor memory investigations.
LEVEL: A LANG: Eng SIRC ARTICLE NO: 108340

Carlton, M.J. Newell, K.M. Carlton, L.G. Predicting individual discrete response outcomes from kinematic characteristics. (Refs: 24)*Journal of human movement studies (Edinburgh, Eng.) 10(2), 1984, 63-82.*
ABST: Three subjects were studied in detail during discrete motor tasks in order to determine the importance of variance parameters as determinants of movement outcome. The results indicate that there is no distinct relationship between response initiation and response outcome in movements as short as 100 msec. and as long as 600 msec. Multiple correlations using kinematic parameters to predict movement time were high, ranging between 0.871 and 0.997, with the highest correlations associated with the shortest movement times. These findings suggest that response tuning makes a significant contribution to the control of even short duration responses.
LEVEL: A LANG: Eng SIRC ARTICLE NO: 096067

Cauraugh, J.H. Toole, T. Lucariello, G. A test of the iris pigmentation - reactivity hypothesis during letter matching. (Refs: 17)*Journal of human movement studies (London) 10(4), 1984, 239-246.*
ABST: The iris pigmentation - reactive behavior hypothesis was further investigated in 2 experiments. Experiment 1 examined the hyothesis during extended simple reaction time practice (80 trials). The findings indicated that eye color effects were still evident even when reaction time stabilized. Light-eyed subjects were slower than dark-eyed subjects. Experiment 2 attempted to answer the question: Is there a relationship between eye color and reaction time during a cognitive task, such as letter matching? The results revealed significant iris pigmentation reaction time differences on the 'different' name responses. Dark-eyed subjects responded faster than light-eyed subjects.
LEVEL: A LANG: Eng SIRC ARTICLE NO: 104162

Fischman, M.G. Programming time as a function of number of connected movement parts and changes in movement direction. Eugene, Ore.: Microform

Publications, University of Oregon, 1984. 2 microfiches : negative, ill. ; 11 x 15 cm. NOTES: Thesis (Ph.D.) - Pennsylvania State University, 1983; (x, 133, (1) leaves); vita; includes bibliography.
LEVEL: A LANG: Eng UO84 389-390

Fischman, M.G. Programming time as a function of number of movement parts and changes in movement direction. (Refs: 30) *Journal of motor behavior (Washington) 16(4), Dec 1984, 405-423.*
ABST: The question of whether changes seen in simple reaction time (SRT) as a function of response complexity (i.e., number of movement parts) should be considered as differences in the time needed to centrally program a motor response was addressed. Using a large-scale tapping response, 14 subjects contacted from one to five targets positioned in a straight line, while a second group of 14 subjects executed 90o changes in direction in striking the targets. Results revealed that mean SRT and mean premotor time increased linearly as the number of movement parts increased, regardless of whether changes in movement direction had to be programmed, with the greatest increase occurring between one-, and two-part responses.
LEVEL: A LANG: Eng SIRC ARTICLE NO: 105358

Gielen, C.C.A.M. van den Heuvel, P.J.M. van der Gon, J.J.D. Modification of muscle activation patterns during fast goal-directed arm movements. (Refs: 29)*Journal of motor behaviour (Washington, D.C.) 16(1), Mar 1984, 2-19.*
ABST: The motor programming of fast goal-directed arm movements was studied in a tracking task. A target jumped once or twice randomly to the left or right direction with an interstimulus interval (ISI) in a range between 50 and 125 msec. Double step stimuli were either two steps in the same direction (C-trial) or in opposite direction (R-trial). Tracking results how that at the beginning average EMG-activity is the same for responses to single step trials, r-trials and C-trials. Differences set in after some time equal to or somewhat shorter than ISI. It was concluded that muscle activation patterns of fast goal-directed movements are not preprogrammed but they can be modified during the movement. The time interval between second target step and the moment when EMG activity of a single step (RT2) could be smaller than the time interval between first target displacement and EMG onset (RT1). If modification of the muscle ativation pattern require a longer or larger activation of the active muscle, RT2 tended to be smaller than RT1, whereas RT2 was about equal to RT1 if the new muscle activation required a termination of the ongoing muscle activation pattern and the activation of another muscle.
LEVEL: A LANG: Eng SIRC ARTICLE NO: 108335

Heurer, H. Binary choice reaction time as a function of the relationship between durations and forms of responses. (Refs: 17 *Journal of motor behavior (Washington) 16(4), Dec 1984, 392-404.*
ABST: In a choice between responding with the left or right hand, some kinds of differences between the movements increase RT (Reaction Time) while others do not. Since there is some indication that a difference in duration is sufficient to lengthen RT, both characteristics were varied separately. It turned out that a difference in form (duration being constant) has essentially the same effects as a difference in duration (form being constant): Mean RT is longer, variability of RT and MT (movement time) is larger, and frequency of choice errors is

smaller than in choice between identical movements. Additional results on the relationship between response duration and RT suggest that RT does not depend on duration (or velocity) per se, but on how much the duration deviates from quickest performance.
LEVEL: A LANG: Eng SIRC ARTICLE NO: 105360

Howard, R.M. The effects of stimulus velocity and stimulus duration on the spatial-temporal structure and response accuracy of coincident timing responses in closed and open environements. Eugene, Ore.: Microform Publications, University of Oregon, 1984. 2 microfiches : negative, ill. ; 11 x 15 cm.
NOTES: Thesis (Ph.D.) - Texas A & M University, 1981; (xii, 164 leaves); vita; includes bibliography.
LEVEL: A LANG: Eng UO84 20-21

Irvine, A.B. Results of studies to measure the potential effects of light spectra on human performance. Eugene, Ore.: Microform Publications, University of Oregon, 1984. 2 microfiches : negative ; 11 x 15 cm.
NOTES: Thesis (M.A.) - University of Florida, 1983; (vii, 42, (78) leaves); vita; includes bibliography.
LEVEL: A LANG: Eng UO84 337-338

Lee, C.L. A study on reaction time and movement time for university athletes. *Asian journal of physical education (Taiwan, China) 7(2), Jul 1984, 89-90.*
LEVEL: I LANG: Eng Chi SIRC ARTICLE NO: 099115

Muller, E. The backswing and pause as determinants of the timing of a rapid forward arm-swing response. Eugene, Ore.: Microform Publications, University of Oregon, 1984. 1 microfiche : negative, ill. ; 11 x 15 cm.
NOTES: Thesis (M.S.) - Pennsylvania State University, 1983; (viii, 74 leaves); includes bibliography.
LEVEL: A LANG: Eng UO84 347

Proteau, L. Girouard, Y. Motor programming: does the choice of the limb which is to carry out the response imply a delay? (Refs: 9)*Journal of motor behavior (Washington) 16(3), Sept 1984, 302-312.*
ABST: In many activities, the human being must quickly decide on the response to be produced. It seems that in these situations, the human being does not take the decrease in movement time into consideration and that the response is carried out with the dominant hand. Why is this so? It may be because the reaction is faster when there doesn't have to be a choice as to which limb will carry out the response. The goal of this study was to check this possibility. The subjects performed a two choice reaction-time task. For this task, some subjects knew beforehand which hand they had to use to carry out the response while other subjects were unaware of this fact. The results of two experiments indicate that the choice of the limb requires no particular delay when the movement to be produced is externally guided.
LEVEL: A LANG: Eng SIRC ARTICLE NO: 104166

Schellekens, J.M.H. Kalverboer, A.F. Scholten, C.A. The micro-structure of tapping movements in children. (Refs: 33)*Journal of motor behavior (Washington, D.C.) 16(1), Mar 1984, 20-39.*
ABST: In order to investigate the development of movement speed in relation to movement organization, children of 5, 6, 7, 8 and 9 years of age and adults carried out a reciprocal tapping task, in which time pressure and distance were manipulated. The duration, velocity, acceleration

and accuracy of the movements were compared between age groups. Age differences appeared mainly in the homing time, not in the duration of the distance covering movement phase. Accuracy and velocity of the distance covering movement phase differed with age. Time pressure affected the homing time, but not the duration of the distance covering phase. Distance manipulation affected mainly the velocity and duration of the distance covering movement phase and the homing time. In the discussion it is contended that age differences in homing time may be related to both the accuracy of the distance covering movement phase and the rate of information processing of the subject.
LEVEL: A LANG: Eng SIRC ARTICLE NO: 108336

Szmodis, I. Szabo, T. Rendi, M. Temesi, Z. Meszaros, J. Performance in plate-tapping and simple serial reaction time of children aged 5-14 years. (Refs: 2)
CONF: Symposium of Paediatric Work Physiology (10th : 1981 : Joutsa, Finland).
NOTES: In, Ilmarinen, J. and Vaelimaeki, I. (eds.), Children and sport: paediatric work physiology, Berlin, Springer-Verlag, 1984, p. 42-45.
ABST: Plate-tapping and response-time measurements are used by Hungarian coaches and trainers to estimate the speed characteristics of trainees. Evaluation is generally restricted to intragroup comparisons. Consequently, the authors developed some basis of reference by which performance observed in children of different ages can be compared.
LEVEL: A LANG: Eng SIRC ARTICLE NO: 102343

REFLEX

Zemke, R. Draper, D.C. Notes on measurement of the magnitude of the asymmetrical tonic neck reflex response in normal preschool children. (Refs: 16)*Journal of motor behavior (Washington) 16(3), Sept 1984, 336-343.*
ABST: This study investigated the magnitude of the asymmetrical tonic neck reflex (ATNR) response in forty preschool children, grouped by age (3 years and 5 years) and sex. Change scores indicating the difference in degrees of elbow flexion before and after head rotation were analyzed. Repetition of the stimulus (head turning) to the left and to the right occurred under two test postures (supine, quadrupedal) with the effect of a lindolf nested within quadruped trials and the effect of added tension nested within supine, totaling 16 trials per child. The magnitude of the ATNR decreased significantly with age, but sex differences were not significant. The quadrupedal test posture produced significantly larger than did the supine test posture.
LEVEL: A LANG: Eng SIRC ARTICLE NO: 104167

REINFORCEMENT

Krampitz, J.B. Knowledge of results in the acquisition of a coincident-timing skill. Eugene, Ore.: Microform Publications, University of Oregon, 1984. 2 microfiches : negative, ill. ; 11 x 15 cm.
NOTES: Thesis (Ph.D.) - Texas A & M University, 1980; (xi, 125 leaves); vita; includes bibliography.
LEVEL: A LANG: Eng UO84 22-23

Krampitz, J.B. Shea, C.H. Post response knowledge of results in anticipation tasks. (Refs: 13)*Journal of human movement studies (Edinburgh, Eng.) 10(3), 1984, 157-164.*
ABST: The present study investigated the effects of post response knowledge of results (KR) and

PERCEPTUAL MOTOR PROCESSES (continued)

inherent task feedback in a complex timing task. Subjects (n,60) were randomly assigned to 1 of 6 groups in a 2 (KR) by 3 (stimulus preview) arrangement. The subjects attempted to terminate a right-to-left 'zig-zag' movement in a criterion time of 1250 msec. The visual stimulus consisted of a Bassin stimulus runway positioned parallel to the movement sequence. The 3 stimulus conditions consisted of presentation of the visual stimulus (coincident with movement initiation) along the entire runway, the first half of the runway or not at all. The KR conditions consisted of providing subjects with no KR or directional msec KR (i.e., early or late'n' msec) following each trial. All subjects received 125 trials with a 2 min rest period following the 75th trial. The analysis indicated comparable response accuracy for the 3 stimulus groups when msec KR was provided but response accuracy increased as the preview of stimulus was increased when no KR was provided.
LEVEL: A LANG: Eng SIRC ARTICLE NO: 108760

SENSORY PERCEPTION

Craske, B. Kenny, F.T. Keith, D. Modifying an underlying component of perceived arm length: adaptation of tactile location induced by spatial discordance. *Journal of experimental psychology: human perception and performance (Washington) 10(2), Apr 1984, 307-317.*
LEVEL: A LANG: Eng SIRC ARTICLE NO: 101007

SPACIAL PERCEPTION

Azemar, G. Vision de l'espace et anticipation. Les conditions visuo-spatiales de l'anticipation du sportif. (Refs: 31)*Dans, Culture technique no. 13, Neuilly-sur-Seine, France, Centre de Recherche sur la Culture Technique, c1984, p. 100-117.*
LEVEL: A LANG: Fr RC1235 20096

Johnson, R.D. Analysis of selected factors related to the element of space in movement creativity. Eugene, Ore.: Microform Publications, University of Oregon, 1984. 2 microfiches : negative, ill. ; 11 x 15 cm.
NOTES: Thesis (Ph.D.) - University of Oregon, 1980; (xiii, 102 leaves); vita; includes bibliography.
LEVEL: A LANG: Eng UO84 134-135

Larish, D.D. Volp, C.M. Wallace, S.A. An empirical note on attaining a spatial target after distorting the initial condition of movement via muscle vibration. (Refs: 23)*Journal of motor behavior (Washington, D.C.) 16(1), Mar 1984, 76-83.*
ABST: Can one's limb be accurately positioned to a spatial location without a veridical estimate of the initial conditions of movement? The experiment reported here examined this question by distorting perception of a limb's starting position via muscle vibration. Subjects executed rapid flexion movements under no-vibration, contralateral arm vibration, and ipsilateral arm vibration conditions. Vibration was applied to the biceps for 10 sec prior to the start of a reproduction movement. The results showed that vibration on the ipsilateral arm caused a significant increase in reproduction error, relative to the no-vibration and contralateral-vibration conditions. This findings provides additional evidence that accurate knowledge about the initial conditions of movement is a necessary component in positioning a limb.
LEVEL: A LANG: Eng SIRC ARTICLE NO: 108339

TEACHING

Daines, D. Mastery learning of motor skills. (Refs: 19)*CAHPERD journal times (Danville, Calif.) 46(4), Jan 1984, 8-9;12.*
LEVEL: B LANG: Eng SIRC ARTICLE NO: 097616

Gallagher, J.D. Making sense of motor development: interfacing research with lesson planning. (Refs: 43)*In, Thomas, J.R. (ed.), Motor development during childhood and adolescence, Minneapolis, Minn., Burgess Publishing Co., 1984, p. 123-138.*
LEVEL: A LANG: Eng BF1 20187

TESTING

Austrew, T. Physical capacities evaluation: the application of corrective therapy evaluation techniques to assist in determining physical abilities after disability. *American corrective therapy journal (San Diego, Calif.) 38(3), May/Jun 1984, 67-68.*
LEVEL: B LANG: Eng SIRC ARTICLE NO: 108152

Liemohn, W. Knapczyk, D.R. An analysis of the Southern California Perceptual Motor Tests. (Refs: 31)*Research quarterly for exercise & sport (Reston, Va.) 55(3), Sept 1984, 248-253.*
ABST: The purpose of this study was to examine the Southern California Perceptual Motor Tests (SCPMT). The subjects were 386 children characterized as having learning and/or perceptual problems. A factor analysis was made based on the subjects' performances on the 42 individual items. The results indicated that the test items generally have good discriminative ability. However, the distribution of items of some of the individual tests across more than one factor suggests that, at least in children with learning disorders, the tests are sampling a wider number of constructs than was intended in their design.
LEVEL: A LANG: Eng SIRC ARTICLE NO: 102620

Petrofsky, J.S. Isaacs, L.D. Construction of an inexpensive response timer. *Research quarterly for exercise & sport (Reston Va.) 55(2), Jun 1984, 195-196.*
ABST: This paper describes how persons with very little knowledge of electronics can construct a response timer for around $85.00. The necessary parts are listed and the associated circuitry is diagrammed.
LEVEL: A LANG: Eng SIRC ARTICLE NO: 096074

VISION

Bailey, J.E. Palmer, J.D. Eland, W.R. Dark adaptation in long-distance runners. (Refs: 3)*Journal of sports medicine and physical fitness (Torino, Italy) 24(2), Jun 1984, 135-138.*
ABST: Transient, abnormal visual dark adaptation has been reported to occur during periods of vigorous exercise. To assess possible chronic impairment in night vision function in a group of long-distance runners, light intensity thresholds were measured at rest during a 35 minute period of darkness following exposure to intense daylight stimulation. The average threshold intensity was consistently 0.1 log unit less than we obtained for an age-matched control group of non-exercising individuals. However, a casual positive relationship between distance run per week and duration of the exercise program and threshold level during the rod receptor phase of dark adaptation was demonstrated.
LEVEL: A LANG: Eng SIRC ARTICLE NO: 102563

Davids, K. The role of peripheral vision in ball games: some theoretical and practical notions. (Refs: 83)*Physical educatio review (Manchester) 7(1), Spring 1984, 26-40.*
ABST: This article reviews the literature on peripheral vision research.
LEVEL: A LANG: Eng SIRC ARTICLE NO: 099337

Davis, W.E. Precise visual target information and throwing accuracy in adults. (Refs: 34)*Perceptual and motor skills (Missoula, Mont.) 59(3), Dec 1984, 759-768.*
ABST: Equal numbers of men and women threw a tennis ball at a target with and without a marking in the centre of a large white target. Women are signicantly more accurate when a dot was visible at the centre of the target.
LEVEL: A LANG: Eng SIRC ARTICLE NO: 102615

Moore, S.P. Systematic removal of visual feedback. (Refs: 11)*Journal of human movement studies (Edinburgh, Eng.) 10(3), 198 165-173.*
ABST: The effects of the systematic removal of visual feedback while performing a time-constrained single-aiming movement were examined. Subjects (n,6). using a joystick, maneuvered a cursor, displayed on an oscilloscope screen, from a starting box to a target positioned at four amplitudes in a movement time of 400 plus or minus 40 msec. Each subject participated in seven blanking conditions during which the time of the initial visible segment was manipulated. Analysis of variance revealed a significant main effect on the two factors manipulated: movement amplitude and blanking or the amount of initial visual feedback available. Trend analysis indicated a significant linear amplitude component which supports previous findings of a positive relationship between amplitude and We. Post hoc analysis investigating the percentage of blanking effect suggested that visual information provided in the first 180 msec of a 400 msec movement is not used.
LEVEL: A LANG: Eng SIRC ARTICLE NO: 108761

Ripoll, H. L'exploration visuelle du sportif en action. (Refs: 7)*Dans, Culture technique no. 13, Neuilly-sur-Seine, France, Centre de Recherche sur la Culture Technique, c1984, p. 94-99.*
LEVEL: A LANG: Fr RC1235 20096

The athletic eye: how to improve your most precious skill. *Executive fitness newsletter (Emmaus, Pa.) 15(6), 17 Mar 1984, 3.*
LEVEL: B LANG: Eng SIRC ARTICLE NO: 094746

VISUAL PERCEPTION

Craske, B. Kenny, F.T. Keith, D. Modifying an underlying component of perceived arm length: adaptation of tactile location induced by spatial discordance. *Journal of experimental psychology: human perception and performance (Washington) 10(2), Apr 1984, 307-317.*
LEVEL: A LANG: Eng SIRC ARTICLE NO: 101007

Honda, H. Eye-position signals in successive saccades. *Perception and psychophysics (Austin, Tex.) 36(1), Jul 1984, 15-20.*
LEVEL: A LANG: Eng

Lyle, J. Cook, M. Non-verbal cues and decision making in games. (Refs: 9)*Momentum: a journal of human movement studies (Edinburgh) 9(1), Spring 1984, 20-25.*
ABST: This paper examines specific sport cues and

the decision making they produce in the behaviour of the opponent. A video taped recording was made from a field hockey goaltender's view of penalty flicks taken by a number of hockey players. 40 flicks in all were evaluated by goaltenders, players, physical education students and non-participants. Subjects were asked to anticipate the eventual direction of the ball. The differences between the four groups were found to be inconclusive in this exploratory investigation.
LEVEL: A LANG: Eng SIRC ARTICLE NO: 099539

Solomon, J. Carello, C. Turvey, M.T. Flow fields: the optical support for skilled activities. (Refs: 17)*In, Straub, W.F. an Williams, J.M. (eds.), Cognitive sport psychology, Lansing, N.Y., Sport Science Associates, c1984, p. 129-139.*
LEVEL: A LANG: Eng GV706.4 20099

PETANQUE

Foyot, M. Dupuy, A. Dalmas, L. La petanque. Paris: Robert Laffont, c1984. 215 p. : ill. (Sports pour tous.)
LEVEL: B LANG: ISBN: 2-221-04434-7 GV910.5.P4 18693

PHILATELY

Loevy, H.T. Kowitz, A. Dentistry on stamps (Dr. Kerstin Palm). *Journal of the American Dental Association (Chicago) 109(5), Nov 1984, 755.*
LEVEL: B LANG: Eng

PHILOSOPHY

Bernard, M.P. Le sport: hedonisme de masse ou priere Paienne? *Loisirs sante (Paris) 10, juin/juil/aout 1984, 31-34.*
LEVEL B LANG: Fr SIRC ARTICLE NO: 104213

Case, B. Eastern thought and movement forms: possible implications for western sport. (Refs: 22)*Physical educator (Indianapolis) 41(4), Dec 1984, 170-175.*
LEVEL: B LANG: Eng SIRC ARTICLE NO: 104215

Geiringer, E. Farewell to arms - and legs. (Refs: 6)*New Zealand journal of health, physical education & recreation (Dunedin New Zealand) 17(2), Aug 1984, 3-6.*
CONF: New Zealand AHPER. Conference (1984).
LEVEL: B LANG: Eng SIRC ARTICLE NO: 099146

Kirsch, K. Schuessler, I. Possibilities of understanding modern sport on the basis of Aristotelian theory. (Refs: 5)*In, Ilmarinen, M. (ed.) et al., Sport and International Understanding: proceedings of the congress held in Helsinki, Finland, July 7-10, 1982, Berlin, Springer-Verlag, 1984, p. 72-77.*
CONF: Congress on Sport and International Understanding (1982 : Helsinki).
LEVEL: A LANG: Eng GV706.8 18979

Lenk, H. Status and development as well as research tendencies and central aspects of sport philosophy. *International journal of physical education (Schorndorf, W. Germany) 21(2), 19-26 Jul 1984, 33-34;36.*
LEVEL: I LANG: Eng SIRC ARTICLE NO: 097645

Nunes, E.L. The gap between the 'intentions' and the 'realities' in sport: a question of education and culture? (Refs: 7) *Bulletin of the Federation internationale d'education physique (Cheltenham, Eng.) 54(1), Jan/Mar 1984, 42-44.*
LEVEL: I LANG: Eng SIRC ARTICLE NO: 094500

Parlebas, P. La dissipation sportive. (Refs: 32)*Dans, Culture technique no. 13, Neuilly-sur-Seine, France, Centre de Recherche sur la Culture Technique, c1984, p. 18-37.*
LEVEL: A LANG: Fr RC1235 20096

Rioux, G. Sport et emotivite. *Cinesiologie (Paris) 95, mai/juin 1984, 219-224.*
LEVEL: I LANG: Fr SIRC ARTICLE NO: 097790

AESTHETICS

Bolwell, J. The aesthetic dimension - it's significance in human movement. (Refs: 4)*New Zealand journal of health, physical education & recreation (Dunedin, New Zealand) 17(2), Aug 1984, 6-8.*
CONF: New Zealand AHPER. Conference (1984).
LEVEL: B LANG: Eng SIRC ARTICLE NO: 099145

Meredith, L. Aesthesis and kinesthesis: meditations on metaphysical education, or, Graffiti in the gameroom. (Refs: 10) *Arete: the journal of sport literature (San Diego, Calif.) 2(1), Fall 1984, 11-24.*
LEVEL: A LANG: Eng SIRC ARTICLE NO: 108404

Pool, J. Aesthetic physical education for elementary schools. *In, Simri, U. (ed.), et al., Preschool and elementary school children and physical activity. Proceedings of the 26th ICHPER World Congress 1983, Wingate Institute, Israel, vol. III, Jerusalem, Israel, 1984, p. 109-121.*
CONF: ICHPER World Congress (26th : 1983 : Wingate Institute, Israel).
LEVEL: I LANG: Eng GV443 20093

COMPETITION

Quilici, J.F. Haute competition: science, technique, societe. *Dans, Culture technique no. 13, Neuilly-sur-Seine, France, Centre de Recherche sur la Culture Technique, c1984, p. 194-199.*
LEVEL: I LANG: Fr RC1235 20096

ETHICS

Arnold, P.J. Sport as fairness. (Refs: 17)*CAHPER journal (Ottawa) 51(1), Sept/Oct 1984, 10-12.*
LEVEL: B LANG: Eng SIRC ARTICLE NO: 100817

Bredemeier, B.J. Sport, gender, and moral growth. NOTES: In, Silva, J.M. and Weinberg, R.S. (eds.), Psychological foundations of sport, Champaign, Ill., Human Kinetics Publishers, c1984, p. 400-413.
LEVEL: A LANG: Eng GV706.4 17779

Bredemeier, B.J. Shields, D.L. Divergence in moral reasoning about sport and everyday life. (Refs: 23)*Sociology of sport journal (Champaign, Ill.) 1(4), Dec 1984, 348-357.*
ABST: The observation that sport represents a unique context has been widely discussed, but social scientists have done little to empirically examine the moral adaptations of sport participants. In the present study, the divergence between levels of moral reasoning used to discuss hypothetical dilemmas set in sport and in everyday life contexts was investigated among 120 high school and collegiate basketball players, swimmers, and nonathletes. Protocols were scored according to

Haan's interactional model of moral development. It was found that levels of moral reasoning used to discuss sport dilemmas were lower than levels characterizing reasoning about issues within an everyday life context. Findings were discussed in terms of the specific social and moral context of sport experience.
LEVEL: A LANG: Eng SIRC ARTICLE NO: 104214

Duquin, M.E. Power and authority: moral consensus and conformity in sport. (Refs: 11)*International review for the sociology of sport (Warszawa, Poland) 19(3/4), 1984, 295-304.*
ABST: This study examined the moral rationales of 109 male and female coaches, athletes and non-athletes. Subjects read a series of sport scenarios in which a conflict arose between an athlete and a member of the athletic establishment. Five categories of moral rationales emerged from the data, two of which, the ethic of care and self-interest, predominated. Females employed the ethic of care significantly more often than males, while males used the self-interest rationale significantly more often than females.
LEVEL: A LANG: Eng SIRC ARTICLE NO: 105391

Fraleigh, W.P. Right actions in sport, ethics for contestants. Champaign, Ill.: Human Kinetics Publishers, c1984. xii, 195 p
NOTES: Includes bibliographical references.
LEVEL: I LANG: Eng ISBN: 0-931250-55-2 LC CARD: 83-083165 GV706.3 18012

Rotella, R.J. Connelly, D. Individual ethics in the application of cognitive sport psychology. (Refs: 11)*In, Straub, W.F. and Williams, J.M. (eds.), Cognitive sport psychology, Lansing, N.Y., Sport Science Associates, c1984, p. 102-112.*
LEVEL: A LANG: Eng GV706.4 20099

Shields, D.L. Bredemeier, B.J. Sport and moral growth: a structural developmental perspective. (Refs: 39)*In, Straub, W.F. and Williams, J.M. (eds.), Cognitive sport psychology, Lansing, N.Y., Sport Science Associates, c1984, p. 89-101.*
LEVEL: A LANG: Eng GV706.4 20099

Underwood, J. Spoiled sport: a fan's notes on the troubles of spectator sports. 1st ed. Boston ; Toronto: Little, Brown, c1984. viii, 287 p.
LEVEL: B LANG: Eng ISBN: 0-316-887331 LC CARD: 84-17182 GV706.3 18195

HUMANISM

Nugent, J.E. The human condition of the game. Eugene, Ore.: Microform Publications, University of Oregon, 1984. 3 microfiche : negative ; 11 x 15 cm.
NOTES: Thesis (Ed.D.) - University of North Carolina at Greensboro, 1982; (iv, 244 leaves); includes bibliography.
LEVEL: A LANG: Eng UO84 136-138

RESEARCH METHODS

Progen, J.L. DeSensi, J.T. The value of theoretical frameworks for exploring the subjective dimension of sport. (Refs: 23) *Quest (Champaign, Ill.) 36(1), 1984, 80-88.*
ABST: This study focuses on the similarities and differences between Martin Buber's I-Thou philosophy and Mihaly Csikszentmihalyi's flow theory.
LEVEL: A LANG: Eng SIRC ARTICLE NO: 099147

PHILOSOPHY (continued)

SPORTSMANSHIP

Camp, W. Walter Camp on sportsmanship.
NOTES: In, Riess, S.A. (ed.), The American sporting experience: a historical anthology of sport in America, New York, Leisure Press, c1984, p. 164-167. Excerpt from: Book of college sports, New York, Century, 1893, p. 1-9.
LEVEL: B LANG: Eng GV583 17631

de Wachter, F. Fairness, democracy and justice. (Refs: 11)*In, Ilmarinen, M. (ed.) et al., Sport and International Understanding: proceedings of the congress held in Helsinki, Finland, July 7-10, 1982, Berlin, Springer-Verlag, 1984, p. 111-114.*
CONF: Congress on Sport and International Understanding (1982 : Helsinki).
LEVEL: I LANG: Eng GV706.8 18979

Guay, D. Sport... and sportsmanship... Le sport... et son esprit. s.l.: s.n., 1984. 24, (24) p.
CONF: Symposium on Research Applied to Hockey (8th : 1984 : Quebec).
NOTES: Photocopie. Photocopy. Resume of a presentation given at the 8th Symposium on Research Applied to Hockey, the 4, 5, 6th of May 1984, at Laval University, Quebec. Texte resume de l'expose presente lors...
LEVEL: A LANG: Eng Fr GV706.3 18577

von Bose, R.C.W. Attention for 'fair play'. *Olympic review (Lausanne, Switzerland) 197, Mar 1984, 173-174.*
LEVEL: B LANG: Eng SIRC ARTICLE NO: 094501

von Bose, R.C.W. Attirer l'attention sur le 'fair play'. *Revue olympique (Lausanne) 197, mars 1984, 173-174.*
LEVEL: B LANG: Fr SIRC ARTICLE NO: 096124

PHOTOGRAPHY

Powell, S. Duffy, T. Nelson, K. Thompson, D. Sports photography. London: Batsford, c1984. 167 p. : ill.
LEVEL: B LANG: Eng ISBN: 0-7134-3740-5 TR821 20401

Scheuer, H.J. Art and sport: sport and photography: movement immobilized. *Olympic review (Lausanne) 200, Jun 1984, 452-457.*
LEVEL: B LANG: Eng SIRC ARTICLE NO: 096432

Stevenson, J.M. New products information: developments in 35mm photography. *CAHPER journal/Revue de l'ACSEPR (Ottawa) 50(6) Jul/Aug 1984, 19-20.*
LEVEL: B LANG: Eng SIRC ARTICLE NO: 099347

Zwingle, E. Motion pictures: three professional strategies for action. *Outside (Chicago) 9(6), Jul 1984, 63-69.*
LEVEL: B LANG: Eng SIRC ARTICLE NO: 104499

PHYSICAL EDUCATION

Andrews, J.C. The future of FIEP and its mission in developing countries. (Refs: 18)*Bulletin of the Federation internationale d'education physique (Cheltenham, Eng.) 54(2), Apr/Jun 1984, 9-18.*
CONF: FIEP International Course-Congress (1984 : Rabat, Morocco).
LEVEL: B LANG: Eng SIRC ARTICLE NO: 102913

Bobson, A. English physical education: not my cup of tea. (England) *Washington journal of health, physical education, recreation and dance (Bellingham, Wash.) 39(1), Winter/Spring 1984, 3-4;9.*
LEVEL: B LANG: Eng SIRC ARTICLE NO: 108731

Buckellew, W. The role of colleges and universities in providing educational programs in health, physical education, and recreation. *Asian journal of physical education (Taipei, Taiwan) 7(3), Oct 1984, 41-42.*
LEVEL: B LANG: Eng Chi SIRC ARTICLE NO: 102654

Cambell, S. The Sports Council and physical education: partners in development. *British journal of physical education (London) 15(1), Mar/Apr 1984, 36-37;45.*
LEVEL: B LANG: Eng SIRC ARTICLE NO: 099150

Church, M.E. Perspectives on the mission of higher education. *NAPEHE proceedings (Champaign, Ill.) 5, 1984, 3-5.*
CONF: National Association for Physical Education in Higher Education. Annual Conference (1984 : College Park, Md.).
NOTES: Conference theme: Current challenge: revitalization or obsolescence?
LEVEL: B LANG: Eng SIRC ARTICLE NO: 102659

Corbin, C.B. The importance of physical education. *Physical educator (Bloomington, Ind.) 41(2), May 1984, 58-59.*
LEVEL: B LANG: Eng SIRC ARTICLE NO: 099152

DePauw, K.P. In pursuit of excellence: health and human movement as a part of basic education. *Washington journal of health physical education, recreation and dance (Bellingham, Wash.) 39(1), Winter/Spring 1984, 2;9.*
LEVEL: B LANG: Eng SIRC ARTICLE NO: 108728

Gagnon Bouchard, I. Guay Boisvert, A. Harvey, G. Activites sensorielles et motrices: education, reeducation. Sillery, Que.: Presses de l'Universite du Quebec, 1984. xiii, 255 p. : ill.
NOTES: Includes indexes. Bibliography: p. (239)-243.
LEVEL: I LANG: Fr ISBN: 2-7605-0356-9 LC CARD: 85-131812 GV443 20836

Gondowidjojo, M. The development of sport and physical education in Indonesia. *Asian journal of physical education (Taiwan, China) 7(1), Apr 1984, 46-54.*
NOTES: Abstract in Chinese.
LEVEL: B LANG: Eng Chi SIRC ARTICLE NO: 096244

Harrington, W.M. Making it happen: connecting theory and practice. (Refs: 2)*Journal of physical education, recreation & dance (Reston, Va.) 55(6), Aug 1984, 32-33.*
LEVEL: B LANG: Eng SIRC ARTICLE NO: 097655

Kemper, H.C.G. Farrally, M.R. Equality for all - assessing the physiological load of physical education lessons. Part I. (Refs: 13)*Scottish journal of physical education (Glasgow, Scotland) 12(4), Nov 1984, 37-40.*
LEVEL: I LANG: Eng SIRC ARTICLE NO: 102671

Lamour, H. Les quatre theorisations de l'education physique. (Refs: 25)*EPS: Education physique et sport (Paris) 187, mai/juin 1984, 10-13.*
LEVEL: B LANG: Fr SIRC ARTICLE NO: 096145

Lawson, H.A. Invitation to physical education. Champaign, Ill.: Human Kinetics, c1984. xxi, 231 p.

: ill.
NOTES: Includes bibliographies.
LEVEL: I LANG: Eng ISBN: 0-931250-47-1 LC CARD: 83-81454 GV341 17778

Mennie, C. Commitment to change. (Refs: 16)
CONF: Physical Education Graduating Seminar Conference (1984 : Footscray Institute of Technology).
NOTES: In, Physical education in Australia: past, present and future directions, s.l., Footscray Institute of Technology, 1984, p. 154-157.
LEVEL: I LANG: Eng SIRC ARTICLE NO: 096156

Moody, P. School physical education is under attack. *ACHPER national journal 103, Mar 1984, 2-3.*
LEVEL: B LANG: Eng SIRC ARTICLE NO: 097664

Musikawan, S. The state of physical education in Thailand. (Refs: 1)*Asian journal of physical education (Taiwan, China) 7(2), Jul 1984, 12-15.*
NOTES: Abstract in Chinese.
LEVEL: B LANG: Eng SIRC ARTICLE NO: 099170

Physical education in Australia: past, present and future directions. s.l.: Footscray Institute of Technology, 1984. 162, 31 p
CONF: Physical Education Graduating Seminar Conference (1984 : Footscray Institute of Technology).
CORP: Footscray Institute of Technology.
NOTES: Cover title. Includes bibliographies.
ABST: A collection of 29 papers on aspects of physical education in Australia, prepared by the June 1984 graduating class of the Dept. of Physical Education and Recreation of the Footscray Institute of Technology. Major themes of the papers include: history, children, special populations, legal liability, employment opportunities and future directions of physical education within the Australian context.
LEVEL: A LANG: Eng GV315 17673

Powell, K.E. Christenson, G.M. Kreuter, M.W. Objectives for the nation: assessing the role physical education must play. (Refs: 9)*Journal of physical education, recreation & dance (Reston, Va.) 55(6), Aug 1984, 18-20.*
LEVEL: B LANG: Eng SIRC ARTICLE NO: 097668

Priest, L. The case for physical education. (Refs: 18)*WAHPERD journal (Milwaukee, Wis.) 13(1), May 1984, 24-25.*
NOTES: Reprinted with permission from ERIC FACT SHEET.
LEVEL: B LANG: Eng SIRC ARTICLE NO: 100843

Rijsdorp, K. Bonnier, B.R.T. Binkhorst, R.A. Bollaert, L. van den Broek, J.A. van Coppenolle, H. Crum, B.J. Laporte, W. van Loon, C. Renson, R. Vermeer, A. Zebregs, A.A.F. Handboek lichamelijke opvoeding en sportbegeleiding. Deventer: Van Loghum Slaterus, 1984. ca. 1200 p.
LEVEL: I

Staffo, D.F. In what direction is physical education really going? *Foil (Indianapolis) Fall 1984, 7-8.*
LEVEL: B LANG: Eng SIRC ARTICLE NO: 173560

Targa, J.F. Physical education in schools in developing countries: the case for a minimum of three weekly classes of physica education in primary and secondary schools. *Bulletin of the Federation internationale d'education physique (Cheltenham, Eng.) 54(2), Apr/Jun 1984, 28-38.*
CONF: FIEP International Course-Congress (1984 : Rabat, Morocco).
LEVEL: B LANG: Eng SIRC ARTICLE NO: 102700

Taylor, M.J. The plight of physically awkward children in our schools or 'why they hate physical education'. Le malaise des etudiants physiquement maladrois ou 'pourquoi ils detestent l'education physique'. (Refs: 15)*CAHPER journal/Revue de l'ACSEPR (Ottawa) 50(5), May/Jun 1984, 26-27;36.*
LEVEL: B LANG: Eng Fr SIRC ARTICLE NO: 096171

ACADEMIC ACHIEVEMENT

Kohen-Raz, R. Hecht, O. Ayalon, T. Possible effects of structured physical education on scholastic progress of culturally disadvantaged first graders. (Refs: 4)*In, Simri, U. (ed.), et al., Preschool and elementary school children and physical activity. Proceedings of the 26th ICHPER World Congress 1983, Wingate Institute, Israel, vol. III, Jerusalem, Israel, 1984, p. 64-68.*
CONF: ICHPER World Congress (26th : 1983 : Wingate Institute, Israel).
LEVEL: A LANG: Eng GV443 20093

Shephard, R.J. Volle, M. Lavallee, H. LaBarre, R. Jequier, J.C. Rajic, M. Required physical activity and academic grades: a controlled study. (Refs: 6)
CONF: Symposium of Paediatric Work Physiology (10th : 1981 : Joutsa, Finland).
NOTES: In, Ilmarinen, J. and Vaelimaeki, I. (eds.), Children and sport: paediatric work physiology, Berlin, Springer-Verlag, 1984, p. 58-63
LEVEL: A LANG: Eng SIRC ARTICLE NO: 102340

ADMINISTRATION

Buturusis, D. Gaining and keeping support for physical education. *Journal of physical education, recreation & dance (Reston Va.) 55(6), Aug 1984, 44-45.*
LEVEL: B LANG: Eng SIRC ARTICLE NO: 097649

Case, B. Program and curriculum trends in sport management. Alexandria, Va.: Computer Microfilm International, 1984. 1 microfiche (18 fr.)
CONF: American Alliance for Health, Physical Education, Recreation and Dance. Convention (1984 : Anaheim, Calif.).
LEVEL: A LANG: Eng EDRS: ED244946

Everett, P.W. Early retirement programs. (Refs: 9)*Journal of physical education, recreation & dance (Reston, Va.) 55(5), May/Jun 1984, 54-58.*
LEVEL: B LANG: Eng SIRC ARTICLE NO: 094514

Glaser, P.A. A rewarding early retirement. *Journal of physical education, recreation & dance (Reston, Va.) 55(5), May/Jun 1984, 58.*
LEVEL: B LANG: Eng SIRC ARTICLE NO: 094516

Griffin, L.E. Resolving conflict. (Refs: 6)*Journal of physical education, recreation & dance 55(1), Jan 1984, 33-34;40.*
LEVEL: B LANG: Eng SIRC ARTICLE NO: 091603

Jones, L. The role of the advisory teacher in physical education *Bulletin of physical education (London) 20(2), Summer 1984 68-74.*
CONF: British Association of Advisers and Lecturers in Physical Education. Congress (64th : 1984 : Cardiff).
LEVEL: I LANG: Eng SIRC ARTICLE NO: 104220

Klappholz, L.A. Securing public support for physical education. *Physical education newsletter (Old Saybrook, Conn.) 165, De 1984, 2-5.*
LEVEL: B LANG: Eng SIRC ARTICLE NO: 173337

Koehler, R.W. Marketing education. Some good ideas. (Refs: 5)*Bulletin of the Federation internationale d'education physique (Toulouse, France)54(3/4), Jul/Dec 1984, 33-35.*
LEVEL: B LANG: Eng SIRC ARTICLE NO: 105409

Lundegren, H.M. Decision making in physical education in higher education: theory and application. (Refs: 10)*NAPEHE proceedings (Champaign, Ill.) 5, 1984, 114-121.*
CONF: National Association for Physical Education in Higher Education. Annual Conference (1984 : College Park, Md.).
NOTES: Conference theme: Current challenge: revitalization or obsolescence?
LEVEL: I LANG: Eng SIRC ARTICLE NO: 102304

Ostro, H. Try the army: a field training exercise. *Scholastic coach (New York) 54(4), Nov 1984, 4;6;8;10.*
LEVEL: B LANG: Eng SIRC ARTICLE NO: 102307

Schraer, R. Higher education and physical education: the perspective of central administration. *NAPEHE proceedings (Champaign, Ill.) 5, 1984, 6-10.*
CONF: National Association for Physical Education in Higher Education. Annual Conference (1984 : College Park, Md.).
NOTES: Conference theme: Current challenge: revitalization or obsolescence?
LEVEL: B LANG: Eng SIRC ARTICLE NO: 102310

Tenoschok, M. Sanders, S. Planning an effective public relations program. *Journal of physical education, recreation & dance 55(1), Jan 1984, 48-49.*
LEVEL: B LANG: Eng SIRC ARTICLE NO: 091641

Tips on conducting a physical education demonstration. *Physical education newsletter (Old Saybrook, Conn.) 158, Apr 1984, 4-6.*
LEVEL: B LANG: Eng SIRC ARTICLE NO: 096172

Training volunteers to help in a perceptual-motor training program. *Physical education newsletter (Old Saybrook, Conn.) 158, Apr 1984, 2-3.*
LEVEL: B LANG: Eng SIRC ARTICLE NO: 096174

ASSOCIATIONS

Dechavanne, N. La Federation francaise d'education physique et de gymnastique volontaire. *Revue de l'education physique (Liege, Belgique) 24(4), 1984, 3-6.*
LEVEL: B LANG: Fr SIRC ARTICLE NO: 104218

Dougherty, N.J. The future of NAPEHE. *NAPEHE proceedings (Champaign, Ill.) 5, 1984, 164-165.*
CONF: National Association for Physical Education in Higher Education. Annual Conference (1984 : College Park, Md.).
NOTES: Conference theme: Current challenge: revitalization or obsolescence?
LEVEL: B LANG: Eng SIRC ARTICLE NO: 102665

Hebbelinck, M. Borms, J. Sport international. *International journal of physical education (Schorndorf, W. Germany) 21(1), 1984, 38.*
LEVEL: B LANG: Eng SIRC ARTICLE NO: 093004

Johnstone, J. The history of the Physical Education Association: 11 a widening influence. (Refs: 8)*British journal of physical education (London) 15(1), Mar/Apr 1984, 50-51.*
LEVEL: B LANG: Eng SIRC ARTICLE NO: 099160

Johnstone, J. The history of the Physical Education Association of GB & NI i)the early years.

(Refs: 5)*British journal of physical education (London) 15(1), Jan/Feb 1984, 13.*
LEVEL: B LANG: Eng SIRC ARTICLE NO: 099161

Poindexter, H.B.W. The future of NAPEHE. *NAPEHE proceedings (Champaign, Ill.). 5, 1984, 166-167.*
CONF: National Association for Physical Education in Higher Education. Annual Conference (1984 : College Park, Md.).
NOTES: Conference theme: Current challenge: revitalization or obsolescence?
LEVEL: B LANG: Eng SIRC ARTICLE NO: 102691

Shea, E.J. The future agenda. (American Academy of Physical Education) (Refs: 11)*American Academy of Physical Education papers (Champaign, Ill.) 17, 1984, 146-151.*
CONF: American Academy of Physical Education. Annual Meeting (54th : 1983 : Minneapolis).
NOTES: Conference theme: Exercise and health.
LEVEL: B LANG: Eng SIRC ARTICLE NO: 104233

ATTITUDE

Berlin, P. Physical education: is it central to the mission of higher education? The teacher's perspective. (Refs: 15)*NAPEH proceedings (Champaign, Ill.) 5, 1984, 22-28.*
CONF: National Association for Physical Education in Higher Education. Annual Conference (1984 : College Park, Md.).
NOTES: Conference theme: Current challenge: revitalization or obsolescence?
LEVEL: I LANG: Eng SIRC ARTICLE NO: 102653

Dodds, P. Locke, L.F. Is physical education in American schools worth saving? Evidence, alternatives, judgement. (Refs: 50) *NAPEHE proceedings (Champaign, Ill.) 5, 1984, 76-90.*
CONF: National Association for Physical Education in Higher Education. Annual Conference (1984 : College Park, Md.).
NOTES: Conference theme: Current Challenge: revitalization or obsolescence.
LEVEL: B LANG: Eng SIRC ARTICLE NO: 102664

Duquin, M.E. Bredemeier, B.J. Oglesby, C. Greendorfer, S.L. Teacher values: political and social justice orientations of physical educators. (Refs: 29)*Journal of teaching in physical education (Blacksburg, Va.) 3(2), Winter 1984, 9-19.*
ABST: Four hundred seventy-nine physical education majors and professionals completed a 30 item questionnaire designed to determine attitudes towards a variety of social, political and professional issues considered to be of special relevance to women. The results support the psychological literature in that women, who experience greater discrimination than men, also give greater support to those social and political justice issues relating to women. Liberals tended to report more supportive attitudes than subjects of other political ideologies.
LEVEL: A LANG: Eng SIRC ARTICLE NO: 092999

Maggard, N.J. Upgrading our image. *Journal of physical education, recreation & dance 55(1), Jan 1984, 17;82.*
LEVEL: B LANG: Eng SIRC ARTICLE NO: 091616

Massey, B.H. Massey, S.R.D. Perceptions of physical education in higher education. (Refs: 9)*NAPEHE proceedings (Champaign, Ill.) 5, 1984, 122-126.*
CONF: National Association for Physical Education in Higher Education. Annual Conference (1984 :

PHYSICAL EDUCATION (continued)

College Park, Md.).
NOTES: Conference theme: Current challenge: revitalization or obsolescence?
LEVEL: I LANG: Eng SIRC ARTICLE NO: 102682

Poitras, J.G. The attitudes of students, parents, and teachers toward physical education in New Brunswick. (Refs: 9)*CAHPER journal/Revue de l'ACSEPR (Ottawa) 50(4), Mar/Apr 1984, 12-14;30.*
ABST: The purpose of this study was to determine the differences, if any, in attitudes toward physical education among French-speaking and English-speaking students and teachers from the province of New Brunswick, Canada. 3600 subjects (1,800 French-speaking and 1,800 English-speaking) were administered the Physical Education Attitude Inventory. Both French-speaking and English-speaking people held a positive or favorable attitude toward physical education regardless of whether they were students, parents, or teachers.
LEVEL: A LANG: Eng SIRC ARTICLE NO: 096165

Poitras, J.G. Les attitudes des eleves, parents et enseignants a l'egard de l'education physique au Nouveau-Brunswick. (Refs 9)*CAHPER journal/ Revue de l'ACSEPR (Ottawa) 50(6), juil/aout 1984, 15-18;20;*
RESUME: L'auteur compare les attitudes des eleves, parents et enseignants francophones et anglophones a l'egard de l'education physique au Nouveau-Brunswick. 3,600 sujets (1,800 francophones et l,800 anglophones) provenant de 48 ecoles secondaires servent de sujets ainsi que leurs parents et professeurs. Tous demontrent une attitude positive a l'egard de l'education physique.
LEVEL: A LANG: Fr SIRC ARTICLE NO: 099176

Ruszovan, V.J. Relationship between program goals and attitudes of instructors and students in general college physical education. Eugene, Ore.: Microform Publications, University of Oregon, 1984. 2 microfiches : negative, ill. ; 11 x 15 cm.
NOTES: Thesis (M.S.) - University of North Carolina at Greensboro, 1980; (viii, 128 leaves); includes bibliography.
LEVEL: A LANG: Eng UO84 3-4

Symonette, P.L. Assessment of the physical fitness of Bahamian youths age 13 thru 17 years, and their attitudes toward physical education. Eugene, Ore.: Microform Publications, University of Oregon, 1984. 1 microfiche : negative ; 11 x 15 cm.
NOTES: Thesis (M.S.) - Howard University, 1983; (x, 52 leaves); vita; includes bibliography.
LEVEL: A LANG: Eng UO84 330

AUDIO-VISUAL AIDS

Begin, L. La diffusion d'une conception de l'education physique 'elargie' aupres des parents. (Refs: 9)*Revue quebecoise de l'activite physique (Trois-Rivieres, Que.) 3(1), oct 1984, 3-6.*
LEVEL: B LANG: Fr SIRC ARTICLE NO: 100820

BIBLIOGRAPHIES

Locke, L.F. References. *Journal of teaching in physical education (Blacksburg, Va.) 2, Summer 1984, 63-85.*
NOTES: Special issue: Research on teaching teachers: where are we now?
ABST: Over 400 references are listed relating to the subject of teaching research.
LEVEL: I LANG: Eng SIRC ARTICLE NO: 102679

BIOGRAPHY AND AUTOBIOGRAPHY

Bennett, B.L. Dudley Allen Sargent: the man and his philosophy. (Refs: 21)*Journal of physical education, recreation & dance (Reston, Va.) 55(9), Nov/Dec 1984, 61-64.*
LEVEL: B LANG: Eng SIRC ARTICLE NO: 102651

Caldwell, S.F. The mind/body problem: quest for accurate terminology in twentieth century American 'physical education': Rosalind Cassidy. (Refs: 10)*CAHPERD journal times (Danville, Calif.) 47(2), Nov 1984, 6-8.*
LEVEL: I LANG: Eng SIRC ARTICLE NO: 108273

Davenport, J. Thomas Denison Wood: physical educator and father of health education. (Refs: 16)*Journal of physical education, recreation and dance (Reston, Va.) 55(8), Oct 1984, 63-65;68.*
LEVEL: B LANG: Eng SIRC ARTICLE NO: 100828

Kozar, A. R. Tait McKenzie: a man of noble achievement. *Journal of physical education, recreation and dance (Reston, Va.) 55(7), Sept 1984, 27-31.*
LEVEL: B LANG: Eng SIRC ARTICLE NO: 100839

Lee, M. Strong Hinman, 1893-1983. *Journal of physical education, recreation & dance (Reston, Va.) 55(5), May/Jun 1984, 16.*
LEVEL: B LANG: Eng SIRC ARTICLE NO: 094524

Mangan, J.A. Hely Hutchinson Almond: iconoclast, anglophile and imperialist. *Scottish journal of physical education (Glasgow, Scotland) 12(3), Aug 1984, 38-41.*
LEVEL: B LANG: Eng SIRC ARTICLE NO: 099165

CAREERS

Bianco, A. Paese, P.C. So you want to be a teacher/coach. (Refs: 1)*Journal of physical education, recreation & dance 55(1), Jan 1984, 55.*
LEVEL: B LANG: Eng SIRC ARTICLE NO: 091595

Drowatzky, J.N. Armstrong, C.W. Physical education: career perspectives and professional foundations. Englewood Cliffs, N.J. Prentice-Hall, c1984. xiv, 289 p. : ill.
NOTES: Includes index. Bibliography: p. 277-283.
LEVEL: I LANG: Eng ISBN: 0136682855 LC CARD: 83-013876 GV362 15884

Kelly, D. To teach or not to teach...that is the answer. (Refs: 8)
CONF: Physical Education Graduating Seminar Conference (1984 : Footscray Institute of Technology).
NOTES: In, Physical education in Australia: past, present and future directions, s.l., Footscray Institute of Technology, 1984, Suppl. p.13-18.
LEVEL: I LANG: Eng SIRC ARTICLE NO: 096144

Kneer, M.E. Help: where to look. (Refs: 11)*Journal of physical education, recreation & dance (Reston, Va.) 55(6), Aug 1984, 50-52.*
LEVEL: B LANG: Eng SIRC ARTICLE NO: 097658

Lehr, C. Meeting staff development needs of teachers. (Refs: 3)*Journal of physical education, recreation & dance (Reston, Va.) 55(6), Aug 1984, 73-75.*
LEVEL: B LANG: Eng SIRC ARTICLE NO: 097660

Pestolesi, R.A. Baker, C. Introduction to physical education: a contemporary careers approach. Glenview, Ill.: Scott, Foresman & Co., c1984. xii, 334 p.
NOTES: Includes bibliographies and index.

LEVEL: I LANG: Eng ISBN: 0673165922 LC CARD: 83-015378 GV362 15950

Priest, L. User's guide for subject, physical education, object, career opportunities. Hanover, N.H.: Houghton Mifflin, c1984-. 1v. (loose-leaf)
NOTES: Spine title: Subject, physical education, object, career opportunities.
LEVEL: B LANG: Eng ISBN: 089466073X LC CARD: 84-154612

Rog, J.A. Teaching and coaching: the ultimate challenge. (Refs: 6)*Journal of physical education, recreation & dance (Reston Va.) 55(6), Aug 1984, 48-49.*
ABST: In the author's opinion, the teaching of physical education and the coaching of a sport are two distinct activities. In a school situation, it is very rare that an individual will only be involved in one or the other - more usual is the hybrid teacher-coach. The author outlines the context differences between teaching physical education and coaching as well as offers suggestions on how best to insure quality performance in both activities.
LEVEL: B LANG: Eng SIRC ARTICLE NO: 097430

COEDUCATION

Griffin, P. Coed physical education: problems and promise. *Journal of physical education, recreation & dance (Reston, Va.) 55(6), Aug 1984, 36-37.*
LEVEL: B LANG: Eng SIRC ARTICLE NO: 097653

DICTIONARIES AND TERMINOLOGY

Cotten, D.J. Gallemore S.L. In quest of practical communication. (Refs: 2)*Quest (Champaigm, Ill.) 36(2), 1984, 177-180.*
ABST: The purpose of this article is to present a tongue-in-cheek look at physical education language. Upon examining the language and terminology used in physical education and research literature, the authors have developed lists of commonly used physical education terminology and explained how to use the lists to make scholarly or research-sounding sentences. The subtle message of the article is 'Stop trying to impress. Speak and write to be understood'.
LEVEL: B LANG: Eng SIRC ARTICLE NO: 102662

Ojeme, E.O. Has the name, physical education, outlived its usefulness? (Refs: 16)*Physical educator (Indianapolis) 41(4), De 1984, 190-194.*
LEVEL: I LANG: Eng SIRC ARTICLE NO: 104226

ECONOMICS

Austin, D.A. Economic impact on physical education. (Refs: 5)*Journal of physical education, recreation & dance (Reston, Va. 55(5), May/Jun 1984, 35-37.*
LEVEL: B LANG: Eng SIRC ARTICLE NO: 094504

Spirduso, W.W. Kennamer, L. The economy and education. (Refs: 9)*Journal of physical education, recreation, & dance (Reston, Va.) 55(5), May/Jun 1984, 19-22;52.*
LEVEL: I LANG: Eng SIRC ARTICLE NO: 094533

EQUIPMENT

Boucher, C. Un materiel d'education physique non conventionnel. (Refs: 20)*Revue quebecoise de l'activite physique (Trois-Rivieres, Que.) 3(1), oct 1984, 7-11.*
LEVEL: B LANG: Fr SIRC ARTICLE NO: 100821

Corbin, D.E. Corbin, C.B. Homemade play equipment for use in physical education classes. (Refs: 7)*Runner (Edmonton) 21(4), Winter 1983/ 1984, 40-42.*
NOTES: Reprinted from, JOPERD, June 1983.
LEVEL: B LANG: Eng SIRC ARTICLE NO: 096134

Dassel, H. The 'Reutlinger Sprungleine' for school and club. La cuerda de salto 'Reutlinger' para e colegio y el club. *International journal of physical education (Schorndorf, W. Germany) 21(2), 19-26 Jul 1984, Special supplement II, 2-5.*
NOTES: Translation of, Die Reutlinger Sprungleine fuer Schule und Verein, Sportuntericht 32(9), 1983, Supp., Lehrhilfen fuer den Sportunterricht 143-144.
LEVEL: B LANG: Eng Spa SIRC ARTICLE NO: 097481

Lewandowski, D.M. Shoestrings and shoeboxes. *Journal of physical education, recreation & dance (Reston, Va.) 55(6), Aug 1984, 34-35.*
LEVEL: B LANG: Eng SIRC ARTICLE NO: 097661

Sharp, B. Paliczka, V. Computing in physical education. (Refs: 7)*Scottish journal of physical education (Glasgow, Scotland) 12(2), Apr 1984, 10-18.*
ABST: This study presents the results of a survey of Scottish secondary school physical education teachers and their interest, knowledge and use of microcomputers. There was a large variety of applications of microcomputers in physical education. However for the most part they were used in record keeping applications and program planning.
LEVEL: A LANG: Eng SIRC ARTICLE NO: 094532

Spicing up the elementary PE program by using homemade equipment. *Physical education newsletter (Old Saybrook, Conn.) 155, Ja 1984, 2-6.*
LEVEL: B LANG: Eng SIRC ARTICLE NO: 097669

EVALUATION

An ungraded physical education report card keeps parents informed of student progress. *Physical education newsletter (Old Saybrook, Conn.) 160, Jun 1984, 3-5.*
LEVEL: B LANG: Eng SIRC ARTICLE NO: 104238

Boulard, R. Morana, M. EPS opinion publique et evaluation. (Refs: 5)*EPS: Education physique et sport (Paris) 189, sept/oct 1984, 40-41.*
LEVEL: B LANG: Fr SIRC ARTICLE NO: 100823

Carroll, R. Developments in C.S.E. and the leisure paradox. (Refs: 5)*British journal of physical education (London) 15(1), Jan/Feb 1984, 25-26.*
LEVEL: B LANG: Eng SIRC ARTICLE NO: 099151

Cleuziou, J.P. Notation et renovation en education physique et sportive. (Paris): (Institut national du sport et de l'education physique), 1984. 255 f.
NOTES: Memoire INSEP : Paris : 1984. Bibliographie. LANG: Fr

de Faria, A.G. Proposition du systeme Famoc comme technique d'analyse du comportement verbal du professeur d'education physique. (Refs: 12)*Revue de l'education physique (Liege, Belgique) 24(1), 1984, 3-8.*
LEVEL: I LANG: Fr SIRC ARTICLE NO: 096136

Delapp, L. Healthy minds, healthy bodies?: a study of the decline of physical education in California's schools. Sacramento, Calif.: AOR, (1984). v, 70 p. : ill.
CORP: California. Legislature. Assembly. Office of Research.
NOTES: Copies may be purchased from the Assembly Publications Office. Bibliography: p. 69-70.
LEVEL: I LANG: Eng LC CARD: 84-622040

Deutsch, H. Sex fair grading in physical education. (Refs: 12)*Physical educator (Indianapolis, Ind.) 3(41), Oct 1984, 137-141.*
LEVEL: I LANG: Eng SIRC ARTICLE NO: 100830

Dodd, G. An evaluation of daily physical education in South Australian primary schools. *ACHPER national journal (Kingswood, Aust.) 105, Spring 1984, 16;49-51.*
LEVEL: I LANG: Eng SIRC ARTICLE NO: 102663

Dunham, P. Systematic evaluation for elementary school physical educators. (Refs: 7)*In, Simri, U. (ed.), et al., Preschool and elementary school children and physical activity. Proceedings of the 26th ICHPER World Congress 1983, Wingate Institute, Israel, vol. III, Jerusalem, Israel, 1984, p. 32-40.*
CONF: ICHPER World Congress (26th : 1983 : Wingate Institute, Israel).
LEVEL: I LANG: Eng GV443 20093

Geron, E. Reches, I. The effect of a self-assessment approach during physical education on the perceptual-motor development of 7-8 year old children. (Refs: 14)*In, Simri, U. (ed.), et al., Preschool and elementary school children and physical activity. Proceedings of the 26th ICHPER World Congress 1983, Wingate Institute, Israel, vol. III, Jerusalem, Israel, 1984, p. 54-63.*
CONF: ICHPER World Congress (26th : 1983 : Wingate Institute, Israel).
LEVEL: A LANG: Eng GV443 20093

Gusthart, J.L. The stability of teaching behavior over a unit of instruction. (Refs: 7)*CAHPER journal/ Revue de l'ACASEPR (Ottawa) 50(4), Mar/Apr 1984, 2-7.*
ABST: The stability of teaching behaviour of three male physical educators over an instructional unit was assessed in this study. Audiotapes were collected in ten lessons in a volleyball unit. Observational data were obtained by using the Observation System For Content Development. Soliciting behaviour (request student to do something) (39%) and initiating behaviour (providing information) (26%) were the most predominant, direct communication behaviours. The most common indirectly contributing behaviour was observing of students (10%). Results indicated that most teaching behaviours were a function of the lesson rather than the unit.
LEVEL: A LANG: Eng SIRC ARTICLE NO: 096140

Hill, C. Criteria for judging a P.E. department. *Bulletin of physical education (London) 20(1), Spring 1984, 13-18.*
LEVEL B LANG: Eng SIRC ARTICLE NO: 102669

Howe, B. The University of Victoria: studies of teaching effectiveness in physical education. (Refs: 10)*In: Internationales Symposium Sportpaedagogik - Koerpererziehung - Persoenlichkeit: Protokoll, Potsdam, Deutsche Demokratische Republik, ICSSPE/CIEPSS, 1984?, p. 226-236.*
CONF: Internationales Symposium Sportpaedagogik - Koerpererziehung - Persoenlichkeit (1983 : Potsdam).
LEVEL: A LANG: Eng GV205 20231

Hullihan, W.F. Physical educators and credibility. *Florida journal of health, physical education,* recreation and dance (Gainsville, Fla.) 22(1), Feb 1984, 3-4.
LEVEL: B LANG: Eng SIRC ARTICLE NO: 096143

Instructional improvement materials for physical education. Alexandria, Va.: Computer Microfilm International, 1984. 1 microfiche (61 fr.)
LEVEL: A LANG: Eng EDRS: ED248214

Lambdin, D. Keeping track. *Journal of physical education, recreation & dance (Reston, Va.) 55(6), Aug 1984, 40-43.*
LEVEL: LANG: Eng SIRC ARTICLE NO: 097659

Lashuk, M. A percentile method of grading physical education. (Refs: 17)*CAHPER journal/Revue de l'ACSEPR (Ottawa) 50(4), Mar/Apr 1984, 8-11.*
LEVEL: I LANG: Eng SIRC ARTICLE NO: 096146

Marsenach, J. L'evaluation en education physique: une recherche de l'INRP. *EPS: Education physique et sport 185, janv/fevr 1984, 52-56.*
LEVEL: B LANG: Fr SIRC ARTICLE NO: 093012

Ne, R. L'evaluation en EPS: nouvelle mode ou exigence necessaire? *EPS: Revue education physique et sport (Paris) 188, juil/aout 1984, 14-18.*
LEVEL: B LANG: FR SIRC ARTICLE NO: 097665

Pieron, M. Evaluation et observation. (Refs: 6)*EPS: Education physique et sport (Paris) 189, sept/oct 1984, 21-23.*
NOTES: Extrait du document: 'Pedagogie des activites physiques et sportives-methodologie et didactique', de Maurice Pieron, Universite de Liege, 1984.
LEVEL: B LANG: Fr SIRC ARTICLE NO: 100842

Pieron, M. Research on teacher effectiveness: the process-product model. (Refs: 18)*In: Internationales Symposium Sportpaedagogik - Koerpererziehung - Persoenlichkeit: Protokoll, Potsdam, Deutsche Demokratische Republik, ICSSPE/CIEPSS, 1984?, p. 212-225.*
CONF: Internationales Symposium Sportpaedagogik - Koerpererziehung - Persoenlichkeit (1983 : Potsdam).
LEVEL: A LANG: Eng GV205 20231

Ratliffe, T. Evaluation of students' skill using generic levels of skill proficiency. (Refs: 3)*Physical educator (Bloomington, Ind.) 41(2), May 1984, 64-68.*
LEVEL: I LANG: Eng SIRC ARTICLE NO: 099178

Reichenbach, M. Helmke, C. Zur Wirksamkeit des Sportpaedagogen aus der Sicht der Schueler. (The efficiency of the sport pedagogue from the pupils' viewpoint). (Refs: 6)*In: Internationales Symposium Sportpaedagogik - Koerpererziehung - Persoenlichkeit: Protokoll, Potsdam, Deutsche Demokratische Republik, ICSSPE/CIEPSS, 1984?, p. 237-244.*
CONF: Internationales Symposium Sportpaedagogik - Koerpererziehung - Persoenlichkeit (1983 : Potsdam).
LEVEL: A LANG: Ger GV205 20231

FACILITIES

Klappholz, L.A. Using community resources for instruction. *Physical education newsletter (Old Saybrook, Conn.) 163, Oct 198 2-4.*
LEVEL: B LANG: Eng SIRC ARTICLE NO: 105408

Larson, G. Fournier, R. Putting a new emphasis on multipurpose. *Athletic administration (Cleveland,*

PHYSICAL EDUCATION (continued)

Ohio.) 19(2), Apr 1984, 10-12.
LEVEL: B LANG: Eng SIRC ARTICLE NO: 094522

Lewandowski, D.M. Shoestrings and shoeboxes.
Journal of physical education, recreation & dance (Reston, Va.) 55(6), Aug 1984, 34-35.
LEVEL: B LANG: Eng SIRC ARTICLE NO: 097661

HEALTH AND HYGIENE

Abrosimova, L.I. Health building effect of children's physical education. (Refs: 16)*In, Idrett for barn. Sport for Children Sport pour les enfants 27.9.-1.10.1982 Tonsberg, Norway. Report. Oslo, Norway, Ministry of Cultural and Scientific Affairs: Norwegian Confederation of Sport, 1984, p. (19)-(20).*
CONF: Idrett for barn. Sport for Children. Sport pour les enfants (1982 : Tonsberg, Norway).
LEVEL: I LANG: Eng GV709.2 20111

Abrosimova, L.I. Effets positifs de l'education physique sur la sante des enfants. (Refs: 16)*Dans, Idrett for barn. Sport for Children. Sport pour les enfants 27.9.-1.10.1982 Tonsberg, Norway. Rapport. Oslo, Norvege, Ministere de la culture et de la science : Confederation norvegienne des sports, 1984, p. (20)-(21).*
CONF: Idrett for barn. Sport for Children. Sport pour les enfants (1982 : Tonsberg, Norway).
LEVEL: I LANG: Fr GV709.2 20112

Jensen, G. Health related physical education.
WAHPERD journal (Milwaukee, Wis.) 13(1), May 1984, 32-33.
LEVEL: B LANG: En SIRC ARTICLE NO: 100837

HISTORY

Jones, J.C. The history of physical activities at an emerging Christian liberal arts college. Eugene, Ore.: Microform Publications, University of Oregon, 1984. 3 microfiches : negative ; 11 x 15 cm.
NOTES: Thesis (M.Ed.) - University of North Carolina at Greensboro, 1982; (vi, 244 leaves); includes bibliography.
LEVEL: A LANG: Eng UO84 323-325

Long, M. Physical education in Australian schools 1865-1965. (Refs: 4)
CONF: Physical Education Graduating Seminar Conferenc (1984 : Footscray Institute of Technology).
NOTES: In, Physical education in Australia: past, present and future directions, s.l., Footscray Institute of Technology, 1984, p. 21-26.
LEVEL: I LANG: Eng SIRC ARTICLE NO: 096148

McCormack, C. Pioneers in physical education in Australia. (Refs: 13)
CONF: Physical Education Graduating Seminar Conference (1984 : Footscray Institute of Technology).
NOTES: In, Physical education in Australia: past, present and future directions, s.l., Footscray Institute of Technology, 1984, p. 6-12.
LEVEL: I LANG: Eng SIRC ARTICLE NO: 096153

McIntosh, P.C. Hieronymus Mercurialis 'de arte gymnastica': classification and dogma in physical education in the sixteenth century. (Refs: 37)*British journal of sports history (London) 1(1), May 1984, 73-84.*
ABST: The author reviews a 16th century work on gymnastics written by an Italian physician. Although there are references to contemporary authors, the influence of classical writers is predominant. The

book underlines the importance of exercise for maintaining health and preventing and curing disease. Athletic training, on the other hand, is considered harmful and athletes socially useless.
LEVEL: A LANG: Eng SIRC ARTICLE NO: 108508

Roberts, M.J. The physical education time line past and present. (Refs: 6)
CONF: Physical Education Graduating Seminar Conference (1984 : Footscray Institute of Technology).
NOTES: In, Physical education in Australia: past, present and future directions, s.l., Footscray Institute of Technology, 1984, Suppl. p. 2-6.
LEVEL: I LANG: Eng SIRC ARTICLE NO: 096166

Ross, J.L. From informal to formal physical education. (Refs: 14)
CONF: Physical Education Graduating Seminar Conference (1984 : Footscray Institute of Technology).
NOTES: In, Physical education in Australia: past, present and future directions, s.l., Footscray Institute of Technology, 1984, p. 13-20.
LEVEL: I LANG: Eng SIRC ARTICLE NO: 096168

Thomson, I. Almond of Loretto: origins and development of his system of health education. (Refs: 26)*Scottish journal of physical education (Glasgow, Scotland) 12(1), Jan 1984, 32-36.*
LEVEL: I LANG: Eng SIRC ARTICLE NO: 094344

Treadwell, P.J. Victorian public school sport. (Refs: 40)*Physical education review (North Humberside, Eng.) 7(2), Autumn 1984, 113-119.*
LEVEL: I LANG: Eng SIRC ARTICLE NO: 105427

Van Dalen, D.B. Bennett, B.L. L'education physique et le naturalisme en education. *Dans, Massicotte, J.P. et Lessard, C. (eds.), Histoire du sport de l'antiquite au XIXe siecle, Sillery, Que., Presses de l'Universite du Quebec, 1984, p. 113-125.*
LEVEL: A LANG: Fr GV571 18971

INJURIES AND ACCIDENTS

Knight, M. Rehabilitation - human movement. (Refs: 2)*ACHPER national journal (Kingswood, Aust.) 104, Winter 1984, 26-27.*
LEVEL: B LANG: Eng SIRC ARTICLE NO: 100838

Rist, M.C. Learn from this school sports tragedy.
Executive educator (Washington) 6(8), Aug 1984, 22.
LEVEL: B LANG: Eng SIRC ARTICLE NO: 104230

LAW AND LEGISLATION

Adams, S.H. Liability and the physical educator. (Refs: 6)*Physical educator (Indianapolis) 41(4), Dec 1984, 200-204.*
LEVEL: B LANG: Eng SIRC ARTICLE NO: 104216

Alabama - 'no amount of evidence would be sufficient to allow the plaintiff to recover'. *Sports and the courts (Winston-Salem N.C.) 5(1), Winter 1984, 9-10.*
LEVEL: B LANG: Eng SIRC ARTICLE NO: 094502

Alexander, B.L. The reasonable prudent physical and health educator. *OPHEA: Ontario Physical and Health Education Association 10(3), Fall 1984, 42-50.*
LEVEL: B LANG: Eng SIRC ARTICLE NO: 102648

Appenzeller, H. Ross, C.T. Louisiana - is the trampoline an inherently dangerous object? *Sports and the courts (Winston-Salem, N.C.) 5(3),*

Summer 1984, 5-8.
LEVEL: B LANG: Eng SIRC ARTICLE NO: 097647

Bullock, L. Norwood, D. Liability in the physical education classroom. (Refs: 45)
NOTES: In, Brown, R. (ed.) et al., Sport, physical activity and the law, Ottawa, Canadian Association for Health, Physical Education, Recreation and Dance, c1984, p. 16-25.
LEVEL: I LANG: Eng GV705 18324

Frank, N.L. Knowledge tests covering selected liabilities of physical educators and coaches. Eugene, Ore.: Microform Publications, University of Oregon, 1984. 2 microfiches : negative ; 11 x 15 cm.
NOTES: Thesis (M.S.) - University of North Carolina at Greensboro, 1982; (vi, 105 leaves); includes bibliography.
LEVEL: A LANG: Eng UO84 198-199

Leach, G.C. Liability in physical education. *In, Della-Guistina, D. and Moore, L.M. (eds.), Proceedings of the National Conference on Liability in the Schools, Reston, Va., American School and Community Safety Association, c1984, p. 1-13.*
CONF: National Conference on Liability in the Schools (1984 : Morgantown, West Virginia).
LEVEL: I LANG: Eng GV705 18960

Louisiana - disciplinarians in the public schools should be encouraged rather than deterred. *Sports and the courts (Winston-Salem, N.C.) 5(4), Fall 1984, 13-14.*
LEVEL: B LANG: Eng SIRC ARTICLE NO: 102557

Massachusetts - denial of tenure to female physical education teacher upheld. *Sports and the courts (Winston, Salem, N.C.) 5(4), Fall 1984, 12.*
LEVEL: B LANG: Eng SIRC ARTICLE NO: 102681

Napier, D.E. Negligence, an application to physical education; potential liabilities and protection methods. (Refs: 17)
CONF Physical Education Graduating Seminar Conference (1984 : Footscray Institute of Technology).
NOTES: In, Physical education in Australia: past, present and future directions, s.l., Footscray Institute of Technology, 1984, p. 104-116.
LEVEL: I LANG: Eng SIRC ARTICLE NO: 096159

MEDICINE

Burdack, S. Sports med for phys ed? (Refs: 8)
CONF: Physical Education Graduating Seminar Conference (1984 : Footscray Institute of Technology).
NOTES: In, Physical education in Australia: past, present and future directions, s.l., Footscray Institute of Technology, 1984, p. 122-127.
LEVEL: I LANG: Eng SIRC ARTICLE NO: 096130

Klimt, F. Schulsportfreistellungen. (Exemption from school sports.) *Oeffentliches Gesundheitswesen (Stuttgart) 46(9), Sept 1984, 419-425.*
LEVEL: I LANG: Ger

MacAuley, D. The physical education teacher: a medical viewpoint. (Refs: 29)*Bulletin of physical education (London) 20(1), Spring 1984, 5-12.*
LEVEL: B LANG: Eng SIRC ARTICLE NO: 102680

Romeo, F. The physical educator and anorexia nervosa. (Refs: 8)*Physical educator (Indianapolis, Ind.) 41(1), Mar 1984, 2-5.*
LEVEL: B LANG: Eng SIRC ARTICLE NO: 096045

MOVEMENT EDUCATION

Cote-Laurence, P. La rythmique a l'elementaire. Montreal ; Sherbrooke: Presses de l'Universite de Montreal : Editions de l'Universite de Sherbrooke, 1984. 133 p. : ill.
NOTES: Bibliography: p. 132-133.
LEVEL: B LANG: Fr ISBN: 2-7606-0651-1 LC CARD: 84-16463-7 GV443 18942

Eldar, D. Movement education, traditional gymnastics and body awareness. (Refs: 16)*In, Simri, U. (ed.), et al., Preschool and elementary school children and physical activity. Proceedings of the 26th ICHPER World Congress 1983, Wingate Institute, Israel, vol. III, Jerusalem, Israel, 1984, p. 41-53.*
CONF: ICHPER World Congress (26th : 1983 : Wingate Institute, Israel).
LEVEL: A LANG: Eng GV443 20093

Kisabeth, K.L. A child's movement performance using Labanotation and referenced to the Laban framework: a case study. Eugene Ore.: Microform Publications, University of Oregon, 1984. 3 microfiches : negative, ill. ; 11 x 15 cm.
NOTES: Thesis (Ed.D.) - University of North Carolina at Greensboro, 1980; (xi, 223 leaves); includes bibliography.
LEVEL: A LANG: Eng UO84 41-43

Laporte, W. The impact of a program of integrated movement education on motor and intellectual behavior of children in the first year of the primary school. (Refs: 7)*In, Simri, U. (ed.), et al., Preschool and elementary school children and physical activity. Proceedings of the 26th ICHPER World Congress 1983, Wingate Institute, Israel, vol. III, Jerusalem, Israel, 1984, p. 69-78.*
CONF: ICHPER World Congress (26th : 1983 : Wingate Institute, Israel).
LEVEL: A LANG: Eng GV443 20093

Movement exploration in the primary grades. *Physical education newsletter (Old Saybrook, Conn.) 164, Nov 1984, 4-5.*
LEVEL: LANG: Eng SIRC ARTICLE NO: 173182

Owen, D. Dyke, S. An example of liaison through dance. *Bulletin of physical education (Leeds, Eng.) 20(3), Autumn/Winter 1984, 33-35.*
LEVEL: B LANG: Eng SIRC ARTICLE NO: 105417

Shochat, E. Early development of movement quality - an important consideration in elementary school physical education. (Refs: 9)*In, Simri, U. (ed.), et al., Preschool and elementary school children and physical activity. Proceedings of the 26th ICHPER World Congress 1983, Wingate Institute, Israel, vol. III, Jerusalem, Israel, 1984, p. 137-142.*
CONF: ICHPER World Congress (26th : 1983 : Wingate Institute, Israel).
LEVEL: I LANG: Eng GV443 20093

PERCEPTUAL MOTOR PROCESSES

Ashy, M.H. Lee, A.M. Applying the mastery learning model to motor skill instruction for children. (Refs: 18)*Physical educator (Bloomington, Ind.) 41(2), May 1984, 60-63.*
LEVEL: I LANG: Eng SIRC ARTICLE NO: 099113

Heyters, C. Appreciation de l'aptitude motrice d'une population sportive pluridisciplinaire. (Refs: 11)*Revue de l'education physique (Liege) 24(2), 1984, 25-31.*

RESUME: L'aptitude motrice de 182 garcons et 143 filles inscrits en education physique ainsi que de 127 garcons et 127 filles inscrits en kinesitherapie est evaluee au cours de cette etude. Les resultats indiquent des differences entre garcons et filles. Les etudiants en kinesitherapie obtiennent dans l'ensemble des resultats plus faibles que leurs homologues d'education physique. Les sujets subissent 11 epreuves differentes permettant d'evaluer l'endurance musculaire des membres superieurs, la puissance musculaire des bras, des jambes, des abdominaux et des dorsaux, la souplesse des epaules, du tronc, et des jambes, la coordination et la vitesse.
LEVEL: A LANG: Fr SIRC ARTICLE NO: 100836

Lydon, M.C. Cheffers, J.T.F. Decision-making in elementary school-age children: effects upon motor learning and self-concept development. (Refs: 19)*Research quarterly for exercise & sport (Reston, Va.) 55(2), Jun 1984, 135-140.*
ABST: This study investigated the effects of variable decision-making models upon the development of body coordination and self-concept of 285 children in grades one through five. The children were from two schools which were equivalent in terms of socioeconomic status. The experimental school received two physical education programs which varied only in the type of teacher behavior exhibited. The control school did not receive any treatment. The results indicate that students can be given decision-making responsibility in physical education class and maintain a level of motor skill achievement equal to that of students who have not been allowed to make decisions in physical education class. There were no conclusions concerning the effects of student decision on self-concept.
LEVEL: A LANG: Eng SIRC ARTICLE NO: 096149

Murdoch, E.B. Motor learning - progression, differentiation and assessment in the teaching of young children. (Refs: 23) *Momentum (Edinburgh, Scotland) 9(3), Autumn 1984, 25-35.*
LEVEL: I LANG: Eng SIRC ARTICLE NO: 105362

Tiainen, J. Tiainen, A. Physical education and its significance on personality development at the sensorimotor period. (Refs 8)*In: Internationales Symposium Sportpaedagogik - Koerpererziehung - Persoenlichkeit: Protokoll, Potsdam, Deutsche Demokratische Republik, ICSSPE/CIEPSS, 1984?, p. 143-149.*
CONF: Internationales Symposium Sportpaedagogik - Koerpererziehung - Persoenlichkeit (1983 : Potsdam).
LEVEL: I LANG: Eng GV205 20231

Training volunteers to help in a perceptual-motor training program. *Physical education newsletter (Old Saybrook, Conn.) 158, Apr 1984, 2-3.*
LEVEL: B LANG: Eng SIRC ARTICLE NO: 096174

Volle, M. Tisal, H. LaBarre, R. Lavallee, H. Shephard, R.J. Jequier, J.C. Rajic, M. Required physical activity and psychomotor development of primary school children. (Refs: 8)
CONF: Symposium of Paediatric Work Physiology (10th : 1981 : Joutsa, Finland).
NOTES: In, Ilmarinen, J. and Vaelimaeki, I. (eds.), Children and sport: paediatric work physiology, Berlin, Springer-Verlag, 1984, p. 53-57.
ABST: School children between the ages of 6 and 11 were studied in 14 schools for 2 years during a program of required physical education. The body schema forms the corner stone of both education and reeducation in the psychomotor domain. This

paper examines such elements as the correct perception of body dimensions, concepts of laterality and verticality, and finger recognition.
LEVEL: A LANG: Eng SIRC ARTICLE NO: 102623

PHILOSOPHY

Barbazanges, J.P. Une education physique pour quel corps. (Refs: 2)*Revue de l'education physique (Liege, Belgique) 24(1), 1984, 9-11.*
LEVEL: B LANG: Fr SIRC ARTICLE NO: 096125

Cagigal, J.M. Sport and education. *Bulletin of the Federation internationale d'education physique (Cheltenham, Eng.) 54(1), Jan/Mar 1984, 16-22.*
NOTES: Reprinted from, FIEP bulletin 46(4), 1976.
LEVEL: I LANG: Eng SIRC ARTICLE NO: 094509

Carpenter, L.J. Physical education, athletics, and the mission of higher education. *NAPEHE proceedings (Champaign, Ill.) 5, 1984, 110-113.*
CONF: National Association for Physical Education in Higher Education. Annual Conference (1984 : College Park, Md.).
NOTES: Conference theme: Current challenge: revitalization or obsolescence?
LEVEL: I LANG: Eng SIRC ARTICLE NO: 102658

Fairs, J.R. Maoism, body puritanism, and physical education: a study of impulse control in a political economy. Part II. (Refs: 78)*Canadian journal of history of sport/Revue canadienne de l'histoire des sports (Windsor) 15(1), May 1984, 1-29.*
ABST: The importance of physical education in Mao Tse-tung's political philosophies is studied. Six of Chairman Mao's aims for the reformation of the proletariat for a Marxist-Leninist society are examined in detail. These aims are 1) training the will, 2) habit formation for social action, 3) disciplinary asceticism, 4) ideological moulding, 5) agent of cultural transformation, and 6) military heroism. In each case physical education was found to play an important role in moulding the socialist man. But these aims were never intended for the benefit of the individual; rather, they were for the benefit of the state. The implications of this were that Mao's China placed great control over the teaching of physical education in order that it conform to Maoist philosophy. This, in turn, meant that self-styled programs were nonexistant.
LEVEL: A LANG: Eng SIRC ARTICLE NO: 108313

Figley, G.E. Moral education through physical education. (Refs: 42)*Quest (Champaign, Ill.) 36(1), 1984, 89-101.*
LEVEL: I LANG: Eng SIRC ARTICLE NO: 099155

Fleischman, T. Le rapport theorie-pratique en education physique. (Paris): (Institut national du sport et de l'education physique), 1984. 138 f.
NOTES: Memoire INSEP : Paris : 1984. Bibliographie.
LEVEL: A LANG: Fr

Harper, W. Self-help. (Refs: 7)*NAPEHE proceedings (Champaign, Ill.) 5, 1984, 29-35.*
CONF: National Association for Physical education in Higher Education. Annual Conference (1984 : College Park, Md.).
NOTES: Conference theme: Current challenge: revitalization or obsolescence?
ABST: The author discusses the role of physical education in the whole process of higher education.
LEVEL: I LANG: Eng SIRC ARTICLE NO: 102668

Kirk, D. Physical education, aesthetics, and education. (Refs: 18)*Physical education review*

(Manchester) 7(1), Spring 1984, 65-72.
LEVEL: I LANG: Eng SIRC ARTICLE NO: 099162

Kretchmar, R.S. Thomas Denison Wood's hope and reality: a philosophic review. (Refs: 10)*Journal of physical education, recreation and dance (Reston, Va.) 55(8), Oct 1984, 66-68.*
LEVEL: B LANG: Eng SIRC ARTICLE NO: 100840

Miller, D.M. Philosophy: whose business? (Refs: 22)*Quest (Champaign, Ill.) 36(1), 1984, 26-36.*
LEVEL: I LANG: Eng SIRC ARTICLE NO: 099169

Mitchell, B. Working towards sport. (Refs: 11)
CONF: Physical Education Graduating Seminar Conference (1984 : Footscray Institute of Technology).
NOTES: In, Physical education in Australia: past, present and future directions, s.l., Footscray Institute of Technology, 1984, p. 64-69.
LEVEL: I LANG: Eng SIRC ARTICLE NO: 096157

Osterhoudt, R.G. Empiricistic dualism: the paradoxical basis/nemesis of modern physical education. (Refs: 8)*Quest (Champaign, Ill.) 36(1), 1984, 61-65.*
LEVEL: I LANG: Eng SIRC ARTICLE NO: 099171

Proctor, N. Physical education in the revised school curriculum. (Refs: 29)*Physical education review (North Humberside, Eng 7(2), Autumn 1984, 106-112.*
LEVEL: B LANG: Eng SIRC ARTICLE NO: 105421

Progen, J.L. DeSensi, J.T. The value of theoretical frameworks for exploring the subjective dimension of sport. (Refs: 23) *Quest (Champaign, Ill.) 36(1), 1984, 80-88.*
ABST: This study focuses on the similarities and differences between Martin Buber's I-Thou philosophy and Mihaly Csikszentmihalyi's flow theory.
LEVEL: A LANG: Eng SIRC ARTICLE NO: 099147

Robb, M. Physical education: is it central to the mission of higher education? *NAPEHE proceedings (Champaign, Ill.) 5, 1984 49-52.*
CONF: National Association for Physical Education in Higher Education. Annual Conference (1984 : College Park, Md.).
NOTES: Conference theme: Current challenge: revitalization or obsolescence?
LEVEL: I LANG: Eng SIRC ARTICLE NO: 102692

Sheehan, T. An alternate perspective of physical education in higher education. (Refs: 6)*NAPEHE proceedings (Champaign, Ill.) 5, 1984, 36-41.*
CONF: National Association for Physical Education in Higher Education. Annual Conference (1984 : College Park, Md.).
NOTES: Conference theme: Current challenge; revitalization or obsolescence?
LEVEL: I LANG: Eng SIRC ARTICLE NO: 102696

Sloan, M.R. Physical education: is it central to the mission of higher education? An administrator's perspective. (Refs: 4) *NAPEHE proceedings (Champaign, Ill.) 5, 1984; 42-48.*
CONF: National Association for Physical Education in Higher Education. Annual Conference (1984 : College Park, Md.).
NOTES: Conference theme: Current challenge: revitalization or obsolescence?
LEVEL: I LANG: Eng SIRC ARTICLE NO: 102697

Sykora, F. Die Wirksamkeit sportbezogener theoretischer Kenntnisse fuer die sportliche Taetigkeit. (The effectiveness of sports-related theoretical knowledge for sports activities.) (Refs:

18)*In: Internationales Symposium Sportpaedagogik - Koerpererziehung - Persoenlichkeit: Protokoll, Potsdam, Deutsche Demokratische Republik, ICSSPE/CIEPSS, 1984?, p. 162-179.*
CONF: Internationales Symposium Sportpaedagogik - Koerpererziehung - Persoenlichkeit (1983 : Potsdam).
LEVEL: A GV205 20231

Taylor, B. Physical education and the community. *Bulletin of physical education (London) 20(2), Summer 1984, 8-10.*
CONF: British Association of Advisers and Lecturers in Physical Education. Congress (64th : 1984 : Cardiff).
NOTES: Summary of the opening address by the Chief Education Officer, Somerset.
LEVEL: B LANG: Eng SIRC ARTICLE NO: 104236

PHYSICAL FITNESS

Blair, S. Values of physical activity as expressed by physical education majors. (Refs: 20)*Physical educator (Indianapolis) 41(4), Dec 1984, 186-189.*
LEVEL: A LANG: Eng SIRC ARTICLE NO: 104217

Conrad, C.C. Physical fitness in the elementary school physical education program. *Physical education newsletter (Old Saybrook, Conn.) 157, Mar 1984, 5-8.*
LEVEL: B LANG: Eng SIRC ARTICLE NO: 096133

Corbin, C.B. Fitness for life - a status report. (Refs: 7)*Physical education newsletter (Old Saybrook, Conn.) 162, Sept 1984, 4-6.*
LEVEL: B LANG: Eng SIRC ARTICLE NO: 102660

Eckert, H.M. Montoye, H.J. Exercise and health: American Academy of Physical Education papers, volume 17. Champaign, Ill.: Human Kinetics Publishers, Inc., 1984?. 160 p.
LEVEL: I LANG: Eng

Field, C.A. Meeting the challenge of physical education. (Refs: 5)*Coaching clinic (Princeton, N.J.) 23(1), Sept 1984, 13-16.*
LEVEL: I LANG: Eng SIRC ARTICLE NO: 099154

Frost, H. Moving for life. (Refs: 5)
CONF: Physical Education Graduating Seminar Conference (1984 : Footscray Institute of Technology).
NOTES: In, Physical education in Australia: past, present and future directions, s.l., Footscray Institute of Technology, 1984, p. 38-44.
LEVEL: I LANG: Eng SIRC ARTICLE NO: 096138

Heyters, C. Appreciation de l'aptitude motrice d'une population sportive pluridisciplinaire. (Refs: 11)*Revue de l'education physique (Liege) 24(2), 1984, 25-31.*
RESUME: L'aptitude motrice de 182 garcons et 143 filles inscrits en education physique ainsi que de 127 garcons et 127 filles inscrits en kinesitherapie est evaluee au cours de cette etude. Les resultats indiquent des differences entre garcons et filles. Les etudiants en kinesitherapie obtiennent dans l'ensemble des resultats plus faibles que leurs homologues d'education physique. Les sujets subissent 11 epreuves differentes permettant d'evaluer l'endurance musculaire des membres superieurs, la puissance musculaire des bras, des jambes, des abdominaux et des dorsaux, la souplesse des epaules, du tronc, et des jambes, la coordination et la vitesse.
LEVEL: A LANG: Fr SIRC ARTICLE NO: 100836

Misner, J.E. Are we fit to educate about fitness? (Refs: 8)*Journal of physical education, recreation & dance (Reston, Va.) 55(9), Nov/Dec 1984, 26-28;40.*
LEVEL: B LANG: Eng SIRC ARTICLE NO: 102730

Morken, C. A revolutionary new concept for school physical education. *Sports retailer (Mt. Prospect, Ill.) 37(8), Aug 1984, 28-30.*
LEVEL: B LANG: Eng SIRC ARTICLE NO: 102731

Physical fitness instruction at the secondary school level. *Physical education newsletter (Old Saybrook, Conn.) 157, Mar 1984 8.*
LEVEL: B LANG: Eng SIRC ARTICLE NO: 096164

Stein, J.U. Personalizing individual fitness programs with microcomputers. *Physical education newsletter (Old Saybrook, Conn.) 155, Jan 1984, 6-8.*
LEVEL: B LANG: Eng SIRC ARTICLE NO: 097703

Uppal, A.K. Singh, R. Effect of training and break in training on flexibility of physical education majors. (Refs: 9)*SNIPES journal (Patiala, India) 7(4), Oct 1984, 49-53.*
ABST: The flexibility of 28 boys and thirteen girls, aged between 16 and 21 years, participating in a regular programme of physical education and conditioning was tested 10 weeks after training and 4 weeks after break in training. Improvements of the flexibility of the hip, trunk, shoulder and spine as measured by Sit and Reach, Standing Bobbing, Shoulder flexibility and Spine flexibility tests respectively were observed following training. Detraining lowered the flexibility of hip, trunk, shoulder and spine.
LEVEL: A LANG: Eng SIRC ARTICLE NO: 171616

PLAY

Miracle, A.W. Rowan, B. Suggs, D.N. Play activities and elementary school peer groups. (Refs: 7)
NOTES: In, Sutton-Smith, B. and Kelly-Byrne, D. (eds.), The masks of play, New York, Leisure Press, c1984, p. 119-124.
LEVEL: I LANG: Eng HQ782 17029

Vinel, C. Les jeux et l'enfant, de 5 a 12 ans. Paris: Amphora, 1984?. 128 p.
LEVEL: B LANG: Fr

PROGRAMS

Boucherin, B. Une meilleure condition physique par les jeux d'agres. (Refs: 1)*Macolin (Berne) 2, fevr 1984, 9-10.*
LEVEL: LANG: Fr SIRC ARTICLE NO: 100822

Chin, M. Physical education in Malaysia for women and children. *Asian journal of physical education (Taiwan, China) 7(1), Apr 1984, 33-35.*
NOTES: Abstract in Chinese.
LEVEL: B LANG: Eng Chi SIRC ARTICLE NO: 096229

Ennis, C.D. A future scenario for physical education. The movement of life curriculum, 2017-2035. (Refs: 4)*Journal of physical education, recreation and dance (Reston, Va.) 55(7), Sept 1984, 4-5.*
LEVEL: B LANG: Eng SIRC ARTICLE NO: 100831

Fong, R.K. State of physical education in Republic of China. *Asian journal of physical education (Taiwan, China) 7(1), Apr 1984, 36-45.*
NOTES: Abstract in Chinese.

LEVEL: I LANG: Eng Chi SIRC ARTICLE NO:
096240

Harageones, M. Curriculum frameworks, what are
they? How were they developed? What are their
implications? *Florida JOHPERD (Gainesville, Fla.)
22(3), Aug 1984, 18-19.*
LEVEL: B LANG: Eng SIRC ARTICLE NO: 099156

Heitmann, H.M. Physical education for survival:
back to basics. (Refs: 1)*Journal of physical
education, recreation & dance (Reston, Va.) 55(6),
Aug 1984, 25-26.*
LEVEL: B LANG: Eng SIRC ARTICLE NO: 097656

Inwood, K. Case study 1. *Bulletin of physical
education (Leeds, Eng.) 20(3), Autumn/Winter
1984, 20-23.*
LEVEL: B LANG: En SIRC ARTICLE NO: 105405

McGuckian, A. The nature of outdoor education
and the role of the physical educator in outdoor
education. (Refs: 10)
CONF: Physical Education Graduating Seminar
Conference (1984 : Footscray Institute of
Technology).
NOTES: In, Physical education in Australia: past,
present and future directions, s.l., Footscray
Institute of Technology, 1984, p. 135-140.
LEVEL: I LANG: Eng SIRC ARTICLE NO: 096154

McIntyre, M. Marketing olympism in the schools.
(Refs: 4)*TAHPERD journal (Austin, Tex.) 52(2), Feb
1984, 8;45.*
LEVEL: B LANG: Eng SIRC ARTICLE NO: 093013

Melograno, V. The balanced curriculum: where is
it? What is it? (Refs: 10)*Journal of physical
education, recreation & dance (Reston, Va.) 55(6),
Aug 1984, 21-24;52.*
LEVEL: I LANG: Eng SIRC ARTICLE NO: 097663

Phillips, R. The physical education curriculum in
schools. *Bulletin of physical education (London)
20(2), Summer 1984, 11-21.*
CONF: British Association of Advisers and
Lecturers in Physical Education. Congress (64th :
1984 : Cardiff).
LEVEL: I LANG: Eng SIRC ARTICLE NO: 104227

Promotion of physical education and sport.
*ACHPER national journal (Kingswood, Aust.) 104,
Winter 1984, 28-29.*
LEVEL: B LANG: Eng SIRC ARTICLE NO: 100844

Sartorius, S. Solberg, E. Physical management -
a class to meet individual needs. (Refs: 10)*Journal
of physical education, recreation and dance
(Reston, Va.) 55(8), Oct 1984, 15-16.*
LEVEL: B LANG: Eng SIRC ARTICLE NO: 100846

Standards for graduate programs in physical
education. *Journal of physical education, recreation
& dance 55(2), Feb 1984, 54-62.*
LEVEL: B LANG: Eng SIRC ARTICLE NO: 091637

Thorpe, R. Bunker, D. Almond, L. Four
fundamentals for planning a games curriculum.
(Refs: 7)*Bulletin of physical education (London)
20(1), Spring 1984, 24-28.*
LEVEL: B LANG: Eng SIRC ARTICLE NO: 102701

Tripps, D.G. Olympic Scientific Congress: sport
science and the physical education curriculum.
(Refs: 2)*Journal of physical education, recreation &
dance 55(2), Feb 1984, 31-33.*
LEVEL: B LANG: Eng SIRC ARTICLE NO: 091645

Turner, L.F. Turner, S.L. Alternative sports and
games for the new physical education. Palo Alto,
Calif.: Peek Publications, c1984. vi, 143 p. : ill.

LEVEL: B LANG: Eng ISBN: 0-917962-76-1 GV341
20754

Virgilio, S.J. A paradigm for curriculum
implementation. (Refs: 10)*Journal of teaching in
physical education (Champaign, Ill.) 4(1), Oct 1984,
57-63.*
ABST: The purpose of this article is twofold: to
discuss some current problems with curriculum
design in physical education, and to offer some
suggestions for model-based attempts to assist the
process of implementing a new curriculum. The
process of curriculum implementation can be
broken into two phases, the preoperational stage
and the operational stage. Several issues within
each of the two stages are discussed, for
curriculum changes in general and specifically for
physical education. The key elements in curriculum
implementation are: support (material and human),
changes strategies, communication channels, staff
development, and instructional planning. Each
element has its own role to play in the process, and
the lack of any single element will severely hinder
the efficacy of the changes desired. The final of the
article presents a model of the curriculum change
process as outlined in the text.
LEVEL: A LANG: Eng SIRC ARTICLE NO: 102702

Willgoose, C.E. Curriculum in physical education.
4th ed. Englewood Cliffs, N.J.: Prentice-Hall,
c1984. x, 406 p.
NOTES: Includes bibliographies and index.
LEVEL: I LANG: Eng ISBN: 0131960725 LC CARD:
83-011159 GV341 17065

Williamson, T. Training the curriculum leader.
*Bulletin of physical education (Leeds, Eng.) 20(3),
Autumn/Winter 1984, 17-20.*
LEVEL: B LANG: Eng SIRC ARTICLE NO: 105430

Wispe, C. Rhythmic movement activities and dance
in education. (Refs: 4)*KAPHER journal (Richmond,
Ky.) 20(1), Winter 1984, 6-7.*
LEVEL: B LANG: Eng SIRC ARTICLE NO: 094539

Wright, J.J. Teaching Olympism in the schools.
(Refs: 5)*WAHPERD, journal (Milwaukee, Wis.)
13(1), May 1984, 6;27.*
LEVEL: LANG: Eng SIRC ARTICLE NO: 100847

PROGRAMS - ELEMENTARY
SCHOOL

Atack, M. Case study 3. *Bulletin of physical
education (Leeds, Eng.) 20(3), Autumn/Winter
1984, 24-26.*
LEVEL: B LANG: Eng SIRC ARTICLE NO: 105394

Bean, D. Program design in teaching games to
children. (Refs: 4)*Asian journal of physical
education (Taiwan, China) 7(2), Jul 1984, 67-75.*
NOTES: Abstract in Chinese.
LEVEL: I LANG: Eng SIRC ARTICLE NO: 099149

Bean, D. Child centered approaches and the
development of quality in primary school physical
education. (Refs: 7)*In, Simri, U. (ed.), et al.,
Preschool and elementary school children and
physical activity. Proceedings of the 26th ICHPER
World Congress 1983, Wingate Institute, Israel, vol.
III, Jerusalem, Israel, 1984, p. 18-22.*
CONF: ICHPER World Congress (26th : 1983 :
Wingate Institute, Israel).
LEVEL: I LANG: Eng GV443 20093

Carson, L. Meeting developmental needs in early
elementary physical education. (Refs:
2)*WVAHPERD journal (Morgantown, W. Va.) 2(1),*

Winter/Spring 1984, 8-9.
LEVEL: B LANG: Eng SIRC ARTICLE NO: 097650

Collins, J. Children's play and its importance in
primary schools. (Refs: 5)
CONF: Physical Education Graduating Seminar
Conference (1984 : Footscray Institute of
Technology).
NOTES: In, Physical education in Australia: past,
present and future directions, s.l., Footscray
Institute of Technology, 1984, p. 34-37.
LEVEL: I LANG: Eng SIRC ARTICLE NO: 096132

Higginbotham, P.E. Philips, K. What's happening
in elementary physical education classes in the
state of Florida? *Florida JOHPERD (Gainesville,
Fla.) 22(3), Aug 1984, 6-8.*
LEVEL: I LANG: Eng SIRC ARTICLE NO: 099157

Innovative tasks and problems solving activities for
elementry (sic) school children. *Physical education
newsletter (Old Saybrook, Conn.) 165, Dec 1984,
5-6.*
LEVEL: B LANG: Eng SIRC ARTICLE NO: 173339

Martinet, P.H. Escalade et grimper. *EPS: Revue
education physique et sport (Paris) 188, juil/aout
1984, 54-55.*
LEVEL: B LANG: Fr SIRC ARTICLE NO: 097662

McKee, D. Daily quality physical education for
elementary students: long overdue. (Refs:
12)*OPHEA: Ontario Physical and Health Education
Association 10(3), 19-22.*
LEVEL: B LANG: Eng SIRC ARTICLE NO: 102685

Mertens, C. A program for training of perception
through movement. (Refs: 29)*In, Simri, U. (ed.), et
al., Preschool and elementary school children and
physical activity. Proceedings of the 26th ICHPER
World Congress 1983, Wingate Institute, Israel, vol.
III, Jerusalem, Israel, 1984, p. 99-108.*
CONF: ICHPER World Congress (26th : 1983 :
Wingate Institute, Israel).
LEVEL: A LANG: Eng GV443 20093

Parachute activities. *OPHEA: Ontario Physical and
Health Education Association (London, Ont.) 10(2),
Spring 1984, 43-48.*
LEVEL: B LANG: Eng SIRC ARTICLE NO: 099173

Physical education for the elementary school child.
(Refs: 7)*Physician and sportsmedicine 12(4), Apr
1984, 98-104;109-111;115.*
LEVEL: B LANG: Eng SIRC ARTICLE NO: 093018

Rose, C. A means of evaluating experiences in
primary physical education. *Bulletin of physical
education (Leeds, Eng.) 20(3), Autumn/Winter
1984, 27-32.*
LEVEL: B LANG: Eng SIRC ARTICLE NO: 105423

Ryan, A.J. Do children need physical education?
Physician and sportsmedicine 12(4), Apr 1984, 41.
LEVEL: B LANG: Eng SIRC ARTICLE NO: 093026

Saccone, P.P. It's 'funner' to be a runner physical
education/classroom program. Alexandria, Va.:
Computer Microform International, 1984. 1
microfiche (31 fr.); 10 x 15 cm.
LEVEL: B LANG: Eng EDRS: ED242660 ERIC
242660

Seefeldt, V. Influence of the content and
methodology in physical activity programs on the
motor, physiological, and psychological
characteristics of children. (Refs: 32)*In, Simri, U.
(ed.), et al., Preschool and elementary school
children and physical activity. Proceedings of the
26th ICHPER World Congress 1983, Wingate*

Institute, Israel, vol. III, Jerusalem, Israel, 1984, p. 7-17.
CONF: ICHPER World Congress (26th : 1983 : Wingate Institute, Israel).
LEVEL: I LANG: Eng GV443 20093

Siedentop, D. Herkowitz, J. Rink, J. Elementary physical education methods. Englewood Cliffs, N.J.: Prentice-Hall, c1984. xix, 491 p.
NOTES: Includes index. Bibliography: p. 479-484.
LEVEL: I LANG: Eng ISBN: 0132593823 LC CARD: 83-004585 GV363 15500

Simri, U. Eldar, D. Lieberman, S. Preschool and elementary school children and physical activity. Proceeding of the 26th ICHPER World Congress 1983, Wingate Institute, Israel, vol. III. Jerusalem, Israel: E. Gill Pub. House : Wingate Institute for Physical Education and Sport, 1984. 171 p. : ill.
CONF: International Council on Health, Physical Education and Recreation World Congress (26th : 1983 : Wingate Institute).
CORP: Wingate Institute for Physical Education and Sport.
NOTES: Includes bibliographies.
LEVEL: A LANG: Eng LC CARD: 85-100427 GV443 20093

Smith, N. The place of physical education in the primary school curriculum. *Bulletin of physical education (Leeds, Eng.) 20(3), Autumn/Winter 1984, 5-15.*
LEVEL: B LANG: Eng SIRC ARTICLE NO: 105425

Smith, T.L. Put some sock into it. (Refs: 6)*Journal of physical education, recreation & dance 55(1), Jan 1984, 52-53.*
LEVEL: B LANG: Eng SIRC ARTICLE NO: 091635

Tillman, K.G. Toner, P.R. You'll never guess what we did in gym today: more new physical education games and activities. Wes Nyack, N.Y.: Parker Pub. Co., c1984. 228 p. : ill.
LEVEL: B LANG: Eng ISBN: 0-13-977075-5 LC CARD: 83-22071 GV443 17973

Wasmund-Bodenstedt, U. Research findings on the impact of a daily physical exercise program on the biological, motor and psycho-social development of children in primary schools. (Refs: 3)*In, Simri, U. (ed.), et al., Preschool and elementary school children and physical activity. Proceedings of the 26th ICHPER World Congress 1983, Wingate Institute, Israel, vol. III, Jerusalem, Israel, 1984, p. 154-162.*
CONF: ICHPER World Congress (26th : 1983 : Wingate Institute, Israel).
LEVEL: A LANG: Eng GV443 20093

PROGRAMS - SECONDARY SCHOOL

Allan, D. Thompson, T. Twenty years of health and P.E. in Queensland State Secondary Schools - will the next twenty be any better? (Refs: 20)*ACHPER national journal (Kingswood, Aust.) 105, Spring 1984, 55-61.*
LEVEL: I LANG: Eng SIRC ARTICLE NO: 102649

Baker, R. Bridging the Gap - an alternative approach to the early years of Secondary School Physical Education. *Bulletin of physical education (Leeds, Eng.) 20(3), Autumn/Winter 1984, 36-37.*
LEVEL: B LANG: Eng SIRC ARTICLE NO: 105395

Bean, D. Program design in teaching games to children. (Refs: 4)*Asian journal of physical education (Taiwan, China) 7(2), Jul 1984, 67-75.*

NOTES: Abstract in Chinese.
LEVEL: I LANG: Eng SIRC ARTICLE NO: 099149

Conducting a junior high elective program in all disciplines. *Physical education newsletter (Old Saybrook, Conn.) 161, Aug 1984, 4-6.*
LEVEL: B LANG: Eng SIRC ARTICLE NO: 100826

Fisher, R. Case study 2. *Bulletin of physical education (Leeds, Eng.) 20(3), Autumn/Winter 1984, 23-24.*
LEVEL: B LANG: En SIRC ARTICLE NO: 105400

Gallois, A. Organisation et evaluation en terminale. *EPS: Education physique et sport (Paris, France) 186, mars/avr 1984, 30-32.*
LEVEL: B LANG: Fr SIRC ARTICLE NO: 094515

Howell, M. Jordan, B.J. Body/mind research: an integrated physical education and science class. (Refs: 1)*Journal of physica education, recreation & dance 55(3), Mar 1984, 80-81.*
LEVEL: B LANG: Eng SIRC ARTICLE NO: 093008

Independent study in high school physical education. *Physical education newsletter (Old Saybrook, Conn.) 163, Oct 1984, 8.*
LEVEL: B LANG: Eng SIRC ARTICLE NO: 105403

Jefferson High School district returns to three year P.E. graduation requirements. Board accepts new competency-based program. *CAHPERD journal times (Danville, Calif.) 46(8), May 1984, 5;7.*
LEVEL: B LANG: Eng SIRC ARTICLE NO: 094520

Lang, L. A course in sports studies. *Scottish journal of physical education (Glasgow, Scotland) 12(1), Jan 1984, 9-13.*
LEVEL: I LANG: Eng SIRC ARTICLE NO: 094521

Nichols, A. Emerging trends in physical education in Australian secondary schools. (Refs: 9)
CONF: Physical Education Graduating Seminar Conference (1984 : Footscray Institute of Technology).
NOTES: In, Physical education in Australia: past, present and future directions, s.l., Footscray Institute of Technology, 1984, p. 142-153.
LEVEL: A LANG: Eng SIRC ARTICLE NO: 096160

Osness, W.H. A response to the national reports. *NASSP bulletin (Reston, Va.) 68(470), Mar 1984, 24-27.*
LEVEL: B LANG: En SIRC ARTICLE NO: 096161

Parrish, B. Reading practices and possibilities in physical education. (Refs: 21)*Journal of physical education, recreation dance 55(3), Mar 1984, 73-77.*
LEVEL: B LANG: Eng SIRC ARTICLE NO: 093017

Petrelli, J.J. Lifting a P.E. program out of the doldrums. An optional choice survey approach to program development. *Scholastic coach (New York) 54(4), Nov 1984, 40;42.*
LEVEL: B LANG: Eng SIRC ARTICLE NO: 102688

Riley, D.R. Ollerup Gymnastics High School: a modern programme built on the spirit of the past. (Refs: 3)*Physical educator (Indianapolis) 41(4), Dec 1984, 179-180.*
LEVEL: B LANG: Eng SIRC ARTICLE NO: 104229

Stimulating student interest in high school physical education. *Physical education newsletter (Old Saybrook, Conn.) 164, Nov 1984, 6-7.*
LEVEL: B LANG: Eng SIRC ARTICLE NO: 173183

The state of the art: California physical education. *CAHPERD journal times (Danville, Calif.) 46(8), May 1984, 8-9.*

ABST: Excerpted from: a study of the decline of physical education in California's schools, March 1984.
LEVEL: B LANG: Eng SIRC ARTICLE NO: 094535

PROGRAMS - UNIVERSITY AND COLLEGE

Butler, K.N. Rejuvenating general education via personalized health fitness. (Refs: 2)*NAPEHE proceedings (Champaign, Ill.) 5, 1984, 152-154.*
CONF: National Association for Physical Education in Higher Education. Annual Conference (1984 : College Park, Md.).
NOTES: Conference theme: Current challenge: revitalization or obsolescence? (Required phys ed.).
LEVEL: B LANG: Eng SIRC ARTICLE NO: 102655

Caporali, J.M. Disc sports in physical education. (Refs: 3)*Journal of physical education, recreation & dance (Reston, Va.) 55(4), Apr 1984, 72-73.*
LEVEL: B LANG: Eng SIRC ARTICLE NO: 094510

Hassen, C. Considerations for maximum utilization of the university program. Pour profiter au maximum de son programme universitaire. *CAHPER journal (Ottawa) 51(2), Nov/Dec 1984, 38-39.*
NOTES: Part of a series of Administrative Tips prepared by the Administration Committee of CAHPER. Ces conseils en administration proviennent de la serie preparee par le comite d'administration de l'ACSEPL.
LEVEL: B LANG: Eng Fr SIRC ARTICLE NO: 102721

Hopper, C. Knowledge - toward an integration. (Refs: 7)*Journal of physical education, recreation & dance 55(3), Mar 1984, 66-68.*
LEVEL: B LANG: Eng SIRC ARTICLE NO: 093006

Mauffrey, D. L'organisation du Bac-EPS au Lycee de Martigues. *EPS: Education physique et sport (Paris) 187, mai/juin 1984, 28-36.*
LEVEL: B LANG: Fr SIRC ARTICLE NO: 096151

Milner, E.K. Baker, J.A.W. Collins, M.S. Skiing for credit: a concentrated program. (Refs: 1)*Journal of physical education, recreation & dance 55(1), Jan 1984, 50-51.*
LEVEL: B LANG: Eng SIRC ARTICLE NO: 092376

Neate, D. The development of a programme. *Bulletin of physical education (London) 20(2), Summer 1984, 27-34.*
CONF: Britis Association of Advisers and Lecturers in Physical Education. Congress (64th : 1984 : Cardiff).
LEVEL: I LANG: Eng SIRC ARTICLE NO: 104225

Pineau, C. Baccalaureat 1984: les nouvelles epreuves d'education physique et sportive. *EPS: Education physique et sport 185 janv/fevr 1984, 38-39.*
LEVEL: B LANG: Fr SIRC ARTICLE NO: 093020

Rousseau, J.J. Le travail collectif preparatoire a l'organisation des nouvelles epreuves d'EPS au baccalaureat dans l'Academie de Paris. *EPS: Education physique et sport 185, janv/fevr 1984, 39-42.*
LEVEL: B LANG: Fr SIRC ARTICLE NO: 093024

Schendel, J.S. Activity courses: changing patterns of support. (Refs: 2)*Journal of physical education, recreation & dance (Reston, Va.) 55(5), May/Jun 1984, 46-48;58.*
LEVEL: B LANG: Eng SIRC ARTICLE NO: 094531

Smith, T. The physical education curriculum - 16 - 19 years age group. *Bulletin of physical education (London) 20(2), Summe 1984, 22-26.* CONF: British Association of Advisers and Lecturers in Physical Education. Congress (64th : 1984 : Cardiff). LEVEL: I LANG: Eng SIRC ARTICLE NO: 104235

Sturtevant, M. Use management techniques to assess programs. *Journal of physical education, recreation & dance (Reston, Va. 55(5), May/Jun 1984, 48.* LEVEL: B LANG: Eng SIRC ARTICLE NO: 094536

Trimble, R.T. Hensley, L.D. The general instruction program in physical education at four-year colleges and universities: 1982. (Refs: 4)*Journal of physical education, recreation & dance (Reston, Va.) 55(5), May/Jun 1984, 82-89.* LEVEL: I LANG: Eng SIRC ARTICLE NO: 094537

Wilke, B.J. The future of the general instruction physical education program in higher education: a delphi study. Eugene, Ore.: Microform Publications, University of Oregon, 1984. 3 microfiches : negative, ill. ; 11 x 15 cm. NOTES: Thesis (Ed.D.) - West Virginia University, 1982; (xiv, 200 leaves); vita; includes bibliography. LEVEL: A LANG: Eng UO84 182-184

PSYCHOLOGY

Arnold, P.J. Personality and the effect of physical education on its development. (Refs: 17)*Bulletin of the Federation internationale d'education physique (Cheltenham, Eng.) 54(2), Apr/Jun 1984, 39-45.* LEVEL: B LANG: Eng SIRC ARTICLE NO: 102650

Carlisle, C. Phillips, D.A. The effects of enthusiasm training on selected teacher and student behaviors in preservice physical education teachers. (Refs: 20)*Journal of teaching in physical education (Champaign, Ill.) 4(1), Oct 1984, 64-75.* ABST: Teacher enthusiasm has long been considered an important part of the teaching process. Twenty-four preservice teachers participated in this study to determine the differences in teacher and student behavior between the levels of enthusiasm in trained and untrained teachers. The experimental group was given 6 hours of enthusiasm training whereas the control group received no such training. Both groups taught a 30-minute Experimental Teacher Unit (ETU) to a total of 120 middle-school students. The observation instrument in this study was the Physical Education Teaching Assessment Instrument (PETAI), while the Collins Enthusiasm Rating Scale was used to measure the teachers' enthusiasm. The trained teachers received much higher ratings on their ETU lessons and were significantly better on three of the PETAI items. The students of the trained teachers also had higher skill achievement gains over their counterparts under the untrained teachers. LEVEL: A LANG: Eng SIRC ARTICLE NO: 102656

Coe, M.J. Children's perception of physical education in the middle school. (Refs: 6)*Physical education review (North Humberside, Eng.) 7(2), Autumn 1984, 120-125.* LEVEL: I LANG: Eng SIRC ARTICLE NO: 105397

Eayrs, M.A. The effect of a creative problem solving instructional unit upon the level of creative productivity of selected physical education and recreation majors. Eugene, Ore.: Microform Publications, University of Oregon, 1984. 2

microfiches : negative, ill. ; 11 x 15 cm. NOTES: Thesis (D.Ed.) - University of Oregon, 1982; (xi, 136 leaves); vita; includes bibliography. LEVEL: A LANG: Eng UO84 62-63

Gmelch, W.H. Sharratt, G. Stress wellness through exercise and physical education. (Refs: 5)*Washington journal of health, physical education, recreation and dance (Bellingham, Wash.) Winter 1983, 8;10.* LEVEL: B LANG: Eng SIRC ARTICLE NO: 104408

Harris, W.H. Kelly, B.J. Teacher stress. (Refs: 10)*TAHPERD journal (Austin, Tex.) 52(2), Feb 1984, 6-7;44-45.* LEVEL: B LANG: Eng SIRC ARTICLE NO: 093003

Hatfield, B.D. Psychological knowledge and its emerging role in the physical education curriculum. (Refs: 25)*NAPEHE proceedings (Champaign, Ill.) 5, 1984, 60-68.* CONF: National Association for Physical Education in Higher Education. Annual Conference (1984 : College Park, Md.) . NOTES: Conference theme: Current challenge: revitalization or obsolescence? LEVEL: I LANG: Eng SIRC ARTICLE NO: 102851

Horton, L. What do we know about teacher burnout? (Refs: 21)*Journal of physical education, recreation & dance 55(3), Mar 1984, 69-71.* LEVEL: B LANG: Eng SIRC ARTICLE NO: 093007

Johnson, S.B. Student expectations and dyadic interactions with physical education teachers of third-grade children. Eugene, Ore.: Microform Publications, University of Oregon, 1984. 3 microfiches : negative, ill. ; 11 x 15 cm. NOTES: Thesis (Ed.D.) - University of North Carolina at Greensboro, 1982; (xi, 192 leaves); includes bibliography. LEVEL: A LANG: Eng UO84 290-292

Kamlesh, M.L. Singh, B. Kaur, K. A peep into personality variables with regard to prospective physical education teachers. (Refs: 45)*SNIPES journal (Patiala, India) 7(4), Oct 1984, 42-48.* ABST: The authors studied the personality traits of 57 physical education student teachers (34 men, 23 women), in the age-group 19-35. Sex differences were observed: women achieved better academic results; men were more extroverted, and women were more neurotic. The Sports Competition Anxiety Test was administered to the subjects. The variables cognitive worry, somatic tension, and self-confidence yielded no significant differences between men and women. LEVEL: A LANG: Eng SIRC ARTICLE NO: 171615

Lydon, M.C. Cheffers, J.T.F. Decision-making in elementary school-age children: effects upon motor learning and self-concept development. (Refs: 19)*Research quarterly for exercise & sport (Reston, Va.) 55(2), Jun 1984, 135-140.* ABST: This study investigated the effects of variable decision-making models upon the development of body coordination and self-concept of 285 children in grades one through five. The children were from two schools which were equivalent in terms of socioeconomic status. The experimental school received two physical education programs which varied only in the type of teacher behavior exhibited. The control school did not receive any treatment. The results indicate that students can be given decision-making responsibility in physical education class and maintain a level of motor skill achievement equal to that of students who have not been allowed to

make decisions in physical education class. There were no conclusions concerning the effects of student decision on self-concept. LEVEL: A LANG: Eng SIRC ARTICLE NO: 096149

Man, F. Hondlik, J. (Use of compulsory lessons of physical training at an elementary school for the stimulation of the achievement motivation of pupils in the socialist school. (Refs: 29)*Ceskoslovenska psychologie (Prague) 28(5), 1984, 411-420.* LEVEL: A LANG: Cze

Man, F. Hondlik, J. Use of compulsory lessons of physical training for the stimulation of achievement motivation of pupils a an elementary school. (Refs: 22)*International journal of sport psychology (Rome, Italy) 15(4), 1984, 259-270.* ABST: This paper presents a motivation training program which was integrated in the normal course of physical education in the 4th forms of the elementary school. This program was based on the application of the following principles: realistic goal-setting; adequate use of the patterns of attribution, also with respect to prospective orientation: individual reference-norm oriented achievement evaluation; cooperation as a factor conditioning a successful result in a number of situations. The program lasted 5 months, two lessons of physical education a week. Total values of achievement motivation for all six spheres did not show any statistically significant difference between the experimental and the control samples. LEVEL: A LANG: Eng SIRC ARTICLE NO: 106670

Mancini, V.H. Wuest, D.A. Vantine, K.W. Clark, E.K. The use of instruction and supervision in interaction analysis on burned out teachers: its effects on teaching behaviors, levels of burn out, and academic learning time. (Refs: 33)*Journal of teaching in physical education (Blacksburg, Va.) 3(2), Winter 1984, 29-46.* ABST: Six teachers, who had been assigned a high burnout score using the Maslach Burnout Inventory (MBI), were divided into control and treatment groups. Treatment consisted of feedback on their teaching performance and instruction and supervision through Cheffers' Adaptation of Flanders' interaction Analysis System (CAFIAS). After five days of treatment, teachers in the treatment group verbally and nonverbally praised and accepted their students ideas and efforts more, used more verbal questions to elicit students' input, and provided students with more information. Academic Learning Time increased in both groups but the increase was larger in the treatment group. The treatment group perceived themselves as less burned out at the conclusion of the study. LEVEL: A LANG: Eng SIRC ARTICLE NO: 093153

Marsh, J.J. Measuring affective objectives in physical education. (Refs: 4)*Physical educator (Bloomington, Ind.) 41(2), May 1984, 77-81.* LEVEL: I LANG: Eng SIRC ARTICLE NO: 099166

Martinek, T.J. Karper, W.G. Multivariate relationships of specific impression, cues with teacher expectations and dyadic interactions in elementary physical education classes. (Refs: 31) *Research quarterly for exercise & sport (Reston, Va.) 55(1), Mar 1984, 32-40.* ABST: The purpose of this study was to investigate the relationship of student physical attractiveness and expression of effort to expectations of the teacher, and to describe how expectations were related to teacher - student interactions. Three elementary physical education teachers and 128 children (K-3) served as subjects. The teachers

were asked to rate their students according to physical attractiveness, expression of effort, and four expectancy variables, while three other observers used a previously described observation system to describe teacher - student interactions. From the results it was determined that for the younger group teachers' expectations for social relations and cooperative behavior were significantly related to teacher praise, direction-giving, criticism, and predictable student response. For the older group the teachers' expectation for cooperative behavior was related to eight behavioral variables.
LEVEL: A LANG: Eng SIRC ARTICLE NO: 096150

Martinek, T.J. Karper, W.B. The effects of noncompetitive and competitive instructional climates on teacher expectancy effects in elementary physical education classes. (Refs: 35)*Journal of sport psychology (Champaign, Ill.) 6(4), Dec 1984, 408-421.*
ABST: The purpose of this study was to describe the operation of teacher expectancy effects within two instructional climates of elementary physical education classes. Specifically, high and low expectancy groups were compared during noncompetitive and competitive instruction in terms of teacher-student interaction and perceived expression of effort. Four alternating experimental phases of instruction were employed. Analysis of the interaction data revealed that low expectancy students perceived significantly more praise and encouragement during the first (noncompetitive) phase and the fourth (competitive) phase than did high expectancy students. They also received significantly more empathy from their teachers during both competitive phases of instruction. High expectancy students were perceived to exhibit significantly more effort than low expectancy students during all four phases.
LEVEL: A LANG: Eng SIRC ARTICLE NO: 104223

Pieron, M. Wauquier, P. Modification de comportements d'enseignement chez des etudiants en education physique en stage d'agregation. (Refs: 21)*Revue de l'education physique (Liege, Belgique) 24(4), 1984, 29-37.*
LEVEL: A LANG: Fr SIRC ARTICLE NO: 104228

Placek, J.H. Involving the nonparticipant: motivation and make-ups. (Refs: 12)*Journal of physical education, recreation & dance (Reston, Va.) 55(6), Aug 1984, 27-29.*
LEVEL: I LANG: Eng SIRC ARTICLE NO: 097667

Rolider, A. Cooper, J. Van Houten, R. Effects of modeling, instruction and grade incentives on supportive verbalizations among peers in a college physical education class. (Refs: 31)*Journal of teaching in physical education (Blacksburg, Va.) 3(3), Spring 1984, 44-50.*
ABST: This study compared the effects of modeling instruction and grade incentives to the rate of positive statements among teammates during game playing in a college basketball class. The results indicate that the grade incentive was very effective in producing positive statements among teammates. Although not as effective as the grade incentive condition the teacher modeling condition produced a large increase in positive statements among teammates over the baseline rate. Least effective in producing positive statements among teammates was the instructional method.
LEVEL: A LANG: Eng SIRC ARTICLE NO: 096339

Williams, L.R.T. Relationships among body-esteem, self-esteem and attitudes of pupils towards

physical education. (Refs: 8) *New Zealand journal of health, physical education & recreation (Wellington, N.Z.) 17(1), May 1984, 10-11.*
LEVEL: I LANG: Eng SIRC ARTICLE NO: 097672

Zakrajsek, D.B. Johnson, R.L. Walker, D.B. Comparison of learning styles between physical education and dance majors. (Refs: 6)*Perceptual and motor skills (Missoula, Mont.) 58(2), Apr 1984, 583-588.*
ABST: This paper investigates the learning styles of 80 dance and 87 physical education majors. Kolb's Learning Style Inventory, which assesses the level of abstractness or concreteness and the level of activity or reflectivity, was used in the assessment. Findings indicate no significant differences between the two majors or between female and male students.
LEVEL: A LANG: Eng SIRC ARTICLE NO: 094540

RESEARCH

Abstracts of research papers 1984. Presented at the Anaheim, California Convention of the American Alliance for Health, Physical Education, Recreation and Dance in the Research Consortium meetings. Reston, Va.: AAHPERD, c1984. 169 p. (Abstracts of research papers 1984.)
CONF: American Alliance for Health, Physical Education, Recreation and Dance. Convention (1984 : Anaheim, Cal.)
CORP: American Alliance for Health, Physical Educaltion, Recreation and Dance.
LEVEL: A LANG: Eng ISBN: 0883142856

Brack, C. Lamon, A. Otter-Schouten, C. Psychomotor research and psychomotor stimulation of pre-school children. (Refs: 7)*In Simri, U. (ed.), et al., Preschool and elementary school children and physical activity. Proceedings of the 26th ICHPER World Congress 1983, Wingate Institute, Israel, vol. III, Jerusalem, Israel, 1984, p. 23-31.*
CONF: ICHPER World Congress (26th : 1983 : Wingate Institute, Israel).
LEVEL: A LANG: Eng GV443 20093

Carlson, B.R. McKenzie, T.L. Computer technology for recording, storing, and analyzing temporal data in physical activity settings. (Refs: 20)*Journal of teaching in physical education (Champaign, Ill.) 4(1), Oct 1984, 24-29.*
ABST: This article addresses one of the most critical problems for doing research on teaching using time based variables. In the past, when duration recording was the observational technique, there were two ways to collect data: either through multiple stop watches or through interval recording. Both methods have their limitations - one in the manipulation of the several watches and the other in converting interval data to accurate units of time. Outlined in this article is a microcomputer program for on-site duration coding, data analysis, permanent storage, and mainframe support for research on teaching physical education. The system is complex by design but practical to use. It produces total observation time, total time by category, frequency by category, mean length of occurrence, and the percent of total time each category was observed.
LEVEL: I LANG: Eng SIRC ARTICLE NO: 102657

Clarke, D.H. Clarke, H.H. Research processes in physical education. 2nd ed. Englewood Cliffs, N.J.: Prentice-Hall, c1984. viii, 472 p.
NOTES: Includes bibliographies and indexes. Rev. ed. of: Research processes in physical education,

recreation, and health, c1970.
LEVEL: A LANG: Eng ISBN: 0137745133 LC CARD: 83-013653 GV361 15615

Entretien avec...Robert Merand. *EPS: Education physique et sport (Paris, France) 186, mars/avr 1984, 5-10.*
LEVEL: B LANG: F SIRC ARTICLE NO: 094513

EPS interroge Joel de Rosnay. (Refs: 5)*EPS: Education physique et sport 185, janv/fevr 1984, 4-10.*
LEVEL: B LANG: Fr SIRC ARTICLE NO: 093224

Locke, L.F. Preface. *Journal of teaching in physical education (Blacksburg, Va.) 2, Summer 1984, 3-11.*
NOTES: Special issue: Research on teaching teachers: where are we now?
LEVEL: I LANG: Eng SIRC ARTICLE NO: 102673

Locke, L.F. Research on preservice teacher education, 1960-1981. *Journal of teaching in physical education (Blacksburg, Va. 2, Summer 1984, 13-21.*
NOTES: Special issue: Research on teaching teachers: where are we now?
LEVEL: I LANG: Eng SIRC ARTICLE NO: 102674

Locke, L.F. Overview of the RTE-PE literature, 1960-1981. *Journal of teaching in physical education (Blacksburg, Va.) 2, Summer 1984, 23-37.*
NOTES: Special issue: Research on teaching teachers: where are we now?
LEVEL: I LANG: Eng SIRC ARTICLE NO: 102675

Locke, L.F. Overview of the RTE-PE literature, 1981-1984. *Journal of teaching in physical education (Blacksburg, Va.) 2, Summer 1984, 39-44.*
NOTES: Special issue: Research on teaching teachers: where are we now?
LEVEL: I LANG: Eng SIRC ARTICLE NO: 102676

Locke, L.F. RTE: a review of reviews. *Journal of teaching in physical education (Blacksburg, Va.) 2, Summer 1984, 45-58.*
NOTES: Special issue: Research on teaching teachers: where are we now?
LEVEL: I LANG: Eng SIRC ARTICLE NO: 102677

Locke, L.F. How to RTE-PE for (both) fun and profit: Popham's poltergeist. *Journal of teaching in physical education (Blacksburg, Va.) 2, Summer 1984, 59-61.*
NOTES: Special issue: Research on teaching teachers: where are we now?
LEVEL: B LANG: Eng SIRC ARTICLE NO: 102678

Locke, L.F. References. *Journal of teaching in physical education (Blacksburg, Va.) 2, Summer 1984, 63-85.*
NOTES: Special issue: Research on teaching teachers: where are we now?
ABST: Over 400 references are listed relating to the subject of teaching research.
LEVEL: I LANG: Eng SIRC ARTICLE NO: 102679

Myors, R. The impact of research on physical education. (Refs: 9)
CONF: Physical Education Graduating Seminar Conference (1984 : Footscray Institute of Technology).
NOTES: In, Physical education in Australia: past, present and future directions, s.l., Footscray Institute of Technology, 1984, p. 27-32.
LEVEL: I LANG: Eng SIRC ARTICLE NO: 096158

Ryu, C.M. Creative pedagogical concepts for physical education. *Asian journal of physical*

education (Taipei, Taiwan) 7(3), Oct 1984, 12-19.
LEVEL: I LANG: Eng Chi SIRC ARTICLE NO: 102693

Wildman, T.M. A perspective on the utilization of research to improve teaching. (Refs: 41)*Journal of teaching in physical education (Blacksburg, Va.) 2, Summer 1984, 87-95.*
NOTES: Special issue: Research on teaching teachers: where are we now?
LEVEL: I LANG: Eng SIRC ARTICLE NO: 102703

Young, J.C. Revitalization through collaboration: instructional analysis in physical education. (Refs: 12)*NAPEHE proceeding (Champaign, Ill.) 5, 1984, 146-151.*
CONF: National Association for Physical Education in Higher Education. Annual Conference (1984 : College Park, Md.).
NOTES: Conference theme: Current challenge: revitalization or obsolescence?
LEVEL: A LANG: Eng SIRC ARTICLE NO: 102704

RESEARCH METHODS

McKinzer, T.L. Carlson, B.R. Computer technology for exercise and sport pedagogy recording, storing and analyzing internal data. (Refs: 18)*Journal of teaching in physical education (Blacksburg, Va.) 3(3), Spring 1984, 17-27.*
ABST: This article discussed the advantages of using a portable briefcase computer in sport pedagogy research. The computer allows complex questions concerning teacher and coach behavior to be addressed with a minimal increase in the time demand of the researcher. The author describes the hardware of the briefcase computer.
LEVEL: A LANG: Eng SIRC ARTICLE NO: 096155

SOCIAL PSYCHOLOGY

Palmer, G.M. A study of the relationships of leadership behavior, organizational climate, and demographic data in physical education departments at selected colleges and universities in Canada and the United States. Eugene, Ore.: Microform Publications, University of Oregon, 1984. 3 microfiches : negative, ill. ; 11 x 15 cm.
NOTES: Thesis (Ph.D.) - University of Oregon, 1982; (xvii, 256 leaves); vita; includes bibliography.
LEVEL: A LANG: Eng UO84 47-49

SOCIOLOGY

Bironneau, M. Pociello, C. L'EPS demain...enquete aupres de nouveaux agreges. *EPS: Revue education physique et sport (Paris 188, juil/aout 1984, 43-45.*
LEVEL: B LANG: Fr SIRC ARTICLE NO: 097648

Buckely, M. Physical education and ethnic participation. (Refs: 9)*Unpublished paper, Physical Education Graduating Seminar Conference, Australia, 1984, 1-4.*
CONF: Physical Education Graduating Seminar Conference (1984 : Footscray Institute of Technology).
LEVEL: B LANG: Eng SIRC ARTICLE NO: 096129

Demers, P.J. La base conceptuelle en education physique: de l'opposition a la complementarite. (Refs: 5)*CAHPER journal/Revu de l'ACSEPR (Vanier, Ont.) 50(3), janv/fevr 1984, 13-15.*
LEVEL: B LANG: Fr SIRC ARTICLE NO: 094511

Figley, G.E. Moral education through physical education. (Refs: 42)*Quest (Champaign, Ill.) 36(1),*

1984, 89-101.
LEVEL: I LANG: Eng SIRC ARTICLE NO: 099155

Griffin, P.S. Girls' participation patterns in a middle school team sports unit. (Refs: 10)*Journal of teaching in physical education (Champaign, Ill.) 4(1), Oct 1984, 30-38.*
ABST: The purpose of the study was to identify girls' participation patterns in a middle school team sport unit. Through class observations, formal interviews, and informal discussions with the physical education teachers, six styles of participation were identified. These were (a) athlete, (b) JV player, (c) cheerleader, (d) femme fatale, (e) lost soul, (f) system beater. A description of behavior, characteristic of the majority of the girls observed, outlined four kinds of nonassertive behaviour: (a) giving up, (b) giving away, (c) hanging back, and (d) acquiescing. Several contextual factors were identified as potentially contributing to the participation patterns identified. These were: availability of out-of-school team sport programs, community racial and socioeconomic status, the age group studied, and interactions with teachers and other students in the class.
LEVEL: A LANG: Eng SIRC ARTICLE NO: 102667

Hollands, R.G. The role of cultural studies and social criticism in the sociological study of sport. (Refs: 66)*Quest (Champaign, Ill.) 36(1), 1984, 66-79.*
LEVEL: I LANG: Eng SIRC ARTICLE NO: 099333

Lawson, H.A. Problem-setting for physical education and sport. (Refs: 59)*Quest (Champaign, Ill.) 36(1), 1984, 48-60.*
LEVEL: I LANG: Eng SIRC ARTICLE NO: 099164

Lindner, K.J. Influence of group-oriented and individual-oriented physical education programs on the social status and socia structure of fourth-grade classes. (Refs: 24)*In, Simri, U. (ed.), et al., Preschool and elementary school children and physical activity. Proceedings of the 26th ICHPER World Congress 1983, Wingate Institute, Israel, vol. III, Jerusalem, Israel, 1984, p. 89-98.*
CONF: ICHPER World Congress (26th : 1983 : Wingate Institute, Israel).
LEVEL: A LANG: Eng GV443 20093

Massengale, J.D. Social process and traditional physical education. (Refs: 15)*NAPEHE proceedings (Champaign, Ill.) 5, 1984, 69-74.*
CONF: National Association for Physical Education in Higher Education. Annual Conference (1984 : College Park, Md.).
NOTES: Conference theme: Current challenge: revitalization or obsolescence?
LEVEL: I LANG: Eng SIRC ARTICLE NO: 102909

Poitras, J.-G. A comparison of the attitudes of French-speaking and English-speaking students, parents, and teachers toward physical education. Eugene, Ore.: Microform Publications, University of Oregon, 1984. 2 microfiches : negative, ill. ; 11 x 15 cm.
NOTES: Thesis (D.P.E.) - Springfield College, 1983; (viii, 103 leaves); includes bibliography.
LEVEL: A LANG: Eng UO84 441-442

Pooley, J.C. Physical education and sport and the quality of life. *Journal of physical education, recreation & dance 55(3), Mar 1984, 45-48.*
LEVEL: B LANG: Eng SIRC ARTICLE NO: 093215

Rees, C.R. Applying sociology to physical education: who needs it? (Refs: 21)*NAPEHE proceedings (Champaign, Ill.) 5, 1984, 54-59.*

CONF: National Association for Physical Education in Higher Education. Annual conference (1984 : College Park, Md.).
NOTES: Conference theme: Current challenge: revitalization or obsolescence?
LEVEL: I LANG: Eng SIRC ARTICLE NO: 102912

Wiseman, E.D. Minimizing sex-role stereotyping in the physical education of young children. (Refs: 3)*In, Simri, U. (ed.), e al., Preschool and elementary school children and physical activity. Proceedings of the 26th ICHPER World Congress 1983, Wingate Institute, Israel, vol. III, Jerusalem, Israel, 1984, p. 163-166.*
CONF: ICHPER World Congress (26th : 1983 : Wingate Institute, Israel).
LEVEL: I LANG: Eng GV443 20093

TEACHER TRAINING

Annarino, A.A Changing times: keeping abreast professionally - a dilemma? (Refs: 6)*Journal of physical education, recreation & dance (Reston, Va.) 55(5), May/Jun 1984, 32-34;52-53.*
LEVEL: B LANG: Eng SIRC ARTICLE NO: 094503

Baeskau, H. Zur Gestaltung effektiver Theorie-Praxis-Beziehungen in der Ausbildung von Sportlehrern. (Effective relations between theory and practice in sports-pedagogic training.) (Refs: 7)*In: Internationales Symposium Sportpaedagogik - Koerpererziehung - Persoenlichkeit: Protokoll, Potsdam, Deutsche Demokratische Republik, ICSSPE/CIEPSS, 1984?, p. 186-192.*
CONF: Internationales Symposium Sportpaedagogik - Koerpererziehung - Persoenlichkeit (1983 : Potsdam).
LEVEL: I LANG: Ger GV205 20231

Beauchamp, L. Helping the weak student teacher. (Refs: 1)*Runner (Edmonton, Alb.) 22(2), Summer 1984, 3-5.*
LEVEL: B LANG: Eng SIRC ARTICLE NO: 100819

Chu, D. Teacher/coach orientation and role socialization: a description and explanation. (Refs: 16)*Journal of teaching in physical education (Blacksburg, Va.) 3(2), Winter 1984, 3-8.*
ABST: The paper examines the consistency of the socialization experience offered in physical education preparation programs and questions the nationality of the preparation programs as they now exist. The author believes that preparation programs do not give the graduate a strong enough background in coaching considering the emphasis the eventual employers place on this role. The author also believes that graduates are not committed to teaching the primary role for which they are trained. The article concludes with a historical background of teacher training colleges.
LEVEL: A LANG: Eng SIRC ARTICLE NO: 092703

Desrosiers, P. Un perfectionnement en milieu universitaire anime par des personnes-ressources du milieu scolaire. (Refs: 6) *Revue quebecoise de l'activite physique (Trois-Rivieres, Que.) 3(1), oct 1984, 21-23.*
LEVEL: B LANG: Fr SIRC ARTICLE NO: 100829

Ferre, J. Leroux, P. Preparation aux brevets d'etat d'educateur sportif: bases physiologiques de l'entrainement. Paris: Editions Amphora, c1984. 349 p. : ill. (Collection sports & loisirs.)
LEVEL: I LANG: Fr ISBN: 2-85180-082-5 RC1235 18963

PHYSICAL EDUCATION (continued)

Gluyas, G. Associate of the College of Preceptors. *Athletics coach (London.) 18(2), Jun 1984, 8-9.*
LEVEL: B LANG: Eng SIR ARTICLE NO: 094517

Hill, P. Gilchrist, J. A pilot study into a collaborative approach to the supervision of physical education students on secondary school teaching practice. (Refs: 4)*Momentum: a journal of human movement studies (Edinburgh) 9(2), Summer 1984, 17-25.*
ABST: 31 supervising teachers and 10 third year physical education students are surveyed on the co-operative approach to supervision. 82.5% (100% of the students and 77% of the teachers) of all respondents preferred this approach. Teacher's evaluation of the suitability of approach to supervision by degree of involvement with student (i.e. less than 4 lessons supervised per week, 5-8 lessons, or 9 or more lessons) is also discussed.
LEVEL: A LANG: Eng SIRC ARTICLE NO: 099158

La formation professionnelle continue des enseignants d'EPS. Changements et perspectives. 7 questions a Gerard Pages. *EPS: Education physique et sport (Paris) 189, sept/oct 1984, 42-44.*
LEVEL: B LANG: Fr SIRC ARTICLE NO: 100833

Locke, L.F. Dodds, P. Is physical education teacher education in American colleges worth saving? Evidence, alternatives, judgment. (Refs: 65)*NAPEHE proceedings (Champaign, Ill.) 5, 1984, 91-107.*
CONF: National Association for Physical Education in Higher education. Annual Conference (1984 : College Park, Md.).
NOTES: Conference theme: Current challenge: revitalization or obsolescence?
LEVEL: I LANG: Eng SIRC ARTICLE NO: 102672

Mawer, M. Rapson, B.H. P.E.A. primary education study group's research. (Refs: 7)*British journal of physical education (London) 15(1), Mar/Apr 1984, 38-39.*
LEVEL: I LANG: Eng SIRC ARTICLE NO: 099167

Mawson, L.M. Insurance against the nation's risk: extended professional preparation for physical education. (Refs: 18)*NAPEH proceedings (Champaign, Ill.) 5, 1984, 138-145.*
CONF: National Association for Physical Education in Higher Education. Annual Conference (1984 : College Park, Md.).
NOTES: Conference theme: Current challenge: revitalization or obsolescence?
LEVEL: I LANG: Eng SIRC ARTICLE NO: 102683

McBride, R.E. Perceived teaching and program concerns among preservice teachers, university supervisors, and cooperating teachers. (Refs: 14)*Journal of teaching in physical education (Blacksburg, Va.) 3(3), Spring 1984, 36-43.*
ABST: This study examined the perceived concerns of six preservice physical education students and compared their concerns with the concerns of their university supervisor and the concerns of their six cooperating teachers. The results indicate that at least some teacher concerns were being considered by those educators responsible for their program.
LEVEL: A LANG: Eng SIRC ARTICLE NO: 096152

McBride, R.E. Some future considerations in the professional preparation of physical education teachers. *Physical educator (Bloomington, Ind.) 41(2), May 1984, 95-99.*
LEVEL: B LANG: Eng SIRC ARTICLE NO: 099168

McBride, R.E. An intensive study of a systematic teacher training model in physical education. (Refs: 26)*Journal of teachin in physical education (Champaign, Ill.) 4(1), Oct 1984, 3-16.*
ABST: This study sought to reduce the practical concerns of six preservice physical education teachers in the Stanford Teacher Education Program (STEP) through adoption of the first six components of the Systematic Teacher Training Model. The study employed an intensive experimental approach emphasizing repeated measures over time and an intervention. A multiple baseline ABABA design ('A' indicating the baseline measures and 'B' the experimental time periods) was used. The teachers were matched by concerns and randomly assigned to either the experimental group or the control group. The analysis indicated that the teachers assigned to the experimental group employing the systematic treatment showed a significantly greater trend toward reduction of teaching concerns and overall increases in observed teacher effectiveness.
LEVEL: A LANG: Eng SIRC ARTICLE NO: 102684

McBride, R.E. Physical education - a profession vs. a non-profession. (Refs: 8)*TAHPERD journal (Austin, Tex.) 52(3), May 1984, 14-15;33-34.*
LEVEL: B LANG: Eng SIRC ARTICLE NO: 109096

Paese, P.C. Student teaching supervision: where we are and where we should be. (Refs: 18)*Physical educator (Bloomington, Ind.) 41(2), May 1984, 90-94.*
LEVEL: B LANG: Eng SIRC ARTICLE NO: 099172

Paese, P.E. The effects of cooperating teacher intervention and a self-assessment technique on the verbal interactions of elementary student teachers. (Refs: 15)*Journal of teaching in physical education (Blacksburg, Va.) 3(3), Spring 1984, 51-58.*
ABST: This study assessed the effect of two interventions on the verbal interaction of three female student teachers with their classes. These two interventions were: 1) cooperating teacher feedback and 2) self-assessment via tape recording of lessons. The results indicate that verbal interaction increased during both intervention phases. The author concludes that both cooperating teachers and student teachers can be trained to systematically observe and record reliable data which will improve the teaching ability of verbal interactions.
LEVEL: A LANG: Eng SIRC ARTICLE NO: 096162

Petray, C. Hennessy, B. Coulter, B. Elementary physical education: a survey of teacher preparation in California colleges an universities. *CAHPERD journal times (Danville, Calif.) 46(8), May 1984, 6.*
LEVEL: B LANG: Eng SIRC ARTICLE NO: 094528

Rolider, A. Siedentop, D. Houten, R.V. Effects of enthusiasm training on subsequent teacher enthusiastic behavior. (Refs: 32 *Journal of teaching in physical education (Blacksburg, Va.) 3(2), Winter 1984, 47-59.*
ABST: Fifteen preservice teachers received enthusiasm training during seven 2-hour training sessions. Non-verbal and verbal enthusiasm measures increased an average of 68% and 213% respectively in the fifteen teachers. These teachers were also rated as enthusiastic by students.
LEVEL: A LANG: Eng SIRC ARTICLE NO: 093022

Rose, D. The position of sports medicine in Australia as a vocation for physical educators. (Refs: 8)

CONF: Physical Education Graduating Seminar Conference (1984 : Footscray Institute of Technology).
NOTES: In, Physical education in Australia: past, present and future directions, s.l., Footscray Institute of Technology, 1984, p. 128-134.
LEVEL: I LANG: Eng SIRC ARTICLE NO: 096167

Svoboda, B. Coaches and physical education teachers training in socialist countries. Prague: Olympia, 1984. 103 p. (A collection of studies in the international scientific cooperation (task no. 6); v. 2.)
CORP: Charles University, Prague. Faculty of Physical Education and Sport.
CORP: Czechoslovak Union of Physical Education. Central Committee.
NOTES: Includes bibliographies.
LEVEL: I LANG: Eng GV361 20849

Thompson, J.G. Logos protreptikos: building pride in the profession. (Refs: 10)*Canadian journal of history of sport/Revue canadienne de l'histoire des sports (Windsor, Ont.) 15(2), Dec 1984, 1-4.*
LEVEL: B LANG: Eng SIRC ARTICLE NO: 104237

Williamson, T. Gill, W. Approaches to in-service training. *Bulletin of physical education (London) 20(2), Summer 1984, 74-78.*
CONF: British Association of Advisers and Lecturers in Physical Education. Congress (64th : 1984 : Cardiff).
LEVEL: I LANG: Eng SIRC ARTICLE NO: 104240

TEACHING

Amirtash, A.M. Determinants of job satisfaction among selected male high school physical educators in the city of Tehran, Iran. Eugene, Ore.: Microform Publications, University of Oregon, 1984. 3 microfiches : negative, ill. ; 11 x 15 cm.
NOTES: Thesis (Ph.D.) - University of Oregon, 1982; (xv, 194 leaves); vita; includes bibliography.
LEVEL: A LANG: Eng UO84 30-32

Arrighi, M.A. Successful teaching: a view from the schools. (Refs: 11)*Physical educator (Bloomington, Ind.) 41(2), May 1984 82-84.*
LEVEL: I LANG: Eng SIRC ARTICLE NO: 099148

Bennett, J.P. The grid system for skillful, fit, joyful movers. *Physical education newsletter (Old Saybrook, Conn.) 162, Sept 1984, 2-4.*
LEVEL: B LANG: Eng SIRC ARTICLE NO: 102652

Biro, E. Die grundlegenden Fragen der sportpaedagogischen wissenschaftlichen Forschungen. (Basic questions of research into scientific problems of sport.) *In: Internationales Symposium Sportpaedagogik - Koerpererziehung - Persoenlichkeit: Protokoll, Potsdam, Deutsche Demokratische Republik, ICSSPE/CIEPSS, 1984?, p. 113-116.*
CONF: Internationales Symposium Sportpaedagogik - Koerpererziehung - Persoenlichkeit (1983 : Potsdam).
LEVEL: I LANG: Ger GV205 20231

Boenisch, S. Bemerkungen zu Bedingungen der Konstitution eines wissenschaftlichen Gegenstandes aus wissenschaftstheoretische Sicht. (Observations on the conditions for solving theoretical problems of sports pedagogics.) *In: Internationales Symposium Sportpaedagogik - Koerpererziehung - Persoenlichkeit: Protokoll, Potsdam, Deutsche Demokratische Republik, ICSSPE/CIEPSS, 1984?, p. 94-104.*
CONF: Internationales Symposium Sportpaedagogik

- Koerpererziehung - Persoenlichkeit (1983 : Potsdam).
LEVEL: A LANG: Ger GV205 20231

Briest, H.D. Wirksamkeit sporttheoretischer Kenntnisse auf die Bereitschaft und Befaehigung zum bewussten und schoepferische Handeln in der sportlichen Taetigkeit. (The contribution of sports-theoretical training to the willingness and ability for conscious and creative action in physical activities.) (Refs: 1)*In: Internationales Symposium Sportpaedagogik - Koerpererziehung - Persoenlichkeit: Protokoll, Potsdam, Deutsche Demokratische Republik, ICSSPE/CIEPSS, 1984?, p. 180-185.*
CONF: Internationales Symposium Sportpaedagogik - Koerpererziehung - Persoenlichkeit (1983 : Potsdam).
LEVEL: I LANG: Ger GV205 20231

Burel, H. L'EPS demain...enquete aupres de nouveaux agreges. (Refs: 4)*EPS: Education phsyique et sport (Paris) 187, mai/jui 1984, 65-67.*
NOTES: Suite du no. 187, p. 42-52.
LEVEL: B LANG: Fr SIRC ARTICLE NO: 096131

Caruso, V.M. Computer literacy and the physical educator. (Refs: 6)*Runner (Edmonton, Alb.) 22(2), Summer 1984, 6-7.*
LEVEL B LANG: Eng SIRC ARTICLE NO: 100825

Corbin, C.B. Lindsey, R. The conceptual approach to teaching physical education. *Physical education newsletter (Old Saybrook, Conn.) 162, Sept 1984, 6-8.*
LEVEL: B LANG: Eng SIRC ARTICLE NO: 102661

Crum, B. Diskrepanzen zwischen paedagogischem Anspruch und Wirklichkeit der schulischen Sporterziehung. (Discrepancies between pedagogical claims and reality in school sport.) (Refs: 5)*In: Internationales Symposium Sportpaedagogik - Koerpererziehung - Persoenlichkeit: Protokoll, Potsdam, Deutsche Demokratische Republik, ICSSPE/CIEPSS, 1984?, p. 199-211.*
CONF: Internationales Symposium Sportpaedagogik - Koerpererziehung - Persoenlichkeit (1983 : Potsdam).
LEVEL: A LANG: Ger GV205 20231

Dewar, A.M. Lawson, H.A. The subjective warrant and recruitment into physical education. (Refs: 32)*Quest (Champaign, Ill.) 36(1), 1984, 15-25.*
ABST: The authors identify the major factors influencing individuals to enter physical education programs. They review the general literature on occupational choice and the professional socialization literature.
LEVEL: A LANG: Eng SIRC ARTICLE NO: 099153

Doering-Paul, L. Wissenschaftstheoretische Oberlegungen zur Herausbildung der Sportpaedagogik als Wissenschaftsdisziplin. (Theoretical reflections on the development of sports pedagogics as a scientific discipline.) (Refs: 14)*In: Internationales Symposium Sportpaedagogik - Koerpererziehung - Persoenlichkeit: Protokoll, Potsdam, Deutsche Demokratische Republik, ICSSPE/CIEPSS, 1984?, p. 83-93.*
CONF: Internationales Symposium Sportpaedagogik - Koerpererziehung - Persoenlichkeit (1983 : Potsdam).
LEVEL: A LANG: Ger GV205 20231

Entretien avec Claude Pujade-Renaud. 1re partie. *EPS: Education physique et sport (Paris) 190, nov/dec 1984, 6-12.*
LEVEL: B LANG: Fr SIRC ARTICLE NO: 102666

Goetze, H. Die paedagogische Fuehrung - wesentliche Bedingung fuer den effektiven Beitrag des Sportunterrichts zur Persoenlichkeitsentwicklung der Kinder und Jugendlichen. (Pedagogic guidance - essential condition for an effective contribution of P.E. lessons to the personality development of children and young people.) (Refs: 4)*In: Internationales Symposium Sportpaedagogik - Koerpererziehung - Persoenlichkeit: Protokoll, Potsdam, Deutsche Demokratische Republik, ICSSPE/CIEPSS, 1984?, p. 118-124.*
CONF: Internationales Symposium Sportpaedagogik - Koerpererziehung - Persoenlichkeit (1983 : Potsdam).
LEVEL: I LANG: Ger GV205 20231

Haag, H. Entwicklung einer Forschungsmethodologie fuer Sportpaedagogik als Theoriefeld der Sportwissenschaften. (The development of a research methodology for sports pedagogics as a theory field of sports sciences.) (Refs: 46)*In: Internationales Symposium Sportpaedagogik - Koerpererziehung - Persoenlichkeit: Protokoll, Potsdam, Deutsche Demokratische Republik, ICSSPE/CIEPSS, 1984?, p. 53-81.*
CONF: Internationales Symposium Sportpaedagogik - Koerpererziehung - Persoenlichkeit (1983 : Potsdam).
LEVEL: A LANG: Ger GV205 20231

Hoffmann, G. Das Normenproblem in der Sportpaedagogik: Fragmente zu grundlagentheoretischen Annaeherungen an ein Problemfeld Koeln: Deutsche Sporthochschule, Paedagogisches Seminar, 1984. 601 p.
NOTES: Bibliography: p. 564-601. Thesis (Ph.D.) - Deutsche Sporthochschule Koeln, 1984.
LEVEL: A LANG: Ger GV361 18378

Imwold, C. Developing feedback behavior through a teach-reteach cycle. (Refs: 16)*Physical educator (Bloomington, Ind.) 41(2), May 1984, 72-76.*
ABST: Feedback behaviors of 28 preservice physical education teachers were examined during an initial and a second microteaching experience. Findings indicated that the number of contacts with students, the average number of repeat contacts and the average length of contact increased from experience 1 to experience 2. Class length from experience 1 to experience 2 increased from 4:38.8 to 5:09.
LEVEL: A LANG: Eng SIRC ARTICLE NO: 099159

Imwold, C.H. Rider, R.A. Twardy, B.M. Oliver, P.S. Griffin, M. Arsenault, D.N. The effect of planning on the teaching behavior of preservice physical education teachers. (Refs: 10)*Journal of teaching in physical education (Champaign, Ill.) 4(1), Oct 1984, 50-56.*
ABST: The purpose of this study was to compare the teaching process interaction behavior of teachers who planned for classes with those who did not plan. Senior physical education majors served as the teaching subjects for this study - six in the planning (experimental) group and six in the no-plan (control) group. Each teacher taught the same lesson content for a 15-minute episode. The planning group spent 1 hour before the lesson writing explicit plans, while the control group was given 2 minutes just before the lesson to gather

their thoughts and be informed of the content to be covered. The behaviours of all teachers were observed by the Cheffers Adaptation of the Flanders' Interaction Analysis System (CAFIAS). The results indicated significant differences in only two interaction categories: amount of directions given and the amount of silence. Both variables were better for the planning group.
LEVEL: A LANG: Eng SIRC ARTICLE NO: 102670

Kareen, B.K.R. Decision-making in teaching a fourth-grade educational games unit: a description and analysis of inexperience and experienced teachers. Eugene, Ore.: Microform Publications, University of Oregon, 1984. 2 microfiches : negative : 11 x 15 cm.
NOTES: Thesis (M.Ed.) - University of North Carolina at Greensboro, 1982; (viii, 144 leaves); includes bibliography.
LEVEL: A LANG: Eng UO84 180-181

Kim, D. Zakrajsek, D.B. Teaching behaviors: a cultural perspective. (Refs: 13)*Foil (Indianapolis) Fall 1984, 10-13.*
ABST: It was the purpose of this study to determine whether significant differences in teaching behaviours existed between Korean and Idaho physical education teachers. The subjects were 15 Korean and 15 Idaho secondary school teachers of both sexes. Ten teaching behaviours were identified, directed at individuals, small groups or the whole class. It was found that Idaho teachers spent more time talking to their students, whereas Korean teachers asked more questions than their American counterparts.
LEVEL: A LANG: Eng SIRC ARTICLE NO: 173561

Kizer, D.L. Piper, D.L. Sauter, W.E. Practical approach to teaching physical education. Ithaca, N.Y.: Mouvement Publications c1984. 291 p. : ill.
NOTES: Bibliography: p. 291.
LEVEL: I LANG: Eng ISBN: 0-932392-18-0 GV361 17723

Kostkova, J. Die Didaktik der Koerpererziehung als wissenschaftliche Disziplin und als integrierender Gegenstand in der Vorbereitung der Sportkader an der Fakultaet fuer Koerpererziehung und Sport der Karls-Universitaet in Prag. (The didactics of physical education as a scientific discipline and integral subject in training sports experts at the Charles University Prague.) In: Internationales Symposium Sportpaedagogik - Koerpererziehung - Persoenlichkeit: Protokoll, Potsdam, Deutsche Demokratische Republik, ICSSPE/CIEPSS, 1984?, p. 105-108.
CONF: Internationales Symposium Sportpaedagogik - Koerpererziehung - Persoenlichkeit (1983 : Potsdam).
LEVEL: I LANG: Ger GV205 20231

Kruse, C.C. Begruendung und Stellenwert des erzieherischen Verhaeltnisses in der paedagogischen und sportpaedagogischen Theoriebildung: dargestellt an ausgewaehlten Beispielen. Koeln: Deutsche Sporthochschule, 1984. 459 p.
NOTES: Thesis (Ph.D.) - Deutsche Sporthochschule Koeln, 1984. Bibliography: p. 431-459.
LEVEL: A LANG: Ger GV361 17683

L'EPS demain... la commission permanente de reflexion sur l'enseignement de l'EPS. *EPS: Education physique et sport (Paris) 189, sept/oct 1984, 6-9.*
LEVEL: B LANG: Fr SIRC ARTICLE NO: 100832

Logsdon, B.J. Physical education for children: a focus on the teaching process. 2nd ed. Philadelphia: Lea & Febiger, 1984. ix, 467 p. : ill. NOTES: Includes index and bibliographies. LEVEL: A LANG: Eng ISBN: 0812108922 LC CARD: 83-011964 GV443 17001

Magnotta, J. Overseas employment opportunities for physical educators. *Physical educator (Indianapolis) 41(4), Dec 1984, 205-208.* LEVEL: B LANG: Eng SIRC ARTICLE NO: 104222

Marrs, L.K. Student teacher as social strategist. Eugene, Ore.: Microform Publications, University of Oregon, 1984. 1 microfiche : negative ; 11 x 15 cm. NOTES: Thesis (M.S.) - Purdue University, 1982; (v, 92 leaves); includes bibliography. LEVEL: A LANG: Eng UO84 309

Marsenach, J. Bertsch, J. L'EPS demain... (Refs: 11)*EPS: Education physique et sport (Paris, France) 186, mars/avr 1984, 42-45.* NOTES: A suivre. LEVEL: B LANG: Fr SIRC ARTICLE NO: 094526

Matwejew, L.P. O pravomernosti vydedeniya 'sportivnoi pedagogiki i ee otnoshenii k sdozivshimsya naukam o sporte. (Reasons for the evolvement of sports pedagogics and its relation to sports sciences.) *In: Internationales Symposium Sportpaedagogik - Koerpererziehung - Persoenlichkeit: Protokoll, Potsdam, Deutsche Demokratische Republik, ICSSPE/CIEPSS, 1984?, p. 50-52.* CONF: Internationales Symposium Sportpaedagogik - Koerpererziehung - Persoenlichkeit (1983 : Potsdam). LEVEL: B LANG: Rus GV205 20231

Metzler, M. Developing teaching skills: a systematic sequence. (Refs: 1)*Journal of physical education, recreation & dance 55(1), Jan 1984, 38-40.* LEVEL: B LANG: Eng SIRC ARTICLE NO: 091622

Metzler, M.W. Young, J.C. The relationship between teachers' preactive planning and student process measures. (Refs: 21) *Research quarterly for exercise and sport (Reston, Va.) 55(4), Dec 1984, 356-364.* ABST: The purpose of this study was to examine the student process behavior differences resulting from divergent lesson planning patterns within an Experimental Teaching Unit (ETU). Two teachers were asked to plan for and implement a 20 minute ETU on three occasions using different groups of 65 fourth grade students. The ETU task, a combination hockey/golf novel skill, was explained to the teachers, as were their identical teaching space and equipment allocations. The two teachers planned and implemented contrasting lessons for this same teaching goal. The Flow of Teacher Organizational Patterns system was used to verify that the teachers consistently and faithfully implemented their intended plans. Student process behavior was analyzed with the Academic Learning Time-Physical Education (ALT-PE) observational system. The data indicate that the students' process behaviors under each teacher were very similar at the main ALT-PE system levels. However, each teaching patterns resulted in markedly different student process behavior in the system subcategories. LEVEL: A LANG: Eng SIRC ARTICLE NO: 104224

Mosston, M. Ashworth, S. From command to discovery: toward a unified theory of teaching. (Refs: 6)*Bulletin of the Federatio internationale d'education physique (Toulouse, France) 54(3/4), Jul/Dec 1984, 5-8.* LEVEL: B LANG: Eng SIRC ARTICLE NO: 105415

Ojeme, E.O. Towards a multi-observation system for supervising physical education student-teachers. (Refs: 11)*International journal of physical education (Schorndorf, W. Germany) 21(3), 1984, 17-22.* LEVEL: I LANG: Eng SIRC ARTICLE NO: 102687

Ostro, H. Of teaching, coaching, and merit pay. *Scholastic coach 53(7), Feb 1984, 4;6;8;10;12.* LEVEL: B LANG: Eng SIRC ARTICLE NO: 093201

Paese, P.C. Academic learning time in physical education. (Refs: 28)*TAHPERD journal (Austin, Tex.) 52(3), May 1985, 16-17;34-35.* LEVEL: I LANG: Eng SIRC ARTICLE NO: 109097

Pare, C. Marchand, A. Analyse des habiletes d'enseignement en situation de stages chez les etudiants-maitres en education physique. (Refs: 16)*CAHPER journal/Revue de l'ACSEPR (Ottawa) 50(6), juil/aout 1984, 10-13.* RESUME: Le but de cette etude est de comparer les habiletes d'enseignement d'etudiants-maitre en education physique en situation de laboratoire et de classe normale. 54 etudiants de troisieme annee sont observes a l'aide du systeme 'analyse des habiletes d'enseignement en education physique'. Les resultats indiquent qu'une periode d'adaptation de 6 semaines en milieu scolaire est necessaire aux etudiants-maitre pour reproduire des comportements semblables a ceux observes en laboratoire. LEVEL: A LANG: Fr SIRC ARTICLE NO: 099174

Pare, C. Lessard, M. Marchand, A. Etude du temps de pratique active des etudiants-maitres en activite physique. (Refs: 19) *Revue quebecoise de l'activite physique (Trois-Rivieres, Que.) 3(1), oct 1984, 13-17.* ABST: Les auteurs analysent les pourcentages du temps alloue au temps de pratique active des eleves des stagiaires en education physique. L'echantillon se compose de 94 stagiaires enseignant a des niveaux scolaires differents; 44 au primaire, 28 au secondaire et 22 au collegial. Les resultats indiquent que les eleves des stagiaires consacrent, en moyenne, 91% de leur temps de classe a des situations d'education physique et 60% a l'engagement moteur. Ces resultats sont superieurs a ceux obtenus en classes regulieres d'education physique. LEVEL: A LANG: Fr SIRC ARTICLE NO: 100841

Pettigrew, F. Zakrajsek, D. A profile of learning style preferences among physical education majors. (Refs: 19)*Physical educator (Bloomington, Ind.) 41(2), May 1984, 85-89.* ABST: This paper investigates the learning style preferences of 104 university's physical education majors. Canfield's Learning Style Inventory is the testing instrument. The authors compare the learning styles of both male and female students. Female majors demonstrate the highest preference for inanimate experience, direct experience, organization, authority, iconics, and peer. Men majors are more interested by people, authority, iconics and direct experience. A low preference in both groups for independence and reading is observed. LEVEL: A LANG: Eng SIRC ARTICLE NO: 099175

Pieron, M. Graham, G. Research on physical education teacher effectiveness: the experimental teaching units. (Refs: 17) *International journal of physical education (Schorndorf, W. Germany) 21(3), 1984, 9-14.* LEVEL: I LANG: Eng SIRC ARTICLE NO: 102689

Pieron, M. Analysis of research based on observation of the teaching of physical education. (Refs: 11)*Bulletin of the Federation internationale d'education physique (Toulouse, France) 54(3/4), Jul/Dec 1984, 39-47.* LEVEL: I LANG: Eng SIRC ARTICLE NO: 105419

Placek, J.H. A multi-case study of teacher planning in physical education. (Refs: 25)*Journal of teaching in physical education (Champaign, Ill.) 4(1), Oct 1984, 39-49.* ABST: The purpose of this study was to examine how four physical education teachers planned lessons. The multi-case approach provided a naturalistic, descriptive account of planning at two levels: daily and yearly plans. Four teachers were observed over an intensive 2-week period for data collection. Data consisted of observations, interviews, and excerpts from documents and records. The results indicated that the four teachers did not use the classical ends/means model for planning but instead employed informal planning habits that typically focused on daily activities, not coherent efforts to match objectives with content. This pattern does not necessarily produce disorganized classes, however, as the researcher described the teachers as having positive in-class instructional behaviors. It is suggested that the teacher did in fact plan for classes, however briefly or informally. LEVEL: A LANG: Eng SIRC ARTICLE NO: 102690

Pranzo, D. Physical education and recreation: seduction and fraud in high school. *Washington journal of health, physical education, recreation and dance (Bellingham, Wash.) 39(1), Winter/Spring 1984, 9;12.* LEVEL: B LANG: Eng SIRC ARTICLE NO: 108732

Proctor, N. Problems facing physical education after the great education debate. (Refs: 39)*Physical education review (Manchester) 7(1), Spring 1984, 4-11.* LEVEL: I LANG: Eng SIRC ARTICLE NO: 099177

Recla, J. Der gute Sportlehrer - ein berufener, wirksamer Menschenbildner. (The good P.E. teacher - a competent and effectiv shaper of human beings.) *In: Internationales Symposium Sportpaedagogik - Koerpererziehung - Persoenlichkeit: Protokoll, Potsdam, Deutsche Demokratische Republik, ICSSPE/CIEPSS, 1984?, p. 245-248.* CONF: Internationales Symposium Sportpaedagogik - Koerpererziehung - Persoenlichkeit (1983 : Potsdam). LEVEL: I LANG: Ger GV205 20231

Riecken, R. Tendenzen und Probleme der Entwicklung der Sportpaedagogik in der DDR. (Tendencies and problems of the develomen of sports pedagogics in the GDR.) (Refs: 17)*In: Internationales Symposium Sportpaedagogik - Koerpererziehung - Persoenlichkeit: Protokoll, Potsdam, Deutsche Demokratische Republik, ICSSPE/CIEPSS, 1984?, p. 31-49.* CONF: Internationales Symposium Sportpaedagogik - Koerpererziehung - Persoenlichkeit (1983 : Potsdam). LEVEL: A LANG: Ger GV205 20231

Sage, G.H. The quest for identity in college physical education. *Quest (Champaign, Ill.) 36(2), 1984, 115-121.* NOTES: The fourth Dudley Allen Sargent

Commemorative lecture: 1984.
LEVEL: B LANG: Eng SIRC ARTICLE NO: 102695

Schempp, P.G. Stability in the gym: a one-year time-series analysis. Alexandria, Va.: Computer Microfilm International, 1984 1 microfiche (12 fr.)
CONF: American Alliance for Health, Physical Education, Recreation and Dance. Convention (1984 : Anaheim, Calif.).
LEVEL: A LANG: Eng EDRS: ED243859

Scranton, S.A. A comparative analysis between physical education majors' perceptions of the physical education teacher, and their satisfaction with selected professional preparation experiences. Eugene, Ore.: Microform Publications, University of Oregon, 1984. 2 microfiches : negative, ill. ; 11 x 15 cm.
NOTES: Thesis (M.S.) - University of North Carolina at Greensboro, 1981; (viii, 113 leaves); includes bibliography.
LEVEL: A LANG: Eng UO84 273-274

Seifert, G. Koerperliche Grundausbildung als Beitrag allseitiger Erziehung der heranwachsenden Persoenlichkeit. (Basic physical training as a contribution to personality development.) (Refs: 7)*In: Internationales Symposium Sportpaedagogik - Koerpererziehung - Persoenlichkeit: Protokoll, Potsdam, Deutsche Demokratische Republik, ICSSPE/CIEPSS, 1984?, p. 125-131.*
CONF: Internationales Symposium Sportpaedagogik - Koerpererziehung - Persoenlichkeit (1983 : Potsdam).
LEVEL: I LANG: Ger GV205 20231

Shields, E. Student ratings of teachers + personnel decision-making
CAUTION. (Refs: 8)*Journal of physical education, recreation & dance 55(1), Jan 1984, 35-37.*
LEVEL: B LANG: Eng SIRC ARTICLE NO: 091634

Silverman, S. Dodds, P. Placek, J. Shute, S. Rife, F. Academic learning time in elementary school physical education (ALTA-PE) for student subgroups and instructional activity units. (Refs: 13)*Research quarterly for exercise and sport (Reston, Va.) 55(4), Dec 1984, 365-370.*
LEVEL: A LANG: Eng SIRC ARTICLE NO: 104234

Spackman, L. Recent changes in the focus of physical education. (Refs: 30)*Bulletin of physical education (London) 20(1), Spring 1984, 19-23.*
LEVEL: B LANG: Eng SIRC ARTICLE NO: 102698

Svoboda, B. Eine Konzeption der Sporterziehung. (A concept of sports education.) *In: Internationales Symposium Sportpaedagogik - Koerpererziehung - Persoenlichkeit: Protokoll, Potsdam, Deutsche Demokratische Republik, ICSSPE/CIEPSS, 1984?, p. 136-142.*
CONF: Internationales Symposium Sportpaedagogik - Koerpererziehung - Persoenlichkeit (1983 : Potsdam).
LEVEL: I LANG: Ger GV205 20231

Tainton, B. Primary physical education teachers: their role through the eyes of principals and classroom teachers. (Refs: 4) *ACHPER national journal (Kingswood, Aust.) 105, Spring 1984, 52-54.*
NOTES: Reprinted from, ACHPER Action Jul/Aug 1983, 5-6.
LEVEL: B LANG: Eng SIRC ARTICLE NO: 102699

Todorov, A. Ekstremadbnye situatsii i formirovanie psikhicheskikh kachestv sportsmena. (Extreme situations in the course of physical educations sic as a special form of external conditions.) (Refs:

4)*In: Internationales Symposium Sportpaedagogik - Koerpererziehung - Persoenlichkeit: Protokoll, Potsdam, Deutsche Demokratische Republik, ICSSPE/CIEPSS, 1984?, p. 132-135.*
CONF: Internationales Symposium Sportpaedagogik - Koerpererziehung - Persoenlichkeit (1983 : Potsdam).
LEVEL: I LANG: Rus GV205 20231

Turner, E.T. Physical education leaders: an innovative teaching approach. *Journal of physical education, recreation & dance 55(1), Jan 1984, 41-42.*
LEVEL: B LANG: Eng SIRC ARTICLE NO: 091646

Van Dyke, S.C. The effects of three different organizing centers on teacher-student behaviors. Eugene, Ore.: Microform Publications, University of Oregon, 1984. 2 microfiches : negative, ill. ; 11 x 15 cm.
NOTES: Thesis (Ph.D.) - Temple University, 1982; (vii, 130 leaves); includes bibliography.
LEVEL: A LANG: Eng UO84 275-276

Vertinsky, P. In search of a gender dimension: an empirical investigation of teacher preferences for teaching strategies in physical education. (Refs: 11)*Journal of curriculum studies (Basingstoke, Eng.) 16(4), 1984, 425-430.*
LEVEL: A LANG: Eng SIRC ARTICLE NO: 104239

Virgilio, S.J. Krebs, P.S. Effective time management techniques. (Refs: 7)*Journal of physical education, recreation & dance (Reston, Va.) 55(4), Apr 1984, 68;73.*
LEVEL: B LANG: Eng SIRC ARTICLE NO: 094538

Williams, L.R.T. Teachers' perceptions of objectives and learning outcomes in physical education. (Refs: 10)*New Zealand journal of health, physical education & recreation (Dunedin, New Zealand) 17(2), Aug 1984, 12-19.*
ABST: This study focuses on the importance assigned by 121 teachers to different objectives for the physical education program and their perceptions of student's learning outcomes. Each teacher is teaching either in primary or secondary school levels. Enjoyment and satisfaction, self-realisation and health education are considered the most important objectives. Differences in the perceptions of learning outcomes (i.e. mainly certain aspects of motor skills, tolerance to exercise and enjoyment and satisfaction) between teachers at the two levels are observed. Perceptions also differ for male and female teachers with the major differentiators being certain aspects of aesthetic appreciation, social competence and enjoyment and satisfaction.
LEVEL: A LANG: Eng SIRC ARTICLE NO: 099180

Zukowska, Z. Entwicklung und Forschungsrichtungen der Sportpaedagogik in Polen. (Development and research branches of sports pedagogics in Poland.) *In: Internationales Symposium Sportpaedagogik - Koerpererziehung - Persoenlichkeit: Protokoll, Potsdam, Deutsche Demokratische Republik, ICSSPE/CIEPSS, 1984?, p. 109-112.*
CONF: Internationales Symposium Sportpaedagogik - Koerpererziehung - Persoenlichkeit (1983 : Potsdam).
LEVEL: I LANG: Ger GV205 20231

TEACHING METHODS

Barlow, D.A. Bayalis, P.A. Computer facilitated learning in physical education.
CONF: National Symposium on Teaching Kinesiology and Biomechanics in Sports (2nd : 1984 : Colorado Springs).
NOTES: In, Shapiro, R. and Marett, J.R. (eds.), Proceedings: Second National Symposium on Teaching Kinesiology and Biomechanics in Sports, Colorado Springs, Colorado, January 12-14, Dekalb, Ill., AAHPERD, 1984, p. 107.
LEVEL: B LANG: Eng SIRC ARTICLE NO: 100818

Bigou, A. Vigouroux, G. Acceleration du jeu. *I.N.S.E.P. dossier documentaire (Paris) 3, 1984, 31-42.*
LEVEL: I LANG: Fr SIRC ARTICLE NO: 094506

Bonnery, L. Continuite du jeu. *I.N.S.E.P. dossier documentaire (Paris) 3, 1984, 8-30.*
NOTES: Aspects reglementaires; aspects theoriques et prolongements pratiques.
LEVEL: I LANG: Fr SIRC ARTICLE NO: 094507

Carlson, J.B. Excel, relate, keep the public up to date. *Physical education newsletter (Old Saybrook, Conn.) 159, May 1984, 2-4.*
LEVEL: B LANG: Eng SIRC ARTICLE NO: 100824

Carlson, R.P. Ideas II: a sharing of teaching practices by secondary school physical education practitioners. Reston, Va.: American Alliance for Health, Physical Education, Recreation and Dance, c1984. x, 144 p. : ill.
CORP: National Association for Sport and Physical Education.
LEVEL: I LANG: Eng ISBN: 0-88314-264-3 GV363 18251

Contract learning - one approach to developing and maintaining physical fitness. *Physical education newsletter (Old Saybrook, Conn.) 159, May 1984, 4-7.*
LEVEL: B LANG: Eng SIRC ARTICLE NO: 100827

Cremers, P. Etude sur la pedagogie appliquee a l'Institut provincial d'enseignement secondaire de Verviers III, dans les cours d'education physique, de technologie et de pratique professionnelle (bois). (Refs: 13)*Revue de l'education physique (Liege, Belgique) 24(1), 1984, 13-16.*
LEVEL: I LANG: Fr SIRC ARTICLE NO: 096135

Freedman, M.S. A model for teaching reading in the physical education content area. (Refs: 15)*Journal of teaching in physical education (Blacksburg, Va.) 3(3), Spring 1984, 28-35.*
ABST: The author proposes a model for teaching reading through physical education content. The model is an interactive system that contains five components. These five components are: 1) Reading Instructional Design. 2) Psychomotor Instructional Design. 3) Practise Style of Teaching. 4) Psychomotor-Cognitive Functioning, and 5) Academic Learning Time. The purpose of the model is to decrease the disparity between the classroom and the gymnasium.
LEVEL: A LANG: Eng SIRC ARTICLE NO: 096137

Gangstead, S.K. Beveridge, S.K. The implementation and evaluation of a methodological approach to qualitative sport skill analysis instruction. (Refs: 20)*Journal of teaching in physical education (Blacksburg, Va.) 3(2), Winter 1984, 60-70.*
ABST: This study investigated the effects of a methodological approach to sport skill analysis

instruction on the analytical proficiency of undergraduates. The experimental group utilized the methodological approach while the control group did not utilize a specific strategy. The experimental group analyzed skills to a significantly better degree than did the control group. The results indicate that systematic qualitative skill analysis instruction can significantly improve the performance of undergraduates on specific perceptual and diagnostic aspects of analysis.
LEVEL: A LANG: Eng SIRC ARTICLE NO: 093001

Garcia, R.A. Time use of nondressers in physical education class. (Refs: 19)*Journal of physical education, recreation and dance (Reston, Va.) 55(8)*, Oct 1984, 74-76.
LEVEL: B LANG: Eng SIRC ARTICLE NO: 100834

Goldberger, M. Effective learning: through a spectrum of teaching styles. (Refs: 19)*Journal of physical education, recreation and dance (Reston, Va.) 55(8)*, Oct 1984, 17-21.
LEVEL: B LANG: Eng SIRC ARTICLE NO: 100835

Jansma, P. French, R. Horvat, M.A. Behavioral engineering in physical education. (Refs: 2)*Journal of physical education, recreation & dance (Reston, Va.) 55(6)*, Aug 1984, 80-81.
LEVEL: B LANG: Eng SIRC ARTICLE NO: 097657

McKenzie, E.K. McKenzie, R. McKenzie, T.L. Instructional strategies: influence on teacher and student behavior. (Refs: 21) *Journal of teaching in physical education (Blacksburg, Va.) 3(2)*, Winter 1984, 20-28.
ABST: A fencing instructor used two different teaching strategies for two separate fencing classes. Data was collected for students and for the instructor. The results indicate that the different teaching strategies placed different requirements on student behavior and on instructor behavior. These requirements resulted in different opportunities for the students to learn. The authors conclude that teachers should examine their teaching strategies to determine how successful they are in reaching instructional goals.
LEVEL: A LANG: Eng SIRC ARTICLE NO: 093014

Olson, J.K. Keeping cool: be a teacher who disciplines least. (Refs: 2)*Journal of physical education, recreation & dance (Reston, Va.) 55(6)*, Aug 1984, 38-39.
LEVEL: B LANG: Eng SIRC ARTICLE NO: 097666

Scheiff, A. Efficacite de deux styles d'enseignement et relation avec certains aspects des strategies d'apprentissage dans des praxies gymniques et athletiques. (Refs: 38)*Revue de l'education physique (Liege, Belgique) 24(4)*, 1984, 7-23.
LEVEL: I LANG: Fr SIRC ARTICLE NO: 104232

Slava, S. Laurie, D.R. Corbin, C.B. Long-term effects of a conceptual physical education program. (Refs: 14)*Research quarterly for exercise & sport (Reston, Va.) 55(2)*, Jun 1984, 161-168.
ABST: This study evaluated the attitudes, knowledge, and activity behaviors of 100 college graduates who completed a lecture - laboratory (concepts) course in physical education during their tenure as undergraduates. These students were compared to 100 students who received advanced credit for the concepts class and therefore did not take the class and to 100 students who transferred from another university with a traditional physical education course instead of the concepts course. The results indicate that the attitude - knowledge - activity profile of the concepts group differed from

the profiles of either of the other groups. The results suggest that a conceptual physical education class can have positive long term effects.
LEVEL: A LANG: Eng SIRC ARTICLE NO: 096169

Stein, J.U. Individualized instruction in physical education. *Physical education newsletter (Old Saybrook, Conn.) 164*, Nov 1984, 2-4.
LEVEL: B LANG: Eng SIRC ARTICLE NO: 173181

WOMEN

Abigail, J. Girls and physical education. (Refs: 10)*New Zealand journal of health, physical education & recreation (Wellington, N.Z.) 17(1)*, May 1984, 1-4.
NOTES: An extract from, Secondary school influences on the training and career aspirations of girls: a study of seventeen Wellington schools, Vocational Training Council, 1983.
LEVEL: I LANG: Eng SIRC ARTICLE NO: 097646

Chin, M. Physical education in Malaysia for women and children. *Asian journal of physical education (Taiwan, China) 7(1)*, Apr 1984, 33-35.
NOTES: Abstract in Chinese.
LEVEL: B LANG: Eng Chi SIRC ARTICLE NO: 096229

Evans, J. Muscle, sweat and showers. Girls' conceptions of physical education and sport: a challenge for research and curriculum reform. (Refs: 17)*Physical education review (Manchester) 7(1)*, Spring 1984, 12-18.
LEVEL: I LANG: Eng SIRC ARTICLE NO: 099364

Heyters, C. Profil morpho-fonctionnel d'etudiantes en education physique. (Refs: 44)*Revue de l'education physique (Liege, Belgique) 24(1)*, 1984, 25-30.
RESUME: Au cours de cette etude, l'auteur evalue les mensurations morphologiques, la capacite vitale, l'indice de Tiffeneau, le debit expiratoire de pointe, la ventilation maximale minute a la cadence de 80 respirations par minute, l'aptitude cardio-circulatoire et l'aptitude motrice d'etudiantes (agees en moyenne de 21.3 ans + - 1.5) en education physique. Les resultats obtenus sont compares a ceux provenant d'etudes realisees aupres de sportives de haut niveau et d'une population generale d'etudiantes.
LEVEL: A LANG: Fr SIRC ARTICLE NO: 096451

Matsumoto, C. A survey on awareness of women leaders of physical education -1983-84, in Japan. *Asian journal of physical education (Taiwan, China) 7(1)*, Apr 1984, 55-63.
NOTES: Abstract in Chinese.
LEVEL: I LANG: Eng Chi SIRC ARTICLE NO: 096278

Ryan, S. The Fritz Duras Memorial Lecture. *ACHPER national journal 103*, Mar 1984, 12-14.
ABST: A speech by the Federal Minister for Education and Youth Affairs.
LEVEL: I LANG: Eng SIRC ARTICLE NO: 097425

Safrit, M.J. Women in research in physical education: A 1984 update. (Refs: 19)*Quest (Champaign, Ill.) 36(2)*, 1984, 103-114.
NOTES: The eighteenth Amy Morris Homans lecture - 1984.
LEVEL: I LANG: Eng SIRC ARTICLE NO: 102694

Setzler, H.A. Attitudes of women physical educators towards feminism. Eugene, Ore.: Microform Publications, University of Oregon, 1984. 3 microfiches : negative ; 11 x 15 cm.

NOTES: Thesis (M.S.) - University of North Carolina at Greensboro, 1982; (ix, 192 leaves); includes bibliography.
LEVEL: A LANG: Eng UO84 316-318

Smith, B.M. The discrimination against women and girls in physical education. (Refs: 9)
CONF: Physical Education Graduating Seminar Conference (1984 : Footscray Institute of Technology).
NOTES: In, Physical education in Australia: past, present and future directions, s.l., Footscray Institute of Technology, 1984, p. 95-102.
LEVEL: I LANG: Eng SIRC ARTICLE NO: 096170

Spence, J. Role model relationship. A support program for female participation in Carleton Board of Education intermediate physical education program. *OPHEA: Ontario Physical and Health Education Association (London, Ont.) 10(2)*, Spring 1984, 29-39.
LEVEL: I LANG: Eng SIRC ARTICLE NO: 099179

Tollich, H. The history of IAPESGW. A contribution to the development of Comparative Physical Education and Sports for Women as a means for international understanding. *ICSSPE/CIEPSS review (Berlin, GDR) 7*, 1984, 32-36.
LEVEL: B LANG: Eng SIRC ARTICLE NO: 096484

PHYSICAL FITNESS

A conversation with the President. Ronald Reagan discusses fitness: his own and that of the nation. *Runner's world (Mountain View, Calif.) 19(10)*, Oct 1984, 24-26;28;30;34;39;40;42.
LEVEL: B LANG: Eng SIRC ARTICLE NO: 099184

Arnot, R. The complete manual of fitness and well-being. 1st American ed. New York: Viking, c1984. 312 p.
NOTES: Includes index. Bibliography: p. 305.
LEVEL: I LANG: Eng ISBN: 0670234311 LC CARD: 84-040259 RA776 18326

Bortz, W.M. The disuse syndrome. *Western journal of medicine (San Francisco) 141(5)*, Nov 1984, 691-694.
LEVEL: I LANG: En

Cassidy, L. Wilkenfeld, T. Findlay, S. Ajoulant, F.S. Thuvs, Y. Broeske, P. Aronson, V. Theavney, A. Rip-offs on the fitness market. Fit looks at 1984's 10 biggest fitness rip-offs - and tells you how to get smart. *Fit (Mountain View, Calif.) 3(8)*, Jan 1984, 26-32;75-77;80-83.
LEVEL: I LANG: Eng SIRC ARTICLE NO: 094550

Cooper, K. Cooper recommends six 'building blocks' to wellness. *Employee health & fitness (Atlanta, Ga.) 6(12)*, Dec 1984, 145-146;148.
LEVEL: B LANG: Eng SIRC ARTICLE NO: 105435

Elson, P.R. Information age makes old definition of library obsolete. L'age de l'information rend perimee l'ancienne definition de la bibliotheque. *CAHPER journal/Revue de l'ACSEPR (Ottawa) 50(5)*, May/Jun 1984, 28-29.
LEVEL: B LANG: Eng Fr SIRC ARTICLE NO: 096185

Fitness. Toronto: PARTICIPaction, c1984. 16 p. : ill.
CORP: PARTICIPaction.
LEVEL: B LANG: Eng GV481 20861

Hatfield, F.C. Sport fitness: feeling fit and looking good are part and parcel of the bodybuilding

lifestyle. Some sports fans want more - they want to play sports with a proficiency that matches their fitness and good looks. Here's how to shape up for any athletic endeavor. *Muscle & fitness (Woodland Hills, Calif.) 45(10), Oct 1984, 90-92;165-166;168;170;172;175.*
LEVEL: B LANG: Eng SIRC ARTICLE NO: 108997

Lagarde, F. Sante et activite physique. Longueuil, Que.: College Edouard-Montpetit, c1984. ix, 127 p. : ill.
CORP: Kino-Quebec.
NOTES: Comprend des bibliographies.
LEVEL: I LANG: Fr ISBN: 2-920411-01-2 GV481 17104

Lee, R.V. The generalist: a jaundiced view. XXXIV. Burnt offerings. (editorial) *American journal of medicine (New York) 77(2), Aug 1984, 197-198.*
LEVEL: B LANG: Eng SIRC ARTICLE NO: 104255

Myths and facts about exercise. *Executive fitness newsletter (Emmaus, Pa.) 15(3), 4 Feb 1984, 1-2.*
NOTES: Excerpted from: Fitness for everyone, Rodale Press.
LEVEL: B LANG: Eng SIRC ARTICLE NO: 094566

Nikolaev, V. Galitsky, A. Health for everyone. *Soviet sports review (Escondido, Calif.) 19(3), Sept 1984, 150-152.*
NOTES: Translated from, Fizkultura i sport 11, 1983, 18-19.
LEVEL: B LANG: Eng SIRC ARTICLE NO: 102733

Optaz, J.P. Wellness promotion strategies. Selected proceedings of the Annual National Wellness Conference. Alexandria, Va.: Computer Microfilm International, 1984. 1 microfiche (158 fr.)
CONF: National Wellness Conference (8th : Stevens Point, Wisc.).
LEVEL: A LANG: Eng EDRS: ED243864

Rogers, C.C. Books by exercise experts: why aren't they working out? (Refs: 8)*Physician and sportsmedicine 12(3), Mar 1984, 143-145;148-150.*
LEVEL: B LANG: Eng SIRC ARTICLE NO: 091690

Serfass, R.C. Gerberich, S.G. Exercise for optimal health: strategies and motivational considerations. (Refs: 119)*Preventiv medicine (New York) 13(1), Jan 1984, 79-99.*
LEVEL: A LANG: Eng SIRC ARTICLE NO: 100874

Sheehan, G.A. The case for exercise. *American journal of cardiology (New York) 53(1), 1 Jan 1984, 260.*
LEVEL: B LANG: Eng SIRC ARTICLE NO: 097701

Shuffield, G. Dana, R.H. Wellness assessment: a rationale, a measure, and physical/psychological components. Alexandria, Va. Computer Microfilm International, 1984. 1 microfiche (7 fr.)
CONF: Society for Personality Assessment. Meeting (1984 : Tampa, Fla.).
LEVEL: A LANG: Eng EDRS: ED248212

Stone, W. Physical fitness for the dentist. *New York State dental journal (New York) 50(5), May 1984, 283-285.*
LEVEL: B LANG: Eng SIRC ARTICLE NO: 100875

Tanner, G. The development of a school based executive fitness group. *British journal of physical education (London) 15(1), Mar/Apr 1984, 56-57.*
LEVEL: B LANG: Eng SIRC ARTICLE NO: 099213

Tinning, R. Social critique in physical education. *ACHPER national journal 103, Mar 1984, 10.*
LEVEL: B LANG: Eng SIRC ARTICLE NO: 097706

Wade, C. How to exercise your way to total fitness. It's the greatest all-natural way to build a youthful body and mind. And it's fun, too. *Muscle training illustrated (New York) 18(6), Aug 1984, 34-37;91-92.*
LEVEL: B LANG: Eng SIRC ARTICLE NO: 104269

Williamson, W.M. Hamley, E.J. Fitness and health measurement in air crew. (Refs: 17)*British journal of sports medicine (Loughborough, Eng.) 18(2), Jun 1984, 110-115.*
ABST: To fulfil the various tasks and roles efficiently in the Royal Air Force good health is implicit but 'fitness' is not so specifically defined. Using a system of submaximal measurement of oxygen uptake (VO2), skinfold thickness, weight and health parameters involving an acturial scaled questionnaire and blood pressure measurement, a fitness profile was developed evaluating health and fitness. The physiologic characteristics of eighty-two aircrew, 90% fast-jet, fixed-wing and 10% rotary wing employed in search and rescue duties, were investigated in evaluating and developing the fitness profile.
LEVEL: A LANG: Eng SIRC ARTICLE NO: 102753

Witczak, T.J. Physical-fitness with a pay incentive. *Police chief (Gaithersburg, Md.) 51(1), 1984, 50-51.*
LEVEL: B LANG: Eng SIRC ARTICLE NO: 099217

ADMINISTRATION

Wankel, L. Exercise goals: keeping task and person goals in balance. *Fitness leader (Ottawa) 2(9), May 1984, 17-18.*
LEVEL B LANG: Eng SIRC ARTICLE NO: 100884

Warnick, R.B. Marketing factors in the evaluation of exercise/fitness programs: an examination of core and fringe participation by importance-performance analysis. Eugene, Ore.: Microform Publications, University of Oregon, 1984. 3 microfiches : negative, ill. ; 11 x 15 cm.
NOTES: Thesis (Ph.D.) - Pennsylvania State University, 1983; (xi, 203, (1) leaves); vita; includes bibliography.
LEVEL: A LANG: Eng UO84 358-360

ASSOCIATIONS

Dechavanne, N. La Federation francaise d'education physique et de gymnastique volontaire. *Revue de l'education physique (Liege, Belgique) 24(4), 1984, 3-6.*
LEVEL: B LANG: Fr SIRC ARTICLE NO: 104218

National group hopes to unite 50 state fitness councils. *Athletic purchasing and facilities (Madison, Wis.) 8(1), Jan 1984, 12-13.*
LEVEL: B LANG: Eng SIRC ARTICLE NO: 094567

ATTITUDE

Bassey, E.J. Fentem, P.H. Skene, P.C. Health professionals view on exercise - a study. *Journal of the Royal Society of Health (London) 194(6), Dec 1984, 225-228.*
LEVEL: A LANG: Eng SIRC ARTICLE NO: 106685

BIBLIOGRAPHIES

Fitness resource list. *Parks & recreation (Alexandria, Va.) 19(12), Dec 1984, 62-63.*
LEVEL: B LANG: Eng SIRC ARTICLE NO: 173260

BIOGRAPHY AND AUTOBIOGRAPHY

Cross, I. Interview with Jack Ramsay. *Running & fitness (Washington, D.C.) 16(4), Jul/Aug 1984, 10-11.*
LEVEL: B LANG: Eng SIRC ARTICLE NO: 105436

CERTIFICATION

Guidelines for the training and recognition of fitness leaders in Canada. Lignes directrices sur la formation et la reconnaissance des moniteurs de conditionnement physique au Canada. Ottawa: Fitness Canada : Interprovincial Sport and Recreation Council, c1984. 16, 20 p. (Cat. no. H93-89/1984.)
CORP: Canada. Fitness and Amateur Sport.
CORP: Canada. Condition physique et Sport amateur.
CORP: Interprovincial Sport and Recreation Council.
CORP: Conseil interprovincial du sport et des loisirs.
NOTES: French and English texts on inverted pages with separate paging. Textes francais et anglais disposes tete-beche avec pagination separee.
LEVEL: B LANG: Eng Fr ISBN: 0-662-53330-5 GV481 18302

Wilson, P.K. Hall, L.K. Industrial fitness, adult fitness, and cardiac rehabilitation: graduate programs specific to trainin exercise specialists. *Journal of physical education, recreation & dance 55(3), Mar 1984, 40-44.*
LEVEL: B LANG: Eng SIRC ARTICLE NO: 093063

ECONOMICS

Mallick, M. Vigor vaults to the top. *Australian business 4(9), 29 Feb 1984, 74-75.*
ABST: Fitness franchisees expect to make more than $100,000 a year, while Vigor's management is driving for a healthy $100 million turnover by 1988. This year's expansion is international.
LEVEL: B LANG: Eng SIRC ARTICLE NO: 093051

EQUIPMENT

At home with exercise. *Fit (Mountain View, Calif.) 3(8), Jan 1984, 60-69.*
LEVEL: B LANG: Eng SIRC ARTICLE NO: 094546

Brodsky, A.B. Health equipment. *Pool & spa news (Los Angeles, Calif.) 23(4), 27 Feb 1984, 30-32;55.*
LEVEL: B LANG: Eng SIRC ARTICLE NO: 097473

Conditioning, training and testing equipment: products used in athletic training, conditioning and testing programs are listed here. The manufacturers and suppliers of each product are listed alphabetically following the heading. *Athletic purchasing and facilities (Madison, Wis.) 8(2), Feb 1984, 147-148;150;152;154.*
NOTES: 1984 buyers guide.
LEVEL: B LANG: Eng SIRC ARTICLE NO: 108283

Dayton, L. Those marvelous machines: assisted by cams, cables and complicated gears, today's technologically advanced machines can help you

slim, trim and get in shape. *Fit (Mountain View, Calif.) 4(4), Sept 1984, 73-77;80.*
LEVEL: B LANG: Eng SIRC ARTICLE NO: 108554

Equipment: the home market. *Fitness industry (Miami, Fla.) 2(2), Mar/Apr 1984, 48-50;52;54;56.*
LEVEL: B LANG: Eng SIRC ARTICLE NO: 097483

Focus on fitness equipment. *Sports trade Canada (Downsview, Ont.) 12(4), May/Jun 1984, 10;12-13;15-16.*
LEVEL: B LANG: Eng SIRC ARTICLE NO: 103910

Growth through diversity. (Weider Sports Equipment) *Sports trade Canada (Downsview, Ont.) 12(4), May/Jun 1984, 19.*
LEVEL: B LANG: Eng SIRC ARTICLE NO: 103911

Jarvis, W. Fitness equipment: the market of the '80s flexes its muscle. *Bicycle dealer showcase (Irvine, Calif.) 13(10), Oc 1984, 10-15;20.*
LEVEL: B LANG: Eng SIRC ARTICLE NO: 108791

Knight, T. Specialization for success. (physical fitness equipment) *Sports retailer (Mt. Prospect, Ill.) 37(5), May 1984, 46-47.*
LEVEL: B LANG: Eng SIRC ARTICLE NO: 100559

Lafavore, M. The home gym: a guide to fitness equipment. New York: Avon, c1984. 175 p. : ill.
LEVEL: B LANG: Eng ISBN: 0-380-87965-4 LC CARD: 84-091117 GV409 20153

Mosher, C. Bringing home the gym. *Women's sports (Palo Alto, Calif.) 6(11), Nov 1984, 35-41.*
LEVEL: B LANG: Eng SIRC ARTICLE NO: 173597

Netter, P. Merfeld, K. Patrick Netter's high-tech fitness. New York: Workman Pub., c1984. 280 p. : ill.
CORP: High-Tech Fitness Team.
LEVEL: B LANG: Eng ISBN: 0-89480-771-4 LC CARD: 84-040317 GV481 18895

Stedman, N. The electric sportsman: technology is becoming the toughest fitness trainer of all. *Health magazine (New York) 16(1), Jan 1984, 28;30-32;62.*
LEVEL: B LANG: Eng SIRC ARTICLE NO: 094578

The fitness revolution: how to make it pay in dollars and sense. *American bicyclist and motorcyclist (New York) 105(2), Feb 1984, 113-115;126-127;131;138.*
LEVEL: B LANG: Eng SIRC ARTICLE NO: 097486

Wiley, J. Make your own exercise equipment. 1st ed. Blue Ridge Summit, Pa.: TAB Books, c1984. vi, 233 p. : ill.
NOTES: Includes index.
LEVEL: I LANG: Eng ISBN: 0-8306-1779-5 LC CARD: 84-016428 GV543 18679

EXERCISE PRESCRIPTION

Hanson, P. Exercise prescription. Part II: Clinical guidelines for exercise training. (Refs: 29)
NOTES: In, Strauss, R.H. (ed.), Sports medicine, Philadelphia ; Toronto, Saunders, 1984, p. 45-56.
LEVEL: A LANG: Eng RC1210 17196

Hartley, L.H. Exercise prescription. Part I: General principles of exercise prescription.
NOTES: In, Strauss, R.H. (ed.), Sports medicine, Philadelphia ; Toronto, Saunders, 1984, p. 41-45.
LEVEL: A LANG: Eng RC1210 17196

Ribisl, P.M. Developing an exercise prescription for health. (Refs: 19)*In, Matarazzo, J.D. (ed.) et al., Behavioral health: a handbook of health enhancement and disease prevention, New York,*

Wiley, c1984, p. 448-466.
LEVEL: I LANG: Eng

Schmidt, L. Practical aspects of exercise prescription and counselling for lifetime health and fitness. (Refs: 6)
CONF: Physical Education Graduating Seminar Conference (1984 : Footscray Institute of Technology).
NOTES: In, Physical education in Australia: past, present and future directions, s.l., Footscray Institute of Technology, 1984, p. 117-121.
LEVEL: I LANG: Eng SIRC ARTICLE NO: 096204

Sharkey, B.J. Physiology of fitness: prescribing exercise for fitness, weight control, and health. 2nd ed. Champaign, Ill.: Human Kinetics Publishers, c1984. xv, 365 p. : ill.
NOTES: Includes index. Bibliography: p. 351-359.
LEVEL: I LANG: Eng ISBN: 0931250668 LC CARD: 84-003850 RC1235 17491

FACILITIES

Barrett, S. How to find a health club fit for you. *Slimmer (Santa Monica, Calif.) 4(4), Jun 1984, 56-58;70.*
LEVEL: B LANG Eng SIRC ARTICLE NO: 100849

Fitness & fittings: everything you need to know about building a dance or health studio. *Sport and leisure (London) 25(2), May/Jun 1984, 36-37.*
LEVEL: B LANG: Eng SIRC ARTICLE NO: 103919

Russell, D.G. Health and fitness: our professional responsibility. (Refs: 2)*New Zealand journal of health, physical education & recreation (Dunedin, New Zealand) 17(2), Aug 1984, 9-11.*
LEVEL: I LANG: Eng SIRC ARTICLE NO: 099205

Selcon, H. Annotation: an open-air running and circuit exercising track in France. *British journal of sports medicine (Loughborough, Eng.) 18(3), Sept 1984, 223-225.*
LEVEL: B LANG: Eng SIRC ARTICLE NO: 102419

Westcott, W.L. Establishing sports conditioning complex is effective. *Journal of physical education and program (Columbus, Ohio) 81(8), Dec 1984, H12-H13.*
LEVEL: B LANG: Eng SIRC ARTICLE NO: 108252

FLEXIBILITY

Borms, J. Importance of flexibility in overall physical fitness. (Refs: 96)*International journal of physical education (Schorndorf, W. Germany) 21(2), 19-26 Jul 1984, 15-26.*
LEVEL: I LANG: Eng SIRC ARTICLE NO: 097677

Loewendahl, E. Body basics: testing your flexibility. *Slimmer (Santa Monica, Calif.) 4(3), May 1984, 17-21.*
LEVEL: B LANG Eng SIRC ARTICLE NO: 100867

Stevenson, E. The trunk twister. (Refs: 4)*CAHPERD journal times (Danville, Calif.) 47(2), Nov 1984, 15.*
LEVEL: B LANG: En SIRC ARTICLE NO: 108274

Uppal, A.K. Singh, R. Effect of training and break in training on flexibility of physical education majors. (Refs: 9)*SNIPES journal (Patiala, India) 7(4), Oct 1984, 49-53.*
ABST: The flexibility of 28 boys and thirteen girls, aged between 16 and 21 years, participating in a regular programme of physical education and conditioning was tested 10 weeks after training and 4 weeks after break in training. Improvements of the

flexibility of the hip, trunk, shoulder and spine as measured by Sit and Reach, Standing Bobbing, Shoulder flexibility and Spine flexibility tests respectively were observed following training. Detraining lowered the flexibility of hip, trunk, shoulder and spine.
LEVEL: A LANG: Eng SIRC ARTICLE NO: 171616

LIFESTYLE

Arends, J. Lifestyle of fitness. *MAHPERD: Michigan journal for health, physical education, recreation, dance (Ypsilanti, Mich.) Spring 1984, 5-6.*
LEVEL: B LANG: Eng SIRC ARTICLE NO: 094545

Arends, J. Lifestyle of fitness. *MAHPERD journal (Yspilanti, Mich.) Winter 1984, 5-6.*
NOTES: Reprinted from, Michigan medicine, May 1983.
LEVEL: B LANG: Eng SIRC ARTICLE NO: 097675

Blair, S.N. Goodyear, N.N. Wynne, K.L. Saunders, R.P. Comparison of dietary and smoking habit changes in physical fitness improvers and nonimprovers. *Preventive medicine (New York) 13(4), Jul 1984, 411-420.*
LEVEL: A LANG: Eng

Matarazzo, J.D. Weiss, S.M. Herd, J.A. Miller, N.E. Behavioral health: a handbook of health enhancement and disease prevention. New York: Wiley, c1984. xx, 1292 p. (A Wiley-Interscience publication.)
LEVEL: A LANG: Eng ISBN: 0-471-86975-9 LC CARD: 84-11906

MEDICINE

Brodzinski, W. Analiza czynnikowa wybranych parametrow psychomotoryki w badaniu wplywow krwawien menstruacyjnych na sprawnos kobiet. (Factor analysis of selected psychomotor indicators in the study of the effect of menstrual bleeding on the physical fitness of women.) *Wiadomosci lekarskie (Warsaw) 37(17), 1 Sept 1984, 1331-1335.*
LEVEL: A LANG: Pol

Buchan, N. Fitness instructing - what a physiotherapist would like to see. *Recreation reporter (Vancouver, B.C.) Mar/Apr 1984, 8.*
LEVEL: B LANG: Eng SIRC ARTICLE NO: 097679

Lack of physical activity can make body grow old faster. *Employee health & fitness (Atlanta, Ga.) 6(3), Mar 1984, 34-35.*
LEVEL: B LANG: Eng SIRC ARTICLE NO: 093048

Macauley, D.C. Promoting exercise from general practice. (editorial) *Practitioner (London) 228(1397), Nov 1984, 991-993.*
LEVEL: B LANG: Eng

Make the goal fitness, not fastness. *Referee (Franksville, Wis.) 9(5), May 1984, 29.*
LEVEL: B LANG: Eng SIRC ARTICLE NO: 097695

Mostafa, S.D. Garrett, H.L. Freeman, R.A. Physical exercise and health: a review study. *Journal of the Mississippi State Medical Association (Jackson) 25(4), Apr 1984, 87-88.*
LEVEL: B LANG: Eng SIRC ARTICLE NO: 102732

Oberman, A. Healthy exercise. *Western journal of medicine (San Francisco) 141(6), Dec 1984, 864-871.*
LEVEL: I LANG: Eng SIRC ARTICLE NO: 106731

Stromme, S.B. Frey, H. Harlem, O.K. Stokke, O. Vellar, O.D. Aaro, L.E. Johnsen, J.E. Sante et activite physique. (Refs: 62)
NOTES: Dans, Lagarde, F. (ed.), Sante et activite physique, Longueuil, Que., College Edouard-Montpetit, c1984, p. 15-33.
LEVEL: I LANG: Fr GV481 17104

The benefits of fitness. *National racquetball (Glenview, Ill.)* 13(10), Oct 1984, 22-23.
LEVEL: B LANG: Eng SIRC ARTICLE NO: 105433

MIDDLE AGED

Cupelli, V. Brettoni, M. Attina, D.A. Laverone, E. Arcangeli, G. Cupelli, G. Bucchino, G. Bini, G. Giuliano, G. Cardiovascular response to maximal exercise in active elderly healthy people. (Refs: 28)*Journal of sports medicine and physical fitness (Torino, Italy)* 24(4), Dec 1984, 273-279.
ABST: The influence of variables (age, sport, degree of training, athletic seniority) on the cardiovascular responses of 216 subjects to maximal cycloergometer tests were examined. Systolic blood pressure (BP) was higher and efficiency (E) better in the groups of subjects over 50. The maximal work load, E and test duration were higher for aerobic sports, diastolic BP after exercise was higher for mixed sports. Trained subjects showed higher double product and better E in contrast to non-athletic subjects showing a higher systolic BP standard and reaching a lower work load. It is maintained that older subjects, particularly those with higher BP, must be started on aerobic sports which, if correctly calibrated, protect them from BP increases.
LEVEL: A LANG: Eng SIRC ARTICLE NO: 106694

Fitness on trial. La condition physique en proces. (Toronto): TV Ontario, Fitness and Amateur Sport Canada, 1984. 1 film, 35 mm.
CORP: Canada. Fitness Canada.
CORP: TV Ontario.
LEVEL: B LANG: Eng Fr

Jerome, J. Staying with it. New York: Viking Press, c1984. xii, 225 p.
NOTES: Portions of this book appeared originally in American health, Car and driver, Harvard magazine, Outside, Running, Sportstyle and United magazine in different form.
LEVEL: B LANG: Eng ISBN: 0670668761 LC CARD: 83-040226 GV711.5 17640

MOTIVATION

Abraham, L. The Expres program and adherence. Le programme Expres et l'assiduite. *Periscope (Ottawa)* 16, 1984, 21-24.
LEVEL: B LANG: Eng Fr SIRC ARTICLE NO: 179915

Howe, M.A. Ogilvie, B.C. The physician as fitness motivator. (Refs: 22)
NOTES: In, Birrer, R.B. (ed.), Sports medicine for the primary care physician, Norwalk, Conn., Appleton-Century-Crofts, c1984, p. 313-325.
LEVEL: I LANG: Eng RC1210 17030

Norton, C.J. Student purposes for engaging in fitness activities. Eugene, Ore.: Microform Publications, University of Oregon 1984. 2 microfiches : negative ; 11 x 15 cm.
NOTES: Thesis (Ed.D.) - University of Georgia, 1982; (viii, 151 leaves); includes bibliography.
LEVEL: A LANG: Eng UO84 268-269

Oatey, J.S. Hammond, M.A. Where do you fit? (Refs: 2)*In, Vendl, B.C. (ed.) et al., Interpretive aspects of intramural-recreational sports: selected proceedings from the Thirty-fifth Annual National Intramural-Recreational Sports Association Conference, Corvallis, Or., Oregon State University, c1984, p. 258-261.*
CONF: National Intramural-Recreational Sports Association Conference (35th : 1984 : Fort Worth, Tex.).
LEVEL: B LANG: Eng GV710 18914

Turock, A. Getting physical: powerful, easy-to-learn techniques for motivating yourself to stick with regular exercise. Seattle, Wash.: Turock Fitness Pub., c1984. 1v.
LEVEL: B LANG: Eng ISBN: 091691500X LC CARD: 84-002726

Wankel, L. Decision-making approaches to increase exercise commitment. *Fitness leader (Ottawa)* 2(10), Jun 1984, 37-38.
LEVEL: B LANG: Eng SIRC ARTICLE NO: 102153

PARTICIPACTION

The Canadian idea: fitness should be fun. *Athletic business (Madison, Wis.)* 8(3), Mar 1985, 12;14;16.
LEVEL: B LANG: Eng SIRC ARTICLE NO: 175919

PARTICIPATION

Dean, P.J. Physical activity patterns in Ontario - IIa. A research report from the Ministry of Tourism and Recreation. 1982-83 update. Toronto: Ministry of Tourism and Recreation, 1984?. 7 leaves
CORP: Ontario. Ministry of Tourism and Recreation.
CORP: Fitness Ontario.
NOTES: Cover title.
LEVEL: B LANG: Eng GV481 17878

PHILOSOPHY

Griffin, J.C. The formula for fitness adherence. La solution pour assurer la fidelite aux programmes de conditionnement physique. (Refs: 10)*CAHPER journal (Ottawa)* 51(1), Sept/Oct 1984, 24-26.
NOTES: Part of a series of Fitness Tips prepared by the CAHPER Fitness Committee. Ces conseils en conditionnement physique proviennent de la serie preparee par le comite de la Condition physique ACESPL.
LEVEL: B LANG: Eng Fr SIRC ARTICLE NO: 100860

POLICY

Wankel, L. Participant goals and leadership roles. *Fitness leader (Ottawa)* 2(9), May 1984, 33-36.
LEVEL: B LANG: Eng SIRC ARTICLE NO: 100883

POSTURE

Back owner's manual. Toronto: PARTICIPaction, c1984. 16 p. ; ill.
CORP: PARTICIPaction.
NOTES: Cover title.
LEVEL: B LANG: Eng RA781.5 20863

Mayo, D. Mayo, J. Perfect posture: correct body alignment is essential to your workout and your well-being. *Fit (Mountain View, Calif.)* 4(4), Sept 1984, 33;88;90;92.
LEVEL: B LANG: Eng SIRC ARTICLE NO: 108551

Your back is always working. Toronto: PARTICIPaction, c1984. 16 p.
CORP: PARTICIPaction.
LEVEL: B LANG: Eng RA781.5 20858

PROMOTION

Bartos, S. Medicina--prevence--pohyb. (Medicine--prevention--exercise.) *Casopis lekaru ceskych (Praha)* 123(29), 20 Jul 1984 890-892.
LEVEL: A LANG: Cze

Feher, A. Lifetime sports. (Refs: 5)
CONF: Physical Education Graduating Seminar Conference (1984 : Footscray Institute of Technology).
NOTES: In, Physical education in Australia: past, present and future direction, s.l., Footscray Institute of Technology, 1984, Suppl. p. 19-22.
LEVEL: I LANG: Eng SIRC ARTICLE NO: 096188

Gross, R. A preliminary evaluation of a health promotion program for the reduction of health-risk behaviors of college students. Eugene, Ore.: Microform Publications, University of Oregon, 1984. 1 microfiche : negative, ill. ; 11 x 15 cm.
NOTES: Thesis (M.S.) - University of Oregon, 1984; (viii, 88 leaves); vita; includes bibliography.
LEVEL: A LANG: Eng UO84 428

Heinila, L. Ways of promoting voluntary physical education activity in present-day society. (Refs: 16)*Bulletin of the Federation internationale d'education physique (Cheltenham, Eng.)* 54(1), Jan/Mar 1984, 45-49.
CONF: Congress on Sport and International Understanding (1982 : Helsinki).
LEVEL: I LANG: Eng SIRC ARTICLE NO: 094561

Keys, C. Fitness and the public health nurse. Le conditionnement physique et les infirmieres de l'hygiene publique. *CPHA health digest/ACHP selection sante (Ottawa)* Apr/avr 1984, 2-5;2-4.
LEVEL: B LANG: Eng Fr SIRC ARTICLE NO: 100864

Melancon, J.G. Marketing fitness: sell the imagery not the agony. Marketing de la pleine forme: une vente de l'imagerie et non de l'agonie. *Periscope (Ottawa)* 16, 1984, 95-98.
LEVEL: B LANG: Eng Fr SIRC ARTICLE NO: 179920

PSYCHOLOGY

Biddle, S. Motivation issues in health-related fitness: a note of caution. *British journal of physical education (London)* 15(1), Jan/Feb 1984, 21-22.
LEVEL: I LANG: Eng SIRC ARTICLE NO: 099182

Chodzko-Zajko, W.J. Ismail, A.H. MMPI interscale relationships in middle-aged males SS before and after an 8-month fitness program. (Refs: 20)*Journal of clinical psychology (Brandon, Vt.)* 40(1), Jan 1984, 163-169.
LEVEL: A LANG: Eng SIRC ARTICLE NO: 109764

Corbin, C.B. Laurie, D.R. Gruger, C. Smiley, B. Vicarious success experience as a factor influencing self-confidence, attitudes, and physical activity of adult women. (Refs: 11)*Journal of teaching in physical education (Champaign, Ill.)* 4(1), Oct 1984, 17-23.
ABST: Recent research indicates that females are particularly likely to lack confidence in their abilities to perform physical activities. One theory of instruction suggests a need for educational support for developing competence, self-confidence, and

PHYSICAL FITNESS (continued)

persistence in physical activities. Thirty-nine adult women participating in an exercise class were studied to determine if vicarious success presented via audiovisuals was effective in altering self-confidence, commitment to physical activity, and physical activity involvement. A discriminant function analysis indicated a significant difference between treatment and control groups on a profile of improved confidence/attitude/activity involvement, with the treatment group showing a more positive profile. Vicarious success experiences enhanced self-confidence, and there was a trend toward greater persistence in activity among those experiencing vicarious success through audiovisual presentations.
LEVEL: A LANG: Eng SIRC ARTICLE NO: 102846

Griffith, L.L. When fitness becomes an obsession. *Fit (Mountain View, Calif.) 3(9), Feb 1984, 42-44;78.*
LEVEL: B LANG: En SIRC ARTICLE NO: 099191

Griffith, L.L. Are you afraid of fitness? *Fit (Mountain View, Calif.) 4(5), Oct 1984, 66-68.*
LEVEL: B LANG: Eng SIRC ARTICLE NO: 106707

Kriz, M. Krizova, M. Balaz, J. Petrik, A. Hajek, T. Vplyv pravidelnej zataze na psychicky stav, vykonnostne a somaticke parametre. (The effect of regular exercise on mental status, performance and somatic parameters.) *Ceskoslovenske zdravotnictvi (Praha) 32(4), Apr 1984, 180-186.*
LEVEL: A LANG: Slo

Short, M.A. DiCarlo, S. Steffee, W.P. Pavlov, K. Effects of physical conditioning on self-concept of adult obese males. *Physical therapy (Alexandria, Va.) 64(2), Feb 1984, 194-198.*
ABST: The purpose of this study was to investigate the possible effects of a supervised physical conditioning program on psychological measures in 45 obese police men. For an eight-week program of instruction regarding physical conditioning and nutrition, 22 randomly selected subjects also participated in an aerobic conditioning program. The remaining 23 subjects were asked to maintain activity habits similar to those before the study. At the end of eight weeks, the exercising group displayed significantly higher measures of maximal oxygen consumption, an index of physical fitness, and higher scores on the Physical Self and Self-satisfaction subscales of the Tennessee Self-concept Scale. These results reinforce the interrelationship between physical exercise and self-concept, as conditioning and diet were associated with greater improvements in obese police men.
LEVEL: A LANG: Eng SIRC ARTICLE NO: 094661

Sothmann, M.S. Ismail, A.H. Chodepkozajiko, W. Influence of catecholamine activity on the hierarchical relationships among physical fitness condition and selected personality characteristics. (Refs: 24)*Journal of clinical psychology (Brandon, Vt.) 40(6), 1984, 1308-1317.*
LEVEL: A LANG: Eng SIRC ARTICLE NO: 104264

Yeager, T. Rewarding yourself for fitness. *Fit (Mountain View, Calif.) 3(11), Apr 1984, 36-37;81-82.*
LEVEL: B LANG: Eng SIRC ARTICLE NO: 099218

PSYCHOPHYSIOLOGY

Buffone, G.W. Exercise as a therapeutic adjunct. NOTES: In, Silva, J.M. and Weinberg, R.S. (eds.), Psychological foundation of sport, Champaign, Ill., Human Kinetics Publishers, c1984, p. 445-451.
LEVEL: A LANG: Eng GV706.4 17779

Sachs, M.L. Psychological well-being and vigorous physical activity. NOTES: In, Silva, J.M. and Weinberg, R.S. (eds.), Psychological foundations of sport, Champaign, Ill., Human Kinetics Publishers, c1984, p. 435-444.
LEVEL: A LANG: Eng GV706.4 17779

Sothmann, M.S. Ismail, A.H. Chodepko-Zajiko, W. Influence of catecholamine activity on the hierarchical relationships among physical fitness condition and selected personality characteristics. *Journal of clinical psychology (Brandon, Va.) 40(6), Nov 1984, 1308-1317.*
LEVEL: A LANG: Eng

RESEARCH

What's going on 1984. Practical research in physical activity: a review of research projects funded by Fitness Canada, Fitness and Amateur Sport. Mise a jour 1984. Recherche appliquee en activite physique: survol des projets de recherche subventionnes par Condition physique Canada, Condition physique et Sport amateur. Ottawa: Fitness and Amateur Sport, 1984. 44, 50 p. : ill.
CORP: Canada. Fitness and Amateur Sport.
CORP: Canada. Condition physique et Sport amateur.
NOTES: French and English texts on inverted pages with separate paging. Textes francais et anglais disposes tete-beche avec pagination separee.
LEVEL: I LANG: Eng Fr GV481 15187

RESEARCH METHODS

Blair, S.N. How to assess exercise habits and physical fitness. (Refs: 30)*In, Matarazzo, J.D. (ed.) et al., Behavioral health: a handbook of health enhancement and disease prevention, New York, Wiley, c1984, p. 424-447.*
LEVEL: I LANG: Eng

Montoye, H.J. Taylor, H.L. Measurement of physical activity in population studies: a review. *Human biology (Detroit) 56(2), May 1984, 195-216.*
LEVEL: A LANG: Eng

SMOKING

Cigarette smoking declining in Canada. L'usage de la cigarette au Canada est en baisse. (Refs: 1)*Highlights/Faits saillants (Ottawa) 21, Jan 1984, 1-2.*
CORP: Canada Fitness Survey.
CORP: Enquete condition physique Canada.
LEVEL: B LANG: Eng Fr SIRC ARTICLE NO: 094331

Do young women start smoking for weight control? Les femmes commencent-elles a fumer pour controler leur poids? *Highlights/Faits saillants (Ottawa) 20, Jan 1984, 1-2.*
CORP: Canada Fitness Survey.
CORP: Enquete condition physique Canada.
LEVEL: B LANG: Eng Fr SIRC ARTICLE NO: 094332

Epstein, L.H. Dickson, B.E. McKenzie, S. Russell, P.O. The effect of smoking on perception of muscle tension. *Psychopharmacology (Berlin) 83(1), 1984, 107-113.*
LEVEL: A LANG: Eng

Larsson, L. Orlander, J. Skeletal muscle morphology, metabolism and function in smokers and non-smokers. A study on smoking-discordant monozygous twins. *Acta physiologica scandinavica (Stockholm) 120(3), Mar 1984, 343-352.*
LEVEL: A LANG: Eng

Stamford, B.A. Matter, S. Fell, R.D. Sady, S. Cresanta, M.K. Papanek, P. Cigarette smoking, physical activity, and alcohol consumption: relationship to blood lipids and lipoproteins in premenopausal females. (Refs: 27)*Metabolism, clinical and experimental (New York) 33(7), Jul 1984, 585-590.*
ABST: 164 premenopausal female subjects were tested. Relationships between blood lipid and lipoprotein levels as dependent variables and cigarette smoking, physical activity, and alcohol consumption were determined from partial regression analyses. Results suggest that cigarette smoking may attenuate the effects of chronic exercise and/or alcohol consumption, to raise HDL-C levels. Chronic exercise and alcohol consumption may also exert an additive effect, raising HDL-C level.
LEVEL: A LANG: Eng SIRC ARTICLE NO: 102831

Tucker, L.A. Cigarette smoking intentions and physcial fitness: a multivariate study of high school males. *Adolescence (Roslyn Heights, N.Y.) 19(74), Summer 1984, 313-321.*
LEVEL: A LANG: Eng SIRC ARTICLE NO: 104268

SOCIAL PSYCHOLOGY

Eagan, M. Why everyone isn't exercising. *Employee services management (Westchester, Ill.) 27(3), Apr 1984, 34-35.*
LEVEL: LANG: Eng SIRC ARTICLE NO: 097682

Gale, J.B. Eckhoff, W.T. Rodnick, J.E. Mogel, S.F. Factors related to adherence to an exercise program for healthy adults. (Refs: 21)*Medicine and science in sports and exercise (Indianapolis) 16(6), Dec 1984, 544-549.*
ABST: Healthy men (N, 33) and women (N, 73) participated in a 6-month exercise program three mornings per week, and their attendance scores were related to a variety of physiological, anthropometric, psychological, and demographic variables which were studied. These subjects were also grouped by adherence patterns; 18 per cent attended less than 10 per cent of the classes (early dropouts), 40 per cent attended between 10 and 50 per cent of the classes (nonadherers), and 42 per cent attended more than 50 per cent (adherers). It was concluded that for healthy volunteers, participant characteristics are not good predictors of compliance to an exercise regimen.
LEVEL: A LANG: Eng SIRC ARTICLE NO: 104246

Keller, S. Seraganian, P. Physical fitness level and autonomic reactivity to psychosocial stress. (Refs: 32)*Journal of psychosomatic research (Oxford) 28(4), 1984, 279-287.*
LEVEL: I LANG: Eng SIRC ARTICLE NO: 104252

Snyder, E.E. Spreitzer, E. Patterns of adherence to a physical conditioning program. (Refs: 32)*Sociology of sport journal (Champaign, Ill.) 1(2), 1984, 103-116.*

ABST: This study analyzes correlates of adherence to a physical fitness regimen. The sample consisted of adults who had volunteered to take a physical fitness stress test at a sports physiology laboratory. A self-administered questionnaire was mailed to persons who had taken the stress test over the past 5 years. The rationale for the study was an attempt to develop a profile of the prospective dropout from a physical fitness program in order to permit special intervention to enhance the probability of adherence. The findings showed that 31% of the persons in our sample were basically inactive subsequent to the stress test. Our set of 11 predictor variables was able to explain 33% of the variance in physical activity.
LEVEL: A LANG: Eng SIRC ARTICLE NO: 102747

SOCIOLOGY

Curtis, J.E. White, P.G. Age and sport participation: decline in participation or increased specialization with age? (Refs: 22)
CONF: North American Society for the Sociology of Sport. Conference (3rd : 1982 : Toronto, Ont.).
NOTES: In, Theberge, N. and Donnelly, P. (eds.), Sport and the sociological imagination: refereed proceedings of the 3rd Annual Conference of the North American Society for the Sociology of Sport, Toronto, Canada, November 1982, Fort Worth, Tex., Texas Christian University Press, c1984, p. 273-293.
ABST: This paper discusses results from a national sample of adult Canadians dealing with patterns of sport participation for various age groups. The findings support both the disengagement theory (which hypothesizes that as age increases so does withdrawal from sport and physical activity) and the continuity and activity theory (which hypothesizes that sport or fitness roles once acquired will be maintained).
LEVEL: A LANG: Eng SIRC ARTICLE NO: 097841

Fasting, K. L'activite physique et la sante chez les chomeurs. (Refs: 17)
NOTES: Dans, Lagarde, F. (ed.), Sante et activite physique, Longueuil, Que., College Edouard-Montpetit, c1984, p. 119-127.
LEVEL: I LANG: Fr GV481 17104

Shephard, R.J. Godin, G. Physical fitness - individual or societal responsibility? (Refs: 35)Canadian journal of public health/Revue canadienne de sante publique (Ottawa) 75(3), May/Jun 1984, 200-203.
LEVEL: B LANG: Eng SIRC ARTICLE NO: 099207

SPORT-FOR-ALL

Background paper for theme 1: 'Promotion and development of sport for all'. Results of the work undertaken by the CDDS in 1981 - 1982 - 1983. Strasbourg: Council of Europe, 1984. i, 74 p.
CONF: Conference of European Ministers Responsible for Sport (4th : 1984 : Malta).
LEVEL: A LANG: Eng GV701 17426

Heinilae, L. Ways of promoting voluntary physical activity in present-day society. (Refs: 16)In, Ilmarinen, M. (ed.) et al. Sport and International Understanding: proceedings of the congress held in Helsinki, Finland, July 7-10, 1982, Berlin, Springer-Verlag, 1984, p. 255-260.
CONF: Congress on Sport and International Understanding (1982 : Helsinki).
LEVEL: I LANG: Eng GV706.8 18979

Matthews, I. Victorian Government Sporting Policy: towards a true 'sport for all'. (Refs: 7)
CONF: Physical Education Graduating Seminar Conference (1984 : Footscray Institute of Technology).
NOTES: In, Physical education in Australia: past, present and future directions, s.l., Footscray Institute of Technology, 1984, Suppl. p. 23-31.
LEVEL: I LANG: Eng SIRC ARTICLE NO: 096425

Recommendations, publications, reports and other results of CDDS work 1975-1984, set out with reference to the European Sport for All Charter. Strasbourg: Council of Europe, Committee for the Development of Sport, 1984. 7 p. (loose-leaf)
CORP: Council of Europe. Committee for the Development of Sport.
LEVEL: B LANG: Eng GV603 20879

Van Lierde, A. Sport pour tous - groupe cible: les enfants. Etude de quelques recommandations existantes sur le sport pour les enfants (6 a 12 ans). (Refs: 18)Dans, Idrett for barn. Sport for Children. Sport pour les enfants 27.9.-1.10.1982 Tonsberg, Norway. Rapport. Oslo, Norvege, Ministere de la culture et de la science : Confederation norvegienne des sports, 1984, p. (48)-(51).
CONF: Idrett for barn. Sport for Children. Sport pour les enfants (1982 : Tonsberg, Norway).
LEVEL: A LANG: Fr GV709.2 20112

Wolanska, T. The extent, content and organisation of international co-operation in the past, present and future in respect o sport for all. (Refs: 10)In, Ilmarinen, M. (ed.) et al., Sport and International Understanding: proceedings of the congress held in Helsinki, Finland, July 7-10, 1982, Berlin, Springer-Verlag, 1984, p. 236-240.
CONF: Congress on Sport and International Understanding (1982 : Helsinki).
LEVEL: I LANG: Eng GV706.8 18979

STATISTICS AND SURVEYS

Activities for summer - and all year-round. Activites d'ete - et pour l'annee entiere. Highlights/Faits saillants (Ottawa) 26 Apr 1984, 1-2.
CORP: Canada Fitness Survey.
CORP: Enquete condition physique Canada.
LEVEL: B LANG: Eng Fr SIRC ARTICLE NO: 094543

Holt, P. Jeune, B. Fysisk inaktivitet blandt yngre voksne. En interviewundsogelse af sundhedsadfaerd blandt 917 personer i alderen 25-44 ar. (Physical inactivity among young adults. An interview of the health activities in 917 individuals aged 25-44 years.) Ugeskrift for laeger (Copenhagen) 146(42), 15 Oct 1984, 3219-3223.
NOTES: English abstract.
LEVEL: A LANG: Dan

How hard do Canadians play? L'intensite de l'activite physique chez les canadiens. Highlights/Faits saillants (Ottawa) 22, Fe 1984, 1-2.
CORP: Canada Fitness Survey.
CORP: Enquete condition physique Canada.
LEVEL: B LANG: Eng Fr SIRC ARTICLE NO: 094563

Summer is coming. A l'approche de l'ete. Highlights/Faits saillants (Ottawa) 25, Apr 1984, 1-2.
CORP: Canada Fitness Survey
CORP: Enquete condition physique Canada.

LEVEL: B LANG: Eng Fr SIRC ARTICLE NO: 094581

STRESS MANAGEMENT

Cox, C. The stress connection: combatting depression with a 20-minute exercise routine from the Nickolaus Technique. Slimme (Santa Monica, Calif.) 4(3), May 1984, 30-32.
LEVEL: B LANG: Eng SIRC ARTICLE NO: 100852

Irvine, P. Introducing college students to stress management. Health education (Reston, Va.) 15(3), May/Jun 1984, 36-37.
LEVEL: B LANG: Eng SIRC ARTICLE NO: 102857

Jaffe, D.T. Scott, C.D. From burnout to balance: a workbook for peak performance and self-renewal. New York; Montreal: McGraw-Hill , c1984. 209 p.
NOTES: Bibliography: p. 193.
LEVEL: I LANG: Eng ISBN: 0-07-032186-8 LC CARD: 84-4395 RA776 20012

Montgomery, B. Doran, R.J. Lum-Doran, P.A. Coping with stress. Toronto: Copp Clark Pitman, c1984. vi, 58 p. (Pitman health information series.)
NOTES: Bibliography: p. 58.
LEVEL: B LANG: Eng ISBN: 0-7730-4061-7 RA776 17544

Pasek, T. Daniel, J. Stress management through relaxation-concentration training. (Refs: 40)CAHPER journal/Revue de l'ACSEP (Ottawa) 50(5), May/Jun 1984, 17-19;36;38.
LEVEL: I LANG: Eng SIRC ARTICLE NO: 096336

Vaz, K. Pacing: how to manage time and stress. Slimmer (Santa Monica, Calif.) 4(2), Apr 1984, 20-21;36.
LEVEL: B LANG: En SIRC ARTICLE NO: 100881

Volkind, N.I. REziztentnost k stressu u studentov, zanimaiushchikhsia i ne zanimaiushchikhsia fizicheskimi uprazhneniiami. (Stress resistance of students who do and do not engage in physical exercises.) Gigiena i sanitariia (Moskva) 5, May 1984, 93-94.
LEVEL: I LANG: Rus

TEACHING

A model fitness program. Parks & recreation (Alexandria, Va.) 19(12), Dec 1984, 58;61.
LEVEL: B LANG: Eng SIRC ARTICLE NO: 173259

Leavitt, J.C. Here's a course outline for fitness leaders workshop. Journal of physical education and program (Columbus, Ohio) 81(3), Feb 1984, C12-C13;C15.
LEVEL: B LANG: Eng SIRC ARTICLE NO: 099195

Paris, B. La pedagogie des situations evolutives par mises en relation, au sein des sections GV. (Refs: 4)Loisirs sante (Paris) 11, sept/oct 1984, 12-14.
NOTES: Communication presentee au colloque 'Anthropologie des techniques du corps' organisee par la revue STAPS (mars 1984).
LEVEL: B LANG: Fr SIRC ARTICLE NO: 100871

Taunton, C. Fitness is fun for everyone but fitness leaders. Recreation reporter (Vancouver, B.C.) Mar/Apr 1984, 14.
LEVEL: B LANG: Eng SIRC ARTICLE NO: 097705

Watts, D.G. Kinnear, G.R. Designing creative exercise movements. (Refs: 2)Runner (Edmonton) 22(3), Fall/Winter 1984, 25-29.
LEVEL: B LANG: Eng SIRC ARTICLE NO: 104270

WEIGHT CONTROL

Collis, M. The phacts of life. Markham, Ont.: Fitzhenry & Whiteside, c1984. 110 p. : ill. LEVEL: B LANG: Eng ISBN: 0-88902-994-6 LC CARD: C85-99283-4 RA781.6 20776

de Mondenard, J.P. Comment maigrir par l'exercice physique. (Refs: 4)*Annales de kinesitherapie (Paris, France) 11(1/2), 1984, 37-40.* LEVEL: I LANG: Fr SIRC ARTICLE NO: 093037

Does concern for weight control influence activity choice? Choisit-on certaines activites pour controler son poids? *Highlights/Faits saillants (Ottawa) 24, Mar 1984, 1-2.* CORP: Canada Fitness Survey. CORP: Enquete condition physique Canada. LEVEL: B LANG: Eng Fr SIRC ARTICLE NO: 094556

Epstein, L.H. Wing, R.R. Koeske, R. Valoski, A. Effects of diet plus exercise on weight change in parents and children. (Refs: 23)*Journal of consulting and clinical psychology (Washington) 52(3), 1984, 429-437.* LEVEL: A LANG: Eng SIRC ARTICLE NO: 096187

Physical activity and weight control. L'activite physique et le controle du poids. *Highlights/Faits saillants (Ottawa) 23, Ma 1984, 1-2.* CORP: Canada Fitness Survey. CORP: Enquete condition physique Canada. LEVEL: B LANG: Eng Fr SIRC ARTICLE NO: 094570

Ross, D. Thinning your waist. Mountain View, Calif.: Anderson World Books, 1984. 1v. (The getting strong book series; bk. 4. LEVEL: B LANG: Eng ISBN: 0890373078 LC CARD: 84-018505

Sander, N. Comment la course vous fait perdre du poids. *Spiridon (Salvan, Suisse) 76, nov/dec 1984, 5-10.* LEVEL: I LANG: SIRC ARTICLE NO: 173525

PHYSICAL FITNESS - EMPLOYEE AND INDUSTRIAL FITNESS

Active rest: an office exercise break. (Refs: 2)*Fit third age/Troisieme age en forme (Ottawa) 2, 1984, 8.* LEVEL: B LANG: En SIRC ARTICLE NO: 173091

Bowman, S. Aguiar, C. Ambitious conference program attracts record attendance in Milwaukee. *AFB action (Stamford, Conn.) 7 (4), Oct/Nov 1984, 1;4-5.* LEVEL: B LANG: Eng SIRC ARTICLE NO: 106686

Break those desk-bound habits. *Executive fitness newsletter (Emmaus, Pa.) 15(13), 23 Jun 1984, 1-2.* LEVEL: B LANG: Eng SIRC ARTICLE NO: 102708

Chantry-Price, A. Fighting fit. *Occupational health (London) 36(8), Aug 1984, 348-355.* LEVEL: I LANG: Eng

Firming up the firm: part I. *Employee services management (Westchester, Ill.) 27(7), Sept 1984, 9-10.* LEVEL: B LANG: Eng SIRC ARTICLE NO: 108430

How can I fit exercise into my busy schedule? *Executive fitness newsletter (Emmaus, Pa.) 15(22), 27 Oct 1984, 1-2.* LEVEL: B LANG: Eng SIRC ARTICLE NO: 108881

Hrcka, J. Connaissance: la culture physique et les travailleurs intellectuels. *Sport & plein air (Paris) 290, oct 1984, 16-17.* LEVEL: B LANG: Fr SIRC ARTICLE NO: 105439

Kurt, T.L. Fitness program should blend prevention with medical care. *Occupational health and safety (Waco, Tex.) May 1984, 56;61.* LEVEL: B LANG: Eng SIRC ARTICLE NO: 102725

Levis Plaza Fitness Center: the people are the program. *Athletic business (Madison, Wis.) 8(3), Mar 1984, 64;66.* LEVEL: B LANG: Eng SIRC ARTICLE NO: 178380

Muir Gray, J.A. Ennis, J.R. Facilitating fitness at work. (Refs: 1)*Journal of the Royal College of Physicians of London (London) 18(3), Jul 1984, 180-181.* LEVEL: B LANG: Eng SIRC ARTICLE NO: 104259

Robinson, M. Becoming fitter at work. (Refs: 2)*Occupational health (London) 36(10), Oct 1984, 456-461.* LEVEL: I LANG: Eng SIRC ARTICLE NO: 174315

Smolander, J. Louhevaara, V. Oja, P. Policemen's physical fitness in relation to the frequency of leisure-time physical exercise. *International archives of occupational and environmental health (Berlin) 54(4), 1984, 295-302.* LEVEL: A LANG: Eng

Smythe, M.A. Fitness in the workplace. How employee-fitness programs are helping to lower stress and raise productivity. *Ottawa business life (Ottawa) Jul/Aug 1984, 8-9;27.* LEVEL: B LANG: Eng SIRC ARTICLE NO: 105447

ADMINISTRATION

Baun, W.B. Baun, M. A corporate health and fitness program: motivation and management by computers. (Refs: 3)*Journal of physical education, recreation & dance (Reston, Va.) 55(4), Apr 1984, 42-45.* LEVEL: B LANG: Eng SIRC ARTICLE NO: 094547

Cooper, K.H. Collingwood, T.R. Physical fitness: programming issues for total well being. (Refs: 3)*Journal of physical education, recreation & dance 55(3), Mar 1984, 35-36;44.* LEVEL: B LANG: Eng SIRC ARTICLE NO: 093036

Flynn, R.B. Berg, K. Community health promotion and wellness: a working model. *Journal of physical education, recreation & dance 55(3), Mar 1984, 37-39.* LEVEL: B LANG: Eng SIRC ARTICLE NO: 093043

Gartska, J.W. Planning the sports award banquet. *Employee services management (Westchester, Ill.) 27(8), Oct 1984, 23-24.* LEVEL: B LANG: Eng SIRC ARTICLE NO: 108428

Preiffer, G. Build program support through involvement, communication. *Employee health & fitness (Atlanta, Ga.) 6(10), Oct 1984, 117-120.* LEVEL: B LANG: Eng SIRC ARTICLE NO: 102739

Shephard, R.J. Practical issues in employee fitness programming. (Refs: 16)*Physician and sportsmedicine (Minneapolis, Minn. 12(6), Jun 1984, 160-166.* LEVEL: I LANG: Eng SIRC ARTICLE NO: 094573

ATTITUDE

Hill, C.S. Employee perceptions of the use of corporate fitness programs in recruitment. Eugene, Ore.: Microform Publications, University of Oregon, 1984. 1 microfiche : negative ; 11 x 15 cm. NOTES: Thesis (M.S.) - North Texas State University, 1982; (v, 85 leaves); includes bibliography. LEVEL: A LANG: Eng UO84 200

Morgan, P.P. Shephard, R.J. Finucane, R. Schimmelfing, L. Jazmaji, V. Health beliefs and exercise habits in an employee fitness programme. (Refs: 24)*Canadian journal of applied sport sciences/Journal canadien des sciences appliquees au sport (Windsor, Ont.) 9(2), Jun 1984, 87-93.* ABST: This prospective study examined the health beliefs and exercise habits of 409 adults who enrolled in a work-place fitness program. Twenty months later, the health beliefs and exercise habits of 263 adults from the original sample were re-assessed. The results indicate that adults in an exercise program believe that exercise contributes to a healthy lifestyle. Also, attitudes towards fitness generally become more positive over the 20 month period. The authors conclude that the retention rate of an exercise program will increase if there are a large number of participants who are ready to change their lifestyle and who believe in the benefits of exercise. LEVEL: A LANG: Eng SIRC ARTICLE NO: 096196

ECONOMICS

Bowne, D.W. Russell, M.L. Optenberg, S.A. Clarke, A.E. Morgan, J.L. Reduced disability and health care costs in an industria fitness program. *Journal of occupational medicine (Chicago) 26(11), Nov 1984, 807-816.* LEVEL: A LANG: Eng

Henson, C.D. An evaluation of an employee health promotion program in a community college setting. Eugene, Ore.: Microform Publications, University of Oregon, 1984. 2 microfiches : negative, ill. ; 11 x 15 cm. NOTES: Thesis (M.A.) - Texas Woman's University, 1982; (vii, 171 leaves); includes bibliography. LEVEL: A LANG: Eng UO84 246-247

Sorian, R. Tax breaks for fitness programs? *Physician and sportsmedicine (Minneapolis, Minn.) 12(6), Jun 1984, 35-36;40.* LEVEL: B LANG: Eng SIRC ARTICLE NO: 094575

EVALUATION

Gray, S.W. A simple procedure for evaluating exercise-based health promotion programs in a worksite. (Refs: 4)*Perceptual an motor skills (Missoula, Mont.) 59(1), Aug 1984, 143-146.* LEVEL: I LANG: Eng SIRC ARTICLE NO: 099190

Urban, S. Pacina, V. Vojanec, V. Vyuziti tristupnoveho zatezoveho testu k posouzeni fyzicke zdatnosti pracovniku uranoveho prumyslu. (The use of the three-stage load test for the evaluation of physical fitness in workers in the uranium industry.) *Pracovni lekarstvi (Prague) 36(3), 1984, 95-98.* ABST: A spiroergometric examination of 84 persons was made using the three-stage load test. The authors compared the values of the observed parameters of individual groups at rest and at the three load degrees. From the observed parameters the most informative ones were: minute ventilation,

respiratory frequency, ventilation volume, heart rate, ventilation equivalent 02 and C02.
LEVEL: A LANG: Cze

FACILITIES

Chivetta, A.J. Hastings, B. Facility design: building for today and tomorrow. *Employee services management (Westchester, Ill.) 27(9), Nov 1984, 14-18.*
LEVEL: B LANG: Eng SIRC ARTICLE NO: 108422

Horton, W. Employee fitness facilities: how much is enough? *Athletic business (Madison, Wis.) 8(3), Mar 1984, 28;30;32.*
LEVEL: I LANG: Eng SIRC ARTICLE NO: 175924

Reaching the upper levels in corporate fitness. *Recreation, sports & leisure (Minneapolis) 4(6), Aug 1984, 87;89.*
NOTES: Special issue: Managed recreation research report.
LEVEL: B LANG: Eng SIRC ARTICLE NO: 103922

Thomas, K.A. The modern path to wellness. *Employee services management (Westchester, Ill.) 27(2), Mar 1984, 22-24.*
LEVEL: LANG: Eng SIRC ARTICLE NO: 099214

Working and working out at Shaklee's Centerra. *Recreation, sports & leisure (Minneapolis) 4(6), Aug 1984, 94-98.*
NOTES: Special issue: Managed recreation research report.
LEVEL: B LANG: Eng SIRC ARTICLE NO: 103923

MEDICINE

Avoid problems in program by prescreening employees. *Employee health & fitness (Atlanta) 6(6), Jun 1984, 67-68.*
LEVEL: B LANG: Eng SIRC ARTICLE NO: 104242

Rickards, G. The remedial gymnast in industry (as related to preventive medicine). *Journal of the Society of Remedial Gymnastics and Recreational Therapy (Manchester) 114, Nov 1984, 13-15.*
LEVEL: B LANG: Eng SIRC ARTICLE NO: 104261

Sands, M.J. Osborn, R.R. Leach, C.N. Lachman, A.S. Industrial fitness programs: the physician's role. *Connecticut medicine (New Haven, Conn.) 48(1), Jan 1984, 1-6.*
LEVEL: B LANG: Eng SIRC ARTICLE NO: 102743

Schmidt, G. Roentgenuntersuchungen bei arbeitsmedizinischen Tauglichkeits und Uberwachungsuntersuchungen und sonstigen Vorsorgeuntersuchungen. (Roentgen studies in occupational fitness and monitoring examinations and in other preventive examinations.) *Radiologia diagnostica (Berlin) 25(4), 1984, 441-446.*
LEVEL: I LANG: Ger

PARTICIPATION

Iverson, D. Alternatives for employees increase program participation. *Employee health & fitness (Atlanta, Ga.) 6(12), Dec 1984, 151-152.*
LEVEL: B LANG: Eng SIRC ARTICLE NO: 105440

PHYSIOLOGY

Maddocks, N.J. Physiological variables as predictors of exercise adherence in an executive population. Eugene, Ore.: Microform Publications, University of Oregon, 1984. 1 microfiche : negative, ill. ; 11 x 15 cm.

NOTES: Thesis (M.S.) - Pennsylvania State University, 1983; (ix, 50 leaves); includes bibliography.
LEVEL: A LANG: Eng UO84 369

PRODUCTIVITY

Bernacki, E.J. Baun, W.B. The relationship of job performance to exercise adherence in a corporate fitness program. (Refs: 1 *Journal of occupational medicine (Chicago) 26(7), Jul 1984, 529-531.*
ABST: An investigation of the relationship between exercise adherence and job performance was conducted over a six-month period among a group of white-collar workers (3,231) eligible to participate in a corporate fitness program. The study population was divided into four job categories and five exercise adherence groups. A strong association was observed between above average performance and increasing adherence levels. An inverse relationship was demonstrated between poor performance and increasing adherence levels. In each adherence group no differences in performance were noted when prior performance was compared with current performance. On the basis of these findings there appears to be a positive although probably noncausal relationship between exercise adherence in a corporate fitness program and above average job performance.
LEVEL: A LANG: Eng SIRC ARTICLE NO: 104243

Sergeev, V.N. Ananev, N.I. Vliianie proizvodstvennoi gimnastiki na proizvoditelnost truda boitsov studencheskikh stroitelnyk otriadov. (Effect of on-the-job gymnastics on work productivity of the lead workers of student construction brigades.) *Gigiena i sanitariia (Moskva) 5, May 1984, 91-93.*
LEVEL: I LANG: Rus

PROGRAMS

Austin, D.K. Tone up at the terminals: an exercise plan you can do sitting down. *Shape (Woodland Hills, Calif.) 3(7), Mar 1984, 70-73.*
LEVEL: B LANG: Eng SIRC ARTICLE NO: 099181

Breuleux, C. A survey of corporate fitness programs. *Employee services management (Westchester, Ill.) 26(10), Dec/Jan 1983/1984, 29.*
LEVEL: B LANG: Eng SIRC ARTICLE NO: 097678

College's faculty and staff benefit from wellness program. *Employee health & fitness (Atlanta) 6(6), Jun 1984, 70-71.*
LEVEL B LANG: Eng SIRC ARTICLE NO: 104244

Collingwood, T.R. This good-health regimen keeps employes fit -- and school budgets trim. *American school board journal (Washington) 171(4), Apr 1984, 48-49.*
ABST: The Dallas Independent School District's staff stress reduction and health awareness program is detailed. This article reports that health and attitudes have significantly improved and absenteeism among participating staff members has been reduced.
LEVEL: I LANG: Eng SIRC ARTICLE NO: 097681

Design fitness programs based on future business trends. *Employee health & fitness (Atlanta, Ga.) 6(11), Nov 1984, 133-135.*
LEVEL: B LANG: Eng SIRC ARTICLE NO: 102709

Firming up the firm: part II. (Refs: 36)*Employee services management (Westchester, Ill.) 27(8), Oct*

1984, 11-14;24.
LEVEL: LANG: Eng SIRC ARTICLE NO: 108425

Gedaliah, R.L. Alicea, S. P.E.P., the productivity effectiveness program. 1st ed. New York: Holt, Rinehart and Winston, c1984. 32 p. : ill. (An Owl book.)
LEVEL: B LANG: Eng ISBN: 0030698669 LC CARD: 83-026667 GV505 18099

Health promotion in the workplace. *Employee services management (Westchester, Ill.) 27(6), Aug 1984, 27-28.*
LEVEL: B LANG: Eng SIRC ARTICLE NO: 104248

Hunter, K.R. A survey of industrial fitness programs in the Pacific Northwest. Eugene, Ore.: Microform Publications, University of Oregon, 1984. 1 microfiche : negative ; 11 x 15 cm.
NOTES: Thesis (M.S.) - University of Oregon, 1982; (ix, 83 leaves); vita; includes bibliography.
LEVEL: A LANG: Eng UO84 201

Kondrasuk, J.N. Corporate physical fitness programs: the role of the personnel department. A survey of the goals, structure, services and results of corporate PFPs. (Refs: 11)*Personnel administrator (Berea, Oh.) 29(12), Dec 1984, 75;78-80.*
LEVEL: B LANG: Eng SIRC ARTICLE NO: 102724

Labour fitness and lifestyle report: a demonstration project conducted by the Canadian Public Health Association in collaboration with Fitness Canada, Fitness and Amateur Sport Canada. Ottawa: Canadian Public Health Association : Fitness and Amateur Sport Canada, 1984. iii, 89 p. : ill.
CORP: Canadian Public Health Association.
CORP: Canada. Fitness and Amateur Sport.
NOTES: Egalement publie en francais sous le titre: Rapport sur le projet condition physique et mode de vie au travail: un projet pilote realise conjointement par l'Association canadienne d'hygiene publique et Condition physique Canada (Condition physique et Sport amateur Canada).
LEVEL: B LANG: Eng GV183.6 17223

Marks, L.N. Martin, F.C. St. Clair, C. Clark, D.W. Patrick, N.H. Guidelines to a fitness program for previously sedentary employees. *Occupational health and safety (Waco, Tex.) Jun 1984, 34;36-38;40-43.*
LEVEL: B LANG: Eng SIRC ARTICLE NO: 102727

Massachusetts resource center coordinates firefighter fitness. *Employee health & fitness (Atlanta, Ga.) 6(10), Oct 1984, 124-125.*
LEVEL: B LANG: Eng SIRC ARTICLE NO: 102728

Nelson, K.H. Is corporate fitness really the career of the future? (Refs: 13)*Physical educator (Bloomington, Ind.) 41(2), May 1984, 100-103.*
ABST: The purpose of this study was: 1) to survey to extent of employee fitness and/or recreation programs in the state of Wisconsin, and 2) to evaluate employer rating of 19 potential professional qualifications for employment as a fitness or recreation director. 75 firms answered the survey: 20% offered programs employing trained personnel, 20% ran limited programs and 60% had no programs presently. Respondents considered experience in recreation related activities (68%), course work in sports/acitvities/exercise (68%), ACSM certification as a fitness instructor (56.3%), and experience within the company (56.3%) to be very important qualifications for employment..
LEVEL: I LANG: Eng SIRC ARTICLE NO: 099201

PHYSICAL FITNESS - EMPLOYEE AND INDUSTRIAL FITNESS (continued)

Pindroh, B. Fitness without facilities. *Employee services management (Westchester, Ill.) 27(1), Feb 1984, 13-14.*
LEVEL: B LANG: Eng SIRC ARTICLE NO: 093057

Rapport sur le projet condition physique et mode de vie au travail: un projet pilote realise conjointement par l'Association canadienne d'hygiene publique et Condition physique Canada (Condition physique et Sport amateur Canada). Ottawa: Association canadienne d'hygiene publique : Condition physique et Sport amateur, 1984. iii, 95 p. : ill.
CORP: Association canadienne d'hygiene publique.
CORP: Canada. Condition physique et Sport amateur.
NOTES: Also published in English under the title: Labour fitness and lifestyle report: a demonstration project conducted by the Canadian Public Health Association in collaboration with Fitness Canada, Fitness and Amateur Sport Canada.
LEVEL: B LANG: Fr GV183.6 17224

Reid, G. Montgomery, D.L. The effects of an exercise program conducted by workshop employees on the physical fitness and absenteeism of mentally retarded workers. Final report to Fitness Canada. Montreal: McGill University, 1984. 26 leaves
NOTES: Report financially assisted by Fitness and Amateur Sport. Bibliography: l. 25-26.
LEVEL: A LANG: Eng GV183.7 18401

Rogers, C.C. Firing up for fitness. *Physician and sportsmedicine 12(4), Apr 1984, 134-140;142.*
LEVEL: B LANG: Eng SIRC ARTICLE NO: 093059

Tishler, J.W. A wellness program for university faculty and staff. Alexandria, Va.: Computer Microfilm International, 1984. microfiche (15 fr.)
CONF: American Alliance for Health, Physical Education, Recreation and Dance. Convention (1984 : Anaheim, Calif.).
LEVEL: I LANG: Eng EDRS: ED246013

PSYCHOLOGY

Finney, C. Boosting productivity. *Employee services management (Westchester, Ill.) 27(2), Mar 1984, 10-13.*
LEVEL: B LANG: Eng SIRC ARTICLE NO: 099187

Murphy, P. Office stress: is a solution shaping up? *Physician and sportsmedicine (Minneapolis, Minn.) 12(12), Dec 1984, 114-118.*
LEVEL: B LANG: Eng SIRC ARTICLE NO: 102864

SOCIAL PSYCHOLOGY

Imrie-Carey, M. A study of selected benefits of a pilot wellness program implemented for Oregon state workers. Eugene, Ore.: Microform Publications, University of Oregon, 1984. 1 microfiche : negative ; 11 x 15 cm.
NOTES: Thesis (M.S.) - University of Oregon, 1984; (xi, 71 leaves); vita; includes bibliography.
LEVEL: A LANG: Eng UO84 429

TESTING

Key, B. Preventive medicine. (Refs: 3)*Journal of the Society of Remedial Gymnastics and Recreational Therapy (Manchester) 114, Nov 1984, 8-13.*
LEVEL: I LANG: Eng SIRC ARTICLE NO: 104253

Optenberg, S.A. Lairson, D.R. Slater, C.H. Russell, M.L. Agreement of self-reported and physiologically estimated fitness status in a symptom-free population. *Preventive medicine (New York) 13(4), Jul 1984, 349-354.*
LEVEL: A LANG: Eng

PHYSICAL FITNESS - PROGRAMS AND ACTIVITIES

10-min qigong exercise. *China sports (Beijing, China) 16(7), Jul 1984, 55-56.*
LEVEL: B LANG: Eng SIRC ARTICLE NO: 102184

Alex, B. Laawrenz, F. Teaming with schools for fitness takes planning. *Journal of physical education and program (Columbus, Oh.) Sept 1984, F-19-F-20.*
LEVEL: B LANG: Eng SIRC ARTICLE NO: 102705

Aquilon, J. Aquilon, N.D. One on one: exercising together: the sensual way to superbly conditioned bodies. New York: Simon and Schuster, c1984. 1v.
LEVEL: B LANG: Eng ISBN: 0671503995 LC CARD: 84-010664

Blais, J. Passeport pour une bonne forme. *Marathon plus (Laval, Que.) 1(2), oct 1984, 42-44.*
LEVEL: B LANG: Fr SIRC ARTICLE NO: 173441

Chuan, Z. 'Dayan Qigong': wild goose breathing exercise (contd). *China sports (Beijing, China) 16(11), 1984, 54-59.*
NOTES To be continued.
LEVEL: B LANG: Eng SIRC ARTICLE NO: 108452

Chuan, Z. Daya qigong: wild goose breathing exercise. (First 64 forms) *China sports (Beijing, China) 16(10), Oct 1984, 43-48.*
NOTES: To be continued in next issue.
LEVEL: B LANG: Eng SIRC ARTICLE NO: 109053

Chuan, Z. 'Dayan Quihong': Wild goose breathing exercise. *China sports (Beijing, China) 16(12), Dec 1984, 57-60.*
NOTES: T be continued.
LEVEL: B LANG: Eng SIRC ARTICLE NO: 173026

Cummings, S. Rating the celebrity fitness books. The coaches look good, but do the programs deliver? *Health magazine (New York) 16(1), Jan 1984, 34;36-38;57;59.*
LEVEL: B LANG: Eng SIRC ARTICLE NO: 094555

Dardik, I. Waitley, D. Quantum fitness: breakthrough to excellence. New York: Pocket Books, c1984. 185 p. : ill.
NOTES: Bibliography: p. 177-179.
LEVEL: B LANG: Eng ISBN: 0671509039 LC CARD: 84-002165 RA781 18240

Dubois, P. Physical fitness for public safety personnel: an opportunity for the profession. (Refs: 13)*NAPEHE proceedings (Champaign, Ill.) 5, 1984, 155-161.*
CONF: National Association for Physical Education in Higher Education. Annual Conference (1984 : College Park, Md.).
NOTES: Conference theme: Current challenge: revitalization or obsolescence?
ABST: This article outlines the design and establishment of a state-supported health fitness agency for firefighters at a Massachusetts university.
LEVEL: A LANG: Eng SIRC ARTICLE NO: 102711

Freifeld, K. Engelmayer, S. The ultimate high-tech workout. *New body (New York) 3(4), Jul 1984, 16;19.*
LEVEL: B LANG: Eng SIRC ARTICLE NO: 100856

Getchell, B. Marshall, M.G. The basic guidelines for being fit. (Refs: 26)
NOTES: In, Strauss, R.H. (ed.), Sports medicine, Philadelphia ; Toronto, Saunders, 1984, p. 457-467.
LEVEL: I LANG: Eng RC1210 17196

Grau, J. A home exercise workout. *Shape (Woodland Hills, Calif.) 3(8), Apr 1984, 40-44.*
LEVEL: B LANG: Eng SIRC ARTICLE NO: 099189

Hagerman, F.C. Row, row, row your way to fitness. *Shape (Woodland Hills, Calif.) 3(5), Jan 1984, 58-60;100;103.*
LEVEL: B LANG: Eng SIRC ARTICLE NO: 097689

LeMay, T. Look before you leap: weighing your fitness options. *Financial post magazine (Toronto, Ont.) 1 Dec 1984, 54-55.*
LEVEL: B LANG: Eng SIRC ARTICLE NO: 100866

Levy, B.S. Goldberg, R. Rippe, J. Love, D. A regular physical exercise program for medical students: learning about prevention through participation. *Journal of medical education (Chicago) 59(7), Jul 1984, 596-598.*
LEVEL: I LANG: Eng SIRC ARTICLE NO: 102726

Lilley, J.H. Greenberg, S.F. Physical-training program addresses long-term attitudes toward fitness. *Police chief (Gaithersburg, Md.) 51(1), 1984, 47-49.*
LEVEL: B LANG: Eng SIRC ARTICLE NO: 099197

Marsden, V. Exercise design: your upper body. *Fitness leader (Ottawa) 2(8), Apr 1984, 29-32.*
LEVEL: B LANG: Eng SIRC ARTICLE NO: 100868

Pinckney, C. Batson, S. Moody, G. 10 years younger in 10 hours with callanetics. New York: W. Morrow, 1984. 1v.
LEVEL: B LANG: Eng ISBN: 0688037879 LC CARD: 84-006565

Pollock, M.L. Recommendations for adults physical fitness programs. (Refs: 4)*Sports medicine digest (Van Nuys, Calif.) 6(10), Oct 1984, 1-3.*
LEVEL: B LANG: Eng SIRC ARTICLE NO: 102737

Strachan, D. Exercise design: your abdominals. *Fitness leader (Ottawa, Ont.) 2(6), Feb 1984, 21-24.*
LEVEL: B LANG: Eng SIRC ARTICLE NO: 099210

Strachan, D. Variations on a leg theme. *Fitness leader (Ottawa) 2(9), May 1984, 17-18.*
LEVEL: B LANG: Eng SIRC ARTICLE NO 100876

Total fitness: getting started. *National racquetball (Glenview, Ill.) 13(10), Oct 1984, 25-28.*
LEVEL: B LANG: Eng SIRC ARTICLE NO: 105455

Travolta, J. Rawles, D. Rawles, S. Isaacson, D. John Travolta's creative exercising. New York: Simon and Schuster, c1984. 1v
LEVEL: B LANG: Eng ISBN: 0671497987 LC CARD: 84-005506

Wagstaff, M. Mattfeldt-Beman, M. The fitness opportunity for dietetic educators and practitioners. *Journal of the American Dietetic Association (Chicago) 84(12), Dec 1984, 1465-1467.*
LEVEL: I LANG: Eng

Warnick, R.B. Marketing factors in the evaluation of exercise/fitness programs: an examination of

core and fringe participation by importance-performance analysis. Eugene, Ore.: Microform Publications, University of Oregon, 1984. 3 microfiches : negative, ill. ; 11 x 15 cm. NOTES: Thesis (Ph.D.) - Pennsylvania State University, 1983; (xi, 203, (1) leaves); vita; includes bibliography.
LEVEL: A LANG: Eng UO84 358-360

Watts, D. Kinnear, G. Activity patterns for fitness classes. *Runner (Edmonton, Alb.) 22(2), Summer 1984, 30-32.*
LEVEL: B LANG: Eng SIRC ARTICLE NO: 100885

Weiss, U. Jogging - stretching - aerobic. *Macolin (Macolin, Suisse) 41(5), mai 1984, 14-16.*
NOTES: Traduction de, Mariann Weber.
LEVEL: B LANG: Fr SIRC ARTICLE NO: 108770

Wheeler, J.R. The medical clearance: essential precautions for runners at risk. *New Zealand runner (Auckland, N.Z.) 32, May/Jun 1984, 26-31.*
NOTES: Reprinted from, The New Zealand road to fitness, Stortford publications, 1984.
LEVEL: B LANG: Eng SIRC ARTICLE NO: 098696

Will the real sit-up please stand up? *Executive fitness newsletter (Emmaus, Pa.) 15(7), 31 Mar 1984, 1-2.*
LEVEL: B LANG: En SIRC ARTICLE NO: 094585

AEROBIC TRAINING

Aroutcheff, P. Pourquoi l'aerobic. *Science et vie (Paris) HS147, 1984, 24-29.*
LEVEL: B LANG: Fr

Burwash, P. Tullius, J. Haase, B. Peter Burwash's aerobic workout book for men. 1st ed. New York: Dodd, Mead, c1984. xvii, 151 p. : ill. NOTES: Includes bibliographical references.
LEVEL: B LANG: Eng ISBN: 0396083803 LC CARD: 84-001684 GV482.5 17844

Esquire ultimate fitness: featuring a new complete aerobics workout. Reading, Mass.: Addison-Wesley, (1984). 1v.
CORP: Esquire.
NOTES: Includes index.
LEVEL: B LANG: Eng ISBN: 0201119900 LC CARD: 84-021695

Exercising in the great indoors. *Your health & fitness (Highland Park, Ill.) 6(5), Oct/Nov 1984, 22-23.*
LEVEL: B LANG: Eng SIRC ARTICLE NO: 100855

Fisher, G.A. Allsen, P.E. Jogging. 2nd ed. Dubuque, Iowa: Wm. C. Brown, c1984. viii, 92 p. : ill. (Exploring sports series.)
NOTES: Bibliography: p. 81-82.
LEVEL: B LANG: Eng ISBN: 0-697-00291-8 LC CARD: 84-070347 GV494 10179

France, K. Body conditioning: a thinking person's guide to aerobic fitness. Atlanta, Ga.: Humanics, c1984.
NOTES: Includes index and bibliography.
LEVEL: I LANG: Eng ISBN: 0893340804 LC CARD: 84-019801

Goodrick, G.K. Warren, D.R. Hartung, G.H. Hoepfel, J.A. Helping adults to stay physically fit. Preventing relapse following aerobic exercise training. (Refs: 13)*Journal of physical education, recreation & dance 55(2), Feb 1984, 48-49.*
LEVEL: B LANG: Eng SIRC ARTICLE NO: 091666

Graham. G.S. Becoming aerobically fit. *Ohio runner (Columbus, Oh.) 6(3), Sept 1984, 12-14.*
LEVEL: B LANG: Eng SIRC ARTICL NO: 100859

Hamilton, I. Traveling. *Fitness leader (Ottawa, Ont.) 2(5), Jan 1984, 9-10.*
LEVEL: B LANG: Eng SIRC ARTICLE NO: 099192

Janklowicz, G. Split your routine. *Shape (Woodland Hills, Calif.) 4(3), Nov 1984, 86-96.*
LEVEL: B LANG: Eng SIRC ARTICLE NO: 173222

Marsden, V. Stride jump jazz. *Fitness leader (Ottawa, Ont.) 2(5), Jan 1984, 9-10.*
LEVEL: B LANG: Eng SIRC ARTICLE NO: 099198

Marsden, V. Aerobic rhythmics: like a sailor. *Fitness leader (Ottawa, Ont.) 2(6), Feb 1984, 11-12.*
LEVEL: B LANG: Eng SIR ARTICLE NO: 099199

O'Neil, K. Exercise bank: wiggle'n move. *Fitness leader (Ottawa) 2(7), Mar 1984, 13-14.*
LEVEL: B LANG: Eng SIRC ARTICLE NO: 096198

O'Neill, K. Aerobic rhythmics: feeling. *Fitness leader (Ottawa) 2(7), Mar 1984, 13-14.*
LEVEL: B LANG: Eng SIRC ARTICLE NO 096199

Patano, P. Savage, L. Muscle aerobics: get the most out of your workout by strapping on some wrist and ankle weights. *Fit (Mountain View, Calif.) 3(12), May 1984, 40-41;94-95.*
LEVEL: B LANG: Eng SIRC ARTICLE NO: 100573

Patano, P. Savage, L. Are you ready for it? Take the test - find out exactly what kind of shape your body is in. *Fit (Mountain View, Calif.) 4(7), Dec 1984, 62-63;76-77.*
LEVEL: B LANG: Eng SIRC ARTICLE NO: 173559

Ross, M. Lightweight aerobics. s.l.: Leisure Press, 1984. 128p. : ill.
LEVEL: B LANG: Eng ISBN: 0-88011-255-7

Running. Putting together a safe program. Toronto: PARTICIPaction, c1984. 8 p. : ill.
CORP: PARTICIPaction.
LEVEL: B LANG: E GV1061 20859

Strachan, D. Let's dance: how sweet. *Fitness leader (Ottawa, Ont.) 2(6), Feb 1984, 11-12.*
LEVEL: B LANG: Eng SIRC ARTICLE NO: 099212

Strachan, D. 'What I want' - a moving needs assessment. *Fitness leader (Ottawa) 3(3), Nov 1984, 5-6.*
LEVEL: B LANG: Eng SIRC ARTICLE NO: 105452

Whittemore, A. Ultimate ball: an aerobic game is fun, plus it works. *Journal of physical education and program (Columbus, Oh.) Sept 1984, F-21;F-23.*
LEVEL: B LANG: Eng SIRC ARTICLE NO: 102752

AQUATIC EXERCISE

Aetna Canada Swimfit instructor manual. s.l.: Canadian Amateur Swimming Association, 1984?. 139 p. : ill.
CORP: Canadian Amateur Swimming Association.
NOTES: Includes bibliographies.
LEVEL: B LANG: Eng GV838.53.P5 18335

Aquafit: water exercise program. Toronto: NC Press Ltd., c1984. 32 p. : ill.
CORP: Canadian Police College.
LEVEL: B LANG: E ISBN: 0-920053-39-4 LC CARD: C85-098384-3 GV838.53.P5 18959

Biegel, L. In the swim. (Refs: 1)
NOTES: In, Biegel, L. (ed.), Physical fitness and the older person: a guide to exercise fo health care

professionals, Rockville, Md., Aspen Systems Corp., 1984, p. 119-128.
LEVEL: I LANG: Eng GV482.6 17754

DeVarona, D. Tarshis, B. Donna DeVarona's hydro-aerobics. New York: Macmillan, c1984. xii, 163 p. : ill.
NOTES: Includes index.
LEVEL: B LANG: Eng ISBN: 0025312502 LC CARD: 84-004421 GV837 17540

Etter, M. Olympiade nautique. *Macolin (Suisse) 8, aout 1984, 11-12.*
NOTES: Traduction de, Marianne Weber.
LEVEL: B LANG: Fr SIRC ARTICLE NO: 100854

Hanson, S.B. Water workout: slim and shape up while you cool down in the pool. *Fit (Mountain View, Calif.) 4(2), Jul 1984, 60-61;85.*
LEVEL: B LANG: Eng SIRC ARTICLE NO: 100861

Johnson, B.M. Aquadynamics: take to the water to firm up. *Slimmer (Santa Monica, Calif.) 4(3), May 1984, 86-90.*
LEVEL: B LANG: Eng SIRC ARTICLE NO: 100863

Kitchen, D. Hushagen, J. Roos, V. Get wet, get fit - aquatic fitness manual. Edmonton, Alta.: Alberta Recreation and Parks, 1984?. 143 leaves : ill.
NOTES: Bibliography: I. 142-143.
LEVEL: I LANG: Eng GV837 17646

Krasevec, J.A. Grimes, D.C. Hydrorobics: a water exercise program for individuals of all ages and fitness levels. New York: Leisure Press, c1984. 176 p. : ill.
NOTES: Includes bibliographies.
LEVEL: B LANG: Eng ISBN: 0880111569 LC CARD: 83-80711 GV838.53.P5 17374

Lee, T. Aquacises: Terri Lee's water workout book. Reston, Va.: Reston Pub. Co., c1984. xiii, 240 p.
NOTES: Includes index. Bibliography: p. 228.
LEVEL: B LANG: Eng ISBN: 0835901521 LC CARD: 83-013651 GV481 16010

Rocan, S. O'Neill, K. Focus (aqua-fitness). *Fitness leader (Ottawa) 2(7), Mar 1984, 25-28.*
LEVEL: B LANG: Eng SIRC ARTICL NO: 096202

Signorile, J. Shields, D. Aerobic swimming: it's no sweat when you're wet. (Refs: 10)*Florida JOHPERD (Gainesville, Fla.) 22(4), Nov 1984, 11-16.*
LEVEL: I LANG: Eng SIRC ARTICLE NO: 106091

White, S.W. Something new for the pool. Individualized instruction in aquatic fitness. *Journal of physical education, recreation & dance 55(2), Feb 1984, 52-53.*
LEVEL: B LANG: Eng SIRC ARTICLE NO: 091705

CIRCUIT TRAINING

Vaz, K. Fitness trails, they're free, fun, and great exercise... *Slimmer (Santa Monica, Calif.) 4(6), Oct 1984, 20-24.*
LEVEL: B LANG: Eng SIRC ARTICLE NO: 173238

EXERCISE ROUTINES

Adcock, S. Bean, J. Steve Adcock's partner workout. New York: M. Evans, c1984. 1v.
NOTES: Includes index.
LEVEL: E LANG: E ISBN: 0871314479 LC CARD: 84-013687

Arsenault, S. En forme avec Sylvie Arsenault. *Marathon, la revue de la bonne forme (Montreal)*

16, mai 1984, 31-34.
LEVEL: LANG: Fr SIRC ARTICLE NO: 108702

Austin, D. Tone up at the terminals: an exercise guide for computer and word processing operators. Sunnyvale, Calif.: Verbatim Corporation, c1984. (11) p. : ill.
NOTES: Cover title. Pamphlet.
LEVEL: B LANG: Eng GV481 20027

Corbin, C.B. Lindsey, R. The ultimate fitness book: physical fitness forever. New York: Leisure Press, c1984. 272 p. : ill.
NOTES: Includes bibliographical references.
LEVEL: I LANG: Eng ISBN: 0880112328 LC CARD: 84-047519 GV481 17752

Drury, N. Bodywork book. Vancouver, B.C.: Raincoast Book, 1984?. 1v.
LEVEL: B LANG: Eng

Erdman, M. Koplan, B.K. Undercover exercise: turn everyday activities into fitness and fun. Englewood Cliffs, N.J.: Prentice-Hall, c1984. xvi, 187 p. : ill. (Spectrum book.)
NOTES: Includes indexes. Bibliography: p. 183-184.
LEVEL: B LANG: Eng ISBN: 0139354468 LC CARD: 84-006772 GV481 17464

Fitness for everyone. Emmaus, Pa.: Rodale Press, c1984. vii, 167 p. : ill. (The Prevention Total Health System.)
CORP: Prevention Magazine.
NOTES: Includes index.
LEVEL: B LANG: Eng ISBN: 0878574670 LC CARD: 83-027037 RA781 18190

Grossfeld, M. Body moves. New York: G.P. Putnam's Sons, c1984. 189 p. : ill.
LEVEL: B LANG: Eng ISBN: 0-399-12942-1 LC CARD 83-020984 GV481 18082

Hutton, D. Vogue exercise book. London: Octopus Books, c1984. 127 p. : ill.
LEVEL: B LANG: Eng ISBN: 0-7064-2077-2 GV481 18799

Kino-memoire. Fit thrid age/Troisieme age en forme (Ottawa) 2, 1984, 8.
LEVEL: B LANG: Fr SIRC ARTICLE NO: 173966

Kravitz, L. Maximize the workout minimize the risk: by correcting your exercise technique, you will always get the most from your workout. Fit (Mountain View, Calif.) 4(6), Nov 1984, 54-59.
LEVEL: B LANG: Eng SIRC ARTICLE NO: 105441

Main, S. Stewart, G.W. Bradshaw, R. Chelle Fit all over: a catalogue of exercises. Ganges, B.C.: 3 S Fitness Group, c1984. 6 p. : ill. (Fitline series booklet.)
LEVEL: B LANG: Eng ISBN: 0-920846-04-1 GV481 17322

Marsden, V. Exercise design: your hips and thighs. Fitness leader (Ottawa) 3(1), Sept 1984, 1-4.
NOTES: 3rd in a series.
LEVEL: B LANG: Eng SIRC ARTICLE NO: 105444

Mayo, D. Mayo, J. The importance of cooldown: don't forget to round out your workout with some easy exercises designed to help your body unwind. Fit (Mountain View, Calif.) 4(5), Oct 1984, 27-30.
LEVEL: B LANG: Eng SIRC ARTICLE NO: 106724

Oldridge, N.B. Adherence to adult exercise fitness programs. (Refs: 72)In, Matarazzo, J.D. (ed.) et al., Behavioral health: a handbook of health enhancement and disease prevention, New York,

Wiley, c1984, p. 467-487.
LEVEL: A LANG: Eng

Playing it safe. A pocket guide to fitness. Chicago, Ill.: National Safety Council, c1984. 15 p. : ill.
CORP: National Safety Council.
NOTES: Cover title. Pamphlet.
LEVEL: B LANG: Eng GV481 20028

Provost, R. Turn your home into a gym. Fit (Mountain View, Calif.) 4(5), Oct 1984, 61-64.
LEVEL: B LANG: Eng SIRC ARTICLE NO: 106738

Richardson, D. The balanced body. New York: Harmony Books, 1984. 1v.
CORP: Body Center.
LEVEL: B LANG: Eng ISBN: 051755497 LC CARD: 84-003801

Ross, D. Thinning your waist. Mountain View, Calif.: Anderson World Books, 1984. 1v. (The getting strong book series; bk. 4.
LEVEL: B LANG: Eng ISBN: 0890373078 LC CARD: 84-018505

Shipman, C. P. Exercise, the new language of love. New York: Leisure Press, 1984. 1v.
LEVEL: B LANG: Eng ISBN: 0880111135 L CARD: 82-083946

Staying in shape on a super-packed schedule. New body (New York) 3(6), Nov 1984, 23-29.
LEVEL: B LANG: Eng SIRC ARTICLE NO: 173273

Steinfeld, J. Miller, M. Ellison, N. Body by Jake. New York: Simon and Schuster, c1984. 1v.
LEVEL: B LANG: Eng ISBN: 0671503219 LC CARD: 84-003909

Strachan, D. Standing warmup. Fitness leader (Ottawa) 3(3), Nov 1984, 5-6.
LEVEL: B LANG: Eng SIRC ARTICLE NO: 105451

Wassersug, J.D. Jarm: how to jog with your arms to live longer. 1st ed. Port Washington, N.Y.: Ashley Books, c1984. 101 p. : ill.
LEVEL: B LANG: Eng ISBN: 0-87949-197-3 LC CARD: 81-10919 GV508 18059

ISOMETRIC, ISOKINETIC AND ISOTONIC TRAINING

Clark, B. Isokinetics. Part III. The last in our series: the benefits of training with uniform resistance. Fit (Mountain View, Calif.) 4(2), Jul 1984, 32-34.
LEVEL: B LANG: Eng SIRC ARTICLE NO: 101021

Clark, B. Isometrics. This form of exercise offers an easy, efficient and effective way to keep your muscles toned. Fit (Mountain View, Calif.) 3(12), May 1984, 54-55;106;111.
NOTES: Part I of a three-part series.
LEVEL: B LANG: Eng SIRC ARTICLE NO: 100851

MILITARY PROGRAMS

Bohannon, R.L. From the founder; physical fitness in the military. Running & fitness (Washington, D.C.) 16(3), May/Jun 1984 4.
LEVEL: B LANG: Eng SIRC ARTICLE NO: 100850

Cox, J.S. Lenz, H.W. Women midshipmen in sports. (Refs: 7)American journal of sports medicine (Baltimore) 12(3), May/Jun 1984, 241-243.
CONF: American Orthopaedic Society for Sports Medicine. Annual Meeting (9th : 1983 : Williamsburg, Va.).
ABST: This report studied the performance and injury rate of seven freshman classes of women

midshipmen, from 1976 (63) to 1983 (88), in comparison to their male counterparts. Comparitive health care statistics for six weeks of each summer were taken, as well as the results of five fitness tests batteries. These included a mile run, flexed arm hang, standing long jump, situps for two minutes, and an obstacle course. Among the trends seen by the authors was that women midshipmen were improving their fitness level more rapidly than the men. Also, women sought more medical attention than the men for stress-related problems, but less often as they became acclimated to a more active lifstyle. The authors indicate that many of the increases in performance and the number of injuries should be attributed to societal conditions and a greater participation in athletics by women.
LEVEL: A LANG: Eng SIRC ARTICLE NO: 102968

Dornan, P. Return to Kokoda. (Refs: 1)Sport health (Pennant Hills, Aust.) 2(1), 1984, 36-38.
LEVEL: I LANG: Eng SIRC ARTICLE NO: 094817

Drews, F.R. The Army's high priority physical fitness program. Journal of physical education, recreation & dance (Reston, Va.) 55(9), Nov/Dec 1984, 47-50.
LEVEL: B LANG: Eng SIRC ARTICLE NO: 102710

Goldstein, J.E. America's defense: America's fitness. Parks & recreation (Alexandria, Va.) 19(12), Dec 1984, 46-48;67.
LEVEL: B LANG: Eng SIRC ARTICLE NO: 173253

Lee, W. Physical fitness training program for CF figher(sic) pilots - phase I. L'entrainement physique des pilotes de chasse des forces canadiennes - phase I. Periscope (Ottawa) 16, 1984, 43-44.
LEVEL: B LANG: Eng Fr SIRC ARTICLE NO: 179916

Lee, W. A comparison between the standard recruit training program and hydraulic resistive training on aerobic power, strength and endurance at CFRS Cornwallis. Comparaison entre le programme regulier d'entrainement physique des recrues et l'entrainement avec un appareil de resistance hydraulique sur la puissance cardio-respiratoire, la force et l'endurance musculaires a l'ERFC Cornwallis. Periscope (Ottawa) 16, 1984, 99-101.
ABST: A comparison is made between regular training methods for recruits and methods using hydra gym equipment. The aspects tested were VO2 max, muscle strength and endurance. There were improvements in all areas in the group using the hydra equipment, due mainly to its capability to produce training results in a minimum time frame. RESUME: Dans cet article on compare la methode d'entrainement physique habituelle pour des recrues a celle qui utilise un appareil de resistance hydraulique. En evaluant la puissance cardio-respiratoire, la force et l'endurance musculaires, on a note une nette amelioration chez les participants qui se servaient de l'appareil hydraulique. Cette amelioration est surtout due a sa qualite d'occasioner des resultats d'entrainement positifs dans un bref delai.
LEVEL: A LANG: Eng Fr SIRC ARTICLE NO: 179921

Poruchikov, E.A. Fenomenon 'beskonechnogo tona' kak pokazatel' fizicheskoi trenirovannosti voennosluzhashchikh. (Phenomenon of 'sustained tone' as an index of the physical training status of servicemen.) Voenno-meditsinskii zhurnal (Moscow) 6, Jun 1984, 41-43.
LEVEL: I LANG: Rus

MINI-TRAMPOLINING

Fisk, J.W. Haldeman, S. Kirkland-Smith, I. A simple answer to fitness for all ages: how to lose weight without dieting--with practical reasons why--easily explainable to laypersons and physicians. Springfield, Ill.: Charles C. Thomas, c1984. xiv, 118 p. : ill.
LEVEL: B LANG: Eng ISBN: 0398049955 LC CARD: 84-000029 RA781 17512

Mini-tramps: they're fun, but are they aerobic? *Executive fitness newsletter (Emmous, Pa.) 15(4), 18 Feb 1984, 4.*
LEVEL: B LANG: Eng SIRC ARTICLE NO: 093056

Warren, S. Bouncing with health: jumping up and down on a trampoline stops you looking old. *Sport & leisure (London, Eng.) Sept/Oct 1984, 34.*
LEVEL: B LANG: Eng SIRC ARTICLE NO: 108897

RELAXATION

Conway, K. Energy training. *Fitness leader (Ottawa, Ont.) 2(5), Jan 1984, 17-19.*
LEVEL: B LANG: Eng SIRC ARTICLE NO: 0991

Strachan, D. Centering. *Fitness leader (Ottawa, Ont.) 2(5), Jan 1984, 9-10.*
LEVEL: B LANG: Eng SIRC ARTICLE NO: 099208

Strachan, D. Slow reach. *Fitness leader (Ottawa, Ont.) 2(5), Jan 1984, 9-10.*
LEVEL: B LANG: Eng SIRC ARTICLE NO: 099209

ROPE SKIPPING

Coccagna, E.M. Selected physiological responses to varied rope skipping intensities. Eugene, Ore.: Microform Publications, University of Oregon, 1984. 1 microfiche : negative, ill. ; 11 x 15 cm.
NOTES: Thesis (M.S.) - Pennsylvania State University, 1981; (viii, 83 leaves); includes bibliography.
LEVEL: A LANG: Eng UO84 78

Newson, O. Bring back the rope... *British journal of physical education (London) 15(1), Jan/Feb 1984, 6-8.*
LEVEL: B LANG: Eng SIRC ARTICLE NO: 099202

Smith Jones, S. Benefits of exercise: jumping into better health. *Muscle & fitness (Woodland Hills, Calif.) 45(1), Jan 1984 11;202;205;228.*
LEVEL: B LANG: Eng SIRC ARTICLE NO: 096205

STRETCHING

Croce, P. Stretching for athletics. 2nd ed. New York: Leisure Press, c1984. 127 p. : ill.
LEVEL: B LANG: Eng ISBN: 08801111 LC CARD: 83-80859 GV505 15870

Leard, J.S. Flexibility and conditioning in the young athlete. (Refs: 29)
NOTES: In, Micheli, L.J. (ed.), Pediatric and adolescent sports medicine, Boston ; Toronto, Little, Brown, c1984, p. 194-210.
LEVEL: I LANG: Eng RC1210 17791

Moreau, J.P. Stretching. (Refs: 7)*EPS: Education physique et sport (Paris) 187, mai/juin 1984, 5-9.*
LEVEL: B LANG: Fr SIR ARTICLE NO: 096195

Moreau, J.P. Le stretching: s'etirer pour mieux vivre. Montreal: Primeur, c1984. 157 p. : ill.
LEVEL: B LANG: Fr ISBN: 2-89286-013-X LC CARD: 85-10102 GV505 18918

Sorine, S.R. Sorine, D.S. Stretch out: warm up and beat stress. 1st ed. New York: Crown, c1984. v, 56 p. : ill. (Prince paperbacks.)
LEVEL: B LANG: Eng ISBN: 0517554763 LC CARD: 84-007823 GV505 18161

Stevenson, E. Hip flexor stretches. *CAHPERD journal times (Danville, Calif.) 46(8), May 1984, 17.*
LEVEL: B LANG: Eng SIRC ARTICLE NO: 094579

Stewart, G.W. Faulkner, R.A. Chelle Taylor, N. Bend and stretch: suppleness and strength exercises. rev. & expanded ed. Ganges, B.C.: 3 S Fitness Group, c1984. 31 p. : ill. (Fitline series booklet.)
LEVEL: B LANG: Eng ISBN: 0-920846-03-3 GV505 17321

Strachan, D. Exercise bank: liftoff. *Fitness leader (Ottawa, Ont.) 2(6), Feb 1984, 11-12.*
LEVEL: B LANG: Eng SIRC ARTICLE NO: 099211

The executive's guide to stretching for relaxation. *Executive fitness newsletter (Emmaus, Pa.) 15(20), 29 Sept 1984, 3-6.*
LEVEL: B LANG: Eng SIRC ARTICLE NO: 102712

WALKING

Biegel, L. Walking: oft neglected highly recommended. (Refs: 6)
NOTES: In, Biegel, L. (ed.), Physical fitness and the older person: a guide to exercise for health care professionals, Rockville, Md., Aspen Systems Corp., 1984, p. 89-99.
LEVEL: I LANG: Eng GV482.6 17754

Get fit fast. *New body (New York) 3(4), Jul 1984, 56-59.*
LEVEL: B LANG: Eng SIRC ARTICLE NO: 100858

On walking...nature's true - and painless - elixir. *Executive health (Sante Fe, Calif.) 20(9), Jun 1984, 1-4.*
LEVEL: I LANG Eng SIRC ARTICLE NO: 094569

Walking your way to health. *Cardiac alert (Potomac, Md.) 7(11), Oct 1984, 4-5.*
LEVEL: B LANG: Eng SIRC ARTICLE NO: 173382

White, M.K. Yeater, R.A. Martin, R.B. Rosenberg, B.S. Sherwood, L. Weber, K.C. Della-Giustina, D.E. Effects of aerobic dancing and walking on cardiovascular function and muscular strength in postmenopausal women. (Refs: 21)*Journal of sports medicine and physical fitness (Torino, Italy) 24(2), Jun 1984, 159-166.*
ABST: The effects of a six month aerobic dancing and walking program were examined in 51 postmenopausal women. A treadmill test to a heart rate of 145 bpm was used to assess changes in cardiovascular fitness. Analysis of variance indicated that both groups showed significant increases in treadmill time and work accomplished while showing decreases in resting heart rate, rate-pressure products and recovery heart rates. The only significant group X test interaction occurred with heart rate during the third minute of recovery, where the members of the dancing group showed a 5% decrease while the walking group remained unchanged. ANOVAs indicated that significant increases occurred in knee extension and ankle plantar flexion strength. A significant group X test interaction for ankle plantar flexion indicated that greater improvement occurred in the walkers. On the other hand, the dancers showed greater improvement in elbow flexion strength (5% dancers,

2% walkers).
LEVEL: A LANG: Eng SIRC ARTICLE NO: 102751

WEIGHT TRAINING

Barry, A. Don't let upper body strength be the forgotten factor in your exercise equation. (Refs: 5)*Cardio gram (La Crosse, Wis.) 11(3), June/July 1984, 4-5.*
LEVEL: B LANG: Eng SIRC ARTICLE NO: 173014

Clark, B. Isotonics. Part II. Of a three-part series. *Fit (Mountain View, Calif.) 4(1), Jun 1984, 70-72.*
LEVEL: B LANG: E SIRC ARTICLE NO: 101022

Dayton, L. Toughening up for aerobics. Get a leg up on your aerobic workout - strengthen your lower body with these exercise that will add a kick to your step. *Fit (Mountain View, Calif.) 4(1), Jun 1984, 54-56;88.*
LEVEL: B LANG: Eng SIRC ARTICLE NO: 101024

Lennon, R. Getting the most from resistance machines. *New body (New York) 3(6), Nov 1984, 44-45;81.*
LEVEL: B LANG: Eng SIRC ARTICLE NO: 173276

Squats: how to perform the 'King of exercise' safety. *Executive fitness newsletter (Emmaus, Pa.) 15(20), 29 Sept 1984, 7.*
LEVEL: B LANG: Eng SIRC ARTICLE NO: 102958

Stamford, B. Exercising with hand and ankle weights. *Physician and sportsmedicine (Minneapolis, Minn.) 12(12), Dec 1984, 139.*
LEVEL: B LANG: Eng SIRC ARTICLE NO: 102748

Yessis, M. Do it right. *Shape (Woodland Hills, Calif.) 4(3), Nov 1984, 22-23.*
LEVEL: B LANG: Eng SIRC ARTICLE NO: 173221

YOGA

Folan, L. Yoga: fitness for mind and body. *Shape (Woodland Hills, Calif.) 4(4), Dec 1984, 82-83;88;114.*
LEVEL: B LANG: En SIRC ARTICLE NO: 173236

How yoga cleans the inner man. *Inside kung-fu (Hollywood, Calif.) 11(4), Apr 1984, 22;24.*
LEVEL: B LANG: Eng SIRC ARTICLE NO: 097098

Yoga: the tranquilizing exercise. *Your health & fitness (Highland Park, Ill.) 6(1), Feb/Mar 1984, 12-13.*
LEVEL: B LANG: Eng SIRC ARTICLE NO: 098856

PHYSICAL FITNESS - TESTING

AR&FA fitness quiz: test your fitness level. *Running & fitness (Washington, D.C.) 16(4), Jul/Aug 1984, 23.*
LEVEL: B LANG: E SIRC ARTICLE NO: 105432

Arnot, R.B. Gaines, C.L. Sportselection. New York: Viking Press, c1984. xiv, 303 p. : ill.
NOTES: Includes index. Bibliography: p. 300-303.
LEVEL: I LANG: Eng ISBN: 0-670-66467-7 LC CARD: 83-047929 GV436 20365

Canada Fitness Award. Jeunesse en forme. (Ottawa): (Fitness and Amateur Sport / Condition physique et Sport amateur), (1984). various pieces
CORP: Canada. Fitness and Amateur Sport.
CORP: Canada. Condition physique et Sport amateur.

PHYSICAL FITNESS - TESTING (continued)

NOTES: Cover title. Titre de la couverture.
LEVEL: B LANG: Eng Fr GV436.5 17986

David, D. Aptitude aux sports. (Refs: 10)*Concours medical (Paris) 106(26), 1984, 2478-2481.*
LEVEL: I LANG: Fr

Dawson, B. Ackland, T. Roberts, C. A new fitness test for team and individual sports. *Sports coach (Wembley, W. Aust.) 8(2) Oct 1984, 42-44.*
LEVEL: B LANG: Eng SIRC ARTICLE NO: 104245

Dean, J.A. FitCirc is model self-testing program. *Journal of physical education and program (Columbus, Ohio) 81(8), Dec 198 H20-H21.*
LEVEL: B LANG: Eng SIRC ARTICLE NO: 108254

Docherty, D. Quinney, A. Evaluating physical fitness with reference to the functional capacities of muscle. (Refs: 30)*CAHPE journal/Revue de l'ACSEPR (Ottawa) 50(4), Mar/Apr 1984, 15-18.*
LEVEL: I LANG: Eng SIRC ARTICLE NO: 096180

Farrally, M.R. Tuxworth, W. Eurofit - an initiative of the Council of Europe. *Scottish journal of physical education (Glasgow, Scotland) 12(4), Nov 1984, 11-13.*
LEVEL: B LANG: Eng SIRC ARTICLE NO: 102714

Gallay, P. Tests d'aptitude physique a l'effort. (Tests for physical exertion endurance.) *Soins. Cardiologie (Paris) 16/17, juin/juil 1984, 49-50.*
LEVEL: I LANG: Fr

Haag, H. Council of Europe, testing physical fitness: Eurofit (experimental battery). Consejo de Europa, probando el estado fisico: Eurofit (bateria experimental). (Refs: 6)*International journal of physical education (Schorndorf, W. Germany) 21(2), 19-26 Jul 1984, Special supplement II, 6-15.*
NOTES: To be continued in issue 21(4), 1984.
LEVEL: I LANG: Eng Spa SIRC ARTICLE NO: 097688

Haag, H. Council of Europe testing physical fitness: Eurofit (experimental battery). Consejo de Europa Probando el estado fisico: Eurofit (bateria experimental). (Refs: 10)*International journal of physical education (Schorndorf, FRG) 21(4), 1984, 2-16.*
NOTES: Continued from no. 2/84, p. 15.
LEVEL: I LANG: Eng Spa SIRC ARTICLE NO: 105437

Hebbelinck, M. The concept of health related to physical fitness. (Refs: 11)*International journal of physical education (Schorndorf, W. Germany) 21(1), 1984, 9-18.*
LEVEL: I LANG: Eng SIRC ARTICLE NO: 093044

Herbert, H.R. Montgomery, L.C. Holland, J.C. Wetzler, H.P. Design and results of retesting in the National Defence Universit Health/Fitness Program. *Military medicine (Washington) 149(7), Jul 1984, 375-378.*
LEVEL: A LANG: Eng SIRC ARTICLE NO: 104249

Heyward, V.H. Designs for fitness: a guide to physical fitness appraisal and exercise prescription. Minneapolis, Minn.: Burgess Pub. Co., c1984. vii, 215 p.
NOTES: Includes bibliographies and index.
LEVEL: I LANG: Eng ISBN: 0-8087-3188-2 LC CARD: 83-010061 GV426 20188

Kuntzleman, C.T. 5 fitness tests: how fit are your kids? *Shape (Woodland Hills, Calif.) 4(4), Dec 1984, 49-50;119-120;122.*
LEVEL: B LANG: Eng SIRC ARTICLE NO: 173233

Lacy, E. Marshall, B. Fitnessgram: an answer to physical fitness improvement for school children. *Journal of physical education, recreation & dance 55(1), Jan 1984, 18-19.*
LEVEL: B LANG: Eng SIRC ARTICLE NO: 091678

Macdonald, R. Fitness and assessment. *Physiotherapy in sport (Dymchurch, Kent) 7(2), Autumn 1984, 2.*
LEVEL: B LANG: Eng SIRC ARTICLE NO: 105443

Montaye, H.J. Age and cardiovascular response to submaximal treadmill exercise in males. (Refs: 33)*Research quarterly for exercise & sport (Reston Va.) 55(1), Mar 1984, 85-88.*
ABST: The purpose of this report was to compare males of various ages with respect to their heart rate and systolic blood pressure in response to submaximal treadmill walking of different intensities. The subjects ranged in age from 10 to 59 years, with no fewer than 30 subjects in each age grouping. The data support the observation of a decrease in heart rate in response to a given submaximal workload children aged from about 10 to 18 and little change thereafter to about the age of 60. Systolic blood pressure increases with an increase in age from about 10 to 60 years. The author states that because the subject population was more clearly defined in this report, the heart rate and systolic blood pressure data, at various workloads, represent better standards than previously reported.
LEVEL: A LANG: Eng SIRC ARTICLE NO: 096194

Mostardi, R.A. Porterfield, J. Urycki, S. Construction of a police physical fitness battery as a substitute for age requirements. *Journal of biomechanics (Elmsford, N.Y.) 17(11), 1984, 873.*
LEVEL: B LANG: Eng SIRC ARTICLE NO: 104258

Promotion kit. Trousse de promotion. (Ottawa): (Fitness and Amateur Sport / Condition physique et Sport amateur), (1984). 36 leaves
CORP: Canada. Fitness and Amateur Sport.
CORP: Canada. Condition physique et Sport amateur.
NOTES: Cover title. Titre de la couverture.
LEVEL: B LANG: Eng Fr GV436.5 17985

Revised Canada Fitness Award manual. Jeunesse en forme Canada: manuel revisee. Ottawa: Fitness and Amateur Sport/Condition physique et Sport amateur, 1984. 22, 22 p. (Cat. No. H93-31/1984)
CORP: Canada. Fitness and Amateur Sport.
CORP: Canada. Condition physique et Sport amateur.
NOTES: Titre de la couverture. Cover title. French and English texts on inverted pages with separate paging. Textes francais et anglais disposes tete-beche avec pagination separee.
LEVEL: B LANG: Eng Fr ISBN: 0-662-52904-9 GV436.5 17978

Shephard, R.J. Tests of maximum oxygen intake: a critical review. (Refs: 280)*Sports medicine (Auckland) 1(2), Mar/Apr 1984, 99-124.*
ABST: The author reviews the determinants of maximum oxygen intake, techniques for measuring maximum oxygen intake, and the interpretation of test results. The author suggests that limitations of methodology and wide interindividual variations of constitutional potential limit the interpretation of test results. The author concludes that the main practical value of VO2 max measurement is in the functional assessment of patients with cardiorespiratory disease.
LEVEL: A LANG: Eng SIRC ARTICLE NO: 094574

Sinclair, J.D. Fitness tests. *New Zealand medical journal (Dunedin) 97(763), 12 Sept 1984, 601-602.*
LEVEL: B LANG: Eng SIRC ARTICLE NO: 104263

The George Mason University computerized physical fitness profile. *Physical education newsletter (Old Saybrook, Conn.) 160, Jun 1984, 6-7.*
LEVEL: B LANG: Eng SIRC ARTICLE NO: 104247

Vuori, I. Fyysisen harjoittelun fysiologisten edellytysten ja vaikutusten mittaaminen. (Assessment of physical condition and the effects of training.) *Duodecim (Helsinki) 100(21), 1984, 1480-1494.*
LEVEL: I LANG: Fin

Wolf, M.D. Conditioning: take-home tests. *Women's sports (Palo Alto, Calif.) 6(11), Nov 1984, 12.*
LEVEL: B LANG: Eng SIRC ARTICLE NO: 173598

Zack, M.B. Cardiopulmonary exercise testing: an integrated approach. (Refs: 6)
NOTES: In, Cantu, R.C. (ed.), Clinical sports medicine, Lexington, Mass. ; Toronto, Collamore Press : D.C. Heath, c1984, p. 109-114.
LEVEL: I LANG: Eng RC1201 15964

AAHPER FITNESS TEST

Health related physical fitness: technical manual. Reston, Va.: American Alliance for Health, Physical Education, Recreation and Dance, c1984. 47 p.
CORP: American Alliance for Health, Physical Education, Recreation and Dance.
NOTES: Bibliography: p. 43-47.
LEVEL: I LANG: Eng ISBN: 0-88314-267-8 GV436.5 19049

Ryan, A.J. Few teachers know of new fitness tests. *Physician and sportsmedicine (Minneapolis, Minn.) 12(6), Jun 1984, 41.*
LEVEL: B LANG: Eng SIRC ARTICLE NO: 094571

AAHPER YOUTH FITNESS TEST

Hall, E.G. Lee, A.M. Sex differences in motor performance of young children: fact or fiction? (Refs: 10)*Sex roles: a journa of research (New York) 10(3/4), Feb 1984, 217-230.*
ABST: Children in grades 3, 4 and 5 who had participated in a coeducational physical fitness program were tested 3 times over a 3 year period with the AAHPER youth fitness test. Girls consistently performed as well or better than boys in the same grade level.
LEVEL: A LANG: Eng SIRC ARTICLE NO: 097690

ASTRAND-RHYMING TEST

Bodelet, J. Boura, M. Trois ans d'entrainement controle par differents tests. Signification et valeurs de ces tests. *Medecine du sport 58(1), 25 janv 1984, 18-22.*
RESUME: Au cours de cette etude, 37 sujets (20 hommes et 17 femmes) ont ete soumis a deux tests d'aptitude physique, le test de Ruffier-Dickson et CT170, lors de leur admission au programme d'education physique de l'U.E.R.E.P. a Nancy et apres trois annees d'entrainement. Une augmentation marquee de la CT170 a ete constatee alors que l'indice de Ruffier-Dickson n'a pas varie de facon significative.
LEVEL: A LANG: Fr SIRC ARTICLE NO: 091656

BRUCE TREADMILL TEST

Saris, W.H.M. de Koning, F. Elvers, J.W.H. deBoo, T. Binkhorst, R.A. Estimation of W170 and maximal oxygen consumption in young children by different treadmill tests. (Refs: 14)
CONF: Symposium of Paediatric Work Physiology (10th : 1981 : Joutsa, Finland).
NOTES: In, Ilmarinen, J. and Vaelimaeki, I. (eds.), Children and sport: paediatric work physiology, Berlin, Springer-Verlag, 1984, p. 86-92.
ABST: Directly measured maximal oxygen uptake is the most precise index of physical performance capacity. However, this method requires the full cooperation and motivation of the subjects, but young children are difficult to motivate. The treadmill is generally used for children under 10 years of age and this study tested 5 year olds using a variety of treadmill procedures in order to establish a suitable nonmaximal treadmill procedure for predicting performance capacity.
LEVEL: A LANG: Eng SIRC ARTICLE NO: 102824

CANADIAN HOME FITNESS TEST

Leger, L. The Canadian Home Fitness Test revisited. (Refs: 15)*CAHPER journal/Revue de l'ACSEPR (Ottawa) 50(6), Jul/Aug 1984 6-8.*
LEVEL: I LANG: Eng SIRC ARTICLE NO: 099196

Morgan, K. Hughes, A.O. Philipp, R. Reliability of a test of cardiovascular fitness. (Canadian Home Fitness Test) (Refs: 17) *International journal of epidemiology (London) 13(1), Mar 1984, 32-37.*
LEVEL: I LANG: Eng SIRC ARTICLE NO: 099200

EVALUATION

Edelman, B. Smits, G. The pedometer: a reassessment of its usefulness in the measurement of activity level. (Refs: 27) *Perceptual and motor skills 58(1), Feb 1984, 151-158.*
ABST: The authors evaluate the reliability of the pedometer as a measuring tool of activity level. Comparisons were made between pedometer, diary and questionnaire scores obtained from 35 male and 49 female subjects. Results indicate that the pedometer is highly reliable and strongly correlated with the diary. The relationships of physical activity to age, sex, and body weight were also examined. A negative relationship was established between percent overweight and activity level. There was no significant correlation between activity level and age or sex.
LEVEL: A LANG: Eng SIRC ARTICLE NO: 093039

Griffiths, A. Decouvrir des athletes talenteux. Talent identification. *Champion (Vanier, Ont.) 8(2), May/mai 1984, 14-17.*
LEVEL: B LANG: Fr Eng SIRC ARTICLE NO: 094753

Myers, D.C. Validation of the military entrance physical strength capacity test. Alexandria, Va.: Computer Microfilm International, 1984. 1 microfiche (194 fr.) (Technical report 610.)
LEVEL: A LANG: Eng EDRS: ED246016

Sanhueza, G. Ibarra, R. Santana, R. Adasme, A. Reyes, J.C. Riquelme, C. Reliability of the multi-trial items of the Santiago Youth Fitness Test. (Refs: 4)*Asian journal of physical education (Taiwan, China) 7(1), Apr 1984, 83-86.*
NOTES: Abstract in Chinese.
LEVEL: I LANG: Eng SIRC ARTICLE NO: 096203

Taylor, C.B. Coffey, T. Berra, K. Iaffaldano, R. Casey, K. Haskell, W.L. Seven-day activity and self-report compared to a direct measure of physical activity. (Refs: 6)*American journal of epidemiology (Baltimore) 120(6), Dec 1984, 818-824.*
LEVEL: A LANG: Eng SIRC ARTICLE NO: 174116

Vogelaere, P. Principales methodes permettant de determiner l'aptitude physique: evolution historique et aspects critiques. (Refs: 44)*Medecine du sport (Paris) 58(3), 25 mai 1984, 4-11.*
RESUME: L'auteur discute des diverses batteries de tests utilisees pour determiner l'aptitude physique. Il subdivise son etude en six genre d'epreuves: epreuves ayant pour critere la recuperation cardiaque a l'effort, determination directe de la consommation d'oxygene, determination indirecte du VO2, determination biometrique, determination biochimique et epreuves ayant pour critere la mesure des dimensions du coeur.
LEVEL: A LANG: Fr SIRC ARTICLE NO: 096209

Wilson, N. Putting the tests to the test: who needs a fitness test and when? and what is the quality of the information provided by the testers? If Neil Wilson's experience is anything to go by, the results can be instructive - but variable. *Running (London) 44, Dec 1984, 44-47.*
LEVEL: B LANG: Eng SIRC ARTICLE NO: 104271

HARVARD STEP TEST

Banerjee, P.K. Chatterjee, S. Harvard step test as a measure of physical fitness in adolescent boys. *Indian journal of medical research (New Delhi) 79, Mar 1984, 413-417.*
LEVEL: A LANG: Eng

PWC TESTS

Bodelet, J. Boura, M. Trois ans d'entrainement controle par differents tests. Signification et valeurs de ces tests. *Medecine du sport 58(1), 25 janv 1984, 18-22.*
RESUME: Au cours de cette etude, 37 sujets (20 hommes et 17 femmes) ont ete soumis a deux tests d'aptitude physique, le test de Ruffier-Dickson et CT170, lors de leur admission au programme d'education physique de l'U.E.R.E.P. a Nancy et apres trois annees d'entrainement. Une augmentation marquee de la CT170 a ete constatee alors que l'indice de Ruffier-Dickson n'a pas varie de facon significative.
LEVEL: A LANG: Fr SIRC ARTICLE NO: 091656

Matsui, K. Iwasaki, I. (A statistical approach to measure fitness by PWC 170.) *Sangyo ika daigaku zasshi (Kitakyushu) 6(2), 1 June 1984, 163-170.*
LEVEL: A LANG: Jpn

STANDARDS AND GUIDELINES

Combs, M.A. Golding, L.A. New guide set for determining ergometer workloads. *Journal of physical education and program (Columbus, Ohio) 81(8), Dec 1984, H14-H15;H17.*
LEVEL: I LANG: Eng SIRC ARTICLE NO: 108253

STEP TESTS

Watkins, J. Ewing, B. The effects of practice and method of scoring on performance in a step test suitable for use in school (Refs: 12)*Scottish journal of physical education (Glasgow, Scotland) 12(3),*

Aug 1984, 12-17.
ABST: The authors compared six step test performance scores of 26 boys (aged 15.8 plus or minus 0.27 yr) over three trials using two methods of scoring. No significant change in performance was observed. Results indicated no correlation between either performance and height or performance and weight.
LEVEL: A LANG: Eng SIRC ARTICLE NO: 099215

Watkins, J. Step tests of cardiorespiratory fitness suitable for mass testing. *British journal of sports medicine (Loughborough, Eng.) 18(2), Jun 1984, 84-89.*
ABST: A review of the literature strongly suggests that step tests can give reliable and valid measures of cardiorespiratory fitness provided that (a) the subjects have received adequate instruction and practice in taking the test prior to the criterion test performance, and (b) the work load is above a certain threshold.
LEVEL: A LANG: Eng SIRC ARTICLE NO: 102750

STRENGTH TESTING

Baumagartner, T.A. East, W.B Hensley, L.D. Knox, D.F. Norton, C.J. Frye, P.A. Equipment improvements and additional norms fo the modified pull-up test. (Refs: 4)*Research quarterly for exercise & sports (Reston, Va.) 55(1), Mar 1984, 64-68.*
ABST: This sport outlines the improvements made in the equipment design of the modified pull-out test, which is a test of shoulder girdle strength and endurance. In addition, evidence is presented in the form of norms that the modified pull-out test can be utilized on a variety of populations. The U.S. college groups and large Canadian public school groups, descriptive statistics and norms are presented. High reliability is reported in all test-retest measures. The authors conclude that the modified pull-out test seems to be a valid and reliable test which is practical to use with both sexes and a variety of age groups.
LEVEL: A LANG: Eng SIRC ARTICLE NO: 096176

Jackson, A.S. Osburn, H.G. Laughery, K.R. Validity of isometric strength tests for predicting performance in physically demanding tasks. *In, Proceedings of the Human Factors Society 28th Annual Meeting 'New Frontiers for Science and Technology', San Antonio, Texas, 22-26 October 1984, edited by M.J. Alluisi, S. De Groot and E.A. Alluisi. The Human Factors Society, Santa Monica, California, 1984, Vol. 1, p. 452-454.*
LEVEL: A LANG: Eng

STRESS TESTING

Stein, R.A. Exercise ECG testing. (Refs: 10)
NOTES: In, Birrer, R.B. (ed.), Sports medicine for the primary care physician, Norwalk, Conn., Appleton-Century-Crofts, c1984, p. 77-84.
LEVEL: I LANG: Eng RC1210 17030

PHYSICAL THERAPY

Caruso, I. Concetti riabilitativi. Concepts of rehabilitation. (Refs: 6)*Italian journal of sports traumatology (Milano, Italy) 6(4), Oct/Dec 1984, 321-324.*
CONF: Italian Society of Sports Traumatology.

Congress (1st : 1983 : Rome)
LEVEL: I LANG: It Eng SIRC ARTICLE NO: 105333

Devine, K.L. Competencies in biomechanics for the physical therapist. (Refs: 7)*Physical therapy (Alexandria, Va.) 64(12), Dec 1984, 1883-1885.*
LEVEL: B LANG: Eng SIRC ARTICLE NO: 102569

Harris, F.A. Facilitation techniques and technological adjuncts in therapeutic exercise. (Refs: 200)
NOTES: In, Basmajian, J.V. (ed.), Therapeutic exercise, 4th ed., Baltimore, Md., Williams & Wilkins, c1984, p. 110-178.
LEVEL: A LANG: Eng RM719 17505

Jull, G.A. Cupit, R.L. Physiotherapy at the XII Commonwealth Games: part 2: injuries and management. (Refs: 1)*Australian journal of physiotherapy 30(1), Feb 1984, 10-14.*
ABST: At the XII Commonwealth Games, Australian physiotherapists treated the injuries of competitors from the 10 sports contested. A high incidence of vertebrogenic pain and knee joint injuries were noted. Percentage of types of injuries treated in each sport is tabulated.
LEVEL: I LANG: Eng SIRC ARTICLE NO: 097573

Jull, G.A. Cupit, R.L. Physiotherapy at the XII Commonwealth Games: part 1: organization and utilization of services. *Australian journal of physiotherapy 30(1), Feb 1984, 3-9.*
ABST: A report on the organizational and administrative aspects of the physiotherapy service provided by 60 Australian physiotherapists at the Commonwealth Games in Brisbane in 1982. A total of 988 individuals were treated over a 5 week period, 80% of whom were competitors. Of 4,427 consultations, 3,536 were for treatment of pain or injury, 891 were for rub downs only.
LEVEL: I LANG: Eng SIRC ARTICLE NO: 097601

Knoeppel, D.E. Suggestions for the clinic: maximizing equipment utilization in orthopedic and sports medicine rehabilitation (Refs: 2)*Journal of orthopaedic and sports physical therapy (Baltimore) 5(6), May/Jun 1984, 373-381.*
ABST: Much of today's rehabilitative equipment is overpriced and underutilized. This paper introduces some alternative equipment combinations and patient-equipment position variations in an effort to increase utilization. The U.B.X.T. and Mini-Gym can be most effectively used in combination for upper extremity rehabilitation while the U.B.X.T. and Orthotron provide numerous possibilities for upper and lower extremity exercising. Position and pattern variations are feasible and offer increased versatility. The clinician is encouraged to experiment with this information and seek out the most efficient and productive use of available equipment.
LEVEL: I LANG: Eng SIRC ARTICLE NO: 100730

Licht, S. History. (Refs: 136)
NOTES: In, Basmajian, J.V. (ed.), Therapeutic exercise, 4th ed., Baltimore, Md., Williams & Wilkins, c1984, p. 1-44.
LEVEL: A LANG: Eng RM719 17505

Moshkov, V.N. Teoreticheskie osnovy lechebnoi fizicheskoi kul'tury. (Theoretical bases of physical therapy.) *Voproso kurortologii, fizioterapii i lechebnoi fizicheskoi kultury (Moscow) 6, Nov/Dec 1984, 52-55.*
LEVEL: I LANG: Rus

Pollock, D.W. Physical therapy in the treatment of athletic injuries. (Refs: 4)

NOTES: In, Birrer, R.B. (ed.), Sports medicine for the primary care physician, Norwalk, Conn., Appleton-Century-Crofts, c1984, p. 259-268.
LEVEL: I LANG: Eng RC1210 17030

Reasoner, A.E. A western states survey of certified athletic trainers' use of joint mobilization in treatment programs. Eugene, Ore.: Microform Publications, University of Oregon, 1984. 2 microfiches : negative, ill. ; 11 x 15 cm.
NOTES: Thesis (M.S.) - University of Oregon, 1982; (xiii, 112 leaves); vita; includes bibliography.
LEVEL: A LANG: Eng UO84 139-140

Schuster, N.D. Nelson, D.L. Quisling, C. Burnout among physical therapists. (Refs: 19)*Physical therapy (Alexandria, Va.) 64(3), Mar 1984, 299-303.*
ABST: One hundred sixty therapists answered a questionnaire designed to assess burnout. Eighty-four (53%) stated that they were currently experiencing feeling of burnout. Data analysis revealed that four of the five symptoms of burnout could be predicted by different potential causes.
LEVEL: A LANG: Eng SIRC ARTICLE NO: 094434

Segal, M. Gaudebert, G. La contactotherapie des verrues dites vulgaires. *Medecine du sport 58(1), 25 janv 1984, 17.*
LEVEL B LANG: Fr SIRC ARTICLE NO: 091775

Sion, D. Medecine physique et sports. (Physical medicine and sports.) *LARC medical (Lille) 4(9), Nov 1984, 568-570.*
LEVEL B LANG: Fr

Sotosky, J.R. Physical therapists' attitude towards teaching. (Refs: 14)*Physical therapy (Alexandria, Va.) 64(3), Mar 1984, 347-349.*
ABST: Fifty-seven physical therapists answered a questionnaire that was designed to determine the attitudes of physical therapists toward teaching as part of their professional role. The results indicate that physical therapists have a strong positive attitude toward teaching. The author suggests that the physical therapy curriculum be assessed regarding the inclusion of educational theory and skills and that continuing education for physical therapists be established.
LEVEL: A LANG: Eng SIRC ARTICLE NO: 094438

Tomberlin, J.P. Eggart, J.S. Callister, L. The use of standardized evaluation forms in physical therapy. (Refs: 13)*Journal of orthopaedic and sports physical therapy (Baltimore) 5(6), May/Jun 1984, 348-372.*
ABST: The need for a consistent and efficient method of patient evaluation is not a new one. Standardized evaluation forms that include body charts can be useful in recording subjective and objective data in a systematic way. At the Physical Therapy Unit - Student Health Center, University of Wisconsin-La Crosse, the authors designed and put into use this type of evaluation form. They feel these evaluation forms allow them to perform consistent and efficient patient evaluations in a short amount of time, especially for acute musculoskeletal injuries.
LEVEL: I LANG: Eng SIRC ARTICLE NO: 100765

Toubiana, L. Pour une approche cybernetique du probleme sportif. (Refs: 12)*Homeopathie francaise (Paris) 72(5), 1984, 333-335.*
LEVEL: I LANG: Fr

Wolf, S.L. Morphological functional considerations for therapeutic exercise. (Refs: 243)
NOTES: In, Basmajian, J.V. (ed.), Therapeutic

exercise, 4th ed., Baltimore, Md., Williams & Wilkins, c1984, p. 45-87.
LEVEL: A LANG: Eng RM719 17505

BALNEOTHERAPY

Vanvooren, P. Lescaudron, A. Bretaudeau, A. Kinebalneotherapie et prevention des accidents musculaires du sportif. *Cinesiologie (Paris) 94, mars/avr 1984, 167-168.*
LEVEL: B LANG: Fr SIRC ARTICLE NO: 096061

CRYOTHERAPY

Cousteau, J.P. Medecine: etre ou ne pas etre de glace. *Tennis de France (Paris) 373, mai 1984, 137-138.*
LEVEL: B LANG: Fr SIRC ARTICLE NO: 100712

Ebrahim, K. The effect of cold application and flexibility techniques on hip extensors and their influence on flexibility in college males. Eugene, Ore.: Microform Publications, University of Oregon, 1984. 1 microfiche : negative, ill. ; 11 x 15 cm.
NOTES: Thesis (Ph.D.) - North Texas State University, 1982; (iii, 75 leaves); includes bibliography.
LEVEL: A LANG: Eng UO84 211

Finke, R.C. Cold as an effective treatment for sports injuries. (Refs: 12)*Sideline view (Minneapolis, Minn.) 5(8), Mar 1984 1-4.*
LEVEL: B LANG: Eng SIRC ARTICLE NO: 092858

Lievens, P. Leduc, A. Cryotherapy and sports. (Refs: 12)*International journal of sports medicine (Stuttgart) Suppl. 5, Nov 1984, 37-39.*
CONF: International Congress on Sports and Health (1983 : Maastricht, Netherlands).
LEVEL: A LANG: Eng SIRC ARTICLE NO: 104122

Vaillant, M. Mette, F. Viel, E. Neiger, H. Mesure de la temperature cutanee pendant l'application d'une source de froid avec enveloppe mouillee et enveloppe seche. (Refs: 15)*Cinesiologie: medecine du sport (Paris) 98, nov/dec 1984, 457-463.*
RESUME: Sur vingt sujets sains, les variations de temperature cutanee ont ete mesurees au cours de l'application d'un cryogene avec enveloppe seche et enveloppe mouillee pendant une duree de 20 min. Les resultats montrent une difference significative entre les deux modes d'application. Seule l'enveloppe mouillee permet d'obtenir un refroidissement important et rapide qui permet d'esperer un effet antalgique. L'humidification de l'enveloppe du cryogene constitue la condition d'efficacite therapeutique du froid.
LEVEL: A LANG: Fr SIRC ARTICLE NO: 104152

Yackzan, L. Adams, C. Francis, K.T. The effects of ice massage on delayed muscle soreness. (Refs: 30)*American journal of sports medicine (Baltimore, Md.) 12(2), Mar/Apr 1984, 159-165.*
ABST: Thirty female subjects performed exhaustive eccentric bilateral arm exercise. Ten subjects had one arm iced immediately following exercise, ten other subjects had one arm iced 24 hours post-exercise, the final ten subjects had ice applied to one arm 48 hours post-exercise. The second arm of all subjects served as an untreated control. The results indicate that cold treatment does not reduce delayed muscle soreness.
LEVEL: A LANG: Eng SIRC ARTICLE NO: 094451

ELECTROTHERAPY AND ELECTRIC STIMULATION

Almekinders, L.C. Transcutaneous muscle stimulation for rehabilitation. (Refs: 22)*Physician and sportsmedicine 12(3), Mar 1984, 118-122;124.*
LEVEL: I LANG: Eng SIRC ARTICLE NO: 091495

Bejor, M. Monti, G. Ruju, A. Dalla Toffola, E. La stimolazione nervosa transcutanea (T.E.N.S.) nel trattamento e nel recuper di atleti affetti da stati di contrattura muscolare. Transcutaneous electric nerve stimulation (TENS) in the treatment and rehabilitation of sportsmen with muscle contractions. (Refs: 16)*Italian journal of sports traumatology (Milan) 6(1), Jan/Mar 1984, 51-61.*
ABST: The purpose of this study was to investigate the usefulness of transcutaneous electric nerve stimulation (TENS) in reducing subjective pain, which affects the hold times of various stretching exercises. A group comprised of 27 males and 28 females was used for the study. Maximum hold times were recorded for three stretching exercises, aimed at the muscle areas of the femoral quadriceps, the ischiocrural muscles and the sural triceps. These were done for both limbs, with and without TENS treatments. The use of TENS increased the average hold times during the preliminary measurement sessions and after 12 stretching sessions, when compared to the hold times without TENS. The authors suggest that this pain reduction is extremely useful as an aid to correct position, since it avoids the transition through incorrect postures.
LEVEL: A LANG: Eng It SIRC ARTICLE NO: 097354

Currier, D.P. Mann, R. Pain complaint: comparison of electrical stimulation with conventional isometric exercise. (Refs: 17) *Journal of orthopaedic and sports physical therapy (Baltimore, Md.) 5(6), May/Jun 1984, 318-323.*
ABST: The purpose of this retrospective study was to assess the pain experiences of 17 healthy subjects who trained with isometric exercise, electrical stimulation, and the combination of isometric exercise and electrical stimulation for 5 weeks. Results indicated that subjects who received the electrical stimulation mode of training experienced similar torque gains but less muscle soreness than those who used conventional isometric exercise. Most subjects of the exercise and electrical stimulation groups experienced pain at the medial aspect of their knee. Those who received electrical stimulation described the greatest amount of transient discomfort. Electrical stimulation does not appear to increase the risk of discomfort more than volitional resistive exercise for achieving similar force-developing capacity of muscle in healthy subjects.
LEVEL: A LANG: Eng SIRC ARTICLE NO: 100713

Gastaldi, B.P. An investigation of the effects of electrical stimulus of muscle in reducing the effects of disuse atrophy. Eugene, Ore.: Microform Publications, University of Oregon, 1984. 1 microfiche : negative, ill. ; 11 x 15 cm.
NOTES: Thesis (M.S.) - University of Oregon, 1982; (viii, 48 leaves); vita; includes bibliography.
LEVEL: A LANG: Eng UO84 33

Houston, M.E. La stimulation electrique des muscles. (Refs: 21)*Nouveautes en science de l'entrainement (Ottawa) 1984, 20-22.*
NOTES: Traduction d'un article redige par Michael E. Houston, qui a paru dans le Canadian journal of applied sport sciences, mars 1983, 8(2), 49-51.
LEVEL: I LANG: Fr SIRC ARTICLE NO: 096254

Kramer, J. Lindsay, D. Magee, D. Mendryk, S. Wall, T. Comparison of voluntary and electrical stimulation contraction torques (Refs: 21)*Journal of orthopaedic and sports physical therapy (Baltimore, Md.) 5(6), May/Jun 1984, 324-331.*
ABST: Informed male volunteers completed maximal isometric knee extension efforts under each of three contraction conditions: 1) voluntary, 2) electrical stimulation (ES) only, and 3) superimposed (ES superimposed onto voluntary). Ten subjects completed the three contraction conditions using each of the following current formats: 1) asymmetrical biphasic rectangular wave, 2) asymmetrical biphasic spike wave, and 3) symmetrical monophasic square wave. Under the ES contraction condition, the torque associated with the symmetrical monophasic square wave was significantly less than that associated with the other two current formats. As well, the torque associated with the asymmetrical biphasic spike wave was significantly less than that associated with the asymmetrical biphasic rectangular wave format. The ES condition was associated with significantly less torque than were the MVC and the superimposed conditions for the asymmetrical biphasic spike and the symmetrical monophasic square wave formats. It is suggested that ES does not recruit more motor units, resulting in a greater force of contraction, than are recruited under MVC.
LEVEL: A LANG: Eng SIRC ARTICLE NO: 100905

Magner, R.L. Determining the effectiveness of electrical stimulation in limiting foot pronation and strengthening the intrinsic adductor muscles of the foot. Eugene, Ore.: Microform Publications, University of Oregon, 1984. 1 microfiche : negative, ill. ; 11 x 15 cm.
NOTES: Thesis (M.S.) - Brigham Young University, 1982; (vii, 74 leaves); includes bibliography.
LEVEL: A LANG: Eng UO84 320

Matteson, J.H. Cybernetic technology and high-performance athletic training. *National Strength & Conditioning Association journal (Lincoln, Neb.) 6(3), Jun/Jul 1984, 32-33;66.*
LEVEL: I LANG: Eng SIRC ARTICLE NO: 096033

Silbuit, D. The shock that heals. *Maclean's (Toronto) 30 Apr 1984, 64.*
LEVEL: B LANG: Eng SIRC ARTICLE NO: 092890

Walmsey, R.P. Vooys, J. Letts, G. A comparison of torque generated by knee extension with a maximal voluntary muscle contraction vis-a-vis electrical stimulation. (Refs: 19)*Journal of orthopaedic and sports physical therapy (Baltimore, Md.) 6(1), Jul/Aug 1984, 10-17.*
ABST: In view of the Russian's claim that electrical stimulation can be used to increase muscle tension above the values generated by a maximum voluntary muscle isometric contraction, two experiments were conducted. Both compared torque values generated around the knee by a maximal voluntary isometric contraction first, to stimulation on its own and second, stimulation in conjunction with voluntary effort. Both experiments contrasted low and medium frequency currents. The first experiment used machines commonly available in therapy departments (12). The second experiment used machines which approximate the Soviets' apparatus (14). Comparisons which were made include: 1) Maximum voluntary contraction. 2) Low frequency current stimulation. 3) Medium frequency current stimulation. 4) '1' plus '2'. 5) '1'

plus '3'. Results showed that no method was superior to maximal voluntary contraction. In each instance, the torque generated solely by any of the electrical devices was significantly inferior to voluntary effort.
LEVEL: A LANG: Eng SIRC ARTICLE NO: 100932

Wong, R.A. Jette, D.U. Changes in sympathetic tone associated with different forms of transcutaneous electrical nerve stimulation in healthy subjects. (Refs: 19)*Physical therapy (Alexandria, Va.) 64(4), Apr 1984, 478-482.*
ABST: This study investigated the effect of four different forms of transcutaneous electrical nerve stimulation (TENS) on sympathetic tone in twelve healthy women. The four treatments consisted of high frequency TENS, low frequency TENS, burst mode TENS, and placebo TENS. Ipsilateral and contralateral fingertip skin temperatures were taken 25 minutes before treatment, immediately after a 25 minute treatment and 25 minutes post-treatment. High, low, and burst mode TENS significantly increased sympathetic tone in the ipsilateral arm immediately after TENS treatment.
LEVEL: A LANG: Eng SIRC ARTICLE NO: 094450

EXERCISE THERAPY

Allman, F.L. Exercise in sports medicine. (Refs: 16)
NOTES: In, Basmajian, J.V. (ed.), Therapeutic exercise, 4th ed., Baltimore, Md., Williams & Wilkins, c1984, p. 485-518.
LEVEL: A LANG: Eng RM719 17505

Basmajian, J.V. Therapeutic exercise. 4th ed. Baltimore, Md.: Williams & Wilkins, c1984. xvii, 622 p. : ill. (Rehabilitation medicine library.)
NOTES: Originally published as part of the Physical medicine library, edited by Sidney Licht. Includes bibliographies.
LEVEL: A LANG: Eng ISBN: 0-683-00434-4 LC CARD: 83-14814 RM719 17505

Basmajian, J.V. Exercises in water. (Refs: 4)
NOTES: In, Basmajian, J.V. (ed.), Therapeutic exercise, 4th ed., Baltimore, Md., Williams & Wilkins, c1984, p. 303-308.
LEVEL: I LANG: Eng RM719 17505

Basmajian, J.V. Exercise in foot disabilities.
NOTES: In, Basmajian, J.V. (ed.), Therapeutic exercise, 4th ed., Baltimore, Md., Williams & Wilkins, c1984, p. 519-528.
LEVEL: I LANG: Eng RM719 17505

Bohannon, R.W. Effect of repeated eight-minute muscle loading on the angle of straight-leg raising. (Refs: 22)*Physical therapy (Alexandria, Va.) 64(4), Apr 1984, 491-497.*
ABST: This investigation determined if a change in the straight leg raise angle could be elicited in ten subjects by passively loading their lower extremities for 8 minutes per day for three days. Twenty-four hours after the third day of loading the straight leg raise angle was 4.4 degrees greater than it was initially, but this effect was not statistically significant. The author suggests that the muscles involved in the passive loading slowly lengthened in response to the treatment.
LEVEL: A LANG: Eng SIRC ARTICLE NO: 094412

Brask, B. Leuke, R.H. Soderberg, G.L. Electromyographic analysis of selected muscles during the latest step-up exercise. (Refs: 22)*Physical therapy (Alexandria, Va.) 64(3), Mar 1984, 324-329.*

ABST: Twenty-nine subjects performed lateral step-up exercise at step heights of 4- and 8in. The results revealed that the average muscular activity, depending on height and direction, ranged from 24-60% maximal voluntary contraction (MVC) for vastus medials, 8-23% MVC for rectus femoris, 3-9% for biceps femoris, and 4-9% for semimembranosus/semitendinosus muscles. The authors conclude that there appears to be insufficient activation of the hamstring muscles to neutralize the anterior shear force produced by the quadriceps femoris muscle. Therapists should consider this finding in relation to anterior ligament rehabilitation.
LEVEL: A LANG: Eng SIRC ARTICLE NO: 094414

Bringmann, W. Gyogykezelesben reszesuelt paciensek sportterapiai gondozasa. (Sports training used in follow-up health care and post-treatment rehabilitation.) (Refs: 35)*Sportorvosi szemle/ Hungarian review of sports medicine (Budapest) 25(3), 1984, 163-172.*
ABST: Considering the fundamental principles of medical treatment and prevention the author points out how important it is to include sports training already in the therapeutic phase. Health and physical fitness can be markedly promoted by exploiting this essential adaptive mechanism also later, namely in the process of rehabilitations as well. Four studies are reported in which patient groups of equal numbers were compared in respect of some selected physiological parameters of performance. One group of each study continued the endurance primed sports training initiated during the treatment for four additional months while the other group did not. Performance capacity improved dynamically in the groups continued sports training, whereas those who stopped endurance training immediately after medical therapy had ended fell back to nearly initial levels by the time of the follow-up investigation. The report closes with helpful suggestions for the continuation of post-treatment sport training and for improving its efficiency.
LEVEL: A LANG: Hun SIRC ARTICLE NO: 100233

Ebel, A. Kim, D.D.J. Exercise in peripheral vascular diseases. (Refs: 52)
NOTES: In, Basmajian, J.V. (ed.), Therapeutic exercise, 4th ed., Baltimore, Md., Williams & Wilkins, c1984, p. 546-564.
LEVEL: A LANG: Eng RM719 17505

Goldberg, L. Elliot, D.L. Prescribing exercise. *Western journal of medicine (San Francisco) 141(3), Sept 1984, 383-386.*
LEVEL: I LANG: Eng

Henderson, A. An introduction to isokinetics. (Refs: 6)*Remedial gymnastics and recreational therapy (Manchester, Eng.) 112, May 1984, 13-15.*
LEVEL: B LANG: Eng SIRC ARTICLE NO: 101029

Hoberman, M. Basmajian, J.V. Crutch and cane exercises and use. (Refs: 14)
NOTES: In, Basmajian, J.V. (ed.), Therapeutic exercise, 4th ed., Baltimore, Md., Williams & Wilkins, c1984, p. 267-284.
LEVEL: A LANG: Eng RM719 17505

Jette, D.U. Physiological effects of exercise in the diabetic. (Refs: 26)*Physical therapy (Alexandria, Va.) 64(3), Mar 1984,339-342.*
ABST: This review article discusses the physiological effects of exercise and training in the diabetic. Exercise treatment can improve glucose tolerance and cardiovascular disease in the diabetic

if it is correctly administered.
LEVEL: A LANG: Eng SIRC ARTICLE NO: 094425

Knapp, M.E. Exercises for lower motor neuron lesions. (Refs: 9)
NOTES: In, Basmajian, J.V. (ed.), Therapeutic exercise, 4th ed., Baltimore, Md., Williams & Wilkins, c1984, p. 381-406.
LEVEL: A LANG: Eng RM719 17505

Liberson, W.T. Brief isometric exercises. (Refs: 31)
NOTES: In, Basmajian, J.V. (ed.), Therapeutic exercise, 4th ed., Baltimore, Md., Williams & Wilkins, c1984, p. 236-256.
LEVEL: A LANG: Eng RM719 17505

Meiguang, H. A study on the therapeutic value of the 'rolling balls'. *China sports (Beijing, China) 16(9), Sept 1984, 8;21.*
LEVEL: I LANG: Eng SIRC ARTICLE NO: 108873

Moshkov, V.N. Lechebnaia fizkultura kak sredstvo vosstanovitelnoi, podderzhivaiushchei i profilakticheskoiterapii. (Exercise therapy as a means of restorative, supporting and preventive treatment.) *Voprosy kurortologii, Fizioterapii i lechebnoi fizicheskoi kultury (Moscow) 2, Mar/Apr 1984, 70-72.*
LEVEL: I LANG: Rus

Muse, M. LeFew, B. Shafiei, M. Frigola, G. Exercise for the chronic pain patient. Ithaca, N.Y.: Mouvement Publications Inc., c1984. iv, 104 p. : ill.
NOTES: Bibliography: p. 104.
LEVEL: B LANG: Eng ISBN: 0-932392-20-2 RA781 18053

O'Sullivan, S.B. Perceived exertion: a review. (Refs: 38)*Physical therapy (Alexandria, Va.) 64(3), Mar 1984, 343-346.*
ABST: This article summarizes the literature on perceived exertion and discusses the therapeutic implications for physical therapy. The author concludes that ratings of perceived exertion appear to be a useful tool for quantifying exercise stress. Further clinical research is needed to assess the usefulness of perceived exertion scales.
LEVEL: A LANG: Eng SIRC ARTICLE NO: 094614

Peninou, G. Dufour, M. Pierron, G. Proposition technologique pour l'entrainement des muscles abdominaux. *Annales de kinesitherapie (Paris) 11(5), 1984, 205-216.*
LEVEL: I LANG: Fr SIRC ARTICLE NO: 096040

Pollock, M.L. Wilmore, J.H. Fox, S.M. Exercise in health and disease: evaluation and prescription for prevention and rehabilitation. Philadelphia ; Toronto: W.B. Saunders, 1984. viii, 471 p. : ill.
NOTES: Includes bibliographical references.
LEVEL: I LANG: Eng ISBN: 0721611478 LC CARD: 83-015270 RM719 17475

Powers, S.K. Baker, B.A. Deason, R. Mangum, M. A trend analysis of steady state oxygen consumption during arm crank ergometr (Refs: 7)*Journal of sports medicine and physical fitness (Torino, Italy) 24(2), Jun 1984, 131-134.*
ABST: The purpose of this investigation was to examine the effects of increasing work rate on oxygen consumption during steady-rate arm crank exercise (ACE). Six males who were not trained specifically for arm work exercised at 50 rpm at power outputs of 15, 30, 45, and 60 watts. Oxygen uptake (VO2) was measured with open-circuit spirometry. Linear, quadratic, and cubic models were computed using a least-squares technique to determine the mathematical model that best

described the increase in VO2 as a function of work rate. It was determined that VO2 increased as a curvilinear function of the work rate. This mathematical model should be useful to the clinician when prescribing exercise for patient rehabilitation and conditioning.
LEVEL: A LANG: Eng SIRC ARTICLE NO: 102817

Renauld, J. Sport et traitement Mezieres. *Homeopathie francaise (Paris) 72(5), 1984, 336-337.*
LEVEL: B LANG: Fr

Russek, A.S. Exercises for amputees. (Refs: 11)
NOTES: In, Basmajian, J.V. (ed.), Therapeutic exercise, 4th ed., Baltimore, Md., Williams & Wilkins, c1984, p. 421-440.
LEVEL: A LANG: Eng RM719 17505

Schram, D.A. Resistance exercise. (Refs: 12)
NOTES: In, Basmajian, J.V. (ed.), Therapeutic exercise, 4th ed., Baltimore, Md. Williams & Wilkins, c1984, p. 225-235.
LEVEL: A LANG: Eng RM719 17505

Schuele, K. Deimel, H. Sport- und Bewegungstherapie in der Rehabilitation - eine empirische Erhebung zum Sportlehrerbedarf. (Sports and exercise therapy in rehabilitation - an empirical survey of requirements for sport teachers.) *Offentliche Gesundheitswesen (Stuttgart) 46(12), Dec 1984, 603-607.*
LEVEL: I LANG: Ger

Symposium on exercise: physiology and clinical applications. *Clinics in chest medicine (Philadelphia) 5(1), Mar 1984, 1-210.*
LEVEL: A LANG: Eng

HYDROTHERAPY

Kirby, R.L. Sacamano, J.T. Balch, D.E. Kriellaars, D.J. Oxygen consumption during exercise in a heated pool. (Refs: 14) *Archives of physical medicine and rehabilitation (Chicago) 65(1), Jan 1984, 21-23.*
ABST: This study determined the oxygen consumption of thirteen healthy subjects during different forms of therapeutic exercise in a heated (36C) hydrotherapy pool. Oxygen consumption was measured in six settings: resting supine; resting seated in shoulder deep water; running at the fastest speed possible in chest-deep water; using hand paddles and running in place at shoulder depth. These exercises produced a graduated oxygen consumption scale with resting supine being the lowest (4.91.ml/kg/min) and running in place at shoulder depth being the highest (29.11.ml/kg/min). These results suggest that the more vigorous exercises stress aerobic capacity heavily but not excessively.
LEVEL: A LANG: Eng SIRC ARTICLE NO: 094604

MASSAGE

Crosman, L.J. Chateauvert, S.R. Weisberg, J. The effects of massage to the hamstring muscle group on range of motion. (Refs: 14)*Journal of orthopaedic and sports physical therapy (Baltimore, Md.) 6(3), Nov/Dec 1984, 168-172.*
ABST: This study was designed to measure the effect on range of motion of a single massage treatment to the hamstring muscle group. Thirty-four normal female subjects between 18 and 35 years of age were given a 9-12 minute massage treatment to the posterior aspect of one randomly assigned lower extremity. Passive range of motion

of both lower extremities was measured. Measurements were taken pre-, and post-, and 7-days postmassage treatment. Immediate postmassage increases in range of motion were noted in the test group (massaged) legs with significance at the 0.05 level.
LEVEL: A LANG: Eng SIRC ARTICLE NO: 102567

Evans, W. Massage. *Strength & health (York, Pa.)* 52(6), Oct/Nov 1984, 30-31.
LEVEL: B LANG: Eng SIRC ARTICLE NO: 099088

Nickel, D.J. Ullis, K.C. Acupressure for athletes: self-help for weekend to professional athletes. Rev. ed. Santa Monica, Calif.: Health-Acu-Press, c1984. xiii, 158 p. : ill.
LEVEL: B LANG: Eng ISBN: 0-9614009-2-7 LC CARD: 84-82068 RC1226 20105

Phaigh, R. Perry, P. Morgan, W. Athletic massage. New York: Simon and Schuster, c1984. 175 p. : ill.
LEVEL: I LANG: Eng ISBN: 0-671-52565-4 LC CARD: 84-014177 RC1226 18934

Viel, E. Donnees recentes concernant le massage du sportif. (Refs: 16)*Cinesiologie (Paris) 95, mai/juin 1984, 263-269.
LEVEL: I LANG: Fr SIRC ARTICLE NO: 097615

SAUNAS

Sobolevski, V.I. Shukhardin, I.O. The sauna as a means of restoration during intense training of swimmers (condensed). *Soviet sports review (Escondido, Calif.)* 19(1), Mar 1984, 49-51.
NOTES: Translated from, Plavanye 1980, 15-17.
LEVEL: I LANG: Eng SIRC ARTICLE NO: 095322

THERMOTHERAPY

Allary, B. Gavrilenko, P. Hummer Crenotherapie et pathologie du sport. (Refs: 30)*Cinesiologie 92/93, nov/dec 1983-janv/fevr 1984, 5-10.
NOTES: Numero special: Medecine du sport et thermalisme.
LEVEL: I LANG: Fr SIRC ARTICLE NO: 092916

Bourbonne-les-Bains ou la renovation exemplaire d'une station. *Cinesiologie 92/93, nov/dec 1983-janv/fevr 1984, 89-95.
NOTES: Numero special: Medecine du sport et thermalisme.
LEVEL: B LANG: Fr SIRC ARTICLE NO: 092917

Dubarry, J.J. Thermalisme dans le 3e age. *Cinesiologie 92/93, nov/dec 1983-janv/fevr 1984, 85-87.
NOTES: Numero special: Medecine du sport et thermalisme.
LEVEL: I LANG: Fr SIRC ARTICLE NO: 092927

Gavrilenko, P. Allary, B. La cure a Bourbonne-les-Bains et ses resultats sur 63 cas d'algodystrophie. *Cinesiologie 92/93, nov/dec 1983-janv/fevr 1984, 13-17.
NOTES: Numero special: Medecine du sport et thermalisme.
LEVEL: A LANG: Fr SIRC ARTICLE NO: 092931

Girault, G. Medecine thermale et sport. *Cinesiologie 92/93, nov/dec 1983-janv/fevr 1984, 19-22.
NOTES: Numero special: Medecine du sport et thermalisme.
LEVEL: I LANG: Fr SIRC ARTICLE NO: 092933

Leglise, M. Delabroise, A.M. Thermalisme et climatisme: interet des activites physiques durant la

cure. Apport du thermalism a la preparation du sportif. *Cinesiologie 92/93, nov/dec 1983-janv/fevr 1984, 23-26.
NOTES: Numero special: Medecine du sport et thermalisme.
LEVEL: I LANG: Fr SIRC ARTICLE NO: 092940

Palmer, M. Forestier, F. Sport et cures thermales. (Refs: 2)*Cinesiologie 92/93, nov/dec 1983-janv/fevr 1984, 35-42.
NOTES Numero special: Medecine du sport et thermalisme.
LEVEL: I LANG: Fr SIRC ARTICLE NO: 092947

Picard, H. Valton, C. Sport, thermalisme et oligo-elements en pathologie osteo-articulaire et O.R.L. (Refs: 10)*Cinesiologie 92/93, nov/dec 1983-janv/fevr 1984, 75-80;83-84.
NOTES: Numero special: Medecine du sport et thermalisme.
RESUME: Les auteurs discutent de l'utilisation des oligo-elements dans le traitements des pathologies osteo-articulaires et musculo-tendineuses. Ils expliquent le role joue par quelques uns de ces elements. La crenotherapie est percue comme le moyen privilegie, simple et facile de la cure par les oligo-elements.
LEVEL: A LANG: Fr SIRC ARTICLE NO: 092884

Toubeau, C. La reeducation des sportifs a Aix-les-Bains. (Refs: 5)*Cinesiologie 92/93, nov/dec 1983-janv/fevr 1984, 43-48.
NOTES: Numero special: Medecine du sport et thermalisme.
LEVEL: I LANG: Fr SIRC ARTICLE NO: 092952

ULTRASONIC THERAPY

Dyson, M. Theory & mechanics of ultrasound. *Physiotherapy in sport (Dymchurch, Kent) 7(2), Autumn 1984, 3-4.
LEVEL: I LANG: Eng SIRC ARTICLE NO: 105337

Jennings, L.R.F. Ultrasound - a guide to use. *Physiotherapy in sport (Kent, Eng.) 7(1), Spring 1984, 8-9.
LEVEL: I LANG: Eng SIRC ARTICLE NO: 099092

Moore, M. Ultrasound: a relief for overuse injuries. *Bicycling (Emmaus, Pa.) 25(9), Nov/Dec 1984, 40-42.
LEVEL: B LANG: E SIRC ARTICLE NO: 100745

Stratton, S.A. Heckmann, R. Francis, R.S. Therapeutic ultrasound: its effects on the integrity of a nonpenetrating wound. (Refs: 14)*Journal of orthopaedic and sports physical therapy (Baltimore, Md.) 5(5), Mar/Apr 1984, 278-281.
ABST: Sixty-six male Holtymann rats were traumatized, treated and sacrificed. The rats were divided into control and experimental groups. The experimental groups received 6 ultrasound treatments of 3 and 7 minutes duration at an intensity of either 0.5 or 1.5 watts per square centimeter. The results indicate that ultrasound promoted healing and that this effect was more noticeable at the higher intensity. The duration mode (pulsed or continuous) of treatment did not affect healing.
LEVEL: A LANG: Eng SIRC ARTICLE NO: 094395

PHYSIOLOGY

Brancazio, P.J. SportScience: physical laws and optimum performance. New York: Simon and Schuster, c1984. 400 p.
NOTES: Includes index. Bibliography: p. 383-386.
LEVEL: I LANG: Eng ISBN: 0671455842 LC CARD: 83-020152 RC1235 17120

Cassidy, W.J. Cassidy, C. Oxygen: the breath of life. *Fit (Mountain View, Calif.) 4(6), Nov 1984, 45-49;75-76.
LEVEL: B LANG: Eng SIRC ARTICLE NO: 105464

Culture technique no. 13. Neuilly-sur-Seine, France: Centre de Recherche sur la Culture Technique, c1984. 327 p. : ill.
NOTES Comprend des bibliographies. ISSN: 0223-4386. Titre de la couverture.
LEVEL: A LANG: Fr RC1235 20096

Environmental factors - genetics and health/nutrition - recreation/leisure. Scientific program abstracts. 1984 Olympic Scientific Congress, July 19-26, University of Oregon, Eugene, Oregon. Eugene, Or.: University of Oregon, Microform Publications, 1984. 48 p.
CONF: Olympic Scientific Congress (1984 : Eugene, Or.).
NOTES: Cover title.
LEVEL: A LANG: Eng RC1201 17865

Ferre, J. Leroux, P. Preparation aux brevets d'etat d'educateur sportif: bases physiologiques de l'entrainement. Paris: Editions Amphora, c1984. 349 p. : ill. (Collection sports & loisirs.)
LEVEL: I LANG: Fr ISBN: 2-85180-082-5 RC1235 18963

Fox, E.L. Close, N.A. Sports physiology. 2nd ed. Philadelphia: Saunders College Pub., c1984. xii, 418 p.
NOTES: Includes bibliographies and index.
LEVEL: A LANG: Eng ISBN: 0030637716 LC CARD: 83-015067 RC1235 15821

Fox, E.L. Mathews, D.K. Peronnet, F. Bases physiologiques de l'activite physique. Montreal: Decarie, c1984. 404 p. : ill.
NOTES: Comprend des bibliographies. Traduit de: Physiological Basis of Physical Education and Athletics, W.B. Saunders, Philadelphia, c1981.
LEVEL: A LANG: Fr ISBN: 2-89137-016-3 RC1235 19077

Legros, P. Pradet, M. L'effort. *EPS: Education physique et sport 185, janv/fevr 1984, 24-29.
LEVEL: B LANG: Fr SIRC ARTICLE NO: 093108

Menard, D. Fat facts. Considerations sur la graisse. *Periscope (Ottawa) 16, 1984, 45-51.
LEVEL: B LANG: Eng Fr SIRC ARTICLE NO: 179917

Milhorn, H.T. Exercise physiology - a primer. *Sports medicine digest (Van Nuys, Calif.) 6(10), Oct 1984, 3-4.
LEVEL: B LANG: Eng SIRC ARTICLE NO: 102806

Pyke, F.S. The role of the physiologist in sport. *Pelops 5, Feb 1984, 1-5.
ABST: Discusses a number of areas of sports development in which the physiologist has become involved: coach education, administrator education, preparation of athletes, testing of athletes and research.
LEVEL: I LANG: Eng SIRC ARTICLE NO: 097755

Schrier, E.W. Allman, W.F. Newton at the bat: the science in sports. New York: Scribner, c1984. xi, 178 p. : ill.
NOTES: Includes index.
LEVEL: I LANG: Eng ISBN: 0684181304 LC CARD: 84-001299 RC1235 18609

Schuerch, P. Perspectives et limites du sport de haut niveau vues sous l'angle medical. *Macolin (Suisse) 9, sept 1984, 12-15.*
LEVEL: I LANG: Fr SIRC ARTICLE NO: 102931

Shephard, R.J. Biochemistry of physical activity. Springfield, Ill.: Charles C. Thomas, 1984. ix, 391 p.
NOTES: Includes bibliographies.
LEVEL: A LANG: Eng ISBN: 0-398-04854-1 LC CARD: 83-4789 RC1235 19082

Southwest Chapter - American College of Sports Medicine: Las Vegas, Nevada, November 18-19, 1983. (abstracts) *International journal of sports medicine (Stuttgart) 5(3), Jun 1984, 156-164.*
LEVEL: A LANG: Eng SIRC ARTICLE NO: 104149

Viru, A. The mechanism of training effects: a hypothesis. (Refs: 122)*International journal of sports medicine (Stuttgart) 5(5), Oct 1984, 219-227.*
LEVEL: A LANG: Eng SIRC ARTICLE NO: 104389

Wirhed, R. Athletic ability: the anatomy of winning. New York: Harmony Books, c1984. 135 p. : ill.
NOTES: Bibliography: p. 135.
LEVEL: I LANG: Eng ISBN: 0517555905 LC CARD: 84-010813 RC1235 18444

Wirhed, R. Athletic ability and the anatomy of motion. London: Wolfe Medical, 1984. 135 p. : ill.
LEVEL: B LANG: Eng

Youth sports - sport for the disabled and sport and gender - sport and aging. Scientific program abstracts: 1984 Olympic Scientific Congress, July 19-26, University of Oregon, Eugene, Oregon. Eugene, Or.: University of Oregon, Microform Publications, 1984. 75 p.
CONF: Olympic Scientific Congress (1984 : Eugene, Or.).
NOTES: Cover title.
LEVEL: A LANG: Eng RC1201 17864

AGING AND AGED

Aniansson, A. Ljungberg, P. Rundgren, A. Wetterqvist, H. Effect of a training programme for pensioners on condition and muscular strength. *Archives of gerontology and geriatrics (Amsterdam) 3(3), Oct 1984, 229-241.*
ABST: Changes in the physical fitness and muscular strength of 15 women (63 to 84 yr) following a 10 mths/twice a week training program were assessed in this study. Improvements of physical fitness as well as increases of static and dynamic muscular strength in the knee-extensors (6-13 per cent) were recorded. Relative FTa fibre area in the vastus lateralis muscle increased.
LEVEL: A LANG: Eng

Brischetto, M.J. Millman, R.P. Peterson, D.D. Silage, D.A. Pack, A.I. Effect of aging on ventilatory response to exercise an CO2. (Refs: 30)*Journal of applied physiology: respiratory, environmental and exercise physiology (Bethesda, Md.) 56(5), May 1984, 1143-1150.*
ABST: This study investigated the relationship between increasing ventilation and increasing CO2 production (VCO2) during steady-state exercise and changes in minute ventilation in response to

progressive hypercapnia during CO2 rebreathing in 10 young subjects (22-37 yr) and 10 elderly subjects (67-79 yr). The results indicate that elderly people have a decreased ventilatory response to hypercapnia than young people. Conversely, the ventilatory response of elderly people to exercise is greater than that of young people. The authors suggest that exercise hyperpnea is produced by neural mechanisms different from those subserving the response of altered activity of the peripheral or central chemoreceptors.
LEVEL: A LANG: Eng SIRC ARTICLE NO: 097716

Bruce, R.A. Exercise, functional aerobic capacity, and aging - another viewpoint. (Refs: 29)*Medicine and science in spots and exercise 16(1), 1984, 8-13.*
ABST: Endurance exercise had been found to increase aerobic metabolism as seen by cardiac output and arterial-mixed venous oxygen differences. The maximal oxygen intake sets the limits of the cardiovascular system and consequently affects the process of aging. The decline of VO2 max with aging has been found to be more dramatic for sedentary individuals than for active individuals. The relationship of cardiovascular disease to exercise is discussed in this review and the author concludes by detailing the need for further research using longitudinal and observational approaches.
LEVEL: A LANG: Eng SIRC ARTICLE NO: 091720

Danneskiold-Samsoe, B. Kofod, V. Munter, J. Grimby, G. Schnohr, P. Jensen, G. Muscle strength and functional capacity in 78-81-year-old-men and women. (Refs: 22)*European journal of applied physiology and occupational physiology (Heidelberg) 52(3), Apr 1984, 310-314.*
ABST: This descriptive study measured muscle strength in 23 men and 29 women of about 80 years of age. Knee-extension strength in this group was about 30% lower than the knee-extension strength of a similar group of 70-year-old subjects. Muscle strength was significantly lower in women than in men in all muscle groups studied except for the plantar-and dorsi-flexor of the foot where the two groups were statistically equal. Body cell mass was reduced in this group compared to younger groups and this reduction was of about the same magnitude as the decrease muscle strength. The results of step tests and walking tests indicated that this age group has a diminished capacity to use public transport and pedestrian street intersections.
LEVEL: A LANG: Eng SIRC ARTICLE NO: 097718

deVries, H.A. Exercise and the physiology of aging. (Refs: 51)*American Academy of Physical Education papers (Champaign, Ill.) 17, 1984, 76-88.*
CONF: American Academy of Physical Education. Annual Meeting (54th : 1983 : Minneapolis).
NOTES: Conference theme: Exercise and health.
LEVEL: A LANG: Eng SIRC ARTICLE NO: 104299

Duncan, J. Exercise: the medicine of choice in aging? *Aerobics (Dallas, Tex.) 5(3), Mar 1984, 5;8.*
NOTES: First part of a two-part series.
LEVEL: I LANG: Eng SIRC ARTICLE NO: 099231

Dustman, R.E. Ruhling, R.O. Russell, E.M. Shearer, D.E. Bonekat, H.W. Shigeoka, J.W. Wood, J.S. Bradford, D.C. Aerobic exercise training and improved neuropsychological function of older individuals. (Refs: 69)*Neurobiology of aging (Fayetteville, N.Y.) 5(1), Spring 1984, 35-42.*
ABST: This study evaluated the effects of a four month aerobic exercise conditioning program on neuropsychological test performance, depression

indices, sensory thresholds, and visual acuity of 55-70 year old sedentary individuals. Aerobically trained subjects were compared with age-matched subjects who trained with strength and flexibility exercises and others who were not engaged in a supervised exercise program. The results led the authors to speculate that aerobic exercise promoted increased cerebral metabolic activity with a resultant improvement in neuropsychological test scores.
LEVEL: A LANG: Eng SIRC ARTICLE NO: 109740

Gauthier, P. L'activite physique et le vieillissement. *Kino-nouvelles (Quebec) 6(4), oct 1984, 4-5.*
LEVEL: I LANG: Fr SIR ARTICLE NO: 100857

Goertzen, D. Serfass, R. Sopko, G. Leon, A. The functional capacity and physical activity levels of women over 60 years of age. (Refs: 25)*Journal of sports medicine and physical fitness (Torino) 24(1), Mar 1984, 30-36.*
ABST: Functional capacity and physical activity levels were compared between 12 female social dancers with an average age of 70 and 12 female cardplayers with an average age of 72.4. The dancers had a significantly lower resting heart rate. However, the non-athletic elderly women had higher predicted functional capacities than any values reported in the literature. Though the dancers scored significantly higher Activity Metabolic Index scores, the two groups of women were not significantly different in estimated functional capacity.
LEVEL: A LANG: Eng SIRC ARTICLE NO: 099236

Haber, P. Hoeniger, B. Klicpera, M. Niederberger, M. Ergebnisse eines 3monatigen Ausdauertrainings auf einem Fahrradergomete bei alten Menschen zwischen 67 und 76 Jahren. (Results of 3 months' endurance training on a bicycle ergometer in people between 67 and 76.) *Acta medica austriaca (Vienna) 11(3/4), 1984, 107-111.*
ABST: 8 healthy women and 4 men with a mean age 71.1 years, took part in a bicycle ergometer training, 3 times a week, for 12 weeks. In order to hold the training heart rate (HR) at the constant level of 60 per cent of maximum, the work load had to be increased systematically during the whole training period up to 180 per cent of the level at the beginning. The working time in each training session was increased from 2 x 10 minutes in the beginning up to 2 x 20 minutes from the 7th week on. The maximum work load and the maximum oxygen uptake increased significantly. The submaximal HR decreased significantly. This study concludes that in healthy people between 67-76 years a significant endurance effect is possible when the training is systematically increased in work load and working time.
LEVEL: A LANG: Ger

Haber, P. Hoeniger, B. Klicpera, M. Niederberger, M. Effects in elderly people 67-76 years of age of three-month endurance training on a bicycle ergometer. (Refs: 7)*European heart journal (London) 5(Suppl E), Nov 1984, 37-39.*
LEVEL: A LANG: Eng SIRC ARTICLE NO: 109719

Holm, K. Kirchhoff, K.T. Perspectives on exercise and aging. (Refs: 47)*Heart and lung (St. Louis) 13(5), Sept 1984, 519-524.*
LEVEL: I LANG: Eng SIRC ARTICLE NO: 104250

Horvath, S.M. Borgia, J.F. Cardiopulmonary gas transport and aging. (Refs: 28)*American review of respiratory disease (New York) 129(2 Pt 2), Feb*

1984, S68-S71.
CONF: Exercise Testing in the Dyspneic Patient Workshop (1982 : Bethesda).
ABST: Exercise performance as modified by age has never been properly defined. Studies that are available in the literature have provided conflicting information due to the small number of studies performed and the absence of longitudinal research in the literature. The studies reviewed in this paper show significant age-related changes in the cardiorespiratory system during exercise. It appears that oxygen uptake and minute ventilation remain constant at fixed submaximal work rates but require progressively greater fractions of the maximal values. Some studies suggest that there is a greater percent contribution of anaerobic oxidative processes than aerobic for a given work rate with increasing age.
LEVEL: A LANG: Eng SIRC ARTICLE NO: 099241

Korkushko, O.V. Iaroshenko I.T. Osobennnsti energeticheskogo i gemodinamicheskogo obespecheniia submaksimal'noi fizickeskoi nagruzki u muzhchin pozhilogo. (Characteristics of the energy and hemodynamic support for submaximal physical loading in elderly men.) *Fiziologiya cheloveka (Moscow) 10(1), Jan/Feb 1984, 120-125.*
LEVEL: A LANG: Rus

Larsson, B. Renstroem, P. Svaerdsudd, K. Welin, L. Grimby, G. Eriksson, H. Ohlson, L.O. Bjoerntorp, P. Health and aging characteristics of highly physically active 65-year-old men. (Refs: 13)*International journal of sports medicine (Stuttgart) 5(6), Dec 1984, 336-340.*
ABST: Eighteen highly physically active men aged 65 years, training since youth, were compared to 67-year-old men from the general population. They characterized themselves as being in a general state of good health and well-being. Plasma insulin values were remarkably low. Blood pressure and resting heart rate were lower and ventilatory capacity better than in controls, and they had fewer heart diseases. The results obtained suggest that physical activity protects against several age-dependent conditions as well as obesity, also at a fairly advanced age.
LEVEL: A LANG: Eng SIRC ARTICLE NO: 104333

Larsson, B. Renstroem, P. Svaerdsudd, K. Welin, L. Grimby, G. Eriksson, H. Ohlson, L.O. Wilhelmsen, L. Bjoerntorp, P. Health and ageing characteristics of highly physically active 65-year-old men. (Refs: 5)*European heart journal (London) 5(Suppl E), Nov 1984, 31-35.*
ABST: A comparative study between 80 highly physically active 65-year-old men and controls in the same age group was the focus of this study. The well-trained subjects were characterized by low body fat, good health, lower plasma insulin, blood pressure, resting heart rate and ventilatory capacity than the controls.
LEVEL: A LANG: Eng SIRC ARTICLE NO: 109718

Miyazawa, K. Yamaguchi, I. Cardiovascular response to exercise in the healthy male septuagenarians: with reference to plasma norepinephrine. *Tohoku journal of experimental medicine (Sendai) 143(2), Jun 1984, 177-183.*
ABST: Hemodynamics during supine graded exercise were measured in 7 healthy aged and 20 young. The maximal work load in the aged was about one half of that in the young. Cardiac output (CO) increased linearly with increasing work load, but its maximal value was markedly lower in the

aged than in the young. Although CO at each level of submaximal exercise was essentially the same in both groups, the aged had smaller increases in stroke volume (SV) and systemic vascular conductance (SC), corresponding to larger increases in heart rate and mean blood pressure. Plasma norepinephrine concentration in the aged was higher than in the young at rest and both groups showed similar high levels at exhaustion.
LEVEL: A LANG: Eng SIRC ARTICLE NO: 104346

Niederberger, M. Detry, J.M. Exercise and old age. London: Academic Press, 1984. viii, 123 p. (European heart journal (London) 5 (Suppl E), Nov 1984.)
CONF: Symposium on Exercise and Old Age (1984 : Wien, Austria).
LEVEL: A LANG: Eng RD795 20687

Ogawa, S. Sports activities and life span. *Asian journal of physical education (Taipei, Taiwan) 7(3), Oct 1984, 20-21.*
LEVEL: B LANG: Eng Chi SIRC ARTICLE NO: 102734

Rodeheffer, R.J. Gerstenblith, G. Becker, L.C. Fleg, J.L. Weisfeldt, M.L. Lakatta, E.G. Exercise cardiac output is maintaine with advancing age in healthy human subjects: cardiac dilatation and increased stroke volume compensate for a diminished heart rate. *Circulation (New York) 69(2), Feb 1984, 203-213.*
ABST: 61 subjects ranging in age from 25 to 79 and free of cardiac disease performed serial gated blood pool scans at rest and during progressive upright bicycle exercise. Age related changes included increases in end-diastolic volume and stroke volume, and a decrease in heart rate. The results indicate that in healthy subjects their hemodynamic profile is changed by an age related decrease in the cardiovascular response to beta-adrenergic stimulation.
LEVEL: A LANG: Eng SIRC ARTICLE NO: 097758

Rowlands, D.B. Stallard, T.J. Littler, W.A. Isaacs, B. Ambulatory blood pressure and its response to exercise in the elderly (Refs: 11)*European heart journal (London) 5(Suppl E), Nov 1984, 13-16.*
LEVEL: A LANG: Eng SIRC ARTICLE NO: 109716

Seals, D.R. Hagberg, J.M. Hurley, B.F. Ehsani, A.A. Holloszy, J.O. Effects of endurance training on glucose tolerance and plasma lipid levels in older men and women. (Refs: 26)*JAMA: Journal of the American Medical Association (Chicago) 252(5), 3 Aug 1984, 645-649.*
ABST: Eleven healthy men and women 62-64 years of age participated in a 12-month endurance-training program to determine the effects of low-intensity and high-intensity training on glucose tolerance and plasma lipids in older persons. The results indicated that older persons respond to prolonged, high-intensity endurance training with an increase in sensitivity to insulin and a favorable alteration in their plasma lipoprotein-lipid profile.
LEVEL: A LANG: Eng SIRC ARTICLE NO: 109729

Seals, D.R. Hagberg, J.M. Hurley, B.F. Ehsani, A.A. Holloszy, J.O. Endurance training in older men and women I. Cardiovascular responses to exercise. (Refs: 37)*Journal of applied physiology: respiratory, environmental and exercise physiology (Bethesda, Md.) 57(4), Oct 1984, 1024-1029.*
ABST: Eleven older individuals 61 to 65 years of age exercised for 6 months at low intensity and for a furhter 6 months at a higher intensity. The

cardiovascular system was monitored and significant improvements were found in most areas with a large increase in overall aerobic power.
LEVEL: A LANG: Eng SIRC ARTICLE NO: 108942

Shephard, R.J. Physical activity for the senior: a role for pool exercises? (Refs: 33)*CAHPER journal/ Revue de l'ACSEPR (Ottawa) 50(6), Jul/Aug 1984, 2-5;20.*
LEVEL: I LANG: Eng SIRC ARTICLE NO: 099206

Siegel, A.J. Exercise and aging. (Refs: 77)
NOTES: In, Strauss, R.H. (ed.), Sports medicine, Philadelphia ; Toronto, Saunders, 1984, p. 270-285.
LEVEL: A LANG: Eng RC1210 17196

Spirduso, W.W. Exercise as a factor in aging motor behavior plasticity. (Refs: 47)*American Academy of Physical Education papers (Champaign, Ill.) 17, 1984, 89-100.*
CONF: American Academy of Physical Education. Annual Meeting (54th : 1983 : Minneapolis).
NOTES: Conference theme: Exercise and health.
LEVEL: A LANG: Eng SIRC ARTICLE NO: 104420

Stamford, B. Exercise and longevity. *Physician and sportsmedicine (Minneapolis, Minn.) 12(6), Jun 1984, 209.*
LEVEL: B LANG: Eng SIRC ARTICLE NO: 094576

Vallbona, C. Baker, S.B. Physical fitness prospects in the elderly. (Refs: 47)*Archives of physical medicine and rehabilitation 65(4), Apr 1984, 194-200.*
LEVEL: I LANG: Eng SIRC ARTICLE NO: 093062

CHILDREN AND ADOLESCENTS

Andersen, K.L. Rutenfranz, J. Ilmarinen, J. Berndt, I. Kylian, H. Ruppel, M. Seliger, V. The growth of lung volumes affected by physical performance capacity in boys and girls during childhood and adolescence. (Refs: 13)*European journal of applied physiology and occupational physiology (Berlin, FRG) 52(4), Jun 1984, 380-384.*
ABST: This longitudinal study compares the rate of lung volume growth to the rate of growth in body height and maximal aerobic power in ordinary boys and girls during childhood and adolescence, in order to test the hypothesis that the growth in lung volume is independent of the growth in physical performance capacity. The results clearly indicate that the growth in lung volume was entirely due to growth in body dimensions, with no additional effect of changes in the development of physical performance capacity.
LEVEL: A LANG: Eng SIRC ARTICLE NO: 097707

Andersen, K.L. Ilmarinen, J. Rutenfranz, J. Ottmann, W. Berndt, I. Kylian, H. Ruppel, M. Leisure time and sport activities and maximal aerobic power during late adolescence. (Refs: 14)*European journal of applied physiology and occupational physiology (Berlin, FRG) 52(4), Jun 1984, 431-436.*
ABST: This longitudinal study of 25 German girls and 27 German boys analyzed the relationship between lifestyle and cardiovascular health in late adolescence. This study lasted five years. Both sexes decreased their activity pattern and fitness level from 14 to 18 years of age. Leisure time sport activities or lack thereof did not affect cardiovascular health as measured by a test of maximal aerobic power. The authors suggest that sports activity, executed for the sake of pleasure, social contacts and play, is not sufficient to prevent

PHYSIOLOGY (continued)

a reduction in fitness during late adolescence in ordinary children.
LEVEL: A LANG: Eng SIRC ARTICLE NO: 097422

Armando, I. Barontini, M. Levin, G. Simsolo, R. Glover, V. Sandler, M. Exercise increases endogenous urinary monoamine oxidase benzodiazepine receptor ligand inhibitory activity in normal children. *Journal of the autonomic nervous system (Amsterdam) 11(1), Jul 1984, 95-100.*
ABST: This study shows that in normal children the stress of maximal exercise induced not only activation of the sympathetic nervous system but also an increased urinary output of both MAO inhibitory activity and (3H) flunitrazepam binding to rat cerebellar membranes inhibitory activity.
LEVEL: A LANG: Eng SIRC ARTICLE NO: 104274

Armstrong, N. Davis, B. The metabolic and physiological responses of children to exercise and training. (Refs: 134)*Physical education review (North Humberside, Eng.) 7(2), Autumn 1984, 90-105.*
ABST: This article reviews the literature on the responses of exercising children. The relationship between physical activity patterns of children and coronary heart disease risk factors is also discussed.
LEVEL: A LANG: Eng SIRC ARTICLE NO: 105163

Attina, D.A. Cupelli, V. Giuliano, G. Galanti, A. Musante, R. Bucchino, G. Frosini, F. Maximal exercise stress testing in evaluation of premature beats in children with normal hearts. (Refs: 20)*International journal of sports cardiology (Torino, Italy) 1(1), Jan/June 1984, 25-30.*
ABST: The authors tested on a bicycle ergometer 97 children aged 10 to 15 years with premature beats (PBs) at rest and 50 control ones without PBs. Heart rate, blood pressure, maximum tolerated work, and total work were monitored. No significant differences were observed between children: 1) with and without PBs; 2) with supraventricular and ventricular PBs; 3) with simple and complex PBs; 4) with suppressed and still present PBs at heart rate greater than 150 beats/min.
LEVEL: A LANG: Eng SIRC ARTICLE NO: 171821

Baldauf, K.L. Swenson, D.K. Medeiros, J.M. Radtka, S.A. Clinical assessment of trunk flexor muscle strength in healthy girls 3 to 7 years of age. (Refs: 35)*Physical therapy (Alexandria, Va.) 64(8), Aug 1984, 1203-1208.*
ABST: The authors' aim was to determine trunk flexor muscle strength in 75 girls 3 to 7 years of age. Findings indicated that the frequency of normal muscle strength first appeared to predominate at age 5 years. At 7 years of age, most children had normal muscle strength. An increase of mean muscle strength with age was also observed.
LEVEL: A LANG: Eng SIRC ARTICLE NO: 097709

Bar-Or, O. The growth and development of children's physiologic and perceptional responses to exercise. (Refs: 59)
CONF: Symposium of Paediatric Work Physiology (10th : 1981 : Joutsa, Finland).
NOTES: In, Ilmarinen, J. and Vaelimaeki, I. (eds.), Children and sport: paediatric work physiology, Berlin, Springer-Verlag, 1984, p. 3-17.
LEVEL: I LANG: Eng SIRC ARTICLE NO: 102328

Beekman, R.H. Katch, V. Marks, C. Rocchini, A.P. Validity of CO2-rebreathing cardiac output during rest and exercise in youn adults. (Refs: 19)*Medicine and science in sports and exercise*

(Indianapolis) 16(3), June 1984, 306-310.
ABST: To validate the C02 rebreathing method (Defare's method) for estimating cardiac output in children and young adults, measurements were compared to thermodilution (TDCO) cardiac output in 16 subjects (age 7-19 yr) with congenital heart disease. Data were collected at rest (N, 11) and during 4-min stages of supine bicycle exercise exercise (N, 13). Estimated arterial-venous (v-a)C02 content differences related linearly to the measured C02 content difference. The correlation between C02 rebreathing cardiac output and the TDCO was higher for exercise than for rest.
LEVEL: A LANG: Eng SIRC ARTICLE NO: 108603

Bendien, C. Bossina, K.K. Buurma, A.E. Gerding, A.M. Kuipers, J.R. Landsman, M.L. Mook, G.A. Zijlstra, W.G. Hemodynamic effects of dynamic exercise in children and adolescents with moderate-to-small ventricular septal defects. *Circulation (Dallas, Tex.) 70(6), Dec 1984, 929-934.*
LEVEL: A LANG: Eng

Bosc, R. Cavalier, B. Exploration chez l'enfant sportif: la force musculaire. (Refs: 10)*Dans, Mandel, C. (ed.), Le medecin, l'enfant et le sport, Paris, (Vigot), c1984, p. 89-95.*
LEVEL: A LANG: Fr RC1218.C45 18886

Chausow, S.A. Riner, W.F. Boileau, R.A. Metabolic and cardiovascular responses of children during prolonged physical activit (Refs: 36)*Research quarterly for exercise & sport (Reston, Va.) 55(1), Mar 1984, 1-7.*
ABST: The purpose of this study was to provide additional information on how children respond physiologically during an extended period of moderate exercise. Eleven children between the ages of 8 and 11 years were each observed during the 45 minutes of continuous treadmill walking. Among six selected points of measurement, oxygen consumption was significantly higher in the first period (0.92 l/min.) than in the five subsequent periods which averaged 0.88 l/min. Changes in pulmonary ventilation, cardiac output, and total peripheral resistance were found to be more nonsignificant. In conclusion, the authors suggest that children respond to prolonged exercise in much the same manner as do adults at an exercise intensity of approximately 50% V02 max.
LEVEL: A LANG: Eng SIRC ARTICLE NO: 095729

Chrustschow, S.W. Medizinische Aspekte im Prozess der langjaehrigen sportlichen Ausbildung von Kindern. *In, Idrett for barn Sport for Children. Sport pour les enfants 27.9.-1.10.1982 Tonsberg, Norway. Report. Oslo, Norway, Ministry of Cultural and Scientific Affairs: Norwegian Confederation of Sport, 1984, p. (21)-(24).*
CONF: Idrett for barn. Sport for Children. Sport pour les enfants (1982 : Tonsberg, Norway).
LEVEL: I LANG: Ger GV709.2 20111

Cooper, D.M. Weiler-Ravell, D. Whipp, B.J. Wasserman. K. Aerobic parameters of exercise as a function of body size during growth in children. (Refs: 34)*Journal of applied physiology: respiratory, environmental and exercise physiology (Bethesda, Md.) 56(3), Mar 1984, 628-634.*
ABST: The purpose of this study was to examine metabolic rates during exercise as a function of the body changes in body weight accompanying growth in children. In a cross-section of 58 boys and 51 girls, aged 6 to 17 years, determinations of anaerobic threshold, maximum O2 uptake, work efficiency, and response time for O2 uptake were

made. Heights and weights were also recorded. Results indicate that anaerobic threshold and maximum O2 uptake increased systematically with body weight, whereas work efficiency and O2 uptake response time were independent of body size. The authors conclude that certain cardiorespiratory responses are optimized relatively early in life in spite of changes in body size during growth.
LEVEL: A LANG: Eng SIRC ARTICLE NO: 095730

Cooper, D.M. Weiler-Ravell, D. Gas exchange response to exercise in children. (Refs: 18)*American review of respiratory disease (New York) 129(2 Pt 2), Feb 1984, S47-S48.*
CONF: Exercise Testing in the Dyspneic Patient Workshop (1982 : Bethesda).
ABST: The gas exchange response to exercise in 109 normal children (aged 6 to 17 years) was measured with noninvasive techniques. Maximal oxygen uptake and anaerobic threshold were highly correlated with increasing height and values were found to be significantly higher in boys. Girls were found to have significantly lower values than girls in earlier studies.
LEVEL: A LANG: Eng SIRC ARTICLE NO: 098882

Cooper, D.M. Weiler-Ravell, D. Whipp, B.J. Wasserman, K. Growth-related changes in oxygen uptake and heart rate during progressive exercise in children. *Pediatric research 18(9), Sept 1984, 845-851.*
LEVEL: A LANG: Eng

Cousteau, J.P. L'entrainement sous surveillance cardiologique. (Refs: 31)*Dans, Mandel, C. (ed.), Le medecin, l'enfant et le sport, Paris, (Vigot), c1984, p. 79-88.*
LEVEL: I LANG: Fr RC1218.C45 18886

Cunningham, D.A. Paterson, D.H. Blimkie, C.J.R. Donner, A.P. Development of cardiorespiratory function in circumpubertal boys: a longitudinal study. (Refs: 33)*Journal of applied physiology: respiratory, environmental and exercise physiology 56(2), Feb 1984, 302-307.*
ABST: Sixty-two boys, aged 9-10 years, were tested annually for six years to investigate cardiorespiratory function during circumpubertal growth. Statistical analysis indicated that VO2 was determined primarily by the size of stroke volume throughout the age range that was studied.
LEVEL: A LANG: Eng SIRC ARTICLE NO: 093078

Cunningham, D.A. Paterson, D.H. Blimkie, C.J.R. The development of the cardiorespiratory system with growth and physical activity. (Refs: 100)*In, Boileau, R.A. (ed.), Advances in pediatric sport sciences. Volume 1: biological issues, Champaign, Ill., Human Kinetics Publishers, c1984, p. 85-116.*
LEVEL: A LANG: Eng RJ125 20044

Demarais Il faut se donner les moyens de surveiller l'enfant sportif. *Generaliste (Paris) 618, 1984, 38-39.*
LEVEL: B LANG Fr

Deroanne, R. Pirnay, F. Crielaard, J.M. Vivegnis, L. Evaluation de la tolerance a l'effort chez des garcons de l'enseignemen primaire superieur. (Refs: 26)*Revue de l'education physique (Liege, Belgique) 24(1), 1984, 35-40.*
RESUME: Cette etude evalue la tolerance a l'effort de deux groupes de garcons ages entre 9 ans 6 mois et 12 ans 6 mois. La premiere population (60 enfants) beneficie de deux heures d'education physique et d'une heure de natation par semaine,

et la deuxieme population (56 enfants) d'une heure d'education physique dont une demi-heure de natation. Les sujets subissent des tests de tolerance a l'effort ainsi que des tests de motricite globale. L'auteur observe un plus grande puissance aerobie et anaerobique des etudiants du premier groupe comparativement a ceux du deuxieme. La difference au niveau de la puissance aerobie s'attenue en fonction de l'age pour devenir nulle a 12 ans. Les enfants du premier group atteignent un 'age moteur' statistiquement superieur a ceux du deuxieme groupe.
LEVEL: A LANG: Fr SIRC ARTICLE NO: 096233

Eston, R.G. A discussion of the concepts: exercise intensity and perceived exertion with reference to the secondary school. (Refs: 30)*Physical education review (Manchester) 7(1), Spring 1984, 19-25.*
ABST: The author reviews the literature on the measurement of exercise intensity and the role of perceived exertion. He suggests a method of measurement of exercise intensity in the secondary school setting. He discusses the Van Der Walt's and Wyndharr's equation for the calculations of exercise intensity by prediction of oxygen uptake at various running speeds.
LEVEL: A LANG: Eng SIRC ARTICLE NO: 098883

Flandrois, R. Capacite physique: aerobie et anaerobie. (Refs: 7)*Dans, Mandel, C. (ed.), Le medecin, l'enfant et le sport, Paris, (Vigot), c1984, p. 43-54.*
LEVEL: A LANG: Fr RC1218.C45 18886

Fontaine, G. Le sport et l'enfant. (Refs: 17)*Larc medical (France) 4(1), 1984, 45-52.*
LEVEL: I LANG: Fr

Frisch, R.E. Body fat, puberty and fertility. (Refs: 128)*Biological reviews (London) 59(2), May 1984, 161-188.*
LEVEL: I LANG: Eng SIRC ARTICLE NO: 102330

Frynas, K. Adaptacja ukladu krazenia do wysilku submaksymalnego u dzieci z otyloscia prosta. (Adaptation of the circulatory system to submaximal exertion in children with simple obesity.) *Pediatria polska (Warsaw) 59(1), Jan 1984, 37-44.*
LEVEL: A LANG: Pol

Herbert, A. The reliability and reproducibility of maximal oxygen consumption in young females, aged 10-13. Eugene, Ore.: Microform Publications, University of Oregon, 1984. 1 microfiche : negative ; 11 x 15 cm.
NOTES: Thesis (M.S.) - University of Wisconsin-La Crosse, 1983; (v, 77 leaves); includes bibliography.
LEVEL: A LANG: Eng UO84 297

Ilmarinen, J. Vaelimaeki, I. Children and sport: paediatric work physiology. Berlin: Springer-Verlag, 1984. xix, 274 p.
CONF: Symposium of Paediatric Work Physiology (10th : 1981 : Joutsa, Finland).
NOTES: Includes index. Includes bibliographies.
LEVEL: A LANG: Eng ISBN: 3-540-13044-6 LC CARD: 84-001363 RC1235 17600

Ilnitskii, V.I. Ekhokardiogramma iunykh sportsmenov. (Echocardiogram of young athletes.) *Kardiologiia (Moscow) 24(3), Mar 1984, 116-117.*
LEVEL: I LANG: Rus

Jost-Relyveld, A. Experience de suivi sur 4 ans de 35 sections sport-etudes. (Refs: 4)*Medecine du sport (Paris) 58(2), 25 mars 1984, 10-16.*
RESUME: Cette enquete longitudinale portait sur 406 enfants et adolescents, ages de 10 a 20 ans, appartenant a 35 sections sports-etudes (S.S.E.)

differentes. La capacite aerobique, le nombre d'heures hebdomadaires d'entrainement, les resultats scolaires, l'equilibre sport-etudes et les causes d'arrets ou d'abandon furent etudiees. Les resultats indiquent: 1) une capacite physique aerobique legerement superieure a la moyenne, 2) un entrainement hebdomadaire entre 13 et 18 heures, 3) de meilleurs resultats scolaires chez les filles et un pourcentage eleve de resultats mauvais ou mediocres (60% des garcons et 50% de filles), et 4) un bon equilibre sport-etudes (43% des garcons et 47% des filles). L'auteur souligne les carences des S.S.E. a leur debut.
LEVEL: A LANG: Fr SIRC ARTICLE NO: 094204

Khroutchev, S. Aspects medicaux de la formation sportive prolongee des enfants 1. *Dans, Idrett for barn. Sport for Children Sport pour les enfants 27.9.-1.10.1982 Tonsberg, Norway. Rapport. Oslo, Norvege, Ministere de la culture et de la science : Confederation norvegienne des sports, 1984, p. (22)-(25).*
CONF: Idrett for barn. Sport for Children. Sport pour les enfants (1982 : Tonsberg, Norway).
LEVEL: I LANG: Fr GV709.2 20112

Koethe, R. Schmidt, H. Adalekok a gerincoszlop biologiai koranak ertekelesere vonatkozoan a pubertas szakaszban edzesben lev gyermekeknel a ifjusagiaknal. (Data for the valuation of the biological age of the vertebral column of trained adolescents and juniors.) (Refs: 32)*Sportorvosi szemle/Hungarian review of sports medicine (Budapest) 25(3), 1984, 173-186.*
ABST: To enable the establishment of individual loading programs for childhood and adolescence, the assessment of the biologic age is taken to be indispensable in sports-medical perspective. Based on given x-ray pictures taken in children and adolescents training several times per week, it has been investigated the development of a possible method, by means of which the biologic age of the vertebral column can be ascertaind for the puberty period proceeding from the marginal ossification of biologic age of the vertebral column can be ascertained for the vertebral column had been evaluated by altogether 742 x-ray pictures of the vertebral column taken in 414 sound sportswomen and sportsmen. This investigation enabled a separate scheduling of maturation formulae for girls and boys. The biologic age can be evaluated by means of these formulae on the basis of marginal vertebral development.
LEVEL: A LANG: Hun SIRC ARTICLE NO: 100234

Lammert, O. A review of the physiological changes related to physical training in 6 to 14 years old children. (Refs: 92)*In, Idrett for barn. Sport for Children. Sport pour les enfants 27.9.-1.10.1982 Tonsberg, Norway. Report. Oslo, Norway, Ministry of Cultural and Scientific Affairs: Norwegian Confederation of Sport, 1984, p. (10)-(17).*
CONF: Idrett for barn. Sport for Children. Sport pour les enfants (1982 : Tonsberg, Norway).
LEVEL: A LANG: Eng GV709.2 20111

Lammert, O. Apercu des modifications physiologiques liees a l'entrainement physique des enfants de 6 a 14 ans. (Refs: 92) *Dans, Idrett for barn. Sport for Children. Sport pour les enfants 27.9.-1.10.1982 Tonsberg, Norway. Rapport. Oslo, Norvege, Ministere de la culture et de la science : Confederation norvegienne des sports, 1984, p. (10)-(18).*
CONF: Idrett for barn. Sport for Children. Sport

pour les enfants (1982 : Tonsberg, Norway).
LEVEL: A LANG: Fr GV709.2 20112

Leger, L. Lambert, J. Goulet, A. Rowan, C. Dinelle, Y. Capacite aerobie des Quebecois de 6 a 17 ans - test navette de 20 metres avec paliers de 1 minute. (Refs: 9)*Canadian journal of applied sport sciences/Journal canadien des sciences appliquees au sport (Windsor, Ont.) 9(2), Jun 1984, 64-69.*
RESUME: Une epreuve de course navette de 20 metres est administree a 3,669 garcons et 3,355 filles, ages de 6 a 17 ans, repartis dans 8 regions du Quebec. Les variables analysees sont le nombre de palier completes (ou vitesse maximale atteinte) lors de l'epreuve, l'age et le niveau scolaire, le poids et la taille, la region et l'ecole, et le type de surface sur lequel se deroule l'epreuve. Les resultats obtenus, dont l'evolution de la puissance aerobie maximale et fonctionnelle en fonction de l'age et du sexe, sont comparables a d'autres indices de capacite aerobie.
LEVEL: A LANG: Fr SIRC ARTICLE NO: 095737

Mandel, C. Le medecin, l'enfant et le sport. Paris: (Vigot), (1984). 253 p. : ill. (Medecine et enfance.)
LEVEL: A LANG: Fr ISBN: 2-904942-00-9 RC1218.C45 18886

Meen, H.D. Oseid, S. L'activite physique chez les enfants et les adolescents en relation avec la croissance et le developpement. (Refs: 63)
NOTES: Dans, Lagarde, F. (ed.), Sante et activite physique, Longueuil, Que., College Edouard-Montpetit, c1984, p. 37-66.
LEVEL: A LANG: Fr GV481 17104

Micheli, L.J. Yost, J.G. Preparticipation evaluation and first aid for sports. (Refs: 11)
NOTES: In, Micheli, L.J. (ed.), Pediatric and adolescent sports medicine, Boston ; Toronto, Little, Brown, c1984, p. 30-48.
LEVEL: I LANG: Eng RC1210 17791

Palgi, Y. Gutin, B. Young, J. Alejandro, D. Physiologic and anthropometric factors underlying endurance performance in children. (Refs: 34)*International journal of sports medicine (Stuttgart, FRG) 5(2), Apr 1984, 67-73.*
ABST: This study investigated the relationship between endurance performance and several measures of aerobic, anaerobic, and morphological fitness in 30 girls and 28 boys, 10 to 14 years of age. A multistage treadmill test was used for assessment of VO2 max and anaerobic threshold (AT) expressed both in absolute (AT-VO2) and relative (percent VO2 max) terms. Anaerobic capacity (AC) was measured in a 30-s cycling task and expressed as kpm.kg of body weight minus 1.min minus 1. Percent fat was estimated from skinfolds. The correlations between these measures and 2-km run time were: minus 0.73, minus 0.73, minus 0.50, minus 0.77, and 0.55 for VO2 max, AT-VO2, AT-percent VO2 max, AC, and percent fat, respectively. When entered into a forward selection multiple regression with run time as the dependent variable. AC accounted for 59.5 percent of the variance and VO2 max accounted for an additional 6.9 percent, with AT and percent fat making no significant additional contribution. When the girls and boys were compared, no reliable differences were found for run time and AC. the boys exhibited reliably higher values for VO2 max and AT-VO2. No reliable difference in percent fat was found for the younger boys and girls, but the older girls were significantly fatter than the older boys.
LEVEL: A LANG: Eng SIRC ARTICLE NO: 108520

PHYSIOLOGY (continued)

Pfeiffer, K.P. Steyer, G.E. Determination of the physical working capacity in children using three different regression models. (Refs: 29)*International journal of sports medicine (Stuttgart, FRG) 5(2), Apr 1984, 83-88.*
ABST: Experimental findings of the working capacity at a heart rate of 170 bts/min (W170) were compared to predicted values. Statistical tests were applied to examine the suitability and the error of prediction of three different regression models: a linear regression line, a polynomial regression model, and a 'break point' regression model, which were compared to the time course of the heart rate during a linearly increasing work load from 0 to 100 W during 10 min. For this study the results of 28 children, 15 and 16 years old, and students of physical education were investigated. When a linear regression line was compared to these data, systematic deviations between measured data and the values estimated by this model were found. When the W170 was predicted using this model from the data collected during the first 10 min of an exercise procedure for the determination of the heart rate index, the physical working capacity was overestimated. The polynomial regression model and the 'break point' regression model agreed with the time course of the heart rate without systematic error and allowed an unbiased prediction of the W170 from the first 10 min of the exercise test.
LEVEL: A LANG: Eng SIRC ARTICLE NO: 171636

Pirnay, F. Crielaard, J.M. Deroanne, R. Croissance et developpement de la puissance musculaire dynamique. (puissance anaerobie) (Refs: 10)*Revue de l'education physique (Liege) 24(3), 1984, 51-53.*
LEVEL: I LANG: Fr SIRC ARTICLE NO: 104357

Robin, M. Les parametres de la croissance. (Refs: 9)*Basketball (Paris) 492, fevr/mars/avr 1984, 23-24;33-36.*
LEVEL: I LANG: Fr SIRC ARTICLE NO: 097757

Rutenfranz, J. Andersen, K.L. Seliger, V. Klimmer, F. Kylian, H. Ruppel, M. Ilmarinen, J. Maximal aerobic power affected by maturation and body growth during childhood and adolescence. (Refs: 27)
CONF: Symposium of Paediatric Work Physiology (10th : 1981 : Joutsa, Finland).
NOTES: In, Ilmarinen, J. and Vaelimaeki, I. (eds.), Children and sport: paediatric work physiology, Berlin, Springer-Verlag, 1984, p. 67-85.
ABST: This paper examines the maximal aerobic power and its rate of change as a function of maturation and body growth in order to test the hypothesis that the differences in maximal aerobic power between the Norwegian and German children are primarily due to differences in growth and maturation.
LEVEL: A LANG: Eng SIRC ARTICLE NO: 102338

Sady, S.P. Berg, K. Beal, D. Smith, J.L. Savage, M.P. Thompson, W.H. Nutter, J. Aerobic fitness and serum high-density lipoprotein cholesterol in young children. *Human biology (Detroit) 56(4), Dec 1984, 771-781.*
LEVEL: A LANG: Eng

Siegel, J.A. Manfredi, T.G. Effects of a ten-month fitness program on children. (Refs: 29)*Physician and sportsmedicine (Minneapolis, Minn.) 12(5), May 1984, 91-94;96-97.*
LEVEL: I LANG: Eng SIRC ARTICLE NO: 094212

Smith, N. Children and parents: growth development, and sports. (Refs: 12)

NOTES: In, Strauss, R.H. (ed.), Sports medicine, Philadelphia ; Toronto, Saunders, 1984, p. 207-217.
LEVEL: I LANG: Eng RC1210 17196

Verit, J. Pasquis, P. Etude des performances de jeunes sportifs de section sport-etudes. (Refs: 5)*Medecine du sport (Paris) 58(2), 25 mars 1984, 27-29.*
RESUME: La morphologie et les performances de 42 filles et 62 garcons, ages de 12 a 18 ans, participants a des sections sport-etudes (soccer, handball olympique, tennis de table et gymnastique) sont etudiees. Les gymnastes et les joueurs de tennis sont plus petits. Dans tous les sports, l'auteur observe des puissances maximales et 170 ainsi que VO2 max kg-1 semblables. Les performances chez les garcons sont en moyenne 20% superieures a celles des filles.
LEVEL: A LANG: Fr SIRC ARTICLE NO: 094215

Viitasalo, M.T. Kala, R. Eisalo, A. Ambulatory electrocardiographic findings in young athletes between 14 and 16 years of ag *European heart journal (London) 5(1), Jan 1984, 2-6.*
ABST: The authors discuss electrocardiographic recordings of 35 male athletes between 14 and 16 years old and of 35 male non-athletes of the same ages. Findings indicate that: 1) the heart rates of athletes are significantly lower than those of non-athletes; 2) sinus intervals over 2.00 s occur in five athletes (14%) and one control (3%); and 3) eight athletes (23%) and four controls (11%) show first-degree atrioventricular block while seven athletes (20%) and one control (3%) have second-degree block.
LEVEL: A LANG: Eng SIRC ARTICLE NO: 100930

Woynarowska, B. Poziom i dynamika zmian wydolnosci fizycznej dzieci i mlodziezy w zeleznosci od rozwoju somatycznego i aktywnosci ruchowej. (Degree and dynamics of changes in physical work capacity of children and adolescents in relation to somatic development and motor activity.) *Problemy medycyny wieku rozwojowego (Warsaw) 13, 1984, 32-49.*
LEVEL: A LANG: Pol

Wright, G. Know your children. (Refs: 10)*Sports coach (Wembley, Australia) 7(4), Mar 1984, 7-10.*
LEVEL: B LANG: Eng SIRC ARTICLE NO: 094218

RESEARCH METHODS

Donner, A. Cunningham, D.A. Regression analysis in physiological research: some comments on the problem of repeated measurements. (Refs: 11)*Medicine and science in sports and exercise (Indianapolis) 16(4), Aug 1984, 422-425.*
ABST: The statistical implications of repeated-measures linear regression, in which each subject contributes several pairs of measurements to the analysis, are discussed in the context of physiological research. The major point of the paper is that standard least-squares procedures cannot be applied without modification to regression problems with repeated measures. An example is given.
LEVEL: A LANG: Eng SIRC ARTICLE NO: 102769

TESTING

Anderson, I. American science takes up sport. *New scientist (London) 1415, 2 Aug 1984, 10-12.*
NOTES: The best rifle shooters use their heartbeat as a cue to fire. If they squeeze the trigger as their

hearts beat, they usually miss. Revelations such as this are the progeny of a new marriage of science to sports fostered by the US Olympic Committee.
LEVEL: I LANG: Eng SIRC ARTICLE NO: 099221

Olszewski, R. Athlete testing. *Athletics (Willowdale, Ont.) Feb/Mar 1984, 30.*
LEVEL: B LANG: Eng SIRC ARTICLE NO: 097752

Sharp, C. It's amazing what they can do these days... Craig Sharp takes a look at the extraordinary ways in which science is being used to improve sporting performance. *Sports and leisure (London) 25(5), Nov/Dec 1984, 22-23.*
LEVEL: B LANG: Eng SIRC ARTICLE NO: 108962

Van Handel, P.J. Bradley, P. Puhl, J. Harms, S. Sports physiology at the USOC training center. *Journal of physical education, recreation & dance (Reston, Va.) 55(4), Apr 1984, 17-22.*
LEVEL: I LANG: Eng SIRC ARTICLE NO: 094631

PHYSIOLOGY - CARDIOVASCULAR

Athlete's heart: is big bad or can it be benign? (editorial) *Lancet (London) 2(8403), 15 Sept 1984, 613-614.*
LEVEL: B LANG: Eng SIRC ARTICLE NO: 104104

Brodan, V. Kolarova, N. Frouz, J. Frekvencni analyza EKG v klidu a pri telesnem zatizeni po podani roztiku glukoza-insulin-kalium a po aplikaci heparinu. (Frequency analysis of the ECG at rest, during physical exercise, after administration of a glucose-insulin-potassium solution and after administration of heparin.) *Casopis lekaru ceskych (Praha) 123(8), 24 Feb 1984, 225-228.*
LEVEL: A LANG: Cze

Delsignore, R. Crotti, G. Dei Cas, L. Manca, C. Francia, M.T. Baroni, M.C. Mineo, F. Tsialtas, D. Butturini, U. Valutazione del comportamento emoreologico durante prova da sforzo al cicloergometro in soggetti normali ed atleti. (Evaluation of hemorrheologic behavior during the bicycle ergometry stress test in normal subjects and athletes) *Giornale di clinica medica (Bologna) 65(11/12), Nov/Dec 1984, 477-487.*
LEVEL: A LANG: It

Ernst, E. Schmid, M. Verbesserung der Blutfluiditaet durch intensives koerperliches Training. (Improvement of blood rheology by intensive physical training) *Fortschritte der Medizin (Leipzig) 102(43), 22 Nov 1984, 1097-1099.*
ABST: In a comparative study of athletes and sedentary normal subjects, it is shown that the former have significantly better hemorrheological factors. In a follow-up study, it is further shown that a three months training program for healthy subjects leads to a lowering of blood viscosity, which is comparable with the effects that can be achieved with suitable hemorrheological treatment.
LEVEL: A LANG: Ger

Graettinger, W.F. The cardiovascular response to chronic physical exertion and exercise training: an echocardiographic revie *American heart journal (St. Louis) 108(4 Pt 1), Oct 1984, 1014-1018.*
LEVEL: A LANG: Eng

Greer, M. Dimick, Burns, S. Heart rate and blood pressure response to several methods of strength training. (Refs: 14) *Physical therapy (Alexandria, Va.) 64(2), Feb 1984, 179-183.*

ABST: This study was done to describe the changes which occur in heart rate, blood pressure and the pressure-rate product during various strength training exercises. Five female subjects performed right elbow flexion exercises, the trials of which were isometric, isokinetic or isotonic in nature. Blood pressure was measured in the left arm by auscultation and heart rate was measured with an electrocardiogram recorder. The results indicated that; i) heart rate and blood pressure responses to heavy resistance exercise increase proportionally to the intensity of effort; ii) heart rate and blood pressure do not always progressively increase during the course of a short exercise session; and iii) in exercises which allow periods of relaxation, lower heart rate and blood pressure elevations are seen than in those of other styles of exercise.
LEVEL: A LANG: Eng SIRC ARTICLE NO: 094645

Hamulyak, K. Brommer, E.J.P. Devilee, P.P. Hemker, H.C. Activation of coagulation and fibrinolysis during maximal physical exercise. (Refs: 15)*International journal of sports medicine (Stuttgart) Suppl. 5, Nov 1984, 64-65.*
CONF: International Congress on Sports and Health (1983 : Maastricht, Netherlands).
LEVEL: A LANG: Eng SIRC ARTICLE NO: 104318

Hietanen, E. Cardiovascular responses to static exercise. *Scandinavian journal of work, environment and health (Helsinki) 1 (6 Spec No), Dec 1984, 397-402.*
LEVEL: I LANG: Eng

Ito, A. (Effect of exercise on plasma cyclic AMP.) *Nippon seirigaku zasshi (Tokyo) 46(7), 1984, 250-268.*
LEVEL: A LANG: J

Kurowski, T.T. Chatterton, R.T. Hickson, R.C. Glucocorticoid-induced cardiac hypertrophy: additive effects of exercise. (Refs: 35)*Journal of applied physiology: respiratory, environmental and exercise physiology (Bethesda, Md.) 57(2), Aug 1984, 514-519.*
LEVEL: A LANG: Eng SIRC ARTICLE NO: 108357

Lehmann, M. Schmid, P. Bergdolt, E. Jakob, E. Spoeri, U. Keul, J. Ist die Alpha-adrenorezeptorendichte an intakten Thrombozyten bei statisch trainierten Athleten erhoeht? (Is the alpha adrenergic receptor density increased in intact thrombocytes in non-isometric trained athletes?) *Klinische Wochenschrift (Berlin) 62(20), 15 Oct 1984, 992-995.*
LEVEL: A LANG: Ger

Linton, R.A. Lim, M. Wolff, C.B. Wilmshurst, P. Band, D.M. Arterial plasma potassium measured continuously during exercise i man. *Clinical science (London) 67(4), Oct 1984, 427-431.*
ABST: Records of arterial plasma potassium were obtained from three normal subjects during brief periods (5-7 min) of exercise (100 W). In two of these subjects hepatic venous blood samples were withdrawn at 0.5-1.0 min intervals and analysed in vitro for plasma potassium. Arterial plasma potassium rose rapidly at the start of exercise from 3.8 plus or minus 0.3 mmol/l to plateau levels of 5.4 plus or minus 0.1 mmol/l. One of the above subjects and a further subject were studied after beta-blockade with propranolol. This resulted in an exaggerated rise in arterial plasma potassium during exercise. Hepatic venous potassium measurements indicated that the liver probably had little effect on potassium changes during exercise.

The changes in arterial plasma potassium during exercise are rapid and substantial.
LEVEL: A LANG: Eng SIRC ARTICLE NO: 104336

Maneval, M.W. The effects of variable resistance circuit weight training on cardiovascular fitness and body composition. Eugene, Ore.: Microform Publications, University of Oregon, 1984. 2 microfiches : negative, ill. ; 11 x 15 cm.
NOTES: Thesis (Ph.D.) - Texas A & M University, 1981; (xii, 91 leaves); vita; includes bibliography.
LEVEL: A LANG: Eng UO84 1-2

Mant, M.J. Kappagoda, C.T. Quinlan, J. Lack of effect of exercise on platelet activation and platelet reactivity. (Refs: 32) *Journal of applied physiology: respiratory, environmental and exercise physiology (Bethesda, Md.) 57(5), Nov 1984, 1333-1337.*
LEVEL: A LANG: Eng SIRC ARTICLE NO: 108909

Marino, N. DePasquale, E. Bruno, M.S. DePasquale, N.P. Cardiovascular system. (Refs: 39)
NOTES: In, Scott, W.N. (ed.) et al. Principles of sports medicine, Baltimore, Williams & Wilkins, c1984, p. 1-14.
LEVEL: A LANG: Eng RC1210 18016

Markarian, S.S. Rol' serdechno-sosudistoi sistemy v adaptatsii k fizicheskoi nagruzke. (Role of the cardiovascular system in adaptation to a physical load.) *Klinicheskaia meditsina (Moscow) 62(11), Nov 1984, 7-11.*
LEVEL: A LANG: Rus

Nielson, B. Rowell, L.B. Bonde-Petersen, F. Cardiovascular responses to heat stress and blood volume displacements during exercise in man. (Refs: 19)*European journal of applied physiology and occupational physiology (Berlin, FRG) 52(4), Jun 1984, 370-374.*
ABST: Eight men exercised in the upright position at approximately 50% of Vo2 max in four situations. These situations were: 1) in 25o air 2) in 45o air, 3) 35oC water immersed to the level of the riphoid process, and 4) wearing a suit perfused with 35o water. Core temperature rose continually in the water immersion condition as did forearm blood flow. The results indicate that the prevention of hydrostatic shifts of peripheral venous volume permits the maintenance of a higher stroke volume and peripheral blood flow and enhances the ability of the circulation to deal with the combined exercise and heat stress.
LEVEL: A LANG: Eng SIRC ARTICLE NO: 097750

Pierce, G.N. Kutryk, M.J.B. Dhalla, K.S. Beamish, R.E. Dhalla, N.S. Biochemical alterations in heart after exhaustive swimming in rats. (Refs: 35)*Journal of applied physiology: respiratory, environmental and exercise physiology (Bethesda, Md.) 57 (2), Aug 1984, 326-331.*
LEVEL: A LANG: Eng SIRC ARTICLE NO: 108349

Ryzhikov, G.V. Dzhebrailova, T.D. Vliianie geomagnitnykh vozmushchenii na sostoianie serdechno-sosudistykh funktsii u sportsmenov. (Effect of geomagnetic disturbances on cardiovascular functions in athletes.) *Fiziologiya cheloveka (Moscow) 10(4), Jul/Aug 1984, 640-646.*
LEVEL: A LANG: Rus

Schmidt, K.G. Rasmussen, J.W. Exercise-induced changes in the in vivo distribution of 111In-labelled platelets. *Scandinavia journal of haematology (Copenhagen) 32(2), Feb 1984, 159-166.*
ABST: This report focuses on the in vivo

distribution of 111In-labelled platelets injected to 15 healthy subjects. Subjects are evaluated one day after injection following a bicycle ergometer test. Findings show that the spleen is the major platelet-releasing organ.
LEVEL: A LANG: Eng SIRC ARTICLE NO: 099265

Schmidt, K.G. Rasmussen, J.W. Are young platelets released in excess from the spleen in response to short-term physical exercise. *Scandinavian journal of haematology (Copenhagen) 32(2), Feb 1984, 207-214.*
LEVEL: A LANG: Eng SIRC ARTICLE NO: 099266

Shapiro, L.M. Physiological left ventricular hypertrophy. *British heart journal (London) 52(2), Aug 1984, 130-135.*
ABST: Echocardiograms were recorded in 154 active athletes (from various sports) and 21 ex-athletes and compared with those in 40 normal control subjects. As a group, athletes had a significantly increased diastolic cavity dimension, posterior wall and septal thickness, and left ventricular mass. Ex-athletes had entirely normal left ventricular dimensions and wall thickness. When athletes are categorised by their standard of competition national standard competitors had a significantly increased posterior wall and septal thickness and left ventricular mass compared with university and non-competitive sportsmen. In conclusion, strenuous activity results in left ventricular hypertrophy which is appropriate to the body size of the athlete and the degree of activity but not to its type.
LEVEL: A LANG: Eng SIRC ARTICLE NO: 104370

Sheldahl, L.M. Wann, L.S. clifford, P.S. Tristani, F.E. Wolf, L.G. Kalbfleisch, J.H. Effect of central hypervolemia on cardiac performance during exercise. (Refs: 30)*Journal of applied physiology: respiratory, environmental and exercise physiology (Bethesda, Md.) 57(6), Dec 1984, 1662-1667.*
ABST: The effects of head-out water immersion (WI) and a change in body posture from upright (UP) to supine (SP) on cardiovascular parameters were compared at rest and two stages of submaximal exercise. Left ventricular end-diastolic (LVD) and end-systolic (LVS) diameter, fractional shortening (FS), heart rate (HR), systolic blood pressure (SBP) and 02 consumption (V02) were measured in twelve young men. Significantly greater mean LVD and LVS dimensions were observed with WI than with UP during exercise. At a mean V02 of 1.8 l/min or less, heart rate was similar between UP, SP, and WI groups at rest or during exercise. Significant higher heart rate was recorded with UP compared with WI and SP at a mean V02 of 2.4 l/min.
LEVEL: A LANG: Eng SIRC ARTICLE NO: 108560

Small, M. Tweddel, A.C. Rankin, A.C. Lowe, G.D. Prentice, C.R. Forbes, C.D. Blood coagulation and platelet function followin maximal exercise: effects of beta-adrenoceptor blockade. *Haemostasis (Basel) 14(3), 1984, 262-268.*
ABST: To determine if beta-blockade could modify exercise-induced changes in haemostatic factors we performed a double-blind study of acute strenuous exercise in normal males with and without beta-blockade. Exercise increased prostacyclin and plasminogen activator levels but there was no evidence of thrombin generation as indicated by unchanged platelet aggregation responses, beta-thromboglobulin and fibrinopeptide A levels. The only alteration in coagulation by beta-blockade was a reduction in the factor VIII:C and

PHYSIOLOGY - CARDIOVASCULAR (continued)

VIII:RAg rise after exercise and this modification may be relevant to the protective effect of these drugs in patients with coronary artery disease.
LEVEL: A LANG: Eng SIRC ARTICLE NO: 104372

Stone, H.L. Liang, I.Y. Cardiovascular response and control during exercise. (Refs: 27)*American review of respiratory disease (New York) 129(2 Pt 2), Feb 1984, S13-S16.*
CONF: Exercise Testing in the Dyspneic Patient Workshop (1982 : Bethesda).
LEVEL: I LANG: Eng SIRC ARTICLE NO: 099270

Symons, J.D. The effect of chronic exercise on norepinephrine and adenosine diphosphate induced aggregation times of blood platelets in vitro.
Eugene, Ore.: Microform Publications, University of Oregon, 1984. 2 microfiches : negative, ill. ; 11 x 15 cm.
NOTES: Thesis (M.S.) - University of Oregon, 1982; (xvi, 144 leaves); vita; includes bibliography.
LEVEL: A LANG: Eng UO84 154-155

Taniguchi, N. Furui, H. Yamauchi, K. Sotobata, I. Effects of treadmill exercise on platelet functions and blood coagulating activities in healthy men. *Japanese heart journal (Tokyo) 25(2), Mar 1984, 167-180.*
ABST: The effects of treadmill exercise (up to 85 per cent of the predicted maximum heart rate) on platelet functions and coagulating activities were studied in 26 normal men. The results indicate that dynamic leg exercise of a moderate to high intensity produced a significantly elevated plasma level of factor VIII, fibrinogen, antithrombin III, and catecholamines without affecting the hemostatic balance in normal subjects.
LEVEL: A LANG: Eng SIRC ARTICLE NO: 104379

Vigyazo, G. Sportsziv vagy szivizom hipertrofia? (Athletes heart or myocardial hypertrophy?) (Refs: 23)*Sportorvosi szemle/Hungarian review of sports medicine (Budapest) 25(1), 1984, 59-65.*
ABST: Regular intense exercise brings about complex adaptation. A part of this complex adaptation involves the increase of heart volume and is associated with a moderate hypertrophy of myocardial fibres. This hypertrophy does not impair myocardial structure, is not a permanent condition, but a reversible one, and is usually a natural, physiological concomitant of regular intense physical training, especially in athletes engaged in endurance events.
LEVEL: A LANG: Hun SIRC ARTICLE NO: 095681

Zalessky, M. Sport and the heart-vascular system. *Soviet sports review (Escondido, Calif.) 19(1), Mar 1984, 1-6.*
NOTES: Translated from, Legkaya atletika 9, 1983, 26-27.
LEVEL: I LANG: Eng SIRC ARTICLE NO: 094638

ACID-BASE BALANCE

Costill, D.L. Verstappen, F. Kuipers, H. Janssen, E. Fink, W. Acid-base balance during repeated bouts of exercise: influence of HCO3. (Refs: 20)*International journal of sports medicine (Stuttgart) 5(5), Oct 1984, 228-231.*
ABST: Ten men and one woman were studied before, during, and following five 1-min cycling bouts 1 h after consuming either 0.2 g/kg B.W. of NaHCO3 or a placebo drink (NaCl). During and following the exercise, blood pH and HCO3 were always higher in the NaHCO3 than placebo trial. Performance times during the fifth cycling bout averaged 113.5 and 160.8 in the NaCl and

NaHCO3 trials, respectively. The blood hydrogen ion to lactic acid ratios measured between each exercise bout and during recovery from the exhaustive fifth bout suggests that the enhanced performance during the NaHCO3 trial was the result of greater buffer capacity.
LEVEL: A LANG: Eng SIRC ARTICLE NO: 104294

Fregosi, R.F. Dempsey, J.A. Arterial blood acid-base regulation during exercise in rats. (Refs: 33)*Journal of applied physiology: respiratory, environmental and exercise physiology (Bethesda, Md.) 57(2), Aug 1984, 396-402.*
LEVEL: A LANG: Eng SIRC ARTICLE NO: 108352

Katz, A. Costill, D.L. King, D.S. Hargreaves, M. Fink, W.J. Maximal exercise tolerance after induced alkalosis. (Refs: 31) *International journal of sports medicine (Stuttgart, FRG) 5(2), Apr 1984, 107-110.*
ABST: Eight healthy males performed two rides to exhaustion at a work load corresponding to 125 VO2 max, 1 h after ingesting either 0.2 g NahCO3/kg body weight (E) or NaCl (C). Mean plus or minus SE pre-exercise blood pH, HCO3, and base excess (BE) values were respectively 7.42 plus or minus 0.01, 28.2 plus or minus 1.5 mmol/l, and 2.02 plus or minus 0.10 mmol/l for the E condition, and 7.39 plus or minus 0.01, 24.4 plus or minus 0.07 mmol/l, and -0.40 plus or minus 0.07 mmol/l for the C condition. Cycling time exhaustion (E, 100.6 plus or minus 6.1; C, 98.6 plus or minus 5.7 s) and total VO2 during recovery (E, 17.7 plus or minus 0.9; C, 17.3 plus or minus 0.8 l/30 min) did not differ significantly between treatments. Blood pH, HCO3, and BE were significantly higher while the hydrogen ion to lactate ratio (nmol/mmol) was significantly lower in E than in C during recovery. Blood LA levels were also greater in E than in C during the latter part of recovery although peak individual values were not significantly different between trials (E, 14.4 plus or minus 0.4; C, 13.3 plus or minus 0.0 mmol.l).
LEVEL: A LANG: Eng SIRC ARTICLE NO: 108527

Kowalchuk, J.M. Heigenhauser, G.J.F. Jones, N.L. Effect of pH on metabolic and cardiorespiratory responses during progressiv exercise. (Refs: 34)*Journal of applied physiology: respiratory, environmental and exercise physiology (Bethesda, Md.) 57(5), Nov 1984, 1558-1563.*
ABST: This study of six healthy males found that acid-base changes influence the maximum power output that may be sustained in incremental dynamic power, but there is little effect on hydrogen ion appearance in plasma.
LEVEL: A LANG: Eng SIRC ARTICLE NO: 108928

BLOOD FLOW

Cowley, A.J. Stainer, K. Rowley, J.M. Hanley, S.P. The effect of aspirin on peripheral haemodynamic changes following submaximal exercise in normal volunteers. *Cardiovascular research (London) 18(8), Aug 1984, 511-513.*
ABST: Eight normal healthy volunteers participated in a study to determine the effect of 1800 mg of aspirin on the peripheral haemodynamic changes that occur following upright exercise. Aspirin reduced the extent of calf hyperaemia and accentuated the reduction in forearm blood flow following exercise. It had no effect on either calf or forearm blood flow at rest.
LEVEL: A LANG: Eng SIRC ARTICLE NO: 104295

Farhi, L.E. Physiologic requirements to perform work. (Refs: 6)*American review of respiratory disease (New York) 129(2 Pt 2), Feb 1984, S4-S5.*
CONF: Exercise Testing in the Dyspneic Patient Workshop (1982 : Bethesda).
ABST: This article discusses the importance of an appropriate blood flow and acceptable blood composition for exercising muscle. The physiologic adaptations involved in accomplishing this are discussed.
LEVEL: I LANG: Eng SIRC ARTICLE NO: 099234

Liang, I.Y.S. Hamra, M. Stone, H.L. Maximum coronary blood flow and minimum coronary resistance in exercise-trained dogs. (Refs: 34)*Journal of applied physiology: respiratory, environmental and exercise physiology (Bethesda, Md.) 56(3), Mar 1984, 641-647.*
ABST: The present study was designed to examine the effect of daily exercise leading to the trained condition on maximum coronary flow caused by the adenosine. Myocardial flow measurements were made in 16 unanesthetized dogs before and after 4 to 5 weeks, as well as 8 to 10 weeks of an exercise training program on a treadmill. Results indicate that maximum coronary flow and minimum coronary resistance were not altered by either 4 to 5 or 8 to 10 weeks of exercise in dogs. Thus, it was indicated that coronary reserve was not altered by daily exercise.
LEVEL: A LANG: Eng SIRC ARTICLE NO: 096272

Ring, E.F.J. Trotman, S. Techniques for measuring skin temperature and blood flow. (Refs: 8)*Journal of the Society of Remedial Gymnastics and Recreational Therapy (Manchester) 114, Nov 1984, 32-34.*
NOTES: Reprinted from, Pharmaceutical journal (London), 1983, 231;236.
LEVEL: I LANG: Eng SIRC ARTICLE NO: 104362

Taylor, W.F. Johnson, J.M. O'Leary, D.S. Park, M.K. Modification of the cutaneous vascular response to exercise by local ski temperature. (Refs: 31)*Journal of applied physiology: respiratory, environmental and exercise physiology (Bethesda, Md.) 57(6), Dec 1984, 1878-1884.*
LEVEL: A LANG: Eng SIRC ARTICLE NO: 108571

BLOOD GAS

Kentala, E. Repo, U.K. Feasibility of cutaneous blood gas monitoring during exercise stress testing. (Refs: 9)*Annals of clinical research (Helsinki) 16(1), 1984, 40-46.*
ABST: The feasibility of cutaneous blood gas monitoring in connection with exercise testing was evaluated in 113 patients. The correlations between transcutaneous and arterial O2 and CO2 values were not statistically significant. The shape of the whole transcutaneous O2-CO2 registration curve is diagnostically more rewarding than single transcutaneous O2 and CO2 values.
LEVEL: A LANG: Eng SIRC ARTICLE NO: 109732

Miller, W.C. Exercise blood gases. (letter) *Chest (Chicago) 85(1), Jan 1984, 140-141.*
LEVEL: I LANG: Eng SIRC ARTICLE NO: 097746

BLOOD PRESSURE

(Changes in the blood pressure and pulse rates upon climbing up or down the stairs in various conditions - an experiment on normal subjects.) *Kurinikaru sutadi 5(8), Aug 1984, 945-953.*
LEVEL: A LANG: Jpn

Cupelli, V. Attina, D.A. Giuliano, G. Brettoni, M. Musante, R. Bini, G. Cupelli, G. Abnormal blood pressure response to the bicycle ergometer maximal stress test in apparently healthy and normotensive middle-aged subjects practising aerobic physical activity in leisure-time. (Refs: 19)*International journal of sports cardiology (Torino, Italy) 1(2), Jul/Dec 1984, 80-83.*
ABST: A bicycle ergometer maximal stress test carried out on 133 middle-aged, apparently healthy and normotensive male subjects was characterized by an abnormal blood response in 38 cases (28.6 percent). Statistically significant differences between these subjects and the ones with normal blood pressure response were found, as to the mean values of baseline systolic and diastolic pressure (tendentially higher, event if still within normal limits) and intensity of physical training (lower). The usefulness of the maximal stress test in sports practising people and the favourable effect of aerobic physical exercise of adequate intensity in possibly preventing arterial hypertension is emphasized.
LEVEL: A LANG: Eng SIRC ARTICLE NO: 179171

Evdokimova, E.V. Evdokimov, V.G. Rannee vyivlenie vzaimosviazi lipidnogo spektra syvorotki krovi i gipertenzivnogo tipa reaktsii arterial'nogo davleniia na fizicheskuiu nagruzku u zdorovykh lits molodogo vozrasta. (Early detection of the relationship between the serum lipid spectrum and the hypertensive response of blood pressure to physical exertion in healthy young persons.) *Kardiologiia (Moscow) 24(11), Nov 1984, 47-49.*
ABST: A comparative study was carried out on the lipid levels in the blood serum and the frequency of hyperlipoproteinemias in 1005 normal subjects of young age (17-29 years) of both sexes with the normo- and hypertensive types of the blood pressure (BP) response to exercise. The subject with the hypertensive type of the BP response to exercise showed a significant elevation in the lipid levels and the rate of hyperlipoproteinemias as against the group with the normotensive type of the BP reaction.
LEVEL: A LANG: Rus

Imachi, Y. Man-I, M. Rebound of blood pressure after exercise. (Refs: 9)*Journal of sports medicine and physical fitness (Torino, Italy) 24(4), Dec 1984, 286-289.*
ABST: This study introduces a phenomenon which was tentatively called 'rebound' of blood pressure. It was an abnormal rise of systolic blood pressure emerged transiently in the post-exercise resting stage on veteran marathoner's measurements. The cause was undetermined but was hypothesized to be due to some composite effects of delayed secretion of uncertain hormonal substances, accompanying rapid decrease of heart rates and cooperation of activities of sympathetic nerve systems. It was concluded that the blood pressure had to be carefully measured especially when it was measured immediately after the exercise.
LEVEL: A LANG: Eng SIRC ARTICLE NO: 106779

Marie, G.V. Lo, C.R. Van Jones, J. Johnston, D.W. The relationship between arterial blood pressure and pulse transit time during dynamic and static exercise. *Psychophysiology (Madison) 21(5), Sept 1984, 521-527.*
LEVEL: A LANG: Eng SIRC ARTICLE NO: 104341

McGarthy, J.P. Hunter, G.R. Blood pressure adaptations to training. (Refs: 36)*National Strength & Conditioning Association journal 5(6), Jan 1984,* 44-47;71.
ABST: The authors explain the effects of various forms of training on blood pressure. They review some of the findings of five investigations on anaerobic training and blood pressure. Anaerobic training was found to increase blood pressure.
LEVEL: A LANG: Eng SIRC ARTICLE NO: 090277

Siconolfi, S.F. Carleton, R.A. Elder, J.P. Bouchard, P.A. Hypotension after exercise and relaxation. (Refs: 11)
NOTES: In, Cantu, R.C. (ed.), Clinical sports medicine, Lexington, Mass. ; Toronto, Collamore Press : D.C. Heath, c1984, p. 129-138.
LEVEL: A LANG: Eng RC1201 15964

Terman, J.W. Blood pressure: The force that's with us, at rest or on the go. *Cardiogram (La Crosse, Wis.) 11(1), Dec 1983/Jan 1984, 4-5;10-11.*
LEVEL: B LANG: Eng SIRC ARTICLE NO: 094442

van Hooff, M.E.J. Rahn, K.H. van Baak, M.A. Effects of acute and chronic administration of propranolol during submaximal exercise in essential hypertension. (Refs: 17)*International journal of sports medicine (Stuttgart) Suppl. 5, Nov 1984, 186-188.*
CONF: International Congress on Sports and Health (1983 : Maastricht, Netherlands).
LEVEL: A LANG: Eng SIRC ARTICLE NO: 103905

Will, J. Plasma renin response to graded exercise in borderline hypertensive young males. Eugene, Ore.: Microform Publications, University of Oregon, 1984. 1 microfiche : negative, ill. ; 11 x 15 cm.
NOTES: Thesis (M.S.) - University of Wisconsin-Madison, 1982; (viii, 55 leaves); includes bibliography.
LEVEL: A LANG: Eng UO84 156

BLOOD VOLUME

Edwards, R.J. Harrison, M.H. Intravascular volume and protein responses to running exercise. (Refs: 28)*Medicine and science in sports and exercise (Indianapolis) 16(3), June 1984, 247-255.*
ABST: The roles of posture and mean skin temperature (T) in determining intravascular volume and protein responses to running exercise were examined in 12 male subjects. Moving from a sitting to a standing position before exercise was always accompanied by a decrease in blood volume (BV), as indicated by increases in the hematocrit and hemoglobin concentration. Althoug neither the onset of running nor alterations in T during runing caused any further consistent change in BV, there was an acceleration of the rate of which protein entered the intravascular space. At the end of exercise and in recovery this led to an augmentation of intravascular protein. It is concluded that intravascular volume responses to running exercise are determined by the accompanying postural hemoconcentration, and that running per se and any imposed thermal stress have minimal effects on BV thereafter.
LEVEL: A LANG: Eng SIRC ARTICLE NO: 108593

Green, H.J. Thomson, J.A. Ball, M.E, Hughson, R.L. Houston, M.E. Sharratt, M.T. Alternations in blood volume following short-term supramaximal exercise. (Refs: 23)*Journal of applied physiology: respiratory, environmental and exercise physiology (Bethesda, Md.) 56(1), Jan 1984, 145-149.*
ABST: High intensity intermittent work on the bicycle ergometer was performed on 3 consecutive days by young adults. The exercise provided a stimulus for the expansion of blood volume. Associated with the increase in blood volume was a decrease in red cell volume and increase in plasma volume. The hemoglobin content was not altered.
LEVEL: A LANG: Eng SIRC ARTICLE NO: 096245

Jensen, P.N. Glud, T.K. Arnfred, T. Platelet number and platelet volume in healthy young men during exercise and changes in posture. *Scandinavian journal of clinical and laboratory investigation (Oslo) 44(8), Dec 1984, 735-738.*
LEVEL: A LANG: Eng

Kanstrup, I.-L. Ekblom, B. Blood volume and hemoglobin concentration as determinants of maximal aerobic power. (Refs: 31) *Medicine and science in sports and exercise (Indianapolis) 16(3), June 1984, 256-262.*
ABST: Changes in blood volume (BV) and hemoglobin concentration (Hb) were induced in five healthy young men. After acute hypovolemic anemia was achieved by blood withdrawal VO2 max values decreased, while the same (Hb) due to acute plasma volume expansion (6 per cent dextran) did not alter VO2 max. After reinfusion of red blood cells, leading to hypervolemia and increased (Hb), VO2 max increased. Plasma volume exapansion in this situation, leading to hypervolemia at normal (Hb), resulted in a slight reduction in VO2 max, which however, remained elevated above control values. Physical performance, measured as time to exhaustion, corresponded to the changes in VO2 max except for the hypervolemic anemic situation, where it decreased. The results point to a significant influence of the total amount of Hb rather than the blood hemoglobin concentration for obtaining a high maximal aerobic power.
LEVEL: A LANG: Eng SIRC ARTICLE NO: 108594

Raven, P.B. Rohm-Young, D. Gunnar, C. Blamqvist, C.G. Physical fitness and cardiovascular response to lower body negative pressure. (Refs: 32)*Journal of applied physiology: respiratory, environmental and exercise physiology (Bethesda, Md.) 56(1), Jan 1984, 138-144.*
ABST: A comparison between high and average male fit subjects was made to determine the hemodynamic response to lower body negative pressure. The highly fit subjects had higher cardiac outputs than the average fit subjects under lower body negative pressure conditions. This appeared to be a diminished ability to vasoconstrict.
LEVEL: A LANG: Eng SIRC ARTICLE NO: 096290

CARDIAC FUNCTION

Danek, V. Poznatky o EKG zmenach po extremne prolongovane fyzicke zatezi. (ECG changes after extremely prolonged physical exertion.) *Casopis lekaru ceskych (Prague) 123(1), 6 Jan 1984, 21-26.*
LEVEL: A LANG: Cze

Furukawa, K. Kitamura, H. Nishida, K. Yamada, C. Niki, S. Sugihara, H. Katsume, H. Tsuji, H. Kunishige, H. Ijichi, H. Simultaneous changes of left ventricular and left atrial size and function in normal subjects during exercise. *Japanese heart journal (Tokyo) 25(4), Jul 1984, 487-497.*
LEVEL: A LANG: Eng

Mizutani, Y. Nakano, S. Ote, N. Iwase, T. Fujinami, T. Evaluation of effects of aging, training and myocardial ischemia on cardiac reserve by exercise echocardiography. (Refs: 25)*Japanese*

PHYSIOLOGY - CARDIOVASCULAR (continued)

circulation journal (Kyoto) 48(9), Sept 1984, 969-979.
LEVEL: A LANG: Eng SIRC ARTICLE NO: 109745

Noreau, L. Theriault, G. La fonction ventriculaire chez le sujet normal et coronarien suite a l'entrainement. (Refs: 49) *Canadian journal of applied sport sciences/Journal canadien des sciences appliquees au sport (Windsor, Ont.) 9(3), sept 1984, 133-140.*
RESUME: Le but de cette revue est de faire etat des connaissances et des donnees recentes sur les adaptations et les modifications de la pompe cardiaque suite a l'entrainement physique chez les sujets normaux et cardiaques.
LEVEL: A LANG: Fr SIRC ARTICLE NO: 102808

Righetti, A. Barthelemy, J.C. Ratib, O. Stucki, V. Bopp, P. Donath, A. Fonction ventriculaire globale et synchronicite de contraction pendant et apres l'effort. (Global ventricular function and synchronism of contraction during and after exertion.) *Schweizerische Medizin Wochenschrift/Journal suisse de medecine (Basel) 114(45), 10 Nov 1984, 1607-1611.*
NOTES: English abstract.
LEVEL: A LANG: Fr

Rost, R. Clinical significance of echocardiographic findings in athletes. (Refs: 6)*International journal of sports cardiology (Torino, Italy) 1(1), Jan/June 1984, 34-40.*
LEVEL: I LANG: Eng SIRC ARTICLE NO: 171823

CARDIAC OUTPUT

Brynjolf, I. Kelbaek, H. Munck, O. Golftfredsen, J. Larsen, S. Eriksen, J. Right and left ventricular ejection fraction and left ventricular volume changes at rest and during exercise in normal subjects. *European heart journal (London) 5(9), Sept 1984, 756-761.*
LEVEL: A LANG: Eng

Green, J.F. Jackman, A.P. Peripheral limitations to exercise. (Refs: 17)*Medicine and science in sports and exercise (Indianapolis) 16(3), June 1984, 299-305.*
ABST: We present a computer simulation of a two-compartment model of the systemic circulation which demonstrates how this model can be used to understand the mechanism (s) for the maximal exercise cardiac output (Q). The model consists of two parallel vascular channels, the splanchnic channel (all blood draining throug the hepatic veins) and the peripheral channel (all other vascular beds). The distinguishing characteristic of each channel is the product of its venous compliance and venous resistance. Model parameters for the human circulation were estimated from similar parameters obtained directly from animal experiments.
LEVEL: A LANG: Eng SIRC ARTICLE NO: 108602

Loucks, A.B. Cardiac output and gonadal steroids. (letter) *Fertility and sterility (Birmingham, Ala.) 42(5), Nov 1984, 810-811.*
LEVEL: A LANG: Eng

Pedoe, D.T. The way to an athlete's heart. *New scientist (London) 1415, 2 Aug 1984, 32-33.*
NOTES: Athletes often have big and slow-beating hearts. But these cardiac adaptations to physical training may not be essential for outstanding performance.
LEVEL: I LANG: Eng SIRC ARTICLE NO: 099258

Smyth, R.J. Gledhill, N. Froese, A.B. Jamnik, V.K. Validation of noninvasive maximal cardiac output measurement. (Refs: 14) *Medicine and science in sports and exercise (Indianapolis) 16(5), Oct 1984, 512-515.*
ABST: The acetylene-rebreathing technique is well-suited for maximal exercise; however, until recent technological advances, difficulties involved in collecting and measuring alveolar acetylene samples have restricted its use. We compared cardiac output values measured via the acetylene-rebreathing technique (Qa) (modified for use with a mass spectrometer) and the dye-dilution technique (Qd) at rest and during light to maximal exercise in six moderately active males. Although Qa consistently underestimated Qd, the two techniques showed a significant correlation of 0.87 throughout all levels of exercise.
LEVEL: A LANG: Eng SIRC ARTICLE NO: 102828

Wang, Y. Gutman, J.M. Heilbron, D. Wahr, D. Schiller, N.B. Atrial volume in a normal adult population by two-dimensional echocardiography. *Chest (Chicago) 86(4), Oct 1984, 595-601.*
LEVEL: A LANG: Eng

HEMODYNAMICS

Cleland, J.G. Dargie, H.J. Robertson, J.I. Ball, S.G. Hodsman, G.P. Renin and angiotensin responses to posture and exercise in elderly patients with heart failure. (Refs: 11)*European heart journal (London) 5(Suppl E), Nov 1984, 9-11.*
LEVEL: A LANG: Eng SIRC ARTICLE NO: 109722

Clements, I.P. Offord, K.P. Baron, D.W. Brown, M.L. Bardsley, W.T. Harrison, C.E. Cardiovascular hemodynamics of bicycle and handgrip exercise in normal subjects before and after administration of propranolol. *Mayo clinic proceedings (Rochester, Minn.) 59(9), Sept 1984, 604-611.*
ABST: This study focused on the effects of supine and upright bicycle exercise and handgrip exercise in 17 normal subjects before (control) and immediately after the administration of propranolol. Control left ventricular volumes and the cardiac index were greater in the supine position than in the upright at rest but resting left ventricular ejection fraction was similar in both positions. Propranolol increased left ventricular end-diastolic volume at rest and at maximal exercise. Left ventricular end-systolic volume, however, was substantially greater only in the upright position both at rest and at maximal exercise when compared with control values. Heart rate, systolic arterial pressure, cardiac index, and pressure volume index were decreased at rest and maximal exercise after treatment with propranolol. Handgrip exercise primarily increased heart rate and arterial pressure and did not affect cardiac volume, and this response was unaffected by propranolol.
LEVEL: A LANG: Eng SIRC ARTICLE NO: 103886

Cokkinos, D.V. Perrakis, C. Diakoumakos, N. Papantonakos, A. Mamaki, S. Cardiac function at treadmill exercise in various ag groups. (Refs: 18)*European heart journal (London) 5(Suppl E), Nov 1984, 41-45.*
LEVEL: A LANG: Eng SIRC ARTICLE NO: 109720

Corbeau, J. Variation de la frequence cardiaque au cours d'une epreuve d'effort standardisee. (Refs: 16)*EPS: Education physique et sport (Paris) 189, sept/oct 1984, 64-69.*
LEVEL: I LANG: Fr SIRC ARTICLE NO: 100891

Dean, J. Target heart rates don't hold water, says study. *Journal of physical education and program (Columbus, Ohio) 81(7), Oct 1984, G15-G17.*
LEVEL: I LANG: Eng SIRC ARTICLE NO: 100853

Dzizinskii, A.A. Cherniak, B.A. Kuklin, S.G. Fedotchenko, A.A. Tolerantnost' k fizicheskoi nagruzke i osobennosti ee gemodinamicheskogo obespecheniia u zdorovykh liudei v zavisimosti ot tipa gemodinamiki. (Physical exertion tolerance and the characteristics of hemodynamics in healthy persons depending on its type.) *Kardiologiia (Moskva) 24(2), Feb 1984, 68-73.*
ABST: Central hemodynamic parameters were studied in 113 normal male subjects, aged 20-59, at rest and during bicycle ergometric exercise. Capacity for physical exercise was shown to depend on both the age and the basic hemodymic type. Subjects with hyperkinetic circulation had the greatest, and those with hypokinetic circulation, the smallest capacity for exercise.
LEVEL: A LANG: Rus

Erikssen, J. Levorstad, K. Aakhus, T. Heart volumes in healthy middle-aged men. A seven-year prospective investigation. (Refs: 17)*Acta radiologica: diagnosis (Stockholm) 25(4), 1984, 277-282.*
LEVEL: A LANG: Eng SIRC ARTICLE NO: 109744

Faraci, F.M. Olsen, S.C. Erickson, H.H. Effect of exercise on oxygen consumption, heart rate, and the electrocardiogram of pigs. (Refs: 22)*Medicine and science in sports and exercise (Indianapolis) 16(4), Aug 1984, 406-410.*
ABST: Pigs were exercised for 5 min at five different treadmill speeds (1.0-1.8 m.s-1) (3o incline), while oxygen consumption (MO2), carbon dioxide production (MCO2), and the electrocardiogram (ECG) were recorded continuously. Data were taken at rest, during exercise, and at 2, 5, 15, and 30 min after exercise. Values for MO2, MCO2, and heart rate (HR) showed progressive increases with increasing treadmill speed. The respiratory exchange ratio (R) increased during exercise and approached 1.0 but peak values were seen shortly after exercise. Heart rate, MO2, MCO2, and R reached steady-state values after 2 min of exercise, which were maintained for the duration of exercise. In most cases, these variables had returned to control levels 15 min after exercise. A high correlation between HR and MO2 was found in these animals.
LEVEL: A LANG: Eng SIRC ARTICLE NO: 102772

Frynas, K. Adaptacja ukladu krazenia do wysilku submaksymalnego u dzieci z otyloscia prosta. (Adaptation of the circulatory system to submaximal exertion in children with simple obesity.) *Pediatria polska (Warsaw) 59(1), Jan 1984, 37-44.*
LEVEL: A LANG: Pol

Gandelsman, A.B. Evdokimova, T.A. Kim, V.V. Ponomarev, V.P. Shanskov, M.A. Integratsii dvigatelnykh i vegetativnykh funktsii pri myshechnoi rabote. (Integration of motor and autonomic functions during muscle work.) *Fiziologicheskii zhurnal SSSR imeni I.M. Sechenova (Leningrad) 70(12), Dec 1984, 1611-1616.*
ABST: In isometric efforts small energy expenditure was found to involve an inadequate increase of the heart rate and blood pressure. In dynamic cyclic loads, the heart rate and blood pressure increase occurs linearly, corresponding to the increase of 02 consumption and systolic index. Voluntary relaxation of muscles in the course of cyclic load involves small values of the 02 consumption and

systolic index, as well as low heart rate and blood pressure. In natural cyclic and noncyclic motor activity, the character of integration of the motor and vegetative functions depends on the relative weight of each of the biomechanical modes.
LEVEL: A LANG: Rus

Hurley, B.F. Seals, D.R. Ehsani, A.A. Cartier, L.-J. Dalsky, G.P. Hagberg, J.M. Holloszy, J.O. Effects of high-intensity strength training on cardiovascular function. (Refs: 27)*Medicine and science in sports and exercise (Indianapolis) 16(5), Oct 1984, 483-488.*
ABST: Thirteen healthy, untrained males (range 40-55 yr) were studied to determine the effects of 16 wk of high-intensity, variable-resistance, Nautilus strength training on cardiovascular function. A control group consisting of 10 untrained males (range 40-64 yr) underwent the same evaluation procedures as the training group. Maximal oxygen uptake (VO2 max) cardiac output during submaximal exercise, and body composition were determined before and after training. Muscular strength increased markedly (a 44% average increase). Body weight and percent body fat did not change with training, though fat-free weight did increase (66.9 plus or minus 2.6 vs 68.8 plus or minus 2.7 kg) significantly. Maximal oxygen uptake did not change significantly in either the training or the control group, and there were no changes in the hemodynamic responses to submaximal exercise after training.
LEVEL: A LANG: Eng SIRC ARTICLE NO: 102788

Jackson, N.C. Silke, B. Verma, S.P. Reynolds, G. Hafizullah, M. Taylor, S.H. Haemodynamic effects of intravenous nicardipine during upright exercise in patients with stable angina pectoris. *Postgraduate medicine (Minneapolis) 60(Suppl 4), 1984, 11-16.*
LEVEL: A LANG: Eng

Keep your heart fit: lower your pulse. *Executive fitness newsletter (Emmaus, Pa.) 15(16), 4 Aug 1984, 1-2.*
LEVEL: B LANG: E SIRC ARTICLE NO: 102792

Krasnikov, N.P. Issledovanie funktsii vneshnego dykhaniia i krovoobrashcheniia, rabotosposobnost' cheloveka. (External respiratory and circulatory functions determining and limiting human physical work capacity.) *Fiziologiya cheloveka (Moscow) 10(6), Nov/Dec 1984, 1036-1041.*
LEVEL: A LANG: Rus

Lai, J.S. Lien, I.N. (Cardiopulmonary functions during maximal exercise in young Chinese athletes and non-athletes.) *Taiwan i hsueh hui tsa chich (Taipei) 83(2), Feb 1984, 196-205.*
LEVEL: A LANG: Chi

Lo, C.R. Johnston, D.W. The self-control of the cardiovascular response to exercise using feedback of the product of interbeat interval and pulse transit time. *Psychosomatic medicine (New York) 46(2), Mar/Apr 1984, 115-125.*
ABST: The authors compared the interbeat interval and pulse transit time of subjects receiving product feedback, relaxation training or simply exercising. 36 subjects were tested at rest and on a bicycle ergometer. The product feedback subjects minimized the decrease in interbeat interval and pulse transit time caused by exercise, while the subjects of the two other groups showed similar changes.
LEVEL: A LANG: Eng SIRC ARTICLE NO: 100911

Lo, C.R. Johnston, D.W. Cardiovascular feedback during dynamic exercise. *Psychophysiology (Madison, Wisc.) 21(2), Mar 1984, 199-206.*
LEVEL: A LANG: Eng SIRC ARTICLE NO: 102797

Louhevaara, V. Tuomi, T. Korhonen, O. Jaakkola, J. Cardiorespiratory effects of respiratory protective devices during exercise in well-trained men. (Refs: 20)*European journal of applied physiology and occupational physiology (Heidelberg) 52(3), Apr 1984, 340-345.*
ABST: This study investigated the effects of a filtering device, an air-line breathing apparatus, and a self-contained breathing apparatus on pulmonary ventilation (Ve), oxygen consumption (VO2) and heart rate (HR) at rest, during progressive submaximal work levels, and during recovery in 12 voluntary firemen. All three devices hampered respiration, resulting in hypoventilation during work. Oxygen consumption was increased at the same work load compared to control values when the respirators were used. This effect was particularly noticeable at higher work loads. The use of the heavy (15 kg) self-contained breathing apparatus imposes a particularly severe stress on the cardiorespiratory system.
LEVEL: A LANG: Eng SIRC ARTICLE NO: 097740

Malini, P.L. Strocchi, E. Ambrosioni, E. Comparison of the effects of prizidilol and propranolol on renal haemodynamics at rest and during exercise. *British journal of clinical pharmacology (London) 17(3), Mar 1984, 251-255.*
ABST: The purpose of this study was to compare the effects of prizidilol and propranolol on renal hemodynamics. 22 hypertensive patients were tested during placebo and following 3 months of treatment with one of the two drugs. Increases in renal plasma flow with prizidolol (9%) and decrease with propranolol (-13.6%) were observed. There was no change in the glomerular filtration rate after both drugs treatment.
LEVEL: A LANG: Eng SIRC ARTICLE NO: 100912

McConnell, T.R. Swett, D.D. Jeresaty, R.M. Missri, J.C. Al-Hani, A.J. The hemodynamic and physiologic differences between exercise modalities. (Refs: 28)*Journal of sports medicine and physical fitness (Torino, Italy) 24(3), Sept 1984, 238-245.*
ABST: Twenty healthy subjects participated to investigate the hemodynamic and physiologic differences between four exercise modalities: treadmill (T), cycle ergometry (C), supine cycle ergometry (S), and arm ergometry (A). Heart rate (HR), blood pressure (BP), rate pressure product (RPP), and oxygen consumption (VO2) were measured. VO2 peak during C, S, and A was 89.9 per cent, 73.6 per cent and 71.4 per cent of that obtained during T, respectively. HR peak was significantly greater during T with C, S, and A values being 96.8 per cent, 88.0 per cent, and 94.0 per cent of the T values, respectively. There were no significant differences in SBP peak between T, C, and S with A values being significantly less. RPP peak was not significantly different between T and C with S and A being 89.5 per cent and 79.6 per cent of that obtained during T.
LEVEL: A LANG: Eng SIRC ARTICLE NO: 105485

McLeod, A.A. Brown, J.E. Kitchell, B.B. Sedor, F.A. Kuhn, C. Shandi, D.G. Williams, R.S. Hemodynamic and metabolic responses to exercise after adrenaceptor blockage in humans. (Refs: 29)*Journal of applied physiology: respiratory, environmental and exercise physiology (Bethesda,*

Md.) 56(3), Mar 1984, 716-722.
ABST: This study was done to examine the effects of acute alpha adrenoreceptor blockade with Prazosin, beta adreno-receptor blockade with atenolol, and nonselective beta adrenoreceptor blockade with propanolol on hemodynamic and metabolic responses to exercise after muscle glycogen depletion. Six male subjects exercised in a bicycle ergometer in four separate occasions, under one of the three treatments or a placebo. The results indicate major differences in both hemodynamic and metabolic responses observed during exercise when alpha and beta antagonists are administered acutely. Both beta blockers reduced free fatty levels, but only propanolol lowered plasma glucose levels relative to the placebo levels. Prazosin resulted in elevated free fatty acid and glucose levels. The authors suggest that the beneficial effects of Prazosin on plasma lipids may be mediated by enhanced peripheral utilization of fat as substrate.
LEVEL: A LANG: Eng SIRC ARTICLE NO: 096283

Miles, D.S. Sawka, M.N. Hanpeter, D.E. Foster, J.E. Doerr, B.M. Frey, M.A.B. Central hemodynamics during progressive upper- and lower-body exercise and recovery. (Refs: 30)*Journal of applied physiology: respiratory, environmental and exercise physiology (Bethesda, Md.) 57(2), Aug 1984, 366-370.*
LEVEL: A LANG: Eng SIRC ARTICLE NO: 108350

Misner, J.E. Bloomfield, D.K. Heart rate and PVCs during exercise. (Refs: 27)*Physician and sportsmedicine 12(2), Feb 1984, 100-104;107;110-111.*
ABST: The heart rate and PVCs of 48 men were assessed before, during and after exercise in this study. Subjects were divided in four groups based on the frequency of ventricular ectopy. The results indicate a significant increase in PVCs per hour and PVCs per 1,000 heart beats during exercise compared with the rest period. No significant difference between exercise and recovery periods was observed.
LEVEL: A LANG: Eng SIRC ARTICLE NO: 091755

Momot, M.D. Usachev, N.K. Pokazateli tsentral'noi gemodinamiki i sokratitel'noi sposobnosti miokarda u zdorovykh lits pri fizicheskoi nagruzke. (Indices of central hemodynamics and contractile function of the myocardium of healthy subjects during physical exertion.) *Voenno-meditsinskii zhurnal (Moscow) 11, Nov 1984, 53-54.*
LEVEL: A LANG: Rus

Nylander, E. Dahlstroem, U. Influence of long-term beta receptor stimulation with prenalterol on intrinsic heart rate in rat (Refs: 22)*European journal of applied physiology and occupational physiology (Berlin, W.G.) 53(1), 1984, 48-52.*
ABST: In this study, rats were subjected to long-term oral treatment with the beta receptor stimulating drug prenalterol. During the treatment period heart rates at rest and during submaximal exercise were measured. Heart rate after 30 min rest and also 2 min after exercise was higher in the treated animals. The treated rats had a significantly lower heart rate increase during exercise than untreated controls, consistent with a partial beta-blocking effect of the drug in states with a high endogenous sympathetic activity. After 25 weeks, prenalterol was withdrawn and the IHR was measured in situ after a denervation procedure. The

treatment with prenalterol had not altered the IHR.
LEVEL: A LANG: Eng SIRC ARTICLE NO: 104350

Ordway, G.A. Floyd, D.L. Longhurst, J.C. Mitchell, J.H. Oxygen consumption and hemodynamic responses during graded treadmill exercise in the dog. (Refs: 25)*Journal of applied physiology: respiratory, environmental and exercise physiology (Bethesda, Md.) 57 (2), Aug 1984, 601-607.*
LEVEL: A LANG: Eng SIRC ARTICLE NO: 108359

Pabst, H. Kleine, M.W. Problematique de la mesure de la frequence cardiaque dans le sport. *Medecine du sport (Paris) 58(2), 25 mars 1984, 39-40.*
LEVEL: I LANG: Fr SIRC ARTICLE NO: 094616

Payrau, B. Les troubles du rythme cardiaque chez les sportifs. (Refs: 6)*Homeopathie francaise (Paris) 72(5), 1984, 324-328.*
LEVEL: I LANG: Fr

Pedoe, D.T. The way to an athlete's heart. *New scientist (London) 1415, 2 Aug 1984, 32-33.*
NOTES: Athletes often have big and slow-beating hearts. But these cardiac adaptations to physical training may not be essential for outstanding performance.
LEVEL: I LANG: Eng SIRC ARTICLE NO: 099258

Reynolds, G. Verifiez leur pouls. C'est en verifiant le pouls de vos athletes que vous decouvrirez si l'entrainement que leur imposez les prepare vraiment aux situations de jeu. *Revue de l'entraineur (Montreal) avr/juin 1984, 32-34.*
NOTES: Traduit de, Coaching review Nov/Dec 1983.
LEVEL: B LANG: Fr SIRC ARTICLE NO: 094622

Rodeheffer, R.J. Gerstenblith, G. Becker, L.C. Fleg, J.L. Weisfeldt, M.L. Lakatta, E.G. Exercise cardiac output is maintaine with advancing age in healthy human subjects: cardiac dilatation and increased stroke volume compensate for a diminished heart rate. *Circulation (New York) 69(2), Feb 1984, 203-213.*
ABST: 61 subjects ranging in age from 25 to 79 and free of cardiac disease performed serial gated blood pool scans at rest and during progressive upright bicycle exercise. Age related changes included increases in end-diastolic volume and stroke volume, and a decrease in heart rate. The results indicate that in healthy subjects their hemodynamic profile is changed by an age related decrease in the cardiovascular response to beta-adrenergic stimulation.
LEVEL: A LANG: Eng SIRC ARTICLE NO: 097758

Rowell, L.B. Blackmon, J.R. Kenny, M.A. Escourrou, P. Splanchnic vasomotor and metabolic adjustments to hypoxia and exercise in humans. *American journal of physiology (Bethesda, Md.) 247(2 Pt 2), Aug 1984, H251-H258.*
LEVEL: A LANG: Eng SIRC ARTICLE NO: 104363

Sidorenko, G.I. Al'khimovich, V.M. Pavlova, A.I. Izmenenie pokazatelei krovoobrashcheniia u zdorovykh lits pri raznykh urovniakh fizicheskoi nagruzki v zavisimosti ot iskhodnogo tipa gemodinamiki. (Changes in the circulatory indices of healthy persons under various levels of physical load in relation to the initial type of hemodynamics. *Kardiologiia (Moscow) 24(6), Jun 1984, 79-84.*
ABST: The parameters of the central hemodynamics were studied in 78 normal subjects at rest and during bicycle ergometry of various intensity, using bipolar chest rheography. Three types of circulation were identified (eu-, hyper-, and hypokinetic) which represent normal variants ensuring (at exercise of various intensity) the constant level of energy required for the transportation of one litre of blood and the mean hemodynamic pressure. Various mechanisms of maintaining the adequate level of the mean hemodynamic pressure during exercise were identified.
LEVEL: A LANG: Rus

Svedenhag, J. Henriksson, J. Juhlin-Dannfelt, A. Asano, K. Beta-adrenergic blockade and training in healthy men--effects on central circulation. *Acta physiologica scandinavica (Stockholm) 120(1), Jan 1984, 77-86.*
ABST: This paper investigated the effects of beta-adrenergic blockade on central circulation prior to and following training on cycle ergometers 40 min/day 4 days a week for 8 weeks. 8 subjects received beta-adrenergic receptor blocker propanolol (160 mg/day) while 8 subjects were given placebo tablets. Similar increase (18%) in vo2 max and decreases in resting heart rate (-4 beats/min) and exercise heart rate at moderate work load (120 W: -11 beats/min) were observed in both groups. At a high work load (180 W), the exercise heart rate decreased more in the placebo group than in the beta-blockade group (-19 vs. - 7 beats/min) and the oxygen pulse only increased in the placebo group (8%).
LEVEL: A LANG: Eng SIRC ARTICLE NO: 100925

van Putten, M. Verstappen, F. Bloemen, L. Physical exercise and industrial respirators. (Refs: 3)*International journal of sports medicine (Stuttgart) Suppl. 5, Nov 1984, 13-14.*
CONF: International Congress on Sports and Health (1983 : Maastricht, Netherlands).
LEVEL: A LANG: Eng SIRC ARTICLE NO: 104386

Vanmeenen, M.T. Ghesquiere, J. Demedts, M. Effects of thoracic or abdominal strapping on exercise performance. *Bulletin europeen de physiopathologie respiratoire (Oxford) 20(2), Mar/Apr 1984, 127-132.*
ABST: 11 young men were tested on hemodynamics and respiratory parameters with abdominal orthoracic strapping. Tidal volume and stroke volume decreased while respiratory frequency and heart rate increased with both types of strapping. Thoracic strapping was significantly more impeding than abdominal strapping.
LEVEL: A LANG: Eng SIRC ARTICLE NO: 102837

Visser, C.A. Jaarsma, W. Kan, G. Lie, K.I. Immediate and longer-term of nicardipine, at rest and during exercise, in patient with coronary artery disease. *Posgraduate medicine (Minneapolis) 60(Suppl 4), 1984, 17-20.*
LEVEL: A LANG: Eng

Warzel, H. Krell, D. Effects of auditory stimulus timing in the respiratory cycle on the evoked cardiac response in man at rest. (Refs: 30)*European journal of applied physiology and occupational physiology (Berlin, W.G.) 53(2), 1984, 144-148.*
ABST: The present experiments were carried out in 21 healthy adults to study the effects of auditory stimulus timing within the respiratory cycle on evoked cardiac response. The mean of interbeat intervals (IBI) and standard deviation (SD) were calculated separately for each IBI of 20 trials for each subject, during both the prestimulus and poststimulus phases. The stimulus effects were expressed as changes from prestimulus conditions, in terms of IBI and SD. Stimulation during early inspiration did not produce any effect. It was not before the beginning of the following expiration that a significant deceleration was evoked, which was associated with an enhanced SD, whereas stimulation during early expiration promptly evoked a biphasic cardiac response of the deceleration - acceleration pattern and an increase and decrease in SD, respectively.
LEVEL: A LANG: Eng SIRC ARTICLE NO: 104391

Wolf, M.D. Conditioning: affairs of the heart. (pulse monitors) *Women's sports (San Francisco) 6(6), Jun 1984, 54.*
LEVEL: LANG: Eng SIRC ARTICLE NO: 104395

Yamamoto, J. Morita, S. Okamoto, U. Clearance of modified plasminogen produced in the circulation after strenuous exercise. *Thrombosis research (Elmsford, N.Y.) 36(1), 1 Oct 1984, 67-71.*
LEVEL: A LANG: Eng

HEMOGLOBIN

Farber, M.O. Sullivan, T.Y. Fineberg, N. Carlone, S. Manfredi, F. Effect of decreased O2 affinity of hemoglobin on work performance during exercise in healthy humans. *Journal of laboratory and clinical medicine (St. Louis) 104(2), Aug 1984, 166-175.*
ABST: In an attempt to induce significant, sustained reductions in O2 affinity of hemoglobin by primary DPG stimulation, six normal humans were given a diphosphonate followed by infusion of 10 per cent fructose with added phosphate and, subsequently, fructose-phosphate by itself. Participants underwent exercise testing (bicycle ergometer) and cardiopulmonary parameters were measured before and after administration of Didronel plus fructose-phosphate infusion alone. The results indicated that with reduced O2 affinity of hemoglobin, participants could perform at comparable work loads and utilize the same amount of O2 with less cardiac work.
LEVEL: A LANG: Eng SIRC ARTICLE NO: 104306

Ivanov, L.A. Chebotarev, N.D. Vliianie maksimal'noi fizicheskoi agruzki na kislorodtransportnye svoistva krovi. (Effect of maximum physical exertion on the oxygen transport system of the blood.) *Kosmicheskaia biologiia i aviakosmicheskaia meditsina (Moscow) 18(4), Jul/Aug 1984, 69-72.*
ABST: Ventilation, gas exchange, gas composition and pH of venous blood, as well as oxyhemoglobin dissociation curves were investigated during exercise tests of 9 healthy volunteers, aged 19-31. During maximal exercises the dissociation curve shifted to the right. The shift was associated with the extraerythrocyte factor, i.e. the Bohr effect due to metabolic acidosis in muscles. The shift which indicates a lower hemoglobin affinity for oxygen and a higher oxygen release by blood is of adaptive importance: during exercises oxygen supply to tissues increases. This shift is also evidenced by an increase of venous p02 during muscle work.
LEVEL: A LANG: Rus

Kanstrup, I.-L. Ekblom, B. Blood volume and hemoglobin concentration as determinants of maximal aerobic power. (Refs: 31) *Medicine and science in sports and exercise (Indianapolis) 16(3), June 1984, 256-262.*
ABST: Changes in blood volume (BV) and hemoglobin concentration (Hb) were induced in five healthy young men. After acute hypovolemic anemia was achieved by blood withdrawal VO2 max values decreased, while the same (Hb) due to

acute plasma volume expansion (6 per cent dextran) did not alter VO2 max. After reinfusion of red blood cells, leading to hypervolemia and increased (Hb), VO2 max increased. Plasma volume exapansion in this situation, leading to hypervolemia at normal (Hb), resulted in a slight reduction in VO2 max, which however, remained elevated above control values. Physical performance, measured as time to exhaustion, corresponded to the changes in VO2 max except for the hypervolemic anemic situation, where it decreased. The results point to a significant influence of the total amount of Hb rather than the blood hemoglobin concentration for obtaining a high maximal aerobic power.
LEVEL: A LANG: Eng SIRC ARTICLE NO: 108594

Katz, A. Sharp, R.L. King, D.S. Costill, D.L. Fink, W.J. Effect of high intensity interval training on 2, 3-diphosphoglycerate at rest and after maximal exercise. (Refs: 27)*European journal of applied physiology and occupational physiology (Heidelberg) 52(3), Apr 1984, 331-335.*
ABST: This investigation studied the effect of intense interval training on erythrocyte 2,3-diphosphoglycerate (2,3-DPG) levels at rest and after maximal exercise. Eight subjects trained on a cycle ergometer 4 days/week, for a period of 8 weeks. The training elicited significant increases in the amount of work done during a 45-5 ride, in VO2 max, and in total recovery VO2 after a graded leg exercise test. Training did not cause significant changes in 2,3-DPG levels at rest, nor did acute exercise change 2,3-DPG levels at exhaustion or during recovery. The role, if any, of 2,3-DPG in enhancing tissue oxygenation during physical work remains to be elucidated.
LEVEL: A LANG: Eng SIRC ARTICLE NO: 097736

Powers, S.K. Dodd, S. Woodyard, J. Beadle, R.E. Church, G. Haemoglobin saturation during incremental arm and leg exercise. (Refs: 12)*British journal of sports medicine (Loughborough, Eng.) 18(3), Sept 1984, 212-216.*
ABST: The purpose of this study was to assess the dynamic changes in %SO2 changes duing incremental arm and leg work. Nine trained subjects (7 males and 2 females) performed incremental arm and leg exercise to exhaustion on an arm crank ergometer and a cycle ergometer, respectively. Ventilation and gas exchange measurements were obtained minute by minute via open circuit spirometry and changes in %SO2 were recorded via an ear oximeter. No significant difference existed between arm and leg work in end-tidal oxygen, end-tidal carbon dioxide, or %SO2 when compared as a function of percent VO2 max. These results provide evidence that arterial O2 desaturation occurs in a similar fashion in both incremental arm and leg work with the greatest changes in %SO2 occurring at work rates greater than 70% VO2 max.
LEVEL: A LANG: Eng SIRC ARTICLE NO: 102816

Tokuda, S. Iiboshi, A. Suenaga, M. Otsuji, S. Changes in erythrocyte carbonic anhydrase activity due to physical exercise. (Refs: 29)*European journal of applied physiology and occupational physiology (Heidelberg) 52(3), Apr 1984, 249-254.*
ABST: In this descriptive study, one hundred forty-two athletes were tested to determine if changes in erythrocyte carbonic anhydrase activity (RBC-CA) are related to physical exercise. Acute aerobic and anaerobic exercise slightly influenced RBC-CA but there were no fixed trends. After three weeks of weight training RBC-CA was not significantly altered

but RBC-CA decreased after one week of recovery. The rest values of RBC-CA were higher in subjects who had undergone long-term strenuous aerobic training.
LEVEL: A LANG: Eng SIRC ARTICLE NO: 097769

Vokal, E. Kriz, M. Goldenberg, A. Studium vztahov COHb k fyzickej zdatnosti a parametrom lipidoveho metabolizmu u brancov. (Relation of COHb to physical fitness and lipid metabolism parameters in recruits.) *Ceskoslovenske zdravotnictvi (Prague) 32(8/9), Sept 1984, 349-355.*
LEVEL: A LANG: Slo

Woodson, R.D. Hemoglobin concentration and exercise capacity. (Refs: 18)*American review of respiratory disease (New York) 129(2 Pt 2), Feb 1984, S72-S75.*
CONF: Exercise Testing in the Dyspneic Patient Workshop (1982 : Bethesda).
ABST: This paper reviews research on the effects of mild to moderate anemia on exercise capacity and hemodynamics. The close relationship between hemoglobin and VO2 max is believed to be part of the reason for sex differences in VO2 max in age matched subjects. Anemia is compensated for in submaximal exercise by relative increases in cardiac output, heart rate and ventilation. Reduced hemoglobin levels result in an almost proportional reduction in maximal exercise capacity.
LEVEL: I LANG: Eng SIRC ARTICLE NO: 099278

MYOCARDIUM

Appell, H.J. Heller-Umpfenbach, B. Feraudi, M. Weicker, H. Ultrastructural and morphometric investigations on the effects of training and administration of anabolic steroids on the myocardium of guinea pigs. (Refs: 31)*International journal of sports medicine (Stuttgart, FRG) 4(4), Dec 1983, 268-274.*
ABST: Twenty male mature guinea pigs were tested in this study for the purpose of demonstrating the effect of a training program, of anabolic steroids, and of both combined on the myocardium. The results show that both anabolic steroids and training have a similar effect on the cellular components but have different influences on mitochondrial proliferation. The combination of the two produces pathological alterations of the cells, a consequence of drug abuse that athletes should be aware of.
LEVEL: A LANG: Eng SIRC ARTICLE NO: 097452

de Knecht, S. Saris, W.H.M. Daniels, O. Elvers, J.W.H. de Boo, Th.M. Echocardiographic study of the left ventricle in sedentary and active boys aged 8 - 9 years. (Refs: 17)
CONF: Symposium of Paediatric Work Physiology (10th : 1981 : Joutsa, Finland).
NOTES: In, Ilmarinen, J. and Vaelimaeki, I. (eds.), Children and sport: paediatric work physiology, Berlin, Springer-Verlag, 1984, p. 170-176.
LEVEL: A LANG: Eng SIRC ARTICLE NO: 102766

Fagard, R. Aubert, A. Staessen, J. Eynde, E.V. Vanhees, L. Amery, A. Cardiac structure and function in cyclists and runners. Comparative echocardiographic study. *British heart journal (London) 52(2), Aug 1984, 124-129.*
ABST: Twelve cyclists and 12 long distance runners matched for age, height, and weight with two control groups of 12 non-athletes were studied echocardiographically to evaluate cardiac structure and function. The athletes' hearts had a larger and

diastolic left ventricular internal diameter, mean wall thickness, and cross sectional area of the left ventricular wall than those of the respective control subjects. Nevertheless, whereas the left ventricular internal diameter was not different between the cyclists and runners, mean wall thickness and cross sectional area of the left ventricular wall were greater in the cyclists even after adjustment for weight. The ratio of wall thickness to left ventricular internal radius was significantly larger in cyclists than in their control group. Systolic left ventricular meridional wall stress was lower in the cyclists than in the runners. The data suggest that runners develop an increase internal diameter but that in cyclists the increase is disproportionate because of the isometric work of the upper part of the body during cycling.
LEVEL: A LANG: Eng SIRC ARTICLE NO: 104304

Nakanishi, N. Konishi, M. Akiyama, M. Takayama, Y. Terao, A. Naito, Y. Ito, H. Iida, M. Doi, M. Shimamoto, T. (Influences of daily physical labor on left ventricular dimensions in normotensive subjects.) *Nippon ronen igakkai zasshi/Japanese journal of geriatrics (Tokyo) 21(5), Sept 1984, 477-484.*
LEVEL: A LANG: Jpn

Small, B.G. Left ventricular dimensions and functions in athletes who train in selected postural positions relative to the force of gravity. Eugene, Ore.: Microform Publications, University of Oregon, 1984. 2 microfiches : negative, ill. ; 11 x 15 cm.
NOTES: Thesis (D.P.E.) - Springfield College, 1983; (vii, 91 leaves); includes bibliography.
LEVEL: A LANG: Eng UO84 423-424

Ward, K. O'Brien, M. Dolphin, C. Knight, D. Allen, J. Rodahl, A. Ward, R. Cahill, N. Left ventricular function in young male and female swimmers. (Refs: 4)
CONF: Symposium of Paediatric Work Physiology (10th : 1981 : Joutsa, Finland).
NOTES: In, Ilmarinen, J. and Vaelimaeki, I. (eds.), Children and sport: paediatric work physiology, Berlin, Springer-Verlag, 1984, p. 177-181.
ABST: Six young male and female swimmers from a group of athletes preparing for the 1980 Olympic Games were studied. Echocardiograms were obtained in the supine position before and after submaximal exercise. This study examines the relationship between left ventricular mass, left ventricular chamber size and wall thickness in systole and diastole, and systolic pressure before and after submaximal exercise.
LEVEL: A LANG: Eng SIRC ARTICLE NO: 103503

TESTING

Balfour, I. Strong, W.B. The pediatric exercise ECG. (Refs: 14)*In, Boileau, R.A. (ed.), Advances in pediatric sport sciences. Volume 1: biological issues, Champaign, Ill., Human Kinetics Publishers, c1984, p. 157-169.*
LEVEL: A LANG: Eng RJ125 20044

Berteau, P. Les pieges de l'examen cardiologique du sportif. *Pratique medicale (Paris) 24, 1984, 35-37.*
LEVEL: B LANG: Fr

Compaigne, B.N. Gilliam. T.B. Spencer, M.L. Gold, E.R. Heart rate Holter monitoring of 6- and 7- year old children with insulin dependent diabetics mellitus cardiovascular and short term metabolic response to exercise: a pilot story. (Refs: 14) *Research quarterly for exercise & sport (Reston,*

Va.) 55(1), Mar 1984, 69-73.
ABST: The purpose of this study was to examine the heart rate of four children with insulin dependent diabetics mellitus during a normal day at camp, and to compare this to a day that included special vigorous physical exercise programs. A heart rate monitoring device was worn by each child from 9:00 AM to 7:00 PM on each day of study. Insulin usage and urine glucose (Clinitest) were also monitored and recorded three times daily. The results showed that the exercise day resulted in 26.3 minutes during which the heart rate was greater than 160 beats per minute in comparison to 1.0 minutes for the normal activity day. Thus, the authors conclude that the children did not participate in vigorous activity on a voluntary basis. However, it is possible to increase physical activity, measured by heart rate, to increase cardiovascular fitness and to establish short-term metabolic control of urine glucose and hypoglycemia.
LEVEL: A LANG: Eng SIRC ARTICLE NO: 096006

Cousteau, J.P. L'entrainement sous surveillance cardiologique. (Refs: 31)Dans, Mandel, C. (ed.), Le medecin, l'enfant et le sport, Paris, (Vigot), c1984, p. 79-88.
LEVEL: I LANG: Fr RC1218.C45 18886

Di Bello, V. Lunardi, M. Santoro, G. Galetta, F. Cini, G. Dini, G. Giusti, C. Analisi delle variazioni del rendimento cardiaco indotte dal tilt e dallhand-grip in atleti ed in soggetti non allenati. (Analysis of variations in cardiac performance induced by tilt and hand-grip in athletes and in untrained subjects.) Gionale italiano di cardiologia (Rome) 14(3), Mar 1984, 188-198.
ABST: This study analyzed variations of external cardiac work and of myocardial oxygen consumption induced by upright tilting and hand-grip in volleyball athletes in comparison with a group of normal subjects.
LEVEL: A LANG: It

Dormer, K.J. Modulation of cardiovascular response to dynamic exercise by fastigial nucleus. (Refs: 36)Journal of applied physiology: respiratory, environmental and exercise physiology (Bethesda, Md.) 56(5), May 1984, 1369-1377.
ABST: This study examined the cardiovascular response of 34 dogs before and after the introduction of lesions in fastigial nucleus. The results indicate that there was a significant reduction in heart rate and mean arterial blood pressure after the introduction of the lesions. The authors conclude that the fastigial nucleus acts as modulator of heart rate and mean arterial blood pressure.
LEVEL: A LANG: Eng SIRC ARTICLE NO: 097722

Hanson, P. Clinical exercise testing. (Refs: 55)
NOTES: In, Strauss, R.H. (ed.), Sports medicine, Philadelphia ; Toronto, Saunders, 1984, p. 13-40.
LEVEL: A LANG: Eng RC1210 17196

Higginbotham, M.B. Morris, K.G. Coleman, R.E. Cobb, F.R. Sex-related differences in the normal cardiac response to upright exercise. Circulation (Dallas) 70(3), Sept 1984, 357-366.
ABST: To examine the hypothesis that apparent abnormality in left ventricular function represents a physiologic difference between men and women, the authors prospectively studied central and peripheral cardiovascular responses to exercise in 31 age-matched healthy volunteers (16 women and 15 men). The results demonstrate a basic difference between men and women with respect to

the mechanism by which they achieve a normal response of stroke volume to exercise: these differences must be taken into account when measurements of cardiac function during exercise stress are used for diagnostic purposes.
LEVEL: A LANG: Eng SIRC ARTICLE NO: 104320

Horstmann, E. Das Impedanzkardiogramm unter Belastung zur Beurteilung der linksventrikulaeren Funktion. (Impedance cardiography during exercise in the evaluation of left-ventricular function.) Zeitschrift fuer Kardiologie (Darmstadt) 73(6), Jun 1984, 374-379.
ABST: Transthoracic impedance cardiography is a method which, by measurement of transthoracic impedance, gives information on hemodynamic events, parameters of contractility, and valvular heart disease. In 50 patients mean pulmonary artery pressure was measured at rest and during exercise and compared to the corresponding changes in the impedance cardiogram. It was examined whether, by means of impedance cardiography, an elevated pulmonary artery pressure could be predicted. The results show that the impedance ratio can be used to assess left ventricular function non-invasively.
LEVEL: A LANG: Ger

Karvonen, J. Chwalbinska-Moneta, J. Saynajakangas, S. Comparison of heart rates measured by ECG and microcomputer. (Refs: 8) Physician and sportsmedicine (Minneapolis, Minn.) 12(6), Jun 1984, 65-66;68-69.
ABST: The authors compared the efficiency of a wrist worn microcomputer and an ECG in measuring the heart rate of 10 men and four women while exercising on a bicycle ergometer and a treadmill. No significant difference was found between the 2 devices.
LEVEL: A LANG: Eng SIRC ARTICLE NO: 094426

Pan, L.G. Forster, H.V. Bisgard, G.E. Dorsey, S.M. Busch, M.A. O2 transport in ponies during treadmill exercise. (Refs: 32) Journal of applied physiology: respiratory, environmental and exercise physiology (Bethesda, Md.) 57(3), Sept 1984, 744-752.
LEVEL: A LANG: Eng SIRC ARTICLE NO: 108935

Squires, R.W. Bove, A.A. Cardiovascular profiling. (Refs: 48)Clinics in sports medicine (Philadelphia) 3(1), Jan 1984, 11-29.
NOTES: Symposium on profiling.
ABST: For cardiovascular profiling of athletes and non-athletes a history of the person is recorded and a physical examination is performed. A graded exercise test is conducted especially for the middle aged or older noncompetitive athlete. Scores of maximal oxygen uptakes are obtained and compared to norms for the respective age group. Individual exercise prescription is determined by the results of the cardiovascular profile.
LEVEL: A LANG: Eng SIRC ARTICLE NO: 092951

Stein, R.A. Cooper, R.S. Cardiovascular evaluation for sports participation. (Refs: 9)
NOTES: In, Birrer, R.B. (ed.), Sports medicine for the primary care physician, Norwalk, Conn., Appleton-Century-Crofts, c1984, p. 65-76.
LEVEL: I LANG: Eng RC1210 17030

Stein, R.A. Exercise ECG testing. (Refs: 10)
NOTES: In, Birrer, R.B. (ed.), Sports medicine for the primary care physician, Norwalk, Conn., Appleton-Century-Crofts, c1984, p. 77-84.
LEVEL: I LANG: Eng RC1210 17030

Sturek, M.L. Bedford, T.G. Tipton, C.M. Newcomer, L. Acute cardiorespiratory responses of hypertensive rats to swimming and treadmill exercise. (Refs: 31)Journal of applied physiology: respiratory, environmental and exercise physiology (Bethesda, Md.) 57 (5), Nov 1984, 1328-1332.
LEVEL: A LANG: Eng SIRC ARTICLE NO: 108906

Thompson, P.D. McGhee, J.R. Cardiac evaluation of the competitive athlete. (Refs: 25)
NOTES: In, Strauss, R.H. (ed.), Sports medicine, Philadelphia ; Toronto, Saunders, 1984, p. 3-12.
LEVEL: A LANG: Eng RC1210 17196

PHYSIOLOGY - ENERGY METABOLISM

Aerobic training in power sports. National Strength & Conditioning Association journal (Lincoln, Neb.) 6(5), Oct/Nov 1984, 10-19.
LEVEL: I LANG: Eng SIRC ARTICLE NO: 102935

Blom, P.C.S. Vollestad, N.K. Hermansen, L. Diet and recovery processes. (Refs: 34)
CONF: International Course on Physiology and Biochemistry of Exercise and Detraining (2nd : 1982 : Nice).
NOTES: In, Marconnet, P. (ed.) et al., Physiological chemistry of training and detraining, New York, Karger, c1984, p. 148-160.
LEVEL: A LANG: Eng RC1235 17596

Brotherhood, J.R. Nutrition and sports performance. (Refs: 268)Sports medicine (Auckland, N.Z.) 1(5), Sept/Oct 1984, 350-389.
ABST: The author reviews the published information on the dietary habits and attitudes of athletes, then examines the specific nutritional stresses associated with sports activity and, finally, states practical recommandations for nutrition and optimal physical performance.
LEVEL: A LANG: Eng SIRC ARTICLE NO: 102625

Calles-Escandon, J. Felig, P. Fuel-hormone metabolism during exercise and after physical training. Clinics in chest medicin (Philadelphia) 5(1), Mar 1984, 3-11.
LEVEL: I LANG: Eng SIRC ARTICLE NO: 102762

Chebotarev, D.F. Korkushko, O.V. Iaroshenko, I.T. Osobennosti anaerobnogo energoobespecheniia fizicheskoi nagruzki v razlichnye vozrastny periody. (Characteristics of anaerobic energy metabolism during physical training of persons of various age groups.) Fiziologicheskii zhurnal (Kiev) 30(1), Jan/Feb 1984, 53-59.
LEVEL: A LANG: Rus

Costill, D.L. Energy supply in endurance activities. (Refs: 27)International journal of sports medicine (Stuttgart) Suppl. 5, Nov 1984, 19-21.
CONF: International Congress on Sports and Health (1983 : Maastricht, Netherlands).
LEVEL: A LANG: Eng SIRC ARTICLE NO: 104293

Energy for exercise. Health letter (San Antonio, Tex.) 24(4), 24 Aug 1984, 2-3.
LEVEL: B LANG: Eng SIRC ARTICLE NO: 103061

Ford, L.E. Some consequences of body size. American journal of physiology (Bethesda, Md.) 7(4 Pt 2), Oct 1984, H495-H507.
LEVEL: A LANG: Eng

Health through knowledge. Part 1. *Sport & fitness (Sunbury, Middlesex) Nov 1984, 57;59-60.*
NOTES: The Sport & Fitness medical series.
LEVEL: B LANG: Eng SIRC ARTICLE NO: 109024

Iurimiae, T.A. Viru, A.A. Vliianie izbytka zhira v tele na fizicheskuiu rabotosposobnost' studentov. (Effect of excess fat i the body on the physical work capacity of students.) *Fiziologiya cheloveka (Moscow) 10(3), May/June 1984, 440-444.*
LEVEL: A LANG: Rus

LeBlanc, J. Diamond, P. Cote, J. Labine, A. Hormome factors in reduced postprandial heat production of exercise-trained subjects. (Refs: 21)*Journal of applied physiology: respiratory, environmental and exercise physiology (Bethesda, Md.) 56(3), Mar 1984, 772-776.*
ABST: The purpose of this study was to examine the influence of exercise training on postprandial heat production in the resting state. Seven trained and seven nontrained men were the subjects of this study, in which determinations of resting metabolic rate (RMR), plasma glucose, insulin, plasma epinephrine and norepinephrine were made after a 755 Kcal meal. The results showed that the elevations of RMR and plasma norepinephrine, after a meal, were significantly greater in the sedentary subjects, The highest values of plasma insulin were found at 30 min, and the levels were significantly lower in the trained subjects throughout the period of study. The authors conclude that exercise training reduces the increase of both glucose oxidation and energy expenditure that is normally observed following a meal, perhaps through the permissive effect of norepinephrine and insulin in these actions.
LEVEL: A LANG: Eng SIRC ARTICLE NO: 096270

Lowe, S.G. Metabolism: it keeps you fat and keeps you thin. Make yours work for you. *Slimmer (Santa Monica, Calif.) 4(6), Oct 1984, 32-35;78.*
LEVEL: B LANG: Eng SIRC ARTICLE NO: 173239

Maddaiah, V.T. Exercise and energy metabolism. *Pediatric annals (New York) 13(7), Jul 1984, 565-572.*
LEVEL: A LANG: Eng SIRC ARTICLE NO: 104339

McKeag, D. Body energy key to good training. *Spotlight (East Lansing, Mich.) 7(2), Summer 1984, 2.*
LEVEL: B LANG: Eng SIR ARTICLE NO: 097744

Parizkova, J. Bunc, V. Havlickova, L. Relation of working energy output to basal metabolic rate and body size in different age groups. (Refs: 8)*Human nutrition. Clinical nutrition (London) 38(3), May 1984, 233-235.*
LEVEL: A LANG: Eng SIRC ARTICLE NO: 104353

Richter, E.A. Sonne, B. Mikkines, K.J. Ploug, T. Galbo, H. Muscle and liver glycogen, protein, and triglyceride in the rat. Effect of exercise and of the sympatho-adrenal system. (Refs: 23)*European journal of applied physiology and occupational physiology (Heidelberg) 52(3), Apr 1984, 346-350.*
ABST: This investigation sought to determine if an increased net breakdown of protein and/or triglyceride accompanies decreased glycogen breakdown in exercising, adrenodemedullated rats. Rats swam to exhaustion or ran for 45 min at 10 and 14 m/min. Adrenomedullated rats had impaired muscle glycogenolysis during both exercise protocols. The results indicate that there was no compensatory increase in breakdown of triglyceride and protein in muscle or liver despite decreased muscle glycogenolysis. Indirect evidence suggests

that fatty acids from adipose tissue were oxidized in lieu of deficient muscle glycogenolysis.
LEVEL: A LANG: Eng SIRC ARTICLE NO: 097756

Vranic, M. Gauthier, C. Bilinski, D. Wasserman, D. El Tayeb, K. Hetenyi, G. Lickley, H.L. Catecholamine responses and their interactions with other glucoregulatory hormones. *American journal of physiology (Bethesda, Md.) 247(2 Pt 1), Aug 1984, E145-E156.*
ABST: We have investigated catecholamine-glucagon-insulin interactions using three stress models: 1) hypoglycemia; 2) exercise; and 3) epinephrine infusion. Glucagon played a role only in the recovery from insulin-induced hypoglycemia, which could reflect increased hepatic sensitivity to glucagon with declining plasma insulin. Exaggerated epinephrine release during hypoglycemic exercise prevented severe hypoglycemia by inhibiting glucose utilization and stimulating glucose production, with an associated increase in lactate and free fatty acid levels. We conclude that, during exercise, glucagon is directly responsible for 80 percent of the increment of glucose production and controls glucose uptake by the muscle indirectly; thus glucagon spares muscle glycogen by increasing hepatic glucose production.
LEVEL: A LANG: Eng SIRC ARTICLE NO: 104390

AEROBIC CAPACITY

Alexander, J.F. Liang, M.T.C. Stull, G.A. Serfass, R.C. Wolfe, D.R. Ewing, J.L. A comparison of the Bruce and Liang equation for predicting VO2 max in young adult males. (Refs: 16)*Research quarterly for exercise and sport (Reston, Va.) 55(4), Dec 1984, 383-387.*
LEVEL: A LANG: Eng SIRC ARTICLE NO: 104272

Bassett, D.R. Smith, P.A. Getchell, L.H. Energy cost of simulated rowing using a wind-resistance device. (Refs: 13)*Physicia and sportsmedicine (Minneapolis, Minn.) 12(8), Aug 1984, 113-116;118.*
ABST: The study compared the maximal aerobic capacity (VO2 max) obtained during treadmill running and simulated rowing. The energy cost (VO2) of rowing was also measured at five work loads. 10 men participated in the study. VO2 max was 10% lower on the rowing ergometer while VO2 increased curvilinearly with the velocity.
LEVEL: A LANG: Eng SIRC ARTICLE NO: 097710

Boileau, R.A. McKeown, B.C. Riner, W.F. Cardiovascular and metabolic contributions to the maximal aerobic power of the arms and legs. (Refs: 29)*International journal of sports cardiology (Torino, Italy) 1(2), Jul/Dec 1984, 67-75.*
ABST: The relative contribution of cardiac output (Qmax), heart rate (HRmax), stroke difference (SVmax) and arteriovenous oxygen (a-v)O2 diff max) to variation in arm and leg VO2 max was assessed in 40 male subjects, age 18-25 years. The VO2 max for each segment was measured by a continuous test with progressive loading of arm cranking and leg cycling. The arm VO2 max was 72 per cent of the leg VO2 max. Analysis of the individual variation in VO2 max indicated that the (a-v)O2 diff max contributed more than either SVmax or HRmax for the arm while SVmax contributed more than (a-v)O2 diff max or HRmax for the leg. The data were then divided into high and low VO2 max groups for the arms and legs to further analyze the Fick relationship within these respective groups. For arm work, the (a-v)O2 diff max contributed more variance than SVmax or HRmax in the low VO2 max group while the high

VO2 max group followed the pattern of the legs with SVmax contributing more to the variance in VO2 max than (a-vO2 diff max or HRmax. This evidence suggests that central factors as opposed to peripheral factors are more important in leg work, whereas, peripheral factors play a primary role in arm work, particularly in arms that are relatively untrained.
LEVEL: A LANG: Eng SIRC ARTICLE NO: 179169

Cerretelli, P. Does muscle blood flow limit maximal aerobic performance? (Refs: 24)*International journal of sports cardiology (Torino, Italy) 1(2), Jul/Dec 1984, 59-66.*
LEVEL: A LANG: Eng SIRC ARTICLE NO: 179168

Denis, C. Dormois, D. Lacour, J.R. Endurance training, VO2 max, and OBLA: a longitudinal study of two different age groups. (Refs: 45)*International journal of sports medicine (Stuttgart) 5(4), Aug 1984, 167-173.*
ABST: This study examined the effect of a 20-week training program of six middle-aged men (33-41 yrs) (GIT) and six young male subjects (19-21 yrs) (GIIT). Measurement of VO2 max, maximal work onset of blood lactate accumulation, absolute (OBLAW), and relative to MWL (OBLA per cent) were made on GIT and GIIT groups and on a third group (19-22 yrs) (GIIC). VO2 max which was initially similar in GIT and GIIT increased significantly by 8 per cent in GIT and by 19 per cent in GIIT. OBLAW increased significantly to the same level in the two groups (38 per cent and 42 per cent, respectively). OBLA per cent increases significantly (20 per cent) in GIT only.
LEVEL: A LANG: Eng SIRC ARTICLE NO: 104297

Dotson, C.O. Caprarola, M.A. Maximal oxygen intake estimated from submaximal heart rate. (Refs: 17)*British journal of sport medicine (Loughborough, Eng.) 18(3), Sept 1984, 191-194.*
ABST: This study investigated the predictability of maximal oxygen intake from three different submaximal heart rates assessed during an initial and follow-up ride on bicycle ergometer. Twenty-four healthy male subjects performed workloads of 600, 750, and 900 kpm's for six minutes on each of two visits to the laboratory. Relationships between the actual and estimated maximal oxygen intakes were determined using the Pearson Product-Moment formula of correlation. The average estimated maximal oxygen intake was significantly increased from the first testing occasion to the second. The correlation coefficients were consistently low at 600 kpm for both testing occasions (0.68 and 0.73, respectively), consistently high at 750 kpm (0.82 and 0.84, respectively), and quite variable at 900 kpm (0.71 and 0.84, respectively), indicated that the validity of the nomogram was not consistent with all workloads or testing occasions. Despite these inconsistencies, the nomogram is, for practical purposes, a valid predictor of maximal oxygen consumption.
LEVEL: A LANG: Eng SIRC ARTICLE NO: 102770

Froberg, K. Pedersen, P.K. Sex differences in endurance capacity and metabolic response in prolonged, heavy exercise. (Refs: 20)*European journal of applied physiology and occupational physiology (Berlin, FRG) 52(4), Jun 1984, 446-450.*
ABST: Six women and seven men performed bicycle ergometer exercise at 80% and 90% of their maximal oxygen uptakes until exhaustion. Women exercised significantly longer than men at 80% VO2 max. There were no significant differences between

the sexes at 90% VO2 max. The authors conclude that the women exercised longer at 80% VO2 max due to a sparing of glycogen in the middle phase of the exhaustive exercise.
LEVEL: A LANG: Eng SIRC ARTICLE NO: 097725

Gaesser, G.A. Poole, D.C. Gardner, B.P. Dissociation between V02max and ventilatory threshold responses to endurance trainin (Refs: 32)*European journal of applied physiology and occupational physiology (Berlin) 53(3), Dec 1984, 242-247.*
ABST: The purpose of this investigation was to determine whether the ventilatory gas exchange threshold (Tvent) changes significantly during the first 1-3 weeks of endurance training. Six men were studied during 3 weeks of training. At the end of each week, VO2 max, Tvent, and maximal and submaximal heart rates were determined during an incremental exercise test on the cycle ergometer. The dissociation between the significant improvement in VO2 max and the lack of a significant increase in Tvent during the first 3 weeks of training indicates that the exercise-induced changes in these two parameters are regulated by different mechanisms.
LEVEL: A LANG: Eng SIRC ARTICLE NO: 104308

Gaesser, G.A. Rich, R.G. Effects of high- and low-intensity exercise training on aerobic capacity and blood lipids. (Refs: 3 *Medicine and science in sports and exercise (Indianapolis) 16(3), June 1984, 269-274.*
ABST: Sixteen non-obese, non-smoking males, ages 20-30 yr, were assigned to one of two training groups, excercising on a cycle ergometer 3 d/wk for 18 wk: high-intensity or low-intensity. Data were obtained at 3-wk intervals for VO2 max, body weight, percent body fat, and 12-h fasting blood levels of cholesterol (CHOL), triglycerides (TG), high-density lipoprotein cholesterol (HDL-C), and low-density lipoprotein cholesterol (LDL-C). The average post-training increase in VO2 max for group H (0.56 l.min-1, 8.5 ml.min-1.kg-1) was not significantly greater than for group L (0.45 l.min-1, 6.5ml.min-1.kg-1). Significant reductions in percent body fat occurred in both groups. No statistically significant changes in CHOL, TG, HDL-C, LDL-C, CHOL/HDL-C, or HDL-C/LDL-C occurred in either group. However, changes in HDL-C after 18 wk of training were inversely correlated with pre-training levels.
LEVEL: A LANG: Eng SIRC ARTICLE NO: 108596

Hardman, A.E. Williams, C. Single leg maximal oxygen uptake and endurance performance before and after short term training. (Refs: 2)*International journal of sports medicine (Stuttgart) Suppl. 5, Nov 1984, 122-123.*
CONF: International Congress on Sports and Health (1983 : Maastricht, Netherlands).
LEVEL: A LANG: Eng SIRC ARTICLE NO: 104319

Humphreys, J.H.L. The application of physiological measurements to training. (Refs: 25)*Carnegie research papers (Beckett Park, Leeds) 1(6), Dec 1984, 4-7.*
ABST: This brief review of the literature focuses in maximum oxygen uptake (V02 max) during physical work, V02 max and distance running performance, and methods of training V02 max for distance running.
LEVEL: A LANG: Eng SIRC ARTICLE NO: 172497

Hurley, B.F. Seals, D.R. Ehsani, A.A. Cartier, L.-J. Dalsky, G.P. Hagberg, J.M. Holloszy, J.O. Effects of high-intensity strength training on

cardiovascular function. (Refs: 27)*Medicine and science in sports and exercise (Indianapolis) 16(5), Oct 1984, 483-488.*
ABST: Thirteen healthy, untrained males (range 40-55 yr) were studied to determine the effects of 16 wk of high-intensity, variable-resistance, Nautilus strength training on cardiovascular function. A control group consisting of 10 untrained males (range 40-64 yr) underwent the same evaluation procedures as the training group. Maximal oxygen uptake (VO2 max) cardiac output during submaximal exercise, and body composition were determined before and after training. Muscular strength increased markedly (a 44% average increase). Body weight and percent body fat did not change with training, though fat-free weight did increase (66.9 plus or minus 2.6 vs 68.8 plus or minus 2.7 kg) significantly. Maximal oxygen uptake did not change significantly in either the training or the control group, and there were no changes in the hemodynamic responses to submaximal exercise after training.
LEVEL: A LANG: Eng SIRC ARTICLE NO: 102788

Jousselin, E. Handschuh, R. Barrault, D. Rieu, M. Maximal aerobic power of French top level competitors. (Refs: 19)*Journal of sports medicine and physical fitness (Torino, Italy) 24(3), Sept 1984, 175-182.*
ABST: The authors studied the maximal aerobic power of a large number of top level French sportsmen belonging to National Teams. They calculated the mean and standard deviation for each sport activity. The comparison between the obtained values and those published in the international literature shows that, in most cases, there is little difference between the French and International top level population. The comparison according to sport activities confirms that the maximal oxygen intake (in ml/min.kg) increases with the aerobic energy requirement.
LEVEL: A LANG: Eng SIRC ARTICLE NO: 105481

Kirby, R.L. Sacamano, J.T. Balch, D.E. Kriellaars, D.J. Oxygen consumption during exercise in a heated pool. (Refs: 14) *Archives of physical medicine and rehabilitation (Chicago) 65(1), Jan 1984, 21-23.*
ABST: This study determined the oxygen consumption of thirteen healthy subjects during different forms of therapeutic exercise in a heated (36C) hydrotherapy pool. Oxygen consumption was measured in six settings: resting supine; resting seated in shoulder deep water; running at the fastest speed possible in chest-deep water; using hand paddles and running in place at shoulder depth. These exercises produced a graduated oxygen consumption scale with resting supine being the lowest (4.91.ml/kg/min) and running in place at shoulder depth being the highest (29.11.ml/kg/min). These results suggest that the more vigorous exercises stress aerobic capacity heavily but not excessively.
LEVEL: A LANG: Eng SIRC ARTICLE NO: 094604

Kriz, M. Krizova, M. Balaz, J. Petrik, A. Hajek, T. Vplyv pravidelnej zataze na psychicky stav, vykonnostne a somaticke parametre. (The effect of regular exercise on mental status, performance and somatic parameters.) *Ceskoslovenske zdravotnictvi (Praha) 32(4), Apr 1984, 180-186.*
LEVEL: A LANG: Slo

Kukkonen-Harjula, K. Rauramaa, R. Oxygen consumption of lumberjacks in logging with a power-saw. *Ergonomics (London) 27(1), Jan 1984,*

59-65.
LEVEL: A LANG: Eng SIRC ARTICLE NO: 100906

Lacour, J.R. Denis, C. Detraining effects on aerobic capacity. (Refs: 16)
CONF: International Course on Physiology and Biochemistry of Exercise and Detraining (2nd : 1982 : Nice).
NOTES: In, Marconnet, P. (ed.) et al., Physiological chemistry of training and detraining, New York, Karger, c1984, p. 230-237.
LEVEL: A LANG: Eng RC1235 17596

Lortie, G. Simoneau, J.A. Hamel, P. Boulay, M.R. Landry, F. Bouchard, C. Responses of maximal aerobic power and capacity to aerobic training. (Refs: 28)*International journal of sports medicine (Stuttgart) 5(5), Oct 1984, 232-236.*
ABST: The purpose of this experiment was to investigate the individual differences and the specificity in the response of maximal aerobic power (MAP) and capacity (MAC) to a 20-week aerobic training program. Twenty-four subjects (21-29 years) participated in this study. The aerobic training program enhanced mean MAP/kg and MAC/kg by 33% and 51%, respectively. There was a sex difference in the response of MAC/kg, men improving 50% more than women. Individual differences in the response to the standardized training program were considerable with training gains ranging from 5% to 88% for MAP/kg and from 16% to 97% for MAC/kg.
LEVEL: A LANG: Eng SIRC ARTICLE NO: 104338

Makowiec-Dabrowska, T. Drewczynski, A. Woskowska, Z. Lewgowd-Chwialkowska, T. Wplyw pracy o roznym charakterze i intensywnosci na zmiany zdolnosci wysilkowej. (Effect of work of different types and intensity on changes in work capacity.) *Medycyna pracy (Lodz) 35(2), 1984, 113-125.*
ABST: Changes in the current effort capacity following 4-hrs' performance of six types of work of different intensity and different muscular system engagement, have been evaluated. The studies involved two groups of women. Group I, consisting of 25 women, performed the dynamic, work on cycle-and manual-ergometers (Rr) and two types of static effort resulting from the shift of the load constituting 20 per cent body weight (N) and maintenance of forced posture during manual weaving (T). Group II, consisting of 9 women, performed the dynamic work on cycle ergometer (R) and dynamic-static work, with an additional load. Whatever the type of the previously performed work, the tolerance of fatigue was found to decrease, which was expressed by lower values of oxygen consumption and heart rate at which the women stopped the test effort.
LEVEL: A LANG: Pol

Moreira-da-Costa, M. Russo, A.K. Picarro, I.C. Silva, A.C. Leite-de-Barros-Neto, T. Tarasantchi, J. Barbosa, A.S. Maximal oxygen uptake during exercise using trained or untrained muscles. *Brazilian journal of medical and biological research (Sao Paulo) 17(2), 1984, 197-202.*
ABST: Maximal oxygen uptake (VO2 max), heart rate (HR), blood lacate and maximal voluntary ventilation were assessed in cyclists, long-distance runners and non-athletes during uphill running (treadmil) and cycling (bicycle ergometre). Runners and non-athletes showed higher VO2 max during the treadmill exercise while cyclists reached higher VO2 max on the bicycle ergometre. Similar increases in HR were obtained for cyclists during

both exercises while higher increases in HR were observed for the other two groups during treadmill exercise. Blood lactate was similar during both exercises for all groups.
LEVEL: A LANG: Eng

Nag, P.K. Circulo-respiratory responses to different muscular exercises. (Refs: 34)*European journal of applied physiology and occupational physiology (Berlin, FRG) 52(4), Jun 1984, 393-399.*
ABST: This study investigated the relationship between bodily reactions and six different muscular exercises performed on a modified ergometer. The six exercises were: pedalling while seated (PS), arm cranking while seated (CS), arm and leg cranking (ALC), pedalling while reclining (PR) and pedalling with back support (PBS). Measurements were taken on five subjects. CST, CS, PR, PS and PBS yielded 76, 72, 72, 87 and 97 per cent of VO2 max (ALC) respectively. Blood pressure was less in arm work than in leg work. The results indicate that CS, PR and PBS have more of an isometric component than CST, PS and ALC.
LEVEL: A LANG: Eng SIRC ARTICLE NO: 097749

Nagle, F.J. Richie, J.P. Giese, M.D. VO2 max responses in separate and combined arm and leg air-braked ergometer exercise. (Refs: 11)*Medicine and science in sports and exercise (Indianapolis) 16(6), Dec 1984, 563-566.*
ABST: Using an air-braked cycle ergometer, we sought to determine the relative contributions of the arms and legs in eliciting the maximal O2 update (VO2 max). Ten healthy, non-armtrained males did progressive exercise to exhaustion on the ergometer instrumented to partition the push-pull arm exercise from the cycling leg exercise. Exercise was done with arms only (100 per cent arms), legs only (100 percent legs, with arms at sides), and in combinations of 10 per cent arms/90 per cent legs, 20 per cent arms/80 per cent legs, and 30 per cent arms/70 per cent legs. The authors conclude that push-pull arm exercise of 10 or 20 per cent, combined with leg cycling of 90 or 80 per cent, respectively, or leg cycling with hands fixed to bars optimize the arm/leg contributions in eliciting VO2 max. Upper-body stabilizing effort in conventional cycling (legs cycling, hands fixed) contributes approximately 10-20 per cent to inducing VO2 max. The use of legs alone, or a proportion of 30 per cent arms/70 per cent legs elicit lower VO2 max values.
LEVEL: A LANG: Eng SIRC ARTICLE NO: 104348

O'Donnell, C. Smith, D.A. O'Donnell, T.V. Stacy, R.J. Physical fitness of New Zealand army personnel; correlation between field tests and direct laboratory assessments - anaerobic threshold and maximum O2 uptake. *New Zealand medical journal (Dunedin) 97(760), 25 Jul 1984, 476-479.*
ABST: Performance in two field tests was compared with maximum oxygen uptake (VO2 max) and anaerobic threshold in 42 male army staff. VO2 max ranged from 39.8 to 66.0 ml kg-1min-1 with a mean of 50.8 ml kg-1 min-1 for the group. Mean anaerobic threshold was 30.7 ml kg-1min-1. These values compare favourably with those for other military populations. The time to run 2.4 km averaged 616 s for the group while the mean distance covered in 12 minutes was 2.78 km. The time for the 2.4 km run showed a significant inverse correlation with both VO2 max and anaerobic threshold. The linear correlations between 12 min run distance and VO2 max or anaerobic threshold were lower.
LEVEL: A LANG: Eng SIRC ARTICLE NO: 104260

Pate, R.R. Krista, A. Physiological basis of the sex difference in cardiorespiratory endurance. (Refs: 45)*Sports medicine (Auckland) 1(2), Mar/Apr 1984, 87-98.*
ABST: This review discussed the physiological basis accounting for male-female differences in endurance performance. The authors draw two conclusions: the cardiorespiratory endurance of the male exceeds that of the female by 5 to 50%, and the sex difference in cardiorespiratory endurance is apparently linked to sex-related variance in maximal aerobic power and work efficiency.
LEVEL: A LANG: Eng SIRC ARTICLE NO: 094618

Peronnet, F. Thibault, G. Consommation maximale d'oxygene endurance et performance. *Revue de l'entraineur (Montreal) oct/de 1984, 20-22.*
LEVEL: I LANG: Fr SIRC ARTICLE NO: 105489

Snell, P.G. Mitchell, J.H. The role of maximal oxygen uptake in exercise performance. (Refs: 92)*Clinics in chest medicine (Philadelphia) 5(1), Mar 1984, 51-62.*
LEVEL: A LANG: Eng SIRC ARTICLE NO: 102829

Thomas, T.R. Adeniran, S.B. Etheridge, G.L. Effects of different running programs on VO2 max, percent fat, and plasma lipids (Refs: 30)*Canadian journal of applied sport sciences/Journal canadien des sciences appliquees au sport (Windsor, Ont.) 9(2), Jun 1984, 55-62.*
ABST: The purpose of this study was to determine the effects of interval and continuous running on factors associated with cardiovascular health in 59 young men and women. The experimental subjects trained three times a week for 12 weeks using either an interval (90% maximal heart rate) or a continuous (75% maximal heart rate) program. All programs utilized approximately 500 cal/session. Only the interval group improved their VO2 max compared to the control group. All experimental groups decreased in percent fat with no method found to be superior to the others in decreasing percent fat. There were no changes in plasma lipids between groups.
LEVEL: A LANG: Eng SIRC ARTICLE NO: 096302

Vogelaere, P. Duquet, W. CT 170: validation en fonction du VO2 max pour une population agee de 6 a 12 ans. (Refs: 29) *Medecine du sport (Paris) 58(5), 25 sept 1984, 6-12.*
RESUME: Cette etude vise a verifier la validite d'une procedure experimentale du CT170 a divers paliers d'intensite sur la base du VO2 max derive du test cyclergometrique (Vita max). 93 enfants ages de 6 a 12 ans classes selon le sexe en trois groupes d'age participent a l'etude. Les variables suivantes sont mesurees: la capacite de travail, le niveau maximal de la charge imposee et VO2 max. Pour l'ensemble de l'echantillon les auteurs observent une forte correlation du CT170 et de la Vita max.
LEVEL: A LANG: Fr SIRC ARTICLE NO: 100882

Wetzler, H.P. Cruess, D.F. Aerobic capacity of selected young air force officers and officer candidates. (Refs: 5)*Physician and sportsmedicine 12(1), Jan 1984, 131-133;136.*
ABST: The aerobic capacity of Air Force officers, officer trainers, and cadets was evaluated during a 1.5-mile run. Women were found to have an higher level of physical fitness than men.
LEVEL: A LANG: Eng SIRC ARTICLE NO: 091787

Wilmore, J.H. The assessment of and variation in aerobic power in world class athletes as related to specific sports. (Refs: 98)*American journal of sports medicine (Baltimore, Md.) 12(2), Mar/Apr 1984, 120-127.*
ABST: This article discusses the different types of devices used to assess the VO2 max of elite athletes. The concept of specificity of training/testing is also covered. The author provides a comprehensive table listing the VO2 max of athletes from a wide range of sports.
LEVEL: A LANG: Eng SIRC ARTICLE NO: 094636

Yazir, Y. Effendi, H. Aerobic capacities and blood pressure responses of five different groups in North Sumatra and Aceh at different workloads. (Refs: 7)*European journal of applied physiology and occupational physiology (Heidelberg) 52(2), Jan 1984, 163-166.*
ABST: Field studies in two northern provinces of the island of Sumatra were done to assess the aerobic capacity and blood pressure response within the individuals of five different sample groups. The multistage submaximal work test on a cycle ergometer and Astrand's Nomogram were implemented to assess VO2 max indirectly, and blood pressure was monitored at different workloads during steady state. It was stated that no other large scale assessment of aerobic capacity has been done in Indonesia. This is a report of the results compiled in the period between December 1977 and December 1980. The results here were also compared to those in other studies.
LEVEL: A LANG: Eng SIRC ARTICLE NO: 096312

Zivanic, S. Zivotic-Vanovic, M. Dimitrijevic, B. Stamenkovic, C. Maksimalna potrosnja kiseonika i opsta misicna snaga zena-regruta. (Maximal oxygen uptake and general muscle strength in female recruits.) *Vojnosanitetski pregled (Belgrad) 41(1), Jan/Feb 1984, 12-14.*
LEVEL: A LANG: Scr

AEROBIC CAPACITY - TESTING

Astrand, P.-O. Principles in ergometry and their implications in sports practice. (Refs: 9)*International journal of sports medicine (Stuttgart) Suppl. 5, Nov 1984, 102-105.*
CONF: International Congress on Sports and Health (1983 : Maastricht, Netherlands).
LEVEL: A LANG: Eng SIRC ARTICLE NO: 104276

Binkhorst, R.A. de Jong-van de Kar, M.C. Vissers, A.C.A. Growth and aerobic power of boys aged 11 - 19 years. (Refs: 6)
CONF Symposium of Paediatric Work Physiology (10th : 1981 : Joutsa, Finland).
NOTES: In, Ilmarinen, J. and Vaelimaeki, I. (eds.), Children and sport: paediatric work physiology, Berlin, Springer-Verlag, 1984, p. 99-105.
ABST: This paper reports the results of a longitudinal study of aerobic power in children during the later stages of growth.
LEVEL: A LANG: Eng SIRC ARTICLE NO: 102759

Boulay, M.R. Hamel, P. Simoneau, J.A. Lortie, G. Prud'homme, D. Bouchard, C. A test of aerobic capacity: description and reliability. (Refs: 19)*Canadian journal of applied sport sciences/Journal canadien des sciences appliquees au sport (Windsor, Ont.) 9(3), Sept 1984, 122-126.*
ABST: The purposes of this study were 1) to describe a maximal aerobic capacity (MAC) test and 2) to report on its reliability. Thirty subjects (16 males and 14 females) were tested for maximal aerobic power (MAP) with a progressive bicycle ergometer test and the ventilatory anaerobic

threshold (VANT) was determined. The same subjects were tested twice for MAC within 7 days. There was a non significant difference between means (p.05) of the first and second test in total work performed in kJ/kg. There was also no difference between variances of both tests. These results suggest that MAC as defined in this study can be measured with a high level of reproducibility.
LEVEL: A LANG: Eng SIRC ARTICLE NO: 102761

Bradley, H.R. A flexible multistage treadmill exercise protocol for prediction of anaerobic threshold and determination of aerobic capacity in young adults. Eugene, Ore.: Microform Publications, University of Oregon, 1984. 2 microfiches : negative, ill. ; 11 x 15 cm.
NOTES: Thesis (M.S.) - Virginia Polytechnic Institute and State University, 1982; (viii, 115 leaves); vita; includes bibliography.
LEVEL: A LANG: Eng UO84 208-209

Davies, B. Daggett, A. Jakeman, P. Mulhall, J. Maximum oxygen uptake utilising different treadmill protocols. (Refs: 19) *British journal of sports medicine (Loughborough, Eng.)* 18(2), Jun 1984, 74-79.
ABST: The study compared five treadmill protocols (four utilising a motorised, and one a non-motorised, treadmill) on maximum oxygen uptake. The five male and five female subjects, all actively engaged in training, were assigned the tests in random order. Statistical analysis revealed no significant differences between the five protocols for maximal oxygen uptake, maximum ventilation, maximum heart rate and blood lactate inflection point, relative to maximal oxygen uptake. Significant differences were observed between the 3' protocol with incline increments of 1.5% and all other protocols on time to exhaustion and maximum blood lactate levels. The resuls indicate that the protocols used in this study did not significantly influence the maximum oxygen uptake attained.
LEVEL: A LANG: Eng SIRC ARTICLE NO: 102764

Foster, C. Jackson, A.S. Pollock, M.L. Taylor, M.M. Hare, J. Sennett, S.M. Rod, J.L. Sarwar, M. Schmidt, D.H. Generalized equations for predicting functional capacity from treadmill performance. *American heart journal (St. Louis)* 107(6), Jun 1984, 1229-1234.
LEVEL: A LANG: Eng SIRC ARTICLE NO: 100895

Hammond, H.K. Froelicher, V.F. Exercising testing for cardiorespiratory fitness. (Refs: 25)*Sports medicine (Auckland, N.Z.)* 1(3), May/Jun 1984, 234-239.
ABST: This review cites maximal oxygen consumption (VO2 max) tests as the best available measure of cardiorespiratory fitness. Although indirect measurements of VO2 max are attractive they are not as accurate as the direct tests. Due to this inaccuracy the indirect tests are not as useful to elite athletes as the direct tests. The authors suggest that the best use of the measurement of VO2 max in athletes is in assessing the success of training programmes in a longitudinal manner.
LEVEL: A LANG: Eng SIRC ARTICLE NO: 096247

Kasch, F.W. The validity of the Astrand and Sjostrand submaximal tests. (Refs: 28)*Physician and sportsmedicine (Minneapolis Minn.)* 12(8), Aug 1984, 47-51;54.
ABST: The purpose of this study was to evaluate the validity of the Astrand and Sjostrand sublimaximal tests for determining maximal oxygen uptake (VO2). 83 males, (aged between 30 and 66

years) served as subjects. Results indicated a standard error of 12% and 16% for the Sjostrand and Astrand tests, respectively. The author concluded that both tests were not adequate substitutes for direct measurement of VO2.
LEVEL: A LANG: Eng SIRC ARTICLE NO: 097735

Kuipers, H. Geurten, P. Verstappen, F.T.J. van Kranenburg, G. Keizer, H.A. Inter-individual variation in heart rate response to exercise and its consequences for the accuracy of estimating VO2max. (Refs: 6)*International journal of sports medicine (Stuttgart) Suppl. 5, Nov 1984, 128-129.
CONF: International Congress on Sports and Health (1983 : Maastricht, Netherlands).
LEVEL: A LANG: Eng SIRC ARTICLE NO: 104331

Norris, C. Measuring physical work capacity (part 11). *Remedial gymnastics and recreational therapy (Northampton, Eng.)* 111 Feb 1984, 4-6.
LEVEL: I LANG: Eng SIRC ARTICLE NO: 096286

Robertshaw, S.A. Reed, J.W. Mortimore, I.L. Cotes, J.E. Afacan, A.S. Grogan, J.B. Submaximal alternatives to the Harvard pac index as guides to maximal oxygen uptake (physical fitness). *Ergonomics (London)* 27(2), Feb 1984, 177-185.
LEVEL: A LANG: Eng SIRC ARTICLE NO: 102820

Verma, S.S. Gupta, R.K. Gypta, J.S. Some simple multiple linear regression equations for estimation of maximal aerobic power in healthy Indian males. (Refs: 30)*European journal of applied physiology and occupational physiology (Heidelberg)* 52(3), Apr 1984, 336-339.
ABST: The maximal aerobic power (VO2 max) was assessed in 320 healthy Indian males. Body weight, time for 3.2 km run, and exercise dysponeic index (DIstd Ex%) were observed to be well correlated with VO2 max. A multiple linear regression containing these variables as predictors of VO2 max yielded a coefficient of 0.658 (p0.001). **The authors feel the simple measurements needed for this equation will make this procedure useful in personnel selection.**
LEVEL: A LANG: Eng SIRC ARTICLE NO: 097773

Washburn, R.A. Montoye, H.J. The validity of predicting VO2 max in males age 10-39. (Refs: 30)*Journal of sports medicine an physical fitness (Torino)* 24(1), Mar 1984, 41-48.
ABST: VO2 max was measured in 474 males age 10-39 classified into 5 year groups. VO2 max was predicted from maximal heart rate and VO2 measured by the Astrand-Rhyming nomogram, Margaria's procedure, and Maritz's method. Significant differences were found in the measurement methods for various age groups. All three methods provide a reasonably accurate estimate of mean VO2 max in groups while estimates for individuals may be subject to large errors.
LEVEL: A LANG: Eng SIRC ARTICLE NO: 099271

Wilmore, J.H. Morphologic and physiologic differences between man and woman relevant to exercise. (Refs: 20)*International journal of sports medicine (Stuttgart) Suppl. 5, Nov 1984, 193-194.
CONF: International Congress on Sports and Health (1983 : Maastricht, Netherlands).
LEVEL: A LANG: Eng SIRC ARTICLE NO: 104393

AEROBIC-ANAEROBIC TRANSITION

Aunola, S. Rusko, H. Reproducibility of aerobic and anaerobic thresholds in 20-50 year old men. (Refs: 37)*European journal of applied physiology and occupational physiology (Berlin)* 53(3), Dec 1984, 260-266.
ABST: The reproducibility of the aerobic (AerT) and the anaerobic (AnT) threshold was studied in 33 men aged 20-50 years. They completed two maximal exercise tests on a bicycle ergometer. The work rate and the measured physiological variables of the AerT and AnT, except for the blood lactate concentration, were very reproducible. The poor reproducibility of blood lactate concentration of the AnT confirmed our previous opinion that the fixed blood lactate levels of 2 and 4 mmol.1-1 are poor indicators of AerT and AnT.
LEVEL: A LANG: Eng SIRC ARTICLE NO: 104277

Black, A. Ribeiro, J.P. Bochese, M.A. Effects of previous exercise on the ventilatory determination of the aerobic threshold (Refs: 20)*European journal of applied physiology and occupational physiology (Heidelberg)* 52(3), Apr 1984, 315-319.
ABST: Sixteen men performed three maximal tests consisting of 3 min pedalling at 25W, followed by 25W increments every minute until volitional fatigue. One test was preceded by 10 min cycling at a power output corresponding to the anaerobic threshold of the individual. This test showed significantly higher anaerobic threshold values compared to the anaerobic thresholds of the other two maximal tests. The authors conclude that the performance of previous exercise can increase the value for the ventilatory determination of the anaerobic threshold due to a faster sub-threshold VO2 response.
LEVEL: A LANG: Eng SIRC ARTICLE NO: 097714

Bradley, H.R. A flexible multistage treadmill exercise protocol for prediction of anaerobic threshold and determination of aerobic capacity in young adults. Eugene, Ore.: Microform Publications, University of Oregon, 1984. 2 microfiches : negative, ill. ; 11 x 15 cm.
NOTES: Thesis (M.S.) - Virginia Polytechnic Institute and State University, 1982; (viii, 115 leaves); vita; includes bibliography.
LEVEL: A LANG: Eng UO84 208-209

Bunc, V. Moznosti vyuziti anaerobniho prahu ve fyziologii prace. II. Metody stanoveni anaerobniho prahu. (Possibilities of application of anaerobic threshold in work physiology: II. Methods of determining anaerobic threshold.) *Pracovni lekarstvi (Prague)* 36(4), 1984, 127-133.
LEVEL: A LANG: Cze

Bunc, V. Sprynarova, S. Heller, J. Zdanowicz, R. Stanoveni anaerobniho prahu s prihlednutim k individualnimu funkcnimu stavu vyuzitim zmen parametru acidobazicke rovnovahy (BE). (Determination of the anaerobic threshold with regard to the individual functional state using changes within the parameters of the acid-base equilibrium.) *Casopis lekaru ceskych (Praha)* 123(29), 20 Jul 1984, 899-903.
LEVEL: A LANG: Cze

Gaisl, G. Buchberger, J. Changes in the aerobic-anaerobic transition in boys after 3 years of special physical education. (Refs: 23)
CONF: Symposium of Paediatric Work Physiology (10th : 1981 : Joutsa, Finland).
NOTES: In, Ilmarinen, J. and Vaelimaeki, I. (eds.),

Children and sport: paediatric work physiology, Berlin, Springer-Verlag, 1984, p. 156-161.
LEVEL: A LANG: Eng SIRC ARTICLE NO: 102779

Gladden, L.B. Current 'anaerobic threshold' controversies. (Refs: 47)*Physiologist (Bethesda, Md.) 27(4), Aug 1984, 312-318.*
LEVEL: I LANG: Eng SIRC ARTICLE NO: 104312

Gleim, G.W. Zabetakis, P.M. DePasquale, E.E. Michelis, M.F. Nicholas, J.A. Plasma osmolality, volume, and renin activity at the 'anaerobic threshold'. (Refs: 28)*Journal of applied physiology: respiratory, environmental and exercise physiology (Bethesda, Md.) 56(1), Jan 1984, 57-63.*
ABST: 8 males exercised progressively on a bicycle ergometer and performed repetitive bouts of unilateral isokinetic knee extension-flexion in this study of the relation of plasma renin activity/volume, osmolality, and hemodynamic parameters to the anaerobics threshold. The results found that at the anaerobic threshold there is an increase in blood lactate, minute ventilation and CO2 production. The anaerobic threshold seems to represent a point at which plasma renin activity increases abruptly as does plasma osmolality. Past this point there is less of a rise in arterial pressure.
LEVEL: A LANG: Eng SIRC ARTICLE NO: 096243

Golden, H.P. Vaccaro, P. The effects of endurance training intensity on the anaerobic threshold. (Refs: 26)*Journal of sport medicine and physical fitness (Torino, Italy) 24(3), Sept 1984, 205-211.*
ABST: The purpose of this investigation was to examine the effect of intensity of endurance training on AT, V02max, PWC, HRrest and HRmax of untrained, male colllege students (18 to 24 years). The experimental groups trained for thirty minutes, three times per week for eight weeks on bicycle ergometers. The low intensity group trained at the AT, and the high intensity group trained at a point halfway between AT and V02max. The pretest revealed a mean AT for all groups between 65 and 66% V02max. The results indicated no significant changes in AT for any groups. A significant increase in PWC was found for both the high and low intensity groups as compared to the control.
LEVEL: A LANG: Eng SIRC ARTICLE NO: 105473

Hughson, R.L. Methodologies for measurement of the anaerobic threshold. (Refs: 24)*Physiologist (Bethesda, Md.) 27(4), Aug 1984, 304-311.*
LEVEL: I LANG: Eng SIRC ARTICLE NO: 104322

Jousselin, E. Handschuh, R. Stephan, H. Determination de la zone de transition aerobie-anaerobie et utilisation pratique pou l'entrainement. (Refs: 9)*Cinesiologie (Paris) 96, juil/aout 1984, 301-303.*
LEVEL: I LANG: Fr SIRC ARTICLE NO: 099244

Kheder, A.B. Bartegi, Z. Nacef, T. Bouzayen, A. Chedly, A. Le seuil anaerobique. Son application dans l'evaluation de la capacite cardio-respiratoire a l'effort chez les athletes de haut niveau. (The anaerobic threshold. Its application in the evaluation of cardiorespiratory capacity under effort in high-caliber athletes.) *Tunisie medicale (Tunis) 62(7), Nov 1984, 547-550.*
LEVEL: A LANG: Fr

Lavoie, J.M. Levesque, R. Acide lactique et seuil anaerobie. (Refs: 6)*Revue de l'entraineur (Montreal) avr/juin 1984, 11-13.*
LEVEL: I LANG: Fr SIRC ARTICLE NO: 094608

McLellan, T.M. Training and the aerobic and anaerobic thresholds: an understanding of the current research. (Refs: 11) *Coaching science update (Ottawa, Ont.) 1984, 27-30.*
LEVEL: I LANG: Eng SIRC ARTICLE NO: 094610

McLellan, T.M. Les seuils aerobie et anaerobie. (Refs: 11)*Nouveautes en science de l'entrainement (Ottawa) 1984, 23-25.*
LEVEL: I LANG: Fr SIRC ARTICLE NO: 096282

Nikolic, Z. Todorovic, B. Anaerobic threshold during arm and leg exercise and cardiorespiratory fitness tests in a group of male and female students. (Refs: 54)*International journal of sports medicine (Stuttgart) 5(6), Dec 1984, 330-335.*
ABST: The anaerobic threshold (AT) was determined in 19 female and 41 male physical education students (mean age 19 yrs) during incremental arm and leg exercise on a bicycle ergometer. The AT values were 62.6 plus or minus 7.3 W and 109.3 plus or minus 17.4 W during arm exercise 136.6 plus or minus 22.8 W and 224.6 plus or minus 41.96 W during leg exercise in female and male subjects, respectively.
LEVEL: A LANG: Eng SIRC ARTICLE NO: 104349

Powers, S.K. Dodd, S. Garner, R. Precision of ventilatory and gas exchange alterations as a predictor of the anaerobic threshold. (Refs: 15)*European journal of applied physiology and occupational physiology (Heidelberg) 52(2), Jan 1984, 173-177.*
ABST: The purpose of this study was to compare ventilatory and gas exchange techniques for determining anaerobic threshold with the technique which uses blood lactate changes to determine anaerobic threshold. From a 30 W incremental cycle ergometer test performed by 13 trained male subjects, the results provide evidence that ventilatory or gas exchange anaerobic thresholds do not always occur simultaneously with blood lactate anaerobic thresholds. Thus, limitations are revealed in using either of these measures to estimate blood lactate anaerobic threshold.
LEVEL: A LANG: Eng SIRC ARTICLE NO: 096289

Reybrouck, T. Ghesquiere, J. Validation and determination of the 'anaerobic threshold'. (Refs: 15)*Journal of applied physiology: respiratory, environmental and exercise physiology (Bethesda, Md.) 57(2), Aug 1984, 610.*
ABST: This letter refers to a study by Yeh, M.P. et al., Anaerobic threshold: problems of determination and validation. J. appl. physiol.: respirat. environ. exercise physiol. 55, p. 1178-1186, 1983. The result of this study is not in agreement with previous research, which prompted the authors of the letter to comment on the research design and the results. Unlike Yeh et al. they believe that a ventilatory threshold can be determined during graded exercise, which is coincidental with the onset of blood lactate accumulation during graded exercise.
LEVEL: A LANG: Eng SIRC ARTICLE NO: 108361

Smith, D.A. O'Donnell, T.V. The time course during 36 weeks' endurance training of changes in VO2 max. and anaerobic threshold as determined with a new computerized method. *Clinical science (London) 67(2), Aug 1984, 229-236.*
ABST: Anaerobic threshold (AT), maximum oxygen uptake (VO2 max) and cardiac frequency at an oxygen uptake of 1.0 litres/min (Fc1.0) of six males following a 36 week endurance training program were evaluated at 12 week intervals. Increases of VO2 max of 13.6 per cent, of AT (32.3 per cent)

and per cent AT/VO2 max (17.0 per cent) and a decrease (10.2 per cent) in Fc1.0 were observed at the end of the program.
LEVEL: A LANG: Eng SIRC ARTICLE NO: 104373

Spynarova, S. Bunc, V. Heller, J. Moznosti vyuziti anaerobniho prahu ve fyziologii Prace. I. Fyziologicke zaklady anaerobnih prahu a jeho vztah k maximalnim funkcnim parametrum. (Possibilities of application of anaerobic threshold in work physiology: I. Physiological basis of anaerobic threshold and its relation to maximal functional parameters.) *Pracovni lekarstvi (Prague) 36(4), 1984, 123-126.*
LEVEL: A LANG: Cze

Van Meerhaeghe, A. Sergysels, R. De Coster, A. Assessment of the anaerobic threshold during exercise in normal man by means of the occlusion pressure as compared to conventional noninvasive techniques. *Respiration (Basel) 46(4), 1984, 346-353.*
LEVEL: A LANG: Eng

Wasserman, K. The anaerobic threshold measurement to evaluate exercise performance. (Refs: 43)*American review of respirator disease (New York) 129(2 Pt 2), Feb 1984, S35-S40.*
CONF: Exercise Testing in the Dyspneic Patient Workshop (1982 : Bethesda).
ABST: The anaerobic threshold has important functional implications since it measures the work rate above which metabolic acidosis accelerates the stimulation to breathing and exercise endurance is reduced. This paper details the means by which lactate increase is related to tissue anaerobiosis during exercise and the methods for measuring the anaerobic threshold. The type of exercise performed affects the anaerobic threshold in that treadmill exercise produces a measure 10 per cent greater than cycling in sedentary subjects. The anaerobic threshold is useful in the prediction of a subject's ability to maintain a given work rate and for measuring VO2 above which the cardiovascular insufficiently meets tissue oxygen requirements.
LEVEL: A LANG: Eng SIRC ARTICLE NO: 099272

ANAEROBIC CAPACITY

Davies, C.T.M. Young, K. Effects of external loading on short term power output in children and young male adults. (Refs: 13 *European journal of applied physiology and occupational physiology (Heidelberg) 52(3), Apr 1984, 351-354.*
ABST: This study assessed the effects of external loading on power output in 10 children and 4 young adults during maximal vertical jumping. During unloaded conditions the absolute peak power output (W) achieved by children and adults was 572 W (45%) and 765 W (25%) respectively higer in cycling than jumping exercise. External loading reduced the generation of W immediately prior to take-off of a maximal jump from a force platform. This decrease in W with external loading is contrary to previous research.
LEVEL: A LANG: Eng SIRC ARTICLE NO: 097719

Dolan, P. Sargeant, A.J. Maximal short-term (anaerobic) power output following submaximal exercise. (Refs: 5)*International journal of sports medicine (Stuttgart) Suppl. 5, Nov 1984, 133-134.*
CONF: International Congress on Sports and Health (1983 : Maastricht, Netherlands).
LEVEL: A LANG: Eng SIRC ARTICLE NO: 104301

Grodjinovsky, A. Bar-Or, O. Influence of added physical education hours upon anaerobic capacity,

adiposity, and grip strengt in 12 - 13 year-old children enrolled in a sports class. (Refs: 15)
CONF: Symposium of Paediatric Work Physiology (10th : 1981 : Joutsa, Finland).
NOTES: In, Ilmarinen, J. and Vaelimaeki, I. (eds.), Children and sport: paediatric work physiology, Berlin, Springer-Verlag, 1984, p. 162-169.
ABST: This study examines whether boys and girls enrolled in a sports class were physically and physiologically superior compared to their peers, and examines the effectiveness of added physical education hours on selected morphological and physiological parameters.
LEVEL: A LANG: Eng SIRC ARTICLE NO: 102783

Parkhouse, W.S. McKenzie, D.C. Possible contribution of skeletal muscle buffers to enhanced anaerobic performance: a brief review. (Refs: 129)*Medicine and science in sports and exercise (Indianapolis) 16(4), Aug 1984, 328-338.*
ABST: Sprint-trained athletes demonstrate a remarkable ability to perform exercise which results in fatigue quickly. Associated with these performances are large accumulations of anaerobic end products which produce decrements in intracellular pH. Because intracellular pH decrements of sufficient magnitude have been shown to inhibit athletic performances, it has been postulated that sprint-trained athletes have an enhanced proton-sequestering capability which would ultimately alter the rate of pH decrement. This would delay the inhibition of the enzymatic and contractile machinery resulting in enhanced performances. The intracellular buffers that are capable of contributing to this enhanced buffering capacity were identified as inorganic phosphate, protein-bound histidine residues, the dipeptide carnosine, bicarbonate, and creatine phosphate.
LEVEL: A LANG: Eng SIRC ARTICLE NO: 102811

Rodgers, C.D. A velocity related means for determining pendulum setting on the Wingate test of anaerobic power: a comparatic study. Ottawa: National Library of Canada, 1984. 1 microfiche (81 fr.) ; 11 x 15 cm.
NOTES: Thesis (M.H.K.) - University of Windsor, 1982. Includes bibliography. Canadian theses on microfiche: 57332.
LEVEL: A LANG: Eng ISBN: 0-315-09415-X LC CARD: 84-22471-0 CAN THESES 57332

Stone, M.H. Wilson, D. Rozenek, R. Newton, H. Physiological basis. (Refs: 34)*National Strength & Conditioning Association journal 5(6), Jan 1984, 40;63-65.*
LEVEL: I LANG: Eng SIRC ARTICLE NO: 090305

ANAEROBIC CAPACITY - TESTING

Astrand, P.-O. Principles in ergometry and their implications in sports practice. (Refs: 9)*International journal of sports medicine (Stuttgart) Suppl. 5, Nov 1984, 102-105.*
CONF: International Congress on Sports and Health (1983 : Maastricht, Netherlands).
LEVEL: A LANG: Eng SIRC ARTICLE NO: 104276

Camus, G. Fossion, A. Juchmes, J. Burette, J.L. Equivalent energetique de la production du lactate plasmatique dans la cours d'intensite supramaximale. (Energetic equivalent of the production of plasma lactate during running of supramaximal intensity.) *Archives internationales de physiologie et de biochimie (Liege) 92(5), dec 1984, 361-367.*
LEVEL: A LANG: Fr

Coggan, A.R. Costill, D.L. Biological and technological variability of three anaerobic ergometer tests. (Refs: 17) *International journal of sports medicine (Stuttgart) 5(3), Jun 1984, 142-145.*
ABST: To assess the relative biological and technological variability of anaerobic testing, 27 male subjects performed either 30- or 60-s sprint bouts on a hydraulically braked, Fitron ergometer or timed rides to exhaustion at 125 per cent VO2 max on an electrically braked Collins ergometer. Each subject performed four trials within a 4-week period. Total variability was estimated from the mean coefficient of variation for each variable. There were no significant differences across the four trials of each test for any of the variables measured (mean power or ride time, peak torque, fatiguability, or blood lactate). There were also no significant differences in test variabilities.
LEVEL: A LANG: Eng SIRC ARTICLE NO: 104291

La Voie, N. Dallaire, J. Brayne, S. Barrett, D. Anaerobic testing using the Wingate and Evans-Quinney protocols with and without toe stirrups. (Refs: 12)*Canadian journal of applied sport sciences/Journal canadien des sciences appliquees au sport 9(1), Mar 1984, 1-5.*
ABST: This study compared the anaerobic power outputs during bicycle ergometer work using the Wingate and Evans-Quinney protocols with and without toe stirrups. Fifty male college students performed a total of four maximal 30-second anaerobic power tests. The authors concluded that the Evans-Quinney protocol with toe stirrups resulted in significantly higher power measures than any of the other treatments tested.
LEVEL: A LANG: Eng SIRC ARTICLE NO: 093106

Norris, C. Measuring physical work capacity (part 11. *Remedial gymnastics and recreational therapy (Northampton, Eng.) 111 Feb 1984, 4-6.*
LEVEL: I LANG: Eng SIRC ARTICLE NO: 096286

Sargeant, A.J. Dolan, P. Thorne, A. Isokinetic measurement of maximal leg force and anaerobic power output in children. (Refs: 14)
CONF: Symposium of Paediatric Work Physiology (10th : 1981 : Joutsa, Finland).
NOTES: In, Ilmarinen, J. and Vaelimaeki, I. (eds.), Children and sport: paediatric work physiology, Berlin, Springer-Verlag, 1984, p.93-98.
ABST: The authors developped a technique based on cycling where maximal leg force and power output are both measured under isokinetic conditions. This technique is applied to a group of 13-year-old boys.
LEVEL: A LANG: Eng SIRC ARTICLE NO: 102823

Semenick, D. An aerobic testing: practical applications. (Refs: 14)*National Strength & Conditioning Association journal (Lincoln, Neb.) 6(5), Oct/Nov 1984, 45;70-73.*
LEVEL: I LANG: Eng SIRC ARTICLE NO: 102826

Tesch, A. An aerobic testing: research basis. (Refs: 13)*National Strength & Conditioning Association journal (Lincoln, Neb. 6(5), Oct/Nov 1984, 44;67-69.*
LEVEL: I LANG: Eng SIRC ARTICLE NO: 102835

CARBOHYDRATES

Fuller, J.L. Utilization of glucose and free fatty acids during exercise under two different oxygen concentrations. Eugene, Ore.: Microform Publications, University of Oregon, 1984. 1 microfiche : negative, ill. ; 11 x 15 cm.

NOTES: Thesis (M.S.) - Pennsylvania State University, 1981; (vii, 85 leaves); includes bibliography.
LEVEL: A LANG: Eng UO84 84

Hasson, S.M. The effect of the ingestion of glucose and fructose on blood glucose concentration of resting and exercising university students. Eugene, Ore.: Microform Publications, University of Oregon, 1984. 2 microfiches : negative, ill. ; 11 x 15 cm.
NOTES: Thesis (Ed.D.) - University of Northern Colorado, 1982; (x, 101 leaves); vita; includes bibliography.
LEVEL: A LANG: Eng UO84 191-192

Holloszy, J.O. Regulation of glucose metabolism and glycogen resynthesis following prolonged strenuous exercise. (Refs: 28)
CONF: International Course on Physiology and Biochemistry of Exercise and Detraining (2nd : 1982 : Nice).
NOTES: In, Marconnet, P. (ed.) et al., Physiological chemistry of training and detraining, New York, Karger, c1984, p. 111-118.
LEVEL: A LANG: Eng RC1235 17596

James, D.E. Kraegen, E.W. Chisholm, D.J. Effect of exercise training on whole-body insulin sensitivity and responsiveness. (Refs: 39)*Journal of applied physiology: respiratory, environmental and exercise physiology (Bethesda, Md.) 56(5), May 1984, 1217-1222.*
ABST: In this study the euglycemic clamp was used to determine the effect of exercise training on the whole-body insulin sensitivity and responsiveness of male Wistar rats. Rats were ran 6 days/wk at 10o incline for 7wk. After 2 weeks the rats ran continuously for 1h/day at 21 m/min and were maintained at this level until they were sacrificed. A sedentary control group and a food restricted sedentary control group were used to control for the effects of exercise and increased caloric intake of the experimental rats. The exercised group exhibited an increase in insulin sensitivity without a change in maximal insulin responsiveness. These results emphasize the potential benefit of moderate exercise in obesity and Type II diabetes.
LEVEL: A LANG: Eng SIRC ARTICLE NO: 097731

Krzentowski, G. Jandrain, B. Pirnay, F. Mosora, F. Lacroix, M. Luyckx, A.S. Lefebvre, P.J. Availability of glucose given orally during exercise. (Refs: 22)*Journal of applied physiology: respiratory, environmental and exercise physiology 56(2), Feb 1984, 315-320.*
ABST: This study investigated whether the time when glucose is ingested during exercise affects exogenous glucose disposal. Nine healthy subjects ingested 100 g of labelled glucose after either 120 min of exercise at 45% VO2 max (5 subjects) or after 15 min of exercise at 45% VO2 max. All subjects exercised for 4 hours. The results indicate that for both groups approximately 55% of the ingested glucose was oxidized within two hours of ingestion.
LEVEL: A LANG: Eng SIRC ARTICLE NO: 093105

Miller, W.J. Sherman, W.M. Ivy, J.L. Effect of strength training on glucose tolerance and post-glucose insulin response. (Refs: 28)*Medicine and science in sports and exercise (Indianapolis) 16(6), Dec 1984, 539-543.*
ABST: The effect of muscle strength training on glucose tolerance and the insulin response after glucose feeding was investigated in eight healthy male subjects. Glucose tolerance and the associated insulin response was assessed using a

standard 100-g oral glucose load before and after a supervised 10-wk high-resistance, isotonic weight-lifting program. Glucose tolerance was not changed by the training program. However a significant reduction in the basal plasma insulin concentration (37.5 per cent) and the area under the insulin response curve (18.0 per cent) was found. This reduction in the insulin response was significantly correlated with the increase in lean body mass.
LEVEL: A LANG: Eng SIRC ARTICLE NO: 104182

Pirnay, F. Krzentowski, G. Luyckx, A. Pallikarakis, N. Mosora, F. Lacroix, M. Lefebvre, P. Glucose ingestion during recovery (Refs: 19)
CONF: International Course on Physiology and Biochemistry of Exercise and Detraining (2nd : 1982 : Nice).
NOTES: In, Marconnet, P. (ed.) et al., Physiological chemistry of training and detraining, New York, Karger, c1984, p. 161-168.
LEVEL: A LANG: Eng RC1235 17596

Procaccini, D.A. Telesforo, P. Zaccaria, N. Pignatelli, P. Del Gaudio, M. Prova di tolleranza al glucosio per via intravenos durante esercizio muscolare. (Intravenous glucose tolerance test during muscular exercise.) *Quaderni sclavo di diagnostica clinica e di laboratorio (Siena) 20(3), Sept 1984, 264-270.*
LEVEL: A LANG: It

Sato, Y. Iguchi, A. Sakamoto, N. Biochemical determination of training effects using insulin clamp technique. *Hormone and metabolic research (Stuttgart) 16(9), Sept 1984, 483-486.*
LEVEL: A LANG: Eng

Seals, D.R. Hagberg, J.M. Allen, W.K. Hurley, B.F. Dalsky, G.P. Ehsani, A.A. Holloszy, J.O. Glucose tolerance in young and older athletes and sedentary men. (Refs: 32) *Journal of applied physiology: respiratory, environmental and exercise physiology (Bethesda, Md.) 56(6), Jun 1984, 1521-1525.*
ABST: This investigation studied the separate effects of age, endurance exercise training, and body fatness on the responses of plasma glucose and insulin to a 100 g. oral glucose load. There were five subject groups: endurance-trained masters athletes, older untrained men, older untrained lean men, endurance trained young athletes and young untrained men. The two endurance-trained groups had significantly blunted plasma insulin responses compared with the other three groups. The results of this study provide evidence that regularly performed vigorous exercise can, in some individuals, prevent the deterioration of glucose tolerance and insulin sensitivity with age.
LEVEL: A LANG: Eng SIRC ARTICLE NO: 097762

Tabata, I. Atomi, Y. Miyashita, M. Blood glucose concentration dependent ACTH and cortisol responses to prolonged exercise. (Refs: 21) *Clinical physiology (Oxford) 4(4), Aug 1984, 299-307.*
ABST: The purpose of this study is to investigate responses of serum ACTH and cortisol concentration to low intensity prolonged exercise. In experiment 1, 10 subjects fasted for 12 h and performed bicycle exercise until exhaustion. Whilst the time to serum ACTH concentration increasing varied among the subjects, the increases of this hormone occurred for all subjects when blood glucose concentration decreased to a critical level of 3.3 mmol/l. At the end of the exercise, blood glucose concentration decreased to 2.60 plus or minus 0.21 mmol/l, and serum ACTH and cortisol concentrations increased to 313 plus or minus 159

ng/l and 371 plus or minus 151 micrograms/l, respectively. In experiment 2, four subjects performed the same intensity exercise until exhaustion, and were then given 600 ml of 20 glucose solution, and asked to repeat the same exercise. During the second exercise, blood glucose concentration increased to the pre-exercise value and simultaneously, serum ACTH concentration decreased considerably.
LEVEL: A LANG: Eng SIRC ARTICLE NO: 104377

ENERGY COST

Cerretelli, P. Oxygen debt: definition, role and significance. (Refs: 40)
CONF: International Course on Physiology and Biochemistry of Exercise and Detraining (2nd : 1982 : Nice).
NOTES: In, Marconnet, P. (ed.) et al., Physiological chemistry of training and detraining, New York, Karger, c1984, p. 68-80.
LEVEL: A LANG: Eng RC1235 17596

Convertino, V.A. Goldwater, D.J. Sandler, H. Oxygen uptake kinetics of constant-load work: upright vs. supine exercise. *Aviation space and environmental medicine (Washington) 55(6), Jun 1984, 501-506.*
ABST: Oxygen uptake (VO2), O2 deficit, steady state VO2, and recovery VO2 of ten men (36-40 yr) were compared during exercise tests in the supine and upright positions. No change was observed in steady state VO2 during both exercises. Total VO2 during upright exercise was 0.30 l greater than during supine. O2 deficit and recovery VO2 were 0.64 l and 022 l less in the upright position than in the supine position.
LEVEL: A LANG: Eng SIRC ARTICLE NO: 104292

Hermansen, L. Medbo, J.I. The relative significance of aerobic and anaerobic processes during maximal exercise of short duration. (Refs: 22)
CONF: International Course on Physiology and Biochemistry of Exercise and Detraining (2nd : 1982 : Nice).
NOTES: In, Marconnet, P. (ed.) et al., Physiological chemistry of training and detraining, New York, Karger, c1984, p. 56-67.
LEVEL: A LANG: Eng RC1235 17596

Hermansen, L. Grandmontagne, M. Moehlum, S. Ingnes, I. Postexercise elevation of resting oxygen uptake: possible mechanisms and physiological significance. (Refs: 29)
CONF: International Course on Physiology and Biochemistry of Exercise and Detraining (2nd : 1982 : Nice).
NOTES: In, Marconnet, P. (ed.) et al., Physiological chemistry of training and detraining, New York, Karger, c1984, p. 119-129.
LEVEL: A LANG: Eng RC1235 17596

Hickson, J.F. Wilmore, J.H. Buono, M.J. Constable, S.H. Energy cost of weight training exercise. (Refs: 19) *National Strengt & Conditioning Association journal (Lincoln, Neb.) 6(5), Oct/Nov 1984, 22-23;66.*
ABST: This paper investigates the energy cost of a weight training program. Four men, aged between 19 and 26 years old, participate in a two part exercise program: 1) part A working the chest, shoulders and arms and 2) part B working the back and legs. Results indicate a mean net energy expenditure for part A of 174 kcals/session and for part B 222 kcals (n.s.). These findings are

compared to those of other investigations. An overall average net energy expenditure across investigating of 179 kcals/36-minute session is obtained.
LEVEL: A LANG: Eng SIRC ARTICLE NO: 102784

Iaruzhnyi, N.V. Dinamika potrebleniia kisloroda v vosstanovitel'nom periode posle kratkovremennykh upraxhnenii predel'noi moshchnosti. (Oxygen consumption dynamics in the recovery period after short-term exercises at threshold capacity.) *Fiziologiya cheloveka (Moscow) 10(6), Nov/Dec 1984, 1042-1044.*
LEVEL: A LANG: Rus

Jones, B.H. Toner, M.M. Daniels, W.L. Knapik, J.J. The energy cost and heart-rate response of trained and untrained subjects walking and running in shoes and boots. *Ergonomics (London) 27(8), Aug 1984, 895-902.*
LEVEL: A LANG: Eng

Morris, A.F. Energy: equating expenditure in different activities. *Running & fitness (Washington, D.C.) 16(3), May/Jun 1984 8-9.*
LEVEL: I LANG: Eng SIRC ARTICLE NO: 100915

Ordway, G.A. Floyd, D.L. Longhurst, J.C. Mitchell, J.H. Oxygen consumption and hemodynamic responses during graded treadmill exercise in the dog. (Refs: 25) *Journal of applied physiology: respiratory, environmental and exercise physiology (Bethesda, Md.) 57 (2), Aug 1984, 601-607.*
LEVEL: A LANG: Eng SIRC ARTICLE NO: 108359

Powers, S.K. Beadle, R.E. Mangum, M. Exercise efficiency during arm ergometry: effects of speed and work rate. (Refs: 14) *Journal of applied physiology: respiratory, environmental and exercise physiology 56(2), Feb 1984, 495-499.*
ABST: This study sought to elucidate the effects of speed and work rate on muscular efficiency during arm crank ergometry (ACE). Ten men exercised at speeds of 50, 70 and 90 rpm at power outputs of 15, 30, 45 and 60 W. Work (unloaded cranking as base-line correction) and delta (measurable work as base-line correction) efficiencies decreased with increases in power output. However, gross (work accomplished/energy expended) efficiency increased with increases in power output. All efficiencies decreased with increasing speed of movement.
LEVEL: A LANG: Eng SIRC ARTICLE NO: 093123

Steinacker, J.M. Wodick, R.E. Transcutaneous PO2 during exercise. *Advances in experimental medicine and biology (New York) 169, 1984, 763-774.*
LEVEL: A LANG: Eng SIRC ARTICLE NO: 102832

Vandewall, H. Sebert, M.P. Alimoradian, S. Monod, H. Bio-energetique du test de Ruffier. (Refs: 9) *Medecine du sport (Paris) 58(5), 25 sept 1984, 14-19.*
RESUME: Les auteurs evaluent la frequence cardiaque et la consommation d'oxygene de 10 sujets, ages de 21 a 34 ans, au cours du test de Ruffier ainsi qu'au cours de tests de flexion sur les jambes. Les resultats indiquent que le cout energetique du test de Ruffier est eleve (en moyenne 1960 ml pour 45 secondes d'exercice) et proche du VO2 max d'un sujet sedentaire.
LEVEL: A LANG: Fr SIRC ARTICLE NO: 100928

Washburn, R.A. Seals, D.R. Peak oxygen uptake during arm cranking for men and women. (Refs: 25) *Journal of applied physiology: respiratory,*

environmental and exercise physiology 56(4), Apr 1984, 954-957.
ABST: Peak values for power output, VO2, minute ventilation, and heart rate were determined for twenty males and twenty females during maximal arm-cranking exercise. In addition, arm-shoulder volume (A-SV) was measured before exercise. The males scored significantly higher than the females on all parameters except peak heart rate where there was a significant difference between the two groups. However, when peak VO2 was corrected for A-SV there was no significant difference between the groups. These results suggest that there are no sex-related differences in the ability of skeletal muscle to utilize O2 during dynamic exercise.
LEVEL: A LANG: Eng SIRC ARTICLE NO: 096307

FATS

Askew, E.W. Role of fat metabolism in exercise. (Refs: 54)*Clinics in sports medicine (Philadelphia) 3(3), Jul 1984, 605-621.*
NOTES: Symposium on nutritional aspects of exercise.
ABST: Fat and carbohydrate are the two main energy sources used during exercise. Either may be the predominant source, depending upon the duration and intensity of exercise, the degree of prior physical conditioning, and the composition of the diet consumed in the days prior to a bout of exercise. Trained individuals oxidize more fat and less carbohydrate than untrained subjects when performing submaximal work of the same absolute intensity. This increased capacity to utilize energy from fat can contribute to increased endurance.
LEVEL: A LANG: Eng SIRC ARTICLE NO: 100887

Despies, J.P. Bouchard, C.B. Savard, R. Tremblay, A. Marcotte, M. Theriault, G. Level of physical fitness and adipocyte lipolysis in humans. (Refs: 41)*Journal of applied physiology: respiratory, environmental and exercise physiology (Bethesda, Md.) 56(5), May 1984, 1157-1161.*
ABST: This study investigated the amount of training which is required to produce maximal adipocyte lipolysis. Fifty-one male subjects were used in the study. The subjects were placed in experimental groups based on their level of training: 1) sedentary 2) trained subjects (4 months of training) 3) experienced marathon runners. The subjects in group 2 exercised 5 days/wk, 45 min/day for 4 months. Basal lipolysis and epinephrine stimulated lipolysis were measured in all groups. The results indicate that training increases suprailiac fat cell lipolysis and that four months of training is sufficient to produce maximal adipocyte lipolysis.
LEVEL: A LANG: Eng SIRC ARTICLE NO: 097720

Lukaski, H.C. Bolonchuk, W.W. Klevay, L.M. Mahalko, J.R. Milne, D.B. Sandstead, H.H. Influence of type and amount of dietary lipid on plasma lipid concentrations in endurance athletes. *American journal of clinical nutrition (Bethesda, Md.) 39(1), Jan 1984, 35-44.*
ABST: 3 male endurance cyclists consumed isoenergetic diets for 3 28-day periods during which carbohydrate, polunsaturated fat or saturated fat were about 50% of the daily energy intake. The polyunsaturated fat diet significantly reduced mean fasting plasma total cholesterol in comparison to the other 2 diets. The polyunsaturated diet significantly depressed mean plasma triglycerides compared to the other 2 diets. The authors

conclude that dietary lipid differences influence fasting serum lipid and lipoprotein levels among men with high energy expenditures. The Key's equation was found to be a useful tool for predicting changes in plasma total cholesterol in these circumstances.
LEVEL: A LANG: Eng SIRC ARTICLE NO: 097626

Scheff, J. Cholesterol blues: diet and exercise fight the killer. *Triathlon (Santa Monica, Calif.) 2(3), Jun/Jul 1984, 26-27.*
LEVEL: B LANG: Eng SIRC ARTICLE NO: 100920

Toriola, A.L. Influence of 12-week jogging on body fat and serum lipids. (Refs: 23)*British journal of sports medicine (Loughborough, Leicestershire) 18(1), Mar 1984, 13-17.*
ABST: This study investigated the influence of different levels of distance running on percent body fat and serum lipids in 40 untrained male university students. The students were randomly assigned to four groups of equal size. These four groups were: control, 1.6 km joggers (3 days/wk), 3.2 km joggers (3 days/wk), 4.8 km joggers (3 days/wk). All exercise groups showed significant decreases in percent body fat in comparison to the control group at the conclusion of the 12 week study. Serum triglycerides were significantly reduced in all exercise groups in comparison to the control group. The author concludes that moderate physical activities of different intensities have lowering effects on body fat and serum lipids.
LEVEL: A LANG: Eng SIRC ARTICLE NO: 097007

Wood, P. The cholesterol controversy is over. Twelve years and $150 million later, the scientific community finally agrees o cholesterol. But what does this mean for runners and their diet? *Runner's world 19(3), Mar 1984, 76-80.*
LEVEL: I LANG: Eng SIRC ARTICLE NO: 091790

FATS - BLOOD LIPIDS

Brilla, L.R. Effects of hypomagnesemia and exercise on total cholesterol, high density lipoprotein cholesterol, and lipoprotein profile in rats. Eugene, Ore.: Microform Publications, University of Oregon, 1984. 2 microfiches : negative, ill. ; 11 x 15 cm.
NOTES: Thesis (Ph.D.) - University of Oregon, 1983; (xiii, 120 leaves); vita; includes bibliography.
LEVEL: A LANG: Eng UO84 400-401

Coleman, E. Fat mobilization in endurance training. *Sports medicine digest (Van Nuys, Calif.) 6(1), Jan 1984, 4-5.*
LEVEL: LANG: Eng SIRC ARTICLE NO: 099225

Danner, S.A. Wieling, W. Havekes, L. Leuven, J.G. Smit, E.M. Dunning, A.J. Effect of physical exercise on blood lipids and adipose tissue composition in young healthy men. *Atherosclerosis (Amsterdam) 53(1), Oct 1984, 83-90.*
LEVEL: A LANG: Eng

Davis, J.R. Exercise and estrus cycle influences on the plasma triglycerides of female rats. Eugene, Ore.: Microform Publications, University of Oregon, 1984. 1 microfiche : negative, ill. ; 11 x 15 cm.
NOTES: Thesis (M.S.) - University of Illinois at Chicago Circle, 1982; (ix, 61 leaves); includes bibliography.
LEVEL: A LANG: Eng UO84 210

Despres, J.P. Bouchard, C. Savard, R. Tremblay, A. Marcotte, M. Theriault, G. Effects of exercise-training and detraining on fat cell lipolysis in men and women. (Refs: 32)*European journal of*

applied physiology and occupational physiology (Berlin, W.G.) 53(1), 1984, 25-30.
ABST: The effects of training and detraining on adipose tissue lipolysis were studied in 19 healthy subjects (7 women and 12 men) who were submitted to a 20-week aerobic training program. Suprailiac fat biopsies were performed before training, after training, and at the end of the detraining period. Mean fat cell diameter and epinephrine stimulated lipolysis (ESL) were assessed on collagenase isolated fat cells. Training significantly increased ESL in men but not in women. No significant changes in female lipolysis were observed under any conditions. Changes in lipolysis were not correlated with changes in body fatness. However, a significant correlation was observed between the increase in ESL produced by training and the subsequent decrease caused by detraining.
LEVEL: A LANG: Eng SIRC ARTICLE NO: 104298

Fort, I.L. The acute response of high-density lipoproteins and psychological stress to aerobic exercise. Eugene, Ore.: Microform Publications, University of Oregon, 1984. 1 microfiche : negative ; 11 x 15 cm.
NOTES: Thesis (Ed.D.) - University of Arkansas, 1982; (vii, 80 leaves); includes bibliography.
LEVEL: A LANG: Eng UO84 171

Fuller, J.L. Utilization of glucose and free fatty acids during exercise under two different oxygen concentrations. Eugene, Ore.: Microform Publications, University of Oregon, 1984. 1 microfiche : negative, ill. ; 11 x 15 cm.
NOTES: Thesis (M.S.) - Pennsylvania State University, 1981; (vii, 85 leaves); includes bibliography.
LEVEL: A LANG: Eng UO84 84

Gaesser, G.A. Rich, R.G. Effects of high- and low-intensity exercise training on aerobic capacity and blood lipids. (Refs: 3 *Medicine and science in sports and exercise (Indianapolis) 16(3), June 1984, 269-274.*
ABST: Sixteen non-obese, non-smoking males, ages 20-30 yr, were assigned to one of two training groups, excercising on a cycle ergometer 3 d/wk for 18 wk: high-intensity or low-intensity. Data were obtained at 3-wk intervals for VO2 max, body weight, percent body fat, and 12-h fasting blood levels of cholesterol (CHOL), triglycerides (TG), high-density lipoprotein cholesterol (HDL-C), and low-density lipoprotein cholesterol (LDL-C). The average post-training increase in VO2 max for group H (0.56 l.min-1, 8.5 ml.min-1.kg-1) was not significantly greater than for group L (0.45 l.min-1, 6.5ml.min-1.kg-1). Significant reductions in percent body fat occurred in both groups. No statistically significant changes in CHOL, TG, HDL-C, LDL-C, CHOL/HDL-C, or HDL-C/LDL-C occurred in either group. However, changes in HDL-C after 18 wk of training were inversely correlated with pre-training levels.
LEVEL: A LANG: Eng SIRC ARTICLE NO: 108596

Goldberg, L. Elliot, D.L. Schutz, R.W. Kloster, F.E. Changes in lipid and lipoprotein levels after weight training. (Refs: 2 *JAMA: Journal of the American Medical Association (Chicago) 252(4), 27 Jul 1984, 504-506.*
ABST: Lipid and lipoprotein levels were studied in previously sedentary men (mean age, 33 years) and women (mean age, 27 years) undergoing 16 weeks of weight-training exercise. Tests at the end of the training period found favorable changes in

lipid and lipoprotein levels in previously sedentary men and women.
LEVEL: A LANG: Eng SIRC ARTICLE NO: 102780

Gorski, J. Wyplyw wysilku miesniowego na metabolizm tluszczow. (Effect of muscular exertion on lipid metabolism.) *Polski tygodnik lekarski (Warsaw) 39(9), 27 Feb 1984, 299-303.*
LEVEL: A LANG: Pol

Harting, G.H. Moore, C.E. Mitchell, R. Kappus, C.M. Relationship of menopausal status and exercise level to HDL-cholesterol in women. *Experimental aging research (Bar Harbor, Mich.) 10(1), Spring 1984, 13-18.*
ABST: This study examined the relationship between exercise habits, menopausal status and HDL cholesterol in 44 long distance runners, 47 joggers, and 45 relatively inactive women. The authors suggest endurance exercise by post-menopausal females may help prevent adverse lipid and lipoprotein changes which give rise to coronary heart disease risks.
LEVEL: A LANG: Eng SIRC ARTICLE NO: 102973

Haskell, W.L. The influence of exercise on the concentrations of triglyceride and cholesterol in human plasma. (Refs: 186) *Exercise and sport sciences reviews (Lexington, Mass.) 12, 1984, 205-244.*
ABST: This paper reviews the acute and chronic effects of exercise on the plasma concentration of lipids and lipoproteins; as well as how this influence might be mediated and the interactive effects of exercise with other determinants of lipoprotein concentration. The review focuses on the plasma cholesterol and triglyceride contents of specific lipoproteins and the changes they undergo with exercise. Triglyceride response to exercise is an acute response, probably resulting from increased lipoprotein lipase activity. The decrease in cholesterol seems to be a more chronic response to exercise. The major exercise effect on plasma cholesterol is an increase in high density lipoprotein-cholesterol, which is thought to protect against coronary heart disease.
LEVEL: A LANG: Eng SIRC ARTICLE NO: 096326

Haskell, W.L. Exercise-induced changes in plasma lipids and lipoproteins. (Refs: 63) *Preventive medicine (New York) 13(1), Jan 1984, 23-36.*
LEVEL: A LANG: Eng SIRC ARTICLE NO: 100899

Herbert, P.N. Bernier, D.N. Cullthane, E.M. Edelstein, L. Kantor, M.A. Thompson, P.D. High-density lipoprotein metabolism in runners and sedentary men. *JAMA. Journal of the American Medical Association (Chicago) 252(8), 24-31 Aug 1984, 1034-1037.*
ABST: The authors studied the high-density lipoprotein (HDL) metabolism of five trained men who ran 16 km daily and five inactive men. Runners were leaner and their aerobic exercise capacity was much greater. The lipid-rich HDL2 species accounted for a much higher proportion of the HDL in runners. Tracer studies of radioiodinated autologous HDL demonstrated that runners did not produce more HDL protein but rather catabolized less. The mean biologic half-life of HDL proteins was 6.2 days in the runners compared with 3.8 days in the sedentary men. The activity of lipoprotein lipase was 80 per cent higher in the postheparin plasma of the runners, whereas the activity of hepatic triglyceride hydrolase was 38 per cent lower. Thus, the prolonged survival of plasma HDL proteins in runners may result from augmented lipid transfer to HDL by lipoprotein lipase or

diminished HDL clearance by hepatic lipase.
LEVEL: A LANG: Eng SIRC ARTICLE NO: 104979

Higuchi, M. Hashimoto, I. Yamakawa, K. Tsuji, E. Nishimuta, M. Suzuki, S. Effects of exercise training on plasma high-densit lipoprotein cholesterol level at constant weight. *Clinical physiology (Oxford) 4(2), Apr 1984, 125-133.*
ABST: The authors' aim was to investigate whether or not elevations of plasma high-density lipoprotein cholesterol (HDL-Chol) as a result of exercise training were due to weight loss or physical training itself. 5 males, aged 28-31 years, followed a 4-week training program while maintaining their weight. The HDL-Chol level increased from 54 to 73 mg/dl and the ratio of low density lipoprotein decreased by 30.8%.
LEVEL: A LANG: Eng SIRC ARTICLE NO: 102785

Kiens, B. Vessby, B. Lithell, H. Further increase in high density lipoprotein in trained males after enhanced training. (Refs: 21) *European journal of applied physiology and occupational physiology (Berlin, FRG) 52(4), Jun 1984, 426-430.*
ABST: This study investigated whether a period of enhanced endurance training could affect the lipoproteins of well-trained subjects with initially high levels of serum HDL-cholesterol. Eight subjects were studied before, during and after 6 months of a progressively increasing endurance training program. The results indicate that this group of well-trained males with high levels of HDL further increased their HDL-cholesterol concentration by 5-15%. This difference was statistically significant.
LEVEL: A LANG: Eng SIRC ARTICLE NO: 097738

Lithell, H. Schele, R. Vessby, B. Jacobs, I. Lipoproteins, lipoprotein lipase, and glycogen after prolonged physical activit (Refs: 30) *Journal of applied physiology: respiratory, environmental and exercise physiology (Bethesda, Md.) 57(3), Sept 1984, 698-702.*
ABST: Sixteen soldiers were tested before and after a day of strenuous field maneuvers. Significant alterations in plasma lipoprotein levels and composition and muscle metabolism occurred with some changes requiring 3 to 5 days of recovery.
LEVEL: A LANG: Eng SIRC ARTICLE NO: 108932

Mondon, C.E. Dolkas, C.B. Tobey, T. Reaven, G.M. Causes of the triglyceride-lowering effect of exercise training in rats. (Refs: 35) *Journal of applied physiology: respiratory, environmental and exercise physiology (Bethesda, Md.) 57(5), Nov 1984, 1466-1471.*
LEVEL: A LANG: Eng SIRC ARTICLE NO: 108923

Nagao, N. Arie, J. Inomoto, T. Sawada, Y. Karatsu, K. Comparison of serum apoproteins between physically active and inactive groups. (Refs: 22) *Journal of sports medicine and physical fitness (Torino, Italy) 24(3), Sept 1984, 219-224.*
ABST: We investigated the effect of long-term exercise on serum TG, T-C, HDL-C apoprotein A-I and apoprotein A-II, as well as T-C/HDL-C and Apo A-I/Apo A-II ratios. The 94 subjects included 28 physically active middle-aged and older males and 17 age-, sex- matched controls who were physically inactive; 13 active young females (6 controls). A training requiring vigorous physical activity seemed to cause an increase in both HDL-C and Apo A-I and a decrease in the T-C/HDL-C ratio. Significant differences between the active and control groups were observed in young females as well as in middle-aged and older males, but not in

middle-aged females.
LEVEL: A LANG: Eng SIRC ARTICLE NO: 105487

Palazzuoli, V. De Stefano, R. Mondillo, S. Kristodhullu, A. Pallasini, A. Fini, F. Napolitano, M. Effetto dell'esercizio fisico sulle lipoproteine sieriche. (Effect of physical exercise on serum lipoprotein.) *Bollettino della societa italiana di cardiologia (Rome) 29(7/8), Jul/Aug 1984, 395-403.*
LEVEL: A LANG: It

Patsch, J.R. Patsch, W. Exercise, high density lipoproteins, and fat tolerance. *Comprehensive therapy (Harvard, Ma.) 10(2), Feb 1984, 29-37.*
LEVEL: A LANG: Eng SIRC ARTICLE NO: 100917

Rauramaa, R. Salonen, J.T. Kukkonen-Harjula, K. Seppaenen, K. Seppaelae, E. Vapaatalo, H. Huttunen, J.K. Effects of mild physical exercise on serum lipoproteins and metabolites of arachidonic acid: a controlled randomised trial in middle aged men. *British medical journal (clinical research) (London) 288(6417), 25 Feb 1984, 603-606.*
ABST: This paper explores the effect of exercise on biochemic risk factors for coronary disease in 31 middle aged men. The authors observe that in the exercising patients serum cholesterol concentrations increase 26% more in the high density lipoprotein susfraction two (HDL2) and decrease 31% more in the susfraction three (HDL3) and 9% more in the low density lipoprotein fraction than in the controls.
LEVEL: A LANG: Eng SIRC ARTICLE NO: 099260

Savard, R. Despres, J.P. Marcotte, M. Bouchard, C. Endurance training and glucose conversion into triglycerides in human fat cells. (Refs: 35) *Journal of applied physiology (Bethesda, Md.) 58(1), Jan 1985, 230-235.*
ABST: 24 sedentary subjects (11 men and 13 women) participated in a 20 week endurance training program using a bicycle ergometer. VO2 max and body density were measured and adipose tissue biopsies were analyzed for fat conversion from glucose. The male subjects showed significant decreases in body fat and significant increases in glucose conversion to triglycerides. The women had no significant changes in these areas.
LEVEL: A LANG: Eng SIRC ARTICLE NO: 108066

Scorpio, R. Rigsby, R.L. Thomas, D.R. Gardner, B.D. Regulation of fatty acid biosynthesis in rats by physical training. (Refs: 21) *Journal of applied physiology: respiratory, environmental and exercise physiology 56(4), Apr 1984, 1060-1064.*
ABST: Male rats were forced to swim for periods up to 90 min/day, 6 day/wk for approximately 11 wk. Hepatic fatty biosynthesis and acetyl-CoA carboxylase activities were lower in the exercised rats at the end of 11 wk than they were in untrained rats. Acutely exercised untrained rats exhibited the same lowered responses but these responses did not persist as long as those of acutely exercised trained rats. The authors implicate acetyl CoA carboxylase as a control site in the regulation of hepatic fatty acid biosynthesis by both physical training and acute exercise in rats.
LEVEL: A LANG: Eng SIRC ARTICLE NO: 096295

Seals, D.R. Allen, W.K. Hurley, B.F. Dalsky, G.P. Ehsani, A.A. Hagberg, J.M. Elevated high-density lipoprotein cholesterol levels in older endurance athletes. *American journal of cardiology (New York) 54(3), 1 Aug 1984, 390-393.*
ABST: Comparisons between 14 endurance trained masters athletes and age matched sedentary men

and young trained and untrained men found the masters athletes to have markedly higher high density lipoprotein cholesterol, and better cholesterol ratios.
LEVEL: A LANG: Eng SIRC ARTICLE NO: 104369

Stamford, B.A. Matter, S. Fell, R.D. Sady, S. Cresanta, M.K. Papanek, P. Cigarette smoking, physical activity, and alcohol consumption: relationship to blood lipids and lipoproteins in premenopausal females. (Refs: 27)*Metabolism, clinical and experimental (New York) 33(7), Jul 1984, 585-590.*
ABST: 164 premenopausal female subjects were tested. Relationships between blood lipid and lipoprotein levels as dependent variables and cigarette smoking, physical activity, and alcohol consumption were determined from partial regression analyses. Results suggest that cigarette smoking may attenuate the effects of chronic exercise and/or alcohol consumption, to raise HDL-C levels. Chronic exercise and alcohol consumption may also exert an additive effect, raising HDL-C level.
LEVEL: A LANG: Eng SIRC ARTICLE NO: 102831

Stamford, B.A. Matter, S. Fell, R.D. Sady, S. Papanek, P. Cresanta, M. Cigarette smoking, exercise and high density lipoprotein cholesterol. *Atherosclerosis (Amsterdam) 52(1), Jul 1984, 73-83.*
LEVEL: A LANG: Eng SIRC ARTICLE NO: 104375

Thomas, T.R. Adeniran, S.B. Etheridge, G.L. Effects of different running programs on VO2 max, percent fat, and plasma lipids (Refs: 30)*Canadian journal of applied sport sciences/Journal canadien des sciences appliquees au sport (Windsor, Ont.) 9(2), Jun 1984, 55-62.*
ABST: The purpose of this study was to determine the effects of interval and continuous running on factors associated with cardiovascular health in 59 young men and women. The experimental subjects trained three times a week for 12 weeks using either an interval (90% maximal heart rate) or a continuous (75% maximal heart rate) program. All programs utilized approximately 500 cal/session. Only the interval group improved their VO2 max compared to the control group. All experimental groups decreased in percent fat with no method found to be superior to the others in decreasing percent fat. There were no changes in plasma lipids between groups.
LEVEL: A LANG: Eng SIRC ARTICLE NO: 096302

Wanne, O. Viikari, J. Valimaki, I. Physical performance and serum lipids in 14 - 16-year-old trained, normally active, and inactive children. (Refs: 16)
CONF: Symposium of Paediatric Work Physiology (10th : 1981 : Joutsa, Finland).
NOTES: In, Ilmarinen, J. and Vaelimaeki, I. (eds.), Children and sport: paediatric work physiology, Berlin, Springer-Verlag, 1984, p. 241-246.
LEVEL: A LANG: Eng SIRC ARTICLE NO: 102839

Watson, M.L. Effects of mild exercise on serum lipoproteins and metabolites of arachidonic acid. (letter) *British medical journal (clinical research) (London) 288(6425), 21 Apr 1984, 1232.*
LEVEL: I LANG: Eng SIRC ARTICLE NO: 100934

GLYCOGEN

Guezemnec, C.Y. Ferre, P. Serrurier, B. Merino, D. Aymonod, M. Pesquies, P.C. Metabolic effects of testosterone during prolonged physical exercise and fasting. (Refs: 19)*European journal of applied physiology and occupational physiology (Heidelberg) 52(3), Apr 1984, 300-304.*
ABST: This study examined the effects of acute and chronic increases in levels of circulating testosterone on the energy metabolism of both fasting and exercising rats. In 72 h fasted rats both acute and chronic increases in testosterone were associated with significant decreases in blood alanine and lactate. Furthermore chronic elevation of testerone also increase muscle glycogen content in 72 h. fasted rats. After 7h of continuous treadmill running at 20m/min acute and chronic elevation of testosterone induced a significant decrease in blood alanine and a slight decrease in blood glucose. The authors conclude that increased levels of testosterone can induce clygoen supercompensation in the fed resting state but cannot counteract the exhaustion of muscle glycogen during running.
LEVEL: A LANG: Eng SIRC ARTICLE NO: 097726

James, D.E. Kraegen, E.W. The effect of exercise training on glycogen, glycogen synthase and phosphorylase in muscle and liver. (Refs: 22)*European journal of applied physiology and occupational physiology (Heidelberg) 52(3), Apr 1984, 276-281.*
ABST: This study examined whether changes in regulatory enzymes of glycogen metabolism occurs with training and whether these changes provide an explanation for the glycogen-sparing which results from exercise training. Endurance trained male rats had increases of 60-150% in glycogen synthase and phosphorylase and an increase of 50-70% in glycogen content in soleus but not in extensor digitorum longus (EDL) or liver. These results do not provide an explanation for the phenomenon of glycogen-sparing but are consistent with an improved capacity in intermediate muscle for improved glycogen mobilisation and repletion following training.
LEVEL: A LANG: Eng SIRC ARTICLE NO: 097730

Kono, N. Mineo, I. Sumi, S. Shimizu, T. Kang, J. Nonaka, K. Tarui, S. Metabolic basis of improved exercise tolerance: muscle phosphorylase deficiency after glucagon administration. *Neurology (New York) 34(11), Nov 1984, 1471-1476.*
LEVEL: A LANG: Eng

Vollestad, N.K. Vaage, O. Hermansen, L. Muscle glycogen depletion patterns in type I and subgroups of type II fibres during prolonged severe exercise in man. *Acta physiologica scandinavica (Stockholm) 122(4), Dec 1984, 433-441.*
ABST: The purpose of this study was to evaluate glycogen depletion of muscle fibre types I, II A, II AB and II B in 5 subjects during exhaustive exercise. From start of exercise, glycogen depletion rates were similar in type I and II A. A decrease of glycogen content in type II AB and finally in II B occurred only during the second part of exercise.
LEVEL: A LANG: Eng SIRC ARTICLE NO: 106814

LACTATE

Denis, C. Dormois, D. Lacour, J.R. Endurance training, VO2 max, and OBLA: a longitudinal study of two different age groups. (Refs: 45)*International journal of sports medicine (Stuttgart) 5(4), Aug 1984, 167-173.*
ABST: This study examined the effect of a 20-week training program of six middle-aged men (33-41 yrs) (GIT) and six young male subjects (19-21 yrs) (GIIT). Measurement of VO2 max, maximal work onset of blood lactate accumulation, absolute (OBLAW), and relative to MWL (OBLA per cent) were made on GIT and GIIT groups and on a third group (19-22 yrs) (GIIC). VO2 max which was initially similar in GIT and GIIT increased significantly by 8 per cent in GIT and by 19 per cent in GIIT. OBLAW increased significantly to the same level in the two groups (38 per cent and 42 per cent, respectively). OBLA per cent increases significantly (20 per cent) in GIT only.
LEVEL: A LANG: Eng SIRC ARTICLE NO: 104297

Dodd, S.L. Blood lactate removal during varying intensities of active recovery following supramaximal work. Eugene, Ore.: Microform Publications, University of Oregon, 1984. 1 microfiche : negative, ill. ; 11 x 15 cm.
NOTES: Thesis (Ph.D.) - Louisianna State University, 1982; (ix, 64 leaves); vita; includes bibliography.
LEVEL: A LANG: Eng UO84 237

Freminet, A. Minaire, Y. On the use of isotopic tracers for the study of lactate metabolism in vivo. (Refs: 80)
CONF: International Course on Physiology and Biochemistry of Exercise and Detraining (2nd : 1982 : Nice).
NOTES: In, Marconnet, P. (ed.) et al., Physiological chemistry of training and detraining, New York, Karger, c1984, p. 25-39.
LEVEL: A LANG: Eng RC1235 17596

Freund, H. Zouloumian, P. Enguelle, S.O. Lampert, E. Lactate kinetics after maximal exercise in man. (Refs: 40)
CONF: International Course on Physiology and Biochemistry of Exercise and Detraining (2nd : 1982 : Nice).
NOTES: In, Marconnet, P. (ed.) et al., Physiological chemistry of training and detraining, New York, Karger, c1984, p. 9-24.
ABST: This paper describes the development and applications of a two-compartment mathematical model which describes the observed lactate kinetics in man after maximal exercise on a bicycle ergometer. The two compartments are the active muscle mass (M) and the remaining body space (S). The model predicts different exponential patterns for the time evolution of lactate concentration in (M) and (S) during recovery. Experimentally, the prediction is supported. The model gives a dynamic view of the lactate disappearance during recovery from maximal exercise in each individual tested.
LEVEL: A LANG: Eng RC1235 17596

Froberg, K. Pedersen, P.K. Sex differences in endurance capacity and metabolic response in prolonged, heavy exercise. (Refs: 20)*European journal of applied physiology and occupational physiology (Berlin, FRG) 52(4), Jun 1984, 446-450.*
ABST: Six women and seven men performed bicycle ergometer exercise at 80% and 90% of their maximal oxygen uptakes until exhaustion. Women

exercised significantly longer than men at 80% VO2 max. There were no significant differences between the sexes at 90% VO2 max. The authors conclude that the women exercised longer at 80% VO2 max due to a sparing of glycogen in the middle phase of the exhaustive exercise.
LEVEL: A LANG: Eng SIRC ARTICLE NO: 097725

Gaesser, G.A. Brooks, G.A. Metabolic bases of excess post-exercise oxygen consumption: a review. (Refs: 129)*Medicine and science in sports and exercise 16(1), 1984, 29-43.*
ABST: This review attempts to clarify the metabolic basis of oxygen debt. Underlying biochemical, physiological and physical factors are found to play a role in the elevation of oxygen uptake after exercise. There does not appear to be a definitive reason for this phenomenon; however it is felt that O2 debt is an inapropriate term. The authors disprove earlier theories which placed a heavy emphasis on the role of lactic acid metabolism in excess post-exercise oxygen consumption.
LEVEL: A LANG: Eng SIRC ARTICLE NO: 091727

Graham, T.E. Mechanisms of blood lactate increase during exercise. *Physiologist (Bethesda, Md.) 27(4), Aug 1984, 299-303.*
LEVEL: I LANG: Eng SIRC ARTICLE NO: 104313

Hagberg, J.M. Physiological implications of the lactate threshold. (Refs: 53)*International journal of sports medicine (Stuttgart) Suppl. 5, Nov 1984, 106-109.*
CONF: International Congress on Sports and Health (1983 : Maastricht, Netherlands).
LEVEL: A LANG: Eng SIRC ARTICLE NO: 104317

Hogan, M.C. Welch, H.G. Effect of varied lactate levels on bicycle ergometer performance. (Refs: 34)*Journal of applied physiology: respiratory, environmental and exercise physiology (Bethesda, Md.) 57(2), Aug 1984, 507-513.*
ABST: Six male subjects exercised on a bicycle ergometer at various levels of inspired 02 fraction during the initial 5-min work period. This task was followed by a 4-min rest and exercise to exhaustion. Whereas power output remained the same during the initial stage, the variations in inspired 02 fraction produced significantly different mean blood lactate and hydrogen ion concentrations at the start of the performance task. It appears that muscle performance is significantly affected by alterations in endogenously produced lactate and hydrogen ion concentration.
LEVEL: A LANG: Eng SIRC ARTICLE NO: 108356

Hurby, B.F. Hagberg, J.M. Allen, W.K. Seals, D.R. Young, J.C. Cuddikee, R.W. Holloszy, J.O. Effect of training on blood lactate levels during submaximal exercise. (Refs: 31)*Journal of applied physiology: respiratory, environmental and exercise physiology (Bethesda, Md.) 56(5), May 1984, 1260-1264.*
ABST: This study examined the effect of a 12 wk training program on blood lactate levels during submaximal exercise. Eight men performed high-intensity interval training on a bicycle ergometer 3 days/wk and continuous running for 40 min 3 days/wk. Training elicited a 26% increase in maximum oxygen uptake. Lactate concentrations at a given exercise intensity were significantly lower after training as opposed to before training. The results also indicate that the training adaptations which result in an increase in VO2 max are, to some degree, independent of those responsible for the lower blood lactate levels during submaximal

exercise.
LEVEL: A LANG: Eng SIRC ARTICLE NO: 097729

Juto, J.E. Lundberg, C. Nasal mucosa reaction, catecholamines and lactate during physical exercise. *Acta otolaryngologica (Stockholm) 98(5/6), Nov/Dec 1984, 533-542.*
ABST: This study examined the effects of exercise on mucosal congestion and blood concentrations of lactate, epinephrine and nor-epinephrine. Of 7 subjects, 6 showed mucosal decongestion during exercise. An increase of nor-epinephrine concentration was observed when half of the mucosal decongestion ability was utilized, while concentration of both lactate and epinephrine did not rise until almost maximal decongestion was established.
LEVEL: A LANG: Eng SIRC ARTICLE NO: 106578

Lavoie, J.M. Levesque, R. Acide lactique et seuil anaerobie. (Refs: 6)*Revue de l'entraineur (Montreal) avr/juin 1984, 11-13.*
LEVEL: I LANG: Fr SIRC ARTICLE NO: 094608

Moritani, T. Tanaka, H. Yoshida, T. Ishii, C. Yoshida, T. Shindo, M. Relationship between myoelectric signals and blood lactate during incremental forearm exercise. (Refs: 37)*American journal of physical medicine (Baltimore) 63(3), Jun 1984, 122-132.*
ABST: Five men performed incremental isometric forearm exercise until volitional fatigue. The results indicate that venous lactate concentration was highly correlated with integrated electromyography measurements (IEMG) during the incremental exercise. This finding was strongly evident after the lactate threshold had been surpassed. The authors conclude that analysis of myo-electric signals may provide a non-invasive measure of lactate threshold after which the dynamic equilibrium of lactate production and utilization becomes unbalanced during incremental forearm exercise.
LEVEL: A LANG: Eng SIRC ARTICLE NO: 097747

Sahlin, K. Henriksson, J. Buffer capacity and lactate accumulation in skeletal muscle of trained and untrained men. *Acta physiologica scandinavica (Stockholm) 122(3), Nov 1984, 331-339.*
LEVEL: A LANG: Eng

Seals, D.R. Hurley, B.F. Schultz, J. Hagberg, J.M. Endurance training in older men and women. II. Blood lactate response to submaximal exercise. (Refs: 14)*Journal of applied physiology: respiratory, environmental and exercise physiology (Bethesda, Md.) 57 (4), Oct 1984, 1030-1033.*
ABST: Eleven older people aged 61 to 65 exercised for 6 months at low intensity and for a further 6 months at a higher intensity. The low intensity exercise yielded significant improvements in lactate while the higher intensity exercise resulted in further improvements, which were however less marked.
LEVEL: A LANG: Eng SIRC ARTICLE NO: 108943

Tan, M.H. Watson-Wright, B.W. Hood, D. Sopper, M. Currie, D. Belcastro, A.N. Pierce, G. Blood lactate disappearance at various intensities of recovery exercise. (Refs: 21)*Journal of applied physiology: respiratory, environmental and exercise physiology (Bethesda, Md.) 57(5), Nov 1984, 1462-1465.*
LEVEL: A LANG: Eng SIRC ARTICLE NO: 108918

Tesch, P.A. Karlsson, J. Effects of exhaustive, isometric training on lactate accumulation in different muscle fiber types. (Refs: 18)*International journal of sports medicine (Stuttgart, FRG) 5(2), Apr

1984, 89-91.*
ABST: Four physically active men took part in a 6-week training program. They performed three sustained leg press contractions at 50 percent maximal isometric strength (MIS) to exhaustion 3-4 times a week. Before training and following performance of 50 percent MIS to exhaustion, muscle biopsies were obtained from m. vastus lateralis for subsequent lactate analysis on freeze-dried fiber fragments. Post-training biopsies were taken (a) after a contraction performed at the same tension level and for the same time period and (b) after an exhaustive contraction held at 50 percent of the post-training MIS. Prior to training, lactate concentration in fast-twitch (FT) and slow-twitch (ST) muscle fibers averaged 29.8 and 28.7 mmol.kg-1 w.w, respectively. After training the values were 16.7 (FT) and 14.1 (ST). Lactate concentration following exhaustive contraction were 21.3 (FT) and 17.8 (ST).
LEVEL: A LANG: Eng SIRC ARTICLE NO: 108523

Yoshida, T. Effect of exercise duration during incremental exercise on the determination of anaerobic threshold and the onse of blood lactate accumulation. (Refs: 24)*European journal of applied physiology and occupational physiology (Berlin) 53(3), Dec 1984, 196-199.*
ABST: To determine the effect of the duration of incremental exercise on the point at which arterial blood lactate concentration (HLa) increases above the resting value (anaerobic threshold: AT) and on the point at which HLa reaches a constant value of 4 mM (onset of blood lactate accumulation: OBLA), eight male students performed two different kinds of incremental exercise. A comparison of arterial HLa and venous HLa was made under both conditions. It was concluded that when arterial blood was used, there was no effect of duration of workload increase in an incremental exercise test on the determination of the AT and OBLA expressed in VO2. On the other hand, when venous HLa was used these points might be overestimated when a fast increase in workload, such as the 1-min test, is used.
LEVEL: A LANG: Eng SIRC ARTICLE NO: 104397

Yoshida, T. Effect of dietary modifications on lactate threshold and onset of blood lactate accumulation during incremental exercise. (Refs: 27)*European journal of applied physiology and occupational physiology (Berlin) 53(3), Dec 1984, 200-205.*
ABST: Five healthy male subjects were put on a mixed diet for 3 days, followed by 4 days of a low carbohydrate diet, and then 3 days of a high carbohydrate diet. Following each type of diet, the subjects performed a progressive bicycle exercise test, during which concentrations of HLa, pyruvate, FFA, and glucose were analyzed. It was concluded that the dietary modifications used in this study had no influence on lactate threshold but did affect the point of OBLA. Therefore, dietary conditions should be considered when OBLA is determined using a fixed 4-mM HLa method.
LEVEL: A LANG: Eng SIRC ARTICLE NO: 104188

METABOLIC ENZYMES

Cucinell, S.A. Wan, S. O'Brien, J. Wade, C. Amylase excretion after exercise. *American journal of gastroenterology (New York) 79(8), Aug 1984, 619-622.*
ABST: Increase in amylase excretion in the urine in response to 8 days of aerobic running is delayed

until after the athletes have rested for 24-48 h. In contrast, the amylase creatinine ratio is increased immediately after intense short-term exercise.
LEVEL: A LANG: Eng SIRC ARTICLE NO: 104296

Gimenez, M. Florentz, M. Serum enzyme variations in men during an exhaustive 'square-wave' endurance exercise test. (Refs: 3 *European journal of applied physiology and occupational physiology (Heidelberg) 52(2), Jan 1984, 219-224.*
ABST: The variations in the activities of seven serum enzymes (CK, PHI, LDH, MDH, ALD, GOT, GPT) were studied before, during and after a 'square wave' endurance exercise test on bicycle ergometer. The aim of the study was to verify increases in serum enzyme activity as a result of an exhaustive exercise, and any differences in these activities which might occur between trained and untrained individuals. Particular enzymes were indicated, from the results, as representative of 'intense muscular exercise' and 'clearly distinguish trained from untrained subjects'. The effects of haemoconcentration and arterial blood acidosis upon enzyme activity was also considered. A brief review of other studies done in the area of serum enzyme measurement during exercise was included in the discussion.
LEVEL: A LANG: Eng SIRC ARTICLE NO: 096241

Goldberg, D.I. The effect of estrogen on lipoprotein lipase activity in the rat heart. Eugene, Ore.: Microform Publications, University of Oregon, 1984. 2 microfiches : negative, ill. ; 11 x 15 cm.
NOTES: Thesis (Ph.D.) - Temple University, 1982; (vi, 148 leaves); leaf 77 missing; includes bibliography.
LEVEL: A LANG: Eng UO84 277-278

Gollnick, P.D. Moore, R.L. Riedy, M. Quintinskie, J.J. Significance of skeletal muscle oxidative enzyme changes with endurance training and detraining. (Refs: 45)
CONF: International Course on Physiology and Biochemistry of Exercise and Detraining (2nd : 1982 : Nice).
NOTES: In, Marconnet, P. (ed.) et al., Physiological chemistry of training and detraining, New York, Karger, c1984, p. 215-229.
LEVEL: A LANG: Eng RC1235 17596

Kettunen, P. Kala, R. Rehunen, S. CK and CK-MB in skeletal muscle of athletes and in serum after thoracic contusion in sport (Refs: 10)*Journal of sports medicine and physical fitness (Torino) 24(1), Mar 1984, 21-25.*
ABST: Creatine kinase and its isoenzyme were measured in 9 national hockey players before and after a match. Before the match the hockey players had higher creatine kinase levels than normal untrained subjects. Creatine kinase activity decreased during exercise. With the data obtained from hockey players the authors compared creatine kinase, ASAT and ALAT enzyme activites in baseball players, boxers, judoists and weightlifters. Creatine kinase was found to increase after exercise. Isoenzyme levels in 2 boxers indicated cardiac muscle injury.
LEVEL: A LANG: Eng SIRC ARTICLE NO: 099248

Kihlstroem, M. Salminen, A. Vihko, V. Prednisolone decreases exercise-induced acid hydrolase response in mouse skeletal muscle. (Refs: 23)*European journal of applied physiology and occupational physiology (Berlin, W.G.) 53(1), 1984, 53-56.*
ABST: Male mice were subjected to exhaustive treadmill exercise. 3 and 6 days after the exertion,

quadriceps femoris muscles were examined histologically and analyzed for acid hydrolases in order to follow the degree and progress of injuries. Prednisolone (PRED), an anti-inflammatory corticosteroid, was given to some of the animals. The activities of both arylsulphatase and B-glycuronidase increased significantly in the exercise control group after 3 and 6 days. The increase in activity correlated with fibre necrosis and an abundant infiltration of inflammatory cells, and was greatest after 3 days. After 6 days the inflammatory response decreased and regenerating muscle fibres were seen. PRED decreased the exercise-induced acid hydrolase response. PRED also diminished degeneration and inflammation.
LEVEL: A LANG: Eng SIRC ARTICLE NO: 104328

Lijnen, P. Groeseneken, D. Fagard, R. Staessen, J. Amery, A. Effect of indomethacin on active and inactive renin in sodium-replete men at rest and during exercise. *Journal of laboratory and clinical medicine (St. Louis) 103(5), May 1984, 677-683.*
ABST: This study examines the effects of the administration of indomethacin on active and inactive renin in nine men with sodium repletion, at rest and during exercise. Indomethacin reduces total, active, and inactive renin levels. Reductions in the plasma concentrations of immunoreactive prostaglandin E2, prostaglandin F2, alpha, and 13,14-dihydro-15-keto-prostaglandin F2 alpha, are also observed.
LEVEL: A LANG: Eng SIRC ARTICLE NO: 100909

Mayer, S.J. Clarkson, P.M. Serum creatine kinase levels following isometric exercise. (Refs: 15)*Research quarterly for exercise & sport (Reston, Va.) 55(2), Jun 1984, 191-194.*
ABST: This investigation studied the effect of varying numbers of isometric muscular contractions on creatine kinase (CK) efflux from skeletal muscle. Nine college-age males performed four series of tests. The first series involved familiarization with equipment and baseline knee extension maximal voluntary contraction (MVC) measurements. In the second series the subjects performed 60s of isometric work at 40% of MVC followed 60s rest until exhaustion (60:60). In the third and fourth series the subjects performed the same amount of work as in the 60:60 series but the work/rest ratio was 15:15 or 30:30. The highest CK efflux occurred in the 60:60 series followed by the 30:30 series and then the 15:15 series. The authors suggest that CK efflux may be influenced by blood pressure.
LEVEL: A LANG: Eng SIRC ARTICLE NO: 096279

Scorpio, R. Rigsby, R.L. Thomas, D.R. Gardner, B.D. Regulation of fatty acid biosynthesis in rats by physical training. (Refs: 21)*Journal of applied physiology: respiratory, environmental and exercise physiology 56(4), Apr 1984, 1060-1064.*
ABST: Male rats were forced to swim for periods up to 90 min/day, 6 day/wk for approximately 11 wk. Hepatic fatty biosynthesis and acetyl-CoA carboxylase activities were lower in the exercised rats at the end of 11 wk than they were in untrained rats. Acutely exercised untrained rats exhibited the same lowered responses but these responses did not persist as long as those of acutely exercised trained rats. The authors implicate acetyl CoA carboxylase as a control site in the regulation of hepatic fatty acid biosynthesis by both physical training and acute exercise in rats.
LEVEL: A LANG: Eng SIRC ARTICLE NO: 096295

Spitler, D.L. Alexander, W.C. Hoffler, G.W. Doerr, D.F. Buchanan, P. Haptoglobin and serum

enzymatic response to maximal exercise in relation to physical fitness. (Refs: 30)*Medicine and science in sports and exercise (Indianapolis) 16(4), Aug 1984, 366-370.*
ABST: Muscle enzymatic and hemolytic responses following a progressive cycle-ergometer test to maximal aerobic capacity were studied in 12 women and 12 men, aged 27 to 55 yr, who had been previously assigned to 'high' and 'low' fitness group. Venous blood samples were obtained at rest prior to the cycle test, immediately following maximal effort, and 1, 2, 4, 6 and 24 h post exercise. The samples were analyzed for hematocrit (Hct), hemoglobin (Hb), lactate dehydrogenase (LDH), serum glutamic oxalacetic transaminase (SGOT), creatine phosphokinase (CK), CK isoenzymes, and haptoglobin (Hapt). Hemoglobin and Hct were the only variables to rise significantly (P0.05) following exercise, and at all sampling times were significantly lower in the women compared with the men; CK was constituted in the MM isoenzyme band at all times; and Hapt levels were significantly lower in high-fitness men and women as compared with low-fitness men and women.
LEVEL: A LANG: Eng SIRC ARTICLE NO: 102830

Toncsev, H. Frenkl, R. Studies on the lysosomal enzyme system of the liver in rats undergoing swimming training. (Refs: 11) *International journal of sports medicine (Stuttgart) 5(3), Jun 1984, 152-155.*
ABST: Lysosomal acid phosphatase, beta-glucuronidase, and cathepsin-D were studied in liver cell fractions of rats regularly exercised by swimming. On the 21st day of the training, enzyme activities in the extralysosomal fraction and in the lysosomal fraction were higher and lower, respectively, than in the untrained controls. On the 40th day an increased enzyme activity was found in both fractions. By the end of the training period (54th and 80th days), a slightly decreased activity was recorded in both fractions. Lysosomal membrane permeability for enzymes was higher during the first period of the training, in particular when estimated under hypotonic conditions. Regular swimming training or 12-day treatment by ACTH stabilized the membrane of the liver lysosomes.
LEVEL: A LANG: Eng SIRC ARTICLE NO: 104384

PROTEINS

Butterfield, G.E. Calloway, D.H. Physical activity improves protein utilization in young men. *British journal of nutrition (London) 51(2), Mar 1984, 171-184.*
ABST: This study concludes that physical activity affects protein utilization negatively by increasing sweat and faecal N losses, and positively by supporting increased energy intake.
LEVEL: A LANG: Eng SIRC ARTICLE NO: 100773

Dufaux, B. Order, U. Geyer, H. Hollmann, W. C-reactive protein serum concentrations in well-trained athletes. (Refs: 27) *International journal of sports medicine (Stuttgart, FRG) 5(2), Apr 1984, 102-106.*
ABST: To evaluate the effect of physical training on the C-reactive protein (CRP) levels, a sensitive enzyme immunoassay was developed and used to assess the basal CRP concentrations in 356 male and 103 female athletes, who trained at least 4 times per week in various disciplines, in 45 male

and 40 female untrained controls, and in 35 elderly coronary patients. In male athletes the lowest CRP values were found in swimmers (median: 102 ng/ml), which were signicantly lower than those of male controls (median: 502 ng/ml). CRP levels in middle-and long-distance runners (median: 315 ng/ml), racing cyclists (median: 660 ng/ml), and soccer players (median: 660 ng/ml) did not differ significantly from those of the controls. In female athletes the lowest CRP concentrations were also found in swimmers (median: 110 ng/ml) which were significantly lower than those of the female controls (median: 396 ng/ml). This results suggest that training induces a suppressive effect upon CRP, responsible for the low serum levels in athletes (particularly swimmers) when compared to controls. CRP has a broad bacteriostatic action, hence low CRP levels intensively training athletes could be implicated in an increased susceptibility for infections.
LEVEL: A SIRC ARTICLE NO: 108526

Edwards, R.J. Harrison, M.H. Intravascular volume and protein responses to running exercise. (Refs: 28)*Medicine and science in sports and exercise (Indianapolis) 16(3), June 1984, 247-255.*
ABST: The roles of posture and mean skin temperature (T) in determining intravascular volume and protein responses to running exercise were examined in 12 male subjects. Moving from a sitting to a standing position before exercise was always accompanied by a decrease in blood volume (BV), as indicated by increases in the hematocrit and hemoglobin concentration. Althoug neither the onset of running nor alterations in T during runing caused any further consistent change in BV, there was an acceleration of the rate of which protein entered the intravascular space. At the end of exercise and in recovery this led to an augmentation of intravascular protein. It is concluded that intravascular volume responses to running exercise are determined by the accompanying postural hemoconcentration, and that running per se and any imposed thermal stress have minimal effects on BV thereafter.
LEVEL: A LANG: Eng SIRC ARTICLE NO: 108593

Magnus, P. Borresen, A.-L. Opstad, P.K. Bugge, J.F. Berg, K. Increase in the ratio of serum levels of apolipoproteins A-I an A-II during prolonged physical strain and calorie deficiency. (Refs: 13)*European journal of applied physiology and occupational physiology (Berlin, W.G.) 53(1), 1984, 21-24.*
ABST: Effects of four days of intense physical activity on serum concentrations of total triglycerides, total cholesterol and apolipoproteins A-I, A-II, and B were studied in 35 well-trained young men. Serum total triglyceride levels decreased to 70 per cent of baseline levels after 24 h, and fell further to 50 per cent of baseline levels after 4 days. Serum levels of total cholesterol fell steadily to about 80 per cent of baseline levels on the 4th day. Apo-B levels fell to 85 per cent of baseline levels after 24 h, and remained at that level. Apo A-I fell to about 90 per cent, and apo A-II to about 80 per cent of baseline levels, causing a significant increase in the ratio of apo A-I to A-II.
LEVEL: A LANG: Eng SIRC ARTICLE NO: 104340

Neumann, G. Schubert, I. Wulf, E. Zimmer, A. A haptoglobin dinamikaja hosszu ideig tarto allokepessegi terhelesek utan. (On haptoglobin dynamics after long-lasting endurance exercise.) (Refs: 37)*Sportorvosi szemle/Hungarian review of sports medicine (Budapest) 25(1), 1984, 7-26.*

ABST: The haptoglobin concentration determined by laser nephelometry is lower in untrained runners than in trained ones or in trained racing cyclists. Haptoglobin levels after long term endurance running dropped by 44 to 82 per cent of pre-start values. The haptoglobin drop depends on the kind of work loads and compared to cycling it is greater after running. The influence of the haptoglobin decrease (haemolysis) on the connective tissue by athletic stress is also discussed.
LEVEL: A LANG: Hun SIRC ARTICLE NO: 095678

Plante, P.D. Houston, M.E. Effects of concentric and eccentric exercise on protein catabolism in man. (Refs: 32) *International journal of sports medicine (Stuttgart) 5(4), Aug 1984, 174-178.*
ABST: To test the effects of different modes of exercise on indices of protein catabolism, eight adult males on a meat-free diet performed single 60-min bouts of concentric and eccentric cycle ergometer exercise in two 7-day periods. The excretion of 3-methylhistidine, creatinine, and urea in 24 h urine samples was constant over the 2 weeks in which exercise was performed. Compared to pre-exercise values, the concentrations of 3-methylhistidien, creatinine, and urea were unchanged in serum samples obtained immediately after and for up to 48 h following eccentric exercise. However, serum urea concentration was elevated by 18 per cent and 21 per cent in samples obtained immediately and 1 h after concentric exercise only.
LEVEL: A LANG: Eng SIRC ARTICLE NO: 104358

Plante, R.I. Houston, M.E. Exercise and protein catabolism in women. *Annals of nutrition and metabolism (Basel) 28(2), 1984 123-129.*
ABST: 8 sedentary young women were tested over 11 days while performing single bouts of prolonged submaximal and intermittent supraximal exercise. 3 - methylhistidine urea and creatinine levels remained constant while plasma urea concentration was elevated following exercise. Acute exercise appears to have a minimal effect on protein metabolism and does not lead to significant changes in myofibrillar protein degradation in young women.
LEVEL: A LANG: Eng SIRC ARTICLE NO: 099259

Poortmans, J.R. Protein turnover and amino acid oxidation during and after exercise. (Refs: 84)
CONF: International Course o Physiology and Biochemistry of Exercise and Detraining (2nd : 1982 : Nice).
NOTES: In, Marconnet, P. (ed.) et al., Physiological chemistry of training and detraining, New York, Karger, c1984, p. 130-147.
LEVEL: A LANG: Eng RC1235 17596

Roxin, L.-E. Venge, P. Friman, G. Variations in serum myoglobin after a 2-min isokinetic exercise test and the effects of training. (Refs: 20)*European journal of applied physiology and occupational physiology (Berlin, W.G.) 53(1), 1984, 43-47.*
ABST: Serum-myoglobin was measured after the completion of three different types of exercise (dynamic, isometric, and isokinetic). The maximal rises in serum-myoglobin levels were 20 percent, 70 percent, and 300 percent, respectively. On the basis of this finding a 2-min isokinetic test was developed. Fourteen healthy men peformed the 2-min test. Blood lactate increased on average eight times with maximal levels obtained 4 min after completed work. S-myoglobin was raised approximately five times after 2 h. The rise in S-myoglobin was significantly related to the loss in

muscle strength during the test. After a training period of 3 weeks comprising 4 min of maximal isokinetic exercise three times a week the rise in S-myoglobin after a 2-min isokinetic test was reduced.
LEVEL: A LANG: Eng SIRC ARTICLE NO: 104364

Rozenek, R. Stone, M.H. Protein metabolism related to athletes. (Refs: 29)*National Strength & Conditioning Association journal (Lincoln, Neb.) 6(2), Apr/May 1984, 42-45;62.*
LEVEL: I LANG: Eng SIRC ARTICLE NO: 094623

Saartok, T. Steroid receptors in two types of rabbit skeletal muscle. (Refs: 45)*International journal of sports medicine (Stuttgart) 5(3), Jun 1984, 130-136.*
ABST: The presence of the cytosolic androgen, glucocorticoid, and estrogen receptors was verified by saturation analysis showing low-capacity, high-affinity binding for the steroid-receptor complexes, specific for each class of steroids. Comparisons of fast-twitch (the gastrocnemius/plantaris complex) and slow-twitch (soleus) muscles revealed that the latter contained higher concentrations (expressed per g of tissue wet weight) of glucocorticoid and estrogen receptors, but not of androgen receptor. Expressed per mg of soluble protein, the slow-twitch muscle contained higher concentrations of all three receptors, but when related to the concentration of DNA, only the concentration of estrogen receptor was higher in the slow-twitch muscle.
LEVEL: A LANG: Eng SIRC ARTICLE NO: 104365

PROTEINS - AMINO ACIDS

Drake, M. Stimulate muscle growth with amino acids. *Muscle digest (San Gabriel, Calif.) 8(4), Aug 1984, 18-19;43;47.*
LEVEL: B LANG: Eng SIRC ARTICLE NO: 104302

Hatfield, F.C. Amino acids: the essence of life. *Muscle & fitness (Woodland Hills, Calif.) 45(1), Jan 1984, 44-45;137-140.*
LEVEL: B LANG: Eng SIRC ARTICLE NO: 096248

Lowry, S.F. Horowitz, G.D. Rose, D. Brennan, M.F. Influence of nutritional status on exertion-induced forearm amino acid metabolism in normal man. *Journal of surgical research: clinical and laboratory investigation (New York) 36(5), May 1984, 438-445.*
LEVEL: A LANG: Eng SIRC ARTICLE NO: 102798

Wolfe, R.R. Wolfe, M.H. Nadel, E.R. Shaw, J.H.F. Isotopic determination of amino acid-urea interactions in exercise in human *Journal of applied physiology: respiratory, environmental and exercise physiology (Bethesda, Md.) 56(1), Jan 1984, 221-229.*
ABST: Previous studies found that with exercise there was an increase in leucine oxidation, but no increase in urea production. This was confirmed in this study. The authors concluded that the production of urea reflected the net protein catabolism, but that transamination reactions may have resulted in the regeneration of other amino acids.
LEVEL: A LANG: Eng SIRC ARTICLE NO: 096310

TESTING

Astrand, P.O. Principles in ergometry and their implications in sports practice. (Refs: 11)*Sports medicine (Auckland) 1(1), Jan/Feb 1984, 1-5.*
ABST: This article provides an overview of recent

research and principles in ergometry in sports practice. The author states that ergometry is usually associated with measurements or prediction of the capacity and efficiency of the oxygen transport system. The related factors which are reviewed are: specificity of training, the concept of anaerobic threshold, and fibre types. Also, tests of aerobic power are reviewed with respect to their advantages and disadvantages. The author recommends repeated submaximal exercise testing, in general, as a decline in heart rate, at a given workload, may be associated with an improved maximal aerobic power.
LEVEL: A LANG: Eng SIRC ARTICLE NO: 094587

Carswell, H. New arm ergometer is sport specific. *Physician and sportsmedicine (Minneapolis, Minn.) 12(6), Jun 1984, 61.*
LEVEL: B LANG: Eng SIRC ARTICLE NO: 094591

de Bruyn-Prevost, P. Sturbois, X. Physiological response of girls to aerobic and anaerobic endurance tests. (Refs: 4)*Journa of sports medicine and physical fitness (Torino, Italy) 24(2), Jun 1984, 149-154.*
ABST: Physiological response to an aerobic and an anaerobic test on a bicycle ergometer was investigated in a group of 70 girls and 74 boys. The aerobic test uses a progressively increasing load. The maximal values of working capacity and VO2 max are lower for the girls even if expressed per kilogram of body weight. The anaerobic endurance test (a sprint against a load of 350 watts for the girls and 400 watts for the boys) gives similar results for girls and boys when the values are expressed per kg of body weight. Factorial analysis allows to compare the response to both tests and shows that the response to aerobic and anaerobic exercises are not necessarily related and suggest that the two tests are necessarily to determine physical fitness.
LEVEL: A LANG: Eng SIRC ARTICLE NO: 102765

Ennis, P. The test Conconi. *Velo-news (Brattleboro, Vt.) 13(18), 14 Dec 1984, 4-6.*
LEVEL: I LANG: Eng SIRC ARTICLE NO: 103095

Massicotte, D. Hillaire-Marcel, C. Ledoux, M. Peronnet, F. The natural isotope tracing with 13C: a non-invasive method for studying the metabolism during exercise. (Refs: 5)*Canadian journal of applied sport sciences/Journal canadien des sciences appliquees au sport (Windsor, Ont.) 9(3), Sept 1984, 164.*
LEVEL: I LANG: Eng SIRC ARTICLE NO: 102801

Weicker, H. Haegele, H. Kornes, B. Werner, A. Determination of alanine, lactate, pyruvate, B-hydroxybutyrate, and acetoacetate by flow injection analysis (FIA). (Refs: 19)*International journal of sportsmedicine 5(1), Feb 1984, 47-54.*
ABST: The purpose of this study was to apply the flow injection analysis (FIA) system to other NAD or NADH-dependent reactions which provide information about metabolic regulation during exercise. The FIA assays, for all the substances tested, had higher sampling rates, lower reagent consumptions, lower coefficients of variation, better reproducibilities, and greater consistency of duplicates than manual enzyme methods.
LEVEL: A LANG: Eng SIRC ARTICLE NO: 093137

Westerterp, K.R. de Boer, J.O. Saris, W.H.M. Schoffelen, P.F.M. ten Hoor, F. Measurement of energy expenditure using doubly labelled water. (Refs: 10)*International journal of sports medicine (Stuttgart) Suppl. 5, Nov 1984, 74-75.*

CONF: International Congress on Sports and Health (1983 : Maastricht, Netherlands).
LEVEL: A LANG: Eng SIRC ARTICLE NO: 104392

PHYSIOLOGY - EXERCISE

1984 American College of Sports Medicine Annual Meeting abstracts. Indianapolis: American College of Sports Medicine, 1984. xx 109 p. (Medicine and science in sports and exercise 16(2), 1984.)
CONF: American College of Sports Medicine. Annual Meeting (1984 : San Diego).
CORP: American College of sports Medicine.
LEVEL: A LANG: Eng

Abraham, F.A. Epstein, Y. Blumenthal, M. The scotopic threshold of the human retina during static physical effort. *Ophthalmic research (Basel) 16(6), 1984, 322-324.*
LEVEL: A LANG: Eng

Alexander, S. Physiologic and biochemical effects of exercise. *Clinical biochemistry (Toronto) 17(2), Apr 1984, 126-131.*
LEVEL: I LANG: Eng

Brancazio, P.J. Sport science. Physical laws and optimum performance. New York: Simon and Schuster, c1984. 400 p. : ill.
NOTES: Bibliography: p. 383-386.
LEVEL: I LANG: Eng ISBN: 0-671-45584-2 LC CARD: 83-20152 RC1235 20729

Chien, I.-H. The effects of professional training on physiological and psychological measures in physical education majors (III). *Asian journal of physical education (Taipei, Taiwan) 7(3), Oct 1984, 55-56.*
LEVEL: I LANG: Eng Chi SIRC ARTICLE NO: 102845

Dehn, M.M. Blomqvist, C.G. Mitchell, J.H. Clinical exercise performance. (Refs: 30)*Clinics in sports medicine (Philadelphia 3(2), Apr 1984, 319-332.*
ABST: This paper discusses the key concepts of exercise performance as they relate to the practise of clinical medicine. The authors discuss types of exercise, skeletal muscle physiology, maximal oxygen uptake, myocardial oxygen demand and supply, and the neural regulation of the cardiovascular response to exercise.
LEVEL: A LANG: Eng SIRC ARTICLE NO: 094593

Fox, E.L. Physiology of exercise and physical fitness. (Refs: 184)
NOTES: In, Strauss, R.H. (ed.), Sports medicine, Philadelphia ; Toronto, Saunders, 1984, p. 381-456.
LEVEL: A LANG: Eng RC1210 17196

Lamb, D.R. Physiology of exercise: responses and adaptations. 2nd ed. New York: Macmillan, c1984. xx, 489 p. : ill.
NOTES: Includes bibliographies.
LEVEL: A LANG: Eng ISBN: 0-02-367210-2 LC CARD: 82-9886 RC1220.E9 18972

Ljunghall, S. Joborn, H. Benson, L. Fellstroem, B. Wide, L. Akerstrom, G. Effects of physical exercise on serum calcium and parathyroid hormone. *European journal of clinical investigation (Oxford) 14(6), Dec 1984, 469-473.*
LEVEL: A LANG: Eng

Matlina, E. Effects of physical activity and other types of stress on catecholamine metabolism in

various animal species. *Journal of neural transmission (Wien) 60(1), 1984, 11-18.*
LEVEL: A LANG: Eng

Nasolodin, V.V. Obmen mikroelementov pri tiazheloi fizicheskoi rabote. (Trace element metabolism during strenuous physical work.) *Gigiena i sanitariia (Moskva) 6, Jun 1984, 81-83.*
LEVEL: A LANG: Rus

Payne, F.E. The physiology of physical fitness. (Refs: 8)
NOTES: In, Birrer, R.B. (ed.), Sports medicine for the primary car physician, Norwalk, Conn., Appleton-Century-Crofts, c1984, p. 42-54.
LEVEL: I LANG: Eng RC1210 17030

Pimental, N.A. Sawka, M.N. Billings, D.S. Trad, L.A. Physiological responses to prolonged upperbody exercise. (Refs: 30) *Medicine and science in sports and exercise (Indianapolis) 16(4), Aug 1984, 360-365.*
ABST: Nine males, with a peak oxygen uptake of 49 plus or minus 7 for cycle (CY) and 35 plus or minus 6 ml.min-1.kg-1 for arm crank (AC) exercise, completed four 60-min exercise tests. The subjects performed AC and CY exercise at the same absolute (ABS) oxygen uptake (1.6 l.min-1) and at the same relative (REL) percent of ergometer-specific peak oxygen uptake (60%). During the ABS tests, AC exercise elicited significantly greater heart rate (HR), ventilatory equivalnet of oxygen (Ve.Vo2-1), blood lactate (La), and percent decrease in plasma volume (PV) than CY exercise. During the REL tests, HR was lower and VE.VO2-1 was higher for AC than CY exercise; there were no differences between AC and CY exercise in La or PV responses.
LEVEL: A LANG: Eng SIRC ARTICLE NO: 102814

Raven, P.B. Smith, M.L. A guideline for cardiopulmonary conditioning in the middle-aged recreational athlete. (Refs: 109) *American journal of sports medicine (Baltimore, Md.) 12(4), Jul/Aug 1984, 268-277.*
ABST: Exercise conditioning can improve the VO2 max by augmenting both the cardiac output and the oxygen extraction within the capillaries. Resting stroke volume is increased by a conditioning effect and resting bradycardia is common. Changes in total peripheral resistance (TPR) and blood pressure are not as readily demonstrable. To produce a conditioning effet and maintain fitness it is recommended that dynamic exercise at intensities of 60 to 90 percent of the maximum heart rate reserve for at least 15 minutes should be performed at least 3 days/week. The total work load (as a function of intensity and duration) appears to be the most important criterion for producing a conditioning effect. Proper testing and evaluation is necessary for a clinician in prescribing an exercise program that is safe and effective. With the middle-aged individual precautions must be taken to discern any risks for a cardiovascular event or structural injury.
LEVEL: A LANG: Eng SIRC ARTICLE NO: 108532

Rybka, J. Novosad, P. Reaction of human organism to exercise. I. Theoretical part. *Acata Universitatis Carolinae, Medica (Prague) 30(5/6), 1984, 251-295.*
LEVEL: I LANG: Eng

Rybka, J. Novosad, P. Reaction of human organism to exercise. II. Experimental part. *Acta Universitatis Carolinaes Medica (Prague) 30(5/6),*

1984, 297-386.
LEVEL: I LANG: Eng

Rybka, J. Novosad, P. Reaction of human organism to exercise. III. Biochemical response to physical loading. *Acta Universitatis Carolinaes Medica (Prague) 30(5/6), 1984, 387-441.*
LEVEL: I LANG: Eng

Torrey, L. How science creates winners. *Science digest (New York) 92(8), Aug 1984, 33-37;40;91.*
LEVEL: B LANG: Eng SIRC ARTICLE NO: 096437

Yulsman, T. The scientific shape-up. You don't have to be an Olympic athlete to benefit from advances in sports science. *Science digest (New York) 92(8), Aug 1984, 41;86-87.*
LEVEL: B LANG: Eng SIRC ARTICLE NO: 096314

ACUTE ADAPTATIONS

Abraham, F.A. Brill, S. Yoran, P. Blumentahl, M. Scotopic threshold of the human retina during dynamic physical effort. *Ophthalmic research (Basel) 16(6), 1984, 334-336.*
LEVEL: A LANG: Eng

Asano, K. Hirakoba, K. Respiratory and circulatory adaption during prolonged exercise in 10 - 12 year-old children and in adults. (Refs: 16)
CONF: Symposium of Paediatric Work Physiology (10th : 1981 : Joutsa, Finland).
NOTES: In, Ilmarinen, J. and Vaelimaeki, I. (eds.), Children and sport: paediatric work physiology, Berlin, Springer-Verlag, 1984, p. 119-128.
ABST: This study examines the difference between children and adults in respiro-circulatory changes during one hour of exercise, and examines the abilities of children in prolonged exercise.
LEVEL: A LANG: Eng SIRC ARTICLE NO: 102755

Asfour, S.S. Ayoub, M.M. Mital, A. Effects of an endurance and strength training programme on lifting capability of males. (Refs: 25)*Ergonomics (London) 27(4), Apr 1984, 435-442.*
LEVEL: A LANG: Eng SIRC ARTICLE NO: 109761

Bandyopadhyay, D.K. Effect of speed and endurance activities on blood pressure, heart rate and blood lactate, and their correlation. (Refs: 8)*Journal of sports medicine and physical fitness (Torino, Italy) 24(2), Jun 1984, 107-111.*
ABST: The study was conducted to find out the changes of blood pressure, heart rate and blood lactate after performing selected speed and endurance activities. Thirty students of Physical Education College were selected randomly forming two groups in order to find out the changes in the selected parameters after exercise. A significant increase was evident in three variables, heart rate, blood pressure (systolic and diastolic) and blood lactate and a significant decrease in diastolic blood pressure during post exercise phase for both speed and endurance groups. The existence of significant correlation of blood lactate on peak heart rate and systolic blood pressure was evident in the speed group and on systolic blood pressure and diastolic blood pressure in the endurance group respectively. A negative correlation was found between blood lactate and peak heart rate in speed performance and between diastolic blood pressure and peak heart rate in endurance performance. A significant relationship of blood lactate was found with peak heart rate and diastolic blood pressure while the effect of diastolic and systolic blood pressure was eliminated separately.
LEVEL: A LANG: Eng SIRC ARTICLE NO: 102756

Bell, P.M. Henry, R.W. Buchanan, K.D. Alberti, K.G. The effect of starvation on the gastro-entero-pancreatic hormonal and metabolic responses to exercise. (GEP hormones in starvation and exercise.) *Diabete et metabolisme (Paris) 10(3), sept 1984, 194-198.*
LEVEL: A LANG: Eng

Berg, A. Keul, J. Validity of predictable effects in metabolic changes. (Refs: 26)
CONF: International Course on Physiology and Biochemistry of Exercise and Detraining (2nd : 1982 : Nice).
NOTES: In, Marconnet, P. (ed.) et al., Physiological chemistry of training and detraining, New York, Karger, c1984, p. 238-249.
LEVEL: A LANG: Eng RC1235 17596

Bjertnaes, L. Hauge, A. Kjekshus, J. Soyland, E. Cardiovascular responses to face immersion and apnea during steady state muscle exercise. A heart catheterization study on humans. *Acta physiologica scandinavica (Stockholm) 120(4), Apr 1984, 605-612.*
LEVEL: A LANG: Eng

Buono, M.J. Clancy, T.R. Cook, J.R. Blood lactate and ammonium ion accumulation during graded exercise in humans. (Refs: 21) *Journal of applied physiology: respiratory, environmental and exercise physiology (Bethesda, Md.) 57(1), Jul 1984, 135-139.*
ABST: Six adult volunteers (2 women, 4 men) performed a maximum 02 uptake (V02 max) test on a bicycle ergometer. It was noted that blood lactate as well as ammonium ion increased exponentially in relation to increased work. At mild exercise both metabolites remained near resting levels, only to increase upruptly at increased work loads. The break point for both occurred in each subject at roughly the same work load. A significant linear relationship between the blood concentrations of ammonium ion and lactate during exercise was also discovered.
LEVEL: A LANG: Eng SIRC ARTICLE NO: 108364

Caldwell, J.E. Ahonen, E. Nousiainen, U. Differential effects of sauna-, diuretic-, and exercise-induced hypohydration. (Refs: 31)*Journal of applied physiology: respiratory, environmental and exercise physiology (Bethesda, Md.) 57(4), Oct 1984, 1018-1023.*
ABST: 62 nonendurance athletes employed either exercise, diuretics, or used a sauna to achieve rapid weight loss. The results indicate that both the quantity of weight loss and the method used to achieve it rapidly may limit physical performance.
LEVEL: A LANG: Eng SIRC ARTICLE NO: 108941

Chirtel, S.J. Barbee, R.W. Stainsby, W.N. Net O2, CO2, lactate, and acid exchange by muscle during progressive working contractions. (Refs: 14)*Journal of applied physiology: respiratory, environmental and exercise physiology (Bethesda, Md.) 56(1), Jan 1984, 161-165.*
ABST: The gastrocnemius - plantaus muscle group of the dog was used to measure lactate during progressively intense contractions. Non-carbon dioxide acid output (HA) was also measured. The levels of lactic acid and HA showed different patterns that appeared to be independent of each other, but related to the muscle-fibre type being utilized.
LEVEL: A LANG: Eng SIRC ARTICLE NO: 096230

Craig, B.W. Foley, P.J. Effects of cell size and exercise on glucose uptake and metabolism in

adipocytes of female rats. (Refs: 32)*Journal of applied physiology: respiratory, environmental and exercise physioloyg (Bethesda, Md.) 57(4), Oct 1984, 1120-1125.*
LEVEL: A LANG: Eng SIRC ARTICLE NO: 108946

Davidson, L. Vandongen, R. Beilin, L.J. Arkwright, P.D. Free and sulfate-conjugated catecholamines during exercise in man. *Journal of clinical endocrinology and metabolism (Philadelphia) 58(3), Mar 1984, 415-418.*
ABST: The plasma concentration of free and sulfate-conjugated norepinephrine and epinephrine at rest and after vigorous exercise was measured. Exercise resulted in a predictable rise in norepinephrine and epinephrine concentration which correlated with hemodynamic changes and resulted in a significant decrease in the levels of catecholamine sulfate conjugate. This study suggests that the degree of conjugation is another factor determining the concentration of free amines in plasma.
LEVEL: A LANG: Eng SIRC ARTICLE NO: 099227

Despres, J.P. Bouchard, C. Savard, R. Tremblay, A. Marcotte, M. Theriault, G. The effect of a 20-week endurance training program on adipose-tissue morphology and lipolysis in men and women. *Metabolism, clinical and experimental (New York) 33(3), Mar 1984, 235-239.*
ABST: 22 adult subjects participated in a 20 week ergocycle training program in order to evaluate the effect of endurance training on adipose tissue and lipolysis. Overall, training significantly reduced fat cell weight, percentage of fat, and increased adipocyte epinephrine maximal stimulated lipolysis. Though the exercise program significantly lowered the adiposity of men, in women training induced no significant changes in the fatness indicators.
LEVEL: A LANG: Eng SIRC ARTICLE NO: 099230

Galbo, H. Gollnick, P.D. Hormonal changes during and after exercise. (Refs: 8)
CONF: International Course on Physiology and Biochemistry of Exercise and Detraining (2nd : 1982 : Nice).
NOTES: In, Marconnet, P. (ed.) et al., Physiological chemistry of training and detraining, New York, Karger, c1984, p. 97-110.
LEVEL: A LANG: Eng RC1235 17596

Hallberg, L. Magnusson, B. The etiology of 'sports anemia'. A physiological adaptation of the oxygen-dissociation curve of hemoglobin to an unphysiological exercise load. (editorial) *Acta medica scandinavica (Stockholm) 216(2), 1984, 147-148.*
LEVEL: A LANG: Eng

Harms, S.J. Mitochondrial and myoglobin adaptations in the different types of skeletal muscle in response to endurance training at three intensities in female rats. Eugene, Ore.: Microform Publications, University of Oregon, 1984. 1 microfiche : negative, ill. ; 11 x 15 cm.
NOTES: Thesis (M.S.) - University of Illinois at Chicago Circle, 1982; (ix, 39 leaves); includes bibliography.
LEVEL: A LANG: Eng UO84 279

Kelso, T.B. Herbert, W.G. Gwazdauskas, F.C. Goss, F.L. Hess, J.L. Exercise-thermoregulatory stress and increased plasma beta-endorphin/beta-lipotropin in humans. (Refs: 26)*Journal of applied physiology: respiratory, environmental and exercise physiology (Bethesda, Md.) 57(2), Aug 1984, 444-449.*

ABST: Six adult males exercised for 120 min. under various temperature/humidity conditions. Beta-endorphin (beta-EN) and beta-lipotropin (beta-LPH) was calculated by radiommunoassay. Beta-EN/beta-LPH levels rose considerably in hot-dehydrated and hot-euhydrated conditions, but the greatest response was produced by a hot-dehydrated environment after 105 min.
LEVEL: A LANG: Eng SIRC ARTICLE NO: 108354

Kjaer, M. Mikines, K.J. Christensen, N.J. Tronier, B. Vinten, J. Sonne, B. Richter, E.A. Galbo, H. Glucose turnover and hormonal changes during insulin-induced hypoglycemia in trained humans. (Refs: 34)*Journal of applied physiology: respiratory, environmental and exercise physiology (Bethesda, Md.) 57(1), Jul 1984, 21-27.*
ABST: Eight elite athletes (T) and seven healthy sedentary subjects (C) had insulin infused until plasma glucose. During and after insulin infusion production, disappearance and clearance of glucose changed identically in T and C subjects. Responses of norepinephrine, cortisol, C-peptide, and lactate were similar. However, epinephrine, somatotropin, and pancreatic polypeptide was higher in group T, whereas glucagon reached lower levels.
LEVEL: A LANG: Eng SIRC ARTICLE NO: 108362

Lewis, S. Nygaard, E. Sanchez, J. Egeblad, H. Saltin, B. Static contraction of the quadriceps muscle in man: cardiovascular control and responses to one-legged strength training. *Acta physiologica scandinavica (Stockholm) 122(3), Nov 1984, 341-353.*
LEVEL: A LANG: Eng

Macek, M. Vavra, J. Benesova, H. Radvansky, J. The adjustment of oxygen uptake at the onset of exercise: relation to age and to work load. (Refs: 7)
CONF: Symposium of Paediatric Work Physiology (10th : 1981 : Joutsa, Finland).
NOTES: In, Ilmarinen, J. and Vaelimaeki, I. (eds.), Children and sport: paediatric work physiology, Berlin, Springer-Verlag, 1984, p. 129-134.
LEVEL: A LANG: Eng SIRC ARTICLE NO: 102799

Mahsenin, V. Gonzalez, R.R. Tissue pressure and plasma oncotic pressure during exercise. (Refs: 28)*Journal of applied physiology: respiratory environmental and exercise physiology (Bethesda, Md.) 56(1), Jan 1984, 102-108.*
ABST: It has been found that some extracellular fluid moves into interstitial and cellular space during exercise. This plasma volume loss appeared to reach a plateau at points greater than 65% of maximal oxygen uptake.This study of 6 healthy male subjects who exercised on a bicycle ergometer found that the excessive loss of plasma volume was prevented by an elevation of transvascular colloid osmotic pressure and increased interstitial fluid pressure.
LEVEL: A LANG: Eng SIRC ARTICLE NO: 096276

Martin, W.H. Coyle, E.F. Ehsani, A.A. Cardiovascular sensitivity to epinephrine in the trained and untrained states. *American journal of cardiology (New York) 54(10), 1 Dec 1984, 1326-1330.*
LEVEL: A LANG: Eng

McConnell, T.R. Sinning, W.E. Exercise and temperature effects on human sperm production and testosterone levels. (Refs: 28) *Medicine and science in sports and exercise 16(1), 1984, 51-55.*
ABST: Three groups of men were formed to study the effects of heavy exercise at different temperatures on sperm production. One group of subjects exercised at 6.2oC, one group exercised at 37.7oC and one group served as controls. Although plasma testosterone levels were elevated in the exercise groups on days 4 and 5 of the exercise period, no significant differences in sperm production were found.
LEVEL: A LANG: Eng SIRC ARTICLE NO: 091752

Michel, G. Vocke, T. Fiehn, W. Weicker, H. Schwarz, W. Bieger, W.P. Bidirectional alteration of insulin receptor affinity by different forms of physical exercise. *American journal of physiology (Bethesda, Md.) 246(2 Pt 1), Feb 1984, E153-E159.*
ABST: Monocyte and erythrocyte insulin binding was studied in untrained males after 15 minutes of exhaustive bicycle exercise and after 90 minutes of moderate exercise. Insulin receptor affinity decreased in monocytes and erythrocytes with no change in receptor number. Binding to monocytes was significantly enhanced after moderate exercise due to increased receptor affinity. The quantity of circulating monocytes was significantly increased after both forms of exercise. These results indicate that physical exercise changes serum insulin levels and cellular hormone sensitivity possibly through the mediation of low-molecular-weight serum components.
LEVEL: A LANG: Eng SIRC ARTICLE NO: 099254

Morrison, J.F. van Malsen, S. Noakes, T.D. Leisure-time physical activity levels, cardiovascular fitness and coronary risk factors in 1015 white Zimbabweans. (Refs: 34)*South African medical journal (Cape Town) 65(7), 18 Feb 1984, 250-256.*
ABST: To determine a 'threshold' level of habitual physical activity for the reduction of coronary risk factors, a cross-sectional study of 646 male and 369 female White Zimbabweans aged 20-70 years was undertaken. The data shows that a 'threshold' level of exercise might exist above which there is a reduction in the percentage of body fat, the incidence of smoking and abnormal ST-segment depression during exercise, increased VO2MAX values and a reduced rate of fall of VO2MAX with age. Whereas participation in only light exercises had little effect, more strenuous exercise was associated with beneficial alterations in all these parameters.
LEVEL: A LANG: Eng SIRC ARTICLE NO: 098916

Nguyen, N.U. Wolf, J.P. Simon, M.L. Henriet, M.T. Dumoulin, G. Berthelay, S. Variations de la prolactine et de l'hormone de croissance circulantes (sic) au cours d'un exercice physique chez l'homme: influence de la puissance du travail fourni. (Variations in circulating levels of prolactin and growth hormone during physical exercise in man: influence of the intensity of the workout.) *Comptes rendus des seances de la Societe de biologie et de ses filiales (Paris) 178(4), 1984, 450-457.*
ABST: Following a 20 minute bicycle ergometry exercise prolactin and growth hormone levels increased significantly. The authors observed an higher increase in growth hormone level after maximal exercise than after submaximal one.
LEVEL: A LANG: Fr

Ohno, H. Yahata, T. Hirata, F. Yamamura, K. Doi, R. Harada, M. Taniguchi, N. Changes in dopamine-beta-hydroxylase, and copper, and catecholamine concentrations in human plasma with physical exercise. (Refs: 30)*Journal of sports medicine and physical fitness (Torino, Italy) 24(4), Dec 1984, 315-320.*

ABST: Seven untrained male volunteers were studied to observe the effects of bicycle exercise (150 W for 30 min) upon the levels of dopamine-beta-hydroxylase (DBH) activity, copper, ceruloplasmin (CP), and 4 catecholamines (dopa, dopamine, norepinephrine (NE), and epinephrine (E)) in plasma. The values of all the parameters except for dopa showed significant increases immediately after exercise. DBH activity seemed to remain high after 30 min of rest. Since the changes in DBH activity did not correlate with those in copper concentration or CP concentration after exercise, it seemed likely that the changes in DBH activity may not be due to those in copper concentration. In addition, this study suggests that plasma DBH activity is a poor index of sympatho-adrenal activity during physical exercise because of its much lesser increase than seen for NE or E. Due to its relatively long biological half-life, however, the activity of DBH in plasma may be a good index of chronic stress.
LEVEL: A LANG: Eng SIRC ARTICLE NO: 106799

Oktedalen, O. Guldvog, I. Opstad, P.K. Berstad, A. Gedde-Dahl, D. Jorde, R. The effect of physical stress on gastric secretion and pancreatic polypeptide levels in man. *Scandinavian journal of gastroenterology (Oslo) 19(6), Sept 1984, 770-778.*
LEVEL: A LANG: Eng

Phillips, C.A. Petrofsky, J.S. Cardiovascular responses to isometric neck muscle contractions: results after dynamic exercis with various headgear loading configurations. *Aviation, space and environmental medicine (Washington) 55(8), Aug 1984, 740-745.*
LEVEL: A LANG: Eng

Pilardeau, P.A. Garnier, M. Fischer, F. Desbleds, M. Vaysse, J. Lesenechal, M. Margo, J.N. Origin of the increase in H.D.L. cholesterol on sportsmen. (Refs: 28)*Journal of sports medicine and physical fitness (Torino, Italy) 24(4), Dec 1984, 311-314.*
ABST: In this study, the authors suggest two experiments on a group of 10 trained cyclists after giving the present facts in specialised works dealing with the increase in H.D.L.c on trained sportsmen. This work puts into light a significant increase of circulating V.L.D.L. and triglycerides at the beginning of the exercise. Using the arguments mispelled by Schefer on the regulation of the synthesis of H.D.L.c they try to explain the two most frequent variations usually noticed in trained sportsmen: an increase in H.D.L.c and a decrease in triglycerides. They give the hypothesis that the repeated increase in triglycerides during heavy exercises could provoke the increase in the synthesis of H.D.L.c and a decrease in the synthesis of V.L.D.L. after several weeks.
LEVEL: A LANG: Eng SIRC ARTICLE NO: 106803

Premel-Cabic, A. Turcant, A. Chaleil, D. Allain, P. Victor, J. Tadei, A. Concentration plasmatique de catecholamines a l'effort chez le sujet non entraine et chez le sportif. (Plasma catecholamine concentrations during exercise in the untrained subject and in the sportsman.) *Pathologie biologie (Paris) 32(6), juin 1984, 702-704.*
LEVEL: A LANG: Fr SIRC ARTICLE NO: 104359

Rieu, M. L'adaptation a l'effort. (Refs: 5)*Science et vie (Paris) HS147, 1984, 80-91.*
LEVEL: A LANG: Fr

Sapov, I.A. Novikov, V.S. Vliianie fizicheskoi trenirovki na nespetsificheskie mekhanizmy adaptatsii. (Effect of physical training on nonspecific

mechanisms of adaptation.) *Voenno-meditsinskii zhurnal (Moscow) 1, Jan 1984, 41-43.*
LEVEL: A LANG: Rus

Sawhney, R.C. Chhabra, P.C. Rai, R.M. Plasma LH, FSH, testosterone & LH response to GnRH during exercise in man. *Indian journal of medical research (New Delhi) 79, Apr 1984, 523-528.*
LEVEL: A LANG: Eng

Scharf, S.M. Bark, H. Heimer, D. Cohen, A. Macklem, P.T. Second wind during inspiratory loading. (Refs: 8)*Medicine and science in sports and exercise 16(1), 1984, 87-91.*
ABST: Second wind as a physiological phenomenon was investigated in 5 subjects exercising until fatigue while breathing through an inspiratory resister. Fatigue of the diaphragm was relieved by a second wind in all subjects. The commencement of the second wind suddenly decreased neural stimulation to the diaphragm muscle. The authors feel a change in the contractile state of this muscle is involved in the second wind phenomenon.
LEVEL: A LANG: Eng SIRC ARTICLE NO: 091774

Schnabel, A. Kindermann, W. Steinkraus, V. Salas-Fraire, O. Biro, G. Metabolic and hormonal responses to exhaustive supramaximal running with and without beta-adrenergic blockade. (Refs: 32)*European journal of applied physiology and occupational physiology (Heidelberg) 52(2), Jan 1984, 214-218.*
ABST: This study was done to determine some possible delayed metabolic and hormonal responses beyond the first minutes after an exhaustive, short-term, supramaximal run on a treadmill. Also, the effects of beta-1-selective and non-selective beta-adrenergic blockade were examined. Among the results it was demonstrated that the strong sympaths-adrenal reponse to exercise of this nature is a major determinant of blood glucose increases at the cessation of exercise. Also, the delayed increase of growth hormone seems to be triggered by the declining glucose levels.
LEVEL: A LANG: Eng SIRC ARTICLE NO: 096294

Shaffrath, J.D. Adams, W.C. Effects of airflow and work load on cardiovascular drift and skin blood flow. (Refs: 33)*Journal of applied physiology: respiratory, environmental and exercise physiology (Bethesda, Md.) 56(5), May 1984, 1411-1417.*
ABST: This study examined the relationship between cardiovascular drift (CVD) and changes in cutaneous blood flow during prolonged exercise. Eight subjects exercised on four occasions for 70 minutes/session. The subjects exercised on an ergometer at two different intensities and in conditions of no airflow (0.2 m/s) or airflow (4.3 m/s). At the high workload with no airflow, heart rate and skin blood flow increased and stroke volume and mean arterial blood pressure decreased as the exercise progressed. There were non-significant changes in these variables in the other exercise conditions. The authors conclude that it is a progressive redistribution of blood volume into cutaneous capacitance vessels which reduces the central blood volume and initiales CVD.
LEVEL: A LANG: Eng SIRC ARTICLE NO: 097764

Stanec, A. Stefano, G. Cyclic AMP in normal and malignant hyperpyrexia susceptible individuals following exercise. *British journal of anaesthesia (London) 56(11), Nov 1984, 1243-1246.*
LEVEL: A LANG: Eng

CHRONIC ADAPTATIONS AND OVERTRAINING

D'Amours, Y. Le surentrainement chez l'athlete. (Refs: 5)*Revue de l'entraineur (Montreal) oct/dec 1984, 10-11.*
LEVEL: B LANG: Fr SIRC ARTICLE NO: 105466

Franklin, B.A. Wrisley, D. Johnson, S. Mitchell, M. Rubenfire, M. Chronic adaptations to physical conditioning in cardiac patients. Implications regarding exercise trainability. (Refs: 168)*Clinics in sports medicine (Philadelphia) 3(2), Apr 1984, 471-512.*
ABST: This article reviews the physiologic basis and rationale for exercise therapy in patients with coronary heart disease with specific reference to potential variables affecting exercise trainability. Regular exercise increases functional capacity, promotes relief of angina pectoris, reduces the 'risk factor' profile, enhances psychologic status and generally improves the quality of the patient's life. The mechanisms underlying these changes are not well understood.
LEVEL: A LANG: Eng SIRC ARTICLE NO: 094249

Markarian, S.S. Rol' serdechno-sosudistoi sistemy v adaptatsii k fizicheskoi nagruzke. (Role of the cardiovascular system in adaptation to a physical load.) *Klinicheskaia meditsina (Moscow) 62(11), Nov 1984, 7-11.*
LEVEL: A LANG: Rus

McDonagh, M.J.N. Davies, C.T.M. Adaptive response of mammalian skeletal muscle to exercise with high loads. (Refs: 101) *European journal of applied physiology and occupational physiology (Heidelberg) 52(2), Jan 1984, 139-155.*
ABST: This is a review of studies concerned with the effects of chronic exercise using high loads on skeletal muscle. Areas of review include: the nature of various training stimuli; hypertrophy of the muscle and muscle fibres; and the other underlying biochemical and neurological mechanisms of the response. Data from both human and animal muscle experiments are included.
LEVEL: A LANG: Eng SIRC ARTICLE NO: 096280

GROWTH AND DEVELOPMENT

Jenoure, P. Physiologie de l'entrainement au debut de la scolarite. (Refs: 7)*Dans, Mandel, C. (ed.), Le medecin, l'enfant e le sport, Paris, (Vigot), c1984, p. 31-41.*
LEVEL: I LANG: Fr RC1218.C45 18886

PRESCRIPTIONS AND TRAINING

Bravaya, D.U. Comparative analysis of the effectiveness of static (isometric) and dynamic (isokinetic) strength training. *Soviet sports review (Escondido, Calif.) 19(4), Dec 1984, 161-164.*
NOTES: Condensed translation from, Teoriya i praktika fizicheskoi kultury 2, 1984, 18-20.
LEVEL: A LANG: Eng SIRC ARTICLE NO: 104500

Burke, E.J. Collins, M.L. Using perceived exertion for the prescription of exercise in healthy adults. (Refs: 31)
NOTES: In, Cantu, R.C. (ed.), Clinical sports medicine, Lexington, Mass. ; Toronto, Collamore Press : D.C. Heath, c1984, p. 93-105.
LEVEL: A LANG: Eng RC1201 15964

Champbell, D.E. Physiological basis for cardiovascular fitness. Effects of training. (Refs: 12)*Women's coaching clinic 7(6) Feb 1984, 14-16.*
LEVEL: I LANG: Eng SIRC ARTICLE NO: 090231

Coyle, E.F. Martin III. W.H. Sinacore, D.R. Joyner, M.J. Hagberg, J.M. Holloszy, J.O. Time course of loss of adaptations after stopping prolonged intense endurance training. (Refs: 23)*Journal of applied physiology: respiratory, environmental and exercise physiology (Bethesda, Md.) 57(6), Dec 1984, 1857-1864.*
ABST: Changes of physiological parameters in 7 endurance trained athletes were assessed after 12, 21, 56, and 84 days of detraining. Experimental subjects reached a maximal 02 uptake level of 16 percent below the initial trained value after 56 days. Following 84 days of detraining, the VO2 max of these subjects were still higher than sedentary control subjects. A decrease of stroke volume was observed during detraining. Skeletal muscle capillarization remained unchanged and 50 percent higher than sedenary control.
LEVEL: A LANG: Eng SIRC ARTICLE NO: 108569

De Lateur, B.J. Exercise for strength and endurance. (Refs: 23)
NOTES: In, Basmajian, J.V. (ed.), Therapeutic exercise, 4th ed., Baltimore, Md., Williams & Wilkins, c1984, p. 88-109.
LEVEL: A LANG: Eng RM719 17505

De Marees, H. Physiologische Aspekte des Ausdauertraining. (Physiological aspects of endurance training.) *Krankenpflege journal (Wurzburg, W. Ger.) 22(11), 1 Nov 1984, 20-25.*
LEVEL: A LANG: Ger

DeMeersman, R.E. Schiltz, J.H. Decreased training frequency and pulmonary function retention in the female athlete. *Journal of sports medicine and physical fitness (Torino, Italy) 24(2), Jun 1984, 155-158.*
ABST: Pulmonary function and body composition retention were observed in 18 female collegiate athletes exposed to a decrease in training frequency while participating in consecutive field hockey and lacrosse competitive seasons. Although one sport season represented 31% fewer workouts than the other, no significant differences were noted in body density, body fat, closing volume, nitrogen delta, closing capacity, residual volumes, functional residual volume, expiratory reserve volume, total lung capacity and vital capacity post-season scores. Results were noted as being in agreement with previous investigations in that the degree of fitness achieved can be maintained despite a substantial decrease in training frequency.
LEVEL: A LANG: Eng SIRC ARTICLE NO: 102768

Hickson, R.C. overland, S.M. Dougherty, K.A. Reduced training frequency effects on aerobic power and muscle adaptations in rats. (Refs: 36)*Journal of applied physiology: respiratory, environmental and exercise physiology (Bethesda, Md.) 57(6), Dec 1984, 1834-1841.*
LEVEL: A LANG: Eng SIRC ARTICLE NO: 108568

Kirkendall, D.T. Exercise prescription for the healthy adult. (Refs: 10)*Primary care: clinics in office practice (Philadelphia) 11(1), Mar 1984, 23-31.*
LEVEL: I LANG: Eng SIRC ARTICLE NO: 100904

Lambert, M. Sports medicine review. *Powerlifting USA (Camarillo, Calif.) 8(3), Oct 1984, 7.*
LEVEL: I LANG: Eng SIRC ARTICLE NO: 173184

PHYSIOLOGY - EXERCISE (continued)

Marconnet, P. Poortmans, J. Hermansen, L.
Physiological chemistry of training and detraining.
New York: Karger, c1984. xii, 262 p. (Medicine and
sport science: v. 17.)
CONF: International Course on Physiology and
Biochemistry of Exercise and Detraining (2nd :
1982 : Nice).
NOTES: Includes index. Includes bibliographies.
LEVEL: A LANG: Eng ISBN: 3-8055-3764-6
RC1235 17596

Marini, J.F. Van Hoecke, J. Mathieu, C.
Adaptation du muscle a l'entrainement. (Refs: 72)
NOTES: Dans, Renforcement musculaire, Paris,
Institut national du sport et de l'education physique,
c1984, p. 55-78.
LEVEL: A LANG: Fr GV711.5 18233

Merten, A.A. Iansone, R.A. Ozolin, P.P.
Effektivnost primeneniia intervalno-krugovogo
metoda obuchnii v fizicheskom vospitanii. (Efficacy
of using the interval-circular method of training in
physical education.) Gigiena i sanitariia (Moscow)
4, Apr 1984, 24-27.
LEVEL: I LANG: Rus

Peres, G. Connaissances medicales et
entrainement sportif. Dans, Culture technique no.
13, Neuilly-sur-Seine, France, Centr de Recherche
sur la Culture Technique, c1984, p. 168-179.
LEVEL: I LANG: Fr RC1235 20096

Peterson, R.A. Generalized physiological principles
which guide conditioning programs. Palaestra
(Macomb, Ill.) 1(1), Fall 1984, 13-15;43.
LEVEL: I LANG: Eng SIRC ARTICLE NO: 171812

Pivarniki, J.M. Leeds, E.M. Wilkerson, J.E. Effect
of endurance exercise on metabolic water
production and plasma volume. (Refs: 34)Journal of
applied physiology: respiratory, environmental and
exercise physiology (Bethesda, Md.) 56(3), Mar
1984, 613-618.
ABST: The purpose of this study was to determine
the effects of three different submaximal exercise
intensities on the metabolic water production and
plasma volume of trained and heat-acclimatized
individuals. Six male subjects ran on a treadmill for
one hour or until exhaustion on three different
occasions. Changes in the measurements of body
weight, blood hemoglobin, hematocrit and
estimates of blood volume, plasma volume, plasma
protein concentration and metabolic water
production were made. Measurements of the body,
rectal and mean skin temperature were monitored
during each session. The results indicate that
metabolic water production increased with
increasing work intensity, while plasma volume was
maintained. The authors suggest that metabolic
water production only plays a minor role in plasma
volume maintenance and thermoregulatory control
during endurance exercise.
LEVEL: A LANG: Eng SIRC ARTICLE NO: 096455

Robbins, F.L. Comparative analysis of Karvonen
and anaerobic threshold methods for prescribing
exercise in healthy adult males. Eugene, Ore.:
Microform Publications, University of Oregon, 1984.
2 microfiches : negative, ill. ; 11 x 15 cm.
NOTES: Thesis (M.S.) - Virginia Polytechnic
Institute and State University, 1982; (vii, 140
leaves); vita; includes bibliography.
LEVEL: A LANG: Eng UO84 152-153

Sleamaker, R.H. Caloric cost of performing the
Perrier Parcourse Fitness Circuit. (Refs:
20)Medicine and science in sports and exercise
(Indianapolis) 16(3), June 1984, 283-286.

ABST: The metabolic cost of performing a Perrier
Parcourse Fitness Circuit was determined in 18
men, ages 18-26 yr. A laboratory simulation of the
Parcourse was conducted using a treadmill for the
running phases between exercise stations, and
apparatus was constructed to stimulate the various
apparatus of each of the specific exercise stations
on the Parcourse. Subjects completed two
simulations on separate days, performing at a pace
that enabled them to maintain a training heart rate
of 70-85 per cent absolute maximum heart rate.
Metabolic data for rest, exercise, and recovery were
collected. With a mean exercise time of 29.6 min,
the average total gross energy expenditure was
394.9 kcal for stimulation I and 38.2 l kcal for
stimulation II. It was concluded that performance of
the Parcourse would be an adequate exercise for
expending energy in programs emphasizing weight
control and would be appropriate for
cardiorespiratory endurance conditioning.
LEVEL: A LANG: Eng SIRC ARTICLE NO: 108599

Stein, R.A. Rohen, A.B. Cardiovascular effects
and complications of exercise and exercise training.
(Refs: 13)
NOTES: In, Birrer, R.B. (ed.), Sports medicine for
the primary care physician, Norwalk, Conn.,
Appleton-Century-Crofts, c1984, p. 55-64.
LEVEL: I LANG: Eng RC1210 17030

Vitti, G.J. The effects of variable training speeds
on leg strength & power. (Refs: 16)Athletic training
19(1), Spring 1984 26-29.
ABST: 30 untrained males under 30 were selected
to determine the effects of variable training speeds
on the strength and power outputs of the
quadriceps femoris and hamstring muscle groups.
The subjects were trained at different speeds on an
Orthotron isokinetic exercising device. Significant
differences were revealed in the experimental
groups from pre- to posttest for both strength and
power output, whereas there were no significant
differences for the control group.
LEVEL: A LANG: Eng SIRC ARTICLE NO: 091891

**Woodhouse, S.P. Sutherland, W.H. Nye, E.R.
Sargent, J. Waite, G. Merhtens, C. Cruickshank
F.M. Belcher, M.R.** Physical training and fasting
serum insulin levels in sedentary men. Clinical
physiology (Oxford) 4(6), Dec 1984, 475-482.
LEVEL: A LANG: Eng

PSYCHOPHYSIOLOGY

Fibiger, W. Singer, G. Miller, A.J. Relationships
between catecholamines in urine and physical and
mental effort. International journal of
psychophysiology (Amsterdam) 1(4), June 1984,
325-333.
LEVEL: A LANG: Eng

TESTING

**Alabouvette, G. Bertholon, M. Helfre, G.
Chatard, J.C. Geyssant, A. Lacour, J.R.** Effort
maximal, frequence cardiaque maximal et
lactacidemie en electrocardiographie d'effort. Etude
comparative. (Maximal effort, maximal heart rate
and serum lactic acid in exercise
electrocardiography. A comparative study.)
Archives des maladies du coeur et des vaisseaux
(Paris) 77(12), nov 1984, 1301-1306.
LEVEL: A LANG: Fr

**Bergert, K.D. Neubert, I. Zehner, C. Schettler,
R.** Die Katecholaminausscheidung im Harn zur

Bewertung koerperlicher Belastungen. (Urinary
catecholamine excretion for the evaluation of
physical stress.) Zeitschrift fuer die gesamte
Hygiene und ihre Grenzgebiete (Berlin) 30(7), Jul
1984, 387-388.
LEVEL: I LANG: Ger

Bruce, R.A. Value and limitations of the
electrocardiogram in progressive exercise testing.
(Refs: 30)American review of respiratory disease
(New York) 129(2 Pt 2), Feb 1984, S28-S30.
CONF: Exercise Testing in the Dyspneic Patient
Workshop (1982 : Bethesda).
ABST: This review of the values of the
electrocardiogram during exercise discusses its
pathophysiologic significance, standards, and
diagnostic and prognostic values.
LEVEL: I LANG: Eng SIRC ARTICLE NO: 098902

**Busse, M.W. Mueller, M. Boening, D. Boecher,
A.** A method of continuous treadmill testing. (Refs:
20)International journal o sports medicine
(Stuttgart) Suppl. 5, Nov 1984, 15-18.
CONF: International Congress on Sports and Health
(1983 : Maastricht, Netherlands).
LEVEL: A LANG: Eng SIRC ARTICLE NO: 104285

Hansen, J.E. Sue, D.Y. Wasserman, K. Predicted
values for clinical exercise testing. (Refs:
47)American review of respiratory disease (New
York) 129(2 Pt 2), Feb 1984, S49-S55.
CONF: Exercise Testing in the Dyspneic Patient
Workshop (1982 : Bethesda).
ABST: 265 current or ex-shipguard workers were
thoroughly evaluated at rest and then exercised on
a bicycle ergometer with equal work increments
each minute to exhaustion while continuous
multiple noninvasive cardiorespiratory and
intermittent blood pressure and blood gas
measures were made. Seventy-seven men, with a
mean age of 54 were judged to have normal
cardiorespiratory systems. The statistical results
are detailed and analyzed. The authors found that
for predicting maximal oxygen uptake and oxygen
pulse in an overweight man, the use of age and
height were preferred to age and weight.
LEVEL: A LANG: Eng SIRC ARTICLE NO: 099239

Jones, N.L. Evaluation of a microprocessor-
controlled exercise testing system. (Refs:
11)Journal of applied physiology: respiratory,
environmental and exercise physiology (Bethesda,
Md.) 57(5), Nov 1984, 1312-1318.
LEVEL: A LANG: Eng SIRC ARTICLE NO: 108904

Mazzeo, R.S. Brooks, G.A. Horvath, S.M. Effects
of age on metabolic responses to endurance
training in rats. (Refs: 39) Journal of applied
physiology: respiratory, environmental and exercise
physiology (Bethesda, Md.) 57(5), Nov 1984, 1369-
1374.
LEVEL: A LANG: Eng SIRC ARTICLE NO: 108911

**McConnell, T.R. Swett, D.D. Missri, J.C.
Jeresaty, R.M. Al-Hani, A.J.** Basic ventilatory
responses to different exercise modalities. (Refs:
21)
NOTES: In, Cantu, R.C. (ed.), Clinical sports
medicine, Lexington, Mass. ; Toronto, Collamore
Press : D.C. Heath, c1984, p. 115-127.
LEVEL: A LANG: Eng RC1201 15964

**Yamaguchi, I. Komatsu, E. Fukuyzawa, H.
Miyazawa, K.** (Theoretical consideration and
clinical applicability of ramp function exercise test.)
Kokyu to junkan. Respiration and circulation
(Tokyo) 32(3), Mar 1984, 269-273.
LEVEL: I LANG: Jpn

WARM-UP AND RECOVERY

Bielinski, R. Schutz, Y. Jequier, E. Metabolisme energetique au cours de la recuperation de l'exercice. (Refs: 13)*Revue medicale de la Suisse romande (Lausanne) 104(10), oct 1984, 771-778.*
RESUME: Dix sujets masculins (20 a 25 ans) sont soumis a une marche de trois heures sur tapis roulant afin d'evaluer les depenses energetiques et l'utilisation des nutriments au cours de la periode de recuperation. Les auteurs observent par calorimetrie indirecte une stimulation de la depense d'energie et une utilisation accrue des lipides plus de dix-sept heures apres l'arret de l'exercise.
LEVEL: A LANG: Fr SIRC ARTICLE NO: 174094

Dimsdale, J.E. Hartley, L.H. Guiney, T. Ruskin, J.N. Greenblatt, D. Postexercise peril. Plasma catecholamines and exercise. *JAMA: Journal of the American Medical Association (Chicago) 251(5), 3 Feb 1984, 620-632.*
ABST: In an attempt to understand the physiology of postexercise cardiac death this study examined plasma catecholamine levels in ten healthy men at each work load during an exercise test and during the recovery period. Both norepinephrine and epinephrine levels increased in response to exercise. They continued to increase in the postexercise recovery period with the norepinephrine level increasing tenfold over the baseline level. These increases may have profound effects on people with existing coronary disease.
LEVEL: A LANG: Eng SIRC ARTICLE NO: 097721

Dimsdale, J.E. Postexercise cool-down. *Sports medicine digest (Van Nuys, Calif.) 6(5), May 1984, 6.*
LEVEL: I LANG: Eng SIRC ARTICLE NO: 100894

Kamen, G. Strength recovery patterns following exercise with an imposed myotatic stretch. (Refs: 22)*Archives of physical medicine and rehabilitation 65(4), Apr 1984, 178-181.*
ABST: This study compared the recovery of strength following isometric exercise with or without an imposed stretch in a group of trained and untrained men. Twenty-four men aged between 19 and 33 years were divided in two groups: 12 untrained subjects and 12 trained subjects (6 weightlifter, four football players, and two track sprinters). Strength recovery patterns were similar for both groups and both exercise conditions. However, both groups recovered faster during the first minute following stretch exercise, than following isometric exercise.
LEVEL: A LANG: Eng SIRC ARTICLE NO: 093101

Luczak, H. Rohmert, W. Zur objektivitaet, validitaet und reliabilitaet der Bestimmung von Erholungsdauern nach Erschoepfungsversuchen bei schwerer dynamischer Muskelarbeit aus Zeitreihen der Herzschlagfrequenz. (Objectivity, validity and reliability of determination of recovery times from time series of heart rate after exhausting ergometer work.) (Refs: 19)*European journal of applied physiology and occupational physiology (Berlin, W.G.) 53(2), 1984, 133-143.*
ABST: Records of heart rate after 152 experiments with exhaustion of three male subjects were rated by three experts to determine the end of the recovery phase. Inter-rater-reliability of recovery times vary between 0.87-0.97 according to the method of calculation. An algorithm for the identification of the end of recovery is developed by approximation of the expert-ratings. The corresponding rater-reliability of the algorithm is

0.9. A stepwise multiple regression shows, that most of the variance of recovery times is explained by heart rate at the end of the working phase (63.8 per cent) and by the conditions of the rest phase (18.9 per cent).
LEVEL: A LANG: Ger

Tan, M.H. Watson-Wright, B.W. Hood, D. Sopper, M. Currie, D. Belcastro, A.N. Pierce, G. Blood lactate disappearance at various intensities of recovery exercise. (Refs: 21)*Journal of applied physiology: respiratory, environmental and exercise physiology (Bethesda, Md.) 57(5), Nov 1984, 1462-1465.*
LEVEL: A LANG: Eng SIRC ARTICLE NO: 108918

Vogelaere, P. S'Jongers, J.J. Relations entre le niveau de condition physique et le temps de recuperation apres effort. (Refs: 35)*Medecine du sport (Paris) 58(5), 25 sept 1984, 36-42.*
RESUME: 60 males ages de 21,6 plus ou moins 1,3 ans sont testes lors d'une epreuve sur cyclergometre. Les parametres etudies sont les temps theoriques de recuperation (alactique et lactique), la consommation d'oxygene, la frequence cardiaque et le pouls d'oxygene. Les resultats indiquent une phase lactique de recuperation plus rapide chez les sujets presentant une bonne capacite aerobie que chez les sujets moins aptes.
LEVEL: A LANG: Fr SIRC ARTICLE NO: 100931

PHYSIOLOGY - FACTORS AFFECTING PERFORMANCE

Bunc, V. Sprynarova, S. Parizkova, J. Leso, J. Effects of adaptation on the mechanical efficiency and energy cost of physica work. *Human nutrition. Clinical nutrition (London) 38(4), Jul 1984, 317-319.*
LEVEL: I LANG: Eng SIRC ARTICLE NO: 104284

Irvine, A.B. Results of studies to measure the potential effects of light spectra on human performance. Eugene, Ore.: Microform Publications, University of Oregon, 1984. 2 microfiches : negative ; 11 x 15 cm.
NOTES: Thesis (M.A.) - University of Florida, 1983; (vii, 42, (78) leaves); vita; includes bibliography.
LEVEL: A LANG: Eng UO84 337-338

BIORHYTHMS AND CIRCADIAN RHYTHMS

Arendt, J. Biorhythms. *Physiotherapy in sport (Dymchurch, Kent) 7(2), Autumn 1984, 7-8;10.*
LEVEL: I LANG: Eng SIRC ARTICL NO: 105457

Graham, H.C. Athletic performance and circadian rhythms. (Refs: 3)*Skating magazine (Colorado Springs, Colo.) 61(6), Jun 1984, 21-22.*
LEVEL: B LANG: Eng SIRC ARTICLE NO: 102781

Hahn, C.K.G. Pre-adaptive circadian rhythm programming for International Canadian Athletes.
NOTES: In: Proceedings of the 1984 International Conference on Occupational Ergonomics, Toronto, Ontario, 7-9th May 1984, Edited by D.A. Attwood and C. McCann, Volume 1, p. 210-214.
ABST: This paper examines the methods and results of the application of a circadian rhythm pre-flight synchronization programme for competitive figure-skaters changing time zones prior to international competition and discusses some possibilities of an appropriate scheduling

programme in other fields.
LEVEL: A LANG: Eng SIRC ARTICLE NO: 103144

Kirkcaldy, B.D. Performance and circadian rhythms. (Refs: 18)*European journal of applied physiology and occupational physiology (Berlin. FRG) 52(4), Jun 1984, 375-379.*
ABST: One hundred-fifty subjects were assigned to a 45-min session between 08:00 and 24:00. Psychophysiological measures and tonic somatic activity were monitored while the subjects executed a visual choice reaction time task, proceeded by a recovery phase and followed by an experimenter paced visual reaction time task. Extraverts exhibited a stability through the day on physiological parameters; while introverts exhibited a complex interaction with time of day. Psychologically stable introverts possessed high heart rates in the early part of the day while psychologically unstable introverts possessed high heart rate in the late evening. The author concludes that personality variables can exercise moderating influences in physiological activity associated with performance.
LEVEL: A LANG: Eng SIRC ARTICLE NO: 097739

Murphy, P. Chronobiology: for athletes it's a matter of time. *Physician and sportsmedicine (Minneapolis, Minn.) 12(9), Sept 1984, 158-159;162;164.*
LEVEL: I LANG: Eng SIRC ARTICLE NO: 099255

Preston, F.S. Travel and performance. *Medicine, science and the law (Brentford, Eng.) 24(4), Oct 1984, 249-253.*
LEVEL: I LANG: Eng

Price, W.J. Jets, jet lag, and sleep: effects on the travelling athlete. *Sports mediscope (Colorado Springs) 4(1), Jan/Mar 1984, 1-10.*
LEVEL: B LANG: Eng SIRC ARTICLE NO: 097754

Reilly, T. Robinson, G. Minors, D.S. Some circulatory responses to exercise at different times of day. (Refs: 25)*Medicine and science in sports and exercise (Indianapolis) 16(5), Oct 1984, 477-482.*
ABST: Circadian rhythms in heart rate were examined at rest, immediately pre-exercise, during submaximal and maximal exercise on a cycle ergometer, and during recovery post-exercise. Observations were made under controlled conditions at 0300, 0900, 1500, and 2100 hours. A significant circadian rhythm was found for resting heart rate lying supine and sitting pre-exercise. The rhythm in heart rate persisted during submaximal exercise (150 W) and at the maximal rate; the amplitude of the rhythm was attenuated at maximum. Ratings of perceived exertion at submaximal and maximal exercise intensities, and time to exhaustion on the ergometic test did not vary significantly with time of day. A significant rhythm was found for recovery heart rates in minutes 2, 3, 4, and 5 post-exercise ($P0.05$).
LEVEL: A LANG: Eng SIRC ARTICLE NO: 102819

Rietveld, W.J. Circadian rhythms. Physical performance as function of the time of the day. (Refs: 8)*International journal o sports medicine (Stuttgart) Suppl. 5, Nov 1984, 25-27.*
CONF: International Congress on Sports and Health (1983 : Maastricht, Netherlands).
LEVEL: I LANG: Eng SIRC ARTICLE NO: 104361

Shephard, R.J. Sleep, biorhythms and human performance. (Refs: 275)*Sports medicine (Auckland) 1(1), Jan/Feb 1984, 11-37.*
ABST: This review of literature defines some of the

terms used in the study of biorhythms and points out the functional importance of biorhythms. Physiological changes and associated variations of performance are explored in the context of daily, weekly, 4-weekly and annual cycles with particular reference to shifts of time zones and sleep deprivation. Finally the impact of regular moderate activity upon disturbances of biorhythm is examined. The author concludes that although performances are relatively small, the margin of success in athletic competition is such that more attention should be given to the optimising of biorhythms.
LEVEL: A LANG: Eng SIRC ARTICLE NO: 094626

Simonson, M. Segal, D.D. Your body rhythms. *Shape (Woodland Hills, Calif.) 4(2), Oct 1984, 74-79;122-123;125.*
LEVEL: B LANG: Eng SIRC ARTICLE NO: 173220

Winget, C.M. Les horaires de voyage et la performance. (Refs: 13)*Science du sport: documents de recherche et de technologie (Ottawa) W-1, oct 1984, 1-5.*
LEVEL: I LANG: Fr SIRC ARTICLE NO: 099276

Winget, C.M. Timing travel and athletic performance. (Refs: 13)*Sports: science periodical on research and technology in sport (Ottawa) Oct 1984, 1-5.*
LEVEL: I LANG: Eng SIRC ARTICLE NO: 099277

Winget, C.M. DeRoshia, C.W. Markley, C.L. Holley, D.C. A review of human physiological and performance changes associated with desynchronosis of biological rhythms. *Aviation, space and environmental medicine (Washington) 55(12), Dec 1984, 1085-1096.*
LEVEL: A LANG: Eng

Zahorska-Markiewicz, B. Markiewicz, A. Circannual rhythm of exercise metabolic rate in humans. (Refs: 12)*European journal o applied physiology and occupational physiology (Heidelberg) 52(3), Apr 1984, 328-330.*
ABST: Eighteen subjects underwent exercise tests and body fat determinations every month for a year. Exercise metabolic rate, respiratory quotient, acceleration of heart rate during exercise, and percentage body fat demonstrated circannual rhythms. These parameters exhibited their acrophases in April, October, February and August respectively.
LEVEL: A LANG: Eng SIRC ARTICLE NO: 097779

Zani, A. Rossi, B. Borriello, A. Mecacci, L. Diurnal interindividual differences in the habitual activity pattern of top level athletes. (Refs: 8)*Journal of sports medicine and physical fitness (Torino, Italy) 24(4), Dec 1984, 307-310.*
ABST: Different sport activities were chosen to verify the hypothesis of an influence of interindividual diurnal differences on the habitual activity pattern of the athletes. Results showed significant differences in the morningness-eveningness expressed preferences among athletes in agreement with their sport activity. Based on these findings a few suggestions for specific training activity programs are given.
LEVEL: A LANG: Eng SIRC ARTICLE NO: 106820

DRUGS, DOPING AND ERGOGENIC AIDS

Ades, P.A. Brammell, H.L. Greenberg, J.H. Horwitz, L.D. Effect of beta blockade and intrinsic sympathomimetic activity on exercise performance.

American journal of cardiology (New York) 54(10), 1 Dec 1984, 1337-1341.
LEVEL: A LANG: Eng

Alen, M. Haekkinen, K. Komi, P.V. Lihaksiston voimantuottokyvyn muutokset androgeenisia steroideja kaeyttaeneillae voimailijoila. (Changes in muscle power production capacity in power athletes self-administering androgenic anabolic steroids.) *Duodecim (Helsinki) 100(17), 1984, 1096-1104.*
LEVEL: A LANG: Fin

Allen, C.J. Craven, M.A. Rosenbloom, D. Sutton, J.R. Beta-blockade and exercise in normal subjects and patients with coronar artery disease. (Refs: 48)*Physician and sportsmedicine (Minneapolis, Minn.) 12(10), Oct 1984, 51-54;56;59-60.*
LEVEL: I LANG: Eng SIRC ARTICLE NO: 098896

Andersen, K. Vik-Mo, H. Increased left ventricular emptying at maximal exercise after reduction in afterload. *Circulation (New York) 69(3), Mar 1984, 492-496.*
ABST: The effect of afterload reduction on left ventricular function during maximal exertion was studied in 12 healthy men during exercise. One maximal exercise bicycle test was performed without drugs and another one was performed 4 hours later with 20 mg nifedipine. The results found increased left ventricle emptying at maximal exercise after nifedipine. This was attributed to a reduction in the afterload.
LEVEL: A LANG: Eng SIRC ARTICLE NO: 099220

Bengtsson, C. Impairment of physical performance after treatment with beta blockers and alpha blockers. *British medical journal (clinical research) (London) 288(6418), 3 Mar 1984, 671-672.*
ABST: This investigation found that the beta blockers, the alpha blocker, and the combined alpha and beta blocker significantly reduce physical performance in the small number of subjects tested.
LEVEL: A LANG: Eng SIRC ARTICLE NO: 099222

Bond, V. Franks, B.D. Howley, E.T. Alcohol, cardiorespiratory function and work performance. (Refs: 13)*British journal of sports medicine (Loughborough, Eng.) 18(3), Sept 1984, 203-206.*
ABST: Twelve males (six moderate drinkers and six abstainers) were studied for the influence of varying dosages of alcohol on cardiorespiratory function and work performance. The subjects underwent three separate maximal exercise tests which consisted of progressive workloads on the bicycle ergometer. Prior to each work bout the subject consumed either a placebo, a small, or a moderate dose of a 95 per cent ethanol solution. Analysis of the results indicated that the ingestion of a small of moderate amount of alcohol had no significant effect on heart rate, blood pressure, ventilation, oxygen uptake or work performance.
LEVEL: A LANG: Eng SIRC ARTICLE NO: 102760

Caldwell, J.E. Ahonen, E. Nousiainen, U. Diuretic therapy, physical performance, and neuromuscular function. (Refs: 25) *Physician and sportsmedicine (Minneapolis, Minn.) 12(6), Jun 1984, 73-76;79-81;85.*
ABST: 46 male athletes were tested before and after a 48 hour weight loss regimen. 15 athletes took furosemide, a diuretic while 16 athletes exercised and 15 others served as controls. Electromyographic examination of the diuretic group showed significant differences in nerve reactivity after diuretic use. Testing on a bicycle ergometer revealed that the diuretic group had

significant decreases in VO2, O2 pulse, work load , respiration and tidal volume compared to the other 2 groups. The authors conclude that diuretic use for rapid weight loss can be hazardous.
LEVEL: A LANG: Eng SIRC ARTICLE NO: 094590

Doyle, W.J. Weber, P.A. Meeks, R.H. Effect of topical timolol maleate on exercise performance. *Archives of ophthalmology (New York) 102(10), Oct 1984, 1517-1518.*
LEVEL: A LANG: Eng

Dragan, I. Contribution a l'augmentation de la capacite d'effort des sportifs par utilisation de facteurs physiologiques ergotropes. Etudes pharmacologiques au sujet de l'efficacite de la L-Carnitine. Contribution to increasing sporting effort capabilities by using ergotrophic physiological factors. Pharmacological studies in the efficiency of L-Carnitine. *Medecine du sport (Paris) 58(5), 25 sept 1984, 26.*
LEVEL: I LANG: Fr Eng SIRC ARTICLE NO: 100536

Hall, P.E. Kendall, M.J. Smith, S.R. Beta blockers and fatigue. *Journal of clinical and hospital pharmacy (Oxford) 9(4), De 1984, 283-291.*
LEVEL: A LANG: Eng

Hare, T.W. Lowenthal, D.T. Hakki, H. Goodwin, M.J. Training effect in elderly patients with coronary artery disease on beta adrenergic blocking drugs. (Refs: 23)*Annals of sports medicine (North Hollywood, Calif.) 2(1), 1984, 36-40.*
ABST: The authors examined 27 patients with cardiac disease, who underwent symptom-limited exercise testing prior to and at the completion of an eight week aerobic activities training program. A training effect was demonstrated for workload and total duration in each of four groups. A: 54 years or younger on beta adrenergic blocking drugs (BABD) (n, 6); B: 54 years or younger off BABD (n, 7): C: older than 54 years on BABD (n, 9); D: older than 54 years off BABD (n, 5). The results demonstrate the neither age (54 years or younger), (older than 54 years) nor drug (off BABD) (on BABD) interfere with benefits derived from an eight week training program.
LEVEL: A LANG: Eng SIRC ARTICLE NO: 103868

Hiatt, W.R. Marsh, R.C. Brammell, H.L. Fee, C. Horwitz, L.D. Effect of aerobic conditioning on the peripheral circulation during chronic beta-adrenergic blockade. *Journal of the American College of Cardiology (New York) 4(5), Nov 1984, 958-963.*
LEVEL: A LANG: Eng

Hughson, R.L. Alterations in the oxygen deficit-oxygen debt relationships with beta-adrenergic receptor blockade in man. *Journal of physiology (Cambridge) 349, Apr 1984, 375-387.*
ABST: The effects of beta-adrenergic receptor blockade (100 mg oral metoprolol) or matched placebo on gas exchange kinetics were studied in six males. Ventilation and gas exchange were monitored in four transitions from loadless pedalling to a selected work rate and back to loadless pedalling.
LEVEL: A LANG: Eng

Ingemann-Hansen, T. Halkjaer-Kristensen, J. Maximum oxygen consumption rate and dihydrogenated ergot alkaloids in humans. (Refs: 11)*British journal of sports medicine (Loughborough, Eng.) 18(2), Jun 1984, 70-73.*
ABST: The relationship of maximal oxygen uptake (VO2 max) with dihydrogenated ergot alkaloids was investigated in twelve young men. They were

subjected to graded bicycle exercise with work loads corresponding to 75% and 120% of the load necessary to elicit VO2 max. The exercise tests were performed after intravenous administration of 2 mg dihydroergostin (DE-145) as well as after saline as control, both preparations were given double-blind. VO2 max averaged (SD) 3.36 (0.41) l/min and no significant difference was disclosed between the DE-145 and the control situation. Normal relationships were observed between VO2 and work load, ventilation, heart rate, cardiac output, central venous pressure and acid-base data, and these relations were unaffected by DE-145 administration.
LEVEL: A LANG: Eng SIRC ARTICLE NO: 102789

Issekutz, B. Effect of ss-adrenergic blockade on lactate turnover in exercising dogs. (Refs: 25)*Journal of applied physiology: respiratory, environmental and exercise physiology (Bethesda, Md.) 57(6), Dec 1984, 1754-1759.*
LEVEL: A LANG: Eng SIRC ARTICLE NO: 108565

Kaiser, P. Physical performance and muscle metabolism during beta-adrenergic blockade in man. *Acta physiologica scandinavic (Stockholm) (Suppl) 536, 1984, 1-53.*
LEVEL: A LANG: Eng

Kindermann, W. Scheerer, W. Salas-Fraire, O. Biro, G. Woelfing, A. Verhalten der koerperlichen Leistungsfaehigkeit und des Metabolismus unter akuter Beta 1- und Beta 1/2-Blockade. (Behavior of physical endurance and metabolism during acute beta 1 and beta 1/2-blockade.) *Zeitschrift fuer Kardiologie (Darmstadt) 73(6), Jun 1984, 380-387.*
ABST: The effect of acute beta 1-blockade (100 mg metoprolol) beta 1/2-blockade (2 mg levobunolol) on exercise performance and metabolism was studied in 16 healthy male physical education students. The study was carried out in a randomized double blind cross-over fashion. The results indicate beta 1-blockade affects exercise performance, especially endurance performance, less than beta 1/2-blockade due to unaffected beta 2-receptors mediating giycogenolysis in the skeletal muscles.
LEVEL: A LANG: Ger

Krasikov, S.I. Boev, V.M. Zheleznov, L.M. Bliianie antioksidante M-1 na soderzhanie dienovykh konjugatov pri predel'noi fizicheskoi nagruzke. (Effect of the antioxidant M-1 on the concentration of diene conjugates after maximal physical exertion.) *Ukrainskii biokhimicheskii zhurnal (Kiev) 56(2), Mar/Apr 1984, 202-204.*
ABST: Diene conjugates, one of lipid peroxidation products, are accumulated in the blood serum of untrained people under maximum physical load. Introduction of antioxidant M-1 prevents their accumulation and enzymia, and promotes a decrease in the intensity of lactate accumulation under physical loads.
LEVEL: A LANG: Rus

Laustiola, K. Seppala, E. Nikkari, T. Vapaatalo, H. Exercise-induced increase in plasma arachidonic acid and thromboxane B2 in healthy men: effect of beta-adrenergic blockade. *Journal of cardiovascular pharmacology (New York) 6(3), May/Jun 1984, 449-454.*
ABST: The authors researched the effects of propranolol, atenolol, and practolol on the levels of free arachidonic acid (AA), thromboxane B2 (TxB2), prostaglandin (PG) E2, and 6-keto-P6F1 alpha in plasma, and TxB2 production by platelets during

clotting in 6 healthy men during exercise. Exercise-induced increase in AA,TxB2, and 6-keto-P6F1 in plasma was observed. All three beta blockers decreased the plasma levels of AA and TxB2 during exercise. The effects of beta blockade were less pronounced on plasma 6-keto-P6F1 alpha and P6E2 levels, and no significant effect was seen on TxB2 formation by platelets.
LEVEL: A LANG: Eng SIRC ARTICLE NO: 102794

Lebrun, P. Guezennec, Y. Bonnet, P. Muh, J.P. Aymonod, M. Morand, P. Influence d'une prise de D.L. carnitine par voie orale sur les parametres physiologiques et biochimiques au cours de deux types d'epreuves d'effort. Interet chez l'athlete d'endurance. (Refs: 18)*Medecine du sport (Paris) 58(5), 25 sept 1984, 20-25.*
RESUME: Les auteurs etudient les effets de l'administration de carnitine sur divers parametres physiologiques et biochimiques lors d'une epreuve d'effort a 80% du VO2 max jusqu'a l'epuisement. 5 sujets ages entre 26 et 52 ans se sont pretes a l'experimentation. Une augmentation de la capacite de travail sous D.L. Carnitine et des modifications des metabolites lipidiques sont observees.
LEVEL: A LANG: Fr SIRC ARTICLE NO: 100907

Lehtonen, A. Huupponen, R. Himanen, P. Effect of the short-term beta-adrenoceptor blockade on exercise metabolism in cold weather. *International journal of clinical pharmacology, therapy and toxicology (Munich) 22(2), Feb 1984, 86-90.*
ABST: The authors researched the effect of 2 days of treatment with either placebo, the non-selective beta-adrenoceptor antagonist with high ISA pindolol (10mg), or the cardioselective drug atenolol (100mg) on carbohydrate and lipid metabolism. Ten males served as subjects. Some results observed: 1) post exercise growth levels increased in placebo (P less than 0.01), in pindolol (P less than 0.01), and in atenolol (P less than 0.05), 2) plasma free fatty acid concentrations increased in placebo and pindolol (P less than 0.05) and in atenolol (p less than 0.01), and 3) serum triglyceride concentrations descreased significantly during exercise in placebo or pindolol (P less than 0.01).
LEVEL: A LANG: Eng SIRC ARTICLE NO: 099252

Mann, S.J. Krakoff, L.R. Felton, K. Yeager, K. Cardiovascular responses to infused epinephrine: effect of the state of physical conditioning. *Journal of cardiovascular pharmacology (New York) 6(2), Mar/Apr 1984, 339-343.*
ABST: The effects of epinephrine infusions on arterial pressure and heart rate responses are determined in 15 healthy subjects. The state of physical fitness of the subjects is assessed. The authors conclude that physical fitness increases the effect of circulating epinephrine on systolic arterial pressure without altering the chronotropic effect of this hormone.
LEVEL: A LANG: Eng SIRC ARTICLE NO: 100913

McLeod, A.A. Brown, J.E. Kitchell, B.B. Sedor, F.A. Kuhn, D.C. Williams, R.S. Shand, D.G. Hemodynamic and metabolic response to exercise after alpha 1-, beta 1-, and nonselective beta-adrenoceptor blockade in man. *American journal of medicine (New York) 76(2A), 27 Feb 1984, 97-100.*
LEVEL: A LANG: Eng SIRC ARTICLE NO: 099253

McLeod, A.A. Kraus, W.E. Williams, R.S. Effects of beta 1-selective and nonselective beta-adrenoceptor blockade during exercise conditioning in healthy adults. *American journal of cardiology (New York) 53(11), 1 Jun 1984, 1656-1661.*
ABST: The exercise tolerance of 30 adults was

evaluated in this study following the administration of atenolol (100 mg/day), propranolol (80 mg twice daily), and placebo before and after a 2-month training program. Findings indicated that only subjects receiving propranolol showed an acutely impaired exercise tolerance after drug administration but before training. Improvements in exercise capacity following training were observed in all 3 groups after drug treatment had stopped.
LEVEL: A LANG: Eng SIRC ARTICLE NO: 102804

Meerson, F.Z. Preduprezhdenie stressovykh povrezhdenii i povyshenie vynosimosti organizma k fizicheskoi nagruzke s pomoshch'iu khimicheskikh faktorov. (Prevention of stress damage and increasing body endurance in physical load by chemical factors.) *Patologicheskaia fiziologiia i eksperimentalnaia terapiia (Moskva) 1, Jan/Feb 1984, 11-19.*
LEVEL: A LANG: Rus

Morano, I. Influence of exercise and dianabol on the degradation rate of myofibrillar proteins of the heart and three fiber types of skeletal muscle of female guinea pigs. (Refs: 16)*International journal of sports medicine (Stuttgart) 5(6), Dec 1984, 317-319.*
ABST: The influence of methandrostenolone (Dianabol) and of a running training program on the degradation rate of myofibrillar proteins of the heart, soleus, red portion of the vastus lateralis, and white portion of the vastus lateralis of female guinea pigs was studied. Some results: 1) a significantly higher myofibrillar protein concentration in the skeletal muscle types than in the heart, and 2) the degradation rate of the myofibrillar proteins decreased in all muscle type in the trained group receiving Dianabol and in the heart of the untrained group receiving Dianabol and in the trained group.
LEVEL: A LANG: Eng SIRC ARTICLE NO: 104347

Ring, E.F.J. Trotman, S. Techniques for measuring skin temperature and blood flow. (Refs: 8)*Journal of the Society of Remedial Gymnastics and Recreational Therapy (Manchester) 114, Nov 1984, 32-34.*
NOTES: Reprinted from, Pharmaceutical journal (London), 1983, 231;236.
LEVEL: I LANG: Eng SIRC ARTICLE NO: 104362

Saurenmann, P. Koller, E.A. The ECG changes due to altitude and to catecholamines. (Refs: 23)*European journal of applied physiology and occupational physiology (Berlin, W.G.) 53(1), 1984, 35-42.*
ABST: In order to distinguish the effects of beta-receptor stimulation on the ECG from other factors during short-term adjustment to hypoxic aerohypoxia, the ECG of 19 volunteers were compared during moderately acute, stepwise exposure to high altitude (6,000 m) in a low pressure chamber, once with and once without beta-receptor blockade (propranolol), and after isoprenaline inhalation at ground level. The results show that beta-receptor stimulation accounts mainly for most ECG changes during altitude exposure. After exclusion of the catecholamines, the minor but still significant ECG changes at altitude may be attributed to other, so far undefined factors, such as cardiac hypoxia, vagal withdrawal, or increase of pulmonary resistance.
LEVEL: A LANG: Eng SIRC ARTICLE NO: 104366

Sawka, M.N. Levine, L. Kolka, M.A. Appleton, B.S. Joyce, B.E. Pandolf, K.B. Effect of atropine on the exercise-heat performance of man. *Fundamental and applied toxicology: official journal*

of the Society of Toxicology (Akron, Oh.) 4(2 Pt 2), Apr 1984, S190-S194.
ABST: This article reviews the findings of two studies on the physiological effects of atropine (0 to 4 mg, im) on soldiers exercising in hot-dry environments. The first study focuses on the threshold of physiological effects and the gradation of these effects with higher dose of atropine. The second study reports on the effects of exercise-heat acclimation on the reduced physical exercise performance following atropine administration.
LEVEL: A LANG: Eng SIRC ARTICLE NO: 102825

Schlaeffer, F. Engelberg, I. Kaplanski, J. Danon, A. Effect of exercise and environmental heat on theophylline kinetics. *Respiration (Basel) 45(4), 1984, 438-442.*
ABST: The pharmacokinetics of theophylline were studied in 6 healthy volunteers at rest, during light and moderate exercise and during exercise in a hot environment. Exercise was performed between 2 and 4 h after oral ingestion of theophylline. Significant prolongations of the half-life of the drug and reductions in its body clearance were observed during exercise to 30 per cent of VO2, max both at 22 and 40 degrees C, as well as during exercise to 50 per cent of VO2, max at 22 degrees C. Plasma clearances at the three exercise sessions were 0.70 plus or minus 0.09, 0.62 plus or mihus 0.1 and 0.75 plus or minus 0.09 ml/min/kg, respectively, compared with 0.99 plus or minus 0.13 ml/min/kg at rest.
LEVEL: A LANG: Eng SIRC ARTICLE NO: 104368

Shashkov, V.S. Lakota, N.G. Farmakologicheskaia korrektsiia rabotosposobnosti v model'nykh issledovaniiakh. (Pharmacological correction of work capacity in simulation studies.) *Farmakologiya i toksikologiya (Moscow) 47(2), Mar/Apr 1984, 5-15.*
LEVEL: A LANG: Rus

Silke, B. Watt, S.J. Taylor, S.H. The circulatory response to lifting and carrying and its modification by beta-adrenoceptor blockade. *International journal of cardiology (Amsterdam) 6(4), Oct 1984, 527-536.*
LEVEL: A LANG: Eng

Small, M. Tweddel, A.C. Rankin, A.C. Lowe, G.D. Prentice, C.R. Forbes, C.D. Blood coagulation and platelet function followin maximal exercise: effects of beta-adrenoceptor blockade. *Haemostasis (Basel) 14(3), 1984, 262-268.*
ABST: To determine if beta-blockade could modify exercise-induced changes in haemostatic factors we performed a double-blind study of acute strenuous exercise in normal males with and without beta-blockade. Exercise increased prostacyclin and plasminogen activator levels but there was no evidence of thrombin generation as indicated by unchanged platelet aggregation responses, beta-thromboglobulin and fibrinopeptide A levels. The only alteration in coagulation by beta-blockade was a reduction in the factor VIII:C and VIII:RAg rise after exercise and this modification may be relevant to the protective effect of these drugs in patients with coronary artery disease.
LEVEL: A LANG: Eng SIRC ARTICLE NO: 104372

Staessen, J. Cattaert, A. Fagard, R. Lijnen, P. Moermam, E. Hemodynamic and humoral effects of prostaglandin inhibition in exercising humans. (Refs: 31)*Journal of applied physiology: respiratory, environmental and exercise physiology (Bethesda, Md.) 56(1), Jan 1984, 39-45.*
ABST: Nine sodium-replete subjects exercised on

the bicycle ergometer after administration of placebo and after indomethacin, a prostaglandin synthetase inhibitor. After prostaglandin inhibition an increase in systolic and diastolic intra-arterial pressure was noted. Plasma renin activity and concentration were reduced at rest and after exercise. However, this study did not find a reduction in exercise capacity with prostaglandin inhibition.
LEVEL: A LANG: Eng SIRC ARTICLE NO: 095802

Stein, D.T. Lowenthal, D.T. Porter, R.S. Falkner, B. Bravo, E.L. Hare, T.W. Effects of nifedipine and verapamil on isometric and dynamic exercise in normal subjects. *American journal of cardiology (New York) 54(3), 1 Aug 1984, 386-389.*
ABST: The authors compared the effects of nifedipine and verapamil in 10 men during static and dynamic exercise. Blood pressure (BP), heart rate (HR), and plasma catecholamine were assessed during placebo, single- and at 2 multiple-dose levels of each of the drugs. Peak BP responses were blunted by a maximal dosage of verapamil administered during static activity. BP and HR did not change significantly at any dosage level of nifedipine during static exercise. During isotonic exercise, a progressive decrease in the peak exercise HR with both verapamil and nifedipine was observed. The plasma potassium level increased with both static and dynamic activity.
LEVEL: A LANG: Eng SIRC ARTICLE NO: 103899

Svedenhag, J. Henriksson, J. Juhlin-Dannfelt, A. Asano, K. Beta-adrenergic blockade and training in healthy men--effects on central circulation. *Acta physiologica scandinavica (Stockholm) 120(1), Jan 1984, 77-86.*
ABST: This paper investigated the effects of beta-adrenergic blockade on central circulation prior to and following training on cycle ergometers 40 min/day 4 days a week for 8 weeks. 8 subjects received beta-adrenergic receptor blocker propanolol (160 mg/day) while 8 subjects were given placebo tablets. Similar increase (18%) in vo2 max and decreases in resting heart rate (-4 beats/min) and exercise heart rate at moderate work load (120 W: -11 beats/min) were observed in both groups. At a high work load (180 W), the exercise heart rate decreased more in the placebo group than in the beta-blockade group (-19 vs. - 7 beats/min) and the oxygen pulse only increased in the placebo group (8%).
LEVEL: A LANG: Eng SIRC ARTICLE NO: 100925

Svedenhag, J. Hewnriksson, J. Juhlin-Dannfelt, A. Beta-adrenergic blockade and training in human subjects: effects on muscle metabolic capacity. *American journal of physiology (Bethesda, Md.) 247(3 Pt 1), Sept 1984, E305-E311.*
ABST: Sixteen male subjects (20-31 yr) trained for 8 wk on cycle ergometers. Eight of the subjects were treated with propranolol (160 mg/day). Training-induced increases in VO2 max and decreases in blood lactate and norepinephrine concentrations at submaximal exercise were not different between the beta-blockade and the placebo groups. The activities of the mitochondrial enzymes citrate synthase (CS), succinate dehydrogenase (SDH), cytochrome c oxidase (Cyt-c-ox), and 3-hydroxyacyl-CoA dehydrogenase (HAD) in the quadriceps femoris muscle increased significantly with training. Cyt-c-ox and HAD increased significantly more in the placebo group than in the beta-blockade group, while a tendency to an increase was noted for SDH. Muscle capillary

density increased similarly with training in the two groups.
LEVEL: A LANG: Eng SIRC ARTICLE NO: 103900

Tesch, P.A. Kaiser, P. Komi, P.V. Effects of beta-adrenergic blockade and EMG signal characteristics during progressive exercise. *Acta physiologica scandinavica (Stockholm) 121(2), Jun 1984, 189-191.*
LEVEL: I LANG: Eng SIRC ARTICLE NO: 103902

Tobin, M.J. Hughes, J.A. Hutchison, D.C. Effects of ipratropium bromide and fenoterol aerosols on exercise tolerance. *European journal of respiratory diseases (Copenhagen) 65(6), Aug 1984, 441-446.*
ABST: Twelve male patients with radiological evidence of pulmonary emphysema performed progressive exercise tests on a cycle ergometer. Ipratropium bromide (Ip), fenoterol (Fen), their combination and placebo were administered in a double-blind crossover study to compare the effects on ventilation (VE), heart rate (fc) and oxygen uptake (VO2) at rest and at maximal and sub-maximal workloads. There were no significant differences in resting VE between the 4 treatment regimes. During submaximal exercise, VE at a given workload was greater after Fen containing treatment regimes than after Ip alone or placebo. With respect to fc and VO2, there were no differences between treatments at rest or on submaximal or maximal exercise.
LEVEL: A LANG: Eng SIRC ARTICLE NO: 103903

van Baak, M.A. Jennen, W.H.J. Verstappen, F.T.J. Metabolic effects of acute and chronic beta-blockade during maximal aerobic exercise. (Refs: 8)*International journal of sports medicine (Stuttgart) Suppl. 5, Nov 1984, 183-185.*
CONF: International Congress on Sports and Health (1983 : Maastricht, Netherlands).
LEVEL: A LANG: Eng SIRC ARTICLE NO: 104385

Vapaatalo, H. Laustiola, K. Seppaelae, E. Rauramaa, R. Kaste, M. Hillbom, M. Kangasaho, M. Exercise, ethanol and arachidonic acid metabolism in healthy men. *Biomedica biochimica acta (Berlin) 43(8/9), 1984, S413-S420.*
LEVEL: A LANG: Eng

Violante, B. Buccheri, G. Brusasco, V. Effects of beta-adrenoceptor blockade on exercise performance and respiratory respons in healthy, physically untrained humans. *British journal of clinical pharmacology (London) 18(6), Dec 1984, 811-815.*
LEVEL: A LANG: Eng

Wijnen, S. Verstappen, F. Kuipers, H. The influence of intravenous NaHCO3-administration on interval exercise: acid-base balance and endurance. (Refs: 4)*International journal of sports medicine (Stuttgart) Suppl. 5, Nov 1984, 130-132.*
CONF: International Congress on Sports and Health (1983 : Maastricht, Netherlands).
LEVEL: A LANG: Eng SIRC ARTICLE NO: 103908

Zaloga, G.P. Dons, R.F. Exercise-induced hypoglycemia following propranolol in a patient after gastric fundoplication surger *Digestive disease and scienes (New York) 29(12), Dec 1984, 1164-1166.*
LEVEL: A LANG: Eng

ENVIRONMENT

Bar-Or, O. Children and physical performance in warm and cold environments. (Refs: 48)*In, Boileau, R.A. (ed.), Advances in pediatric sport sciences. Volume 1: biological issues, Champaign, Ill.,*

Human Kinetics Publishers, c1984, p. 117-129.
LEVEL: A LANG: Eng RJ125 20044

Gibbons, S.I. Adams, W.C. Combined effects of ozone exposure and ambient heat on exercising females. (Refs: 30)*Journal of applied physiology: respiratory, environmental and exercise physiology (Bethesda, Md.) 57(2), Aug 1984, 450-456.*
ABST: The present study investigated the effect of ozone and heat during simulated aerobic training. The subjects were ten aerobically trained young females. Higher ozone exposure induced significant impairment of pulmonary function variables. Furthermore, subjective discomfort increased with both ozone and heat exposure. The mechanisms for these reactions remain unclear.
LEVEL: A LANG: Eng SIRC ARTICLE NO: 108355

Marron, J.T. Tucker, J.B. Environmental factors. (Refs: 44)
NOTES: In, Birrer, R.B. (ed.), Sports medicine for the primary care physician, Norwalk, Conn., Appleton-Century-Crofts, c1984, p. 91-104.
LEVEL: I LANG: Eng RC1210 17030

Shephard, R.J. Athletic performance and urban air pollution. (Refs: 19)*Canadian Medical Association journal/Journal de l'Association medicale canadienne (Ottawa) 131(2), 15 Jul 1984, 105-109.*
LEVEL: I LANG: Eng SIRC ARTICLE NO: 096297

ENVIRONMENT - ALTITUDE

Boutellier, U. Giezendanner, D. Cerretelli, P. di Prampero, P.E. After effects of chronic hypoxia on VO2 kinetics and on O2 deficit and debt. (Refs: 11)*European journal of applied physiology and occupational physiology (Berlin, W.G.) 53(2), 1984, 87-91.*
ABST: Single breath O2 consumption was measured at rest, during 10 min cycloergometric exercise at 125 W, and in the following recovery phase in seven subjects before, and 12 days after 6 weeks at 5,200 m or above. Peak blood lactate after exercise was measured. O2 deficits and debts and half times of the VO2 on- and off-kinetics were calculated. Before acclimatization, the VO2 on- and off-responses were close to a single exponential. After return to sea level, the VO2 on-response curves were less steep in the initial phase, becoming closer to sigmoid. The VO2 off-responses during the initial 4 min of recovery were the same before and after acclimatization. Average O2 deficit was approx 320 ml larger after acclimatization: the fast component of O2 debt was similar.
LEVEL: A LANG: Eng SIRC ARTICLE NO: 104283

Cerretelli, P. Marconi, C. Deriaz, O. Giezendanner, D. After effects of chronic hypoxia on cardiac output and muscle blood flow at rest and exercise. (Refs: 17)*European journal of applied physiology and occupational physiology (Berlin, W.G.) 53(2), 1984, 92-96.*
ABST: Cardiac output (Q) and limb muscle blood flow were determined in eight male subjects at rest and during cycloergometric loads immediately before and 12 days after return from the 1981 Swiss Lhotse Shar (8,398 m) Expedition. Compared to control conditions, after exposure to hypoxia: 1) Q was unchanged at rest and at 75 watts (W) but was 18 per cent less at 150 W with a constant heart rate of 140 beats per min; 2) qm in the vastus lateralis was identical at rest but 26 per cent and 39 per cent less at two submaximal leg work loads (75 and 125 W); 3) qm in the biceps at 50 W was 34

per cent less; 4) hemoglobin flow, similarly to blood flow, was significantly reduced; 5) the qm adjustment rate was slower, particularly at the lower work loads.
LEVEL: A LANG: Eng SIRC ARTICLE NO: 104290

Escourrou, P. Johnson, D.G. Rowell, L.B. Hypoxemia increases plasma catecholamine concentrations in exercising humans. (Refs 20)*Journal of applied physiology: respiratory, environmental and exercise physiology (Bethesda, Md.) 57(5), Nov 1984, 1507-1511.*
LEVEL: A LANG: Eng SIRC ARTICLE NO: 108925

Filcescu, V. Groza, P. Vrancianu, R. Pintilie, I. Stoian, M. Ionescu, V. Dinu, C. Nicolae, A. Boanta, F. Modifications cardiodynamiques determinees par l'effort physique a l'altitude simulee (4000 m) et sous l'influence de l'inhalation de l'oxygene avec hyperpression intrapulmonaire. (Cardiodynamic changes caused by physical exertion at simulated altitude (4000 m) and under the influence of oxygen inhalation with intrapulmonary hyperpressure.) *Physiologie (Bucharest) 21(2), Apr/Jun 1984, 127-132.*
LEVEL: A LANG: Fr SIRC ARTICLE NO: 102774

Greksa, L.P. Haas, J.D. Leatherman, T.L. Thomas, R.B. Spielvogel, H. Work performance of high-altitude Aymara males. *Annals of human biology (London) 11(3), May/Jun 1984, 227-233.*
ABST: The sample for this study were 28 Aymara males between the ages of 15 and 43 years who were temporarily working as porters in La Paz, Bolivia (3700 m). There was a significant negative relationship between VO2 max and age in adult porters. However, there was also a significant positive relationship between maximal work output and age and a significant negative relationship between VO2 during submaximal exercise and age. Relative work intensity during submaximal exercise did not change significantly with age. Thus, even though VO2 max decreased significantly with age, these data suggest that there may not be a substantial decrease with age in the adaptive status of these men. Minimal support was found for the hypothesis that chest size in Andean highlanders influences the effectiveness of the oxygen transport system.
LEVEL: A LANG: Eng SIRC ARTICLE NO: 102782

Houston, C.S. Man at altitude. (Refs: 7)
NOTES: In, Strauss, R.H. (ed.), Sports medicine, Philadelphia ; Toronto, Saunders, 1984, p. 344-360.
LEVEL: A LANG: Eng RC1210 17196

Katch, V. Katch, F. Inside exercise. (high-altitude exercise) *Shape (Woodland Hills, Calif.) 4(2), Oct 1984, 18.*
LEVEL: B LANG: Eng SIRC ARTICLE NO: 173219

Lange, V. Diamox - a potential aid in acclimatization. (Refs: 7)*Climbing (Aspen, Colo.) 85, Jun 1984, 58.*
LEVEL: I LANG: Eng SIRC ARTICLE NO: 099251

Maresh, C.M. Noble, B.J. Robertson, K.L. Seip, R.L. Adrenocortical responses to maximal exercise in moderate-altitude native at 447 Torr. (Refs: 29)*Journal of applied physiology: respiratory, environmental and exercise physiology 56(2), Feb 1984, 482-488.*
ABST: Six low-altitude natives (LAN) (373 m or less) and eight moderate-altitude natives (MAN) (1,830-2200 m) exercised to exhaustion at their home altitudes and at a simulated altitude of 4,270 m (447 Torr). Maximal exercise at 447 Torr

resulted in a reduction of exercise performance in both LAN and MAN; however the decrease in exercise performance was greater at 447 Torr decreased the aldosterone concentration in both groups but this decrease was pronounced in the LAN group. The authors suggested that high altitude aldosterone concentrations are more like resident altitude values in MAN than in LAN.
LEVEL: A LANG: Eng SIRC ARTICLE NO: 093111

Nizovtsev, V.P. Zvarich, L.F. Otsenka effektivnosti vnutrilegochnogo gazoobmena pri myshechnoi rabote v usloviiakh gipoksicheskoi gipoksii. (Evaluation of the efficiency of intrapulmonary gas exchange during muscular work under hypoxic hypoxia.) *Fiziologicheskii zhurnal (Kiev) 30(4), Jul/Aug 1984, 494-498.*
LEVEL: A LANG: Rus

Oberneder, V. Understanding altitude physiology. *Sportsmedicine digest (Van Nuys, Calif.) 6(3), Mar 1984, 7.*
LEVEL: B LANG: Eng SIRC ARTICLE NO: 097751

Pootmans, J.R. Transport de l'oxygene et adaptations metaboliques lors de l'exercice en altitude. *Revue de l'Amicale des entraineurs francais d'athletisme (Paris) 89, oct/nov/dec 1984, 13-14.*
LEVEL: I LANG: Fr SIRC ARTICLE NO: 102815

Richalet, J.P. Les reactions de l'organisme a l'altitude. (Refs: 53)
NOTES: Dans, Richalet, J.P. (ed.) et al., Medecine de l'alpinisme, Paris, Masson, 1984, p. 30-55.
LEVEL: A LANG: Fr RC1220.M6 17787

Salzano, J.V. Camporesi, E.M. Stolp, B.W. Moon, R.E. Physiological responses to exercise at 47 and 66 ATA. (Refs: 31)*Journa of applied physiology: respiratory, environmental and exercise physioloyg (Bethesda, Md.) 57(4), Oct 1984, 1055-1068.*
LEVEL: A LANG: Eng SIRC ARTICLE NO: 108945

Smith, M.H. Sharkey, B.J. Altitude training: who benefits? *Physician and sportsmedicine 12(4), Apr 1984, 48-50;53-56;59;62.*
LEVEL: I LANG: Eng SIRC ARTICLE NO: 093131

Usha Singh, R.G. Agrawal, N.K. Singh, K.G. Histological changes in lungs at high altitude. (Refs: 18)*Journal of sports medicine and physical fitness (Torino, Italy) 24(3), Sept 1984, 225-229.*
ABST: Twenty Albino rats were taken to the high altitude. They were sacrificed in 4 sets of 5 rats each at 4 different altitudes. Autopsy study of lungs were done. Grossly, lungs showed marked congestion and peticheal haemorrhages at 12,000 feet and above. Light microscopy revealed marked passive congestion of the lungs, perivascular haemorrhages, features of pulmonary hypertension, emphysematous changes and mild bronchiolitis at the higher altitudes. No evidence of pulmonary oedema fluid could be noticed in any of the lung sections up to the height of 16,500 feet.
LEVEL: A LANG: Eng SIRC ARTICLE NO: 105497

Utsunomiya, T. Kadota, T. Yanaga, T. (Pituitary hormone responses to exercise at high altitudes.) *Nippon naibunpi gakkai zasshi/Folia endocrinologica japonica (Kyoto) 60(10), 20 Oct 1984, 1214-1226.*
LEVEL: A LANG: Jpn

ENVIRONMENT - COLD

Bangs, C.C. Cold injuries. (Refs: 6)
NOTES: In, Strauss, R.H. (ed.), Sports medicine, Philadelphia ; Toronto, Saunders, 1984 p. 323-343.
LEVEL: A LANG: Eng RC1210 17196

Houdas, Y. Carette, G. L'organisme au froid: echanges thermiques, reactions physiologiques et protection vestimentaire. (Refs: 15)
NOTES: Dans, Richalet, J.P. (ed.) et al., Medecine de l'alpinisme, Paris, Masson, 1984, p. 56-69.
LEVEL: I LANG: Fr RC1220.M6 17787

Jacobs, I. Romet, T. Frim, J. Hynes, A. Effects of endurance fitness on response to cold water immersion. *Aviation, space and environmental medicine (Washington) 55(8), Aug 1984, 715-720.*
LEVEL: A LANG: Eng

Jerome, J. Liquid heat: in winter, water can save your life - if it doesn't kill you first. *Outside (Chicago, Ill.) 9(9), Oct 1984, 29-30;32.*
LEVEL: I LANG: Eng SIRC ARTICLE NO: 108735

Kolka, M.A. Martin, B.J. Elizondo, R.S. Exercise in a cold environment after sleep deprivation. (Refs: 22)*European journal of applied physiology and occupational physiology (Berlin) 53(3), Dec 1984, 282-285.*
ABST: Seven subjects exercised to thermal comfort in cold environment after normal sleep (control) and following a 50-h period of sleep deprivation. Resting core temperature taken before the subject entered the cold environment was significantly lower following the 50-h period of wakefulness. Fifty hours of sleep deprivation failed to alter the core temperature response during exercise in severe cold stress, and subjects chose identical work rates to minimize fatigue and cold sensation. The results suggest that the 50-h sleep deprivation period was not a true physiological stress during exercise in a cold environment.
LEVEL: A LANG: Eng SIRC ARTICLE NO: 104329

Mackova, J. Sturmova, M. Macek, M. Prolonged exercise in prepubertal boys in warm and cold environments. (Refs: 5)
CONF: Symposium of Paediatric Work Physiology (10th : 1981 : Joutsa, Finland).
NOTES: In, Ilmarinen, J. and Vaelimaeki, I. (eds.), Children and sport: paediatric work physiology, Berlin, Springer-Verlag, 1984, p. 135-141.
ABST: In order to determine the most suitable temperature of the environment for school gymnastics ten prepubertal boys were studied on a bicycle ergometer at a workload of 50 per cent of aerobic capacity in 25 degrees Celcius and 10 degrees Celsius. The results indicated that there were significantly greater physiological strains in the warm environment than in the cold one.
LEVEL: A LANG: Eng SIRC ARTICLE NO: 102800

Nogaller, A.M. Butov, M.A. Kalygina, T.A. Immunologicheskaia rezistentnost i adaptatsionnye reaktsii pri zakalivanii kholodo (Immunological resistance and adaptational reactions to hardiness training against cold.) *Sovetskaia meditsina (Moscow) 1, 1984, 92-95.*
LEVEL: A LANG: Rus

Park, Y.S. Pendergast, D.R. Rennie, D.W. Decrease in body insulation with exercise in cool water. *Undersea biomedical research (Bethesda, Md.) 11(2), June 1984, 159-168.*
LEVEL: A LANG: Eng

Patton, J.F. Vogel, J.A. Effects of acute cold exposure on submaximal endurance performance. (Refs: 12)*Medicine and science in sports and exercise (Indianapolis) 16(5), Oct 1984, 494-497.*
ABST: The purposes of this study were to assess VO2 max and submaximal endurance time to exhaustion (ET) during acute cold-air exposure. Eight male subjects (X age is 19.9 yr) were alternately exposed in groups of four to chamber temperarures of plus 20oC and minus 20oC for 30 h each. Maximum oxygen uptake was not significantly different between conditions 3.43 plus or minus 0.09 l.min-1 at plus 20oC and 3.35 plus or minus 0.10 l.min-1 at minus 20oC. During endurance exercise, intensities equaled 77.1 plus or minus 1.4% and 78.9 plus or minus 2.0% of VO2 max at plus or minus 20oC and minus 20oC, respectively. Heart rate and VO2 values obtained between 8 and 10 min of the endurance run were not significantly different (156 plus or minus 2 bpm and 2.63 plus or minus 0.08 l.min-1 at plus 20oC and 158 plus or minus 3 bpm and 2.65 plus or minus 0.11 l.min-1 at minus 20oC). Endurance time to exhaustion however, decreased 38% (P0.05) from 111.9 plus or minus 22.8 min at plus 20oC to 66.9 plus or minus 13.6 min at minus 20oC.
LEVEL: A LANG: Eng SIRC ARTICLE NO: 102812

Soroko, S.I. Matusov, A.L. Sidorov, I.A. Adaptatsiia cheloveka k ekstremal'nym usloviiam Antarktidy. (Human adaptation to th extreme conditions of the Antarctic.) *Fiziologiya cheloveka (Moscow) 10(6), Nov/Dec 1984, 907-920.*
LEVEL: A LANG: Rus

Storlie, J. Adapting to cold weather exercise. *Aerobics (Dallas, Tex.) 5(2), Feb 1984, 5;8.*
LEVEL: B LANG: Eng SIRC ARTICLE NO: 097767

ENVIRONMENT - GAS MIXTURE

Avol, E.L. Linn, W.S. Venet, T.G. Shamoo, D.A. Hackney, J.D. Comparative respiratory effects of ozone and ambient oxidant pollution exposure during heavy exercise. *Journal of the Air Pollution Control Association (Pittsburgh, Pa.) 34(8), Aug 1984, 804-809.*
LEVEL: A LANG: Eng

Byrnes, W.C. Mihevic, P.M. Freedson, P.S. Horvath, S.M. Submaximal exercise quantified as percent of normoxic and hyperoxic maximum oxygen uptakes. (Refs: 26)*Medicine and science in sports and exercise (Indianapolis) 16(6), Dec 1984, 572-577.*
ABST: Maximum oxygen uptake (VO2 max) was measured in six college-aged males under normoxic (NVO2 max) and hyperoxic (HVO2 max; 70 per cent oxygen) conditions. Subjects then randomly performed three 20-min submaximal exercise bouts. Hyperoxia resulted in a 13 per cent increase in VO2 max. Significant decreases were observed in VE (ventilation) (13 per cent), epinephrine (37 per cent), norepinephrine (26 per cent), and blood lactate (28 per cent), with no change in oxygen uptake (VO2), carbon dioxide production (VCO2), or respiratory exchange ratio (R) during hyperoxia at the same absolute power output.
LEVEL: A LANG: Eng SIRC ARTICLE NO: 104286

Drechsler, D.M. Airway gas mixing during rest and bicycle exercise. Eugene, Ore.: Microform Publications, University of Oregon, 1984. 1 microfiche : negative, ill. ; 11 x 15 cm.

NOTES: Thesis (Ph.D.) - Pennsylvania State University, 1981; (ix, 86, 1 leaves); vita; includes bibliography.
LEVEL: A LANG: Eng UO84 83

Eiken, O. Tesch, P.A. Effects of hyperoxia and hypoxia on dynamic and sustained static performance of the human quadriceps muscle. *Acta physiologica scandinavica (Stockholm) 122(4), Dec 1984, 629-633.*
ABST: Quadriceps muscle performance during dynamic and sustained static exercise was compared in eight men breathing 11 per cent, 21 per cent or 99 per cent O2 mixtures. Subjects performed (1) 60 maximal consecutive dynamic contractions and (2) one sustained exhaustive static contration at 22 per cent of maximal voluntary contraction. During dynamic exercise, mean peak torque was as follows: 104 plus or minus 4 Nm (hyperoxia); 95 plus or minus 5 Nm (hypoxia); and 98 plus or minus 4 Nm (normoxia). Reductions of static endurance time were observed during hypoxia (152 plus or minus 12s) as compared to normoxia (189 plus or minus 13s) and hyperoxia (169 plus or minus 11s).
LEVEL: A LANG: Eng

Folinsbee, L.J. Bedi, J.F. Horvath, S.M. Pulmonary function changes after 1 h continuous heavy exercise in 0.21 ppm ozone. (Refs: 12)*Journal of applied physiology: respiratory, environmental and exercise physiology (Bethesda, Md.) 57(4), Oct 1984, 984-988.*
ABST: Seven trained athletes exercised for one hour at 75 percent of their maximum oxygen consumption in both room air and in a 0.21 ppm ozone environment. Following the ozone environment exercise the athletes reported laryngeal soreness, tracked uritation, and chest tightness on taking a deep breath. Compared to an earlier study with moderate exercise, it appears that people performing heavy exercise are affected more readily by lower ozone levels.
LEVEL: A LANG: Eng SIRC ARTICLE NO: 108940

ENVIRONMENT - HEAT

AbuSaleh, A.M. Physiological responses to heat stress of Arabs and Americans. Eugene, Ore.: Microform Publications, University of Oregon, 1984. 2 microfiches : negative, ill. ; 11 x 15 cm.
NOTES: Thesis (Ph.D.) - University of Oregon, 1983; (xi, 122 leaves); vita; includes bibliography.
LEVEL: A LANG: Eng UO84 396-397

Armstrong, L.E. Muscle potassium levels during training in the heat. (Refs: 17)*Track and field quarterly review (Kalamazoo, Mich.) 84(3), Fall 1984, 39-41.*
LEVEL: I LANG: Eng SIRC ARTICLE NO: 096213

Barnes, G. Wilson, A. The effect of a new glucose-electrolyte fluid on blood electrolyte levels, gastric emptying and work performance. (Refs: 32)*Australian journal of science & medicine in sport (Kingston, Aust.) 16(1), Jun 1984, 25-30.*
ABST: Plasma volume, plasma and urine electrolytes, heart rates, body weight and gastric emptying were measured in twelve male and one female subjects during rest, work and recovery in a hot environment in an environmental chamber, following the ingestion of either demineralised water (DW) or a glucose-electrolyte solution (GE). Despite the fact that DW was emptied more efficiently than GE, plasma volumes and work heart rates did not differ significantly between the two drinks. The

results of this study suggest that there is little difference in the physiologic effects induced through the ingestion of either a GE or DW drink before, during and after work of this intensity and duration in the heat.
LEVEL: A LANG: Eng SIRC ARTICLE NO: 104168

Cloud, E.V. Steady state VO2 responses to exercise in two thermal environments. Eugene, Ore.: Microform Publications, University of Oregon, 1984. 1 microfiche : negative, ill. ; 11 x 15 cm.
NOTES: Thesis (M.S.) - Auburn University, 1982; (viii, 60 leaves); vita; includes bibliography.
LEVEL: A LANG: Eng UO84 148

Francesconi, R.P. Sawka, M.N. Pandolf, K.B. Hypohydration and acclimation: effects on hormone responses to exercise/heat stress. *Avitation space and environmental medicine (Washington) 55(5), May 1984, 365-369.*
LEVEL: A LANG: Eng SIRC ARTICLE NO: 102775

Gregory, W.B. Thermoregulatory boundaries to exercise in hot, humid environments. Eugene, Ore.: Microform Publications, University of Oregon, 1984. 2 microfiches : negative, ill.; 11 x 15 cm.
NOTES: Thesis (Ph.D.) - Texas A & M University, 1979; (x, 102 leaves); vita; includes bibliography.
LEVEL: A LANG: Eng UO84 9-10

Haymes, E.M. Physiological responses of female athletes to heat stress: a review. (Refs: 36)*Physician and sportsmedicine (Minneapolis, Minn.) 12(3), Mar 1984, 45-48;51-53;56;59.*
ABST: This article reviews studies dealing with men's and women's responses to heat stress. Findings indicate few differences in their responses to exercise in hot, dry environments. Women show a higher tolerance for exercise in the heat than men. Higher rectal temperatures and heart rates were observed among women at higher relative exercise intensity.
LEVEL: A LANG: Eng SIRC ARTICLE NO: 091734

Kachanovskii, K.N. Vliianie kratkovremennoi teplovoi adaptatsii na nekotorye pokazateli fizicheskoi rabotosposobnosti. (Effect of short-term thermal adaptation on indices of physical work capacity.) *Fiziologiya cheloveka (Moscow) 10(1), Jan/Feb 1984, 163-165.*
LEVEL: A LANG: Rus

Kivett, L.D. Physiological responses to exercise in a hot-dry versus a hot-humid environment. Eugene, Ore.: Microform Publication, University of Oregon, 1984. 2 microfiches : negative, ill. ; 11 x 15 cm.
NOTES: Thesis (M.S.) - Western Illinois University, 1981; (viii, 98 leaves); includes bibliography.
LEVEL: A LANG: Eng UO84 150-151

Kolka, M.A. Levine, L. Cadarette, B.S. Rock, P.B. Sawka, M.N. Pandolf, K.B. Effects of heat acclimation on atropine-impaired thermoregulation. *Aviation, space and environmental medicine (Washington) 55(12), Dec 1984, 1107-1110.*
LEVEL: A LANG: Eng

Kratzing, C.C. Cross, R.B. Effects of facial cooling during exercise at high temperature. (Refs: 6)*European journal of applied physiology and occupational physiology (Berlin, W.G.) 53(2), 1984, 118-120.*
ABST: Healthy men and women were exercised on a cycle ergometer in a hot environment (46o C). Cold air (5o C) was blown onto the face either as a jet from the tube directed towards the nose or being introduced under a face mask. There was a subjective feeling of increased comfort although the temperature under the mask decreased to only 28o C-32o C. Facial cooling did not cause any changes in either blood pressure or heart rate.
LEVEL: A LANG: Eng SIRC ARTICLE NO: 104330

Levin, L. Sawka, M.N. Joyce, B.E. Cadarette, B.S. Pandolf, K.B. Varied and repeated atropine dosages and exercise-heat stres (Refs: 19)*European journal of applied physiology and occupational physiology (Berlin, W.G.) 53(1), 1984, 12-16.*
ABST: Comparisons of physiological responses to 0, 0.5, 1, and 2 mg of atropine were made in seven males while they exercised in a hot-dry environment. Responses to 4 mg, as well repeatability of responses to 2 mg, were studied in two and six of these subjects, respectively. On 8 test days an intramuscular injection of atropine or saline control was administered 20 min before subjects walked on a treadmill for two 50-min bouts. Heart rate (HR) during exercise did not change in the control trial but by min 50 increased during all atropine trials. Rectal temperature (Tre) increased in all trials by min 50 and continued increasing in the 2-mg trial during the second exercise bout. For the two subjects tested with all dosages, the change in HR and Tre between the atropine and control trials at 50 min of exercise was regressed against the various atropine dosages.
LEVEL: A LANG: Eng SIRC ARTICLE NO: 104335

Loesel, H. Important medical aspects on sport referring to the Olympic Games in Summer 1984. (Part 5) Sportmedizinisch relevante Aspekte bezueglich der Olympischen Spiele im Sommer 1984. (5. Teil) Aspects importants du point de vue de la medecine du sport pour les Jeux olympiques d'ete 1984. (5ieme partie) Aspectos importantes de la medicina y del deporte para los Juegos Olimpicos de verano de 1984. (5a parte) *UIT shooting sport journal (Muenchen, FRG) 24(3), May/Jun 1984, 13-14;16-19;40-43.*
LEVEL: Eng Ger Fr Spa SIRC ARTICLE NO: 098447

Mackova, J. Sturmova, M. Macek, M. Prolonged exercise in prepubertal boys in warm and cold environments. (Refs: 5)
CONF: Symposium of Paediatric Work Physiology (10th : 1981 : Joutsa, Finland).
NOTES: In, Ilmarinen, J. and Vaelimaeki, I. (eds.), Children and sport: paediatric work physiology, Berlin, Springer-Verlag, 1984, p. 135-141.
ABST: In order to determine the most suitable temperature of the environment for school gymnastics ten prepubertal boys were studied on a bicycle ergometer at a workload of 50 per cent of aerobic capacity in 25 degrees Celcius and 10 degrees Celsius. The results indicated that there were significantly greater physiological strains in the warm environment than in the cold one.
LEVEL: A LANG: Eng SIRC ARTICLE NO: 102800

Murakami, N. Effects of prolonged exercise on behavioral responses to heat stress. *International journal of biometeorology (Amsterdam) 28(4), 1984, 349.*
LEVEL: I LANG: Eng SIRC ARTICLE NO: 104066

Sawka, M.N. Francesconi, R.P. Pimental, N.A. Pendolf, K.B. Hydration and vascular fluid shifts during exercise in the heat. (Refs: 27)*Journal of applied physiology: respiratory, environmental and exercise physiology (Bethesda, Md.) 56(1), Jan 1984, 91-96.*
ABST: Six male and six female subjects were euhydrated and hypohydrated consequently serving as their own controls, to determine the effects of hydration level on vascular fluid shifts during exercise in the heat. Hemodilution occurred when euhydrated and hemoconcentration occurred when hypohydrated. With hypohydration, the total plasma protein also decreased. These fluid shifts were not affected by the sex of the subject.
LEVEL: A LANG: Eng SIRC ARTICLE NO: 096292

Sawka, M.N. Francesconi, R.P. Young, A.J. Pandolf, K.B. Influence of hydration level and body fluids on exercise performance in the heat. *JAMA. Journal of the American Medical Association (Chicago) 252(9), 7 Sept 1984, 1165-1169.*
ABST: During exercise in the heat, sweat output often exceeds water intake, resulting in hypohydration, which is defined as a body fluid deficit. This fluid deficit is comprised of water loss from both the intracellular and extracellular fluid compartments. Hypohydration during exercise causes a greater heat storage and reduces endurance in comparison with euhydration levels. The greater heat storage is attributed to a decreased sweating rate (evaporative heat loss) as well as a decreased cutaneous blood flow (dry heat loss). These response decrements have been attributed to both plasma hyperosmolality and a plasma hypovolemia.
LEVEL: A LANG: Eng SIRC ARTICLE NO: 104367

Schiltz, J. Heat: the athlete killer. Coaches must understand the dangers involved in playing in hot weather and be prepared to cope with heat stress in their athletes. *Athletic journal 64(8), Mar 1984, 14;60-62.*
LEVEL: B LANG: Eng SIRC ARTICLE NO: 093127

Sen Gupta, J. Swamy, Y.V. Pichan, G. Dimri, G.P. Physiological responses during continuous work in hot dry and hot humid environments in Indians. *International journal of biometeorology (Amsterdam) 28(2), May 1984, 137-146.*
LEVEL: A LANG: Eng

Sutton, J.R. Heat illness. (Refs: 57)
NOTES: In, Strauss, R.H. (ed.), Sports medicine, Philadelphia ; Toronto, Saunders, 1984, p. 307-322.
LEVEL: A LANG: Eng RC1210 17196

Tochihara, Y. Physiological responses of men and women during prolonged 40 percent VO2 max exercise at different ambient temperatures. *Journal of the anthropological society of Nippon (Tokyo) 92(1), 1984, 1-11.*
LEVEL: A LANG: Eng SIRC ARTICLE NO: 096303

Wells, T.D. Jessup, G.T. Langlotz, K.S. Effects of sunscreen use during exercise in the heat. (Refs: 18)*Physician and sportsmedicine (Minneapolis, Minn.) 12(6), Jun 1984, 132-137;141;144.*
ABST: 16 men exercised in an environmental chamber using a sunscreen during both hot day and hot humid environment conditions. The results found that during hot day conditions mean skin temperature was significantly increased, however no such results were found during hot humid exercise. The authors conclude that use of a sunscreen on hot days sweat evaporation.
LEVEL: A LANG: Eng SIRC ARTICLE NO: 094635

PHYSIOLOGY - FACTORS AFFECTING PERFORMANCE (continued)

ENVIRONMENT - WATER

Lecomte, J. Sur quelques effets cardio-vasculaires de l'immersion chez l'homme normal. (Refs: 3)*Revue de l'education physique (Liege) 24(2), 1984, 3-9.*
LEVEL: I LANG: Fr SIRC ARTICLE NO: 100908

Toxer, M.M. Sawka, M.N. Pandolf, K.B. Thermal responses during arm and leg and combined arm-leg exercise in water. (Refs: 22 *Journal of applied physiology: respiratory, environmental and exercise physiology (Bethesda, Md.) 56(5), May 1984, 1355-1360.*
ABST: This investigation studied the effects of arm, leg, and combined arm-leg exercise on selected thermoregulatory responses to exercise in water. Eight subjects performed ergometer work at different intensities in water with a temperature of 20, 26 or 33oC. Rectal temperature was significantly higher during leg exercise compared to arm or combined arm-leg exercise at any water temperature. The authors suggest that there is a greater conductive and convective heat loss during exercise utilizing the arms when compared to legs-only exercise.
LEVEL: A LANG: Eng SIRC ARTICLE NO: 097770

FATIGUE

DeMeersman, R.E. Schaefer, D.C. Miller, W.W. Personality and self-motivation during biochemical fatigue. *Journal of human stress (Shelburne Falls, Mass.) 10(3), Fall 1984, 146-150.*
ABST: This study compared the physical endurance during an ergometer test of 10 females exhibiting the Type A behaviour pattern and 10 with type B pattern. Two experimental sessions were provided: 1) a nonmotivated session and 2) a session with encouragement given by the experimenter to exercise until exhaustion.
LEVEL: A LANG: Eng

Duchateau, J. Hainaut, K. Training effects on muscle fatigue in man. (Refs: 19)*European journal of applied physiology and occupational physiology (Berlin) 53(3), Dec 1984, 248-252.*
ABST: Effects of 3 months training, on electrical and mechanical failures during fatigue, were studied in human adductor pollicis muscle. Eight subjects carried out a daily training program of 10 series of 20 fast (0.5s) voluntary contractions. No significant change of surface muscle action potential (SAP) is observed after training. The considerable loss of force recorded during fatigue in control muscles (minus 36 per cent) is significantly smaller after training (minus 17 per cent). Slowing of tension development and of tension relaxation, observed during fatigue in control muscles (respectively minus 47 per cent and minus 79 per cent) is smaller after training (respectively minus 28 per cent and minus 65 per cent). Analysis of electrical failure indicates that training significantly reduces augmentation of muscle SAP duration and area recorded during fatigue.
LEVEL: A LANG: Eng SIRC ARTICLE NO: 104303

Ewing, J.L. Stull, G.A. Rate of force development in the handgripping muscles by females as a function of fatigue level. (Refs: 14)*Research quarterly for exercise & sport (Reston, Va.) 55(1), Mar 1984, 17-23.*
ABST: The purpose of this study was to ascertain the effects on the rate at which the handgripping muscles in 28 females develop force when they are

fatigued to 80%, 60%, and 40% of their original maximal strength level. Handgrip forces were recorded from a handgripping device and a strain gauge. As expected in this study, regardless of the level of fatigue, the absolute force generated during contraction tended to increase over time. The sigmoidal pattern of the absolute force-time curve at all levels of fatigue was noted. In addition, throughout the duration of the contraction, the amount of force developed decreased with progressive increases in fatigue. The findings of this study conflict with another finding that females generate maximal isometric forces faster than do males.
LEVEL: A LANG: Eng SIRC ARTICLE NO: 096239

Franks, B.D. Myers, B.C. Effects of talking on exercise tolerance. (Refs: 23)*Research quarterly for exercise & sport (Reston, Va.) 55(3), Sept 1984, 237-241.*
ABST: Two studies determined the effects of responding to questions on heart rate (HR), rating of perceived exertion (RPE), and time to voluntary exhaustion on a graded treadmill walking/running test in college students. The first study used 16 (8 female and 8 male) volunteers; each subject was tested both without talking and while responding to 3 questions during each exercise stage. The second study had independent groups (n, 10 females each): (1) no talking during the early exercise stages (two walking stages), but answering questions during the later (running) stages until exhaustion, and (2) answering questions during the walking stages, but not talking during the running stages. Exercise tolerance, HR, and RPE were generally not affected by the tester asking subjects questions about subjects' physical activity habits, with the following exceptions: the first study found a lower HR response to light work when the subjects were responding to questions. In the second study, the subjects perceived the work to be harder with no talking during the second (walking) stage, and while talking during the third (running) stage.
LEVEL: A LANG: Eng SIRC ARTICLE NO: 102776

Hughes, J.R. Crow, R.S. Jacobs, D.. Mittlemark, M.B. Leon, A.S. Physical activity, smoking, and exercise-induced fatigue. *Journal of behavioral medicine (New York) 7(2), Jun 1984, 217-230.*
LEVEL: A LANG: Eng SIRC ARTICLE NO: 104321

Jannuzzi, L. The chemistry of fatigue. *Runner's world (Mountain View, Calif.) 19(8), Aug 1984, 54-57.*
LEVEL: B LANG: Eng SIRC ARTICLE NO: 096258

Ji, L.L. The relationship of maximal oxygen uptake to endurance performance at maximal and submaximal work loads. Eugene, Ore.: Microform Publications, University of Oregon, 1984. 1 microfiche : negative, ill. ; 11 x 15 cm.
NOTES: Thesis (M.S.) - University of Wisconsin-Madison, 1982; (vii, 62, 6 leaves); includes bibliography.
LEVEL: A LANG: Eng UO84 149

Kahn, J.F. Monod, H. A study of fatigue during repetitive static work performed in two different segmental positions. (Refs: 20)*European journal of applied physiology and occupational physiology (Berlin, W.G.) 53(2), 1984, 169-174.*
ABST: Sixteen subjects, nine women and seven men, aged between 19 and 35 years , performed three series of isometric contractions of the flexor muscles of the forearm. Each series consisted of four isometric contractions sustained until

exhaustion. The position of the arm was variable according to the series. Under these conditions, study of heart rate (HR), systolic blood pressure (SBP) and limit-time showed that: 1. HR and SBP were not affected by the arm position even when fatigue was important; 2. for a given load with a progressive appearance of fatigue, the limit-time in female subjects was higher; and 3. in both groups, in spite of the fatigue appearing after several isometric contractions performed in the upper position, movement of the arm to the lower position was sufficient to significantly increase the time-limit of another isometric contraction at 40 per cent MVC without concomitant increase in cardiac work.
LEVEL: A LANG: Eng SIRC ARTICLE NO: 104326

Katch, F.I. Katch, V.L. Solve the mystery of fatigue. *Joe Weider's muscle & fitness (Woodland Hills, Calif.) 45(8), Aug 1984, 126-127;238.*
LEVEL: I LANG: Eng SIRC ARTICLE NO: 096261

Makowicki, D. The influence of individualized music on fatigue during a graded exercise test. Eugene, Ore.: Microform Publications, University of Oregon, 1984. 1 microfiche : negative, ill. ; 11 x 15 cm.
NOTES: Thesis (M.S.) - Springfield College, 1982; (vii, 52 leaves); includes bibliography.
LEVEL: A LANG: Eng UO84 257

Protasov, V.N. Sposoby profilaktiki pereutomleniia (obzor literatury). (Methods of preventing overfatigue (a review of the literature).) *Voenno-meditsinskii zhurnal (Moscow) 2, Feb 1984, 36-39.*
LEVEL: A LANG: Rus

Schochina, M. Magora, A. Gonen, B. Wolf, E. Electrophysiological study of the development of fatigue in the opponens pollici muscle. *Electromyography and clinical neurophysiology (Louvain) 24(1/2), Jan/Feb 1984, 155-160.*
LEVEL: A LANG: Eng SIRC ARTICLE NO: 099267

Sologub, E.B. Tsoneva, T.N. Petrov, I.A. Pavlov, O.G. Dakhab, T.V. Dinamika sverhmedlennogo omega-potetsiala i prostranstvennoi sinkhronizatsii EEG pri myshechnom utomlenii. (Dynamics of the infraslow omega potential and of the spatial synchronization of the EEG in muscle fatigue.) *Fiziologicheskii zhurnal SSSR imeni I.M. Sechenova (Leningrad) 70(12), Dec 1984, 1617-1623.*
ABST: The object of the present study was the dynamics of infraslow omega-potentials and EEG interrelated activity modifications in young and adult (19-25 years old) sportsmen during strenuous endurance exercise on a cycle-ergometer. Correlation and coherence analysis revealed at the initial stage of muscle fatigue an increase of close relationship (synchronization and in phase readjustment) of different cortical areas potentials mainly between the prefrontal and precentral cortex. It becomes more pronounced with age and improvement in professional skill. A reliable correlation between omega-potential dynamics and spatial EEG synchronization was found.
LEVEL: A LANG: Rus

Wolf, E. Blank, A. Schochina, M. Gonen, B. Effect of exercise of the lower limbs on the non-exercised biceps brachii muscle. (Refs: 29)*American journal of physical medicine (Baltimore) 63(3), Jun 1984, 113-121.*
ABST: The purpose of this study was to examine the electrophysiological pattern of fatigue of the biceps brachii (BB) in 12 subjects before and after bicycle leg exercise (LE). The results indicate that a potentiating transfer effect in BB may occur as a

result of the LE. There was no correlation between electromyographic changes and lactic acid concentrations.
LEVEL: A LANG: Eng SIRC ARTICLE NO: 097778

Zauner, C.W. Theories of fatigue. *Sportsmedicine digest (Van Nuys, Calif.)* 6(3), Mar 1984, 4-6.
LEVEL: B LANG: Eng SIRC ARTICLE NO: 097780

Zimkin, N.V. O variativnosti struktury funktsionalnoi sistemyu v protsesse deiatelnosti i pri utomlenii. (Structural variability of the functional system during activity and fatigue.) *Fiziologicheskii zhurnal SSSR Imeni, I.M. Sechenova (Leningrad)* 70(12), Dec 1984, 1593-1599.
ABST: The object of the present paper is an analysis of factors causing considerable variability of functional systems (P. K. Anokhin) in their efferent part. This variability concerns the structure not only of different movements but has been established as well for similar repeated (cyclic, in particular) movements during work performed with the same working power. The problem of variability of the functional systems in fatigue is discussed.
LEVEL: A LANG: Rus

GENETICS

Bouchard, C. Lortie, G. Heredity and endurance performance. (Refs: 151)*Sports medicine (Auckland)* 1(1), Jan/Feb 1984, 38-64.
ABST: This review considers the evidence in the existing literature for genetic effects in several determinants of endurance performance, namely: body measurements and physique, body fat, pulmonary functions, cardiac and circulatory functions, muscle characteristics, substrate utilization, and maximal aerobic power. Also, the response to aerobic training of indicators of aerobic work metabolism and endurance performance is reviewed, with emphasis on the specificity of the response and the individual differences observed in trainability. The authors conclude that there are considerable differences in the level of endowment for endurance performance and in the sensitivity to endurance training. However, the genetic effects are modest in comparison to other phenotypes, such as skeletal dimensions of the body.
LEVEL: A LANG: Eng SIRC ARTICLE NO: 094588

Bouchard, C. Malina, R.M. Genetics and Olympic athletes: a discussion of methods and issues. (Refs: 29)
NOTES: In, Carter, J.E.L. (ed.), Physical structure of Olympic athletes. Part II. Kinanthropometry of Olympic athletes, Basel, Karger, c1984, p. 28-38.
LEVEL: A LANG: Eng RC1235 12672

Despres, J.P. Bouchard, C. Savard, R. Prud'homme, D. Bukowiecki, L. Theriault, G. Adaptive changes to training in adipose tissue lipolysis are genotype dependent. (Refs: 35)*International journal of obesity (London)* 8(1), 1984, 87-95.
ABST: The authors evaluate the effects of heredity and training on adipose tissue morphology and metabolism. 15 pairs of monozygotic twins (MZ), aged from 16 to 24 years, are submitted to a biopsy of adipose tissue while 8 pairs of twins participate in a 20-week training program, five days a week, 40 min a day. Significant increases of VO2 max, basal lipolysis, epinephrine submaximal lipolysis (ESML), and epinephrine maximal stimulated lipolysis (EML) are observed. Percent body fat and adipocyte diameter do not change. The training effect on ESML and EML are similar for twins of the same

MZ pair.
LEVEL: A LANG: Eng SIRC ARTICLE NO: 100893

Kagamimori, S. Robson, J.M. Heywood, C. Cotes, J.E. Genetic and environmental determinants of the cardio-respiratory respons to submaximal exercise--a six-year follow-up study of twins. *Annals of human biology (London)* 11(1), Jan/Feb 1984, 29-38.
ABST: This longitudinal study evaluated the fat-free mass and the cardio-respiratory response of a total of 65 identical and non-identical boy and girl twin pairs. Both fat-free mass and the exercise cardiac frequency were influenced by genetic and environmental factors. Non-identical twins and boys were subject to a greater environmental component than their counterparts.
LEVEL: A LANG: Eng SIRC ARTICLE NO: 099245

Prud'Homme, D. Bouchard, C. Leblanc, C. Landry, L.F. Fontaine, E. Sensitivity of maximal aerobic power to training is genotype-dependent. *Medicine and science in sports and exercise (Indianapolis)* 16(5), Oct 1984, 489-493.
ABST: Ten pairs of monozygotic twins of both sexes were submitted to a 20-wk endurance-training program, four and five times per week, 40 min per session, at an average of 80% of the maximal heart rate reserve. Maximal aerobic power (MAP) and ventilatory aerobic (VAT) and anaerobic (VANT) thresholds were measured before and after the training program, as well as during the 7th and 14th week to adjust training to changes in maximal heart rate. Training significantly increased MAP (from 44 plus or minus 6 to 50 plus or minus 6), VAT (25 plus or minus 3 to 30 plus or minus 4), and VANT (36 plus or minus 5 to 42 plus or minus 6). Differences in the MAP response to training were not distributed randomly among the twin pairs. Results suggest that there are considerable individual differences in the adaptive capacity to short-term endurance training.
LEVEL: A LANG: Eng SIRC ARTICLE NO: 102818

NUTRITION

Bjoerkman, O. Sahlin, K. Hagenfeldt, L. Wahren, J. Influence of glucose and fructose ingestion on the capacity for long-term exercise in well-trained men. *Clinical physiology (Oxford)* 4(6), Dec 1984, 483-494.
ABST: This study focuses on the influence of glucose and fructose ingestion on endurance performance. Eight men perform bicycle ergometry exercises until exhaustion while taking either glucose, fructose, or water in a double-blind study. Findings indicate that subjects ingesting glucose exercise longer (137 plus or minus 13 min) than subjects ingesting either fructose (114 plus or minus 12 min) or water (116 plus or minus 13 min).
LEVEL: A LANG: Eng

Brilla, L.R. Effects of hypomagnesemia and exercise on total cholesterol, high density lipoprotein cholesterol, and lipoprotein profile in rats. Eugene, Ore.: Microform Publications, University of Oregon, 1984. 2 microfiches : negative, ill. ; 11 x 15 cm.
NOTES: Thesis (Ph.D.) - University of Oregon, 1983; (xiii, 120 leaves); vita; includes bibliography.
LEVEL: A LANG: Eng UO84 400-401

Bruce, V. Crosby, L.O. Reicheck, N. Pertschuk, M. Lusk, E. Mullen, J.L. Energy expenditure in primary malnutrition during standardized exercise. *American journal of physical medicine (Baltimore)*

63(4), Aug 1984, 165-174.
ABST: Energy metabolism of 8 malnourished females was assessed during exercise and compared to control subjects. The malnourished subjects consumed less oxygen and had a resting energy expenditure less than predicted values. Body composition, total body water and thyroxine levels were within normal limits.
LEVEL: A LANG: Eng SIRC ARTICLE NO: 104170

Coyle, E.F. Coggan, A.R. Effectiveness of carbohydrate feeding in delaying fatigue during prolonged exercise. (Refs: 49) *Sports medicine (Auckland, N.Z.)* 1(6), Nov/Dec 1984, 446-458.
ABST: Carbohydrate feeding during moderate intensity exercise postpones the development of fatigue by approximately 15 to 30 minutes, yet it does not prevent fatigue. This observation agrees with data suggesting that carbohydrate supplementation reduces muscle glycogen depletion. In contrast to moderate intensity exercise, carbohydrate feeding during low intensity exercise results in hyperinsulinaemia. Consequently, muscle glucose uptake and total carbohydrate oxidation are increased by approximately the same amount. The amount of ingested glucose which is oxidised is greater than the increase in total carbohydrate oxidation and therefore endogenous carbohydrate is spared. The majority of sparing appears to occur in the liver, which is reasonable since muscle glycogen is not utilised to a large extent during mild exercise.
LEVEL: A LANG: Eng SIRC ARTICLE NO: 102628

Elia, M. Lammert, O. Zed, C. Neale, G. Energy metabolism during exercise in normal subjects undergoing total starvation. *Human nutrition. Clinical nutrition (London)* 38(5), Sept 1984, 355-362.
LEVEL: A LANG: Eng

Falecka-Wieczorek, I. Kaciuba-Uscilko, H. Metabolic and hormonal responses to prolonged physical exercise in dogs after a single fat-enriched meal. (Refs: 28)*European journal of applied physiology and occupational physiology (Berlin)* 53(3), Dec 1984, 267-273.
ABST: Metabolic and hormonal responses to prolonged physical exercise in dogs fed a fat-enriched meal 4 h prior to the exercise were compared to those measured 4 h after a mixed meal or in the postabsorptive state. It is concluded that ingestion of a single fat-enriched meal considerably modifies the exercise-induced changes in lipid metabolism. The pattern of changes in plasma TG, FFA, and glycerol concentrations indicates an enhanced hydrolysis of plasma chylomicron-TG, suggesting that this lipid source may contribute markedly to exercise metabolism.
LEVEL: A LANG: Eng SIRC ARTICLE NO: 104305

Francesconi, R. Hubbard, R. Exercise in the heat: effects of saline or bicarbonate infusion. *Journal of applied physiology: respiratory, environmental and exercise physiology (Bethesda, Md.)* 57(3), Sept 1984, 733-738.
LEVEL: A LANG: Eng SIRC ARTICLE NO: 108934

Gissal, W. Analysis of urinary hydroxyproline levels and delayed muscle soreness resulting from high and low intensity step testing under gelatin-free and gelatin-loading dietary regimens. Eugene, Ore.: Microform Publications, University of Oregon, 1984. 1 microfiche : negative ; 11 x 15 cm.
NOTES: Thesis (M.S.) - University of Wisconsin-La Crosse, 1982; (vi, 89 leaves); includes bibliography.
LEVEL: A LANG: Eng UO84 296

PHYSIOLOGY - FACTORS AFFECTING PERFORMANCE (continued)

Gollnick, P.D. Matoba, H. Role of carbohydrate in exercise. (Refs: 31)*Clinics in sports medicine (Philadelphia) 3(3), Jul 1984, 583-593.*
NOTES: Symposium on nutritional aspects of exercise.
ABST: Carbohydrate is an important source of energy during exercise. During short, heavy exercise, it may be the only energy source for the working muscle and may be derived solely from the glycogen stored within the muscle fibers themselves. During prolonged, submaximal exercise, the extent of the contribution that carbohydrate makes to the total fuel consumed depends upon several factors, which are discussed in detail in this article.
LEVEL: I LANG: Eng SIRC ARTICLE NO: 100778

Guezemnec, C.Y. Ferre, P. Serrurier, B. Merino, D. Aymonod, M. Pesquies, P.C. Metabolic effects of testosterone during prolonged physical exercise and fasting. (Refs: 19)*European journal of applied physiology and occupational physiology (Heidelberg) 52(3), Apr 1984, 300-304.*
ABST: This study examined the effects of acute and chronic increases in levels of circulating testosterone on the energy metabolism of both fasting and exercising rats. In 72 h fasted rats both acute and chronic increases in testosterone were associated with significant decreases in blood alanine and lactate. Furthermore chronic elevation of testerone also increased muscle glycogen content in 72 h. fasted rats. After 7h of continuous treadmill running at 20m/min acute and chronic elevation of testosterone induced a significant decrease in blood alanine and a slight decrease in blood glucose. The authors conclude that increased levels of testosterone can induce clygoen supercompensation in the fed resting state but cannot counteract the exhaustion of muscle glycogen during running.
LEVEL: A LANG: Eng SIRC ARTICLE NO: 097726

Hargreaves, M. Costill, D.L. Coggan, A. Fink, W.J. Nishibata, I. Effect of carbohydrate feedings on muscle glycogen utilization and exercise performance. (Refs: 27)*Medicine and science in sports and exercise (Indianapolis) 16(3), June 1984, 219-222.*
ABST: Ten men were studied during 4 h of cycling to determine the effect of solid carbohydrate (CHO) feedings on muscle glycogen utilization and exercise performance. In the experimental trial (E) the subjects ingested 43 g of sucrose in solid form along with 400 ml of water at 0, 1, 2 and 3 h of exercise. During the control trial (C) they received 400 ml of an artificially sweetened drink without solid CHO. No differences in VO2, heart rate, or total energy expenditure were observed between trials; however, respiratory exchange ratios were significantly higher during E. Blood glucose was significantly elevated 20 min post-feeding in E; however, by 50 min no differences were observed between trials until 230 min. Muscle glycogen utilization was significantly lower during E than C. During a sprint (100 per cent VO2 max) ride to exhaustion at the end of each trial, subjects performed 45 per cent longer when fed CHO.
LEVEL: A LANG: Eng SIRC ARTICLE NO: 108588

Jandrain, B. Krzentowski, G. Pirnay, F. Mosora, F. Lacroix, M. Luyckx, A. Lefebvre, P. Metabolic availability of glucose ingested 3h before prolonged exercise in humans. (Refs: 35)*Journal of applied physiology: respiratory, environmental and exercise physiology (Bethesda, Md.) 56(5), May 1984, 1314-1319.*

ABST: This study investigated the extent to which 100g of glucose dissolved in 400 ml of water is available as an energy source during 4h of moderate exercise if it is ingested 3h before the exercise. Five healthy subjects drank the glucose solution, rested for 3h and then exercised on a treadmill at 45% of their individual maximal oxygen consumption for 4h. The results indicate that the ingested glucose represents a readily available energy substrate. Throughout the entire period of exercise blood glucose concentrations remained between 3.5 and 4.0 mmol/l. The average total amount of exogenous glucose oxidized during the exercise was 67.5g.
LEVEL: A LANG: Eng SIRC ARTICLE NO: 097732

Keller, K. Schwarzkopf, R. Preexercise snacks may decrease exercise performance. (Refs: 21)*Physician and sportsmedicine 12(4), Apr 1984, 89-91.*
LEVEL: I LANG: Eng SIRC ARTICLE NO: 093103

Lafontaine, P. Eterradossi, J. Tanche, M. Effets d'une ingestion de glucose avant l'exercice sur l'utilisation des substrats et l'adaptation hormonale au cours de l'effort. (Refs: 11)*Medecine du sport (Paris) 58(3), 25 mai 1984, 44-48.*
RESUME: Les auteurs comparent les parametres physiques et les modifications biologiques des substrats et des hormones dans deux epreuves precedees ou non d'une ingestion glucosee. 6 hommes, ages de 25 a 32 ans, pratiquant en amateur un sport d'endurance depuis plusieur annees participent a l'etude. Aucune variation n'est observee d'une epreuve a l'autre au niveau de la frequence cardiaque, la fraction de VO2 max, le quotient et equivalent respiratoire. L'absorption de glucose avant l'epreuve entraine: 1) une augmentation importante de la glycemie avant l'effort, puis une chute dans les 20 premieres minutes suivant le debut de l'exercice et 2) une mobilisation moins importante des acides gras libres.
LEVEL: A LANG: Fr SIRC ARTICLE NO: 096268

Lavoie, J.M. Peronnet, F. Cousineau, D. Provencher, P.J. Effects of a 24-h CHO-poor diet on metabolic and hormonal responses during prolonged CHO-loaded leg exercise. (Refs: 30)*International journal of sports medicine (Stuttgart) 5(3), Jun 1984, 146-151.*
ABST: This study examined the effects of the pre-experimental period of arm exercise followed by a 24-h carbohydrate (CHO)-poor intake, intended to reduce initial hepatic glycogen levels, on substrate and endocrine responses during prolonged CHO-loaded leg exercise. Seven subjects pedaled a cycle ergometer for 60 min at 62 per cent VO2 max in the two following conditions: 1) after leg CHO loading followed by a 60-min arm exercise and a 24-h CHO-poor diet and 2) after leg CHO loading only. There were no significant differences during exercise between the two conditions in blood glucose, lactate, glucagon, and cortisol concentrations.
LEVEL: A LANG: Eng SIRC ARTICLE NO: 104178

Lukaski, H.C. Bolonchuk, W.W. Klevay, L.M. Mahalko, J.R. Milne, D.B. Sandstead, H.H. Influence of type and amount of dietary lipid on plasma lipid concentrations in endurance athletes. *American journal of clinical nutrition (Bethesda, Md.) 39(1), Jan 1984, 35-44.*
ABST: 3 male endurance cyclists consumed isoenergetic diets for 3 28-day periods during which carbohydrate, polunsaturated fat or saturated fat

were about 50% of the daily energy intake. The polyunsaturated fat diet significantly reduced mean fasting plasma total cholesterol in comparison to the other 2 diets. The polyunsaturated diet significantly depressed mean plasma triglycerides compared to the other 2 diets. The authors conclude that dietary lipid differences influence fasting serum lipid and lipoprotein levels among men with high energy expenditures. The Key's equation was found to be a useful tool for predicting changes in plasma total cholesterol in these circumstances.
LEVEL: A LANG: Eng SIRC ARTICLE NO: 097626

Lukaski, H.C. Bolonchuk, W.W. Klevay, L.M. Milne, D.B. Sandstead, H.H. Changes in plasma zinc content after exercise in men fed a low-zinc diet. *American journal of physiology (Bethesda, Md.) 247(1 Pt 1), Jul 1984, E88-E93.*
ABST: For 30 days five healthy men aged 23-57 yr consumed a diet adequate in zinc (8.6 mg/day); they ate a low-zinc diet (3.6 mg/day) for the next 120 days and then received a zinc-supplemented (33.6 mg/day) diet for 30 days. Aerobic capacity was determined periodically during each diet period. Relative zinc balance declined during depletion. Pre- and postexercise zinc concentrations decreased when dietary zinc was restricted and increased with supplementation. Both plasma zinc and hematocrit increased after maximal exercise. To minimize the effect of hemoconcentration during exercise, the van Beaumont quotient was calculated using pre- and postexercise hematocrit and plasma zinc. The initial quotient declined during depletion. With zinc repletion, the quotient increased to levels greater than the quotient in depletion but similar to the initial quotient. The quotient was a strong predictor of the change in relative zinc balance during zinc depletion.
LEVEL: A LANG: Eng SIRC ARTICLE NO: 102633

MacLaren, D. Reilly, T. Ireland, J. A nutritional aid to recovery from strenuous exercise. (Refs: 16)*International journal of sports medicine (Stuttgart) Suppl. 5, Nov 1984, 32-34.*
CONF: International Congress on Sports and Health (1983 : Maastricht, Netherlands).
LEVEL: A LANG: Eng SIRC ARTICLE NO: 104180

Marniemi, J. Vuori, I. Kinnunen, V. Rahkila, P. Vainikka, M. Peltonen, P. Metabolic changes induced by combined prolonged exercise and low-calorie intake in man. (Refs: 35)*European journal of applied physiology and occupational physiology (Berlin, W.G.) 53(2), 1984, 121-127.*
ABST: Thirteen middle-aged women and 10 men walked 344 km during 7 days. Except for some natural products, no food intake was allowed. During the hike the body weight and serum protein concentration of the subjects decreased by about 7 per cent, on average. Serum triglyceride and total cholesterol decreased drastically, about 30-40 per cent during the hike, but HDL-cholesterol showed a tendency to increase. Serum free fatty acids rose 1.5-2 times above the starting level. Serum glucose and evening insulin levels decreased significantly during the hike. Serum cortisol in evening samples after the daily walking and plasma norepinephrine concentrations were significantly increased. Serum testosterone levels decreased in men but not in women.
LEVEL: A LANG: Eng SIRC ARTICLE NO: 104342

Nice, C. Reeves, A.G. Brinck-Johnsen, T. Noll, W. The effects of pantothenic acid on human exercise capacity. (Refs: 14) *Journal of sports*

medicine and physical fitness (Torino) 24(1), Mar 1984, 26-29.
ABST: 9 highly trained distance runners consumed one gram of panthothenic acid per day for two weeks while 9 others took a placebo in this double blind study. Both groups were exercised to exhaustion on a treadmill before and after the two week period. No significant effects on human exercise capacity were observed.
LEVEL: A LANG: Eng SIRC ARTICLE NO: 099256

Spurr, G.B. Barac-Nieto, M. Reina, J.C. Ramirez, R. Marginal malnutrition in school-aged Colombian boys: efficiency of treadmill walking in submaximal exercise. *American journal of clinical nutrition (Bethesda, Md.) 39(3), Mar 1984, 452-459.*
ABST: Testing of 658 boys 6 to 16 years of age found that marginal malnutrition has no effect on the efficiency of submaximal work during treadmill walking.
LEVEL: A LANG: Eng SIRC ARTICLE NO: 099129

Suboticanec-Buzina, K. Buzina, R. Brubacher, G. Sapunar, J. Christeller, S. Vitamin C status and physical working capacity i adolescents. (Refs: 9)*International journal for vitamin and nutrition research (Berne) 54(1), 1984, 55-60.*
ABST: The effect of ascorbic acid supplementation on physical working capacity was studied in 49 young adolescent boys. After daily administration for two months of 70 mg ascorbic acid, mean plasma vitamin C levels in the experimental group rose from 0.33 to 1.49 mg/dl and the prevalence of deficient plasma vitamin C values decreased from 52.3 percent to zero. The improvement in vitamin C biochemical status was also accompanied by a statistically significant increase in VO2 max.
LEVEL: A LANG: Eng SIRC ARTICLE NO: 102634

van der Beek, E.J. van Dokkum, W. Schrijver, J. Wesstra, J.A. van de Weerd, H. Hermus, R.J.J. Effect of marginal vitamin intake on physical performance of man. (Refs: 37)*International journal of sports medicine (Stuttgart) Suppl. 5, Nov 1984, 28-31.*
CONF: International Congress on Sports and Health (1983 : Maastricht, Netherlands).
LEVEL: A LANG: Eng SIRC ARTICLE NO: 104186

Welle, S. Metabolic responses to a meal during rest and low-intensity exercise. *American journal of clinical nutrition (Bethesda, Md.) 40(5), Nov 1984, 990-994.*
LEVEL: A LANG: Eng

Williams, M.H. Vitamin and mineral supplements to athletes: do they help? (Refs: 85)*Clinics in sports medicine (Philadelphia) 3(3), Jul 1984, 623-637.*
NOTES: Symposium on nutritional aspects of exercise.
ABST: Vitamins and minerals are essential for the regulation of many metabolic processes involved in exercise. Consequently, vitamin and mineral supplements have been utilized by a number of athletes in attempts to increase physical performance. However, research has, in general, revealed that such supplementation will not be effective if given to an athlete who is already receiving an adequate supply of nutrients.
LEVEL: I LANG: Eng SIRC ARTICLE NO: 100793

Wootton, S.A. Williams, C. Influence of carbohydrate-status on performance during maximal exercise. (Refs: 4)*International journal of sports medicine (Stuttgart) Suppl. 5, Nov 1984, 126-127.*
CONF: International Congress on Sports and Health

(1983 : Maastricht, Netherlands).
LEVEL: A LANG: Eng SIRC ARTICLE NO: 104396

PHYSIOLOGY - MUSCLE

Baldwin, K.M. Muscle development: neonatal to adult. (Refs: 68)*Exercise and sport sciences reviews (Lexington, Mass.) 12, 1984, 1-19.*
ABST: This paper reviews the physiological, biochemical, and histological changes that occur in developing muscles of mammals, beginning at birth and continuing through maturation. In both human and rodent muscle, fiber type differentiation occurs relatively early in life. The major change which occurs is a loss of Type IIc fibers and an increase in Type I, Type IIa, and Type IIb fibers. Training effects on neonatal muscle are briefly discussed.
LEVEL: A LANG: Eng SIRC ARTICLE NO: 096217

Bobet, J. Norman, R.W. Effects of load placement on back muscle activity in load carriage. (Refs: 8)*European journal of applied physiology and occupational physiology (Berlin, W.G.) 53(1), 1984, 71-75.*
ABST: The effect of two different load placements (just below mid-back or just above shoulder level) on erector spinae EMG, trapezius EMG, and heart rate were investigated during load carriage. The EMG and heart rates were telemetered from 11 subjects while they walked on a smooth level surface carrying a load of 19.5 kg in a specially designed backpack. The high load placement resulted in significantly higher levels of muscle activity than did the lower placement. Heart rate was not significantly different between the two placements. A qualitative biomechanical analysis suggests that the EMG differences are primarily due to differences in the moments and forces arising from the angular and linear accelerations of the load and trunk.
LEVEL: A LANG: Eng SIRC ARTICLE NO: 104282

Caix, M. Outrequin, G. Descottes, B. Kalfon, M. Pouget, X. The muscles of the abdominal wall: a new functional approach with anatomoclinical deductions. *Anatomica clinica (New York) 6(2), 1984, 101-108.*
LEVEL: A LANG: Eng

Friden, J. Changes in human skeletal muscle induced by long-term eccentric exercise. *Cell and tissue research (Berlin) 236(2), 1984, 365-372.*
ABST: The fine structure of muscle fibres from the vastus lateralis of nine healthy males (mean age 26 years) was investigated. Four individuals constituted non-exercised controls while five subjects participated in a two-months eccentric muscular training program. It is concluded that muscular work of high tension can induce fine-structural alterations. When repeated over a long period of time, extreme tension demands seem to initiate reorganization in the muscle fibres, predominantly in the Type-2 fibres. This adaptation probably results in a better stretchability of the muscle fibres, reduces the risk of mechanical damage and brings about an optimal overlap between actin and myosin filaments.
LEVEL: A LANG: Eng SIRC ARTICLE NO: 102777

Gregoire, L. Veeger, H.E. Huijing, P.A. van Ingen Schenau, G.J. Role of mono- and biarticular muscles in explosive movements (Refs: 18)*International journal of sports medicine (Stuttgart) 5(6), Dec 1984, 301-305.*

ABST: From 24 vertical jumps (eight subjects, three jumps each), calculation of forces, torques, and power per joint were combined with EMG data of eight leg muscles and with estimations of their contraction velocities. In the second part of the push-off, a high power output of 3000-4000 W was delivered in the ankle joints during plantar flexion. During the high plantar flexion velocity at the end of the push-off, hip and knee joints showed high extension velocities resulting in relatively low contraction velocities for the biarticular muscles.
LEVEL: A LANG: Eng SIRC ARTICLE NO: 104315

Hort, W. Floethner, R. Etore, J. Heudes, A.M. Les bases scientifiques de la musculation et de la traumatologie musculaire. Paris: Vigot, 1984. 173 p. : ill. (Collection sport & enseignement; 75.)
NOTES: Bibliographie: p. 165-173. Traduit de: Die Muskulatur des Leistungssportlers, Erlangen, Perimed, c1983.
LEVEL: I LANG: Fr ISBN: 2-7114-0912-0 RC1235 19036

Lindstedt, S. That marvellous machine: what you need to know about muscles. *Bicycling 25(1), Jan/Feb 1984, 28;31.*
LEVEL: LANG: Eng SIRC ARTICLE NO: 090265

Loos, T. Boelens, P. The effect of ankle-tape on lower limb muscle-activity. *International journal of sports medicine (Stuttgart) Suppl. 5, Nov 1984, 45-46.*
CONF: International Congress on Sports and Health (1983 : Maastricht, Netherlands).
LEVEL: A LANG: Eng SIRC ARTICLE NO: 104337

McDonagh, M.J.N. Davies, C.T.M. Adaptive response of mammalian skeletal muscle to exercise with high loads. (Refs: 101) *European journal of applied physiology and occupational physiology (Heidelberg) 52(2), Jan 1984, 139-155.*
ABST: This is a review of studies concerned with the effects of chronic exercise using high loads on skeletal muscle. Areas of review include: the nature of various training stimuli; hypertrophy of the muscle and muscle fibres; and the other underlying biochemical and neurological mechanisms of the response. Data from both human and animal muscle experiments are included.
LEVEL: A LANG: Eng SIRC ARTICLE NO: 096280

Roldan Villalobos, R. Pena Amaro, J. Vaamonde Lemos, R. Alvarez, J.M. Carabot, L. del Castillo, G. La biopsie musculaire methode d'etude en medecine du sport. (Refs: 34)*Medecine du sport (Paris) 58(6), nov 1984, 31-37.*
LEVEL: I LANG: Fr SIRC ARTICLE NO: 102822

Sargeant, A.J. Dolan, P. Young, A. Optimal velocity for maximal short-term (Anaerobic) power output in cycling. (Refs: 8) *International journal of sports medicine (Stuttgart) Suppl. 5, Nov 1984, 124-125.*
CONF: International Congress on Sports and Health (1983 : Maastricht, Netherlands).
LEVEL: I LANG: Eng SIRC ARTICLE NO: 104650

Tarkka, I.M. Power spectrum of electromyography in arm and leg muscles during isometric contractions and fatigue. (Refs: 16) *Journal of sports medicine and physical fitness (Torino, Italy) 24(3), Sept 1984, 189-194.*
ABST: The electromyography of eight muscles were investigated in nine men to find out whether predominantly fast or slow muscles have different power spectral density function (PSDF). The PSDF was described as mean power frequency (MPF). The MPF in maximal isometric contractions was

significantly lower in triceps brachii compared to biceps brachii or soleus, gastrocnemius and tibialis anterior. The quadriceps muscles did not differ from each other or from arm or shank muscles. During submaximal fatigueing contraction the shift of MPF to lower frequencies was evident in all the muscles investigated.
LEVEL: A LANG: Eng SIRC ARTICLE NO: 105495

EXCITATION-CONTRACTION

Anderson, D.S. Jackson, M.F. Kropf, D.S. Soderberg, G.L. Electromyographic analysis of selected muscles during sitting push-ups: effects of position and sex. (Refs: 15)*Physical therapy 64(1), Jan 1984, 24-28.*
ABST: EMG activity of selected muscles was monitored in 16 men and 16 women in various exercise positions. It was the purpose of the study to detect differences due to sex and/or position. Results showed that women had greater EMG activity in all positions.
LEVEL: A LANG: Eng SIRC ARTICLE NO: 091710

Camus, G. Thys, H. Lhermerout, C. Pigeon, G. Modifications de l'electromyogramme global lors de l'exercice statique: effets de l'age. (Changes in the global electromyogram during static exercise; effect of age.) *Comptes rendus des seances de la Societe de biologie et de ses filiales (Paris) 178(5), 1984, 567-571.*
LEVEL: A LANG: Fr

De Koning, F.L. Binkhorst, R.A. Vissers, A.C.A. Vos, J.A. The influence of static strength training on the force-velocity relationship of the arm flexors of 16-year-old boys. (Refs: 7)
CONF: Symposium of Paediatric Work Physiology (10th : 1981 : Joutsa, Finland).
NOTES: In, Ilmarinen, J. and Vaelimaeki, I. (eds.), Children and sport: paediatric work physiology, Berlin, Springer-Verlag, 1984, p. 201-205.
LEVEL: A LANG: Eng SIRC ARTICLE NO: 102767

Duchateau, J. Hainaut, K. Isometric or dynamic training: differential effects on mechanical properties of a human muscle. (Refs: 27)*Journal of applied physiology: respiratory, environmental and exercise physiology 56(2), Feb 1984, 296-301.*
ABST: Twenty normal subjects exercised the adductor pollicus muscle of the nondominant hand 10 min/day for 3 mo. These subjects were divided into two equal groups; one group trained isometrically while the second group trained dynamically. Both training programs produced increases in maximal tetanic tension and in peak rate of tension development but the changes in intrinsic contractile properties were significantly different between the two training programs. The authors suggest that human muscle adapts differently to isometric or to dynamic training programs and that its contractile kinetics can be altered by such exercise.
LEVEL: A LANG: Eng SIRC ARTICLE NO: 093085

Duvillard, S.P. Basic physiology of skeletal muscle contraction. *Texas coach (Austin, Tex.) 28(1), Aug 1984, 60-61.*
LEVEL B LANG: Eng SIRC ARTICLE NO: 102771

Ekholm, J. Nisell, R. Arborelius, U.P. Hammerberg, C. Nemeth, G. Load on knee joint structures and muscular activity during lifting. (Refs: 33)*Scandinavian journal of rehabilitation medicine (Stockholm) 16(1), 1984, 1-9.*
LEVEL: I LANG: Eng SIRC ARTICLE NO: 100470

Gandelsman, A.B. Evdokimova, T.A. Kim, V.V. Ponomarev, V.P. Shanskov, M.A. Integratsii dvigatelnykh i vegetativnykh funktsii pri myshechnoi rabote. (Integration of motor and autonomic functions during muscle work.) *Fiziologicheskii zhurnal SSSR imeni I.M. Sechenova (Leningrad) 70(12), Dec 1984, 1611-1616.*
ABST: In isometric efforts small energy expenditure was found to involve an inadequate increase of the heart rate and blood pressure. In dynamic cyclic loads, the heart rate and blood pressure increase occurs linearly, corresponding to the increase of 02 consumption and systolic index. Voluntary relaxation of muscles in the course of cyclic load involves small values of the 02 consumption and systolic index, as well as low heart rate and blood pressure. In natural cyclic and noncyclic motor activity, the character of integration of the motor and vegetative functions depends on the relative weight of each of the biomechanical modes.
LEVEL: A LANG: Rus

Gardner, V.O. Caiozzo, V.J. Long, S.T. Stoffel, J. McMaster, W.C. Prietto, C.A. Contractile properties of slow and fast muscle following tourniquet ischemia. (Refs: 11)*American journal of sports medicine (Baltimore) 12(6), Nov/Dec 1984, 417-423.*
ABST: This study examines the influence of tourniquet ischemia on the contractile properties of muscle and also determines whether slow and fast muscles exhibit a differential response. In adult male guinea pigs, the plantaris and soleus muscles of control and experimental legs were tested for time-peak-tension, one-half relaxation tetanic tension. The results indicate that the contractile properties of both the soleus and plantaris are dramatically effected by a 2 hour tourniquet. They further suggest that there may be a differential response based upon fiber type.
LEVEL: A LANG: Eng SIRC ARTICLE NO: 104309

Gollhofer, A. Schmidtbleicher, D. Dietz, V. Regulation of muscle stiffness in human locomotion. (Refs: 28)*International journal of sports medicine 5(1), Feb 1984, 19-22.*
ABST: Force-time curves, angular displacements, film analyses, innervation patterns and Achilles tendon tensions were taken from 10 subjects as they walked or ran at various speeds. The main finding of this study was the temporal coincidence of maximal dorsiflexion, maximal Achilles tendon tension, transition from amortization to acceleration phase, and projection of the center of gravity to the supporting leg. During running, the gastrocnemius was slightly preactivated before impact with the ground. The authors suggest two functions for the preactivation of the triceps surae muscle: 1) to buffer high initial force peaks and 2) to trigger an adequate segmental reflex activity for producing a corresponding muscle stiffness to support and push off the body.
LEVEL: A LANG: Eng SIRC ARTICLE NO: 093092

Hart, D.L. Stobbe, T.J. Till, C.W. Plummer, R.W. Effect of trunk stabilization on quadriceps femoris muscle torque. (Refs: 2 *Physical therapy (Alexandria, Va.) 64(9), Sept 1984, 1375-1380.*
ABST: This article examines the differences in 1) angle-specific torque, 1) torque-velocity relationships, and 3) power-velocity relationships of the quadriceps femoris muscle group when the trunk is and is not stabilized. Seven men (20 to 32 years old) are tested at various starting positions (40, 60, and 100o of knee flexion) and velocities of movement (0,30, and 105o/sec). Findings indicate

that 1) angle-specific maximum torque and power are greater when trunk is stabilized, and 2) the influence of trunk stabilization is greater at 105o sec than 30o/sec.
LEVEL: A LANG: Eng SIRC ARTICLE NO: 099240

Kaneko, M. Komi, P.V. Aura, O. Mechanical efficiency of concentric and eccentric exercises performed with medium to fast contraction rates. (Refs: 18)*Scandinavian journal of sports science (Helsinki, Finland) 6(1), Jul 1984, 15-20.*
ABST: By utilizing a special 'sledge' apparatus which was connected to a forceplate, eccentric and concentric exercises were isolated so that only one form of contraction of the leg extensor muscles (either eccentric or concentric) was performed in a single exercise set of 80 contractions. A total of four submaximal energy levels were investigated in both exercise types and the peak knee angular velocities ranged from 14 rad x s-1 to 28 rad x s-1, respectively during the lowest, and highest exercise levels. The results indicate that under all exercise conditions the net mechanical efficiency of the concentric exercise stayed relatively constant with a mean of 19.4 plus or minus 2.0%. In eccentric exercise the corresponding value was 85.2 plus or minus 36.8%, but varied greatly, the highest individual value being 190.6%. In the whole group of six subjects the net mechanical efficiency of eccentric exercise was significantly (p.01) related **to the peak knee angular velocity, indicating higher efficiency values with increased stretch velocities of the knee extensor muscles.**
LEVEL: A LANG: Eng SIRC ARTICLE NO: 102790

Koerner, L. Parker, P. Almstroem, C. Herberts, P. Kadefors, R. The relation between spectral changes of the myoelectric signal and the intramuscular pressure of human skeletal muscle. (Refs: 20)*European journal of applied physiology and occupational physiology (Heidelberg) 52(2), Jan 1984, 202-206.*
ABST: This study investigated the hypothesis that spectral EMG changes are elicited only at intramuscular pressure levels high enough to affect muscular blood perfusion. Spectral changes of the EMG signal were observed as a function of the intramuscular pressures generated during an isometric contraction. Significant recoveries of the mean frequency occurred at intramuscular pressures below about 2.7 KPa 920 mm Hg). It was suggested that fatigue development is more specifically determined by the intramuscular pressure generated by the contraction, rather than the external load itself.
LEVEL: A LANG: Eng SIRC ARTICLE NO: 096265

Lakomy, H.K.A. Williams, C. Measurement of isokinetic concentric and eccentric muscle imbalance. (Refs: 3)*International journal of sports medicine (Stuttgart) Suppl. 5, Nov 1984, 40-41.*
CONF: International Congress on Sports and Health (1983 : Maastricht, Netherlands).
LEVEL: A LANG: Eng SIRC ARTICLE NO: 104332

Osternig, L.R. Hamill, J. Corcos, D.M. Lander, J. Electromyographic patterns accompanying isokinetic exercise under varying speed and sequencing conditions. (Refs: 9)*American journal of physical medicine (Baltimore) 63(6), Dec 1984, 289-297.*
ABST: Five male adults performed knee extensions on an isokinetic dynamometer at four speeds and under two counterbalanced conditions. No consistent electromyographic patterns were found

to infer intermittent surges of muscular activity. The findings suggest that the inertia of the limb/lever system and gravity were largely responsible for limb deceleration.
LEVEL: A LANG: Eng SIRC ARTICLE NO: 102809

Stanhope, S.J. Electromyographic analysis of Molbech's two-joint muscle model. Eugene, Ore.: Microform Publications, University of Oregon, 1984.
1 microfiche : negative, ill. ; 11 x 15 cm.
NOTES: Thesis (M.A.) - University of Maryland, 1982; (viii, 85 leaves); vita; includes bibliography.
LEVEL: A LANG: Eng UO84 145

Tanaka, M. McDonagh, M.J.N. Davies, C.T.M. A comparison of the mechanical properties of the first dorsal interosseous in the dominant and non-dominant hand. (Refs: 9)*European journal of applied physiology and occupational physiology (Berlin, W.G.) 53(1), 1984, 17-20.*
ABST: The electrically evoked and voluntary contractile properties of the first dorsal interosseous muscle were measured on both hands in 10 healthy adults. The mean values of time to peak tension measured on the dominant hands were significantly slower than the values on the non-dominant hand in a paired t-test. Maximal tetanic tension, maximal voluntary contraction strength, and maximal twitch tension were not significantly different. Fatigue indices on the dominant hands in each subject were higher than those on the non-dominant hands.
LEVEL: A LANG: Eng SIRC ARTICLE NO: 104378

Urazaeva, Z.V. Denisenko, I.P. Dubilei, P.V. Novak, O.A. Metodika otsenki funktsional'nogo sostoianiia oporno-dvigatel'nogo apparata u sportsmenov. (Method of evaluating musculoskeletal function in sportsmen.) *Gigiena i sanitariia (Moscow) 8, Aug 1984, 55-58.*
LEVEL: A LANG: Rus

van Boxtel, A. Schomaker, L.R.B. Influence of motor unit firing statistics on the median frequency of the EMG power spectrum (Refs: 42)*European journal of applied physiology and occupational physiology (Heidelberg) 52(2), Jan 1984, 207-213.*
ABST: This investigation observed the influence of firing rate peaks on the change of the median frequency of the EMG power spectrum during static fatiguing contractions for two facial muscles (frontalis and corrugator supercilii). Also, the influence of firing rate peaks on the median frequency, during nonfatiguing contractions of varying strength, was observed for the frontalis muscle. The results demonstrated that the change in the median frequency during fatigue is partly affected by variations in the magnitude of the firing rate peak. Effects upon the median frequency were also shown during relatively short, nonfatiguing contractions. In view of these results, it is indicated that the influence of firing rate peaks on central tendency measures of the EMG power spectral density function should not be neglected.
LEVEL: A LANG: Eng SIRC ARTICLE NO: 096305

Vandewalle, H. Peres, G. Flouret, A. Etude de la contractilite du muscle triceps sural par l'enregistrement de la secousse maximale isometrique. (Refs: 18)*Cinesiologie (Paris) 95, mai/juin 1984, 229-234.*
RESUME: Les auteurs etudient la secousse du triceps sural avec le genou a 90o et a 180o chez 3 joueurs de water-polo, un coureur de demi-fond, un educateur physique, et 3 non-athletes. L'influence de l'angulation du genou ainsi que de l'intensite de la stimulation sur la secousse musculaire sont analysees. Une secousse plus ample et plus breve

est observee a 180o comparativement a 90o. Les auteurs constatent que l'etude de la secousse musculaire isometrique ne permet pas d'apprecier les proprietes contractiles du muscles triceps sural aussi precisement qu'avec des tests tels la detente verticale, l'ergometrie et la dynanometrie isocinetique.
LEVEL: A LANG: Fr SIRC ARTICLE NO: 097771

Winkel, J. Bendix, T. A method for electromyographic analysis of muscular contraction frequencies. (Refs: 20)*European journal of applied physiology and occupational physiology (Berlin, W.G.) 53(2), 1984, 112-117.*
ABST: A method for evaluation of muscular contraction frequencies during prolonged work is presented. It is based upon computer-aided electromyographic (EMG) analyses. Variations in muscular tension, expressed as the relative force of contraction or torque in the joint, are followed using previously described EMG techniques. The number of times muscular tension crosses an amplitude band from below is then estimated. The band represents a predetermined range of amplitude. It is moved in steps from the lowest to the highest force level which occurred during the work task, and the frequency of band-crossings is computed for each band position. The frequencies are then plotted against the force levels at which the upper limit of the band was placed.
LEVEL: A LANG: Eng SIRC ARTICLE NO: 104394

FIBRE TYPES

Citterio, G. Agostoni, E. Selective activation of quadriceps muscle fibers according to bicycling rate. (Refs: 36)*Journal o applied physiology: respiratory, environmental and exercise physiology (Bethesda, Md.) 57(2), Aug 1984, 371-379.*
ABST: For this study the electromyography of the quadriceps muscle was recorded during cycling at various rates with constant force. Whereas the moving average electromyography (MA) during pedal downstroke always increased at power increments achieved by increasing force at constant rate, the results for similar power increments achieved by increasing the rate at constant force varied considerably. It appears that fibers of quadriceps muscle of humans are selectively activated according to movement speed.
LEVEL: A LANG: Eng SIRC ARTICLE NO: 108351

Friden, J. Sjoestreom, M. Ekblom, B. Muscle fibre type characteristics in endurance trained and untrained individuals. (Refs 15)*European journal of applied physiology and occupational physiology (Heidelberg) 52(3), Apr 1984, 266-271.*
ABST: Muscle biopsies were obtained from six trained and four untrained males. The main fibre types were quantitatively determined according to the M-band appearance. The volume of mitochondria (Vmit) was higher in Type 1 fibres than in Type 2 fibres; although results indicate that this is not a satisfactory criterion to distinguish between fibre types. Z band width was larger in Type 1 fibres than in Type 2 fibres. The classification of fibres based on ultrastructural criteria (Vmit, Zband width, lipid droplets) was found to be useful but not entirely specific.
LEVEL: A LANG: Eng SIRC ARTICLE NO: 097724

Gollnick, P.D. Matoba, H. The muscle fiber composition of skeletal muscle as a predictor of athletic success. (Refs: 55) *American journal of sports medicine (Baltimore) 12(3), May/Jun 1984, 212-217.*

ABST: The purpose of this paper was to review the current status of knowledge regarding the importance of characteristics of muscle as predictors of successful athletic performance. Areas of review include: fibre type identification, the distribution in human muscle, fibre composition in muscles of athletes with different abilities, and the influence of training on muscle fibre composition. However, the authors stress that when one considers all of the systems that must be coordinated to produce peak performance, it cannot be concluded that the fibre composition of the muscle, alone, is the determinant of success.
LEVEL: A LANG: Eng SIRC ARTICLE NO: 102585

Green, H.J. Houston, M.E. Thomson, J.A. Fraser, I.G. Fiber type distribution and maximal activities of enzymes involved in energy metabolism following short-term supramaximal exercise. (Refs: 32)*International journal of sports medicine (Stuttgart) 5(4), Aug 1984, 198-201.*
ABST: Alterations in enzyme activities involved in muscle energy metabolism and the muscle fiber type distribution were investigated in six subjects, ranging in age from 9-23 years, following short-term, high intensity exercise. Changes in the vastus lateralis muscle were studied prior to exercise and approximately 24 h after each of 2 consecutive days of supramaximal cycling exercise. Results indicated that supramaximal exercise performed on a short-term basis does not alter the enzymatic profile or the fiber type distribution when measured 24 h following the activity.
LEVEL: A LANG: Eng SIRC ARTICLE NO: 104314

Howald, H. Transformations morphologiques et fonctionnelles des fibres musculaires, provoquees par l'entrainement. (Refs: 36 *Revue medicale de la Suisse romande (Lausanne) 104(10), oct 1984, 757-769.*
RESUME: L'auteur discute des proprietes contractiles des fibres musculaires de type I et de type II. Il compare les repercussions de differentes formes d'entrainement (endurance, anaerobie et force), de l'electrostimulation et de l'immobilisation sur les caracteristiques structurales et fonctionnelles des fibres musculaires. Un entrainement d'endurance intense et de longue duree amene une transformation des fibres de type II en celles de type I. Apres des entrainements par intevalles ou de force, des modifications de la composition ultrastructurale (par ex. le rapport myofibrilles a mitochondries) et des proprietes metaboliques sont observees dans les differents fibres.
LEVEL: A LANG: Fr SIRC ARTICLE NO: 174093

Lindstedt, S. That marvellous machine: what you need to know about muscles. *Bicycling 25(1), Jan/Feb 1984, 28;31.*
LEVEL: LANG: Eng SIRC ARTICLE NO: 090265

MacDougall, J.D. Sale, D.G. Alway, S.E. Sutton, J.R. Muscle fiber number in biceps brachii in bodybuilders and control subjects. (Refs: 20)*Journal of applied physiology: respiratory, environmental and exercise physiology (Bethesda, Md.) 57(5), Nov 1984, 1399-1403.*
ABST: Muscle fiber quantities were estimated in biceps brachii in 5 elite bodybuilders, 7 intermediate bodybuilders and 13 age matched controls. These was a wide range in individual fiber numbers but despite these and muscle size differences the two bodybuilding groups and the controls had the same number of muscle fibres. The authors conclude that heavy resistance training performed for maximizing

PHYSIOLOGY - MUSCLE (continued)

muscle size does not increase muscle fiber numbers. Differences in muscle fiber numbers are more likely due to genetic factors.
LEVEL: A LANG: Eng SIRC ARTICLE NO: 108915

Maughan, R.J. Relationship between muscle strength and muscle cross-sectional area: implications for training. (Refs: 27) *Sports medicine (Auckland, N.Z.) 1(4), Jul/Aug 1984, 263-269.*
LEVEL: I LANG: Eng SIRC ARTICLE NO: 102802

Meacci, C. Alterations in human skeletal muscle properties through isokinetic cycle ergometry. Eugene, Ore.: Microform Publications, University of Oregon, 1984. 2 microfiches : negative, ill. ; 11 x 15 cm.
NOTES: Thesis (Ed.D.) - West Virginia University, 1982; (viii, 134 leaves); vita; includes bibliography.
LEVEL: A LANG: Eng UO84 193-194

Pette, D. Activity-induced fast to slow transitions in mamalian muscle. (Refs: 73)*Medicine and science in sports and exercise (Indianapolis) 16(6), Dec 1984, 517-528.*
ABST: Chronically increased contractile activity by low-frequency stimulation induces a transformation of fast- into slow-twitch muscle fibers in the rabbit. Early changes in enzyme activities and isozymes of energy metabolism result in a 'white to red' metabolic transformation. Simultaneously, cytosolic Ca2 plus-binding and Ca2 plus-sequestration are reduced by a decrease in parvalbumin and a transformation of the sarcoplasmic reticulum membranes. The fast to slow transformation is completed by an exchange of fast with slow-type myosin isoforms. Changes in total RNA and qualitative and quantitative alterations in translatable mRNA indicate that the various transitions result from altered translational and transcriptional activities.
LEVEL: A LANG: Eng SIRC ARTICLE NO: 104356

Riedy, M. Matoba, H. Vollestad, N.K. Oakley, C.R. Blank, S. Hermansen, L. Gollnick, P.D. Influence of exercise on the fiber composition of skeletal muscle. *Histochemistry (Berlin) 80(6), 1984, 553-557.*
ABST: Biopsy samples from the vastus lateralis muscle (VLM) of man were examined for fiber composition at rest and at selected intervals during prolonged exercise. Studies were also completed where the effect of exercise on the fiber composition of the rat soleus muscle (SM) was examined. Exercise reduced muscle glycogen in all experiments. In the studies with man, blood lactate exceeded 17 mmoles/l after heavy exercise. In studies where fibers were identified only as type I and type II, type II fibers in the VLM of all samples (16) taken at rest averaged 61.2 plus or minus 12.5 per cent as compared to 59.0 plus or minus 12.0 per cent after exercise (54 biopsy samples). In a second series of studies with man where the subtypes of type II fibers were identified, there were also no differences in fiber composition of the VLM after varying periods of exercise. Exercise (30 to 40 min) did not alter the fiber composition of the rat SM.
LEVEL: A LANG: Eng SIRC ARTICLE NO: 104360

Secher, N.H. Mizuno, M. Saltin, B. Adaptation of skeletal muscles to training. *Bulletin europeen de physiopathologie respiratoire/Clinical respiratory physiology (Oxford) 20(5), Sept/Oct 1984, 453-457.*
LEVEL: A LANG: Eng

Staron, R.S. Hikida, R.S. Hagerman, F.C. Dudley, G.A. Murray, T.F. Human skeletal muscle fiber type adaptability to various workloads. *Journal of histochemistry and cytochemistry (Baltimore) 32(2), Feb 1984, 146-152.*
ABST: Muscle biopsy specimens were removed from the vastus lateralis muscles of controls, weight lifters, and distance runners. A histochemical analysis of the biopsy specimens revealed that the runners had a significantly higher percentage of fiber types I and IIC than either the controls or the weight lifters. The results of volume-percent mitochondria analysis demonstrated a strong relationship between the ATPase activity and oxidative potential of the fiber types for all three groups. Irrespective of fiber type, there were significant differences between the groups with regard to muscle-fiber mitochondrial (runners greater than lifters greater than controls) and lipid content (runners greater than controls greater than lifters). The lifters had a significantly greater content of mitochondria than the controls, which may suggest that inactivity rather than the lifting exercise contributes to a low volume-percent mitochondria and a high percentage of type IIB fibers.
LEVEL: A LANG: Eng SIRC ARTICLE NO: 099269

Tesch, A. Thorsson, A. Kraiser, P. Muscle capillary supply and fiber type characteristics in weight and power lifters. (Refs 25)*Journal of applied physiology: respiratory environmental and exercise physiology (Bethesda, Md.) 56(1), Jan 1984, 35-38.*
ABST: A comparison was made between 8 weight and power lifters, 8 endurance athletes and 8 untrained individuals to determine the differences in capillary density, fibre type distribution and fibre size of the vastus lateralis muscle. This study found that the weight and power lifters had reduced capillary density compared to the other 2 groups. The heavy resistance training of these athletes resulted in fast-twitch fibre hypertrophy with a reduction in the number of capillaries per square millimeter.
LEVEL: A LANG: Eng SIRC ARTICLE NO: 097042

FLEXIBILITY

Carty, B.S. P.N.F. stretching and local skin temperature regulation as affected by EMG and thermal biofeedback. *Journal of the Canadian Athletic Therapists Association (Oakville, Ont.) 11(2), Fall 1984, 13-15.*
LEVEL: A LANG: Eng SIRC ARTICLE NO: 104288

Corbin, C.B. Flexibility. (Refs: 24)*Clinics in sports medicine (Philadelphia) 3(1), Jan 1984, 101-117.*
NOTES: Symposium o profiling.
ABST: Flexibility is important for optimal performance and for prevention of injury. Measurement allows a profile to be constructed of the individuals selection of exercises to improve it. Basic guidelines for increasing flexibility are outlined. Exercises should be progressive with passive stretching preceding active stretching.
LEVEL: I LANG: Eng SIRC ARTICLE NO: 092923

Cornelius, W. Jackson, A. The effects of cryotherapy and PNF on hip extensor flexibility. (Refs: 11)*Athletic training (Greenville, N.C.) 19(3), Fall 1984, 183-184;199.*
ABST: The purpose of this study was to determine if the use of Proprioceptive Neuromuscular Facilitation (PNF) in conjunction with cryotherapy improves hip extensor flexibility. 30 male subjects

between the ages of 17 and 26 years served as subjects. Subjects first received the cryotherapy treatment following by one of two PNF techniques. Findings indicated that both techniques used with cryotherapy are more effective than static stretch technique.
LEVEL: A LANG: Eng SIRC ARTICLE NO: 099226

Ebrahim, K. The effect of cold application and flexibility techniques on hip extensors and their influence on flexibility in college males. Eugene, Ore.: Microform Publications, University of Oregon, 1984. 1 microfiche : negative, ill. ; 11 x 15 cm.
NOTES: Thesis (Ph.D.) - North Texas State University, 1982; (iii, 75 leaves); includes bibliography.
LEVEL: A LANG: Eng UO84 211

Henricson, A.S. Fredriksson, K. Persson, I. Pereira, R. Rostedt, Y. Westlin, N.E. The effect of heat and stretching on the range of hip motion. (Refs: 28)*Journal of orthopaedic and sports physical therapy (Baltimore, Md.) 6(2), Sept/Oct 1984, 110-115.*
ABST: Flexion, abduction, and external rotation of the hip joint were recorded in 30 volunteers randomized into three groups of 10. The measurements were taken before, immediately after, and 30 minutes after treatment of heat, stretching and a combination of heat plus stretching. Heat only did not improve the range of motion of the hip joint. Stretching increased flexion and external rotation, and heat plus stretching in combination gave the greatest increase in flexion motion, and also significantly increased abduction. External rotation after stretching treatment, and flexion and abduction after heat plus stretching treatment were still significantly increased after 30 minutes.
LEVEL: A LANG: Eng SIRC ARTICLE NO: 100722

Hubley, C.L. Kozey, J.W. Stanish, W,D. The effects of static stretching exercises and stationary cycling on range of motion at the hip joint. (Refs: 41)*Journal of orthopaedic and sports physical therapy (Baltimore, Md.) 6(2), Sept/Oct 1984, 104-109.*
ABST: The objective of this study was to compare the effects of static stretching exercises and stationary cycling on hip range of motion measures immediately following exercise and after a 15-min period of rest or continued activity. The results showed that both exercises performed for equal time periods resulted in hip range of motion increases with no significant difference between the immediate effects of the two exercises. Fifteen minutes of cycling or inactivity did not result in significant differences from the initial gains resulting from the stretching, but did result in significant increases in hip flexion for the group that continued cycling. Based on the results of this study, static stretching and cycling were equally effective for increasing range of motion and retaining the increase for a 15-min period in a controlled environment, independent of activity.
LEVEL: A LANG: Eng SIRC ARTICLE NO: 100725

METABOLISM

Bastien, C. Sanchez, J. Phosphagens and glycogen content in skeletal muscle after treadmill training in young and old rats. (Refs: 13)*European journal of applied physiology and occupational physiology (Heidelberg) 52(3), Apr 1984, 291-295.*
ABST: Young (3 months) and old (24 months) rats were trained for 12 weeks, 3 days a week, with a

progressive running program. Aging caused a significant decrease in total adenosine nucleotides (TAN) whereas training increased TAN in both young and old groups. Although aging decreased and training increased TAN the energy charge of muscle was constant throughout the aging process and was decreased with training. These results support the hypothesis that the control of ATP regenerating reactions responds to the energy balance of the cell. Creatine phosphate and glycogen content decreased with age whereas training increased these parameters.
LEVEL: A LANG: Eng SIRC ARTICLE NO: 097711

Blomstrand, E. Bergh, U. Essen-Gustavsson, B. Ekblom, B. Influence of low muscle temperature on muscle metabolism during intense dynamic exercise. *Acta physiologica scandinavica (Stockholm) 120(2), Feb 1984, 229-236.*
ABST: Eight males exercised on a bicycle ergometer during three different protocols: 1) 'cold exhaustive' exercise (initial muscle temperature of 29 degrees); 2) 'warm non-exhaustive' exercise (temperature of 34 degrees C) for the same period of time as in 1), and 3) 'warm exhaustive' (temperature of 34 degrees C). Oxygen deficit and decrease in ATP and CP content were similar in experiments 1 and 2. Higher concentration of glucose-6-phosphate (7.5 to 27.7 and 2.2 to 14.2 mmol x kg dw -1, respectively) and higher lactate concentration (24 to 96 and 19 to 47 mmol x kg dw -1, respectively) were observed following exercise in the 'cold exhaustive exercise'.
LEVEL: A LANG: Eng SIRC ARTICLE NO: 100889

Brotzu, G. Carta, M. Cherchi, R. D'Alia, G. Deriu, I.P. Diaz, G. Draetta, G. Montisci, R. Savona, G. Testa Riva, F. The stereomorphologic disposition of the muscular capillary network. Experimental research into the effect of training, age, arterial insufficiency and chronic treatment with EPL. (Refs: 14)*Journal of sports medicine and physical fitness (Torino) 24(1), Mar 1984, 1-12.*
ABST: This paper examines the causes of any modification in the stereo-morphology in the capillary network of the skeletal muscles. Arterial stenosis was found to produce different age related responses. In young animals capillaries prevailed parallel to the muscle fibres while in adult animals the opposite occurred. Pharmacological treatment with poly-unsaturated phosphodiethylcholine (EPL) during a 9 month period found that the EPL disposed itself on the membrane of the endothelial cells and probably provokes some modifications of the stereomorphologic disposition of the capillaries.
LEVEL: A LANG: Eng SIRC ARTICLE NO: 099223

Essen-Gustavsson, B. Henriksson, J. Enzyme levels in pools of microdissected human muscle fibres of identified type. Adaptiv response to exercise. *Acta physiologica scandinavica (Stockholm) 120(4), Apr 1984, 505-515.*
LEVEL: A LANG: Eng

Green, H.J. Houston, M.E. Thomson, J.A. Fraser, I.G. Fiber type distribution and maximal activities of enzymes involved in energy metabolism following short-term supramaximal exercise. (Refs: 32)*International journal of sports medicine (Stuttgart) 5(4), Aug 1984, 198-201.*
ABST: Alterations in enzyme activities involved in muscle energy metabolism and the muscle fiber type distribution were investigated in six subjects, ranging in age from 9-23 years, following short-term, high intensity exercise. Changes in the vastus lateralis muscle were studied prior to exercise and

approximately 24 h after each of 2 consecutive days of supramaximal cycling exercise. Results indicated that supramaximal exercise performed on a short-term basis does not alter the enzymatic profile or the fiber type distribution when measured 24 h following the activity.
LEVEL: A LANG: Eng SIRC ARTICLE NO: 104314

Harkness, R.A. Simmonds, R.J. Coade, S.B. Effect of hypoxia and exercise on nucleotide metabolism in man. (Refs: 6)*Advances in experimental medicine and biology (New York) 165(Pt B), 1984, 437-442.*
LEVEL: A LANG: Eng SIRC ARTICLE NO: 100898

Jansson, E. Kaijser, L. Leg citrate metabolism at rest and during exercise in relation to diet and substrate utilization in man. *Acta physiologica scandinavica (Stockholm) 122(2), Oct 1984, 145-153.*
LEVEL: A LANG: Eng

Jenkins, R.R. Friedland, R. Howald, H. The relationship of oxygen uptake to superoxide dismutase and catalase activity in human skeletal muscle. (Refs: 35)*International journal of sports medicine 5(1), Feb 1984, 11-14.*
ABST: The authors conducted a cross-sectional study on the hydroperoxide enzyme activity of human muscle and an animal study on the relationship between tissue oxygen consumption and enzyme activity in order to gain insight into the effect of exercise on these enzymes. The main findings showed that subjects with a high aerobic capacity had significantly greater levels of both superoxide dismutase and catalase than subjects with low aerobic capacity. The animal study showed a significant rank order correlation between tissue VO2 and tissue enzyme activity of both superoxide dismutase and catalase.
LEVEL: A LANG: Eng SIRC ARTICLE NO: 093098

Joreteg, T. Jogestrand, T. Physical exercise and binding of digoxin to skeletal muscle - effect of muscle activation frequency. *European journal of clinical pharmacology (Berlin) 27(5), 1984, 567-570.*
ABST: Digoxin in the thigh muscle and serum digoxin concentrations were measured in ten men during an 1-hour bicycle exercise test at two pedalling rates, 40 and 80 rpm. Subjects had ingested 0.5 mg digoxin daily for at least 10 days prior to exercising. Digoxin concentrations increased by 8 per cent at 40 rpm and by 29 per cent at 80 rpm. The serum digoxin concentrations decreasd by 39 per cent at both cadences.
LEVEL: A LANG: Eng

Lavoie, J.-M. Helie, R. Cousineau, D. Effects of a rapid change in muscle glycogen availability on metabolic and hormonal responses during exercise. (Refs: 23)*European journal of applied physiology and occupational physiology (Berlin, W.G.) 53(1), 1984, 57-62.*
ABST: To evaluate the metabolic and hormonal adaptations following a rapid change in muscle glycogen availability, 14 subjects had their muscle glycogen content increased in one leg (IG) and decreased in the other (DG). In group A subjects exercised on a bicycle ergometer for 20 min using the DG leg. Without resting these same subjects exercised another 20 min using the IG leg. 7 subjects in group B followed the same single-leg exercise protocol but in the reverse order. Results indicated that 5 min after the switch from the DG leg to the IG leg transient increases in plasma free fatty acids and serum insulin concentrations

occured. Between minute 25 and 40 of exercise, the DG to IG switch ws accompanied by a degree in free fatty acids and glycerol concentrations as well as an increase in lactate levels. An opposite response was observed in the IG to DG condition during the same time span.
LEVEL: A LANG: Eng SIRC ARTICLE NO: 104334

Layzer, R.B. Lewis, S.F. Clinical disorders of muscle energy metabolism. (Refs: 34)*Medicine and science in sports and exercise (Indianapolis) 16(5), Oct 1984, 451-455.*
CONF: American College of Sports Medicine. Meeting (30th : 1983 : Montreal).
ABST: The disorders of muscle energy metabolism can be classified into degenerative (myopathic) and dynamic syndromes. Four dynamic syndromes are currently recognized: 1) defective carbohydrate utilization, due to block of glycogenolysis of glycolysis; 2) defective lipid utilization, due to deficiency of the mitochondrial translocation of long-chain fatty acids (carnitine palmityltransferase deficiency); 3) lactic acidosis, due to defects of mitochondrial electron transport enzymes and possibly other unidentified defects; and 4) abnormal adenine nucleotide metabolism, exemplified by adenylate deaminase deficiency.
LEVEL: A LANG: Eng SIRC ARTICLE NO: 102795

Lowry, S.F. Horowitz, G.D. Rose, D. Brennan, M.F. Influence of nutritional status on exertion-induced forearm amino acid metabolism in normal man. *Journal of surgical research: clinical and laboratory investigation (New York) 36(5), May 1984, 438-445.*
LEVEL: A LANG: Eng SIRC ARTICLE NO: 102798

Mader, A. Eine Theorie zur Berechnung der Dynamik und des steady state von Phosphorylierungszustand und Stoffwechselaktivitaet der Muskelzelle als Folge des Energiebedarfs. Koeln: Deutsche Sporthochschule Koeln, Institut fuer Kreislaufforschung und Sportmedizin, 1984. 264 p.
NOTES: Bibliography: p. 246-264.
LEVEL: A LANG: Ger RC1235 20576

Matoba, H. Gollnick, P.D. Response of skeletal muscle to training. (Refs: 89)*Sports medicine (Auckland, N.Z.) 1(3), May/Jun 1984, 240-251.*
ABST: This review discusses the fuels for muscular contraction, the metabolic modifications of muscle with training, the significance of the enhanced oxidative potential in skeletal muscle, the mechanism for enhanced exercise capacity after endurance training, and the effects of training on muscular strength and muscle size. The most noticeable adaptations of skeletal muscle to endurance training are the increased concentrations of mitochondria and glycogen. The increased concentration of mitochondria with endurance training is related to the enhanced oxidative potential of muscle which in turn allows glycogen to be spared at a given exercise intensity.
LEVEL: A LANG: Eng SIRC ARTICLE NO: 096277

Richter, E.A. Sonne, B. Mikkines, K.J. Ploug, T. Galbo, H. Muscle and liver glycogen, protein, and triglyceride in the rat. Effect of exercise and of the sympatho-adrenal system. (Refs: 23)*European journal of applied physiology and occupational physiology (Heidelberg) 52(3), Apr 1984, 346-350.*
ABST: This investigation sought to determine if an increased net breakdown of protein and/or triglyceride accompanies decreased glycogen breakdown in exercising, adrenodemedullated rats. Rats swam to exhaustion or ran for 45 min at 10

and 14 m/min. Adrenomedullated rats had impaired muscle glycogenolysis during both exercise protocols. The results indicate that there was no compensatory increase in breakdown of triglyceride and protein in muscle or liver despite decreased muscle glycogenolysis. Indirect evidence suggests that fatty acids from adipose tissue were oxidized in lieu of deficient muscle glycogenolysis.
LEVEL: A LANG: Eng SIRC ARTICLE NO: 097756

Sabina, R.L. Swain, J.L. Bradley, W.G. Holmes, E.W. Quantitation of metabolites in human skeletal muscle during rest and exercise: a comparison of methods. *Muscle and nerve (Boston) 7(1), Jan 1984, 77-82.*
ABST: This study evaluated quantitation of metabolites in vastus lateralis at rest and following exercise using the following methods of normalization of the data: total protein, total creatine, and NAD plus. All methods proved to be adequate, but the total creatine and NAD plus methods yielded better results.
LEVEL: A LANG: Eng SIRC ARTICLE NO: 099262

Salminen, A. Kihlstroem, M. Kainulainen, H. Takala, T. Vihko, V. Endurance training decreases the alkaline proteolytic activity in mouse skeletal muscles. (Refs: 31)*European journal of applied physiology and occupational physiology (Heidelberg) 52(3), Apr 1984, 287-290.*
ABST: Alkaline and myofibrillar protease activities of rectus femoris, soleus, and tibialis anterior muscles and pooled samples of gastrocnemius and plantaris muscles were analyzed in mice which underwent a running program of 3, 10, or 20 daily 1h. sessions at 25 m/min. Endurance training produced similar decreases in alkaline and myofibrillar protease activities. However, beta-glucoronidase activity (a lysosomal hydrolase marker) increased in all muscles, especially at the beginning of training. These results indicate that there are differences in the function of different proteolytic systems.
LEVEL: A LANG: Eng SIRC ARTICLE NO: 097759

Sjogaard, G. Changes in skeletal muscles capillarity and enzyme activity with training and detraining. (Refs: 35)
CONF: International Course on Physiology and Biochemistry of Exercise and Detraining (2nd : 1982 : Nice).
NOTES: In, Marconnet, P. (ed.) et al., Physiological chemistry of training and detraining, New York, Karger, c1984, p. 202-214.
LEVEL: A LANG: Eng RC1235 17596

Sylven, C. Jansson, E. Boeoek, K. Myoglobin content in human skeletal muscle and myocardium: relation to fibre size and oxidative capacity. *Cardiovascular research (London) 18(7), Jul 1984, 443-446.*
ABST: Myoglobin, muscle fibre diameter, and citrate synthase activity were measured in leg muscle of untrained and trained men and in the myocardium from the apex of the left ventricle and from papillary muscle in patients subjected to open heart surgery. The citrate synthase activity was 60 per cent higher in trained than in untrained skeletal muscle. The diffusion distance in terms of fibre diameter decreases with increased oxidative capacity (CS activity), when comparing the statistical means of the four different groups. The capacity for oxygen diffusion in relation to oxygen demand measured as the ratio of myoglobin to fibre diameter appeared to be of similar magnitude in skeletal muscle and left ventricle but was higher in

papillary muscle.
LEVEL: A LANG: Eng SIRC ARTICLE NO: 104376

Thimm, F. zu Verl, E.M. Muscular metabolic acidosis as a heart rate drive. (Refs: 7)*International journal of sports medicin (Stuttgart) Suppl. 5, Nov 1984, 116-117.*
CONF: International Congress on Sports and Health (1983 : Maastricht, Netherlands).
LEVEL: A LANG: Eng SIRC ARTICLE NO: 104383

NEURO-MUSCULAR PHYSIOLOGY

Appell, H.-J. Proliferation of motor end-plates induced by increased muscular activity. (Refs: 36)*International journal of sports medicine (Stuttgart) 5(3), Jun 1984, 125-129.*
ABST: The effects of muscular activity on the motor end-plates were studied. To stimulate an overload training on the diaphragm, Japanese waltzer mice were subjected to hypobaric hypoxia (simulated altitude of 3000 m) for 7 and 14 days. After demonstration of the end-plates by AChE-staining, their size and total number in the sternal part of the diaphragm were measured at the light microscopic level. The end-plate regions were enlarged after 7 days and were increased in number after 14 days. The electron-microscopic examination showed no ultrastructural peculiarities in either of the experimental groups. The muscle fibers of the trained animals showed a strong reaction of AChE; thus, it was suggested that end-plate proliferation was myogenically induced.
LEVEL: A LANG: Eng SIRC ARTICLE NO: 104273

Conte, G. Marcacci, M. Spinelli, M. Girolami, M. Caporali, R. Rossi, A. Meccanorecettori nel legamento collaterale medicale del ginocchio umano (meccanorecettori nel gionocchio umano). Mechanoreceptors in the medial collateral ligament of the human knee (mechanoreceptors in the human knee). (Refs: 51)*Italian journal of sports traumatology (Milan) 6(1), Jan/Mar 1984, 63-72.*
ABST: This investigation examines the nervous structures within the capsular-ligamental components of the human knee. In particular, six medial collateral ligaments were taken from the knee joints of young adult male cadavers shortly after death. The ligaments, stained by the gold chloride method according to Ruffini were dissociated and studied after crushing. In all cases, Ruffini corpuscles, Golgi-Mazzoni corpuscles, Pacini corpuscles, Krause end bulbs, and Golgi tendon organs were observed. In the midst of differing opinions, the authors believe that the encapsulated receptors serve to receive nerve impulses and coordinate the contraction of the knee stabilizers.
LEVEL: A LANG: Eng It SIRC ARTICLE NO: 097355

Ishikawa, T. Miyazawa, T. Fujiwara, T. Characteristics of the spino-bulbo-spinal reflex with evoked EMGs in human subjects. (Refs: 22)*International journal of sports medicine (Stuttgart) 5(4), Aug 1984, 187-192.*
ABST: The late spinal reflexes appearing after conditioning were resolved into a stretch reflex and a spino-bulbo-spinal (SBS) reflex. H and M waves on the tibialis anterior muscle induced by tibial nerve stimulation were determined from the escape potential of the triceps sural muscle contraction. The tibial nerve and peroneal nerve were stimulated bilaterally, and H and M waves from the triceps sural muscle and tibialis anterior muscle were recorded bilaterally. The complete separation method of the late response and the time course of

the stretch reflex and SBS reflex that composed the late response are described.
LEVEL: A LANG: Eng SIRC ARTICLE NO: 104323

Jerome, J. The heart of the muscle: fine control of motor units is the key to athletics. *Outside (Chicago) 9(6), Jul 1984, 27-28.*
LEVEL: B LANG: Eng SIRC ARTICLE NO: 104324

Komi, P.V. Biomechanics and neuromuscular performance. (Refs: 26)*Medicine and science in sports and exercise 16(1), 1984, 26-28.*
ABST: Fast-twitch muscle is innervated by fast motor units and slow-twitch muscle is innervated by slow motor units. This demonstrated how biomechanics and the neuromuscular system overlap in the study of neuromuscular performance. The author discusses the case of the stretch-shortening cycle with reference to mechanical efficiency. Such areas of research must be further studied in order to better understand neuromuscular performance.
LEVEL: A LANG: Eng SIRC ARTICLE NO: 091741

Komi, P.V. Fatigue and recovery of neuromuscular function. (Refs: 32)
CONF: International Course on Physiology and Biochemistry of Exercise and Detraining (2nd : 1982 : Nice).
NOTES: In, Marconnet, P. (ed.) et al., Physiological chemistry of training and detraining, New York, Karger, c1984, p. 187-201.
LEVEL: A LANG: Eng RC1235 17596

Loeb, G.E. The control and responses of mammalian muscle spindles during normally executed motor tasks. (Refs: 142)*Exercise and sport sciences reviews (Lexington, Mass.) 12, 1984, 157-204.*
ABST: This paper considers the general scope of the kinematic control problems that emerge during normal skeletal muscle function. This general synopsis is followed by a theoretical examination of the problem of optimizing the sensory information obtained under varying conditions. This theoretical examination suggests a new way of thinking about the fusimotor control of spindles. Spindle function during normal movement is reviewed. Finally, the author proposes a new term, task groups to describe patterns of task-dependent sensorimotor recruitment that are consistent with optimal control principles.
LEVEL: A LANG: Eng SIRC ARTICLE NO: 096273

MacDonald, M.L. Stanish, W.D. Neuromuscular system. (Refs: 89)
NOTES: In, Scott, W.N. (ed.) et al., Principles of sports medicine, Baltimore, Williams & Wilkins, c1984, p. 15-26.
LEVEL: A LANG: Eng RC1210 18016

Shields, R.W. Robbins, N. Verrilli, A.A. The effects of chronic muscular activity on age-related changes in single fiber electromyography. (Refs: 22)*Muscle and nerve (New York) 7(4), May 1984, 273-277.*
ABST: Active elderly men (66-77 years old) underwent electromyography of the extensor digitorum communis muscle and nerve conduction studies to assess age related changes in neuromuscular physiology and the effect of long-term increased muscular activity on these changes. Two groups served as subjects: a control group and a group of men with occupationally greater usage of hand extensors. Greater variability in mean jitter and a significant increase in the prevalence of potential pairs with increased jitter or

blocking were observed on the hard-user group.
LEVEL: A LANG: Eng SIRC ARTICLE NO: 102827

Svedenhag, J. Wallin, B.G. Sundloef, G. Henriksson, J. Skeletal muscle sympathetic activity at rest in trained and untrained subjects. *Acta physiologica scandinavica (Stockholm) 120(4), Apr 1984, 499-504.*
LEVEL: A LANG: Eng

Wickiewicz, T.L. Roy, R.R. Powell, P.L. Perrine, J.J. Edgerton, V.R. Muscle architecture and force-velocity relationships in humans. (Refs: 37)*Journal of applied physiology: respiratory, environmental and exercise physiology (Bethesda, Md.) 57(2), Aug 1984, 435-443.*
ABST: Twelve untrained subjects (eight males, four females) underwent isokinetic exercise in order to investigate the force-relocity relationship and the influence of the architectural features of flexor and extensor muscles of the lower limb on this relationship. The results suggest that architecture does play a major role and furthermore that some neural inhibitory mechanism limits the maximum forces that could be produced under optimal stimulating conditions.
LEVEL: A LANG: Eng SIRC ARTICLE NO: 108353

RESEARCH METHODS

Bankoff, A.D. Furlani, J. Electromyographic study of the rectus abdominis and external oblique muscles during exercises. *Electroencephalography and clinical neurophysiology (Louvain) 24(6), Aug/ Sept 1984, 501-510.*
LEVEL: A LANG: Eng

STRENGTH AND ENDURANCE

Aubier, M. La fatigue des muscles respiratoires. (Fatigue of the respiratory muscles.) *Presse medicale (Paris) 13(33), 29 sept 1984, 2009-2012.*
LEVEL: A LANG: Fr

Barter, T.J. Freer, P.C. Effect of temperature on handgrip holding time. (Refs: 28)*British journal of sports medicine (Loughborough, Eng.) 18(2), Jun 1984, 91-95.*
ABST: The effects of intramuscular temperature upon the holding time of 70% MVC handgrip contraction was studied in 12 college-age men. The intramuscular temperature was regulated by 30 minutes immersion of the forearm and hand in a waterbath at 18oC, 35oC, or 45oC. Elevating intramuscular temperature significantly reduced the holding time duration, (25.7 plus or minus 6.2 vis 38.3 plus or minus 8.1, while reducing the temperature had no significant effect (37.5 plus or minus 9.4 vis 38.3 plus or minus 8.1, N.S.).
LEVEL: A LANG: Eng SIRC ARTICLE NO: 102757

Brown, B.S. Daniel, M. Gorman, D.R. Visual feedback and strength improvement. (Refs: 10)*National Strength & Conditioning Association journal 6(1), Feb/Mar 1984, 22-24.*
ABST: Strength improvement of a control group and two experimental groups of young men, 18-25 years of age, was assessed in this study. The first experimental group performed a static leg squat exercise for one repetition per day, five days per week, for five weeks. The second experimental group performed the same exercise with the following exceptions: 1) a force meter displaying the amount of effort was in direct view of the subjects, 2) subjects were required to maintain a force equal to, or greater than, 75% of their maximum efforts.

The greatest gain was observed in the second group with a 98.6% increase in strength.
LEVEL: A LANG: Eng SIRC ARTICLE NO: 093070

Cornwall, M.W. Leveau, B. The effect of physical activity on ligamentous strength: an overview. (Refs: 18)*Journal of orthopaedic and sports physical therapy (Baltimore, Md.) 5(5), Mar/Apr 1984, 275-277.*
ABST: The authors note that there have not been any studies regarding this topic which have adequately controlled all variables. However, despite methodological flaws, most studies seem to indicate that systematic exercise strengthens the bone-ligament-bone complex. The actual mechanism of this increase in strength remains to be elucidated.
LEVEL: I LANG: Eng SIRC ARTICLE NO: 094592

Drew, D.L. Effects of a prolonged low carbohydrate diet on liver glycogen and endurance in rats. Eugene, Ore.: Microform Publications, University of Oregon, 1984. 1 microfiche : negative ; 11 x 15 cm. NOTES: Thesis (M.S.) - Brigham young University, 1982; (vi, 54 leaves); includes bibliography.
LEVEL: A LANG: Eng UO84 319

Figoni, S.F. Morris, A.F. Effects of knowledge of results on reciprocal, isokinetic strength and fatigue. (Refs: 33)*Journal of orthopaedic and sports physical therapy (Baltimore, Md.) 6(3), Nov/Dec 1984, 190-197.*
ABST: The purpose of this study was to determine the effects of knowledge of results, i.e., visual feedback from watching the torque curve on the Cybex II recorder, on knee extensor and flexor strength, and fatigue during reciprocal, isokinetic testing at speeds of 15o/sec (slow) and 300o/sec (fast). Knowledge of results induced higher strength and fatigue values in both muscle groups during slow, but not fast, speed tests. The greater amount of fatigue resulted from elevated initial strength levels at the beginning of the slow speed fatigue tests.
LEVEL: A LANG: Eng SIRC ARTICLE NO: 102773

Gillespie, J. Gabbard, C. A test of three theories of strength and muscular endurance development. (Refs: 21)*Journal of human movement studies (London) 10(4), 1984, 213-223.*
ABST: The present investigation examined the relative effects on strength and endurance of weight training programs on 62 male college students. Prior to and after 9 weeks of training, strength was determined by each subject's 1-RM on the bench press exercise and divided by body weight to give a strength/kilogram of body weight ratio. Muscular endurance was measured by the number of correct repetitions that could be performed with a load of 60 per cent of the pretest 1-RM at a frequency of 30 repetitions per minute. Three treatments were randomly assigned to 3 groups who trained at a frequency of 3 times per week. One group trained with 3 sets of 6- to 8-RM (HR-LR), a second group trained with 3 sets of 15- to 20-RM (LR-HR), and a third group trained with 3 sets of 6- to 8-RM followed by a burn-out set until exhaustion (combination of HR-LR and LR-HR). Results indicated that all groups increased significantly in strength and muscular endurance with no between group differences.
LEVEL: A LANG: Eng SIRC ARTICLE NO: 104311

Gissaigne, C. An investigation into the effects on leg power of varying depth jump training programmes. (abstract) *Carnegie research papers (Beckett Park, Leeds) 1(6), Dec 1984, 29.*
CONF: Carnegie Undergraduate Research

Symposium (1984 : Leeds, Eng.).
LEVEL: I LANG: Eng SIRC ARTICLE NO: 172505

Gobelet, C. Monnier, B. Leyvraz, P.F. Force isocinetique et sport. (Refs: 5)*Medecine du sport 58(1), 25 janv 1984, 51-56.*
RESUME: Cette etude visait a comparer la force musculaire isocinetique du quadriceps et les ischio-jambiers a 3oo et 300o/sec chez 13 sujets sedentaires, 15 joueurs de soccer et 15 patients ayant subi une chirurgie reconstructive du ligament croise anterieur (LCA). Les auteurs constatent, que la perte de force est liee a l'accroissement de la vitesse du mouvement. Cette perte de force se manifeste essentiellement a basse vitesse chez les sujets ayant subi une plastie de la LCA.
LEVEL: A LANG: Fr SIRC ARTICLE NO: 091729

Hackney, A.C. Gilliam, T.B. Assessment of maximum isometric isotonic and isokinetic leg extensor strength in young adult females. (Refs: 36)*National Strength & Conditioning Association journal (Lincoln, Neb.) 6(4), Aug/Sept 1984, 28-31.*
ABST: This report focuses on the evaluation of maximum isometric, isotonic and isokinetic left leg extensors strength of sixty-three adult females. Findings are compared with those reported for males in previous studies. No major strength characteristic differences are observed between genders in relationship to the development of maximum force. Maximum isokinetic contractions at 30o/sec produces greater force development than isometric contractions.
LEVEL: A LANG: Eng SIRC ARTICLE NO: 099365

Holmes, J.R. Isokinetic strength characteristics of the quadriceps femoris and hamstring muscles in high school students. (Refs: 25)*Physical therapy (Alexandria, Va.) 64(6), Jun 1984, 914-918.*
ABST: The isokinetic strength of the quadriceps femoris and hamstring muscles of forty-seven 15- and 18-year old students was determined in this study. No significant age effect in peak isokinetic testing was performed at 60o/sec and 180o/sec. torque and no differences between dominant and nondominant limbs for male and female students were observed. Findings indicated significant differences between the isokinetric strength of male and female students. Torque ratio of hamstring to quadriceps femoris muscle increased with increasing testing velocity.
LEVEL: A LANG: Eng SIRC ARTICLE NO: 096253

Jette, M. Sidney, K. Cicutti, N. A critical analysis of sit-ups: a case for the partial curl-up as a test of abdominal muscular endurance. (Refs: 22)*CAHPER journal (Ottawa) 51(1), Sept/Oct 1984, 4-9.*
LEVEL: I LANG: Eng SIRC ARTICLE NO: 100900

Komi, P.V. Physiological and biomechanical correlates of muscle function: effects of muscle structure and stretch-shortening cycle on force and speed. (Refs: 121)*Exercise and sports sciences reviews (Lexington, Mass.) 12, 1984, 81-121.*
ABST: The paper examines some of the integrative functions of physiology and biomechanics, with a primary focus on how force and speed are influenced by the structure and mechanics of intact human skeletal muscles. The review is quite detailed; covering a large portion of the research in this area. In the future if researchers obtain appropriate methods of integrating sensory information with central processing and muscle mechanics, empirical data can be obtained over the entire physiological range of force and speed production.
LEVEL: A LANG: Eng SIRC ARTICLE NO: 096266

PHYSIOLOGY - MUSCLE (continued)

Kulig, K. Andrews, J.G. Hay, J.G. Human strength curves. (Refs: 56)*Exercise and sport sciences reviews (Lexington, Mass.)* 12, 1984, 417-466.
ABST: This paper reviews the literature related to strength curves. The paper deals with: 1) factors influencing strength curves, 2) strength curves for single-joint exercise, 3) strength curves for multiple-joint exercise and 4) a discussion of these studies.
LEVEL: A LANG: Eng SIRC ARTICLE NO: 096267

Langrana, N.A. Lee, C.K. Isokinetic evaluation of trunk muscles. *Spine (Hagerstown, Md.)* 9(2), Mar 1984, 171-175.
LEVEL: LANG: Eng SIRC ARTICLE NO: 102793

Langridge, J.C. A simple pilot study to evaluate the use of a myometer for research measurement of muscle force output. (Refs: 2)*Journal of the society of remedial gymnastics and recreational therapy (Manchester)* 113, Aug 1984, 11-14.
LEVEL: I LANG: Eng SIRC ARTICLE NO: 108556

Maughan, R.J. Relationship between muscle strength and muscle cross-sectional area: implications for training. (Refs: 27) *Sports medicine (Auckland, N.Z.)* 1(4), Jul/Aug 1984, 263-269.
LEVEL: I LANG: Eng SIRC ARTICLE NO: 102802

Maughan, R.J. Watson, J.S. Weir, J. Muscle strength and cross-section area in man: a comparison of strength-trained and untrained subjects. (Refs: 31)*British journal of sports medicine (Loughborough, Eng.)* 18(3), Sept 1984, 149-157.
ABST: This study has examined muscle strength and cross-sectional area in a group of 35 healthy untrained male subjects and 8 subjects who had been engaged in a strenuous weight-training programme. The maximum voluntary knee extension force which could be produced by the untrained subjects was 742 plus or minus 100. The trained subjects could produce a significantly greater force (992 plus or minus 162 N). Cross-sectional area of the knee-extensor muscle group was 81.6 plus or minus 11.8 cm2 in the untrained subjects and 104.1 plus or minus 12.3 cm2 in the trained subjects. In the untrained subjects, a significant correlation existed between strength and muscle cross-sectional area. In the same group of subjects, there was a significant inverse relationship between muscle cross-sectional area and the ratio of strength to cross-sectional area.
LEVEL: A LANG: Eng SIRC ARTICLE NO: 102803

Muscular endurance: after 15 it's all downhill for most Canadians. L'endurance musculaire: apres 15 ans, c'est le declin chez la plupart des canadiens. *Highlights/Faits saillants (Ottawa)* 36, Sept 1984, 1-2.
CORP: Canada Fitness Survey.
CORP: Enquete condition physique Canada.
LEVEL: B LANG: Eng Fr SIRC ARTICLE NO: 100870

Petrofsky, J.S. Hendershot, D.M. The interrelationship between blood pressure, intramuscular pressure, and isometric endurance in fast and slow twitch skeletal muscle in the cat. (Refs: 26)*European journal of applied physiology and occupational physiology (Berlin, W.G.)* 53(2), 1984, 106-111.
ABST: Two series of experiments were performed to examine the interrelationships between blood pressure, intramuscular pressure, muscle blood flow, and the endurance for isometric exercise in a fast (medial gastrocnemius) and a slow (soleus)

twitch muscle of the cat. In the first series of experiments, the relationship between tension and intramuscular pressure was examined. It was found that intramuscular pressure was linearly related to tension in both muscles. A second series of experiments was conducted in which blood pressure was increased above intramuscular pressure and the effect of blood pressure on isometric endurance was measured. It was found that increased perfusion of the muscle resulted in a dramatic increase in the endurance for contractions sustained at isometric tensions below 60 per cent of the muscle's initial strength.
LEVEL: A LANG: Eng SIRC ARTICLE NO: 104355

Scharf, S. Bye, P. Pardy, R. Macklem, P.T. Dyspnea, fatigue, and second wind. (Refs: 3)*American review of respiratory disease (New York)* 129(2 Pt 2), Feb 1984, S88-S89.
CONF: Exercise Testing in the Dyspneic Patient Workshop (1982 : Bethesda).
ABST: This paper addresses the question of different testing dyspnea from fatigue by examining the concept of 'second wind' Diaphragmatic fatigue has been associated with the sensation of dyspnea when fatigue was expressed by Diaphragmatic EMG. This sensation of dyspnea disappeared with the appearance of 'second wind' and a change in the EMG spectrum to normal. This provides an important tool for the evaluation of respiratory muscle fatigue.
LEVEL: A LANG: Eng SIRC ARTICLE NO: 099264

Seaborne, D. Taylor, A.W. The effect of speed of isokinetic exercise on training transfer to isometric strength in the quadriceps muscle. (Refs: 24)*Journal of sports medicine and physical fitness (Torino, Italy)* 24(3), Sept 1984, 183-188.
ABST: The possibility of a transfer of effect from isokinetic to isometric activities was investigated in this study. The female subjects followed a six-week program of quadriceps training at two different speeds, on an isokinetic dynamometer. Functional tests for static strength and endurance were performed before and after the training program, and the findings compared to a control group of five subjects. The results indicated no significant transfer of effect, but rather supported the concept of specificity of training. The group exercising at high speed made significantly greater gains in mean peak torque per minute of exercise, compared to the group exercising at low speed.
LEVEL: A LANG: Eng SIRC ARTICLE NO: 105493

Smolander, J. Louhevaara, V. Tuomi, T. Korhonen, O. Jaakkola, J. Reduction of isometric muscle endurance after wearing impermeable gas protective clothing. (Refs: 13)*European journal of applied physiology and occupational physiology (Berlin, W.G.)* 53(1), 1984, 76-80.
ABST: The isometric endurance of forearm muscles at 40 percent maximum voluntary contraction was measured in six healthy male subjects, after they had walked for 25-30 min on a treadmill while wearing an impermeable gas protective suit and a self-contained breathing apparatus at a light and a moderate work level. The mean endurance times were 12 percent (NS) and 24 percent shorter than the average control value after exercise for the light and moderate work levels, respectively. These changes were accompanied by an increased heart rate, and rectal and skin temperatures.
LEVEL: A LANG: Eng SIRC ARTICLE NO: 104374

Solgaard, S. Kristiansen, B. Jensen, J.S. Evaluation of instruments for measuring grip

strength. *Acta orthopaedica scandinavica (Copenhagen)* 55(5), Oct 1984, 569-572.
LEVEL: A LANG: Eng

Stonecipher, D.R. Catlin, P.A. The effect of a forearm strap on wrist extensor strength. (Refs: 23)*Journal of orthopaedic and sports physical therapy (Baltimore, Md.)* 6(3), Nov/Dec 1984, 184-189.
ABST: Thirty subjects with no pathology of the right elbow were tested using an isokinetic dynamometer to measure wrist extensor strength. Subjects were tested under control and experimental conditions with and without a forearm strap. Tests were conducted at 30 and 120o/sec. No difference in strength was noted at the slower speed. A statistically significant increase in strength with the strap was found at 120o/sec. Facilitation due to sensory stimulation of the skin and pressure on the muscle belly was offered as an explanation.
LEVEL: A LANG: Eng SIRC ARTICLE NO: 102833

Strength fitness of Canadians: 'true north strong,' or...? Le Canada: une super-puissance de la condition physique? *Highlights/Faits saillants (Ottawa)* 35, Sept 1984, 1-2.
CORP: Canada Fitness Survey.
CORP: Enquete condition physique Canada.
LEVEL: B LANG: Eng Fr SIRC ARTICLE NO: 100880

Thomas, L.E. Isokinetic torque for adult females: effects of age and body size. (Refs: 12)*Journal of orthopaedic and sports physical therapy (Baltimore, Md.)* 6(1), Jul/Aug 1984, 21-24.
ABST: The effects of age and body size on isokinetic torque levels for adult females were statistically analyzed. Results indicate that age and to a lesser extent weight and height can account for torque differences in adult women. Additionally, this relationship exists regardless of speed of movement.
LEVEL: A LANG: Eng SIRC ARTICLE NO: 100926

Wahbeh-Foster, E. A comparison of selected muscle strength tests and endurance in children with vestibular deficits and children with normal vestibular functions. Eugene, Ore.: Microform Publications, University of Oregon, 1984. 2 microfiches : negative, ill. ; 11 x 15 cm.
NOTES: Thesis (M.S.) - University of Kansas, 1981; (ix, 148 leaves); includes bibliography.
LEVEL: A LANG: Eng UO84 413-414

Wilmore, J.H. Morphologic and physiologic differences between man and woman relevant to exercise. (Refs: 20)*International journal of sports medicine (Stuttgart)* Suppl. 5, Nov 1984, 193-194.
CONF: International Congress on Sports and Health (1983 : Maastricht, Netherlands).
LEVEL: A LANG: Eng SIRC ARTICLE NO: 104393

Wong, D.L.K. Glasheen-Wray, M. Andrews, L.F. Isokinetic evaluation of the ankle invertors and evertors. (Refs: 26)*Journal o orthopaedic and sports physical therapy (Baltimore, Md.)* 5(5), Mar/Apr 1984, 246-252.
ABST: In order to develop normative strength values (absolute peak torque and relative peak torque) for the ankle invertors and evertors 21 men and 23 women were tested on a Cybex II dynamometer. Men had significantly stronger invertors and evertors when the values were reported in absolute terms. However, when the values were reported in relative terms only the left evertors in men were significantly stronger than the corresponding evertors in women. The authors

suggest that the data presented could provide a guideline for the rehabilitation of patients.
LEVEL: A LANG: Eng SIRC ARTICLE NO: 094637

Young, K. Davies, C.T.M. Effect of diet on human muscle weakness following prolonged exercise. (Refs: 21)*European journal o applied physiology and occupational physiology (Berlin, W.G.) 53(1), 1984, 81-85.*
ABST: The effect of altering muscle glycogen on the ability of skeletal muscle to generate voluntary and electrically evoked isometric force following prolonged exercise has been investigated in five healthy male subjects. Measurements from the tricpes surae were made at rest, and before and after prolonged exercise (uphill walking) at approximately 75 percent VO2 max in low muscle glycogen (low CHO) and high muscle glycogen (high CHO) conditions. It is concluded that changes in muscle glycogen alone do not alter the isometric force generating capacity of human muscle, but when combined with prolonged exercise low muscle glycogen enhances exercise-induced muscle weakness.
LEVEL: A LANG: Eng SIRC ARTICLE NO: 104398

Zivanic, S. Zivotic-Vanovic, M. Dimitrijevic, B. Stamenkovic, C. Maksimalna potrosnja kiseonika i opsta misicna snaga zena-regruta. (Maximal oxygen uptake and general muscle strength in female recruits.) *Vojnosanitetski pregled (Belgrad) 41(1), Jan/Feb 1984, 12-14.*
LEVEL: A LANG: Scr

TESTING

Clayton, J.A. Power output at different areas in the range of motion. (Refs: 2)
NOTES: In, Cantu, R.C. (ed.), Clinical sport medicine, Lexington, Mass. ; Toronto, Collamore Press : D.C. Heath, c1984, p. 163-167.
LEVEL: A LANG: Eng RC1201 15964

DeLacerda, F.G. Claypool, L.P. Determination of a fatigue curve as a function of electromyography and mechanical work. *Journal of orthopaedic and sports physical therapy (Baltimore, Md.) 5(6), May/Jun 1984, 332-335.*
ABST: The purpose of this study was to identify a fatigue curve in which muscle electrical activity was a function of the mechanical work performed by the anterior tibialis muscle. A work fatigue curve was determined to be the function of a cubic regression equation. The work fatigue curve was compatible with the accepted physiological concept of at least two different muscle fiber types.
LEVEL: A LANG: Eng SIRC ARTICLE NO: 100892

Genot, C. Neiger, H. Etude comparative du travail isocinetique maximal des muscles rotateurs internes et externes de l'epaul (Refs: 12)*Medecine du sport 58(1), 25 janv 1984, 28-32.*
RESUME: Cette etude mesure le travail isocinetique des rotateurs internes et externes de l'epaule a diverses positions (abduction de 90o, flexion de 90o et en position fonctionnelle associant 45o d'abduction et 45o de flexion) et a diverses vitesses d'execution. 13 sujets masculins participent a l'etude. Quelques resultats observes: 1) les muscles rotateurs internes sont toujours plus forts que les rotateurs externes, 2) le travail fournit a la vitesse de 60o/seconde est superieure a celui fourni a 120o/seconde, et ce, chez les deux groupes rotateurs.
LEVEL: A LANG: Fr SIRC ARTICLE NO: 091728

Hicks, J.E. Shwaker, T.H. Jones, B.L. Linzer, M. Gerber, L.H. Diagnostic ultrasound: its use in the evaluation of muscle. (Refs: 8)*Archives of physical medicine and rehabilitation 65(3), Mar 1984, 129-131.*
ABST: The authors determine the reliability and reproducibility of diagnostic ultrasound data obtained when evaluating muscle. Echo amplitudes were recorded from the quadriceps femoris muscle of 10 runners and 6 non-runners in a contracted and relaxed state. The study shows that: 1) values of echo amplitudes are reproducible, 2) echo amplitude of muscle has significantly decreased in the contracted state, and 3) echo amplitude value of muscle in the relaxed and contracted state in runners is not significantly different from the relaxed and contracted state in the non-runners.
LEVEL: A LANG: Eng SIRC ARTICLE NO: 093895

Leyvraz, P.F. Gobelet, C. Qu'est-ce que le Cybex? Que permet-il de faire? (Refs: 4)*Revue medicale de la Suisse romande (Lausanne) 104(10), oct 1984, 795-799.*
LEVEL: I LANG: Fr SIRC ARTICLE NO: 174098

Marino, M. Gleim, G.W. Muscle strength and fiber typing. (Refs: 78)*Clinics in sports medicine (Philadelphia) 3(1), Jan 1984 85-100.*
NOTES: Symposium on profiling.
ABST: The composition of an athlete's muscle and its fibre types is influenced by training. Slow-twitch muscle is related to endurance performance; whereas, fast-twitch muscle is related to strength performance. This is found in the trained population, but is not as consistent in the untrained. An evaluation of strength can help the coach determine the best team position for the athlete as well as aid in the design of a training program to prevent injury and increase specific strength needs.
LEVEL: A LANG: Eng SIRC ARTICLE NO: 093112

Mathiowetz, V. Weber, K. Volland, G. Kashman, N. Reliability and validity of grip and pinch strength evaluations. *Journal o hand surgery (St. Louis) 9(2), Mar 1984, 222-226.*
LEVEL: A LANG: Eng SIRC ARTICLE NO: 100914

Patterson, M.E. Nelson, S.G. Duncan, P.W. Effects of stabilizing the nontested lower extremity during isokinetic evaluation of the quadriceps and hamstrings. (Refs: 9)*Journal of orthopaedic and sports physical therapy (Baltimore, Md.) 6(1), Jul/Aug 1984, 18-20.*
ABST: The purpose of this investigation was to determine if stabilization of the nontested lower extremity influences the peak torque generated by the knee musculature of the opposite extremity during isokinetic testing. The subjects included 15 males and 15 females, between 18 to 30 years of age, who had no history of right knee pain or pathology. A Cybex I isokinetic dynamometer was used to measure the torques generated by the quadriceps and hamstring muscles of the right lower extremity during flexion and extension. Each subject performed two trials of extension and flexion of the right knee; each trial consisted of one set of three contractions at 60o/sec and one set at 180o/sec. One trial was performed with the left lower extremity stabilized and the second trial was performed without stabilization. The results demonstrate that the peak torques generated by the quadriceps and hamstrings of the tested extremity are not significantly influenced by stabilization of the opposite lower extremity at the speeds tested.
LEVEL: A LANG: Eng SIRC ARTICLE NO: 100747

Poty, P. Roattino, J.P. Chabanne, G. Le dynamometre isokinetique. Interets et limites. (Refs: 4)*Cinesiologie (Paris) 94, mars/avr 1984, 155-159.*
LEVEL: I LANG: Fr SIRC ARTICLE NO: 095719

Rogers, B.L. The development of an interphase connector to isokinetically evaluate rotary cervical spine musculature using the Cybex II dynamometer. (Refs: 20)*Athletic training 19(1), Spring 1984, 16-18.*
ABST: 54 high school football players were selected for a study to evaluate cervical spine musculature. In order to use the CYBEX, the authors fabricated an interphase connection between the head appliance (Southern Bike football helmets) and the CYBEX input shaft. The equipment proved durable and reusable.
LEVEL: A LANG: Eng SIRC ARTICLE NO: 091767

Weiss, L.W. The use of B-mode ultrasound for measuring the thickness of skeletal muscle at two upper leg sites. (Refs: 24) *Journal of orthopaedic and sports physical therapy (Baltimore, Md.) 6(3), Nov/Dec 1984, 163-167.*
ABST: Preliminary information regarding the use of B-mode ultrasound for measuring the thickness of skeletal muscle on the anterior and posterior sides of the upper leg was evaluated. Subjects were volunteers, including 15 men and 15 women college students. The average weight of the men was 26% more than that of the women. On an absolute basis, men had larger muscle thicknesses including the anterior site (19%) and posterior site (10%). It was concluded that B-mode ultrasound can be used to reliably measure the thickness of skeletal muscle on the upper legs.
LEVEL: A LANG: Eng SIRC ARTICLE NO: 102840

PHYSIOLOGY - NEURAL

Bennett, F.M. A role for neural pathways in exercise hyperpnea. (Refs: 30)*Journal of applied physiology: respiratory, environmental and exercise physiology (Bethesda, Md.) 56(6), Jun 1984, 1559-1564.*
ABST: This study reexamined the role of humoral pathways in mediating the ventilatory response to electrically induced exercise. The method of this study involved the stimulation of the peripheral ends of severed sciatic nerves in seven anesthetized dogs. After stimulation there were increases in expired minute ventilation, arterial CO2 partial pressure and carotid artery temperature. The results indicate that humoral factors cannot maintain an isocapnic hyperpnea. Thus, neural pathways may play a fundamental role in the ventilatory response to exercise in intact animals.
LEVEL: A LANG: Eng SIRC ARTICLE NO: 097713

Casanueva, F.F. Villanueva, L. Cabranes, J.A. Cabezas-Cerrato, J. Fernandez-Cruz, A. Cholinergic mediation of growth hormone secretion elicited by arginine, clonidine, and physical exercise in man. *Journal of clinical endocrinology and metabolism (Baltimore) 59(3), Sept 1984, 526-530.*
ABST: The role of acetylcholine in human growth hormone secretion was studied with atropine, which selectively blocks cholinergic muscarinic receptors and crosses the blood-brain barrier. The results of paired tests in 4 groups of subjects during 20 min of physical exercise, or while employing arginine or clonidine suggest that acetylcholine plays an important role in the regulation of growth hormone

secretion.
LEVEL: A LANG: Eng SIRC ARTICLE NO: 103885

Dustman, R.E. Ruhling, R.O. Russell, E.M. Shearer, D.E. Bonekat, H.W. Shigeoka, J.W. Wood, J.S. Bradford, D.C. Aerobic exercise training and improved neuropsychological function of older individuals. (Refs: 69)*Neurobiology of aging (Fayetteville, N.Y.) 5(1), Spring 1984, 35-42.*
ABST: This study evaluated the effects of a four month aerobic exercise conditioning program on neuropsychological test performance, depression indices, sensory thresholds, and visual acuity of 55-70 year old sedentary individuals. Aerobically trained subjects were compared with age-matched subjects who trained with strength and flexibility exercises and others who were not engaged in a supervised exercise program. The results led the authors to speculate that aerobic exercise promoted increased cerebral metabolic activity with a resultant improvement in neuropsychological test scores.
LEVEL: A LANG: Eng SIRC ARTICLE NO: 109740

Grossman, A. Bouloux, P. Price, P. Drury, P.L. Lam, K.S. Turner, T. Thomas, J. Besser, G.M. Sutton, J. The role of opioid peptides in the hormonal responses to acute exercise in man. *Clinical science (London) 67(5), Nov 1984, 483-491.*
LEVEL: A LANG: Eng

Kamen, G. Taylor, P. Beehler, P.J. Ulnar and posterior tibial nerve conduction velocity in athletes. (Refs: 43)*Internationa journal of sports medicine 5(1), Feb 1984, 26-30.*
ABST: Nerve conduction velocity (NCV) of weight lifters was observed to be significantly faster than the NCV of swimmers, jumpers, sprinters and distance runners. Male marathoners had the slowest posterior tibial NCV of all the athletes. A discriminant function analysis correctly classified 50.6% of the 91 subjects into power-type, endurance-type, or untrained categories on the basis of ulnar and posterior nerve conduction velocities. The authors suggest that both genetic and environmental factors are important determinants of motor nerve conduction velocity.
LEVEL: A LANG: Eng SIRC ARTICLE NO: 093102

Kogan, A.B. Ermakov, P.N. Poroshenko, A.B. O neirofiziologicheskikh korreliatakh idomotornogo napriazheniia sportsmena. (Neurophysiological correlates of ideomotor tension in the athlete.) *Doklady Akademii Nauk SSSR (Moscow) 278(5), 1984, 1263-1264.*
LEVEL: I LANG: Rus

Lehmann, M. Schmid, P. Keul, J. Age- and exercise-related sympathetic activity in untrained volunteers, trained athletes and patients with impaired left-ventricular contractility. (Refs: 44)*European heart journal (London) 5(Suppl E), Nov 1984, 1-7.*
LEVEL: A LANG: Eng SIRC ARTICLE NO: 109711

Petrov, I.A. Izmenenie sootnosheniia biopotentialov zon mozga pri razlichnykh urovniakh rabotosopsobnosti. (Changes in the biopotential ratio of brain areas at different levels of work capacity.) *Fiziologiya cheloveka (Moscow) 10(3), May/June 1984, 370-374.*
LEVEL: A LANG: Rus

ENDORPHINS

Elliot, D.L. Goldberg, L. Watts, W.J. Orwoll, E. Resistance exercise and plasma beta-endorphin/ beta-lipotrophin immunoreactivity. *Life sciences (Oxford) 34(6), 6 Feb 1984, 515-518.*
ABST: 5 men were tested for serum cortisol and plasma beta-endorphin/beta-lipotrophin hormone immunoreactivity before and after treadmill endurance exercise and burst activity resistance exercise (weight training). Mean beta-endorphin/ beta-lipotrophin hormone immunoactivity increases significantly following both exercise protocols. Post-exercise hormonal values were similar for both exercise activities.
LEVEL: A LANG: Eng SIRC ARTICLE NO: 099233

Grossman, A. Endorphins and exercise. (Refs: 23)*Clinical cardiology (New York) 7(5), May 1984, 255-260.*
LEVEL: A LANG: En SIRC ARTICLE NO: 100720

Harber, V.J. Sutton, J.R. Endorphins and exercise. (Refs: 102)*Sports medicine (Auckland) 1(2), Mar/Apr 1984, 154-171.*
ABST: This article reviews the research on endorphins and exercise and examines their involvement in a number of widely disparate physiological processes. Elevated endorphin concentrations induced by exercise have been implicated in mood state changes and exercise induced euphoria: altered pain perception, menstrual disturbances in female athletes, and the stress responses of numerous hormones. Recent evidence also indicates exercise-induced elevated endorphin concentrations in ventilatory regulation and perception of fatigue.
LEVEL: A LANG: Eng SIRC ARTICLE NO: 094600

Howlett, T.A. Tomlin, S. Ngahfoong, L. Rees, L.H. Bullen, B.A. Skrinar, G.S. McArthur, J.W. Release of beta endorphin and met-enkephalin during exercise in normal women: response to training. *British medical journal (Clinical research) (London) 288(6435), 30 Jun 1984, 1950-1952.*
ABST: Endorphin and met-enkephalin concentrations were measured in response to treadmill exercises in 15 women before, during, and after an exercise training program. Significant release of beta endorphin occurred in all test runs, and the pattern and amount of release were not altered by training. Endogenous opioid peptides play a part in adaptive changes to exercise training and probably contribute to the menstrual disturbances of women athletes.
LEVEL: A LANG: Eng SIRC ARTICLE NO: 102787

PHYSIOLOGY - PULMONARY

Agadzhanian, N.A. Elfimov, A.I. Severin, A.E. Pas, I.A. Gazobmen i fizicheskaia rabotosposobnost' u urozhentsev razlichnykh geograficheskikh regionov. (Gas exchange and physical work capacity of natives of different geographical regions.) *Kosmicheskaia biologiia i aviakosmicheskaia meditsina (Moscow) 18(3), May/Jun 1984, 65-68.*
ABST: A study was carried out to investigate exercise tolerance, gas exchange and external respiration of Latin-American students who lived in Moscow for a year. As controls Soviet students residing in and around Moscow were used. In the evening the Latin-American students showed a trend towards an increase of the cardiorespiratory activity and exercise tolerance. The Soviet students did not display changes in exercise tolerance. The Latin-American students showed an increase in the morning and a decrease in the evening of external respiration reactions. The Soviet students exhibited opposite variations. Direct alveolar measurements demonstrated an increase of pCO_2 in the alveolar air in the Latin-American students in the evening and a decrease of the parameter in the Soviet students. It is suggested that cyclic changes in external respiration in response to hypercapnia are associated with exercise tolerance.
LEVEL: A LANG: Rus

Brischetto, M.J. Millman, R.P. Peterson, D.D. Silage, D.A. Pack, A.I. Effect of aging on ventilatory response to exercise an CO2. (Refs: 30)*Journal of applied physiology: respiratory, environmental and exercise physiology (Bethesda, Md.) 56(5), May 1984, 1143-1150.*
ABST: This study investigated the relationship between increasing ventilation and increasing CO_2 production (VCO2) during steady-state exercise and changes in minute ventilation in response to progressive hypercapnia during CO_2 rebreathing in 10 young subjects (22-37 yr) and 10 elderly subjects (67-79 yr). The results indicate that elderly people have a decreased ventilatory response to hypercapnia than young people. Conversely, the ventilatory response of elderly people to exercise is greater than that of young people. The authors suggest that exercise hyperpnea is produced by neural mechanisms different from those subserving the response of altered activity of the peripheral or central chemoreceptors.
LEVEL: A LANG: Eng SIRC ARTICLE NO: 097716

Gaesser, G.A. Brooks, G.A. Metabolic bases of excess post-exercise oxygen consumption: a review. (Refs: 129)*Medicine and science in sports and exercise 16(1), 1984, 29-43.*
ABST: This review attempts to clarify the metabolic basis of oxygen debt. Underlying biochemical, physiological and physical factors are found to play a role in the elevation of oxygen uptake after exercise. There does not appear to be a definitive reason for this phenomenon; however it is felt that O2 debt is an inapropriate term. The authors disprove earlier theories which placed a heavy emphasis on the role of lactic acid metabolism in excess post-exercise oxygen consumption.
LEVEL: A LANG: Eng SIRC ARTICLE NO: 091727

Grassino, A. A rationale for training respiratory muscles. *International rehabilitation medicine (Basel) 6(4), 1984, 175-178.*
LEVEL: I LANG: Eng

Horvath, S.M. Borgia, J.F. Cardiopulmonary gas transport and aging. (Refs: 28)*American review of respiratory disease (New York) 129(2 Pt 2), Feb 1984, S68-S71.*
CONF: Exercise Testing in the Dyspneic Patient Workshop (1982 : Bethesda).
ABST: Exercise performance as modified by age has never been properly defined. Studies that are available in the literature have provided conflicting information due to the small number of studies performed and the absence of longitudinal research in the literature. The studies reviewed in this paper show significant age-related changes in the cardiorespiratory system during exercise. It appears that oxygen uptake and minute ventilation remain constant at fixed submaximal work rates but require

progressively greater fractions of the maximal values. Some studies suggest that there is a greater percent contribution of anaerobic oxidative processes than aerobic for a given work rate with increasing age.
LEVEL: A LANG: Eng SIRC ARTICLE NO: 099241

Killian, K.J. Gandevia, S.C. Summers, E. Campbell, E.J.M. Effect of increased lung volume on perception of breathlessness, effort, and tension. (Refs: 21)*Journal of applied physiology: respiratory, environmental and exercise physiology (Bethesda, Md.) 57 (3), Sept 1984, 686-691.*
LEVEL: A LANG: Eng SIRC ARTICLE NO: 108931

Krasnikov, N.P. Issledovanie funktsii vneshnego dykhaniia i krovoobrashcheniia, rabotosposobnost' cheloveka. (External respiratory and circulatory functions determining and limiting human physical work capacity.) *Fiziologiya cheloveka (Moscow) 10(6), Nov/Dec 1984, 1036-1041.*
LEVEL: A LANG: Rus

Kuchkin, S.N. Faktory, opredeliaiushchie 'effektivnost' proizvol'nogo snizheniia ventiliatsii pri myshechnoi rabote s ispol'zovaniem instrumental'noi obratnoi sviazi. (Factors determining the efficiency of voluntary decreased ventilation during muscle work by using instrumental feedback.) *Fiziologiya cheloveka (Moscow) 10(4), Jul/Aug 1984, 623-630.*
LEVEL: A LANG: Rus

Lind, F. Hesser, C.M. Breathing pattern and occlusion pressure during moderate and heavy exercise. *Acta physiologica scandinavica (Stockholm) 122(1), Sept 1984, 61-69.*
LEVEL: A LANG: Eng

Louhevaara, V. Tuomi, T. Korhonen, O. Jaakkola, J. Cardiorespiratory effects of respiratory protective devices during exercise in well-trained men. (Refs: 20)*European journal of applied physiology and occupational physiology (Heidelberg) 52(3), Apr 1984, 340-345.*
ABST: This study investigated the effects of a filtering device, an air-line breathing apparatus, and a self-contained breathing apparatus on pulmonary ventilation (Ve), oxygen consumption (VO2) and heart rate (HR) at rest, during progressive submaximal work levels, and during recovery in 12 voluntary firemen. All three devices hampered respiration, resulting in hypoventilation during work. Oxygen consumption was increased at the same work load compared to control values when the respirators were used. This effect was particularly noticeable at higher work loads. The use of the heavy (15 kg) self-contained breathing apparatus imposes a particularly severe stress on the cardiorespiratory system.
LEVEL: A LANG: Eng SIRC ARTICLE NO: 097740

Turner, C.R. The effects of one-sided resistance breathing on cardio-respiratory responses. Eugene, Ore.: Microform Publications, University of Oregon, 1984. 1 microfiche : negative, ill, ; 11 x 15 cm. NOTES: Thesis (M.S.) - Pennsylvania State University, 1983; (ix, 46 leaves); includes bibliography.
LEVEL: A LANG: Eng UO84 373

VanBenthuysen, K.M. Swanson, G.D. Weil, J.V. Temporal delay of venous blood correlates with onset of exercise hyperpnea. (Refs: 24)*Journal of applied physiology: respiratory, environmental and exercise physiology (Bethesda, Md.) 57(3), Sept 1984, 874-880.*
LEVEL: A LANG: Eng SIRC ARTICLE NO: 108938

Whipp, B.J. Ward, S.A. Wasserman, K. Ventilatory responses to exercise and their control in man. (Refs: 64)*American review of respiratory disease (New York) 129(2 Pt 2), Feb 1984, S17-S20.*
CONF: Exercise Testing in the Dyspneic Patient Workshop (1982 : Bethesda).
LEVEL: I LANG: Eng SIRC ARTICLE NO: 099274

DIFFUSION

Diffusing capacity to predict arterial desaturation during exercise. (letter) *New England journal of medicine (Boston) 311(11), 13 Sept 1984, 735-737.*
LEVEL: I LANG: Eng SIRC ARTICLE NO: 104300

Saito, G. (A study on pulmonary gas exchange during muscular exercise by patients with idiopathic interstitial pneumonia.) *Nippon kyobu shikkan gakkai zasshi/Japanese journal of thoracic diseases (Tokyo) 22(9), Sept 1984, 733-741.*
LEVEL: A LANG: Jpn

Yasukouchi, A. Uniformity of increase in pulmonary diffusing capacity during submaximal exercise in normal young adults. *Industrial health (Kawasaki) 22(3), 1984, 137-151.*
LEVEL: A LANG: Eng

FUNCTION

Belman, M.J. King, R.R. Pulmonary profiling in exercise. (Refs: 39)*Clinics in sports medicine (Philadelphia, Pa.) 3(1), Jan 1984, 119-136.*
NOTES: Symposium on profiling.
ABST: Research has found that ventilatory muscle endurance can be improved with training, however, lung volumes do not change significantly in the normal population. The authors discuss the effect of exercise on ventilation and gas exchange in the functioning of the lung. Attention is also given the role of exercise in improving asthma and chronic obstructive pulmonary disease.
LEVEL: A LANG: Eng SIRC ARTICLE NO: 093066

Cooper, D.M. Weiler-Ravell, D. Gas exchange response to exercise in children. (Refs: 18)*American review of respiratory disease (New York) 129(2 Pt 2), Feb 1984, S47-S48.*
CONF: Exercise Testing in the Dyspneic Patient Workshop (1982 : Bethesda).
ABST: The gas exchange response to exercise in 109 normal children (aged 6 to 17 years) was measured with noninvasive techniques. Maximal oxygen uptake and anaerobic threshold were highly correlated with increasing height and values were found to be significantly higher in boys. Girls were found to have significantly lower values than girls in earlier studies.
LEVEL: A LANG: Eng SIRC ARTICLE NO: 098882

Forster, H.V. Pan, L.G. Bisgard, G.E. Dorsey, S.M. Britton, M.S. Temporal pattern of pulmonary gas exchange during exercise in ponies. (Refs: 26)*Journal of applied physiology: respiratory, environmental and exercise physiology (Bethesda, Md.) 57(3), Sept 1984, 760-767.*
LEVEL: A LANG: Eng SIRC ARTICLE NO: 108937

Harm, D.L. Marion, R.J. Kotses, H. Creer, T.L. Effect of subjects effort on pulmonary function measures: a preliminary investigation. *Journal of asthma (Ossining, N.Y.) 21(5), 1984, 295-298.*
LEVEL: A LANG: Eng

He, D. (Testing of lung function during exercise in health adults.) *Chung-hua chieh ho ho hu hsi hsi chi ping tsa chih (Peking) 7(3), Jun 1984, 162-165;192.*
LEVEL: A LANG: Chi

Jones, N.L. Normal values for pulmonary gas exchange during exercise. (Refs: 33)*American review of respiratory disease (New York) 129(2 Pt 2), Feb 1984, S44-S46.*
CONF: Exercise Testing in the Dyspneic Patient Workshop (1982 : Bethesda).
LEVEL: I LANG: Eng SIRC ARTICLE NO: 099242

Lai, J.S. Lien, I.N. (Cardiopulmonary functions during maximal exercise in young Chinese athletes and non-athletes.) *Taiwan i hsueh hui tsa chich (Taipei) 83(2), Feb 1984, 196-205.*
LEVEL: A LANG: Chi

Lakhera, S.C. Mathew, L. Rastogi, S.K. Sen Gupta, J. Pulmonary function of Indian athletes and sportsmen: comparison with American athletes. *Indian journal of physiology and pharmacology (New Delhi) 28(3), Jul/Sept 1984, 187-194.*
ABST: Pulmonary functions of Indian athletes and sportsmen were evaluated. Swimmers were found to have higher vital capacity and forced expiratory volume than all other athletes studied. A comparative study between Indian and American athletes indicated superior lung volumes and capacities in US athletes.
LEVEL: A LANG: Eng

Mertz, J.S. McCaffrey, T.V. Kern, E.B. Role of the nasal airway in regulation of airway resistance during hypercapnia and exercise. Second-Place Resident Award at 1982 Research Forum. *Otolaryngology and head and neck surgery (Rochester, Minn.) 92(3), Jun 1984, 302-307.*
ABST: Posterior mask rhinomanometry was used to measure nasal resistance during exercise and hypercapnia in 10 healthy adult volunteers. Exercise was produced by pedaling a stationary bicycle at three loads. The results showed that nasal resistance decreases linearly as expired CO2 levels and exercise levels increase, minute ventilation increases linearly as expired CO2 levels and exercise levels increase, and nasal resistance varies inversely with minute ventilation during both hypercapnia and exercise. The constant relationship between nasal resistance and minute ventilation during hypercapnia and exercise suggests that nasal resistance is regulated by the respiratory center to match the level of respiratory demand.
LEVEL: A LANG: Eng SIRC ARTICLE NO: 104345

Pan, L.G. Forster, H.V. Bisgard, G.E. Dorsey, S.M. Busch, M.A. Cardiodynamic variables and ventilation during treadmill exercise in ponies. (Refs: 23)*Journal of applied physiology: respiratory, environmental and exercise physiology (Bethesda, Md.) 57 (3), Sept 1984, 753-759.*
LEVEL: A LANG: Eng SIRC ARTICLE NO: 108936

Wasserman, K. Coupling of external to internal respiration. (Refs: 11)*American review of respiratory disease (New York) 129(2 Pt 2), Feb 1984, S21-S24.*
CONF: Exercise testing in the Dyspneic Patient Workshop (1982 : Bethesda).
ABST: Oxygen is required to generate chemical energy to allow muscle contraction to occur during exercise. This paper details the role of respiration in the performance of exercise through the examination of bioenergetics and gas exchange, and the coupling of external to internal respiration. The pattern of external respiration (gas exchange at

the lungs) is defined in its three phases.
LEVEL: A LANG: Eng SIRC ARTICLE NO: 099273

RESPIRATORY PHYSIOLOGY

Allen, C.J. Jones, N.L. Killian, K.J. Alveolar gas exchange during exercise: a single-breath analysis. (Refs: 31)*Journal of applied physiology: respiratory, environmental and exercise physiology (Bethesda, Md.) 57(6), Dec 1984, 1704-1709.*
LEVEL: A LANG: Eng SIRC ARTICLE NO: 108562

Banner, A.S. Green, J. O'Connor, M. Relation of respiratory water loss to coughing after exercise. *New England journal of medicine (Boston) 311(14), 4 Oct 1984, 883-886.*
ABST: Some normal subjects report coughing after exercise, and to determine whether this might also be related to respiratory heat loss, we monitored cough frequency after hyperpnea with air of varying temperature and water content in seven such subjects. Hyperpnea with dry air at 37 degrees C resulted in more water loss, less heat loss, and more coughing than hyperpnea with subfreezing air. Hyperpnea with ambient air was associated with a similar cough frequency and water loss but with less heat loss than hyperpnea with subfreezing air. There was a direct relation between cough frequency and respiratory water loss but no consistent relation between cough frequency and respiratory heat loss. This study indicates that coughing after hyperpnea with poorly conditioned air is related to the overall rate of respiratory water loss.
LEVEL: A LANG: Eng SIRC ARTICLE NO: 104280

Bruce, R.A. Normal values for VO2 and the VO2-HR relationship. (Refs: 14)*American review of respiratory disease (New York) 129(2 Pt 2), Feb 1984, S41-S43.*
CONF: Exercise Testing in the Dyspneic Patient Workshop (1982 : Bethesda).
ABST: Heart rate responses to exercise are related to oxygen requirements but this varies according to individual oxygen consumption variance due to various factors. Coronary heart disease patients who are limited by dyspnea and have chest pain, have diminished exercise capacity and cardiac function and have greater risk of secondary events than do coronary patients without dyspnea.
LEVEL: A LANG: Eng SIRC ARTICLE NO: 098903

Bye, P.T.P. Esau, S.A. Walley, K.R. Macklem, P.T. Pardy, R.L. Ventilatory muscle during exercise in air and oxygen in normal men. (Refs: 26)*Journal of applied physiology: respiratory, environmental and exercise physiology 56(2), Feb 1984, 464-471.*
ABST: Seven healthy males performed exercise to exhaustion at 80% of maximum power output inspiring air or 40% O2. Electromyography predicted diaphragmatic fatigue in dive of the subjects. The inspiration of O2 increased the duration of the exercise by reducing the ventilation rate, delaying the onset of diaphragmatic fatigue and/or altering the pattern of ventilatory muscle recruitment. The authors conclude that diaphragmatic fatigue occurs during high intensity short-term exercise in air at a constant work load in some normal men.
LEVEL: A LANG: Eng SIRC ARTICLE NO: 093073

Bylund-Fellenius, A.C. Idstroem, J.P. Holm, S. Muscle respiration during exercise. (Refs: 4)*American review of respiratory disease (New York) 129(2 Pt 2), Feb 1984, S10-S12*

CONF: Exercise Testing in the Dyspneic Patient Workshop (1982 : Bethesda).
ABST: The importance of oxygen as a limiting factor for the mitochondrial respiration in contracting skeletal muscle was studied in ten male patients with peripheral vascular disease and ten normal subjects. The oxygen tension was found to decrease in human gastrocnemius muscle during leg ergometry exercise, and the magnitude of the decrease was a function of the intensity as well as the frequency of the muscle contractions. Significant relationships were found between the intramuscular oxygen tension and various muscle metabolites. This suggests that the oxygen tension measured in the extracellular compartment is of importance for the intracellular energy, and redox state, in exercising muscle. These findings were further confirmed in a second study of rats where the oxygen delivery was varied in a more predictable way.
LEVEL: A LANG: Eng SIRC ARTICLE NO: 099224

Delhez, L. Influence de l'entrainement sur la force des muscles respiratoires. (Refs: 33)*Annales de kinesitherapie (Paris) 11(6), 1984, 249-258.*
RESUME: L'auteur discute de trois methodes utilisees pour mesurer les forces maximales developpees par les muscles respiratoires: la mesure des variations de pression alveolaire en conditions statiques, de pression intrathoracique, en conditions dynamiques et de pression alveolaire en conditions statico-dynamiques. Il analyse l'evolution de la force des muscles respiratoires chez des sujets normaux et chez des handicapes pulmonaires chroniques apres entrainement. Un renforcement musculaire respiratoire est observee chez les deux groupes.
LEVEL: A LANG: Fr SIRC ARTICLE NO: 099228

Duvallet, A. Terreros, J.L. Dessanges, J.F. Rieu, M. Giraud-Chauveau, M. La courbe debit-volume chez le sujet sportif. Etablissement de valeurs normales pour les etudiants en education physique. (Refs: 13)*Cinesiologie (Paris) 96, juil/aout 1984, 295-300.*
RESUME: Les auteurs ont mesures la courbe debit-volume chez 204 etudiants en education physique. Les valeurs respiratoires obtenues sont comparees aux tables des 'valeurs normales' de l'American Thorax Society (A.T.S.) et de la Communaute Europeenne du Charbon et de l'Acier (C.E.C.A.). Les valeurs de l'A.T.S. et de la C.E.C.A. sont inferieures aux valeurs moyennes de la population etudiee. L'etude a demontre egalement qu'il existe une forte correlation entre la capacity vitale et la taille des sujets.
LEVEL: A LANG: Fr SIRC ARTICLE NO: 099232

Faraci, F.M. Olsen, S.C. Erickson, H.H. Effect of exercise on oxygen consumption, heart rate, and the electrocardiogram of pigs. (Refs: 22)*Medicine and science in sports and exercise (Indianapolis) 16(4), Aug 1984, 406-410.*
ABST: Pigs were exercised for 5 min at five different treadmill speeds (1.0-1.8 m.s-1) (3o incline), while oxygen consumption (MO2), carbon dioxide production (MCO2), and the electrocardiogram (ECG) were recorded continuously. Data were taken at rest, during exercise, and at 2, 5, 15, and 30 min after exercise. Values for MO2, MCO2, and heart rate (HR) showed progressive increases with increasing treadmill speed. The respiratory exchange ratio (R) increased during exercise and approached 1.0 but peak values were seen shortly after exercise. Heart rate, MO2, MCO2, and R reached steady-state

values after 2 min of exercise, which were maintained for the duration of exercise. In most cases, these variables had returned to control levels 15 min after exercise. A high correlation between HR and MO2 was found in these animals.
LEVEL: A LANG: Eng SIRC ARTICLE NO: 102772

Gaesser, G.A. Poole, D.C. Gardner, B.P. Dissociation between V02max and ventilatory threshold responses to endurance trainin (Refs: 32)*European journal of applied physiology and occupational physiology (Berlin) 53(3), Dec 1984, 242-247.*
ABST: The purpose of this investigation was to determine whether the ventilatory gas exchange threshold (Tvent) changes significantly during the first 1-3 weeks of endurance training. Six men were studied during 3 weeks of training. At the end of each week, VO2 max, Tvent, and maximal and submaximal heart rates were determined during an incremental exercise test on the cycle ergometer. The dissociation between the significant improvement in VO2 max and the lack of a significant increase in Tvent during the first 3 weeks of training indicates that the exercise-induced changes in these two parameters are regulated by different mechanisms.
LEVEL: A LANG: Eng SIRC ARTICLE NO: 104308

Ghosh, A.K. Ahuja, A. Khanna, G.L. Bhatnagar, S. Lung volumes and physique: intercorrelation in sportsmen. (Refs: 15)*Snipes journal (Patiala, India) 7(3), Jul 1984, 45-49.*
ABST: Intercorrelations between vital capacity (VC), maximum voluntary ventilation (MVV), forced expiratory volume at 1.0 sec (FEV 1.0) were determined in 58 males, aged between 23 and 34 years, playing soccer, basketball, volleyball and field hockey. A multiple correlation was observed among the variables studied. Separate correlations between VC and body height as well as between VC and body surface area showed that VC was more dependent on height.
LEVEL: A LANG: Eng SIRC ARTICLE NO: 099235

Gluskowski, J. Hawrylkiewicz, I. Zych, D. Wojtczak, A. Zielinski, J. Pulmonary haemodynamics at rest and during exercise in patients with sarcoidosis. *Respiration (Basel) 46(1), 1984, 26-32.*
LEVEL: A LANG: Eng

Grassino, A. Macklem, P.A. Respiratory muscle fatigue and ventilatory failure. *Annual review of medicine 35, 1984, 625-647.*
ABST: A review of the major mechanisms of respiratory muscle fatigue is provided in this paper.
LEVEL: A LANG: Eng SIRC ARTICLE NO: 100896

Hagan, R.D. Smith, M.G. Pulmonary ventilation in relation to oxygen uptake and carbon dioxide production during incremental load work. (Refs: 25)*International journal of sports medicine (Stuttgart) 5(4), Aug 1984, 193-197.*
ABST: The purpose of the present investigation was: (1) to describe the relationships between exercise pulmonary ventilation (VE) and oxygen uptake (V02) and VE and carbon dioxide production (VCO2), (2) to determine the per cent VO2 max at the lower ventilatory equivalent of oxygen (VEO2), and (3) to examine the relationship between the per cent VO2 max at the lowest VEO2 and maximal aerobic power (VO2 max). During incremental load work, VE increased exponentially in relation to elevations in VO2 and VCO2.
LEVEL: A LANG: Eng SIRC ARTICLE NO: 104316

Harber, P. Tamimie, J. Emory, J. Bhattacharya, A. Barber, M. Effects of exercise using industrial respirators. *American Industrial Hygiene Association journal (Detroit) 45(9)*, Sept 1984, 603-609.
LEVEL: A LANG: Eng

Hoffmann, U. Dynamische Analyse der Ventilations-Kinetik bei kombinierten Leistungs- und PCO2-Aenderungen. Koeln: Deutsche Sporthochschule, Physiologisches Institut, 1984. 107 p.
NOTES: Bibliography: p. 90-102. Thesis (Ph.D.) - Deutsche Sporthochschule Koeln, 1984.
LEVEL: A LANG: Ger RC1235 19008

Jammes, Y. Askanazi, J. Weissman, C. Milic-Emili, J. Ventilatory effects of biceps vibration during leg exercise in healthy humans. *Clinical physiology (Oxford) 4(5)*, Oct 1984, 379-391.
LEVEL: A LANG: Eng

Kelley, M.A. Laufe, M.D. Millman, R.P. Peterson, D.D. Ventilatory response to hypercapnia before and after athletic training *Respiration physiology (Amsterdam) 55(3)*, Mar 1984, 393-400.
ABST: 13 untrained young men were prospectively studied to assess the effect of athletic training on the slope (S) of the hypercapnic ventilatory response at rest. Six of the subjects trained for seven months as intercollegiate rowers while the remaining subjects underwent no training and served as controls. After training, the rowers had a significant increase in S during hypercapnia. No change was seen in the untrained controls. These data suggest that athletic training in normal subjects increases CO2 sensitivity at rest.
LEVEL: A LANG: Eng

Kennard, C.D. Martin, B.J. Respiratory frequency and the oxygen cost of exercise. (Refs: 18)*European journal of applied physiology and occupational physiology (Heidelberg) 52(3)*, Apr 1984, 320-323.
ABST: This study investigated the effect of several breathing frequencies on VO2 during treadmill walking at a speed associated with 2/3 of the individual's VO2 max. Oxygen consumption was constant regardless of breathing frequency in each of the eight subjects participating in the study. The authors conclude that spontaneous exercise breathing frequency fails to minimize VO2 during either exercise or resting reproduction of exercise ventilation.
LEVEL: A LANG: Eng SIRC ARTICLE NO: 097737

Kuo, C.H. A study on the relationship between sprinter start-dash and the regulation of respiration. (Refs: 5)*Asian journal of physical education (Taiwan, China) 7(2)*, Jul 1984, 76-80.
ABST: The respiration of 71 men, aged between 18 and 22 years old, is recorded at the starting stage of a 50 meters run. The subjects are divided in three groups: 1) 10 sprinters; 2) 4 non-athletes, and 3) 57 sportsmen with no experience in start-dash. Findings show that sprinters have smooth respiration, non-athletes have unregulated respiration, and ordinary sportsmen have ill-prepared regulation respiration for start-dash moment.
LEVEL: A LANG: Eng Chi SIRC ARTICLE NO: 100063

Lind, F. Hesser, C.M. Breathing pattern and lung volumes during exercise. *Acta physiologica scandinavica (Stockholm) 120(1)* Jan 1984, 123-129.
ABST: This paper investigated the interrelationships

between ventilation, tidal volume, inspiratory, expiratory and total breath durations, mean inspiratory and expiratory flows, and lung volumes at rest and during exercise on a cycle ergometer.
LEVEL: A LANG: Eng SIRC ARTICLE NO: 100910

Lind, F.G. Respiratory drive and breathing pattern during exercise in man. *Acta physiologica scandinavica. Supplement (Stockholm) 533, 1984, 1-47.*
LEVEL: A LANG: Eng

Magnin, P. Simon-Rigaud, M.L. Cornu, J.Y. Rouillon, J.D. De la physiopathologie respiratoire au suivi de l'elite sportive. *Pratique medicale (Paris) 24, 1984, 45-52.*
LEVEL: I LANG: Fr

Martin, B.J. Chen, H.I. Kolka, M.A. Anaerobic metabolism of the respiratory muscles during exercise. (Refs: 26)*Medicine and science in sports and exercise 16(1), 1984, 82-86.*
ABST: Strenuous exercise affects the respiratory muscles as well as the large muscle groups involved in the exercise. Elevated blood lactate levels are seen when peak exercise ventilation is maintained for a short period of time. The fatigue of the ventilatory muscles can influence exercise tolerance as is indicated by this study.
LEVEL: A LANG: Eng SIRC ARTICLE NO: 091749

Mertzlufft, F. Thews, G. Determination of pulmonary parameters (VA, DLO2) from arterial O2 and CO2 partial pressures during exercise. *Advances in experimental medicine and biology (New York) 180, 1984, 393-402.*
LEVEL: A LANG: Eng

Muir, A.L. Cruz, M. Martin, B.A. thommasen, H. Belzberg, A. Hogg, J.C. Leukocyte kinetics in the human lung: role of exercis and catecholamines. (Refs: 16)*Journal of applied physiology: respiratory, environmental and exercise physiology (Bethesda, Md.) 57 (3), Sept 1984, 711-719.*
LEVEL: A LANG: Eng SIRC ARTICLE NO: 108933

Nag, P.K. Circulo-respiratory responses to different muscular exercises. (Refs: 34)*European journal of applied physiology and occupational physiology (Berlin, FRG) 52(4), Jun 1984, 393-399.*
ABST: This study investigated the relationship between bodily reactions and six different muscular exercises performed on a modified ergometer. The six exercises were: pedalling while seated (PS), arm cranking while seated (CS), arm and leg cranking (ALC), pedalling while reclining (PR) and pedalling with back support (PBS). Measurements were taken on five subjects. CST, CS, PR, PS and PBS yielded 76, 72, 72, 87 and 97 per cent of VO2 max (ALC) respectively. Blood pressure was less in arm work than in leg work. The results indicate that CS, PR and PBS have more of an isometric component than CST, PS and ALC.
LEVEL: A LANG: Eng SIRC ARTICLE NO: 097749

Pardy, R.L. Hussain, S.N. Macklem, P.T. The ventilatory pump in exercise. *Clinics in chest medicine (Philadelphia) 5(1), Ma 1984, 35-49.*
ABST: The authors review the response of the ventilatory pump during exercise in healthy and obstructive lung disease patients.
LEVEL: A LANG: Eng SIRC ARTICLE NO: 102810

Rochester, D.F. Respiratory muscle function in health. *Heart and lung (St. Louis) 13(4), Jul 1984, 349-354.*
LEVEL: I LANG Eng SIRC ARTICLE NO: 102821

Roger, J.M. La respiration (suite). *Loisirs sante (Paris) 9, avr/mai 1984, 24-25.*
LEVEL: B LANG: Fr SIRC ARTICLE NO: 1009

Scharf, S.M. Bark, H. Heimer, D. Cohen, A. Macklem, P.T. Second wind during inspiratory loading. (Refs: 8)*Medicine and science in sports and exercise 16(1), 1984, 87-91.*
ABST: Second wind as a physiological phenomenon was investigated in 5 subjects exercising until fatigue while breathing through an inspiratory resister. Fatigue of the diaphragm was relieved by a second wind in all subjects. The commencement of the second wind suddenly decreased neural stimulation to the diaphragm muscle. The authors feel a change in the contractile state of this muscle is involved in the second wind phenomenon.
LEVEL: A LANG: Eng SIRC ARTICLE NO: 091774

Schonfeld, S.A. Dixon, G.F. The respiratory system. (Refs: 37)
NOTES: In, Strauss, R.H. (ed.), Sports medicine, Philadelphia ; Toronto, Saunders, 1984, p. 105-119.
LEVEL: A LANG: Eng RC1210 17196

Terreros, J.L. Duvallet, A. La courbe debit-volume comme exploration fonctionnelle respiratoire. Interet en medecine et biologie du sport. (Refs: 6)*Medecine du sport (Paris) 58(2), 25 mars 1984, 17-21.*
LEVEL: I LANG: Fr SIRC ARTICLE NO: 094628

Thews, G. Theoretical analysis of the pulmonary gas exchange at rest and during exercise. (Refs: 51)*International journal o sports medicine (Stuttgart) 5(3), Jun 1984, 113-119.*
LEVEL: A LANG: Eng SIRC ARTICLE NO: 104381

Thews, G. Thews, O. Nomograms for the pulmonary gas exchange at rest and during exercise. (Refs: 12)*International journal o sports medicine (Stuttgart) 5(3), Jun 1984, 120-124.*
LEVEL: A LANG: Eng SIRC ARTICLE NO: 104382

van Putten, M. Verstappen, F. Bloemen, L. Physical exercise and industrial respirators. (Refs: 3)*International journal of sports medicine (Stuttgart) Suppl. 5, Nov 1984, 13-14.*
CONF: International Congress on Sports and Health (1983 : Maastricht, Netherlands).
LEVEL: A LANG: Eng SIRC ARTICLE NO: 104386

Vanmeenen, M.T. Ghesquiere, J. Demedts, M. Effects of thoracic or abdominal strapping on exercise performance. *Bulletin europeen de physiopathologie respiratoire (Oxford) 20(2), Mar/Apr 1984, 127-132.*
ABST: 11 young men were tested on hemodynamics and respiratory parameters with abdominal orthoracic strapping. Tidal volume and stroke volume decreased while respiratory frequency and heart rate increased with both types of strapping. Thoracic strapping was significantly more impeding than abdominal strapping.
LEVEL: A LANG: Eng SIRC ARTICLE NO: 102837

Warren, J. Jennings, S. Normal human airway response to exercise. (letter) (Refs: 8)*Journal of applied physiology: respiratory, environmental and exercise physiology (Bethesda, Md.) 56(6), Jun 1984, 1686.*
ABST: This letter discusses the question of whether or not airway resistance changes during exercise in normal subjects. Recent studies indicate that airway resistance does not change during exercise. However, these studies observed ventilation during

spontaneous respiration. The authors contend that any decrease in resistance caused by exercise will be obscured by the artifactual rise in resistance arising from the increase in flow that occurs during exercise. The authors cite their research which shows decreased airway resistance with exercise when breathing frequency is standarized.
LEVEL: I LANG: Eng SIRC ARTICLE NO: 097775

Warren, J.B. Jennings, S.J. Clark, T.J. Effect of adrenergic and vagal blockade on the normal human airway response to exercise. *Clinical science (London) 66(1), Jan 1984, 79-85.*
ABST: Ten normal subjects performed a progressive exercise bicycle test on 3 separate days using either no medication, propranolol, or ipratropium bromide. With no medication, transpulmonary index (TPI), a measure of airway resistance, fell linearly during exercise and returned to baseline values 2 to 4 minutes after exercise. Propranolol elevated TPI before exercise and it fell linearly during exercise before returning to the elevated levels after exercise. Ipratropium bromide decreased TPI prior to exercise and these values showed little change during and after exercise. These results indicate that normal subjects show considerable airway dilatation during exercise which appears to result from inhibition of resting vagal tone.
LEVEL: A LANG: Eng SIRC ARTICLE NO: 097776

Younes, M. Kivinen, G. Respiratory mechanics and breathing pattern during and following maximal exercise. (Refs: 29)*Journal of applied physiology: respiratory, environemental and exercise physiology (Bethesda, Md.) 57(6), Dec 1984, 1773-1782.*
ABST: The authors researched wheter there were any changes in lung elastic recoil and inspiratory muscle fatigue at maximal exercise in 7 men aged from 25 to 42 yr. Findings indicated no changes of static elastic recoil and no evidence that mechanical fatigue develops at maximal exercise.
LEVEL: A LANG: Eng SIRC ARTICLE NO: 108566

VENTILATORY CONTROL

Bennett, F.M. A role for neural pathways in exercise hyperpnea. (Refs: 30)*Journal of applied physiology: respiratory, environmental and exercise physiology (Bethesda, Md.) 56(6), Jun 1984, 1559-1564.*
ABST: This study reexamined the role of humoral pathways in mediating the ventilatory response to electrically induced exercise. The method of this study involved the stimulation of the peripheral ends of severed sciatic nerves in seven anesthetized dogs. After stimulation there were increases in expired minute ventilation, arterial CO2 partial pressure and carotid artery temperature. The results indicate that humoral factors cannot maintain an isocapnic hyperpnea. Thus, neural pathways may play a fundamental role in the ventilatory response to exercise in intact animals.
LEVEL: A LANG: Eng SIRC ARTICLE NO: 097713

Hesser, C.M. Lind, F. Role of airway resistance in the control of ventilation during exercise. *Acta physiologica scandinavica (Stockholm) 120(4), Apr 1984, 557-565.*
LEVEL: A LANG: Eng

WORK OF BREATHING

Chonan, T. Kikuchi, Y. Hida, W. Shindoh, C. Inoue, H. Sasaki, H. Takishima, T. Response to hypercapnia and exercise hyperpne in graded anesthesia. (Refs: 31)*Journal of applied physiology: respiratory, environmental and exercise physiology (Bethesda, Md.) 57(6), Dec 1984, 1796-1802.*
LEVEL: A SIRC ARTICLE NO: 108567

Dempsey, J.A. Mitchell, G.S. Smith, C.A. Exercise and chemoreception. (Refs: 27)*American review of respiratory disease (New York) 129(2 Pt 2), Feb 1984, S31-S34.*
CONF: Exercise Testing in the Dyspneic Patient Workshop (1982 : Bethesda).
LEVEL: I LANG: Eng SIRC ARTICLE NO: 099229

Menitone, S.M. Rapoport, D.M. Epstein, H. Sorkin, B. Goldring, R.M. CO2 rebreathing and exercise ventilatory responses in humans. (Refs: 18)*Journal of applied physiology: respiratory, environmental and exercise physiology 56(4), Apr 1984, 1039-1044.*
ABST: This study assessed the correlation between the resting CO2 rebreathing response and exercise rebreathing response in 20 normal subjects and in 6 patients with obesity hypoventilation syndrome. The results indicate that there is no correlation between these two parameters in either group. The exercise ventilatory response and the CO2 rebreathing response were independent of each other which suggests that the CO2 rebreathing response does not measure the relevant parameters of ventilatory control during exercise.
LEVEL: A LANG: Eng SIRC ARTICLE NO: 096284

Muza, S.R. Zechman, F.W. Scaling of added loads to breathing: magnitude estimation vs. handgrip matching. (Refs: 17)*Journal of applied physiology: respiratory, environmental and exercise physiology (Bethesda, Md.) 57(3), Sept 1984, 888-891.*
LEVEL: A LANG: Eng SIRC ARTICLE NO: 108939

PHYSIOLOGY - THERMOREGULATION

Baker, M.A. Thermoregulatory responses to exercise in dehydrated dogs. (Refs: 32)*Journal of applied physiology: respiratory environmental and exercise physiology (Bethesda, Md.) 56(3), Mar 1984, 635-640.*
ABST: The purpose of this study was to determine how dehydration affects thermoregulatory and circulatory adjustments to mild exercise in dogs. Seven dogs were studied on two occasions as they ran on a treadmill in a hydrated state, and then in a dehydrated state. Measurements of rectal temperature (Tre), water lost by evaporation (Eresp) and drooling, cardic output (Co), and common cartied blood flow (CCBF) were monitored during each run. Results indicated that during the exercise periods in a dehydrated state, significantly higher Tre and lower rates of Eresp, Co, and CCBF were attained. These observations suggest that dehydration leads to a reduction in thermal sensitivity of central neural structure which controls heat dissipation responses.
LEVEL: A LANG: Eng SIRC ARTICLE NO: 096216

Ballosso, H.M. James, W.P. Whole-body calorimetry studies in adult men. 2. The interaction of exercise and over-feeding on the thermic effect of a meal. *British journal of nutrition (London) 52(1),* Jul 1984, 65-72.
ABST: Eight normal-weight young men were studied during 1 week on a weight-maintenance diet and again during 1 week when they were over-fed by 50 per cent with fat. During each experimental week, the subject occupied a whole-body indirect calorimeter at 26 degrees for two separate periods of 36 h. The thermic responses to the identical meals were measured during rest on one occasion and during exercise on a bicycle ergometer on the other. On the maintenance diet the absolute TEM (kJ/min) was 1.51 at rest and 1.31 during exercise. The equivalent values (kJ/min) on the over-feeding diet were 2.2 and 1.97.
LEVEL: A LANG: Eng SIRC ARTICLE NO: 104278

Cadarette, B.S. Sawka, M.N. Toner, M.M. Pandolf, K.B. Aerobic fitness and the hypohydration response to exercise-heat stress *Aviation space and environmental medicine (Washington) 55(6), Jun 1984, 507-512.*
ABST: This study examined the influence that aerobic fitness had on final heart rate, final rectal temperature, and total body sweat rate when subjects exercised while euhydrated and hypohydrated. The results indicate that, when euhydrated in the heat, aerobic fitness provides cardiovascular and thermoregulatory benefits before acclimatization, but only cardiovascular benefits after acclimatization. However, when hypohydrated in the heat, cardiovascular benefits are present for fit subjects both before and after acclimatization, but thermoregulatory benefits are not associated with fitness.
LEVEL: A LANG: Eng SIRC ARTICLE NO: 104287

Feistkorn, G. Nagel, A. Jessen, C. Circulation and acid-base balance in exercising goats at different body temperatures. (Refs: 29)*Journal of applied physiology: respiratory, environmental and exercise physiology (Bethesda, Md.) 57(6), Dec 1984, 1655-1661.*
LEVEL: A LANG: Eng SIRC ARTICLE NO: 108559

Fujita, T. A study on temperature changes of body surface when using the ultra-red ray-menter during the light exercise. *Asian journal of physical education (Taipei, Taiwan) 7(3), Oct 1984, 23-25.*
LEVEL: I LANG: Eng Chi SIRC ARTICLE NO: 102778

Garby, L. Lammert, O. Nielsen, E. Within-subjects between-weeks variation in 24-hour energy expenditure for fixed physical activity. *Human nutrition. Clinical nutrition (London) 38(5), Sept 1984, 391-394.*
LEVEL: A LANG: Eng

Gisolfi, C.V. Wenger, C.B. Temperature regulation during exercise: old concepts, new ideas. (Refs: 124)*Exercise and sport reviews (Lexington, Mass.) 12, 339-372.*
ABST: This paper describes how the rise in core temperature associated with exercise relates to heat production, heat transfer within the body, and heat exchange with the environment. The paper also proposes a vigorous definition of the concept of set point in thermoregulation and reviews the importance of thermal and nonthermal factors in the control of thermoregulatory effector responses. The set point function of the sodium/calcium ratio in the brain is also evaluated.
LEVEL: A LANG: Eng SIRC ARTICLE NO: 096242

Greenleaf, J.E. Physiology of fluid and electrolyte responses during inactivity: water immersion and bed rest. (Refs: 68) *Medicine and science in sports*

and exercise 16(1), 1984, 20-25.
ABST: Changes in fluid volumes and electrolyte balances have been found to occur with water immersion and bed rest. Humoral mechanisms appear to influence these conditions but further research is needed in this area. Most physiological systems show adaptation to immersion and bed rest with emphasis on the vestibular, immune, thermoregulatory and fluid-electrolyte systems. It is hoped such research will provide further information on how the human body adapts to exercise.
LEVEL: A LANG: Eng SIRC ARTICLE NO: 091730

Jones, R.L. Fever. Running & fitness (Washington, D.C.) 16(3), May/Jun 1984, 18.
LEVEL: B LANG: Eng SIRC ARTICLE NO: 1009

LeBlanc, J. Mercier, P. Samson, P. Diet-induced thermogenesis with relation to training state in female subjects. (Refs: 24) Canadian journal of physiology and pharmacology (Ottawa) 62(3), Mar 1984, 334-337.
ABST: This paper investigates the effects of training level on meal-induced thermogenesis in 30 female subjects (10 competition athletes, 10 moderately active subjects, and 10 sedentary subjects). Oxygen uptake (VO2), respiratory quotient (R), and heart rate (HR) are assessed 45 min before and 120 min after a 800 kCal meal. A diminished meal-induced thermogenesis in well-trained subjects is observed.
LEVEL: A LANG: Eng SIRC ARTICLE NO: 102796

McArdle, W.D. Magel, J.R. Spina, R.J. Gergley, T.J. Toner, M.M. Thermal adjustment to cold-water exposure in exercising men and women. (Refs: 23) Journal of applied physiology: respiratory, environmental and exercise physiology (Bethesda, Md.) 56(6), Jun 1984, 1572-1577.
ABST: Ten men and eight women were classified in terms of body fat. The subjects performed cycle ergometry at 36W for one hour periods in air and water at 20, 24 and 28oC. The exercise prevented or retarded the fall in rectal temperature observed in subjects resting in the water. Lean subjects exhibited the greatest thermal strain. Both sexes had a similar thermoregulatory response to exercise in the water.
LEVEL: A LANG: Eng SIRC ARTICLE NO: 097743

McDonald, A. Goode, R.C. Livingstone, S.D. Duffin, J. Body cooling in human males by cold-water immersion after vigorous exercise. Undersea biomedical research (Bethesda, Md.) 11(1), Mar 1984, 81-90.
ABST: 5 male subjects were immersed to neck level in cold water (19 degrees C) after two different bouts of exercise. The results indicate that vigorous pre-immersion exercise may shorten cold water survival time due to an increase in the cooling rate.
LEVEL: A LANG: Eng

Nadel, E.R. Temperature regulation and hyperthermia during exercise. Clinics in chest medicine (Philadelphia) 5(1), Mar 1984, 13-20.
LEVEL: I LANG: Eng SIRC ARTICLE NO: 102807

Nielsen, B. Dehydration, redehydration and thermoregulation. (Refs: 47)
CONF: International Course on Physiology and Biochemistry of Exercise and Detraining (2nd : 1982 : Nice).
NOTES: In, Marconnet, P. (ed.) et al., Physiological chemistry of training and detraining, New York, Karger, c1984, p. 81-96.
LEVEL: A LANG: Eng RC1235 17596

Sawka, M.N. Pimental, N.A. Pandolf, K.B. Thermoregulatory responses to upper body exercise. (Refs: 19) European journal of applied physiology and occupational physiology (Heidelberg) 52(2), Jan 1984, 230-234.
ABST: This study was designed to compare and describe the thermoregulatory responses for subjects performing upper and lower body exercise at the same absolute and relative exercise intensities. Esophogeal temperature, rectal temperature, mean skin temperature and sweat loss were monitored during the tests. The results indicated that thermoregulatory responses are independent of the skeletal muscle mass employed and dependent upon the absolute metabolic intensity of the exercise. Some of the practical implications are also discussed.
LEVEL: A LANG: Eng SIRC ARTICLE NO: 096291

Sawka, M.N. Gonzalez, R.R. Drolet, L.L. Pandolf, K.B. Heat exchange during upper- and lower-body exercise. (Refs: 26) Journa of applied physiology: respiratory, environmental and exercise physiology (Bethesda, Md.) 57(4), Oct 1984, 1050-1054.
LEVEL: A LANG: Eng SIRC ARTICLE NO: 108944

Shellock, F.G. Rubin, S.A. Temperature regulation during treadmill exercise in the rat. (Refs: 41) Journal of applied physiology: respiratory, environmental and exercise physiology (Bethesda, Md.) 57(6), Dec 1984, 1872-1877.
LEVEL: A LANG: Eng SIRC ARTICLE NO: 108570

FLUID-ELECTROLYTE BALANCE

Costill, D.L. Water and electrolyte requirements during exercise. Clinics in sports medicine (Philadelphia) 3(3), Jul 1984, 639-648.
NOTES: Symposium on nutritional aspects of exercise.
ABST: In general, it appears that the extensive losses of sweat incurred during training and competition are adequately tolerated by athletes, with concomitant adjustments in the water and electrolyte distribution of their fluid compartments. Despite the sizable excretion of ions and sweat, the athletes' large caloric intake and renal conservation of sodium minimize the threat of chronic dehydration or electrolyte deficits, or both.
LEVEL: I LANG: Eng SIRC ARTICLE NO: 100775

Loesel, H. Important medical aspects on sport referring to the Olympic Games in Summer 1984. (Part 2, continued) Sportmedizinisch relevante Aspekte bezueglich der Olympischen Spiele im Sommer 1984. (2. Teil Fortsetzung) Aspects importants du point de vue de la medecine et du sport pour les Jeux olympiques d'ete 1984. (suite de la 2ieme partie) Aspectos importantes de la medicina y del deporte para los Juegos Olimpicos de verano de 1984. (2a parte/continuacion) UIT shooting sport journal (Muenchen, FRG) 24(1), Jan/Feb 1984, 12-14.
LEVEL: B LANG: Eng Ger Fr Spa SIRC ARTICLE NO: 098449

Pivarniki, J.M. Leeds, E.M. Wilkerson, J.E. Effect of endurance exercise on metabolic water production and plasma volume. (Refs: 34) Journal of applied physiology: respiratory, environmental and exercise physiology (Bethesda, Md.) 56(3), Mar 1984, 613-618.
ABST: The purpose of this study was to determine the effects of three different submaximal exercise intensities on the metabolic water production and plasma volume of trained and heat-acclimatized individuals. Six male subjects ran on a treadmill for one hour or until exhaustion on three different occasions. Changes in the measurements of body weight, blood hemoglobin, hematocrit and estimates of blood volume, plasma volume, plasma protein concentration and metabolic water production were made. Measurements of the body, rectal and mean skin temperature were monitored during each session. The results indicate that metabolic water production increased with increasing work intensity, while plasma volume was maintained. The authors suggest that metabolic water production only plays a minor role in plasma volume maintenance and thermoregulatory control during endurance exercise.
LEVEL: A LANG: Eng SIRC ARTICLE NO: 096455

Sejersted, O.M. Medbo, J.I. Orheim, A. Hermansen, L. Relationship between acid-base status and electrolyte balance after maximal work of short duration. (Refs: 30)
CONF: International Course on Physiology and Biochemistry of Exercise and Detraining (2nd : 1982 : Nice).
NOTES: In, Marconnet, P. (ed.) et al., Physiological chemistry of training and detraining, New York, Karger, c1984, p. 40-55.
LEVEL: A LANG: Eng RC1235 17596

SWEATING

Boysen, J.C. Yanagawa, S. Sato, F. Sato, K. A modified anaerobic method of sweat collection. (Refs: 22) Journal of applied physiology: respiratory, environmental and exercise physiology (Bethesda, Md.) 56(5), May 1984, 1302-1307.
ABST: This paper reports a simple method of modified anaerobic sweat collection. This method was performed on six healthy men. The study also reports on the components of sweat collected by this method. Finally, the authors estimate the extent of epidermal contamination of sweat samples collected with conventional methods.
LEVEL: A LANG: Eng SIRC ARTICLE NO: 097715

Johnson, J.M. O'Leary, D.S. Taylor, W.F. Park, M.K. Reflex regulation of sweat rate of skin temperature in exercising humans (Refs: 26) Journal of applied physiology: respiratory, environmental and exercise physiology (Bethesda, Md.) 56(5), May 1984, 1283-1288.
ABST: This study sought to determine if sweat rate (SR) and forearm skin blood flow (SkBF) were reflexly affected by skin temperature (Tsk). Four men exercised on a bicycle ergometer at loads ranging between 50-125 W for approximately 50 minutes. After 10-15 minutes of exercise the Tsk of the subject was raised to 37oC using a water perfused suit. The increase in Tsk was associated with increases in Sr and SkBF. A role for Tsk in the regulation of Sr and SkBF was also apparent at low Tsk.
LEVEL: A LANG: Eng SIRC ARTICLE NO: 097733

POLE VAULT

BIOGRAPHY AND AUTOBIOGRAPHY

Olson, B. Stowers, C. Reaching higher. Waco, Tex.: Word Books, c1984. 1v.
LEVEL: B LANG: Eng ISBN: 0849903874 LC CARD: 84-007560

POLE VAULT (continued)

Varzhapetian, V. Nearing the 6-metre goal: twenty-year-old pole vaulter Sergei Bubka from the Ukrainian town of Donetsk held the limelight in American sports news... *Sport in the USSR (Moscow, USSR)* Jun 1984, 13-15.
LEVEL: B LANG: Eng SIRC ARTICLE NO: 104953

BIOMECHANICS

Jerome, J. Pole vaulting: biomechanics at the bar. In, Schrier, E.W. and Allman, W.F. (eds.), *Newton at the bat: the scienc in sports,* New York, Scribner, c1984, p. 150-153.
LEVEL: I LANG: Eng RC1235 18609

CHILDREN

Lease, D. Pole vault introductory lesson. *Athletics coach (London) 18(2),* Jun 1984, 3-5.
LEVEL: B LANG: Eng SIRC ARTICLE NO: 095386

EQUIPMENT

Defrance, J. L'adoption de la perche en fibre de verre. (Refs: 18)*Dans, Culture technique no. 13,* Neuilly-sur-Seine, France Centre de Recherche sur la Culture Technique, c1984, p. 256-263.
LEVEL: I LANG: Fr RC1235 20096

National racquetball's annual ball guide: your one stop comparison guide. *National Racquetball (Glenview, Ill.) 13(12),* Dec 1984, 14.
LEVEL: B LANG: Eng SIRC ARTICLE NO: 106007

Reader survey: what you told us about your racquetballs. *National racquetball (Glenview, Ill.) 13(12),* Dec 1984, 16-17.
LEVEL: B LANG: Eng SIRC ARTICLE NO: 106012

INJURIES AND ACCIDENTS

Attig, R. Vaulting higher and safer. Coach and athlete must understand proper technique, conditioning and supervision if the goal of vaulting higher and safer is to be achieved. *Athletic journal 64(8),* Mar 1984, 50-53;66-68.
LEVEL: B LANG: Eng SIRC ARTICLE NO: 093854

TECHNIQUES AND SKILLS

Cox, D. Mechanics of the pole vault. *Track and field quarterly review (Kalamazoo, Mich.) 84(4),* Winter 1984, 29-32.
LEVEL I LANG: Eng SIRC ARTICLE NO: 101630

Kostic, V. Your guide to better pole vaulting. (Refs: 14)*Track & field journal (Ottawa) 28,* Nov 1984, 4-8.
LEVEL: B LANG: Eng SIRC ARTICLE NO: 103544

TRAINING AND CONDITIONING

Mahr, J. Training the pole vaulter. Selection of vaulters-to-be is a systematic process involving physical, often psychological criteria. *Athletic journal (Evanston, Ill.) 65(5),* Dec 1984, 18-21;35.
LEVEL: B LANG: Eng SIRC ARTICLE NO: 104949

TRAINING AND CONDITIONING - DRILLS

Stahly, K. Perfect the swing drill. *Athletic journal 64(9),* Apr 1984, 54-55;67.
LEVEL: B LANG: Eng SIRC ARTICLE NO: 09386

TRAINING AND CONDITIONING - STRETCHING AND FLEXIBILITY EXERCISES

Sutcliffe, P. A mobility programme for pole vaulters. *Athletics coach (Halesowen, England) 18(1),* Mar 1984, 20.
LEVEL: B LANG: Eng SIRC ARTICLE NO: 093862

TRAINING AND CONDITIONING - WEIGHT AND STRENGTH TRAINING

Houvion, M. Perfectionnement du perchiste. *EPS: Education physique et sport (Paris) 187, mai/juin 1984,* 49-64.
LEVEL: B LANG: Fr SIRC ARTICLE NO: 096941

Houvion, M. Perfectionnement du perchiste musculation.
NOTES: Dans, Renforcement musculaire, Paris, Institut national du sport et de l'education physique, c1984, p. 157-168.
LEVEL: I LANG: Fr GV711.5 18233

Kostic, V. Your guide to better pole vaulting. (Refs: 14)*Track & field journal (Ottawa) 28,* Nov 1984, 4-8.
LEVEL: B LANG: Eng SIRC ARTICLE NO: 103544

POLITICS AND GOVERNMENT

Hoberman, J.M. Sport and political ideology. 1st ed. Austin: University of Texas Press, c1984. ix, 315 p.
NOTES: Includes index. Bibliography: p. 285-303.
LEVEL: A LANG: Eng ISBN: 0292775881 LC CARD: 83-027415 GV706.8 17720

Iqbal, A. Sport, race and all that. *Cricketer Pakistan (Karachi) 13(4),* Aug 1984, 24-25.
LEVEL: B LANG: Eng SIRC ARTICLE NO: 101009

Read, K. Conseil consultatif des athletes. Athletes' advisory council: boycott lesson unlearned. *Champion (Ottawa) 8(3),* Au 1984, 84;91.
LEVEL: B LANG: Fr Eng SIRC ARTICLE NO: 096429

ACTIVISM

Laitinen, A. Marathon Peace March: a demonstration of international understanding. (Refs: 14)*In, Ilmarinen, M. (ed.) et al. Sport and International Understanding: proceedings of the congress held in Helsinki, Finland, July 7-10, 1982,* Berlin, Springer-Verlag, 1984, p. 248-254.
CONF: Congress on Sport and International Understanding (1982 : Helsinki).
LEVEL: I LANG: Eng GV706.8 18979

APARTHEID

Brown, J. Attitude of the Australian government to sporting contact with South Africa. *ACHPER national journal 103,* Mar 1984, 11.
LEVEL: B LANG: Eng SIRC ARTICLE NO: 097853

Wheatley, J. Briefing. *Sport & leisure (London, Eng.)* Sept/Oct 1984, 10-11.
LEVEL: B LANG: Eng SIRC ARTICLE NO: 108894

CAPITALISM

Keil, T. Sport in advanced capitalism. (Refs: 40)*Arena review (Boston) 8(3),* Nov 1984, 15-29.
LEVEL: I LANG: Eng SIRC ARTICLE NO: 104488

GOVERNMENT - POLICY

Australian Sports Commission information and background: a report to national sporting and recreation organisations. s.l.: ACHP, 1984. 22 leaves (loose-leaf)
NOTES: Cover title.
ABST: The Australian Sports Commission was established to increase coordination and effectiveness of sports development policies and programs in Australia. 21 members have been appointed, many transferring from the Federal Dept. of Sport, Recreation and Tourism. The objectives of the Commission are to sustain and improve on Australia's level of achievement in international sporting competition and to increase the level of participation in sport by all Australians. Legislation has been drafted to establish the commission as a statutory authority.
LEVEL: B LANG: Eng GV675 18660

Brown, J. Review of sporting contact with South Africa. *Minister for Sport, Recreation and Tourism letter (Canberra) 1984,* 1-3.
LEVEL: B LANG: Eng SIRC ARTICLE NO: 092653

Godbout, L. Un defi de taille. *Revue de l'entraineur (Montreal)* avr/juin 1984, 30.
LEVEL: B LANG: Fr SIRC ARTICLE NO: 094752

Laird, D. There is no such thing as sport free from politics. (Refs: 4)*Scottish journal of physical education (Glasgow, Scotland) 12(3),* Aug 1984, 4-10.
LEVEL: B LANG: Eng SIRC ARTICLE NO: 099342

Marcotte, G. La politique quebecoise du sport d'elite: champions des mots? (Refs: 8)*Revue de l'entraineur (Montreal)* avr/juin 1984, 8.
LEVEL: B LANG: Fr SIRC ARTICLE NO: 094761

Progressive Conservative Fitness and Amateur Sport Policy for Canada. Politique nationale du Parti progressiste-conservateur concernant la condition physique et le sport amateur. *Aim (Ottawa) 11,* Autumn/automne 1984, 40-42.
LEVEL: B LANG: Eng Fr SIRC ARTICLE NO: 106910

Sport Canada applied sport research program: policy and guidelines 1984-1985. Sport Canada programme de recherche appliquee dans le sport: politique et lignes directrices 1984-1985. Ottawa: Supply and Services Canada, c1984. 12, 12 p. (Cat. no. H93-85/1984.)
CORP: Canada. Fitness and Amateur Sport.
CORP: Canada. Condition physique et sport amateur.
NOTES: French and English texts on inverted pages with separate paging. Textes francais et anglais disposes tete-beche avec pagination separee. Includes Application form for the Sport Canada applied Sport Research Program 1984-85. Comprend le Formulaire de demande de contribution du Programme de recherche appliquee dans le sport de Sport Canada 1984-1985.
LEVEL: B LANG: Eng Fr ISBN: 0-662-52887-5 GV585 17021

Sport Canada contributions program 1985-1986. Sport Canada programme de contributions 1985-1986. (Ottawa): Minister of Supply and Services, c1984. 42, 46 p.
CORP: Canada. Fitness and Amateur Sport.
CORP: Canada. Condition physique et Sport amateur.
NOTES: French and English texts on inverted pages with separate paging. Textes francais et anglais disposes tete-beche avec pagination separee.
LEVEL: B LANG: Eng Fr ISBN: 0-662-53376-3 GV716 18851

INTERNATIONAL RELATIONS

Ajisafe, M.O. Co-operation between developing countries and advanced countries in respect of sport. (Refs: 4)*In, Ilmarinen, M. (ed.) et al., Sport and International Understanding: proceedings of the congress held in Helsinki, Finland, July 7-10, 1982, Berlin, Springer-Verlag, 1984, p. 298-303.*
CONF: Congress on Sport and International Understanding (1982 : Helsinki).
LEVEL: I LANG: Eng GV706.8 18979

Bedecki, T. International sport relations. (Refs: 14)*In, Ilmarinen, M. (ed.) et al., Sport and International Understanding: proceedings of the congress held in Helsinki, Finland, July 7-10, 1982, Berlin, Springer-Verlag, 1984, p. 312-315.*
CONF: Congress on Sport and International Understanding (1982 : Helsinki).
LEVEL: I LANG: Eng GV706.8 18979

Booth, B.F. Sport, political autonomy and international understanding. (Refs: 8)*In, Ilmarinen, M. (ed.) et al., Sport and International Understanding: proceedings of the congress held in Helsinki, Finland, July 7-10, 1982, Berlin, Springer-Verlag, 1984, p. 92-98.*
CONF: Congress on Sport and International Understanding (1982 : Helsinki).
LEVEL: A LANG: Eng GV706.8 18979

Erbach, G. On the character and contents of sport and international sporting activities at present and in the future. (Refs: 4)*In, Ilmarinen, M. (ed.) et al., Sport and International Understanding: proceedings of the congress held in Helsinki, Finland, July 7-10, 1982, Berlin, Springer-Verlag, 1984, p. 31-37.*
CONF: Congress on Sport and International Understanding (1982 : Helsinki).
LEVEL: A LANG: Eng GV706.8 18979

Galtung, J. Sport and international understanding: sport as a carrier of deep culture and structure. (Refs: 1)*In, Ilmarinen M. (ed.) et al., Sport and International Understanding: proceedings of the congress held in Helsinki, Finland, July 7-10, 1982, Berlin, Springer-Verlag, 1984, p. 12-19.*
CONF: Congress on Sport and International Understanding (1982 : Helsinki).
LEVEL: A LANG: Eng GV706.8 18979

Happel, D. Kramer, R. The objectives of sport and international understanding. *In, Ilmarinen, M. (ed.) et al., Sport and International Understanding: proceedings of the congress held in Helsinki, Finland, July 7-10, 1982, Berlin, Springer-Verlag, 1984, p. 108-110.*
CONF: Congress on Sport and International Understanding (1982 : Helsinki).
LEVEL: B LANG: Eng GV706.8 18979

Heinilae, K. The totalisation process in international sport. (Refs: 14)*In, Ilmarinen, M. (ed.)*

et al., Sport and International Understanding: proceedings of the congress held in Helsinki, Finland, July 7-10, 1982, Berlin, Springer-Verlag, 1984, p. 20-30.
CONF: Congress on Sport and International Understanding (1982 : Helsinki).
LEVEL: A LANG: Eng GV706.8 18979

Hietanen, A. The new international sports order: an appraisal. (Refs: 8)*In, Ilmarinen, M. (ed.) et al., Sport and International Understanding: proceedings of the congress held in Helsinki, Finland, July 7-10, 1982, Berlin, Springer-Verlag, 1984, p. 104-107.*
CONF: Congress on Sport and International Understanding (1982 : Helsinki).
LEVEL: I LANG: Eng GV706.8 18979

Hietanen, A. On the history of international sporting co-operation: some trends. (Refs: 16)*In, Ilmarinen, M. (ed.) et al., Sport and International Understanding: proceedings of the congress held in Helsinki, Finland, July 7-10, 1982, Berlin, Springer-Verlag, 1984, p. 208-212.*
CONF: Congress on Sport and International Understanding (1982 : Helsinki).
LEVEL: I LANG: Eng GV706.8 18979

Hietanen, A. Varis, T. Sport and international understanding: a survey of the structure and trends of international sporting co-operation. (Refs: 36)*In, Ilmarinen, M. (ed.) et al., Sport and International Understanding: proceedings of the congress held in Helsinki, Finland, July 7-10, 1982, Berlin, Springer-Verlag, 1984, p. 213-230.*
CONF: Congress on Sport and International Understanding (1982 : Helsinki).
LEVEL: A LANG: Eng GV706.8 18979

Ilmarinen, M. Komi, P. Koskela, A. Seppaenen, P. Telama, R. Vuolle, P. Sport and International Understanding: proceedings of the congress held in Helsinki, Finland, July 7-10, 1982. Berlin: Springer-Verlag, 1984. xxi, 372 p.
CONF: Congress on Sport and International Understanding (1982 : Helsinki).
CORP: Finnish Society for Research in Sport and Physical Education.
CORP: Finnish Central Sport Federation.
CORP: Worker's Sport Federation.
NOTES: Includes index and bibliographies.
LEVEL: A LANG: Eng ISBN: 3-540-13801-3 LC CARD: 84-023526 GV706.8 18979

Kirvesniemi, H. The importance of the international sports movement in promoting international understanding - the viewpoint of an olympic athlete. *In, Ilmarinen, M. (ed.) et al., Sport and International Understanding: proceedings of the congress held in Helsinki, Finland, July 7-10, 1982, Berlin, Springer-Verlag, 1984, p. 132-137.*
CONF: Congress on Sport and International Understanding (1982 : Helsinki).
LEVEL: I LANG: Eng GV706.8 18979

Klemola, H. The state as sponsor of international sports. *In, Ilmarinen, M. (ed.) et al., Sport and International Understanding: proceedings of the congress held in Helsinki, Finland, July 7-10, 1982, Berlin, Springer-Verlag, 1984, p. 323-326.*
CONF: Congress on Sport and International Understanding (1982 : Helsinki).
LEVEL: B LANG: Eng GV706.8 18979

Lueschen, G. Sport, international conflict and conflict resolution. (Refs: 39)*In, Ilmarinen, M. (ed.) et al., Sport and International Understanding: proceedings of the congress held in Helsinki, Finland, July 7-10, 1982, Berlin, Springer-Verlag,*

1984, p. 47-56.
CONF: Congress on Sport and International Understanding (1982 : Helsinki).
LEVEL: A LANG: Eng GV706.8 18979

McIntosh, P.C. International communication, sport and international understanding. (Refs: 33)*In, Ilmarinen, M. (ed.) et al. Sport and International Understanding: proceedings of the congress held in Helsinki, Finland, July 7-10, 1982, Berlin, Springer-Verlag, 1984, p. 276-284.*
CONF: Congress on Sport and International Understanding (1982 : Helsinki).
LEVEL: I LANG: Eng GV706.8 18979

Milshtein, O. Sport in Europe and the Helsinki agreements. (Refs: 15)*In, Ilmarinen, M. (ed.) et al., Sport and Internationa Understanding: proceedings of the congress held in Helsinki, Finland, July 7-10, 1982, Berlin, Springer-Verlag, 1984, p. 82-91.*
CONF: Congress on Sport and International Understanding (1982 : Helsinki).
LEVEL: A LANG: Eng GV706.8 18979

Petrova, N. The social significance of international sporting activity. (Refs: 5)*In, Ilmarinen, M. (ed.) et al., Sport and International Understanding: proceedings of the congress held in Helsinki, Finland, July 7-10, 1982, Berlin, Springer-Verlag, 1984, p. 78-80.*
CONF: Congress on Sport and International Understanding (1982 : Helsinki).
LEVEL: I LANG: Eng GV706.8 18979

Petrovic, K. Zvan, M. Sugman, R. Sport and non-alignment: dilemmas and prospects. (Refs: 10)*In, Ilmarinen, M. (ed.) et al., Sport and International Understanding: proceedings of the congress held in Helsinki, Finland, July 7-10, 1982, Berlin, Springer-Verlag, 1984, p. 319-322.*
CONF: Congress on Sport and International Understanding (1982 : Helsinki).
LEVEL: I LANG: Eng GV706.8 18979

Seppaenen, P. The idealistic and factual role of sport in international understanding. (Refs: 36)*In, Ilmarinen, M. (ed.) et al., Sport and International Understanding: proceedings of the congress held in Helsinki, Finland, July 7-10, 1982, Berlin, Springer-Verlag, 1984, p. 57-63.*
CONF: Congress on Sport and International Understanding (1982 : Helsinki).
LEVEL: A LANG: Eng GV706.8 18979

Stolyarov, V. Sanadze, L. The role of international sporting ties in strengthening peace and understanding between nations. (Refs: 25)*In, Ilmarinen, M. (ed.) et al., Sport and International Understanding: proceedings of the congress held in Helsinki, Finland, July 7-10, 1982, Berlin, Springer-Verlag, 1984, p. 38-46.*
CONF: Congress on Sport and International Understanding (1982 : Helsinki).
LEVEL: A LANG: Eng GV706.8 18979

Sykora, F. The significance of international co-operation in the field of physical culture sciences for international understanding. *In, Ilmarinen, M. (ed.) et al., Sport and International Understanding: proceedings of the congress held in Helsinki, Finland, July 7-10, 1982, Berlin, Springer-Verlag, 1984, p. 316-318.*
CONF: Congress on Sport and International Understanding (1982 : Helsinki).
LEVEL: B LANG: Eng GV706.8 18979

Varis, T. Co-operation with developing countries in matters of sport. (Refs: 6)*In, Ilmarinen, M. (ed.) et*

POLITICS AND GOVERNMENT (continued)

al., Sport and International Understanding: proceedings of the congress held in Helsinki, Finland, July 7-10, 1982, Berlin, Springer-Verlag, 1984, p. 304-306.
CONF: Congress on Sport and International Understanding (1982 : Helsinki).
LEVEL: B LANG: Eng GV706.8 18979

Wohl, A. The integrational functions of competitive sport and its role in shaping international competition, co-operation an mutual understanding. In, Ilmarinen, M. (ed.) et al., Sport and International Understanding: proceedings of the congress held in Helsinki, Finland, July 7-10, 1982, Berlin, Springer-Verlag, 1984, p. 99-103.
CONF: Congress on Sport and International Understanding (1982 : Helsinki).
LEVEL: I LANG: Eng GV706.8 18979

Zachariev, Z. UNESCO's role in the field of sport and physical education and the challenge facing international sporting links in the future. In, Ilmarinen, M. (ed.) et al., Sport and International Understanding: proceedings of the congress held in Helsinki, Finland, July 7-10, 1982, Berlin, Springer-Verlag, 1984, p. 160-166.
CONF: Congress on Sport and International Understanding (1982 : Helsinki).
LEVEL: I LANG: Eng GV706.8 18979

NATIONALISM

Griffiths, A. La fierte nationale. National pride. Champion (Ottawa) 8(3), Aug 1984, 2-5.
LEVEL: B LANG: Fr Eng SIRC ARTICLE NO: 096418

Vaeyrynen, R. Nationalism and internationalism in sport. (Refs: 19)In, Ilmarinen, M. (ed.) et al., Sport and International Understanding: proceedings of the congress held in Helsinki, Finland, July 7-10, 1982, Berlin, Springer-Verlag, 1984, 64-71.
CONF: Congress on Sport and International Understanding (1982 : Helsinki).
LEVEL: A LANG: Eng GV706.8 18979

SOCIALISM

Jarvie, G. Scientific socialism through sport. (Refs: 25)Canadian journal of history of sport/Revue canadienne de l'histoir des sports (Windsor, Ont.) 15(2), Dec 1984, 5-18.
LEVEL: A LANG: Eng SIRC ARTICLE NO: 104487

POLO

Dawnay, H. Polo vision. Learn to play polo with Hugh Dawnay. London: J.A. Allen, c1984. 143 p. : ill.
LEVEL: B LANG: Eng ISBN: 0-85131-381-7
GV1011 17968

Dawnay, H. Polo vision: the Major's method hits the bookshelves. Polo (Gaithersburg, Md.) 10(1), May 1984, 21-22.
NOTES: An abridged version of chapter 2 'Play for fun' of polo vision by Hugh Dawney.
LEVEL: B LANG: Eng SIRC ARTICLE NO: 096790

AUDIO VISUAL MATERIAL

Kaplan, J.K. The video camera - a tool, a weapon. Polo (Gaithersburg, Md.) 10(1), May 1984, 60.
LEVEL: B LANG: Eng SIRC ARTICLE NO: 096792

BIOGRAPHY AND AUTOBIOGRAPHY

Alexander, B. Bart Evans - pony man: an interview with one of America's top trainers. Polo (Gaithersburg, Md.) 9(8), Apr 1984, 36-37.
LEVEL: B LANG: Eng SIRC ARTICLE NO: 101452

Hamilton, S. The secret of success after seventy: get in the game and keep going. (Fred Zeller) Polo (Gaithersburg, Md.) 10(3), Aug 1984, 16-18.
LEVEL: B LANG: Eng SIRC ARTICLE NO: 103362

Smalley, A. War games in white britches: General George S. Patton. Polo (Gaithersburg, Md.) 9(6), Jan/Feb 1984, 38-39.
LEVEL: B LANG: Eng SIRC ARTICLE NO: 098398

DIRECTORIES

The 1984 Polo Club Directory. Polo (Gaithersburg, Md.) 10(1), May 1984, 16-19.
LEVEL: B LANG: Eng SIRC ARTICLE NO: 096788

HISTORY

Griswold, F.G. Yesteryears: polo in America. Polo (Gaithersburg, Md.) 9(7), Mar 1984, 6-7.
NOTES: Reprinted from, The International Polo Cup, New York, Duttons, 1928.
LEVEL: B LANG: Eng SIRC ARTICLE NO: 098396

INJURIES AND ACCIDENTS

Wilkinson, T.S. Of gear and gray matter. Polo (Gaithersburg, Md.) 10(2), June/Jul 1984, 20.
LEVEL: B LANG: Eng SIRC ARTICLE NO: 173188

OFFICIATING

Hetherington, C. Umpiring: more tips for the polo umpire. Polo (Gaithersburg, Md.) 10(1), May 1984, 54.
LEVEL: B LANG: En SIRC ARTICLE NO: 096791

Hetherington, C. Protecting the pony, and other reminders. Polo (Gaithersburg, Md.) 10(2), June/Jul 1984, 64.
LEVEL: B LANG: Eng SIRC ARTICLE NO: 173191

Rizzo, P.J. The polo umpire - a vote of confidence. Polo (Gaithersburg, Md.) 9(8), Apr 1984, 9.
LEVEL: B LANG: Eng SIRC ARTICLE NO: 101455

PROTECTIVE DEVICES

Wilkinson, T.S. Medic: more notes on protection. Polo (Gaithersburg, Md.) 10(5), Oct 1984, 12.
LEVEL: B LANG: Eng SIRC ARTICLE NO: 105992

RULES AND REGULATIONS

Baker, J. Baker, O. Polo fundamentals: the all-important line. Polo (Gaithersburg, Md.) 10(4), Sept 1984, 18.
LEVEL: B LANG: Eng SIRC ARTICLE NO: 105917

Yesteryears: professionalism in polo. Polo (Gaithersburg, Md.) 10(5), Oct 1984, 10-11.
LEVEL: B LANG: Eng SIRC ARTICLE NO: 105994

SPORTING EVENTS

Butler, M. Iglehart, S. The 'open' debate: should there be a handicap ceiling on the U.S. Open? Polo (Gaithersburg, Md.) 9(8), Apr 1984, 23-25.
LEVEL: B LANG: Eng SIRC ARTICLE NO: 101454

Kaplan, J. Gold medal polo: when polo was an olympic game. Polo (Gaithersburg, Md.) 10(3), Aug 1984, 25-27.
LEVEL: B LANG Eng SIRC ARTICLE NO: 103363

STRATEGY

Markham, J. Position by position: the back - guardian of the goal. Polo (Gaithersburg, Md.) 10(2), June/Jul 1984, 26-27.
NOTES: Four-part series.
LEVEL: B LANG: Eng SIRC ARTICLE NO: 173187

Position by position: No. 3 - the playmaker. Polo (Gaithersburg, Md.) 10(4), Sept 1984, 24-25.
LEVEL: B LANG: Eng SIRC ARTICLE NO: 105950

TECHNIQUES AND SKILLS

Baker, J. Baker, O. Polo fundamentals: the fine art of hitting. Polo (Gaithersburg, Md.) 10(1), May 1984, 52-53.
LEVEL: B LANG: Eng SIRC ARTICLE NO: 096789

Baker, J. Baker, O. Beginning polo: more basics. Polo (Gaithersburg, Md.) 9(7), Mar 1984, 24.
LEVEL: B LANG: Eng SIRC ARTICLE NO: 098395

Baker, J. Baker, O. Beginning polo: the mallet and finding your hitting groove. Polo (Gaithersburg, Md.) 9(8), Apr 1984, 44-45.
LEVEL: B LANG: Eng SIRC ARTICLE NO: 101453

Baker, J. Baker, O. The near-side shots. Polo (Gaithersburg, Md.) 10(2), June/Jul 1984, 62-63.
LEVEL: B LANG: Eng SIRC ARTICLE NO: 173190

Markhan, J. Hitting techniques: the windup. Polo (Gaithersburg, Md.) 9(7), Mar 1984, 32-33.
LEVEL: B LANG: Eng SIRC ARTICLE NO: 098397

Tibetts, S. Getting the job done: polo equitation. Polo (Gaithersburg, Md.) 9(6), Jan/Feb 1984, 40-41;62.
LEVEL: B LANG: Eng SIRC ARTICLE NO: 098399

TRAINING AND CONDITIONING

Lieberman, B. Mackay-Smith, M. Mechanical exercise: bane or benefit? Polo (Gaithersburg, Md.) 10(2), June/Jul 1984, 60-61.
LEVEL: B LANG: Eng SIRC ARTICLE NO: 173189

VETERINARY MEDICINE

Wollenman, P. Vet notes: preventing heatstroke. Polo (Gaithersburg, Md.) 10(4), Sept 1984, 58.
LEVEL: B LANG: Eng SIRC ARTICLE NO: 105993

POLYNESIA

Isaacs, T. Pinaud, Y. Pacific Islands athletics annual 1984: Melanesia, Polynesia, Micronesia. Trowbridge, Wiltshire: Tony Isaacs : Association of Track and Field Statisticians, 1984. 92 p. : ill.
LEVEL: B LANG: Eng GV687 18409

POWERLIFTING

Cassidy, H. Ban the squat. *Powerlifting U S A (Camarillo, Calif.) 7(10), May 1984, 9.*
LEVEL: B LANG: Eng SIRC ARTICLE NO 097038

BIOGRAPHY AND AUTOBIOGRAPHY

Everson, J. The man is an animal...what makes Freddy run? *Powerlifting USA (Camarillo, Calif.) 7(11), Jun 1984, 8.*
LEVEL: LANG: Eng SIRC ARTICLE NO: 101772

Fernando, R. Ed Coan, the wonder of nature. *Powerlifting USA (Camarillo, Calif.) 7(9), Apr 1984, 22-23.*
LEVEL: B LANG: En SIRC ARTICLE NO: 101773

Fernando, R. Joe Ladnier the young Hercules. *Powerlifting USA (Camarillo, Calif.) 7(11), Jun 1984, 14-15.*
LEVEL: B LANG: Eng SIRC ARTICLE NO: 101774

Krall, D. Dave Schneider. *Powerlifting USA (Camarillo, Calif.) 7(12), Jul 1984, 12-13.*
LEVEL: B LANG: Eng SIRC ARTICLE NO 103657

Krall, D. Bob Wahl. *Powerlifting USA (Camarillo, Calif.) 7(12), Jul 1984, 24-25.*
LEVEL: B LANG: Eng SIRC ARTICLE NO: 1036

Krall, D. John Black profile. The man who loves to lift. *Powerlifting USA (Camarillo, Calif.) 8(1), Aug 1984, 12-13.*
LEVEL: B LANG: Eng SIRC ARTICLE NO: 102091

Todd, T. He bends but he doesn't break. (Lamar Gant) *Sports illustrated (Chicago, Ill.) 61(19), 22 Oct 1984, 46-48;51;54-55;58;61-62.*
LEVEL: B LANG: Eng SIRC ARTICLE NO: 100174

Vuono, P. Pioneers of power. Part 10 Chuck Fish. *Powerlifting USA (Camarillo, Calif.) 7(6), Jan 1984, 80.*
LEVEL: B LANG: Eng SIRC ARTICLE NO: 094017

Vuono, P. Pioneers of power (Bob Peoples) (Refs: 1) *Powerlifting U.S.A. (Camarillo, Calif.) 7(7), Feb 1984, 72.*
LEVEL: B LANG: Eng SIRC ARTICLE NO: 095537

BIOMECHANICS

McLaughlin, T. The biomechanics of powerlifting. Assistance exercises, developing the chest and lats. *Powerlifting USA (Camarillo, Calif.) 7(9), Apr 1984, 20-21.*
LEVEL: I LANG: Eng SIRC ARTICLE NO: 101778

McLaughlin, T.M. Madsen, N.H. Bench press techniques of elite heavyweight powerlifters. (Refs: 6) *National Strength & Conditioning Association journal (Lincoln, Neb.) 6(4), Aug/Sept 1984, 44;62-65.*
ABST: The purpose of this study was to analyse kinetic and kinematic values of bench press performances by powerlifters. Three groups of lifters served as subjects: 9 heavy experts, 19 light experts, and 17 light novices. The results indicated that elite heavyweight powerlifters used similar techniques to elite lighter powerlifters. One notable difference observed was that torques about the shoulder were larger for bigger athletes.
LEVEL: A LANG: Eng SIRC ARTICLE NO: 100169

McLaughlin, T.M. Bar path and the bench press. *Powerlifting USA (Camarillo, Calif.) 8(5), Dec 1984, 19-20.*

NOTES: Excerpt from, Mclaughlin, T.M., Bench press more now: breakthroughs in biomechanics and training methods, 1984.
LEVEL: I LANG: Eng SIRC ARTICLE NO: 108868

DRUGS, DOPING AND ERGOGENIC AIDS

Hurley, B.F. Seals, D.R. Hagberg, J.M. Goldberg, A.C. Ostrove, S.M. Holloszy, J.O. Wiest, W.G. Goldberg, A.P. High-density-lipoprotein cholesterol in bodybuilders v powerlifters. Negative effects of androgen use. (Refs: 21) *JAMA: Journal of the American Medical Association (Chicago) 252(4), 27 Jul 1984, 507-513.*
ABST: 8 bodybuilders and 4 powerlifters were tested before and after androgen use to evaluate the effects of anabolic-androgenic steroids on lipids and the relationship to type of weight training. Androgen use by the bodybuilders and powerlifters lowered values of both HDL-Cholesterol and HDL2-C by 55 percent and raised values of LDL-C 61 percent and LDL-C/HDL-C ratios 280 percent. The training regimen of bodybuilders is associated with a more favorable lipid profile than the training use by powerlifters.
LEVEL: A LANG: Eng SIRC ARTICLE NO: 103058

INJURIES AND ACCIDENTS

Everson, J. Treatment and prevention of chronic shoulder injuries. *Powerlifting USA (Camarillo, Calif.) 8(4), Nov 1984, 26.*
LEVEL: B LANG: Eng SIRC ARTICLE NO: 173482

Everson, J. The powerlifter and chronic shoulder injuries. *Powerlifting USA (Camarillo, Calif.) 8(2), Sept 1984, 22.*
LEVEL: B LANG: Eng SIRC ARTICLE NO: 173487

McLaughlin, T. Injury proofing. *Powerlifting USA (Camarillo, Calif.) 7(6), Jan 1984, 26-27.*
LEVEL: B LANG: Eng SIRC ARTICLE NO: 094011

Medical aspects of adolescent powerlifting. *Sportsmedicine digest (Van Nuys, Calif.) 6(2), Feb 1984, 3-4.*
LEVEL: B LANG: En SIRC ARTICLE NO: 100170

MEDICINE

Hatfield, F.C. Power-research. Thoughts on how to solve a grip problem...and other things. *Powerlifting U.S.A. (Camarillo, Calif.) 7(7), Feb 1984, 12.*
LEVEL: B LANG: Eng SIRC ARTICLE NO: 095530

NUTRITION

Digangi, J. Nutrition corner. Do you need more calcium? *Powerlifting USA (Camarillo, Calif.) 7(9), Apr 1984, 29.*
LEVEL: B LANG: Eng SIRC ARTICLE NO: 101771

Digangi, J. Making weight. *Powerlifting USA (Camarillo, Calif.) 8(1), Aug 1984, 26-27.*
LEVEL: B LANG: Eng SIRC ARTICLE NO 102090

PHYSIOLOGY

Boyle, M. Overtraining & powerlifting. (Refs: 3) *Powerlifting U.S.A. (Camarillo, Calif.) 7(7), Feb 1984, 29.*
LEVEL: B LANG Eng SIRC ARTICLE NO: 095527

PHYSIOLOGY - MUSCLE

Tesch, A. Thorsson, A. Kraiser, P. Muscle capillary supply and fiber type characteristics in weight and power lifters. (Refs 25) *Journal of applied physiology: respiratory environmental and exercise physiology (Bethesda, Md.) 56(1), Jan 1984, 35-38.*
ABST: A comparison was made between 8 weight and power lifters, 8 endurance athletes and 8 untrained individuals to determine the differences in capillary density, fibre type distribution and fibre size of the vastus lateralis muscle. This study found that the weight and power lifters had reduced capillary density compared to the other 2 groups. The heavy resistance training of these athletes resulted in fast-twitch fibre hypertrophy with a reduction in the number of capillaries per square millimeter.
LEVEL: A LANG: Eng SIRC ARTICLE NO: 097042

PSYCHOLOGY - MENTAL TRAINING

Biasiotto, J. Palmer, L. Psychological aspects of powerlifting. *Powerlifting USA (Camarillo, Calif.) 8(4), Nov 1984, 28.*
LEVEL: B LANG: Eng SIRC ARTICLE NO: 173483

TECHNIQUES AND SKILLS

Lambert, M. Power technique: a photo-sequence analysis of championship powerlifting technique, squat-bench press-deadlift. Camarillo, Calif.: Powerlifting USA Magazine, c1984. 71 p.
LEVEL: B LANG: Eng LC CARD: 84-200632

TESTING AND EVALUATION

Sale, D.G. MacDougall, J.D. Isokinetic strength in weight-trainers. (Refs: 18) *European journal of applied physiology and occupational physiology (Berlin, W.G.) 53(2), 1984, 128-132.*
ABST: Isokinetic strength of ankle plantarflexion (APF), knee extension (KE) and elbow extension (EE) was measured in male weight-trainers (6 power-lifters and 7 bodybuilders) and 25 untrained men of similar age and height. The weight-trainers exceeded control subjects by 21 per cent, 25 per cent and 73 per cent in APF, KE and EE strength respectively. The relatively greater enhancement of upper versus lower limb strength and muscle mass in the weight-trainers was considered in respect to training habits, trainability of different muscle groups and the state of training of muscle groups in untrained men.
LEVEL: A LANG: Eng SIRC ARTICLE NO: 104602

TRAINING AND CONDITIONING

Fernando, R. Startin' out: forced reps. *Powerlifting USA (Camarillo, Calif.) 8(4), Nov 1984, 30.*
LEVEL: B LANG: Eng SIRC ARTICLE NO: 173484

Kuc, J. Training: deadlift assistance work by 4 time world champion. *Powerlifting U S A (Camarillo, Calif.) 7(10), May 1984 18-19.*
LEVEL: B LANG: Eng SIRC ARTICLE NO: 097040

Kuc, J. Workout of the month. *Powerlifting USA (Camarillo, Calif.) 8(1), Aug 1984, 20.*
LEVEL: B LANG: Eng SIRC ARTICLE NO 102092

Ladnier, J. Workout of the month: Joe Ladnier's bench press routine. *Powerlifting USA (Camarillo,*

Calif.) 7(11), Jun 1984, 15.
LEVEL: B LANG: Eng SIRC ARTICLE NO: 101776

McCain, C. Workout of the month. Chip McCain on deadlifting. *Powerlifting USA (Camarillo, Calif.) 7(9), Apr 1984, 18-19.*
LEVEL: B LANG: Eng SIRC ARTICLE NO: 101777

McLaughlin, T. Biomechanics of powerlifting. (Refs: 3)*Powerlifting U.S.A. (Camarillo, Calif.) 7(7), Feb 1984, 30-31.*
LEVEL: B LANG: Eng SIRC ARTICLE NO: 095532

McLauglin, T. Power research: the biomechanics of powerlifting. (Refs: 7)*Powerlifting U S A (Camarillo, Calif.) 7(10), May 1984, 28-29.*
LEVEL: I LANG: Eng SIRC ARTICLE NO: 097041

Parviainen, J. The Finnish deadlift routine, number two. *Powerlifting USA (Camarillo, Calif.) 7(6), Jan 1984, 17.*
LEVEL: LANG: Eng SIRC ARTICLE NO: 094015

Pfeiffer, D. Pre workout considerations. *Powerlifting USA (Camarillo, Calif.) 7(6), Jan 1984, 29.*
LEVEL: B LANG: Eng SIRC ARTICLE NO: 094016

TRAINING AND CONDITIONING - WEIGHT AND STRENGTH TRAINING

Cash, J. Deadlift power. *Powerlifting USA (Camarillo, Calif.) 7(12), Jul 1984, 11.*
LEVEL: B LANG: Eng SIRC ARTICLE NO: 103650

WOMEN

Dayton, L. Powerful yet feminine. (powerlifting) *Fit (Mountain View, Calif.) 3(10), Mar 1984, 45-49.*
LEVEL: B LANG: Eng SIRC ARTICLE NO: 100164

PSYCHOLOGY

Aggression/violence - aesthetics and elite athletes - sport and politics. Scientific program abstracts. Eugene, Or.: Universit of Oregon, Microform Publications, 1984. 66 p.
CONF: Olympic Scientific Congress (1984 : Eugene, Or.).
NOTES: Cover title.
LEVEL: A LANG: Eng GV701 17862

Alderman, R.B. The future of sport psychology. NOTES: In, Silva, J.M. and Weinberg, R.S. (eds.), Psychological foundations of sport, Champaign, Ill., Human Kinetics Publishers, c1984, p. 45-54.
LEVEL: I LANG: Eng GV706.4 17779

Botterill, C. Winston, G. Psychological skill development. (Refs: 4)*Sports: science periodical on research and technology i sport (Ottawa) BU-1, Aug 1984, 1-5.*
LEVEL: I LANG: Eng SIRC ARTICLE NO: 096317

Botterill, C. Winston, G. Le developpement des aptitudes psychologiques. (Refs: 4)*Science du sport: documents de recherche et de technologie (Ottawa) BU-1, aout 1984, 1-7.*
LEVEL: I LANG: Fr SIRC ARTICLE NO: 096318

Brito, A.D. Aspect psychologique: etude et accompagnement de l'athlete pendant l'entrainement et les periodes pre-competitives, competitives et post-competitives. Fichier et preuves de controles. Preparation psychologique pour competitions. (table des matieres) *Revue de l'education physique (Liege) 24(3), 1984, 59.*
LEVEL: B LANG: Fr SIRC ARTICLE NO: 104399

Browne, M.A. Mahoney, M.J. Sport psychology. (Refs: 100)*Annual review of psychology (Palo Alto, Calif.) 35, 1984, 605-625.*
LEVEL: I LANG: Eng SIRC ARTICLE NO: 096319

Clarke, K.S. The USOC Sports Psychology Registry: a clarification. *Journal of sport psychology (Champaign, Ill.) 6(4), Dec 1984, 365-366.*
LEVEL: B LANG: Eng SIRC ARTICLE NO: 104402

Cratty, B.J. Piggot, R.E. Student projects in sport psychology. Ithaca, N.Y.: Mouvement Publications, c1984. xix, 141 p.
NOTES: Includes bibliographies.
LEVEL: I LANG: Eng ISBN: 0-932392-15-6
GV706.4 18756

Dasilva, A.R. (Some aspects of sports psychology revisited.) (Refs: 4)*Arquivos brasileiros de psicologia (Rio de Janeiro) 36(1), 1984, 113-120.*
LEVEL: I LANG: Por

Griffin, N.S. Keogh, J.F. Maybee, R. Performer perceptions of movement confidence. (Refs: 12)*Journal of sport psychology (Champaign, Ill.) 6(4), Dec 1984, 395-407.*
ABST: The initial study of movement confidence as a construct attempted to answer the research questions of whether confidence is more than competence and whether the determinants of confidence vary in relation to the movement situation. The study was designed as a preliminary examination of these two concerns in terms of the three components - competence, potential for enjoying moving sensations, and potential for harm - which were proposed in the model for movement confidence. Factor and regression analyses of data from 352 college students indicated that movement confidence is more than competence, and the determinants of movement confidence seem to vary in relation to movement situations and possibly in relation to gender. The major contribution of perceived level of confidence generally is a personal feeling of competence. The precise contributions of additional modifiers cannot be specified at present.
LEVEL: A LANG: Eng SIRC ARTICLE NO: 104219

Grimmer, D. J. Psychology and sports performance. (Refs: 4)*Sideline view (Minneapolis) 6(5), Dec 1984, 1-4.*
LEVEL: I LANG Eng SIRC ARTICLE NO: 104409

Harris, D.V. Harris, B.L. Athlete's guide to sports psychology: mental skills for physical people. New York: Leisure Press, c1984. 200 p. : ill.
NOTES: Bibliography: p. 200.
LEVEL: I LANG: Eng ISBN: 0880112069 LC CARD: 83-80735 GV706.4 17028

Heazlewood, I. Sport psychology in track and field. (Refs: 21)*Modern athlete and coach (Athelstone, Aust.) 22(2), Apr 1984, 11-14.*
LEVEL: I LANG: Eng SIRC ARTICLE NO: 096327

Hughes, J.R. Psychological effects of habitual aerobic exercise: a critical review. (Refs: 67)*Preventive medicine (New York 13(1), Jan 1984, 66-78.*
ABST: The author reviews experiments on the effects of habitual exercise on mood, personality, and cognition. Findings show improvements of self-concept but no significant changes in anxiety, depression, body image, personality or cognition.
LEVEL: A LANG: Eng SIRC ARTICLE NO: 100938

Kerr, J.H. Reversal theory - a new direction for sports psychology. *Bulletin of the British psychological society (Leicester) 37, Feb 1984, 45.*
LEVEL: B LANG: Eng SIRC ARTICLE NO: 096330

Kirkcaldy, B.D. Clinical psychology in sport. (Refs: 15)*International journal of sport psychology (Rome, Italy) 15(2), 1984 127-136.*
LEVEL: I LANG: Eng SIRC ARTICLE NO: 099289

Leveque, M. Le psychologue en milieu sportif: une implication singuliere. (Refs: 8)*Bulletin de psychologie (Paris) 37(364), jan/fevr 1984, 359-369.*
LEVEL: I LANG: Fr SIRC ARTICLE NO: 102859

Lewis, C.B. The relationship between posture and psychological variables in students age 18-25. Eugene, Ore.: Microform Publications, University of Oregon, 1984. 2 microfiches : negative, ill. ; 11 x 15 cm.
NOTES: Thesis (Ph.D.) - University of Maryland, 1983; (viii, 117 leaves); vita; includes bibliography.
LEVEL: A LANG: Eng UO84 127-128

Mackenzie, M.M. The metaskills model of sports counseling: helping athletes achieve excellence. (Refs: 8)*Quest (Champaign, Ill.) 36(2), 1984, 122-133.*
ABST: This paper contains a description of a new model of sports counseling which evolved from the use of Neuro-Linguistic Programming and Ericksonian communication patterns with amateur and professional athletes. The first part of the paper explicates the theoretical perspectives of human behavior upon which the model is based. The second section of the paper describes the overall counseling process and its parts. Examples of the model in action are presented to clarify the theoretical perspective and the counseling process.
LEVEL: A LANG: Eng SIRC ARTICLE NO: 102860

Nideffer, R.M. Applied sport psychology. (Refs: 6)
NOTES: In, Strauss, R.H. (ed.), Sports medicine, Philadelphia ; Toronto, Saunders, 1984, p. 501-509.
LEVEL: I LANG: Eng RC1210 17196

Nideffer, R.M. Current concerns in sport psychology.
NOTES: In, Silva, J.M. and Weinberg, R.S. (eds.), Psychological foundations of sport, Champaign, Ill., Human Kinetics Publishers, c1984, p. 35-44.
LEVEL: I LANG: Eng GV706.4 17779

Ogilvie, B. Psychology: looking past the finish line. *Women's sports (Palo Alto, Calif.) 6(1), Jan 1984, 51.*
LEVEL: B LANG: Eng SIRC ARTICLE NO: 097787

Oglivie, B. Building a trust fund. (psychology) *Women's sports (Palo Alto, Calif.) 6(5), May 1984, 58.*
LEVEL: B LANG: Eng SIRC ARTICLE NO: 099294

Schell, B. Hunt, J. Lloyd, C. An investigation of future market opportunities for sport psychologists. (Refs: 11)*Journal of sport psychology (Champaign, Ill.) 6(3), 1984, 335-350.*
ABST: For this study, questionnaires were distributed to 607 elite athletes, coaches, officials, administrators, and sport psychologists in Canada. Variables were examined to predict the development of the sport psychology profession. It was hypothesized that elite athletes had sport-specific psychological needs requiring the services of sport psychologists. This proposition was supported by the athlete population. The perception of sport psychology services was found to be more

positive the more the services were employed. All subgroups tested felt that the role of the sport psychologist is growing in importance and is becoming essential to the elite sporting environment.
LEVEL: A LANG: Eng SIRC ARTICLE NO: 102867

Silva, J.M. Weinberg, R.S. Psychological foundations of sport. Champaign, III.: Human Kinetics Publishers, c1984. xxiv, 528
NOTES: Bibliography: p. 463-515.
LEVEL: A LANG: Eng ISBN: 0-931250-59-5 LC CARD: 83-083239 GV706.4 17779

Silva, J.M. Weinberg, R.S. Psychological foundations of sport. Champaign, III.: Human Kinetics Pub., Inc., 1984. 552 p.
LEVEL: I LANG: Eng

Sime, W.E. Psychological benefits of exercise training in the healthy individual. (Refs: 100)*In, Matarazzo, J.D. (ed.) et al., Behavioral health: a handbook of health enhancement and disease prevention, New York, Wiley, c1984, p. 488-508.*
LEVEL: A LANG: Eng

Singer, R.N. What sport psychology can do for the athlete and coach. (Refs: 15)*International journal of sport psychology (Rome) 15(1), 1984, 52-61.*
LEVEL: B LANG: Eng SIRC ARTICLE NO: 094664

Sport and psychology: what ethics suggest about practice. (Refs: 13)*Sports: Science periodical on research and technology in sport BU-1, Feb 1984, 1-8.*
LEVEL: I LANG: Eng SIRC ARTICLE NO: 091811

Sport et psychologie: l'ethique et la pratique. (Refs: 13)*Science du sport: Documents de recherche et de technologie BU-1, fevr 1984, 1-8.*
LEVEL: I LANG: Fr SIRC ARTICLE NO: 091812

Straub, W.F. Williams, J.M. Cognitive sport psychology: historical, contemporary, and future perspectives. (Refs: 33)*In, Straub, W.F. and Williams, J.M. (eds.), Cognitive sport psychology, Lansing, N.Y., Sport Science Associates, c1984, p. 3-10.*
LEVEL: A LANG: Eng GV706.4 20099

Tutko, T. Sports psychology. *New Zealand gliding kiwi (Tauranga, N.Z.) 16(4), Aug/Sept 1984, 42-43;45.*
LEVEL: B LANG: Eng SIRC ARTICLE NO: 102871

ACTIVATION

Regnier, G. Niveau d'activation et performance sportive. *Revue de l'entraineur (Montreal) oct/dec 1984, 19.*
LEVEL: B LANG Fr SIRC ARTICLE NO: 105516

AGGRESSION

Hagell, A. Brawl games: the perception of aggression in sport. *Bulletin of the British Psychological Society (Leicester) 37 May 1984, 82.*
LEVEL: I LANG: Eng SIRC ARTICLE NO: 096325

Husman, B.F. Silva, J.M. Aggression in sport: definitional and theoretical considerations.
NOTES: In, Silva, J.M. and Weinberg, R.S. (eds.), Psychological foundations of sport, Champaign, III., Human Kinetics Publishers, c1984, p. 246-260.
LEVEL: A LANG: Eng GV706.4 17779

Russell, G.W. Russell, A.M. Sports penalties: an alternative means of measuring aggression. (Refs: 10)*Social behavior and personality (Sudbury) 12(1),*

1984, 69-74.
LEVEL: I LANG: Eng SIRC ARTICLE NO: 104417

Shcherbakov, E.L. Use of the terms 'agressiveness' and 'agressive qualities'. *Soviet sports review (Escondido, Calif.) 19(2), Jun 1984, 72-74.*
NOTES: Translated from, Teoriya i praktika fizicheskoi kultury, 9: 43-44, 1982.
LEVEL: I LANG: Eng SIRC ARTICLE NO: 099300

Silva, J.M. Factors related to the acquisition and exhibition of aggressive sport behavior.
NOTES: In, Silva, J.M. and Weinberg, R.S. (eds.), Psychological foundations of sport, Champaign, III., Human Kinetics Publishers, c1984, p. 261-273.
LEVEL: A LANG: Eng GV706.4 17779

Widmeyer, W.N. Aggression-performance relationships in sport.
NOTES: In, Silva, J.M. and Weinberg, R.S. (eds.), Psychological foundations of sport, Champaign, III., Human Kinetics Publishers, c1984, p. 274-286.
LEVEL: A LANG: Eng GV706.4 17779

ANXIETY

Furst, D.M. Tenenbaum, G. A correlation of body-cathexis and anxiety in athletes and nonathletes. (Refs: 20)*International journal of sport psychology (Rome) 15(3), 1984, 160-168.*
ABST: Participation in a physical activity such as athletics has been assumed to be intrinsically satisfying, associated with a positive body-image, and with lower anxiety. Male athletes (n, 35) and nonathletes (n, 24) were measured on body cathexis, manifest anxiety, and perceived satisfaction in physical activity. The hypotheses were only partially supported, but subjectively perceived satisfaction helped explain the body-cathexis participation relationship.
LEVEL: A LANG: Eng SIRC ARTICLE NO: 104406

Georges, G. L'anxiete en milieu sportif. (Refs: 11)*Revue de l'education physique (Liege, Belgique) 24(1), 1984, 17-20.*
LEVEL: B LANG: Fr SIRC ARTICLE NO: 096324

Gould, D. Petlichkoff, L. Weinberg, R.S. Antecedents of, temporal changes in, and relationships between CSAI-2 Subcomponents (Refs: 26)*Journal of sport psychology (Champaign, III.) 6(3), 1984, 289-304.*
ABST: Two studies were conducted to examine antecedents of, relationships between, and temporal changes in the cognitive anxiety, somatic anxiety, and the self-confidence components of the Martens, Burton, Vealey, Bump, and Smith (1983) newly developed Competitive State Anxiety Inventory-2 (CSAI-2). In addition, the prediction that cognitive and somatic anxiety should differentially influence performance was examined. In Study 1, 37 elite intercollegiate wrestlers were administered the CSAI-2 immediately before two different competitions, whereas in Study 2, 63 female high school volleyball players completed the CSAI-2 on five different occasions (1 week, 48 hrs, 25 hrs, 2 hrs, and 20 min) prior to major tournament. The findings supported the scale development work of Martens and his colleagues by verifying that the CSAI-2 assesses three separate components of state anxiety.
LEVEL: A LANG: Eng SIRC ARTICLE NO: 102850

Hayden, R.M. Allen, G.J. Relationship between aerobic exercise, anxiety, and depression: convergent validation by knowledgeable informants.

(Refs: 17)*Journal of sports medicine and physical fitness (Torino) 24(1), Mar 1984, 69-74.*
ABST: 98 college students who were committed runners, physically active non-runners or sedentary subjects had trait and state anxiety levels measured as well as depression levels. Reports of subjective stress were confirmed by knowledgeable informants. Aerobic activity was associated with significantly less subjective anxiety and depression, both by the subjects and by informants.
LEVEL: A LANG: Eng SIRC ARTICLE NO: 099286

Her, M. Chi, P.L. Effects of motivation level, task difficulty, cooperation and competition on task performance and anxiety state. *Asian journal of physical education (Taipei, Taiwan) 7(3), Oct 1984, 60-61.*
LEVEL: I LANG: Eng Chi SIRC ARTICLE NO: 102852

John, L. The development and evaluation of self-regulation programmes to overcome the disposition of anxiety in student sports performers. (abstract) *Carnegie research papers (Beckett Park, Leeds) 1(6), Dec 1984, 34-35.*
CONF: Carnegie Undergraduate Research Symposium (1984 : Leeds, Eng.).
LEVEL: I LANG: Eng SIRC ARTICLE NO: 172511

Krebs, P. Hoffpauir, D. Mind and body as one in athletic performance. (Refs: 8)*Coaching clinic 22(7), Mar 1984, 12-14.*
LEVEL: B LANG: Eng SIRC ARTICLE NO: 093151

Monteson, P.A. Pechar, G.S. Welsh, H. Y study proves stress can be controlled by exercise. *Journal of physical education an program (Columbus, Oh.) 81(5), Jun 1984, 9-10.*
LEVEL: I LANG: Eng SIRC ARTICLE NO: 096334

Passer, M.W. Competitive trait anxiety in children and adolescents.
NOTES: In, Silva, J.M. and Weinberg, R.S. (eds.), Psychological foundations of sport, Champaign, III., Human Kinetics Publishers, c1984, p. 130-144.
LEVEL: A LANG: Eng GV706.4 17779

Regnier, G. L'anxiete et la performance sportive. (Refs: 1)*Revue de l'entraineur (Montreal) juil/sept 1984, 8-9*
LEVEL: B LANG: Fr SIRC ARTICLE NO: 102865

Smith, R.E. Theoretical and treatment approaches to anxiety reduction.
NOTES: In, Silva, J.M. and Weinberg, R.S. (eds.), Psychological foundations of sport, Champaign, III., Human Kinetics Publishers, c1984, p. 157-170.
LEVEL: A LANG: Eng GV706.4 17779

Sonstroem, R.J. An overview of anxiety in sport.
NOTES: In, Silva, J.M. and Weinberg, R.S. (eds.), Psychological foundation of sport, Champaign, III., Human Kinetics Publishers, c1984, p. 104-117.
LEVEL: A LANG: Eng GV706.4 17779

Taylor, J. Six productive strategies for coping with anxiety. *Sport-talk (Toronto) 13(3), Oct 1984, 1;4-5.*
LEVEL: B LANG: Eng SIRC ARTICLE NO: 102870

Tenenbaum, G. A note on the measurement and relationships of physiological and psychological components and anxiety. (Refs: 28)*International journal of sport psychology (Rome, Italy) 15(2), 1984, 88-97.*
ABST: The effort to validate subjective feelings of anxiety, by physiological indices, has been found to be unsatisfactory. Part of the criticism was focused on inappropriate methodological techniques. The low and significant correlations between the two

variables suggest that indeed the autonomic system does not function monotonically and does not have a linear relationship to what one feels. This paper suggests an improved technique which estimates changes into the autonomic function with respect to psychological characteristics. An improved methodological technique is suggested in order to eliminate misfit responses. It is also suggested that the structure, intensity, duration and form of the stimuli be taken into consideration through on-line analysis as well as the instructions given to subjects during experimentation.
LEVEL: A LANG: Eng SIRC ARTICLE NO: 099302

Watson, G.G. Intrinsic motivation and competitive anxiety in sport: some guidelines for coaches and administrators. (Refs: 3 *Australian journal of science & medicine in sport (Kingston, Aust.) 16(4), Dec 1984, 14-20.*
ABST: In this paper the relationship between intrinsic motivation and the competitive process is examined. When the evaluative influence of competition is perceived as a potential source of interference in the flow of motivated behaviour, stress and psychological conflict then become the inevitable outcome. To examine this basic proposition several theories of play and intrinsic motivation are examined, in terms of the impact of the influence of competition, to identify those conditions under which stress is likely to eventuate. A number of clinical procedures are then identified which may be appropriate in the management of stress resulting from a breakdown in the competitive process.
LEVEL: A LANG: Eng SIRC ARTICLE NO: 105521

Weingarten, G. Dlin, R.A. Karlsson, J. The relationship between state anxiety, muscularity and metabolic responses at the OBLA point. (Refs: 18)*International journal of sport psychology (Rome, Italy) 15(2), 1984, 110-116.*
ABST: The A-State scores of National Water Polo players, taken prior to needle muscle biopsy were related to muscularity, blood pressure and metabolic responses. In the post hoc analysis some possible logical connections were found between subjective anxiety scores and several muscular measurements, autonomic reactivity (SBP) and aerobic efficiency at the onset of blood lactate accumulation (the OBLA point).
LEVEL: A LANG: Eng SIRC ARTICLE NO: 099303

Wittig, A.F. Sport competition anxiety and sex role. *Sex roles: a journal of research (New York) 10(5/6), Mar 1984, 569-573.*
ABST: Athletes tested for competitive trait anxiety were classified into sex role categories. The results found 'masculine' males to be less anxious than other subjects while 'feminine' males were more anxious. No significant differences were found among the female group.
LEVEL: A LANG: Eng SIRC ARTICLE NO: 097793

AROUSAL

Blundell, N. Hype tripe. *Sports world Australia 1(3), Sept 1984, 60-62.*
ABST: Varying levels of arousal/anxiety affect sporting performance in 3 ways: (1) concentration; (2) rhythm, timing and coordination; (3) amount of energy available. Different sports as well as different people require varying levels of arousal for maximum performance, thus the psyching up process practiced by some coaches may be detrimental to some players.
LEVEL: I LANG: Eng SIRC ARTICLE NO: 105505

Creekmore, C.R. Games athletes play. One way to beat your opponents is by using their heads. *Psychology today (New York, N.Y.) 18(7), Jul 1984, 40-44.*
LEVEL: B LANG: Eng SIRC ARTICLE NO: 094641

Melton, J.R. Motivation: how arousal levels affect simple & complex skills - your performance or don't let the inverted-U ge to you. *Kick illustrated (Hollywood, Calif.) 5(2), Feb 1984, 60-61;79.*
LEVEL: I LANG: Eng SIRC ARTICLE NO: 097786

Spink, K.S. Making the athlete the master of his destiny. (self-management techniques) (Refs: 22)*Sports coach (Wembley, W. Aust.) 8(2), Oct 1984, 50-55.*
LEVEL: B LANG: Eng SIRC ARTICLE NO: 104419

Zaichkowsky, L.D. Attentional styles. (Refs: 52)*In, Straub, W.F. and Williams, J.M. (eds.), Cognitive sport psychology, Lansing, N.Y., Sport Science Associates, c1984, p. 140-150.*
LEVEL: A LANG: Eng GV706.4 20099

ASSOCIATIONS

Gilbert, M.A. La SCAPPS et l'avenir. SCAPPS and the future. (Trois-Rivieres): Universite du Quebec a Trois-Rivieres, 1984. 2 leaves
CORP: Societe canadienne d'apprentissage psychomoteur et de psychologie du sport.
CORP: Canadian Society for Psychomotor Learning and Sport Psychology.
LEVEL: I LANG: Eng Fr LC CARD: 84-14386-9 GV706.4 18800

ATTITUDE

Bhullar, J. Personality factors as correlates of attitudes toward physical activity. (Refs: 5)*Snipes journal (Patiala, India) 7(3), Jul 1984, 30-35.*
ABST: The author researched the relationship between personality factors and attitudes toward physical activity. A sample of 100 male post-graduate students served as subjects. Data were obtained through the Cattell's Sixteen Personality Questionnaire and a 70-item attitude scale (known as Pa-as) toward physical activity. Significant correlations were observed between three personality factors (reserved/outgoing, placid/apprehensive, and undisciplined self conflict/controlled) and three sub-domains of attitude (ascetic experience, social experience, and ascetic experience) respectively.
LEVEL: A LANG: Eng SIRC ARTICLE NO: 099281

Corbin, C.B. Laurie, D.R. Gruger, C. Smiley, B. Vicarious success experience as a factor influencing self-confidence, attitudes, and physical activity of adult women. (Refs: 11)*Journal of teaching in physical education (Champaign, Ill.) 4(1), Oct 1984, 17-23.*
ABST: Recent research indicates that females are particularly likely to lack confidence in their abilities to perform physical activities. One theory of instruction suggests a need for educational support for developing competence, self-confidence, and persistence in physical activities. Thirty-nine adult women participating in an exercise class were studied to determine if vicarious success presented via audiovisuals was effective in altering self-confidence, commitment to physical activity, and physical activity involvement. A discriminant function analysis indicated a significant difference between treatment and control groups on a profile of improved confidence/attitude/activity

involvement, with the treatment group showing a more positive profile. Vicarious success experiences enhanced self-confidence, and there was a trend toward greater persistence in activity among those experiencing vicarious success through audiovisual presentations.
LEVEL: A LANG: Eng SIRC ARTICLE NO: 102846

Ogilvie, B. Psychology: semi-tough is not enough. *Women's sports (Palo Alto, Calif.) 6(3), Mar 1984, 50-51.*
LEVEL: B LANG Eng SIRC ARTICLE NO: 097788

Swartz, D. The magic word is attitude. *Swim Canada 98, Feb 1984, 19.*
LEVEL: B LANG: Eng SIRC ARTICLE NO: 090337

ATTRIBUTION

Biddle, S.J.H. Attribution theory in sport and recreation: origins, developments and future directions. (Refs: 71)*Physical education review (North Humberside, Eng.) 7(2), Autumn 1984, 145-159.*
LEVEL: I LANG: Eng SIRC ARTICLE NO: 105504

Brawley, L.R. Roberts, G.C. Attributions in sport: research foundations, characteristics, and limitations.
NOTES: In, Silva J.M. and Weinberg, R.S. (eds.), Psychological foundations of sport, Champaign, Ill., Human Kinetics Publishers, c1984, p. 197-213.
LEVEL: A LANG: Eng GV706.4 17779

Brawley, L.R. Uninentional egocentric biases in attributions. (Refs: 16)*Journal of sport psychology (Champaign, Ill.) 6(3), 1984, 264-278.*
ABST: Two studies were conducted to investigate biases (a) in the available information used to make attributions, and (b) in the attributions of responsibility for actions or events. The subject samples examined were 12 men's doubles tennis teams and 32 coach-athlete pairs. Subjects responded to questions requiring recall of either important events and turning points during tennis matches (Study 1) or examples of joint interaction inputs (Study 2). Estimates of perceived responsibility for both dyad members were gathered from each subject. The data provided evidence for egocentric biases in available information and in responsibility attributions. Subjects consistently remembered more of their personal contributions than those of others, and accepted more responsibility for joint efforts than granted them by others regardless of event outcomes.
LEVEL: A LANG: Eng SIRC ARTICLE NO: 102843

Brawley, L.R. Attributions as social cognitions: contemporary perspectives in sport. (Refs: 85)*In, Straub, W.F. and Williams, J.M. (eds.), Cognitive sport psychology, Lansing, N.Y., Sport Science Associates, c1984, p. 212-230.*
LEVEL: A LANG: Eng GV706.4 20099

Carron, A.V. Attributing causes to success and failure. (Refs: 18)*Australian journal of science & medicine in sport (Kingston, Aust.) 16(2), Aug 1984, 11-15.*
ABST: The general purpose of the present paper was to discuss the implications from attributional research for coaching and teaching. Specifically, this was carried out in three ways. First, the general framework within which attributional research has been undertaken in sport and physical activity was discussed. Second, an overview of the attribution process was outlined. And finally, individual difference considerations (age, sex, task type) were

discussed.
LEVEL: A LANG: Eng SIRC ARTICLE NO: 104401

Tenenbaum, G. Furst, D. Weingarten, G.
Attribution of causality in sport events: validation of the Wingate Sport Achievement Responsibility Scale. (Refs: 30)*Journal of sport psychology (Champaign, Ill.) 6(4), Dec 1984, 430-439.*
ABST: Attribution of causality, based on Rotter's (1966) and Weiner's (1979) models, was investigated in sport setting. The Wingate Sport Achievement Responsibility Scale (WSARS) was developed in order to examine attribution of causality separately for individual and team athletes after successful and unsuccessful events. The scale included feedback from the coach, audience, and teammates. Additional attributions were added in order to examine sport related properties of attributions. In order to examine the distinction between sport-specific attributions and general locus of control (LOC), 69 team athletes and 38 individual athletes were administered the Rotter I-E LOC Scale and the WSARS (Tenenbaum & Weingarten, 1983). Both Rotter's Scale and the WSARS were found to be reliable and valid scales through the probabilistic Rasch Model. Correlational analysis of both scales showed that attribution of causality in team and individual sports were positively related but produced low correlations, which suggests that sport attribution should be examined separately from general LOC.
LEVEL: A LANG: Eng SIRC ARTICLE NO: 104422

AUTOGENIC TRAINING

Kappas, J.G. Self-hypnosis: the key to athletic success. Englewood Cliffs, N.J.: Prentice-Hall, c1984. 168 p. (A Spectrum book.)
NOTES: Includes index.
LEVEL: B LANG: Eng ISBN: 0138033137 LC CARD: 84-011617 GV706.4 18019

Krenz, E.W. Improving competitive performance with hypnotic suggestions and modified autogenic training: case reports. (Refs 21)*American journal of clinical hypnosis (Phoenix, Ariz.) 27(1), Jul 1984, 58-63.*
LEVEL: A LANG: Eng SIRC ARTICLE NO: 174114

BEHAVIOUR

Kirschenbaum, D.S. Self-regulation and sport psychology: nurturing an emerging symbiosis. (Refs: 103)*Sport psychology (Champaign, Ill.) 6(2), 1984, 159-183.*
ABST: This paper attempts to demonstrate the interdependence of research and theorizing on self-regulation and sport psychology. The process of maximizing sport performance was conceptualized as a self-regulatory problem. A five-stage model of self-regulation was presented to show the usefulness of this perspective. In particular, the model of self-regulation applied to this problem indicated that athletes should: specify their goals, establish commitments to change, manage their physical and social environments to facilitate pursuit of goals, execute the components of self-regulation to achieve goals (self-monitor, self-evaluation, self-consequate), and attempt to generalize changes achieved via the development of obsessive-compulsive styles of self-regulation. Recent findings in the self-regulation literature were reviewed to show how ths conceptualization should be refined. Several applications in sport psychology were then described. This analysis supports the conclusion

that (a) sport psychology provides an excellent medium for testing principles of self-regulation, and conversely, (b) self-regulatory models and principes can lead to effective interventions in sport psychology.
LEVEL: A LANG: Eng SIRC ARTICLE NO: 108491

Nelson, C. Schantz, J. Bratton, B. Problem athlete or problem coach: two points of view. *Runner (Edmonton) 21(4), Winter 1983/1984, 20-21.*
LEVEL: I LANG: Eng SIRC ARTICLE NO: 096335

BEHAVIOUR MODIFICATION

Kirschenbaum, D.S. Wittrock, D.A. Cognitive-behavioral interventions in sport: a self-regulatory perspective.
NOTES: In, Silva, J.M. and Weinberg, R.S. (eds.), Psychological foundations of sport, Champaign, Ill., Human Kinetics Publishers, c1984, p. 81-97.
LEVEL: A LANG: Eng GV706.4 17779

Martin, J.E. Dubbert, P.M. Katell, A.D. Thompson, J.K. Raczynski, J.R. Lake, M. Smith, P.O. Webster, J.S. Sikora, T. Cohen, R.E. Behavioral control of exercise in sedentary adults: studies 1 through 6. *Journal of consulting and clinical psychology (Washington) 52(5), Oct 1984, 795-811.*
LEVEL: A LANG: Eng

Zimmerman, R.S. Behavior coaching: some practical aspects in the new health psychology. (Refs: 17)
NOTES: In, Cantu, R.C. (ed.), Clinical sports medicine, Lexington, Mass. ; Toronto, Collamore Press : D.C. Heath, c1984, p. 73-92.
LEVEL: I LANG: Eng RC1201 15964

BIBLIOGRAPHIES

Sachs, M.L. Buffone, G.W. Bibliography: psychological considerations in exercise, including exercise as psychotherapy, exercise addiction, and the psychology of running. s.l.: s.n., 1984. 1v. (loose-leaf)
NOTES: Volume 6, number 1, Summer, 1984.
LEVEL: I LANG: Eng GV706.4 20273

BIOFEEDBACK

Basmajian, J.V. Biofeedback in therapeutic exercise. (Refs: 18)
NOTES: In, Basmajian, J.V. (ed.), Therapeutic exercise, 4th ed., Baltimore, Md., Williams & Wilkins, c1984, p. 257-266.
LEVEL: A LANG: Eng RM719 17505

Chen, W. Lafferty, J. Biofeedback training as an adjunct to a behavioral modification weight reduction program. (Refs: 16) *Florida JOHPERD (Gainesville, Fla.) 22(4), Nov 1984, 5-8.*
ABST: In this study the effect of biofeedback training was tested with the help of 24 volunteers whose average body weight was 49% above ideal weight. While there was no significant difference of weight loss with the addition of biofeedback training, the authors point out that subjects with an extended history of being overweight may require a longer training period. Further studies with a larger sample size and restricted criteria in selecting experimental subjects are recommended.
LEVEL: A LANG: Eng SIRC ARTICLE NO: 105334

Costa, A. Bonaccorsi, M. Scrimali, T. Biofeedback and control of anxiety preceding

athletic competition. (Refs: 46) *International journal of sports psychology (Rome, Italy) 15(2), 1984, 98-109.*
ABST: The authors discuss the theory of pre-start anxiety in the context of athletic preparation, using a technique known as biofeedback training. This therapeutic technique applies the theoretical principles of biofeedback by means of an electronic device, the stress reducer. Based on the findings of research studies in this field, the authors conducted an experiment on a handball team and were able to confirm that biofeedback training in the self-control of anxiety was able to decrease pre-competition anxiety. This result lends support to the hypothesis of a psychophysical genesis of the syndrome.
LEVEL: A LANG: Eng SIRC ARTICLE NO: 099283

Kappes, B.M. Chapman, S.J. The effects of indoor versus outdoor thermal biofeedback training in cold-weather sports. (Refs: 21)*Journal of sport psychology (Champaign, Ill.) 6(3), 1984, 305-311.*
CONF: Biofeedback Society of America: Meeting (1983 : Denver).
ABST: This field study examined the effects of indoor versus outdoor thermal biofeedback training on digital skin temperature for outdoor sports, and also tested the accuracy of estimating one's skin temperature in an outdoor environment. A sample of 25 university student volunteers (14 males and 11 females) were randomly distributed across three groups. All pre- and posttests for all groups were conducted outdoors in an unheated tent. Results indicated the post-period change scores of the outdoor trained group to be superior to indoor trained subjects and controls when all groups were asked to perform outdoors. Indoor subjects were only able to maintain their temperature outdoors, whereas control subjects continued to lose temperature as they did during the pretest. There was no significant overall temperature difference between groups.
LEVEL: A LANG: Eng SIRC ARTICLE NO: 102858

McKee, P. Effects of using enjoyable imagery with biofeedback induced relaxation for chronic pain patients. (Refs: 22) *Therapeutic recreation journal (Alexandria, Va.) 18(1), 1984, 50-61.*
ABST: Twenty patients with chronic back pain took part in a nine week treatment program using biofeedback - assisted deep relaxation and enjoyable or play imagery. The subjects were assigned to one of the following groups: 1) imagery with biofeedback, 2) biofeedback 3) day treatment only, and 4) a no-treatment waiting list control. The imagery-biofeedback and biofeedback groups reported less pain and showed greater increases in amount of daily activity enjoyed than the other groups. Patients in the biofeedback groups showed a greater ability to relax as indicated by EMG ratings.
LEVEL: A LANG: Eng SIRC ARTICLE NO: 094711

Stephens, J. Biofeedback: stress management in the workplace. (Refs: 7)*Employee services management (Westchester, Ill.) 27(1), Feb 1984, 24-27.*
LEVEL: B LANG: Eng SIRC ARTICLE NO: 093156

Woehl, Le biofeedback. *Loisirs sante (Paris) 10, juin/juil/aout 1984, 25-26.*
LEVEL: B LANG: Fr SIRC ARTICLE NO: 104424

PSYCHOLOGY (continued)

BIOGRAPHY AND AUTOBIOGRAPHY

Hempel, L.S. The effect of the Nautilus Express Circuit on cardiorespiratory response. Eugene, Ore.: Microform Publications, university of Oregon, 1984. 1 microfiche : negative, ill. ; 11 x 15 cm.
NOTES: Thesis (M.S.) - Arizona State University, 1982; (vii, 69, (1) leaves); vita; includes bibliography.
LEVEL: A LANG: Eng UO84 327

Reichenbach, A. Entretien avec Monsieur Pal Rokusfalvy. *Macolin (Macolin, Suisse) 41(12), dec 1984, 12-13.*
LEVEL: B LANG: Fr SIRC ARTICLE NO: 108765

BODY IMAGE

Eldar, D. Movement education, traditional gymnastics and body awareness. (Refs: 16)*In, Simri, U. (ed.), et al., Preschool and elementary school children and physical activity. Proceedings of the 26th ICHPER World Congress 1983, Wingate Institute, Israel, vol. III, Jerusalem, Israel, 1984, p. 41-53.*
CONF: ICHPER World Congress (26th : 1983 : Wingate Institute, Israel).
LEVEL: A LANG: Eng GV443 20093

Furst, D.M. Tenenbaum, G. A correlation of body-cathexis and anxiety in athletes and nonathletes. (Refs: 20)*International journal of sport psychology (Rome) 15(3), 1984, 160-168.*
ABST: Participation in a physical activity such as athletics has been assumed to be intrinsically satisfying, associated with a positive body-image, and with lower anxiety. Male athletes (n, 35) and nonathletes (n, 24) were measured on body cathexis, manifest anxiety, and perceived satisfaction in physical activity. The hypotheses were only partially supported, but subjectively perceived satisfaction helped explain the body-cathexis participation relationship.
LEVEL: A LANG: Eng SIRC ARTICLE NO: 104406

Messadie, G. La conquete du corps. *Science et vie (Paris) 147, 1984, 4-7.*
LEVEL: B LANG: Fr

Missoum, G. Le corps 'roi'. Phenomene de culture. (Refs: 9)*Loisirs sante (Paris) 9, avr/mai 1984, 10-12.*
LEVEL: B LANG: F SIRC ARTICLE NO: 100941

CAREERS

Heyman, S.R. The development of models for sport psychology: examing the USOC guidelines. (Refs: 20)*Sport psychology (Champaign, Ill.) 6(2), 1984, 125-132.*
ABST: A review of the literature finds a series of articles discussing developmental problems in the field of sport psychology, particularly regarding the definition of professional roles and the establishment of credentialing criteria for these roles. A committee formed by the United States Olympic Committee was the first to establish concrete guidelines, which are reviewed here for their potential positive and negative effects as a model for sport psychology.
LEVEL: I LANG: Eng SIRC ARTICLE NO: 108489

COMPETITION

Fabian, L. Ross, M. The development of the sports competition trait inventory. (Refs: 20)*Journal of sport behavior (Mobile, Ala.) 7(1), Feb 1984, 13-27.*
ABST: The article describes the Sports Competitive Trait Inventory (SCTI). The SCTI is composed of 17 items with a seven-point rating scale. The validity and reliability of the SCTI was tested using 389 high school and university students. The SCTI was found to be both valid and reliable over a seven to nine week period.
LEVEL: A LANG: Eng SIRC ARTICLE NO: 096323

Gill, D.L. Gross, J.B. Huddleston, S. Shifflett, B. Sex differences in achievement cognitions and performance in competition *Research quarterly for exercise and sport (Reston, Va.) 55(4), Dec 1984, 340-346.*
ABST: Expectancies, performance, perceived ability, and causal attributions of 20 males and 20 females who competed on a motor task after being matched with a same- or opposite-sex opponent of similar ability were examined. Males were more likely than females to predict a win in competition, but actual performance measures, postcompetition ability ratings, and attributions revealed more positive responses to competition by females than males. Females improved their performance times and raised their ability ratings from the initial noncompetitive session more than males and placed more importance on effort attributions than males did. The findings suggest that competition is not necessarily detrimental and can have a positive influence on females' achievement cognitions and behaviors when the competitive task and situation are clearly appropriate for females.
LEVEL: A LANG: Eng SIRC ARTICLE NO: 104407

Grove, J.R. Pargman, D. Behavioural consequences of effort versus ability orientations to interpersonal competition. (Refs: 35)*Australian journal of science & medicine in sport (Kingston, Aust.) 16(2), Aug 1984, 16-20.*
ABST: Subjects experienced three successive wins or three successive losses under effort-oriented or ability-oriented instructional sets. Dependent variables included the number of practice throws made during a five-minute practice period prior to each trial of competition and the number of points scored on each competitive trial. The results indicated that an effort orientation enhanced the practice behaviour of subjects with low achievement tendencies. In addition, both low and high achievers scored more points across the last two trials of competition when given an effort orientation rather than an ability orientation.
LEVEL: A LANG: Eng SIRC ARTICLE NO: 104411

Silva, J.M. Hardy, C.J. Precompetitive affect and athletic performance. (Refs: 57)*In, Straub, W.F. and Williams, J.M. (eds.), Cognitive sport psychology, Lansing, N.Y., Sport Science Associates, c1984, p. 79-88.*
LEVEL: A LANG: Eng GV706.4 20099

Tiainen, J. Telama, R. Children and parents in skiing competitions. (Refs: 3)
CONF: Symposium of Paediatric Work Physiology (10th : 1981 : Joutsa, Finland).
NOTES: In, Ilmarinen, J. and Vaelimaeki, I. (eds.), Children and sport: paediatric work physiology, Berlin, Springer-Verlag, 1984, p. 196-200.
ABST: This study examined competitive cross-country skiing among 8 to 12 year old children. The authors investigated the quantity and quality of training among children, parents' participation in the training, parents' attitudes towards their children's interest in competitive skiing and anxiety in children caused by competition.
LEVEL: A LANG: Eng SIRC ARTICLE NO: 103448

CONCENTRATION

Spink, K. Learning the art of concentration. (Refs: 11)*Sports coach (Wembley, Australia) 7(4), Mar 1984, 19-22.*
ABST: The author provides several descriptions of what 'concentration' is perceived to be as well as its effect on performance. Orlick's concept of 'an uninterrupted connection between two things' as well as Gallwey's inner game approach are examined. Samples of concentration exercises as well as a short supplementary reading list are provided.
LEVEL: B LANG: Eng SIRC ARTICLE NO: 094666

COUNTRIES AND REGIONS

Salmela, J.H. Comparative sport psychology.
NOTES: In, Silva, J.M. and Weinberg, R.S. (eds.), Psychological foundations of sport, Champaign, Ill., Human Kinetics Publishers, c1984, p. 23-34.
LEVEL: I LANG: Eng GV706.4 17779

Schilling, G. Evolution et situation actuelle de la psychologie du sport en Europe. *Macolin (Macolin, Suisse) 41(12), dec 1984, 11-12.*
NOTES: Traduction de, Marianne Weber.
LEVEL: B LANG: Fr SIRC ARTICLE NO: 108764

CREATIVITY

Jeanrenaud, C. Bishop, D. Extraversion and creative regression during playful painting. (Refs: 28)*Recreation research revie (Concord, Ont.) 11(1), Mar 1984, 6-10.*
LEVEL: A LANG: Eng SIRC ARTICLE NO: 105509

Johnson, R.D. Analysis of selected factors related to the element of space in movement creativity. Eugene, Ore.: Microform Publications, University of Oregon, 1984. 2 microfiches : negative, ill. ; 11 x 15 cm.
NOTES: Thesis (Ph.D.) - University of Oregon, 1980; (xiii, 102 leaves); vita; includes bibliography.
LEVEL: A LANG: Eng UO84 134-135

CROSS-CULTURAL STUDIES

Barson, W. Equipment for irrigation. *Groundsman (London, Eng.) 37(5), May 1984, 17-18;20.*
LEVEL: B LANG: Eng SIRC ARTICLE NO: 102124

DEPRESSION

McCann, L. Holmes, D.S. Influence of aerobic exercise on depression. (Refs: 20)*Journal of personality and social psychology (Washington, D.C.) 46(5), May 1984, 1142-1147.*
ABST: Depression levels and aerobic capacity of forty-three depressed women, assigned either to A) an aerobic exercise treatment program, b) a relaxation session, or c) non treatment conditions, were compared in this study. Subjects in the aerobic exercise program showed greater improvements in aerobic capacity than their counterparts. Greater decreases in depression were also observed in aerobic exercise subjects.
LEVEL: A LANG: Eng SIRC ARTICLE NO: 094657

Nichter, D.J. The relationship between cardiovascular fitness and depression in middle-age men as a result of an aerobic conditioning program. Eugene, Ore.: Microform Publications, University of Oregon, 1984. 2 microfiches : negative, ill. ; 11 x 15 cm.
NOTES: Thesis (M.S.) - Pennsylvania State University, 1983; (viii, 103 leaves); includes bibliography.
LEVEL: A LANG: Eng UO84 370-371

Sothmann, M.S. Ismail, A.H. Relationships between urinary catecholamine metabolites, particularly, MHPG, and selected personality and physical fitness characteristics in normal subjects. *Psychosomatic medicine (New York) 46(6), Nov/ Dec 1984, 523-533.*
LEVEL: A LANG: Eng

Stark, E. Exercising away depression. *Psychology today (Boulder, Colo.) 18(12), Dec 1984, 68.*
LEVEL: B LANG: Eng SIRC ARTICLE NO: 102868

EGO

Scheibe, K. The construction of selves in the context of the sporting life. *Bulletin of the British Psychological Society (Leicester, Eng.) 37, Sept 1984, A121.*
LEVEL: B LANG: Eng SIRC ARTICLE NO: 099297

EMOTION

Ewing, J.H. Scott, D.G. Effects of aerobic exercise upon affect and cognition. (Refs: 43)*Perceptual and motor skills (Missoula, Mont.) 59(2), Oct 1984, 407-414.*
ABST: Mood and cognition were assessed in 52 subjects (26 men and 26 women), aged from 18 to 35, during pretest, exercise, and posttest. Half the subjects ran on a treadmill while the others served as controls. Negative mood decreased in both groups, but enhanced positive mood was experienced only by the exercising subjects. There was no effect of aerobic exercise upon subjects' cognitive states.
LEVEL: A LANG: Eng SIRC ARTICLE NO: 102848

Holbrook, M.B. Chestnut, R.W. Greenleaf, E.A. Oliva, T.A. Play as a consumption experience - the roles of emotions, performance, and personality in the enjoyment of games. (Refs: 61)*Journal of consumer research (Los Angeles) 11(2), 1984, 728-739.*
LEVEL: A LANG: Eng SIRC ARTICLE NO: 099287

Jerome, J. Form vs. Dignity: holding it together... and letting yourself go. *Outside (Chicago, Ill.) 9(10), Nov 1984, 35;37-38.*
LEVEL: B LANG: Eng SIRC ARTICLE NO: 173266

Kiester, E. The uses of anger. Winning athletes turn rage into motivation and concentration. *Psychology today (New York, N.Y.) 18(7), Jul 1984, 26.*
LEVEL: B LANG: Eng SIRC ARTICLE NO: 094652

Rioux, G. Sport et emotivite. *Cinesiologie (Paris) 95, mai/juin 1984, 219-224.*
LEVEL: I LANG: Fr SIRC ARTICLE NO: 097790

Tavris, C. Exercise and emotions. *New body (New York) 3(3), May 1984, 14;20.*
NOTES: Reprinted from, Tavris, C., Anger, Simon & Schuster, 1983.
LEVEL: B LANG: Eng SIRC ARTICLE NO: 099301

Vallerand, R.J. Emotion in sport: definitional, historical, and social psychological perspectives. (Refs: 76)*In, Straub, W.F. and Williams, J.M. (eds.), Cognitive sport psychology, Lansing, N.Y., Sport Science Associates, c1984, p. 65-78.*
LEVEL: A LANG: Eng GV706.4 20099

Wughalter, E.H. Love and intimacy through physical activity. (Refs: 5)*Leisure information (New York) 11(2), Fall 1984, 7-8.*
LEVEL: B LANG: Eng SIRC ARTICLE NO: 102876

FATIGUE

Rozenblat, V.V. Vozmozhna li integral'naia otsenka utomleniia? (Is an integral evaluation of fatigue possible?) *Gigiena i sanitariia (Moscow) 7, Jul 1984, 58-59.*
LEVEL: B LANG: Rus

FEAR

Nelson, M.B. Training tips for beginners. *Women's sports and fitness (Palo Alto, Calif.) 6(8), Aug 1984, 42-43.*
LEVEL: B LANG: Eng SIRC ARTICLE NO: 100943

Richardson, P.A. Jackson, A. Albury, K.W. Measurement of fear of failure using the Self-Deprecation and Insecurity Scale. (Refs: 12)*Journal of sport behavior (Mobile, Ala.) 7(3), Sept 1984, 115-119.*
ABST: In 1978 an objective measure of fear of failure entitled the Self-deprecation and Insecurity Scale (SDIS) was developed. This instrument has not been employed extensively in research, therefore the present study was conducted to establish reliability for the instrument. The subjects were 94 male and female college students enrolled in physical education. The Fear of Success Scale (FOSS), developed in 1976, and the SDIS were administered on consecutive days. The split-half method was used to estimate the internal consistency reliability of the SDIS. The zero order correlation between the two scales was .26 with a shared variance of 7 per cent, thus the two scales appear to measure unique constructs. It is therefore hypothesized that the SDIS is an acceptable instrument for assessing the relationship of fear of failure to physical performance despite the fact that it measures other qualities. More research is needed to test this hypothesis.
LEVEL: A LANG: Eng SIRC ARTICLE NO: 100945

FRUSTRATION

Creekmore, C.R. Games athletes play. One way to beat your opponents is by using their heads. *Psychology today (New York, N.Y.) 18(7), Jul 1984, 40-44.*
LEVEL: B LANG: Eng SIRC ARTICLE NO: 094641

GOAL-SETTING

O'Block, F.R. Evans, F.H. Goal-setting as a motivational technique.
NOTES: In, Silva, J.M. and Weinberg, R.S. (eds.), Psychological foundations of sport, Champaign, Ill., Human Kinetics Publishers, c1984, p. 188-196.
LEVEL: A LANG: Eng GV706.4 17779

Rice, H.C. Leadership for leaders: No. 3, goal planning. *Scholastic coach (New York) 54(4), Nov 1984, 56-57.*
LEVEL: B LANG: Eng SIRC ARTICLE NO: 102866

HISTORY

Wiggins, D.K. The history of sport psychology in North America.
NOTES: In, Silva, J.M. and Weinberg, R.S. (eds.), Psychological foundations of sport, Champaign, Ill., Human Kinetics Publishers, c1984, p. 9-22.
LEVEL: I LANG: Eng GV706.4 17779

HYPNOSIS

Krenz, E.W. Improving competitive performance with hypnotic suggestions and modified autogenic training: case reports. (Refs 21)*American journal of clinical hypnosis (Phoenix, Ariz.) 27(1), Jul 1984, 58-63.*
LEVEL: A LANG: Eng SIRC ARTICLE NO: 174114

Russell, R.J. Hypnosis and recall in cognitive sport psychology. (Refs: 31)*In, Straub, W.F. and Williams, J.M. (eds.), Cognitive sport psychology, Lansing, N.Y., Sport Science Associates, c1984, p. 304-310.*
LEVEL: A LANG: Eng GV706.4 20099

INTELLIGENCE

Charreton, P. Sport et intelligence. (Refs: 14)*Macolin (Suisse) 10, oct 1984, 10-13.*
LEVEL: B LANG: Fr SIRC ARTICLE NO: 102914

Fisher, A.C. Sport intelligence. (Refs: 21)*In, Straub, W.F. and Williams, J.M. (eds.), Cognitive sport psychology, Lansing, N.Y., Sport Science Associates, c1984, p. 42-50.*
LEVEL: A LANG: Eng GV706.4 20099

Levin, Z. Intelligence structure of elementary school age athletes. (Refs: 15)*In, Simri, U. (ed.), et al., Preschool and elementary school children and physical activity. Proceedings of the 26th ICHPER World Congress 1983, Wingate Institute, Israel, vol. III, Jerusalem, Israel, 1984, p. 79-88.*
CONF: ICHPER World Congress (26th : 1983 : Wingate Institute, Israel).
LEVEL: A LANG: Eng GV443 20093

MEDITATION

Wolkove, N. Kriesman, H. Darragh, D. Cohen, C. Frank, H. Effect of transcendental meditation in breathing and respiratory control. (Refs: 20)*Journal of applied physiology: respiratory, environment and exercise physiology (Bethesda, Md.) 56(3), Mar 1984, 607-612.*
ABST: The purpose of this study was to study the effect of transcendental meditation (TM) on breathing and respiratory control. Sixteen male and female subjects, who regularly practiced TM, were compared with sixteen controls under progressive hypercapnic and normal condition. In the meditation, VE and VT decreased significantly as they went into meditation. Also, in the same group, VE was significantly less at PACO2 of 55 Torr with meditation than while they were awake. Thus, it was demonstrated that TM can significantly influence quiet breathing and chemosensitivity as measured by the ventilatory response to CO2. The authors conclude that changes in mental state, but not necessarily loss of consciousness, may be associated with alterations in neural drive and central chemosensitivity.
LEVEL: A LANG: Eng SIRC ARTICLE NO: 096311

PSYCHOLOGY (continued)

MENTAL HEALTH

Morgan, W.P. Physical activity and mental health. (Refs: 42)*American Academy of Physical Education papers (Champaign, Ill.) 17, 1984, 132-145.*
CONF: American Academy of Physical Education. Annual Meeting (54th : 1983 : Minneapolis).
NOTES: Conference theme: Exercise and health.
LEVEL: I LANG: Eng SIRC ARTICLE NO: 104413

Railo, W.S. La relation entre le sport et la sante mentale et sociale chez les enfants et les adolescents. (Refs: 32)
NOTES: Dans, Lagarde, F. (ed.), Sante et activite physique, Longueuil, Que., College Edouard-Montpetit, c1984, p. 67-82.
LEVEL: A LANG: Fr GV481 17104

Van Andel, G.E. Austin, D.R. Physical fitness and mental health: a review of the literature. (Refs: 76)*Adapted physical activity quarterly (Champaign, Ill.) 1(3), 1984, 207-220.*
ABST: Empirical evidence has shown a positive relationship between physical training and selected mental health variables. In nonclinical studies the most significant effects of physical exercise have been on self-concept and body image. Two affective variables, depression and anxiety, also seem to be influenced by physical activity but to a lesser degree in this population than with clinical populations. Certain clinical populations appear to benefit cognitively and socially from exercise even though the activity may not be aerobically stressful. Theories that attempt to explain the relationship between fitness and mental health are discussed.
LEVEL: A LANG: Eng SIRC ARTICLE NO: 102873

MENTAL PROCESS

Ewing, J.H. Scott, D.G. Effects of aerobic exercise upon affect and cognition. (Refs: 43)*Perceptual and motor skills (Missoula, Mont.) 59(2), Oct 1984, 407-414.*
ABST: Mood and cognition were assessed in 52 subjects (26 men and 26 women), aged from 18 to 35, during pretest, exercise, and posttest. Half the subjects ran on a treadmill while the others served as controls. Negative mood decreased in both groups, but enhanced positive mood was experienced only by the exercising subjects. There was no effect of aerobic exercise upon subjects' cognitive states.
LEVEL: A LANG: Eng SIRC ARTICLE NO: 102848

Vankersschaver, J. (Information-processing capacities in a sensorimotor skill - a sport skill example). (Refs: 16)*Travail humain (Paris) 47(3), 1984, 281-286.*
LEVEL: A LANG: Fr

Weinberg, R.S. Smith, J. Jackson, A. Gould, D. Effect of association, dissociation and positive self-talk strategies on endurance performance. (Refs: 28)*Canadian journal of applied sport sciences/ Journal canadien des sciences appliquees au sport 9(1), Mar 1984, 25-32.*
ABST: This study compared associative, dissociative and positive self-talk strategies in the performance of two endurance tasks. In the first task, 60 subjects employed one of these strategies during a 30 min. run. There were no significant objective or subjective differences between any of the three groups or the control group. In the second task, 230 subjects employed the same strategies during a muscular leg-endurance task. The results of this second task indicated that dissociation and positive self-talk strategies produced significantly greater endurance than the association or control groups. This study demonstrates that psychological strategies to increase performance are task specific.
LEVEL: A LANG: Eng SIRC ARTICLE NO: 093159

MENTAL TRAINING

Bird, E.I. EMG quantification of mental rehearsal. (Refs: 20)*Perceptual and motor skills (Missoula, Mont.) 59(3), Dec 1984, 899-906.*
ABST: 5 athletes with the ability to visualize internally were tested for EMG response to such training. EMG levels relative to resting levels increased 45 to 178 per cent. Configuration of the EMG profile was highly congruent with the visualized event. Methods are suggested for assessing mental rehearsal processes.
LEVEL: A LANG: Eng SIRC ARTICLE NO: 102842

Bird, E.I. EMG quantification of mental rehearsal. (Refs: 20)*Perceptual and motor skills (Missoula, Mont.) 59(3), Dec 1984, 899-906.*
ABST: 5 athletes who reported the ability to image 'internally' were measured for EMG response to mental rehearsal. The EMG profile was very similar to that taken from an actual performance.
LEVEL: A LANG: Eng SIRC ARTICLE NO: 106279

Botterill, C. Performance enhancement. *Counter attack (Vanier, Ont.) 4(1), Apr 1984, 2-8.*
LEVEL: B LANG: Eng SIRC ARTICLE NO: 097782

Cratty, B.J. Psychological preparation and athletic excellence. Ithaca, N.Y.: Mouvement Publications, c1984. vii, 184 p. : ill.
NOTES: Includes bibliographies.
LEVEL: I LANG: Eng ISBN: 0-932392-17-2
GV706.4 18185

Cratty, B.J. Davis, P.A. The content of athletes' mental lives: process decisions when considering modifications. (Refs: 55) *In, Straub, W.F. and Williams, J.M. (eds.), Cognitive sport psychology, Lansing, N.Y., Sport Science Associates, c1984, p. 317-330.*
LEVEL: A LANG: Eng GV706.4 20099

Garfield, C.A. Bennett, H.Z. Peak performance: mental training techniques of the world's greatest athletes. 1st ed. Los Angeles: J.P. Tarcher, c1984. 219 p.
NOTES: Includes index. Bibliography: p. 203-209.
LEVEL: I LANG: Eng ISBN: 0874772141 LC CARD: 84-000071 GV706.4 17318

Gray, J.J. Haring, M.J. Banks, N.M. Mental rehearsal for sport performance: exploring the relaxation-imagery paradigm. (Refs 24)*Journal of sport behavior (Mobile, Ala.) 7(2), Jun 1984, 68-78.*
ABST: Although practitioners in sport psychology commonly employ relaxation training and covert mental rehearsal as primary interventions to assist athletic performance, the interaction of these procedures remains relatively unexplored. The purpose of this exploratory study was to investigate the effects of preparatory arousal manipulation (relaxation, arousal induction, or control), and two rehearsal strategy factors (physically active vs. sedentary; coping vs. mastery) on: (a) physiological arousal, (b) self-reported state anxiety, (c) imagery vividness and controllability, and (d) personal efficacy expectations for future (actual) sport performance. A single subject (college varsity football player) participated in the study. In preparation for a bowl game, three sessions were conducted, one for each arousal condition. It was found that physiological arousal increased during mental rehearsal for all sessions. Arousal induction and control sessions were associated with higher ratings of imagery vividness and increased efficacy expectations compared to the relaxation session. Implications regarding the appropriateness of inducing relaxation prior to conducting mental rehearsal for activities requiring heightened arousal levels are discussed. Considerations regarding procedural strategies are also addressed.
LEVEL: A LANG: Eng SIRC ARTICLE NO: 099285

Hale, B. No sweat practice: mental imagery. *Rugby (New York) 10(4), Jul 1984, 29.*
LEVEL: B LANG: Eng SIRC ARTICLE NO: 097783

Heyman, S.R. Cognitive interventions: theories, applications, and cautions. (Refs: 74)*In, Straub, W.F. and Williams, J.M. (eds.), Cognitive sport psychology, Lansing, N.Y., Sport Science Associates, c1984, p. 289-303.*
LEVEL: A LANG: Eng GV706.4 20099

Kiester, E. The playing fields of the mind. Our Olympic hopefuls look to psychology for the winning edge. *Psychology today (New York, N.Y.) 18(7), Jul 1984, 18-24.*
ABST: This article examines what is being done in the United States to fine tune the mental state of elite athletes for international competition. It is a general overview of the various methods being employed such as positive feedback, goal-setting, visualization, imagery, relaxation and self-hypnosis. The focus is on sport psychologists such as Robert Nideffer of San Diego who consult with elite athletes at special training camps or elsewhere in order to evaluate and improve the athlete's mental preparation.
LEVEL: B LANG: Eng SIRC ARTICLE NO: 094651

Kirschenbaum, D.S. Bale, R.M. Cognitive - behavioral skills in sports. Application to golf and speculations about soccer. (Refs: 45)*In, Straub, W.F. and Williams, J.M. (eds.), Cognitive sport psychology, Lansing, N.Y., Sport Science Associates, c1984, p. 275-288.*
NOTES: Version of this paper presented at the International Symposium on Sports Psychology, University of Nuevo Leon, Monterrey, Mexico, July 27, 1978.
LEVEL: A LANG: Eng GV706.4 20099

Krebs, P. Hoffpauir, D. Mind and body as one in athletic performance. (Refs: 8)*Coaching clinic 22(7), Mar 1984, 12-14.*
LEVEL: B LANG: Eng SIRC ARTICLE NO: 093151

Krecklow, D. Hartfield, D.J. Visualization motivation. *Coaching clinic 22(7), Mar 1984, 15-16.*
LEVEL: B LANG: Eng SIRC ARTICLE NO: 093152

Mahoney, M.J. Cognitive skills and athletic performance. (Refs: 61)*In, Straub, W.F. and Williams, J.M. (eds.), Cognitive sport psychology, Lansing, N.Y., Sport Science Associates, c1984, p. 11-27.*
LEVEL: A LANG: Eng GV706.4 20099

Meaney, P.H. The use of mental rehearsal in sport. (Refs: 14)*Sports coach (Wembley, Aust.) 8(1), 1984, 3-6.*
ABST: Mental training should be viewed as another useful training method which can further aid in the preparation of the athlete for competitive performance. Examples of successful athletes who have employed these techniques are detailed. The author also delineates the main theoretical

explanations for the functioning of mental rehearsal. This article is particularly good in focusing on what exactly mental rehearsal is and how the coach can develop its use for the maximum benefit of the athlete.
LEVEL: I LANG: Eng SIRC ARTICLE NO: 096333

Miller, B. Mental preparation and performance enhancement in sport. (Refs: 5)*Hockey field (Truro, Eng.) 71(8), 28 Apr 1984, 204-205.*
LEVEL: B LANG: Eng SIRC ARTICLE NO: 099291

Morgan, W.P. Mind over matter. (Refs: 8)*In, Straub, W.F. and Williams, J.M. (eds.), Cognitive sport psychology, Lansing, N.Y., Sport Science Associates, c1984, p. 311-316.*
LEVEL: A LANG: Eng GV706.4 20099

Nelson, M.B. Mental workout: what you see is what you get. *Women's sports (Palo Alto, Calif.) 6(5), May 1984, 22-25.*
LEVEL: B LANG: Eng SIRC ARTICLE NO: 099292

Nelson, M.B. Mental training. *Women's sport and fitness (Palo Alto, Calif.) 6(8), Aug 1984, 40-41.*
LEVEL: B LANG: Eng SIR ARTICLE NO: 100942

Ogilvie, B. Mastering mental moves. (mental training) *Women's sports (San Francisco) 6(6), Jun 1984, 56-57.*
LEVEL: B LANG Eng SIRC ARTICLE NO: 104415

Ostermann, G. Talmud, J. Relaxation and the practice of sport. (Refs: 9)*Olympic review (Lausanne) 206, Dec 1984, 981-985.*
LEVEL: B LANG: Eng SIRC ARTICLE NO: 105514

Rushall, B.S. The content of competition thinkings. (Refs: 49)*In, Straub, W.F. and Williams, J.M. (eds.), Cognitive sport psychology, Lansing, N.Y., Sport Science Associates, c1984, p. 51-62.*
LEVEL: A LANG: Eng GV706.4 20099

Smith, C. The inner race for excellence. Psychologists take a key role in helping Canada's athletes attain calmness and a bevy of medals. *Globe and mail 141(41,894), 15 Mar 1984, 18.*
LEVEL: B LANG: Eng SIRC ARTICLE NO: 091809

Surgent, F.C. A summary of familiar mental imagery programs as they relate to sport and physical activity. (Refs: 8)*Coachin clinic (Princeton, N.J.) 23(4), Dec 1984, 11-15.*
LEVEL: I LANG: Eng SIRC ARTICLE NO: 102869

Syer, J. Connolly, C. Sporting body sporting mind: an athlete's guide to mental training. Cambridge: Cambridge University Press, c1984. 160 p. : ill.
LEVEL: I LANG: Eng ISBN: 0-521-26935-0 LC CARD: 84-004946 GV706.4 17768

Tabor, J. The new psych. Training is a complex equation. The body's capacities are limited, the environment is beyond control. The new frontier is the mind. *Ultrasport (Boston) 1(4), Jul/Aug 1984, 72-77.*
LEVEL: B LANG: Eng SIRC ARTICLE NO: 097792

Thill, E. La preparation psychologique des athletes. *Revue de l'Amicale des entraineurs francais d'athletisme (Paris) 86, janv/fevr/mars 1984, 17-19.*
LEVEL: B LANG: Fr SIRC ARTICLE NO: 094667

Weinberg, R.S. Mental preparation strategies. NOTES: In, Silva, J.M. and Weinberg, R.S. (eds.), Psychological foundations o sport, Champaign, Ill., Human Kinetics Publishers, c1984, p. 145-156.
LEVEL: A LANG: Eng GV706.4 17779

Wilkes, R.L. Summers, J.J. Cognitions, mediating variables, and strength performance. (Refs: 15)*Journal of sport psychology (Champaign, Ill.) 6(3), 1984, 351-359.*
ABST: The effectiveness of five types of cognitive preparation on strength performance was examined in a 2 x 5 (Pre- and Posttest x Mental Preparation Condition) design. The mental preparation conditions were: arousal, attention, imagery, self-efficacy, and a control read condition. The results showed that preparatory arousal and self-efficacy techniques produced significantly greater posttest strength performance than the control group. It was concluded that the effectiveness of a particular cognitive strategy may depend on the nature of the task to be performed and the particular aspects of the task to which attention is directed.
LEVEL: A LANG: Eng SIRC ARTICLE NO: 102875

Zimmer, J. Mental gymnastics: in a real workout, your brain shouldn't come to a standstill. *Health (New York) 16(8), Aug 1984, 50-53.*
LEVEL: B LANG: Eng SIRC ARTICLE NO: 102877

MOTIVATION

Byrne, A.T. The effect of competition on intrinsic motivation. Urbana, Ill.: University of Illinois, 1984. 1v.
NOTES: Thesi (M.S.) - University of Illinois.
LEVEL: A LANG: Eng

Carron, A.V. Motivation: implications for coaching and teaching. London, Ont.: Sports Dynamics, c1984. vi, 191 p.
NOTES: Includes bibliographies.
LEVEL: B LANG: Eng ISBN: 0-9691619-0-5 LC CARD: C84-098180-5 GV706.4 17217

Dishman, R.K. Qu'est-ce qui motive les gens a etre actifs? (Refs: 36)
NOTES: Dans, Lagarde, F. (ed.), Sante et activite physique, Longueuil, Que., College Edouard-Montpetit, c1984, p. 83-96.
LEVEL: I LANG: Fr GV481 17104

Dishman, R.K. Motivation and exercise adherence. NOTES: In, Silva, J.M. and Weinberg, R.S. (eds.), Psychological foundation of sport, Champaign, Ill., Human Kinetics Publishers, c1984, p. 420-434.
LEVEL: I LANG: Eng GV706.4 17779

Duff, S. A comparison of motivational differences between the sexes with respect to participation and performance in sportin activities. *Carnegie research papers (Beckett Park, Leeds) 1(6), Dec 1984, 32-33.*
CONF: Carnegie Undergraduate Research Symposium (1984 : Leeds, Eng.).
LEVEL: I LANG: Eng SIRC ARTICLE NO: 172509

Gould, D. Horn, T. Participation motivation in young athletes.
NOTES: In, Silva, J.M. and Weinberg, R.S. (eds.), Psychological foundations of sport, Champaign, Ill., Human Kinetics Publishers, c1984, p. 359-370.
LEVEL: A LANG: Eng GV706.4 17779

Roberts, G.C. Toward a new theory of motivation in sport: the role of perceived ability.
NOTES: In, Silva, J.M. and Weinberg, R.S. (eds.), Psychological foundations of sport, Champaign, Ill., Human Kinetics Publishers, c1984, p. 214-228.
LEVEL: A LANG: Eng GV706.4 17779

Ruskin, H. Shamir, B. Motivation as a factor affecting males participation in physical activity during leisure time. (Refs: 29)*Loisir & societe/ Society and leisure (Trois-Rivieres, Que.) 7(1), printemps 1984, 141-161.*
ABST: 482 males, aged between 22 and 46, were surveyed on the motivational factors affecting their participation to physical activity during leisure time. Subjects were presented a list of 33 sport activities. The most important motivational factors were 1) physical activity as supplying tension and excitement; 2) physical activity as supplying and facilitating relaxation, release and an inner feeling of psychological well-being; and 3) physical fitness as improving health, physical fitness and physical appearance.
LEVEL: A LANG: Eng SIRC ARTICLE NO: 100946

Ryan, R.M. Vallerand, R.J. Deci, E.L. Intrinsic motivation in sport: a cognitive evaluation theory interpretation. (Refs: 49 In, Straub, W.F. and Williams, J.M. (eds.), Cognitive sport psychology, Lansing, N.Y., Sport Science Associates, c1984, p. 231-242.
LEVEL: A LANG: Eng GV706.4 20099

Silvennoinen, M. On leisure-time physical activity, participation in sports clubs, and motives for physical activity interests among Finnish school children - some aspects of the development of the research on children's motivation for sport. (Refs: 8)*In, Idrett for barn. Sport for Children. Sport pour les enfants 27.9.-1.10.1982 Tonsberg, Norway. Report. Oslo, Norway, Ministry of Cultural and Scientific Affairs: Norwegian Confederation of Sport, 1984, p. (46)-(48).*
CONF: Idrett for barn. Sport for Children. Sport pour les enfants (1982 : Tonsberg, Norway).
LEVEL: A LANG: Eng GV709.2 20111

Silvennoinen, M. Les activites physiques de loisir, la participation aux clubs sportifs et les raisons de l'interet pour les activites physiques chez les ecoliers finlandais; quelques aspects de la recherche sur les motivations des enfants pour le sport. (Refs: 8)*Dans, Idrett for barn. Sport for Children. Sport pour les enfants 27.9.-1.10.1982 Tonsberg, Norway. Rapport. Oslo, Norvege, Ministere de la culture et de la science : Confederation norvegienne des sports, 1984, p. (52)-(55).*
CONF: Idrett for barn. Sport for Children. Sport pour les enfants (1982 : Tonsberg, Norway).
LEVEL: A LANG: Fr GV709.2 20112

Singer, R.N. Sustaining motivation in sport. Tallahassee, Fla.: Sport Consultants International, c1984. iii, 104 p. : ill. (Youth in sport, psychological considerations.)
NOTES: Bibliography: p. 103-104.
LEVEL: B LANG: Eng ISBN: 0-915503-00-X LC CARD: 83-051213 GV706.4 18953

Watson, G.G. Intrinsic motivation and competitive anxiety in sport: some guidelines for coaches and administrators. (Refs: 3 *Australian journal of science & medicine in sport (Kingston, Aust.) 16(4), Dec 1984, 14-20.*
ABST: In this paper the relationship between intrinsic motivation and the competitive process is examined. When the evaluative influence of competition is perceived as a potential source of interference in the flow of motivated behaviour, stress and psychological conflict then become the inevitable outcome. To examine this basic proposition several theories of play and intrinsic motivation are examined, in terms of the impact of the influence of competition, to identify those conditions under which stress is likely to eventuate.

PSYCHOLOGY (continued)

A number of clinical procedures are then identified which may be appropriate in the management of stress resulting from a breakdown in the competitive process.
LEVEL: A LANG: Eng SIRC ARTICLE NO: 105521

Weinberg, R.S. The relationship between extrinsic rewards and intrinsic motivation in sport.
NOTES: In, Silva, J.M. and Weinberg, R.S. (eds.), Psychological foundations of sport, Champaign, Ill., Human Kinetics Publishers, c1984, p. 177-187.
LEVEL: A LANG: Eng GV706.4 17779

Weissinger, E. Iso-Ahola, S.E. Intrinsic leisure motivation, personality and physical health. (Refs: 25)*Loisir & societe/Society and leisure (Trois-Rivieres, Que.) 7(1), printemps 1984, 217-228.*
LEVEL: I LANG: Eng SIRC ARTICLE NO: 100951

Yukelson, D.P. Group motivation in sport teams.
NOTES: In, Silva, J.M. and Weinberg, R.S. (eds.), Psychological foundations of sport, Champaign, Ill., Human Kinetics Publishers, c1984, p. 229-240.
LEVEL: A LANG: Eng GV706.4 17779

PEAKING AND PEAK EXPERIENCE

Bompa, T. Peaking for the major competition(s). Part one. (Refs: 5)*Sports: science periodical on research and technology in sport (Ottawa) W-1, Apr 1984, 1-6.*
ABST: The author discusses the three levels of training i.e. degree of training, athletic shape and peaking, and the following factors that affect peaking: high working potential and quick rate of recovery, neuro-muscular coordination, unloading, overcompensation, recovery, motivation, arousal and psychological relaxation, and nerve cell working capacity.
LEVEL: I LANG: Eng SIRC ARTICLE NO: 093139

Bompa, T. Peaking for the major competition(s). Part two. *Sports: science periodical on research and technology in sport (Ottawa) W-1, May 1984, 1-6.*
ABST: In this article, the author explains how to plan and select competitions so as to enhance proper peaking at the proper time. Methods of identifying peaking, coach/athlete relationship in peaking, duration of peaking and factors which might adversely affect peaking are also discussed.
LEVEL: I LANG: Eng SIRC ARTICLE NO: 093140

Bompa, T. Pour atteindre la forme sportive optimale. Deuxieme partie. (Refs: 5)*Science du sport: documents de recherche et de technologie (Ottawa, Ont.) W-1, juin 1984, 1-6.*
LEVEL: I LANG: Fr SIRC ARTICLE NO: 094639

Bompa, T. Pour atteindre la forme sportive optimale. Premiere partie. (Refs: 7)*Science du sport: documents de recherche et de technologie (Ottawa) W-1, avr 1984, 1-6.*
LEVEL: I LANG: Fr SIRC ARTICLE NO: 094640

Ravizza, K. Qualities of the peak experience in sport.
NOTES: In, Silva, J.M. and Weinberg, R.S. (eds.), Psychological foundations of sport, Champaign, Ill., Human Kinetics Publishers, c1984, p. 452-461.
LEVEL: A LANG: Eng GV706.4 17779

PERSONALITY

Amusa, L.O. Udoh, C.O. Multivariate personality profile analysis of athletes and nonathletes. (Refs: 20)*Snipes journal (Patiala, India) 7(3), Jul 1984, 12-18.*

ABST: This study compares the personality traits of 160 athletes and non-athletes using the Cattell 16 Personality Factor Test. Results show significant differences between male and female subjects as well as between athletes and non-athletes.
LEVEL: A LANG: Eng SIRC ARTICLE NO: 099279

Bhullar, J. Personality factors as correlates of attitudes toward physical activity. (Refs: 5)*Snipes journal (Patiala, India) 7(3), Jul 1984, 30-35.*
ABST: The author researched the relationship between personality factors and attitudes toward physical activity. A sample of 100 male post-graduate students served as subjects. Data were obtained through the Cattell's Sixteen Personality Questionnaire and a 70-item attitude scale (known as Pa-as) toward physical activity. Significant correlations were observed between three personality factors (reserved/outgoing, placid/apprehensive, and undisciplined self conflict/controlled) and three sub-domains of attitude (ascetic experience, social experience, and ascetic experience) respectively.
LEVEL: A LANG: Eng SIRC ARTICLE NO: 099281

Fisher, A.C. New directions in sport personality research.
NOTES: In, Silva, J.M. and Weinberg, R.S. (eds.), Psychological foundations of sport, Champaign, Ill., Human Kinetics Publishers, c1984, p. 70-80.
LEVEL: I LANG: Eng GV706.4 17779

Kirkcaldy, B.D. Individual differences in time estimation. (Refs: 25)*International journal of sport psychology (Rome) 15(1) 1984, 11-24.*
ABST: This article examines the relationship between personality and time estimation. 105 subjects (61 females and 44 males) were involved in the investigation. The time of the day of test administration was noted. Findings indicate that psychoticism and time estimates were negatively correlated. Greater negative time errors and variation in time estimation were observed among extroverts than among introverts. Accurate estimators were less extroverted and neurotic than under- and over-estimators. Time of day did not influence time estimation.
LEVEL: A LANG: Eng SIRC ARTICLE NO: 094653

Krebs, P. Hoffpauir, D. Mind and body as one in athletic performance. (Refs: 8)*Coaching clinic 22(7), Mar 1984, 12-14.*
LEVEL: B LANG: Eng SIRC ARTICLE NO: 093151

Missoum, G. Laforestrie, R. Psychologie du sport, approche des mecanismes psychologiques lies a la detection des jeunes sportifs et a l'optimisation des performances. (Refs: 14)*Bulletin de psychologie (France) 37(364), 1984, 347-357.*
LEVEL: A LANG: Fr

Silva, J.M. Personality and sport performance: controversy and challenge.
NOTES: In, Silva, J.M. and Weinberg, R.S. (eds.), Psychological foundations of sport, Champaign, Ill., Human Kinetics Publishers, c1984, p. 59-69.
LEVEL: I LANG: Eng GV706.4 17779

Sothmann, M.S. Ismail, A.H. Chodepkozajiko, W. Influence of catecholamine activity on the hierarchical relationships among physical fitness condition and selected personality characteristics. (Refs: 24)*Journal of clinical psychology (Brandon, Vt.) 40(6), 1984, 1308-1317.*
LEVEL: A LANG: Eng SIRC ARTICLE NO: 104264

Tucker, L.A. Trait psychology and performance: a credulous viewpoint. (Refs: 38)*Journal of human

movement studies (Edinburgh) 10(1), 1984, 53-62*
ABST: This study investigated the relationship between personality and performance during a four-month weight training program. The results indicate that a significant proportion of performance in a weight training program can be explained by measures of extraversion, neuroticism, body cathexis and self-concept. These results support the assumption that physical performance is a function of selected psychological traits.
LEVEL: A LANG: Eng SIRC ARTICLE NO: 094786

Tzeng, S.-L. Wang, T.-M. Investigation of personality traits in male and female athletes in National Taiwan University. *Asian journal of physical education (Taipei, Taiwan) 7(3), Oct 1984, 62-63.*
LEVEL: I LANG: Eng Chi SIRC ARTICLE NO: 102872

PERSONALITY TESTING

Miller, B.P. Edgington, G.P. Psychological mood state distortion in a sporting context. (Refs: 9)*Journal of sport behavior (Mobile, Ala.) 7(3), Sept 1984, 91-94.*
ABST: Undergraduate students (24) completed the Profile of Mood States (POMS) questionnaire on two separate occasions. They were asked to respond as naturally as possible on one occasion, and one week later they were asked to imagine that they were elite athletes who suspected that data from this questionnaire would be a contributing factor in team selection. Results indicated that there were significant differences between results obtained on the two occasions for Vigour, Depression, Fatigue and Confusion dimensions. Subjects were able to 'fake good' and present themselves in a favourable light. It was concluded that the POMS is a 'transparent' questionnaire and should be used in a limited context only.
LEVEL: A LANG: Eng SIRC ARTICLE NO: 100940

PSYCHOTHERAPY

Stanton, H. 'When all else fails, try this'. (Refs: 16)*Sports coach (Wembley, W. Aust.) 8(2), Oct 1984, 26-28.*
LEVEL: B LANG: Eng SIRC ARTICLE NO: 104421

RELAXATION

Benson, H. The relaxation response and stress. (Refs: 70)*In, Matarazzo, J.D. (ed.) et al., Behavioral health: a handbook of health enhancement and disease prevention, New York, Wiley, c1984, p. 326-337.*
LEVEL: I LANG: Eng

Ostermann, G. Talmud, J. Relaxation et pratique sportive. (Refs: 9)*Revue olympique (Lausanne) 206, dec 1984, 981-985.*
LEVEL: B LANG: Fr SIRC ARTICLE NO: 105515

Sullivan, S. City fitness: think tank. (sensory deprivation) *Running news (New York) 29(5), Jun/Jul 1984, 20.*
LEVEL: B LANG: Eng SIRC ARTICLE NO: 097791

RESEARCH

Silva, J.M. The emergence of applied sport psychology contemporary trends - future issues. (Refs: 35)*International journal of sport psychology (Rome) 15(1), 1984, 40-51.*
LEVEL: I LANG: Eng SIRC ARTICLE NO: 094662

RESEARCH METHODS

Bar-Eli, M. Zur Diagnostik individueller psychischer Krisen im sportlichen Wettkampf: eine wahrscheinlichkeitsorientierte, theoretische und empirische Studie unter besonderer Beruecksichtigung des Basketballspiels. Koeln: Deutsche Sporthochschule, Psychologisches Institut, 1984. viii, 366 p.
NOTES: Thesis (Ph.D.) - Deutsche Sporthochschule Koeln, 1984. Bibliography: p. 306-343.
LEVEL: A LANG: Ger GV706.4 17550

Wood, T.M. Safrit, M.J. A model for estimating the reliability of psychomotor test batteries. (Refs: 27)*Research quarterly for exercise & sport (Reston, Va.) 55(1), Mar 1984, 53-63.*
ABST: This paper describes a proposed model for estimating test battery reliability based upon canonical correlation analysis (CAA). Descriptive statistics from previous investigations and nonempirical data are used to exemplify the procedure. The authors conclude that when the restrictions regarding the use of CCA are observed, CCA is a variable statistical technique for determining the test retest reliability of psychomotor test batteries. The technique lends itself to subtest by subtest analysis and ease of interpretation.
LEVEL: A LANG: Eng SIRC ARTICLE NO: 096347

SELF CONCEPT

Feltz, D.L. Self-efficacy as a cognitive mediator of athletic performance. (Refs: 35)*In, Straub, W.F. and Williams, J.M. (eds.), Cognitive sport psychology, Lansing, N.Y., Sport Science Associates, c1984, p. 191-198.*
LEVEL: A LANG: Eng GV706.4 20099

Rhodewalt, F. Saltzman, A.T. Wittner, J. Self-handicapping among competitive athletes - the role of practice in self-esteem protection. (Refs: 11)*Basic and applied social psychology (Hillsdale, N.J.) 5(3), 1984, 197-209.*
LEVEL: A LANG: Eng SIRC ARTICLE NO: 099295

Shewchuk, R.M. Self-concept and physical performance of preadolescent children: a causal analysis. Eugene, Ore.: Microform Publications, University of Oregon, 1984. 2 microfiches : negative, ill. ; 11 x 15 cm.
NOTES: Thesis (Ph.D.) - University of Oregon, 1983; (xi, 125 leaves); vita; includes bibliography.
LEVEL: A LANG: Eng UO84 129-130

Sonstroem, R.J. Exercise and self-esteem. (Refs: 112)*Exercise and sport sciences reviews (Lexington, Mass.) 12, 1984, 123-155.*
ABST: The paper reviews the importance, structure and development of self-esteem. A rationale for the influence of exercise on self-esteem is presented. Sixteen studies which have stated or implied hypotheses of enhanced self-esteem from exercise training are included in this review.
Recommendations for future research are given.
LEVEL: A LANG: Eng SIRC ARTICLE NO: 096345

SEXUALITY

Tordjman, G. La sexualite est-elle incompatible avec le sport? *Generaliste (Paris) 637, 1984, 24-25.*
LEVEL: B LANG: Fr

SPECTATORS

Wankel, L. Audience effects in sport.
NOTES: In, Silva, J.M. and Weinberg, R.S. (eds.), Psychological foundations of sport, Champaign, Ill., Human Kinetics Publishers, c1984, p. 293-314.
LEVEL: A LANG: Eng GV706.4 17779

STRESS

Collins, D.J. Physological correlates of coping skills and their development through training. Eugene, Ore.: Microform Publications, University of Oregon, 1984. 1 microfiche : negative, ill. ; 11 x 15 cm.
NOTES: Thesis (M.S.) - Pennsylvania State University, 1982; (ix, 69 leaves); includes bibliography.
LEVEL: A LANG: Eng UO84 388

Cooper, C.L. Melhuish, A. Executive stress and health. Differences between men and women. *Journal of occupational medicine (Chicago) 26(2), Feb 1984, 99-104.*
LEVEL: A LANG: Eng SIRC ARTICLE NO: 100936

Eliot, R.S. Breo, D.L. Are you a hot reactor? Is it worth dying for? *Executive health (Santa Fe, Calif.) 20(10), Jul 1984, 1-4.*
LEVEL: I LANG: Eng SIRC ARTICLE NO: 096322

Feigley, D.A. Psychological burnout in high-level athletes. (Refs: 9)*Physician and sportsmedicine (Minneapolis, Minn.) 12(10), Oct 1984, 108-112;115-119.*
LEVEL: I LANG: Eng SIRC ARTICLE NO: 099284

Feigley, D.A. Psychological burnout in high-level athletes. (Refs: 9)*Swimming technique (Inglewood, Calif.) 21(3), Nov 1984/Jan 1985, 19-24.*
LEVEL: I LANG: Eng SIRC ARTICLE NO: 102849

Fort, I.L. The acute response of high-density lipoproteins and psychological stress to aerobic exercise. Eugene, Ore.: Microform Publications, University of Oregon, 1984. 1 microfiche : negative ; 11 x 15 cm.
NOTES: Thesis (Ed.D.) - University of Arkansas, 1982; (vii, 80 leaves); includes bibliography.
LEVEL: A LANG: Eng UO84 171

Franks, B.D. Physical activity and stress: part 1. Acute effects. *International journal of physical education (Schorndorf, FRG) 21(4), 1984, 9-12.*
LEVEL: I LANG: Eng SIRC ARTICLE NO: 105506

Franks, B.D. Physical activity and stress: part 2. Chronic effects. *International journal of physical education (Schorndorf FRG) 21(4), 1984, 13-16.*
LEVEL: I LANG: Eng SIRC ARTICLE NO: 105507

Georges, G. L'anxiete en milieu sportif. (Refs: 11)*Revue de l'education physique (Liege, Belgique) 24(1), 1984, 17-20.*
LEVEL: B LANG: Fr SIRC ARTICLE NO: 096324

Howard, J.H. Cunningham, D.A. Rechnitzer, P.A. Physical activity as a moderator of life events and somatic complaints: a longitudinal study. (Refs: 61)*Canadian journal of applied sport sciences/ Journal canadien des sciences appliquees au sport (Windsor, Ont.) 9(4), Dec 1984, 194-200.*
ABST: The study was longitudinal involving 278 managers from 12 different corporations. All participants were men. Data have been collected at entry, two years later, and four years later. This provides two test periods in which the data are analysed. Analyses are by way of multiple regression and in both time periods the change data support the hypothesis that somatic complaints are significantly related to both life events and physical activity. The results also show that physical activity has a significant buffering effect on the relationship between life events and somatic complaints.
LEVEL: A LANG: Eng SIRC ARTICLE NO: 102854

Keller, S. Seraganian, P. Physical fitness level and autonomic reactivity to psychosocial stress. *Journal of psychosomatic research (Oxford) 28(4), 1984, 279-287.*
LEVEL: A LANG: Eng

Oglivie, B.C. Howe, M.A. Beating slumps at their own game. Well-tested psychological techniques help athletes end the dreade 'prolonged performance decrement'. *Psychology today (New York, N.Y.) 18(7), Jul 1984, 28-32.*
LEVEL: B LANG: Eng SIRC ARTICLE NO: 094658

Ostermann, G. Talmud, J. Relaxation et pratique sportive. (Refs: 9)*Est-medecine (France) 4(67), 1984, 383-387.*
LEVEL: B LANG: Fr

Scanlan, T.K. Competitive stress and the child athlete.
NOTES: In, Silva, J.M. and Weinberg, R.S. (eds.), Psychological foundations of sport, Champaign, Ill., Human Kinetics Publishers, c1984, p. 118-129.
LEVEL: A LANG: Eng GV706.4 17779

Siegl, P. Schultz, K. Die Borg-Skale als Instrument zur Erfassung subjektiv erlebter Beanspruchung in arbeitsmedizinischen Labor- und Felduntersuchungen. (The Borg Scale as an instrument for the detection of subjectively experienced stress in industrial medicine laboratory and field studies.) *Zeitschrift fuer die gesamte Hygiene undihre Grenzgebiete (Berlin) 30(7), Jul 1984, 383-386.*
LEVEL: A LANG: Ger

Smith, R.E. The dynamics and prevention of stress-induced burnout in athletics. (Refs: 10)*Primary care: clinics in office practice (Philadelphia) 11(1), Mar 1984, 115-127.*
LEVEL: I LANG: Eng SIRC ARTICLE NO: 100949

Sothmann, M.S. Ismail, A.H. Chodepko-Zajiko, W. Influence of catecholamine activity on the hierarchical relationships among physical fitness condition and selected personality characteristics. *Journal of clinical psychology (Brandon, Va.) 40(6), Nov 1984, 1308-1317.*
LEVEL: A LANG: Eng

Stavitskii, K.R. Gosudarev, N.A. Metody kontrolia psikhicheskoi rabotosposobnosti i emotsional'noi aktivnosti. (Methods of monitoring psychological work capacity and emotional activity.) *Gigiena i sanitariia (Moscow) 11, Nov 1984, 48-49.*
LEVEL: I LANG: Rus

van den Eynde, E. Stress and pre-race nerves. *Track and field quarterly review (Kalamazoo, Mich.) 84(3), Fall 1984, 29-30.*
NOTES: Translated by, Robin Sykes.
LEVEL: B LANG: Eng SIRC ARTICLE NO: 096346

SUCCESS

Ogilvie, B. Psychology: the press of success. *Women's sports and fitness (Palo Alto, Calif.) 6(7), Jul 1984, 16;18.*
LEVEL B LANG: Eng SIRC ARTICLE NO: 100944

PSYCHOLOGY (continued)

TEACHING

Edwards, S.W. Huston, S.A. The clinical aspects of sport psychology. (Refs: 8)*Physical educator (Indianapolis, Ind.) 3(41), Oct 1984, 142-148.*
LEVEL: I LANG: Eng SIRC ARTICLE NO: 100937

Horn, T.S. The expectancy process: causes and consequences. (Refs: 50)*In, Straub, W.F. and Williams, J.M. (eds.), Cognitive sport psychology, Lansing, N.Y., Sport Science Associates, c1984, p. 199-211.*
LEVEL: A LANG: Eng GV706.4 20099

TESTING AND EVALUATION

Adair, J.D. Construction and validation of an instrument designed to assess states of consciousness during movement activity Eugene, Ore.: Microform Publications, University of Oregon, 1984. 3 microfiches : negative, ill. ; 11 x 15 cm. NOTES: Thesis (Ph.D.) - Temple University, 1982; (xi, 222 leaves); includes bibliography.
LEVEL: A LANG: Eng UO84 281-283

Bird, A.M. Ross, D. Current methodological problems and future directions for theory development in the psychology of sport and motor behavior. (Refs: 19)*Quest (Champaign, Ill.) 36(1), 1984, 1-6.*
LEVEL: I LANG: Eng SIRC ARTICLE NO: 099282

Crampton, J. The use of micro-computers in applied sport psychology. *Sports sciences & medicine quarterly (Australia) 1(2), Oct 1984, 5-7.*
LEVEL: B LANG: Eng SIRC ARTICLE NO: 102847

Khan, H.A. Utility of psychological assessment in selection of top level sportsmen and sportswomen. *Snipes journal (Patiala India) 7(3), Jul 1984, 21-25.*
LEVEL: I LANG: Eng SIRC ARTICLE NO: 099288

Miller, B.P. Edgington, G.P. Psychological mood state distortion in a sporting context. (Refs: 9)*Journal of sport behavior (Mobile, Ala.) 7(3), Sept 1984, 91-94.*
ABST: Undergraduate students (24) completed the Profile of Mood States (POMS) questionnaire on two separate occasions. They were asked to respond as naturally as possible on one occasion, and one week later they were asked to imagine that they were elite athletes who suspected that data from this questionnaire would be a contributing factor in team selection. Results indicated that there were significant differences between results obtained on the two occasions for Vigour, Depression, Fatigue and Confusion dimensions. Subjects were able to 'fake good' and present themselves in a favourable light. It was concluded that the POMS is a 'transparent' questionnaire and should be used in a limited context only.
LEVEL: A LANG: Eng SIRC ARTICLE NO: 100940

WINNING

Segal, E. To win or die: a taxonomy of sporting attitudes. (Refs: 29)*Journal of sport history (University Park, Pa.) 11(2), Summer 1984, 25-31.*
LEVEL: I LANG: Eng SIRC ARTICLE NO: 099298

PSYCHOPHYSIOLOGY

Brown, B.S. Daniel, M. Gorman, D.R. Visual feedback and strength improvement. (Refs: 10)*National Strength & Conditioning Association journal 6(1), Feb/Mar 1984, 22-24.*
ABST: Strength improvement of a control group and two experimental groups of young men, 18-25 years of age, was assessed in this study. The first experimental group performed a static leg squat exercise for one repetition per day, five days per week, for five weeks. The second experimental group performed the same exercise with the following exceptions: 1) a force meter displaying the amount of effort was in direct view of the subjects, 2) subjects were required to maintain a force equal to, or greater than, 75% of their maximum efforts. The greatest gain was observed in the second group with a 98.6% increase in strength.
LEVEL: A LANG: Eng SIRC ARTICLE NO: 093070

Hull, E.M. Young, S.H. Ziegler, M.G. Aerobic fitness affects cardiovascular and catecholamine responses to stressors. *Psychophysiology (Madison, Wisc.) 21(3), May 1984, 353-360.*
LEVEL: I LANG: Eng SIRC ARTICLE NO: 102855

Offenloch, K. Vigilanz und Motorik. (Vigilance and motor activity.) *EEG/EMG (Stuttgart) 15(4), Dec 1984, 203-205.*
LEVEL: LANG: Ger

Sothmann, M.S. Ismail, A.H. Relationships between urinary catecholamine metabolites, particularly, MHPG, and selected personality and physical fitness characteristics in normal subjects. *Psychosomatic medicine (New York) 46(6), Nov/Dec 1984, 523-533.*
LEVEL: A LANG: Eng

Weingarten, G. Dlin, R.A. Karlsson, J. The relationship between state anxiety, muscularity and metabolic responses at the OBLA point. (Refs: 18)*International journal of sport psychology (Rome, Italy) 15(2), 1984, 110-116.*
ABST: The A-State scores of National Water Polo players, taken prior to needle muscle biopsy were related to musculature, blood pressure and metabolic responses. In the post hoc analysis some possible logical connections were found between subjective anxiety scores and several muscular measurements, autonomic reactivity (SBP) and aerobic efficiency at the onset of blood lactate accumulation (the OBLA point).
LEVEL: A LANG: Eng SIRC ARTICLE NO: 099303

RACE WALKING

Laird, R. Racewalking for fitness. *Winged foot (New York) 95(10), Oct 1984, 21-23;56.*
LEVEL: B LANG: Eng SIRC ARTICLE NO: 100031

Racewalking: the competitive sport whose time has come. *Executive fitness newsletter (Emmaus, Pa.) 15(24), 24 Nov 1984, 1-2..*
LEVEL: B LANG: Eng SIRC ARTICLE NO: 106122

BIOGRAPHY AND AUTOBIOGRAPHY

Ackermann-Blount, J. Great feats on foot: from humble beginnings walking for 18 straight hours on a high school track, Jesse Castaneda, here before Red Rock Cliff in New Mexico, has set world records and gained renown as a formidable perambulator. *Sports illustrated 60(13), 26 Mar 1984, 58-62;64;66;68-72.*
LEVEL: B LANG: Eng SIRC ARTICLE NO: 093866

BIOMECHANICS

Turblin, J. Oui pour le footing, non pour le jogging. *Revue de l'Amicale des entraineurs francais d'athletisme (Paris) 86, janv/fevr/mars 1984, 7;9.*
LEVEL: I LANG: Fr SIRC ARTICLE NO: 095471

PHYSIOLOGY

Davies, B. Shapiro, C.M. Daggett, A. Gatt, J.A. Jakeman, P. Physiological changes and sleep responses during and following a world record continuous walking record. (Refs: 42)*British journal of sports medicine (Loughborough, Eng.) 18(3), Sept 1984, 173-180.*
ABST: Physiological changes, and subsequent sleep responses, were recorded in a male subject during and following 338 miles of continuous walking and consequent sleep deprivation. The subject walked at approximately 55% of maximum oxygen update (VO2 max), heart rate ranged between 102-106 b/min, and blood lactate (LA) remained below the 2 mmol/l level. Creatine kinase (CK) and creatine kinase isoenzyme (CK-MB) levels rose throughout the walk. The ratio of CK-MB to CK (MB/CK%) did not exceed levels which are suggestive of myocardial ischaemia. Haematological variables demonstrated signs of anaemia towards the end of the walk. Catecholamine levels rose throughout the walk, with greater rises being observed in nor-adrenaline and dopamine. During the post-walk recovery phase, adrenaline concentration remained elevated. Following this extreme period of exertion, the subject demonstrated very short sleep latency and rapid entry into slow wave sleep (SWS).
LEVEL: A LANG: Eng SIRC ARTICLE NO: 103538

Galun, E. Epstein, Y. Serum creatine kinase activity following a 120-km march. *Clinica chimica acta (Amsterdam) 143(3), 30 Nov 1984, 281-283.*
LEVEL: A LANG: Eng

Guglielmini, C. Paolini, A.R. Conconi, F. Variations of serum testosterone concentrations after physical exercises of different duration. (Refs: 20)*International journal of sports medicine (Stuttgart) 5(5), Oct 1984, 246-249.*
ABST: Serum testosterone concentration was determined before and after physical activities of different duration. The subjects under study were: (1) 7 competitive walkers before and after a 20-km race; (2) 9 middle-distance runners before and after 1-h training; (3) 16 marathon runners before and after a marathon run; (4) 30 ultramarathon runners before and after a 107-km race. Serum testosterone increased by 51.8 per cent in competitive walkers, by 38.2 per cent in middle-distance runners, and by 44.9 per cent marathon runners: it decreased by 31.9 per cent in the ultramarathon runners.
LEVEL: A LANG: Eng SIRC ARTICLE NO: 104978

Hagberg, J.M. Coyle, E.F. Physiological comparison of competitive racewalking and running. (Refs: 16)*International journal of sports medicine (Stuttgart, FRG) 5(2), Apr 1984, 74-77.*
ABST: Eight competitive racewalkers were studied to determine a) the speed where running and racewalking become equally efficient, b) if, at a similar VO2, the physiologic responses to submaximal exercise differ between running and

racewalking, and c) if VO2 max can be attained during racewalking. The speed at which running and racewalking elicited the same VO2 was between 8 and 9 km.h-1. Racewalking was more efficient at slower speeds, and running was more efficient at faster velocities. When running and racewalking were compared at similar oxygen consumptions, heart rate, ventilation, perceived exertion, and respiratory exchange ratio responses were identical. During maximal exercise, running and racewalking resulted in a similar VO2 max, heart rate, ventilation and post-exercise blood lactic acid concentration. These results indicate that the speed where racewalking and running become equally efficient is similar to the crossover speed for conventional walking and running.
LEVEL: A LANG: Eng SIRC ARTICLE NO: 108521

RULES AND REGULATIONS

Jeudy, S. Marrone, N. Archambault, M. Faisons de la marche athletique. *Track and field journal (Ottawa, Ont.) 27, Aug 1984, 13-14.*
LEVEL: B LANG: Fr SIRC ARTICLE NO: 100030

McGuire, F. Food for thought on race walking rules. *Modern athlete and coach (Athelstone, Aust.) 22(1), Jan 1984, 37-39.*
LEVEL: B LANG: Eng SIRC ARTICLE NO: 096933

TECHNIQUES AND SKILLS

Fruktov, A. Ozerov, V. Korolyov, G. Technique and faults in race walking. *Modern athlete and coach (Athelstone, Aust.) 22(3), Jul 1984, 35-37.*
NOTES: Condensed translated from, Legkaya Atletika (Moscow) 1, 1983.
LEVEL: B LANG: Eng SIRC ARTICLE NO: 101623

Pollet, L.S. Racewalking: give it a shot, you may like it. *Scholastic coach (New York) 53(9), Apr 1984, 65-67.*
LEVEL: B LANG: Eng SIRC ARTICLE NO: 095381

RACQUET SPORTS

Special sports de raquette. *Marathon plus (Laval, Que.) 1(2), oct 1984, 27-30;35-37.*
LEVEL: B LANG: Fr SIRC ARTICLE NO: 173445

Zimmer, J. String quartet: whether you want to burn off calories - or steam - one of these four racquet sports is just made for you. *Health (New York) 16(9), Sept 1984, 48-50;52;67.*
LEVEL: B LANG: Eng SIRC ARTICLE NO: 101456

EQUIPMENT

Investigating the professional stringing machine. *Stringer's assistant (Del Mar, Calif.) 10(11), Nov 1984, 1-2;4;6;8.*
LEVEL B LANG: Eng SIRC ARTICLE NO: 107622

The do's & don'ts of racquet stringing. *Stringer's assistant (Del Mar, Calif.) 10(4), Apr 1984, 1;4-5.*
LEVEL: B LANG: Eng SIRC ARTICLE NO: 095173

PROTECTIVE DEVICES

Racquet-sport eyeguards: your eyes' shield against a speeding ball. *Executive fitness newsletter (Emmaus, Pa.) 15(11), 26 May 1984, 4.*
LEVEL: B LANG: Eng SIRC ARTICLE NO: 095174

VARIATIONS

McTavish, B. McTavish, R. Pickle ball. *OPHEA: Ontario Physical and Health Education Association (London, Ont.) 10(2), Sprin 1984, 21-25.*
LEVEL: B LANG: Eng SIRC ARTICLE NO: 099345

RACQUETBALL

Adams, L. Getting ready for a tournament match. *National racquetball (Glenview, Ill) 13(5), May 1984, 24-25.*
LEVEL: B LANG: Eng SIRC ARTICLE NO: 101457

Henkin, M. Racquetball primer. Washington, D.C.: National Press, c1984. 1v. (A full court press book.)
LEVEL: B LANG: Eng ISBN: 0915765039 LC CARD: 84-014883

Mills, J.H. How handball can help your racquetball game. *National racquetball (Glenview, Ill.) 13(7), Jul 1984, 19-21.*
LEVEL: B LANG: Eng SIRC ARTICLE NO: 103374

Mondry, S. 5 reasons a league will help your game. *National racquetball (Glenview, Ill.) 13(5), May 1984, 22-23.*
LEVEL: B LANG: Eng SIRC ARTICLE NO: 101462

ADMINISTRATION

Leve, C. Pro racquetball: the race for sponsorship. *National racquetball (Glenview, Ill.) 13(5), May 1984, 6-8.*
LEVEL: B LANG: Eng SIRC ARTICLE NO: 101461

Leve, M. Larry Lee: racquetball impresario. *National racquetball (Glenview, Ill.) 13(8), Aug 1984, 10-11.*
LEVEL: B LANG: Eng SIRC ARTICLE NO: 103373

Peterson, C. Programming the low level racquetball player. *Fitness industry (Miami, Fla.) 2(2), Mar/Apr 1984, 11-14.*
LEVEL: B LANG: Eng SIRC ARTICLE NO: 098409

ANTHROPOMETRY

Finn, J.A. Put your bathroom scale in its proper place. *National racquetball (Glenview, Ill.) 13(5), May 1984, 30-31.*
LEVEL: B LANG: Eng SIRC ARTICLE NO: 101459

BIOGRAPHY AND AUTOBIOGRAPHY

Robert MacDonald: this is no mistake. *National racquetball (Glenview, Ill.) 13(12), Dec 1984, 9-11.*
LEVEL: B LANG: Eng SIRC ARTICLE NO: 106014

Wilson, R. All in the family: famous racquetball families share their secrets of success. *Racquetball illustrated (Hollywood, Calif.) 7(1), Dec/Jan 1984, 10-15.*
LEVEL: B LANG: Eng SIRC ARTICLE NO: 099844

CERTIFICATION

Level 2 coaching certification program; course conductor manual. Ottawa: Canadian Racquetball Association, c1984. 96 leaves (National Coaching Certification Program.)
CORP: Canadian Racquetball Association.
NOTES: Cover title: Racquetball level 2 technical. Course conductor manual.
LEVEL: B LANG: Eng GV1003.34 17912

Ness, G. Coaching Certification Program level 2 racquetball coaching certification manual. (Ottawa): Canadian Racquetball Association, c1984. 1v. in various pagings (National Coaching Certification Program.)
CORP: Canadian Racquetball Association.
LEVEL: B LANG: Eng GV1003.34 18362

CLOTHING

Courting court apparel. *Fitness industry (Miami, Fla.) 2(1), Jan/Feb 1984, 16-17;19-20;22;24;26.*
LEVEL: B LANG: Eng SIRC ARTICLE NO: 097480

National Racquetball's annual shoe guide. *National racquetball (Glenview, Ill.) 13(10), Oct 1984, 8-9.*
LEVEL: B LANG: Eng SIRC ARTICLE NO: 106008

National racquetball's second annual guide: your exclusive one-step shopping list. (glove) *National racquetball (Glenview, Ill.) 13(5), May 1984, 10-13.*
LEVEL: B LANG: Eng SIRC ARTICLE NO: 100571

Reader survey results: what you told us about your shoes. *National racquetball (Glenview, Ill.) 13(10), Oct 1984, 12-13.*
LEVEL: B LANG: Eng SIRC ARTICLE NO: 106011

CLUBS

Leve, C. What ever happened to my racquetball club? *National racquetball (Glenview, Ill.) 13(9), Sept 1984, 16-18.*
LEVEL: LANG: Eng SIRC ARTICLE NO: 106003

Sauser, J. How to choose a club: get the most for your money. *National racquetball (Glenview, Ill.) 13(9), Sept 1984, 10-11*
LEVEL: B LANG: Eng SIRC ARTICLE NO: 106015

What you told us about your clubs. *National racquetball (Glenview, Ill.) 13(9), Sept 1984, 12-13.*
LEVEL: B LANG: Eng SIRC ARTICLE NO: 106017

COUNTRIES AND REGIONS

Interview: Al Walker. Important insights from the man who is pulling South American Racquetball up by its bootstraps. *International racquetball (Reno, Nevada) 2(10), Dec 1984, 32-33;36.*
LEVEL: B LANG: Eng SIRC ARTICLE NO: 107407

Sheftel, C. Racquetball the Japanese way. *National racquetball (Glenview, Ill.) 13(3), Mar 1984, 10-13.*
LEVEL: B LANG: En SIRC ARTICLE NO: 099841

DISABLED

Boberg, L.C. Sounds of silence: deaf racquetball. *National racquetball (Glenview, Ill.) 13(6), Jun 1984, 10-13.*
LEVEL: B LANG: Eng SIRC ARTICLE NO: 102443

EQUIPMENT

Foes, D. What you told us about your racquetball strings. *National racquetball (Glenview, Ill.) 13(6), Jun 1984, 34-35.*
LEVEL: B LANG: Eng SIRC ARTICLE NO: 103368

National racquetball's annual racquet guide: your one-stop comparison shopping list. *National racquetball (Glenview, Ill.) 13(8), Aug 1984, 16-20.*
LEVEL: B LANG: Eng SIRC ARTICLE NO: 103377

What you told us about your racquet. *National racquetball (Glenview, Ill.) 13(8), Aug 1984, 13-15.*
LEVEL: B LANG: Eng SIRC ARTICLE NO: 103384

RACQUETBALL (continued)

EQUIPMENT - MAINTENANCE

Daigle, R.J. 5 easy steps to a 'quickie' handle repair. *National racquetball (Glenview, Ill.) 13(2), Feb 1984, 26-27.*
LEVEL: B LANG: Eng SIRC ARTICLE NO: 099827

EQUIPMENT - RETAILING

Where is the racquetball market headed? *International racquetball (Reno, Nevada) 2(10), Dec 1984, 29-30.*
LEVEL: B LANG: Eng SIRC ARTICLE NO: 107420

FACILITIES

Haber, R. Portable glass: yes. *National racquetball (Glenview, Ill.) 13(6), Jun 1984, 44.*
LEVEL: B LANG: Eng SIRC ARTICLE NO: 103372

Planning and flexibility: the keys to multi-service success? *Recreation, sports & leisure (Minneapolis) 4(6), Aug 1984, 90;92-93.*
NOTES: Special issue: Managed recreation research report.
LEVEL: B LANG: Eng SIRC ARTICLE NO: 103938

Tekulsky, M. 20 x 40 x 20: in an age of fitness first, many players are building their own racquetball courts. *Racquetball illustrated (Hollywood, Calif.) 7(1), Dec/Jan 1984, 38-41.*
NOTES: Special home fitness section.
LEVEL: B LANG: Eng SIRC ARTICLE NO: 098974

HANDICAPPING

AARA adopts new ARHS ranking system. *National racquetball (Glenview, Ill.) 13(12), Dec 1984, 18-20.*
LEVEL: B LANG: Eng SIRC ARTICLE NO: 105996

INJURIES AND ACCIDENTS

Baum, G. Tennis elbow revisited. *National racquetball (Glenview, Ill.) 13(6), Jun 1984, 30-31.*
LEVEL: B LANG: Eng SIRC ARTICLE NO: 102493

Bayless, M.A. Racquetball. *In, Adams, S.H. (ed.), et al., Catastrophic injuries in sports: avoidance strategies, Salinas, Calif., Cayote Press, c1984, p. 64-69.*
LEVEL: B LANG: Eng RD97 19088

Easterbrook, M. Eye injuries in squash and racquetball players: an update. Blessures oculaires attribuables au squash et au racquetball. (Refs: 5)*Canadian Intramural Recreation Association/Association canadienne de loisirs-intramuros bulletin (Ottawa) 9(5), Feb/fevr 1984, 8-10.*
NOTES: Reprinted from, Campus Recreation, The Faculty of Physical Education, Winter 1984. Tire de, Campus Recreation, Faculte d'education physique, hiver 1984.
LEVEL: I LANG: Eng Fr SIRC ARTICLE NO: 099936

Sabet, D. A step in the right direction. Many players can avoid racquetball injuries by putting their best foot forward. *Racquetball illustrated (Burbank, Calif.) 7(2), Feb/Mar 1984, 19-21.*
LEVEL: B LANG: Eng SIRC ARTICLE NO: 095186

Trifunov, P. Racquetball injuries: a guide to available medical care. *National racquetball (Glenview, Ill.) 13(7), Jul 1984 28-29.*
LEVEL: B LANG: Eng SIRC ARTICLE NO: 103383

NUTRITION

Horn, G. Feeling fit with proper food. *National racquetball (Glenview, Ill.) 13(12), Dec 1984, 38-41.*
LEVEL: B LANG: Eng SIRC ARTICLE NO: 106001

OFFICIATING

Mondry, S. 5 tips to the first-time referee. *National racquetball (Glenview, Ill.) 13(6), Jun 1984, 22-23.*
LEVEL: B LANG: Eng SIRC ARTICLE NO: 103375

PHYSICAL FITNESS

Fitness testing with stationary bikes. *National racquetball (Glenview, Ill.) 13(11), Nov 1984, 40-42.*
LEVEL: B LANG: Eng SIRC ARTICLE NO: 109062

PHYSIOLOGY

Morgans, L.F. Scovil, J.A. Bass, K.M. Heart rate responses during singles and doubles competition in racquetball. (Refs: 20) *Physician and sportsmedicine (Minneapolis, Minn.) 12(11), Nov 1984, 64-68;71-72.*
ABST: This study focused on the heart rates (HR) of 15 male racquetball players, aged between 22 and 46, during singles and doubles matches. In singles, the average HR of subjects was 83% of the maximum heart rate reserve (MHRR). In doubles, the average HR was 67% of the MHRR.
LEVEL: A LANG: Eng SIRC ARTICLE NO: 101463

Stoke, S.A. A comparison of racquetball and jogging training programs and their effects on cardiorespiratory fitness. Eugene Ore.: Microform Publications, University of Oregon, 1984. 1 microfiche : negative, ill. ; 11 x 15 cm.
NOTES: Thesis (M.S.) - University of Arizona, 1983; (viii, 61 leaves); includes bibliography.
LEVEL: A LANG: Eng UO84 395

PROTECTIVE DEVICES

Boberg, L.C. ASTM eyeguard specs: throw away your open frames. *National racquetball (Glenview, Ill.) 13(2), Feb 1984, 6-7.*
LEVEL: B LANG: Eng SIRC ARTICLE NO: 099825

Boberg, L.C. New test, same result: open eyeguards flunk. *National racquetball (Glenview, Ill.) 13(3), Mar 1984, 4.*
LEVEL B LANG: Eng SIRC ARTICLE NO: 099826

National racquetball's annual eyeguard guide. *National racquetball (Glenview, Ill.) 13(2), Feb 1984, 12-16.*
LEVEL: B LANG: Eng SIRC ARTICLE NO: 099838

The eyes have it: eyeguard survey results. *National racquetball (Glenview, Ill.) 13(2), Feb 1984, 8-11.*
LEVEL: B LANG: Eng SIRC ARTICLE NO: 099828

PSYCHOLOGY

Adams, V.S. Personality profiles of highly skilled male and female amateur racquetball players. Eugene, Ore.: Microform Publications, University of Oregon, 1984. 2 microfiches : negative ; 11 x 15 cm.
NOTES: Thesis (Ed.D.) - University of Georgia, 1982; (ix, 102 leaves); includes bibliography.
LEVEL: A LANG: Eng UO84 284-285

Kimiecik, J.C. Getting more enjoyment from your game. *National racquetball (Glenview, Ill.) 13(11), Nov 1984, 32-33.*
LEVEL: B LANG: Eng SIRC ARTICLE NO: 109057

Mark, M.M. Mutrie, N. Brooks, D.R. Harris, D.V. Causal attributions of winners and losers in individual competitive sports: toward a reformulation of the self-serving bias. (Refs: 32)*Sport psychology (Champaign, Ill.) 6(2), 1984, 184-196.*
ABST: The achievement oriented world of sport has been a frequent setting for the study of attributions for success and failure. However, it may be inappropriate to generalize from previous research to attributions made in actual, organized, competitive, individual sports because previous studies suffer from one or more of three characteristics which may limit their generalizability to such settings: previous studies have employed novel tasks, staged the competition for research purposes, or examined attribution about team success or failure. The present research was conducted (a) to avoid these limitations to generalizability, (b) to examine whether competitors who differ in experience or ability make different attributions for success and failure, (c) to employee an attribution measure that does not rely too much on the researchers' interpretation of the subjects' attributions as past techniques have done. Two studies were conducted examining attributions made by winners and losers in the second round of organized squash (Study 1) and racquetball (Study 2) tournaments. Results indicate no difference between players of different experience/ability levels. In addition, winners and losers did not differ in the locus of causality of their attributions, but winners, relative to losers, made more stable and controllable attributions.
LEVEL: A LANG: Eng SIRC ARTICLE NO: 108492

Mondry, S. 4 steps to better consistency. *National racquetball (Skokie, Ill.) 13(4), Apr 1984, 20-21.*
LEVEL: B LANG: Eng SIRC ARTICLE NO: 095183

Mondry, S. 6 ways to avoid choking. *National racquetball (Glenview, Ill.) 13(9), Sept 1984, 24-25.*
LEVEL: B LANG: Eng SIR ARTICLE NO: 106006

Roberts, G.C. Duda, J.L. Motivation in sport: the mediating role of perceived ability. (Refs: 38)*Journal of sport psycholog (Champaign, Ill.) 6(3), 1984, 312-324.*
ABST: The major purpose of this study was to determine the importance of being able to assign ability to self interpreting outcomes as success or failure in a sport context. A field study was conducted with men and women racquetball players. Prior to a two-person racquetball game, subjects were given a questionnaire assessing their own and opponent's perceived ability, self-confidence, reasons for enrolling in racquetball class, and the importance placed on winning. Immediately after the contest a second questionnaire was administered which tapped perceived satisfaction in the game (subjective success and failure), perceptions of own and opponent's demonstrated ability, and the causal attributions of winners and losers. Regression analyses revealed that perception of demonstrated ability was significantly related to perceptions of success and failure for both men and women.
LEVEL: A LANG: Eng SIRC ARTICLE NO: 103378

PSYCHOLOGY - MENTAL TRAINING

Sherry, C.J. Mental practice: racquetball without a racquet or ball. *National racquetball (Glenview, Ill.) 13(11), Nov 1984 29.*
LEVEL: B LANG: Eng SIRC ARTICLE NO: 109055

RULES AND REGULATIONS

Cassell, H. Change serve rules for a better game. *National racquetball (Glenview, Ill.) 13(5), May 1984, 44.*
LEVEL: B LANG: Eng SIRC ARTICLE NO: 101458

Kruger, B. The avoidable hinder: point or ploy? An inside look at the unwritten rules of no man's land. *Racquetball illustrated (Burbank, Calif.) 7(2), Feb/Mar 1984, 36-40.*
LEVEL: B LANG: Eng SIRC ARTICLE NO: 095181

SPORTING EVENTS

Boberg, L.C. In search of olympic gold. *National racquetball (Glenview, Ill.) 13(7), Jul 1984, 6-8.*
LEVEL: B LANG: Eng SIRC ARTICLE NO: 103366

Murphy, M. The growing pains of an olympic sport. *Olympian (Colorado Springs, Colo.) 11(3), Sept 1984, 10-11.*
LEVEL: B LANG: Eng SIRC ARTICLE NO: 108607

SPORTSMANSHIP

Mondry, S. 5 tips for more fun on the court. *National racquetball (Glenview, Ill.) 13(3), Mar 1984, 28-29.*
LEVEL: B LANG: Eng SIRC ARTICLE NO: 099837

STRATEGY

Brouwer, S. Loveday, C. The secret of front court coverage. *National racquetball (Skokie, Ill.) 13(4), Apr 1984, 24-25.*
LEVEL: B LANG: Eng SIRC ARTICLE NO: 095176

Garfinkel, C. 10 shots to combat the ceiling ball. *National racquetball (Skokie, Ill.) 13(1), Jan 1984, 20-23.*
LEVEL: B LANG: Eng SIRC ARTICLE NO: 095179

Garfinkel, C. Playing against the lefthander. *National racquetball (Glenview, Ill.) 13(8), Aug 1984, 21-23.*
LEVEL: B LANG Eng SIRC ARTICLE NO: 103370

Garfinkel, C. Playing the shooter. *National racquetball (Glenview, Ill.) 13(10), Oct 1984, 34-36.*
LEVEL: B LANG: Eng SIRC ARTICLE NO: 105999

Garfinkel, C. Beating the power player. *National racquetball (Glenview, Ill.) 13(9), Sept 1984, 20-23.*
LEVEL: B LANG: Eng SIRC ARTICLE NO: 106000

Garfinkel, C. How to beat the squash player. *National racquetball (Glenview, Ill.) 13(11), Nov 1984, 26-28.*
LEVEL: B LANG Eng SIRC ARTICLE NO: 109054

Keeley, S. 5 simple shot selection strategies. *Racquetball illustrated (Hollywood, Calif.) 7(1), Dec/Jan 1984, 24-26.*
LEVEL: B LANG: Eng SIRC ARTICLE NO: 099834

Thaler, H. Making a comeback. *National racquetball (Glenview, Ill.) 13(2), Feb 1984, 28-29.*
LEVEL: B LANG: Eng SIRC ARTICLE NO: 099843

STRATEGY - DEFENSIVE

Harnett, B. Surprise Southpaw strategies. *Racquetball illustrated (Hollywood, Calif.) 7(1), Dec/Jan 1984, 29-30.*
LEVEL: B LANG: Eng SIRC ARTICLE NO: 099831

Strandemo, S. Learning to cover the cross-court pass. *National racquetball (Glenview, Ill.) 13(6), Jun 1984, 20-21.*
LEVEL B LANG: Eng SIRC ARTICLE NO: 103381

STRATEGY - DOUBLES

Adams, L. How to win at mixed doubles. *Racquetball illustrated (Burbank, Calif.) 7(2), Feb/Mar 1984, 24-25.*
LEVEL: B LANG Eng SIRC ARTICLE NO: 095175

Fleming, K. Garrigus, K. Liefer, M. How to stop a slump. *Racquetball illustrated (Burbank, Calif.) 7(2), Feb/Mar 1984, 26-27.*
LEVEL: B LANG: Eng SIRC ARTICLE NO: 095177

Garfinkel, C. Serve and serve returns in doubles. *National racquetball (Glenview, Ill.) 13(6), Jun 1984, 17-19.*
LEVEL: B LANG: Eng SIRC ARTICLE NO: 103369

Garfinkel, C. Doubles play: follow the spot. *National racquetball (Glenview, Ill.) 13(7), Jul 1984, 24-26.*
LEVEL: B LANG: Eng SIRC ARTICLE NO: 103371

Kruger, B. Court coverage. *Racquetball illustrated (Burbank, Calif.) 7(2), Feb/Mar 1984, 28-30.*
LEVEL: B LANG: Eng SIRC ARTICLE NO: 095182

Trent, S. Wright, S. Doubles do's and don'ts. *Racquetball illustrated (Burbank, Calif.) 7(2), Feb/Mar 1984, 22-23.*
LEVEL: LANG: Eng SIRC ARTICLE NO: 095187

STRATEGY - OFFENSIVE

Garfinkel, C. Use the volley to score points. *National racquetball (Glenview, Ill.) 13(5), May 1984, 16-18.*
LEVEL: B LANG Eng SIRC ARTICLE NO: 101460

TECHNIQUES AND SKILLS

Adams, L. Magic overhead shots. *National racquetball (Glenview, Ill.) 13(6), Jun 1984, 26-28.*
LEVEL: B LANG: Eng SIRC ARTICLE NO: 103365

Mondry, S. 5 keys to hitting the ball harder. *National racquetball (Skokie, Ill.) 13(1), Jan 1984, 24-26.*
LEVEL: B LANG: Eng SIRC ARTICLE NO: 095184

Mondry, S. 5 ways to improve back wall play. *National racquetball (Glenview, Ill.) 13(2), Feb 1984, 22-23.*
LEVEL: B LANG: Eng SIRC ARTICLE NO: 099836

Mondry, S. In a pinch? Pinch. *National racquetball (Glenview, Ill.) 13(10), Oct 1984, 32-33.*
LEVEL: B LANG: Eng SIRC ARTICLE NO: 106005

Mondry, S. How the Z ball can help you win. *National racquetball (Glenview, Ill.) 13(11), Nov 1984, 30-31.*
LEVEL: B LANG: Eng SIRC ARTICLE NO: 109056

Ness, G. 'Getting down' on kill shots. *First service (Vanier, Ont.) 2(1), Jul 1984, 5-6.*
NOTES: Excerpt from the Level 2 Technical

Coaching Manual by Dr. Gary Ness.
LEVEL: B LANG: Eng SIRC ARTICLE NO: 101464

Pizarro, D.C. Pinpointing ball placement: the zone method for beginners. *National racquetball (Glenview, Ill.) 13(12), Dec 1984, 30-32.*
LEVEL: B LANG: Eng SIRC ARTICLE NO: 106010

Sauser, J. Shots on the future: use them today. *National racquetball (Glenview, Ill.) 13(3), Mar 1984, 30-32.*
LEVEL: B LANG: Eng SIRC ARTICLE NO: 099840

Yellen, M. Wide-angle passing shots. *Racquetball illustrated (Hollywood, Calif.) 7(1), Dec/Jan 1984, 28-29.*
LEVEL: B LANG Eng SIRC ARTICLE NO: 099845

TECHNIQUES AND SKILLS - BACKHAND

Garfinkel, C. Using your backhand. *National racquetball (Glenview, Ill.) 13(3), Mar 1984, 23-27.*
LEVEL: B LANG: Eng SIRC ARTICLE NO: 099830

Hogan, M. 4 fast formulas for a better backhand. *Racquetball illustrated (Hollywood, Calif.) 7(1), Dec/Jan 1984, 27.*
LEVEL: B LANG: Eng SIRC ARTICLE NO: 099833

TECHNIQUES AND SKILLS - FOREHAND

Garfinkel C. Using your forehand like the champions. *National racquetball (Glenview, Ill.) 13(2), Feb 1984, 18-21.*
LEVEL: LANG: Eng SIRC ARTICLE NO: 099829

TECHNIQUES AND SKILLS - SERVE RETURN

Strandemo, S. Bruns, B. Advanced racquetball. Part five: return of serve. *International racquetball (Reno, Nevada) 2(10), Dec 1984, 39;41-43.*
LEVEL: B LANG: Eng SIRC ARTICLE NO: 107418

TECHNIQUES AND SKILLS - SERVING

Garfinkel, C. Improve your serve by watching your opponent. *National racquetball (Skokie, Ill.) 13(4), Apr 1984, 16-19.*
LEVEL: B LANG: Eng SIRC ARTICLE NO: 095178

Garfinkel, C. New 5 foot rule bodes well for lobs. *National racquetball (Glenview, Ill.) 13(12), Dec 1984, 22-24.*
LEVEL: LANG: Eng SIRC ARTICLE NO: 105998

Keeley, S. The highs and lows of service. *National racquetball (Skokie, Ill.) 13(1), Jan 1984, 27-29.*
LEVEL: B LANG: Eng SIRC ARTICLE NO: 095180

Sauser, J. Second serves: make them count. *National racquetball (Glenview, Ill.) 13(2), Feb 1984, 24-25.*
LEVEL: B LANG: E SIRC ARTICLE NO: 099839

Strandemo, S. Discover your low drive serve target. *National racquetball (Glenview, Ill.) 13(3), Mar 1984, 20-22.*
LEVEL: LANG: Eng SIRC ARTICLE NO: 099842

Strandemo, S. Hitting a legal screen serve. *National racquetball (Glenview, Ill.) 13(5), May 1984, 19-21.*
LEVEL: B LANG: Eng SIRC ARTICLE NO: 101466

RACQUETBALL (continued)

TECHNIQUES AND SKILLS - STANCE

Hilecher, J. Advanced instruction guide: flawless footwork. *Racquetball illustrated (Hollywood, Calif.) 7(1), Dec/Jan 1984, 22-23.*
LEVEL: B LANG: Eng SIRC ARTICLE NO: 099832

TESTING AND EVALUATION

New rating system gaining momentum. *National racquetball (Skokie, Ill.) 13(4), Apr 1984, 12-15.*
LEVEL: B LANG: Eng SIRC ARTICLE NO: 095185

Valcourt, D.P. Development of a racquetball skills test battery for male and female beginner and intermediate players. Eugene, Ore.: Microform Publications, University of Oregon, 1984. 2 microfiches : negative, ill. ; 11 x 15 cm.
NOTES: Thesis (M.S.) - Springfield College, 1982; (ix, 88 leaves); includes bibliography.
LEVEL: A LANG: Eng UO84 233-234

TRAINING AND CONDITIONING

Fabian, L. O'Brien, M. Training aids for racquetball - part II. *National racquetball (Glenview, Ill.) 13(11), Nov 1984, 23-25.*
LEVEL: B LANG: Eng SIRC ARTICLE NO: 109052

Mondry, S. 5 Summer activities to improve your game. *National racquetball (Glenview, Ill.) 13(8), Aug 1984, 24-25.*
LEVEL: LANG: Eng SIRC ARTICLE NO: 103376

Mondry, S. Getting the most out of watching a match. *National racquetball (Glenview, Ill.) 13(12), Dec 1984, 28-29.*
LEVEL B LANG: Eng SIRC ARTICLE NO: 106004

Sauser, J. Workouts for women: stomach exercises. *National racquetball (Glenview, Ill.) 13(7), Jul 1984, 22-23.*
LEVEL: B LANG: Eng SIRC ARTICLE NO: 103380

TRAINING AND CONDITIONING - AEROBIC TRAINING

Endurance demands of racquetball. *First serve (Vanier, Ont.) 2(2), Sept 1984, 5-6.*
NOTES: Second of a series of excerpts from the Level 2 Technical Coaching Manual.
LEVEL: B LANG: Eng SIRC ARTICLE NO: 173016

Stationary bikes and aerobic fitness for racquetball. *National racquetball (Glenview, Ill.) 13(11), Nov 1984, 38-40.*
LEVEL: LANG: Eng SIRC ARTICLE NO: 109060

TRAINING AND CONDITIONING - DRILLS

Fabian, L. O'Brien, M. Training aids for racquetball: part I. *National racquetball (Glenview, Ill.) 13(10), Oct 1984, 29-31*
LEVEL: B LANG: Eng SIRC ARTICLE NO: 105997

Kessinger, M. Improving the practice court. *National racquetball (Glenview, Ill.) 13(12), Dec 1984, 25-27.*
LEVEL: B LANG: Eng SIRC ARTICLE NO: 106002

TRAINING AND CONDITIONING - STRETCHING AND FLEXIBILITY EXERCISES

Strandberg, K.W. Stretching for racquetball. *National racquetball (Glenview, Ill.) 13(11), Nov 1984, 34-36.*
LEVEL: B LANG Eng SIRC ARTICLE NO: 109059

TRAINING AND CONDITIONING - TRAINING CAMPS

Thumlert, I. Racquetball camps: are they worth it and what could I expect? *First service (Vanier, Ont.) 2(1), Jul 1984, 3-4.*
LEVEL: B LANG: Eng SIRC ARTICLE NO: 101467

TRAINING AND CONDITIONING - WEIGHT AND STRENGTH TRAINING

Muscles and machines mean a better game for you. *National racquetball (Glenview, Ill.) 13(11), Nov 1984, 42-44.*
LEVEL: B LANG: Eng SIRC ARTICLE NO: 109063

Nolan, B. Upper body workouts: weight machines. *National racquetball (Glenview, Ill.) 13(12), Dec 1984, 41-44.*
LEVEL: B LANG: Eng SIRC ARTICLE NO: 106009

Sauser, J. Giarriante, J. Berg, J. Weight training for women in racquetball. *National racquetball (Glenview, Ill.) 13(5), May 1984, 26-28.*
LEVEL: B LANG: Eng SIRC ARTICLE NO: 101465

Sauser, J. Workouts for women: back exercises. *National racquetball (Glenview, Ill.) 13(8), Aug 1984, 26-27.*
LEVEL: B LANG: Eng SIRC ARTICLE NO: 103379

Sauser, J. Workouts for women: exercises for arm strength & tone. *National racquetball (Glenview, Ill.) 13(9), Sept 1984, 26-28.*
LEVEL: B LANG: Eng SIRC ARTICLE NO: 106016

Suaser, J. Workouts for women: free weights for upper body. *National racquetball (Glenview, Ill.) 13(6), Jun 1984, 24-25.*
LEVEL: B LANG: Eng SIRC ARTICLE NO: 103382

WOMEN

Finn, J.A. Taking on breast support myths. *National racquetball (Glenview, Ill.) 13(8), Aug 1984, 30-31.*
LEVEL: B LANG: E SIRC ARTICLE NO: 103367

Keteyian, A. Women's racquetball serves up a new hit: the Lynn and Heather show. *Sports illustrated (Los Angeles, Calif.) 61(20), 29 Oct 1984, 10;14.*
LEVEL: B LANG: Eng SIRC ARTICLE NO: 099835

RAFTING

COUNTRIES AND REGIONS

Wilkinson, K. Whitewater rafting in Eastern Canada. Commentary. (Refs: 1)*Physican and sportsmedicine (Minneapolis, Minn.) 12(6), Jun 1984, 198-200;205.*
LEVEL: B LANG: Eng SIRC ARTICLE NO: 095189

DIRECTORIES

VanDine, D. Fandrich, B. Rafting in British Columbia: featuring the lower Thompson River. Surrey, B.C.: Hancock House, c1984 70 p. : ill.
LEVEL: B LANG: Eng ISBN: 0-88839-985-5 GV776.15.B74 18982

EQUIPMENT - MAINTENANCE

Mills, J.C. A step-by-step guide to raft repair. *River runner (Vista, Calif.) 4(2), Mar/Apr 1984, 35-36.*
LEVEL: B LANG: E SIRC ARTICLE NO: 097960

REFERENCE WORKS

AUDIO-VISUAL MATERIALS

8mm and 16mm cameras/projectors. *Scholastic coach 53(8), Mar 1984, 62-64.*
LEVEL: B LANG: Eng SIRC ARTICLE NO: 093217

Lovece, F. Video cameras and cassette recorders. *Scholastic coach 53(8), Mar 1984, 57-58.*
NOTES: Portions of article adapted from articles by Frank Lovece in the March 1983 and October 1983 issues of Electronic Learning magazine.
LEVEL: B LANG: Eng SIRC ARTICLE NO: 093228

BIBLIOGRAPHIES

Cox, R.W. Annual bibliography of publications on the history of sport in Britain, 1982/83. *British journal of sports histor (London) 1(3), Dec 1984, 318-334.*
LEVEL: B LANG: Eng SIRC ARTICLE NO: 105276

Runcianu-Versteegen, A. World index of sportsperiodicals. The Hague: International Association for Sports Information, 1984. 74 p.
CORP: International Association for Sports Information. Commission Information Sources.
LEVEL: B LANG: Eng GV561 17876

DICTIONARIES AND TERMINOLOGY

Blair, S. Sports talk in everyday life. *TAHPERD journal (Austin, Tex.) 52(2), Feb 1984, 14.*
LEVEL: B LANG: Eng SIRC ARTICLE NO: 093219

Kneyer, W. Possibilities and foundations of comparative physical education and sport through language and terminology. (Refs 12)*IASI Kommission Thesaurus rundbrief/circular letter (Kiel) 1(4), 1984, 23-42.*
CONF: International Symposium for Comparative Physical Education and Sport (4th : 1984 : Kiel, F.R.G.).
ABST: The theoretical foundations of linguistics and terminology are defined and discussed. The limitations of multilinguality within languages are examined along with limiting factors for a comparative sport pedagogy within terminology. The principle structure and function of the IASI sport thesaurus are analyzed and its benefits for sport research are detailed.
LEVEL: A LANG: Eng SIRC ARTICLE NO: 102381

DIRECTORIES

Colgate, C. Freedman, S.J. National recreational, sporting & hobby organizations of the United States. 4th ed. Washington, D.C.: Columbia Books Inc., 1984. 136 p.
LEVEL: I LANG: Eng ISBN: 0910416486 LC CARD: 80-70429 GV53 10891

Lipsey, R.A. Sports market place 1984. January ed. Princeton, N.J.: Sportsguide, 1984. ca. 500 p. in various pagings
NOTES: ISSN: 0277-0296.
LEVEL: B LANG: Eng ISBN: 0-935644-03-2 GV569 17305

Sincennes, J. Winch, M. Sports directory. Repertoire recreation. Ottawa: Sports Federation of Canada : Federation des sports du Canada, c1984. 195 p.
CORP: Sports Federation of Canada.
CORP: Federation des sports du Canada.
LEVEL: B LANG: Eng Fr GV585 12260

Timmer, R. Recla, J. International directory of sports organizations. Haarlem, The Netherlands: De Vrieseborch, c1984. 429 p
LEVEL: I LANG: Eng ISBN: 9060761979 GV569 17650

Winch, M. Sincennes, J. Sports directory 1985. Repertoire recreation 1985. Ottawa: Sports Federation of Canada : Federation des sports du Canada, (1984). 193 p.
CORP: Sports Federation of Canada.
CORP: Federation des sports du Canada.
NOTES: Cover title. Titre de la couverture.
LEVEL: B LANG: Eng Fr GV585 20691

DOCUMENTATION

Olsen, A.M. International sport information and documentation: principles for further development. (Refs: 10)*IASI international bulletin of sport information (The Hague, The Netherlands) 6(3), 1984, 6-14.*
NOTES: Presented to the ESC Working Group 'Sport for the World', Oslo, March 14-15, 1984.
LEVEL: B LANG: Eng SIRC ARTICLE NO: 102926

ENCYCLOPEDIAS

Beclier, D. Sportsguide Solar. Paris: Solar, c1984. 379 p.
CORP: Solar.
NOTES: Includes index. Sur la couverture: Tous les sports de A a Z: les regles, les champions, les resultats.
LEVEL: B LANG: Fr ISBN: 2-263-00818-7 LC CARD: 85-145156 GV567 20819

Fisher, D. Bragonier, R. What's what in sports: the visual glossary of the sports world. Maplewood, N.J.: Hammond, c1984. 24 p. : ill.
NOTES: Includes index.
LEVEL: B LANG: Eng ISBN: 0843735287 LC CARD: 84-009032 GV567 18278

INFORMATION RETRIEVAL SYSTEMS

Belna, A.M. Spala, J.L. Stark, R.W. Olympic Information in the Sport database. *Database (Weston, Conn.) 7(3), Aug 1984, 20-26.*
LEVEL: B LANG: Eng SIRC ARTICLE NO: 095779

Center keeps tabs on fitness research. (ACCESS) *Athletic business (Madison, Wis.) 8(3), Mar 1984, 33.*
LEVEL: B LANG: Eng SIRC ARTICLE NO: 178382

International Association For Sports Information (IASI) coordinating committee of heads on National Sports Information Centers (COCO) 3rd COCO meeting, Cologne (F.R.G.) 3-7 October 1983, provisional minutes. *International bulletin of sports information (The Hague, Netherlands) 6, 1984, 19-27.*
LEVEL: B LANG: Eng SIRC ARTICLE NO: 095780

Neufeld, M.L. Indexing for retrieval: a pragmatic approach. *Unpublished Olympic Scientific Congress paper 1984, 1-18.*
CONF: Olympic Scientific Congress (1984 : Eugene, Ore.).
LEVEL: I LANG: Eng SIRC ARTICLE NO: 097451

Remans, A. The exchange of information within the framework of the Council of Europe. *International bulletin of sports information (The Hague, Netherlands) 6, 1984, 9-16.*
LEVEL: B LANG: Eng SIRC ARTICLE NO: 095783

Sachs, M.L. Exercise, sport, and mental health: a retrieval system. Reisterstown, Md.: Michael L. Sachs, 1984. ca. 30 leaves
CONF: Coping with mental stress: The Potential and Limits of Exercise Intervention (1984 : Washington, D.C.).
CORP: National Institute of Mental Health.
NOTES: Paper presented at a state-of-the-art workshop funded by the National Institute of Mental Health on 'Coping with mental stress: the potential and limits of exercise intervention,' April 27, 1984, Washington, D.C. Bibliography: leaves 11-12.
LEVEL: A LANG: Eng GV567.5 17281

INFORMATION SERVICES

Facts for all: how to trap Britain's biggest reserves of sports information. *Sport and leisure (London) 25(5), Nov/Dec 1984, 24.*
LEVEL: B LANG: Eng SIRC ARTICLE NO: 108963

Lemke, K.H. The development of a microfiche archive parallel to the international data base of SIRC. *International bulletin of sports information (The Hague, Netherlands) 6, 1984, 6-8.*
LEVEL: B LANG: Eng SIRC ARTICLE NO: 095782

LITERATURE REVIEWS

Cleland, N.D. Comparison of sports coverage in Book Review Digest and Book Review Index. (Refs: 8)*Reference quarterly (Chicago) 23(4), 1984, 451-459.*
LEVEL: I LANG: Eng SIRC ARTICLE NO: 097450

QUIZZES

Dolan, E.F. The Simon and Schuster sports question and answer book. New York: Wanderer Books, c1984. 1v.
NOTES: Includes index.
LEVEL: B LANG: Eng ISBN: 0671477498 LC CARD: 84-007457

QUOTATIONS AND MAXIMS

Maikovich, A.J. Sports quotations: maxims, quips and pronouncements for writers and fans. Jefferson, N.C.: McFarland, c1984. vi, 168 p.
NOTES: Includes index.

LEVEL: B LANG: Eng ISBN: 0899501001 LC CARD: 83-020005 GV706.8 17240

RULES

Moore, R. Official rules of sports and games 1985-86. 16th ed. Kingswood, Surrey: Kaye & Ward, c1984. 723 p.
LEVEL: B LANG: Eng ISBN: 0-7182-3961-X GV731 20422

STATISTICS AND RECORDS

McWhirter, N.D. Guinness book of records 1985. 31st ed. Enfield: Guinness Superlatives, c1984. 352 p. : ill.
LEVEL: B LANG: Eng ISBN: 0-85112-419-4 GV741 18199

RELAY RACE

BIBLIOGRAPHIES

Dates, G.G. Theses and dissertations in track & field. *Track & field quarterly review (Kalamazoo, Mich.) 84(2), Summer 1984 60-62.*
LEVEL: B LANG: Eng SIRC ARTICLE NO: 095402

Sport bibliography. *Track and field journal 25, Feb 1984, 33-35.*
LEVEL: B LANG: Eng SIRC ARTICLE NO: 093947

INJURIES AND ACCIDENTS

Teich, M. Tale of the tape. Protection: for legs and feet, it's a wrap. *Runner (Boulder, Colo.) 6(7), Apr 1984, 12;14;16.*
LEVEL: B LANG: Eng SIRC ARTICLE NO: 098689

SPORTING EVENTS

Relays. *Athletics coach (London) 18(4), Dec 1984, 30-34.*
LEVEL: B LANG: Eng SIRC ARTICLE NO: 105017

TRAINING AND CONDITIONING

Goldsmith, M. Relay exchanges and training: 1600 meter relay. *Texas coach (Austin, Tex.) 28(4), Nov 1984, 58-59.*
LEVEL: B LANG: Eng SIRC ARTICLE NO: 173449

Schuster, W. Track talk...relay work. *Coaching clinic (Princeton, N.J.) 23(2), Oct 1984, 11-15.*
LEVEL: B LANG: Eng SIRC ARTICLE NO: 101711

TRAINING AND CONDITIONING - DRILLS

Groves, H. Hot passes for the sprint relays-update. *Track & field quarterly review (Kalamazoo, Mich.) 84(2), Summer 1984, 24-25.*
LEVEL: B LANG: Eng SIRC ARTICLE NO: 095411

Gumb, J. Put some intensity in those exchange work outs. *Athletic journal 64(9), Apr 1984, 58-59;71.*
LEVEL: B LANG: Eng SIRC ARTICLE NO: 093890

RELIGION

Jones, N. Sport and religion: a socio-historic analysis, outlined from a functionalist perspective. (abstract) *Carnegie research papers (Beckett Park, Leeds) 1(6), Dec 1984, 36-37.*
CONF: Carnegie Undergraduate Research Symposium (1984 : Leeds, Eng.).
LEVEL: I LANG: Eng SIRC ARTICLE NO: 172514

CHRISTIANITY

Blankenbaker, J. YMCA fitness: there's a spiritual basis for it. (Refs: 14)*Journal of physical education and program (Columbus, Oh.) Sept 1984, F-15-F-17.*
LEVEL: B LANG: Eng SIRC ARTICLE NO: 102707

Higginson, T.W. Saints and their bodies.
NOTES: In, Riess, S.A. (ed.), The American sporting experience: a historical anthology of sport in America, New York, Leisure Press, c1984, p. 80-90. Reprinted from, Atlantic monthly 1, March 1858, p. 82-95.
LEVEL: I LANG: Eng GV583 17631

RESEARCH AND RESEARCH METHODS

Abstracts of research papers 1984. Presented at the Anaheim, California Convention of the American Alliance for Health, Physical Education, Recreation and Dance in the Research Consortium meetings. Reston, Va.: AAHPERD, c1984. 169 p. (Abstracts of research papers 1984.)
CONF: American Alliance for Health, Physical Education, Recreation and Dance. Convention (1984 : Anaheim, Cal.)
CORP: American Alliance for Health, Physical Educaltion, Recreation and Dance.
LEVEL: A LANG: Eng ISBN: 0883142856

Beckett, A. Philosophy, chemistry and the athlete. *New scientist (London) 103(1415), 1984, 18.*
LEVEL: B LANG: Eng SIRC ARTICLE NO: 097852

Kirsch, A. BISp-News. Federal Institute of Sport Science, Cologne, Federal Republic of Germany. *International journal of physical education (Schorndorf, FRG) 21(4), 1984, 31-33.*
NOTES: Symposium in Magglingen, Switzerland, Sept 17-21, 1984.
LEVEL: B LANG: Eng SIRC ARTICLE NO: 105595

Morton, R.H. Comment on 'an analysis of world records in three types of locomotion'. (Refs: 21)*European journal of applied physiology and occupational physiology (Heidelberg) 52(3), Apr 1984, 324-327.*
ABST: This paper is a critical review of a previous paper published in the European Journal of Applied Physiology. The author discusses a number of methodological flaws in the article under consideration. The most glaring flaw is the interpretation of polynomial second derivatives.
LEVEL: A LANG: Eng SIRC ARTICLE NO: 097868

RESEARCH

EPS interroge Joel de Rosnay. (Refs: 5)*EPS: Education physique et sport 185, janv/fevr 1984, 4-10.*
LEVEL: B LANG: Fr SIRC ARTICLE NO: 093224

The tasks of research and its practical application in mass and recreation sports. Report miscellany of the 10th International Seminar of CIEPSS 'Sports and Leisure' Committee, Piestany, 26-30 Sept. 1983. Prague: Czechoslovak Association of Physical Culture, 1984. 357 p.
CONF: International Seminar of CIEPSS 'Sports and Leisure' Committee (10th : 1983 : Piestani, Czechoslovakia).
CORP: Czechoslovak Association of Physical culture. Scientific and Methodological Department.
LEVEL: A LANG: Eng GV701 20848

RESEARCH METHODS

Shephard, R.J. The challenge of multi-disciplinary studies. (Refs: 9)*Journal of sports medicine and physical fitness (Torino, Italy) 24(2), Jun 1984, 83-89.*
ABST: The growth of inter-disciplinary research is set in its historical perspective. Challenges and opportunities of inter-disciplinary work are discussed in the context of both personal experience and a more general assessment of large-scale trials.
LEVEL: I LANG: Eng SIRC ARTICLE NO: 102609

Sifft, J.M. Guidelines for selecting a sample. *National Strength & Conditioning Association journal 6(1), Feb/Mar 1984, 26-27.*
LEVEL: B LANG: Eng SIRC ARTICLE NO: 093233

RINGETTE

Marcotte, G. A plea for change. Comment renouveler la ringuette. *Ringette review/Revue ringuette (Ottawa) 6(3), Oct 1984, 10-13.*
LEVEL: B LANG: Eng Fr SIRC ARTICLE NO: 101469

Marcotte, G. A plea for change. Invitation au changement. Quebec: s.n., 1984. 9 p. : 10 p.
NOTES: French and English texts on inverted pages with separate paging. Textes francais et anglais disposes tete-beche avec pagination separee.
LEVEL: B LANG: Eng Fr GV857.R5 20183

ADMINISTRATION

Clark, W. Targets in marketing. *Ringette review/ Revue ringuette (Ottawa) 6(3), Oct 1984, 28-29.*
LEVEL: B LANG: Eng SIRC ARTICLE NO: 101468

Clark, W. Focus on marketing (part three). *Ringette review/Revue ringuette (Vanier) 6(4), Dec 1984, 24-25.*
LEVEL: B LANG: Eng SIRC ARTICLE NO: 108855

Clark, W. Corbett, M. Pharmaprix certificat d'aptitude: manuel d'administration. s.l.: Micron & Lange, c1984. i, 27 feuillet
NOTES: Titre de la couverture. Also published in English under the title: Shoppers Drug Mart Skill Awards administration manual.
LEVEL: B LANG: Fr GV857.R5 20340

Clark, W. Focus on management: marketing. *Ringette review/Revue ringuette (Ottawa) 6(2), Mar 1984, 53.*
LEVEL: B LANG: Eng SIRC ARTICLE NO: 181616

Manuel de politiques administratives. Vanier, Ont.: Ringuette Canada, 1984?. 92 feuillets
CORP: Ringuette Canada.

NOTES: Titre de la couverture. Comprend aussi: Reglements administratifs.
LEVEL: B LANG: Fr GV857.R5 18876

National Leadership Seminar Ringette Canada, July 5-8, 1984, Haliburton, Ontario: leaders handbook and seminar summary. Vanier Ont.: Ringette Canada, 1984. ca. 80 p.
CONF: National Leadership Development Seminar (1st : 1984 : Haliburton, Ont.).
CORP: Ringette Canada.
NOTES: Cover title.
LEVEL: I LANG: Eng GV857.R5 18398

Nowosad, M. Fund-raising: approaching corporate sponsors. *Ringette review/Revue ringuette (Ottawa) 6(3), Oct 1984, 30.*
LEVEL: B LANG: Eng SIRC ARTICLE NO: 101471

EQUIPMENT - REGAILING

Huras, L. MacAuley, M. Parkhill, S. McLachlin, H. Niccols, K. Marketing report on ringette skates. Canada?: Bauer Skate Co. Ltd., 1984. ii, 33 leaves
LEVEL: I LANG: Eng GV857.R5 17880

PROTECTIVE DEVICES

Helmets and facemasks. Casques et protecteurs faciaux. *Ringette review/Revue ringuette (Ottawa) 6(1), Jan/Feb-janv/fevr 1984, 26-29.*
LEVEL: B LANG: Eng Fr SIRC ARTICLE NO: 099846

MacQuarrie, D. Playing it safe. Knee protection for ringette. Jouez gagnante. Protection des genoux a la ringuette. *Ringett review/Revue ringuette (Vanier) 6(4), Dec 1984, 30-31.*
LEVEL: B LANG: Eng SIRC ARTICLE NO: 108858

The protective pelvic girdle. La gaine pelviere. *Ringette review/Revue ringuette (Ottawa) 6(2), Mar/mars 1984, 48;49.*
LEVEL B LANG: Eng Fr SIRC ARTICLE NO: 099849

PSYCHOLOGY

Corbett, M. An examination of the relationship between instrumentally and hostilely aggressive behaviours and performance variables in ringette. Waterloo, Ont.: University of Waterloo, 1984. 63, 6 leaves
NOTES: Cover title. Presented to the Department of Kinesiology in fulfillment of the requirements for Kinesiology 431. Bibliography: l. 59-63.
LEVEL: A LANG: Eng GV857.R5 17851

Searle, R.Q. Assessment of reactions to playing ringette using the key zone system. Ottawa: University of Ottawa, 1984. 52 leaves
CORP: Gloucester Ringette Association.
NOTES: A Gloucester Ringette Association Project.
LEVEL: A LANG: Eng GV857.R5 17850

RULES AND REGULATIONS

Rules casebook 1984-1986. Vanier: Ringette Canada, 1984. 46 p.
CORP: Ringette Canada.
NOTES: Cover title. Aussi publie en francais sous le titre: Reglements 1984-1986. Manuel des cas.
LEVEL: B LANG: Eng GV857.R5 20348

STRATEGY

Lamontagne, S. Boyd, F. Team play. *Coaching review (Ottawa) 7, Sept/Oct 1984, 59-61.*
LEVEL: B LANG: Eng SIRC ARTICLE NO: 098415

STRATEGY - OFFENSIVE

LaMontagne, S. Breaking out of the defensive zone. Sortie de la zone defensive. *Ringette review/ Revue ringuette (Ottawa) 6(2), Mar/mars 1984, 44.*
LEVEL: B LANG: Eng Fr SIRC ARTICLE NO: 099847

TECHNIQUES AND SKILLS

Marcotte, G. Cross-over start. Depart croise. *Ringette review/Revue ringuette (Ottawa) 6(3), Oct 1984, 33.*
LEVEL: B LANG: Eng Fr SIRC ARTICLE NO: 101470

TECHNIQUES AND SKILLS - SHOOTING

Marcotte, G. The backland *sic* sweep shot. Lancer revers balaye. *Ringette review/Revue ringuette (Ottawa) 6(2), Mar/mars 1984, 43.*
LEVEL: B LANG: Eng Fr SIRC ARTICLE NO: 099848

ROCK CLIMBING

BIOGRAPHY AND AUTOBIOGRAPHY

Krakauer, J. Zone three. John Bachar is a master of free soloing - rock climbing's high wire act without a net. *Ultrasport (Boston, Mass.) 1(3), May/ Jun 1984, 26-32.*
LEVEL: B LANG: Eng SIRC ARTICLE NO: 096769

Roberts, D. Rock steady. *Ultrasport (San Diego, Calif.) 1(1), Jan/Feb 1984, 33-36.*
LEVEL: B LANG: Eng SIRC ARTICLE NO: 095157

COUNTRIES AND REGIONS

Harlin, J. Hammond, A. West Coast rock climbs. Denver, Colo.: Chockstone Press, 1984. 1v. (The climber's guide to North America; v.1.)
NOTES: Includes bibliographical references and index.
LEVEL: B LANG: Eng ISBN: 0960945229 LC CARD: 84-015598

EQUIPMENT

Ashton, S. Gear special: sit harnesses. *Climber & rambler (Glasgow, Scotland) 23(9), Sept 1984, 36- 38.*
LEVEL: B LANG: Eng SIRC ARTICLE NO: 104853

Microys, H.F. A short course in rope physics - a rebuttal. *Climbing (Aspen, Colo.) 85, Aug 1984, 61- 62.*
LEVEL: B LANG: En SIRC ARTICLE NO: 103351

JUVENILE LITERATURE

Hyden, T. Anderson, T. Wolfe, B. Wolfe, D. Rock climbing is for me. Minneapolis: Lerner Pub. Co., c1984. 1v.
LEVEL: B LANG: Eng ISBN: 0822511479 LC CARD: 84-002906

SAFETY

McGinnis, M. McEwen, D. Making rappelling safer. (Refs: 2)*Journal of physical education, recreation & dance (Reston, Va.) 55(4), Apr 1984, 69-71.*
LEVEL: B LANG: Eng SIRC ARTICLE NO: 095156

TECHNIQUES AND SKILLS

Higgins, T. Tricksters and traditionalists: a look at conflicting climbing styles. *Climbing (Aspen, Colo.) 86, Oct 1984, 18-20;22-25.*
NOTES: Excerpted from: Ascent 1984.
LEVEL: B LANG: Eng SIRC ARTICLE NO: 173563

Walker, J.A. A manual for basic mountaineering and technical climbing. 1st ed. Laramie, Wysc. : Markleeville, Calif.: Jelm Mountain Press ; Dist. by Green Mountain Book Co., 1984. 1v.
LEVEL: B LANG: Eng ISBN: 0936204512 LC CARD: 84-015471

VARIATIONS

Jouty, S. Bompard, P. Place aux murs. (Refs: 21)*Alpirando (Paris) 71, 1984, 20-25.*
LEVEL: I LANG: Fr

RODEO

Byrd, A. Team roping: first things first. A roper has to start somewhere, and it's best to know where that place is. *Wester horseman (Colorado Springs, Colo.) 49(11), Nov 1984, 21-22.*
LEVEL: b LANG: Eng SIRC ARTICLE NO: 108807

Jennings, J. Team penning. *Quarter horse journal (Amarillo, Tex.) 37(3), Dec 1984, 274-277.*
LEVEL: B LANG: Eng SIRC ARTICLE NO: 103254

BIOGRAPHY AND AUTOBIOGRAPHY

Lidz, F. J.C. Trujillo may be a bareback ace, but a pack animal can throw him. *Sports illustrated (Los Angeles, Calif.) 61(24), 26 Nov 1984, 6.*
LEVEL: B LANG: Eng SIRC ARTICLE NO: 101352

INJURIES AND ACCIDENTS

Morgan, R.F. Nichter, L.S. Friedman, H.I. McCue, F.C. Rodeo roping thumb injuries. *Journal of hand surgery (St. Louis) 9(2) Mar 1984, 178-180.*
LEVEL: I LANG: Eng SIRC ARTICLE NO: 101355

JUVENILE LITERATURE

Bellville, C.W. Rodeo. Minneapolis: Carolrhoda Books, c1984. 1v.
LEVEL: B LANG: Eng ISBN: 0876142722 LC CARD: 84-014981

TEACHING

Rowan, L. Rodeo: the heritage sport of Alberta. *Runner (Edmonton, Alb.) 22(2), Summer 1984, 36- 38.*
LEVEL: B LANG: Eng SIR ARTICLE NO: 101359

TECHNIQUES AND SKILLS

Camarillo, L. Heading & heeling. *Western horseman (Colorado Springs, Colo.) 49(3), Mar 1984, 36-44;68.*
NOTES: Condensed and adapted from, Team roping, by Leo Camarillo.
LEVEL: B LANG: Eng SIRC ARTICLE NO: 098185

TRAINING AND CONDITIONING

Josey, M. Running the barrels: a contest countdown. *Performance horseman (Unionville, Pa.) 3(12), Nov 1984, 4-9.*
LEVEL: B LANG: Eng SIRC ARTICLE NO: 105936

TRAINING AND CONDITIONING - TRAINING CAMPS

Kirby, C. Barrel racing clinics: how to prepare for, and how to profit from, a good clinic. *Western horseman (Colorado Springs, Colo.) 49(9), Sept 1984, 32;34.*
LEVEL: B LANG: Eng SIRC ARTICLE NO: 099729

ROLLER HOCKEY

Dupertuis, P.A. Le rink-hockey. *Macolin (Suisse) 10, oct 1984, 4-6.*
LEVEL: B LANG: Fr SIRC ARTICLE NO: 103387

TECHNIQUES AND SKILLS - PASSING

Hemphill, B. Passing, catching: the key to good hockey. *Skate (Lincoln, Neb.) 47(1), Winter 1984, 10.*
LEVEL: B LANG: Eng SIRC ARTICLE NO: 098169

ROLLER SKATING

DIRECTORIES

1984 USAC/RS club directory. Lincoln, Nebr.: United States Amateur Confederation of Roller Skating, 1984. 32 p.
CORP: United States Amateur Confederation of Roller Skating.
NOTES: Cover title.
LEVEL: B LANG: Eng GV859 20062

INJURIES AND ACCIDENTS

Glickman, S. Below the knee: can it be injury free? *Skate (Lincoln, Neb.) 67(4), Fall 1984, 21-23.*
LEVEL: B LANG: Eng SIR ARTICLE NO: 099850

Horner, C. McCabe, M.J. Ice-skating and roller disco injuries in Dublin. (Refs: 9)*British journal of sports medicine (Loughborough, Eng.) 18(3), Sept 1984, 207-211.*
ABST: A comparative study was carried out on a series of 72 ice-skating and 57 roller skating injuries

over a sixteen month period. The average patient age was 20.5 years in the ice-skating group and 16.5 years in the roller skating group. Females predominated in both groups accounting for 72% of ice-skaters injured and 77% of roller skaters injured. Ice-skating fractures accounted for 40% of all injuries while roller skating fractures were only 14% of their total injuries. The majority of ice-skating fractures occurred in females. As a result of their study, the authors recommend several preventative measures.
LEVEL: A LANG: Eng SIRC ARTICLE NO: 103388

Sedlin, E.D. Zitner, D.T. McGuinniss, G. Roller skating accidents and injuries. *Journal of trauma (Baltimore) 24(2), Feb 1984, 136-139.*
ABST: This paper reviews 65 consecutive fractures, dislocations and ligament tears produced by roller skating accidents treated at a hospital in New York. Injuries resulting from collisions occurring in a skating rink were more serious than street accident injuries. Lack of expertise is a significant factor in the cause of injuries, though the sport contains inherent risk. Recommendations are presented for the reduction of injuries.
LEVEL: A LANG: Eng SIRC ARTICLE NO: 099851

JUDGING

Just good judgement. There should be no mystery when it comes to evaluating American or international dance. *Skate (Lincoln, Neb.) 47(1), Winter 1984, 13.*
LEVEL: B LANG: Eng SIRC ARTICLE NO: 098417

MEDICINE

Stevens, P. Glickman, S. Sports medicine and the skater. *Skate (Lincoln, Neb.) 47(2), Spring 1984, 13;15.*
LEVEL: B LANG: Eng SIRC ARTICLE NO: 098419

TECHNIQUES AND SKILLS

Burton, J. Original set pattern. *Skate (Lincoln, Neb.) 67(3), Summer 1984, 12-13.*
LEVEL: B LANG: Eng SIRC ARTICLE NO: 103385

Castro, G. Dance tip: cornering symmetry. *Skate (Lincoln, Neb.) 67(3), Summer 1984, 11.*
NOTES: From Gary Castro's America Dance Seminar presented at the 1983 SRSTA/SCA Convention in Las Vegas, Nevada.
LEVEL: B LANG: Eng SIRC ARTICLE NO: 103386

TRAINING AND CONDITIONING

Merrell, G. Huffman, D. Outdoor training vs. training outdoors: there is a difference. *Skate (Lincoln, Neb.) 47(2), Spring 1984, 23.*
LEVEL: B LANG: Eng SIRC ARTICLE NO: 098418

TRAINING AND CONDITIONING - STRETCHING AND FLEXIBILITY EXERCISES

Glickman, S. Sports medicine: stretching. *Skate (Lincoln, Neb.) 47(1), Winter 1984, 33;35.*
LEVEL: B LANG: Eng SIRC ARTICL NO: 098416

ROWING

Leyniers, J. Prague: XIIe Colloque international des entraineurs d'aviron. *Sport: Communaute francaise de Belgique (Bruxelles) 106, 1984, 111-115.*
LEVEL: B LANG: Fr SIRC ARTICLE NO: 098422

ADMINISTRATION

Chuter, P. A blueprint for the future? *Rowing (Thames, Eng.) 27(297), Mar 1984, 16.*
LEVEL: B LANG: Eng SIRC ARTICLE NO: 101473

King, P. Promotion in rowing. *Catch (Ottawa) Jul/Aug 1984, 13-14.*
LEVEL: B LANG: Eng SIRC ARTICLE NO: 109075

ASSOCIATIONS

Rey, L. West of England ARA: rowing history - 111. *ARA club news (Bedford) 7(4), Apr 1984, 10.*
LEVEL: B LANG: Eng SIRC ARTICLE NO: 101479

BIOGRAPHY AND AUTOBIOGRAPHY

Aviron: Mark and Mike Evans. Rowing: Mark and Mike Evans. *Champion (Ottawa) 8(3), Aug 1984, 52-53.*
LEVEL: B LANG: Fr Eng SIRC ARTICLE NO: 096793

Campbell, R.L. Carol Brown: perspective on women's rowing. *Rowing U S A (Philadelphia) 16(1), Feb/Mar 1984, 9-13.*
LEVEL: LANG: Eng SIRC ARTICLE NO: 096794

Croot, D. Personality profile. (Jim Battersby) *Australian rowing (Perth, Wash.) 7(4), Dec 1984, 22-23.*
LEVEL: B LANG: Eng SIRC ARTICLE NO: 107427

Dodd, C. Anglo File. (Eric & Ted Phelps) *Rowing USA (Philadelphia, Pa.) 16(6), Dec 1984/Jan 1985, 26-27.*
LEVEL: B LANG: E SIRC ARTICLE NO: 103390

Macfarlane, D. Twin allegiances. Mark and Michael Evans are among the best Canadian oarsmen. By rowing for Oxford in the rac against Cambridge they've disrupted the training program of Canada's Olympic eight. *Saturday night (Toronto) 99(5), May 1984, 75-76.*
LEVEL: B LANG: Eng SIRC ARTICLE NO: 104862

Markey, E. Tiff Wood: on crash-B course. *Olympian (Colorado Springs, Colo.) 11(1), Jun 1984, 6-8.*
LEVEL: B LANG: Eng SIRC ARTICLE NO: 101476

Pileggi, S. Perspective. Ginny Gilder's finally going to the games, but not the way she planned. *Sports illustrated (Los Angeles, Calif.) 60(26), 25 Jun 1984, 86;88.*
LEVEL: B LANG: Eng SIRC ARTICLE NO: 095209

Raymond, P. The revenge of the hammer. *Ultrasport (San Diego, Calif.) 1(1), Jan/Feb 1984, 38-43;46.*
LEVEL: B LANG: Eng SIRC ARTICLE NO: 095210

U.S. athlete profiles. *Rowing USA (Philadelphia, Pa.) 16(3), Jun/Jul 1984, 43-47;49.*
LEVEL: B LANG: Eng SIRC ARTICLE NO: 099861

West, T. Donnelly: Olympian rower. Jack Donnelly, rameur et athlete olympique. *Champion (Ottawa) 8(3), Aug 1984, 85;90.*

LEVEL: B LANG: Eng Fr SIRC ARTICLE NO: 096800

BIOMECHANICS

Gjessing, E. Activite musculaire et deroulement des mouvements dans le domaine de l'aviron: une analyse de forces. *Aviron (Paris) 493, mai 1984, 19-22.*
NOTES: Source: Colloque des entraineurs FISA, Tata (Hongrie), 1979. Document de l'entraineur, D56. 2eme partie.
LEVEL: I LANG: Fr SIRC ARTICLE NO: 096796

Gjessing, E. Activite musculaire et deroulement des mouvements dans le domaine de l'aviron: une analyse de forces. *Aviron (Paris) 492, avr 1984, 15-18.*
NOTES: Source: Colloque des entraineurs FISA, Tata (Hongrie), 1979. Document de l'entraineur, D55. 1ere partie.
LEVEL: I LANG: Fr SIRC ARTICLE NO: 096797

Mahler, D.A. Nelson, W.N. Hagerman, F.C. Mechanical and physiological evaluation of exercise performance in elite national rowers. (Refs: 23)*JAMA: Journal of the American Medical Association (Chicago) 252(4), 27 Jul 1984, 496-499.*
ABST: This study details the scientific basis for evaluating the biomechanics and associated physiological requirements of exercise performance in elite national rowers.
LEVEL: A LANG: Eng SIRC ARTICLE NO: 103392

Martindale, W.O. Robertson, D.G.E. Mechanical energy in sculling and in rowing an ergometer. (Refs: 22)*Canadian journal of applied sport sciences/Journal canadien des sciences appliquees au sport (Windsor, Ont.) 9(3), Sept 1984, 153-163.*
ABST: The purpose of this study was to quantify and contrast the instantaneous segmental and total body energy patterns of rowing a single scull racing shell with rowing a rowing ergometer (RE), and to contrast energy savings through exchanges of mechanical energy among segments and conversions of energy within segments. Four scullers, two male and two female, were filmed at three stroke rates while rowing on a stationary and a wheeled RE, and rowing in single sculls racing shells. The internal work was least in the wheeled RE and greatest in the boat. Savings of energy through exchanges were greatest in the boat, and least in the stationary RE. Savings of energy through inter-conversion were greatest in the wheeled RE. The interconversions (expressed as a percentage of total work) were quite similar for both the boat and the stationary RE.
LEVEL: A LANG: Eng SIRC ARTICLE NO: 103393

Rogers, H. A theoretical study of rowing. *Human power (Cambridge, Mass.) 3(2), Winter 1984, 3;6.*
LEVEL: B LANG: Eng SIRC ARTICLE NO: 106026

CLUBS AND TEAMS

Arellano, J. Organization profile: Miami Rowing Club. *Rowing USA (Philadelphia) 16(2), Apr/May 1984, 19;21.*
LEVEL: B LANG Eng SIRC ARTICLE NO: 095191

Campbell, R. Organization profile: Lake Washington Rowing club. *Rowing USA (Philadelphia, Pa.) 16(3), Jun/Jul 1984, 51-52.*
LEVEL: B LANG: Eng SIRC ARTICLE NO: 099853

Club histories: 1 - The Globe Rowing Club, a far cry from Greenwich reach... *ARA club news (London)* 7(2), Feb 1984, 3.
LEVEL: B LANG: Eng SIRC ARTICLE NO: 099855

Doell, K. Profile: Mendota Rowing Club. *Rowing U S A (Philadelphia)* 16(1), Feb/Mar 1984, 31-36.
LEVEL: B LANG: Eng SIRC ARTICLE NO: 096795

Klein, H. McDonnell, A. Organization profile: the Baltimore Rowing Club. *Rowing USA (Philadelphia, Pa.)* 16(4), Aug/Sept 1984, 11-12.
LEVEL: B LANG: Eng SIRC ARTICLE NO: 099856

COACHING

Deschenes, G. Atalibio Magioni. *Revue de l'entraineur janv/mars 1984*, 18-19.
LEVEL: B LANG: Fr SIRC ARTICLE NO: 092346

Evans, E. Harry Parker: he's arguably the most successful coach in collegiate sports - a demigod in a sport steeped in tradition. *Ultrasport (Boston, Mass.)* 1(2), Apr 1984, 6-10.
LEVEL: B LANG: Eng SIRC ARTICLE NO: 098421

Guinness, R. Personality profile. (Phil Cayzer) *Australian rowing (Perth)* 7(1), Mar 1984, 34-35.
LEVEL: B LANG: Eng SIRC ARTICLE NO: 095196

Klavora, P. Implication of feedback in effective coaching for rowing. *Catch (Ottawa)* Feb 1984, 38-41.
LEVEL: I LANG: Eng SIRC ARTICLE NO: 095204

COUNTRIES AND REGIONS

Sculling in the USSR. *Rowing (London)* 27(303), Oct 1984, 19.
LEVEL: B LANG: Eng SIRC ARTICLE NO: 107439

The State of U.S.: rowing - 1984. *Rowing USA (Philadelphia, Pa.)* 16(2), Oct/Nov 1984, 42-43.
LEVEL: B LANG: Eng SIRC ARTICL NO: 103397

DRUGS, DOPING AND ERGOGENIC AIDS

Thomas, P. Amateur Rowing Association: random drugs testing Winter 1981/82. (letter) *British journal of sports medicine (Loughborough, Leicestershire)* 18(1), Mar 1984, 48.
LEVEL: I LANG: Eng SIRC ARTICLE NO: 096799

EQUIPMENT

Japersohn, W. Dreissigacker synthetic oars have swept by the traditional woodies. *Sports illustrated (Los Angeles, Calif.)* 61(22), 12 Nov 1984, 122-124.
LEVEL: B LANG: Eng SIRC ARTICLE NO: 101474

Klavora, P. Who built the boats for worldclass crews in 1983. *Catch (Ottawa, Ont.)* Feb 1984, 44.
NOTES: Translated from, Rudersport 33, Dec 1983.
LEVEL: B LANG: Eng SIRC ARTICLE NO: 095203

Lawrence, N. The winged keel of rowing. (Sargent and Burton) *Australian rowing (Perth, Wash.)* 7(4), Dec 1984, 15-16.
LEVEL: B LANG: Eng SIRC ARTICLE NO: 107434

Spero, D. Melch Buergin: co-owner of Stampfli Bootswerft. *Rowing U.S.A. (Philadelphia, Pa.)* 15(6), Dec 1983/Jan 1984, 32-33.
LEVEL: B LANG: Eng SIRC ARTICLE NO: 093679

Ziel, R. 60 years of Empacher boats. *Rowing USA (Philadelphia, Pa.)* 16(2), Apr/May 1984, 22-23.
NOTES: Translated from, Rudersport 34, 1983, by Suzanne Wamsler.
LEVEL: B LANG: Eng SIRC ARTICLE NO: 095214

FACILITIES

Chuter, P. National land centre for rowing. *ARA club news (London)* 7(2), Feb 1984, 6.
NOTES: To be continued.
LEVEL: B LANG: Eng SIRC ARTICLE NO: 099854

HISTORY

L'aviron et l'olympisme. *Revue olympique (Lausanne)* 205, nov 1984, 901-948.
LEVEL: B LANG: Fr SIRC ARTICLE NO: 104860

Mol, C. Profile: early Victoria rowing history. *Catch (Ottawa)* Nov 1984, 40-41.
NOTES: Reprinted from an unpublished manuscript.
LEVEL: B LANG: Eng SIRC ARTICLE NO: 109078

Rowing and Olympism. *Olympic review (Lausanne)* 205, Nov 1984, 901-948.
LEVEL: B LANG: Eng SIRC ARTICLE NO: 104864

INJURIES AND ACCIDENTS

Howell, D.W. Musculoskeletal profile and incidence of musculoskeletal injuries in lightweight women rowers. *American journa of sports medicine (Baltimore, Md.)* 12(4), Jul/Aug 1984, 278-282.
ABST: There is a lack of information dealing with the musculoskeletal profile of common injuries in women rowers. Strength and flexibility of trunk/ pelvic muscles were qualitatively described in 17 elite lightweight women rowers. Questionnaires regarding incidence of musculoskeletal injuries in this population were completed. Correlations between musculoskeletal profiles and incidence of injury were determined. Results indicate elite lightweight women rowers have a high incidence of low back pain and discomfort. Seventy-five percent of the sample demonstrated hyperflexion of the lumbar spine. There was a high positive correlation between hyperflexion motion of the lumbar spine and incidence of low back pain. There was a high negative correlation between adherence to a regular stretching program and incidence of low back pain.
LEVEL: A LANG: Eng SIRC ARTICLE NO: 108533

Martin, R. Application de la mesotherapie a la pratique de l'aviron. (Refs: 8)*Medecine du sport (Paris)* 58(4), 25 juil 1984 10-14.
LEVEL: I LANG: Fr SIRC ARTICLE NO: 098423

MEDICINE

Walenting, C. Roethle, J. Damken, M.A. Rowing study yields data for an upper body rehabilitation and training method. *CardioGram (La Crosse, Wis.)* 11(5), Oct/Nov 1984, 10.
LEVEL: B LANG: Eng SIRC ARTICLE NO: 173569

NUTRITION

Hagerman, F.C. Sawyer, R.H. Gundy, D. Fuel for crew. *Rowing (Surrey, Eng.)* 27(305), Dec 1984, 19.
NOTES: Part 1.
LEVEL: LANG: Eng SIRC ARTICLE NO: 109037

PHYSIOLOGY

Dorschner, F. L'objectivation des phases de charge et de recuperation. *Aviron (Paris)* 499, dec 1984, 11-14.
NOTES: Colloque des entraineurs F.I.S.A. 1979.
LEVEL: I LANG: Fr SIRC ARTICLE NO: 107428

Hagerman, F.C. Applied physiology of rowing. (Refs: 96)*Sports medicine (Auckland, N.Z.)* 1(4), Jul/Aug 1984, 303-326.
ABST The author reviews the literature on the physiological responses among oarsmen. Elite oarsmen and oarswomen possess large body dimensions and show outstanding aerobic and anaerobic qualities. Rowers also exhibit excellent isokinetic leg strength and power when compared with other elite athletes and oarswomen produced higher relative leg strength values than men when lean body mass is considered. Muscle fibre type distributions in oarsmen resemble those of distance runners while women tend to have a slightly higher proportion of fast-twitch fibres. Oarsmen also achieve very high ventilation volumes being able to average above 200 L/min BTPS for 6 minutes of simulated rowing; women ventilate 170 L/min BTPS for 3 minutes of this exercise.
LEVEL: A LANG: Eng SIRC ARTICLE NO: 103391

Hoyt, R.W. Greenbaum, B. Santilli, T.F. Emmi, R.P. Kinkead, J.A. McGlensy, M.J. Marley, W.P. Asakura, T. Resting echocardiography and metabolic responses to stimulated rowing. (Refs: 32)*Annals of sports medicine (North Hollywood, Calif.)* 2(1), 1984, 30-35.
ABST: We investigated the physiologic differences between a group of 8 competitively successful rowers (Group 1) and a slightly younger, but morphologically similar group of significantly less successful rowers (Group 2). Physical performance during a simulated race on a rowing ergometer was related to oxygen consumption (Vo2), heart rate (HR), venous lactate accumulation, standard hemoglobin-oxygen affinity (std HOA), and the resting echocardiogram. Although initial power production was similar, mean power outout for the race was 361 plus or minus 6 W for Group 1 and 313 plus or minus 5 W (SEM) for Group 2. Mean exercise HR was similar; however, the maximal absolute Vo2 ml of O2 per heart beat (O2 pulse), ventilation, and post-exercise systolic blood pressure of Group 1 exceeded that of Group 2 did not. The blood lactate accumulation of Group 1 at 3 and 15 min after exercise was half that of Group 2.
LEVEL: A LANG: Eng SIRC ARTICLE NO: 104861

Kelley, M.A. Laufe, M.D. Millman, R.P. Peterson, D.D. Ventilatory response to hypercapnia before and after athletic training *Respiration physiology (Amsterdam)* 55(3), Mar 1984, 393-400.
ABST: 13 untrained young men were prospectively studied to assess the effect of athletic training on the slope (S) of the hypercapnic ventilatory response at rest. Six of the subjects trained for seven months as intercollegiate rowers while the remaining subjects underwent no training and served as controls. After training, the rowers had a significant increase in S during hypercapnia. No change was seen in the untrained controls. These data suggest that athletic training in normal subjects increases CO_2 sensitivity at rest.
LEVEL: A LANG: Eng

Kiefer, J. The backward physiology of crew. In, Schrier, E.W. and Allman, W.F. (eds.), Newton at the bat: the science in sports, New York, Scribner,

ROWING (continued)

c1984, p. 154-157.
LEVEL: B LANG: Eng RC1235 18609

Mahler, D.A. Andrea, B.E. Andresen, D.C.
Comparison of 6-min 'all-out' and incremental
exercise tests in elite oarsmen. (Refs: 12)*Medicine
and science in sports and exercise (Indianapolis)
16(6), Dec 1984, 567-571.*
ABST: Heart rate (HR), minute ventilation (VE),
oxygen consumption (VO2), and carbon dioxide
production (VCO2) every 30 s, and obtained ratings
of perceived exertion (RPE) from 12 elite oarsmen
(aged between 21 and 25 years) were measured.
Each oarsman performed either the 6-min 'all-out'
(6M-AO) or the progressive incremental (PI) test on
the rowing ergometer on consecutive days. Peak
physiological values were achieved in the first 2 min
of exercise for the 6M-AO test, but in the last 2 min
for the PI test. There were no statistically significant
differences among peak values for HR, VE, VO2,
VCO2, and RPE with each test. The authors
conclude that physiological values at peak exercise
were similar for the 6M-AO and PI tests.
LEVEL: A LANG: Eng SIRC ARTICLE NO: 104863

**Morton, A.R. Lawrence, S.R. Blanksby, B.A.
Bloomfield, J.** A report of profiles of elite
Australian oarsmen. (Refs: 14) *Australian rowing
(Claremont, Aust.) 7(3), Sept 1984, 21-23.*
LEVEL: I LANG: Eng SIRC ARTICLE NO: 109033

**Premel-Cabic, A. Turcant, A. Chaleil, D. Allain,
P. Victor, J. Tadei, A.** Concentration plasmatique
de catecholamines a l'effort chez le sujet non
entraine et chez le sportif. (Plasma catecholamine
concentrations during exercise in the untrained
subject and in the sportsman.) *Pathologie biologie
(Paris) 32(6), juin 1984, 702-704.*
LEVEL: A LANG: Fr SIRC ARTICLE NO: 104359

Wenderoth, M.P. Snyder, A.C. Steinrauf, L.K.
Physiological testing: a case for its use in rowing.
(Refs: 12)*Rowing USA (Philadelphia, Pa.) 16(2),
Apr/May 1984, 15;17-18;25-27.*
LEVEL: I LANG: Eng SIRC ARTICLE NO: 095213

PHYSIOLOGY - MUSCLE

**Clarkson, P.M. Graves, J. Melchionda, A.M.
Johnson, J.** Isokinetic strength and endurance and
muscle fiber type of elite oarswomen. (Refs:
25)*Canadian journal of applied sport sciences/
Journal canadien des sciences appliquees au sport
(Windsor, Ont.) 9(3), Sept 1984, 127-132.*
ABST: Knee extension (KE) and elbow flexion (EF)
isokinetic strength and fatigue were examined in ten
elite oarswomen and ten untrained subjects. Muscle
fiber types of the corresponding muscles were
determined for the oarswomen. The oarswomen
had a lower slow twitch percentage than previously
reported values for oarsmen. A marked similarity
was found between untrained subjects and
oarswomen in 1) the patterns of the torque velocity
curves of the strength measurements and 2) the
patterns of the fatigue curves of the isokinetic
endurance measurements. For each group,
patterns of both the KE torque velocity and the
isokinetic fatigue curves differed from the patterns
of the corresponding curves for EF.
LEVEL: A LANG: Eng SIRC ARTICLE NO: 103389

**de Koning, F.L. Vos, J.A. Binkhorst, R.A.
Vissers, A.C.A.** Influence of training on the force-
velocity relationship of the ar flexors of active
sportsmen. (Refs: 12)*International journal of sports
medicine 5(1), Feb 1984, 43-46.*
ABST: The force-velocity curve of the arm flexors

of four rowers, five athletes competing in the tug-of-
war, and six runners was established and
periodically re-assessed throughout a year of
training and competition. The results showed very
few changes in the force-velocity curve of these
athletes. The authors conclude that variation in
type, intensity, and volume of arm training
throughout a year hardly affected the course of the
force-velocity curve of the arm flexors of well-
trained athletes.
LEVEL: A LANG: Eng SIRC ARTICLE NO: 093670

Gjessing, E. Activite musculaire et deroulement
des mouvements dans le domaine de l'aviron: une
analyse de forces. *Aviron (Paris) 493, mai 1984,
19-22.*
NOTES: Source: Colloque des entraineurs FISA,
Tata (Hongrie), 1979. Document de l'entraineur,
D56. 2eme partie.
LEVEL: I LANG: Fr SIRC ARTICLE NO: 096796

Gjessing, E. Activite musculaire et deroulement
des mouvements dans le domaine de l'aviron: une
analyse de forces. *Aviron (Paris) 492, avr 1984, 15-
18.*
NOTES: Source: Colloque des entraineurs FISA,
Tata (Hongrie), 1979. Document de l'entraineur,
D55. 1ere partie.
LEVEL: I LANG: Fr SIRC ARTICLE NO: 096797

Herland, J.S. Sculling: an electromyographic
analysis. (Refs: 4)
NOTES: In, Cantu, R.C. (ed.), Clinical sports
medicine, Lexington, Mass. ; Toronto, Collamore
Press : D.C. Heath, c1984, p. 169-175.
LEVEL: A LANG: Eng RC1201 15964

RULES AND REGULATIONS

Martin, A. Racing recreational shells. *Rowing USA
(Philadelphia, Pa.) 16(3), Jun/Jul 1984, 55-56.*
LEVEL: B LANG: Eng SIRC ARTICLE NO: 099858

SPORTING EVENTS

Adler, B. Barry Berkus, Olympic rowing
commissioner. *Rowing USA (Philadelphia, Pa.)
16(3), Jun/Jul 1984, 27;29.*
LEVEL: B LANG: Eng SIRC ARTICLE NO: 099852

L'aviron et l'olympisme. *Revue olympique
(Lausanne) 205, nov 1984, 901-948.*
LEVEL: B LANG: Fr SIRC ARTICLE NO: 106019

Olympic rowing: facts and figures. *Rowing USA
(Philadelphia, Pa.) 16(3), Jun/Jul 1984, 30-31.*
LEVEL: B LANG: Eng SIRC ARTICLE NO: 099860

Rowing and Olympism. *Olympic review (Lausanne)
205, Nov 1984, 901-948.*
LEVEL: B LANG: Eng SIRC ARTICLE NO: 106027

West, T. Donnelly: Olympian rower. Jack Donnelly,
rameur et athlete olympique. *Champion (Ottawa)
8(3), Aug 1984, 85;90.*
LEVEL: B LANG: Eng Fr SIRC ARTICLE NO:
096800

TECHNIQUES AND SKILLS

Korzeniowski, K. Nilsen, T. Rowing techniques.
*Rowing USA (Philadelphia, Pa.) 16(3), Jun/Jul
1984, 59.*
LEVEL: B LANG: Eng SIRC ARTICLE NO: 099857

Rowing fundamentals: the catch. *Rowing USA
(Philadelphia, Pa.) 16(2), Apr/May 1984, 45.*
LEVEL: B LANG: Eng SIRC ARTICLE NO: 095211

Rowing fundamentals: the release. *Rowing USA
(Philadelphia, Pa.) 16(2), Oct/Nov 1984, 45.*
LEVEL: B LANG: Eng SIRC ARTICLE NO: 103395

Smith, J. Measurements of style: 1983 men's
lightweight eight. *Rowing USA (Philadelphia, Pa.)
16(2), Oct/Nov 1984, 11-13.*
LEVEL: I LANG: Eng SIRC ARTICLE NO: 103396

TESTING AND EVALUATION

Marlow, R. Testing: reliability with the ergometer.
Coaching review 7, Mar/Apr 1984, 51-52.
LEVEL: B LANG: Eng SIRC ARTICLE NO: 093674

Stuart, D. A comparison of test scores for elite
rowers: using a Repco amd Gjessing rowing
ergometer. (Refs: 1)*Australian rowing (Claremont,
Aust.) 7(3), Sept 1984, 25-27.*
LEVEL: I LANG: Eng SIRC ARTICLE NO: 109035

TRAINING AND CONDITIONING

Angst, F. L'aviron, sport de performance et sport
de loisir. *Macolin (Suisse) 8, aout 1984, 4-7.*
LEVEL: B LANG: Fr SIRC ARTICLE NO: 101472

Coaching advisory service. *Rowing (Surrey, Eng.)
27(298), Apr/May 1984, 23.*
LEVEL: B LANG: Eng SIRC ARTICLE NO: 098420

Joy, J. Technique modification: some
considerations for the fall training. *Catch (Ottawa)
Nov 1984, 37-38.*
LEVEL: B LANG: Eng SIRC ARTICLE NO: 109077

Leroy, B. Plan-cadre d'entrainement 'juniors'
Saison 1984-85. *Aviron (Paris) 497, oct 1984, 17-
24.*
LEVEL: B LANG: Fr SIRC ARTICLE NO: 107435

Preparing for racing. *Rowing (Thames, Eng.)
27(297), Mar 1984, 11-12.*
LEVEL: B LANG: Eng SIRC ARTICLE NO: 101477

TRAINING AND CONDITIONING - DRYLAND TRAINING

Starting the season. *Rowing (Surrey, Eng.) 27(304),
Nov 1984, 15.*
LEVEL: B LANG: Eng SIRC ARTICLE NO: 106028

TRAINING AND CONDITIONING - STRETCHING AND FLEXIBILITY EXERCISES

Getting the novices going. *Rowing (London)
27(303), Oct 1984, 13.*
LEVEL: B LANG: Eng SIRC ARTICLE NO: 107430

TRAINING AND CONDITIONING - WARM-UPS, WARM-DOWNS, LEAD-UP GAMES

Hagerman, F. Mickelson, T. Warm-down. (Refs:
5)*Rowing (Surrey, Eng.) 27(304), Nov 1984, 21.*
LEVEL: B LANG: Eng SIRC ARTICLE NO: 106020

Marlow, R.G. Doing it right from the start. (Refs:
10)*Coaching review (Ottawa, Ont.) 7, Jul/Aug
1984, 50-51.*
LEVEL: B LANG: Eng SIRC ARTICLE NO: 095207

Mickelson, T. Hagerman, F. Warming up: part
one. *Rowing (Surrey, Eng.) 27(299), May/Jun
1984, 21.*

NOTES: To be concluded next month.
LEVEL: B LANG: Eng SIRC ARTICLE NO: 098424

Mickelson, T. Hagerman, F. Warming up: concluding part two. *Rowing (London, Eng.) 300, Jul 1984, 21.*
LEVEL: B LANG: Eng SIRC ARTICLE NO: 099859

WOMEN

Huisveld, I.A. Kluft, C. Hospers, J.H. Bernink, M.J.E. Erich, W.B.M. Bouma, B.N. Effect of exercise and oral contraceptive agents on fibrinolytic potential in trained females. (Refs: 33)*Journal of applied physiology: respiratory, environmental and exercise physiology 56(4), Apr 1984, 906-913.*
ABST: Ten female competitive rowers who used oral contraceptives and ten female competitive rowers who did not use oral contraceptives performed exhaustive exercise to determine the effect of exercise and oral contraceptive agents on fibrinolytic potential. The preexercise data revealed that the user group had higher levels of factor XII, total plasminogen, and free plasminogen levels along with lower C1-inactivator level. Exercise decreased all factors under study but increased all fibrinolytic activities. The effects of exercise were superimposed on the changes induced by oral contraceptive use.
LEVEL: A LANG: Eng SIRC ARTICLE NO: 096798

Kirby, S. Careers in sport: women rowing. Carrieres en sport: l'aviron et les femmes. *Catch (Ottawa) Summer/ete 1984, 22-24*
LEVEL: B LANG: Eng Fr SIRC ARTICLE NO: 173399

Lisy, Z. Hormonalni kontraceptiva u veslarek. (Hormonal contraceptives in female rowers.) *Casopis lekaru ceskych (Praha) 12 (35), 31 Aug 1984, 1086-1090.*
LEVEL: A LANG: Cze

Pridham, E. Women in rowing. *Rowing (Thames, Eng.) 27(297), Mar 1984, 23.*
LEVEL: B LANG: Eng SIRC ARTICLE NO: 101478

RUGBY

Bouthier, D. Sports collectifs: contribution a l'analyse de l'activite et elements pour une formation tactique essentielle: l'exemple du rugby. (Paris): (Institut national du sport et de l'education physique), 1984. 224 f.
NOTES: Memoire INSEP : Paris : 1984. Bibliographie.
LEVEL: A LANG: Fr

Haden, A. Book excerpt. Boots n'all: the professional approach. *Rugby (New York) 10(1), 5 Mar 1984, 14-15.*
LEVEL: B LANG: Eng SIRC ARTICLE NO: 098430

ADMINISTRATION

Levitan, T. Professional administration needed. *Rugby (New York) 9(8), 16 Jan 1984, 29.*
LEVEL: B LANG: Eng SIRC ARTICLE NO: 098433

von Lichtenberg, A. Running a successful big event. Part 111: publicity. *Rugby (New York) 10(1), 5 Mar 1984, 12-13;20.*
LEVEL: B LANG: Eng SIRC ARTICLE NO: 098439

von Lichtenberg, A. Running a successful big event: part IV. *Rugby (New York) 10(2), 16 Apr 1984, 16-17.*
NOTES: Fourth an final in a series.
LEVEL: B LANG: Eng SIRC ARTICLE NO: 101491

ANTHROPOMETRY

Maud, P.J. Shultz, B.B. The US National Rugby Team: a physiological and anthropometric assessment. (Refs: 32)*Physician and sportsmedicine (Minneapolis, Minn.) 12(9), Sept 1984, 86-94;99.*
ABST: Various physiological and anthropometric variables of 20 forward and back-line players of the US national rugby team were compared. A comparison was also established between these athletes and other rugby players as elite athletes from football, basketball, soccer, baseball, and ice hockey teams. The study showed that the forwards were taller and heavier, had greater lean body weight and a higher percent body fat, and had greater anaerobic power and capacity than the back-line players. Professional soccer players and national representative ice hockey players had higher aerobic fitness scores than rugby players.
LEVEL: A LANG: Eng SIRC ARTICLE NO: 099867

BIOGRAPHY AND AUTOBIOGRAPHY

Cain, N. RFU President Albert Agar: 'there has to be give and take.' *Rugby post (London) Oct 1984, 28-30.*
LEVEL: B LANG: Eng SIRC ARTICLE NO: 107443

CERTIFICATION

Mayes, R. Perkins, J. The seven year plan: 18 month progress report. *Rugby (New York) 10(6), 24 Sept 1984, 25-26.*
LEVEL: LANG: Eng SIRC ARTICLE NO: 107451

CLOTHING

Rugby boots: what's available, how much they cost. *Rugby world (Sutton, Eng.) 24(9), Sept 1984, 58-59;61-62.*
LEVEL: B LANG: Eng SIRC ARTICLE NO: 100576

COACHING

Club coaching guidelines for the implementation of U.S.A.R.F.U. philosophy and style. Berkeley, Calif.: U.S.A.R.F.U., 1984?. ii, 59 p.
LEVEL: B LANG: Eng GV945.75 17947

Dwyer, B. Interview Bob Dwyer: Australian Nat'l Coach. *Rugby (New York) 9(8), 16 Jan 1984, 14-15.*
LEVEL: B LANG: Eng SIRC ARTICLE NO: 098429

Mottram, B. Correcting weaknessess in the U.S. game. *Rugby (New York) 9(8), 16 Jan 1984, 26.*
LEVEL: B LANG: Eng SIRC ARTICLE NO: 098435

Wyatt, D. Coaching in crisis - an investigation, part 2. Time to take P.E. out of the schools. *Rugby world (Sutton, Eng.) 24(2), Feb 1984, 16-19.*
LEVEL: B LANG: Eng SIRC ARTICLE NO: 096802

Wyatt, D. Coaching - where do we go now? *Rugby world (Sutton, Eng.) 24(3), Mar 1984, 15-16.*
NOTES: Third in a three-part series.
LEVEL: B LANG: Eng SIRC ARTICLE NO: 099871

COUNTRIES AND REGIONS

Gray, S. Rugby: a multi-faceted approach to promoting team sports. (Refs: 11)*Florida JOHPERD (Gainesville, Fla.) 22(3), Aug 1984, 3-4.*
LEVEL: B LANG: Eng SIRC ARTICLE NO: 099864

Smith, M. Rugby in Southeast Asia. *Rugby (New York) 9(8), 16 Jan 1984, 16-17;25.*
LEVEL: B LANG: Eng SIRC ARTICLE NO: 0984

DISABLED

Simpson, A. Fighter. (Chris Burns) *Rugby post (London) Feb 1984, 41.*
LEVEL: B LANG: Eng SIRC ARTICLE NO: 099017

ECONOMICS

Halphen, A. Prends l'oseille et tais-toi. *Equipe magazine (Paris) 196, 26 mai 1984, 60-63;65.*
LEVEL: B LANG: Fr SIRC ARTICLE NO: 104865

White, B. 'The man who pays the piper calls the tune.' *Rugby post (London) Oct 1984, 8-10.*
LEVEL: B LANG: Eng SIRC ARTICL NO: 107458

HISTORY

Andrew, P. Rugby on America's Pacific Coast. *Rugby (New York) 1984, 34.*
NOTES: 10th Anniversary issue
LEVEL: B LANG: Eng SIRC ARTICLE NO: 106029

Park, R.J. From football to rugby - and back, 1906-1919: the University of California-Stanford University response to the 'football crisis of 1905'. (Refs: 101)*Journal of sport history (Pennsylvania) 11(3), Winter 1984, 5-40.*
LEVEL: I LANG: Eng SIRC ARTICLE NO: 106032

Ray, D. The way we were. *Rugby post (London) Feb 1984, 38.*
LEVEL: B LANG: Eng SIRC ARTICLE NO: 099870

INJURIES AND ACCIDENTS

Cervical spine injuries and Rugby Union. (editorial) (Refs: 24)*Lancet (London) 1(8386), 19 May 1984, 1108.*
LEVEL: I LANG: E SIRC ARTICLE NO: 103400

Chase, J. Medical care in U.S. Rugby: an evaluation. *Rugby (New York) 10(7), 29 Oct 1984, 26.*
LEVEL: B LANG: Eng SIRC ARTICLE NO: 107445

Cleary, M. The safety factor: Mike Cleary takes stock of a thorny issue confronting the game's administration. *Rugby post (London) Nov 1984, 8-9.*
LEVEL: B LANG: Eng SIRC ARTICLE NO: 107446

Collinson, D. Rugby injuries. *Australian family physician (Sydney) 13(8), Aug 1984, 565-569.*
LEVEL: A LANG: Eng

Glaun, R. Egnal, A. Allen, J. Noakes, T.D. Are high schools adequately prepared to cope with serious rugby injuries? *South African medical journal (Cape Town) 66(20), 17 Nov 1984, 768-770.*
LEVEL: I LANG: Eng

Horan, F.T. Injuries to the cervical spine in schoolboys playing rugby football. (Refs: 7)*Journal of bone and joint surgery British volume*

RUGBY (continued)

(Edinburgh) 66(4), Aug 1984, 470-471.
LEVEL: I LANG: Eng SIRC ARTICLE NO: 104866

Jack, P.D. Bad breaks in football. *Sports world Australia 1(3), Sept 1984, 71-73.*
LEVEL: B LANG: Eng SIRC ARTICLE NO: 106031

Lamid, S. El Ghatit, A.Z. Quadriplegia following rugby football injury. (Refs: 5)*Journal of the American Paraplegia Society 7(1), Jan 1984, 12-14.*
LEVEL: I LANG: Eng SIRC ARTICLE NO: 101485

McCoy, G.F. Piggot, J. Macafee, A.L. Adair, I.V. Injuries of the cervical spine in schoolboy rugby football. (Refs: 21) *Journal of bone and joint surgery: British volume (Edinburgh) 66(4), Aug 1984, 500-503.*
LEVEL: I LANG: Eng SIRC ARTICLE NO: 104867

Micheli, L.J. Injuries in the football sports. (Refs: 25)
NOTES: In, Cantu, R.C. (ed.), Clinical sports medicine, Lexington, Mass. ; Toronto, Collamore Press : D.C. Heath, c1984, p. 203-210.
LEVEL: I LANG: Eng RC1201 15964

Patel, M.K. Burt, A.A. Bradbury, J.A. Are spinal injuries more common in rugby union than in rugby league football? (letter) *British medical journal (clinical research) (London) 288(6426), 28 Apr 1984, 1308.*
LEVEL: B LANG: Eng SIRC ARTICLE NO: 101488

Polson, A. Cervical spine injuries in rugby players. (Refs: 1)*Canadian Medical Association journal/ Journal de l'Association medicale canadienne (Ottawa) 131(8), 15 Oct 1984, 849.*
LEVEL: B LANG: Eng SIRC ARTICLE NO: 099869

Rees, D. Thompson, S.K. Traumatic dislocation of the hip in mini rugby. *British medical journal (Clinical research) (London 289(6436), 7 Jul 1984, 19-20.*
LEVEL: I LANG: Eng SIRC ARTICLE NO: 103404

Silver, J.R. Injuries of the spine sustained in rugby. *British medical journal (clinical research) (London) 288(6410), 7 Ja 1984, 37-43.*
ABST: 67 spinal injuries were recorded between 1952 and 1982 of which 48 lead to paralysis and total incapacity. The injuries occurred predominantly at the lower cervical spine. Such injuries have increased in recent years particularly among schoolboys. However, it is hoped recent changes in rules and player attitude will lower the incidence of such injuries.
LEVEL: A LANG: Eng SIRC ARTICLE NO: 098437

Sovio, O.M. Van Peteghem, P.K. Schweigel, J.F. Cervical spine injuries in rugby players. (Refs: 7)*Canadian Medical Association journal/Journal de l'Association medicale canadienne (Ottawa, Ont.) 130(6), 15 Mar 1984, 735-736.*
LEVEL: I LANG: Eng SIRC ARTICLE NO: 095224

LAW AND LEGISLATION

The player and the law. *Rugby world (Sutton, Eng.) 24(8), Aug 1984, 45-47.*
LEVEL: B LANG: Eng SIRC ARTICLE NO: 101489

MASS MEDIA

Lawrenson, D. Behind the scenes with rugby special. *Rugby world (Sutton, Eng.) 24(4), Apr 1984, 20-24;51-52.*
LEVEL: B LANG: Eng SIRC ARTICLE NO: 099866

MEDICINE

Chase, J. New Zealand's view of sports medicine. *Rugby (New York) 10(2), 16 Apr 1984, 29.*
LEVEL: B LANG: Eng SIRC ARTICLE NO: 101481

White, W.B. Grant-Kels, J.M. Transmission of herpes simplex virus tye 1 infection in rugby players. (Refs: 14)*JAMA: Journal of the American Medical Association (Chicago) 252(4), 27 Jul 1984, 533-535.*
ABST: Four cases of extensive cutaneous herpes simplex virus in players on a rugby team are detailed. All players had a prodrome of fever, malaise, and anorexia with a weight loss of 3.6 to 9.0 kg. All infected players on the team were forwards or members of the 'scrum', which suggests a field-acquired infection.
LEVEL: A LANG: Eng SIRC ARTICLE NO: 103406

OFFICIATING

Fletcher, J. Reducing conflict. (rugby refereeing) *Rugby (New York) 10(7), 29 Oct 1984, 25.*
LEVEL: B LANG: Eng SIRC ARTICLE NO: 107449

Hollands, M. Cut out the rough stuff. (Clive Norling) *Rugby post (London) Mar 1984, 9-11.*
LEVEL: B LANG: Eng SIRC ARTICLE NO: 099865

Morrison, D. Identifying recruiting and retaining referees. *Rugby (New York) 10(8), 30 Nov 1984, 30.*
LEVEL: B LANG: Eng SIRC ARTICLE NO: 103403

Peytavin, A. Les gestes de l'arbitre et des juges de touche. *EPS: Education physique et sport 185, janv/fevr 1984, 34-37.*
LEVEL: B LANG: Fr SIRC ARTICLE NO: 093681

PHYSIOLOGY

Brayne, C.E. Dow, L. Calloway, S.P. Creatine kinease BB isoenzyme in rugby football players. (letter) *Journal of neurology, neurosurgery and psychiatry (London) 47(5), May 1984, 568-569.*
LEVEL: I LANG: Eng SIRC ARTICLE NO: 103399

Kelly, A.E. An assessment of physiological profiles of middle-distance athletes and rugby players. (abstract) *Carnegie research papers (Beckett Park, Leeds) 1(6), Dec 1984, 35.*
CONF: Carnegie Undergraduate Research Symposium (1984 : Leeds, Eng.).
LEVEL: I LANG: Eng SIRC ARTICLE NO: 172512

Maud, P.J. Shultz, B.B. The US National Rugby Team: a physiological and anthropometric assessment. (Refs: 32)*Physician and sportsmedicine (Minneapolis, Minn.) 12(9), Sept 1984, 86-94;99.*
ABST: Various physiological and anthropometric variables of 20 forward and back-line players of the US national rugby team were compared. A comparison was also established between these athletes and other rugby players as elite athletes from football, basketball, soccer, baseball, and ice hockey teams. The study showed that the forwards were taller and heavier, had greater lean body weight and a higher percent body fat, and had greater anaerobic power and capacity than the back-line players. Professional soccer players and national representative ice hockey players had higher aerobic fitness scores than rugby players.
LEVEL: A LANG: Eng SIRC ARTICLE NO: 099867

POLITICS

Chalfont, L. Should we tour South Africa? *Rugby post (London) Apr 1984, 14-15;17.*
LEVEL: B LANG: Eng SIRC ARTICLE NO: 098426

PROTECTIVE DEVICES

Mouthguards and dental injuries. (Refs: 3)*Rugby world (Sutton, Eng.) 24(8), Aug 1984, 43;45.*
LEVEL: B LANG: Eng SIRC ARTICL NO: 101486

PSYCHOLOGY

Hale, B. Stress and relaxation. *Rugby (New York) 10(1), 5 Mar 1984, 30.*
LEVEL: B LANG: Eng SIRC ARTICLE NO: 098431

Hale, B. Slumps and plateaus. *Rugby (New York) 10(8), 30 Nov 1984, 28.*
LEVEL: B LANG: Eng SIRC ARTICLE NO: 103401

PSYCHOLOGY - MENTAL TRAINING

Hale, B. Concentration and attentional focus. *Rugby (New York) 10(2), 16 Apr 1984, 31.*
LEVEL: B LANG: Eng SIRC ARTICLE NO 101484

Hale, B. Improving concentration. *Rugby (New York) 10(3), 28 May 1984, 39.*
LEVEL: B LANG: Eng SIRC ARTICLE NO: 108688

RULES AND REGULATIONS

Diemer, J. Off-side on kicks. *Rugby (New York) 10(2), 16 Apr 1984, 26.*
LEVEL: B LANG: Eng SIRC ARTICLE NO: 101483

Middleton, G. Forward rule changes for under-19s. *Rugby weekly (New South Wales) 2(31), Dec 1984, 2;10-11.*
LEVEL: B LANG: Eng SIRC ARTICLE NO: 173174

SPORTING EVENTS

Cleaveland, N. Glarner, A. A player recalls the 1924 olympics. *Rugby (New York) 10(6), 24 Sept 1984, 6-7.*
LEVEL: B LANG: Eng SIRC ARTICLE NO: 107447

Tournaments. *Rugby (New York) 10(7), 29 Oct 1984, 20.*
LEVEL: B LANG: Eng SIRC ARTICLE NO: 107456

STATISTICS AND RECORDS

Rees, W. 100 years of the international championship. *Rugby world (Sutton, Eng.) 24(1), Jan 1984, 29;31-35;37.*
LEVEL: B LANG: Eng SIRC ARTICLE NO: 098436

STRATEGY - OFFENSIVE

Savoyant, B.A. A contribution to the learning of a collective action: the counter-attack in rugby. (Refs: 9)*International journal of sport psychology (Rome) 15(1), 1984, 25-34.*
LEVEL: I LANG: Eng SIRC ARTICLE NO: 095220

Wynn, J. Transitional rugby. *Rugby (New York) 10(2), 16 Apr 1984, 27.*
LEVEL: B LANG: Eng SIRC ARTICLE NO: 101492

TEACHING

Stein, J.F. Une planification d'objectifs par niveau d'exigence. (Refs: 2)*EPS: Education physique et sport (Paris) 190, nov/dec 1984, 26-28.*
LEVEL: B LANG: Fr SIRC ARTICLE NO: 103405

TECHNIQUES AND SKILLS

John, B. Use your loaf: that's the secret of fly-half play. *Rugby post (London) Apr 1984, 34-35.*
LEVEL: B LANG: Eng SIRC ARTICLE NO: 098432

Luke, M. Captaincy. (leadership skills) *Coaching review (Ottawa, Ont.) 7, May/Jun 1984, 37-38.*
LEVEL: B LANG: Eng SIRC ARTICLE NO: 095218

TECHNIQUES AND SKILLS - BACK

Davies, G. Playing on the wing. *Rugby post (London) Jan 1984, 42-43.*
LEVEL: B LANG: Eng SIRC ARTICLE NO: 098427

TECHNIQUES AND SKILLS - CENTRE

Gibson, M. Playing in the centre...part 2. *Rugby post (London) Mar 1984, 38-39.*
LEVEL: B LANG: Eng SIRC ARTICLE NO: 09986

TECHNIQUES AND SKILLS - FORWARD

Cotton, F. Coaching 1: propping. Tight and loose. *Rugby world (Sutton, Eng.) 24(9), Sept 1984, 16-18.*
LEVEL: B LANG: Eng SIRC ARTICLE NO: 101482

Slattery, F. Follow the ball. (wing forward) *Rugby post (London) Jul 1984, 40-41.*
LEVEL: B LANG: Eng SIRC ARTICLE NO: 101490

Ward, A. The number 8. *Rugby (New York) 10(4), Jul 1984, 27.*
LEVEL: B LANG: Eng SIRC ARTICLE NO: 098440

Wilson, G. The prop. *Rugby (New York) 9(8), 16 Jan 1984, 27.*
LEVEL: B LANG: Eng SIRC ARTICLE NO: 098441

TECHNIQUES AND SKILLS - FULLBACK

Armstrong, W.R. The fullback. *Rugby (New York) 10(1), 5 Mar 1984, 31.*
LEVEL: B LANG: Eng SIRC ARTICLE NO: 098425

Irvine, A. Coaching 4: full back. Positional play must be your first priority. *Rugby world (Sutton, Surrey) 24(12), Dec 198 32-34.*
LEVEL: B LANG: Eng SIRC ARTICLE NO: 173167

TECHNIQUES AND SKILLS - HALFBACK

Gray, S. The flyhalf. *Rugby (New York) 10(7), 29 Oct 1984, 29-30.*
LEVEL: B LANG: Eng SIRC ARTICLE NO: 107450

TESTING AND EVALUATION

Perkins, J.E. The Midwest tour: an assessment. *Rugby (New York) 10(3), 28 May 1984, 36-37.*
LEVEL: B LANG: Eng SIRC ARTICL NO: 108687

TRAINING AND CONDITIONING

Bauer, T. Rationale, design and development of rugby training programs. (Refs: 5)*National Strength & Conditioning Association journal (Lincoln, Neb.) 6(5), Oct/Nov 1984, 61-62;64.*
LEVEL: B LANG: Eng SIRC ARTICLE NO: 103398

Beaumont, B. Coaching 2: the second row. locking and jumping. *Rugby world (Sutton, Eng.) 24(10), Oct 1984, 24-26.*
LEVEL: B LANG: Eng SIRC ARTICLE NO: 101480

Docherty, D. Preparing for the rugby season. (Refs: 10)*New Zealand journal of health, physical education & recreation (Wellington, N.Z.) 17(1), May 1984, 7-10.*
LEVEL: B LANG: Eng SIRC ARTICLE NO: 098428

TRAINING AND CONDITIONING - DRILLS

Corless, B. Rugby: introducing contact. *British journal of physical education (London) 15(1), Mar/Apr 1984, 58-59.*
LEVEL: LANG: Eng SIRC ARTICLE NO: 099862

Old, A. Corless, B. Coaching: improving the player. (back play) *Rugby post (London) Aug 1984, 38-39.*
LEVEL: B LANG: Eng SIRC ARTICLE NO: 101487

Old, A.G.B. Some ideas on introducing handling. *British journal of physical education (London) 15(1), Jan/Feb 1984, 23-24.*
LEVEL: B LANG: Eng SIRC ARTICLE NO: 099868

VARIATIONS

Webb, P. Coffey, D. Touch - Australia's fastest growing team sport. (Refs: 4)*Sports coach (Wembley, Australia) 7(4), Mar 1984, 58-61.*
LEVEL: B LANG: Eng SIRC ARTICLE NO: 095226

WOMEN

Moore, T. Women's rugby comes of age. *Rugby world (Sutton, Eng.) 24(5), May 1984, 18-20.*
LEVEL: B LANG: Eng SIRC ARTICLE NO: 098434

RUMANIA

Bucur, C.I. Peut-on parler de 'miracle sportif roumain' apres les succes remportes par ce pays aux Jeux olympiques de Los Angeles? *Macolin (Macolin, Suisse) 41(12), dec 1984, 14-15.*
LEVEL: B LANG: Fr SIRC ARTICLE NO: 108766

Noran, S. Daciada: an inexhaustible source of gifted athletes. *Sports in Romania/Sport en Roumanie (Bucarest, Romania) 2/3, 1984, 44-45.*
NOTES: Special issue, The Los Angeles Olympic Games.
LEVEL: B LANG: Eng SIRC ARTICLE NO: 109029

Stoian, V. The Romanians' National Sports. *Sports in Romania (Bucharest, Romania) 2/3, 1984, 46-47.*
LEVEL: B LANG: Eng SIRC ARTICLE NO: 105603

OLYMPIC GAMES

Noran, S. Romania at the Olympic Games (IV). *Sports in Romania (Bucharest, Romania) 1, 1984, 16-21.*
LEVEL: B LANG: Eng SIRC ARTICLE NO: 099139

Romania at the Olympic Games. *Sports in Romania (Bucharest, Romania) 2/3, 1984, 5-6.*
LEVEL: B LANG: Eng SIRC ARTICLE NO: 105385

Romania at the Olympic Games. *Sports in Romania/Sport en Roumanie (Bucarest, Romania) 2/3, 1984, 5-6.*
NOTES: Special issue, The Los Angeles Olympic Games.
LEVEL: B LANG: Eng SIRC ARTICLE NO: 109027

RUNNING

Cross, I. Elliott, L. Merhar, G. Dr. Sheehan on running. *Running & fitness (Washington, D.C.) 16(5), Sept/Oct 1984, 1;17-18.*
LEVEL: B LANG: Eng SIRC ARTICLE NO: 098623

Durden, B. Efficient running: it's not so much what you have but how you use it that lets you get the most out of your running. *Runner's world (Mountain View, Calif.) 19(6), Jun 1984, 44-47.*
LEVEL: B LANG: Eng SIRC ARTICLE NO: 095405

Henderson, J. The 10 questions I hear most often: on the running-clinic tour, all the questions I must face are usually the same - it's the answers that change. *Runner's world (Mountain View, Calif.) 19(6), Jun 1984, 54-57.*
LEVEL: B LANG: Eng SIRC ARTICLE NO: 095416

Henderson, J. In the beginning. *Runner's world (Mountain View, Calif.) 19(8), Aug 1984, 138-143.*
LEVEL: B LANG: Eng SIRC ARTICLE NO: 096966

Higdon, H. How to run forever: a ten-point running program to last you a lifetime. *Runner (New York) 6(12), Sept 1984, 36-38;40;95.*
LEVEL: B LANG: Eng SIRC ARTICLE NO: 103573

Olsen, E. On the right track: a spectators' guide to the Olympic running events. Indianapolis: Bobbs-Merrill Co., c1984. xiv 225 p. : ill.
NOTES: Bibliography: p. 219-220.
LEVEL: B LANG: Eng ISBN: 0-672-52807-X LC CARD: 83-21415 GV1060.5 17487

Olsen, E. What's so terrific it feels good even when it feels bad? *Runner (New York) 6(6), Mar 1984, 38-40;42;46-47.*
LEVEL: B LANG: Eng SIRC ARTICLE NO: 100074

Parker, J.L. Again to Carthage. A comeback stirs the soul with the romantic notion that what once was can be again. And, in the comebacks of our heroes, however fleeting, our own phoenix rises from the ashes. *Ultrasport (Boston, Mass.) 1(2), Apr 1984, 32-36.*
LEVEL: B LANG: Eng SIRC ARTICLE NO: 098672

Tulloh, B. Beginners special: stepping out. *Running (London, Eng.) 36, Apr 1984, 62-63;79.*
NOTES: Extracted from, Tulloh, B., The complete distance runner.
LEVEL: B LANG: Eng SIRC ARTICLE NO: 097008

Wenzel, M.M. 10K runs promote increased involvement. *Journal of physical education and program (Columbus, Oh.) 81(4), Apr 1984, D20-D21.*
LEVEL: B LANG: Eng SIRC ARTICLE NO: 095478

RUNNING (continued)

ADMINISTRATION

Jones, A. Scoring races with a personal computer. *Footnotes (Reston, Va.) 12(1), Spring 1984, 16;20.* LEVEL: B LANG: Eng SIRC ARTICLE NO: 098644

King, L.T. Improved record-keeping for track & cross-country. *Scholastic coach (New York) 53(9), Apr 1984, 68-69.* LEVEL: LANG: Eng SIRC ARTICLE NO: 095428

AGED

Fixx, J. Older women. *Running times (Woodbridge, Va.) 92, Sept 1984, 66.* NOTES: Excerpted from, The 1985 runner's day by day log and calendar. LEVEL: B LANG: Eng SIRC ARTICLE NO: 101673

Fixx, J.F. The test of time: John A. Kelly has been a runner for 62 years. New research shows he has the physical condition of a fit 40 year old. What does this mean for the rest of us? *Runner (New York) 6(8), May 1984, 58-62.* LEVEL: I LANG: Eng SIRC ARTICLE NO: 101674

Jokl, P. Aging and athletic performance. *AMJA newsletter (Hollywood, Calif.) Jul/Aug 1984, 10-11.* LEVEL: I LANG: Eng SIRC ARTICLE NO: 101683

Ratelle, A. Fedo, M. Racing fitness after 50. If the only thing keeping you from running is the notion that you're too old, think again. With the proper training, you'll keep up with those half your age. *Runner's world (Mountain View, Calif.) 19(9), Sept 1984, 60-64;94.* LEVEL: B LANG: Eng SIRC ARTICLE NO: 098678

Watson, R. Running after forty: discovering your second wind. Taking stock in your 40s? It's never too late for you to start running and learn how to take middle age in stride. *Runner's world 19(1), Jan 1984, 44-47;67.* LEVEL: B LANG: Eng SIRC ARTICLE NO: 091122

ANTHROPOMETRY

Housh, T.J. Thorland, W.G. Johnson, G.O. Tharp, G.D. Cisar, C.J. Refsell, M.J. Ansorge, C.J. Body composition variables as discriminators of sports participation of elite adolescent female athletes. (Refs: 22)*Research quarterly for exercise & sport (Reston, Va.) 55(3), Sept 1984, 302-304.* ABST: The purpose of this study was to determine the degree to which body composition variables (relative fat, body weight, fat weight, and lean body weight) discriminate between successful participants of different sports. 110 elite female athletes (age 16.08 plus or minus 1.53 years) participated in the study: 64 swimmers (10 distance swimmers and 54 sprinters) and 46 runners (12 distance runners and 34 sprinters). Multiple discriminant analysis was used. The discriminant function correctly classified 87.3% of the subjects in their respective sports. LEVEL: A LANG: Eng SIRC ARTICLE NO: 103491

ART

Blaikie, D. Footloose: an artist's wall. (Claude Dupuis) *Canadian runner Apr 1984, 10.* LEVEL: B LANG: Eng SIRC ARTICLE NO 093875

AUDIO VISUAL MATERIAL

Shyne, K. Picture yourself video analysis as a training aid. *Runner (Boulder, Colo.) 6(10), Jul 1984, 16.* LEVEL: B LANG: Eng SIRC ARTICLE NO: 101712

BIBLIOGRAPHIES

Dales, G.G. A bibliography of theses and dissertations related to track and field. *Track and field quarterly review (Kalamazoo, Mich.) 84(3), Fall 1984, 59-64.* LEVEL: B LANG: Eng SIRC ARTICLE NO: 096958

Sachs, M.L. Buffone, G.W. Bibliography: psychological considerations in exercise, including exercise as psychotherapy, exercise addiction, and the psychology of running. s.l.: s.n., 1984. 1v. (loose-leaf) NOTES: Volume 6, number 1, Summer, 1984. LEVEL: I LANG: Eng GV706.4 20273

BIOGRAPHY AND AUTOBIOGRAPHY

Cottrell, S. No mountain too high. Old Tappan, N.J.: F.H. Revell, c1984. 1v. LEVEL: B LANG: Eng ISBN: 0800712064 LC CARD: 84-006775

Finkel, A. Lenore Marvin. *Canadian runner (Toronto, Ont.) Jun 1984, 24-25.* LEVEL: B LANG: Eng SIRC ARTICLE NO: 095407

Gilmour, G. Former boxer John Hughes is now ultra tough. *New Zealand Runner (Auckland, N.Z.) 35, Nov/Dec 1984, 24-27;31-32.* LEVEL: B LANG: Eng SIRC ARTICLE NO: 109296

Higdon, H. Jim Fixx: how he lived, why de died. He ran, he watched his diet, he was thin and 'fit'. He died running at age 52. What happended? *Runner (New York) 7(2), Nov 1984, 32-38.* LEVEL: B LANG: Eng SIRC ARTICLE NO: 108623

Parker, J. All in the family. (Tom and Ruth Wysocki) *Running times (Woodbridge, Va.) 86, Mar 1984, 14;16;18-19.* LEVEL: B LANG: Eng SIRC ARTICLE NO: 096990

Roberts, D. George Sheehan. *Ultrasport (Boston, Mass.) 1(6), Nov/Dec 1984, 8-12;14-15.* LEVEL: B LANG: Eng SIRC ARTICLE NO 172952

BIOMECHANICS

Clarke, T.E. Frederick, E.C. Hamill, C. The study of rearfoot movement in running. (Refs: 20) NOTES: In, Frederick, E.C. (ed.), Sport shoes and playing surfaces: biomechanical properties, Champaign, Ill., Human Kinetics Publishers, c1984, p. 166-189. LEVEL: A LANG: Eng QP302 17870

De Moya, R.G. A biomechanical comparison of the military boot and the running shoe. Eugene, Ore.: Microform Publications, University of Oregon, 1984. 2 microfiches : negative, ill. ; 11 x 15 cm. NOTES: Thesis (M.S.) - Pennsylvania State University, 1981; (x, 119 leaves); includes bibliography. LEVEL: A LANG: Eng UO84 81-82

From the research lab. (Running and pronation) *Racing South magazine (Hermitage, Tenn.) 6(9), Mar 1984, 27.* LEVEL: I LANG: Eng SIRC ARTICLE NO: 098632

Hinrichs, R.N. Upper extremity function in running. Eugene, Ore: Microform Publications, University of Oregon, 1984. 4 microfiches : negative, ill. ; 11 x 15 cm. NOTES: Thesis (Ph.D.) - Pennsylvania State University, 1982; (xix, 285, (1) leaves); vita; includes bibliography. LEVEL: A LANG: Eng UO84 333-336

Martin, P.E. A biomechanical and physiological evaluation of the effect of lower extremity loading on running performance. Eugene, Ore.: Microform Publications, University of Oregon, 1984. 3 microfiches : negative, ill. ; 11 x 15 cm NOTES: Thesis (Ph.D.) - Pennsylvania State University, 1983; (xiii, 213, (1) leaves); vita; includes bibliography. LEVEL: A LANG: Eng UO84 342-344

Prokop, D. All about rearfoot control. Everybody's feet pound the ground differently, so run in shoes that match your strike Cushioning is important, but there are other factors. *Runners world (Mountain View, Calif.) 19(12), Dec 1984, 44-46;91.* LEVEL: I LANG: Eng SIRC ARTICLE NO: 101704

Turblin, J. Oui pour le footing, non pour le jogging. *Revue de l'Amicale des entraineurs francais d'athletisme (Paris) 86, janv/fevr/mars 1984, 7;9.* LEVEL: I LANG: Fr SIRC ARTICLE NO: 095471

Turblin, J. Walking yes, jogging no. *Olympic review (Lausanne) 201/202, Jul/Aug 1984, 526-529.* LEVEL: I LANG: Eng SIRC ARTICLE NO: 097010

Turblin, J. Oui pour le footing, non pour le jogging. *Revue olympique (Lausanne) 201/202, juil/aout 1984, 526-529.* LEVEL: LANG: Fr SIRC ARTICLE NO: 105032

Vaughan, C.L. Biomechanics of running gait. *Critical reviews in biomedical engineering (Boca Raton, Fla.) 12(1), 1984, 1-48* ABST: This paper reviews the literature on the biomechanics of sprinting, middle and long distance running, and jogging. Some of the topics discussed include: the class of running gait; electromyography; kinematics; kinetics; mathematical models; and sports footwear and surfaces. LEVEL: A LANG: Eng

BIORHYTHM

Prokop, D. The facts on foot impact. Running styles vary from the soft footfall to the hacker's slap, and it's important to regularly monitor your technique. *Runner's world (Mountain View, Calif.) 19(10), Oct 1984, 50-52.* LEVEL: I LANG: Eng SIRC ARTICLE NO: 100083

CHILDREN

Caulfield, B. Young runners: they train, they achieve. Sometimes they get hurt. *New York running times (New York) 27(4), Ma 1984, 56-58;60;74-75.* LEVEL: B LANG: Eng SIRC ARTICLE NO: 101664

Chanon, R. Entrainement a la course des enfants et des jeunes. (Refs: 17)*Revue de l'Amicale des*

entraineurs francais d'athletisme (Paris) 87, avr/
mai/juin 1984, 39-42.
LEVEL: I LANG: Fr SIRC ARTICLE NO: 096957

Egger, K. What can we demand? *Modern athlete
and coach (Athelstone, Aust.)* 22(1), Jan 1984, 23-
25.
NOTES: Based on translated summarised extracts
from, Die Lehre der Leichtathletik 2, 1978.
LEVEL: B LANG: Eng SIRC ARTICLE NO: 095734

Petit, J. La course en aerobie. *EPS: Education
physique et sport (Paris, France)* 186, mars/avr
1984, 39-41.
LEVEL: B LANG Fr SIRC ARTICLE NO: 094206

CLOTHING

10th Annual Runner's World 5-star shoe survey.
Culminating a decade of innovative testing of
running shoes to determine which is best for you,
and which allows you to run injury-free. *Runner's
world (Mountain View, Calif.)* 19(10), Oct 1984, 82-
101.
LEVEL: B LANG: Eng SIRC ARTICLE NO: 098932

Burfoot, A. Inside the modern running shoe. An
exhaustive look at the stitch-by-stitch creation of
the runner's most important piece of equipment.
Runner's world (Mountain View, Calif.) 19(9), Sept
1984, 54-59.
LEVEL: B LANG: Eng SIRC ARTICLE NO: 097474

Cavanagh, P.R. Valiant, G.A. Misevich, K.W.
Biological aspects of modeling shoe/foot interaction
during running. (Refs: 13)
NOTES: In, Frederick, E.C. (ed.), Sport shoes and
playing surfaces: biomechanical properties,
Champaign, Ill., Human Kinetics Publishers, c1984,
p. 24-46.
LEVEL: A LANG: Eng QP302 17870

Drez, D. Running shoes and orthotic devices.
(Refs: 7)
NOTES: In, Scott, W.N. (ed.) et al., Principles of
sports medicine, Baltimore, Williams & Wilkins,
c1984, p. 393-395.
LEVEL: B LANG: Eng RC1210 18016

Fazey, I.H. For whom does the bell toll? *Running
magazine (London)* 42, Oct 1984, 45-47.
LEVEL: B LANG: Eng SIRC ARTICLE NO: 173169

Frederick, E.C. Clarke, T.E. Hamill, C.L. The
effect of running shoe design on shock attenuation.
(Refs: 18)
NOTES: In, Frederick, E.C. (ed.), Sport shoes and
playing surfaces: biomechanical properties,
Champaign, Ill., Human Kinetics Publishers, c1984,
p. 190-198.
LEVEL: A LANG: Eng QP302 17870

Frederick, E.C. Physiological and ergonomics
factors in running shoe design. (Refs: 36)*Applied
ergonomics (Surrey, Eng.)* 15(4), 1984, 281-287.
LEVEL: A LANG: Eng SIRC ARTICLE NO: 104971

Frederick, E.C. Physiological and ergonomics
factors in running shoe design. *Applied ergonomics
(Surrey, Eng.)* 15(4), 1984, 281-287.
LEVEL: A LANG: Eng

Johnson, A. Prevent injury: choose the correct
running shoes. *Marathon (Charleville, Co. Cork,
Ireland)* 22(4), June 1984, 7
LEVEL: B LANG: Eng SIRC ARTICLE NO: 109115

Kerasote, T. Off-season running: the proper
trappings for sleet, snow, and dead of night.

Outside (Chicago, Ill.) 9(9), Oct 1984, 87-89.
LEVEL: B LANG: Eng SIRC ARTICLE NO: 108737

Lees, A. McCullagh, P.J. A preliminary
investigation into the shock absorbency of running
shoes and shoe inserts. (Refs: 5) *Journal of human
movement studies (Edinburgh, Eng.)* 10(2), 1984,
95-106.
ABST: This study measured the differences in the
vertical force record which occur during foot
contact in athletes running at a constant speed
wearing different types of shoe and shoe insert
combinations. The results indicate that the rate of
force loading rather than force magnitudes is the
variable most affected by shoes and inserts.
Although a reduction in the forces or rates of
loading of force could be achieved by using
different shoes or combinations of shoes and
inserts these reductions also brought about an
increase in foot contact time. This increased foot
contact time implies a slower running speed. Shoe
construction is a complex matter but the current
data suggest that optimal shoes can be developed.
LEVEL: A LANG: Eng SIRC ARTICLE NO: 095812

Meister, K. What your old shoes say about your
running. *Runner's world (Mountain View, Calif.)*
19(11), Nov 1984, 45-47;80.
LEVEL: B LANG: Eng SIRC ARTICLE NO: 100068

Misevich, K.W. Cavanagh, P.R. Material aspects
of modeling shoe/foot interaction. (Refs: 54)
NOTES: In, Frederick, E.C. (ed.), Sport shoes and
playing surfaces: biomechanical properties,
Champaign, Ill., Human Kinetics Publishers, c1984,
p. 47-75.
LEVEL: A LANG: Eng QP302 17870

No-bull guide to foul weather gear. How gore-tex,
polypropylene, lycra, and good common sense can
save you from the grip of sweat'n freeze syndrome.
Running times (Woodbridge, Va.) 94, Nov 1984,
37-38;40.
LEVEL: B LANG: Eng SIRC ARTICLE NO: 100572

O'Brien, R. Hot lines: new fabrics and new designs
help today's running tights blend fashion and
function. *Runner (New York* 7(3), Dec 1984, 57-61.
LEVEL: B LANG: Eng SIRC ARTICLE NO: 105007

O'Brien, R. Running shoes for '85: a complete list.
Runner (New York) 7(2), Nov 1984, 115-
116;118;120-122.
LEVEL: B LANG: Eng SIRC ARTICLE NO: 108632

Perlman, E. Soul of a running shoe. *In, Schrier,
E.W. and Allman, W.F. (eds.), Newton at the bat:
the science in sports, Ne York, Scribner, c1984, p.
55-58.
LEVEL: B LANG: Eng RC1235 18609

Personal running profile. *Runner (New York)* 7(2),
Nov 1984, 101-102.
LEVEL: B LANG: Eng SIRC ARTICLE NO: 108629

Previewing the new shoes: a collection of new
models from 26 manufacturers reflects the quality
and diversity in today's marke *Runner (New York)*
7(2), Nov 1984, 104-110.
LEVEL: B LANG: Eng SIRC ARTICLE NO: 108631

Running and common sense. *Hospital for sick
children information handout (Toronto)* 1984?, 1-5.
LEVEL: B LANG: Eng SIRC ARTICLE NO: 106190

Running clothing through the ages. *Running &
fitness (Washington, D.C.)* 16(2), Apr 1984, 14-15..
LEVEL: B LANG: Eng SIRC ARTICLE NO: 098680

RW 5-star quarterly shoe rankings. *Runner's world
(Mountain View, Calif.)* 19(7), Jul 1984, 151-152.
LEVEL: B LANG: Eng SIRC ARTICLE NO: 094289

Schuster, R. The state of the art: patterns of
progress in the development of better running
shoes. *Runner (New York)* 7(2), Nov 1984, 96-98.
LEVEL: B LANG: Eng SIRC ARTICLE NO: 108628

Stamford, B. Choosing shoes for your sport.
Physician and sportsmedicine (Minneapolis, Minn.)
12(10), Oct 1984, 191.
LEVEL: B LANG: Eng SIRC ARTICLE NO: 098959

Subotnick, S.I. Shoes: it's all in the last. *California
track & field running news (Fresno, Calif.)* 95, Sept/
Oct 1984, 16-17.
LEVEL: B LANG: Eng SIRC ARTICLE NO: 173546

The 7th annual review of shoes. *Running times
(Woodbridge, Va.)* 93, Oct 1984, 13-18;20-24;26-
27.
LEVEL: B LANG: Eng SIRC ARTICLE NO: 098933

The inside line on running gear: active sportswear
for active sports. *Runner's world* 19(5), May 1984,
90-92.
LEVEL: B LANG: Eng SIRC ARTICLE NO: 093898

Turnbull, A. Shoe buyer's guide. *Running
magazine (London)* 42, Oct 1984, 38-44.
LEVEL: B LANG: Eng SIRC ARTICLE NO: 17316

Turnbull, A. How your shoes are made. *Running
magazine (London)* 42, Oct 1984, 48-51.
LEVEL: B LANG: Eng SIRC ARTICLE NO: 173170

White, D. Are we becoming a (pro)nation of heels?
Some observations on running shoe design over
the past decade. *Fun runner (Rose Bay)* 6(2), Jun/
Jul 1984, 14-15.
LEVEL: B LANG: Eng SIRC ARTICLE NO: 103918

CLUBS AND TEAMS

Perry, P. The Eugene edge: the path to glory is
paved with redwood chips. *Outside (Chicago)* 9(6),
Jul 1984, 40-46.
LEVEL: LANG: Eng SIRC ARTICLE NO: 105014

Turnbull, A. Downes, S. Club choice. *Running
magazine (London)* 42, Oct 1984, 72-74.
LEVEL: B LANG: Eng SIRC ARTICLE NO: 173173

COACHING

Berenyi, I. Nichols, R. Cracking the secrets of the
Eastern Bloc: are the Eastern European athletes
supermen or do they just know something we
don't? *Runner's world (Mountain View, Calif.)*
19(6), Jun 1984, 72-74;76.
LEVEL: B LANG: Eng SIRC ARTICLE NO: 095393

Burles, J. Interview with Jimmy Hedley. *Athletics
weekly (Rochester, Kent)* 38(11), 17 Mar 1984,
54;56-59.
LEVEL: B LANG: Eng SIRC ARTICLE NO: 093878

Downes, S. The lady is a coach. (Ann Hill) *Running
magazine (London)* 42, Oct 1984, 54-57.
LEVEL: B LANG: Eng SIRC ARTICLE NO: 173171

Lenton, B. Pat Clohessy. *Fun runner (Rose Bay,
Aust.)* 5(5), Dec 1983/Jan 1984, 31-32.
NOTES: Extracted from, Brian Lenton's Through
the tape.
LEVEL: B LANG: Eng SIRC ARTICLE NO: 098650

Myers, L. Stotan gold. *California track & running
news (Fresno, Calif.)* 95, Sept/Oct 1984, 20-23.
LEVEL: B LANG: Eng SIRC ARTICLE NO: 173547

RUNNING (continued)

Shupe, M. Nova Scotia report: Al Yarr: The philosopher coach. *Canadian runner (Toronto, Ont.)* Jun 1984, 28-29.
LEVEL: B LANG: Eng SIRC ARTICLE NO: 095462

Stein, J.U. Track, microcomputers, and you. *Physical education newsletter (Old Saybrook, Conn.)* 159, May 1984, 7-8.
LEVEL B LANG: Eng SIRC ARTICLE NO: 101714

Stifler, J. Hey coach. Behind every good runner, there is usually some good advice. *Runner (New York)* 7(2), Nov 1984, 16;18
LEVEL: B LANG: Eng SIRC ARTICLE NO: 108633

Tutton, M. Amateur coaches: molding muscle and mind. (Duane Jones, John Fitzgerald and John ApSimon) *Ottawa magazine* 4(1), Apr 1984, 12-13;45-50;52-53.
LEVEL: B LANG: Eng SIRC ARTICLE NO: 092712

Van Dyk, J. Ladies' man. (Fred Thompson) *Runner (New York)* 6(6), Mar 1984, 48-49;52-55.
LEVEL: B LANG: Eng SIRC ARTICLE NO: 100100

Whitefield, N. The wizard of Loughborough. George Gandy is interviewed by Nigel Whitefield. *Athletics weekly (Rochester, Kent)* 38(13), 31 Mar 1984, 52-55;57.
LEVEL: B LANG: Eng SIRC ARTICLE NO: 093964

COUNTRIES AND REGIONS

Annerino, J. Running against time. *Running times (Woodbridge, Va.)* 88, May 1984, 28-30;33-35.
LEVEL: B LANG: Eng SIRC ARTICLE NO: 095388

Clark, B. Israeli running. *Running & fitness (Washington, D.C.)* 16(4), Jul/Aug 1984, 25-26.
LEVEL: B LANG: Eng SIRC ARTICLE NO: 106153

Hunt, P.L. Running in China. *Running & fitness (Washington, D.C.)* 16(2), Apr 1984, 22-23.
LEVEL: B LANG: Eng SIRC ARTICLE NO: 098643

Kidane, F. Un africain parle des africains. *Spiridon (Salvan, Suisse)* 74, juil/aout 1984, 5-7;9-11;13.
LEVEL: B LANG: Fr SIRC ARTICLE NO: 104990

Olsen, E. Running in paradise. *Runner (Boulder, Colo.)* 6(7), Apr 1984, 58;62;64.
LEVEL: B LANG: Eng SIRC ARTICLE NO: 0986

DIRECTORIES

Sheahen, A. Guest spot. The ABCs (and TACs) of running: a guide to the governing bodies. *Runner's world (Mountain View, Calif.)* 19(8), Aug 1984, 196.
LEVEL: B LANG: Eng SIRC ARTICLE NO: 096998

DRUGS, DOPING AND ERGOGENIC AIDS

Farrell, S. Artificial aids & athletic performance. *Aerobics (Dallas, Tex.)* 5(1), Jan 1984, 5.
LEVEL: I LANG: Eng SIRC ARTICLE NO: 097456

Pietschmann, R. Running from heroin: an addict's story. A junkie's journey from the needle to the road proves that addiction can be healing. *Runner's world* 19(3), Mar 1984, 89-90;102;104.
LEVEL: B LANG: Eng SIRC ARTICLE NO: 092516

ENVIRONMENT

Harmon, J. Making the most of winter. *Runner's world (Mountain View, Calif.)* 19(11), Nov 1984, 66-68.
LEVEL: B LANG: Eng SIRC ARTICLE NO: 100051

Marwick, C. Olympic athletes may face extra challenge - pollution. (news) *JAMA: Journal of the American Medical Association (Chicago)* 251(19), 18 May 1984, 2495-2497.
LEVEL: B LANG: Eng SIRC ARTICLE NO: 101689

Sutton, J.R. Heat illness. (Refs: 57)
NOTES: In, Strauss, R.H. (ed.), Sports medicine, Philadelphia ; Toronto, Saunders, 1984, p. 307-322.
LEVEL: A LANG: Eng RC1210 17196

EQUIPMENT - RETAILING

Edwards, S. How to promote running shoe sales. *Sports retailer (Mt. Prospect, Ill.)* 37(5), May 1984, 12;61.
LEVEL: B LANG Eng SIRC ARTICLE NO: 100553

FACILITIES - DESIGN, CONSTRUCTION AND PLANNING

Chase, A. Tuning the track. *In, Schrier, E.W. and Allman, W.F. (eds.), Newton at the bat: the science in sports, New York, Scribner, c1984, p. 59-62.*
LEVEL: B LANG: Eng RC1235 18609

Cuin, D.E. Design and construction of a tuned track.
NOTES: In, Frederick, E.C. (ed.), Sport shoes and playing surfaces: biomechanical properties, Champaign, Ill., Human Kinetics Publishers, c1984, p. 163-165.
LEVEL: I LANG: Eng QP302 17870

Higdon, H. Going underground: how to build a 'runner's basement' for your every fitness need. *Runner (Boulder, Colo.)* 6(7) Apr 1984, 40-44.
LEVEL: B LANG: Eng SIRC ARTICLE NO: 098641

HISTORY

Donaldson, G. The running footmen: these super fit servants were the forerunners of the ultra marathon men. *Athletics (Willowdale, Ont.)* Jul 1984, 22-23;49.
LEVEL: B LANG: Eng SIRC ARTICLE NO: 098625

Henderson, J. The 10 greatest advantages in running. *Runners world (Mountain View, Calif.)* 19(12), Dec 1984, 70-72.
LEVEL B LANG: Eng SIRC ARTICLE NO: 101679

Kayser, D. Stars of summers past. *Running times (Woodbridge, Va.)* 89, June 1984, 14-16;19-20;22-23;.
LEVEL: B LANG: Eng SIRC ARTICLE NO: 095427

HUMOUR

Burfoot, A. The running numbers game: are runners fond of figures? Let me count the ways. *Runner's world* 18(13), 1984 Annual, 86-88.
LEVEL: B LANG: Eng SIRC ARTICLE NO: 092473

INJURIES AND ACCIDENTS

Andersen, C.B. Andersen, J.W. Danielsen, C.G. Tibialis anterior syndrome - Muskellogesyndrom. Akut behandlingskraevende tilstand. (Tibial anterior syndrome or compartment syndrome. An acute treatment - demanding condition.) *Ugeskrift for laeger (Copenhagen)* 146(15), 9 Apr 1984, 1134-1136.
LEVEL: I LANG: Dan

Apple, D. Heal thyself: at-home treatment for injuries. *Bicycling (Emmaus, Pa.)* 25(9), Nov/Dec 1984, 34-37.
LEVEL: B LANG Eng SIRC ARTICLE NO: 100672

Ayres, E. 7 ways to beat the heat. *Running times (Woodbridge, Va.)* 91, Aug 1984, 20;23-24.
LEVEL: B LANG: Eng SIRC ARTICL NO: 101653

Baxter, K. Is there life after knee surgery: a battered runner learns the true meaning of rehabilitation. *Runner (New York)* 6(12), Sept 1984, 71-73.
LEVEL: B LANG: Eng SIRC ARTICLE NO: 103559

Bernstein, D.A. The running body: shin splints. *Running & fitness (Washington, D.C.)* 16(2), Apr 1984, 13.
NOTES: Ninth in a series.
LEVEL: B LANG: Eng SIRC ARTICLE NO: 098612

Boesen, K. Hansen, B.F. Thomsen, J.L. Drenck, N.E. Holten, I. Nielsen, N.H. Dodsfald hos kondilobere. (Deaths among joggers. *Ugeskrift for laeger (Copenhagen)* 147(1), 31 Dec 1984, 5-8.
LEVEL: A LANG: Dan

de Mondenard, J.P. Un dossier brulant: la chaleur. Il fait trop chaud pour... courir. *Annales de kinesitherapie (Paris)* 11(7/8), 1984, 349-357.
LEVEL: I LANG: Fr SIRC ARTICLE NO: 101668

de Mondenard, J.P. Dix trucs pour avoir des tendons d'Achille inusables. *Macolin (Macolin, Suisse)* 41(11), nov 1984, 10-12.
LEVEL: B LANG: Fr SIRC ARTICLE NO: 108754

Diekhoff, G.M. Running amok: injuries in compulsive runners. (Refs: 14)*Journal of sport behavior (Mobile, Ala.)* 7(3), Sept 1984, 120-129.
ABST: Questionnaires completed by 68 runners (69% male, mean age 31) who had run for an average of 57 months measured demographic variables, personal compulsivity (Type A/B scale, Addiction to Running, Commitment to Running), running injuries (number of reported injuries, number of doctor visits, and use of drugs and/or physical therapy for running injuries), and six training style variables. Each compulsivity measure was significantly correlated with a different injury measure (Type A/B with reported injuries; Addiction to Running with doctor visits; Commitment to Running with use of drugs and/or physical therapy). Three training variables (length of average run, weekly mileage, and participation in fun runs and races) were also significantly correlated with the injury measures, but partial correlations showed that training and compulsivity variables explained different components of injury variance. In general injured runners tended to be Type A, addicted to running, highly committed to running, ran more miles, and were more likely than uninjured runners to participate in fun runs and races. It was concluded that compulsivity measures are a useful adjunct to training variables in predicting running injuries.
LEVEL: A LANG: Eng SIRC ARTICLE NO: 101669

Dowey, K.E. Moore, G.W. Stress fractures in athletes. *Ulster medical journal (Belfast)* 53(2), 1984, 121-124.
LEVEL: A LANG: Eng

Fassett, R. Exercise haematuria. *Australian family physician (Sydney)* 13(7), Jul 1984, 518-519.
LEVEL: I LANG: Eng

Fazey, I.H. The injury debate: hacking through the private clinic jungle. *Running magazine (London)*

35, Mar 1984, 60-61;63.
NOTES: Second in a series.
LEVEL: B LANG: Eng SIRC ARTICLE NO: 098628

Fitch, K.D. Stress fractures of the lower limbs in runners. *Australian family physician (Sydney) 13(7), Jul 1984, 511-515.*
LEVEL: I LANG: Eng

Geldwert, J. Dunnett, B. Four misunderstood injuries. Just when you thought it was safe to go back on the roads, these little-understood but common problems wait to mount a sneak attack on your body-and your sanity. *Runner's world (Mountain View, Calif.) 19(7), Jul 1984, 98-101;128.*
LEVEL: I LANG: Eng SIRC ARTICLE NO: 094360

Grisogono, V. The running body: 25 the lower back. *Running magazine (London) 35, Mar 1984, 66-67.*
LEVEL: B LANG: Eng SIRC ARTICLE NO: 098636

Grisogono, V. The running body: 24. The pelvis. This month we look at groin pain and injury, particularly hernias and pelvic stress fractures, and at some of the rehabilitative measures that follow treatment. *Running magazine (London) 34, Feb 1984, 81;83;85.*
LEVEL: B LANG: Eng SIRC ARTICLE NO: 097571

Hackney, A.C. Water running: the injured runner's alternative. *Ohio runner (Columbus, Ohio) 5(7), Feb/Mar 1984, 10.*
LEVEL B LANG: Eng SIRC ARTICLE NO: 108667

Heaslet, M.W. Shin splints. *Fun runner (Rose Bay) 6(2), Jun/Jul 1984, 48.*
LEVEL: B LANG: Eng SIRC ARTICLE NO: 104036

Jones, D.C. James, S.L. Partial calcaneal ostectomy by retrocalcaneal bursitis. (Refs: 4)*American journal of sports medicin (Baltimore, Md.) 12(1), Jan/Feb 1984, 72-73.*
ABST: Posterior heel pain caused by running could be due to Achilles tendinitis, Achilles tenosynovitis or retrocalcaneal bursitis. Pinching between the os calcis and the Achilles tendon indicates the latter condition. When this condition does not respond to conservative treatment, surgery to remove part of the calcaneus can be quite successful. This article outlines the surgical techniques employed in treating ten patients.
LEVEL: A LANG: Eng SIRC ARTICLE NO: 095423

Larkins, P.A. Evaluating runners' injuries. *Australian family physician (Sydney) 13(7), Jul 1984, 503-506.*
LEVEL: I LANG: Eng

Leach, R.E. Achilles tendinitis. *Sportsmedicine digest (Van Nuys, Calif.) 6(3), Mar 1984, 6-7.*
LEVEL: B LANG: Eng SIRC ARTICLE NO: 098646

Lehman, W.L. Overuse syndromes in runners. *American family physician (Kansas City) 29(1), Jan 1984, 157-161.*
ABST: Common overuse injuries in running include iliotibial tract tendinitis, chondromdacia patella shin splints, stress fractures and various heel and foot syndromes. Most causes are due to training errors, anatomy factors, inadequate footwear, or poor running surfaces. These injuries are generally treated by exercise program modifications, anti-inflammatory drugs, and orthotic correction of lower limb malalignment.
LEVEL: I LANG: Eng SIRC ARTICLE NO: 100065

Lightbourne, L. Runner, heal thyself: listen to your body. *New Zealand Runner (Auckland, N.Z.) 35,*

Nov/Dec 1984, 54-55;57.
LEVEL: B LANG: Eng SIRC ARTICLE NO: 109297

Linde, F. Lobeidraetsskader. Erhvervsfravaer blandt elitelobere. (Athletic injuries in runners. Sick leave among elite runners.) *Ugeskrift for laeger (Copenhagen) 146(15), 9 Apr 1984, 1166-1168.*
LEVEL: I LANG: Dan

Lindsay, H. Hip to the problem: some causes and effects of piriformis syndrome. *Runner (New York) 6(9), Jun 1984, 20;22.*
LEVEL: B LANG: Eng SIRC ARTICLE NO: 100685

Mirkin, G. Gut reactions: when running brings on stomach pain. *Runner (New York) 6(8), May 1984, 17.*
LEVEL: B LANG: Eng SIRC ARTICLE NO: 101691

Mozee, G. Prokop, D. You can fight lower-back pain: the constant jarring of running can be hard on the back, but there are tried and true methods to strengthen the back against injury. *Runner's world 19(5), May 1984, 66-69;130.*
LEVEL: B LANG: Eng SIRC ARTICLE NO: 093922

Newell, S.G. Bramwell, S.T. Overuse injuries to the knee in runners. (Refs: 15)*Physician and sportsmedicine 12(3), Mar 1984 80-85;88;90-92.*
ABST: In this paper, the different kinds of overuse injuries of the knee are described. The authors also discussed the treatment of 329 patients with knee injuries over an 11-month period. The medical history and the cause of injury of the patients as well as types of shoes worn were factors investigated.
LEVEL: A LANG: Eng SIRC ARTICLE NO: 092510

Newman, N.M. Fowles, J.V. A case of 'trigger toe'. *Canadian journal of surgery (Ottawa) 27(4), Jul 1984, 378-379.*
ABST: Triggering of the toes, in which local tendon hypertrophy prevents the smooth movement of the tendon, has been described as a problem more theoretical than real and only three cases have been reported. The authors report a case of partial tethering of the flexor hallucis longus tendon just distal to the medial malleolus in a 28-year-old jogger who had painful triggering of the great toe on plantar flexion of the ankle and great toe. Division of the flexor hallucis longus tendon pulley distal and posterior to the medial malleolus cured the patient.
LEVEL: I LANG: Eng SIRC ARTICLE NO: 105005

Nielsen, B.M. Flintholm, J. Stress-fraktuere af tibia hos kondilobere. (Stress fractures of the tibia in runners.) *Ugeskrif for laeger (Copenhagen) 146(46), 12 Nov 1984, 3545-3546.*
NOTES: Includes English abstract.
LEVEL: I LANG: Dan

Nilsson, S. Overuse knee injuries in runners. (Refs: 20)*International journal of sports medicine (Stuttgart) Suppl. 5, Nov 1984, 145-148.*
CONF: International Congress on Sports and Health (1983 : Maastricht, Netherlands).
LEVEL: A LANG: Eng SIRC ARTICLE NO: 105006

Olsen, E. Miracle worker? The jury is still out on the Electro-acuscope, but some injured runners aren't waiting for the verdict. *Runner (New York) 6(12), Sept 1984, 42-44.*
LEVEL: B LANG: Eng SIRC ARTICLE NO: 103600

Olsen, E. A real pain in the... if it hurts in the buttocks, you may have an increasingly common lower-back injury known as sciatica. *Runner (New York) 7(3), Dec 1984, 72-76;78-79.*
LEVEL: B LANG: Eng SIRC ARTICLE NO: 105009

Paty, J.G. Swafford, D. Adolescent running injuries. (Refs: 12)*Journal of adolescent health care (New York) 5(2), Apr 1984, 87-90.*
ABST: Nineteen adolescent runners, aged between 13 and 18, were treated for 25 musculoskeletal injuries. Over 70% of the injuries involved the knee or leg. Knee injuries were more common in boys while girls suffered more from leg injuries. Methods for diagnosis, treatment, and prevention of injuries were examined.
LEVEL: A LANG: Eng SIRC ARTICLE NO: 101700

Paul, G.R. Injury prevention and rehabilitation in track. (Refs: 14)
NOTES: In, Cantu, R.C. (ed.), Clinical sports medicine, Lexington, Mass. ; Toronto, Collamore Press : D.C. Heath, c1984, p. 193-201.
LEVEL: I LANG: Eng RC1201 15964

Payne, F.E. The runner: a profile of problems. (Refs: 40)
NOTES: In, Birrer, R.B. (ed.), Sports medicine for the primary car physician, Norwalk, Conn., Appleton-Century-Crofts, c1984, p. 273-278.
LEVEL: I LANG: Eng RC1210 17030

Pietschmann, R.J. Probing death on the run. (Jim Fixx) *Runner's world (Mountain View, Calif.) 19(11), Nov 1984, 38-42;44;90-92;94.*
LEVEL: B LANG: Eng SIRC ARTICLE NO: 100078

Pinshaw, R. Atlas, V. Noakes, T.D. The nature and response to therapy of 196 consecutive injuries seen at a runners' clinic. (Refs: 34)*South African medical journal (Cape Town) 65(8), 25 Feb 1984, 291-298.*
ABST: 196 running injuries were studied. The four commonest injuries were 'runner's knee (22%), shin splints (18%), iliotibial band friction syndrome (12%), and chronic muscle injuries (11%). Within 8 weeks of following a biomechanically based treatment regimen, between 62% and 77% of the runners with the commonest injuries were completely pain-free. Only 13% of runners were not helped at all, but most of these had not adhered to the prescribed treatment. The response of the iliotibial band syndrome to treatment was less predictable.
LEVEL: A LANG: Eng SIRC ARTICLE NO: 100079

Prichard, B. A new twist. Upper body torque and its effects on running. *Runner (New York) 6(11), Aug 1984, 20.*
LEVEL: B LANG: Eng SIRC ARTICLE NO: 106186

Roberson, M. Roberson, E. Heat or ice? When you injure yourself, should you freeze it or warm it up? Your recovery time depends on judicious use of heat and cold. *Runner's world (Mountain View, Calif.) 19(10), Oct 1984, 56-57;114-116;118.*
LEVEL: B LANG: Eng SIRC ARTICLE NO: 099064

Roncarati, Dr. Common running injuries: causes, prevention and treatment. (Refs: 2)*Track and field quarterly review (Kalamazoo, Mich.) 84(3), Fall 1984, 48-50.*
LEVEL: B LANG: Eng SIRC ARTICLE NO: 096996

Ryan, A.J. Sudden death: running is not the culprit. *Physician and sportsmedicine (Minneapolis, Minn.) 12(9), Sept 1984, 29.*
LEVEL: B LANG: Eng SIRC ARTICLE NO: 100085

Sagnet, P. Une blessure frequente: les periostites. *Athletisme et course sur route (Montreal) 4(63), fevr 1984, 6.*
NOTES: Extrait de la revue 'Courir' juin 1983.
LEVEL: B LANG: Fr SIRC ARTICLE NO: 098681

RUNNING (continued)

Schuster, R. The trouble with orthotics. Although a boon to injured runners, they are far from foolproof. *Runner (Boulder, Colo.) 6(4), Jan 1984, 16.*
LEVEL: B LANG: Eng SIRC ARTICLE NO: 093942

Schuster, R. Wear patterns. *Runner (Boulder, Colo.) 6(5), Feb 1984, 14.*
LEVEL: B LANG: Eng SIRC ARTICLE NO: 095459

Schuster, R. Case histories: treatments that worked. *Runner (New York) 6(6), Mar 1984, 16.*
LEVEL: B LANG: Eng SIRC ARTICL NO: 100087

Schuster, R. All the wrong moves: more bad habits that can lead to running injuries. *Runner (New York) 6(8), May 1984, 28.*
LEVEL: B LANG: Eng SIRC ARTICLE NO: 101710

Schuster, R. Injury of the year: if your plantar fascia hurts, you're not alone. *Runner (New York) 6(9), Jun 1984, 26.*
LEVEL: B LANG: Eng SIRC ARTICLE NO: 100696

Schuster, R. Morton's neuralgia: advice for curing metatarsal pain. *Runner (New York) 6(12), Sept 1984, 16.*
LEVEL: B LANG Eng SIRC ARTICLE NO: 102543

Stamford, B. Sportsmedicine advisor: training distance and injury in runners. *Physician and sportsmedicine (Minneapolis, Minn.) 12(8), Aug 1984, 160.*
LEVEL: B LANG: Eng SIRC ARTICLE NO: 098683

Subotnick, S.I. Medical notes for runners: achilles tendinitis. *California track & running news (Fresno, Calif.) 92, Jun 1984, 14-15.*
LEVEL: B LANG: Eng SIRC ARTICLE NO: 098685

Subotnick, S.I. The running body: achilles tendinitis. *Running & fitness (Washington, D.C.) 16(5), Sept/Oct 1984, 15.*
NOTES: 12th in a series.
LEVEL: B LANG: Eng SIRC ARTICLE NO: 098686

Subotnick, S.I. The Plica syndrome: a new cause of knee pain in the athlete. *California track & running news (Fresno, Calif.) 96, Oct 1984, 16.*
LEVEL: B LANG: Eng SIRC ARTICLE NO: 100701

Subotnick, S.I. Leg pain in runners chronic compartment syndrome. *California track & running news (Fresno, Calif.) 91, May 1984, 18-19.*
LEVEL: B LANG: Eng SIRC ARTICLE NO: 101717

Subotnick, S.I. The meniscoid ankle: a new entity or pain in the ankle. *California track & running news (Fresno, Calif.) 98 Dec 1984, 12.*
LEVEL: B LANG: Eng SIRC ARTICLE NO: 173564

Sullivan, D. Warren, R.F. Pavlov, H. Kelman, G. Stress fractures in 51 runners. *Clinical orthopaedics and related research (Philadelphia) 187, Jul/Aug 1984, 188-192.*
ABST: A prospective study was initiated in 1976 to investigate runners who are at risk for incurring stress fractures and how these fractures can be prevented. Fifty-one runners incurred 57 stress fractures. Stress fracture development was positively correlated with the presence of pes planus, weekly training distances greater than 20 miles, hard training surfaces, and training regimen modifications. The incidence did not correlate with generalized musculoskeletal laxity or tightness. Forty-four of 51 patients had initially positive roentgenograms. Five of five bone scans were positive. The average duration of rest before running was resumed was 7.4 weeks.
LEVEL: A LANG: Eng SIRC ARTICLE NO: 105027

Sutton, J.R. Fun runs, safe runs. *Physician and sportsmedicine (Minneapolis, Minn.) 12(7), Jul 1984, 38;40.*
LEVEL: B LANG Eng SIRC ARTICLE NO: 097004

Tasker, J. Stanish, W.D. The cause and cure: runner's knee. (Refs: 7)*Canadian runner (Toronto) Nov 1984, 10-14.*
LEVEL: I LANG: Eng SIRC ARTICLE NO: 100093

Taylor, P.M. Ankle sprains. *Running & fitness (Washington, D.C.) 16(4), Jul/Aug 1984, 15.*
LEVEL: B LANG: Eng SIRC ARTICLE NO: 106198

Tehranzadeh, J. Stoll, D.A. Gabriele, O.M. Case report 271. Posterior migration of the os peroneum of the left foot, indicating a tear of the peroneal tendon. *Skeletal radiology (Berlin) 12(1), 1984, 44-47.*
LEVEL: A LANG: Eng SIRC ARTICLE NO: 105030

Thompson, W.R. Maintaining fitness in the injured athlete. *Running & fitness (Washington, D.C.) 16(2), Apr 1984, 19.*
LEVEL: B LANG: Eng SIRC ARTICLE NO: 098690

Vasyli, P. Achilles tendinitis. *Fun runner (Rose Bay, Aust.) 5(6), Feb/Mar 1984, 46-47.*
LEVEL: B LANG: Eng SIRC ARTICLE NO: 100102

Vasyli, P. Heel pain. *Fun runner (Rose Bay, N.S.W.) 6(1), Apr/May 1984, 24-25.*
LEVEL: B LANG: Eng SIRC ARTICLE NO: 108663

Villarosa, L. Water works: new advances in hydrotherapy can keep a runner afloat when injury strikes. *Runner (New York) 7(2 Nov 1984, 124-126.*
LEVEL: B LANG: Eng SIRC ARTICLE NO: 108637

Wheeler, J.R. Shin splints: cause and cure. *New Zealand runner (Auckland, N.Z.) 30, Jan/Feb 1984, 20-23.*
LEVEL: I LANG: E SIRC ARTICLE NO: 093962

Wischnia, B. Runners who never get injured: for most of us, injuries are a constant running companion, yet there are secrets to avoiding them. *Runner's world 19(5), May 1984, 59-62.*
LEVEL: B LANG: Eng SIRC ARTICLE NO: 093965

MEDICINE

Averbuch, G. Anorexia and compulsion. There's a thin line between dieting to win and starving for attention. *New York running news (New York) 29(6), Aug/Sept 1984, 58-60;81.*
LEVEL: B LANG: Eng SIRC ARTICLE NO: 106138

Blanding, F.H. Adding years to your life: a look at the evidence shows what we thought all along: not only will running make your life better, but it can also add years to your life. *Runner's world 19(4), Apr 1984, 81-84;117.*
LEVEL: B LANG: Eng SIRC ARTICLE NO: 092726

Bone mineral content of female athletes. (letter) *New England journal of medicine (Boston) 311(20), 15 Nov 1984, 1320-1321.*
LEVEL: I LANG: Eng

Bortz, W. Running from infection. *Runner's world (Mountain View, Calif.) 19(11), Nov 1984, 78-79.*
LEVEL: B LANG: Eng SIRC ARTICLE NO: 100040

Caldwell, F. Running-arthritis link discounted. *Physician and sportsmedicine (Minneapolis, Minn.) 12(8), Aug 1984, 25.*
LEVEL: B LANG: Eng SIRC ARTICLE NO: 098617

Colt, E. Heyman, B. Low ferritin levels in runners. (Refs: 17)*Journal of sports medicine and physical fitness (Torino) 24(1), Mar 1984, 13-17.*
ABST: This survey of 86 male and 32 female runners found 3 males and 9 females who had iron deficiency. The distribution of serum ferritin concentrations in this group of runners indicates lower levels than those found in control populations. This is attributed to increased iron losses through sweating and hemolysis, and possibly decreased absorption of iron due to binding in the intestine of high fiber foods.
LEVEL: A LANG: Eng SIRC ARTICLE NO: 100045

Cornwell, G.J. What every runner should know about podiatric biomechanics and orthotics. *Canadian runner Apr 1984, 8.*
LEVEL: B LANG: Eng SIRC ARTICLE NO: 093881

Dobken, J.H. Breathless: shortness of breath, coughing, fatigue and stomach aches may all be signs of exercise-induced asthma, a condition that can be easier for runners to control than to detect. *Runner (Boulder, Colo.) 6(10), Jul 1984, 51-52;57.*
LEVEL: B LANG: Eng SIRC ARTICLE NO: 100714

Dodek, A. Hypertension in the runner. (Refs: 32)*Canadian journal of applied sport sciences/ Journal canadien des sciences appliquees au sport (Windsor, Ont.) 9(4), Dec 1984, 169-175.*
ABST: A therapeutic game plan is important for the management of hypertension in the runner. Participation in physical training programs may result in lower resting blood pressure in mild hypertension. Maximal exercise tests can be used to identify those hypertensive patients with a dangerously high exercise blood pressure. Most antihypertensive drugs can be used for the treatment of hypertension which is refractory to exercise training. Atenolol, a cardioselective beta blocker has minimal side effects and the least risk of impairing performance. Calcium channel blockers effectively lower exercise blood pressure and should be used when side effects of beta blockers contraindicate their use in patients.
LEVEL: A LANG: Eng SIRC ARTICLE NO: 102571

Elliott, L. Jim Fixx: the legend and the legacy. *Running & fitness (Washington, D.C.) 16(5), Sept/ Oct 1984, 1;11;27.*
LEVEL: B LANG: Eng SIRC ARTICLE NO: 098627

Fazey, I.H. NHS-adding insult to injury? *Running magazine (London) 34, Feb 1984, 51-53.*
NOTES: First of a series.
LEVEL: LANG: Eng SIRC ARTICLE NO: 097593

Feigel, W. Wischnia, B. Keeping on the straight & narrow. You may not know what pronation and supination mean, but your feet do. Every runner does one or both to some extent-but hopefully not to excess. *Runner's world (Mountain View, Calif.) 19(9), Sept 1984, 42-44;105-106;108.*
LEVEL: B LANG: Eng SIRC ARTICLE NO: 098629

Gluckson, J. Bio-logic: the body has it's ways; so do those who treat it. (podiatry) *New York running times (New York) 27(4), May 1984, 52-55;66.*
LEVEL: B LANG: Eng SIRC ARTICLE NO: 101677

Grimshaw, P. The effects of running shoe design on the problems of pronation while running. (abstract) *Carnegie research papers (Beckett Park, Leeds) 1(6), Dec 1984, 30.*
CONF: Carnegie Undergraduate Research Symposium (1984 : Leeds, Eng.).
LEVEL: I LANG: Eng SIRC ARTICLE NO: 172506

Israel, S.R. Sports medicine & jogging. *Fun runner (Rose Bay, Aust.) 5(6), Feb/Mar 1984, 27;29.*
NOTES: Reprinted from, Sports in the GDR, May

1982.
LEVEL: B LANG: Eng SIRC ARTICLE NO: 099091

Jenoure, P.J. Reflexions medicales sur la course a pied. *Spiridon (Salvan, Suisse) 72, fevr/mars 1984, 60-62.*
LEVEL: B LANG: Fr SIRC ARTICLE NO: 100056

Knox, H. The massage treatment: giving the feet and legs a good rubdown. *Runner (New York) 6(6), Mar 1984, 24-25.*
ABST: Increasingly, foot and leg massage is being used by competitive runners not only as an aid in injury rehabilitation but also to improve performance. The benefits of deep pressure massage techniques and foot massage are outlined. A brief description of 3 foot massage methods is provided.
LEVEL: B LANG: Eng SIRC ARTICLE NO: 100060

Larsen, J.C. Pedersen, N.T. Wahlin, A. Shocklever og encefalopati hos motionslober. (Liver shock and encephalopathy in an amateur runner.) *Ugeskrift for laeger (Copenhagen) 147(1), 31 Dec 1984, 23-24.*
LEVEL: I LANG: Dan

Liberman, R.B. Palek, J. Hematologic abnormalities simulating anorexia nervosa in an obligatory athlete. (Refs: 24)*American journal of medicine (New York) 76(5), May 1984, 950-952.*
LEVEL: I LANG: Eng SIRC ARTICLE NO: 101686

McDonald, K. Wired: electric muscle stimulation for runners. *Runner (New York) 7(2), Nov 1984, 22.*
LEVEL: B LANG: Eng SIR ARTICLE NO: 108634

Morton, C. Wood, P. Henderson, J. The second annual sportsmedicine special. *Runners world (Mountain View, Calif.) 19(12), Dec 1984, 36-43;87.*
LEVEL: I LANG: Eng SIRC ARTICLE NO: 101692

Morton, C. Runner's world exclusive: a conversation with Gabe Mirkin, the outspoken Maryland doctor who helps runners stay healthy. *Runners world (Mountain View, Calif.) 19(12), Dec 1984, 23-24;27;30;32.*
LEVEL: B LANG: Eng SIRC ARTICLE NO: 101693

Oja, D.E. Everything you always wanted to know about rest. *Footnotes (Reston, Va.) 12(1), Spring 1984, 14-15.*
LEVEL: B LANG: Eng SIRC ARTICLE NO: 098668

Olkin, R.J. Corns, calluses, and warts. *Running & fitness (Washington, D.C.) 16(3), May/Jun 1984, 13.*
NOTES: 10th in a series.
LEVEL: B LANG: Eng SIRC ARTICLE NO: 100746

Olsen, E. Getting the treatment: rolfing can change your shoe size... and more. *Runner (New York) 7(2), Nov 1984, 24;26.*
LEVEL: B LANG: Eng SIRC ARTICLE NO: 108635

Pavela, S.L. Gabster, A.A. DeVoll, C. Runners' myths must be measured against the reality of risk factors, La Crosse authorities say. *CardioGram (La Crosse, Wis.) 11(5), Oct/Nov 1984, 4-5;12.*
LEVEL: B LANG: Eng SIRC ARTICLE NO: 173568

Running and arthritis. *Health letter (San Antonio, Tex.) 24(8), 26 Oct 1984, 2-3.*
LEVEL: B LANG: Eng SIRC ARTICLE NO: 10260

Snell, E. Fluid replacement for the athlete. *Canadian runner (Toronto) Sept/Oct 1984, 16;18.*
LEVEL: B LANG: Eng SIRC ARTICLE NO: 100090

Steinmetz, M. Le pied, le rachis, la course et la chaussure. (Refs: 8)*Medecine du sport 58(1), 25*

janv 1984, 37-45.
LEVEL I LANG: Fr SIRC ARTICLE NO: 092534

Temple, C. The laying - on of hands. (massage) *Running (London) 40, Aug 1984, 62-64.*
ABST: Elite athletes such as Mary Decker and Alberto Salazar have recognized the importance of massage as a regular part of their training regimen. Guy Ogden, veteran cross-country champion and qualified masseur presents some of his views on the necessity of massage.
LEVEL: B LANG: Eng SIRC ARTICLE NO: 100094

Van Camp, S.P. The Fixx tragedy: a cardiologist's perspective. (Refs: 13)*Physician and sportsmedicine (Minneapolis, Minn.) 12(9), Sept 1984, 153-154;157.*
LEVEL: I LANG: Eng SIRC ARTICLE NO: 100099

NUTRITION

Aronson, V. Effective weight control. Pay attention to details: a few calories here and there can bring your weight under control or send scales soaring. *Runner's world 19(3), Mar 1984, 58-65.*
NOTES: Second of two parts.
LEVEL: B LANG: Eng SIRC ARTICLE NO: 091550

Aronson, V. A healthy high-calorie diet. *Runner's world (Mountain View, Calif.) 19(11), Nov 1984, 53-55;82;84-85.*
LEVEL: LANG: Eng SIRC ARTICLE NO: 100037

Barnett, D.W. Conlee, R.K. The effects of a commercial dietary supplement on human performance. (Refs: 20)*American journal of clinical nutrition (Bethesda, Md.) 40(3), Sept 1984, 586-590.*
ABST: Twenty male runners were tested as to whether a commercial ergogenic supplement was of any physiological benefit to their endurance performance. Either a placebo or the supplement (a vitamin, mineral, amino acid, and unsaturated fatty acid complex) was administered to the subjects daily over a 4 week period in a double-blind design. The authors conclude that the supplement had no beneficial effect on performance as indicated by its inability to alter significantly any of the metabolic or physiological parameters, and the supplements of this nature are of no physiological value to the athlete who consumes a normal nutritionally balanced diet.
LEVEL: A LANG: Eng SIRC ARTICLE NO: 104956

Barnett, R. The vegetarian alternative. *Runner (Boulder, Colo.) 6(5), Feb 1984, 18.*
LEVEL: B LANG: Eng SIRC ARTICLE NO: 095390

Clark, N. Fructose-a sweet advantage. *Racing South magazine (Hermitage, Tenn.) 6(8), Feb 1984, 20.*
LEVEL: I LANG: Eng SIR ARTICLE NO: 097621

Henry, S. Breakfast of champions. *Runner (Boulder, Colo.) 6(7), Apr 1984, 80-82.*
LEVEL: B LANG: Eng SIRC ARTICLE NO: 0986

Herrmann, E. How to avoid those racing pit stops. Running to the lead is one thing, but to the head is another. *Runner's world (Mountain View, Calif.) 19(9), Sept 1984, 38-41;90.*
LEVEL: B LANG: Eng SIRC ARTICLE NO: 098639

Mirkin, G. Trace minerals. Your body does need them, but beware of the myths. *Runner (Boulder, Colo.) 6(4), Jan 1984, 14.*
LEVEL: B LANG: Eng SIRC ARTICLE NO: 093920

Mirkin, G. Meal ticket: knowing how the body fuels itself can aid performance. *Runner (New York) 6(6), Mar 1984, 18.*
LEVEL: B LANG: Eng SIRC ARTICLE NO: 100070

Mirkin, G. Pill popping: do runners need vitamin supplements? *Runner (Boulder, Colo.) 6(10), Jul 1984, 20.*
LEVEL: B LANG: Eng SIRC ARTICLE NO: 100784

Mosher, C. Are you eating right? Only a good nutritional counselor knows for sure. *Runner (New York) 6(8), May 1984, 80-82.*
LEVEL: B LANG: Eng SIRC ARTICLE NO: 101694

Nasolodin, V.V. Rusin, V.I. Gladkin, I.P. Sravnitel'naia effektivnost' mikroelementnykh dobavok k pitaniiu sportsmenov pri trenirovke v raznoe vremia goda. (Comparative effectiveness of microelements added to the diet of athletes during training in different seasons.) *Voprosy pitaniia (Moscow) 6, Nov/Dec 1984, 33-38.*
ABST: Twenty-five athletes were entered into this study. Emission spectral analysis employed in the study demonstrated that during the spring-autumn months, there was a considerable decrease in the blood content of iron, copper and manganese as compared to that seen during autumn and winter. This decrease was associated with a negative trace elements balance in the body and a low content thereof in the athletes' diet. Enrichment of the diets with iron, copper and manganese combined with vitamin C during winter was followed by a less marked effect on trace elements metabolism, the growing red fiber of the blood, working capacity and immune resistance, versus the use of the same trace elements in the athletes' diet during summer. The greatest effect was attained upon the intake of trace elements in combination with ascorbic acid and dibazol.
LEVEL: A LANG: Rus

Powell, R. The life of the meatless runners: are vegetarians a step ahead in the search for the perfect diet for runners? *Runner's world 19(5), May 1984, 63-65;128.*
LEVEL: B LANG: Eng SIRC ARTICLE NO: 093933

Wootton, S. The meat question: yes or no? *Running magazine (London) 42, Oct 1984, 63-64.*
LEVEL: B LANG: Eng SIRC ARTICLE NO: 173172

PERCEPTUAL MOTOR PROCESSES

Shyne, K. Body control: how to better coordinate your running. *Runner (Boulder, Colo.) 6(5), Feb 1984, 12.*
LEVEL: B LANG: Eng SIRC ARTICLE NO: 095463

PHYSICAL FITNESS

Agostini, M. How much is too much? *Fun runner (Rose Bay, Aust.) 5(5), Dec 1983/Jan 1984, 29;66.*
LEVEL: B LANG: Eng SIRC ARTICLE NO: 097674

Callahan, C. Winter workouts: stay creative and stay in shape. (Refs: 5)*CardioGram (La Crosse, Wis.) 11(2), Feb/Mar 1984, 9.*
LEVEL: B LANG: Eng SIRC ARTICLE NO: 097680

Canada's runners and joggers: a massive movement. Les coureurs et les joggeurs du Canada: un mouvement de masse. *Highlights/Faits saillants (Ottawa) 33, Aug/aout 1984, 1-2.*
LEVEL: B LANG: Eng Fr SIRC ARTICLE NO: 099183

RUNNING (continued)

Curley, D.K. Running renaissance. *California parks & recreation (Sacramento, Calif.) 39(3), Summer 1983, 10-13.*
LEVEL: B LANG: Eng SIRC ARTICLE NO: 095401

Henderson, J. Running your way to fitness: take that first step to good health. *Fit (Mountain View, Calif.) 3(11), Apr 1984 66-68;70;72;74.*
LEVEL: B LANG: Eng SIRC ARTICLE NO: 099193

Kaplan, N.M. Joggers may live longer. (editorial) (Refs: 6)*JAMA: Journal of the American Medical Association (Chicago) 252(4), 27 Jul 1984, 528.*
LEVEL: B LANG: Eng SIRC ARTICLE NO: 103578

Merhar, G. Bob Glover: professor of fitness. *Running & fitness (Washington, D.C.) 16(2), Apr 1984, 1;20-21.*
LEVEL: B LANG Eng SIRC ARTICLE NO: 098659

Moskovites, J.P. Jogging: Americans are running to catch up. *Military medicine (Washington) 149(7), Jul 1984, 379-382.*
LEVEL: B LANG: Eng SIRC ARTICLE NO: 104257

Roberts, W.C. An agent with lipid-lowering, antihypertensive, positive inotropic, negative chronotropic, vasodilating, diuretic, anorexigenic, weight-reducing, cathartic, hypoglycemic, tranquilizing, hypnotic and antidepressive qualities. (editorial) *American journal of cardiology (New York) 53(1), 1 Jan 1984, 261-262.*
LEVEL: B LANG: Eng SIRC ARTICLE NO: 097698

Running. Putting together a safe program. Toronto: PARTICIPaction, c1984. 8 p. : ill.
CORP: PARTICIPaction.
LEVEL: B LANG: E GV1061 20859

Sander, N. Comment la course vous fait perdre du poids. *Spiridon (Salvan, Suisse) 76, nov/dec 1984, 5-10.*
LEVEL: I LANG: SIRC ARTICLE NO: 173525

PHYSIOLOGY

Brouns, F. Nutrition and running performance. (Refs: 23)*Track and field journal (Ottawa, Ont.) 27, Aug 1984, 6-12.*
CONF: European Athletics Coaches Association. Congress (12th : 1983 : Portugal).
LEVEL: I LANG: Eng SIRC ARTICLE NO: 100041

Child, J.S. Barnard, R.J. Taw, R.L. Cardiac hypertrophy and function in master endurance runners and sprinters. (Refs: 33) *Journal of applied physiology: respiratory, environmental and exercise physiology (Bethesda, Md.) 57(1), Jul 1984, 176-181.*
ABST: Nine long distance runners (E) and eleven sprinters (S) were studied by echocardiography, systolic time intervals and treadmill testing with measurement of oxygen consumption. The subjects were all master athletes, some of them national or world record holders. Oxygen consumption was greater in E than S, but greater in both groups than in non-athletic controls of the same age groups. The same conclusion was reached for left ventricular mass index.
LEVEL: A LANG: Eng SIRC ARTICLE NO: 108366

Costill, D.L. Use it or lost it: a leading physiologist examines the effects of 'de-training' on a runner's fitness level. *Runner (New York) 7(2), Nov 1984, 41-42;59.*
LEVEL: I LANG: Eng SIRC ARTICLE NO: 108624

Ernst, E. Matrai, A. Hematocrit and plasma volume in runners. (letter) *Annals of internal medicine (Philadelphia) 101(4), Oct 1984, 571.*
LEVEL: B LANG: Eng SIRC ARTICLE NO: 104969

Herbert, P.N. Bernier, D.N. Cullthane, E.M. Edelstein, L. Kantor, M.A. Thompson, P.D. High-density lipoprotein metabolism in runners and sedentary men. *JAMA. Journal of the American Medical Association (Chicago) 252(8), 24-31 Aug 1984, 1034-1037.*
ABST: The authors studied the high-density lipoprotein (HDL) metabolism of five trained men who ran 16 km daily and five inactive men. Runners were leaner and their aerobic exercise capacity was much greater. The lipid-rich HDL2 species accounted for a much higher proportion of the HDL in runners. Tracer studies of radioiodinated autologous HDL demonstrated that runners did not produce more HDL protein but rather catabolized less. The mean biologic half-life of HDL proteins was 6.2 days in the runners compared with 3.8 days in the sedentary men. The activity of lipoprotein lipase was 80 per cent higher in the postheparin plasma of the runners, whereas the activity of hepatic triglyceride hydrolase was 38 per cent lower. Thus, the prolonged survival of plasma HDL proteins in runners may result from augmented lipid transfer to HDL by lipoprotein lipase or diminished HDL clearance by hepatic lipase.
LEVEL: A LANG: Eng SIRC ARTICLE NO: 104979

Humphreys, J. Newman, S. Getting there with the help of a physiologist. *Coaching review (Ottawa) 7, Sept/Oct 1984, 48-52.*
LEVEL: B LANG: Eng SIRC ARTICLE NO: 098642

Iltis, P.W. Thomas, T.R. Adeniran, S.B. Aguiar, C.A. Albers, J.J. Different running programs: plasma lipids, apoproteins, an lecithin: cholesterol acyltransferase in middle-aged men. (Refs: 55)*Annals of sports medicine (North Hollywood, Calif.) 2(1), 1984, 16-22.*
ABST: Forty-eight untrained middle-aged men volunteered for a 13 week training study to investigate effects of different running programs on plasma levels of total cholesterol, HDL-C, apo A-I, apo B, and LCAT activity. The subjects were randomly assigned to either a 4-mile (4M), 2-mile (2M), 2-minute interval (I), or control (C) group. Training intensities were prescribed at 80 per cent of maximal heart rate for the distance groups, and at 90 per cent of maximal heart rate for the I group. Significant improvements in TT90 per cent were exclusively achieved in the exercise groups, but no running program was significantly more effective than the others. None of the blood lipid changes were significant. Apo B showed a trend toward increased post-training levels, and LCAT activity also increased. However, for the blood variables in which changes were found, post-hoc comparisons failed to exclusively link the changes to exercise.
LEVEL: A LANG: Eng SIRC ARTICLE NO: 104983

Leger, L. Mercier, D. Gross energy cost of horizontal treadmill and track running. (Refs: 28)*Sports medicine (Auckland, N.Z.) 1(4), Jul/Aug 1984, 270-277.*
ABST: The gross energy cost of treadmill and track running is re-investigated from data published in the literature. An average equation was found: VO2 (ml/kg/min), 2.209 plus 3.163 speed (km/h) for 130 subjects (trained and untrained males and females) and 10 treadmill studies. On the track, wind resistance was added to the treadmill cost of running and yielded the following equation for adults of average weight and height: VO2, 2.209 plus 3.163 speed plus 0.000525542 speed.
LEVEL: A LANG: Eng SIRC ARTICLE NO: 103583

Loucks, A.B. Horvath, S.M. Exercise-induced stress responses of amenorrheic and eumenorrheic runners. *Journal of clinical endocrinology and metabolism (Baltimore) 59(6), Dec 1984, 1109-1120.*
LEVEL: A LANG: Eng

Martin, W.H. Coyle, E.F. Joyner, M. Santeusanio, D. Ehsani, A.A. Holloszy, J.O. Effects of stopping exercise training on epinephrine-induced lipolysis in humans. (Refs: 28)*Journal of applied physiology: respiratory, environmental and exercise physiology 56(4), Apr 1984, 845-848.*
ABST: Six highly trained male athletes stopped exercise training for two months. Four days after the cessation of training there was a significantly smaller increase in serum free fatty acids and blood glycerol and a greater rise in blood lactate in response to a constant infusion of epinephrine. These parameters did not exhibit further change in the two months study period. The authors suggest that epinephrine-induced lipolysis is enhanced in endurance-exercise-trained individuals but that this adaptation is lost very rapidly after cessation of exercise training.
LEVEL: A LANG: Eng SIRC ARTICLE NO: 096983

McKain, V.M. The effect of relaxation training on oxygen consumption, heart rate, and stride length during running. Eugene, Ore.: Microform Publications, University of Oregon, 1984. 1 microfiche : negative, ill. ; 11 x 15 cm.
NOTES: Thesis (M.S.) - Pennsylvania State University, 1983; (viii, 64 leaves); includes bibliography.
LEVEL: A LANG: Eng UO84 368

Miller, T.S. Programming improved running performance. (Refs: 4)*Utah journal of health, physical education, recreation and dance (Provo, Utah) 16, Autumn 1984, 20-24.*
LEVEL: I LANG: Eng SIRC ARTICLE NO: 103594

Newsholme, E.A. Metabolic control and its importance in sprinting and endurance running. (Refs: 5)
CONF: International Cours on Physiology and Biochemistry of Exercise and Detraining (2nd : 1982 : Nice).
NOTES: In, Marconnet, P. (ed.) et al., Physiological chemistry of training and detraining, New York, Karger, c1984, p. 1-8.
ABST: This brief review discusses the biochemical mechanisms that control energy production in sprinting and marathon running. In the sprint the role of substrate cycling is thought to be very important in providing a means of energy production that is exceptionally quick. By cycling substrates in key reactions the body is kept in a state of readiness; the explosive power of a sprint can be attained quickly when necessary. In the marathon the author feels that the importance of the glucose-fatty acid cycle cannot be understated. This cycle allows the conservation of glycogen at the expense of fatty acids. This allows the body to work at a higher rate for a longer period of time.
LEVEL: A LANG: Eng RC1235 17596

Ohkuwa, T. Miyamura, M. Peak blood lactate after 400 m sprinting in sprinters and long-distance runners. *Japanese journal o physiology (Tokyo) 34(3), 1984, 553-556.*
LEVEL: A LANG: Eng

Pimm, P. Science corner: breaking wind. (Refs: 1)*Athletics (Willowdale, Ont.) Jul 1984*, 30-31.
LEVEL: I LANG: Eng SIRC ARTICLE NO: 098675

Rivera Cisneros, A.E. Diaz Cisneros, F.J. Lopez Ortega, H. Efectos del ortostatismo sobre la frecuencia cardiaca y presion arterial en sujetos sedentario y en los fisicamente acondicionados. (Effects of orthostatism on heart rate and arterial pressure in sedentary subjects and in those in good physical conditon.) *Archives del Instituto de Cardiologia de Mexico (Mexico) 54(6), Nov/Dec 1984*, 585-592.
ABST: Measurements of heart rate (HR), systolic (SBP), diastolic (DBP), and mean blood pressures (MBP) were recorded during resting, sitting and upright positions. The subjects were 57 highly trained runners and 57 sedentary untrained men. Significantly lower DBP and MBP were observed in the runners compared with the sedentary group in the sitting position. The upright posture yielded significant decreases of SBP, DBP and MBP in the runners.
LEVEL: A LANG: Spa

Stoke, S.A. A comparison of racquetball and jogging training programs and their effects on cardiorespiratory fitness. Eugene Ore.: Microform Publications, University of Oregon, 1984. 1 microfiche : negative, ill. ; 11 x 15 cm.
NOTES: Thesis (M.S.) - University of Arizona, 1983; (viii, 61 leaves); includes bibliography.
LEVEL: A LANG: Eng UO84 395

Tharp, G.D. Johnson, G.O. Thorland, W.G. Measurement of anaerobic power and capacity in elite young track athletes using the Wingate test. (Refs: 12)*Journal of sports medicine and physical fitness (Torino, Italy) 24(2), Jun 1984*, 100-106.
ABST: Elite male and female track athletes (ages 10-15) from a national championship team were tested for their anaerobic power and capacity, using the Wingate bicycle test. The anaerobic power and capacity were found to be significantly correlated with age, weight, lean body weight and surface area. It appears that the Wingate test can distinguish between sprint and distance running ability, but is a more sensitive index of anaerobic ability when it is expressed relative to body weight or lean body weight.
LEVEL: A LANG: Eng SIRC ARTICLE NO: 103612

Thompson, P.D. Cullinane, E.M. Eshleman, R. Sady, S.P. Herbert, P.N. The effects of caloric restriction or exercise cessatio on the serum lipid and lipoprotein concentrations of endurance athletes. *Metabolism, clinical and experimental (New York) 33(10), Oct 1984*, 943-950.
LEVEL: A LANG: Eng

Turblin, J. Walking yes, jogging no. *Olympic review (Lausanne) 201/202, Jul/Aug 1984*, 526-529.
LEVEL: I LANG: Eng SIRC ARTICLE NO: 097010

Turblin, J. Oui pour le footing, non pour le jogging. *Revue olympique (Lausanne) 201/202, juil/aout 1984*, 526-529.
LEVEL: LANG: Fr SIRC ARTICLE NO: 105032

Wheeler, J.R. Coronary disease can strike the fit athlete: running away from the heart attack. *New Zealand runner (Auckland N.Z.) 35, Nov/Dec 1984*, 58-63.
LEVEL: B LANG: Eng SIRC ARTICLE NO: 109298

PHYSIOLOGY - MUSCLE

Harvey, B.M. The relationship between selected muscle strength imbalance ratio changes and changes in total pseudwork per stride in running. Eugene, Ore.: Microform Publications, University of Oregon, 1984. 2 microfiches : negative ; 11 x 15 cm.
NOTES: Thesis (D.P.E.) - Springfield College, 1982; (vi, 118 leaves); includes bibliography.
LEVEL: A LANG: Eng UO84 421-422

Hicks, J.E. Shwaker, T.H. Jones, B.L. Linzer, M. Gerber, L.H. Diagnostic ultrasound: its use in the evaluation of muscle. (Refs: 8)*Archives of physical medicine and rehabilitation 65(3), Mar 1984*, 129-131.
ABST: The authors determine the reliability and reproducibility of diagnostic ultrasound data obtained when evaluating muscle. Echo amplitudes were recorded from the quadriceps femoris muscle of 10 runners and 6 non-runners in a contracted and relaxed state. The study shows that: 1) values of echo amplitudes are reproducible, 2) echo amplitude of muscle has significantly decreased in the contracted state, and 3) echo amplitude value of muscle in the relaxed and contracted state in runners is not significantly different from the relaxed and contracted state in the non-runners.
LEVEL: A LANG: Eng SIRC ARTICLE NO: 093895

Hughson, R.L. Muscle fibre types: a 1984 look. *Canadian runner (Toronto, Ont.) Jun 1984*, 9-10.
LEVEL: B LANG: Eng SIRC ARTICLE NO: 095420

Kotz, Y.M. Koryak, Y.A. Strength and speed-strength of antagonist muscles in sprinters and long-distance runners. *Soviet sports review (Escondido, Calif.) 19(3), Sept 1984*, 109-112.
NOTES: Translated from, Teoriya i praktika fizicheskoi kultury 11, 1979, 17-19.
LEVEL: I LANG: Eng SIRC ARTICLE NO: 103579

PHYSIOLOGY - TEMPERATURE

Fujita, T. An examination on running by using thermograph. *Asian journal of physical education (Taiwan, China) 7(1), Apr 1984*, 90.
LEVEL: I LANG: Eng Chi SIRC ARTICLE NO: 096962

Martin, D. Riding the heat wave: if you're not cautious, heat injury can cool your summer running in a hurry. *Runner's worl (Mountain View, Calif.) 19(6), Jun 1984*, 66-67;90.
LEVEL: B LANG: Eng SIRC ARTICLE NO: 095434

PSYCHOLOGY

Caldwell, F. Runners vs anorectics - no contest. *Physician and sportsmedicine (Minneapolis, Minn.) 12(8), Aug 1984*, 21-22;25.
LEVEL: I LANG: Eng SIRC ARTICLE NO: 098616

Dielens, S. Narcissisme et activites physiques a la mode. Profil psychologique des pratiquants d'aerobic, de jogging et de bodybuilding. (Refs: 13)*Revue de l'education physique (Liege, Belgique) 24(1), 1984*, 21-24.
LEVEL: I LANG: Fr SIRC ARTICLE NO: 096321

Guyot, G.W. Fairchild, L. Nickens, J. Death concerns of runners and nonrunners. (Refs: 30)*Journal of sports medicine and physical fitness (Torino, Italy) 24(2), Jun 1984*, 139-143.
ABST: This study assessed the death concerns of 64 runners and 62 nonrunners using Dickstein's Death Concern Scale. It was found that runners scored significantly higher than nonrunners on Factor I - thinking about death, whereas, nonrunners scored significantly higher than runners on Factor II - anxiety about death. Parallels were drawn between these results and behavior therapy approaches to anxiety reduction.
LEVEL: A LANG: Eng SIRC ARTICLE NO: 103570

Hathaway B. Running to ruin. *Psychology today (New York, N.Y.) 18(7), Jul 1984*, 14-15.
LEVEL: B LANG: Eng SIRC ARTICLE NO 095414

Lewis, R. Exercise addiction. *Women's sports (Palo Alto, Calif.) 6(1), Jan 1984*, 14-17.
LEVEL: B LANG: Eng SIRC ARTICLE NO: 097785

Lynch, J. Fear of success. *Runner (Boulder, Colo.) 6(5), Feb 1984*, 20-21.
LEVEL: B LANG: Eng SIRC ARTICLE NO: 095433

McKay, D. Running and mental health. *Fun runner (Rose Bay, Aust.) 5(6), Feb/Mar 1984*, 40;82.
LEVEL: B LANG: Eng SIRC ARTICLE NO: 099290

Oja, D.E. Making your goals work for you. *Footnotes (Reston, Va.) 12(2), Summer 1984*, 10.
LEVEL: B LANG: Eng SIRC ARTICLE NO: 109176

Yetman, W. Choke. *Canadian runner Jan/Feb 1984*, 18-21.
LEVEL: B LANG: Eng SIRC ARTICLE NO: 091127

PSYCHOLOGY - MENTAL TRAINING

Surgent, F.C. Visualization training for track events: specific strategies for attaining a peak performance. *Coaching clini (Princeton, N.J.) 23(3), Nov 1984*, 13-16.
LEVEL: B LANG: Eng SIRC ARTICLE NO: 103610

Wischnia, B. How to be your mental best on race day. As any world-class runner can tell you, when it comes to race preparation, the psychological side is every bit as important as the physical, and you don't need a shrink as much as you need a healthy attitude. *Runner's world (Mountain View, Calif.) 19(10), Oct 1984*, 78-81;126;128;130;132-133.
LEVEL: B LANG: Eng SIRC ARTICLE NO: 100105

RULES AND REGULATIONS

Rottenburg, T. The problem of pacemaking. *S.A. atleet/athlete (Pretoria, S.A.) 11(4), Mar 1984*, 8-9.
LEVEL: B LANG: Eng SIRC ARTICLE NO: 171575

SAFETY

Merhar, G. Safety on the run. *Running & fitness (Washington, D.C.) 16(5), Sept/Oct 1984*, 8-10.
LEVEL: B LANG: Eng SIRC ARTICLE NO: 098661

Runner's world guide to safety gear. Tender is the night for runners with the latest gear for visibility and security - so be prepared and be seen when you head out after sunset. *Runner's world 19(2), Feb 1984*, 103-108.
LEVEL: B LANG: Eng SIRC ARTICLE NO: 091112

SEXUALITY

Ayres, A. Androgyny. *Running times (Woodbridge, Va.) 88, May 1984*, 18;23-24;26.
NOTES: Running and sexuality: part 2.
LEVEL: B LANG: Eng SIRC ARTICLE NO: 095389

Ayres, A. Running and sexuality. *Running times (Woodbridge, Va.) 87, Apr 1984*, 12;15-18;20;22.

NOTES: Part 1.
LEVEL: I LANG: Eng SIRC ARTICLE NO: 100038

SOCIOLOGY

Brant, J. Marriage and running: for better or for worse? Running and marriage go together like a horse and carriage, as long as the carriage doesn't get itself before the horse. *Runner's world 19(2), Feb 1984, 88-89;114;118.*
LEVEL: B LANG: Eng SIRC ARTICLE NO: 091072

Brown, B.A. Curtis, J.E. Does running go against the family grain? National survey results on marital status and running. (Refs: 7)
CONF: North American Society for the Sociology of Sport. Conference (3rd : 1982 : Toronto, Ont.).
NOTES: In, Theberge, N. and Donnelly, P. (eds.), Sport and the sociological imagination: refereed proceedings of the 3rd Annual Conference of the North American Society for the Sociology of Sport, Toronto, Canada, November 1982, Fort Worth, Tex., Texas Christian University Press, c1984, p. 352-367.
ABST: This study was based on secondary analyses of the data derived in the 1976 Canadian survey of fitness, physical recreation and sport. 3,481 runners responded in this survey. The results indicate that runners are more likely to be unmarried, younger, and have a higher education and a higher status than the general population. They are also more likely to be male.
LEVEL: A LANG: Eng SIRC ARTICLE NO: 098615

Rozek, M. Running down the aisle: thoughts on keeping a marriage on the right track. *Runner (New York) 6(8), May 1984, 32.*
LEVEL: B LANG: Eng SIRC ARTICLE NO: 101706

Slenker, S.E. Price, J.H. Roberts, S.M. Jurs, S.G. Joggers versus nonexercisers: an analysis of knowledge, attitudes and beliefs about jogging. (Refs: 34)*Research quarterly for exercise and sport (Reston, Va.) 55(4), Dec 1984, 371-378.*
ABST: The Health Belief Model was utilized to examine the knowledge, attitudes and beliefs of individuals regarding regular jogging.Based on an elicitation procedure developed by Martin Fishbein, a questionnaire was developed according to the theoretical tenets of the Health Belief Model and was found to be valid and reliable. Responses from 124 joggers and 96 nonexercisers were analyzed, and significant differences were found. Factors which accounted for the largest portion of predictable variance (40 per cent) were barriers to action such as lack of time, job or family responsibilities, or weather constraints. As a whole, the results provided support for the Health Belief Model in that 61 per cent of the variance in jogging behavior was determined. The study suggests that physical and health educators might more effectively change the behavior of sedentary individuals by utilizing strategies which address perceived obstacles to jogging.
LEVEL: A LANG: Eng SIRC ARTICLE NO: 105024

SPORTING EVENTS

Heidenstrom, P.N. The line of succession: notes on New Zealand's Olympic beginnings. *New Zealand runner (Auckland) 33, Jul/Aug 1984, 50-54.*
LEVEL: B LANG: Eng SIRC ARTICLE NO: 103571

Hersh, B. A track fan's lament. Once again a boycott has denied us something precious. *Runner*

(New York) 6(11), Aug 1984, 60-63.
LEVEL: B LANG: Eng SIRC ARTICLE NO: 106166

STATISTICS AND RECORDS

Matthews, P. Vital statistics: what are the chances of seeing a world best time at any particular track meet? *Running (London) 44, Dec 1984, 63.*
LEVEL: B LANG: Eng SIRC ARTICLE NO: 104998

Morton, R.H. The supreme runner: a theory of running and some of his physiological attributes. (Refs: 10)*Australian journal of science & medicine in sport (Kingston, Aust.) 16(2), Aug 1984, 26-28.*
ABST: Analysis of athletic world records is of continuing interest in many quarters. Estimates of physiological constants and predictive analyses have been performed. This paper combines both approaches and examines an earlier theory of competitive running with reference to ultimate projected records obtained under simple assumptions. The theory stands the test, lending credence to both aspects of this paper, and in so doing, ultimate projections of various physiological constants are obtained.
LEVEL: A LANG: Eng SIRC ARTICLE NO: 105004

STATISTICS AND RECORDS - PARTICIPATION

Who is the American runner? *Runner's world (Mountain View, Calif.) 19(8), Aug 1984, 46-51;156;158;160;162;164;167-168.*
LEVEL: B LANG: Eng SIRC ARTICLE NO: 097018

TECHNIQUES AND SKILLS

Galloway, J. How to run better: tip on proper running form by a former distance runner. *Runner (New York) 7(3), Dec 1984, 62-65.*
LEVEL: B LANG: Eng SIRC ARTICLE NO: 104973

Special Book Excerpt. Chapter 3. The five basic movements. *Runner's gazette (Lewisburg, Pa.) Mar 1984, 22-24.*
NOTES: To be continued.
LEVEL: B LANG: Eng SIRC ARTICLE NO: 093945

TESTING AND EVALUATION

Kudinov, A. Determination of running time from a flying start. *Soviet sports review (Escondido, Calif.) 19(1), Mar 1984, 51.*
NOTES: Translated from, Legkaya atletika 3, 1983, 5.
LEVEL: B LANG: Eng SIRC ARTICLE NO: 095429

Measuring up for the trials. *Runner's world 18(13), 1984 Annual, 90.*
LEVEL: B LANG: Eng SIRC ARTICLE NO: 092501

TRAINING AND CONDITIONING

A high-tech takeoff: the runner's world guide to helpful accessories. *Runner's world (Mountain View, Calif.) 19(8), Aug 1984, 58-60.*
LEVEL: B LANG: Eng SIRC ARTICLE NO: 096968

Caulfield, B. Both sides now: for runnees, a strong stomach is only half of the solution. *Runner (New York) 7(3), Dec 1984, 88-89.*
LEVEL: B LANG: Eng SIRC ARTICLE NO: 104959

Clinical corner: becoming an efficient runner. *Ohio runner (Columbus, Oh.) 6(1), Jul 1984, 7.*

CORP: Bank of Boulder..
LEVEL: B LANG: Eng SIRC ARTICLE NO: 101666

Costill, D.L. Quality training: LSD is nice, but you have to run faster - to be able to run faster. Here's how... *Runner (New York) 6(8), May 1984, 50-54.*
LEVEL: B LANG: Eng SIRC ARTICLE NO: 101667

Dellinger, B. Freeman, B. Salazar, A. The competitive runner's training book. New York: Collier Books, c1984. 160 p. : ill. (A Runner's World book.)
LEVEL: B LANG: Eng ISBN: 0020283407 LC CARD: 84-015436 GV1061.5 18055

Flippin, R. The runner's total fitness training schedule. *Runner (Boulder, Colo.) 6(7), Apr 1984, 84-86.*
LEVEL: B LANG: E SIRC ARTICLE NO: 098630

Galloway, J. Peaking for top performance. *Running & fitness (Washington, D.C.) 16(5), Sept/Oct 1984, 5.*
LEVEL: B LANG: En SIRC ARTICLE NO: 098633

Galloway, J. In training: training for reduced injuries and speed. *Running & fitness (Washington, D.C.) 16(3), May/Jun 1984 25.*
LEVEL: B LANG: Eng SIRC ARTICLE NO: 101676

Galloway, J. Galloway's book on running. New and rev. Bolinas, Calif. : New York: Shelter Publications ; Random House, c1984 1v.
NOTES: Includes index.
LEVEL: I LANG: Eng ISBN: 093607003X LC CARD: 84-005585

Grisogono, V. The running body: 29 - trunk exercises. *Running (London) 39, Jul 1984, 70.*
NOTES: Last in a series.
LEVEL: LANG: Eng SIRC ARTICLE NO: 103569

Heffner, K. Patton, R. Balancing your workouts: the art and science of training. *Runner (New York) 6(8), May 1984, 24;26.*
LEVEL: B LANG: Eng SIRC ARTICLE NO: 101028

Higdon, D. Higdon, H. Programmed for performance: a home computer can put better running at your fingertips. *Runner (New York) 6(6), Mar 1984, 32-33;35-37.*
LEVEL: B LANG: Eng SIRC ARTICLE NO: 100054

Judy, V. A successful track program. *Texas coach (Austin, Tex.) 28(4), Nov 1984, 61.*
LEVEL: B LANG: Eng SIRC ARTICLE NO: 173450

L'ordinateur Hermann au service des coureurs. *Revue de l'entraineur janv/mars 1984, 28-29.*
LEVEL: B LANG: Fr SIRC ARTICLE NO: 092513

Marsh, H. Going nowhere fast: an Olympian shares the joys of his treadmill - an indoor or training device fit for all reason *Runner's world 19(1), Jan 1984, 38-41.*
LEVEL: B LANG: Eng SIRC ARTICLE NO: 091098

Miller, J. Burst of speed: 5 proven techniques to increase your speed. South Bend, Ind.: Icarus Press, 1984. 106 p. : ill.
NOTES: Includes index.
LEVEL: B LANG: Eng ISBN: 0896517063 LC CARD: 84-003802 GV1061.5 18421

Mitchell, B. How does an athlete improve? Progression and progress. *Athletics weekly (Kent, Eng.) 38(45), 10 Nov 1984, 26-27.*
LEVEL: B LANG: Eng SIRC ARTICLE NO: 102954

Mozee, G. The ultimate abdominal workout: strengthening the midsection isn't just for the spa set; a strong middle is an important tool for better

posture and faster running. *Runner's world (Mountain View, Calif.)* 19(7), Jul 1984, 102-105;126.
LEVEL: B LANG: Eng SIRC ARTICLE NO: 095442

Nelson, C. Vandewalle, P. Billouin, A. Courir. Paris: Robert Laffont, c1984. 244 p. : ill. (Sports pour tous.)
NOTES: Bibliographie: p. (235)-244.
LEVEL: I LANG: Fr ISBN: 2-221-04000-3 GV1061.5 18946

O'Brien, R. Gym class: using gymnastics to improve your running. *Runner (Boulder, Colo.)* 6(10), Jul 1984, 24;26.
LEVEL: B LANG: Eng SIRC ARTICLE NO: 101695

Olser, T.J. The conditioning of distance runners: part 1. *Runners world (Mountain View, Calif.)* 19(12), Dec 1984, 52-57;87.
NOTES: Originally published in 1967.
LEVEL: I LANG: Eng SIRC ARTICLE NO: 101699

Pimm, P. Biking for running. Cycling can be a valuable tool for both the injured and healthy runner. (Refs: 5)*Athletics (Willowdale, Ont.)* Jun 1984, 18-20.
LEVEL: B LANG: Eng SIRC ARTICLE NO: 098674

Smaller, F.G. Coaching the co-ed track team. *Coaching clinic (Princeton, N.J.)* 22(9), May 1984, 15-16.
LEVEL: B LANG: Eng SIRC ARTICLE NO: 095464

Speed development. *National Strength & Conditioning Association journal* 5(6), Jan 1984, 12-20;72-73.
LEVEL: I LANG: Eng SIR ARTICLE NO: 091116

Stifler, J. Hard pedaling: state-of-the-art workouts for stationary bikes. *Runner (Boulder, Colo.)* 6(7), Apr 1984, 24;26.
LEVEL: B LANG: Eng SIRC ARTICLE NO: 098684

Stifler, J. Abdominal games: one runner's quest for the perfect sit-up. *Runner (New York)* 6(8), May 1984, 34-35.
LEVEL: B LANG: Eng SIRC ARTICLE NO: 101716

Switzer, K. Peterson, J.A. Fit to run: a conditioning handbook for runners. El Cerrito, Calif.: Leisure Press, 1984. 160 p. ill.
LEVEL: B LANG: Eng ISBN: 0-88011-019-8 LC CARD: 81-85636

Temple, C. Searching for secrets of success. *Runner (New York)* 6(6), Mar 1984, 61-63;67.
LEVEL: B LANG: Eng SIRC ARTICLE NO: 100095

Thibault, G. Votre programme d'entrainement a la course. *Marathon, la revue de la bonne forme (Montreal)* 16, mai 1984, 36-37.
LEVEL: B LANG: Fr SIRC ARTICLE NO: 108705

Wardlaw, C. Working out the system: Chris Wardlaw reviews training methods and systems for better running in '84. *Australia runner* 2(8), Mar 1984, 12-14;17.
LEVEL: B LANG: Eng

Wischnia, B. 20 top runners and coaches give advice on how you can improve your running in 1984. *Runner's world* 18(13), 198 Annual, 45-49;94-95.
LEVEL: B LANG: Eng SIRC ARTICLE NO: 092545

TRAINING AND CONDITIONING - DRILLS

Bridges, D.A. Ferrara, D. Think wet. Forced off the road with an injury? Swimming pool running-using water to absorb shock-i one way to keep your head above water. *Runner's world (Mountain View, Calif.)* 19(9), Sept 1984, 82-84;86;88.
LEVEL: B LANG: Eng SIRC ARTICLE NO: 098614

TRAINING AND CONDITIONING - INTERVAL TRAINING

Becoming an efficient runner: part two. *Ohio runner (Columbus, Ohio)* 6(2), Aug 1984, 6.
LEVEL: B LANG: Eng SIRC ARTICLE NO: 103560

Boggis, D.E. Improve your running events: training sense is the key to improve. (Refs: 2)*Athletic journal* 64(6), Jan 1984, 14;64.
LEVEL: B LANG: Eng SIRC ARTICLE NO: 091071

TRAINING AND CONDITIONING - STRETCHING AND FLEXIBILITY EXERCISES

Running and common sense. *Hospital for sick children information handout (Toronto)* 1984?, 1-5.
LEVEL: B LANG: Eng SIRC ARTICLE NO: 106190

Tamini, N. Le cas du chat. (exercices d'elongation) *Spiridon (Salvan, Suisse)* 71, janv 1984, 41-44.
NOTES: Adapte d'un chapitre a paraitre dans, Coureurs, si vous saviez..., de Noel Tamani.
LEVEL: B LANG: Fr SIRC ARTICLE NO: 098687

TRAINING AND CONDITIONING - WARM-UPS, WARM-DOWNS, LEAD-UP GAMES

McFarlane, B. A continuous warm-up. *Modern athlete and coach (Athelstone, Aust.)* 22(3), Jul 1984, 27-28.
LEVEL: B LANG: E SIRC ARTICLE NO: 101690

Nichols, R.M. Warm-up cool-down exercises. *Runner's world (Mountain View, Calif.)* 19(11), Nov 1984, 56-59.
LEVEL: B LANG: Eng SIRC ARTICLE NO: 100072

Standberg, K. Spice up your exercises. *Running & fitness (Washington, D.C.)* 16(3), May/Jun 1984, 10-11.
LEVEL: B LANG: En SIRC ARTICLE NO: 101032

TRAINING AND CONDITIONING - WEIGHT AND STRENGTH TRAINING

Mozee, G. Prokop, D. Don't forget the upper body. Your upper half needs your help to shoulder its share of the fitness load. *Runner's world* 19(3), Mar 1984, 54-57.
LEVEL: B LANG: Eng SIRC ARTICLE NO: 092509

Olsen, E. Weight training: how much strength do runners really need? (Refs: 10)*Runner (Boulder, Colo.)* 6(7), Apr 1984, 46-54;56.
LEVEL: B LANG: Eng SIRC ARTICLE NO: 098669

Pagliano, J. Wischnia, B. Fabulous feet: the foundation of good running. *Runner's world (Mountain View, Calif.)* 19(8), Aug 1984, 39-41.
LEVEL: B LANG: Eng SIRC ARTICLE NO: 096989

VIOLENCE

Connelly, P. A long day's journey into night. Reflections on a dangerous pastime: with a little caution, after-sunset runner don't have to be afraid of the dark. *Runner's world* 19(2), Feb 1984, 100-102.
LEVEL: B LANG: Eng SIRC ARTICLE NO: 091079

WOMEN

Averbuch, G. The woman runner: free to be the complete athlete. New York: Cornerstone Library, c1984. x, 213 p. : ill.
NOTES: Includes index. Bibliography: p. 202-207.
LEVEL: I LANG: Eng ISBN: 0-346-12644-4 LC CARD: 84-009528 GV1061.18.W6 17762

Averbuch, G. Women, defend thyself. It's better to be safe than sorry, but it's best to be prepared for every eventuality. *New York running news (New York)* 29(6), Aug/Sept 1984, 46-48.
LEVEL: B LANG: Eng SIRC ARTICLE NO: 106137

Caldwell, F. Light-boned and lean athletes: does the penalty outweigh the reward? (Refs: 22)*Physician and sportsmedicine (Minneapolis, Minn.)* 12(9), Sept 1984, 139-145;149.
ABST: Recent research has found an association between reduced bone mineral content and amenorrhea in elite female athletes. The fact that estrogen protects bone has long been an established fact and further research in this area has widened interest into possible ramifications of amenorrhea on female physiology. The results from one recent study suggests that the bone density of a 25 year old amenorrheic woman is similar to that of a 50 year old woman. This article goes on to detail methods employed in the measurement of bone density and possible reasons for wide variations in recent studies. The role of nutrition and diet in female runners and ballet dancers with amenorrhea are also reviewed. The author concludes by stressing the fact that even though many factors have come to be associated with amenorrhea we still do not know the reasons why it occurs.
LEVEL: I LANG: Eng SIRC ARTICLE NO: 100044

Caulfield, B. Men coaching women. Women are relatively new to the sports arena - they have different concerns and problems than men. Is male coaching doing them a disservice? *Ultrasport (Boston, Mass.)* 1(2), Apr 1984, 53-58.
LEVEL: B LANG: Eng SIRC ARTICLE NO: 098619

Dyer, K. Catching up the men. *New scientist (London)* 1415, 2 Aug 1984, 25-26.
NOTES: A statistical look at the progressio of world records in sport shows that women are closing the gender gap. Can the trend continue?
LEVEL: B LANG: Eng SIRC ARTICLE NO: 100049

Harting, G.H. Moore, C.E. Mitchell, R. Kappus, C.M. Relationship of menopausal status and exercise level to HDL-cholesterol in women. *Experimental aging research (Bar Harbor, Mich.)* 10(1), Spring 1984, 13-18.
ABST: This study examined the relationship between exercise habits, menopausal status and HDL cholesterol in 44 long distance runners, 47 joggers, and 45 relatively inactive women. The authors suggest endurance exercise by post-menopausal females may help prevent adverse lipid and lipoprotein changes which give rise to coronary

heart disease risks.
LEVEL: A LANG: Eng SIRC ARTICLE NO: 102973

Kevles, B. The forty-week workout. What science says and fails to say about running during pregnancy. *New York running news (New York) 29(6), Aug/Sept 1984, 50-55.*
LEVEL: B LANG: Eng SIRC ARTICLE NO: 106167

Kort, M. Preview '84: track and field, part 1. *Women's sports (Palo Alto, Calif.) 6(5), May 1984, 27;29-31 .*
LEVEL: B LANG: Eng SIRC ARTICLE NO: 100062

Legal battle over women's Olympic races. *New Zealand runner (Auckland, N.Z.) 31, Mar/Apr 1984, 11-12;14.*
NOTES: Reprinted from, International Runners Committee Newsletter, Mar 1984.
LEVEL: B LANG: Eng SIRC ARTICLE NO: 101685

Lenskyj, H. A kind of precipitate waddle: early opposition to women running. (Refs: 18)
CONF: North American Society for the Sociology of Sport. Conference (3rd : 1982 : Toronto, Ont.).
NOTES: In, Theberge, N. and Donnelly, P. (eds.), Sport and the sociological imagination: refereed proceedings of the 3rd Annual Conference of the North American Society for the Sociology of Sport, Toronto, Canada, November 1982, Fort Worth, Tex., Texas Christian University Press, c1984, p. 153-161.
ABST: Society opposed the participation of women in running in the late nineteenth and early twentieth centuries on medical, aesthetic and social grounds. Femininity was a function of child bearing and the ability to please men, and had nothing to do with physical activities.
LEVEL: A LANG: Eng SIRC ARTICLE NO: 098649

Linnell, S.L. Stager, J.M. Blue, P.W. Oyster, N. Robertshaw, D. Bone mineral content and menstrual regularity in female runners. (Refs: 35)*Medicine and science in sports and exercise (Indianapolis) 16(4), Aug 1984, 343-348.*
ABST: The relationship between bone mineral content and menstrual regularity in 10 amenorrheic runners (0-3 menses during the past year), 12 runners with regular menstrual cycles (10-12 menses during the past year), and 15 non-athletic women with regular menstrual cycles was investigated. Comparisons of the two groups of runners indicated no significant differences in body fatness, average weekly running distance, or average daily intake of calcium (Ca), phosphorus (P), and Ca/P ratios. Mean bone mineral content for the three groups, measured by photon absorptiometry, was 0.508, 0.529, and 0.544 g.cm-2, respectively, at 3 cm distal radius, and 0.707, 0.700, and 0.707 g.cm-2, respectively, at one-third distal radius, indicating no significant differences among the groups (P0.05). **However, a significant relationship (r, 0.77) was noted between bone mineral content and body fatness only in the amenorrheic runners.**
LEVEL: A LANG: Eng SIRC ARTICLE NO: 103587

McNulty, B. Bill McNulty (Canada) speaks out on women's athletics. *Pan athlete (San Juan, Puerto Rico) 2(7), 1984, 23.*
LEVEL: B LANG: Eng SIRC ARTICLE NO: 097894

Rios, J.C. Jogging strengthens women's bones. *Cardiac alert (Bethesda, Md.) 6(3), Mar 1984, 8.*
LEVEL: B LANG: Eng SIRC ARTICLE NO: 097896

Simri, U. Women's races in mediaeval and early modern times. *ICSSPE/CIEPSS review (Berlin, GDR) 7, 1984, 29-32.*
LEVEL: I LANG: Eng SIRC ARTICLE NO: 096481

Stephens, M. Nice girls finish first. *Runner (New York) 6(8), May 1984, 38-46;48.*
LEVEL: B LANG: Eng SIRC ARTICLE NO: 101715

Taylor, W.N. Can a woman ever win a major marathon? an ultra marathon? *AMJA newsletter (Hollywood, Calif.) Mar 1984, 4.*
LEVEL: B LANG: Eng SIRC ARTICLE NO: 098688

Ullyot, J. New women's running. Brattleboro, Vt.: Stephen Greene Press, c1984. xii, 162 p. : ill.
NOTES: Rev. ed. of: Women's running, c1976. Bibliography: p. 161.
LEVEL: B LANG: Eng ISBN: 0-8289-05363 LC CARD: 84-006153 GV1061.18.W6 17798

Women's running. Wide hips and running: how a woman's anatomy affects her stride. *Runner's world (Mountain View, Calif.) 19(8), Aug 1984, 194.*
LEVEL: B LANG: Eng SIRC ARTICLE NO: 097021

Wurster, K.G. Zwirner, M. Keller, E. Schindler, A.E. Schrode, M. Heitkamp, H. Discipline specific differences in the responses of pituitary, gonadal, and adrenal to maximal physical exercise in female top athletes. (Refs: 16)*International journal of sports medicine (Stuttgart) Suppl. 5, Nov 1984, 203-205.*
CONF: International Congress on Sports and Health (1983 : Maastricht, Netherlands).
LEVEL: A LANG: Eng SIRC ARTICLE NO: 105038

SCANDINAVIA

Staehlberg, M. Nordic co-operation in sports. *In, Ilmarinen, M. (ed.) et al., Sport and International Understanding: proceedings of the congress held in Helsinki, Finland, July 7-10, 1982, Berlin, Springer-Verlag, 1984, p. 186-188.*
CONF: Congress on Sport and International Understanding (1982 : Helsinki).
LEVEL: B LANG: Eng GV706.8 18979

SCHOOL SPORT

Bjornaraa, B. Apple Valley high school pentathlon. *National Strength & Conditioning Association journal 6(1), Feb/Mar 1984, 21;54-58.*
LEVEL: B LANG: Eng SIRC ARTICLE NO: 093188

Durbin, B.B. National Federation Research Center proposed to provide outreach services. *Interscholastic athletic administration 10(3), Spring 1984, 3;32.*
LEVEL: B LANG: Eng SIRC ARTICLE NO: 093191

Hughes, C. Athletics in the school program. *Saskatchewan High Schools Athletic Association bulletin (Regina, Sask.) 9(4), Dec/Jan 1984, 5.*
LEVEL: B LANG: Eng SIRC ARTICLE NO: 173493

McCutcheon, L.E. The home advantage in high school athletics. (Refs: 5)*Journal of sport behavior (Mobile, Ala.) 7(4), Dec 1984, 135-138.*
ABST: Several studies have shown that the home team seems to have a slight advantage in sports. A number of explanations have been offered in order to account for this advantage. They include genetic programming to defend home territory, altering the playing conditions to favor the home team, the fact that the home team is more familiar with the idiosyncrasies of the arena, and the verbal support given by fans to the home team. A study of the home advantage in selected high school sports showed home football teams with no statistically significant win-loss advantage, although they scored significantly more points in two of three samples. In basketball, a home advantage was found in one of two samples. In cross-country home teams did not win significantly more often than visitors, but they did have a significantly greater advantage in scoring. The home advantage in high school sports was relatively weak by comparison with college and professional sports.
LEVEL: A LANG: Eng SIRC ARTICLE NO: 100999

Roberts, W.O. Before the season preparation. (Refs: 6)*Sideline view (Minneapolis, Minn.) 6(1), Aug 1984, 1-4.*
LEVEL: B LANG: Eng SIRC ARTICLE NO: 097836

Schoolympics. Alexandria, Va.: Computer Microfilm International, 1984. 1 microfiche (53 fr.); 10 x 15 cm.
CORP: Burlingame Elementary School District, California.
LEVEL: B LANG: Eng EDRS: ED240134 ERIC 240134

Should each player selected to be on the team have an opportunity to play in the game? *Stopwatch (Fredericton, N.B.) 12(3), June 1984, 5-7.*
LEVEL: B LANG: Eng SIRC ARTICLE NO: 108880

Sports participation, high school sports attract five million. Football remains most popular boys sport; basketball draws most girls. *Washington coach (Seattle, Wash.) Winter 1984, 42.*
NOTES: Excerpts from, The National Federation news, Dec 1984.
LEVEL: B LANG: Eng SIRC ARTICLE NO: 102906

ACADEMIC ACHIEVEMENT

Benedict, G.C. Gerardi, R.J. Asmann, G. Everyone is not equal academically or on the playing field. (Refs: 2)*Coaching clini (Princeton, N.J.) 23(1), Sept 1984, 11-13.*
LEVEL: I LANG: Eng SIRC ARTICLE NO: 099327

Benedict, G.C. Gerardi, R.J. Asmann, G. Academic guidelines: a fair standard for participation in high school athletics. (Refs: 2)*Interscholastic athletic administration (Kansas City) 10(4), Summer 1984, 10-13;31.*
LEVEL: B LANG: Eng SIRC ARTICLE NO: 108256

Berenshtein, G.F. Nurbaeva, M.N. Medvedev, P.A. Karavaev, A.G. K otsenke uspevaemosti i fizicheskogo razvitiia selskikh shkolnikov. (Evaluation of the educational achievement and pysical development of rural schoolchildren.) *Gigiena i sanitariia (Moscow) 10, Oct 1984, 72-73.*
LEVEL: I LANG: Rus

Feltz, D.L. Weiss, M.R. The impact of girls' interscholastic sport participation on academic orientation. (Refs: 23)*Researc quarterly for exercise and sport (Reston, Va.) 55(4), Dec 1984, 332-339.*
ABST: This study was designed to assess the influence of athletics and other extracurricular activities on the academic orientation of female high school students. Senior girls were categorized into groups - labeled athlete-only, service activities only, athlete-service and neither. Those taking the ACT college entrance exam (487) were compared on composite and English scores to the other groups, and to national and state averages. Analyses of

covariance, controlling for SES and extent of activity involvement revealed that the athlete-only group recorded the lowest average scores, but these could not be attributed to the participation category to which they belonged. Rather, socioeconomic level and extent of activity involvement were factors contributing to most of the differences between groups in which higher SES levels and higher levels of involvement were predictive of higher ACT scores.
LEVEL: A LANG: Eng SIRC ARTICLE NO: 104463

Jost-Relyveld, A. Experience de suivi sur 4 ans de 35 sections sport-etudes. (Refs: 4)*Medecine du sport (Paris) 58(2), 25 mars 1984, 10-16.*
RESUME: Cette enquete longitudinale portait sur 406 enfants et adolescents, ages de 10 a 20 ans, appartenant a 35 sections sports-etudes (S.S.E.) differentes. La capacite aerobique, le nombre d'heures hebdomadaires d'entrainement, les resultats scolaires, l'equilibre sport-etudes et les causes d'arrets ou d'abandon furent etudiees. Les resultats indiquent: 1) une capacite physique aerobique legerement superieure a la moyenne, 2) un entrainement hebdomadaire entre 13 et 18 heures, 3) de meilleurs resultats scolaires chez les filles et un pourcentage eleve de resultats mauvais ou mediocres (60% des garcons et 50% de filles), et 4) un bon equilibre sport-etudes (43% des garcons et 47% des filles). L'auteur souligne les carences des S.S.E. a leur debut.
LEVEL: A LANG: Fr SIRC ARTICLE NO: 094204

Kanaby, R.F. Athletics & academics: accept the challenge... change the perception... promote the truth. *Interscholastic athletic administration (Kansas City) 11(1), Fall 1984, 4-7;9..*
NOTES: Reprint of the text of a speech delivered at the National Federation of State High School Associations, Annual Summer Meeting, Arlington, Va., July 4, 1984.
LEVEL: B LANG: Eng SIRC ARTICLE NO: 105571

Soltz, D.F. Scholastic guidelines: athletes and achievement - making the grade. (Refs: 2)*Interscholastic athletic administration (Kansas City) 11(2), Winter 1984, 4-5;7.*
LEVEL: B LANG: Eng SIRC ARTICLE NO: 108261

ADMINISTRATION

Andrews, D. The athletic director and public relations. *Athletic journal (Evanston, Ill.) 65(2), Sept 1984, 26;57.*
LEVEL: LANG: Eng SIRC ARTICLE NO: 099325

Barber, R. Mills, T. Organizational guidelines: a cooperative model for state athletic governance. *Interscholastic athletic administration (Kansas City) 10(4), Summer 1984, 14-15.*
LEVEL: B LANG: Eng SIRC ARTICLE NO: 108257

Campbell, N. Auction is crack fund raiser. *Athletic journal (Evanston, Ill.) 65(3), Oct 1984, 36;53.*
LEVEL: B LANG: Eng SIRC ARTICLE NO: 099328

Keller, I.A. Forsythe, C.E. Administration of high school athletics. 7th ed. Englewood Cliffs, N.J.: Prentice-Hall, c1984. viii, 408 p.
NOTES: Includes index. Includes bibliographies.
LEVEL: I LANG: Eng ISBN: 0130057282 LC CARD: 83-017636 GV713 15940

Mendez, R. Extracurricular activities in today's school - have we gone too far? *NASSP bulletin (Reston Va.) 68(470), Mar 1984, 60-64.*
LEVEL: B LANG: Eng SIRC ARTICLE NO: 096388

Olson, J.R. Athletic administration: a three-phase planning guide for spectator safety and comfort. *Interscholastic athleti administration 10(3), Spring 1984, 10-13;15.*
LEVEL: B LANG: Eng SIRC ARTICLE NO: 093200

Ostro, H. Team rules and personal freedom. *Scholastic coach (New York) 54(1), Aug 1984, 10;12;14;16;18.*
LEVEL: B LANG: En SIRC ARTICLE NO: 099330

Ostro, H. Organizing and chairing a meeting or conference. *Scholastic coach (New York) 54(2), Sept 1984, 6;8;10;12.*
LEVEL B LANG: Eng SIRC ARTICLE NO: 099331

Ostro, H. Respect for duly constituted authority. *Scholastic coach (New York) 54(5), Dec 1984, 8;10-12.*
LEVEL: B LANG: En SIRC ARTICLE NO: 102903

Pence, L.S. Youngblood, J. Administration: alternatives to filling coaching position vacancies. *Interscholastic athletic administration (Kansas City) 11(1), Fall 1984, 14-15;29.*
LEVEL: B LANG: Eng SIRC ARTICLE NO: 105575

Teaching/coaching: where it is and where it's going. Six top administrators tell it as it is to Scholastic Coach. *Scholastic coach 53(7), Feb 1984, 62-68.*
ABST: This roundtable discussion by six secondary school athletic directors focuses on the current state of coaching in the American school system. The directors' discussions include the teacher situation, non-staff coaches, merit pay, budget making, equipment purchasing and coaching certification. High schools have a difficult time attracting coaches to support their athletic programmes and they must frequently rely on non-staff coaches who are holding down other jobs. There is currently no standards for high school coaches though certification is seen as an ideal method of rectifying this. However, the administrators largely feel that certification would unduely limit the number of available coaches for the high schools when it is already difficult to attract and find enough coaches for high school programs since many coaches leave these programs each year.
LEVEL: B LANG: Eng SIRC ARTICLE NO: 093205

Vanderzwaag, H.J. Sport management in schools and colleges. New York ; Toronto: Wiley, c1984. xviii, 265 p.
NOTES: Includes bibliographical references and index.
LEVEL: I LANG: Eng ISBN: 0471871354 LC CARD: 83-014763 GV346 15866

ASSOCIATIONS

Sastamala, A. School sport across borders - education in internationalism. (Refs: 4)*In, Ilmarinen, M. (ed.) et al., Sport and International Understanding: proceedings of the congress held in Helsinki, Finland, July 7-10, 1982, Berlin, Springer-Verlag, 1984, p. 189-192.*
CONF: Congress on Sport and International Understanding (1982 : Helsinki).
LEVEL: I LANG: Eng GV706.8 18979

COACHING

Broderick, R. Noncertified coaches. (Refs: 2)*Journal of physical education, recreation & dance (Reston, Va.) 55(5), May/Jun`1984, 38-39;53.*
LEVEL: B LANG: Eng SIRC ARTICLE NO: 094737

Buckelew, S.M. 11 hard facts in coaching H.S. athletes. *Scholastic coach 53(8), Mar 1984, 77.*
LEVEL: B LANG: Eng SIRC ARTICLE NO: 092702

Cassidy, T.P. Guidelines for recruiting high school athletes. *Texas coach 27(4), Jan 1984, 58-61.*
LEVEL: B LANG: Eng SIRC ARTICLE NO: 093190

Cassidy, T.P. Guidelines for recruiting high school athletes. *Coaching clinic (Englewood Cliffs, N.J.) 22(10), Jun 1984, 12-16.*
LEVEL: B LANG: Eng SIRC ARTICLE NO: 094738

Evaluating your coaches. *Physical education newsletter (Old Saybrook, Conn.) 165, Dec 1984, 7.*
LEVEL: B LANG: Eng SIRC ARTICLE NO: 173340

Hattlestad, N. The systematic evaluation of coaches. (Refs: 3)*Physical education newsletter (Old Saybrook, Conn.) 158, Apr 1984, 6-8.*
LEVEL: B LANG: Eng SIRC ARTICLE NO: 095754

Kelley, E.J. Brightwell, S. Should interscholastic coaches be certified? (Refs: 6)*Journal of physical education, recreation & dance 55(3), Mar 1984, 49-50.*
LEVEL: I LANG: Eng SIRC ARTICLE NO: 093196

Ostro, H. Of teaching, coaching, and merit pay. *Scholastic coach 53(7), Feb 1984, 4;6;8;10;12.*
LEVEL: B LANG: Eng SIRC ARTICLE NO: 093201

Stapleton, K.L. Tomlinson, C.M. Shepard, K.F. Coon, V.A. High school coaches' perceptions of their responsibilities in managing their athletes' injuries. (Refs: 17)*Journal of orthopaedic and sports physical therapy (Baltimore, Md.) 5(5), Mar/Apr 1984, 253-260.*
ABST: Thirty coaches were asked six open-ended questions regarding their responsibilities and abilities for athletic health care and opinions about certification and liability. The results indicate that coaches currently assume the major responsibility of athletic health care although the coaches felt that they lacked the knowledge to manage athletic injuries. The authors conclude that more involvement by health care professionals is needed to assist coaches in carrying out the responsibilities of athletic injury management. The coaches were in favour of coaching certification.
LEVEL: A LANG: Eng SIRC ARTICLE NO: 094240

Texas High School Coaches Association. *Texas coach (Austin, Tex.) 28(4), Nov 1984, 12-15.*
LEVEL: B LANG: Eng SIRC ARTICLE NO: 173452

Tonelli, J. An extra tryout may be the answer. *Interscholastic athletic administration (Kansas City) 10(4), Summer 1984, 23;25.*
LEVEL: B LANG: Eng SIRC ARTICLE NO: 108260

ECONOMICS

Frey, J.H. Gambling and college sports: views of coaches and athletic directors. (Refs: 15)*Sociology of sport journal (Champaign, Ill.) 1(1), 1984, 36-45.*
ABST: In light of the pervasiveness of sport betting this paper summarizes and presents data from a national study conducted by the Commission of the review of the National Policy Toward Gambling. Data were collected from 214 coaches and 127

SCHOOL SPORT (continued)

athletic directors from a sample of NCAA schools. Responses to questionnaire items provided information on the perceived impact of betting and publicized point spreads on sport in general and on the behavior of coaches and players in particular. The phenomenon of sport betting is discussed in light of these attitudes.
LEVEL: A LANG: Eng SIRC ARTICLE NO: 108344

Whiddon, S. Supplementing your athletic budget. *Women's coaching clinic 7(6), feb 1984, 13.*
LEVEL: B LANG: Eng SIRC ARTICLE NO: 089874

Yiannakis, A. Survival strategy for high school sports. *Journal of physical education, recreation and dance (Reston, Va.) 55(7), Sept 1984, 20-22.*
LEVEL: B LANG: Eng SIRC ARTICLE NO: 101000

HISTORY

Armstrong, C.F. The lessons of sports: class socialization in British and American boarding schools. (Refs: 25)*Sociology of sport journal (Champaign, Ill.) 1(4), Dec 1984, 314-331.*
ABST: This paper examines five critical functions of team games: the extension of institutional control, their roles as molder of 'manly Christian character', the importance of closer involvement of faculties in games as surrogate parents, the emergence of school leaders from the successful athletes, and their preparation of athletes for elite colleges and universities. Team sports in boarding schools in both England and New England were introduced to teach boys to be gentle men, which is what most of their parents hoped they would become. Team sports socialized boys into class and gender roles that corresponded to moral expectations of legitimate behavior. Success in sports became a crucial prerequisite for acceptance at school; the sports also fostered powerful bonds between classmates and inculcated a strong attachment to the school.
LEVEL: A LANG: Eng SIRC ARTICLE NO: 104459

Goodwin, P.J. Thomas Arnold: so what? (Refs: 22)*Physical education review (North Humberside, Eng.) 7(2), Autumn 1984, 126-131.*
LEVEL: B LANG: Eng SIRC ARTICLE NO: 105570

Jable, J.T. The public schools athletic league of New York City: organized athletics for city schoolchildren, 1903-1914. (Refs: 79)
NOTES: In, Riess, S.A. (ed.), The American sporting experience: a historical anthology of sport in America, New York, Leisure Press, c1984, p. 219-238. Originally published in: Ladd, W.M., and Lumpkin, A. (eds.), Sport and American education: history and perspectives, Washington, D.C., 1979, p. ix;1-18.
LEVEL: A LANG: Eng GV583 17631

INJURIES AND ACCIDENTS

Camp, F.A. Ear and nose trauma in high school sports. *Saskatchewan High Schools Athletic Association bulletin (Regina, Sask 9(4), Dec/Jan 1984, 7-8.*
NOTES: Reprinted from: Oregon School Activities Assn. bulletin.
LEVEL: B LANG: Eng SIRC ARTICLE NO: 173494

Hodgson, C. Woodward, C.A. Feldman, W. A descriptive study of school injuries in a Canadian region. (Refs: 26)*Pediatric nursing (Pitman, N.J.) 10(3), May/Jun 1984, 215-220.*
LEVEL: I LANG: Eng SIRC ARTICLE NO: 102512

Mueller, F.O. Blyth, C.S. Report from National Center for Catastrophic Sports Injury Research. *Ohio high school athlete (Columbus, Oh.) 43(6), Sept 1984, 5-6.*
LEVEL: I LANG: Eng SIRC ARTICLE NO: 100689

Rice, S.G. Heads up: keep sports safe. *Executive educator (Washington) 6(8), Aug 1984, 19-22;30.*
LEVEL: I LANG: Eng SIRC ARTICLE NO: 104466

Robinson, G.E. Wilkerson, G.B. Bailey, R.Q. High school athletic injuries. An unrecognized need for specialized care. *Journal of the Kentucky Medical Association (Louisville) 82(8), Aug 1984, 383-386.*
LEVEL: I LANG: Eng

LAW AND LEGISLATION

Appenzeller, H. Ross, C.T. New York - administrator assigned new duties and reprimanded for failure to supervise sports program. *Sports and the courts (Winston-Salem, N.C.) 5(3), Summer 1984, 8-9.*
LEVEL: B LANG: Eng SIRC ARTICLE NO: 097832

Appenzeller, H. Ross, C.T. Alabama - board of education guilty of employment discrimination against black coach. *Sports and the courts (Winston-Salem, N.C.) 5(3), Summer 1984, 11.*
LEVEL: B LANG: Eng SIRC ARTICLE NO: 097833

Arizona - court disallows school district's advertising biology teaching and football coaching as single position. *Sports and the courts (Winston-Salem, N.C.) 5(4), Fall 1984, 9-10.*
LEVEL: B LANG: Eng SIRC ARTICLE NO: 102554

Della-Giustina, D. Moore, L.M. Proceedings of the National Conference on Liability in the Schools. Reston, Va.: American School and Community Safety Association, c1984. iii, 67 p.
CONF: National Conference on Liability in the Schools (1984 : Morgantown, West Virginia).
CORP: American School and Community Safety Association.
CORP: American Alliance for Health, Physical Education, Recreation and Dance. Midwest District.
CORP: West Virginia University. Dept. of Safety Studies.
LEVEL: I LANG: Eng GV705 18960

Kozlowski, J.C. Two cases of 'crack-the-whip' playground liability. *Parks & recreation (Arlington, Va.) 19(1), Jan 1984, 28-30.*
LEVEL: B LANG: Eng SIRC ARTICLE NO: 092910

Mallios, H.G. In defense of athletic administrators facing litigation. *Athletic administration 19(1), Feb 1984, 17-19.*
LEVEL: B LANG: Eng SIRC ARTICLE NO: 092912

Minnesota - student injured on vaulting horse sues for damages. *Sports and the courts (Winston-Salem, N.C.) 5(1), Winter 1984 2.*
LEVEL: B LANG: Eng SIRC ARTICLE NO: 095063

Ostro, H. About the rights of search & seizure. *Scholastic coach (New York) 54(3), Oct 1984, 8;10;12;14.*
LEVEL: B LANG: E SIRC ARTICLE NO: 100459

Pennsylvania - court grants injunction to allow students to participate in sports. *Sports and the courts (Winston-Salem, N.C. 5(4), Fall 1984, 10-11.*
LEVEL: B LANG: Eng SIRC ARTICLE NO: 102905

Roundy, E. Legal liability - no laughing matter. (Refs: 2)*Utah journal of health, physical education, recreation and dance (Provo, Utah) 16, Autumn*

1984, 6-7.
LEVEL: B LANG: Eng SIRC ARTICLE NO: 102558

Texas - sanctions against high school teams denied by court. *Sports and the courts (Winston-Salem, N.C.) 5(2), Spring 1984, 4-5.*
LEVEL: B LANG: Eng SIRC ARTICLE NO: 094410

Texas - student burned at pep rally not entitled to damages. *Sports and the courts (Winston-Salem, N.C.) 5(4), Fall 1984, 4-5.*
LEVEL: B LANG: Eng SIRC ARTICLE NO: 102559

van der Smissen, B. Liability concerns in the recreational setting under school auspices. (Refs: 5)*In, Della-Giustina, D. and Moore, L.M. (eds.), Proceedings of the National Conference on Liability in the Schools, Reston, Va., American School and Community Safety Association, c1984, p. 39-62.*
CONF: National Conference on Liability in the Schools (1984 : Morgantown, West Virginia).
LEVEL: I LANG: Eng GV705 18960

MEDICINE

Brunet, M.E. Giardina, D. Sports medicine in Louisiana: a survey of 242 high schools. *Journal of Louisiana State Medical Society (New Orleans) 136(8), Aug 1984, 25-27.*
LEVEL: A LANG: Eng

Farmer, M. Sports medicine: forming a sport health team to meet community needs. *Interscholastic athletic administration 10(3), Spring 1984, 22-24.*
LEVEL: B LANG: Eng SIRC ARTICLE NO: 093192

Krueger, P. A community's solution to chemical abuse. *Interscholastic athletic administration (Kansas City) 11(1), Fall 198 19-20.*
LEVEL: B LANG: Eng SIRC ARTICLE NO: 105192

Sandago, M.P. Athletic trainers: a wise investment. *First aider (Gardner, Kans.) 54(3), Nov 1984, 13.*
LEVEL: B LANG: Eng SIRC ARTICLE NO: 108462

OFFICIATING

Laws, J. Bridging the gap to high school officiating. *Referee (Franksville, Wis.) 9(9), Sept 1984, 54.*
LEVEL: B LANG: Eng SIRC ARTICLE NO: 100998

Special report: a survey of assigning practices. *Referee (Franksville, Wis.) 9(2), Feb 1984, 29.*
LEVEL: B LANG: Eng SIRC ARTICLE NO: 097636

Staffo, D.F. Officiating can be thankless job. *Saskatchewan High Schools Athletic Association bulletin (Regina, Sask.) 9(4) Dec/Jan 1984, 3-4.*
LEVEL: B LANG: ng SIRC ARTICLE NO: 173492

Young, R. Attracting and retaining quality sports officials. *Interscholastic athletic administration (Kansas City) 10(4), Summer 1984, 20-21.*
LEVEL: B LANG: Eng SIRC ARTICLE NO: 108259

PHILOSOPHY

Kadingo, C.J. An assessment of female high school varsity athletes' attitudes toward ethical considerations in competitive sports situations. Eugene, Ore.: Microform Publications, University of Oregon, 1984. 2 microfiches : negative ; 11 x 15 cm.
NOTES: Thesis (M.S.) - Pennsylvania State University, 1983; (viii, 92 leaves); includes bibliography.
LEVEL: A LANG: Eng UO84 339-340

PROGRAMS

Bean, D. So you think you have a good primary school programme. *British journal of physical education (London) 15(1), Jan/Feb 1984, 5-6.*
LEVEL: B LANG: Eng SIRC ARTICLE NO: 099326

Evaluating your athletic program. *Physical education newsletter (Old Saybrook, Conn.) 160, Jun 1984, 7-8.*
LEVEL: B LANG: En SIRC ARTICLE NO: 104462

SAFETY

Parsons, T.W. Risk-management: sport administrators' assessment of reality. (Refs: 1)*NIRSA journal (Corvallis, Ore.) 9(1), Fall 1984, 8;10-13.*
LEVEL: I LANG: Eng SIRC ARTICLE NO: 105574

SOCIAL PSYCHOLOGY

Jost-Relyveld, A. Experience de suivi sur 4 ans de 35 sections sport-etudes. (Refs: 4)*Medecine du sport (Paris) 58(2), 25 mars 1984, 10-16.*
RESUME: Cette enquete longitudinale portait sur 406 enfants et adolescents, ages de 10 a 20 ans, appartenant a 35 sections sports-etudes (S.S.E.) differentes. La capacite aerobique, le nombre d'heures hebdomadaires d'entrainement, les resultats scolaires, l'equilibre sport-etudes et les causes d'arrets ou d'abandon furent etudiees. Les resultats indiquent: 1) une capacite physique aerobique legerement superieure a la moyenne, 2) un entrainement hebdomadaire entre 13 et 18 heures, 3) de meilleurs resultats scolaires chez les filles et un pourcentage eleve de resultats mauvais ou mediocres (60% des garcons et 50% de filles), et 4) un bon equilibre sport-etudes (43% des garcons et 47% des filles). L'auteur souligne les carences des S.S.E. a leur debut.
LEVEL: A LANG: Fr SIRC ARTICLE NO: 094204

Kyte, A. Recreation: competition play and our psycho-social objectives. (Refs: 3)*CAHPERD journal times (Danville, Calif.) 46(4), Jan 1984, 4-5.*
LEVEL: B LANG: Eng SIRC ARTICLE NO: 097835

Rice, L. International competition: a great opportunity can be a huge embarrassment. *Interscholastic athletic administratio (Kansas City) 11(2), Winter 1984, 8-9;30-31.*
LEVEL: B LANG: Eng SIRC ARTICLE NO: 108262

St. Clair, R. Athletic administration: athletes, parents, coaches - raise your expectations. *Interscholastic athletic administration (Kansas City) 10(4), Summer 1984, 6-9.*
LEVEL: B LANG: Eng SIRC ARTICLE NO: 108255

SOCIOLOGY

Duquin, M.E. Social justice in sport: the norm of expected inequity. (Refs: 17)
CONF: North American Society for the Sociology of Sport. Conference (3rd : 1982 : Toronto, Ont.).
NOTES: In, Theberge, N. and Donnelly, P. (eds.), Sport and the sociological imagination: refereed proceedings of the 3rd Annual Conference of the North American Society for the Sociology of Sport, Toronto, Canada, November 1982, Fort Worth, Tex., Texas Christian University Press, c1984, p. 177-189.
ABST: 128 middle class high school students aged 14 to 18 equally divided between male and female athletes and non-athletes evaluated 6 sport

scenarios depicting conflict between a member of an athletic department and an athlete. The results shed light on how students perceive social justice in the field of sports. Injustice was viewed as less serious if an athlete was a willing participant while injustice was felt to be more serious when a formal law or rule was violated.
LEVEL: A LANG: Eng SIRC ARTICLE NO: 097842

Edwards, M. Interscholastic athletics: is it an important part of the educational process today? (Refs: 8)*Texas coach (Austin, Tex.) 28(1), Aug 1984, 22-24.*
LEVEL: B LANG: Eng SIRC ARTICLE NO: 102901

Hastad, D.N. Segrave, J.O. Pangrazi, R. Petersen, G. Youth sport participation and deviant behavior. (Refs: 15)*Sociology of sport journal (Champaign, Ill.) 1(4), Dec 1984, 366-373.*
ABST: The purpose of this study was to investigate the relationship between youth sport participation and deviant behavior among elementary school children. The study ascertained deviancy among youth sport participants and nonparticipants, and compared the profiles of youth sport participants and deviants on a selected cluster of eight sociopsychological variables. Of a total sample of 381 sixth-grade students, 278 (146 boys and 132 girls) were classified as youth sport participants. Overall, the results indicated a negative association between youth sport participation and deviancy. Although the study showed some similarities in the profiles of youth sport participants and deviants, important distinctions were found regarding the variables delinquent associates, peer status, and personal values.
LEVEL: A LANG: Eng SIRC ARTICLE NO: 104464

Howell, F.M. Miracle, A.W. Rees, C.R. Do high school athletics pay?: the effects of varsity participation on socioeconomic attainment. (Refs: 9)*Sociology of sport journal (Champaign, Ill.) 1(1), 1984, 15-25.*
CONF: North American Society for the Sociology of Sport. Meeting (1983 : St. Louis).
ABST: It has been reported that participation in high school athletics has a positive effect on education, occupational status attainment, and earnings. (Otto and Alwin, 1977; Howell and Picou, 1983). The findings regarding the economical benefits of sport participation have emerged from the two regional panel studies and need to be examined for generalizability beyond local labor markets. We test this hypothesis using the five-wave Youth in Transition panel based on a national sample of 1,628 males. The respondents were surveyed repeatedly during their high school years (1966-69). They were follow-up 1 year posthigh school (1970) and again 5 years (1974) after graduation. Our results do not support the hypothesis. However, we suggest that the lack of supportive findings may be explained by the stage in the life cycle at which the follow-up was completed.
LEVEL: A LANG: Eng SIRC ARTICLE NO: 108342

Okihiro, N.R. Extracurricular participation, educational destinies and early job outcomes. (Refs: 19)
CONF: North American Society for the Sociology of Sport. Conference (3rd : 1982 : Toronto, Ont.).
NOTES: In, Theberge, N. and Donnelly, P. (eds.), Sport and the sociological imagination: refereed proceedings of the 3rd Annual Conference of the North American Society for the Sociology of Sport, Toronto, Canada, November 1982, Fort Worth, Tex., Texas Christian University Press, c1984, p.

334-349.
ABST: This study assesses the effects of high school athletic and social activities participation on eventual occupational outcomes. 2555 Ontario Grade 12 students contacted in 1973 as a part of an educational intention survey were re-contacted in 1979. 69 per cent were successfully contacted and responded for this survey. The survey considered a number of factors which largely indicated in the results that athletic and social involvement in extracurricular activities play an important role in the process of education and early job attainment.
LEVEL: A LANG: Eng SIRC ARTICLE NO: 097847

Thirer, J. Wieczorek, P.J. On and off field social interaction patterns of black and white high school athletes. (Refs: 19) *Journal of sport behavior (Mobile, Ala.) 7(3), Sept 1984, 105-114.*
ABST: The present study focused on the socialization patterns of high school subjects, relative to sport related activities. The results indicated that very little social interaction between Blacks and Whites occur during or away from team related activites. The implications of this study are that interracial social interaction habits that exist in later life may in fact have been firmly established at the high school level, if not earlier.
LEVEL: A LANG: Eng SIRC ARTICLE NO: 101004

William, G. Sport should become a fundamental right in education. *Olympic review (Lausanne, Switzerland) 195/196, Jan/Feb 1984, 42-43.*
NOTES: Extracted from, Frankfurter Allgemeine Zeitung, 21 Sept 1983.
LEVEL: B LANG: Eng SIRC ARTICLE NO: 094217

William, G. Le sport doit devenir un droit fondamental dans l'education. *Revue olympique (Lausanne) 195/196, janv/fevr 1984 42-43.*
NOTES: Extraits ci-dessus, a ete publie dans le Frankfurter Allgemeine Zeitung, 21 Sept 1983.
LEVEL: B LANG: Fr SIRC ARTICLE NO: 095744

SCOTLAND

Halkett, J. Further education, physical education and the youth training scheme. (Refs: 7)*Scottish journal of physical education (Glasgow, Scotland) 12(1), Jan 1984, 37-43.*
LEVEL: I LANG: Eng SIRC ARTICLE NO: 094519

SHOOTING

Baxter, M. Running boar target shooting. Die Schiessdisziplin: Laufende Scheibe. Le tir a la cible courante. El tiro de jabali. *UIT shooting sport journal (Muenchen, FRG) 24(4), Jul/Aug 1984, 31-33.*
LEVEL: B LANG: Eng Ger Fr Spa SIRC ARTICLE NO: 099873

Blair, W. The complete book of target shooting. Harrisburg, Pa.: Stackpole Books, c1984. x, 405 p. : ill.
LEVEL: I LANG: En ISBN: 0-8117-0427-0 LC CARD: 84-142 GV1153 17621

Blatt, A. Gun Digest book of trap and skeet shooting. Northfield, Ill.: DBI Books, c1984. 256 p. : ill.
LEVEL: I LANG: Eng ISBN: 0910676666 LC CARD: 83-070143 GV1153 17047

SHOOTING (continued)

Rees, C.F. Be an expert shot with rifle, handgun, or shotgun. Piscataway, N.J.: Winchester Press, c1984. 1v.
NOTES: Include index.
LEVEL: I LANG: Eng ISBN: 0832903582 LC CARD: 84-019590

Suleimanov, R. The analysis of the shooting events. (Part 2) Analyse der Schiesswettbewerbe. (2. Teil) L'analyse des epreuve de tir. (2ieme partie) El analisis de los eventos de tiro. (2a parte) *UIT shooting sport journal (Muenchen, FRG) 24(2), Mar/Apr 1984, 49.*
NOTES: To be continued.
LEVEL: B LANG: Eng Ger Fr Spa SIRC ARTICLE NO: 098459

Suleimanov, R. The analysis of shooting events. Analyse der Schiesswettbewerbe. L'analyse des epreuves de tir. El analisis d los eventos de tiro. *UIT shooting sport journal (Muenchen, FRG) 24(1), Jan/Feb 1984, 33-34.*
NOTES: To be continued.
LEVEL: B LANG: Eng Ger Fr Spa SIRC ARTICLE NO: 098460

ADMINISTRATION

Lyons, M. A computer for benchrest matches. *Precision shooting (New York) 30(4), Aug 1984, 18-19.*
LEVEL: B LANG: Eng SIRC ARTICLE NO: 099877

ASSOCIATIONS

Nussbaumer, H. The foundation of the UIT was difficult. UIT-Gruendung war eine schwere Geburt. La fondation de l'UIT fut tre difficile. La fundacion de la UIT fue bastante dificil. *UIT shooting sport journal (Munich, FRG) 24(5), Sept/Oct 1984, 41-42.*
LEVEL: B LANG: Eng Ger Fr Spa SIRC ARTICLE NO: 173529

BALLISTICS AND AMMUNITION

Audette, C. Commentary. *Precision shooting (Elmira, N.Y.) 30(2), Jun 1984, 5-10;32.*
LEVEL: I LANG: Eng SIRC ARTICLE NO: 103407

Bolger, L. Efficiency and bore capacity. *Australian shooters journal (Adelaide, South Aust.) Jun 1984, 41-46.*
LEVEL: B LANG: Eng SIRC ARTICLE NO: 103409

Browne, P. Shotshell reloading: part 3. *Australian shooters journal (Adelaide, South Aust.) Jul 1984, 33-36.*
LEVEL: B LANG: Eng SIRC ARTICLE NO: 103411

Browne, P. Shotshell reloading: part 2. *Australian shooters journal (Adelaide, South Aust.) Jun 1984, 36-39.*
LEVEL: B LANG: Eng SIRC ARTICLE NO: 103412

Browne, P. Shotshell reloading: part one. The basics. *Australian shooters journal (Adelaide, Aust.) May 1984, 24-27;68.*
LEVEL: B LANG: Eng SIRC ARTICLE NO: 103413

Jamison, R. Compact handtools: handy alternatives for beginning reloaders. *Shooting times (Peoria, Ill.) 25(3), Mar 1984, 58-61.*
LEVEL: B LANG: Eng SIRC ARTICLE NO: 099874

BIOGRAPHY AND AUTOBIOGRAPHY

Bullseye: family helped Thom make dream real. (Linda Thom) *Aim (Ottawa) 11, Autumn/automne 1984, 3-6.*
LEVEL: B LANG: Eng Fr SIRC ARTICLE NO: 107462

McCrea, M. Entrevue de champion avec Linda Thom. Champion interview with Linda Thom. *Champion (Ottawa) 8(4), Nov 1984, 11-14.*
LEVEL: B LANG: Fr Eng SIRC ARTICLE NO: 101497

Stroup, L.W. The Wiggers: Olympics could be a family affair. *Olympian (Colorado Springs, Colo.) 11(1), Jun 1984, 22-23.*
LEVEL: B LANG: Eng SIRC ARTICLE NO: 101500

CERTIFICATION

N.S.R.A. coaching scheme revised. *Rifleman (London) 657, Apr 1984, 21-22.*
LEVEL: B LANG: Eng SIRC ARTICLE NO: 098451

The rifle coach: level I technical. Vanier, Ont.: Shooting Federation of Canada, c1984. ca. 50 p. : ill. (National Coaching Certification Program.)
CORP: Shooting Federation of Canada.
NOTES: Cover title: Rifle shooting: level I technical.
LEVEL: B LANG: Eng GV1177 17930

CLOTHING

Loesel, H. Important medical aspects on sport referring to the Olympic Games in Summer 1984. (Part 4) Sportmedizinisch relevante Aspekte bezueglich der Olympischen Spiele im Sommer 1984. (4. Teil) Aspects importants du point de vue de la medecine du sport pour les Jeux olympiques d'ete 1984. (4ieme partie) Aspectos importantes de la medicina y del deporte para los Juegos Olimpicos de verano de 1984. (4a parte) *UIT shoothing sport journal (Muenchen, FRG) 24(2), Mar/Apr 1984, 18-20;51-54.*
LEVEL: B LANG: Eng Ger Fr Spa SIRC ARTICLE NO: 098448

CLUBS

Adelaide Pistol Club. *Australian pistol shooter's bulletin (Australia) 27(2), Mar 1984, 12-13.*
LEVEL: B LANG: Eng SIRC ARTICLE NO: 101493

COACHING

Egolf, R.M. Coaching the highpower team... *American rifleman (Washington) 132(2), Feb 1984, 34-35;74.*
LEVEL: B LANG: Eng SIRC ARTICLE NO: 172194

DISABLED

Bowen, R.W. On target again: after fourteen years, the development of a rest for a rifle made shooting safe and fun. *Paraplegia (Phoenix, Ariz.) 38(8), Aug 1984, 16-17.*
LEVEL: B LANG: Eng SIRC ARTICLE NO: 173365

ENVIRONMENT

Antal, L.C. The problems of smog and the shooting events in Los Angeles. Die Probleme verursacht durch Smog und die Schiesswettbewerbe in Los Angeles. Les problemes du smog et les epreuves de tir a Los Angeles. Los Problemas de Smog y los Eventos de Tiro en Los Angeles. *UIT shooting sport journal (Muenchen, FRG) 24(2), Mar/Apr 1984, 37-38.*
LEVEL: B LANG: Eng Ger Fr Spa SIRC ARTICLE NO: 098442

EQUIPMENT

Brennan, D. The evolution of benchrest equipment. *Precision shooting (Elmira, N.Y.) 30(2), Jun 1984, 12-16.*
LEVEL: B LANG: Eng SIRC ARTICLE NO: 103410

Gascoigne, K. Binoculars - the forgotten accessory or the missing link. *Australian shooters' journal (Adelaide, South Australia) Jan 1984, 36-39.*
LEVEL: B LANG: Eng SIRC ARTICLE NO: 093686

Jamison, R. Lightweight vs. heavyweight varmint rifles. *Shooting times (Pioria, Ill.) 25(5), May 1984, 36-39;80.*
LEVEL: B LANG: Eng SIRC ARTICLE NO: 101495

Langford, G. Air weapons: setting the sights to...trigger your profits. *Sports trader (London) 145(1008), 5 Apr 1984, 19;21-23;25.*
LEVEL: B LANG: Eng SIRC ARTICLE NO: 101496

Robinson, J. Unique rimfire rifles. *Australian shooters journal (Adelaide, South Aust.) Jul 1984, 24-31.*
LEVEL: B LANG: E SIRC ARTICLE NO: 103417

Robinson, J. Centrefires. *Australian shooters journal (Adelaide, South Aust.) Jun 1984, 48-52.*
LEVEL: B LANG: Eng SIRC ARTICLE NO: 103418

Robinson, J. Winchester: westerner model 70. *Australian shooters journal (Adelaide, Aust.) May 1984, 33-36.*
LEVEL: B LANG: Eng SIRC ARTICLE NO: 103419

Robinson, J. Zeiss 'C' series: scopes. *Australian shooters journal (Adelaide, Aust.) Apr 1984, 45-47.*
LEVEL: B LANG: Eng SIRC ARTICLE NO: 103420

EQUIPMENT - MAINTENANCE

Dunlap, R. Gun care & cleaning. *American rifleman (Washington) 132(10), Oct 1984, 32-33;71-74.*
LEVEL: B LANG: Eng SIRC ARTICLE NO: 103414

HISTORY

Brennan, D. The evolution of the benchrest rifle 1947-1950. The pioneer era. Part II. *Precision shooting (Akron, Ohio) 29(10), Feb 1984, 12-13.*
LEVEL: B LANG: Eng SIRC ARTICLE NO: 098444

Brennan, D. The evolution of the benchrest rifle 1947-1950. The pioneer era. Part I. *Precision shooting (Akron, Ohio) 29(9) Jan 1984, 10-12.*
LEVEL: B LANG: Eng SIRC ARTICLE NO: 098445

INJURIES AND ACCIDENTS

Rogers, C.C. Shooters aim to score with beta-blockers. *Physician and sportsmedicine (Minneapolis, Minn.) 12(6), Jun 1984, 35.*
LEVEL: B LANG: Eng SIRC ARTICLE NO: 095228

MASTERS COMPETITION

Robinson, J. Pistol powders. *Australian pistol shooters' bulletin (Eastwood, Aust.) 27(1), Jan 1984, 15;17-20;22-26.*
LEVEL: B LANG: Eng SIRC ARTICLE NO: 096804

MATHEMATICS

Suleimanov, R. The analysis of the shooting events (part 3). Analyse der Schiesswettbewerbe (3. Teil). L'analyse des epreuve de tir (3ieme partie). El analisis de los eventos de tiro (3a parte). *UIT shooting sport journal (Muenchen, FRG) 24(4), Jul/Aug 1984, 35.*
NOTES: To be continued.
LEVEL: I LANG: Eng Ger Fr Spa SIRC ARTICLE NO: 099882

MEDICINE

Hatfield, B.D. Landers, D.M. Ray, W.J. Cognitive processes during self-paced motor performance: an electroencephalographic profile of skilled marksmen. (Refs: 35)*Sport psychology (Champaign, Ill.) 6(1), 1984, 42-59.*
ABST: In the initial phase of the study (Study 1) electrocortical arousal (EEG alpha activity) was assessed at four standardized sites (T3, T4, O1, and O2) from male and female (N, 17) international-caliber marksmen during rifle shooting performance. The task consited of the execution of 40 shots at a conventional indoor target from the standing position. During each shot preparation, a significant increase in left temporal and occipital alpha activity was demonstrated, while the right hemispheric activity remained constant. Hemispheric laterality ratios (Tr:T3) evidenced a significant shift toward right-brain dominance as the time to trigger pull approached. In the second phase of the study (Study 2) male and female (N, 15) marksmen performed patterns the same shooting task and, additionally, the resultant EEG performance patterns were contrasted to those observed during the mental processing of sterotyped left-brain and right-brain mental tasks. Observed EEG patterns, that is, temporal ratios, during shooting replicated the results of Study 1.
LEVEL: A LANG: Eng SIRC ARTICLE NO: 108484

MacDaniel, D.L. Pistol shooter's Rx for tired eyes. *American rifleman (Washington) 132(5), May 1984, 37-39;79.*
LEVEL: B LANG: Eng SIRC ARTICLE NO: 104868

PHYSIOLOGY

Dion, M. La respiration, une technique pour ameliorer vos resultats au tir. (Refs: 17)*Aim (Ottawa) 10, hiver 1984, 6-7.*
LEVEL: I LANG: Fr SIRC ARTICLE NO: 093685

PROTECTIVE DEVICES

Aagaard, F. Shoother eye and ear protection. *American rifleman (Washington, D.C.) 132(6), Jun 1984, 34-35;71.*
LEVEL: B LANG: Eng SIRC ARTICLE NO: 102167

PSYCHOLOGY

Fenk, A. Two different explanations for the alteration of performance on high levels of activation. (Refs: 32)*International journal of sport psychology (Rome) 15(3), 1984, 169-178.*
ABST: In experiments on the level of aspiration during sports activities the correlations between series of predictions and series of subsequent performances, computed for single subjects, were generally positive in shot putting but negative in pilot study with shooting. The predominance of low

or even negative coefficients in subjects with high goal discrepancies and weak performance within their reference group (Fenk, 1981) may be interpreted in terms of the shaped function between levels of activation and performance. Some other authors explained comparable findings - not (only) on the basis of different intensities but different qualities of motivation states.
LEVEL: A LANG: Eng SIRC ARTICLE NO: 105043

PSYCHOLOGY - MENTAL TRAINING

Pelton, T. Straight shooting. *In, Schrier, E.W. and Allman, W.F. (eds.), Newton at the bat: the science in sports, New York Scribner, c1984, p. 158-162.*
LEVEL: I LANG: Eng RC1235 18609

PSYCHOPHYSIOLOGY

Daniels, F.S. Biofeedback training and performance in rifle marksmen. Eugene, Ore.: Microform Publications, University of Oregon, 1984. 2 microfiches : negative, ill. ; 11 x 15 cm.
NOTES: Thesis (M.S.) - Pennsylvania State University, 1981; (ix, 107 leaves); includes bibliography.
LEVEL: A LANG: Eng UO84 79-80

Grant, G. Arousal in competitive pistol shooting. *Australian pistol shooter's bulletin (Australia) 27(3), May 1984, 7-9;11-12.*
LEVEL: I LANG: Eng SIRC ARTICLE NO: 101494

RULES AND REGULATIONS

Monk, J. The clay target game. *Guns Australia Mar/Apr 1984, 34;40-41.*
NOTES: Shotguns and the shotgunning sports.
ABST: The main clay target games, in order of difficulty, are trench, ball-trap, trap (or down-the-line) Olympic (or International Shooting Union) and American skeet. There are also Tower events, walk-up competitions and simulated shooting. Techniques and rules of competition vary widely for each type. The over under or any double barrelled gun is more popular in Australia than the autoloader or repeating gun when shooting trap or skeet.
LEVEL: I LANG: Eng SIRC ARTICLE NO: 102114

Notes on scoring. *Rifleman (London) 657, Apr 1984, 4.*
LEVEL: B LANG: Eng SIRC ARTICLE NO: 098452

SPORTING EVENTS

Anderson, G. How can a shotgun shooter get to the Olympic Games? *Trap & field (Indianapolis, Ind.) 160(3), Mar 1984, 36-38.*
LEVEL: B LANG: Eng SIRC ARTICLE NO: 099872

Banks, A.G. Looking back - the Queen Alexandra's Cup competition 1907. *Rifleman (London) 656, Feb 1984, 18-19.*
LEVEL: B LANG: Eng SIRC ARTICLE NO: 098443

Hunnicutt, R.W. American rifleman guide to the Olympic Games. *American rifleman (Washington) 132(7), Jul 1984, 32-47.*
LEVEL: B LANG: Eng SIRC ARTICLE NO: 103415

Sherling, A. Olympic Games, Paris 1900 - a shooting of a fair. Olympische Spiele, Paris 1900 - ein Jahrmarktsschiessen. Les Jeux olympiques, Paris 1900 - une foire de tir. Los Juegos Olimpicos, Paris 1900 - una feria del tiro. *UIT shooting sport journal (Muenchen, FRG) 24(3), May/Jun 1984, 8-10;40-43.*

LEVEL: B LANG: Eng Ger Fr Spa SIRC ARTICLE NO: 098456

Sherling, A. London 1908 - gold-medals for Grand-fathers. Curiosities of former Olympic shooting competitions. London 1908 - Gold-medaillen fuer Grossvaeter. Merkwuerdigkeiten olympischer Schiesswettbewerbe III. Londres 1908 - medailles en or pour des Grands-peres. Des choses remarquables des Jeux olympiques d'autrefois III. Londres 1908 - medallas de oro para abuelos. Cosas natables en los Juegos Olimpicos anteriores III. *UIT shooting sport journal (Muenchen, FRG) 24(4), Jul/Aug 1984, 20-22;36-39.*
LEVEL: B LANG: Eng Ger Fr Spa SIRC ARTICLE NO: 099880

TECHNIQUES AND SKILLS

Suleimanov, R. The analysis of the shooting events. (part 4) Analyse der Schiesswettbewerbe. (4. Teil) L'analyse des epreuve de tir. (4ieme partie) El analisis de los eventos de tiro. (4a parte) *UIT shooting sport journal (Munich, FRG) 24(5), Sept/Oct 1984, 50-55.*
LEVEL: I LANG: Eng Ger Fr Spa SIRC ARTICLE NO: 173532

TECHNIQUES AND SKILLS - STANCE

Todd, A.R. Principles of sporting rifle shooting. *Aim (Ottawa) 10, Winter 1984, 9.*
LEVEL: B LANG: Eng SIRC ARTICLE NO: 093687

Todd, A.R. The standing position. *Aim (Ottawa) 11, Autumn/automne 1984, 55-56.*
LEVEL: B LANG: Eng SIRC ARTICLE NO: 107467

TESTING AND EVALUATION

Koyler, J.M. Practical target statistics: playing the odds wisely. *Precision shooting (New York) 30(4), Aug 1984, 14-17.*
LEVEL: I LANG: Eng SIRC ARTICLE NO: 099875

Koyler, J.M. Inherent variability of target groups. (Refs: 4)*Precision shooting (New York) 30(1), May 1984, 8-12.*
LEVEL: LANG: Eng SIRC ARTICLE NO: 099876

Stevens, T.S. Hunter class performance evaluation. *Precision shooting (Akron, Ohio) 29(11), Mar 1984, 19-23.*
LEVEL: I LANG: Eng SIRC ARTICLE NO: 098458

VISION

Guidelines for shooting and archery eyewear. *Sports mediscope (Colorado Springs) 4(2), Summer 1984, 13-14.*
CORP: United States. Olympic Committee. Vision Performance and Safety Advisory Committee.
LEVEL: B LANG: Eng SIRC ARTICLE NO: 096803

WOMEN

Beasley, M. Women's Olympic shooting events. *Journal of physical education, recreation & dance (Reston, Va.) 55(5), May/Jun 1984, 68-69.*
LEVEL: B LANG: Eng SIRC ARTICLE NO: 095227

SHOT PUT THROW

BIOGRAPHY AND AUTOBIOGRAPHY

Profile: Myrtle Augee (Cambridge Harriers). *Thrower (West Midlands, Eng.) 28, Feb 1984, 40.*
LEVEL: B LANG: Eng SIRC ARTICLE NO: 095499

Profile: Rosemarie Hauch. *Track and field journal (Ottawa) 26, May 1984, 17-18.*
LEVEL: B LANG: Eng Fr SIRC ARTICLE NO: 0987

Rees, D.P. Simon Rodhouse story. Part III. *Thrower (West Midlands, Eng.) 28, Feb 1984, 28-31.*
LEVEL: B LANG: Eng SIRC ARTICLE NO: 095500

Steen, D. Well put: a one-time Canadian champion questions the meaning of his glory days. *Athletics (Willowdale, Ont.) Nov/Dec 1984, 14-15.*
LEVEL: B LANG: Eng SIRC ARTICLE NO: 177572

BIOMECHANICS

Grigalka, O. Papanov, V. Edward Sarule in the shot put. *Soviet sports review (Escondido, Calif.) 19(2), Jun 1984, 75-77.*
NOTES: Translated from, Legkaya atletika, 2: 15-16, 1984.
LEVEL: B LANG: Eng SIRC ARTICLE NO: 100109

HISTORY

Shot putting technique as it has changed over the years. *Thrower (West Midlands, Eng.) 29, May 1984, 37-42.*
LEVEL: B LANG: Eng SIRC ARTICLE NO: 098719

PSYCHOLOGY

Fenk, A. Two different explanations for the alteration of performance on high levels of activation. (Refs: 32)*International journal of sport psychology (Rome) 15(3), 1984, 169-178.*
ABST: In experiments on the level of aspiration during sports activities the correlations between series of predictions and series of subsequent performances, computed for single subjects, were generally positive in shot putting but negative in pilot study with shooting. The predominance of low or even negative coefficients in subjects with high goal discrepancies and weak performance within their reference group (Fenk, 1981) may be interpreted in terms of the shaped function between levels of activation and performance. Some other authors explained comparable findings - not (only) on the basis of different intensities but different qualities of motivation states.
LEVEL: A LANG: Eng SIRC ARTICLE NO: 105043

TECHNIQUES AND SKILLS

Bosen, K. A comparison between the orthodox and rotation shot put techniques. *Track & field quarterly review (Kalamazoo, Mich.) 84(1), Spring 1984, 24.*
LEVEL: B LANG: Eng SIRC ARTICLE NO: 095481

Bosen, K. A comparison between the orthodox and rotation shot put techniques. *Thrower (West Midlands, Eng.) 31, Dec 1984, 50-51.*
NOTES: Reprinted from: Track & field quarterly review.
LEVEL: B LANG: Eng SIRC ARTICLE NO: 173500

Delavan, P. The shot put. *Track & field quarterly review (Kalamazoo, Mich.) 84(1), Spring 1984, 19-20.*
CONF: Michigan Interscholastic Track Coaches Association Clinic (1981 : Midland, Mich.).
LEVEL: I LANG: Eng SIRC ARTICLE NO: 095485

Grigalka, O. Edward Sarul' - shotputter. *Thrower (West Midlands, Eng.) 30, Aug 1984, 33-35.*
LEVEL: B LANG: Eng SIRC ARTICLE NO: 098706

Jones, M. Sequence analysis. *Thrower (West Midlands, Eng.) 31, Dec 1984, 54-55.*
LEVEL: B LANG: Eng SIRC ARTICLE NO: 17350

O'Shea, P. Elam, R. The shot put - mechanics, techniques, strength and conditioning programs. (Refs: 5)*National Strength & Conditioning Association journal (Lincoln, Neb.) 6(5), Oct/Nov 1984, 4-5;74-76;78-79.*
LEVEL: I LANG: Eng SIRC ARTICLE NO: 103627

Stenlund, G.M. Shot put (part II). *Sports (Kallang, Singapore) 12(10), Nov/Dec 1984, 50-51.*
NOTES: Final instalment of a five-part series on throwing events..
LEVEL: B LANG: Eng SIRC ARTICLE NO: 109004

Wofford, J.C. Developing high school shot putters. *Coaching clinic (Englewood Cliffs, N.J.) 22(10), Jun 1984, 7-9.*
LEVEL: LANG: Eng SIRC ARTICLE NO: 095509

TESTING AND EVALUATION

Krieger, D. Analysis sheet for review of movement quality in the shot. *Track & field quarterly review (Kalamazoo, Mich.) 84(1), Spring 1984, 21.*
NOTES: Translated by, Kevin McGill.
LEVEL: B LANG: Eng SIRC ARTICLE NO: 095494

TRAINING AND CONDITIONING

Baert, J.P. Shot put. *Track and field journal (Ottawa) 26, May 1984, 22-24.*
LEVEL: B LANG: Eng SIRC ARTICLE NO: 098700

Ceronie, R. Torok, D. Pre-season training for shot put & discus throwers. Movement and medicine ball routines provide an effective method of preseason training for throwers. (Refs: 1)*Athletic journal 64(7), Feb 1984, 48;68.*
LEVEL: B LANG: Eng SIRC ARTICLE NO: 092548

Daszkiewicz, A. Edward Sarul: training towards the world championships. *Athletics coach (Halesowen, England) 18(1), Mar 1984, 24-25.*
LEVEL: B LANG: Eng SIRC ARTICLE NO: 093969

Kanishevsky, S. A universal shot. *Soviet sports review (Escondido, Calif.) 19(4), Dec 1984, 207-208.*
NOTES: Translated from, Legkaya atletika 9, 1982, 15.
LEVEL: B LANG: Eng SIRC ARTICLE NO: 105044

Kerr, J. Observations of Edward Sarul's training and methods from his personal coach Alexander Daszkiewicz. *Thrower (West Midlands, Eng.) 30, Aug 1984, 36-43.*
LEVEL: B LANG: Eng SIRC ARTICLE NO: 098713

Marks, R. Specialized strength & technique training for shot put and discus. *Thrower (West Midlands, Eng.) 30, Aug 1984, 26-28.*
LEVEL: B LANG: Eng SIRC ARTICLE NO: 098714

Rees, D.P. Diary of an athlete. (Simon Rodhouse) *Thrower (West Midlands, Eng.) 28, Feb 1984, 32-36.*
LEVEL: B LANG: Eng SIRC ARTICLE NO: 095501

TRAINING AND CONDITIONING - DRILLS

Shannon, K. Shot put and discus drills. *Track & field quarterly review (Kalamazoo, Mich.) 84(1), Spring 1984, 25-26.*
LEVEL: B LANG: Eng SIRC ARTICLE NO: 095503

TRAINING AND CONDITIONING - WEIGHT AND STRENGTH TRAINING

O'Shea, P. Elam, R. The shot put - mechanics, techniques, strength and conditioning programs. (Refs: 5)*National Strength & Conditioning Association journal (Lincoln, Neb.) 6(5), Oct/Nov 1984, 4-5;74-76;78-79.*
LEVEL: I LANG: Eng SIRC ARTICLE NO: 103627

SHOW JUMPING

BIOGRAPHY AND AUTOBIOGRAPHY

Laskin, M. The key to Damuraz. *Practical horseman (Unionville, Pa.) 12(2), Feb 1984, 6-12;46-B.*
LEVEL: B LANG: Eng SIRC ARTICLE NO: 098219

Martin, A. The Edgars forever. London: Pelham Books : Everest Double Glazing, 1984. 215 p., (8) p. of plates : ill.
LEVEL: LANG: Eng ISBN: 0720715040 LC CARD: 84-102559

Mason, H. The pink coat fits him now. (Mario Deslauriers) *Chronicle of the horse (Middleburg, Va.) 47(29), 20 Jul 1984, 78-80.*
LEVEL: B LANG: Eng SIRC ARTICLE NO: 099739

Peddicord, R. Ball, S. John Ammerman's gold medal jumps. *Maryland horse (Lutherville-Timonium, Md.) 50(8), Jul 1984, 38-44.*
LEVEL: B LANG: Eng SIRC ARTICLE NO: 098228

Sports equestres: Mario Deslauriers. Equestrian: Mario Deslauriers. *Champion (Ottawa) 8(3), Aug 1984, 60.*
LEVEL: B LANG: Fr Eng SIRC ARTICLE NO: 096711

BIOMECHANICS

Lieberman, B. Mackay-Smith, M. See how they jump: what it takes to make the great leap upward. *Equus (Gaithersburg, Md.) Au 1984, 21-22;24.*
LEVEL: B LANG: Eng SIRC ARTICLE NO: 103255

FACILITIES - DESIGN, CONSTRUCTION AND PLANNING

Watts, A. A course of your own. *Horse and rider (Surrey, Eng.) 34(385), May 1984, 28.*
LEVEL: B LANG: Eng SIRC ARTICLE NO: 098976

TECHNIQUES AND SKILLS

Hadley, S. Make the difficult fences easy: part seven. *Riding (London) 49(3), Mar 1984, 21-22.*
LEVEL: B LANG: Eng SIRC ARTICLE NO: 098204

Harper, L. We have lift off. Part 4: the careless horse. *Equi (Warrington, Eng.) 20, Jan/Feb 1984, 27-28.*
NOTES: To be continued.
LEVEL: B LANG: Eng SIRC ARTICLE NO: 095105

Hogo-Vidal, H. Learning to ride over fences. Lesson two: poles on the ground. *Practical horseman (Unionville, Pa.) 12(9), Sept 1984, 46-D-46-G;49-52;57;60.*
LEVEL: B LANG: Eng SIRC ARTICLE NO: 105933

Hugo-Vidal, H. Learning to ride over fences. Lesson three: real fences. *Practical horseman (Unionville, Pa.) 12(11), Nov 1984, 46-D-46-F;46-H;48;50;52;54;56.*
LEVEL: B LANG: Eng SIRC ARTICLE NO: 105935

Hugo-Vidal, H. Learning to ride over fences. You can have a good fence every time if you follow this proven system taught by a leading trainer of winning hunt-seat riders. Lesson four: practicing a line. *Practical horseman (Unionville, Pa.) 12(12), Dec 1984, 6-12.*
LEVEL: B LANG: Eng SIRC ARTICLE NO: 108097

TRAINING AND CONDITIONING

Get into your stride. *Riding (London) 49(4), Apr 1984, 36-38.*
LEVEL: B LANG: Eng SIRC ARTICLE NO: 098202

Holly Hugo-Vidal: learning to ride over fences. You can have a good fence every time if you follow this proven system taught b a leading trainer of winning hunt-seat riders. *Practical horseman (Unionville, Pa.) 12(8), Aug 1984, 46-D-46-F.*
NOTES: Lesson one: brushing up your flatwork.
LEVEL: B LANG: Eng SIRC ARTICLE NO: 103253

Taurig, B. Training your horse to jump his best: lesson four: advanced control and combinations. *Practical horseman (Unionville, Pa.) 12(4), Apr 1984, 46-J-46-L;48-52;57-58.*
LEVEL: B LANG: Eng SIRC ARTICLE NO: 098248

Traurig, B. Training your horse to jump his best: lesson three: correcting form faults. *Practical horseman (Unionville, Pa. 12(3), Mar 1984, 49-52;54-55.*
LEVEL: B LANG: Eng SIRC ARTICLE NO: 098251

Traurig, B. Training your horse to jump his best. Lesson five: advanced combinations and natural obstacles. *Practical horseman (Unionville, Pa.) 12(5), May 1984, 46-J-46-K;49;54;57.*
LEVEL: B LANG: Eng SIRC ARTICLE NO: 099756

Valliere, P. Paul Valliere: tools for training. *Practical horseman (Unionville, Pa.) 12(6), June 1984, 5-7;9-10;12;14-A;14-C-14-D;60.*
LEVEL: B LANG: ENg SIRC ARTICLE NO: 108810

TRAINING AND CONDITIONING - DRILLS

Traurig, B. Training your horse to jump his best. Lesson two: introduction to jumping. *Practical horseman (Unionville, Pa.) 12(2), Feb 1984, 49-52;54;57;60.*
LEVEL: B LANG: Eng SIRC ARTICLE NO: 098250

Traurig, B. Bernie Traurig: training your horse to jump his best. The famous trainer of hunters and jumpers shares his uniqu system for maximizing jumping performance, in a series of lessons you can apply to your own horse. Lesson six: winning turns. *Practical horseman (Unionville, Pa.) 12(6), June 1984, 46-A-46-E;46-H;49-50;52;55.*
LEVEL: B LANG: Eng SIRC ARTICLE NO: 108812

TRAINING AND CONDITIONING - WARM-UPS, WARM-DOWNS, LEAD-UP GAMES

Fleischmann, T. The warm-up: preparing the novice/training horse for cross-country and show jumping at a one-day-event. *USCTA news (South Hamilton, Mass.) 13(3), Jun 1984, 14-15;48.*
LEVEL: B LANG: Eng SIRC ARTICLE NO: 098197

SINGAPORE

From spectating to participation. *Sports (Kallang, Singapore) 12(10), Nov/Dec 1984, 39.*
LEVEL: B LANG: Eng SIRC ARTICLE NO: 108995

Wilson, L.R. Leisure and recreation in Singapore and Japan. *WLRA journal (New York) 26(2), Mar/Apr 1984, 12-13.*
NOTES: Excerpt from presentation at the 1982 United States Mediterranean Sports Congress in Monte Carlo.
LEVEL: B LANG: Eng SIRC ARTICLE NO: 097877

SKATING

Katz, D.R. Ice skating: moments of grace. *Outside 9(1), Jan/Feb 1984, 67-69.*
LEVEL: B LANG: Eng SIRC ARTICLE NO: 093405

BIOGRAPHY AND AUTOBIOGRAPHY

Boucher, G. Gaetan, l'histoire de notre heros. Montreal: Quebecor, c1984. 93 p. : ill. (Collection sport.)
LEVEL: B LANG: F ISBN: 2-89089-268-9 LC CARD: 84-6382-2 GV850.3 18025

ENVIRONMENT

Leads from MMWR. Carbon monoxide intoxication associated with use of a resurfacing machine at an ice-skating rink. *JAMA: Journal of the American Medical Association (Chicago) 251(8), 24 Feb 1984, 1016.*
LEVEL: B LANG: Eng SIRC ARTICLE NO: 098971

FACILITIES - MAINTENANCE

Ice cap puts your ice to bed at night. *American hockey & arena (Colorado Springs, Colo.) 5(2), Feb 1984, 5-6.*
LEVEL: B LANG Eng SIRC ARTICLE NO: 097521

HISTORY

Long, S. Magical gliding. (Refs: 13)*Gamut (Cleveland) 11, Winter 1984, 87-96.*
ABST: A brief history of ice skating.
LEVEL: I LANG: Eng

INJURIES AND ACCIDENTS

Cummings, T. Lace-bite padding. *Physician and sportsmedicine 12(2), Feb 1984, 166.*
LEVEL: B LANG: Eng SIRC ARTICLE NO: 092192

Horner, C. McCabe, M.J. Ice-skating and roller disco injuries in Dublin. (Refs: 9)*British journal of sports medicine (Loughborough, Eng.) 18(3), Sept 1984, 207-211.*
ABST: A comparative study was carried out on a series of 72 ice-skating and 57 roller skating injuries over a sixteen month period. The average patient age was 20.5 years in the ice-skating group and 16.5 years in the roller skating group. Females predominated in both groups accounting for 72% of ice-skaters injured and 77% of roller skaters injured. Ice-skating fractures accounted for 40% of all injuries while roller skating fractures were only 14% of their total injuries. The majority of ice-skating fractures occurred in females. As a result of their study, the authors recommend several preventative measures.
LEVEL: A LANG: Eng SIRC ARTICLE NO: 103388

Thomas, J. Haynes, P. Morton, A. Skating on thin ice (interview with Alison Morton). *Nursing mirror (Surrey, Eng.) 158(4), 25 Jan 1984, 22-23.*
LEVEL: B LANG: Eng SIRC ARTICLE NO: 099074

JUVENILE LITERATURE

MacLean, N. Gow, B. Ice skating basics. Englewood Cliffs, N.J.: Prentice-Hall, c1984. 1v.
LEVEL: B LANG: Eng ISBN: 01344876 LC CARD: 84-006933

MEDICINE

Jenkins, G. Skin problems related to skating. *Skating magazine (Colorado Springs, Colo.) 61(5), May 1984, 18-20;24.*
NOTES To be continued.
LEVEL: B LANG: Eng SIRC ARTICLE NO: 097599

STATISTICS AND RECORDS - PARTICIPATION

Ice skating: Canada's number one winter activity. Le patin sur glace: l'activite d'hiver la plus populaire au Canada. *Highlights/Faits saillants (Ottawa, Ont.) 42, Dec 1984, 1;1.*
LEVEL: B LANG: Eng Fr SIRC ARTICLE NO: 102920

TECHNIQUES AND SKILLS

Mason, A. Get ready for CANFIGURESKATE: stroking. *Skater 2(1), Winter 1984, 11;13-14.*
LEVEL: B LANG: Eng SIRC ARTICLE NO: 092056

SKEET SHOOTING

Jones, R.F. Being good at skeet puts you in an exclusive club, not a snobby one. *Sports illustrated (Los Angeles, Calif.) 61(28), 24-31 Dec 1984, 124-127.*
LEVEL: B LANG: Eng SIRC ARTICLE NO: 103416

Sisley, N. How to achieve your top capabilities in the shortest time. Pointers from Dave Starrett. *Skeet shooting review (San Antonio, Tex.) 38(7), Jun 1984, 15-16;18;24.*
LEVEL: B LANG: Eng SIRC ARTICLE NO: 103423

SKEET SHOOTING (continued)

BALLISTICS AND AMMUNITION

Roster,T. Reloading: standardizing components for skeet loads - Part 1. *Skeet shooting review (San Antonio, Tex.) 3(4), Mar 1984, 8.*
LEVEL: B LANG: Eng SIRC ARTICLE NO: 098453

Shoot more for less - reload. *Skeet shooting review (San Antonio, Tex.) 38(10), Sept 1984, 59.*
LEVEL: B LANG: Eng SIRC ARTICLE NO: 173159

Thompson, J.O. Recoil tables. *Skeet shooting review (San Antonio, Tex.) 38(7), Jun 1984, 22-23.*
LEVEL: B LANG: Eng SIRC ARTICLE NO: 103426

BIOGRAPHY AND AUTOBIOGRAPHY

Sisley, N. A skeet shooting lesson with Grant Ilseng. *Skeet shooting review (San Antonio, Tex.) 38(12), Nov 1984, 14-17.*
LEVEL: B LANG: Eng SIRC ARTICLE NO: 107466

CLUBS

Scherer, E. Ed Scherer's club reports: 108 shooters become charter members: Old Hickory comes to life. *Skeet shooting revie (San Antonio, Tex.) 38(13), Dec 1984, 16-17.*
LEVEL: B LANG: Eng SIRC ARTICLE NO: 107463

EQUIPMENT

Sisley, N. One gun. *Skeet shooting review (San Antonio, Tex.) 3(4), Mar 1984, 31;33-35.*
LEVEL: B LANG: Eng SIRC ARTICLE NO: 098457

RULES AND REGULATIONS

Clarke, R. Skeet: participant sport. *Guns Australia Mar/Apr 1984, 30-33.*
NOTES: Shotguns and the shotgunning sports.
ABST: Skeet shooting was developed in 1926 in the United States. The 2 types of competitions shot in Australia are America rules and International Shooting Union (ISU) rules as shot at the Olympic and Commonwealth Games. Both use a semi-circular field with a trap firing clay targets at each end of the diameter. The shooter fires from 7 positions on the radius. The concept of 'lead' can be worked out scientifically before each shot is taken. In ISU rules targets move faster, can be delayed up to 3 seconds and the gun must be held with the stock touching the hip.
LEVEL: I LANG: Eng SIRC ARTICLE NO: 102112

TECHNIQUES AND SKILLS

Horst, G.L. Iron nutrition for warm season grasses. *Grounds maintenance (Overland Park, Kans.) 19(7), Jul 1984, 44;46;48;70*
LEVEL: B LANG: Eng SIRC ARTICLE NO: 106033

Scherer, E. Skeet fundamentals: that elusive station one. *Skeet shooting review (San Antonio, Tex.) 3(4), Mar 1984, 28-30.*
LEVEL: B LANG: Eng SIRC ARTICLE NO: 098455

Scherer, E. Skeet fundamentals. Station two. *Skeet shooting review (San Antonio, Tex.) 38(5), Apr 1984, 34-35.*
LEVEL: B LANG: Eng SIRC ARTICLE NO: 099878

Scherer, E. Skeet fundamentals: station three. *Skeet shooting review (San Antonio, Tex.) 38(6), May 1984, 24-25.*
LEVEL: B LANG: Eng SIRC ARTICLE NO: 099879

Scherer, E. Skeet fundamentals: station four. *Skeet shooting review (San Antonio, Tex.) 38(7), Jun 1984, 21.*
LEVEL: B LANG: Eng SIRC ARTICLE NO: 103421

Scherer, E. Skeet fundamentals: station five. *Skeet shooting review (San Antonio, Tex.) 38(8), Jul 1984, 15-16.*
LEVEL: B LANG: Eng SIRC ARTICLE NO: 103422

Scherer, E. Ed Scherer's skeet fundamentals: station 6. *Skeet shooting review (San Antonio, Tex.) 38(9), Aug 1984, 15;17.*
LEVEL: B LANG: Eng SIRC ARTICLE NO: 106034

Scherer, E. Ed Scherer's skeet fundamentals: doubles at 3, 4 and 5. *Skeet shooting review (San Antonio, Tex.) 38(12), Nov 1984, 40.*
LEVEL: B LANG: Eng SIRC ARTICLE NO: 107464

Scherer, E. Skeet fundamentals: station 8. *Skeet shooting review (San Antonio, Tex.) 38(11), Oct 1984, 51.*
LEVEL: B LANG: Eng SIRC ARTICLE NO: 173160

Sisley, N. A skeet shooting lesson with Dave Starrett. *Skeet shooting review (San Antonio, Tex.) 38(8), Jul 1984, 6-7;27.*
LEVEL: B LANG: Eng SIRC ARTICLE NO: 103424

Sisley, N. A skeet shooting lesson with Ed Scherer. *Skeet shooting review (San Antonio, Tex.) 38(9), Aug 1984, 12-14.*
LEVEL: B LANG: Eng SIRC ARTICLE NO: 106035

Sisley, N. A skeet shooting lesson with Phil Murray. *Skeet shooting review (San Antonio, Tex.) 38(13), Dec 1984, 7-11.*
LEVEL: B LANG: Eng SIRC ARTICLE NO: 107465

TECHNIQUES AND SKILLS - AIMING

Scherer, E. One eyed or two? *Skeet shooting review (San Antonio, Tex.) 38(1), Jan 1984, 17;33.*
LEVEL: B LANG: Eng SIRC ARTICLE NO: 098454

TRAINING AND CONDITIONING

Sisley, N. More productive practice produces more productive shooting. *Skeet shooting review (San Antonio, Tex.) 38(10), Sept 1984, 8-11.*
LEVEL: B LANG: Eng SIRC ARTICLE NO: 173158

SKI JUMPING

AERODYNAMICS

Epstein, S.H. Skiing on air. *In, Schrier, E.W. and Allman, W.F. (eds.), Newton at the bat: the science in sports, New York, Scribner, c1984, p. 134-139.*
LEVEL: B LANG: Eng RC1235 18609

Remizov, L.P. Biomechanics of optimal flight in ski-jumping. (Refs: 8)*Journal of biomechanics (Elmsford, N.Y.) 17(3), 1984, 167-171.*
ABST: Through data obtained in wind tunnel experiments and the application of the basic theorem of the optimal control theory the author determined that the maximum flight distance is achieved when the angle of attack is gradually increased according to a convex function the form of which depends on the individual aerodynamic parameters.
LEVEL: A LANG: Eng SIRC ARTICLE NO: 096826

BIOGRAPHY AND AUTOBIOGRAPHY

Hobson, A. Jon Servold, quelques annees trop tot. Jon Servold, four years too soon. *Champion 8(1), Feb 1984, 42-43.*
LEVEL B LANG: Eng Fr SIRC ARTICLE NO: 090918

Loertscher, H. Une fille sur le tremplin. Karin Grossen, de Kandersteg, premiere sauteuse a skis de Suisse. *Macolin (Macolin, Suisse) 41(11), nov 1984, 2-3.*
NOTES: Adaptation de, Yves Jeannotat.
LEVEL: B LANG: Fr SIRC ARTICLE NO: 108752

Ottum, B. A man of many parts. Kerry Lynch, impressionist, drummer and double-duty skier, is a favorite to win the Nordic combined at Sarajevo. *Sports illustrated 60(5), 6 Feb 1984, 52-54;56;61.*
LEVEL: B LANG: Eng SIRC ARTICLE NO: 090919

Stubbs, D. Horst Bulau, le sauteur sans peur. Horst Bulau, fearless flyer. *Champion 8(1), Feb 1984, 26-27.*
LEVEL: B LANG: Eng Fr SIRC ARTICLE NO: 090917

INJURIES AND ACCIDENTS

Wester, K. Alvorlige skader ved skihopping i Norge 1977-81. (Serious injuries caused by ski jumping in Norway 1977-81.) *Tidsskrift for den norske laegeforening (Oslo) 104(33), 30 Nov 1984, 2317-2319.*
LEVEL: A LANG: Nor

PSYCHOLOGY

von Gruenigen, E. Le saut a skis et la peur. Le point de vue d'un athlete sur la psychologie du sauteur. *Macolin (Macolin, Suisse) 41(12), dec 1984, 4-7.*
NOTES: Traduction de, Marianne Honegger.
LEVEL: B LANG: Fr SIRC ARTICLE NO: 108757

SKIING

Casewit, C.W. The skier's companion. 1st ed. Brattleboro, Vt.: S. Greene Press, c1984. 1v.
NOTES: Includes index and bibliography.
LEVEL: B LANG: Eng ISBN: 0828905495 LC CARD: 84-018733

Kasper, G.F. Les competitions de ski. The ski competitions. *Message olympique/Olympic message (Lausanne) 7, juin/Jun 1984, 15-19.*
LEVEL: B LANG: Fr Eng SIRC ARTICLE NO: 104869

Spring, J. The Brand study: an analysis. 'If nothing more comes of the Brand study of skier-consumer behavior, one lesson is clear: the ski industry does not know or understand its customer.' *Ski area management (North Salem, N.Y.) 23(5), Sept 1984, 69;86-87.*
LEVEL: B LANG: Eng SIRC ARTICLE NO: 103431

ADMINISTRATION

Hewett, J.K. Ski area management at college: a variety of educational opportunities provide a variety of graduates in the field of ski area management. *Ski area management (New York) 23(2), Mar 1984, 70-72;75-76.*
LEVEL: B LANG: Eng SIRC ARTICLE NO: 098463

Kagi, F.R. Micro computers for micro ski areas. *Ski area management (North Salem, N.Y.)* 23(3), May 1984, 104-105;146.
LEVEL: B LANG: Eng SIRC ARTICLE NO: 099888

Millican, M.M. The marketplace: TV promotions. *Ski area management (North Salem, N.Y.)* 23(1), Jan 1984, 44-45;77.
LEVEL: LANG: Eng SIRC ARTICLE NO: 096813

Nelson, J. Phi Beta skia: a ski-college education may give you the inside track on a ski resort job, but there's plenty of hard work behind the glory. *Ski (Los Angeles)* 48(4), Dec 1984, 80;82;84.
LEVEL: B LANG: Eng SIRC ARTICLE NO: 107480

Rowan, D. Skiing as a national policy: government funding and support, localized autonomy and an umbrella council co-exist t successfully promote skiing. *Ski area management (North Salem, N.Y.)* 23(5), Sept 1984, 59;89-93.
LEVEL: B LANG: Eng SIRC ARTICLE NO: 103430

The changing ski industry. *Ski area management (North Salem, N.Y.)* 23(1), Jan 1984, 66-67;89.
NOTES: Part II of a marketing panel.
LEVEL: B LANG: Eng SIRC ARTICLE NO: 096806

ANTHROPOMETRY

Jost-Relyveld, A. Sempe, M. Morphologie comparee de jeunes gymnastes et skieurs de haut niveau. (Refs: 4)*Cinesiologie (Paris)* 95, mai/juin 1984, 241-247.
RESUME: Le but de cette etude consiste a comparer les mensurations de 45 filles gymnastes, 11 etudiantes de gymnastique rythmique sportive, 9 skieuses alpines juniors, 35 garcons gymnastes et 8 skieurs de fond juniors. Les resultats indiquent: 1) des retards pubertaires chez les gymnastes comparativement aux autres groupes et 2) un developpement normal chez les sujets pratiquant la gymnastique rythmique sportive en classe.
LEVEL: A LANG: Fr SIRC ARTICLE NO: 098141

ASSOCIATIONS

Le ski et l'Olympisme. *Revue olympique (Lausanne)* 195/196, janv/fevr 1984, 51-98.
LEVEL: I LANG: Fr SIRC ARTICLE NO: 096814

Ski-ing and Olympsm. *Olympic review (Lausanne, Switzerland)* 195/196, Jan/Feb 1984, 51-98.
LEVEL: I LANG: Eng SIRC ARTICLE NO: 095231

CLOTHING

Auran, J.H. Ettlinger, C. Killham, D. Boots: high tech at $225. Here are test reports on five state-of-the-art models for skiers ready to move out of the intermediate ranks. *Skiing* 36(5), Jan 1984, 56-58;60;63-64;67-68;70.
LEVEL: B LANG: Eng SIRC ARTICLE NO: 093690

McCoy, S. Understanding the words you wear. *Ski (Buyer's guide '85) (New York)* 49(1), 31 Dec 1984, 199.
LEVEL: B LANG: En SIRC ARTICLE NO: 100567

McCoy, S. The sweet yodel of success. (Klaus Obermeyer) *Ski (Buyer's guide '85) (New York)* 49(1), 31 Dec 1984, 196.
LEVEL: B LANG: Eng SIRC ARTICLE NO: 100568

McCoy, S. C.B.: 'it's the Super Bowl every year'. (Charles Bird Vaughan) *Ski (Buyer's guide '85) (New York)* 49(1), 31 Dec 1984, 198.
LEVEL: B LANG: Eng SIRC ARTICLE NO: 100569

Ross, J. Cohen, S. If the boot fits... you probably have a custom insole: or a ski orthotic. Now available in many ski shops these custom-fit footbeds can make you a better more comfortable skier. *Ski (Los Angeles)* 49(2), Oct 1984, 184-186.
LEVEL: B LANG: Eng SIRC ARTICLE NO: 103429

COUNTRIES AND REGIONS

Patterson, S. Forrest, K. Rio Grande ski train. Denver, Colo.: Tramway Press, (1984). 1v.
LEVEL: I LANG: Eng LC CARD: 84-024082

DIRECTORIES

Directory and guide to the ski industry 1984-1985. Repertoire et guide de registerie industrie du ski 1984-1985. Willowdale, Ont.: Canadian Ski Council : Conseil canadien du ski, 1984. 173 p.
CORP: Canadian Ski Council.
CORP: Conseil canadien du ski.
NOTES: Cover title. Titre de la couverture.
LEVEL: B LANG: Eng Fr GV854.A2 18229

Enzel, R.G. The white book of ski areas; U.S. and Canada. 9th ed. Washington, D.C.: Inter-Ski Services, c1984. xxii, 405 p. ill.
LEVEL: B LANG: Eng ISBN: 0-931636-05-1 LC CARD: 77-88510 GV854.4 18607

Jacobsen, B. Riggs, R. The rites of winter: a budget guide to making it on the slopes. New York: Arbor House, c1984. 1v.
LEVEL: B LANG: Eng ISBN: 0877956405 LC CARD: 84-018453

Supplier directory: listing limited to SAM advertisers of the past year. *Ski area management (North Salem, N.Y.)* 23(6), Nov 1984, 84-101.
LEVEL: B LANG: Eng SIRC ARTICLE NO: 107482

DISABLED

Axelson, P. Sit-skiing: part II. *Sports 'n spokes (Phoenix, Ariz.)* 9(6), Mar/Apr 1984, 34-40.
LEVEL: B LANG: Eng SIRC ARTICLE NO: 094307

Axelson, P. Sit-skiing. *Sports 'n spokes (Phoenix, Ariz.)* 9(5), Jan/Feb 1984, 28-31.
NOTES: To be continued.
LEVEL: B LANG: Eng SIRC ARTICLE NO: 094308

McCormick, D.P. Handicapped skiing: an overview. (Refs: 4)
NOTES: In, Cantu, R.C. (ed.), Clinical sports medicine, Lexington Mass. ; Toronto, Collamore Press : D.C. Heath, c1984, p. 63-70.
LEVEL: I LANG: Eng RC1201 15964

ECONOMICS

Farwell, T. The 1982/83 economic study: a gentle drop in skier visits, weather or not. *Ski area management (North Salem, N.Y.)* 23(1), Jan 1984, 56-57.
LEVEL: B LANG: Eng SIRC ARTICLE NO: 096808

Goeldner, C.R. Duea, K. Colorado ski industry characteristics and financial analysis: 1982-83 season. Boulder, Colo.: University of Colorado, Business Research Division, c1984. iv, 93 leaves
NOTES: Bibliography: leaves 92-93.
LEVEL: I LANG: Eng ISBN: 0-89478-107-3 GV854.5.C6 17245

Wigle, D.T. Morgan, P.P. The tobacco industry: still resourceful in recruiting smokers. (Refs: 6)*Canadian Medical Association journal (Ottawa,*

Ont.) 130(12), 15 Jun 1984, 1537-1539.
LEVEL: B LANG: Eng SIRC ARTICLE NO: 094189

EQUIPMENT

Geng, H. Ski linings made from ultrahigh molecular weight polyethylene. (Refs: 1)*Kunststoffe - German plastics (Munich)* 74(1), Jan 1984, 34-35.
LEVEL: I LANG: Eng SIRC ARTICLE NO: 098462

Glenne, B. Vandergrift, J. New bases: faster, harder, longer-lasting. *Skiing (Los Angeles)* 37(4), Dec 1984, 62;67.
LEVEL: LANG: Eng SIRC ARTICLE NO: 107475

Lifts 1983: economic upturn and sunny prospects spur lift building. *Ski area management (North Salem, N.Y.)* 23(1), Jan 1984, 64-65.
LEVEL: I LANG: Eng SIRC ARTICLE NO: 096810

Masia, S. The man who gave skiing the shaft. (Ed Scott) *Ski (Buyer's guide '85) (New York)* 49(1), 31 Dec 1984, 184;186.
LEVEL: B LANG: Eng SIRC ARTICLE NO: 100566

EQUIPMENT - MAINTENANCE

Matlock, D.K. Lift fatigue. *Ski area management (North Salem, N.Y.)* 23(1), Jan 1984, 62-63;80.
LEVEL: I LANG: Eng SIRC ARTICLE NO: 095813

FACILITIES

Collin, A.G. A brilliant idea. *Ski area management (North Salem, N.Y.)* 23(1), Jan 1984, 54-55;78-79.
LEVEL: B LANG: Eng SIRC ARTICLE NO: 095826

Collins, M. The density/capacity conundrum: an industry standard is needed to define these important statistics. *Ski area management (North Salem, N.Y.)* 23(4), Jul 1984, 58.
LEVEL: B LANG: Eng SIRC ARTICLE NO: 099885

Houlihan, R. The transformation of Triple-A ski area into Mountain Empire Resort, Ltd. *Ski area management (North Salem, N.Y.)* 23(3), May 1984, 94-96;137.
LEVEL: B LANG: Eng SIRC ARTICLE NO: 098969

Murphy, G. Murphy, M. The image is the index: a research study among 2,000 skiers points to specific factors for the upswing or decline of ski resorts. *Ski area management (North Salem, N.Y.)* 23(3), May 1984, 106;136.
LEVEL: B LANG: Eng SIRC ARTICLE NO: 098972

Proposed night light recommendation. *Ski area management (North Salem, N.Y.)* 23(1), Jan 1984, 52.
LEVEL: B LANG: Eng SIRC ARTICLE NO: 095834

Schultz, L.W. Umbricht, D.L. Night lights - new look, new code. *Ski area management (North Salem, N.Y.)* 23(1), Jan 1984, 51,53.
LEVEL: B LANG: Eng SIRC ARTICLE NO: 095835

Youds, M. Closing its doors: Hollywood Ski Lodge, once the centre of Lower Mainland winter recreation, is now locked and empty, awaiting a new suitor in the provincial government's move to privatization. *B.C. outdoors (Vancouver, B.C.)* 40(4), May 1984, 32-33;44.
LEVEL: B LANG: Eng SIRC ARTICLE NO: 098466

SKIING (continued)

FACILITIES - DESIGN, CONSTRUCTION AND PLANNING

Fry, J. Emile Allais returns... and unflinchingly reminds us how ski resorts ought to be designed. *Ski area management (North Salem, N.Y.) 23(4), Jul 1984, 45-46;66-67.*
LEVEL: B LANG: Eng SIRC ARTICLE NO: 099887

Hemlock Recreational Resort, B.C. Canada. *Sportstaettenbau und Baederanlagen (Cologne, W. Germany) 18(6), Nov/Dec 1984, 302-307.* LANG: Eng SIRC ARTICLE NO: 173527

FACILITIES - MAINTENANCE

Carey, C. The care and selection of snowmakers. *Ski area management (North Salem, N.Y.) 23(6), Nov 1984, 67;105.*
LEVEL: B LANG: Eng SIRC ARTICLE NO: 107472

HALLS OF FAME AND MUSEUMS

Cuyler, L. History as a marketing tool. *Ski area management (North Salem, N.Y.) 23(6), Nov 1984, 70-71.*
LEVEL: B LANG: En SIRC ARTICLE NO: 107473

INJURIES AND ACCIDENTS

Bracker, M.D. New treatment for dislocated shoulders. *Physician and sportsmedicine (Minneapolis, Minn.) 12(7), Jul 1984, 155.*
LEVEL: B LANG: Eng SIRC ARTICLE NO: 095907

Caldwell, F. Making sense of ski injury statistics. (Refs: 4)*Physician and sportsmedicine 12(2), Feb 1984, 155-157;160;162-163.*
LEVEL: I LANG: Eng SIRC ARTICLE NO: 092355

Campbell, D. Winter breaks. *Nursing mirror (Surrey, Eng.) 158(4), 25 Jan 1984, 16-19.*
LEVEL: B LANG: Eng SIRC ARTICLE NO: 099884

Elliott, B.G. Sherry, E. Common snow skiing injuries. *Australian family physician (Sydney) 13(8), Aug 1984, 570-574.*
LEVEL: A LANG: Eng

Gjuric, M. Korda, A. Gjuric, Z. Promjene u strukturi skijaskih ozljeda u nas. (Changes in the structure of skiing injuries i Yugoslavia.) *Lijecnicki vjesnik (Zagreb) 106(10), Oct 1984, 411-413.*
LEVEL: I LANG: Scr

Johnson, R.J. Pope, M.H. Safety in skiing. (Refs: 54)
NOTES: In, Scott, W.N. (ed.) et al., Principles of sports medicine, Baltimore, Williams & Wilkins, c1984, p. 367-374.
LEVEL: A LANG: Eng RC1210 18016

Kuriyama, S. Fujimaki, E. Katagiri, T. Uemura, S. Anterior dislocation of the shoulder joint sustained through skiing. (Refs 17)*American journal of sports medicine (Baltimore, Md.) 12(5), Sept/Oct 1984, 339-346.*
ABST: Over a period of 10 years the authors have studied 14,952 cases of skiing injuries. Of these, 660 cases (4.5 per cent) were injuries to the shoulder with 291 cases (44.1 per cent) being anterior dislocations of the shoulder. One hundred forty-three cases revealed an initial dislocation (49.1 per cent) and 148 cases were recurrent dislocations (50.9 per cent). The arthrography of the dislocated shoulder in 89 cases was examined. Of these initial dislocations, one-half of the capsular detachment type were redislocated, but no redislocation had occurred in the capsular tear type.
LEVEL: A LANG: Eng SIRC ARTICLE NO: 104870

Lisagor, P. Sports medicine: misdiagnosis in catastrophic ski injuries. (letter) *Journal of trauma (Baltimore) 24(12), Dec 1984, 1065-1066.*
LEVEL: I LANG: Eng

Massart, P. Bezes, H. Severe metacarpophalangeal sprain of the thumb in ski accidents. 125 surgical repairs in group of 340 cases of metacarpophalangeal sprains from ski accidents. *Annales de chirurgie de la main: organe officiel des Societes de chirurgie de la main (Paris) 3(2), 1984, 101-112.*
ABST: From 1968 to 1983, 340 cases of metacarpophalangeal sprains were recorded in skiers. Three types of anatomic lesions were diagnosed: capsulo-ligamentous lesions (70 percent), alvusions of large fragments from the base of the first phalanx (30 percent), and the two fracture of B. Sener (1 in 125). Operatives procedures and long terms results are discussed.
LEVEL: A LANG: Eng

Massart, P. Bezes, H. L'entorse grave metacarpophalangienne du pouce au cours des accidents de ski. (Refs: 20)*Annales de chirurgie de la main (Paris) 3(2), 1984, 101-112.*
LEVEL: I LANG: Fr

McGee, P. Cold comforts - ammunition against the elements. *Ski Canada 12(5), Jan 1984, 67-68.*
LEVEL: B LANG: Eng SIRC ARTICLE NO: 092375

Mote, C.D. Snow falls: the mechanics of skiing injuries. (Refs: 31)*Mechanical engineering (New York) 106(9), Sept 1984, 94-102.*
LEVEL: A LANG: Eng SIRC ARTICLE NO: 104871

Oh, S. Cervical injury from skiing. (Refs: 12)*International journal of sports medicine (Stuttgart) 5(5), Oct 1984, 268-271.*
ABST: A retrospective study of 18 patients with cervical spine injuries from skiing accidents is presented. Four patients were treated surgically because of instabilities. Twelve patients had associated head injuries, two of whom were operated on. One patient died from severe craniocervical injury caused by collision with another skier. The cause of the cervical spine injuries are analyzed and the possibilities for preventing them are presented.
LEVEL: A LANG: Eng SIRC ARTICLE NO: 104872

Pain, C. Accidents will happen. *Nursing mirror (Surrey, Eng.) 158(4), 25 Jan 1984, 20-22.*
LEVEL: B LANG: Eng SIRC ARTICLE NO: 099890

Prince, P. Document de travail. Releve des blessures survenues en ski 1979-1983. Trois-Rivieres: Regie de la securite dans les sports, 1984. 1v.
CORP: Regie de la securite dans les sports. Service de la recherche.
LEVEL: A LANG: Fr RC1220.S5 20602

Sherry, E. Skiing injuries in Australia. *Medical journal of Australia (Sydney) 140(9), 28 Apr 1984, 530-531.*
ABST: A prospective study of 1850 skiing injuries during the 1983 skiing season in Australia is the topic of this paper. Occurrence of injuries is of 36% for upper extremity; 42% for lower extremity, and 17% for head, face and neck. The injury rate is of 3.80 per 1000 skiers.
LEVEL: A LANG: Eng SIRC ARTICLE NO: 101502

Waslen, G. Skier's thumb. (Ulnar collateral ligament tear) - Surgical repair. (Refs: 2)*Canadian Academy of Sport Medicine newsletter (Ottawa) 5(4), 1984, 41-42.*
LEVEL: I LANG: Eng SIRC ARTICLE NO: 106041

Wolter, D. Kortmann, H.R. Eggers, C. Die hintere Schulterverrenkung--eine haeufig uebersehene Luxationsform. (Posterior dislocation of the shoulder--a frequently missed form of luxation.) *Hefte zur Unfallheilkunde (Berlin) 170, 1984, 135-141.*
LEVEL: A LANG: Ger

Yvars, M.F. Kanner, H.R. Ski fractures of the femur. (Refs: 11)*American journal of sports medicine (Baltimore, Md.) 12(5), Sept/Oct 1984, 386-390.*
ABST: Twenty-four cases of femoral ski fractures (as well as one dislocation), collected over 8 years, are presented. Two-thirds of the patients were under 30 years of age. The largest single cause of injury (one-third of the cases) involved collision. High speed skiing with loss of control and falling on icy surfaces were other frequent causes of injury. Internal fixation methods were usually chosen for skeletally mature patients, with traction and casting used in children.
LEVEL: A LANG: Eng SIRC ARTICLE NO: 104873

LAW AND LEGISLATION

Moore, J. Are we properly prepared for courtroom battles? *NSAA news (Springfield, Mass.) 10(1), Oct/Nov 1984, 11.*
LEVEL: LANG: Eng SIRC ARTICLE NO: 100707

PHYSIOLOGY

de Swiniarski, R. Eterradossi, J. Erk Tanche, M. Courbes debit-volume chez de jeunes skieurs de haut-niveau ages de 10 a 20 ans. (Refs: 7)*Medecine du sport (Paris) 58(3), 25 mai 1984, 49-51.*
RESUME: Le but de cette etude etait d'analyser les courbes debit-volume de 110 skieurs males de haut niveau ages de 10 a 20 ans. 19 sujets presentent une courbe avec plateau d'environ V50. Une augmentation significative de PF surtout V50 et V25 est observee (20-30%, x
0.05). L'auteur conclue que le plateau de V50 peut s'observer chez tous les sportifs de haut niveau en excellente condition physique.
LEVEL: A LANG: Fr SIRC ARTICLE NO: 096807

SAFETY

Mathieu, R. Zuanon, J.P. Ski alpinisme: la prevention du risque d'avalanche et le sauvetage des victimes (2e partie). (Refs: 8)*Montagne & alpinisme (Paris) 135, 1984, 278-284.*
LEVEL: I LANG: Fr SIRC ARTICLE NO: 096771

SPORTING EVENTS

Falconnet, G. Ski - XIVe JO, Sarajevo 84. *EPS: Education physique et sport (Paris, France) 186, mars/avr 1984, 26-29.*
LEVEL: B LANG: Fr SIRC ARTICLE NO: 095236

Friedland, L. Nelson, J. Six regions eye future Olympics. *Ski area management (North Salem, N.Y.) 23(4), Jul 1984, 31-33;68.*
LEVEL: B LANG: Eng SIRC ARTICLE NO: 099886

Le ski et l'Olympisme. *Revue olympique (Lausanne)* 195/196, janv/fevr 1984, 51-98.
LEVEL: I LANG: Fr SIRC ARTICLE NO: 096814

Ski-ing and Olympism. *Olympic review (Lausanne, Switzerland)* 195/196, Jan/Feb 1984, 51-98.
LEVEL: I LANG: Eng SIRC ARTICLE NO: 095231

STATISTICS AND RECORDS

Van Doren, C.S. Skiing. *In, Clawson, M. and Van Doren, C.S.* (eds.), Statistics on outdoor recreation, Washington, Resources for the Future, c1984, p. 277-287.
LEVEL: I LANG: Eng GV191.4 20254

TECHNIQUES AND SKILLS

Gaudez, Y. Ski efficace avec la methode de l'ecole du ski francais. Paris: Chiron Sports, c1984. 158 p. : ill.
LEVEL: B LANG: Fr ISBN: 2-7027-03313 GV854 20049

TRAINING AND CONDITIONING

How to get in shape for the skiing season. *Executive fitness newsletter (Emmaus, Pa.)* 15(21), 13 Oct 1984, 3..
LEVEL: B LANG: Eng SIRC ARTICLE NO: 106039

Lloyd-Smith, R. Pre-ski season preparation: conditioning and equipment. *Canadian Academy of Sport Medicine newsletter (Ottawa)* 5(4), 1984, 37-40.
NOTES: Reprinted from: Canadian family physician vol. 29, October 1983.
LEVEL: B LANG: Eng SIRC ARTICLE NO: 106040

Serez-vous prets? *Ski Quebec (Montreal)* 10(2), nov 1984, 90-91;94.
LEVEL: B LANG: Fr SIRC ARTICLE NO: 179531

Vannini, C. En forme pour le ski et... pour la vie. *Macolin (Macolin, Suisse)* 41(12), dec 1984, 8-10.
NOTES: Traduction e adaptation de, Yves Jeannotat.
LEVEL: B LANG: Fr SIRC ARTICLE NO: 108763

TRAINING AND CONDITIONING - WEIGHT AND STRENGTH TRAINING

Lhomme, R. Partez du bon pied. *Sante et sport (Paris)* 214, janv 1984, 34-36.
LEVEL: B LANG: Fr SIRC ARTICLE NO: 098464

VARIATIONS

Mohler, C. On a wind and a prayer. *Powder (San Juan Capistrano, Calif.)* 13(4), Dec 1984, 122-128.
LEVEL: B LANG: Eng SIRC ARTICLE NO: 107479

Para ski: the combined art of gate crashing and hill hammering. *Canpara (Vanier, Ont.)* 16(2), Mar/Apr 1984, 19.
LEVEL: B LANG: Eng SIRC ARTICLE NO: 093650

SLALOM SKIING

BIOGRAPHY AND AUTOBIOGRAPHY

Howe, N. A natural force named Armstrong: Debbie Armstrong grew up believing anything was possible - and her first world-class win was the Olympic GS gold. *Skiing (Boulder, Colo.)* 37(3), Nov 1984, 117-119;121;123.
LEVEL: B LANG: Eng SIRC ARTICLE NO: 099899

Johnson, W.O. Here's a hero for the home folks. (Bojan Krizaj) *Sports illustrated* 60(5), 6 Feb 1984, 69-71.
LEVEL: B LANG Eng SIRC ARTICLE NO: 090886

EQUIPMENT

Doran, J. Ski Canada's fourth annual on-slope test. *Ski Canada magazine (Toronto)* 13(2), Oct 1984, 17;21-22;28;30;32;34;36-38;40;42;44-46;48;50-52.
LEVEL: B LANG: Eng SIRC ARTICLE NO: 106045

Grout, B. Slalom skis. *Skiing (Boulder, Colo.)* 37(3), Nov 1984, 124-133;260-261;264-265.
LEVEL: B LANG: Eng SIRC ARTICLE NO: 098946

Grout, B. Giant slalom skis. *Skiing (Los Angeles)* 37(4), Dec 1984, 146-150;153;155;157-158.
LEVEL: B LANG: Eng SIRC ARTICLE NO: 107499

Grout, W. The super G's: the new World Cup even has spawned a new generation of high-speed cruisers. Here are reports on ten notable models, with slop- and bench-test results. *Skiing* 36(6), Feb 1984, 94;96-98.
LEVEL: B LANG: Eng SIRC ARTICLE NO: 093711

Joubert, G. Hodesseaux, B. Dynastar 'courses' deux skis performants mais faciles. *Ski magazine (Neuilly, Cedex)* 65, nov 198 120-123.
LEVEL: B LANG: Fr SIRC ARTICLE NO: 173524

Masia, S. How a ski comes to market. *Ski (Buyer's guide '85) (New York)* 49(1), 31 Dec 1984, 98;100;102;108.
LEVEL: B LANG Eng SIRC ARTICLE NO: 100564

PHYSIOLOGY

Veicsteinas, A. Ferretti, G. Margonato, V. Rosa, G. Fagliabue, D. Energy cost of and energy sources for alpine skiing in top athletics. (Refs: 13)*Journal of applied physiology: respiratory, environmental and exercise physiology (Bethesda, Md.)* 56(5), May 1984, 1187-1190.
ABST: This study investigated the aerobic and anaerobic metabolism of 8 elite skiers and 5 non-elite skiers during the slalom and giant slalom ski events. For all subjects and in both ski events the energy sources were about 40% aerobic, 20% alactic and 40% lactic metabolism. In all subjects and in both ski events heart rate reached maximal values in 30-40s.
LEVEL: A LANG: Eng SIRC ARTICLE NO: 098482

SPORTING EVENTS

Kidd, B. The Aspen Winternational: with an outstanding GS course and a technically difficult downhill that challenges the world's best, Aspen, Colo., has become a key stop on the World Cup circuit. *Skiing* 36(5), Jan 1984, 67-68;70.
LEVEL: B LANG: Eng SIRC ARTICLE NO: 093722

TECHNIQUES AND SKILLS

Campbell, S. Beat the clock: the key to winning ski races is simple: ski the best line, carry your speed and trick the clock at the start and finish. Here's how. *Ski (New York)* 49(3), Nov 1984, 241-244;246-247.
LEVEL: B LANG: Eng SIRC ARTICLE NO: 099892

Joubert, G. Techniques nouvelles... le choc des piquets. *Ski magazine (Neuilly, Cedex)* 65, nov 1984, 130-131.
LEVEL: B LANG: Fr SIRC ARTICLE NO: 173521

Schoenhaar, H. Racing tactics: from the club level to the World Cup, knowing where to start your turns - and what is the fastest line in a course - is critical to racing success. *Skiing* 36(5), Jan 1984, 134-137.
LEVEL: B LANG: Eng SIRC ARTICLE NO: 093731

SLED DOG RACING

Ritchie, S. It's a dog's life and they love it. So do the growing number of Canadians who have discovered sled-dog racing. *Canadian living* 9(2), Feb 1984, 017;019;021.
LEVEL: B LANG: Eng SIRC ARTICLE NO: 090920

Shields, M. Sled dog trails. Anchorage, Alaska: Alaska Northwest Pub. Co., c1984. 1v.
LEVEL: B LANG: Eng ISBN: 0882402587 L CARD: 83-027548

SPORTING EVENTS

Kizzia, T. Loneliness at its heart. The Iditarod is a 1200-mile sled-dog race from Anchorage to Nome that has 'revived the lore of man (or woman) and dog in the wilderness'. *Ultrasport (Boston, Mass.)* 1(2), Apr 1984, 46-51.
LEVEL: B LANG: Eng SIRC ARTICLE NO: 098488

SNORKELLING

Blount, S. Taylor, H. The joy of snorkeling: an illustrated guide. New York: Collier Books, c1984. 112 p. : ill.
NOTES: Includes index. Bibliography: p. 84-87. 'An International Oceanographic Foundation selection'. 'A Pisces book'.
LEVEL: B LANG: Eng ISBN: 0020281102 LC CARD: 83-063487

EQUIPMENT

Baz, A.M. Optimum design of diving snorkels. (Refs: 7)*Medicine and science in sports and exercise (Indianapolis)* 16(4), Aug 1984, 415-421.
ABST: This manuscript deals with the development of theoretical and experimental procedures for investigating the flow phenomena associated with the clearing and breathing phases of the simple J-type snorkel. Special test stands have been built to monitor the effect of changing the snorkel geometrical parameters on its clearing efficiency and breathing resistance characteristics. The experimental results are used to check the validity of the mathematically-developed models that simulate the flow during the clearing and breathing phases. These models are then used as a basis for the development of a rational design procedure that would enable snorkel designers to select the

optimum geometrical parameters in a way that guarantees a balance between the breathing and clearing requirements in snorkels.
LEVEL: A LANG: Eng SIRC ARTICLE NO: 103633

PHYSIOLOGY

Rouchon, A.M. Adaptation cardiaque et nage avec palmes. *Etudes et sports sous-marins, l'aventure sous-marine (Paris) 73, mars/avr 1984, 40-41.*
LEVEL: B LANG: Fr SIRC ARTICLE NO: 098736

SNOWMOBILING

EQUIPMENT

Specifications des modeles 1985. *Vie en plein air (Montreal) oct 1984, 30-33.*
LEVEL: B LANG: Fr SIRC ARTICLE NO: 173139

FACILITIES

Snowmobiling in Ontario: coming or going? *Recreational vehicle life (Mississauga, Ont.) 16(2), Nov 1984, 18-20;22.*
LEVEL: B LANG: Eng SIRC ARTICLE NO: 173175

SNOWSHOEING

EQUIPMENT

Prater, G. Present 'state of the art' in snowshoes. *Summit (Big Bear Lake, Calif.) 30(2), Mar/Apr 1984, 2-5.*
LEVEL: B LANG: Eng SIRC ARTICLE NO: 103449

EQUIPMENT - MAINTENANCE

Roach, P. The care and feeding of snowshoes. *Outdoor Canada (Toronto) 13(1), Dec/Jan 1985, 60-61.*
LEVEL: B LANG: Eng SIRC ARTICLE NO: 101513

SOAPBOX RACING

RULES AND REGULATIONS

Soap box derby: 1984 rules. Akron, Ohio: All-American Soap Box Derby, National Control Board, 1984. 64 p. : ill.
NOTES: Cover title.
LEVEL: B LANG: Eng GV1029.7 17680

SOCCER

Herbst, D. College soccer keeps growing - against all odds. More and more schools are constructing soccer stadiums, despite the obstacles put in the way by administrators. *Soccer digest 6(6), Feb/Mar 1984, 24-30.*
LEVEL: B LANG: Eng SIRC ARTICLE NO: 092390

Houghton, B. Toye, C. How to play soccer: a guide for every coach, a must for every player. Markham, Ont.: Penguin Books, c1984. 160 p. : ill.
LEVEL: B LANG: Eng ISBN: 0-14-007129-6 LC CARD: C83-098943-9 GV943 17509

Sheldon, T. Minisoccer. *Soccer journal (SUNY-Bringhamton, N.Y.) 29(6), Nov/Dec 1984, 41-42.*
LEVEL: A LANG: Eng SIRC ARTICLE NO: 107549

Soccer development manual. Overview. Ottawa: Canadian Soccer Association, 1984. 45 p. : ill.
CORP: Canadian Soccer Association.
NOTES: Cover title. Bibliography: p. 45.
LEVEL: B LANG: Eng GV943 18301

ADMINISTRATION

Mathurin, D.C.E. A portrait: Sir Stanley Rous, C.B.E. *Can-so-ref (Markham, Ont.) 4, 1984, 6-9.*
LEVEL: B LANG: Eng SIRC ARTICLE NO: 109005

Reguly, E. How pro soccer turned go-go growth into disaster. *Financial times (Toronto) 73(16), 8 Oct 1984, 4-5.*
LEVEL: B LANG: Eng SIRC ARTICLE NO: 099928

ANTHROPOMETRY

Farmosi, I. Apor, P. Mecseki, S. Haasz, S. Body composition of notable soccer players. (Refs: 14)*Sportorvosi szemle/Hungarian review of sports medicine (Budapest) 25(2), 1984, 91-96.*
ABST: The body composition of 22 first-class soccer players were tested. Body density was determined by method of mass measurement under the water, the relative body fat by the Brozek (1963) relationship. The soccer players examined can be characterized by high stature, proportional body weight and low relative body fat. By analysis of the correlation of the parameters of the skinfolds and body composition it was defined that the sum of the hip and the frontal thigh skinfolds are in a very close connection with the body composition and the relative body fat. Completing the two skinfolds with that of the subscapula, relationship of the density and the body fat (%) with the skinfolds were pesented by a multivariate regression equation. This multivariate equation estimating the density, as a consequence of the low residual dispersation, is suitable for the estimation of the soccer players' density.
LEVEL: A LANG: Eng SIRC ARTICLE NO: 099922

BIOGRAPHY AND AUTOBIOGRAPHY

Jose, C. Paolo Rossi: small man making big impact. *Soccer news (Willowdale, Ont.) 2(4), Jun/Jul 1984, 21-22.*
LEVEL: B LANG: Eng SIRC ARTICLE NO: 095249

Lidz, F. A very rare bird indeed. If Tino Lettieri is the NASL's best goalie, he owes it all to Ozzie and his friends of the parrot persuasion. *Sports illustrated (Chicago) 61(11), 3 Sept 1984, 32-34;38.*
LEVEL: B LANG: Eng SIRC ARTICLE NO: 098504

CERTIFICATION

Butts, J.L. Soccer resources for teachers and coaches. (Refs: 5)*TAHPERD journal (Austin, Tex.) 52(3), May 1985, 12.*
LEVEL B LANG: Eng SIRC ARTICLE NO: 109095

Level III coaching course. s.l.: Canadian Soccer Association, 1984?. 136 p. : ill. (National Coaching Certification Program.)
CORP: Canadian Soccer Association.
NOTES: Cover title.
LEVEL: I LANG: Eng GV943.8 18368

CHILDREN

Bardon, C. Jeux d'equipe de 6 a 12 ans. (Refs: 7)*EPS: Education physique et sport (Paris, France) 186, mars/avr 1984, 54-57.*
NOTES: 1er article d'une serie de trois.
LEVEL: B LANG: Fr SIRC ARTICLE NO: 095246

Bean, D. A conceptual approach to beginning soccer. (Refs: 2)*Runner (Edmonton, Alb.) 22(2), Summer 1984, 17-23.*
LEVEL: B LANG: Eng SIRC ARTICLE NO: 101515

DuBois, N. The role of the high school or collegiate coach in the development and/or operation of a youth soccer program. *Soccer journal (Binghamton, N.Y.) 29(4), Jul/Aug 1984, 41;43-45.*
LEVEL: B LANG: Eng SIRC ARTICLE NO: 099921

Mallory, K. Hoehn, A.J. Practice soccer by yourself. South Bend, Ind.: Icarus Press, 1984. 263 p. : ill.
LEVEL: B LANG: Eng ISBN: 0-89651-606-7 LC CARD: 84-015854 GV943.9.T7 20907

Quinn, R.W. A beginning philosophy. (Refs: 3)*Soccer journal (Wayne, Pa.) 29(3), May/Jun 1984, 55-56.*
LEVEL: B LANG: Eng SIRC ARTICLE NO: 095254

Vecchierini-Blineau, M.F. Corbe, S. Ginet, J.D. Analyse des motivations a la pratique du football chez l'enfant. Enquete aupres de 23 garcons de 8 a 10 ans. (Refs: 14)*Cinesiologie (Paris) 94, mars/avr 1984, 149-154.*
LEVEL: I LANG: Fr SIRC ARTICLE NO: 096839

Waiters, T. Coaching to win: soccer for the young player. Toronto: Totem Books, c1984. 320 p. : ill.
LEVEL: B LANG: Eng ISBN: 0-00-217126-0 LC CARD: C84-98379-4 GV944.2 17523

CHILDREN - MINI-SPORT

Baumgarten, S. It can be done. A model youth sports program. (Refs: 4)*Journal of physical education, recreation and dance (Reston, Va.) 55(7), Sept 1984, 55-58.*
LEVEL: B LANG: Eng SIRC ARTICLE NO: 101514

Parkyn, J. Mini soccer: the better way. *Soccer news (Willowdale, Ont.) 2(4), Jun/Jul 1984,12-15.*
LEVEL: B LANG: Eng SIRC ARTICLE NO: 095253

CLOTHING

Vogelsinger, H. The care and fitting of soccer shoes. *Soccer journal (Binghamton, N.Y.) 29(4), Jul/Aug 1984, 46-47.*
LEVEL B LANG: Eng SIRC ARTICLE NO: 099930

CLUBS AND TEAMS

Associations sportives: les difficultes financieres. *Juris associations (France) 9, 1984, 49-51.*
LEVEL: B LANG: Fr

DuBois, N. The role of the high school or collegiate coach in the development and/or operation of a youth soccer program. (part 11) *Soccer journal (New York) 29(5), Sept/Oct 1984, 41-44.*
LEVEL: B LANG: Eng SIRC ARTICLE NO: 103456

Gammon, C. The NASL: it's alive but on death row: a salary cap has served the soccer league from complete collapse, but its future looks

forbidding indeed. *Sports illustrated (Chicago, Ill.)* 60(19), 7 May 1984, 74;76;78;80-81.
LEVEL: B LANG: Eng SIRC ARTICLE NO: 095248

Hall, D. Major indoor soccer league: tailor - made for North Americans. *Soccer news (Willowdale, Ont.)* 2(2), Jan/Mar 1984, 6-7.
LEVEL: B LANG: Eng SIRC ARTICLE NO: 103458

Lewis, M. The NASL: the incredible shrinking league. *Soccer digest (Des Moines, Iowa)* 7(1), Apr/Mar 1984, 48-51.
LEVEL: B LANG: Eng SIRC ARTICLE NO: 093758

Mott, S. Bell, J. The upside-world of the North American soccer league. *Soccer news (Willowdale, Ont.)* 2(4), Jun/Jul 1984, 8-11.
LEVEL: B LANG: Eng SIRC ARTICLE NO: 095252

Sperber, M. Montreal's soccer war ...the results. *Soccer news (Willowdale, Ont.)* 2(3), Apr/May 1984, 10-11.
LEVEL: B LANG: Eng SIRC ARTICLE NO: 095258

COACHING

Charles, J.M. Humanistic soccer coaching. *Soccer journal (New York)* 29(5), Sept/Oct 1984, 49-50.
LEVEL: B LANG: Eng SIRC ARTICLE NO: 103453

Douglas, C.M. You too can coach like a pro with Roy Turner: tips to better coaching. *Soccer America (Berkeley, Calif.)* 26(12), 22 Mar 1984, 12.
LEVEL: B LANG: Eng SIRC ARTICLE NO: 098494

Douglas, C.M. You too can coach like a pro with Willie Roy. *Soccer American (Berkeley, Calif.)* 27(17), 25 Oct 1984, 19.
LEVEL: B LANG: Eng SIRC ARTICLE NO: 103454

Douglas, C.M. You too can coach like a pro: with Pat McBride. *Soccer America (Berkeley, Calif.)* 27(19), 8 Nov 1984, 25.
LEVEL: B LANG: Eng SIRC ARTICLE NO: 103455

Lehrer, S.J. What to look for when scouting a soccer opponent. *Athletic journal (Evanston, Ill.)* 65(4), Nov 1984, 20-21;46.
LEVEL: B LANG: Eng SIRC ARTICLE NO: 101522

Lennox, J. Tactical progressions. *Soccer journal (Wayne, Pa.)* 29(3), May/Jun 1984, 51-54.
LEVEL: B LANG: Eng SIRC ARTICLE NO: 095250

Rosenthal, G. Soccer skills and drills. New York: Scribner, c1984. 1v. (xiii, 226 p. : ill.)
NOTES: Includes index. Originally published under the title: Everybody's soccer book.
LEVEL: B LANG: Eng ISBN: 0-684-18217-3 LC CARD: 84-010623 GV943 20785

Rush, D.B. Ayllon, T. Peer behavioral coaching: soccer. (Refs: 21)*Journal of sport psychology (Champaign, Ill.)* 6(3), 1984, 325-334.
ABST: The subjects were nine boys, ages 8 to 10, identified by the head coach as being deficient in three soccer skills: heading the ball, throw-ins, and goal kicking. The effects of a conventional form of coaching was compared to the behavioral one when each was conducted by the peer coach. The behavioral method included: (a) systematic use of verbal instructions and feedback, (b) positive and negative reinforcement, (c) positive practice, and (d) time out. The results show a two- or threefold increase in soccer skill performance when behavioral coaching was used.
LEVEL: A LANG: Eng SIRC ARTICLE NO: 103465

Thomson, B. How to coach winning soccer. *Coaching review (Ottawa, Ont.)* 7, Nov/Dec 1984,

51-52.
LEVEL: B LANG: Eng SIRC ARTICLE NO: 099929

Whitehead, N.J. Cook, M. Atkinson, R. Games, drills, and fitness practices for soccer coaching. London: A. & C. Black, c1984 128 p. : ill.
NOTES: Includes index.
LEVEL: B LANG: Eng ISBN: 0-7136-2443-4 LC CARD: 84-670236 GV943.8 18762

Woog, D. Common coaching problems: courses of action. *Soccer journal (SUNY-Bringhamton, N.Y.)* 29(6), Nov/Dec 1984, 23-24;26-27.
NOTES: Reprinted from, Soccer letter, issues 60 and 63.
LEVEL: B LANG: Eng SIRC ARTICLE NO: 107553

COUNTRIES AND REGIONS

Marchand, C.-A. Une nouvelle ligue canadienne se pointe: le soccer canadien a perdu ses complexes. *Quebec soccer (Montreal) (9), sept 1984, 8-9.*
LEVEL: B LANG: Fr SIRC ARTICLE NO: 173510

Zieminski, G. How not to celebrate fifty years. *World soccer (London, Eng.)* 24(8), May 1984, 20-21.
LEVEL: B LANG: Eng SIRC ARTICLE NO: 095267

DIRECTORIES

Soccer America 1984 camp directory. *Soccer America (Berkeley, Calif.)* 26(10), 8 Mar 1984, 7-10;12;14-20;22-23.
LEVEL: B LANG: Eng SIRC ARTICLE NO: 103466

DISABLED

Cowin, L. Sibille, J. O'Riain, M.D. The electric connection. *Sports 'n spokes (Phoenix, Ariz.)* 10(4), Nov/Dec 1984, 43-44.
LEVEL: B LANG: Eng SIRC ARTICLE NO: 107535

FACILITIES

Roberts, J. Performance tests in need of development. (Refs: 6)*Turf management (Surrey, Eng.)* 3(7), Jul 1984, 26-27;29.
LEVEL: B LANG: Eng SIRC ARTICLE NO: 102151

Sand football pitches. *Sports turf bulletin (Bingley, Eng.)* 147, Oct/Dec 1984, 5-7.
LEVEL: B LANG: Eng SIRC ARTICLE NO: 100621

FACILITIES - DESIGN, CONSTRUCTION AND PLANNING

Un terrain de football suspendu. *Paysages - actualites (France)* 71, 1984, 21-23.
LEVEL: B LANG: Fr

FACILITIES - MAINTENANCE

Renovation needs more planning. *Turf management (Surrey, Eng.)* 3(6), Jun 1984, 9-10.
LEVEL: B LANG: Eng SIRC ARTICLE NO: 102157

HEALTH AND HYGIENE

Vrillac, M. Sereni, J.P. Quelques elements de l'hygiene de vie du footballeur. *Cinesiologie 92/93, nov/dec 1983-janv/fevr 1984, 27-34.*
NOTES: Numero special: Medecine du sport et thermalisme.
LEVEL: I LANG: Fr SIRC ARTICLE NO: 093761

HISTORY

Foulds, S. Echos from the past speak truth. *Soccer America (Berkeley, Calif.)* 27(3), 19 Jul 1984, 21.
LEVEL: B LANG: Eng SIRC ARTICLE NO: 098499

Jones, S.G. The economic aspects of association football in England, 1918-39. (Refs: 67)*British journal of sports history (London)* 1(3), Dec 1984, 286-299.
ABST: The author examines the development of English association football in the inter-war period from an economic point of view.
LEVEL: A LANG: Eng SIRC ARTICLE NO: 106054

Jose, C. Who is professional? Olympic soccer tournaments have been plagued with controversy since World War 11 - this year's appears to be no exception. *Soccer America (Berkeley, Calif.)* 27(3), 19 Jul 1984, 23.
LEVEL: B LANG: Eng SIRC ARTICLE NO: 098502

Smith, D. Soccer milestones. *Can so ref (Burlington, Ont.)* 3, 1984, 20-21.
LEVEL: B LANG: Eng SIRC ARTICLE NO: 101523

Vamplew, W. Borderline differences? A comparative analysis of shareholders and directors in English and Scottish football before 1914. *Flanders University occasional papers in economics history 2, Feb 1984.*
LEVEL: A LANG: Eng

Weil, E. First time Olimpia. *World soccer (London, Eng.)* 24(8), May 1984, 24-25.
LEVEL: B LANG: Eng SIRC ARTICLE NO: 0952

Weil, E. Independiente carry on. *World soccer (London, Eng.)* 24(5), Feb 1984, 14.
LEVEL: B LANG: Eng SIRC ARTICLE NO: 095264

INJURIES AND ACCIDENTS

Collins, W.J. Hofner, R.G. A lower leg epiphyseal plate injury in a young athlete. (Refs: 6)*Athletic training 19(1), Spring 1984, 61-62.*
LEVEL: I LANG: Eng SIRC ARTICLE NO: 092388

Ekstand, J. Gillquist, J. Prevention of sport injuries in football players. (Refs: 19)*International journal of sports medicine (Stuttgart) Suppl. 5, Nov 1984, 140-144.*
CONF: International Congress on Sports and Health (1983 : Maastricht, Netherlands).
LEVEL: A LANG: Eng SIRC ARTICLE NO: 104884

Gabard, G. Berger-Vachon, C. Ferret, J.M. Panorama des accidents d'une saison (1980-81) dans la ligue de football Rhone-Alpe (Refs: 14)*Cinesiologie (Paris)* 94, mars/avr 1984, 177-182.
LEVEL: I LANG: Fr SIRC ARTICLE NO: 096830

Gabard, G. Berger-Vachon, C. Ferret, J.M. Football. Etude des matches a accidents multiples en Drome-Ardeche et Haute-Savoie sur une saison sportive. Pathologie. Facteurs de risque. (Refs: 9)*Medecine du sport (Paris)* 58(3), 25 mai 1984, 36-43.
RESUME: Le but de cette etude consistait en l'analyse de matches a accidents multiples au cours de la saison 1980-1981 de la Ligue Rhone-Alpes. 1215 declarations d'accidents provenant des districts de Drome-Ardeche et de Haute-Savoie furent retenues. Les resultats indiquent: 1) un risque d'exposition moyen de 5,2 blesses pour 100 matches, 2) qu'un match sur 200 conduit a 2 blesses et un match sur 2000 a 3 blesses, et 3)

SOCCER (continued)

que les novices sont 25 fois moins exposes que les seniors. Les circonstances, la pathologie, le facteur geographique et le niveau de pratique ont la meme incidence sur les matches ayant donne lieu a une ou plusieurs declarations. La frequence des accidents multiples est superieure au cours de la periode hivernale et en fin de championnats.
LEVEL: A LANG: Fr SIRC ARTICLE NO: 096831

Gerwatowska, W. Markucki, S. Przypadek obustronnego przewodzeniowego uposledzenia sluchu po urazie glowy pilka. (Case of bilateral conductive hearing loss after head injury with a ball.) *Otolaryngologia polska (Warsaw) 38(4), 1984, 327-331.*
LEVEL: A LANG: Pol

Golabek, R. Karwowski, B. Czlonkowska, A. Pourazowe zamkniecie tetnicy szyjnej wewnetrznej u mlodocianych. (Post-traumatic occlusion of the internal carotid artery in adolescents.) *Wiadomosci lekarskie (Warsaw) 37(18), 15 Sept 1984, 1447-1452.*
LEVEL: A LANG: Pol

Helman, L. Lymphorragie mortelle. (Fatal lymphorrhagia.) *Cahiers d'anesthesiologie (Paris) 32(1), janv/fevr 1984, 65.*
LEVEL: I LANG: Fr

Hinge, H.H. Brassoe, J.O. Fodboldskader hos old boys fodboldspillere. (Soccer injuries in old boys' games.) *Ugeskrift for laeger (Copenhagen) 146(16), 16 Apr 1984, 1253-1256.*
LEVEL: I LANG: Dan

Huard, G. Maintien en condition physique du joueur blesse en vue d'une reprise acceleree du travail normal. *Cinesiologie (Paris) 94, mars/avr 1984, 169-171.*
LEVEL: B LANG: Fr SIRC ARTICLE NO: 096835

Johannessen, A.C. Frandsen, P. Fedtinfiltration i hjertet. Arsag til pludselig dod i forbindelse med fysisk anstrengelse. (Fatty infiltration of the heart. Cause of sudden death in connection with physical exertion.) *Ugeskrift for laeger (Copenhagen) 147(1), 31 Dec 1984, 25.*
LEVEL: I LANG: Dan

Jorgensen, U. Epidemiology of injuries in typical Scandinavian team sports. (Refs: 6)*British journal of sports medicine (Loughborough, Eng.) 18(2), Jun 1984, 59-63.*
ABST: An investigation by questionnaire was undertaken in a group of 480 football players and 288 handball players (768 players). Of these 803 were injured, giving a player incidence of 4.1 injury/1000 football hours and 8.3 injury/1000 handball hours. The lower extremities were involved in 82% of the football injuries, whereas handball injuries were evenly distributed on both upper and lower extremities. The football injury prevalence was 0.36 per player, the handball injury prevalence 0.71 per player. Medical attention was given to 62% of the injured footballers and 47% of the injured handballers.
LEVEL: A LANG: Eng SIRC ARTICLE NO: 103508

Klasen, H.J. Acute soccer injuries. (Refs: 6)*International journal of sports medicine (Stuttgart) Suppl. 5, Nov 1984, 156-158.*
CONF: International Congress on Sports and Health (1983 : Maastricht, Netherlands).
LEVEL: A LANG: Eng SIRC ARTICLE NO: 104887

Maehlum, S. Daljord, O.A. Football injuries in Olso: a one-year study. (Refs: 20)*British journal of sports medicine (Loughborough, Eng.) 18(3), Sept 1984, 186-190.*
ABST: All football injuries treated at the Emergency Department, Oslo City Hospital, 1329 patients, 1167 males and 162 females, were recorded for one year, accounting for 28.4% of all sports injuries. Most injuries seen were in the 15-19 years age group in females and 20-24 years age group in males. During matches, 695 players were injured giving an incidence of 34.5 injuries/10,000 player matches. Sprains accounted for 41% of the injuries, 23% were contusions and 19% fractures. Most injuries (59%) affected the legs. The football injuries required 1966 consultations and necessitated that 349 patients had to stay away from work for a total of 6137 days.
LEVEL: A LANG: Eng SIRC ARTICLE NO: 103460

McCarroll, J.R. Meaney, C. Sieber, J.M. Profile of youth soccer injuries. (Refs: 8)*Physician and sportsmedicine 12(2), Feb 1984, 113-115;117.*
LEVEL: I LANG: Eng SIRC ARTICLE NO: 092393

Menck, H. Jorgensen, U. Friktionsfrakturer under sportsudovelse. (Friction fractures during sport.) *Ugeskrift for laeger (Copenhagen) 146(46), 12 Nov 1984, 3544-3545.*
NOTES: Includes English abstract.
LEVEL: I LANG: Dan

Micheli, L.J. Injuries in the football sports. (Refs: 25)
NOTES: In, Cantu, R.C. (ed.), Clinical sports medicine, Lexington, Mass. ; Toronto, Collamore Press : D.C. Heath, c1984, p. 203-210.
LEVEL: I LANG: Eng RC1201 15964

Moore, S. Soccer. *In, Adams, S.H. (ed.), et al., Catastrophic injuries in sports: avoidance strategies, Salinas, Calif., Cayote Press, c1984, p. 96-101.*
LEVEL: B LANG: Eng RD97 19088

Mozes, M. Papa, M.Z. Zweig, A. Bass, A. Horoszowsky, H. (Iliopsoas injury in soccer players.) *Harefuah (Tel Aviv) 106(9), 1 May 1984, 396-398.*
LEVEL: A LANG: Heb

Musierowicz, A. Chodkowski, M. Bocianski, W. Labedzki, A. Urazowe pekniecie jadra. (Traumatic rupture of the testis.) *Wiadomosci lekarskie (Warsaw) 37(3), 1 Feb 1984, 227-229.*
LEVEL: I LANG: Pol

Street, F. Treatment goals of the soccer physiotherapist. *Journal of the Society of Remedial Gymnastics and Recreation Therapy (Manchester) 114, Nov 1984, 15-18.*
NOTES: Reprinted from, Therapy weekly, June 28th 1984.
LEVEL: B LANG: Eng SIRC ARTICLE NO: 104894

Tropp, H. Ekstrand, J. Gillquist, J. Stabilometry in functional instability of the ankle and its value in predicting injury. (Refs: 17)*Medicine and science in sports and exercise 16(1), 1984, 64-66.*
ABST: Stabilometry was used to determine whether the incidence of ankle injuries affected postural sway and whether ankle injuries were affected by postural sway. This study tested 127 soccer players and found that those who showed poor stabilometry scores ran a higher risk of ankle injury. This suggests that these players may have underlying balance problems. Players with a previous ankle injury did not run a higher risk of injury than the other players.
LEVEL: A LANG: Eng SIRC ARTICLE NO: 092398

Viola, R. Rigon, A. Considerazioni sulla lassita posteriore 'isolata'. Notes on 'isolated' posterior laxity of the knee. (Refs: 16)*Italian journal of sports traumatology (Milano, Italy) 6(4), Oct/Dec 1984, 257-263.*
ABST: Following the observation of a persistently high level of performance in athletes with chronic posterior laxity, it was decided to study the stages of their running action by means of several series of photographs. An anteroposterior shift was noted in the instable knee. This abnormal movement, however, began and ended in the aerial stage. The profiles of both knees were fully comparable in complete extension, even before the foot touched the ground.
LEVEL: A LANG: It Eng SIRC ARTICLE NO: 106061

Vrillac, M. Sereni, J.P. Traumatismes du sport et Elastocapsil. *Medecine du sport (Paris) 58(5), 25 sept 1984, 63.*
LEVEL: LANG: Fr SIRC ARTICLE NO: 101524

Young, T.B. Tapping fracture of tibia. *British medical journal (clinical research ed.) (London) 289(6460), 22-29 Dec 1984, 1743.*
LEVEL: I LANG: Eng SIRC ARTICLE NO: 107554

JUVENILE LITERATURE

Summer, A. Baldwin, H. Mott, P.B. The official soccer rules. New York: Arco, 1984. 1v.
NOTES: Rev. ed. of: Let's play soccer, c1979.
LEVEL: B LANG: Eng ISBN: 0668061413 LC CARD: 84-014571

Verhees, V.P. Soccer, do you know the rules? (Santa Barbara, Calif.): (Soccer Book Co.), (c1984). 1v.
NOTES: Includes index
LEVEL: B LANG: Eng LC CARD: 83-020440

LAW AND LEGISLATION

Virginia suits filed against soccer clubs. *Referee (Franksville, Wis.) 9(3), Mar 1984, 54.*
LEVEL: B LANG: Eng SIRC ARTICLE NO: 098509

MASS MEDIA

Soccer: the media's viewpoint. *Soccer news (Willowdale, Ont.) 2(3), Apr/May 1984, 17-19;21.*
LEVEL: B LANG: Eng SIRC ARTICLE NO: 095257

Thibert, J. 1946-1984: toujours plus. *France football (Paris) 2000, 7 aout 1984, 6-7.*
LEVEL: B LANG: Fr SIRC ARTICLE NO: 098508

MEDICINE

Aguehounde, C. Richard-Kadio, M. Douane, G. Roux, C. N'Guessan, A. Cornet, L. L'osteome musculaire chez le jeune footballeur en milieu ivoirien. (Refs: 9)*Medecine du sport (Paris) 58(4), 25 juil 1984, 3-9.*
RESUME: Les auteurs presentent quatre cas d'osteome musculaire chez les jeunes footballeurs. L'exerese chirurgicale de l'osteome est le traitement applique. Les resultats obtenus sont bons. Les autres traitements possibles sont discutes.
LEVEL: A LANG: Fr SIRC ARTICLE NO: 098489

Smodlaka, V.N. Medical aspects of heading the ball in soccer. (Refs: 21)*Physician and sportsmedicine 12(2), Feb 1984, 127-128;131.*
LEVEL: I LANG: Eng SIRC ARTICLE NO: 092397

Szczerbi'nski, A. Zawal serca u sportowca. (Myocardial infarction in an athlete.) *Wiadomoscie lekarskie (Warsaw)* 37(24), 15 Dec 1984, 1961-1963.
LEVEL: I LANG: Pol

OFFICIATING

25 years young: Ontario Soccer Referees Association. *Can so ref (Markham, Ont.)* 4, 1984, 12-46.
LEVEL: B LANG: Eng SIRC ARTICLE NO: 109007

Beavis, L. Soccer: the drop ball. *Referee (Franksville, Wis.)* 9(5), May 1984, 42-43.
LEVEL: B LANG: Eng SIRC ARTICLE NO: 098490

Bomboy, R. Miracle Mike and the soccer docs. *Referee (Franksville, Wis.)* 9(9), Sept 1984, 24-28.
LEVEL: B LANG: Eng SIRC ARTICLE NO: 101516

Candler, K. On becoming a referee and getting to the top. *Football referee (Sheffield, Eng.)* 7, Mar 1984, 3.
LEVEL: B LANG: Eng SIRC ARTICLE NO: 098491

Conklin, H. Soccer: administering penalty kicks. *Referee (Franksville, Wis.)* 9(4), Apr 1984, 42-43.
LEVEL: B LANG: Eng SIRC ARTICLE NO: 098492

Dubsky, H. Referee assaults: the Toronto branch experience. *Can so ref (Burlington, Ont.)* 2, 1984, 20-23.
LEVEL: I LANG: Eng SIRC ARTICLE NO: 101519

Focus on...the hour before the kick-off. *Football referee (Sheffield, Eng.)* 6, Feb 1984, 4-5.
LEVEL: B LANG: Eng SIRC ARTICLE NO: 098498

Kovalakides, N. Making a good first impression. *Referee (Franksville, Wis.)* 9(2), Feb 1984, 42-43.
LEVEL: B LANG: Eng SIR ARTICLE NO: 098503

Kovalakides, N. Soccer official's manual: toward better soccer officiating; official rules; referee's responsibilities; official's mechanics. 2nd ed. New York: Leisure Press, c1984. 104 p. : ill.
LEVEL: B LANG: Eng ISBN: 0-88011-242-5 GV943.9.R43 18689

van Galen, W. Diederiks, J.P.M. Offences in amateur soccer: an analysis of 2723 cases. (Refs: 5)*International journal of sports medicine (Stuttgart)* Suppl. 5, Nov 1984, 214-215.
CONF: International Congress on Sports and Health (1983 : Maastricht, Netherlands).
LEVEL: A LANG: Eng SIRC ARTICLE NO: 104897

PHYSIOLOGY

Boeda, A. Corbeau, J. Gillet, J. Pasquis, P. Un test de forme chez les footballeurs. (Refs: 12)*Cinesiologie (Paris)* 94, mars/avr 1984, 145-147.
LEVEL: I LANG: Fr SIRC ARTICLE NO: 096827

Corbeau, J. Variation de la frequence cardiaque au cours d'une epreuve d'effort standardisee. (Refs: 16)*EPS: Education physique et sport (Paris)* 189, sept/oct 1984, 64-69.
LEVEL: I LANG: Fr SIRC ARTICLE NO: 100891

Dufaux, B. Order, U. Hollmann, W. Can physical exercise induce an effective fibrinolysis? *Thrombosis research (Elmsford, N.Y.)* 36(1), 1 Oct 1984, 37-43.
LEVEL: A LANG: Eng

Eisenberg, J.N. Moore, N.A. Plasma MB creatine kinase in soccer players. (letter) *American journal of cardiology (New York)* 54(7), 1 Oct 1984, 941.
LEVEL: I LANG: Eng

Gorostiaga, E. Ferret, J.M. Eclache, J.P. Influence de trois types d'echauffement progressif sur un exercice sous-maximal. (Refs: 66)*Cinesiologie (Paris)* 94, mars/avr 1984, 131-140.
RESUME: Au cours de cette etude, trois varietes d'echauffements de types triangulaire sont analyses: d'une duree nulle Eo; de 8 min E1; et de 16 min E2. Quatre joueurs de soccer agee de 17,6 + - 0,52 ans participent a trois epreuves-tests de 20 minutes a 80% de VO2 max apres Eo, E1 et E2. La consommation d'oxygene, le debit ventilatoire, la frequence cardiaque, la lactacidemie, la glycemie et la glycerolemie sont les variables mesurees. Les auteurs constatent qu'une amelioration de la performance ne peut etre obtenue que lorsque la puissance de l'echauffement est inferieure a 80% de VO2 max.
LEVEL: A LANG: Fr SIRC ARTICLE NO: 096832

Gorostiaga, E. Ferret, J.M. Eclache, J.P. Entrainement fractionne. *Cinesiologie (Paris)* 94, mars/avr 1984, 143-144.
LEVEL I LANG: Fr SIRC ARTICLE NO: 096833

Jako, P. Szabo, G. Bodnar, L. Hajos, M. Ifjusagi labdarugok es oekoelvivok nehany fizikai karakterisztikumanak vizsgalata. (Some physical characteristics of junior football players and boxers.) (Refs: 13)*Sportorvosi szemle/Hungarian review of sports medicine (Budapest)* 25(1), 1984, 43-51.
ABST: The purpose of the present paper was to study and compare the physical abilities in two events which though technically different, both require an alternation between aerobic and anaerobic energy sources. Anthropometry, spiroergometry, dynamometry, body composition, and reaction time was studied in soccer players and boxers of the national junior teams, each group consisting of 30 subjects. The obtained results were compared to the respective means of the senior national teams. No characteristic differences were found between the two events, and junior competitors did not differ significantly from the adult ones either.
LEVEL: A LANG: Hun SIRC ARTICLE NO: 095679

Lacourt, J.R. Chatard, J.C. Aspects physiologiques du football. (Refs: 13)*Cinesiologie (Paris)* 94, mars/avr 1984, 123-130.
LEVEL: I LANG: Fr SIRC ARTICLE NO: 096836

Reilly, T. Bowen, T. Exertional costs of changes in directional modes of running. (Refs: 4)*Perceptual and motor skills* 58(1), Feb 1984, 149-150.
ABST: The energy cost and perceived exertion of 9 male soccer players were assessed while running forwards, backwards and sideways at three different speeds. The energy cost increased linearly with speed of motion for each of the directional modes. Both running backwards and sideways elicited similar perceived exertion. Running forwards elevated the perceived exertion 2.3, and 4 units of the Borg Scale with increasing speeds.
LEVEL: A LANG: Eng SIRC ARTICLE NO: 093760

Reilly, T. Ball, D. The net physiological cost of dribbling a soccer ball. (Refs: 15)*Research quarterly for exercise & spor (Reston, Va.)* 55(3), Sept 1984, 267-271.
ABST: Eight male footballers ran for 5 min on a treadmill at speeds of 9, 10.5, 12 and 13.5km .h-1 while dribbling a football against a rebound box; running at each of these speeds without the ball constituted controls. Oxygen uptake (VO2), perceived exertion (RPE) and blood lactate levels were measured and compared between the two conditions. The energy expended increased linearly with speed for both exercise modes. Similarly, RPE showed a constant elevation for dribbling over running at each speed, and a linear increase with speed of motion for both modes. Blood lactate increased disproprotionately with speed for dribbling, onset of metabolic acidosis being attained at a lower speed for the experimental task.
LEVEL: A LANG: Eng SIRC ARTICLE NO: 103464

PHYSIOLOGY - MUSCLE

Costain, R. Williams, A.K. Isokinetic quadriceps and hamstring torque levels of adolescent, female soccer players. (Refs: 17 *Journal of orthopaedic and sports physical therapy (Baltimore)* 5(4), Jan/Feb 1984, 196-200.
ABST: This study was undertaken to measure the isokinetic properties of knee flexion and extension in adolescent, female soccer players, with the use of a Cybex II dynamometer. It was found that: 1) Extension torque was significantly greater than flexion torque; 2) There was no significant difference between dominant and non-dominant legs for either flexion or extension torque; 3) At 30 degrees per second, peak quadriceps torque occurred at about 73o of extension, and peak flexion torque was achieved at about 38o of flexion; and 4) slow speed flexion and extension resulted in greater torque levels than fast speed contractions.
LEVEL: A LANG: Eng SIRC ARTICLE NO: 093753

Oeberg, B. Ekstrand, J. Moeller, M. Gillquist, J. Muscle strength and flexibility in different positions of soccer players. (Refs: 19)*International journal of sports medicine (Stuttgart)* 5(4), Aug 1984, 213-216.
ABST: One-hundred eighty soccer players were tested for muscle strength in knee extension and knee flexion and for flexibility in the lower extremity. The players were divided into groups according to their player position: goalkeepers, defenders, midfielders, and forwards. The results showed a significantly higher knee extensor torque in goalkeepers and defenders than in forwards. The knee flexion/knee extension ratio was significantly higher for forwards compared to goalkeepers and defenders. The goalkeepers were significantly more flexible than the other players in hip flexion, knee flexion and ankle dorsiflexion.
LEVEL: A LANG: Eng SIRC ARTICLE NO: 104891

PICTORIAL WORKS

McCarra, K. Scottish football: a pictorial history from 1867 to the present day. s.l.: Third Eye Centre/Polygon, (1984?). 1v
LEVEL: B LANG: Eng ISBN: 0-904919-89-7

PSYCHOLOGY

Dowthwaite, P.K. Armstrong, M.R. An investigation into the anxiety levels of soccer players. (Refs: 13)*International journa of sport psychology (Rome)* 15(3), 1984, 149-159.
ABST: The primary purpose of this investigation was to determine the effect of a soccer game on the anxiety levels of individual players. Eleven male college soccer players acted as experimental subjects. The adult version of the Sport Competition Anxiety Test (SCAT) was administered ten minutes

before the first and immediately after the last match. The competitive short form of Spielberger's State Anxiety Inventory (CSAI) was administered ten minutes before and immediately after each game. The CSAI was applied to three matches. Scores on the instrument were indicative of changes in anxiety states before and after competition.
LEVEL: A LANG: Eng SIRC ARTICLE NO: 104883

RULES AND REGULATIONS

Fairbanks, J. Injury stoppages: ruling on the letter and intent of the laws. *Referee (Franksville, Wis.) 9(9), Sept 1984, 46-47.*
LEVEL: B LANG: Eng SIRC ARTICLE NO: 101520

Hill, G. Hill's law of soccer. South Bend, Ind.: Icarus Press, 1984. 1v.
LEVEL: B LANG: Eng ISBN: 0896513033 LC CARD: 84-020510

O'Keefe, J. Why use different high school rules. *Soccer journal (SUNY-Bringhamton, N.Y.) 29(6), Nov/Dec 1984, 39-40.*
LEVEL: B LANG: Eng SIRC ARTICLE NO: 107545

SOCIAL PSYCHOLOGY

Jennett, N. Attendances, uncertainty of outcome and policy in Scottish league football. (Refs: 16)*Scottish journal of political economy (Harlow, Essex) 31(2), 1984, 176-198.*
LEVEL: A LANG: Eng SIRC ARTICLE NO: 098500

Narciso, M. Otto, S. Mielke, D. An analysis of reasons for athletic dropouts in youth soccer programs. (Refs: 2)*Soccer journal (New York) 29(5), Sept/Oct 1984, 33-34;39.*
LEVEL: I LANG: Eng SIRC ARTICLE NO: 103463

SOCIOLOGY

Dawson, S.C. Malmisur, M.C. Lewis, J.M. A comparative analysis of professional soccer in the United States and England. (Refs: 10)*Journal of sport behavior (Mobile, Ala.) 7(3), Sept 1984, 95-104.*
ABST: Soccer is the leading international spectator team sport in the world. This paper compares, using the theoretical work of Talcott Parsons, patterns of social organization (governing bodies, rules and regulations, goals, and fans) of professional soccer in the United States and England. Parsons' LIGA paradigm is used in analyzing soccer in each country.
LEVEL: A LANG: Eng SIRC ARTICLE NO: 101518

Houlston, D.R. Social mobility of professional soccer players in Great Britain. (Refs: 7)*Physical education review (Manchester) 7(1, Spring 1984, 56-64.*
ABST: The author set up to test the hypothesis that professional soccer players in Great Britain would experience downward social mobility at the end of their career. 52 former English Football League players served as subjects. Post-soccer career employment and income levels were the variables analysed. The initial hypothesis was corroborated: more than 75% of the subjects experienced downward mobility.
LEVEL: A LANG: Eng SIRC ARTICLE NO: 099924

Moorhouse, H.F. Professional football and working-class culture: English theories and Scottish evidence. (Refs: 51) *Sociological review*

(Staffordshire, Eng.) 32(2), 1984, 285-315.
LEVEL: A LANG: Eng SIRC ARTICLE NO: 098506

Semyonov, M. Sport and beyond: ethnic inequalities in attainment. (Refs: 33)*Sociology of sport journal (Champaign, Ill.) 1(4), Dec 1984, 358-365.*
ABST: This paper challenges the popular argument that sport is an effective channel for upward mobility, especially for ethnic minorities. The study of retired professional soccer players in Israel establishes the following findings: First, members of the subordinate ethnic group are disadvantaged in attainment of status not only in schools and labor markets but also in and via sport. Second, a professional career in sport does not intervene between background variables and later occupational attainment. Third, both ethnicity and educational level are the most significant determinants of post-retirement occupational attainment; higher education and higher ethnic status improve opportunities for later occupational success. On the basis of these findings it is suggested that the same rules of inequality that push individuals to seek alternative routes of mobility, such as professional sport, continued to operate in and beyond sport.
LEVEL: A LANG: Eng SIRC ARTICLE NO: 104893

Taylor, I. Professional sport and the recession: the case of British soccer. (Refs: 20)*International review for the sociology of sport (Munich) 19(1), 1984, 7-30.*
ABST: This paper attempts to summarise the available evidence on the economic crisis currently affecting Professional Soccer in England and Wales. Various economic and social aspects of soccer's post-war decline are discussed, as well as the inadequacy of the analyses of soccer's current situation offered by economists. The paper proceeds to examine the ways in which individual clubs and the football league as a whole are now engaged in the search for new sources of capital. This forms the basis for an analysis of the contradictory tendencies and pressures towards 'retrenchment' and 'reconstruction' in the game's traditional relationship to the broader society.
LEVEL: A LANG: Eng SIRC ARTICLE NO: 104895

Wagg, S. The football world: a contemporary social history. Brighton, Sussex: Harvester Press, c1984. xv, 252 p.
NOTES: Includes bibliographical references.
LEVEL: I LANG: Eng ISBN: 0-7108-0620-5 GV944.G7 18221

SPECTATORS

Dunning, E. Murphy, P. Williams, J. Maguire, J. Football hooliganism in Britain before the First World War. (Refs: 14) *International review for the sociology of sport (Warszawa, Poland) 19(3/4), 1984, 215-240.*
ABST: This paper summarizes some preliminary findings of a three-year research project carried out at the University of Leicester. Based on historical research and a content analysis of selected reports of football hooliganism before the First World War, the paper shows that, contrary to common opinion, football hooliganism is by no means an entirely new phenomenon. It also examines the sociological implications of this findings and suggests that the major sociological explanations of football hooliganism offered so far will have to be substantially revised.
LEVEL: A LANG: Eng SIRC ARTICLE NO: 106051

Walker, S. Coalter, F. Foley, M. Moorhouse, B. Crowd behaviour at football matches: a study in Scotland. Edinburgh: Centre for Leisure Research, 1984. 182 p.
LEVEL: A LANG: Eng

Williams, J. Dunning, E. Murphy, P. Hooligans abroad: the behaviour and control of English fans in continental Europe. London: Routledge & Kegan Paul, c1984. xiv, 230 p. : ill.
NOTES: Includes bibliographical references and index.
LEVEL: I LANG: Eng ISBN: 0710201435 LC CARD: 83-026988 GV943.9.S64 17622

SPORTING EVENTS

Weil, E. Libertadores Cup story...part eight. Independiente's record sweep. *World soccer (London, Eng.) 24(4), Jan 1984, 22-23;37.*
LEVEL: B LANG: Eng SIRC ARTICLE NO: 095262

STRATEGY

Duvillard, S.P. Important technical and tactical foundations of the soccer game. *Texas coach (Austin, Tex.) 28(1), Aug 1984 30-31.*
LEVEL: B LANG: Eng SIRC ARTICLE NO: 103457

STRATEGY - DEFENSIVE

Miller, J. High pressure vs. low pressure. (defence) *Soccer journal (Binghamton, N.Y.) 29(4), Jul/Aug 1984, 39-40.*
LEVEL: LANG: Eng SIRC ARTICLE NO: 099926

Tipping, J. The coach's survival kit: defensive preparation. *Soccer journal (Philadelphia, Pa.) 29(2), Mar/Apr 1984, 41-44.*
LEVEL: B LANG: Eng SIRC ARTICLE NO: 095261

STRATEGY - OFFENSIVE

Givens, D. Exploiting the dead ball situation. *Athletic journal 64(6), Jan 1984, 38-39.*
LEVEL: B LANG: Eng SIRC ARTICLE NO: 090931

Johnson, J. Think offense. *Soccer journal (Binghamton, N.J.) 29(4), Jul/Aug 1984, 49.*
LEVEL: B LANG: Eng SIRC ARTICLE NO: 099925

Maher, A. Converting the sweeper into a libero. *Scholastic coach (New York) 54(4), Nov 1984, 30-32;14;16.*
LEVEL: B LANG: Eng SIRC ARTICLE NO: 103461

Martin, T. Tactics - beating the offside trap. (Refs: 7)*Soccer journal (New York) 29(5), Sept/Oct 1984, 45-48.*
LEVEL: B LANG: Eng SIRC ARTICLE NO: 103462

Radakovich, M. Counter attack scoring. *Athletic journal (Evanston, Ill.) 65(2), Sept 1984, 34-36.*
LEVEL: B LANG: Eng SIRC ARTICLE NO: 099927

TEACHING

Brown, E.W. Teaching the instep kick to beginning soccer players. *Spotlight on youth sports (East Lansing, Mich.) 7(1), Spring 1984, 3-4.*
LEVEL: B LANG: Eng SIRC ARTICLE NO: 103452

TECHNIQUES AND SKILLS

Coerver, W. Rethacker, J.P. Technique du footballeur. Paris: Robert Laffont, (1984). 200 p. : ill. (Sports pour tous.)
NOTES: Traduit de: Voetbal, leerplan voor de ideale voetballer, Amsterdam/Bruxelles, Uitgeversmaatschappij, Elsevier, c1983.
LEVEL: B LANG: Fr ISBN: 2-221-04453-3 GV943 17820

TECHNIQUES AND SKILLS - GOALTENDER AND GOALTENDING

DiCicco, T. Gaspar, D. Saving the break-away. *Soccer journal (Philadelphia, Pa.) 29(2), Mar/Apr 1984, 37-40.*
LEVEL: B LANG: Eng SIRC ARTICLE NO: 095247

Hopper, C.A. Analyzing the soccer goalie's distribution. *Scholastic coach (New York) 54(2), Sept 1984, 78-79.*
LEVEL: B LANG: Eng SIRC ARTICLE NO: 099923

TESTING AND EVALUATION

Crevoisier, J. Football: l'evaluation en sports collectifs. (Refs: 1)*EPS: Education physique et sport (Paris) 189, sept/oct 1984, 25-30.*
LEVEL: B LANG: Fr SIRC ARTICLE NO: 101517

Feltz, D.L. Brown, E.W. Perceived competence in soccer skills among young soccer players. (Refs: 15)*Journal of sport psychology (Champaign, Ill.) 6(4), Dec 1984, 385-394.*
ABST: Harter's (1979) perceived competence subscale was modified to specifically apply to soccer in order to compare young soccer players' general self-esteem, perceived physical competence, and perceived soccer competence scores in predicting players' actual soccer ability. Young soccer players (218), 8 to 13 years of age, were tested on five soccer skill tests. Players also completed Harter's (1979) Perceived Competence Scale for Children and our perceived soccer competence subscale. We hypothesized that perceived soccer competence would have high internal consistency and would be a better predictor of soccer ability than either perceived physical competence or general self-esteem. Results indicated that the perceived soccer competence subscale had the highest internal consistency reliability coefficient, and that it was also slightly more predictive of soccer ability than perceived physical competence as indicated by multivariate multiple regression analysis and canonical correlation analysis.
LEVEL: A LANG: Eng SIRC ARTICLE NO: 104886

Philipsen, H. Joosten, J. Diederiks, J.P.M. Perceived severity of offences in professional soccer. (Refs: 3)*International journal of sports medicine (Stuttgart) Suppl. 5, Nov 1984, 209-211.*
CONF: International Congress on Sports and Health (1983 : Maastricht, Netherlands).
LEVEL: A LANG: Eng SIRC ARTICLE NO: 104892

TRAINING AND CONDITIONING

Canon-Remley, C. Conditioning to prevent soccer injuries. *Texas coach (Austin, Tex.) 28(4), Nov 1984, 46-47.*
LEVEL: B LANG: Eng SIRC ARTICLE NO: 173442

L'academie internationale FIFA/Coca-Cola IIe partie. Preparation de l'equipe en relation avec le football de competition. Zurich, Suisse: Federation internationale de football association, c1984. 135 p. : ill.
CORP: Federation internationale de football association.
NOTES: Traduit de l'allemand.
LEVEL: B LANG: Fr GV943.9.T7 20318

Luxbacher, J. Fun games for soccer. *Scholastic coach (New York) 53(10), May/Jun 1984, 86-87;103.*
LEVEL: B LANG: Eng SIRC ARTICLE NO: 095251

TRAINING AND CONDITIONING - DRILLS

Bailey, R. Soccer fun games: a midseason break from monotonous practice. *Scholastic coach (New York) 54(5), Dec 1984, 16-17;64.*
LEVEL: B LANG: Eng SIRC ARTICLE NO: 103450

DeLorenzo, D. The corner kick: an offensive weapon. The corner kick can be a powerful offensive weapon - so coaches should try to make it more than a '50-50' ball. *Athletic journal 64(8), Mar 1984, 12-13;72-73.*
LEVEL: B LANG: Eng SIRC ARTICLE NO: 093754

Ford, G. Kane, J. Go for goal: winning drills and exercises for soccer. Boston ; Toronto: Allyn and Bacon, c1984. xii, 174 p : ill.
NOTES: Includes index.
LEVEL: B LANG: Eng ISBN: 0205080650 LC CARD: 83-022303 GV943.9.T7 17327

Guffy, T. 5 vs. 2: key to winning soccer. *Athletic journal (Evanston, Ill.) 65(1), Aug 1984, 32;59.*
LEVEL: B LANG: Eng SIRC ARTICLE NO: 096834

Hawken, C.R. Forging a shooting psyche with a 6-vs-6 drill. *Scholastic coach (New York) 54(3), Oct 1984, 20;22;62.*
LEVEL: LANG: Eng SIRC ARTICLE NO: 101521

Herrick, G. Shooting drills; drills for teaching shooting skills must follow a progression that emphasizes fundamentals. *Athletic journal 64(9), Apr 1984, 49-50;68-69.*
LEVEL: B LANG: Eng SIRC ARTICLE NO: 093755

Herrick, G. A shooting progression for your team, part 1. *Soccer journal (New York) 29(5), Sept/Oct 1984, 37-39.*
LEVEL: B LANG: Eng SIRC ARTICLE NO: 103459

Herrick, G. A shooting progression for your team, Part II. *Soccer journal (SUNY-Bringhamton, N.Y.) 29(6), Nov/Dec 1984, 33;35;37-38.*
LEVEL: B LANG: Eng SIRC ARTICLE NO: 107540

How to shoot the penalty. *Sports (Kallang, Singapore) 12(10), Nov/Dec 1984, 49.*
LEVEL: B LANG: Eng SIRC ARTICLE NO: 108998

Juventeny Verges, P.M. Utilisation des haies: une experience didactique. *EPS: Education physique et sport 185, janv/fevr 1984, 21-23.*
LEVEL: B LANG: Fr SIRC ARTICLE NO: 093756

McNaughton, L. Shoot on sight. *Sports coach (Wembley, W. Aust.) 8(2), Oct 1984, 8-9.*
LEVEL: B LANG: Eng SIRC ARTICLE NO: 104889

Mungioli, S.R. Helpful attacking soccer drills. *Texas coach (Austin, Tex.) 28(3), Oct 1984, 14-17.*
LEVEL: B LANG: Eng SIR ARTICLE NO: 173199

Nicholas, D. Developing passing skill: 5 v. 2 (part 2). *Soccer journal (SUNY-Bringhamton, N.Y.) 29(6), Nov/Dec 1984, 29;31-32.*

NOTES: Reprinted from, Goalines.
LEVEL: B LANG: Eng SIRC ARTICLE NO: 107544

Stewart, C. Winning soccer drills. Soccer practices must be organized in such a way that players' individual skills are enhanced. *Athletic journal (Evanston, Ill.) 64(10), May 1984, 24;66.*
LEVEL: B LANG: Eng SIRC ARTICLE NO: 095259

Warming, B. Soccer conditioning: 'oscar' your way to match fitness. *Women's coaching clinic 7(8), Apr 1984, 12-13.*
LEVEL: LANG: Eng SIRC ARTICLE NO: 093762

VARIATIONS

Bardon, C. Jeux d'equipe de 6 a 12 ans. 2e partie. Equipe contre equipe. *EPS: Education physique et sport (Paris) 187, mai/juin 1984, 14-16.*
LEVEL: B LANG: Fr SIRC ARTICLE NO: 095723

Easley, R.C. Two-ball soccer: a fast moving, everyone involved activity. (Refs: 4)*In, Vendl, B.C. (ed.) et al., Interpretiv aspects of intramural-recreational sports: selected proceedings from the Thirty-fifth Annual National Intramural-Recreational Sports Association Conference, Corvallis, Or., Oregon State University, c1984, p. 49-52.*
CONF: National Intramural-Recreational Sports Association Conference (35th : 1984 : Fort Worth, Tex.).
LEVEL: B LANG: Eng GV710 18914

VIOLENCE

Daniel, C. Violence. *Forum: Council of Europe (Strasbourg) 1, 1984, 12-15.*
LEVEL: B LANG: Eng SIRC ARTICLE NO: 098493

Pratt, J. Salter, M. A fresh look at football hooliganism. (Refs: 18)*Leisure studies (London) 3(2), May 1984, 201-219.*
ABST: The authors present a sociological analysis of hooliganism in soccer. Their findings are based principally on two research reports: 1) on MA dissertation which consisted of observation of soccer matches at Cardiff City of a six-month priod in 1977/8 and series of interview with a group of 'hooligans' and 2) a PHD thesis which involved observation of Milwall and Portsmouth home and away games (around 80) between 1978 and 1982 and interviews with 'hooligans' from these clubs. The historical dimension of this phenomenon in England is discussed.
LEVEL: A LANG: Eng SIRC ARTICLE NO: 108548

Trivizas, E. Disturbances associated with football matches: types of incidents and selection of charges. (Refs: 18)*British journal of criminology (London) 24(4), 1984, 361-383.*
LEVEL: A LANG: Eng SIRC ARTICLE NO: 104896

VISION

Nettleton, B. Shoulder, J. Smith, B.A. Smith, R. Analysis of visual functioning in fast ball team games. (Refs: 24)*Journal of sports medicine and physical fitness (Torino, Italy) 24(4), Dec 1984, 327-336.*
ABST: Following a discussion of visual functioning in fast ball team games, a number of approaches focussing upon measuring attentional style are briefly outlined. One method of constructing a 'Visual Functioning Profile' is then described along with the results of administering this profile to a group of young elite soccer players attending the

Australian Institute of Sport.
LEVEL: A LANG: Eng SIRC ARTICLE NO: 107543

SOCIAL PSYCHOLOGY

Nixon, H.L. Sport and the American dream. New York: Leisure Press, c1984. 264 p.
LEVEL: I LANG: Eng ISBN: 0880111127 LC CARD: 82-83943 GV706.5 15948

DROP-OUT

Lee, C. Owen, N. Preventing dropout - a psychological viewpoint. (Refs: 13)*Sports coach (Wembley, Aust.) 8(1), 1984, 20-23.*
LEVEL: I LANG: Eng SIRC ARTICLE NO: 096331

Olsen, A.M. The consequences of early specialisation and competition on later participation and non-participation: the drop out methodological considerations. (Refs: 35)*In, Idrett for barn. Sport for Children. Sport pour les enfants 27.9.-1.10.1982 Tonsberg, Norway. Report. Oslo, Norway, Ministry of Cultural and Scientific Affairs: Norwegian Confederation of Sport, 1984, p. (36)-(43).*
CONF: Idrett for barn. Sport for Children. Sport pour les enfants (1982 : Tonsberg, Norway).
LEVEL: A LANG: Eng GV709.2 20111

Olsen, A.M. Consecquences (sic) de la specialisation et de competition sur la prarique (sic) ulterieure de l'activite sportive: le phenomene de l'abandon. (Refs: 35)*Dans, Idrett for barn. Sport for Children. Sport pour les enfants 27.9.-1.10.1982 Tonsberg, Norway. Rapport. Oslo, Norvege, Ministere de la culture et de la science : Confederation norvegienne des sports, 1984, p. (37)-(45).*
CONF: Idrett for barn. Sport for Children. Sport pour les enfants (1982 : Tonsberg, Norway).
LEVEL: A LANG: Fr GV709.2 20112

GROUP DYNAMICS

Carron, A.V. Cohesion in sport teams.
NOTES: In, Silva, J.M. and Weinberg, R.S. (eds.), Psychological foundations of sport, Champaign, Ill., Human Kinetics Publishers, c1984, p. 340-351.
LEVEL: A LANG: Eng GV706.4 17779

Gill, D.L. Individual and group performance in sport.
NOTES: In, Silva, J.M. and Weinberg, R.S. (eds.), Psychological foundations of sport, Champaign, Ill., Human Kinetics Publishers, c1984, p. 315-328.
LEVEL: A LANG: Eng GV706.4 17779

INTERPERSONAL RELATIONS

Chauvier, R. Effect of early specialisation on the social life of children aged 6-12. (Refs: 3)*In, Idrett for barn. Sport for Children. Sport pour les enfants 27.9.-1.10.1982 Tonsberg, Norway. Report. Oslo, Norway, Ministry of Cultural and Scientific Affairs: Norwegian Confederation of Sport, 1984, p. (34)-(35).*
CONF: Idrett for barn. Sport for Children. Sport pour les enfants (1982 : Tonsberg, Norway).
LEVEL: I LANG: Eng GV709.2 20111

Chauvier, R. Repercussion d'une specialisation precoce sur la vie sociale d'enfants ages de 6 a 12 ans. (Refs: 5)*Dans, Idrett for barn. Sport for Children. Sport pour les enfants 27.9.-1.10.1982*

Tonsberg, Norway. Rapport. Oslo, Norvege, Ministere de la culture et de la science : Confederation norvegienne des sports, 1984, p. (35)-(36).
CONF: Idrett for barn. Sport for Children. Sport pour les enfants (1982 : Tonsberg, Norway).
LEVEL: I LANG: Fr GV709.2 20112

Redekop, P. Sport and the masculine ethos: some implications for family interaction. (Refs: 11)*International journal of comparative sociology (Leiden, Neth.) 25(3/4), 1984, 262-269.*
LEVEL: A LANG: Eng SIRC ARTICLE NO: 104475

LEADERSHIP

Chelladurai, P. Leadership in sports.
NOTES: In, Silva, J.M. and Weinberg, R.S. (eds.), Psychological foundations of sport, Champaign, Ill., Human Kinetics Publishers, c1984, p. 329-339.
LEVEL: A LANG: Eng GV706.4 17779

Rice, H. Leadership for leaders. Part 1: 'attitude training,' the beginning. *Scholastic coach (New York) 54(2), Sept 1984, 14;16;18.*
LEVEL: B LANG: Eng SIRC ARTICLE NO: 099296

SOCIAL BEHAVIOUR

Rees, C.R. Miracle, A.W. Conflict resolution in games and sports. (Refs: 29)*International review for the sociology of sport (Munich) 19(2), 1984, 145-156.*
CONF: Olympic Scientific Congress (1984 : Eugene, Ore.).
ABST: Structural elements which seem to limit and control conflicts in games and sports are examined. How these elements may be developed within sport environments is then discussed. Valuable lessons can be learned (a) from sports and games in non-Western societies where conflict is often controlled by ritual, (b) from the informal games of children, where the play element is maintained, and (c) from the concept of subordinate goals, developed as a way of ensuring association. Finally, these three forms of conflict resolution are demonstrated in the game of rugby football.
LEVEL: A LANG: Eng SIRC ARTICLE NO: 104476

SOCIAL FACILITATION

Jones, J.G. Problems in social facilitation research: an examination of post-1965 studies which have examined audience effects on performance. (Refs: 9)*Physical education review (Manchester) 7(1), Spring 1984, 41-46.*
ABST: The author analyses 35 post-1965 papers published on the social facilitation phenomenon. The main concern of the author is to evaluate the experimental design adopted in each studies. Results indicate a lack of well designed studies. Problems arise in the following categories: a) alone condition, b) questionnaire/interview, c) personality test, and d) level of skills of subjects.
LEVEL: A LANG: Eng SIRC ARTICLE NO: 099334

SPECTATORS

Ryan, A.J. Fans need protection. *Physician and sportsmedicine 12(2), Feb 1984, 43.*
LEVEL: B LANG: Eng SIRC ARTICLE NO: 091857

Shamir, B. Ruskin, H. Sport participation vs. sport spectatorship: two modes of leisure behavior. (Refs: 19)*Journal of leisure research (Alexandria, Va.) 16(1), 1984, 9-21.*

ABST: This paper compares and contrasts sport participation and sport spectatorship in a sample of 480 subjects. The results indicate that the two parameters are unrelated; although there seems to be a trend towards a negative correlation between the two parameters. The results indicate that there are different socialization patterns for participation and for spectatorship. The authors suggest that physical education would contribute to higher levels of physical activity if it became less competitive and more cooperative.
LEVEL: A LANG: Eng SIRC ARTICLE NO: 096381

SUPERSTITION

Zimmer, J. Courting the gods of sport. Athletes use superstition to ward off the devils of injury and bad luck. *Psychology today (New York, N.Y.) 18(7), Jul 1984, 36-39.*
LEVEL: B LANG: Eng SIRC ARTICLE NO: 094669

VIOLENCE

Allard, R. Violence dans la pratique sportive et le droit. (Refs: 21)*Dans, Barnes, J. (ed.), La violence dans les sports et la reforme du droit. Proces-verbal d'une consultation organisee par l'Institute for Studies in Policy, Ethics & Law (I.S.P.E.L.) et la Commission de reforme du droit du Canada..., Ottawa, Carleton University, 1984?, p. 20-26.*
CONF: La violence dans les sports et la reforme du droit (1984 : Ottawa).
LEVEL: I LANG: Fr GV706.7 20192

Brunon, M. La violence et le fair-play: vues theologiques et pastorales. *Jeunes (Paris) 2322, 1984, 12-13.*
LEVEL: B LANG: Fr

Ferreira, F. Violence in sport: lacking of sporting spirit and ethics: the principal reasons for violence. *Bulletin of the Federation internationale d'education physique (Cheltenham, Eng.) 54(1), Jan/Mar 1984, 39-41.*
NOTES: Paper presented at the FIEP-IOA Congress, Olympia, July 1983.
LEVEL: B LANG: Eng SIRC ARTICLE NO: 094742

Gautheron, J. Olivier, G. Borotra, J. Vautrot, J. Vintzel, J. Clare, M. Ostric, A. Piewcewicz, J. Catelin, A. La violence et le fair-play dans le sport, officiels, entraineurs, pratiquants, media: meme combat. *Jeunes (Paris) 2324, 1984, 9-12.*
NOTES: A suivre.
LEVEL: I LANG: Fr

Gautheron, J. Olivier, G. Borotra, J. Vautrot, J. Vintzel, J. Clare, M. Ostric, A. Piewcewicz, J. Catelin, A. La violence et le fair-play dans le sport, officiels, entraineurs, pratiquants, media: meme combat. *Jeunes (Paris) 2325, 1984, 7-8.*
LEVEL: B LANG: Fr

Kamuti, J. Medical aspects of violence at sports events. *Olympic review (Lausanne, Switzerland) 195/196, Jan/Feb 1984, 36-41.*
LEVEL: B LANG: Eng SIRC ARTICLE NO: 094370

Kamuti, J. Aspects medicaux de la violence dans les manifestations sportives. *Revue olympique (Lausanne) 195/196, janv/fevr 1984, 36-41.*
LEVEL: B LANG: Fr SIRC ARTICLE NO: 095935

Letourneau, G. Le role du droit criminel face a la violence sportive. (Refs: 23)*Dans, Barnes, J. (ed.), La violence dans le sports, et la reforme du droit. Proces-verbal d'une consultation organisee par l'Institute for Studies in Policy, Ethics & Law*

(I.S.P.E.L.) et la Commission de reforme du droit du Canada..., Ottawa, Carleton University, 1984?, p. 3-7.
CONF: La violence dans les sports et la reforme du droit (1984 : Ottawa).
LEVEL: I LANG: Fr GV706.7 20192

Marcotte, G. Les medias sportifs et la violence. (Refs: 3)*Revue de l'entraineur (Montreal) juil/sept 1984, 12.*
LEVEL: B LANG: Fr SIRC ARTICLE NO: 102908

Meaney, P. Aggression in sport. (Refs: 10)*Sports coach (Wembley, Australia) 7(4), Mar 1984, 27-30.*
ABST: There is too muc emphasis on winning at all costs rather than on the benefits of sport participation. Such emphasis results in violent aggression. The author classifies aggression into two categories: 1) reactive aggression and 2) instrumental aggression which often involves frustration and anger. The author examines contributing factors to this second type of aggression and suggests several methods which might be used to control the increase of violent aggression in sport.
LEVEL: B LANG: Eng SIRC ARTICLE NO: 094743

Smith, M.D. A typology of sports violence. (Refs: 22)*In, Barnes, J. (ed.), Sports Violence and Law Reform. Proceedings of a consultation organized by the Institute for Studies in Policy, Ethics & Law (I.S.P.E.L.) and the Law Reform Commission of Canada..., Ottawa, Carleton University, 1984?, p. 8-19.*
CONF: Sports Violence and Law Reform (1984 : Ottawa).
LEVEL: A LANG: Eng GV706.7 20192

SOCIAL SCIENCE

Sport history - sport pedagogy and sport philosophy - sport sociology. Scientific program abstracts. Eugene, Or.: University o Oregon, Microform Publications, 1984. 144 p.
CONF: Olympic Scientific Congress (1984 : Eugene, Or.).
NOTES: Cover title.
LEVEL: A LANG: Eng GV701 17863

SOCIOLOGY

Barwick, N.J. Sport - the modern omnibus. The public vehicle for all people. *Sports coach (Wembley, Aust.) 8(1), 1984, 61-62.*
NOTES: An extract from, the Melbourne University Blues address, December 1983.
LEVEL: B LANG: Eng SIRC ARTICLE NO: 096389

Blanc, J. L'etre humain - le jeu - le sport. *Macolin (Suisse) 8, aout 1984, 18-19.*
LEVEL: B LANG: Fr SIRC ARTICLE NO: 101001

Booth, B. Sport and political autonomy. *OPHEA: Ontario Physical and Health Education Association (London, Ont.) 10(2), Spring 1984, 57-75.*
LEVEL: I LANG: Eng SIRC ARTICLE NO: 099332

Center for the Study of Sport in Society. *Arena review (Boston) 8(3), Nov 1984, 70-75.*
LEVEL: B LANG: Eng SIRC ARTICLE NO: 104467

Chorbajian, L. Toward a marxist sociology of sport: an assessment and a preliminary agenda. (Refs: 32)*Arena review (Boston) 8(3), Nov 1984,* 55-69.
LEVEL: I LANG: Eng SIRC ARTICLE NO: 104468

Curry, T.J. Jiobu, R.M. Sports: a social perspective. Englewood Cliffs, N.J.: Prentice-Hall, c1984. xii, 260 p. : ill.
NOTES: Includes bibliographical references and index.
LEVEL: I LANG: Eng ISBN: 0138378231 LC CARD: 83-013750 GV706.5 17141

Delaunay, M. Voyage au centre de la sociologie du sport. *Loisirs sante (Paris) 10, juin/juil/aout 1984, 10-13.*
LEVEL: B LANG: Fr SIRC ARTICLE NO: 104469

Drake, G.A. Deminoff, W. Sports and the national character: proceedings of a symposium held at Grinnell College. Grinnell, Iowa: Grinnell College, 1984?. vii, 133 p.
CONF: Symposium on Sports and the National Character (1984 : Grinnell, Iowa).
NOTES: Cover title.
LEVEL: I LANG: Eng LC CARD: 85-117536 GV706.5 20741

Eichberg, H. Olympic sport - neocolonization and alternatives. *International review for the sociology of sport (Munich) 19(1), 1984, 97-106.*
ABST: Olympism is more than just an ideology or organizational concept of international sport, also more than the economic interests connected with it. In it a social pattern materializes which forms everyday life above and beyond sport - the everyday culture of the western (and east European) industrial society. However, it fails to reckon with extra-European peoples. If today a new anticolonial movement emerges in the name of 'cultural identity', what does that mean for sport? In four areas of physical culture, so it seems, alternatives are developing: national cultural games, the open air movement, expressional activities and meditative exercises.
LEVEL: I LANG: Eng SIRC ARTICLE NO: 104471

Eitzen, D.S. Conflict theory and the sociology of sport. (Refs: 52)*Arena review (Boston) 8(3), Nov 1984, 45-54.*
LEVEL: I LANG: Eng SIRC ARTICLE NO: 104472

Guttmann, A. The sociological imagination and the imaginative sociologist.
CONF: North American Society for the Sociology o Sport. Conference (3rd : 1982 : Toronto, Ont.).
NOTES: In, Theberge, N. and Donnelly, P. (eds.), Sport and the sociological imagination: refereed proceedings of the 3rd Annual Conference of the North American Society for the Sociology of Sport, Toronto, Canada, November 1982, Fort Worth, Tex., Texas Christian University Press, c1984, p. 4-20.
LEVEL: I LANG: Eng SIRC ARTICLE NO: 097844

Hughes, R. Coakley, J. Mass society and the commercialization of sport. (Refs: 7)*Sociology of sport journal (Champaign, III 1(1), 1984, 57-63.*
LEVEL: I LANG: Eng SIRC ARTICLE NO: 108347

Linhart, J. (Contemporary bourgeois sociology of sports.) (Refs: 57)*Sociologicky casopis (Prague) 20(2), 1984, 156-173.*
LEVEL: I LANG: Cze

McKay, J. Pearson, K. Objectives, strategies, and ethics in teaching introductory courses in sociology of sport. (Refs: 95) *Quest (Champaign, III.) 36(2), 1984, 134-146.*
ABST: This paper presents strategies that have been useful in helping undergraduates develop a critical view of sport. This is usually a difficult taks in teaching introductory students with backgrounds in physical education, kinesiology, and human movement studies because they tend to have a positive, uncritical perspective of sport. Such students often react in an incredulous or hostile fashion when sociologists present evidence that questions or contradicts typical assumptions about sport. It is argued that the fundamental objective in teaching sociology of sport and sociology through sport is to help students develop what Bierstedt terms the 'liberated mind'. Some teaching strategies are then presented to help students grasp the rudimentary principles of thinking critically about sport. Finally, some ethical problems that arise from teaching sociology of sport in this way are discussed.
LEVEL: I LANG: Eng SIRC ARTICLE NO: 102910

Pereira Da Costa, L. Once and for all, what is sports for all? *World leisure and recreation association journal (New York) 26(4), Jul 1984, 16-19.*
LEVEL: B LANG: Eng SIRC ARTICLE NO: 101014

Sansot, P. (Sociology based on sporting emotions). *Cahiers internationaux de sociologie (Paris) 77, juil 1984, 323-338.*
LEVEL: I LANG: Fr

Theberge, N. Donnelly, P. Sport and the sociological imagination: refereed proceedings of the 3rd Annual Conference of the North American Society for the Sociology of Sport, Toronto, Canada, November 1982. Fort Worth, Tex.: Texas Christian University Press, c1984. xv, 384 p.
CONF: North American Society for the Sociology of Sport. Conference (3rd : 1982 : Toronto, Ont.)
CORP: North American Society for the Sociology of Sport.
NOTES: Includes bibliographical references.
LEVEL: A LANG: Eng ISBN: 0912646837 LC CARD: 83-018123 GV706.5 17842

Theberge, N. On the need for a more adequate theory of sport participation. (Refs: 35)*Sociology of sport journal (Champaign III.) 1(1), 1984, 26-35.*
ABST: The purpose of this paper is to review and critique the major approaches to the analysis of participation in sport, and to present suggestions for new approaches offering more useful bases for the explanation and understanding of the participation phenomenon. Past research has focused on the characteristics and backgrounds of sport participants or on the process of socialization into sport roles. Emplying the thecretical guidelines provided by Giddens, it is recommended that future research be based on a conceptualization of participation as a process by which men and women actively create their sporting lives within the constraints of participantion as a process by which men and women actively create their sporting lives within the constraints of particular social and political structures. Examples of this approach are provided and the implications of the approach are discussed.
LEVEL: A LANG: Eng SIRC ARTICLE NO: 108343

Young, T.R. The sociology of sport: a critical overview. (Refs: 15)*Arena review (Boston) 8(3), Nov 1984, 1-14.*
LEVEL: I LANG: Eng SIRC ARTICLE NO: 104481

SOCIOLOGY (continued)

ATTITUDE AND PUBLIC OPINION

Duquin, M.E. Social justice in sport: the norm of expected inequity. (Refs: 17)
CONF: North American Society for the Sociology of Sport. Conference (3rd : 1982 : Toronto, Ont.).
NOTES: In, Theberge, N. and Donnelly, P. (eds.), Sport and the sociological imagination: refereed proceedings of the 3rd Annual Conference of the North American Society for the Sociology of Sport, Toronto, Canada, November 1982, Fort Worth, Tex., Texas Christian University Press, c1984, p. 177-189.
ABST: 128 middle class high school students aged 14 to 18 equally divided between male and female athletes and non-athletes evaluated 6 sport scenarios depicting conflict between a member of an athletic department and an athlete. The results shed light on how students perceive social justice in the field of sports. Injustice was viewed as less serious if an athlete was a willing participant while injustice was felt to be more serious when a formal law or rule was violated.
LEVEL: A LANG: Eng SIRC ARTICLE NO: 097842

BIBLIOGRAPHIES

Annotated bibliography: sport and social stratification, 1976-1983. *Sociology of sport journal (Champaign, Ill.) 1(2), 1984, 201-211.*
LEVEL: B LANG: Eng SIRC ARTICLE NO: 102907

CROSS-CULTURAL STUDIES

Chick, G.E. The cross-cultural study of games. (Refs: 104)*Exercise and sport sciences reviews (Lexington, Mass.) 12, 1984, 307-337.*
ABST: This paper deals with the cross-cultural comparative study of games, emphasizing those played by adults. The history, theoretical developments, and problems of cross-cultural comparative game research are addressed. The author believes that the cross-cultural study of games has reflected the changing theory, methods, and substantive interests of the field of anthropology over approximately the last century. The major finding of this research has been the observation of a positive correlation between the number and complexity of games in a culture and various measures of the complexity of the culture.
LEVEL: A LANG: Eng SIRC ARTICLE NO: 096390

ETHNIC GROUPS

Cheska, A.T. Sport as ethnic boundary maintenance: a case of the American Indian. (Refs: 45)*International review for the sociology of sport (Warszawa, Poland) 19(3/4), 1984, 241-257.*
ABST: An ethnic group's members select and translate into social boundaries cultural behaviors that support the group's values. By using sport contact situations between Navajo Indians and Euro-Americans in a 1903 Fourth of July festival and present basketball participation, it is shown that the content and form signaling ethnic boundaries changed over time from traditional Indian sports to Euro-American sport participation. An analysis of these inter-ethnic sports encounters showed that the ethnic group members' perception, selection, and expression of changing behavioral content continually reinforced ethnic diversity.
LEVEL: A LANG: Eng SIRC ARTICLE NO: 105578

Cowan, W. Papers of the fifteenth Algonquian Conference. Ottawa: Carleton University, 1984. viii, 467 p.
CONF: Algonquian Conference (15th : 1983 : Cambridge, Mass.).
LEVEL: A LANG: Eng ISBN: 0-7709-0165-4 GV585 18629

Scholtz, G.J.L. Olivier, J.L. Attitude of urban South Africans toward non-racial sport and their expectations of future race relations - a comparative study. (Refs: 20)*International review for the sociology of sport (Munich) 19(2), 1984, 129-143.*
CONF: Olympic Scientific Congress (1984 : Eugene, Ore.).
ABST: In 1983 a random sample drawn from the larger urban communities and including 962 Blacks, 943 Indians, 789 Coloureds and 697 Whites, revealed that the majority of urban South Africans strongly favoured non-racial sport at national and club competition levels. For the first time in history, differences occurring between the attitude profile of the four main ethnic groups were non-significant. Attitudes of Whites still tended to be more conservative and have regressed since 1980/81. The attitude pattern of Blacks, Coloureds and Indians was the most homogeneous. A certain amount of ambivalence became evident between present attitudes and more positive expectations of change within the country.
LEVEL: A LANG: Eng SIRC ARTICLE NO: 104477

EX-ATHLETES

Dickie, D. Le defi d'une carriere. Meeting the employment challenge. *Champion (Ottawa) 8(4),* Nov 1984, 46-49.
LEVEL: B LANG: Fr Eng SIRC ARTICLE NO: 101008

Lerch, S. Athletic retirement as social death: an overview. (Refs: 13)
CONF: North American Society for the Sociology of Sport. Conference (3rd : 1982 : Toronto, Ont.).
NOTES: In, Theberge, N. and Donnelly, P. (eds.), Sport and the sociological imagination: refereed proceedings of the 3rd Annual Conference of the North American Society for the Sociology of Sport, Toronto, Canada, November 1982, Fort Worth, Tex., Texas Christian University Press, c1984, p. 259-272.
ABST: This paper examines the issue of athletic retirement through an analogy with death and its various stages.
LEVEL: A LANG: Eng SIRC ARTICLE NO: 097846

Lerch, S. The adjustment of athletes to career ending injuries. (Refs: 23)*Arena review 8(1), Mar 1984, 54-67.*
NOTES: Special issue: sport and disability.
LEVEL: A LANG: Eng SIRC ARTICLE NO: 103711

Pawlak, A. The status and style of life of Polish Olympians after completion of their sports careers. (Refs: 22) *International review for the sociology of sport (Munich) 19(2), 1984, 169-183.*
ABST: The private and professional lives of 240 out of a total of 838 Polish Olympians who participated in the Olympics from 1948 to 1972 were studied in detail. Different types of relationships between educational advancement and a career in sport are outlined. Three types of former Olympians are described with reference to the way in which they perceive their role as athletes and representatives of the Polish society. Former top athletes retain a

high social status and engage in notable activities in social and cultural life. The tendency to compare the current social position with that attained as an Olympian permeates all spheres of life.
LEVEL: A LANG: Eng SIRC ARTICLE NO: 104474

Rosenberg, E. Athletic retirement as social death: concepts and perspectives. (Refs: 27)
CONF: North American Society for th Sociology of Sport. Conference (3rd : 1982 : Toronto, Ont.).
NOTES: In, Theberge, N. and Donnelly, P. (eds.), Sport and the sociological imagination: refereed proceedings of the 3rd Annual Conference of the North American Society for the Sociology of Sport, Toronto, Canada, November 1982, Fort Worth, Tex., Texas Christian University Press, c1984, p. 245-258.
ABST: This article focuses on the treatment of an athlete upon retiring, being cut, or finally waived. Social, structural and psychological forces are discussed along with counseling strategies.
LEVEL: A LANG: Eng SIRC ARTICLE NO: 097850

Vamplew, W. Close of play: career termination in English professional sport 1870-1914. (Refs: 54)*Canadian journal of histor of sport/Revue canadienne de l'histoire des sports (Windsor) 15(1), May 1984, 64-79.*
ABST: This paper is a study of the causes of career cessation, the career lengths, and the post-playing problems of English professional athletes in horse racing, football, soccer, and cricket for the years 1870-1914. Athletes had very little job security because their contracts were usually only one year in length or, as in the case of jockeys, were nonexistent. There were three main causes for a career to end: injury, usurpation by competing athletes, and misbehaviour of the athlete, such as drunkeness, breaking club rules, and criticizing superiors. Football players had the shortest careers, half lasting only one year, while nearly half of the rugby players lasted over three seasons. Cricket was comparable to rugby in that approximately 50 percent of players played for over 3 years. But the upper limit of a career for cricket was 20 years or more, while rugby players rarely lasted over 12 years. Only 40 percent of jockeys became licensed and of these only about 30 percent lasted for over 3 years of a licensed career, although 8 percent lasted for over 20 years. Little is known of the post-play lives of the athletes except that most were forgotten, many went broke and with poor chances of employment, particularly if injured, and only a few remained in the sport as coaches, trainers and assistants.
LEVEL: A LANG: Eng SIRC ARTICLE NO: 108316

LIFESTYLE

Blair, S. Sport permeates all lifestyles - it may be our lifestyle. *Journal of physical education and program (Columbus, Oh.) 81(4), Apr 1984, D12-D13.*
LEVEL: B LANG: Eng SIRC ARTICLE NO: 094741

MARRIAGE

Foeldesi, T. Marriage chances and social status of top female athletes in Hungary. (Refs: 32)*International review for the sociology of sport (Munich) 19(1), 1984, 47-61.*
ABST: The significance of the study of marriage chances of top female athletes extends beyond the private sphere. Marriage chances may influence the probability of reaching the status of top athlete, the

early conclusion of sports careers and the course of life subsequent to such careers. They may indirectly affect even the quality of top female sport in a given country. The marriage chances of top female athletes were analyzed on the basis of complex empirical study carried out among Hungarian participants in the Olympic Games between 1948 and 1976. This analysis concludes with a comparison of the marriage opportunities for top female and male athletes.
LEVEL: A LANG: Eng SIRC ARTICLE NO: 104473

RACE RELATIONS

Dickey, G. The professor of protest: Harry Edwards speaks truth, but it's too painful for whites - and many blacks. *Inside sports (Evanston, III.)* 6, Nov 1984, 78-84;86-87.
LEVEL: B LANG: Eng SIRC ARTICLE NO: 102916

Edwards, H. The black 'Dumb Jock': an American sports tragedy. *College board review (New York)* 131, Spring 1984, 8-13.
LEVEL: I LANG: Eng SIRC ARTICLE NO: 104470

Gilmore, A.T. Jack Johnson: a magnificent black anachronism of the early twentieth century. (Refs: 45)
NOTES: In, Riess, S.A (ed.), The American sporting experience: a historical anthology of sport in America, New York, Leisure Press, c1984, p. 306-315. Previously published in, Journal of social and behavioural sciences 19, Winter 1973, p. 35-42.
LEVEL: I LANG: Eng GV583 17631

Janis, L. Annotated bibliography on minority women in athletics. Alexandria, Va.: Computer Microfilm International, 1984. 1 microfiche (13 fr.)
NOTES: Bibliography: (131).
LEVEL: A LANG: Eng EDRS: ED246010

Lapchick, R.E. Broken promises: racism in American sports. 1st ed. New York: St. Martin's/ Marek, c1984. x, 257 p.
LEVEL: B LANG: Eng ISBN: 0312105924 LC CARD: 83-024803 GV706.8 17654

Rees, C.R. Miracle, A.W. Participation in sport and the reduction of racial prejudices: contact theory, superordinate goals hypothesis or wishful thinking?
CONF: North American Society for the Sociology of Sport. Conference (3rd : 1982 : Toronto, Ont.).
NOTES: In, Theberge, N. and Donnelly, P. (eds.), Sport and the sociological imagination: refereed proceedings of the 3rd Annual Conference of the North American Society for the Sociology of Sport, Toronto, Canada, November 1982, Fort Worth, Tex., Texas Christian University Press, c1984, p. 140-152.
ABST: The authors examine two theories which have been used to suggest that participation on a biracial team leads to a reduction in racial prejudice. The contact theory has been empirically tested with mixed results in non-sport settings and this paper discusses the difficulty of meeting the conditions of forming a group to reduce prejudice when a team is formed with the primary goal of winning competitions. The second theory, the superordinate goal, if applicable to the sport situation has the potential to increase racial tension through spacegoaling as well as reduce it through the satisfaction of seeing the goal achieved. The paper ends by examining the implications of using these methodologies in the measurement of racial tolerance in sport.
LEVEL: A LANG: Eng SIRC ARTICLE NO: 097849

Robinson, J. Smith, W. Jackie Robinson's first spring training.
NOTES: In, Riess, S.A. (ed.), The American sporting experience: a historical anthology of sport in America, New York, Leisure Press, c1984, p. 365-370. Excerpt from: Jackie Robinson: my own story, by Jack R. Robinson and Wendell Smith, New York, Greenberg, 1948, p. 65-68;70-75;79-80.
LEVEL: B LANG: Eng GV583 17631

RESEARCH

Hollands, R.G. The role of cultural studies and social criticism in the sociological study of sport. (Refs: 66)*Quest (Champaign, III.)* 36(1), 1984, 66-79.
LEVEL: I LANG: Eng SIRC ARTICLE NO: 099333

Tomlinson, A. The sociological imagination, the new journalism, and sport. (Refs: 24)
CONF: North American Society for the Sociology of Sport. Conference (3rd : 1982 : Toronto, Ont.).
NOTES: In, Theberge, N. and Donnelly, P. (eds.), Sport and the sociological imagination: refereed proceedings of the 3rd Annual Conference of the North American Society for the Sociology of Sport, Toronto, Canada, November 1982, Fort Worth, Tex., Texas Christian University Press, c1984, p. 21-39.
ABST: The author attempts to show how far-reaching the sociological imagination is and demonstrates some of the qualities and defects of the new journalism as a source of information.
LEVEL: A LANG: Eng SIRC ARTICLE NO: 097851

RESEARCH METHODS

Perun, R. Career contingencies: examining patterns of involvement. (Refs: 65)
CONF: North American Society for the Sociology of Sport. Conference (3rd : 1982 : Toronto, Ont.).
NOTES: In, Theberge, N. and Donnelly, P. (eds.), Sport and the sociological imagination: refereed proceedings of the 3rd Annual Conference of the North American Society for the Sociology of Sport, Toronto, Canada, November 1982, Fort Worth, Tex., Texas Christian University Press, c1984, p. 297-317.
ABST: This paper discusses the contingencies affecting initial involvement, continuities and disinvolvements of people within roles or careers. It provides a theoretical outline of the concept of career contingencies which lends itself to sport and leisure applications.
LEVEL: A LANG: Eng SIRC ARTICLE NO: 097848

RITUAL

Park, R.J. Boys into men - state into nation: rites de passage in student life and college athletics, 1890-1905. (Refs: 22)
NOTES: In, Sutton-Smith, B. and Kelly-Byrne, D. (eds.), The masks of play, New York, Leisure Press, c1984, p. 51-62.
LEVEL: I LANG: Eng HQ782 17029

SEX ROLES

Beamish, R. Materialism and the comprehension of gender-related issues in sport. (Refs: 41)
CONF: North American Society for the Sociology of Sport. Conference (3rd : 1982 : Toronto, Ont.).
NOTES: In, Theberge, N. and Donnelly, P. (eds.), Sport and the sociological imagination: refereed proceedings of the 3rd Annual Conference of the

North American Society for the Sociology of Sport, Toronto, Canada, November 1982, Fort Worth, Tex., Texas Christian University Press, c1984, p. 60-81.
ABST: This paper discusses the theoretical implications of materialism, and the notions of a theoretical or problematic tableau and of dialectic. These are applied to three issues of gender and sport participation opportunity: value-form of production; social class and, the media image of sport.
LEVEL: A LANG: Eng SIRC ARTICLE NO: 097839

Oglesby, C.A. Interactions between gender identity and sport.
NOTES: In, Silva, J.M. and Weinberg, R.S. (eds.), Psychological foundations of sport, Champaign, III., Human Kinetics Publishers, c1984, p. 387-399.
LEVEL: A LANG: Eng GV706.4 17779

Rao, V.V.P. Overman, S.J. Sex role perceptions among black female athletes and nonathletes. (Refs: 20)*Sex roles (New York)* 11(7/8), 1984, 601-614.
LEVEL: A LANG: Eng SIRC ARTICLE NO: 104523

Segal, J.D. Weinberg, R.S. Sex, sex role orientation and competitive trait anxiety. (Refs: 16)*Journal of sport behavior (Mobile, Ala.)* 7(4), Dec 1984, 153-159.
ABST: The purpose of the present investigation was to provide a more definitive assessment of the relationship between sex, sex role orientation and CTA. Subjects were 166 female and 125 male undergraduates who completed the Bem Sex Role Inventory and the SCAT with the order of administration of these two scales counter-balanced. Results indicated no significant order effect, and, therefore, a 2 x 4 (sex by sex role) ANOVA was conducted with SCAT serving as the dependent measure. Results yielded a main effect for sex with females exhibiting significantly higher levels of CTA than males. However, the main effect of sex role orientation and the sex x sex role orientation interaction did not reach significance. The finding that females exhibit higher levels of CTA than males consonants with previous literature and may reflect a difference in socialization into competitive sports. Although statistically significant, both male and female mean scores for competitive trait anxiety fell within the moderate range. Future directions for research are offered.
LEVEL: A LANG: Eng SIRC ARTICLE NO: 100947

SOCIAL CLASS

Ahde, M. International workers' sport as a means of bringing people together. *In, Ilmarinen, M. (ed.) et al., Sport and International Understanding: proceedings of the congress held in Helsinki, Finland, July 7-10, 1982, Berlin, Springer-Verlag, 1984, p. 180-185.*
CONF: Congress on Sport and International Understanding (1982 : Helsinki).
LEVEL: I LANG: Eng GV706.8 18979

Dixon, M.J. Participation in physical activity: option or privilege? (Refs: 20)*CAHPER journal (Ottawa)* 51(1), Sept/Oct 1984 13-17.
LEVEL: I LANG: Eng SIRC ARTICLE NO: 101003

Riordan, J. The Workers' Olympics. *In, Tomlinson, A. and Whannel, G. (eds.), Five-ring circus. Money, power and politics at the Olympic Games, London, Pluto Press, c1984, p. 98-112.*
LEVEL: B LANG: Eng GV721.5 18892

SOCIOLOGY (continued)

Wanat, S. Sociological research on the physical culture of the Polish working class. (Refs: 30)*International review for the sociology of sport (Munich) 19(1), 1984, 83-96.*
ABST: This report deals with Polish sociological research on working class physical culture. Its development after the last World War is compared with the period between the two World Wars, information about the latter being available mainly from memoirs. Modern findings in the sociology of sport are often a by-product of research in cultural or industrial sociology. The significance of physical culture and sport for the working class subculture, in consideration of its relative disinterest in other cultural opportunities, is discussed, as well as the interest and participation of today's Polish labor force in sports activities.
LEVEL: A LANG: Eng SIRC ARTICLE NO: 104478

SOCIAL STATUS

Luechen, G. Status crystallization, social class, integration and sport. (Refs: 26)*International review for the sociology o sport (Warszawa, Poland) 19(3/4), 1984, 283-294.*
ABST: Consistent with Lenski's theory of status crystallization, a pilot study shows that athletes have comparatively low status crystallization; moreover, those with high levels of performance crystallize even lower. Contary to Lenski, low-crystallized individuals try to gain influence in their groups and clubs, while the high-crystallized show more general social contacts and enjoy higher prestige. Athletes make criticisms of the existing social class system, particularly among those with low status crystallization.
LEVEL: A LANG: Eng SIRC ARTICLE NO: 105583

SOCIALIZATION

McPherson, B.D. Sport participation across the life cycle: a review of the literature and suggestions for future research. (Refs: 66)*Sociology of sport journal (Champaign, Ill.) 1(3), 1984, 213-230.*
ABST: To provide baseline information for futures studies pertaining to sport participation and aging, this paper summarizes the literature on sport participation patterns across the life cycle, briefly describes the importance of analyzing aging as a social process, and argues that alternative theoretical frameworks including a life-span developmental perspective should be utilized in future studies. The paper also introduces a number of theoretical and methodological issues that should be addressed concerning research in this area, and raises a variety of research questions that must be pursued in order to better understand sport phenomena from a life cycle perspective, especially during the middle and later years of life.
LEVEL: A LANG: Eng SIRC ARTICLE NO: 102911

Yamaguchi, Y. A comparative study of adolescent socialization into sport: the case of Japan and Canada. (Refs: 29) *International review for the sociology of sport (Munich) 19(1), 1984, 63-82.*
ABST: This paper compares the process of adolescent socialization into sport in Japan and Canada, focussing on the structural and cultural differences and similarities. Results from national survey data indicate that the school is a strong socializing agent in Japan, while the sport system within the community has more influence on sport involvement in Canada. It is suggested that sport socialization in Japan is unique in that it arises from a closed structure, as compared to the open

structure in Canada.
LEVEL: A LANG: Eng SIRC ARTICLE NO: 104480

SOCIOCULTURAL FACTORS

de Noblet, J. Sport et deregulation. *Dans, Culture technique no. 13, Neuilly-sur-Seine, France, Centre de Recherche sur la Culture Technique, c1984, p. 8-16.*
LEVEL: I LANG: Fr RC1235 20096

Mandell, R.D. Sport: a cultural history. New York: Columbia University Press, 1984. xx, 340 p. : ill.
NOTES: Includes index Bibliography: p. 305-330.
LEVEL: I LANG: Eng ISBN: 023105470X LC CARD: 83-020017 GV706.5 17103

Mandell, R.D. Sport - a cultural history. New York: Colombia University Press, c1984. xx, 340 p.
NOTES: Includes bibliographical essays.
LEVEL: A LANG: Eng ISBN: 0-231-05470-X LC CARD: 83-20017 GV706.5 21001

Whitson, D. Sport and hegemony: on the construction of the dominant culture. (Refs: 46)*Sociology of sport journal (Champaign, Ill.) 1(1), 1984, 64-78.*
NOTES: Revised version of a paper delivered to the 7th Commonwealth Conference on Sport, Physical Education and Recreation, Brisbane, Australia.
ABST: This paper seeks to analyze the contribution of sport to a common sense acceptance of the performance principles, and its associated discipline and accountability, as natural and indeed valuable features of social life. It will be our purpose, furthermore, to argue that a conceptual framework incorporating the ideas of 'hegemony', structure of feeling', and 'dominant, residual, and emergent' cultures, offers significant analytical advantages over frameworks based on more straightforward notions of socialization and social control.
LEVEL: A LANG: Eng SIRC ARTICLE NO: 108348

THEORY

Goodger, J. Sport as a sociological concept, an old discussion revisited. (Refs: 6)*International journal of physical education (Schorndorf, W. Germany) 21(2), 19-26 Jul 1984, 32-33.*
LEVEL: I LANG: Eng SIRC ARTICLE NO: 097843

VALUES

Cagigal, J.M. The educational values of Olympism. *Bulletin of the Federation internationale d'education physique (Cheltenham, Eng.) 54(1), Jan/Mar 1984, 31-36.*
LEVEL: I LANG: Eng SIRC ARTICLE NO: 094478

Pooley, J.C. Physical education and sport and the quality of life. *Journal of physical education, recreation & dance 55(3), Mar 1984, 45-48.*
LEVEL: B LANG: Eng SIRC ARTICLE NO: 093215

SOFTBALL

Meyer, R.G. Complete book of softball: the loonies' guide to playing and enjoying the game. New York: Leisure Press, c1984. 191 p. : ill.
NOTES: Bibliography: p. 190.
LEVEL: B LANG: Eng ISBN: 0880112123 LC CARD: 83-80707 GV881 15868

Wolcott, B. Albrecht, R. Baseball and softball: a mid-season update. *Spotlight (East Lansing, Mich.)*

7(2), Summer 1984, 3-4.
LEVEL: B LANG: Eng SIRC ARTICLE NO: 097932

BIOGRAPHY AND AUTOBIOGRAPHY

Ellerbee, T. Darby's dream: What's left? Now that Darby Cottle has captured every softball award possible, what is there lef for her in the sport? The chance to compete, and the opportunity to do it all over again. *Olympian (Colorado Springs, Colo.) 9(2), Jul/Aug 1984, 12-13.*
LEVEL: B LANG: Eng SIRC ARTICLE NO: 104899

Newman, S. Polishing a diamond in the rough. How a teenage farm girl has developed into one of the best softball pitchers in Canada. *Coaching review (Ottawa, Ont.) 7, May/Jun 1984, 27-29.*
LEVEL: B LANG: Eng SIRC ARTICLE NO: 095275

BIOMECHANICS

Messier, S. Biomechanical analysis of the softball stride. This analysis of three types of batting strides supports the theory that differences in performance may be related to the method of striding the batter uses. (Refs: 2)*Athletic journal (Evanston, Ill.) 65(1), Aug 1984, 42-43.*
LEVEL: I LANG: Eng SIRC ARTICLE NO: 096840

Messier, S.P. Owen, M.G. Bat dynamics of female fast pitch softball batters. (Refs: 15)*Research quarterly for exercise & sport (Reston, Va.) 55(2), Jun 1984, 141-145.*
ABST: This descriptive study examined the bat dynamics of eight female fast pitch softball batters. The swings of these eight batters were recorded for later analyses using three-dimensional cinematography. The results suggest that there may be a difference between optimal baseball and softball batting techniques, a smaller reaction as a result of the shorter pitching difference in softball as compared to baseball.
LEVEL: A LANG: Eng SIRC ARTICLE NO: 096841

CHILDREN

Jouons a la balle. s.l.: Maple Leaf : Softball Canada, 1984?. (16) p. : ill. (Programme d'initiation au softball.)
CORP: Softball Canada.
CORP: Maple Leaf.
NOTES: Titre de la couverture. Also published in English under the title: Let's play ball.
LEVEL: B LANG: Fr GV881 18496

Let's play ball. s.l.: Maple Leaf : Softball Canada, 1984?. (16) p. : ill. (Softball skills program.)
CORP: Maple Leaf.
CORP Softball Canada.
NOTES: Cover title. Aussi publie en francais sous le titre: Jouons a la balle.
LEVEL: B LANG: Eng GV881 18497

COACHING

Ferris, W.N. Saving split-seconds in the field. *Scholastic coach (New York) 54(5), Dec 1984, 60-61.*
LEVEL: B LANG: Eng SIRC ARTICLE NO: 103467

Hendon, C.F. Job satisfaction of softball coaches at California two-year colleges. Eugene, Ore.: Microform Publications, Univeristy of Oregon, 1984. 1 microfiche : negative ; 11 x 15 cm.
NOTES: Thesis (M.S.) - University of Oregon, 1983;

(ix, 67 leaves); vita; includes bibliography.
LEVEL: A LANG: Eng UO84 394

Laschen, D. Winning softball ideas. *Women's coaching clinic 7(7), Mar 1984, 9-12.*
LEVEL: B LANG: Eng SIRC ARTICLE NO: 092400

Pastore, D. Hesse, H. The softball switch: slowpitch to fastpitch. (Refs: 3)*Florida JOHPERD (Gainesville, Fla.) 22(4), Nov 1984, 3-4;25.*
LEVEL: B LANG: Eng SIRC ARTICLE NO: 106066

Wenk, R.B. Coaching youth softball. New York: Leisure Press, c1984. 368 p. : ill.
LEVEL: I LANG: Eng ISBN: 0880111968 LC CARD: 83-80784 GV881.4.C6 18011

EQUIPMENT - RETAILING

Marnell, G. Softball bat market is 'go' for growth: softball sheds its 'second cousin' status in the team goods business. *Sports merchandiser (Atlanta, Ga.) 16(12), Dec 1984, 36-38;40-41.*
LEVEL: B LANG: Eng SIRC ARTICLE NO: 104903

Picking up speed. (slow pitch) *Sports trade Canada (Downsview, Ont.) 12(8), Nov/Dec 1984, 14;16.*
LEVEL: B LANG: Eng SIRC ARTICLE NO: 173161

FACILITIES - DESIGN, CONSTRUCTION AND PLANNING

Ball fields. Winnipeg?: Department of Culture, Heritage and Recreation, (1984). 1 kit
CORP: Manitoba. Department of Culture, Heritage and Recreation.
NOTES: Cover title.
LEVEL: B LANG: Eng GV413 17371

HISTORY

Porter, D.E. Le softball. *Revue olympique (Lausanne) 198, avr 1984, 265-266.*
LEVEL: B LANG: Fr SIRC ARTICLE NO: 096842

Porter, D.E. Softball. *Olympic review (Lausanne) 198, Apr 1984, 265-266.*
LEVEL: B LANG: Eng SIRC ARTICLE NO: 096843

INJURIES AND ACCIDENTS

Alabama - 'no amount of evidence would be sufficient to allow the plaintiff to recover'. *Sports and the courts (Winston-Salem N.C.) 5(1), Winter 1984, 9-10.*
LEVEL: B LANG: Eng SIRC ARTICLE NO: 094502

Coblentz, T. Softball. *In, Adams, S.H. (ed.), et al., Catastrophic injuries in sports: avoidance strategies, Salinas, Calif., Cayote Press, c1984, p. 53-58.*
LEVEL: B LANG: Eng RD97 19088

Ichioka, T. Hara, T. Tashiro, T. (A case of subretinal hemorrhage due to a softball injury.) *Josai shika daigaku kiyo/Bulletin of the Josai Dental University (Sakado) 13(3), 1984, 668-674.*
NOTES: English abstract.
LEVEL: A LANG: Jpn

Wheeler, B.R. Slow-pitch softball injuries. (Refs: 5)*American journal of sports medicine (Baltimore) 12(3), May/Jun 1984, 237-240.*
ABST: This investigation was done to describe the nature of injuries which occur in league, slow-pitch baseball, and analyze their causes. Information on 93 injuries, in 83 athletes, referred to an orthopaedic clinic, were recorded for one year. The results indicated that 84 per cent of the total number of injuries to slow-pitch softball athletes could be classified into three types; sliding injuries (42 per cent) jamming injuries (25 per cent), and falling injuries (17 per cent). A review of inpatient data from the Army from 1975 to 1981 was also included. The author suggested that many of these injuries are preventable through a number of possible equipment changes, as well as, better coaching of techniques.
LEVEL: A LANG: Eng SIRC ARTICLE NO: 103469

OFFICIATING

Krause, K. On dealing with umpires. *Softball world (Oakland, Calif.) 8(4), Aug 1984, 7.*
LEVEL: B LANG: Eng SIRC ARTICLE NO: 098512

Narol, M. Recent cases: player injuries and the official. *Referee (Franksville, Wis.) 9(9), Sept 1984, 14.*
LEVEL: B LANG: Eng SIRC ARTICLE NO: 101525

Tapp, G. A dollar short. When denied a 1$ fee hike, the Racine Umpires' Assn. struck the city. A few days later a meeting wa held at which Jim Molbeck urged the RUA to return to work. They did not until the group's president, Earl Hearn resigned. *Referee (Franksville, Wis.) 9(8), Aug 1984, 48-53;59.*
LEVEL: B LANG: Eng SIRC ARTICLE NO: 098514

PSYCHOLOGY

Horn, T.S. Expectancy effects in the interscholastic athletic setting: metodological considerations. (Refs: 26)*Sport psychology (Champaign, Ill.) 6(1), 1984, 60-76.*
ABST: Researchers investigating expectancy effects in academic as well as motor skills contexts have consistently found differences in instructors' behavior towards high-and low-expectancy children. However, certain methodological problems which have recently been identified may limit the interpretation of such differential behaviors as evidence of instructor bias. The present study was conducted to examine expectancy effects in the athletic setting by directly testing three of these methodological issues. The instructional behaviors of five junior high softball coaches were recorded seperately for practice and game situations using the Coaching Behavior Assessment System. Multivariate statistical analyses of coaching behaviors revealed that low-expectancy athletes received more praise for success and more general and corrective instruction in game situations than did high-expectancy athletes.
LEVEL: A LANG: Eng SIRC ARTICLE NO: 108485

STRATEGY - DEFENSIVE

Vance, K.A. Executing the rundown play. The idea is to put out the runner and prevent other runners from advancing. *Scholastic coach (New York) 53(10), May/Jun 1984, 90-92.*
LEVEL: B LANG: Eng SIRC ARTICLE NO: 095278

STRATEGY - OFFENSIVE

Zwingraf, B. Eleven offensive plays for winning softball. *Women's coaching clinic (Princeton, N.J.) 7(9), May 1984, 10-12.*
LEVEL: B LANG: Eng SIRC ARTICLE NO: 095280

TECHNIQUES AND SKILLS - BASERUNNING

King, M.A. Steal: your way to victory. *Athletic journal (Evanston, Ill.), 65(5), Dec 1984, 24;47.*
LEVEL: B LANG: Eng SIRC ARTICLE NO: 104902

Stock, P. Advanced baserunning in fastpitch softball. *Scholastic coach 53(7), Feb 1984, 56-58;80.*
LEVEL: B LANG: Eng SIRC ARTICLE NO: 093763

TECHNIQUES AND SKILLS - BATTER AND BATTING

Matz, D. How to treat that slow-bat syndrome. *Scholastic coach (New York) 54(4), Nov 1984, 54-55.*
LEVEL: B LANG: Eng SIRC ARTICLE NO: 103468

TECHNIQUES AND SKILLS - CATCHER

Cullinane, E. Kennedy, K. Syllabus for the softball catcher. *Scholastic coach (New York) 53(9), Apr 1984, 44;46.*
LEVEL: B LANG: Eng SIRC ARTICLE NO: 095269

Webb, J. Neuman, K. Softball's martyr: the catcher. The trials and tribulations of the catcher in softball are unlike those of any other position. *Athletic journal (Evanston, Ill.) 64(10), May 1984, 46;56-57.*
LEVEL: B LANG: Eng SIRC ARTICLE NO: 095279

TECHNIQUES AND SKILLS - PITCHER AND PITCHING

Hoehn, R.G. Developing championship calibre softball pitchers. (training methods) *Coaching review (Ottawa, Ont.) 7, May/Jun 1984, 40-42.*
LEVEL: B LANG: Eng SIRC ARTICLE NO: 095271

Jilek, B. Drills for windmill. *Women's coaching clinic 7(6), Feb 1984, 8-9.*
LEVEL: B LANG: Eng SIRC ARTICLE NO: 090952

Mogill, A.T. Developing the softball pitcher. Windmill is most effective delivery, but it doesn't come easy; pick your pitchers while they're young. *Athletic journal (Evanston, Ill.) 65(5), Dec 1984, 8-11;42.*
LEVEL: B LANG: Eng SIRC ARTICLE NO: 104904

TESTING AND EVALUATION

Le programme d'initiation au softball. Manuel des entraineurs et des instructeurs. s.l.: Maple Leaf : Softball Canada, 1984?. 16 p. (Programme d'initiation au softball.)
CORP: Softball Canada.
CORP: Maple Leaf.
NOTES: Titre de la couverture. Also published in English under the title: Softball skills program: coaches'/instructor's manual.
LEVEL: B LANG: Fr ISBN: 0-920816-921 GV881 18495

Miller, J. The poor man's speed gun. *Scholastic coach (New York) 53(9), Apr 1984, 82.*
LEVEL: B LANG: Eng SIRC ARTICLE NO: 095273

Softball skills program. Coaches'/instructor's manual. s.l.: Softball Canada : Maple Leaf, 1984?. 16 p. (Softball skills program.)
CORP: Maple Leaf.

SOFTBALL (continued)

CORP: Softball Canada.
NOTES: Cover title. Aussi publie en francais sous le titre: Le programme d'initiation au softball.
LEVEL: B LANG: Eng ISBN: 0-920816-920 GV881 18494

Weismeyer, H. Picture analysis: for classroom instruction or testing. *Journal of physical education, recreation and dance (Reston, Va.) 55(8), Oct 1984, 72-73.*
LEVEL: B LANG: Eng SIRC ARTICLE NO: 101526

TRAINING AND CONDITIONING

Lazar, D.J. Critical phases of indoor softball workouts. *Women's coaching clinic 7(6), Feb 1984, 9-11.*
LEVEL: B LANG: Eng SIRC ARTICLE NO: 090953

TRAINING AND CONDITIONING - DRILLS

Fitzwater, C.H. Making the most of rainy day practices. *Women's coaching clinic 7(7), Mar 1984, 8-9.*
LEVEL: B LANG: Eng SIRC ARTICLE NO: 092399

Lazar, D.J. Critical phases of indoor softball workouts. *Women's coaching clinic (Princeton, N.J.) 7(9), May 1984, 12-14.*
LEVEL: B LANG: Eng SIRC ARTICLE NO: 095272

SOMALIA

OLYMPIC GAMES

Somalia and Olympism. *Olympic review (Lausanne) 200, Jun 1984, 459-462.*
LEVEL: B LANG: Eng SIRC ARTICLE NO: 096113

SOUTH AFRICA

Martin, P. South African sport: apartheid's Achilles heel. (Refs: 7)*World today (London) 40(6), 1984, 234-243.*
LEVEL: I LANG: Eng SIRC ARTICLE NO: 096424

Principles for sports provision. Pretoria, South Africa: Human Sciences Research Council, c1984. xxi, 63 p. (Report of the Wor Committee: Philosophy of sport no.2.)
NOTES: Bibliography: p. 49.
LEVEL: I LANG: Eng ISBN: 0 7969 0127 9 GV667 18622

Scholtz, G.J.L. Olivier, J.L. Attitude of urban South Africans toward non-racial sport and their expectations of future race relations - a comparative study. (Refs: 20)*International review for the sociology of sport (Munich) 19(2), 1984, 129-143.*
CONF: Olympic Scientific Congress (1984 : Eugene, Ore.).
ABST: In 1983 a random sample drawn from the larger urban communities and including 962 Blacks, 943 Indians, 789 Coloureds and 697 Whites, revealed that the majority of urban South Africans strongly favoured non-racial sport at national and club competition levels. For the first time in history, differences occurring between the attitude profile of the four main ethnic groups were non-significant. Attitudes of Whites still tended to be more

conservative and have regressed since 1980/81. The attitude pattern of Blacks, Coloureds and Indians was the most homogeneous. A certain amount of ambivalence became evident between present attitudes and more positive expectations of change within the country.
LEVEL: A LANG: Eng SIRC ARTICLE NO: 104477

SOVIET UNION

Abrosimova, L.I. On some organisational moments of child and adolescent physical education and sports in the USSR. *In, Idrett for barn. Sport for Children. Sport pour les enfants 27.9.-1.10.1982 Tonsberg, Norway. Report. Oslo, Norway, Ministry of Cultural and Scientific Affairs: Norwegian Confederation of Sport, 1984, p. (18).*
CONF: Idrett for barn. Sport for Children. Sport pour les enfants (1982 : Tonsberg, Norway).
LEVEL: B LANG: Eng GV709.2 20111

Abrosimova, L.I. A propos de quelques questions de l'education physique et du sport des enfants et des adolescents en USSR. *Dans, Idrett for barn. Sport for Children. Sport pour les enfants 27.9.-1.10.1982 Tonsberg, Norway. Rapport. Oslo, Norvege, Ministere de la culture et de la science : Confederation norvegienne des sports, 1984, p. (19).*
CONF: Idrett for barn. Sport for Children. Sport pour les enfants (1982 : Tonsberg, Norway).
LEVEL: B LANG: Fr GV709.2 20112

Groves, B.R. Borden, G. Is the Soviet sport system superior? (Refs: 8)*Virginia journal (Harrisonburg, Va.) 6(2), Apr 1984, 9;19.*
LEVEL: B LANG: Eng SIRC ARTICLE NO: 099339

Jefferies, S.C. Sport and education: theory and practice in the USSR. (Refs: 12)*Quest (Champaign, Ill.) 36(2), 1984, 164-176.*
ABST: This paper examines the complex relationship between education and athletics in the USSR. Young athletes throughout the world face many difficulties in dividing their attention between education and sport. In the USSR, the state has taken the initiative in helping young athletes to resolve this dilemma, due to the significance of sport in Soviet society. The importance of sport may in part explain Soviet determination to tackle the education/athletics problem. The paper then describes the organization of youth sport and the training demands expected of school-age athletes, as well as the structure and organization of the sports boarding school and the specialist class.
LEVEL: I LANG: Eng SIRC ARTICLE NO: 102921

Melnikov, V.M. (The problem of reliability in sports in the USSR.) *Psikhologicheskii zhurnal 5(5), 1984, 160-161.*
LEVEL: LANG: Rus

Ryan, A.J. Sports and physical education in the USSR. (Refs: 1)*Physician and sportsmedicine (Minneapolis, Minn.) 12(11), No 1984, 27.*
LEVEL: B LANG: Eng SIRC ARTICLE NO: 100845

Uvarov, V.N. State administration of physical culture and sports. (Refs: 7)*Soviet law and government (Armonk, N.Y.) 22(3), 1984, 74-85.*
LEVEL: I LANG: Eng SIRC ARTICLE NO: 095708

Ziberman, V. Physical education in USSR schools. (Refs: 12)*Journal of physical education, recreation & dance (Reston, Va.) 55(6), Aug 1984, 64-68.*
LEVEL: I LANG: Eng SIRC ARTICLE NO: 097673

HISTORY

Kolmakova, M.N. Kuzin, N.P. The twenty-sixth congress of the CPSU and the development of public education in the USSR. Part III. *Soviet education (Armonk, N.Y.) 26(4), Feb 1984, 5-104.*
LEVEL: I LANG: Eng

OLYMPIC GAMES

Steinbah, V. Kopytkin, Y. Timofeyev, A. 638 Olympic champions: three decades in the Olympic movement. Moscow: Raduga Publishers, 1984. 270 p. : ill. ; 17 cm.
LEVEL: B LANG: Eng LC CARD: 84-212787

SPECIAL OLYMPICS

Brickey, M. Normalizing the Special Olympics. (Refs: 19)*Journal of physical education, recreation and dance (Reston, Va.) 55(8), Oct 1984, 28-29;75-76.*
LEVEL: B LANG: Eng SIRC ARTICLE NO: 100646

Stevens, J. Special Olympics. *Journal of physical education, recreation & dance 55(2), Feb 1984, 42-43.*
LEVEL: B LANG: En SIRC ARTICLE NO: 091431

ADMINISTRATION

Lamunyon, R.E. Wichita police support Special Olympics. *Police chief (Gaithersburg, Md.) 51(12), 1984, 48.*
LEVEL: B LANG: Eng SIRC ARTICLE NO: 103967

ECONOMICS - FUNDING AND FUND RAISING

Kontor, K. LiftAmerica - athletes giving athletes a lift. *National Strength & Conditioning Association journal (Lincoln, Neb.) 6(3), Jun/Jul 1984, 42.*
LEVEL: B LANG: Eng SIRC ARTICLE NO: 096423

Waters, J.V. Big Foot's big event: a LiftAmerica success story. (Refs: 2)*National Strength & Conditioning Association journal (Lincoln, Neb.) 6(3), Jun/Jul 1984, 46-48.*
LEVEL: B LANG: Eng SIRC ARTICLE NO: 096439

MEDICINE

Birrer, R.B. The special olympics: an injury overview. (Refs: 5)*Physician and sportsmedicine 12(4), Apr 1984, 95-97.*
LEVEL: I LANG: Eng SIRC ARTICLE NO: 092802

SOCIOLOGY

Orelove, F.P. Moon, M.S. The Special Olympic program: effects on retarded persons and society. (Refs: 5)*Arena review 8(1), Mar 1984, 41-45.*
NOTES: Special issue: Sport and disability.
ABST: This article examines the detrimental effects of such programs as the Special Olympics which promotes handicapism and segregation.
LEVEL: A LANG: Eng SIRC ARTICLE NO: 103709

SPEED SKATING

Barron, A. Overend, C. Overend, T. Theriault, L. Williamson, L. Ca file bien. Ottawa: Association canadienne de patinage de vitesse amateur, c1984. 15 p. ill.
CORP: Association canadienne de patinage de vitesse amateur.
NOTES: Titre de la couverture. Also published in English under the title: Fast is fun.
LEVEL: B LANG: Fr GV850.3 20135

Barron, A. Overend, C. Overend, T. Theriault, L. Williamson, L. Fast is fun. Ottawa: Canadian Amateur Speed Skating Association, c1984. 15 p. : ill.
CORP: Canadian Amateur Speed Skating Association.
NOTES: Publie aussi en francais sous le titre: Ca file bien. Cover title.
LEVEL: B LANG: Eng GV850.3 20134

ADMINISTRATION

Gazdewich, A. Llewellyn, E.J. The personal computer for sport. *Coaching review (Ottawa, Ont.) 7, Nov/Dec 1984, 40-43.*
LEVEL: B LANG: Eng SIRC ARTICLE NO: 099931

BIOGRAPHY AND AUTOBIOGRAPHY

Chartier, R. Gaetan Boucher: l'aigle de Sarajevo. Montreal: La Presse, c1984. 121 p. : ill.
LEVEL: B LANG: Fr ISBN: 2-89043-121-5 LC CARD: 84-8214-5 GV850.3 18567

Dickie, D. Gaetan Boucher, une medaille d'or a sa portee. Gaetan Boucher, prime time for gold. *Champion 8(1), Feb 1984, 28-29.*
LEVEL: B LANG: Eng Fr SIRC ARTICLE NO: 090955

Verschoth, A. Meet Fraeulein longlegs. (Karin Enke) *Sports illustrated 60(5), 6 Feb 1984, 68-69.*
LEVEL: B LANG: Eng SIRC ARTICLE NO: 090958

COACHING

Newman, S. Joining forces to remain a force: proof cooperation and competition can live side-by-side - even in coaching. *Coaching review (Ottawa, Ont.) 7, Nov/Dec 1984, 45-47.*
LEVEL: B LANG: Eng SIRC ARTICLE NO: 099932

COUNTRIES AND REGIONS

Sevack, M. Patinage de vitesse: la route s'annonce longue d'ici 1988. Speed skaters face long road to '88. *Champion 8(1), Feb 1984, 8-11.*
LEVEL: B LANG: Eng Fr SIRC ARTICLE NO: 090957

EQUIPMENT - MAINTENANCE

Care of speed skates. *On thin ice (Ottawa, Ont.) 6(4), Dec 1984, 10.*
LEVEL: B LANG: Eng SIRC ARTICLE NO: 103470

HISTORY

Levy, M. Speed skating. *Women's sports (Palo Alto, Calif.) 6(1), Jan 1984, 34-35.*
LEVEL: B LANG: Eng SIRC ARTICLE NO: 098516

INJURIES AND ACCIDENTS

Bolduc, R. Injuries on ice. *Coaching review 7, Jan/Feb 1984, 44-46.*
LEVEL: B LANG: Eng SIRC ARTICLE NO: 092401

PHYSIOLOGY

Geijsel, J. Bomhoff, G. van Velzen, J. de Groot, G. van Ingen Schenau, G.J. Bicycle ergometry and speed skating performance. (Refs: 30)*International journal of sports medicine (Stuttgart) 5(5), Oct 1984, 241-245.*
ABST: A comparison between maximal power output during cycling and skating was made, and correlates of skating performance with bicycle performance and skating technique were investigated. Twenty-five well-trained speed skaters performed two bicycle tests and a 500-m and 1500-m ice skating race. The power (P) during skating is calculated from ice and air friction losses: at 500 m P_{500}, 344 plus or minus 60 W and at 1500 m P_{1500}, 283 plus or minus 65 W. The highest correlate of P_{500} as well as P_{1500} appeared to be P_{30C}, respectively, 0.78 and 0.85. The correlation of P_{30C} suggests that the interindividual differences of skating performance at 500-m and 1500-m distances can be attributed substantially to differences in anaerobic power.
LEVEL: A LANG: Eng SIRC ARTICLE NO: 104906

Rasin, M.S. Speed-strength of young speed skaters. *Soviet sports review (Escondido, Calif.) 19(3), Sept 1984, 156.*
LEVEL: B LANG: Eng SIRC ARTICLE NO: 103472

PSYCHOLOGY

Gutmann, M.C. Pollock, M.L. Foster, C. Schmidt, D. Training stress in Olympic speed skaters: a psychological perspective. (Refs: 24)*Physician and sportsmedicine (Minneapolis, Minn.) 12(12), Dec 1984, 45-48;51-54;57.*
ABST: The authors tested 11 male contenders for the 1980 US Olympic Speed Skating Team six months before the December 1979 Olympic Winter Trials (June), at the end of summer training (October), and immediately before and after the trials. Subjects were interviewed on their personal background, motivation, stressors and coping strategies in training and competition. They were administered the Profile of Mood States rating scale. Findings indicated that the skaters who made the team responded positively to training and achieved a psychological peak just before the trials.
LEVEL: A LANG: Eng SIRC ARTICLE NO: 103471

RULES AND REGULATIONS

How the game is played. *Women's sports (Palo Alto, Calif.) 6(1), Jan 1984, 40.*
LEVEL: B LANG: Eng SIRC ARTICLE NO: 098515

SPORTING EVENTS

Le patinage et l'olympisme. *Revue olympique (Lausanne) 199, mai 1984, 345-387.*
LEVEL: B LANG: Fr SIRC ARTICLE NO: 102132

Poulsen, O. Le patinage, des origines a nos jours. Skating from its origins to the present day. *Message olympique/Olympic message (Lausanne) 7, juin/Jun 1984, 33-44.*
LEVEL: B LANG: Fr Eng SIRC ARTICLE NO: 104678

STATISTICS AND RECORDS

Poulsen, O. Skating and Olympism. *Olympic review (Lausanne) 199, May 1984, 345-348.*
LEVEL: B LANG: Eng SIRC ARTICLE NO: 096648

Poulsen, O. Le patinage et l'olympisme. *Revue olympique (Lausanne) 199, mai 1984, 345-348.*
LEVEL: B LANG: Fr SIRC ARTICLE NO: 104679

TRAINING AND CONDITIONING

Holum, D. Johnson, P. Complete handbook of speed skating. Hillside, N.J.: Enslow Publishers, c1984. 256 p. : ill.
LEVEL: I LANG: Eng ISBN: 089490051X LC CARD: 82-018174 GV850.3 17229

SPELEOLOGY

Farr, M. The great caving adventure. Sparkford, Yeovil, Somerset: Oxford Illustrated Press, c1984. v, 229 p., (8) p. of plat (Great Adventure series; no. 2.)
LEVEL: B LANG: Eng ISBN: 0946609101 LC CARD: 84-191983

Lamarre, J. Speleologie: du plein air au service de la science. *Science loisir (Montreal) 3(4), dec 1984, 11-12.*
LEVEL: B LANG: Fr SIRC ARTICLE NO: 173509

BIBLIOGRAPHIES

Mansfield, R. Current titles in speleology 1983. Rhychydwr, Crymych, Dyfed, U.K.: Anne Oldham, 1984. viii, 142 p.
NOTES: A Manol production.
LEVEL: I LANG: Eng GV200.6 12272

Szentes, G. Bibliography of the Colombian speleological literature until 1st May 1984. *British caver (Dyfed, U.K.) 91, Summer 1984, 27-30.*
LEVEL: B LANG: Eng SIRC ARTICLE NO: 099933

CHILDREN

Mercier, M. Une sortie speleologie. *EPS: Revue education physique et sport (Paris) 188, juil/aout 1984, 50-51.*
LEVEL: B LANG: Fr SIRC ARTICLE NO: 098517

SPELEOLOGY (continued)

COUNTRIES AND REGIONS

Cohen, L. Illinois caverns: a history. (Refs: 14)*Journal of Spelean history (Knoxville, Tenn.) 18(1), Jan/Mar 1984, 17-21.*
LEVEL: B LANG: Eng SIRC ARTICLE NO: 109049

The history of Hungarian cave research. *British caver (Dyfed, U.K.) 93, Winter 1984, 25-29.*
NOTES: Translated from, Magyarorzag Barlangjai (Hungarian caves) by Gyula Hegedues.
LEVEL: I LANG: Eng SIRC ARTICLE NO: 108851

EQUIPMENT

Elliot, D. Equipment column. *Caves & caving (Somerset, Eng.) 26, Nov 1984, 28-30.*
LEVEL: B LANG: Eng SIRC ARTICLE NO: 107559

Romford, P. A new look at ropewalking. (Refs: 2)*Descent (Gloucester, Eng.) 61, Nov 1984, 25-27.*
LEVEL: B LANG: Eng SIRC ARTICLE NO: 108478

SOCIAL PSYCHOLOGY

Elements pour une deontologie des expeditions speleologiques a l'etranger. (Refs: 10)*Spelunca (Paris) 15, juil/sept 1984, 21-24.*
LEVEL: B LANG: Fr SIRC ARTICLE NO: 101528

TECHNIQUES AND SKILLS

Sewell, R. Basic SRT pitch rigging techniques. (Refs: 5)*Caves & caving (Somerset, U.K.) 25, Aug 1984, 6-7.*
LEVEL: I LANG: Eng SIRC ARTICLE NO: 101529

SPORT INSTITUTES

ADMINISTRATION

Daly, J.A. The Australian Institute of Sport and its decentralisation. (Refs: 17)*Sports coach (Wembley, W. Aust.) 8(3), Jan 1985, 9-12.*
NOTES: Modified and edited version of a paper presented at the 15th National Biennial Conference of the Australian Council for Health, Physical Education and Recreation, Sydney, January 1984.
LEVEL: B LANG: Eng SIRC ARTICLE NO: 103802

Ou va la Societe des sports du Quebec? *Revue de l'entraineur (Montreal) juil/sept 1984, 24-25.*
LEVEL: B LANG: Fr SIRC ARTICLE NO: 102927

Pearce, W. The Victorian Sports Institute, and its relationship with the existing physical education system in Victoria. (Refs: 3)
CONF: Physical Education Graduating Seminar Conference (1984 : Footscray Institute of Technology).
NOTES: In, Physical education in Australia: past, present and future directions, s.l., Footscray Institute of Technology, 1984, p. 51-54.
LEVEL: I LANG: Eng SIRC ARTICLE NO: 096163

SPRINT SWIMMING

BIOGRAPHY AND AUTOBIOGRAPHY

Chaffin, T. Yesterday's heroes. *Women's sports (Palo Alto, Calif.) 6(9), Sept 1984, 31-33.*
LEVEL: B LANG: Eng SIRC ARTICL NO: 173592

Crouse, K. Mark Kerry: Australia's model swimmer. *Swimming world and junior swimmer (Englewood, Calif.) 25(11), Nov 1984, 35-38.*
LEVEL: B LANG: Eng SIRC ARTICLE NO: 103485

Ewald, E. Prado's learned well. *Swimming world and junior swimmer (Los Angeles, Calif.) 25(6), Jun 1984, 21-24.*
LEVEL: B LANG: Eng SIRC ARTICLE NO: 095296

Ewald, R. Canada's female star. (Ann Ottenbrite) *Swimming world and junior swimmer (Inglewood, Calif.) 25(7), Jul 1984, 34-35.*
LEVEL: B LANG: Eng SIRC ARTICLE NO: 099947

Ewald, R. The next Mark Spitz: Aka Pablo. (Pablo Morales) *Swimming world and junior swimmer (Englewood, Calif.) 25(11), Nov 1984, 20-25.*
LEVEL: B LANG: Eng SIRC ARTICLE NO: 103486

Hart, R. The eyes of the world are on Texas' Carey. (Rick Carey) *Swimming world and junior swimmer (Los Angeles, Calif.) 25(3), Mar 1984, 24-27.*
LEVEL: B LANG: Eng SIRC ARTICLE NO: 098532

Ingram, B. Sippy. *Swimming world and junior swimmer (Los Angeles, Calif.) 25(6), Jun 1984, 28-35.*
LEVEL: B LANG: Eng SIRC ARTICLE NO: 095307

Kelso, J. 1968 Olympian recalls the experience. (Elaine Tanner) *Swim Canada (Toronto) 11(7), Jul 1984, 13.*
LEVEL: B LANG: Eng SIRC ARTICLE NO: 101552

Pursley, D. Inside Mary T. (Mary T. Meagher) *Swimming world and junior swimmer (Inglewood, Calif.) 25(7), Jul 1984, 27-28.*
LEVEL: B LANG: Eng SIRC ARTICLE NO: 099954

Pursley, D. Madam Butterfly. (Mary T. Meagher) *International swimming and water polo (Budapest, Hungary) 14, 1984, 20-21.*
LEVEL: B LANG: Eng SIRC ARTICLE NO: 108479

TECHNIQUES AND SKILLS - BUTTERFLY

Thornton, K.M. Learning from the Olympians: sprint and distance butterfly. *Swimming world and junior swimmer (Los Angeles, Calif.) 25(4), Apr 1984, 28-30.*
LEVEL: B LANG: Eng SIRC ARTICLE NO: 095326

TRAINING AND CONDITIONING

MacDonald, B. Sprint training and tapering Dave Churchill. *Swim Canada (Toronto) 11(9), Oct 1984, 28.*
LEVEL: B LANG: Eng SIRC ARTICLE NO: 103493

SPRINTING

BIBLIOGRAPHIES

Dates, G.G. Theses and dissertations in track & field. *Track & field quarterly review (Kalamazoo, Mich.) 84(2), Summer 1984 60-62.*
LEVEL: B LANG: Eng SIRC ARTICLE NO: 095402

Sport bibliography. *Track and field journal 25, Feb 1984, 33-35.*
LEVEL: B LANG: Eng SIRC ARTICLE NO: 093947

BIOGRAPHY AND AUTOBIOGRAPHY

Athletics: Marita Payne. Athletisme: Marita Payne. *Champion (Ottawa) 8(3), Aug 1984, 44-45.*
LEVEL: B LANG: Eng Fr SIRC ARTICLE NO: 096948

Battersby, E. How Caroline's experimental gamble paid off: Eileen Battersby profiles Ireland's first female olympic finalist *Athletics weekly (Kent, Eng.) 38(51), 22 Dec 1984, 12-14.*
LEVEL: B LANG: Eng SIRC ARTICLE NO: 103558

Burfoot, A. Jarmila. Speedster Jarmila Kratochvilova of Czechoslovakia is tearing up women's track on both sides of the iron curtain. *Runner's world (Mountain View, Calif.) 19(7), Jul 1984, 85-88;110-112;114.*
LEVEL: B LANG: Eng SIRC ARTICLE NO: 095397

Chaffin, T. Yesterday's heroes. *Women's sports (Palo Alto, Calif.) 6(9), Sept 1984, 31-33.*
LEVEL: B LANG: Eng SIRC ARTICL NO: 173592

Hadley, T. European junior gold medallists - Lincoln Asquith. *Athletics coach (London) 18(2), Jun 1984, 14.*
LEVEL: B LANG Eng SIRC ARTICLE NO: 095413

Hendershott, J. Athlete of-the-year: Ashford gets gold, and more. *Track & field news (Los Altos, Calif.) 37(11), Dec 1984, 8-9.*
LEVEL: B LANG: Eng SIRC ARTICLE NO: 103572

Herdershott, J. Athlete of the year. Carl Lewis: more in '84. *Track & field news 36(12), Jan 1984, 9-10.*
LEVEL: B LANG: E SIRC ARTICLE NO: 092467

McIntyre, P. Mel Lattany. T&FN interview. *Track & field news (Los Altos, Calif.) 37(5), Jun 1984, 66-67.*
LEVEL: B LANG: E SIRC ARTICLE NO: 095441

Nichols, P. A spilling over of dreams: he'll be at his peak for the 1992 Olympics, and he says he won't mind missing LA. But life has a habit of speeding up for sprint sensation Ade Mafe. *Running (London) 39, Jul 1984, 52-55.*
LEVEL: B LANG: Eng SIRC ARTICLE NO: 103596

Nightingale, D. Carl Lewis: all this 'superman' is trying to do is to be the best that he can be. *Sporting news (St. Louis) 198(5), 30 Jul 1984, 3;11.*
LEVEL: B LANG: Eng SIRC ARTICLE NO: 096988

Profile: Angela Bailey. *Track and field journal 25, Feb 1984, 17-18.*
LEVEL: B LANG: Eng SIRC ARTICLE NO: 093934

Profile: Ben Johnson. *Track and field journal 25, Feb 1984, 19-20.*
LEVEL: B LANG: Eng SIRC ARTICLE NO: 093935

Rick Mitchell's long road to Los Angeles. (interview) *Sports coach (Wembley, Aust.) 8(1), 1984, 35-39.*
LEVEL: B LANG: Eng SIRC ARTICLE NO: 096995

Riding a long winning streak, Greg Foster enters the Olympic season short on publicity and long on confidence. *Runner's world 19(3), Mar 1984, 23-24;26;30;32;34;36;38.*
LEVEL: B LANG: Eng SIRC ARTICLE NO: 092522

Runner's World gold medal exclusive: America's No. 1 woman sprinter, Evelyn Ashford, talks about her training and going for th gold. *Runner's world 19(4), Apr 1984, 27-28;30;32;34;37-38.*
LEVEL: B LANG: Eng SIRC ARTICLE NO: 093938

Smith, G. 'I do what I want to do' (Carl Lewis) *Sports illustrated (Chicago, Ill.) 61(4), 18 Jul 1984, 22-26;29-30;32;34;36-39.*
LEVEL: B LANG: Eng SIRC ARTICLE NO: 097000

Smith, J. Running with a dream. *California history 63(1), Winter 1984, 22-25.*
LEVEL: I LANG: Eng SIRC ARTICLE NO: 106193

Stump, A.J. Charley Paddock's sprint around the world. *Olympic review (Lausanne, Switzerland) 197, Mar 1984, 170-172.*
LEVEL: B LANG: Eng SIRC ARTICLE NO: 095467

Stump, A.J. Le sprint autour du monde de Charley Paddock. *Revue olympique (Lausanne) 197, mars 1984, 170-172.*
LEVEL: B LANG: Fr SIRC ARTICLE NO: 097001

Van Dyk, J. The start of something big. A proud town and strong family values gave Carl Lewis a head start, and he ran with it. *Runner (New York) 6(11), Aug 1984, 54-59.*
LEVEL: B LANG: Eng SIRC ARTICLE NO: 106199

Watman, M. Britain's most capped international. Mel Watman reviews the career of Verona Elder. *Athletics weekly (Rochester, Kent) 38(11), 17 Mar 1984, 21-22;24-26;28-29.*
LEVEL: B LANG: Eng SIRC ARTICLE NO: 093960

Whitefield, N. Fastest 400m runner in Southampton: Nigel Whitefield looks at the meteoric rise to the top of Britain's current fastest quarter miler, Kriss Akabusi. *Athletics weekly (Kent, Eng.) 38(42), 20 Oct 1984, 34-35;37-39.*
LEVEL: B LANG: Eng SIRC ARTICLE NO: 103619

Who's who in British athletics. Jayne Andrews. *Athletics weekly (Kent, Eng.) 38(48), 1 Dec 1984, 42;45-46.*
LEVEL: B LANG: E SIRC ARTICLE NO: 103621

Wilma Rudolph: polio didn't stop her from achieving stardom. *Sporting news (St. Louis) 198(4), 23 Jul 1984, Olympic special insert, 12;14.*
LEVEL: B LANG: Eng SIRC ARTICLE NO: 097020

BIOMECHANICS

Ariel, G. Biomechanics and athletic achievement. *Scholastic coach (New York) 53(9), Apr 1984, 70-72;74-75.*
LEVEL: B LANG: Eng SIRC ARTICLE NO: 094190

Chapman, A.E. Lonergan, R. Caldwell, G.E. Kinetic sources of lower-limb angular displacement in the recovery phase of sprinting. (Refs: 9)*Medicine and science in sports and exercise (Indianapolis) 16(4), Aug 1984, 382-388.*
ABST: One female sprinter was filmed at the 100-m mark (speed 6.5 m.s-1) of a 400-m run. Four moments occurring at each end of the thigh and shank segments during lower-limb recovery were

calculated. These were: proximal and distal net muscle moments, a moment due to proximal joint accelerative force and, a moment due to distal joint-force resulting from motion and inertia of the distal connected segment. Individual contributions of each moment to segmental angular displacement were calculated by double integration, and angular velocity at toe-off was multiplied by time to yield its contribution. Contributions of the proximal muscle moments throughout recovery were 21 rad and 7.5 rad for the thigh and shank segments, respectively. Such large angular displacements did not occur because the three remaining moments opposed the proximal muscle moment.
LEVEL: A LANG: Eng SIRC ARTICLE NO: 103564

Doolittle, D. Tellez, T. Sprinting - from start to finish. (Refs: 6)*Track & field quarterly review (Kalamazoo, Mich.) 84(2) Summer 1984, 5-8.*
LEVEL: I LANG: Eng SIRC ARTICLE NO: 095404

Giordano, S. Quantitative investigation by photographic-stroboscopic method on the athlete during the first meters of sprint running. *Track & field quarterly review (Kalamazoo, Mich.) 84(2), Summer 1984, 23.*
CONF: ELLV Conference (11th : 1981 : Venice, Italy).
LEVEL: I LANG: Eng SIRC ARTICLE NO: 095408

Plamondon, A. Roy, B. Cinematique et cinetique de la course acceleree. (Refs: 38)*Canadian journal of applied sport sciences/Journal canadien des sciences appliquees au sport 9(1), Mar 1984, 42-52.*
RESUME: Cette etude visait a analyser les facteurs biomecaniques de la course d'acceleration. Dix sujets masculins participerent a l'etude. Les variables suivantes furent prelevees a l'aide de la cinematographie: frequence et longueur d'enjambee, duree des differentes phases et angles posturaux au cours de certaines phases de la course. Force, impulsion et duree d'application des forces furent obtenues a l'aide d'une plate-forme de marque Kistler. Les resultats obtenus indiquent une association etroite entre la majorite des parametres cinematiques et cinetiques et la variation de velocite au cours de 18 premieres enjambees.
LEVEL: A LANG: Fr SIRC ARTICLE NO: 093930

Tupa, V. Chistyakov, V. Aleshinsky, S. Korneluk, A. Yarmulnik, D. Zhukov, I. Guseinov, F. Biomechanics of the take-off in running. *Soviet sports review (Escondido, Calif.) 19(1), Mar 1984, 19-23.*
NOTES: Translated from, Legkaya atletika 9, 1981, 10-11. To be continued in vol. 19, no. 2.
LEVEL: I LANG: Eng SIRC ARTICLE NO: 095470

Tupa, V. Korneluk, A. Chistyakov, V. Aleshinsky, S. Yarmulnik, D. Zukov, I. Guseinov, F. Biomechanics of the take-off in running. *Soviet sports review (Escondido, Calif.) 19(2), Jun 1984, 78-82.*
NOTES: Translated from Legkaya atletika, 9: 10-11, 1981. (continuation from volume 19, number 1.)
LEVEL: I LANG: Eng SIRC ARTICLE NO: 100097

COACHING

Groseclose, B. Track and field coaching hints. *Texas coach (Austin, Tex.) 28(3), Oct 1984, 44-46.*
LEVEL: B LANG: Eng SIRC ARTICLE NO: 173208

Honz, K. De la solitude et de l'autonomie de l'athlete. *Macolin (Suisse) 9, sept 1984, 3.*
NOTES: Traduction et adaptation de, Francoise

Huguening et Yves Jeannotat.
LEVEL: B LANG: Fr SIRC ARTICLE NO: 103574

Interview with potential summer olympic coaches: Charlie Francis. *Coaching review 7, Mar/Apr 1984, 15-17.*
LEVEL: B LANG: En SIRC ARTICLE NO: 093899

ECONOMICS

Newman, S. The good and the not so good. Two Canadian athletes' experiences on U.S. athletic scholarships and what other Canadians may learn from their experiences. *Coaching review (Ottawa) 7, Sept/Oct 1984, 24-27.*
LEVEL: B LANG: Eng SIRC ARTICLE NO: 098664

EQUIPMENT

Krysanov, V. Vasyuk, V. An exerciser for sprinters. *Soviet sports review (Escondido, Calif.) 19(3), Sept 1984, 137-138.*
NOTES: Translated from, Legkaya atletika 2, 1982, 10.
LEVEL: I LANG: Eng SIRC ARTICLE NO: 103580

MEDICINE

Kuoppasalmi, K. Effects of side stress on human plasma hormone levels. *Track and field quarterly review (Kalamazoo, Mich.) 84(3), Fall 1984, 56-58.*
NOTES: Abstracted from the Academic Dissertation presented at the XIth European Track & Field Coaches Association Congress, Venice, Italy, March 17-20, 1981.
LEVEL: I LANG: Eng SIRC ARTICLE NO: 096980

NUTRITION

Zalessky, M. The doctor answers. (Post-training appetite) *Soviet sports review (Escondido, Calif.) 19(1), Mar 1984, 52.*
NOTES: Translated from, Legkaya atletika 2, 1983, 15.
LEVEL: B LANG: Eng SIRC ARTICLE NO: 095479

PHYSIOLOGY

Crielaard, J.M. Mouton, G. Boudart, J. Pirnay, F. Etude longitudinale de l'aptitude physique en athletisme. (Refs: 10)*Sport Communaute francaise de belgique (Bruxelles) 108, 1984, 218-221.*
LEVEL: I LANG: Fr SIRC ARTICLE NO: 103565

Kuo, C.H. A study on the relationship between sprinter start-dash and the regulation of respiration. (Refs: 5)*Asian journal of physical education (Taiwan, China) 7(2), Jul 1984, 76-80.*
ABST: The respiration of 71 men, aged between 18 and 22 years old, is recorded at the starting stage of a 50 meters run. The subjects are divided in three groups: 1) 10 sprinters; 2) 4 non-athletes, and 3) 57 sportsmen with no experience in start-dash. Findings show that sprinters have smooth respiration, non-athletes have unregulated respiration, and ordinary sportsmen have ill-prepared regulation respiration for start-dash moment.
LEVEL: A LANG: Eng Chi SIRC ARTICLE NO: 100063

Ohkuwa, T. Saito, M. Miyamura, M. Plasma LDH and CK activities after 400 m sprinting by well-trained sprint runners. (Refs: 28)*European journal of applied physiology and occupational physiology (Heidelberg) 52(3), Apr 1984, 296-299.*

SPRINTING (continued)

ABST: Blood samples obtained immediately after a maximal 400-m sprint from 13 well-trained middle distance runners were analyzed for blood lactate and plasma LDH and CK activities. Blood samples were taken at 1, 3, 5, 7.5 and 10 min following the 400-m sprint. Significant relationships were observed between mean velocity in the 400-m sprint and plasma CK activity, mean velocity and H type LDH isozyme activity, and mean velocity and M type LDh isozyme activity. The authors suggest that training may depress enzyme efflux from tissue to blood and that in well-trained sprinters plasma CK and LDH isozymes may be suitable indicators of training stress.
LEVEL: A LANG: Eng SIRC ARTICLE NO: 098667

Ohkuwa, T. Kato, Y. Katsumata, K. Nakao, T. Miyamura, M. Blood lactate and glycerol after 400-m and 3,000-m runs in sprint and long distance runners. (Refs: 27)*European journal of applied physiology and occupational physiology (Berlin) 53(3), Dec 1984, 213-218.*
ABST: Lactate, glycerol, and catecholamine in the venous blood after 400-m and 3,000-m runs were determined in eight sprint runners, eight long distance runners, and seven untrained students. In 400-m sprinting, average values of velocity, peak blood lactate, and adrenaline were significantly higher in the sprint group than in the long distance and untrained groups. In the 3,000-m run, on the other hand, average values of velocity and glycerol were significantly higher in the long distance group than in the sprint and untrained groups, but there are no significant differences in lactate levels between the three groups.
LEVEL: A LANG: Eng SIRC ARTICLE NO: 105008

Schnabel, A. Kindermann, W. Keul, J. Schmitt, W.M. Appreciation de l'endurance anaerobie ('resistance') en laboratoire. (Refs: 18)*Revue de l'Amicale des entraineurs francais d'athletisme (Paris) 89, oct/nov/dec 1984, 29-31.*
NOTES: Traduit de, Leistungssport 9(6), 1979, 503/507.
LEVEL: I LANG: Fr SIRC ARTICLE NO: 103605

PHYSIOLOGY - MUSCLE

Radford, P. The nature and nurture of a sprinter. *New scientist (London) 1415, 2 Aug 1984, 13-15.*
NOTES: In the first few seconds of a sprint, runners achieve an intensity of muscular activity unparalleled in the world of sport. Success depends on a fortuitous choice of both coach and parents.
LEVEL: I LANG: Eng SIRC ARTICLE NO: 100084

Zalessky, M. Restoration in the sprint and hurdles. *Soviet sports review (Escondido, Calif.) 19(2), Jun 1984, 53-58.*
NOTES: Translated from, Legkaya atletika, 4: 6-7, 1981.
LEVEL: I LANG: Eng SIRC ARTICLE NO: 100107

SPORTING EVENTS

Smith, J. Running with a dream. *California history 63(1), Winter 1984, 22-25.*
LEVEL: I LANG: Eng SIRC ARTICLE NO: 106193

Sprints and hurdles. *Athletics coach (London) 18(4), Dec 1984, 18-29.*
LEVEL: B LANG: Eng SIRC ARTICLE NO: 105025

TECHNIQUES AND SKILLS

Goldsmith, M. Developing sprinters. *Texas coach (Austin, Tex.) 28(2), Sept 1984, 60-62.*
LEVEL: B LANG: Eng SIRC ARTICLE NO: 106163

TECHNIQUES AND SKILLS - START

Best, D. The sprint start. Developing an effective sprint start must combine proper techniques with individual preference. *Athletic journal 64(7), Feb 1984, 30-31.*
LEVEL: B LANG: Eng SIRC ARTICLE NO: 092470

Embling, S. The sprint start. *Modern athlete and coach (Athelstone, Aust.) 22(4), Oct 1984, 30-31.*
LEVEL: B LANG: Eng SIR ARTICLE NO: 104966

Glover, D. Stand-up starts. For younger or less powerful sprinters and hurdlers, the stand-up start may be of great benefit. *Athletic journal (Evanston, Ill.) 64(10), May 1984, 16;69;71.*
LEVEL: B LANG: Eng SIRC ARTICLE NO: 095409

Smaller, F.G. Coaching the co-ed track team. *Coaching clinic (Princeton, N.J.) 22(9), May 1984, 15-16.*
LEVEL: B LANG: Eng SIRC ARTICLE NO: 095464

TESTING AND EVALUATION

de Vodi, B. Le probleme de la selection des futurs sprinters. *Revue de l'Amicale des entraineurs francais d'athletisme (Paris) 89, oct/nov/dec 1984, 27-28.*
NOTES: Traduit par P.E. Brown, extrait de la revue Athletic coach.
LEVEL: B LANG: Fr SIRC ARTICLE NO: 103566

Radford, P. The nature and nurture of a sprinter. *New scientist (London) 1415, 2 Aug 1984, 13-15.*
NOTES: In the first few seconds of a sprint, runners achieve an intensity of muscular activity unparalleled in the world of sport. Success depends on a fortuitous choice of both coach and parents.
LEVEL: I LANG: Eng SIRC ARTICLE NO: 100084

TRAINING AND CONDITIONING

Baughman, M. Takaha, M. Sprint training - including strength training. *Track & field quarterly review (Kalamazoo, Mich.) 84(2), Summer 1984, 9-12.*
LEVEL: I LANG: Eng SIRC ARTICLE NO: 095392

Borzov, V. Training procedures in sprinting. *Modern athlete and coach (Athelstone, Aust.) 22(2), Apr 1984, 15-17.*
NOTES: Based on translated extracts from, 10 seconds - a lifetime, Perioodika, tallinn, Estonia.
LEVEL: B LANG: Eng SIRC ARTICLE NO: 096952

Hawkins, J.D. Specificity strength training as a factor in the improvement of shoulder strength and sprinting speed. (Refs: 22)*Track & field quarterly review (Kalamazoo, Mich.) 84(2), Summer 1984, 55-59.*
LEVEL: I LANG: Eng SIRC ARTICLE NO: 095415

Jarver, J. Basic sprinting. *Modern athlete and coach (Athelstone, Aust.) 22(4), Oct 1984, 26-29.*
NOTES: Extract from: Athletics fundamentals, published by A.H. & A. W. Reed Pty. Ltd.
LEVEL: B LANG: Eng SIRC ARTICLE NO: 104988

Kvac, M. Training of 400m runner Jarmila Kratochilova for the 1980 Moscow Olympic Games. *Track & field quarterly review (Kalamazoo, Mich.)*

84(2), Summer 1984, 18-22.
NOTES: Presented by Dr. Emil Dostal at the XIth European Track Coaches' Congress, Venice, Italy, March 17-20, 1981.
LEVEL: I LANG: Eng SIRC ARTICLE NO: 095430

Levchenko, A. The sprint. *Soviet sports review (Escondido, Calif.) 19(4), Dec 1984, 203-207.*
NOTES: To be continued in vol. 20, no. 1. Translated from, Legkaya atletika 3, 1984, 6-8.
LEVEL: I LANG: Eng SIRC ARTICLE NO: 104992

McFarlane, B. Developing maximum running speed. (Refs: 1)*Sports: science periodical on research and technology in sport (Ottawa) W-1, Sept 1984, 1-7.*
LEVEL: I LANG: Eng SIRC ARTICLE NO: 098654

McFarlane, B. Le developpemment d'une vitesse de course maximale. (Refs: 1)*Science du sport: documents de recherche et de technologie (Ottawa) W-1, sept 1984, 1-7.*
LEVEL: I LANG: Fr SIRC ARTICLE NO: 098655

McFarlane, B. Developing maximum running speed. *National Strength & Conditioning Association journal (Lincoln, Neb.) 6(5), Oct/Nov 1984, 24-26;28.*
LEVEL: B LANG: Eng SIRC ARTICLE NO: 103591

Ontl, K. L'entrainement du sprint long feminin en altitude. *Revue de l'Amicale des entraineurs francais d'athletisme (Paris 89, oct/nov/dec 1984, 23-25.*
LEVEL: B LANG: Fr SIRC ARTICLE NO: 103601

Rogers, J. Planning training for sprinters. (Refs: 4)*Track & field quarterly review (Kalamazoo, Mich.) 84(2), Summer 1984, 13-17.*
LEVEL: I LANG: Eng SIRC ARTICLE NO: 095452

Tabatshnik, B. Mehrikadze, V. The aims and planning of sprint training. *Modern athlete and coach (Athelstone, Aust.) 22(3), Jul 1984, 15-17.*
NOTES: Based on translated extracts from, Legkaja Atletika (Moscow) 9, Sept 1984.
LEVEL: B LANG: Eng SIRC ARTICLE NO: 101718

Valsevich, V. Multiyear preparation of sprinters. *Soviet sports review (Escondido, Calif.) 19(2), Jun 1984, 58-63.*
NOTES: Translated from, Legkaya atletika, 5: 6-7, 1983.
LEVEL: I LANG: Eng SIRC ARTICLE NO: 100098

TRAINING AND CONDITIONING - ISOKINETIC, ISOMETRIC AND ISOTONIC TRAINING

Mumford, J. Uses and training methods for the Excelerator sprint machine. *Track and field journal 25, Feb 1984, 30-31.*
LEVEL: B LANG: Eng SIRC ARTICLE NO: 093923

TRAINING AND CONDITIONING - STRETCHING AND FLEXIBILITY EXERCISES

Cummings, M.S. Wilson, V.E. Bird, E.I. Flexibility development in sprinters using EMG biofeedback and relaxation training. (Refs: 20)*Biofeedback and self regulation (New York) 9(3), 1984, 395-405.*
LEVEL: A LANG: Eng SIRC ARTICLE NO: 174381

TRAINING AND CONDITIONING - WARM-UPS, WARM-DOWNS, LEAD-UP GAMES

Bourbeillon, P. Stephan, H. Quelques conseils pour une prevention des claquages des muscles posterieurs de la cuisse chez le sprinters. *Revue de l'Amicale des entraineurs francais d'athletisme (Paris) 86, janv/fevr/mars 1984, 5-6.*
LEVEL: B LANG: Fr SIRC ARTICLE NO: 095395

WOMEN

Sultanov, N. Training problems in women's sprinting. *Modern athlete and coach (Athelstone, Aust.) 22(1), Jan 1984, 17-19.*
NOTES: Based on a condensed translation from, Legkaya Atletika 9, 1982.
LEVEL: B LANG: Eng SIRC ARTICLE NO: 097003

SQUARE DANCE

TECHNIQUES AND SKILLS

Napier, P.E. Square dancing - Kentucky Mountain style. (Refs: 1)*Journal of physical education, recreation and dance (Reston Va.) 55(7), Sept 1984, 39-42.*
LEVEL: B LANG: Eng SIRC ARTICLE NO: 101205

SQUASH RACQUETS

Colburn, A. Squash. Winchester, Mass.: Faber and Faber, Inc., 1984. 1v.
LEVEL: I LANG: Eng

Endemann, C. Ready for squash? How to's on safety, equipment, exercise, clubs. *Racquets Canada (Toronto) Oct/Nov 1984, 28-30;32.*
LEVEL: B LANG: Eng SIRC ARTICLE NO: 109110

Funston, S. Squash: winning the racquets race. Topical trivia for the typical squash player. *Squash life (Willowdale, Ont.) 8(1), Jan/Feb 1984, 19-22.*
LEVEL: B LANG: Eng SIRC ARTICLE NO: 098519

Squash rackets. London: A. & C. Black Ltd., (1984). 48 p. : ill. (KTG know the game.)
CORP: Squash Rackets Association.
LEVEL: B LANG: Eng ISBN: 0-7136-2571-6
GV1004 18770

AGED

Easter, J. Killer squash? Don't believe everything you read. *Squash player international (London) 13(4), Jan 1984, 6-7.*
LEVEL: B LANG: Eng SIRC ARTICLE NO: 098518

ASSOCIATIONS

United States Squash Racquets Association official yearbook 1984-1985. Bala-Cynwyd, Pa.: United States Squash Racquets Association, 1984. 180 p. : ill.
CORP: United States Squash Racquets Association.
NOTES: Cover title.
LEVEL: B LANG: Eng GV1004 18065

BIOGRAPHY AND AUTOBIOGRAPHY

Bell, G. The wrath of Khan: Only 20 years old, the newest superstar of squash's first family dominates his sport with a vengeance. *Ultrasport (Boston, Mass.) 1(5), Sept/Oct 1984, 70-74.*
LEVEL: B LANG: Eng SIRC ARTICLE NO: 173305

Blanks, T. Squash goest public: Heather McKay and Clive Caldwell - two champions working to bring squash out of the private clubs and into the public domain. *Racquets Canada (Toronto) Oct/Nov 1984, 14-18.*
LEVEL: B LANG: Eng SIRC ARTICLE NO: 109109

Bronstein, M. Khan dynasty rules squash. Jahangir carries on tradition of family by dominating his days in the courts. *Glob and mail (Toronto) 22 May 1984, 20;22.*
LEVEL: B LANG: Eng SIRC ARTICLE NO: 095281

COACHING

Denis, R. Fault diagnosis. *Coaching review (Ottawa, Ont.) 7, Nov/Dec 1984, 53-54.*
LEVEL: B LANG: Eng SIRC ARTICLE NO: 099934

EQUIPMENT

Badminton & squash: product action on the courts. *Sports trader (London) 145(1009), 19 Apr 1984, 14-15;17.*
LEVEL: B LANG: E SIRC ARTICLE NO: 101872

EQUIPMENT - RETAILING

No change at the top: our survey reveals that established names still dominate badminton and squash. *Sports trader (London) 145(1009), 19 Apr 1984, 10-11.*
LEVEL: B LANG: Eng SIRC ARTICLE NO: 101871

The Pro's progress. Badminton & squash. (Pro-Kennex) *Sports trader (London) 145(1009), 19 Apr 1984, 19;22-23.*
LEVEL: B LANG Eng SIRC ARTICLE NO: 101873

FACILITIES - MAINTENANCE

Buzzolini, S. Construction des courts de squash. *Macolin (Suisse) 4, avr 1984, 16-17.*
LEVEL: B LANG: Fr SIRC ARTICLE NO: 100582

INJURIES AND ACCIDENTS

Easterbrook, M. Eye injuries in squash and racquetball players: an update. Blessures oculaires attribuables au squash et au racquetball. (Refs: 5)*Canadian Intramural Recreation Association/Association canadienne de loisirs-intramuros bulletin (Ottawa) 9(5), Feb/fevr 1984, 8-10.*
NOTES: Reprinted from, Campus Recreation, The Faculty of Physical Education, Winter 1984. Tire de, Campus Recreation, Faculte d'education physique, hiver 1984.
LEVEL: I LANG: Eng Fr SIRC ARTICLE NO: 099936

Fowler, A.W. Cox, J. Sudden death in squash players. (letters) *Lancet (London) 1(8373), 18 Feb 1984, 393-394.*
LEVEL: I LANG: Eng SIRC ARTICLE NO: 099938

Northcote, R.J. Evanst, A.D. Ballantyne, D. Sudden death in squash players. (Refs: 6)*Lancet (London) 1(8369), 21 Jan 1984, 148-150.*
ABST: 30 sudden deaths (29 men, 1 woman) associated with playing squash are studied. The subjects' age range was 22 to 66 with a mean of 46.7. Of the known causes of death, coronary heart disease was found in 23, valvular heart disease in 3, hypertrophic obstructive cardiomyopathy in 1, cardiac arrhythmia in 2, and one death from intracerebral hemorrhage. 22 subjects had reported symptoms prior to death, and 12 subjects had been known by their physician to have a cardiovascular disorder.
LEVEL: A LANG: Eng SIRC ARTICLE NO: 098522

Sudden death in squash players. *Sports medicine digest (Van Nuys, Calif.) 6(6), Jun 1984, 5-6.*
LEVEL: B LANG: Eng SIRC ARTICLE NO: 102144

OFFICIATING

Hawkey, D. Refereeing: it's never been more difficult. *Squash player international (London) 12(12), Sept 1984, 12.*
LEVEL: LANG: Eng SIRC ARTICLE NO: 173475

PERCEPTUAL MOTOR PROCESSES

Howarth, C. Walsh, W.D. Abernethy, B. A field examination of anticipation in squash: some preliminary data. (Refs: 26) *Australian journal of science & medicine in sport (Kingston, Aust.) 16(3), Oct 1984, 6-10.*
ABST: The initial anticipatory movements of two high level and two lower level squash players were examined during competition. Cinematographic analysis revealed that although the overall speed of the game was similar for both skill groups, the highly skilled players made their initial anticipatory movements significantly earlier than did the lower grade players. Estimation of the completion times for initial movement selection indicated a reliance of the highly skilled players upon advance information alone, whereas the lesser skilled appeared to wait until later ball flight information was available before selecting their return stroke.
LEVEL: A LANG: Eng SIRC ARTICLE NO: 106067

PHYSICAL FITNESS

Vigorous athletics after 40. *Health letter (San Antonio, Tex.) 23(12), 22 Jun 1984, 3.*
LEVEL: B LANG: Eng SIRC ARTICLE NO: 095282

PROTECTIVE DEVICES

Eye safety campaign gains ally. *Squash life (Willowdale, Ont.) 8(5), Sept/Oct 1984, 8-9.*
LEVEL: B LANG: Eng SIRC ARTICLE NO 101530

Funston, S. There are none so blind. (eyeguards) *Squash life (Willowdale, Ont.) 8(3), May/Jun 1984, 11;13.*
LEVEL: B LANG: Eng SIRC ARTICLE NO: 099937

PSYCHOLOGY

Mark, M.M. Mutrie, N. Brooks, D.R. Harris, D.V. Causal attributions of winners and losers in individual competitive sports: toward a reformulation of the self-serving bias. (Refs: 32)*Sport psychology (Champaign, Ill.) 6(2), 1984, 184-196.*
ABST: The achievement oriented world of sport has been a frequent setting for the study of attributions for success and failure. However, it may be inappropriate to generalize from previous research to attributions made in actual, organized,

SQUASH RACQUETS (continued)

competitive, individual sports because previous studies suffer from one or more of three characteristics which may limit their generalizability to such settings: previous studies have employed novel tasks, staged the competition for research purposes, or examined attribution about team success or failure. The present research was conducted (a) to avoid these limitations to generalizability, (b) to examine whether competitors who differ in experience or ability make different attributions for success and failure, (c) to employee an attribution measure that does not rely too much on the researchers' interpretation of the subjects' attributions as past techniques have done. Two studies were conducted examining attributions made by winners and losers in the second round of organized squash (Study 1) and racquetball (Study 2) tournaments. Results indicate no difference between players of different experience/ability levels. In addition, winners and losers did not differ in the locus of causality of their attributions, but winners, relative to losers, made more stable and controllable attributions.
LEVEL: A LANG: Eng SIRC ARTICLE NO: 108492

SPORTING EVENTS

Dinerman, R. A history of the Nationals. *Squash news (New York) 7(1), Apr 1984, 24;26-28.*
LEVEL: B LANG: Eng SIRC ARTICLE NO: 099935

SPORTSMANSHIP

Putting the 'sport' back into sportsmanship. *Squash life (Willowdale, Ont.) 8(5), Sept/Oct 1984, 6.*
LEVEL: B LANG: Eng SIRC ARTICLE NO: 101534

STRATEGY

Beddington, J. Keeping command of the T spot. *Racquets Canada (Toronto) Oct/Nov 1984, 20-21.*
LEVEL: B LANG: Eng SIRC ARTICLE NO: 109111

Fairs, J. Shaping strategy and tactics for effective squash. *Squash life (Willowdale, Ont.) 8(5), Sept/Oct 1984, 14-19.*
LEVEL: B LANG: Eng SIRC ARTICLE NO: 101531

STRATEGY - OFFENSIVE

Truby, J.O. Truby, J.O. The secret of squash: how to win using the 4-CRO system. 1st ed. Boston ; Toronto: Little, Brown & Co., c1984. 146, (32) p. : ill.
LEVEL: B LANG: Eng ISBN: 0-316-853534 LC CARD: 84-17187 GV1004 18193

TEACHING

Siegel, D. I teach squash. (Refs: 1)*Journal of physical education, recreation and dance (Reston, Va.) 55(7), Sept 1984, 59-60.*
LEVEL: B LANG: Eng SIRC ARTICLE NO: 101535

TECHNIQUES AND SKILLS

Denis, R. Uses of the boast. *Canadian squash (Ottawa) 3(4), Oct/Dec 1984, 9.*
LEVEL: B LANG: Eng SIRC ARTICLE NO: 107560

Shmerler, C. Squash your fears for better tennis. *World tennis (Los Angeles) 32(7), Dec 1984, 60-61.*
LEVEL: B LANG: Eng SIRC ARTICLE NO: 173590

TRAINING AND CONDITIONING

Harris, B. Keep fit with Bomber Harris. *Squash player international (London) 12(10), Jul 1984, 17.*
LEVEL: B LANG: Eng SIR ARTICLE NO: 101532

Harris, B. Keep fit with Bomber Harris. *Squash player international (London) 12((9), Jun 1984, 11.*
LEVEL: B LANG: Eng SIR ARTICLE NO: 101533

Harris, B. Keep fit with Bomber Harris: keep on running. *Squash player international (London) 12(12), Sept 1984, 14.*
LEVEL: B LANG: Eng SIRC ARTICLE NO: 173476

TRAINING AND CONDITIONING - DRILLS

Goodfellow, D. Winning is not a hit and miss affair. *Squash life (Willowdale, Ont.) 8(1), Jan/Feb 1984, 35.*
LEVEL: B LANG Eng SIRC ARTICLE NO: 098520

Instructional squash: some drills to improve your shots. *Sports (Kallang, Singapore) 12(3), Mar 1984, 32.*
LEVEL: B LANG: En SIRC ARTICLE NO: 098521

TRAINING AND CONDITIONING - WEIGHT AND STRENGTH TRAINING

Harris, B. Keep fit: National squad trainer Bomber Harris continues his series. *Squash player international (Survey, Eng.) (1), Oct 1984, 14.*
LEVEL: B LANG: Eng SIRC ARTICLE NO: 173368

Wong, H. An intelligent approach to working with weights. *Squash life (Willowdale, Ont.) 8(6), Nov/Dec 1984, 13-14.*
LEVEL B LANG: Eng SIRC ARTICLE NO: 173480

STEEPLECHASE

BIOGRAPHY AND AUTOBIOGRAPHY

Burfoot, A. Where were you in '32? One olympian took the long way to a bronze medal. (Joseph P. McCluskey) *Runner's world 18(13), 1984 Annual, 9-11;92-93.*
LEVEL: B LANG: Eng SIRC ARTICLE NO: 092472

Higdon, H. Life in the pits. (Henry Marsh) *Runner (Boulder, Colo.) 6(5), Feb 1984, 76-81.*
LEVEL: B LANG: Eng SIRC ARTICLE NO: 095417

Runner's world gold medal exclusive: Henry Marsh, a man of faith, optimism and determination, faces his greatest challenge in LA. *Runner's world 19(5), May 1984, 25-26;29;32;34;36;40.*
LEVEL: B LANG: Eng SIRC ARTICLE NO: 093939

BIOMECHANICS

Gartland, J. Henson, P. A comparison of the hurdle steeplechase water barrier technique with the conventional water barrier technique. *Track and field quarterly review (Kalamazoo, Mich.) 84(3), Fall 1984, 26-28.*
LEVEL: I LANG: Eng SIRC ARTICLE NO: 096963

ECONOMICS

Newman, S. The good and the not so good. Two Canadian athletes' experiences on U.S. athletic scholarships and what other Canadians may learn from their experiences. *Coaching review (Ottawa) 7, Sept/Oct 1984, 24-27.*
LEVEL: B LANG: Eng SIRC ARTICLE NO: 098664

SPORTING EVENTS

Wischnia, B. The long distances: will the Yanks get kicked again in the steeple, 5000 and 10,000? *Runner's world 19(4), Apr 1984, 40-47.*
LEVEL: B LANG: Eng SIRC ARTICLE NO: 093966

TECHNIQUES AND SKILLS

Fix, D. Smith, N. Analysis chart for steeplechase waterjumping. *Track and field review (Kalamazoo, Mich.) 84(3), Fall 1984, 23-25.*
LEVEL: B LANG: Eng SIRC ARTICLE NO: 096960

Higdon, H. Steeplechasing. *Runner (Boulder, Colo.) 6(5), Feb 1984, 82.*
LEVEL: B LANG: Eng SIRC ARTICLE NO: 095418

TRAINING AND CONDITIONING

Wilczinski, G. Analyse du processus annuel d'entrainement (saison 1982-1983) de Boguslaw Maminski, vice-champion du monde du 3000 m steeple. *Revue de l'Amicale des entraineurs francais d'athletisme (Paris) 87, avr/mai/juin 1984, 14-21.*
LEVEL: B LANG: Fr SIRC ARTICLE NO: 097019

SURFING

Lueras, L. Bechlen, F. Surfing: the ultimate pleasure. New York: Workman Publishing, c1984. 236 p. : ill. (An Emphasis International book.) NOTES: Bibliography: p. 222-227.
LEVEL: I LANG: Eng ISBN: 0-89480-708-0 LC CARD: 83-40541 GV840.S8 17485

BIOGRAPHY AND AUTOBIOGRAPHY

Carter, C. Alex Cooke: on the line Chris Carter and Alex Cooke 10/5/83. *Surfing (San Diego) 20(2), Feb 1984, 81;83.*
LEVEL B LANG: Eng SIRC ARTICLE NO: 102106

George, S. Tom Curren: on the line Tom Curren and Sam George. *Surfing magazine (San Clemente, Calif.) 20(3), Mar 1984, 163;165.*
LEVEL: B LANG: Eng SIRC ARTICLE NO: 108638

George, S. Mark Richards: on the line Mark Richards and Sam George. *Surfing magazine (San Clemente, Calif.) 20(3), Mar 1984 158;160.*
LEVEL: B LANG: Eng SIRC ARTICLE NO: 108639

George, S. Shaun Tomson: on the line Shaun Tomson and Sam George. *Surfing magazine (Can Clemente, Calif.) 20(3), Mar 1984, 155;157.*
LEVEL: B LANG: Eng SIRC ARTICLE NO: 108640

George, S. Nat Young: on the line Nat Young and Sam George. *Surfing magazine (San Clemente, Calif.) 20(3), Mar 1984, 150;152.*
LEVEL: B LANG: Eng SIRC ARTICLE NO: 108642

Hodge, H. Kong uncaged: profile of Gary (Kong) Elkerton. *Surfer (Dana Point, Calif.) 25(6), Jun*

1984, 42-49.
LEVEL: B LANG: Eng SIRC ARTICLE NO: 099940

Kampion, D. David Nuuhiwa: on the line David Nuuhiwa and Drew Kampion. *Surfing magazine (San Clemente, Calif.) 20(3), Mar 1984, 147;149.*
LEVEL: B LANG: Eng SIRC ARTICLE NO: 108641

ECONOMICS

Hurley, B. Knoernschild, J. Tips. Part two: how to find (and keep) a sponsor. *Surfer (Dana Point, Calif.) 25(4), Apr 1984, 33.*
LEVEL: B LANG: Eng SIRC ARTICLE NO: 098523

Hurley, B. Knoernschild, J. There's no such thing as a free lunch: or how to find (and keep) a sponsor. *Surfer (Dana Point, Calif.) 25(3), Mar 1984, 23.*
LEVEL: B LANG: Eng SIRC ARTICLE NO: 098524

EQUIPMENT

Baker, B. Mark Richards performance tests twins vs. fours. (multi-fins) *Surfer (Dana Point, Calif.) 25(6), Jun 1984, 52-53.*
LEVEL: B LANG: Eng SIRC ARTICLE NO: 099939

Holmes, P. Cheyne Horan tests new hull/keel concept. *Surfer (Dana Point, Calif.) 25(6), Jun 1984, 50-51.*
LEVEL: B LANG: E SIRC ARTICLE NO: 099941

Sharp, B. Soft core: bodyboarders explore new surfing limits. *Surfing (San Clemente, Calif.) 20(9), Sept 1984, 56-63.*
LEVEL: B LANG: Eng SIRC ARTICLE NO: 103478

HISTORY

Aaberg, D. Long boards. 1964-1966. *Surfing magazine (San Clemente, Calif.) 20(3), Mar 1984, 74-87.*
LEVEL: B LANG: Eng SIR ARTICLE NO: 108643

Bartholomew, W. Wave rebeles: 1971 to 1976. *Surfing magazine (San Clemente, Calif.) 20(3), Mar 1984, 100-116;168;172.*
LEVEL: B LANG: Eng SIRC ARTICLE NO: 108646

Kampion, D. Short boards. 1967-1970. *Surfing magazine (San Clemente, Calif.) 20(3), Mar 1984, 88-89.*
LEVEL: B LANG: Eng SIRC ARTICLE NO: 108644

Tomson, M. Professional: 1977-1982. *Surfing magazine (San Clemente, Calif.) 20(3), Mar 1984, 118-130;166.*
LEVEL: B LANG: Eng SIRC ARTICLE NO: 108648

INJURIES AND ACCIDENTS

Hypothermia: the winter surfer's biggest worry. *Surfer (San Juan Capistrano, Calif.) 25(11), Nov 1984, 20.*
LEVEL: B LANG: E SIRC ARTICLE NO: 103477

Lowdon, B.J. Surfing injuries: Immediate and long term problems and prevention. (Refs: 11)*Athletic training (Greenville, N.C.) 19(2), Summer 1984, 105-108.*
LEVEL: I LANG: Eng SIRC ARTICLE NO: 095283

Pritchard, B. Media release: surfboard riding injuries. *ACHPER national journal (Kingswood, Aust.) 104, Winter 1984, 32.*
LEVEL: I LANG: Eng SIRC ARTICLE NO: 101538

Surfboard-riding injuries. (letter) *Medical journal Australia (Sydney) 140(9), 28 Apr 1984, 562-563.*
LEVEL: B LANG: Eng SIR ARTICLE NO: 101539

MEDICINE

Surfing with heart and soul. Heart transplant patient surfs to recovery. *Surfing (San Clemente, Calif.) 20(9), Sept 1984, 30;35.*
LEVEL: B LANG: Eng SIRC ARTICLE NO: 103479

SPORTING EVENTS

Holmes, P. The '84 summer Olympics: why surfers won't be there... *Surfer (Dana Point, Calif.) 25(9), Sept 1984, 94-97.*
LEVEL: B LANG: Eng SIRC ARTICLE NO: 101536

The world contest: twenty years 1964 to 1984. *Surfing magazine (San Clemente, Calif.) 20(3), Mar 1984, 63-66;71.*
LEVEL: B LANG: Eng SIRC ARTICLE NO: 108645

TECHNIQUES AND SKILLS

Curren, T. Curren on Curren. *Surfing (San Diego) 20(2), Feb 1984, 36-43.*
LEVEL: B LANG: Eng SIRC ARTICLE NO: 102105

McClure, J. Tips: aerials. *Surfer (Dana Point, Calif.) 25(9), Sept 1984, 38.*
LEVEL: B LANG: Eng SIRC ARTICLE NO: 101537

Stokes, G. Switchfoot surfing. *Surfer (Dana Point, Calif.) 25(7), Jul 1984, 32;34;36.*
LEVEL: B LANG: Eng SIRC ARTICLE NO: 099942

SWEDEN

Silletta, T. Sweden's sport school system. *Coaching review (Ottawa, Ont.) 7, Nov/Dec 1984, 60-61.*
LEVEL: B LANG: Eng SIRC ARTICLE NO: 099346

HISTORY

Van Dalen, D.B. Bennett, B.L. L'education physique et le nationalisme pedagogique en Suede. *Dans, Massicotte, J.P. et Lessard, C. (eds.), Histoire du sport de l'antiquite au XIXe siecle, Sillery, Que., Presses de l'Universite du Quebec, 1984, p. 155-160.*
LEVEL: I LANG: Fr GV571 18971

PHYSICAL FITNESS

Friskvaerd i Vattenfall. Stockholm, Sweden?: s.n., (1984). 19 p. : ill.
LEVEL: B LANG: Swe ISBN: 91-7186-236-6 GV481 20229

Haglund, B.J. Geographical and socioeconomic distribution of physical activity at work and leisure time and its relation to morbidity in a Swedish rural county. *Scandinavian journal of social medicine (Stockholm) 12(4), 1984, 155-164.*
LEVEL: I LANG: Eng

SWIMMING

Jerome, J. Propellers, paddlewheels, and swimming faster. *In, Schrier, E.W. and Allman, W.F. (eds.), Newton at the bat: the science in sports, New York, Scribner, c1984, p. 140-144.*
LEVEL: B LANG: Eng RC1235 18609

Krotee, B. Swimming slick. (shaving) *Triathlon (Santa Monica, Calif.) 2(3), Jun/Jul 1984, 21.*
LEVEL: B LANG: Eng SIRC ARTICLE NO: 101553

Odent, M. Bastin, P. Vio, P.M. Dieulouard, C. Quilez, M. Le Camus, J. Folliard, R. Fluck, R. Fernandez, P. Dion, C. Tarting, Coupry, A. Fourcade, J.M. de Hodeau, H. L'eau: une nouvelle vague de pratiques en piscine II. (Refs: 31)*Pratiques corporelles (France) 63, 1984, 3-36.*
NOTES: Suite du numero de mars 83.
LEVEL: I LANG: Fr

Pursley, D. Let the coaches have their say: AIS update. *International swimmer Jan/Feb 1984, 16-17.*
LEVEL: B LANG: Eng SIR ARTICLE NO: 098541

Vickers, B.J. Vincent, W.J. Swimming. 4th ed. Dubuque, Iowa: W.C. Brown Co., c1984. vii, 84 p. : ill. (Exploring sports series.)
NOTES: Bibliography: p. 73-74. Includes index.
LEVEL: B LANG: Eng ISBN: 0-697-09977-6 LC CARD: 83-70269 GV837 18952

ADMINISTRATION

Kaslik. P.J. Computerizing your swimmers: now you can keep your swimmers up-to-date on how they stack up with the best of their competitors. *Swimming technique (Los Angeles, Calif.) 21(2), Aug/Oct 1984, 21-22.*
LEVEL: B LANG: Eng SIRC ARTICLE NO: 098534

AGED

Biegel, L. In the swim. (Refs: 1)
NOTES: In, Biegel, L. (ed.), Physical fitness and the older person: a guide to exercise fo health care professionals, Rockville, Md., Aspen Systems Corp., 1984, p. 119-128.
LEVEL: I LANG: Eng GV482.6 17754

Firsov, Z. Swimming old. *International swimming and water polo (Budapest, Hungary) 4(16), 1984, 46-47.*
LEVEL: B LANG: Eng SIRC ARTICLE NO: 108652

Hartley, A.A. Hartley, J.T. Performance changes in champion swimmers aged 30 to 84 years. *Experimental aging research (Bar Harbor, Mich.) 10(3), Autumn 1984, 141-150.*
ABST: Cross-sectional studies revealed performance decrements in swimmers with age while follow-up studies indicated substantially smaller changes in performance.
LEVEL: A LANG: Eng

Hogan, P.I. Santomier, J.P. Effect of mastering swim skills on older adults' self-efficacy. (Refs: 9)*Research quarterly for exercise & sport (Reston, Va.) 55(3), Sept 1984, 294-296.*
LEVEL: I LANG: Eng SIRC ARTICLE NO: 103490

SWIMMING (continued)

ANTHROPOMETRY

Bloomfield, J. Blansby, B.A. Ackland, T.R.
Analysis of the swimming profiles. *International swimmer Jan/Feb 1984, 38.*
ABST: A method to profile pulmonary function, flexibility, body composition and somatotype for individual swimmers to enable coaches to identify areas of improvement.
LEVEL: I LANG: Eng SIRC ARTICLE NO: 098526

Housh, T.J. Thorland, W.G. Johnson, G.O. Tharp, G.D. Cisar, C.J. Refsell, M.J. Ansorge, C.J. Body composition variables as discriminators of sports participation of elite adolescent female athletes. (Refs: 22)*Research quarterly for exercise & sport (Reston, Va.) 55(3), Sept 1984, 302-304.*
ABST: The purpose of this study was to determine the degree to which body composition variables (relative fat, body weight, fat weight, and lean body weight) discriminate between successful participants of different sports. 110 elite female athletes (age 16.08 plus or minus 1.53 years) participated in the study: 64 swimmers (10 distance swimmers and 54 sprinters) and 46 runners (12 distance runners and 34 sprinters). Multiple discriminant analysis was used. The discriminant function correctly classified 87.3% of the subjects in their respective sports.
LEVEL: A LANG: Eng SIRC ARTICLE NO: 103491

McGarty, J.M. Comparison of three hydrostatic weighing methods. Eugene, Ore.: Microform Publications, University of Oregon, 1984. 1 microfiche : negative, ill. ; 11 x 15 cm.
NOTES: Thesis (M.S.) - University of Wisconsin-La Crosse, 1982; (viii, 65 leaves); includes bibliography.
LEVEL: A LANG: Eng UO84 295

Peltenburg, A.L. Erich, W.B.M. Zonderland, M.L. Bernink, M.J.E. VanDenBrande, J.L. Huisveld, I.A. A retrospective growth study of female gymnasts and girl swimmers. (Refs: 13)*International journal of sports medicine (Stuttgart) 5(5), Oct 1984, 262-267.*
ABST: The aim of this investigation was to retrospectively evaluate growth patterns of different groups of gymnasts as compared to schoolgirls and girl swimmers from 1 until 11 years of age. The differences in body height between the groups of sports participants and schoolgirls in the prepubertal period appeared to be mainly based on the genetic growth regulation and seemed to be largely dependent in the gymnastic groups on inheritance of the mothers' height. Significant differences existed in weight as percentage of normal weight for height between the gymnasts and the swimmers.
LEVEL: A LANG: Eng SIRC ARTICLE NO: 104774

Spurgeon, J.H. Giese, W.K. Physique of world-class female swimmers. (Refs: 16)*Scandinavian journal of sports science (Helsinki, Finland) 6(1), Jul 1984, 11-14.*
ABST: This study pertains to body size, form, and composition of world-class predominantly white female swimmers. The subjects were specialists in breaststroke, backstroke, sprint, and distance swimming. On each subject, data were collected for 10 measures of body size, 7 indices of body form, and a measure of body composition. It was found: 1) the 'sprint' group was tallest and the 'sprint butterfly' group shortest 2) lower limb length relative to sitting height was similar for the 'sprint' and 'long distance' groups, and lowest for the

'sprint butterfly' group 3) all groups were similar in respect to body composition fat (% body weight) and 4) discriminant function analyses correctly classified (100%) the 'sprint butterfly' group as differing in physique from all other groups.
LEVEL: A LANG: Eng SIRC ARTICLE NO: 103501

Vaccaro, P. Ostrove, S.M. Vandervelden, L. Goldfarb, A.H. Clarke, D.H. Dummer, G.M. Body composition and physiological responses of masters female swimmers 20 to 70 years of age. (Refs: 34)*Research quarterly for exercise & sport (Reston, Va.) 55(3), Sept 1984, 278-284.*
ABST: Eighty-seven female masters swimmers ranging in age from 20 to 69 were selected for a detailed study of their body composition and physiological responses at rest and during exercise. These women were then placed into two subsets, a highly trained group and a not highly trained group. Both the highly trained and not highly trained swimmers were considerably lower in percent fat than previously reported data for normal untrained women of similar ages. In both groups, however, percent fat across age levels within each training group showed significant increases at approximately 40 years of age. In the highly trained swimmers, VO2 max (ml.kg-1.min-1) decreased at a mean rate of about 7% per decade, while in the not highly trained swimmers the decline was approximately 8% per decade.
LEVEL: A LANG: Eng SIRC ARTICLE NO: 103502

BIOGRAPHY AND AUTOBIOGRAPHY

Aquatics: Alex Baumann. Sports nautiques: Alex Baumann. *Champion (Ottawa) 8(3), Aug 1984, 40-41.*
LEVEL: B LANG: Eng Fr SIRC ARTICLE NO: 096848

Dawson, B. The real life of Tarzan. (Johnny Weissmuller) *Swimming world and junior swimmer (Los Angeles, Calif.) 25(3), Mar 1984, 36-41.*
LEVEL: B LANG: Eng SIRC ARTICLE NO: 098528

Dawson, B. Legend of Tarzan. (Johnny Weissmuller) *International swimming and water polo (Budapest, Hungary) 4(16), 1984, 40-43.*
LEVEL: B LANG: Eng SIRC ARTICLE NO: 108649

de Lamare, G. Pradinho: a quartet played by one. (Ricardo Prado) *International swimming and water polo (Budapest, Hungary) 14, 1984, 22-23.*
LEVEL: B LANG: Eng SIRC ARTICLE NO: 108480

Ewald, R. Footloose Linehan couldn't stay away. *Swimming world and junior swimmer (Los Angeles, Calif.) 25(6), Jun 1984, 25-27.*
LEVEL: B LANG: Eng SIRC ARTICLE NO: 095297

Johnson, W.O. A star was born. (Buster Crabbe) *Sports illustrated (Chicago, Ill.) 61(4), 18 Jul 1984, 137-138;143;146;151;152-154;156;159.*
NOTES: Special preview: the 1984 Olympics.
LEVEL: B LANG: Eng SIRC ARTICLE NO: 096867

Levin, D. She's set her sights on L.A. Dara Torres, the world's best in the 50 freestyle, is stretching to make the U.S. Olympic team in the 100. *Sports illustrated (Chicago, Ill.) 60(25), 18 Jun 1984, 40;42;46;48.*
LEVEL: B LANG: Eng SIRC ARTICLE NO: 095311

Mullins, D. A giant, but gentle man. (Johnny Weissmuller) *Swimming world and junior swimmer (Los Angeles, Calif.) 25(3), Ma 1984, 43-46.*
LEVEL: B LANG: Eng SIRC ARTICLE NO: 098538

Neff, C. Putting his back into his work: intense, driven Rick Carey, a world record backstroker, goes all out for perfection in everything he does. *Sports illustrated 60(13), 26 Mar 1984, 28-30;34;38.*
LEVEL: B LANG: Eng SIRC ARTICLE NO: 093779

Neff, C. The albatross will fly. (Michael Gross) *Sports illustrated (Chicago, Ill.) 61(4), 18 Jul 1984, 74-76;78;80;84;87;88;90.*
NOTES: Special preview: the 1984 Olympics.
LEVEL: B LANG: Eng SIRC ARTICLE NO: 096876

Your Naber, the swimmer. The quadruple gold-medalist of the 1976 Olympics assesses America's chances in L.A. *Scholastic coach (New York) 53(10), May/Jun 1984, 26-27;98-99.*
LEVEL: B LANG: Eng SIRC ARTICLE NO: 095328

BIOMECHANICS

Adams, T.A. Martin, R.B. Yeater, R.A. Gilson, K.A. Tethered force and velocity relationships. (Refs: 16)*Swimming technique (Los Angeles, Calif.) 20(3), Nov 1983/Jan 1984, 21-22;24-26.*
ABST: The author evaluated the relationship between tethered force, stroke rate and velocity in college varsity male and female swimmers performing the front crawl. Fully tethered and partially thethered swimming was examined. The results indicated tethered force and free swimming velocity to be a direct function of stroke rate. The tethered experiments confirmed a negative linear relationship between tethered force and release velocity.
LEVEL: A LANG: Eng SIRC ARTICLE NO: 095285

Adams, T.M. A biomechanical analysis of the interrelationships of tethered forces, velocity, and stroke rate in the front crawl stroke. Eugene, Ore.: Microform Publications, University of Oregon, 1984. 2 mirofiches : negative, ill. : 11 x 15 cm.
NOTES: Thesis (Ed.D.) - West Virginia University, 1981; (vii, 143 leaves); vita; includes bibliography.
LEVEL: A LANG: Eng UO84 176-177

Colwin, C. Kinetic streamlining. *Swimming world and junior swimmer (Los Angeles, Calif.) 25(2), Feb 1984, 47-51.*
LEVEL: I LANG: Eng SIRC ARTICLE NO: 095289

Griffiths, J. A biomechanical analysis of racing dives in swimming. *Carnegie research papers (Beckett Park, Leeds) 1(6), De 1984, 32.*
CONF: Carnegie Undergraduate Research Symposium (1984 : Leeds, Eng.).
LEVEL: I LANG: Eng SIRC ARTICLE NO: 172508

Mason, B. Problems in stroke mechanics amongst swimmers. *Sports sciences & medicine quarterly (Australia) 1(2), Oct 1984, 2-5.*
NOTES: First article in a two part series.
LEVEL: I LANG: Eng SIRC ARTICLE NO: 103495

Newman, S. At the zoo: a lesson in mechanics. (biomechanics) *Coaching review (Ottawa, Ont.) 7, Jul/Aug 1984, 40-41.*
LEVEL B LANG: Eng SIRC ARTICLE NO: 095314

Rodeo, S. Sports performance series: swimming the breaststroke - a kinesiological analysis and considerations for strength training. *National Strength & Conditioning Association journal (Lincoln, Neb.) 6(4), Aug/Sept 1984, 4-6;74-76;80.*
LEVEL: I LANG: Eng SIRC ARTICLE NO: 099956

CHILDREN

An eight year training plan. *Swim Canada 97, 11(1), Jan 1984, 8.*
LEVEL: B LANG: Eng SIRC ARTICLE NO: 092420

Bolduc, D. Glou. Glou. Demarche d'acclimatation a l'eau pour des enfants de maternelle et du premier cycle du primaire. (Refs: 16)*Revue quebecoise de l'activite physique (Trois-Rivieres, Que.) 3(1), oct 1984, 25-28.*
LEVEL: B LANG: Fr SIRC ARTICLE NO: 101541

Denis, B. A l'eau bebe. Quebec: Utilis, c1984. 123 p.
LEVEL: B LANG: Fr ISBN: 2-8930-0006-1 GV837.25 18947

Hoch, M. Swimming young. *International swimming and water polo (Budapest, Hungary) 4(16), 1984, 44-45.*
LEVEL: B LANG: Eng SIRC ARTICLE NO: 108650

Katz, J. No more water wings. *Shape (Woodland Hills, Calif.) 4(4), Dec 1984, 52;124.*
LEVEL: B LANG: Eng SIRC ARTICLE NO: 173235

Lassota, M. Allow parents to watch swim lessons; there are pay-offs. *Journal of physical education and program (Columbus, Oh.) Sept 1984, F-10-F-11.*
LEVEL: B LANG: Eng SIRC ARTICLE NO: 103492

Mileikovskaia, M.V. Plavanie detei rannego vozrasta -- effektivnyi metod zakalivaniia. (Swimming for young children - an effective method of hardiness training.) *Meditsinskaya sestra (Moscow) 43(10), Oct 1984, 35-36.*
LEVEL: B LANG: Rus

Watson, G.G. Blanksby, B.A. Bloomfield, J. Children and competitive swimming. (Refs: 3)*International swimmer (N.S.W., Aust. 21(3), May/Jun 1984, 27-30.*
LEVEL: I LANG: Eng SIRC ARTICLE NO: 101559

CLOTHING

Performance swimwear. *Fitness industry (Miami, Fla.) 2(2), Mar/Apr 1984, 32-34;36.*
LEVEL: B LANG: Eng SIRC ARTICLE NO: 0975

CLUBS AND TEAMS

A look at Canadian swim clubs. *Swim Canada 97, 11(1), Jan 1984, 20.*
LEVEL: B LANG: Eng SIRC ARTICLE NO: 092427

Balmain makes it a century. (Balmain Swimming Club) *International swimmer (N.S.W., Aust.) 21(3), May/Jun 1984, 15-16.*
LEVEL B LANG: Eng SIRC ARTICLE NO: 101540

Gambril, D. Bay, A. From the ground up. (building a swim club) *Swimming technique (Los Angeles, Calif.) 21(2), Aug/Oct 1984 9-14.*
NOTES: Reprinted from, Swimmer and team, by Don Gambril and Alfred Bay, Icarus Press, South Bend, Ind., 1984.
ABST: Gambril, a respected American swimming coach, describes step-by-step the planning and organization of a new competitive swimming club. He outlines the necessity of market research prior to establishing a new club: available facilities, community need, community support and then the stpes involved after a club is incorporated as a non-profit organization. This article is invaluable reading for all those planning a new sport club.
LEVEL: B LANG: Eng SIRC ARTICLE NO: 098531

COACHING

Bance, D. The American coaching system (part 1). *Swimming times (Loughborough, Eng.) 61(11), Nov 1984, 14;20.*
LEVEL: B LANG: Eng SIRC ARTICLE NO: 173505

Benson, R.A. The art and science of swim coaching. (Refs: 7)*Swimming technique (Los Angeles, Calif.) 21(1), May/Jul 1984, 25-28.*
LEVEL: I LANG: Eng SIRC ARTICLE NO: 095286

Colwin, C. Colwin talks with Bouws. (Niels Bouws) *Swim Canada 98, Feb 1984, 20-21.*
LEVEL: B LANG: Eng SIRC ARTICLE NO: 090972

Crossman, J. Effective feedback. (Refs: 16)*Coaching review (Ottawa, Ont.) 7, Jul/Aug 1984, 45-46.*
LEVEL: B LANG: Eng SIRC ARTICLE NO: 095292

Essick, R. My involvement in US swimming. *International swimmer (N.S.W., Aust.) Jul/Aug 1984, 8-11.*
LEVEL: B LANG: Eng SIRC ARTICLE NO: 101548

Interview: Colwin talks with Talbot. (Don Talbot) *Swim Canada (Toronto) 11(6), Jun 1984, 32-34.*
LEVEL: B LANG: Eng SIRC ARTICLE NO: 095308

Interview: Paul Meronen. *Coaching review (Ottawa, Ont.) 7, Nov/Dec 1984, 8-16.*
LEVEL: B LANG: Eng SIRC ARTICLE NO: 099950

Swartz, D. Hopper, B. Experiential coaching. *Swimming technique (Los Angeles, Calif.) 20(3), Nov 1983/Jan 1984, 12;14.*
LEVEL: B LANG: Eng SIRC ARTICLE NO: 095323

Tutton, M. Amateur coaches: molding muscle and mind. (Duane Jones, John Fitzgerald and John ApSimon) *Ottawa magazine 4(1), Apr 1984, 12-13;45-50;52-53.*
LEVEL: B LANG: Eng SIRC ARTICLE NO: 092712

COUNTRIES AND REGIONS

Xiaofei, L. Homes of swimming: swimming standards are inexplicably low in this country with a huge swimming population. But things are changing for the better now. *China sports (Beijing, China) 16(8), Aug 1984, 18-20.*
LEVEL: B LANG: Eng SIRC ARTICLE NO: 101561

DIRECTORIES

1985 buyer's digest. *Pool & spa marketing (Thornhill, Ont.) 8(4), Dec 1984, 25-27;30-31;34-36;38-40;42-43;46-48;50-52;54-55;57-58;60;62-64;66-67;69-70;72;74-76;78-79;82-83;85-86;88-94;96;98;102.*
LEVEL: B LANG: Eng SIRC ARTICLE NO: 105216

DISABLED

Bell, G.H. Gunsten, P.H. A recreational swim program for the educable mentally retarded. (Refs: 6)*NIRSA journal (Mt. Pleasant, Mich.) 8(2), Winter 1984, 40-41.*
LEVEL: B LANG: Eng SIRC ARTICLE NO: 097529

Natation Canada Esso programme pour les personnes handicapees: manuel de l'instructeur. Programme de perfectionnement des habiletes, Federation canadienne des organisations sportives pour personnes handicapees. Ottawa: Federation canadienne des organisations sportives pour personnes handicapees, c1984. 90 p. : ill.
CORP: Federation canadienne des organisations sportives pour personnes handicapees..
NOTES: Bibliographie: p. 90. Also published in English under the title: The Esso Swim Canada Program for the physically disabled: instructor manual. A skill development program of the Canadian Federation of Sport Organizations for the Disabled.
LEVEL: B LANG: Fr ISBN: 0-9691953-0-3 GV837.4 18861

Penny, P. Swimming and asthma wheeze. *Sport and leisure (London) 25(2), May/Jun 1984, 28-29.*
NOTES: Reprinted from, British medical journal.
LEVEL: B LANG: Eng SIRC ARTICLE NO: 103973

The Esso Swim Canada Program for the physically disabled: instructor manual. A skill development program of the Canadian Federation of Sport Organizations for the Disabled. Ottawa: Canadian Federation of Sport Organizations for the Disabled, c1984. 82 p. : ill.
CORP: Canadian Federation of Sport Organizations for the Disabled.
NOTES: Bibliography: p. 82. Aussi publie en francais sous le titre: Natation Canada Esso programme pour les personnes handicapees: manuel de l'instructeur. Programme de perfectionnement des habiletes, Federation canadienne des organisations sportives pour personnes handicapees.
LEVEL: B LANG: Eng ISBN: 0-9691953-0-3 GV837.4 18860

Wright, M.L.C. Halliwick method: teaching disabled individuals to become water free. (Refs: 4)*WAHPERD journal (Milwaukee, Wis.) 13(1), May 1984, 30-31.*
LEVEL: B LANG: Eng SIRC ARTICLE NO: 100664

DRUGS, DOPING AND ERGOGENIC AIDS

Singh, H. Bambah, S. Singh, G. Action of drugs on movements of the rat during swimming. (Refs: 10)*Journal of human movement studies (London) 10(4), 1984, 225-230.*
ABST: An account is given of the experimental evaluation of 3 drugs: ephedrine, pemoline and d-amphetamine on the motor activity of the rat during swimming. Ephedrine (5mg/kg) and pemoline (10 mg/kg) reduce the motor activity of the rat, whereas d-amphetamine (2 mg/kg) increases the activity of rats which show low activity in the control experiment and decreases the activity of those which show high activity. A toxic dose of ephedrine (20 mg/kg) produces similar effects on the motor activity of the rat to those of d-amphetamine (2 mg/kg) during swimming.
LEVEL: A LANG: Eng SIRC ARTICLE NO: 103898

EQUIPMENT

1984 Swimming Technique buying guide. *Swimming technique (Los Angeles) 20(4), Feb/Apr 1984, 29-35.*
LEVEL: B LANG: Eng SIRC ARTICLE NO: 095284

Elliott, R.S. Pool industry trends. *Swimming technique (Los Angeles, Calif.) 20(3), Nov 1983/Jan 1984, 39;41-42.*
LEVEL: B LANG: Eng SIRC ARTICLE NO: 094295

SWIMMING (continued)

EQUIPMENT - RETAILING

Bonne, K. Established sport offers new opportunities... (swimming) *Action sports retailer (South Laguna, Calif.) 5(7), Jul 1984, 8;10;12;14;18;20;22.*
LEVEL: B LANG: Eng SIRC ARTICLE NO: 103510

Canadian Swimming Pool Industry: reflecting business activity for 1983. A synopsis of 1984. *Pool & spa marketing (Thornhill, Ont.) 8(4), Dec 1984, 9;11;14-15;17-19.*
LEVEL: B LANG: Eng SIRC ARTICLE NO: 105219

FACILITIES

Desmarais, H. Les couvertures de piscine. *Alerte (Montreal) 19, dec 1984, 26-29.*
LEVEL: B LANG: Fr SIRC ARTICLE NO: 10642

Downes, C.J. Mitchell, J.W. Viotto, E.S. Eggers, N.J. Determination of cyanuric acid levels in swimming pool waters by u. v. absorbance, HPLC and melamine cyanurate precipitation. (Refs: 3)*Water research (Elmsford, N.Y.) 18(3), 1984, 277-280.*
LEVEL: I LANG: Eng SIRC ARTICLE NO: 095827

Govaer, D. Determining the solar heating of swimming pools by the utilizability method. (Refs: 10)*Solar energy (Elmsford, N.Y.) 32(5), 1984, 667-669.*
LEVEL: A LANG: Eng SIRC ARTICLE NO: 095828

Korinek, C. Shedding light on the purpose of the ground fault circuit interrupter. *Pool & spa marketing (Thornhill, Ont.) 8(2), Summer 1984, 8-10;12.*
LEVEL: B LANG: Eng SIRC ARTICLE NO: 100585

Neuburger, D. Promoting and marketing public aquatic facilities. *Parks & recreation (Arlington, Va.) 19(4), Apr 1984, 43-47.*
LEVEL: B LANG: Eng SIRC ARTICLE NO: 093780

Ross, B. Pool complex creates a splash in Bernards Township. *Parks & recreation (Arlington, Va.) 19(4), Apr 1984, 38-42;67.*
LEVEL: B LANG: Eng SIRC ARTICLE NO: 093783

Terminologie 'Baeder' (Entwurf). Terminologie 'piscines' (esquisse). Terminology 'swimming pools' (draft). Terminologia sobre 'piscinas' (borrador). *Sportstaettenbau und Baederanlagen (Cologne, W. Germany) 18(4), Jul/Aug 1984,M83-M108.*
LEVEL: B LANG: Ger Fr Eng Spa SIRC ARTICLE NO: 101558

FACILITIES - DESIGN, CONSTRUCTION AND PLANNING

Bosman, D.E. Scholtz, D.J.P. Survey of man-made tidal swimming pools along the South Africa Coast. *Shore and beach (Berkeley, Calif.) 52(2), Apr 1984, 26-30.*
LEVEL: I LANG: Eng

Butler, D. Thomson, N. Swimming pools. NOTES: In, Thomson, N. (ed.) et al., Sports and recreation provision for disabled people, London, Architectural Press, c1984, p. 25-39.
LEVEL: I LANG: Eng GV433.G7 17991

Corso, M. Bryn Mawr pool features movable bulkhead. *Park maintenance (Appleton, Wis.) 37(3), Mar 1984, 26-30.*
LEVEL: B LANG: Eng SIRC ARTICLE NO: 098966

Johannsson, R. Energy saving in indoor swimming pools. *Sportstaettenbau + Baederanlagen (Cologne, W. Germany) 18(1), Jan/Fe 1984, M102-M106.*
LEVEL: B LANG: Eng SIRC ARTICLE NO: 094297

FACILITIES - MAINTENANCE

Beasley, W. Ford Dodge updates two pools. *Park maintenance (Appleton, Wis.) 37(6), June 1984, 14-15.*
LEVEL: B LANG: Eng SIRC ARTICLE NO: 108907

Debergue, S. Faut-il transformer les piscines de plein air en piscines couvertes? *Piscines (Paris) 90, 1984, 82-87.*
LEVEL B LANG: Fr

Desmarais, H. La brome. *Alerte (Montreal) 17, juin 1984, 26-27.*
LEVEL: B LANG: Fr SIRC ARTICLE NO: 109093

Elliott, R.S. Automation in pool care. *Swimming technique (Los Angeles, Calif.) 20(4), Feb/Apr 1984, 36-40.*
LEVEL: B LANG Eng SIRC ARTICLE NO: 094294

Elliott, R.S. Terminal confusion. Pool operators are often hit with a barrage of murky terms essential to keeping their wate clear. *Swimming technique (Inglewood, Calif.) 21(3), Nov 1984/Jan 1985, 31-33.*
LEVEL: B LANG: Eng SIRC ARTICLE NO: 102423

Pope, J.R. Here's a job description for swimming pool personnel. *Journal of physical education and program (Columbus, Ohio) 81(8), Dec 1984, H6-H7.*
LEVEL: B LANG: Eng SIRC ARTICLE NO: 108249

Sobotka, J. Kryzystofik, B. Biochemical changes occurring in swimming pool water during UV disinfection. (Refs: 13)*Aqua (Oxford) 3, 1984, 170-172.*
LEVEL: A LANG: Eng SIRC ARTICLE NO: 103939

The leak detective: good investigative techniques pay off. *Pool & spa marketing (Thornhill, Ont.) 8(2), Summer 1984, 13-14.*
LEVEL: B LANG: Eng SIRC ARTICLE NO: 100586

Tolotta, F. Pool renovation was best way for Phillipsburg. *Park maintenance (Appleton, Wis.) 37(3), Mar 1984, 12-13.*
LEVEL: B LANG: Eng SIRC ARTICLE NO: 098975

HISTORY

Baotian, Y. Underwater swimming in ancient China. *China sports (Beijing, China) 16(9), Sept 1984, 33-35.*
LEVEL: I LANG: E SIRC ARTICLE NO: 108875

HYDRODYNAMICS

Colwin, C. Fluid dynamics: vortex circulation in swimming propulsion. (Refs: 15)*American Swimming Coaches Association yearbook (Ft. Lauderdale, Fla.) 1984, 38-46.*
LEVEL: I LANG: Eng SIRC ARTICLE NO: 181607

Colwin, C. The significance of vortex circulation in swimming propulsion: a study showing two different lift-producing mechanisms. *Unpublished World Clinic notes 1984, 1-36.*
CONF: American Swimming Coaches' Association. World Clinic (1984 : Chicago).
ABST: The study sought to identify flow reactions common to the stroke mechanics of world-class swimmers. Methodical analysis of underwater movies, slides and photographs consistently revealed similar patterns of vorticity. The application of lift force in swimming propulsion is dependent upon vortex circulation round a hand, foot or limb. A vortex is a rotating flow in which the streamlines are concentric circles. Vortex rings and filaments frequently become visible through accidental flow-aeration in the swimming stroke. Vortex patterns provide a 'history' of a swimming stroke because each propulsive impulse produces a distinctive type of vortex as its 'signature'. Recognizable patterns indicate how individual swimmers apply their power. Vortex patterns in the flow-field show that swimmers use two different mechanisms of creating lift-circulation (the foil-type mechanism during steady flow and quasi-steady flow, and the fling-ring mechanism during unsteady flow.) The analysis of vortex formations provides a new perspective for evaluating swimming efficiency.
LEVEL: A LANG: Eng SIRC ARTICLE NO: 181612

INJURIES AND ACCIDENTS

Aquatic deaths and injuries. *Sportsmedicine digest (Van Nuys, Calif.) 6(4), Apr 1984, 1.*
LEVEL: B LANG: Eng SIRC ARTICLE NO 099943

Bernett, P. Haas, W. Ertrinken, Badetod und andere Zwischenfaelle beim Schwimmsport. (Drowning, swimming pool death and othe emergencies related to swimming.) *Fortschritte der Medizin (Leipzig) 102(29/30), 16 Aug 1984, 752-754.*
LEVEL: I LANG: Ger

Bracewell, M. Survival in cold water - some implications for teachers. (Refs: 19)*British journal of physical education (London) 15(1), Mar/Apr 1984, 40.*
LEVEL: I LANG: Eng SIRC ARTICLE NO: 099945

DeMers, G. Competitive diving and swimming. *In, Adams, S.H. (ed.), et al., Catastrophic injuries in sports: avoidance strategies, Salinas, Calif., Cayote Press, c1984, p. 22-37.*
LEVEL: I LANG: Eng RD97 19088

Ebben, A. Hypothermia. (Refs: 6)*Swimming times (Loughborough, Eng.) 61(10), Oct 1984, 44-45.*
LEVEL: B LANG: Eng SIRC ARTICLE NO: 101546

Fricker, P. Purdam, C. Sweetenham, B. Mahoney, A. Swimmer's shoulder. (Refs: 7)*Sports sciences & medicine quarterly (Australia) 1(2), Oct 1984, 8-12.*
LEVEL: I LANG: Eng SIRC ARTICLE NO: 103487

Guerrin, F. Natation et medecine. (Swimming and medicine.) *LARC medical (Lille) 4(4), avr 1984, 247-248.*
LEVEL: I LANG: F SIRC ARTICLE NO: 103489

Lartigue, G. Lederer, R. Comment eviter l'hydrocution. *EPS: Revue education physique et sport (Paris) 188, juil/aout 1984, 34-36.*
LEVEL: B LANG: Fr SIRC ARTICLE NO: 098535

Lemenager, J. Fabre, J. Sesboue, B. Laryngospasme et noyade. (Refs: 8)*Medecine du sport 58(1), 25 janv 1984, 25-27.*
LEVEL I LANG: Fr SIRC ARTICLE NO: 092426

Mahoney, A. Purdam, C. Fricker, P. Swimmer's shoulder. (Refs: 7)*International swimmer (Artarmon, N.S.W. Aust.) Jan/Feb 1984 23-26.*
LEVEL: I LANG: Eng SIRC ARTICLE NO: 096872

McLean, I.D. Swimmers' injuries. *Australian family physician (Sydney) 13(7), Jul 1984, 499-502.*
LEVEL: I LANG: Eng

Pelck, R. Reimer, E. Luxatio testis traumatica. (Traumatic dislocation of the testis.) *Ugeskrift for laeger (Copenhagen) 14 (25), 18 June 1984, 1860-1861.*
LEVEL: I LANG: Dan

Podolsky, M.L. Otitis externa: immersion ears-swimmer's ears hot tub ears-pseudomonas folliculitis. (Refs: 4)*Sportsmedicine digest (Van Nuys, Calif.) 6(4), Apr 1984, 1-3.*
LEVEL: I LANG: Eng SIRC ARTICLE NO: 099953

Prince, P. Releve des blessures survenues dans des piscines publiques au Quebec 1980-1983. Trois-Rivieres: Regie de la securite dans les sports, 1984. (11) feuillets
CORP: Regie de la securite dans les sports. Service de la recherche.
LEVEL: I LANG: Fr RC1220.S8 20604

LAW AND LEGISLATION

Johnson, R.L. What is your aquatics liability IQ? *Parks & recreation (Arlington, Va.) 19(4), Apr 1984, 48-52.*
LEVEL: B LANG: Eng SIRC ARTICLE NO: 092909

Kozlowski, J.C. Runner-up decisions in RPLR swim suit competition. *Parks & recreation (Arlington, Va.) 19(4), Apr 1984, 33-35;67.*
LEVEL: B LANG: Eng SIRC ARTICLE NO: 092911

MASTERS COMPETITION

Novak, J. Masters of competition in swimming in Czechoslavakia. *Wave lengths (Schomberg, Ont.) 1(4), Fall 1984, 10-11.*
NOTES: Reprinted from, A.U.S.S.I. magazine.
LEVEL: B LANG: Eng SIRC ARTICLE NO: 173024

Radetsky, P. Master strokes: masters swimming encompasses nearly all ages and competitive ambitions. But all participants paint it in glowing terms. *Ultrasport (Boston, Mass.) 1(5), Sept/Oct 1984, 30-37.*
LEVEL: B LANG: Eng SIRC ARTICLE NO: 173302

MATHEMATICS

Craig, A.B. The basics of swimming. (Refs: 7)*Swimming technique (Los Angeles, Calif.) 20(4), Feb/Apr 1984, 22-27.*
ABST: The author presents a mathematical evaluation of the role of drag, energy production and efficiency in affecting the speed and performance of the swimmer.
LEVEL: A LANG: Eng SIRC ARTICLE NO: 095291

MEDICINE

Caldwell, F. Running-arthritis link discounted. *Physician and sportsmedicine (Minneapolis, Minn.) 12(8), Aug 1984, 25.*
LEVEL: I LANG: Eng SIRC ARTICLE NO: 098617

Joles, J.A. Nicaise, E. Saunders, M. Schot, A. Effects of NaHCO3, a-, and b-adrenergic blockade on albuminuria after swimmin in splenectomized dogs. (Refs: 17)*International journal of sports medicine (Stuttgart) 5(6), Dec 1984, 306-310.*
ABST: The albuminuria occurring after swimming in splenectomized dogs was investigated. Swimming in splenectomized dogs induces metabolic acidosis,

a decrease in renal vascular conductance, and an increase in plasma renin activity, all three factors possibly implicated in the occurrence of albuminuria. The administration of sodium bicarbonate prior to swimming reduced the magnitude of the acidosis and eliminated the increase in albuminuria after swimming. Phenoxybenzamine maintains the renal blood flow during exercise and blocks the increase in albuminuria despite a decrease of blood pH during swimming.
LEVEL: A LANG: Eng SIRC ARTICLE NO: 103891

Joles, J.A. Sanders, M. Velthuizen, J. Den Hertog, J.M. van Dijk, C. Proteinuria in intact and splenecotomized dogs after running and swimming. (Refs: 29)*International journal of sports medicine (Stuttgart) 5(6), Dec 1984, 311-316.*
ABST: The occurrence of post-exercise proteinuria was investigated in intact and splenectomized dogs after treadmill running and swimming and compared to control experiments. Swimming in the spelectomized dogs increased the albumin excretion in the first 30 min after exercise from 0.03 to 0.22 mg.min-1 and the lysozyme excretion in the same period from 0.11 to 0.75 mg.min-1. Swimming in intact dogs caused smaller increase in the lysozyme and albumin excretions during the exercise period itself as well as in the albumin excretion in the first 30 min after exercise. Running had no effect on urinary albumin or lysozyme but increased the low molecular weight protein fraction in the splenectomized dogs.
LEVEL: A LANG: Eng SIRC ARTICLE NO: 103892

Lamb, L.E. Swimming causes tooth damage. *Health letter (San Antonio, Tex.) 24(1), 13 Jul 1984, 4.*
LEVEL: I LANG: Eng SIRC ARTICLE NO: 099951

Sobolevski, V.I. Shukhardin, I.O. The sauna as a means of restoration during intense training of swimmers (condensed). *Soviet sports review (Escondido, Calif.) 19(1), Mar 1984, 49-51.*
NOTES: Translated from, Plavanye 1980, 15-17.
LEVEL: I LANG: Eng SIRC ARTICLE NO: 095322

Soft contact lenses and water sports. *Sportsmedicine digest (Van Nuys, Calif.) 6(4), Apr 1984, 4.*
LEVEL: B LANG: Eng SIRC ARTICLE NO: 099957

Tympanic ventilation tube and swimming recommendations. *Sportsmedicine digest (Van Nuys, Calif.) 6(4), Apr 1984, 3-4.*
LEVEL B LANG: Eng SIRC ARTICLE NO: 099961

NUTRITION

Adams, B. Gronbech, C.E. Moran, E. Endurance through adjusted pH. Can eating foods like these increase the endurance of your swimmers? Research, past and present, suggests that it can. (Refs: 11)*Swimming technique (Inglewood, Calif.) 21(3), Nov 1984/Jan 1985, 15-18.*
LEVEL: I LANG: Eng SIRC ARTICLE NO: 103480

Benson, R.A. Keeping your swimmers on the losing end. (Refs: 6)*Swimming technique (Inglewood, Calif.) 21(3), Nov 1984/Jan 1985, 34-35.*
LEVEL: B LANG: Eng SIRC ARTICLE NO: 103481

Houtkooper, L. Food and folklore. *Swimming world and junior swimmer (Los Angeles, Calif.) 25(4), Apr 1984, 20-21;23-26.*
LEVEL: B LANG: Eng SIRC ARTICLE NO: 095305

Houtkooper, L. Food power: high performance diet for swimmers. *Swimming world and junior swimmer (Los Angeles, Calif.) 25(6), Jun 1984, 38-39;41-46.*
LEVEL: I LANG: Eng SIRC ARTICLE NO: 095306

Houtkooper, L. Food power: vitamin and minerals requirements. *Swimming world and junior swimmer (Inglewood, Calif.) 25(8), Aug 1984, 27-28;30.*
NOTES: Third in a series.
LEVEL: B LANG: Eng SIRC ARTICLE NO: 099949

Whetton, J. Nutrition for swimming. *Swimming times (Loughborough, Eng.) 61(9), Sept 1984, 10-11.*
LEVEL: B LANG: Eng SIRC ARTICLE NO: 099963

Whetton, j. Nutrition for swimming. *Swimming times (Loughborough, Eng.) 61(11), Nov 1984, 10-12.*
NOTES: Second of a serie of three articles.
LEVEL: B LANG: Eng SIRC ARTICLE NO: 173504

OFFICIATING

Dwyre, B. Doing the unthinkable: the Hopping affair. *Referee (Franksville, Wis.) 9(9), Sept 1984, 20.*
LEVEL: B LANG: Eng SIRC ARTICLE NO: 101545

PERCEPTUAL MOTOR PROCESSES

Allen, J.G. Differentiated perceptions of exertion and their relative influence during swimming. Eugene, Ore.: Microform Publications, University of Oregon, 1984. 1 microfiche : negative, ill. ; 11 x 15 cm.
NOTES: Thesis (M.S.) - University of Wyoming, 1982; ((9), 45 leaves); includes bibliography.
LEVEL: A LANG: Eng UO84 251

PHILATELY, NUMISMATICS AND COLLECTIONS

Gurney, J.D. Swimmerabilia. *Swimming teacher (West Bronwich, Eng.) 11, Nov 1984, 4-9.*
NOTES: Reprinted from, Antique Collecting, Jun 1984.
LEVEL: B LANG: Eng SIRC ARTICLE NO: 101549

PHILOSOPHY

Bonhomme, G. La natation entre l'utile et l'agreable. *Loisirs sante (Paris) 11, sept/oct 1984, 32-34.*
LEVEL: B LANG: Fr SIRC ARTICLE NO: 101542

Bredemeier, B.J. Shields, D.L. Divergence in moral reasoning about sport and everyday life. (Refs: 23)*Sociology of sport journal (Champaign, Ill.) 1(4), Dec 1984, 348-357.*
ABST: The observation that sport represents a unique context has been widely discussed, but social scientists have done little to empirically examine the moral adaptations of sport participants. In the present study, the divergence between levels of moral reasoning used to discuss hypothetical dilemmas set in sport and in everyday life contexts was investigated among 120 high school and collegiate basketball players, swimmers, and nonathletes. Protocols were scored according to Haan's interactional model of moral development. It was found that levels of moral reasoning used to discuss sport dilemmas were lower than levels characterizing reasoning about issues within an everyday life context. Findings were discussed in terms of the specific social and moral context of

SWIMMING (continued)

sport experience.
LEVEL: A LANG: Eng SIRC ARTICLE NO: 104214

PHYSICAL FITNESS

Beaudet, S.M. Comparison of swimming with running as training stimuli. *Ergonomics (London) 27(9), 1984, 955-957.*
ABST: Th cardiovascular training effect was compared between swimming and running. Twenty-two healthy young women trained for six weeks either swimming or running with the same frequency, duration and intensity (as judged by heart rate). Both groups showed significant improvement in cardiovascular fitness after training, assessed on a bicycle ergometer, with no significant difference between the two groups before or after training.
LEVEL: A LANG: Eng

DeVarona, D. Tarshis, B. Donna DeVarona's hydro-aerobics. New York: Macmillan, c1984. xii, 163 p. : ill.
NOTES: Includes index.
LEVEL: B LANG: Eng ISBN: 0025312502 LC CARD: 84-004421 GV837 17540

Signorile, J. Shields, D. Aerobic swimming: it's no sweat when you're wet. (Refs: 10)*Florida JOHPERD (Gainesville, Fla.) 22(4), Nov 1984, 11-16.*
LEVEL: I LANG: Eng SIRC ARTICLE NO: 106091

Stamford, B. Swimming for fitness. *Physician and sportsmedicine (Minneapolis, Minn.) 12(7), Jul 1984, 158.*
LEVEL: B LANG: Eng SIRC ARTICLE NO: 096894

Swimming - head-to-toe sport for head-to-toe fitness. *Your health & fitness (Highland Park, Ill.) 6(3), Jun/Jul 1984, 8-9.*
LEVEL: B LANG: Eng SIRC ARTICLE NO: 096896

Theoret, E. Aetnatation Canada. *Alerte (Montreal) 19, dec 1984, 33-34.*
LEVEL: B LANG: Fr SIRC ARTICLE NO: 107598

PHYSICS

Huberdeau, S. Teaching fundamental physics in swimming & life-saving. *Alterte (Montreal) 17, mars 1984, 8-9.*
LEVEL: B LANG: Eng SIRC ARTICLE NO: 098533

PHYSIOLOGY

Allen, G. Energy delivery for muscular activity with specific reference to swimming: Part two. *International swimmer (Artarmon, N.S.W. Aust.) Jan/Feb 1984, 21.*
LEVEL: I LANG: Eng SIRC ARTICLE NO: 096847

Armstrong, N. Ellard, R. The measurement of alactacid anaerobic power in trained and untrained adolescent boys. (Refs: 38) *Physical education review (Manchester) 7(1), Spring 1984, 73-79.*
ABST: The anaerobic capacity of 7 male swimmers and of 28 male non-athletes were compared in this study. Modified versions of the Margaria Step Test and the Wingate Anaerobic Test were used and proved to be appropriate in the testing of adolescent boys.
LEVEL: A LANG: Eng SIRC ARTICLE NO: 099944

Bloomfield, J. Blansby, B.A. Ackland, T.R. Analysis of the swimming profiles. *International swimmer Jan/Feb 1984, 38.*
ABST: A method to profile pulmonary function,
flexibility, body composition and somatotype for individual swimmers to enable coaches to identify areas of improvement.
LEVEL: I LANG: Eng SIRC ARTICLE NO: 098526

Bloomfield, J. Blanksby, B.A. Beard, D.F. Ackland, T.R. Elliott, B.C. Biological characteristics of young swimmers, tennis players and non-competitors. (Refs: 27)*British journal of sports medicine (Loughborough, Eng.) 18(2), Jun 1984, 97-103.*
ABST: One hundred and twelve finalists in the State Swimming Championships aged between seven and twelve years and 65 ranked tennis players of similar age were selected on the basis of their sporting performances. A third group comprised children of similar socio-economic status who only took part in casual sport. A multifactorial analysis of variance and post-hoc t-tests were applied of the data to determine if any statistical differences were apparent between the three groups. The results demonstrated that no size, body shape, flexibility, strength or lung function differences were evident between the competitors and non-competitors, but that the swimmers and tennis players were superior to the non-competitors in cardiovascular endurance.
LEVEL: A LANG: Eng SIRC ARTICLE NO: 103482

Burke, E.J. Keenan, T.J. Energy cost, heart rate, and perceived exertion during the elementary backstroke. (Refs: 11) *Physician and sportsmedicine (Minneapolis, Minn.) 12(12), Dec 1984, 75-78;80.*
ABST: The authors evaluate the energy cost, heart rate, perceived exertion, and velocity of five men and five women performing the elementary backstroke at four different intensities. Significant increases of the dependent variables are observed with increasing intensity. Average energy cost ranges from 0.097 Kcal-Kg-1-min-1 at 1.1 to 1.4 Km-hr-1 to 0.17 Kcal-kg-1 min-1 at 1.8 to 2.0 km-hr-1.
LEVEL: A LANG: Eng SIRC ARTICLE NO: 103483

Cazorla, G. Montpetit, R. Chatard, J.C. Aspects biologiques de la natation de competition. (Refs: 91)*Dans, Culture techniqu no. 13, Neuilly-sur-Seine, France, Centre de Recherche sur la Culture Technique, c1984, p. 126-157.*
LEVEL: A LANG: Fr RC1235 20096

Cheremisin, A.P. Kosinsky, V.I. Rozman, A.M. Use of imitational electrostimulation in the training of high level swimmers. *Soviet sports review (Escondido, Calif.) 19(3), Sept 1984, 135-136.*
NOTES: Translated from, Plavanye 1, 1983, 56.
LEVEL: I LANG: Eng SIRC ARTICLE NO: 103484

Madrigal, R. Problems with overtraining. Rest can be just as important as high-intensity workouts in competitive swimming. (Refs: 24)*Swimming technique (Inglewood, Calif.) 21(3), Nov 1984/Jan 1985, 25-30.*
LEVEL: I LANG: Eng SIRC ARTICLE NO: 103494

Marconnet, P. Slaoui, F. Gastaud, M. Ardisson, J.L. Preexercise, exercise and early post exercise arterial blood pressure in young competitive swimmers versus non swimmers. (Refs: 13)*Journal of sports medicine and physical fitness (Torino, Italy) 24(3), Sept 1984, 252-258.*
ABST: Arterial blood pressure (ABP) has been measured non invasively on 243 highly trained athletes (132 females, 111 males) before, during and after standard exercise on cycloergometer. Swimmers'(s) data were compared with non
swimmers (NS): runners, skiers and soccers' ones. In both sexes in spite of lower ages, (S) demonstrated higher ABP (mean and systolic) than (NS) whose activity was mainly focused on legs. Several possible etiologies are evoked as: ages, training (volume and intensity), type of activity, actual weight excess (FAT), muscular hypertrophy, type of test for the exercise and recovery results.
LEVEL: A LANG: Eng SIRC ARTICLE NO: 106084

Marino, M. Profiling swimmers. (Refs: 86)*Clinics in sports medicine (Philadelphia) 3(1), Jan 1984, 211-229.*
NOTES: Symposium on profiling.
ABST: The winning of 89 medals in swimming by the East Germans at the Montreal Olympics made much of the rest of the world realize that there was more than talent and training involved in winning medals. Profiling of swimming now considers the mechanics of the strokes, the fitness of the individual and the injuries due to overtraining. Such information can result in the designing of individual training programs.
LEVEL: A LANG: Eng SIRC ARTICLE NO: 093778

Monpetit, R. Lactate testing: relevance and suggested protocol. (Refs: 13)*Swim Canada (Toronto) 11(5), May 1984, 20-21.*
LEVEL: I LANG: Eng SIRC ARTICLE NO: 095313

Nielsen, B. Sjogaard, G. Bonde-Petersen, F. Cardiovascular, hormonal and body fluid changes during prolonged exercise. (Refs 29)*European journal of applied physiology and occupational physiology (Berlin, W.G.) 53(1), 1984, 63-70.*
ABST: During prolonged heavy exercise a gradual upward drift in heart rate (HR) is seen after the first 10 min of exercise. Swimming and bicycling differ with respect to hydrostatic pressure and to water loss, due to sweating. Five subjects were studied during 90 min of bicycle exercise, and swimming the leg kick of free style. After the initial rise in heart rate the 'secondary rise' followed parallel courses in the two situations. The secondary rise in HR could not be explained by changes in plasma volume or in water balance, nor by changes in plasma (K). The plasma volume decreased 5-6 percent within the first 5 to 10 min of exercise both in bicycling and swimming, but thereafter remained virtually unchanged. The total water loss during swimming was 25 percent less than during bicycling.
LEVEL: A LANG: Eng SIRC ARTICLE NO: 104912

Noble, B.J. Allen, J.G. Perceived extertion in swimming. (Refs: 8)*Swimming technique (Los Angeles, Calif.) 21(1), May/Jul 1984, 11-15.*
ABST: Two experiments conducted on swimmers at the University of Wyoming found that ratings of perceived swimming effort increase in a relatively linear fashion with swimming intensity. The results indicate that more emphasis should be placed on the training of arms. Other training and teaching implications are discussed.
LEVEL: A LANG: Eng SIRC ARTICLE NO: 095315

Perkins, D.R. Circadian rhythms in swimming. (Refs: 9)*Swimming technique (Los Angeles, Calif.) 21(1), May/Jul 1984, 37-38.*
LEVEL: I LANG: Eng SIRC ARTICLE NO: 095316

Pierce, G.N. Kutryk, M.J.B. Dhalla, K.S. Beamish, R.E. Dhalla, N.S. Biochemical alterations in heart after exhaustive swimming in rats. (Refs: 35)*Journal of applied physiology: respiratory, environmental and exercise physiology*

(Bethesda, Md.) 57 (2), Aug 1984, 326-331.
LEVEL: A LANG: Eng SIRC ARTICLE NO: 108349

Smith, B.W. McMurray, R.G. Symanski, J.D. A comparison of the anaerobic threshold of sprint and endurance trained swimmers. (Refs: 28)*Journal of sports medicine and physical fitness (Torino, Italy) 24(2), Jun 1984, 94-99.*
ABST: Anaerobic threshold was evaluated in twelve competitive swimmers: six whose primary events were 200 m or less and six whose primary events were 400 m or greater. Each subject was tested using a discontinuous, tethered swim protocol consisting of incremental three minute work stages until exhaustion. The endurance swimmers were able to sustain a greater propelling force than the sprinters at the same maximal oxygen uptake, therefore indicating a greater stroke efficiency. The results indicate that sprint trained swimmers, although possessing a similar aerobic capacity to endurance swimmers, have a lower anaerobic threshold.
LEVEL: A LANG: Eng SIRC ARTICLE NO: 103500

Telford, R. Lactic acid measurements - are they useful? (Refs: 9)*Sports science & medicine quarterly 1(1), Jun 1984, 2-7.*
ABST: Blood lactic acid measures are used to gauge the level of anaerobic output. However there are difficulties in interpreting these measurements. Some of the factors responsible for these difficulties include variations in the diffusion and metabolism of lactic acid, sampling techniques, exercise modes and the fact that blood level is really being used to assess what is happening to muscle. This article describes the methods of blood lactate measurement used at the Australian Institute of Sport with particular reference to swimmers.
LEVEL: A LANG: Eng SIRC ARTICLE NO: 097768

Vaccaro, P. Ostrove, S.M. Vandervelden, L. Goldfarb, A.H. Clarke, D.H. Dummer, G.M. Body composition and physiological responses of masters female swimmers 20 to 70 years of age. (Refs: 34)*Research quarterly for exercise & sport (Reston, Va.) 55(3), Sept 1984, 278-284.*
ABST: Eighty-seven female masters swimmers ranging in age from 20 to 69 were selected for a detailed study of their body composition and physiological responses at rest and during exercise. These women were then placed into two subsets, a highly trained group and a not highly trained group. Both the highly trained and not highly trained swimmers were considerably lower in percent fat than previously reported data for normal untrained women of similar ages. In both groups, however, percent fat across age levels within each training group showed significant increases at approximately 40 years of age. In the highly trained swimmers, VO2 max (ml.kg-1.min-1) decreased at a mean rate of about 7% per decade, while in the not highly trained swimmers the decline was approximately 8% per decade.
LEVEL: A LANG: Eng SIRC ARTICLE NO: 103502

Ward, K. O'Brien, M. Dolphin, C. Knight, D. Allen, J. Rodahl, A. Ward, R. Cahill, N. Left ventricular function in young male and female swimmers. (Refs: 4)
CONF: Symposium of Paediatric Work Physiology (10th : 1981 : Joutsa, Finland).
NOTES: In, Ilmarinen, J. and Vaelimaeki, I. (eds.), Children and sport: paediatric work physiology, Berlin, Springer-Verlag, 1984, p. 177-181.
ABST: Six young male and female swimmers from a group of athletes preparing for the 1980 Olympic Games were studied. Echocardiograms were obtained in the supine position before and after submaximal exercise. This study examines the relationship between left ventricular mass, left ventricular chamber size and wall thickness in systole and diastole, and systolic pressure before and after submaximal exercise.
LEVEL: A LANG: Eng SIRC ARTICLE NO: 103503

Zonderland, M.L. Erich, W.B.M. Peltenburg, A.L. Havekes, L. Bernink, M.J.E. Huisveld, I.A. Apolipoprotein and lipid profiles in young female athletes. (Refs: 34)*International journal of sports medicine (Stuttgart, FRG) 5(2), Apr 1984, 78-82.*
ABST: The apolipoprotein and lipid profiles were investigated in 22 female gymnasts, 20 girl swimmers, and 12 controls. The average age of all groups was about 12 years, and the girls were matched for sexual development. The gymnasts appeared to have the highest level of HDL cholesterol and the highest HDL cholesterol / total cholesterol, HDL cholesterol / LDL cholesterol and HDL cholesterol/apo A-I ratios in comparison to both the swimmers and the control group. The swimmers had the highest level of apo A-I, but a lipid profile similar to that of the controls. It is concluded that in children, as in adults, regular physical activity affect the lipid and apolipoprotein profiles. In addition, it appears that the apolipoproteins discriminate between trained and nontrained subjects as well as (apo B) or better (apo A-I) than the lipid components of the corresponding lipoproteins (LDL cholesterol or HDL cholesterol).
LEVEL: A LANG: Eng SIRC ARTICLE NO: 108522

PHYSIOLOGY - MUSCLE

Petersen, S.R. Miller, G.D. Wenger, H.A. Quinney, H.A. The acquisition of muscular strength: the influence of training velocity and initial VO2 max. (Refs: 11)*Canadian journal of applied sport sciences/Journal canadien des sciences appliquees au sport (Windsor, Ont.) 9(4), Dec 1984, 176-180.*
ABST: To examine velocity specific training and to determine if VO2 max is related to the increase in muscular strength and power, 12 elite male swimmers (x age is 18.8 years) were blocked on VO2 max and assigned high intensity, high velocity training. Subjects performed 2 or 3 circuits of two 20s sets at each of six variable resistance stations at a work relief ratio of 1:3. Subjects trained four times weekly, for five weeks. Loads were set to achieve limb velocities of approximately 180o.s-1. Increases (p0.001) in all knee peak torques at 180o.s-1 were observed. A decrease (p0.02) was noted in right knee extension at 30o.s-1, while other peak torques at that velocity remained constant. Anaerobic power increased (p0.001) across the training programme.
LEVEL: A LANG: Eng SIRC ARTICLE NO: 103497

PSYCHOLOGY

Burton, D. Goal setting: a secret to success. *Swimming world and junior swimmer (Los Angeles, Calif.) 25(2), Feb 1984, 25-29.*
ABST: The author suggests that an athlete's goals must be kept realistic and should be based on the individual's personal performance standards rather than on a comparison with other athletes' performance. He feels that goal setting skill, like physical skill, must be developed and provides some suggestions for this. An article written for swimmers and their coaches, but useful for all sports.
LEVEL: B LANG: Eng SIRC ARTICLE NO: 095287

Fernandez, K.R. Think short-term. *Swimming world and junior swimmer (Los Angeles, Calif.) 25(4), Apr 1984, 51-52.*
LEVEL: A LANG: Eng SIRC ARTICLE NO: 095298

Riddick, C.C. Comparative psychological profiles of three groups of female collegians: competitive swimmers, recreational swimmers, and inactive swimmers. (Refs: 21)*Journal of sport behavior (Mobile, Ala.) 7(4), Dec 1984, 160-174.*
ABST: Personality characteristics of 26 female, collegiate, varsity swim team members were compared to 28 female recreational swimmers and 25 physically inactive peers. Characteristics were measured by Profiles of Mood States (POMS), Levenson's Multi-dimensional Locus of Control (LOC), the California F-Scale, and the Sports Competition Anxiety Test (SCAT). Results revealed that recreational swimmers had the lowest total mood disturbance. The two swimming groups had substantially more vigor than the non-athletes, and the varsity swimmers were significantly more fatigued than their classmates. Concerning authoritarianism, competitive swimmers had a significantly elevated score compared to recreational swimmers and non-athletes. For the SCAT, varsity swimmers and inactive students experienced the greatest pre-competition anxiety. Overall, the results suggest that recreational swimmers, more so than competitive swimmers or inactive women, had the most positive personality characteristics. Because the athletes were undergoing intensive training for an important regional swim meet, however, results could reflect state versus personality characteristics.
LEVEL: A LANG: Eng SIRC ARTICLE NO: 101556

Swartz, D. Mental focus. *Swimming world and junior swimmer (Los Angeles, Calif.) 25(1), Jan 1984, 54-55.*
LEVEL: B LANG: E SIRC ARTICLE NO: 093785

Swartz, D. Mental focus. (goal setting) *Swimming world and junior swimmer (Inglewood, Calif.) 25(7), Jul 1984, 98-99.*
LEVEL: B LANG: Eng SIRC ARTICLE NO: 099959

Watson, A. Getting into flow. *International swimmer Jan/Feb 1984, 30.*
ABST: In Garry Egger's book 'the Sport Drug' he refers to peak experiences or flow. This article considers the implications of flow for swim coaches and their swimmers.
LEVEL: I LANG: Eng SIRC ARTICLE NO: 098545

Watson, G.G. Blanksby, B.A. Bloomfield, J. Reward systems in children's sport: perceptions and evaluations of elite junior swimmers. (Refs: 35)*Journal of human movement studies (Edinburgh, Eng.) 10(3), 1984, 123-156.*
ABST: In this paper we consider the elements of Intrinsic Reward experienced by children as the attractive components of competitive swimming. The sample for this study was taken from participants in the Australian National Junior Swimming Championships, Perth, 1981. After examining the ingredients of intrinsic motivation based on the work of Deci et al., this theory is applied to a model of the attraction of games. Three elements of attraction are identified including: 1)the potential availability of intrinsic reward; 2)the attraction of co-operative relations with others; and

3)the attraction of achievement and task mastery. When this model is applied to a comparison of the two prevailing ideologies found in competitive sport contrasting the point of view of the child with that of the adult, we are able to identify two conflicting themes. Intrinsic Reward is replaced by training and discipline; co-operation is replaced by a need to cope with competitive anxiety; and finally, task mastery is replaced by the influence of extrinsic reward.
LEVEL: A LANG: Eng SIRC ARTICLE NO: 108759

PSYCHOLOGY - MENTAL TRAINING

Evans, J. Feeling great and swimming fast. *Swim Canada (Toronto) 11(5),* May 1984, 10-11.
LEVEL: B LANG: Eng SIRC ARTICLE NO: 095295

Holmes, T. Mental training. *Swim Canada (Toronto) 11(8),* Aug/Sept 1984, 24.
LEVEL: B LANG: Eng SIRC ARTICLE NO: 101550

Swartz, D. Mental focus. *Swimming world and junior swimmer (Los Angeles, Calif.) 25(3),* Mar 1984, 67-68.
LEVEL: B LANG: E SIRC ARTICLE NO: 098542

RULES AND REGULATIONS

How the game is played. (Swimming) *Women's sports (Palo Alto, Calif.) 6(4),* Apr 1984, 43.
LEVEL: B LANG: Eng SIRC ARTICLE NO: 101551

SAFETY

Palm, J. Educating the public in the risks of cold water immersion. *Swimming teacher (West Bromwich, Eng.) 1,* Jan 1984, 9-11.
LEVEL: B LANG: Eng SIRC ARTICLE NO: 093781

Rogers, C.C. Swimming safety hitting home with pool owners. *Physician and sportsmedicine (Minneapolis, Minn.) 12(7),* Jul 1984, 107-110;112-113.
LEVEL: B LANG: Eng SIRC ARTICLE NO: 096887

SPORTING EVENTS

Freifeld, K. Lucky stroke. (swimming) *Health (New York) 16(5),* May 1984, 64;66-67.
LEVEL: B LANG: Eng SIRC ARTICLE NO: 099948

Kemp, N. Looking back at the Montreal Games. *Swim Canada (Toronto) 11(7),* Jul 1984, 14.
LEVEL: B LANG: Eng SIRC ARTICLE NO: 100805

STATISTICS AND RECORDS

Chiang, M. A comparative study of the paces achieved in competition by top-level Republic of China and European swimmers. *Asian journal of physical education (Taiwan, China) 7(2),* Jul 1984, 81-84.
ABST: The purposes of this study was to compare the different paces achieved respectively by R.O.C. and European swimmers during the 1983 Taiwan Sports Festival and the 1983 European Cup, to compare time records in various events, and to compare the height, weight and age of the swimmers studied.
LEVEL: A LANG: Eng Chi SIRC ARTICLE NO: 099946

Jokl, E. The future of athletic records. (Refs: 20)*Track & field quarterly review (Kalamazoo, Mich.) 84(1),* Spring 1984, 5-16.
LEVEL: I LANG: Eng SIRC ARTICLE NO: 095375

King, H.A. Black, D.G. Analysis of Olympic and world records in track and field and swimming: past, present, and future. (Refs: 29)
NOTES: In, Carter, J.E.L. (ed.), Physical structure of Olympic athletes. Part II. Kinanthropometry of Olympic athletes, Basel, Karger, c1984, p. 212-230.
LEVEL: A LANG: Eng RC1235 12672

STATISTICS AND RECORDS - PARTICIPATION

Chase, D.R. Harada, M. Response error in self-reported recreation participation. (Refs: 7)*Journal of leisure research (Alexandria, Va.) 16(4),* 1984, 322-329.
ABST: The research reported in this paper addresses a fundamental question underlying self-report surveys; how accurately do individuals recall the recreation activities in which they have participated? The three research questions were: (1) What is the pattern and amount of response error? (2) What are some explanatory factors for response error? (3) To what extent does survey (self-reported) response predict actual swimming frequency? The results indicate a large amount of response overestimation of actual participation. An important finding concerning the distribution of self-reports is that almost all estimates of frequency of participation, except for very small estimates, were numbers ending in 0 or 5. With regard to the second research question, the results indicate that the importance of swimming as to leisure activity to the respondent is moderately and positively related to the percent error of estimation. The prediction of actual participation from self-reports of participation, the third research question, produced mixed results.
LEVEL: A LANG: Eng SIRC ARTICLE NO: 106073

Swimming at a pool -- popular at all ages. La natation en piscine -- activite populaire a tout age. *Highlights/Faits saillant (Ottawa) 28,* May 1984, 1-2.
CORP: Canada Fitness Survey.
CORP: Enquete condition physique Canada.
LEVEL: B LANG: Eng Fr SIRC ARTICLE NO: 095324

STRATEGY

Hencken, J. Breaststroke strategy and pacing. *Swimming world and junior swimmer (Los Angeles, Calif.) 25(1),* Jan 1984, 18-20.
NOTES: Third in a series.
LEVEL: B LANG: Eng SIRC ARTICLE NO: 093776

Van Der Meer, D. 5 ways to foil a net rusher. *Tennis (Norwalk, Conn.) 20(2),* Jun 1984, 104-107.
LEVEL: B LANG: Eng SIRC ARTICLE NO: 101615

TEACHING

Aetna Canada Swimfit instructor manual. s.l.: Canadian Amateur Swimming Association, 1984?. 139 p. : ill.
CORP: Canadian Amateur Swimming Association.
NOTES: Includes bibliographies.
LEVEL: B LANG: Eng GV838.53.P5 18335

Workman, C.L. Shank, C.B. Operation F.E.A.R. N.O.T. Fun enrichment activities to reduce negative overpowering tension. (Refs 9)*Journal of physical education, recreation & dance (Reston, Va.) 55(6),* Aug 1984, 60-63.
LEVEL: I LANG: Eng SIRC ARTICLE NO: 098547

TECHNIQUES AND SKILLS

Furniss, B. Learning from the Olympians: freestyle turns. *Swimming world and junior swimmer (Los Angeles, Calif.) 25(3),* Mar 1984, 20-23.
LEVEL: B LANG: Eng SIRC ARTICLE NO: 098530

Prins, J. The power's in the pull: a step-by-step guide to perfect technique. *Triathlon magazine (Santa Monica, Calif.) 2(4 Aug/Sept 1984, 46-52.
NOTES: Excerpted from, Prins, J. , The Illustrated Swimmer.
LEVEL: B LANG: Eng SIRC ARTICLE NO: 108921

TECHNIQUES AND SKILLS - BACKSTROKE

Dubois, C. Robin, J.P. Le dos. (natation) *EPS: Education physique et sport (Paris) 187, mai/juin 1984,* 17-21.
LEVEL: B LANG: Fr SIRC ARTICLE NO: 096859

Hamlin, M.B. Learning from the Olympians: backstroke starts and finishes. *Swimming world and junior swimmer (Los Angeles, Calif.) 25(2),* Feb 1984, 21-24.
NOTES: Third in a series.
LEVEL: B LANG: Eng SIRC ARTICLE NO: 095301

Hamlin, M.B. Backstroke flip turns. *Swimming world and junior swimmer (Los Angeles, Calif.) 25(6),* Jun 1984, 18-20.
LEVEL B LANG: Eng SIRC ARTICLE NO: 095302

TECHNIQUES AND SKILLS - BREASTSTROKE

Hencken, J. Learning from the Olympians: breaststroke underwater stroke. *Swimming world and junior swimmer (Los Angeles, Calif.) 25(5),* May 1984, 20-22.
NOTES: Fourth in a series.
LEVEL: B LANG: Eng SIRC ARTICLE NO: 095303

Minxing, C. An added kick for breaststrokers. *Swimming technique (Los Angeles, Calif.) 21(2),* Aug/Oct 1984, 15-19.
LEVEL: LANG: Eng SIRC ARTICLE NO: 098537

Prins, J. The breaststroke. *Wave lengths (Schomberg, Ont.) 1(4),* Fall 1984, 18-25.
NOTES: Excerpted from, the Illustrated Swimmer.
LEVEL: B LANG: Eng SIRC ARTICLE NO: 173025

Rodeo, S. Breaking down the breaststroke. *Swimming technique (Inglewood Calif.) 21(3),* Nov 1984/Jan 1985, 8-10;12-14.
LEVEL: I LANG: Eng SIRC ARTICLE NO: 103498

Shrugging off water resistance. *Swimming technique (Inglewood, Calif.) 21(3),* Nov 1984/Jan 1985, 11.
LEVEL: B LANG: Eng SIR ARTICLE NO: 103499

TECHNIQUES AND SKILLS - BUTTERFLY

Dubois, C. Robin, J.P. Le papillon. *EPS: Education physique et sport (Paris, France) 186, mars/avr 1984,* 11-15.
LEVEL: B LANG: Fr SIRC ARTICLE NO: 095294

TECHNIQUES AND SKILLS - CRAWL

Colwin, C. Kinetic streamlining and the phenomenon of prolonged momentum in the crawl swimming stroke. (Refs: 8)*Swim Canada 97, 11(1), Jan 1984, 12-15.*
LEVEL: I LANG: Eng SIRC ARTICLE NO: 092417

TESTING AND EVALUATION

Hamilton, R. Predicting meet times. (Refs: 4)*Swimming technique (Los Angeles, Calif.) 20(4), Feb/Apr 1984, 43-44.*
LEVEL: LANG: Eng SIRC ARTICLE NO: 095300

Jorgensen, L.W. An endurance test for swimmers. (Refs: 2)*Swimming technique (Los Angeles, Calif.) 21(1), May/Jul 1984, 17-18.*
ABST: The author tested the endurance of 14 East Carolina University swimmers by measuring their heart rate at 30 second sequences after a 25 yard sprint and a 100 yard sprint. The results found that a 30 second pulse recovery count 2 and a half minutes after an all out 25 yard sprint provided the best indication of swimming endurance.
LEVEL: A LANG: Eng SIRC ARTICLE NO: 095309

Mesteganot, D. Natation: evaluation motrice. *EPS: Education physique et sport (Paris) 189, sept/oct 1984, 30-33.*
LEVEL: B LANG: Fr SIRC ARTICLE NO: 101554

Miliski, S. Johns, R. Testing swimmers' progress. (Refs: 3)*International swimmer (Artarmon, N.S.W. Aust.) Jan/Feb 1984, 19-20.*
LEVEL: I LANG: Eng SIRC ARTICLE NO: 096873

Rispin, P.D. Velocity fluctuations in single-stroke cycles of the breast stroke in competitive swimming. Eugene, Ore.: Microform Publications University of Oregon, 1984. 1 microfiche : negative, ill. ; 11 x 15 cm.
NOTES: Thesis (M.S.) - Pennsylvania State University, 1981; (ix, 77 leaves); includes bibliography.
LEVEL: A LANG: Eng UO84 75

Thayer, A.L. Hay, J.G. Motivating start and turn improvement. (Refs: 2)*Swimming technique (Los Angeles, Calif.) 20(4), Feb/Apr 1984, 17-20.*
ABST: The starts and turns of Iowa swimmers were timed at three selected meets during the season. The results were given to the coaches after each competition and were used to improve the swimmers techniques in these areas. Noticeable improvements were seen after the swimmers were able to compare their second set of times with their beginning season times. This was further reflected in the third set of times.
LEVEL: A LANG: Eng SIRC ARTICLE NO: 095325

TRAINING AND CONDITIONING

Brems, M. The fit swimmer, 120 workouts and training tips. Chicago: Contemporary Books, c1984. ix, 115 p. : ill.
NOTES: Bibliography: p. 115.
LEVEL: B LANG: Eng ISBN: 0-8092-5454-9 LC CARD: 84-004355 GV837.7 17592

Colwin, C. Tethered swimming. *Swim Canada (Toronto) 99, 11(3), Mar 1984, 20-21.*
LEVEL: B LANG: Eng SIRC ARTICLE NO: 09377

Distance training: Rod Archibald. *Swim Canada (Toronto) 11(6), Jun 1984, 36-37.*
LEVEL: B LANG: Eng SIRC ARTICLE NO: 095293

Gambril, D. A swimming season. A complete season's training from day one through the taper. s.l.: Alabama University, 1984. 317 p.
LEVEL: I LANG: Eng

Gergley, T.J. McArdle, W.D. DeJesus, P. Toner, M.M. Jacobowitz, S. Spina, R.J. Specificity of arm training on aerobic power during swimming and running. (Refs: 27)*Medicine and science in sports and exercise (Indianapolis) 16(4), Aug 1984, 349-354.*
ABST: The specificity of aerobic training for upper-body exercise requiring differing amounts of muscle mass was evaluated in 25 college-aged male recreational swimmers who were randomly assigned to either a non-training control group (N,9) a 10-wk swim(S)-training group (N,9), or a group that trained with a standard swim-bench pulley system (SB; N,7). Significant increases of peak VO2 in tethered swimming (11%) and SB (21%) were observed for the SB-trained group, while the S-trained group improved 18% and 19% on the tethered swimming and SB tests, respectively. No changes were observed during treadmill running, and the control subjects remained unchanged on all measures. Comparisons between training groups indicated that although both groups improved to a similar extent when measured on the swim bench, the 0.53 l.min-1 improvement in tethered-swimming peak VO2 for the S-trained group was greater than the 0.32 l.min-1 increase noted for the SB-trained group.
LEVEL: A LANG: Eng SIRC ARTICLE NO: 103488

Gibson, R.L. Tapering: a small college perspective. *Women's coaching clinic (Princeton, N.J.) 7(9), May 1984, 15-16.*
LEVEL: B LANG: Eng SIRC ARTICLE NO: 095299

Madrigal, R. Sprint-assisted towing: rather than making it harder to swim fast, try giving your swimmers a boost in their maximal workout speed. (Refs: 23)*Swimming technique (Los Angeles, Calif.) 20(3), Nov 1983/Jan 1984, 33-36.*
LEVEL: I LANG: Eng SIRC ARTICLE NO: 095312

Salo, D.C. High-intensity training and freestyle performance. *Swimming technique (Los Angeles, Calif.) 21(1), May/Jul 1984, 20-23.*
ABST: An untrained ex-collegiate swimmer sprint trained over a ten week period and was weekly tested at 25, 100 and 500 yards. The subject progressively improved in the 100 and 500 distances but not the 25 yard sprint. He was also able to better or nearly equal his previous collegiate best times for various distances and strokes. The results further validate previous findings on the effectiveness of velocity-overload training.
LEVEL: I LANG: Eng SIRC ARTICLE NO: 095318

Schubert, M. Our philosophy is to make it fun. *Internationl swimmer (N.S.W., Aust.) Jul/Aug 1984, 12-14.*
LEVEL: B LANG: E SIRC ARTICLE NO: 101557

Swimming aids. *Swimming times (Loughborough, Eng.) 61(6), Jun 1984, 36-37.*
LEVEL: B LANG: Eng SIRC ARTICLE NO: 099960

Yancher, R. Larsen, O. Baer, C.L.H. Sprint recovery times: determining how much rest is necessary after a maximal effort can help establish training bases. (Refs: 5)*Swimming technique (Los Angeles, Calif.) 20(3), Nov 1983/Jan 1984, 27-28.*
LEVEL: I LANG: Eng SIRC ARTICLE NO: 095327

TRAINING AND CONDITIONING - DRILLS

Engesvik, F. Getting your freestyle rolling: a step-by-step progression of drills for teaching the freestyle body roll. *Swimming Technique (Los Angeles, Calif.) 21(2), Aug/Oct 1984, 32-33;35.*
LEVEL: B LANG: Eng SIRC ARTICLE NO: 098529

Wolf, M.D. Conditioning: different strokes. *Women's sports and fitness (Palo Alto, Calif.) 6(7), Jul 1984, 114.*
LEVEL: B LANG: Eng SIRC ARTICLE NO: 101560

TRAINING AND CONDITIONING - DRYLAND TRAINING

Schulz, S. Rodeo, S. Stanford University dryland training program. *National Strength & Conditioning Association journal (Lincoln, Neb.) 6(2), Apr/May 1984, 48-49;56-57.*
LEVEL: B LANG: Eng SIRC ARTICLE NO: 095319

Terry, J. Approaching the bench: specific event-time training can increase your swimmer's performance. (Refs: 6)*Swimming technique (Los Angeles, Calif.) 21(2), Aug/Oct 1984, 28-31.*
LEVEL: I LANG: Eng SIRC ARTICLE NO: 098543

TRAINING AND CONDITIONING - STRETCHING AND FLEXIBILITY EXERCISES

Maksimov, N.M. Exercises for development of joint mobility in swimmers. *Soviet sports review (Escondido, Calif.) 19(2), Jun 1984, 69-71.*
NOTES: Translated from, Plavanye, 1-15, 1980.
LEVEL: B LANG: Eng SIRC ARTICLE NO: 099952

TRAINING AND CONDITIONING - WEIGHT AND STRENGTH TRAINING

Rodeo, S. Sports performance series: swimming the breaststroke - a kinesiological analysis and considerations for strength training. *National Strength & Conditioning Association journal (Lincoln, Neb.) 6(4), Aug/Sept 1984, 4-6;74-76;80.*
LEVEL: I LANG: Eng SIRC ARTICLE NO: 099956

WOMEN

Peltenburg, A.L. Erich, W.B.M. Thijssen, J.J.H. Zonderland, M.L. Veeman, W. Jansen, M. Bernink, M.J.E. van den Brande, J.L. Huisveld, I.A. Sex hormones profiles of premenarcheal athletes. (Refs: 34)*European journal of applied physiology and occupational physiology (Berlin, FRG) 52(4), Jun 1984, 385-392.*
ABST: This study tested the hypothesis that the delay in onset of puberty in gymnasts as compared to girl swimmers is modulated by a lower estrone level due to a smaller amount of body fat. Sex-hormone and gonadotropin levels were measured in 46 gymnasts and 37 swimmers. The subjects were at a similar stage of biological maturation. There is a clear relationship between estrone levels and the levels of testosterone and androstenedione but not between estrone levels and fat mass. The authors conclude that the testosterone and androstenedione levels are responsible for differences in estrone levels between the two groups rather than the amount of body fat.
LEVEL: A LANG: Eng SIRC ARTICLE NO: 097895

Annen-Ruf, M. L'importance de la competition hier et aujourd'hui. *Macolin (Macolin, Suisse) 41(11), nov 1984, 13-15.*
NOTES: Traduction de, Marianne Weber.
LEVEL: B LANG: Fr SIRC ARTICLE NO: 108755

SYNCHRONIZED SWIMMING

ADMINISTRATION

Charte et reglements operationnels. **Ottawa:** Association canadienne de nage synchronisee amateur, 1984. 49 p.
CORP: Association canadienne de nage synchronisee amateur.
NOTES: Titre de la couverture. Also published in English under the title: Constitution and operational by-laws.
LEVEL: B LANG: Fr ISBN: 0-920194-50-8
GV838.53.S95 18124

Royer, B. Rose, M. Public relations and promotion. *Synchro (Santa Ana, Calif.) 22(2), Apr 1984, 18-21.*
LEVEL: B LANG: Eng SIRC ARTICLE NO: 095333

BIOGRAPHY AND AUTOBIOGRAPHY

Martin, K. In Sync: champion synchronized swimmers Tracie Ruiz and Candy Costie will show off their talents in the Summer Olympics. *Fit (Mountain View, Calif.) 4(2), Jul 1984, 70-71;88;93.*
LEVEL: B LANG: Eng SIRC ARTICLE NO: 101564

Merfeld, M. Making ends meet: Candy Costie and Tracie Ruiz make it look simple, but it took years of mirrored efforts to fin their perfect match - the Olympic gold medal. *Swimming world and junior swimmer (Inglewood, Calif.) 25(10), Oct 1984, 25-26;28;30.*
LEVEL: B LANG: Eng SIRC ARTICLE NO: 107605

CERTIFICATION

Forbes, M.S. Kane, D.T. Bean, D. Coaching synchronized swimming effectively. Champaign, Ill.: Human Kinetics, c1984. viii, 126 p. : ill.
NOTES: Bibliography: p. 126.
LEVEL: B LANG: Eng ISBN: 0931250803 LC CARD: 84-015853 GV838.53.S95 18181

CHOREOGRAPHY AND MUSIC

Bean, R. Music lessons from the Olympics. *Synchro (Santa Ana, Calif.) 22(6), Dec 1984, 18;28.*
LEVEL: B LANG: Eng SIRC ARTICLE NO: 107603

Davis, C. Choreographic critique of national routines. *Synchro (Santa Ana, Calif.) 22(2), Apr 1984, 22-23.*
LEVEL: B LANG: Eng SIRC ARTICLE NO: 095329

Emery, G. Choreography critique of national routines. *Synchro (Santa Ana, Calif.) 22(1), Feb 1984, 18.*
LEVEL: B LANG: Eng SIRC ARTICLE NO: 098549

COACHING

Carver, C. Age group organization and coaching. *Synchro (Santa Ana, Calif.) 22(1), Feb 1984, 20-22.*
LEVEL: B LANG: Eng SIRC ARTICLE NO: 098548

Dickie, D. The coaches: Debbie Muir, Jack Donohue, Ken Maeda, and Marina van der Merwe. Les entraineurs: Debbie Muir, Jack Donohue, Ken Maeda, et Marina van der Merwe. *Champion (Ottawa) 8(3), Aug 1984, 61-65.*
LEVEL: B LANG: Eng Fr SIRC ARTICLE NO: 095750

Interview with potential summer olympic coaches: Debbie Muir. *Coaching review 7, Mar/Apr 1984, 12-15.*
LEVEL: B LANG: Eng SIRC ARTICLE NO: 093786

ECONOMICS

Powley, I. Funding fun. *Synchro Canada (Nepean, Ont.) 14(3), 1984, 32-33.*
LEVEL: B LANG: Eng SIRC ARTICLE NO: 101565

INJURIES AND ACCIDENTS

Tucker, M. Weinberg, S. Injuries and problems common to synchronized swimmers. *Synchro (Santa Ana, Calif.) 22(1), Feb 1984, 22-23.*
LEVEL: B LANG: Eng SIRC ARTICLE NO: 098551

JUDGING

Jasontek, G. Forbes, M. McGowan, J. Judging contest. *Synchro (Santa Ana, Calif.) 22(1), Feb 1984, 19-20.*
LEVEL: B LANG: E SIRC ARTICLE NO: 098550

Judges training and accreditation program Canada Synchro. Policies, procedures, and administration manual. (Ottawa): Canadian Amateur Synchronized Swimming Association Inc., c1984. 1v. in various pagings
LEVEL: B LANG: Eng ISBN: 0-920194-70-2
GV838.53.S95 18372

Kretschmer, M. Mackellar, B. Eytchison, I. Sowers, D. Judging content. *Synchro (Santa Ana, Calif.) 22(2), Apr 1984, 16-18*
LEVEL: B LANG: Eng SIRC ARTICLE NO: 095332

PSYCHOLOGY

Dawn, B. Motivating the swimmer. *Synchro (Santa Ana, Calif.) 22(2), Apr 1984, 11-13.*
LEVEL: B LANG: Eng SIRC ARTICLE NO: 095330

SPORTING EVENTS

Ruggieri, M.J. United States synchronized swimming. *Journal of physical education, recreation & dance 55(3), Mar 1984, 29.*
LEVEL: B LANG: Eng SIRC ARTICLE NO: 093788

TECHNIQUES AND SKILLS

Bean, D. Do it where they'll see it. *Synchro (Santa Ana, Calif.) 22(3), Jun 1984, 3-4.*
LEVEL: B LANG: Eng SIRC ARTICLE NO 103504

Haeberli, M. La natation synchronisee: un sport de competition, mais aussi une matiere d'enseignement. *Macolin (Suisse) 6, juin 1984, 4-8.*
NOTES: Traduction de, Margaret Biderbost.
LEVEL: B LANG: Fr SIRC ARTICLE NO: 103505

TRAINING AND CONDITIONING

Fraser, L. Training: general to specific. *Synchro Canada (Nepean, Ont.) 14(3), 1984, 20-22.*
LEVEL: B LANG: Eng SIRC ARTICLE NO: 101563

Hambrook, G. Synchro for adults. (teaching methods) *Coaching review (Ottawa, Ont.) 7, May/Jun 1984, 49-51.*
LEVEL: B LANG: Eng SIRC ARTICLE NO: 095331

Vandal, J. Outdoor synchro. *Synchro Canada (Ottawa, Ont.) 14(1), 1984, 9.*
LEVEL: B LANG: Eng SIRC ARTICLE NO: 099964

TRAINING AND CONDITIONING - DRILLS

Donahue, G. How to improve your routine practice sessions. *Synchro Canada (Nepean, Ont.) 14(3), 1984, 22-24.*
LEVEL: B LANG: Eng SIRC ARTICLE NO: 101562

TABLE TENNIS

ANTHROPOMETRY

Holzer, E. Kauser, G. Prokop, L. The physique of Austrian table-tennis players, sociodemographic and ergometric aspects. (Refs: 8)*Sportorvosi szemle/Hungarian review of sports medicine (Budapest) 25(1), 1984, 27-41.*
ABST: Anthropometric, sportspecific and sociodemographic investigation of 51 male high level Austrian table tennis players ranging between 18 and 48 years of age was carried out. The results were compared with those from corresponding studies on European and Swiss table tennis players. They are in good agreement with each other indicating less marked limitation to a certain physique as is the case for other athletes, though endomesomorphic and meso-endomorphic somatotypes might be regarded as optimal; also the limitation to younger age-groups typical for other sports is missing. In addition laterality effects are discussed, pointing to an advantage of left handed players over right handed ones.
LEVEL: A LANG: Eng SIRC ARTICLE NO: 098560

BIOGRAPHY AND AUTOBIOGRAPHY

Boggan, T. Seeing the world. (Scott Boggan) *Olympian (Colorado Springs, Colo.) 9(2), Jul/Aug 1984, 20-21.*
LEVEL: B LANG: Eng SIRC ARTICLE NO: 104917

CHILDREN

Taylor, G. Coaching juniors in China. *Australian table tennis (Wagga Wagga, N.S.W.) 24(1), Apr 1984, 7.*
LEVEL: B LANG: En SIRC ARTICLE NO: 108782

DIRECTORIES

Directory - annuaire 1984. Vanier: Canadian Table Tennis Association, 1984. 31 p.
CORP: Canadian Table Tennis Association.
CORP: Association canadienne de tennis de table.
NOTES: Cover title.
LEVEL: B LANG: Eng GV1005 15855

ECONOMICS

Stewart, D. Sponsorship - getting it ...and keeping it. *Sports coach (Wembley, W. Aust.) 8(2), Oct 1984, 56-60.*
LEVEL: B LANG: Eng SIRC ARTICLE NO: 104919

EQUIPMENT

Schwartzberg, P. Attributes of different rubber surfaces. *Spin (Colorado Springs) 2(8), Oct 1984, 22-23.*
LEVEL: B LANG: E SIRC ARTICLE NO: 099968

PHYSIOLOGY

Duquette, J. Les qualites physiques de l'athlete de haut niveau. (Refs: 13)*Revue de l'entraineur (Montreal) avr/juin 1984, 15-22.*
LEVEL: I LANG: Fr SIRC ARTICLE NO: 095334

Palierne, C. Chronique medico-pongiste. *France tennis de table (Paris) 404, dec 1984, 29.*
NOTES: A suivre.
LEVEL: B LANG Fr SIRC ARTICLE NO: 173417

STRATEGY

Canor, J. Leroy, G. Prat, P. Communiquer a la balle une grande vitesse (attaquer). *France tennis de table (Paris) 401, sept 1984, 23-24;33-34.*
LEVEL: B LANG: Fr SIRC ARTICLE NO: 101566

Hodges, L. Combination rackets: the competitive challenge. *Spin (Colorado Springs, Colo.) 2(3), Mar 1984, 26.*
LEVEL: B LANG: Eng SIRC ARTICLE NO: 093789

STRATEGY - OFFENSIVE

Schwartzberg, P. Attacking your opponent's middle. *Spin (Colorado Springs, Colo.) 2(3), Mar 1984, 26.*
LEVEL: B LANG: Eng SIRC ARTICLE NO: 093791

TEACHING

Barbereau, G. Tennis de table a Roussillon. Une experience de penetration du tennis de table en milieu scolaire. *France tennis de table (Paris) 395, fevr 1984, 69-70.*
NOTES: Suite du no. 394, janv 1984.
LEVEL: B LANG: Fr SIRC ARTICLE NO: 098552

Barbereau, G. Tennis de table a Roussillon: une experience de penetration du tennis de table en milieu scolaire. *France tennis de table (Paris) 396, mars 1984, 77.*
NOTES: Suite du no 395, Fev 1984.
LEVEL: B LANG: Fr SIRC ARTICLE NO: 098553

Canor, J. Leroy, G. Prat, P. Remettre une balle attaquee ou liftee (bloc). *France tennis de table (Paris) 402, oct 1984, 19-20;25-26.*
LEVEL: B LANG: Fr SIRC ARTICLE NO: 173421

George, W. Les fondamentaux, themes permanentes de l'entrainement en tennis de table. *Sport: Communaute francaise de Belgiqu (Bruxelles) 106, 1984, 67-73.*
LEVEL: B LANG: Fr SIRC ARTICLE NO: 098558

Mallen, R. Returning spin - a teaching method that works. *Australian table tennis (Wagga Wagga, N.S.W.) 24(1), Apr 1984, 26*
LEVEL: B LANG: Eng SIRC ARTICLE NO: 108783

TECHNIQUES AND SKILLS

Zhengxian, L. How to make loops powerful. *China sports (Beijing, China) 16(11), 1984, 21-23.*
LEVEL: B LANG: Eng SIRC ARTICLE NO: 108449

TECHNIQUES AND SKILLS - SERVE RETURN

Hodges, L. Returning short serves. *Spin (Colorado Springs, Colo.) 2(5), May/Jun 1984, 14;16.*
NOTES: A follow-up of 'Serving short' which appeared in Spin Apr 1984, 15.
LEVEL: B LANG: Eng SIRC ARTICLE NO: 099966

TECHNIQUES AND SKILLS - SERVING

Hodges, L. Serving short. *Spin (Colorado Springs) 2(4), Apr 1984, 15.*
LEVEL: B LANG: Eng SIRC ARTICLE NO: 098559

TRAINING AND CONDITIONING

Barbereau, G. L'entrainement de la base. *France tennis de table (Paris) 404, dec 1984, 40.*
NOTES: Suite du no. 402, octobre 1984. A suivre.
LEVEL: B LANG: Fr SIRC ARTICLE NO: 173418

Canor, J. Leroy, G. Prat, P. A la decouverte du tennis de table. *France tennis de table (Paris) 396, mars 1984, 39-41.*
LEVEL: B LANG: Fr SIRC ARTICLE NO: 098555

Madhosingh, C. Exercise and human condition. *OTTA update (Willowdale, Ont.) Aug/Sept 1984, 19-20.*
LEVEL: B LANG: Eng SIRC ARTICLE NO: 099967

TRAINING AND CONDITIONING - DRILLS

Canor, J. Leroy, G. Prat, P. A la decouverte du tennis de table. *France tennis de table (Paris) 395, fevr 1984, 35-38.*
LEVEL: B LANG: Fr SIRC ARTICLE NO: 098554

Canor, J. Leroy, G. Prat, P. Maitriser la direction du renvoi de la balle dans le plan horizontal (a droite ou a gauche). *France tennis de table (Paris) 397, avr 1984, 31-34.*
LEVEL: B LANG: Fr SIRC ARTICLE NO: 098556

Canor, J. Leroy, G. Prat, P. A la decouverte du tennis de table. *France tennis de table (Paris) 394, janv 1984, 31-34.*
LEVEL: B LANG: Fr SIRC ARTICLE NO: 098557

Canor, J. Leroy, G. Prat, P. Communiquer a la balle une rotation arriere (coupe). *France tennis de table (Paris) 398, mai 1984, 39-42.*
LEVEL: B LANG: Fr SIRC ARTICLE NO: 099965

Canor, J. Leroy, G. Prat, P. Communiquer a la balle une rotation avant (lift). *France tennis de table (Paris) 399, juin 1984, 27-30.*
LEVEL: B LANG: Fr SIRC ARTICLE NO: 104918

TRAINING AND CONDITIONING - INTERVAL TRAINING

Sharara, A. Training methods: motor ball. *Coaching review (Ottawa, Ont.) 7, May/Jun 1984, 56-59.*
LEVEL: B LANG: Eng SIRC ARTICLE NO: 095336

TAE KWON DO

INJURIES AND ACCIDENTS

Kryger, H. Siana, J.E. Bojsen, P.B. Skader ved verdensmesterskabet i sportsgrenen Taekwondo. (Injuries sustained in the worl championship in the sport Taekwondo.) *Ugeskrift for laeger (Copenhagen) 146(44), 29 Oct 1984, 3371-3372.*
LEVEL: I LANG: Dan

STRATEGY - DEFENSIVE

McCarthy, M. Parulski, G.R. Taekwon-do: a guide to the theories of defensive movement. Chicago: Contemporary Books, 1984. 1v
NOTES: Includes index.
LEVEL: B LANG: Eng ISBN: 0809254042 LC CARD: 84-017532

TECHNIQUES AND SKILLS

Cater, D. Modified Tae Kwon Do: quicker, smoother - and better? *Black belt magazine (Burbank, Calif.) 22(11), Nov 1984, 28-32.*
LEVEL: B LANG: Eng SIRC ARTICLE NO: 107337

Gonzalez, M.J. Tae Kwon Do: the fighting kicks, the forms kicks. *Black belt (Burbank, Calif.) 22(1), Jan 1984, 48-52;109.*
LEVEL: B LANG: Eng SIRC ARTICLE NO: 108610

Gwon, P.G. Taegeuk: the new forms of tae kwon do. Burbank, Calif.: Ohara Publications, Inc., c1984. 223 p. : ill.
LEVEL: B LANG: Eng ISBN: 0-89750-097-0 LC CARD: 83-63602 GV1112 18909

Hallander, J. Kung fu vs. Tae kwon do: which approach to kicking strategy and tactics is really more effective? *Inside karate (Burbank, Calif.) 5(9), Sept 1984, 48-51.*
LEVEL: B LANG: Eng SIRC ARTICLE NO: 107353

TAICHICHUAN

Kotsias, J. The essential movement of tai chi. Brookline, Mass.: Paradigm Publications, c1984. 1v.
LEVEL: B LANG: Eng ISBN: 0912111046 LC CARD: 84-011335

COUNTRIES AND REGIONS

Kelly, B.J. Taichiquan, the gentle martial art. *TAHPERD journal (Austin, Tex.) 52(2), Feb 1984, 12-13.*
LEVEL: B LANG: Eng SIRC ARTICLE NO: 093594

PHYSIOLOGY

Zhuo, D. Shephard, R.J. Plyley, M.J. Davis, G.M. Cardiorespiratory and metabolic responses during Tai Chi Chuan exercise. (Refs: 16)*Canadian journal of applied sport sciences/Journal canadien des sciences appliquees au sport 9(1), Mar 1984, 7-10.*
ABST: Eleven healthy males were studied for oxygen cost and related metabolic variables heart rate, and blood pressure during the performance of Tai Chai Chuan; a form of shadow boxing of Chinese tradition. All subjects had been practising Tai Chai Chuan regularly for 3-8 years. The results

TAICHICHUAN (continued)

indicate that performance of 17-25 minutes of Tai Chai Chuan places a moderate exercise stress on the body.
LEVEL: A LANG: Eng SIRC ARTICLE NO: 093619

TECHNIQUES AND SKILLS

Barnes, S. Locking and trapping techniques of Tai Chi Chuan. *Black belt (Burbank, Calif.) 22(7), Jul 1984, 54-56;105-108.*
LEVEL: B LANG: Eng SIRC ARTICLE NO: 103283

Carrabis, J.D. Combined tai chi in the U.S.: stepping out of China's shadow. *Black belt (Burbank, Calif.) 22(4), Apr 1984, 28-32;72-73.*
LEVEL: B LANG: Eng SIRC ARTICLE NO: 099795

Danks, B. Tai Chi Chuan: who says it can't work on the street? *Black belt magazine (Burbank, Calif.) 22(12), Dec 1984, 50-54.*
LEVEL: B LANG: Eng SIRC ARTICLE NO: 107344

Meehan, J.J. The combat secrets of Chen Tai Chi. *Inside kung-fu (Burbank, Calif.) 11(8), Aug 1984, 69-73.*
LEVEL: B LANG: Eng SIRC ARTICLE NO: 105971

TEAM HANDBALL

BIOGRAPHY AND AUTOBIOGRAPHY

Maxant, C. Andre Sannier ou les souvenirs d'un pionnier. *Sante et sport (Paris) 217, avr 1984, 28-29.*
LEVEL: B LANG: Fr SIRC ARTICLE NO: 098562

CHILDREN - MINI-SPORT

Whitfield, B. Mini-handball: a primary viewpoint. *British journal of physical education (London) 15(1), Mar/Apr 1984, 55.*
LEVEL: B LANG: Eng SIRC ARTICLE NO: 099971

COUNTRIES AND REGIONS

Edwards, R.W. Team handball: a familiar name but a different game. *Journal of physical education, recreation & dance 55(2), Feb 1984, 27-28.*
LEVEL: B LANG: Eng SIRC ARTICLE NO: 092437

INJURIES AND ACCIDENTS

Jorgensen, U. Epidemiology of injuries in typical Scandinavian team sports. (Refs: 6)*British journal of sports medicine (Loughborough, Eng.) 18(2), Jun 1984, 59-63.*
ABST: An investigation by questionnaire was undertaken in a group of 480 football players and 288 handball players (768 players). Of these 803 were injured, giving a player incidence of 4.1 injury/1000 football hours and 8.3 injury/1000 handball hours. The lower extremities were involved in 82% of the football injuries, whereas handball injuries were evenly distributed on both upper and lower extremities. The football injury prevalence was 0.36 per player, the handball injury prevalence 0.71 per player. Medical attention was given to 62% of the injured footballers and 47% of the injured handballers.
LEVEL: A LANG: Eng SIRC ARTICLE NO: 103508

Roattino, J.P. Hand-ball risque traumatique: resultats de l'observation de deux echantillons. Problemes methodologiques. (Refs: 19)*Medecine*

du sport 58(1), 25 janv 1984, 12-16.
LEVEL: I LANG: Fr SIRC ARTICLE NO: 092439

MEDICINE

Csanady, M. Gruber, N. Comparative echocardiographic studies in leading canoe-kayak and handball sportsmen. (Refs: 15)*Cor et vasa (Prague) 26(1), 1984, 32-37.*
ABST: The purpose of this study was to compare echocardiographic data of 21 elite kayak-canoeists and 16 elite handball players. A thicker posterior wall and interventricular system as well as a greater left ventricular mass were observed in the kayak-canoeists.
LEVEL: A LANG: Eng SIRC ARTICLE NO: 103507

PSYCHOLOGY - MENTAL TRAINING

Costa, A. Bonaccorsi, M. Scrimali, T. Biofeedback and control of anxiety preceding athletic competition. (Refs: 46) *International journal of sports psychology (Rome, Italy) 15(2), 1984, 98-109.*
ABST: The authors discuss the theory of pre-start anxiety in the context of athletic preparation, using a technique known as biofeedback training. This therapeutic technique applies the theoretical principles of biofeedback by means of an electronic device, the stress reducer. Based on the findings of research studies in this field, the authors conducted an experiment on a handball team and were able to confirm that biofeedback training in the self-control of anxiety was able to decrease pre-competition anxiety. This result lends support to the hypothesis of a psychophysical genesis of the syndrome.
LEVEL: A LANG: Eng SIRC ARTICLE NO: 099283

RULES AND REGULATIONS

Homsy, M. Team handball: a budget sport for any program. *Journal of physical education, recreation & dance (Reston, Va.) 55(5), May/Jun 1984, 90.*
LEVEL: B LANG: Eng SIRC ARTICLE NO: 095338

Regles du jeu, statuts et reglements. 20e ed. 1984-1985. Montreal: La Federation, 1984. 71 p. : ill.
CORP: Federation quebecoise handball olympique.
LEVEL: B LANG: Fr GV1017.F5 18138

STRATEGY

Marique, T. Gerard, P. Dedoyard, E. Handball: initiation et apprentissage (2e partie). Apprentissage des fondamentaux techniques et tactiques. (Refs: 6)*Sport: Communaute francaise de Belgique (Bruxelles) 27(3), 1984, 156-169.*
LEVEL: B LANG: Fr SIRC ARTICLE NO: 099969

STRATEGY - OFFENSIVE

Alba, P. Approche du 'un contre un'. *EPS: Education physique et sport (Paris) 190, nov/dec 1984, 17-21.*
NOTES: Tire et modifie de, Handazur 12, avr 1981.
LEVEL: B LANG: Fr SIRC ARTICLE NO: 103506

TEACHING

Marique, T. Gerard, P. Dedoyard, E. Hand-ball: initiation et apprentissage (1e partie). (Refs: 4)*Sport: Communaute francais de Belgique (Bruxelles) 106, 1984, 81-90.*
LEVEL: B LANG: Fr SIRC ARTICLE NO: 098561

Preira, A. Les principes de base regissant l'entrainement de l'attaque et de la defense chez le debutant - lere partie. *Handball magazine (Montreal) 8(2), avr 1984, 7-8;10.*
LEVEL: B LANG: Fr SIRC ARTICLE NO: 095340

TECHNIQUES AND SKILLS - SHOOTING

Bayer, C. Mauvoisin, M. Les tirs a distances. 1re partie. (Refs: 4)*EPS: Education physique et sport 185, janv/fevr 1984, 46-51.*
LEVEL: B LANG: Fr SIRC ARTICLE NO: 093792

TESTING AND EVALUATION

Gallois, A. Gayraud, J. Handball: un exemple d'evaluation. *EPS: Education physique et sport (Paris) 189, sept/oct 1984, 34-39.*
LEVEL: B LANG: Fr SIRC ARTICLE NO: 101567

TRAINING AND CONDITIONING

Cercel, P. Handballtraining. Berlin: Sportverlag, c1984. 212 p. : ill.
NOTES: Translated from Rumanian.
LEVEL: I LANG: Ger GV1017.F5 18150

TRAINING AND CONDITIONING - DRILLS

Bayer, C. Mauvoisin, M. Handball: le tir de loin: ameliorer la puissance et la precision. 2e partie. (Refs: 6)*EPS: Educatio physique et sport (Paris, France) 186, mars/avr 1984, 21-25.*
NOTES: A suivre.
LEVEL: B LANG: Fr SIRC ARTICLE NO: 095337

Bayer, C. Mauvoisin, M. Tirs a distance: les tirs en suspension. 3e partie. *EPS: Education physique et sport (Paris) 187, mai/juin 1984, 69-72.*
LEVEL: B LANG: Fr SIRC ARTICLE NO: 096910

Newnhan, P. The teaching of handball. *British journal of physical education (London) 15(1), Jan/Feb 1984, 28-29.*
LEVEL: B LANG: Eng SIRC ARTICLE NO: 099970

WOMEN

Senlanne, Y. Horvath, S. Preparation de la force specifique de l'equipe de France juniors de hand-ball pour les championnats du monde de 1983.
NOTES: Dans, Renforcement musculaire, Paris, Institut national du sport et de l'education physique, c1984, p. 36.
LEVEL: I LANG: Fr GV711.5 18233

TEAM SPORTS

Chen, E. The cause for the preparatory commission of the R.O.C. Korfball Association. *Asian journal of physical education (Taipei, Taiwan) 7(3), Oct 1984, 43-44.*
LEVEL: B LANG: Eng Chi SIRC ARTICLE NO: 102915

Lambert, P. Treadwell, T.W. Kumar, V.K. Popular games, where did they originate. (Refs: 1)*International journal of sport psychology (Rome) 15(1), 1984, 35-39.*
LEVEL: I LANG: Eng SIRC ARTICLE NO: 094758

Smith, R.G. Decision-making in high level sport. (Refs: 35)*Sports coach (Wembley, Aust.) 8(1), 1984, 24-30.*
LEVEL: I LANG: Eng SIRC ARTICLE NO: 096433

Vincelette, B. La aki, un jeu de mains. *Velimag (Dorval, Que.) 1(4), juin 1984, 17.*
LEVEL: B LANG: Fr SIRC ARTICLE NO: 173430

Zhenrong, Y. Shuttlecock kicking. *China sports (Beijing, China) 16(7), Jul 1984, 26.*
LEVEL: B LANG: Eng SIRC ARTICLE NO: 102181

ADMINISTRATION

Houston, W. Ballard: a portrait of Canada's most controversial sports figure. Toronto: Summerhill Press, c1984. 256 p. : ill
LEVEL: B LANG: Eng ISBN: 0-920197-05-1 LC CARD: C84-099445-1 GV848.5.B34 18062

Martini, S. Team sports management: instant scheduling and the computer. *NIRSA journal (Corvallis, Ore.) 9(1), Fall 1984, 58-60.*
LEVEL: B LANG: Eng SIRC ARTICLE NO: 105154

CHILDREN

Villeneuve, M.J. Jeu traditionnel modifie: le ballon prisonnier. *Canadian Intramural Recreation Association (Vanier, Ont.) (8), May/June 1984, 4.*
NOTES: Tire de, Villeneuve, M.J., Viens jouer: 146 jeux cooperatifs pour s'amuser et se detendre en groupe, Editions de l'homme, 1983.
LEVEL: B LANG: Eng SIRC ARTICLE NO: 108660

COACHING

MacDonald, N. Avoiding the pitfalls in player selection. (Refs: 9)*Ringette review/Revue ringuette (Vanier) 6(4), Dec 1984, 27-28.*
LEVEL: B LANG: Eng SIRC ARTICLE NO: 108857

Yukelson, D.P. Group motivation in sport teams. NOTES: In, Silva, J.M. and Weinberg, R.S. (eds.), Psychological foundations of sport, Champaign, Ill., Human Kinetics Publishers, c1984, p. 229-240.
LEVEL: A LANG: Eng GV706.4 17779

ECONOMICS

Raber, T.R. How to...raise money for your team. *Sports now (St. Louis, Mo.) 2(8), Aug 1984, 22.*
LEVEL: B LANG: Eng SIRC ARTICLE NO: 097414

EQUIPMENT

Oliver, P. A buyer's guide to inflatable balls. What to look for in purchasing your footballs, basketballs, soccer balls, an volleyballs. But, remember, performance is the ultimate measure of excellence for all equipment. *Scholastic coach (New York) 54(4), Nov 1984, 58-63.*
LEVEL: B LANG: Eng SIRC ARTICLE NO: 102408

Oliver, P. A buyer's guide to non-inflatable balls: surprise, the old horsehide is really made out of cowhide. *Scholastic coach (New York) 54(5), Dec 1984, 48-51;63.*
LEVEL: B LANG: Eng SIRC ARTICLE NO: 102409

INJURIES AND ACCIDENTS

Diederiks, J. van Galen, W. Philipsen, H. Injuries in indoor korfball. (Refs: 6)*International journal of sports medicine (Stuttgart) Suppl. 5, Nov 1984, 216-217.*

CONF: International Congress on Sports and Health (1983 : Maastricht, Netherlands).
LEVEL: A LANG: Eng SIRC ARTICLE NO: 104028

JUVENILE LITERATURE

Dickmeyer, L.A. Humphreys, M. Teamwork. New York: F. Watts, 1984. 1v. (An easy-read sports book.)
NOTES: Includes index.
LEVEL: B LANG: Eng ISBN: 0531047148 LC CARD: 83-021718

OFFICIATING

Tapp, J. Profile: the CCSOO. The Chester County Sports Officials' Organization had made significant inroads since being formed in June of 1982. *Referee (Franksville, Wisc.) 9(10), Oct 1984, 56-57.*
LEVEL: B LANG: Eng SIRC ARTICLE NO: 105375

PERCEPTUAL MOTOR PROCESSES

Dunnet, J.D. The teaching of games - feedback and environmental conditions. (Refs: 8)*Momentum (Edinburgh, Scotland) 9(3), Autumn 1984, 7-13.*
LEVEL: I LANG: Eng SIRC ARTICLE NO: 105357

PSYCHOLOGY

Carron, A.V. Cohesion in sport teams. NOTES: In, Silva, J.M. and Weinberg, R.S. (eds.), Psychological foundations of sport, Champaign, Ill., Human Kinetics Publishers, c1984, p. 340-351.
LEVEL: A LANG: Eng GV706.4 17779

Fielding, L.W. The 'I' in team sports. (Refs: 32)*Physical educator (Indianapolis) 41(4), Dec 1984, 181-185.*
LEVEL: I LANG: Eng SIRC ARTICLE NO: 104404

Gross, J.B. Perception: seeing things that others don't see. (Refs: 6)*Sports coach (Wembley, W. Aust.) 8(2), Oct 1984, 15-17.*
CONF: ACHPER Bicentennial. Conference (1984 : Sydney).
LEVEL: B LANG: Eng SIRC ARTICLE NO: 104410

Nettleton, B. Barras, N. Ways to talk out the biggest problems. (verbal report techniques) (Refs: 16)*Sports coach (Wembley, W. Aust.) 8(2), Oct 1984, 36-41.*
LEVEL: I LANG: Eng SIRC ARTICLE NO: 104414

RULES AND REGULATIONS

Bin, Z. Jianqiu: a new game. *China sports (Beijing, China) 16(7), Jul 1984, 27-28.*
LEVEL: B LANG: Eng SIRC ARTICLE NO: 102182

Stoian, V. The romanians' national sports: a 'brother' of basse-ball. *Sports in Romania/Sport en Roumanie (Bucarest, Romani 2/3, 1984, 46-47.*
NOTES: Special issue, The Los Angeles Olympic Games.
LEVEL: B LANG: Eng SIRC ARTICLE NO: 109030

Swinny, S.R. Korfball - the Netherlands answer to recreational basketball. (Refs: 2)*NIRSA journal (Mt. Pleasant, Mich.) 8(2), Winter 1984, 44-46.*
LEVEL: B LANG: Eng SIRC ARTICLE NO: 097874

SOCIAL PSYCHOLOGY

Watson, G.G. Social motivation in games: toward a conceptual framework of game attraction. (Refs: 36)*Journal of human movement studies (Edinburgh) 10(1), 1984, 1-19.*
ABST: This review examined the attractions of games and applied this knowledge towards the construction of a conceptual framework of game attraction. The central components of game attractions included: 1) 'intrinsic rewards' interpretations; 2) co-operative interaction or social reciprocity interpretations, and 3) goal attainment or 'achievement mastery' interpretation. These components paralleled Miyomoto's conceptual framework of social motivation. Thus the conceptual framework of game attraction was based on Miyomoto's model. The authors consider the application of this model to human movement studies and leisure administration to be of central importance in meeting the needs of the participants.
LEVEL: A LANG: Eng SIRC ARTICLE NO: 094668

STATISTICS AND RECORDS

Frazier, C.S. Hatfield, A.B. Computerize your sports statistics. *Texas coach (Austin, Tex.) 28(2), Sept 1984, 22-24.*
LEVEL: B LANG: Eng SIRC ARTICLE NO: 105591

TEACHING

Bigou, A. Vigouroux, G. Acceleration du jeu. *I.N.S.E.P. dossier documentaire (Paris) 3, 1984, 31-42.*
LEVEL: I LANG: Fr SIRC ARTICLE NO: 094506

Bonnery, L. Continuite du jeu. *I.N.S.E.P. dossier documentaire (Paris) 3, 1984, 8-30.*
NOTES: Aspects reglementaires; aspects theoriques et prolongements pratiques.
LEVEL: I LANG: Fr SIRC ARTICLE NO: 094507

TENNIS

Austin, T. Tracy Austin's 8-point program to help you move up a level. *Tennis (Norwalk, Conn.) 20(6), Oct 1984, 48-49;51-52;54;56;59.*
LEVEL: B LANG: Eng SIRC ARTICLE NO: 108886

Barrett, J. Tingay, L. Flink, S. World of tennis 1984: the official yearbook of the International Tennis Federation. London: Willow Books, 1984. 416 p. : ill.
CORP: International Tennis Federation.
LEVEL: B LANG: Eng ISBN: 0-00-218122-3 GV995 18048

Flink, S. College tennis: older and wiser. *World tennis (Los Angeles, Calif.) 32(1), Jun 1984, 23-25.*
LEVEL: B LANG: Eng SIRC ARTICLE NO: 101591

Groppel, J.L. Tennis for advanced players, and those who would like to be. Champaign, Ill.: Human Kinetics Publishers, c1984 xv, 187 p. : ill.
NOTES: Includes bibliographies.
LEVEL: I LANG: Eng ISBN: 0-931250-57-9 LC CARD: 83-083164 GV995 18013

Hutchins, P. Guide to better tennis: from clay to grass. *Tennis world (London) Jun 1984, 78-79.*
LEVEL: B LANG: Eng SIRC ARTICLE NO: 101595

Instruction: an 11-step program for winning a match. *Tennis (Norwalk, Conn.) 19(10), Feb 1984,*

23-34.
LEVEL: B LANG: Eng SIRC ARTICLE NO: 093803

Lambert, P. Treadwell, T.W. Kumar, V.K.
Popular games, where did they originate. (Refs:
1)*International journal of sport psychology (Rome)*
15(1), 1984, 35-39.
LEVEL: I LANG: Eng SIRC ARTICLE NO: 094758

Master the indoor game: how to make the transition
from out to in an easy one. *World tennis (Los*
Angeles) 32(6), Nov 1984, 23-25.
LEVEL: B LANG: Eng SIRC ARTICLE NO: 108576

Navratilova, M. Carilo, M. Mathieu, P. Mon tennis
a votre service. Paris: Solar, 1984. 128 p. : ill.
(Sports 2014.)
NOTES: Traduit de: Tennis my way.
LEVEL: B LANG: Fr ISBN: 2-263-00841-1

Seiden, M. The business of tennis. *Dissent (New*
York) 31(4), 1984, 487-491.
LEVEL: B LANG: Eng SIRC ARTICLE NO: 100012

Tennis, a professional guide. 1st ed. New York:
Kodansha International, c1984. 326 p. : ill.
CORP: United States Professional Tennis
Association.
LEVEL: I LANG: Eng ISBN: 0870116827 LC CARD:
84-000846 GV995 18015

ADMINISTRATION

Berst, J. On line: what computers can do for a
tennis club. *Tennis industry (N. Miami, Fla.) 12(2),*
Feb 1984, 7-8;11;41;43.
NOTES: First of a twelve - part series.
ABST: A properly chosen computer system can
assist in tennis club management. Computers can
help automate member accounts, provide word
processing capabilities for the production of
newsletters, promotional material, a club
handbooks as well as keep track of delinquent
memberships. In a profit-making enterprise, the
computer can also help to monitor shop inventory
as well as keep track of items which are not selling
well.
LEVEL: B LANG: Eng SIRC ARTICLE NO: 099976

Berst, J. A computer shopping list: part 1. *Tennis*
industry (N. Miami, Fla.) 12(6), Jun 1984, 36-40.
ABST: Before purchasing any computer system, a
club should carefully examine its needs and desires
as well as investigate appropriate software
packages. Guidelines for evaluating software in
general (e.g. english-language operator prompts,
menu-driven) as well as detailed suggestions for
necessary components for accounting software
packages are provided.
LEVEL: B LANG: Eng SIRC ARTICLE NO: 101572

Caltabiano, J. A look into the future management
controls. Part III. *Tennis industry (Miami, Fla.)*
12(9), Sept 1984, 24;26.
LEVEL: B LANG: Eng SIRC ARTICLE NO: 173216

Garman, B. Applications: applying a linear function
to schedule tennis matches. *Mathematics teacher*
(Reston, Va.) 77(7), Oc 1984, 544-547.
LEVEL: I LANG: Eng SIRC ARTICLE NO: 104924

Interview: Lamar Hunt. *Tennis world (London) Apr*
1984, 16-18.
LEVEL: B LANG: Eng SIRC ARTICLE NO: 100001

King, J. Programming tournaments. *In, Level one*
coaching course 1983. Tennis coaching manual,
Wembley, W.A., Western Australian Lawn Tennis

Association et al., 1984, p. 25-28.
LEVEL: B LANG: Eng GV1002.9.C6 18656

Mewshaw, M. True confessions. An anonymous
umpire, John McEnroe Sr., and Arthur Ashe engage
in some straight talk about what's crooked in men's
tennis. *Racquets Canada (Toronto) Apr 1984, 18-*
20;22;24;26;28;30;32-33.
LEVEL: B LANG: Eng SIRC ARTICLE NO: 095358

Velasco, F. Tournament organization.
NOTES: In, United States Professional Tennis
Association, Tennis, a professional guide 1st ed.,
New York, Kodansha International, c1984, p. 230-
232.
LEVEL: B LANG: Eng GV995 18015

Wancke, H. Interview: Buzzer Hadingham. *Tennis*
world (London) Jul 1984, 22-23;25.
LEVEL: B LANG: Eng SIRC ARTICLE NO: 101618

AGED

Branham, G. Pettrone, F.A. Tennis for senior
citizens. Pilot program to promote fitness.
Postgraduate medicine (Minneapolis Minn.) 75(6),
May 1984, 199;202-203.
LEVEL: B LANG: Eng SIRC ARTICLE NO: 101576

ANTHROPOMETRY

Buti, T. Elliott, B. Morton, A. Physiological and
anthropometric profiles of elite prepubescent tennis
players. *Physician and sportsmedicine 12(1), Jan*
1984, 111-116.
ABST: Physiological and anthropometric
parameters of eight male and eight female tennis
players were measured in this study. No significant
differences were found between girls and boys.
However, girls had an higher level of fat.
LEVEL: A LANG: Eng SIRC ARTICLE NO: 092445

Carlson, J.S. Cera, M.A. Cardiorespiratory,
muscular strength and anthropometric
characteristics of elite Australian junior male and
female tennis players. (Refs: 21)*Australian journal*
of science & medicine in sport (Kingston, Aust.)
16(4), Dec 1984, 7-13.
ABST: Six male and six female elite junior tennis
players (10-1/years) were tested for
cardiorespiratory characteristics, body fat, grip
strength, isokinetic strength and power, selected
skinfolds, bone diameters and circumferences and
anaerobic power and capacity. The males were
found to have significantly higher VO2 max values
than the females. Body fat (per cent) of the males
(11.40) was significantly lower than that of the
females (18.96). The males were found to be
significantly stronger than the females in all
measures of grip and isokinetic strength and power.
The males exhibited significantly smaller tricep,
bicep, iliac and axilla skinfold than the females.
Measures of anaerobic power and capacity also
significantly differentiated between the sexes.
LEVEL: A LANG: Eng SIRC ARTICLE NO: 106100

Morton, A.R. Physical training for elite pre-
adolescent tennis players. (Refs: 25)*Australian*
journal of science & medicine in sport (Kingston,
Aust.) 16(3), Oct 1984, 2-5.
ABST: Anthropometric and physiological changes
following a 10-week physical fitness program are
evaluated for eight elite pre-adolescent tennis
players with a mean age of 11.7 years. A control
group of eight pre-adolescent tennis players with
a mean age of 11.8 years who continued to
play tennis but did not take part in the training

program were also tested. The experimental group
recorded a significant reduction of from 106.9mm to
94.4mm in sum of skinfold thickness following the
training, while the control group was unchanged.
Maximal aerobic performance (12-minute run,
2178m to 2489.3m), glycolytic capacity (400, run,
83.4s to 79.7s) and agility (Illinois agility run, 18.4s
to 16.6s) all improved in the experimental group
following the training while the control group
recorded no significant changes.
LEVEL: A LANG: Eng SIRC ARTICLE NO: 106106

ASSOCIATIONS

1984 Wheelchair Tennis Players Association. s.l.:
National Foundation of Wheelchair Tennis, 1984.
38 p.
CORP: National Foundation of Wheelchair Tennis.
CORP: Everest & Jennings.
NOTES: Cover title.
LEVEL: B LANG: Eng GV1001.4.D5 18433

BIOGRAPHY AND AUTOBIOGRAPHY

Adams, S.B. Lacoste & Head: they changed the
shape of tennis. *World tennis (Los Angeles) 32(7),*
Dec 1984, 25-26.
LEVEL: B LANG: Eng SIRC ARTICLE NO: 173586

Bodo, P. Scott Davies: the game's new all-
American boy. *Tennis (Norwalk, Conn.) 19(11), Mar*
1984, 52-54;56;59;61;65.
LEVEL: B LANG: Eng SIRC ARTICLE NO: 098567

Bodo, P. Hana Mandlikova: her battle with her
private fears. *Tennis (Norwalk, Conn.) 20(1), May*
1984, 58-62;65;67;69;71.
LEVEL: B LANG: Eng SIRC ARTICLE NO: 099980

Bodo, P. Yannick Noah: a champion in turmoil.
Tennis (Norwalk, Conn.) 20(2), Jun 1984, 34-39.
LEVEL: B LANG: Eng SIRC ARTICLE NO: 101573

Bureau, M. Pauvre petite fille riche. (Carling
Bassett) *Tennis magazine (Paris) 98, mai 1984,*
128-130.
LEVEL: B LANG: Fr SIRC ARTICLE NO: 099984

Bureau, M. La femme qui en cachait une autre ou
la prodigieuse metamorphose de Martina
Navratilova. *Tennis magazine (Paris) 100, juil 1984,*
126-129.
LEVEL: B LANG: Fr SIRC ARTICLE NO: 101577

Bureau, M. Entretien avec... Colin Dowdeswell.
Tennis magazine (Paris) 101, aout 1984, 60-68.
LEVEL: B LANG: Fr SIRC ARTICLE NO: 106098

Clerici, G. La reine Marguerite. (Marguerite
Broquedis) *Tennis de France (Paris) 374, juin 1984,*
275;277;279.
LEVEL: B LANG: Fr SIRC ARTICLE NO: 109163

Collins, B. Chrissie, jusqu'a la solitude. *Tennis*
magazine (Paris) 99, juin 1984, 148-151.
LEVEL: B LANG: Fr SIRC ARTICLE NO: 101578

Deford, F. So why can't you smile? If he did, then
he would no longer be the raging genius that is
John McEnroe. *Sports illustrated (Los Angeles,*
Calif.) 60(26), 25 Jun 1984, 70-74;76;78;80;82-84.
LEVEL: B LANG: Eng SIRC ARTICLE NO: 095349

Deford, F. A head to heed. Since the days when
peach ice cream tasted like peach ice cream,
Teddy Tinling's grace and sense of history have
meant as much to tennis as his dress designs.
Sports illustrated (Chicago, Ill.) 61(2), 9 Jul 1984,

72-76;78;80;82;84;86.
LEVEL: B LANG: Eng SIRC ARTICLE NO: 095350

Endemann, C. Carling Bassett: history is made as Canada's star shines in the top ten. *Racquets Canada (Toronto) Winter 1984 10-11.*
LEVEL: B LANG: Eng SIRC ARTICLE NO: 109112

Entretien avec... Scott Davis. *Tennis magazine (Neuilly Cedex, France) 103, oct 1984, 68-75.*
LEVEL: B LANG: Fr SIRC ARTICLE NO: 173456

Entretien avec... Vitas Gerulaitis. *Tennis magazine (Neuilly Cedex, France) 102, sept 1984, 44-50.*
LEVEL: B LANG: Fr SIRC ARTICLE NO: 108905

Entretien avec...Martina Navratilova. *Tennis magazine (Paris) 96, mars 1984, 46-52.*
LEVEL: B LANG: Fr SIRC ARTICLE NO: 0999

Hayes, A.S. Pam Shriver: coming of age. *Tennis (Norwalk, Conn.) 20(4), Aug 1984, 34-39.*
LEVEL: B LANG: Eng SIRC ARTICLE NO: 101593

Hayes, A.S. Mac the mouth: next time, ban him for a year. *Tennis (Norwalk, Conn.) 20(7), Nov 1984, 34-39.*
LEVEL: B LANG: Eng SIRC ARTICLE NO: 108583

Lorge, B. The future is now: for Noelle Porter and other talented teens, who dream of stardom. *World tennis (Los Angeles, Calif.) 32(3), Aug 1984, 26-33.*
LEVEL: B LANG: Eng SIRC ARTICLE NO: 101604

Lorge, B. Sport interview: John McEnroe. Tennis' top winner and sinner tries out a new racket - Mr. Nice Guy. *Sport (New York) 75(7), Jul 1984, 13;16;20-21.*
LEVEL: B LANG: Eng SIRC ARTICLE NO: 103516

Macfarlane, D. Darling Carling. At sixteen Carling Bassett is an international celebrity, a marketer's delight, and the sixteenth best female tennis player in the world. Even her parents don't know what drives this precocious daughter of the Canadian establishment. *Saturday night Jan 1984, 22-30;32.*
LEVEL: B LANG: Eng SIRC ARTICLE NO: 092449

McDermott, B. Oh, were it only the racket. (Andrea Jaeger) *Sports illustrated 60(15), 9 Apr 1984, 34-36;38;40-41;44.*
LEVEL: B LANG: Eng SIRC ARTICLE NO: 093807

McGregor, C. Profile : a weighty problem. Can Carling Bassett beat her biggest foes? *Racquets Canada (Toronto) Aug/Sept 1984, 12-13.*
LEVEL: B LANG: Eng SIRC ARTICLE NO: 098587

Steinberg, A. Andrea Jaeger: the real story. *Inside sports (Evanston, Ill.) 6, Jul 1984, 76-78;80-86.*
LEVEL: B LANG: Eng SIRC ARTICLE NO: 095363

Tangay, L. All time greats: William Renshaw. *Tennis world (London) Jun 1984, 81.*
LEVEL: B LANG: Eng SIRC ARTICLE NO: 1016

Tebbutt, T. The man and the myth. (Ivan Lendl) *Racquets Canada (Toronto) May 1984, 10-19.*
LEVEL: B LANG: Eng SIRC ARTICLE NO: 095365

Tebbutt, T. The decline and rise of Glenn Michibata. *Racquets Canada (Toronto) Mar 1984, 16-18;20.*
LEVEL: B LANG: Eng SIR ARTICLE NO: 096920

Tingay, L. Pauline Betz. *Tennis world (London) Mar 1984, 36.*
LEVEL: B LANG: Eng SIRC ARTICLE NO: 098595

Wade, V. Rafferty, J. Ladies of the court. London: Michael Joseph, c1984. 192 p. : ill. (Pavilion books.)

LEVEL: B LANG: En ISBN: 0-907516-45-9
GV994.A1 18962

Wancke, H. Interview: Mrs. Kitty Godfree. Twice Wimbledon women's champion - 1924 & 1926. *Tennis world (London) Jun 1984, 14-16;18;22.*
LEVEL: B LANG: Eng SIRC ARTICLE NO: 101617

Wilson, S. How they put Martina together. *Sport (New York) 75(6), Jun 1984, 42-43;45;47;50.*
LEVEL: B LANG: Eng SIRC ARTICLE NO: 093813

Wilson, S. The trials of a tennis brat: at 11, he was a tennis prodigy. At 15, he was the prized product of a Florida tennis factory. At 20, he stands on the verge of breaking up the Big Three. Unless he's too late. (Jimmy Arias) *Sport (New York) 75(9), Sept 1984, 49;51-52;54;59.*
LEVEL: B LANG: Eng SIRC ARTICLE NO: 103524

BIOMECHANICS

Durey, A. De Kermadec, G. Tous les coups du tennis et leurs effets. *Science et vie (Paris) HS147, 1984, 44-69.*
LEVEL: I LANG: Fr

Groppel, J.L. Improving your tennis through biomechanics.
NOTES: In, United States Professional Tennis Association, Tennis, a professional guide. 1st ed., New York, Kodansha International, c1984, p. 200-211.
LEVEL: I LANG: Eng GV995 18015

Howell, R.C. A biomechanical analysis of the flat and topspin serves in tennis. Eugene, Ore.: Microform Publications, University of Oregon, 1984. 1 microfiche : negative ; 11 x 15 cm.
NOTES: Thesis (M.S.) - Purdue University, 1982; (vi, 45 leaves); includes bibliography.
LEVEL: A LANG: Eng UO84 308

Picchio, A.A. Dall'Acqua, E. Sorbini, S. Zini, R. Biomeccanica della spalla nel tennis. Biomechanics of the shoulder in tennis. (Refs: 7)*Italian journal of sports traumatology (Milano, Italy) 6(3), Jul/Sept 1984, 197-206.*
CONF: Italian Society of Sports Traumatology. Congress (1st : 1983 : Rome).
ABST: In tennis the upper limb is the most stressed: the biomechanical study of the shoulder by Roentgen-cinematography and electromyography permits differentiating the functions according to the main athletic movements. The study of six sample muscles led to an outlining of the typical movements and to the understanding of the biomechanical stresses present in each phase of the game. From this is derived the therapeutical indication or better still preventive approach to avoiding possible stress-caused articular diseases.
LEVEL: A LANG: Eng It SIRC ARTICLE NO: 103518

Ricciardi-Pollini, P.T. Ronconi, P. La patologia dell' avampiede nel tennista. Forefoot pathology in tennis. (Refs: 6) *Italian journal of sports traumatology (Milano, Italy) 6(4), Oct/Dec 1984, 303-309.*
CONF: Italian Society of Sports Traumatology. Congress (1st : 1983 : Rome)
ABST: The various movements involved in tennis are discussed. A study of these movements using televideopodometry (TVP) was conducted in order to reveal modifications in pressure on both feet during the various phases of the game. Characteristic aspects of forefoot pathology in

tennis are also discussed.
LEVEL: A LANG: It Eng SIRC ARTICLE NO: 106108

CAREERS

Bacso, G. How to become a teaching professional.
NOTES: In, United States Professional Tennis Association, Tennis, a professional guide. 1st ed., New York, Kodansha International, c1984, p. 221-226.
LEVEL: B LANG: Eng GV995 18015

CERTIFICATION

Casey, R. The national coaching accreditation scheme. *In, Level one coaching course 1983. Tennis coaching manual, Wembley, W.A., Western Australian Lawn Tennis Association et al., 1984, p. 1.*
LEVEL: B LANG: Eng GV1002.9.C6 18656

Level one coaching course 1983. Tennis coaching manual. Wembley, W.A.: Western Australian Lawn Tennis Ass. : Tennis Professionals : Dept. for Youth, Sport & Rec. Ass., 1984. 31 p.
CORP: Western Australia. Department for Youth, Sport & Recreation.
CORP: Western Australian Lawn Tennis Association.
CORP: Tennis Professionals Association.
NOTES: Cover title.
LEVEL: B LANG: Eng GV1002.9.C6 18656

CHILDREN

Alsheimer, D. Use your young players effectively. *Women's coaching clinic 7(8), Apr 1984, 13-16.*
LEVEL: B LANG: Eng SIRC ARTICLE NO: 093793

Barbier, G. Papa, maman, le tennis et moi. *Tennis magazine (Paris) 97, avr 1984, 108-115.*
LEVEL: B LANG: Fr SIRC ARTICLE NO: 101571

Bollettieri, N. How do you start your child playing tennis? *World tennis (Los Angeles, Calif.) 31(8), Jan 1984, 26-27.*
LEVEL: B LANG: Eng SIRC ARTICLE NO: 098568

Giang, F. Vega, A. Savoir prescrire le tennis aux enfants. *Impact medecin (Puteaux, France) 107, 1984, 58-60.*
LEVEL: B LANG: Fr

Gueniot, C. L'enfant ne doit pas jouer un tennis d'adulte. *Generaliste (Paris) 618, 1984, 40.*
LEVEL: B LANG: Fr

Hannoun, M. Les revers du tennis chez l'enfant. *Pratique medicale, le journal (Paris) 110, 1984, 1-2.*
LEVEL: B LANG: Fr

Lichtenstein, G. Too much too soon...the teen pros: or a unique opportunity for young talent to cash in? The answer must probe tender muscles and minds as well as pocketbooks. *World tennis (Los Angeles, Calif.) 31(8), Jan 1984, 28-34.*
LEVEL: B LANG: Eng SIRC ARTICLE NO: 098583

CHILDREN - MINI-SPORT

Jaquet, G. Le mini tennis a l'ecole. *EPS: Education physique et sport 185, janv/fevr 1984, 11-15.*
LEVEL: B LANG: Fr SIRC ARTICLE NO: 092696

CLOTHING

1984 merchandiser for shoe buyers. *Tennis industry (Miami, Fla.) 12(9), Sept 1984, 29-45.*
LEVEL: B LANG: Eng SIRC ARTICLE NO: 173213

1984 shoe market report. *Tennis industry (N. Miami, Fla.) 12(2), Feb 1984, 16-17;20-22;24-28.*
LEVEL: B LANG: Eng SIRC ARTICLE NO: 099972

Courting court apparel. *Fitness industry (Miami, Fla.) 2(1), Jan/Feb 1984, 16-17;19-20;22;24;26.*
LEVEL: B LANG: Eng SIRC ARTICLE NO: 097480

Fiber facts. *Tennis industry (N. Miami, Fla.) 12(6), Jun 1984, 32-35.*
LEVEL: B LANG: Eng SIRC ARTICLE NO: 100554

LaMarche, R.J. Mesh shoes are cooler, but are they better? *Tennis (Norwalk, Conn.) 20(6), Oct 1984, 46-47.*
LEVEL: B LANG: Eng SIRC ARTICLE NO: 108890

Leonard, T. Answers to the 9 most-asked questions about equipment. *Tennis (Norwalk, Conn.) 19(10), Feb 1984, 40-42;44;46;48.*
LEVEL: B LANG: Eng SIRC ARTICLE NO: 093804

Levisohn, S.R. Simon, H.B. How to cure and prevent foot problems. *Tennis (Norwalk, Conn.) 19(12), Apr 1984, 110-111.*
LEVEL: B LANG: Eng SIRC ARTICLE NO: 100004

Target: court shoes. *Fitness industry (Miami, Fla.) 2(1), Jan/Feb 1984, 52-54;56;60-63.*
LEVEL: B LANG: Eng SIRC ARTICLE NO: 097503

Tennis shoe promotion kit. *Tennis industry (N. Miami, Fla.) 12(2), Feb 1984, 29-39.*
LEVEL: B LANG: Eng SIRC ARTICLE NO: 100014

The best of the Class of '84. (shoes) *World tennis (Los Angeles, Calif.) 31(12), May 1984, 48;54;56;58;61-62;64;66.*
LEVEL: LANG: Eng SIRC ARTICLE NO: 099978

COACHING

Ashe, A. Arthur Ashe: de l'utilite des coaches. *Tennis de France (Paris) 369, janv 1984, 62-65.*
LEVEL: B LANG: Fr SIRC ARTICLE NO: 099975

Colwin, C. Colwin talks with Chavoor. (Sherman Chavoor) *Swim Canada (Toronto) 99, 11(3), Mar 1984, 12-13.*
LEVEL: B LANG: Eng SIRC ARTICLE NO: 093771

Doherty, D. Dennis Ralston: from menace to mentor. *Tennis (Norwalk, Conn.) 20(2), Jun 1984, 112;114;116;118;120.*
LEVEL: B LANG: Eng SIRC ARTICLE NO: 101588

Eikenberry, M. Choosing a tennis pro and a camp.
NOTES: In, United States Professional Tennis Association, Tennis, a professional guide. 1st ed., New York, Kodansha International, c1984, p. 196-199.
LEVEL: B LANG: Eng GV995 18015

Hayes, A.S. Why more pros are hiring coaches. *Tennis (Norwalk, Conn.) 19(12), Apr 1984, 54-56;58;60;62-64.*
LEVEL: B LANG: Eng SIRC ARTICLE NO: 099999

Heldman, G.M. WT looks at the great coaches. What is the key fundamental to matchplay? *World tennis (Los Angeles, Calif.) 31(10), Mar 1984, 61-66.*
LEVEL: B LANG: Eng SIRC ARTICLE NO: 100000

Huber, M. Nick Bollettieri. The self assured coach of Carling Bassett, Canada's best known tennis player, talks about his teaching methods, his highs and lows and the Nick Bolletieri Tennis Academy. *Coaching review (Ottawa, Ont.) 7, Jul/Aug 1984, 8-15.*
LEVEL: B LANG: Eng SIRC ARTICLE NO: 095353

Reid, P.A. Tennis coaching at club level. (Refs: 9)*Momentum: a journal of human movement studies (Edinburgh) 9(1), Spring 1984, 2-19.*
ABST: This paper examines and evaluates the structure of tennis coaching in clubs in the light of modern coaching theory and to suggest how club coaching could be made more effective. The principles of a sound coaching structure are examined, the features of an ideal club coaching structure are noticed and finally alterations to the club structure are suggested which take account of the constraints which are likely to prevent a club achieving the ideal. The conclusion is reached that despite the constraints many useful steps can be taken to make the coaching of tennis more effective at club level.
LEVEL: A LANG: Eng SIRC ARTICLE NO: 099955

Si vous voulez devenir un champion... ne manquez pas le coach. *Tennis de France (Paris) 374, juin 1984, 98-99;101;103;105-106*
LEVEL: B LANG: Fr SIRC ARTICLE NO: 109153

Singer, R.N. A psychological intervention program: tips for tennis instructors...and coaches. *Addvantage (Cleveland, Ohio) 8(3), May/Jun 1984, 4-5.*
LEVEL: B LANG: Eng SIRC ARTICLE NO: 098591

COUNTRIES AND REGIONS

Evans, R. The barren state of British tennis. *Tennis World (London) Jul 1984, 26-27.*
LEVEL: B LANG: Eng SIRC ARTICLE NO: 101590

Le blanc et le noir: a la decouverte du tennis africain. *Tennis magazine (Paris) 96, mars 1984, 144-156.*
LEVEL: B LANG: Fr SIRC ARTICLE NO: 099979

DIRECTORIES

1984 tennis camp directory: where to improve your game. *World tennis (Los Angeles, Calif.) 31(8), Jan 1984, 68-69;71-76;78-81;84.*
LEVEL: B LANG: Eng SIRC ARTICLE NO: 098563

Cox, R. Playing paradises: 50 greatest U.S. tennis resorts. *Tennis (Norwalk, Conn.) 20, Nov 1984, 52-55;57-58.*
LEVEL: B LANG: Eng SIRC ARTICLE NO: 108584

Doherty, D. The best buys in tennis videocassettes. *Tennis (Norwalk, Conn.) 19(9), Jan 1984, 42-44.*
LEVEL: B LANG: Eng SIRC ARTICLE NO: 098575

Preston, M. The 17th annual directory of tennis camps & clinics. *Tennis (Norwalk, Conn.) 19(9), Jan 1984, 60-67.*
LEVEL: B LANG: Eng SIRC ARTICLE NO: 098589

Resorts in the Caribbean: a selective guide. *World tennis (Los Angeles, Calif.) 32(6), Nov 1984, 49-50;52.*
LEVEL: B LANG: Eng SIRC ARTICLE NO: 108578

Ross, J.P. 50 vacations for 50 states. *World tennis (Los Angeles, Calif.) 31(10), Mar 1984, 74-83.*
LEVEL: B LANG: Eng SIR ARTICLE NO: 100010

WT's annual five-star guide. *World tennis (Los Angeles) 32(6), Nov 1984, 42-43.*
LEVEL: B LANG: Eng SIRC ARTICLE NO: 108577

DISABLED

1984 Wheelchair Tennis Players Association. s.l.: National Foundation of Wheelchair Tennis, 1984. 38 p.
CORP: National Foundation of Wheelchair Tennis.
CORP: Everest & Jennings.
NOTES: Cover title.
LEVEL: B LANG: Eng GV1001.4.D5 18433

Tennis programs for the disabled. Princeton, N.J.: United States Tennis Association, c1984. v, 46 p. : ill.
CORP: United States Tennis Association. Education and Research Center.
LEVEL: B LANG: Eng ISBN: 0-938822-18-7 GV1001.4.D5 18021

Thompson, G. Tennis tips: quadriplegic tennis? you bet. *Sports 'n spokes (Phoenix, Ariz.) 10(2), Jul/Aug 1984, 8.*
LEVEL: LANG: Eng SIRC ARTICLE NO: 097551

ECONOMICS

Delamarre, G. Dossier: le tennis et l'argent: toujours plus? *Tennis magazine (Paris) 98, mai 1984, 134-141.*
LEVEL: B LANG Fr SIRC ARTICLE NO: 099990

Lorge, B. Dollars and sense at Flushing. *World tennis (Los Angeles) 32(4), Sept 1984, 46-48.*
LEVEL: B LANG: Eng SIRC ARTICLE NO: 173387

Sahota, G.S. Sahota, C.K. A theory of human investment in physical skills and its application to achievement in tennis. (Refs: 1)*Southern economic journal (Chapel Hill, N.C.) 50(3), 1984, 642-664.*
LEVEL: I LANG: Eng SIRC ARTICLE NO: 096919

Trial and tribulations. *World tennis (Los Angeles, Calif.) 31(10), Mar 1984, 57-59.*
LEVEL: B LANG: Eng SIRC ARTICLE NO: 100015

Wheeler, E. Why tennis stars are so product pitchmen. *Tennis (Norwalk, Conn.) 20(1), May 1984, 38-43.*
LEVEL: B LANG: Eng SIRC ARTICLE NO: 100019

EQUIPMENT

A midsummer's trio of midsizes. *World tennis (Los Angeles, Calif.) 32(1), Jun 1984, 50-51.*
LEVEL: B LANG: Eng SIRC ARTICLE NO: 101606

Barbier, G. La corde sensible. *Tennis magazine (Paris) 101, aout 1984, 84-87.*
LEVEL: B LANG: Fr SIRC ARTICLE NO: 106096

Cleary, S. Hedrick, K. An end of string confusion, part 2. Does string tension really matter? Yes. But new research now show that a lot more factors go into creating your racket's most effective hitting area. *World tennis (Los Angeles, Calif.) 31(7), Dec 1983, 56-57.*
LEVEL: B LANG: Eng SIRC ARTICLE NO: 098572

Dereix, A.J. L'empire de M. Lo. (Lo Kunnan) *Tennis de France (Paris) 374, juin 1984, 256-259;261-262.*
LEVEL: B LANG: Fr SIRC ARTICLE NO: 109161

Gagon, P. How to choose your first string. *World tennis (Los Angeles) 32(7),* Dec 1984, 28-29.
LEVEL: B LANG: Eng SIRC ARTICLE NO: 173587

Gour, G. Tennis racquets: which is your racquet? To find out, you will have to consider your style of playing as well as the racquet's construction. *Protect yourself (Montreal)* Jul 1984, 21-25.
LEVEL: B LANG: Eng SIRC ARTICLE NO: 103512

Hedrick, K. Mikic, B. Rammath, R. How to read the lab test numbers. *World tennis (Los Angeles, Calif.) 31(7),* Dec 1983, 58-62.
LEVEL: B LANG: Eng SIRC ARTICLE NO: 098579

How they tested on the court. *World tennis (Los Angeles, Calif.) 31(7),* Dec 1983, 63-64.
LEVEL: B LANG: Eng SIRC ARTICLE NO 098580

In search of 'the racket of the year'. *World tennis (Los Angeles, Calif.) 32(3),* Aug 1984, 57-59.
LEVEL: B LANG: Eng SIRC ARTICLE NO: 101597

Internal frame damage. *Stringer's assistant (Del Mar, Calif.) 10(7),* Jul 1984, 1;8;14.
LEVEL: B LANG: Eng SIRC ARTICLE NO: 106104

Keep pace with the latest in tennis court products. *Athletic purchasing and facilities (Madison, Wis.) 8(1),* Jan 1984, 44-48;54-57.
LEVEL: B LANG: Eng SIRC ARTICLE NO: 095355

Knots. *Stringer's assistant (Del Mar, Calif.) 10(9),* Sept 1984, 1;4-6.
LEVEL: B LANG: Eng SIRC ARTICLE NO: 108758

LaMarche, R.J. The dawn of a new racquet era: introducing 8 top-line graphite composites. *Tennis (Norwalk, Conn.) 19(11),* Mar 1984, 42-45.
LEVEL: B LANG: Eng SIRC ARTICLE NO: 097494

LaMarche, R.J. 6 boron composites: what these new racquets offer you. *Tennis (Norwalk, Conn.) 20(1),* May 1984, 50-53.
LEVEL: B LANG: Eng SIRC ARTICLE NO: 100003

LaMarche, R.J. Is the wood racquet obsolete? *Tennis (Norwalk, Conn.) 20(2),* Jun 1984, 40-43.
LEVEL: B LANG: Eng SIRC ARTICLE NO: 101599

LaMarche, R.J. Are metal racquets on the verge of a new breakthrough? *Tennis (Norwalk, Conn.) 20(7),* Nov 1984, 68-71.
LEVEL: B LANG: Eng SIRC ARTICLE NO: 108585

Lansberry, R. The great debate: midsize vs. oversize. *World tennis (Los Angeles) 32(4),* Sept 1984, 26-29.
LEVEL: B LANG: Eng SIRC ARTICLE NO: 173385

Leonard, T. Answers to the 9 most-asked questions about equipment. *Tennis (Norwalk, Conn.) 19(10),* Feb 1984, 40-42;44;46;48.
LEVEL: B LANG: Eng SIRC ARTICLE NO: 093804

Levy, M. Racquets: the midsize makes its move. *Women's sports and fitness (Palo Alto, Calif.) 6(8),* Aug 1984, 56-58.
LEVEL: B LANG: Eng SIRC ARTICLE NO: 101602

Parier, J. Van Hoeck, J. Le couple homme-raquette. *Science et vie (Paris) HS147,* 1984, 71-75.
LEVEL: B LANG: Eng

Power zone tests can help your game. *World tennis (Los Angeles) 32(4),* Sept 1984, 81-83.
LEVEL: B LANG: Eng SIRC ARTICLE NO 173388

Pro Kennex Dominator Composite. *World tennis (Los Angeles, Calif.) 31(10),* Mar 1984, 41.
LEVEL: B LANG: Eng SIRC ARTICLE NO 100008

Racket of the year '84. *World tennis (Los Angeles) 32(7),* Dec 1984, 33-40;42-57.
LEVEL: B LANG: Eng SIRC ARTICLE NO: 173588

Racket research: the top-of-the-lines. *Tennis industry (Miami, Fla.) 12(11),* Nov 1984, 8-12;15-21.
LEVEL: B LANG: Eng SIRC ARTICLE NO: 173217

Racket review: Avant Garde graphite. *World tennis (Los Angeles, Calif.) 31(11),* Apr 1984, 69.
LEVEL: B LANG: Eng SIRC ARTICLE NO: 100009

Racket review: how stiffness affects your game. *World tennis (Los Angeles) 32(5),* Oct 1984, 63.
LEVEL: B LANG: Eng SIRC ARTICLE NO: 108729

Racquet review: stability and your racket. *World tennis (Los Angeles) 32(6),* Nov 1984, 57-59.
LEVEL: B LANG: Eng SIRC ARTICLE NO: 108579

Randall, J. The tennis racquet. In, Schrier, E.W. and Allman, W.F. (eds.), *Newton at the bat: the science in sports,* New York, Scribner, c1984, p. 67-70.
LEVEL: B LANG: Eng RC1235 18609

Rothstein, J. Polyester is one of the latest synthetic materials to be used in the manufacture of tennis strings. A successful emergence among nylon competitors, polyester strings are appearing under several labels in the marketplace. *Stringer's assistant (Del Mar, Calif.) 10(4),* Apr 1984, 11-12.
LEVEL: B LANG: Eng SIRC ARTICLE NO: 095361

Six new midsize frames. *World tennis (Los Angeles) 32(4),* Sept 1984, 82-83.
LEVEL: B LANG: Eng SIRC ARTICLE NO: 173389

String gauge & playability. *Stringer's assistant (Del Mar, Calif.) 10(5),* May 1984, 1;4-5.
LEVEL: I LANG: Eng SIRC ARTICLE NO: 100013

String survey results 8: welcome to the USRSA's 8th annual string survey tally. *Stringer's assistant (Del Mar, Calif.) 10(12),* Dec 1984, 1;5-8.
LEVEL: B LANG: Eng SIRC ARTICLE NO: 104926

String technology for the twenty-first century. *Tennis industry (Miami, Fla.) 12(8),* Aug 1984, 16-17;19;22;24;27-28.
LEVEL: LANG: Eng SIRC ARTICLE NO: 106110

Tension testers: tools of the trade, or tricks of the trade? *Stringer's assistant (Del Mar, Calif.) 10(7),* Jul 1984, 1;4;15.
LEVEL: B LANG: Eng SIRC ARTICLE NO: 106111

Testing tennis string (Part 1). *Stringer's assistant (Del Mar, Calif.) 10(6),* Jun 1984, 1;3-6;8.
LEVEL: I LANG: Eng SIRC ARTICLE NO: 094290

Testing tennis string (part 2). *Stringer's assistant (Del Mar, Calif.) 10(8),* Aug 1984, 1;4-5.
LEVEL: B LANG: Eng SIRC ARTICLE NO: 103522

Testing tennis string (part 3). *Stringer's assistant (Del Mar, Calif.) 10(10),* Oct 1984, 1-2;4;7.
LEVEL: B LANG: Eng SIRC ARTICLE NO: 109050

The do's & don't of racquet stringing. *Stringer's assistant (Del Mar, Calif.) 10(4),* Apr 1984, 1;4-5.
LEVEL: B LANG: Eng SIRC ARTICLE NO: 101587

The guess factor. (stringing the unknown frame) *Stringer's assistant (Del Mar, Calif.) 10(8),* Aug 1984, 1-2.
LEVEL: B LANG: Eng SIRC ARTICLE NO: 103514

The new technology in tennis. *Tennis industry (Miami, Fla.) 12(9),* Sept 1984, 10;13-15.
LEVEL: B LANG: Eng SIRC ARTICLE NO: 173212

Tym, A. Your gut tennis strings...from Ferninand sic to forehand. *Addvantage (Cleveland, Ohio) 8(3),* May/Jun 1984, 16-17.
LEVEL: B LANG: Eng SIRC ARTICLE NO: 098596

USRA interview with Dr. Jack Groppel. Meet the man who's taken the scientific approach to tennis. He's changing the way both pro's and amateurs are playing, thinking, and choosing their equipment. *Stringer's assistant (Del Mar, Calif.) 10(6),* Jun 1984, 10-11;19-20.
LEVEL: B LANG: Eng SIRC ARTICLE NO: 095367

EQUIPMENT - MAINTENANCE

Sikowitz, P. Get a grip on racket care. *World tennis (Los Angeles) 32(7),* Dec 1984, 58.
LEVEL: B LANG: Eng SIRC ARTICLE NO: 173589

Sports shops dominate as tennis racket boom approaches. *Sports trader (Kent, Eng.) 146(1024),* 15 Nov 1984, 14-17.
LEVEL: B LANG: Eng SIRC ARTICLE NO: 173350

Stencil your way to fame and fortune. *Stringer's assistant (Del Mar, Calif.) 10(6),* Jun 1984, 14;17.
LEVEL: B LANG: Eng SIR ARTICLE NO: 095364

The advanced stringer. *Stringer's assistant (Del Mar, Calif.) 10(6),* Jun 1984, 15-16.
LEVEL: B LANG: Eng SIRC ARTICLE NO: 095341

EQUIPMENT - RETAILING

Apparel: 1984 market report. *Tennis industry (N. Miami, Fla.) 12(4),* Apr 1984, 46-50.
LEVEL: B LANG: Eng SIRC ARTICLE NO: 100549

Berst, J. A computer shopping list. Part II. *Tennis industry (Miami, Fla.) 12(9),* Sept 1984, 16.
LEVEL: B LANG: Eng SIRC ARTICLE NO: 173215

Heckler, T. Pro shop development and management.
NOTES: In, United States Professional Tennis Association, Tennis, a professional guide. 1st ed., New York, Kodansha International, c1984, p. 247-254.
LEVEL: B LANG: Eng GV995 18015

How big is the string market? *Stringer's assistant (Del Mar, Calif.) 10(7),* Jul 1984, 1-2.
LEVEL: B LANG: Eng SIRC ARTICLE NO: 106102

String technology for the twenty-first century. *Tennis industry (Miami, Fla.) 12(8),* Aug 1984, 16-17;19;22;24;27-28.
LEVEL: LANG: Eng SIRC ARTICLE NO: 104927

Tech demo days. *Tennis industry (Miami, Fla.) 12(9),* Sept 1984, 50-55.
LEVEL: B LANG: Eng SIRC ARTICLE NO: 173214

FACILITIES

Technical sports data, July 1984 No. 15: outdoor lawn tennis. *Sport and leisure (London) 25(3),* Jul/Aug 1984, 51-54.
LEVEL: LANG: Eng SIRC ARTICLE NO: 100589

Tennis courts 1984-1985: construction, maintenance, equipment, guideline specifications. Lynn, Mass.: H.O. Zimman, c1984. 144
CORP: United States Tennis Association.
CORP: United States Tennis Court and Track Builders Association.
LEVEL: B LANG: Eng GV1002 1495

FACILITIES - DESIGN, CONSTRUCTION AND PLANNING

Construction update. *Tennis industry (N. Miami, Fla.) 12(6), Jun 1984, 18-19;21-22;24-26;61.*
LEVEL: B LANG: Eng SIRC ARTICL NO: 100583

Dereix, A.J. Elle se fume pas, elle se broute pas...c'est l'herbe synthetique. *Tennis de France (Paris) 371, mars 1984, 36-37.*
LEVEL: B LANG: Fr SIRC ARTICLE NO: 094303

Fahmy, A.H. Computer-aided optimal lighting systems design. (Refs: 7)*Lighting research and technology (London) 16(1), 1984, 42-51.*
ABST: This paper details a computer design package for the design of an optimal lighting system or for the evaluation of an existing system. The lighting for a tennis court and for a street are used as illustrative examples.
LEVEL: A LANG: Eng SIRC ARTICLE NO: 097506

Sprague, J. Tennis court contractors. (part II) *Tennis industry (N. Miami, Fla.) 12(1), Dec/Jan 1984, 39-40;42;44;49.*
LEVEL: B LANG: Eng SIRC ARTICLE NO: 092774

Sprague, J. Tennis court construction. *Tennis industry (N. Miami, Fla.) 12(4), Apr 1984, 34;36;39-41.*
LEVEL: B LANG: Eng SIRC ARTICLE NO: 100588

Sprague, J. Construction today - Part two: Impact of landscaping. *Tennis industry (Miami, Fla.) 12(8), Aug 1984, 30;32;37-38.*
LEVEL: B LANG: Eng SIRC ARTICLE NO: 103940

Sprague, J. Construction today. Part II - impact of landscaping. *Tennis industry (Miami, Fla.) 12(8), Aug 1984, 30;32;37-38.*
LEVEL: B LANG: Eng SIRC ARTICLE NO: 106109

FACILITIES - MAINTENANCE

Autumn care of tennis courts. *Sports turf bulletin (West Yorkshire, Eng.) 146, Jul/Sept 1984, 10-12.*
LEVEL: B LANG: Eng SIR ARTICLE NO: 102428

Grass tennis courts. *Groundsman (London) 37(6), Jun 1984, 8.*
LEVEL: B LANG: Eng SIRC ARTICLE NO: 100607

Green, L. Managing grass tennis courts is an art. *Turf management (Surrey, Eng.) 3(6), Jun 1984, 24-26.*
LEVEL: B LANG: En SIRC ARTICLE NO: 102159

Perris, J. Tennis courts: providing a surface worthy of champions. *Parks, golf courses & sports grounds (Middlesex, Eng.) 49(11), Aug 1984, 81-82;84.*
LEVEL: B LANG: Eng SIRC ARTICLE NO: 102433

Sprague, J. Construction today. Solutions to water problems: part I. *Tennis industry (Miami, Fla.) 12(11), Nov 1984, 29-30;35.*
LEVEL: B LANG: Eng SIRC ARTICLE NO: 173218

HISTORY

Fein, P. David and Goliath revisited: is bigger better in tennis? *Addvantage (Cleveland, Oh.) 8(2), Mar/Apr 1984, 8-13.*
LEVEL: B LANG: Eng SIRC ARTICLE NO: 096914

Fiott, S. Frames of reference. *World tennis (Los Angeles) 32(7), Dec 1984, 20-23.*
LEVEL: B LANG: Eng SIRC ARTICLE NO: 173585

Lalanne, D. Trente ans de Wimbledon. *Tennis magazine (Paris) 100, juil 1984, 116-119.*
LEVEL: B LANG: Fr SIRC ARTICLE NO: 101598

Little, A. Tingay, L. Wimbledon ladies, a centenary record 1884-1984, the singles champions. London: Wimbledon Lawn Tennis Museum, 1984. 80 p.
LEVEL: B LANG: Eng ISBN: 0-906741-13-0 GV993 17681

INJURIES AND ACCIDENTS

Aglietti, P. Buzzi, R. De Faveri Tron, M. Saggini, R. Il gomito del tennista, aspetti clinici ed anatomici. Tennis elbow, clinical and anatomical aspects. (Refs: 28)*Italian journal of sports traumatology (Milano, Italy) 6(2), Apr/Jun 1984, 113-124.*
CONF: Italian Society of Sports Traumatology. Congress (1st : 1983 : Rome).
ABST: A clinical analysis was made of 87 tennis players suffering from tennis elbow. The epicondyle was affected in 70 cases while the epitrochlea was in 12. The subjects were largely male averaging between 30 and 50 years of age. The injury lasted an average of 9 months. Errors in stroke technique were found in the majority of the cases analyzed.
LEVEL: A LANG: It Eng SIRC ARTICLE NO: 099973

Baudel, F. Comment les lombalgiques peuvent-ils jouer au tennis en epargnant leur rachis? *Cinesiologie (Paris) 95, mai/juin 1984, 257-260.*
LEVEL: B LANG: Fr SIRC ARTICLE NO: 098565

Bocchi, L. Fontanesi, G. Orso, C.A. Camurri, G.B. La patologia del piede nel tennis in rapporto al terreno di gioco. Foot pathology in tennis in relation to playing surface. (Refs: 8)*Italian journal of sports traumatology (Milano, Italy) 6(4), Oct/Dec 1984, 325-332.*
CONF: Italian Society of Sports Traumatology. Congress (1st : 1983 : Rome)
ABST: The interrelation of the primary aetiological factors involved (foot morphology, playing surfaces and shoes) in chronic foot disease are analysed. For the purpose of effective prophylaxis, improved shoe design with the adoption of build-in or removeable supports is recommended.
LEVEL: A LANG: It Eng SIRC ARTICLE NO: 106097

Davis, R. Tennis. *In, Adams, S.H. (ed.), et al., Catastrophic injuries in sports: avoidance strategies, Salinas, Calif., Cayote Press, c1984, p. 70-72.*
LEVEL: B LANG: Eng RD97 19088

Dueben, W. Putzki, H. Dueben, G. Beidseitige Ermeudungsfraktur der Tibia. (Bilateral fatigue fracture of the tibia.) *Unfallheilkunde (Berlin) 87(8), Aug 1984, 354-356.*
LEVEL: I LANG: Ger

Elstein, R. Collins, J. Four steps to avoiding painful cramps. *World tennis (Los Angeles, Calif.) 31(8), Jan 1984, 23.*
LEVEL: B LANG: Eng SIRC ARTICLE NO: 098576

Grillo, G. Rocco, P. Rosa, D. Aspetti fisiopatologici della seconda articolazione della spalla. Physiopathologic aspects of the second shoulder joint. (Refs: 10)*Italian journal of sports traumatology (Milano, Italy) 6(3), Jul/Sept 1984, 187-196.*
CONF: Italian Society of Sports Traumatology. Congress (1st : 1983 : Rome).
ABST: Following some anatomopathological observations on the second shoulder joint, the pathology of this joint has been studied in tennis players. Diagnostic methods are analysed and work

on thermography for patients suffering from tennis shoulder is reported.
LEVEL: A LANG: Eng It SIRC ARTICLE NO: 103513

Hang, Y.S. Peng, S.M. An epidemiologic study of upper extremity injury in tennis players with a particular reference to tennis elbow. *Taiwan i hsueh hui tsa chih (Taipei) 83(3), Mar 1984, 307-316.*
LEVEL: A LANG: Eng

Kovalik, A.T. The tennis player's guide to sports medicine. New York: Leisure Press, 1984. 176 p. : ill.
LEVEL: B LANG: Eng ISBN: 0-88011-155-0 LC CARD: 83-80729

Lanzetta, A. Meani, E. Instabilita inveterata della caviglia in esiti di lesioni capsulo-legamentose. Inveterate instability of the ankle as an outcome of capsulo-ligamentous lesions. *Italian journal of sports traumatology (Milano, Italy) 6(4), Oct/Dec 1984, 311-319.*
CONF: Italian Society of Sports Traumatology. Congress (1st : 1983 : Rome)
ABST: Non-recognition of knee ligamentous lesions often leads to a chronic instability of this joint. Diagnosis of lesions of this kind make use of both functional radiograms and sometimes subtalar arthrography. Treatment of inveterate instabilities, depending on seriousness, can be proprioceptive functional re-education, re-tension surgery or external ligament plasty.
LEVEL: A LANG: It Eng SIRC ARTICLE NO: 105304

Legwold G. The pros face the cons of constant play. *Physician and sportsmedicine (Minneapolis, Minn.) 12(6), Jun 1984, 187-189.*
NOTES: Tennis update, part 2.
LEVEL: B LANG: Eng SIRC ARTICLE NO: 095356

Legwold, G. Tennis elbow: joint resolution by conservative treatment and improved technique. *Physician and sportsmedicine (Minneapolis, Minn.) 12(6), Jun 1984, 168-169;172;174;176;179;182.*
NOTES: Tennis update, part 1.
LEVEL: I LANG: Eng SIRC ARTICLE NO: 095357

Levisohn, S.R. Simon, H.B. Smith, S. Terizian, B. Tennis medic: conditioning, sports medicine, and total fitness for every player. St. Louis ; Toronto: Mosby, c1984. xiii, 226 p. : ill.
NOTES: Includes index.
LEVEL: I LANG: Eng ISBN: 0801646693 LC CARD: 84-014910 RC1220.T4 18081

Levisohn, S.R. Simon, H.B. Brace yourself: how wraps, bandages & braces can help. *Tennis (Norwalk, Conn.) 20(2), Jun 1984, 108-111.*
LEVEL: B LANG: Eng SIRC ARTICLE NO: 101601

Nirschl, R.P. Fitness, conditioning, injury prevention and treatment.
NOTES: In, United States Professional Tennis Association, Tennis, a professional guide. 1st ed., New York, Kodansha International, c1984, p. 117-123.
LEVEL: B LANG: Eng GV995 18015

Parier, J. Combelles, F. Lecoz, J. Dacruz, B. Tennis elbow: finis les vains maux. *Tennis magazine (Neuilly Cedex, France) 104, nov 1984, 80-84.*
LEVEL: I LANG: Fr SIRC ARTICLE NO: 109168

Paulsen, J. Paar, O. Bernett, P. Tennisspezifische Verletzungen und Schaeden an der unteren Extremitaet. (Tennis-specific injuries and lesions of the lower extremity.) *Munchener Medizinische*

Wochenschrift (Munchen) 126(5), 3 Feb 1984, 106-108.
LEVEL: A LANG: Ger

Saggini, R. Colotto, S. Innocenti, M. Cantalamessa, G. La tendinite dell'estensore e del flessore ulnare del carpo nel tennista. Tendinitis of the extensor and flexor carpi ulnaris in tennis players. (Refs: 7)*Italian journal of sports traumatology (Milano, Italy) 6(3), Jul/Sept 1984, 171-175.*
CONF: Italian Society of Sports Traumatology. Congress (1st : 1983 : Rome).
ABST: Tendinitis of the extensor and flexor carpi ulnaris is fairly common among tennis players. Together the ulnar extensor and flexor are responsible for ulnar wrist deviation. In isolation, the extensor is responsible for the stability of the wrist, while the flexor flattens the ulnar edge of the hand.
LEVEL: A LANG: Eng It SIRC ARTICLE NO: 103520

Santilli, G. Bagarone, A. Bonsignore, D. Candela, V. Dragoni, S. Ferretti, A. Epicondilite omerale: terapia medica e fisica. Medical and physical treatment of tennis elbow. (Refs: 37)*Italian journal of sports traumatology (Milano, Italy) 6(2), Apr/Jun 1984, 125-132.*
CONF: Italian Society of Sports Traumatology. Congress (1st : 1983 : Rome).
ABST: This retrospective study examines 141 cases of tennis elbow. Statistical analysis showed that goal-directed therapy in association with telethermography was significantly better than other methods in treating tennis elbow. Recurrence may be prevented by changing the type of racquet one uses in playing tennis.
LEVEL: A LANG: It Eng SIRC ARTICLE NO: 100011

Sartori, E. Cantalamessa, G. Carosella, A. Innocenti, M. Le lesioni delle strutture anteriori della spalla nel tennista. Damage to the anterior shoulder structures in tennis players. (Refs: 16)*Italian journal of sports traumatology (Milano, Italy) 6(3), Jul/Sept 1984, 177-181.*
CONF: Italian Society of Sports Traumatology. Congress (1st : 1983 : Rome).
ABST: A tennis player's shoulder is subject to considerable functional overloading, particularly during a match play. The damage this may cause to the anterior structures over the course of time was examined in 30 young subjects who had been engaged in competitive tennis for some time. Chronic lesions of the distal insertion of the subscapular muscle were common, whereas chronic damage to the anterior capsular structures was less frequent.
LEVEL: A LANG: Eng It SIRC ARTICLE NO: 103521

Weiker, G. Ankle injuries in tennis. *Tennis industry (N. Miami, Fla.) 12(4), Apr 1984, 71-73.*
LEVEL: B LANG: Eng SIRC ARTICLE NO: 101620

JUVENILE LITERATURE

Rich, S. Tennis. Cambridge ; New York: Cambridge University Press, 1984. 1v.
LEVEL: B LANG: Eng ISBN: 0521275369 LC CARD: 84-005911

LAW AND LEGISLATION

Pennsylvania - top ranked tennis player challenges bylaws of the NCAA and ECAC in court. *Sports and the courts (Winston-Salem N.C.) 5(1), Winter 1984, 2-4.*
LEVEL: B LANG: Eng SIRC ARTICLE NO: 094245

MASS MEDIA

Hilliard, D.C. Media images of male and female professional athletes: an interpretive analysis of magazine articles. (Refs: 39)*Sociology of sport journal (Champaign, Ill.) 1(3), 1984, 251-262.*
ABST: An interpretive analysis of mass circulation magazine articles on leading male and female professional tennis players indicates that both groups are treated in terms of a 'debunking motif' which reveals their imperfections and character flaws. The flaws identified among the women are closely associated with stereotypically feminine gender roles, while the flaws observed among the men are associated with stereotypically masculine gender roles. Thus, the articles reinforce the concept of professional sport as a male preserve, while suggesting an underlying traditionally feminine gender role for the female athletes. It is argued that this construction of the female athlete role derives from the commercial sponsorship of professional tennis.
LEVEL: A LANG: Eng SIRC ARTICLE NO: 103515

MEDICINE

Boissinot, P. Role du medecin du sport dans l'education preventive des joueurs de tennis a l'approche des competitions. *Medecine du sport 58(1), 25 janv 1984, 6-8.*
LEVEL: B LANG: Fr SIRC ARTICLE NO: 092442

McKaba, D. The big sneeze: rub, scratch, and blow. If it's your routine on the court, there's relief on the way for those nagging allergies. *World tennis (Los Angeles, Calif.) 32(2), Jul 1984, 38-40.*
LEVEL: B LANG: Eng SIRC ARTICLE NO: 101605

Nash, D.B. Medical care at tournaments. *Physician and sportsmedicine (Minneapolis, Minn.) 12(6), Jun 1984, 193.*
NOTES: Tennis update, part 3.
LEVEL: B LANG: Eng SIRC ARTICLE NO: 095359

NUTRITION

Haas, R. Eating for peak performance.
NOTES: In, United States Professional Tennis Association, Tennis, a professional guide. 1st ed., New York, Kodansha International, c1984, p. 111-116.
LEVEL: B LANG: Eng GV995 18015

Rafaitin, G. Les raisons de la colere. *Tennis de France (Paris) 371, mars 1984, 46-48.*
LEVEL: B LANG: Fr SIRC ARTICLE NO: 095360

OFFICIATING

Carlock, M. Tennis anyone? Interested in working pro tennis? If you have experience working other sports, you may have a leg up on your competition. *Referee (Franksville, Wis.) 9(3), Mar 1984, 56-57.*
LEVEL: B LANG: Eng SIRC ARTICLE NO: 098571

Frank Hammond finally speaks out. *World tennis (Los Angeles) 32(4), Sept 1984, 40-42;44.*
LEVEL: B LANG: Eng SIRC ARTICLE NO 173386

Vincent, R. Bonne ou faute? Seriez-vous capable de juger cette balle? *Tennis de France (Paris) 373, mai 1984, 195-197.*
LEVEL: B LANG: Fr SIRC ARTICLE NO: 101616

PERCEPTUAL MOTOR PROCESSES

Adenis, J.P. Prise d'informations visuelles et tennis. (Refs: 5)*Medecine du sport (Paris) 58(5), 25 sept 1984, 55-57.*
LEVEL: I LANG: Fr SIRC ARTICLE NO: 101570

PHYSICAL FITNESS

Gray, J.M. Fitness: walk-don't run-to better tennis. *Tennis (Norwalk, Conn.) 20(4), Aug 1984, 64-66.*
LEVEL: B LANG: Eng SIRC ARTICLE NO: 101592

Horan, J. If the sport fits, play it: being an all-aroung jock can improve your game. *World tennis (Los Angeles) 32(5), Oct 1984, 59-62.*
LEVEL: B LANG: Eng SIRC ARTICLE NO: 108727

Pilardeau, P. Jones, A. Garner, M. Prillard, X. Un test d'effort specifique. (Refs: 8)*EPS: Education physique et sport 185, janv/fevr 1984, 57-59.*
LEVEL: I LANG: Fr SIRC ARTICLE NO: 093809

Vega, A. La surveillance medicale du tennisman. *Impact medecin (Puteaux, France) 103, 1984, 65-71.*
LEVEL: B LANG: Fr

PHYSICS

Missavage, R.J. Baker, J.A.W. Putnam, C.A. Theoretical modeling of grip firmness during ball-racket impact. (Refs: 9) *Research quarterly for exercise & sport (Reston, Va.) 55(3), Sept 1984, 254-260.*
ABST: This study was undertaken to establish theoretical bases for the experimental results reported by Baker and Putnam (1979), and Watanabe, Ikegami and Miyashita (1979), concerning grip firmness on a tennis racket and its effect on the ratio of post- to pre-impact ball velocity. The model predicted that, for central impacts, there was no change in the ball velocity ratio when a regular tennis racket was rightly clamped at the grip or allowed to freely stand on its butt. To validate the model further, alterations were made to two parameters of the racket - a tennis racket was modified to increase the stiffness, and a racketball racket was used to simulate a shortened tennis racket. It was found that shortening the length and greatly increasing the stiffness was required before the effect of grip firmness was noticeable.
LEVEL: A LANG: Eng SIRC ARTICLE NO: 103517

Putnam, C.A. Baker, J.A.W. Spin imparted to a tennis ball during impact with conventionally and diagonally strung rackets. (Refs: 7)*Research quarterly for exercise & sport (Reston, Va.) 55(3), Sept 1984, 261-266.*
ABST: This study compared the amount of spin imparted to a tennis ball during impact with conventionally and diagonally strung tennis rackets. Balls were projected at the rackets at an angle of approximately 45o. Ten multiple-image photographs were taken of a ball approaching, striking and leaving the rackets. For similar pre-impact conditions, it was found that the angular impulse of the contact force applied to the ball (and hence the amount of spin) was almost identical for the two

string configurations.
LEVEL: A LANG: Eng SIRC ARTICLE NO: 103519

PHYSIOLOGY

Anjuere, J. Collin, J.P. Pillet, J. Etude comparative, sur trois mois, de 8 intervalles de temps systoliques, chez les sportifs. Proposition d'un 'indice de forme cardiaque' fiable. (Refs: 16)*Medecine du sport (Paris) 58(6), nov 1984, 22-25.*
LEVEL: I LANG: Fr SIRC ARTICLE NO: 103079

Bloomfield, J. Blanksby, B.A. Beard, D.F. Ackland, T.R. Elliott, B.C. Biological characteristics of young swimmers, tennis players and non-competitors. (Refs: 27)*British journal of sports medicine (Loughborough, Eng.) 18(2), Jun 1984, 97-103.*
ABST: One hundred and twelve finalists in the State Swimming Championships aged between seven and twelve years and 65 ranked tennis players of similar age were selected on the basis of their sporting performances. A third group comprised children of similar socio-economic status who only took part in casual sport. A multifactorial analysis of variance and post-hoc t-tests were applied of the data to determine if any statistical differences were apparent between the three groups. The results demonstrated that no size, body shape, flexibility, strength or lung function differences were evident between the competitors and non-competitors, but that the swimmers and tennis players were superior to the non-competitors in cardiovascular endurance.
LEVEL: A LANG: Eng SIRC ARTICLE NO: 103482

Buti, T. Elliott, B. Morton, A. Physiological and anthropometric profiles of elite prepubescent tennis players. *Physician and sportsmedicine 12(1), Jan 1984, 111-116.*
ABST: Physiological and anthropometric parameters of eight male and eight female tennis players were measured in this study. No significant differences were found between girls and boys. However, girls had an higher level of fat.
LEVEL: A LANG: Eng SIRC ARTICLE NO: 092445

Cantalamessa, G. Sartori, E. Piscini, S. Saggini, R. Variazioni del contenuto menerale dell'osso nei tennisti. Changes in bone mineral content in tennis players. (Refs: 22)*Italian journal of sports traumatology (Milano, Italy) 6(2), Apr/Jun 1984, 143-148.*
CONF: Italian Society of Sports Traumatology. Congress (1st : 1983 : Rome).
ABST: Bone mineral content was studied in both forearms of 20 professional male tennis players with an average age of 25 years who had been playing tennis for 6 to 15 years. The results indicate that heavy use of the dominant forearm is certain to lead to both bone and muscle hypertrophy.
LEVEL: A LANG: It Eng SIRC ARTICLE NO: 099986

Carlson, J.S. Cera, M.A. Cardiorespiratory, muscular strength and anthropometric characteristics of elite Australian junior male and female tennis players. (Refs: 21)*Australian journal of science & medicine in sport (Kingston, Aust.) 16(4), Dec 1984, 7-13.*
ABST: Six male and six female elite junior tennis players (10-1/years) were tested for cardiorespiratory characteristics, body fat, grip strength, isokinetic strength and power, selected skinfolds, bone diameters and circumferences and anaerobic power and capacity. The males were

found to have significantly higher VO2 max values than the females. Body fat (per cent) of the males (11.40) was significantly lower than that of the females (18.96). The males were found to be significantly stronger than the females in all measures of grip and isokinetic strength and power. The males exhibited significantly smaller tricep, bicep, iliac and axilla skinfold than the females. Measures of anaerobic power and capacity also significantly differentiated between the sexes.
LEVEL: A LANG: Eng SIRC ARTICLE NO: 106100

De la sueur et des armes. *Tennis magazine (Neuilly Cedex, France) 103, oct 1984, 98-100.*
LEVEL: B LANG: Fr SIRC ARTICLE NO: 173460

Friedman, D.B. Ramo, B.W. Gray, G.J. Tennis and cardiovascular fitness in middle-aged men. (Refs: 10)*Physician and sportsmedicine (Minneapolis, Minn.) 12(7), Jul 1984, 87-90;92.*
ABST: During this study, the heart rate and cardiac rhythm of 28 intermediate male players between the ages of 45 and 72 were monitored before, during, and after singles tennis. 13 of the subjects were also tested on a treadmill to examine their oxygen consumption and physical fitness levels. Results indicated that subjects achieved heart rates between 60% and 100% of age-predicted maximum. Subjects also demonstrated high fitness levels.
LEVEL: A LANG: Eng SIRC ARTICLE NO: 096915

Morton, A.R. Physical training for elite pre-adolescent tennis players. (Refs: 25)*Australian journal of science & medicine in sport (Kingston, Aust.) 16(3), Oct 1984, 2-5.*
ABST: Anthropometric and physiological changes following a 10-week physical fitness program are evaluated for eight elite pre-adolescent tennis players with a mean age of 11.7 years. A control group of eight elite pre-adolescent tennis players with a mean age of 11.8 years who continued to play tennis but did not take part in the training program were also tested. The experimental group recorded a significant reduction of from 106.9mm to 94.4mm in sum of skinfold thickness following the training, while the control group was unchanged. Maximal aerobic performance (12-minute run, 2178m to 2489.3m), glycolytic capacity (400, run, 83.4s to 79.7s) and agility (Illinois agility run, 18.4s to 16.6s) all improved in the experimental group following the training while the control group recorded no significant changes.
LEVEL: A LANG: Eng SIRC ARTICLE NO: 106106

PSYCHOLOGY

Bollettieri, N. Kids clutch too: take a cue from Arias, Krickstein, Bassett and Casale. Overcome your fear of failure. *Worl tennis (Los Angeles, Calif.) 32(1), Jun 1984, 39.*
LEVEL: B LANG: Eng SIRC ARTICLE NO: 101574

Cunningham, K. Choking blood, sweat & fears. *World tennis (Los Angeles, Calif.) 32(1), Jun 1984, 34-38.*
LEVEL: B LANG: En SIRC ARTICLE NO: 101581

Davidson, W.B. Teaching the control of...temper. (Refs: 4)*Addvantage (Cleveland, Ohio) 8(3), May/Jun 1984, 20-21.*
LEVEL: LANG: Eng SIRC ARTICLE NO: 098574

Davidson, W.B. How to control your temper. *Sports (Kallang, Singapore) 12(10), Nov/Dec 1984, 44-45;53.*
LEVEL: B LANG: Eng SIRC ARTICLE NO: 108996

Fox, A. The power of positive tennis. *Tennis (Norwalk, Conn.) 19(12), Apr 1984, 66;68;70.*
LEVEL: B LANG: Eng SIRC ARTICLE NO: 099996

Griffith, L.L. How to break out of a tennis slump. *Tennis (Norwalk, Conn.) 20(1), May 1984, 84;86;88.*
LEVEL: B LANG: Eng SIRC ARTICLE NO: 099998

Heath, K.F. A study of sex role, sex differences, locus of control, and expectancy of success in tennis among college students. Eugene, Ore.: Microform Publications, University of Oregon, 1984. 5 microfiches : negative, ill. ; 11 x 15 cm.
NOTES: Thesis (Ph.D.) - University of Oregon, 1982; (xii, 401 leaves); vita; includes bibliography.
LEVEL: A LANG: Eng UO84 34-38

Loehr, J. Be cool on court: avoiding the apple can be as easy as pie. *World tennis (Los Angeles, Calif.) 32(1), Jun 1984, 40-41.*
LEVEL: B LANG: Eng SIRC ARTICLE NO: 101603

Loehr, J.E. Groppel, J. Emotions of power: you can will yourself to play your best-or worst-by how you control your emotions Some upbeat advice to bring out the champion in you. *World tennis (Los Angeles, Calif.) 31(8), Jan 1984, 36-37.*
LEVEL: B LANG: Eng SIRC ARTICLE NO: 098584

Loehr, J.E. How to overcome tension & play at your peak all the time. *Tennis (Norwalk, Conn.) 19(11), Mar 1984, 66-70;72-74;76.*
LEVEL: B LANG: Eng SIRC ARTICLE NO: 098585

Ramo, S. Tennis by Machiavelli. 1st ed. New York: Rawson, c1984. xiv, 174 p.
LEVEL: B LANG: Eng ISBN: 0-89256-269-2 LC CARD 84-42504 GV1002.9.P75 17845

Secunda, A. Ultimate tennis: the pleasure game. Englewood Cliffs, N.J.: Prentice-Hall, c1984. 1v.
NOTES: Includes index.
LEVEL: B LANG: Eng ISBN: 0139354387 LC CARD: 84-015107

Singer, R.N. Mental readiness to execute self-paced tennis strokes. *Addvantage (Cleveland, Oh.) 8(5), Sept/Oct 1984, 8-9.*
LEVEL: B LANG: Eng SIRC ARTICLE NO: 101610

Steinbaum, E. The many faces of rage in tennis: broken rackets, frayed tempers and shouting matches become common. *Sports now (St. Louis, Mo.) 2(5), May 1984, 1.*
LEVEL: B LANG: Eng SIRC ARTICLE NO: 098592

Vous avez dit sophrologie? *Tennis magazine (Paris) 98, mai 1984, 101-102.*
LEVEL: B LANG: Fr SIRC ARTICLE NO: 100017

Woods, R. There are no key points in tennis. *Addvantage (Cleveland, Ohio) 8(3), May/Jun 1984, 14.*
LEVEL: B LANG: Eng SIRC ARTICLE NO: 098598

PSYCHOLOGY - MENTAL TRAINING

Chien, I.-H. Jwo, J.-L. Effects of mental practice on learning tennis forehand groundstroke. *Asian journal of physical education (Taipei, Taiwan) 7(3), Oct 1984, 56-57.*
LEVEL: I LANG: Eng Chi SIRC ARTICLE NO: 103511

Gallwey, T. Lalanne, L.B. Gagner le match. Montreal: Le Jour, c1984. 237 p.
NOTES: Traduit de: Inner tennis, Random House.
LEVEL: B LANG: Fr ISBN: 2-89044-178-4 LC CARD: 85-10088-7 GV1002.9.P75 18944

RULES AND REGULATIONS

LaMarche, R.J. Col. Nick Powel: the man who makes the rules. *Tennis (Norwalk, Conn.) 20(6),* Oct 1984, 64;67-68;70;72.
LEVEL: B LANG: Eng SIRC ARTICLE NO: 108891

Mansell, J.R. The yardstick: the rules and regulations of tennis. Vanier, Ont.: Tennis Canada, (1984). 78 p.
CORP: Tennis Canada.
NOTES: Cover title.
LEVEL: B LANG: Eng ISBN: 0-9691122-3-8
GV1001 18042

SOCIAL PSYCHOLOGY

Champion et pere: plus dur encore. *Tennis magazine (Paris) 98, mai 1984, 117-119.*
LEVEL: B LANG: Fr SIRC ARTICLE NO: 099987

Stark, E. Woman's tennis: friends vs.foes. *Psychology today (New York, N.Y.) 18(7), Jul 1984, 17.*
LEVEL: B LANG: ENG SIRC ARTICLE NO: 095362

SPORTING EVENTS

Freed, D.A. The Royal Court: a glimpse into the charmed circle of Wimbledon. *Racquets Canada (Toronto) Jun/Jul 1984, 10-12;14;16;18;20-21.*
LEVEL: B LANG: Eng SIRC ARTICLE NO: 104923

Raising the winning cup. (Wimbledon) *Tennis world (London) Jun 1984, 73;76.*
LEVEL: B LANG: Eng SIRC ARTICLE NO: 101608

SPORTSMANSHIP

Endemann, C. A bitter victory: today's breed of tennis stars have lost the panache of the gentlemen of yesteryear. *Racquets Canada (Toronto) Winter 1984, 12-18.*
LEVEL: B LANG: Eng SIRC ARTICLE NO: 109113

STATISTICS AND RECORDS

Heath, E.H. Tennis. *In, Clawson, M. and Van Doren, C.S. (eds.), Statistics on outdoor recreation, Washington, Resources for the Future, c1984, p. 272-273.*
LEVEL: B LANG: Eng GV191.4 20254

STATISTICS AND RECORDS - PARTICIPATION

Tennis -- worth the wait for many. Le tennis - un sport plus populaire chez les adultes. *Highlights/ Faits saillants (Ottawa) 29, Jun 1984, 1-2.*
CORP: Canada Fitness Survey.
CORP: Enquete condition physique Canada.
LEVEL: B LANG: Eng Fr SIRC ARTICLE NO: 095366

STRATEGY

Connors, J. Jimmy Connors: change pace to add a new dimension to your attack. *Tennis (Norwalk, Conn.) 20(2), Jun 1984, 44-47.*
LEVEL: B LANG: Eng SIRC ARTICLE NO: 101580

Fein, P. Advanced strategy in tennis. *Scholastic coach (New York) 53(9), Apr 1984, 42-43.*
LEVEL: B LANG: Eng SIRC ARTICLE NO: 095351

Fein, P. Clever counters. *Coaching review (Ottawa, Ont.) 7, Jul/Aug 1984, 42-43.*
LEVEL: B LANG: Eng SIRC ARTICLE NO: 0953

Fein, P. Clever counters. *Addvantage (Cleveland, Ohio) 8(3), May/Jun 1984, 22-23.*
LEVEL: B LANG: Eng SIRC ARTICLE NO: 098577

Gottfried, B. Be a winner on all surfaces. *Tennis (Norwalk, Conn.) 20(1), May 1984, 104-107.*
LEVEL: B LANG: Eng SIRC ARTICLE NO: 099997

Navratilova, M. Solving the mystery of an unknown opponent: when you are playing someone for the first time, look for these keys in the warmup and beyond-they'll reduce your fear of the unknown and give you the upper hand. *World tennis (Los Angeles, Calif.) 31(8), Jan 1984, 48-49.*
LEVEL: B LANG: Eng SIRC ARTICLE NO: 098588

Smith, S. Stan Smith's inside moves: adjusting your game to indoor play. *Tennis (Norwalk, Conn.) 20, Nov 1984, 40-43.*
LEVEL: B LANG: Eng SIRC ARTICLE NO: 108582

STRATEGY - DEFENSIVE

Verdieck, J. Van der Meer, D. Manual IV: how to play the court personalities. *Tennispro (Hilton Head Island, S.C.) 4(1), Feb/Mar 1984, 3;10.*
LEVEL: B LANG: Eng SIRC ARTICLE NO: 098597

STRATEGY - DOUBLES

Alsheimer, D. The trenches: the battle. *Coaching clinic (Princeton, N.J.) 22(8), Apr 1984, 13-15.*
LEVEL: B LANG: Eng SIRC ARTICLE NO: 095344

Bodo, P. Pro mixed doubles: how different is it from the club game? *Tennis (Norwalk, Conn.) 20(6), Oct 1984, 34-37.*
LEVEL B LANG: Eng SIRC ARTICLE NO: 108889

Braden, V. Vic Braden's 8 rules for success in doubles. *Tennis (Norwalk, Conn.) 19(11), Mar 1984, 98-101.*
LEVEL: B LANG: Eng SIRC ARTICLE NO: 098570

How to win the battle of the sexes. *World tennis (Los Angeles) 32(4), Sept 1984, 85-87.*
LEVEL: B LANG: Eng SIRC ARTICLE NO: 173390

Hutchins, P. Guide to better tennis: mixed doubles. *Tennis world (London) Jul 1984, 30-31.*
LEVEL: B LANG: Eng SIRC ARTICL NO: 101596

Love, R.C. Two-way tandem in tennis doubles. *Scholastic coach 53(7), Feb 1984, 32;79.*
LEVEL: B LANG: Eng SIRC ARTICLE NO: 093806

Navratilova, M. Dynamic doubles. *World tennis (Los Angeles, Calif.) 31(12), Apr 1984, 37-39.*
LEVEL: B LANG: Eng SIRC ARTICLE NO: 100007

Stolle, F. Kramer, J. Drysdale, C. Ralston, D. Cohen, P. Heldman, G.M. How to build your doubles game. What aspect of double must be worked on the most? *World tennis (Los Angeles, Calif.) 31(8), Jan 1984, 51-56.*
LEVEL: B LANG: Eng SIRC ARTICLE NO: 098593

TEACHING

Baldwin, M. Advanced planning of lessons No. 2. *Addvantage (Cleveland) 8(4), Jul/Aug 1984, 18-19.*
LEVEL: B LANG: Eng SIRC ARTICLE NO: 103509

Casey, R. Teaching skills. Summary sheet. *In, Level one coaching course 1983. Tennis coaching manual, Wembley, W.A., Wester Australian Lawn*

Tennis Association et al., 1984, p. 7.
LEVEL: B LANG: Eng GV1002.9.C6 18656

Ehrhardt, K. Twenty ways to relieve the teaching pro syndrome. *Addvantage (Cleveland, Oh.) 8(5), Sept/Oct 1984, 14-16.*
LEVEL: B LANG: Eng SIRC ARTICLE NO: 101589

Hatt, P. Activities and games for groups. *In, Level one coaching course 1983. Tennis coaching manual, Wembley, W.A., Wester Australian Lawn Tennis Association et al., 1984, p. 14-18.*
LEVEL: B LANG: Eng GV1002.9.C6 18656

Hatt, P. Ball games for groups. *In, Level one coaching course 1983. Tennis coaching manual, Wembley, W.A., Western Australian Lawn Tennis Association et al., 1984, p. 19-22.*
LEVEL: B LANG: Eng GV1002.9.C6 18656

Katz, L. The planning of group lessons. *Addvantage (Cleveland, Oh.) 8(1), Jan/Feb 1984, 22-23.*
LEVEL: B LANG: Eng SIRC ARTICLE NO: 096916

Le Grand, Y. Le tennis, un jeu a la portee des enfants. *Macolin (Suisse) 4, avr 1984, 8-10.*
NOTES: Traduction de, Mariann Weber.
LEVEL: B LANG: Fr SIRC ARTICLE NO: 101600

Massias, J.C. Tennis: la section sport-etudes de l'INSEP. *EPS: Revue education physique et sport (Paris) 188, juil/aout 1984, 19-23.*
NOTES: A suivre.
LEVEL: B LANG: Fr SIRC ARTICLE NO: 098586

Meadow, B. The speed doctor. (footwork) *World tennis (Los Angeles, Calif.) 31(10), Mar 1984, 46-48.*
LEVEL: B LANG: Eng SIRC ARTICLE NO: 100005

Meinhardt, T. Brown, J. Tennis group instruction II. Reston, Va.: American Alliance for Health, Physical Education, Recreation and Dance, c1984. 64 p. : ill.
CORP: United States Tennis Association.
CORP: National Association for Sport and Physical Education.
NOTES: Bibliography: p. 64.
LEVEL: B LANG: Eng ISBN: 0-88314-263-5
GV991.5 18250

Metzler, M.W. A tennis unit for individualizing instruction. *Virginia journal (Harrisonburg, Va.) 6(2), Apr 1984, 17-19.*
LEVEL: B LANG: Eng SIRC ARTICLE NO: 100006

Murton, R. Psychology of teaching. *In, Level one coaching course 1983. Tennis coaching manual, Wembley, W.A., Western Australian Lawn Tennis Association et al., 1984, p. 3-5.*
LEVEL: I LANG: Eng GV1002.9.C6 18656

Tabak, L. Put that Olympic spirit into your junior lessons. *Addvantage (Cleveland, Ohio) 8(3), May/ Jun 1984, 13.*
LEVEL: B LANG: Eng SIRC ARTICLE NO: 098594

Tennis: la section sport-etudes de l'INSEP. *EPS: Education physique et sport (Paris) 189, sept/oct 1984, 60-63.*
LEVEL: B LANG: Fr SIRC ARTICLE NO: 101613

VanderGriend, M. Interviewing prospective tennis teachers for your tennis program. *Utah journal of health, physical education, recreation and dance (Provo, Utah) 16, Autumn 1984, 8-9.*
LEVEL: B LANG: Eng SIRC ARTICLE NO: 103523

TECHNIQUES AND SKILLS

Alsheimer, D. Drop that opponent. *Women's coaching clinic (Princeton, N.J.) 8(1), Sept 1984, 11-13.*
LEVEL: B LANG: Eng SIRC ARTICLE NO: 099974

Ashe, A. Arthur Ashe: les qualites de Jaeger, sa patience et son physique. *Tennis de France (Paris) 370, fevr 1984, 106-109.*
LEVEL: B LANG: Fr SIRC ARTICLE NO: 095345

Bollettieri, N. Le smash. *Tennis magazine (Paris) 98, mai 1984, 93-96.*
LEVEL: B LANG: Fr SIRC ARTICLE NO: 099981

Bollettieri, N. L'amortie. *Tennis magazine (Paris) 95, fevr 1984, 105-108.*
LEVEL: B LANG: Fr SIRC ARTICLE NO: 099982

Braden, V. Vic Braden unravels the mysteries of spin. *Tennis (Norwalk, Conn.) 20(6), Oct 1984, 60-62.*
LEVEL: B LANG: Eng SIRC ARTICLE NO: 108887

de Kermadec, G. McNamara-Lendl: smash de volee et smash apres rebond. *Tennis de France (Paris) 374, juin 1984, 217-219.*
LEVEL: B LANG: Fr SIRC ARTICLE NO: 109157

Delaney, B. Get the drop on your opponent: in order to master the drop shot, the player must understand the technical and tactical aspects of its execution and apply them in drills and competition. *Athletic journal 64(9), Apr 1984, 28-30;78-79.*
LEVEL: B LANG: Eng SIRC ARTICLE NO: 093797

Delaney, B. A special shot: the kneeling overhead. *Addvantage (Cleveland, Oh.) 8(5), Sept/Oct 1984, 12-13.*
LEVEL: B LANG: Eng SIRC ARTICLE NO: 101583

Deniau, G. Un champion a votre portee. 29. John McEnroe, la volee basse. *Tennis magazine (Paris) 98, mai 1984, 105-110.*
LEVEL: B LANG: Fr SIRC ARTICLE NO: 099991

Deniau, G. Un champion a votre portee. 30. Yannick Noah, service-volee. *Tennis magazine (Paris) 99, juin 1984, 155-160.*
LEVEL: B LANG: Fr SIRC ARTICLE NO: 101586

Deniau, G. Un champion a votre portee. 35. Guillermo Vilas: le smash apres rebond. *Tennis magazine (Neuilly Cedex, France) 104, nov 1984, 71-76.*
LEVEL: B LANG: Fr SIRC ARTICLE NO: 109166

Ford, S. Design B: how to play tennis in the zone. South Bend, Ind.: Icarus Press, 1984. 125 p.
NOTES: Includes index.
LEVEL: B LANG: Eng ISBN: 0896511537 LC CARD: 84-004677 GV995 17719

How to win on clay: what should a club player do on clay? *World tennis (Los Angeles, Calif.) 32(1), Jun 1984, 71-76.*
LEVEL: LANG: Eng SIRC ARTICLE NO: 101594

Le Goulven, F. Le Guen, A. Le tennis. Comment devenir meilleur. Artigues-pres-Bordeaux: Delmas, 1984. 40 p. : ill.
LEVEL: B LANG: Fr

McCullough, J. Traendly, C. Rinaldi, K. Two-handed tennis: how to play a winner's game. New York: M. Evans, c1984. xi, 176 p : ill.
NOTES: Includes index.
LEVEL: B LANG: Eng ISBN: 0871314258 LC CARD: 83-020759 GV1002.9.T86 17301

Navratilova, M. The forehand slice approach: handle with care. *World tennis (Los Angeles, Calif.) 32(3), Aug 1984, 40-41.*
LEVEL: B LANG: Eng SIRC ARTICLE NO: 101607

Professeur Ashe: six enseignements du jeu de Yannick Noah. *Tennis de France (Paris) 374, juin 1984, 212-215.*
LEVEL: B LANG: Fr SIRC ARTICLE NO: 109155

Shmerler, C. Squash your fears for better tennis. *World tennis (Los Angeles) 32(7), Dec 1984, 60-61.*
LEVEL: B LANG: Eng SIRC ARTICLE NO: 173590

Speciality shots: when and why. *World tennis (Los Angeles, Calif.) 32(3), Aug 1984, 35-37.*
LEVEL: B LANG: Eng SIRC ARTICLE NO: 101611

The fine art of spin. *World tennis (Los Angeles) 32(5), Oct 1984, 69-71.*
LEVEL: B LANG: Eng SIRC ARTICLE NO: 108734

TECHNIQUES AND SKILLS - BACKHAND

Bollettieri, N. Le revers a deux mains (accompagne a une main). *Tennis magazine (Paris) 94, janv 1984, 65-68.*
LEVEL: B LANG: Fr SIRC ARTICLE NO: 099983

de Kermadec, G. Leconte-Noah: passing shots de revers. *Tennis de France (Paris) 369, janv 1984, 67-69.*
LEVEL: B LANG: Fr SIRC ARTICLE NO: 099989

Deniau, G. Un champion a votre portee. 26. Henri Leconte, le revers d'approche. *Tennis magazine (Paris) 95, fevr 1984, 91-96.*
LEVEL: B LANG: Fr SIRC ARTICLE NO: 099992

Deniau, G. Un champion a votre portee. 31. Mats Wilander, l'acceleration de revers. *Tennis magazine (Paris) 100, juil 1984, 151-156.*
LEVEL: B LANG: Fr SIRC ARTICLE NO: 101585

Deniau, G. Un champion a votre portee. 34. Ivan Lendl: le revers coupe. *Tennis magazine (Neuilly Cedex, France) 103, oct 1984, 89-94.*
LEVEL: B LANG: Fr SIRC ARTICLE NO: 173458

Helfrich, J. Topspin backhand made easy. *Athletic journal 64(8), Mar 1984, 8-9;65-66.*
LEVEL: B LANG: Eng SIRC ARTICLE NO: 093800

The evolution of style: backhand. How do today's top backhand differ from 20 years ago? *World tennis (Los Angeles, Calif.) 31(12), May 1984, 37-42.*
LEVEL: B LANG: Eng SIRC ARTICLE NO: 099995

TECHNIQUES AND SKILLS - FOREHAND

de Kermadec, G. E. Goolagong Cawley - J. Durie: coups droits coupes. *Tennis de France (Paris) 370, fevr 1984, 111-113.*
LEVEL: B LANG: Fr SIRC ARTICLE NO: 095348

Deniau, G. Un champion a votre portee. 28. Vitas Gerulaitis, le coup droit d'attente. *Tennis magazine (Paris) 97, avr 1984, 85-90.*
LEVEL: B LANG: Fr SIRC ARTICLE NO: 101584

Deniau, G. Un champion a votre portee. 36. Jimmy Arias, le coup droit lifte. *Tennis magazine (Neuilly Cedex, France) 105, dec 1984, 59-64.*
LEVEL: B LANG: Fr SIRC ARTICLE NO: 108903

Love, B. Parks 11, G.W. The three stroke model: finish to start. *Addvantage (Cleveland, Oh.) 8(1),*

Jan/Feb 1984, 8-11.
LEVEL: B LANG: Eng SIRC ARTICLE NO: 096918

van der Meer, D. Simplify your forehand volley for success. *Tennis (Norwalk, Conn.) 20(6), Oct 1984, 78-81.*
LEVEL: B LANG Eng SIRC ARTICLE NO: 108888

TECHNIQUES AND SKILLS - GRIP

Van Der Meer, D. All about grips. *Tennis (Norwalk, Conn.) 19(12), Apr 1984, 48-53.*
LEVEL: B LANG: Eng SIRC ARTICLE NO: 100016

TECHNIQUES AND SKILLS - SERVING

Connors, J. Jimmy Connors: how I improved my serve. *Tennis (Norwalk, Conn.) 19(12), Apr 1984, 37-41.*
LEVEL: B LANG: Eng SIRC ARTICLE NO: 099988

Deniau, G. Un champion a votre portee. 25. Martina Navratilova, le service (suivi au filet). *Tennis magazine (Paris) 94, janv 1984, 55-60.*
LEVEL: B LANG: Fr SIRC ARTICLE NO: 099993

Jimmy Connors: comment j'ai ameliore mon service. *Tennis de France (Paris) 374, juin 1984, 221-225.*
LEVEL: B LANG: Fr SIRC ARTICLE NO: 109159

Serve - and - volley: an analysis. *World tennis (Los Angeles, Calif.) 32(2), Jul 1984, 51-54.*
LEVEL: B LANG: Eng SIRC ARTICLE NO: 101609

Trabert, T. Hook, J. The serve: key to winning tennis. New York: Dodd, Mead, c1984. xiii, 140 p. : ill.
LEVEL: B LANG: Eng ISBN: 0-396-08299-8 LC CARD: 84-1510 GV1002.9.S47 18277

TECHNIQUES AND SKILLS - STANCE

Connors, J. Jimmy Connors: how to be quicker on court. *Tennis (Norwalk, Conn.) 20(4), Aug 1984, 68-70.*
LEVEL: B LANG: Eng SIRC ARTICLE NO: 101579

Ehrhardt, K.W. Innovative footwork for every advancing player. *Addvantage (Cleveland, Oh.) 8(1), Jan/Feb 1984, 4-5.*
LEVEL B LANG: Eng SIRC ARTICLE NO: 096913

Hopkins, P.W. A comparison of movement times between the open and the closed stance for the tennis forehand groundstroke. Eugene, Ore.: Microform Publications, University of Oregon, 1984. 1 microfiche : negative, ill. ; 11 x 15 cm.
NOTES: Thesis (M.S.) - Pennsylvania States University, 1981; (viii, 56 leaves); includes bibliography.
LEVEL: A LANG: Eng UO84 126

Wall, P. Ghost drills and improving on footwork. *Women's coaching clinic (Princeton, N.J.) 8(2), Oct 1984, 8-11.*
LEVEL: B LANG: Eng SIRC ARTICLE NO: 100018

TESTING AND EVALUATION

Braden, V. Can a computer develop a champion? *Tennis (Norwalk, Conn.) 20(2), Jun 1984, 48-51.*
LEVEL: B LANG: Eng SIRC ARTICLE NO: 101575

Schechter, A. A computer service scores points with a good many tennis players. *Sports illustrated*

(Chicago, Ill.) 6(14), 1 Sept 1984, 6;8-9.
LEVEL: B LANG: Eng SIRC ARTICLE NO: 098590

Wancke, H. High technology in tennis. *Tennis world (London) Jul 1984, 46-47.*
LEVEL: B LANG: Eng SIRC ARTICLE NO: 101619

TRAINING AND CONDITIONING

Alsheimer, D. Practice makes perfect. *Coaching clinic (Princeton, N.J.) 22(8), Apr 1984, 9-10.*
LEVEL: B LANG: Eng SIRC ARTICLE NO: 095342

Buckett, B.J. Paddle through indoor tennis. (Refs: 2)*Women's coaching clinic 7(7), Mar 1984, 12-13.*
LEVEL: B LANG: Eng SIRC ARTICLE NO: 092444

Burke, M.S. You can practice tennis in the gym. *Scholastic coach (New York) 53(10), May/Jun 1984, 36;38.*
LEVEL: B LANG: E SIRC ARTICLE NO: 095346

Cobb, L.G. Wired for success: the new programmable tennis player. (Refs: 5)*Addvantage (Cleveland) 8(6), Nov/Dec 1984, 14-16.*
LEVEL: B LANG: Eng SIRC ARTICLE NO: 104920

Goffi, C. McEnroe, J. Tournament tough. 1st ed. New York: Holt, Rinehart, and Winston, c1984. 1v.
LEVEL: B LANG: Eng ISBN: 0030715989 LC CARD: 84-019741

Gould, D. Gould, A. Conditioning for tennis: a guide for players and coaches. s.l.: Leisure Press, 1984. 192 p. : ill.
LEVEL: B LANG: Eng ISBN: 0-88011-030-9 LC CARD: 81-86513

Grosse, S.J. Dorow, K.M. Krueger, R.J. Aerobic-dance your team into condition. *Scholastic coach (New York) 54(4), Nov 1984, 64-65;71.*
LEVEL: B LANG: Eng SIRC ARTICLE NO: 102944

TRAINING AND CONDITIONING - DRILLS

Alsheimer, D. Spin to victory. *Coaching clinic (Princeton, N.J.) 22(8), Apr 1984, 11-13.*
LEVEL: B LANG: Eng SIRC ARTICLE NO: 095343

Braden, V. Find your window to hit better strokes. *Tennis (Norwalk, Conn.) 19(9), Jan 1984, 54-55.*
LEVEL: B LANG: Eng SIR ARTICLE NO: 098569

Burke, M.S. A simple service return drill. *Athletic journal (Evanston, Ill.) 65(3), Oct 1984, 10.*
LEVEL: B LANG: Eng SIRC ARTICLE NO: 099985

Jeffries, E. Transitional drills: baseline-approach-volley. *Athletic journal (Evanston, Ill.) 64(10), May 1984, 8-9.*
LEVEL: B LANG: Eng SIRC ARTICLE NO: 095354

Kinlund, N. A day with a winner. Drills for success. *Women's coaching clinic (Princeton, N.J.) 8(1), Sept 1984, 8-11.*
LEVEL: B LANG: Eng SIRC ARTICLE NO: 100002

Kozlowski, D. Making practice fun...through competition. *Addvantage (Cleveland, Oh.) 8(2), Mar/Apr 1984, 20-22.*
LEVEL: B LANG: Eng SIRC ARTICLE NO: 096917

Murphy, C. Effective planning and drills for improvement.
NOTES: In, United States Professional Tennis Association, Tennis, a professional guide. 1st ed., New York, Kodansha International, c1984, p. 124-134.
LEVEL: B LANG: Eng GV995 18015

The best drills you'll ever use. *World tennis (Los Angeles, Calif.) 31(11), Apr 1984, 61-66.*
LEVEL: B LANG: Eng SIRC ARTICL NO: 099977

Tym, A. Designing practice routines for different student levels. *Addvantage (Cleveland, Oh.) 8(5), Sept/Oct 1984, 6-7.*
LEVEL: B LANG: Eng SIRC ARTICLE NO: 101614

TRAINING AND CONDITIONING - STRETCHING AND FLEXIBILITY EXERCISES

Cousteau, J.P. Medecine: il faut vous e-ti-rer. *Tennis de France (Paris) 370, fevr 1984, 97.*
LEVEL: B LANG: Fr SIRC ARTICLE NO: 095347

Detrich, R.P. 'Stretching' more than just injury prevention. *Addvantage (Cleveland, Oh.) 8(2), Mar/Apr 1984, 14-17.*
LEVEL B LANG: Eng SIRC ARTICLE NO: 096912

TRAINING AND CONDITIONING - TRAINING CAMPS

Ackerman, L. The 17th annual directory of tennis camps & clinics: what you can expect at todays tennis camps & clinics. *Tennis (Norwalk, Conn.) 19(9), Jan 1984, 57-59.*
LEVEL: B LANG: Eng SIRC ARTICLE NO: 098564

TRAINING AND CONDITIONING - WARM-UPS, WARM-DOWNS, LEAD-UP GAMES

Auclair, J. Une nouvelle methode d'introduction au tennis cela s'imposait. *Marathon plus (Laval, Que.) 2(1), dec 1984/janv 1985, 11-12.*
LEVEL: B LANG: Fr SIRC ARTICLE NO: 173448

Levisohn, S.R. Simon, H.B. Warming down: 10 minutes that make a difference. *Tennis (Norwalk, Conn.) 19(11), Mar 1984, 102;106.*
LEVEL: B LANG: Eng SIRC ARTICLE NO: 098582

TRAINING AND CONDITIONING - WEIGHT AND STRENGTH TRAINING

Dardik, I. Waitley, D. Body work: exercise your options. *World tennis (Los Angeles, Calif.) 32(3), Aug 1984, 60-61.*
LEVEL: B LANG: Eng SIRC ARTICLE NO: 101582

Levisohn, S.R. Simon, H.B. How to strengthen your game with weight machines. *Tennis (Norwalk, Conn.) 19(10), Feb 1984, 36-39.*
LEVEL: B LANG: Eng SIRC ARTICLE NO: 093805

VARIATIONS

Half court tennis. *Ilam: Institute of leisure & amenity management (London) 2(2), Feb 1984, 25-26.*
LEVEL: B LANG: Eng SIRC ARTICLE NO: 098578

McTavish, B. McTavish, R. Pickle ball. *OPHEA: Ontario Physical and Health Education Association (London, Ont.) 10(2), Sprin 1984, 21-25.*
LEVEL: B LANG: Eng SIRC ARTICLE NO: 099345

TENPIN BOWLING

Kouros, T. Getting ready for a new season: you could be in for a shock if you plunge into the new bowling season unprepared. *Bowlers journal (Chicago, Ill.) 71(8), Aug 1984, 38.*
LEVEL: B LANG: Eng SIRC ARTICLE NO: 106114

Semenik, J. A bowling bible for beginners and the average bowler. (s.l.): J. Semenik, c1984. 76 p. : ill.
NOTES: Spine title: A bowling bible.
LEVEL: B LANG: Eng LC CARD: 84-135968

ADMINISTRATION

Baker, F. Frank reflections of bowling's past: Frank Baker, chief of the American Bowling Congress during its biggest years of growth and, perhaps, its stormiest years, looks back at some of bowling's biggest crises and the personal stake he had in making some of the Congress' decisions. *Bowlers journal (Chicago, Ill.) 71(12), Dec 1984, 38;41-42;44;46-49.*
LEVEL: B LANG: Eng SIRC ARTICLE NO: 107635

Conversation with a bowling pioneer. (Raymond R. Woodruff) *Bowlers journal (Chicago, Ill.) 71(4), Apr 1984, 52;55-56;58;60-61;64-66.*
LEVEL: B LANG: Eng SIRC ARTICLE NO: 100020

Gillespie, R. 'Ya gotta believe': when you need something done and the odds seem hopelessly stacked against - call Falzone. (John Falzone) *Bowling (Greendale, Wis.) 51(2), Sept 1984, 28-31.*
LEVEL: B LANG: Eng SIRC ARTICLE NO: 103526

The empire builder. (John Powell Jr.) *Bowlers journal (Chicago, Ill.) 71(2), Feb 1984, 44;47;48;50;52-57.*
LEVEL: B LANG: En SIRC ARTICLE NO: 100022

BIOGRAPHY AND AUTOBIOGRAPHY

Interview: all the signs are 'go'. (Nikki Gianulias) *Bowlers journal (Chicago, Ill.) 71(3), Mar 1984, 51-58.*
LEVEL: B LANG: Eng SIRC ARTICLE NO: 100023

Janka, F. Bowling's first olympic flirtation: a quiet, unassuming cigar owner was the big giant-killer when bowling staged its own exhibition at the 1936 Olympic Games. (Karl Goldhammer) *Bowlers journal (Chicago, Ill.) 71(9), Sept 1984, 82-83.*
LEVEL: B LANG: Eng SIRC ARTICLE NO: 103529

Lichstein, L. If Gil Sliker ever gets mean, watch out. *Bowlers journal (Chicago, Ill) 71(10), Oct 1984, 23.*
LEVEL: B LANG Eng SIRC ARTICLE NO: 108738

Roth, M. The granddaddy of the modern game. *Bowlers journal (Chicago, Ill.) 71(8), Aug 1984, 68;77;79-81.*
LEVEL: B LANG: Eng SIRC ARTICLE NO: 106117

BIOMECHANICS

Martin, C.L. Generating bowling ball speed. *Athletic coach (Evanston, Ill.) 65(3), Oct 1984, 38-39;54.*
LEVEL: I LANG: Eng SIRC ARTICLE NO: 100027

TENPIN BOWLING (continued)

CERTIFICATION

Mitchell, R. Tenpin bowling. Level 1 technical. Coaching certification. s.l.: Canadian Tenpin Federation, 1984?. 80 p. : ill (loose-leaf) (National Coaching Certification Program.)
CORP: Canadian Tenpin Federation.
NOTES: Cover title.
LEVEL: B LANG: Eng GV903 20079

CHILDREN

Bowling: is it losing the pitch for the Jr. Market? *Bowlers journal (Chicago) 71(7), Jul 1984, 62-64.*
LEVEL: B LANG: Eng SIRC ARTICLE NO: 104929

Hall, C. A chat with YABA's main man. (Chuck Hall) *Bowlers journal (Chicago) 71(7), Jul 1984, 46;49-50;52;54;56;61.*
LEVEL B LANG: Eng SIRC ARTICLE NO: 104930

EQUIPMENT

Kelley, G. Customizing your equipment: fitting a ball to your game is no accident if you know what you're looking for. *Bowlers journal (Chicago, Ill.) 71(10), Oct 1984, 78-79.*
LEVEL: B LANG: Eng SIRC ARTICLE NO: 108740

Lichstein, L. Tricks of the ball trade: every little tool helps, and the pros today sand or resurface their bowling equipmen to keep or find that competitive edge. *Bowlers journal (Chicago, Ill.) 71(1), Jan 1984, 16-18.*
LEVEL: B LANG: Eng SIRC ARTICLE NO: 098600

Schroeder, J. The keys to customizing equipment. *Bowlers journal (Chicago, Ill.) 71(11), Nov 1984, 78-79.*
LEVEL: B LANG: Eng SIRC ARTICLE NO: 107646

Strickland, B. Controlling your equipment experiments: the key to narrowing your search for the perfect ball is standardizin your experiments. *Bowlers journal (Chicago, Ill.) 71(12), Dec 1984, 70-71.*
LEVEL: B LANG: Eng SIRC ARTICLE NO: 107648

EQUIPMENT - MAINTENANCE

Dresset, J. The search for true bowling grit. *Bowlers journal (Chicago, Ill.) 71(5), May 1984, 94-99.*
LEVEL: B LANG: Eng SIRC ARTICLE NO: 100021

FACILITIES

Kiefer, J. Bowling: the great oil debate. *In, Schrier, E.W. and Allman, W.F. (eds.), Newton at the bat: the science in sports, New York, Scribner, c1984, p. 33-37.*
LEVEL: B LANG: Eng RC1235 18609

Schulty, D. Lane problems may be answered with new device to measure dressing. *Bowling (Greendale, Wis.) 51(2), Sept 1984, 8-10.*
LEVEL: B LANG: Eng SIRC ARTICLE NO: 103534

FACILITIES - DESIGN, CONSTRUCTION AND PLANNING

Whitten, R.E. Bringing the game down to earth. *Golf course management (Lawrence, Kans.) 52(11), Nov 1984, 6-7;10;12-14;16;18-19.*
LEVEL: B LANG: Eng SIRC ARTICLE NO: 172998

HISTORY

Hills, E. Bowling a part of West Point history. *Bowling (Greendale, Wis.) 51(2), sept 1984, 12-14.*
LEVEL: B LANG: Eng SIR ARTICLE NO: 103528

JUVENILE LITERATURE

Pezzano, C. Knudsen, A. Gow, B. Bowling basics. Englewood Cliffs, N.J.: Prentice-Hall, c1984. 1v.
LEVEL: B LANG: Eng ISBN: 0130805165 LC CARD: 83-022893

PHYSICS

Farnall, O. Equipment specifications begins study of bowling pin dynamics. *Bowling (Greendale, Wis.) 51(3), Dec 1984, 10-11*
LEVEL: B LANG: Eng SIRC ARTICLE NO: 107637

Judging ball reaction by CG weight: the center of gravity can produce effects which don't show up on your ball scale. *Bowlers journal (Chicago) 71(7), Jul 1984, 76-77.*
LEVEL: I LANG: Eng SIRC ARTICLE NO: 104931

Kouros, T. The friction and elasticity factors: the two chief architects of the game's environment today. *Bowlers journal (Chicago, Ill.) 71(6), Jun 1984, 12.*
LEVEL: I LANG: Eng SIRC ARTICLE NO: 103530

PSYCHOLOGY

Mazzio, J. The flaws you can't feel: to correct faulty technique, a student first must be convinced that he's doing it wrong *Bowlers journal (Chicago, Ill.) 71(10), Oct 1984, 72-73.*
LEVEL: B LANG: Eng SIRC ARTICLE NO: 108739

PSYCHOLOGY - MENTAL TRAINING

Martin, C.L. Imaginary wall boosts scores. *Coaching clinic (Princeton, N.J.) 22(9), May 1984, 7-8.*
LEVEL: B LANG: Eng SIR ARTICLE NO: 095368

RULES AND REGULATIONS

Common sense guides conduct. *Women bowler (Greendale, Wis.) 49(10), Nov 1984, 38;40.*
LEVEL: B LANG: Eng SIRC ARTICLE NO: 173579

Here's a short course in how to score. *Woman bowler (Greendale, Wis.) 49(8), Sept 1984, 50.*
LEVEL: B LANG: Eng SIRC ARTICLE NO: 103527

SOCIOLOGY

Yarnold, P. The total image picture. *Bowlers journal (Chicago, Ill.) 71(2), Feb 1984, 58-61.*
NOTES: Part III of a three-part series.
LEVEL: B LANG: Eng SIRC ARTICLE NO: 100029

TEACHING

Kouros, T. Learning, the active process: it is good learning that defines good teaching, not vice versa. *Bowlers journal (Chicago) 71(7), Jul 1984, 40.*
LEVEL: B LANG: Eng SIRC ARTICLE NO: 104932

TECHNIQUES AND SKILLS

Kouros, T. Re-examining three controversial tenets. *Bowlers journal (Chicago, Ill.) 71(1), Jan 1984, 14.*
LEVEL: B LANG: E SIRC ARTICLE NO: 098599

Kouros, T. Playing the percentages. *Bowlers journal (Chicago, Ill.) 71(4), Apr 1984, 38-40.*
LEVEL: B LANG: Eng SIRC ARTICLE NO: 100024

Kouros, T. You can't afford to ignore spares: even strike artists eventually pay a price for spare shooting deficiencies. *Bowlers journal (Chicago, Ill.) 71(5), May 1984, 36.*
LEVEL: B LANG: Eng SIRC ARTICLE NO: 100026

Martin, C.L. Learn to read the bowling arm. *Scholastic coach (New York) 54(4), Nov 1984, 39.*
LEVEL: B LANG: Eng SIRC ARTICLE NO: 103532

McGrath, M. How to increase your equipment juggling effectiveness. *Bowlers journal (Chicago, Ill.) 71(9), Sept 1984, 44.*
LEVEL: B LANG: Eng SIRC ARTICLE NO: 103533

Schroeder, J. Thar's gold in them thar holes: the profitable pro shop operation must keep up with bowling's constant evolution. *Bowlers journal (Chicago, Ill.) 71(5), May 1984, 52-53.*
LEVEL: B LANG: Eng SIRC ARTICLE NO: 100028

Taylor, B. The swing in the park. *Bowlers journal (Chicago, Ill.) 71(9), Sept 1984, 100-103.*
LEVEL: B LANG: Eng SIRC ARTICLE NO: 103536

TECHNIQUES AND SKILLS - AIMING

Kouros, T. The ins & outs of lane alignment. *Bowlers journal (Chicago, Ill.) 71(3), Mar 1984, 35.*
LEVEL: B LANG: Eng SIRC ARTICLE NO: 100025

TECHNIQUES AND SKILLS - GRIP

Lastowski, M. The 4-hole grip explained. *Bowlers journal (Chicago, Ill.) 71(8), Aug 1984, 30-31.*
LEVEL: B LANG: Eng SIRC ARTICLE NO: 106115

Strickland, B. The windup is the pitch: never lose sight of the overall pitch relationships when making spec changes. *Bowlers journal (Chicago, Ill.) 71(6), Jun 1984, 24-25.*
LEVEL: B LANG: Eng SIRC ARTICLE NO: 103535

TECHNIQUES AND SKILLS - STANCE

Kouros, T. How to line up the feet for more strikes. *Bowlers journal (Chicago, Ill.) 71(9), Sept 1984, 17.*
LEVEL: B LANG: Eng SIRC ARTICLE NO: 103531

TESTING AND MEASUREMENT

Baranowski, T. Dworkin, R.J. Cieslik, C.J. Hooks, P. Clearman, D.R. Ray, L. Dunn, J.K. Nader, P.R. Reliability and validity of self report of aerobic activity: family health project. (Refs: 26)*Research quarterly for exercise and sport (Reston, Va.) 55(4), Dec 1984, 309-317.*
ABST: Two studies are presented which deal with the reliability and validity of self-reports of aerobic activity. The first study compared two forms of self-report data obtained as part of a study of intervention strategy. The two forms were daily self-report and weekly retrospective report. The need

for the development and testing of self-report forms among children was noted, and was the subject of the second study. In Study II, six different forms on which third to sixth grade children recorded their aerobic activity were compared against two days of continuous observations of their behavior. The six forms varied along two dimensions, the time period of reporting and the response format. The segmented day forms resulted in significantly higher agreement with the observers' report of activity.
LEVEL: A LANG: Eng SIRC ARTICLE NO: 104482

Kirkland, R. Agility and quickness formula. *Coaching clinic (Princeton, N.J.) 22(8), Apr 1984, 16.*
LEVEL: B LANG: Eng SIR ARTICLE NO: 094756

Nicholas, J.A. The value of sports profiling. (Refs: 6)*Clinics in sports medicine (Philadelphia) 3(1), Jan 1984, 3-10.*
NOTES: Symposium on profiling.
ABST: The interaction between the fields of anatomy, pathology, physiology and biochemistry provides information on the physical attributes and deficiencies of an athlete. This information gathering process is called profiling. Profiling is done on individuals and groups to determine what capabilities are needed for a particular sport and whether or not an individual can participate in a given sport without injury. Profile studies are conducted on athletes and potential athletes of all ages and abilities.
LEVEL: I LANG: Eng SIRC ARTICLE NO: 092943

Yetman, W. La science et le sport: la cle du succes. Science and sport bring success. *Champion (Vanier, Ont.) 8(2), May/mai 1984, 6-9.*
LEVEL: B LANG: Fr Eng SIRC ARTICLE NO: 094765

EQUIPMENT

Conditioning, training and testing equipment: products used in athletic training, conditioning and testing programs are listed here. The manufacturers and suppliers of each product are listed alphabetically following the heading. *Athletic purchasing and facilities (Madison, Wis.) 8(2), Feb 1984, 147-148;150;152;154.*
NOTES: 1984 buyers guide.
LEVEL: B LANG: Eng SIRC ARTICLE NO: 108283

Horvat, M.A. Golding, L.A. Beutel-Horvat, T. McConnell, T.J. A treadmill modification for wheelchairs. (Refs: 18)*Research quarterly for exercise & sport (Reston, Va.) 55(3), Sept 1984, 297-301.*
LEVEL: I LANG: Eng SIRC ARTICLE NO: 102455

MEASUREMENT

Newell, K.M. Hancock, P.A. Forgotten moments: a note on skewness and kurtosis as influential factors in inferences extrapolated from response distributions. (Refs: 26)*Journal of motor behavior (Washington) 16(3), Sept 1984, 320-335.*
ABST: It is proposed that reliance on only the mean and standard deviation of a distribution to describe response frequency may lead to erroneous inferences concerning such distributions when skewness and kurtosis are present. After defining the first four moments of a distribution, it is demonstrated analytically that skewness and kurtosis may vary to systematically influence the mean and standard deviation of a set of related distributions. The significance of these relationships

for the interpretation of differing response distributions is advanced through examples gleaned from the movement control literature.
LEVEL: A LANG: Eng SIRC ARTICLE NO: 104491

THAILAND

PHYSICAL FITNESS

Torranin, C. Physical working capacity and fitness norms of Thai men from various occupations in Bangkok, 1977-1983. *Asian journal of physical education (Taiwan, China) 7(1), Apr 1984, 87-89.*
NOTES: Abstract in Chinese.
LEVEL: I LANG: Eng SIRC ARTICLE NO: 096207

THREE-DAY EVENT

Lefaive, M. The three day event: could you meet the challenge? *Horse sense (Elora, Ont.) 3(5), Aug/Sept 1984, 12-13.*
LEVEL: B LANG: Eng SIRC ARTICLE NO: 099733

Smith, A. Giles, B. The SR direct mail book of eventing. London: Stanley Paul, c1984. 222 p. : ill.
LEVEL: B LANG: Eng ISBN 0091551803 SF295.7 17872

Treviranus, C. Preparation and transport for the first event. *Dressage & CT (Cleveland Heights, Ohio) 21(3), Mar 1984, 10;12.*
LEVEL: B LANG: Eng SIRC ARTICLE NO: 171489

Vincent, L. Combined training seminar: eventing tips for lower level competitors. *USCTA news (South Hamilton, Mass.) 13(3), Jun 1984, 21-23.*
LEVEL: B LANG: Eng SIRC ARTICLE NO: 098253

FACILITIES

Ayer, N.R. A preview of the Olympic three day event course: an informative description of the 34 obstacles, the terrain and climate. *USCTA news (South Hamilton, Mass.) 13(1), Feb 1984, 12-13.*
LEVEL: B LANG: Eng SIRC ARTICLE NO: 097518

FACILITIES - DESIGN, CONSTRUCTION AND PLANNING

Another dimension in golf course grooming: the golf community showed its stuff in accommodating one '84 Olympic event. *Golf course management (Kansas) 52(10), Oct 1984, 38-39;42;44.*
LEVEL: B LANG: Eng SIRC ARTICLE NO: 105222

Coles, F. The olympic course: the philosophy behind it, the actual plan, and how it measured up to the expectations. *USCTA news (Hamilton, Mass.) 13(5), Oct 1984, 21-25.*
LEVEL: B LANG: Eng SIRC ARTICLE NO: 173391

PSYCHOLOGY

Struby, J. The psychological factors of the three day event. *USCTA news (Hamilton, Mass.) 13(6), Dec 1984, 15-16.*
LEVEL: LANG: Eng SIRC ARTICLE NO: 173394

RULES AND REGULATIONS

1984-1985 rule book. New York: American Horse Shows Association, 1984. 544 p.
CORP: American Horse Shows Association.
LEVEL: LANG: Eng SF294.5 17830

Burton, J.R. Explanation of the new combined training rules. *USCTA news (South Hamilton, Mass.) 13(1), Feb 1984, 14;16-17.*
LEVEL: B LANG: Eng SIRC ARTICLE NO: 098184

SPORTING EVENTS

Bliss, M. Introductory three-day eventing at the training level yea or neigh? *USCTA news (Hamilton, Mass.) 13(6), Dec 1984, 18-20.*
LEVEL: B LANG: Eng SIRC ARTICLE NO: 173395

TESTING AND EVALUATION

Treviranus, C. The making of a prospect. Final two weeks before first event. *Dressage & CT (Cleveland, Ohio) 21(2), Feb 1984, 4-6;8-10.*
LEVEL: B LANG: Eng SIRC ARTICLE NO: 098252

TRAINING AND CONDITIONING

Coffin, T. Conditioning the novice and training level horse. *USCTA news (South Hamilton, Mass.) 13(3), Jun 1984, 6-7.*
LEVEL: B LANG: Eng SIRC ARTICLE NO: 098187

Coles, F. Helpful hints from a USET training session. *USCTA news (Hamilton, Ma.) 13(2), Apr 1984, 8-10.*
LEVEL: B LANG: En SIRC ARTICLE NO: 099712

Lieberman, B. A month in the life... Three horses, three sports, three programs. *Equus (Farmingdale, N.Y.) 79, May 1984, 28-29;33.*
LEVEL: B LANG: Eng SIRC ARTICLE NO: 099734

O'Connor, S. Starting the young event prospect over cavaletti. *USCTA news (Hamilton, Mass.) 13(6), Dec 1984, 6-9.*
LEVEL: LANG: Eng SIRC ARTICLE NO: 173392

TRAINING AND CONDITIONING - TRAINING CAMPS

Rodenas, P. Combined training. Linda Smith discusses combined training clinics. *Chronicle of the horse (Middleburg, Va.) 47(8), 24 Feb 1984, 10;12.*
LEVEL: B LANG: Eng SIRC ARTICLE NO: 098233

TOBOGGANING

Norman, G. Sledding: the short course to becoming a kid again. *Outside 9(1), Jan/Feb 1984, 61-62;69.*
LEVEL: B LANG: Eng SIRC ARTICLE NO: 093841

TOUCH FOOTBALL

STRATEGY - OFFENSIVE

Valeriote, S. A triple option offense for touch football. *Audible (Willowdale, Ont.) Summer 1984, 10-11.*
LEVEL: B LANG: E SIRC ARTICLE NO: 099610

TRACK AND FIELD

DeKunder, T. Marion track: a small school track program. *Texas coach 27(5), Feb 1984, 30-31.*
LEVEL: B LANG: Eng SIRC ARTICLE NO: 092459

Webb, E.J. Track and field at Borger High School. *Texas coach (Austin, Tex.) 28(2), Sept 1984, 43-45.*
LEVEL: B LANG: Eng SIRC ARTICLE NO: 106124

ADMINISTRATION

Holliday, C. Building, selling, and motivating championship track teams. *Coaching clinic (Englewood Cliffs, N.J.) 22(10), Jun 1984, 9-11.*
LEVEL: B LANG: Eng SIRC ARTICLE NO: 095373

AGED

Stones, M.J. Kozma, A. Longitudinal trends in track and field performances. *Experimental aging research (Bar Harbor, Mich.) 10(2), Summer 1984, 107-110.*
ABST: Longitudinal performances on age curves from 81 older, elite, male athletes were recorded over a mean period of 5.3 years in 6 different events. Attenuated decline for the earlier portion of the longitudinal span, due to the effects of accumulated training, was observed. The shape of the curves differed between the long jump and running events.
LEVEL: A LANG: Eng SIRC ARTICLE NO: 174151

ASSOCIATIONS

Dickie, D. Le syndicat des athletes deconcerte l'association. Athletes' union baffles association. *Champion (Vanier, Ont.) 8(2), May/mai 1984, 10-13.*
LEVEL: B LANG: Fr Eng SIRC ARTICLE NO: 095371

I.A.A.F. directory 1984. Repertoire F.I.A.A. 1984. London: International Amateur Athletic Federation, 1984. 57 p.
CORP: International Amateur Athletic Federation.
CORP: Federation internationale d'athletisme amateur.
NOTES: Cover title.
LEVEL: B LANG: Eng GV1060.5 18105

MacWilliam, T. Bedard, B. Alleyn, J. Canadian athletics annual 1983. Annuaire de l'athletisme canadienne. Ottawa, Ont.: Canadian Track & Field Association, c1984. vii, 159 p. : ill.
CORP: Canadian Track and Field Association.
CORP: Association canadienne d'athletisme.
LEVEL: B LANG: Eng Fr ISBN: 0919375-06-5 GV1060.65.C3 18736

Wigley, J.V. I.A.A.F. Bureau - London - Center of International Track and Field. *Pan athlete (San Juan, Puerto Rico) 2(6), 1984, 24-25.*
LEVEL: B LANG: Eng SIRC ARTICLE NO: 098607

BIBLIOGRAPHIES

Dales, G.G. A bibliography of theses and dissertations relating to track and field. *Track & field quarterly review (Kalamazoo, Mich.) 84(1), Spring 1984, 61-62.*
LEVEL: B LANG: Eng SIRC ARTICLE NO: 095484

BIOGRAPHY AND AUTOBIOGRAPHY

Babe Didrikson: the 'Texas Tornado' could do it all. *Sporting news (St. Louis) 198(4), 23 Jul 1984, Olympic special insert, 19;22.*
LEVEL: B LANG: Eng SIRC ARTICLE NO: 096923

Jesse Owens: he captured America's fancy at '36 games. *Sporting news (St. Louis) 198(4), 23 Jul 1984, Olympic special insert, 23-24.*
LEVEL: B LANG: Eng SIRC ARTICLE NO: 096929

Jim Thorpe: he always did - and always will - stand alone. *Sporting news (St. Louis) 198(4), 23 Jul 1984, Olympic special insert, 22-23.*
LEVEL: B LANG: Eng SIRC ARTICLE NO: 096930

McLean, J. The golden age of women's sport. (Fanny Rosenfeld; Ethel Catherwood) *Canadian runner (Toronto) May 1984, 26;29;38.*
LEVEL: B LANG: Eng SIRC ARTICLE NO: 094798

BIOMECHANICS

Morgan, W.R. Garrett, G.E. A developmental biomechanics instructional approach - learning basic track & field skills (ages 5-12). (Refs: 17)
CONF: National Symposium on Teaching Kinesiology and Biomechanics in Sports (2nd : 1984 : Colorado Springs).
NOTES: In, Shapiro, R. and Marett, J.R. (eds.), Proceedings: Second National Symposium on Teaching Kinesiology and Biomechanics in Sports, Colorado Springs, Colorado, January 12-14, Dekalb, Ill., AAHPERD, 1984, p. 97-104.
LEVEL: I LANG: Eng SIRC ARTICLE NO: 100491

CHILDREN

Dhellemmes, R. Reflexion sur les pratiques athletiques...comme contenu d'enseignement. 1re partie. (Refs: 12)*EPS: Revue education physique et sport (Paris) 188, juil/aout 1984, 24-29.*
LEVEL: B LANG: Fr SIRC ARTICLE NO: 098603

Dick, F.W. Coaching the young athlete. *Modern athlete and coach (Athelstone, Aust.) 22(1), Jan 1984, 25-27.*
NOTES: Based on extracts from the author's address to the Ontario Track and Field Association's symposium in Toronto, Canada.
LEVEL: B LANG: Eng SIRC ARTICLE NO: 095733

Handley, K. Peck, B. Is there life after age group? *Starting line (Reseda, Calif.) 13(75), Fall 1984, 3.*
LEVEL: B LANG: E SIRC ARTICLE NO: 173506

Hershey track and field: ongoing attention to fitness. *Parks & recreation (Alexandria, Va.) 19(6), Jun 1984, 46-47;67.*
LEVEL: B LANG: Eng SIRC ARTICLE NO: 095372

COACHING

Coach of the year: Tom Tellez. *Runner's world 19(1), Jan 1984, 36-37.*
LEVEL: B LANG: Eng SIRC ARTICLE NO: 091029

Collins, D. Coaching a championship high school track and field team. West Nyack, N.Y.: Parker Pub. Co., c1984. 230 p. : ill
NOTES: Includes index.
LEVEL: I LANG: Eng ISBN: 013138967X LC CARD: 83-019385 GV1060.675.C6 17466

Dick, F.W. Coaching in the club. *Athletics coach (Halesowen, England) 18(1), Mar 1984, 2-6.*
LEVEL: B LANG: Eng SIRC ARTICLE NO: 093842

Ehrler, W. Liebscher, C. Leichtathletik. Anleitung fuer den Uebungsleiter. Berlin: Sportverlag, 1984. (222) p. : ill.
NOTES Bibliography: p. (220)-(222).
LEVEL: I LANG: Ger GV1060.675.C6 18129

Johnson, C. Coaching - still an 'art'. *Track & field quarterly review (Kalamazoo, Mich.) 84(1), Spring 1984, 17-18.*
LEVEL B LANG: Eng SIRC ARTICLE NO: 095374

Larry Ellis talks Olympics: 'I think that nationalism is a positive element of the Olympics. It involves people who have done something for their country.' *Scholastic coach (New York) 53(9), Apr 1984, 38-39;41;84-85.*
LEVEL: B LANG: Eng SIRC ARTICLE NO: 095378

Launder, A. Coaching in Australia. *Modern athlete and coach (Athelstone, Aust.) 22(1), Jan 1984, 34-36.*
LEVEL: B LANG: En SIRC ARTICLE NO: 096932

Ward, I. The work of a national coach - 1962. *Athletics coach (London) 18(2), Jun 1984, 17-18.*
LEVEL: B LANG: Eng SIRC ARTICLE NO: 095383

INJURIES AND ACCIDENTS

Casselman, R. Track and field. *In, Adams, S.H. (ed.), et al., Catastrophic injuries in sports: avoidance strategies, Salinas, Calif., Cayote Press, c1984, p. 102-108.*
LEVEL: B LANG: Eng RD97 19088

Gaines, R. Track season brings strains, pains. Help prevent troublesome injuries with proper conditioning warm-up. *First aider (Gardner, Kan.) 53(5), Feb 1984, 1;4-5.*
LEVEL: B LANG: Eng SIRC ARTICLE NO: 096925

Grogan, D.P. Bobechko, W.P. Pathogenesis of a fracture of the distal femoral epiphysis. A case report. *Journal of bone and joint surgery (Boston) 66(4), Apr 1984, 621-622.*
LEVEL: I LANG: Eng SIRC ARTICLE NO: 101624

MEDICINE

Training supplies for track kits. *First aider (Gardner, Kan.) 53(5), Feb 1984, 7.*
LEVEL: B LANG: Eng SIRC ARTICLE NO: 09693

OFFICIATING

Hansen, L. Profile: Larry Houston. If it can be accomplished by a track and field arbiter, Larry Houston has probably done i *Referee (Franksville, Wis.) 9(7), Jul 1984, 25-28.*
LEVEL: B LANG: Eng SIRC ARTICLE NO: 101625

PHOTOGRAPHY

Chadez, D. Track & field photography. Part two: exposure & composition. *Starting line (Reseda, Calif.) 13(74), Summer 1984, 8-9.*
LEVEL: B LANG: Eng SIRC ARTICLE NO: 101622

Chadez, D. Track and field photography. Part one: equipment and film. *Starting line (Reseda, Calif.) 13(72), Spring 1984, 8.*
LEVEL: B LANG: Eng SIRC ARTICLE NO: 104934

PHYSIOLOGY

Hong, C.Z. Lien, I.N. Metabolic effects of exhaustive training of athletes. (Refs: 40)*Archives of physical medicine and rehabilitation (Chicago, Ill.) 65(7), Jul 1984, 362-365.*
ABST: Blood chemistries of elite track and field athletes (11 males and females) were compared before and after four weeks of exhaustive training. The authors observed 1) significant decrease of body weight, 2) no significant changes of resting and maximal heart rate, 3) significant increase in hematocrit, concentrations of serum free fatty acid, serum Na plus, serum glutamic - oxaloacetic transaminase, and significant decreases in the concentrations of blood glucose, total serum lipids, serum triglycerides, and cholesterol and, 4) no significant changes in serum phospholipids, serum glutamic - pyruvic transamimase, serum albumen, serum globulin, serum C1-, and serum creatinine.
LEVEL: A LANG: Eng SIRC ARTICLE NO: 096927

PHYSIOLOGY - MUSCLE

Kuznetsov, S.P. Koryak, U.A. Kosheleva, L.A. Speed and speed-strength properties of muscles and their relationship to beginning track and field athletes. (Condensed) *Soviet sports review (Escondido, Calif.) 19(1), Mar 1984, 26-29.*
NOTES: Translated from, Teoriya i praktika fizicheskoi kultury 6, 1979, 37-39.
LEVEL: I LANG: Eng SIRC ARTICLE NO: 095377

Thorland, W.G. Tharp, G.D. Johnson, G.O. Cisar, G.J. Housh, T.J. Isokinetic leg flexion and extension strength of elite adolescent female track and field athletes. (Refs: 25)*Research quarterly for exercise and sport (Reston, Va.) 55(4), Dec 1984, 347-350.*
ABST: Sixty-two elite adolescent female track and field athletes volunteered to be measured isokinetically for peak torque of the leg flexors and extensors. The sample included 16 throwers, 11 jumpers, 12 middle-distance runners, and 23 sprinters. Scheffe post-hoc comparisons showed that, for absolute leg extension strength, throwers were stronger than middle-distance runners (by 54.4 per cent), sprinters (35.6 per cent), and jumpers (23.6 per cent). For absolute leg flexion movements, throwers were stronger than middle distance runners (37.4 per cent) and sprinters (32.1 per cent). Jumpers had greater extension peak torque values than middle-distance runners relative to body weight (14.0 per cent), and throwers were stronger than middle-distance runners for extension/lean body weight (14.9 per cent). No other comparisons were significant. However, when strength was expressed relative to body weight and lean body weight, there were few differences between events for flexion or extension.
LEVEL: A LANG: Eng SIRC ARTICLE NO: 104943

PSYCHOLOGY

Heazlewood, I. Sport psychology in track and field. (Refs: 21)*Modern athlete and coach (Athelstone, Aust.) 22(2), Apr 1984, 11-14.*
LEVEL: I LANG: Eng SIRC ARTICLE NO: 096327

Poole, R.C. Henschen, K. Brigham Young's psychological program for women's cross-country and track. (Refs: 9)*Scholastic coach 53(8), Mar 1984, 52-53;73-75.*
LEVEL: B LANG: Eng SIRC ARTICLE NO: 093848

Ross, R. Psychological preparation for high-level track competition. *Scholastic coach 53(7), Feb 1984, 54-55;73-74.*
LEVEL B LANG: Eng SIRC ARTICLE NO: 093849

RULES AND REGULATIONS

How the game is played. *Women's sports (San Francisco) 6(6), Jun 1984, 34-36.*
LEVEL: B LANG: Eng SIRC ARTICLE NO: 104937

SAFETY

Simpson, S. For a safe track meet, plan ahead. *First aider (Gardner, Kan.) 53(5), Feb 1984, 6.*
LEVEL: B LANG: Eng SIRC ARTICLE NO: 096936

SOCIAL PSYCHOLOGY

Groseclose, B. Motivating track and field athletes. *Texas coach (Austin, Tex.) 28(2), Sept 1984, 46-48.*
LEVEL: B LANG: En SIRC ARTICLE NO: 106120

Launder, A. Let us retain our champions. *Modern athlete and coach (Athelstone, Aust.) 22(4), Oct 1984, 34-35.*
LEVEL: B LANG: Eng SIRC ARTICLE NO: 104939

SPORTING EVENTS

Bedard, B. Palmason, D. Brockington, C. Cournoyer, M. Whiting, K. 1984 Canadian track and field team guide. Guide de l'equip canadienne d'athletisme. Ottawa: Canadian Track and Field Association, 1984. 74 p.
CORP: Canadian Track and Field Association.
CORP: Association canadienne d'athletisme.
LEVEL: B LANG: Eng Fr ISBN: 0-919375-04-9 GV1060.65.C3 17692

Coaching and preparation of the olympic team. *Athletics coach (London) 18(4), Dec 1984, 5-17.*
LEVEL: B LANG: Eng SIRC ARTICLE NO: 104935

Lucas, J. The greatest gathering of olympians: an historical flashback. *Olympian (Colorado Springs, Colo.) 9(2), Jul/Aug 1984, 6-8.*
LEVEL: B LANG: Eng SIRC ARTICLE NO: 104940

MacWilliam, T. Commentary. Commentaire. *Track & field journal (Ottawa) 28, Nov 1984, 2-3.*
LEVEL: B LANG: Eng Fr SIRC ARTICLE NO: 103539

U.K. performance analysis. *Athletics coach (London) 18(4), Dec 1984, 3-4.*
LEVEL: B LANG: Eng SIRC ARTICLE NO: 104944

STATISTICS AND RECORDS

Epstein, S.H. World records: the limits of human performance. *In, Schrier, E.W. and Allman, W.F. (eds.), Newton at the bat: the science in sports, New York, Scribner, c1984, p. 123-127.*
LEVEL: B LANG: Eng RC1235 18609

Gupta, R.K. Bhatnagar, S. Camparison (sic) of national athletic records of three leading Asian countries in track and field events over a decade. (Refs: 6)*SNIPES journal (Patiala, India) 7(4), Oct 1984, 22-31.*
ABST: The authors compared the improvements of national track and field records of Japan, China, and Indian between 1972 and 1983.
LEVEL: A LANG: Eng SIRC ARTICLE NO: 171612

Jokl, E. The future of athletic records. (Refs: 20)*Track & field quarterly review (Kalamazoo, Mich.) 84(1), Spring 1984, 5-16.*
LEVEL: I LANG: Eng SIRC ARTICLE NO: 095375

Jokl, E. Future of athletic records. *Running & fitness (Washington, D.C.) 16(2), Apr 1984, 1;10-11.*
LEVEL: B LANG: Eng SIRC ARTICLE NO: 098604

King, H.A. Black, D.G. Analysis of Olympic and world records in track and field and swimming: past, present, and future. (Refs: 29)
NOTES: In, Carter, J.E.L. (ed.), Physical structure of Olympic athletes. Part II. Kinanthropometry of Olympic athletes, Basel, Karger, c1984, p. 212-230.
LEVEL: A LANG: Eng RC1235 12672

Olszewski, R. Technically speaking: Canada vs the world. *Athletics (Willowdale, Ont.) Jun 1984, 40;52.*
LEVEL: B LANG: Eng SIRC ARTICLE NO: 098605

TESTING AND EVALUATION

Sitler, S.E. Peak torque and subsequent strength ratios about the knee determined isokinetically among track and field athletes. Eugene, Ore.: Microform Publications, University of Oregon, 1984. 2 microfiches : negative, ill. ; 11 x 15 cm.
NOTES: Thesis (M.S.) - University of Kansas, 1981; (xiv, 136 leaves); appendix J ommitted; includes bibliography.
LEVEL: A LANG: Eng UO84 407-408

Sohi, A.S. Relationship between performance in propulsive cyclic and acyclic activities in track and field. (Refs: 9)*Asian journal of physical education (Taipei, Taiwan) 7(3), Oct 1984, 72-79.*
ABST: A random sample of 50 boys aged 10-11 were tested performing a 40 metre sprint, the standing long jump and the vertical jump. This study provides relationships between these activities and provides clues as to concomitants and adjuncts in training and talent identification in track and field.
LEVEL: A LANG: Eng SIRC ARTICLE NO: 103540

Stones, M.J. Kozma, A. Longitudinal trends in track and field performances. (Refs: 16)*Experimental aging research (Bar Harbour, Mich.) 10(2), 1984, 107-110.*
LEVEL: A LANG: Eng SIRC ARTICLE NO: 104942

Whitby, D. The use of black and white photography. (Refs: 1)*Athletics coach (Halesowen, England) 18(1), Mar 1984, 6-8.*
LEVEL: B LANG: Eng SIRC ARTICLE NO: 093852

TRAINING AND CONDITIONING

Green, D. Off season program for track and field. *Texas coach (Austin, Tex.) 28(4), Nov 1984, 51.*
LEVEL: B LANG: Eng SIRC ARTICLE NO: 173446

Kachaev, S.V. Methods of developing speed-strength (explosiveness) in young track and field athletes. *Soviet sports review (Escondido, Calif.) 19(1), Mar 1984, 44-48.*
NOTES: Translated from, Teoriya i praktika fizicheskoi kultury 8, 1982, 32-34.
LEVEL: I LANG: Eng SIRC ARTICLE NO: 095376

Lynch, R.L. Winning at track and field. *Coaching clinic (Princeton, N.J.) 22(9), May 1984, 13-14.*
LEVEL: B LANG: Eng SIRC ARTICLE NO: 095379

Maccolini, J. The multi-event intra-squad track meet: a practice alternative. *Coaching clinic 22(7),*

Mar 1984, 10-12.
LEVEL: B LANG: Eng SIRC ARTICLE NO: 093845

Sitz, J.K. Bounding beyond strength to power (bound for success). *Track and field quarterly review (Kalamazoo, Mich.) 84(4) Winter 1984, 40-42.*
LEVEL: B LANG: Eng SIRC ARTICLE NO: 101626

Verkhoshansky, Y. Modeling the training: in speed-strength events. *Soviet sports review (Escondido, Calif.) 19(3), Sept 1984, 130-135.*
NOTES: Translated from, Legkaya atletika 9, 1980, 10-11.
LEVEL: I LANG: Eng SIRC ARTICLE NO: 102961

TRAINING AND CONDITIONING - WEIGHT AND STRENGTH TRAINING

Crossley, G. Megacircuits: an alternative to strength training. (Refs: 1)*Technical bulletin - Ontario Track and Field Association (Willowdale, Ont.) 43, Fall 1984, 1-3.*
LEVEL: B LANG: Eng SIRC ARTICLE NO: 102940

Marks, M. Weight training for track and field. *Track & field quarterly review (Kalamazoo, Mich.) 84(1), Spring 1984, 57-58.*
CONF: Olympic Development Coaches' Clinic (1978 : Colorado Springs).
LEVEL: B LANG: Eng SIRC ARTICLE NO: 095380

WOMEN

Levy, M. All-time greats. *Women's sports (San Francisco) 6(6), Jun 1984, 37-40.*
LEVEL: B LANG: Eng SIRC ARTICLE NO: 10451

Tenisci, T. Women at the olympics. *S.A. atleet/ athlete (Pretoria, S.A.) 11(4), Mar 1984, 4;12-13;20.*
NOTES: This article is reprinted from, Women's track world, Mar 1981.
LEVEL: B LANG: Eng SIRC ARTICLE NO: 171574

TRACK AND FIELD - JUMPING

AUDIO VISUAL MATERIAL

Mahon, T. Videotaping the field events. The video recorder provides an effective, cost-efficient coaching aid. *Athletic journal 64(8), Mar 1984, 48;68-69.*
LEVEL: B LANG: Eng SIRC ARTICLE NO: 093860

BIBLIOGRAPHIES

Dales, G.G. A bibliography of theses and dissertations related to track and field. *Track and field quarterly review (Kalamazoo, Mich.) 84(4), Winter 1984, 43-45.*
LEVEL: B LANG: Eng SIRC ARTICLE NO: 101631

Sport bibliography. *Track and field journal (Ottawa) 28, Nov 1984, 34-36.*
LEVEL: B LANG: Eng SIRC ARTICLE NO: 103550

SPORTING EVENTS

Jumps. *Athletics coach (London) 18(4), Dec 1984, 45-51.*
LEVEL: B LANG: Eng SIRC ARTICLE NO: 104948

TECHNIQUES AND SKILLS

Tellez, T. The jumping events. *Track and field quarterly review (Kalamazoo, Mich.) 84(4), Winter 1984, 5-6.*
NOTES: Presented at the NCAA Division 1 Indoor Track Coaches' Clinic, Syracuse University, March 1984.
LEVEL: B LANG: Eng SIRC ARTICLE NO: 101648

Young, W. Marino, W. The takeoff in the long and triple jumps. (Refs: 13)*Modern athlete and coach (Athelstone, Aust.) 22(4) Oct 1984, 11-14.*
LEVEL: I LANG: Eng SIRC ARTICLE NO: 104954

TESTING AND EVALUATION

Bosco, C. Zanon, S. Rusko, H. Dal Monte, A. Bellotti, P. Latteri, F. Candeloro, N. Locatelli, E. Azzaro, E. Pozzo, R. Bonomi, S. The influence of extra load on the mechanical behavior of skeletal muscle. (Refs: 31)*European journal of applied physiology and occupational physiology (Berlin, W.G.) 53(2), 1984, 149-154.*
ABST: Eleven international jumpers and throwers engaged in year round training were divided into experimental and control groups. The experimental group was tested before and after a 3 weeks simulated hypergravity period. The high gravity condition was created by wearing a vest weighing about 13 per cent of the subjects body weight. Vertical jumps, drop jumps and a 15 s continuous jumping test were used to measure the explosive power characteristics of the subjects. After the hypergravity period the experimental subjects demonstrated significant improvements in most of the variables studied: however, 4 weeks after cessation of the high gravity period they tended to return towards the starting values.
LEVEL: A LANG: Eng SIRC ARTICLE NO: 104945

TRAINING AND CONDITIONING

Mekhonoshin, S.A. Jumping power for the young. *Modern athlete and coach (Athelstone, Aust.) 22(2), Apr 1984, 31-32.*
NOTES A series of exercises extracted from Mekhonashin's power development program published in Physical Culture for School, U.S.S.R., 9, 1980.
LEVEL: B LANG: Eng SIRC ARTICLE NO: 096944

von Arx, F. Comment ameliorer la force specifique des sauteurs? *Macolin (Suisse) 7, juil 1984, 4-10.*
LEVEL: B LANG: Fr SIRC ARTICLE NO: 101649

TRACK AND FIELD - THROWING

AUDIO VISUAL MATERIAL

Mahon, T. Videotaping the field events. The video recorder provides an effective, cost-efficient coaching aid. *Athletic journal 64(8), Mar 1984, 48;68-69.*
LEVEL: B LANG: Eng SIRC ARTICLE NO: 093860

BIBLIOGRAPHIES

Dales, G.G. A bibliography of theses and dissertations relating to track and field. *Track & field quarterly review (Kalamazoo, Mich.) 84(1), Spring 1984, 61-62.*
LEVEL: B LANG: Eng SIRC ARTICLE NO: 095484

Sport bibliography. *Track and field journal (Ottawa) 26, May 1984, 32-36.*
LEVEL: B LANG: Eng Fr SIRC ARTICLE NO: 098720

BIOMECHANICS

Biomechanical analysis of the hammer. *Thrower (West Midlands, Eng.) 28, Feb 1984, 4-9.*
LEVEL: I LANG: Eng SIRC ARTICLE NO: 095480

COACHING

Miller, B. Anthropomaximology and the throws coach. *Thrower (West Midlands, Eng.) 31, Dec 1984, 52-53.*
LEVEL: B LANG: Eng SIRC ARTICLE NO: 173501

Stewart, J. Even when no one is watching. *Athletic journal (Evanston, Ill.) 65(2), Sept 1984, 32-33.*
LEVEL: B LANG: Eng SIRC ARTICLE NO: 100112

HISTORY

Tanner, G. The development of athletic throwing - part 1. *Thrower (West Midlands, Eng.) 30, Aug 1984, 14-18.*
NOTES: To be continued in next issue.
LEVEL: B LANG: Eng SIRC ARTICLE NO: 098721

PSYCHOLOGY

Jones, M. Coming good - on the day. *Thrower (West Midlands, Eng.) 30, Aug 1984, 8-12.*
LEVEL: B LANG: Eng SIRC ARTICLE NO: 098711

PSYCHOLOGY - MENTAL TRAINING

Jones, M. Coming good - on the day. *Athletics coach (London) 18(2), Jun 1984, 29-30.*
LEVEL: B LANG: Eng SIRC ARTICLE NO: 095491

SPORTING EVENTS

Throws. *Athletics coach (London) 18(4), Dec 1984, 52-60.*
LEVEL: B LANG: Eng SIRC ARTICLE NO: 105047

STATISTICS AND RECORDS

Hodge, I. World age bests. *Thrower (West Midlands, Eng.) 29, May 1984, 30.*
LEVEL: B LANG: Eng SIRC ARTICLE NO: 098707

TEACHING

The test of equivalence. *Track & field quarterly review (Kalamazoo, Mich.) 84(1), Spring 1984, 50-53.*
NOTES: Translated by, Kevin McGill from, Amicale des entraineurs francais d'athletisme.
LEVEL: I LANG: Eng SIRC ARTICLE NO: 095505

TECHNIQUES AND SKILLS

Bosen, K.O. Latest material on throwing events shot-put, hammer, javelin, discus. *Athletic Asia (Patiala, India) 13(2), Sep 1984, 10-22.*
LEVEL: I LANG: Eng SIRC ARTICLE NO: 106212

Jones, M. Trends in throws. *Athletics coach (London) 18(3), Sept 1984, 12.*
LEVEL: B LANG: Eng SIRC ARTICLE NO: 100111

TESTING AND EVALUATION

Bosco, C. Zanon, S. Rusko, H. Dal Monte, A. Bellotti, P. Latteri, F. Candeloro, N. Locatelli, E. Azzaro, E. Pozzo, R. Bonomi, S. The influence of extra load on the mechanical behavior of skeletal muscle. (Refs: 31)*European journal of applied physiology and occupational physiology (Berlin, W.G.) 53(2), 1984, 149-154.*
ABST: Eleven international jumpers and throwers engaged in year round training were divided into experimental and control groups. The experimental group was tested before and after a 3 weeks simulated hypergravity period. The high gravity condition was created by wearing a vest weighing about 13 per cent of the subjects body weight. Vertical jumps, drop jumps and a 15 s continuous jumping test were used to measure the explosive power characteristics of the subjects. After the hypergravity period the experimental subjects demonstrated significant improvements in most of the variables studied; however, 4 weeks after cessation of the high gravity period they tended to return towards the starting values.
LEVEL: A LANG: Eng SIRC ARTICLE NO: 104945

Jones, M. Test quadathlon. *Thrower (West Midlands, Eng.) 30, Aug 1984, 29-32.*
LEVEL: B LANG: Eng SIRC ARTICLE NO: 098712

Komarova, A. Ruderman, G. Selection of young throwers. *Modern athlete and coach (Athelstone, Aust.) 22(1), Jan 1984, 9-11.*
NOTES: Translated and condensed from, Legkaya Atletika 4, 1983.
LEVEL: I LANG: Eng SIRC ARTICLE NO: 097026

TRAINING AND CONDITIONING

Chabrier, M. L'entrainement des lanceurs: un cycle de 6 semaines. *EPS: Education physique et sport (Paris, France) 186, mars/avr 1984, 58-60.*
LEVEL: B LANG: Fr SIRC ARTICLE NO: 095483

Goriot, G. La pedagogie des lancers. *Revue de l'Amicale des entraineurs francais d'athletisme (Paris) 87, avr/mai/juin 1984 27-30.*
LEVEL: B LANG: Fr SIRC ARTICLE NO: 097024

Ionesco, T. La philosophie de la premiere sortie (chez les lanceurs). *Track and field journal (Ottawa) 26, May 1984, 16;21.*
LEVEL: B LANG: Fr SIRC ARTICLE NO: 098708

TRAINING AND CONDITIONING - CIRCUIT TRAINING

Jones, M. Preventing injuries. *Thrower (West Midlands, Eng.) 30, Aug 1984, 4-7.*
LEVEL: B LANG: Eng SIRC ARTICLE NO: 09871

TRAINING AND CONDITIONING - DRILLS

Pedemonte, J. Teaching the throws via 'imitative drills'. *Scholastic coach 53(7), Feb 1984, 44-45.*
LEVEL: B LANG: Eng SIR ARTICLE NO: 093971

TRAINING AND CONDITIONING - WEIGHT AND STRENGTH TRAINING

Bielik, E. Diagonal-rotational strength training for the trunk: a track and field throwers' program. *National Strength & Conditioning Association journal 6(1), Feb/Mar 1984, 36-37;45-49.*
LEVEL: B LANG: Eng SIRC ARTICLE NO: 093968

Egger, J.P. La musculation dans la planification annuelle de l'entrainement des lanceurs. (Refs: 3)*Macolin (Suisse) 6, juin 1984, 9-11.*
LEVEL: B LANG: Fr SIRC ARTICLE NO: 103626

Pedemonte, J. Specific strength in throwing events. *Thrower (West Midlands, Eng.) 28, Feb 1984, 15-20.*
LEVEL: I LANG: Eng SIRC ARTICLE NO: 095498

TRAINING AND CONDITIONING

Condor, B. Computerfit: technology helps you train. *Bicycling (Emmaus, Pa.) 25(9), Nov/Dec 1984, 14-16;18-19.*
LEVEL: B LANG: Eng SIRC ARTICLE NO: 101023

Elson, P.R. How to make your off-season sport work for you. *Sport-talk (Toronto) 13(2), May 1984, 4-5.*
LEVEL: B LANG: Eng SIRC ARTICLE NO: 097880

Jerome, J. The high-tech workout: training by computer. *Outside 9(1), Jan/Feb 1984, 25-26;28.*
LEVEL: B LANG: Eng SIRC ARTICLE NO: 093241

O'Callaghan, C. Sport and the 10 S's. *Grasp (Leicestershire, Eng.) 3(4/5), Mar/Apr 1984, 2-4.*
NOTES: Reprinted from, Coaching today.
LEVEL: B LANG: Eng SIRC ARTICLE NO: 173118

TRAINING CAMPS

1984 Camp guide and scholarship program by the Women's Sports Foundation. *Women's sports (Palo Alto, Calif.) 6(4), Apr 1984, 57;59-63;66-71.*
LEVEL: B LANG: Eng SIRC ARTICLE NO: 101037

Moffit, D. Olympic training centers: a first for the U.S. *Journal of physical education, recreation & dance (Reston, Va.) 55(4), Apr 1984, 16;28.*
ABST: The United States first Olympic Training Centre was opened in 1977 in Squaw Valley. Due to the remoteness of this location it was closed in 1980 in favour of new expanded facilities in Colorado Springs. This center can house and feed 500 athletes at any one time training in all Olympic events. It is interesting to note though that less than 10 per cent of the athletes who train and compete here are considered elite level. This article provides further details about the center's facilities and also looks at the newer facility at Lake Placid, New York.
LEVEL: B LANG: Eng SIRC ARTICLE NO: 094780

TRAINING THEORY

Dick, F. Trends in training theory. *Athletics coach (London) 18(3), Sept 1984, 22-29.*
LEVEL: I LANG: Eng SIRC ARTICLE NO: 099349

Nesbitt, R. Periodization: a coach's example. Coaches have to understand their sport's physical demands, in addition to its psychological, tactical and technical aspects, before they can properly plan an annual training program. *Coaching review (Ottawa, Ont.) 7, May/Jun 1984, 16-18.*
LEVEL: B LANG: Eng SIRC ARTICLE NO: 094781

Newman, S. Tudor Bompa: the untapped wealth of an international sport genius. *Coaching review (Ottawa, Ont.) 7, May/Jun 1984, 8-14.*
LEVEL: B LANG: Eng SIRC ARTICLE NO: 094782

Verkhoshansky, Y. Modeling the training: in speed-strength events. *Soviet sports review (Escondido, Calif.) 19(3), Sept 1984, 130-135.*
NOTES: Translated from, Legkaya atletika 9, 1980, 10-11.
LEVEL: I LANG: Eng SIRC ARTICLE NO: 102961

TRAINING METHODS

Baughman, M. Takaha, M. Tellez, T. Sprint training. *National Strength & Conditioning Association journal (Lincoln, Neb.) 6(3), Jun/Jul 1984, 34-36;66.*
LEVEL: B LANG: Eng SIRC ARTICLE NO: 096441

Freischlag, J. Freischlag, S. Winning with speed training. *Coaching clinic (Princeton, N.J.) 23(1), Sept 1984, 8-11.*
LEVEL: B LANG: Eng SIRC ARTICLE NO: 099353

Goodger, M.J. Training methods: getting ready for the season. (Refs: 4)*Coaching review 7, Mar/Apr 1984, 54-56.*
LEVEL: B LANG: Eng SIRC ARTICLE NO: 093240

Holland, R.G. Speed training. A new device - the sprint master - helps improve towing as a method of speed training. (Refs: *Athletic journal 64(7), Feb 1984, 50-51.*
LEVEL: B LANG: Eng SIRC ARTICLE NO: 091883

Improving jumping ability. *National Strength & Conditioning Association journal (Lincoln, Neb.) 6(2), Apr/May 1984, 10-20.*
LEVEL: I LANG: Eng SIRC ARTICLE NO: 094774

Klinzing, J. Improving sprint speed for all athletes. *National Strength & Conditioning Association journal (Lincoln, Neb.) 6(4), Aug/Sept 1984, 32-33.*
LEVEL: B LANG: Eng SIRC ARTICLE NO: 099356

McKeag, D. Training guidelines. *Spotlight on youth sports (East Lansing, Mich.) 7(4), Winter 1984, 2.*
NOTES: Reprinted from, Lansing State Journal, 26 Apr 1981. Seventh in a series of articles on sports medicine.
LEVEL: B LANG: Eng SIRC ARTICLE NO: 108877

Methodes et types d'entrainement. (Refs: 18)*Revue de l'entraineur (Montreal) juil/sept 1984, 13-22.*
LEVEL: I LANG: Fr SIRC ARTICLE NO: 102953

Vaz, K. Cross training: the winning combination. *Slimmer (Santa Monica, Calif.) 4(6), Oct 1984, 66-68;76.*
LEVEL: B LANG: Eng SIRC ARTICLE NO: 173240

TRAINING METHODS (continued)

AEROBIC TRAINING

Aerobic training in power sports. *National Strength & Conditioning Association journal (Lincoln, Neb.) 6(5), Oct/Nov 1984, 10-19.*
LEVEL: I LANG: Eng SIRC ARTICLE NO: 102935

Avoid cold weather layoffs with in-home aerobic training. *Ontario water skier (Willowdale, Ont.) 11(4), Winter 1984, 32-33.*
NOTES: Reproduced from, Fitness bulletin.
LEVEL: B LANG: Eng SIRC ARTICLE NO: 173334

Pavlovic, B. Une nouvelle culture physique: l'aerobic. Paris: Amphora, c1984. 167 p. : ill. (Sports & loisirs.)
LEVEL: B LANG: Fr ISBN: 2-85180-071-X GV481 17484

ANAEROBIC TRAINING

Brook, N.D. Current trends in endurance training. *Athletics coach (London) 18(2), Jun 1984, 18-24.*
LEVEL: I LANG: Eng SIR ARTICLE NO: 094767

Hale, T. Kox, W. Murrie, D. Athlete and the specificity of training: maximal oxygen uptake, the endurance. (Refs: 5) *Athletics coach (London) 18(2), Jun 1984, 25-26.*
LEVEL: I LANG: Eng SIRC ARTICLE NO: 094771

CIRCUIT TRAINING

Thompson, D.C. Obstacle courses. *Texas coach (Austin, Tex.) 28(1), Aug 1984, 46-48.*
LEVEL: B LANG: Eng SIRC ARTICLE NO: 102960

INTERVAL TRAINING

Daniels, J. Scardina, N. Interval training and performance. (Refs: 12)*Sports medicine (Auckland, N.Z.) 1(4), Jul/Aug 1984, 327-334.*
LEVEL: I LANG: Eng SIRC ARTICLE NO: 102941

Jerome, J. Fascinating rhythms: interval training makes every moment count. *Outside (Chicago, Ill.) 9(3), Apr 1984, 29-30.*
LEVEL: B LANG: Eng SIRC ARTICLE NO: 099354

RITE: the easy, efficient way to exercise. (rhythmic interval training exercise) *Executive fitness newsletter (Emmaus, Pa.) 15(18), 1 Sept 1984, 1-2.*
LEVEL: B LANG: Eng SIRC ARTICLE NO: 102957

PLYOMETRIC TRAINING

Adams, T.M. An investigation of selected plyometric training exercises on muscular leg strength and power. (Refs: 12)*Track and field quarterly review (Kalamazoo, Mich.) 84(4), Winter 1984, 36-39.*
LEVEL: I LANG: Eng SIRC ARTICLE NO: 101020

Chu, D. Plyometric exercise. *National Strength & Conditioning Association journal 5(6), Jan 1984, 56-59;61-63.*
LEVEL: B LANG: Eng SIRC ARTICLE NO: 090410

Chu, D.A. Plummer, L. The language of plyometrics. *National Strength & Conditioning Association journal (Lincoln, Neb.) 6(5), Oct/Nov 1984, 30-31.*
LEVEL: B LANG: Eng SIRC ARTICLE NO: 102938

Jones, J. Plyometrics: light weights for quick results. *New body (New York) 3(3), May 1984, 28-32.*
LEVEL: B LANG: Eng SIR ARTICLE NO: 099355

STRENGTH TRAINING

Ankle weights: handle with care. *Executive fitness newsletter (Emmaus, Pa.) 15(15), 21 Jul 1984, 4.*
LEVEL: B LANG: Eng SIRC ARTICLE NO: 102399

Babish, G. Use volunteers to monitor strength-training programs. *Journal of physical education and program (Columbus, Oh.) 81(4), Apr 1984, D11-D12.*
LEVEL: B LANG: Eng SIRC ARTICLE NO: 094766

Baechle, T.R. Women in resistance training. (Refs: 53)*Clinics in sports medicine (Philadelphia) 3(4), Oct 1984, 791-808.*
NOTES: Symposium on the athletic woman.
ABST: This article presents a factual and revealing analysis of the values of resistance training for female athletes. Discussions on training principles, equipment, and exercise prescription, including special considerations for women, provide a comprehensive approach to this topic.
LEVEL: A LANG: Eng SIRC ARTICLE NO: 101038

Bell, E. The start of the demise of athletics. *Texas coach (Austin, Tex.) 28(2), Sept 1984, 20-21.*
LEVEL: B LANG: Eng SIR ARTICLE NO: 105609

Berger, R.A. Introduction to weight training. Englewood Cliffs, N.J.: Prentice-Hall, c1984. xii, 179 p. : ill.
NOTES: Includes bibliographical references and index.
LEVEL: B LANG: Eng ISBN: 0135007453 LC CARD: 83-019204 GV546.5 17140

Bielik, E. The speed-strength macrocycle with specialized exercises for volleyball, softball and sprinting. *National Strength & Conditioning Association journal (Lincoln, Neb.) 6(5), Oct/Nov 1984, 56-59.*
LEVEL: B LANG: Eng SIRC ARTICLE NO: 102936

Buffier, M. Charge libre ou guidee? *Sante et sport (Paris) 215, fevr 1984, 22-25.*
LEVEL: B LANG: Fr SIRC ARTICLE NO: 0993

Christie, B. Strength training. *In, Adams, S.H. (ed.), et al., Catastrophic injuries in sports: avoidance strategies, Salinas, Calif., Cayote Press, c1984, p. 16-21.*
LEVEL: B LANG: Eng RD97 19088

Coaches roundtable: the squat and its application to athletic performance. *National Strength & Conditioning Association journal (Lincoln, Neb) 6(3), Jun/Jul 1984, 10-22;68.*
LEVEL: B LANG: Eng SIRC ARTICLE NO: 096442

Connelly, L. Woodworth, W. Lean & firm: the no-nonsense Nautilus and universal body shaping program. New York: Putnam Pub. Group, 1984. 1v.
LEVEL: B LANG: Eng ISBN: 0399510745 LC CARD: 84-020785

Curry, L. Body sculpting & design: a capsulized program. *Strength & health (York, Pa.) 52(5), Aug/Sept 1984, 49-52.*
LEVEL B LANG: Eng SIRC ARTICLE NO: 173478

Darden, E. The Nautilus handbook for young athletes. New York: Wanderer Books, c1984. 128 p. : ill.
LEVEL: B LANG: Eng ISBN 0671496883 LC CARD: 83-026029 GV546.5 17471

Darden, E. Building bigger arms: building larger and stronger muscles requires harder, briefer exercise. *Athletic journal (Evanston, Ill.) 64(10), May 1984, 10;58.*
LEVEL: B LANG: Eng SIRC ARTICLE NO: 094768

De Koning, F.L. Binkhorst, R.A. Vissers, A.C.A. Vos, J.A. The influence of static strength training on the force-velocity relationship of the arm flexors of 16-year-old boys. (Refs: 7)
CONF: Symposium of Paediatric Work Physiology (10th : 1981 : Joutsa, Finland).
NOTES: In, Ilmarinen, J. and Vaelimaeki, I. (eds.), Children and sport: paediatric work physiology, Berlin, Springer-Verlag, 1984, p. 201-205.
LEVEL: A LANG: Eng SIRC ARTICLE NO: 102767

Diange, J. Developing maximum strength with maximum intensity. *Scholastic coach 53(8), Mar 1984, 14;16;75-76.*
LEVEL: B LANG: Eng SIRC ARTICLE NO: 093239

Elder, G. Strength training methods: system critique 5 - cycling. *Muscular development (York, Pa.) 21(5), Sept/Oct 1984, 43;56-58.*
LEVEL: B LANG: Eng SIRC ARTICLE NO: 173295

Elder, G.E. The 5x5 method system critique 3. *Muscular development (York, Pa.) 21(3), May/Jun 1984, 29;56.*
LEVEL: B LANG Eng SIRC ARTICLE NO: 101026

Everson, J.M. Nagle, F. The twin study: variable resistance vs isotonic weight training in monozygotic male twins. (Refs: 24) *Powerlifting U.S.A. (Camarillo, Calif.) 7(7), Feb 1984, 5-8.*
LEVEL: I LANG: Eng SIRC ARTICLE NO: 094769

Foran, B. Uebel, R. Strength development in Germany. (Refs: 7)*National Strength & Conditioning Association journal (Lincoln Neb.) 6(3), Jun/Jul 1984, 50-51;59-60.*
LEVEL: I LANG: Eng SIRC ARTICLE NO: 096445

Fowler, J.A. Progressive resisted exercise. (Refs: 31)*Physiotherapy in sport (Kent, Eng.) 7(1), Spring 1984, 2-8.*
LEVEL: LANG: Eng SIRC ARTICLE NO: 099352

Friedman, M.J. Nicholas, J.A. Conditioning and rehabilitation. (Refs: 34)
NOTES: In, Scott, W.N. (ed.) et al., Principles of sports medicine, Baltimore, Williams & Wilkins, c1984, p. 396-402.
LEVEL: I LANG: Eng RC1210 18016

Fuller, J. White House symposium deals with strength and training. *Journal of physical education and program (Columbus, Oh. 81(4), Apr 1984, D10-D11.*
LEVEL: B LANG: Eng SIRC ARTICLE NO: 094770

Garhammer, J. Power clean: kinesiological evaluation. (Refs: 8)*National Strength & Conditioning Association journal (Lincoln, Neb.) 6(3), Jun/Jul 1984, 40;61-63.*
LEVEL: I LANG: Eng SIRC ARTICLE NO: 096446

Gates, R.D. Muscles by micro. The computerized exercise machine has added a sophisticated dimension to strength training. *Coaching review 7, Jan/Feb 1984, 20-23.*
LEVEL: I LANG: Eng SIRC ARTICLE NO: 091880

Glickstein, E. Computer-age weight lifting: trainer created software to match his program. *Athletic business (Madison, Wis. 8(3), Mar 1984, 52-53.*
LEVEL: B LANG: Eng SIRC ARTICLE NO: 175926

Gotshalk, L. Analysis of the deadlift. *National Strength & Conditioning Association journal (Lincoln, Neb.) 6(6), Jan 1985, 4-5;74-76;78.*
LEVEL: B LANG: Eng SIRC ARTICLE NO: 102943

Hatfield, F.C. High-tech equipment: which shapes your body best? *Shape (Woodland Hills, Calif.) 3(5), Jan 1984, 46-56;104.*
LEVEL: B LANG: Eng SIRC ARTICLE NO: 097488

Hatfield, F.C. Krotee, M.L. Personalized weight training for fitness and athletics: from theory to practice. 2nd ed. Dubuque Iowa: Kendall/Hunt Pub. Co., c1984. x, 191 p. : ill.
NOTES: Bibliography: p. 188-191.
LEVEL: B LANG: Eng ISBN: 084033219X LC CARD: 83-082908

Hemba, G.D. Why not use 1(RM)s in strength training? *Scholastic coach (New York) 53(10), May/Jun 1984, 20.*
LEVEL: B LANG: Eng SIRC ARTICLE NO: 094772

Henderson, A. An introduction to isokinetics. (Refs: 6)*Remedial gymnastics and recreational therapy (Manchester, Eng.) 112, May 1984, 13-15.*
LEVEL: B LANG: Eng SIRC ARTICLE NO: 101029

Hickson, J.F. Wilmore, J.H. Buono, M.J. Constable, S.H. Energy cost of weight training exercise. (Refs: 19)*National Strengt & Conditioning Association journal (Lincoln, Neb.) 6(5), Oct/Nov 1984, 22-23;66.*
ABST: This paper investigates the energy cost of a weight training program. Four men, aged between 19 and 26 years old, participate in a two part exercise program: 1) part A working the chest, shoulders and arms and 2) part B working the back and legs. Results indicate a mean net energy expenditure for part A of 174 kcals/session and for part B 222 kcals (n.s.). These findings are compared to those of other investigations. An overall average net energy expenditure across investigating of 179 kcals/36-minute session is obtained.
LEVEL: A LANG: Eng SIRC ARTICLE NO: 102784

Hommel, H. Current trends in strength training. (Refs: 9)*Track & field quarterly review (Kalamazoo, Mich.) 84(1), Spring 1984, 54-56.*
CONF: International Coaches Convention (7th : Edinburgh, Scotland).
LEVEL: I LANG: Eng SIRC ARTICLE NO: 094773

Horvath, L. L'evolution historique des methodes de musculation. (Refs: 18)
NOTES: Dans, Renforcement musculaire, Paris, Institut national du sport et de l'education physique, c1984, p. 7-35.
LEVEL: A LANG: Fr GV711.5 18233

Hunter, E.D. Give a lift to your weightroom facilities. (Refs: 3)*In, Vendl, B.C. (ed.) et al., Interpretive aspects of intramural-recreational sports: selected proceedings from the Thirty-fifth Annual National Intramural-Recreational Sports Association Conference, Corvallis, Or., Oregon State University, c1984, p. 191-206.*
CONF: National Intramural-Recreational Sports Association Conference (35th : 1984 : Fort Worth, Tex.)
LEVEL: I LANG: Eng GV710 18914

Jenkins, W.L. Thackaberry, M. Killian, C. Speed-specific isokinetic training. (Refs: 7)*Journal of orthopaedic and sports physical therapy (Baltimore, Md.) 6(3), Nov/Dec 1984, 181-183.*
ABST: The authors studied the effects of high speed (240o/sec) and low speed (60o/sec) isokinetic exercise. Twenty-four subjects were randomly selected into one high speed and one low speed treatment group; treatments consisted of one set of 15 repetitions, 3 times a week for 6 weeks.

Pre- and post-testing with a Cybex II isokinetic dynamometer was performed to determine if significant strength gains were elicited at 30, 60, 180, 240, or 300o/sec. Both low and high speed groups produced significant strength gains (0.01 significance level) at their treatment speed and at one testing speed higher. However, this study indicates that the range of this carry over is not sufficient enough to replace speed-specific training.
LEVEL: A LANG: Eng SIRC ARTICLE NO: 102945

Katch, V. Get into the act. *Shape (Woodland Hills, Calif.) 3(6), Feb 1984, 70-77.*
LEVEL: B LANG: Eng SIRC ARTICLE NO: 097882

Kindig, L.E. Soares, P.L. Wisenbaker, J.M. Mrvos, S.R. Standard scores for women's weight training. (Refs: 9)*Physician and sportsmedicine (Minneapolis, Minn.) 12(10), Oct 1984, 67-74.*
ABST: This report focuses on the standard scores for women on the bench press, bent-arm pullover, dead lift, half squat, and military press following a ten week beginning weight-training course. 221 young (20.4 plus or minus 2.12 years) females divided in seven body-weight classifications served as subjects.
LEVEL: A LANG: Eng SIRC ARTICLE NO: 099369

Kinnear, G.R. Watts, D.G. Strengthening exercises with a partner. *Runner (Edmonton) 21(4), Winter 1983/1984, 8-12.*
LEVEL: LANG: Eng SIRC ARTICLE NO: 096452

Kontor, K. 1 RM mania. *National Strength & Conditioning Association journal 5(6), Jan 1984, 42.*
LEVEL: B LANG: Eng SIRC ARTICLE NO: 090413

Kraemer, W.J. Exercise prescription: rest periods. *National Strength & Conditioning Association journal 6(1), Feb/Mar 1984, 43.*
LEVEL: B LANG: Eng SIRC ARTICLE NO: 093245

Kraemer, W.J. Exercise prescription: isotonic loading. *National Strength & Conditioning Association journal (Lincoln, Neb.) 6(2), Apr/May 1984, 47.*
LEVEL: B LANG: Eng SIRC ARTICLE NO: 094775

Kraemer, W.J. Variables in successful program design. (Refs: 4)*National Strength & Conditioning Association journal (Lincoln, Neb.) 6(2), Apr/May 1984, 54-55.*
LEVEL: B LANG: Eng SIRC ARTICLE NO: 094776

Kraemer, W.J. Exercise prescription: choice of exercise. *National Strength & Conditioning Association journal (Lincoln, Neb.) 6(3), Jun/Jul 1984, 43.*
LEVEL: B LANG: Eng SIRC ARTICLE NO: 096453

Kraemer, W.J. Exercise prescription: order of exercises. *National Strength & Conditioning Association journal (Lincoln, Neb.) 6(4), Aug/Sept 1984, 47.*
LEVEL: B LANG: Eng SIRC ARTICLE NO: 099357

Kraemer, W.J. Exercise prescription: needs analysis. (Refs: 1)*National Strength & Conditioning Association journal (Lincoln Neb.) 6(5), Oct/Nov 1984, 47.*
LEVEL: B LANG: Eng SIRC ARTICLE NO: 102947

Kraemer, W.J. The challenge of training the three sport athlete. (Refs: 16)*National Strength & Conditioning Association journal (Lincoln, Neb.) 6(5), Oct/Nov 1984, 50-52.*
ABST: This article outlines guidelines to be used in the strength and power training of the three sport high school athlete. General strength and power design and scheduling is discussed. Some sample

programs are also provided. Different programming methods must not be employed so that there will be an easy transition from the strength and power training program of one sport to the next. This will result in the most effective development of the athlete's potential.
LEVEL: B LANG: Eng SIRC ARTICLE NO: 102948

Lambert, G. Le renforcement musculaire de compensation.
NOTES: Dans, Renforcement musculaire, Paris, Institut national du sport et de l'education physique, c1984, p. 87-96.
LEVEL: A LANG: Fr GV711.5 18233

Mamaliga, E. Basic weight training program. *Track & field quarterly review (Kalamazoo, Mich.) 84(1), Spring 1984, 63.*
CONF: U.S. Marine Corps Track & Field Clinic (5th : 1981 : Houston).
LEVEL: B LANG: Eng SIRC ARTICLE NO: 094777

Maneval, M.W. The effects of variable resistance circuit weight training on cardiovascular fitness and body composition. Eugene, Ore.: Microform Publications, University of Oregon, 1984. 2 microfiches : negative, ill. ; 11 x 15 cm.
NOTES: Thesis (Ph.D.) - Texas A & M University, 1981; (xii, 91 leaves); vita; includes bibliography.
LEVEL: A LANG: Eng UO84 1-2

Mannie, K. Basic strength training principles. *Coaching clinic (Princeton, N.J.) 22(9), May 1984, 9-11.*
LEVEL: B LANG: En SIRC ARTICLE NO: 094778

Mannie, K. Organizational considerations for the high school strength program. *Texas coach (Austin, Tex.) 28(1), Aug 1984, 36-37.*
LEVEL: B LANG: Eng SIRC ARTICLE NO: 102950

Mannie, K. Shoulder development through manual resistance. *Athletic journal (Evanston, Ill.) 65(5), Dec 1984, 28-29.*
LEVEL: B LANG: Eng SIRC ARTICLE NO: 104504

Mathes, M. Year-round weight training for multi-sport athletes. *Coaching clinic (Princeton, N.J.) 22(9), May 1984, 8-9.*
LEVEL: B LANG: Eng SIRC ARTICLE NO: 094779

Mecozzi, M. Using conditioning components to motivate the high school athlete. *National Strength & Conditioning Association journal (Lincoln, Neb.) 6(4), Aug/Sept 1984, 34-35.*
LEVEL: B LANG: Eng SIRC ARTICLE NO: 099358

Mottin, A. Analyse musculaire et musculation.
NOTES: Dans, Renforcement musculaire, Paris, Institut national du sport et de l'education physique, c1984, p. 79-86.
LEVEL: A LANG: Fr GV711.5 18233

New Eagle variable resistance abdominal machine. *Journal of the Canadian Athletic Therapists Association (Oakville, Ont.) 11(2), Fall 1984, 22.*
LEVEL: B LANG: Eng SIRC ARTICLE NO: 104505

Newton, H. Power clean: teaching the beginner practical applications. *National Strength & Conditioning Association journal (Lincoln, Neb.) 6(3), Jun/Jul 1984, 41;65-66.*
LEVEL: B LANG: Eng SIRC ARTICLE NO: 096454

O'Bryant, H.S. Periodization: a hypothetical training model for strength and power. Eugene, Ore.: Microform Publications, University of Oregon, 1984. 2 microfiches : negative, ill. ; 11 x 15 cm.
NOTES: Thesis (Ph.D.) - Louisiana State University,

TRAINING METHODS (continued)

1982; (x, 99 leaves); includes bibliography.
LEVEL: A LANG: Eng UO84 238-239

Rankin, S.R. A comparison of the use of Nautilus apparatus and Universal Gym equipment for the development of strength and flexibility. Eugene, Ore.: Microform Publications, University of Oregon, 1984. 1 microfiche : negative, ill. ; 11 x 15 cm.
NOTES: Thesis (M.S.) - Pennsylvania State University, 1981; (viii, 64 leaves); includes bibliography.
LEVEL: A LANG: Eng UO84 86

Reifkin, M. Developing your chest. Mountain View, Calif.: Anderson World Books, 1984. 1v. (The getting strong book series; bk. 3.)
LEVEL: B LANG: Eng ISBN: 089037306X LC CARD: 84-016904

Renforcement musculaire. Paris: Institut national du sport et de l'education physique, c1984. 177 p. : ill. (Les dossiers de l'entraineur.)
CORP: Institut national du sport et de l'education physique.
CORP: France. Ministere du temps libre, de la jeunesse et des sports.
LEVEL: I LANG: Fr ISBN: 2-86580-011-3 GV711.5 18233

Rosentswieg, J. Homemade strength equipment. *Journal of physical education, recreation & dance* 55(1), Jan 1984, 45-47.
LEVEL: B LANG: Eng SIRC ARTICLE NO: 091887

Serafini, A. The 24-hour workout: a guide to the latest family fitness equipment. *Racquetball illustrated (Hollywood, Calif.)* 7(1), Dec/Jan 1984, 32-37.
NOTES: Special home fitness section.
LEVEL: B LANG: Eng SIRC ARTICLE NO: 098958

Smith, M.L. A review of the need for assistant strength coaches in good athletic programs. *National Strength & Conditioning Association journal (Lincoln, Neb.)* 6(4), Aug/Sept 1984, 52.
LEVEL: B LANG: Eng SIRC ARTICLE NO: 098891

Smith, T.K. Preadolescent strength training: some considerations. (Refs: 14)*Journal of physical education, recreation & dance* 55(1), Jan 1984, 43-44;80.
LEVEL: B LANG: Eng SIRC ARTICLE NO: 091292

Stamford, B. Weight-training principles. *Physician and sportsmedicine* 12(3), Mar 1984, 195.
LEVEL: B LANG: Eng SIRC ARTICLE NO: 091890

Stiggins, C. Allsen, P. Exercise methods notebook 10. *National Strength & Conditioning Association journal* 5(6), Jan 1984, 69.
LEVEL: B LANG: Eng SIRC ARTICLE NO: 090419

Stiggins, C. Exercise methods notebook 11: front squat. *National Strength & Conditioning Association journal* 6(1), Feb/Mar 1984, 69.
LEVEL: B LANG: Eng SIRC ARTICLE NO: 093235

Stiggins, C. Allsen, P. Exercise method notebook 12: bent arm pull-over. *National Strength & Conditioning Association journal (Lincoln, Neb.)* 6(2), Apr/May 1984, 69.
LEVEL: B LANG: Eng SIRC ARTICLE NO: 094785

Stiggins, C. Allsen, P. Exercise methods notebook 13: leg extensions. *National Strength & Conditioning Association journal (Lincoln, Neb.)* 6(3), Jun/Jul 1984, 69.
LEVEL: B LANG: Eng SIRC ARTICLE NO: 096456

Stiggins, C. Allsen, P. Exercise methods notebook 15: sealed dumbbell press. *National Strength &*

Conditioning Association journal (Lincoln, Neb.) 6(5), Oct/Nov 1984, 77.
LEVEL: B LANG: Eng SIRC ARTICLE NO: 102959

Stratton, G. The use of isokinetics as a training mode to increase the strength, work capacity, power, power endurance and flexibility of quadriceps and hamstrings muscle groups in the preferred legs of trained and untrained college students. *Carnegie research papers (Beckett Park, Leeds)* 1(6), Dec 1984, 24-26.
CONF: Carnegie Undergraduate Research Symposium (1984 : Leeds, Eng.).
ABST: The purpose of this study was to assess strength, power, work, power endurance and flexibility gains of the quadriceps and hamstrings muscle groups following a five week isokinetic and power endurance training programme. Twenty-four (11 trained, 13 untrained) college males served as subjects. Improvements were observed in all variables for both groups.
LEVEL: A LANG: Eng SIRC ARTICLE NO: 172502

Tancred, W.R. Power training - a must for all athletes. *Athletics coach (Halesowen, England)* 18(1), Mar 1984, 21-22.
LEVEL: B LANG: Eng SIRC ARTICLE NO: 093248

Todd, T. Karl Klein and the squat. (Refs: 71)*National Strength & Conditioning Association journal (Lincoln, Neb.)* 6(3), Jun/Jul 1984, 26-31;67.
LEVEL: I LANG: Eng SIRC ARTICLE NO: 096457

Tucker, L.A. Trait psychology and performance: a credulous viewpoint. (Refs: 38)*Journal of human movement studies (Edinburgh)* 10(1), 1984, 53-62
ABST: This study investigated the relationship between personality and performance during a four-month weight training program. The results indicate that a significant proportion of performance in a weight training program can be explained by measures of extraversion, neuroticism, body cathexis and self-concept. These results support the assumption that physical performance is a function of selected psychological traits.
LEVEL: A LANG: Eng SIRC ARTICLE NO: 094786

Villenave, J. Saviez-vous que...? *Sante et sport (Paris)* 221, sept 1984, 20-21.
LEVEL: B LANG: Fr SIRC ARTICLE NO: 105210

Villenave, J. Saviez-vous que...? *Sante et sport (Paris)* 224, dec 1984, 22-23.
LEVEL: B LANG: Fr SIRC ARTICLE NO: 173513

Villenave, J. Saviez-vous que...? *Sante et sport (Paris)* 223, nov 1984, 20-22.
LEVEL: B LANG: Fr SIRC ARTICLE NO: 173515

Vitti, G.J. The effects of variable training speeds on leg strength & power. (Refs: 16)*Athletic training* 19(1), Spring 1984 26-29.
ABST: 30 untrained males under 30 were selected to determine the effects of variable training speeds on the strength and power outputs of the quadriceps femoris and hamstring muscle groups. The subjects were trained at different speeds on an Orthotron isokinetic exercising device. Significant differences were revealed in the experimental groups from pre- to posttest for both strength and power output, whereas there were no significant differences for the control group.
LEVEL: A LANG: Eng SIRC ARTICLE NO: 091891

Weight training - bench press 'safety'. Halterophilie - securite au banc d'exercice. *Periscope (Ottawa)* 16, 1984, 52-53.

LEVEL: B LANG: Eng Fr SIRC ARTICLE NO: 179918

Weight training for women: a manual for leaders. Toronto: YWCA of Canada, 1984. 77 p. : ill.
CORP: YWCA of Canada.
NOTES: Bibliography: p. 76-77.
LEVEL: B LANG: Eng ISBN: 0-919313-16-7 GV546.6.W64 18832

Westcott, W. Croteau, K. Whittaker, L. Effects of strength training on women studied by YMCA *Journal of physical education and program (Columbus, Ohio)* 81(8), Dec 1984, H8-H9.
LEVEL: I LANG: Eng SIRC ARTICLE NO: 108250

Westcott, W.L. The case for slow weight-training technique. (Refs: 2)*Scholastic coach (New York)* 54(1), Aug 1984, 42-44.
LEVEL: I LANG: Eng SIRC ARTICLE NO: 099359

Westcott, W.L. Modern currents in weight training. *Scholastic coach (New York)* 54(4), Nov 1984, 52-53;12.
LEVEL: B LANG: Eng SIRC ARTICLE NO: 102965

Wilmore, J. Strength training for female athletes. Chicago: Teach'em Inc., 1984?. 2 sound cassettes : 31 35mm slides (Audio cassette series on sports medicine: Sportsmedicine for female athletes, SM-36.)
NOTES: Cassettes recorded and produced by Teach'em Inc. in cooperation with the Physician and Sportsmedicine.
LEVEL: I LANG: Eng

Wolf, M.D. The complete book of Nautilus training. Chicago: Contemporary Books, c1984. vi, 122 p. : ill.
NOTES: Includes index.
LEVEL: B LANG: Eng ISBN: 0809254557 LC CARD: 83-027310 GV546 17306

Wolfe, M.D. Be-twitched. (strength training) *Women's sports (Palo Alto, Calif.)* 6(5), May 1984, 60.
LEVEL: B LANG: Eng SIRC ARTICLE NO: 099360

Yessis, M. Sports medicine. General and specialized workouts: a Weider research clinic report. *Muscle & fitness (Woodland Hills, Calif.)* 45(1), Jan 1984, 13;228.
LEVEL: B LANG: Eng SIRC ARTICLE NO: 096458

Yessis, M. Glute-ham-gastroc raises. *National Strength & Conditioning Association journal (Lincoln, Neb.)* 6(3), Jun/Jul 1984, 54-57.
LEVEL: B LANG: Eng SIRC ARTICLE NO: 096459

Yessis, M. Sports medicine: which is the best exercise regimen for you? *Joe Weider's muscle & fitness (Woodland Hills, Calif.)* 45(8), Aug 1984, 13;142;145-146.
LEVEL: B LANG: Eng SIRC ARTICLE NO: 096460

Yessis, M. Kinesiology: leg press. *Joe Weider's muscle & fitness (Woodland Hills, Calif.)* 45(8), Aug 1984, 22;149.
LEVEL: LANG: Eng SIRC ARTICLE NO: 096461

Yessis, M. Intensity training. How hard should you push yourself? *Shape (Woodland Hills, Calif.)* 3(5), Jan 1984, 57;97-98.
LEVEL: B LANG: Eng SIRC ARTICLE NO: 097886

Yessis, M. Biceps curl. *Muscle & fitness (Woodland Hills, Calif.)* 45(6), Jun 1984, 24-25.
LEVEL: B LANG: Eng SIRC ARTICLE NO: 101034

Yessis, M. Kinesiology: bent-arm pullover. *Muscle & fitness (Woodland Hills, Calif.)* 45(11), Nov 1984,

26-27;190;192.
LEVEL: B LANG: Eng SIRC ARTICLE NO: 101035

Yessis, M. Kinesiology: the squat. *Muscle & fitness (Woodland Hills, Calif.) 4(9), Sept 1984, 22-23;184.*
LEVEL: B LANG: E SIRC ARTICLE NO: 101036

Yessis, M. Leg (knee-joint) extensions. *Muscle & fitness (Woodland Hills, Calif.) 45(10), Oct 1984, 20-21;208;216-217.*
LEVEL: B LANG: Eng SIRC ARTICLE NO: 109003

Yessis, M. The last pulldown. *Muscle & fitness (Woodland Hills, Calif.) 45(12), Dec 1984, 22-23;217.*
LEVEL: B LANG: Eng SIRC ARTICLE NO: 109038

STRETCHING AND FLEXIBILITY EXERCISES

Cornelius, W.L. Exercise beneficial to the hip but questionable for the knee. *National Strength & Conditioning Association journal (Lincoln, Neb.) 6(5), Oct/Nov 1984, 40-41.*
LEVEL: B LANG: Eng SIRC ARTICLE NO: 102939

Downie, A. Stretching: regularity & relaxation. *Counter attack (Ottawa) 4(2), Aug 1984, 15-18.*
LEVEL: B LANG: Eng SIRC ARTICLE NO: 101025

Durey Stretching: generalites. *Cinesiologie (Paris) 94, mars/avr 1984, 186-188;190.*
LEVEL: B LANG: Fr SIRC ARTICLE NO: 096443

Flexibility. *National Strength & Conditioning Association journal (Lincoln, Neb.) 6(4), Aug/Sept 1984, 10-22;71-73.*
LEVEL: LANG: Eng SIRC ARTICLE NO: 099351

L'etirement: une possibilite de recuperation active et de prevention des blessures. *Macolin (Suisse) 1, janv 1984, 8.*
NOTES Tire de 'Stretching', depliant edite par la 'Praxisklinik Rennbahn' de medecine du sport, Muttenz.
LEVEL: B LANG: Fr SIRC ARTICLE NO: 096444

La flexibilite. *Revue de l'entraineur janv/mars 1984, 35.*
LEVEL: B LANG: Fr SIRC ARTICLE NO: 091879

Stamford, B. Flexibility and stretching. *Physician and sportsmedicine 12(2), Feb 1984, 171.*
LEVEL: B LANG: Eng SIRC ARTICLE NO: 091889

Werthner, P. The stretch. *OPHEA: Ontario Physical and Health Education Association 10(3), Fall 1984, 10-17.*
LEVEL: B LANG Eng SIRC ARTICLE NO: 102964

WARM-UPS AND WARM-DOWNS

Arsenault, S. Votre programme de musculation. *Marathon, la revue de la bonne forme (Montreal) 15, avr 1984, 30-34;40-41.*
LEVEL: B LANG: Fr SIRC ARTICLE NO: 108698

Duxbury, P.R. Prepare for exercise. (Refs: 8)*Sideline view (Minneapolis, Minn.) 6(3), Oct 1984, 1-3.*
LEVEL: B LANG: Eng SIRC ARTICLE NO: 099350

Hemstrom, C. Why, when and how to use exercise to warm-up for game preparation. (Refs: 16)*Sports coach (Wembley, Aust.) 8(1), 1984, 16-19.*
LEVEL: I LANG: Eng SIRC ARTICLE NO: 096450

Jerome, J. The essential warm-up: you always knew it was good - but not this good. *Outside*

(Chicago, Ill.) 9(2), Mar 1984, 29;31-32.
LEVEL: B LANG: Eng SIRC ARTICLE NO: 097881

Mayo, D. Mayo, J. The wonders of warmup: give your body a break and avoid injury by easing into your workout with these simple, yet effective, exercises. *Fit (Mountain View, Calif.) 4(4), Sept 1984, 44-46;100.*
LEVEL: B LANG: Eng SIRC ARTICLE NO: 108552

Thorson, J. Cool-down: how and why. *Fitness industry (Miami, Fla.) 2(2), Mar/Apr 1984, 30.*
LEVEL: B LANG: Eng SIRC ARTICL NO: 097885

TRAMPOLINING

Riviere, H. Le trampoline: et que ca saute. *Generaliste (Paris) 640, 1984, 47-49.*
LEVEL: B LANG: Fr

DISABLED

Williams, D. Rebound education therapy (RBT). *Bulletin of physical education (London) 20(2), Summer 1984, 45-53.*
CONF: British Association of Advisers and Lecturers in Physical Education. Congress (64th : 1984 : Cardiff).
LEVEL: I LANG: Eng SIRC ARTICLE NO: 104785

INJURIES AND ACCIDENTS

Torg, J.S. Das, M. Trampoline-related quadriplegia: review of the literature and reflections on the American Academy of Pediatrics' position statement. *Pediatrics (Evanston, Ill.) 74(5), Nov 1984, 804-812.*
LEVEL: A LANG: Eng

PHYSIOLOGY

Rezette, D. Le controle des sauts acrobatiques. *Science et vie (Paris) HS147, 1984, 104-109.*
LEVEL: B LANG: Fr

TECHNIQUES AND SKILLS

Hery, G. 'No flip' trampoline program. *International gymnast magazine (Santa Monica, Calif.) 26(12), Dec 1984, 46-47.*
LEVEL: B LANG: Eng SIRC ARTICLE NO: 109322

TESTING AND EVALUATION

Moreaux, A. Mesure de la performance en trampoline. Mise au point et consequences. (Refs: 6)*Dans, Culture technique no. 13, Neuilly-sur-Seine, France, Centre de Recherche sur la Culture Technique, c1984, p. 218-219.*
LEVEL: I LANG: Fr RC1235 20096

TRAP SHOOTING

Zutz, D. The role of rhythm and imtimidation in erratic scoring. *Trap & field (Indianapolis) 160(6), Jun 1984, 54-55.*
LEVEL: B LANG: Eng SIRC ARTICLE NO: 103427

BIOGRAPHY AND AUTOBIOGRAPHY

Shooting: John Primrose. Tir: John Primrose. *Champion (Ottawa) 8(3), Aug 1984, 54-55.*
LEVEL: B LANG: Eng Fr SIRC ARTICLE NO 096805

EQUIPMENT

Birnbaum, H. Trapguns: a breed apart. Visiting a trapshoot can be a shock for the average field gunner. Devotees of claybird dusting are never afraid to try the new and unusual. *American rifleman (Washington) 132(8), Aug 1984, 40-43;78-79.*
LEVEL: B LANG: Eng SIRC ARTICLE NO: 103408

Sterett, L. Test report: Rottweil 720 Super Trap. *Trap & field (Indianapolis, Ind.) 160(3), Mar 1984, 32-34.*
LEVEL: B LANG: Eng SIRC ARTICLE NO: 099881

Sterett, L. Winchester diamond grade unsingle. *Trap & field (Indianapolis, Ind.) 160(8), Aug 1984, 66-69.*
LEVEL: B LANG: Eng SIRC ARTICLE NO: 101498

Sterett, L. Test report: Ithaca-SKB century trap. *Trap & field (Indianapolis, Ind.) 160(4), Apr 1984, 28-30.*
LEVEL: B LANG: Eng SIRC ARTICLE NO: 101499

Sterett, L. Test report: Laurona 82 Super Trap. *Trap & field (Indianapolis) 160(6), Jun 1984, 44-47.*
LEVEL: B LANG: Eng SIRC ARTICLE NO: 103425

Sterett, L. Baker bore 84. *Trap & field (Indianapolis) 160(9), Sept 1984, 76-79.*
LEVEL: B LANG: Eng SIRC ARTICLE NO: 1060

Zutz, D. Competition triggers: do you have one? *Trap & field (Indianapolis, Ind.) 160(5), May 1984, 22-24.*
LEVEL: B LANG: Eng SIRC ARTICLE NO: 099883

PSYCHOLOGY

Zutz, D. Anticipation can help overcome common errors. *Trap & field (Indianapolis, Ind.) 160(4), Apr 1984, 36-38.*
LEVEL: LANG: Eng SIRC ARTICLE NO: 101501

TECHNIQUES AND SKILLS

Monk, J. How to improve your field shooting. *Guns Australia Mar/Apr 1984, 42-45.*
LEVEL: B LANG: Eng SIRC ARTICLE NO: 1729

TRIATHLON

Cattran, D.E. Fitting bicycling into the triathlon. *Ohio runner (Columbus, Oh.) 5(9), Jun 1984, 24-26.*
LEVEL: B LANG: Eng SIRC ARTICLE NO: 096570

Delorme, D. Triathlon. *Marathon, la revue de la bonne forme (Montreal) 15, avr 1984, 23-24.*
LEVEL: B LANG: Fr SIRC ARTICL NO: 108695

Edwards, S. Your day at the triathlon: how to make the most of it. *Running & fitness (Washington, D.C.) 16(5), Sept/Oct 1984, 12-13.*
LEVEL: B LANG: Eng SIRC ARTICLE NO: 097858

Gross, A. Is the triathlon for you? (Refs: 9)*Runner (Boulder, Colo.) 6(7), Apr 1984, 34-39.*
LEVEL: B LANG: Eng SIRC ARTICLE NO: 097860

King, W.H. Triathlete's balance. *Aerobics (Dallas, Tex.)* 5(8), Aug 1984, 4;8.
LEVEL: B LANG: Eng SIRC ARTICLE NO: 101010

Stuller, J. Beyond tough: it's time to end the bickering. What's really the hardest, sickest ultra-endurance event of them all? *Outside 9(1), Jan/Feb 1984, 39-43;76-77.*
LEVEL: B LANG: Eng SIRC ARTICLE NO: 093237

Trick of the trade: how to shave valuable minutes from your time in the transition area. *Triathlon (Santa Monica, Calif.) 2(3), Jun/Jul 1984, 30-34.*
LEVEL: B LANG: Eng SIRC ARTICLE NO: 101016

Vaz, K. Cross-training: the complete book of the triathlon. New York: Avon Books, 1984. 1v.
CORP: Triathlon Magazine.
LEVEL: I LANG: Eng ISBN: 0380879573 LC CARD: 84-045252

Zimmer, J. What's in it for you? You don't have to be a fanatic to enjoy the triple (swim-bike-run) sport. *Health (New York 16(8), Aug 1984, 22-24.*
LEVEL: B LANG: Eng SIRC ARTICLE NO: 102934

ADMINISTRATION

Hutchinson, B. Organizing an intramural triathlon. *Journal of physical education, recreation and dance (Reston, Va.) 55(7), Sept 1984, 66-67.*
LEVEL: B LANG: Eng SIRC ARTICLE NO: 100518

Millinder, L. Triathlon: state of the sport. The sport of the '80s may be growing too fast for its own good. The issues that must be addressed: organization, safety, and money. *Ultrasport (Boston, Mass.) 1(2), Apr 1984, 12;14-15.*
LEVEL: B LANG: Eng SIRC ARTICLE NO: 097867

Twitchell, R.W. Feigley, D.A. A recreational approach to triathlon programming. *NIRSA journal (Mt. Pleasant, Mich.) 8(2), Winter 1984, 47-49;54.*
LEVEL: B LANG: Eng SIRC ARTICLE NO: 097875

BIOGRAPHY AND AUTOBIOGRAPHY

Armstrong, S. Will two tie for gold. Montreal's Puntous twins are so in tune with each other, they may cross the Olympic finish line hand in hand. *Canadian living 9(4), Apr 1984, 40-44;46;49.*
LEVEL: B LANG: Eng SIRC ARTICLE NO: 091860

Holman, M. Sylviane & Patricia Puntous. *Sports people (Toronto) 4(1), Jan 1984, 10.*
LEVEL: B LANG: Eng SIRC ARTICLE NO: 097862

Howard, J. John Howard: from high school runner, to elite cyclist to triathlete - Howard reveals the evolution of his holistic training philosophy, and the benefits any athlete can accrue from diversity. *Ultrasport (Boston) 1(4), Jul/Aug 1984, 16;18-19.*
LEVEL: B LANG: Eng SIRC ARTICLE NO: 097863

Kort, M. Sibling revelry: together the Puntous twins swim, bike, run and win. *Women's sport and fitness (Palo Alto, Calif.) 6(8), Aug 1984, 22-25.*
LEVEL: B LANG: Eng SIRC ARTICLE NO: 101047

Kort, M. The Puntous twins: double trouble for everyone else. *Triathlon (Santa Monica, Calif.) 2(3), Jun/Jul 1984, 36-38;108.*
LEVEL: B LANG: Eng SIRC ARTICLE NO: 101048

Marchand, P. Canada's Puntous twins. *Chatelaine (Toronto) 57(5), May 1984, 66-67;177-181.*
LEVEL: B LANG: Eng SIRC ARTICLE NO: 093229

Rozek, M. Body & soul: Joe Oakes. *Ultrasport (Boston, Mass.) 1(3), May/Jun 1984, 16-18.*
LEVEL: B LANG: Eng SIRC ARTICLE NO: 096430

CLOTHING

Edwards, S. Triathlon clothing. *Sports retailer (Mt. Prospect, Ill.) 37(2), Feb 1984, 16.*
LEVEL: B LANG: Eng SIRC ARTICLE NO: 098939

ECONOMICS

Ritter, A. Sponsorship growing with athlete participation. *Sport style (New York) 6(19), 22 Oct 1984, 80.*
LEVEL: B LANG: Eng SIRC ARTICLE NO: 099501

EQUIPMENT

Hosler, R. Lehrer, J. The triathlon machine: a complete guide to picking the right bicycle for a successful triathloning debut. *Runner's world 19(4), Apr 1984, 86-92;94.*
LEVEL: B LANG: Eng SIRC ARTICLE NO: 092750

Kranzley, G. Best buys in triathlon bikes: mean machines to get you started. *Bicycling (Emmaus, Pa.) 25(9), Nov/Dec 1984, 50;52-63.*
LEVEL: B LANG: Eng SIRC ARTICLE NO: 100560

Kruse, B. Sewn-up or clinched: Barclay Kruse on choosing tires. *Triathlon magazine (Santa Monica, Calif.) 2(5), Oct/Nov 198 18.*
LEVEL: B LANG: Eng SIRC ARTICLE NO: 107116

EQUIPMENT - RETAILING

Triathlons: triple profit potential. *Fitness industry (Miami, Fla.) 2(6), Oct 1984, 16-17;19-22.*
LEVEL: B LANG: Eng SIRC ARTICLE NO: 106916

INJURIES AND ACCIDENTS

Shyne, K. Triathlon organizers help minimize injuries. *Physician and sportsmedicine 12(1), Jan 1984, 26.*
LEVEL: B LANG: E SIRC ARTICLE NO: 091486

NUTRITION

Forsythe, K. So long solids: drink your way to better endurance. *Triathlon magazine (Santa Monica, Calif.) 2(4), Aug/Sept 1984, 18-19.*
LEVEL: B LANG: Eng SIRC ARTICLE NO: 108922

Vaz, K. Pritkin's promise for ultra-fit endurance athletes. *Triathlon magazine (Santa Monica, Calif.) 2(4), Aug/Sept 1984, 34-38;93.*
LEVEL: B LANG: Eng SIRC ARTICLE NO: 108920

PHYSIOLOGY

Scheff, J. Maxing out: VO2 max reflects your endurance potential. *Triathlon magazine (Santa Monica, Calif.) 2(5), Oct/Nov 1984, 24-25.*
LEVEL: B LANG: Eng SIRC ARTICLE NO: 106805

Thomas, B.D. Motley, C.P. Myoglobinemia and endurance exercise: a study of twenty-five participants in a triathlon competition. (Refs: 30)*American journal of sports medicine (Baltimore, Md.) 12(2), May/Apr 1984, 113-119.*
ABST: The highest level of serum myoglobin occured just after completion of the triathlon. The average peak level was 842 mg/ml. The serum myoglobin level slowly fell to near resting values over the following 24 hours. There was a significant correlation between average serum myoglobin and finishing time (P0.0125) and between average serum myoglobin and postexercise temperature (P0.05).
LEVEL: A LANG: Eng SIRC ARTICLE NO: 094629

van Rensburg, J.P. Kielblock, A.J. van der Walt, W.H. Maximal aerobic capacity and endurance fitness as determinants of rowing, cycling and running performance during a triathlon competition. (Refs: 20)*Australian journal of science & medicine in sport (Kingston, Aust.) 16(3), Oct 1984, 11-15.*
ABST: To assess the major physiological determinants of success in a triathlon consisting of canoeing (28km), cycling (90 km) and running (42km), a correlation matrix was drawn to relate performance in each of the individual events, as well as overall performance, to respectively, body mass, maximal aerobic capacity and the lactic acid turnpoint. The results revealed that rowing performance (canoeing) was best correlated with V02 max in absolute and relative terms as well as on V02 at LATP. Running time was related primarily to V02max relative to body mass. The latter attribute was also most significantly related to overall performance.
LEVEL: A LANG: Eng SIRC ARTICLE NO: 105498

TRAINING AND CONDITIONING

Davis, D. How to train triathlon program. *Fun runner (Rose Bay, NSW) 6(5), Dec 1984/Jan 1985, 36-38.*
LEVEL: B LANG: Eng SIRC ARTICLE NO: 173029

Edwards. S. First-rate fitness means getting all wet. *Running & fitness (Washington, D.C.) 16(3), May/Jun 1984, 19;27.*
LEVEL: B LANG: Eng SIRC ARTICLE NO: 101547

Jonas, S. Triathloning: getting started - 1. *AMJA newsletter (Hollywood, Calif.) Jul/Aug 1984, 5.*
NOTES: Based on an article published in The Beast Feb/Mar 1984.
LEVEL: B LANG: Eng SIRC ARTICLE NO: 101030

Perry, P. Cross-training: when one sport just isn't enough. *Bicycling (Emmaus, Pa.) 25(9), Nov/Dec 1984, 44-47.*
LEVEL: B LANG: Eng SIRC ARTICLE NO: 101031

Puntous, P. Puntous, S. Wischnia, B. Your first triathlon: tried and true method. Tips for making your excursion into triathloning a triple treat. *Runner's world (Mountain View, Calif.) 19(6), Jun 1984, 48-49;84;86-88.*
LEVEL: B LANG: Eng SIRC ARTICLE NO: 094783

Smith, R. Quality, not quantity. (running workouts) *Triathlon (Santa Monica, Calif.) 2(3), Jun/Jul 1984, 24.*
LEVEL: B LANG: Eng SIRC ARTICLE NO: 101713

Stuller, K.J. Hi-tech sweat: triathletes are going on-line with computer-programmed training. *Triathlon magazine (Santa Monica, Calif.) 2(5), Oct/Nov 1984, 48-50;52.*
LEVEL: B LANG: Eng SIRC ARTICLE NO: 106926

VARIATIONS

Wallace, D. Coolangatta Gold. (Tri-Aquathon) *Triathlon (Santa Monica, Calif.) 2(3), Jun/Jul 1984, 44-49.*
LEVEL: B LANG: E SIRC ARTICLE NO: 101017

TRIPLE JUMP

TECHNIQUES AND SKILLS

Heal, A. The importance of maintaining velocity in triple jump. (Refs: 6)*Technical bulletin - Ontario Track and Field Association (Willowdale, Ont.) 43, Fall 1984, 21-26.*
LEVEL: B LANG: Eng SIRC ARTICLE NO: 103543

Jarver, J. Boase, G. Helsinki observations - horizontal jumps. *Modern athlete and coach (Athelstone, Aust.) 22(1), Jan 1984 3-7.*
LEVEL: B LANG: Eng SIRC ARTICLE NO: 096942

Javer, J. Boase, G. Helsinki observations - horizontal jumps. *Track and field journal (Ottawa) 28, Nov 1984, 31-33.*
LEVEL B LANG: Eng SIRC ARTICLE NO: 109769

Sidorenko, S. The sprint and the jump. *Soviet sports review (Escondido, Calif.) 19(4), Dec 1984, 182-184.*
NOTES: Translated from, Legkaya atletika 7, 1984, 18.
LEVEL: I LANG: Eng SIRC ARTICLE NO: 104952

TESTING AND EVALUATION

Verbitski, G. Bekker, H. The triple jump from place as an exercise and as a test. *Soviet sports review (Escondido, Calif.) 19(2), Jun 1984, 100-102.*
NOTES: Translated from, Legkaya atletika, 3:5, 1983.
LEVEL: I LANG: Eng SIRC ARTICLE NO: 100035

TRAINING AND CONDITIONING

Kreyer, V. Long term periodisation of triple jump training. *Athletic coach (London) 18(2), Jun 1984, 11-13.*
LEVEL: B LANG Eng SIRC ARTICLE NO: 095385

Prost, R. Pliometrie pour tous.
NOTES: Dans, Renforcement musculaire, Paris, Institut national du sport et de l'education physique, c1984, p. 173-177.
LEVEL: B LANG: Fr GV711.5 18233

Prost, R. L'entrainement des sauteurs en longueur et des triple-sauteurs en altitude. *Revue de l'Amicale des entraineurs francais d'athletisme (Paris) 89, oct/nov/dec 1984, 19-21.*
LEVEL: B LANG: Fr SIRC ARTICLE NO: 103548

Tenke, Z. Preparation of long and triple-jumpers. (Refs: 2)*Track and field journal (Ottawa) 28, Nov 1984, 15-19.*
LEVEL: B LANG: Eng SIRC ARTICLE NO: 103551

Yuchkevitsh, T. Training suggestions for young horizontal jumpers. *Modern athlete and coach (Athelstone, Aust.) 2(3), Jul 1984, 18-20.*
NOTES: Translated and condensed from Legkaja Atletika (Moscow) 3, Mar 1983.
LEVEL: B LANG: Eng SIRC ARTICLE NO: 101650

TRAINING AND CONDITIONING - DRILLS

Hayes, D. The beginning triple jumper. *Track and field quarterly review (Kalamazoo, Mich.) 84(4), Winter 1984, 9-10.*
LEVEL: B LANG: Eng SIRC ARTICLE NO: 101638

TUMBLING

TECHNIQUES AND SKILLS

Tonry, D. Beginning tumbling. *New Zealand gymnast (New Plymouth, N.Z.) 9(3), Jun 1984, 13-14.*
LEVEL: B LANG: Eng SIRC ARTICLE NO: 098154

Tonry, D. Coaching tumbling. *New Zealand gymnast (New Plymouth, N.Z.) 9(5), Oct 1984, 9-10.*
LEVEL: B LANG: Eng SIRC ARTICLE NO: 109008

ULTRALIGHT FLYING

Ultralight owner's survey. (Refs: 2)*Glider rider (Chattanooga, Tenn.) 9(8), Oct 1984, 62-73.*
LEVEL: B LANG: Eng SIRC ARTICL NO: 109146

ADMINISTRATION

Meadowcroft, W.J. Let's not regulate ultralights out of business. *Gllder rider magazine (Chattanooga, Tenn.) 9(4), Jun 1984 47-48.*
NOTES: Reprinted from Special Report SR 83-7, courtesy of the National Business Aircraft Association.
LEVEL: B LANG: Eng SIRC ARTICLE NO: 098077

Steenblik, J.W. A conversation with Donald D. Engen. *Glider rider magazine (Chattanooga, Tenn.) 9(6), Aug 1984, 20-21.*
LEVEL: B LANG: Eng SIRC ARTICLE NO: 098081

DISABLED

Heinrich, M. Shapcott, N. Adapting ultralights for disabled pilots. *Paraplegia news (Phoenix, Ariz.) 38(5), May 1984, 65-67.*
LEVEL: B LANG: Eng SIRC ARTICLE NO: 095860

DRUGS, DOPING AND ERGOGENIC AIDS

Farrell, S. Artificial aids & athletic performance. *Aerobics (Dallas, Tex.) 5(1), Jan 1984, 5.*
LEVEL: I LANG: Eng SIRC ARTICLE NO: 097456

ENVIRONMENT

Lert, P. Everything you ever wanted to know about ultralight flying in winter. *Air progress ultralights (Canoga Park, Calif.) 2(1), Jan/Feb 1984, 16-21.*
LEVEL: B LANG: Eng SIRC ARTICLE NO: 098071

Pagen, D. At home in the air: part IV. *Glider rider 8(12), Feb 1984, 39-41.*
LEVEL: B LANG: Eng SIRC ARTICLE NO: 090624

Pagen, D. Winter flying... *Glider rider 8(11), Jan 1984, 38-39.*
LEVEL: B LANG: Eng SIRC ARTICLE NO: 090626

Pagen, D. At home in the air. Part VI - watching the weather. *Glider rider magazine 9(2), Apr 1984, 37-39.*
LEVEL: B LANG: Eng SIRC ARTICLE NO: 093415

Pagen, D. At home in the air. Part V. *Glider rider magazine 9(1), Mar 1984, 53-55.*
LEVEL: I LANG: Eng SIRC ARTICLE NO: 093416

Stull, R. Turbulence in the atmospheric boundry layer: understanding this meteorological condition will lead to better fligh planning. *Air progress ultralights (Canoga Park, Calif.) 2(7), Sept/Oct 1984, 70-73.*
LEVEL: B LANG: Eng SIRC ARTICLE NO: 173426

EQUIPMENT

Air test... on inflatable wings. *Air progress ultralights (Canoga Park, Calif.) 2(7), Sept/Oct 1984, 26;28-32.*
LEVEL: B LANG: Eng SIRC ARTICLE NO: 173419

Air test: the Challenger. *Air progress ultralights (Canoga Park, Calif.) 2(7), Sept/Oct 1984, 34-40.*
LEVEL: B LANG: Eng SIR ARTICLE NO: 173420

Aupetit, H. L'U.L.M. Du gadget au sport. *Dans, Culture technique no. 13, Neuilly-sur-Seine, France, Centre de Recherche sur la Culture Technique, c1984, p. 298-307.*
LEVEL: I LANG: Fr RC1235 20096

Bradford, M. Hangar and trailer buyer's guide. *Glider rider 8(12), Feb 1984, 47-51.*
LEVEL: B LANG: Eng SIRC ARTICLE NO: 090617

Bradford, M. How to buy an ultralight: part III. *Glider rider 8(11), Jan 1984, 41;43.*
LEVEL: B LANG: Eng SIRC ARTICLE NO: 090619

Bradford, M. Putting on the ritz. (Standard Model A.) *Glider rider magazine 9(3), May 1984, 40-43.*
LEVEL: B LANG: Eng SIR ARTICLE NO: 093406

Bradford, M. Quad City Ultralight contender...Taking on the Challenger. *Glider rider magazine (Chattanooga, Tenn.) 9(6), Au 1984, 39-41;43.*
LEVEL: B LANG: Eng SIRC ARTICLE NO: 098067

Bradford, M. The Drifter DR277: steady as she goes - rock or roll. *Glider rider magazine (Chattanooga, Tenn.) 9(9), Nov 198 40-45.*
LEVEL: B LANG: Eng SIRC ARTICLE NO: 108815

Bradford, M. 'Essence of replicas': the Parasol. *Glider rider magazine (Chattanooga, Tenn.) 9(10), Dec 1984, 36-41.*
LEVEL B LANG: Eng SIRC ARTICLE NO: 108818

Campbell, J. Float flying accessories. With a raft of convertible ultralights on the market we look at pontoons and props to help keep you high and dry. *Air progress ultralights (Canoga Park, Calif.) 2(6), Jul/Aug 1984, 28-32;74-77.*
LEVEL: B LANG: Eng SIRC ARTICLE NO: 104680

Campbell, J. Star wars fantasy: the Sun Ray. *Air progress ultralights (Canoga Park, Calif.) 2(6), Jul/Aug 1984, 50-56.*
LEVEL: B LANG: Eng SIRC ARTICLE NO: 104681

Campbell, J. Another new star from middle America: the Starflight XC. *Air progress ultralights (Canoga Park, Calif.) 2(7), Spet/Oct 1984, 42-48.*
LEVEL: B LANG: Eng SIRC ARTICLE NO: 173422

Cry, Buccaneer. Available as a bare-bones landplane, an enclosed luxury model, a seaplane, or a full-feature amphibian, the Buccaneer may not be 'all things to all people' - but it sure comes close. *Air progress ultralights (Canoga Park, Calif.) 2(6), Jul/Aug 1984, 42-49;66.*
LEVEL: B LANG: Eng SIRC ARTICLE NO: 104682

Glider's rider's summer'84 ultralight buyers guide. *Glider rider (Chattanooga, Tenn.) 9(5), Jul 1984, 37-39;41;43-46;49;51;53;55-61.*
LEVEL: B LANG: Eng SIRC ARTICLE NO: 099554

ULTRALIGHT FLYING (continued)

Lanier, E. How to make your own wheel pants. The author shows off his handiwork on his Eagle ultralight. *Glider rider magazine 9(3), May 1984, 37-39.*
LEVEL: B LANG: Eng SIRC ARTICLE NO: 093408

Lert, P. The remarkable Avid Flyer: our intrepid ultralight airman puts an intriguing new design through its pace. *Air progress ultralights (Canoga Park, Calif.) 2(1), Jan/Feb 1984, 40-46;66-67.*
LEVEL: B LANG: Eng SIRC ARTICLE NO: 098072

Lert, P. XTC ecstasy afloat. The Diehl XTC with its all composite, Canard configuration is light years away from tube and ra foot launched vehicle, but on land or sea it's still an Ultralight and a pleasant one to fly at that. *Air progress ultralights (Canoga Park, Calif.) 2(6), Jul/Aug 1984, 33-41.*
LEVEL: B LANG: Eng SIRC ARTICLE NO: 104686

Lert, P. Teratorn Tierra: we put tierra to the test and it fairs very well indeed. More improvements are promised for 1984. *Air progress ultralights (Canoga Park, Calif.) 2(3), Apr 1984, 50-57;81.*
LEVEL: B LANG: Eng SIRC ARTICLE NO: 104688

Lert, P. Ultralight communications... *Air progress ultralights (Canoga Park, Calif.) 2(3), Apr 1984, 62-65;72.*
LEVEL: B LANG: Eng SIRC ARTICLE NO: 104689

Lert. P. Air test: Eipper Quicksilver GT. *Air progress ultralights (Canoga Park, Calif.) 2(2), Mar 1984, 34-39;41.*
LEVEL B LANG: Eng SIRC ARTICLE NO: 098073

MacFarlane, M.G. Glider's rider's ultralight radio buyer's guide. *Glider rider magazine (Chattanooga, Tenn.) 9(4), Jun 1984 32-33;35-37.*
LEVEL: B LANG: Eng SIRC ARTICLE NO: 098074

Macfarlane, M.G. Instrument deck: buyer's guide. *Glider rider magazine (Chattanooga, Tenn.) 9, Nov 1984, 48-53.*
LEVEL: B LANG: Eng SIRC ARTICLE NO: 108816

Martin, D. Will the Eagle be forgotten in...the age of the Falcon? *Glider rider magazine 9(2), Apr 1984, 40-45.*
LEVEL: B LANG: Eng SIRC ARTICLE NO: 093409

Martin, D. Flying Bob Hovey's Delta Hawk. *Glider rider magazine 9(1), Mar 1984, 40-43.*
LEVEL: B LANG: Eng SIRC ARTICLE NO 093410

Martin, D. Aircraft radios for ultralight pilots. In an ultralight? Who needs it? Glider Rider evaluates three hand-held VHF transceivers for those who do. *Glider rider magazine 9(1), Mar 1984, 35-39.*
LEVEL: B LANG: Eng SIRC ARTICLE NO: 093411

Martin, D. First of a new line: Eipper's GT series. *Glider rider magazine (Chattanooga, Tenn.) 9(7), Sept 1984, 31-33;35.*
LEVEL: B LANG: Eng SIRC ARTICLE NO: 098075

Martin, D. The hiperlight: an ultralight among airplanes. *Glider rider magazine (Chattanooga, Tenn.) 9(4), Jun 1984, 39-41;43-45.*
LEVEL: B LANG: Eng SIRC ARTICLE NO: 098076

Martin, D. The Moni motorglider: it's no ultralight and not meant to be. *Glider rider (Chattanooga, Tenn.) 9(5), Jul 1984, 27-29;31.*
LEVEL: B LANG: Eng SIRC ARTICLE NO: 099555

Martin, D. Ultralight testing and evaluation. *Glider rider (Chattanooga, Tenn.) 9(8), Oct 1984, 51;53;74-75.*
LEVEL: B LANG: Eng SIRC ARTICLE NO: 109149

Pagen, D. Combating corrosion: just as tooth decay attacks our teeth, corrosion eats away our aluminum. In both cases the cure is preventive maintenance. *Glider rider magazine (Chattanooga, Tenn.) 9(7), Sept 1984, 43-45.*
LEVEL: B LANG: Eng SIRC ARTICLE NO: 098079

Pagen, D. Wire wisdom: engineers will tell you that a cable and spar system has the best strength-to-weight ratio, followed by pure truss construction, then cantilever construction. *Glider rider magazine (Chattanooga, Tenn.) 9(4), Jun 1984, 57-59.*
LEVEL: B LANG: Eng SIRC ARTICLE NO: 098080

Pagen, D. Aluminum in the air. *Glider rider (Chattanooga, Tenn.) 9(5), Jul 1984, 65-67.*
LEVEL: I LANG: Eng SIRC ARTICLE NO: 099556

Pagen, D. More on structure. *Glider rider (Chattanooga, Tenn.) 9(8), Oct 1984, 39-41;76.*
LEVEL: B LANG: Eng SIRC ARTICLE NO: 109151

Roberts, C. Bionic Bat: with the potential for staying aloft for days at a time this latest development of Dr. Paul MacCread is hot on the heels of the latest Kremer prize for high speed human powered flight... *Air progress ultralights (Canoga Park, Calif.) 2(3), Apr 1984, 42-43;45-46;48.*
LEVEL: B LANG: Eng SIRC ARTICLE NO: 104691

Roberts, C. Taras Kiceniuk: the Icarus II was one of the great landmarks in hang gliding. It's concept served as a precursor for modern day ultralights... *Air progress ultralights (Canoga Park, Calif.) 2(3), Apr 1984, 74-79.*
LEVEL: B LANG: Eng SIRC ARTICLE NO: 104692

Steenblik, J.W. Flying the Kolb UltraStar: lawn chair on the edge of eternity. *Glider rider (Chattanooga, Tenn.) 9(8), Oct 1984, 43-50.*
LEVEL: B LANG: Eng SIRC ARTICLE NO: 109145

Ultralight buyer's guide. *Glider rider magazine (Chattanooga, Tenn.) 9(10), Dec 1984, 44-51;55-59;61-69.*
LEVEL: B LANG: Eng SIRC ARTICLE NO: 108820

Whittall, N. Back to basics. (Pixie trike) *Whole air (Lookout Mountain, Tenn.) 7(2), May 1984, 12-13.*
LEVEL: B LANG: Eng SIRC ARTICLE NO: 099558

EQUIPMENT - MAINTENANCE

Pagen, D. Sail repair. Can you repair your own sail? The answer is a qualified yes, if you have: (1) the right materials; (2 an understanding of what you are doing; and (3) patience. *Glider rider magazine 9(3), May 1984, 61-63.*
LEVEL: B LANG: Eng SIRC ARTICLE NO: 093414

Pagen, D. Ultralight maintenance: a poem by Oliver Wendell Holmes gives food advice to ultralight owners: you must practice preventive maintenance. *Glider rider magazine (Chattanooga, Tenn.) 9(9), Nov 1984, 54-55;63..*
LEVEL: B LANG: Eng SIRC ARTICLE NO: 108817

EQUIPMENT - RETAILING

Meier, R. Profile: Culver's prop shop. *Glider rider magazine 9(3), May 1984, 53-54.*
LEVEL: B LANG: Eng SIRC ARTICLE NO: 093413

Weeks, D. Diary of a dealership: living within the system. *Glider rider magazine 9(2), Apr 1984, 32-34.*
LEVEL: B LANG: En SIRC ARTICLE NO: 093417

FACILITIES

Sheehan, J.J. Obtaining and keeping ultralight flying sites. *Glider rider (Chattanooga, Tenn.) 9(5), Jul 1984, 33-35.*
LEVEL: B LANG: Eng SIRC ARTICLE NO: 099557

HISTORY

Lert, P. Path to the future...paving the way. Five machines which mark significant milestones in the ultralight movement. *Air progress ultralights (Canoga Park, Calif.) 2(2), Mar 1984, 50-55;68-69;78.*
LEVEL: B LANG: Eng SIRC ARTICLE NO: 098070

INJURIES AND ACCIDENTS

DeLacerda, F.G. Potential hearing loss. *Glider rider magazine (Chattanooga, Tenn.) 9(7), Sept 1984, 21-22.*
LEVEL: B LANG: Eng SIRC ARTICLE NO: 098068

LAW AND LEGISLATION

Lert, P. Trespass. *Air progress ultralights (Canoga Park, Calif.) 2(3), Apr 1984, 28-29;31-32.*
LEVEL: B LANG: Eng SIRC ARTICLE NO: 104687

PHYSICS

Pagen, D. Wingtips: the threat of vibration. *Glider rider magazine (Chattanooga, Tenn.) 9(6), Aug 1984, 57-59.*
LEVEL: I LANG: Eng SIRC ARTICLE NO: 098078

PSYCHOLOGY - MENTAL TRAINING

James, G. Visualization in ultralight flight training. *Air progress ultralights (Canoga Park, Calif.) 2(1), Jan/Feb 1984, 48-49;64-65.*
LEVEL: B LANG: Eng SIRC ARTICLE NO: 098069

SAFETY

Rawson, J. TCA operations. *Air progress ultralights (Canoga Park, Calif.) 2(3), Apr 1984, 18-21.*
LEVEL: B LANG: Eng SIRC ARTICLE NO: 104690

TEACHING

Bradford, M. Your first flight in an ultralight. Sometime the next day, or the next, it hits you: I can fly. At that moment you begin to become a pilot. *Glider rider magazine 9(1), Mar 1984, 47;49.*
LEVEL: B LANG: Eng SIRC ARTICLE NO: 093407

Campbell, J. The 2-seater exemption. *Air progress ultralights (Canoga Park, Calif.) 2(7), Sept/Oct 1984, 18-21;74-75.*
LEVEL: B LANG: Eng SIRC ARTICLE NO: 173415

Martin, D. A step in the right direction: two-place ultralight training. *Glider rider magazine 9(1), Mar 1984, 31-33.*
LEVEL: B LANG: Eng SIRC ARTICLE NO: 093412

UNDERWATER DIVING

Brylske, A. Boat diving: supervision and control. *Undersea journal (Santa Ana, Calif.) 1984, 5;8-9;36.*
LEVEL: B LANG: Eng SIRC ARTICLE NO: 105049

Hardy, J. Sportdivers doing work underwater are the benefits worth the risk? *Diver magazine (Vancouver) 10(9), Dec 1984, 6-7.*
LEVEL: B LANG: Eng SIRC ARTICLE NO: 108474

Nadler, J. PADI's impact on the diving industry. *Undersea journal (Santa Ana, Calif.) 1984, 14-15.*
LEVEL: I LANG: Eng SIR ARTICLE NO: 108573

AGED

McCutcheon, E. The elder aquanaut: diving after 50. *Diver magazine (Vancouver) 10(7), Oct/Nov 1984, 17-19.*
LEVEL: B LANG: Eng SIRC ARTICLE NO: 108477

ASSOCIATIONS

Bove, F. Rx for divers. (Divers Alert Network) *Skin diver (Los Angeles, Calif.) 33(1), Jan 1984, 46-48.*
LEVEL: B LANG: En SIRC ARTICLE NO: 095510

BIOGRAPHY AND AUTOBIOGRAPHY

Fine, J.C. Profil: Philippe Taillez, pionnier de l'ocean. *Plongee (Montreal) 11(2), mai/juin 1984, 15-18.*
LEVEL: B LANG: SIRC ARTICLE NO: 100126

CERTIFICATION

Hamel, F.A. La carte quebecoise de plongee: un systeme de formation et de developpement (2e partie). *Plongee (Montreal) 11(4), sept/oct 1984, 26-27.*
LEVEL: B LANG: Fr SIRC ARTICLE NO: 101733

CHILDREN

Gauthier, J.J. Une experience du C.I.S.N.: l'enfant plongeur. *Etudes et sports sous-marins, l'aventure sous-marine (Paris) 76, sept/oct 1984, 40-42.*
LEVEL: I LANG: Fr SIRC ARTICLE NO: 100128

Missirliu, C. Bernus, J.P. Preparation et initiation a la plongee chez l'enfant prepubere. (Refs: 5)*Medecine du sport (Paris) 58(4), 25 juil 1984, 43-45.*
LEVEL: I LANG: Fr SIRC ARTICLE NO: 098734

CLOTHING

Drysuit survey - Part II. Whatever happened to 'required training'? *Undercurrent (Sausalito, Calif.) 9(2), Feb 1984, 8-10.*
LEVEL: B LANG: Eng SIRC ARTICLE NO: 093982

McDaniel, N. Drysuit roundup. *Diver magazine (Vancouver, B.C.) 10(2), Mar 1984, 14-21.*
LEVEL: B LANG: Eng SIRC ARTICLE NO 095518

Undercurrent wet suit survey: part II. Would you recommend your suit to a friend? *Undercurrent (New York) 9(11/12), Nov/Dec 1984, 10-13.*
LEVEL: B LANG: Eng SIRC ARTICLE NO: 103643

White, J.S. The Nautilus drysuit. *Diver magazine (Vancouver, B.C.) 10(3), Apr/May 1984, 18-19.*
LEVEL: B LANG: Eng SIRC ARTICLE NO: 100137

White, J.S. Seatec's ultralight drysuit. *Diver magazine (Vancouver) 10(9), Dec 1984, 12.*
LEVEL: B LANG: Eng SIRC ARTICLE NO: 108473

COUNTRIES AND REGIONS

Farley, M.B. Farley, L.K. Baja California diver's guide. Rev. ed. Port Hueneme, Calif.: Marcor Pub., (1984). 220 p. : ill.
NOTES: Rev. ed. of: Diving Mexico's Baja California, c1978. Includes index.
LEVEL: B LANG: Eng ISBN: 0932248055 LC CARD: 84-061084

Leonard, T. The Grand Raid expedition. *Diver magazine (Vancouver, B.C.) 10(3), Apr/May 1984, 24-27.*
LEVEL: B LANG: Eng SIRC ARTICLE NO: 100132

Lewbel, G.S. Diving and snorkeling guide to Curacao and Bonaire with information on Aruba. Locust Valley, N.Y.: Pisces Books (1984). 1v.
LEVEL: B LANG: Eng ISBN: 0866360352 LC CARD: 84-001179

Muller, R.E. Diving in Japan. *Scottish diver (Glasgow, Scotland) 23(5), Sept/Oct 1984, 99-101.*
LEVEL: B LANG: Eng SIRC ARTICLE NO: 173488

DISABLED

Bove, F. Rx for divers. (Epilepsy and diving) *Skin diver (Los Angeles, Calif.) 33(2), Feb 1984, 44;58;60;62.*
LEVEL: B LANG: Eng SIRC ARTICLE NO: 094310

DRUGS, DOPING AND ERGOGENIC AIDS

Mansky, W. Drugs and the diver. *Man underwater (Winnipeg, Man.) Jul 1984, 12-13.*
LEVEL: B LANG: Eng SIRC ARTICLE NO: 0987

EQUIPMENT

Addy, P. A pony tank rig: Patrick Addy on his search for a safe air supply for an emergency ascent. *Diver (London) 29(12), Dec 1984, 28.*
LEVEL: B LANG: Eng SIRC ARTICLE NO: 108465

Analog and digital dive watches: the U.S. Navy tests six. *Undercurrent (Sausalito, Calif.) 9(2), Feb 1984, 6-8.*
LEVEL: B LANG: Eng SIRC ARTICLE NO: 093978

Charles Jehle retires. *Skin diver (Los Angeles, Calif.) 33(2), Feb 1984, 132-134.*
LEVEL: B LANG: Eng SIRC ARTICLE NO: 09551

Cozens, G. SDM special series in regulators: cressi-sib polaris 1V. *Skin diver (Los Angeles, Calif.) 33(5), May 1984, 66-67.*
LEVEL: B LANG: Eng SIRC ARTICLE NO: 100122

Cozens, G. SDM special series on regulations: Sherwood Selpac Brut. *Skin diver (Los Angeles, Calif.) 33(4), Apr 1984, 50-51.*
LEVEL: B LANG: Eng SIRC ARTICLE NO: 101730

Cozens, G. U.S. divers conshelf 30. *Skin diver (Los Angeles, Calif.) 33(7), Jul 1984, 50-51.*
NOTES: SDM special series on regulators.
LEVEL: B LANG: Eng SIRC ARTICLE NO: 103634

Cozens, G. Dacor AERO 35OA. *Skin diver (Los Angeles, Calif.) 33(6), Jun 1984, 50-51.*
NOTES: SDM special series on regulators.
LEVEL: B LANG: Eng SIRC ARTICLE NO: 103635

Crocker, T. Get the gear that can banish fear: report on years-long tests of octopus rigs. *Diver (London) 29(2), Feb 1984, 40-41.*
LEVEL: B LANG: Eng SIRC ARTICLE NO: 100123

Cross, E.R. Technifacts. *Skin diver (Los Angeles, Calif.) 33(2), Feb 1984, 24-26;134.*
LEVEL: B LANG: Eng SIRC ARTICLE NO: 095513

Davison, B. The personal diving computer - see how impressive it looks. *Undercurrent (Sausalito, Calif.) 9(4), Apr 1984, 7-8.*
LEVEL: B LANG: Eng SIRC ARTICLE NO: 098724

Diver surveys diving inflatables. *Diver (London, Eng.) 29(1), Jan 1984, 18-20.*
LEVEL: B LANG: Eng SIRC ARTICLE NO: 095515

Fryer, M. Simon Fraser University's hypo/hyperbaric research facility. *Diver magazine (Vancouver, B.C.) 10(4), Jun 1984, 31.*
LEVEL: B LANG: Eng SIRC ARTICLE NO: 100127

Hanauer, E. Force fin pro: new model for more kick. *Skin diver (Los Angeles, Calif.) 33(5), May 1984, 65.*
LEVEL: B LANG: Eng SIRC ARTICLE NO: 100129

Houston, J. An aid to mid-water decompression. *Scottish diver (Glasgow, Scotland) 23(5), Sept/Oct 1984, 114.*
LEVEL: B LANG: Eng SIRC ARTICLE NO: 173491

Mansky, B. Canadian air purity inspection program. *Man underwater (Winnipeg, Man.) Sept 1984, 9.*
LEVEL: B LANG: Eng SIRC ARTICLE NO: 101734

Murphy, G. The mini pony: strap on one of these ponies and be prepared for anything. *Skin diver (Los Angeles, Calif.) 33(7) Jul 1984, 54-55.*
LEVEL: B LANG: Eng SIRC ARTICLE NO: 103640

Octopus rigs - second thoughts? *Scottish diver (Glasgow, Scotland) 23(5), Sept/Oct 1984, 102-103;106.*
LEVEL: B LANG: Eng SIRC ARTICLE NO: 173489

Pharo, C. Wardell Aqua Comfort's self-entry suit. *Diver magazine (Vancouver) 10(1), Jan/Feb 1984, 14-15.*
LEVEL: B LANG: E SIRC ARTICLE NO: 095519

Regulation issues. *Diver (London) 29(9), Sept 1984, 17.*
LEVEL: B LANG: Eng SIRC ARTICLE NO: 108470

Vassilopoulos, P. Inflatable dive boat review. *Diver magazine (Vancouver, B.C.) 10(4), Jun 1984, 24-27.*
LEVEL: B LANG: En SIRC ARTICLE NO: 100135

Vassilopoulos, P. Tekna's T-2100BX regulator. *Diver magazine (Vancouver) 10(9), Dec 1984, 28-29.*
LEVEL: B LANG: Eng SIRC ARTICLE NO: 108475

EQUIPMENT - MAINTENANCE

Shave, P.R. Practical aspects of hot dip galvanising and zinc spraying. *Scottish diver (Glasgow, Scotland) 23(5), Sept/Oct 1984, 109-110.*
LEVEL: B LANG: Eng SIRC ARTICLE NO: 173490

INJURIES AND ACCIDENTS

Bove, F. Rx for divers. (ear squeeze) *Skin diver (Los Angeles, Calif.) 33(5), May 1984, 26;28-29;128-129.*
LEVEL: B LANG: Eng SIRC ARTICLE NO: 100118

Bove, F. RX for divers. (hyperthermia) *Skin diver (Los Angeles, Calif.) 33(8), Aug 1984, 29-30;112.*
LEVEL: B LANG: Eng SIRC ARTICLE NO: 101729

UNDERWATER DIVING (continued)

Dickey, L.S. Diving injuries. *Journal of emergency medicine (Elmsford, N.Y.) 1(3), 1984, 249-262.*
LEVEL: A LANG: Eng

Dueker, C.W. Deep diving. *Undersea journal (Santa Ana, Calif.) 1984, 16-17.*
LEVEL: B LANG: Eng SIRC ARTICLE NO: 105053

Hardy, J. The human side of a diving accident. *Diver magazine (Vancouver) 10(1), Jan/Feb 1984, 8.*
LEVEL: B LANG: Eng SIRC ARTICLE NO: 095516

Jacquin, M. Fredenucci, P. Gourmelen, E. Amoros, J.F. Monin, P. Duflot, J.C. Epreuves de remontees rapides et accidents: a propos de deux cas. *Medsubhyp (France) 3(1), 1984, 9-16.*
LEVEL: I LANG: Fr

Kizer, K. Flying after diving. *Underwater reporter (Daly City, Calif.) 14(1), 1984, 18-19.*
LEVEL: B LANG: Eng SIRC ARTICL NO: 105059

Lartigue, G. Lederer, R. Comment eviter l'hydrocution. *EPS: Revue education physique et sport (Paris) 188, juil/aout 1984, 34-36.*
LEVEL: B LANG: Fr SIRC ARTICLE NO: 098535

Lederer, R.J. Sciarli, R. Urgences et traumatologie en plongee. (Refs: 4)*Medecine du sport (Paris) 58(4), 25 juil 1984, 58-64.*
LEVEL: I LANG: Fr SIRC ARTICLE NO: 098731

Lederer, R.J. Sciarli, R. Urgences et traumatologie en plongee. *Medecine du sport (Paris) 58(6), nov 1984, 43-50.*
NOTES: Cet article annule et remplace celui paru sous le no. 84025 le 25 juillet 1984 dans le tome 58/4.
LEVEL: I LANG: Fr SIRC ARTICLE NO: 103639

Marks, M. Safety rules - OK? One up, all up. *Diver (London) 29(7), Jul 1984, 22.*
NOTES: Second part of a series.
LEVEL: LANG: Eng SIRC ARTICLE NO: 100133

Orr, D. Swimming emergency ascent: an unassisted (?) option. *Institute of Diving newsletter (Panama City, Fla.) Spring 1984 5.*
LEVEL: B LANG: Eng SIRC ARTICLE NO: 098539

Re, G. Borgogna, E. Fogliano, F. Scotto, G. Patologia e traumatologia dento-maxillo-facciale nella pratica del nuoto subacqueo e del wind-surf. (Maxillodentofacial pathology and traumatology in skin diving and wind surfing.) *Minerva stomatologia (Turin) 33(2), Mar/Apr 1984, 375-376.*
LEVEL: I LANG: It

Streid, R.B. Avoid decompression stops: how sport divers should use the dive tables. *Skin diver (Los Angeles) 33(10), Oct 1984, 90-92;94.*
LEVEL: I LANG: Eng SIRC ARTICLE NO: 107798

The diving accident victim - how DAN saves lives. *Undercurrent (Sausalito, Calif.) 9(4), Apr 1984, 9-11.*
LEVEL: B LANG: Eng SIRC ARTICLE NO: 098725

Watskinson, A. Danger. 'Plumbers' at work. *Diver (London) 29(11), Nov 1984, 14-15.*
LEVEL: B LANG: Eng SIRC ARTICLE NO: 108466

JUVENILE LITERATURE

McGovern, A. Night dive. New York: MacMillan, c1984. 1v.
LEVEL: B LANG: Eng ISBN: 0027657108 LC
CARD: 84-007163

LAW AND LEGISLATION

Normes d'encadrement en milieu naturel. *Etudes et sports sous-marins, l'aventure sous-marine (Paris) 75, 1984, 27-29.*
LEVEL B LANG: Fr

MEDICINE

Bassett, B.E. Medical fitness for sport diving: a guide for instructors, part 1. *Undersea journal (Santa Ana, Calif.) 1984, 16-18.*
LEVEL: I LANG: Eng SIRC ARTICLE NO: 100114

Becker, G.D. Parell, G.J. Medical examination of the sport scuba diver. *Sportsmedicine digest (Van Nuys, Calif.) 6(4), Apr 1984, 4-5.*
LEVEL: B LANG: Eng SIRC ARTICLE NO: 100115

Bennett, P.B. McLeod, M. Probing the limits of human deep diving. *Philosophical transactions of the Royal Society of London Serie B: Biological sciences (London) 304(1118), 7 Jan 1984, 105-117.*
LEVEL: A LANG: Eng SIRC ARTICLE NO: 100116

Betts, J. Vision under. *Diver (London) 29(7), Jul 1984, 11.*
LEVEL: B LANG: Eng SIRC ARTICLE NO: 100117

Betts, J. Water shortage. (dehydration) *Diver (London) 29(10), Oct 1984, 10.*
LEVEL: B LANG: Eng SIRC ARTICLE NO: 108467

Bove, F. RX for divers. (coronary artery diseases) *Skin diver (Los Angeles, Calif.) 33(4), Apr 1984, 118-119;122-123.*
LEVEL: B LANG: Eng SIRC ARTICLE NO: 101728

Cardone, B.J. DAN needs you. *Skin diver (Los Angeles) 33(12), Dec 1984, 110.*
LEVEL: B LANG: Eng SIRC ARTICLE NO: 107787

D.A.N.: le reseau americain d'urgence-sante. *Plongee (Montreal) 11(4), sept/oct 1984, 28-29.*
LEVEL: B LANG: Fr SIRC ARTICLE NO: 101731

Davis, J.C. Appendix A: medical examination of sport scuba divers.
NOTES: In, Strauss, R.H. (ed.), Sports medicine, Philadelphia ; Toronto, Saunders, 1984, p. 513-523.
LEVEL: I LANG: Eng RC1210 17196

Dueker, C.W. Drugs and diving. *Undersea journal (Santa Ana, Calif.) 1984, 16-17.*
LEVEL: B LANG: Eng SIRC ARTICLE NO: 1085

Hempleman, V. O2: is it OK? (decompression sickness) *Diver (London) 29(10), Oct 1984, 19.*
LEVEL: B LANG: Eng SIRC ARTICLE NO: 108468

Ibrahimoff, O. Naissance et croissance. La plongee hyperbare en question. (Refs: 36)*Medecine du sport (Paris) 58(4), 25 jui 1984, 26-35.*
RESUME: L'auteur passe en revue les etudes effectuees entre 1972 et 1983 sur la fertilite et la plongee, la gestation et la plongee, le nouveau-ne et l'oxygene, et les effets de la plongee sur la croissance.
LEVEL: A LANG: Fr SIRC ARTICLE NO: 098729

King, R. In the spot. *Skindiving in Australia and New Zealand 14(3), June 1984, 71-73.*
ABST: An account by a decompressio chamber attendant of a patient treated for neurological decompression sickness.
LEVEL: I LANG: Eng

Kizer, K. Diving doctor: the bends - some long-term considerations. *Diver magazine (Vancouver, B.C.) 10(2), Mar 1984, 12;46.*
LEVEL: B LANG: Eng SIRC ARTICLE NO: 095517

Kizer, K. Diabetes and diving. *Diver magazine (Vancouver, B.C.) 10(3), Apr/May 1984, 10-11.*
LEVEL: B LANG: Eng SIRC ARTICLE NO: 099007

Kizer, K. Nitrogen narcosis more questions than answers. *Diver magazine (Vancouver) 10(6), Sept 1984, 8.*
LEVEL: B LANG: E SIRC ARTICLE NO: 108472

Lederer, R.J. Aptitude et contre indications a la plongee sportive. *Medecine du sport (Paris) 58(4), 25 juil 1984, 51-57.*
LEVEL: B LANG: Fr SIRC ARTICLE NO: 098730

Sands, R.L. Oxygen therapy: Australia leads the way. *Skindiving in Australia and the South Pacific 14(2), Apr 1984, 97.*
ABST: 100 per cent oxygen is the single most effective treatment for decompression sickness and air embolism other than recompression. Gives details of a new technique for administering oxygen which requires no special training and is unique to Australia.
LEVEL: I LANG: Eng

Splichal, P. Allegre, G. Examens electro-encephalo-graphiques et electro-myo-graphiques associes, executes systematiquement sur des moniteurs de plongee sub-aquatique. Premiers resultats. (Refs: 6)*Medecine du sport (Paris) 58(4), 25 juil 1984, 36-42.*
RESUME: Les auteurs comparent les resultats d'examens electroencephalographique et electromyographique effectues chez 15 moniteurs de plongee, 15 plongeurs et 15 non plongeurs, non sportifs presentant des signes de spasmophilie.
LEVEL: A LANG: Fr SIRC ARTICLE NO: 098738

Tonjum, S. Norwegian deep diving trials. *Philosphical transactions of the Royal Society of London. Series B: Biological Sciences (London) 304(1118), 7 Jan 1984, 143-149.*
LEVEL: A LANG: Eng SIRC ARTICLE NO: 100134

Unsworth, I.P. Oxygen breathing as a first aid measure in decompression sickness and diving related accidents. (Refs: 10) *Skindiving in Australia and New Zealand 14(3), June 1984, 36-37.*
ABST: A director of diving and hyperbaric medicine considers the efficacy of oxygen inhalation in the interval from surfacing with decompression sickness (DCS) to the commencement of curative recompression.
LEVEL: I LANG: Eng

Wachholz, C. Guidelines for teaching emergency procedures. *Undersea journal (Santa Ana, Calif.) 1984, 32-33.*
LEVEL: B LANG: Eng SIRC ARTICLE NO: 100136

NAVIGATION

Cross, E.R. Technifacts. (Diver navigation) *Skin diver (Los Angeles, Calif.) 33(1), Jan 1984, 20;24;26;32;34.*
LEVEL: B LANG: Eng SIRC ARTICLE NO: 095514

Cross, E.R. More on magnetic compasses. *Skin diver (Los Angeles, Calif.) 33(5), May 1984, 22;39;42.*
LEVEL: B LANG: Eng SIRC ARTICLE NO: 100124

PHOTOGRAPHY

Church, J. Church, C. Get snapping with a disc: super simple U/W photography for beginners. *Diver magazine (Vancouver, B.C. 10(3), Apr/May 1984, 14-15;17.*
LEVEL: B LANG: Eng SIRC ARTICLE NO: 100121

Gilbert, M. Les objectifs. Photographie sous-marine. *Plongee (Montreal) 11(5), nov/dec 1984, 34-36.*
LEVEL: B LANG: Fr SIR ARTICLE NO: 101732

PHYSICAL FITNESS

Cotes, J.E. Reed, J.W. North Sea divers are no fitter than sedentary men. (letter) *Lancet (London) 2(8398), 11 Aug 1984, 348-349.*
LEVEL: I LANG: Eng SIRC ARTICLE NO: 105051

Crosbie, W.A. Fitness of North Sea divers. (letter) *Lancet (London) 2(8400), 25 Aug 1984, 471-472.*
LEVEL: B LANG: Eng SIR ARTICLE NO: 105052

Missirliu, C. Foy, B. Chauvire, D. Test de Ruffier-Dickson accelere chez le plongeur. Validation et calibrage au moyen de calculatrices programmables de poche. (Refs: 3)*Medecine du sport (Paris) 58(4), 25 juil 1984, 46-50.*
RESUME: Les auteurs discutent des trois methodes permettant le depistage des insuffisances d'entrainement des candidats a la plongee: l'indice corporel, le test de Ruffier-Dickson et le test de Flack. 30 candidats et 12 moniteurs de plongee servent de sujets. Un Ruffier moyen de l'order de 7 avec un ecart type de 2,9 et un indice corporel de 413 sont observes chez les postulants. Les moniteurs presentent un Ruffier de 5 avec ecart type de 2,3 et un indice corporel moyen de 376.
LEVEL: A LANG: Fr SIRC ARTICLE NO: 098735

Thompson, J. Barr, D. Rennie, M.J. Fitness of North Sea divers. (letter) *Lancet (London) 2(8406), 6 Oct 1984, 806.*
LEVEL: LANG: Eng

Tibika, B. La plongee sous-marine. *Pratique medicale (Paris) 38, 1984, 9-33.*
LEVEL: I LANG: Fr

PHYSICS

Craig, A.B. Physics and physiology of swimming goggles. (Refs: 1)*Physician and sportsmedicine (Minneapolis, Minn.) 12(12), Dec 1984, 107-109;112.*
LEVEL: I LANG: Eng SIRC ARTICLE NO: 103636

PHYSIOLOGY

Carsac, J.L. Vaultier, R. Anatomie et physiologie humaines appliquees a la plongee. Paris: Editions Amphora, c1984. 119 p. : ill. (Sports & loisirs.)
LEVEL: B LANG: Fr ISBN: 2-85180-078-7
GV840.S78 18024

Daney, I.S. Cotes, J.E. Reed, J.W. Relationship of ventilatory capacity to hyperbaric exposure in divers. (Refs: 14)*Journal of applied physiology: respiratory, environmental and exercise physiology (Bethesda, Md.) 56(6), Jun 1984, 1655-1658.*
ABST: The purpose of this study was to assess the effects of diving exposure on forced vital capacity (FVC) and forced expiratory volume in 1s (FEV1). 858 divers served as subjects. Findings indicated a significant positive association of maximal depth

with FVC and negative association with FEV1/FVC%. FEV1/FVC% was also positively correlated with years of diving exposure. No association with FEV1 was observed. A longitudinal study of 255 of the divers surveyed over a minimum period of 5 years showed that changes in FVC per annum was correlated with change in maximal depth.
LEVEL: A LANG: Eng SIRC ARTICLE NO: 098723

Foex, J.A. Plongee profonde. L'hydrogene au banc d'essai: 6 hommes ont passe 18 jours en immersion fictive jusqu'a 300 metre de profondeur. *Etudes et sports sous-marins, l'aventure sous-marine (Paris) 73, mars/avr 1984, 32-35.*
LEVEL: B LANG: Fr SIRC ARTICLE NO: 098726

Hempleman, H.V. Florio, J.T. Garrard, M.P. Harris, D.J. Hayes, P.A. Hennessy, T.R. Nichols, G. Toeroek, Z. Winsborough, M.M. U.K. deep diving trials. *Philosophical transactions of the Royal Society of London. Series B: Biological Sciences (London) 304(1118), 7 Jan 1984, 119-141.*
LEVEL: A LANG: Eng SIRC ARTICLE NO: 100130

Hemplemann, V. Will gill change diving? *Diver (London) 29(5), May 1984, 14.*
LEVEL: B LANG: Eng SIRC ARTICLE NO: 098727

Hentsch, U. Ulmer, H.V. Trainability of underwater breath-holding time. (Refs: 13)*International journal of sports medicine (Stuttgart) 5(6), Dec 1984, 343-347.*
CONF: Deutsche Physiologische Gesellschaft. Meeting (57th : 1982 : Gieben).
ABST: Breath-holding time (BHT) and the 'onset point' of involuntary respiratory movements of 64 subjects were registered after deep inspiration and immersion in ca. 1 m. Two different tests were set up: (I) 2 breath-holds per day on 5 consecutive days, (II) 5 repeated breath-holds with pauses of 3 min in between. BHT of the first test was shorter underwater than in similar experiments in air: the increase of BHT underwater was distinctly higher (series II: 160 per cent). Thirty percent of the subjects inequivocally showed respiratory movements (group 1), 31 per cent did not reach the 'onset point' (group 3). In group 1 BHT was considerably higher than in group 3. Results confirm and quantify the good trainability of BHT underwater.
LEVEL: A LANG: Eng SIRC ARTICLE NO: 105056

Mukhtar, M.R. Patrick, J.M. Bronchoconstriction: a component of the 'diving response' in man. (Refs: 13)*European journal of applied physiology and occupational physiology (Berlin, W.G.) 53(2), 1984, 155-158.*
ABST: We have investigated the possibility that a bronchoconstriction accompanies the vagally-mediated bradycardia induced in man by immersion of the face in cold water. Forced expiratory flows (FEF) at 40 per cent and 25 per cent of vital capacity (VC) have been measured from partial flow-volume curves obtained during forced expirations starting at 70 per cent VC. These were performed immediately after 15 s apnoea with or without face immersion. Five of the 10 subjects showed evidence of a greater than 10 per cent reduction in FEF, which averaged 17 per cent. Half the response was attributable to the apnoea alone and the other half, to cold face immersion.
LEVEL: A LANG: Eng SIRC ARTICLE NO: 105060

Smeland, E.B. Owe, J.O. Andersen, H.T. Modification of the 'dividing bradycardia' by hypoxia or exercise. *Respiration physiology (Amsterdam) 56(2), May 1984, 245-251.*

ABST: The authors report a study in which either hypoxia or exercise has been imposed as an additional stress on human subjects performing apneic face immersion in order to determine any early changes in the reflex rate of onset and/or the final level of cardiovascular adjustment. It is concluded that the rate of onset of the diving reflex varies with the stresses imposed whereas the final level of adjustment does not.
LEVEL: A LANG: Eng SIRC ARTICLE NO: 105061

Strauss, R.H. Medical aspects of scuba and breath-hold diving. (Refs: 15)
NOTES: In, Strauss, R.H. (ed.), Sports medicine, Philadelphia ; Toronto, Saunders, 1984, p. 361-377.
LEVEL: A LANG: Eng RC1210 17196

PHYSIOLOGY - ALTITUDE

Salzano, J.V. Camporesi, E.M. Stolp, B.W. Moon, R.E. Physiological responses to exercise at 47 and 66 ATA. (Refs: 31)*Journa of applied physiology: respiratory, environmental and exercise physioloyg (Bethesda, Md.) 57(4), Oct 1984, 1055-1068.*
LEVEL: A LANG: Eng SIRC ARTICLE NO: 108945

PSYCHOLOGY

Burgess, L.G. The effects of teaching coping strategies on the performance of beginning scuba divers. Eugene, Ore.: Microfor Publications, University of Oregon, 1984. 2 microfiches : negative, ill. ; 11 x 15 cm.
NOTES: Thesis (M.S.) - Pennsylvania State University, 1983; (ix, 92 leaves); includes bibliography.
LEVEL: A LANG: Eng UO84 362-363

Phillips, C.J. Cognitive performance in sports scuba divers. (Refs: 1)*Perceptual and motor skills (Missoula, Mont.) 59(2), Oct 1984, 645-646.*
ABST: The author evaluates the cognitive performance of seven scuba divers (four men, three women), aged between 21 and 33 yr., during one month of work at an underwater archeology site. Findings indicate that cognitive impairment can occur at depths experienced by divers.
LEVEL: A LANG: Eng SIRC ARTICLE NO: 103641

SAFETY

Always use an ABLJ. Survival rules, OK? Part four. (adjustable buoyancy life jacket) *Diver (London) 29, Sept 1984, 38.*
LEVEL: B LANG: Eng SIRC ARTICLE NO: 108471

Boyd, E. Diver's rally saves flag. *Skin diver (Los Angeles) 33(9), Sept 1984, 30-31;38-39.*
LEVEL: B LANG: Eng SIRC ARTICL NO: 107785

Existe-t-il vraiment un drapeau de plongee sportive? *Plongee (Montreal) 11(2), mai/juin 1984, 10-14.*
LEVEL: B LANG: Fr SIRC ARTICLE NO: 100125

Gruber, S.H. Shark repellents: perspectives for the future. *Hart House newsletter (Toronto) Jan 1984, 19-21.*
NOTES: Excerpted from, Oceanus 24(4), Winter 1981-82, 72-78.
LEVEL: B LANG: Eng SIRC ARTICLE NO: 103637

Sharing air: standardizing an emergency procedure. *Undercurrent (New York) 9(11/12), Nov/Dec 1984,*

UNDERWATER DIVING (continued)

14-16.
LEVEL: B LANG: En SIRC ARTICLE NO: 103642

Todd, M. The buoyancy business. *Diver (London) 29(5), May 1984, 15.*
LEVEL: B LANG: Eng SIRC ARTICLE NO: 098739

TEACHING

Brylske, A. Teaching psychomotor skills: a perspective for the diving educator. *Undersea journal (Santa Ana, Calif.) 1984, 29-31;35.*
LEVEL: B LANG: Eng SIRC ARTICLE NO: 100119

Brylske, A. PADI's divemaster course: a giant step forward. *Undersea journal (Santa Ana, Calif.) 1984, 4-7;20.*
LEVEL: B LANG: Eng SIRC ARTICLE NO: 105048

Brylske, A. The PADI system: toward an educational technology of diver training. *Undersea journal (Santa Ana, Calif.) 1984, 13;38-39;42.*
LEVEL: B LANG: Eng SIRC ARTICLE NO: 105050

Brylske, A. The PADI instructor development course: an overview. *Undersea journal (Santa Ana, Calif.) 1984, 5-7.*
LEVEL: B LANG: Eng SIRC ARTICLE NO: 108572

Brylski, A. Knowledge vs. learning: a choice of approach. *Undersea journal (Santa Ana, Calif.) 1984, 12-13;21.*
LEVEL: B LANG: Eng SIRC ARTICLE NO: 100120

Hornsby, A. What you want to happen. What you expect to happen. *Undersea journal (Santa Ana, Calif.) 1984, 14-15;21.*
LEVEL: B LANG: Eng SIRC ARTICLE NO: 105057

Walker, J. PADI: dedicated to making diving better for everyone. *Skin diver (Los Angeles, Calif.) 33(1), Jan 1984, 56-58;126.*
LEVEL: B LANG: Eng SIRC ARTICLE NO: 095521

TECHNIQUES AND SKILLS

Brylske, A. Instructional systems development: the PADI approach. *Undersea journal (Santa Ana, Calif.) 1984, 24-27.*
LEVEL B LANG: Eng SIRC ARTICLE NO: 108575

Hardy, J. Mastering buoyancy control. *Diver magazine (Greenville, Island, B.C.) 10(5), Jul/Aug 1984, 8-9.*
LEVEL: B LANG: Eng SIRC ARTICLE NO: 103638

Hardy, J. Clearing your ears. *Diver magazine (Vancouver) 10(7), Oct/Nov 1984, 6-7.*
LEVEL: B LANG: Eng SIRC ARTICLE NO: 108476

Hobson, B. Safety with an Octopus rig - fact or fantasy? *Scottish diver (Glasgow, Scotland) 23(3), May/Jun 1984, 54-55.*
LEVEL: B LANG: Eng SIRC ARTICLE NO: 100131

Schnabel, J. How to clear your mask. *Skin diver (Los Angeles, Calif.) 33(1), Jan 1984, 122-124;127.*
LEVEL: B LANG: Eng SIRC ARTICLE NO: 095520

TESTING AND EVALUATION

Hennessy, T.R. Towse, E.J. Diving the decompression computer: results at sea and in chamber tests. *Diver (London) 29(4), Ap 1984, 24-25.*
LEVEL: B LANG: Eng SIRC ARTICLE NO: 098728

VARIATIONS - CAVE DIVING

Horne, P. A report on the fatal cave-diving accident at Piccaninnie Ponds 7 April 1984. *Skindiving in Australia and New Zealand 14(3), June 1984, 68-70.*
ABST: The Cave Divers Association of Australia is a self regulating body established in 1973 which tests cave divers and assesses their knowledge of the cave environments and proves their in-water competence and capabilities before issuing certificates in different categories. This is a committee report on the first caving accident in 10 years which resulted in 2 deaths on 7 April 1984. The significant cause of the accident was the apparent deliberate breaking of strict safety rules and the extreme depth of the dive with attendent danger of nitrogen narcosis. Conclusions are drawn and recommendations made.
LEVEL: I LANG: Eng

Lloyd, O. The physiology of training. *Caves & caving (Lancs, Eng.) 24, May 1984, 20.*
LEVEL: B LANG: Eng SIRC ARTICLE NO: 103473

Sheffe, E. Black holes in the sea. Cave diving combines the dangers of rock climbing, cave exploration and scuba diving. Its few practitioners aren't crazy - just careful. Very, very careful. *Ultrasport (Boston) 1(3), May/Jun 1984, 67-70.*
LEVEL: B LANG: Eng SIRC ARTICLE NO: 097035

Vergier, F. Accidents et maladies de decompression. *Spelunca (Paris) 15, juil/sept 1984, 42-43.*
LEVEL: I LANG: Fr SIRC ARTICLE NO: 101735

VARIATIONS - ICE DIVING

Lefebvre, P. D'Amours, M. Dossier special: Super. Plongee sous-glace. Une specialite du Quebec decrite par les moniteurs et plongeurs du club de plongee sous-glace BAISER-BLANC. *Plongee (Montreal) 11(1), hiver 1984, 17-24.*
LEVEL: B LANG: Fr SIRC ARTICLE NO: 098732

UNITED STATES OF AMERICA

Leonard, W.M. Sociological perspective of sport. 2nd ed. Minneapolis: Burgess Pub. Co., c1984. viii, 360 p.
NOTES: Includes index.
LEVEL: I LANG: Eng ISBN: 0808738631 LC CARD: 83-010158 GV706.5 15955

Lupton, C.H. Ostrove, N.M. Bozzo, R.M. Participation in leisure-time physical activity: a comparison of the existing data. (Refs: 13)*Journal of physical education, recreation & dance (Reston, Va.) 55(9), Nov/Dec 1984, 19-23.*
LEVEL: I LANG: Eng SIRC ARTICLE NO: 102922

Nixon, H.L. Sport and the American dream. New York: Leisure Press, c1984. 264 p.
LEVEL: I LANG: Eng ISBN: 0880111127 LC CARD: 82-83943 GV706.5 15948

Van Doren, C.S. Sport participation, sporting goods sales, and recreation expenditures. *In, Clawson, M. and Van Doren, C.S. (eds.), Statistics on outdoor recreation, Washington, Resources for the Future, c1984, p. 288-296.*
LEVEL: I LANG: Eng GV191.4 20254

HISTORY

Breen, T.H. Horses and gentlemen: the cultural significance of gambling among the gentry of Virginia. (Refs: 70)
NOTES: In, Riess, S.A. (ed.), The American sporting experience: a historical anthology of sport in America, New York, Leisure Press, c1984, p. 35-54. Reprinted from, William & Mary quarterly 34, April 1977, p. 329-347.
LEVEL: A LANG: Eng GV583 17631

Bruce, H.A. Baseball and the national life.
NOTES: In, Riess, S.A. (ed.), The American sporting experience: a historical anthology of sport in America, New York, Leisure Press, c1984, p. 264-270. Previously published in, Outlook 104, May 1913, p. 104-107.
LEVEL: I LANG: Eng GV583 17631

Camp, W. Walter Camp on sportsmanship.
NOTES: In, Riess, S.A. (ed.), The American sporting experience: a historical anthology of sport in America, New York, Leisure Press, c1984, p. 164-167. Excerpt from: Book of college sports, New York, Century, 1893, p. 1-9.
LEVEL: B LANG: Eng GV583 17631

Dolan, G.K. Athletes and athletics: sports almanac, USA. 1st ed. Loma Linda, Calif.: Footprint Pub. Co., c1984. 397 p. ; 23 cm.
NOTES: Bibliography: p. 396-397.
LEVEL: B LANG: Eng LC CARD: 84-090369

Gilmore, A.T. Jack Johnson: a magnificent black anachronism of the early twentieth century. (Refs: 45)
NOTES: In, Riess, S.A (ed.), The American sporting experience: a historical anthology of sport in America, New York, Leisure Press, c1984, p. 306-315. Previously published in, Journal of social and behavioural sciences 19, Winter 1973, p. 35-42.
LEVEL: I LANG: Eng GV583 17631

Higginson, T.W. Saints and their bodies.
NOTES: In, Riess, S.A. (ed.), The American sporting experience: a historical anthology of sport in America, New York, Leisure Press, c1984, p. 80-90. Reprinted from, Atlantic monthly 1, March 1858, p. 82-95.
LEVEL: I LANG: Eng GV583 17631

Holmes, J. Texas sport: the illustrated history. Austin, Tex.: Texas Monthly Press, c1984. 1v.
NOTES: Includes index.
LEVEL: B LANG: Eng ISBN: 0932012728 LC CARD: 84-008448

Jable, J.T. The public schools athletic league of New York City: organized athletics for city schoolchildren, 1903-1914. (Refs: 79)
NOTES: In, Riess, S.A. (ed.), The American sporting experience: a historical anthology of sport in America, New York, Leisure Press, c1984, p. 219-238. Originally published in: Ladd, W.M., and Lumpkin, A. (eds.), Sport and American education: history and perspectives, Washington, D.C., 1979, p. ix;1-18.
LEVEL: A LANG: Eng GV583 17631

Park, R.J. British sports and pastimes in San Francisco, 1848-1900. (Refs: 54)*British journal of sports history (London) 1(3), Dec 1984, 300-317.*
ABST: This study focuses on the recreational and sporting activities from 1848 to 1900 of English, Scottish and Irish immigrants living in San Francisco.
LEVEL: A LANG: Eng SIRC ARTICLE NO: 105277

Riess, S.A. The American sporting experience: a historical anthology of sport in America. New York: Leisure Press, c1984. 40 p.
NOTES: Includes bibliographies.
LEVEL: A LANG: Eng ISBN: 0880112107 LC CARD: 84-7188 GV583 17631

Robinson, J. Smith, W. Jackie Robinson's first spring training.
NOTES: In, Riess, S.A. (ed.), The American sporting experience: a historical anthology of sport in America, New York, Leisure Press, c1984, p. 365-370. Excerpt from: Jackie Robinson: my own story, by Jack R. Robinson and Wendell Smith, New York, Greenberg, 1948, p. 65-68;70-75;79-80.
LEVEL: B LANG: Eng GV583 17631

Sargent, D.A. Are athletics making girls masculine? A practical answer to a question every girl asks.
NOTES: In, Riess, S.A (ed.), The American sproting experience: a historical anthology of sport in America, New York, Leisure Press, c1984, p. 255-263. Previously published in, Ladies home journal 29, March 1912, p. 11;71;73.
LEVEL: I LANG: Eng GV583 17631

Smith, R.A. The rise of basketball for women in colleges. (Refs: 66)
NOTES: In, Riess, S.A. (ed.), The American sporting experience: a historical anthology of sport in America, New York, Leisure Press, c1984, p. 239-254. Originally published in, Canadian journal of history of sport and physical education 1, December 1970, p. 18-36.
LEVEL: A LANG: Eng GV583 17631

Smith, R.A. Sports and games in Western Iowa in the early 1880s. *Palimpsest (Iowa City) 65(1), Jan/Feb 1984, 9-15;25.*
LEVEL: I LANG: Eng

Starr, K. The sporting life. *California history (San Francisco) 63(1), Winter 1984, 26-31.*
ABST: A history of sport in Lo Angeles.
LEVEL: B LANG: Eng

The great contest: Fashion v. Peytona (1845).
NOTES: In, Riess, S.A. (ed.), The American sporting experience: a historical anthology of sport in America, New York, Leisure Press, c1984, p. 91-103. Reprinted from, New York herald, 5 May 1845.
LEVEL: B LANG: Eng GV583 17631

Uminowicz, G. Sport in a middle-class Utopia: Asbury Park, New Jersey, 1871-1895. *Journal of sport history (Seattle, Wash.) 11(1), Spring 1984, 51-73.*
ABST: An historical look of Asbury Park, a New Jersey seaside resort, is provided in this paper. The author discusses the life of its founder, James A. Bradley. The role of sport in the resort is also examined.
LEVEL: A LANG: Eng SIRC ARTICLE NO: 095901

Wiggins, D.K. Smith, R.A. North American Society for Sport History proceedings and newsletter 1984.
s.l.: North American Society for Sport History, c1984. 76 p. : ill.
CONF: North American Society for Sport History Conference (12th : 1984 : Louisville, Ky.).
CORP: North American Society for Sport History.
NOTES: ISSN: 0093-6235.
LEVEL: I LANG: Eng LC CARD: 74-642308 GV571 18383

OLYMPIC GAMES

Davenport, J. The American Alliance/U.S. Olympic Committee relationship. *Journal of physical education, recreation & dance 55(3), Mar 1984, 18-19;30.*
LEVEL: B LANG: Eng SIRC ARTICLE NO: 092978

Osness, W.H. The American Alliance role in Olympic sport: a present assessment. *Journal of physical education, recreation & dance 55(3), Mar 1984, 20;30.*
LEVEL: B LANG: Eng SIRC ARTICLE NO: 092988

PHYSICAL FITNESS

Blumenthal, K.J. Long, P.T. A recreation and park perspective on fitness and health. *Parks & recreation (Alexandria, Va.) 1 (12), Dec 1984, 38;40.*
LEVEL: B LANG: Eng SIRC ARTICLE NO: 173250

Cato, B. Research update: promoting fitness. (Refs: 11)*Parks and recreation (Alexandria, Va.) 19(7), Jul 1984, 53-54;61.*
LEVEL: B LANG: Eng SIRC ARTICLE NO: 096178

Day, W.C. Health and fitness of Americans: the state of the union. *Parks & recreation (Alexandria, Va.) 19(12), Dec 1984, 28-31.*
LEVEL: B LANG: Eng SIRC ARTICLE NO: 173246

Fitness in America--The Perrier study: a national research report of behavior, knowledge and opinions concerning the taking up of sports and exercise. New York: Garland Pub., 1984. 58, (1) p. (Garland reference library of social science; v.141.)
CORP: Louis Harris & Ass., Inc..
NOTES: Originally published as: The Perrier study.
LEVEL: A LANG: Eng ISBN: 0824091434 LC CARD: 82-049184 GV481 17539

Golding, L.A. Partnership for the fit. (YMCA) (Refs: 2)*Journal of physical education, recreation & dance (Reston, Va.) 55(9), Nov/Dec 1984, 51-53.*
LEVEL: B LANG: Eng SIRC ARTICLE NO: 102719

Lupton, C.H. Ostrove, N.M. Bozzo, R.M. Participation in leisure-time physical activity: a comparison of the existing data. (Refs: 13)*Journal of physical education, recreation & dance (Reston, Va.) 55(9), Nov/Dec 1984, 19-23.*
LEVEL: I LANG: Eng SIRC ARTICLE NO: 102922

Razor, J.E. AAHPERD and a fit America. (Refs: 1)*Journal of physical education, recreation & dance (Reston, Va.) 55(9), Nov/Dec 1984, 54-60.*
LEVEL: B LANG: Eng SIRC ARTICLE NO: 102740

VOLLEYBALL

ADMINISTRATION

Kent, J. Strachan, D. Grandir dans le sport: un guide pour l'elaboration d'une perspective de developpement dans le sport. Ottawa: Condition physique et Sport amateur, 1984. vi, 105 feuillets
CORP: Canada. Condition physique et Sport amateur.
CORP: Canada. Fitness and Amateur Sport.
NOTES: Also published in English under the title: Growing in sport: a handbook for creating a sport development perspective. Bibliographie: feuillets 104-105. Comprend aussi: Modele de perfectionnement par etapes des volleyeurs, par

Lorne Sawula et Terry Valeriote.
LEVEL: I LANG: Fr GV713 17283

Kent, J. Strachan, D. Growing in sport: a handbook for creating a sport development perspective. Ottawa: Fitness and Amateur Sport, 1984. vi, 99 leaves
CORP: Canada. Fitness and Amateur Sport.
CORP: Canada. Condition physique et Sport amateur.
NOTES: Egalement publie en francais sous le titre: Grandir dans le sport: un guide pour l'elaboration d'une perspective de developpement dans le sport. Bibliography: leaves 98-99. Includes: Volleyball development model, 2nd ed., by Lorne Sawula and Terry Valeriote, and Fair play codes for children in sport, by the National Task Force on Children's Play.
LEVEL: I LANG: Eng GV713 17282

ANTHROPOMETRY

Grewal, R. Sidhu, L.S. Effect of training on subcutaneous and lean tissues of top class Indian female volleyball players. (Refs: 9)*Sportorvosi szemle/Hungarian review of sports medicine (Budapest) 25(2), 1984, 85-89.*
ABST: The present study was conducted to investigate the effect of training on subcutaneous and lean tissues of 12 outstanding Indian female volleyball players, who attended a training camp at Netaji Subhas National Institute of Sports, Patiala, in October-November, 1979, before participating in the World Cup competition held at Hong Kong. Six circumferences and six skinfold measurements were taken on each subject initially at the start of the camp and then after a gap of 42 days of intense training. It has been observed that there is an increase in the muscle mass with a decrease in the subcutaneous tissue, after the training period.
LEVEL: A LANG: Eng SIRC ARTICLE NO: 100144

BIOMECHANICS

Fellows, P.J. Biomechanical analyses of the volleyball front and back sets. Eugene, Ore.: Microform Publications, University of Oregon, 1984. 1 microfiche : negative, ill. ; 11 x 15 cm.
NOTES: Thesis (M.S.) - Purdue University, 1982; (v, 48 leaves); includes bibliography.
LEVEL: A LANG: Eng UO84 301

Iwoilow, A.W. Volleyball - Biomechanik und Methodik. Berlin: Sportverlag, 1984. 147 p. : ill.
NOTES: Translated from Russia Bibliography: p. 141-145.
LEVEL: I LANG: Ger GV1015.3 18151

Saunders, H.L. A cinematographical study of the relationship between speed of movement and available force. Eugene, Ore.: Microform Publications, University of Oregon, 1984. 3 microfiches : negative, ill. ; 11 x 15 cm.
NOTES: Thesis (Ph.D.) - Texas A & M University, 1980; (xvi, 204 leaves); vita; includes bibliography.
LEVEL: A LANG: Eng UO84 5-7

VOLLEYBALL (continued)

CHILDREN

Volleyball development model. Age group: 13-14. *Sports (Kallang, Singapore) 12(1), Jan 1984, 32-33.* LEVEL: B LANG: Eng SIRC ARTICLE NO: 101744

CHILDREN - MINI-SPORT

Pittera, C. Vancondio, O. Minivolley story. Fipav, Milan: Arnoldo Mondadori Editore, 1984. 66 p. : ill. LEVEL: B LANG: It

COACHING

Dickie, D. The coaches: Debbie Muir, Jack Donohue, Ken Maeda, and Marina van der Merwe. Les entraineurs: Debbie Muir, Jack Donohue, Ken Maeda, et Marina van der Merwe. *Champion (Ottawa) 8(3), Aug 1984, 61-65.* LEVEL: B LANG: Eng Fr SIRC ARTICLE NO: 095750

Martinez, C. The volleyball court... a classroom? *Texas coach (Austin, Tex.) 28(3), Oct 1984, 42-43.* LEVEL: B LANG: Eng SIRC ARTICLE NO: 173207

Money, J. The recruiting of Nancy Reno. *Women's sports (Palo Alto, Calif.) 6(9), Sept 1984, 36-39.* LEVEL: B LANG: Eng SIR ARTICLE NO: 173593

Scates, A.E. Winning volleyball. 3rd ed. Boston ; Toronto: Allyn & Bacon, c1984. xvii, 345 p. : ill. NOTES: Bibliography: p 331-332. LEVEL: I LANG: Eng ISBN: 0-205-08110-X LC CARD: 83-26567 GV1015.5.C63 17520

COUNTRIES AND REGIONS

El Nagar, R. Les volleyball dans le monde arabe. Volleyball in the Arab world. Voleibol en el mundo arabe. *Volleyball (Rome 3, May/Jun 1984, 10-15.* LEVEL: B LANG: Fr Eng Spa SIRC ARTICLE NO: 100142

INJURIES AND ACCIDENTS

Coleman, J. Volleyball. *In, Adams, S.H. (ed.), et al., Catastrophic injuries in sports: avoidance strategies, Salinas, Calif., Cayote Press, c1984, p. 87-90.* LEVEL: B LANG: Eng RD97 19088

Ferretti, A. Puddu, G. Mariani, P.P. Neri, M. Jumper's knee: an epidemiological study of volleyball players. (Refs: 9) *Physician and sportsmedicine (Minneapolis, Minn.) 12(10), Oct 1984, 97-99;101;104;106.* ABST: The incidence of jumper's knee in 407 volleyball players was investigated in this study. The controlled variables were age and sex, years of play, frequency of training sessions and games, type of playing surface, and type of training. 93 (22.8%) of the subjects had experienced symptoms related to jumper's knee or were currently experiencing pain. Both frequency of play and floor surface were significant factors in the incidence of jumper's knee. LEVEL: A LANG: Eng SIRC ARTICLE NO: 100143

Mattison, R. U.B.C. mens volleyball prevention program for ankle injuries. *Journal of the Canadian Athletic Therapists Association (Oakville, Ont.) 11(2), Fall 1984, 17-18.* LEVEL: B LANG: Eng SIRC ARTICLE NO: 105066

MASS MEDIA

Berruti, G. Lettre ouverte aux federations: les prix de Sportfest. Open lettre to the federations: Sportfest's prizes. Carta abierta a las federaciones: los premios de Sportfest. *Volleyball (Rome) 3, May/Jun 1984, 18-20.* LEVEL: B LANG: Fr Eng Spa SIRC ARTICLE NO: 100140

NUTRITION

Bombardieri, E. Battistessa, R. Crippa, F. Esposito, G. The effects of an energy stimulator on blood electrolyte and lactate levels in athletes under training. (Refs: 8)*Acta vitaminologica et enzymologica (Milano) 6(1), 1984, 57-61.* ABST: The effects of a mineral-vitamin-sugar preparation has been tested on a group of volleyball players under training. Plasma electrolytes (Na, K, Cl), erythrocyte electrolyte content, plasma lactate concentration and erythrocyte water content have been determined before and after a training session in three different experimental situations: a) controls ; b) acute treatment with the energy stimulator; c) chronic treatment (8 days) with a similar preparation of the energy stimulator. The results are indicative of a significantly lower lactate production and a more stable electrolyte concentration after treatment with respect to the control data. LEVEL: A LANG: Eng SIRC ARTICLE NO: 105062

PERCEPTUAL MOTOR PROCESSES

Hansen, J. Few Americans can focus on vision training. *Volleyball monthly (San Luis Obispo, Calif.) 3(1), Jan 1984, 19-20.* LEVEL: B LANG: Eng SIRC ARTICLE NO: 100146

PHYSICAL FITNESS

Elenkov, E. Tests d'evaluation. Evaluation tests. Tests de evaluacion. *Volleyball (Roma) 4, Jul/Aug 1984, 21-24.* LEVEL: I LANG: Fr Eng Spa SIRC ARTICLE NO: 101737

PHYSIOLOGY

Belyaev, A.V. Methods of developing work capacity in volleyball. *Soviet sports review (Escondido, Calif.) 19(1), Mar 1984, 7-10.* NOTES: Translated from, Volleyball 1983, 54-58. To be continued in volume 19 no. 2. LEVEL: I LANG: Eng SIRC ARTICLE NO: 095522

Bosco, C. Physiologie et entrainement. Physiology and training. Fisiologia y entrenamiento. (Refs: 4)*Volleyball (Roma) 4, Jul/Aug 1984, 5-8.* LEVEL: I LANG: Fr Eng Spa SIRC ARTICLE NO: 101736

Di Bello, V. Lunardi, M. Santoro, G. Galetta, F. Cini, G. Dini, G. Giusti, C. Analisi delle variazioni del rendimento cardiaco indotte dal tilt e dallhand-grip in atleti ed in soggetti non allenati. (Analysis of variations in cardiac performance induced by tilt and hand-grip in athletes and in untrained subjects.) *Gionale italiano di cardiologia (Rome) 14(3), Mar 1984, 188-198.* ABST: This study analyzed variations of external cardiac work and of myocardial oxygen consumption induced by upright tilting and hand-grip in volleyball athletes in comparison with a

group of normal subjects. LEVEL: A LANG: It

Tihanyi, J. La vitesse du saut. Jumping speed. La velocidad del salto. (Refs: 6)*Volleyball (Roma) 4, Jul/Aug 1984, 9-12.* LEVEL: I LANG: Fr Eng Spa SIRC ARTICLE NO: 101741

PSYCHOLOGY

Aguglia, E. Sapienza, S. Locus of control according to Rotter's S.R.I. in volleyball players. (Refs: 16)*International journal of sport psychology (Rome, Italy) 15(4), 1984, 250-258.* ABST: The authors, using a new personality test called the Locus of Control, have observed 30 subjects - 24 volleyball players and 6 volleyball team captains registered with the F.I.P.A.V. - to study their group dynamics. It was shown that the women have an E-type LC, and captains an I-type LC. In conclusion, the volleyball player group showed an E-type LC, with a low degree of adaptability, an impressionability, weak group contractuality, and more difficult interpersonal relationships. LEVEL: A LANG: Eng SIRC ARTICLE NO: 107799

Petersen, J.R. Interaction among personality, anxiety, situational criticality, and athletic performance. Eugene, Ore.: Microform Publication, University of Oregon, 1984. 1 microfiche : negative, ill. ; 11 x 15 cm. NOTES: Thesis (M.S.) - Pennsylvania State University, 1983; (ix, 80 leaves); includes bibliography. LEVEL: A LANG: Eng UO84 391

STRATEGY

Shockey, S. Volleyball tips... Specialized positions on offense and defense. *Women's coaching clinic (Princeton, N.J.) 8(3) Nov 1984, 8-12.* LEVEL: B LANG: Eng SIRC ARTICLE NO: 103648

STRATEGY - DEFENSIVE

Petit, D. La defense basse. Methodologie d'une recherche analyse des resultats. Utilisation pour l'entrainement. 1re partie. (Refs: 1)*EPS: Revue education physique et sport (Paris) 188, juil/aout 1984, 60-63.* LEVEL: B LANG: Fr SIRC ARTICLE NO: 098743

STRATEGY - OFFENSIVE

Hartfiel, S.M. Single blocker in a 5-1 offense in volleyball. *Scholastic coach (New York) 54(3), Oct 1984, 76-77.* LEVEL: LANG: Eng SIRC ARTICLE NO: 101738

Schreurs, P. The 5-1 offense. *Women's coaching clinic 7(7), Mar 1984, 15-16.* LEVEL: B LANG: Eng SIRC ARTICLE NO: 092570

Shockey, S. For a winning team... Getting the most out of your better players. *Women's coaching clinic (Princeton, N.J.) 8(3), Nov 1984, 12-16.* LEVEL: B LANG: Eng SIRC ARTICLE NO: 103649

TECHNIQUES AND SKILLS - SERVING

Banachowski, A. Serving can give you the jump on competition. *Volleyball monthly (San Luis Obispo, Calif.) 26, Oct 1984, 13-14.*
LEVEL: B LANG: Eng SIRC ARTICLE NO: 100138

TESTING AND EVALUATION

Belyaev, A.V. Methods of developing work capacity in volleyball. (III) *Soviet sports review (Escondido, Calif.) 19(3), Sept 1984, 139-141.*
NOTES: Translated from, Kleschev, Y., ed., Volleyball, 1983, 54-58. Third part in a continuing series.
LEVEL: I LANG: Eng SIRC ARTICLE NO: 103644

Byra, M. Scott, A. Using statistics to analyze the opponent's play in volleyball. *Women's coaching clinic (Princeton, N.J.) 8(4), Dec 1984, 9-12.*
LEVEL: B LANG: Eng SIRC ARTICLE NO: 103645

Weismeyer, H. Picture analysis: for classroom instruction or testing. *Journal of physical education, recreation and dance (Reston, Va.) 55(8), Oct 1984, 72-73.*
LEVEL: B LANG: Eng SIRC ARTICLE NO: 101526

TRAINING AND CONDITIONING

Belyaev, A.V. Methods of developing work capacity in volleyball. *Soviet sports review (Escondido, Calif.) 19(2), Jun 1984, 95-100.*
NOTES: Translated from, Volleyball (edited by Yuri Kleshchev), 54-58, 1983. (continuation from volume 19, No.1).
LEVEL: I LANG: Eng SIRC ARTICLE NO: 100139

Iams, J. Too quick a start may result in too quick a finish. (training) *Volleyball monthly (San Luis Obispo, Calif.) 3(1), Jan 1984, 8;20.*
LEVEL: B LANG: Eng SIRC ARTICLE NO: 100147

Martinez, C. Volleyball: off-season program to meet the individual's needs. *Texas coach (Austin, Tex.) 28(2), Sept 1984, 30-31.*
LEVEL: B LANG: Eng SIRC ARTICLE NO: 106223

Petit, D. La defense basse: methodologie d'une recherche analyse des resultats utilisation pour l'entrainement. Deuxieme partie. (Refs: 3)*EPS: Education physique et sport (Paris) 189, sept/oct 1984, 53-55.*
LEVEL: B LANG: Fr SIRC ARTICLE NO: 101739

Preston, K. Solo training regimen deserves a second look. *Volleyball monthly (San Luis Obispo, Calif.) 3(3), Mar 1984, 10-11.*
LEVEL: B LANG: Eng SIRC ARTICLE NO: 100149

Sevciuc, P. L'entrainement des bresiliens. Brazilians' training. El entrenamiento de los brasilenos. (Refs: 7)*Volleyball (Roma) 4, Jul/Aug 1984, 16-20.*
LEVEL: Fr Eng Spa SIRC ARTICLE NO: 101740

Tschiene, P. Comment s'entrainer en vitesse. How to train quickly. Como entrenarse de priesa. *Volleyball (Roma) 4, Jul/Aug 1984, 13-15.*
LEVEL: B LANG: Fr Eng Spa SIRC ARTICLE NO: 101742

Viitasalo, J. Bandes elastiques pour le saut. Rubber bands in jumping. Elasticos para saltar. (Refs: 4)*Volleyball (Roma) 4, Jul/Aug 1984, 25-28.*

LEVEL: I LANG: Fr Eng Spa SIRC ARTICLE NO: 101743

TRAINING AND CONDITIONING - CIRCUIT TRAINING

Yonker, D. How to organize a large volleyball turnout. *Athletic journal (Evanston, Ill.) 65(3), Oct 1984, 26-29.*
LEVEL: B LANG: Eng SIRC ARTICLE NO: 100152

TRAINING AND CONDITIONING - DRILLS

Bertucci, B. Hippolyte, R. Championship volleyball drills: vol. 1 - individual skill training. New York: Leisure Press, c1984. 112 p.
NOTES: Contents: Vol. 1: Individual skill training. - Vol. 2: Combination and complex training. isbn: 088011035X.
LEVEL: B LANG: Eng ISBN: 0880110341 LC CARD: 81-86508 GV1015.5.T73 17075

Cothren, B. Volleyball drills to add variety to your practices. *Women's coaching clinic 7(7), Mar 1984, 13-15.*
LEVEL: B LANG: Eng SIRC ARTICLE NO: 092564

Daniels-Oleksak, S. Volleyball transition drill for setters: set/cover/retreat to defense. *Women's coaching clinic (Princeton, N.J.) 8(1), Sept 1984, 13-16.*
LEVEL: B LANG: Eng SIRC ARTICLE NO: 100141

Genevieve, P. Reagir ou agir: comment enseigner l'anticipation. *EPS: Education physique et sport 185, janv/fevr 1984, 60-63.*
LEVEL: B LANG: Fr SIRC ARTICLE NO: 093998

Scates, A. Winning volleyball drills: the coach of the highly successful UCLA Bruins describes some volleyball drills that are sure to improve your program. *Athletic journal 64(7), Feb 1984, 8-11;70.*
LEVEL: B LANG: Eng SIRC ARTICLE NO: 092569

Scates, A.E. UCLA winning volley ball drills. *Scholastic coach 53(7), Feb 1984, 16-18;69.*
LEVEL: B LANG: Eng SIRC ARTICLE NO: 094001

Wilks, M. A complete volleyball skill drill. *Athletic journal (Evanston, Ill.) 65(2), Sept 1984, 38-39.*
LEVEL: B LANG: En SIRC ARTICLE NO: 100151

TRAINING AND CONDITIONING - WARM-UPS, WARM-DOWNS, LEAD-UP GAMES

Hammer, R.L. The effects of selected warm-up procedures on internal core temperature. Eugene, Ore.: Microform Publication, University of Oregon, 1984. 1 microfiche : negative, ill. ; 11 x 15 cm.
NOTES: Thesis (M.S.) - Brigham Young University, 1982; (ix, 55 leaves); includes bibliography.
LEVEL: A LANG: Eng UO84 404

TRAINING AND CONDITIONING - WEIGHT AND STRENGTH TRAINING

Butler, R. Rogness, K. Strength training for the advanced volleyball player. *National Strength & Conditioning Association journal 5(6), Jan 1984, 34-37.*
LEVEL: B LANG: Eng SIRC ARTICLE NO: 091161

Ces, D. Doffe, P. Programme de musculation realise durant la saison 80/81 par l'equipe Espoir de France feminine de volley-ball.

NOTES: Dans, Renforcement musculaire, Paris, Institut national du sport et de l'education physique, c1984, p. 125-136.
LEVEL: A LANG: Fr GV711.5 18233

Kolb, J.J. Don't let your shoulder shoulder all the work. *Volleyball monthly (San Luis Obispo, Calif.) 26, Oct 1984, 14.*
LEVEL: B LANG: Eng SIRC ARTICLE NO: 100148

Simmons, J. Hille, T. Year round strength and conditioning program for volleyball at the University of Southern California. *National Strength & Conditioning Association journal (Lincoln, Neb.) 6(4), Aug/Sept 1984, 57-58.*
LEVEL: B LANG: Eng SIRC ARTICLE NO: 100150

VARIATIONS

Cross, D. Trim volley: the answer to your scheduling problems? (Refs: 3)*NIRSA journal (Mt. Pleasant, Mich.) 8(2), Winter 1984, 56.*
LEVEL: B LANG: Eng SIRC ARTICLE NO: 098741

Cross, D. Trim volley: the answer to your scheduling problems? (Refs: 3)*Runner (Edmonton) 22(3), Fall/Winter 1984, 16-17.*
LEVEL: B LANG: Eng SIRC ARTICLE NO: 105063

WATER POLO

Bouchard, C. Interview. (Skok Viatcheslav) *Poloiste (Montreal) 6(2), hiver 1984, 11.*
LEVEL: B LANG: Fr SIRC ARTICLE NO: 098744

COACHING

Glover, J.M. Introducing water polo. *Swimming times (Loughborough, Eng.) 61(7), Jul 1984, 46-49.*
LEVEL: B LANG: Eng SIRC ARTICLE NO: 100153

DISABLED

Orr, R.E. Sheffield, J. Innertube water polo: more than just a non-swimmers' recreation, it can be used to get the disabled into action. *Swimming technique (Los Angeles, Calif.) 20(3), Nov 1983/ Jan 1984, 37-38.*
LEVEL: B LANG: Eng SIRC ARTICLE NO: 094323

OFFICIATING

Rajki, B. Responsibility of the referee: to what extent is refereeing to blame for the deterioration of the level of water polo? *International swimming and water polo (Budapest, Hungary) 1(13), 1984, 28-29.*
LEVEL: B LANG: Eng SIRC ARTICLE NO: 098746

PHYSIOLOGY

Dlin, R.A. Dotan, R. Inbar, O. Rotstein, A. Jacobs, I. Karlson, J. Exaggerated systolic blood pressure response to exercise in a water polo team. (Refs: 20)*Medicine and science in sports and exercise (Indianapolis) 16(3), June 1984, 294-298.*
ABST: Twenty-three top-level water polo players (WP) were examined for blood pressure (BP) response to graded and continuous cycle ergometry. Testing also included resting muscle biopsy for fiber typing, exercise ECG recording for heart rate (HR), exercise concentrations of blood lactate (LA), measured VO2 max, and ratings of perceived exertion (RPE). A control group (C), whose subjects were physically active in endurance

WATER POLO (continued)

sports, but were older and less fit than the experimental subjects, was tested by an identical protocol. The BP response to exercise was significantly higher in the WP group at all comparison criteria including onset of blood lactate accumulation, absolute HR percent of HR max, and power loads (including loadless pedaling).
LEVEL: A LANG: Eng SIRC ARTICLE NO: 108601

RULES AND REGULATIONS

Rajki, B. History of the rules. *International swimming and water polo (Budapest, Hungary) 14, 1984, 40-41.*
LEVEL: B LANG: Eng SIRC ARTICLE NO: 108482

Rajki, B. History of the rules. Part II. *International swimming and water polo (Budapest, Hungary) 4(16), 1984, 36-39.*
LEVEL: B LANG: Eng SIRC ARTICLE NO: 108647

STRATEGY

Csepregi, G. Developing tactics in water polo. (Refs: 7)*Swimming technique (Los Angeles, Calif.) 21(1), May/Jul 1984, 29-34.*
LEVEL: I LANG: Eng SIRC ARTICLE NO: 095524

Konya, I.K. Water-polo. L'attaque avec un homme en plus. La defense avec un homme en moins. *Macolin (Suisse) 8, aout 1984, 8-10.*
NOTES: Traduction de, Yves Jeannotat.
LEVEL: B LANG: Fr SIRC ARTICLE NO: 101745

TESTING AND EVALUATION

Water Polo Canada game analysis report. Ottawa: Canadian Water Polo Association Inc., 1984. 1 v. (loose-leaf)
CORP: Canadian Water Polo Association.
NOTES: Cover title.
LEVEL: I LANG: Eng GV839 20880

TRAINING AND CONDITIONING - DRILLS

Couillard, R. Exercice du mois. (la passe) *Poloiste (Montreal) 6(2), hiver 1984, 10.*
LEVEL: B LANG: Fr SIRC ARTICLE NO: 098745

WOMEN

Keen, L. Women's water polo. *International swimming and water polo (Budapest, Hungary) 14, 1984, 32-33.*
LEVEL: B LANG: En SIRC ARTICLE NO: 108481

WATER SKIING

de Man, E. Water when it burns... Drag. Circle. Marathon. The ultimate skiing rush. *World water skiing (Winter Park, Fla.) 6(6), Oct 1984, 46-50;52.*
LEVEL: B LANG: Eng SIRC ARTICLE NO: 106230

Dorner, T. Driving patterns for open-water skiing. Driving a pre-set pattern in open-water skiing will help keep your ski area from getting too rough. *Spray's water ski (Brattleboro, Vt.) 8(6), Sept 1984, 19.*
LEVEL: B LANG: Eng SIRC ARTICLE NO: 106231

Hansen, A. Tips for the novice driver: slalom skiers' special requirements. *World water skiing (Winter Park, Fla.) 6(5), Au 1984, 21.*
LEVEL: B LANG: Eng SIRC ARTICLE NO: 105074

Hansen, A. Freestyle jumping: expert boat driving required. *World water skiing (Winter Park, Fla.) 6(4), Jul 1984, 21.*
LEVEL: B LANG: Eng SIRC ARTICLE NO: 102118

Rathbun, G. How to drive shortline slalom--a skier's perspective. *Water skier (Winter Haven, Fla.) 34(4), Jul/Aug 1984, 60-61.*
LEVEL: B LANG: Eng SIRC ARTICLE NO: 098756

Swann, C. Growing into slalom: style first, then strength. *World water skiing (Winter Park, Fla.) 6(7), Winter 1984, 22-23.*
LEVEL: B LANG: Eng SIRC ARTICLE NO: 106243

Witherell, W. From water skiing to snow skiing: training tips to ease the transition. *World water skiing (Winter Park, Fla. 6(7), Winter 1984, 24-25.*
LEVEL: B LANG: Eng SIRC ARTICLE NO: 106246

ADMINISTRATION

AWSA Quick Count Slalom Buoy chart. *Water skier (Winter Haven, Fla.) 34(5), Sept/Oct 1984, 49.*
LEVEL: B LANG: Eng SIRC ARTICLE NO: 106226

BIOGRAPHY AND AUTOBIOGRAPHY

Dorner, T. Spray's Water Ski 1984 skier of the year, Cory Pickos. *Water ski (Brattleboro, Vt.) 8(2), Apr 1984, 40-45.*
LEVEL: B LANG: Eng SIRC ARTICLE NO: 100154

Massey, G.H. Deena Brush: spray's water ski 1984 women's skier of the year. *Water ski (Holmes, Penn.) 8(1), Mar 1984, 30-37.*
LEVEL: B LANG: Eng SIRC ARTICLE NO: 098753

CERTIFICATION

Canadian Water Ski Association: level I coaching certification. Ottawa: Canadian Water Ski Association, c1984. iv, (38) p. : ill. (National Coaching Certification Program.)
CORP: Canadian Water Ski Association.
NOTES: Cover title.
LEVEL: B LANG: Eng GV840.S5 17934

CHILDREN

Schoen, L. Kids on skis: teaching children to ski is fun and rewarding. *World water skiing (Winter Park, Fla.) 6(4), Jul 1984, 36-43.*
LEVEL: B LANG: Eng SIRC ARTICLE NO: 102116

CLOTHING

Wetsuits '84: high fashion for low temperatures. Technology and styling combine to give warmth and good looks. *Water ski (Holmes, Penn.) 8(1), Mar 1984, 40-46.*
LEVEL: B LANG: Eng SIRC ARTICLE NO: 098758

DIRECTORIES

1984 ski school directory. *World water skiing (Winter Park, Fla.) 6(1), Apr 1984, 94-99.*
LEVEL: B LANG: Eng SIRC ARTICLE NO 108970

DISABLED

Baker, J. An AWSA instruction guide: teaching the blind to ski. *Water skier (Winter Haven, Fla.) 34(2), May 1984, 44-48.*
LEVEL: B LANG: Eng SIRC ARTICLE NO: 100644

EQUIPMENT

Baker, J. Evolution of the toe strap. *Water skier (Winter Haven, Fla.) 34(5), Sept/Oct 1984, 36-40.*
LEVEL: B LANG: Eng SIRC ARTICLE NO: 106227

Briggs, S. Breakthroughs: two decades of high technology. *World water skiing (Winter Park, Fla.) 6(5), Aug 1984, 40-42;44;46.*
LEVEL: B LANG: Eng SIRC ARTICLE NO: 105070

Brown, B. The outboard answer: when the question is which rig to buy, we've got the answer. Outboard rigs come in four price/performance categories. One of them is right for you. *Spray's water ski magazine (Brattleboro, Vt.) 8(4), Jun 1984, 56-62.*
LEVEL: B LANG: Eng SIRC ARTICLE NO: 105071

Cozier, A. Tournament towboats: an indepth review of nine of the champions' choices. *World water skiing (Winter Park, Fla.) 6(2), May 1984, 56-58;60;62;64.*
LEVEL: B LANG: Eng SIRC ARTICLE NO: 101748

Crone, M. Flex and the single ski: the effect of stiffness on a ski's performance. *World Water skiing (Winter Park, Fla.) 6(2), May 1984, 85.*
LEVEL: B LANG: Eng SIRC ARTICLE NO: 101749

Crone, M. All about bevels: a major part of slalom ski design. *World water skiing (Winter Park, Fla.) 6(3), Jun 1984, 85.*
LEVEL: B LANG: Eng SIRC ARTICLE NO: 101750

Crone, M. All about bevels, part two. The skis are compared. *World water skiing (Winter Park, Fla.) 6(4), Jul 1984, 77.*
LEVEL: B LANG: Eng SIRC ARTICLE NO: 102123

Crone, M. Slalom ski construction: the inner workings of fiberglass skis. *World water skiing (Winter Park, Fla.) 65(1), Apr 1984, 85.*
LEVEL: B LANG: Eng SIRC ARTICLE NO: 108975

Dorner, T. Performance boards: today's kneeboards have performance built in. Learn what they are to help you make the right selection. *Spray's water ski magazine (Brattleboro, Vt.) 8(4), Jun 1984, 31-35.*
LEVEL: B LANG: Eng SIRC ARTICLE NO: 105072

Hardman, T. Like rock & roll: wood skis are here to stay. *Water skier (Winter Haven, Fla.) 34(1), Mar/Apr 1984, 42-45;48-49.*
LEVEL: B LANG: Eng SIRC ARTICLE NO: 098752

Intermediate slalom skis: the facts on upper level skis. *World water skiing (Winter Park, Fla.) 6(3), Jun 1984, 76-77;79.*
LEVEL: B LANG: Eng SIRC ARTICLE NO: 101758

Jobe, J. Repair or replace your ski? Take an end of season inspection. *World water skiing (Winter Park, Fla.) 6(6), Oct 1984, 74.*
LEVEL: B LANG: Eng SIRC ARTICLE NO: 106234

McClintock, J. The right ski for the right person -
it's important. *Ontario water skier (Toronto) 11(1),
Spring 1984, 17-18.*
LEVEL: B LANG: Eng SIRC ARTICLE NO: 097037

Peak performers: lab tests results on twelve
slaloms that guarantee high performance. *World
water skiing (Winter Park, Fla.) 6(2), May 1984, 76-
82.*
LEVEL: B LANG: Eng SIRC ARTICLE NO: 101766

Ricketts, R. Towlines: a long and winding rope.
*World water skiing (Winter Park, Fla.) 6(3), Jun
1984, 64-67;71-74.*
LEVEL B LANG: Eng SIRC ARTICLE NO: 100574

Ricketts, R. Bindings: the essence of control.
*World water skiing (Winter Park, Fla.) 6(4), Jul
1984, 60-61;63-66.*
LEVEL: LANG: Eng SIRC ARTICLE NO: 102117

Spray's Water Ski Magazine's 1984 tow boat
performance tests. *Water ski (Brattleboro, Vt.) 8(2),
Apr 1984, 28-39.*
LEVEL: B LANG: Eng SIRC ARTICLE NO: 100161

Suyderhoud, M. Where design meets
performance: slalom skis. *Water ski (Brattleboro,
Vt.) 8(2), Apr 1984, 49-55.*
LEVEL: B LANG: Eng SIRC ARTICLE NO: 100162

Suyderhoud, M. Bindings. *Spray's water ski
magazine (Holmes, Penn.) 8(5), Jul 1984, 36-41.*
LEVEL: B LANG: Eng SIRC ARTICL NO: 101767

Suyderhoud, M. The evolution of trick skis. From a
tennis shoe nailed on a board to a high-tech water
ski tool, here's the story of the evolution of trick
skis and a buyer's guide to the right one for you.
*Spray's water ski (Brattleboro, Vt.) 8(6), Sept 1984,
48-53.*
LEVEL: B LANG: Eng SIRC ARTICLE NO: 106242

Teeter, R. Rocker: degree and location predicts
performance. *World water skiing (Winter Park, Fla.)
6(5), Aug 1984, 69.*
LEVEL: B LANG: Eng SIRC ARTICLE NO: 105085

Teeter, R. At the core of it: the innards of skis.
*World water skiing (Winter Park, Fla.) 6(7), Winter
1984, 28.*
LEVEL: B LANG: Eng SIRC ARTICLE NO: 106244

EQUIPMENT - MAINTENANCE

Jobe, J. Rubber edge repair: don't ignore signs of
structural damage. *World water skiing (Winter Park,
Fla.) 6(3), Jun 1984 92.*
LEVEL: B LANG: Eng SIRC ARTICLE NO: 101760

Jobe, J. Rope repair: how to use a 'fid'. *World
water skiing (Winter Park, Fla.) 6(5), Aug 1984, 76.*
LEVEL: B LANG: Eng SIRC ARTICLE NO: 105078

Teeter, R. Bottom surface condition: rough and
fast. *World water skiing (Winter Park, Fla.) 6(6), Oct
1984, 69.*
LEVEL: B LANG: Eng SIRC ARTICLE NO: 106245

FACILITIES

Crosby, A. Rigging your own outboard: your skiing
needs dictate your setup. *World water skiing
(Winter Park, Fla.) 6(3), Ju 1984, 36-37;39-43.*
LEVEL: B LANG: Eng SIRC ARTICLE NO: 101751

Smith, W.K. The cable connection: Part II. An
update of the Ski Rixen Cableway, one year later.
*World water skiing (Winter Park, Fla.) 6(1), Apr
1984, 60-61;63-66.*
LEVEL: B LANG: Eng SIRC ARTICLE NO: 108969

FACILITIES - DESIGN,
CONSTRUCTION AND PLANNING

Brazil, E. Slalom course on a budget: time a
money saving ideas for that first slalom course.
*World water skiing (Winter Park, Fla.) 6(1), Apr
1984, 44-45;47-50.*
LEVEL: B LANG: Eng SIRC ARTICLE NO: 108967

INJURIES AND ACCIDENTS

Don't get burned. Sunburn is an injury that can
have a cumulative effect. Prevention is the best
remedy. *Spray's water ski magazine (Brattleboro,
Vt.) 8(4), Jun 1984, 23;25.*
LEVEL: B LANG: Eng SIRC ARTICLE NO: 104029

Key, J. Strains, sprains and pains. The lowdown,
part II. *World water skiing (Winter Park, Fla.) 6(7),
Winter 1984, 12.*
LEVEL: B LANG: Eng SIRC ARTICLE NO: 106235

Key, J. Back strains: where, what and why. *World
water skiing (Winter Park, Fla.) 6(6), Oct 1984, 12.*
LEVEL: B LANG: Eng SIRC ARTICLE NO: 106236

Mavrelis, P.G. Wylie, R.R. Water-ski colon. (letter)
*New England journal of medicine (Boston) 311(17),
25 Oct 1984, 1128.*
LEVEL: B LANG: Eng

JUDGING

Canadian Water Ski Association official's handbook.
Levels one - two - three. Ottawa: Canadian Water
Ski Association, 1984?. 2 p.
CORP: Canadian Water Ski Association.
NOTES: Cover title.
LEVEL: B LANG: Eng GV840.S5 18628

MASTERS COMPETITION

Wilkening, D. Better with ace: seniors and
veterans are still hot competitors. *World water
skiing (Winter Park, Fla.) 6(5), Aug 1984, 30-
34;36;38.*
LEVEL: B LANG: Eng SIRC ARTICLE NO: 105087

MEDICINE

Bundgaard, A. Jarnum, S. Water-ski spill and
ulcerative colotis. (letter) *Lancet (London) 2(8412),
17 Nov 1984, 1157.*
LEVEL: I LANG: Eng

Horn, G. Water. Water. Staying ahead of the fluid
game. *Water skier (Winter Haven, Fla.) 34(5), Sept/
Oct 1984, 16;18.*
LEVEL: B LANG: Eng SIRC ARTICLE NO: 106233

Morgan, J.D. Handling your hands: ski longer by
learning to care for hand calluses and blisters.
*Spray's water ski magazine (Holmes, Penn.) 8(5),
Jul 1984, 15-16;19.*
LEVEL: B LANG: Eng SIRC ARTICLE NO: 101764

Soft contact lenses and water sports.
*Sportsmedicine digest (Van Nuys, Calif.) 6(4), Apr
1984, 4.*
LEVEL: B LANG: Eng SIRC ARTICLE NO: 099957

NUTRITION

Horn, G. Nutrition tips for water skiers: for top
energy & performance, your body demands
premium fuel. *Water skier (Winter Haven, Fla.)
34(3), Jun 1984, 14-16.*
LEVEL: B LANG: Eng SIRC ARTICLE NO: 105076

PHYSIOLOGY

Figar, S. Horak, J. PUlec, Z. Albrecht, V.
Abnrmalni cevni reflexy u vodnich slalomaru.
(Abnormal vascular reflexes in water slalom
competitors.) *Ceskolovenska fysiologie (Prague)
33(3), 1984, 246-254.*
LEVEL: A LANG: Cze

PSYCHOLOGY

Mondor, J. Climbing out of a slump: the secret to
breaking a plateau and improving performance.
*World water skiing (Winter Park, Fla.) 6(5), Aug
1984, 18.*
LEVEL: B LANG: Eng SIRC ARTICLE NO: 105080

PSYCHOLOGY - MENTAL TRAINING

Barnes, R. Psychology in training: relaxation
summary. (Refs: 3)*Ski nautique news (Ottawa)
Jun/juin 1984, 11.*
LEVEL: B LANG: Eng SIRC ARTICLE NO: 098749

Barnes, R. Psychology in training water skiers.
*Water skier (Winter Haven, Fla.) 34(6), Nov/Dec
1984, 24-25.*
LEVEL: B LANG: Eng SIRC ARTICLE NO: 106229

RULES AND REGULATIONS

Reglements officiels de l'Association de ski
nautique du Canada. Ottawa: Association de ski
nautique du Canada, (1984). 53 p.
CORP: Association de ski nautique du Canada.
NOTES: Also published in English under the title:
The official rule book of the Canadian Water Ski
Association.
LEVEL: B LANG: Fr GV840.S5 18626

The official rule book of the Canadian Water Ski
Association. Ottawa: Canadian Water Ski
Association, (1984). 55 p.
CORP: Canadian Water Ski Association.
NOTES: Aussi publie en francais sous le titre:
Reglements officiels de l'Association de ski
nautique du Canada.
LEVEL: B LANG: Eng GV840.S5 18625

SAFETY

Hansen, A. Boat driving: responsibility and
judgement. Insuring a safe, successful ski ride.
*World water skiing (Winter Park, Fla.) 6(2), May
1984, 21.*
LEVEL: B LANG: Eng SIRC ARTICLE NO: 101755

Hansen, A. Retrieving the fallen skier: a proven
procedure for safety. *World water skiing (Winter
Park, Fla.) 6(3), Jun 1984, 21.*
LEVEL: B LANG: Eng SIRC ARTICLE NO: 101756

WATER SKIING (continued)

SPORTING EVENTS

Hardman, T. Water skiing & the Olympic Games. A review of the present status of water skiing in its quest to be recognized a an Olympic sport. *Water skier (Winter Haven, Fla.) 34(4), Jul/Aug 1984, 36-38.*
LEVEL: B LANG: Eng SIRC ARTICLE NO: 098751

TECHNIQUES AND SKILLS

Brazil, E. The next steps. (water ski jumping) *World water skiing (Winter Park, Fla.) 6(3), Jun 1984, 58-59.*
LEVEL: B LANG: Eng SIRC ARTICLE NO: 101747

Dorner, T. The whip-finish: timing and coordination between driver and skier make shortening the slalom rope or finishing a ski ride quick and easy. *Spray's water ski magazine (Holmes, Penn.) 8(5), Jul 1984, 13.*
LEVEL: B LANG: Eng SIRC ARTICLE NO: 101752

Duvall, S. The acceleration stage: face away from the boat for maximum angle. *World water skiing (Winter Park, Fla.) 6(4), Jul 1984, 22-23.*
LEVEL: B LANG: Eng SIRC ARTICLE NO: 102120

Ferraro, M. Trick clinic for beginners. Head off numerous falls and frustration by following these basic instructions of learning to trick ski. *Spray's water ski (Brattleboro, Vt.) 8(3), May 1984, 57-61.*
LEVEL: B LANG: Eng SIRC ARTICLE NO: 100156

Ferraro, M. 'Toe back - toe front': first step to higher trick runs. *World water skiing (Winter Park, Fla.) 6(2), May 1984, 24-27.*
LEVEL: B LANG: Eng SIRC ARTICLE NO: 101753

Hillier, R. 3, 2, 1, ignition... Blast Off. *Spray's water ski magazine (Brattleboro, Vt.) 8(4), Jun 1984, 45-48.*
LEVEL: B LANG: Eng SIRC ARTICLE NO: 105075

Jackson, M. Stibbe, L. The drape: mastering the art of adagio doubles. *World water skiing (Winter Park, Fla.) 6(3), Jun 1984, 24-25.*
LEVEL: B LANG: Eng SIRC ARTICLE NO: 101759

Jackson, M. Learn the helicopter spin. *Water skier (Winter Haven, Fla.) 34(3), Jun 1984, 33-35.*
LEVEL: B LANG: Eng SIRC ARTICLE NO: 105077

McClintock, J. Rhythm and timing: ease into an aggressive slalom style. *World water skiing (Winter Park, Fla.) 6(5), Aug 1984, 22-23.*
LEVEL: B LANG: Eng SIRC ARTICLE NO: 105079

McClintock, J. Heads or tails? You call the wind condition (even if it's a crosswind), and we'll tell you how to slalom in i *Spray's water ski (Brattleboro, Vt.) 8(6), Sept 1984, 20-25.*
LEVEL: B LANG: Eng SIRC ARTICLE NO: 106237

McElyea, J. The big turn: how to correct your mistakes. *World water skiing (Winter Park, Fla.) 6(6), Oct 1984, 22-23.*
LEVEL: B LANG: Eng SIRC ARTICLE NO: 106238

Mondor, J. Back to basics: piecing together the fundamentals of water skiing. *World water skiing (Winter Park, Fla.) 6(4), Jul 1984, 68-69;71-74;90.*
LEVEL: B LANG: Eng SIRC ARTICLE NO: 102119

Mondor, J. The elements of style: a study of top skiers' slalom styles that will help improve your skiing. *World water skiing (Winter Park, Fla.) 6(1), Apr 1984, 52-58;103.*
LEVEL: B LANG: Eng SIRC ARTICLE NO: 108968

Morgan, M. One-hand turn: a three step process to advance your style. *World water skiing (Winter Park, Fla.) 6(2), May 1984 36-37;39-42.*
LEVEL: B LANG: Eng SIRC ARTICLE NO: 101765

Pickos, C. Skills--advanced tricks: learn to wake line 5 back. *Water skier (Winter Haven, Fla.) 34(4), Jul/Aug 1984, 56-57.*
LEVEL: B LANG: Eng SIRC ARTICLE NO: 098754

Pickos, C. Skills--advanced tricks: learn the one-ski wrap-in toehold 360. *Water skier (Winter Haven, Fla.) 34(1), Mar/Apr 1984, 58-59.*
LEVEL: B LANG: Eng SIRC ARTICLE NO: 098755

Pickos, C. Wake back-to-back & reverse. *Water skier (Winter Haven, Fla.) 34(3), Jun 1984, 62-64.*
LEVEL: B LANG: Eng SIRC ARTICLE NO: 105081

Pickos, C. Learn the toe-wake back, front. *Water skier (Winter Haven, Fla.) 34(5), Sept/Oct 1984, 54-55.*
LEVEL: B LANG: E SIRC ARTICLE NO: 106240

Roberge, C. Speeding is the ticket. *Water ski (Brattleboro, Vt.) 8(2), Apr 1984, 62-65.*
LEVEL: B LANG: Eng SIRC ARTICLE NO: 100159

Roberts, P. Helicopter: wake 360 degrees. *World water skiing (Winter Park, Fla.) 6(5), Aug 1984, 24-25.*
LEVEL: B LANG: En SIRC ARTICLE NO: 105082

Stiffler, R. Beginning tricks: a five step foundation. *World water skiing (Winter Park, Fla.) 6(5), Aug 1984, 56-60;62.*
LEVEL: B LANG: Eng SIRC ARTICLE NO: 105083

Suyderhoud, M. In slow motion: dissection of the slalom turn 1. *World water skiing (Winter Park, Fla.) 6(3), Jun 1984, 28.*
LEVEL: B LANG: Eng SIRC ARTICLE NO: 101768

Suyderhoud, M. Rope handling: overcoming your initial instincts. *World water skiing (Winter Park, Fla.) 6(5), Aug 1984, 28.*
LEVEL: B LANG: Eng SIRC ARTICLE NO: 105084

Suyderhoud, M. Overcoming slalom plateaus: how to quicken your slalom progression - part 1. *World water skiing (Winter Park Fla.) 6(1), Apr 1984, 28.*
LEVEL: B LANG: Eng SIRC ARTICLE NO: 108973

Thurlow, G. Advanced slalom, the right start: getting the gates down. *World water skiing (Winter Park, Fla.) 6(3), Jun 1984 22-23.*
LEVEL: B LANG: Eng SIRC ARTICLE NO: 101770

TECHNIQUES AND SKILLS - START

McCormick, R. The two-ski back start: a fun and exciting start method. *World water skiing (Winter Park, Fla.) 6(1), Apr 198 24-25.*
LEVEL: B LANG: Eng SIRC ARTICLE NO: 108972

TESTING AND EVALUATION

Segal, K.R. Tests for training: evaluate your strength and weakness. *World water skiing (Winter Park, Fla.) 6(7), Winter 1984, 18-19.*
LEVEL: B LANG: Eng SIRC ARTICLE NO: 106241

TRAINING AND CONDITIONING

Hazelwood, M. Advanced slalom: tournament training. Getting ready for the competition. *World water skiing (Winter Park, Fla.) 6(2), May 1984, 22-23.*
LEVEL: B LANG: Eng SIRC ARTICLE NO: 101757

Key, J. Bernardo, C. Overtraining: when more is not better. *World water skiing (Winter Park, Fla.) 6(2), May 1984, 18.*
LEVEL: B LANG: Eng SIRC ARTICLE NO: 101762

McClintock, J. Pre season slaloming: tips to ease your way back into slalom shape. *World water skiing (Winter Park, Fla.) 6 (1), Apr 1984, 22-23.*
LEVEL: B LANG: Eng SIRC ARTICLE NO: 108971

Mondor, J. Skill and strength training: achieving the proper balance. *World water skiing (Winter Park, Fla.) 6(2), May 1984 32-33.*
LEVEL: B LANG: Eng SIRC ARTICLE NO: 101763

Mondor, J. Pre season shape up: four areas to work on for skill improvement. *World water skiing (Winter Park, Fla.) 6(1), Apr 1984, 32-33.*
LEVEL: B LANG: Eng SIRC ARTICLE NO: 108974

Segal, K.R. Tune it up. *Water ski (Brattleboro, Vt.) 8(2), Apr 1984, 19-21.*
LEVEL: B LANG: Eng SIRC ARTICLE NO: 100160

TRAINING AND CONDITIONING - DRILLS

Winter, S. Bemman, R. Losen up: proper stretching before your skin can help prevent injury and increase the quality of your performance. All you need are these five easy stretches. *Spray's water ski magazine (Brattleboro, Vt.) 8(4), Jun 1984, 49-53.*
LEVEL: B LANG: Eng SIRC ARTICLE NO: 105088

TRAINING AND CONDITIONING - WEIGHT AND STRENGTH TRAINING

Eberhardt, T. Get a grip. Whether you use the overhand or baseball bat technique, you'll get a stronger grip with these tailormade exercises. *Spray's water ski (Brattleboro, Vt.) 8(3), May 1984, 19;21.*
LEVEL: B LANG: Eng SIRC ARTICLE NO: 100155

Mondor, J. Winding down in off season: thoughts turn to staying fit. *World water skiing (Winter Park, Fla.) 6(6), Oct 1984, 18-19.*
LEVEL: B LANG: Eng SIRC ARTICLE NO: 106239

VARIATIONS

Temple, T. Kneeboarding: then and now. *World water skiing (Winter Park, Fla.) 6(3), Jun 1984, 44-50;52.*
LEVEL: B LANG: En SIRC ARTICLE NO: 101769

VARIATIONS - BAREFOOT WATERSKIING

Baker, J. Scarpa, R. Backward tricks--the basics. *Water skier (Winter Haven, Fla.) 34(4), Jul/Aug 1984, 62;64.*
LEVEL: B LANG: Eng SIRC ARTICLE NO: 098747

Baker, J. Scarpa, R. Improving barefoot skills: the winter workout--staying in shape. *Water skier (Winter Haven, Fla.) 34(1), Mar/Apr 1984, 69-70.*
LEVEL: B LANG: Eng SIRC ARTICLE NO: 098748

Baker, J. Scarpa, R. Establishing a tournament regimen. *Water skier (Winter Haven, Fla.) 34(2), May 1984, 28;30.*
LEVEL: B LANG: Eng SIRC ARTICLE NO: 101746

Baker, J. Scarpa, R. Basic forward tricks - a solid foundation. *Water skier (Winter Haven, Fla.) 34(3),*

Jun 1984, 29-32.
LEVEL: B LANG: Eng SIRC ARTICLE NO: 105069

Baker, J. Scarpa, R. The back step-off. *Water skier (Winter Haven, Fla.) 34(5), Sept/Oct 1984, 68-69.*
LEVEL: B LANG: Eng SIRC ARTICLE NO: 106228

Gillette, J. Look ma, no hands. (barefoot water skiing) *Water ski (Holmes, Penn.) 8(1), Mar 1984, 69-71.*
LEVEL: B LANG: E SIRC ARTICLE NO: 098750

Gillette, J. Stand up for yourself. (barefoot water skiing) *Water ski (Brattleboro, Vt.) 8(2), Apr 1984, 73-74.*
LEVEL: B LANG: Eng SIRC ARTICLE NO: 100157

Gillette, J. Shopping for a barefoot wetsuit? Barefoot wetsuit technology has brought about a variety of styles and features Learn how to determine your needs to make the right selection. *Spray's water ski (Brattleboro, Vt.) 8(3), May 1984, 71-73.*
LEVEL: B LANG: Eng SIRC ARTICLE NO: 100158

Gillette, J. The tumbleturn: this versatile trick only looks hard. Here's the technique that makes learning it easy. *Spray' water ski magazine (Holmes, Penn.) 8(5), Jul 1984, 57-58.*
LEVEL: B LANG: Eng SIRC ARTICLE NO: 101754

Gillette, J. How fast is fast? It's a myth that the only speed for barefooting is wide open. Here's how to avoid hard falls by determining the proper speed for you. *Spray's water ski magazine (Brattleboro, Vt.) 8(4), Jun 1984, 75-76.*
LEVEL: B LANG: Eng SIRC ARTICLE NO: 105073

Gillette, J. How to fall. Yes, there is a proper technique for falling...and it can save you from the pain you always though you had to take. *Spray's water ski (Brattleboro, Vt.) 8(6), Sept 1984, 55.*
LEVEL: B LANG: Eng SIRC ARTICLE NO: 106232

Johnson, W. Step by step: tricks for the intermediate barefooter. *World water skiing (Winter Park, Fla.) 6(2), May 1984, 66-68;71-72;74;95-96;98.*
LEVEL: B LANG: Eng SIRC ARTICLE NO: 101761

Seipel, M. Pointers for advancing barefooters. *Water skier (Winter Haven, Fla.) 23(7), Jan/Feb 1984, 58-59;61.*
LEVEL: B LANG: Eng SIRC ARTICLE NO: 098757

Seipel, M. The flying dock start: fast and furious barefooting fun. *World water skiing (Winter Park, Fla.) 6(4), Jul 1984, 24-25.*
LEVEL: B LANG: Eng SIRC ARTICLE NO: 102121

WEIGHTLIFTING

Worobjow, A.N. Gewichtheben. Berlin: Sportverlag, 1984. 336 p. : ill.
NOTES: Translated from Russian.
LEVEL: I LANG: Ger GV546.3 18152

ANTHROPOMETRY

Sosnovsky, I. The desire to be copied. *Soviet sports review (Escondido, Calif.) 19(4), Dec 1984, 167-170.*
NOTES: Translated from, Fizkulturi i sport 8, 1984, 6-7.
LEVEL: B LANG: Eng SIRC ARTICLE NO: 105093

BIOGRAPHY AND AUTOBIOGRAPHY

Krall, D. Bob Bridges. *Powerlifting U.S.A. (Camarillo, Calif.) 7(8), Mar 1984, 27.*
LEVEL: B LANG: Eng SIRC ARTICLE NO: 098764

Todd, T. Behold Bulgaria's vest-pocket Hercules. Pound for 123 pounds, 16-year-old Naim Suleimanov is now the world's greatest weightlifter and clearly the driving force of his country's lifting revolution. *Sports illustrated (Chicago, Ill.) 60(24), 11 Jun 1984, 32-34;36;38;41-42;44;46.*
LEVEL: B LANG: Eng SIRC ARTICLE NO: 095536

Vuono, P. Pioneers of power: part 12: Paul Anderson. *Powerlifting U.S.A. (Camarillo, Calif.) 7(8), Mar 1984, 68.*
LEVEL: B LANG: Eng SIRC ARTICLE NO: 098770

Weightlifting: Jacques Demers. Halterophilie: Jacques Demers. *Champion (Ottawa) 8(3), Aug 1984, 56-57.*
LEVEL: B LANG: Eng F SIRC ARTICLE NO: 097043

BIOMECHANICS

Haekkinen, K. Kauhanen, H. Komi, P.V. Biomechanical changes in the olympic weightlifting technique of the snatch and clean & jerk from submaximal to maximal loads. (Refs: 7)*Scandinavian journal of sports sciences (Helsinki, Finland) 6(2), Dec 1984, 57-66.*
ABST: Various dynamic kinematic, kinetic and electromyographic characteristics of the olympic weightlifting technique of the snatch and clean & jerk from submaximal to maximal loads were investigated in seven weightlifters of Finnish national level (ELI group) and in six weightlifters of the district level (DIS group). Greater maximal relative ground reaction forces were recorded in both groups at submaximal (70, 80, 90 per cent) loads than at maximal (100 per cent) loads during first and third pulls of the snatch and clean. During the first pull of the lifts the ELI group produced greater reaction forces at all loads than the DIS group. During the third pulls of both lifts the velocities of the barbell decreased significantly in the two groups when the load of the barbell increased. The average durations of the drop under the bar phases in the snatch, clean and jerk were in both groups significantly longer at 100 per cent loads than at 70 per cent loads.
LEVEL: A LANG: Eng SIRC ARTICLE NO: 107806

Kauhanen, H. Haekkinen, K. Komi, P.V. A biomechanical analysis of the snatch and clean & jerk techniques of Finnish elite an district level weightlifters. (Refs: 14)*Scandinavian journal of sports sciences (Helsinki, Finland) 6(2), Dec 1984, 47-56.*
ABST: Seven Finnish elite national level weightlifters (ELI group) and six district level weightlifters (DIS group) were used as subjects in a biomechanical study to investigate dynamic, kinematic, kinetic and electromyographic characteristics of the olympic lifting technique. The ELI group tended to produce greater relative maximal ground reaction forces during each phase of the snatch and clean & jerk, and a significant difference between the two groups was observed in this force during the first pull phase of the clean. The duration of the drop under the bar phase of the jerk was significantly shorther for the ELI group. The maximal barbell heights of the snatch-lift were 119.7 plus or minus 8.1 and 130.5 plus or minus 8.6 cm for the two groups, respectively. In other

kinematics parameters no significant differences between the two groups were observed.
LEVEL: A LANG: Eng SIRC ARTICLE NO: 107807

Livanoc, O.I. Falameyev, A.I. Technique and methods of learning the classical exercises. *Soviet sports review (Escondido, Calif.) 19(3), Sept 1984, 117-121.*
NOTES: Translated from, Tyazhelaya atletika 1, 1983, 16-18. ,1
LEVEL: I LANG: Eng SIRC ARTICLE NO: 103660

Madsen, N. McLaughlin, T. Kinematic factors influencing performance and injury risk in the bench press exercise. (Refs: 5) *Medicine and science in sports and exercise (Indianapolis) 16(4), Aug 1984, 376-381.*
ABST: The purpose of this research was to identify kinematic factors that could be relevant to performance and injury risk in the bench press. Kinematic and kinetic differences between 19 experts and 17 novices were investigated. In addition to the fact that experts were able to lift 79% more weight than the novices, the pertinent kinetic differences included the following: 1) the difference in peak force exerted while lowering the bar was only 43%; 2) the difference in peak force exerted while raising the bar was only 45%; and 3) the difference in minimum force exerted while raising the bar was 87%. The relevant kinematic differences were: 1) the expert group maintained a smaller bar speed while lowering the bar; 2) the expert group used a bar path closer to the shoulders; and 3) the expert group used a different sequence of bar movements.
LEVEL: A LANG: Eng SIRC ARTICLE NO: 103661

Roman, R.A. Treskov, V.V. Snatch technique of world record holder U. Zakharevich. *Soviet sports review (Escondido, Calif.) 19(3), Sept 1984, 113-117.*
NOTES: Translated from, Tyazhelaya atletika 1, 1983, 10-16. To be continued.
LEVEL: I LANG: Eng SIRC ARTICLE NO: 103663

CHILDREN

Dvorkin, L.S. The young weightlifter. Part IV: preparation of weightlifters 12-13 years old. *Soviet sports review (Escondido, Calif.) 19(1), Mar 1984, 37-41.*
NOTES: Continuation from vol. 18, no. 4.
LEVEL: B LANG: Eng SIRC ARTICLE NO: 095529

Dvorkin, L.S. The young weightlifter: part VII. Physical capabilities of young weightlifters during beginning prepation. *Soviet sports review (Escondido, Calif.) 19(4), Dec 1984, 193-198.*
NOTES: Continued from volume 19, No. 3. Translated from Russian.
LEVEL: I LANG: Eng SIRC ARTICLE NO: 105089

COACHING

St-Cyr, S. Cahier pedagogie de l'enseignement de l'halterophilie. *Coup d'oeil sur l'halterophilie (Montreal) dec 1984/janv 1985, 5-7.*
NOTES: Suite du precedent numero.
LEVEL: B LANG: Fr SIRC ARTICLE NO: 107809

DRUGS, DOPING AND ERGOGENIC AIDS

Bond, V. Gresham, K.E. Balkissoon, B. Clearwater, H.E. Effects of small and moderate doses of alcohol on peak torque and average

WEIGHTLIFTING (continued)

torque in an isokinetic contraction. (Refs: 10)*Scandinavian journal of sports science (Helsinki, Finland) 6(1), Jul 1984, 1-5.*
ABST: Twelve college male athletes were evaluated isokinetically for their elbow flexor, extensor, and knee extensor torque generating capabilities after the ingestion of alcohol. Each subject was tested on a Cybex II dynamometer at the following speeds to evaluate peak and average peak torque: (1) dominant arm flexor, 0, 60, 90, 120 and 150o .s-1, (2) dominant arm extensor, 60, 90, 120 and 150o .s-1, and (3) dominant leg extensor, 0, 30, 102, 210 and 300o .s-1. Prior to each experimental test the subject consumed either a placebo (.0g.Kg-1), small (.34g.Kg-1), or a moderate (.69g.Kg-1) dose of pure ethanol. Analysis of the results by a one-way ANOVA indicated that the ingestion of a small or moderate amount of alcohol had no significant effect on the peak and average torque generating capabilities during elbow flexion, extension and knee extension.
LEVEL: A LANG: Eng SIRC ARTICLE NO: 102383

Brassard, A. La stimulation electrique. *Coup d'oeil sur l'halterophilie (Montreal) 17(1), mars 1984, 5-6.*
LEVEL: I LANG: SIRC ARTICLE NO: 100163

De Coste, J. Ciavattone, F. Doping - l'opinion de quelques americains. *Coup d'oeil sur l'halterophilie (Montreal) 17(1), mars 1984, 17-18.*
LEVEL: B LANG: Fr SIRC ARTICLE NO: 098923

Jelinek, O. Declaration de l'honorable Otto Jelinek Ministre d'Etat a la condition physique et au sport amateur sur l'usage de drogues dans le sport. *Condition physique et sport amateur declaration du ministre (Ottawa) 10 dec 1984, 1-3.*
CORP: Canada. Condition physique et sport amateur.
LEVEL: B LANG: Fr SIRC ARTICLE NO: 102391

Jelinek, O. Statement by Otto Jelinek, Minister of State for Fitness and Amateur Sport, on use of drugs in sport. *Fitness and Amateur Sport ministerial statement (Ottawa) 10 Dec 1984, 1-3.*
CORP: Canada. Fitness and Amateur Sport.
LEVEL: B LANG: Eng SIRC ARTICLE NO: 102392

Overly, W.L. Dankoff, J.A. Wang, B.K. Singh, U.D. Androgens and hepatocellular carcinoma in an athlete. (letter) (Refs: 5) *Annals of internal medicine (Philadelphia) 100(1), Jan 1984, 158-159.*
LEVEL: I LANG: Eng SIRC ARTICLE NO: 098766

INJURIES AND ACCIDENTS

Griffin, A.B. Troup, J.D. Lloyd, D.C. Tests of lifting and handling capacity. Their repeatability and relationship to back symptoms. *Ergonomics (London) 27(3), Mar 1984, 305-320.*
LEVEL: A LANG: Eng SIRC ARTICLE NO: 103655

Ludolph, E. Das 'Verhebetrauma' in der Unfallversicherung. (Injury from lifting heavy weights and accident insurance.) *Unfallheilkunde (Berlin) 87(9), Sept 1984, 390-392.*
LEVEL: I LANG: Ger

Valk, P. Muscle localization of Tc-99m MDP after exertion. *Clinical nuclear medicine (Philadelphia) 9(9), Sept 1984, 493-494.*
LEVEL: A LANG: Eng

MEDICINE

Cleveland, H.C. Headaches: a weighty problem for lifters. *Physician and sportsmedicine (Minneapolis, Minn.) 12(7), Jul 1984 23.*
LEVEL: B LANG: Eng SIRC ARTICLE NO: 097039

Legwold, G. More on hypertension and weight lifting. *Physician and sportsmedicine (Minneapolis, Minn.) 12(10), Oct 1984, 21.*
LEVEL: I LANG: Eng SIRC ARTICLE NO: 100168

PHYSIOLOGY

Lehmann, M. Schmid, P. Keul, J. Age- and exercise-related sympathetic activity in untrained volunteers, trained athletes and patients with impaired left-ventricular contractility. (Refs: 44)*European heart journal (London) 5(Suppl E), Nov 1984, 1-7.*
LEVEL: A LANG: Eng SIRC ARTICLE NO: 109711

McBurney, E.I. Rosen, D.A. Elevated creatine phosphokinase with isotretinoin. (letter) *Journal of the American Academy of Dermatology (St. Louis) 10(3), Mar 1984, 528-529.*
LEVEL: I LANG: Eng SIRC ARTICLE NO: 103662

Stepanova, S.V. Sinyakov, A.F. Belina, O.N. Body composition and physical work capacity of the strongest weightlifters in th USSR. *Soviet sports review (Escondido, Calif.) 19(2), Jun 1984, 90-92.*
NOTES: Translated from, Tyazhelaya atletika, 29-31, 1983.
LEVEL: I LANG: Eng SIRC ARTICLE NO: 100173

Stone, M.H. Wilson, D. Rozenek, R. Newton, H. Physiological basis. (Refs: 34)*National Strength & Conditioning Association journal 5(6), Jan 1984, 40;63-65.*
LEVEL: I LANG: Eng SIRC ARTICLE NO: 090305

PHYSIOLOGY - MUSCLE

Foucart, S. Brassard, L. Taylor, A.W. Peronnet, F. Caracteristiques du tissu musculaire et performances de six halterophiles de haut-niveau. (Refs: 14)*Medecine du sport (Paris) 58(6), nov 1984, 3-7.*
RESUME: Le but de cette etude est d'analyser le tissu musculaire de six halterophiles de haut niveau, ages de 17 a 24 ans. Les resultats indiquent que ces athletes possedent en moyenne un pourcentage eleve de fibres a secousse rapide.
LEVEL: A LANG: Fr SIRC ARTICLE NO: 103654

Gonyea, W.J. Physiology of exercise-induced muscle hyperplasia and hypertrophy. (Refs: 4)*Sportsmedicine digest (Van Nuys, Calif.) 6(2), Feb 1984, 1-3.*
LEVEL: I LANG: Eng SIRC ARTICLE NO: 099237

Kovalik, A.V. Prevention of overstress in the skeletal-joint system of weightlifters. (condensed) *Soviet sports review (Escondido, Calif.) 19(3), Sept 1984, 121-124.*
NOTES: Translated from, Teoriya i praktika fizicheskoi kultury 4, 1978, 36-39.
LEVEL: I LANG: Eng SIRC ARTICLE NO: 103656

Legg, S.J. Pateman, C.M. A physiological study of the repetitive lifting capabilities of healthy young males. (Refs: 28) *Ergonomics (London) 27(3), Mar 1984, 259-272.*
LEVEL: A LANG: Eng SIRC ARTICLE NO: 103659

Staron, R.S. Hikida, R.S. Hagerman, F.C. Dudley, G.A. Murray, T.F. Human skeletal muscle

fiber type adaptability to various workloads. *Journal of histochemistry and cytochemistry (Baltimore) 32(2), Feb 1984, 146-152.*
ABST: Muscle biopsy specimens were removed from the vastus lateralis muscles of controls, weight lifters, and distance runners. A histochemical analysis of the biopsy specimens revealed that the runners had a significantly higher percentage of fiber types I and IIC than either the controls or the weight lifters. The results of volume-percent mitochondria analysis demonstrated a strong relationship between the ATPase activity and oxidative potential of the fiber types for all three groups. Irrespective of fiber type, there were significant differences between the groups with regard to muscle-fiber mitochondrial (runners greater than lifters greater than controls) and lipid content (runners greater than controls greater than lifters). The lifters had a significantly greater content of mitochondria than the controls, which may suggest that inactivity rather than the lifting exercise contributes to a low volume-percent mitochondria and a high percentage of type IIB fibers.
LEVEL: A LANG: Eng SIRC ARTICLE NO: 099269

Tesch, A. Thorsson, A. Kraiser, P. Muscle capillary supply and fiber type characteristics in weight and power lifters. (Refs 25)*Journal of applied physiology: respiratory environmental and exercise physiology (Bethesda, Md.) 56(1), Jan 1984, 35-38.*
ABST: A comparison was made between 8 weight and power lifters, 8 endurance athletes and 8 untrained individuals to determine the differences in capillary density, fibre type distribution and fibre size of the vastus lateralis muscle. This study found that the weight and power lifters had reduced capillary density compared to the other 2 groups. The heavy resistance training of these athletes resulted in fast-twitch fibre hypertrophy with a reduction in the number of capillaries per square millimeter.
LEVEL: A LANG: Eng SIRC ARTICLE NO: 097042

PSYCHOLOGY

Filanovsky, S.G. Bonch-Bruevicha, M.A. Anikin, L.P. The post-competitive stage of training weightlifters. *Soviet sports review (Escondido, Calif.) 19(2), Jun 1984, 92-94.*
NOTES: Translated from, Tyazhelaya atletika, 1: 19-20, 1983.
LEVEL: I LANG: Eng SIRC ARTICLE NO: 100166

PSYCHOLOGY - MENTAL TRAINING

Bond, J. Psychological skills training for peak performance. *Sports science & medicine quarterly 1(1), Jun 1984, 10-12.*
LEVEL: I LANG: Eng SIRC ARTICLE NO: 098759

STATISTICS AND RECORDS

Croucher, J.S. An analysis of world weightlifting records. (Refs: 6)*Research quarterly for exercise & sport (Reston, Va.) 55(3), Sept 1984, 285-288.*
ABST: The author analyses the world weightlifting records for both the snatch and the jerk from 1956 until 1982. He discusses the relationship between the 1982 world records in snatch and jerk and body weight. Projections for 1988 are given.
LEVEL: A LANG: Eng SIRC ARTICLE NO: 103651

TEACHING

St-Cyr, S. Cahier pedagogique de l'enseignement de l'halterophilie. *Coup d'oeil sur l'halterophilie (Montreal) 17(4), oct/nov 1984, 7-8.*
NOTES: Suite au prochain numero.
LEVEL: B LANG: Fr SIRC ARTICLE NO: 101779

TECHNIQUES AND SKILLS

Dvorkin, L.S. The young weightlifter. Part V. Technique of executing weightlifting exercises. *Soviet sports review (Escondido, Calif.) 19(2), Jun 1984, 85-90.*
NOTES: Continuation from volume 19, No.1. To be continued.
LEVEL: I LANG: Eng SIRC ARTICLE NO: 100165

Roman, R.A. Treskov, V.V. Snatch technique of world record holder U. Zakharevich. *Soviet sports review (Escondido, Calif.) 19(4), Dec 1984, 199-203.*
NOTES: Continued from volume 19, number 3. Translated from, Tyayhelaya atletika 1, 1983, 10-16.
LEVEL: I LANG: Eng SIRC ARTICLE NO: 105092

Spitz, L. Pietka, L. Snatch technique. *Track & field quarterly review (Kalamazoo, Mich.) 84(1), Spring 1984, 59-60.*
NOTES Translated by Keven McGill.
LEVEL: B LANG: Eng SIRC ARTICLE NO: 095535

TESTING AND EVALUATION

Dvorkin, L.S. The young weightlifter: part VI. Evaluation of technical preparation. *Soviet sports review (Escondido, Calif. 19(3), Sept 1984, 142-145.*
NOTES: Continuing series.
LEVEL: I LANG: Eng SIRC ARTICLE NO: 103652

Medvedev, A.S. Marchenko, V.V. Fomichenko, S.V. Speed-strength structure of vertical jumps by qualified weightlifters in different take-off conditions. *Soviet sports review (Escondido, Calif.) 19(4), Dec 1984, 164-167.*
NOTES: Condensed translation from, Teoriya i praktika fizicheskoi kultury 12, 1983, 8-10.
LEVEL: I LANG: Eng SIRC ARTICLE NO: 105091

TRAINING AND CONDITIONING

DeMarco, L. Coaching clinic: training system for American lifters. *Weightlifters newsletter (West Newton, Mass.) 110, 5 May 1984, 4-5;10-11.*
LEVEL: B LANG: Eng SIRC ARTICLE NO: 098761

Deniskin, V.N. Verhoshansky, U.V. Medvedev, A.S. Speed-strength preparation of weightlifters in the pre-competitive stage. *Soviet sports review (Escondido, Calif.) 19(1), Mar 1984, 15-17.*
NOTES: Translated from, Tyazhelaya atletika 1982, 17-19.
LEVEL: I LANG: Eng SIRC ARTICLE NO: 095528

Filanovsky, S.G. Bonch-Bruevicha, M.A. Anikin, L.P. The post-competitive stage of training weightlifters. *Soviet sports review (Escondido, Calif.) 19(2), Jun 1984, 92-94.*
NOTES: Translated from, Tyazhelaya atletika, 1: 19-20, 1983.
LEVEL: I LANG: Eng SIRC ARTICLE NO: 100166

Kuzmin, V.F. Roman, R.A. Risin, E.E. Training loads of weightlifters in different weight categories, ages and levels of mastery. *Soviet sports review*

(Escondido, Calif.) 19(4), Dec 1984, 171-175.
NOTES: Translated from, Tyayhelaya atletika 1, 1983, 20-27. To be continued.
LEVEL: A LANG: Eng SIRC ARTICLE NO: 105090

Medvedev, A.S. Classification and ranking of weightlifting exercises. *Soviet sports review (Escondido, Calif.) 19(1), Mar 1984, 11-14*
NOTES: Translated from, Tyazhelaya atletika 1982, 19-23. To be concluded in vol. 19, no. 2.
LEVEL: I LANG: Eng SIRC ARTICLE NO: 095533

Medvedev, A.S. Periodization of training in weightlifting (preparatory plan for a base mesocycle). *Soviet sports review (Escondido, Calif.) 19(1), Mar 1984, 30-32.*
NOTES: Translated from, Tyazhelaya atletika 1, 1980, 11-15. Continuation from vol. 18, no. 4.
LEVEL: I LANG: Eng SIRC ARTICLE NO: 095534

Medvedev, A.S. Classification and ranking of weightlifting exercises. *Soviet sports review (Escondido, Calif.) 19(2), Jun 1984, 64-66.*
NOTES: Translated from, Tyazhelaya atletika, 19-23, 1982. (continuation from volume 19, No.1.)
LEVEL: B LANG: Eng SIRC ARTICLE NO: 100171

Mihailuk, M.P. Bashkorov, P.P. Modeling speed-strength preparation of weightlifters. *Soviet sports review (Escondido, Calif.) 19(2), Jun 1984, 66-68.*
NOTES: Translated from, Tyazahelaya atletika, 1: 28-29, 1983.
LEVEL: I LANG: Eng SIRC ARTICLE NO: 100172

Yessis, M. Soviet training concepts: GPP in the USSR. *Strength & health (York, Pa.) 52(3), Apr/May 1984, 60-62.*
LEVEL: B LANG: Eng SIRC ARTICLE NO: 100175

Yessis, M. Soviet training concepts: supplementary exercises. *Strength & health (York, Pa.) 52(6), Oct/Nov 1984, 56-58.*
LEVEL: B LANG: Eng SIRC ARTICLE NO: 100176

Yessis, M. Cycling and periodization Soviet style. *Muscle & fitness (Woodland Hills, Calif.) 45(11), Nov 1984, 104-106;148-149.*
LEVEL: B LANG: Eng SIRC ARTICLE NO: 101782

Yessis, M. Soviet training concepts: SPP in the USSR. (specialized physical preparation) *Strength & health (York, Pa.) 52(4), Jun/Jul 1984, 62-64.*
LEVEL: B LANG: Eng SIRC ARTICLE NO: 103664

Zeinalov, A.A. Developing leg strength. *Soviet sports review (Escondido, Calif.) 19(1), Mar 1984, 33-36.*
NOTES: Translate from, Tyazhelaya atletika 1976, 29-31.
LEVEL: I LANG: Eng SIRC ARTICLE NO: 095538

TRAINING AND CONDITIONING - TRAINING CAMPS

Zuffellato, R. Apres tout, c'est quoi un camp d'entrainement? *Coup d'oeil sur l'halterophilie (Montreal) 17(2), avr/mai 198 23-24.*
LEVEL: B LANG: Fr SIRC ARTICLE NO: 109107

TRAINING AND CONDITIONING - WEIGHT AND STRENGTH TRAINING

A non-olympian's guide to olympic training techniques. *Executive fitness newsletter (Emmaus, Pa.) 15(1), 7 Jan 1984, 1-2.*
LEVEL: B LANG: Eng SIRC ARTICLE NO: 094014

Allman, W.F. Weight lifting: what makes muscles work. In, Schrier, E.W. and Allman, W.F. (eds.),

Newton at the bat: the science in sports, New York, Scribner, c1984, p. 110-113.
LEVEL: B LANG: Eng RC1235 18609

Hatfield, F.C. Adapting Russian speed/strength training methods to powerlifting. *Powerlifting U.S.A. (Camarillo, Calif.) 7(8), Mar 1984, 28.*
LEVEL: B LANG: Eng SIRC ARTICLE NO: 098762

Kelso, P. The Kelso shrug system. *Powerlifting U.S.A. (Camarillo, Calif.) 7(8), Mar 1984, 22.*
LEVEL: B LANG: Eng SIRC ARTICLE NO: 098763

Kuc, J. The bench press 16 week intermediate program. *Powerlifting U.S.A. (Camarillo, Calif.) 7(8), Mar 1984, 11.*
LEVEL: LANG: Eng SIRC ARTICLE NO: 098765

Sword, W.L. Belt squats. *Powerlifting U.S.A. (Camarillo, Calif.) 7(8), Mar 1984, 20.*
LEVEL: B LANG: Eng SIRC ARTICLE NO: 098768

Weis, D.B. Preparation for competition. *Powerlifting U.S.A. (Camarillo, Calif.) 7(8), Mar 1984, 26.*
LEVEL: B LANG: Eng SIRC ARTICLE NO: 098771

Yessis, M. Soviet training concepts: speed-strength training. *Strength & health (York, Pa.) 52(5), Aug/Sept 1984, 28-30.*
LEVEL: B LANG: Eng SIRC ARTICLE NO: 173477

WOMEN

L'halterophilie au feminin: les Etats-Unis s'organisent. *Coup d'oeil sur l'halterophilie (Montreal) 17(1), mars 1984, 15.*
LEVEL: B LANG: Fr SIRC ARTICLE NO: 099366

WEIGHTLIFTING AND BODYBUILDING

CHILDREN

Carroll, J. At what age should youngsters begin training? *Muscular development (York, Pa.) 21(3), May/Jun 1984, 14-15;58-59.*
LEVEL: B LANG: Eng SIRC ARTICLE NO: 101114

PHYSIOLOGY

Alen, M. Rahkila, P. Reduced high-density lipoprotein-cholesterol in power athletes: use of male sex hormone derivates, an atherogenic factor. (Refs: 9)*International journal of sports medicine (Stuttgart) 5(6), Dec 1984, 341-342.*
ABST: The effect of androgenic steroids on plasma lipids was studied in seven power athletes who self-administered androgenic steroids on the average 45 mg/day during an 8-week strength training period. After 8 weeks of strength training, the androgen users had reduced the HDL-cholesterol by 54 per cent (from 1.47 to 0.67 mmol/l). The difference when compared to controls was highly significant.
LEVEL: A LANG: Eng SIRC ARTICLE NO: 104595

Haekkinen, K. Alen, M. Komi, P.V. Neuromuscular, anaerobic, and aerobic performance characteristics of elite power athletes. (Refs: 43)*European journal of applied physiology and occupational physiology (Berlin, W.G.) 53(2), 1984, 97-105.*
ABST: Various aspects of neuromuscular, anaerobic, and aerobic performance capacity were investigated in four powerlifters, seven bodybuilders, and three wrestlers with a history of

specific training for several years. The data showed that the three subject groups possessed similar values for maximal isometric force per unit bodyweight. However, significant differences were observed in the times for isometric force production. No differences were observed between the groups in anaerobic power in a 1-min maximal test, but the values for VO2 max were higher among the wrestlers and bodybuilders as compared to the powerlifters. No differences of a statistical significancy were observed between the groups in fibre distribution, fibre areas, or the area ratio of fast (FT) and slow (ST) twitch fibres in vastus lateralis.
LEVEL: A LANG: Eng SIRC ARTICLE NO: 104599

Hatfield, F.C. Estep, R. Aerobic vs weight-trained hearts. Debunking another myth. NASA's chief flight surgeon says heavy weight training is bad for the heart, but our experts' state-of-the-art research shows the truth. *Muscle & fitness (Woodland Hills, Calif.) 45(6), Jun 1984, 82-83;209-210;212-213;215.*
LEVEL: I LANG: Eng SIRC ARTICLE NO: 101775

Tesch, P.A. Lindeberg, S. Blood lactate accumulation during arm exercise in world class kayak paddlers and strength trained athletes. (Refs: 28)*European journal of applied physiology and occupational physiology (Berlin, FRG) 52(4), Jun 1984, 441-445.*
ABST: Blood lactate accumulation during continuous arm cranking of progressively increasing intensity was compared in 11 elite flat water kayakers, 6 elite weight-/power-lifters, 8 body-builders and 6 physically active non-athletes. Blood lactate concentrations were significantly lower in the kayakers compared to the other groups at low submaximal exercise intensities. At higher work outputs the differences between male kayakers and non-kayakers increased while the differences between female kayakers and non-kayakers decreased. The results suggest that factors other than muscle mass per se are responsible for the blood lactate response during progressive arm-cranking exercise.
LEVEL: A LANG: Eng SIRC ARTICLE NO: 098769

Webb, O.L. Laskarzewski, P.M. Glueck, C.J. Severe depression of high-density lipoprotein cholesterol levels in weight lifter and body builders by self-administered exogenous testosterone and anabolic-androgenic steroids. *Metabolism, clinical and experimental (New York) 33(11), Nov 1984, 971-975.*
LEVEL: A LANG: Eng

WEST INDIES

OLYMPIC GAMES

Les Antilles Neerlandaises et l'olympisme. *Revue olympique (Lausanne) 204, oct 1984, 839-841.*
LEVEL: B LANG: Fr SIRC ARTICL NO: 100800

The Netherlands Antilles and Olympism. *Olympic review (Lausanne) 204, Oct 1984, 839-841.*
LEVEL: B LANG: Eng SIRC ARTICLE NO 100807

WESTERN RIDING

TECHNIQUES AND SKILLS

Hank Clason: putting on a headset. The top-winning pleasure rider gets lasting results with a head-to-tail method of training in five easy-to-follow steps. *Performance horseman (Unionville, Pa.) 3(9), Aug 1984, 5-9;59-60.*
LEVEL: B LANG: Eng SIRC ARTICLE NO: 103252

Hyland, A. Introduction to Western reining. *Equi (Cheshire, Eng.) 23, Aug/Sept 1984, 9-11.*
LEVEL: B LANG: Eng SIRC ARTICL NO: 101350

Rocky Dare: system for a winning stop. The leading reining horse rider describes his unique method of teaching a sliding stop in details you can apply to your own horse. *Performance horseman (Unionville, Pa.) 3(7), Jun 1984, 4-11.*
LEVEL: B LANG: Eng SIRC ARTICLE NO: 103262

TRAINING AND CONDITIONING

Manion, T. Take one part showmanship, add one part horsemanship, mix and you have Tommy Manion's recipe for winning Western pleasure. The famous horseman talks about his training techniques and show-ring strategies. *Performance horseman (Unionville, Pa.) 3(6), May 1984, 5-7;10-11;13;60.*
LEVEL: B LANG: Eng SIRC ARTICLE NO: 099738

Milholland, D. Chamberlain, R. Training reining horses: Part 1. *Quarter horse journal (Amarillo, Tex.) 36(10), Jul 1984, 138-146.*
LEVEL: B LANG: Eng SIRC ARTICLE NO: 096708

Milholland, D. Chamberlain, R. Training running horses. Part II. *Quarter horse journal (Amarillo, Tex.) 36(11), Aug 1984, 180-188.*
LEVEL: B LANG: Eng SIRC ARTICLE NO: 096709

WILDERNESS SURVIVAL

Grenier, J. La survie en plein air: illusion ou realite. *CAHPER journal/Revue de l'ACSEPR (Ottawa) 50(4), Mar/Apr 1984, 23-24.*
LEVEL: B LANG: Fr SIRC ARTICLE NO: 096779

Tomikel, J. Short term survival techniques. Elgin, Pa.: Allegheny Press, c1984. 144 p. : ill. ; 21 cm.
NOTES: Includes inde
LEVEL: B LANG: Eng ISBN: 0910042454 LC CARD: 84-070534

PSYCHOLOGY

Raines, J.T. The impact of a 24-hour wilderness isolation on the expressed fear and anxiety of 10-, 11-, and 13-year-old boy Eugene, Ore.: Microform Publications, University of Oregon, 1984. 1 microfiche : negative, ill. ; 11 x 15 cm.
NOTES: Thesis (M.S.) - Pennsylvania State University, 1981; (viii, 80 leaves); includes bibliography.
LEVEL: A LANG: Eng UO84 104

WINTER CAMPING

EQUIPMENT

Townsend, C. Winter gear for winter camping. (Refs: 6)*Scottish journal of physical education (Glasglow, Scotland) 12(2), Ap 1984, 5-9.*
LEVEL: B LANG: Eng SIRC ARTICLE NO: 094911

TECHNIQUES AND SKILLS

Woodward, B. Topheavy touring. A simple guide to skiing with a pack on your back. *Backpacker (Los Angeles) 12(6), Nov 1984, 36;38-39;43.*
LEVEL: B LANG: Eng SIRC ARTICLE NO: 104881

WINTER SPORTS

HISTORY

Beattie, B. The Queen City celebrates winter: the Burlington Coasting Club and the Burlington Carnival of winter sports, 1886-1887. (Refs: 17)*Vermont history (Montpelier) 52(1), Winter 1984, 5-16.*
LEVEL: A LANG: Eng

INJURIES AND ACCIDENTS

Petit, M. Raveno, M. Pilardeau, P. Vaysse, J. Garnier, M. Influence de la preparation physique et du suivi dietetique sur la traumatologie observee lors des classes de neige. (Refs: 15)*Medecine du sport (Paris) 58(2), 25 mars 1984, 4-8*
RESUME: Les auteurs proposent un programme d'entrainement physique pour les enfants participant aux classes de neige. Ils soulignent l'importance d'une bonne alimentation lors de la duree des activites. L'etude de 4,300 enfants en 1979-1980 et 4,330 enfants en 1980-1981 dont l'age varie de 9 a 11 ans, indique une diminution de la frequence des accidents suite a la mise en place du programme de prevention.
LEVEL: A LANG: Fr SIRC ARTICLE NO: 094207

STATISTICS AND RECORDS - PARTICIPATION

Fitting fitness into the Canadian winter. En bonne condition par conditions difficiles. *Highlight/Faits saillants (Ottawa, Ont.) 41, Dec 1984, 1;1.*
LEVEL: B LANG: Eng Fr SIRC ARTICLE NO: 102918

TRAINING AND CONDITIONING - WARM-UPS, WARM-DOWNS, LEAD-UP GAMES

Martin, K. Warming up for winter sports: don't exercise 'cold'-prepare yourself for winter activity with these stretching exercises to warm you up. *Fit (Mountain View, Calif.) 4(7), Dec 1984, 50-55;65.*
LEVEL: B LANG: Eng SIRC ARTICLE NO: 173558

WOMEN

Adedeji, J.A. Women's sport in developing countries. (Refs: 9)*ICSSPE/CIEPSS review (Berlin, GDR) 7, 1984, 36-43.*
LEVEL: I LANG: Eng SIRC ARTICLE NO: 096463

Adrian, M. Biomechanics of female athletes. *ICSSPE/CIEPSS review (Berlin, GDR) 7, 1984, 24-29.*
ABST: This review of the literature focuses on biomechanical research on women participating in the following sports: swimming, running, jumping and gymnastics.
LEVEL: A LANG: Eng SIRC ARTICLE NO: 096464

Bentz, G. Frauensport in der Bundesrepublik Deutschland - eine positive und negative Bilanz. (Women's sport in the German Democratic Republic - positive and negative aspects.) (Refs: 17)*ICSSPE/CIEPSS review (Berlin, GDR) 7, 1984, 57-61.*
LEVEL: I LANG: Ger SIRC ARTICLE NO: 095657

Dickie, D. Les femmes ont fait bien du chemin, mais sont-elles allees assez loin? You've come a long way, but have you gone far enough? *Champion 8(1), Feb 1984, 54-58.*
LEVEL: B LANG: Eng Fr SIRC ARTICLE NO: 090422

Hubert-Rafin, C. Sport feminin. (Refs: 15)*Revue de l'education physique (Liege) 24(2), 1984, 11-17.*
RESUME: L'auteur expose les differences physiologiques et psycho-sociales entre les sexes. Il rapporte les resultats d'une enquete sur la pratique sportive feminine belge en 1980-1981. Un sondage fut effectue aupres de 200 federations sportives belges ainsi qu'en milieu parascolaire.
LEVEL: A LANG: Fr SIRC ARTICLE NO: 101046

Jones, J. Women in motion. *In, Boston Women's Health Book Collective, The new our bodies, ourselves, New York, Simon & Schuster, 1984, p. 41-53.*
LEVEL: I LANG: Eng

Kleiber, D.A. Kane, M.J. Sex differences and the use of leisure as adaptive potentiation. (Refs: 42)*Loisir & societe/Societ and leisure (Trois-Rivieres, Que.) 7(1), printemps 1984, 165-173.*
LEVEL: I LANG: Eng SIRC ARTICLE NO: 100968

Kostkova, J. Koerpererziehung der Frauen in der CSSR. (The physical education of women in the CSSR.) *ICSSPE/CIEPSS review (Berlin, GDR) 7, 1984, 61-65.*
LEVEL: I LANG: Ger SIRC ARTICLE NO: 095658

Lenskyj, H. A discussion paper. Female participation in sport: the issue of integration versus separate-but-equal. s.l.: s.n., 1984. i, 103 leaves
CORP: Canadian Association for the Advancement of Women in Sport.
CORP: Canada. Sport Canada.
NOTES: Includes bibliographical references.
LEVEL: A LANG: Eng GV709 20587

Treble, G. Sex differences in athletic performance: if boys can, girls can. *Sports coach (Wembley, W. Aust.) 8(2), Oct 1984 5-7;17.*
LEVEL: B LANG: Eng SIRC ARTICLE NO: 104525

Wonneberger, I. Frau und Sport in der DDR. (Women and sport in the GDR.) (Refs: 19)*ICSSPE/CIEPSS review (Berlin, GDR) 7, 1984, 43-48.*
LEVEL: I LANG: Ger SIRC ARTICLE NO: 095655

ADMINISTRATION

Grant, C.H.B. The gender gap in sport: from Olympic to intercollegiate level. (Refs: 12)*Arena review (Boston, Ma.) 8(2), Ju 1984, 31-47.*
LEVEL: I LANG: Eng SIRC ARTICLE NO: 101044

ASSOCIATIONS

Grant, C.H.B. The gender gap in sport: from Olympic to intercollegiate level. (Refs: 12)*Arena review (Boston, Ma.) 8(2), Ju 1984, 31-47.*
LEVEL: I LANG: Eng SIRC ARTICLE NO: 101044

Tollich, H. The history of IAPESGW. A contribution to the development of Comparative Physical Education and Sports for Women as a means for international understanding. *ICSSPE/CIEPSS review (Berlin, GDR) 7, 1984, 32-36.*
LEVEL: B LANG: Eng SIRC ARTICLE NO: 096484

ATTITUDE

Michael, M.E. Gilroy, F.D. Sherman, M.F. Athletic similarity and attitudes towards women as factors in the perceived physica attractiveness and liking of female varsity athletes. (Refs: 21)*Perceptual and motor skills (Missoula, Mont. 59(2), Oct 1984, 511-518.*
ABST: 120 male and female athletes and non-athletes were asked questions pertaining to the description of a hypothetical female college student who was characterized as being either athletic or non-athletic. The Attitudes Toward Women Scale was also used to measure subjects' attitudes toward women. Athletes found the female athlete more attractive than the non-athlete one while the opposite was true for the non athletes. Athletic similarity was also related to perceived liking but only for the athletic subjects. Women were significantly more liberal than the men in their attitudes toward women.
LEVEL: A LANG: Eng SIRC ARTICLE NO: 102975

BIBLIOGRAPHIES

Paelvimaeki, A. Women and sport. La femme et le sport. La mujer y el deporte. Frau und Sport. *ICSSPE/CIEPSS review (Berlin, GDR) 7, 1984, 80-96.*
LEVEL: B LANG: Eng Fr Spa Ger SIRC ARTICLE NO: 096477

BIOGRAPHY AND AUTOBIOGRAPHY

Canada's Olympic women think gold. *Chatelaine (Toronto) 57(8), Aug 1984, 46-49;65-66;68-69.*
LEVEL: B LANG: Fr SIRC ARTICLE NO: 101005

Casabona, H. Dawson, A. Winner's circle. *Women's sport and fitness (Palo Alto, Calif.) 6(8), Aug 1984, 34-39.*
LEVEL: B LANG: Eng SIRC ARTICLE NO: 101040

Gray, C. The emergence of the female jock. *Chatelaine 57(4), Apr 1984, 98-99;118;120-122.*
LEVEL: B LANG: Eng SIRC ARTICLE NO: 091901

CLOTHING

Siegel, D. Sport bras (abstract). (Refs: 9)*Sports physiotherapy division (Victoria, B.C.) 9(2), Mar/Apr 1984, 30.*
LEVEL: LANG: Eng SIRC ARTICLE NO: 097502

HISTORY

Diem, L. Frau und Sport - eine kritische Studie. (Women and sport - a critical study.) (Refs: 10)*ICSSPE/CIEPSS review (Berlin, GDR) 7, 1984, 11-15.*
LEVEL: I LANG: Ger SIRC ARTICLE NO: 095654

Hay, E. Evolution de la femme dans le sport. *Ligne d'arret (France) 20, 1984, 15-19.*
LEVEL: B LANG: Fr

Lumpkin, A. Historical perspectives of female participation in youth sport. Alexandria, Va.: Computer Microfilm International, 1984. 1 microfiche (13 fr.)
CONF: American Alliance for Health, Physical Education, Recreation and Dance. Convention (1984 : Anaheim, Calif.)
LEVEL: A LANG: Eng EDRS: ED243878

Sargent, D.A. Are athletics making girls masculine? A practical answer to a question every girl asks.
NOTES: In, Riess, S.A (ed.), The American sproting experience: a historical anthology of sport in America, New York, Leisure Press, c1984, p. 255-263. Previously published in, Ladies home journal 29, March 1912, p. 11;71;73.
LEVEL: I LANG: Eng GV583 17631

Spears, B. A perspective of the history of women's sport in Ancient Greece. (Refs: 59)*Journal of sport history (University Park, Pa.) 11(2), Summer 1984, 32-47.*
ABST: The author examines the history of women's sport in ancient Greece during four periods: the Archaic Period (c.800 B.C. - c.500 B.C.); the Classical Period (c.500 B.C. - c.323 B.C.); the Hellenestic Period (c.323 B.C. - c.146 B.C.) and the Roman Period (c.146 B.C. - c.400 A.D.).
LEVEL: A LANG: Eng SIRC ARTICLE NO: 099378

Stuna, N.L. Beyond mapping experience: the need for understanding in the history of American sporting women. *Journal of sport history (Seattle, Wash.) 11(1), Spring 1984, 120-133.*
LEVEL: I LANG: Eng SIRC ARTICLE NO: 096483

LAW AND LEGISLATION

Lenskyj, H. Equal opportunity for girls and women in sport. (Refs: 20)*In, Canadian Intramural Recreation Association, Sixth National Conference Proceedings, (Geneva Park, Ont.), C.I.R.A., 1984, p. 63-76.*
CONF: Canadian Intramural Recreation Association. National Conference (6th : 1984 : Geneva Park, Ont.).
ABST: Research into human rights legislation in Canada and strategies for achieving sex equality in relation to female participation in sport is outlined in this paper.
LEVEL: I LANG: Eng SIRC ARTICLE NO: 107959

MASS MEDIA

Rintala, J. Birrell, S. Fair treatment for the active female: a content analysis of Young Athlete magazine. (Refs: 46) *Sociology of sport journal (Champaign, Ill.) 1(3), 1984, 231-250.*
ABST: The availability of female role models is examined through a content analysis of Young Athlete magazine. Two research questions are posed: Do males and females receive differential treatment in Young Athlete? Does the

WOMEN (continued)

representation of males and females in Young Athlete reflect actual participation rates? Young Athlete depicts sport as a male activity. For example, less than one-third of all photographs depict females, and the percentage decreases with the prominence of the photograph. Compared to actual participation rates, Young Athlete subtly distorts girls involvement. Girls are markedly under-represented in team sports, even those they dominate numerically. Discussion focuses upon the issue of fair treatment.
LEVEL: A LANG: Eng SIRC ARTICLE NO: 102976

MEDICINE

Bullen, B.A. Skrinar, G.S. Beitins, I.Z. Carr, D.B. Reppert, S.M. Gervino, E.V. McArthur, J.W. Dotson, C.O. Fencel, M. de M. Endurance training effects on plasma hormonal responsiveness and sex hormone excretions. (Refs: 59)*Journal of applied physiology: respiratory environmental and exercise physiology (Bethesda, Md.) 56(6), Jun 1984, 1453-1463.*
ABST: This study investigated the effects of moderate physical training on plasma hormonal responsiveness and sex hormone excretion. Seven young women exercised at 85% of their maximum heart rate 20-45 min/day, 6 days/week for 8 weeks. Acute exercise induced the release of a wide array of hormones, several of which possess antireproductive properties. A mild impairment in ovarian excretion was noted in some, but not all, subjects.
LEVEL: A LANG: Eng SIRC ARTICLE NO: 097890

Fibiger, W. Singer, G. Urinary dopamine in physical and mental effort. (Refs: 12)*European journal of applied physiology and occupational physiology (Berlin, FRG) 52(4), Jun 1984, 437-440.*
ABST: Twelve subjects performed six separate tasks spaced approximately one week apart. Three tasks were physical in nature requiring the subject to exercise at 35, 50 and 75% VO2 max. The other three tasks were mental in nature requiring the subjects to perform tasks involving delayed auditory feedback (DAF), vigilance or arithmetic. There was a significant difference in dopamine excretion for the physical tasks and the DAF task. In addition, the response patterns (ratios of noradrenaline (dopamine and adrenaline) dopamine) differ after physical and mental stress. The authors suggest that this result could be refined and eventually be used to differentiate between mental and physical effort.
LEVEL: A LANG: Eng SIRC ARTICLE NO: 097594

Frisch, R.E. Body fat, puberty and fertility. (Refs: 128)*Biological reviews (London) 59(2), May 1984, 161-188.*
LEVEL: I LANG: Eng SIRC ARTICLE NO: 102330

Jacobson, P.C. Beaver, W. Grubb, S.A. Taft, T.N. Talmage, R.V. Bone density in women: college athletes and older athletic women. *Journal of orthopeadic research (New York) 2(4), 1984, 328-332.*
LEVEL: A LANG: Eng

Jools, N. Are we looking after our 'women in sport'. (Refs: 11)*Sport health (Pennant Hills, Aust.) 2(1), 1984, 12-13.*
ABST: Defines a possible role for the gynaecologist in the management of some of the more common problems faced by women in sport. The following are outlined: (1) management of the menstrual cycle; (2) emotional stress and gynaecology; (3)

prophylaxis and prevention; (4) counselling; (5) management of gynaecological surgery; (6) pregnancy and sport. Concludes that there is a place for the medical profession to reassess its attitudes to women in sport.
LEVEL: B LANG: Eng SIRC ARTICLE NO: 094796

Otis, C.L. Women and athletic participation. (Refs: 4)*CAHPERD journal times (Danville, Calif.) 47(2), Nov 1984, 20-21.*
LEVEL: B LANG: Eng SIRC ARTICLE NO: 108275

Rougier, G. Roger, J.M. Garrigues, R. Menopause et GV. *Loisirs sante (Paris) 9, avr/mai 1984, 26-29.*
LEVEL: I LANG: Fr SIRC ARTICLE NO: 101051

Saya, T. Le sport de haut niveau est-il compatible avec la 'feminite'? *Generaliste (Paris) 640, 1984, 1820.*
LEVEL: B LANG Fr

Schilling, J.A. Molen, M.T. Physical fitness and its relationship to postoperative recovery in abdominal hysterectomy patients. *Heart and lung (St. Louis) 13(6), Nov 1984, 639-644.*
LEVEL: A LANG: Eng

Telesna vychova a rehabilitacia v gynekologii a porodnictve. (Physical training and rehabilitation in gynecology and obstetrics.) *Ceskoslovenska gynekologie (Prague) 49(2), Mar 1984, 136-158.*
LEVEL: A LANG: Slo Cze

Verstraete, Peut-on prevenir les troubles de la menopause? *Loisirs sante (Paris) 10, juin/juil/aout 1984, 24;26.*
LEVEL: B LANG: Fr SIRC ARTICLE NO: 104526

Wallace, J.P. Serum concentrations of sex hormones during exercise in pre-, peri-, and post-menopausal women. Eugene, Ore.: Microform Publications, University of Oregon, 1984. 2 microfiches : negative, ill. ; 11 x 15 cm.
NOTES: Thesis (Ph.D.) - Pennsylvania State University, 1981; (xv, 174, 1 leaves); vita; includes bibliography.
LEVEL: A LANG: Eng UO84 87-88

Walsh, B.T. Puig-Antich, J. Goetz, R. Gladis, M. Novacenko, H. Glassman, A.H. Sleep and growth hormone secretion in women athletes. *Electromyography and clinical neurophysiology (Louvain) 57(6), Jun 1984, 528-531.*
ABST: Assessments of growth hormone secretion and sleep pattern of six women athletes were performed in this study. More stage 4 sleep, less REM activity and a similar REM density were observed in athletes when compared with 5 normal women. The nocturnal secretion of growth hormone was higher in the first hour following sleep onset in the athletes.
LEVEL: A LANG: Eng SIRC ARTICLE NO: 102980

Weicker, H. Barwich, D. Bauer, D. Zachmann, L. Changes in sexual hormones with female top athletes. (Refs: 15)*International journal of sports medicine (Stuttgart) Suppl. 5, Nov 1984, 200-202.*
CONF: International Congress on Sports and Health (1983 : Maastricht, Netherlands).
LEVEL: A LANG: Eng SIRC ARTICLE NO: 104528

White, M.K. Martin, R.B. Yeater, R.A. Butcher, R.L. Radin, E.L. The effects of exercise on the bones of postmenopausal women (Refs: 36)*International orthopaedics (New York) 7(4), 1984, 209-214.*
ABST: The effects of walking and aerobic dancing on the bones of 73 recently postmenopausal

women have been compared with a control group who did not exercise. The period of observation was six months. Results showed that the control group and the walking group lost statistically significant amounts of bone mineral content (1.6 per cent, and 1.7 per cent respectively), but that the dancing group did not (0.8 per cent). The control group did not show a significant increase in the bone width (0.9 per cent), but both the dancing (1.3 per cent) and walking (1.6 per cent) groups did.
LEVEL: A LANG: Eng SIRC ARTICLE NO: 104529

Wilmore, J.H. Maxwell, B.D. Constable, S.H. Atwater, A.E. Rotkis, T.C. A water displacement method for the determination of breast volume. (Refs: 5)*Research quarterly for exercise and sport (Reston, Va.) 55(4), Dec 1984, 388-389.*
LEVEL: A LANG: Eng SIRC ARTICLE NO: 104156

MEDICINE - MENSTRUATION

Bonen, A. Menstrual cycle irregularities in athletes (AMI). (Refs: 5)*Coaching science update (Ottawa, Ont.) 1984, 21-22.*
LEVEL: B LANG: Eng SIRC ARTICLE NO: 094788

Bonen, A. L'amenorrhee chez les athletes. (Refs: 5)*Nouveautes en science de l'entrainement (Ottawa) 1984, 18-19.*
LEVEL: I LANG: Fr SIRC ARTICLE NO: 096467

Bonen, A. Keizer, H.A. Athletic menstrual cycle irregularity: endocrine response to exercise and training. (Refs: 60) *Physician and sportsmedicine (Minneapolis, Minn.) 12(8), Aug 1984, 78-82;84-90;93-94.*
ABST: The authors (1) review the literature on menstrual disorder in female athletes, 2) compare the menstrual cycle hormone patterns of women with normal and abnormal cycles, 3) discuss the hormone responses to exercise, and 4) explain the sex-steroid metabolism during exercise.
LEVEL: A LANG: Eng SIRC ARTICLE NO: 097889

Bonen, A. Effect of exercise and training on reproductive hormones. (Refs: 14)*International journal of sports medicine (Stuttgart) Suppl. 5, Nov 1984, 195-197.*
CONF: International Congress on Sports and Health (1983 : Maastricht, Netherlands).
LEVEL: A LANG: Eng SIRC ARTICLE NO: 104512

Brodzinski, W. Analiza czynnikowa wybranych parametrow psychomotoryki w badaniu wplywow krwawien menstruacyjnych na sprawnos kobiet. (Factor analysis of selected psychomotor indicators in the study of the effect of menstrual bleeding on the physical fitness of women.) *Wiadomosci lekarskie (Warsaw) 37(17), 1 Sept 1984, 1331-1335.*
LEVEL: A LANG: Pol

Bruno, B. Moscardelli, S. Disfunzioni mestruali nelle atlete. (Menstruation disorders in athletes.) *Recenti progressi in medicina (Rome) 75(6), Jun 1984, 531-539.*
LEVEL: I LANG: It

Caldwell, F. PMS symptoms are relieved by exercise. *Physician and sportsmedicine (Minneapolis, Minn.) 12(5), May 1984, 23-24.*
LEVEL: B LANG: Eng SIRC ARTICLE NO: 094789

Canty, A.P. Can aerobic exercise releive the symptoms of premenstrual syndrome (PMS)? (Refs: 20)*Journal of school health (Kent, Ohio) 54(10), Nov 1984, 410-411.*
LEVEL: I LANG: Eng SIRC ARTICLE NO: 108222

Canu, M.F. Chez les jeunes sportives: problemes gynecologiques. (Refs: 10)*Dans, Mandel, C. (ed.), Le medecin, l'enfant et l sport, Paris, (Vigot), c1984, p. 153-162.*
LEVEL: I LANG: Fr RC1218.C45 18886

Carlin, N. Menarche. (Refs: 5)*Athletic training (Greenville, N.C.) 19(4), Winter 1984, 303-304.*
LEVEL: I LANG: Eng SIRC ARTICLE NO: 104513

Dauwalter, T.P. Finke, C.K. Woman in sports. (Refs: 16)*Sideline view (Minneapolis, Minn.) 5(10), May 1984, 1-4.*
LEVEL: I LANG: Eng SIRC ARTICLE NO: 094790

de Bruyn-Prevost, P. Masset, C. Sturbois, X. Physiological response from 18-25 years women to aerobic and anaerobic physical fitness tests at different periods during the menstrual cycle. (Refs: 8)*Journal of sports medicine and physical fitness (Torino, Italy) 24(2), Jun 1984, 144-148.*
ABST: A question which frequently arises about sports practice by women is to know whether it is suitable to have important physical activities or any competition during the menstruation. This study investigates the possible influence of the period during the menstrual cycle on the physiological response of young women to aerobic and anaerobic physical fitness tests. Two groups participate at the experiments: 7 women taking regularly oral contraceptives and 7 women not taking any medication. For both groups, the response seems not to be influenced by the period of the cycle and the two groups show similar results for the two tests.
LEVEL: A LANG: Eng SIRC ARTICLE NO: 102969

Drinkwater, B.L. Nilson, K. Chesnut, C.H. Bremner, W.J. Shainholtz, S. Southworth, M.B. Bone mineral content of amenorrheic and eumonorrheic athletes. *New England journal of medicine (Boston) 311(5), 2 Aug 1984, 277-281.*
ABST: This study examined whether the hypoestrogenic status of 14 amenorrheic athletes was associated with a decrease in regional bone mass relative to that of 14 of their eumenorrheic peers. The results indicate that amenorrhea in female athletes may be accompanied by a decrease in mineral density of the lumbar vertebrae.
LEVEL: A LANG: Eng SIRC ARTICLE NO: 102971

Drinkwater, B.L. Athletic amenorrhea: a review. (Refs: 48)*American Academy of Physical Education papers (Champaign, Ill.) 17, 1984, 120-131.*
CONF: American Academy of Physical Education. Annual Meeting (54th : 1983 : Minneapolis).
NOTES: Conference theme: Exercise and health.
LEVEL: I LANG: Eng SIRC ARTICLE NO: 104515

Emans, S.J. The athletic adolescent with amenorrhea. *Pediatric annals (New York) 13(8), Aug 1984, 605;612.*
LEVEL: B LANG: Eng

Eston, R.G. The regular menstrual cycle and athletic performance. (Refs: 106)*Sports medicine (Auckland, N.Z.) 1(6), Nov/Dec 1984, 431-445.*
ABST: This review considers the evidence for the cyclic effects of the regular or normal menstrual cycle on performance. It examines surveyed evidence of the effects of the regular menstrual cycle on athletic performance, effects on psychological and perceptual factors, maximum oxygen uptake, endurance and time to fatigue, temperature, sweating, body-weight, respiratory drive, blood lactate, carbohydrate and lipid metabolism, and cardiovascular parameters. It is concluded that there is considerable variation in the

findings of the literature and that any reported variations in performance may well be greatly influenced by intersubject variability, the nature of the exercise, and the nutritional status of the athlete, as well as minor changes that could be attributable to the menstrual cycle.
LEVEL: A LANG: Eng SIRC ARTICLE NO: 102972

Eston, R.G. Physiological and psychophysiological parameters during exercise across four phases of the menstrual cycle. Eugene, Ore.: Microform Publications, University of Oregon, 1984. 2 microfiches : negative, ill. ; 11 x 15 cm.
NOTES: Thesis (D.P.E.) - Springfield College, 1983; (xii, 149 leaves); includes bibliography.
LEVEL: A LANG: Eng UO84 426-427

Frisch, R.E. Amenorrhoea, vegetarianism, and/or low fat. (letter) *Lancet (London) 1(8384), 5 May 1984, 1024.*
LEVEL: B LANG: Eng SIRC ARTICLE NO: 100718

Frisch, R.E. Delayed menarche and amenorrhea of athletes: significance for fertility and reproductive health. *Population index (Princeton, N.J.) 50(3), 1984, 382.*
LEVEL: I LANG: Eng SIRC ARTICLE NO: 104517

Goodyear, C. Prostaglandin inhibitors: a better treatment for dysmenorrhea. (Refs: 6)*Coaching science update (Ottawa, Ont.) 1984, 19-21.*
LEVEL: I LANG: Eng SIRC ARTICLE NO: 094420

Goodyear, C. Les inhibiteurs de prostaglandine: meilleur traitement pour la dysmenorrhee. (Refs: 6)*Nouveautes en science de l'entrainement (Ottawa) 1984, 16-18.*
LEVEL: I LANG: Fr SIRC ARTICLE NO: 096018

Hansen, I.L. Larsen, L.O. Udholdenhedstraening og menstruation. (Endurance training and menstruation.) *Ugeskrift for laeger (Copenhagen) 146(27), 2 Jul 1984, 2004-2005.*
NOTES: Includes English abstract.
LEVEL: I LANG: Dan

Haycock, C.E. Amenorrhea linked to stress of training, competition. *First aider (Gardner, Kan.) 53(7), Summer 1984, 6-7.*
ABST: A major factor in menstrual dysfunction is stress associated with such hormonal changes as the lowering of estrogen levels. Physical and psychological stress interferes with the functioning of the hypothalamus which controls the release of hormones required to maintain the normal menstrual cycle. Amenorrhea in athletes is usually temporary and can often be corrected by a reduction in training load. The author advises that the athlete be examined by a gynecological endocrinologist if the dysfunction occurs and that all female athletes have a thorough medical exam, including pap smear and pelvic exam, on a yearly basis.
LEVEL: B LANG: Eng SIRC ARTICLE NO: 096474

Janess, S.R. Amenorrhea among sedentary women, physically active women, and varsity team athletes. Eugene, Ore.: Microform Publications, University of Oregon, 1984. 1 microfiche : negative ; 11 x 15 cm.
NOTES: Thesis (M.S.) - Pennsylvania State University, 1983; ((9), 78 leaves); includes bibliography.
LEVEL: A LANG: Eng UO84 261

Lindberg, J.S. Fears, W.B. Hunt, M.M. Powell, M.R. Boll, D. Wade, C.E. Exercise-induced amenorrhea and bone density. *Annals of internal*

medicine (Philadelphia) 101(5), Nov 1984, 647-648.
LEVEL: I LANG: Eng

Loucks, A.B. Horvath, S.M. Freedson, P.S. Menstrual status and validation of body fat prediction in athletes. *Human biology (Detroit) 56(2), May 1984, 383-392.*
LEVEL: A LANG: Eng

Loucks, A.B. Horvath, S.M. Exercise-induced stress responses of amenorrheic and eumenorrheic runners. *Journal of clinical endocrinology and metabolism (Baltimore) 59(6), Dec 1984, 1109-1120.*
LEVEL: A LANG: Eng

McArthur, J. Amenorrhoeic athletes: at risk of developing osteoporosis? (Refs: 9)*British journal of sports medicine (Loughborough, Eng.) 18(4), Dec 1984, 253-255.*
CONF: London Marathon Conference (1984 : London).
LEVEL: I LANG: Eng SIRC ARTICLE NO: 104522

Mesaki, N. Sasaki, J. Shoji, M. Iwasaki, H. (Delayed menarche following early onset of athletic sports training.) *Nippon Sanka Fujinka Gakkai Zasshi. Acta obstetrica et gynaecologica Japonica (Tokyo) 36(1), Jan 1984, 49-56.*
ABST: This study investigates the onset of menarche of 174 college and 137 non-athlete control students (group C). The athletes are divided into hard physical activity (group A) and moderate physical activity (group B) groups. No significant difference among the three groups are observed. Morever, group A athletes who begin training before menarche have a later menarcheal age averaging 13.1 years.
LEVEL: A LANG: Jpn

Mesaki, N. Sasaki, J. Shoji, M. Iwasaki, H. Eda, M. (Menstrual characteristics in college athletes.) *Nippon Sanka Fujinka Gakkai Zasshi. Acta obstetrica et gynaecologica Japonica (Tokyo) 36(2), Feb 1984, 247-254.*
ABST: Menstrual characteristics of 174 college athletes and 137 non-athlete control students (group C) were compared in this study. The athletes were divided into hard physical activity (group A) and moderate physical acitivty (group B) groups. Prolonged menstruation and hypomenorrhea were more common in athletes than in non-athletes. There was no significant difference in the incidence of oligomenorrhea and polymenorrhea in the three groups. Findings showed that an higher incidence of irregular menstrual cycles in group A than in group C.
LEVEL: A LANG: Jpn

Oian, P. Augestad, L.B. Molne, K. Oseid, S. Aakvaag, A. Menstrual dysfunction in Norwegian top athletes. *Acta obstetricia e gynecologica scandinavica (Stockholm) 63(8), 1984, 693-697.*
ABST: This paper outlined the data obtained from 18 Norwegian female top athletes suffering from secondary amenorrhea. Their mean age was 20.8 years (range 18-27) and their mean age at menarche 14.6 years (13-16.5), significantly older than that of the other top athletes: 13.5 years. Hormonal changes were consistent with simple normoprolactinemic hypothalamic suppression, characterized by low values of FSH, estradiol-17 beta and prolactin.
LEVEL: A LANG: Eng

Parr, R.B. Bachman, L.A. Moss, R.A. Iron deficiency in female athletes. (Refs: 24)*Physician and sportsmedicine (Minneapolis Minn.) 12(4), Apr*

WOMEN (continued)

1984, 81-86.
ABST: The authors compare three stages of iron deficiency immediately after menstruation and at midcycle, within a group of 29 athletes (track and field, softball, and field hockey) and a group of 8 sedentary controls. All athletes were stage 1 iron deficient and two were stage 2 iron deficient. No deficiency existed in non-athletes. Nutrition counseling is suggested within sport programs.
LEVEL: A LANG: Eng SIRC ARTICLE NO: 093254

Ronkainen, H. Pakarinen, A. Kauppila, A. Pubertal and menstrual disorders of female runners, skiers and volleyball players. *Gynecologic and obstetric investigation (Basel) 18(4), 1984, 183-189.*
LEVEL: A LANG: Eng

Rosenstein, M. Menstrual cramps. *Skating magazine (Colorado Springs, Colo.) 61(10), Dec 1984, 13-14.*
LEVEL: B LANG: Eng SIRC ARTICLE NO: 105635

Russell, J.B. Mitchell, D. Musey, P.I. Collins, D.C. The relationship of exercise to anovulatory cycles in female athletes: hormonal and physical characteristics. *Obstetrics and gynecology (New York) 63(4), Apr 1984, 452-456.*
ABST: The authors compared the menstrual cycle of women with high, medium, and low levels of physical activity. Results indicated a correlation between anovulatory cycles and the amount of exercise and increased levels of catechol estrogens.
LEVEL: A LANG: Eng SIRC ARTICLE NO: 099375

Russell, J.B. Mitchell, D.E. Musey, P.I. Collins, D.C. The role of beta-endorphins and catechol estrogens on the hypothalamic-pituitary axis in female athletes. *Fertility and sterility (Birmingham, Ala.) 42(5), Nov 1984, 690-695.*
LEVEL: A LANG: Eng

Shangold, M.M. Exercise and the adult female: hormonal and endocrine effects. (Refs: 105)*Exercise and sport sciences review (Lexington, Mass.) 12, 1984, 53-79.*
ABST: This paper reviews existing literature and research on menstrual physiology in the female athlete. This examination focuses on hormonal changes, however, hormone levels are affected by many variable factors such as diet, temperature and emotion, which are difficult to study separately. Furthermore the hormonal response to exercise is influenced by a subject's fitness, her training loads and the amount of time spent exercising. Acute hormone changes during exercise are reviewed but such changes have not yet been found to produce any long term effects. Research into chronic hormone and menstrual alterations in female athletes have found long term effects on menstruation. In particular, a number of studies have found a significant relation between the leaness of a women and the occurrence of menstrual disfunction. Menstrual cycles have also been found to be adversely affected by training. Though this article reports no new information on research in this area it is nevertheless a useful review of recent findings.
LEVEL: A LANG: Eng SIRC ARTICLE NO: 096480

Shangold, M.M. Menstrual disturbances in the athlete. (Refs: 18)*Primary care: clinics in office practice (Philadelphia) 11(1), Mar 1984, 109-114.*
LEVEL: I LANG: Eng SIRC ARTICLE NO: 101052

Shangold, M.M. Gynecologic concerns in the woman athlete. (Refs: 16)*Clinics in sports medicine*

(Philadelphia) 3(4), Oct 1984, 869-879.
NOTES: Symposium on the athletic woman.
ABST: Many athletes question how exercise and certain gynecologic conditions may affect each other. Among the issues of greatest concern are menstrual irregularity and amenorrhea, delay of puberty, menopause, menstrual cramps, premenstrual syndrome, contraception, infertility, urinary incontinence, pelvic and vaginal infections, sanitary protection, heavy bleeding, breast problems, and postoperative and postpartum training. Any gynecologic problems that arise should be evaluated and treated appropriately, with regard to the importance of exercise in the lifestyle of the woman.
LEVEL: I LANG: Eng SIRC ARTICLE NO: 101053

Slavin, J. Lutter, J. Cushman, S. Amenorrhoea in vegetarian athletes. (letter) *Lancet (London) 1(8392), 30 Jun 1984, 1474-1475.*
LEVEL: B LANG: Eng SIRC ARTICLE NO: 102977

Stager, J.M. Reversibility of amenorrhoea in athletes. (Refs: 19)*Sports medicine (Auckland, N.Z.) 1(5), Sept/Oct 1984, 337-340.*
ABST: Though athletic amenorrhea has been studied extensively very little documentation exists with respect to the effects of routine exercise upon ovulation or subsequent fertility. This review of the existing literature finds that amenorrhea associated with physical training generally persists for less than 2 months once training has either been reduced or discontinued. This may be good news for amenorrheic athletes but the author does point to a need for further study into the long term impact of sport participation on fertility which up until now has not been researched.
LEVEL: I LANG: Eng SIRC ARTICLE NO: 102979

Wilkerson, L.A. The female athlete. *American family physician (Kansas City, Mo.) 29(5), May 1984, 233-237.*
LEVEL: I LANG: Eng SIRC ARTICLE NO: 102981

Williams, M. Oligomenorrhoea and amenorrhoea associated with exercise. A literature review. *Australian family physician (Sydney) 13(9), Sept 1984, 659-663.*
LEVEL: A LANG: Eng

Wilson, C. Emans, S.J. Mansfield, J. Podolsky, C. Grace, E. The relationships of calculated percent body fat, sports participation, age, and place of residence on menstrual patterns in healthy adolescent girls at an independent New England high school. *Journal of adolescent health care (New York) 5(4), Oct 1984, 248-253.*
LEVEL: A LANG: Eng

Ziporyn, T. Latest clue to exercise-induced amenorrhea. (news) *JAMA. Journal of the American Medical Association (Chicago) 252(10), 14 Sept 1984, 1258-1259;1263.*
LEVEL: I LANG: Eng SIRC ARTICLE NO: 104530

MEDICINE - PREGNANCY

Artal, R. Romem, Y. Paul, R.H. Wiswell, R. Fetal bradycardia induced by maternal exercise. (Refs: 14)*Lancet (London) 2(8397), 4 Aug 1984, 258-260.*
ABST: Fetal bradycardia seen in three healthy women during a treadmill test appears to be transitory and is apparently compensated for by an increase in fetal heart rate after the cessation of exercise.
LEVEL: A LANG: Eng SIRC ARTICLE NO: 104511

Brodzinski, W. Metabolizm wysilkowy wykladnia dynamiki zmian stezenia glukozy we krwi kobiet w porodach fizjologicznych. (Exertion metabolism as an indicator of changes in blood glucose level in physiological labor.) *Wiadomosci lekarski (Warsaw) 37 (15), 1 Aug 1984, 1184-1190.*
NOTES: Includes English abstract.
LEVEL: A LANG: Pol

Clapp, J.F. Dickstein, S. Endurance exercise and pregnancy outcome. (Refs: 14)*Medicine and science in sports and exercise (Indianapolis) 16(6), Dec 1984, 556-562.*
ABST: The interaction between maternal endurance exercise at or above a minimal conditioning level, prior to and during pregnancy, and pregnancy outcome was examined prospectively. Over a 3-month interval all women registering for antepartum care were interviewed. Those planning to continue exercise during pregnancy were re-interviewed between the 28th and 34th gestational weeks. Women who continued endurance exercise at or near preconceptual levels during pregnancy gained less weight (minus 4.6 kg), delivered earlier (minus 8 d), and had lighter-weight offspring (minus 500 g) than those who stopped exercising prior to the 28th week. The latter group gained 2.2 kg more weight but delivered similar birthweight infants at a similar gestational age as their sedentary controls.
LEVEL: A LANG: Eng SIRC ARTICLE NO: 104514

Dale, E. Exercise and sports during pregnancy. Chicago: Teach'em Inc., 1984?. 1 sound cassette : study guide (Audio cassette series on sports medicine : Sportsmedicine for female athletes, SM-39.)
NOTES: Cassettes recorded and produced by Teach'em Inc. in cooperation with the Physician and Sportsmedicine.
LEVEL: I LANG: Eng

Diddle, A.W. Interrelationship of pregnancy and athletic performance. *Journal of the Tennessee Medical Association (Nashville) 77(5), May 1984, 265-269.*
LEVEL: I LANG: Eng SIRC ARTICLE NO: 102970

Erkkola, R. Physical work capacity and training in pregnancy. (Refs: 9)*International journal of sports medicine (Stuttgart) Suppl. 5, Nov 1984, 198-199.*
CONF: International Congress on Sports and Health (1983 : Maastricht, Netherlands).
LEVEL: A LANG: Eng SIRC ARTICLE NO: 104516

Fukuoa, M. (Ms. Elisabeth Bing and her books: 'The Complete Pregnancy Exercise' and 'Making Love During Pregnancy'.) *Josanp Zasshi/Japanese journal for the midwife (Tokyo) 38(1), Jan 1984, 54-59.*
LEVEL: I LANG: Jpn

Goodlin, R.C. Buckley, K.K. Maternal exercise. (Refs: 42)*Clinics in sports medicine (Philadelphia) 3(4), Oct 1984, 881-894.*
NOTES: Symposium on the athletic woman.
ABST: Additional maternal exercise is associated with a feeling of well-being, although there is no consistent evidence that it contributes to an improved pregnancy outcome.
LEVEL: I LANG: Eng SIRC ARTICLE NO: 101042

Ketter, D.E. Shelton, B.J. Pregnant and physically fit, too. *Medical center news (Detroit) 9(2), Mar/Apr 1984, 120-122.*
LEVEL: B LANG: Eng SIRC ARTICLE NO: 099368

Lotgering, F.K. Gilbert, R.D. Longo, L.D. The interactions of exercise and pregnancy: a review.

(Refs: 78)*American journal of obstetrics and gynecology (St. Louis) 149(5), 1 Jul 1984, 560-568.*
LEVEL: I LANG: Eng SIRC ARTICLE NO: 102974

Mamelle, N. Laumon, B. Lazar, P. Prematurity and occupational activity during pregnancy. (Refs: 28)*American journal of epidemiology (Baltimore) 119(3), Mar 1984, 309-322.*
LEVEL: A LANG: Eng SIRC ARTICLE NO: 099371

Massey, J.B. Reproductive effects of aerobic exercise in women. *Journal of the Medical Association of Georgia (Atlanta) 73(7), Jul 1984, 457-459.*
LEVEL: I LANG: Eng SIRC ARTICLE NO: 104521

Matsumoto, J. Kaji, T. Takahashi, T. Kikuchi, S. (The effect of maternal exercise on the fetal heart rate.) *Nippon Sanka Fujinka Gakkai Zasshi/Acta obstetrica et gynaelogica japonica (Tokyo) 36(7), Jul 1984, 1057-1063.*
LEVEL: A LANG: Jpn

Metcalfe, J. Catz, C. Clapp, J.F. Cureton, K.J. Fabro, S.E. Longo, L.D. McNellis, D. Summary report on the NICHD research planning Workshop on Physical activity in Pregnancy. *American journal of pernatalogy (New York) 1(3), Apr 1984, 276-279.*
LEVEL: I LANG: Eng

Pijpers, L. Wladimiroff, J.W. McGhie, J. Effect of short-term maternal exercise on maternal and fetal cardiovascular dynamic *British journal of obstetrics and gynaecology (London) 91(11), Nov 1984, 1081-1086.*
LEVEL: A LANG: Eng

References from Workshop on Physical Activity in Pregnancy, Chantilly, Virginia, September 29-October 1, 1982. *American journal of perinatalogy (New York) 1(3), Apr 1984, 272-275.*
LEVEL: I LANG: Eng

Telesna vychova a rehabilitacia v gynekologii a porodnictve. (Physical training and rehabilitation in gynecology and obstetrics.) *Ceskoslovenska gynekologie (Prague) 49(2), Mar 1984, 136-158.*
LEVEL: A LANG: Slo Cze

Zak, B. Nowotny, J. Brudnik, A. Uczeszczanie kobiet do szkoly rodzenia a czynniki ryzyka u ich dzieci. (Participation of pregnant women in prenatal care programs and risk factors in their children.) *Polski tygodnik lekarski (Warsaw) 39(13), 26 Mar 1984, 429-431.*
LEVEL: I LANG: Pol

NUTRITION

Grandjean, A.C. Nutritional concerns for the woman athlete. (Refs: 62)*Clinics in sports medicine (Philadelphia) 3(4), Oct 1984, 923-938.*
NOTES: Symposium on the athletic woman.
ABST: There are no major differences between female and male athletes in such areas as precompetition meals, weight control, and fluid balance. The female athlete does, however, present additional nutritional concerns. These include the nutritional demands of pregnancy and lactation, iron requirements, nutritional aberrations attributed to contraceptive steroids, and dietary modifications for treatment of premenstrual syndrome.
LEVEL: I LANG: Eng SIRC ARTICLE NO: 101043

Steinbaugh, M. Nutritional needs of female athletes. (Refs: 57)*Clinics in sports medicine (Philadelphia) 3(3), Jul 1984, 649-670.*
NOTES: Symposium on nutritional aspects of exercise.

ABST: Nutrition is an important component of physical performance for women as well as men in that it helps to maintain physical stamina and endurance. As a result, athletes may turn to nutrition, appropriately or inappropriately, as a means of providing the 'competitive edge'. Nutritional advice that will best serve female athletes in their physical endeavors and general health is (1) nutrients needed by the athlete are the same as those needed by the nonathlete: however, (2) the athlete will need larger amounts of certain nutrients. Special dietary adjustments by the female athlete are generally not needed to meet these elevated nutritional needs.
LEVEL: A LANG: Eng SIRC ARTICLE NO: 100791

PHILOSOPHY

Bandy, S.J. Equality and sport: a philosophic view. *Unpublished conference paper 1984, 1-10.*
CONF: American Alliance for Health, Physical Education, Recreation and Dance. National Convention (99th: 1984 : Anaheim, Calif.).
LEVEL: A LANG: Eng

Theberge, N. Joining social theory to social action: some marxist principles. (Refs: 4)*Arena review (Boston, Ma.) 8(2), Jul 1984, 11-19.*
NOTES: Edited version of a paper presented at the 'Feminism and sport: connections and directions' workshop, the 1982 Women as Leaders in Physical Education Workshop, sponsored by the Department of Physical Education and Dance, University of Iowa.
LEVEL: I LANG: Eng SIRC ARTICLE NO: 101054

PHYSICAL FITNESS

Biegel, L. Sex, attitudes, aging processes, and exercise guideline. (Refs: 9)
NOTES: In, Biegel, L. (ed.), Physical fitness and the older person: a guide to exercise for health care professionals, Rockville, Md., Aspen Systems Corp., 1984, p. 13-26.
LEVEL: I LANG: Eng GV482.6 17754

Changing times: women and physical activity. En evolution: la femme et l'activite physique. Ottawa: Canada Fitness Survey : Enquete condition physique Canada, 1984. 46, 47 p. : ill.
CORP: Canada. Fitness and Amateur Sport. Women's Program.
CORP: Canada Fitness Survey.
CORP: Canada. Condition physique et Sport amateur. Programme pour les femmes.
CORP: Enquete condition physique Canada.
NOTES: Bibliography: p. 42. Bibliographie: p. 43. French and English texts on inverted pages with separate paging. Textes francais et anglais disposes tete-beche avec pagination separee.
LEVEL: I LANG: Eng Fr GV482 18389

Cook, J. Wolf, M.D. Body type beautiful. Chicago: Contemporary Books, c1984. 1v.
NOTES: Includes index.
LEVEL: B LANG: Eng ISBN: 0809254115 LC CARD: 84-014954

Cox, J.S. Lenz, H.W. Women midshipmen in sports. (Refs: 7)*American journal of sports medicine (Baltimore) 12(3), May/Jun 1984, 241-243.*
CONF: American Orthopaedic Society for Sports Medicine. Annual Meeting (9th : 1983 : Williamsburg, Va.).
ABST: This report studied the performance and injury rate of seven freshman classes of women

midshipmen, from 1976 (63) to 1983 (88), in comparison to their male counterparts. Comparitive health care statistics for six weeks of each summer were taken, as well as the results of five fitness tests batteries. These included a mile run, flexed arm hang, standing long jump, situps for two minutes, and an obstacle course. Among the trends seen by the authors was that women midshipmen were improving their fitness level more rapidly than the men. Also, women sought more medical attention than the men for stress-related problems, but less often as they became acclimated to a more active lifstyle. The authors indicate that many of the increases in performance and the number of injuries should be attributed to societal conditions and a greater participation in athletics by women.
LEVEL: A LANG: Eng SIRC ARTICLE NO: 102968

Dean, L. Women's fitness camps expand across nation. *Journal of physical education and program (Columbus, Oh.) 81(5), Jun 1984, 15-17.*
LEVEL: B LANG: Eng SIRC ARTICLE NO: 096179

Dimitrijevic, B. Zivotic-Vanovic, M. Zivanic, S. Marisavljevic, T. Savic, S. Jorga, V. Banovic, I. Uticaj vojne obuke na maksimalnu potrosnju kiseonika, opstu misicnu snagu i telesnu masu zena-vojnika. (The effect of military training on maximal oxygen consumption, general muscle strength and body mass of female soldiers.) *Vojnosanitetski pregled (Belgrad) 41(5), Sept/Oct 1984, 393-396.*
NOTES: English abstract.
LEVEL: A LANG: Scr

Doelen, J.V. Women perform well in physically demanding jobs. *Employee health & fitness (Atlanta, Ga.) 6(2), Feb 1984, 13-16.*
LEVEL: B LANG: Eng SIRC ARTICLE NO: 099363

Knibbs, A.V. Some physiologic effects of social acceptable exercise on young female adults. (Refs: 12)
CONF: Symposium of Paediatric Work Physiology (10th : 1981 : Joutsa, Finland).
NOTES: In, Ilmarinen, J. and Vaelimaeki, I. (eds.), Children and sport: paediatric work physiology, Berlin, Springer-Verlag, 1984, p. 206-216.
ABST: This study investigated the physiologic effects of exercise intensity and frequency in order to determine those amounts of activity to nonathletes and necessary for cardiorespiratory fitness. The authors also provide some indication of the expectations of improvement which might result from short term physical activity above the training threshold.
LEVEL: A LANG: Eng SIRC ARTICLE NO: 102723

Lutter, J.M. Lutter, L.D. Exercise patterns of women aged 46-76: current physical activity compared with youthful patterns. *Maturitas (Amsterdam) 6(2), 1984, 143-144.*
LEVEL: B LANG: Eng SIRC ARTICLE NO: 104256

Marshall, J.L. Barbash, H. How fit are you? *Shape (Woodland Hills, Calif.) 3(6), Feb 1984, 34-43.*
LEVEL: B LANG: Eng SIRC ARTICLE NO: 097696

O'Seen, M. Bell, D. Faulkner, B. Evaluation de la condition physique des femmes du milieu rural en Saskatchewan. Fitness evaluation in rural Saskatchewan females. (Refs: 7)*Recreation Canada (Ottawa) 42(4), Sept/sept 1984, 30-32.*
LEVEL: I LANG: Fr Eng SIRC ARTICLE NO: 099203

Pierce, E.E. The effect of a health promotion program on the wellness behavior and self-esteem upon behavior change. Eugene, Ore.: Microform

Publications, University of Oregon, 1984. 2
microfiches : negative, ill. ; 11 x 15 cm.
NOTES: Thesis (M.S.) - University of Wisconsin-La
Crosse, 1982; (viii, 170 leaves); includes
bibliography.
LEVEL: A LANG: Eng UO84 300-301

Rogers, C.C. Fitness may be a woman's best
defense. (Refs: 5)*Physician and sportsmedicine
(Minneapolis, Minn.) 12(10), Oct 1984, 146-151-
154;156.*
LEVEL: B LANG: Eng SIRC ARTICLE NO: 099374

Snyder, D.K. Carruth, B.R. Current controversies:
exercising during pregnancy. (Refs: 23)*Journal of
adolescent health care (New York) 5(1), Jan 1984,
34-36.*
ABST: This paper points out that the implications of
exercise during pregnancy for the 'trained' woman
and the 'untrained' woman need to be further
studied.
LEVEL: I LANG: Eng SIRC ARTICLE NO: 099377

PHYSICAL FITNESS - PROGRAMS

Berger, B.G. Schneck, P. Free weights for
women. New York: Simon & Schuster, c1984. 127
p. : ill. (A Wallaby book.)
NOTES: Bibliography: p. 126.
LEVEL: B LANG: Eng ISBN: 0671497103 LC
CARD: 84-003542 GV482 17508

Burstein, N. The executive body: a working
woman's guide to life style and total fitness. New
York: Simon and Schuster, c1984. 223 p. : ill.
NOTES: Bibliography: p. 207.
LEVEL: B LANG: Eng ISBN: 0671494376 LC
CARD: 84-005507 GV482 18346

Comite d'etude Kino-Quebec sur l'activite physique
et la femme enceinte: rapport final. Quebec, Que.:
Ministere du loisir, de la chasse et de la peche,
1984. 39 p.
CORP: Kino-Quebec. Comite d'etude sur l'activite
physique et la femme enceinte.
NOTES: Comprend des references
bibliographiques.
LEVEL: B LANG: Fr GV482 17713

Comite d'etude Kino-Quebec sur l'activite physique
et la femme enceinte: annexe au rapport final,
fevrier 1984. (Quebec): Ministere du loisir, de la
chasse et de la peche, 1984. iii, 195 p. : ill.
CORP: Quebec. Ministere du loisir, de la chasse et
de la peche.
NOTES: Comprend des references
bibliographiques.
LEVEL: A LANG: Fr GV482 17714

Connelly, L. Woodworth, W. Lean & firm: the no-
nonsense Nautilus and universal body shaping
program. New York: Putnam Pub. Group, 1984. 1v.
LEVEL: B LANG: Eng ISBN: 0399510745 LC
CARD: 84-020785

DeLyser, F. Schapiro, S. Martineau, C. La
methode Jane Fonda pour la grossesse,
l'accouchement...et apres. Paris?: Seuil, c1984.
237 p. : ill.
NOTES: Traduit de: The Jane Fonda workout book
for pregnancy, birth, and recovery, New York,
Simon & Schuster, c1982.
LEVEL: B LANG: Fr ISBN: 2-02-006830-3 GV482
17841

Greggains, J. Foreman, J. Jensen, J. Joanie
Greggains' total shape-up. New York: New
American Library, c1984. 1v.

NOTES: Includes index. NAL books.
LEVEL: B LANG: Eng ISBN: 0453004555 LC
CARD: 83-025448

Gregor, C. Samon, K.A. Joseph, M. Carol
Gregor's body type workout book. New York: Dodd,
Mead & Co., c1984. 113 p. : ill.
LEVEL: B LANG: Eng ISBN: 0-396-08423-0 LC
CARD: 84-8077 RA781.6 18182

Mantell, S. Fit to be pregnant. *Women's sports
(San Francisco) 6(6), Jun 1984, 43-45;62.*
LEVEL: B LANG: Eng SIRC ARTICLE NO: 104520

Marx, G. Body by Gilda: the ultimate program for a
beautiful figure. New York: Putnam, c1984. 1v.
LEVEL: B LANG: Eng ISBN: 0399129189 LC
CARD: 83-023007

Mayo, D. Yoga for 2. *Fit (Mountain View, Calif.)
3(11), Apr 1984, 44-47.*
LEVEL: B LANG: Eng SIRC ARTICLE NO: 099372

McWilliams, S. Hospital finds pregnagym adds to
its health promotion menu. *Employee health &
fitness (Atlanta, Ga.) 6(12), Dec 1984, 157-158.*
LEVEL: B LANG: Eng SIRC ARTICLE NO: 105445

Roberts, L. Pastor, M. Computercise: Lucille
Roberts' 21-day personalized body-shaping
program. New York: Simon and Schuster c1984.
1v.
LEVEL: B LANG: Eng ISBN: 0671467735 LC
CARD: 83-020153

Roger, G. Van Ceunebroek, R. Retrouver sa
forme apres l'accouchement: quelles
kinesitherapies? (Regaining one's shape after labor:
which exercise therapy?) *Soins gynecologie
obstetrique et la puericulture (Paris) 35, Apr 1984,
43-48.*
LEVEL: I LANG: Fr

Saubert, C. W. Water exercise effective for
pregnant woman. *Journal of physical education and
program (Columbus, Oh.) 81(4) Apr 1984, D16-
D18.*
LEVEL: B LANG: Eng SIRC ARTICLE NO: 094800

Smith, A. The gifted figure: proportioning exercises
for large women. Santa Barbara: Capra Press,
1984. 85, (10) p. : ill.
LEVEL: B LANG: Eng ISBN: 0884962210 LC
CARD: 84-007710 GV482 18217

Weaver, N. Your fit pregnancy book. Mountain
View, Calif.: Anderson World Books, c1984. 208 p.
: ill.
NOTES: Bibliography: p. 207.
LEVEL: B LANG: Eng ISBN: 0-89037-285-3 GV482
17765

Welch, R. Raquel: the Raquel Welch total beauty &
fitness program. 1st ed. New York: Holt, Rinehart
and Winston, c1984. 1v.
LEVEL: B LANG: Eng LC CARD: 84-004574

Whiteford, B. Polden, M. Postnatal exercises: a
six-month fitness programme for mother and baby.
London: Century Publishing, c1984. 128 p.
LEVEL: B LANG: Eng

Young, K. Exercise can be child's play: playtime
workout for mothers and babies. Nashville: T.
Nelson Publishers, c1984. 112 p. : ill.
LEVEL: B LANG: Eng ISBN: 0840758928 LC
CARD: 84-002156 GV482 18241

PHYSIOLOGY

Baechle, T.R. Women in resistance training. (Refs:
53)*Clinics in sports medicine (Philadelphia) 3(4),
Oct 1984, 791-808.*
NOTES: Symposium on the athletic woman.
ABST: This article presents a factual and revealing
analysis of the values of resistance training for
female athletes. Discussions on training principles,
equipment, and exercise prescription, including
special considerations for women, provide a
comprehensive approach to this topic.
LEVEL: A LANG: Eng SIRC ARTICLE NO: 101038

Berg, K. Aerobic function in female athletes. (Refs:
69)*Clinics in sports medicine (Philadelphia) 3(4),
Oct 1984, 779-789.*
NOTES: Symposium on the athletic woman.
ABST: The capacity of female athletes to perform
endurance exercise is described. Physiologic
comparisons are made between males and females
on body composition, cardiovascular function,
muscle fiber type, bioenergetics, and movement
efficiency. It is concluded that, although inherent
physiologic differences exist, females are as
trainable as males and, with a larger pool of talent
to draw upon, will continue to reduce the gap in
endurance performance.
LEVEL: I LANG: Eng SIRC ARTICLE NO: 100888

Dauwalter, T.P. Finke, C.K. Woman in sports.
(Refs: 16)*Sideline view (Minneapolis, Minn.) 5(10),
May 1984, 1-4.*
LEVEL: I LANG: Eng SIRC ARTICLE NO: 094790

de Bruyn-Prevost, P. Masset, C. Sturbois, X.
Physiological response from 18-25 years women to
aerobic and anaerobic physical fitness tests at
different periods during the menstrual cycle. (Refs:
8)*Journal of sports medicine and physical fitness
(Torino, Italy) 24(2), Jun 1984, 144-148.*
ABST: A question which frequently arises about
sports practice by women is to know whether it is
suitable to have important physical activities or any
competition during the menstruation. This study
investigates the possible influence of the period
during the menstrual cycle on the physiological
response of young women to aerobic and anaerobic
physical fitness tests. Two groups participate at the
experiments: 7 women taking regularly oral
contraceptives and 7 women not taking any
medication. For both groups, the response seems
not to be influenced by the period of the cycle and
the two groups show similar results for the two
tests.
LEVEL: A LANG: Eng SIRC ARTICLE NO: 102969

de Mondenard, J.P. La femme peut-elle depasser
l'homme? (Refs: 27)*Dans, Culture technique no.
13, Neuilly-sur-Seine, France Centre de Recherche
sur la Culture Technique, c1984, p. 158-167.*
LEVEL: A LANG: Fr RC1235 20096

Drinkwater, B.L. Women and exercise:
physiological aspects. (Refs: 146)*Exercise and
sport sciences reviews (Lexington, Mass.) 12,
1984, 21-51.*
ABST: This paper reviews the physiological aspects
of the exercising woman over the period 1973 to
1983. The review contains descriptive and
histochemical studies. This period of research
showed that differences in aerobic capacity
between the sexes were much less than originally
believed. Histochemical evidence indicates men
and women have similar muscle fiber composition.
One problem with this period of research is the

large number of descriptive studies and the paucity of experimental studies.
LEVEL: A LANG: Eng SIRC ARTICLE NO: 096469

Drinkwater, B.L. Women's physiological response to exercise - selected topics. (Refs: 36)*ICSSPE/CIEPSS review (Berlin, GDR) 7, 1984, 19-24.*
ABST: The author reviews the literature on exercise physiology and women. Aerobic power, strength, body composition, iron deficiency and amenorrhea are the topics discussed.
LEVEL: A LANG: Eng SIRC ARTICLE NO: 096470

Freedson, P.S. Endurance training for girls and women. Chicago: Teach'em Inc., 1984?. 1 sound cassette (Audio cassette serie on sports medicine: Sportsmedicine for female athletes, SM-35.)
NOTES: Cassettes recorded and produced by Teach'em Inc. in cooperation with the Physician and Sportsmedicine.
LEVEL: I LANG: Eng

Gibbons, E.S. The effects of various training intensity levels on anaerobic threshold, aerobic power, and aerobic capacity i young females. Eugene, Ore.: Microform Publications, University of Oregon, 1984. 1 microfiche : negative, ill. ; 11 x 15 cm.
NOTES: Thesis (Ph.D.) - Texas A & M University, 1981; (x, 60 leaves); vita; includes bibliography.
LEVEL: A LANG: Eng UO84 8

Hale, R.W. Factors important to women engaged in vigorous physical activity. (Refs: 16)
NOTES: In, Strauss, R.H. (ed.), Sports medicine, Philadelphia ; Toronto, Saunders, 1984, p. 250-269.
LEVEL: A LANG: Eng RC1210 17196

Haymes, E.M. Physiological responses of female athletes to heat stress: a review. (Refs: 36)*Physician and sportsmedicine (Minneapolis, Minn.) 12(3), Mar 1984, 45-48;51-53;56;59.*
ABST: This article reviews studies dealing with men's and women's responses to heat stress. Findings indicate few differences in their responses to exercise in hot, dry environments. Women show a higher tolerance for exercise in the heat than men. Higher rectal temperatures and heart rates were observed among women at higher relative exercise intensity.
LEVEL: A LANG: Eng SIRC ARTICLE NO: 091734

Heyters, C. Profil morpho-fonctionnel d'etudiantes en education physique. (Refs: 44)*Revue de l'education physique (Liege, Belgique) 24(1), 1984, 25-30.*
RESUME: Au cours de cette etude, l'auteur evalue les mensurations morphologiques, la capacite vitale, l'indice de Tiffeneau, le debit expiratoire de pointe, la ventilation maximale minute a la cadence de 80 respirations par minute, l'aptitude cardio-circulatoire et l'aptitude motrice d'etudiantes (agees en moyenne de 21.3 ans + - 1.5) en education physique. Les resultats obtenus sont compares a ceux provenant d'etudes realisees aupres de sportives de haut niveau et d'une population generale d'etudiantes.
LEVEL: A LANG: Fr SIRC ARTICLE NO: 096451

Hubert-Rafin, C. Sport feminin. (Refs: 15)*Revue de l'education physique (Liege) 24(2), 1984, 11-17.*
RESUME: L'auteur expose les differences physiologiques et psycho-sociales entre les sexes. Il rapporte les resultats d'une enquete sur la pratique sportive feminine belge en 1980-1981. Un sondage fut effectue aupres de 200 federations

sportives belges ainsi qu'en milieu parascolaire.
LEVEL: A LANG: Fr SIRC ARTICLE NO: 101046

Keizer, H.A. Bonen, A. Exercise-induced changes in gonadotropin secretion patterns. (Refs: 10)*International journal of sports medicine (Stuttgart) Suppl. 5, Nov 1984, 206-208.*
CONF: International Congress on Sports and Health (1983 : Maastricht, Netherlands).
LEVEL: A LANG: Eng SIRC ARTICLE NO: 104327

Sharp, C. Physiology and the woman athlete. *New scientist (London) 1415, 2 Aug 1984, 22-24.*
NOTES: Women might outperform men if only competitions involved a cross-Channel swim followed by a long run through deserts and mountains.
LEVEL: I LANG: Eng SIRC ARTICLE NO: 099376

Vander, L.B. Franklin, B.A. Wrisley, D. Rubenfire, M. Cardiorespiratory responses to arm and leg ergometry in women. (Refs: 17)*Physician and sportsmedicine (Minneapolis, Minn.) 12(5), May 1984, 101-106.*
LEVEL: I LANG: Eng SIRC ARTICLE NO: 094632

White, M.K. The effects of walking and aerobic dancing on the skeletal and cardiovascular systems of post-menopausal females Eugene, Ore.: Microform Publications, University of Oregon, 1984. 2 microfiches : negative, ill. ; 11 x 15 cm.
NOTES: Thesis (Ed.D.) - West Virginia University, 1981; (x, 156 leaves); vita; includes bibliography.
LEVEL: A LANG: Eng UO84 195-196

Zauner, C.W. Notelovitz, M. Fields, C.D. Clair, K.M. Clair, W.J. Vogel, R.B. Cardiorespiratory efficiency at submaximal work in young and middle-aged women. *American journal of obstetrics and gynecology (St. Louis) 150(6), 15 Nov 1984, 712-715.*
LEVEL: A LANG: Eng

PSYCHOLOGY

Abood, D.A. The effects of acute physical exercise on the state anxiety and mental performance of college women. (Refs: 25) *American corrective therapy journal (San Diego, Calif.) 38(3), May/Jun 1984, 69-74.*
LEVEL: I LANG: Eng SIRC ARTICLE NO: 108153

Corbin, C.B. Self-confidence of females in sports and physical activity. (Refs: 39)*Clinics in sports medicine (Philadelphia 3(4), Oct 1984, 895-908.*
NOTES: Symposium on the athletic woman.
ABST: The research evidence suggests that many females lack confidence in sports and physical activities. When the activities are judged to be sex-role inappropriate, to be self-evaluative or competitive, or to be lacking in positive feedback, confidence among females is especially likely to be low. Guidelines for building self-confidence - including insuring successful performance, using positive reinforcement, providing positive role models, improving communications, and reducing anxiety - are presented.
LEVEL: I LANG: Eng SIRC ARTICLE NO: 101041

Lan, L.Y. Gill, D.L. The relationship among self-efficacy, stress responses, and a cognitive feedback manipulation. (Refs: 1 *Sport psychology (Champaign, Ill.) 6(2), 1984, 227-238.*
ABST: The influence of self-efficacy on physiological arousal and self-reported anxiety was examined in the first phase of this study. All 32 undergraduate females in the study performed five trials of both an easy task and a difficult task, with

half of them performing the easy task first and half performing the difficult task first. A manipulation check revealed that the easy task clearly elicited higher self-efficacy than the difficult task. Individuals reported lower cognitive and somatic anxiety and higher self-confidence, as assessed with the CSAI-2, and had lower heartrate increases when performing the easy (high-efficacious) task. After the subjects finished both the easy and difficult tasks, half of them were given a cognitive feedback manipulation suggesting that elevated arousal levels were typical responses of good competitors under stress. Contary to predictions, the manipulation did not induce higher self-efficacy and the manipulation group did not differ from the no-manipulation group on self-reported anxiety scores or heart rates.
LEVEL: A LANG: Eng SIRC ARTICLE NO: 108495

Lazier, M.M. Sports psychology: examining motivational tendencies of the female athlete. (Refs: 4)*Interscholastic athletic administration (Kansas City) 10(4), Summer 1984, 16-17;19.*
LEVEL: I LANG: Eng SIRC ARTICLE NO: 108258

Lenskyj, H. Sport, femininity and sexuality. *Resources for feminist research/Documentation sur la recherche feministe (Toronto) 13(2), 1984, 66-68.*
LEVEL: I LANG: Eng

Linde, C.A. A female athlete's perception of self and others in relationship to her psychological reaction to injury. Eugene Ore.: Microform Publications, University of Oregon, 1984. 2 microfiches : negative, ill. ; 11 x 15 cm.
NOTES: Thesis (M.S.) - Brigham Young University, 1982; (vii, 153 leaves); includes bibliography.
LEVEL: A LANG: Eng UO84 314-315

Lovell, S.S. Deconditioning: the effects of adherence on selected physiological and anthropometric variables and the relationship with attitude towards physical activity and perceptions of self-motivation. Eugene, Ore.: Microform Publications, University of Oregon, 1984. 1 microfiche : negative ; 11 x 15 cm.
NOTES: Thesis (M.S.) - Pennsylvania State University, 1983; (ix, 84 leaves) includes bibliography.
LEVEL: A LANG: Eng UO84 367

McCabe, N. Burnout: women athletes more susceptible to stress effects. *Globe and mail 140(41,932), 28 Apr 1984, S1-S2.*
LEVEL: B LANG: Eng SIRC ARTICLE NO: 093253

Mogil, V.P. Self concept in early adolescent female athletes and nonathletes. Eugene, Ore.: Microform Publications, University of Oregon, 1984. 1 microfiche : negative ; 11 x 15 cm.
NOTES: Thesis (M.S.) - University of Illinois at Chicago, 1983; (ix, 68 leaves); includes bibliography.
LEVEL: A LANG: Eng UO84 221

Segal, J.D. Weinberg, R.S. Sex, sex role orientation and competitive trait anxiety. (Refs: 16)*Journal of sport behavior (Mobile, Ala.) 7(4), Dec 1984, 153-159.*
ABST: The purpose of the present investigation was to provide a more definitive assessment of the relationship between sex, sex role orientation and CTA. Subjects were 166 female and 125 male undergraduates who completed the Bem Sex Role Inventory and the SCAT with the order of administration of these two scales counter-balanced. Results indicated no significant order

effect, and, therefore, a 2 x 4 (sex by sex role) ANOVA was conducted with SCAT serving as the dependent measure. Results yielded a main effect for sex with females exhibiting significantly higher levels of CTA than males. However, the main effect of sex role orientation and the sex x sex role orientation interaction did not reach significance. The finding that females exhibit higher levels of CTA than males consonants with previous literature and may reflect a difference in socialization into competitive sports. Although statistically significant, both male and female mean scores for competitive trait anxiety fell within the moderate range. Future directions for research are offered.
LEVEL: A LANG: Eng SIRC ARTICLE NO: 100947

Stark, J.A. Toulouse, A. The young female athlete: psychological considerations. (Refs: 43)*Clinics in sports medicine (Philadelphia) 3(4), oct 1984, 909-921.*
NOTES: Symposium on the athletic woman.
ABST: This article provides a much-needed analysis of those critical psychological variables of the young female athlete and is as comprehensive as the limited research on this topic allows. The three major sections of this article cover the psychological aspects of competing, psychological assessment of female athletic behavior, and treatment strategies designed to enhance performance and psychological well-being. Further considerations and recommendations are also provided as a blueprint for the future.
LEVEL: I LANG: Eng SIRC ARTICLE NO: 100950

Watson, G.G. Brien, A. Physical activity and identity formation among inactive married women. (Refs: 48)*Australian journal of science & medicine in sport (Kingston, Aust.) 16(1), Jun 1984, 17-24.*
ABST: A conceptual framework based on the socialisation function and attraction of games was applied to the involvement of inactive married women in a program of physical fitness training. Three orientations to self, based on Miyomoto's interpretation of 'social motivation' were employed: the cognitive (fitness), the evaluative (appearance) and the affective (pleasure) orientations of the activity outcomes to self. It was found that rankings of orientations vary systematically with: activity type (in this instance squash, swimming, calisthenics); age; years married; and the perception of female role (as wife or mother).
LEVEL: A LANG: Eng SIRC ARTICLE NO: 104527

RESEARCH

Zukowska, Z. Der Frauensport in polnischen Untersuchungen. (Women's sport in Polish research.) (Refs: 34)*ICSSPE/CIEPSS review (Berlin, GDR) 7, 1984, 48-57.*
LEVEL: I LANG: Ger SIRC ARTICLE NO: 095656

SEX DISCRIMINATION

Jarvie, G. Women in sport: a dialectical process. (Refs: 9)*Scottish journal of physical education (Glasgow, Scotland) 12(3) Aug 1984, 42-44.*
LEVEL: B LANG: Eng SIRC ARTICLE NO: 099367

Kidd, B. Lenskyj, H. Can he play? Can she play? *Mudpie 4(1), 1984, 12;19.*
LEVEL: B LANG: Eng SIRC ARTICLE NO: 183306

Laliberte, V. La discrimination sexuelle en sport: mythe ou realite? s.l.: s.n., 1984.
NOTES: These (M.Sc.) non publiee - Universite de Laval, 1984.
LEVEL: A LANG: Fr

Lenskyj, H. No sporting chance. *Broadside: a feminist review (Toronto) 5 Feb 1984, 5.*
LEVEL: B LANG: Eng SIRC ARTICLE NO: 183328

Theberge, N. Some evidence on the existence of a sexual double standard in mobility to leadership positions in sport. (Refs: 19)*International review for the sociology of sport (Munich) 19(2), 1984, 185-197.*
ABST: This is an analysis of a survey of executive boards in five amateur sport organizations in Ontario, Canada, concerning a possible sexual double standard in requirements for mobility to leadership positions. Variables examined include prior experiences in sport and other voluntary organizations, orientations toward the sport volunteer role, and family and social status. Results provide little evidence of a sexual double standard. However, social status is higher in the case of men. Organizational structure and history greatly influence patterns of recruitment and mobility to leadership positions. Possibly the underrepresentation of, and sexual discrimination against women increase with the level of the position.
LEVEL: A LANG: Eng SIRC ARTICLE NO: 104524

SOCIAL PSYCHOLOGY

Hubert-Rafin, C. Sport feminin. (Refs: 15)*Revue de l'education physique (Liege) 24(2), 1984, 11-17.*
RESUME: L'auteur expose les differences physiologiques et psycho-sociales entre les sexes. Il rapporte les resultats d'une enquete sur la pratique sportive feminine belge en 1980-1981. Un sondage fut effectue aupres de 200 federations sportives belges ainsi qu'en milieu parascolaire.
LEVEL: A LANG: Fr SIRC ARTICLE NO: 101046

Nagy, M.C. Attributional differences in health status and life satisfactions of older women: a comparison between widows and non-widows. Eugene, Ore.: Microform Publications, University of Oregon, 1984. 2 microfiches: negative, ill. ; 11 x 15 cm.
NOTES: Thesis (Ph.D.) - University of Oregon, 1982; (xii, 138 leaves); vita; includes bibliography.
LEVEL: A LANG: Eng UO84 162-163

Noland, M.P. Feldman, R.H.L. Factors related to the lesiure exercise behavior of 'returning' women college students. (Refs: 19)*Health education (Reston, Va.) 15(2), Mar/Apr 1984, 32-36.*
ABST: The purpose of this study was to determine the correlations between the participation of adult women in exercise and their (1) exercise locus of control, (2) health values, (3) physical appearance values, (4) physical fitness values, and (5) attitudes toward physical activity. 64 women enrolled in undergraduate health education classes served as subjects. Exercise behaviour was highly correlated to attitude toward physical activity (r, .315, p.05) and environment (r, .332, p.01).
LEVEL: A LANG: Eng SIRC ARTICLE NO: 099373

Rogers, C.C. Fitness may be a woman's best defense. (Refs: 5)*Physician and sportsmedicine (Minneapolis, Minn.) 12(10), Oct 1984, 146-151-154;156.*
LEVEL: B LANG: Eng SIRC ARTICLE NO: 099374

SOCIOLOGY

Allison, M.T. Butler, B. Role conflict and the elite female athlete: empirical findings and conceptual dilemmas. (Refs: 23) *International review for the sociology of sport (Munich) 19(2), 1984, 157-168.*
ABST: Whereas gender-related literature portrays an image of psychological struggle, role conflict and identity crisis for the female athlete, empirical studies indicate that female athletes perceive and experience a relatively low level of conflict, regardless of their age, level of competitive experience and the sport in which they compete. This study further supports these findings. 44 female powerlifters competing at the 1981 National US championship were administered questionnaires including a role conflict instrument. Factor analysis identified the four factors of emotion, attraction, the sport-performance component and the significant other component and showed the multidimensionality of the construct of role conflict. Further differentiation of this concept is necessary.
LEVEL: A LANG: Eng SIRC ARTICLE NO: 104510

Birrell, S. Studying gender in sport: a feminist perspective. (Refs: 10)
CONF: North American Society for the Sociology of Sport. Conference (3rd : 1982 : Toronto, Ont.).
NOTES: In, Theberge, N. and Donnelly, P. (eds.), Sport and the sociological imagination: refereed proceedings of the 3rd Annual Conference of the North American Society for the Sociology of Sport, Toronto, Canada, November 1982, Fort Worth, Tex., Texas Christian University Press, c1984, p. 125-135.
ABST: This paper examines past and present sociological research on sport and women. New methods need to be established in the use of gender as a variable in sociology of sport research, but more importantly theoretical assumptions must be critically appraised.
LEVEL: A LANG: Eng SIRC ARTICLE NO: 097888

Birrell, S. Separatism as an issue in women's sport. (Refs: 11)*Arena review (Boston, Ma.) 8(2), Jul 1984, 21-29.*
NOTES: Originally presented at the 'Feminity and sport: continuity and change' workshop, the 1983 Women as Leaders in Physical Education Workshop, sponsored by the Department of Physical Education and Dance, University of Iowa.
LEVEL: I LANG: Eng SIRC ARTICLE NO: 101039

Bray, C. Gender and the political economy of Canadian sport. (Refs: 40)
CONF: North American Society for the Sociology of Sport. Conference (3rd : 1982 : Toronto, Ont.).
NOTES: In, Theberge, N. and Donnelly, P. (eds.), Sport and the sociological imagination: refereed proceedings of the 3rd Annual Conference of the North American Society for the Sociology of Sport, Toronto, Canada, November 1982, Fort Worth, Tex., Texas Christian University Press, c1984, p. 104-124.
ABST: This paper critiques two prominent themes within Canadian political economy: dependency theory and elite studies. The author contends that by largely concentrating on these two issues sociologists have failed to properly analyze the role of gender relations in Canadian society and its influences on political economy. This is examined in works which analyze sport within this tradition.
LEVEL: A LANG: Eng SIRC ARTICLE NO: 097840

Hall, M.A. On the importance of taking account of gender. (Refs: 13)*ICSSPE/CIEPSS review (Berlin,*

GDR) 7, 1984, 15-18.
LEVEL: I LANG: Eng SIRC ARTICLE NO: 096473

Hall, M.A. Towards a feminist analysis of gender inequality in sport. (Refs: 47)
CONF: North American Society for the Sociology of Sport. Conference (3rd : 1982 : Toronto, Ont.).
NOTES: In, Theberge, N. and Donnelly, P. (eds.), Sport and the sociological imagination: refereed proceedings of the 3rd Annual Conference of the North American Society for the Sociology of Sport, Toronto, Canada, November 1982, Fort Worth, Tex., Texas Christian University Press, c1984, p. 82-103.
ABST: This paper describes feminism as a systematic theoretical analysis and examines the current strands of feminist social theory in which the central focus is sexuality, referred to as Marxist-feminist analysis. These perspectives are used in the comprehension of gender inequality in sport.
LEVEL: A LANG: Eng SIRC ARTICLE NO: 097891

Hall, M.A. Feminist prospects for the sociology of sport. (Refs: 7)*Arena review (Boston, Ma.) 8(2), Jul 1984, 1-9.*
NOTES: Edited version of a speech presented at the 'Feminism and sport: connections and directions' workshop, the 1982 Women as Leaders in Physical Education Workshop, sponsored by the Department of Physical Education and Dance, University of Iowa.
LEVEL: I LANG: Eng SIRC ARTICLE NO: 101045

Hall, M.A. Females, sport, and biosocial explanations. *In, Vickers, J. (ed.), Taking gender into account, Ottawa, Carleton Univ. Press, 1984, p. 73-84.*
LEVEL: I LANG: Eng

Higginson, D. Social class background implications in the female sport participation process. (Refs: 31)*Australian journal of science & medicine in sport (Kingston, Aust.) 16(2), Aug 1984, 21-25.*
ABST: This study investigated the social class background information of elite female athletes who participated in the Empire State Games at Syracuse, New York (N, 587). More specifically, it was the intent of this study to examine the conceptual link between social class background and sport participation represented by types of sports and selected sports.
LEVEL: A LANG: Eng SIRC ARTICLE NO: 104518

Jokl, E. The athletic status of women. *Running & fitness (Washington, D.C.) 16(5), Sept/Oct 1984, 19-20.*
LEVEL: B LANG: E SIRC ARTICLE NO: 097893

Krebs, P. At the starting blocks: women athletes' new agenda. *Off our backs (Washington) 14(1), Jan 1984, 1-3.*
LEVEL: B LANG: Eng SIRC ARTICLE NO: 183315

Laberge, S. Rousseau, P. Sankoff, D. Sociocultural aspects of regular physical activity of non-athlete women. *Unpublished paper 1984, 1-12.*
LEVEL: I LANG: Eng SIRC ARTICLE NO: 183320

Lenskyj, H. Sport, femininity and sexuality. (Refs: 8)*Resources for feminist research/Documentation sur la recherche feministe (Toronto) 13(2), Jul 1984, 66-68.*
LEVEL: I LANG: Eng SIRC ARTICLE NO: 183319

Lenskyj, H. Myth making spoils sports. *Broadside: a feminist review (Toronto) 6(8), June 1984, 4.*
LEVEL: B LANG: Eng SIRC ARTICLE NO: 183322

May, J.R. Veach, T.L. Furman, G. Daily-McKee, D. A preliminary study of elite adolescent women athletes and their attitudes towards training and femininity. *Journal of professional ski coaching and instruction (Boulder, Colo.) May 1984, 29-30.*
LEVEL: I LANG: Eng SIRC ARTICLE NO: 096475

Rao, V.V.P. Overman, S.J. Sex role perceptions among black female athletes and nonathletes. (Refs: 20)*Sex roles (New York) 11(7/8), 1984, 601-614.*
LEVEL: A LANG: Eng SIRC ARTICLE NO: 104523

Talbot, M. Women and sport: a gender contradiction in terms? (Refs: 41)*Unpublished conference paper 1984, 1-25.*
CONF: International Conference of the Leisure Studies Association (1984 : Palmer, Sussex).
LEVEL: I LANG: Eng SIRC ARTICLE NO: 183305

Walters, J. An examination of attitudes in society towards female participation in sport. (abstract) *Carnegie research papers (Beckett Park, Leeds) 1(6), Dec 1984, 31.*
CONF: Carnegie Undergraduate Research Symposium (1984 : Leeds, Eng.).
LEVEL: I LANG: Eng SIRC ARTICLE NO: 172507

Zechetmeyr, M. Toward a marxist feminist perspective in the sociology of sport. (Refs: 35)*Unpublished conference paper 1984 1-13.*
CONF: Conference on Sport and Society (1984 : Clemson, S.C.).
LEVEL: A LANG: Eng

TITLE IX

The impact of Title IX. Participation in high school and college competitive athletics.
NOTES: In, Riess, S.A. (ed.), The American sporting experience: a historical anthology of sport in America, New York, Leisure Press, c1984, p. 386-397. Reprinted from, U.S. Commission on Civil Rights, more hurdles to clear: women and girls in competitive athletics, Washington, D.C., U.S. Government Printing Office, 1980, p. 7-36.
LEVEL: I LANG: Eng GV583 17631

Title IX update. *Sports and the courts (Winston-Salem, N.C.) 5(2), Spring 1984, 9-10.*
LEVEL: B LANG: Eng SIRC ARTICLE NO: 094801

WORLD UNIVERSITY GAMES

Universiade d'hiver 85, Belluno, Italie, 1-24 fevrier. Winter Universiade 85, Belluno, Italy, February 1-24. *Bulletin of the International University Sports Federation/Bulletin de la Federation internationale du sport universitaire (Bruxelles, Belgique) Jun/juin 1984, 8-11.*
LEVEL: B LANG: Fr Eng SIRC ARTICLE NO: 102932

MEDICINE

Brukner, P. The role of the team doctor: a report from the World University Games, Edmonton, Canada. (Refs: 6)*Sport health (Pennant Hills, Aust.) 2(1), 1984, 21-22.*
ABST: A report from the World University Games, Edmonton, Canada 1983, by the doctor for the Australian team. The following are included: preparation on arrival, training, competition,

femininity testing, drug testing, injuries, illness, professional contact, conference, the games, the doctor. Includes a list of equipment and medications required by the team doctor.
LEVEL: B LANG: Eng SIRC ARTICLE NO: 094415

WRESTLING

Cipriano, N. A wrestler's rights. *Ontario wrestler (Toronto) Jun/Jul 1984, 14-15.*
LEVEL: B LANG: Eng SIRC ARTICLE NO: 097045

Gillot, L. Galceran, R. Lutte et gymnastique. Paris: Hachette, 1984. 95 p.
LEVEL: B LANG: Fr

Holt, M.E. Robinson, J.E. Introducing parents to wrestling. *Wrestling USA (Missoula, Tenn.) 19(8), 1 Mar 1984, 17.*
LEVEL: LANG: Eng SIRC ARTICLE NO: 100186

Leyshon, G.A. On the way to the forum. A bus ride is a bus ride. Not quite. Not quite, for what happens on the way to a competition sit during a bus ride can have debilitating effects on athletic performance. *Coaching review (Ottawa) 7, Sept/Oct 1984, 22-24.*
LEVEL: B LANG: Eng SIRC ARTICLE NO: 098774

Welker, B. Wrestling: a sport where excuses are useless. Part I. *Wrestling USA (Bozeman, Mont.) 20(1), 20 Sept 1984, 42-43.*
NOTES: First in a two-part series.
LEVEL: B LANG: Eng SIRC ARTICLE NO: 103671

ANTHROPOMETRY

Freischlag, J. Weight loss, body composition, and health of high school wrestlers. (Refs: 10)*Physician and sportsmedicine 12(1), Jan 1984, 121-123;126.*
ABST: This study compares the body weight, percent body fat, the grip strength, illnesses, the energy level, the emotional stability, and the bowel habits of 104 wrestlers and 73 non wrestlers. Decreases of body fat, grip strength and energy levels in wrestlers were more significant than the ones in controls. Illnesses and emotional stability in both groups were similar, but wrestler's bowel habits were more regular. Changes between weight classes were also analysed.
LEVEL: A LANG: Eng SIRC ARTICLE NO: 092603

Huff, D. Limiting weight-cutting high school wrestling. *Wrestling USA (Missoula, Mont.) 21(10), 15 Apr 1984, 9-10.*
LEVEL: LANG: Eng SIRC ARTICLE NO: 100187

Pierro, F. Developing a good wrestling diet. *Wrestling USA (Missoula, Mont.) 21(10), 15 Apr 1984, 5;7.*
LEVEL: B LANG: Eng SIRC ARTICLE NO: 100190

Scott, J.R. The wrestler's approach to weight control. *Wrestling USA (Missoula, Mont.) 19(7), 15 Feb 1984, 5-6.*
LEVEL: B LANG: Eng SIRC ARTICLE NO: 100192

Tipton, C.M. Oppliger, R.A. The Iowa wrestling study: lessons for physicians. *Iowa medicine (Des Moines) 74(9), Sept 1984, 381-385.*
LEVEL: I LANG: Eng

Vollrath, W.A. Body composition among college wrestlers and sedentary college-aged students with emphasis on 3-mythlhistidine excretion and calculations of muscle mass. Eugene, Ore.: Microform Publications, University of Oregon, 1984. 1 microfiche : negative, ill. ; 11 x 15 cm.

WRESTLING (continued)

NOTES: Thesis (M.S.) - Pennsylvania State University, 1983; (ix, 36 leaves); includes bibliography.
LEVEL: A LANG: Eng UO84 372

Weight loss can be dangerous. *Wrestling USA (Missoula, Mont.) 21(10), 15 Apr 1984, 21.*
LEVEL: B LANG: Eng SIRC ARTICLE NO: 100196

BIOGRAPHY AND AUTOBIOGRAPHY

Dexter, P. Mad dog uncaged. He tries to be polite, but his public makes him rude. (Maurice Vachon) *Esquire (New York) 102(2), Aug 1984, 131-132.*
LEVEL: B LANG: Eng SIRC ARTICLE NO: 097046

Howell, F.R. A tribute to: Walter 'Golden Superman' Podolak in his final bout. *Muscle development (York, Pa.) 21(4), Jul/Au 1984, 44-45;59-63.*
LEVEL: B LANG: Eng SIRC ARTICLE NO: 105097

Kluge, V. Werner Seelenbinder - lutteur pour l'ideal olympique. Werner Seelenbinder: a fighter for the Olympic ideal. *Comit national olympique de la Republique democratique allemande bulletin (Berlin, GDR) 29(2), 1984, 28-31.*
LEVEL: B LANG: Fr Eng SIRC ARTICLE NO: 108725

Moross, D. Double trouble on the mats. (Steve Fraser) *Olympian (Colorado Springs, Colo.) 11(1), Jun 1984, 18-20.*
LEVEL: B LANG: Eng SIRC ARTICLE NO: 101786

Neff, C. Brothers and brawlers. Wrestlers Dave and Mark Schultz aren't afraid to shed each other's blood training for the Olympics. *Sports illustrated (Chicago, Ill.) 61(3), 16 Jul 1984, 32-34;38.*
LEVEL: B LANG: Eng SIRC ARTICLE NO: 097053

CHILD DEVELOPMENT

Gardiner, G. The paradox of weight classification. (growth and development) *Coaching review (Ottawa, Ont.) 7, May/Jun 1984, 45-47.*
LEVEL: B LANG: Eng SIRC ARTICLE NO: 095540

CHILDREN

Kid wrestling. Starting a kid wrestling program. Part II. *Wrestling USA (Bozeman, Mont.) 20(4), 15 Nov 1984, 20-21.*
LEVEL: LANG: Eng SIRC ARTICLE NO: 173875

Mikles, G. Youth Sports Institute initates longitudinal study on young wrestlers. *Spotlight on youth sports (East Lansing, Mich.) 7(1), Spring 1984, 1;5.*
LEVEL: I LANG: Eng SIRC ARTICLE NO: 103665

Moore, R. Introduction to wrestling - the elementary school program. *Ontario wrestler (Toronto) Apr/May 1984, 10-11.*
LEVEL: B LANG: Eng SIRC ARTICLE NO: 097051

Petrov, R. Kid wrestling: starting a kid wrestling program. *Wrestling USA (Bozeman, Mont.) 20(5), 15 Dec 1984, 24-25.*
LEVEL: B LANG: Eng SIRC ARTICLE NO: 173870

CHILDREN - MINI-SPORT

Gachoud, J.D. La mini-lutte a l'ecole. *Macolin (Suisse) 1, janv 1984, 4-7.*
LEVEL: B LANG: Fr SIRC ARTICLE NO: 097047

COACHING

Can wrestling take a hold? (interview) (Fred Powell) *Sports coach (Wembley, Aust.) 8(1), 1984, 51-55.*
LEVEL: B LANG: Eng SIRC ARTICLE NO: 097044

Looney, D.S. The ultimate winner. Dan Gable willed himself to become the best U.S. wrestler ever. Now he's applying his singular dedication to coaching the American team in L.A. *Sports illustrated (Chicago, Ill.) 61(4), 18 Jul 1984, 496-500;503;506;509-510;513;515;518.*
NOTES: Special preview: the 1984 Olympics.
LEVEL: B LANG: Eng SIRC ARTICLE NO: 097049

Scott, M.D. Pelliccioni, L. Understanding coaching style and performance. *Wrestling USA (Missoula, Tenn.) 19(9), 15 Mar 1984, 5-8.*
LEVEL: B LANG: Eng SIRC ARTICLE NO: 100193

Wrestling; a coach's planning manual. (Willowdale, Ont.): (Ontario Amateur Wrestling Association), (c1984). 1v. (loose-leaf)
CORP: Ontario Amateur Wrestling Association.
NOTES: Includes bibliographical references. Cover title.
LEVEL: I LANG: Eng GV1196.3 20254

COUNTRIES AND REGIONS

Cooper, K. The Soviet sports wrestling system. *Wrestling USA (Missoula, Tenn.) 19(6), 15 Jan 1984, 4-7;9.*
LEVEL: B LANG: Eng SIRC ARTICLE NO: 100178

Petrov, R. Wrestling in Bulgaria. *Olympic review (Lausanne) 199, May 1984, 341-343.*
LEVEL: B LANG: Eng SIRC ARTICLE NO: 097054

Petrov, R. Les lutteurs bulgares. *Revue olympique (Lausanne) 199, mai 1984, 341-343.*
LEVEL: B LANG: Fr SIRC ARTICLE NO: 105099

Petrov, R. Les lutteurs bulgares. *Revue olympique (Lausanne) 199, mai 1984, 341-343.*
LEVEL: B LANG: Fr SIRC ARTICLE NO: 102131

DISABLED

Wrestling for the blind. Coaching manual level 1. Ottawa: Canadian Blind Sports Association, c1984. 25 p. : ill. (National Coaching Certification Program.)
CORP: Canadian Blind Sports Association.
LEVEL: B LANG: Eng GV1196.2.H3 18543

HEALTH AND HYGIENE

Palov, D. Keep it clean. (hygiene) (Refs: 5)*Coaching review (Ottawa, Ont.) 7, Jul/Aug 1984, 44.*
LEVEL: B LANG: Eng SIRC ARTICLE NO: 095543

HISTORY

Leyshon, G. New wrestling book. (Chapter I) *Ontario wrestler (Toronto) Jun/Jul 1984, 11-13.*
NOTES: To be continued.
LEVEL: B LANG: Eng SIRC ARTICLE NO: 097048

Leyshon, G. Of mice and men: chapter II. *Ontario wrestler newsletter (Willowdale, Ont.) Aug/Sept 1984, 13-14.*
NOTES: To b continued, Excerpts from Dr. Glynn Leyshon's book, Of mice and men.
LEVEL: B LANG: Eng SIRC ARTICLE NO: 101785

Leyshon, G.A. Of mats and men. The story of Canadian amateur and olympic wrestling from 1600 to 1984. London, Ont.: Sports Dynamics, c1984. viii, 148 p. : ill.
LEVEL: I LANG: Eng ISBN: 0-9691619-1-3 LC CARD: 84-090225-5 GV1198.15.A2 18928

Sayenga, D. The oldest sport: Greek myths. (Refs: 2)*Amateur wrestling news (Oklahoma City) 30(1), 24 Sept 1984, 12-13.*
LEVEL: B LANG: Eng SIRC ARTICLE NO: 103666

Shuai, J. Wrestling contest before the emperor. *China sports (Beijing, China) 16(7), Jul 1984, 60.*
LEVEL: B LANG: Eng SIR ARTICLE NO: 102186

INJURIES AND ACCIDENTS

Hogan, L. Wrestling. In, Adams, S.H. (ed.), et al., *Catastrophic injuries in sports: avoidance strategies, Salinas, Calif., Cayote Press, c1984, p. 112-116.*
LEVEL: B LANG: Eng RD97 19088

Marti, S. On-the-mat evaluation of injuries.: coaches need to make quick, but knowledgeable, decisions. *Wrestling USA (Missoula, Tenn.) 19(8), 1 Mar 1984, 18-20.*
LEVEL: B LANG: Eng SIRC ARTICLE NO: 100189

Snook, G.A. How I manage skin problems in wrestling. (Refs: 2)*Physician and sportsmedicine 12(3), Mar 1984, 97-98.*
LEVEL: LANG: Eng SIRC ARTICLE NO: 092611

LAW AND LEGISLATION

Appenzeller, H. Ross, C.T. New York - wrestler with learning disability challenges state association's regulations. *Sports and the courts (Winston-Salem, N.C.) 5(3), Summer 1984, 13-14.*
LEVEL: B LANG: Eng SIRC ARTICLE NO: 097527

Ohio - wrestling coach fired for instructing student-athlete to 'lie and cheat'. *Sports and the courts (Winston-Salem, N.C.) 5(2), Spring 1984, 3-4.*
LEVEL: B LANG: Eng SIRC ARTICLE NO: 095542

MEDICINE

Berkes, I. A sportorvos feladata a birkozo sportban. (The task of the sports physician in wrestling.) *Sportorvosi szemle/Hungarian review of sports medicine (Budapest) 25(2), 1984, 133-135.*
LEVEL: B LANG: Hun SIRC ARTICLE NO: 097261

Freischlag, J. Weight loss, body composition, and health of high school wrestlers. (Refs: 10)*Physician and sportsmedicine 12(1), Jan 1984, 121-123;126.*
ABST: This study compares the body weight, percent body fat, the grip strength, illnesses, and the energy level, the emotional stability, and the bowel habits of 104 wrestlers and 73 non wrestlers. Decreases of body fat, grip strength and energy levels in wrestlers were more significant than the ones in controls. Illnesses and emotional stability in both groups were similar, but wrestler's bowel habits were more regular. Changes between weight classes were also analysed.
LEVEL: A LANG: Eng SIRC ARTICLE NO: 092603

Glanzer, J.M. Richards, M. Chronic subdural hematoma in a wrestler. (Refs: 2)*Physician and sportsmedicine 12(2), Feb 1984, 121-122.*
LEVEL: I LANG: Eng SIRC ARTICLE NO: 092605

Mnatzakanian, P.A. Vaccaro, P. Effects of 4% thermal dehydration and rehydration of hematologic and urinary profiles of college wrestlers. (Refs: 41)*Annals of sports medicine (North Hollywood, Calif.) 2(1), 1984, 41-46.*
ABST: The authors investigated fluctuations in wrestlers' hematologic profiles and urinary profiles in the normal state, after 4 per cent dehydration, and after 5 hours of subsequent rehydration. Seventeen University of Maryland varsity wrestlers were studied. The hematologic profiles indicated changes in serum sodium, serum potassium, hematocrit, and plasma volume from the normal state to the dehydrated state. All other hematologic changes were not significant. Urinary profiles showed significant changes in sodium and specific gravity. No significant changes were found for potassium levels and osmolality.
LEVEL: A LANG: Eng SIRC ARTICLE NO: 105098

Sahin, I. Kilic, H. Ozcan, M. Orhan, R. Milli guresciler uzerinde kopro - parazitolojik bir aurastirma. (A copro-parasitological study on the wrestlers of the national team.) *Mikrobiyologii bulteni (Ankara, Turkey) 18(2), Apr 1984, 114-118.*
ABST: This copro-parasitological research was made on the 18 wrestlers of the national team in the Talas training camp in Kayseri. The majority of them came with gastro-intestinal complaints such as nausea, colicky pains, anorexia and dyspepsia and other complaints such as exhaustion and fatigue and 16 of them were found infested with one or more than one parasites. 11 of the total wrestlers were found infected with one kind, 4 of them were found infected with two kinds and 1 was found infested with three kinds parasites.
LEVEL: A LANG: Tur

Vance, N.S. Amateur wrestling...making weight: wrestlers' habit of shedding weight, then adding it back before matches, alarms physicians, coaches. *NAIA news (Kansas, Mo.) 34(1), Aug/Sept 1984, 8-9.*
LEVEL: B LANG: Eng SIRC ARTICLE NO: 101788

NUTRITION

Cipriano, N. Temporary weight loss for the high school wrestler. *Wrestling USA (Bozeman, Mont.) 20(4), 15 Nov 1984, 7;9.*
LEVEL: B LANG: Eng SIRC ARTICLE NO: 173871

Coleman, E. Nutrition aids for wrestlers. *Sports medicine digest (Van Nuys, Calif.) 6(9), Sept 1984, 5.*
LEVEL: B LANG: En SIRC ARTICLE NO: 108773

Dziedzic, S. Nutrition and weight control. *Wrestling USA (Missoula, Tenn.) 19(8), 1 Mar 1984, 5;7.*
LEVEL: B LANG: Eng SIR ARTICLE NO: 100183

Gold, M. Wrestling with weight loss. *In, Schrier, E.W. and Allman, W.F. (eds.), Newton at the bat: the science in sports, New York, Scribner, c1984, p. 97-100.*
LEVEL: B LANG: Eng RC1235 18609

Lincoln, A. Eat better. Compete better. *Wrestling USA (Bozeman, Mont.) 20(4), 15 Nov 1984, 7;9.*
LEVEL: B LANG: Eng SIRC ARTICLE NO: 173872

Shubin, V.I. Laricheva, K.A. Yalovaya, N.I. Lobas, N.M. Shamarina, T.M. Regulating body weight by means of a hypocaloric die (condensed). *Soviet sports review (Escondido, Calif.) 19(1), Mar 1984, 41-43.*
NOTES: Translated from, Voprosy pitanie 1, 1981, 11-15.
LEVEL: I LANG: Eng SIRC ARTICLE NO: 095545

Tipton, C.M. Weight loss hazards and male high school wrestlers. (Refs: 6)*Sports medicine digest (Van Nuys, Calif.) 6(9), Sept 1984, 1-3.*
LEVEL: I LANG: Eng SIRC ARTICLE NO: 108772

PERCEPTUAL MOTOR PROCESSES

Williford, H.N. Wrestling: use of the kinesthetic sense. *Wrestling USA (Bozeman, Mont.) 20(1), 20 Sept 1984, 42-43.*
LEVEL B LANG: Eng SIRC ARTICLE NO: 103672

PHYSIOLOGY

Alen, M. Rahkila, P. Reduced high-density lipoprotein-cholesterol in power athletes: use of male sex hormone derivates, an atherogenic factor. (Refs: 9)*International journal of sports medicine (Stuttgart) 5(6), Dec 1984, 341-342.*
ABST: The effect of androgenic steroids on plasma lipids was studied in seven power athletes who self-administered androgenic steroids on the average 45 mg/day during an 8-week strength training period. After 8 weeks of strength training, the androgen users had reduced the HDL-cholesterol by 54 per cent (from 1.47 to 0.67 mmol/l). The difference when compared to controls was highly significant.
LEVEL: A LANG: Eng SIRC ARTICLE NO: 104595

Birukov, A.A. Pogosyan, M.M. Special means of restoration of work capacity of wrestlers in the periods between competitive bouts. *Soviet sports review (Escondido, Calif.) 19(4), Dec 1984, 191-192.*
NOTES: Condensed translation from, Teoriya i praktika fizicheskoi kultury 3, 1983, 49-50.
LEVEL: B LANG: Eng SIRC ARTICLE NO: 105094

Clarke, D.H. Vaccaro, P. Andresen, N.M. Physiological alterations in 7- to 9-year-old boys following a season of competitive wrestling. (Refs: 31)*Research quarterly for exercise and sport (Reston, Va.) 55(4), Dec 1984, 318-322.*
ABST: Muscular and aerobic capacity changes resulting from three months of wrestling training were examined in a group of normally active 7- to 9-year-old boys (23) who competed in a intramural league tournament. A nontraining group of twenty-two boys of similar age, height, and weight served as control subjects. The subjects were measured for body dimensions and skinfolds, and were given measures of back lift, leg press, and arm endurance (dips and chins). They were also measured for VE max, VO2 max, and HR max employing a progressive treadmill protocol. Results of ANCOVA analyses indicated that (1) the mean improvement in VE max and in VO2 max were not significantly greater than control, nor was HR max; (2) arm endurance improved significantly over control, as did the leg press, but the back lift was not improved significantly; (3) no significant change occurred in height, weight, or in some of skinfolds, but the wrestlers were less endomorphic and more ectomorphic than their control counterparts, and were judged essentially equivalent in mesomorphy.
LEVEL: A LANG: Eng SIRC ARTICLE NO: 105096

Haeekkinen, K. Alen, M. Komi, P.V. Neuromuscular, anaerobic, and aerobic performance characteristics of elite power athletes. (Refs: 43)*European journal of applied physiology and occupational physiology (Berlin, W.G.) 53(2), 1984, 97-105.*
ABST: Various aspects of neuromuscular, anaerobic, and aerobic performance capacity were investigated in four powerlifters, seven bodybuilders, and three wrestlers with a history of specific training for several years. The data showed that the three subject groups possessed similar values for maximal isometric force per unit bodyweight. However, significant differences were observed in the times for isometric force production. No differences were observed between the groups in anaerobic power in a 1-min maximal test, but the values for VO2 max were higher among the wrestlers and bodybuilders as compared to the powerlifters. No differences of a statistical significance were observed between the groups in fibre distribution, fibre areas, or the area ratio of fast (FT) and slow (ST) twitch fibres in vastus lateralis.
LEVEL: A LANG: Eng SIRC ARTICLE NO: 104599

Jako, P. Birkozok es oekoelvivok sulyszabalyozasanak nehany kerdese. (The weight control of wrestlers and boxers.) (Refs: 20 *Sportorvosi szemle/Hungarian review of sports medicine (Budapest) 25(1), 1984, 53-58.*
ABST: Wrestlers and boxers usually reduce their body weight before weighing in by forced dehydration. The need for that arises in part from the existing system of weight categories, and in part from the inadequacy of conditioning. Dehydration obviously will reduce the athlete's performance capacity, primarily by affecting his blood composition and circulation. The right answer to this problem is to help competitors maintain their optimum - individually assessed - weight by bringing their physical activity in harmony with a suitably diet. In this way, only a minimum weight reduction is necessary before weighing in. Diuretics should be avoided, and after weighing in care should be taken to supply the necessary kind and amount of fluids and food.
LEVEL: A LANG: Hun SIRC ARTICLE NO: 095680

Kraemer, W.J. Wrestling: physiological aspects for conditioning. (Refs: 22)*National Strength & Conditioning Association journal 6(1), Feb/Mar 1984, 40;66-67.*
LEVEL: I LANG: Eng SIRC ARTICLE NO: 094021

Sady, S.P. Thomson, W.H. Berg, K. Savage, M. Physiological characteristics of high-ability prepubescent wrestlers. (Refs: 36 *Medicine and science in sports and exercise 16(1), 1984, 72-76.*
ABST: The cardiorespiratory fitness, anaerobic capacity and body composition of 15 pre-pubescent wrestlers and a matched non-wrestling group were compared. The fitness parameters for the wrestling group were higher than the age matched non-wrestling group. The wrestlers also had higher body densities and lower skinfold scores.
LEVEL: A LANG: Eng SIRC ARTICLE NO: 092609

Sharratt, M. A systematic application of science to sport: the Canadian Amateur Wrestling Association (CAWA) model. (Refs: 4 *Coaching science update (Ottawa, Ont.) 1984, 31-34.*
LEVEL: I LANG: Eng SIRC ARTICLE NO: 095544

Sharratt, M. La science appliquee a la lutte. (Refs: 4)*Nouveautes en science de l'entrainement (Ottawa) 1984, 26-28.*
LEVEL: I LANG: Fr SIRC ARTICLE NO: 097056

Sharratt, M.T. Wrestling profile. (Refs: 34)*Clinics in sports medicine (Philadelphia) 3(1), Jan 1984, 273-289.*
NOTES: Symposium on profiling.
ABST: The complete profile of a wrestler consists of anthropometric, cardiovascular, flexibility, nutrition, strength, psychological, sociological and injury frequency profiles. The intent of the profile is to determine success. This is aimed at the eight to thirty year age group, due to the extreme physiological demands of the sport.
LEVEL: A LANG: Eng SIRC ARTICLE NO: 094025

Song, T.M.K. Cipriano, N. Effects of seasonal training on physical and physiological function on elite varsity wrestlers. (Refs: 39)*Journal of sports medicine and physical fitness (Torino, Italy) 24(2), Jun 1984, 123-130.*
ABST: The purpose of this study was to establish the initial status and the training effects during the competitive season on the anthropometry, flexibility, strength, and cardiorespiratory function of 11 members of the elite varsity wrestlers ranging in age from 18 to 24 years. Total mass and lean body mass decreased significantly. No changes of resting or maximum heart rate, blood pressure, and pulmonary function occurred. Forced vital capacity, VO2 max, anaerobic capacity, the strength of the flexion and extension of the elbow, knee, trunk, and neck improved significantly. The flexibility of the neck and shoulder also improved significantly. The lack of significant improvement in some variables may be due to the initial high level of fitness and/or the nature of the training regimen.
LEVEL: A LANG: Eng SIRC ARTICLE NO: 103667

PHYSIOLOGY - MUSCLE

Serfass, R.C. Stull, G.A. Alexander, J.F. Ewing, J.L. The effects of rapid weight loss and attempted rehydration on strength and endurance of the handgripping muscles in college wrestlers. (Refs: 34)*Research quarterly for exercise & sport (Reston, Va.) 55(1), Mar 1984, 46-52.*
ABST: The purpose of this study was to determine if strength and muscular endurance are affected by either dehydration or rehydration in college wrestlers. Testing took place on three separate occasions during which the subject squeezed a hand dynamometer maximally and then relaxed every other second for a total of 180 contractions. This test was repeated (1) following a 5% reduction of body weight within a three day period prior to testing, (2) following a reduction of 5% of body weight, followed by an attempt to rehydrate to the original weight, and (3) under a control condition with no weight loss. Analyses of the results failed to show any affects of rapid weight loss or attempted rehydration on initial strength, final strength, or the force-time integrals. The authors conclude by comparing these results with those of similar studies.
LEVEL: A LANG: Eng SIRC ARTICLE NO: 097055

PSYCHOLOGY

Miller, R. Gruber, J.I. Using the competitive state anxiety inventory on an intact intercollegiate wrestling team. (Refs: 12 *KAHPER journal (Richmond, Ky.) 20(1), Winter 1984, 2-4.*
LEVEL: I LANG: Eng SIRC ARTICLE NO: 095541

Scanlan, T.K. Lewthwaite, R. Jackson, B.L. Social psychological aspects of competition for male youth sport participants: II Predictors of performance outcomes. (Refs: 20)*Journal of sport psychology (Champaign, Ill.) 6(4), Dec 1984, 422-429.*
ABST: This field study investigated sport-related and psychological predictors of children's performance outcomes (win-loss) across two consecutive rounds of a competitive wrestling tournament. The 76 wrestlers studied were 9- to 14-year-old boys, and the sport-related variable examined involved their years of competitive wrestling experience. The psychological predictors investigated were the participants' prematch performance expectancies and their characteristic prematch cognitions including: (a) worries about failure and (b) concerns about the performance expectations and evaluative reactions of their parents and coach. The most influential and stable predictors of performance outcomes across both tournament rounds were competitive experience and prematch performance expectancies. In addition, characteristic failure cognitions significantly predicted win-loss in the first round of the tournament. In total, win-loss was successfully predicted in 78 and 80 per cent of the cases for round 1 and 2, respectively, by these predictors.
LEVEL: A LANG: Eng SIRC ARTICLE NO: 105101

Scanlan, T.K. Lewthwaite, R. Social psychological aspects of competition for male youth sport participants: I. Predictors of competitive stress. (Refs: 32)*Sport psychology (Champaign, Ill.) 6(2), 1984, 208-226.*
ABST: This field study investigated that influence and stability of individual difference and situational factors on the competitive stress experienced by 9- to 14-year-old wrestlers. Stress was assessed by the childrfen's form of the Competitive State Anxiety Inventory and was measured immediately before and after each of two consecutive tournament matches. Wrestlers' dispositions, characteristic precompetition cognitions, perceptions of significant adult influences, psychological states, self-perceptions, and competitive outcomes were examined as predictors of pre- and postmatch anxiety in separate multiple regression analyses for each tournament round. The most influential and stable predictors of prematch stress for both matches were competitive trait anxiety and personal performance expectancies, while win-loss and fun experienced during the match predicted postmatch stress for both rounds. In addition, prematch worries about failure and perceived parental pressure to participate were predictive of round 1 prematch stress. Round 1 postmatch stress levels predicted stress after round 2, suggesting some connsistency in children's stress responses. In total, 61 and 35 percent of prematch and 41 and 32 percent of postmatch state anxiety variance was explained for rounds 1 and 2, respectively.
LEVEL: A LANG: Eng SIRC ARTICLE NO: 108494

Welker, B. Wrestling a sport where excuses are useless: part II. *Wrestling USA (Bozeman, Mont.) 20(2), 1 Oct 1984, 4;6.*
NOTES: Second in a two-part series.
LEVEL: B LANG: Eng SIRC ARTICLE NO: 173400

RULES AND REGULATIONS

Hassman, G. A new stature for wrestling. *Wrestling USA (Missoula, Tenn.) 19(11), 1 May 1984, 9;12.*
LEVEL: B LANG: Eng SIR ARTICLE NO: 100185

Murphy, P. Rule change limits weight of wrestlers. *Physician and sportsmedicine (Minneapolis, Minn.)* 12(7), Jul 1984, 25.
LEVEL: B LANG: Eng SIRC ARTICLE NO: 097052

SPORTING EVENTS

Sayenga, D. Collegians and the Olympics. *Wrestling USA (Missoula, Tenn.) 19(11), 1 May 1984, 25-27.*
LEVEL: B LANG: Eng SIRC ARTICLE NO: 100191

STRATEGY

Siddens, B. Pinning. *Wrestling USA (Missoula, Mont.) 19(7), 15 Feb 1984, 19.*
LEVEL: B LANG: Eng SIRC ARTICLE NO: 100194

STRATEGY - DEFENSIVE

Action - reaction: stalling. *Wrestling USA (Missoula, Mont.) 19(7), 15 Feb 1984, 13-14.*
LEVEL: B LANG: ENG SIRC ARTICLE NO: 100177

Humphrey, J. Big bird. *Canadian wrestler (Vanier, Ont.) 8(2), Summer 1984, 13.*
LEVEL: B LANG: Eng SIRC ARTICLE NO: 098772

TEACHING

Texier, A. Le combat a l'ecole. *EPS: Education physique et sport (Paris) 190, nov/dec 1984, 23-25.*
LEVEL: B LANG: Fr SIRC ARTICLE NO: 103668

TECHNIQUES AND SKILLS

Cox, K. Inside standup series. *Wrestling USA (Missoula, Tenn.) 19(11), 1 May 1984, 9-11.*
LEVEL: B LANG: Eng SIRC ARTICLE NO: 100180

Cox, K. 'Knee pick series'. *Wrestling USA (Missoula, Mont.) 21(10), 15 Apr 1984, 5-6.*
LEVEL: B LANG: Eng SIRC ARTICLE NO: 100181

Dominick, J.J. Inside wrist series. *Wrestling USA (Missoula, Tenn.) 19(8), 1 Mar 1984, 5-6.*
LEVEL: B LANG: Eng SIRC ARTICLE NO: 100182

Groves, R. Leg torque turn sticktly for the gutsy wrestler. *Wrestling USA (Bozeman, Mont.) 20(2), 1 Oct 1984, 4-6.*
LEVEL: LANG: Eng SIRC ARTICLE NO: 173397

Kid wrestling: starting a kid wrestling program. *Wrestling USA (Bozeman, Mont.) 20(3), 15 Oct 1984, 36-39.*
LEVEL: B LANG: E SIRC ARTICLE NO: 173413

Kornhauser, S. Gillman, J. Sit-out series: easy as one, two, five. *Scholastic coach (New York) 54(2), Sept 1984, 72-74.*
LEVEL: B LANG: Eng SIRC ARTICLE NO: 100188

Sacchi, J. The Russian variation of the firemans carry. *Wrestling USA (Bozeman, Mont.) 20(3), 15 Oct 1984, 6-7.*
LEVEL: B LANG: Eng SIRC ARTICLE NO: 173407

Schalles, W. Reverse turk craddle. *Wresling USA (Bozeman, Mont.) 20(4), 15 Nov 1984, 26.*
LEVEL: B LANG: Eng SIRC ARTICLE NO: 173876

The seven basic skills: 2. motion. *Wrestling USA (Bozeman, Mont.) 20(4), 15 Nov 1984, 14.*
LEVEL: B LANG: Eng SIRC ARTICLE NO: 173874

The seven basic skills: 3. changing levels. *Wrestling USA (Bozeman, Mont.) 20(5), 15 Dec 1984, 5.*
LEVEL: B LANG: Eng SIRC ARTICLE NO: 173867

Wrestling skill awards program; standardized approach to teaching wrestling. Willowdale, Ont.: Ontario Amateur Wrestling Association, c1984. ii, 84, (3) p. : ill.
CORP: Ontario Amateur Wrestling Association.
NOTES: Cover title. Bibliography: p. (87).
LEVEL: B LANG: Eng ISBN: 0-920385-00-1 LC CARD: 84-10150-3 GV1195 18910

TRAINING AND CONDITIONING

Marcil, S. Querelles autour d'un centre national d'entrainement. Revue de l'entraineur janv/mars 1984, 26-27.
LEVEL: B LANG: Fr SIRC ARTICLE NO: 092607

Siddens, B. Wrestlers corner. (off-season training program) Wrestling USA (Missoula, Tenn.) 19(11), 1 May 1984, 21.
LEVEL B LANG: Eng SIRC ARTICLE NO: 100195

Tips and secrets: weight training and conditioning for wrestling. Wrestling USA (Bozeman, Mont.) 20(2), 1 Oct 1984, 7;9-10.
LEVEL: B LANG: Eng SIRC ARTICLE NO: 173401

TRAINING AND CONDITIONING - DRILLS

Cox, K. Mat drill. Wrestling USA (Bozeman, Mont.) 20(5), 15 Dec 1984, 6-7;9.
LEVEL: B LANG: Eng SIRC ARTICLE NO: 173868

TRAINING AND CONDITIONING - STRETCHING AND FLEXIBILITY EXERCISES

Tumanyan, G.S. Dzhanyan, S.M. Strength exercises as a means of improving active flexibility of wrestlers. Soviet sports review (Escondido, Calif.) 19(3), Sept 1984, 146-150.
NOTES: Translated from, Teoriya i praktika fizicheskoi kultury 10, 1980, 10-11.
LEVEL: I LANG: Eng SIRC ARTICLE NO: 103669

TRAINING AND CONDITIONING - WEIGHT AND STRENGTH TRAINING

Bean, D. It's in the bag. (weight training) Wrestling USA (Bozeman, Mont.) 20(5), 15 Dec 1984, 6;9-11.
LEVEL: B LANG: Eng SIRC ARTICLE NO: 173402

Brzycki, M. Strength and conditioning for wrestling: the Princeton way. Athletic journal (Evanston, Ill.) 65(4), Nov 1984, 12-14;44-45.
LEVEL: B LANG: Eng SIRC ARTICLE NO: 101783

Cottrell, R.W. Strength training: some ideas, theories and facts. Wrestling USA (Missoula, Mont.) 19(7), 15 Feb 1984, 5-8;26.
LEVEL: B LANG: Eng SIRC ARTICLE NO: 100179

O'Bryant, H.S. Programs for basketball, wrestling, football. (Refs: 5)National Strength & Conditioning Association journal 5(6), Jan 1984, 41;66-67.
ABST: Weight training is an important training method for pre-season strength-power development in athletes. The role of circuit and non-circuit weight training programs are discussed for basketball, wrestling and football. Ten week programs are outlined with specific phases of development being used to attain specific physical goals. This article is extremely useful in planning the progression of a pre-season circuit training program.
LEVEL: B LANG: Eng SIRC ARTICLE NO: 090414

Richardson, T. Wrestling: practical aspects for strength programming. (Refs: 5)National Strength & Conditioning Association journal 6(1), Feb/Mar 1984, 41;70.
LEVEL: B LANG: Eng SIRC ARTICLE NO: 094024

Taberna, P. Musculation des lutteurs.
NOTES: Dans, Renforcement musculaire, Paris, Institut national du sport et de l'education physique, c1984, p. 169-172.
LEVEL: B LANG: Fr GV711.5 18233

WU SHU

Gast, P. Wushu: is it real martial art - or mere acrobatics? Inside kung-fu (Burbank, Calif.) 11(12), Dec 1984, 28-33.
LEVEL: B LANG: Eng SIRC ARTICLE NO: 107347

Gee, C. Funk, J. Could you be a Wushu star? Inside kung-fu (Hollywood, Calif.) 11(4), Apr 1984, 50-51.
LEVEL: B LANG: Eng SIRC ARTICLE NO: 096736

Hallander, J. Why wushu? A woman's point of view. Karate illustrated (Burbank, Calif.) 15(9), Sept 1984, 38-41.
LEVEL: B LANG: Eng SIRC ARTICLE NO: 103300

McCutcheon, S. Pioneers of Wushu: how spirited Canadians transplant the Wushu spirit of China. Inside kung-fu (Hollywood, Calif.) 11(2), Feb 1984, 53-57.
LEVEL: B LANG: Eng SIRC ARTICLE NO: 098319

Taiji swordplay. (contd) China sports (Beijing, China) 16(2), Feb 1984, 27-29.
LEVEL: B LANG: Eng SIRC ARTICLE NO: 098330

Tremblay, J. Le wu shu, art martial chinois. Revue de l'entraineur (Montreal) avr/juin 1984, 25-28.
LEVEL: B LANG: Fr SIR ARTICLE NO: 095151

Wushu: teach yourself. 'Taiji' swordplay. China sports (Beijing, China) 16(1), Jan 1984, 26-29.
NOTES: To be continued in next issue.
LEVEL: B LANG: Eng SIRC ARTICLE NO: 098333

BIOGRAPHY AND AUTOBIOGRAPHY

Huo, Z. Venerable master Wang Qingzhai. China sports (Beijing, China) 16(6), Jun 1984, 53.
LEVEL: B LANG: Eng ARTICL NO: 102188

COUNTRIES AND REGIONS

Meibin, L. Wushu: nation wide systematization. China sports (Bijing, China) 16(11), 1984, 37-39.
LEVEL: B LANG: Eng SIRC ARTICLE NO: 108450

Zhou, H. Wushu: the next Olympic martial arts event? Black belt (Burbank, Calif.) 22(6), Jun 1984, 32-36.
LEVEL: B LANG: Eng SIRC ARTICLE NO: 096751

HISTORY

Tremblay, J. Le wu shu, art martial chinois. Revue de l'entraineur (Montreal) avr/juin 1984, 25-28.
LEVEL: B LANG: Fr SIR ARTICLE NO: 095151

RULES AND REGULATIONS

Wenying, L. How is Wushu contested? China sports (Beijing, China) 16(1), Jan 1984, 24-25.
LEVEL: B LANG: Eng SIRC ARTICLE NO: 098332

Zhou, H. Wushu: the next Olympic martial arts event? Black belt (Burbank, Calif.) 22(6), Jun 1984, 32-36.
LEVEL: B LANG: Eng SIRC ARTICLE NO: 096751

TEACHING

Wen-Chung, W. A brief talk on Kuo-Shu professional education in Chinese Culture University -the tradition and renewal of Chinese Kuo-Shu. Asian journal of physical education (Taiwan, China) 7(1), Apr 1984, 24-31.
LEVEL: B LANG: Eng Chi SIRC ARTICLE NO: 096748

TECHNIQUES AND SKILLS

'Taiji' swordplay. China sports (Beijing, China) 16(3), Mar 1984, 27-31.
LEVEL: B LANG: Eng SIRC ARTICLE NO: 099788

Hallander, J. Revamping the traditional wushu forms: older doesn't necessarily mean better. Black belt (Burbank, Calif.) 22(7), Jul 1984, 20-24.
LEVEL: B LANG: Eng SIRC ARTICLE NO: 103299

YACHTING

Boat trim. Yachts and yachting (Southend-on-sea, Eng.) 982, 21 Sept 1984, 10-12.
NOTES: Second excerpt from, Brooke-Houghton, J., Dinghy crewing, London, Fernhurst Books.
LEVEL: B LANG: Eng SIRC ARTICLE NO: 106250

Creagh-Osborne, R. Milne, P.A.G. Sleight, S. This is sailing: a complete course. 2nd ed. New York: Hearst Marine Books, (1984?). 215 p.
LEVEL: B LANG: Eng ISBN: 0688054293 LC CARD: 84-062460

Dashew, S. Working aloft. Yachting (Los Angeles) 156(4), Oct 1984, 44;46;48.
LEVEL: B LANG: Eng SIRC ARTICLE NO: 106252

Davids, K. International optimist dinghy. Yacht racing & cruising (Philadelphia, Pa.) 23(2), Feb 1984, 55-57.
LEVEL: B LANG: Eng SIRC ARTICLE NO: 098788

Davison, T. Moving offshore. Yachts and yachting (Southend-on-Sea, Eng.) 964, 13 Jan 1984, 20-21.
NOTES: Second article o a series.
LEVEL: B LANG: Eng SIRC ARTICLE NO: 098789

George, M.B. Barlow, P. Iken, H. Basic sailing. New York: Hearst Marine Books, 1984. 112 p. : ill.
LEVEL: B LANG: Eng ISBN: 0-688-03567-1 LC CARD: 78-184227 GV811 18347

James, R.A. Multihulls offshore. 1st ed. New York: Dodd, Mead, 1984, c1983. 279 p. : ill.
LEVEL: B LANG: Eng ISBN: 03960828 LC CARD: 83-072344

Kirby, B. Canada 1. The impertinent challenge for the America's Cup that raised the self-esteem of all Canadians. *Canadian geographic 104(1), Feb/Mar 1984, 10-20.*
LEVEL: B LANG: Eng SIRC ARTICLE NO: 091220

Kostecki, J. Winning in one-designs: getting into a new class. *Yacht racing & cruising (Philadelphia, Pa.) 23(3), Mar 1984, 40;42.*
LEVEL: B LANG: Eng SIRC ARTICLE NO: 098804

Marshall, R. Racing at night. *Sail (Boston, Mass.) 15(6), Jun 1984, 37-38;40.*
LEVEL: B LANG: Eng SIRC ARTICLE NO: 101807

Massey, K. Winning in one-designs: smallboat campaign management. *Yacht racing & cruising (Philadelphia, Pa.) 23(2), Feb 1984, 30;32.*
LEVEL: B LANG: Eng SIRC ARTICLE NO: 098810

Pavot, H. L'heure de la meridienne du soleil. *Quebec yachting (Montreal) 7(1), fevr 1984, 20.*
LEVEL: B LANG: Fr SIRC ARTICLE NO: 100207

Powlison, D. On being a better crew. *Yacht racing & cruising (Philadelphia, Pa.) 23(9), Oct 1984, 61-63.*
LEVEL: B LANG: E SIRC ARTICLE NO: 107885

Pugh, J. The race course. Part 10: crew work. *Yachting world (Surrey, Eng.) 136(2906), Oct 1984, 73-76.*
LEVEL: B LANG: En SIRC ARTICLE NO: 106257

Walker, G. The race course: part 1 - Commissioning and campaigning a grand-prix yacht. *Yachting world (London) 136(2897), Jan 1984, 74-75;77-78.*
LEVEL: B LANG: Eng SIRC ARTICLE NO: 095569

ADMINISTRATION

Dellenbaugh, D. Profile: Sam Merrick. The motivating force behind the American Olympic yachting effort is a hard-working sco sailor from Washington, D.C. *Yacht racing & cruising (Philadelphia) 23(6), Jun 1984, 64-66.*
LEVEL: B LANG: Eng SIRC ARTICLE NO: 097065

Newton, A. Profile: Don Green. *Sailing (Toronto) Jul 1984, 38-46.*
LEVEL: B LANG: Eng SIRC ARTICLE NO: 100206

AERODYNAMICS

Beck, D. Keels: everything you always wanted to know, but were afraid you would't understand. *Yacht racing & cruising (Philadelphia, Pa.) 23(1), Jan 1984, 50-55.*
LEVEL: I LANG: Eng SIRC ARTICLE NO: 098778

Sloof, J. Water wings. *Yachting world (London) 136(2898), Feb 1984, 67-69.*
LEVEL: I LANG: Eng SIRC ARTICLE NO: 098823

Sponberg, E. Rigs: measuring and reducing windage. *Sail (Des Moines, Iowa) 15(3), Mar 1984, 191-192;195-196;198.*
LEVEL: I LANG: Eng SIRC ARTICLE NO: 098827

The ancient interface XIV. Proceedings of the fourteenth AIAA Symposium on the Aero/Hydronautics of Sailing. North Hollywood, Calif.: Weston Periodicals, c1984. v, 125 p. (American Institute of Aeronautics and Astronautics. Monographs, vol. 30.)
CONF: American Institute of Aeronautics and Astronautics Symposium of Sailing. Annual (14th : 1984 : Long Beach, Calif.).
CORP: American Institute of Aeronautics and Astronautics. Orange County Section.
CORP: Society of Naval Architects and Marine Engineers. Los Angeles Section.
LEVEL: A LANG: Eng

ASSOCIATIONS

Ogilvy, S. 1984 log of the Star Class. Official rule book. Glenview, Ill.: International Star Class Yacht Racing Association 1984. 272 p. : ill.
CORP: International Star Class Yacht Racing Association.
LEVEL: B LANG: Eng GV826.5 11830

BIOGRAPHY AND AUTOBIOGRAPHY

Dennis Conner looks ahead. The man who wrote the book on 12-meter sailing talks about his future and the next America's Cup in this interview with Peter Isler. *Yacht racing & cruising (Philadelphia, Pa.) 23(3), Mar 1984, 48-51.*
LEVEL: B LANG: Eng SIRC ARTICLE NO: 098791

Howard, P. Profile: Terry McLaughlin. *Sailing Canada (Toronto, Ont.) 6(2), Mar 1984, 26;30-35.*
LEVEL: B LANG: Eng SIRC ARTICLE NO: 095558

Kolius, J. What it takes to win... *Yacht racing & cruising (Philadelphia, Pa.) 23(10), Nov 1984, 36-39.*
LEVEL: B LANG: En SIRC ARTICLE NO: 106254

Soames, S. Jo Richards: a profile of Jo Richards, our brightest hope for the '84 Olympics and designer of the illusion mini-keelboat. *Yachts and yachting (Southend-on-Sea, Eng.) 964, 13 Jan 1984, 15-18.*
LEVEL: B LANG: Eng SIRC ARTICLE NO: 098826

Soames, S. Graham Walker. *Yachts and yachting (Southend-on-Sea, Eng.) 963, 2 Jan 1984, 25-27.*
LEVEL: B LANG: Eng SIRC ARTICLE NO: 100213

Soames, S. Kenneth Gumley. *Yachts and yachting (Southend-on-Sea, Eng.) 971, 20 Apr 1984, 29-31.*
LEVEL: B LANG: Eng SIRC ARTICLE NO: 101828

Soames, S. Bill Anderson. *Yachts and yachting (Southend-on-sea, Eng.) 986, 16 Nov 1984, 11-13.*
LEVEL: B LANG: Eng SIRC ARTICLE NO: 107894

Soames, S. Dr. Robin Steavenson. *Yachts and yachting (Southend-on-sea, Eng.) 987, 1 Dec 1984, 58-61.*
LEVEL: B LANG: Eng SIRC ARTICLE NO: 109048

The world according to Ted Turner: a conversation about life & sailboat racing. *Yacht racing & cruising (Philadelphia, Pa.) 2 (9), Oct 1984, 56-60.*
LEVEL: B LANG: Eng SIRC ARTICLE NO: 107912

Yachting: Hans Fogh. Voile: Hans Fogh. *Champion (Ottawa) 8(3), Aug 1984, 58-59.*
LEVEL: B LANG: Eng Fr SIRC ARTICLE NO: 0970

CHILDREN

Lotimer, G. Water babies: with only a few adjustments and some extra planning, babies can go sailing too. *Canadian yachting power & sail (Toronto) 9(5), May 1984, 26-27.*
LEVEL: B LANG: Eng SIRC ARTICLE NO: 101805

CLOTHING

Brantley, D. Ullrich, A. Shoes and boots: secrets of the sole. *Sail (Boston, Mass.) 15(5), May 1984, 21-24.*
LEVEL: B LANG Eng SIRC ARTICLE NO: 100550

Johannessen, C. The drysuits are here. *Yacht racing & cruising (Philadelphia, Pa.) 23(3), Mar 1984, 43-46.*
LEVEL: B LANG: Eng SIRC ARTICLE NO: 098803

Johannessen, C. Inner layers: Chris Johannessen provides an insider's look at the latest in clothing that will keep you warm in wet and chilly weather. *Yacht racing & cruising (Philadelphia, Pa.) 23(10), Nov 1984, 45-48.*
LEVEL: B LANG: Eng SIRC ARTICLE NO: 106253

Linskey, T. Drysuits and wetsuits: the new cold remedies. *Sail (Boston, Mass.) 15(5), May 1984, 8-13.*
LEVEL: B LANG: Eng SIRC ARTICLE NO: 100562

Rousmaniere, J. Dry technology: foul-weather gear. *Sail (Boston, Mass.) 15(5), May 1984, 4-7.*
LEVEL: B LANG: Eng SIRC ARTICLE NO: 100575

CLUBS AND TEAMS

Shellbacks Club 50 years of tradition. For some hearty Canadian sailors the season never ends. *Gam on yachting (Toronto) 28(30, Mar 1984, 11.*
LEVEL: B LANG: Eng SIRC ARTICLE NO: 100212

The Royal Canadian Yacht Club. *Sailing Canada (Toronto) 6(7), Aug 1984, 12-14;16.*
LEVEL: B LANG: Eng SIRC ARTICLE NO: 10368

COACHING

Miller, D. Getting a good crew. (team selection) *Coaching review (Ottawa, Ont.) 7, Jul/Aug 1984, 52-53.*
LEVEL: B LANG: En SIRC ARTICLE NO: 095564

COUNTRIES AND REGIONS

Loory, A. Soviet sailing. *Yacht racing & cruising (Philadelphia, Pa.) 23(10), Nov 1984, 55-58.*
LEVEL: B LANG: Eng SIRC ARTICLE NO: 106255

Voile et olympisme. *Quebec yachting (Dorval, Que.) 7(8), sept 1984, 18-19.*
LEVEL: B LANG: Fr SIRC ARTICLE NO: 173425

DICTIONARIES AND TERMINOLOGY

Pengelley, H. Small sailboats: which small day-sailer has the design and quality construction to meet your performance needs *Protect yourself (Montreal) Jun 1984, 21-28.*
LEVEL: B LANG: Eng SIRC ARTICLE NO: 097080

DIRECTORIES

Annuaire de la voile 1984. Montreal: Federation de voile du Quebec, (1984). 52 p.
CORP: Federation de voile du Quebec.
NOTES Titre de la couverture.
LEVEL: B LANG: Fr ISBN: 2-89252-009-6 GV810 17685

Meyer, K. YR&C goes to the movies. YR&C presents the movie guide for people who love the look of sailing. *Yacht racing & cruising (Philadelphia, Pa.) 23(4), Apr 1984, 77-80.*
LEVEL: B LANG: Eng SIRC ARTICLE NO: 098812

ECONOMICS

Buying a boat abroad: low price, high overhead. *Practical sailor (Riverside, Conn.) 10(16), 15 Aug 1984, 1;3-5.*
LEVEL: B LANG: Eng SIRC ARTICLE NO: 098785

Evans, E. Alternative purchase plans. *Sailing Canada (Toronto) 6(1), Jan/Feb 1984, 14-15;17-22.*
LEVEL: B LANG: Eng SIRC ARTICLE NO: 098795

Perry, R. Big corporate money sails with transAtlantic race. *Financial post (Toronto) 78(35), 1 Sept 1984, 4.*
LEVEL: B LANG: Eng SIRC ARTICLE NO: 097081

ENVIRONMENT

Baird, L.P. Weather revisited: Mike Baird begins a two-part series with a new look at the fundamentals of meteorology. *Yach racing & cruising (Philadelphia, Pa.) 23(4), Apr 1984, 57-61.*
NOTES: First of a two-part series.
LEVEL: B LANG: Eng SIRC ARTICLE NO: 098777

Baird, M. Weather revisited, part 11: a fresh look at wind. *Yacht racing & cruising (Philadelphia, Pa.) 23(5), May 1984, 92-95.*
LEVEL: B LANG: Eng SIRC ARTICLE NO: 101789

Gouard, P. Recherches sur le vent et applications dans l'entrainement assiste par ordinateur des equipes de France de voile. *Dans, Culture technique no. 13, Neuilly-sur-Seine, France, Centre de Recherche sur la Culture Technique, c1984, p. 252-255.*
LEVEL: I LANG: Fr RC1235 20096

Moorhouse, D. Windy old weather. *Yachts and yachting(Southend-on-Sea, Eng.) Mid Apr 1984, 25-27.*
LEVEL: B LANG: Eng SIRC ARTICLE NO: 097075

Pavot, H. L'information meteo. *Quebec yachting (Dorval, Que.) 7(4), mai 1984, 44-45.*
LEVEL: B LANG: Fr SIRC ARTICLE NO: 101815

Perrin, C. Mettez-vous aux courants. *Cahiers du yachting (Paris) 257, mai 1984, 104-109.*
LEVEL: I LANG: Fr SIRC ARTICLE NO: 101817

Pocock, M. The breaking wave. *Yachts and yachting (Southend-on-Sea, Eng.) 971, 20 Apr 1984, 34-37.*
LEVEL: I LANG: Eng SIR ARTICLE NO: 101818

Watts, A. The Nor' Westerly. *Yachts and yachting (Southend-on-Sea, Eng.) Late Mar 1984, 25-27.*
LEVEL: B LANG: Eng SIRC ARTICLE NO: 097087

Watts, A. Predicting shoreline shifts. *Sail (Boston, Ma.) 15(8), Aug 1984, 35-36;38.*
LEVEL: B LANG: Eng SIRC ARTICLE NO: 103688

EQUIPMENT

A resounding endorsement for wheel steering systems. *Practical sailor (Riverside, Conn.) 10(8), 15 Apr 1984, 1;5-6.*
LEVEL: LANG: Eng SIRC ARTICLE NO: 100210

All right, who's going up this time? (an evaluation of nine bosun's chairs). *Practical sailor (Riverside, Conn.) 10(11), 1 Ju 1984, 1;6-13.*
LEVEL: B LANG: Eng SIRC ARTICLE NO: 100197

Bakeman, P. Metal boats: Some questions answered. *Sailing Canada (Toronto) 6(3), Apr 1984, 50-60.*
LEVEL: B LANG: Eng SIRC ARTICLE NO: 095548

Benjamin, S. Speed development: Steve Benjamin, Olympic silver medalist, takes a look at what's involved in the boatspeed development process. *Yachts and yachting (Southend-on-sea, Eng.) 986, 16 Nov 1984, 16-18.*
LEVEL: B LANG: Eng SIRC ARTICLE NO: 107818

Boatpox: scratching the surface of a perplexing problem. (blistering) *Practical sailor (Riverside, Conn.) 10(15), 1 Aug 1984, 1;4-6.*
LEVEL: B LANG: Eng SIRC ARTICLE NO: 104593

Burke, K. What does it take to break a mast? A California sparmaker conducts destruction tests under 'controlled' conditions *Cruising world (Newport, R.I.) 10(10), 1984, 130;132;134.*
LEVEL: B LANG: Eng SIRC ARTICLE NO: 100199

Callahan, S. Rigs: wings and wire. *Sail (Boston, Mass.) 15(6), Jun 1984, 151-152;154;156-158.*
LEVEL: B LANG: Eng SIRC ARTICLE NO: 101790

Carden, G. CLASS-C (5m). *Downeast sailor (Concord, Ma.) 19, Apr 1984, 2-4.*
LEVEL: B LANG: Eng SIRC ARTICLE NO: 103675

Chesterton, D. Timbers, taffails & truck. (laying a teak deck) *Gam on yachting (Toronto) 28(6), Jun 1984, 25-33.*
LEVEL: I LANG: Eng SIRC ARTICLE NO: 101792

Cracknell, B. Laminate sails. *Yachting world (London, Eng.) 136(2900), Apr 1984, 69-71.*
LEVEL: B LANG: Eng SIRC ARTICLE NO: 097062

Crawford, L. Knock on wood. (wooden sailboats) *Sailing Canada (Toronto) 6(7), Aug 1984, 14-19.*
LEVEL: B LANG: Eng SIRC ARTICLE NO: 103677

Cruse, S. Trimming the mylar headsail. *Sail (Boston, Mass.) 15(1), Jan 1984, 29-30;32.*
LEVEL: B LANG: Eng SIRC ARTICLE NO 098787

Donaldson, S. Outboard engines. Equipment focus. A review of outboard basics and the state of the art for sailors interested in relating better with their machines. *Yacht racing & cruising (Philadelphia) 23(6), Jun 1984, 60-63.*
LEVEL: B LANG: Eng SIRC ARTICLE NO: 097066

Donaldson, S. State of the art boatbuilding: Part 1. an introduction to materials and structures. *Pacific yachting (Vancouver, B.C.) 25(8), Aug 1984, 36;38-41.*
LEVEL: B LANG: Eng SIRC ARTICLE NO: 098792

Donaldson, S. Rigging alternatives make tacks easier. *Pacific yachting (Vancouver, B.C.) 25(8), Aug 1984, 19-21.*
LEVEL: B LANG: Eng SIRC ARTICLE NO: 098793

Donaldson, S. State of the art boatbuilding, Part 11: fibre and plastic composites. *Pacific yachting (Vancouver, B.C.) 25(9), Sept 1984, 47-49;51-53.*
LEVEL: B LANG: Eng SIRC ARTICLE NO: 100200

Endean, K. Folding dinghies. *Yachts and yachting (Southend-on-Sea, Eng.) Mid Mar 1984, 46-48.*
LEVEL: B LANG: Eng SIRC ARTICLE NO: 097067

Garland, P. Wire halyards. *Yacht racing & cruising (Philadelphia, Pa.) 23(1), Jan 1984, 84.*
LEVEL: B LANG: Eng SIRC ARTICLE NO: 098796

Gautron, D. L'innovation en poupe. *Dans, Culture technique no. 13, Neuilly-sur-Seine, France, Centre de Recherche sur la Culture Technique, c1984, p. 246-249.*
LEVEL: I LANG: Fr RC1235 20096

Gendron, M. Aspects techniques du 470. *Quebec yachting (Montreal) 6(8), dec 1983/janv 1984, 14-15.*
LEVEL: B LANG: Fr SIRC ARTICLE NO: 095556

Grube, J. The quest for the 'unsinkable' boat: practicing the principals of flotation will keep your boat above water. *Cruising world (Newport, R.I.) 10(10), 1984, 125-127;129.*
LEVEL: B LANG: Eng SIRC ARTICLE NO: 100201

Gurney, G. Kevlar offshore: now only small amounts of the material may be used on offshore racing yachts - except maxis, which enjoy unlimited use. *Yachting (New York) 155(2), Feb 1984, 74-75.*
LEVEL: B LANG: Eng SIRC ARTICLE NO: 095557

Gurney, G. The hot designers: Bruce Farr. The leader of the 'New Zealand School' of yacht design is producing winners again from waterfront office in Annapolis. *Yachting (Los Angeles, Calif.) 156(1), Jul 1984, 72-75;106-108.*
LEVEL: B LANG: Eng SIRC ARTICLE NO: 101797

Gutelle, P. Dubois, E. The design of sailing yachts. London: Nautical Books, c1984. 207 p. : ill.
NOTES: Translated from French.
LEVEL: I LANG: Eng ISBN: 0-333-322681 GV811 17780

Hard data for seven brands of soft dinghy. *Practical sailor (Riverside, Conn.) 1984, 4-5.*
NOTES: 1984 gear buying guide.
LEVEL: B LANG: Eng SIRC ARTICLE NO: 101798

Henkel, S. Boat closeup: Bill Dunlop's Wind's Will. *Yacht racing & cruising (Philadelphia, Pa.) 23(2), Feb 1984, 62-63.*
LEVEL: B LANG: Eng SIRC ARTICLE NO: 098799

Howard, P. Sailmaking revolution. The traditional hands-on approach to sail making relied on the experience of a master sailmaker. Now, with computers, sailmaking is an increasingly exact science and you can get precisely what you want in a sail. *Sailing Canada (Toronto) 6(4), May 1984, 57-61.*
LEVEL: B LANG: Eng SIRC ARTICLE NO: 102102

Hunter, D. Sails: the new technology. *Gam on yachting (Toronto, Ont.) 28(1), Jan 1984, 9-18.*
LEVEL: I LANG: Eng SIRC ARTICLE NO: 095559

Jeffery, T. Light fantastic. (Aluminium yachts) *Yachting world (London) 136(2898), Feb 1984, 70-72.*
LEVEL: B LANG: Eng SIRC ARTICLE NO: 098802

Johnstone, R. Coming to terms with the IOR. *Yachting (New York) May 1984, 82-86;122;124.*
LEVEL: B LANG: Eng SIRC ARTICLE NO: 097071

Kattel, E. Swan: 5 meter sailing canoe. *Downeast sailor (Concord, Mass.) 18, Feb 1984, 3.*
LEVEL: B LANG: Eng SIRC ARTICLE NO: 094914

Kelley, B. Design forum: the semi-production one tons. *Yacht racing & cruising (Philadelphia, Pa.) 23(5), May 1984, 102-103.*
LEVEL: B LANG: Eng SIRC ARTICLE NO: 101802

Kirby, B. Technically speaking: winged victory. *Canadian yachting power & sail (Toronto) 9(2), Feb 1984, 14-17.*
LEVEL: B LANG: Eng SIRC ARTICLE NO: 097072

Linskey, T. Cruising sails: spinnakers and drifters. *Yacht racing & cruising (Philadelphia, Pa.) 23(5), May 1984, 88-91.*
LEVEL: B LANG: Eng SIRC ARTICLE NO: 101804

Love, R. The race course. Part 2: spars and rigs. *Yachting world (London) 136(2898), Feb 1984, 62-65.*
LEVEL: B LANG: Eng SIRC ARTICLE NO: 098806

Lush, B. Roller headsail systems. *Sailing Canada (Toronto, Ont.) 6(8), Sept/Oct 1984, 14-19.*
LEVEL: B LANG: Eng SIRC ARTICLE NO: 173224

Macdonald-Smith, I. The race course part 4: headsail trim. *Yachting world (London, Eng.) 136(2900), Apr 1984, 54-57.*
LEVEL: B LANG: Eng SIRC ARTICLE NO: 097073

Macdonald-Smith, I. The race course. Part 3: mainsail trim. *Yachting world (London) 136(2899), Mar 1984, 59-61;63.*
LEVEL: B LANG: Eng SIRC ARTICLE NO: 098807

Marshall, J. America's Cup 1983: sailmaker's laboratory. *Yachting (New York) 155(2), Feb 1984, 66-70.*
LEVEL: B LANG: Eng SIRC ARTICLE NO: 095560

Marshall, J. 12-metre sail revolution. *Yacht racing & cruising (Philadelphia, Pa.) 23(2), Feb 1984, 42-46.*
LEVEL: B LANG: Eng SIRC ARTICLE NO: 098808

Mason, C. High-tech and 12-meters; what's in it for us? *Sail (Boston, Mass.) 15(1), Jan 1984, 103-108.*
LEVEL: B LANG: Eng SIRC ARTICLE NO: 098809

Mazza, R. Racing deck layout. *Canadian yachting power & sail 9(1), Jan 1984, 16-19.*
LEVEL: B LANG: Eng SIRC ARTICLE NO: 092629

Mazza, R. The latest last words on rigs: a discussion on the science of spars. *Canadian yachting power & sail (Toronto, Ont.) 9(6), Jun 1984, 18-23.*
LEVEL: B LANG: Eng SIRC ARTICLE NO: 100202

McKeag, M. White-sail reaching. *Yachts and yachting (Southend-on-Sea, Eng.) 976, 29 Jun 1984, 10-11.*
LEVEL: B LANG: Eng SIRC ARTICLE NO: 101808

McKeag, M. Changing the spinnaker. *Yachts and yachting (Southend-on-Sea, Eng.) 977, 13 Jul 1984, 14-16.*
NOTES: Third and final excerpt from, McKeag, M., Yacht creiving.
LEVEL: B LANG: Eng SIRC ARTICLE NO: 101809

Mercier, G. Voiles et reglages. *Quebec yachting (Montreal) 7(7), aout 1984, 14-18;20;51.*
LEVEL: B LANG: Fr SIRC ARTICLE NO: 100203

Mercier, G. Concept et performances des bateaux a voile. *Quebec yachting (Montreal) 7(1), fevr 1984, 35-37.*
LEVEL: I LANG Fr SIRC ARTICLE NO: 100204

Mercier, G. Le Laser 28. *Quebec yachting (Montreal) 7(1), fevr 1984, 15-17.*
LEVEL: B LANG: Fr SIRC ARTICLE NO: 100205

Mercier, G. Mats et greements (1re partie). *Quebec yachting (Dorval, Que.) 7(3), avr 1984, 20-23.*
LEVEL: B LANG: Fr SIRC ARTICLE NO: 101811

Mercier, G. Mats et greements. 2e partie. *Quebec yachting (Dorval, Que.) 7(4), mai 1984, 20-21;23-25;46-47.*
LEVEL: B LANG Fr SIRC ARTICLE NO: 101812

Milne, P. Light, bright and strong. (aluminium construction) *Yachting world (Surrey, Eng.) 136(2902), Jun 1984, 102-103;105.*
LEVEL: B LANG: Eng SIRC ARTICLE NO: 101813

Naranjo, R. Offshore voyaging: staying afloat. *Sail (Des Moines, Iowa) 15(3), Mar 1984, 43-44;47-48;50.*
LEVEL: B LANG: En SIRC ARTICLE NO: 098814

Nickle, C. Gooderham, B. Luna 24/SL: a measure of comfort added without subtracting racing excitement. *Canadian yachting magazine (Toronto) 9(10), Oct 1984, 32-35.*
LEVEL: B LANG: Eng SIRC ARTICLE NO: 108784

Pattison, D.R. Design of a sailing hydrofoil - Force 8. (Refs: 26)*Naval architect (London) Apr 1984, 73-91.*
ABST: Description of the design and development of the sailing hydrofoil Force 8 as a challenger for the world sailing speed record.
LEVEL: I LANG: Eng SIRC ARTICLE NO: 098815

Pavot, H. La radio amateur: des ondes sur la mer. *Quebec yachting (Montreal) 6(8), dec 1983/janv 1984, 13.*
LEVEL: B LANG: Fr SIRC ARTICLE NO: 095566

Pazereskis, J. A look at four tiller tenders. *Practical sailor (Riverside, Conn.) 1984, 6-8.*
NOTES: 1984 gear buying guid
LEVEL: B LANG: Eng SIRC ARTICLE NO: 101816

Pengelley, H. Small sailboats: which small day-sailer has the design and quality construction to meet your performance needs *Protect yourself (Montreal) Jun 1984, 21-28.*
LEVEL: B LANG: Eng SIRC ARTICLE NO: 097080

Perrin, C. Reglages. *Cahiers du yachting (Paris) 255, mars 1984, 64-67;131.*
LEVEL: B LANG: Fr SIRC ARTICLE NO: 100208

Popular electronics (and not so): PS reader survey report. *Practical sailor (Riverside, Conn.) 1984, 11-14.*
NOTES: 1984 gea buying guide.
LEVEL: B LANG: Eng SIRC ARTICLE NO: 101819

Powlison, D. La mystique de Mark Lindsay: les nouveaux materiaux de construction nautique. *Traduction INSEP (Paris) 421, 1-4.*
NOTES: Traduit par, Patricia Vandewalle. Traduit de, Document exterieur.
LEVEL: B LANG: Fr SIRC ARTICLE NO: 101820

Preece, A. Hi-tech low-down. *Yachts and yachting (Southend-on-sea, Eng.) 987, 1 Dec 1984, 22-26;29.*
NOTES: First of two articles
LEVEL: B LANG: Eng SIRC ARTICLE NO: 109044

Priedkalns, J. Wary wing - part 1: protecting and preserving electrical power. *Gam on yachting (Toronto) 28(5), May 1984, 18-20.*
LEVEL: I LANG: Eng SIRC ARTICLE NO: 100209

Racing classes review. *Yachts and yachting (Southend-on-sea, Eng.) 987, 1 Dec 1984, 43-52;54-55.*
LEVEL: B LANG: Eng SIRC ARTICLE NO: 109046

Read, K. Winning in one-designs: everything you wanted to know about telltales. *Yacht racing & cruising (Philadelphia, Pa.) 23(5), May 1984, 42;45-46.*
LEVEL: B LANG: Eng SIRC ARTICLE NO: 101821

Robinson, B. America's Cup: sailing's new tacks. In, Schrier, E.W. and Allman, W.F. (eds.), Newton at the bat: the science in sports, New York, Scribner, c1984, p. 87-90.
LEVEL: B LANG: Eng RC1235 18609

Rudoff, H. Construction: plastics onboard. *Sail (Boston, Mass.) 15(5), May 1984, 135-136;138;140.*
LEVEL: B LANG: Eng SIRC ARTICLE NO: 101824

Short test X-95. *Yachting world (London) 136(2898), Feb 1984, 96-97.*
LEVEL: B LANG: Eng SIRC ARTICLE NO: 098821

Sigma 292. *Yachting world (London) 136(2898), Feb 1984, 90-91;93-95.*
LEVEL: B LANG: Eng SIRC ARTICLE NO: 098822

Simmer, G. Australia II's computer brain. *Australian sailing Jan 1984, 29-31;65-67.*
ABST: The instrument and computer package developed for Australia II is one of the most advanced systems of its type in the world. A fully expanded Ockam system, it uses standard type sensors being masthead unit, paddle wheel boatspeed transducers, keel potentiometer, and an electric compass.
LEVEL: I LANG: Eng SIRC ARTICLE NO: 094080

Smith, D. Barberhauling for speed. *Sail (Boston, Mass.) 15(6), Jun 1984, 43-44;46;48;50.*
LEVEL: B LANG: Eng SIRC ARTICLE NO: 101827

Smyth, R. Alexander, D. Multihulls rudder tuning: Part 1. *Yacht racing & cruising (Philadelphia, Pa.) 23(3), Mar 1984, 36;38.*
LEVEL: B LANG: Eng SIRC ARTICLE NO: 098825

Spar power. *Yachts and yachting (Southend-on-Sea, Eng.) Late Mar 1984, 50-52.*
LEVEL: B LANG: Eng SIRC ARTICLE NO: 097084

Steel for strength. *Yachting world (Surrey, Eng.) 136(2905), Sept 1984, 126-128.*
LEVEL: B LANG: Eng SIRC ARTICLE NO: 108814

Stollery, R. Swing Rig. *Yachting world (Surrey, Eng.) 136(2907), Nov 1984, 84-85;87.*
LEVEL: B LANG: Eng SIRC ARTICLE NO: 106259

Street, D. Cruising rigs - part 1: sailplan. *Yachting world (London) 136(2897), Jan 1984, 110-112.*
LEVEL: B LANG: Eng SIR ARTICLE NO: 095568

Terbeest, R. International 14: the dinghy of dinghies that packs the fun. *Sailing (Port Washington, Wis.) 19(2), Oct 1984, 36-40.*
LEVEL: B LANG: Eng SIRC ARTICLE NO: 100215

The classics - Scows. *Yachting world (London) 136(2897), Jan 1984, 100-101;103.*
LEVEL: B LANG: Eng SIRC ARTICLE NO: 095554

Three new tiller extensions for big boats. *Practical sailor (Riverside, Conn.) 1984, 9-10.*
NOTES: 1984 gear buying guide.
LEVEL: B LANG: Eng SIRC ARTICLE NO: 101831

Trimble, N. Boats for beginners: your child hopes to find a sailboat under the Christmas tree? Before Santa goes shopping, here are some points and some new designs to consider. *Yachting (Los Angeles) 156(5), Nov 1984, 78-80.*
LEVEL: B LANG: Eng SIRC ARTICLE NO: 109043

Underwood, D. Electronics: a look at what's new. *Sailing Canada (Toronto) 6(5), Jun 1984, 102141.*
LEVEL: B LANG: Eng SIRC ARTICLE NO: 102141

Warner, R. The case for roller furling: racers and cruisers alike are drawn to the latest in furling technology. *Canadian yachting power & sail (Toronto, Ont.) 9(6), Jun 1984, 24-26;58;60.*
LEVEL: B LANG: Eng SIRC ARTICLE NO: 100216

Wilson, D.G. Human auxiliary power in a transatlantic sailing race. *Human power*

(Cambridge, Mass.) 3(2), Winter 1984, 13-14.
LEVEL: B LANG: Eng SIRC ARTICLE NO: 106262

Wormwood, P. Eliminating the boom. *Yacht racing & cruising (Philadelphia, Pa.) 23(8), Sept 1984, 44-45.*
LEVEL: B LANG: En SIRC ARTICLE NO: 103691

EQUIPMENT - MAINTENANCE

Caswell, C. The art of sail repair: the proper knowledge and the right tools can make all the difference. *Yachting (New York) 155(2), Feb 1984, 7173.*
LEVEL: B LANG: Eng SIRC ARTICLE NO: 095552

Crawford, L. Winter lay-up. *Sailing Canada (Toronto, Ont.) 6(8), Sept/Oct 1984, 54-59.*
LEVEL: B LANG: Eng SIRC ARTICLE NO 173227

Dougherty, R. How to evaluate old sails: a sailmaker tells when it's time to buy new ones. *Cruising world (Newport, R.I.) 10(9), Sept 1984, 30;32;34.*
LEVEL: B LANG: Eng SIRC ARTICLE NO: 098794

Hall, B. Replacing halyards. *Yacht racing & cruising (Philadelphia, Pa.) 23(2), Feb 1984, 100.*
LEVEL: B LANG: Eng SIRC ARTICLE NO: 098797

Harris, D. Cold storage: don't wait till spring, do it now - this is the season for preventive maintenance. *Canadian yachting magazine (Toronto) 9(10), Oct 1984, 18-21.*
LEVEL: B LANG: Eng SIRC ARTICLE NO: 108781

Mate, F. Shipshape. The complete book of sailing maintenance. s.l.: Hearst Marine, 1984. 416 p. : ill.
LEVEL: I LANG: Eng ISBN: 0-688-047025

Mellor, J. Damage control: it's more effective to stop the water coming in than it is to pump it out. *Canadian yachting magazine (Toronto, Ont.) 9(11), Nov 1984, 17-19.*
LEVEL: B LANG: Eng SIRC ARTICLE NO: 173565

Nicholson, I. Stiffening alloy repairs. *Yachts and yachting (Southend-on-Sea, Eng.) Late Mar 1984, 43-45.*
LEVEL: B LANG: Eng SIRC ARTICLE NO: 097078

Rejuvenating topsides: awlgrip, imron, and brushable polyurethanes. *Practical sailor (Riverside, Conn.) 1984, 25-29.*
NOTES: 1984 gear buying guide.
LEVEL: B LANG: Eng SIRC ARTICLE NO: 101822

Spranger, J. Anti-fouling is not the only factor. *Practical sailor (Riverside, Conn.) 1984, 22-24.*
NOTES: 1984 gear buyin guide.
LEVEL: B LANG: Eng SIRC ARTICLE NO: 101829

Staton-Bevan, T. Fiberglass upkeep. *Sailing (Port Washington, Wis.) 19(1), Sept 1984, 45.*
LEVEL: B LANG: Eng SIRC ARTICLE NO: 100214

Walcoff, H. Curtis, D. From the experts J/24. One of the most successful J/24 skipper-crew combinations details their approach to tuning, preparation, sail trim and boathandling for this popular one-design keelboat. *Yacht racing & cruising (Philadelphia) 23(6), Jun 1984, 67-72.*
NOTES: Parts of this article appear in more detail on the Horizon Sails' J/24 tuning sheet.
LEVEL: B LANG: Eng SIRC ARTICLE NO: 097085

EQUIPMENT - RETAILING

Spranger, J. Buying or selling a used boat, part 2: now it's the buyer's turn. *Practical sailor (Riverside, Conn.) 10(10), 15 May 1984, 1;4-6.*
LEVEL: B LANG: Eng SIRC ARTICLE NO: 101830

FACILITIES

Chamier, J. John Chamier's anchor watch: improve the Olympic course - cut starting time. *Yachts and yachting (Southend-on-Sea, Eng.) Mid Mar 1984, 32.*
LEVEL: I LANG: Eng SIRC ARTICLE NO: 097060

The National Sailing Centre Cowes, Great Britain. *Sportstaettenbau + Baederanlagen (Cologne, W. Germany) 18(2), Mar/Apr 1984, 77-78.*
LEVEL: B LANG: Eng SIRC ARTICLE NO: 097076

FACILITIES - DESIGN, CONSTRUCTION AND PLANNING

Architecture of docks, harbor buildings, harbors and marinas: a bibliography. Monticello, Ill.: Vance Bibliographies, 1984. 10 p. (Architecture series: bibliography; A-1190.)
CORP: Coppa and Avery Consultants.
NOTES: ISSN: 0194-1356.
LEVEL: I LANG: Eng ISBN: 0-88066-980-2
GV770.7 17745

HANDICAPPING

Blais, A. La regate: notions des jauges ou handicaps. *Ecoute (Montreal) 39, printemps 1984, 22-23.*
LEVEL: B LANG: Fr SIRC ARTICLE NO: 105104

Mercier, G. Jauges, handicaps, et equite. *Quebec yachting (Montreal) 7(5), juin 1984, 20-21.*
LEVEL: B LANG: Fr SIRC ARTICLE NO: 095562

HISTORY

Cameron, S.D. Schooner: one of the last in long line of magnificent sailing ships, Bluenose was Canada's pride and glory of the open seas. *Canadian yachting power & sail (Toronto) 9(4), Apr 1984, 34-41;75-78.*
LEVEL: B LANG: Eng SIRC ARTICLE NO: 101791

de Toma, E. Les rubans bleus de la voile. *Dans, Culture technique no. 13, Neuilly-sur-Seine, France, Centre de Recherche su la Culture Technique, c1984, p. 234-245.*
LEVEL: I LANG: Fr RC1235 20096

Guex, A. Meltzer, C. Wirz, M. Yachting 1890. L'ephemere et l'immuable. Geneve: Societe nautique, 1984. 52 p. : ill.
LEVEL: LANG: Fr

Martin, G. The sporting life. The exploits of the Canadian team at Newport last summer are now a part of the America's Cup lore. *Saturday night Apr 1984, 34-43.*
LEVEL: B LANG: Eng SIRC ARTICLE NO: 092628

Michael, J. The keel controversy: a member of the America's Cup Committee scrutinizes the legalities of the super keel and suggests that the Cup might well have stayed here. *Yachting (New York) 155(1), Jan 1984, 80-84;144;146;148;150;152;154;156.*
LEVEL: B LANG: Eng SIRC ARTICLE NO: 095563

Parker, S. Distant thunder. Unforgettable, perhaps a little crazy and absolutely unrepeatable, the J-boats were perfect symbols of an extraordinary era. *Canadian yachting power & sail (Toronto) 9(3), Mar 1984, 26-30;61;66;68.*
LEVEL: B LANG: Eng SIRC ARTICLE NO: 097079

HYDRODYNAMICS

Sloof, J.W. On wings and keels. (Refs: 15)*International shipbuilding progress 31(357), May 1984, 94-104.*
ABST: This paper details the physical mechanisms governing the hydrodynamics and performance of yacht keels. The presence of free water surface dictates that the optimum keel shape will differ from optimum aircraft wings. Through the use of computational fluid dynamic analysis and optimization methods the performance of conventional keels have been found to improve significantly through the reduction of taper or even by the application of inverse taper. Performance can be significantly improved as in the case of Australia II which used a keel with winglets in the 1983 America's Cup.
LEVEL: A LANG: Eng SIRC ARTICLE NO: 098824

INJURIES AND ACCIDENTS

Simonnet, J. Kinesitherapie et preparation olympique en voile. (Kinesitherapy and preparation for Olympic sailing.) *Union medicale du Canada (Montreal) 113(8), aout 1984, 648-650.*
LEVEL: I LANG: Fr

MATHEMATICS

Edgerton, B. The race course. Part 12: optimisation. *Yachting world (Surrey, Eng.) 136(2908), Dec 1984, 70-73.*
LEVEL: I LANG: Eng SIRC ARTICLE NO: 108558

Wilson, P. Calculated speed: part one. Canada 1's navigator explains the use of the pocket calculator in around-the-buoys racing. *Canadian yachting, power & sail (Toronto) 9(7), Jul 1984, 16-18;55.*
LEVEL: I LANG: Eng SIRC ARTICLE NO: 103689

Wilson, P. Calculated speed: part two. A review of vector arithmetic, the basis of dead-reckoning navigation. *Canadian yachting, power & sail (Toronto) 9(8), Aug 1984, 16-18.*
LEVEL: I LANG: Eng SIRC ARTICLE NO: 103690

MEDICINE

Blondelle, P. Simonnet, J. Un kinesitherapeute a l'America's Cup de 1983. (A physical therapist at the America's Cup in 1983 *Union medicale du Canada (Montreal) 113(8), aout 1984, 637-639.*
LEVEL: I LANG: Fr

Tacher, J. L'ecole nationale de voile, St-Pierre-Quiberon (Bretagne-Sud): son role medico-sportif. (The National sailing school, St-Pierre-Quiberon (South Britany): its role in sports medicine.) *Union medicale du Canada (Montreal) 113(8), aout 1984, 627-631.*
LEVEL: I LANG: Fr

Young, J. Prevent physical problems. Ways to avoid overuse and overexposure. *Sail (Des Moines, Iowa) 15(4), Apr 1984, 51-52;54;56.*
LEVEL: B LANG: Eng SIRC ARTICLE NO: 095570

NAVIGATION

Allison, D. Celestial navigation and the pocket computer: a simple program unlocks a two-body fix and a running sun fix. *Cruising world (Newport, R.I.) 10(10), 1984, 79-83.*
LEVEL: I LANG: Eng SIRC ARTICLE NO: 100198

Bowker, P. Racing in fog. *Yacht racing & cruising (Philadelphia, Pa.) 23(3), Mar 1984, 100.*
LEVEL: B LANG: Eng SIRC ARTICLE NO: 098782

Campbell, S. Cruising yachtsman/the practical navigator: compass error. *Yachting (New York) May 1984, 48;50-51.*
LEVEL: B LANG: Eng SIRC ARTICLE NO: 097059

Campbell, S. The yachting book of coastwise navigation. New York: Dodd, Mead, 1984. 1v.
NOTES: Includes index.
LEVEL: I LANG: Eng ISBN: 0396083560 LC CARD: 84-013827

Comparison of pedestal-mount compasses. *Practical sailor (Riverside, Conn.) 10(7), 1 Sept 1984, 7-10.*
LEVEL: B LANG: Eng SIRC ARTICLE NO: 103676

Cronier, R. The noon sight: a simple lesson in using the sextant. *Canadian yachting power & sail (Toronto) 9(4), Apr 1984, 16-18.*
LEVEL: I LANG: Eng SIRC ARTICLE NO: 101793

Donaldson, S. Loran C: the Loran C computer is providing easy answers to the question 'where are we?'. *Yacht racing & cruising (Philadelphia, Pa.) 23(8), Sept 1984, 63-67.*
LEVEL: B LANG: Eng SIRC ARTICLE NO: 103679

Ellis, A. Computers aboard: an instrument maker extols the uses of onboard computers and includes some that software writers haven't thought of. *Yachting (Los Angeles) 156(6), Dec 1984, 72-74.*
LEVEL: B LANG: Eng SIRC ARTICLE NO: 107844

Kelsey, M.C. Lorsat arrives: when the loran and the satnav can 'talk' to each other, you know precisely where you are. *Yachting (New York) 155(6), Jun 1984, 123-125.*
LEVEL: B LANG: Eng SIRC ARTICLE NO: 101803

Macaulay, B. Loran: while the instruments are getting more sophisticated, their price is falling - for yachtsmen, there's no time like the present. *Canadian yachting, power & sail (Toronto) 9(7), Jul 1984, 34-37;45.*
LEVEL: B LANG: Eng SIRC ARTICLE NO: 103682

Mellor, J. Dead reckoning. *Sailing Canada (Toronto) 6(3), Apr 1984, 14-18.*
LEVEL: B LANG: Eng SIRC ARTICLE NO: 095561

Pavot, H. Donnees sur la carte marine. *Ciel et mer. Quebec yachting (Dorval, Que.) 7(3), avr 1984, 13.*
LEVEL: B LANG: Fr SIRC ARTICLE NO: 101814

Pavot, H. Compas magnetique et declinaison magnetique. *Quebec yachting (Dorval, Que.) 7(8), sept 1984, 31.*
LEVEL: B LANG: Fr SIRC ARTICLE NO: 173427

Rousmaniere, J. Piloting review 1: dead reckoning. *Yacht racing & cruising (Philadelphia, Pa.) 23(2), Feb 1984, 58-61.*
NOTES: First article of a two-part series. Excerpted from, The Annapolis book of seasmanship, by John Rousmaniere.
LEVEL: I LANG: Eng SIRC ARTICLE NO: 098817

Rousmaniere, J. Piloting review 11: positions. *Yacht racing & cruising (Philadelphia, Pa.) 23(3),*

Mar 1984, 60-63.
NOTES: Second of a two-part series. Excerpted from, The Annapolis book of Seamanship, by John Rousmaniere.
LEVEL: B LANG: Eng SIRC ARTICLE NO: 098818

Tellet, G.G. Marine electronics '85: with new efficiency and reliability, modern electronic instruments have improved navigation, performance, communications and safety. This special section looks at today's marine electronics and to the trend toward more efficiency and economical equipment tommorow. *Yachting (Los Angeles) 156(6), Dec 1984, 68-71.*
LEVEL: B LANG: Eng SIRC ARTICLE NO: 107898

Wardrop, P. The race course. Part 11: navigation. *Yachting world (Surrey, Eng.) 136(2907), Nov 1984, 70-73.*
LEVEL: B LANG Eng SIRC ARTICLE NO: 106261

OFFICIATING

Dellenbaugh, D. The Finn controversy: what really happened... (U.S. Finn Olympic Trials) *Yacht racing & cruising (Philadelphia, Pa.) 23(8), Sept 1984, 77-81.*
LEVEL: B LANG: Eng SIRC ARTICLE NO: 103678

PHYSICS

Pocock, M. Maintaining control. *Yachts and yachting (Southend-on-Sea, Eng.) Late Mar 1984, 29-32.*
NOTES: First of two articles.
LEVEL: B LANG: Eng SIRC ARTICLE NO: 097082

Pocock, M. Losing control. *Yachts and yachting (Southend-on-Sea) Mid Apr 1984, 21-23.*
NOTES: Second of two articles.
LEVEL: B LANG: Eng SIRC ARTICLE NO: 097083

Woods, R. Feet first: catamaran stability. *Yacht and yachting (Southend-on-Sea, Eng.) 1 Jun 1984, 35-37.*
LEVEL: I LANG: E SIRC ARTICLE NO: 101835

PHYSIOLOGY

Bachemont, F. Fouillot, J.P. Terkaia, M.A. Brobzowski, T. Etude de la frequence cardiaque en deriveur et en planche a voile par monitoring ambulatoire. (Study of the heart rate while sailing or windsurfing by ambulatory monitoring.) *Union medicale du Canada (Montreal) 113(8), aout 1984, 644-647.*
LEVEL: A LANG: Fr

PHYSIOLOGY - MENTAL TRAINING

Young, J. Winning with the mind. *Sail (Des Moines, Iowa) 15(3), Mar 1984, 35-36;38;40.*
ABST: Concentration is the most important mental skill used in sailing, however, distractions are the main pitfall of concentration and can easily lead to stress. Relaxation must be used to minimize stress in sailing competition. A sailor needs these mental skills on the water, but he can also improve them with imagery training. An athlete uses imagery to visually rehearse his sport performance and prepare for competition. Imagery training will improve a sailor's important mental skills such as concentration and will lead to better competitive performance.
LEVEL: B LANG: Eng SIRC ARTICLE NO: 098836

PICTORIAL WORKS

Rosenfeld, M. Rosenfeld, S. A century under sail. Reading, Mass.: Addison-Wesley, 1984. 1v.
LEVEL: B LANG: Eng ISBN: 0201065711 LC CARD: 84-006411

PSYCHOLOGY

Baird, E. Regatta psyche: the head game of consistent championship performance. *Yachting (New York) 155(2), Feb 1984, 136-138.*
LEVEL: B LANG: Eng SIRC ARTICLE NO: 095547

RULES AND REGULATIONS

Chamier, J. John Chamier's anchor watch: improve the Olympic course - cut starting time. *Yachts and yachting (Southend-on-Sea, Eng.) Mid Mar 1984, 32.*
LEVEL: I LANG: Eng SIRC ARTICLE NO: 097060

Lamarque, B. Forest, A. Berthier, M.P.G. Les regles de course de l'I.Y.R.U. Paris: Voiles/Gallimard, 1984. 285 p. : ill. (Collection 'Le savoir marin'.)
NOTES: Includes index.
LEVEL: I LANG: Fr ISBN: 2070600629 LC CARD: 82-233305 GV826.7 17234

McLaughlin, F. Winning by the book. *Canadian yachting power & sail (Toronto) 9(5), May 1984, 37-40;44;46;64-65.*
LEVEL: B LANG: Eng SIRC ARTICLE NO: 101810

Orrell, J. Proper course. *Australian sailing Jan 1984, 46-49;68.*
ABST: The concept of a proper course as it appears in th rule book is not easy to define. This article interprets the position throughout a race.
LEVEL: I LANG: Eng SIRC ARTICLE NO: 094064

Rose, D. Rules corner: rounding the weather mark - part 111. *Yacht racing & cruising (Philadelphia, Pa.) 23(7), Aug 1984, 36-37.*
LEVEL: B LANG: Eng SIRC ARTICLE NO: 101823

Rose, D. Rules corner: 'predictable' alternations of course. *Yacht racing & cruising (Philadelphia, Pa.) 23(9), Oct 1984, 32;34.*
LEVEL: B LANG: Eng SIRC ARTICLE NO: 107888

Sambrooke-Sturgess, G. All change. *Yachts and yachting (Southend-on-Sea, Eng.) 964, 13 Jan 1984, 22-23.*
LEVEL: B LANG: En SIRC ARTICLE NO: 098819

Sambrooke-Sturgess, G. Abandon? *Yachts and yachting (Southend-on-Sea, Eng.) 966, 10 Feb 1984, 18-20.*
LEVEL: B LANG: Eng SIRC ARTICLE NO: 098820

Sambrooke-Sturgess, G. Which rules rule? *Yachts and yachting (Southend-on-Sea, Eng.) 963, 2 Jan 1984, 41.*
LEVEL: B LANG: Eng SIRC ARTICLE NO: 100211

Sambrooke-Sturgess, G. Drifting astern. *Yachts and yachting (Southend-on-Sea, Eng.) 978, 27 Jul 1984, 23-25.*
LEVEL: B LANG: Eng SIRC ARTICLE NO: 101825

Sambrooke-Sturgess, G. Poking your nose in. *Yacht and yachting (Southend-on-Sea, Essex) 5 Oct 1984, 28-29.*
LEVEL: B LANG: Eng SIRC ARTICLE NO: 109125

Walker, S. Port end start - Part 1: the rules. *Yacht racing & cruising (Philadelphia, Pa.) 23(2), Feb*

1984, 14D;18.
NOTES First of a three-part series.
LEVEL: B LANG: Eng SIRC ARTICLE NO: 098830

Willis, B. The race course. Part 9: the rules.
Yachting world (Surrey, Eng.) 136(2905), Sept 1984, 99;101-102;104.
LEVEL: LANG: Eng SIRC ARTICLE NO: 108813

Yoakum, J. Racing rules: pumping the butterfly syndrome. *Wind Rider (Winter Park, Fla.) 3(5), Oct 1984, 20-21;25.*
LEVEL: LANG: Eng SIRC ARTICLE NO: 098835

SAFETY

Bingham, B. Bingham, S. Lifelines you can trust. *Sail (Des Moines, Iowa) 15(3), Mar 1984, 82-87.*
LEVEL: B LANG: Eng SIRC ARTICLE NO: 098780

Caswell, C. Equipment '84. Taking safety personally: many crews are taking safety into their own hands and are making a practice of supplying their own emergency gear. *Yachting (New York) 155(1), Jan 1984, 89-91;165-166.*
LEVEL: B LANG: Eng SIRC ARTICLE NO: 095553

Harnden, T.S. Electrocution from powerline contact: it can happen to anyone. *Sail (Des Moines, Iowa) 15(3), Mar 1984, 78-81.*
LEVEL: B LANG: Eng SIRC ARTICLE NO: 098798

Jordan, D.J. Preventing capsize in breaking waves. *Sail (Boston) 15(9), Sept 1984, 72-75.*
LEVEL: B LANG: Eng SIRC ARTICLE NO: 105106

Man overboard: a retrieval system that works. *Practical sailor (Riverside, Conn.) 10(23), 1 Dec 1984, 12-14.*
LEVEL: B LANG: Eng SIRC ARTICLE NO: 103683

McCurdy, D. Second capsizing research progress report issued. *American sailor (Newport, R.I.) 9(7), Jul 1984, 1;3.*
LEVEL: LANG: Eng SIRC ARTICLE NO: 098811

SPORTING EVENTS

Blackaller, T. Why we lost the America's Cup. The author, who skippered Defender in the trials, says the U.S. had charted a fatal course before the races began. *Sports illustrated 60(11), 12 Mar 1984, 66-70;72-73;76-77;79-80.*
LEVEL: B LANG: Eng SIRC ARTICLE NO: 092614

Boyd, J. Hunter. D. Trials: Canada I and the 1983 America's Cup. Toronto: Macmillan of Canada, c1984. xiv, 330 p. : ill.
LEVEL: I LANG: Eng ISBN: 0-7715-9805-X LC CARD: C84-099001-4 GV830.1983 18086

Brown, B.C. Big boat series. (St. Francis Perpetual Trophy Regatta) *Yacht racing & cruising (Philadelphia, Pa.) 23(1), Jan 1984, 36-39.*
LEVEL: B LANG: Eng SIRC ARTICLE NO: 098784

Callahan, S. Adventure racing. (Transat TAG Quebec - St. Malo) *Canadian yachting, power & sail (Toronto) 9(7), Jul 1984, 26-27;29-32.*
LEVEL: B LANG: Eng SIRC ARTICLE NO: 103674

Fisher, B. Great yacht races. New York: Stewart, Tabori & Chang, c1984. 256 p. : ill.
NOTES: Includes index. Bibliography: p. 255.
LEVEL: I LANG: Eng ISBN: 0941434575 LC CARD: 84-000234 GV827 18095

Hollins, H. Racing Tall Ships. *Yachting world (London, Eng.) 136(2900), Apr 1984, 48-51;53.*
LEVEL: B LANG: Eng SIRC ARTICLE NO: 097069

Hundred Guinea Cup. (Canada's Cup) *Sailing Canada (Toronto) 6(7), Aug 1984, 6-8;10.*
LEVEL: B LANG: Eng SIRC ARTICLE NO: 103646

Kemp, B. Port Huron to Mackinac: the secret's out. *Sailing Canada (Toronto, Ont.) 6(8), Sept/Oct 1984, 26-27;29-31.*
LEVEL B LANG: Eng SIRC ARTICLE NO: 173226

Littlepage, D. Thunderbirds in flight: a return of the roost. *Yacht racing & cruising (Philadelphia, Pa.) 23(1), Jan 1984, 44-46.*
LEVEL: B LANG: Eng SIRC ARTICLE NO: 098805

Shute, N. Laser power: hanging it out on a small boat meant for the serious - minded sailor. *Outside 9(4), May 1984, 37-41;71-72.*
LEVEL: B LANG: Eng SIRC ARTICLE NO: 094079

Trimble, N. Thirty years of MORC: founded in 1954 by cost-conscious sailors on Long Island Sound, the Midget Ocean Racing Club has come of age. *Yachting (Los Angeles) 156(5), Nov 1984, 56-59;118.*
LEVEL: B LANG: Eng SIRC ARTICLE NO: 109042

Weston, V.L. Olympic sailors triumph. *Sailing Canada (Toronto, Ont.) 6(8), Sept/Oct 1984, 21-25.*
LEVEL: B LANG: Eng SIRC ARTICLE NO: 173225

SPORTSMANSHIP

Dellenbaugh, D. The issue of sportsmanship: reader survey results. *Yacht racing & cruising (Philadelphia, Pa.) 23(2), Feb 1984, 67-70.*
LEVEL: B LANG: Eng SIRC ARTICLE NO: 098790

STRATEGY

Baird, E. Grinding down the competition. *Sail boarder international (Dana Point, Calif.) 4(3), May 1984, 29;33.*
LEVEL: B LANG: Eng SIRC ARTICLE NO: 095546

Baird, E. Catching the boat ahead: grinding down the opposition requires concentration. *Sail (Des Moines, Iowa) 15(3), Mar 1984, 25-26;28-30.*
LEVEL: B LANG: Eng SIRC ARTICLE NO: 098776

Bell, M. Guay, S. Le pres: une allure technique. *Quebec yachting (Montreal) 6(8), dec 1983/janv 1984, 35.*
LEVEL: B LANG: SIRC ARTICLE NO: 095549

Benjamin, S. Ocean racing: lessons from the Admiral's Cup. *Sail (Boston, Mass.) 15(1), Jan 1984, 37-38;40;42.*
LEVEL: B LANG: Eng SIRC ARTICLE NO: 098779

Davidson, T. Sizing up the situation. *Yachts and yachting (Southend-on-Sea, Eng.) Late Feb 1984. 21-22.*
LEVEL: B LANG: En SIRC ARTICLE NO: 097063

Davison, T. Sizing up the situation. *Yachts and yachting (Southend-on-Sea, Eng.) 976, 29 Jun 1984, 15-16.*
LEVEL: B LANG: Eng SIRC ARTICLE NO: 101794

Davison, T. Sizing up the situation: Tim Davison ponders the eternal problem of which side of the beat will pay. *Yachts and yachting (Southend-on-sea, Eng.) 988, 15 Dec 1984, 53-54.*
LEVEL: B LANG: Eng SIRC ARTICLE NO: 107830

Davison, T. Sizing up the situation. (close reaching) *Yachts and yachting (Southend-on-sea, Eng.) 986, 16 Nov 1984, 43-48.*
LEVEL: B LANG: Eng SIRC ARTICLE NO: 107831

Isler, P. Winning in one-designs: strategy on the run. *Yacht racing & cruising (Philadelphia, Pa.) 23(7), Aug 1984, 44-46;49.*
LEVEL: B LANG: Eng SIRC ARTICLE NO: 101800

Isler, P. Tactics on the run. *Yacht racing & cruising (Philadelphia, Pa.) 23(8), Sept 1984, 50;54;56.*
LEVEL: B LANG: Eng SIRC ARTICLE NO: 103680

Jobson, G. The race course part 5: upwind sailing. *Yachting world (London, Eng.) 136(2901), May 1984, 59-61;63.*
LEVEL: B LANG: Eng SIRC ARTICLE NO: 097070

McKee, J. Winning in one-designs: speed on the run. *Yacht racing & cruising (Philadelphia) 23(6), Jun 1984, 37;39;41.*
LEVEL: B LANG: Eng SIRC ARTICLE NO: 097074

Miller, D. Tactics on the reaching leg... *Pacific yachting (Vancouver, B.C.) 25(12), Dec 1984, 20-21.*
LEVEL: B LANG: Eng SIRC ARTICLE NO: 173345

Perry, D. Everything you always wanted to know about finishing upwind. *Beam reach (Hawkesbury, Ont.) 19, Dec 1984, 4-6.*
LEVEL: B LANG: Eng SIRC ARTICLE NO: 105107

Tupper, S. Tactician's role critical to winning. *Pacific yachting (Vancouver, B.C.) 25(4), Apr 1984, 25-27.*
LEVEL: B LANG Eng SIRC ARTICLE NO: 098828

Walker, S. Port end starts - the conservative alternative. *Yacht racing & cruising (Philadelphia, Pa.) 23(4), Apr 1984, 18;22;26.*
LEVEL: B LANG: Eng SIRC ARTICLE NO: 098829

Walker, S. Port end starts - Part 11: the offense. *Yacht racing & cruising (Philadelphia, Pa.) 23(3), Mar 1984, 16;20;22.*
NOTES: Second part of a three-part series.
LEVEL: B LANG: Eng SIRC ARTICLE NO: 098831

Walker, S. The run that won the cup. *Yacht racing & cruising (Philadelphia, Pa.) 23(1), Jan 1984, 14;16-17.*
LEVEL: B LANG Eng SIRC ARTICLE NO: 098832

Walker, S. Tactics: windward leg strategy, part 1. *Yacht racing & cruising (Philadelphia, Pa.) 23(7), Aug 1984, 12;14.*
NOTES: First of a two-part series.
LEVEL: B LANG: Eng SIRC ARTICLE NO: 101833

Walker, S. Tactics: big vs. small fleets. *Yacht racing & cruising (Philadelphia, Pa.) 23(5), May 1984, 14;16-17.*
LEVEL: B LANG: Eng SIRC ARTICLE NO: 101834

Walker, S. Windward leg strategy: part 2. *Yacht racing & cruising (Philadelphia, Pa.) 23(8), Sept 1984, 10;14;18;20.*
LEVEL: B LANG: Eng SIRC ARTICLE NO: 103687

Walker, S. Conservatism in oscillating winds. *Yacht racing & cruising (Philadelphia, Pa.) 23(10), Nov 1984, 8;12.*
LEVEL: B LANG: Eng SIRC ARTICLE NO: 106260

Walker, S. Tactics: downwind strategy. *Yacht racing & cruising (Philadelphia, Pa.) 23(9), Oct 1984, 14;16;18.*
LEVEL: B LANG: Eng SIRC ARTICLE NO: 107903

Wefer, D. Winning in one-designs: frostbiting tips. *Yacht racing & cruising (Philadelphia, Pa.) 23(1), Jan 1984, 32;34.*
LEVEL: B LANG: Eng SIRC ARTICLE NO: 098833

YACHTING (continued)

TEACHING

Barta, E. Sailing 'The Annapolis Way': how to master the basic techniques for ocean, lake, and river, as taught at the Nation's Famous Sailing school. Harrisburg, Pa.: Stackpole Books, c1984. 1v.
LEVEL: B LANG: Eng ISBN: 0811722627 LC CARD: 84-000051

Robinson, B. Sail training: bound for better weather. *Sail (Des Moines, Iowa) 15(3), Mar 1984, 73-77.*
LEVEL: B LANG: Eng SIRC ARTICLE NO: 098816

TECHNIQUES AND SKILLS

Blackaller, T. The race course Part 8: helming technique. *Yachting world (London) 136(2904), Aug 1984, 78-80;82.*
LEVEL: B LANG: Eng SIRC ARTICLE NO: 098781

Brantley, D. Reefing pointers. When the wind's up, know how to reduce sail. *Sail (Des Moines, Iowa) 15(2), Feb 1984, 43-44;46.*
LEVEL: B LANG: Eng SIRC ARTICLE NO: 095550

Brantley, D. Learning from your mistakes. Five common problems. *Sail (Des Moines, Iowa) 15(4), Apr 1984, 25-26;28;30.*
LEVEL: B LANG: Eng SIRC ARTICLE NO: 095551

Brantley, D. Surfing and planing: speed sailing adds to your skills. *Sail (Boston, Mass.) 15(1), Jan 1984, 47-48;50.*
LEVEL: B LANG: Eng SIRC ARTICLE NO: 098783

Brantley, D. Docking under sail. *Sail (Boston, Ma.) 15(8), Aug 1984, 17-18;20;23-24.*
LEVEL: B LANG: Eng SIRC ARTICLE NO: 103673

Brownell, D. Roll tacking: when you have to get from one tack to the other, rolling is the quickest way to go... *Yacht racing & cruising (Philadelphia, Pa.) 23(10), Nov 1984, 52-54.*
LEVEL: B LANG: Eng SIRC ARTICLE NO: 106251

Cheret, B. Le jeu du vent et des voiles. *Neptune yachting (Neuilly/Seine, Cedex, France) 7, dec 1984, 98-101.*
NOTES: 7 em partie.
LEVEL: B LANG: Fr SIRC ARTICLE NO: 109123

Clegg, H. Dealing with eyes. (knot) *Sailing Canada (Toronto) 6(1), Jan/Feb 1984, 25-27.*
LEVEL: B LANG: Eng SIRC ARTICLE NO: 098786

Davison, T. Sizing up the situation. *Yacht and yachting (Southend-on-Sea, Essex) 5 Oct 1984, 31-32.*
LEVEL: B LANG: Eng SIRC ARTICLE NO: 109128

Fisher, G. Changing gears. (sail trim) *Yacht racing & cruising (Philadelphia, Pa.) 23(7), Aug 1984, 62-65.*
LEVEL: B LANG: Eng SIRC ARTICLE NO: 101795

Fowler, N. Basics of boat speed part IV. Preparation and tuning can tie all the boat speed elements into a single, winning package. *Yachting (New York) 155(1), Jan 1984, 68;70.*
LEVEL: B LANG: Eng SIRC ARTICLE NO: 095555

Fries, D. Successful Sunfish racing. Clinton Corners, N.Y.: John de Graff, Inc., 1984. xii, 147 p. : ill.
LEVEL: B LANG: En ISBN: 0-8286-0095-3 LC CARD: 83-72325 GV811.63.S94 20009

Hoffman, R. Getting off: the difference between a nudge on a sand bank and the loss of a boat may be as simple as one, two, three. Randy Hoffman looks at the steps involved in refloating a sailboat after grounding out. *Sailing Canada (Toronto) 6(1), Jan/Feb 1984, 58-61.*
LEVEL: B LANG: Eng SIRC ARTICLE NO: 098800

Holmes, R. Oh 'Chute: don't let the fear of spinnaker foul-ups prevent the exhilaration of heavy weather kite flying. *Sailing Canada (Toronto, Ont.) 6(9), Nov/Dec 1984, 13;15-17.*
LEVEL: B LANG: Eng SIRC ARTICLE NO: 173223

Isler, P. Steering big boats upwind: the art of sailing fast and pointing high - or is it a science? An analytical look from the helm of an offshore racer. *Yachting (New York) 156(2), Aug 1984, 45-46;48-49;109.*
LEVEL: B LANG: Eng SIRC ARTICLE NO: 101799

Jobson, G. The race course, part 6: downsailing. *Yachting world (Surrey, Eng.) 136(2902), Jun 1984, 83-85;87.*
NOTES: Second article of a series.
LEVEL: B LANG: Eng SIRC ARTICLE NO: 101801

MacLane, D. Multihulls: sailing with a wing. *Yacht racing & cruising (Philadelphia, Pa.) 23(5), May 1984, 26;28.*
LEVEL: B LANG: Eng SIRC ARTICLE NO: 101806

MacLeod, R. Graver, D. Sailing fundamentals. Marina del Rey, Calif.: America Sailing Association, c1984. vii, 112, (9) p. : ill.
NOTES: On cover: Official learn-to-sail manual of the American Sailing Association. Includes index. Bibliograhy: p. (6).
LEVEL: B LANG: Eng LC CARD: 84-195980

Martin-Raget, G. Technique habitables: a vos marques. *Yachting a voile (Paris) 86, aout/sept 1984, 67-68.*
LEVEL: B LANG: SIRC ARTICLE NO: 173367

Perry, D. Winning in one-designs. New York: Dodd, Mead, (1984). 1v.
NOTES: Includes index.
LEVEL: I LANG: Eng ISBN: 0396082009 LC CARD: 83-011583

Pfuntner, A. Mastering the mast maneuver. *Sail (Boston, Ma.) 15(8), Aug 1984, 27-28;31-32.*
LEVEL: B LANG: Eng SIRC ARTICL NO: 103684

Pilon, A. Le cercle navigable. *Quebec yachting (Dorval, Que.) 7(8), sept 1984, 12-13.*
LEVEL: B LANG: Fr SIRC ARTICLE NO: 173424

Roy, A. Laser: Canadian Laser Champion, Andy Roy explains his approach to preparation, boathandling and sail trim for this popular singlehander. *Yacht racing & cruising (Philadelphia, Pa.) 23(8), Sept 1984, 68-72.*
LEVEL: B LANG: Eng SIRC ARTICLE NO: 103685

Shute, N. Laser power: hanging it out on a small boat meant for the serious - minded sailor. *Outside 9(4), May 1984, 37-41;71-72.*
LEVEL: B LANG: Eng SIRC ARTICLE NO: 094079

Shute, N. Laser power: hanging it out on a small boat meant for the serious-minded sailor. *Outside (Chicago, Ill.) 9(4), Ma 1984, 37-41;71-72.*
LEVEL: B LANG: Eng SIRC ARTICLE NO: 101826

Tillman, D. Advanced techniques offwind: reaching. *Beam reach (Hawkesbury, Ont.) 19, Dec 1984, 10-11.*
LEVEL: B LANG: Eng SIRC ARTICLE NO: 105109

Toss, B. A turn around the cook's leg. (belaying) *Sail (Boston, Mass.) 15(6), Jun 1984, 80-81.*
LEVEL: B LANG: Eng SIRC ARTICLE NO: 101832

Walker, S. Tactics. Importance of stability. *Yacht racing & cruising (Philadelphia) 23(6), Jun 1984, 12;14.*
LEVEL: B LANG Eng SIRC ARTICLE NO: 097086

White, R. Multihulls: getting the right 'attitude'. *Yacht racing & cruising (Philadelphia, Pa.) 23(2), Feb 1984, 76;78.*
LEVEL: B LANG: Eng SIRC ARTICLE NO: 098834

TECHNIQUES AND SKILLS - START

deCamp, W. Curing recall mania: one sailor's solution for limiting time-wasting recalls on the starting line. *Yachting (New York) May 1984, 62;64;66.*
LEVEL: B LANG: Eng SIRC ARTICLE NO: 097064

Miller, D. Good starts win races. *Pacific yachting (Vancouver, B.C.) 25(3), Mar 1984, 27-29.*
LEVEL: B LANG: Eng SIRC ARTICLE NO: 098813

TRAINING AND CONDITIONING

Anderson, G. Fitness guidelines for Laser sailors. *Beam reach (Hawkesbury, Ont.) 19, Dec 1984, 8-9.*
LEVEL: B LANG: Eng SIRC ARTICLE NO: 105102

Cooper, D. Machine fit. *Yachting world (London, Eng.) 136(2900), Apr 1984, 64-65.*
LEVEL: B LANG: Eng SIRC ARTICLE NO: 097061

TRAINING AND CONDITIONING - DRILLS

Isler, P. Clinic drills. *Yacht racing & cruising (Philadelphia, Pa.) 23(1), Jan 1984, 47-49.*
LEVEL: B LANG: Eng SIRC ARTICLE NO: 098801

Legler, K. Bringing the best to the basics. *Sail (Boston, Mass.) 15(7), Jul 1984, 29-30;32;34.*
LEVEL: B LANG: Eng SIRC ARTICLE NO: 103681

TRAINING AND CONDITIONING - TRAINING CAMPS

Rice, C.J. Which sailing camp? Here are some things to consider when selecting one for your child. *Yachting (New York) 155(2), Feb 1984, 123124;126;128.*
LEVEL: B LANG: Eng SIRC ARTICLE NO: 095567

TRANSPORTATION

Burgess, R.F. Handbook of trailer sailing. New York: Dodd, Mead, 1984. 1 v.
LEVEL: B LANG: Eng ISBN: 039608303X LC CARD: 84-008007

YUGOSLAVIA

Berkovic, L. Olympism and physical education in Yugoslavia. *Bulletin of the Federation internationale d'education physique (Cheltenham, Eng.) 54(1), Jan/Mar 1984, 37-38.*
LEVEL: B LANG: Eng SIRC ARTICLE NO: 094505

INDEX EN FRANÇAIS

Acrobatie, 1
Acrobatie au sol, 499
Administration, 1-4
Afrique, 6
Afrique du sud, 458
Aiki-do, 8
Allemagne, 168
Alpinisme, 274-276
Angleterre, 144
Anneaux (gymnastique), 183
Anthropologie, 12
Anthropométrie, 12-17
Antigua, 17
Antilles, 514
Art, 19
Arts martiaux, 251-254
Associations, 19-20
Athlétisme, 490-492
Athlétisme—lancer, 492-493
Athlétisme—sauts, 492
Attelage, 137-138
Australie, 20-21
Aviron, 418-421
Badminton, 23-24
Balle au mur, 185
Balle-molle, 456-458
Ballet, 24-25
Ballet jazz, 232
Ballon dirigeable, 25
Ballon sur glace, 62
Bandy, 25
Barre fixe (gymnastique), 183
Barres asymétriques (gymnastique), 184
Barres parallèles (gymnastique), 183
Baseball, 25-33
Basket-ball, 33-42
Bateau, 56-57
Biathlon, 42
Bicyclette, 43-44
Bicyclette et cyclisme, 44-47
Billard et pool, 47-48
Biographie et autobiographie, 48
Biomécanique, 48-52
Blessures et accidents, 204-228
Bobsled, 57
Boccie, 57
Boomerang, 60
Boulingrin, 242-243
Boxe, 60-62
Boxe française, 237
Brésil, 62
Bulgarie, 63
Camping, 63-64
Camping—hiver, 514
Canada, 64-66
Canotage, 66-68
Carrières dans le sport, 282
Cerf-volant, 239
Cheval d'arçons (gymnastique), 183
Chili, 75
Cinésiologie, 237-238
Cinésiologie—interactions structurales, 238-239
Claque, 68
Clubs, 75
Concours complet (sport équestre), 489
Condition physique, 322-328
Condition physique—au travail, 328-330
Condition physique—programmes et activités, 330-333
Condition physique—testing, 333-335
Côte d'Ivoire, 231
Cotswold Games, 83
Course, 423-434
Course—cross-country, 86-87

Course automobile, 21-22
Course d'orientation, 291
Course de boîtes à savon, 446
Course de fond et de demi-fond, 262-269
Course de haies, 202-203
Course de relais, 415
Course de vitesse, 460-463
Courses de traîneaux à chiens, 445
Cricket, 83-86
Croissance et développement, 178
Crosse, 240
Cuba, 89
Culturisme, 57-60
Curling, 89-90
Cyclisme, 90-93
Cyclisme—course sur piste, 95
Cyclisme—course sur route, 93-95
Cyclisme sur parcours accidenté, 86
Cyclocross et bi-cross, 95
Cyclotourisme, 42-43
Danemark, 98
Danse, 96-98
Danse aérobique, 4-6
Danse carrée, 463
Danse du ventre, 42
Danse folklorique, 156-157
Danse moderne, 269-270
Décathlon, 98
Déficience mentale, 105-106
Deltaplane, 185-187
Dressage, 136-137
Drogues et doping, 138-142
Dynamophilie, 399-400
Economie et finance, 142-143
Écosse, 437
Education en plein air, 291-292
Education physique, 306-322
Education sanitaire, 188-190
Egypte, 143
Enfance et adolescence, 68-75
Entraînement, 76-80
Entraînement et conditionnement, 493
Équipement, 144-146
Équitation, 199-202
Équitation western, 514
Ergogènes, 146
Escalade, 417
Escrime, 151-153
États-Unis d'Amérique, 504-505
Europe, 146
Excursion sac-au-dos, 22-23
Exercices au sol (gymnastique), 183
Femmes, 515-523
Fers à cheval, 202
Festivals, 153
Finlande, 156
Fléchettes, 98
Football, 157-167; 446-452
Football au drapeau, 156
Football australien, 21
Football canadien, 66
Football gaélique, 167
Football-toucher, 489
France, 167
Frisbee, 167
Golf, 171-177
Grande-Bretagne, 177-178
Gymnastique, 178-183
Gymnastique rhythmique moderne, 270
Haltérophilie, 511-513
Haltérophilie et culturisme, 513-514
Handball olympique, 476
Heptathlon, 190
Highland Games, 191
Hippisme, 196-199
Histoire, 191-192

Hockey, 192-196
Hockey sur gazon, 153-154
Hockey sur patins à roulettes, 417
Hockey sur plancher, 156
Humour et satire, 202
Inde, 203
Indonésie, 204
Installations, 146-151
Instituts de sport, 460
Iraq, 231
Jai-alai, 231
Japon, 231
Jeu à dix quilles, 487-488
Jeux, 168
Jeux d'équipe, 476-477
Jeux de boules, 60
Jeux de hasard, 167-168
Jeux de l'Asie, 19
Jeux du Commonwealth, 83
Jeux du Québec, 232
Jeux olympiques, 283-291
Jeux olympiques spéciaux, 458
Judo, 232
Jui-jitsu, 232
Karate, 232-235
Karting, 171
Kayak, 235-236
Kendo, 237
Kung-fu, 239-240
Lancer de disque, 106-107
Lancer de javelot, 231-232
Lancer de marteau, 184
Lancer de poids, 440
Littérature, 243-244
Loi et législation, 240-242
Luge, 244
Lutte, 523-527
Maladies et troubles, 107-134
Marathon et ultramarathon, 245-251
Marche, 410-411
Médecine, 255-262
Média, 254-255
Méthodes d'entraînement, 493-497
Mini-trampoline, 269
Motocross, 270-272
Motocyclisme, 272-274
Motonautisme, 272
Motoneige, 446
Nage de vitesse, 460
Nage synchronisée, 474
Natation, 465-473
Natation—distance, 134
Natation—groupe d'âge, 6
Netball, 276-277
Neuro-endocrinologie, 277-278
Niger, 278
Nouvelle-Zélande, 278
Nutrition, 278-282
Officiels, 282-283
Ouvrages de référence, 414-415
Paddle-ball, 293
Parachutisme, 293-295
Participation, 295
Patin à roulettes, 417-418
Patinage, 441
Patinage artistique, 155-156
Patinage de vitesse, 459
Pays-Bas, 277
Pentathlon, 295
Pentathlon moderne, 270
Personnes âgées, 6-8
Personnes handicapées, 98-105
Pétanque, 305
Philatélie, 305
Philosophie, 305-306
Photographie, 306

Physiologie, 339-344
Physiologie—exercice, 366-371
Physiologie—facteurs influençant la
  performance, 371-381
Physiologie—métabolisme de l'énergie, 352-366
Physiologie—muscle, 381-389
Physiologie—neurale, 389-390
Physiologie—thermorégulation, 394-395
Physiologie cardiovasculaire, 344-352
Physiologie pulmonaire, 390-394
Physiothérapie, 335-339
Planche à voile, 52-56
Plongée libre, 445-446
Plongée sous-marine, 500-504
Plongeon, 134-136
Politique et gouvernement, 396-398
Polo, 398
Polynésie, 398
Poutre d'équilibre (gymnastique), 183
Processus moteurs perceptuels, 296-305
Psychologie, 400-410
Psychologie—anomalies, 1
Psychologie sociale, 452-453
Psychophysiologie, 410
Racquetball, 411-414
Radeau, 414
Randonnée d'endurance (équitation), 143-144
Raquette, 446
Recherche et méthodes de recherche, 416
Recherche historique et historiographie, 191
Religion, 416
République démocratique allemande, 168
République fédérale allemande, 151
République populaire de Chine, 295
Ringette, 416-417
Rodéo, 417
Roumanie, 423
Rugby, 421-423
Santé et hygiène, 187-188
Saut à la perche, 395-396
Saut d'obstacles (sport équestre), 440-441
Saut de cheval (gymnastique), 184
Saut en hauteur, 190-191
Saut en longueur, 244
Saut en ski, 442
Sauvetage, 243
Scandinavie, 434
Sciences sociales, 453
Singapour, 441
Skeet, 441-442
Ski, 442-445
Ski—slalom, 445
Ski—style libre, 167
Ski alpin, 8-12
Ski de descente, 136
Ski de fond, 87-89
Ski nautique, 508-511
Soccer, 446-452
Sociologie, 453-456
Soigneur, 20
Somalie, 458
Souvenirs, 262
Spéléologie, 459-460
Sport de maîtres, 255
Sport équestre, 144
Sport équestre—cross, 86
Sport scolaire, 434-437
Sports aéronautiques, 6
Sports aquatiques, 17
Sports d'hiver, 514
Sports de combat, 83
Sports de raquette, 411
Sports en bateau, 57
Sports et activités de plein-air, 292-293
Sports intramuraux, 228-231
Sports sur glace, 203
Sports universitaires et collégiaux, 80-83

Squash-racquets, 463-464
Steeple, 464
Steeplechase (hippisme), 199
Suède, 465
Suisse, 474
Surf, 464-465
Survie en régions désertes, 514
Taekwon-do, 475
Tai-chi-chuan, 475-476
Tchécoslovaquie, 96
Temples de la renommée et musées, 184
Tennis, 477-487
Tennis de table, 474-475
Testing et mesure, 488-489
Thaïlande, 489
Tir, 437-439
Tir à l'arc, 17-19
Tir à l'arc—tir en campagne, 153
Tir au pigeon d'argile, 497
Tir au poignet, 19
Toboggan, 489
Trampoline, 497
Triathlon, 497-498
Triple saut, 499
Trot attelé, 187
Union soviétique, 458
Universiades, 523
Vêtements, 75
Voile, 527-534
Voile sur glace, 203
Vol, 156
Vol en avion ultraléger, 499-500
Vol plané et vol à voile, 168-171
Volleyball, 505-507
Water polo, 507-508
Wu shu, 527
Yugoslavie, 534

INDICE EN ESPAÑOL

Acampado, 63-64
Acampado de invierno, 514
Acrobacia, 1
Administración, 1-4
Africa, 6
Africa del Sur, 458
Aikido, 8
Alemania, 168
Alpinismo, 274-276; 417
Anillas (gimnasia), 183
Antigua, 17
Antropología, 12
Antropometria, 12-17
Aptitud física, 322-328
Aptitud física—empleados, 328-330
Arbitraje, 282-283
Arte, 19
Artes marciales, 251-254
Ascensión en globo, 25
Asociaciones, 19-20
Athletic trainer, 20
Atletismo, 490-492
Atletismo—pruebas de lanzamiento, 492-493
Australia, 20-21
Badminton, 23-24
Baile de jazz, 232
Baile moderno, 269-270
Baile popular, 156-157
Ballet, 24-25
Balon escoba, 62
Baloncesto, 33-42
Balonmano, 185

Balonmano por equipos, 476
Bandy, 25
Barra de equilibrio (gimnasia), 183
Barra fija (gimnasia), 183
Béisbol, 25-33
Béisbol de pelota blanda, 456-458
Biatlón, 42
Billares, 47-48
Biografía y autobiografía, 48
Biomecánica, 48-52
Boardsailing, 52-56
Boliche de 10 bolos, 487-488
Bolos sobre pasto, 242-243
Boxeo, 60-62
Boxeo de pines y manos, 237
Brasil, 62
Brujulismo, 291
Bulgaria, 63
Canada, 64-66
Carrera, 423-434
Carrera a campo traviesa, 86-87
Carrera ciclista en carretera, 93-95
Carrera ciclista en pista, 95
Carrera de caballos, 196-199
Carrera de marcha, 410-411
Carrera de media y larga distancia, 262-269
Carrera de obstáculos, 464
Carrera de relevos, 415
Carrera de vallas, 202-203
Carrera de velocidad, 460-463
Carreras de automóviles, 21-22
Carreras de cajones con ruedas, 446
Carreras de mini-automóviles, 171
Carreras de motonieves, 446
Carreras de obstáculos (equitación), 199
Carreras de trineos, 57
Carreras de trineos con perros, 445
Carreras de trotones, 187
Checoslavaquia, 96
Cheerleading, 68
Chile, 75
Ciclismo, 43-44; 44-47; 90-93
Ciclismo—cyclo-cross y bicycle moto-cross, 95
Ciclismo a campo traviesa, 86
Ciencias sociales, 453
Clubes, 75
Concurso completo de equitación, 489
Conduccion de carruajes, 137-138
Contradanza, 463
Costa del Marfil, 231
Crecimiento y desarrollo, 178
Criquet, 83-86
Cuba, 89
Curling, 89-90
Danza, 96-98
Danza aerobica, 4-6
Danza oriental, 42
Dardos, 98
Decatlón, 98
Deporte ecuestre, 144
Deportes acuáticos, 17
Deportes aeronauticos, 6
Deportes de bolos, 60
Deportes de combate, 83
Deportes de equipo, 476-477
Deportes de invierno, 514
Deportes de raqueta, 411
Deportes de veteranos, 255
Deportes escolares, 434-437
Deportes intramuros, 228-231
Deportes sobre hielo, 203
Deportes universitarios, 80-83
Deportes y actividades al aire libre, 292-293
Desarrollo muscular, 57-60
Descenso en tobogan, 489
Descenso sobre esquís, 136
Desliz amiento en luge, 244

Dinamarca, 98
Doma, 136-137
Economía y finanzas, 142-143
Educación física, 306-322
Egipto, 143
Ejercicios con mini-tramplín, 269
Ejercicios sobre pista (gimnasia), 183
Enfermedades y desórdenes, 107-134
Enseñanza al aire libre, 291-292
Enseñanza sanitaria, 188-190
Entrenamiento atlético, 20
Entrenamiento y preparación, 493
Entrenar, 76-80
Equipo, 144-146
Equitación, 199-202
Equitación de resistencia, 143-144
Equitación en campo, 86
Ergogenic aids, 146
Escandinavia, 434
Escocia, 437
Esgrima, 151-153
Espeleologia, 459-460
Esquí, 442-445
Esquí a campo traviesa, 87-89
Esquí acuático, 508-511
Esquí alpino, 8-12
Esquí estilo libre, 167
Estados Unidos de América, 504-505
Europa, 146
Excursionismo en bicicleta, 42-43
Festivales, 153
Filatelia, 305
Filosofía, 305-306
Finlandia, 156
Fisiología, 339-344
Fisiología—cardiovascular, 344-352
Fisiología—ejercicio, 366-371
Fisiología—factores que afectan el rendimiento, 371-381
Fisiología—metabolismo de la energía, 352-366
Fisiología—muscular, 381-389
Fisiología—pulmonar, 390-394
Fisiología—termoregulación, 394-395
Fisioterapia, 335-339
Fotografia, 306
Francia, 167
Fútbol, 157-167; 446-452
Fútbol australiano, 21
Fútbol canadiense, 66
Fútbol de pañuelo, 156
Fútbol de toque, 489
Fútbol galés, 167
Galerías y museos, 184
Gimnasia, 178-183
Gimnasia rítmica moderna, 270
Golf, 171-177
Gran Bretaña, 177-178
Heptatlón, 190
Heridas y accidentes, 204-228
Highland Games, 191
Historia, 191-192
Hockey, 192-196
Hockey—patin de ruedas, 417
Hockey con aro, 416-417
Hockey de salón, 156
Hockey sobre hierba, 153-154
Humor y sátira, 202
India, 203
Indias Occidentales, 514
Indonesia, 204
Inglaterra, 144
Instalaciones, 146-151
Institutos de deportes, 460
Investigación histórica e historiografía, 191
Investigación y métodos investigativos, 416
Iraq, 231
Jai alai, 231

Japón, 231
Jeux du Québec, 232
Ju jitsu, 232
Judo, 232
Juego de azar, 167-168
Juego de bochas, 57
Juegos, 168
Juegos Asiáticos, 19
Juegos Cotswold, 83
Juegos de la Commonwealth, 83
Juegos de Quebec, 232
Juegos Olímpicos, 283-291
Juegos Olímpicos Especiales, 458
Karate, 233-235
Kayak, 235-236
Kendo, 237
Kinesiología, 237-238
Kinesiología—anatomía funcional, 238-239
Kung fu, 239-240
Lacrosse, 240
Lanzamiento de bumerang, 60
Lanzamiento de disco, 106-107
Lazamiento de disco volante, 167
Lazamiento de herradura, 202
Lanzamiento de jabalina, 231-232
Lanzamiento de martillo, 184
Lanzamiento del peso, 440
Levantamiento de pesas, 511-513
Levantamiento de peso y desarrollo muscular, 513-514
Leyes y legislación, 240-242
Literatura, 243-244
Lucha libre, 523-527
Maratón, 245-251
Marcha con raquetas sobre nieve, 446
Medicina, 20; 255-262
Métodos de entrenamiento, 493-497
Minusválidos, 98-106
Monta estilo oeste, 514
Montañismo, 22-23
Motociclismo, 272-274
Motociclismo—motocross, 270-272
Mujeres, 515-523
Narcoticos y drogadictos, 138-142
Natación, 465-473
Natación con tubo respiratorio, 445-446
Natación de fondo, 134
Natación de velocidad, 460
Natación en Grupo, 6
Natación sincronizada, 474
Navegación a vela, 527-534
Navegación a vela sobre hielo, 203
Navegación de recreo, 56-57
Navegación deportiva, 57
Navegación en lancha a motor, 272
Netball, 276-277
Neuroendocrinología, 277-278
Neurofisiología, 389-390
Niger, 278
Niños y adolescentes, 68-75
Nueva Zelandia, 278
Nutrición, 278-282
Obras de referencia, 414-415
Paddleball, 293
Paises bajos, 277
Paracaidismo, 293-295
Paralelas (gimnasia), 183
Paralelas asimétricas (gimnasia), 184
Participación, 295
Patinaje, 441
Patinaje artistico, 155-156
Patinaje de fondo, 459
Patinaje de ruedas, 417-418
Pelota a raqueta, 411-414
Pentatlón, 295
Pentatlón moderno, 270
Petanca, 305

Piragüismo, 66-68
Planeo colgado, 185-187
Planeo y vuelo a vela, 168-171
Polinesia, 398
Política y gobierno, 396-398
Polo, 398
Polo acuático, 507-508
Pontón, 414
Potro con arzón (gimnasia), 183
Powerlifting, 399-400
Prendas de vestido, 75
Prensa, 254-255
Procesos motores de la percepción, 296-305
Profesiones deportivas, 282
Programas y actividades de aptitud física, 330-333
Pruebas de aptitud física, 333-335
Pruebas y medidas, 488-489
Pulso y lucha de brazo, 19
Raquetas de squash, 463-464
Recuerdos, 262
Religión, 416
Remo, 418-421
República Democrática Alemana, 168
República Federal Alemana, 151
República Popular China, 295
Retraso mental, 105-106
Rodeo, 417
Rugby, 421-423
Rumania, 423
Salto (gimnasia), 184
Salto con esquis, 442
Salto con pértiga, 395-396
Salto con trampolín, 497
Salto de altura, 190-191
Salto de longitud, 244
Salto de obstáculos (equitación), 440-441
Saltos, 134-136
Saltos de atletismo, 492
Saltos de palanca, 500-504
Salud e higiene, 187-188
Salvamento, 243
Sicofisiología, 410
Sicologia, 400-410
Sicología de subnormales, 1
Sicología social, 452-453
Singapur, 441
Slalon (esquí), 445
Sociología, 453-456
Somalia, 458
Suecia, 465
Suiza, 474
Supervivencia en la selva, 514
Surfing, 464-465
Tae kwon do, 475
Tai chi chuan, 475-476
Tailandia, 489
Tenis, 477-487
Tenis de mesa, 474-475
Tiro, 437-439
Tiro al arco, 17-19
Tiro al plato, 441-442
Tiro con arco en campo abierto, 153
Tiro de pichon, 497
Triatlón, 497-498
Triple salto, 499
Unión Soviética, 458
Universiada, 523
Viejo, 6-8
Vitorear, 68
Voleibol, 505-507
Volteo, 499
Vuelo, 156
Vuelo con máquinas ultraligeras, 499-500
Vuelo de cometas, 239
Wu shu, 527
Yugoslavia, 534

DEUTSCHES INHALTSVERZEICHNIS

Abfahrtslauf, 136
Ägypten, 143
Aerobic, 4-6
Afrika, 6
Aikido, 8
Akrobatik, 1
Alpiner Skilauf, 8-12
Altersgruppenprogramm (Schwimmen), 6
Alterssport, 6-8
Amerikanischer Fußball, 157-167
Amtieren, 282-283
Andenken, 262
Anthropologie, 12
Anthropometrie, 12-17
Antigua, 17
Arbeitnehmerfitneß, 328-330
Arm wrestling und Wrist wrestling, 19
Asiatische Spiele, 19
Athletic trainer, 20
Ausdauerreiten, 143
Ausrüstung, 144-146
Australien, 20-21
Australischer Fußball, 21
Automobilrennen, 21-22
Badminton, 23-24
Bahnrennsport (Radsport), 95
Ballett, 24-25
Bandy, 25
Barren (Turnen), 183
Baseball, 25-33
Basketball, 33-42
Bauchtanz, 42
Behindertensport, 98-105
Bergsteigen, 274-276
Berufe im Sportbereich, 282
Biathlon, 42
Billard und Pool, 47-48
Biographie und Autobiographie, 48
Biomechanik, 48-52
Bobsport, 57
Boccia, 57
Bodenturnen, 183; 499
Bogenschießen, 17-19
Bootfahren, 56-57
Bootssportarten, 57
Bowling, 487-488
Bowlingsportarten, 60
Boxen, 60-62
Brasilien, 62
Broomball, 62
Bulgarien, 63
Bumerangwerfen, 60
Bundesrepublik Deutschland, 151
Camping, 63-64
Cheerleading, 68
Chile, 75
Commonwealth-Spiele, 83
Cotswold Games, 83
Curling, 89-90
Cyclo-cross und Bicycle moto-cross, 95
Dänemark, 98
Darts, 98
Deutsche Demokratische Republik, 168
Deutschland, 168
Diskuswerfen, 106-107
Drachenfliegen, 185-187
Dreisprung, 499
Dressurreiten, 136-137
Driving (Pferdesport), 137-138
Eishockey, 192-196
Eiskunstlauf, 155-156
Eislaufen, 441
Eisschnellauf, 459

Eissegeln, 203
Eissportarten, 203
Elfenbeinküste, 231
England, 144
Ergogenic aids, 146
Ernährung, 278-282
Europa, 146
Fahrradfahren, 43-44
Fahrradfahren und Radsport, 44-47
Fallschirmsport, 293-295
Fechten, 151-153
Feldbogenschießen, 153
Feldhockey, 153-154
Feste und Festspiele, 153
Finnland, 156
Fitneß, 322-328; 328-330
Fitneß—Programme und Betätigungen, 330-333
Fitneß—Testing, 333-335
Flag football, 156
Flugsport, 156
Forschung und Forschungsmethoden, 416
Frankreich, 167
Frauen und Sport, 515-523
Freiballonsport, 25
Freiluftsportarten und Betätigungen, 292-293
Freistilskilauf, 167
Frisbeewerfen, 167
Fünfkampf, 295
Fußball, 446-452
Gälischer Fußball, 167
Gehen, 410-411
Geländelauf, 86-87
Geländeritt, 86
Geschichte, 191-192
Gesetz und Gesetzgebung, 240-242
Gesundheit und Hygiene, 187-188
Gesundheitsaufklärung, 188-190
Gewichtheben, 511-513
Gewichtheben und Körperkulturistik, 513-514
Golf, 171-177
Großbritannien, 177-178
Hallenhockey, 156
Hammerwerfen, 184
Handball, 476
Handball (Zweikampfsportart), 185
Highland Games, 191
Hindernislauf (Leichtathletik), 464
Hindernisrennen (Pferderennen), 199
Historische Forschung und
    Geschichtsschreibung, 191
Hochsprung, 190-191
Horseshoe pitching, 202
Hürdenlauf, 202-203
Humor und Satire, 202
Indien, 203
Indonesien, 204
Intramural sports, 228-231
Irak, 231
Jai Alai, 231
Japan, 231
Jazztanz, 232
Jeux du Québec, 232
Judo, 232
Jugoslawien, 534
Jui-Jitsu, 232
Kajaksport, 235-236
Kampfsportarten, 83
Kanada, 64-66
Kanadischer Fußball, 66
Kanusport, 66-68
Karate, 233-235
Karting, 171
Kendo, 237
Kickboxing, 237
Kinder und Jugendliche, 68-75
Kinesiologie, 237-238

Kinesiologie—Funktionelle Anatomie, 238-239
Kiteflying, 239
Kleidung, 75
Klettern, 417
Körperkulturistik, 57-60
Korbball, 276-277
Krankheiten und Störungen, 107-134
Kricket, 83-86
Kuba, 89
Kugelstoßen, 440
Kung-fu, 239-240
Kunst, 19
Kurzstreckenlaufen, 460-463
Kurzstreckenschwimmen, 460
Lacrosse, 240
Langlauf, 87-89
Langstreckenschwimmen, 134
Laufen, 423-434
Lawn bowling, 242-243
Leibesübungen, 306-322
Leichtathletik, 490-492
Literatur, 243-244
Lungenphysiologie, 390-394
Mannschaftsspiele, 476-477
Marathonlauf und Ultramarathonlauf, 245-251
Massenmedien, 254-255
Medikamente und Doping, 138-142
Medizin, 20; 255-262
Mini-Trampolinturnen, 269
Mittelstreckenlauf und Langstreckenlauf, 262-269
Modern dance, 269-270
Moderne rhythmische Gymnastik, 270
Moderner Fünfkampf, 270
Motorbootsport, 272
Motorflugsportarten, 6
Motorradsport, 272-274
Motorradsport—Moto-Cross, 270-272
Muskelphysiologie, 381-389
Nachschlagewerke, 414-415
Nervenphysiologie, 389-390
Neuroendokrinologie, 277-278
Neuseeland, 278
Niederlande, 277
Niger, 278
Olympische Spiele, 283-291
Orientierungslauf, 291
Outdoor education, 291-292
Paddleball, 293
Pathologische Psychologie, 1
Perzeptionsmotorik, 296-305
Petanque, 305
Pferderennen, 196-199
Pferdesportarten, 144
Philatelie, 305
Philosophie, 305-306
Photographie, 306
Physiologie, 339-344
Physiologie—Energiestoffwechsel, 352-366
Physiologie—Faktoren welche die Leistung
    beeinflussen, 371-381
Physiologie—Kardiovaskulär, 344-352
Physiologie—Leibesübungen, 366-371
Physiologie—Wärmeregulation, 394-395
Physiotherapie, 335-339
Politik und Regierung, 396-398
Polo, 398
Polynesien, 398
Powerlifting, 399-400
Psychologie, 400-410
Psychophysiologie, 410
Querfeldeinrennen, 86
Racquet sports, 411
Racquetball, 411-414
Radsport, 90-93
Radwandern, 42-43
Rafting, 414

Reckturnen, 183
Reiten—Westernreiten, 514
Reiten und Reitkunst, 199-202
Religion, 416
Rennschlittensport, 244
Retardierung, 105-106
Rettungsschwimmen, 243
Ringen, 523-527
Ringette, 416-417
Ringeturnen, 183
Rodeln, 489
Rodeo, 417
Rollhockey, 417
Rollschuhlaufen, 417-418
Rudern, 418-421
Rugby, 421-423
Ruhmeshallen und Museen, 184
Rumänien, 423
Schießsport, 437-439
Schlittenhunderennen, 445
Schneemobilfahren, 446
Schneeschuhwandern, 446
Schnorcheln, 445-446
Schottland, 437
Schulsport, 434-437
Schwebebalken (Turnen), 183
Schweden, 465
Schweiz, 474
Schwimmen, 465-473
Segelfliegen, 168-171
Segeln, 527-534
Seifenkistenrennen, 446
Seitpferd, 183
Selbstverteidigungssportarten, 251-254
Seniorensport, 255
Siebenkampf, 190
Singapur, 441
Skandinavien, 434
Skeetschießen, 441-442
Skilaufen, 442-445
Skispringen, 442
Slalom (Skisport), 445
Softball, 456-458
Somalia, 458
Sowjetunion, 458
Sozialpsychologie, 452-453
Sozialwissenschaft, 453
Soziologie, 453-456
Special Olympics, 458
Speerwerfen, 231-232
Speläologie, 459-460
Spiele, 168
Spiele und Wetten, 167-168
Sportinstitute, 460
Sportstätten, 146-151
Springen (Leichtathletik), 492
Springreiten, 440-441
Square-Dance, 463
Squash racquets, 463-464
Stabhochsprung, 395-396
Staffellauf, 415
Straßenrennsport (Radsport), 93-95
Stufenbarren, 184
Südafrika, 458
Synchronschwimmen, 474
Taekwon-Do, 475
Tai chi chuan, 475-476
Tanz, 96-98
Tauchsport, 500-504
Teilnahme, 295
Tennis, 477-487
Testen und Messungen, 488-489
Thailand, 489
Tischtennis, 474-475
Touch football, 489
Trabrennen, 187

Trainieren, 493
Trainingslehre, 76-80
Trainingsmethoden, 493-497
Trampolinturnen, 497
Triathlon, 497-498
Tschechoslowakei, 96
Turnen, 178-183
Überlebensschulung (Wildnis), 514
Ultralight flying, 499-500
Universiaden, 523
Universitätssport, 80-83
Verbände, 19-20
Vereine, 75
Vereinigten Staaten, 504-505
Verletzungen und Unfälle, 204-228
Verwaltung, 1-4
Vielseitigkeitsprüfung, 489
Volksrepublik China, 295
Volkstanz, 156-157
Volleyball, 505-507
Voltigieren (Turnen), 184
Wachstum und Entwicklung, 178
Wandern, 22-23
Wasserball, 507-508
Wasserskilaufen, 508-511
Wassersportarten, 17
Wasserspringen, 134-136
Weitsprung, 244
Wellenreiten, 464-465
Werfen (Leichtathletik), 492-493
Westindische Inseln, 514
Windsurfing, 52-56
Winter camping, 514
Wintersportarten, 514
Wirtschaft und Finanz, 142-143
Wu shu, 527
Wurftaubenschießen, 497
Zehnkampf, 98

РУССКИЙ УКАЗАТЕЛЬ

Австралийский Футбол, 21
Австралия, 20-21
Автомобильные гонки, 21-22
Администрация, 1-4
Азартные игры, 167-168
Азиатские игры, 19
Аики-до, 8
Акробатика, 1; 499
Альпинизм, 274-276
Американский Футбол, 157-167
Англия, 144
Антигва, 17
Антропология, 12
Антропометрия, 12-17
Ассоциации, 19-20
Африка, 6
Аэробическая гимнастика, 4-6
Аэросани, 446
Бадминтон, 23-24
Балет, 24-25
Бальные танцы, 232
Баскетбол, 33-42
Барьерный бег, 202-203
Бег, 423-434
Бег на средние и длинные дистанции, 262-269
Бег по пересечённой местности, 86-87
Бег с препятствиями, 464
Бейсбол, 25-33
Берег слоновой кости, 231
Биатлон, 42

Биллиард, 47-48
Биография и автобиография, 48
Биомеханика, 48-52
Бобслей, 57
Бодибилдинг, 57-60
Бокс, 60-62
Болезни и расстройства, 107-134
Болгария, 63
Борьба, 523-527
Борьба рук и борьба кистей, 19
Бочи, 57
Бразилия, 62
Бревно, 183
Брусья параллельные, 183
Брусья параллельные, разной высоты, 184
Буерный спорт, 203
Бумеранг, 60
Великобритания, 177-178
Велосипедный спорт, 44-47
Велосипедные гонки, 93-95
Велосипедные гонки на треке, 95
Велокросс, 95
Велоспорт, 43-44; 90-93
Велотуризм, 42-43
Верховая езда в западом стиле, 514
Верховая езда—длинные дистанции, 143-144
Верховая езда и искусство верховой езды, 199-202
Вест—Индия, 514
Виды спорта на открытом воздухе, 292-293
Виды спорта с ракеткой, 411
Воздушные змеи, 239
Воздушный шар, 25
Всеобщие игры, 83
Водное поло, 507-508
Водные виды спорта, 17
Водные лыжи, 508-511
Военизированные виды спорта, 251-254
Волейбол, 505-507
Вольная гимнастика, 183
Воспринимаемые мото процессы, 296-305
Восьмиборье, 190
Ву-схху, 527
Выездка, 136-137
Выживание в дикой местности, 514
Гаэльский футбол, 167
Германия, 168
Германская Демократическая Республика, 168
Гимнастика, 178-183
Гольф, 171-177
Гонки «соупбокс», 446
Горнолыжый спорт, 8-12
Гребля, 418-421
Дания, 98
Дельта-планеризм, 185-187
Десятиборье, 98
Дети и юношество, 68-75
Джаи-алаи, 231
Джиу-джица, 232
Дзю-до, 232
Доска с парусом, 52-56
Достопамятность, 262
Европа, 146
Египет, 143
Езда на велосипеде по пересечённой местности, 86
Езда по пересечённой местности, 86
Женщины, 515-523
Закон и законодательство, 240-242
Залы славы и музеи, 184
Здоровье и гигиена, 187-188
Здравоохранение, 188-190
Зимние виды спорта, 514
Зимние туристские походы, 514

Игра в мяч на льду, 62
Игра в мяч с сеткой, 276-277
Игры, 168
Игры «Котсволд», 83
Игры нагорья, 191
Инвалиды, 98-106
Индия, 203
Индонезия, 204
Ирак, 231
Искусство, 19
Исследование и методы исследования, 416
История, 191-192
Исторические исследования и
   историография, 191
Канада, 64-66
Канадский футбол, 66
Каноэ, 66-68
Карате, 233-235
Картинг, 171
Катание на лодках, 56-57
Катание на роликовых коньках, 417-418
Каякинг, 235-236
Кегли, 60
Кегли на траве, 242-243
Кегли с десятью фигурами, 487-488
Кемпинг, 63-64
Кендо, 237
Кикбоксинг, 237
Кинециология, 237-238
Кинециология—функциональная
   анатомия, 238-239
Китайская Народная Республика, 295
Клубы, 75
Кольца (гимнастика), 183
Командные состязания, 476-477
Конный спорт, 137-138; 144
Конь с ручками (гимнастика), 183
Коньки, 441
Корейская борьба, 475
Крикет, 83-86
Куба, 89
Кунг-фу, 239-240
Кэрлинг, 89-90
Лакросс, 240
Легкая атлетика, 490-492
Легкая атлетика—соревнования по
   прыжкам, 492
Литература, 243-244
Лодочные виды спорта, 57
Лудж, 244
Лыжный спорт, 442-445
Лыжные гонки, 87-89
Малый трамплин, 269
Марафон и ультрамарафон, 245-251
Медицина, 20; 255-262
Метание диска, 106-107
Метание копья, 231-232
Метание молота, 184
Методы тренировки, 493-497
Моторные лодки, 272
Мотоспорт, 272-274
Мотоспорт—мотокросс, 270-272
Наркотики, 138-142
Народные танцы, 156-157
Настольный теннис, 474-475
Народные танцы, 463
Нигер, 278
Нидерланды, 277
Новая Зеландия, 278
Оборудование, 144-146
Обучение на открытом воздухе, 291-292
Общественная психология, 452-453
Одежда, 75
Олимпийские Игры, 283-291
Опорный прыжок, 184
Ориентирование, 291

Падлбол, 293
Параллельные брусья разной высоты, 184
Парашютный спорт, 293-295
Парусный спорт, 527-534
Перекладина (гимнастика), 183
Петакю, 305
Питание, 278-282
Плавание, 465-473
Плавание в разных возрастных группах, 6
Плавание на длинные дистанции, 134
Плавание с маской под водой, 445-446
Плавание—спринт, 460
Планеризм и парящие полеты, 168-171
Плоты, 414
Подача подков, 202
Подводное ныряние, 500-504
Пожилой возраст, 6-8
Полевая стрельба из лука, 153
Полёты, 156
Полинезия, 398
Политика и правительство, 396-398
Поло, 398
Преодоление препятствий, 440-441
Проверка и измерение, 488-489
Прыжки в воду, 134-136
Прыжки в высоту, 190-191
Прыжки в длину, 244
Прыжки на лыжах с трамплина, 442
Прыжки с трамплина, 497
Прыжки с шестом, 395-396
Психология, 400-410
Психопатология, 1
Психофизиология, 410
Пятиборье, 295
Ракетбол, 411-414
Ракетки для игры в мяч (сквош), 463-464
Ранения и аварии, 204-228
Регби, 421-423
Религия, 416
Рингетте, 416-417
Родео, 460
Рост и развитие, 178
Румыния, 423
Ручной мяч, 185
Ручной мяч (соревнования команд), 476
Сверхлегкие полеты, 499-500
Серфинг, 464-465
Силовая атлетика, 399-400
Скачки с препятствиями, 199
Скоростной бег на коньках, 459
Скоростной спуск на лыжах, 136
Слалом (лыжах), 445
Служебная и профессинальная
   пригодность, 328-330
Советский Союз, 458
Современное пятиборье, 270
Современные танцы, 269-270
Соединённые Штаты Америки, 504-505
Сомали, 458
Сооружения, 146-151
Соревнование по метанию (легкая
   атлетика), 492-493
Соревнование по прыжкам (легкая
   атлетика), 492
Соревнования собачьих упряжек, 445
Софтбол, 456-458
Социология, 453; 453-456
Спасение утопающих, 243
Спелеология, 459-460
Специализированные Олимпиады, 458
Спорт в рамках предприятия, города, т.д.,
   228-231
Спорт мастеров, 255
Спорт на льду, 203
Спортивная аэронавтика, 6
Спортивная тренировка, 20

Спортивная ходьба, 410-411
Спортивное единоборство, 83
Спортивные занятия, 282
Спортивные институты, 460
Спортивные сани, 489
Справочники, 414-415
Спринт (легкая атлетика), 460-463
Средства массовой информации, 254-255
Стендовая стрельба на круглом стенде, 441-442
Стрелы, 98
Стрельба из лука, 17-19
Стрельба по движущей мишени, 497
Студенческий спорт, 80-83
Судейство, 282-283
Таиланд, 489
Танец живота, 42
Танцы, 96-98
Та-чи-чан, 475-476
Теннис, 477-487
Толкание ядра, 440
Тренировка, 76-80
Тренировка и подготовка, 493
Троеборье, 497-498
Троеборье—конный спорт, 489
Тройной прыжок, 499
Туризм, 22-23
Тяжелая атлетика, 511-513
Тяжелая атлетика и бодибилдинг, 513-514
Умственная отсталость, 105-106
Универсиада, 523
Участие, 295
Федеративная Республика Германия,
   151
Фестивали, 153
Фехтование, 151-153
Фигурное катание на коньках, 155-156
Фигурное катание на лыжах, 167
Фигурное плавание, 474
Физиология, 339-344
Физиология—кардиососудистая система,
   344-352
Физиология—лёгочная, 390-394
Физиология—метаболизм энергии, 352-366
Физиология—мускулы, 381-389
Физиология—невралгия, 389-390
Физиология—невроендекринология, 277-278
Физиология—терморегуляция, 394-395
Физиология—упражнения, 366-371
Физиология—факторы, влияющие на
   выступление, 371-381
Физиотерапия, 335-339
Физическая форма, 322-328
Физическая форма—проверка, 333-335
Физическая форма—программы и
   деятельность, 330-333
Физическое воспитание, 306-322
Филателия, 305
Философия, 305-306
Финляндия, 156
Флажковый футбол, 156
Фотография, 306
Франция, 167
Фризби, 167
Футбол, 446-452
Фубол «тач», 489
Ходьба на снегоступах, 446
Хоккей, 192-196
Хоккей в закрытом помещении, 156
Хоккей на траве, 153-154
Хоккей с мячом, 25
Художественная гимнастика, 270
Чиэлидинг, 68
Швейцария, 474
Швеция, 465
Школьный спорт, 434-437
Шотландия, 437

Экономика и финансы, 142-143
Эстафета (легкая атлетика), 415
Югославия, 534
Южно-Африканская Республика, 458
Юмор и сатира, 202
Япония, 231